W9-BEJ-769

ADAMS

EXECUTIVE RECRUITERS ALMANAC

2nd Edition

Managing Editor
Steven Graber

Assistant Managing Editor
Michelle Roy Kelly

Editor
Anne M. Grignon

Senior Associate Editors
Heidi E. Sampson • Heather L. Vinhateiro

Editorial Assistants
Thom Blackett • Michelle M. Lang
Michael Paydos • Elizabeth Washer
Jennifer M. Wood

Adams Media Corporation
HOLBROOK, MASSACHUSETTS

Published by Adams Media Corporation
260 Center Street, Holbrook, MA 02343. USA.
http://www.adamsmedia.com

Manufactured in Canada.

A B C D E F G H I J

Copyright © 2000 by Adams Media Corporation. All rights reserved. No part of the material printed may be reproduced or used in any form or by any means, electronic or mechanical, including photocopying, recording, or by any information storage retrieval system without permission from the publisher.

The *Adams Executive Recruiters Almanac, 2nd Edition* and its cover design are trademarks of Adams Media Corporation.

Brand name products in the agency listings are proprietary property of the applicable firm, subject to trademark protection, and registered with government offices.

While the publisher has made every reasonable effort to obtain and verify accurate information, occasional errors are inevitable due to the magnitude of the database. Should you discover an error, or if an agency is missing, please write the editors at the above address so that we may update future editions.

"This publication is designed to provide accurate and authoritative information with regard to the subject matter covered. It is sold with the understanding that the publisher is not engaged in rendering legal, accounting, or other professional advice. If legal advice or other expert assistance is required, the services of a competent professional person should be sought."
--From a *Declaration of Principles* jointly adopted by a Committee of the American Bar Association and a Committee of Publishers and Associations

The appearance of a listing in the book does not constitute an endorsement from the publisher.

ISBN: 1-58062-332-8
ISSN: 1099-0216

This book is available at quantity discounts for bulk purchases.
This book is also available on standing order.
For information, call 800/872-5627.

Visit our exciting job and career site at http://www.careercity.com

TABLE OF CONTENTS

SECTION ONE: EMPLOYMENT SERVICES LISTINGS

INTRODUCTION/5

EMPLOYMENT SERVICES LISTINGS/11

SECTION TWO: EMPLOYMENT SERVICES INDEXES

Many jobseekers turn to temporary agencies, permanent employment agencies, or executive recruiters to assist them in their respective job searches. At their best, these resources can be a valuable friend -- it's comforting to know that someone is putting his or her wealth of experience and contacts to work for you. At their worst, however, they are more of a friend to the employer, or to more experienced recruits, than to you personally, and it is best not to rely on them exclusively.

That said, there are several types of employment services for jobseekers to check out as part of their job search efforts:

EXECUTIVE SEARCH FIRMS

Also known as "headhunters," these firms consist of recruiters who are paid by client companies that hire them to fill a specific position. Executive search firms seek out and carefully screen (and weed out) candidates for high-salaried technical, executive, and managerial positions and are paid by the employer. The prospective employee is generally not charged a fee. Unlike permanent employment agencies, they often approach viable candidates directly, rather than waiting for candidates to approach them. Some prefer to deal with already employed candidates. Whether you are employed or not, do not contact an executive search firm if you aren't ready to look for a job. If a recruiter tries to place you right away and finds out you are not really looking yet, it is unlikely they will spend much time with you in the future.

Many search firms specialize in particular industries, while generalist firms typically provide placements in a wide range of industries. Look for firms that specialize in your field of interest or expertise, as well as generalist firms that conduct searches in a variety of fields. While you should concentrate on firms in your geographic area, you do not have to limit yourself to these as many firms operate nationally or internationally.

There are two basic types of executive search firms -- retainer-based and contingency-based. Note, however, that some firms conduct searches of both types. Essentially, retainer firms are hired by a client company for a search and paid a fee by the client company regardless of whether or not a placement is made. Conversely, contingency firms receive payment from the client company only when their candidate is hired. Fees are typically based on the position's first-year salary. The range is usually between 20 and 35 percent, and retainer firm fees tend to be at the higher end of that scale, according to Ivan Samuels, President of Abbott's of Boston, an executive search firm that conducts both types of searches.

Generally, companies use retainer firms to fill senior-level positions, with salaries over $60,000. In most cases, a company will hire only one retainer firm to fill a given position, and part of the process is a thorough, on-site visit by the search firm to the client company so that the recruiter may check out the operation. These search firms are recommended for a highly experienced professional seeking a job in his or her current field. Confidentiality is more secure with these firms, since a recruiter may only use your file in consideration for one job at a time, and most retainer firms will not freely circulate your resume without permission. This is particularly important to a jobseeker who is currently employed and insists on absolute discretion. If that's the case, however, make sure you do not contact a retainer firm used by your current employer.

Contingency firms make placements that cover a broader salary range, so these firms are more ideal for someone seeking a junior or mid-level position. Unlike retainer firms, contingency firms may be competing with other firms to fill a particular opening. As a result, these firms can be quicker and more responsive to your job search. In addition, a contingency firm will distribute your resume more widely. Some firms require your permission before sending your resume to any given company, while others ask that you trust their discretion. You should inquire about this with your recruiter at the outset, and choose according to your needs.

That said, once you've chosen the specific recruiter or recruiters that you will contact, keep in mind that recruiters are working for the companies that hire them, not for you, the jobseeker. Attempting to fill a position -- especially amongst fierce competition with other firms -- means your best interests may not be the recruiter's only priority. For this reason, you should contact as many search firms as possible in order to increase your chances of finding your ideal position.

A phone call is your first step, during which you should speak with a recruiter and exchange all relevant information. Ask questions about whether they operate on a retainer or contingency basis (or both), and any and all questions you have regarding the firm's procedures. Offer the recruiter information about your employment history, as well as what type of work you are seeking. Make sure you sound enthusiastic, but not pushy. The recruiter will ask that you send a resume and cover letter as soon as possible.

Occasionally, the recruiter will arrange to meet with you, but most often this will not occur until he or she has received your resume and has found a potential match. James E. Slate, President of F-O-R-T-U-N-E Personnel Consultants in Topsfield, Massachusetts, advises that you generally not expect an abundance of personal attention at the beginning of the relationship with your recruiter, particularly with a large firm that works nationally and does most of its work over the phone. You should, however, use your recruiter's inside knowledge to your best advantage. Some recruiters will help coach you before an interview and many are open about giving you all the facts they know about a client company.

In addition, do your own research on the company before your first interview, although you should never contact a company directly that is considering you for a position through an executive search firm. The recruiter acts as a go-between, and all salary and benefits negotiations are handled by him or her as well.

Not all executive search firms are licensed, so make sure those you plan to deal with have solid reputations and don't hesitate to check with the Better Business Bureau. Also keep in mind that it is common for recruiters to search for positions in other states. For example, recruiters in Boston sometimes look for candidates to fill positions in New York City, and the reverse is true as well.

Names of search firms nationwide can be found in *The JobBank Guide to Employment Services* (Adams Media Corporation), or by contacting:

Association of Executive Search Consultants (AESC)
500 Fifth Avenue, Suite 930, New York NY 10110. 212/398-9556.

Top Echelon, Inc.
World Wide Web address: http://www.topechelon.com.
A cooperative placement networking service of recruiting firms.

PERMANENT EMPLOYMENT AGENCIES

Permanent employment agencies are commissioned by employers to find qualified candidates for job openings. The catch is that their main responsibility is to meet the employer's needs -- not necessarily to find a suitable job for the candidate.

This is not to say that permanent employment agencies should be ruled out altogether. There are permanent employment agencies specializing in specific industries that can be useful for experienced professionals. However, permanent employment agencies are not always a good choice for entry-level jobseekers. Some will try to steer inexperienced candidates in an unwanted direction or offer little more than clerical placements to experienced applicants. Others charge a fee for their services -- a condition that jobseekers should always ask about up front.

Some permanent employment agencies dispute the criticisms mentioned above. As one recruiter puts it, "Our responsibilities are to the applicant and the employer equally, because without one, we'll lose the other." She also maintains that entry-level people are desirable, saying that "as they grow, we grow, too, so we aim to move them up the ranks."

In short, as that recruiter states, "All services are not the same." If you decide to register with an agency, your best bet is to find one that is recommended by a friend or associate. Barring that, names of agencies across the country can be found in *The JobBank Guide to Employment Services* (Adams Media Corporation). Or you can contact:

National Association of Personnel Services (NAPS)
3133 Mount Vernon Avenue
Alexandria VA 22305
703/684-0180

Be aware that there are an increasing number of bogus employment service firms, often advertising in newspapers and magazines. These "services" promise even inexperienced jobseekers top salaries in exciting careers -- all for a sizable fee. Others use expensive 900 numbers that jobseekers are encouraged to call. Unfortunately, most people find out too late that the jobs they have been promised do not exist.

As a general rule, most legitimate permanent employment agencies will never guarantee a job and will not seek payment until after the candidate has been placed. Even so, every agency you are interested in should be checked out with the local chapter of the Better Business Bureau.

If everything checks out, call the firm to find out if it specializes in your area of expertise and how it will go about marketing your qualifications. After you have selected a few agencies (three to five is best), send each one a resume with a cover letter. Make a follow-up phone call a week or two later, and try to schedule an interview. Once again, be prepared to take a battery of tests at the interview.

Above all, do not expect too much. Only a small portion of all professional, managerial, and executive jobs are listed with these agencies. Use them as an addition to your job search campaign, not a centerpiece.

TEMPORARY EMPLOYMENT AGENCIES

Temporary or "temp" agencies can be a viable option. Often these agencies specialize in clerical and support work, but it's becoming increasingly common to find temporary assignments in areas like accounting or computer programming. Working on temporary assignments will provide you with additional income during your job search and will add experience to your resume. It may also provide valuable business contacts or lead to permanent job opportunities.

Temporary agencies are listed in your local telephone directory and in *The JobBank Guide to Employment Services* (Adams Media Corporation), found in your local public library. Send a resume and cover letter to the agency, and call to schedule an interview. Be prepared to take a number of tests at the interview.

CONTRACT SERVICES FIRMS

Firms that place individuals on a contract basis commonly receive job orders from client companies that can last anywhere from a month to over a year. The function of these firms differs from that of a temporary agency in that the candidate has specific, marketable skills they wish to put to work, and the contract recruiter interviews the candidate extensively. Most often, contract services firms specialize in placing technical professionals, though some do specialize in other fields including clerical and office support. The use of these firms is increasing in popularity, as jobseekers with technical skills recognize the benefit of utilizing and demonstrating their talents at a sampling of different companies, and establishing contacts along the way that could lead to a permanent position, if desired. Most contract services firms do not charge a fee to the candidate.

For more information on contract services, contact:

C.E. Publications, Inc.
Contract Employment Weekly Magazine
P.O. Box 3006, Bothell WA 98041-3006. 425/806-5200.
World Wide Web address: http://www.ceweekly.com.

CAREER/OUTPLACEMENT COUNSELING FIRMS

These firms are very diverse in the services they provide. Many nonprofit organizations -- colleges, universities, private associations -- offer free or very inexpensive counseling services. For-profit career/outplacement counseling services, on the other hand, can charge a broad range of fees, depending on what services they provide. Services offered include career counseling, outplacement, resume development/writing, interview preparation, assessment testing, and various workshops. Upon contacting one of these firms, you should ask about the specific services that firm provides. Some firms provide career counseling only, teaching you how to conduct your own job search, while others also provide outplacement services. The difference here is that those which provide outplacement will conduct a job search for you, in addition to the counseling services. Firms like these are sometimes referred to as "marketing firms."

According to a representative at Career Ventures Counseling Services in Salem, Massachusetts, fees for career counseling average about $85 per hour. Furthermore, outplacement fees can range from $170 to over $7,000! As results are not guaranteed, you may want to check on a firm's reputation through the local Better Business Bureau.

For more information on resume services, contact:

Professional Association of Resume Writers
3637 Fourth Street, Suite 330, St. Petersburg FL 33704.
Attention: Mr. Frank Fox, Executive Director.

EXPLANATION OF LISTINGS

Employment service listings are presented in alphabetical order by state, and by agency type (temporary, permanent, executive search, contract services, and career/outplacement counseling) within each state.

Each listing contains some or all of the following types of information:

- Name of employment service
- Mailing address
- Phone, toll-free phone, and fax number
- Recorded jobline
- Contact person and title or department
- E-mail address
- World Wide Web address
- Employment service profile
- Areas of specialization
- Positions commonly filled
- Benefits available
- Corporate headquarters location
- Other area, national, and international locations
- Average salary range of placements
- Number of placements per year

Visit our exciting job and career site at http://www.careercity.com

ACT PERSONNEL SERVICE
4900 University Square, Suite 34, Huntsville AL 35816. 256/830-5228. **Contact:** Manager. **Description:** An executive search firm that also provides some temporary placements. **Positions commonly filled include:** Account Manager; Accountant/Auditor; Accounting Clerk; Administrative Assistant; Clerk; Computer Operator; Computer Programmer.

ALLGOOD ASSOCIATES
P.O. Box 310399, Enterprise AL 36331. 334/393-3334. **Fax:** 334/347-7829. **Contact:** Manager. **E-mail address:** arecruit@alaweb.com. **World Wide Web address:** http://www.allgoodjobs.com. **Description:** An executive search firm. **Specializes in the areas of:** Engineering; Manufacturing; Quality Assurance.

BRADLEY PERSONNEL CONSULTANTS
2421 Presidents Drive, Suite B8, Montgomery AL 36116. 334/272-3539. **Fax:** 334/272-7032. **Contact:** Manager. **Description:** An executive search firm. **Positions commonly filled include:** Clerk; Office Manager.

BREEN PERSONNEL, INC.
P.O. Box 1413, Huntsville AL 35807. 256/536-4431. **Fax:** 256/539-0583. **Contact:** Bill Breen, President. **Description:** An executive search firm operating on both retainer and contingency bases. **Specializes in the areas of:** Computer Science/Software; Engineering; Personnel/Labor Relations. **Positions commonly filled include:** Accountant/Auditor; Buyer; Chief Financial Officer; Computer Programmer; Controller; Credit Manager; Database Manager; Design Engineer; Electrical/Electronics Engineer; Finance Director; Human Resources Manager; Industrial Engineer; Industrial Production Manager; Manufacturing Engineer; Mechanical Engineer; MIS Specialist; Operations/Production Manager; Purchasing Agent/Manager; Quality Control Supervisor; Sales Engineer; Sales Executive; Sales Manager; Software Engineer; Systems Analyst; Telecommunications Manager. **Other U.S. locations:** Nationwide. **Average salary range of placements:** More than $50,000. **Number of placements per year:** 200 - 499.

CARTER GROUP
6420 Hillcrest Park Court, Suite A, Mobile AL 36608. 334/342-0999. **Fax:** 334/342-7999. **Contact:** Torrie Pierce, Manager. **Description:** An executive search firm that conducts searches in the South and the Northeast.

MARY CHEEK & ASSOCIATES, INC.
11991 Knollwood Road, Northport AL 35475. 205/333-8550. **Fax:** 205/333-9440. **Contact:** Mary Cheek, President. **Description:** An executive search firm operating on both retainer and contingency bases. **Specializes in the areas of:** Accounting/Auditing; Engineering; Industrial; Personnel/Labor Relations; Technical. **Positions commonly filled include:** Accountant/Auditor; Buyer; Chief Financial Officer; Controller; Design Engineer; Draftsperson; Electrical/ Electronics Engineer; General Manager; Human Resources Manager; Industrial Engineer; Industrial Production Manager; Management Trainee; Manufacturing Engineer; Mechanical Engineer; Operations/Production Manager; Purchasing Agent/ Manager; Quality Control Supervisor; Transportation/ Traffic Specialist. **Number of placements per year:** 1 - 49.

CLARK PERSONNEL SERVICE OF MOBILE, INC.
P.O. Box 991850, Mobile AL 36691-1850. 334/342-5511. **Physical address:** 4317 Downtowner Loop North, Mobile AL 36609. **Fax:** 334/343-5588. **Contact:** Donna Clark, President. **Description:** An executive search firm operating on a contingency basis. **Specializes in the** areas of: Accounting/Auditing; Computer Science/ Software; Engineering; Industrial; Manufacturing; Personnel/Labor Relations; Sales; Transportation. **Positions commonly filled include:** Accountant/Auditor; Administrative Manager; Aerospace Engineer; Agricultural Engineer; Architect; Bank Officer/Manager; Biological Scientist; Biomedical Engineer; Blue-Collar Worker Supervisor; Branch Manager; Chemical Engineer; Chemist; Civil Engineer; Clerical Supervisor; Computer Programmer; Credit Manager; Draftsperson; Electrical/Electronics Engineer; Human Resources Manager; Industrial Engineer; Manufacturer's/ Wholesaler's Sales Rep.; Mechanical Engineer; Metallurgical Engineer; Mining Engineer; Nuclear Engineer; Operations/Production Manager; Petroleum Engineer; Purchasing Agent/Manager; Quality Control Supervisor; Software Engineer; Stationary Engineer; Structural Engineer; Systems Analyst. **Corporate headquarters location:** This Location. **Average salary range of placements:** $30,000 - $50,000. **Number of placements per year:** 200 - 499.

DUNHILL OF SOUTH BIRMINGHAM
2738 18th Street South, Birmingham AL 35209. 205/877-4580. **Toll-free phone:** 800/548-0116. **Fax:** 205/877-4590. **Contact:** Peggy Clarke, President. **Description:** An executive search firm operating on a contingency basis. The firm also provides some temporary and contract placements. **Specializes in the areas of:** Accounting/Auditing; Administration; Banking; Computer Science/Software; Finance; Manufacturing; Personnel/Labor Relations; Secretarial; Technical. **Positions commonly filled include:** Accountant/Auditor; Administrative Manager; Bank Officer/Manager; Budget Analyst; Computer Programmer; Credit Manager; Financial Analyst; Health Services Manager; Human Resources Manager; Market Research Analyst; MIS Specialist; Operations/Production Manager; Purchasing Agent/Manager; Quality Control Supervisor; Software Engineer; Systems Analyst; Telecommunications Manager. **Benefits available to temporary workers:** Bonus Award/Plan; Medical Insurance; Paid Holidays; Paid Vacation. **Corporate headquarters location:** Woodbury NY. **Other U.S. locations:** Nationwide. **Number of placements per year:** 50 - 99.

F-O-R-T-u-N-E PERSONNEL CONSULTANTS
1414 Fifth Avenue SE, Suite A, Decatur AL 35601. 256/341-0400. **Fax:** 256/341-0444. **Contact:** Branch Manager. **E-mail address:** decatur@fpcweb.com. **World Wide Web address:** http://www. fortunerecruiting.com. **Description:** An executive search firm. **Specializes in the areas of:** Automotive; Chemicals; Plastics. **Positions commonly filled include:** Engineer; Facilities Engineer; Financial Analyst; Management; Quality Control Supervisor. **Corporate headquarters location:** New York NY.

F-O-R-T-u-N-E PERSONNEL CONSULTANTS
3311 Bob Wallace Avenue, Suite 204, Huntsville AL 35805. 256/534-7282. **Contact:** Bob Langford, President. **Description:** An executive search firm operating on a contingency basis. **Specializes in the areas of:** Accounting/Auditing; Administration; Computer Science/Software; Engineering; Finance; General Management; Industrial; Manufacturing; Personnel/Labor Relations. **Positions commonly filled include:** Accountant/Auditor; Buyer; Ceramics Engineer; Computer Programmer; Design Engineer; Designer; Electrical/Electronics Engineer; Environmental Engineer; Financial Analyst; General Manager; Human Resources Specialist; Industrial Engineer; Industrial Production Manager; Materials Engineer; Mechanical Engineer; Metallurgical Engineer; MIS Specialist; Pharmacist; Quality Control Supervisor; Telecommunications Manager; Transportation/Traffic Specialist. **Corporate**

headquarters location: New York NY. **Other U.S. locations:** Nationwide. **Average salary range of placements:** More than $50,000. **Number of placements per year:** 100 - 199.

THE HRM GROUP
321 Lorna Square, Birmingham AL 35216. 205/978-7181. **Fax:** 205/978-7616. **Contact:** Manager. **World Wide Web address:** http://www.hrmgroup.com. **Description:** An executive search firm that also offers some Human Resources management services. Founded in 1992. **Corporate headquarters location:** This Location.

ROBERT HALF INTERNATIONAL ACCOUNTEMPS
2000A Southbridge Parkway, Suite 430, Birmingham AL 35209. 205/879-4000. **World Wide Web address:** http://www.roberthalf.com. **Description:** An executive search firm. Accountemps (also at this location) provides temporary placements. **Specializes in the areas of:** Accounting/Auditing. **Corporate headquarters location:** Menlo Park CA. **Other U.S. locations:** Nationwide.

HEALTHCARE RECRUITERS OF ALABAMA
1945 Hoover Court, Suite 205, Birmingham AL 35226. 205/979-9840. **Fax:** 205/979-5879. **Contact:** Frank Johnson, President. **Description:** An executive search firm operating on both retainer and contingency bases. **Specializes in the areas of:** Health/Medical; Management; Marketing; Sales; Technical. **Positions commonly filled include:** Biological Scientist; Biomedical Engineer; Chemist; Clinical Lab Technician; Dental Assistant/Dental Hygienist; Dentist; Dietician/Nutritionist; EEG Technologist; EKG Technician; General Manager; Health Services Manager; Licensed Practical Nurse; Manufacturer's/Wholesaler's Sales Rep.; Market Research Analyst; MIS Specialist; Nuclear Medicine Technologist; Pharmacist; Physical Therapist; Physician; Psychologist; Recreational Therapist; Registered Nurse; Respiratory Therapist; Science Technologist; Software Engineer; Surgical Technician; Veterinarian. **Corporate headquarters location:** Dallas TX. **Other U.S. locations:** Nationwide. **Number of placements per year:** 1 - 49.

HUGHES & ASSOCIATES
3737 Government Boulevard, Suite 304B, Mobile AL 36693. 334/661-8888. **Contact:** Manager. **Description:** An executive search firm. **Specializes in the areas of:** Chemicals; Petrochemical.

INFORMATION TECHNOLOGY SERVICES
P.O. Box 7107, Huntsville AL 35807. 256/533-9800. **Contact:** Manager. **Description:** An executive search firm. **Specializes in the areas of:** Computer Science/Software.

INTERIM EXECUTIVE RECRUITING
100 Riverpoint Corporate Center, Birmingham AL 35243. 205/969-6700. **Contact:** Manager. **Description:** An executive search firm.

LANGFORD SEARCH
2025 Third Avenue North, Suite 301, Birmingham AL 35203. 205/328-5477. **Contact:** Manager. **Description:** An executive search firm. **Specializes in the areas of:** Accounting/Auditing; Finance; Information Technology.

LEED STAFFING SERVICE
100 Smothers Road, Montgomery AL 36117. 334/215-3200. **Fax:** 334/215-3210. **Contact:** Office Manager. **Description:** An executive search firm. **Positions commonly filled include:** Clerk; Data Entry Clerk; Engineer; Industrial Engineer.

LOCKE & ASSOCIATES
4144 Carmichael Road, Suite 19, Montgomery AL 36106. 334/272-7400. **Fax:** 334/272-6106. **Contact:** Manager. **Description:** An executive search firm. **Specializes in the areas of:** Construction; Engineering.

MANAGEMENT RECRUITERS INTERNATIONAL
3263 Demetropolis Road, Suite 6-C, Mobile AL 36693. 334/602-0104. **Contact:** Mr. R.C. Brock, Manager. **Description:** An executive search firm. **Specializes in the areas of:** Accounting/Auditing; Administration; Advertising; Architecture/Construction; Banking; Chemicals; Communications; Computer Hardware/Software; Design; Electrical; Engineering; Food; General Management; Health/Medical; Insurance; Legal; Manufacturing; Operations Management; Personnel/Labor Relations; Procurement; Publishing; Retail; Sales; Technical; Textiles; Transportation. **Positions commonly filled include:** Chemical Engineer; Chemist; Computer Programmer; Electrical/Electronics Engineer; Health Care Administrator; Industrial Engineer; Mechanical Engineer; Registered Nurse; Systems Analyst. **Corporate headquarters location:** Cleveland OH. **Other U.S. locations:** Nationwide.

MANAGEMENT RECRUITERS OF DAPHNE SALES CONSULTANTS
P.O. Box 2784, Daphne AL 36526. 334/625-0200. **Fax:** 334/625-0203. **Contact:** Manager. **Description:** An executive search firm. **Specializes in the areas of:** Automotive; Automotive Retailing; Banking. **Corporate headquarters location:** Cleveland OH. **Other U.S. locations:** Nationwide.

MANAGEMENT RECRUITERS OF DECATUR
401 Lee Street, Suite 301, Decatur AL 35601. 256/341-0140. **Fax:** 256/341-0041. **Contact:** Branch Manager. **Description:** An executive search firm. **Specializes in the areas of:** Packaging; Printing.

MANAGEMENT RECRUITERS OF NORTH ALABAMA
2004 Poole Drive NW, Huntsville AL 35810. 256/858-9494. **Contact:** Manager. **Description:** An executive search firm. **Specializes in the areas of:** Accounting/Auditing; Administration; Advertising; Architecture/Construction; Banking; Chemicals; Communications; Computer Hardware/Software; Design; Electrical; Engineering; Food; General Management; Health/Medical; Insurance; Legal; Manufacturing; Operations Management; Personnel/Labor Relations; Procurement; Publishing; Retail; Sales; Technical; Textiles; Transportation. **Positions commonly filled include:** Chemical Engineer; Chemist; Computer Programmer; Electrical/Electronics Engineer; Health Care Administrator; Industrial Engineer; Mechanical Engineer; Registered Nurse; Systems Analyst.

MILLMAN SEARCH GROUP INCORPORATED
28651 U.S. Highway 98, Suite A5, Daphne AL 36526. 334/626-5513. **Contact:** Manager. **Description:** An executive search firm. **Specializes in the areas of:** Retail.

PERSONNEL CONNECTION
One Office Park, Suite 404E, Mobile AL 36609. 334/343-9300. **Fax:** 334/343-9300. **Contact:** Manager. **Description:** An executive search firm. **Specializes in the areas of:** Chemical Engineering; Chemicals; Engineering; Paper; Printing; Restaurant.

PERSONNEL INC.
917 Merchants Walk SW, Suite D, Huntsville AL 35801. 256/536-4431. **Contact:** Manager. **Description:** An executive search firm. **Average salary range of placements:** More than $50,000.

PROSEARCH
578 Azalea Road, Suite 109, Mobile AL 36609. 334/660-7077. **Fax:** 334/666-0118. **Contact:** Branch Manager. **Description:** An executive search firm. **Specializes in the areas of:** Engineering; Information Systems; Information Technology.

SANFORD ROSE ASSOCIATES - FAIRHOPE
22873 US Highway 98, Building 1, Fairhope AL 36532. 334/928-7072. **Contact:** Manager. **Description:** An executive search firm. **Specializes in the areas of:** Printing.

SANFORD ROSE ASSOCIATES - MOBILE
4321 Downtower Loop North, Suite 201, Mobile AL 36609. 334/414-5551. **Fax:** 334/414-5141. **Contact:** Manager. **World Wide Web address:** http://www. sanfordrose.com. **Description:** An executive search firm. **Specializes in the areas of:** Engineering; General Management; Information Technology; Sales.

SAVELA AND ASSOCIATES
One Chase Corporate Drive, Suite 490, Birmingham AL 35244. 205/444-0080. **Contact:** Manager. **Description:** An executive search firm.

SEARCH SOUTH INC.
P.O. Box 2224, Anniston AL 36202. 256/237-1868. **Contact:** Manager. **Description:** An executive search firm.

J.L. SMALL ASSOCIATES
3201 Lorna Road, Birmingham AL 35216. 205/823-4545. **Contact:** Jim Small, Owner. **Description:** An executive search firm operating on a contingency basis. Founded in 1989. **Specializes in the areas of:** Accounting/Auditing; Administration; Engineering; Industrial; Personnel/Labor Relations. **Positions commonly filled include:** Accountant/Auditor; Budget Analyst; Chemical Engineer; Chemist; Chief Financial Officer; Civil Engineer; Computer Programmer; Controller; Environmental Engineer; Financial Analyst;

General Manager; Human Resources Manager; Industrial Engineer; Industrial Production Manager; Manufacturing Engineer; Mechanical Engineer; Metallurgical Engineer; MIS Specialist; Operations Manager; Purchasing Agent/Manager; Quality Control Supervisor; Systems Analyst. **Corporate headquarters location:** This Location. **Average salary range of placements:** $30,000 - $50,000. **Number of placements per year:** 1 - 49.

SNELLING PERSONNEL SERVICES
400 East 14th Street, Suite E, Decatur AL 35601. 256/355-5424. **Fax:** 256/355-2298. **Contact:** Jorge Valdes, Manager. **Description:** An executive search firm operating on a contingency basis. **Specializes in the areas of:** Computer Science/Software; Engineering; Health/Medical; Sales. **Positions commonly filled include:** Applications Engineer; Chemical Engineer; Civil Engineer; Computer Programmer; Database Manager; Design Engineer; Electrical/Electronics Engineer; Environmental Engineer; Industrial Engineer; Manufacturer's/Wholesaler's Sales Rep.; Mechanical Engineer; Metallurgical Engineer; Physical Therapist; Software Engineer; Structural Engineer. **Corporate headquarters location:** Dallas TX. **Other U.S. locations:** Nationwide. **Average salary range of placements:** $30,000 - $50,000. **Number of placements per year:** 1 - 49.

PERMANENT EMPLOYMENT AGENCIES

AEROTEK, INC.
4910 Corporate Drive, Suite G, Huntsville AL 35805. 256/721-4520. **Toll-free phone:** 800/377-3144. **Contact:** Manager. **World Wide Web address:** http://www. aerotek.com. **Description:** A permanent employment agency that also provides some contract placements. **Specializes in the areas of:** Computer Science/ Software; Engineering; Industrial; Manufacturing; Telecommunications. **Positions commonly filled include:** Aerospace Engineer; Aircraft Mechanic/Engine Specialist; Chemical Engineer; Civil Engineer; Computer Programmer; Cost Estimator; Design Engineer; Designer; Draftsperson; Electrical/Electronics Engineer; Environmental Engineer; Industrial Engineer; Industrial Production Manager; Mechanical Engineer; Metallurgical Engineer; MIS Specialist; Nuclear Engineer; Quality Control Supervisor; Software Engineer; Structural Engineer; Systems Analyst; Technical Writer/Editor. **Corporate headquarters location:** Baltimore MD. **Other U.S. locations:** Nationwide. **Average salary range of placements:** $30,000 - $50,000. **Number of placements per year:** 100 - 199.

ALABAMA NANNIES, INC.
15 Office Park Circle, Suite 209-A, Birmingham AL 35223. 205/871-2032. **Contact:** President. **Description:** A permanent employment agency engaged in the placement of live-in and live-out nannies and governesses. **Positions commonly filled include:** Nanny. **Number of placements per year:** 1 - 49.

EMPLOYMENT CONSULTANTS INC.
649 South McDonough Street, Montgomery AL 36104. 334/264-0649. **Fax:** 334/263-7413. **Contact:** Janet Hutto, President. **Description:** A permanent employment agency that concentrates on mid-level executive positions. The company also places entry-level accounting, engineering, management, and sales professionals, as well as upper-level office and administrative personnel. **Specializes in the areas of:** Accounting/Auditing; Administration; Computer Science/Software; Engineering; Finance; Health/Medical; Industrial; Legal; Manufacturing; Sales; Secretarial. **Positions commonly filled include:** Accountant/Auditor; Adjuster; Administrative Manager; Agricultural Engineer; Bank Officer/Manager; Biological Scientist; Budget Analyst; Chemist; Civil Engineer; Claim Representative;

Clerical Supervisor; Clinical Lab Technician; Computer Programmer; Cost Estimator; Counselor; Credit Manager; Customer Service Representative; Designer; Dietician/ Nutritionist; Draftsperson; Economist; Editor; Electrical/ Electronics Engineer; Financial Aid Officer; Food Scientist/ Technologist; Forester/Conservation Scientist; General Manager; Health Services Manager; Hotel Manager; Human Resources Manager; Industrial Engineer; Industrial Production Manager; Landscape Architect; Management Analyst/Consultant; Management Trainee; Manufacturer's/ Wholesaler's Sales Rep.; Mechanical Engineer; Medical Records Technician; Occupational Therapist; Paralegal; Physical Therapist; Property and Real Estate Manager; Public Relations Specialist; Quality Control Supervisor; Radiological Technologist; Registered Nurse; Respiratory Therapist; Restaurant/Food Service Manager; Securities Sales Representative; Social Worker; Speech-Language Pathologist; Structural Engineer; Systems Analyst; Technical Writer/Editor; Transportation/Traffic Specialist; Underwriter; Urban/Regional Planner. **Average salary range of placements:** $30,000 - $50,000. **Number of placements per year:** 100 - 199.

EXECUTIVE STAFFING INC.
1025 Montgomery Highway, Suite 103, Montgomery AL 35216. 205/979-6505. **Contact:** Manager. **Description:** A permanent employment agency that also provides some temporary placements. **Specializes in the areas of:** Administration; Clerical; Health/Medical; Legal.

GENERAL PERSONNEL CORPORATION
616 Gadsden Highway, Suite B, Birmingham AL 35235. 205/833-3467. **Fax:** 205/836-6802. **Contact:** James L. Gilbert, Jr., Recruiter. **Description:** A permanent employment agency. **Specializes in the areas of:** Apparel; Textiles.

INITIAL STAFFING
The Galleries at Riverchase, 3075 Highway 150, Birmingham AL 35244. 205/444-8733. **Contact:** Manager. **Description:** A permanent employment agency. **Specializes in the areas of:** Accounting/ Auditing; Banking; Secretarial. **Positions commonly filled include:** Claim Representative. **Corporate headquarters location:** Houston TX. **Average salary range of placements:** Less than $20,000. **Number of placements per year:** 1000+.

JOB REFERRALS
3600 Debby Drive, Montgomery AL 36111. 334/288-2080. **Contact:** Manager. **Description:** A permanent placement agency that also provides some temporary placements. **Positions commonly filled include:** Warehouse Manager; Warehouse/Distribution Worker.

MARINE JOBS, INC.
800 Downtowner Boulevard, Suite 111, Mobile AL 36609. 334/380-0765. **Fax:** 334/380-0571. **Contact:** Wendy Sullivan, President. **Description:** A permanent employment agency. **Specializes in the areas of:** Maritime. **Corporate headquarters location:** This Location. **Average salary range of placements:** $20,000 - $29,999. **Number of placements per year:** 1000+.

PERFORM STAFFING SERVICE
3107 Independence Drive, Birmingham AL 35209. 205/870-8170. **Contact:** Jerry Sulzby, Vice President/General Manager. **Description:** A permanent employment agency. **Specializes in the areas of:** Accounting/Auditing; Banking; Computer Hardware/Software. **Positions commonly filled include:** Bookkeeper; Clerk; Data Entry Clerk; EDP Specialist; Factory Worker; Light Industrial Worker; Nurse; Receptionist; Secretary; Stenographer; Typist/Word Processor. **Number of placements per year:** 50 - 99.

PERSONNEL WORLD, INC.
3125 Independence Drive, Suite 119, Birmingham AL 35209. 205/870-5862. **Contact:** Manager. **Description:** A permanent employment agency. **Positions commonly filled include:** Controller; Office Manager; Receptionist.

PLACERS, INC.
1686 Creely Drive, Birmingham AL 35235. 205/856-0646. **Fax:** 205/856-3387. **Contact:** Gina Wilson, President. **Description:** A permanent employment agency. **Specializes in the areas of:** Accounting/Auditing; Engineering; Insurance; Manufacturing; Secretarial. **Positions commonly filled include:** Accountant/Auditor; Adjuster; Chemist; Customer Service Representative; Design Engineer; Industrial Engineer; Insurance Agent/Broker; Manufacturer's/Wholesaler's Sales Rep.; Mechanical Engineer; Metallurgical Engineer; Operations/Production Manager; Purchasing Agent/Manager. **Corporate headquarters location:** This Location. **Average salary range of placements:** $30,000 - $50,000. **Number of placements per year:** 1 - 49.

SNELLING PERSONNEL SERVICES
1813 University Drive, Huntsville AL 35801. 256/382-3000. **Toll-free phone:** 888/562-6683. **Fax:** 256/382-6691. **Contact:** George Barnes, Owner. **E-mail address:** gbarnes172@aol.com. **Description:** A permanent employment agency. **Specializes in the areas of:** Computer Science/Software; Engineering; Health/Medical; Sales. **Positions commonly filled include:** Accountant/Auditor; Aerospace Engineer; Civil Engineer; Computer Programmer; Customer Service Rep.; Electrical/Electronics Engineer; Industrial Engineer; Manufacturer's/Wholesaler's Sales Rep.; Mechanical Engineer; Nuclear Medicine Technologist; Occupational Therapist; Pharmacist; Physical Therapist; Physicist; Registered Nurse; Software Engineer; Speech-Language Pathologist; Systems Analyst. **Corporate headquarters location:** Dallas TX. **Other U.S. locations:** Nationwide. **Number of placements per year:** 100 - 199.

VIP PERSONNEL, INC.
P.O. Box 361925, Birmingham AL 35236-1925. 205/733-8889. **Fax:** 205/733-8817. **Contact:** Bonnie Wainwright, Owner. **Description:** A permanent employment agency. Founded in 1981. **Specializes in the areas of:** Accounting/Auditing; Administration; Advertising; Banking; Broadcasting; Computer Science/Software; Finance; General Management; Health/Medical; Industrial; Insurance; Legal; Nonprofit; Personnel/Labor Relations; Sales; Secretarial. **Positions commonly filled include:** Account Manager; Accountant/Auditor; Adjuster; Administrative Assistant; Administrative Manager; Advertising Clerk; Auditor; Bank Officer/Manager; Branch Manager; Budget Analyst; Buyer; Chief Financial Officer; Clerical Supervisor; Computer Programmer; Credit Manager; Customer Service Representative; Database Manager; Finance Director; Financial Analyst; General Manager; Graphic Artist; Graphic Designer; Health Services Manager; Hotel Manager; Human Resources Specialist; Industrial Production Manager; Management Analyst/Consultant; Management Trainee; Manufacturer's/Wholesaler's Sales Rep.; Production Manager; Public Relations Specialist; Purchasing Agent/Manager; Quality Control Supervisor; Sales Engineer; Sales Manager; Sales Rep.; Systems Analyst; Typist/Word Processor; Underwriter. **Corporate headquarters location:** This Location. **Average salary range of placements:** $20,000 - $29,999. **Number of placements per year:** 1000+.

TEMPORARY EMPLOYMENT AGENCIES

EAI HEALTH CARE STAFFING
500 Southland Drive, Suite 155-D, Birmingham AL 35226. 205/823-5032. **Fax:** 205/823-5232. **Contact:** Manager. **Description:** A temporary agency that provides clerical and clinical placements for the medical industry. **Specializes in the areas of:** Health/Medical. **Positions commonly filled include:** Clerical Supervisor; Clinical Lab Technician; Medical Records Technician; Pharmacist; Physician; Registered Nurse. **Corporate headquarters location:** This Location. **Average salary range of placements:** Less than $20,000. **Number of placements per year:** 100 - 199.

LABOR FINDERS
P.O. Box 2843, Tuscaloosa AL 35404. 205/750-0059. **Physical address:** 1120 35th Street, Suite A, Tuscaloosa AL 35401. **Fax:** 205/752-0056. **Contact:** Manager. **Description:** A temporary agency. **Specializes in the areas of:** Food; Industrial; Manufacturing; Retail; Secretarial; Transportation. **Positions commonly filled include:** Automotive Mechanic; Blue-Collar Worker Supervisor; Branch Manager; Clerical Supervisor; Construction Contractor; Customer Service Rep.; Electrician; Landscape Architect; Operations/Production Manager; Typist/Word Processor. **Corporate headquarters location:** Mobile AL. **Other U.S. locations:** FL; LA; MI; TN; TX. **Average salary range of placements:** Less than $20,000. **Number of placements per year:** 500 - 999.

SPECIAL COUNSEL
2340 Woodcrest Place, Suite 210, Birmingham AL 35209. 205/870-3330. **Fax:** 205/870-3337. **Contact:** Manager. **World Wide Web address:** http://www.specialcounsel.com. **Description:** A temporary agency that also provides some permanent placements. **Specializes in the areas of:** Legal.

WORKFORCE ENTERPRISES
1355 South Eufaula Avenue, Suite E, Eufaula AL 36027. 334/687-4222. **Fax:** 334/687-4228. **Contact:** Rachel Britt, Accounts Manager. **E-mail address:** workforce@zebra.net. **Description:** A temporary agency. **Specializes in the areas of:** Accounting/Auditing; Administration; Advertising; Engineering; Food; Industrial; Manufacturing; Personnel/Labor Relations; Retail; Sales; Secretarial. **Positions commonly filled include:** Accountant/Auditor; Administrative Manager; Blue-Collar Worker Supervisor; Buyer; Computer Programmer; Customer Service Representative; Design Engineer; Draftsperson; Electrician; General Manager; Management Trainee; Manufacturer's/Wholesaler's Sales

Rep.; Operations/Production Manager; Purchasing Agent/Manager; Quality Control Supervisor; Services Sales Representative; Typist/Word Processor. **Other**

U.S. locations: AR; MS; TN. **Average salary range of placements:** Less than $20,000. **Number of placements per year:** 200 - 499.

CONTRACT SERVICES FIRMS

INTELLI MARK
One Perimeter Park South, Suite 400-N, Birmingham AL 35243. 205/969-1099. **Contact:** Manager. **Description:** A contract services firm that also provides some permanent placements. All positions are exclusively in computer-related occupations. **Positions commonly filled include:** Computer Operator; Computer Support Technician; Computer Technician.

SEATEC, INC.
P.O. Box 127, Warrior AL 35180. 205/647-4224. **Fax:** 205/647-7677. **Contact:** Ray Seaver, Manager of Recruiting. **Description:** A contract services firm. Founded in 1979. **Specializes in the areas of:** Architecture/Construction; Computer Science/Software; Engineering; Manufacturing; Technical. **Positions commonly filled include:** Architect; Chemical Engineer; Chemist; Civil Engineer; Computer Programmer; Cost Estimator; Design Engineer; Designer; Draftsperson; Electrical/Electronics Engineer; Environmental Engineer; Geologist/Geophysicist; Mechanical Engineer; Metallurgical Engineer; MIS Specialist; Science Technologist; Software Engineer; Structural Engineer; Systems Analyst; Technical Writer/Editor. **Corporate headquarters location:** Huntsville AL. **Other U.S. locations:** Pensacola FL. **Average salary range of placements:** More than $50,000. **Number of placements per year:** 200 - 499.

VIATECH NORTHSTAR
2200 Woodcrest Place, Suite 300, Birmingham AL 35209. 205/871-4321. **Fax:** 205/871-4378. **Contact:** Manager. **World Wide Web address:** http://www. callviatech.com. **Description:** A contract services firm.

VIATECH SERVICES
150 West Park Loop, Suite 105, Huntsville AL 35806. 256/721-4500. **Fax:** 256/721-1552. **Contact:** Manager. **World Wide Web address:** http://www.callviatech.com. **Description:** A contract services firm.

CAREER/OUTPLACEMENT COUNSELING FIRMS

HIGHLANDS PROGRAM
5901 Airport Boulevard, Suite B, Mobile AL 36608. 334/343-2597. **Contact:** Dr. Kent Welsh, Counselor. **World Wide Web address:** http://www.highlandsprogram.com.

Description: Provides career counseling to students and adults, and training and development services to corporations.

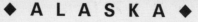

EXECUTIVE SEARCH FIRMS

ALASKA EXECUTIVE SEARCH (AES)
821 N Street, Suite 204, Anchorage AK 99501. 907/276-5707. **Fax:** 907/279-3731. **Contact:** Manager. **Description:** An executive search firm. **Specializes in the areas of:** Administration; Banking; Clerical; Health/Medical; Professional; Technical.

THE GROWTH COMPANY
2221 East Northern Lights Boulevard, Suite 107, Anchorage AK 99508. 907/276-4769. **Contact:** Manager. **Description:** An executive search firm.

MANAGEMENT RECRUITERS INTERNATIONAL
154 East Redoubt Avenue, Soldotna AK 99669. 907/283-5633. **Contact:** Manager. **Description:** An executive search firm.

PERMANENT EMPLOYMENT AGENCIES

ADAMS & ASSOCIATES INC.
3201 C Street, Suite 402, Anchorage AK 99503. 907/561-5161. **Fax:** 907/563-7417. **Contact:** Staffing Specialist. **Description:** A permanent employment agency that also provides some temporary placements.

ALASKA DEPARTMENT OF LABOR AND WORKFORCE DEVELOPMENT
3301 Eagle Street, Anchorage AK 99503. 907/269-4800. **Contact:** Manager. **World Wide Web address:** http://www.labor.state.ak.us. **Description:** A state-operated permanent employment agency. **Specializes in the areas of:** Clerical; Food; Technical.

ALASKA DEPARTMENT OF LABOR AND WORKFORCE DEVELOPMENT
10002 Glacier Highway, Suite 200, Juneau AK 99801. 907/465-4562. **Contact:** Recruiter. **World Wide Web address:** http://www.labor.state.ak.us. **Description:** A state-operated permanent employment agency.

CHUGACH NORTH EMPLOYMENT
3601 C Street, Anchorage AK 99503. 907/561-4321. **Contact:** Manager. **Description:** A permanent employment agency.

KODIAK EMPLOYMENT OFFICE
309 Center Street, Kodiak AK 99615. 907/486-3105. **Contact:** Manager. **Description:** A permanent employment agency.

MIDNIGHT SUN MANAGEMENT
12871 Johns Road, Anchorage AK 99515. 907/345-9542. **Contact:** Manager. **Description:** A permanent employment agency.

PERSONNEL PLUS
3335 Arctic Boulevard, Suite 200, Anchorage AK 99503. 907/563-7587. **Contact:** Manager. **Description:** A permanent employment agency that also provides some temporary placements.

TEMPORARY EMPLOYMENT AGENCIES

CHUGACH NORTH TECHNICAL SERVICE
59 College Road, Suite 102, Fairbanks AK 99701. 907/451-6393. **Contact:** Manager. **Description:** A temporary employment agency. **Specializes in the areas of:** Administration; General Labor.

ELITE EMPLOYMENT SERVICE
1113 West Fireweed Lane, Suite 200, Anchorage AK 99503. 907/276-8367. **Fax:** 907/276-5172. **Contact:** Manager. **Description:** A temporary agency that also provides some permanent placements. **Specializes in the areas of:** Administration; Clerical; Secretarial.

MANPOWER TEMPORARY SERVICES
4300 B Street, Suite 103, Anchorage AK 99503. 907/562-1440. **Fax:** 907/562-7080. **Contact:** Branch Manager. **World Wide Web address:** http://www.manpower.com. **Description:** A temporary agency. Client company pays fee. **Specializes in the areas of:** Clerical; Data Processing; Industrial; Light Industrial; Marketing; Office Support; Technical. **Benefits available to temporary workers:** Computer Training; Paid Holidays; Paid Vacation; Referral Bonus Plan.

MANPOWER TEMPORARY SERVICES
714 Fourth Avenue, Suite 302A, Fairbanks AK 99701. 907/474-8875. **Fax:** 907/479-8272. **Contact:** Manager. **Description:** A temporary agency. **Specializes in the areas of:** Clerical; Light Industrial; Office Support; Technical.

OLSTEN STAFFING SERVICES
341 West Tudor Road, Suite 106, Anchorage AK 99503. 907/563-0090. **Fax:** 907/563-1080. **Contact:** Manager. **Description:** A temporary agency. Founded in 1950. **Specializes in the areas of:** Accounting/Auditing; Assembly; Distribution; Engineering; Entry-Level; Finance; Legal Secretarial; Marketing; MIS/EDP; Office Automation; Office Support; Production; Professional; Technical; Telemarketing; Telephone Technical Support. **Positions commonly filled include:** Clerk. **Benefits available to temporary workers:** Bonus Award/Plan; Health Benefits; Paid Holidays; Paid Vacation; Training.

PROFESSIONAL BUSINESS SERVICE, INC.
807 G Street, Suite 200, Anchorage AK 99501. 907/279-7679. **Fax:** 907/276-5758. **Contact:** Manager. **Description:** A temporary agency that also provides some permanent placements. **Specializes in the areas of:** Accounting/Auditing; Engineering; Secretarial. **Positions commonly filled include:** Administrative Assistant; Civil Engineer; Computer Operator; Draftsperson; Financial Analyst; Geologist/Geophysicist; Secretary; Technical Writer/Editor; Typist/Word Processor. **Benefits available to temporary workers:** Medical Insurance; Profit Sharing.

CONTRACT SERVICES FIRMS

NORTHWEST TECHNICAL SERVICES (NTS)
P.O. Box 241921, Anchorage AK 99524. 907/562-1633. **Contact:** Manager. **Description:** A contract services firm.

◆ A R I Z O N A ◆

ACCOUNTANTS EXECUTIVE SEARCH
ACCOUNTANTS ON CALL
2111 East Highland Avenue, Suite B420, Phoenix AZ 85016. 602/957-1200. **Contact:** Manager. **Description:** An executive search firm. Accountants on Call (also at this location) is a temporary agency. **Specializes in the areas of:** Accounting/Auditing; Finance.

ACCOUNTING & FINANCE PERSONNEL, INC.
1702 East Highland Avenue, Suite 200, Phoenix AZ 85016. 602/277-3700. **Fax:** 602/277-8212. **Contact:** Mike Nolan, Owner. **Description:** An executive search firm that also provides some temporary and permanent placements. Founded in 1990. **Specializes in the areas of:** Accounting/Auditing; Bookkeeping; Finance. **Positions commonly filled include:** Accountant/Auditor; Budget Analyst; Credit Manager; Financial Analyst. **Corporate headquarters location:** This Location. **Other area locations:** Tucson AZ. **Number of placements per year:** 200 - 499.

ACCOUNTING & FINANCE PERSONNEL, INC.
4400 East Broadway Boulevard, Suite 600, Tucson AZ 85711. 520/323-3600. **Fax:** 520/795-4753. **Contact:** Recruiter. **Description:** An executive search firm that also provides some temporary and permanent placements. **Specializes in the areas of:** Accounting/ Auditing; Bookkeeping; Finance. **Positions commonly filled include:** Accountant/Auditor; Budget Analyst; Credit Manager; Financial Analyst. **Corporate headquarters location:** Phoenix AZ.

ACCOUNTING QUEST
3101 North Central Avenue, Suite 1240, Phoenix AZ 85012. 602/351-1700. **Fax:** 602/351-2255. **Contact:** Kimberly Thompson, Director. **E-mail address:** kimberlyt@accountingquest.com. **World Wide Web address:** http://www.accountingquest.com. **Description:** An executive search firm operating on a contingency basis. Accounting Quest also provides some temporary, permanent, and contract placements. **Specializes in the areas of:** Accounting; Finance; Tax. **Other U.S. locations:** Denver CO; Portland OR; Seattle WA. **Number of placements per year:** 100 - 199.

AZTECH RECRUITMENT COMPANY
4131 North 24th Street, Suite A122, Phoenix AZ 85016. 602/955-8080. **Contact:** Manager. **Description:** An executive search firm. **Specializes in the areas of:** Computer Science/Software; Engineering; Technical.

BJB MEDICAL ASSOCIATES
4325 North Wells Fargo Avenue, Suite 3, Scottsdale AZ 85251. 480/421-1801. **Contact:** Manager. **Description:** An executive search firm. **Specializes in the areas of:** Health/Medical. **Positions commonly filled include:** Physician.

BARTHOLDI & COMPANY
10040 East Happy Valley Road, Suite 244, Scottsdale AZ 85255. 480/502-2178. **Contact:** Office Manager. **Description:** An executive search firm. **Specializes in the areas of:** High-Tech.

DAN BOLEN & ASSOCIATES
9741 North 90th Place, Suite 200, Scottsdale AZ 85258. 480/767-9000. **Contact:** Dan Bolen, Owner. **Description:** An executive search firm focusing on making placements in the rotating machinery field. **Specializes in the areas of:** Industrial.

THE BREN GROUP
13951 North Scottsdale Road, Suite 111A, Scottsdale AZ 85254. 480/951-2736. **Fax:** 480/951-5881. **Contact:** Michael S. Mudge, Director of Business Development. **E-mail address:** bren@brengroup.com. **Description:** An executive search firm operating on a contingency basis.

Client company pays fee. **Specializes in the areas of:** Banking; Computer Science/Software; Internet Development; Internet Marketing; Marketing; MIS/EDP; Sales; Transportation; Travel. **Positions commonly filled include:** Account Manager; Account Representative; Accountant; Administrative Manager; Aircraft Mechanic/Engine Specialist; Applications Engineer; AS400 Programmer Analyst; Auditor; Branch Manager; Budget Analyst; Chief Financial Officer; Computer Programmer; Computer Support Technician; Consultant; Content Developer; Controller; Customer Service Representative; Database Administrator; Database Manager; Finance Director; Financial Analyst; General Manager; Human Resources Manager; Internet Services Manager; Management Analyst/Consultant; Market Research Analyst; Marketing Manager; Marketing Specialist; MIS Specialist; Multimedia Designer; Network/Systems Administrator; Operations Manager; Project Manager; Purchasing Agent/Manager; Quality Control Supervisor; Sales Executive; Sales Manager; Sales Rep.; Software Engineer; SQL Programmer; Systems Analyst; Systems Manager; Technical Writer/ Editor; Telecommunications Manager; Transportation/ Traffic Specialist; Vice President of Operations; Vice President of Sales; Webmaster. **Corporate headquarters location:** This Location. **Other U.S. locations:** Nationwide. **International locations:** Worldwide. **Average salary range of placements:** $50,000 - $100,000. **Number of placements per year:** 100 - 199.

C.S. ASSOCIATES, LLC
P.O. Box 30926, Tucson AZ 85751. 520/327-7999. **Contact:** J.B. Connelly, Owner. **World Wide Web address:** http://www.csassoc.com. **Description:** An executive search firm. **Specializes in the areas of:** Architecture/Construction; Engineering. **Positions commonly filled include:** Architect; Civil Engineer; Design Engineer; Designer; Draftsperson; Electrical/ Electronics Engineer; Environmental Engineer; Geologist/Geophysicist; Landscape Architect; Mechanical Engineer; Mining Engineer; Structural Engineer; Surveyor; Transportation/Traffic Specialist. **Number of placements per year:** 1 - 49.

CIRCUIT TECHNOLOGY SEARCH INC.
P.O. Box 44168, Tucson AZ 85733. 520/292-9122. **Fax:** 520/292-9221. **Contact:** Rick Greenwald, President. **E-mail address:** circuit@azstarnet.com. **World Wide Web address:** http://www.circuit-tech-search.com. **Description:** An executive search firm operating on a contingency basis. **Specializes in the areas of:** Electronics; Engineering; Manufacturing; Technical. **Positions commonly filled include:** Chemical Engineer; Chemist; Environmental Engineer; Industrial Production Manager; Materials Engineer; Mechanical Engineer; Metallurgical Engineer. **Number of placements per year:** 1 - 49.

CIZEK ASSOCIATES INC.
2390 East Camelback Road, Suite 300, Phoenix AZ 85016. 602/553-1066. **Contact:** Research Director. **E-mail address:** cizekassoc@aol.com. **Description:** A generalist executive search firm operating on a retainer basis. Cizek Associates recruits only senior level executives. Client company pays fee. **NOTE:** This firm does not accept unsolicited resumes. Please respond only to advertised openings. **Specializes in the areas of:** Banking; Consumer Package Goods; Health/Medical; Manufacturing; Nonprofit; Technical. **Corporate headquarters location:** This Location. **Other U.S. locations:** Oak Brook IL. **Average salary range of placements:** More than $100,000.

COMPUTECH CORPORATION
4375 North 75th Street, Scottsdale AZ 85251. 480/947-7534. **Fax:** 480/947-7537. **Contact:** Bob Dirickson,

President. **Description:** An executive search firm. **Specializes in the areas of:** Computer Science/Software. **Positions commonly filled include:** Computer Programmer; Consultant; Software Engineer; Systems Analyst; Technical Writer/Editor. **Number of placements per year:** 100 - 199.

CONFIDENTIAL SEARCH INC.
1553 West Todd Drive, Suite 210, Tempe AZ 85283. 480/820-8663. **Fax:** 480/820-8709. **Contact:** Manager. **Description:** Confidential Search Inc. is an executive search firm.

CORPORATE DYNAMIX
6619 North Scottsdale Road, Scottsdale AZ 85250. 480/607-0040. **Fax:** 480/607-0054. **Contact:** Manager. **Description:** An executive search firm. **Specializes in the areas of:** High-Tech.

DHR INTERNATIONAL INC.
11811 North Tatum Boulevard, Suite 3031, Phoenix AZ 85028. 602/953-7810. **Contact:** Office Manager. **Description:** DHR International is an executive search firm.

THE DORFMAN GROUP
12005 East Mission Lane, Scottsdale AZ 85259. 480/860-8820. **Fax:** 480/860-0888. **Contact:** Mike Flamer, Vice President. **E-mail address:** dorfgrp@getnet.com. **World Wide Web address:** http://gn2.getnet.com/dorfman. **Description:** An executive search firm operating on both retainer and contingency bases. **Specializes in the areas of:** Engineering; Logistics; Materials; Packaging. **Positions commonly filled include:** Applications Engineer; Civil Engineer; Design Engineer; Electrical/Electronics Engineer; General Manager; Industrial Engineer; Logistics Manager; Manufacturing Engineer; Mechanical Engineer; Project Engineer; Project Manager; Sales Engineer; Sales Executive; Sales Representative; Software Engineer. **Average salary range of placements:** More than $50,000. **Number of placements per year:** 1 - 49.

EFL INTERNATIONAL
8777 East Via de Ventura, Suite 300, Scottsdale AZ 85258. 480/483-0496. **Fax:** 480/483-2832. **Contact:** Manager. **World Wide Web address:** http://www.eflinternational.com. **Description:** An executive search firm.

ELECTRONIC POWER SOURCE
1507 West Loughlin Drive, Chandler AZ 85224. 480/821-1946. **Fax:** 413/208-6859. **Contact:** Garry Moore, Owner. **Description:** An executive search firm specializing in analog design, power supplies, ballasts, magnetics, and other high-tech industries. Electronic Power Source operates on both retainer and contingency bases. Founded in 1985. **Specializes in the areas of:** Aerospace; Computer Science/Software; Engineering; Light Industrial. **Positions commonly filled include:** Aerospace Engineer; Applications Engineer; Buyer; Computer Programmer; Database Manager; Designer; Electrical/Electronics Engineer; Industrial Engineer; Manufacturing Engineer; Mechanical Engineer; Software Engineer. **Corporate headquarters location:** This Location. **Other U.S. locations:** Nationwide. **Average salary range of placements:** $30,000 - $50,000. **Number of placements per year:** 1 - 49.

EXECUTEMPS, INC.
7330 North 16th Street, Suite C117, Phoenix AZ 85020. 602/861-1200. **Contact:** Manager. **Description:** Executemps is an executive search firm. **Specializes in the areas of:** Food.

FISHEL HUMAN RESOURCES ASSOCIATES
5125 North 16th Street, Suite B-125, Phoenix AZ 85016. 602/266-5600. **Contact:** Richard A. Fishel, President. **Description:** Fishel Human Resources Associates is an executive search firm. **Specializes in the areas of:** Accounting/Auditing; Administration; Banking; General Management; Human Resources. **Positions commonly**

filled include: Accountant/Auditor; Administrative Manager; Bank Officer/Manager; Buyer; Computer Programmer; Human Resources Manager. **Number of placements per year:** 200 - 499.

FOODSTAFF 2000, INC.
6774 East Gelding Drive, Scottsdale AZ 85254. 480/607-9555. **Contact:** Manager. **World Wide Web address:** http://www.foodstaff2000.com. **Description:** Foodstaff 2000, Inc. is an executive search firm. **Specializes in the areas of:** Food. **Corporate headquarters location:** Franklin WI.

H&M RECRUITERS
P.O. Box 7496, Mesa AZ 85216. 480/357-1717. **Contact:** Recruiter. **Description:** H&M Recruiters is an executive search firm operating on a contingency basis. Founded in 1986. **Specializes in the areas of:** Chemicals; Engineering; Industrial; Manufacturing; Plastics; Rubber; Technical. **Positions commonly filled include:** Biochemist; Chemical Engineer; Chemist; Design Engineer; Industrial Engineer; Mechanical Engineer. **Average salary range of placements:** More than $50,000. **Number of placements per year:** 1 - 49.

ROBERT HALF INTERNATIONAL ACCOUNTEMPS
100 West Clarendon Avenue, Suite 1520, Phoenix AZ 85013. 602/264-6488. **Contact:** Branch Manager. **World Wide Web address:** http://www.roberthalf.com. **Description:** Robert Half International is an executive search firm. Accountemps (also at this location) provides temporary placements. **Specializes in the areas of:** Accounting/Auditing. **Corporate headquarters location:** Menlo Park CA. **Other U.S. locations:** Nationwide.

PHYLLIS HAWKINS & ASSOCIATES
5025 North Central, Suite 611, Phoenix AZ 85012. 602/263-0248. **Fax:** 602/678-1564. **Contact:** Office Manager. **Description:** Phyllis Hawkins & Associates is an executive search firm. **Specializes in the areas of:** Legal. **Positions commonly filled include:** Attorney. **Average salary range of placements:** More than $50,000. **Number of placements per year:** 1 - 49.

MANAGEMENT RECRUITERS INTERNATIONAL
6262 North Swan Road, Suite 125, Tucson AZ 85718-3600. 520/529-6818. **Fax:** 520/529-6877. **Contact:** Ms. Lorian E. Roethlein, President. **World Wide Web address:** http://www.mrihitech.com. **Description:** Management Recruiters International is an executive search firm. **Specializes in the areas of:** Computer Science/Software; Engineering; Manufacturing. **Positions commonly filled include:** Computer Programmer; Design Engineer; Electrical/Electronics Engineer; General Manager; Industrial Engineer; MIS Specialist; Software Engineer; Systems Analyst. **Corporate headquarters location:** Cleveland OH. **Other U.S. locations:** Nationwide. **International locations:** Worldwide. **Average salary range of placements:** More than $50,000. **Number of placements per year:** 1 - 49.

MANAGEMENT RECRUITERS OF SCOTTSDALE
6900 East Camelback Road, Suite 935, Scottsdale AZ 85251. 480/941-1515. **Fax:** 480/941-1430. **Contact:** Manager. **E-mail address:** resume@mriscottsdale.com. **World Wide Web address:** http://www.BrilliantPeople.com. **Description:** An executive search firm. **NOTE:** Resumes are only accepted when submitted by e-mail. **Specializes in the areas of:** Accounting/Auditing; Administration; Advertising; Architecture/Construction; Banking; Communications; Computer Hardware/Software; Electrical; Engineering; Finance; Food; General Management; Health/Medical; Insurance; Legal; Manufacturing; Personnel/Labor Relations; Procurement; Publishing; Real Estate; Sales; Technical; Textiles; Transportation. **Corporate headquarters location:**

Cleveland OH. **Other U.S. locations:** Nationwide. **International locations:** Worldwide.

MANAGEMENT RECRUITERS OF TUCSON
310 South Williams Boulevard, Suite 300, Tucson AZ 85711. 520/745-2270. **Fax:** 520/745-2820. **Contact:** Jack DeJong, Manager. **E-mail address:** careers@ mroftucson.com. **World Wide Web address:** http://www.mroftucson.com. **Description:** An executive search firm operating on both retainer and contingency bases. Client company pays fee. **Specializes in the areas of:** Engineering; Telecommunications. **Positions commonly filled include:** Design Engineer; Electrical/Electronics Engineer; Industrial Engineer; Manufacturing Engineer; Mechanical Engineer; Quality Assurance Engineer; Sales Engineer; Sales Executive; Sales Manager; Sales Representative. **Corporate headquarters location:** Cleveland OH. **Other U.S. locations:** Nationwide. **International locations:** Worldwide. **Average salary range of placements:** $50,000 - $100,000. **Number of placements per year:** 1 - 49.

MILLER & WIMER, LLC
11022 South 51st Street, Suite 101B, Phoenix AZ 85044. 602/496-4989. **Fax:** 602/496-8421. **Contact:** Manager. **Description:** An executive search firm.

OLSTEN FINANCIAL STAFFING
3550 North Central Avenue, Suite 1407, Phoenix AZ 85012. 602/287-8663. **Toll-free phone:** 888/222-8693. **Fax:** 602/266-4033. **Contact:** Jonathan Thom, Regional Vice President. **E-mail address:** ofs.phoenix@ olsten.com. **World Wide Web address:** http://www. olsten.com/ofs. **Description:** An executive search firm operating on a contingency basis. Olsten Financial Staffing also provides some temporary and permanent placements. **Specializes in the areas of:** Accounting; Banking; Finance. **Positions commonly filled include:** Accountant; Auditor; Budget Analyst; Chief Financial Officer; Controller; Credit Manager; Finance Director; Financial Analyst. **Corporate headquarters location:** Melville NY. **Other U.S. locations:** Nationwide. **Average salary range of placements:** $50,000 - $100,000. **Number of placements per year:** 200 - 499.

PEARSON & ASSOCIATES, INC.
7400 East McDonald Drive, Suite 121, Scottsdale AZ 85250. 602/953-9783. **Fax:** 602/996-1261. **Contact:** Bill Haugen, Director of Health Care. **E-mail address:** contact@pearson-assoc.com. **World Wide Web address:** http://www.pearson-assoc.com. **Description:** An executive search firm operating on both retainer and contingency bases. Pearson & Associates specializes in the nationwide recruitment and placement of management professionals in a variety of health care settings. **Specializes in the areas of:** Health/Medical. **Positions commonly filled include:** Administrative Manager; Branch Manager; Chief Financial Officer; Controller; Dietician/Nutritionist; Finance Director; General Manager; Human Resources Manager; Medical Records Technician; Nuclear Medicine Technologist; Nurse Practitioner; Occupational Therapist; Operations Manager; Pharmacist; Physical Therapist; Physician Assistant; Radiological Technologist; Registered Nurse; Respiratory Therapist; Social Worker; Speech-Language Pathologist. **Corporate headquarters location:** This Location. **Average salary range of placements:** More than $50,000. **Number of placements per year:** 100 - 199.

PROFESSIONAL PLACEMENT INC.
3900 East Camelback Road, Suite 500, Phoenix AZ 85018. 602/955-0870. **Contact:** Jeff Seifert, Manager. **World Wide Web address:** http://www.proplacement. com. **Description:** An executive search firm.

PROFESSIONAL SEARCH
7434 East Stetson Drive, Suite 144, Scottsdale AZ 85251. 480/994-4400. **Contact:** Chris Siller, Office Administrator. **Description:** An executive search firm for professionals with AS/400, PC client/server

mainframe experience. **Specializes in** Computer Science/Software. **Positions co** **include:** Computer Programmer; Syste Systems Manager. **Number of placements** 100 - 199.

ROMAC INTERNATIONAL
5343 North 16th Street, Suite 270, Phoenix AZ 602/230-0220. **Fax:** 602/248-4204. **Contact:** Man. **Description:** An executive search firm. **Specializes** **the areas of:** Accounting/Auditing; Comput Hardware/Software; Information Technology.

SALES CONSULTANTS
12005 North Panorama Drive, Suite 102, Fountain Hills AZ 85268. 480/816-4526. **Fax:** 480/816-4973. **Contact:** Manager. **Description:** An executive search firm. **Specializes in the areas of:** Computer Science/Software; Health/Medical; Medical Technology; Publishing; Sales. **Positions commonly filled include:** Branch Manager; General Manager; Health Services Manager; Product Manager; Sales Manager; Sales Representative; Services Sales Representative. **Number of placements per year:** 50 - 99.

SAXON ASSOCIATES
13430 North Scottsdale Road, Suite 203, Scottsdale AZ 85254. 480/991-4460. **Fax:** 480/991-2006. **Contact:** Manager. **E-mail address:** admin@saxonassoc.com. **World Wide Web address:** http://www.saxonassoc. com. **Description:** An executive search firm. **Specializes in the areas of:** Human Resources; Information Systems; Sales; Secretarial.

SUSAN SCHULTZ & ASSOCIATES
4350 East Camelback Road, Suite B-200, Phoenix AZ 85018. 480/998-1744. **Contact:** Susan Schultz, President. **Description:** An executive search firm. **Number of placements per year:** 1 - 49.

SEARCH MASTERS INTERNATIONAL
500 Foothills South, Suite 2, Sedona AZ 86336. 520/282-3553. **Fax:** 520/282-5881. **Contact:** Office Manager. **Description:** An executive search firm. **Specializes in the areas of:** Biotechnology; Pharmaceuticals.

SEARCHAMERICA INC.
459 North Gilbert Road, Suite B-140, Gilbert AZ 85234. 480/632-8452. **Contact:** Manager. **World Wide Web address:** http://www.searchamerica.net. **Description:** An executive search firm. **Specializes in the areas of:** Computer Science/Software; Engineering; Information Technology. **Positions commonly filled include:** Applications Engineer; Biomedical Engineer; Chemical Engineer; Civil Engineer; Computer Programmer; Database Manager; Design Engineer; Electrical/ Electronics Engineer; Human Resources Manager; Industrial Engineer; Industrial Production Manager; Internet Services Manager; Manufacturing Engineer; Mechanical Engineer; Operations Manager; Production Manager; Project Manager; Sales Engineer; Software Engineer; Systems Analyst. **Average salary range of placements:** More than $50,000. **Number of placements per year:** 50 - 99.

SOUTHWEST SEARCH AND CONSULTING
4500 South Lakeshore Drive, Suite 520, Tempe AZ 85282. 480/838-0333. **Fax:** 480/838-0368. **Contact:** Manager. **Description:** An executive search firm. **Specializes in the areas of:** Information Systems.

SPECTRA INTERNATIONAL
3200 North Hayden, Suite 210, Scottsdale AZ 85251. 480/481-0411. **Fax:** 480/481-0525. **Contact:** Sybil Goldberg, CEO/President. **Description:** An executive search firm that also provides contract and temporary placements. **Specializes in the areas of:** Accounting/ Auditing; Administration; Computer Science/Software; Engineering; Finance; General Management; Manufacturing; Personnel/Labor Relations; Retail; Sales; Technical; Transportation. **Positions commonly filled include:** Accountant/Auditor; Administrative Manager;

lue-Collar Worker Supervisor; Branch Manager; Budget Analyst; Buyer; Clerical Supervisor; Computer Programmer; Customer Service Representative; Electrical/Electronics Engineer; General Manager; Human Resources Manager; Network Engineer; Operations/Production Manager; Purchasing Agent/ Manager; Quality Control Supervisor; Retail Manager; Software Engineer. **Number of placements per year:** 200 - 499.

STAFF ONE SEARCH
2800 North 44th Street, Suite 340, Phoenix AZ 85008. 602/952-9060. **Contact:** William French, Office Administrator. **Description:** An executive search firm that also provides some temporary placements. **Specializes in the areas of:** Accounting/Auditing; Sales; Secretarial. **Positions commonly filled include:** Accountant/Auditor; Construction Contractor; Customer Service Representative; Human Resources Specialist; Restaurant/Food Service Manager; Services Sales Representative; Travel Agent; Typist/Word Processor.

STAFFMARK
3140 North 35th Avenue, Phoenix AZ 85017. 602/957-4799. **Contact:** Manager. **Description:** An executive search firm.

MARJORIE STARR & ASSOCIATES
2266 South Dobson Road, Suite 273, Mesa AZ 85202. 480/730-6050. **Contact:** Marjorie Starr, Owner. **E-mail address:** mstarr273@aol.com. **Description:** An executive search firm. **Specializes in the areas of:** Health/Medical; Industrial Sales and Marketing; Medical Sales and Marketing; Sales. **Positions commonly filled include:** Account Manager; Account Representative; Database Manager; Electrical/Electronics Engineer; Health Services Manager; Home Health Aide; Internet Services Manager; Manufacturer's/Wholesaler's Sales Rep.; Occupational Therapist; Pharmacist; Physical Therapist; Respiratory Therapist; Sales Representative; Services Sales Representative; Telecommunications Manager. **Average salary range of placements:** $30,000 - $50,000.

TSS CONSULTING, LTD.
2525 East Camelback Road, Suite 560, Phoenix AZ 85016. 602/955-7000. **Toll-free phone:** 800/489-2425. **Fax:** 602/957-3948. **Contact:** Recruiter. **Description:** An executive search firm. **Specializes in the areas of:** Aerospace; Chemicals; Computer Science/Software; Electronics; Engineering; High-Tech; Information Technology; Telecommunications. **Positions commonly filled include:** Electrical/Electronics Engineer; MIS Manager; Software Engineer; Telecommunications Manager. **Number of placements per year:** 1 - 49.

TELE-SOLUTION SEARCH
8655 East Via De Ventura, Suite F-127, Scottsdale AZ 85258. 480/483-1300. **Fax:** 480/483-7221. **Contact:**

Carole Wichansky, Manager. **Description:** An executive search firm. **NOTE:** Technical backgrounds, particularly in UNIX and Windows NT applications, are preferred. **Specializes in the areas of:** Computer Hardware/ Software; Engineering; Telecommunications. **Positions commonly filled include:** Software Engineer; Telecommunications Manager. **Average salary range of placements:** More than $50,000. **Number of placements per year:** 50 - 99.

TORRANCE RECRUITING, INC.
P.O. Box 1984, Scottsdale AZ 85252. 480/946-9024. **Contact:** Matthew Torrance, Manager. **Description:** An executive search firm. **Specializes in the areas of:** Publishing. **Positions commonly filled include:** Chief Financial Officer; Cost Estimator; Engineer; General Manager; Production Manager; Quality Control Supervisor; Sales and Marketing Manager. **Average salary range of placements:** More than $50,000. **Number of placements per year:** 1 - 49.

WSA ASSOCIATES
2361 Hyde Park Boulevard, Lake Havasu City AZ 86404. 520/764-2200. **Fax:** 800/489-9192. **Contact:** Jeff Stone, General Manager. **E-mail address:** lhcstone@ interworldnet.net. **Description:** An executive search firm operating on both retainer and contingency bases. **Specializes in the areas of:** Restaurant. **Positions commonly filled include:** Hotel Manager; Human Resources Manager; Restaurant/Food Service Manager. **Average salary range of placements:** $30,000 - $50,000. **Number of placements per year:** 100 - 199.

WEINMAN & ASSOCIATES
7110 East McDonald Drive, Suite B-6, Scottsdale AZ 85253. **Fax:** 480/922-9248. **Contact:** Mary Weinman, President. **Description:** An executive search firm. Founded in 1993. **Specializes in the areas of:** Food; Hotel/Restaurant; Manufacturing; MIS/EDP; Personnel/ Labor Relations. **Positions commonly filled include:** Computer Programmer; Hotel Manager; Human Resources Specialist; Purchasing Agent/Manager; Restaurant/Food Service Manager. **Average salary range of placements:** More than $50,000. **Number of placements per year:** 1 - 49.

WITT/KIEFFER, FORD, HADELMAN & LLOYD
432 North 44th Street, Suite 360, Phoenix AZ 85008. 602/267-1370. **Fax:** 602/244-2722. **Contact:** Michelle Meyer, Senior Vice President. **World Wide Web address:** http://www.wittkieffer.com. **Description:** An executive search firm. Client company pays fee. **Specializes in the areas of:** Health/Medical. **Corporate headquarters location:** Oak Brook IL. **Other U.S. locations:** Nationwide. **Average salary range of placements:** More than $100,000. **Number of placements per year:** 200 - 499.

PERMANENT EMPLOYMENT AGENCIES

ACCUSTAFF INCORPORATED
7840 East Broadway, Suite 100, Tucson AZ 85710. 520/751-8775. **Contact:** Manager. **Description:** A permanent employment agency. **Specializes in the areas of:** Administration; Banking. **Positions commonly filled include:** Accountant/Auditor; Administrator; Clerk; Management; Secretary; Typist/Word Processor.

ACCUSTAFF INCORPORATED
1400 East Southern Avenue, Suite 345, Tempe AZ 85202. 480/345-2633. **Fax:** 480/345-2613. **Contact:** Manager. **Description:** A permanent employment agency. **Specializes in the areas of:** Accounting/ Auditing; Data Processing; Finance.

ARIZONA MEDICAL EXCHANGE
777 East Missouri Avenue, Suite 207, Phoenix AZ 85014. 602/246-4906. **Contact:** Manager. **Description:**

A permanent employment agency. **Specializes in the areas of:** Health/Medical. **Positions commonly filled include:** Claim Representative; Clinical Lab Technician; Credit Manager; Customer Service Representative; EEG Technologist; EKG Technician; Health Services Manager; Licensed Practical Nurse; Medical Records Technician; Physical Therapist; Registered Nurse; Respiratory Therapist; Surgical Technician. **Number of placements per year:** 100 - 199.

CLIFFORD & ASSOCIATES
16042 North 32nd Street, Suite D-14, Phoenix AZ 85032. 602/992-1477. **Fax:** 602/992-7017. **Contact:** Dennis Clifford, Owner. **Description:** A permanent employment agency. Founded in 1992. **Specializes in the areas of:** Automotive; Finance; Personnel/Labor Relations; Retail; Sales; Secretarial; Transportation. **Positions commonly filled include:** Accountant/Auditor;

Administrative Manager; Automotive Mechanic; Blue-Collar Worker Supervisor; Credit Manager; Services Sales Representative. **Average salary range of placements:** $30,000 - $50,000. **Number of placements per year:** 50 - 99.

COMPUTER STRATEGIES, INC.
5620 North Kolb Road, Suite 225, Tucson AZ 85750. 520/577-7117. **Contact:** Manager. **Description:** A permanent employment agency. **Specializes in the areas of:** Data Processing.

CONSTRUCTION SECRETARIES
1250 East Baseline Road, Suite 104, Tempe AZ 85283. 480/345-1282. **Contact:** Susan Sabato, President. **Description:** A permanent employment agency. **Specializes in the areas of:** Accounting/Auditing; Administration; General Management; Legal; Personnel/Labor Relations; Secretarial. **Positions commonly filled include:** Accountant/Auditor; Administrative Manager; Branch Manager; Clerical Supervisor; Construction Contractor; Credit Manager; Customer Service Representative; General Manager; Human Resources Specialist; Management Analyst/Consultant; Operations/Production Manager; Purchasing Agent/Manager; Typist/Word Processor; Underwriter/Assistant Underwriter. **Corporate headquarters location:** This Location. **Average salary range of placements:** Less than $20,000. **Number of placements per year:** 500 - 999.

DEALER CONNECTION
7500 East Butherus Drive, Suite Q, Scottsdale AZ 85260. 480/607-6996. **Fax:** 800/252-3947. **Contact:** Ivan L. Sells, President/CEO. **E-mail address:** dealerc@dancris.com. **Description:** A permanent employment agency. Dealer Connection specializes in providing placements to auto dealers, auto manufacturers, and the heavy-duty truck industry. Founded in 1992. **Specializes in the areas of:** Automotive; General Management; Personnel/Labor Relations; Retail; Transportation. **Positions commonly filled include:** Accountant/Auditor; Administrative Manager; Automotive Mechanic; Claim Representative; Clerical Supervisor; Cost Estimator; Customer Service Rep.; General Manager; Management Analyst/Consultant; Manufacturer's/Wholesaler's Sales Rep.; Public Relations Specialist; Quality Control Supervisor; Services Sales Representative; Transportation/Traffic Specialist. **Corporate headquarters location:** This Location. **Other U.S. locations:** Kansas City MO. **Average salary range of placements:** More than $50,000. **Number of placements per year:** 50 - 99.

GENERAL EMPLOYMENT ENTERPRISES, INC.
100 West Clarendon Avenue, Suite 1700, Phoenix AZ 85013. 602/265-7800. **Fax:** 602/265-1779. **Contact:** Manager. **Description:** A permanent employment agency. **Specializes in the areas of:** Computer Science/Software; Engineering; Manufacturing; Technical. **Positions commonly filled include:** Aerospace Engineer; Biochemist; Biomedical Engineer; Chemical Engineer; Chemist; Civil Engineer; Computer Programmer; Designer; Draftsperson; Electrical/Electronics Engineer; Geologist/Geophysicist; Industrial Engineer; Internet Services Manager; Mechanical Engineer; Metallurgical Engineer; MIS Specialist; Operations/Production Manager; Quality Control Supervisor; Software Engineer; Structural Engineer; Systems Analyst; Technical Writer/Editor; Telecommunications Manager. **Corporate headquarters location:** Oakbrook Terrace IL. **Other U.S. locations:** Nationwide. **Average salary range of placements:** $30,000 - $50,000. **Number of placements per year:** 100 - 199.

HUMAN RESOURCE NETWORK, INC.
6045 North Scottsdale Road, Suite 108, Scottsdale AZ 85250. 480/948-1991. **Fax:** 480/948-1667. **Contact:** Diana L. Doss, President. **E-mail address:** staffing@hrminc.com. **World Wide Web address:** http://www.hrminc.com. **Description:** A permanent employment agency that also provides some temporary placements.

Founded in 1987. **Specializes in the areas of:** Health/Medical. **Positions commonly filled include:** Licensed Practical Nurse; Medical Assistant; Radiological Technologist; Registered Nurse; Typist/Word Processor. **Benefits available to temporary workers:** Dental Insurance; Medical Insurance; Paid Holidays; Referral Bonus Plan; Vision Insurance. **Corporate headquarters location:** This Location. **Other area locations:** Tucson AZ. **Average salary range of placements:** $20,000 - $29,999. **Number of placements per year:** 200 - 499.

HUMAN RESOURCE NETWORK, INC.
6369 East Tangue Verde, Suite 180, Tucson AZ 85715. 520/722-8227. **Fax:** 520/722-8188. **Contact:** Manager. **E-mail address:** staffing@hrminc.com. **World Wide Web address:** http://www.hrminc.com. **Description:** A permanent employment agency that also provides some temporary placements. Founded in 1987. **Specializes in the areas of:** Health/Medical. **Corporate headquarters location:** Scottsdale AZ.

HUNTER TECHNICAL SERVICES
1232 East Broadway Road, Suite 202, Tempe AZ 85282. 480/966-7000. **Contact:** Manager. **Description:** A permanent employment agency that also provides some temporary placements. **Specializes in the areas of:** Computer Hardware/Software; Technical. **Positions commonly filled include:** Mechanical Engineer.

KERRY'S REFERRALS
11225 North 28th Drive, Suite B-201, Phoenix AZ 85029-5613. 602/548-8777. **Fax:** 602/548-9453. **Contact:** Linda Watrons, Vice President. **E-mail address:** kerrysref@msn.com. **Description:** Kerry's Referrals is a permanent employment agency that also provides some temporary placements. Founded in 1985. Client company pays fee. **Specializes in the areas of:** Administration; General Management; Insurance; Legal; Personnel/Labor Relations; Secretarial. **Positions commonly filled include:** Accountant; Administrative Assistant; Administrative Manager; Assistant Manager; Attorney; Branch Manager; Claim Representative; Clerical Supervisor; Computer Operator; Customer Service Representative; Human Resources Manager; MIS Specialist; Network/Systems Administrator; Paralegal; Secretary; Typist/Word Processor. **Average salary range of placements:** $30,000 - $49,999. **Number of placements per year:** 1000+.

LDS EMPLOYMENT CENTER
4333 North Central Avenue, Phoenix AZ 85012. 602/241-9444. **Fax:** 602/234-3613. **Contact:** Frank Bailey, Employment Coordinator. **Description:** A permanent employment agency. The LDS Employment Center is a nonprofit endeavor operated by full-time missionaries for the Latter-Day-Saints Church. There is no fee to jobseekers or employers.

McEVOY & JOHNSON ASSOCIATES, INC.
10535 North 96th Place, Scottsdale AZ 85258. 480/661-9422. **Fax:** 480/661-6932. **Contact:** Donna Johnson, President. **E-mail address:** mjassoc@primenet.com. **Description:** A permanent employment agency. Client company pays fee. **Specializes in the areas of:** Information Technology. **Positions commonly filled include:** AS400 Programmer Analyst; Computer Programmer; Computer Support Technician; Database Administrator; Database Manager; MIS Specialist; Network/Systems Administrator; SQL Programmer; Systems Analyst; Systems Manager. **Corporate headquarters location:** This Location. **Average salary range of placements:** $50,000 - $100,000. **Number of placements per year:** 50 - 99.

PRIORITY STAFFING, INC.
7850 South Hardy Drive, Suite 112, Tempe AZ 85282. 480/491-2191. **Fax:** 480/491-5702. **Contact:** Jill Zahn, Director of Recruiting. **E-mail address:** mail@prioritystaffing.com. **World Wide Web address:** http://www.prioritystaffing.com. **Description:** Priority Staffing is a permanent employment agency that also

provides some temporary placements. Founded in 1993. **Specializes in the areas of:** Clerical; Technical. **Positions commonly filled include:** Account Manager; Account Representative; Accountant; Adjuster; Administrative Assistant; Administrative Manager; Applications Engineer; Architect; Auditor; Bank Officer/Manager; Blue-Collar Worker Supervisor; Buyer; Chemical Engineer; Chemist; Civil Engineer; Claim Representative; Clerical Supervisor; Customer Service Representative; Database Manager; Electrical/Electronics Engineer; Electrician; Graphic Artist; Human Resources Manager; Industrial Engineer; Internet Services Manager; Librarian; Management Trainee; Purchasing Agent/Manager; Sales Executive; Sales Manager; Sales Representative; Secretary; Software Engineer; Systems Analyst; Systems Manager; Technical Writer/Editor; Telecommunications Manager; Typist/Word Processor. **Benefits available to temporary workers:** Bonus Award/Plan; Health Benefits; Paid Holidays; Paid Vacation. **Corporate headquarters location:** This Location. **Other U.S. locations:** Las Vegas NV. **Average salary range of placements:** $20,000 - $29,999. **Number of placements per year:** 1000+.

SNELLING PERSONNEL SERVICES
310 South Williams Boulevard, Suite 255, Tucson AZ 85711. **Fax:** 520/790-3901. **Contact:** Recruiter. **Description:** A permanent employment agency that also

provides some temporary and contract placements. **Specializes in the areas of:** Accounting/Auditing; Administration; Computer Science/Software; Engineering; Sales; Secretarial; Technical. **Positions commonly filled include:** Accountant/Auditor; Ceramics Engineer; Industrial Engineer; Materials Engineer; Metallurgical Engineer; Mining Engineer; Technical Writer/Editor; Typist/Word Processor. **Benefits available to temporary workers:** Medical Insurance; Paid Holidays; Paid Vacation. **Average salary range of placements:** $20,000 - $29,999.

TECH/AID OF ARIZONA
1438 West Broadway, Suite B-225, Tempe AZ 85282. 480/894-6161. **Contact:** Manager. **Description:** A permanent employment agency. **Specializes in the areas of:** Architecture/Construction; Cable TV; Computer Hardware/Software; Construction; Engineering; Manufacturing; Technical. **Positions commonly filled include:** Aerospace Engineer; Architect; Buyer; Ceramics Engineer; Draftsperson; Electrical/Electronics Engineer; Estimator; Factory Worker; Industrial Engineer; Mechanical Engineer; Metallurgical Engineer; Mining Engineer; Operations/Production Manager; Petroleum Engineer; Purchasing Agent/Manager; Quality Control Supervisor; Technical Writer/Editor; Technician. **Number of placements per year:** 1000+.

TEMPORARY EMPLOYMENT AGENCIES

ACCOUNTANTS INC.
1400 East Southern Avenue, Suite 910, Tempe AZ 85282. 480/730-1110. **Fax:** 480/730-1123. **Contact:** Manager. **E-mail address:** tempe@accountantsinc.com. **World Wide Web address:** http://www.accountantsinc.com. **Description:** A temporary employment agency that also offers some permanent placements. **Specializes in the areas of:** Accounting; Finance. **Corporate headquarters location:** Burlingame CA. **Other U.S. locations:** Nationwide.

ACCUSTAFF INCORPORATED
4747 North Seventh Street, Suite 140, Phoenix AZ 85014. 602/200-3910. **Contact:** Branch Manager. **Description:** A temporary agency that also provides some temp-to-perm placements. **Specializes in the areas of:** Accounting/Auditing; Banking; Personnel/Labor Relations; Secretarial. **Positions commonly filled include:** Accountant/Auditor; Clerical Supervisor; Cost Estimator; Credit Manager; Customer Service Rep.; Human Resources Specialist; Management Trainee; Paralegal; Services Sales Representative; Technical Writer/Editor; Typist/Word Processor. **Average salary range of placements:** $20,000 - $29,999. **Number of placements per year:** 500 - 999.

ADECCO
931 East Southern Avenue, Suite 207, Mesa AZ 85204. 480/497-2260. **Contact:** Technical Recruiter. **Description:** A temporary agency. **Specializes in the areas of:** Art/Design; Computer Science/Software; Engineering. **Positions commonly filled include:** Aerospace Engineer; Architect; Computer Programmer; Designer; Draftsperson; Electrical/Electronics Engineer; Industrial Engineer; Mechanical Engineer; Metallurgical Engineer; Quality Control Supervisor; Sales Representative; Systems Analyst; Technical Writer/Editor.

ADECCO
333 East Osborn, Suite 370, Phoenix AZ 85012. 602/246-1143. **Contact:** Manager. **Description:** A temporary agency. **Specializes in the areas of:** Clerical; Legal; Manufacturing; Personnel/Labor Relations; Publishing. **Positions commonly filled include:** Administrative Assistant; Bookkeeper; Clerk; Computer Operator; Computer Programmer; Construction Trade Worker; Customer Service Representative; Human Resources Manager; Legal Secretary; Light Industrial

Worker; Quality Control Supervisor; Receptionist; Sales Representative; Secretary; Typist/Word Processor. **Number of placements per year:** 1000+.

ADECCO/TAD TECHNICAL SERVICES
411 North Central Avenue, Suite 720, Phoenix AZ 85004. 602/267-7254. **Fax:** 602/256-7586. **Contact:** Manager. **Description:** A temporary agency. Founded in 1956. **Specializes in the areas of:** Architecture/Construction; Computer Science/Software; Engineering; Industrial; Manufacturing; Personnel/Labor Relations; Technical. **Positions commonly filled include:** Aerospace Engineer; Aircraft Mechanic/Engine Specialist; Architect; Blue-Collar Worker Supervisor; Branch Manager; Budget Analyst; Buyer; Chemical Engineer; Civil Engineer; Computer Programmer; Construction Contractor; Design Engineer; Designer; Editor; Electrical/Electronics Engineer; Environmental Engineer; Human Resources Specialist; Industrial Engineer; Industrial Production Manager; Landscape Architect; Mechanical Engineer; Mining Engineer; MIS Specialist; Operations/Production Manager; Petroleum Engineer; Purchasing Agent/Manager; Quality Control Supervisor; Science Technologist; Software Engineer; Structural Engineer; Systems Analyst; Technical Writer/Editor; Telecommunications Manager. **Benefits available to temporary workers:** 401(k); Medical Insurance; Paid Holidays; Paid Vacation. **Other U.S. locations:** Nationwide. **International locations:** Worldwide. **Average salary range of placements:** $30,000 - $50,000. **Number of placements per year:** 1000+.

AQUENT PARTNERS
2525 East Camelback Road, Suite 265, Phoenix AZ 85016. 602/957-1100. **Toll-free phone:** 877/PARTNER. **Fax:** 602/957-9200. **Contact:** Rudy Munoz, Office Manager Recruiter. **World Wide Web address:** http://www.aquent.com. **Description:** A temporary agency that provides placements for creative, Web, and technical professionals. Aquent Partners also provides some temp-to-perm, permanent, and contract placements. **Specializes in the areas of:** Administration; Art/Design; Computer Science/Software; Marketing. **Positions commonly filled include:** Computer Animator; Computer Engineer; Computer Operator; Computer Programmer; Computer Support Technician; Computer Technician; Content Developer; Database Administrator; Database Manager; Desktop Publishing Specialist;

Editor; Editorial Assistant; Graphic Artist; Graphic Designer; Internet Services Manager; Managing Editor; MIS Specialist; Multimedia Designer; Network/Systems Administrator; Production Manager; Project Manager; Software Engineer; SQL Programmer; Systems Analyst; Systems Manager; Technical Writer/Editor; Webmaster. **Benefits available to temporary workers:** 401(k); Dental Insurance; Disability Coverage; Medical Insurance. **CEO:** John Chuang.

DEVAU HUMAN RESOURCES
2131 East Broadway, Suite 34, Tempe AZ 85282. 480/921-3688. **Fax:** 480/968-2396. **Contact:** Terry Wilkey, President. **Description:** A temporary agency that also provides some temp-to-perm placements. Founded in 1984. **Specializes in the areas of:** Accounting/Auditing; Administration; Clerical; Industrial; Light Industrial; Manufacturing; Retail; Secretarial; Technical. **Average salary range of placements:** Less than $20,000. **Number of placements per year:** 500 - 999.

EAI HEALTHCARE STAFFING SOLUTIONS
3800 North Central Avenue, Suite 800, Phoenix AZ 85012. 602/266-7400. **Toll-free phone:** 800/736-8066. **Fax:** 602/266-7020. **Contact:** Ellen B. Echales, President. **World Wide Web address:** http://www.eai-healthcare.com. **Description:** A temporary agency that also provides some temp-to-perm placements. Founded in 1986. **Specializes in the areas of:** Health/Medical. **Positions commonly filled include:** Administrative Assistant; Biomedical Engineer; Certified Nurses Aide; Clerical Supervisor; Clinical Lab Technician; Computer Programmer; Customer Service Representative; EEG Technologist; EKG Technician; Licensed Practical Nurse; Medical Records Technician; Nuclear Medicine Technologist; Occupational Therapist; Pharmacist; Physical Therapist; Radiological Technologist; Registered Nurse; Respiratory Therapist; Secretary; Software Engineer; Surgical Technician; Typist/Word Processor. **Corporate headquarters location:** This Location. **Other U.S. locations:** Tucson AZ; San Diego CA; Chicago IL; Las Vegas NV; Nashville TN; Dallas TX; Fort Worth TX; Houston TX; San Antonio TX; Seattle WA. **Average salary range of placements:** $20,000 - $29,999. **Number of placements per year:** 100 - 199.

FAVORITE NURSES INC.
727 East Bethany Home Road, Suite A-104, Phoenix AZ 85014. 602/265-7440. **Contact:** Manager. **Description:** A temporary agency. **Specializes in the areas of:** Health/Medical. **Positions commonly filled include:** Nurse.

INSURANCE SUPPORT SERVICES
207 West Southern Avenue, Tempe AZ 85282. 480/967-3075. **Contact:** President. **Description:** A temporary agency that also provides some contract services, primarily to property and casualty insurance agents. Founded in 1992. **Specializes in the areas of:** Insurance; Secretarial. **Positions commonly filled include:** Customer Service Representative. **Number of placements per year:** 1 - 49.

MANPOWER TECHNICAL SERVICES
645 East Missouri Avenue, Suite 260, Phoenix AZ 85012. 602/264-0871. **Contact:** Branch Manager. **Description:** A temporary agency. **Specializes in the areas of:** Data Processing; Industrial; Office Support; Word Processing. **Positions commonly filled include:** Accountant/Auditor; Accounting Clerk; Administrative Assistant; Assembler; Biological Scientist; Bookkeeper; Chemist; Computer Operator; Customer Service Representative; Designer; Desktop Publishing Specialist; Electrical/Electronics Engineer; Inspector/Tester/Grader; Inventory Control Specialist; Machine Operator; Order Clerk; Packaging/Processing Worker; Project Engineer; Proofreader; Receptionist; Records Manager; Research Assistant; Secretary; Software Engineer; Stenographer; Systems Analyst; Technical Writer/Editor; Technician; Telemarketer; Typist/Word Processor. **Benefits available**

to **temporary workers:** Life Insurance; Medical Insurance; Paid Holidays; Paid Vacation. **Corporate headquarters location:** Milwaukee WI. **Other U.S. locations:** Nationwide. **Number of placements per year:** 1000+.

NORRELL INTERIM SERVICES
3923 South McClintock, Suite 404, Tempe AZ 85282. 480/831-0064. **Contact:** Branch Manager. **Description:** A temporary agency. **Specializes in the areas of:** Clerical; Construction; Manufacturing; Sales. **Positions commonly filled include:** Administrative Assistant; Clerk; Computer Operator; Construction Trade Worker; Customer Service Representative; Data Entry Clerk; Draftsperson; Driver; Factory Worker; Legal Secretary; Light Industrial Worker; Receptionist. **Corporate headquarters location:** Atlanta GA. **Number of placements per year:** 500 - 999.

RETIREE SKILLS INC.
1475 West Prince Road, Tucson AZ 85705. 520/888-8310. **Contact:** Manager. **Description:** A temporary agency. **Specializes in the areas of:** Accounting/Auditing; Engineering; Secretarial. **Positions commonly filled include:** Accountant/Auditor; Civil Engineer; Computer Programmer; Design Engineer; Electrical/Electronics Engineer; Industrial Engineer; Mechanical Engineer; Purchasing Agent/Manager; Technical Writer/Editor; Typist/Word Processor. **Corporate headquarters location:** This Location. **Average salary range of placements:** Less than $20,000. **Number of placements per year:** 100 - 199.

STIVERS TEMPORARY PERSONNEL, INC.
1717 West Northern Avenue, Suite 117, Phoenix AZ 85021. 602/264-4580. **Fax:** 602/678-0771. **Contact:** Manager. **Description:** A temporary agency. **Specializes in the areas of:** Accounting/Auditing; Administration; Advertising; Banking; Broadcasting; Computer Science/Software; Engineering; Finance; Health/Medical; Industrial; Insurance; Legal; Manufacturing; Nonprofit; Personnel/Labor Relations; Publishing; Retail; Sales; Secretarial; Technical. **Positions commonly filled include:** Accountant/Auditor; Administrative Assistant; Administrative Manager; Advertising Clerk; Brokerage Clerk; Budget Analyst; Claim Representative; Clerical Supervisor; Computer Operator; Computer Programmer; Credit Manager; Customer Service Representative; Database Manager; Graphic Artist; Graphic Designer; Human Resources Specialist; Insurance Agent/Broker; Management Trainee; Market Research Analyst; Marketing Specialist; Medical Records Technician; Paralegal; Property and Real Estate Manager; Purchasing Agent/Manager; Quality Control Supervisor; Secretary; Statistician; Surveyor; Technical Writer/Editor; Typist/Word Processor; Underwriter/Assistant Underwriter. **Benefits available to temporary workers:** Dental Insurance; Medical Insurance; Paid Vacation; Vision Plan. **Corporate headquarters location:** Chicago IL. **Other U.S. locations:** Nationwide. **Average salary range of placements:** Less than $20,000. **Number of placements per year:** 1000+.

TAYLOR DESIGN RECRUITING
6155 East Indian School Road, Suite 100B, Scottsdale AZ 85251. 480/423-5056. **Fax:** 480/423-8595. **Contact:** Steve Tweito, Operations Manager. **E-mail address:** stweito@taylordesign.net. **World Wide Web address:** http://www.taylordesign.net. **Description:** A temporary agency that also provides some permanent placements. Founded in 1990. Client company pays fee. **Specializes in the areas of:** Advertising; Architecture/Construction; Art/Design; Computer Science/Software; Engineering; Internet Development; Internet Marketing; Marketing; Printing; Publishing; Sales; Transportation. **Positions commonly filled include:** Administrative Assistant; Advertising Clerk; Advertising Executive; Architect; Civil Engineer; Computer Animator; Computer Engineer; Computer Operator; Computer Programmer; Computer Support Technician; Computer Technician; Content Developer; Database Administrator; Database Manager; Design Engineer; Desktop Publishing Specialist;

Draftsperson; Editor; Editorial Assistant; Electrical/ Electronics Engineer; Environmental Engineer; Graphic Artist; Graphic Designer; Internet Services Manager; Marketing Manager; Marketing Specialist; Mechanical Engineer; MIS Specialist; Multimedia Designer; Network/Systems Administrator; Operations Manager; Production Manager; Project Manager; Quality Control Supervisor; Systems Manager; Technical Writer/Editor; Telecommunications Manager; Transportation/Traffic Specialist; Webmaster. **Benefits available to temporary workers:** Dental Insurance; Medical Insurance. **Corporate headquarters location:** This Location. **Other U.S. locations:** Los Angeles CA. **Average salary range of placements:** $20,000 - $100,000. **Number of placements per year:** 200 - 499.

CONTRACT SERVICES FIRMS

ANDREWS, STEVENS & ASSOCIATES
4110 North Scottsdale Road, Suite 115, Scottsdale AZ 85251. 480/970-9962. **Contact:** Managing Director. **Description:** A contract services firm. **Specializes in the areas of:** Accounting/Auditing; Administration; Economics; General Management; Legal; Manufacturing; Sales. **Positions commonly filled include:** Accountant/Auditor; Administrative Assistant; Attorney; Bank Officer/Manager; Branch Manager; Financial Analyst; Hotel Manager; Operations/ Production Manager. **Corporate headquarters location:** Phoenix AZ. **Average salary range of placements:** More than $50,000. **Number of placements per year:** 100 - 199.

CDI CORPORATION
2800 North 44th Street, Suite 700, Phoenix AZ 85008. 602/508-6402. **Toll-free phone:** 800/878-9686. **Fax:** 602/508-9200. **Contact:** Recruiter. **World Wide Web address:** http://www.cdicorp.com. **Description:** A contract services firm. **Specializes in the areas of:** Administration; Computer Science/Software; Engineering; Industrial; Manufacturing; Technical. **Positions commonly filled include:** Accountant/Auditor; Aerospace Engineer; Aircraft Mechanic/Engine Specialist; Buyer; Chemical Engineer; Computer Programmer; Cost Estimator; Design Engineer; Designer; Draftsperson; Electrical/Electronics Engineer; Financial Analyst; Industrial Engineer; Internet Services Manager; Mechanical Engineer; MIS Specialist; Purchasing Agent/Manager; Quality Control Supervisor; Software Engineer; Statistician; Structural Engineer; Technical Writer/Editor; Telecommunications Manager. **Corporate headquarters location:** Philadelphia PA. **Other U.S. locations:** Nationwide. **International locations:** Worldwide. **Number of placements per year:** 1000+.

CDI CORPORATION
4400 East Broadway Boulevard, Suite 512, Tucson AZ 85711. 520/795-6900. **Fax:** 520/323-4495. **Contact:** Manager. **World Wide Web address:** http://www. cdicorp.com. **Description:** A contract services firm. **Specializes in the areas of:** Computer Science/Software; Engineering; Manufacturing; Technical. **Positions commonly filled include:** Aerospace Engineer; Agricultural Engineer; Architect; Biomedical Engineer; Budget Analyst; Buyer; Chemical Engineer; Civil Engineer; Clinical Lab Technician; Computer Programmer; Cost Estimator; Design Engineer; Designer; Draftsperson; Electrical/Electronics Engineer; Environmental Engineer; Industrial Engineer; Industrial Production Manager; Internet Services Manager; Landscape Architect; Mechanical Engineer; Metallurgical Engineer; Mining Engineer; MIS Specialist; Software Engineer; Structural Engineer; Systems Analyst; Technical Writer/Editor; Telecommunications Analyst. **Corporate headquarters location:** Philadelphia PA. **Other U.S. locations:** Nationwide. **International locations:** Worldwide. **Average salary range of placements:** $30,000 - $50,000. **Number of placements per year:** 100 - 199.

COMFORCE TECHNICAL SERVICES, INC.
1858 East Southern Avenue, Tempe AZ 85282. 480/897-2479. **Toll-free phone:** 800/543-6076. **Fax:** 480/345-2471. **Contact:** Tom Diaz, IT Director. **World Wide Web address:** http://www.comforce.com. **Description:** A contract services firm. **Specializes in the areas of:** Administration; Advertising; Clerical; Communications; Computer Science/Software; Construction; Consulting; Design; Economics; Engineering; Finance; Management; Marketing; Publishing; Scientific. **Corporate headquarters location:** This Location. **Average salary range of placements:** $50,000 - $100,000. **Number of placements per year:** 200 - 499.

CONTRACT PROFESSIONALS INCORPORATED
1855 West Baseline Road, Suite 210, Mesa AZ 85202. **Fax:** 480/839-6700. **Contact:** Recruiter. **Description:** A contract services firm. **Average salary range of placements:** $30,000 - $100,000. **Number of placements per year:** 200 - 499.

CROWN TECHNICAL SERVICE
504 East Southern Avenue, Tempe AZ 85282. 480/966-8686. **Contact:** Manager. **Description:** A contract services firm. **Specializes in the areas of:** Construction.

DVA CONSULTING
1661 North Swan Road, Suite 210, Tucson AZ 85712. 520/320-5301. **Contact:** Manager. **Description:** A contract services firm. **Specializes in the areas of:** Computer Science/Software; High-Tech.

PAUL DICKEN ASSOCIATES, INC.
1930 South Alma School Road, Suite D-207, Mesa AZ 85210. 480/345-2036. **Toll-free phone:** 800/658-5954. **Fax:** 480/345-2997. **Contact:** Manager. **Description:** A contract services firm that also provides some temporary placements. Founded in 1985. **Specializes in the areas of:** Computer Science/Software; Engineering; Manufacturing. **Positions commonly filled include:** Aerospace Engineer; Buyer; Computer Programmer; Customer Service Representative; Design Engineer; Designer; Draftsperson; Electrical/Electronics Engineer; Human Resources Specialist; Mechanical Engineer; MIS Specialist; Quality Control Supervisor; Software Engineer; Technical Writer/Editor; Typist/Word Processor. **Benefits available to temporary workers:** Medical Insurance; Paid Holidays; Paid Vacation. **Corporate headquarters location:** This Location. **Number of placements per year:** 1000+.

HALL KINION
1201 South Alma School Road, Suite 4450, Mesa AZ 85210. **Toll-free phone:** 888/833-3308. **Fax:** 480/833-3877. **Contact:** Branch Manager. **World Wide Web address:** http://www.hallkinion.com. **Description:** Hall Kinion is a contract services firm that also provides some permanent placements. **Specializes in the areas of:** Information Systems; Information Technology; Internet Development; Network Administration; Quality Assurance; Systems Administration; Systems Design; Technical Writing.

PDS TECHNICAL SERVICES
5150 North 16th Street, Suite C266, Phoenix AZ 85016. 602/280-9777. **Toll-free phone:** 800/456-8644. **Contact:** Peter Janes, Branch Manager. **World Wide Web address:** http://www.pdstech.com. **Description:** A contract services firm. **Specializes in the areas of:** Architecture/Construction; Computer Science/Software; Engineering; Manufacturing; Technical. **Positions commonly filled include:** Aerospace Engineer; Aircraft Mechanic/Engine Specialist; Buyer; Chemical Engineer; Civil Engineer; Computer Programmer; Construction and Building Inspector; Design Engineer; Designer; Draftsperson; Electrical/Electronics Engineer; Industrial

Engineer; Landscape Architect; Mechanical Engineer; Metallurgical Engineer; MIS Specialist; Petroleum Engineer; Software Engineer; Structural Engineer; Surveyor; Systems Analyst; Technical Writer/Editor; Urban/Regional Planner. **Corporate headquarters location:** Irving TX. **Other U.S. locations:** Anchorage AK; Costa Mesa CA; Miami FL; Atlanta GA; Wichita KS; St. Louis MO; Tulsa OK; Nashville TN; Austin TX; Houston TX; San Antonio TX; Seattle WA; Green Bay WI; Milwaukee WI. **Average salary range of placements:** $20,000 - $140,000. **Number of placements per year:** 50 - 99.

VOLT TECHNICAL SERVICES
3020 East Camelback Road, Suite 365, Phoenix AZ 85016. 602/955-7750. **Contact:** Regional Manager. **Description:** A contract services firm that also provides some temporary and permanent placements. **Specializes in the areas of:** Computer Science/Software; Engineering; Scientific; Technical. **Positions commonly filled include:** Applications Engineer; AS400 Programmer Analyst; Biochemist; Biological Scientist; Biomedical Engineer; Chemical Engineer; Chemist; Civil Engineer; Clinical Lab Technician; Computer Animator; Computer Engineer; Computer Operator; Computer Programmer; Computer Scientist; Computer Support Technician; Computer Technician; Content Developer;

Database Administrator; Database Manager; Design Engineer; Desktop Publishing Specialist; Draftsperson; Editor; Electrical/Electronics Engineer; Environmental Engineer; Geologist/Geophysicist; Graphic Artist; Graphic Designer; Industrial Engineer; Internet Services Manager; Manufacturing Engineer; Mechanical Engineer; Metallurgical Engineer; MIS Specialist; Multimedia Designer; Network/Systems Administrator; Quality Assurance Engineer; Software Engineer; SQL Programmer; Statistician; Systems Analyst; Systems Manager; Technical Writer/Editor; Webmaster. **Corporate headquarters location:** Orange CA. **Other U.S. locations:** Nationwide. **International locations:** United Kingdom. **Number of placements per year:** 500 - 999.

H.L. YOH COMPANY
100 West Clarendon, Suite 1450, Phoenix AZ 85013. 602/235-9739. **Contact:** Manager. **Description:** A contract services firm. **Specializes in the areas of:** Computer Science/Software; Information Technology.

H.L. YOH COMPANY
1325 North Wilmot Road, Suite 320, Tucson AZ 85712. 520/886-2723. **Contact:** Manager. **Description:** A contract services firm. **Specializes in the areas of:** Computer Science/Software; Information Technology.

CAREER/OUTPLACEMENT COUNSELING FIRMS

ALLEN AND ASSOCIATES
4725 North Scottsdale Road, Suite 200, Scottsdale AZ 85251. **Toll-free phone:** 800/562-7602. **Fax:** 480/423-1661. **Contact:** Manager. **World Wide Web address:** http://www.allenandassociates.com. **Description:** A career/outplacement counseling firm. **Corporate headquarters location:** Maitland FL. **Other U.S. locations:** Nationwide.

AMERICAN CAREER EXECUTIVES
2400 East Arizona Biltmore Circle, Suite 2250, Phoenix AZ 85016. 602/381-1667. **Fax:** 602/381-8146. **Contact:** Linda J. Baugh, President. **E-mail address:** amcareer@abilnet.com. **World Wide Web address:** http://www.amcareer.com. **Description:** American Career Executives is a career/outplacement counseling firm. **Specializes in the areas of:** Accounting; Advertising; Banking; Biology; Broadcasting; Economics; Education; Engineering; Finance; Food; General Management; Health/Medical; Industrial; Insurance; Internet Development; Internet Marketing; Marketing; Nonprofit; Personnel/Labor Relations; Printing; Publishing; Real Estate; Retail; Sales; Scientific; Technical; Transportation. **Positions commonly filled include:** Account Manager; Account Representative; Accountant; Adjuster; Administrative Manager; Advertising Executive; Architect; Assistant Manager; Attorney; Auditor; Bank Officer/Manager; Biochemist; Biological Scientist; Biomedical Engineer; Branch Manager; Budget Analyst; Buyer; Chemical Engineer; Chemist; Civil Engineer; Claim Representative; Clinical Lab Technician; Computer Animator; Computer Engineer; Computer Scientist; Controller; Counselor; Credit Manager; Customer Service Rep.; Database Administrator; Database Manager; Design Engineer; Dietician/Nutritionist; Draftsperson; Economist; Editor; Education Administrator; Electrical/Electronics Engineer; Environmental Engineer; ESL Teacher; Finance Director; Financial Analyst; Food Scientist/Technologist; Fund Manager; General Manager; Geographer; Geologist/ Geophysicist; Graphic Designer; Human Resources Manager; Industrial Designer; Industrial Production

Manager; Instructional Technologist; Insurance Agent/ Broker; Intellectual Property Lawyer; Internet Services Manager; Librarian; Management Trainee; Managing Editor; Manufacturing Engineer; Market Research Analyst; Marketing Manager; Marketing Specialist; Mechanical Engineer; Metallurgical Engineer; MIS Specialist; Multimedia Designer; Network/Systems Administrator; Operations Manager; Pharmacist; Physical Therapist; Production Manager; Psychologist; Public Relations Specialist; Purchasing Agent/Manager; Quality Assurance Engineer; Quality Control Supervisor; Radio/TV Announcer/Broadcaster; Reporter; Sales Engineer; Sales Executive; Sales Manager; Sales Representative; Social Worker; Special Education Teacher; Speech-Language Pathologist; Statistician; Systems Analyst; Systems Manager; Teacher/Professor; Technical Writer/Editor; Telecommunications Manager; Transportation/Traffic Specialist; Underwriter/Assistant Underwriter; Vice President; Video Production Coordinator. **Corporate headquarters location:** This Location. **Average salary range of placements:** $50,000 - $100,000. **Number of placements per year:** 1 - 49.

FRANKLIN COVEY
350 East Elliot Road, Chandler AZ 85225. 480/539-3800. **Contact:** Account Executive. **Description:** A career/outplacement counseling firm that provides information to individuals seeking career opportunities in the sports industry. Franklin Covey offers products for jobseekers including an audiocassette tape series, a regular newsletter with job listings, a career enhancement software test, a resume development kit, and a resume bank service. **Positions commonly filled include:** Accountant/Auditor; Administrator; Customer Service Representative; Marketing Specialist; Public Relations Specialist; Services Sales Representative.

BERNARD HALDANE ASSOCIATES
5151 East Broadway Boulevard, Suite 390, Tucson AZ 85711. 520/790-2767. **Contact:** Manager. **Description:** A career/outplacement counseling firm.

◆ ARKANSAS ◆

CLINTON STREET PROFESSIONAL RECRUITERS
708 Clinton Street, Arkadelphia AR 71923. 870/230-1200. **Fax:** 870/230-1880. **Contact:** Manager. **Description:** An executive search firm. Client company pays fee. **Specializes in the areas of:** Manufacturing. **Positions commonly filled include:** Engineer; Human Resources Generalist; Management; Material Control Specialist; Materials Engineer; Materials Manager; Quality Control Supervisor. **Average salary range of placements:** More than $50,000.

EDP STAFFING SOLUTIONS, INC.
2024 Arkansas Valley Drive, Suite 206, Little Rock AR 72212. 501/223-4733. **Fax:** 501/223-4735. **Contact:** Manager. **World Wide Web address:** http://www.recruitme.com. **Description:** EDP Staffing Solutions is an executive search firm. **Specializes in the areas of:** Information Technology.

EXECUTIVE RECRUITERS AGENCY, INC.
P.O. Box 21810, Little Rock AR 72221. 501/224-7000. **Fax:** 501/224-8534. **Contact:** Greg Downs, Vice President. **E-mail address:** gtdowns@execrecruit.com. **World Wide Web address:** http://www.execrecruit.com. **Description:** An executive search firm operating on both retainer and contingency bases. This firm also provides some contract, resume, and career counseling services. Client company pays fee. **Specializes in the areas of:** Accounting; Computer Science/Software; Engineering; Marketing; MIS/EDP; Sales; Scientific; Technical. **Positions commonly filled include:** Account Manager; Account Representative; Accountant; AS400 Programmer Analyst; Chemical Engineer; Chief Financial Officer; Computer Engineer; Computer Programmer; Computer Scientist; Controller; Database Administrator; Database Manager; Design Engineer; Electrical/Electronics Engineer; Environmental Engineer; General Manager; Human Resources Manager; Industrial Engineer; Industrial Production Manager; Manufacturing Engineer; Mechanical Engineer; MIS Specialist; Network/Systems Administrator; Operations Manager; Production Manager; Project Manager; Purchasing Agent/Manager; Quality Assurance Engineer; Quality Control Supervisor; Sales Engineer; Sales Executive; Sales Manager; Sales Representative; Software Engineer; SQL Programmer; Systems Analyst; Systems Manager; Webmaster. **Average salary range of placements:** $50,000 - $100,000. **Number of placements per year:** 50 - 99.

FOSTER PROFESSIONAL SEARCH INC.
1821 Phoenix Avenue, Fort Smith AR 72901. 501/646-1413. **Contact:** Manager. **Description:** An executive search firm dealing exclusively in computer-related occupations. **Specializes in the areas of:** Computer Hardware/Software; Computer Operations; Computer Programming; Computer Science/Software.

HERRING & ASSOCIATES INC.
600 Pine Forest Drive, Suite 130, Maumelle AR 72113. 501/851-1234. **Fax:** 501/851-7753. **Contact:** Manager. **Description:** An executive search firm. **Specializes in the areas of:** Distribution.

MDR & ASSOCIATES, INC.
11 Ontur Lane, Hot Springs Village AR 71909. 501/915-0244. **Fax:** 501/915-0240. **Contact:** Mel Robinson, President. **Description:** An executive search firm operating on both retainer and contingency bases. **Specializes in the areas of:** Engineering; Hotel/Restaurant.

MANAGEMENT RECRUITERS OF LITTLE ROCK
Redding Building, 1701 Centerview Drive, Suite 314, Little Rock AR 72211. 501/224-0801. **Fax:** 501/224-0798. **Contact:** Noel K. Hall, Managing Partner. **Description:** An executive search firm operating on a contingency basis. **Specializes in the areas of:** Accounting/Auditing; Administration; Advertising; Architecture/Construction; Banking; Chemicals; Communications; Computer Hardware/Software; Design; Electrical; Engineering; Food; General Management; Health/Medical; Insurance; Legal; Manufacturing; Operations Management; Personnel/Labor Relations; Procurement; Publishing; Retail; Sales; Technical; Textiles; Transportation. **Positions commonly filled include:** Accountant/Auditor; Agricultural Engineer; Computer Programmer; Design Engineer; Electrical/Electronics Engineer; Environmental Engineer; Industrial Engineer; Industrial Production Manager; Mechanical Engineer; MIS Specialist; Physical Therapist; Physician; Quality Control Supervisor; Registered Nurse; Systems Analyst. **Corporate headquarters location:** Cleveland OH. **Average salary range of placements:** More than $50,000. **Number of placements per year:** 50 - 99.

MOORE & ASSOCIATES
5111 Rogers Avenue, Suite 514, Fort Smith AR 72903. 501/478-7052. **Fax:** 501/478-7053. **Contact:** Noel Moore, Owner/Manager. **Description:** An executive search firm operating on a contingency basis. This firm also provides some resume and career counseling services. Moore & Associates networks with more than 400 firms, providing jobseekers with nationwide opportunities. Client company pays fee. **Specializes in the areas of:** Accounting; Engineering; General Management; Manufacturing. **Positions commonly filled include:** Accountant; AS400 Programmer Analyst; Blue-Collar Worker Supervisor; Chemical Engineer; Chief Financial Officer; Controller; Database Administrator; Design Engineer; Draftsperson; Electrical/Electronics Engineer; Environmental Engineer; General Manager; Human Resources Manager; Industrial Engineer; Industrial Production Manager; Manufacturing Engineer; Mechanical Engineer; Metallurgical Engineer; MIS Specialist; Operations Manager; Production Manager; Purchasing Agent/Manager; Quality Assurance Engineer; Quality Control Supervisor; Sales Engineer; Sales Manager; Software Engineer; SQL Programmer; Vice President; Vice President of Finance; Vice President of Operations. **Average salary range of placements:** $50,000 - $100,000. **Number of placements per year:** 1 - 49.

SALES CONSULTANTS OF NORTHWEST ARKANSAS
One West Mountain Street, Fayetteville AR 72701. 501/521-9700. **Contact:** Manager. **Description:** An executive search firm.

SANFORD ROSE ASSOCIATES
810-D NW Third Street, Suite D, Bentonville AR 72712. 501/271-9288. **Fax:** 501/271-9260. **Contact:** Manager. **World Wide Web address:** http://www.sanfordrose.com. **Description:** An executive search firm. **Specializes in the areas of:** Automotive; Electronics; Engineering; Finance; General Management; Operations Management.

SEARCH ASSOCIATES
P.O. Box 10703, Fort Smith AR 72917. 501/452-0005. **Contact:** Jennie Little, President. **Description:** An executive search firm. Ms. Little is a founding member of the Council of Medical Recruiters and Consultants, a national network of executive recruiters. **Specializes in the areas of:** Health/Medical.

SEARCH ONE
P.O. Box 17407, Little Rock AR 72222-7407. 501/868-8992. **Fax:** 501/218-2679. **Contact:** Manager. **Description:** An executive search firm. **Specializes in the areas of:** Engineering; Information Systems.

SNELLING SEARCH
3901 Rogers Avenue, Fort Smith AR 72903. 501/782-4911. **Fax:** 501/782-4916. **Contact:** Office Manager.

Description: An executive search firm operating on both retainer and contingency bases. **Specializes in the areas of:** Accounting/Auditing; Administration; Banking; Engineering; Finance; General Management; Insurance; Manufacturing; Personnel/Labor Relations. **Positions commonly filled include:** Accountant/Auditor; Adjuster; Bookkeeper; Claim Representative; Credit Manager; Customer Service Representative; Financial Analyst; General Manager; Industrial Engineer; Industrial Production Manager; Management Trainee; Manufacturer's/Wholesaler's Sales Rep.; Mechanical Engineer; Operations/Production Manager; Purchasing Agent/Manager; Quality Control Supervisor; Services Sales Rep.; Statistician. **Corporate headquarters location:** Dallas TX. **Average salary range of placements:** $30,000 - $49,999. **Number of placements per year:** 200 - 499.

SNELLING SEARCH
P.O. Box 1627, Bentonville AR 72712. 501/271-0505. **Contact:** Manager. **Description:** An executive search firm. **Specializes in the areas of:** Transportation. **Corporate headquarters location:** Dallas TX.

SPENCER CAREERS
212 North 34th Street, Rogers AR 72756. 501/631-1300. **Toll-free phone:** 800/562-7266. **Fax:** 501/631-1551. **Contact:** James Spencer, Manager. **E-mail address:** jspencer@staffing.net. **Description:** An executive search firm operating on a contingency basis. Spencer Careers also provides some contract services. Founded in 1988. **Specializes in the areas of:** Banking; Computer Science/Software. **Positions commonly filled include:** Computer Programmer; Database Manager; Software Engineer; Systems Analyst; Systems Manager. **Average salary range of placements:** $30,000 - $49,999.

TURNAGE EMPLOYMENT SERVICE GROUP
1225 Breckenridge Drive, Suite 206, Little Rock AR 72205. 501/224-6870. **Fax:** 501/224-5709. **Contact:** Office Manager. **Description:** An executive search firm operating on a contingency basis. **Specializes in the areas of:** Administration; Computer Science/Software; Engineering; General Management; Health/Medical; Industrial; Insurance; Legal; Manufacturing; Personnel/Labor Relations; Sales; Secretarial; Technical. **Positions commonly filled include:** Accountant/Auditor; Administrative Manager; Bank Officer/Manager; Blue-Collar Worker Supervisor; Branch Manager; Buyer; Chemical Engineer; Clerical Supervisor; Computer Programmer; Cost Estimator; Credit Manager; Dental Assistant/Dental Hygienist; Design Engineer; Draftsperson; Electrical/Electronics Engineer; Environmental Engineer; Financial Analyst; General Manager; Health Services Manager; Hotel Manager; Human Resources Specialist; Industrial Production Manager; Licensed Practical Nurse; Management Analyst/Consultant; Management Trainee; Metallurgical Engineer; MIS Specialist; Operations/Production Manager; Paralegal; Property and Real Estate Manager; Public Relations Specialist; Purchasing Agent/Manager; Quality Control Supervisor; Registered Nurse; Restaurant/Food Service Manager; Services Sales Representative; Software Engineer; Systems Analyst; Technical Writer/Editor; Travel Agent; Typist/Word Processor; Underwriter. **Corporate headquarters location:** This Location. **Other area locations:** Conway AR; Russellville AR. **Average salary range of placements:** $20,000 - $70,000.

UTOPIA, INC.
P.O. Box 1010, Melbourne AR 72556. 870/368-3000. **Fax:** 870/368-3010. **Contact:** Steve Miller, President. **Description:** An executive search firm operating on a contingency basis. The firm focuses on placing management and engineering personnel in manufacturing industries. **Specializes in the areas of:** Engineering; General Management; Industrial; Manufacturing; Personnel/Labor Relations. **Positions commonly filled include:** Buyer; Chemical Engineer; Chemist; Civil Engineer; Computer Programmer; Design Engineer; Electrical/Electronics Engineer; Industrial Designer; Industrial Engineer; Mechanical Engineer; Metallurgical Engineer; MIS Specialist; Operations/Production Manager; Plant Manager; Purchasing Agent/Manager; Quality Control Supervisor; Statistician; Transportation/Traffic Specialist; Vice President. **Corporate headquarters location:** This Location. **Average salary range of placements:** More than $50,000. **Number of placements per year:** 1 - 49.

PERMANENT EMPLOYMENT AGENCIES

ACCUSTAFF
3301 South 70th Street, Suite B, Fort Smith AR 72903. 501/452-7315. **Contact:** Manager. **Description:** A permanent employment agency.

EAGLE PERSONNEL SERVICE
1431 Merrill Drive, Little Rock AR 72211. 501/223-9400. **Fax:** 501/223-0234. **Contact:** Office Manager. **Description:** Eagle Personnel Service is a permanent employment agency that also provides some temporary placements.

ECHOLS AND ASSOCIATES
P.O. Box 1050, Monticello AR 71657. 870/367-3401. **Fax:** 870/367-6058. **Contact:** Manager. **Description:** A permanent employment agency that also provides some temporary placements.

EMPLOYERS SERVICES OF AMERICA, INC.
310 West McCoy, Monticello AR 71655. 870/367-3401. **Contact:** Office Manager. **World Wide Web address:** http://www.employers-inc.com. **Description:** Employers Services of America, Inc. is a permanent employment agency that also offers some temporary placements.

EMPLOYMENT WORLD, INC.
5111 JFK Boulevard, Suite 3, North Little Rock AR 72116. 501/758-7307. **Contact:** Office Manager. **Description:** Employment World is a permanent employment agency.

EXPRESS PERSONNEL SERVICE
2608 Olive Street, Pine Bluff AR 71601. 870/535-3330. **Contact:** Manager. **Description:** A permanent employment agency.

PENMAC PERSONNEL SERVICE
109 East 11th Street, Russellville AR 72801. 501/967-8827. **Fax:** 501/967-9822. **Contact:** Manager. **Description:** A permanent employment agency that also provides some temp-to-perm placements. **Specializes in the areas of:** Clerical; Construction; Transportation.

PROMAX - EMPLOYEE ASSISTANCE
650 South Shackleford Road, Little Rock AR 72211. 501/224-6688. **Contact:** Manager. **Description:** An employment agency which provides jobs for people with mental health needs or disabilities.

SNELLING GROUP
125 East Township Street, Fayetteville AR 72703. 501/444-0111. **Fax:** 501/444-0464. **Contact:** Manager. **Description:** A permanent employment agency.

SNELLING PERSONNEL SERVICE
601 East Eighth Street, Pine Bluff AR 71601. 870/535-5500. **Fax:** 870/535-5502. **Contact:** Manager. **Description:** A permanent employment agency.

SNELLING PERSONNEL SERVICE
650 South Shackleford Road, Suite 312, Little Rock AR 72211. 501/223-2069. **Contact:** Manager. **Description:** A permanent employment agency.

TEMPORARY EMPLOYMENT AGENCIES

PREMIER STAFFING, INC.
10110 West Markham, Little Rock AR 72205. 501/223-8367. **Fax:** 501/223-8368. **Contact:** Office Manager. **Description:** A temporary agency. **Specializes in the areas of:** Accounting/Auditing; Banking; General Management; Insurance; Personnel/Labor Relations; Sales; Secretarial. **Positions commonly filled include:** Accountant/Auditor; Actuary; Administrative Manager; Advertising Clerk; Bank Officer/Manager; Branch Manager; Brokerage Clerk; Budget Analyst; Buyer; Claim Representative; Clerical Supervisor; Customer Service Representative; Financial Analyst; General Manager; Human Resources Specialist; Management Trainee; Operations/Production Manager; Paralegal; Property and Real Estate Manager; Purchasing Agent/Manager; Quality Control Supervisor; Securities Sales Representative; Services Sales Representative; Typist/Word Processor; Underwriter/Assistant Underwriter. **Corporate headquarters location:** This Location. **Number of placements per year:** 200 - 499.

SEARK BUSINESS SERVICES
205 Fairview Road, Crossett AR 71635. 870/364-6873. **Contact:** Debbie Barnett, President. **Description:** A temporary agency focusing on technical placements. Founded in 1983. **Specializes in the areas of:** Accounting/Auditing; Secretarial; Technical. **Positions commonly filled include:** Accountant/Auditor; Clinical Lab Technician; Purchasing Agent/Manager; Typist/Word Processor.

STAFFMARK
2024 Arkansas Valley Drive, Suite 701, Little Rock AR 72212. 501/225-8080. **Contact:** Cindy Prusf, Manager. **Description:** A temporary agency. **Specializes in the areas of:** Computer Hardware/Software; Office Support; Technical. **Positions commonly filled include:** Administrative Assistant; Computer Operator; Computer Programmer; Data Entry Clerk; Secretary; Systems Analyst; Technician.

CONTRACT SERVICES FIRMS

SEATEC
124 West Capital Avenue, Suite 106, Little Rock AR 72201. **Toll-free phone:** 800/581-9175. **Fax:** 501/801-0201. **Contact:** Manager. **Description:** A contract services firm. **Specializes in the areas of:** Engineering; Information Technology.

◆ CALIFORNIA ◆

AAA McKINSTRY PERSONNEL CONSULTANTS & RESUME SERVICES
1450 North Tustin Avenue, Suite 130, Santa Ana CA 92705. 949/646-9090. **Contact:** Manager. **Description:** A generalist executive search firm that also provides resume writing services.

ABA STAFFING, INC.
690 Market Street, Suite 800, San Francisco CA 94104. 415/434-4222. **Fax:** 415/434-3958. **Contact:** Staffing Manager. **E-mail address:** info@abastaff.com. **World Wide Web address:** http://www.abastaff.com. **Description:** An executive search firm operating on a contingency basis. ABA Staffing also provides some temporary and contract placements. **Specializes in areas of:** Accounting; Administration; Banking; Computer Science/Software; Finance; Health/Medical; Legal; MIS/EDP; Personnel/Labor Relations; Retail; Sales; Secretarial; Technical. **Positions commonly filled include:** Account Manager; Account Representative; Administrative Assistant; Administrative Manager; Applications Engineer; Computer Operator; Customer Service Representative; Database Manager; Financial Analyst; Fund Manager; Management Trainee; MIS Specialist; Online Content Specialist; Personnel Manager; Project Manager; Quality Control Supervisor; Software Engineer; Systems Analyst; Systems Manager; Technical Writer/Editor; Typist/Word Processor. **Benefits available to temporary workers:** Holiday Bonus; Vacation Pay. **Corporate headquarters location:** This Location. **Other area locations:** San Mateo CA. **Average salary range of placements:** $30,000 - $50,000. **Number of placements per year:** 100 - 199.

ABA STAFFING, INC.
2121 South El Camino Real, Suite 605, San Mateo CA 94403. 650/349-9200. **Fax:** 650/349-9721. **Contact:** Employment Specialist. **Description:** An executive search firm that focuses on administrative placements for human resource professionals. ABA Staffing also provides some temporary placements. **Specializes in the areas of:** Accounting/Auditing; Advertising; Finance; Health/Medical; Insurance; Legal; Nonprofit; Personnel/Labor Relations; Publishing; Sales; Secretarial; Technical. **Positions commonly filled include:** Accountant/Auditor; Administrative Manager; Branch Manager; Brokerage Clerk; Buyer; Customer Service Rep.; Financial Analyst; General Manager; Human Resources Specialist; Internet Services Manager; MIS Specialist; Operations/Production Manager; Paralegal; Public Relations Specialist; Purchasing Agent/Manager; Software Engineer; Technical Writer/Editor; Typist/Word Processor; Underwriter/Assistant Underwriter. **Corporate headquarters location:** San Francisco CA. **Average salary range of placements:** $30,000 - $50,000. **Number of placements per year:** 1 - 49.

ARI INTERNATIONAL
1501 Ocean Avenue, Seal Beach CA 90740. 562/795-5111. **Contact:** Ron Curci, President. **E-mail address:** rlcurci@worldnet.att.net. **Description:** An executive search firm operating on a retainer basis. **Specializes in the areas of:** Health/Medical. **Positions commonly filled include:** Biological Scientist; Biomedical Engineer; Chemical Engineer; Chemist; Controller; Design Engineer; General Manager; Marketing Manager; Mechanical Engineer; Production Manager; Project Manager; Sales Executive; Sales Manager; Vice President. **Corporate headquarters location:** This Location. **Other U.S. locations:** Nationwide. **Average salary range of placements:** More than $50,000. **Number of placements per year:** 1 - 49.

ABACUS STAFFING FOR ACCOUNTING
4100 Newport Place, Suite 770, Newport Beach CA 92660. 949/752-7676. **Fax:** 949/752-1447. **Contact:**

Account Executive. **Description:** An executive search firm that also provides some temporary placements. **Specializes in the areas of:** Accounting/Auditing; Finance. **Positions commonly filled include:** Accountant/Auditor; Credit Manager; Financial Analyst. **Other area locations:** Brea CA; Long Beach CA. **Average salary range of placements:** $30,000 - $50,000. **Number of placements per year:** 200 - 499.

ACCESS TECHNOLOGY
4000 Barranca Parkway, Suite 250, Irvine CA 92604. 714/850-1000. **Fax:** 949/262-0386. **Contact:** R.J. Nadel, Principal. **E-mail address:** hightechjobs@earthlink.com. **Description:** An executive search firm operating on a retainer basis. Client company pays fee. **Specializes in the areas of:** Computer Science/Software; Engineering; Internet Development; Scientific; Technical. **Positions commonly filled include:** Account Manager; Applications Engineer; Computer Engineer; Computer Programmer; Content Developer; Database Manager; Human Resources Manager; MIS Specialist; Network Engineer; Network/Systems Administrator; Project Manager; Sales Engineer; Sales Executive; Sales Manager; Sales Representative; Software Engineer; SQL Programmer; Systems Manager; Vice President; Webmaster. **Corporate headquarters location:** This Location. **Average salary range of placements:** $50,000 - $100,000. **Number of placements per year:** 50 - 99.

ACCOUNTANTS EXECUTIVE SEARCH
ACCOUNTANTS ON CALL
970 West 190th Street, Suite 870, Torrance CA 90502. 310/527-2777. **Contact:** Randy Wagaman, Branch Manager. **Description:** An executive search firm operating on a contingency basis. Accountants On Call (also at this location) is a temporary agency. **Specializes in the areas of:** Accounting/Auditing; Finance. **Positions commonly filled include:** Accountant/Auditor; Financial Analyst. **Corporate headquarters location:** Saddle Brook NJ. **Other U.S. locations:** Nationwide. **International locations:** Worldwide. **Average salary range of placements:** $30,000 - $50,000. **Number of placements per year:** 100 - 199.

ACCOUNTANTS EXECUTIVE SEARCH
ACCOUNTANTS ON CALL
21800 Oxnard Street, Suite 750, Woodland Hills CA 91367. 818/992-7676. **Fax:** 818/348-8871. **Contact:** Area Manager. **Description:** An executive search firm operating on a contingency basis. Accountants On Call (also at this location) is a temporary agency that also provides some permanent placements. Client company pays fee. **Specializes in the areas of:** Accounting/Auditing; Finance. **Positions commonly filled include:** Accountant/Auditor; Budget Analyst; Credit Manager; Human Resources Specialist. **Benefits available to temporary workers:** Medical Insurance; Paid Vacation. **Corporate headquarters location:** Saddle Brook NJ. **Other U.S. locations:** Nationwide. **International locations:** Worldwide. **Number of placements per year:** 200 - 499.

ACCOUNTANTS EXECUTIVE SEARCH
ACCOUNTANTS ON CALL
3500 West Olive Avenue, Suite 550, Burbank CA 91505. 818/845-6700. **Fax:** 818/845-3237. **Contact:** Kyle Grimes, Manager. **Description:** An executive search firm operating on a contingency basis. Accountants On Call (also at this location) is a temporary agency. **Specializes in the areas of:** Accounting/Auditing; Finance; Tax. **Positions commonly filled include:** Accountant/Auditor; Finance Director; Financial Analyst. **Corporate headquarters location:** Saddle Brook NJ. **Other U.S. locations:** Nationwide. **International locations:** Worldwide. **Number of placements per year:** 100 - 199.

ACCOUNTANTS EXECUTIVE SEARCH
ACCOUNTANTS ON CALL
1650 Spruce Street, Suite 412, Riverside CA 92507. 909/686-2100. **Contact:** Manager. **Description:** An executive search firm. Accountants On Call (also at this location) is a temporary agency that also provides some permanent placements. **Specializes in the areas of:** Accounting/Auditing; Banking; Finance. **Corporate headquarters location:** Saddle Brook NJ. **Other U.S. locations:** Nationwide. **International locations:** Worldwide.

ACCOUNTANTS EXECUTIVE SEARCH
ACCOUNTANTS ON CALL
100 Howe Avenue, Suite 210 North, Sacramento CA 95825. 916/483-6666. **Contact:** Brad Garner, Manager. **Description:** An executive search firm. Accountants On Call (also at this location) is a temporary agency that also provides some permanent placements. **Specializes in the areas of:** Accounting/Auditing; Finance. **Corporate headquarters location:** Saddle Brook NJ. **Other U.S. locations:** Nationwide. **International locations:** Worldwide.

ACCOUNTANTS EXECUTIVE SEARCH
ACCOUNTANTS ON CALL
10960 Wilshire Boulevard, Suite 1115, Los Angeles CA 90024. 310/312-3330. **Fax:** 310/444-0606. **Contact:** Manager. **E-mail address:** losangeles@aocnet.com. **Description:** An executive search firm. Accountants On Call (also at this location) is a temporary agency that also provides some permanent placements. **Specializes in the areas of:** Accounting/Auditing; Finance. **Positions commonly filled include:** Accountant; Auditor; Budget Analyst; Chief Financial Officer; Controller; Credit Manager; Financial Analyst. **Benefits available to temporary workers:** Medical Insurance; Paid Holidays; Paid Vacation. **Corporate headquarters location:** Saddle Brook NJ. **Other U.S. locations:** Nationwide. **International locations:** Worldwide. **Average salary range of placements:** $30,000 - $50,000.

ACCOUNTANTS EXECUTIVE SEARCH
ACCOUNTANTS ON CALL
2001 Gateway Place, Suite 200, San Jose CA 95110. 408/437-9779. **Fax:** 408/437-0716. **Contact:** Manager. **Description:** An executive search firm. Accountants On Call (also at this location) is a temporary agency that also provides some permanent placements. **Specializes in the areas of:** Accounting/Auditing; Banking; Finance. **Corporate headquarters location:** Saddle Brook NJ. **Other U.S. locations:** Nationwide. **International locations:** Worldwide.

ACCOUNTANTS EXECUTIVE SEARCH
ACCOUNTANTS ON CALL
One Kaiser Plaza, Suite 1030, Oakland CA 94612. 510/986-1800. **Contact:** Manager. **Description:** An executive search firm. Accountants On Call (also at this location) is a temporary agency that also provides some permanent placements. **Specializes in the areas of:** Accounting/Auditing; Banking; Finance. **Corporate headquarters location:** Saddle Brook NJ. **Other U.S. locations:** Nationwide. **International locations:** Worldwide.

ACCOUNTANTS EXECUTIVE SEARCH
ACCOUNTANTS ON CALL
6140 Stone Ridge Mall Road, Suite 360, Pleasanton CA 94588. 925/734-8666. **Contact:** Manager. **Description:** An executive search firm. Accountants On Call (also at this location) is a temporary agency that also provides some permanent placements. **Specializes in the areas of:** Accounting/Auditing; Banking; Finance. **Corporate headquarters location:** Saddle Brook NJ. **Other U.S. locations:** Nationwide. **International locations:** Worldwide.

ACCOUNTANTS EXECUTIVE SEARCH
ACCOUNTANTS ON CALL
17700 Castleton Street, Suite 305, City of Industry CA 91748. 626/912-0090. **Contact:** Manager. **Description:** An executive search firm. Accountants on Call (also at this location) is a temporary agency. **Specializes in the areas of:** Accounting/Auditing; Finance. **Corporate headquarters location:** Saddle Brook NJ. **Other U.S. locations:** Nationwide. **International locations:** Worldwide.

ACCOUNTANTS EXECUTIVE SEARCH
ACCOUNTANTS ON CALL
5000 Birch Street, Suite 550, Newport Beach CA 92660. 949/955-0100. **Contact:** Manager. **Description:** An executive search firm. Accountants on Call (also at this location) is a temporary agency. **Specializes in the areas of:** Accounting; Finance. **Corporate headquarters location:** Saddle Brook NJ. **Other U.S. locations:** Nationwide. **International locations:** Worldwide.

ACCOUNTANTS EXECUTIVE SEARCH
ACCOUNTANTS ON CALL
44 Montgomery Street, Suite 2310, San Francisco CA 94104. 415/398-3366. **Contact:** Manager. **Description:** An executive search firm. Accountants on Call (also at this location) is a temporary agency. **Specializes in the areas of:** Accounting/Auditing; Finance. **Corporate headquarters location:** Saddle Brook NJ. **Other U.S. locations:** Nationwide. **International locations:** Worldwide.

ACCOUNTING ADVANTAGE
11444 West Olympic Boulevard, Suite 260, Los Angeles CA 90064. 310/445-4111. **Fax:** 310/312-8722. **Contact:** Recruiter. **Description:** An executive search firm. **Specializes in the areas of:** Accounting/Auditing; Finance. **Positions commonly filled include:** Accountant; Budget Analyst; Credit Manager; Financial Analyst. **Corporate headquarters location:** Brentwood CA. **Number of placements per year:** 200 - 499.

ACSYS, INC.
3160 Crow Canyon Road, Suite 230, San Ramon CA 94583. 925/543-0233. **Fax:** 925/543-0234. **Contact:** Manager. **World Wide Web address:** http://www.acsysinc.com. **Description:** An executive search firm. **Specializes in the areas of:** Accounting; Finance; Personnel/Labor Relations. **Positions commonly filled include:** Accountant/Auditor; Budget Analyst; Chief Financial Officer; Controller; Credit Manager; Financial Analyst; Human Resources Manager.

ACTIVE SEARCH AND PLACEMENT INC.
2041 Business Center Drive, Suite 102, Irvine CA 92612. 949/833-9900. **Fax:** 949/833-7988. **Contact:** Nada D. Williston, Partner. **World Wide Web address:** http://www.asapemployment.com. **Description:** An executive search firm focusing on investment management, trust, and mutual fund industry placement. The firm operates on both retainer and contingency bases. Client company pays fee. **Specializes in the areas of:** Accounting; Finance; Investment. **Positions commonly filled include:** Accountant; Budget Analyst; Financial Analyst; Fund Manager. **Corporate headquarters location:** This Location. **Average salary range of placements:** $50,000 - $100,000. **Number of placements per year:** 50 - 99.

ACTUARIAL SEARCH ASSOCIATES
1107 Venice Boulevard, Venice CA 90291. **Toll-free phone:** 800/776-6415. **Fax:** 310/391-7612. **Contact:** Manager. **E-mail address:** actuarialsearch@att.net. **World Wide Web address:** http://www.actuarialsearch.com. **Description:** An executive search firm. Founded in 1971. **Specializes in the areas of:** Insurance. **Positions commonly filled include:** Actuary.

ADDLEMAN & JENKINS ASSOCIATES
4460 Redwood Highway, Suite 13, San Rafael CA 94903. 415/491-8980. **Contact:** Manager. **Description:** An executive search firm. **Specializes in the areas of:** Computer Hardware/Software. **Positions commonly filled include:** Hardware Engineer; Software Engineer.

ADLER-BROWN ASSOCIATES
2672 Bayshore Parkway, Suite 524, Mountain View CA 94043. 650/960-7101. **Contact:** Manager. **Description:** An executive search firm. **Specializes in the areas of:** Data Communications.

ADMINISTRATIVE EXECUTIVE SEARCH (AES)
3600 Wilshire Boulevard, Suite 2120, Los Angeles CA 90010. 213/368-6960. **Contact:** Manager. **Description:** An executive search firm. **Specializes in the areas of:** Administration.

ADVANCED TECHNOLOGY CONSULTANTS, INC.
536 Weddell Drive, Suite 7, Sunnyvale CA 94089. 408/734-0635. **Fax:** 408/734-5833. **Contact:** Reza Vakili, Professional Staffing Manager. **E-mail address:** atci@ix.netcom.com. **Description:** An executive search firm. **Specializes in the areas of:** Computer Science/ Software; Software Engineering. **Positions commonly filled include:** Applications Engineer; Computer Programmer; Consultant; Database Manager; Design Engineer; Marketing Manager; MIS Specialist; Online Content Specialist; Sales Engineer; Sales Manager; Software Engineer; Technical Writer/Editor; Vice President of Project Development; Webmaster. **Benefits available to temporary workers:** Workers' Compensation Plan. **Corporate headquarters location:** This Location. **Average salary range of placements:** More than $50,000. **Number of placements per year:** 100 - 199.

ADVANCEMENT PERSONNEL SERVICES (APS)
13123 Whistler Avenue, Granada Hills CA 91344. 818/366-2738. **Fax:** 818/366-9618. **Contact:** Manager. **Description:** A generalist executive search firm.

THE AFFILIATES
5151 South Figueroa Street, Suite 650, Los Angeles CA 90071. 213/624-8335. **Contact:** Manager. **Description:** An executive search firm. **Specializes in the areas of:** Legal. **Positions commonly filled include:** Attorney; Legal Secretary; Paralegal.

AFFORDABLE EXECUTIVE RECRUITERS
5518 Lemona Avenue, Sherman Oaks CA 91411. 818/782-8554. **Contact:** Fred Gerson, President. **Description:** An executive search firm. **Specializes in the areas of:** Accounting/Auditing; Banking; Computer Science/Software; Engineering; Finance; General Management; Sales. **Positions commonly filled include:** Accountant/Auditor; Bank Officer/Manager; Computer Programmer; Human Resources Manager; Internet Services Manager; Software Engineer; Systems Analyst; Typist/Word Processor. **Number of placements per year:** 1 - 49.

AGRI SEARCH INTERNATIONAL
P.O. Box 775, Elk Grove CA 95759-0775. 916/689-6400. **Contact:** Ken Yelle, Director. **Description:** An executive search firm operating on both retainer and contingency bases. The firm also provides some career counseling and outplacement services. Client company pays fee. **Specializes in the areas of:** Agriculture. **Positions commonly filled include:** Agricultural Scientist; Sales Manager; Sales Rep.; Veterinarian. **Corporate headquarters location:** This Location. **Average salary range of placements:** $30,000 - $100,000.

AGRIESTI & ASSOCIATES
16291 Country Day Road, Poway CA 92064. 858/451-7766. **Fax:** 858/451-7843. **Contact:** Kay Agriesti, Owner. **Description:** An executive search firm that recruits sales management and marketing professionals nationwide, primarily in the consumer products and medical industries. The firm operates on both retainer and contingency bases. **Specializes in the areas of:** Sales. **Positions commonly filled include:** Manufacturer's/Wholesaler's Sales Rep. **Corporate headquarters location:** This Location. **Other U.S. locations:** Nationwide. **Number of placements per year:** 50 - 99.

ALERT STAFFING
1801 Avenue of the Stars, Suite 430, Los Angeles CA 90067. 310/788-0911. **Fax:** 310/788-0736. **Contact:** Carin Maher, Vice President of Operations. **Description:** An executive search firm that also offers contract services. **Specializes in the areas of:** Accounting/ Auditing; Administration; Banking; Computer Hardware/ Software; Finance; Legal; Personnel/Labor Relations; Sales; Secretarial; Technical. **Positions commonly filled include:** Accountant/Auditor; Administrative Manager; Blue-Collar Worker Supervisor; Branch Manager; Brokerage Clerk; Budget Analyst; Clerical Supervisor; Computer Programmer; Design Engineer; Financial Analyst; Human Resources Specialist; Internet Services Manager; MIS Specialist; Multimedia Designer; Paralegal; Services Sales Representative; Software Engineer; Typist/Word Processor. **Benefits available to temporary workers:** Dental Insurance; Medical Insurance; Paid Vacation. **Corporate headquarters location:** This Location. **Other U.S. locations:** El Segundo CA; Woodland Hills CA. **Number of placements per year:** 200 - 499.

ALLARD ASSOCIATES
425 Market Street, Suite 2200, San Francisco CA 94105. **Toll-free phone:** 800/291-5279. **Fax:** 800/526-7791. **Contact:** Susan Allard, Partner. **Description:** An executive search firm. NOTE: Resumes should be sent to Allard Associates, Operations Center, 1059 Court Street, Suite 114, Woodland CA 95695. **Specializes in the areas of:** Banking; Retail. **Positions commonly filled include:** Credit Manager; Customer Service Manager; Database Manager; Economist; Marketing Manager; Mathematician; Operations/Production Manager; Product Manager; Statistician. **Number of placements per year:** 50 - 99.

ALLARD ASSOCIATES
1059 Court Street, Suite 114, Woodland CA 95695. 530/757-2176. **Contact:** Manager. **Description:** An executive search firm providing placements to the credit card industry nationwide.

ALLIED SEARCH, INC.
2030 Union Street, Suite 206, San Francisco CA 94123. 415/921-2200. **Contact:** Manager. **Description:** An executive search firm. **Specializes in the areas of:** Accounting; Administration; Banking; Computer Science/Software; Finance; General Management; Health/Medical; Legal; Personnel/Labor Relations; Retail. **Average salary range of placements:** More than $50,000. **Number of placements per year:** 200 - 499.

ALPHA-NET CONSULTING GROUP
3838 Carson Street, 3rd Floor, Torrance CA 90503. 310/792-1994. **Contact:** Miyoko Sasagie, Consultant. **Description:** An executive search firm focusing on the placement of people who are bilingual in Japanese and English. Alpha-Net Consulting Group also places non-bilingual applicants. **Specializes in the areas of:** Accounting/Auditing; Administration; Banking; Computer Science/Software; Engineering; Finance; Food; General Management; Industrial; Manufacturing; Personnel/Labor Relations; Sales; Secretarial; Technical; Transportation.

AMARX SEARCH
9524 Kearny Villa Road, Suite 205, San Diego CA 92126. 858/578-6050. **Contact:** Manager. **Description:** An executive search firm. **Specializes in the areas of:** Computer Hardware/Software.

AMATO & ASSOCIATES OF CALIFORNIA, INC.
388 Market Street, Suite 500, San Francisco CA 94111. 415/781-7664. **Contact:** Joe Amato, President. **Description:** An executive search firm. **Specializes in the areas of:** Insurance. **Number of placements per year:** 100 - 199.

AMERICAN MAGNA SEARCH
P.O. Box 12197, Marina Del Rey CA 90295. 310/306-3973. **Fax:** 888/447-3968. **Contact:** Branch Manager.

Description: An executive search firm. **Specializes in the areas of:** Apparel; Fashion.

ANDERA & ASSOCIATES, INC.
2115 West Crescent Avenue, Suite A, Anaheim CA 92801. 714/776-2179. **Contact:** Office Manager. **E-mail address:** gandera@idt.net. **World Wide Web address:** http://www.anderajobs.com. **Description:** An executive search firm. **Specializes in the areas of:** Accounting; Finance.

ANKENBRANDT GROUP
4685 MacArthur Court, Suite 480, Newport Beach CA 92660. 949/955-1455. **Fax:** 949/955-2029. **Contact:** Office Manager. **E-mail address:** resumes@ankgrp.com. **World Wide Web address:** http://www.ankgrp.com. **Description:** An executive search firm. **Specializes in the areas of:** Accounting/Auditing; Administration; Computer Science/Software; Sales; Technical. **Positions commonly filled include:** Accountant/Auditor; Internet Services Manager; Management Analyst/Consultant; Marketing Specialist; Sales Representative; Systems Analyst. **Number of placements per year:** 100 - 199.

ARAN ROCK
318 Utah Street, San Francisco CA 94103. 415/255-1717. **Contact:** Colom Byrne, Manager. **World Wide Web address:** http://www.aranrock.com. **Description:** An executive search firm operating on a contingency basis. Aran Rock also provides some temporary and contract placements. Founded in 1989. **Specializes in the areas of:** Computer Science/Software. **Positions commonly filled include:** Computer Animator; Computer Operator; Computer Programmer; Consultant; Database Manager; MIS Specialist; Multimedia Designer; Project Manager; Software Developer; Software Engineer; Systems Analyst; Systems Manager; Telecommunications Manager; Webmaster. **Benefits available to temporary workers:** 401(k); Health Benefits. **Corporate headquarters location:** This Location. **Average salary range of placements:** More than $50,000. **Number of placements per year:** 200 - 499.

AUSTIN & ASSOCIATES
215 North Marengo Avenue, 2nd Floor, Pasadena CA 91101. 626/793-4807. **Contact:** Manager. **Description:** An executive search firm.

AUTOMOTIVE CAREER PLACEMENT COUNSELORS
P.O. Box 2163, Orinda CA 94563-6563. 925/734-8111. **Fax:** 510/360-8690. **Contact:** Manager. **Description:** An executive search firm that focuses on the automotive industry. **Specializes in the areas of:** Accounting/Auditing; Automotive; Finance; Sales. **Positions commonly filled include:** Accountant/Auditor; Adjuster; General Manager.

AVERY ASSOCIATES, INC.
3 1/2 North Santa Cruz Avenue, Suite B, Los Gatos CA 95030. 408/399-4424. **Contact:** Manager. **Description:** An executive search firm.

BDP MANAGEMENT CONSULTING GROUP
1800 Century Park East, Suite 600, Los Angeles CA 90067. 310/229-5999. **Contact:** Manager. **World Wide Web address:** http://www.bdpmgmt.com. **Description:** An executive search firm. **Specializes in the areas of:** Advertising; Entertainment; High-Tech; Marketing.

THE BADGER GROUP
4125 Blackhawk Plaza Circle, Suite 270, Danville CA 94506. 925/736-5553. **Fax:** 925/736-5554. **Contact:** Fred Badger, President. **E-mail address:** info@badgergroup.com. **World Wide Web address:** http://www.badgergroup.com. **Description:** The Badger Group is an executive search firm operating on a retainer basis. Client company pays fee. **Specializes in the areas of:** Computer Science/Software; Engineering; General Management; Internet Development; Marketing; MIS/EDP; Sales; Scientific; Technical. **Positions commonly filled include:** CEO; Director; General Manager; Senior Management; Vice President. **Corporate headquarters location:** This Location. **President:** Fred Badger. **Average salary range of placements:** More than $100,000. **Number of placements per year:** 1 - 49.

BARNES & ASSOCIATES
1101 Dove Street, Suite 200, Newport Beach CA 92660. 949/253-6750. **Fax:** 949/253-6753. **Contact:** Meredith Schwarz, Partner. **E-mail address:** msbarnes@ix.netcom.com. **Description:** An executive search firm. Founded in 1988. **Specializes in the areas of:** Computer Hardware/Software; Sales. **Positions commonly filled include:** Computer Programmer; Internet Services Manager; Manufacturer's/Wholesaler's Sales Rep.; Software Engineer; Strategic Relations Manager; Systems Analyst. **Corporate headquarters location:** This Location. **Other U.S. locations:** Nationwide. **Average salary range of placements:** More than $50,000. **Number of placements per year:** 50 - 99.

BAST & ASSOCIATES, INC.
11726 San Vicente Boulevard, Suite 200, Los Angeles CA 90049. 310/207-2100. **Fax:** 310/207-3003. **Contact:** Larry C. Bast, Managing Director. **Description:** An executive search firm focusing on marketing, advertising, and marketing research staffing for consumer goods and service companies. **Specializes in the areas of:** Advertising; Marketing. **Average salary range of placements:** More than $50,000. **Number of placements per year:** 1 - 49.

BATTALIA WINSTON INTERNATIONAL
1888 Century Park East, Suite 1150, Los Angeles CA 90067. 310/284-8080. **Contact:** Office Manager. **World Wide Web address:** http://www.battaliawinston.com. **Description:** An executive search firm. **Specializes in the areas of:** Consumer Products; Finance; Health/Medical; Industrial; Nonprofit; Professional; Technical. **Other area locations:** San Francisco CA. **Other U.S. locations:** Chicago IL; Boston MA; Edison NJ; New York NY.

BAY RESOURCES INC.
519 17th Street, Suite 510, Oakland CA 94612. 510/465-2781. **Contact:** Sandra Adams, President. **Description:** An executive search firm. **Specializes in the areas of:** Accounting/Auditing; Banking; Finance. **Positions commonly filled include:** Accountant/Auditor; Budget Analyst; Financial Analyst. **Corporate headquarters location:** This Location. **Average salary range of placements:** More than $50,000. **Number of placements per year:** 100 - 199.

THOMAS BECK INC.
P.O. Box 789, Sausalito CA 94966-0789. 415/331-1555. **Fax:** 415/381-1608. **Contact:** Thomas Beck, CEO. **Description:** An executive search firm. **Specializes in the areas of:** Electronics; Engineering; Sales. **Number of placements per year:** 1 - 49.

BECK/EASTWOOD RECRUITMENT SOLUTIONS
28170 Avenue Crocker, Suite 202, Valencia CA 91355. 661/295-6666. **Fax:** 661/295-5153. **Contact:** Manager. **E-mail address:** info@beckeastwood.com. **World Wide Web address:** http://beckeastwood.com. **Description:** An executive search firm. **Specializes in the areas of:** Marketing; Sales.

ROBERT BEECH INC.
383 South Palm Canyon Drive, Palm Springs CA 92262. 760/864-1380. **Fax:** 760/864-1382. **Contact:** Robert Beech, Director. **Description:** An executive search firm that places sales and marketing professionals in the computer software industry. **NOTE:** Applicants must have at least four years of experience in sales or marketing. **Specializes in the areas of:** Computer Science/Software; Sales. **Positions commonly filled include:** Customer Service Rep.; Manufacturer's/Wholesaler's Sales Rep.; Sales Representative; Software Engineer. **Average salary range of placements:** More than $50,000. **Number of placements per year:** 50 - 99.

HARVEY BELL & ASSOCIATES
700 Lindsay Avenue, Rohnert Park CA 94928. 707/795-0650. **Contact:** Harvey Bell, Owner. **Description:** An executive search firm. **Specializes in the areas of:** Administration; Banking; Computer Science/Software; Education; Engineering; Finance; General Management; Health/Medical; Legal; Sales. **Positions commonly filled include:** Attorney; Bank Officer/Manager; Biomedical Engineer; Branch Manager; Computer Programmer; Economist; Education Administrator; Electrical/Electronics Engineer; General Manager; Geologist/Geophysicist; Health Services Manager; Instrument Engineer; Licensed Practical Nurse; Management Analyst/Consultant; Manufacturer's/Wholesaler's Sales Rep.; Operations/Production Manager; Physician; Quality Control Supervisor; Registered Nurse; Securities Sales Representative; Services Sales Representative; Software Engineer; Systems Analyst; Teacher/Professor.

EDWARD BELL ASSOCIATES
50 First Street, Suite 320, San Francisco CA 94105. 415/442-0270. **Fax:** 415/442-1862. **Contact:** Professional Recruiter. **E-mail address:** pres@ebajobs.com. **Description:** An executive search firm operating on both retainer and contingency bases. The firm also provides temporary placements for accounting, finance, clerical, data processing, and real estate professionals. **Specializes in the areas of:** Accounting/Auditing; Administration; Computer Science/Software; Finance; Secretarial. **Positions commonly filled include:** Accountant/Auditor; Clerical Supervisor; Computer Programmer; Credit Manager; Financial Analyst; Internet Services Manager; Multimedia Designer; Paralegal; Property and Real Estate Manager; Software Engineer; Systems Analyst. **Corporate headquarters location:** This Location. **Average salary range of placements:** More than $50,000. **Number of placements per year:** 100 - 199.

BENCH INTERNATIONAL SEARCH INC.
116 North Robertson Boulevard, Suite 800, Los Angeles CA 90048. 310/854-9900. **Contact:** Office Manager. **Description:** An executive search firm. **Specializes in the areas of:** Biotechnology; Pharmaceuticals.

BENNETT & COMPANY CONSULTING GROUP
2135 Manzanita Drive, Oakland CA 94611-1134. 510/339-3175. **Fax:** 510/339-2162. **Contact:** Linda Bennett, Principal. **E-mail address:** lindabennett@earthlink.net. **Description:** An executive search firm operating on both retainer and contingency bases. Bennett & Company Consulting group also provides interview coaching. **Specializes in the areas of:** General Management; Nonprofit; Personnel/Labor Relations; Sales. **Positions commonly filled include:** Account Manager; Accountant; Administrative Manager; Applications Engineer; Credit Manager; Database Manager; Human Resources Manager; Management Analyst/Consultant; MIS Specialist; Operations Manager; Project Manager; Public Relations Manager; Quality Control Supervisor; Sales Engineer; Sales Representative; Software Engineer; Systems Analyst; Systems Manager; Technical Writer/Editor. **Average salary range of placements:** More than $50,000. **Number of placements per year:** 1 - 49.

BENTLEY PRICE ASSOCIATES, INC.
3541 West Oak Trail Road, Santa Ynez CA 93460. 805/686-1234. **Contact:** Dennis P. Rizzo, President. **Description:** An executive search firm that places management consultants in the hospitality industry. **Specializes in the areas of:** Hotel/Restaurant. **Number of placements per year:** 200 - 499.

BERKHEMER/CLAYTON, INC.
221 South Figueroa Street, Suite 240, Los Angeles CA 90012. 213/621-2300. **Contact:** Manager. **Description:** An executive search firm.

BIALLA & ASSOCIATES, INC.
4000 Bridgeway, Suite 201, Sausalito CA 94965. 415/332-7111. **Fax:** 415/332-3964. **Contact:** H. Scott

Thomson, Partner and General Manager. **Description:** An executive search firm. **Specializes in the areas of:** Advertising; General Management; Sales. **Number of placements per year:** 50 - 99.

BILLINGTON & ASSOCIATES, INC.
3250 Wilshire Boulevard, Suite 900, Los Angeles CA 90010. 213/386-7511. **Fax:** 213/386-7025. **Contact:** B.J. Billington, Principal. **Description:** An executive search firm operating on a retainer basis. **Specializes in the areas of:** Accounting/Auditing; Finance. **Positions commonly filled include:** Accountant/Auditor; Administrative Manager; CFO; Clerical Supervisor; Controller; Credit Manager; Customer Service Rep.; Economist; Financial Analyst; MIS Specialist. **Average salary range of placements:** More than $50,000. **Number of placements per year:** 1 - 49.

DEBORAH BISHOP & ASSOCIATES
1070 Marina Village Parkway, Suite 203, Alameda CA 94501. 510/523-2305. **Contact:** Owner. **Description:** An executive search firm that places senior-level managers. **Specializes in the areas of:** Computer Hardware/Software; High-Tech. **Average salary range of placements:** More than $100,000.

THE BLACK LEOPARD
79180 Fox Run, La Quinta CA 92253. 760/771-8400. **Toll-free phone:** 800/360-4191. **Fax:** 760/771-9300. **Contact:** Lauren Kurbatoff, Owner. **E-mail address:** tbleopard@aol.com. **World Wide Web address:** http://www.blackleopard.com. **Description:** The Black Leopard is an executive search firm operating on both retainer and contingency bases. Founded in 1984. **Specializes in the areas of:** Food; Manufacturing; Personnel/Labor Relations; Publishing; Sales. **Positions commonly filled include:** Accountant/Auditor; Agricultural Engineer; Blue-Collar Worker Supervisor; Buyer; Chemical Engineer; Chemist; Civil Engineer; Computer Programmer; Design Engineer; Electrical/Electronics Engineer; Environmental Engineer; Financial Analyst; Food Scientist/Technologist; General Manager; Health Services Manager; Human Service Worker; Industrial Engineer; Industrial Production Manager; Management Trainee; Manufacturer's/Wholesaler's Sales Representative; Market Research Analyst; Mechanical Engineer; MIS Specialist; Operations/Production Manager; Personnel Specialist; Purchasing Agent/Manager; Quality Control Supervisor; Services Sales Rep.; Software Engineer; Strategic Relations Manager; Systems Analyst; Telecommunications Manager; Transportation/Traffic Specialist. **Average salary range of placements:** $30,000 - $50,000. **Number of placements per year:** 50 - 99.

BLACKHAWK ADVANTAGE, INC.
P.O. Box 6226, Irvine CA 92616. 714/731-9400. **Fax:** 714/731-8400. **Contact:** Phil Andersen, Director. **E-mail address:** phil@blackhawkusa.com. **Description:** An executive search firm. **Specializes in the areas of:** Banking; Insurance. **Positions commonly filled include:** Accountant/Auditor; Trust Officer. **Average salary range of placements:** More than $50,000. **Number of placements per year:** 50 - 99.

BLANCHARD, ZUFALL AND ASSOCIATES
P.O. Box 66815, Scotts Valley CA 95066. 831/438-7388. **Fax:** 831/438-1520. **Contact:** Manager. **World Wide Web address:** http://www.bzasearch.com. **Description:** An executive search firm.

BLUE, GARNI & COMPANY
111 Pine Street, Suite 1620, San Francisco CA 94111. 415/986-1110. **Fax:** 415/986-2595. **Contact:** Patricia Blue, Principal. **Description:** Blue, Garni & Company is an executive search firm. **Specializes in the areas of:** Accounting/Auditing; Advertising; Banking; Computer Science/Software; Engineering; Finance; General Management; Transportation. **Positions commonly filled include:** Financial Analyst; General Manager; Industrial Engineer; Internet Services Manager; Management Analyst/Consultant; Management Trainee; Mechanical

Engineer; Public Relations Specialist; Purchasing Agent/ Manager; Strategic Relations Manager; Transportation/ Traffic Specialist; Urban/Regional Planner. **Corporate headquarters location:** This Location. **Other area locations:** San Francisco CA. **Average salary range of placements:** More than $50,000. **Number of placements per year:** 1 - 49.

J. BORAGINE & ASSOCIATES
207 Powell Street, 7th Floor, San Francisco CA 94102. 415/433-1143. **Contact:** Area Manager. **Description:** An executive search firm.

BORDWELL & ASSOCIATES
1400 Quail Street, Suite 100, Newport Beach CA 92660. 949/724-1466. **Contact:** Manager. **Description:** An executive search firm. **Specializes in the areas of:** Legal.

BOWERS THOMAS
11150 West Olympic Boulevard, Suite 805, Los Angeles CA 90064. 310/477-3244. **Fax:** 310/444-1885. **Contact:** Manager. **Description:** An executive search firm operating on both retainer and contingency bases. Bowers Thomas offers placement in traditional legal practice areas such as litigation, corporate transactions, and real estate, and also provides expertise in practices such as patient/IP, employment/labor, and tax. **NOTE:** At least one year of practice experience, following passage of the U.S. Bar exam, is required for placement consideration. **Specializes in the areas of:** Legal. **Positions commonly filled include:** Attorney. **Corporate headquarters location:** This Location. **Other area locations:** San Diego CA. **Other U.S. locations:** Washington DC; Chicago IL; Boston MA; New York NY; Austin TX; Dallas TX; Houston TX; Seattle WA. **International locations:** Vancouver, British Columbia; Sydney, Australia; London, England.

BOWMAN ASSOCIATES
1660 South Amphlett Boulevard, Suite 245, San Mateo CA 94402. 650/573-0188. **Contact:** Office Manager. **Description:** An executive search firm. **Specializes in the areas of:** Hotel/Restaurant.

BOYDEN
Embarcadero Center West Tower, 275 Battery Street, Suite 420, San Francisco CA 94111. 415/981-7900. **Contact:** Manager. **E-mail address:** boydensf@aol.com. **World Wide Web address:** http://www.boyden.com. **Description:** Boyden is a generalist executive search firm. **Corporate headquarters location:** New York NY. **Other U.S. locations:** Washington DC; Chicago IL; Bloomfield Hills MI; Chesterfield MO; Morristown NJ; Hawthorne NY; New York NY; Pittsburgh PA; Houston TX. **International locations:** Worldwide.

BOYLE OGATA
18301 Von Karman Drive, Suite 810, Irvine CA 92612. 949/474-3354. **Fax:** 949/474-2204. **Contact:** Michael Boyle, Partner. **E-mail address:** info@boyleogata.com. **World Wide Web address:** http://www.boyleogata.com. **Description:** An executive search firm. Founded in 1979. **Specializes in the areas of:** Aerospace; Chemicals; Computer Hardware/Software; High-Tech; Medical Devices; Pharmaceuticals; Telecommunications.

BOZICH & CRUZ
2540 North First Street, Suite 309, San Jose CA 95131. 408/955-9800. **Contact:** Area Manager. **Description:** An executive search firm. **Specializes in the areas of:** Computer Science/Software.

BRANDENBURG SMITH & ASSOCIATES
4633 Old Ironsides Drive, Suite 400, Santa Clara CA 95054. 408/727-5554. **Contact:** Manager. **Description:** An executive search firm. **Specializes in the areas of:** Engineering; High-Tech.

BRENNAN ASSOCIATES
19531 Ventura Boulevard, Suite 7, Los Angeles CA 91356. 818/881-3046. **Contact:** Mike Brennan, Branch

Manager. **Description:** An executive search firm. **Specializes in the areas of:** Real Estate.

BRIDGECREEK & ASSOCIATES
12792 Valley View Street, Suite 202, Garden Grove CA 92845. 714/891-1771. **Fax:** 714/892-1567. **Contact:** W.A. (Bill) Foster, President. **Description:** An executive search firm. **Specializes in the areas of:** Distribution; Manufacturing; Plastics. **Positions commonly filled include:** Biological Scientist; Biomedical Engineer; Buyer; Chemical Engineer; Chemist; Civil Engineer; Customer Service Representative; Designer; Electrical/ Electronics Engineer; Environmental Scientist; Food Scientist/Technologist; General Manager; Geologist/ Geophysicist; Industrial Engineer; Industrial Production Manager; Management Analyst/Consultant; Management Trainee; Manufacturer's/Wholesaler's Sales Rep.; Mechanical Engineer; Operations/Production Manager; Personnel Manager; Petroleum Engineer; Purchasing Agent/Manager; Quality Control Supervisor; Services Sales Representative; Software Engineer. **Number of placements per year:** 50 - 99.

BRIDGEGATE LLC
18401 Von Karman, Suite 440, Irvine CA 92612. 949/553-9200. **Fax:** 949/852-0749. **Contact:** Kevin M. Rosenberg, Managing Director. **E-mail address:** info@ bridgegate.com. **World Wide Web address:** http://www.bridgegate.com. **Description:** An executive search firm operating on both retainer and contingency bases. The firm focuses on mid- to senior-level placements in high-tech industries. Founded in 1967. Client company pays fee. **Specializes in the areas of:** Accounting; Computer Science/Software; Consulting; Finance; General Management; Internet Development; Internet Marketing; Marketing; MIS/EDP; Personnel/ Labor Relations; Sales; Scientific; Technical. **Positions commonly filled include:** Account Manager; Account Representative; Accountant; Applications Engineer; AS400 Programmer Analyst; Bank Officer/Manager; Chief Financial Officer; Computer Animator; Computer Engineer; Computer Programmer; Computer Scientist; Consultant; Content Developer; Controller; Cost Estimator; Database Administrator; Database Manager; Finance Director; Financial Analyst; General Manager; Human Resources Manager; Internet Services Manager; Market Research Analyst; Marketing Manager; Marketing Specialist; MIS Specialist; Multimedia Designer; Network/Systems Administrator; Public Relations Specialist; Sales Engineer; Sales Executive; Sales Manager; Sales Representative; Software Engineer; SQL Programmer; Systems Analyst; Systems Manager; Vice President of Finance; Vice President of Marketing and Sales; Webmaster. **Corporate headquarters location:** This Location. **Other area locations:** 10585 Santa Monica Boulevard, Suite 135, Los Angeles CA 90025. **Other U.S. locations:** Nationwide. **Average salary range of placements:** More than $50,000. **Number of placements per year:** 200 - 499.

BRISTOL ASSOCIATES
5757 West Century Boulevard, Suite 628, Los Angeles CA 90045. 310/670-0525. **Contact:** Branch Manager. **Description:** An executive search firm. **Specializes in the areas of:** Direct Marketing; Food; Health/Medical; Hotel/Restaurant.

BROOK-BLAIR LTD.
15970 High Knoll Road, Encino CA 91436. 818/981-9888. **Contact:** President. **Description:** An executive search firm operating on both retainer and contingency bases. **Specializes in the areas of:** Banking. **Positions commonly filled include:** Bank Officer/Manager; Financial Analyst. **Average salary range of placements:** More than $50,000. **Number of placements per year:** 1 - 49.

BROOKS ASSOCIATES
610 Anekapa Street, Santa Barbara CA 93101. 805/963-5858. **Contact:** President. **Description:** An executive search firm operating on both retainer and contingency bases. **Specializes in the areas of:** Advertising;

Cosmetics; General Management; Sales. **Corporate headquarters location:** This Location. **Other U.S. locations:** Nationwide. **Number of placements per year:** 1 - 49.

A.J. BROWN & ASSOCIATES
P.O. Box 61151, Pasadena CA 91106-1151. 626/793-1193. **Contact:** Manager. **Description:** An executive search firm. **Specializes in the areas of:** Technical.

BRYSON MYERS COMPANY
2083 Old Middlefield Way, Suite 206, Mountain View CA 94043. 650/964-7600. **Fax:** 650/964-7655. **Contact:** Partner. **Description:** An executive search firm. **Specializes in the areas of:** Computer Hardware/Software; Engineering; Health/Medical; Technical. **Positions commonly filled include:** Biomedical Engineer; Ceramics Engineer; Computer Programmer; Electrical/Electronics Engineer; Industrial Designer; Industrial Engineer; Manufacturing Engineer; MIS Specialist; Software Engineer; Technical Writer/Editor. **Number of placements per year:** 50 - 99.

BUFF & ASSOCIATES
4539 Canoga Drive, Woodland Hills CA 91367. 818/340-6300. **Contact:** Area Manager. **Description:** An executive search firm. **Specializes in the areas of:** Home Furnishings.

BULLIS & COMPANY, INC.
120 Quintara Street, San Francisco CA 94116. 415/753-6140. **Fax:** 415/753-6653. **Contact:** Richard Bullis, President. **Description:** An executive search firm. **Specializes in the areas of:** Architecture/Construction; Computer Science/Software; Engineering; Finance; General Management; Manufacturing. **Average salary range of placements:** More than $50,000. **Number of placements per year:** 1 - 49.

BUSINESS AND PROFESSIONAL CONSULTANTS
3255 Wilshire Boulevard, Suite 1732, Los Angeles CA 90010. 213/380-8200. **Contact:** Manager. **Description:** An executive search firm. **Number of placements per year:** 1 - 49.

C&C ASSOCIATES
27001 La Paz Road, Suite 400, Mission Viejo CA 92691. 949/859-6733. **Contact:** Manager. **Description:** C&C Associates is an executive search firm. **Specializes in the areas of:** Sales. **Positions commonly filled include:** Sales Manager.

C-E SEARCH
42335 Washington Street, Suite F312, Palm Desert CA 92211. 760/568-3060. **Contact:** Manager. **Description:** An executive search firm, specializing in construction and engineering. Client company pays fee. **Specializes in the areas of:** Construction.

CBA
400 Capital Mall, Suite 900, Sacramento CA 95814. 916/449-3922. **Contact:** Manager. **Description:** An executive search firm that places upper-level managers in a variety of fields.

CN ASSOCIATES
4040 Civic Center Drive, San Rafael CA 94903. 415/883-1114. **Fax:** 415/883-3321. **Contact:** Charles Nicolosi, Principal. **E-mail address:** chasn@earthlink.net. **World Wide Web address:** http://www.cnassociates.com. **Description:** An executive search firm. **Specializes in the areas of:** Administration; Computer Science/Software; Engineering; Sales; Technical. **Positions commonly filled include:** Branch Manager; Computer Programmer; Internet Services Manager; Management Analyst/Consultant; MIS Specialist; Multimedia Designer; Radio/TV Announcer/Broadcaster; Software Engineer; Systems Analyst; Telecommunications Manager. **Average salary range of placements:** More than $50,000. **Number of placements per year:** 1 - 49.

C.R. ASSOCIATES
P.O. Box 60998, Palo Alto CA 94306. 650/324-9000. **Contact:** Harold Stephenson, Owner. **Description:** An executive search firm. **Specializes in the areas of:** Banking; Finance.

CRI PROFESSIONAL SEARCH
1784 Leimert Boulevard, Oakland CA 94602-1930. 510/531-1681. **Toll-free phone:** 800/528-1991. **Fax:** 510/531-9599. **Contact:** Chuck Acridge, Owner. **E-mail address:** chuck@california.com. **Description:** CRI Professional Search is an executive search firm. **Specializes in the areas of:** Health/Medical; Insurance. **Positions commonly filled include:** Physician. **Average salary range of placements:** More than $50,000. **Number of placements per year:** 1 - 49.

CALIFORNIA MANAGEMENT SEARCH (CMS)
881 11th Street, Suite 117, Lakeport CA 95453. 707/263-6000. **Fax:** 707/263-6800. **Contact:** Randy Marsh, Manager/Owner. **Description:** An executive search firm operating on a contingency basis. **Specializes in the areas of:** Insurance. **Positions commonly filled include:** Actuary; Adjuster; Branch Manager; Loss Prevention Specialist; Underwriter. **Corporate headquarters location:** This Location. **Average salary range of placements:** $30,000 - $50,000. **Number of placements per year:** 1 - 49.

CALIFORNIA SEARCH AGENCY, INC. (CSA)
2603 Main Street, Suite 550, Irvine CA 92614-6232. 949/475-0790. **Fax:** 949/475-0796. **Contact:** Don Crane, President. **E-mail address:** dcrane@jobagency.com. **World Wide Web address:** http://www.jobagency.com. **Description:** An executive search firm operating on both retainer and contingency bases. **Specializes in the areas of:** Accounting/Auditing; Administration; Architecture/Construction; Biology; Computer Science/Software; Engineering; Food; General Management; Industrial; Manufacturing; Marketing; Personnel/Labor Relations; Sales; Scientific; Technical; Transportation. **Positions commonly filled include:** Applications Engineer; Biomedical Engineer; Buyer; Chemical Engineer; Chemist; Chief Financial Officer; Civil Engineer; Computer Programmer; Controller; Cost Estimator; Design Engineer; Draftsperson; Electrical/Electronics Engineer; Environmental Engineer; General Manager; Geologist/Geophysicist; Graphic Artist; Graphic Designer; Human Resources Manager; Industrial Engineer; Industrial Production Manager; Manufacturing Engineer; Marketing Manager; Mechanical Engineer; Metallurgical Engineer; MIS Specialist; Operations Manager; Production Manager; Project Manager; Purchasing Agent/Manager; Quality Control Supervisor; Sales Engineer; Sales Executive; Sales Manager; Sales Rep.; Software Engineer; Systems Analyst; Systems Manager; Technical Writer/Editor; Transportation/Traffic Specialist. **Average salary range of placements:** More than $30,000. **Number of placements per year:** 50 - 99.

CALIFORNIA SEARCH CONSULTANTS (CSC)
2103 El Camino Real, Suite 202, Oceanside CA 92054. 760/439-5511. **Fax:** 760/439-0751. **Contact:** Manager. **Description:** An executive search firm. **Specializes in the areas of:** Electronics; Engineering.

CANON BROWER
15315 Magnolia Boulevard, Suite 418, Sherman Oaks CA 91403. 818/501-8088. **Contact:** Branch Manager. **Description:** An executive search firm.

CAREER ADVANTAGE
1215 East Airport Drive, Suite 125, Ontario CA 91761. 909/466-9232. **Fax:** 909/948-1165. **Contact:** Brynda Woods, President. **E-mail address:** resumes@careeradvantage.net. **Description:** An executive search firm. **Specializes in the areas of:** Accounting/Auditing; Administration; Banking; Engineering; Finance; Food; Manufacturing; Personnel/Labor Relations; Sales. **Positions commonly filled include:** Accountant/Auditor; Administrative Manager; Aerospace Engineer; Bank Officer/Manager; Biochemist; Branch Manager; Buyer;

Chemical Engineer; Computer Programmer; Design Engineer; Financial Analyst; General Manager; Human Resources Manager; Industrial Engineer; Industrial Production Manager; Market Research Analyst; Mechanical Engineer; MIS Specialist; Operations/Production Manager; Paralegal; Purchasing Agent/Manager; Registered Nurse; Software Engineer; Systems Analyst; Telecommunications Manager; Transportation/Traffic Specialist; Typist/Word Processor. **Corporate headquarters location:** This Location. **Average salary range of placements:** More than $50,000. **Number of placements per year:** 100 - 199.

CAREER CONSULTANTS INTERNATIONAL (CCI)
620 Newport Center Drive, Newport Beach CA 92660. 949/721-1166. **Fax:** 949/721-8963. **Contact:** Manager. **Description:** An executive search firm. **Specializes in the areas of:** Accounting; Human Resources; Information Technology; Telecommunications.

CARLSON & ASSOCIATES
11400 West Olympic Boulevard, Suite 200, Los Angeles CA 90064. 310/445-1915. **Contact:** Branch Manager. **Description:** An executive search firm. **Specializes in the areas of:** Health/Medical.

J. CARSON & ASSOCIATES
16200 Ventura Boulevard, Suite 228, Encino CA 91436. 818/906-3312. **Fax:** 818/728-6630. **Contact:** Jeannea Nightingale, President. **Description:** An executive search firm. **Specializes in the areas of:** Market Research. **Positions commonly filled include:** Management Analyst/Consultant; Market Research Analyst; Statistician. **Average salary range of placements:** More than $50,000. **Number of placements per year:** 1 - 49.

CARTER & ASSOCIATES
P.O. Box 21444, El Cajon CA 92021. 619/588-5339. **Contact:** Manager. **Description:** An executive search firm. **Specializes in the areas of:** Publishing.

CERTIFIED HEALTH AND PERSONNEL SERVICES
3418 Loma Vista Road, Suite G, Ventura CA 93003. 805/339-2968. **Contact:** Area Manager. **Description:** An executive search firm.

CHAITIN & ASSOCIATES
22543 Ventura Boulevard, Suite 220, Woodland Hills CA 91364. 818/225-8655. **Fax:** 818/225-8660. **Contact:** Chuck Hayes, Sales Manager. **Description:** An executive search firm. **Specializes in the areas of:** Accounting/Auditing; Administration; Broadcasting; Finance; Retail; Sales. **Positions commonly filled include:** Buyer; Credit Manager; General Manager; Human Resources Manager; Manufacturer's/Wholesaler's Sales Rep. **Average salary range of placements:** More than $50,000. **Number of placements per year:** 50 - 99.

WAYNE CHAMBERLAIN & ASSOCIATES
25835 Narbonne Avenue, Suite 280-C, Lomita CA 90717. 310/534-4840. **Fax:** 310/539-9885. **Contact:** Wayne Chamberlain, Owner. **Description:** An executive search firm. **Specializes in the areas of:** Electronics; Engineering; Industrial; Manufacturing; Marketing; Sales. **Positions commonly filled include:** Electrical/Electronics Engineer; Mechanical Engineer. **Number of placements per year:** 1 - 49.

ELSIE CHAN & ASSOCIATES INC.
5751 Palmer Way, Carlsbad CA 92008. 760/944-9478. **Contact:** Manager. **Description:** An executive search firm. **Specializes in the areas of:** Information Systems.

CHRISTIAN & TIMBERS
701 Sutter, 6th Floor, San Francisco CA 94109. 415/885-8004. **Contact:** Manager. **World Wide Web address:** http://www.ctnet.com. **Description:** An executive search firm. **Specializes in the areas of:** Accounting; Banking; Chemicals; Computer Hardware/Software; Consulting; Consumer Package Goods; Consumer Products; Electrical; Electronics; Finance; Information Technology; Insurance; Internet Marketing; Investment; Medical Devices; New Media; Petrochemical; Pharmaceuticals; Restaurant; Retail; Technical; Telecommunications.

CLAIMSEARCH/THE SEARCH GROUP
P.O. Box 357, Fort Bragg CA 95437. 707/964-1795. **Fax:** 707/964-1555. **Contact:** Thomas Bayard, Manager. **E-mail address:** tbayard@mcn.org. **Description:** An executive search firm focusing on property and casualty insurance, claims, and risk management industries. The firm operates on both retainer and contingency bases. **Specializes in the areas of:** Insurance; Risk Management. **Positions commonly filled include:** Adjuster; Claim Representative; Risk Manager. **Other U.S. locations:** Nationwide. **Average salary range of placements:** $30,000 - $50,000. **Number of placements per year:** 1 - 49.

CLARIA CORPORATION
1861 Landings Drive, Mountain View CA 94043. 650/966-1200. **Fax:** 650/966-1450. **Contact:** Manager. **World Wide Web address:** http://www.claria.com. **Description:** An executive search firm. **Specializes in the areas of:** Computer Science/Software; High-Tech; Internet Marketing; Start-up Organizations.

COAST TO COAST EXECUTIVE SEARCH
4040 Civic Center Drive, Suite 200, San Rafael CA 94903. 415/492-2870. **Fax:** 415/491-4710. **Contact:** Alan Horowitz, President. **Description:** An executive search firm. **Specializes in the areas of:** Banking; Computer Science/Software; Consumer Products; Food; Health/Medical; Sales; Technical. **Positions commonly filled include:** Food Scientist/Technologist. **Corporate headquarters location:** This Location. **Average salary range of placements:** More than $50,000. **Number of placements per year:** 1 - 49.

THE COELYN GROUP
Western Business Center of Irvine, One Park Plaza, Irvine CA 92614. 949/553-8855. **Contact:** Manager. **Description:** An executive search firm.

COHEN ASSOCIATES
23801 Calabasas Road, Suite 2032, Calabasas CA 91302. 818/222-6600. **Contact:** Nancy Cohen, Owner. **Description:** An executive search firm. **Specializes in the areas of:** Wireless Communications.

LARRY COMBS EXECUTIVE SEARCH
4909 Stockdale Highway, Suite 289, Bakersfield CA 93309. 661/831-0149. **Contact:** Manager. **Description:** An executive search firm.

COMPUTER NETWORK RESOURCES INC.
28231 Tinajo, Mission Viejo CA 92692. 949/951-5929. **Fax:** 949/951-6013. **Contact:** Ken Miller, President. **Description:** An executive search firm. **Specializes in the areas of:** Computer Science/Software; Information Technology; Insurance; Sales. **Positions commonly filled include:** Systems Analyst; Technical Writer/Editor. **Number of placements per year:** 1 - 49.

COMPUTER PROFESSIONALS UNLIMITED
P.O. Box 4455, Huntington Beach CA 92605-4455. 714/891-1244. **Contact:** Area Manager. **Description:** An executive search firm. **Specializes in the areas of:** Computer Programming; Computer Science/Software.

COMPUTER RECRUITERS, INC.
22276 Buenaventura Street, Woodland Hills CA 91364. 818/704-7722. **Fax:** 818/704-7724. **Contact:** Bob Moore, President. **E-mail address:** b.moore@usa.net. **World Wide Web address:** http://www.tekjobs.com. **Description:** An executive search firm. Computer Recruiters also provides some contract and contract-to-hire placements. Founded in 1980. **Specializes in the areas of:** Information Systems. **Positions commonly filled include:** Computer Programmer; Data Analyst; Database Specialist; Information Systems Director; Network Administrator; Project Manager; Systems Specialist.

CORPORATE DYNAMIX
222 North Sepulveda Boulevard, Suite 2000, El Segundo CA 90245. 310/260-1390. **Fax:** 310/662-4771. **Contact:** Office Manager. **E-mail address:** corpdyn@aol.com. **Description:** An executive search firm. **Specializes in the areas of:** Computer Hardware/Software; Sales. **Positions commonly filled include:** Sales and Marketing Manager; Software Engineer; Systems Analyst. **Average salary range of placements:** More than $50,000. **Number of placements per year:** 100 - 199.

CORPORATE RESOURCES
30220 Rancho Viejo Road, Suite E, San Juan Capistrano CA 92675. 949/248-9655. **Contact:** Nigel McClurg, Owner. **Description:** Corporate Resources is an executive search firm. **Specializes in the areas of:** Computer Programming.

CORPORATE SEARCH
36 Harold Avenue, Suite 11, San Jose CA 95117. 408/985-9500. **Fax:** 408/985-9500. **Contact:** Hal Wilson, President. **Description:** Corporate Search is an executive search firm. **Specializes in the areas of:** Computer Science/Software; Design; Engineering; Technical. **Positions commonly filled include:** Aerospace Engineer; Biomedical Engineer; Chemical Engineer; Computer Programmer; Electrical/Electronics Engineer; Financial Analyst; Industrial Engineer; Management Analyst/Consultant; Mechanical Engineer; Metallurgical Engineer; Nuclear Engineer; Systems Analyst; Technical Writer/Editor; Travel Agent. **Number of placements per year:** 1 - 49.

CORPORATE TECHNOLOGY INC.
P.O. Box 70310, Sunnyvale CA 94086. 408/735-1690. **Fax:** 650/949-0448. **Contact:** John Reinhardt, President. **E-mail address:** corptech@ix.netcom.com. **Description:** An executive search firm. **Specializes in the areas of:** Engineering. **Positions commonly filled include:** Ceramics Engineer; Chemical Engineer; Design Engineer; Electrical/Electronics Engineer; Mechanical Engineer. **Corporate headquarters location:** This Location. **Average salary range of placements:** More than $50,000. **Number of placements per year:** 1 - 49.

CORY ASSOCIATES AGENCY INC.
18500 Von Karman Avenue, Suite 720, Irvine CA 92612. 949/261-1988. **Contact:** Candidate Relations Manager. **Description:** An executive search firm operating on a retainer basis. **Specializes in the areas of:** Sales.

CORY ASSOCIATES AGENCY INC.
16255 Ventura Boulevard, Suite 710, Encino CA 91436. 818/995-7755. **Contact:** Manager. **Description:** An executive search firm. **Specializes in the areas of:** Sales.

CREATIVE LEADERSHIP CONSULTANTS
11777 Bernardo Plaza Court, Suite 101, San Diego CA 92128. 858/592-0506. **Fax:** 858/592-0413. **Contact:** Bob Spence, President/CEO. **Description:** An executive search firm operating on a retainer basis. **Positions commonly filled include:** Branch Manager; Education Administrator; General Manager; Health Services Manager; Operations/Production Manager; Personnel Manager; Software Engineer; Structural Engineer; Technical Writer/Editor. **Other U.S. locations:** Irvine CA; Denver CO. **Average salary range of placements:** More than $50,000. **Number of placements per year:** 50 - 99.

CROWE-INNES & ASSOCIATES
100 Mar West, Suite D, Tiburon CA 94920. 415/435-6211. **Fax:** 415/435-6867. **Contact:** Manager. **World Wide Web address:** http://www.executiverecruit.com. **Description:** An executive search firm.

THE CULVER GROUP
111 North Market Street, Suite 420, San Jose CA 95113. 408/918-0820. **Fax:** 408/918-0827. **Contact:** Patrick Casey, Account Executive. **Description:** An executive search firm operating on a contingency basis. **Specializes**

in the areas of: Computer Science/Software; Engineering; Health/Medical; Marketing; Sales; Technical; Transportation. **Positions commonly filled include:** Account Manager; Account Representative; Applications Engineer; Branch Manager; Computer Programmer; Consultant; Electrical/Electronics Engineer; Management Trainee; Marketing Manager; Sales Engineer; Sales Executive; Sales Manager; Sales Representative; Software Engineer; Systems Analyst; Systems Manager; Vice President of Marketing and Sales. **Corporate headquarters location:** San Diego CA. **Average salary range of placements:** $50,000 - $100,000. **Number of placements per year:** 50 - 99.

THE CULVER GROUP
19700 Fairchild Road, Suite 146, Irvine CA 92612. 949/476-3224. **Fax:** 949/476-8725. **Contact:** Dale Johnson, Branch Manager. **World Wide Web address:** http://www.culvercorp.com. **Description:** An executive search firm. **Specializes in the areas of:** Biotechnology; Finance; General Management; Health/Medical; Insurance; Nonprofit; Retail; Sales; Transportation. **Corporate headquarters location:** San Diego CA.

THE CULVER GROUP
3900 Kilroy Airport Way, Suite 260, Long Beach CA 90807. 562/427-0069. **Fax:** 562/427-3506. **Contact:** George Kaszacs, Branch Manager. **World Wide Web address:** http://www.culvercorp.com. **Description:** An executive search firm operating on a contingency basis. **Specializes in the areas of:** Advertising; Engineering; Finance; Personnel; Sales; Transportation. **Positions commonly filled include:** Account Manager; Account Representative; Advertising Executive; Applications Engineer; Assistant Manager; Management Trainee; Operations Manager; Sales Engineer; Sales Executive; Sales Manager; Sales Representative; Software Engineer; Telecommunications Manager. **Corporate headquarters location:** San Diego CA. **Average salary range of placements:** $30,000 - $50,000. **Number of placements per year:** 50 - 99.

THE CULVER GROUP
3 Pointe Drive, Suite 100, Brea CA 92821. 714/990-4459. **Contact:** Vice President. **World Wide Web address:** http://www.culvercorp.com. **Description:** An executive search firm. **Specializes in the areas of:** Sales. **Positions commonly filled include:** Account Manager; Account Representative; Management Trainee; Sales Executive; Sales Manager; Sales Representative. **Corporate headquarters location:** San Diego CA. **Number of placements per year:** 200 - 499.

THE CULVER GROUP
5994 West Las Positas Boulevard, Suite 111, Pleasanton CA 94588. 510/416-9400. **Fax:** 510/416-9401. **Contact:** Diane Friedenbach, Senior Manager. **E-mail address:** dfbach@pacbell.net. **Description:** An executive search firm. **Specializes in the areas of:** Marketing; Sales. **Positions commonly filled include:** Account Manager; Account Representative; General Manager; Management Trainee; Operations Manager; Sales Engineer; Sales Executive; Sales Manager; Sales Representative. **Corporate headquarters location:** San Diego CA. **Average salary range of placements:** $50,000 - $100,000. **Number of placements per year:** 200 - 499.

CURPHEY & MALKIN ASSOCIATES INC.
13011 West Washington Boulevard, Los Angeles CA 90066. 310/822-7555. **Fax:** 310/305-0467. **Contact:** Area Manager. **Description:** An executive search firm. **Specializes in the areas of:** Data Processing; Sales; Technical.

DBL ASSOCIATES
1334 Park View Avenue, Suite 100, Manhattan Beach CA 90266. 310/546-8121. **Fax:** 310/546-8122. **Contact:** David Long, President. **E-mail address:** davelong@ix.netcom.com. **Description:** An executive search firm. **Specializes in the areas of:** Accounting/Auditing; Administration; Finance; Personnel/Labor Relations. **Positions commonly filled include:** Accountant/Auditor;

CFO; Controller; Finance Director; Financial Analyst; General Manager; MIS Manager; Personnel Manager; Tax Specialist. **Average salary range of placements:** More than $50,000.

DMG-MAXIMUS, INC.
4320 Auburn Boulevard, Suite 2000, Sacramento CA 95841. 916/485-8102. **Contact:** Manager. **Description:** An executive search firm.

DMG-MAXIMUS, INC.
1800 Century Park East, Suite 430, Los Angeles CA 90067. 310/552-1112. **Contact:** Manager. **Description:** An executive search firm.

DNA MEDICAL SEARCH
16133 Ventura Boulevard, Suite 805, Encino CA 91436. 818/986-6300. **Toll-free phone:** 800/434-8687. **Fax:** 818/981-1105. **Contact:** Branch Manager. **World Wide Web address:** http://www.dnasrch.com. **Description:** An executive search firm. **Specializes in the areas of:** Administration; Health/Medical. **Positions commonly filled include:** Health Services Manager. **Number of placements per year:** 50 - 99.

DACO RECRUITING INC.
9852 West Katella Avenue, Suite 254, Anaheim CA 92804. 714/533-2274. **Contact:** Manager. **Description:** An executive search firm. **Specializes in the areas of:** Insurance.

DALEY CONSULTING & SEARCH
1866 Clayton Road, Suite 211, Concord CA 94520. 925/798-3866. **Contact:** Mike Daley, Owner. **E-mail address:** mdaley@dpsearch.com. **World Wide Web address:** http://www.dpsearch.com. **Description:** Daley Consulting & Search is an executive search firm. **Specializes in the areas of:** Computer Science/Software; Data Processing; Information Systems; MIS/EDP. **Positions commonly filled include:** Computer Operator; Computer Programmer; MIS Specialist; Software Engineer; Systems Analyst; Systems Manager; Telecommunications Analyst. **Corporate headquarters location:** This Location. **Other area locations:** Sacramento CA. **Average salary range of placements:** More than $50,000.

DATA CENTER PERSONNEL
24007 Ventura Boulevard, Suite 240, Calabasas CA 91302. 818/225-2830. **Fax:** 818/225-2840. **Contact:** Jim Auld, President. **E-mail address:** datacenter@earthlink. net. **Description:** An executive search firm. **Specializes in the areas of:** Administration; Computer Science/ Software; Information Systems. **Positions commonly filled include:** Computer Programmer; Software Engineer; Systems Analyst; Telecommunications Manager. **Average salary range of placements:** More than $50,000. **Number of placements per year:** 50 - 99.

DAVIDSON & ASSOCIATES
1453 North Benton Way, Los Angeles CA 90026. 213/413-2613. **Fax:** 213/413-2663. **Contact:** Manager. **Description:** An executive search firm. **Specializes in the areas of:** Legal. **Positions commonly filled include:** Attorney.

DELTA FINANCIAL SEARCH
137 South Fuller Avenue, Los Angeles CA 90036. 323/954-1700. **Fax:** 323/954-0104. **Contact:** Manager. **Description:** An executive search firm. **Specializes in the areas of:** Accounting; Finance.

ROBERT W. DINGMAN COMPANY
650 Hampshire Road, Suite 116, Westlake Village CA 91361. 805/778-1777. **Fax:** 805/778-9288. **Contact:** Office Manager. **E-mail address:** info@dingman.com. **Description:** An executive search firm that places senior-level managers with corporations, nonprofit organizations, and educational institutions. The Robert W. Dingman Company operates on a retainer basis. **Specializes in the areas of:** Finance; General Management; Health/Medical; Manufacturing; Sales.

Positions commonly filled include: General Manager; President; Vice President.

DOMINGUEZ METZ & ASSOCIATES
12 Geary Street, Suite 604, San Francisco CA 94108. 415/765-1505. **Contact:** Office Manager. **Description:** An executive search firm. **Specializes in the areas of:** Distribution; Retail.

DOUGLAS DORFLINGER & ASSOCIATES
9171 Wilshire Boulevard, Suite 510, Beverly Hills CA 90210. 310/276-7091. **Contact:** Manager. **Description:** An executive search firm. **Specializes in the areas of:** Construction.

DOUGLAS PERSONNEL ASSOCIATES, INC.
4444 Riverside Drive, Suite 204, Toluca Lake CA 91505. 818/842-2477. **Fax:** 818/842-3874. **Contact:** Leslie Klein, Owner. **Description:** An executive search firm. **Specializes in the areas of:** Management; Retail. **Positions commonly filled include:** Buyer; Designer; General Manager; Human Resources Manager; Merchandiser; MIS Specialist. **Other U.S. locations:** Fort Lee NJ; Manhattan NY. **Average salary range of placements:** More than $50,000.

DRESSLER ASSOCIATES
526 Ramona Street, Palo Alto CA 94301. 650/323-0456. **Contact:** Manager. **Description:** An executive search firm. **Specializes in the areas of:** High-Tech.

DRUMMER PERSONNEL, INC.
700 South Claremont, Suite 103, San Mateo CA 94402. 650/685-1000. **Fax:** 650/685-1007. **Contact:** Geri Geller, Consultant. **Description:** An executive search firm operating on a contingency basis. The firm also provides some permanent placements. **Specializes in the areas of:** Internet Marketing; Marketing; Sales. **Positions commonly filled include:** Account Manager; Account Representative; Administrative Assistant; Advertising Executive; Graphic Designer; Internet Services Manager; Management Trainee; Sales Engineer; Sales Executive; Sales Manager; Sales Rep.; Webmaster. **Corporate headquarters location:** This Location. **Average salary range of placements:** $50,000 - $75,000. **Number of placements per year:** 50 - 99.

J.H. DUGAN & ASSOCIATES
225 Crossroads Boulevard, Suite 416, Carmel CA 93923. 831/625-5880. **Fax:** 831/625-2504. **Contact:** John Dugan, President. **E-mail address:** plastic-recruiter@ jhdugan.com. **World Wide Web address:** http://www. jhdugan.com. **Description:** An executive search firm focusing on market research and acquisitions placements in the plastics industry. **Specializes in the areas of:** Plastics. **Positions commonly filled include:** Chemical Engineer; Chemist; General Manager; Industrial Engineer; Industrial Production Manager; Manufacturer's/Wholesaler's Sales Rep. **Average salary range of placements:** More than $50,000. **Number of placements per year:** 100 - 199.

DUNHILL EXECUTIVE SEARCH OF LOS ANGELES
4727 Wilshire Boulevard, Suite 410, Los Angeles CA 90010. 323/931-1311. **Fax:** 323/931-0565. **Contact:** Branch Manager. **Description:** An executive search firm. **Specializes in the areas of:** Computer Operations; Entertainment; Finance; Government; Health/Medical; Legal; Manufacturing; Nonprofit; Real Estate. **Positions commonly filled include:** Accountant/Auditor; Administrative Assistant; Bookkeeper; Clerk; Customer Service Rep.; Legal Secretary; Sales and Marketing Manager; Secretary; Systems Analyst; Typist/Word Processor. **Number of placements per year:** 200 - 499.

DUNHILL OF SAN FRANCISCO, INC.
268 Bush Street, Suite 2909, San Francisco CA 94104. 415/956-3700. **Toll-free phone:** 800/798-7675. **Fax:** 415/956-3702. **Contact:** George R. Curtiss, President. **E-mail address:** dunhills@pacbell.net. **World Wide Web address:** http://www.dunhillstaff.com. **Description:** An executive search firm operating on a contingency basis.

The firm also provides some permanent placements. Client company pays fee. **Specializes in the areas of:** Engineering; General Management; Industrial; Marketing; Sales; Scientific; Technical. **Positions commonly filled include:** Account Manager; Account Representative; Chemical Engineer; Chemist; Civil Engineer; Design Engineer; Electrical/Electronics Engineer; Environmental Engineer; General Manager; Human Resources Manager; Industrial Engineer; Industrial Production Manager; Manufacturing Engineer; Marketing Manager; Mechanical Engineer; Metallurgical Engineer; Operations Manager; Production Manager; Project Manager; Quality Assurance Engineer; Quality Control Supervisor; Sales Engineer; Sales Executive; Sales Manager; Sales Representative; Vice President. **Other U.S. locations:** Nationwide. **Average salary range of placements:** $50,000 - $100,000.

DUNHILL PROFESSIONAL SEARCH OF OAKLAND, INC.
3732 Mount Diablo Boulevard, Suite 375, Lafayette CA 94549. 925/283-5300. **Fax:** 925/283-5310. **Contact:** John Tierney, President. **Description:** An executive search firm that focuses on high-end engineering and manufacturing management positions in the chemical industry. Searches are conducted on both retainer and contingency bases and candidates are placed with companies throughout the nation. **Specializes in the areas of:** Engineering; Food; Industrial Sales and Marketing; Manufacturing. **Positions commonly filled include:** Biomedical Engineer; Chemical Engineer; Civil Engineer; Electrical/Electronics Engineer; Food Scientist/Technologist; Industrial Engineer; Mechanical Engineer; Metallurgical Engineer; Nuclear Engineer; Petroleum Engineer; President; Project Engineer; Software Engineer; Stationary Engineer; Vice President. **Other U.S. locations:** Nationwide. **Average salary range of placements:** More than $50,000. **Number of placements per year:** 50 - 99.

JOANNE DUNN & ASSOCIATES
824 Moraga Drive, Los Angeles CA 90049. 310/471-5991. **Contact:** Joanne Dunn, Owner. **Description:** An executive search firm.

DUVALL & ASSOCIATES
10 Emerald Glen, Suite 100, Laguna Niguel CA 92677. 949/488-8790. **Fax:** 949/488-8793. **Contact:** Manager. **Description:** An executive search firm. **Specializes in the areas of:** Computer Hardware/Software.

DYNAMIC SYNERGY CORPORATION
2730 Wilshire Boulevard, Suite 550, Santa Monica CA 90403. 310/586-1000. **Contact:** Manager. **Description:** An executive search firm. **Specializes in the areas of:** Computer Science/Software; Sales. **Positions commonly filled include:** Computer Programmer; Database Manager; Marketing Manager; Sales Engineer; Software Engineer; Technical Writer/Editor; Webmaster. **Average salary range of placements:** More than $50,000.

E.C. INTERNATIONAL
16000 Ventura Boulevard, Suite 500, Encino CA 91436. 818/905-7779. **Contact:** Evan Cohn, Owner. **E-mail address:** searcheci@aol.com. **Description:** An executive search firm operating on a contingency basis. The firm places claims adjusters, underwriters, and loss control engineers in the property/casualty insurance industry. **Specializes in the areas of:** Insurance. **Average salary range of placements:** $30,000 - $49,999.

ET SEARCH INC.
1250 Prospect Street, Suite 101, La Jolla CA 92037-3618. 858/459-3443. **Fax:** 858/459-4147. **Contact:** Kathleen Jennings, President. **World Wide Web address:** http://www.etsearch.com. **Description:** An executive search firm that specializes in placing tax executives with *Fortune* 1000 companies and public accounting firms. The firm operates on a retainer basis.

EAGLE SEARCH ASSOCIATES
PMB 295, 336 Bon Air Center, Greenbrae CA 94904. 415/398-6066. **Fax:** 415/924-8996. **Contact:** Mark Gideon, Executive Director. **World Wide Web address:** http://www.eaglesearch.com. **Description:** An executive search firm. **Specializes in the areas of:** Computer Science/Software; Sales. **Positions commonly filled include:** Account Manager; Account Representative; Sales Engineer; Sales Executive; Sales Representative; Systems Analyst; Systems Engineer. **Average salary range of placements:** More than $50,000. **Number of placements per year:** 50 - 99.

EATON & ASSOCIATES
23161 Lake Center Drive, Suite 201, Lake Forest CA 92630. 949/586-3898. **Contact:** Manager. **Description:** An executive search firm. **Specializes in the areas of:** Health/Medical; Plastics.

EDWARDS SEARCH GROUP
769 Monterey Boulevard, Suite 4, San Francisco CA 94127. 415/585-1900. **Contact:** Manager. **Description:** An executive search firm.

ENLOW & ASSOCIATES
P.O. Box 7888, Santa Rosa CA 95407. 707/824-0500. **Contact:** Office Manager. **Description:** An executive search firm.

ENSEARCH MANAGEMENT CONSULTANTS
921 Transport Way, Suite 29, Petaluma CA 94954. 707/766-8700. **Toll-free phone:** 800/473-6776. **Fax:** 707/778-1555. **Contact:** Tim Mattis, Principal. **E-mail address:** headhtr@rpnet.net. **World Wide Web address:** http://www.ensearch.com. **Description:** An executive search firm. **Specializes in the areas of:** Health/Medical. **Positions commonly filled include:** Nurse Practitioner. **Corporate headquarters location:** This Location. **Average salary range of placements:** More than $50,000. **Number of placements per year:** 1 - 49.

ETHOS CONSULTING, INC.
100 Drake's Landing Road, Suite 100, Greenbrae CA 94904. 415/925-0211. **Fax:** 415/925-0688. **Contact:** Conrad E. Prusak, President. **E-mail address:** inquiry@ensearch.com. **Description:** An executive search firm providing senior-level placements. **Specializes in the areas of:** Banking; Computer Programming; Finance; Food; General Management; Health/Medical; Retail; Sales; Transportation. **Positions commonly filled include:** Bank Officer/Manager; General Manager; Management Analyst/Consultant. **Average salary range of placements:** More than $50,000. **Number of placements per year:** 1 - 49.

EXCEL TECHNICAL SERVICES, INC.
30100 Town Center Drive, Suite 129, Laguna Niguel CA 92677. 949/240-0438. **Fax:** 949/240-0817. **Contact:** Bob Langieri, Director. **E-mail address:** excel@excelsearch.com. **World Wide Web address:** http://www.excelsearch.com. **Description:** An executive search firm. The firm also places contract programmers. Founded in 1973. **Specializes in the areas of:** Administration; Computer Science/Software. **Positions commonly filled include:** Systems Analyst; Technical Support Rep. **Average salary range of placements:** More than $50,000. **Number of placements per year:** 100 - 199.

EXECUTIVE DIRECTIONS
155 Sansome Street, Suite 400, San Francisco CA 94104. 415/394-5500. **Contact:** Fred Naderi, President. **World Wide Web address:** http://www.exdir.com. **Description:** Executive Directions is an executive search firm. **Specializes in the areas of:** Computer Hardware/Software; Engineering. **Positions commonly filled include:** Computer Programmer; General Manager; Management Analyst/Consultant; MIS Manager; Multimedia Designer; Science Technologist; Software Engineer; Systems Analyst. **Average salary range of placements:** More than $50,000.

EXECUTIVE DYNAMICS, INC.
330 Washington Boulevard, Suite 713, Marina Del Rey CA 90292. 310/821-6155. **Contact:** Office Manager.

Description: An executive search firm. **Specializes in the areas of:** Computer Science/Software.

THE EXECUTIVE GROUP
9191 Towne Center Drive, Suite 105, San Diego CA 92122. 858/457-8100. **Contact:** Manager. **Description:** An executive search firm.

EXECUTIVE GROUP WEST
369 San Miguel Drive, Suite 200, Newport Beach CA 92660. 949/759-9000. **Contact:** Manager. **Description:** An executive search firm. **Specializes in the areas of:** Sales.

EXECUTIVE MEDICAL SEARCH
111 Pacifica Street, Suite 250, Irvine CA 92618. 949/770-9022. **Fax:** 949/770-5658. **Contact:** Diana Brewer, President. **Description:** An executive search firm operating on a contingency basis. **Specializes in the areas of:** Health/Medical. **Positions commonly filled include:** Administrator; Department Manager; Dietician/Nutritionist; Marketing Manager; Occupational Therapist; Pharmacist; Physical Therapist; Regional Manager; Registered Nurse; Respiratory Therapist; Sales Manager; Vice President. **Other U.S. locations:** AZ; OR; WA. **Number of placements per year:** 1 - 49.

EXECUTIVE RECRUITERS OF DANVILLE
3840 Blackhawk Road, Suite 160, Danville CA 94506. 925/736-1700. **Contact:** Manager. **Description:** An executive search firm. **Specializes in the areas of:** Retail.

EXECUTIVE RESOURCE SYSTEMS
P.O. Box 2992, Capistrano Beach CA 92624. 949/248-3800. **Fax:** 949/496-4407. **Contact:** Steve Brody, President. **E-mail address:** brody@erscareers.com. **World Wide Web address:** http://www.erscareers.com. **Description:** An executive search firm operating on both retainer and contingency bases. **Specializes in the areas of:** Accounting/Auditing; Computer Science/Software; Engineering; Finance; Personnel/Labor Relations; Sales. **Positions commonly filled include:** Accountant; Attorney; Auditor; Budget Analyst; CFO; Computer Programmer; Controller; Cost Estimator; CPA; Credit Manager; Design Engineer; Finance Director; Financial Analyst; Human Resources Manager; Manufacturing Engineer; Sales Executive; Tax Specialist; Webmaster. **Corporate headquarters location:** This Location. **Other U.S. locations:** Nationwide. **Average salary range of placements:** More than $50,000. **Number of placements per year:** 50 - 99.

EXECUTIVE SEARCH CONSULTANTS
21241 Ventura Boulevard, Suite 190, Woodland Hills CA 91364. 818/999-9891. **Contact:** Branch Manager. **Description:** An executive search firm that provides placements in New York and Chicago in financial risk management.

EXECUTIVE SEARCH CONSULTANTS
2108 Appaloosa Circle, Petaluma CA 94954-4643. 707/763-0100. **Fax:** 707/765-6963. **Contact:** Peg Iversen-Grubb, Owner. **Description:** An executive search firm operating on both retainer and contingency bases. **Specializes in the areas of:** Computer Science/Software; Engineering; Technical. **Positions commonly filled include:** Computer Programmer; Electrical/Electronics Engineer; Multimedia Designer; Software Engineer. **Average salary range of placements:** More than $50,000. **Number of placements per year:** 1 - 49.

EXTRACT & ASSOCIATES
7337 Hyannis Drive, West Hills CA 91307. 818/999-2837. **Contact:** Manager. **Description:** An executive search firm. **Specializes in the areas of:** Manufacturing.

FARGO AGENCY
7801 Mission Center Court, Suite 200, San Diego CA 92108. 619/299-9734. **Contact:** Manager. **Description:** An executive search firm.

LEON A. FARLEY ASSOCIATES
468 Jackson Street, San Francisco CA 94111. 415/989-0989. **Contact:** Manager. **Description:** An executive search firm that provides senior-level placements. **Average salary range of placements:** More than $50,000.

FERNEBORG & ASSOCIATES
1450 Fashion Island Boulevard, Suite 650, San Mateo CA 94404. 650/577-0100. **Contact:** Office Manager. **Description:** An executive search firm.

FINESSE PERSONNEL ASSOCIATES
11030 Arrow Route, Suite 204, Rancho Cucamonga CA 91730. 909/980-8765. **Fax:** 909/980-4081. **Contact:** Manager. **Description:** An executive search firm. **Specializes in the areas of:** Accounting/Auditing; Administration; Computer Hardware/Software; Food; General Management; Insurance; Manufacturing; Personnel/Labor Relations; Sales; Secretarial. **Positions commonly filled include:** Accountant/Auditor; Administrative Manager; Biomedical Engineer; Budget Analyst; Buyer; Computer Programmer; Credit Manager; Draftsperson; Environmental Engineer; Financial Analyst; General Manager; Human Resources Manager; Industrial Engineer; Manufacturer's/Wholesaler's Sales Rep.; Market Research Analyst; MIS Specialist; Operations/Production Manager; Systems Analyst; Typist/Word Processor. **Number of placements per year:** 500 - 999.

NEIL FINK & ASSOCIATES
900 North Point Street, Suite 410, San Francisco CA 94109. 415/441-3777. **Contact:** Manager. **Description:** An executive search firm operating on a retainer basis. **Specializes in the areas of:** New Media.

FISHER & ASSOCIATES
1063 Lenor Way, San Jose CA 95128. 408/554-0156. **Fax:** 408/246-7807. **Contact:** Gary Fisher, Owner. **Description:** An executive search firm operating on a retainer basis. **Specializes in the areas of:** Computer Science/Software; Engineering; General Management; Sales. **Positions commonly filled include:** General Manager; Marketing Manager; Sales Executive. **Average salary range of placements:** More than $50,000. **Number of placements per year:** 1 - 49.

FISHER PERSONNEL MANAGEMENT SERVICES
1219 Morningside Drive, Manhattan Beach CA 90266. 310/546-7507. **Fax:** 310/546-7574. **Contact:** Neal Fisher, President. **Description:** A generalist executive search firm operating on a retainer basis for all industries involved in manufacturing operations. The firm also provides other related services including career development, compensation planning, management audit, management consulting, organization planning, and succession planning counsel. Founded in 1986. **Specializes in the areas of:** Engineering; Food; General Management; Industrial; Manufacturing; Personnel/Labor Relations; Publishing; Sales; Technical; Transportation. **Positions commonly filled include:** Administrative Manager; Aerospace Engineer; Branch Manager; Ceramics Engineer; Chemical Engineer; Computer Programmer; Cost Estimator; Customer Service Rep.; Design Engineer; Designer; Environmental Engineer; Financial Analyst; General Manager; Human Resources Specialist; Industrial Engineer; Industrial Production Manager; Management Analyst/Consultant; Management Trainee; Manufacturer's/Wholesaler's Sales Rep.; Market Research Analyst; Materials Engineer; Mechanical Engineer; Metallurgical Engineer; MIS Specialist; Multimedia Designer; Nuclear Engineer; Operations/Production Manager; Purchasing Agent/Manager; Quality Control Supervisor; Securities Sales Representative; Services Sales Representative; Software Engineer; Strategic Relations Manager; Structural Engineer; Systems Analyst; Technical Writer/Editor; Telecommunications Manager. **Average salary range of placements:** More than $50,000. **Number of placements per year:** 1 - 49.

GAVIN FORBES & ASSOCIATES
2207 Garnet Avenue, Suite F, San Diego CA 92109. 858/581-2025. **Fax:** 858/581-2025. **Contact:** Manager. **Description:** An executive search firm. **Specializes in the areas of:** Banking. **Positions commonly filled include:** Bank Officer/Manager. **Other U.S. locations:** Nationwide. **Average salary range of placements:** More than $50,000. **Number of placements per year:** 1 - 49.

F-O-R-T-U-N-E PERSONNEL CONSULTANTS
332 Encinitas Boulevard, Suite 200, Encinitas CA 92024. 760/944-8980. **Fax:** 760/944-0075. **Contact:** Mr. Carmine Furioso, President. **Description:** An executive search firm. **Specializes in the areas of:** Biotechnology; Health/Medical; Pharmaceuticals; Technical. **Positions commonly filled include:** Biomedical Engineer; Quality Control Supervisor; Statistician. **Corporate headquarters location:** New York NY. **Other U.S. locations:** Nationwide. **Average salary range of placements:** More than $50,000.

F-O-R-T-U-N-E PERSONNEL CONSULTANTS
2527 Carmino Ramon, Suite 110, San Ramon CA 94583. 925/461-0170. **Toll-free phone:** 800/291-9229. **Fax:** 925/461-0270. **Contact:** Branch Manager. **Description:** An executive search firm. **Specializes in the areas of:** Computer Hardware/Software; Engineering; Marketing; Sales. **Corporate headquarters location:** New York NY. **Other U.S. locations:** Nationwide.

F-O-R-T-U-N-E PERSONNEL CONSULTANTS
18552 MacArthur Boulevard, Suite 345, Irvine CA 92715. 949/250-0650. **Fax:** 949/250-8535. **Contact:** Manager. **World Wide Web address:** http://www. fortunecom.com. **Description:** An executive search firm. **Specializes in the areas of:** Design; Electrical; Engineering; Marketing; Sales; Telecommunications. **Corporate headquarters location:** New York NY.

F-O-R-T-U-N-E PERSONNEL CONSULTANTS OF BEVERLY HILLS
2615 Pacific Coast Highway, Suite 330, Hermosa Beach CA 90254. 310/376-6964. **Fax:** 310/376-7173. **Contact:** Marc Kasten, President. **Description:** An executive search firm operating on both contingency and retainer bases. **Specializes in the areas of:** Biology; Biotechnology; Engineering; General Management; Health/Medical; Manufacturing; Medical Devices; Pharmaceuticals. **Positions commonly filled include:** Biological Scientist; Biomedical Engineer; Chemical Engineer; Chemist; Electrical/Electronics Engineer; Industrial Engineer; Industrial Production Manager; Mechanical Engineer; Metallurgical Engineer; Pharmacist; Quality Control Supervisor; Research Scientist. **Corporate headquarters location:** New York NY. **Other U.S. locations:** Nationwide. **Number of placements per year:** 50 - 99.

FOX-MORRIS ASSOCIATES
1940 West Orangewood Avenue, Suite 207, Orange CA 92868. 714/634-2600. **Contact:** Manager. **Description:** An executive search firm.

CHARLES FRALICK ASSOCIATES
1766 Lacassie Avenue, Suite 103, Walnut Creek CA 94596. 925/946-0817. **Contact:** Charles Fralick, Owner. **Description:** An executive search firm. **Specializes in the areas of:** Computer Hardware/Software.

FRESQUEZ AND ASSOCIATES
405 14th Street, Suite 208, Oakland CA 94612. 925/274-9360. **Fax:** 925/274-1875. **Contact:** Ernesto Fresquez, Principal. **E-mail address:** ernesto@fresquez.com. **World Wide Web address:** http://www.fresquez.com. **Description:** An executive search firm that focuses on the recruitment of Hispanic and bilingual professionals. **Specializes in the areas of:** Accounting/Auditing; Administration; Advertising; Engineering; Finance; Food; General Management; Information Systems; Latin America; Manufacturing; Personnel/Labor Relations; Sales. **Positions commonly filled include:** Accountant/

Auditor; Budget Analyst; Civil Engineer; Computer Programmer; Customer Service Rep.; Human Resources Manager; Industrial Engineer; Management Analyst/ Consultant; Market Research Analyst; Mechanical Engineer; Operations/Production Manager; Public Relations Specialist; Software Engineer. **Average salary range of placements:** More than $50,000. **Number of placements per year:** 1 - 49.

GM MANAGEMENT SERVICES
2760-7 Tapo Canyon Road, PMB 120, Simi Valley CA 93063. 805/526-0303. **Contact:** Manager. **Description:** An executive search firm. **Specializes in the areas of:** Insurance.

GAGE & ASSOCIATES
5887 Brockton Avenue, Suite 200, Riverside CA 92507. 909/684-4200. **Toll-free phone:** 800/916-4243. **Fax:** 909/684-6138. **Contact:** Art Gage, President. **Description:** An executive search firm. **Positions commonly filled include:** Account Manager; Account Rep.; Buyer; Real Estate Agent; Sales Engineer; Sales Executive; Sales Manager; Sales Representative.

GAJEK KYLE & ASSOCIATES
2600 Michelson Drive, 17th Floor, Irvine CA 92612. 949/852-3600. **Contact:** Office Manager. **Description:** An executive search firm. **Specializes in the areas of:** Accounting/Auditing; Finance.

GARB & ASSOCIATES
2001 Wilshire Boulevard, Suite 510, Santa Monica CA 90403. 310/998-3388. **Contact:** Manager. **Description:** An executive search firm. **Specializes in the areas of:** Legal.

GARRISON-RANDALL INC.
480 Second Street, Suite 304, San Francisco CA 94107. 415/433-2330. **Contact:** Rita Fornino, Vice President. **Description:** An executive search firm operating on both retainer and contingency bases. **Specializes in the areas of:** Health/Medical; Nursing Administration. **Positions commonly filled include:** Accountant/Auditor; Clinical Lab Technician; EEG Technologist; EKG Technician; Medical Records Technician; MIS Specialist; Nuclear Medicine Technologist; Occupational Therapist; Personnel Manager; Physical Therapist; Physician; Psychologist; Registered Nurse; Social Worker; Speech-Language Pathologist; Surgical Technician. **Average salary range of placements:** More than $60,000.

RICHARD GAST & ASSOCIATES
15550-B Rockfield Boulevard, Suite 100, Irvine CA 92618. 949/472-1130. **Fax:** 949/472-0403. **Contact:** Richard Gast, President. **E-mail address:** rgaltd@ deltanet.com. **World Wide Web address:** http://www. rgaltd.com. **Description:** An executive search firm operating on both retainer and contingency bases. Client company pays fee. **Specializes in the areas of:** Personnel/Labor Relations. **Corporate headquarters location:** This Location. **Average salary range of placements:** $50,000 - $100,000.

DIANNE GAUGER & ASSOCIATES
8573 Buena Tierra Place, Buena Park CA 90621-1001. 714/522-4300. **Fax:** 714/522-4338. **Contact:** Dianne Gauger, President. **Description:** An executive search firm. **Specializes in the areas of:** Computer Science/ Software; Engineering; General Management; Industrial; Marketing; Sales; Technical. **Positions commonly filled include:** Chemical Engineer; Computer Programmer; Customer Service Rep.; Design Engineer; Electrical/ Electronics Engineer; General Manager; Manufacturer's/ Wholesaler's Sales Representative; Mechanical Engineer; Operations/Production Manager; Services Sales Rep.; Software Engineer. **Average salary range of placements:** More than $50,000. **Number of placements per year:** 50 - 99.

GENEVAGROUP INTERNATIONAL
4 Embarcadero Center, Suite 1400, San Francisco CA 94111. 415/433-4646. **Fax:** 415/433-6635. **Contact:**

Manager. **World Wide Web address:** http://www.
genevagroup.com. **Description:** An executive search
firm. Founded in 1984. **Specializes in the areas of:**
Computer Hardware/Software; Internet Development;
Internet Marketing.

GLOBAL RESOURCES LTD.
27520 Hawthorne Boulevard, Suite 150, Rolling Hills
Estates CA 90274. 310/544-7145. **Fax:** 310/544-7148.
Contact: Don Gertner, Manager. **Description:** An
executive search firm operating on a retainer basis.
Global Resources also provides some contract
placements. Client company pays fee. **Specializes in the
areas of:** Accounting; Advertising; Banking;
Engineering; Finance; General Management; Industrial;
Marketing; Personnel/Labor Relations; Printing;
Publishing; Retail; Sales; Scientific; Technical. **Positions
commonly filled include:** Account Manager; Account
Rep.; Accountant; Applications Engineer; Bank Officer/
Manager; Biochemist; Biomedical Engineer; Chemical
Engineer; Chief Financial Officer; Computer Scientist;
Controller; Cost Estimator; Credit Manager; Customer
Service Representative; Design Engineer; Finance
Director; Financial Analyst; General Manager; Graphic
Designer; Human Resources Manager; Industrial
Production Manager; Management Analyst/Consultant;
Managing Editor; Manufacturing Engineer; Marketing
Manager; Marketing Specialist; MIS Specialist;
Operations Manager; Production Manager; Project
Manager; Purchasing Agent/Manager; Sales Executive;
Sales Manager; Sales Representative; Transportation/
Traffic Specialist; Vice President of Marketing and
Sales. **Corporate headquarters location:** Los Angeles
CA. **Other U.S. locations:** San Diego CA; San
Francisco CA; Washington DC; Chicago IL; New York
NY. **International locations:** London, England; Odessa,
Ukraine. **Average salary range of placements:** More
than $100,000. **Number of placements per year:** 100 -
199.

BARRY GOLDBERG & ASSOCIATES, INC.
2049 Century Park East, Suite 1100, Los Angeles CA
90067. 310/277-5800. **Contact:** Manager. **Description:**
An executive search firm. **Specializes in the areas of:**
Legal. **Positions commonly filled include:** Attorney.

THE GOODMAN GROUP
P.O. Box G, San Rafael CA 94913-3908. 415/472-6500.
Contact: Office Manager. **E-mail address:** mail@
goodmangroup.com. **World Wide Web address:**
http://www.goodmangroup.com. **Description:** An
executive search firm operating on a retainer basis.
Client company pays fee. **Specializes in the areas of:**
Computer Science/Software; Health/Medical; Insurance.
Positions commonly filled include: Aerospace
Engineer; Biomedical Engineer; Civil Engineer;
Computer Programmer; Consultant - Computer; EDP
Specialist; Electrical/Electronics Engineer; General
Manager; Management Analyst/Consultant; Physician;
Sales Executive; Sales Manager; Sales Rep.; Systems
Analyst. **Corporate headquarters location:** This
Location. **Average salary range of placements:** More
than $100,000. **Number of placements per year:** 50 -
99.

GORELICK & ASSOCIATES
1971 East Fourth Street, Suite 100, Santa Ana CA 92705.
714/667-5050. **Fax:** 714/571-1830. **Contact:** Michael
Gorelick, Vice President. **Description:** An executive
search firm. **Specializes in the areas of:** Computer
Science/Software; Consumer Package Goods; Food;
General Management; Sales; Telecommunications.
Positions commonly filled include: Branch Manager;
Management Analyst/Consultant; Manufacturer's/
Wholesaler's Sales Rep. **Number of placements per
year:** 50 - 99.

GRANT & ASSOCIATES
417 Montgomery Street, Suite 910, San Francisco CA
94104. 415/986-1500. **Fax:** 415/986-1630. **Contact:**
Susan Grant, President. **Description:** An executive
search firm operating on a retainer basis. **Specializes in

the areas of: Computer Science/Software; Engineering;
General Management; Manufacturing; Sales; Technical.
Positions commonly filled include: Aerospace
Engineer; Biochemist; Biomedical Engineer; Branch
Manager; Chemical Engineer; Electrical/Electronics
Engineer; General Manager; Human Resources Manager;
Internet Services Manager; Management Analyst/
Consultant; Manufacturer's/Wholesaler's Sales Rep.;
Mechanical Engineer; MIS Specialist; Multimedia
Designer; Operations/Production Manager; Science
Technologist; Services Sales Representative; Software
Engineer; Strategic Relations Manager; Systems Analyst;
Telecommunications Manager. **Average salary range of
placements:** More than $50,000. **Number of
placements per year:** 1 - 49.

GREEN ROBERTS & ASSOCIATES
One Sansome Street, Suite 2100, San Francisco CA
94104. 415/951-1012. **Contact:** Manager. **Description:**
An executive search firm.

GREGORY & LEIGH
450 San Antonio Road, Suite 20, Palo Alto CA 94306.
650/493-9066. **Contact:** Office Manager. **Description:**
An executive search firm.

GRIFFITH & ASSOCIATES
1001 Reno Avenue, Suite 2B, Modesto CA 95351.
209/521-2898. **Contact:** Manager. **Description:** An
executive search firm that also provides business analysis
and motivational speaking services. **Specializes in the
areas of:** Construction; Engineering; Food; Health/
Medical; Industrial.

GROENEKAMP & ASSOCIATES
P.O. Box 2308, Beverly Hills CA 90213. 310/855-0119.
Contact: Manager. **Description:** An executive search
firm.

ALICE GUNDERSON & ASSOCIATES
5757 West Century Boulevard, Suite 700, Los Angeles
CA 90045. 310/530-1942. **Fax:** 310/530-1737. **Contact:**
Alice Gunderson, Manager. **Description:** An executive
search firm. **Specializes in the areas of:** Retail.

BERNARD HALDANE ASSOCIATES
1340 Treat Boulevard, Suite 220, Walnut Creek CA
94596. 925/945-0776. **Contact:** Manager. **Description:**
An executive search firm. **Other U.S. locations:**
Nationwide.

ROBERT HALF INTERNATIONAL
ACCOUNTEMPS
10877 Wilshire Boulevard, Suite 1605, Los Angeles CA
90024. 310/286-6800. **Contact:** Recruiter. **Description:**
An executive search firm. **Specializes in the areas of:**
Accounting/Auditing; Banking; Computer Hardware/
Software; Finance; MIS/EDP. **Positions commonly
filled include:** Accountant/Auditor; Bank Officer/
Manager; Bookkeeper; Computer Programmer; Credit
Manager; Data Entry Clerk; EDP Specialist; Financial
Analyst; Human Resources Manager; Systems Analyst.
Corporate headquarters location: Menlo Park CA.
International locations: Worldwide. **Number of
placements per year:** 500 - 999.

HARLEY ASSOCIATES
1370 Brea Boulevard, Suite 130, Fullerton CA 92835-
4125. 714/441-0223. **Fax:** 714/441-0224. **Contact:**
Wayne Harley, President. **Description:** An executive
search firm. **Specializes in the areas of:** Engineering;
Technical; Wireless Communications. **Positions
commonly filled include:** Construction and Building
Inspector; Construction Contractor; Design Engineer;
Electrical/Electronics Engineer; Software Engineer;
Structural Engineer; Telecommunications Manager.
Average salary range of placements: More than
$50,000.

HARMELING & ASSOCIATES
3232 Governor Drive, Suite J, San Diego CA 92122.
858/455-6212. **Contact:** Manager. **Description:** An

executive search firm. **Specializes in the areas of:** Architecture/Construction.

HARRISON GLENN & ASSOCIATES
801 East Katella Avenue, Suite 210, Anaheim CA 92805. 714/939-2849. **Contact:** Manager. **Description:** An executive search firm.

HEALTHCARE EXECUTIVE RECRUITERS INC.
17003 Ventura Boulevard, Suite E-1, Encino CA 91316. 818/788-0150. **Fax:** 818/788-6549. **Contact:** Manager. **Description:** An executive search firm operating on both retainer and contingency bases. **Specializes in the areas of:** Health/Medical. **Positions commonly filled include:** Chief Financial Officer; Health Care Administrator; Health Services Manager; Physician; Registered Nurse. **Corporate headquarters location:** Dallas TX. **Average salary range of placements:** More than $50,000. **Number of placements per year:** 50 - 99.

HEALTHCARE RECRUITERS OF LOS ANGELES
15300 Ventura Boulevard, Suite 207, Sherman Oaks CA 91403. 818/981-9510. **Fax:** 818/981-9523. **Contact:** Deborah Wilson, Vice President of Operations. **E-mail address:** hcrla@aol.com. **World Wide Web address:** http://www.hcrintl.com. **Description:** An executive search firm. **Specializes in the areas of:** Engineering; Health/Medical; Technical. **Positions commonly filled include:** Account Manager; Account Representative; Advertising Executive; Applications Engineer; Biochemist; Biological Scientist; Biomedical Engineer; Branch Manager; Budget Analyst; Buyer; Chemical Engineer; Chemist; Chief Financial Officer; Clinical Lab Technician; Computer Programmer; Controller; Database Manager; Design Engineer; Dietician/Nutritionist; Electrical/Electronics Engineer; Finance Director; General Manager; Human Resources Manager; Industrial Engineer; Industrial Production Manager; Internet Services Manager; Management Analyst/Consultant; Manufacturer's/Wholesaler's Sales Rep.; Market Research Analyst; Marketing Manager; Marketing Specialist; Mechanical Engineer; MIS Specialist; Nuclear Engineer; Nuclear Medicine Technologist; Online Content Specialist; Operations/Production Manager; Pharmacist; Physician; Production Manager; Project Manager; Quality Control Supervisor; Radiological Technologist; Registered Nurse; Respiratory Therapist; Sales Engineer; Sales Executive; Sales Manager; Sales Rep.; Services Sales Representative; Software Engineer; Systems Analyst; Systems Manager; Vice President; Webmaster. **Corporate headquarters location:** Dallas TX. **Other U.S. locations:** Nationwide. **Average salary range of placements:** More than $50,000.

HEALTHCARE RECRUITERS OF ORANGE COUNTY
26361 Crown Valley Parkway, Suite 150, Mission Viejo CA 92691. 949/367-7888. **Fax:** 949/367-7881. **Contact:** Manager. **Description:** An executive search firm. **Specializes in the areas of:** Health/Medical. **Corporate headquarters location:** Dallas TX.

HEALTHCARE RECRUITERS OF SAN DIEGO
701 Palomar Airport Road, Suite 300, Carlsbad CA 92009. 760/931-4790. **Fax:** 760/931-9979. **Contact:** Judy Thurmond, Owner. **Description:** An executive search firm operating on both retainer and contingency bases. **Specializes in the areas of:** Biotechnology; Health/Medical. **Positions commonly filled include:** Account Manager; Account Representative; Applications Engineer; Biochemist; Biomedical Engineer; Branch Manager; CFO; Computer Programmer; Controller; Customer Service Representative; Dietician/Nutritionist; Financial Analyst; General Manager; Health Services Manager; Industrial Production Manager; Manufacturing Engineer; Market Research Analyst; Mechanical Engineer; Medical Records Technician; MIS Specialist; Operations/Production Manager; Pharmacist; Physical Therapist; Physician; Production Manager; Project Manager; Quality Control Supervisor; Registered Nurse; Sales Executive; Sales Representative; Software Engineer; Systems Manager. **Corporate headquarters location:** Dallas TX. **Average salary range of**

placements: More than $50,000. **Number of placements per year:** 50 - 99.

HEIDRICK & STRUGGLES
2740 Sand Hill Road, Menlo Park CA 94025. 650/234-1500. **Fax:** 650/854-4191. **Contact:** Branch Manager. **Description:** An executive search firm.

HEIDRICK & STRUGGLES
18101 Von Karman Avenue, Suite 1050, Irvine CA 92612. 949/475-6500. **Fax:** 949/475-6525. **Contact:** Manager. **Description:** An executive search firm.

HEIDRICK & STRUGGLES
300 South Grand Avenue, Suite 2400, Los Angeles CA 90071. 213/625-8811. **Fax:** 213/617-7216. **Contact:** Manager. **Description:** An executive search firm.

HEIDRICK & STRUGGLES
4 Embarcadero Center, Suite 3570, San Francisco CA 94111. 415/981-2854. **Fax:** 415/981-0482. **Contact:** Manager. **Description:** An executive search firm.

BRUCE HENRY ASSOCIATES
465 California Street, Suite 450, San Francisco CA 94104. 415/438-2110. **Fax:** 415/438-2112. **Contact:** Bruce Henry, President. **E-mail address:** bh@brucehenry.com. **World Wide Web address:** http://www.brucehenry.com. **Description:** An executive search firm operating on a retainer basis. **Specializes in the areas of:** Health/Medical. **Positions commonly filled include:** Administrative Manager; Assistant Manager; Auditor; Biochemist; Branch Manager; Budget Analyst; Buyer; Chief Financial Officer; Computer Programmer; Controller; Database Manager; Dietician/Nutritionist; Finance Director; Financial Analyst; Health Care Risk Consultant; Human Resources Manager; Industrial Engineer; Licensed Practical Nurse; Marketing Manager; Medical Records Technician; MIS Specialist; Operations Manager; Pharmacist; Physical Therapist; Physician; Psychologist; Registered Nurse; Sales Manager; Software Engineer; Systems Analyst; Systems Manager; Technical Writer/Editor; Veterinarian. **Average salary range of placements:** More than $50,000. **Number of placements per year:** 1 - 49.

HERITAGE PACIFIC CORPORATION
14172 Klee Drive, Suite 500, Irvine CA 92606. 949/559-1166. **Contact:** Gary Draper, Manager. **Description:** An executive search firm focusing on the placement of experienced professionals in the paper industry. **Positions commonly filled include:** Chemical Engineer; Chemist; Civil Engineer; Electrical/Electronics Engineer; Industrial Production Manager; Multimedia Designer; Operations/Production Manager; Quality Control Supervisor. **Average salary range of placements:** More than $50,000. **Number of placements per year:** 1 - 49.

HERRERIAS & ASSOCIATES
330 Sir Francis Drake Boulevard, Suite E, San Anselmo CA 94960. 415/398-1001. **Contact:** Paul Herrerias, Executive Director. **E-mail address:** recruit@herrerias.com. **World Wide Web address:** http://www.herrerias.com. **Description:** An executive search firm operating on a retainer basis. **Specializes in the areas of:** Accounting/Auditing; Administration; Advertising; Banking; Finance; General Management; Personnel/Labor Relations; Sales. **Positions commonly filled include:** Accountant/Auditor; Bank Officer/Manager; Financial Analyst; Management Analyst/Consultant; Telecommunications Manager. **Average salary range of placements:** More than $50,000.

HEURISTICS SEARCH INC.
160 West Santa Clara Street, Suite 1200, San Jose CA 95113. 408/925-9300. **Contact:** Manager. **Description:** An executive search firm. **Specializes in the areas of:** High-Tech.

HOCHMAN & ASSOCIATES
1801 Avenue of the Stars, Suite 420, Los Angeles CA 90067. 310/552-0662. **Fax:** 310/552-4650. **Contact:** Judi

L. Hochman, President. **Description:** An executive search firm operating on both retainer and contingency bases. The firm provides placements in investment banking and portfolio management. **Specializes in the areas of:** Banking; Legal; Personnel/Labor Relations. **Positions commonly filled include:** Customer Service Representative; Financial Analyst; Human Service Worker. **Average salary range of placements:** More than $50,000. **Number of placements per year:** 50 - 99.

HOCKETT ASSOCIATES INC.
P.O. Box 1765, Los Altos CA 94023. 650/941-8815. **Contact:** Manager. **Description:** An executive search firm. **Specializes in the areas of:** Biotechnology.

HOLLAND EXECUTIVE SEARCH
P.O. Box 9774, Marina Del Rey CA 90295. 310/459-1802. **Contact:** Joy Spencer, Office Manager. **Description:** An executive search firm. Client company pays fee. **Specializes in the areas of:** Technical. **Positions commonly filled include:** Attorney; Design Engineer; General Manager. **International locations:** Worldwide.

HOLLANDER HORIZON INTERNATIONAL
1617 South Pacific Coast Highway, Suite C, Redondo Beach CA 90277. 310/540-3231. **Fax:** 310/540-4230. **Contact:** Arnold Zimmerman, Senior Partner. **Description:** An executive search firm. **Specializes in the areas of:** Consumer Products; Food. **Positions commonly filled include:** Agricultural Engineer; Biological Scientist; Chemical Engineer; Food Scientist/Technologist; Industrial Engineer; Market Research Analyst; Mechanical Engineer; Operations/Production Manager; Quality Control Supervisor. **Other U.S. locations:** MN; NJ. **Average salary range of placements:** More than $50,000. **Number of placements per year:** 1 - 49.

HONEYCUTT INTERNATIONAL
1935 North Marshall Avenue, Suite C, El Cajon CA 92202. 619/258-7404. **Toll-free phone:** 800/407-5700. **Fax:** 619/258-2139. **Contact:** Recruiter. **E-mail address:** headhunters@worldnet.att.net. **Description:** Honeycutt International is an executive search firm that also offers career consultation services. **Corporate headquarters location:** This Location. **Other U.S. locations:** Nationwide. **International locations:** Worldwide.

FRED L. HOOD & ASSOCIATES
23801 Calabasas Road, Suite 2034, Calabasas CA 91302. 818/222-6222. **Contact:** Manager. **Description:** An executive search firm operating on both retainer and contingency bases. **Specializes in the areas of:** Consumer Package Goods; Food; Marketing; Sales. **Positions commonly filled include:** Account Manager; Account Representative; Advertising Executive; General Manager; Marketing Manager; MIS Specialist; Sales Executive; Sales Manager; Sales Rep. **Average salary range of placements:** $50,000 - $100,000. **Number of placements per year:** 50 - 99.

R.H. HORTON INTERNATIONAL
24405 Chestnut Street, Suite 107, Santa Clarita CA 91321. 661/222-2272. **Contact:** Manager. **Description:** An executive search firm.

HUGHES PERRY & ASSOCIATES
P.O. Box 384, Sea Ranch CA 95497. 707/785-3083. **Contact:** Manager. **E-mail address:** hpa@mcn.org. **Description:** An executive search firm. **Specializes in the areas of:** Government. **Other area locations:** San Francisco CA.

HUTTON BARNES & ASSOCIATES
5900 Sepulveda Boulevard, Suite 104, Sherman Oaks CA 91411. 818/989-2500. **Contact:** Manager. **Description:** An executive search firm. **Specializes in the areas of:** Computer Hardware/Software; Technical.

IMPACT, INC.
1000 Fremont Avenue, Suite 210, Los Altos CA 94024. 650/941-9400. **Fax:** 650/917-1424. **Contact:** Mary Voss, President. **Description:** An executive search firm operating on a retainer basis. **Specializes in the areas of:** Computer Science/Software; Engineering; Personnel/Labor Relations. **Positions commonly filled include:** Computer Programmer; Design Engineer; Designer; Electrical/Electronics Engineer; Human Resources Manager; Industrial Engineer; Mathematician; Mechanical Engineer; MIS Specialist; Multimedia Designer; Quality Control Supervisor; Software Engineer; Systems Analyst; Telecommunications Manager. **Benefits available to temporary workers:** 401(k). **Average salary range of placements:** More than $50,000. **Number of placements per year:** 1000+.

INDEPENDENT RESOURCE SYSTEMS, INC.
28222 Agoura Road, Suite 201, Agoura Hills CA 91301. 818/999-5690. **Fax:** 818/865-3155. **Contact:** Don Speth, President. **Description:** Independent Resource Systems is an executive search firm operating on both retainer and contingency bases. **Specializes in the areas of:** Administration; Engineering; High-Tech; Sales; Technical. **Positions commonly filled include:** Mechanical Engineer; MIS Specialist; Multimedia Designer; Software Engineer; Technical Writer/Editor; Telecommunications Manager. **Average salary range of placements:** More than $50,000.

INFOSYS
2377 Gold Meadow Way, Gold River CA 95670. 916/526-2760. **Contact:** Manager. **World Wide Web address:** http://www.istechstaff.com. **Description:** An executive search firm. **Specializes in the areas of:** Information Technology.

INNOVATIVE SEARCH ASSOCIATES (ISA)
P.O. Box 6955, Laguna Niguel CA 92607. 949/488-0010. **Contact:** Manager. **Description:** An executive search firm.

INTECH SUMMIT GROUP, INC.
5075 Shoreham Place, Suite 280, San Diego CA 92122. 619/452-2100. **Fax:** 619/452-8500. **Contact:** Manager. **Description:** An executive search firm. **Specializes in the areas of:** Health/Medical; Human Resources.

INTERACTIVE SEARCH NETWORK
3330 Pierce Street, Suite 305, San Francisco CA 94123. 415/921-0663. **Fax:** 415/776-9361. **Contact:** Doug Perlstadt, Manager. **E-mail address:** dougexecs@aol.com. **Description:** Interactive Search Network is an executive search firm operating on a retainer basis. Founded in 1996. Client company pays fee. **Specializes in the areas of:** Administration; Fashion; General Management; Internet Marketing; Marketing; Retail; Sales. **Positions commonly filled include:** Account Manager; Advertising Executive; Branch Manager; Buyer; Chief Financial Officer; Controller; Marketing Manager; Sales Executive; Sales Manager. **Average salary range of placements:** More than $100,000. **Number of placements per year:** 1 - 49.

INTERNATIONAL STAFFING CONSULTANTS
2010 Main Street, Suite 840, Irvine CA 92614. 949/263-5200. **Fax:** 949/263-5201. **Contact:** James Gettys, President. **E-mail address:** iscinc@iscworld.com. **World Wide Web address:** http://www.iscworld.com. **Description:** An executive search firm operating on a contingency basis. International Staffing Consultants also provides contract services. **Specializes in the areas of:** Architecture/Construction; Computer Science/Software; Engineering; Industrial; Marketing; Personnel/Labor Relations; Sales; Scientific; Technical; Transportation. **Positions commonly filled include:** Administrative Manager; Applications Engineer; Architect; Chemical Engineer; Chemist; Civil Engineer; Computer Animator; Computer Operator; Computer Programmer; Controller; Cost Estimator; Database Manager; Design Engineer; Draftsperson; Electrical/Electronics Engineer; ESL Teacher; General Manager; Geologist/Geophysicist;

Human Resources Manager; Industrial Engineer; Industrial Production Manager; Management Analyst/Consultant; Manufacturing Engineer; Market Research Analyst; Marketing Manager; Marketing Specialist; Mechanical Engineer; Metallurgical Engineer; MIS Specialist; Multimedia Designer; Operations Manager; Production Manager; Project Manager; Purchasing Agent/Manager; Quality Control Supervisor; Sales Engineer; Sales Executive; Sales Manager; Software Engineer; Systems Analyst; Systems Manager; Telecommunications Manager; Transportation/Traffic Specialist. **Benefits available to temporary workers:** 401(k). **Corporate headquarters location:** This Location. **International locations:** England; Saudi Arabia. **Average salary range of placements:** More than $50,000. **Number of placements per year:** 100 - 199.

INTERSTATE RECRUITERS CORPORATION
5126 Clareton Drive, Suite 204, Agoura Hills CA 91301. 818/706-3737. **Contact:** Office Manager. **Description:** An executive search firm. **Specializes in the areas of:** Engineering; Health/Medical.

BETH ISABELLE & ASSOCIATES INC.
374 F Avenue, Coronado CA 92118. 619/437-8436. **Contact:** Beth Isabelle, Manager. **Description:** An executive search firm that focuses on providing placements in Mexico. **Specializes in the areas of:** Banking; Manufacturing.

ALAN ISRAEL EXECUTIVE SEARCH
3655 Torrance Boulevard, Suite 316, Torrance CA 90503. 310/370-0144. **Fax:** 310/370-8868. **Contact:** Alan Israel, Manager. **Description:** An executive search firm. **Specializes in the areas of:** Computer Science/Software.

JPM INTERNATIONAL
26034 Acero, Mission Viejo CA 92691. 949/955-2545. **Fax:** 949/699-4333. **Contact:** Trish Ryan, Vice President. **Description:** An executive search firm. **Specializes in the areas of:** Engineering; Environmental; Health/Medical; Industrial; Insurance; Manufacturing; Sales; Technical; Telecommunications. **Positions commonly filled include:** Accountant/Auditor; Biological Scientist; Biomedical Engineer; Chemical Engineer; Electrical/Electronics Engineer; Emergency Medical Technician; Health Services Manager; Manufacturer's/Wholesaler's Sales Rep.; Mechanical Engineer; Medical Records Technician; Metallurgical Engineer; Nuclear Engineer; Nuclear Medicine Technologist; Occupational Therapist; Pharmacist; Physical Therapist; Radiological Technologist; Registered Nurse; Respiratory Therapist; Services Sales Rep.; Software Engineer; Structural Engineer; Systems Analyst. **Corporate headquarters location:** This Location. **Number of placements per year:** 500 - 999.

CINDY JACKSON SEARCH INTERNATIONAL (CJSI)
3031 Tisch Way, Suite 700, San Jose CA 95128. 408/247-6767. **Contact:** Manager. **Description:** An executive search firm. **Specializes in the areas of:** Computer Hardware/Software; Electronics; Sales.

DAVID JAMES SEARCH
27315 Jefferson Avenue, Suite J, Temecula CA 92590. 909/693-2555. **Fax:** 909/693-2881. **Contact:** David James, President. **E-mail address:** mail@davidjamessearch.com. **World Wide Web address:** http://www.davidjamessearch.com. **Description:** David James Search is an executive search firm operating on both retainer and contingency bases. The firm places internal auditors with *Fortune* 500 companies. **Positions commonly filled include:** Auditor. **Average salary range of placements:** $50,000 - $100,000. **Number of placements per year:** 50 - 99.

THE JAMESON GROUP
1900 Avenue of the Stars, Suite 670, Los Angeles CA 90067-4301. **Contact:** John B. Jameson, President. **E-mail address:** tjg@thejamesongroup.com. **Description:**

An executive search firm operating on both retainer and contingency bases. **Specializes in the areas of:** Legal. **Positions commonly filled include:** Attorney. **Average salary range of placements:** More than $50,000. **Number of placements per year:** 50 - 99.

JATINEN & ASSOCIATES
20422 Beach Boulevard, Suite 235, Huntington Beach CA 92648. 714/960-9082. **Fax:** 714/960-1772. **Contact:** Manager. **Description:** An executive search firm focusing on placements in the title insurance industry. **Specializes in the areas of:** Insurance. **Number of placements per year:** 1 - 49.

AARON JENSEN ASSOCIATES INC.
275 North Ola Vista, San Clemente CA 92672. 949/498-6050. **Contact:** Manager. **Description:** An executive search firm. **Specializes in the areas of:** Computer Hardware/Software; Paper.

JEROME & COMPANY
211 Culver Boulevard, Suite R, Playa Del Ray CA 90293. 310/305-1812. **Fax:** 310/305-8678. **Contact:** Gerald E. Jerome, President. **Description:** An executive search firm. **Specializes in the areas of:** Engineering; General Management; Industrial; Manufacturing. **Positions commonly filled include:** Aerospace Engineer; Electrical/Electronics Engineer; General Manager; Industrial Engineer; Industrial Production Manager; Mechanical Engineer; Metallurgical Engineer; Operations/Production Manager; Personnel Manager; Purchasing Agent/Manager; Quality Control Supervisor. **Number of placements per year:** 1 - 49.

JOB LINK INC.
7060 Miramar Road, Suite 205, San Diego CA 92121. 858/695-1100. **Contact:** Manager. **Description:** An executive search firm. **Specializes in the areas of:** High-Tech; Manufacturing; Professional; Technical.

JOB SEARCH
137 East Thousand Oaks Boulevard, Suite 203, Thousand Oaks CA 91360. 805/496-9908. **Fax:** 805/496-5512. **Contact:** Peter H. Wolf, President. **E-mail address:** jobsearch@jsearch.com. **World Wide Web address:** http://www.jsearch.com. **Description:** An executive search firm operating on both retainer and contingency bases. **Positions commonly filled include:** Accountant/Auditor; Aerospace Engineer; Biological Scientist; Biomedical Engineer; Chemist; Computer Operator; Computer Programmer; Construction Trade Worker; Electrical/Electronics Engineer; Industrial Designer; Industrial Engineer; Manufacturing Engineer; Marketing Specialist; Mechanical Engineer; MIS Specialist; Operations/Production Manager; Public Relations Specialist; Purchasing Agent/Manager; Quality Control Supervisor; Sales Rep.; Software Engineer; Systems Analyst. **Average salary range of placements:** More than $50,000. **Number of placements per year:** 500 - 999.

JOHN ANTHONY & ASSOCIATES
P.O. Box 12291, La Jolla CA 92039-2291. 858/457-1116. **Contact:** John A. Muller, Jr., Principal Recruiter. **Description:** John Anthony & Associates is an executive search firm that operates on both contingency and retainer bases. **Specializes in the areas of:** Accounting/Auditing; Administration; Biotechnology; Computer Science/Software; Engineering; Finance; General Management; Insurance; Management; Sales; Secretarial; Telecommunications. **Positions commonly filled include:** Accountant; Actuary; Administrative Assistant; Administrative Manager; Auditor; Bank Officer/Manager; Biological Scientist; Biomedical Engineer; Budget Analyst; Chemical Engineer; Chemist; Chief Financial Officer; Computer Programmer; Controller; Credit Manager; Database Manager; Finance Director; Financial Analyst; General Manager; Human Resources Manager; Internet Services Manager; Marketing Manager; Marketing Specialist; Mechanical Engineer; MIS Specialist; Nuclear Engineer; Operations Manager; Sales Executive; Sales Manager; Science

Technologist; Secretary; Software Engineer; Systems Analyst; Systems Manager; Telecommunications Manager; Typist/Word Processor; Underwriter/Assistant Underwriter. **Average salary range of placements:** More than $50,000.

JOHNSTON ASSOCIATES
2680 Mary Lane, Escondido CA 92025. 858/487-5200. **Contact:** Manager. **Description:** An executive search firm. **Specializes in the areas of:** Health/Medical. **Positions commonly filled include:** Nurse; Physician.

PETER JOSEPH ASSOCIATES
40038 Corte Fortuna, Murrieta CA 92562. 909/600-9700. **Contact:** Manager. **Description:** An executive search firm. **Specializes in the areas of:** Hotel/Restaurant.

K&M INTERNATIONAL, INC.
One Park Plaza Drive, 6th Floor, Irvine CA 92614. 949/770-1477. **Fax:** 949/770-4707. **Contact:** Chris Miller, Managing Consultant. **Description:** An executive search firm operating on both retainer and contingency bases. **Specializes in the areas of:** Accounting/Auditing; Finance; Marketing; Sales. **Positions commonly filled include:** Accountant; Auditor; Budget Analyst; Chief Financial Officer; Controller; Cost Estimator; Credit Manager; Finance Director; Financial Analyst; General Manager; Management Analyst/Consultant; Marketing Manager; Personnel Manager; Project Manager. **Average salary range of placements:** $30,000 - $50,000. **Number of placements per year:** 100 - 199.

KABL ABILITY NETWORK
1727 State Street, Santa Barbara CA 93101. 805/563-2398. **Contact:** Brad Naegle, President. **Description:** An executive search firm. **Specializes in the areas of:** Computer Science/Software; Executives; General Management; Nonprofit; Personnel/Labor Relations; Technical; Telecommunications. **Positions commonly filled include:** Computer Programmer; Electrical/Electronics Engineer; General Manager; Human Resources Manager; Software Engineer; Systems Analyst. **Average salary range of placements:** More than $50,000. **Number of placements per year:** 1 - 49.

GARY KAPLAN & ASSOCIATES
201 South Lake Avenue, Suite 600, Pasadena CA 91101. 626/796-8100. **Fax:** 626/796-1003. **Contact:** Gary Kaplan, President. **E-mail address:** general@gkasearch. com. **World Wide Web address:** http://www.gkasearch. com. **Description:** An executive search firm operating on a retained basis. Founded in 1984.

HOWARD KARR & ASSOCIATES
1777 Borel Place, Suite 408, San Mateo CA 94402. 650/574-5277. **Contact:** Manager. **Description:** An executive search firm. **Positions commonly filled include:** Chief Financial Officer.

KARSCH/CARD
2049 Century Park East, Suite 1200, Los Angeles CA 90067. 310/556-8866. **Contact:** Cris Card, Owner. **Description:** An executive search firm. **Specializes in the areas of:** Advertising; Marketing.

KASS ABELL & ASSOCIATES
10780 Santa Monica Boulevard, Suite 200, Los Angeles CA 90049. 310/475-4666. **Contact:** Office Manager. **Description:** An executive search firm. **Specializes in the areas of:** Legal.

KAUFMAN & HUNT
6320 Canoga Avenue, Suite 1500, Woodland Hills CA 91367. 818/227-5086. **Contact:** President. **Description:** An executive search firm. **Positions commonly filled include:** Tax Specialist. **Average salary range of placements:** More than $50,000.

A.T. KEARNEY EXECUTIVE SEARCH
500 South Grand Avenue, Suite 1780, Los Angeles CA 90071. 213/689-6800. **Contact:** Manager. **Description:** An executive search firm.

A.T. KEARNEY EXECUTIVE SEARCH
3 Lagoon Drive, Suite 160, Redwood Shores CA 94065. 650/637-6600. **Contact:** Manager. **Description:** An executive search firm. **Specializes in the areas of:** High-Tech.

KEARNEY BOYLE & ASSOCIATES
336 Bon Air Center, Suite 106, Greenbrae CA 94904. 415/925-0397. **Contact:** Manager. **Description:** An executive search firm. **Specializes in the areas of:** Finance; Legal.

KEIFER PROFESSIONAL SEARCH
1475 South Bascom Avenue, Suite 202, Campbell CA 95008-0629. 408/559-7377. **Fax:** 408/558-8100. **Contact:** Kevin Keifer, President. **Description:** An executive search firm. **Specializes in the areas of:** Chemicals; Computer Science/Software; Engineering; Industrial; Manufacturing; Network Administration; Sales; Technical. **Positions commonly filled include:** Chemical Engineer; Computer Programmer; Customer Service Representative; Electrical/Electronics Engineer; Manufacturer's/Wholesaler's Sales Rep.; Mechanical Engineer; Network/Systems Administrator; Operations/Production Manager; Quality Control Supervisor; Software Engineer. **Other U.S. locations:** Nationwide. **Number of placements per year:** 1 - 49.

KENNETH, GEORGE, & ASSOCIATES
6818 Burke Court, Chino CA 91710. 909/591-1980. **Fax:** 909/591-7599. **Contact:** James Kenneth, Managing Partner. **Description:** Kenneth, George, & Associates is an executive search firm. **Specializes in the areas of:** Accounting/Auditing; Banking; Finance; Health/Medical; Manufacturing; Retail. **Positions commonly filled include:** Accountant/Auditor; Budget Analyst; Cost Estimator; Credit Manager; Financial Analyst. **Corporate headquarters location:** This Location. **Other U.S. locations:** Nationwide. **Number of placements per year:** 50 - 99.

KIZER ASHLYN EXECUTIVE SEARCH
21032 Devonshire Street, Suite 214, Chatsworth CA 91311. 818/709-9821. **Contact:** Manager. **Description:** An executive search firm. **Specializes in the areas of:** Finance.

BARRY C. KLEINMAN & ASSOCIATES
2936 Domingo Avenue, Suite 5, Berkeley CA 94705. 510/549-7300. **Fax:** 510/549-7306. **Contact:** Manager. **Description:** An executive search firm. **Specializes in the areas of:** High-Tech.

KLENIN GROUP
32107 West Lindero Canyon Road, Suite 108, Westlake Village CA 91361. 818/597-3434. **Fax:** 818/597-3438. **Contact:** Larry Klenin, President. **Description:** An executive search firm. **Specializes in the areas of:** Computer Science/Software; Sales. **Positions commonly filled include:** Systems Analyst. **Average salary range of placements:** More than $50,000. **Number of placements per year:** 50 - 99.

KORN/FERRY INTERNATIONAL
1800 Century Park East, Suite 900, Los Angeles CA 90067. 310/552-1834. **Fax:** 310/553-6452. **Contact:** Manager. **World Wide Web address:** http://www. kornferry.com. **Description:** A generalist executive search firm. Founded in 1969. **Corporate headquarters location:** This Location. **International locations:** Worldwide. **Average salary range of placements:** More than $50,000.

KORN/FERRY INTERNATIONAL
2600 Michelson Drive, Suite 720, Irvine CA 92612. 949/851-1834. **Fax:** 949/833-7608. **Contact:** Manager. **World Wide Web address:** http://www.kornferry.com. **Description:** A generalist executive search firm. **Corporate headquarters location:** Los Angeles CA. **International locations:** Worldwide. **Average salary range of placements:** More than $50,000.

KORN/FERRY INTERNATIONAL
One Embarcadero Center, Suite 2101, San Francisco CA 94111. 415/956-1834. **Fax:** 415/956-8265. **Contact:** Manager. **World Wide Web address:** http://www. kornferry.com. **Description:** A generalist executive search firm that specializes in the placement of upper-level management. **Corporate headquarters location:** Los Angeles CA. **International locations:** Worldwide. **Average salary range of placements:** More than $50,000.

KORN/FERRY INTERNATIONAL
3 Lagoon Drive, Suite 280, Redwood City CA 95014. 650/632-1834. **Fax:** 650/632-1835. **Contact:** Manager. **World Wide Web address:** http://www.kornferry.com. **Description:** A generalist executive search firm that specializes in the placement of upper-level management. **Corporate headquarters location:** Los Angeles CA. **International locations:** Worldwide. **Average salary range of placements:** More than $50,000.

EVIE KREISLER & ASSOCIATES
865 South Figueroa Street, Suite 950, Los Angeles CA 90017. 213/622-8994. **Fax:** 213/622-9660. **Contact:** Manager. **Description:** An executive search firm operating on both retainer and contingency bases. **Specializes in the areas of:** Fashion; Manufacturing; Retail; Wholesaling. **Positions commonly filled include:** Account Manager; Account Rep.; Chief Financial Officer; Controller; Finance Director; Sales Executive; Sales Manager. **Corporate headquarters location:** This Location. **Other U.S. locations:** Nationwide. **Average salary range of placements:** More than $50,000. **Number of placements per year:** 100 - 199.

KREUZBERGER RAND
1000 Fourth Street, Suite 150, San Rafael CA 94901. 415/459-2300. **Fax:** 415/459-2471. **Contact:** Neil Kreuzberger, President. **Description:** An executive search firm operating on both retainer and contingency bases. The firm also provides some career/outplacement counseling and contract services. **Specializes in the areas of:** Accounting/Auditing; Finance. **Positions commonly filled include:** Accountant/Auditor; Financial Analyst. **Number of placements per year:** 50 - 99.

JEFF KROH ASSOCIATES
11400 West Olympic Boulevard, Suite 760, Los Angeles CA 90064. 310/231-0313. **Fax:** 310/231-9232. **Contact:** Manager. **Description:** Jeff Kroh Associates is an executive search firm. **Specializes in the areas of:** Manufacturing; Pharmaceuticals.

KUHN MED-TECH
27128-B Paseo Espada, Suite 623, San Juan Capistrano CA 92675. 949/496-3500. **Fax:** 949/496-1716. **Contact:** Larry Kuhn, President. **Description:** An executive search firm. **Specializes in the areas of:** Engineering; General Management; Health/Medical; Manufacturing; Sales; Technical. **Positions commonly filled include:** Biological Scientist; Biomedical Engineer; Chemical Engineer; Chemist; Electrical/Electronics Engineer; Industrial Engineer; Manufacturing Engineer; Marketing Specialist; Mechanical Engineer; Metallurgical Engineer; Nurse; Operations/Production Manager; Plastics Engineer; Quality Control Supervisor; Sales Rep. **Number of placements per year:** 50 - 99.

JOHN KUROSKY & ASSOCIATES
3 Corporate Park Drive, Suite 210, Irvine CA 92606. 949/851-6370. **Fax:** 949/851-8465. **Contact:** John Kurosky, President. **E-mail address:** jka@ix.netcom. com. **Description:** An executive search firm. **Specializes in the areas of:** Accounting/Auditing; Administration; Biology; Computer Science/Software; Engineering; Finance; Food; General Management; Health/Medical; Industrial; Legal; Sales; Technical. **Positions commonly filled include:** Abstractor/Indexer; Account Manager; Accountant; Applications Engineer; Attorney; Biochemist; Biomedical Engineer; Buyer; Chemical Engineer; Chemist; CFO; Civil Engineer; Computer Programmer; Controller; Credit Manager; Database

Manager; Design Engineer; Electrical/Electronics Engineer; Finance Director; Food Scientist/Technologist; General Manager; Industrial Engineer; Industrial Production Manager; Intellectual Property Lawyer; Internet Services Manager; Manufacturing Engineer; Marketing Manager; Mechanical Engineer; Metallurgical Engineer; MIS Manager; Operations Manager; Personnel Manager; Production Manager; Project Manager; Purchasing Agent/Manager; Quality Control Supervisor; Sales Executive; Sales Manager; Software Engineer; Systems Manager; Telecommunications Manager. **Corporate headquarters location:** This Location. **Other U.S. locations:** Nationwide. **Average salary range of placements:** More than $50,000. **Number of placements per year:** 100 - 199.

MARVIN LABA & ASSOCIATES
6255 West Sunset Boulevard, Suite 617, Los Angeles CA 90028. 323/464-1355. **Fax:** 323/465-0330. **Contact:** Manager. **Description:** An executive search firm. **Specializes in the areas of:** Finance; Human Resources; MIS/EDP; Operations Management; Retail. **Average salary range of placements:** More than $50,000. **Number of placements per year:** 1 - 49.

LaCOSTA & ASSOCIATES
6727 Flanders Drive, Suite 108, San Diego CA 92121. 858/457-1377. **Fax:** 858/457-0971. **Contact:** Paul LaCosta, President. **Description:** LaCosta & Associates is an executive search firm. **Specializes in the areas of:** Wireless Communications. **Positions commonly filled include:** Accountant/Auditor; Branch Manager; Customer Service Representative; Electrical/Electronics Engineer; General Manager; Human Resources Manager; Manufacturer's/Wholesaler's Sales Rep.; Operations/Production Manager; Public Relations Specialist; Purchasing Agent/Manager. **Number of placements per year:** 1 - 49.

LANDER INTERNATIONAL
P.O. Box 1370, El Cerrito CA 94530. **Toll-free phone:** 800/548-5318. **Fax:** 510/232-6795. **Contact:** Richard Tuck, President. **World Wide Web address:** http://www.landerint.com. **Description:** An executive search firm. Client company pays fee. **Specializes in the areas of:** Accounting/Auditing; Computer Science/Software. **Positions commonly filled include:** Auditor; Computer Programmer; Consultant; Information Systems Consultant; Systems Specialist. **Corporate headquarters location:** This Location. **Average salary range of placements:** More than $50,000. **Number of placements per year:** 500 - 999.

LARKIN GROUP
9343 Culver Boulevard, Culver City CA 90232. 310/260-0080. **Contact:** Managing Director. **Description:** An executive search firm. **Specializes in the areas of:** Art/Design; Interactive Entertainment; Multimedia; Sales; Software Development; Technical. **Positions commonly filled include:** Computer Programmer; Multimedia Designer. **Average salary range of placements:** More than $50,000. **Number of placements per year:** 1 - 49.

LeBLANC & ASSOCIATES
P.O. Box 571151, Tarzana CA 91357. 818/705-5619. **Contact:** Manager. **Description:** An executive search firm. **Specializes in the areas of:** Transportation.

LEFEBER & ASSOCIATES
One Almaden Boulevard, Suite 701, San Jose CA 95113. 408/271-1300. **Contact:** Manager. **Description:** An executive search firm. **Specializes in the areas of:** High-Tech.

LEINOW ASSOCIATES
P.O. Box 154, Woodacre CA 94973. 415/488-4885. **Fax:** 415/488-4886. **Contact:** Leonard Leinow, President. **Description:** An executive search firm. **Specializes in the areas of:** Health/Medical. **Positions commonly filled include:** Computer Programmer; Design Engineer; MIS Specialist; Software Engineer; Systems Analyst.

Average salary range of placements: More than $50,000.

LENDING PERSONNEL SERVICES
2938 Daimler Street, Santa Ana CA 92705. 949/250-8133. **Fax:** 949/250-7180. **Contact:** Carla Bloch, Owner. **Description:** An executive search firm. **Specializes in the areas of:** Accounting/Auditing; Banking; Computer Science/Software; Finance; General Management; High-Tech; Insurance; Manufacturing; Personnel/Labor Relations; Sales. **Positions commonly filled include:** Accountant/Auditor; Adjuster; Bank Officer/Manager; Branch Manager; Budget Analyst; Claim Representative; Computer Programmer; Construction and Building Inspector; Counselor; Credit Manager; Customer Service Representative; Financial Analyst; General Manager; Human Resources Manager; Insurance Agent/Broker; Internet Services Manager; MIS Specialist; Operations/Production Manager; Property and Real Estate Manager; Real Estate Agent; Securities Sales Rep.; Systems Analyst; Telecommunications Manager; Underwriter/Assistant Underwriter. **Average salary range of placements:** More than $50,000. **Number of placements per year:** 1 - 49.

BYRON LEONARD INTERNATIONAL, INC.
2659 Townsgate Road, Suite 100, Westlake Village CA 91361. 805/373-7500. **Fax:** 805/373-5531. **Contact:** Branch Manager. **E-mail address:** bli@bli-inc.com. **World Wide Web address:** http://www.bli-inc.com. **Description:** An executive search firm.

LEWIS & BLANK INTERNATIONAL, LLC
520 South El Camino Real, Suite 342, San Mateo CA 94402-1716. 650/685-6855. **Fax:** 650/685-0671. **Contact:** Branch Manager. **World Wide Web address:** http://www.lewis-blank.com. **Description:** An executive search firm. **Specializes in the areas of:** Biotechnology; Health/Medical; Medical Devices; Pharmaceuticals; Start-up Organizations.

LIFTER & ASSOCIATES
10918 Lurline Avenue, Chatsworth CA 91311. 818/998-0283. **Fax:** 818/341-7979. **Contact:** Barbara or Jay Lifter, Principals. **Description:** An executive search firm. **Specializes in the areas of:** Administration; Banking; Computer Science/Software; Consulting; Finance; Information Technology; Insurance; Manufacturing. **Positions commonly filled include:** Computer Programmer; Database Manager; Internet Services Manager; Management Analyst/Consultant; MIS Manager; Multimedia Designer; Project Manager; Software Engineer; Systems Analyst; Systems Manager; Telecommunications Manager; Webmaster. **Average salary range of placements:** More than $50,000. **Number of placements per year:** 1 - 49.

J.H. LINDELL & COMPANY
560 First Street East, Sonoma CA 95476. **Contact:** John Lindell, President. **Description:** An executive search firm that provides senior-level management placements. **Specializes in the areas of:** Architecture/Construction; Real Estate. **Number of placements per year:** 1 - 49.

THE LONDON ASSOCIATES
12424 Wilshire Boulevard, Suite 1270, Los Angeles CA 90025. 310/826-6060. **Fax:** 310/207-4447. **Contact:** Greg Inguagiato, Manager. **Description:** The London Associates is an executive search firm operating on a contingency basis. **Specializes in the areas of:** Accounting/Auditing; Advertising; Architecture/Construction; Banking; Broadcasting; Computer Science/Software; Finance; General Management; Health/Medical; Legal; Nonprofit; Retail; Sales; Secretarial. **Positions commonly filled include:** Administrative Assistant; Advertising Executive; Budget Analyst; Controller; Financial Analyst; Human Resources Manager; Sales Representative; Secretary; Typist/Word Processor. **Average salary range of placements:** $30,000 - $50,000. **Number of placements per year:** 200 - 499.

C.L. LOVICK & ASSOCIATES
P.O. Box 9402, Inglewood CA 90305. 310/330-3670. **Contact:** Manager. **Description:** An executive search firm.

MIS SEARCH
2099 Gateway Place, Suite 120, San Jose CA 95110. 408/437-0800. **Contact:** Manager. **Description:** An executive search firm. **Specializes in the areas of:** Administration; Computer Hardware/Software.

MRI RETAIL SEARCH
350 Crown Point Circle, Suite 125, Grass Valley CA 95945. 530/273-0200. **Fax:** 530/273-0364. **Contact:** Ridge Eagan, President. **E-mail address:** ridge@mriretailsearch.com. **World Wide Web address:** http://www.mriretailsearch.com. **Description:** An executive search firm operating on both retainer and contingency bases. MRI Retail Search is an affiliate of Management Recruiters International and focuses on placing individuals in all levels of the retail industry. **Specializes in the areas of:** Retail. **Corporate headquarters location:** Cleveland OH. **Other U.S. locations:** Nationwide. **Average salary range of placements:** $50,000 - $100,000. **Number of placements per year:** 100 - 199.

MACNAUGHTON ASSOCIATES
3600 Lime Street, Suite 323, Riverside CA 92501-2974. 909/788-4951. **Fax:** 909/788-4953. **Contact:** Sperry MacNaughton, President. **E-mail address:** sperrym@pacbell.net. **Description:** An executive search firm. **Specializes in the areas of:** Education; Health/Medical; Human Resources; Nonprofit. **Positions commonly filled include:** Director; President; Vice President. **Average salary range of placements:** More than $50,000. **Number of placements per year:** 1 - 49.

MADDEN ASSOCIATES
P.O. Box 6775, Morgana CA 94570. 925/284-3634. **Fax:** 925/284-8286. **Contact:** Office Manager. **Description:** An executive search firm. **Specializes in the areas of:** General Management; Real Estate.

JUDY MADRIGAL & ASSOCIATES
66 Bovet Road, Suite 390, San Mateo CA 94402. 510/795-8121. **Contact:** Office Manager. **Description:** An executive search firm. **Specializes in the areas of:** Health/Medical.

MAGENTA GROUP
15707 Rockfield Boulevard, Irvine CA 92718. 949/582-0600. **Fax:** 949/457-9136. **Contact:** General Manager. **Description:** An executive search firm that focuses on placement in the commercial printing, business forms, prepress, digital printing, and publishing industries. **Specializes in the areas of:** Graphic Arts; Printing; Publishing. **Positions commonly filled include:** Production Worker; Sales Manager; Sales Rep. **Corporate headquarters location:** Mission Viejo CA. **Average salary range of placements:** $50,000 - $150,000. **Number of placements per year:** 50 - 99.

MAHONEY BREWER ASSOCIATES INC.
2001 Union Street, Suite 640, San Francisco CA 94123. 415/771-3725. **Contact:** Manager. **Description:** An executive search firm. **Specializes in the areas of:** Finance; Government; Health/Medical; High-Tech. **Other U.S. locations:** Atlanta GA. **International locations:** Belgium.

MAJOR, HAGEN & AFRICA
500 Washington Street, 5th Floor, San Francisco CA 94111. 415/956-1010. **Fax:** 415/398-2425. **Contact:** Recruiter. **Description:** An executive search firm. **Specializes in the areas of:** Legal. **Positions commonly filled include:** Attorney.

MANAGEMENT RECRUITERS INLAND EMPIRE AGENCY
19 East Citrus Avenue, Suite 201, Redlands CA 92373. 909/335-2055. **Fax:** 909/792-4194. **Contact:** M.R.

Meyers, Manager. **Description:** Management Recruiters is an executive search firm. **Specializes in the areas of:** Architecture/Construction; Engineering; Finance; General Management; Manufacturing; Personnel/ Labor Relations; Sales; Transportation. **Corporate headquarters location:** Cleveland OH.

MANAGEMENT RECRUITERS INTERNATIONAL SALES CONSULTANTS
100 Corporate Pointe, Suite 380, Culver City CA 90230. 310/670-3040. **Fax:** 310/670-2981. **Contact:** Manager. **Description:** An executive search firm. **Specializes in the areas of:** Sales. **Positions commonly filled include:** Biomedical Engineer; Branch Manager; Electrical/ Electronics Engineer; Environmental Engineer; Human Resources Manager; Industrial Engineer; Industrial Production Manager; Licensed Practical Nurse; Manufacturer's/Wholesaler's Sales Rep.; Restaurant/Food Service Manager; Software Engineer. **Average salary range of placements:** $30,000 - $50,000. **Number of placements per year:** 100 - 199.

MANAGEMENT RECRUITERS INTERNATIONAL, INC.
150 Clovis Avenue, Suite 205, Clovis CA 93612. 559/299-7992. **Fax:** 559/299-2167. **Contact:** Gary Hendrickson, Manager. **E-mail address:** food@jx. netcom.com. **World Wide Web address:** http://www. mrinet.com. **Description:** An executive search firm. **Specializes in the areas of:** Food. **Positions commonly filled include:** Computer Programmer; Electrical/ Electronics Engineer; Food Scientist/Technologist; Human Resources Manager; Industrial Engineer; Industrial Production Manager; Manufacturing Engineer; Mechanical Engineer; Production Manager; Quality Control Supervisor; Systems Analyst; Transportation/ Traffic Specialist. **Corporate headquarters location:** Cleveland OH. **Other U.S. locations:** Nationwide. **Average salary range of placements:** More than $50,000. **Number of placements per year:** 1 - 49.

MANAGEMENT RECRUITERS INTERNATIONAL, INC.
126 West 25th Avenue, San Mateo CA 94403. 650/548-4800. **Fax:** 650/548-4805. **Contact:** Don Hirschbein, President. **Description:** An executive search firm. **Specializes in the areas of:** Accounting/Auditing; Administration; Architecture/Construction; Banking; Communications; Computer Hardware/Software; Construction; Electrical; Engineering; Finance; Food; General Management; Health/Medical; Insurance; Manufacturing; Operations Management; Personnel/ Labor Relations; Pharmaceuticals; Procurement; Publishing; Retail; Sales; Technical; Textiles. **Corporate headquarters location:** Cleveland OH. **Other U.S. locations:** Nationwide. **Number of placements per year:** 100 - 199.

MANAGEMENT RECRUITERS INTERNATIONAL, INC.
4125 Mohr Avenue, Suite M, Pleasanton CA 94566. 925/462-8579. **Fax:** 925/462-0208. **Contact:** Michael Machi, General Manager. **E-mail address:** confidential@mricareers.com. **World Wide Web address:** http://www.mricareers.com. **Description:** An executive search firm operating on both retainer and contingency bases. **Specializes in the areas of:** Accounting/Auditing; Administration; Computer Science/Software; Electronics; Engineering; Finance; Industrial; Information Systems; Marketing; Personnel/ Labor Relations; Plastics; Sales; Transportation. **Positions commonly filled include:** Accountant; Chief Financial Officer; Computer Programmer; Controller; Credit Manager; Customer Service Representative; Design Engineer; Electrical/Electronics Engineer; Electrician; Finance Director; Financial Analyst; Fund Manager; Human Resources Manager; Industrial Engineer; Industrial Production Manager; Manufacturing Engineer; Mechanical Engineer; MIS Specialist; Production Manager; Quality Control Supervisor; Sales Engineer; Sales Manager; Sales Representative; Software Engineer; Statistician; Systems Analyst; Systems Manager; Transportation/Traffic Specialist. **Corporate headquarters location:** Cleveland OH. **Other U.S. locations:** Nationwide.

MANAGEMENT RECRUITERS INTERNATIONAL, INC.
494 Alvarado Street, Suite F, Monterey CA 93940. 831/649-0737. **Contact:** Manager. **World Wide Web address:** http://www.mrinet.com. **Description:** An executive search firm. **Specializes in the areas of:** Health/Medical. **Corporate headquarters location:** Cleveland OH. **Other U.S. locations:** Nationwide.

MANAGEMENT RECRUITERS INTERNATIONAL, INC.
2316 Bell Executive Way, Suite 100, Sacramento CA 95825. 916/565-2700. **Fax:** 916/565-2828. **Contact:** Manager. **World Wide Web address:** http://www. mrinet.com. **Description:** An executive search firm. **Specializes in the areas of:** Accounting; Banking; Construction; Engineering; Finance; Manufacturing. **Corporate headquarters location:** Cleveland OH. **Other U.S. locations:** Nationwide.

MANAGEMENT RECRUITERS INTERNATIONAL, INC.
591 Redwood Highway, Suite 2225, Mill Valley CA 94941. 415/383-7044. **Contact:** Manager. **World Wide Web address:** http://www.mrinet.com. **Description:** An executive search firm. **Specializes in the areas of:** High-Tech. **Corporate headquarters location:** Cleveland OH. **Other U.S. locations:** Nationwide.

MANAGEMENT RECRUITERS INTERNATIONAL, INC.
2222 Francisco Drive, Suite 430, El Dorado Hills CA 95762. 916/939-9780. **Contact:** Manager. **World Wide Web address:** http://www.mrinet.com. **Description:** An executive search firm. **Specializes in the areas of:** Food. **Corporate headquarters location:** Cleveland OH. **Other U.S. locations:** Nationwide.

MANAGEMENT RECRUITERS INTERNATIONAL, INC.
SALES CONSULTANTS OF OAKLAND
480 Roland Way, Suite 103, Oakland CA 94621. 510/635-7901. **Toll-free phone:** 800/581-7901. **Fax:** 510/562-7237. **Contact:** Branch Manager. **World Wide Web address:** http://www.mrinet.com. **Description:** An executive search firm. **Specializes in the areas of:** Administration; Computer Science/Software; Engineering; Finance; Food; General Management; Health/Medical; Industrial; Manufacturing; Sales; Technical. **Positions commonly filled include:** Administrative Manager; Biochemist; Biological Scientist; Biomedical Engineer; Branch Manager; Chemical Engineer; Chemist; Computer Programmer; Construction and Building Inspector; Construction Contractor; Credit Manager; Design Engineer; Dietician/ Nutritionist; EEG Technologist; EKG Technician; Electrical/Electronics Engineer; Environmental Engineer; Food Scientist/Technologist; General Manager; Health Services Manager; Hotel Manager; Industrial Engineer; Industrial Production Manager; Internet Services Manager; Management Analyst/Consultant; Management Trainee; Manufacturer's/Wholesaler's Sales Rep.; Market Research Analyst; Mechanical Engineer; Metallurgical Engineer; Mining Engineer; MIS Specialist; Multimedia Designer; Nuclear Engineer; Nuclear Medicine Technologist; Occupational Therapist; Operations/ Production Manager; Personnel Manager; Petroleum Engineer; Pharmacist; Physical Therapist; Physician; Psychologist; Public Relations Specialist; Purchasing Agent/Manager; Quality Control Supervisor; Radiological Technologist; Recreational Therapist; Respiratory Therapist; Restaurant/Food Service Manager; Science Technologist; Services Sales Representative; Software Engineer; Speech-Language Pathologist; Stationary Engineer; Strategic Relations Manager; Surgical Technician; Systems Analyst; Telecommunications Manager. **Corporate headquarters location:** Cleveland OH. **Other U.S. locations:** Nationwide. **Average salary range of placements:** $30,000 - $50,000. **Number of placements per year:** 500 - 999.

MANAGEMENT RECRUITERS INTERNATIONAL, INC.
SALES CONSULTANTS OF SACRAMENTO
4320 Auburn Boulevard, Suite 2100, Sacramento CA 95841. 916/481-7000. **Fax:** 916/481-7099. **Contact:** Ron Whitney, Manager. **E-mail address:** resumes@

scsacramento.com. **Description:** An executive search firm operating on both retainer and contingency bases. **Specializes in the areas of:** Computer Science/Software; Engineering; Industrial; Sales; Technical. **Positions commonly filled include:** Marketing Manager; Marketing Specialist; Sales Engineer; Sales Executive; Sales Manager; Sales Rep. **Other U.S. locations:** Nationwide. **International locations:** Worldwide. **Average salary range of placements:** More than $50,000. **Number of placements per year:** 50 - 99.

MANAGEMENT RECRUITERS OF BERKELEY
2150 Shattuck Avenue, Suite 704, Berkeley CA 94704. 510/486-8100. **Fax:** 510/486-8189. **Contact:** Richard Howard, General Manager. **E-mail address:** rhoward@mri-berkeley.com. **World Wide Web address:** http://www.mri-berkeley.com. **Description:** An executive search firm. Client company pays fee. **Specializes in the areas of:** Architecture/Construction; Banking; Engineering; Finance; Food; Transportation. **Positions commonly filled include:** Architect; Bank Officer/Manager; Chief Financial Officer; Construction Contractor; Controller; Cost Estimator; Credit Manager; Design Engineer; Electrical/Electronics Engineer; Environmental Engineer; Food Scientist/Technologist; Human Resources Manager; Mechanical Engineer; Nurse Practitioner; Operations Manager; Registered Nurse; Systems Manager; Transportation/Traffic Specialist; Vice President of Operations. **Corporate headquarters location:** Cleveland OH. **Other U.S. locations:** Nationwide. **Average salary range of placements:** $50,000 - $100,000.

MANAGEMENT RECRUITERS OF ENCINO
16027 Ventura Boulevard, Suite 320, Encino CA 91436. 818/906-3155. **Fax:** 818/906-0642. **Contact:** Manager. **E-mail address:** consult@MRI-LA.com. **Description:** Management Recruiters of Encino is an executive search firm. **Specializes in the areas of:** Accounting/Auditing; Administration; Advertising; Architecture/Construction; Banking; Chemicals; Communications; Computer Hardware/Software; Construction; Electrical; Engineering; Finance; Food; General Management; Health/Medical; Insurance; Legal; Manufacturing; Operations Management; Personnel/Labor Relations; Pharmaceuticals; Procurement; Publishing; Real Estate; Retail; Sales; Technical; Textiles; Transportation. **Positions commonly filled include:** Accountant/Auditor; Administrative Manager; Bank Officer/Manager; Biochemist; Biological Scientist; Biomedical Engineer; Computer Programmer; Construction and Building Inspector; Cost Estimator; Engineer; Financial Analyst; General Manager; Health Services Manager; Internet Services Manager; MIS Specialist; Occupational Therapist; Operations/Production Manager; Recreational Therapist; Registered Nurse; Respiratory Therapist; Securities Sales Representative; Software Engineer; Systems Analyst; Telecommunications Manager. **Corporate headquarters location:** Cleveland OH. **Average salary range of placements:** More than $50,000. **Number of placements per year:** 100 - 199.

MANAGEMENT RECRUITERS OF LAGUNA HILLS
23461 South Pointe Drive, Suite 390, Laguna Hills CA 92653. 949/768-9112. **Fax:** 949/768-6135. **Contact:** Thomas J. Toole, President. **Description:** An executive search firm. **Specializes in the areas of:** Accounting/Auditing; Advertising; Biology; Computer Science/Software; Engineering; Finance; Food; General Management; Industrial; Manufacturing; Personnel/Labor Relations; Sales; Technical; Transportation. **Positions commonly filled include:** Accountant/Auditor; Attorney; Biological Scientist; Biomedical Engineer; Branch Manager; Chemical Engineer; Chemist; Electrical/Electronics Engineer; General Manager; Geologist/Geophysicist; Hotel Manager; Human Resources Manager; Industrial Engineer; Manufacturer's/Wholesaler's Sales Rep.; Mechanical Engineer; Metallurgical Engineer; Operations/Production Manager; Pharmacist; Physical Therapist; Quality Control Supervisor; Restaurant/Food Service Manager; Software Engineer; Systems Analyst. **Corporate headquarters**

location: Cleveland OH. **Number of placements per year:** 50 - 99.

MANAGEMENT RECRUITERS OF ORANGE SALES CONSULTANTS
One City Boulevard West, Suite 710, Orange CA 92868. 714/978-0500. **Fax:** 714/978-8064. **Contact:** Manager. **Description:** An executive search firm. **Specializes in the areas of:** Administration; Computer Science/Software; Health/Medical; Publishing; Sales. **Positions commonly filled include:** Computer Programmer; EDP Specialist; Health Services Manager; Insurance Agent/Broker; Nurse; Physician; Software Engineer; Surgical Technician; Systems Analyst; Telecommunications Manager; Underwriter/Assistant Underwriter. **Corporate headquarters location:** Cleveland OH. **Number of placements per year:** 200 - 499.

MANAGEMENT RECRUITERS OF ROSEVILLE
3001 Douglas Boulevard, Suite 230, Roseville CA 95661. 916/781-8110. **Fax:** 916/781-6719. **Contact:** Manager. **E-mail address:** mri@mriexec.com. **World Wide Web address:** http://www.mriexec.com. **Description:** An executive search firm operating on both retainer and contingency bases. Client company pays fee. **Specializes in the areas of:** Information Technology. **Positions commonly filled include:** Account Rep.; Database Administrator; MIS Specialist; Sales Exec.; Sales Manager; Sales Rep.; Software Engineer; Systems Analyst; Systems Manager. **Corporate headquarters location:** Cleveland OH. **Average salary range of placements:** $50,000 - $100,000.

MANAGEMENT RECRUITERS OF SAN LUIS OBISPO
7360 El Camino Real, Suite A, Atascadero CA 93422. 805/462-8044. **Contact:** Manager. **World Wide Web address:** http://www.mrinet.com. **Description:** An executive search firm. **Specializes in the areas of:** Biotechnology; Pharmaceuticals; Research and Development. **Corporate headquarters location:** Cleveland OH.

MANAGEMENT SOLUTIONS INC.
595 Market Street, Suite 1100, San Francisco CA 94123. 415/357-0300. **Contact:** Manager. **World Wide Web address:** http://www.mgmtsolutions.com. **Description:** An executive search firm that also offers some temporary placements. **Specializes in the areas of:** Accounting; Finance; Human Resources; Information Technology. **Corporate headquarters location:** San Jose CA. **Other U.S. locations:** Santa Ana CA; Torrance CA; Walnut Creek CA; Portland OR; Bellevue WA.

MANAGEMENT SOLUTIONS INC.
99 Almaden Boulevard, Suite 600, San Jose CA 95113. 408/292-6600. **Fax:** 408/298-5714. **Contact:** Rich Williams, President. **World Wide Web address:** http://www.mgmtsolutions.com. **Description:** An executive search firm operating on both retainer and contingency bases. The firm also provides some temporary and contract placements. **Specializes in the areas of:** Accounting/Auditing; Computer Science/Software; Engineering; Finance; Manufacturing; Personnel/Labor Relations. **Positions commonly filled include:** Accountant/Auditor; Budget Analyst; Computer Programmer; Credit Manager; Design Engineer; Draftsperson; Electrical/Electronics Engineer; Environmental Engineer; Financial Analyst; Human Resources Manager; Industrial Engineer; Internet Services Manager; Mechanical Engineer; Metallurgical Engineer; MIS Specialist; Multimedia Designer; Operations/Production Manager; Quality Control Supervisor; Systems Analyst; Technical Writer/Editor; Telecommunications Manager. **Corporate headquarters location:** This Location. **Other U.S. locations:** San Francisco CA; Santa Ana CA; Torrance CA; Walnut Creek CA; Portland OR; Bellevue WA. **Number of placements per year:** 1000+.

MANAGEMENT SOLUTIONS INC.
6 Hutton Centre Drive, Suite 1150, Santa Ana CA 92707. 714/979-2900. **Contact:** Manager. **World Wide Web**

address: http://www.mgmtsolutions.com. **Description:** An executive search firm. **Specializes in the areas of:** Accounting/Auditing; Computer Hardware/Software; Finance; High-Tech; Real Estate. **Corporate headquarters location:** San Jose CA. **Other U.S. locations:** San Francisco CA; Torrance CA; Walnut Creek CA; Portland OR; Bellevue WA.

MANAGEMENT SOLUTIONS INC.
PROFILES EXECUTIVE SEARCH
970 West 190th Street, Suite 600, Torrance CA 90502-1000. 310/523-3455. **Contact:** Office Manager. **World Wide Web address:** http://www.mgmtsolutions.com. **Description:** An executive search firm. Profiles Executive Search (also at this location, 310/523-3400) is an executive search firm that also provides some contract placements. **Corporate headquarters location:** San Jose CA. **Other U.S. locations:** San Francisco CA; Santa Ana CA; Walnut Creek CA; Portland OR; Bellevue WA.

MARKAR ASSOCIATES
940 South Coast Drive, Suite 175, Costa Mesa CA 92626. 714/433-0100. **Fax:** 714/549-1838. **Contact:** Mike Chitjian, President. **Description:** An executive search firm operating on both retainer and contingency bases. Client company pays fee. **Specializes in the areas of:** Accounting; Administration; Engineering; Scientific; Technical. **Positions commonly filled include:** Accountant; Administrative Assistant; Administrative Manager; Chemical Engineer; Civil Engineer; Controller; Environmental Engineer; Financial Analyst; Geologist/Geophysicist; Graphic Artist; Graphic Designer; Human Resources Manager; Marketing Specialist. **Corporate headquarters location:** This Location. **Average salary range of placements:** $50,000 - $100,000. **Number of placements per year:** 50 - 99.

BRAD MARKS INTERNATIONAL
1888 Century Park East, 20th Floor, Los Angeles CA 90067. 310/286-0600. **Contact:** Manager. **World Wide Web address:** http://www.bradmarks.com. **Description:** An executive search firm. **Specializes in the areas of:** Accounting; Advertising; Communications; Consulting; Entertainment; High-Tech; Legal; Media Sales; New Media; Publishing.

MARSHALL CONSULTANTS
1800 Century Park East, Suite 600, Los Angeles CA 90067. 310/456-0666. **Fax:** 310/456-8886. **Contact:** Larry Marshall, President/CEO. **World Wide Web address:** http://www.marshallconsultants.com. **Description:** An executive search firm. Founded in 1967. **Specializes in the areas of:** Communications. **Corporate headquarters location:** New York NY.

THE MARSHALL GROUP
316 Mid Valley Center, Suite 226, Carmel CA 93923. 831/620-1144. **Fax:** 831/620-0984. **Contact:** Lois Vana Marshall, President. **World Wide Web address:** http://www.the-marshall-group.com. **Description:** An executive search firm that specializes in the franchising industry.

MASON CONCEPTS
6380 Wilshire Boulevard, Suite 1000, Los Angeles CA 90048. 323/655-7555. **Contact:** Attilio Armeni, President. **E-mail address:** attilio@masonconcepts.com. **World Wide Web address:** http://www.masonconcepts.com. **Description:** An executive search firm. **Specializes in the areas of:** Computer Science/Software. **Positions commonly filled include:** Computer Programmer; Graphic Artist; Graphic Designer; Internet Services Manager; MIS Specialist; Software Engineer; Systems Analyst; Systems Manager; Technical Writer/Editor; Webmaster. **Average salary range of placements:** More than $50,000. **Number of placements per year:** 500 - 999.

MASTER CONSULTANTS ASSOCIATION AGENCY INC.
851 Burlway Road, Suite 618, Burlingame CA 94010. 650/340-0416. **Fax:** 650/340-7156. **Contact:** Steven

Anderson, President. **Description:** An executive search firm. **Specializes in the areas of:** Sales. **Positions commonly filled include:** Sales and Marketing Representative. **Average salary range of placements:** $30,000 - $50,000. **Number of placements per year:** 100 - 199.

MASTER SEARCH
P.O. Box 9070, Santa Rosa CA 95405. 707/538-4000. **Fax:** 707/539-4567. **Contact:** Barbara Masters, President. **World Wide Web address:** http://www.mastersearch.com. **Description:** An executive search firm operating on both retainer and contingency bases. **Specializes in the areas of:** Computer Science/Software; Engineering. **Positions commonly filled include:** Database Manager; Design Engineer; Electrical/Electronics Engineer; Internet Services Manager; Manufacturing Engineer; Sales Engineer; Software Engineer; Systems Analyst; Systems Manager; Telecommunications Manager; Webmaster. **Other U.S. locations:** Nationwide.

MATA & ASSOCIATES
180 Harbor Drive, Suite 208, Sausalito CA 94965. 415/332-2893. **Fax:** 415/332-3916. **Contact:** Dick Mata, Owner. **Description:** An executive search firm. **Specializes in the areas of:** Computer Science/Software. **Positions commonly filled include:** Computer Programmer; Software Engineer; Systems Analyst; Technical Writer/Editor; Telecommunications Manager. **Average salary range of placements:** More than $50,000. **Number of placements per year:** 1 - 49.

K.E. McCARTHY & ASSOCIATES
9800 South Sepulveda Boulevard, Suite 720, Los Angeles CA 90045. 310/568-4070. **Fax:** 310/568-4077. **Contact:** Kevin McCarthy, Principal. **Description:** An executive search firm operating on a retainer basis. **Specializes in the areas of:** Accounting/Auditing; Administration; Banking; Computer Science/Software; Finance; General Management. **Positions commonly filled include:** Account Manager; Accountant; Applications Engineer; Bank Officer/Manager; Budget Analyst; Chief Financial Officer; Computer Programmer; Consultant; Controller; Database Manager; Economist; Finance Director; Financial Analyst; Fund Manager; General Manager; Management Analyst/Consultant; MIS Specialist; Project Manager; Sales Executive; Software Engineer; Systems Analyst; Systems Manager; Technical Writer/Editor; Telecommunications Manager. **Average salary range of placements:** More than $50,000.

ROBERT McCONNELL & ASSOCIATES
205 East Commonwealth, Suite A, Alhambra CA 91801-4206. 626/289-8764. **Contact:** Robert McConnell, Owner. **Description:** An executive search firm. **Number of placements per year:** 50 - 99.

LYNN McINTOSH EXECUTIVE SEARCH
21535 Hawthorne Boulevard, Suite 501, Torrance CA 90503. 310/792-2028. **Contact:** Manager. **Description:** An executive search firm.

McKAVIS & ASSOCIATES
3724 Clove Way, Oceanside CA 92057. 760/966-1292. **Contact:** Manager. **Description:** A generalist executive search firm.

SABINE McMANUS & ASSOCIATES
433 North Camden Drive, Suite 600, Beverly Hills CA 90210. 310/205-2006. **Fax:** 310/559-9883. **Contact:** Sabine McManus, President. **Description:** An executive search firm that places financial and operational candidates in hospitals, managed care companies, and other health care organizations. **Specializes in the areas of:** Accounting/Auditing; Finance; Health/Medical. **Positions commonly filled include:** Accounting Supervisor; Budget Analyst; Chief Financial Officer; Controller; Financial Analyst; Health Services Manager; Systems Analyst. **Average salary range of placements:** More than $50,000. **Number of placements per year:** 100 - 199.

MED EXEC INTERNATIONAL
100 North Brand Boulevard, Suite 200, Glendale CA 91203-2614. **Toll-free phone:** 800/507-5277. **Fax:** 818/552-2475. **Contact:** Rosemarie Christopher, Principal. **E-mail address:** rosechristopher@sprintmail. com. **World Wide Web address:** http://www. medexecintl.com. **Description:** An executive search firm operating on a contingency basis. **Specializes in the areas of:** Biology; Biotechnology; Clinical Research; Diagnostic Imaging; Health/Medical; Medical Devices; Pharmaceuticals; Quality Assurance; Regulatory Affairs. **Positions commonly filled include:** Auditor; Biochemist; Biological Scientist; Biomedical Engineer; Chemical Engineer; Chemist; Clinical Applications Specialist; Clinician; Computer Programmer; Design Engineer; Electrical/Electronics Engineer; Manufacturing Engineer; Mechanical Engineer; Metallurgical Engineer; Operations/Production Manager; Pharmacist; Production Manager; Project Manager; Quality Assurance Engineer; Quality Control Supervisor; Software Engineer; Statistician; Systems Analyst. **Corporate headquarters location:** This Location. **Average salary range of placements:** More than $50,000. **Number of placements per year:** 50 - 99.

MED QUEST
655 Skyway, San Carlos CA 94070-2709. 650/593-3103. **Contact:** Lynn Brodhead, President. **Description:** An executive search firm. **Specializes in the areas of:** Biology; Engineering; Health/Medical; Manufacturing; Pharmaceuticals. **Positions commonly filled include:** Biochemist; Biological Scientist; Biomedical Engineer; Chemical Engineer; Chemist; Clinical Lab Technician; Design Engineer; Electrical/Electronics Engineer; Industrial Engineer; Mechanical Engineer; Operations/ Production Manager; Quality Control Supervisor; Science Technologist; Statistician. **Average salary range of placements:** More than $50,000. **Number of placements per year:** 1 - 49.

MEDICAL EXECUTIVE RECRUITERS
1198 Melody Lane, Suite 109, Roseville CA 95678. 916/786-8615. **Fax:** 916/786-8609. **Contact:** Manager. **E-mail address:** medexec@pacbell.net. **Description:** An executive search firm. **Specializes in the areas of:** Biology; Biotechnology; Computer Science/Software; Health/Medical; Pharmaceuticals. **Positions commonly filled include:** General Manager; Marketing Manager; Marketing Specialist; Sales Executive; Sales Manager; Sales Rep. **Average salary range of placements:** More than $50,000. **Number of placements per year:** 100 - 199.

EDWARD MEISTER EXECUTIVE SEARCH
100 Bush Street, Suite 2102, San Francisco CA 94104. 415/362-6262. **Contact:** Manager. **Description:** An executive search firm. **Specializes in the areas of:** Banking.

J.M. MEREDITH & ASSOCIATES
2240 North Rodeo Gulch Road, Soquel CA 95073. 831/479-7522. **Contact:** Manager. **Description:** An executive search firm. **Specializes in the areas of:** Computer Hardware/Software; High-Tech.

MESA INTERNATIONAL
7777 Greenback Lane, Suite 100A, Citrus Heights CA 95610. 916/729-7700. **Fax:** 916/729-1135. **Contact:** President. **E-mail address:** mesa@mesaint.com. **World Wide Web address:** http://www.mesaint.com. **Description:** An executive search firm operating on both retainer and contingency bases. **Specializes in the areas of:** Administration; Computer Science/Software; Engineering; Food; Marketing; MIS/EDP; Packaging; Retail; Sales. **Positions commonly filled include:** Applications Engineer; Chemical Engineer; Computer Programmer; Controller; Database Manager; Design Engineer; Electrical/Electronics Engineer; Food Scientist/ Technologist; General Manager; Graphic Designer; Human Resources Manager; Industrial Engineer; Industrial Production Manager; Internet Services Manager; Management Trainee; Manufacturing Engineer; Mechanical Engineer; Metallurgical Engineer; MIS Specialist; Operations Manager; Packaging Engineer; Production Manager; Project Manager; Quality Assurance Engineer; Quality Control Supervisor; Sales Engineer; Sales Executive; Sales Manager; Sales Representative; Software Engineer; Systems Analyst; Systems Manager; Technical Writer/Editor; Telecommunications Manager; Transportation/Traffic Specialist; Vice President of Marketing and Sales; Webmaster. **Corporate headquarters location:** Astoria OR. **Average salary range of placements:** More than $50,000. **Number of placements per year:** 100 - 199.

MILESTONE PROFESSIONAL SEARCH
1474 Kings Lane, Palo Alto CA 94303-2836. 650/321-8994. **Fax:** 650/321-8995. **Contact:** President. **Description:** An executive search firm operating on a retainer basis. **Specializes in the areas of:** Computer Science/Software; Engineering; General Management; Legal; Manufacturing; Personnel/Labor Relations; Sales. **Positions commonly filled include:** Design Engineer; Electrical/Electronics Engineer; General Manager; Industrial Production Manager; MIS Specialist; Multimedia Designer; Operations/Production Manager; Personnel Manager; Public Relations Specialist; Purchasing Agent/Manager; Quality Control Supervisor. **Corporate headquarters location:** This Location. **Average salary range of placements:** More than $50,000. **Number of placements per year:** 1 - 49.

CRAIG MILLER ASSOCIATES
1720 East Garry Avenue, Suite 207, Santa Ana CA 92705. 949/261-6246. **Fax:** 949/261-9539. **Contact:** Manager. **Description:** An executive search firm. **Specializes in the areas of:** High-Tech.

MIND FINDERS INC.
3235 Kifer Road, Santa Clara CA 95051. 408/481-0100. **Contact:** Manager. **Description:** An executive search firm.

MIXTEC GROUP
31255 Cedar Valley Drive, Suite 317, Westlake Village CA 91362. 818/889-8819. **Fax:** 818/889-9025. **Contact:** Ward A. Fredericks, Chairman. **E-mail address:** MIXTEC@mixtec.net. **World Wide Web address:** http://mixtec.net. **Description:** An executive search firm. Founded in 1984. **Specializes in the areas of:** Executives; Food; Health/Medical; Manufacturing. **Positions commonly filled include:** Biological Scientist; President; Vice President. **Number of placements per year:** 50 - 99.

JAMES MOORE & ASSOCIATES
90 New Montgomery, Suite 412, San Francisco CA 94105. 415/392-3933. **Fax:** 415/896-0931. **Contact:** Terry Kain, Director of Research. **Description:** An executive search firm that focuses on client/server networking, GUI, and object-oriented technology. **Specializes in the areas of:** Computer Hardware/ Software. **Positions commonly filled include:** Computer Programmer; Internet Services Manager; Software Engineer; Systems Analyst. **Other area locations:** Mountain View CA. **Average salary range of placements:** More than $50,000.

MORRIS & WOLF
2120 Wilshire Boulevard, Suite 310, Santa Monica CA 90403. 310/792-1777. **Contact:** Manager. **Description:** An executive search firm.

J.R. MORRISON & ASSOCIATES
43 Kinross Drive, San Rafael CA 94901. 415/453-1139. **Contact:** Manager. **Description:** An executive search firm.

MULTISEARCH RECRUITERS
P.O. Box 309, Ballico CA 95303. 209/634-5814. **Fax:** 209/634-2648. **Contact:** Dennis Gallagher, Owner. **Description:** An executive search firm operating on a contingency basis. **Specializes in the areas of:** Engineering; Industrial; Manufacturing; Plastics; Sales;

Technical. **Positions commonly filled include:** Account Manager; Account Representative; Applications Engineer; Chemical Engineer; Controller; Industrial Engineer; Industrial Production Manager; Manufacturing Engineer; Operations Manager; Production Manager; Quality Control Supervisor; Sales Executive; Sales Manager; Software Engineer. **Other U.S. locations:** Nationwide. **Number of placements per year:** 1 - 49.

MUSICK & ASSOCIATES
2812 Vista Mar Drive, Malibu CA 90265. 310/456-8252. **Fax:** 310/456-5783. **Contact:** Stephen Musick, President. **World Wide Web address:** http://www. professionalplacement.com. **Description:** An executive search firm that operates on both retainer and contingency bases. The firm also provides some contract placements. **Specializes in the areas of:** Accounting/ Auditing; Art/Design; Banking; Computer Science/ Software; Finance; General Management; Insurance; MIS/EDP; Personnel/Labor Relations. **Positions commonly filled include:** Accountant; Auditor; Budget Analyst; Chief Financial Officer; Claim Representative; Computer Animator; Controller; Cost Estimator; Credit Manager; Database Manager; Financial Analyst; Fund Manager; Graphic Artist; Graphic Designer; Human Resources Manager; Management Analyst/Consultant; Market Research Analyst; MIS Specialist; Multimedia Designer; Operations Manager; Project Manager; Sales Executive; Sales Manager; Sales Representative; Software Engineer; Statistician; Systems Analyst; Systems Manager; Underwriter/Assistant Underwriter. **Corporate headquarters location:** This Location. **Average salary range of placements:** $30,000 - $50,000. **Number of placements per year:** 50 - 99.

J.A. MYRBEN & ASSOCIATES
5334 North Marina Pacifica Drive, Long Beach CA 90803. 562/431-2584. **Contact:** Manager. **Description:** An executive search firm. **Specializes in the areas of:** Accounting/Auditing; Finance.

NADZAM, LUSK, HORGAN & ASSOCIATES
3211 Scott Boulevard, Suite 205, Santa Clara CA 95054. 408/727-6601. **Fax:** 408/727-6605. **Contact:** Office Manager. **World Wide Web address:** http://www.nlh. com. **Description:** An executive search firm.

NATIONAL CAREER CHOICES (NCC)
1300-B Santa Barbara Street, Santa Barbara CA 93101. 805/963-0433. **Toll-free phone:** 800/622-0431. **Fax:** 805/966-9857. **Contact:** Manager. **E-mail address:** ncc@west.net. **Description:** An executive search firm. Founded in 1984. **Specializes in the areas of:** Computer Hardware/Software; Electronics; Engineering; Executives; Finance; Pharmaceuticals; Sales; Software Development; Technical; Telecommunications. **Office hours:** Monday - Friday, 8:00 a.m. - 5:00 p.m. **Corporate headquarters location:** This Location.

NATIONAL CAREER CHOICES (NCC)
1655 Mesa Verde Avenue, Suite 120, Ventura CA 93003. **Toll-free phone:** 800/639-3640. **Fax:** 805/639-2015. **Contact:** Manager. **E-mail address:** ncc@west. net. **Description:** An executive search firm. Founded in 1984. **Specializes in the areas of:** Executives; Technical. **Office hours:** Monday - Friday, 8:00 a.m. - 5:00 p.m. **Corporate headquarters location:** Santa Barbara CA.

NATIONAL CAREER CHOICES (NCC)
560 Farallon Avenue, Pacifica CA 94044. 650/738-0887. **Contact:** Manager. **Description:** An executive search firm. **Specializes in the areas of:** Biotechnology; Pharmaceuticals. **Corporate headquarters location:** Santa Barbara CA.

NATIONAL HOSPITALITY RECRUITERS
1426 Louisiana Street, Vallejo CA 94590. 925/825-5400. **Fax:** 707/553-2195. **Contact:** Debbie Blanchard, Owner. **Description:** An executive search firm. **Specializes in the areas of:** Food; Hotel/Restaurant. **Positions commonly filled include:** Chef/Cook/Kitchen Worker; Dietician/Nutritionist; Food Scientist/Technologist; Hotel Manager; Restaurant/Food Service Manager. **Number of placements per year:** 200 - 499.

NATIONAL RESOURCES
23901 Calabasas Road, Suite 2024, Calabasas CA 91302. 818/703-1994. **Fax:** 818/703-1915. **Contact:** Manager. **Description:** An executive search firm. **Specializes in the areas of:** Computer Science/Software. **Positions commonly filled include:** Computer Programmer; Software Engineer; Systems Analyst. **Number of placements per year:** 100 - 199.

NATIONAL SEARCH ASSOCIATES
2035 Corte Del Nogal, Suite 100, Carlsbad CA 92009. 760/431-1115. **Fax:** 760/431-0660. **Contact:** Philip Peluso, President. **Description:** An executive search firm. **Specializes in the areas of:** Biology; Computer Science/Software. **Positions commonly filled include:** Biological Scientist; Biomedical Engineer; Chemist; Software Engineer.

NATIONAL STAFFING BY NOELLE & ASSOCIATES
3518 Cahuenga Boulevard West, Suite 314, Los Angeles CA 90068. 323/874-3663. **Fax:** 323/851-8767. **Contact:** Noelle Lea King, Owner. **Description:** An executive search firm. **Specializes in the areas of:** Health/Medical. **Positions commonly filled include:** Physician; Physician Assistant. **Number of placements per year:** 100 - 199.

NATIONS STAFFING SOLUTIONS INC.
18952 MacArthur Boulevard, Suite 1000, Irvine CA 92612. 949/252-1515. **Toll-free phone:** 888/252-2520. **Fax:** 949/252-1313. **Contact:** M.J. Houge, Manager. **E-mail address:** hotjobs@natstaff.com. **Description:** An executive search firm that also offers some temporary and contract placements. Client company pays fee. **Specializes in the areas of:** Administration; Banking; Finance; Information Systems; Mortgage. **Positions commonly filled include:** Accountant; Administrative Assistant; Administrative Manager; Applications Engineer; AS400 Programmer Analyst; Assistant Manager; Auditor; Bank Officer/Manager; Branch Manager; Budget Analyst; Chief Financial Officer; Clerical Supervisor; Computer Animator; Computer Engineer; Computer Operator; Computer Programmer; Computer Scientist; Computer Support Technician; Computer Technician; Content Developer; Controller; Credit Manager; Customer Service Representative; Database Administrator; Database Manager; Desktop Publishing Specialist; Finance Director; Financial Analyst; Fund Manager; Graphic Artist; Graphic Designer; Internet Services Manager; Management Trainee; MIS Specialist; Multimedia Designer; Network/Systems Administrator; Operations Manager; Production Manager; Project Manager; Purchasing Agent/Manager; Quality Control Supervisor; Secretary; SQL Programmer; Systems Analyst; Systems Manager; Typist/Word Processor; Webmaster. **Corporate headquarters location:** Irvine CA. **Average salary range of placements:** $30,000 - $49,999. **Number of placements per year:** 1000+.

NETWORK RESOURCE GROUP
P.O. Box 25253, San Mateo CA 94102. 650/344-5550. **Fax:** 650/347-2415. **Contact:** Bob Read, Senior Consultant. **Description:** An executive search firm operating on a retainer basis. Network Resource Group focuses on placing upper-level management. **Specializes in the areas of:** Engineering; General Management. **Positions commonly filled include:** Administrative Manager; Chief Financial Officer; Controller; General Manager; Human Resources Manager; Industrial Production Manager; Manufacturing Engineer; Mechanical Engineer; Network/Systems Administrator; Production Manager; Quality Assurance Engineer; Sales Engineer; Sales Executive; Sales Manager; Software Engineer. **Corporate headquarters location:** This Location. **Average salary range of placements:** $50,000 - $100,000. **Number of placements per year:** 1 - 49.

NEW VENTURE DEVELOPMENT, INC.
596 Canyon Vista Drive, Thousand Oaks CA 91320. 805/498-8506. **Fax:** 805/498-2735. **Contact:** David R. Du Ket, President. **E-mail address:** duketnvd@gte.net. **Description:** An executive search firm operating on both retainer and contingency bases. Founded in 1985. Client company pays fee. **NOTE:** The firm prefers to be contacted by e-mail. **Specializes in the areas of:** Computer Science/Software; Engineering; Marketing; Sales; Scientific; Technical. **Positions commonly filled include:** Account Manager; Account Representative; Applications Engineer; Attorney; Biochemist; Biological Scientist; Biomedical Engineer; Buyer; Chemical Engineer; Chemist; Chief Financial Officer; Clinical Lab Technician; Computer Engineer; Computer Programming Manager; Computer Scientist; Computer Support Technician; Computer Technician; Controller; Cost Estimator; Database Administrator; Database Manager; Design Engineer; Electrical/Electronics Engineer; Environmental Engineer; Manufacturing Engineer; Marketing Manager; Marketing Specialist; Mechanical Engineer; Metallurgical Engineer; MIS Specialist; Multimedia Designer; Network/Systems Administrator; Operations Manager; Production Manager; Project Manager; Purchasing Agent/Manager; Quality Assurance Engineer; Quality Control Supervisor; Sales Engineer; Sales Executive; Sales Manager; Sales Representative; Software Engineer; SQL Programmer; Systems Analyst; Systems Manager; Telecommunications Manager; Vice President. **Average salary range of placements:** $50,000 - $100,000. **Number of placements per year:** 50 - 99.

C. NEWELL & ASSOCIATES
18101 Von Karman Avenue, Suite 350, Irvine CA 92612. 949/251-6560. **Contact:** Manager. **Description:** An executive search firm. **Specializes in the areas of:** Legal. **Positions commonly filled include:** Attorney.

NEWPORT STRATEGIC SEARCH LLC
3088 Pio Pico Drive, Suite 203, Carlsbad CA 92008. 760/434-9940. **Fax:** 760/434-9896. **Contact:** John C. Fitzpatrick, President. **Description:** Newport Strategic Search is an executive search firm. **Specializes in the areas of:** Accounting/Auditing; Computer Science/Software; Finance; Telecommunications. **Positions commonly filled include:** Accountant/Auditor; Financial Analyst; Telecommunications Manager. **Average salary range of placements:** More than $50,000. **Number of placements per year:** 100 - 199.

NICHOLS & ASSOCIATES
1211 West Imperial Highway, Suite 202, Brea CA 92821. 714/680-8380. **Contact:** Manager. **Description:** An executive search firm.

NORSELL & ASSOCIATES, INC.
P.O. Box 6686, Auburn CA 95604-6686. 530/269-0121. **Fax:** 530/268-3202. **Contact:** Paul Norsell, President. **Description:** An executive search firm. **Specializes in the areas of:** Biotechnology; General Management; Manufacturing; Pharmaceuticals; Sales; Technical. **Positions commonly filled include:** Attorney; Biological Scientist; Biomedical Engineer; Chemical Engineer; Chemist; Electrical/Electronics Engineer; General Manager; Geologist/Geophysicist; Industrial Production Manager; Management Analyst/Consultant; Mechanical Engineer; Operations/Production Manager; Petroleum Engineer; Physician; Science Technologist; Software Engineer.

NYBORG-DOW ASSOCIATES INC.
12781 Woodlake Road, Grass Valley CA 95949. 530/477-7817. **Fax:** 530/477-0745. **Contact:** Marilyn Nyborg, Manager. **Description:** An executive search firm operating on a contingency basis. **Specializes in the areas of:** Engineering. **Positions commonly filled include:** Electrical/Electronics Engineer; Software Engineer. **Average salary range of placements:** More than $50,000. **Number of placements per year:** 1 - 49.

O'CROWLEY & O'TOOLE EXECUTIVE SEARCH
4071 Avenida Sevilla, Cypress CA 90630-3411. 714/816-0286. **Contact:** Manager. **Description:** An executive search firm. **Specializes in the areas of:** Finance; Insurance. **Positions commonly filled include:** Accountant/Auditor; Bank Officer/Manager; Branch Manager; Financial Analyst; Loan Officer; Underwriter/Assistant Underwriter. **Number of placements per year:** 1 - 49.

OLSTEN FINANCIAL STAFFING
90 New Montgomery Street, Suite 1420, San Francisco CA 94105. 415/234-7800. **Toll-free phone:** 888/222-8693. **Fax:** 415/284-7808. **Contact:** Jonathan Thom, Region Vice President. **E-mail address:** ofs.hq@olsten.com. **World Wide Web address:** http://www.olsten.com/ofs. **Description:** An executive search firm operating on a contingency basis that also offers some temporary placements. Client company pays fee. **Specializes in the areas of:** Accounting; Banking; Finance. **Positions commonly filled include:** Accountant; Auditor; Budget Analyst; Chief Financial Officer; Controller; Credit Manager; Finance Director; Financial Analyst. **Corporate headquarters location:** Melville NY. **Other U.S. locations:** Nationwide. **Average salary range of placements:** $50,000 - $100,000. **Number of placements per year:** 200 - 499.

OMNI SEARCH INC.
31225 La Baya Drive, Suite 100, Westlake Village CA 91362. 818/707-4500. **Contact:** Mr. Lory Goldstein, President. **Description:** An executive search firm. **Number of placements per year:** 50 - 99.

ONLINE PROFESSIONAL SEARCH
1030 Trellis Lane, Alameda CA 94502-7053. 510/769-7111. **Contact:** Anita Ho, President. **Description:** An executive search firm that places candidates with a minimum of five years experience in data processing. **Specializes in the areas of:** Administration; Banking; Computer Science/Software. **Positions commonly filled include:** Computer Programmer; Systems Analyst. **Average salary range of placements:** More than $50,000. **Number of placements per year:** 1 - 49.

OPEN SYSTEMS CONSULTANTS
2850 Pio Pico Drive, Suite K, Carlsbad CA 92008. 760/729-2224. **Fax:** 760/729-2225. **Contact:** Manager. **Description:** An executive search firm. **Specializes in the areas of:** Telecommunications.

OPTIMUM EXECUTIVE SEARCH
600 Townsend Street, Suite 410 West, San Francisco CA 94103. 415/863-2700. **Contact:** Manager. **Description:** An executive search firm. **Specializes in the areas of:** Computer Hardware/Software.

ORTMAN RECRUITING INTERNATIONAL
1101 Sylvan Avenue, Building B, Suite B20, Modesto CA 95350. 209/529-5051. **Fax:** 209/529-5054. **Contact:** Jim Ortman, Owner. **Description:** An executive search firm. **Specializes in the areas of:** Biology; Engineering; Food; Industrial; Light Industrial; Manufacturing; Marketing; Sales; Scientific; Technical. **Positions commonly filled include:** Biochemist; Biological Scientist; Biomedical Engineer; Branch Manager; Chemical Engineer; Chemist; Design Engineer; Electrical/Electronics Engineer; General Manager; Industrial Engineer; Industrial Production Manager; Mechanical Engineer; Nuclear Engineer; Operations Manager; Production Manager; Project Manager; Sales Engineer; Sales Executive; Sales Manager; Sales Representative; Vice President; Wastewater Specialist. **Other U.S. locations:** Nationwide. **Average salary range of placements:** More than $50,000. **Number of placements per year:** 50 - 99.

DOUGLAS OWEN SEARCH CONSULTANTS
2814 South Court, Palo Alto CA 94306. 650/321-0193. **Contact:** Manager. **Description:** An executive search firm that specializes in the placement of senior-level

management professionals. **Specializes in the areas of:** Technical.

PAAR & ASSOCIATES
1440 North Harbor Boulevard, Suite 900, Fullerton CA 92835. 714/579-1465. **Fax:** 714/579-7921. **Contact:** Fred H. Paar, President. **E-mail address:** fredpaar@ msn.com. **World Wide Web address:** http://www. paar.com. **Description:** An executive search firm operating on a retainer basis. The firm provides placements for senior-level managers and also offers outplacement services. **Specializes in the areas of:** Management. **Positions commonly filled include:** Chief Executive Officer; Chief Financial Officer; General Manager; President; Vice President. **Number of placements per year:** 1 - 49.

PACIFIC CROSSING
27141 Aliso Creek Road, Suite 260, Aliso Viejo CA 92656. 949/360-5888. **Fax:** 949/360-5898. **Contact:** Manager. **Description:** An executive search firm.

PACIFIC RECRUITING OFFICES
2102 Business Center Drive, Suite 130, Irvine CA 92612. 949/253-4646. **Contact:** Harvey Dorland, President. **Description:** An executive search firm. **Specializes in the areas of:** Insurance. **Positions commonly filled include:** Account Representative; Claim Rep.; Management; Sales Rep.; Underwriter/ Assistant Underwriter. **Number of placements per year:** 50 - 99.

PACIFIC SEARCH GROUP
1801 Century Park East, Suite 1801, Los Angeles CA 90067. 310/286-6921. **Fax:** 310/712-0777. **Contact:** Nick Roberts, President. **E-mail address:** nickerpsg@ aol.com. **Description:** An executive search firm operating on both retainer and contingency bases. **Specializes in the areas of:** Accounting/Auditing; Banking; Computer Science/Software; Finance; Food; General Management; Health/Medical; Insurance; Marketing; MIS/EDP; Printing; Publishing; Retail; Sales. **Positions commonly filled include:** Accountant/Auditor; Auditor; Chief Financial Officer; Controller; Credit Manager; Finance Director; Financial Analyst; Human Resources Manager; Internet Services Manager; Marketing Manager; MIS Specialist; Purchasing Agent/ Manager; Sales Executive; Software Engineer; Systems Manager; Telecommunications Manager. **Average salary range of placements:** More than $50,000. **Number of placements per year:** 50 - 99.

PACIFIC SYSTEMS SEARCH
7011 Knoll Center Parkway, Suite 270, Pleasanton CA 94566. 925/426-9910. **Fax:** 925/426-9310. **Contact:** Manager. **Description:** An executive search firm. **Specializes in the areas of:** MIS/EDP.

PALERMO & ASSOCIATES
24596 Cronas, Mission Viejo CA 92691. 949/458-1123. **Contact:** Manager. **Description:** An executive search firm.

FRANK PARILLO & ASSOCIATES
1801 East Heim Avenue, Suite 200, Orange CA 92865. 714/921-8008. **Contact:** Manager. **Description:** An executive search firm. **Specializes in the areas of:** Biomedical; Biotechnology.

PARKER & LYNCH EXECUTIVE SEARCH
260 California Street, Suite 400, San Francisco CA 94111. 415/956-6700. **Fax:** 415/956-5642. **Contact:** Montie Parker, Partner. **Description:** An executive search firm. **Specializes in the areas of:** Accounting/Auditing; Finance; Personnel/Labor Relations. **Positions commonly filled include:** Accountant/Auditor; Budget Analyst; Credit Manager; Economist; Financial Analyst; Human Resources Manager; Management Analyst/Consultant; Management Trainee. **Average salary range of placements:** More than $50,000. **Number of placements per year:** 50 - 99.

PASTER & ASSOCIATES
9025 Wilshire Boulevard, Suite 301, Beverly Hills CA 90211. 310/273-5424. **Fax:** 310/273-8378. **Contact:** Steve Paster, President. **Description:** An executive search firm. **Specializes in the areas of:** Health/Medical; Pharmaceuticals; Sales. **Number of placements per year:** 50 - 99.

PEDEN & ASSOCIATES
2000 Broadway Street, Redwood City CA 94063. 650/367-1181. **Fax:** 650/367-7525. **Contact:** Ann Peden, President. **E-mail address:** apeden@pedenassoc.com. **World Wide Web address:** http://www.pedenassoc. com. **Description:** An executive search firm that places software developers in start-up companies throughout the San Francisco Bay Area. **NOTE:** A minimum of two years experience in the industry is required, as well as experience with various software applications. **Specializes in the areas of:** Computer Science/Software. **Positions commonly filled include:** Electrical/ Electronics Engineer; Software Engineer. **Average salary range of placements:** More than $50,000. **Number of placements per year:** 1 - 49.

PERKISS & ASSOCIATES
3470 Mount Diablo Boulevard, Suite A-150, Lafayette CA 94549. 925/284-5310. **Contact:** Dave Perkiss, Owner. **Description:** An executive search firm. **Specializes in the areas of:** Sales.

PERSONNEL STRATEGIES INC.
23141 Verdugo Drive, Suite 204, Laguna Hills CA 92653. 949/597-8293. **Fax:** 949/597-8094. **Contact:** George Coccas, President. **E-mail address:** hirethem@ aol.com. **Description:** An executive search firm operating on both retainer and contingency bases. Personnel Strategies specializes in the placement of financial professionals within the high-tech, biotech, telecommunications, and real estate industries in the San Francisco, San Jose, and Los Angeles metropolitan areas. Client company pays fee. **Specializes in the areas of:** Accounting; Computer Science/Software; Finance; High-Tech. **Positions commonly filled include:** Accountant; Auditor; Budget Analyst; Chief Financial Officer; Controller; Credit Manager; Economist; Finance Director; Financial Analyst; Management Analyst/ Consultant; MIS Specialist; Systems Analyst; Telecommunications Manager; Vice President of Finance. **Average salary range of placements:** More than $50,000. **Number of placements per year:** 50 - 99.

TOM PEZMAN & ASSOCIATES
P.O. Box 3175, San Clemente CA 92674. 949/661-6637. **Fax:** 949/661-6965. **Contact:** Tom Pezman, President. **Description:** An executive search firm. **Specializes in the areas of:** Broadcasting; Sales; Technical; Telecommunications; Wireless Communications. **Positions commonly filled include:** Computer Programmer; Customer Service Rep.; Electrical/ Electronics Engineer; Financial Analyst; General Manager; Software Engineer. **Number of placements per year:** 50 - 99.

PHYSICIANS SEARCH ASSOCIATES
1224 East Katella Avenue, Suite 202, Orange CA 92687. 714/288-8350. **Toll-free phone:** 800/748-6320. **Fax:** 714/288-8345. **Contact:** Office Manager. **E-mail address:** info@physicianssearch.com. **World Wide Web address:** http://www.physicianssearch.com. **Description:** An executive search firm. **Specializes in the areas of:** Health/Medical. **Positions commonly filled include:** Physician. **Number of placements per year:** 100 - 199.

PIERCE & ASSOCIATES
255 South Grand Avenue, Suite 513, Los Angeles CA 90012. 213/626-6711. **Contact:** Lisa Pierce, Owner. **Description:** An executive search firm. **Specializes in the areas of:** Legal. **Positions commonly filled include:** Attorney. **Other U.S. locations:** Washington DC.

PINSKER & COMPANY
P.O. Box 3269, Saratoga CA 95070. 408/867-5161. **Contact:** Manager. **Description:** An executive search firm. **Specializes in the areas of:** High-Tech; Manufacturing.

PLANTING & ASSOCIATES
220 State Street, Suite H, Los Altos CA 94022. 650/949-2002. **Contact:** Office Manager. **Description:** Planting & Associates is an executive search firm. **Specializes in the areas of:** Information Technology.

BOB POLINE ASSOCIATES INC.
12625 High Bluff Drive, Suite 114, San Diego CA 92130. 858/481-3700. **Contact:** Office Manager. **Description:** Bob Poline Associates Inc. is an executive search firm. **Specializes in the areas of:** Real Estate.

DAVID POWELL, INC. (DPI)
2995 Woodside Road, Suite 150, Woodside CA 94062. 650/851-6000. **Fax:** 650/851-5514. **Contact:** Office Manager. **E-mail address:** DPI@davidpowell.com. **World Wide Web address:** http://www.davidpowell.com. **Description:** David Powell, Inc. is an executive search firm. Founded in 1976. **Specializes in the areas of:** High-Tech.

POWER 2000+
1400 Coleman Avenue, Suite G13, Santa Clara CA 95050. 408/970-9919. **Fax:** 408/970-8818. **Contact:** Manager. **World Wide Web address:** http://www.power2000.net. **Description:** Power 2000+ is an executive search firm operating on a retainer basis. Founded in 1970. **Specializes in the areas of:** Engineering; Management; Marketing; Sales; Scientific; Technical.

PREMIER RESOURCES
28202 Cabot Road, Suite 300, Laguna Niguel CA 92677. 949/365-5699. **Contact:** Jerry Thomas, Owner. **Description:** An executive search firm. **Specializes in the areas of:** Administration; Information Technology. **Positions commonly filled include:** Computer Programmer; MIS Specialist; Software Engineer; Systems Analyst. **Average salary range of placements:** More than $50,000. **Number of placements per year:** 1 - 49.

PRESLEY CONSULTANTS, INC.
812 Third Street, Norco CA 91760. 909/734-2237. **Fax:** 909/734-1775. **Contact:** Philip E. Presley, Principal. **E-mail address:** phil@presleyconsultants.com. **World Wide Web address:** http://www.presleyconsultants.com. **Description:** Presley Consultants, Inc. is an executive search firm. Founded in 1972. **Specializes in the areas of:** Hotel/Restaurant. **Corporate headquarters location:** This Location.

PRINCETON CORPORATE CONSULTANTS
16830 Ventura Boulevard, Suite 346, Encino CA 91436-1707. 818/784-8989. **Contact:** Manager. **Description:** Princeton Corporate Consultants is an executive search firm. **Specializes in the areas of:** Engineering; Health/Medical; Manufacturing; Technical. **Number of placements per year:** 200 - 499.

PRISM GROUP
475 Sansome Street, Suite 1850, San Francisco CA 94111. 415/394-7171. **Contact:** Office Manager. **Description:** Prism Group is an executive search firm. **Specializes in the areas of:** Information Systems.

PROBUS EXECUTIVE SEARCH
4962 El Camino Real, Suite 126, Los Altos CA 94022. 650/960-3756. **Fax:** 650/960-0331. **Contact:** Office Manager. **World Wide Web address:** http://www.probus-exec.com. **Description:** Probus Executive Search is an executive search firm. **Specializes in the areas of:** Accounting; Finance.

PROFESSIONAL DENTAL NETWORK
P.O. Box 84748, San Diego CA 92138. 619/284-2706. **Contact:** Linda Turner, Owner. **Description:** An executive search firm that also provides some temporary placements. **Positions commonly filled include:** Dental Assistant/Dental Hygienist; Office Manager; Receptionist.

PROFESSIONAL RECRUITERS INC.
19671 Beach Boulevard, Suite 203, Huntington Beach CA 92648-5901. 714/963-0034. **Fax:** 714/969-0072. **Contact:** Chuck Bechtloff, Owner. **Description:** Professional Recruiters Inc. is an executive search firm that focuses on placing personnel in the paper and packaging industry with an emphasis on companies that manufacture corrugated boxes and folding cartons. **Specializes in the areas of:** Art/Design; Engineering; General Management; Manufacturing; Publishing; Sales. **Positions commonly filled include:** Blue-Collar Worker Supervisor; Buyer; Cost Estimator; Customer Service Representative; Designer; Electrical/Electronics Engineer; Electrician; General Manager; Human Resources Manager; Industrial Engineer; Industrial Production Manager; Manufacturer's/Wholesaler's Sales Rep.; Mechanical Engineer; Purchasing Agent/Manager; Quality Control Supervisor. **Average salary range of placements:** $30,000 - $50,000. **Number of placements per year:** 1 - 49.

PROFESSIONAL SEARCH INC.
5480 Baltimore Drive, Suite 201, La Mesa CA 91942. 619/697-2138. **Fax:** 619/697-2139. **Contact:** Vernon E. Kleist, President. **E-mail address:** vk@recruitwest.com. **Description:** An executive search firm operating on both retainer and contingency bases. **Specializes in the areas of:** Computer Science/Software; Engineering; Manufacturing. **Positions commonly filled include:** Computer Programmer; Electrical/Electronics Engineer; Industrial Engineer; Mechanical Engineer; Metallurgical Engineer; Multimedia Designer; Science Technologist; Software Engineer; Systems Analyst. **Number of placements per year:** 1 - 49.

PROFILER
12400 Wilshire Boulevard, Suite 1460, Los Angeles CA 90025. 310/820-2393. **Fax:** 310/820-3093. **Contact:** Manager. **World Wide Web address:** http://www.profilerusa.com. **Description:** Profiler is an executive search firm that provides placements for digital media companies.

PROGRESSIVE SEARCH & CONSULTING
1320 Mount Diablo Boulevard, Suite D, Walnut Creek CA 94596. 925/930-6340. **Fax:** 925/930-8142. **Contact:** Office Manager. **Description:** Progressive Search & Consulting is an executive search firm. **Specializes in the areas of:** Consumer Package Goods; Sales.

PROGRESSIVE SEARCH ASSOCIATES
12526 High Bluff Drive, Suite 300, San Diego CA 92130. 858/457-7818. **Contact:** Manager. **Description:** Progressive Search Associates is an executive search firm.

PROSEARCH & ASSOCIATES
27302 Becedas, Mission Viejo CA 92691. 949/452-0630. **Fax:** 949/951-2602. **Contact:** Sharon Dodson, Owner. **Description:** Prosearch & Associates is an executive search firm operating on both retainer and contingency bases. The firm also provides some temporary placements. **Specializes in the areas of:** Accounting/Auditing; Administration; Computer Science/Software; Personnel/Labor Relations; Sales; Secretarial; Technical. **Positions commonly filled include:** Accountant/Auditor; Administrative Manager; Bank Officer/Manager; Branch Manager; Clinical Lab Technician; Computer Programmer; MIS Specialist; Registered Nurse; Software Engineer; Systems Analyst; Technical Writer/Editor. **Average salary range of placements:** $30,000 - $50,000.

PROTOCOL SEARCH & SELECTION
650 Hampshire Road, Suite 100, Westlake Village CA 91361. 805/371-0069. **Fax:** 805/371-0048. **Contact:** Chris Salcido, Branch Manager. **Description:** An executive search firm. **Specializes in the areas of:** Computer Hardware/Software. **Positions commonly filled include:** Computer Programmer; MIS Specialist; Systems Analyst. **Average salary range of placements:** More than $50,000. **Number of placements per year:** 100 - 199.

PROTOCOL SEARCH & SELECTION
300 North Lake Avenue, Suite 208, Pasadena CA 91101. 626/449-2214. **Fax:** 626/577-0484. **Contact:** Kelly J. Lucas, Vice President/Branch Manager. **Description:** An executive search firm that also provides some temporary placements. **Specializes in the areas of:** Accounting/ Auditing; Secretarial. **Positions commonly filled include:** Accountant/Auditor; Administrative Manager; Clerical Supervisor; Data Entry Clerk; Human Resources Manager; Paralegal. **Average salary range of placements:** $30,000 - $50,000. **Number of placements per year:** 1000+.

THE PROVEN EDGE EXECUTIVE RECRUITERS
12616 Springbrook Drive, Suite D, San Diego CA 92128. 909/303-2221. **Contact:** Walter Gold, Executive Officer. **Description:** An executive search firm operating on a contingency basis. The company also provides career/outplacement counseling services. **Specializes in the areas of:** Accounting; Administration; Biology; Chemicals; Computer Science/Software; Finance; General Management; Marketing; MIS/EDP; Pharmaceuticals; Plastics; Printing; Publishing; Sales; Scientific; Technical. **Positions commonly filled include:** Accountant; Administrative Manager; Biochemist; Biological Scientist; Biomedical Engineer; Chemist; Chief Financial Officer; Computer Programmer; Editor; Finance Director; General Manager; Geologist/Geophysicist; Graphic Artist; Graphic Designer; Human Resources Manager; Industrial Production Manager; Managing Editor; Manufacturing Engineer; Marketing Manager; MIS Specialist; Multimedia Designer; Operations Manager; Production Manager; Sales Executive; Sales Manager; Technical Writer/Editor. **Corporate headquarters location:** This Location. **Average salary range of placements:** More than $50,000. **Number of placements per year:** 1 - 49.

QUEST SEARCH ASSOCIATES INC.
1901 South Bascom Avenue, Suite 1525, Campbell CA 95008. 408/371-8313. **Contact:** Manager. **Description:** An executive search firm that provides placements for mid- to senior-level management professionals.

RGA ASSOCIATES
465 California Street, Suite 830, San Francisco CA 94104. 415/397-4646. **Contact:** Manager. **Description:** An executive search firm. **Specializes in the areas of:** Computer Hardware/Software. **Positions commonly filled include:** Computer Programmer.

RJ ASSOCIATES
23730 Canzonet Street, Woodland Hills CA 91367. 818/715-7121. **Contact:** President. **Description:** An executive search firm. **Specializes in the areas of:** Accounting/Auditing; Finance; Information Technology. **Positions commonly filled include:** Controller; Finance Director; MIS Specialist. **Average salary range of placements:** More than $50,000. **Number of placements per year:** 50 - 99.

RABER ASSOCIATES
523 West Sixth Street, Suite 520, Los Angeles CA 90014. 213/622-0505. **Contact:** Manager. **Description:** An executive search firm.

RADOSEVIC ASSOCIATES
4350 La Jolla Village Drive, Suite 870, San Diego CA 92122-1247. 858/642-0900. **Contact:** Frank Radosevic, Owner. **Description:** An executive search firm operating on a retainer basis. The firm provides placements for upper-level managers. **Average salary range of placements:** More than $50,000.

RALEIGH & COMPANY
611 Washington Street, Suite 2206, San Francisco CA 94111. 415/362-7550. **Contact:** Manager. **Description:** An executive search firm.

JAMES RANDALL & ASSOCIATES
29021 Bouquet Canyon Road, Saugus CA 91350. **Toll-free phone:** 800/829-6269. **Fax:** 661/613-9832. **Contact:** Manager. **Description:** An executive search firm. **Specializes in the areas of:** Computer Science/ Software; High-Tech.

EDWARD RAST AND COMPANY
235 Montgomery Street, Suite 901, San Francisco CA 94104. 415/986-1710. **Fax:** 415/986-1711. **Contact:** Edward Rast, Managing Director. **Description:** An executive search firm. **Specializes in the areas of:** Accounting/Auditing; Administration; Biology; Biotechnology; Computer Science/Software; Finance; General Management; Health/Medical; Multimedia; Nonprofit; Retail; Sales; Technical; Transportation. **Positions commonly filled include:** Accountant/Auditor; Biological Scientist; Biomedical Engineer; Budget Analyst; Buyer; Clinical Lab Technician; Computer Programmer; Credit Manager; Economist; Financial Analyst; General Manager; Health Services Manager; Human Resources Manager; Management Analyst/ Consultant; Operations/Production Manager; Public Relations Specialist; Software Engineer; Systems Analyst; Technical Writer/Editor; Wholesale and Retail Buyer. **Number of placements per year:** 50 - 99.

RAY & BERNDTSON, INC.
2029 Century Park East, Suite 1000, Los Angeles CA 90067. 310/557-2828. **Fax:** 310/227-0674. **Contact:** Manager. **World Wide Web address:** http://www. rayberndtson.com. **Description:** An executive search firm. **Positions commonly filled include:** Senior Management. **International locations:** Worldwide.

RAY & BERNDTSON, INC.
2479 East Bayshore Road., Suite 801, Palo Alto CA 94303. 650/494-2500. **Fax:** 650/494-3800. **Contact:** Manager. **World Wide Web address:** http://www. rayberndtson.com. **Description:** An executive search firm. **Positions commonly filled include:** Senior Management. **International locations:** Worldwide.

RAYCOR SEARCH
1874 South Pacific Coast Highway, Suite 180, Redondo Beach CA 90277. 310/791-5090. **Toll-free phone:** 800/472-9267. **Fax:** 310/791-5089. **Contact:** R.H. DeFeo, Manager. **E-mail address:** rcsraycor@aol.com. **Description:** An executive search firm. **Specializes in the areas of:** Accounting/Auditing; Computer Science/ Software. **Positions commonly filled include:** Computer Programmer; Consultant; Database Manager; Management Analyst/Consultant; Software Engineer; Systems Analyst; Systems Manager; Technical Writer/Editor; Webmaster. **Corporate headquarters location:** This Location. **Other U.S. locations:** Nationwide. **Average salary range of placements:** More than $50,000. **Number of placements per year:** 1 - 49.

REED GROUP, LLC
1241 Adams Street, Suite 1142, St. Helena CA 94574. 415/732-6158. **Contact:** Manager. **World Wide Web address:** http://www.reedgroup.com. **Description:** An executive search firm. Founded in 1984. **Specializes in the areas of:** Internet Development; Internet Marketing.

RESOURCE PERSPECTIVES, INC.
535 Anton Boulevard, Suite 860, Costa Mesa CA 92626. 714/662-4947. **Fax:** 714/662-4953. **Contact:** Steven Cherney, Ph.D., President. **Description:** An executive search firm operating on a retainer basis. **Specializes in the areas of:** Consumer Products; Engineering; Food; General Management; Industrial; Manufacturing;

Marketing; Sales; Technical. **Positions commonly filled include:** Agricultural Engineer; Agricultural Scientist; Applications Engineer; Biochemist; Biological Scientist; Biomedical Engineer; Chemical Engineer; Chemist; Civil Engineer; Electrical/Electronics Engineer; Environmental Engineer; Food Scientist/Technologist; General Manager; Industrial Engineer; Manufacturing Engineer; Market Research Analyst; Marketing Manager; Marketing Specialist; Mechanical Engineer; Metallurgical Engineer; Operations Manager; Production Manager; Project Manager; Restaurant/Food Service Manager. **Average salary range of placements:** More than $50,000. **Number of placements per year:** 1 - 49.

RICCI LEE ASSOCIATES, INC.
100 Spear Street, Suite 1810, San Francisco CA 94105. 415/247-2980. **Fax:** 415/247-2985. **Contact:** Carol Ricci Lee, President. **Description:** An executive search firm. **Specializes in the areas of:** Advertising; Communications; Direct Marketing; Marketing; Public Relations. **Positions commonly filled include:** Marketing/Public Relations Manager; Public Relations Specialist. **Number of placements per year:** 100 - 199.

RILEY-COLE
P.O. Box 10635, Oakland CA 94610-0635. 510/428-2022. **Fax:** 510/428-2072. **Contact:** Jim Riley or Don Cole, Partners. **Description:** An executive search firm that places mid- to senior-level professionals. Riley-Cole operates on a contingency basis. **Specializes in the areas of:** Accounting/Auditing; Consumer Package Goods; Engineering; Fashion; Finance; Food; General Management; Industrial; Manufacturing; Personnel/Labor Relations; Retail; Sales; Technical. **Positions commonly filled include:** Buyer; Chemical Engineer; Chemist; Customer Service Representative; Electrical/Electronics Engineer; Financial Analyst; Food Scientist/Technologist; General Manager; Human Resources Manager; Industrial Engineer; Industrial Production Manager; Management Analyst/Consultant; Manufacturer's/Wholesaler's Sales Rep.; Market Research Analyst; Mechanical Engineer; Purchasing Agent/Manager; Quality Control Supervisor; Science Technologist; Transportation/Traffic Specialist; Wholesale and Retail Buyer. **Average salary range of placements:** More than $50,000. **Number of placements per year:** 1 - 49.

RITTER & ASSOCIATES
1190 Saratoga Avenue, Suite 140, San Jose CA 95129. 408/551-6144. **Contact:** Willis Ritter, President. **Description:** An executive search firm. **Specializes in the areas of:** Accounting/Auditing; Administration; Computer Science/Software; Engineering; Finance; General Management; Legal; Manufacturing; Sales. **Positions commonly filled include:** Accountant/Auditor; Administrative Manager; Aerospace Engineer; Attorney; Branch Manager; Electrical/Electronics Engineer; Financial Analyst; General Manager; Human Resources Manager; Industrial Engineer; Management Analyst/Consultant; Manufacturer's/Wholesaler's Sales Rep.; Property and Real Estate Manager; Real Estate Agent; Science Technologist; Software Engineer; Systems Analyst. **Number of placements per year:** 1 - 49.

THE ROGAN GROUP
2900 Bristol Street, Suite H-204, Costa Mesa CA 92626. 443/394-8100. **Contact:** Manager. **Description:** An executive search firm. **Specializes in the areas of:** Insurance. **Positions commonly filled include:** Claim Representative; Insurance Agent/Broker; MIS Specialist; Underwriter/Assistant Underwriter. **Number of placements per year:** 1 - 49.

ROLLINS & ASSOCIATES PERSONNEL SERVICE, INC.
4010 Watson Plaza Drive, Suite 105, Lakewood CA 90712. 562/421-6649. **Contact:** Joan Rollins, President. **Description:** An executive search firm. **Specializes in the areas of:** Import/Export. **Number of placements per year:** 100 - 199.

R. ROLLO ASSOCIATES
725 South Figueroa Street, Suite 440, Los Angeles CA 90017. 213/688-9444. **Fax:** 213/688-8358. **Contact:** Manager. **Description:** An executive search firm.

ROMAC INTERNATIONAL
15260 Ventura Boulevard, Suite 380, Sherman Oaks CA 91403-5307. 818/905-7300. **Fax:** 818/905-8260. **Contact:** Recruiter. **Description:** An executive search firm. **Specializes in the areas of:** Accounting/Auditing; Computer Science/Software; Finance. **Positions commonly filled include:** Accountant/Auditor; Computer Programmer; Credit Manager; Financial Analyst; Internet Services Manager; Licensed Practical Nurse; Registered Nurse; Systems Analyst. **Benefits available to temporary workers:** Medical Insurance. **Other U.S. locations:** Nationwide. **Average salary range of placements:** More than $50,000. **Number of placements per year:** 100 - 199.

ROMAC INTERNATIONAL
101 Metro Drive, Suite 680, San Jose CA 95110. 408/437-2440. **Fax:** 408/437-7534. **Contact:** Manager. **Description:** An executive search firm. **Specializes in the areas of:** Accounting/Auditing; Finance.

ROMAC INTERNATIONAL
3 Lagoon Drive, Redwood City CA 94065. 650/628-1850. **Contact:** Nancy Baltzer, Division Manager. **Description:** An executive search firm. **Specializes in the areas of:** Accounting/Auditing; Finance.

ROMAC INTERNATIONAL
180 Montgomery Street, Suite 1860, San Francisco CA 94104. 415/788-2815. **Contact:** Manager. **Description:** An executive search firm. **Specializes in the areas of:** Accounting/Auditing; Finance.

ROMAC INTERNATIONAL
879 West 190th Street, Suite 300, Gardena CA 90248. 310/323-0808. **Fax:** 310/323-1101. **Contact:** Manager. **Description:** An executive search firm. **Specializes in the areas of:** Accounting/Auditing; Computer Hardware/Software; Finance; Information Technology.

ROMAC INTERNATIONAL
2603 Main Street, Suite 1100, Irvine CA 92614. 949/660-1666. **Fax:** 949/660-1815. **Contact:** Bob Gennawey, Regional Vice President. **World Wide Web address:** http://www.romac.com. **Description:** An executive search firm that also offers some career and resume counseling. Client company pays fee. **Specializes in the areas of:** Accounting; Computer Hardware/Software; Finance; Information Technology; MIS/EDP. **Positions commonly filled include:** Accountant; Adjuster; Applications Engineer; AS400 Programmer Analyst; Auditor; Bank Officer/Manager; Budget Analyst; Chief Financial Officer; Computer Animator; Computer Engineer; Computer Operator; Computer Programmer; Computer Scientist; Computer Support Technician; Computer Technician; Content Developer; Controller; Cost Estimator; Credit Manager; Database Administrator; Database Manager; Economist; Finance Director; Financial Analyst; Fund Manager; Internet Services Manager; MIS Specialist; Multimedia Designer; Network/Systems Administrator; Purchasing Agent/Manager; Software Engineer; SQL Programmer; Systems Analyst; Systems Manager; Webmaster. **Other U.S. locations:** Nationwide. **Average salary range of placements:** $50,000 - $100,000. **Number of placements per year:** 1000+.

ROMAC INTERNATIONAL
4510 Executive Drive, Suite 325, San Diego CA 92121. 858/552-0300. **Fax:** 858/452-7011. **Contact:** Manager. **Description:** An executive search firm. **Specializes in the areas of:** Accounting/Auditing; Computer Hardware/Software; Engineering; Information Technology.

ROMAC INTERNATIONAL
425 California Street, Suite 1200, San Francisco CA 94104. 415/591-1700. **Fax:** 415/296-9843. **Contact:**

Manager. **Description:** An executive search firm. **Specializes in the areas of:** Computer Hardware/Software; Information Technology; Legal.

LARRY ROSENTHAL & ASSOCIATES
2333 Camino del Rio South, Suite 110, San Diego CA 92108. **Contact:** Manager. **Description:** Larry Rosenthal & Associates is an executive search firm. **Specializes in the areas of:** Computer Hardware/Software; Engineering.

ROWLAND ASSOCIATES
7840 Madison Avenue, Suite 185, Fair Oaks CA 95628. 916/961-3632. **Fax:** 916/962-2938. **Contact:** John R. Rowland, President. **Description:** Rowland Associates is an executive search firm. **Specializes in the areas of:** Accounting/Auditing; Architecture/Construction; Banking; Computer Hardware/Software; Engineering; Finance; Manufacturing; Technical. **Positions commonly filled include:** Accountant/Auditor; Aerospace Engineer; Architect; Biomedical Engineer; Chemical Engineer; Civil Engineer; Claim Representative; Computer Programmer; Electrical/Electronics Engineer; Industrial Engineer; Manufacturing Engineer; Mechanical Engineer; MIS Specialist; Quality Control Supervisor; Software Engineer; Systems Analyst. **Corporate headquarters location:** This Location. **Number of placements per year:** 1 - 49.

ROYAL STAFFING SERVICES
14011 Ventura Boulevard, Suite 214 W, Sherman Oaks CA 91423. 818/981-1080. **Fax:** 818/981-1338. **Contact:** Rosemarie Wolff, President. **Description:** An executive search firm. **Specializes in the areas of:** Accounting; Auditing; Administration; Advertising; Computer Hardware/Software; Economics; Engineering; Finance; Food; Legal; Manufacturing; Nonprofit; Personnel/Labor Relations; Publishing; Sales; Secretarial; Technical. **Positions commonly filled include:** Accountant/Auditor; Aerospace Engineer; Budget Analyst; Buyer; Claim Representative; Clerical Supervisor; Computer Programmer; Credit Manager; Dentist; Design Engineer; Draftsperson; Electrical/Electronics Engineer; Financial Analyst; General Manager; Health Services Manager; Human Resources Specialist; Internet Services Manager; Management Analyst/Consultant; Manufacturer's/Wholesaler's Sales Rep.; Medical Records Technician; MIS Specialist; Paralegal; Property and Real Estate Manager; Public Relations Specialist; Purchasing Agent/Manager; Quality Control Supervisor; Securities Sales Representative; Services Sales Rep.; Technical Writer/Editor; Telecommunications Manager; Transportation/Traffic Specialist; Typist/Word Processor; Underwriter/Assistant Underwriter. **Benefits available to temporary workers:** Bonus Award/Plan; Medical Insurance; Paid Holidays. **Corporate headquarters location:** This Location. **Number of placements per year:** 50 - 99.

RUSHER, LOSCAVIO, AND LOPRESTO
2479 East Bayshore Road, Suite 700, Palo Alto CA 94303. 650/494-0883. **Fax:** 650/494-7231. **Contact:** Manager. **Description:** Rusher, Loscavio, and Lopresto is an executive search firm. **Specializes in the areas of:** Executives; General Management; High-Tech; Information Systems; Insurance; Manufacturing; Marketing; Nonprofit; Sales.

RUSHER, LOSCAVIO, AND LOPRESTO
142 Sansome Street, 5th Floor, San Francisco CA 94104. 415/765-6600. **Fax:** 415/397-2842. **Contact:** Manager. **Description:** An executive search firm. Founded in 1977. **Specializes in the areas of:** Executives; Finance; General Management; High-Tech; Human Resources; Information Systems; Insurance; Manufacturing; Marketing; Nonprofit; Sales.

RUSSELL REYNOLDS ASSOCIATES, INC.
333 South Grand Avenue, Suite 3500, Los Angeles CA 90071. 213/489-1520. **Fax:** 213/253-4444. **Contact:** Manager. **Description:** A generalist executive search firm.

RUSSELL REYNOLDS ASSOCIATES, INC.
2500 Sands Hill Road, Suite 105, Menlo Park CA 94025. 650/233-2400. **Fax:** 650/233-2499. **Contact:** Manager. **World Wide Web address:** http://www.russreyn.com. **Description:** A generalist executive search firm.

RUSSELL REYNOLDS ASSOCIATES, INC.
101 California Street, Suite 3140, San Francisco CA 94111. 415/352-3300. **Fax:** 415/781-7690. **Contact:** Manager. **World Wide Web address:** http://www.russreyn.com. **Description:** A generalist executive search firm.

RYAN, MILLER & ASSOCIATES
4601 Wilshire Boulevard, Suite 225, Los Angeles CA 90010. 323/938-4768. **Fax:** 323/857-7009. **Contact:** Lee Ryan, Partner. **Description:** An executive search firm. **Specializes in the areas of:** Accounting/Auditing; Banking; Finance; Investment; Real Estate. **Number of placements per year:** 100 - 199.

RYAN, MILLER & ASSOCIATES
790 East Colorado Boulevard, Suite 506, Pasadena CA 91101-2113. 626/568-3100. **Fax:** 626/568-3772. **Contact:** Roger Miller, Partner. **E-mail address:** rma111@aol.com. **Description:** An executive search firm specializing in the recruitment and placement of financial professionals. The firm represents the investment banking, investment management, and commercial banking industries and works with entrepreneurial companies placing CFO and treasury positions throughout the United States. **Specializes in the areas of:** Banking; Finance; Personnel/Labor Relations. **Positions commonly filled include:** Accountant/Auditor; Bank Officer/Manager; Budget Analyst; Financial Analyst; Internet Services Manager; Securities Sales Representative. **Average salary range of placements:** More than $50,000. **Number of placements per year:** 100 - 199.

SAI (SLOAN ASSOCIATES INC.)
2855 Mitchell Drive, Suite 117, Walnut Creek CA 94598. 925/932-3000. **Fax:** 925/932-3857. **Contact:** Steve Sloan, President. **Description:** An executive search firm. **Specializes in the areas of:** Computer Science/Software. **Positions commonly filled include:** Branch Manager; Systems Analyst. **Number of placements per year:** 50 - 99.

SMC GROUP
26772 Vista Terrace, Lake Forest CA 92630-8110. 949/855-4545. **Contact:** Shala Shashani, President. **E-mail address:** shala@smcgroup.com. **World Wide Web address:** http://www.smcgroup.com. **Description:** An executive search firm focusing on the placement of LAN/WAN professionals. **Specializes in the areas of:** Computer Hardware/Software. **Positions commonly filled include:** MIS Manager; Software Engineer; Telecommunications Manager. **Number of placements per year:** 50 - 99.

S.R. & ASSOCIATES
5001 Birch Street, Newport Beach CA 92660. 949/756-3271. **Fax:** 949/640-7268. **Contact:** Steve Ross, President. **Description:** An executive search firm that also develops and markets software applications for recruiting firms. **Specializes in the areas of:** Accounting/Auditing; Computer Science/Software; Sales. **Positions commonly filled include:** Accountant/Auditor; Computer Programmer; Credit Manager; Human Resources Manager; Management Analyst/Consultant; Manufacturer's/Wholesaler's Sales Rep.; Services Sales Representative; Systems Analyst. **Average salary range of placements:** More than $50,000. **Number of placements per year:** 50 - 99.

PENNI SAFFORD & ASSOCIATES
6939 Sunrise Boulevard, Suite 119, Citrus Heights CA 95610. 916/723-5939. **Contact:** Manager. **Description:** An executive search firm. **Specializes in the areas of:** Computer Hardware/Software. **Positions commonly filled include:** Database Manager; Software Engineer.

SALES PROFESSIONALS PERSONNEL SERVICES
595 Market Street, Suite 2500, San Francisco CA 94105. 415/543-2828. **Contact:** Linda Glover, President. **Description:** An executive search firm. **Specializes in the areas of:** Marketing; Sales; Sales Management. **Positions commonly filled include:** Manufacturer's/ Wholesaler's Sales Rep.; Marketing Manager; Sales Manager; Services Sales Representative.

SAMPSON MEDICAL SEARCH
22330 Hawthorne Boulevard, Suite 207, Torrance CA 90505. 310/791-1744. **Fax:** 310/791-0684. **Contact:** Judie Sampson, President. **World Wide Web address:** http://www.sampsonmed.com. **Description:** Sampson Medical Search is an executive search firm operating on a contingency basis. **Specializes in the areas of:** Biotechnology; Clinical Research; Health/Medical; Information Systems; Information Technology; Pharmaceuticals; Regulatory Affairs. **Positions commonly filled include:** Chief Executive Officer; Clinical Applications Specialist; Computer Programmer; Human Resources Manager; Medical Records Technician; MIS Specialist; Product Manager; Project Manager; Sales Executive; Sales Manager; Sales Representative; Statistician. **Average salary range of placements:** More than $50,000. **Number of placements per year:** 100 - 199.

SANFORD ROSE ASSOCIATES
748 Dos Hermanos Road, Santa Barbara CA 93111. 805/966-1846. **Contact:** Manager. **World Wide Web address:** http://www.sanfordrose.com. **Description:** An executive search firm. **Specializes in the areas of:** Engineering; General Management; High-Tech; Sales Management.

SANFORD ROSE ASSOCIATES
9 St. Francis Court, Suite D, Monarch Beach CA 92629. 949/487-9055. **Fax:** 949/487-9214. **Contact:** Bob Dudley, President. **World Wide Web address:** http://www.sanfordrose.com. **Description:** An executive search firm. **Specializes in the areas of:** Computer Science/Software. **Positions commonly filled include:** Computer Programmer; Electrical/Electronics Engineer; MIS Specialist; Purchasing Agent/Manager; Software Engineer; Systems Analyst. **Average salary range of placements:** More than $50,000. **Number of placements per year:** 1 - 49.

SANFORD ROSE ASSOCIATES
2030 East Fourth Street, Suite 140, Santa Ana CA 92705. 714/558-1622. **Contact:** Manager. **World Wide Web address:** http://www.sanfordrose.com. **Description:** An executive search firm that places individuals in the semiconductor industry. **Specializes in the areas of:** Electronics.

SANFORD ROSE ASSOCIATES
9471 Florence Circle, Villa Park CA 92861. 714/289-9460. **Contact:** Manager. **World Wide Web address:** http://www.sanfordrose.com. **Description:** An executive search firm that places individuals in the semiconductor industry. **Specializes in the areas of:** Electronics.

SANFORD ROSE ASSOCIATES - SAN FRANCISCO
1415 Oakland Boulevard, Suite 215, Walnut Creek CA 94596. 925/974-1760. **Fax:** 925/974-1763. **Contact:** Manager. **World Wide Web address:** http://www. sanfordrose.com. **Description:** An executive search firm. **Specializes in the areas of:** Biology; Biotechnology; Health/Medical; Investment; Medical Devices; Pharmaceuticals.

SCHLATTER & ASSOCIATES
388 Market Street, Suite 500, San Francisco CA 94111. 415/433-8100. **Fax:** 415/421-4176. **Contact:** Craig Schlatter, President. **Description:** An executive search firm. **Specializes in the areas of:** Accounting/Auditing; Finance; MIS/EDP. **Positions commonly filled include:** Accountant/Auditor; Budget Analyst; Chief Financial Officer; Controller; Finance Director; Financial Analyst;

Management Analyst/Consultant. **Number of placements per year:** 100 - 199.

AVERY SCHLUETER EXECUTIVE SEARCH
2 Annabel Lane, Suite 260, San Ramon CA 94583. 925/866-8660. **Contact:** Manager. **Description:** An executive search firm that focuses on placing sales professionals in the food processing and packaging machinery industries. **Specializes in the areas of:** Food.

SCHWEICHLER ASSOCIATES INC.
200 Tamal Vista, Building 200, Suite 100, Corte Madera CA 94925. 415/924-7200. **Fax:** 415/924-9152. **Contact:** Manager. **Description:** An executive search firm. **Specializes in the areas of:** Computer Hardware/ Software; Data Communications; Internet Development; Network Administration; Start-up Organizations; Telecommunications; Wireless Communications.

SCOTT-THALER ASSOCIATES, INC.
86 Brookhollow Drive, Santa Ana CA 92705. 714/966-1671. **Fax:** 714/755-7101. **Contact:** Brian D. Thaler, President. **Description:** An executive search firm operating on both retainer and contingency bases. **Specializes in the areas of:** Fashion; Transportation. **Positions commonly filled include:** Account Representative; Buyer; Industrial Engineer; Operations/ Production Manager; Production Manager; Purchasing Agent/Manager; Sales Executive; Sales Manager; Sales Rep.; Transportation/Traffic Specialist; Wholesale and Retail Buyer. **Corporate headquarters location:** This Location. **Average salary range of placements:** More than $50,000. **Number of placements per year:** 100 - 199.

THE SEARCH GROUP
1328 Sierra Alta Way, Los Angeles CA 90069. 310/550-0292. **Contact:** Manager. **World Wide Web address:** http://www.jobsearch4you.com. **Description:** The Search Group is an executive search firm. **Specializes in the areas of:** Engineering.

THE SEARCH NETWORK
5755 Oberlin Drive, Suite 312, San Diego CA 92121. 858/535-0015. **Fax:** 858/535-0152. **Contact:** Manager. **E-mail address:** snet@pacbell.net. **Description:** An executive search firm. **Specializes in the areas of:** Engineering; Manufacturing. **Positions commonly filled include:** Design Engineer; Electrical/Electronics Engineer; Internet Services Manager; Mechanical Engineer; MIS Specialist; Multimedia Designer; Nuclear Engineer; Software Engineer. **Average salary range of placements:** More than $50,000. **Number of placements per year:** 50 - 99.

SEARCH WEST
2049 Century Park East, Suite 650, Los Angeles CA 90067. 310/284-8888. **Contact:** General Manager. **Description:** An executive search firm. **Specializes in the areas of:** Accounting/Auditing; Advertising; Banking; Computer Hardware/Software; Engineering; Finance; Food; Health/Medical; Insurance; MIS/EDP; Real Estate; Sales; Technical. **Positions commonly filled include:** Accountant/Auditor; Administrative Assistant; Aerospace Engineer; Bank Officer/Manager; Biomedical Engineer; Bookkeeper; Chemical Engineer; Civil Engineer; Computer Operator; Computer Programmer; Credit Manager; Customer Service Representative; Draftsperson; Economist; EDP Specialist; Electrical/ Electronics Engineer; Financial Analyst; Hotel Manager; Human Resources Manager; Industrial Designer; Industrial Engineer; Insurance Agent/Broker; Marketing Specialist; Nurse; Operations/Production Manager; Purchasing Agent/Manager; Quality Control Supervisor; Sales Rep.; Systems Analyst; Technician; Underwriter/ Assistant Underwriter. **Number of placements per year:** 1000+.

SEARCH WEST OF ONTARIO
2151 Convention Center Way, Suite 121-B, Ontario CA 91764. 909/937-0100. **Contact:** Nate Reddicks, General Manager. **Description:** An executive search firm.

Specializes in the areas of: Accounting/Auditing; Architecture/Construction; Banking; Computer Hardware/Software; Construction; Engineering; Finance; Food; Health/Medical; Insurance; Manufacturing; Personnel/Labor Relations; Publishing; Sales; Technical. **Positions commonly filled include:** Accountant/Auditor; Actuary; Aerospace Engineer; Agricultural Engineer; Architect; Attorney; Bank Officer/Manager; Biological Scientist; Biomedical Engineer; Buyer; Ceramics Engineer; Chemical Engineer; Chemist; Civil Engineer; Computer Programmer; Credit Manager; Dietician/Nutritionist; Draftsperson; Economist; EDP Specialist; Electrical/Electronics Engineer; Financial Analyst; Food Scientist/Technologist; General Manager; Hotel Manager; Human Resources Manager; Industrial Designer; Marketing Specialist; Mechanical Engineer; Metallurgical Engineer; Mining Engineer; MIS Specialist; Petroleum Engineer; Physicist; Purchasing Agent/Manager; Quality Control Supervisor; Sales Representative; Statistician; Systems Analyst; Technical Writer/Editor; Underwriter/Assistant Underwriter. **Number of placements per year:** 1000+.

SEITCHIK, CORWIN AND SEITCHIK, INC.
3443 Clay Street, San Francisco CA 94118-2008. 415/928-5717. **Contact:** Bill Seitchik, Vice President. **Description:** An executive search firm. **Specializes in the areas of:** Fashion; Manufacturing.

SELTZER FONTAINE BECKWITH
2999 Overland Avenue, Suite 120, Los Angeles CA 90064-4243. 310/839-6000. **Fax:** 310/839-4408. **Contact:** Valerie A. Fontaine, Partner. **E-mail address:** sfbsearch@aol.com. **World Wide Web address:** http://www.sfbsearch.com. **Description:** An executive search firm operating on both retainer and contingency bases. **Specializes in the areas of:** Legal. **Positions commonly filled include:** Attorney. **Number of placements per year:** 1 - 49.

THE SEPTEMBER GROUP, INC.
11611 San Vicente Boulevard, Suite 840, Los Angeles CA 90049. 310/207-0444. **Fax:** 310/826-2023. **Contact:** President. **Description:** An executive search firm operating on a retainer basis. **Specializes in the areas of:** Banking; Finance. **Positions commonly filled include:** Bank Officer/Manager; Chief Financial Officer; Economist; Finance Director; Financial Analyst; Fund Manager; Human Resources Manager. **Other U.S. locations:** San Francisco CA; New York NY. **International locations:** London, England; Mexico City, Mexico. **Average salary range of placements:** More than $50,000. **Number of placements per year:** 1 - 49.

SHARP PERSONNEL & SEARCH
1665 East Fourth Street, Suite 204, Santa Ana CA 92706. 714/667-6909. **Fax:** 714/667-2916. **Contact:** Manager. **Description:** An executive search firm that also provides some temporary placements. **Specializes in the areas of:** Accounting/Auditing; Banking; Computer Science/Software; Finance; Health/Medical; Insurance; Personnel/Labor Relations; Secretarial. **Positions commonly filled include:** Accountant/Auditor; Bank Officer/Manager; Financial Analyst; Human Resources Manager; Software Engineer; Systems Analyst; Underwriter/Assistant Underwriter. **Benefits available to temporary workers:** Credit Union; Dental Insurance; Paid Holidays; Paid Vacation. **Average salary range of placements:** $30,000 - $50,000. **Number of placements per year:** 100 - 199.

PEGGY SHEA & ASSOCIATES
2660 Townsgate Road, Suite 800, Westlake Village CA 91361. 818/889-5350. **Contact:** Peggy Shea, Owner. **Description:** An executive search firm.

DAVID SHIPLACOFF & ASSOCIATES
2030 Fairburn Avenue, Suite 100, Los Angeles CA 90025-5914. 310/474-3600. **Fax:** 310/474-2680. **Contact:** David Shiplacoff, Principal. **E-mail address:** david@dsasearch.com. **World Wide Web address:**

http://www.dsasearch.com. **Description:** A generalist executive search firm. Founded in 1979.

J.W. SILVERIA & COMPANY
1058 Cass Street, Suite A, Monterey CA 93940. 831/646-8811. **Contact:** James Silveria, Owner. **Description:** An executive search firm. **Positions commonly filled include:** Accountant/Auditor; Administrative Manager; Agricultural Engineer; Architect; Attorney; Bank Officer/Manager; Biochemist; Branch Manager; Budget Analyst; Buyer; Chemical Engineer; Clerical Supervisor; Computer Programmer; Design Engineer; Financial Analyst; Health Services Manager; Hotel Manager; Human Resources Manager; MIS Specialist; Software Engineer; Systems Analyst. **Average salary range of placements:** $30,000 - $50,000. **Number of placements per year:** 1 - 49.

SINGER STROUSE
1865 California Street, San Francisco CA 94109-4541. 415/781-6444. **Contact:** Pamela Singer, Owner. **Description:** An executive search firm operating on both retainer and contingency bases for *Fortune* 500 companies in California. **Specializes in the areas of:** Accounting/Auditing; Legal; Tax. **Positions commonly filled include:** Accountant; Attorney. **Average salary range of placements:** More than $50,000. **Number of placements per year:** 1 - 49.

SOLUTION MARKETING
5371 Wilshire Boulevard, Suite 203, Los Angeles CA 90036. 323/935-3053. **Fax:** 323/932-6138. **Contact:** Jennifer Rosky, President. **E-mail address:** mktmstr@mediaone.net. **Description:** An executive search firm. **Specializes in the areas of:** Advertising; Marketing; Public Relations. **Average salary range of placements:** More than $50,000.

SOUTHWEST SEARCH ASSOCIATES
10226 Buena Vista Avenue, Santee CA 92071. 619/562-1103. **Fax:** 619/562-1104. **Contact:** Linda Shaw, Owner. **E-mail address:** shawsearch@msn.com. **Description:** An executive search firm operating on both retainer and contingency bases. **Specializes in the areas of:** Engineering. **Positions commonly filled include:** Chemical Engineer; Chemist; Design Engineer; Electrical/Electronics Engineer; Environmental Engineer; General Manager; Industrial Engineer; Industrial Production Manager; Manufacturing Engineer; Marketing Manager; Marketing Specialist; Mechanical Engineer; MIS Specialist; Operations Manager; Product Manager; Project Manager; Quality Control Supervisor; Sales Engineer; Sales Executive; Sales Manager; Sales Representative; Systems Manager. **Average salary range of placements:** More than $50,000. **Number of placements per year:** 1 - 49.

SPECTRAWEST
38193 Martha Avenue, Fremont CA 94536. 510/791-1700. **Fax:** 510/791-8900. **Contact:** Fred Arredondo, Director. **Description:** An executive search firm. **Specializes in the areas of:** Computer Hardware/Software; Software Engineering. **Positions commonly filled include:** Chemical Engineer; Design Engineer; Electrical/Electronics Engineer; Software Engineer. **Average salary range of placements:** More than $50,000. **Number of placements per year:** 1 - 49.

SPECTRUM SEARCH AGENCY
60 East Highland Avenue, Sierra Madre CA 91024. 323/256-4564. **Contact:** Joe Florence, Employment. **Description:** An executive search firm. **Specializes in the areas of:** Sales; Telecommunications. **Positions commonly filled include:** Marketing Specialist; Sales Representative.

SPLAINE & ASSOCIATES INC.
15951 Los Gatos Boulevard, Los Gatos CA 95032-3488. 408/354-3664. **Fax:** 408/356-6329. **Contact:** Charles Splaine, President. **E-mail address:** info@exec-search.com. **World Wide Web address:** http://www.exec-search.com. **Description:** An executive search firm

operating on a retainer basis. Founded in 1982. Client company pays fee. **Specializes in the areas of:** Communications; Computer Science/Software; High-Tech; Internet Development; Internet Marketing. **Corporate headquarters location:** This Location. **Average salary range of placements:** More than $100,000. **Number of placements per year:** 1 - 49.

M.H. SPRINGER & ASSOCIATES
5855 Topanga Canyon Boulevard, Suite 230, Woodland Hills CA 91367. 818/710-8955. **Contact:** Manager. **Description:** An executive search firm. **Specializes in the areas of:** Finance.

STAFF SEEKERS
1850 East 17th Street, Suite 214, Santa Ana CA 92705. 714/796-1580. **Fax:** 714/796-1585. **Contact:** Manager. **Description:** An executive search firm operating on both retainer and contingency bases. **Specializes in the areas of:** Health/Medical. **Positions commonly filled include:** Dental Assistant/Dental Hygienist; Licensed Practical Nurse; Medical Assistant; Medical Records Technician; Office Manager. **Average salary range of placements:** $30,000 - $50,000. **Number of placements per year:** 200 - 499.

STAFFMARK
14150 Vine Place, Cerritos CA 90703. 562/407-3700. **Contact:** Manager. **Description:** An executive search firm.

STEINBRUN, HUGHES AND ASSOCIATES
10866 Wilshire Boulevard, Suite 360, Los Angeles CA 90024. 310/474-9495. **Fax:** 310/474-0255. **Contact:** Manager. **Description:** An executive search firm operating on a retainer basis. **Specializes in the areas of:** Accounting/Auditing; Administration; Banking; Finance; Food; General Management; Personnel/Labor Relations; Sales. **Positions commonly filled include:** Accountant/Auditor; Budget Analyst; Chief Financial Officer; Controller; Finance Director; Financial Analyst; Fund Manager; General Manager; Human Resources Manager; Management Analyst/Consultant; Market Research Analyst; Marketing Manager; Marketing Specialist; MIS Specialist; Operations Manager; Production Manager; Project Manager; Strategy Consultant; Systems Analyst. **Average salary range of placements:** More than $50,000. **Number of placements per year:** 50 - 99.

ADELE STEINMETZ EXECUTIVE SEARCH
365 D Tyrella Avenue, Mountain View CA 94043. 650/965-9138. **Contact:** Adele Steinmetz, Owner. **Description:** An executive search firm. **Specializes in the areas of:** Computer Science/Software; Engineering; Light Industrial; Manufacturing; Sales; Technical. **Positions commonly filled include:** Account Manager; Advertising Executive; Applications Engineer; Architect; Buyer; Chemical Engineer; Chemist; Chief Financial Officer; Computer Programmer; Customer Service Representative; Database Manager; Design Engineer; Electrical/Electronics Engineer; General Manager; Industrial Engineer; Internet Services Manager; Manufacturing Engineer; Marketing Manager; Marketing Specialist; Mechanical Engineer; Metallurgical Engineer; MIS Specialist; Multimedia Designer; Online Content Specialist; Operations Manager; Product Manager; Project Manager; Purchasing Agent/Manager; Quality Control Supervisor; Sales Engineer; Sales Executive; Sales Manager; Sales Representative; Software Engineer; Statistician; Systems Analyst; Systems Manager; Technical Writer/Editor; Telecommunications Manager; Vice President; Webmaster. **Corporate headquarters location:** This Location. **International locations:** Japan; United Kingdom. **Average salary range of placements:** More than $50,000. **Number of placements per year:** 1 - 49.

STONE & ASSOCIATES
10850 Wilshire Boulevard, Suite 600, Los Angeles CA 90024. 310/475-7433. **Contact:** Manager. **Description:**

An executive search firm. **Specializes in the areas of:** Insurance.

D.M. STONE PROFESSIONAL STAFFING
100 Bush Street, Suite 650, San Francisco CA 94104. 415/391-5151. **Toll-free phone:** 800/391-1726. **Fax:** 415/391-5536. **Contact:** David Stone, CPA/President. **E-mail address:** dave@dmstone.com. **World Wide Web address:** http://www.dmstone.com. **Description:** An executive search firm. Founded in 1987. **Specializes in the areas of:** Administration; Banking; Finance; Insurance; Investment. **Positions commonly filled include:** Account Representative; Administrative Assistant; Bank Officer/Manager; Branch Manager; Customer Service Representative; Financial Analyst; Fund Manager; Management Trainee; Marketing Manager; Paralegal; Project Manager; Sales Executive; Sales Manager; Sales Rep.; Secretary; Underwriter/Assistant Underwriter. **Corporate headquarters location:** This Location. **Average salary range of placements:** More than $50,000.

STRATEGIC ALTERNATIVES
3 Portola Road, Portola Valley CA 94028. 650/851-2211. **Contact:** Manager. **World Wide Web address:** http://www.strategicalternatives.com. **Description:** An executive search firm that operates on a retainer basis. Founded in 1986. **Specializes in the areas of:** Computer Hardware/Software; Marketing; Operations Management; Research and Development; Sales.

SYSTEMS CAREERS
211 Sutter Street, Suite 607, San Francisco CA 94108. 415/434-4770. **Contact:** Wayne Sarchett, Principal. **Description:** An executive search firm operating on a contingency basis. Client company pays fee. **Specializes in the areas of:** Computer Science/Software; Consulting; Software Development. **Positions commonly filled include:** Applications Engineer; Architect; Computer Animator; Computer Programmer; Consultant; Management Analyst/Consultant; Marketing Manager; Project Manager; Software Engineer; Systems Analyst; Systems Manager; Telecommunications Manager; Vice President. **Corporate headquarters location:** This Location. **Average salary range of placements:** $50,000 - $100,000. **Number of placements per year:** 1 - 49.

SYSTEMS RESEARCH GROUP
162 South Rancho Santa Fe Road, Suite B80, Encinitas CA 92024-4365. 760/436-1575. **Fax:** 760/634-3614. **Contact:** Stephen Gebler, President. **E-mail address:** jobs@systemsresearchgroup.com. **World Wide Web address:** http://www.systemsresearchgroup.com. **Description:** An executive search firm concentrating on the placement of CAD/CAM/CAE, rapid prototyping, product data management, and computer graphics personnel. The firm operates on both retainer and contingency bases. **Specializes in the areas of:** Administration; Computer Science/Software; Marketing; MIS/EDP; Sales; Scientific; Technical. **Positions commonly filled include:** Account Manager; Account Representative; Applications Engineer; Branch Manager; Database Manager; Design Engineer; Draftsperson; Graphic Artist; Graphic Designer; Manufacturing Engineer; Market Research Analyst; Marketing Manager; Mechanical Engineer; Sales Engineer; Sales Executive; Sales Manager; Sales Representative; Software Engineer; Technical Writer/Editor; Telecommunications Manager. **Corporate headquarters location:** This Location. **Average salary range of placements:** More than $50,000. **Number of placements per year:** 50 - 99.

TMP EXECUTIVE RESOURCES
One Lower Ragsdale Drive, Building One, Suite 150, Monterey CA 93940-5741. 831/375-2676. **Fax:** 831/375-2841. **Contact:** Ronald W. Sills, Partner. **World Wide Web address:** http://www.tmpw.com. **Description:** An executive search firm. **Specializes in the areas of:** Biotechnology; Consumer Products; Finance; Health/Medical; Industrial; Pharmaceuticals; Technical. **Other U.S. locations:** Nationwide.

TMP WORLDWIDE
1801 Century Park East, Suite 2300, Los Angeles CA 90067-2325. 310/277-0550. **Fax:** 310/277-0538. **Contact:** Branch Manager. **World Wide Web address:** http://www.tmpw.com. **Description:** TMP Worldwide is an executive search firm. **Specializes in the areas of:** Biotechnology; Consumer Products; Finance; Health/Medical; Industrial; Pharmaceuticals; Technical. **Other U.S. locations:** Nationwide.

TMP WORLDWIDE
44 Montgomery Street, Suite 3060, San Francisco CA 94104. 415/296-0600. **Contact:** David M. de Wilde, Managing Partner. **World Wide Web address:** http://www.tmpw.com. **Description:** An executive search firm. **Specializes in the areas of:** Biotechnology; Consumer Products; Finance; Health/Medical; Industrial; Pharmaceuticals; Technical. **Other U.S. locations:** Nationwide.

TMP WORLDWIDE
16255 Ventura Boulevard, Suite 400, Encino CA 91436-2394. 818/905-6010. **Contact:** Branch Manager. **World Wide Web address:** http://www.tmpw.com. **Description:** TMP Worldwide is an executive search firm. **Specializes in the areas of:** Biotechnology; Consumer Products; Finance; Health/Medical; Industrial; Pharmaceuticals; Technical. **Other U.S. locations:** Nationwide.

TAX EXECUTIVE SEARCH, INC.
842 South Orange Grove Boulevard, Pasadena CA 91105-1742. 626/403-1522. **Fax:** 603/658-2817. **Contact:** Charles Heil, Principal Recruiter. **Description:** Tax Executive Search, Inc. is an executive search firm focusing on the placement of tax accountants, tax attorneys, appraisers, and business valuation financial consultants. **Specializes in the areas of:** Accounting/Auditing; Appraisal; Economics; Finance; Legal; Professional; Sales; Tax; Technical; Valuation. **Positions commonly filled include:** Attorney; Economist; Mathematician; Securities Sales Representative; Services Sales Representative. **Number of placements per year:** 1 - 49.

TECHNICAL SEARCH CONSULTANTS
32732 Johnathan Circle, Dana Point CA 92629. 949/493-5488. **Contact:** Manager. **Description:** Technical Search Consultants is an executive search firm. **Specializes in the areas of:** Computer Science/Software; Electronics; Engineering.

TECHNIQUEST
P.O. Box 548, San Jose CA 95106-0548. 408/293-1122. **Fax:** 408/293-1223. **Contact:** Claudia Lindquist, General Manager. **E-mail address:** claudia@techniquest.com. **Description:** Techniquest is an executive search firm. **Specializes in the areas of:** Biology; Biotechnology; Electronics; Engineering; Medical Devices. **Positions commonly filled include:** Biochemist; Biological Scientist; Biomedical Engineer; Design Engineer; Electrical/Electronics Engineer; Mechanical Engineer; Metallurgical Engineer; Quality Control Supervisor; Science Technologist; Software Engineer. **Average salary range of placements:** More than $50,000. **Number of placements per year:** 50 - 99.

TECHSTAFF WEST INC.
1200 West Hillcrest Drive, Suite 201, Thousand Oaks CA 91320-2734. 805/376-2250. **Contact:** Sue Duffy, Recruiter. **Description:** An executive search firm. **Specializes in the areas of:** Administration; Engineering; Information Technology. **Positions commonly filled include:** Account Manager; Account Representative; Accountant; Adjuster; Administrative Assistant; Applications Engineer; AS400 Programmer Analyst; Auditor; Bank Officer/Manager; Budget Analyst; Buyer; Chief Financial Officer; Computer Animator; Computer Engineer; Computer Operator; Computer Programmer; Computer Scientist; Computer Support Technician; Computer Technician; Content Developer; Controller; Cost Estimator; Credit Manager; Customer Service Representative; Database Administrator; Database Manager; Design Engineer; Draftsperson; Economist; Electrical/Electronics Engineer; Electrician; Environmental Engineer; Finance Director; Financial Analyst; Fund Manager; General Manager; Human Resources Manager; Industrial Engineer; Internet Services Manager; Management Analyst/Consultant; Management Trainee; Manufacturing Engineer; Mechanical Engineer; Metallurgical Engineer; MIS Specialist; Multimedia Designer; Network/Systems Administrator; Operations Manager; Production Manager; Project Manager; Purchasing Agent/Manager; Quality Assurance Engineer; Quality Control Supervisor; Real Estate Agent; Sales Engineer; Sales Executive; Sales Manager; Sales Representative; Secretary; Software Engineer; SQL Programmer; Systems Analyst; Systems Manager; Typist/Word Processor; Vice President; Webmaster. **Corporate headquarters location:** Milwaukee WI. **Average salary range of placements:** More than $50,000. **Number of placements per year:** 200 - 499.

TELEFORCE INTERNATIONAL
P.O. Box 3175, San Clemente CA 92674-3175. 949/661-3337. **Fax:** 949/661-6965. **Contact:** Joseph Barrigas, President. **Description:** An executive search firm operating on both retainer and contingency bases. **Specializes in the areas of:** Accounting/Auditing; Administration; Computer Science/Software; Engineering; Finance; General Management; Personnel/Labor Relations; Sales; Telecommunications. **Positions commonly filled include:** Accountant/Auditor; Broadcast Technician; Computer Programmer; Customer Service Representative; Electrical/Electronics Engineer; Financial Analyst; Internet Services Manager; Management Analyst/Consultant; Market Research Analyst; MIS Specialist; Systems Analyst; Telecommunications Manager. **Number of placements per year:** 1 - 49.

TELFORD, ADAMS & ALEXANDER
402 West Broadway, Suite 900, San Diego CA 92101-3542. 619/238-5686. **Fax:** 619/687-0002. **Contact:** John T. Alexander, Managing Principal. **E-mail address:** jahrstaa@aol.com. **Description:** Telford, Adams, & Alexander is an executive search firm. **Specializes in the areas of:** Accounting/Auditing; Banking; Computer Science/Software; Electronics; Finance; General Management; Health/Medical; Insurance; Manufacturing; Personnel/Labor Relations; Real Estate; Retail; Sales. **Positions commonly filled include:** General Manager; Health Services Manager; Human Resources Manager. **Other U.S. locations:** Costa Mesa CA; San Francisco CA. **Average salary range of placements:** More than $50,000. **Number of placements per year:** 50 - 99.

TELFORD, ADAMS, & ALEXANDER
455 Market Street, Suite 1910, San Francisco CA 94105. 415/546-4150. **Fax:** 415/882-3232. **Contact:** Jeffrey C. Adams, Managing Principal. **E-mail address:** jefadams@concentric.net. **Description:** Telford, Adams, & Alexander is an executive search firm. **Other U.S. locations:** Costa Mesa CA; San Diego CA. **Average salary range of placements:** More than $50,000. **Number of placements per year:** 50 - 99.

JUDY THOMPSON & ASSOCIATES
3727 Camino Del Rio South, Suite 200, San Diego CA 92108-4005. 619/281-2626. **Fax:** 619/281-2671. **Contact:** Megan Shirk, Recruiter. **E-mail address:** megan@jtaa.net. **Description:** Judy Thompson & Associates is an executive search firm operating on both retainer and contingency bases. **Specializes in the areas of:** Accounting/Auditing; Finance. **Positions commonly filled include:** Accountant/Auditor; Accounting Supervisor; Budget Analyst; Chief Financial Officer; Controller; Financial Analyst; Litigation Support Consultant; Vice President of Finance. **Average salary range of placements:** More than $50,000.

THORNTON ASSOCIATES
2040 Avenue of the Stars, Suite 400, Los Angeles CA 90067-4703. 310/553-1773. **Fax:** 310/284-8202. **Contact:** Raphaelle Thornton, President. **Description:** An executive search firm operating on both retainer and contingency bases. **Specializes in the areas of:** Health/Medical. **Positions commonly filled include:** Human Resources Manager; Registered Nurse. **Average salary range of placements:** More than $50,000. **Number of placements per year:** 1 - 49.

TOPS TECHNICAL STAFFING
1455 Frazee Road, Suite 102, San Diego CA 92108. 619/686-5228. **Contact:** Manager. **Description:** An executive search firm. **Specializes in the areas of:** Technical.

TRIPLE-J SERVICES
P.O. Box 10105, Bakersfield CA 93389-0105. 661/321-0695. **Fax:** 661/321-0882. **Contact:** Manager. **E-mail address:** tjservices@ncinternet.net. **Description:** An executive search firm. **Specializes in the areas of:** Computer Science/Software; Engineering; Food; Oil and Gas; Technical. **Positions commonly filled include:** Agricultural Engineer; Chemical Engineer; Civil Engineer; Computer Programmer; Cost Estimator; Design Engineer; Designer; Draftsperson; Electrical/Electronics Engineer; Environmental Engineer; Industrial Engineer; Mechanical Engineer; MIS Specialist; Petroleum Engineer; Software Engineer; Structural Engineer; Systems Analyst. **Average salary range of placements:** More than $50,000. **Number of placements per year:** 50 - 99.

TRUEX ASSOCIATES
332 Pine Street, Suite 400, San Francisco CA 94104. 415/433-6222. **Fax:** 415/781-6607. **Contact:** Renee Labourdette, Office Manager. **World Wide Web address:** http://www.truexassociates.com. **Description:** An executive search firm that also provides some temporary placements. **Specializes in the areas of:** Administration; Advertising; Architecture/Construction; Banking; Broadcasting; Finance; General Management; Insurance; Personnel/Labor Relations; Sales; Secretarial. **Positions commonly filled include:** Administrative Assistant; Administrative Manager; Advertising Clerk; Human Resources Manager; Secretary. **Benefits available to temporary workers:** Bonus Award/Plan; Medical Insurance; Paid Vacation. **Corporate headquarters location:** This Location. **Other area locations:** Newport Beach CA; Palo Alto CA; San Jose CA. **Average salary range of placements:** $30,000 - $50,000. **Number of placements per year:** 100 - 199.

UNISEARCH
790 The City Drive South, Suite 150, Orange CA 92868. 714/748-0700. **Fax:** 714/748-7234. **Contact:** James L. Rose, President. **Description:** An executive search firm operating on a contingency basis. **Specializes in the areas of:** Accounting/Auditing; Banking; Biology; Engineering; Finance; Food; General Management; Health/Medical; Marketing; Printing; Publishing; Sales; Scientific; Technical. **Positions commonly filled include:** Accountant; Applications Engineer; Assistant Manager; Attorney; Auditor; Bank Officer/Manager; Biochemist; Biological Scientist; Biomedical Engineer; Buyer; Chemical Engineer; Computer Programmer; Controller; Credit Manager; Design Engineer; Electrical/Electronics Engineer; Finance Director; Financial Analyst; Food Scientist/Technologist; General Manager; Human Resources Manager; Manufacturing Engineer; Marketing Manager; Mechanical Engineer; Occupational Therapist; Operations Manager; Physical Therapist; Production Manager; Purchasing Agent/Manager; Registered Nurse; Sales Engineer; Sales Executive; Sales Manager; Sales Rep.; Software Engineer; Technical Writer/Editor. **Corporate headquarters location:** This Location. **Other U.S. locations:** Nationwide. **Average salary range of placements:** More than $50,000. **Number of placements per year:** 100 - 199.

UNITED STAFFING SOLUTIONS
14240 St. Andrews, Suite 201, Victorville CA 92392. **Toll-free phone:** 800/363-4233. **Contact:** Manager. **Description:** An executive search firm that also provides some temporary placements. **Specializes in the areas of:** Accounting/Auditing; Administration; Advertising; Banking; Biology; Computer Science/Software; Education; Engineering; Finance; Food; General Management; Health/Medical; Industrial; Insurance; Manufacturing; Personnel/Labor Relations; Retail; Sales; Secretarial; Technical. **Positions commonly filled include:** Accountant/Auditor; Administrative Manager; Advertising Clerk; Aerospace Engineer; Agricultural Engineer; Aircraft Mechanic/Engine Specialist; Architect; Attorney; Automotive Mechanic; Bank Officer/Manager; Biochemist; Blue-Collar Worker Supervisor; Branch Manager; Broadcast Technician; Brokerage Clerk; Budget Analyst; Buyer; Chemical Engineer; Chemist; Civil Engineer; Claim Representative; Clerical Supervisor; Clinical Lab Technician; Computer Programmer; Construction and Building Inspector; Counselor; Credit Manager; Customer Service Rep.; Draftsperson; Economist; Education Administrator; Electrical/Electronics Engineer; Environmental Engineer; Financial Analyst; Food Scientist/Technologist; General Manager; Health Services Manager; Human Resources Specialist; Industrial Engineer; Librarian; Management Analyst/Consultant; Management Trainee; Medical Records Technician; Mining Engineer; Multimedia Designer; Operations/Production Manager; Paralegal; Pharmacist; Quality Control Supervisor; Real Estate Agent; Registered Nurse; Respiratory Therapist; Securities Sales Representative; Services Sales Representative; Social Worker; Sociologist; Structural Engineer; Surveyor; Systems Analyst; Technical Writer/Editor; Telecommunications Manager; Travel Agent; Typist/Word Processor; Underwriter/Assistant Underwriter. **Benefits available to temporary workers:** Dental Insurance; Medical Insurance. **Corporate headquarters location:** This Location. **Average salary range of placements:** $30,000 - $50,000. **Number of placements per year:** 1000+.

VAUGHAN & COMPANY EXECUTIVE SEARCH, INC.
9 Executive Circle, Suite 240, Irvine CA 92614. 949/474-6666. **Fax:** 949/474-6674. **Contact:** David Vaughan, President. **E-mail address:** recruiters@vaughanandcompany.com. **World Wide Web address:** http://www.vaughanandcompany.com. **Description:** An executive search firm operating on both retainer and contingency bases. Client company pays fee. **Specializes in the areas of:** Engineering; General Management; Industrial; Marketing; Sales. **Positions commonly filled include:** Account Manager; Account Representative; Applications Engineer; Branch Manager; Buyer; Chemical Engineer; Chief Financial Officer; Electrical/Electronics Engineer; Industrial Engineer; Manufacturing Engineer; Mechanical Engineer; Operations Manager; Production Manager; Project Manager; Purchasing Agent/Manager; Quality Assurance Engineer; Quality Control Supervisor; Sales Engineer; Sales Executive; Sales Manager; Sales Representative. **Corporate headquarters location:** This Location. **Other U.S. locations:** Nationwide. **International locations:** Worldwide. **Average salary range of placements:** $50,000 - $100,000. **Number of placements per year:** 50 - 99.

LARRY WADE & ASSOCIATES
P.O. Box 9105, Rancho Santa Fe CA 92067. 858/481-8300. **Contact:** Manager. **Description:** An executive search firm. **Specializes in the areas of:** Computer Hardware/Software.

WALDORF ASSOCIATES, INC.
11400 West Olympic Boulevard, Suite 200, Los Angeles CA 90064. 310/445-8886. **Fax:** 310/445-8810. **Contact:** Michael Waldorf, President. **Description:** An executive search firm operating on both retainer and contingency bases. **Specializes in the areas of:** Legal. **Positions commonly filled include:** Attorney; Vice President.

Average salary range of placements: More than $50,000.

WALKER & TORRENTE
P.O. Box 707, Belvedere CA 94920-0707. 415/435-9178. **Fax:** 415/435-9144. **Contact:** William T. Walker, Partner. **E-mail address:** info@walker-torrente.com. **World Wide Web address:** http://www.walker-torrente.com. **Description:** An executive search firm operating on both retainer and contingency bases. **Specializes in the areas of:** Accounting/Auditing; Administration; Banking; Economics; Finance; General Management; Legal. **Positions commonly filled include:** Accountant/Auditor; Attorney; Bank Officer/Manager; Budget Analyst; Chief Financial Officer; Computer Programmer; Controller; Database Manager; Economist; Financial Analyst; General Manager; Human Resources Manager; Industrial Engineer; Management Analyst/Consultant; MIS Specialist; Project Manager; Systems Analyst; Telecommunications Manager; Underwriter/Assistant Underwriter. **Corporate headquarters location:** This Location. **Average salary range of placements:** More than $50,000. **Number of placements per year:** 1 - 49.

K.K. WALKER PROFESSIONAL RECRUITMENT
7308 Madison Avenue, Citrus Heights CA 95610. 916/863-6363. **Fax:** 916/863-3224. **Contact:** Karen Walker, Owner. **Description:** An executive search firm operating on a contingency basis. **Specializes in the areas of:** Health/Medical. **Positions commonly filled include:** Administrative Manager; Branch Manager; Medical Technologist; Physical Therapist; Registered Nurse; X-ray Technician. **Corporate headquarters location:** This Location. **Average salary range of placements:** More than $50,000. **Number of placements per year:** 1 - 49.

WARREN, MORRIS & MADISON, LTD.
2190 Carmel Valley Road, Del Mar CA 92014. 858/481-3388. **Fax:** 858/481-6221. **Contact:** Manager. **E-mail address:** info@wmmltd.com. **World Wide Web address:** http://www.wmmltd.com. **Description:** An executive search firm operating on both retainer and contingency bases. **Specializes in the areas of:** Telecommunications; Wireless Communications. **Positions commonly filled include:** Account Manager; Account Rep.; Accountant; Advertising Executive; Chief Financial Officer; Computer Programmer; ESL Teacher; Finance Director; Financial Analyst; General Manager; Human Resources Manager; Management Analyst/Consultant; Marketing Manager; MIS Specialist; Multimedia Designer; Operations Manager; Purchasing Agent/Manager; Sales Executive; Systems Analyst; Telecommunications Manager. **Corporate headquarters location:** This Location. **Other U.S. locations:** Durham NH; Portsmouth NH; Virginia Beach VA. **Average salary range of placements:** More than $50,000. **Number of placements per year:** 100 - 199.

R.J. WATKINS & COMPANY
3104 Fourth Avenue, San Diego CA 92103. 619/299-3094. **Contact:** Manager. **Description:** An executive search firm operating on a retainer basis. **Specializes in the areas of:** Biotechnology; High-Tech.

WELDON EDWARDS
18627 Brookhurst Street, Fountain Valley CA 92708. 714/963-9632. **Contact:** Manager. **World Wide Web address:** http://www.weldonedwards.com. **Description:** An executive search firm that operates on a retainer basis. **Specializes in the areas of:** Computer Hardware/Software; Computer Science/Software; Marketing; Sales.

WENTWORTH COMPANY, INC.
The Arcade Building, 479 West Sixth Street, San Pedro CA 90731. 310/519-0113. **Toll-free phone:** 800/995-9678. **Fax:** 310/519-8402. **Contact:** John Wentworth, President. **E-mail address:** wentco@wentco.com. **Description:** An executive search firm. **Number of placements per year:** 200 - 499.

WESTERN TECHNICAL RESOURCES
2033 Gateway Boulevard, Suite 600, San Jose CA 95110. **Toll-free phone:** 800/600-8970. **Fax:** 800/600-5351. **Contact:** Bruce West, Principal. **E-mail address:** wtr@wtrusa.com. **World Wide Web address:** http://www.wtrusa.com. **Description:** An executive search firm that also provides contract placements in a variety of technical disciplines. **Specializes in the areas of:** Administration; Computer Science/Software; Engineering; Health/Medical; Sales; Technical. **Positions commonly filled include:** Account Manager; Applications Engineer; Biochemist; Biological Scientist; Biomedical Engineer; Chemical Engineer; Chemist; Clinical Lab Technician; Computer Operator; Computer Programmer; Database Manager; Design Engineer; Draftsperson; Electrical/Electronics Engineer; Environmental Engineer; Industrial Engineer; Mathematician; Mechanical Engineer; MIS Specialist; Nuclear Engineer; Petroleum Engineer; Software Engineer; Structural Engineer; Systems Analyst; Technical Writer/Editor. **Benefits available to temporary workers:** Flight Benefits; Medical Insurance; Paid Holidays; Paid Vacation. **Average salary range of placements:** More than $50,000.

WESTPACIFIC NATIONAL SEARCH INC.
23421 South Pointe Drive, Suite 270, Laguna Hills CA 92653. 949/830-8780. **Fax:** 949/830-8781. **Contact:** Monique Grimaud, Office Manager. **E-mail address:** wstpac@ix.netcom.com. **Description:** An executive search firm. **Specializes in the areas of:** Finance; Health/Medical; Marketing; Sales. **Positions commonly filled include:** Account Manager; Actuary; Administrative Manager; Chief Financial Officer; Claim Rep.; Finance Director; Health Services Manager; Insurance Agent/Broker; Licensed Practical Nurse; Market Research Analyst; Marketing Manager; Nurse; Occupational Therapist; Pharmacist; Physical Therapist; Physician; Quality Control Supervisor; Registered Nurse; Sales Executive; Sales Manager; Services Sales Representative; Systems Analyst; Underwriter/Assistant Underwriter. **Corporate headquarters location:** This Location. **Other U.S. locations:** Nationwide. **Average salary range of placements:** More than $50,000. **Number of placements per year:** 50 - 99.

DANIEL WIER & ASSOCIATES
333 South Grand Avenue, Suite 1880, Los Angeles CA 90071. 213/628-2580. **Contact:** Manager. **Description:** An executive search firm.

S.R. WILSON INC.
520 Mendicino Avenue, Suite 263, Santa Rosa CA 95401. 707/571-5990. **Contact:** Manager. **Description:** An executive search firm. **Specializes in the areas of:** Engineering; Legal.

WINSER EXECUTIVE SEARCH
30290 Rancho Viejo Road, San Juan Capistrano CA 92675. 949/443-0225. **Contact:** Manager. **Description:** An executive search firm. **Specializes in the areas of:** Consumer Package Goods; Sales.

WITT/KIEFFER, FORD, HADELMAN & LLOYD
2200 Powell Street, Suite 890, Emeryville CA 94608. 510/420-1370. **Fax:** 510/420-0363. **Contact:** Manager. **World Wide Web address:** http://www.wittkieffer.com. **Description:** An executive search firm. **Specializes in the areas of:** Health/Medical. **Other area locations:** Irvine CA. **Other U.S. locations:** Nationwide.

WITT/KIEFFER, FORD, HADELMAN & LLOYD
1920 Main Street, Suite 310, Irvine CA 92614. 949/851-5070. **Fax:** 949/851-2412. **Contact:** Manager. **World Wide Web address:** http://www.wittkieffer.com. **Description:** An executive search firm. **Specializes in the areas of:** Health/Medical. **Other area locations:** Emeryville CA. **Other U.S. locations:** Nationwide.

WORLDWIDE EXECUTIVE SEARCH
620 Newport Center Drive, Suite 1100, Newport Beach CA 92660. 949/721-6603. **Fax:** 949/640-1044. **Contact:**

Jim Ginther, President. **Description:** An executive search firm operating on both retainer and contingency bases. **Specializes in the areas of:** Finance; Hotel/Restaurant; Retail. **Positions commonly filled include:** Controller; Credit Manager; Finance Director; Human Resources Manager; Marketing Manager; Sales Executive; Sales Manager. **Corporate headquarters location:** Phoenix AZ. **Average salary range of placements:** More than $50,000. **Number of placements per year:** 50 - 99.

DON ZEE ASSOCIATES
6 South Portola, Laguna Beach CA 92651. 949/499-0917. **Contact:** Don Zee, President. **Description:** An executive search firm that provides placement in the industrial measurement and control engineering markets worldwide for sales, marketing, engineering, and operations positions. The firm operates on both retainer and contingency bases. **Specializes in the areas of:** Engineering; Manufacturing; Sales. **Positions commonly filled include:** Chemical Engineer; Chemist; Computer Programmer; Design Engineer; Human Resources Manager; Manufacturing Engineer; Marketing Manager; Sales Engineer; Sales Executive; Sales Manager; Sales Representative; Software Engineer. **Corporate headquarters location:** This Location. **Average salary range of placements:** More than $50,000. **Number of placements per year:** 1 - 49.

ZEIGER & ASSOCIATES
4766 Park Granada Boulevard, Suite 211, Calabasas CA 91302. 818/222-0052. **Contact:** Stephen A. Zeiger, President/CEO. **E-mail address:** szeiger147@aol.com. **Description:** An executive search firm operating on a contingency basis that focuses on placing technical executives with computer disk drive knowledge. The firm also provides career/outplacement counseling. **Specializes in the areas of:** Computer Science/Software; General Management. **Positions commonly filled include:** Applications Engineer; Biomedical Engineer; Computer Programmer; Design Engineer; Electrical/Electronics Engineer; General Manager; Industrial Engineer; Industrial Production Manager; Internet Services Manager; Management Analyst/Consultant; Manufacturing Engineer; Mechanical Engineer; MIS Specialist; Operations Manager; Personnel Manager; Production Manager; Project Manager; Purchasing Agent/Manager; Service Engineer; Software Engineer; Systems Manager; Telecommunications Manager; Vice President. **Corporate headquarters location:** This Location. **Average salary range of placements:** More than $50,000.

PERMANENT EMPLOYMENT AGENCIES

A PERMANENT SUCCESS EMPLOYMENT SERVICE
12658 Washington Boulevard, Suite 104, Los Angeles CA 90066. 310/305-7376. **Fax:** 310/306-2929. **Contact:** Darrell W. Gurney, Owner. **E-mail address:** aps@apscareersearch.com. **World Wide Web address:** http://www.apscareersearch.com. **Description:** A permanent employment agency focusing on the nationwide placement of career professionals in sales/marketing, accounting/finance, human resource, and MIS/computer fields. **Specializes in the areas of:** Accounting/Auditing; Administration; Computer Science/Software; Finance; Marketing; Personnel/Labor Relations; Sales; Secretarial. **Positions commonly filled include:** Accountant/Auditor; Administrative Manager; Budget Analyst; Claim Rep.; Clerical Supervisor; Computer Programmer; Credit Manager; Customer Service Representative; Financial Analyst; Human Resources Specialist; Manufacturer's/Wholesaler's Sales Rep.; MIS Specialist; Multimedia Designer; Public Relations Specialist; Services Sales Rep.; Systems Analyst; Technical Writer/Editor; Telecommunications Manager; Typist/Word Processor. **Average salary range of placements:** More than $50,000. **Number of placements per year:** 50 - 99.

ACS TECHNOLOGY SOLUTIONS
8880 Rio San Diego Drive, Suite 925, San Diego CA 92108. 619/297-5611. **Contact:** Office Manager. **Description:** A permanent employment agency. **Specializes in the areas of:** Banking; Computer Hardware/Software; Finance; Manufacturing; MIS/EDP; Technical. **Positions commonly filled include:** Computer Programmer; EDP Specialist; Systems Analyst; Technical Writer/Editor. **Number of placements per year:** 50 - 99.

A.S.A.P. EMPLOYMENT SERVICE
13 Commons Lane, Foster City CA 94404. 650/345-2727. **Fax:** 650/349-1900. **Contact:** Bonnie Marsh, President. **Description:** A permanent employment agency. **Specializes in the areas of:** Administration; Art/Design; Banking; Engineering; General Management; Insurance; Legal; Manufacturing; Personnel/Labor Relations; Sales; Technical. **Positions commonly filled include:** Accountant/Auditor; Administrative Manager; Architect; Attorney; Bank Officer/Manager; Budget Analyst; Claim Rep.; Cost Estimator; Design Engineer; Draftsperson; Editor; Financial Analyst; General Manager; Industrial Production Manager; Management Analyst/Consultant; Occupational Therapist; Paralegal; Physical Therapist; Quality Control Supervisor; Services

Sales Rep.; Software Engineer; Systems Analyst; Technical Writer/Editor; Typist/Word Processor. **Average salary range of placements:** More than $50,000. **Number of placements per year:** 1 - 49.

AW DATA PROCESSING PERSONNEL
P.O. Box 4176, Ventura CA 93004. **Contact:** Manager. **Description:** A permanent employment agency that also provides some temporary placements. **Specializes in the areas of:** Computer Hardware/Software; Data Processing; Management.

THE ACCOUNTING GUILD INITIAL FINANCIAL
12400 Wilshire Boulevard, Suite 1275, Los Angeles CA 90025. **Contact:** Manager. **Description:** A permanent employment agency that also provides some temporary placements. **Specializes in the areas of:** Accounting/Auditing; Administration; Legal.

ACCOUNTING PARTNERS
2041 Mission College Boulevard, Suite 200, Santa Clara CA 95054. **Contact:** Office Manager. **Description:** A permanent employment agency that also provides some temp-to-perm and temporary placements. **Specializes in the areas of:** Accounting/Auditing.

ACCUSTAFF INCORPORATED
16501 Ventura Boulevard, Suite 104, Encino CA 91436-2064. 818/905-5522. **Fax:** 818/905-9411. **Contact:** Patti Taylor, Senior Consultant. **Description:** A permanent placement agency that also provides some temporary placements. **Specializes in the areas of:** Accounting/Auditing; Computer Science/Software; Finance; Legal; Office Support; Personnel/Labor Relations; Sales; Secretarial. **Positions commonly filled include:** Accountant/Auditor; Financial Analyst; MIS Specialist; Paralegal; Personnel Manager; Software Engineer; Typist/Word Processor. **Corporate headquarters location:** This Location. **Other U.S. locations:** Nationwide. **Number of placements per year:** 1000+.

ACT 1 PERSONNEL SERVICES
647 Main Street, Pleasanton CA 94566. 925/462-8550. **Fax:** 925/426-0689. **Contact:** Manager. **Description:** A permanent employment agency that also provides some temporary placements. Founded in 1978. **Specializes in the areas of:** Personnel/Labor Relations; Sales; Secretarial. **Positions commonly filled include:** Administrative Assistant; Branch Manager; Claim Rep.; Clerical Supervisor; Computer Programmer; Credit

Manager; Customer Service Rep.; Financial Analyst; Human Resources Specialist; Management Trainee; Services Sales Rep.; Systems Analyst; Typist/Word Processor. **Benefits available to temporary workers:** 401(k); Bonus Award/Plan; Medical Insurance; Vision Insurance. **Corporate headquarters location:** Torrance CA. **Other U.S. locations:** AZ; CO; NC. **Average salary range of placements:** $20,000 - $29,999. **Number of placements per year:** 1000+.

ACT 1 PERSONNEL SERVICES
720 North Archibald Avenue, Suite C, Ontario CA 91764. 909/987-8679. **Contact:** Manager. **Description:** A permanent employment agency that also provides some temporary placements. **Specializes in the areas of:** Administration; Clerical. **Corporate headquarters location:** Torrance CA. **Other U.S. locations:** AZ; CO; NC.

ACTION PERSONNEL
THE WALLACE/WHALEN AGENCY, INC.
601 Daily Drive, Suite 300, Camarillo CA 93010. 805/389-3663. **Fax:** 805/389-3672. **Contact:** Office Manager. **Description:** A permanent placement agency that also provides some temporary placements. **Specializes in the areas of:** Accounting; Administration; Legal; Office Support.

ADECCO/TAD TECHNICAL SERVICES
17310 Redhill Avenue, Suite 100, Irvine CA 92614. 949/851-1010. **Contact:** Manager. **Description:** A permanent employment agency that also provides some temporary placements. **Specializes in the areas of:** Engineering; Technical. **Positions commonly filled include:** Buyer; Chemical Engineer; Chemist; Civil Engineer; Design Engineer; Designer; Draftsperson; Electrical/Electronics Engineer; Environmental Engineer; Financial Analyst; Industrial Engineer; Market Research Analyst; Mechanical Engineer; MIS Specialist; Multimedia Designer; Nuclear Engineer; Software Engineer; Structural Engineer; Technical Writer/Editor. **Other U.S. locations:** Nationwide. **International locations:** Worldwide. **Number of placements per year:** 500 - 999.

ADECCO/TAD TECHNICAL SERVICES
2900 Gordon Avenue, Suite 207, Santa Clara CA 95051. 408/328-0760. **Contact:** Manager. **Description:** A permanent employment agency. **Other U.S. locations:** Nationwide.

ADECCO/TAD TECHNICAL SERVICES
200 Corporate Pointe, Suite 120, Culver City CA 90230. 310/410-6740. **Contact:** Teri Miglin, Senior Recruiter. **Description:** A permanent employment agency. **Specializes in the areas of:** Engineering; Technical.

ADVANTAGE PERSONNEL INC.
19925 Stevens Creek Boulevard, Suite 141, Cupertino CA 95014. 408/252-0400. **Fax:** 408/252-0101. **Contact:** Cristina Gomez, Owner. **Description:** A permanent employment agency. **Specializes in the areas of:** Accounting/Auditing; Administration; Advertising; Computer Science/Software; Legal; Manufacturing; Personnel/Labor Relations; Sales; Secretarial. **Positions commonly filled include:** Accountant/Auditor; Administrative Manager; Advertising Clerk; Bank Officer/Manager; Branch Manager; Brokerage Clerk; Budget Analyst; Buyer; Claim Representative; Clerical Supervisor; Credit Manager; Customer Service Rep.; Financial Analyst; Human Resources Specialist; Management Analyst/Consultant; Market Research Analyst; MIS Specialist; Operations/Production Manager; Public Relations Specialist; Purchasing Agent/Manager; Quality Control Supervisor; Systems Analyst; Technical Writer/Editor; Typist/Word Processor.

AMTEC ENGINEERING CORPORATION
2749 Saturn Street, Brea CA 92821. 714/993-1900. **Fax:** 714/993-2419. **Contact:** Shawn Byrne, CFO. **E-mail address:** staffing@amtec-eng.com. **World Wide Web address:** http://www.amtec-eng.com. **Description:** A

permanent employment agency. **Specializes in the areas of:** Computer Science/Software; Engineering; High-Tech; Manufacturing; Technical. **Positions commonly filled include:** Aerospace Engineer; Agricultural Engineer; Aircraft Mechanic/Engine Specialist; Applications Engineer; Architect; Biological Scientist; Biomedical Engineer; Buyer; Chemical Engineer; Chemist; Civil Engineer; Clinical Lab Technician; Computer Operator; Computer Programmer; Consultant; Cost Estimator; Database Manager; Design Engineer; Designer; Draftsperson; Editor; Electrical/Electronics Engineer; Electrician; Environmental Engineer; Graphic Artist; Graphic Designer; Industrial Engineer; Industrial Production Manager; Manufacturing Engineer; Mechanical Engineer; Metallurgical Engineer; Mining Engineer; MIS Specialist; Nuclear Engineer; Operations Manager; Project Manager; Purchasing Agent/Manager; Quality Control Supervisor; Sales Engineer; Science Technologist; Software Engineer; Structural Engineer; Systems Analyst; Systems Manager; Technical Writer/Editor. **Benefits available to temporary workers:** Dental Insurance; Medical Insurance; Paid Holidays; Paid Vacation. **Average salary range of placements:** $30,000 - $50,000. **Number of placements per year:** 500 - 999.

ANDREW & POTTER, LTD.
P.O. Box 50707, Santa Barbara CA 93150. 805/565-4444. **Fax:** 805/565-4446. **Contact:** Heather Irena Anand, CEO. **World Wide Web address:** http://www.andrewandpotter.com. **Description:** Andrew & Potter is a permanent employment agency. **Positions commonly filled include:** Chef/Cook/Kitchen Worker; Gardener; Nanny. **Number of placements per year:** 1000+.

APPLE ONE EMPLOYMENT SERVICES
1295 North Euclid, Anaheim CA 92801. 714/956-5180. **Contact:** Sales Manager. **Description:** A permanent employment agency. **Specializes in the areas of:** Accounting/Auditing; Clerical; Finance; Personnel/Labor Relations; Sales. **Corporate headquarters location:** Glendale CA. **Other U.S. locations:** Nationwide. **Number of placements per year:** 1000+.

APPLE ONE EMPLOYMENT SERVICES
18538 Hawthorne Boulevard, Torrance CA 90504. 310/542-8534. **Contact:** Manager. **Description:** A permanent employment agency. **Specializes in the areas of:** Accounting/Auditing; Banking; Clerical; Finance; Health/Medical. **Positions commonly filled include:** Administrative Assistant; Bank Officer/Manager; Bookkeeper; Buyer; Clerk; Customer Service Rep.; Data Entry Clerk; Legal Secretary; Medical Secretary; Personnel Manager; Receptionist; Secretary; Typist/Word Processor. **Corporate headquarters location:** Glendale CA. **Other U.S. locations:** Nationwide. **Number of placements per year:** 1000+.

APPLE ONE EMPLOYMENT SERVICES
1970 Broadway, Suite 110, Oakland CA 94612. 510/835-0217. **Contact:** General Manager. **Description:** A permanent employment agency. **Specializes in the areas of:** Accounting/Auditing; Clerical; Finance. **Positions commonly filled include:** Accountant/Auditor; Administrative Assistant; Aerospace Engineer; Bank Officer/Manager; Bookkeeper; Buyer; Civil Engineer; Claim Representative; Clerk; Computer Operator; Computer Programmer; Credit Manager; Customer Service Rep.; Data Entry Clerk; Draftsperson; Economist; Electrical/Electronics Engineer; Factory Worker; Financial Analyst; Human Resources Manager; Industrial Engineer; Legal Secretary; Marketing Specialist; Mechanical Engineer; Medical Secretary; Operations/Production Manager; Quality Control Supervisor; Sales Rep.; Secretary; Stenographer; Typist/Word Processor. **Corporate headquarters location:** Glendale CA. **Other U.S. locations:** Nationwide. **Number of placements per year:** 1000+.

APPLE ONE EMPLOYMENT SERVICES
11352 East 183rd Street, Cerritos CA 90703-5419. 562/924-7009. **Fax:** 562/924-3025. **Contact:** Branch

Manager. **Description:** A permanent employment agency that also provides some temporary placements. **Specializes in the areas of:** Accounting/Auditing; Advertising; Fashion; Food; Health/Medical; Industrial; Manufacturing; Personnel/Labor Relations; Secretarial. **Positions commonly filled include:** Accountant/Auditor; Computer Programmer; Credit Manager; Customer Service Representative; Electrical/Electronics Engineer; Financial Analyst; Human Resources Manager; Management Trainee; MIS Specialist; Quality Control Supervisor; Software Engineer; Systems Analyst; Typist/Word Processor. **Corporate headquarters location:** Glendale CA. **Other U.S. locations:** Nationwide. **Number of placements per year:** 1000+.

APPLE ONE EMPLOYMENT SERVICES
44 Montgomery Street, Suite 150, San Francisco CA 94104. 415/397-3201. **Contact:** Amber Ash, Account Executive. **Description:** A permanent employment agency that also provides some temporary placements. **Specializes in the areas of:** Accounting/Auditing; Administration; Computer Science/Software; General Management; Health/Medical; Legal; Personnel/Labor Relations; Publishing; Sales; Secretarial. **Positions commonly filled include:** Accountant/Auditor; Administrative Manager; Clerical Supervisor; Computer Programmer; Counselor; Customer Service Rep.; General Manager; Human Resources Specialist; Insurance Agent/Broker; Internet Services Manager; Management Trainee; Manufacturer's/Wholesaler's Sales Rep.; Market Research Analyst; Medical Records Technician; MIS Specialist; Multimedia Designer; Operations/Production Manager; Paralegal; Property and Real Estate Manager; Public Relations Specialist; Purchasing Agent/Manager; Securities Sales Rep.; Services Sales Representative; Telecommunications Manager; Typist/Word Processor. **Corporate headquarters location:** Glendale CA. **Other U.S. locations:** Nationwide. **Average salary range of placements:** $20,000 - $40,000. **Number of placements per year:** 500 - 999.

APPLE ONE EMPLOYMENT SERVICES
225 South Sepulveda Boulevard, Suite 100, Manhattan Beach CA 90266. 310/318-9912. **Fax:** 310/372-8356. **Contact:** Samantha Suarez, Branch Manager. **Description:** A permanent employment agency that also provides some temporary placements. Founded in 1964. **Specializes in the areas of:** Sales; Secretarial. **Positions commonly filled include:** Accountant/Auditor; Advertising Clerk; Clerical Supervisor; Customer Service Rep.; Human Resources Specialist; Management Trainee; MIS Specialist; Paralegal; Purchasing Agent/Manager; Technical Writer/Editor; Typist/Word Processor. **Benefits available to temporary workers:** 401(k); Bonus Award/Plan; Dental Insurance; Medical Insurance. **Corporate headquarters location:** Glendale CA. **Other U.S. locations:** Nationwide. **Number of placements per year:** 500 - 999.

APPLE ONE EMPLOYMENT SERVICES
8421 Wilshire Boulevard, Suite 100, Beverly Hills CA 90211. 323/653-6727. **Contact:** Manager. **Description:** A permanent employment agency that also provides some temporary placements. **Corporate headquarters location:** Glendale CA. **Other U.S. locations:** Nationwide.

APPLE ONE EMPLOYMENT SERVICES
327 West Broadway, Glendale CA 91204. 818/240-8688. **Toll-free phone:** 800/872-2677. **Contact:** Manager. **Description:** This location houses the corporate offices only. Overall, Apple One Employment Services is a permanent employment agency that also provides some temporary and career/outplacement counseling placements. **Specializes in the areas of:** Accounting/Auditing; Administration; Computer Hardware/Software; Engineering; Industrial; Manufacturing; Personnel/Labor Relations; Sales; Secretarial; Technical. **Positions commonly filled include:** Accountant/Auditor; Administrative Manager; Advertising Clerk; Biochemist; Biomedical Engineer; Blue-Collar Worker Supervisor; Brokerage Clerk; Budget Analyst; Buyer; Chemical Engineer; Chemist; Claim Representative; Clerical Supervisor; Clinical Lab Technician; Computer Programmer; Credit Manager; Customer Service Representative; Design Engineer; Designer; Draftsperson; Electrical/Electronics Engineer; Financial Analyst; Human Resources Specialist; Industrial Engineer; Industrial Production Manager; Internet Services Manager; Mechanical Engineer; Medical Records Technician; MIS Specialist; Paralegal; Securities Sales Rep.; Services Sales Representative; Software Engineer; Technical Writer/Editor; Typist/Word Processor. **Corporate headquarters location:** This Location. **Other U.S. locations:** Nationwide. **Number of placements per year:** 1000+.

APROPOS EMPLOYMENT AGENCY
1661 Botelho Drive, Suite 297, Walnut Creek CA 94596. 925/937-3540. **Fax:** 925/937-3542. **Contact:** Dori Val, President. **E-mail address:** dorival2@aol.com. **Description:** A permanent employment agency. **Specializes in the areas of:** Accounting/Auditing; Administration; Banking; Biology; Computer Science/Software; Finance; General Management; Health/Medical; Industrial; Insurance; Legal; Manufacturing; Personnel/Labor Relations; Sales; Secretarial; Technical; Transportation. **Positions commonly filled include:** Accountant/Auditor; Actuary; Adjuster; Administrative Manager; Architect; Attorney; Bank Officer/Manager; Biochemist; Branch Manager; Buyer; Chemist; Claim Rep.; Clerical Supervisor; Computer Programmer; Cost Estimator; Credit Manager; Customer Service Representative; Draftsperson; Financial Analyst; General Manager; Health Services Manager; Management Trainee; Manufacturer's/Wholesaler's Sales Rep.; Mathematician; MIS Specialist; Operations/Production Manager; Paralegal; Property and Real Estate Manager; Purchasing Agent/Manager; Quality Control Supervisor; Software Engineer; Systems Analyst; Technical Writer/Editor; Telecommunications Manager; Typist/Word Processor; Underwriter/Assistant Underwriter. **Average salary range of placements:** $50,000 - $80,000. **Number of placements per year:** 100 - 199.

BARBARA ARDEN INC.
236 West Portal Avenue, Suite 385, San Francisco CA 94127. 415/585-4900. **Fax:** 415/585-4955. **Contact:** Manager. **Description:** A permanent employment agency that also provides some executive searches. **Specializes in the areas of:** Legal. **Positions commonly filled include:** Legal Secretary; Paralegal.

ARROWSTAFF SERVICES, INC.
2010 North First Street, Suite 300, San Jose CA 95131. 408/437-8989. **Fax:** 408/437-7547. **Contact:** Recruiter. **E-mail address:** info@arrowstaff.com. **World Wide Web address:** http://www.arrowstaff.com. **Description:** A permanent employment agency that also provides some temporary placements, executive searches on a contingency basis, and contract services. Founded in 1981. Client company pays fee. **Specializes in the areas of:** Computer Science/Software; Engineering; Internet Development; Scientific; Technical. **Positions commonly filled include:** Account Manager; Administrative Assistant; Administrative Manager; Applications Engineer; Buyer; Computer Engineer; Computer Operator; Computer Programmer; Computer Support Technician; Computer Technician; Content Developer; Customer Service Representative; Database Administrator; Database Manager; General Manager; Marketing Specialist; MIS Specialist; Multimedia Designer; Network/Systems Administrator; Production Manager; Secretary; Software Engineer; Systems Analyst; Systems Manager; Typist/Word Processor; Webmaster. **Benefits available to temporary workers:** Dental Insurance; Medical Insurance; Paid Holidays. **Corporate headquarters location:** This Location. **Average salary range of placements:** $40,000 - $60,000. **Number of placements per year:** 500 - 999.

ART LINKS STAFFING
1450 Fourth Street, Suite 10, Berkeley CA 94710. 510/528-2668. **Fax:** 510/528-0521. **Contact:** Ms. Marti

Stites, Owner. **World Wide Web address:** http://www.artlinks-staffing.com. **Description:** Art Links Staffing is a permanent employment agency that also provides some temporary placements. **Specializes in the areas of:** Art/Design; Multimedia; Publishing. **Positions commonly filled include:** Editor; Editorial Assistant; Graphic Artist; Graphic Designer; Webmaster. **Benefits available to temporary workers:** Direct Deposit. **Corporate headquarters location:** This Location. **Average salary range of placements:** More than $50,000.

ASSURED PERSONNEL SERVICES, INC.
1301 South Beach Boulevard, Suite M, La Habra CA 90631. 562/691-3258. **Contact:** Don Rains, Administrator. **Description:** A permanent employment agency. **Specializes in the areas of:** Accounting/Auditing; Clerical; Health/Medical; Secretarial. **Positions commonly filled include:** Accountant/Auditor; Administrative Assistant; Advertising Executive; Bookkeeper; Clerk; Computer Programmer; Credit Manager; Data Entry Clerk; Draftsperson; EDP Specialist; Electrical/Electronics Engineer; Financial Analyst; General Manager; Human Resources Manager; Legal Secretary; Marketing Specialist; Mechanical Engineer; Medical Secretary; Metallurgical Engineer; Nurse; Petroleum Engineer; Receptionist; Secretary; Stenographer; Systems Analyst; Technical Writer/Editor; Technician; Typist/Word Processor. **Number of placements per year:** 500 - 999.

ASTRA WEST PERSONNEL SERVICES
12304 Santa Monica Boulevard, Suite 108, Los Angeles CA 90025. 310/442-6650. **Fax:** 310/979-4419. **Contact:** Manager. **E-mail address:** staffup@astrawest.com. **Description:** A permanent employment agency that also provides some temporary and contract placements. Astra West offers training and consulting services in such areas as disability awareness and school-to-work transition. Client company pays fee. **Specializes in the areas of:** Accounting; Administration; Banking; Computer Science/Software; Engineering; Finance; General Management; Health/Medical; Insurance; Legal; Marketing; Personnel/Labor Relations; Publishing; Sales; Secretarial; Technical. **Positions commonly filled include:** Account Manager; Account Representative; Accountant; Adjuster; Administrative Assistant; Administrative Manager; Assistant Manager; Auditor; Bank Officer/Manager; Budget Analyst; Chief Financial Officer; Civil Engineer; Claim Representative; Clerical Supervisor; Computer Animator; Computer Operator; Computer Programmer; Controller; Customer Service Representative; Database Manager; Design Engineer; Editor; Editorial Assistant; Electrical/Electronics Engineer; Finance Director; Financial Analyst; Fund Manager; General Manager; Graphic Artist; Graphic Designer; Human Resources Manager; Internet Services Manager; Manufacturing Engineer; Market Research Analyst; Marketing Manager; Marketing Specialist; Mechanical Engineer; Medical Records Technician; MIS Specialist; Multimedia Designer; Operations Manager; Paralegal; Production Manager; Project Manager; Public Relations Specialist; Purchasing Agent/Manager; Quality Control Supervisor; Sales Engineer; Sales Executive; Sales Manager; Sales Representative; Secretary; Software Engineer; Systems Analyst; Systems Manager; Technical Writer/Editor; Telecommunications Manager; Typist/Word Processor; Underwriter. **Average salary range of placements:** More than $50,000. **Number of placements per year:** 50 - 99.

BSA PERSONNEL CENTER
16531 Bolsa Chica Street, Suite 315, Huntington Beach CA 92649-3596. 714/377-1182. **Fax:** 714/377-1184. **Contact:** Barbara Sue Miller, President. **Description:** A permanent employment agency that also provides some temporary placements. **Specializes in the areas of:** Accounting/Auditing; Administration; Advertising; Food; General Management; Health/Medical; Insurance; Legal; Personnel/Labor Relations; Real Estate; Retail; Secretarial. **Positions commonly filled include:** Accountant/Auditor; Administrative Manager; Advertising Clerk; Attorney; Blue-Collar Worker

Supervisor; Branch Manager; Budget Analyst; Buyer; Claim Representative; Clerical Supervisor; Clinical Lab Technician; Computer Programmer; Cost Estimator; Credit Manager; Customer Service Rep.; Dental Assistant/Dental Hygienist; Dentist; Editor; Emergency Medical Technician; Financial Analyst; General Manager; Health Services Manager; Human Resources Specialist; Human Service Worker; Insurance Agent/Broker; Management Analyst/Consultant; Management Trainee; Manufacturer's/Wholesaler's Sales Rep.; Market Research Analyst; Medical Records Technician; MIS Specialist; Operations/Production Manager; Paralegal; Physical Therapist; Physician; Property and Real Estate Manager; Public Relations Specialist; Purchasing Agent/Manager; Real Estate Agent; Registered Nurse; Restaurant/Food Service Manager; Securities Sales Representative; Services Sales Representative; Social Worker; Systems Analyst; Teacher/Professor; Technical Writer/Editor; Telecommunications Manager; Travel Agent; Typist/Word Processor; Underwriter/Assistant Underwriter; Veterinarian. **Corporate headquarters location:** This Location. **Other U.S. locations:** Nationwide. **Average salary range of placements:** More than $50,000. **Number of placements per year:** 1000+.

BEVERLY HILLS BAR ASSOCIATION PERSONNEL SERVICE
300 South Beverly Drive, Suite 214, Beverly Hills CA 90212. 310/553-4575. **Contact:** Manager. **Description:** A permanent employment agency. **Specializes in the areas of:** Legal. **Positions commonly filled include:** Attorney; Legal Secretary; Receptionist; Typist/Word Processor. **Number of placements per year:** 50 - 99.

BUSINESS SYSTEMS SUPPORT
10680 West Pico Boulevard, Suite 210, Los Angeles CA 90064. 310/204-6711. **Fax:** 310/204-2941. **Contact:** Vivian Hotchkiss, Owner. **E-mail address:** lajobline@aol.com. **Description:** A permanent employment agency. **Specializes in the areas of:** Accounting/Auditing; Administration; Advertising; Architecture/Construction; Communications; Computer Science/Software; Engineering; Entertainment; Fashion; General Management; Insurance; Legal; Nonprofit; Personnel/Labor Relations; Sales; Secretarial; Transportation. **Positions commonly filled include:** Accountant/Auditor; Advertising Clerk; Bank Officer/Manager; Buyer; Civil Engineer; Claim Representative; Clerical Supervisor; Clinical Lab Technician; Construction and Building Inspector; Credit Manager; Customer Service Rep.; Electrical/Electronics Engineer; Financial Analyst; General Manager; Human Resources Manager; Human Service Worker; Industrial Engineer; Manufacturer's/Wholesaler's Sales Rep.; Mechanical Engineer; Metallurgical Engineer; Operations/Production Manager; Paralegal; Property and Real Estate Manager; Social Worker; Software Engineer; Structural Engineer; Systems Analyst. **Benefits available to temporary workers:** Bonus Award/Plan; Credit Union. **Average salary range of placements:** $30,000 - $50,000. **Number of placements per year:** 200 - 499.

CT PERSONNEL SERVICES
2221 Rosecrans Avenue, Suite 131, El Segundo CA 90245. 310/643-8333. **Fax:** 310/643-7151. **Contact:** Guy Schepis, President. **World Wide Web address:** http://www.cteng.com. **Description:** A permanent employment agency that also provides some temporary placements. Founded in 1956. **Specializes in the areas of:** Accounting/Auditing; Administration; Architecture/Construction; Computer Science/Software; Engineering; MIS/EDP; Personnel/Labor Relations; Scientific; Secretarial; Technical. **Positions commonly filled include:** Accountant; Administrative Assistant; Architect; Buyer; Chemical Engineer; Chemist; Civil Engineer; Computer Operator; Computer Programmer; Construction Contractor; Controller; Cost Estimator; Customer Service Representative; Database Manager; Design Engineer; Draftsperson; Editor; Editorial Assistant; Electrical/Electronics Engineer; Environmental Engineer; Finance Director; Financial Analyst;

Geologist/Geophysicist; Graphic Artist; Graphic Designer; Human Resources Manager; Industrial Engineer; Internet Services Manager; Managing Editor; Manufacturing Engineer; Mechanical Engineer; Metallurgical Engineer; MIS Specialist; Production Manager; Project Manager; Purchasing Agent/Manager; Quality Control Supervisor; Secretary; Software Engineer; Statistician; Systems Analyst; Systems Manager; Technical Writer/Editor; Telecommunications Manager; Typist/Word Processor. **Benefits available to temporary workers:** 401(k). **Corporate headquarters location:** This Location. **Average salary range of placements:** $30,000 - $50,000. **Number of placements per year:** 200 - 499.

CALIFORNIA JOB CONNECTION
11825 Del Amo Boulevard, Cerritos CA 90703. 562/809-7785. **Toll-free phone:** 800/645-2971. **Fax:** 562/403-3427. **Contact:** Brenda Sanchez, Branch Manager. **Description:** A permanent employment agency. Founded in 1988. **Specializes in the areas of:** Banking; Computer Science/Software; Industrial; Manufacturing; Personnel/Labor Relations; Sales; Secretarial. **Positions commonly filled include:** Accountant/Auditor; Administrative Manager; Advertising Clerk; Blue-Collar Worker Supervisor; Branch Manager; Buyer; Civil Engineer; Clerical Supervisor; Computer Programmer; Customer Service Rep.; General Manager; Management Trainee; Public Relations Specialist; Personnel Specialist; Purchasing Agent/Manager; Quality Control Supervisor; Technical Writer/Editor; Telecommunications Manager; Typist/Word Processor. **Benefits available to temporary workers:** Medical Insurance; Paid Holidays; Paid Vacation. **Other U.S. locations:** Newport Beach CA. **Average salary range of placements:** $30,000 - $50,000. **Number of placements per year:** 100 - 199.

CAREER PARTNERS
1231 South Gerhart Street, City of Commerce CA 90022. 323/727-7988. **Contact:** Manager. **Description:** A government-funded, permanent employment agency.

CHOICE PERSONNEL
800 Wilshire Boulevard, Suite 1475, Los Angeles CA 90017. 213/489-3260. **Fax:** 213/624-7318. **Contact:** Donnae Callaway, Owner. **Description:** A permanent employment agency that also provides some temporary placements. **Specializes in the areas of:** Accounting/Auditing; Administration; Banking; Computer Science/Software; Finance; Insurance; Legal; Personnel/Labor Relations; Secretarial. **Positions commonly filled include:** Accountant/Auditor; Computer Programmer; Credit Manager; Customer Service Rep.; Human Resources Manager; Paralegal; Systems Analyst; Typist/Word Processor. **Average salary range of placements:** $30,000 - $50,000. **Number of placements per year:** 200 - 499.

CHOSEN FEW PERSONNEL SERVICES
911 Wilshire Boulevard, Suite 1880, Los Angeles CA 90017. 213/689-9400. **Contact:** Kim Walker, Owner. **Description:** A permanent employment agency that also provides some temporary placements. **Specializes in the areas of:** Legal. **Positions commonly filled include:** Accountant/Auditor; Bookkeeper; Clerk; Data Entry Clerk; Legal Secretary; Paralegal; Typist/Word Processor. **Number of placements per year:** 1000+.

COLE VOCATIONAL SERVICES
1174 Nevada Street, Redlands CA 92374. 909/307-6584. **Contact:** Office Manager. **Description:** A permanent employment agency that also provides vocational training. **Specializes in the areas of:** Social Services. **Positions commonly filled include:** Human Service Worker. **Average salary range of placements:** Less than $20,000. **Number of placements per year:** 100 - 199.

COLT SYSTEMS PROFESSIONAL PERSONNEL SERVICES
1880 Century Park East, Suite 208, Los Angeles CA 90067. 310/277-4741. **Fax:** 310/277-8317. **Contact:**

Manager. **Description:** A permanent employment agency. **Specializes in the areas of:** Accounting/Auditing; Administration; Clerical; Data Processing; Executives; Finance; Technical. **Positions commonly filled include:** Account Manager; Accountant/Auditor; Administrative Assistant; Bookkeeper; Clerical Supervisor; Collector; Computer Programmer; Controller; Credit Manager; Customer Service Rep.; Data Entry Clerk; Engineer; Financial Analyst; Human Resources Manager; Secretary. **Number of placements per year:** 50 - 99.

COMPLETE STAFFING RESOURCES, INC.
12110 East Slauson Avenue, Santa Fe Springs CA 90670. 562/945-8885. **Fax:** 562/945-7445. **Contact:** Manager. **Description:** A permanent placement agency that also provides temporary placements. **Specializes in the areas of:** Accounting; Administration; Assembly; Customer Service; Data Entry; General Labor; Light Industrial; Manufacturing; Office Support; Secretarial; Warehousing; Word Processing.

THE COMPUTER RESOURCES GROUP, INC.
275 Battery Street, Suite 800, San Francisco CA 94111. 415/398-3535. **Contact:** Jackie Autry, President. **Description:** A permanent employment agency. **Specializes in the areas of:** Computer Hardware/Software; MIS/EDP. **Positions commonly filled include:** Computer Programmer; EDP Specialist; MIS Specialist; Systems Analyst. **Number of placements per year:** 1000+.

CORESTAFF SERVICES
5000 East Spring Street, Suite 320, Long Beach CA 90815. 562/420-7616. **Contact:** Manager. **Description:** A permanent employment agency. **Specializes in the areas of:** Accounting/Auditing; Computer Science/Software; Engineering; Industrial; Legal; Personnel/Labor Relations; Secretarial; Technical. **Positions commonly filled include:** Accountant/Auditor; Aerospace Engineer; Aircraft Mechanic/Engine Specialist; Automotive Mechanic; Civil Engineer; Computer Programmer; Customer Service Representative; Draftsperson; Electrical/Electronics Engineer; Electrician; Human Resources Manager; Mechanical Engineer; MIS Specialist; Quality Control Supervisor; Software Engineer; Structural Engineer; Technical Writer/Editor; Typist/Word Processor. **Corporate headquarters location:** Brea CA. **Other U.S. locations:** Nationwide.

CORESTAFF SERVICES
1700 South El Camino Real, Suite 410, San Mateo CA 94403. 650/340-6999. **Contact:** Manager. **Description:** A permanent employment agency. **Corporate headquarters location:** Brea CA. **Other U.S. locations:** Nationwide.

CORESTAFF SERVICES
275 Saratoga Avenue, Suite 150, Santa Clara CA 95050. 408/984-7203. **Contact:** Manager. **Description:** A permanent employment agency that also offers contract services. **Specializes in the areas of:** Accounting/Auditing; Administration; Computer Science/Software; Engineering; Finance; General Management; Industrial; Manufacturing; Personnel/Labor Relations; Publishing; Retail; Sales; Technical. **Positions commonly filled include:** Administrative Manager; Blue-Collar Worker Supervisor; Buyer; Claim Rep.; Clerical Supervisor; Customer Service Rep.; Designer; Electrical/Electronics Engineer; Environmental Engineer; Human Resources Specialist; Management Trainee; Mechanical Engineer; Quality Control Supervisor. **Benefits available to temporary workers:** Bonus Award/Plan; Dental Insurance; Medical Insurance. **Corporate headquarters location:** Brea CA. **Other U.S. locations:** Nationwide. **Average salary range of placements:** $30,000 - $50,000. **Number of placements per year:** 1000+.

CORPORATE SOLUTIONS
99 Pacific Street, Suite 155C, Monterey CA 93940. 831/646-0779. **Contact:** Judy Marra, CPC/Owner.

Description: A permanent employment agency.
Specializes in the areas of: Accounting/Auditing;
Finance. **Positions commonly filled include:**
Accountant/Auditor; Budget Analyst; Financial Analyst.
Number of placements per year: 1 - 49.

MARLENE CRITCHFIELD COMPANY
P.O. Box 122, Salinas CA 93902. 831/753-2466. **Fax:**
831/753-2467. **Contact:** Marlene Critchfield, Owner.
Description: A permanent employment agency.
Specializes in the areas of: Accounting/Auditing; Food;
General Management; Manufacturing; Sales. **Positions
commonly filled include:** Accountant/Auditor;
Aerospace Engineer; Agricultural Scientist; Budget
Analyst; Financial Analyst; Food Scientist/Technologist;
General Manager; Human Resources Manager; Industrial
Engineer; Mechanical Engineer; Operations/Production
Manager; Quality Control Supervisor; Transportation/
Traffic Specialist.

CULVER PERSONNEL SERVICES
1660 Amphlett Boulevard, Suite 325, San Mateo
CA 94402-2509. 650/356-1100. **Fax:** 650/692-6618.
Contact: Ryan Eberhard, Branch Manager. **E-mail
address:** culverbg@pacbell.net. **World Wide Web
address:** http://www.culvercorp.com. **Description:** A
permanent employment agency. **Specializes in the areas
of:** Advertising; Broadcasting; Computer Science/
Software; Finance; Food; General Management;
Health/Medical; Industrial; Insurance; Legal;
Personnel/Labor Relations; Publishing; Retail; Sales;
Transportation. **Positions commonly filled include:**
Account Manager; Account Representative; Advertising
Executive; Branch Manager; Claim Representative;
Customer Service Representative; General Manager;
Internet Services Manager; Management Analyst/
Consultant; Management Trainee; Marketing Manager;
Marketing Specialist; Online Content Specialist;
Operations/Production Manager; Real Estate Agent;
Sales Engineer; Sales Executive; Sales Manager; Sales
Representative; Telecommunications Manager; Vice
President of Marketing and Sales; Wholesale and Retail
Buyer. **Corporate headquarters location:** San Diego
CA. **Average salary range of placements:** More than
$50,000. **Number of placements per year:** 100 - 199.

CULVER PERSONNEL SERVICES
3625 Del Amo Boulevard, Suite 110, Torrance CA
90503. 310/793-1164. **Fax:** 310/793-1170. **Contact:**
Catherine Geis, Branch Manager. **World Wide Web
address:** http://www.culvercorp.com. **Description:**
Culver Personnel Services is a permanent employment
agency. **Specializes in the areas of:** Management; Sales.
Positions commonly filled include: Branch Manager;
Management Trainee; Manufacturer's/Wholesaler's Sales
Rep.; Services Sales Representative. **Corporate
headquarters location:** San Diego CA. **Number of
placements per year:** 100 - 199.

CULVER PERSONNEL SERVICES
8599 Haven Avenue, Suite 205, Rancho Cucamonga
CA 91730. 909/989-3333. **Fax:** 909/989-3962. **Contact:**
General Manager. **World Wide Web address:**
http://www.culvercorp.com. **Description:** A permanent
employment agency that also provides some temporary
and temp-to-hire placements. **Specializes in the areas
of:** Accounting; Administration; Banking; Biology;
Computer Science/Software; Economics; Engineering;
Finance; Food; General Management; Health/Medical;
Legal; Light Industrial; Retail; Sales; Secretarial.
Positions commonly filled include: Account Manager;
Account Representative; Accountant; Administrative
Assistant; Administrative Manager; Applications
Engineer; Assistant Manager; Bank Officer/Manager;
Biological Scientist; Blue-Collar Worker Supervisor;
Branch Manager; Claim Representative; Computer
Operator; Computer Programmer; Controller; Credit
Manager; Customer Service Representative; Electrical/
Electronics Engineer; General Manager; Human
Resources Manager; Industrial Production Manager;
Management Trainee; Marketing Specialist; MIS
Specialist; Production Manager; Project Manager; Sales

Engineer; Sales Executive; Sales Manager; Sales
Representative; Secretary; Software Engineer; Systems
Analyst; Systems Manager; Telecommunications
Manager; Typist/Word Processor; Underwriter/Assistant
Underwriter. **Benefits available to temporary workers:**
Medical Insurance; Paid Holidays; Paid Vacation.
Corporate headquarters location: San Diego CA.
Other U.S. locations: Nationwide. **Average salary
range of placements:** $30,000 - $50,000. **Number of
placements per year:** 1000+.

**DATA CAREERS PERSONNEL SERVICES &
SEARCH GROUP**
3320 Fourth Avenue, San Diego CA 92103-5704.
619/291-9994. **Fax:** 619/291-9835. **Contact:** Recruiter.
Description: Data Careers Personnel Services & Search
Group is a permanent employment agency that also
provides some temporary and contract placements.
Specializes in the areas of: Computer
Hardware/Software. **Positions commonly filled include:**
Computer Engineer; Computer Operator; Computer
Programmer; Customer Service Representative; Financial
Analyst; Graphic Designer; Internet Services Manager;
Network/Systems Administrator; Operations Manager;
Project Manager; Software Engineer; Systems Analyst.
Average salary range of placements: $30,000 -
$80,000. **Number of placements per year:** 50 - 99.

DATA SYSTEMS SEARCH CONSULTANTS
1756 Lacassie Avenue, Suite 202, Walnut Creek CA
94596. 925/256-0635. **Contact:** John R. Martinez,
President. **Description:** A permanent employment
agency that also provides some temporary, executive,
and contract placements. **Specializes in the areas
of:** Computer Hardware/Software. **Positions commonly
filled include:** Computer Operator; Computer
Programmer; MIS Specialist; Network Engineer;
Operations/Production Manager; Systems Analyst;
Telecommunications Analyst; UNIX System
Administrator; Voice/Data Engineer. **Average salary
range of placements:** More than $50,000. **Number of
placements per year:** 200 - 499.

DENT-ASSIST PERSONNEL SERVICE
2331 L Street, Suite B, Sacramento CA 95816. 916/443-
1113. **Contact:** Lisa Saiia, Director. **Description:** A
permanent placement agency that also provides some
temporary placements. **Specializes in the areas of:**
Dental.

DENTAL STATEWIDE STAFFING
P.O. Box 2051, El Cajon CA 92021-0051. 619/443-7252.
Fax: 619/443-0881. **Contact:** Bonnie Romano, Owner.
Description: A permanent employment agency that also
provides some temporary placements. **Specializes in the
areas of:** Dental. **Corporate headquarters location:**
This Location. **Number of placements per year:** 500 -
999.

**DEPENDABLE EMPLOYMENT AGENCY
NETWORK**
9301 Wilshire Boulevard, Suite 403, Beverly Hills
CA 90210-5424. 310/274-3434. **Fax:** 310/274-8440.
Contact: Randy Hudnutt, Account Manager.
Description: A permanent employment agency that also
provides some temporary placements. **Specializes in
the areas of:** Accounting/Auditing; Administration;
Banking; Computer Science/Software; Education;
Finance; Insurance; Legal; Personnel/Labor Relations;
Secretarial. **Positions commonly filled include:**
Accountant; Administrative Assistant; Administrative
Manager; Advertising Clerk; Brokerage Clerk; Clerical
Supervisor; Computer Operator; Computer Programmer;
Customer Service Representative; Database Manager;
Editorial Assistant; Financial Analyst; Graphic Artist;
Graphic Designer; Human Resources Manager; Human
Resources Specialist; Librarian; Library Technician;
Management Trainee; Market Research Analyst;
Marketing Specialist; MIS Specialist; Paralegal;
Secretary; Securities Sales Representative; Software
Engineer; Statistician; Systems Analyst; Technical
Writer/Editor; Typist/Word Processor; Underwriter/

Assistant Underwriter. **Corporate headquarters location:** This Location. **Average salary range of placements:** $30,000 - $50,000. **Number of placements per year:** 1 - 49.

DESERT PERSONNEL SERVICE, INC.
DESERT TEMPS
73-350 El Paseo, Suite 205, Palm Desert CA 92260-4240. 760/346-3945. **Fax:** 619/346-2455. **Contact:** Manager. **E-mail address:** jobs@desertpersonnel.com. **World Wide Web address:** http://www.desertpersonnel.com. **Description:** A permanent employment agency that also provides some temporary placements. **Specializes in the areas of:** Accounting/Auditing; General Management; Personnel/Labor Relations; Secretarial. **Positions commonly filled include:** Account Manager; Accountant; Computer Programmer; Consultant; Controller; Finance Director; MIS Specialist; Sales Executive; Sales Manager; Sales Representative. **Benefits available to temporary workers:** Medical Insurance; Paid Holidays; Paid Vacation; Profit Sharing; Referral Bonus Plan. **Corporate headquarters location:** This Location. **Average salary range of placements:** $30,000 - $50,000. **Number of placements per year:** 50 - 99.

THE DIAL GROUP
14522 East Whittier Boulevard, Whittier CA 90605. 562/945-1071. **Contact:** Doug Lopez, Owner. **Description:** A permanent employment agency. **Specializes in the areas of:** Accounting/Auditing; Banking; Clerical; Finance. **Positions commonly filled include:** Accountant/Auditor; Administrative Assistant; Bookkeeper; Buyer; Clerk; Computer Operator; Credit Manager; Customer Service Representative; Data Entry Clerk; Human Resources Manager; Legal Secretary; Medical Secretary; Sales Representative; Secretary; Stenographer. **Other U.S. locations:** Brea CA; Newport Beach CA. **Number of placements per year:** 500 - 999.

CATHY DUNN'S ASSOCIATED PERSONNEL SERVICES INC.
800 North Harbor Boulevard, Suite B, La Habra CA 90631. 562/690-6693. **Fax:** 562/690-8107. **Contact:** Manager. **Description:** A permanent placement agency that also provides some temporary placements. Founded in 1985. Client company pays fee. **Specializes in the areas of:** Automotive; Bookkeeping; Clerical; Dental; Health/Medical; Secretarial.

EASTRIDGE INFOTECH
2355 Northside Drive, Suite 180, San Diego CA 92108. 619/260-2109. **Fax:** 619/280-0843. **Contact:** Joanne Kinsey, Recruiter. **Description:** Eastridge Infotech is a permanent employment agency that also provides some temporary placements. Founded in 1971. **Specializes in the areas of:** Computer Science/Software; Technical. **Positions commonly filled include:** Computer Programmer; Draftsperson; Internet Services Manager; Software Engineer; Systems Analyst. **Corporate headquarters location:** This Location. **Other U.S. locations:** Nationwide. **Number of placements per year:** 1 - 49.

EMCO PERSONNEL SERVICE
27575 Via Montoya, San Juan Capistrano CA 92675-5366. 949/487-6870. **Contact:** Dick Tinlin, President. **Description:** A permanent employment agency. **Specializes in the areas of:** Banking; Finance. **Positions commonly filled include:** Credit Manager. **Number of placements per year:** 50 - 99.

THE EMERALD AGENCY
P.O. Box 91705, Los Angeles CA 90009. 310/643-8900. **Fax:** 310/643-8749. **Contact:** Janelle Jenkins, President. **World Wide Web address:** http://www.emeraldagency.com. **Description:** A permanent employment agency that also provides some temporary placements. The Emerald Agency also offers resume development services. **Specializes in the areas of:** Legal. **Positions commonly filled include:** Attorney; Engineer; Human Resources Specialist; Legal Secretary; Legal Writer/Editor; MIS

Specialist; Systems Analyst. **Corporate headquarters location:** This Location. **Average salary range of placements:** More than $50,000. **Number of placements per year:** 50 - 99.

EMPLOYMENT SERVICE AGENCY
8423 Florence Avenue, Suite C, Downey CA 90240. 562/869-8811. **Fax:** 562/869-7952. **Contact:** Owner. **Description:** A permanent employment agency that also provides some temporary placements. **Specializes in the areas of:** Industrial; Manufacturing; Secretarial. **Positions commonly filled include:** Administrative Assistant; Clerical Supervisor; Credit Manager; Customer Service Representative; Secretary; Typist/Word Processor. **Average salary range of placements:** $20,000 - $29,999. **Number of placements per year:** 200 - 499.

ESSENTIAL SOLUTIONS, INC.
2542 South Bascom Avenue, Suite 100, Campbell CA 95008. 408/369-9500. **Fax:** 408/369-9595. **Contact:** Manager. **E-mail address:** openings@esiweb.com. **World Wide Web address:** http://www.esiweb.com. **Description:** A permanent employment agency that also provides some contract services. **Specializes in the areas of:** Computer Science/Software; Engineering; Internet Development; MIS/EDP; Scientific; Technical. **Positions commonly filled include:** Applications Engineer; Computer Engineer; Computer Programmer; Computer Scientist; Computer Support Technician; Consultant; Content Developer; Database Administrator; Database Manager; Electrical/Electronics Engineer; Internet Services Manager; Management Analyst/Consultant; Manufacturing Engineer; Marketing Manager; Mechanical Engineer; MIS Specialist; Multimedia Designer; Network/Systems Administrator; Project Manager; Quality Assurance Engineer; Sales Executive; Sales Manager; Sales Representative; Software Developer; SQL Programmer; Systems Analyst; Systems Manager; Technical Writer/Editor; Vice President of Marketing; Vice President of Operations; Webmaster. **Corporate headquarters location:** This Location. **Average salary range of placements:** $50,000 - $100,000. **Number of placements per year:** 100 - 199.

FASTEK TECHNICAL SERVICES
4479 Stoneridge Drive, Pleasanton CA 94588. 925/462-1050. **Fax:** 925/462-1139. **Contact:** Kelly Union, Technical Recruiter. **E-mail address:** fastek1@mindspring.com. **Description:** A permanent employment agency. **Specializes in the areas of:** Accounting/Auditing; Administration; Art/Design; Biology; Computer Science/Software; Engineering; High-Tech; Manufacturing; Sales; Technical. **Positions commonly filled include:** Aerospace Engineer; Agricultural Scientist; Architect; Biological Scientist; Biomedical Engineer; Broadcast Technician; Buyer; Chemical Engineer; Chemist; Civil Engineer; Clinical Lab Technician; Computer Programmer; Cost Estimator; Designer; Draftsperson; Editor; Electrical/Electronics Engineer; Electrician; Industrial Engineer; Internet Services Manager; Landscape Architect; Mechanical Engineer; Metallurgical Engineer; Physicist; Purchasing Agent/Manager; Quality Control Supervisor; Science Technologist; Software Engineer; Stationary Engineer; Structural Engineer; Systems Analyst; Technical Writer/Editor; Transportation/Traffic Specialist. **Benefits available to temporary workers:** Medical Insurance. **Corporate headquarters location:** This Location. **Other U.S. locations:** Orange County CA. **Average salary range of placements:** More than $50,000. **Number of placements per year:** 200 - 499.

FAY TECH SERVICES
P.O. Box 1615, Lomita CA 90717. 310/325-8744. **Fax:** 310/325-8782. **Contact:** Nasser Yazdanpanah, Partner. **Description:** A permanent employment agency. **Specializes in the areas of:** Administration; Architecture/Construction; Computer Science/Software; Economics; Engineering; Finance; Manufacturing; Personnel/Labor Relations. **Positions commonly filled include:** Administrative Manager; Advertising Clerk;

Aerospace Engineer; Agricultural Engineer; Aircraft Mechanic/Engine Specialist; Chemical Engineer; Civil Engineer; Clerical Supervisor; Computer Programmer; Construction and Building Inspector; Construction Contractor; Cost Estimator; Design Engineer; Designer; Electrical/Electronics Engineer; Emergency Medical Technician; Environmental Engineer; Financial Analyst; Geologist/Geophysicist; Human Resources Specialist; Industrial Engineer; Industrial Production Manager; Landscape Architect; Mechanical Engineer; Metallurgical Engineer; Nuclear Engineer; Nuclear Medicine Technologist; Operations/Production Manager; Petroleum Engineer; Software Engineer; Structural Engineer; Systems Analyst; Technical Writer/Editor; Transportation/Traffic Specialist; Typist/Word Processor.

FIRST CALL STAFFING
1811 Wilshire Boulevard, Santa Monica CA 90403. 310/264-9914. **Fax:** 310/998-9217. **Contact:** Branch Manager. **Description:** A permanent employment agency. **Specializes in the areas of:** Administration. **Positions commonly filled include:** Administrative Manager; Advertising Clerk; Branch Manager; Brokerage Clerk; Clerical Supervisor; Customer Service Representative; Human Resources Specialist; Purchasing Agent/Manager; Secretary. **Corporate headquarters location:** Torrance CA. **Other U.S. locations:** Glendale CA. **Average salary range of placements:** $20,000 - $29,999. **Number of placements per year:** 1000+.

GPL ENGINEERING
3031 Tisch Way, Suite 810, San Jose CA 95128. 408/243-1077. **Fax:** 408/241-2652. **Contact:** Guy Leo, Owner. **Description:** A permanent employment agency. **Specializes in the areas of:** Computer Science/Software; Electrical; Engineering. **Positions commonly filled include:** Electrical/Electronics Engineer; Software Engineer. **Number of placements per year:** 1 - 49.

GENERAL EMPLOYMENT ENTERPRISES INC.
21535 Hawthorne Boulevard, Suite 330, Torrance CA 90503. 310/540-9151. **Fax:** 310/316-2095. **Contact:** Agency Manager. **Description:** A permanent employment agency. **Specializes in the areas of:** Computer Science/Software; Information Technology. **Positions commonly filled include:** Internet Services Manager; MIS Specialist; Multimedia Designer; Software Engineer; Systems Analyst; Technical Writer/Editor; Telecommunications Manager. **Corporate headquarters location:** Oakbrook Terrace IL. **Other U.S. locations:** Nationwide. **Number of placements per year:** 100 - 199.

GENERAL EMPLOYMENT ENTERPRISES INC.
2540 North First Street, Suite 110, San Jose CA 95131. 408/954-9000. **Fax:** 408/943-0404. **Contact:** Albert C. Cato, Agency Manager. **Description:** A permanent employment agency. **Positions commonly filled include:** Aerospace Engineer; Computer Programmer; Design Engineer; Electrical/Electronics Engineer; Human Resources Specialist; Industrial Engineer; Management Analyst/Consultant; Mathematician; Mechanical Engineer; MIS Specialist; Multimedia Designer; Systems Analyst. **Corporate headquarters location:** Oakbrook Terrace IL. **Other U.S. locations:** Nationwide. **Average salary range of placements:** More than $50,000. **Number of placements per year:** 1000+.

GOULD PERSONNEL SERVICES
850 Colorado Boulevard, Suite 104, Los Angeles CA 90041. 323/256-5800. **Fax:** 323/255-0414. **Contact:** Warren Gould, President. **Description:** A permanent employment agency. **Specializes in the areas of:** Accounting/Auditing; Advertising; Architecture/Construction; Banking; Computer Science/Software; Economics; Finance; General Management; Health/Medical; Insurance; Legal; Manufacturing; Nonprofit; Personnel/Labor Relations; Publishing; Sales; Secretarial. **Positions commonly filled include:** Accountant/Auditor; Adjuster; Administrative Manager; Bank Officer/Manager; Branch Manager; Buyer;

Chiropractor; Claim Representative; Clerical Supervisor; Collector; Computer Programmer; Counselor; Credit Manager; Customer Service Rep.; Draftsperson; EKG Technician; Investigator; Licensed Practical Nurse; Management Trainee; Physical Therapist; Registered Nurse. **Average salary range of placements:** $20,000 - $29,999. **Number of placements per year:** 100 - 199.

INITIAL STAFFING SERVICES
601 University Avenue, Suite 103, Sacramento CA 95825. 916/568-0343. **Fax:** 916/568-1880. **Contact:** Beth Noseworthy, Market Manager. **Description:** A permanent employment agency that also provides some temporary placements. Founded in 1976. **Specializes in the areas of:** Banking; Personnel/Labor Relations; Secretarial. **Positions commonly filled include:** Customer Service Rep.; Typist/Word Processor. **Benefits available to temporary workers:** 401(k); Dental Insurance; Medical Insurance; Vision Plan. **Corporate headquarters location:** Houston TX. **Other U.S. locations:** Nationwide. **Average salary range of placements:** $30,000 - $50,000. **Number of placements per year:** 50 - 99.

INITIAL STAFFING SERVICES
343 Sansome Street, Suite 170, San Francisco CA 94104. 415/391-2333. **Fax:** 415/391-2270. **Contact:** John St. Germain, Service Manager. **Description:** A permanent employment agency that also provides some temporary placements. Founded in 1976. **Specializes in the areas of:** Banking; Finance; Personnel/Labor Relations; Secretarial. **Positions commonly filled include:** Customer Service Rep.; Typist/Word Processor. **Benefits available to temporary workers:** 401(k); Dental Insurance; Medical Insurance; Vision Plan. **Corporate headquarters location:** Houston TX. **Other U.S. locations:** Nationwide. **Average salary range of placements:** $30,000 - $50,000. **Number of placements per year:** 50 - 99.

INITIAL STAFFING SERVICES
500 Ygnacio Valley Road, Suite 160, Walnut Creek CA 94596. 925/937-4550. **Fax:** 925/937-4552. **Contact:** Leigh Shughrou, Service Manager. **Description:** A permanent employment agency that also provides some temporary placements. Founded in 1976. **Specializes in the areas of:** Banking; Finance; Personnel/Labor Relations; Secretarial. **Positions commonly filled include:** Customer Service Representative; Typist/Word Processor. **Benefits available to temporary workers:** 401(k); Dental Insurance; Medical Insurance; Vision Plan. **Corporate headquarters location:** Houston TX. **Other U.S. locations:** Nationwide. **Average salary range of placements:** $30,000 - $50,000. **Number of placements per year:** 50 - 99.

INITIAL STAFFING SERVICES
2600 El Camino Real, Suite 415, Palo Alto CA 94306. 650/813-8310. **Fax:** 650/813-8312. **Contact:** Kurt Chou, Senior Staffing Consultant. **Description:** A permanent employment agency that also provides some temporary placements. Founded in 1976. **Specializes in the areas of:** Accounting/Auditing; Administration; Banking; Computer Science/Software; Finance; Health/Medical; Personnel/Labor Relations; Sales; Secretarial. **Positions commonly filled include:** Accountant/Auditor; Administrative Manager; Buyer; Clerical Supervisor; Customer Service Representative; Financial Analyst; Human Resources Specialist; Management Trainee; Medical Secretary; Typist/Word Processor. **Benefits available to temporary workers:** 401(k); Dental Insurance; Medical Insurance; Paid Holidays; Referral Bonus Plan; Vision Plan. **Corporate headquarters location:** Houston TX. **Other U.S. locations:** Nationwide. **Average salary range of placements:** $20,000 - $29,999. **Number of placements per year:** 500 - 999.

INTERIM FINANCIAL SOLUTIONS
18500 Von Karman Avenue, Suite 510, Irvine CA 92612. 949/756-1028. **Fax:** 949/756-1225. **Contact:** Michelle Fenstermaker, Financial Recruiter.

Description: A permanent employment agency that also provides some temporary placements. **Specializes in the areas of:** Accounting/Auditing; Administration; Banking; Finance. **Positions commonly filled include:** Accountant/Auditor; Chief Financial Officer; Controller; Credit Manager; Financial Analyst.

INTERNATIONAL SEARCH CONSULTANTS
30827 Mainmast Drive, Agoura Hills CA 91301. 818/706-2635. **Fax:** 818/706-1358. **Contact:** George Schortz, President. **E-mail address:** george@isccnc. com. **Description:** A permanent employment agency. **Specializes in the areas of:** Engineering; Manufacturing; Sales; Technical. **Positions commonly filled include:** Aerospace Engineer; Consultant; Electrical/Electronics Engineer; Manufacturer's/Wholesaler's Sales Rep.; Marketing Specialist; Materials Engineer; Mechanical Engineer; Sales Rep. **Corporate headquarters location:** This Location. **Other U.S. locations:** Nationwide. **Average salary range of placements:** $30,000 - $50,000. **Number of placements per year:** 1 - 49.

INTERTEC DESIGN, INC.
6290 Sunset Boulevard, Suite 1104, Hollywood CA 90028. 323/466-4388. **Fax:** 323/466-4723. **Contact:** Darian James, Branch Manager. **Description:** A permanent employment agency. **Specializes in the areas of:** Advertising; Banking; Light Industrial; Nonprofit; Printing; Retail; Sales; Secretarial. **Positions commonly filled include:** Account Representative; Administrative Assistant; Administrative Manager; Editorial Assistant; Graphic Artist; Receptionist; Sales Rep.; Secretary. **Corporate headquarters location:** Pennsauken NJ. **Other U.S. locations:** Nationwide. **Average salary range of placements:** $30,000 - $50,000. **Number of placements per year:** 1 - 49.

JAA EMPLOYMENT AGENCY
6404 Wilshire Boulevard, Suite 1230, Los Angeles CA 90048. 323/655-0285. **Fax:** 800/818-9991. **Contact:** Arthur White, President. **Description:** A permanent employment agency. **Specializes in the areas of:** Entry-Level Management; Sales. **Positions commonly filled include:** Bank Officer/Manager; Claim Representative; Customer Service Representative; Management Trainee; Underwriter/Assistant Underwriter.

JACKSON PERSONNEL
717 Market Street, Suite 224, San Francisco CA 94103. 415/546-4500. **Fax:** 415/546-0926. **Contact:** Emily Wilson, Operations Manager. **Description:** A permanent employment agency. **Specializes in the areas of:** Accounting/Auditing; Administration; Computer Science/Software; Insurance; Legal; Manufacturing; Personnel/Labor Relations; Sales; Secretarial; Technical. **Positions commonly filled include:** Accountant/Auditor; Administrative Manager; Advertising Clerk; Bank Officer/Manager; Blue-Collar Worker Supervisor; Branch Manager; Claim Representative; Clerical Supervisor; Clinical Lab Technician; Computer Programmer; Construction and Building Inspector; Counselor; Credit Manager; Designer; Editor; Financial Analyst; Food Scientist/Technologist; Health Services Manager; Hotel Manager; Human Resources Specialist; Library Technician; Management Analyst/Consultant; Management Trainee; Market Research Analyst; Medical Records Technician; Paralegal; Property and Real Estate Manager; Public Relations Specialist; Purchasing Agent/Manager; Quality Control Supervisor; Securities Sales Representative; Services Sales Representative; Software Engineer; Statistician; Telecommunications Manager; Transportation/Traffic Specialist; Travel Agent; Typist/Word Processor. **Benefits available to temporary workers:** Bonus Award/Plan. **Average salary range of placements:** $20,000 - $29,999. **Number of placements per year:** 200 - 499.

JASON BEST AGENCY
10940 Wilshire Boulevard, Los Angeles CA 90024. 310/209-7500. **Fax:** 310/209-7501. **Contact:** Manager. **E-mail address:** jasonbest@worldnet.att.net. **World Wide Web address:** http://gtesupersite.com/jasonbest.

Description: A permanent employment agency that also provides some temporary placements. Founded in 1973. Client company pays fee. **Specializes in the areas of:** Accounting/Auditing; Administration; Office Support; Operations Management; Secretarial; Word Processing. **Positions commonly filled include:** Administrative Assistant; Bookkeeper; Executive Assistant; Secretary. **Office hours:** Monday - Friday, 8:00 a.m. - 5:30 p.m.

KELCH & SHEA ASSOCIATES
401 Boyd Street, Vacaville CA 95688. 925/932-6011. **Contact:** Manager. **Description:** Kelch & Shea Associates is a permanent employment agency. **Specializes in the areas of:** Automotive Retailing.

LANDMARK MANAGEMENT SERVICES
1123 Chapala Street, Suite 201, Santa Barbara CA 93101. 805/965-7300. **Fax:** 805/967-6337. **Contact:** Manager. **Description:** A permanent placement agency. Founded in 1987. **Specializes in the areas of:** Administration; Legal; Technical. **Office hours:** Monday - Friday, 9:00 a.m. - 5:00 p.m.

MS DATA SERVICE CORPORATION
4030 Birch Street, Suite 101, Newport Beach CA 92660. 714/540-4430. **Contact:** Personnel Manager. **Description:** A permanent employment agency. **Specializes in the areas of:** Computer Hardware/Software; MIS/EDP; Technical. **Positions commonly filled include:** Computer Operator; Computer Programmer; Data Entry Clerk; EDP Specialist; MIS Specialist; Receptionist; Systems Analyst; Typist/Word Processor.

MACIEJEWSKI & ASSOCIATES
883 Sneath Lane, Suite 217, San Bruno CA 94066. 650/871-0373. **Contact:** Theresa Altvater, Office Manager. **Description:** A permanent employment agency that places senior-level developers and mid- to senior-level executives. Maciejewski & Associates also offers some temporary placements and contract services. Client company pays fee. **Specializes in the areas of:** Computer Science/Software; Internet Development; MIS/EDP; Software Development. **Positions commonly filled include:** Applications Engineer; AS400 Programmer Analyst; Computer Programmer; Computer Support Technician; Content Developer; Database Administrator; Database Manager; Internet Services Manager; MIS Specialist; Network/Systems Administrator; Software Engineer; SQL Programmer; Systems Analyst; Systems Manager; Webmaster. **Corporate headquarters location:** This Location. **Other U.S. locations:** Nationwide. **Average salary range of placements:** $50,000 - $100,000. **Number of placements per year:** 50 - 99.

RICHARD MARIE'S STAFFING CENTER
200 West Pondera Street, Lancaster CA 93534. 661/942-0466. **Contact:** Office Manager. **Description:** Richard Marie's Staffing Center is a permanent employment agency. **Specializes in the areas of:** Accounting/Auditing; Clerical; Computer Hardware/Software; Health/Medical; Secretarial. **Positions commonly filled include:** Accountant/Auditor; Administrative Assistant; Aerospace Engineer; Bookkeeper; Claim Representative; Clerk; Customer Service Representative; Data Entry Clerk; General Manager; Hotel Manager; Insurance Agent/Broker; Legal Secretary; Medical Secretary; Purchasing Agent/Manager; Receptionist; Secretary; Typist/Word Processor. **Number of placements per year:** 50 - 99.

MARTIN STAFFING RESOURCES
7901 Stoneridge Drive, Suite 599, Pleasanton CA 94588. 925/225-0900. **Contact:** Peggy Johnston, Administrative Assistant. **Description:** A permanent employment agency that also provides some temporary placements. **Specializes in the areas of:** Accounting/Auditing; Administration; Computer Science/Software; Personnel/Labor Relations; Sales; Secretarial; Technical. **Positions commonly filled include:** Accountant/Auditor; Administrative Manager; Advertising Clerk; Branch

Manager; Buyer; Computer Programmer; Credit Manager; Customer Service Rep.; Financial Analyst; Human Resources Specialist; Internet Services Manager; Management Trainee; MIS Specialist; Purchasing Agent/Manager; Services Sales Representative; Software Engineer; Systems Analyst; Technical Writer/Editor; Telecommunications Manager; Typist/Word Processor. **Benefits available to temporary workers:** 401(k); Paid Holidays. **Other U.S. locations:** Santa Clara CA; Walnut Creek CA. **Average salary range of placements:** $30,000 - $50,000. **Number of placements per year:** 100 - 199.

McCALL STAFFING SERVICES
351 California Street, Suite 1200, San Francisco CA 94104. 415/981-3400. **Fax:** 415/397-8349. **Contact:** Tess Genato, Vice President/General Manager. **E-mail address:** staff@mccall-sf.com. **World Wide Web address:** http://www.mccall-sf.com. **Description:** A permanent employment agency that also provides some temporary and temp-to-perm placements. Client company pays fee. **Specializes in the areas of:** Administration; Office Support. **Positions commonly filled include:** Accounting Clerk; Administrative Assistant; Bookkeeper; Clerk; Data Entry Clerk; Executive Assistant; Legal Secretary; Receptionist. **Number of placements per year:** 200 - 499.

MEDICAL STAFF UNLIMITED
3517 Marconi Avenue, Suite 207, Sacramento CA 95821. 916/485-1986. **Fax:** 916/485-4022. **Contact:** Donna Starr, Director. **E-mail address:** msu207@ns.net. **Description:** A permanent employment agency that also provides some temporary placements. **Specializes in the areas of:** Health/Medical; Insurance; Secretarial. **Positions commonly filled include:** EEG Technologist; EKG Technician; Medical Assistant; Medical Records Technician; Medical Secretary; Registered Nurse; Surgical Technician. **Average salary range of placements:** $20,000 - $29,999. **Number of placements per year:** 50 - 99.

JOSEPH MICHAELS INC.
120 Montgomery Street, Suite 1260, San Francisco CA 94104. **Toll-free phone:** 800/786-1099. **Fax:** 415/434-1165. **Contact:** Dennis Billingsley, Vice President. **Description:** A permanent employment agency. **Specializes in the areas of:** Accounting/Auditing; Finance. **Positions commonly filled include:** Accountant/Auditor; Bookkeeper. **Number of placements per year:** 200 - 499.

MONROE PERSONNEL SERVICES
TEMPTIME
333 Market Street, Suite 3320, San Francisco CA 94105. 415/882-7100. **Fax:** 415/882-7145. **Contact:** Debra Monroe, Owner. **E-mail address:** monroe@temptime. com. **Description:** A permanent employment agency whose clients include international firms. Temptime (also at this location) provides temporary placements. **Specializes in the areas of:** Engineering; Legal; Printing; Secretarial. **Positions commonly filled include:** Administrative Assistant; Advertising Clerk; Clerical Supervisor; Secretary; Typist/Word Processor. **Benefits available to temporary workers:** Paid Vacation. **Corporate headquarters location:** This Location. **Average salary range of placements:** $30,000 - $50,000. **Number of placements per year:** 50 - 99.

M.O.R.E. EMPLOYMENT SERVICES
344 Placerville Drive, Placerville CA 95667. 530/621-4027. **Fax:** 530/622-0204. **Contact:** Suzanne Miller, Supported Employment Coordinator. **Description:** A private, nonprofit permanent employment agency that offers counseling, training, and job search assistance for people with developmental disabilities. **Specializes in the areas of:** Food; Health/Medical. **Positions commonly filled include:** Preschool Worker. **Corporate headquarters location:** This Location. **Other U.S. locations:** South Lake Tahoe CA. **Average salary range of placements:** Less than $20,000. **Number of placements per year:** 1 - 49.

MULTAX SYSTEMS, INC.
505 North Sepulveda Boulevard, Suite 7, Manhattan Beach CA 90266-6743. 310/379-8398. **Fax:** 310/379-1142. **Contact:** Randy Heinesh, General Manager. **Description:** A permanent employment agency. **Specializes in the areas of:** Computer Science/Software; Engineering. **Positions commonly filled include:** Aerospace Engineer; Computer Programmer; Designer; Draftsperson; Software Engineer; Structural Engineer; Systems Analyst. **Number of placements per year:** 200 - 499.

NELSON HUMAN RESOURCE SOLUTIONS
P.O. Box 1546, Sonoma CA 95476. 707/935-6113. **Fax:** 707/935-6124. **Contact:** Manager. **World Wide Web address:** http://www.nelsonjobs.com. **Description:** A permanent employment agency that also provides temporary and contract positions, executive searches on both retainer and contingency bases, and career counseling. Nelson Human Resource Solutions operates through four divisions: Nelson Staffing Solutions, Accountants Plus, Nelson Associates, and TechSource. Founded in 1970. **Specializes in the areas of:** Accounting/Auditing; Administration; Banking; Computer Science/Software; Engineering; Finance; General Management; Industrial; Insurance; Legal; Light Industrial; MIS/EDP; Office Support; Production; Sales; Scientific; Secretarial; Technical. **Positions commonly filled include:** Account Representative; Accountant; Administrative Assistant; Administrative Manager; Applications Engineer; Assistant Manager; Auditor; Branch Manager; Budget Analyst; Buyer; Chief Financial Officer; Clerical Supervisor; Computer Operator; Computer Programmer; Controller; Credit Manager; Customer Service Representative; Database Manager; Design Engineer; Electrical/Electronics Engineer; Finance Director; Financial Analyst; General Manager; Human Resources Manager; Industrial Engineer; Internet Services Manager; Management Trainee; Manufacturing Engineer; Market Research Analyst; Marketing Manager; Marketing Specialist; Mechanical Engineer; MIS Specialist; Operations Manager; Paralegal; Production Manager; Project Manager; Public Relations Specialist; Purchasing Agent/Manager; Quality Control Supervisor; Sales Executive; Sales Manager; Sales Representative; Secretary; Software Engineer; Systems Analyst; Systems Manager; Technical Writer/Editor; Vice President of Finance. **Benefits available to temporary workers:** Bonus Award/Plan; Medical Insurance; Paid Holidays; Training. **Corporate headquarters location:** This Location. **Number of placements per year:** 1000+.

NELSON STAFFING SOLUTIONS
3478 Buskirk Avenue, Suite 105, Pleasant Hill CA 94523. 925/933-0505. **Contact:** Manager. **Description:** A permanent employment agency that also provides some temporary placements. **Specializes in the areas of:** Administration; Manufacturing; Office Support; Secretarial; Technical. **Corporate headquarters location:** Sonoma CA.

NELSON STAFFING SOLUTIONS
425 California Street, Suite 600, San Francisco CA 94104. 415/989-9911. **Contact:** Manager. **Description:** A permanent employment agency that also provides some temporary placements. **Specializes in the areas of:** Administration; Manufacturing; Office Support; Secretarial; Technical. **Corporate headquarters location:** Sonoma CA.

NESCO SERVICE COMPANY
2431 North Tustin Avenue, Suite H, Santa Ana CA 92705-1660. 714/973-1303. **Fax:** 714/972-8947. **Contact:** Manager. **Description:** A permanent employment agency. **Specializes in the areas of:** Accounting/Auditing; Administration; Food; General Management; Manufacturing; Personnel/Labor Relations; Secretarial. **Positions commonly filled include:** Administrative Manager; Blue-Collar Worker Supervisor; Branch Manager; Buyer; Claim Rep.; Clerical Supervisor; Computer Programmer; Customer

Service Rep.; General Manager; Human Resources Specialist; Manufacturer's/Wholesaler's Sales Rep.; Purchasing Agent/Manager; Quality Control Supervisor; Restaurant/Food Service Manager; Services Sales Rep.; Typist/Word Processor. **Benefits available to temporary workers:** 401(k); Medical Insurance; Paid Holidays; Paid Vacation. **Corporate headquarters location:** Tampa FL. **Other U.S. locations:** Nationwide. **Average salary range of placements:** $20,000 - $29,999. **Number of placements per year:** 1000+.

NURSES INTERNATIONAL
3319 Glendale Boulevard, Suite E, Los Angeles CA 90039. 323/913-2836. **Contact:** Manager. **Description:** A permanent employment agency. **Specializes in the areas of:** Health/Medical. **Positions commonly filled include:** Registered Nurse. **Number of placements per year:** 100 - 199.

OFFICEMATES5 (OM5)
DAYSTAR TEMPORARY SERVICES
3031 Tisch Way, San Jose CA 95128. 408/246-9696. **Fax:** 408/246-2423. **Contact:** Ms. Verna File, Regional Manager. **Description:** A permanent employment agency. Daystar Temporary Services (also at this location) provides temporary placements. **Specializes in the areas of:** Accounting/Auditing; Administration; Personnel/Labor Relations; Sales; Secretarial. **Positions commonly filled include:** Accountant/Auditor; Administrative Assistant; Administrative Manager; Advertising Clerk; Branch Manager; Credit Manager; Customer Service Representative; Financial Analyst; Human Resources Manager; Human Resources Specialist; Management Trainee; Marketing Specialist; Operations Manager; Property and Real Estate Manager; Purchasing Agent/Manager; Secretary; Services Sales Representative; Typist/Word Processor. **Benefits available to temporary workers:** Dental Insurance; Medical Insurance. **Corporate headquarters location:** Cleveland OH. **Other U.S. locations:** Nationwide. **Average salary range of placements:** $20,000 - $50,000. **Number of placements per year:** 200 - 499.

PARAGON TECHNICAL STAFFING
100 North Barranca, Suite 820, West Covina CA 91791. 626/966-7811. **Fax:** 626/966-9620. **Contact:** Manager. **E-mail address:** jobs@paragonstaff.com. **World Wide Web address:** http://paragonstaff.com. **Description:** A permanent placement agency that also provides some temporary placements. **Positions commonly filled include:** Buyer; Chemist; Computer Operator; Computer Programmer; Draftsperson; Electrician; Electronics Technician; Engineer; Graphic Artist; Inventory Control Specialist; IT Specialist; Laboratory Technician; Machine Operator; Machinist; Maintenance Technician; Planner; Product Manager; Purchasing Agent/Manager; Quality Control Supervisor; Systems Analyst; Technical Writer/Editor; Warehouse Manager; Welder.

PIPS PERSONNEL SERVICES
5000 East Spring, Suite 380, Long Beach CA 90815. 562/425-8282. **Contact:** Ernie Davis, Owner/General Manager. **Description:** A permanent employment agency. **Specializes in the areas of:** Accounting/Auditing; Clerical; Finance; Sales. **Positions commonly filled include:** Accountant/Auditor; Administrative Assistant; Bookkeeper; Buyer; Claim Representative; Clerk; Computer Operator; Computer Programmer; Credit Manager; Customer Service Representative; Data Entry Clerk; EDP Specialist; Legal Secretary; Marketing Specialist; Medical Secretary; Packaging Technologist; Public Relations Specialist; Purchasing Agent/Manager; Receptionist; Sales Rep.; Secretary; Statistician; Stenographer; Support Personnel; Systems Analyst; Technical Writer/Editor; Typist/Word Processor; Underwriter/Assistant Underwriter. **Number of placements per year:** 100 - 199.

PREMIER NURSING SERVICE
444 West Ocean Boulevard, Suite 1050, Long Beach CA 90802. 562/437-4313. **Fax:** 562/495-1508. **Contact:** Manager. **Description:** A permanent employment

agency. **Specializes in the areas of:** Health/Medical. **Positions commonly filled include:** Nurse. **Number of placements per year:** 1000+.

PREMIER STAFFING
500 Esplanade Drive, Suite 990, Oxnard CA 93030. 805/485-3006. **Fax:** 805/485-4979. **Contact:** Manager. **Description:** A permanent employment agency. **Specializes in the areas of:** Accounting; Clerical; Human Resources; Industrial; Marketing; Sales; Technical. **Positions commonly filled include:** Accountant; Accounting Clerk; Administrative Assistant; Assembler; Bookkeeper; Computer Programmer; Data Entry Clerk; Designer; Draftsperson; Engineer; Inspector/Tester/Grader; Office Manager; Receptionist; Secretary; Shipping and Receiving Clerk; Switchboard Operator; Technician; Warehouse/Distribution Worker; Writer.

PRESTIGE PERSONNEL SERVICE
P.O. Box 8751, Rowland Heights CA 91748-8751. 626/964-1082. **Contact:** Ms. Toni Shores, President. **Description:** A permanent employment agency. **Specializes in the areas of:** Clerical; Manufacturing; Secretarial. **Positions commonly filled include:** Administrative Assistant; Bookkeeper; Clerk; Customer Service Representative; Data Entry Clerk; Human Resources Manager; Legal Secretary; Light Industrial Worker; Sales Representative; Secretary; Stenographer; Typist/Word Processor. **Number of placements per year:** 200 - 499.

PRO STAFF PERSONNEL SERVICES
879 West 190th Street, Suite 935, Torrance CA 90248. 310/353-2411. **Fax:** 310/353-2416. **Contact:** Staffing Supervisor. **World Wide Web address:** http://www.prostaff.com. **Description:** A permanent employment agency that also provides some temporary placements. **Specializes in the areas of:** Accounting/Auditing; Administration; Computer Science/Software; Industrial; Personnel/Labor Relations. **Positions commonly filled include:** Accountant/Auditor; Administrative Manager; Bank Officer/Manager; Blue-Collar Worker Supervisor; Branch Manager; Claim Rep.; Computer Programmer; Customer Service Rep.; Environmental Engineer; Financial Analyst; Human Resources Manager; Internet Services Manager; MIS Specialist; Paralegal; Purchasing Agent/Manager; Services Sales Rep. **Corporate headquarters location:** Minneapolis MN. **Other U.S. locations:** Nationwide. **Number of placements per year:** 1000+.

PRO STAFF PERSONNEL SERVICES
225 West Broadway, Suite 103, Glendale CA 91204-1331. 818/551-9145. **Fax:** 818/551-1284. **Contact:** Manager. **World Wide Web address:** http://www.prostaff.com. **Description:** A permanent employment agency that also provides some temporary placements. **Specializes in the areas of:** Accounting/Auditing; Administration; Banking; Computer Science/Software; Engineering; Finance; Industrial; Insurance; Legal; Manufacturing; Personnel/Labor Relations; Secretarial; Technical. **Positions commonly filled include:** Accountant/Auditor; Administrative Manager; Clerical Supervisor; Computer Programmer; Human Resources Specialist; MIS Specialist; Quality Control Supervisor; Typist/Word Processor. **Benefits available to temporary workers:** 401(k); Dental Insurance; Medical Insurance; Referral Bonus Plan. **Corporate headquarters location:** Minneapolis MN. **Other U.S. locations:** Nationwide. **Average salary range of placements:** $30,000 - $50,000. **Number of placements per year:** 1000+.

PRO STAFF PERSONNEL SERVICES
18300 Von Karman Avenue, Suite 710, Irvine CA 92612. 949/250-8850. **Toll-free phone:** 800/979-2100. **Fax:** 949/250-8862. **Contact:** Manager. **World Wide Web address:** http://www.prostaff.com. **Description:** A permanent employment agency that also provides some temporary and contract placements and career/outplacement counseling services. **Specializes in the**

areas of: Accounting/Auditing; Administration; Computer Science/Software; Fashion; General Management; MIS/EDP; Nonprofit; Personnel/Labor Relations. **Positions commonly filled include:** Account Manager; Account Representative; Administrative Assistant; Administrative Manager; Advertising Clerk; Advertising Executive; Applications Engineer; Blue-Collar Worker Supervisor; Branch Manager; Claim Representative; Clerical Supervisor; Computer Animator; Computer Operator; Computer Programmer; Controller; Credit Manager; Customer Service Representative; General Manager; Graphic Artist; Graphic Designer; Human Resources Manager; Market Research Analyst; Paralegal; Sales Executive; Sales Manager; Sales Representative; Secretary; Systems Analyst; Systems Manager; Telecommunications Manager; Typist/Word Processor. **Benefits available to temporary workers:** Medical Insurance; Paid Holidays; Referral Bonus Plan; Scholarship Program; Service Award. **Corporate headquarters location:** Minneapolis MN. **Other U.S. locations:** Nationwide. **Number of placements per year:** 500 - 999.

PROFOUND
180 Seventh Avenue, Suite 201, Santa Cruz CA 95062. 831/461-7000. **Contact:** Manager. **Description:** A permanent employment agency. **Specializes in the areas of:** Engineering; Sales.

PRYOR & ASSOCIATES
90 New Montgomery, Suite 401, San Francisco CA 94105. 415/908-1388. **Contact:** Jo-Ann Pryor, Managing Partner. **Description:** A permanent employment agency. **Positions commonly filled include:** Accountant/Auditor; Actuary; Adjuster; Administrative Manager; Claim Rep.; Insurance Agent/Broker; Underwriter/Assistant Underwriter. **Number of placements per year:** 50 - 99.

PYRAMID PLACEMENT
5850 Thille Street, Suite 100, Ventura CA 93003. 805/644-7491. **Fax:** 805/642-6910. **Contact:** Manager. **Description:** A permanent placement agency that also provides some temporary placements. Founded in 1977. **Specializes in the areas of:** Accounting; Administration; Clerical; Engineering; General Labor; Light Industrial; Manufacturing; Sales; Technical.

QUORUM/LANIER LEGAL PROFESSIONALS
650 Castro Street, Suite 250, Mountain View CA 94041-2056. 650/964-2060. **Fax:** 650/964-2332. **Contact:** Joseph Machbitz, Client Relations Representative. **E-mail address:** jmachbitz@qlanier.com. **World Wide Web address:** http://www.lanier.com/legal. **Description:** A permanent employment agency. Founded in 1993. **Specializes in the areas of:** Legal. **Positions commonly filled include:** Attorney; Paralegal. **Benefits available to temporary workers:** 401(k); Medical Insurance; Paid Holidays. **Corporate headquarters location:** Bloomington MN. **Other U.S. locations:** Los Angeles CA; San Francisco CA; Chicago IL; Minneapolis MN. **Average salary range of placements:** $30,000 - $50,000. **Number of placements per year:** 200 - 499.

RAND PERSONNEL
1200 Truxtun Avenue, Suite 130, Bakersfield CA 93301. 661/325-0751. **Contact:** Manager. **Description:** A permanent employment agency. **Positions commonly filled include:** Accountant/Auditor; Administrative Assistant; Bookkeeper; Clerk; Computer Operator; Computer Programmer; Credit Manager; Customer Service Representative; Data Entry Clerk; Draftsperson; EDP Specialist; Legal Secretary; Medical Secretary; Receptionist; Sales Rep.; Secretary; Stenographer; Typist/Word Processor. **Number of placements per year:** 100 - 199.

RELISTAFF
201 South Lake Avenue, Suite 507, Pasadena CA 91101. 626/583-4703. **Fax:** 626/583-4760. **Contact:** Renee Dominique, Branch Service Manager. **Description:** A permanent employment agency that also offers temporary placements and resume and career counseling services. Client company pays fee. **Specializes in the areas of:** Light Industrial; Manufacturing; Marketing; Printing; Sales; Secretarial; Technical. **Positions commonly filled include:** Account Manager; Accountant; Administrative Assistant; Clerical Supervisor; Credit Manager; Customer Service Rep.; Financial Analyst; Human Resources Generalist; Paralegal; Purchasing Agent/Manager; Receptionist; Secretary; Typist/Word Processor. **Benefits available to temporary workers:** Dental Insurance; Holiday Bonus; Life Insurance; Medical Insurance; Vision Insurance. **Corporate headquarters location:** Los Angeles CA. **Average salary range of placements:** $20,000 - $49,999. **Number of placements per year:** 200 - 499.

RENOIR STAFFING SERVICES INC.
3710 Grand Avenue, Oakland CA 94610. 510/836-2220. **Fax:** 510/836-0321. **Contact:** Manager. **Description:** A permanent employment agency. **Specializes in the areas of:** Banking; Computer Science/Software; Personnel/Labor Relations; Real Estate. **Positions commonly filled include:** Accountant/Auditor; Administrative Manager; Architect; Attorney; Computer Programmer; Construction and Building Inspector; Cost Estimator; Customer Service Representative; Design Engineer; Electrical/Electronics Engineer; Environmental Engineer; General Manager; Human Resources Specialist; Human Service Worker; Management Analyst/Consultant; Mining Engineer; Property and Real Estate Manager; Real Estate Agent; Services Sales Representative; Software Engineer. **Average salary range of placements:** $20,000 - $29,999. **Number of placements per year:** 1000+.

ELIZABETH ROSE AGENCY
1434 Sixth Street, Santa Monica CA 90401. 310/451-4866. **Fax:** 310/451-3786. **Contact:** Recruiter. **Description:** A permanent employment agency. **Specializes in the areas of:** Personnel/Labor Relations. **Positions commonly filled include:** Chef/Cook/Kitchen Worker; Licensed Practical Nurse; Nanny; Preschool Worker; Registered Nurse; Speech-Language Pathologist; Teacher/Professor. **Number of placements per year:** 100 - 199.

SANTA BARBARA STAFFING
1300 Santa Barbara Street, Suite B, Santa Barbara CA 93101. 805/965-0511. **Fax:** 805/966-9857. **Contact:** Recruiter. **Description:** A permanent employment agency that also provides some temporary placements and career/outplacement counseling services. **Specializes in the areas of:** Accounting/Auditing; Administration; Advertising; Architecture/Construction; Art/Design; Banking; Biology; Computer Science/Software; Engineering; Finance; General Management; Industrial; Insurance; Legal; Light Industrial; Manufacturing; Nonprofit; Personnel/Labor Relations; Sales; Secretarial; Technical. **Positions commonly filled include:** Account Manager; Account Representative; Accountant; Administrative Assistant; Administrative Manager; Chief Financial Officer; Clinical Lab Technician; Computer Operator; Computer Programmer; Controller; Database Manager; Design Engineer; Draftsperson; Electrical/Electronics Engineer; Electrician; Finance Director; Financial Analyst; Graphic Artist; Graphic Designer; Human Resources Manager; Internet Services Manager; Manufacturing Engineer; Marketing Manager; Marketing Specialist; Mechanical Engineer; MIS Specialist; Purchasing Agent/Manager; Quality Control Supervisor; Sales Engineer; Sales Executive; Sales Manager; Sales Rep.; Software Engineer; Technical Writer/Editor; Typist/Word Processor. **Corporate headquarters location:** This Location. **Other U.S. locations:** Ventura CA. **Average salary range of placements:** $30,000 - $50,000. **Number of placements per year:** 1000+.

SHARF, WOODWARD & ASSOCIATES
5900 Sepulveda Boulevard, Suite 104, Sherman Oaks CA 91411. 818/989-2200. **Fax:** 818/781-5554. **Contact:** Office Manager. **Description:** A permanent employment

agency. **Specializes in the areas of:** Computer Science/Software. **Positions commonly filled include:** Computer Programmer; MIS Specialist; Software Engineer; Systems Analyst. **Average salary range of placements:** More than $50,000. **Number of placements per year:** 200 - 499.

DAVID SHARP & ASSOCIATES
800 Wilshire Boulevard, Suite 1475, Los Angeles CA 90017-2604. 213/486-9801. **Fax:** 213/486-9874. **Contact:** David Sharp, Owner. **E-mail address:** sharpjobs@earthlink.net. **World Wide Web address:** http://www.sharpjobs.com. **Description:** A permanent employment agency. **Specializes in the areas of:** Accounting/Auditing; Administration; Advertising; Banking; Clerical; Computer Science/Software; Economics; Finance; General Management; Health/Medical; Legal; Personnel/Labor Relations; Secretarial; Technical. **Positions commonly filled include:** Account Manager; Account Representative; Accountant; Administrative Assistant; Advertising Clerk; Advertising Executive; Applications Engineer; Auditor; Bank Officer/Manager; Budget Analyst; Chief Financial Officer; Civil Engineer; Computer Operator; Computer Programmer; Controller; Customer Service Rep.; Editorial Assistant; Financial Analyst; Fund Manager; Graphic Artist; Human Resources Manager; Librarian; Management Analyst/Consultant; Marketing Specialist; MIS Specialist; Paralegal; Secretary; Statistician. **Average salary range of placements:** $30,000 - $50,000. **Number of placements per year:** 500 - 999.

SNELLING PERSONNEL INC.
26229 Eden Landing Road, Suite 3, Hayward CA 94545. 510/887-8210. **Fax:** 510/887-8533. **Contact:** Branch Manager. **E-mail address:** haysnell@tdl.com. **World Wide Web address:** http://www.snelling.com/hayward. **Description:** A permanent employment agency that also provides some temporary placements. **Specializes in the areas of:** Accounting/Auditing; Clerical; Legal; Personnel/Labor Relations; Secretarial. **Positions commonly filled include:** Accountant/Auditor; Administrative Assistant; Bookkeeper; Clerical Supervisor; Credit Manager; Customer Service Representative; Data Entry Clerk; Human Resources Specialist; Human Service Worker; Legal Secretary; Purchasing Agent/Manager; Receptionist; Secretary; Typist/Word Processor. **Number of placements per year:** 200 - 499.

DANIELLE STEVENS & ASSOCIATES
14801 Pacific Avenue, Suite 27, Baldwin Park CA 91706. 626/338-1257. **Contact:** Manager. **Description:** A permanent employment agency. **Specializes in the areas of:** Legal.

FRED STUART CONSULTING/PERSONNEL SERVICES
5855 East Naples Plaza, Suite 310, Long Beach CA 90803-5091. 562/439-0921. **Toll-free phone:** 800/298-3021. **Fax:** 562/439-2750. **Contact:** Fred Stuart, Owner. **E-mail address:** fredstuart@globalpac.com. **World Wide Web address:** http://www.fredstuart.com. **Description:** A permanent employment agency that also provides some executive searches. **Specializes in the areas of:** Administration; Computer Hardware/Software; General Management; Personnel/Labor Relations. **Positions commonly filled include:** Branch Manager; Chemical Engineer; Civil Engineer; Computer Programmer; EDP Specialist; Financial Analyst; Human Resources Specialist; Management Analyst/Consultant; MIS Specialist; Multimedia Designer; Software Engineer; Systems Analyst; Technical Writer/Editor; Telecommunications Manager; Webmaster. **Average salary range of placements:** More than $50,000. **Number of placements per year:** 1 - 49.

SUNDAY & ASSOCIATES, INC.
P.O. Box 847, Petaluma CA 94953. 510/644-0440. **Contact:** Michael Sunday, Owner. **Description:** A permanent employment agency. **Specializes in the areas of:** Computer Hardware/Software; Technical. **Positions commonly filled include:** Computer Programmer;

Software Engineer; Systems Analyst; Technical Writer/Editor.

SYSTEM ONE
3021 Citrus Circle, Suite 230, Walnut Creek CA 94598. 925/932-8801. **Fax:** 925/932-3651. **Contact:** Dave Doyle, Owner. **E-mail address:** system1search@ccnet.com. **Description:** A permanent employment agency. **Specializes in the areas of:** Computer Science/Software; Engineering; Manufacturing; Technical. **Positions commonly filled include:** Chemical Engineer; Electrical/Electronics Engineer; Industrial Engineer; Manufacturing Engineer; Mechanical Engineer. **Number of placements per year:** 1 - 49.

SYSTEMATICS AGENCY INC.
1448 15th Street, Suite 202, Santa Monica CA 90404. 310/395-4991. **Contact:** Peter J. Locke, Owner. **Description:** A permanent employment agency that also provides some temporary placements. **Specializes in the areas of:** Administration; Computer Science/Software. **Positions commonly filled include:** Computer Programmer; MIS Specialist; Software Engineer; Systems Analyst; Telecommunications Manager. **Average salary range of placements:** $35,000 - $100,000. **Number of placements per year:** 100 - 199.

T.R. EMPLOYMENT AGENCY
2800 28th Street, Suite 330, Santa Monica CA 90405. 310/399-6107. **Fax:** 310/399-7302. **Contact:** Tel Ramon, Manager. **Description:** A permanent employment agency that also provides executive searches on a retainer basis. **Specializes in the areas of:** Accounting/Auditing; Administration; Advertising; Engineering; General Management; Industrial; Marketing; Sales. **Positions commonly filled include:** Account Manager; Account Representative; Accountant; Administrative Assistant; Administrative Manager; Advertising Executive; Applications Engineer; Architect; Assistant Manager; Auditor; Biochemist; Biological Scientist; Biomedical Engineer; Blue-Collar Worker Supervisor; Chemical Engineer; Chemist; Civil Engineer; Computer Programmer; Daycare Worker; Design Engineer; Electrical/Electronics Engineer; Environmental Engineer; Financial Analyst; General Manager; Geologist/Geophysicist; Human Resources Manager; Industrial Engineer; Industrial Production Manager; Manufacturing Engineer; Market Research Analyst; Marketing Manager; Mechanical Engineer; Production Manager; Project Manager; Purchasing Agent/Manager; Quality Control Supervisor; Sales Executive; Software Engineer. **Number of placements per year:** 1000+.

TRC STAFFING SERVICES, INC.
11300 West Olympic Boulevard, Suite 650, West Los Angeles CA 90064. 310/473-4161. **Fax:** 310/445-9243. **Contact:** Branch Manager. **E-mail address:** trcwestla@aol.com. **World Wide Web address:** http://www.trcstaff.com. **Description:** A permanent employment agency that also provides some temporary placements. Founded in 1986. **Specializes in the areas of:** Accounting/Auditing; Administration; Banking; Computer Science/Software; Education; Finance; Health/Medical; Insurance; Legal; Light Industrial; Marketing; Nonprofit; Personnel/Labor Relations; Sales; Secretarial; Technical. **Positions commonly filled include:** Accountant/Auditor; Administrative Manager; Advertising Clerk; Branch Manager; Computer Programmer; Financial Analyst; General Manager; Human Resources Specialist; Human Service Worker; Paralegal; Systems Analyst. **Benefits available to temporary workers:** Medical Insurance; Paid Holidays; Paid Vacation. **Corporate headquarters location:** Atlanta GA. **Other U.S. locations:** Nationwide. **Average salary range of placements:** $20,000 - $29,999. **Number of placements per year:** 500 - 999.

TRC STAFFING SERVICES, INC.
1337 East Thousand Oaks Boulevard, Suite 110, Thousand Oaks CA 91362. 805/497-9051. **Fax:** 805/497-4093. **Contact:** Denise Figueiredo, President. **World Wide Web address:** http://www.trcstaff.com.

Description: A permanent employment agency that also provides some temporary placements. **Specializes in the areas of:** Accounting; Administration; Art/Design; Banking; Computer Science/Software; Engineering; Finance; Health/Medical; Internet Development; Legal; Light Industrial; Marketing; Nonprofit; Personnel/Labor Relations; Sales; Scientific; Secretarial; Technical. **Positions commonly filled include:** Account Rep.; Accountant; Administrative Assistant; AS400 Programmer Analyst; Biochemist; Blue-Collar Worker Supervisor; Buyer; Computer Animator; Computer Operator; Computer Programmer; Computer Support Technician; Computer Technician; Controller; Design Engineer; Draftsperson; Graphic Artist; Graphic Designer; Human Resources Manager; Industrial Production Manager; Manufacturing Engineer; Marketing Manager; Mechanical Engineer; MIS Specialist; Network/Systems Administrator; Paralegal; Production Manager; Purchasing Agent/Manager; Quality Control Supervisor; Sales Representative; Software Engineer; Systems Analyst; Systems Manager; Technical Writer/Editor; Webmaster. **Benefits available to temporary workers:** Medical Insurance; Paid Holidays; Paid Vacation. **Corporate headquarters location:** Atlanta GA. **Other U.S. locations:** Nationwide. **Average salary range of placements:** $50,000 - $100,000. **Number of placements per year:** 1000+.

TECHSEARCH
Three Harbor Drive, Suite 201, Sausalito CA 94965. 415/332-1282. **Fax:** 415/332-1285. **Contact:** Roger King, President. **E-mail address:** resume@jobsight.com. **World Wide Web address:** http://www.jobsight.com. **Description:** A permanent employment agency that also provides temporary and contract placements, and executive searches on both retainer and contingency bases. **Specializes in the areas of:** Computer Science/Software. **Positions commonly filled include:** Account Manager; Computer Animator; Computer Programmer; Consultant; Database Manager; Graphic Artist; Graphic Designer; Marketing Manager; MIS Specialist; Multimedia Designer; Online Content Specialist; Project Manager; Sales Engineer; Sales Executive; Sales Manager; Software Engineer; Systems Analyst; Systems Manager; Technical Writer/Editor; Telecommunications Manager; Vice President; Webmaster. **Other U.S. locations:** Nationwide. **Average salary range of placements:** More than $50,000. **Number of placements per year:** 200 - 499.

TODAY PERSONNEL SERVICES
98 Battery Street, Suite 603, San Francisco CA 94111. 415/788-2150. **Fax:** 415/788-3197. **Contact:** Pat Hurley, Owner. **E-mail address:** pathurley@todaypersonnel.com. **World Wide Web address:** http://www.todaypersonnel.com. **Description:** Today Personnel Services is a permanent employment agency. Client company pays fee. **Specializes in the areas of:** Accounting; Administration; Banking; Computer Science/Software; Finance; General Management; Insurance; Legal; Light Industrial; Personnel/Labor Relations; Sales; Secretarial. **Positions commonly filled include:** Accountant; Administrative Assistant; Administrative Manager; Assistant Manager; Bank Officer/Manager; Branch Manager; Budget Analyst; Chief Financial Officer; Claim Representative; Clerical Supervisor; Controller; Financial Analyst; General Manager; Graphic Designer; Human Resources Manager; Internet Services Manager; Management Trainee; Market Research Analyst; Operations Manager; Purchasing Agent/Manager; Sales Manager; Sales Rep.; Secretary; Transportation/Traffic Specialist; Typist; Word Processor; Underwriter/Assistant Underwriter. **Corporate headquarters location:** This Location. **Average salary range of placements:** $30,000 - $50,000. **Number of placements per year:** 1 - 49.

TOWN & COUNTRY RESOURCES
425 Sherman Avenue, Suite 130, Palo Alto CA 94306. 650/326-8570. **Fax:** 650/326-1556. **Contact:** Recruiter. **Description:** A permanent employment agency.

Specializes in the areas of: Child Care, In-Home. **Positions commonly filled include:** Nanny. **Number of placements per year:** 200 - 499.

TRANS U.S., INC.
2500 Wilshire Boulevard, Suite 838, Los Angeles CA 90057. 213/384-8288. **Contact:** Manager. **Description:** A permanent employment agency that also provides some temporary and contract placements. **Specializes in the areas of:** Accounting/Auditing; Banking; Education; Health/Medical; Insurance; Legal; Retail; Secretarial. **Positions commonly filled include:** Accountant/Auditor; Administrative Assistant; Legal Secretary; Marketing Specialist; Medical Secretary; Nurse; Sales Representative. **Corporate headquarters location:** This Location. **Average salary range of placements:** $30,000 - $50,000. **Number of placements per year:** 500 - 999.

TRATTNER NETWORK
101 Larkspur Landing Circle, Suite 215, Larkspur CA 94939. 415/464-5555. **Contact:** Manager. **World Wide Web address:** http://www.tratnet.com. **Description:** A permanent employment agency. **Specializes in the areas of:** Computer Science/Software; Engineering; High-Tech. **Positions commonly filled include:** Computer Programmer; Internet Services Manager; MIS Specialist; Software Engineer; Systems Analyst. **Corporate headquarters location:** Los Altos CA. **Average salary range of placements:** More than $50,000. **Number of placements per year:** 100 - 199.

THE TRUMAN AGENCY
13200 Crossroads Parkway North, Suite 470, City of Industry CA 91746. 562/908-1233. **Fax:** 562/908-1238. **Contact:** Robert Truman, Vice President. **Description:** A permanent employment agency. **Specializes in the areas of:** Accounting/Auditing; Administration; Engineering; Finance; General Management; Manufacturing; Personnel/Labor Relations; Sales; Secretarial; Technical; Transportation. **Positions commonly filled include:** Accountant/Auditor; Actuary; Administrative Manager; Advertising Clerk; Attorney; Blue-Collar Worker Supervisor; Branch Manager; Buyer; Chemical Engineer; Chemist; Clerical Supervisor; Credit Manager; Customer Service Representative; Designer; Draftsperson; Electrical/Electronics Engineer; Financial Analyst; General Manager; Human Resources Manager; Industrial Engineer; Industrial Production Manager; Manufacturer's/Wholesaler's Sales Rep.; Mechanical Engineer; Occupational Therapist; Physical Therapist; Purchasing Agent/Manager; Quality Control Supervisor; Services Sales Representative; Software Engineer; Stationary Engineer; Transportation/Traffic Specialist; Wholesale and Retail Buyer. **Average salary range of placements:** $30,000 - $100,000. **Number of placements per year:** 50 - 99.

TUSTIN PERSONNEL SERVICES, INC.
17702 Irvine Boulevard, Suite 101, Tustin CA 92780. 714/544-6141. **Contact:** JoAnn Manion, Owner. **Description:** Tustin Personnel Services is a permanent placement agency. **Specializes in the areas of:** Accounting/Auditing; Clerical; Engineering; Finance; Manufacturing; Personnel/Labor Relations; Technical. **Positions commonly filled include:** Accountant/Auditor; Administrative Assistant; Aerospace Engineer; Bookkeeper; Buyer; Computer Operator; Credit Manager; Data Entry Clerk; Draftsperson; Electrical/Electronics Engineer; Factory Worker; Financial Analyst; Human Resources Manager; Industrial Engineer; Light Industrial Worker; Mechanical Engineer; Purchasing Agent/Manager; Receptionist; Secretary; Stenographer; Technical Writer/Editor; Technician; Typist/Word Processor. **Number of placements per year:** 100 - 199.

UAW LABOR EMPLOYMENT AND TRAINING CORPORATION
790 East Willow Street, Suite 150, Long Beach CA 90806. 562/989-7700. **Fax:** 562/989-7728. **Contact:** Patricia Williams, President. **Description:** A permanent employment agency that also provides some temporary

placements. Founded in 1984. **Specializes in the areas of:** Education; Finance; Health/Medical; Marketing; Nonprofit; Personnel/Labor Relations; Sales; Scientific; Secretarial; Technical. **Positions commonly filled include:** Administrative Assistant; Blue-Collar Worker Supervisor; Claim Representative; Clerical Supervisor; Computer Operator; Computer Programmer; Consultant; Customer Service Representative; Daycare Worker; Education Administrator; ESL Teacher; General Manager; Grant Writer; Human Resources Manager; Internet Services Manager; Management Analyst/ Consultant; Management Trainee; Market Research Analyst; Marketing Specialist; MIS Specialist; Multimedia Designer; Occupational Therapist; Operations Manager; Paralegal; Preschool Worker; Project Manager; Public Relations Specialist; Purchasing Agent/Manager; Quality Control Supervisor; Sales Engineer; Sales Executive; Sales Manager; Sales Rep.; Secretary; Social Worker; Telecommunications Manager; Typist/Word Processor. **Corporate headquarters location:** This Location. **Other U.S. locations:** KY; MI; NY; OH; TN; UT. **Average salary range of placements:** $30,000 - $50,000. **Number of placements per year:** 200 - 499.

VISUALS
101 California Street, Suite 950, San Francisco CA 94111. 415/434-2020. **Fax:** 415/434-2021. **Contact:** Simone da Rosa, Manager. **E-mail address:** info@ visualsonline.com. **World Wide Web address:** http://www.visualsonline.com. **Description:** A permanent placement agency that also provides some temporary placements. Client company pays fee. **Specializes in the areas of:** Art/Design; Digital Arts; New Media. **Positions commonly filled include:** Computer Animator; Graphic Designer; Multimedia Designer; Online Content Specialist; Prepress Worker; Presentation Specialist. **Benefits available to temporary workers:** Medical Insurance. **Corporate headquarters location:** This Location. **Average salary range of placements:** $30,000 - $50,000. **Number of placements per year:** 200 - 499.

VOLT ACCOUNTING SPECIALISTS
3055 Wilshire Boulevard, Suite 100, Los Angeles CA 90010. 213/487-3493. **Fax:** 213/487-0186. **Contact:** Manager. **Description:** A permanent employment agency. **Specializes in the areas of:** Accounting/ Auditing. **Positions commonly filled include:** Accountant/Auditor; Cost Estimator. **Benefits available to temporary workers:** Medical Insurance; Paid Holidays; Paid Vacation; Reimbursement Accounts. **Corporate headquarters location:** Orange CA. **Other U.S. locations:** Nationwide. **Average salary range of placements:** $30,000 - $50,000. **Number of placements per year:** 100 - 199.

THE WINDSOR GROUP
700 South Flower Street, Suite 1100, Los Angeles CA 90017. 213/892-6347. **Fax:** 213/651-2273. **Contact:** Recruiter. **Description:** A permanent employment agency. **Specializes in the areas of:** Accounting/ Auditing; Administration; Banking; Personnel/Labor Relations; Secretarial. **Positions commonly filled include:** Accountant/Auditor; Administrative Manager; Customer Service Representative; Human Resources Specialist; Internet Services Manager; Services Sales Representative; Typist/Word Processor. **Average salary range of placements:** $30,000 - $50,000. **Number of placements per year:** 50 - 99.

WOLLBORG-MICHELSON PERSONNEL SERVICE
3480 Buskirk Avenue, Suite 100, Pleasant Hill CA 94523. 925/946-0200. **Contact:** Tom Bruce, Branch Manager. **Description:** A permanent employment agency. **Specializes in the areas of:** Clerical; General Labor. **Positions commonly filled include:** Administrative Worker/Clerk; Bookkeeper; Clerk; Data Entry Clerk; Receptionist; Sales Representative; Secretary; Stenographer; Typist/Word Processor.

WOLLBORG-MICHELSON PERSONNEL SERVICE
400 South El Camino Real, Suite 120, San Mateo CA 94402. 650/342-7600. **Contact:** Manager. **Description:** A permanent employment agency. **Specializes in the areas of:** Administration; General Management; Secretarial; Word Processing. **Positions commonly filled include:** Customer Service Representative. **Average salary range of placements:** $30,000 - $50,000. **Number of placements per year:** 1 - 49.

YOLANDA'S AGENCY
5534 Encino Avenue, Suite 112, Encino CA 91316-1784. 323/872-0083. **Contact:** Daniel A. Guerra, Manager. **Description:** A permanent employment agency. **Specializes in the areas of:** Domestic Help. **Positions commonly filled include:** Housekeeper; Nanny. **Number of placements per year:** 200 - 499.

YOUR PEOPLE PROFESSIONALS
P.O. Box 5609, Santa Maria CA 93456-5609. 805/928-5725. **Toll-free phone:** 800/445-4737. **Fax:** 805/928-9763. **Contact:** Ross Griego, Senior Recruiting Specialist. **E-mail address:** ypp@ypp.com. **Description:** A permanent employment agency that also provides some temporary placements. Client company pays fee. **Specializes in the areas of:** Accounting; Administration; Computer Science/Software; Economics; Engineering; Food; General Management; Insurance; Light Industrial; Marketing; Nonprofit; Personnel/Labor Relations; Printing; Publishing; Retail; Sales; Secretarial. **Positions commonly filled include:** Account Manager; Account Representative; Accountant; Administrative Assistant; Administrative Manager; Advertising Clerk; Advertising Executive; Auditor; Bank Officer/Manager; Blue-Collar Worker Supervisor; Branch Manager; Budget Analyst; Claim Representative; Clerical Supervisor; Computer Engineer; Computer Operator; Computer Programmer; Computer Support Technician; Computer Technician; Credit Manager; Customer Service Representative; Design Engineer; Electrical/Electronics Engineer; Electrician; Environmental Engineer; Financial Analyst; General Manager; Graphic Artist; Graphic Designer; Human Resources Manager; Industrial Production Manager; Insurance Agent/Broker; Management Analyst/Consultant; Management Trainee; Marketing Manager; Marketing Specialist; Medical Assistant; MIS Specialist; Network/Systems Administrator; Operations Manager; Production Manager; Project Manager; Public Relations Specialist; Purchasing Agent/Manager; Quality Control Supervisor; Sales Executive; Sales Manager; Sales Representative; Secretary; Software Engineer; Systems Analyst; Systems Manager; Technical Writer/ Editor; Typist/Word Processor. **Benefits available to temporary workers:** Paid Vacation. **Corporate headquarters location:** This Location. **Number of placements per year:** 500 - 999.

AMY ZIMMERMAN & ASSOCIATES
111 North Sepulveda Boulevard, Suite 243, Manhattan Beach CA 90266. 310/798-6979. **Fax:** 310/798-0019. **Contact:** Manager. **E-mail address:** amyzimm@ earthlink.net. **Description:** A permanent employment agency that also provides some temporary placements and executive searches on a contingency basis. Client company pays fee. **Specializes in the areas of:** Accounting; Administration; Advertising; Computer Science/Software; Finance; Internet Development; Marketing; MIS/EDP; Personnel/Labor Relations; Sales; Scientific; Secretarial; Technical. **Positions commonly filled include:** Account Manager; Account Rep.; Accountant; Administrative Assistant; Administrative Manager; Advertising Clerk; Advertising Executive; AS400 Programmer Analyst; Buyer; Clerical Supervisor; Computer Programmer; Computer Support Technician; Computer Technician; Content Developer; Credit Manager; Customer Service Representative; Database Administrator; Database Manager; Desktop Publishing Specialist; Financial Analyst; Human Resources Manager; Internet Services Manager; Management Trainee; Marketing Manager; Marketing Specialist; MIS Specialist; Network/Systems Administrator; Operations Manager; Public Relations Specialist; Purchasing

Agent/Manager; Sales Executive; Sales Manager; Sales Representative; Secretary; Systems Analyst; Technical Writer/Editor; Typist/Word Processor; Webmaster. **Benefits available to temporary workers:** Bonus Award/Plan. **Corporate headquarters location:** This Location. **Average salary range of placements:** $20,000 - $49,999. **Number of placements per year:** 100 - 199.

TEMPORARY EMPLOYMENT AGENCIES

ACCOUNTANTS EXCHANGE
7100 Hayvenhurst Avenue, Suite 109, Van Nuys CA 91406. 323/933-7411. **Fax:** 818/780-9223. **Contact:** Mark Jay. **Description:** A temporary agency that also provides some permanent placements. **Specializes in the areas of:** Accounting/Auditing. **Positions commonly filled include:** Accountant/Auditor. **Average salary range of placements:** $30,000 - $50,000. **Number of placements per year:** 200 - 499.

ACCOUNTANTS INC.
111 Anza Boulevard, Suite 400, Burlingame CA 94010. 650/579-1111. **Fax:** 650/579-1927. **Contact:** Ursula Williams, Vice President of Marketing. **Description:** A temporary agency that also provides some permanent placements. Founded in 1987. **Specializes in the areas of:** Accounting/Auditing; Finance. **Positions commonly filled include:** Accountant/Auditor; Budget Analyst; Financial Analyst. **Corporate headquarters location:** This Location. **Other U.S. locations:** Nationwide.

ACCOUNTANTS INC.
2200 Powell Street, Suite 1280, Emeryville CA 94608. 510/601-1111. **Contact:** Manager. **Description:** A temporary agency that also provides some temp-to-perm and permanent placements. **Specializes in the areas of:** Accounting/Auditing.

ACCOUNTANTS INC.
555 Montgomery Street, Suite 811, San Francisco CA 94111. 415/434-1411. **Contact:** Manager. **Description:** A temporary agency that also provides some permanent placements. **Specializes in the areas of:** Accounting; Finance.

ACCOUNTING PRINCIPALS
4660 La Jolla Village Drive, Suite 550, San Diego CA 92122. 760/632-1804. **Contact:** Manager. **Description:** A temporary agency. **Specializes in the areas of:** Accounting/Auditing.

ACCUSTAFF INCORPORATED
39899 Balentine Drive, Suite 265, Newark CA 94560. 510/651-7055. **Fax:** 510/657-6389. **Contact:** Manager. **Description:** A temporary agency. **Specializes in the areas of:** Accounting/Auditing; Administration; Engineering; Industrial; Manufacturing; Personnel/Labor Relations; Sales; Secretarial. **Number of placements per year:** 500 - 999.

ACCUSTAFF INCORPORATED
2901 Tasman Drive, Suite 100, Santa Clara CA 95054. 408/727-1782. **Fax:** 408/727-6434. **Contact:** Manager. **Description:** A temporary agency. **Specializes in the areas of:** Accounting/Auditing; Administration; Computer Science/Software; Engineering; Finance; Manufacturing; Technical. **Positions commonly filled include:** Accountant/Auditor; Buyer; Computer Programmer; Design Engineer; Designer; Draftsperson; Electrical/Electronics Engineer; Financial Analyst; Internet Services Manager; Mechanical Engineer; Metallurgical Engineer; Purchasing Agent/Manager; Quality Control Supervisor; Software Engineer; Technical Writer/Editor. **Benefits available to temporary workers:** 401(k); Medical Insurance; Savings Plan. **Average salary range of placements:** More than $50,000. **Number of placements per year:** 1000+.

ALFANO TEMPORARY PERSONNEL
11750 Sorrento Valley Road, San Diego CA 92121. 858/453-9580. **Contact:** Vincent Alfano, Manager. **Description:** A temporary agency. **Specializes in the** areas of: Engineering; Industrial; Manufacturing; Office Support; Technical. **Positions commonly filled include:** Accountant/Auditor; Aerospace Engineer; Ceramics Engineer; Chemical Engineer; Computer Programmer; Design Engineer; Designer; Dietician/Nutritionist; Draftsperson; Electrical/Electronics Engineer; Industrial Engineer; Materials Engineer; Mechanical Engineer; Metallurgical Engineer; MIS Specialist; Science Technologist; Software Engineer. **Average salary range of placements:** $30,000 - $50,000. **Number of placements per year:** 500 - 999.

ANSWERS UNLIMITED
920 South Robertson Boulevard, Suite 3, Los Angeles CA 90035. 310/360-0303. **Contact:** Christine Lieber, President. **Description:** A temporary agency that also offers some permanent placements. **Specializes in the areas of:** Accounting/Auditing; Administration; Advertising; Art/Design; Computer Science/Software; Finance; General Management; Insurance; Legal; Manufacturing; Nonprofit; Personnel/Labor Relations; Publishing; Secretarial. **Positions commonly filled include:** Accountant/Auditor; Administrative Manager; Advertising Clerk; Attorney; Bank Officer/Manager; Branch Manager; Budget Analyst; Buyer; Claim Representative; Clerical Supervisor; Computer Programmer; Credit Manager; Customer Service Representative; Editor; Financial Analyst; General Manager; Human Resources Specialist; Internet Services Manager; Management Trainee; Manufacturer's/ Wholesaler's Sales Rep.; Market Research Analyst; MIS Specialist; Multimedia Designer; Operations/Production Manager; Paralegal; Physician; Purchasing Agent/ Manager; Securities Sales Representative; Services Sales Representative; Software Engineer; Technical Writer/ Editor; Telecommunications Manager; Transportation/ Traffic Specialist; Travel Agent; Typist/Word Processor. **Number of placements per year:** 200 - 499.

AQUENT PARTNERS
3961 MacArthur Boulevard, Suite 109, Newport Beach CA 92660-3015. 949/476-9900. **Toll-free phone:** 877/PARTNER. **Contact:** Brian Guidry, Manager. **World Wide Web address:** http://www.aquent.com. **Description:** A temporary agency that provides placements for creative, Web, and technical professionals. Aquent Partners also provides some temp-to-perm, permanent, and contract placements. **Specializes in the areas of:** Administration; Art/Design; Computer Science/Software; Multimedia; Publishing. **Positions commonly filled include:** Computer Programmer; Graphic Designer; Internet Services Manager; MIS Specialist; Multimedia Designer; Software Engineer; Systems Analyst; Typist/Word Processor; Video Production Coordinator. **Benefits available to temporary workers:** 401(k); Dental Insurance; Medical Insurance. **Other U.S. locations:** Nationwide. **CEO:** John Chuang. **Average salary range of placements:** $30,000 - $50,000. **Number of placements per year:** 200 - 499.

AQUENT PARTNERS
6100 Wilshire Boulevard, Suite 410, Los Angeles CA 90048. 323/634-7000. **Toll-free phone:** 877/PARTNER. **Contact:** Manager. **World Wide Web address:** http://www.aquentpartners.com. **Description:** Aquent Partners is a temporary agency that provides placements for creative, Web, and technical professionals. Aquent Partners also provides some temp-to-perm, permanent, and contract placements. **Specializes in the areas of:** Administration; Art/Design; Computer Science/Software; Marketing. **Positions commonly filled include:** Computer Animator; Computer Engineer; Computer

Operator; Computer Programmer; Computer Support Technician; Computer Technician; Content Developer; Database Administrator; Database Manager; Desktop Publishing Specialist; Editor; Editorial Assistant; Graphic Artist; Graphic Designer; Internet Services Manager; Managing Editor; MIS Specialist; Multimedia Designer; Network/Systems Administrator; Production Manager; Project Manager; Software Engineer; SQL Programmer; Systems Analyst; Systems Manager; Technical Writer/ Editor; Webmaster. **Benefits available to temporary workers:** 401(k); Dental Insurance; Disability Coverage; Medical Insurance. **CEO:** John Chuang.

AQUENT PARTNERS
220 Sansome Street, 2nd Floor, San Francisco CA 94104-4711. 415/399-8800. **Toll-free phone:** 877/PARTNER. **Fax:** 415/399-8804. **Contact:** Lisa Herbinger, Manager. **World Wide Web address:** http://www.aquentpartner.com. **Description:** Aquent Partners is a temporary agency that provides placements for creative, Web, and technical professionals. Aquent Partners also provides some temp-to-perm, permanent, and contract placements. **Specializes in the areas of:** Administration; Art/Design; Computer Science/Software; Marketing. **Positions commonly filled include:** Computer Animator; Computer Engineer; Computer Operator; Computer Programmer; Computer Support Technician; Computer Technician; Content Developer; Database Administrator; Database Manager; Desktop Publishing Specialist; Editor; Editorial Assistant; Graphic Artist; Graphic Designer; Internet Services Manager; Managing Editor; MIS Specialist; Multimedia Designer; Network/Systems Administrator; Production Manager; Project Manager; Software Engineer; SQL Programmer; Systems Analyst; Systems Manager; Technical Writer/Editor; Webmaster. **Benefits available to temporary workers:** 401(k); Dental Insurance; Disability Coverage; Medical Insurance. **CEO:** John Chuang.

AROSE RECRUITING COMPANY, INC.
P.O. Box 2945, Newport Beach CA 92663. 949/642-2696. **Fax:** 949/642-2694. **Contact:** Deborah Prestia, President. **Description:** A temporary agency. **Specializes in the areas of:** Computer Science/Software; Information Technology. **Positions commonly filled include:** Computer Programmer; Internet Services Manager; Management Analyst/Consultant; Multimedia Designer; Software Engineer; Systems Analyst; Technical Writer/Editor; Telecommunications Manager. **Corporate headquarters location:** This Location. **Average salary range of placements:** More than $50,000. **Number of placements per year:** 1 - 49.

ASSOCIATED SOFTWARE CONSULTANTS, INC.
1509 North Sepulveda Boulevard, Manhattan Beach CA 90266-5109. 310/545-5646. **Contact:** Marshall Biggs, President. **E-mail address:** ascboss@deltanet.com. **Description:** A temporary agency that also provides some contract placements. **Specializes in the areas of:** Accounting; Advertising; Banking; Computer Science/ Software; Finance; Insurance. **Positions commonly filled include:** Applications Engineer; AS400 Programmer Analyst; Computer Operator; Computer Programmer; Computer Scientist; Computer Support Technician; Computer Technician; Database Administrator; Database Manager; Desktop Publishing Specialist; Editor; MIS Specialist; Network/Systems Administrator; Software Engineer; SQL Programmer; Systems Analyst; Systems Manager; Technical Writer/Editor; Webmaster. **Average salary range of placements:** More than $50,000. **Number of placements per year:** 50 - 99.

B&M ASSOCIATES INC.
4180 Ruffin Road, Suite 255, San Diego CA 92123-1834. 858/627-9675. **Toll-free phone:** 888/713-9675. **Fax:** 858/627-0703. **Contact:** Cydney Runions, Branch Manager. **E-mail address:** resume-sd@bmanet.com. **World Wide Web address:** http://www.bmanet.com. **Description:** A temporary agency that also provides some permanent placements. **Specializes in the areas of:**

Computer Programming; Computer Science/Software; Engineering; Information Technology; MIS/EDP. **Positions commonly filled include:** Applications Engineer; Computer Engineer; Computer Programmer; Computer Scientist; Computer Support Technician; Computer Technician; Content Developer; Database Administrator; Database Manager; Design Engineer; Draftsperson; Electrical/Electronics Engineer; Electrician; Industrial Engineer; Internet Services Manager; Manufacturing Engineer; Mechanical Engineer; MIS Specialist; Network/Systems Administrator; Quality Assurance Engineer; Software Engineer; SQL Programmer; Systems Analyst; Systems Manager; Webmaster.

B&M ASSOCIATES INC.
3130 South Harbor Boulevard, Suite 360, Santa Ana CA 92704. 714/556-9675. **Contact:** Manager. **World Wide Web address:** http://www.bmanet.com. **Description:** A temporary agency. **Specializes in the areas of:** Computer Science/Software; Engineering; Technical.

BEST TEMPORARY SERVICE
1410 Third Street, Suite 1, Riverside CA 92507. 909/369-1111. **Fax:** 909/369-8291. **Contact:** Marty Ferguson, Vice President. **Description:** A temporary agency that also provides some temp-to-perm and permanent placements. Client company pays fee. **Specializes in the areas of:** Clerical; Industrial; Light Industrial; Scientific; Technical. **Positions commonly filled include:** Account Representative; Administrative Assistant; Blue-Collar Worker Supervisor; Branch Manager; Clerical Supervisor; Computer Engineer; Computer Operator; Construction Contractor; Customer Service Representative; Desktop Publishing Specialist; Draftsperson; Electrician; Human Resources Manager; Mechanical Engineer; Production Manager; Secretary; Typist/Word Processor. **Benefits available to temporary workers:** Bonus Award/Plan; Medical Insurance. **Corporate headquarters location:** This Location. **Other U.S. locations:** Corona CA; Ontario CA. **Average salary range of placements:** $20,000 - $29,999. **Number of placements per year:** 500 - 999.

BLAINE & ASSOCIATES
2029 Century Park East, Suite 1080, Los Angeles CA 90067. 310/785-0560. **Fax:** 310/785-9670. **Contact:** Carrie Blaine, President. **World Wide Web address:** http://www.blaineandassociates.com. **Description:** Blaine & Associates is a temporary agency. **Specializes in the areas of:** Accounting; Administration; Advertising; Secretarial. **Positions commonly filled include:** Account Manager; Account Representative; Administrative Assistant; Administrative Manager; Advertising Clerk; Clerical Supervisor; Desktop Publishing Specialist; Editorial Assistant; General Manager; Graphic Artist; Graphic Designer; Human Resources Manager; Management Trainee; MIS Specialist; Paralegal; Secretary; Systems Analyst; Typist/Word Processor; Webmaster. **Corporate headquarters location:** This Location. **Other U.S. locations:** Phoenix AZ; Las Vegas NV. **Average salary range of placements:** $30,000 - $49,999. **Number of placements per year:** 100 - 199.

BLUE MOON PERSONNEL INC.
369 Pine Street, Suite 200, San Francisco CA 94104. 415/394-9500. **Fax:** 415/394-9540. **Contact:** Manager. **Description:** A temporary agency. **Specializes in the areas of:** Nonprofit; Office Support. **Positions commonly filled include:** Administrative Assistant; Typist/Word Processor. **Corporate headquarters location:** This Location. **Average salary range of placements:** $20,000 - $29,999. **Number of placements per year:** 1 - 49.

BRADFORD STAFF, INC.
100 California Street, 14th Floor, San Francisco CA 94111. 415/362-0435. **Fax:** 415/362-4735. **Contact:** Manager. **E-mail address:** sf@bradfordstaff.com. **World Wide Web address:** http://www.bradfordstaff. com. **Description:** A temporary agency that also

provides some permanent and temp-to-perm placements. **Specializes in the areas of:** Accounting/Auditing; Administration; General Management; Legal; Manufacturing; Secretarial; Technical. **Positions commonly filled include:** Abstractor/Indexer; Account Representative; Accountant; Administrative Assistant; Administrative Manager; Assistant Manager; Bank Officer/Manager; Brokerage Clerk; Claim Rep.; Clerical Supervisor; Computer Programmer; Customer Service Representative; Database Manager; Design Engineer; Editorial Assistant; General Manager; Human Resources Manager; Management Trainee; Managing Editor; Market Research Analyst; Marketing Manager; Marketing Specialist; Operations Manager; Paralegal; Project Manager; Quality Control Supervisor; Sales Executive; Secretary; Securities Sales Representative; Services Sales Representative; Software Engineer; Systems Analyst; Technical Writer/Editor; Typist/Word Processor; Underwriter/Assistant Underwriter. **Benefits available to temporary workers:** 401(k); Bonus Award/Plan; Credit Union; Dental Insurance; Medical Insurance; Paid Holidays; Profit Sharing. **Corporate headquarters location:** This Location. **Other U.S. locations:** Oakland CA; Palo Alto CA; San Rafael CA; Walnut Creek CA. **Average salary range of placements:** $30,000 - $50,000. **Number of placements per year:** 500 - 999.

CDI TECHNICAL SERVICES
3401 West Sunflower Avenue, Suite 225, Santa Ana CA 92704. 714/556-8022. **Fax:** 714/641-0621. **Contact:** Maria Kludt, Recruiter. **E-mail address:** mkludt@cdicorp.com. **World Wide Web address:** http://www.cdicorp.com. **Description:** A temporary agency. **Specializes in the areas of:** Administration; Architecture/Construction; Art/Design; Biology; Computer Science/Software; Economics; Engineering; Industrial; Manufacturing; Personnel/Labor Relations; Technical. **Positions commonly filled include:** Aerospace Engineer; Agricultural Engineer; Aircraft Mechanic/Engine Specialist; Architect; Biochemist; Biological Scientist; Biomedical Engineer; Buyer; Chemical Engineer; Chemist; Civil Engineer; Clinical Lab Technician; Computer Programmer; Construction Contractor; Cost Estimator; Customer Service Representative; Design Engineer; Designer; Draftsperson; Editor; Electrical/Electronics Engineer; Electrician; Environmental Engineer; Financial Analyst; Geographer; Geologist/Geophysicist; Industrial Engineer; Industrial Production Manager; Internet Services Manager; Landscape Architect; Librarian; Management Analyst/Consultant; Mathematician; Mechanical Engineer; Metallurgical Engineer; MIS Specialist; Multimedia Designer; Operations/Production Manager; Petroleum Engineer; Purchasing Agent/Manager; Quality Control Supervisor; Science Technologist; Software Engineer; Stationary Engineer; Statistician; Surveyor; Systems Analyst; Technical Writer/Editor; Telecommunications Manager; Transportation/Traffic Specialist; Urban/Regional Planner. **Corporate headquarters location:** Philadelphia PA. **Other U.S. locations:** Nationwide. **International locations:** Worldwide. **Average salary range of placements:** $30,000 - $50,000. **Number of placements per year:** 100 - 199.

CAREER IMAGES
2049 Century Park East, Suite 3730, Los Angeles CA 90067. 310/553-5208. **Fax:** 310/553-8098. **Contact:** Ms. Chris Donaldson, President. **Description:** A temporary agency that also provides some permanent placements. The company focuses on entry-level to middle management staffing for law firms, corporations, and the entertainment industry. **Specializes in the areas of:** Accounting/Auditing; Clerical; Legal; Secretarial. **Positions commonly filled include:** Accountant/Auditor; Human Resources Specialist; Legal Secretary; Management Trainee; Paralegal; Receptionist; Typist/Word Processor. **Average salary range of placements:** $25,000 - $65,000. **Number of placements per year:** 1 - 49.

CHAMPAGNE PERSONNEL
3849 Birch Street, Newport Beach CA 92660. 949/756-1844. **Fax:** 949/756-0904. **Contact:** Pat Hutt, Assignment Supervisor. **Description:** A temporary agency that also provides some temp-to-perm and permanent placements. **Specializes in the areas of:** Accounting/Auditing; Administration; Banking; Finance; Human Resources; Insurance; Marketing; MIS/EDP; Nonprofit; Office Support; Sales; Secretarial. **Positions commonly filled include:** Accountant; Administrative Assistant; Administrative Manager; Buyer; Computer Operator; Customer Service Representative; Human Resources Manager; Secretary; Technical Writer/Editor; Typist/Word Processor. **Corporate headquarters location:** This Location. **Average salary range of placements:** $30,000 - $50,000. **Number of placements per year:** 1000+.

CHIPTON-ROSS
343 Main Street, El Segundo CA 90245. 310/414-7800. **Contact:** Manager. **Description:** A temporary agency. **Specializes in the areas of:** Technical.

COAST PERSONNEL
2295 De La Cruz Boulevard, Santa Clara CA 95050-3020. 408/653-2100. **Fax:** 408/653-2109. **Contact:** Recruiting Manager. **Description:** A temporary agency. **Specializes in the areas of:** Accounting/Auditing; Engineering; Technical. **Positions commonly filled include:** Accountant/Auditor; Aerospace Engineer; Buyer; Chemical Engineer; Chemist; Civil Engineer; Computer Programmer; Design Engineer; Designer; Draftsperson; Editor; Electrical/Electronics Engineer; Electrician; Financial Analyst; Human Resources Specialist; Mechanical Engineer; MIS Specialist; Purchasing Agent/Manager; Quality Control Supervisor; Software Engineer; Structural Engineer; Typist/Word Processor. **Benefits available to temporary workers:** Dental Insurance; Medical Insurance; Paid Holidays; Paid Vacation. **Corporate headquarters location:** This Location. **Average salary range of placements:** $30,000 - $50,000. **Number of placements per year:** 500 - 999.

COMPLIMATE TECHNICAL STAFFING
150 West Iowa Avenue, Suite 203, Sunnyvale CA 94086. 408/733-8994. **Fax:** 408/773-0968. **Contact:** Manager. **E-mail address:** careerdesk@complimate.com. **World Wide Web address:** http://www.complimate.com. **Description:** A temporary agency that provides personnel for electronic equipment manufacturers and information technology companies. The agency also provides some permanent placements. **Specializes in the areas of:** Technical. **Positions commonly filled include:** Computer Programmer; Design Engineer; Internet Services Manager; MIS Specialist; Multimedia Designer; Software Engineer; Systems Analyst; Technical Writer/Editor; Telecommunications Manager. **Average salary range of placements:** $30,000 - $50,000. **Number of placements per year:** 1000+.

CONTRACTORS LABOR POOL
1504 East Katella Avenue, Anaheim CA 92805. 714/456-0999. **Fax:** 714/456-0996. **Contact:** Dan Cekosh, Manager. **World Wide Web address:** http://www.clp.com. **Description:** A temporary agency that places construction personnel with licensed contractors. Founded in 1987. **Specializes in the areas of:** Administration; Construction. **Positions commonly filled include:** Administrative Manager; Construction Contractor; Construction Manager; Electrician. **Benefits available to temporary workers:** Dental Insurance; Medical Insurance. **Corporate headquarters location:** Reno NV. **Other U.S. locations:** Altadena CA; Emeryville CA; Sacramento CA; San Jose CA; Tarzana CA; Everett WA; Seattle WA; Tacoma WA.

CREATIVE ASSETS - SAN FRANCISCO
562 Mission Street, Suite 601, San Francisco CA 94105. 415/357-0900. **Toll-free phone:** 888/304-9600. **Fax:** 415/357-0901. **Contact:** Lara Thurman, Recruiting

Assistant. **E-mail address:** lara@creativeassets.com. **World Wide Web address:** http://www.creativeassets. com. **Description:** A temporary agency focusing on the placement of freelance graphic and digital professionals. Creative Assets also provides some permanent placements. Founded in 1990. Client company pays fee. **Specializes in the areas of:** Art/Design. **Positions commonly filled include:** Computer Animator; Graphic Artist; Graphic Designer; Multimedia Designer; Photographer; Prepress Worker; Program Manager; Project Manager. **Benefits available to temporary workers:** 401(k); Health Benefits. **Corporate headquarters location:** Seattle WA. **Other area locations:** Los Angeles CA. **Other U.S. locations:** Portland OR.

CROSSROADS STAFFING SERVICE

820 Bay Avenue, Suite 144, Capitola CA 95010. 831/476-8367. **Contact:** Catherine Patterson, Branch Manager. **Description:** A temporary agency. **Specializes in the areas of:** Accounting/Auditing; Administration; Computer Science/Software; Engineering; Finance; Food; General Management; Industrial; Insurance; Legal; Manufacturing; Personnel/Labor Relations; Publishing; Secretarial; Technical. **Positions commonly filled include:** Accountant/Auditor; Blue-Collar Worker Supervisor; Branch Manager; Buyer; Chemical Engineer; Civil Engineer; Clerical Supervisor; Computer Programmer; Credit Manager; Customer Service Rep.; Design Engineer; Designer; Draftsperson; Electrical/ Electronics Engineer; Environmental Engineer; General Manager; Human Resources Specialist; Industrial Engineer; Industrial Production Manager; Mechanical Engineer; MIS Specialist; Operations/Production Manager; Purchasing Agent/Manager; Quality Control Supervisor; Services Sales Representative; Systems Analyst; Typist/Word Processor. **Benefits available to temporary workers:** Medical Insurance; Paid Holidays. **Corporate headquarters location:** San Jose CA.

CULVER STAFFING RESOURCES

8885 Rio San Diego Drive, Suite 320, San Diego CA 92108. 619/297-6400. **Fax:** 619/297-5288. **Contact:** Angela Vasquez, Area Manager. **Description:** A temporary agency. **Specializes in the areas of:** Accounting/Auditing; Administration; Computer Science/Software; Food; General Management; Health/ Medical; Insurance; Secretarial. **Positions commonly filled include:** Administrative Assistant; Administrative Manager; Advertising Clerk; Assistant Manager; Blue-Collar Worker Supervisor; Branch Manager; Claim Rep.; Clerical Supervisor; Computer Operator; Computer Programmer; Credit Manager; Customer Service Rep.; Database Manager; General Manager; Graphic Artist; Graphic Designer; Human Resources Manager; Internet Services Manager; Management Trainee; Medical Records Technician; Secretary; Software Engineer; Technical Writer/Editor; Typist/Word Processor; Underwriter/Assistant Underwriter. **Benefits available to temporary workers:** Medical Insurance; Paid Vacation. **Other U.S. locations:** Salt Lake City UT. **Average salary range of placements:** $30,000 - $50,000. **Number of placements per year:** 1 - 49.

DEC HEALTHCARE PERSONNEL

1601 East Chapman Avenue, Fullerton CA 92831. 714/447-0826. **Fax:** 714/447-0280. **Contact:** Owner. **Description:** A temporary agency that also provides some contract services. **Specializes in the areas of:** Health/Medical. **Positions commonly filled include:** Chiropractor; Claim Representative; Clinical Lab Technician; Counselor; Customer Service Rep.; Dental Assistant/Dental Hygienist; Dentist; EEG Technologist; EKG Technician; Emergency Medical Technician; Health Services Manager; Human Resources Specialist; Licensed Practical Nurse; Medical Assistant; Medical Records Technician; Nuclear Medicine Technologist; Occupational Therapist; Pharmacist; Physical Therapist; Physician Assistant; Radiological Technologist; Registered Nurse; Respiratory Therapist; Surgical Technician; Typist/Word Processor. **Number of placements per year:** 500 - 999.

DENTAL PLUS MEDICAL (DPM)

490 Post Street, Suite 1701, San Francisco CA 94102. 415/677-0961. **Contact:** Beverly Davis, Owner. **Description:** A temporary agency that also provides some permanent placements. **Specializes in the areas of:** Health/Medical. **Positions commonly filled include:** Dental Assistant/Dental Hygienist; Dentist. **Average salary range of placements:** $30,000 - $50,000. **Number of placements per year:** 100 - 199.

DRAKE OFFICE OVERLOAD

17744 Skypark Circle, Suite 290, Irvine CA 92614. 949/474-2974. **Contact:** Office Manager. **Description:** A temporary agency that also provides some permanent placements. **Specializes in the areas of:** Clerical; Data Processing. **Positions commonly filled include:** Bookkeeper; Clerk; Computer Operator; Data Entry Clerk; Legal Secretary; Receptionist; Secretary; Stenographer; Typist/Word Processor. **Number of placements per year:** 500 - 999.

DRAKE OFFICE OVERLOAD

19401 South Vermont Avenue, Suite I-102, Torrance CA 90502. 310/515-4800. **Contact:** Manager. **Description:** A temporary agency. Drake Office Overload also provides some temp-to-perm placements of clerical, word processing, accounting, customer service, MIS, and light industrial personnel. **Specializes in the areas of:** Accounting/Auditing; Administration; Computer Science/Software; Engineering; General Management; Health/Medical; Industrial; Manufacturing; Personnel/ Labor Relations; Publishing; Sales; Secretarial; Technical; Transportation. **Positions commonly filled include:** Accountant/Auditor; Administrative Manager; Blue-Collar Worker Supervisor; Branch Manager; Buyer; Chemist; Clerical Supervisor; Computer Programmer; Credit Manager; Customer Service Representative; Electrical/Electronics Engineer; General Manager; Health Services Manager; Human Resources Specialist; Industrial Production Manager; Medical Records Technician; MIS Specialist; Operations/Production Manager; Quality Assurance Engineer; Quality Control Supervisor; Services Sales Representative; Software Engineer; Systems Analyst; Technical Writer/Editor; Telecommunications Manager; Transportation/Traffic Specialist; Typist/Word Processor. **Other U.S. locations:** FL; NC; VA; WA. **Number of placements per year:** 1000+.

ENGINEERING TECHNICAL SERVICE (ETS)

194-B Wikiup Drive, Santa Rosa CA 95403-7757. 707/546-4300. **Fax:** 707/546-2444. **Contact:** President. **Description:** A temporary agency. **Specializes in the areas of:** Engineering; Manufacturing; Technical. **Positions commonly filled include:** Aerospace Engineer; Biomedical Engineer; Ceramics Engineer; Chemical Engineer; Chemist; Civil Engineer; Design Engineer; Designer; Draftsperson; EKG Technician; Electrical/Electronics Engineer; Environmental Engineer; Industrial Engineer; Landscape Architect; Materials Engineer; Mechanical Engineer; Metallurgical Engineer; Physicist; Software Engineer; Structural Engineer; Technical Writer/Editor. **Average salary range of placements:** $30,000 - $50,000. **Number of placements per year:** 50 - 99.

EXECUTIVE TEMPS

2321 West Olive, Suite F, Burbank CA 91506. 818/563-2939. **Contact:** Manager. **Description:** A temporary agency. **Specializes in the areas of:** Entertainment.

EXPRESS PERSONNEL SERVICES

11870 Santa Monica Boulevard, Suite 208, Los Angeles CA 90025. 310/571-2200. **Fax:** 310/571-2202. **Contact:** Manager. **E-mail address:** temps4you@aol.com. **Description:** A temporary agency that also provides some direct-hire placements. **Specializes in the areas of:** Accounting/Auditing; Administration; Finance; General Management; Personnel/Labor Relations; Secretarial. **Positions commonly filled include:** Accountant/Auditor; Brokerage Clerk; Buyer; Clerical Supervisor; Financial Analyst; General Manager; Human Resources

Generalist; Property and Real Estate Manager; Secretary; Typist/Word Processor. **Number of placements per year:** 50 - 99.

FAITHFUL SUPPORT SYSTEMS
2245 First Street, Suite 101, Simi Valley CA 93065-1987. 805/522-8812. **Fax:** 805/522-8826. **Contact:** Manager. **Description:** A temporary agency focusing on medical billing and collections positions. The agency also provides placements in middle management, accounting, legal, and clerical professions. **Specializes in the areas of:** Accounting; Health/Medical; Legal; Secretarial. **Positions commonly filled include:** Billing Clerk; Claim Representative; Collections Agent; Financial Analyst; Paralegal. **Number of placements per year:** 1 - 49.

PAT FRANKLYN ASSOCIATES INC.
655 Redwood Highway, Suite 2739, Mill Valley CA 94941. 415/388-1894. **Fax:** 415/388-1897. **Contact:** Rhona Leibof, Partner. **Description:** A temporary agency. **Specializes in the areas of:** Accounting/Auditing; Administration; Computer Science/Software; Legal; Secretarial. **Positions commonly filled include:** Attorney; Computer Programmer; Credit Manager; Customer Service Representative; Human Resources Specialist; Internet Services Manager; MIS Specialist; Paralegal; Software Engineer; Systems Analyst; Typist/Word Processor. **Average salary range of placements:** $20,000 - $29,999. **Number of placements per year:** 100 - 199.

FULL SERVICE TEMPORARIES
255 North Market Street, Suite 248, San Jose CA 95110. 408/295-6350. **Fax:** 408/295-6355. **Contact:** Operations Manager. **Description:** A temporary agency that also provides some permanent placements. **Specializes in the areas of:** Clerical; Computer Hardware/Software; Design; Light Industrial; Professional; Publishing; Technical. **Positions commonly filled include:** Assembler; Clerical Supervisor; Design Engineer; Draftsperson; Inspector/Tester/Grader; Light Industrial Worker; Purchasing Agent/Manager; Software Engineer; Technician. **Benefits available to temporary workers:** Medical Insurance; Paid Holidays; Paid Vacation. **Number of placements per year:** 1000+.

GARNETT STAFFING
16195 Monterey Road, Morgan Hill CA 95037. 408/778-0729. **Fax:** 408/779-9154. **Contact:** Ernie Filice, Manager. **Description:** A temporary agency that also provides some permanent placements. **Specializes in the areas of:** Engineering; Food; General Management; Manufacturing; Sales; Secretarial; Technical; Transportation. **Positions commonly filled include:** Accountant/Auditor; Administrative Manager; Blue-Collar Worker Supervisor; Clerical Supervisor; Customer Service Representative; General Manager; Industrial Production Manager; Restaurant/Food Service Manager; Services Sales Representative; Transportation/Traffic Specialist; Truck Driver; Typist/Word Processor. **Average salary range of placements:** $20,000 - $29,999. **Number of placements per year:** 500 - 999.

GOLDSTEIN & ASSOCIATES
8601 Wilshire Boulevard, Suite 1101, Beverly Hills CA 90211. 310/657-7161. **Fax:** 310/657-7166. **Contact:** David Goldstein, Owner. **Description:** A temporary agency that also provides some permanent and contract placements. **Specializes in the areas of:** Accounting/Auditing; Administration; Advertising; Architecture/Construction; Art/Design; Banking; Computer Science/Software; General Management; Health/Medical; Insurance; Legal; Nonprofit; Personnel/Labor Relations; Publishing; Retail; Sales; Secretarial. **Positions commonly filled include:** Accountant/Auditor; Attorney; Branch Manager; Brokerage Clerk; Budget Analyst; Buyer; Clerical Supervisor; Computer Programmer; Counselor; Credit Manager; Customer Service Representative; Designer; Financial Analyst; Human Resources Specialist; Internet Services Manager; Management Analyst/Consultant; Management Trainee;

Medical Records Technician; MIS Specialist; Paralegal; Property and Real Estate Manager; Purchasing Agent/Manager; Securities Sales Representative; Software Engineer; Systems Analyst; Technical Writer/Editor; Telecommunications Manager; Typist/Word Processor. **Average salary range of placements:** $30,000 - $50,000. **Number of placements per year:** 1 - 49.

HIREKNOWLEDGE
118 King Street, Suite 525, San Francisco CA 94107. 415/538-7892. **Toll-free phone:** 800/937-3622. **Fax:** 415/538-7893. **Contact:** Recruiter. **World Wide Web address:** http://www.hireknowledge.com. **Description:** A temporary agency that also provides some permanent placements. Client company pays fee. **Specializes in the areas of:** Advertising; Art/Design; Computer Science/Software; Internet Development; Internet Marketing; MIS/EDP; Printing; Publishing. **Positions commonly filled include:** Applications Engineer; AS400 Programmer Analyst; Computer Animator; Computer Engineer; Computer Operator; Computer Programmer; Computer Scientist; Computer Support Technician; Content Developer; Database Administrator; Editor; Editorial Assistant; Graphic Artist; Graphic Designer; Internet Services Manager; Managing Editor; MIS Specialist; Multimedia Designer; Network/Systems Administrator; Software Engineer; SQL Programmer; Systems Analyst; Systems Manager; Technical Writer/Editor; Webmaster. **Benefits available to temporary workers:** 401(k); Direct Deposit; Health Benefits; Vacation Days (1 - 5). **Corporate headquarters location:** Providence RI. **Other U.S. locations:** Nationwide. **Average salary range of placements:** $30,000 - $49,999. **Number of placements per year:** 200 - 499.

INDUSTRIAL SERVICES COMPANY
1070 Concord Avenue, Suite 112, Concord CA 94520. 925/680-4422. **Fax:** 925/680-4482. **Contact:** Jim Stielow, Manager. **World Wide Web address:** http://www.workers.com. **Description:** A temporary agency. **Specializes in the areas of:** Architecture/Construction; Engineering; Industrial; Manufacturing. **Positions commonly filled include:** Aircraft Mechanic/Engine Specialist; Architect; Automotive Mechanic; Blue-Collar Worker Supervisor; Civil Engineer; Construction and Building Inspector; Design Engineer; Draftsperson; Electrical/Electronics Engineer; Electrician; Environmental Engineer; Industrial Production Manager; Mechanical Engineer; Petroleum Engineer; Structural Engineer. **Benefits available to temporary workers:** Paid Holidays. **Average salary range of placements:** $20,000 - $29,999. **Number of placements per year:** 1000+.

INITIAL FINANCIAL STAFFING
17800 Castleton Street, Suite 100, City of Industry CA 91748. 626/912-0231. **Contact:** Manager. **Description:** A temporary agency. **Specializes in the areas of:** Finance.

INTERIM PERSONNEL
15260 Ventura Boulevard, Suite 1220, Sherman Oaks CA 91403-5347. 818/789-8211. **Contact:** Manager. **Description:** A temporary agency. **Specializes in the areas of:** Industrial; Manufacturing; Personnel/Labor Relations. **Positions commonly filled include:** Administrative Manager; Bookkeeper; Buyer; Clerical Supervisor; Clerk; Computer Operator; Customer Service Representative; Factory Worker; Human Resources Specialist; Legal Secretary; Medical Secretary; Quality Control Supervisor; Receptionist; Stenographer; Technician; Typist/Word Processor. **Benefits available to temporary workers:** Dental Insurance; Medical Insurance. **Corporate headquarters location:** Fort Lauderdale FL. **Other U.S. locations:** Nationwide. **Number of placements per year:** 500 - 999.

INTERIM PERSONNEL
2377 North Oxnard Boulevard, Oxnard CA 93030. 805/983-2000. **Contact:** Manager. **Description:** A

temporary agency. **Specializes in the areas of:** Architecture/Construction; Clerical; Food; Health/ Medical; Manufacturing; Personnel/Labor Relations; Sales; Technical. **Positions commonly filled include:** Accountant/Auditor; Buyer; Clerk; Computer Operator; Computer Programmer; Data Entry Clerk; Draftsperson; Factory Worker; Human Resources Manager; Nurse; Petroleum Engineer; Physicist; Purchasing Agent/ Manager; Receptionist; Secretary; Statistician; Stenographer; Support Personnel; Systems Analyst; Typist/Word Processor; Waitstaff. **Corporate headquarters location:** Fort Lauderdale FL. **Other U.S. locations:** Nationwide. **Number of placements per year:** 1000+.

INTERIM PERSONNEL
475 Sansome Street, Suite 730, San Francisco CA 94111. 415/391-5979. **Contact:** Branch Manager. **Description:** A temporary agency. **Specializes in the areas of:** Accounting/Auditing; Clerical; MIS/EDP; Sales; Secretarial. **Positions commonly filled include:** Administrative Assistant; Clerk; Human Resources Manager; Legal Secretary; Receptionist; Secretary; Stenographer; Typist/Word Processor. **Corporate headquarters location:** Fort Lauderdale FL. **Other U.S. locations:** Nationwide. **Number of placements per year:** 200 - 499.

INTERIM PERSONNEL
1610 Arden Way, Suite 287, Sacramento CA 95815. 916/927-7789. **Contact:** Manager. **Description:** A temporary agency. **Specializes in the areas of:** Clerical; Construction; Food; Health/Medical; Industrial; Insurance; Legal; Manufacturing; MIS/EDP; Sales. **Positions commonly filled include:** Administrative Assistant; Bookkeeper; Clerk; Computer Programmer; Construction Trade Worker; Customer Service Representative; Data Entry Clerk; Draftsperson; Driver; Editor; EDP Specialist; Factory Worker; Food Production Worker; Legal Secretary; Light Industrial Worker; Medical Secretary; Receptionist; Sales Representative; Secretary; Statistician; Stenographer; Transcriptionist; Typist/Word Processor. **Number of placements per year:** 1000+.

INTERIM PERSONNEL
2615 Pacific Coast Highway, Suite 120, Hermosa Beach CA 90254. 310/318-1561. **Fax:** 310/318-1776. **Contact:** Jeri McKay, Manager. **Description:** A temporary agency that also provides some permanent placements. **Specializes in the areas of:** Light Industrial; Manufacturing; Office Support. **Positions commonly filled include:** Administrative Assistant; Executive Assistant. **Corporate headquarters location:** Fort Lauderdale FL. **Other U.S. locations:** Nationwide. **Number of placements per year:** 1000+.

INTERIM PERSONNEL
75 South Milpitas Boulevard, Suite 107, Milpitas CA 95035. **Fax:** 408/934-9981. **Contact:** Branch Manager. **Description:** A temporary agency. **Specializes in the areas of:** Administration; Engineering; General Management; Manufacturing; Personnel/Labor Relations; Sales; Technical. **Positions commonly filled include:** Administrative Manager; Automotive Mechanic; Branch Manager; Budget Analyst; Buyer; Claim Rep.; Credit Manager; Customer Service Rep.; Editor; Electrician; Environmental Engineer; Human Resources Specialist; Human Service Worker; Internet Services Manager; Management Trainee; Public Relations Specialist; Purchasing Agent/Manager; Restaurant/Food Service Manager; Software Engineer; Structural Engineer; Technical Writer/Editor; Telecommunications Manager. **Corporate headquarters location:** Fort Lauderdale FL. **Other U.S. locations:** Nationwide.

INTERTEC PERSONNEL
1045 East Green Street, Pasadena CA 91106. 626/584-1043. **Fax:** 626/584-1941. **Contact:** Lisa Perez, Branch Manager. **Description:** A temporary agency. **Specializes in the areas of:** Accounting/Auditing; Industrial;

Personnel/Labor Relations; Secretarial. **Positions commonly filled include:** Accountant/Auditor; Administrative Manager; Clerical Supervisor; Customer Service Representative; Human Service Worker; Purchasing Agent/Manager. **Number of placements per year:** 1000+.

ANITA R. JOHNSON & ASSOCIATES
2131 Capitol Avenue, Suite 305, Sacramento CA 95816. 916/329-9100. **Contact:** Cordelia R. Kirkland, Associate. **Description:** Anita R. Johnson & Associates is a temporary agency. **Specializes in the areas of:** Accounting/Auditing; Bookkeeping. **Benefits available to temporary workers:** Paid Vacation. **Number of placements per year:** 1 - 49.

KELLY IT RESOURCES
3031 Tisch Way, Suite 300, San Jose CA 95128. 408/557-4900. **Contact:** Chuck Sproat, Manager. **Description:** A temporary agency. **Specializes in the areas of:** Accounting/Auditing; Administration; Biology; Engineering; Finance; Manufacturing; Personnel/Labor Relations; Secretarial; Technical. **Positions commonly filled include:** Accountant/Auditor; Administrative Manager; Agricultural Engineer; Biochemist; Biomedical Engineer; Chemical Engineer; Chemist; Clinical Lab Technician; Computer Programmer; Credit Manager; Design Engineer; Designer; Draftsperson; Electrical/Electronics Engineer; Environmental Engineer; Financial Analyst; Human Resources Specialist; Management Analyst/Consultant; MIS Specialist; Multimedia Designer; Purchasing Agent/Manager; Quality Control Supervisor; Software Engineer; Systems Analyst; Technical Writer/Editor; Telecommunications Manager. **Benefits available to temporary workers:** 401(k); Dental Insurance; Medical Insurance; Paid Holidays; Paid Vacation. **Corporate headquarters location:** Troy MI.

KELLY SCIENTIFIC RESOURCES
625 The City Drive, Suite 375, Orange CA 92868. 714/971-0721. **Fax:** 714/971-2443. **Contact:** Branch Manager. **World Wide Web address:** http://www. kellyscientific.com. **Description:** A temporary agency. **Specializes in the areas of:** Biomedical; Biotechnology; Chemicals; Environmental; Food; Petrochemical; Pharmaceuticals.

KELLY SERVICES, INC.
21250 Hawthorne Boulevard, Suite 750, Torrance CA 90503. 310/543-3589. **Fax:** 310/316-6145. **Contact:** Ms. Pat Georgen, Senior Evaluation Manager. **World Wide Web address:** http://www.kellyservices.com. **Description:** A temporary agency. **Specializes in the areas of:** Clerical; Light Industrial; Manufacturing; Office Support; Secretarial; Technical. **Positions commonly filled include:** Accountant/Auditor; Administrative Manager; Aerospace Engineer; Biochemist; Blue-Collar Worker Supervisor; Branch Manager; Buyer; Chemical Engineer; Clerical Supervisor; Computer Programmer; Design Engineer; Designer; Human Resources Specialist; Industrial Engineer; Internet Services Manager; Management Analyst/Consultant; Management Trainee; Paralegal; Software Engineer; Systems Analyst; Technical Writer/Editor; Telecommunications Manager; Typist/Word Processor. **Benefits available to temporary workers:** Credit Union; Paid Holidays; Paid Vacation. **Corporate headquarters location:** Troy MI.

KELLY TECHNICAL SERVICES
1400 North Harbor Boulevard, Suite 103, Fullerton CA 92835. 714/879-9763. **Toll-free phone:** 800/659-1401. **Fax:** 714/525-6980. **Contact:** Greg Inguagiato, Technical Recruiting Manager. **World Wide Web address:** http://www.dice.com/kts1. **Description:** A temporary agency that also provides some contract services. Client company pays fee. **Specializes in the areas of:** Accounting/Auditing; Personnel/Labor Relations; Technical. **Positions commonly filled include:** Accountant; Applications Engineer; Architect; AS400 Programmer Analyst; Auditor; Budget Analyst;

Civil Engineer; Computer Animator; Computer Engineer; Computer Operator; Computer Programmer; Computer Scientist; Computer Support Technician; Computer Technician; Construction Contractor; Content Developer; Database Administrator; Database Manager; Design Engineer; Desktop Publishing Specialist; Draftsperson; Electrical/Electronics Engineer; Graphic Artist; Graphic Designer; Human Resources Manager; Industrial Engineer; Internet Services Manager; Manufacturing Engineer; Mechanical Engineer; Metallurgical Engineer; MIS Specialist; Multimedia Designer; Network/Systems Administrator; Project Manager; Purchasing Agent/ Manager; Quality Assurance Engineer; Quality Control Supervisor; Software Engineer; SQL Programmer; Systems Analyst; Systems Manager; Technical Writer/Editor; Telecommunications Manager; Transportation/Traffic Specialist; Webmaster. **Benefits available to temporary workers:** 401(k); Paid Holidays; Vacation Pay. **Corporate headquarters location:** Troy MI. **Number of placements per year:** 200 - 499.

KLEIN & ASSOCIATES
3510 Torrance Boulevard, Suite 112, Torrance CA 90503. 310/540-3140. **Toll-free phone:** 800/475-5346. **Fax:** 310/540-5030. **Contact:** Robert Klein, Owner. **Description:** A temporary agency that also provides some permanent placements. **Specializes in the areas of:** Accounting/Auditing; Administration; Architecture/ Construction; Banking; Computer Science/Software; Economics; Engineering; Finance; Industrial; Legal; Light Industrial; Nonprofit; Personnel/Labor Relations; Sales; Secretarial; Technical. **Positions commonly filled include:** Accountant/Auditor; Buyer; Civil Engineer; Clerical Supervisor; Computer Operator; Computer Programmer; Controller; Cost Estimator; Design Engineer; Draftsperson; Economist; Editor; Editorial Assistant; Electrician; Geologist/Geophysicist; Graphic Artist; Graphic Designer; Human Resources Manager; Industrial Engineer; Internet Services Manager; Manufacturing Engineer; MIS Specialist; Operations Manager; Paralegal; Purchasing Agent/Manager; Sales Engineer; Sales Executive; Sales Manager; Sales Rep.; Secretary; Software Engineer; Statistician; Systems Analyst; Systems Manager; Teacher/Professor; Technical Writer/Editor; Telecommunications Manager; Typist/ Word Processor; Webmaster. **Benefits available to temporary workers:** Medical Insurance; Paid Holidays; Paid Vacation. **Corporate headquarters location:** This Location. **Average salary range of placements:** $30,000 - $50,000. **Number of placements per year:** 200 - 499.

LAB SUPPORT INC.
7901 Stoneridge Drive, Suite 526, Pleasanton CA 94588-3600. 925/416-0840. **Toll-free phone:** 800/995-7378. **Contact:** Angela Gatewood, Account Manager. **Description:** A temporary agency. **Specializes in the areas of:** Biology; Health/Medical; Industrial; Manufacturing; Personnel/Labor Relations; Scientific; Technical. **Positions commonly filled include:** Agricultural Engineer; Biochemist; Biological Scientist; Biomedical Engineer; Chemist; Food Scientist/ Technologist; Petroleum Engineer; Quality Control Supervisor; Science Technologist. **Benefits available to temporary workers:** 401(k); Bonus Award/Plan; Medical Insurance; Paid Holidays; Stock Purchase. **Corporate headquarters location:** Calabasas CA. **Other U.S. locations:** Nationwide. **Average salary range of placements:** $20,000 - $29,999. **Number of placements per year:** 100 - 199.

LAB SUPPORT INC.
HEALTHCARE FINANCIAL STAFFING
26651 West Agoura Road, Calabasas CA 91302. **Toll-free phone:** 800/998-3332. **Fax:** 818/878-7940. **Contact:** Manager. **E-mail address:** mail@labsupport. com. **World Wide Web address:** http://www. labsupport.com. **Description:** A temporary agency that also provides some temp-to-perm placements for scientific personnel. **NOTE:** Healthcare Financial Staffing (also at this location) is a temporary agency that

also provides some temp-to-perm placements for health care billing and collection professionals. The agency can be contacted by phone at 800/269-5172 or through the Internet at http://www.healthcarefinancial.com. EnviroStaff (also at this location) is a temporary agency that also provides some temp-to-perm placements for environmental and health safety professionals. The agency can be contacted by phone at 800/521-4801 or through the Internet at http://www.envirostaff.com **Specializes in the areas of:** Biology; Food; Industrial; Manufacturing; Scientific; Technical. **Positions commonly filled include:** Biochemist; Biological Scientist; Chemical Engineer; Chemist; Environmental Engineer; Food Scientist/Technologist; Mechanical Engineer; Metallurgical Engineer; Quality Control Supervisor; Technical Writer/Editor. **Benefits available to temporary workers:** 401(k); Bonus Award/Plan; Dental Insurance; Medical Insurance; Stock Purchase. **Corporate headquarters location:** This Location. **Other U.S. locations:** Nationwide. **Average salary range of placements:** $20,000 - $29,999. **Number of placements per year:** 1000+.

LEIGH & ASSOCIATES
18552 MacArthur Boulevard, Suite 200, Irvine CA 92612. 949/756-0388. **Fax:** 949/756-0397. **Contact:** Cindy Leigh, President. **Description:** A temporary agency that also provides some permanent placements. **Specializes in the areas of:** Legal; Secretarial. **Positions commonly filled include:** Attorney; Human Resources Specialist; Legal Secretary; Library Technician; MIS Specialist; Paralegal; Typist/Word Processor. **Corporate headquarters location:** This Location. **Other U.S. locations:** Los Angeles CA.

LEIGH & ASSOCIATES
444 South Flower Street, Suite 1500, Los Angeles CA 90071. 213/612-4411. **Fax:** 213/612-4433. **Contact:** Recruiter. **Description:** A temporary agency that also provides some permanent placements. **Specializes in the areas of:** Legal; Secretarial. **Positions commonly filled include:** Attorney; Human Resources Specialist; Legal Secretary; Librarian; MIS Specialist; Paralegal; Typist/ Word Processor. **Corporate headquarters location:** Irvine CA.

LONDON TEMPORARY SERVICES
5670 Wilshire Boulevard, Suite 880, Los Angeles CA 90036. 323/931-9400. **Contact:** Human Resources. **Description:** A temporary agency. **Specializes in the areas of:** Accounting/Auditing; Administration; Advertising; Banking; Broadcasting; Computer Hardware/Software; Engineering; Finance; Health/ Medical; Insurance; Legal; Nonprofit; Personnel/Labor Relations; Publishing; Secretarial. **Positions commonly filled include:** Accountant/Auditor; Administrative Assistant; Bookkeeper; Clerk; Computer Operator; Computer Programmer; Customer Service Rep.; Data Entry Clerk; Legal Secretary; Receptionist; Secretary; Typist/Word Processor. **Number of placements per year:** 200 - 499.

MK TECHNICAL SERVICES, INC.
1620 Oakland Road, Suite D100, San Jose CA 95131. 408/453-2562. **Fax:** 408/453-0958. **Contact:** Manager. **World Wide Web address:** http://www.mktech.com. **Description:** A temporary agency. **Specializes in the areas of:** Engineering; Industrial; Manufacturing; Technical. **Positions commonly filled include:** Buyer; Computer Programmer; Design Engineer; Designer; Draftsperson; Editor; Electrical/Electronics Engineer; Mechanical Engineer; Software Engineer; Technical Writer/Editor. **Benefits available to temporary workers:** Medical Insurance; Paid Holidays. **Number of placements per year:** 500 - 999.

MANPOWER STAFFING SERVICES
1600 State Street, Santa Barbara CA 93101. 805/569-2081. **Contact:** Irene Solovij, Branch Manager. **Description:** A temporary agency. **Specializes in the areas of:** Clerical; Data Security; Industrial; Word Processing. **Positions commonly filled include:**

Administrative Assistant; Bookkeeper; Clerk; Computer Operator; Construction Trade Worker; Customer Service Representative; Data Entry Clerk; Draftsperson; Driver; Factory Worker; Legal Secretary; Light Industrial Worker; Medical Secretary; Receptionist; Secretary; Stenographer; Technical Writer/Editor; Typist/Word Processor. **Corporate headquarters location:** Milwaukee WI. **Number of placements per year:** 1000+.

MANPOWER STAFFING SERVICES
355 South Grand Avenue, Suite 3275, Los Angeles CA 90017. 213/745-6500. **Contact:** Branch Manager. **Description:** A temporary agency. **Specializes in the areas of:** Data Processing; Industrial; Office Support; Word Processing. **Positions commonly filled include:** Accountant/Auditor; Accounting Clerk; Administrative Assistant; Biological Scientist; Bookkeeper; Chemist; Computer Operator; Customer Service Representative; Designer; Desktop Publishing Specialist; Electrician; Inspector/Tester/Grader; Inventory Control Specialist; Machine Operator; Packaging Engineer; Painter; Project Engineer; Proofreader; Receptionist; Records Manager; Research Assistant; Secretary; Software Engineer; Stenographer; Systems Analyst; Technical Writer/Editor; Telemarketer; Transcriptionist; Typist/Word Processor; Welder. **Corporate headquarters location:** Milwaukee WI. **Number of placements per year:** 1000+.

MANPOWER STAFFING SERVICES
One World Trade Center, Suite 208, Long Beach CA 90831-0208. 562/432-8582. **Fax:** 562/432-4482. **Contact:** Christy Littauer, Branch Supervisor. **Description:** A temporary agency. **Specializes in the areas of:** Administration; Banking; Industrial; Manufacturing; Marketing; Personnel/Labor Relations; Sales; Secretarial; Technical. **Positions commonly filled include:** Accountant/Auditor; Customer Service Rep. **Benefits available to temporary workers:** 401(k); Life Insurance; Medical Insurance; Paid Holidays; Paid Vacation; Referral Bonus Plan. **Corporate headquarters location:** Milwaukee WI. **Other U.S. locations:** Nationwide. **Average salary range of placements:** Less than $20,000. **Number of placements per year:** 200 - 499.

MANPOWER STAFFING SERVICES
39650 Liberty Street, Suite 130, Fremont CA 94538. 510/440-9040. **Fax:** 510/440-9048. **Contact:** Charlene Ritchie, Service Supervisor. **Description:** A temporary agency that also provides some permanent placements. **Specializes in the areas of:** Administration; Computer Science/Software; Economics; Engineering; Finance; General Management; Industrial; Light Industrial; Marketing; MIS/EDP; Sales; Scientific; Technical. **Positions commonly filled include:** Account Manager; Account Representative; Administrative Assistant; Administrative Manager; Advertising Clerk; Advertising Executive; Applications Engineer; Assistant Manager; Auditor; Bank Officer/Manager; Biological Scientist; Blue-Collar Worker Supervisor; Branch Manager; Budget Analyst; Buyer; Chemical Engineer; Chemist; Chief Financial Officer; Civil Engineer; Claim Representative; Clerical Supervisor; Clinical Lab Technician; Computer Animator; Computer Operator; Computer Programmer; Controller; Cost Estimator; Counselor; Credit Manager; Customer Service Representative; Database Manager; Design Engineer; Draftsperson; Economist; Editor; Editorial Assistant; Electrical/Electronics Engineer; Environmental Engineer; Finance Director; Financial Analyst; General Manager; Geologist/Geophysicist; Graphic Artist; Graphic Designer; Human Resources Manager; Industrial Engineer; Industrial Production Manager; Internet Services Manager; Management Trainee; Managing Editor; Manufacturing Engineer; Market Research Analyst; Marketing Manager; Marketing Specialist; Mechanical Engineer; MIS Specialist; Operations Manager; Production Manager; Project Manager; Purchasing Agent/Manager; Quality Control Supervisor; Sales Engineer; Sales Executive; Sales Manager; Sales Rep.; Secretary; Software Engineer; Statistician; Systems Analyst; Systems Manager; Technical Writer/Editor; Transportation/Traffic Specialist; Typist/Word Processor; Underwriter/Assistant Underwriter. **Benefits available to temporary workers:** 401(k); Medical Insurance; Paid Holidays; Paid Vacation; Referral Bonus Plan; Stock Purchase. **Corporate headquarters location:** Milwaukee WI. **Other U.S. locations:** Nationwide. **International locations:** Worldwide. **Average salary range of placements:** $30,000 - $50,000. **Number of placements per year:** 500 - 999.

MANPOWER STAFFING SERVICES
50 California Street, Suite 835, San Francisco CA 94111. 415/781-7171. **Contact:** Branch Manager. **Description:** A temporary agency that also provides some permanent placements. **Specializes in the areas of:** Industrial; Office Support; Telemarketing; Word Processing. **Positions commonly filled include:** Accountant/Auditor; Accounting Clerk; Administrative Assistant; Assembler; Biological Scientist; Bookkeeper; Chemist; Computer Operator; Customer Service Representative; Designer; Desktop Publishing Specialist; Electrician; Inventory Control Specialist; Machine Operator; Materials Manager; Project Engineer; Secretary; Software Engineer; Systems Analyst; Technical Writer/Editor; Telemarketer; Typist/Word Processor. **Benefits available to temporary workers:** Life Insurance; Medical Insurance; Paid Holidays; Paid Vacation. **Corporate headquarters location:** Milwaukee WI. **Other U.S. locations:** Nationwide. **International locations:** Worldwide. **Number of placements per year:** 1000+.

MARK ASSOCIATES
300 Montgomery Street, Suite 860, San Francisco CA 94104. 415/392-1835. **Fax:** 415/392-7338. **Contact:** Judith Chapman, President. **E-mail address:** markassociates@pacbell.net. **Description:** A temporary agency that also provides some permanent placements. **Specializes in the areas of:** Legal. **Positions commonly filled include:** Computer Operator; Legal Secretary; MIS Specialist; Paralegal. **Average salary range of placements:** $30,000 - $75,000. **Number of placements per year:** 100 - 199.

MICRO TRACK TEMPORARY SERVICES
4450 California Avenue, Suite K260, Bakersfield CA 93309. 661/871-9529. **Contact:** Scott Hurlbert, President. **Description:** A temporary agency. **Specializes in the areas of:** Computer Science/Software. **Positions commonly filled include:** Computer Programmer; Systems Analyst. **Benefits available to temporary workers:** Dental Insurance; Medical Insurance; Paid Holidays; Paid Vacation. **Average salary range of placements:** $30,000 - $50,000. **Number of placements per year:** 1 - 49.

MURRAY ENTERPRISES STAFFING SERVICES, INC.
P.O. Box 1136, Santa Clara CA 95052. 408/557-1320. **Fax:** 408/557-8863. **Contact:** Office Administrator. **Description:** A temporary agency. **Specializes in the areas of:** Accounting/Auditing; Administration; Computer Science/Software; Engineering; Industrial; Manufacturing; Personnel/Labor Relations; Sales; Secretarial; Technical. **Positions commonly filled include:** Accountant/Auditor; Administrative Manager; Buyer; Clerical Supervisor; Computer Programmer; Systems Analyst; Technical Writer/Editor; Telecommunications Manager; Typist/Word Processor; Urban/Regional Planner. **Benefits available to temporary workers:** Dental Insurance; Medical Insurance; Paid Holidays. **Average salary range of placements:** $30,000 - $50,000. **Number of placements per year:** 200 - 499.

NORRELL TEMPORARY SERVICES, INC. OF CALIFORNIA
3460 Torrance Boulevard, Suite 302, Torrance CA 90503. 310/543-2405. **Fax:** 310/543-9364. **Contact:** Manager. **Description:** A temporary agency that also provides some permanent placements. The agency focuses on clerical, technical, industrial, and managerial marketing placements. **Specializes in the areas of:** Accounting/Auditing; Administration; Banking;

Industrial; Manufacturing; Personnel/Labor Relations; Sales; Secretarial. **Positions commonly filled include:** Accountant/Auditor; Advertising Clerk; Budget Analyst; Computer Programmer; Customer Service Rep.; Editor; Management Trainee; Secretary; Support Personnel; Systems Analyst; Technical Writer/Editor; Transportation/Traffic Specialist; Typist/Word Processor. **Corporate headquarters location:** Atlanta GA. **Other U.S. locations:** Nationwide. **Number of placements per year:** 500 - 999.

NORRELL TEMPORARY SERVICES, INC. OF CALIFORNIA
4751 Wilshire Boulevard, Suite 130, Los Angeles CA 90010. 323/964-9566. **Toll-free phone:** 800/579-3332. **Contact:** Manager. **Description:** A temporary agency. **Specializes in the areas of:** Bilingual; Clerical; Computer Science/Software; Word Processing. **Positions commonly filled include:** Accountant/Auditor; Administrative Assistant; Clerk; Computer Operator; Customer Service Representative; Data Entry Clerk; Legal Secretary; Light Industrial Worker; MIS Specialist; Receptionist; Stenographer; Support Personnel; Typist/ Word Processor. **Corporate headquarters location:** Atlanta GA. **Other U.S. locations:** Nationwide. **Number of placements per year:** 1000+.

NORRELL TEMPORARY SERVICES, INC. OF CALIFORNIA
2001 Gateway Place, Suite 120, San Jose CA 95110. 408/441-6841. **Fax:** 408/441-6840. **Contact:** D. Lynn Ward, Manager. **Description:** A temporary agency that also provides some temp-to-perm and permanent placements. **Specializes in the areas of:** Administration; Computer Science/Software; Personnel/Labor Relations; Secretarial. **Positions commonly filled include:** Administrative Assistant; Clerical Supervisor; Customer Service Representative; Human Resources Specialist; Public Relations Specialist; Purchasing Agent/Manager; Secretary; Systems Analyst; Telecommunications Manager; Typist/Word Processor. **Benefits available to temporary workers:** 401(k); Medical Insurance; Paid Holidays; Paid Vacation. **Corporate headquarters location:** Atlanta GA. **Other U.S. locations:** Nationwide. **Average salary range of placements:** $20,000 - $29,999.

O'BRIEN EMPLOYMENT SERVICES
5510 Birdcage Street, Suite 210, Citrus Heights CA 95610. 916/961-2778. **Contact:** Manager. **Description:** A temporary agency. **Specializes in the areas of:** Clerical; Health/Medical. **Positions commonly filled include:** Dental Assistant/Dental Hygienist; Medical Assistant; Secretary.

OLSTEN STAFFING SERVICES
800 East Colorado Boulevard, Suite 120, Pasadena CA 91101. 626/449-1342. **Contact:** Manager. **Description:** A temporary agency. **Specializes in the areas of:** Accounting/Auditing; Advertising; Banking; Clerical; Finance; Health/Medical; Insurance; Legal; Manufacturing; Real Estate. **Positions commonly filled include:** Accountant/Auditor; Actuary; Administrative Assistant; Administrative Worker/Clerk; Bank Officer/Manager; Bookkeeper; Claim Representative; Clerk; Computer Operator; Computer Programmer; Credit Manager; Customer Service Representative; Data Entry Clerk; Driver; EDP Specialist; Financial Analyst; General Manager; Insurance Agent/Broker; Legal Secretary; Medical Secretary; Purchasing Agent/ Manager; Quality Control Supervisor; Receptionist; Sales Rep.; Secretary; Statistician; Stenographer; Support Personnel; Typist/Word Processor; Underwriter/Assistant Underwriter. **Corporate headquarters location:** Melville NY. **Number of placements per year:** 1000+.

OLSTEN STAFFING SERVICES
1000 Broadway, Suite 400, Oakland CA 94607. 510/987-7555. **Fax:** 510/987-7553. **Contact:** Eva Gonzalez, Team Leader. **World Wide Web address:** http://www. olsten.com. **Description:** A temporary agency. Founded in 1950. **Specializes in the areas of:** Accounting/ Auditing; Clerical; Legal; Secretarial. **Positions commonly filled include:** Administrative Assistant;

Bookkeeper; Claim Representative; Clerk; Customer Service Representative; Data Entry Clerk; Driver; Legal Secretary; Light Industrial Worker; Medical Secretary; Receptionist; Secretary; Typist/Word Processor. **Corporate headquarters location:** Melville NY. **Number of placements per year:** 1000+.

OLSTEN STAFFING SERVICES
32990 Alvarado Niles Road, Suite 970, Union City CA 94587-3106. 510/429-8995. **Fax:** 510/429-8909. **Contact:** Joe Hasselwander, Account Representative. **Description:** A temporary agency that also provides some permanent placements. Founded in 1950. **Specializes in the areas of:** Accounting/Auditing; Administration; Personnel/Labor Relations; Secretarial. **Positions commonly filled include:** Accountant/Auditor; Blue-Collar Worker Supervisor; Branch Manager; Clerical Supervisor; Customer Service Representative; General Manager; Human Resources Specialist; Typist/ Word Processor. **Benefits available to temporary workers:** Dental Insurance; Medical Insurance. **Corporate headquarters location:** Melville NY. **Average salary range of placements:** $20,000 - $29,999. **Number of placements per year:** 200 - 499.

OMNI EXPRESS TEMPS
2185 Faraday Avenue, Suite 120, Carlsbad CA 92008. 760/438-4405. **Fax:** 760/438-4482. **Contact:** Jennifer Mendenhall, Vice President. **Description:** A temporary agency. **Specializes in the areas of:** Accounting/ Auditing; Administration; Computer Science/Software; Engineering; Finance; Industrial; Manufacturing; Personnel/Labor Relations; Sales; Technical. **Positions commonly filled include:** Accountant/Auditor; Advertising Clerk; Aerospace Engineer; Aircraft Mechanic/Engine Specialist; Bank Officer/Manager; Blue-Collar Worker Supervisor; Branch Manager; Budget Analyst; Buyer; Chemical Engineer; Chemist; Civil Engineer; Clerical Supervisor; Clinical Lab Technician; Computer Programmer; Credit Manager; Customer Service Manager; Design Engineer; Designer; Draftsperson; Electrical/Electronics Engineer; Financial Analyst; General Manager; Human Resources Specialist; Industrial Engineer; Industrial Production Manager; Internet Services Manager; Mechanical Engineer; Metallurgical Engineer; MIS Specialist; Property and Real Estate Manager; Purchasing Agent/Manager; Quality Control Supervisor; Software Engineer; Structural Engineer; Systems Analyst; Technical Writer/ Editor; Typist/Word Processor. **Benefits available to temporary workers:** 401(k); Dental Insurance; Medical Insurance; Paid Holidays. **Corporate headquarters location:** This Location. **Other U.S. locations:** Escondido CA; San Diego CA; Tustin CA. **Number of placements per year:** 1000+.

ON ASSIGNMENT, INC.
26651 West Agoura Road, Calabasas CA 91302. 818/878-7900. **Fax:** 818/878-7930. **Contact:** Jackie Hoofring, Training and Recruitment Director. **Description:** A temporary agency that provides placements in laboratories through its Lab Support Division and in financial institutions through its Finance Support Division. **Specializes in the areas of:** Banking; Finance; Health/Medical. **Positions commonly filled include:** Bank Officer/Manager; Biological Scientist; Biomedical Engineer; Chemical Engineer; Environmental Engineer; Financial Analyst; Food Scientist/Technologist; Lender; Machinist. **Number of placements per year:** 1000+.

PACIFIC PLACEMENT GROUP
180 Sutter, 4th Floor, San Francisco CA 94104. 415/989-0542. **Fax:** 415/394-5966. **Contact:** Jane Groner, President. **E-mail address:** resume@pacificplacement. com. **Description:** A temporary agency that also provides some permanent placements. **Specializes in the areas of:** Administration; Graphic Arts. **Positions commonly filled include:** Administrative Assistant; Graphic Designer. **Average salary range of placements:** $30,000 - $50,000. **Number of placements per year:** 200 - 499.

PASONA PACIFIC
777 South Figueroa Street, Suite 2900, Los Angeles CA 90017. 213/489-2989. **Contact:** Consultants. **Description:** A temporary agency that also provides some permanent placements and career/outplacement counseling. **Specializes in the areas of:** Accounting/Auditing; Administration; Computer Science/Software; Economics; Engineering; General Management; Insurance; Sales; Technical. **Positions commonly filled include:** Account Manager; Accountant; Administrative Assistant; Administrative Manager; Assistant Manager; Bank Officer/Manager; Budget Analyst; Buyer; Chief Financial Officer; Clerical Supervisor; Computer Operator; Computer Programmer; Controller; Customer Service Rep.; Database Manager; Editorial Assistant; Finance Director; Financial Analyst; Graphic Designer; Human Resources Manager; Management Analyst/Consultant; Management Trainee; Manufacturing Engineer; Market Research Analyst; Marketing Manager; Mechanical Engineer; MIS Specialist; Operations Manager; Production Manager; Project Manager; Purchasing Agent/Manager; Quality Control Supervisor; Sales Engineer; Sales Executive; Sales Manager; Sales Representative; Secretary; Software Engineer; Systems Analyst; Systems Manager; Technical Writer/Editor; Telecommunications Manager; Typist/Word Processor. **Benefits available to temporary workers:** Health Benefits. **Corporate headquarters location:** This Location. **Other U.S. locations:** Irvine CA; Torrance CA; New York NY. **Average salary range of placements:** $30,000 - $50,000. **Number of placements per year:** 500 - 999.

PERSONALIZED PLACEMENT AGENCY
1605 West El Camino, Suite 101, Mountain View CA 94040. 650/968-4436. **Fax:** 650/968-4436. **Contact:** Gerry Harrison, Owner. **Description:** A temporary agency that also provides some permanent placements. **Specializes in the areas of:** Accounting/Auditing; Secretarial; Technical. **Positions commonly filled include:** Accountant/Auditor; Administrative Manager; Advertising Clerk; Biochemist; Buyer; Chemist; Clerical Supervisor; Computer Programmer; Customer Service Representative; Human Resources Specialist; Librarian; MIS Specialist; Operations/Production Manager; Paralegal; Purchasing Agent/Manager; Systems Analyst; Technical Writer/Editor; Typist/Word Processor. **Average salary range of placements:** $20,000 - $29,999. **Number of placements per year:** 500 - 999.

PREMIER PERSONNEL SERVICES
2463 208th Street, Suite 200, Torrance CA 90501. 310/320-1023. **Fax:** 310/320-5456. **Contact:** Anne Kocsis, Owner. **Description:** A temporary agency that also provides some permanent placements. **Specializes in the areas of:** Accounting/Auditing; Administration; General Management; Industrial; Insurance; Marketing; MIS/EDP; Personnel/Labor Relations; Sales; Secretarial. **Positions commonly filled include:** Account Manager; Account Representative; Administrative Assistant; Administrative Manager; Buyer; Chief Financial Officer; Clerical Supervisor; Controller; Credit Manager; Customer Service Rep.; Environmental Engineer; Financial Analyst; Human Resources Manager; Manufacturing Engineer; Market Research Analyst; Marketing Manager; Mechanical Engineer; MIS Specialist; Purchasing Agent/Manager; Quality Control Supervisor; Sales Engineer; Sales Executive; Sales Manager; Sales Rep.; Secretary; Software Engineer; Systems Analyst; Telecommunications Manager. **Average salary range of placements:** $20,000 - $30,000. **Number of placements per year:** 500 - 999.

PRESIDIO PERSONNEL
3710 State Street, Suite C, Santa Barbara CA 93105. 805/682-2848. **Fax:** 805/682-5211. **Contact:** Gloria Radley, President. **E-mail address:** jobs@presidio-jobs.com. **World Wide Web address:** http://www.presidio-jobs.com. **Description:** A temporary agency that also provides some permanent placements. **Specializes in the areas of:** Accounting/Auditing; Administration; Computer Science/Software; General Management; Industrial; Insurance; Legal; Manufacturing; Nonprofit; Personnel/Labor Relations; Retail; Sales; Secretarial. **Positions commonly filled include:** Accountant/Auditor; Administrative Manager; Advertising Clerk; Aerospace Engineer; Bank Officer/Manager; Branch Manager; Buyer; Claim Representative; Clerical Supervisor; Computer Programmer; Counselor; Credit Manager; Customer Service Rep.; Design Engineer; Designer; Draftsperson; Editor; Education Administrator; Electrical/Electronics Engineer; Environmental Engineer; Financial Analyst; General Manager; Hotel Manager; Human Resources Specialist; Human Service Worker; Industrial Engineer; Industrial Production Manager; Insurance Agent/Broker; Internet Services Manager; Landscape Architect; Management Analyst/Consultant; Management Trainee; Manufacturer's/Wholesaler's Sales Rep.; Market Research Analyst; Mechanical Engineer; MIS Specialist; Multimedia Designer; Paralegal; Public Relations Specialist; Purchasing Agent/Manager; Quality Control Supervisor; Software Engineer; Statistician; Strategic Relations Manager; Systems Analyst; Technical Writer/Editor; Telecommunications Manager; Travel Agent; Typist/Word Processor; Underwriter/Assistant Underwriter. **Average salary range of placements:** $20,000 - $45,000. **Number of placements per year:** 1000+.

PRIDESTAFF
Three Pointe Drive, Suite 305, Brea CA 92821. 714/255-1400. **Fax:** 714/255-9465. **Contact:** Melissa Marques, Recruiter. **World Wide Web address:** http://www.pridestaff.com. **Description:** A temporary agency that also provides some permanent placements. **Specializes in the areas of:** Accounting; Administration; Finance; General Management; Industrial; Light Industrial; Secretarial. **Positions commonly filled include:** Account Manager; Account Representative; Accountant; Adjuster; Administrative Assistant; Administrative Manager; AS400 Programmer Analyst; Assistant Manager; Blue-Collar Worker Supervisor; Branch Manager; Buyer; Claim Representative; Clerical Supervisor; Computer Programmer; Computer Support Technician; Credit Manager; Customer Service Representative; General Manager; Graphic Designer; Human Resources Manager; Industrial Production Manager; Insurance Agent/Broker; Management Trainee; MIS Specialist; Operations Manager; Project Manager; Purchasing Agent/Manager; Quality Control Supervisor; Sales Manager; Sales Rep.; Secretary; Transportation/Traffic Specialist; Typist/Word Processor. **Benefits available to temporary workers:** 401(k); Dental Insurance; Medical Insurance. **Other U.S. locations:** AZ; GA. **Average salary range of placements:** $20,000 - $49,999. **Number of placements per year:** 1000+.

QUESTEMPS
405 Esplanade Drive, Suite 101, Oxnard CA 93030. 805/983-3959. **Fax:** 805/983-6939. **Contact:** Sonia Robles, Operations Manager. **Description:** A temporary agency. **Specializes in the areas of:** Accounting/Auditing; Administration; Engineering; Finance; Industrial; Personnel/Labor Relations; Secretarial. **Positions commonly filled include:** Accountant/Auditor; Buyer; Customer Service Representative; Electrical/Electronics Engineer; Human Resources Specialist; Mechanical Engineer; MIS Specialist; Purchasing Agent/Manager; Quality Control Supervisor; Typist/Word Processor. **Average salary range of placements:** $20,000 - $29,999. **Number of placements per year:** 1000+.

Rx RELIEF
6780 North West Avenue, Suite 102, Fresno CA 93711. **Toll-free phone:** 800/797-3543. **Fax:** 559/432-2349. **Contact:** Manager. **Description:** A temporary agency. Founded in 1978. **Specializes in the areas of:** Health/Medical. **Positions commonly filled include:** Pharmacist. **Benefits available to temporary workers:** Bonus Award/Plan; Medical Insurance. **Average salary range of placements:** More than $50,000. **Number of placements per year:** 100 - 199.

REMEDY CALLER ACCESS
146 South Main Street, Suite S, Orange CA 92868. 714/938-0800. **Toll-free phone:** 800/338-8367x6140. **Fax:** 714/939-9933. **Contact:** Rick Nolan, Caller Access Placement Specialist. **E-mail address:** rickn@remedystaff.com. **World Wide Web address:** http://www.remedystaff.com. **Description:** A temporary agency that also provides some permanent placements. Remedy Caller Access specializes in placing individuals in high-volume call centers. Client company pays fee. **Specializes in the areas of:** Accounting/Auditing; Banking; Computer Hardware/Software; Engineering; Finance; General Management; Health/Medical; Industrial; Insurance; Manufacturing; Publishing; Retail; Sales; Secretarial. **Positions commonly filled include:** Customer Service Representative; Sales Representative; Telemarketer. **Benefits available to temporary workers:** 401(k); Dental Insurance; Medical Insurance; Vision Insurance. **Corporate headquarters location:** Aliso Viejo CA. **Other U.S. locations:** Nationwide. **Average salary range of placements:** $20,000 - $29,999. **Number of placements per year:** 200 - 499.

REMEDY INTELLIGENT STAFFING
4371 Glencoe Avenue, Suite B7, Marina Del Rey CA 90292. 310/826-5065. **Fax:** 310/827-2292. **Contact:** Manager. **World Wide Web address:** http://www.remedystaff.cm. **Description:** A temporary agency. **Specializes in the areas of:** Personnel/Labor Relations; Retail; Sales; Secretarial; Word Processing. **Positions commonly filled include:** Customer Service Rep. **Corporate headquarters location:** Aliso Viejo CA. **Other U.S. locations:** Nationwide. **Number of placements per year:** 500 - 999.

REMEDY INTELLIGENT STAFFING
18500 Van Karman Avenue, Suite 140, Irvine CA 92612. 949/477-3027. **Fax:** 949/756-1200. **Contact:** Debbie Neal, Senior Placement Consultant. **World Wide Web address:** http://www.remedystaff.com. **Description:** A temporary agency that also provides some permanent placements. **Specializes in the areas of:** Administration; General Management; Marketing; Sales; Secretarial. **Positions commonly filled include:** Account Manager; Account Rep.; Accountant; Administrative Assistant; Administrative Manager; Assistant Manager; Computer Programmer; Credit Manager; Customer Service Representative; Sales Executive; Secretary. **Benefits available to temporary workers:** 401(k); Dental Insurance; Medical Insurance; Vision Insurance. **Corporate headquarters location:** Aliso Viejo CA. **Other U.S. locations:** Nationwide. **International locations:** Worldwide. **Average salary range of placements:** $30,000 - $49,999. **Number of placements per year:** 500 - 999.

REMEDY INTELLIGENT STAFFING
820 Myrtle Avenue, Monrovia CA 91016. 626/301-9204. **Fax:** 626/303-2433. **Contact:** Branch Leader. **World Wide Web address:** http://www.remedystaff.com. **Description:** A temporary agency that also provides some permanent placements. **Specializes in the areas of:** Engineering; Light Industrial; Manufacturing. **Positions commonly filled include:** Aerospace Engineer; Aircraft Mechanic/Engine Specialist; Automotive Mechanic; Blue-Collar Worker Supervisor; Cost Estimator; Design Engineer; Draftsperson; Electrical/Electronics Engineer; Electrician; Industrial Engineer; Industrial Production Manager; Light Industrial Worker; Mechanical Engineer; Operations/Production Manager. **Corporate headquarters location:** Aliso Viejo CA. **Other U.S. locations:** Nationwide. **Average salary range of placements:** Less than $20,000. **Number of placements per year:** 500 - 999.

REMEDY INTELLIGENT STAFFING
4340 Stevens Creek Boulevard, Suite 168, San Jose CA 95127. 408/554-8174. **Contact:** Recruiter. **Description:** A temporary agency. Founded in 1965. **Specializes in the areas of:** Administration; Industrial; Manufacturing; Personnel/Labor Relations; Sales; Secretarial. **Positions commonly filled include:** Buyer; Customer Service Representative; Management Trainee. **Benefits available to temporary workers:** Dental Insurance; Medical Insurance; Vision Insurance. **Corporate headquarters location:** Aliso Viejo CA. **Other U.S. locations:** Nationwide. **Average salary range of placements:** $20,000 - $29,999.

REMEDY INTELLIGENT STAFFING
402 West Broadway, Suite 2150, San Diego CA 92101. 619/702-0730. **Contact:** Manager. **World Wide Web address:** http://www.remedystaff.com. **Description:** A temporary agency that also provides some temp-to-perm placements. **Specializes in the areas of:** Administration; Clerical; Secretarial. **Corporate headquarters location:** Aliso Viejo CA. **Other U.S. locations:** Nationwide.

RICHMAR ASSOCIATES INC.
283 Brokaw Road, Santa Clara CA 95050. 408/727-6070. **Fax:** 408/727-4465. **Contact:** Office Manager. **Description:** A temporary agency that also provides some temp-to-perm placements. **Specializes in the areas of:** Administration; Engineering; Manufacturing; Technical.

SAN DIEGO PERSONNEL & EMPLOYMENT
9474 Kearney Villa Road, Suite 104, San Diego CA 92126. 858/689-8500. **Toll-free phone:** 888/685-8500. **Fax:** 858/689-8587. **Contact:** Coordinator. **Description:** A temporary agency. **Specializes in the areas of:** Accounting/Auditing; Industrial; Manufacturing; Personnel/Labor Relations; Secretarial. **Positions commonly filled include:** Accountant/Auditor; Administrative Manager; Clerical Supervisor; Customer Service Representative; Electrician; Human Resources Specialist; Purchasing Agent/Manager; Quality Control Supervisor; Travel Agent; Typist/Word Processor. **Average salary range of placements:** $20,000 - $29,999. **Number of placements per year:** 1000+.

SELECT PERSONNEL SERVICES
1528 Chapala Street, Santa Barbara CA 93101. 805/882-2200. **Fax:** 805/882-2210. **Contact:** Office Manager. **Description:** A temporary agency. **Specializes in the areas of:** Accounting; Administration; Banking; Computer Science/Software; Economics; Engineering; Finance; General Management; Industrial; Light Industrial; Marketing; MIS/EDP; Personnel/Labor Relations; Printing; Publishing; Retail; Sales; Scientific; Secretarial; Technical. **Positions commonly filled include:** Account Manager; Account Representative; Accountant; Administrative Assistant; Administrative Manager; Advertising Clerk; Advertising Executive; Assistant Manager; Auditor; Bank Officer/Manager; Biochemist; Biomedical Engineer; Blue-Collar Worker Supervisor; Branch Manager; Budget Analyst; Buyer; Chemical Engineer; Chemist; CFO; Civil Engineer; Claim Rep.; Clerical Supervisor; Computer Operator; Computer Programmer; Draftsperson; Economist; Editor; Editorial Assistant; Education Administrator; Electrical/Electronics Engineer; Emergency Medical Technician; Environmental Engineer; ESL Teacher; Finance Director; Financial Analyst; General Manager; Geographer; Geologist/Geophysicist; Graphic Artist; Graphic Designer; Human Resources Manager; Industrial Engineer; Industrial Production Manager; Internet Services Manager; Librarian; Management Analyst/Consultant; Management Trainee; Managing Editor; Manufacturing Engineer; Market Research Analyst; Marketing Manager; Marketing Specialist; Mechanical Engineer; Medical Records Technician; MIS Specialist; Operations Manager; Paralegal; Production Manager; Project Manager; Public Relations Specialist; Purchasing Agent/Manager; Quality Control Supervisor; Sales Executive; Sales Manager; Sales Representative; Secretary; Software Engineer; Systems Analyst; Systems Manager; Technical Writer/Editor; Telecommunications Manager; Typist/Word Processor. **Benefits available to temporary workers:** 401(k); Medical Insurance; Paid Holidays; Paid Vacation. **Corporate headquarters location:** This Location. **Average salary range of placements:** $30,000 - $50,000. **Number of placements per year:** 1000+.

Representative; Management Trainee. **Benefits available to temporary workers:** Dental Insurance; Medical Insurance; Vision Insurance. **Corporate headquarters location:** Aliso Viejo CA. **Other U.S. locations:** Nationwide. **Average salary range of placements:** $20,000 - $29,999.

SELECT PERSONNEL SERVICES
325 North Azusa Avenue, West Covina CA 91791-1146.
626/331-6339. **Fax:** 626/331-7229. **Contact:** Manager.
Description: A temporary agency. **Specializes in the areas of:** Accounting/Auditing; Manufacturing; Retail; Secretarial. **Positions commonly filled include:** Blue-Collar Worker Supervisor; Typist/Word Processor. **Corporate headquarters location:** This Location. **Average salary range of placements:** Less than $20,000. **Number of placements per year:** 1000+.

SPECTRUM PERSONNEL
2130 Geer Road, Suite C, Turlock CA 95380. 209/667-8367. **Fax:** 209/667-4510. **Contact:** Branch Manager. **Description:** A temporary agency that also provides some permanent placements. **Specializes in the areas of:** Accounting/Auditing; Industrial; Manufacturing; Personnel/Labor Relations; Secretarial. **Positions commonly filled include:** Accountant/Auditor; Blue-Collar Worker Supervisor; Clerical Supervisor; Customer Service Representative; Operations/Production Manager; Personnel Specialist. **Corporate headquarters location:** Campbell CA. **Other area locations:** Hayward CA; Milpitas CA; Newark CA; Sacramento CA.

STAFF SEARCH
4047 Clipper Court, Fremont CA 94538. 510/249-1300. **Contact:** Manager. **Description:** A temporary agency. **Specializes in the areas of:** Manufacturing; Technical. **Other area locations:** Tracy CA. **Average salary range of placements:** Less than $20,000. **Number of placements per year:** 1000+.

STAR MED STAFF
400 30th Street, Suite 202, Oakland CA 94609. 510/834-8065. **Fax:** 510/834-0760. **Contact:** Office Manager. **Description:** A temporary agency. **Specializes in the areas of:** Health/Medical. **Positions commonly filled include:** Dental Assistant/Dental Hygienist; EKG Technician; Emergency Medical Technician; Registered Nurse; Respiratory Therapist. **Benefits available to temporary workers:** Medical Insurance; Paid Vacation.

STIVERS TEMPORARY PERSONNEL INC.
55 South Lake Avenue, Suite 100, Pasadena CA 91101. 626/796-8559. **Contact:** Manager. **Description:** A temporary agency. **Specializes in the areas of:** Accounting/Auditing; Banking; Clerical; Finance; Health/Medical; Insurance; Legal. **Positions commonly filled include:** Accountant/Auditor; Actuary; Administrative Assistant; Advertising Clerk; Bookkeeper; Claim Rep.; Clerk; Computer Operator; Data Entry Clerk; Legal Secretary.

STIVERS TEMPORARY PERSONNEL INC.
16633 Ventura Boulevard, Encino CA 91436. 818/906-1145. **Contact:** Manager. **Description:** A temporary agency. **Specializes in the areas of:** Accounting/Auditing; Banking; Clerical; Health/Medical; Insurance; Legal. **Positions commonly filled include:** Account Representative; Actuary; Administrative Assistant; Advertising Clerk; Bookkeeper; Claim Representative; Computer Operator; Data Entry Clerk; Legal Secretary; Medical Secretary; Receptionist; Secretary; Statistician; Stenographer; Typist/Word Processor; Underwriter/Assistant Underwriter.

STRATEGIC STAFFING, INC.
369 Pine Street, Mezzanine Level, San Francisco CA 94104. 415/616-6300. **Fax:** 415/616-6306. **Contact:** Office Manager. **World Wide Web address:** http://www.strategic-staffing.com. **Description:** A temporary agency that also provides some temp-to-perm and permanent placements. **Specializes in the areas of:** Accounting/Auditing; Administration; Advertising; Computer Science/Software; Personnel/Labor Relations; Secretarial; Technical. **Positions commonly filled include:** Accountant/Auditor; Administrative Manager; Advertising Clerk; Branch Manager; Budget Analyst; Claim Representative; Clerical Supervisor; Computer Programmer; Customer Service Representative; Financial Analyst; General Manager; Human Resources Specialist;

Librarian; Management Trainee; Market Research Analyst; MIS Specialist; Purchasing Agent/Manager; Software Engineer; Systems Analyst; Technical Writer/Editor; Travel Agent; Typist/Word Processor. **Number of placements per year:** 1000+.

SUN PERSONNEL SERVICES
915 River Street, Santa Cruz CA 95060. 831/458-5301. **Fax:** 831/458-0950. **Contact:** Richard Huffman, Owner. **Description:** A temporary agency that also provides some permanent placements and career/outplacement counseling. **Specializes in the areas of:** Accounting/Auditing; Computer Science/Software; Engineering; Industrial; Manufacturing; Personnel/Labor Relations; Publishing; Sales; Secretarial. **Positions commonly filled include:** Accountant/Auditor; Administrative Manager; Advertising Clerk; Branch Manager; Budget Analyst; Buyer; Claim Representative; Clerical Supervisor; Computer Programmer; Credit Manager; Customer Service Representative; Design Engineer; Designer; Draftsperson; Editor; Electrical/Electronics Engineer; Financial Analyst; Human Resources Specialist; Industrial Engineer; Industrial Production Manager; Management Trainee; Market Research Analyst; Mechanical Engineer; Medical Records Technician; MIS Specialist; Preschool Worker; Purchasing Agent/Manager; Quality Control Supervisor; Restaurant/Food Service Manager; Services Sales Rep.; Software Engineer; Structural Engineer; Systems Analyst; Teacher/Professor; Telecommunications Manager; Typist/Word Processor. **Benefits available to temporary workers:** Medical Insurance; Paid Vacation. **Average salary range of placements:** $20,000 - $29,999. **Number of placements per year:** 100 - 199.

TLC STAFFING
8788 Balboa Avenue, San Diego CA 92123. 858/569-6260. **Toll-free phone:** 800/834-4576. **Fax:** 858/569-8026. **Contact:** Kay Christian, Vice President of Operations. **E-mail address:** tlc@tlc-staffing.com. **World Wide Web address:** http://www.tlc-staffing.com. **Description:** TLC Staffing is a temporary agency that also provides some contract services. **Specializes in the areas of:** Administration; Computer Science/Software; Engineering; Human Resources; Sales; Secretarial. **Positions commonly filled include:** Administrative Manager; Buyer; Chemical Engineer; Chemist; Civil Engineer; Clerical Supervisor; Computer Programmer; Customer Service Rep.; Draftsperson; Electrical/Electronics Engineer; Human Resources Manager; Human Resources Specialist; Mechanical Engineer; MIS Specialist; Software Engineer; Systems Analyst; Technical Writer/Editor; Typist/Word Processor. **Benefits available to temporary workers:** 401(k); Direct Deposit; Paid Holidays. **Corporate headquarters location:** This Location. **Other U.S. locations:** Ontario CA. **Average salary range of placements:** $30,000 - $50,000. **Number of placements per year:** 1000+.

TRC STAFFING SERVICES
1000 North Central Avenue, Suite 203, Glendale CA 91202. 818/548-3597. **Fax:** 818/548-1016. **Contact:** Nancy Clark, Vice President of Marketing. **World Wide Web address:** http://www.trcstaff.com. **Description:** A temporary agency that also provides some permanent placements. **Specializes in the areas of:** Administration; Light Industrial; Secretarial. **Positions commonly filled include:** Account Manager; Administrative Assistant; Clerical Supervisor; Computer Operator; Customer Service Rep.; Database Administrator; Human Resources Manager; Secretary. **Corporate headquarters location:** Atlanta GA. **Other U.S. locations:** Nationwide. **Number of placements per year:** 200 - 499.

TAC ENGINEERING RESOURCES
17320 Red Hill Avenue, Suite 320, Irvine CA 92614. 949/263-1500. **Toll-free phone:** 800/896-8452. **Contact:** Branch Manager. **Description:** A temporary agency. **Specializes in the areas of:** Software Engineering; Technical. **Positions commonly filled include:** Computer Programmer; Database Manager; Graphic Artist; Graphic Designer; Software Engineer; Systems

Analyst; Systems Manager; Technical Writer/Editor; Telecommunications Manager; Webmaster. **Benefits available to temporary workers:** 401(k); Dental Insurance; Medical Insurance. **Corporate headquarters location:** Newton Upper Falls MA. **Other U.S. locations:** Nationwide. **International locations:** Worldwide. **Average salary range of placements:** More than $50,000. **Number of placements per year:** 200 - 499.

TAC ENGINEERING RESOURCES
1733 North First Street, San Jose CA 95112. 408/324-0345. **Toll-free phone:** 888/547-6904. **Fax:** 408/324-0355. **Contact:** Recruiter. **Description:** A temporary agency. **Specializes in the areas of:** Computer Science/Software.

TAC STAFFING SERVICES
39159 Paseo Padre Parkway, Suite 107, Fremont CA 94538. 510/797-6444. **Contact:** Manager. **World Wide Web address:** http://www.tacstaffing.com. **Description:** A temporary agency. **Specializes in the areas of:** Administration. **Other U.S. locations:** Nationwide.

TAC STAFFING SERVICES
2001 Gateway Place, Suite 350, San Jose CA 95110. 408/437-0260. **Contact:** Manager. **World Wide Web address:** http://www.tacstaffing.com. **Description:** A temporary agency. **Specializes in the areas of:** Administration.

TAC STAFFING SERVICES
1801 Oakland Boulevard, Suite 225, Walnut Creek CA 94596. 925/935-9450. **Contact:** Manager. **World Wide Web address:** http://www.tacstaffing.com. **Description:** A temporary agency. **Specializes in the areas of:** Administration; Clerical; Light Industrial; Office Support.

TAC STAFFING SERVICES
120 Montgomery Street, Suite 1390, San Francisco CA 94104. 415/391-9933. **Contact:** Manager. **World Wide Web address:** http://www.tacstaffing.com. **Description:** A temporary agency. **Specializes in the areas of:** Administration; Clerical; Office Support; Secretarial. **Positions commonly filled include:** Administrative Assistant.

TECH/AID
6345 Balboa Boulevard, Suite 186, Encino CA 91316. 818/995-2910. **Contact:** Manager. **World Wide Web address:** http://www.techaid.com. **Description:** A temporary agency. **Specializes in the areas of:** Computer Hardware/Software; Design; Engineering; Manufacturing. **Positions commonly filled include:** Aerospace Engineer; Architect; Biological Scientist; Chemist; Civil Engineer; Commercial Artist; Draftsperson; Electrical/Electronics Engineer; Industrial Designer; Industrial Engineer; Mechanical Engineer; Physicist; Quality Control Supervisor; Technical Writer/Editor; Technician. **Corporate headquarters location:** Newton MA. **Other U.S. locations:** Nationwide. **Number of placements per year:** 1000+.

TECH/AID
7700 Edgewater Drive, Suite 543, Oakland CA 94621. 510/577-6700. **Contact:** Office Manager. **Description:** A temporary agency. **Specializes in the areas of:** Computer Hardware/Software; Design; Engineering; Manufacturing. **Positions commonly filled include:** Aerospace Engineer; Architect; Biological Scientist; Chemist; Civil Engineer; Commercial Artist; Designer; Draftsperson; Electrical/Electronics Engineer; Industrial Designer; Industrial Engineer; Light Industrial Worker; Mechanical Engineer; Physicist; Quality Control Supervisor; Technical Writer/Editor; Technician. **Number of placements per year:** 1000+.

TECH/AID
P.O. Box 3190, Tustin CA 92780. 714/573-9111. **Fax:** 714/573-9565. **Contact:** Branch Manager. **E-mail address:** tustin@techaid.com. **World Wide Web**

address: http://www.techaid.com. **Description:** A temporary agency that also provides some contract services. **Specializes in the areas of:** Architecture/Construction; Art/Design; Biology; Engineering; Industrial; Manufacturing; Technical. **Positions commonly filled include:** Aerospace Engineer; Aircraft Mechanic/Engine Specialist; Architect; Biochemist; Biological Scientist; Biomedical Engineer; Buyer; Chemical Engineer; Chemist; Civil Engineer; Clinical Lab Technician; Construction and Building Inspector; Cost Estimator; Design Engineer; Designer; Draftsperson; Editor; Electrical/Electronics Engineer; Electrician; Environmental Engineer; Industrial Engineer; Landscape Architect; Mechanical Engineer; Metallurgical Engineer; Multimedia Designer; Petroleum Engineer; Purchasing Agent/Manager; Quality Control Supervisor; Structural Engineer; Surveyor; Technical Writer/Editor; Telecommunications Manager; Urban/Regional Planner. **Corporate headquarters location:** Newton MA. **Other U.S. locations:** Nationwide. **Average salary range of placements:** $30,000 - $50,000. **Number of placements per year:** 1000+.

TECH/AID
1733 North First Street, San Jose CA 95112. 408/434-9800. **Fax:** 408/232-7660. **Contact:** Steve Lion, Branch Manager. **E-mail address:** sanjose@techaid.com. **World Wide Web address:** http://www.techaid.com. **Description:** A temporary agency. **Specializes in the areas of:** Engineering; Manufacturing; Technical. **Positions commonly filled include:** Aerospace Engineer; Architect; Biochemist; Buyer; Chemical Engineer; Chemist; Civil Engineer; Clinical Lab Technician; Design Engineer; Designer; Draftsperson; Editor; Electrical/Electronics Engineer; Environmental Engineer; Financial Analyst; Industrial Engineer; Industrial Production Manager; Mechanical Engineer; Multimedia Designer; Nuclear Engineer; Purchasing Agent/Manager; Quality Control Supervisor; Structural Engineer; Technical Writer/Editor; Telecommunications Manager. **Benefits available to temporary workers:** 401(k); Medical Insurance; Paid Holidays. **Other U.S. locations:** Nationwide. **Average salary range of placements:** $30,000 - $50,000. **Number of placements per year:** 1000+.

TECH/AID
One Civic Plaza Drive, Suite 335, Carson CA 90745. 310/952-9527. **Fax:** 310/952-0728. **Contact:** Lead Recruiter. **World Wide Web address:** http://www.techaid.com. **Description:** Tech/Aid is a temporary agency. **Specializes in the areas of:** Art/Design; Engineering; Manufacturing; Technical. **Positions commonly filled include:** Aerospace Engineer; Buyer; Chemical Engineer; Civil Engineer; Design Engineer; Designer; Draftsperson; Electrical/Electronics Engineer; Environmental Engineer; Industrial Engineer; Mechanical Engineer; Nuclear Engineer; Purchasing Agent/Manager; Structural Engineer; Technical Writer/Editor. **Benefits available to temporary workers:** 401(k); Medical Insurance. **Corporate headquarters location:** Newton MA. **Other U.S. locations:** Nationwide. **International locations:** Worldwide. **Average salary range of placements:** $30,000 - $50,000. **Number of placements per year:** 1000+.

TEMPS UNLIMITED, INC.
17411 Chatsworth Street, Suite 103, Granada Hills CA 91344. 818/363-2345. **Fax:** 818/363-3683. **Contact:** Manager. **Description:** A temporary agency. **Specializes in the areas of:** Industrial; Manufacturing; Personnel/Labor Relations; Secretarial. **Positions commonly filled include:** Cable TV Installer; Customer Service Rep.; Receptionist; Typist/Word Processor. **Benefits available to temporary workers:** Paid Holidays. **Average salary range of placements:** $20,000 - $29,999. **Number of placements per year:** 500 - 999.

THOMAS STAFFING
1450 Frazee Road, Suite 312, San Diego CA 92108. 619/285-9800. **Fax:** 619/688-9188. **Contact:** Manager. **E-mail address:** partners@thomas-staffing.com. **World**

Wide Web address: http://www.thomas-staffing.com. Description: A temporary agency that also provides some temp-to-perm and direct hire placements. Founded in 1969. Specializes in the areas of: Retail; Sales; Secretarial. Positions commonly filled include: Accountant/Auditor; Administrative Assistant; Customer Service Rep.; Management Trainee; Typist/Word Processor. Benefits available to temporary workers: 401(k); Medical Insurance; Paid Holidays. Corporate headquarters location: Irvine CA. Average salary range of placements: $20,000 - $50,000. Number of placements per year: 500 - 999.

THOR TEMPORARY SERVICES
3601 Aviation Boulevard, Manhattan Beach CA 90266. 310/373-0922. Contact: Manager. Description: Thor Temporary Services is a temporary agency. Specializes in the areas of: Accounting/Auditing; Advertising; Architecture/Construction; Banking; Clerical; Computer Hardware/Software; Construction; Finance; Food; Health/Medical; Insurance; Legal; Manufacturing; MIS/EDP; Publishing; Real Estate; Secretarial; Technical; Transportation. Positions commonly filled include: Accountant/Auditor; Administrative Assistant; Bookkeeper; Computer Programmer; Credit Manager; Customer Service Representative; Data Entry Clerk; EDP Specialist; Financial Analyst; Legal Secretary; Medical Secretary; Receptionist; Secretary; Stenographer; Systems Analyst; Technical Writer/Editor; Typist/Word Processor. Number of placements per year: 1000+.

TOD STAFFING
32 West 25th Avenue, Suite 201, San Mateo CA 94403. 650/574-8900. Fax: 650/574-2636. Contact: Manager. Description: A temporary agency that also provides some temp-to-perm placements. Specializes in the areas of: Legal. Positions commonly filled include: Accountant; Administrative Manager; Advertising Clerk; Branch Manager; Budget Analyst; Buyer; Claim Rep.; Clerical Supervisor; Computer Programmer; Cost Estimator; Credit Manager; Customer Service Representative; Financial Analyst; Management Trainee; Paralegal; Purchasing Agent/Manager; Services Sales Rep.; Statistician; Systems Analyst; Technical Writer/ Editor. Number of placements per year: 500 - 999.

TOD STAFFING
690 Market Street, Suite 100, San Francisco CA 94104. 415/392-0700. Fax: 415/392-0752. Contact: David Adcock, Branch Administration Manager. Description: A temporary agency that also provides some temp-to-perm placements. Both jobseeker and client company share fee. Specializes in the areas of: Accounting/ Auditing; Banking; Computer Science/Software; Finance; Insurance; Legal; Manufacturing; Personnel/ Labor Relations; Sales; Secretarial. Positions commonly filled include: Accountant/Auditor; Administrative Manager; Bank Officer/Manager; Buyer; Claim Representative; Clerical Supervisor; Clinical Lab Technician; Computer Programmer; Counselor; Credit Manager; Customer Service Rep.; Draftsperson; Financial Analyst; Human Resources Specialist; Internet Services Manager; Librarian; Market Research Analyst; Medical Records Technician; MIS Specialist; Multimedia Designer; Paralegal; Purchasing Agent/ Manager; Quality Control Supervisor; Securities Sales Rep.; Services Sales Representative; Software Engineer; Statistician; Systems Analyst; Technical Writer/Editor; Typist/Word Processor; Video Production Coordinator. Average salary range of placements: $30,000 - $50,000. Number of placements per year: 1000+.

TREND WESTERN TECHNICAL CORPORATION
4128 West Commonwealth Avenue, Fullerton CA 92833. 714/525-0134. Contact: Manager. Description: A temporary agency. Specializes in the areas of: Computer Hardware/Software; Engineering; Publishing. Positions commonly filled include: Aerospace Engineer; Agricultural Engineer; Biological Scientist; Biomedical Engineer; Buyer; Ceramics Engineer; Chemical Engineer; Chemist; Civil Engineer; Clerk; Commercial Artist; Computer Operator; Computer

Programmer; Data Entry Clerk; Draftsperson; Electrical/Electronics Engineer; Human Resources Manager; Industrial Engineer; Marketing Specialist; Mechanical Engineer; Metallurgical Engineer; Mining Engineer; Petroleum Engineer; Physicist; Purchasing Agent/Manager; Receptionist; Sales Representative; Systems Analyst; Technical Writer/Editor; Technician; Typist/Word Processor. Number of placements per year: 500 - 999.

TRENDTEC INC.
1620 Zanker Road, San Jose CA 95112. 408/436-1200. Fax: 408/436-0626. Contact: Bonnie Werley, Vice President. Description: A temporary agency. Specializes in the areas of: Computer Science/Software; Engineering; Industrial; Manufacturing. Positions commonly filled include: Accountant/Auditor; Architect; Buyer; Chemical Engineer; Civil Engineer; Computer Programmer; Customer Service Rep.; Design Engineer; Designer; Draftsperson; Editor; Electrical/ Electronics Engineer; Electrician; Environmental Engineer; Financial Analyst; Human Resources Specialist; Industrial Engineer; Internet Services Manager; Mechanical Engineer; Metallurgical Engineer; MIS Specialist; Operations/Production Manager; Purchasing Agent/Manager; Quality Control Supervisor; Software Engineer; Structural Engineer; Systems Analyst; Technical Writer/Editor; Transportation/Traffic Specialist; Typist/Word Processor. Average salary range of placements: $20,000 - $29,999. Number of placements per year: 1000+.

VOLT SERVICES GROUP
6130 Stoneridge Mall Road, Suite 150, Pleasanton CA 94588. 925/463-2800. Fax: 925/463-2807. Contact: Carol Brokens, Branch Manager. World Wide Web address: http://www.volt.com. Description: A temporary agency that also provides some permanent placements. Specializes in the areas of: Accounting/ Auditing; Computer Science/Software; Industrial; Manufacturing; Personnel/Labor Relations; Publishing; Secretarial. Positions commonly filled include: Administrative Assistant; Bookkeeper; Clerk; Customer Service Representative; Data Entry Clerk; Driver; Factory Worker; Legal Secretary; Light Industrial Worker; Medical Secretary; Receptionist; Secretary; Typist/Word Processor. Corporate headquarters location: Orange CA. Other U.S. locations: Nationwide. Average salary range of placements: $20,000 - $29,999. Number of placements per year: 1000+.

VOLT SERVICES GROUP
3031 Tisch Way, Suite 600, San Jose CA 95128. 408/247-9777. Fax: 408/247-9778. Contact: Chris Robinson, Branch Manager. World Wide Web address: http://www.volt.com. Description: A temporary agency. Specializes in the areas of: Accounting/Auditing; Banking; Computer Science/Software; Education; Engineering; Finance; Industrial; Insurance; Legal; Manufacturing; Personnel/Labor Relations; Retail; Sales; Secretarial. Positions commonly filled include: Accountant; Administrative Assistant; Customer Service Representative; Secretary; Typist/Word Processor. Benefits available to temporary workers: Dental Insurance; Medical Insurance; Referral Bonus Plan. Corporate headquarters location: Orange CA. Other U.S. locations: Nationwide. Average salary range of placements: $20,000 - $29,999.

WESTAFF
301 Lennon Lane, Walnut Creek CA 94598. 925/930-5300. Contact: Administrator. Description: Westaff is a temporary agency. Specializes in the areas of: Accounting/Auditing; Banking; Clerical; Computer Hardware/Software; Health/Medical; MIS/EDP; Sales; Secretarial; Technical. Positions commonly filled include: Accountant/Auditor; Actuary; Administrative Assistant; Aerospace Engineer; Agricultural Engineer; Architect; Attorney; Bank Teller; Biological Scientist; Biomedical Engineer; Bookkeeper; Ceramics Engineer; Civil Engineer; Claim Representative; Clerk; Clinical

Lab Technician; Commercial Artist; Computer Programmer; Customer Service Representative; Data Entry Clerk; Dietician/Nutritionist; Draftsperson; Economist; EDP Specialist; Electrical/Electronics Engineer; Electronics Technician; Emergency Medical Technician; Factory Worker; Financial Analyst; Industrial Designer; Industrial Engineer; Interior Designer; Legal Assistant; Licensed Practical Nurse; Light Industrial Worker; Marketing Specialist; Mechanical Engineer; Medical Records Technician; Medical Secretary; Metallurgical Engineer; Mining Engineer; Nurse; Petroleum Engineer; Pharmacist; Physicist; Public Relations Specialist; Purchasing Agent/Manager; Receptionist; Registered Nurse; Reporter; Respiratory Therapist; Sales Representative; Secretary; Security Officer; Statistician; Stenographer; Systems Analyst; Technical Writer/Editor; Technician; Typist/Word Processor; Underwriter. **Corporate headquarters location:** This Location. **Average salary range of placements:** $30,000 - $50,000. **Number of placements per year:** 1000+.

WESTAFF
1214 Apollo Way, Suite 404-1, Sunnyvale CA 94086. 408/245-4850. **Fax:** 408/245-4858. **Contact:** Patty Pratt, Manager. **Description:** A temporary agency. **Specializes in the areas of:** Accounting/Auditing; Personnel/Labor Relations; Sales; Secretarial. **Positions commonly filled include:** Human Resources Specialist; Management Trainee; Services Sales Rep.; Travel Agent; Typist/Word Processor. **Corporate headquarters location:** Walnut Creek CA. **Average salary range of placements:** $20,000 - $29,999. **Number of placements per year:** 500 - 999.

WESTAFF
23030 Lake Forest Drive, Suite 204, Laguna Hills CA 92653. 949/855-4011. **Fax:** 949/859-1897. **Contact:** Area Manager. **Description:** Westaff is a temporary agency. **Specializes in the areas of:** Accounting/ Auditing; Administration; Computer Science/Software; Engineering; Finance; Industrial; Legal; Personnel/Labor Relations; Sales; Secretarial; Technical. **Positions commonly filled include:** Accountant/Auditor; Administrative Manager; Aerospace Engineer; Blue-Collar Worker Supervisor; Budget Analyst; Buyer; Chemist; Clerical Supervisor; Customer Service Representative; Draftsperson; Electrical/Electronics Engineer; Electrician; Human Resources Specialist; Industrial Production Manager; Insurance Agent/Broker; Management Analyst/Consultant; Management Trainee; MIS Specialist; Paralegal; Software Engineer; Technical Writer/Editor; Telecommunications Manager. **Benefits available to temporary workers:** Dental Insurance;

Medical Insurance. **Corporate headquarters location:** Walnut Creek CA. **Other U.S. locations:** Nationwide. **Number of placements per year:** 1000+.

WESTAFF
1213 State Street, Suite L, Santa Barbara CA 93101. 805/962-5229. **Fax:** 805/965-3567. **Contact:** April Goddard, Branch Manager. **Description:** A temporary agency that also provides some permanent placements. Jobseeker pays fee. **Specializes in the areas of:** Accounting/Auditing; Administration; Advertising; Architecture/Construction; Computer Science/Software; Engineering; Finance; General Management; Industrial; Legal; Manufacturing; Personnel/Labor Relations; Publishing; Retail; Sales; Secretarial; Technical; Transportation. **Positions commonly filled include:** Accountant/Auditor; Administrative Manager; Advertising Clerk; Aerospace Engineer; Agricultural Engineer; Aircraft Mechanic/Engine Specialist; Architect; Attorney; Automotive Mechanic; Bank Officer/Manager; Blue-Collar Worker Supervisor; Branch Manager; Brokerage Clerk; Budget Analyst; Buyer; Chemical Engineer; Claim Representative; Clerical Supervisor; Clinical Lab Technician; Computer Programmer; Cost Estimator; Credit Manager; Customer Service Representative; Design Engineer; Draftsperson; Editor; Education Administrator; Electrical/Electronics Engineer; Electrician; Environmental Engineer; Financial Analyst; General Manager; Geographer; Geologist/ Geophysicist; Hotel Manager; Human Resources Specialist; Human Service Worker; Industrial Engineer; Industrial Production Manager; Insurance Agent/ Broker; Internet Services Manager; Landscape Architect; Librarian; Management Analyst/Consultant; Management Trainee; Market Research Analyst; Mechanical Engineer; Metallurgical Engineer; Multimedia Designer; Paralegal; Property and Real Estate Manager; Public Relations Specialist; Purchasing Agent/Manager; Quality Control Supervisor; Reporter; Restaurant/Food Service Manager; Services Sales Representative; Software Engineer; Systems Analyst; Technical Writer/Editor; Telecommunications Manager; Travel Agent; Typist/Word Processor. **Corporate headquarters location:** Walnut Creek CA. **International locations:** Worldwide. **Number of placements per year:** 200 - 499.

WORK LOAD INC.
629 El Portal Center, San Pablo CA 94806. 510/233-7363. **Contact:** Ed Lane, Owner. **Description:** A temporary agency. **Specializes in the areas of:** Industrial; Warehousing. **Number of placements per year:** 500 - 999.

CONTRACT SERVICES FIRMS

ACCESS IT RESOURCES
100 Pine Street, Suite 1950, San Francisco CA 94111. 415/901-5007. **Toll-free phone:** 800/287-5977. **Fax:** 415/781-6226. **Contact:** Senior Technical Recruiter. **E-mail address:** access@accstaff.com. **Description:** A contract services firm that places technical consultants with expertise in mainframe and personal computing platforms. **Specializes in the areas of:** Administration; Computer Science/Software. **Positions commonly filled include:** Computer Programmer; Internet Services Manager; Management Analyst/Consultant; MIS Specialist; Multimedia Designer; Systems Analyst. **Average salary range of placements:** More than $50,000. **Number of placements per year:** 100 - 199.

BIOSOURCE TECHNICAL SERVICE
333 West El Camino Real, Suite 210, Sunnyvale CA 94087. 408/738-4300. **Fax:** 408/733-3305. **Contact:** Pam Albo, Manager of Business Development. **Description:** A contract services firm. **Specializes in the areas of:** Biology; Food; Pharmaceuticals; Technical. **Positions commonly filled include:** Biochemist; Biological Scientist; Biomedical Engineer; Chemical

Engineer; Chemist; Clinical Lab Technician; Environmental Engineer; Food Scientist/Technologist; Quality Control Supervisor; Science Technologist; Veterinarian. **Corporate headquarters location:** This Location. **Average salary range of placements:** $30,000 - $50,000. **Number of placements per year:** 100 - 199.

CDI INFORMATION SERVICES
44 Montgomery Street, Suite 2120, San Francisco CA 94104. 415/434-1846. **Contact:** Branch Manager. **World Wide Web address:** http://www.cdicorp.com. **Description:** A contract services firm. **Specializes in the areas of:** Secretarial; Word Processing. **Corporate headquarters location:** Philadelphia PA. **Other U.S. locations:** Nationwide. **International locations:** Worldwide. **Number of placements per year:** 500 - 999.

CDS STAFFING SERVICES
1636 East 14th Street, San Leandro CA 94577. 415/975-3970. **Toll-free phone:** 800/498-4237. **Contact:** Office Manager. **Description:** A contract services firm.

Specializes in the areas of: Transportation. Positions commonly filled include: Accountant/Auditor; Administrative Manager; Driver; Human Resources Specialist. Corporate headquarters location: This Location. Other U.S. locations: Seattle WA. Average salary range of placements: Less than $20,000. Number of placements per year: 100 - 199.

CAREER QUEST INTERNATIONAL
1901 Avenue of the Stars, Suite 920, Los Angeles CA 90067-6001. 310/282-8505. Fax: 310/282-0514. Contact: Office Manager. World Wide Web address: http://www.careerquest.com. Description: A contract services firm that also provides some permanent and temporary placements. Specializes in the areas of: Accounting; Administration; Advertising; Art/Design; Banking; Computer Science/Software; Finance; Food; General Management; Health/Medical; Industrial; Insurance; Legal; Light Industrial; Marketing; MIS/EDP; Nonprofit; Personnel/Labor Relations; Printing; Publishing; Retail; Sales; Scientific; Technical; Transportation. Positions commonly filled include: Account Manager; Account Representative; Accountant; Adjuster; Administrative Assistant; Administrative Manager; Advertising Clerk; Advertising Executive; Applications Engineer; Architect; Assistant Manager; Auditor; Bank Officer/Manager; Blue-Collar Worker Supervisor; Branch Manager; Broadcast Technician; Budget Analyst; Buyer; Chief Financial Officer; Claim Representative; Clerical Supervisor; Computer Animator; Computer Operator; Computer Programmer; Consultant; Controller; Cost Estimator; Counselor; Credit Manager; Customer Service Representative; Database Manager; Dietician/Nutritionist; Draftsperson; Finance Director; Financial Analyst; Fund Manager; General Manager; Graphic Artist; Graphic Designer; Human Resources Manager; Industrial Agent/Broker; Internet Services Manager; Management Analyst/Consultant; Management Trainee; Market Research Analyst; Marketing Manager; Marketing Specialist; Mechanical Engineer; MIS Specialist; Multimedia Designer; Operations Manager; Paralegal; Production Manager; Project Manager; Purchasing Agent/Manager; Quality Control Supervisor; Sales Executive; Sales Manager; Sales Representative; Secretary; Software Engineer; Systems Analyst; Systems Manager; Technical Writer/Editor; Telecommunications Manager; Typist/Word Processor; Underwriter/Assistant Underwriter; Vice President; Vice President of Finance; Video Production Coordinator; Webmaster. Corporate headquarters location: This Location. Other U.S. locations: Universal City CA.

THE CARL GROUP
21710 Stevens Creek Boulevard, Suite 110, Cupertino CA 95014. 408/255-9171. Fax: 408/255-9170. Contact: Tim Carl, President. E-mail address: jobs@carlgrp.com. World Wide Web address: http://www.carlgrp.com. Description: A contract services firm that places engineering, documentation, and Internet professionals. Positions commonly filled include: Computer Programmer; Multimedia Designer; Software Engineer; Systems Analyst; Technical Writer/Editor. Benefits available to temporary workers: 401(k). Number of placements per year: 50 - 99.

COMFORCE TECHNICAL SERVICES, INC.
17682 Mitchell North, Suite 100, Irvine CA 92614. 949/660-9544. Contact: Manager. Description: A contract services firm. Specializes in the areas of: Light Industrial; Technical.

COMFORCE TECHNICAL SERVICES, INC.
2672 Bay Shore Pkwy, Suite 514, Mount View CA 94043. 650/938-6605. Fax: 650/938-6172. Contact: Manager. Description: A contract services firm. Specializes in the areas of: Technical.

COMFORCE TECHNICAL SERVICES, INC.
5220 Pacific Concourse Drive, Suite 135, Los Angeles CA 90045. 310/643-2682. Fax: 310/643-8656. Contact: Manager. Description: A contract services firm that also

offers some permanent placements. Specializes in the areas of: Technical.

COMFORCE TECHNICAL SERVICES, INC.
9449 Balboa Avenue, Suite 204, San Diego CA 92123. 858/565-4992. Fax: 858/292-8561. Contact: Manager. Description: A contract services firm that also offers some temp-to-perm placements. Specializes in the areas of: Clerical; Electronics; Light Industrial; Pharmaceuticals; Technical.

EDP CONTRACT SERVICES
800 South Figueroa Street, Suite 790, Los Angeles CA 90017. 213/624-9810. Toll-free phone: 888/877-5054. Fax: 213/624-9786. Contact: Branch Manager. E-mail address: la@edpcs.com. World Wide Web address: http://www.edpcs.com. Description: A contract services firm. Positions commonly filled include: Computer Operator; Computer Programmer; Consultant; Database Manager; EDP Specialist; MIS Specialist; Network Support Technician; Software Engineer; Systems Analyst; Systems Manager; Webmaster. Benefits available to temporary workers: 401(k); Medical Insurance. Corporate headquarters location: Newton MA. Other U.S. locations: Nationwide. Average salary range of placements: More than $50,000. Number of placements per year: 200 - 499.

EDP CONTRACT SERVICES
685 Market Street, Suite 470, San Francisco CA 94105. 650/952-5010. Contact: Technical Recruiter. World Wide Web address: http://www.edpcs.com. Description: A contract services firm that also provides some temporary placements. Specializes in the areas of: Computer Science/Software; Engineering; Internet Development; MIS/EDP; Publishing; Technical. Positions commonly filled include: Applications Engineer; AS400 Programmer Analyst; Computer Animator; Computer Engineer; Computer Operator; Computer Programmer; Computer Scientist; Computer Support Technician; Computer Technician; Content Developer; Database Administrator; Database Manager; Desktop Publishing Specialist; EDP Specialist; Internet Services Manager; MIS Specialist; Multimedia Designer; Network/Systems Administrator; Software Engineer; SQL Programmer; Systems Analyst; Systems Manager; Technical Writer/Editor; Telecommunications Manager; Webmaster. Corporate headquarters location: Newton MA. Other U.S. locations: Nationwide. Number of placements per year: 1000+.

EDP CONTRACT SERVICES
3180 Crow Canyon Place, Suite 100, San Ramon CA 94583. 925/866-1030. Contact: Mr. Chris Pankey, Branch Manager. World Wide Web address: http://www.edpcs.com. Description: A contract services firm. Specializes in the areas of: Computer Science/Software; Engineering; Scientific; Technical. Positions commonly filled include: Computer Animator; Database Manager; Design Engineer; Electrical/Electronics Engineer; Graphic Artist; Graphic Designer; Internet Services Manager; MIS Specialist; Multimedia Designer; Online Content Specialist; Quality Control Supervisor; Software Engineer; Systems Analyst; Systems Manager; Technical Writer/Editor; Telecommunications Manager; Video Production Coordinator; Webmaster. Benefits available to temporary workers: 401(k); Dental Insurance; Direct Deposit; Medical Insurance. Corporate headquarters location: Newton MA. Other U.S. locations: Nationwide. Average salary range of placements: More than $50,000. Number of placements per year: 1000+.

HALL KINION
1900 McCarthy Boulevard, Suite 420, Milpitas CA 95035. 408/435-8367. Fax: 408/428-6484. Contact: Loretta Roslund, Account Manager. E-mail address: fmresume@hallkinion.com. World Wide Web address: http://www.hallkinion.com. Description: A contract services firm. Founded in 1987. Specializes in the areas of: Accounting/Auditing; Administration; Personnel/Labor Relations; Sales; Secretarial. Positions commonly

filled include: Accountant/Auditor; Administrative Manager; Buyer; Clerical Supervisor; Computer Programmer; Customer Service Representative; Financial Analyst; Human Resources Specialist; MIS Specialist; Multimedia Designer; Systems Analyst; Typist/Word Processor. **Benefits available to temporary workers:** Dental Insurance; Medical Insurance; Paid Holidays. **Other U.S. locations:** Nationwide. **Average salary range of placements:** $20,000 - $49,999. **Number of placements per year:** 500 - 999.

HALL KINION
1435 River Park Drive, Suite 510, Sacramento CA 95815. 916/646-3000. **Fax:** 916/646-3202. **Contact:** Manager. **E-mail address:** saresume@hallkinion.com. **World Wide Web address:** http://www.hallkinion.com. **Description:** A contract services firm that also provides some permanent placements. **Specializes in the areas of:** Aerospace; High-Tech; Information Systems; Information Technology; Internet Development; Network Administration; Quality Assurance; Systems Administration; Systems Design; Technical Writing.

HALL KINION
19925 Stevens Creek Boulevard, Suite 180, Cupertino CA 95014. **Toll-free phone:** 800/603-6602. **Fax:** 408/863-5707. **Contact:** Manager. **E-mail address:** sjresume@hallkinion.com. **World Wide Web address:** http://www.hallkinion.com. **Description:** A contract services firm that also offers some permanent placements. **Specializes in the areas of:** Computer Hardware/Software; Information Systems; Information Technology; Internet Development; Network Administration; Quality Assurance; Systems Administration; Technical Writing.

HALL KINION
China Basin Landing, 185 Berry Street, Suite 6440, San Francisco CA 94107. **Toll-free phone:** 888/757-4254. **Fax:** 415/974-1354. **Contact:** Manager. **E-mail address:** sfresume@hallkinion.com. **World Wide Web address:** http://www.hallkinion.com. **Description:** A contract services firm that also provides some permanent placements. **Specializes in the areas of:** Information Systems; Information Technology; Internet Development; Network Administration; Quality Assurance; Systems Administration; Systems Design; Technical Writing.

HALL KINION
3675 Mount Diablo Boulevard, Suite 270, Lafayette CA 94549. **Toll-free phone:** 888/770-4254. **Fax:** 925/962-1136. **Contact:** Manager. **E-mail address:** lfyresume@hallkinion.com. **World Wide Web address:** http://www.hallkinion.com. **Description:** A contract services firm that also provides some permanent placements. **Specializes in the areas of:** Information Systems; Information Technology; Internet Development; Network Administration; Quality Assurance; Systems Administration; Systems Design; Technical Writing.

LLOYD-RITTER CONSULTING, INC.
1043 North Shoreline Boulevard, Suite 101, Mountain View CA 94043. 650/964-6644. **Fax:** 650/964-8719. **Contact:** Manager. **Description:** A contract services firm. **Specializes in the areas of:** High-Tech. **Positions commonly filled include:** Computer Programmer; MIS Specialist.

MEDICAL FINANCIAL SERVICES
1060 Willow Street, San Jose CA 95125-2350. 408/280-7309. **Fax:** 408/280-6965. **Contact:** Joanne Hernandez, Sourcer. **Description:** A contract services firm that places medical accountants. **Specializes in the areas of:** Accounting/Auditing; Health/Medical. **Positions commonly filled include:** Accountant/Auditor; Claim Representative; Clerical Supervisor; Health Services Manager; Human Resources Specialist; Medical Records Technician. **Average salary range of placements:** $20,000 - $29,999. **Number of placements per year:** 200 - 499.

MINDSOURCE SOFTWARE ENGINEERS, INC.
2685 Marine Way, Suite 1305, Mountain View CA 94043-1115. 650/254-8909. **Fax:** 650/254-8907. **Contact:** Manager. **E-mail address:** info@mindsrc.com. **World Wide Web address:** http://www.mindsrc.com. **Description:** A contract services firm providing placements in UNIX system administration, Web engineering, and networking. Mindsource Software Engineers also provides some temporary and permanent placements. **Specializes in the areas of:** Computer Science/Software; Network Administration. **Positions commonly filled include:** Computer Programmer; Internet Services Manager; Software Engineer; Systems Analyst; Telecommunications Manager; Webmaster. **Benefits available to temporary workers:** 401(k); Dental Insurance; Medical Insurance. **Average salary range of placements:** More than $50,000. **Number of placements per year:** 200 - 499.

MORGEN DESIGN INC.
310 Via Vera Cruz, Suite 205, San Marcos CA 92069. 760/591-7975. **Contact:** Manager. **Description:** A contract services firm. **Specializes in the areas of:** Engineering. **Positions commonly filled include:** Biomedical Engineer; Chemical Engineer; Civil Engineer; Clinical Lab Technician; Computer Programmer; Design Engineer; Designer; Draftsperson; Electrical/Electronics Engineer; Environmental Engineer; Health Services Manager; Industrial Engineer; Mechanical Engineer; Metallurgical Engineer; MIS Specialist; Petroleum Engineer; Quality Control Supervisor; Registered Nurse; Respiratory Therapist; Software Engineer; Structural Engineer; Systems Analyst; Technical Writer/Editor; Typist/Word Processor. **Corporate headquarters location:** This Location. **Other U.S. locations:** Salt Lake City UT; Seattle WA. **Average salary range of placements:** $30,000 - $50,000. **Number of placements per year:** 50 - 99.

BREN NORRIS ASSOCIATES INC.
100 Ulloa Street, San Francisco CA 94127. 415/564-7440. **Toll-free phone:** 800/765-2736. **Fax:** 415/664-1035. **Contact:** Bren Norris, President. **E-mail address:** bren-bna@ix.netcom.com. **World Wide Web address:** http://www.bren-bna.com. **Description:** A contract services firm that also provides some career/outplacement counseling services. **Specializes in the areas of:** Administration; Computer Science/Software; Technical. **Positions commonly filled include:** Computer Animator; Computer Programmer; Consultant; Database Manager; Design Engineer; Designer; Electrical/Electronics Engineer; Internet Services Manager; Management Analyst/Consultant; Mechanical Engineer; MIS Specialist; Multimedia Designer; Software Engineer; Systems Analyst; Systems Manager; Technical Writer/Editor; Telecommunications Manager; Webmaster. **Benefits available to temporary workers:** Medical Insurance. **Average salary range of placements:** More than $50,000. **Number of placements per year:** 50 - 99.

PC PERSONNEL
101 California Street, Suite 950, San Francisco CA 94111-5866. 415/956-0500. **Fax:** 415/956-1956. **Contact:** Raymond O. Lee, President. **E-mail address:** info@pcpersonnel.com. **World Wide Web address:** http://www.pcpersonnel.com. **Description:** A contract services firm. **Specializes in the areas of:** Administration; Network Administration. **Positions commonly filled include:** Administrative Assistant; LAN/WAN Designer/Developer; MIS Specialist; Systems Analyst; Technical Support Representative; Typist/Word Processor. **Corporate headquarters location:** This Location. **Other area locations:** San Jose CA. **Average salary range of placements:** $30,000 - $50,000. **Number of placements per year:** 200 - 499.

PEOPLEWARE TECHNICAL RESOURCES, INC.
302 West Grand Avenue, Suite 4, El Segundo CA 90245. 310/640-2406. **Fax:** 310/640-2629. **Contact:** Sheryl Rooker, President. **World Wide Web address:**

http://www.peopleware.com. **Description:** A contract services firm. **Specializes in the areas of:** Network Administration; Software Development; Technical. **Positions commonly filled include:** Computer Programmer; Graphic Artist; Graphic Designer; Internet Services Manager; MIS Specialist; Multimedia Designer; Software Developer; Technical Writer/Editor. **Number of placements per year:** 100 - 199.

QUALITY IMAGING SERVICES
P.O. Box 7604, Northridge CA 91327. 818/609-7697. **Fax:** 818/831-1126. **Recorded jobline:** 818/349-7337. **Contact:** Joe Alas, President. **Description:** A contract services firm that provides placements in nuclear medicine, ultrasound, and radiology. The company also places medical and general clerical personnel. **Specializes in the areas of:** Health/Medical; Personnel/Labor Relations; Secretarial; Technical. **Positions commonly filled include:** Accountant/Auditor; Administrative Manager; Advertising Clerk; Clerical Supervisor; Computer Programmer; General Manager; Medical Records Technician; Nuclear Medicine Technologist; Radiological Technologist; Systems Analyst; Typist/Word Processor. **Average salary range of placements:** $30,000 - $50,000. **Number of placements per year:** 50 - 99.

SIERRA TECHNOLOGY CORPORATION
4141 Manzanita Avenue, Suite 200, Carmichael CA 95608. 916/488-4960. **Fax:** 916/488-7058. **Contact:** Jackie Russell, Area Manager. **E-mail address:** resumes@volt-sierra.com. **World Wide Web address:** http://www.volt-west.com. **Description:** A contract services firm. Sierra Technology is a division of Volt Information Sciences. **Specializes in the areas of:** Computer Science/Software; Engineering; Industrial; Manufacturing; Technical. **Positions commonly filled include:** Aerospace Engineer; Agricultural Engineer; Aircraft Mechanic/Engine Specialist; Biochemist; Biological Scientist; Biomedical Engineer; Buyer; Chemical Engineer; Chemist; Civil Engineer; Computer Programmer; Construction and Building Inspector; Cost Estimator; Design Engineer; Designer; Draftsperson; Electrical/Electronics Engineer; Electrician; Environmental Engineer; Industrial Engineer; Mechanical Engineer; Metallurgical Engineer; MIS Specialist; Science Technologist; Software Engineer; Structural Engineer; Technical Writer/Editor; Telecommunications Manager. **Benefits available to temporary workers:** 401(k); Dental Insurance; Medical Insurance; Paid Holidays. **Corporate headquarters location:** Orange CA. **Other U.S. locations:** Nationwide. **Average salary range of placements:** $30,000 - $50,000. **Number of placements per year:** 1000+.

SMARTSOURCE INCORPORATED
500 Ygnacio Valley Road, Suite 390, Walnut Creek CA 94596. 925/935-4200. **Fax:** 925/935-0645. **Contact:** Patty Taylor, Partner. **E-mail address:** resume@smartsourceinc.com. **World Wide Web address:** http://www.smartsourceinc.com. **Description:** A contract services firm. **Specializes in the areas of:** Information Systems; Network Administration; Technical; Telecommunications. **Corporate headquarters location:** This Location. **Other area locations:** Gold River CA; Marina Del Rey CA; Sacramento CA. **Number of placements per year:** 200 - 499.

SOFTWARE ENGINEERING SOLUTIONS
914 North Rengstorff Avenue, Suite F, Mountain View CA 94043. 650/969-0141. **Contact:** Manager. **Description:** A contract services firm. **Specializes in the areas of:** Computer Programming; Engineering.

SYNERGY PERSONNEL SERVICES, INC.
66 Bovet Road, Suite 375, San Mateo CA 94402. 650/341-7777. **Fax:** 650/341-7778. **Contact:** Recruiter. **Description:** A contract services firm that also provides temporary and permanent placements in administrative, office automation, and computer technical areas. **Specializes in the areas of:** Administration. **Positions**

commonly filled include: Clerical Supervisor; Computer Programmer; MIS Specialist; Systems Analyst; Technical Writer/Editor; Typist/Word Processor. **Average salary range of placements:** $30,000 - $50,000. **Number of placements per year:** 1 - 49.

TECHNOLOGY LOCATOR
6480 Weathers Place, Suite 200, San Diego CA 92121-3912. **Toll-free phone:** 800/275-4852. **Fax:** 858/552-6820. **Contact:** Manager. **World Wide Web address:** http://www.tlcsd.com. **Description:** A contract services firm focusing on consulting assignments in engineering, software development, information technology, and network administration. Founded in 1983. **Specializes in the areas of:** Computer Science/Software; Engineering. **Positions commonly filled include:** Computer Programmer; Design Engineer; Electrical/Electronics Engineer; Internet Services Manager; Mechanical Engineer; MIS Specialist; Software Engineer; Systems Analyst. **Benefits available to temporary workers:** 401(k); Cafeteria; Medical Insurance. **Corporate headquarters location:** This Location. **Other U.S. locations:** Mountain View CA. **Average salary range of placements:** More than $50,000. **Number of placements per year:** 200 - 499.

TECHSOURCE
4010 Moorpark Avenue, Suite 208, San Jose CA 95117. 408/345-3077. **Contact:** Manager. **Description:** A contract services firm. **Specializes in the areas of:** Engineering; Information Technology; Technical. **Corporate headquarters location:** Sonoma CA.

VOLT SERVICES GROUP
500 South Douglas Street, El Segundo CA 90245. 310/640-1170. **Fax:** 310/640-1563. **Contact:** Manager. **E-mail address:** voltels@ix.netcom.com. **World Wide Web address:** http://www.volt.com. **Description:** A contract services firm. **Specializes in the areas of:** Computer Science/Software; Engineering; Technical. **Positions commonly filled include:** Aerospace Engineer; Architect; Buyer; Chemical Engineer; Computer Programmer; Cost Estimator; Design Engineer; Designer; Draftsperson; Editor; Electrical/Electronics Engineer; Industrial Engineer; Mechanical Engineer; MIS Specialist; Purchasing Agent/Manager; Software Engineer; Structural Engineer; Systems Analyst; Technical Writer/Editor. **Benefits available to temporary workers:** 401(k); Medical Insurance. **Corporate headquarters location:** Orange CA. **Other U.S. locations:** Nationwide. **Average salary range of placements:** $30,000 - $50,000. **Number of placements per year:** 500 - 999.

VOLT SERVICES GROUP
20545 Valley Green Drive, Cupertino CA 95014. 408/366-5000. **Fax:** 408/366-5005. **Contact:** Manager. **E-mail address:** volt_sj@volt.com. **World Wide Web address:** http://www.volt.com. **Description:** A contract services firm. **Specializes in the areas of:** Computer Science/Software; Engineering; Technical. **Positions commonly filled include:** Buyer; Computer Operator; Computer Programmer; Database Manager; Design Engineer; Draftsperson; Electrical/Electronics Engineer; Electrician; Financial Analyst; Industrial Engineer; Industrial Production Manager; Internet Services Manager; Manufacturing Engineer; Mechanical Engineer; MIS Specialist; Multimedia Designer; Purchasing Agent/Manager; Science Technologist; Software Engineer; Structural Engineer; Technical Writer/Editor; Webmaster. **Benefits available to temporary workers:** 401(k); Direct Deposit; Medical Insurance. **Corporate headquarters location:** Orange CA. **Average salary range of placements:** More than $50,000. **Number of placements per year:** 200 - 499.

WESTERN LABOR LEASING
5555 East Stearns Plaza, Suite 201, Long Beach CA 90815. 562/430-6403. **Toll-free phone:** 800/805-5555. **Fax:** 562/493-5165. **Contact:** Manager. **E-mail address:** wll@aol.com. **World Wide Web address:** http://www.gtesupersite.com/westernlabor. **Description:** A contract

services firm that also provides some temporary placements. **Specializes in the areas of:** Clerical; Light Industrial; Management; Technical. **Office hours:** Monday - Friday, 8:00 a.m. - 5:00 p.m.

H.L. YOH COMPANY
9710 Scranton Street, Suite 250, San Diego CA 92121. 858/622-9005. **Contact:** Manager. **Description:** A contract services firm. **Specializes in the areas of:** Biotechnology; Engineering; Information Systems; Information Technology.

CAREER/OUTPLACEMENT COUNSELING FIRMS

EFFORTLESS RESUMES
151 Deepstone Drive, San Rafael CA 94903. 415/479-6531. **Contact:** Karen Baird, CPRW. **E-mail address:** kb@effortlessresumes.com. **World Wide Web address:** http://www.effortlessresumes.com. **Description:** A professional resume writing service that also provides job search and interview counseling services. Jobseeker pays fee. **Corporate headquarters location:** This Location. **Average salary range of placements:** $50,000 - $100,000. **Number of placements per year:** 500 - 999.

HUMAN RESOURCE MARKETING SERVICES
3600 Wilshire Boulevard, Suite 228, Los Angeles CA 90010. 310/855-1064. **Contact:** Richard Katz, President. **Description:** A career/outplacement counseling service. **Specializes in the areas of:** Personnel/Labor Relations. **Positions commonly filled include:** Radio/TV Announcer/Broadcaster; Video Production Coordinator. **Average salary range of placements:** $30,000 - $50,000. **Number of placements per year:** 50 - 99.

L.A. WORKS
5200 Irwindale Avenue, Irwindale CA 91706. 626/960-3964. **Fax:** 626/962-0064. **Contact:** Traci Smith, Reemployment Center Training Specialist. **E-mail address:** info@laworks.org. **World Wide Web address:** http://www.laworks.org. **Description:** A federally-funded, nonprofit government agency offering resume preparation assistance, mock interviews, transition workshops, and placement in a variety of fields with no cost to the individual. **Positions commonly filled include:** Advertising Clerk; Automotive Mechanic; Bank Officer/Manager; Blue-Collar Worker Supervisor; Claim Representative; Clerical Supervisor; Customer Service Representative; Draftsperson; Human Service Worker; Medical Records Technician; Preschool Worker. **Number of placements per year:** 100 - 199.

LINK BUSINESS & PERSONNEL SERVICES
LINK CAREER CENTER
154 East Gobbi, Ukiah CA 95482. 707/468-5465. **Fax:** 707/468-1171. **Contact:** Rachel Peugh, Owner. **Description:** A small, service-oriented agency that provides skills testing; resume services; word processing projects; bookkeeping; and some temporary and temp-to-

perm placements. LINK Career Center (also at this location) is a vocational school offering computer training, business courses, and basic skills classes. **Specializes in the areas of:** Accounting/Auditing; Bookkeeping; Computer Science/Software; Office Support; Secretarial. **Positions commonly filled include:** Clerical Supervisor; Customer Service Representative; Medical Records Technician; Services Sales Representative; Typist/Word Processor. **Average salary range of placements:** $20,000 - $29,999. **Number of placements per year:** 50 - 99.

STANLEY, BARBER & ASSOCIATES
10050 North Wolfe Road, SW1-160, Cupertino CA 95014. 408/725-1440. **Fax:** 408/725-1461. **Contact:** Nancy Bergman, Vice President. **E-mail address:** info@stanleybarber.com. **World Wide Web address:** http://www.stanleyb.com. **Description:** A career/outplacement counseling firm. **Positions commonly filled include:** Account Manager; Account Representative; Accountant; Administrative Manager; Advertising Executive; Applications Engineer; Assistant Manager; Attorney; Bank Officer/Manager; Biochemist; Branch Manager; Brokerage Clerk; Budget Analyst; Chemical Engineer; Chemist; Chief Financial Officer; Civil Engineer; Computer Programmer; Customer Service Representative; Database Manager; Design Engineer; Editor; Education Administrator; Electrical/Electronics Engineer; Environmental Engineer; Finance Director; Financial Analyst; Fund Manager; General Manager; Human Resources Manager; Industrial Engineer; Industrial Production Manager; Internet Services Manager; Management Analyst/Consultant; Managing Editor; Manufacturing Engineer; Marketing Manager; Marketing Specialist; Mechanical Engineer; MIS Specialist; Operations/Production Manager; Production Manager; Project Manager; Public Relations Specialist; Purchasing Agent/Manager; Quality Control Supervisor; Sales Engineer; Sales Executive; Sales Manager; Sales Representative; Statistician; Systems Analyst; Systems Manager; Technical Writer/Editor; Telecommunications Manager; Vice President; Webmaster. **Average salary range of placements:** More than $50,000.

◆ C O L O R A D O ◆

AAFA
ROCKY MOUNTAIN RECRUITERS
2000 South Colorado Boulevard, The Annex Building, Suite 200, Denver CO 80222. 303/296-2000. **Contact:** Manager. **Description:** An executive search firm. **Specializes in the areas of:** Finance.

ACCOUNTANTS CHOICE PERSONNEL
5600 Greenwood Plaza Boulevard, Suite 208, Englewood CO 80111. 303/741-6494. **Fax:** 303/741-6499. **Contact:** Ginny Matthes, President/Owner. **Description:** An executive search firm operating on both retainer and contingency bases. The firm also provides some temporary placements. **Specializes in the areas of:** Accounting/Auditing; Administration; Banking; Finance. **Positions commonly filled include:** Accountant/Auditor; Bank Officer/Manager; Budget Analyst; Cost Estimator; Credit Manager; Financial Analyst; Management Analyst/Consultant. **Number of placements per year:** 200 - 499.

ACCOUNTANTS EXECUTIVE SEARCH
ACCOUNTANTS ON CALL
1099 18th Street, Suite 2820, Denver CO 80202. 303/571-1116. **Fax:** 303/291-1055. **Contact:** Manager. **Description:** An executive search firm. Accountants On Call (also at this location) is a temporary agency. **Specializes in the areas of:** Accounting/Auditing; Finance.

ACCOUNTING PARTNERS
1200 17th Street, Suite 2630, Denver CO 80202. 303/820-3400. **Fax:** 303/820-3450. **Contact:** Charlene Landers, Office Manager. **Description:** An executive search firm. **Specializes in the areas of:** Accounting; Finance.

ACCOUNTING QUEST
7951 East Maplewood, Suite 250, Englewood CO 80111. 303/773-6100. **Fax:** 303/773-9225. **Contact:** Kristin Schott, Project Manager. **E-mail address:** kristins@accountingquest.com. **World Wide Web address:** http://www.accountingquest.com. **Description:** An executive search firm operating on a contingency basis. Accounting Quest also provides some temporary, permanent, and contract placements. Client company pays fee. **Specializes in the areas of:** Accounting; Finance; Tax. **Other U.S. locations:** Phoenix AZ; Portland OR; Seattle WA. **Average salary range of placements:** $30,000 - $49,999.

ACCOUNTING SOLUTIONS
410 17th Street, Suite 1700, Denver CO 80202. 303/534-1950. **Fax:** 303/534-4850. **Contact:** Branch Manager. **Description:** An executive search firm. **Specializes in the areas of:** Accounting. **Positions commonly filled include:** Accountant.

ADAM JAMES COMPANY
400 Inverness Drive South, Suite 200, Englewood CO 80112. 303/791-9670. **Contact:** Manager. **Description:** A generalist executive search firm.

ADTECH RESOURCES INC.
1665 Grant Street, Denver CO 80203. 303/831-9045. **Contact:** Manager. **Description:** An executive search firm. **Positions commonly filled include:** IT Specialist.

ALEXANDER GROUP
4575 Hilton Parkway, Suite 102, Colorado Springs CO 80907. 719/528-5700. **Contact:** Manager. **Description:** An executive search firm. **Specializes in the areas of:** Information Technology.

ALPHA GROUP
311 1/2 Eighth Street, Suite 600, Glenwood Springs CO 81601. 970/945-2336. **Contact:** J. Astrach, President.

Description: An executive search firm that places individuals in the area of advanced composite materials. **Specializes in the areas of:** Materials.

AMERICAN MEDICAL RECRUITERS
325 Krameria Street, Denver CO 80220. 303/393-0791. **Contact:** Manager. **Description:** An executive search firm. **Specializes in the areas of:** Administration; Health/Medical.

THE ARDENT GROUP
3131 South Vaughn Way, Suite 524, Aurora CO 80014. 303/745-6355. **Fax:** 303/745-6356. **Contact:** Office Manager. **E-mail address:** info@ardentgroup.com. **World Wide Web address:** http://www.ardentgroup.com. **Description:** An executive search firm. Founded in 1991. **Specializes in the areas of:** Communications; Computer Hardware/Software.

WILLIAM B. ARNOLD ASSOCIATES, INC.
Cherry Creek Plaza, 600 South Cherry Street, Suite 1105, Denver CO 80246. 303/393-6662. **Contact:** William B. Arnold, President. **Description:** An executive search firm operating on a retainer basis. Founded in 1964.

AUTOMOTIVE MANAGEMENT CAREERS
2135 Burgess Creek Road, P.O. Box 774711, Steamboat Springs CO 80477. 970/879-4743. **Fax:** 970/879-3710. **Contact:** Dave Miller, President. **Description:** An executive search firm. **Specializes in the areas of:** Automotive.

BADER AND COMPANY
1200 17th Street, Suite 1000, Denver CO 80202. 303/572-6028. **Contact:** Geri Bader, Owner. **Description:** An executive search firm. **Positions commonly filled include:** Attorney; Human Resources Manager. **Average salary range of placements:** More than $50,000. **Number of placements per year:** 1 - 49.

BARTHOLDI & COMPANY
1515 Arapahoe Street, Suite 450, Denver CO 80202. 303/606-4782. **Contact:** Manager. **Description:** An executive search firm.

BECKETT BROWN INTERNATIONAL INC.
1660 South Albion Street, Suite 309, Denver CO 80222. 303/691-2096. **Fax:** 303/691-6210. **Contact:** Manager. **Description:** An executive search firm.

BOLING & ASSOCIATES
55 Madison Street, Suite 735, Denver CO 80206. 303/320-4755. **Fax:** 303/320-5619. **Contact:** Manager. **Description:** An executive search firm.

THE BRIDGE
P.O. Box 777, Westcliffe CO 81252. 719/783-4128. **Fax:** 719/783-4129. **Contact:** Alex B. Wilcox, Principal. **E-mail address:** alex@bridgesearch.com. **World Wide Web address:** http://www.bridgesearch.com. **Description:** An executive search firm. **Specializes in the areas of:** Accounting/Auditing; Administration; Chemicals; Computer Science/Software; Engineering; Environmental; Manufacturing; Personnel/Labor Relations; Sales. **Positions commonly filled include:** Accountant/Auditor; Chemist; Computer Programmer; Engineer; Forester/Conservation Scientist; General Manager; Geologist/Geophysicist; Human Resources Manager; Purchasing Agent/Manager; Quality Control Supervisor; Technical Writer/Editor. **Corporate headquarters location:** This Location. **Average salary range of placements:** More than $50,000. **Number of placements per year:** 1 - 49.

CAREER CONNECTIONS
2404 Sheffield Circle East, Fort Collins CO 80526. 970/221-3511. **Fax:** 970/221-2766. **Contact:** Nancy

Valentine, Owner. **E-mail address:** nancy@ careerdesign.com. **World Wide Web address:** http://www.careerdesign.com. **Description:** Career Connections is an executive search firm operating on a contingency basis. This firm also provides some permanent placements and resume and career counseling services. Client company pays fee. **Specializes in the areas of:** Computer Science/Software; Marketing; Sales; Secretarial; Technical. **Positions commonly filled include:** Account Manager; Account Representative; Accountant; Administrative Assistant; Administrative Manager; Advertising Executive; Assistant Manager; Buyer; Chief Financial Officer; Clerical Supervisor; Computer Engineer; Computer Programmer; Computer Support Technician; Content Developer; Customer Service Rep.; Database Administrator; Database Manager; Desktop Publishing Specialist; Electrical/ Electronics Engineer; Electrician; Graphic Artist; Graphic Designer; Human Resources Manager; Insurance Agent/Broker; Marketing Manager; Marketing Specialist; Network/Systems Administrator; Paralegal; Public Relations Specialist; Real Estate Agent; Sales Engineer; Sales Executive; Sales Manager; Sales Representative; Software Engineer; SQL Programmer; Systems Manager; Technical Writer/Editor. **Corporate headquarters location:** This Location. **Average salary range of placements:** $50,000 - $100,000. **Number of placements per year:** 100 - 199.

CAREER CONNECTIONS
1375 South Ivanhoe Way, Suite B, Denver CO 80224. 303/584-9745. **Contact:** Manager. **Description:** An executive search firm.

CAREER FORUM, INC.
350 Indiana Street, Suite 500, Golden CO 80401. 303/279-9200. **Fax:** 303/279-9296. **Contact:** Stan Grebe, President. **E-mail address:** careerfm@aol.com. **World Wide Web address:** http://www.careerforum.com. **Description:** An executive search firm operating on both retainer and contingency bases. Founded in 1969. **Specializes in the areas of:** Accounting/Auditing; Administration; Advertising; Architecture/Construction; Computer Science/Software; Engineering; General Management; Industrial; Publishing; Sales; Technical. **Positions commonly filled include:** Account Manager; Account Representative; Administrative Manager; Advertising Executive; Applications Engineer; Bank Officer/Manager; Branch Manager; Buyer; Chemical Engineer; Civil Engineer; Computer Operator; Computer Programmer; Construction Contractor; Electrical/ Electronics Engineer; General Manager; Human Resources Manager; Industrial Engineer; Insurance Agent/Broker; Internet Services Manager; Management Trainee; Manufacturing Engineer; Marketing Manager; Marketing Specialist; Mechanical Engineer; MIS Specialist; Operations Manager; Purchasing Agent/ Manager; Quality Control Supervisor; Sales Engineer; Sales Executive; Sales Manager; Sales Representative; Software Engineer; Systems Analyst; Systems Manager; Telecommunications Manager. **Corporate headquarters location:** This Location. **Other U.S. locations:** Nationwide. **Average salary range of placements:** $30,000 - $50,000. **Number of placements per year:** 200 - 499.

CAREER MARKETING ASSOCIATES (CMA)
7100 East Belleview Avenue, Suite 102, Greenwood Village CO 80111. 303/779-8890. **Fax:** 303/779-8139. **Contact:** Jan Sather, President. **E-mail address:** cma@cmagroup.com. **World Wide Web address:** http://www.cmagroup.com. **Description:** An executive search firm operating on both retainer and contingency bases. **Specializes in the areas of:** Computer Science/Software; Engineering; Technical. **Positions commonly filled include:** Biomedical Engineer; Computer Programmer; Database Manager; Electrical/ Electronics Engineer; Internet Services Manager; Manufacturing Engineer; Mechanical Engineer; MIS Specialist; Multimedia Designer; Production Manager; Risk Manager; Sales Engineer; Software Engineer; Systems Analyst; Toxicologist. **Benefits available to** temporary workers: Incentive Plan; Medical Insurance; Paid Vacation. **Corporate headquarters location:** This Location. **Average salary range of placements:** More than $50,000. **Number of placements per year:** 100 - 199.

CAREERS LIMITED
1700 Lincoln Street, Denver CO 80203. 303/832-5200. **Fax:** 303/832-5200. **Contact:** Office Manager. **Description:** An executive search firm. **Specializes in the areas of:** Engineering; Information Technology; Insurance; Office Support; Sales. **Positions commonly filled include:** Benefit Analyst; Engineer; IT Specialist; Sales and Marketing Representative.

CARLSEN RESOURCES, INC.
800 Belford Avenue, Suite 200, Grand Junction CO 81501. 970/242-9462. **Contact:** Manager. **Description:** An executive search firm. **Specializes in the areas of:** Telecommunications.

CARLSON, BENTLEY ASSOCIATES
3889 Promontory Court, Boulder CO 80304. 303/443-6500. **Contact:** Donald E. Miller, President. **Description:** An executive search firm. **Specializes in the areas of:** Computer Science/Software; Data Processing. **Positions commonly filled include:** AS400 Programmer Analyst; Computer Programmer; Systems Analyst. **Number of placements per year:** 1 - 49.

CASEY SERVICES, INC. (CSI)
5300 DTC Parkway, Suite 370, Englewood CO 80111. 303/721-9211. **Fax:** 303/721-9508. **Contact:** Kerrie Hall, Placement Manager. **E-mail address:** csijob@ caseystaffing.com. **Description:** An executive search firm operating on a contingency basis. Casey Services also provides some temporary placements. **Specializes in the areas of:** Accounting/Auditing; Administration; Banking; Computer Science/Software; Finance; General Management; Health/Medical; Sales; Secretarial. **Positions commonly filled include:** Accountant/Auditor; Bank Officer/Manager; Budget Analyst; Clerical Supervisor; Computer Programmer; Cost Estimator; Credit Manager; Customer Service Representative; General Manager; MIS Specialist; Operations/Production Manager; Quality Control Supervisor; Services Sales Representative; Software Engineer; Systems Analyst; Telecommunications Manager. **Benefits available to temporary workers:** Dental Insurance; Medical Insurance. **Corporate headquarters location:** Denver CO. **Other U.S. locations:** Chicago IL. **Number of placements per year:** 200 - 499.

CLOCKWISE PARTNERS
P.O. Box 327, Boulder CO 80306. 303/444-3678. **Contact:** Manager. **Description:** An executive search firm. **Specializes in the areas of:** Engineering. **Positions commonly filled include:** Construction Engineer; Hardware Engineer; Sales Engineer; Software Engineer.

COAST TO COAST EXECUTIVE SEARCH
9769 West 119th Drive, Suite 14, Broomfield CO 80021. 303/464-1704. **Fax:** 303/464-1553. **Contact:** Dennis Updyke, Principal. **E-mail address:** exsrch1@aol.com. **Description:** An executive search firm operating on both retainer and contingency bases. **Specializes in the areas of:** Hotel/Restaurant. **Positions commonly filled include:** Hotel Manager; Restaurant/Food Service Manager. **Average salary range of placements:** More than $50,000. **Number of placements per year:** 1 - 49.

DANIELS & PATTERSON CORPORATE SEARCH, INC.
1732 Marion Street, Denver CO 80218. 303/830-1230. **Contact:** Ruby Chavez Patterson, President. **E-mail address:** dpsearch@nilenet.com. **Description:** An executive search firm that also provides some permanent and contract placements. **Specializes in the areas of:** Computer Hardware/Software; Computer Science/ Software; Information Systems; MIS/EDP; Telecommunications. **Positions commonly filled include:** Administrative Assistant; Computer Programmer; Data Analyst; Data Entry Clerk; MIS

Specialist; Secretary; Software Engineer; Systems Analyst. **Corporate headquarters location:** This Location. **Other U.S. locations:** Nationwide. **Average salary range of placements:** $30,000 - $50,000. **Number of placements per year:** 1 - 49.

DUNHILL OF FORT COLLINS
2120 South College Avenue, Suite 3, Fort Collins CO 80525. 970/221-5630. **Fax:** 970/221-5692. **Contact:** Jerold Lyons, President. **E-mail address:** dfc@frii.com. **World Wide Web address:** http://www.dunhillstaff. com. **Description:** An executive search firm. **Specializes in the areas of:** Agri-Business; Banking; Electrical; Engineering; Wire and Cable. **Positions commonly filled include:** Bank Officer/Manager; Electrical/Electronics Engineer; Mechanical Engineer. **Corporate headquarters location:** Happauge NY. **Average salary range of placements:** More than $50,000. **Number of placements per year:** 1 - 49.

DUNHILL PERSONNEL OF BOULDER
P.O. Box 488, Niwot CO 80544. 303/652-8370. **Fax:** 303/652-8369. **Contact:** Fran Boruff, President. **World Wide Web address:** http://www.dunhillstaff.com. **Description:** An executive search firm. **Specializes in the areas of:** Engineering; Food; General Management; Personnel/Labor Relations; Technical. **Positions commonly filled include:** Account Manager; Administrative Assistant; Chemical Engineer; Civil Engineer; Controller; Electrician; Food Scientist/ Technologist; Human Resources Manager; Industrial Engineer; Industrial Production Manager; Manufacturing Engineer; Mechanical Engineer; Product Manager; Transportation/Traffic Specialist; Vice President. **Corporate headquarters location:** Happauge NY. **Other U.S. locations:** Nationwide. **Average salary range of placements:** $30,000 - $50,000. **Number of placements per year:** 1 - 49.

EDP RECRUITING SERVICES
7340 East Caley Avenue, Suite 230, Englewood CO 80112. 303/694-2222. **Contact:** Manager. **Description:** An executive search firm. **Specializes in the areas of:** Computer Hardware/Software.

EFL ASSOCIATES
7120 East Orchard Road, Suite 240, Englewood CO 80111. 303/779-1724. **Contact:** Manager. **Description:** An executive search firm operating on a retainer basis.

EXECUTIVE CAREER CONSULTANTS (ECC)
1240 South Parker Road, Denver CO 80231. 303/337-9344. **Fax:** 303/337-0693. **Contact:** Office Manager. **Description:** An executive search firm. **Specializes in the areas of:** Administration; Light Industrial; Marketing; MIS/EDP; Sales; Technical.

EXECUTIVE CASINO PLACEMENT SERVICES INC.
387 Monte Vista Road, Golden CO 80401. 303/526-1052. **Contact:** Manager. **Description:** An executive search firm specializing in casino placements.

EXECUTIVE PERSONNEL
4155 East Jewell Avenue, Suite 218, Denver CO 80222. 303/758-4602. **Fax:** 303/782-4982. **Contact:** Susan MacKey, President. **Description:** An executive search firm. **Specializes in the areas of:** Sales. **Positions commonly filled include:** Account Manager; Account Representative; Management Trainee; Sales Manager; Sales Representative. **Average salary range of placements:** $30,000 - $50,000. **Number of placements per year:** 1 - 49.

EXECUTIVE SEARCH PLACEMENTS (ESP)
P.O. Box 17403, Boulder CO 80308. 303/776-0094. **Contact:** Manager. **Description:** An executive search firm. **Specializes in the areas of:** Banking.

EXECUTIVES BY STERLING, INC.
1880 South Pierce Street, Suite 16E, Lakewood CO 80232. 303/934-7343. **Fax:** 303/934-8411. **Contact:** Art Mangual, Principal. **Description:** An executive search

firm operating on both retainer and contingency bases. Executives by Sterling also provides resume consulting services. Founded in 1986. Client company pays fee. **Specializes in the areas of:** Food; Hotel/Restaurant; Marketing; Sales. **Positions commonly filled include:** Account Manager; Account Representative; Chief Financial Officer; Controller; General Manager; Human Resources Manager; Sales Executive; Sales Manager; Sales Representative; Vice President. **Corporate headquarters location:** This Location. **Number of placements per year:** 100 - 199.

F-O-R-T-U-N-E PERSONNEL CONSULTANTS
885 Arapahoe Avenue, Boulder CO 80302. 303/541-9840. **Fax:** 303/541-9841. **Contact:** Branch Manager. **Description:** An executive search firm. **Specializes in the areas of:** Computer Science/Software; High-Tech. **Corporate headquarters location:** New York NY. **Other U.S. locations:** Nationwide.

F-O-R-T-U-N-E PERSONNEL CONSULTANTS
6165 Lehman Drive, Suite 202, Colorado Springs CO 80918. 719/599-7353. **Contact:** David Zolowicz, President. **E-mail address:** david@fpccos.com. **World Wide Web address:** http://www.fpccos.com. **Description:** An executive search firm. **Specializes in the areas of:** Computer Hardware/Software; Manufacturing; Sales; Software Engineering; Warehousing. **Corporate headquarters location:** New York NY. **Other U.S. locations:** Nationwide.

F-O-R-T-U-N-E PERSONNEL CONSULTANTS
7400 East Arapahoe Road, Suite 200, Greenwood Village CO 80112. 303/773-0047. **Contact:** Manager. **Description:** An executive search firm.

F-O-R-T-U-N-E PERSONNEL CONSULTANTS
390 Union Boulevard, Suite 250, Lakewood CO 80228. 303/989-1544. **Fax:** 303/989-1506. **Contact:** Manager. **Description:** An executive search firm.

F-O-R-T-U-N-E PERSONNEL CONSULTANTS OF DENVER
7800 South Elati Street, Suite 319, Littleton CO 80120. 303/795-9210. **Fax:** 303/795-9215. **Contact:** Jan L. Dorfman, President. **E-mail address:** mail@fpcdenver. com. **World Wide Web address:** http://www.fpcdenver. com. **Description:** An executive search firm. **Specializes in the areas of:** Biotechnology; Computer Science/ Software; Engineering; Health/Medical; Manufacturing; Medical Technology; Pharmaceuticals. **Positions commonly filled include:** Biochemist; Biological Scientist; Biomedical Engineer; Chemical Engineer; Chemist; Clinical Lab Technician; Computer Programmer; Design Engineer; Designer; Electrical/ Electronics Engineer; General Manager; Industrial Engineer; Industrial Production Manager; Materials Engineer; Mathematician; Mechanical Engineer; Metallurgical Engineer; MIS Specialist; Operations/ Production Manager; Pharmacist; Quality Assurance Engineer; Quality Control Supervisor; Regulatory Affairs Director; Software Engineer. **Corporate headquarters location:** New York NY. **Other U.S. locations:** Nationwide. **Average salary range of placements:** More than $50,000. **Number of placements per year:** 50 - 99.

GEOSEARCH, INC.
P.O. Box 62129, Colorado Springs CO 80962-2129. 719/260-7087. **Fax:** 719/260-7389. **Contact:** Richard Serby, President. **E-mail address:** resumes@geosearch. com. **World Wide Web address:** http://www.geosearch. com. **Description:** An executive search firm operating on both retainer and contingency bases. **Specializes in the areas of:** Computer Science/Software; Engineering; Technical. **Positions commonly filled include:** Civil Engineer; Computer Programmer; Environmental Engineer; Forester/Conservation Scientist; Geographer; Landscape Architect; Market Research Analyst; Software Engineer; Surveyor; Systems Analyst; Technical Writer/Editor; Urban/Regional Planner. **Average salary**

range of placements: $30,000 - $50,000. **Number of placements per year:** 200 - 499.

GIMBLE & NICOL EXECUTIVE SEARCH
1675 Broadway, Suite 1800, Denver CO 80202. 303/892-6400. **Contact:** Manager. **Description:** An executive search firm. **Specializes in the areas of:** Engineering; Legal.

ROBERT HALF INTERNATIONAL ACCOUNTEMPS
1225 17th Street, Suite 1450, Denver CO 80202. 303/296-1010. **Fax:** 303/292-9403. **Contact:** Staffing Manager. **E-mail address:** denver@accountemps.com. **World Wide Web address:** http://www.rhii.com. **Description:** An executive search firm that also provides some temporary and contract placements. Accountemps (also at this location) provides temporary placements. Client company pays fee. **Specializes in the areas of:** Accounting; Computer Science/Software; Secretarial. **Positions commonly filled include:** Accountant; Administrative Assistant; Applications Engineer; AS400 Programmer Analyst; Auditor; Chief Financial Officer; Computer Engineer; Computer Operator; Computer Programmer; Computer Scientist; Computer Support Technician; Controller; Credit Manager; Customer Service Representative; Database Administrator; Database Manager; Financial Analyst; Internet Services Manager; MIS Specialist; Multimedia Designer; Network/Systems Administrator; Secretary; Software Engineer; SQL Programmer; Systems Analyst; Systems Manager; Typist/Word Processor; Webmaster. **Benefits available to temporary workers:** Medical Insurance; Paid Holidays; Tuition Assistance. **Corporate headquarters location:** Menlo Park CA. **Other U.S. locations:** Nationwide. **International locations:** Canada; Europe; Israel; Australia. **Average salary range of placements:** $30,000 - $49,999. **Number of placements per year:** 500 - 999.

HALLMARK PERSONNEL SYSTEMS, INC.
6825 East Tennessee Avenue, Denver CO 80224. 303/388-6190. **Fax:** 303/355-3760. **Contact:** Joe Sweeney, CPC, General Manager. **Description:** An executive search firm. **Specializes in the areas of:** Computer Science/Software; Engineering; Food; Personnel/Labor Relations; Technical. **Positions commonly filled include:** Applications Engineer; Biochemist; Biological Scientist; Biomedical Engineer; Chemical Engineer; Computer Programmer; Database Manager; Design Engineer; Electrical/Electronics Engineer; Food Scientist/Technologist; Human Resources Manager; Industrial Engineer; Industrial Production Manager; Manufacturing Engineer; Mechanical Engineer; Metallurgical Engineer; MIS Specialist; Operations Manager; Production Manager; Quality Control Supervisor; Software Engineer; Structural Engineer; Systems Analyst; Telecommunications Manager. **Average salary range of placements:** More than $50,000. **Number of placements per year:** 1 - 49.

HEALTH INDUSTRY CONSULTANTS, INC.
MEDQUEST ASSOCIATES
9250 East Costilla Avenue, Suite 600, Englewood CO 80112. 303/790-2009. **Contact:** Jon K. Fitzgerald, President. **Description:** An executive search firm. MedQuest Associates (also at this location) provides medical sales placements. **Specializes in the areas of:** Medical Sales and Marketing. **Average salary range of placements:** More than $50,000.

HEALTHCARE RECRUITERS OF THE ROCKIES, INC.
6860 South Yosemite Court, Suite 200, Englewood CO 80112. 303/779-8570. **Fax:** 303/779-7974. **Contact:** Richard Moore, President. **Description:** An executive search firm. **Specializes in the areas of:** Computer Science/Software; Health/Medical; Sales; Technical. **Positions commonly filled include:** Biomedical Engineer; Clinical Lab Technician; Design Engineer; Dietician/Nutritionist; Health Services Manager; Industrial Engineer; Industrial Production Manager;

Manufacturer's/Wholesaler's Sales Rep.; Marketing Manager; Mechanical Engineer; MIS Specialist; Occupational Therapist; Pharmacist; Physical Therapist; Physician; Registered Nurse; Sales Executive; Sales Manager; Sales Representative; Services Sales Representative; Software Engineer; Systems Analyst. **Corporate headquarters location:** Dallas TX. **Average salary range of placements:** More than $50,000. **Number of placements per year:** 50 - 99.

I.J. & ASSOCIATES, INC.
2525 South Wadsworth Boulevard, Suite 106, Lakewood CO 80227. 303/984-2585. **Fax:** 303/984-2589. **Contact:** Ila Larson, President. **E-mail address:** ilarson@ ijassoc.com. **World Wide Web address:** http://www. ijassoc.com. **Description:** An executive search firm. **Specializes in the areas of:** Computer Science/Software. **Positions commonly filled include:** Computer Operator; Computer Programmer; Database Manager; Internet Services Manager; Project Manager; Systems Analyst; Telecommunications Manager; Webmaster. **Average salary range of placements:** More than $50,000. **Number of placements per year:** 1 - 49.

INFORMATION SYSTEMS CONSULTING CORPORATION
2851 South Parker Road, Suite 730, Aurora CO 80014. 303/283-4800. **Fax:** 303/283-8006. **Contact:** Ron Brennan, Manager. **E-mail address:** opportunities@ iscc.com. **World Wide Web address:** http://www.iscc. com. **Description:** An executive search firm. **Specializes in the areas of:** Accounting; Computer Hardware/ Software; Food; Telecommunications; Transportation. **Other U.S. locations:** Kansas City MO; Dallas TX; Reston VA.

INFORMATION TECHNOLOGIES RESOURCES
370 17th Street, Suite 3170, Denver CO 80202. 303/446-9006. **Fax:** 303/446-9177. **Contact:** Michelle O'Mahoney, President. **Description:** An executive search firm operating on a contingency basis. **Average salary range of placements:** $30,000 - $50,000. **Number of placements per year:** 100 - 199.

INTEGRITY NETWORK INC.
400 Inverness Drive South, Suite 200, Englewood CO 80112. 303/220-9752. **Contact:** Manager. **Description:** An executive search firm. **Specializes in the areas of:** Computer Science/Software; Sales.

JACKSON GROUP INTERNATIONAL
650 South Cherry Street, Suite 610, Denver CO 80246. 303/321-3844. **Fax:** 303/321-3551. **Contact:** Manager. **Description:** An executive search firm.

KUTT, INC.
2336 Canyon Boulevard, Suite 202, Boulder CO 80302. 303/440-6111. **Fax:** 303/440-9582. **Contact:** Greg Neighbors, Partner. **Description:** An executive search firm. **Specializes in the areas of:** Printing; Publishing. **Positions commonly filled include:** Blue-Collar Worker Supervisor; Buyer; Cost Estimator; Customer Service Rep.; General Manager; Industrial Engineer; Industrial Production Manager; Manufacturer's/Wholesaler's Sales Rep.; Mechanical Engineer; Operations/Production Manager; Purchasing Agent/Manager; Quality Control Supervisor; Services Sales Rep. **Average salary range of placements:** $30,000 - $50,000. **Number of placements per year:** 1 - 49.

LEADING EDGE MEDICAL SEARCH
609 Quince Circle, Boulder CO 80304. 303/449-9300. **Fax:** 303/449-2472. **Contact:** Roger Brooks, President. **World Wide Web address:** http://www. leadingedgemedical.com. **Description:** An executive search firm operating on a contingency basis. **Specializes in the areas of:** Executives; Health/Medical; Medical Devices; Start-up Organizations.

MANAGEMENT RECRUITERS OF BOULDER, INC.
P.O. Box 4657, Boulder CO 80306. 303/447-9900. **Fax:** 303/447-9536. **Contact:** Manager. **World Wide Web address:** http://www.mrboulder.com. **Description:** An

executive search firm operating on a contingency basis. **Specializes in the areas of:** Administration; Banking; Engineering. **Positions commonly filled include:** Electrical/Electronics Engineer; Systems Analyst. **Corporate headquarters location:** Cleveland OH. **Other U.S. locations:** Nationwide. **Average salary range of placements:** More than $50,000. **Number of placements per year:** 50 - 99.

MANAGEMENT RECRUITERS OF COLORADO dba THE WESTMINSTER GROUP
8791 Wolff Court, Suite 200, Westminster CO 80031. 303/650-8870. **Fax:** 303/650-8871. **Contact:** Gloria Kellerhals, Managing Partner. **World Wide Web address:** http://www.mrwestminster.com. **Description:** An executive search firm operating on both retainer and contingency bases. **Specializes in the areas of:** Health/Medical; Sales. **Positions commonly filled include:** Account Manager; Account Representative; Computer Programmer; Database Manager; Financial Analyst; Fund Manager; Health Services Manager; Management Analyst/Consultant; Registered Nurse; Sales Executive; Sales Manager; Sales Representative; Systems Analyst; Systems Manager; Technical Writer/Editor. **Corporate headquarters location:** Cleveland OH. **Other U.S. locations:** Nationwide. **Average salary range of placements:** $20,000 - $29,999. **Number of placements per year:** 50 - 99.

MANAGEMENT RECRUITERS OF COLORADO SPRINGS
13 South Tejon, Suite 501, Colorado Springs CO 80903. 719/575-0500. **Contact:** Mark Merriman, Office Manager. **World Wide Web address:** http://www.mrcosprings.com. **Description:** An executive search firm. **Specializes in the areas of:** Administration; Architecture/Construction; Electrical; Engineering; Finance; Food; General Management; Health/Medical; Manufacturing; Operations Management; Personnel/Labor Relations; Procurement; Sales; Technical. **Corporate headquarters location:** Cleveland OH. **Other U.S. locations:** Nationwide.

MANAGEMENT RECRUITERS OF DENVER-DOWNTOWN, INC.
1888 Sherman Street, Suite 600, Denver CO 80203-1159. 303/832-5250. **Toll-free phone:** 800/933-5250. **Fax:** 303/832-5211. **Contact:** Manager. **E-mail address:** mridenver@mridenver.com. **World Wide Web address:** http://www.mridenver.com. **Description:** An executive search firm. **Specializes in the areas of:** Chemicals; Computer Science/Software; Internet Development; Plastics; Sales; Telecommunications. **Positions commonly filled include:** Account Manager; Applications Engineer; AS400 Programmer Analyst; Computer Engineer; Computer Operator; Computer Programmer; Computer Support Technician; Consultant; Database Administrator; Management Analyst/Consultant; MIS Specialist; Network/Systems Administrator; Project Manager; Sales Engineer; Sales Executive; Sales Manager; Sales Representative; Software Engineer; SQL Programmer; Systems Analyst; Webmaster. **Corporate headquarters location:** Cleveland OH. **Other U.S. locations:** Nationwide. **Average salary range of placements:** $50,000 - $100,000. **Number of placements per year:** 200 - 499.

MANAGEMENT RECRUITERS OF GOLDEN HILL
12600 West Colfax Avenue, Suite C-440, Lakewood CO 80215. 303/233-8600. **Contact:** Rodney Bonner, Coordinator. **Description:** An executive search firm. **Specializes in the areas of:** Manufacturing. **Positions commonly filled include:** Electrical/Electronics Engineer; Mechanical Engineer. **Corporate headquarters location:** Cleveland OH. **Other U.S. locations:** Nationwide. **Number of placements per year:** 50 - 99.

WILLIAM K. McLAUGHLIN ASSOCIATES
P.O. Box 1718, Edwards CO 81632. **Toll-free phone:** 800/618-0715. **Contact:** Manager. **Description:** An executive search firm that provides only patent and trademark law placements.

MILLER DENVER
P.O. Box 340, Castle Rock CO 80104. 303/688-6630. **Fax:** 303/688-4334. **Contact:** Eric Miller, Owner. **Description:** An executive search firm operating on a contingency basis. **Specializes in the areas of:** Computer Science/Software; Engineering; Manufacturing; Technical. **Positions commonly filled include:** Applications Engineer; Biomedical Engineer; Buyer; Chemical Engineer; Civil Engineer; Design Engineer; Electrical/Electronics Engineer; General Manager; Industrial Engineer; Industrial Production Manager; Manufacturing Engineer; Mechanical Engineer; Metallurgical Engineer; Operations/Production Manager; Purchasing Agent/Manager; Quality Control Supervisor; Sales Engineer; Software Engineer; Structural Engineer. **Average salary range of placements:** More than $50,000. **Number of placements per year:** 1 - 49.

NATIONAL AFFIRMATIVE ACTION CAREER NETWORK, INC.
4255 South Buckley Road, Suite 299, Aurora CO 80013. 303/699-8599. **Fax:** 303/699-8525. **Contact:** Calvin Booker, President. **Description:** An executive search firm operating on both retainer and contingency bases. **Specializes in the areas of:** Accounting/Auditing; Banking; Engineering; Finance; Food; Manufacturing; Nonprofit; Personnel/Labor Relations. **Positions commonly filled include:** Accountant/Auditor; Attorney; Bank Officer/Manager; Buyer; Ceramics Engineer; Chemical Engineer; Chemist; Computer Programmer; Design Engineer; Financial Analyst; Food Scientist/Technologist; Industrial Engineer; Materials Engineer; Mathematician; Mechanical Engineer; Metallurgical Engineer; MIS Specialist; Purchasing Agent/Manager; Reporter; Software Engineer; Technical Writer/Editor; Telecommunications Manager. **Number of placements per year:** 1 - 49.

NATIONAL EXECUTIVE RESOURCES, INC. (NERI)
5445 DTC Parkway, Englewood CO 80111. 303/721-7672. **Contact:** Manager. **Description:** An executive search firm. **Specializes in the areas of:** Technical.

NELSON COULSON & ASSOCIATES INC.
4830 Rusina Road, Colorado Springs CO 80907. 719/593-9580. **Toll-free phone:** 800/593-9580. **Contact:** Manager. **Description:** An executive search firm that also provides temporary and permanent placements. **Average salary range of placements:** $20,000 - $29,999. **Number of placements per year:** 500 - 999.

NETWORK SEARCH INC.
4625 15th Street, Boulder CO 80304. 303/444-8600. **Contact:** Manager. **Description:** An executive search firm. **Specializes in the areas of:** High-Tech.

PEAK LTD.
3810 McKay Road, Colorado Springs CO 80906. 719/578-1814. **Contact:** Manager. **Description:** An executive search firm. **Specializes in the areas of:** Insurance.

PENDLETON RESOURCES
1301 Pennsylvania Street, Suite 240, Denver CO 80203. 303/832-8100. **Contact:** Manager. **Description:** An executive search firm. **Specializes in the areas of:** Computer Science/Software; Construction; Engineering; Information Systems.

THE PINNACLE SOURCE
4600 South Ulster Street, Suite 975, Denver CO 80237. 303/796-9900. **Contact:** Jordan Greenberg, President. **Description:** An executive search firm operating on both retainer and contingency bases. **Specializes in the areas of:** Computer Science/Software; Sales; Technical. **Positions commonly filled include:** Branch Manager; Computer Programmer; MIS Specialist; Services Sales Representative; Software Engineer; Systems Analyst. **Average salary range of placements:** More than $50,000. **Number of placements per year:** 50 - 99.

PLACEMENT PROFESSIONALS INC.
7700 East Arapahoe Road, Suite 200, Englewood CO 80112. 303/721-8308. **Contact:** Manager. **Description:** An executive search firm. **Specializes in the areas of:** Accounting/Auditing; Legal; Sales.

PREMIER CONSULTING
8400 East Prentice Avenue, Suite 1380, Englewood CO 80111. 303/779-1006. **Contact:** Manager. **Description:** An executive search firm. **Specializes in the areas of:** Computer Hardware/Software.

PROFESSIONAL SEARCH AND PLACEMENT
4901 East Dry Creek Road, Littleton CO 80122-4010. 303/779-8004. **Contact:** John Turner, President. **E-mail address:** pspinc@pspjobs.com. **World Wide Web address:** http://www.pspjobs.com. **Description:** An executive search firm that also provides some contract placements. Founded in 1979. **Specializes in the areas of:** Computer Science/Software. **Positions commonly filled include:** Computer Programmer; Software Engineer; Systems Analyst; Technical Writer/Editor. **Benefits available to temporary workers:** Medical Insurance. **Average salary range of placements:** More than $50,000. **Number of placements per year:** 200 - 499.

REAL ESTATE PERSONNEL
1762 Emerson Street, Denver CO 80218. 303/832-2380. **Fax:** 303/832-2330. **Contact:** Dan Grantham, Owner. **E-mail address:** dangrant@realtyjobs.com. **Description:** An executive search firm that also provides some temporary placements. **Specializes in the areas of:** Accounting/Auditing; Architecture/Construction; Engineering; General Management; Sales. **Positions commonly filled include:** Accountant/Auditor; Administrative Manager; Architect; Buyer; Civil Engineer; Construction and Building Inspector; Construction Contractor; Cost Estimator; Credit Manager; Draftsperson; Electrical/Electronics Engineer; Financial Analyst; General Manager; Human Resources Manager; Landscape Architect; Property and Real Estate Manager; Purchasing Agent/Manager; Urban/Regional Planner. **Number of placements per year:** 50 - 99.

ROMAC INTERNATIONAL
7730 East Belleview Avenue, Suite 302, Englewood CO 80111. 303/773-3700. **Toll-free phone:** 888/883-1936. **Fax:** 303/773-8201. **Contact:** Kellie Hudut, Administrative Service Manager. **World Wide Web address:** http://www.romac.com. **Description:** An executive search firm that provides contract and temporary placements as well as consulting services. The divisions at this location include IT Consulting, IT Placements, Finance, Accounting, Accounting Temps, Engineering, and Scientific. Client company pays fee. **Specializes in the areas of:** Accounting; Computer Science/Software; Engineering; Finance; MIS/EDP; Scientific; Technical. **Positions commonly filled include:** Accountant; Applications Engineer; AS400 Programmer Analyst; Auditor; Budget Analyst; Chief Financial Officer; Computer Engineer; Computer Programmer; Computer Support Technician; Consultant - Technical; Controller; Cost Estimator; Credit Manager; Database Administrator; Database Manager; Economist; Electrical/Electronics Engineer; Finance Director; Financial Analyst; Fund Manager; Internet Services Manager; Manufacturing Engineer; MIS Specialist; Multimedia Designer; Network/Systems Administrator; Operations Manager; Project Manager; Purchasing Agent/Manager; Quality Assurance Engineer; Quality Control Supervisor; Software Engineer; SQL Programmer; Systems Analyst; Systems Manager; Vice President; Vice President of Finance; Webmaster. **Benefits available to temporary workers:** 401(k); Medical Insurance; Paid Holidays. **Corporate headquarters location:** Tampa FL. **Other U.S. locations:** Nationwide. **Average salary range of placements:** $50,000 - $100,000. **Number of placements per year:** 200 - 499.

SALES CONSULTANTS OF DENVER
13111 East Briarwood Avenue, Suite 350, Englewood CO 80112. 303/706-0123. **Contact:** Manager. **World Wide Web address:** http://www.scdenver.com. **Description:** Sales Consultants is an executive search firm. **Specializes in the areas of:** Accounting/Auditing; Administration; Advertising; Architecture/Construction; Banking; Communications; Computer Hardware/Software; Construction; Design; Electrical; Engineering; Finance; Food; General Management; Health/Medical; Insurance; Legal; Manufacturing; Operations Management; Personnel/Labor Relations; Pharmaceuticals; Procurement; Publishing; Retail; Sales; Technical; Textiles; Transportation.

SCHEER & ASSOCIATES
1873 South Bellaire, Suite 900, Denver CO 80222. 303/757-7357. **Contact:** Manager. **Description:** An executive search firm. **Specializes in the areas of:** Sales.

SNELLING PERSONNEL SERVICES
2460 West 26th Avenue, Suite 360-C, Denver CO 80211. 303/964-8200. **Fax:** 303/964-9312. **Contact:** F. Daryl Gatewood, President. **World Wide Web address:** http://www.snelling.com. **Description:** An executive search firm operating on a contingency basis. Snelling Personnel Services also offers some temporary placements. **Specializes in the areas of:** Accounting/Auditing; Administration; Computer Science/Software; Engineering; Finance; Personnel/Labor Relations; Sales; Secretarial; Technical. **Positions commonly filled include:** Accountant/Auditor; Administrative Manager; Aerospace Engineer; Bank Officer/Manager; Clerical Supervisor; Computer Programmer; Electrical/Electronics Engineer; Financial Analyst; Human Resources Manager; Public Relations Specialist; Securities Sales Representative; Services Sales Representative; Systems Analyst; Typist/Word Processor. **Benefits available to temporary workers:** 401(k); Medical Insurance; Paid Holidays; Paid Vacation. **Corporate headquarters location:** Dallas TX. **International locations:** Worldwide. **Average salary range of placements:** $30,000 - $50,000. **Number of placements per year:** 100 - 199.

STAR PERSONNEL SERVICE, INC.
2600 South Parker Road, Building 6, Suite 163, Aurora CO 80014. 303/695-1161. **Fax:** 303/695-1058. **Contact:** Paul Staffieri, Owner. **Description:** An executive search firm that also provides some temporary placements. **Specializes in the areas of:** Accounting/Auditing; Computer Science/Software; Engineering; Finance; General Management; Industrial; Manufacturing; Personnel/Labor Relations; Retail; Sales. **Positions commonly filled include:** Accountant/Auditor; Computer Programmer; Credit Manager; Draftsperson; General Manager; Health Services Manager; Management Trainee; Mechanical Engineer; Property and Real Estate Manager; Purchasing Agent/Manager; Quality Control Supervisor; Software Engineer; Structural Engineer; Underwriter/Assistant Underwriter. **Average salary range of placements:** $30,000 - $50,000. **Number of placements per year:** 50 - 99.

R.W. SWANSON & ASSOCIATES, INC.
10200 East Girard Avenue, Suite 225-B, Denver CO 80231. 303/695-0978. **Contact:** Richard Swanson, President. **Description:** An executive search firm. **Positions commonly filled include:** Accountant/Auditor; Actuary; Adjuster; Administrative Manager; Aerospace Engineer; Agricultural Engineer; Agricultural Scientist; Architect; Attorney; Bank Officer/Manager; Biological Scientist; Branch Manager; Budget Analyst; Buyer; Chemical Engineer; Chemist; Chiropractor; Civil Engineer; Claim Representative; Clinical Lab Technician; Computer Programmer; Construction and Building Inspector; Construction Contractor; Cost Estimator; Counselor; Credit Manager; Customer Service Rep.; Designer; Dietician/Nutritionist; Draftsperson; Economist; Editor; Education Administrator; EEG Technologist; EKG Technician; Electrical/Electronics Engineer; Financial Analyst; Geographer; Geologist/

Geophysicist; Health Services Manager; Human Resources Manager; Industrial Engineer; Industrial Production Manager; Insurance Agent/Broker; Library Technician; Management Analyst/Consultant; Management Trainee; Manufacturer's/Wholesaler's Sales Representative; Mathematician; Mechanical Engineer; Metallurgical Engineer; Meteorologist; Mining Engineer; Nuclear Engineer; Nuclear Medicine Technologist; Operations/Production Manager; Paralegal; Petroleum Engineer; Pharmacist; Physical Therapist; Physician; Physicist; Property and Real Estate Manager; Psychologist; Public Relations Specialist; Purchasing Agent/Manager; Quality Control Supervisor; Radio/TV Announcer/Broadcaster; Radiological Technologist; Real Estate Agent; Restaurant/Food Service Manager; Securities Sales Representative; Services Sales Representative; Software Engineer; Stationary Engineer; Statistician; Structural Engineer; Surgical Technician; Surveyor; Systems Analyst; Technical Writer/Editor; Transportation/Traffic Specialist; Travel Agent; Underwriter/Assistant Underwriter; Urban/Regional Planner; Wholesale and Retail Buyer. **Average salary range of placements:** More than $50,000. **Number of placements per year:** 100 - 199.

TECHNICAL RECRUITERS OF COLORADO SPRINGS
3322 Water Street, Colorado Springs CO 80904. 719/632-3835. **Contact:** Manager. **Description:** An executive search firm. **Specializes in the areas of:** Engineering.

TECHNICAL RESOURCE CONSULTANTS
2851 South Parker Street, Suite 780, Aurora CO 80014. 303/337-2700. **Fax:** 303/283-1854. **Contact:** Manager. **E-mail address:** opportunities@trcdenver.com. **World Wide Web address:** http://www.trcdenver.com. **Description:** An executive search firm. Technical Resource Consultants is a division of MAGIC (Management Alliance Group of Independent Companies). **Specializes in the areas of:** Software Engineering.

TECHNICAL STAFF RECRUITERS
2851 South Parker Road, Suite 780, Aurora CO 80014. 303/283-1600. **Contact:** Michael Birch-Jones, Manager. **E-mail address:** opportunities@tsrdenver.com. **World Wide Web address:** http://www.tsrdenver.com. **Description:** An executive search firm. Technical Staff Recruiters is a division of MAGIC (Management Alliance Group of Independent Companies). Founded in 1976. **Specializes in the areas of:** Computer Hardware/Software; Sales; Telecommunications.

TRIAD CONSULTANTS
8101 East Prentice Avenue, Suite 610, Englewood CO 80111. 303/220-8516. **Fax:** 303/220-5265. **Contact:** Ronald Burgy, Partner. **E-mail address:** ronburgy@tci-colorado.com. **World Wide Web address:** http://www.tci-colorado.com. **Description:** An executive search firm. **Specializes in the areas of:** Administration; Computer Science/Software; Sales. **Positions commonly filled include:** Computer Programmer; MIS Specialist; Software Engineer; Systems Analyst. **Corporate headquarters location:** This Location. **Average salary range of placements:** More than $50,000. **Number of placements per year:** 100 - 199.

J.Q. TURNER & ASSOCIATES, INC.
200 South Wilcox Street, PMB 217, Castle Rock CO 80104-1913. 303/671-0800. **Contact:** Jim Turner, President. **E-mail address:** jqt@jqt.com. **World Wide Web address:** http://www.jqt.com. **Description:** An executive search firm. **Specializes in the areas of:** Biomedical; Computer Hardware/Software; Computer Operations; Computer Science/Software; Engineering; Industrial; Manufacturing; Technical; Telecommunications. **Positions commonly filled include:** Biomedical Engineer; Chemical Engineer; Electrical/Electronics Engineer; Industrial Engineer; Industrial Production Manager; Manufacturing Engineer; Manufacturing Manager; Mechanical Engineer; Optical Engineer; Quality Assurance Engineer; Quality Control

Supervisor; Software Engineer. **Average salary range of placements:** More than $50,000. **Number of placements per year:** 1 - 49.

TWO DEGREES
7951 East Maplewood, Suite 250, Englewood CO 80111. 303/773-6100. **Fax:** 303/773-9225. **Contact:** Keith Pykkonen, Senior Project Manager. **E-mail address:** keithp@twodegrees.com. **World Wide Web address:** http://www.twodegrees.com. **Description:** An executive search firm operating on a retainer basis that also provides contract placements. The agency only works with experienced accounting and finance professionals. Client company pays fee. **Specializes in the areas of:** Accounting; Finance; Tax. **Corporate headquarters location:** Seattle WA. **Other area locations:** Denver CO. **Other U.S. locations:** Chicago IL. **Average salary range of placements:** $50,000 - $100,000.

WELZIG, LOWE & ASSOCIATES
761 West Birch Court, Louisville CO 80027. 303/666-4195. **Contact:** Frank Welzig, President. **Description:** An executive search firm operating on both retainer and contingency bases. **Specializes in the areas of:** Computer Science/Software; Engineering; Oil and Gas; Technical. **Positions commonly filled include:** Aerospace Engineer; Computer Programmer; Design Engineer; Electrical/Electronics Engineer; MIS Specialist; Software Engineer; Systems Analyst.

JULIE WEST & ASSOCIATES
4155 East Jewell Avenue, Suite 210, Denver CO 80222. 303/759-1622. **Fax:** 303/691-8069. **Contact:** Julie West, Owner. **Description:** An executive search firm. **Specializes in the areas of:** General Management; Sales; Sales Promotion. **Positions commonly filled include:** Sales and Marketing Representative; Sales Engineer; Sales Executive; Sales Manager.

WOODMOOR GROUP
P.O. Box 1383, Monument CO 80132. 719/488-8589. **Fax:** 719/488-9043. **Contact:** Ray Bedingfield, President. **E-mail address:** woodmoor@woodmoor.com. **Description:** An executive search firm. **Specializes in the areas of:** Administration; Automotive; Chemicals; Engineering; Finance; Food; Heavy Equipment; Industrial; Manufacturing; Oil and Gas; Technical; Transportation. **Positions commonly filled include:** Accountant; Administrative Worker/Clerk; Agricultural Engineer; Biochemist; Biological Scientist; Biomedical Engineer; Budget Analyst; Ceramics Engineer; Chemical Engineer; Chemist; Chief Financial Officer; Computer Programmer; Controller; Corrosion Engineer; Customer Service Representative; Design Engineer; EDP Specialist; Facilities Engineer; Food Scientist/Technologist; General Manager; Industrial Engineer; Industrial Production Manager; Materials Engineer; Mechanical Engineer; Metallurgical Engineer; Mining Engineer; MIS Manager; MIS Specialist; Petroleum Engineer; Software Engineer; Statistician; Structural Engineer; Systems Analyst; Transportation/Traffic Specialist. **Average salary range of placements:** More than $50,000. **Number of placements per year:** 50 - 99.

THE WOODSTONE CONSULTING COMPANY, INC.
43500 Elk River Road, Steamboat Springs CO 80487. 970/879-1079. **Fax:** 970/879-2345. **Contact:** President. **Description:** An executive search firm operating on a retainer basis. The Woodstone Consulting Company also provides human resources management consulting, executive coaching, and management development services. **Specializes in the areas of:** Food; Operations Management; Personnel/Labor Relations; Sales. **Average salary range of placements:** More than $50,000. **Number of placements per year:** 1 - 49.

YORK & ASSOCIATES
1019 Ninth Street, Greeley CO 80631. 970/352-3086. **Fax:** 970/352-3087. **Contact:** Teri F. York, President. **Description:** An executive search firm. **Specializes in the areas of:** Construction. **Positions commonly filled include:** Civil Engineer; Construction Contractor;

Construction Manager; Cost Estimator; Environmental Engineer; Industrial Engineer; Mechanical Engineer; Mining Engineer; Operations Manager; Petroleum Engineer; Project Manager; Quality Control Supervisor; Structural Engineer; Vice President of Marketing; Vice President of Operations. **Average salary range of** **placements:** More than $50,000. **Number of** **placements per year:** 1 - 49.

YOUNG & THULIN
555 Clover Lane, Suite 100, Boulder CO 80303. 303/499-7242. **Contact:** Manager. **Description:** An executive search firm operating on a retainer basis. **Specializes in the areas of:** High-Tech.

PERMANENT EMPLOYMENT AGENCIES

A TO Z BUSINESS SERVICES
415 East Hyman Avenue, Suite 204, Aspen CO 81611. 970/925-4787. **Fax:** 970/920-1876. **Contact:** Nancy K. Bosshard, Principal. **E-mail address:** a2z@sopris.net. **Description:** A permanent employment agency that also provides some temporary placements. Founded in 1984. **Specializes in the areas of:** Legal; Nonprofit; Secretarial. **Positions commonly filled include:** Administrative Assistant; Clerical Supervisor; Computer Operator; Computer Programmer; Controller; Database Manager; Paralegal; Real Estate Agent; Secretary; Typist/Word Processor. **Average salary range of placements:** $20,000 - $29,999. **Number of placements per year:** 500 - 999.

ABC NANNIES
425 South Cherry Street, Suite 290, Denver CO 80246. 303/321-3866. **Contact:** Ginger Swift, Owner. **World Wide Web address:** http://www.abcnannies.com. **Description:** A permanent employment agency. Founded in 1994. **NOTE:** Candidates should have a minimum of two years of child care experience. **Positions commonly filled include:** Nanny. **Average salary range of placements:** Less than $20,000. **Number of placements per year:** 100 - 199.

ABSOLUTE STAFFING SOLUTIONS
2222 South Havanna, Aurora CO 80203. 303/743-0222. **Contact:** Manager. **Description:** A permanent employment agency. **Specializes in the areas of:** Clerical; Light Industrial; Manufacturing; Sales; Secretarial. **Positions commonly filled include:** Automotive Mechanic; Clerical Supervisor; Customer Service Representative. **Corporate headquarters location:** This Location. **Number of placements per year:** 1000+.

ADD STAFF, INC.
2118 Hollow Brook Drive, Suite 100, Colorado Springs CO 80918. 719/528-8888. **Fax:** 719/528-8890. **Contact:** Manager. **Description:** A permanent employment agency that also provides some temporary placements. **Specializes in the areas of:** Accounting; Clerical; Technical.

AHRNSBRAK AND ASSOCIATES, INC.
14666 East Stanford Place, Aurora CO 80222. 303/693-5403. **Fax:** 303/690-4964. **Contact:** Manager. **Description:** A permanent employment agency. Founded in 1986. **Specializes in the areas of:** Accounting/ Auditing; Administration; Advertising; Banking/ Computer Science/Software; Engineering; Finance; General Management; Insurance; Legal; Marketing; Printing; Publishing; Sales; Secretarial. **Positions commonly filled include:** Account Manager; Account Representative; Administrative Assistant; Administrative Manager; Advertising Clerk; Advertising Executive; Assistant Manager; Bank Officer/Manager; Branch Manager; Budget Analyst; Buyer; Chemical Engineer; Chief Financial Officer; Civil Engineer; Claim Representative; Clerical Supervisor; Computer Animator; Computer Operator; Computer Programmer; Controller; Cost Estimator; Credit Manager; Customer Service Rep.; Design Engineer; Draftsperson; Education Administrator; Electrical/Electronics Engineer; Environmental Engineer; Finance Director; Financial Analyst; General Manager; Graphic Artist; Graphic Designer; Human Resources Manager; Industrial Engineer; Industrial Production Manager; Insurance Agent/Broker; Internet Services Manager; Librarian; Management Analyst/Consultant; Management Trainee; Managing Editor; Manufacturing Engineer; Market Research Analyst; Marketing Manager; Marketing Specialist; Mechanical Engineer; Medical Records Technician; Operations/Production Manager; Paralegal; Production Manager; Project Manager; Public Relations Specialist; Purchasing Agent/Manager; Quality Control Supervisor; Radio/TV Announcer/Broadcaster; Sales Engineer; Sales Executive; Sales Manager; Sales Representative; Secretary; Software Engineer; Statistician; Systems Analyst; Systems Manager; Technical Writer/Editor; Telecommunications Manager; Typist/Word Processor; Underwriter/Assistant Underwriter; Video Production Coordinator.

ASPEN PERSONNEL SERVICES, INC.
1155 South Main Street, Suite 4, Longmont CO 80501. 303/776-9661. **Fax:** 303/776-0195. **Contact:** Manager. **Description:** A permanent employment agency that also provides some temporary and temp-to-perm placements. Founded in 1994. **Specializes in the areas of:** Clerical; General Labor; Industrial; Manufacturing. **Positions commonly filled include:** Typist/Word Processor. **Average salary range of placements:** Less than $20,000. **Number of placements per year:** 200 - 499.

CORESTAFF SERVICES
7355 West 88th Avenue, Suite V, Westminster CO 80021. 303/425-6646. **Fax:** 303/425-1101. **Contact:** Maggie Torres, Branch Manager. **World Wide Web address:** http://www.corestaffservices.com. **Description:** A permanent employment agency that also provides some temporary placements. Founded in 1983. **Specializes in the areas of:** Secretarial. **Positions commonly filled include:** Customer Service Representative; Human Resources Specialist; Typist/ Word Processor. **Benefits available to temporary workers:** 401(k); Medical Insurance; Paid Holidays; Stock Purchase. **Corporate headquarters location:** Houston TX. **Other U.S. locations:** Nationwide. **Number of placements per year:** 1000+.

CORESTAFF SERVICES
303 16th Street, Suite 220, Denver CO 80202. 303/825-1500. **Contact:** Manager. **World Wide Web address:** http://www.corestaffservices.com. **Description:** A permanent employment agency that also provides some temporary placements. **Specializes in the areas of:** Accounting/Auditing; Administration; Manufacturing; Personnel/Labor Relations; Secretarial; Technical. **Positions commonly filled include:** Accountant/Auditor; Claim Representative; Customer Service Representative; Electrician; Human Resources Specialist; Quality Control Supervisor; Technical Writer/Editor; Typist/ Word Processor. **Corporate headquarters location:** Houston TX. **Other U.S. locations:** Nationwide. **Number of placements per year:** 1000+.

GOODWIN PERSONNEL, INC.
800 Grant Street, Suite 110, Denver CO 80203. 303/863-1500. **Fax:** 303/863-1664. **Contact:** President. **Description:** A permanent employment agency. Founded in 1983. **Specializes in the areas of:** Accounting/ Auditing; Administration; Clerical; Consulting; Health/ Medical; Legal; Light Industrial; Technical.

MARGARET HOOK'S PERSONNEL
7800 East Union Avenue, Suite 120, Denver CO 80237. 303/770-2100. **Contact:** Margaret Hook. **Description:** A

permanent employment agency. **Specializes in the areas of:** Administration.

INITIAL STAFFING SERVICES
5299 DTC Boulevard, Suite 340, Englewood CO 80111. 303/694-4522. **Fax:** 303/796-9651. **Contact:** Accounting Specialist. **Description:** A permanent employment agency that also provides some temporary placements. **Specializes in the areas of:** Accounting/Auditing; Finance. **Positions commonly filled include:** Accountant/Auditor; Financial Analyst. **Benefits available to temporary workers:** 401(k); Dental Insurance; Medical Insurance. **Corporate headquarters location:** Houston TX. **Average salary range of placements:** $20,000 - $29,999. **Number of placements per year:** 200 - 499.

INITIAL STAFFING SERVICES
717 17th Street, Suite 140, Denver CO 80202. 303/296-1700. **Fax:** 303/296-1848. **Contact:** Service Manager. **Description:** A permanent agency that also provides some temporary placements. **Specializes in the areas of:** Accounting/Auditing; Administration; Banking; Computer Science/Software; Engineering; Finance; Health/Medical; Insurance; Legal; Personnel/Labor Relations; Secretarial. **Positions commonly filled include:** Accountant/Auditor; Human Resources Specialist; MIS Specialist; Technical Writer/Editor; Typist/Word Processor. **Other U.S. locations:** Nationwide. **Average salary range of placements:** $20,000 - $29,999. **Number of placements per year:** 100 - 199.

JOB STORE STAFFING
7100 East Hampden Avenue, Denver CO 80224. 303/757-7801. **Fax:** 303/757-5604. **Contact:** Dorothy Grandbois, President. **Description:** A permanent employment agency that also provides some temporary placements. **Specializes in the areas of:** Accounting; Administration; Legal; Light Industrial. **Benefits available to temporary workers:** Dental Insurance; Medical Insurance; Paid Holidays; Paid Vacation. **Average salary range of placements:** $20,000 - $30,000. **Number of placements per year:** 1000+.

MEDICAL PERSONNEL RESOURCES
3333 South Bannock Street, Suite 930, Englewood CO 80110. 303/762-0806. **Fax:** 303/762-0875. **Contact:** Ronald Robacker, President. **Description:** A permanent employment agency. Founded in 1981. **Specializes in the areas of:** Health/Medical. **Positions commonly filled include:** Administrative Manager; Bookkeeper; Claim Rep.; Clerical Supervisor; Clinical Lab Technician; EKG Technician; Health Services Manager; Licensed Practical Nurse; Medical Assistant; Medical Records Technician; Radiological Technologist; Registered Nurse; Surgical Technician.

MILE HIGH EMPLOYMENT
7475 Dakin Street, Suite 120, Denver CO 80221. 303/650-0332. **Contact:** President. **Description:** A permanent employment agency.

PAYROLL PRINCIPALS, INC.
118 West Sixth Street, Suite 202, Glenwood Springs CO 81601. 970/945-2433. **Fax:** 970/945-1106. **Contact:** President. **Description:** A permanent employment agency that also provides some temporary placements. Founded in 1979. **Specializes in the areas of:** Clerical; Construction; Light Industrial. **Positions commonly filled include:** Construction Contractor; Construction

Manager. **Benefits available to temporary workers:** Medical Insurance; Paid Vacation. **Average salary range of placements:** $20,000 - $29,999. **Number of placements per year:** 50 - 99.

SURGICAL ASSOCIATED SERVICES, INC.
6825 East Tennessee Avenue, Suite 407, Denver CO 80224. 303/322-9111. **Fax:** 303/322-1529. **Contact:** Ron Johnson, Corporate Office Manager/Vice President. **E-mail address:** rjohnson@surgicalassociated.com. **Description:** A permanent employment agency that also provides some temporary placements. **Specializes in the areas of:** Health/Medical. **Positions commonly filled include:** Registered Nurse; Surgical Technician. **Benefits available to temporary workers:** 401(k); Bonus Award/Plan; Dental Insurance; Disability Coverage; Life Insurance; Medical Insurance; Vacation Pay; Vision Insurance. **Corporate headquarters location:** This Location. **Average salary range of placements:** $30,000 - $49,999. **Number of placements per year:** 50 - 99.

TPM STAFFING SERVICE
6021 South Syracuse, Suite 210, Englewood CO 80111. 303/771-7208. **Fax:** 303/771-7217. **Contact:** Jody Audet, President. **Description:** TPM Staffing Service is a permanent employment agency. **Specializes in the areas of:** Administration; Food; Light Industrial; Retail; Secretarial. **Positions commonly filled include:** Administrative Assistant; Blue-Collar Worker Supervisor; Claim Representative; Clerical Supervisor; Customer Service Representative; Industrial Engineer; Industrial Production Manager; Operations Manager; Project Manager; Secretary; Typist/Word Processor. **Other U.S. locations:** Phoenix AZ; Anaheim CA; Santa Ana CA. **Average salary range of placements:** $20,000 - $29,999. **Number of placements per year:** 1000+.

TERRY PERSONNEL
8958 North Washington Street, Thornton CO 80229. 303/286-8333. **Contact:** Tim Matlick, CEO. **Description:** A permanent employment agency. **Specializes in the areas of:** Clerical; Construction; Manufacturing; Secretarial. **Positions commonly filled include:** Administrative Assistant; Bookkeeper; Buyer; Civil Engineer; Clerk; Computer Operator; Computer Programmer; Credit Manager; Data Entry Clerk; Draftsperson; EDP Specialist; Factory Worker; Insurance Agent/Broker; Legal Secretary; Light Industrial Worker; Mechanical Engineer; Nurse; Public Relations Specialist; Receptionist; Sales Representative; Secretary; Stenographer; Typist/Word Processor. **Number of placements per year:** 200 - 499.

WSI PERSONNEL SERVICE INC.
3400 East Bayaud Avenue, Suite 290, Denver CO 80209. 303/322-8300. **Toll-free phone:** 800/585-2697. **Fax:** 303/322-0233. **Contact:** Shari Donnelly, President. **E-mail address:** sdonne43@aol.com. **Description:** A permanent employment agency that also provides some temporary placements. **Specializes in the areas of:** Accounting/Auditing; Administration; Health/Medical. **Positions commonly filled include:** Accountant/Auditor; Administrative Manager; Claim Representative; Clerical Supervisor; Clinical Lab Technician; Computer Programmer; Customer Service Representative; EEG Technologist; EKG Technician; Emergency Medical Technician; General Manager; Health Services Manager; Licensed Practical Nurse; Nuclear Medicine Technologist; Physical Therapist; Radiological Technologist; Registered Nurse; Services Sales Rep.

TEMPORARY EMPLOYMENT AGENCIES

ATA STAFFING
350 Indiana Street, Suite 800, Golden CO 80401. 303/278-9900. **Fax:** 303/278-7500. **Contact:** Ms. Kari Knowles, Recruiter. **Description:** A temporary agency. **Specializes in the areas of:** Administration; Computer Science/Software; Environmental.

ADECCO
44 Cook Street, Denver CO 80206. 303/399-7706. **Contact:** Manager. **Description:** A temporary agency. **Specializes in the areas of:** Accounting/Auditing; Banking; Clerical; Data Processing; Finance; Insurance; Legal; Secretarial; Technical; Word Processing.

Positions commonly filled include: Administrative Assistant; Bookkeeper; Claim Representative; Computer Operator; Customer Service Representative; Data Entry Clerk; Factory Worker; Legal Secretary; Light Industrial Worker; Medical Secretary; Public Relations Specialist; Receptionist; Typist/Word Processor. **Number of placements per year: 50 - 99.**

AQUENT PARTNERS
6300 South Syracuse Way, Suite 470, Englewood CO 80111-6724. 303/721-6360. **Toll-free phone: 877/PARTNER. Fax:** 303/721-0464. **Contact:** Cheryl Jackson, Manager. **E-mail address:** cherylj@aquent.com. **World Wide Web address:** http://www.aquentpartners.com. **Description:** A temporary agency that provides placements for creative, Web, and technical professionals. Aquent Partners also provides some temp-to-perm, permanent, and contract placements. **Specializes in the areas of:** Administration; Art/Design; Computer Science/Software; Marketing. **Positions commonly filled include:** Computer Animator; Computer Engineer; Computer Operator; Computer Programmer; Content Developer; Database Administrator; Database Manager; Desktop Publishing Specialist; Editor; Editorial Assistant; Graphic Artist; Graphic Designer; Internet Services Manager; Managing Editor; MIS Specialist; Multimedia Designer; Network/Systems Administrator; Production Manager; Project Manager; Software Engineer; SQL Programmer; Systems Analyst; Systems Manager; Technical Writer/Editor; Webmaster. **Benefits available to temporary workers:** 401(k); Dental Insurance; Disability Coverage; Medical Insurance. **CEO:** John Chuang.

ASSISTANCE ON CALL, INC.
7220 West Jefferson Avenue, Suite 127, Lakewood CO 80235-2015. 303/989-5199. **Contact:** Heidi Donckels, Placement Specialist. **Description:** A temporary agency that also provides some permanent placements. Founded in 1983. **Specializes in the areas of:** Dental. **Positions commonly filled include:** Dental Assistant/Dental Hygienist; Receptionist. **Benefits available to temporary workers:** Medical Insurance. **Number of placements per year:** 100 - 199.

BANKTEMPS, INC.
600 Grant Street, Suite 500, Denver CO 80203. 303/861-4115. **Fax:** 303/861-0377. **Contact:** Alice Swanson. **Description:** A temporary agency that also provides some permanent placements. BankTemps employees work at such institutions as banks, credit unions, savings and loans, and brokerage and insurance companies. **Specializes in the areas of:** Banking; Credit and Collection; Personnel/Labor Relations; Secretarial. **Positions commonly filled include:** Bank Officer/Manager; Bank Teller; Branch Manager; Credit Manager; Customer Service Rep.; Human Resources Specialist; Management Trainee; Securities Sales Rep.; Services Sales Representative; Typist/Word Processor; Underwriter/Assistant Underwriter. **Benefits available to temporary workers:** 401(k); Dental Insurance; Medical Insurance; Paid Holidays; Paid Vacation. **Corporate headquarters location:** This Location. **Other area locations:** Colorado Springs CO. **Other U.S. locations:** Chicago IL. **Average salary range of placements:** Less than $20,000. **Number of placements per year:** 1000+.

EAGLE VALLEY TEMPS
P.O. Box 1469, Avon CO 81620. 970/748-1000. **Contact:** Caroline Houston, President. **E-mail address:** evtemps@vail.net. **Description:** A temporary agency that also provides some temp-to-perm placements. Founded in 1989. **Specializes in the areas of:** Accounting; Clerical; Construction; Secretarial. **Average salary range of placements:** Less than $30,000. **Number of placements per year:** 500 - 999.

EXECUTEMPS, INC.
8801 East Hampden Avenue, Suite 210, Bridgecreek Plaza, Denver CO 80231. 303/696-6868. **Contact:** Patricia J. Rostvedt, President. **Description:** A temporary agency that also provides some permanent placements.

Specializes in the areas of: Legal; Office Support; Personnel/Labor Relations; Secretarial. **Positions commonly filled include:** Administrative Assistant; Clerical Supervisor; Legal Secretary; Paralegal; Receptionist; Typist/Word Processor. **Average salary range of placements:** $20,000 - $29,999. **Number of placements per year:** 200 - 499.

THE FIRM
5555 DTC Parkway, Suite C-3210, Englewood CO 80111-3020. 303/889-0000. **Contact:** Office Manager. **World Wide Web address:** http://www.thefirm-us.com. **Description:** A temporary agency that also provides some temp-to-perm placements. **Specializes in the areas of:** Administration. **Positions commonly filled include:** Administrative Assistant; Executive Assistant. **Average salary range of placements:** $30,000 - $50,000. **Number of placements per year:** 100 - 199.

INTELLIMARK
3850 North Grant Avenue, Loveland CO 80538. 970/667-3559. **Toll-free phone:** 800/555-8593. **Fax:** 970/667-8966. **Contact:** Technical Division Manager. **Description:** A temporary agency. **Specializes in the areas of:** Accounting/Auditing; Computer Science/Software; Engineering; Finance; General Management; Industrial; Manufacturing; Technical. **Positions commonly filled include:** Accountant/Auditor; Aerospace Engineer; Architect; Biomedical Engineer; Buyer; Civil Engineer; Clinical Lab Technician; Computer Programmer; Design Engineer; Designer; Draftsperson; Editor; Electrical/Electronics Engineer; Electrician; Environmental Engineer; Financial Analyst; Geologist/Geophysicist; Human Resources Specialist; Industrial Engineer; Internet Services Manager; Market Research Analyst; Mechanical Engineer; MIS Specialist; Operations/Production Manager; Paralegal; Purchasing Agent/Manager; Quality Control Supervisor; Software Engineer; Structural Engineer; Surveyor; Systems Analyst; Technical Writer/Editor; Transportation/Traffic Specialist. **Average salary range of placements:** $30,000 - $50,000. **Number of placements per year:** 1000+.

INTERIM PERSONNEL
8101 East Belleview, Unit W, Denver CO 80237. 303/694-0936. **Fax:** 303/721-8973. **Contact:** Area Manager. **World Wide Web address:** http://www.interim.com. **Description:** A temporary agency that also provides some temp-to-perm placements. **Specializes in the areas of:** Accounting; Banking; Computer Science/Software; Health/Medical; Secretarial. **Positions commonly filled include:** Administrative Assistant; Computer Operator; Customer Service Representative; Design Engineer; Financial Analyst; Human Resources Manager; Secretary; Typist/Word Processor. **Benefits available to temporary workers:** Bonus Award/Plan; Credit Union; Health Benefits; Medical Insurance; Scholarship Program; Training. **Number of placements per year:** 500 - 999.

INTERIM PERSONNEL
1901 North Union Boulevard, Suite 105, Colorado Springs CO 80909. 719/636-1606. **Fax:** 719/636-2705. **Contact:** Area Manager. **World Wide Web address:** http://www.interim.com. **Description:** A temporary agency. Founded in 1946. **Specializes in the areas of:** Administration; Manufacturing; Secretarial. **Positions commonly filled include:** Administrative Manager; Advertising Clerk; Branch Manager; Brokerage Clerk; Buyer; Claim Rep.; Clerical Supervisor; Customer Service Rep.; Human Resources Specialist; Management Trainee; Medical Records Technician; Public Relations Specialist; Purchasing Agent/Manager; Restaurant/Food Service Manager; Typist/Word Processor. **Corporate headquarters location:** Fort Lauderdale FL. **Average salary range of placements:** $20,000 - $29,999. **Number of placements per year:** 1000+.

JOBSEARCH
1107 South Nevada Avenue, Suite 115, Colorado Springs CO 80903. 719/475-9755. **Fax:** 719/575-9585. **Contact:**

Michael Bram, President. **Description:** A temporary employment agency that also provides some contract services. Founded in 1989. **Specializes in the areas of:** Accounting/Auditing; Administration; Advertising; Architecture/Construction; Banking; Broadcasting; Computer Science/Software; Economics; Education; Engineering; Finance; Food; General Management; Health/Medical; Industrial; Insurance; Legal; Manufacturing; Nonprofit; Personnel/Labor Relations; Publishing; Retail; Sales; Secretarial; Technical; Transportation. **Positions commonly filled include:** Accountant/Auditor; Administrative Manager; Advertising Clerk; Architect; Bank Officer/Manager; Branch Manager; Buyer; Claim Representative; Clerical Supervisor; Clinical Lab Technician; Computer Programmer; Construction Contractor; Customer Service Representative; Dental Assistant/Dental Hygienist; Design Engineer; Dietician/Nutritionist; Economist; Editor; Education Administrator; EEG Technologist; EKG Technician; Electrical/Electronics Engineer; Electrician; Environmental Engineer; General Manager; Health Services Manager; Hotel Manager; Human Resources Specialist; Industrial Engineer; Industrial Production Manager; Internet Services Manager; Licensed Practical Nurse; Management Analyst/ Consultant; Management Trainee; Manufacturer's/ Wholesaler's Sales Rep.; Market Research Analyst; Mechanical Engineer; Multimedia Designer; Occupational Therapist; Operations/Production Manager; Paralegal; Pharmacist; Physical Therapist; Property and Real Estate Manager; Public Relations Specialist; Purchasing Agent/Manager; Quality Control Supervisor; Radio/TV Announcer/Broadcaster; Registered Nurse; Reporter; Respiratory Therapist; Securities Sales Representative; Services Sales Rep.; Sociologist; Software Engineer; Teacher/Professor; Technical Writer/Editor; Telecommunications Manager; Typist/ Word Processor. **Number of placements per year:** 1000+.

KELLY IT RESOURCES
6760 Corporate Drive, Suite 100, Colorado Springs CO 80919. **Toll-free phone:** 800/590-2850. **Fax:** 719/528-5603. **Contact:** Branch Manager. **Description:** A temporary agency that also provides some permanent placements. **Specializes in the areas of:** Computer Science/Software; Engineering; Manufacturing; Secretarial. **Positions commonly filled include:** Computer Programmer; Customer Service Rep.; Design Engineer; Draftsperson; Electrical/Electronics Engineer; Mechanical Engineer; MIS Specialist. **Benefits available to temporary workers:** Paid Holidays; Paid Vacation. **Corporate headquarters location:** Troy MI. **Other U.S. locations:** Nationwide. **Number of placements per year:** 1000+.

KELLY SCIENTIFIC RESOURCES
8753 Yates Drive, Suite 105, Westminster CO 80031-3679. 303/427-4140. **Fax:** 303/427-4875. **Contact:** Manager. **World Wide Web address:** http://www.kellyscientific.com. **Description:** A temporary agency. **Specializes in the areas of:** Biomedical; Biotechnology; Chemicals; Environmental; Food; Petrochemical.

KELLY SERVICES, INC.
3500 John F. Kennedy Parkway, Suite 206, Fort Collins CO 80525. 970/223-3955. **Fax:** 970/223-0217. **Contact:** Marianne Godwin, Manager. **Description:** A temporary agency that also provides some permanent placements. Founded in 1946. **Specializes in the areas of:** Clerical; Light Industrial; Marketing; Technical. **Benefits available to temporary workers:** Medical Insurance; Paid Holidays; Paid Vacation. **Corporate headquarters location:** Troy MI. **Other U.S. locations:** Nationwide. **Average salary range of placements:** $15,000 - $35,000. **Number of placements per year:** 1000+.

KELLY SERVICES, INC.
3025 South Parker Road, Suite 101, Aurora CO 80014. 303/695-9292. **Contact:** Manager. **Description:** A temporary agency. **Specializes in the areas of:** Accounting/Auditing; Administration; Banking;

Computer Science/Software; Education; Engineering; Finance; General Management; Industrial; Legal; Personnel/Labor Relations; Retail; Sales; Secretarial. **Positions commonly filled include:** Claim Representative; Clerical Supervisor; Management Trainee; Quality Control Supervisor. **Corporate headquarters location:** Troy MI. **Other U.S. locations:** Nationwide. **Average salary range of placements:** Less than $20,000. **Number of placements per year:** 1000+.

LAB SUPPORT, INC.
600 South Cherry Street, Suite 1125, Denver CO 80222. 303/388-3869. **Fax:** 303/388-3844. **Contact:** Rene Fager, Account Manager. **World Wide Web address:** http://www.labsupport.com. **Description:** A temporary agency. **Specializes in the areas of:** Biology; Technical. **Positions commonly filled include:** Biochemist; Biological Scientist; Chemist; Food Scientist/ Technologist. **Benefits available to temporary workers:** 401(k); Medical Insurance; Paid Holidays; Stock Purchase. **Corporate headquarters location:** Calabasas CA. **Other U.S. locations:** Nationwide. **Average salary range of placements:** $20,000 - $29,999. **Number of placements per year:** 1000+.

LABOR READY, INC.
8840 West Colfax Avenue, Lakewood CO 80215. 303/274-1466. **Contact:** Manager. **Description:** A temporary agency. **Specializes in the areas of:** Industrial; Manufacturing; Personnel/Labor Relations; Publishing; Technical; Transportation. **Positions commonly filled include:** Customer Service Representative; Electrician. **Corporate headquarters location:** Tacoma WA. **Other U.S. locations:** Nationwide. **Number of placements per year:** 1000+.

MANPOWER INTERNATIONAL INC.
5445 DTC Parkway, Suite 925, Englewood CO 80111. 303/740-7310. **Fax:** 303/740-0053. **Contact:** Branch Manager. **Description:** A temporary agency. **Specializes in the areas of:** Administration; Architecture/ Construction; Banking; Computer Science/Software; Engineering; Finance; Industrial; Insurance; Legal; Manufacturing; Personnel/Labor Relations; Publishing; Retail; Sales; Secretarial; Technical. **Positions commonly filled include:** Administrative Manager; Aerospace Engineer; Agricultural Engineer; Aircraft Mechanic/Engine Specialist; Architect; Bank Officer/ Manager; Biomedical Engineer; Blue-Collar Worker Supervisor; Branch Manager; Budget Analyst; Chemical Engineer; Chemist; Civil Engineer; Claim Representative; Clerical Supervisor; Clinical Lab Technician; Computer Programmer; Design Engineer; Electrical/Electronics Engineer; Electrician; Environmental Engineer; Financial Analyst; Human Resources Specialist; Human Service Worker; Industrial Engineer; Mechanical Engineer; MIS Specialist; Quality Control Supervisor; Services Sales Rep.; Systems Analyst; Technical Writer/Editor; Telecommunications Manager; Typist/Word Processor. **Corporate headquarters location:** Milwaukee WI. **International locations:** Worldwide. **Average salary range of placements:** $20,000 - $29,999. **Number of placements per year:** 1000+.

NORRELL INTERIM
4500 Cherry Creek South Drive, Suite 1050, Denver CO 80246-1535. 303/337-6306. **Contact:** Recruiter. **Description:** A temporary agency. **Specializes in the areas of:** Accounting/Auditing; Finance; Personnel/ Labor Relations; Secretarial. **Positions commonly filled include:** Accountant/Auditor; Budget Analyst; Customer Service Representative; Financial Analyst; Human Resources Specialist; Medical Records Technician; Typist/Word Processor. **Benefits available to temporary workers:** Medical Insurance; Paid Holidays; Paid Vacation.

OFFICE SPECIALISTS INC.
11990 Grant Street, Northglenn CO 80233. 303/451-0700. **Contact:** Kelli Squire, Branch Manager. **World Wide Web address:** http://www.officespec.com.

Description: A temporary agency that also provides some temp-to-perm placements. **Specializes in the areas of:** Accounting; Administration; Health/Medical; Personnel/Labor Relations; Secretarial. **Positions commonly filled include:** Accountant; Administrative Assistant; Claim Representative; Clerical Supervisor; Clerk; Customer Service Rep.; Data Entry Clerk; Database Manager; Graphic Artist; Graphic Designer; Medical Records Technician; Personnel Manager; Secretary; Typist/Word Processor. **Benefits available to temporary workers:** Health Benefits; Training. **Corporate headquarters location:** Peabody MA. **Average salary range of placements:** $20,000 - $29,999. **Number of placements per year:** 1000+.

OLSTEN STAFFING SERVICES
6025 South Quebec Street, Suite 250, Englewood CO 80111. 303/793-0330. **Fax:** 303/721-6418. **Contact:** Recruitment Specialist. **Description:** A temporary agency that also provides some contract services. **Specializes in the areas of:** Office Support; Personnel/Labor Relations; Secretarial. **Positions commonly filled include:** Administrative Assistant; Clerk; Customer Service Representative; Data Entry Clerk; Receptionist; Typist/Word Processor. **Corporate headquarters location:** Melville NY. **Other U.S. locations:** Nationwide. **Average salary range of placements:** Less than $20,000. **Number of placements per year:** 1000+.

OLSTEN STAFFING SERVICES
10701 Melody Drive, Suite 425, Northglenn CO 80234. 303/252-8458. **Fax:** 303/252-8511. **Contact:** Manager. **Description:** A temporary agency. Founded in 1950. **NOTE:** Technical and computer training is available. **Specializes in the areas of:** Administration; Engineering; Industrial; Manufacturing; Secretarial; Technical. **Positions commonly filled include:** Administrative Manager; Blue-Collar Worker Supervisor; Clerical Supervisor; Computer Programmer; Customer Service Rep.; Draftsperson; Electrical/Electronics Engineer; Electrician; Mechanical Engineer; MIS Specialist; Software Engineer; Typist/Word Processor. **Benefits available to temporary workers:** Dental Insurance; Medical Insurance; Paid Holidays; Paid Vacation. **Corporate headquarters location:** Melville NY. **Other U.S. locations:** Nationwide. **Average salary range of placements:** Less than $20,000. **Number of placements per year:** 50 - 99.

SOS STAFFING SERVICES
1111 West Victory Way, Suite 108, Craig CO 81625. 970/824-0033. **Fax:** 970/824-0034. **Contact:** Manager. **Description:** A temporary agency. **Specializes in the areas of:** Accounting/Auditing; Banking; Food; General Management; Industrial; Insurance; Manufacturing; Retail; Sales; Secretarial; Technical; Transportation. **Positions commonly filled include:** Accountant/Auditor; Automotive Mechanic; Bank Officer/Manager; Customer Service Representative; Geologist/Geophysicist; Medical Records Technician; Typist/Word Processor. **Corporate headquarters location:** Salt Lake City UT. **Other U.S. locations:** AZ; ID; NM; NV; WY. **Average salary range of placements:** Less than $20,000. **Number of placements per year:** 100 - 199.

SOS STAFFING SERVICES
344 East Foothills Parkway, Suite 24E, Fort Collins CO 80525. 970/282-4401. **Contact:** Branch Manager. **Description:** A temporary agency that also provides career/outplacement counseling. **Specializes in the areas of:** Accounting/Auditing; Food; Industrial; Manufacturing; Personnel/Labor Relations; Publishing; Retail; Secretarial; Technical. **Benefits available to temporary workers:** 401(k); Paid Vacation. **Corporate headquarters location:** Salt Lake City UT. **Other U.S. locations:** AZ; ID; NM; NV; WY. **Average salary range of placements:** $20,000 - $29,999.

STAFF WORKS
2696 South Colorado Boulevard, Suite 555, Denver CO 80222. 303/756-4440. **Fax:** 303/756-0409. **Contact:**

Recruiter. **Description:** A temporary agency that also provides some permanent placements. **Specializes in the areas of:** Clerical; Data Processing; Office Support; Word Processing. **Average salary range of placements:** $20,000 - $29,999. **Number of placements per year:** 100 - 199.

STIVERS TEMPORARY PERSONNEL
2490 West 26th Avenue, Suite A5, Denver CO 80211. 303/458-1441. **Fax:** 303/477-8069. **Contact:** Sandra Nickerson, Regional Manager. **Description:** A temporary agency. **Specializes in the areas of:** Accounting/Auditing; Administration; Insurance; Legal; Office Support; Personnel/Labor Relations; Secretarial. **Positions commonly filled include:** Customer Service Representative; Typist/Word Processor. **Corporate headquarters location:** Chicago IL. **Other U.S. locations:** Nationwide. **Average salary range of placements:** $20,000 - $29,999. **Number of placements per year:** 1000+.

TECH STAFFING
7222 Commerce Center Drive, Suite 102, Colorado Springs CO 80919. 719/592-1133. **Fax:** 719/598-4193. **Contact:** David Landdeck, Accounts Manager. **Description:** A temporary agency that also provides some contract services. Founded in 1969. **Specializes in the areas of:** Administration; Computer Science/Software; Engineering; Industrial; Manufacturing; Personnel/Labor Relations. **Positions commonly filled include:** Administrative Manager; Aerospace Engineer; Agricultural Engineer; Architect; Biomedical Engineer; Buyer; Chemical Engineer; Chemist; Civil Engineer; Computer Programmer; Cost Estimator; Design Engineer; Designer; Draftsperson; Editor; Electrical/Electronics Engineer; Electrician; Environmental Engineer; Human Resources Specialist; Industrial Engineer; Industrial Production Manager; Management Analyst/Consultant; Mechanical Engineer; MIS Specialist; Multimedia Designer; Operations/Production Manager; Petroleum Engineer; Purchasing Agent/Manager; Quality Control Supervisor; Software Engineer; Statistician; Structural Engineer; Technical Writer/Editor; Telecommunications Manager; Typist/Word Processor. **Benefits available to temporary workers:** 401(k). **Corporate headquarters location:** Boston MA. **Average salary range of placements:** $30,000 - $50,000. **Number of placements per year:** 500 - 999.

TEMPORARY ACCOUNTING PERSONNEL, INC.
1801 Broadway, Suite 810, Denver CO 80202. 303/297-8367. **Fax:** 303/296-2223. **Contact:** Marilyn Turner, President. **E-mail address:** taprocky@compuserve.com. **Description:** A temporary agency. Founded in 1985. Client company pays fee. **Specializes in the areas of:** Accounting; Finance. **Positions commonly filled include:** Account Manager; Accountant; Accounting Clerk; Auditor; Budget Analyst; Chief Financial Officer; Controller; Cost Estimator; CPA; Credit Manager; Finance Director; Financial Analyst; Fund Manager. **Benefits available to temporary workers:** 401(k); Health Benefits; Vacation Pay. **Other U.S. locations:** Nationwide. **International locations:** Canada; Europe. **Number of placements per year:** 1000+.

TODAYS TEMPORARY
1099 18th Street, Suite 1820, Denver CO 80202. 303/294-0055. **Fax:** 303/296-6373. **Contact:** Office Manager. **Description:** A temporary agency. **Specializes in the areas of:** Accounting/Auditing; Administration; Advertising; Architecture/Construction; Banking; Broadcasting; Computer Science/Software; Engineering; Finance; General Management; Industrial; Legal; Manufacturing; Nonprofit; Personnel/Labor Relations; Sales; Secretarial; Technical; Transportation. **Positions commonly filled include:** Administrative Manager; Advertising Clerk; Brokerage Clerk; Clerical Supervisor; Credit Manager; Paralegal; Services Sales Rep.; Typist/Word Processor. **Corporate headquarters location:** Dallas TX. **Other U.S. locations:** Nationwide. **Number of placements per year:** 200 - 499.

CONTRACT SERVICES FIRMS

CDI CORPORATION
1115 Elkton Drive, Suite 101, Colorado Springs CO 80907. 719/592-0890. **Contact:** Manager. **World Wide Web address:** http://www.cdicorp.com. **Description:** A contract services firm. **Specializes in the areas of:** Engineering; Technical. **Corporate headquarters location:** Philadelphia PA. **Other U.S. locations:** Nationwide. **International locations:** Worldwide.

CHUCK'S CONTRACT LABOR SERVICE, INC.
707 17th Street, MCI Tower, Suite 100, Denver CO 80201. 303/295-7336. **Contact:** Chuck Harbargh, President. **Description:** A contract services firm. **Specializes in the areas of:** Construction; Food; General Labor; Manufacturing. **Positions commonly filled include:** Construction Trade Worker; Driver; Factory Worker; Light Industrial Worker; Distribution Worker.

HALL KINION
370 Interlocken Boulevard, Suite 150, Broomfield CO 80021. **Toll-free phone:** 888/990-4254. **Fax:** 303/462-0148. **Contact:** Manager. **World Wide Web address:** http://www.hallkinion.com. **Description:** Hall Kinion is a contract services firm that also provides some permanent placements. **Specializes in the areas of:** Computer Hardware/Software; Information Systems; Information Technology; Internet Development; Network Administration; Quality Assurance; Systems Administration; Systems Design; Technical Writing.

HALL KINION
5613 DTC Parkway, Suite 830, Englewood CO 80111. **Toll-free phone:** 800/425-5764. **Fax:** 303/741-9986. **Contact:** Manager. **E-mail address:** coresume@hallkinion.com. **World Wide Web address:** http://www.hallkinion.com. **Description:** Hall Kinion is a contract services firm that also provides some permanent placements. **Specializes in the areas of:** Computer Hardware/Software; Internet Development; Network Administration; Quality Assurance; Systems Administration; Systems Design; Technical Writing.

INTELLIENT
1777 South Harrison Street, Suite 404, Denver CO 80210. 303/759-5064. **Contact:** Manager. **Description:** A contract services firm that also provides some permanent placements. **Positions commonly filled include:** IT Specialist.

INTERIM TECHNOLOGY
1155 Kelly Johnson Boulevard, Suite 110, Colorado Springs CO 80920. 719/522-1616. **Contact:** Manager.

Description: A contract services firm. **Specializes in the areas of:** Information Technology.

MARTINEZ & HROMADA ASSOCIATES, INC.
P.O. Box 21876, Denver CO 80221. 303/428-1728. **Fax:** 303/428-1769. **Contact:** Thomas Albert, Technical Support Specialist. **Description:** A contract services firm. **Specializes in the areas of:** Engineering; Personnel/Labor Relations; Technical. **Positions commonly filled include:** Aerospace Engineer; Architect; Biomedical Engineer; Ceramics Engineer; Chemical Engineer; Chemist; Civil Engineer; Computer Programmer; Construction Contractor; Cost Estimator; Design Engineer; Designer; Draftsperson; Editor; Electrical/Electronics Engineer; Environmental Engineer; Geologist/Geophysicist; Industrial Engineer; Industrial Production Manager; Landscape Architect; Materials Engineer; Mechanical Engineer; Metallurgical Engineer; Mining Engineer; MIS Specialist; Nuclear Engineer; Petroleum Engineer; Purchasing Agent/Manager; Software Engineer; Stationary Engineer; Structural Engineer; Systems Analyst; Technical Writer/Editor. **Average salary range of placements:** $30,000 - $50,000. **Number of placements per year:** 100 - 199.

SOUTHWEST TECHNICAL CONSULTANTS, INC.
120 North Tejon Street, Suite 201, Colorado Springs CO 80903. 719/473-5950. **Fax:** 719/473-5434. **Contact:** Office Manager. **E-mail address:** swtci@swtci.com. **World Wide Web address:** http://www.swtci.com. **Description:** A contract services firm that also provides some temporary and permanent placements. Client company pays fee. **Specializes in the areas of:** Administration; Computer Science/Software; Engineering; MIS/EDP; Technical. **Positions commonly filled include:** Computer Operator; Computer Programmer; Database Manager; Electrical/Electronics Engineer; Industrial Engineer; Internet Services Manager; Manufacturing Engineer; Mechanical Engineer; MIS Specialist; Project Manager; Sales Engineer; Software Engineer; Systems Analyst; Systems Manager; Technical Writer/Editor; Telecommunications Manager. **Corporate headquarters location:** This Location. **Other area locations:** Denver CO.

H.L. YOH COMPANY
1801 Broadway, Suite 920, Denver CO 80202. 303/280-9000. **Contact:** Manager. **Description:** A contract services firm. **Specializes in the areas of:** Computer Hardware/Software; Engineering. **Positions commonly filled include:** Computer Operator; Computer Programmer; Designer; Draftsperson; Engineer.

CAREER/OUTPLACEMENT COUNSELING FIRMS

ABOVE AND BEYOND RESUMES
1660 South Albion Street, Suite 309, Denver CO 80222. 303/782-5447. **Contact:** President. **Description:** A resume writing service.

ALLEN & ASSOCIATES
2000 South Colorado Boulevard, Suite 3000, Denver CO 80222. **Toll-free phone:** 800/562-7303. **Fax:** 303/691-

2662. **Contact:** Office Manager. **World Wide Web address:** http://www.allenandassociates.com. **Description:** Allen & Associates is a career/outplacement counseling firm. **Corporate headquarters location:** Maitland FL. **Other U.S. locations:** Nationwide.

◆ C O N N E C T I C U T ◆

RYAN ABBOTT SEARCH ASSOCIATES
250 West Main Street, Branford CT 06405. 203/488-7245. **Contact:** Manager. **Description:** An executive search firm. **Specializes in the areas of:** Finance; Pharmaceuticals.

ABRAHAM & LONDON, LTD.
7 Old Sherman Turnpike, Suite 209, Danbury CT 06810. 203/730-4000. **Fax:** 203/798-1784. **Contact:** Stuart R. Laub, President. **Description:** A worldwide executive search firm operating on a contingency basis. **Specializes in the areas of:** Computer Science/Software; Marketing; Sales; Scientific; Technical; Telecommunications. **Positions commonly filled include:** Account Manager; Account Rep.; Branch Manager; Management Analyst/ Consultant; Market Research Analyst; Marketing Manager; Marketing Specialist; Online Content Specialist; Project Manager; Sales Engineer; Sales Executive; Sales Manager; Sales Representative; Telecommunications Manager; Vice President of Marketing; Vice President of Sales; Webmaster. **Corporate headquarters location:** This Location. **Other area locations:** Wilton CT. **Average salary range of placements:** More than $50,000. **Number of placements per year:** 200 - 499.

ACCESS FINANCIAL
700 Canal Street, Harbour Square, Stamford CT 06902. **Contact:** Anthony E. Granger, Principal. **E-mail address:** acc.fin@snet.net. **World Wide Web address:** http://www.accfin.com. **Description:** An executive search firm. **Specializes in the areas of:** Accounting; Finance; Tax.

ACCOUNTANTS EXECUTIVE SEARCH
ACCOUNTANTS ON CALL
2777 Summer Street, Stamford CT 06905. 203/327-5100. **Contact:** Manager. **Description:** An executive search firm. Accountants On Call (also at this location) is a temporary agency. **Specializes in the areas of:** Accounting/Auditing. **Positions commonly filled include:** Accountant.

ANDERSON GROUP
P.O. Box 1067, Old Saybrook CT 06475. 860/399-0365. **Fax:** 860/399-0368. **Contact:** James L. Anderson, President. **E-mail address:** anderson.j.l@ worldnet.att.net. **Description:** An executive search firm. **Specializes in the areas of:** Health/Medical; Manufacturing; Marketing. **Positions commonly filled include:** Biological Scientist; Biomedical Engineer; Chemical Engineer; Chemist; Designer; Mechanical Engineer; Metallurgical Engineer; Quality Control Supervisor.

ANDEX EXECUTIVE SEARCH
65 High Ridge Road, Suite 505, Stamford CT 06905. 203/783-1616. **Fax:** 203/783-3939. **Contact:** Manager. **E-mail address:** jobs@andex.com. **World Wide Web address:** http://www.andex.com. **Description:** An executive search firm. **Specializes in the areas of:** Computer Hardware/Software; Computer Science/ Software; Technical.

ANDREWS & MAHON
P.O. Box 97, East Haddam CT 06423. 860/345-4778. **Fax:** 860/345-3944. **Contact:** Marj Andrews, CPC/ Principal. **Description:** An executive search firm. **Specializes in the areas of:** Insurance; Manufacturing. **Positions commonly filled include:** Accountant/Auditor; Adjuster; Administrative Manager; Budget Analyst; Claim Representative; Computer Programmer; Credit Manager; Financial Analyst; General Manager; Health Services Manager; Human Resources Manager; Insurance Agent/Broker; Mechanical Engineer; MIS Specialist; Operations/Production Manager; Quality Control Supervisor; Transportation/Traffic Specialist;

Underwriter/Assistant Underwriter. **Number of placements per year:** 1 - 49.

ATLANTIC SEARCH GROUP
1100 Summer Street, Stamford CT 06905. 203/356-9540. **Contact:** Manager. **Description:** An executive search firm. **Specializes in the areas of:** Computer Programming.

BADAL ASSOCIATES INC.
1155 East Putnam Avenue, Riverside CT 06878. 203/637-3822. **Fax:** 203/637-4815. **Contact:** Manager. **Description:** A generalist executive search firm.

BALDWIN ASSOCIATES INC.
39 Locust Avenue, New Canaan CT 06840. 203/966-5355. **Contact:** Manager. **Description:** An executive search firm operating on a retainer basis. **Specializes in the areas of:** Computer Hardware/Software; Telecommunications.

BANKERS SEARCH
P.O. Box 854, Madison CT 06443. 203/245-0694. **Contact:** Manager. **Description:** An executive search firm. **Specializes in the areas of:** Banking.

BLACKWOOD ASSOCIATES INC.
P.O. Box 1131, Torrington CT 06790. 860/489-0494. **Contact:** Manager. **Description:** An executive search firm. **Specializes in the areas of:** Accounting/Auditing; Banking; Engineering; Health/Medical.

BOEHMER TOMASCO & ALEXANDER (BT&A)
6527 Main Street, Trumbull CT 06611. 203/452-3660. **Contact:** Manager. **Description:** An executive search firm. **Specializes in the areas of:** Technical.

BOND & COMPANY
10 Saugatuck Avenue, Westport CT 06880. 203/221-3233. **Contact:** Manager. **Description:** An executive search firm.

BONNELL ASSOCIATES LTD.
2960 Post Road, Suite 200, Southport CT 06490. 203/319-7214. **Contact:** Manager. **Description:** An executive search firm. **Specializes in the areas of:** Health/Medical.

BRANDYWINE RETAINED VENTURES, INC.
75 Glen Road, Suite 301, Sandy Hook CT 06482. 203/270-6355. **Fax:** 203/270-6369. **Contact:** Branch Manager. **E-mail address:** info@brv-inc.com. **World Wide Web address:** http://www.brv-inc.com. **Description:** An executive search firm. **Specializes in the areas of:** Apparel; Computer Hardware/Software; Consumer Products; Finance; Pharmaceuticals; Telecommunications; Transportation.

BURKE AND ASSOCIATES
THE WESTFIELD GROUP
1010 Washington Boulevard, Stamford CT 06901. 203/406-2300. **Fax:** 203/406-2315. **Contact:** Joanne Fiala, President. **Description:** An executive search firm operating on both retainer and contingency bases. **Specializes in the areas of:** Accounting; Economics; Finance; Personnel/Labor Relations. **Positions commonly filled include:** Accountant; Budget Analyst; Computer Programmer; Financial Analyst; Human Resources Manager; MIS Specialist; Software Engineer; Systems Analyst. **Corporate headquarters location:** This Location. **Other U.S. locations:** White Plains NY. **Average salary range of placements:** More than $50,000. **Number of placements per year:** 200 - 499.

BUXBAUM/RINK CONSULTING
One Bradley Road, Suite 901, Woodbridge CT 06525. 203/389-5949. **Fax:** 203/397-0615. **Contact:** Sherrie

Rink, Partner. **Description:** An executive search firm. **Specializes in the areas of:** Accounting/Auditing; Finance; General Management; Personnel/Labor Relations; Sales. **Positions commonly filled include:** Accountant/Auditor; Controller; Credit Manager; Human Resources Manager; Marketing Specialist. **Number of placements per year:** 1 - 49.

CAHILL ASSOCIATES
P.O. Box 401, 100 Main Street, 2nd Floor, Southington CT 06489. 860/628-3963. **Contact:** Peter M. Cahill, President. **Description:** An executive search firm. **Specializes in the areas of:** Engineering; General Management; Industrial; Manufacturing; Personnel/Labor Relations; Sales; Technical. **Positions commonly filled include:** Buyer; Chemical Engineer; Chemist; Designer; Electrical/Electronics Engineer; Environmental Engineer; General Manager; Human Resources Manager; Industrial Engineer; Industrial Production Manager; Market Research Analyst; Metallurgical Engineer; Operations/Production Manager; Software Engineer. **Average salary range of placements:** More than $50,000.

THE CAMBRIDGE GROUP LTD.
1175 Post Road East, Westport CT 06880. 203/226-4243. **Fax:** 203/226-3856. **Contact:** Mike Salvagno, Executive Vice President. **E-mail address:** msalvagno@cambridgegroup.com. **World Wide Web address:** http://www.cambridgegroup.com. **Description:** An executive search firm operating on both retainer and contingency bases. Founded in 1976. Client company pays fee. **Specializes in the areas of:** Accounting; Computer Science/Software; Finance; General Management; Health/Medical; Internet Development; MIS/EDP. **Positions commonly filled include:** Account Manager; Accountant; Applications Engineer; AS400 Programmer Analyst; CFO; Computer Programmer; Computer Support Technician; Controller; Database Administrator; Database Manager; Finance Director; Financial Analyst; General Manager; Human Resources Manager; Internet Services Manager; MIS Specialist; Network/Systems Administrator; Sales Manager; Software Engineer; SQL Programmer; Statistician; Systems Analyst; Systems Manager; Webmaster. **Corporate headquarters location:** This Location. **Other U.S. locations:** Flemington NJ; Williamsburg VA. **Average salary range of placements:** More than $50,000. **Number of placements per year:** 200 - 499.

CAREER PROSPECTS
991 Main Street, Suite 3D, East Hartford CT 06108. 860/291-9817. **Contact:** Manager. **Description:** An executive search firm. **Specializes in the areas of:** Data Processing.

CHARTER PERSONNEL SERVICES
P.O. Box 1070, Danbury CT 06813-1070. 203/744-6440. **Physical address:** 52 Federal Road, Danbury CT. **Fax:** 203/748-2122. **Contact:** James T. Fornabaio, President. **Description:** An executive search firm that also provides some temporary and contract placements. **Specializes in the areas of:** Accounting; Administration; Biology; Computer Science/Software; Engineering; General Management; Health/Medical; Industrial; Legal; Manufacturing; Pharmaceuticals; Scientific; Secretarial; Technical. **Positions commonly filled include:** Accountant; Administrative Assistant; Administrative Manager; Biochemist; Biological Scientist; Biomedical Engineer; Chemical Engineer; Chemist; Customer Service Rep.; Database Manager; Electrical/Electronics Engineer; Industrial Engineer; Manufacturing Engineer; Mechanical Engineer; MIS Specialist; Paralegal; Pharmacist; Physician; Production Manager; Quality Control Supervisor; Software Engineer; Statistician; Typist/Word Processor; Veterinarian. **Benefits available to temporary workers:** Cafeteria Plan; Medical Insurance. **Number of placements per year:** 200 - 499.

CHARTER PERSONNEL SERVICES
33 Wolcott Road, Suite 6A, Wolcott CT 06716. 203/573-1471. **Contact:** Manager. **Description:** An executive

search firm that also provides some temporary and contract placements. **Specializes in the areas of:** Biomedical; Clerical; General Management; Light Industrial; Technical.

CHAVES & ASSOCIATES
7 Whitney Street Extention, Westport CT 06880. 203/222-2222. **Fax:** 203/222-2223. **Contact:** Victor Chaves, CPC/President. **World Wide Web address:** http://www.chaves.com. **Description:** An executive search firm. **Specializes in the areas of:** Computer Science/Software. **Positions commonly filled include:** Computer Programmer; Database Manager; Internet Services Manager; MIS Specialist; Multimedia Designer; Software Engineer; Systems Analyst. **Other U.S. locations:** Nationwide. **Average salary range of placements:** More than $50,000. **Number of placements per year:** 200 - 499.

CHENEY ASSOCIATES
One Laurel Square, 3190 Whitney Avenue, Hamden CT 06518. 203/281-3736. **Fax:** 203/281-6881. **Contact:** Manager. **E-mail address:** webmaster@cheney.com. **World Wide Web address:** http://www.cheney.com. **Description:** An executive search firm. **Specializes in the areas of:** Administration; Engineering; Information Technology.

CLIFFORD GARZONE ASSOCIATES
321 Main Street, Farmington CT 06032. 860/675-7054. **Fax:** 860/673-5459. **Contact:** Dawn Garzone, CPC/Search Consultant. **Description:** An executive search firm operating on both retainer and contingency bases. Client company pays fee. **Specializes in the areas of:** Insurance. **Positions commonly filled include:** Chief Financial Officer; Marketing Manager; Underwriter/Assistant Underwriter; Vice President. **Average salary range of placements:** $70,000 - $100,000. **Number of placements per year:** 1 - 49.

CUPPLES CONSULTING SERVICES
P.O. Box 2526, Stamford CT 06906-0526. 203/327-4406. **Fax:** 203/327-4688. **Contact:** Gerard A. Cupples, Owner. **Description:** An executive search firm operating on a retainer basis. **Specializes in the areas of:** Engineering; General Management; Manufacturing; Sales. **Positions commonly filled include:** Biomedical Engineer; Electrical/Electronics Engineer; Nuclear Medicine Technologist; Radiological Technologist. **Corporate headquarters location:** This Location. **International locations:** Worldwide. **Average salary range of placements:** More than $50,000. **Number of placements per year:** 1 - 49.

DATA CAREERS
98 Washington Street, Suite 222, Middletown CT 06457. 860/346-1213. **Contact:** Manager. **World Wide Web address:** http://www.datacareers.com. **Description:** An executive search firm. **Specializes in the areas of:** Information Technology. **Positions commonly filled include:** Applications Engineer; Database Administrator; Management; Network Administrator; Network Manager.

DATA TRENDS INC.
4133 Whitney Avenue, Suite 1, Hamden CT 06518. 203/287-8485. **Fax:** 203/248-8138. **Contact:** George Flohr, Manager. **E-mail address:** careers@datatrendsinc.com. **Description:** An executive search firm operating on a contingency basis. Data Trends specializes in placing professionals in Connecticut, suburban New York, and western Massachusetts. **Specializes in the areas of:** Administration; Computer Science/Software. **Positions commonly filled include:** Computer Programmer; Internet Services Manager; MIS Specialist; Software Engineer; Systems Analyst. **Average salary range of placements:** $30,000 - $100,000. **Number of placements per year:** 100 - 199.

DATAPATH SEARCH CORPORATION
32 Sherwood Place, Greenwich CT 06830. 203/869-3536. **Contact:** Manager. **Description:** An executive

search firm. **Specializes in the areas of:** Computer Programming; MIS/EDP. **Positions commonly filled include:** Computer Programmer.

DEVELOPMENT SYSTEMS, INC.
The Highland Building, 402 Highland Avenue, Suite 7, Cheshire CT 06410. 203/271-3705. **Fax:** 203/272-0429. **Contact:** Arnold Bernstein, President. **E-mail address:** developmentsystems@compuserve.com. **World Wide Web address:** http://www.developmentsystems.com. **Description:** An executive search firm. **Specializes in the areas of:** Administration; Computer Hardware/ Software; Personnel/Labor Relations; Retail. **Number of placements per year:** 1 - 49.

DREW PROFESSIONAL RECRUITERS
15 Pepper Ridge Circle, Stratford CT 06614-1000. 203/377-7566. **Contact:** Manager. **Description:** An executive search firm. **Specializes in the areas of:** Health/Medical.

ESA PROFESSIONAL CONSULTANTS
141 Durham Road, Suite 16, Madison CT 06443. 203/245-1983. **Fax:** 203/245-8428. **Contact:** Manager. **World Wide Web address:** http://www.esa-search.com. **Description:** An executive search firm. Founded in 1983.

ENGINEERING RESOURCE GROUP, LLC
37 Cherry Blossom Lane, Shelton CT 06484. 203/922-8198. **Fax:** 203/922-8239. **Contact:** Manager. **E-mail address:** engrgroup@aol.com. **World Wide Web address:** http://www.engrgroup.com. **Description:** An executive search firm. **Specializes in the areas of:** Plastics.

ENGINEERING RESOURCE RECRUITERS
270 Farmington Avenue, Suite 306, Farmington CT 06032. 860/674-0366. **Fax:** 860/674-1267. **Contact:** Manager. **Description:** An executive search firm. **Specializes in the areas of:** Engineering.

EXECUTIVE REGISTER INC.
34 Mill Plain Road, Danbury CT 06811. 203/743-5542. **Fax:** 203/794-1689. **Contact:** J. Scott Williams, President. **World Wide Web address:** http://www.exec-reg.com. **Description:** An executive search firm. Founded in 1978. **Specializes in the areas of:** Accounting/Auditing; Computer Science/Software; Engineering; Finance; Information Systems; Manufacturing. **Positions commonly filled include:** Accountant/Auditor; Chemical Engineer; Computer Programmer; Electrical/Electronics Engineer; Financial Analyst; Mechanical Engineer; MIS Specialist; Multimedia Designer; Software Engineer; Systems Analyst. **Number of placements per year:** 50 - 99.

FAIRFAXX CORPORATION
17 High Street, Norwalk CT 06851. 203/838-8300. **Fax:** 203/851-5844. **Contact:** Jeff Thomas, Owner. **Description:** An executive search firm that also offers some temporary placements.

FINANCIAL CAREERS
Silas Deane Highway, Rocky Hill CT 06067. 860/563-9991. **Fax:** 860/529-1652. **Contact:** Manager. **Description:** An executive search firm. **Specializes in the areas of:** Accounting/Auditing; Banking; Finance.

FINANCIAL EXECUTIVE SEARCH
474 Maple Avenue, Old Saybrook CT 06475. 860/395-5679. **Contact:** Manager. **Description:** An executive search firm. **Specializes in the areas of:** Banking; Finance. **Positions commonly filled include:** Bank Officer/Manager.

FLYNN HANNOCK, INC.
1001 Farmington Avenue, West Hartford CT 06107. 860/521-5005. **Fax:** 860/561-5294. **Contact:** Manager. **Description:** An executive search firm operating on a retainer basis. **Specializes in the areas of:** General Management; Marketing; Personnel/Labor Relations;

Sales. **Positions commonly filled include:** General Manager; Human Resources Manager. **Corporate headquarters location:** This Location. **Other U.S. locations:** Stamford CT. **Average salary range of placements:** More than $100,000. **Number of placements per year:** 1 - 49.

FRIEDMAN ASSOCIATES
129 Main Street, Old Saybrook CT 06475. 860/388-9400. **Fax:** 860/388-6900. **Contact:** Manager. **Description:** An executive search firm. **Specializes in the areas of:** Engineering.

GATFIELD GREENWICH & ASSOCIATES
537 Steamboat Road, Suite 400, Greenwich CT 06830. 203/622-9191. **Contact:** Manager. **Description:** An executive search firm.

GOODRICH & SHERWOOD ASSOCIATES, INC.
401 Merritt 7, Corporate Park, 5th Floor, Norwalk CT 06851. 203/847-2525. **Fax:** 203/846-2880. **Contact:** Manager. **World Wide Web address:** http://www. goodrichsherwood.com. **Description:** An executive search firm that also offers outplacement/career transition counseling, executive coaching, and Human Resources consulting. **Specializes in the areas of:** Human Resources. **Corporate headquarters location:** New York NY. **Other U.S. locations:** Shelton CT; Parsippany NJ; Princeton NJ; Rochester NY.

GREY ASSOCIATES
21 Eastwood Road, Norwalk CT 06851. 203/849-9291. **Contact:** Manager. **Description:** An executive search firm. **Specializes in the areas of:** Information Systems.

ALICE GROVES CO.
700 Canal Street, Stamford CT 06902. 203/324-3225. **Contact:** Ken Leavee, President. **Description:** An executive search firm. **Specializes in the areas of:** Retail. **Positions commonly filled include:** Human Resources Manager; Marketing Specialist; Merchandiser; MIS Specialist; Operations/Production Manager. **Average salary range of placements:** More than $50,000. **Number of placements per year:** 1 - 49.

ROBERT HALF INTERNATIONAL ACCOUNTEMPS
One Corporate Drive, Suite 118, Shelton CT 06484. 203/929-2600. **Contact:** Manager. **World Wide Web address:** http://www.roberthalf.com. **Description:** An executive search firm. Accountemps (also at this location) provides temporary placements. **Specializes in the areas of:** Accounting. **Corporate headquarters location:** Menlo Park CA. **Other U.S. locations:** Nationwide. **International locations:** Worldwide.

ROBERT HALF INTERNATIONAL ACCOUNTEMPS
One Canterbury Green, 4th Floor, Stamford CT 06901. 203/324-3399. **Contact:** Manager. **E-mail address:** stamford@roberthalf.com. **World Wide Web address:** http://www.roberthalf.com. **Description:** An executive search firm. Accountemps (also at this location) provides temporary placements. **Specializes in the areas of:** Accounting/Auditing. **Corporate headquarters location:** Menlo Park CA. **Other U.S. locations:** Nationwide. **International locations:** Worldwide.

ROBERT HALF INTERNATIONAL, INC. ACCOUNTEMPS
555 Long Wharf Drive, New Haven CT 06511. 203/562-9262. **Toll-free phone:** 800/803-8367. **Fax:** 203/624-3247. **Contact:** Manager. **World Wide Web address:** http://www.accountemps.com. **Description:** An executive search firm. Accountemps (also at this location) provides temporary placements. Client company pays fee. **Specializes in the areas of:** Accounting; Finance. **Positions commonly filled include:** Accountant; Adjuster; Auditor; Bank Officer/ Manager; Budget Analyst; Chief Financial Officer; Controller; Cost Estimator; Credit Manager; Finance Director; Financial Analyst; Fund Manager; Purchasing

Agent/Manager. **Corporate headquarters location:** Menlo Park CA. **Other U.S. locations:** Nationwide. **International locations:** Worldwide. **Average salary range of placements:** $30,000 - $49,999.

HALLMARK TOTALTECH, INC.
1155 Silas Deane Highway, Wethersfield CT 06109. 860/529-7500. **Toll-free phone:** 800/876-4255. **Fax:** 860/529-9800. **Contact:** Andrew Parker, President. **E-mail address:** jobs@hallmarkit.com. **World Wide Web address:** http://www.hallmarkit.com. **Description:** An executive search firm operating on a contingency basis. The firm also offers some temporary and contract placements. **Specializes in the areas of:** Administration; Computer Science/Software; Consulting; Engineering; Industrial; Internet Development; MIS/EDP; Scientific; Secretarial; Technical. **Positions commonly filled include:** Administrative Assistant; Applications Engineer; AS400 Programmer Analyst; Biochemist; Biological Scientist; Biomedical Engineer; Chemical Engineer; Chemist; Civil Engineer; Claim Rep.; Clinical Lab Technician; Computer Animator; Computer Engineer; Computer Operator; Computer Programmer; Computer Scientist; Computer Support Technician; Computer Technician; Customer Service Rep.; Database Administrator; Database Manager; Design Engineer; Draftsperson; Electrical/Electronics Engineer; Electrician; Environmental Engineer; Geologist/ Geophysicist; Industrial Engineer; Internet Services Manager; Manufacturing Engineer; Metallurgical Engineer; MIS Specialist; Multimedia Designer; Network/Systems Administrator; Quality Assurance Engineer; Secretary; Software Engineer; SQL Programmer; Statistician; Systems Analyst; Systems Manager; Transportation/Traffic Specialist; Webmaster. **Corporate headquarters location:** This Location. **Average salary range of placements:** $50,000 - $100,000. **Number of placements per year:** 500 - 999.

HARBOR ASSOCIATES
70 New Canaan Avenue, Norwalk CT 06850. 203/849-0863. **Contact:** Manager. **Description:** An executive search firm. **Specializes in the areas of:** Accounting/Auditing; Finance. **Positions commonly filled include:** Accountant/Auditor; Tax Specialist.

HARRIS HEERY EXECUTIVE RESOURCE CONSULTANTS
One Norwalk West, 40 Richards Avenue, Norwalk CT 06854. 203/857-0808. **Fax:** 203/857-0822. **Contact:** William Heery, Partner. **World Wide Web address:** http://www.marketingrecruiter.com. **Description:** An executive search firm that operates on a retainer basis. Founded in 1981. **Specializes in the areas of:** Marketing.

HARVARD AIMES GROUP
6 Holcomb Street, P.O. Box 16006, West Haven CT 06516. 203/933-1976. **Fax:** 203/933-0281. **Contact:** Manager. **Description:** An executive search firm that is engaged exclusively in the placement of corporate risk management professionals. **Specializes in the areas of:** Risk Management.

HEIDRICK & STRUGGLES
3 Greenwich Office Park, 2nd Floor, Greenwich CT 06831. 203/862-4600. **Fax:** 203/629-1331. **Contact:** Manager. **Description:** An executive search firm.

HIGBEE ASSOCIATES
112 Rowayton Avenue, Rowayton CT 06853. 203/853-7600. **Fax:** 203/853-2426. **Contact:** R. Higbee, President. **Description:** Higbee Associates is an executive search firm operating on a retainer basis. **Specializes in the areas of:** Banking; Health/Medical; Technical; Telecommunications. **Positions commonly filled include:** Human Resources Manager; Market Research Analyst; Marketing Manager; Pharmacist; Physician; Sales Executive; Sales Manager; Software Engineer; Systems Analyst. **Average salary range of placements:** More than $50,000. **Number of placements per year:** 50 - 99.

HIPP WATERS PROFESSIONAL SEARCH
777 Summer Street, Stamford CT 06901. 203/357-8400. **Contact:** Manager. **Description:** An executive search firm. **Specializes in the areas of:** Accounting/Auditing; Computer Science/Software; Finance; Information Systems; Insurance.

HOBSON ASSOCIATES
P.O. Box 278, Cheshire CT 06410. 203/272-0227. **Contact:** Manager. **Description:** An executive search firm. **Specializes in the areas of:** Sales.

HUMAN RESOURCE CONSULTANTS LTD.
350 Silas Deane Highway, Suite 303, Wethersfield CT 06109. 860/257-7300. **Contact:** Joseph Koneski, CPC/President. **Description:** An executive search firm operating on both retainer and contingency bases. **Specializes in the areas of:** Engineering; Industrial; Personnel/Labor Relations; Scientific; Technical. **Positions commonly filled include:** Buyer; Chemical Engineer; Chemist; Design Engineer; Electrical/ Electronics Engineer; Environmental Engineer; General Manager; Human Resources Manager; Industrial Engineer; Industrial Production Manager; Management Analyst/Consultant; Manufacturing Engineer; Mechanical Engineer; Metallurgical Engineer; Production Manager; Project Manager; Purchasing Agent/Manager; Quality Control Supervisor; Software Engineer. **Average salary range of placements:** More than $50,000. **Number of placements per year:** 100 - 199.

HUNTINGTON GROUP
6527 Main Street, Trumbull CT 06611. 203/261-1166. **Fax:** 203/452-9153. **Contact:** Rose Rutledge, Associate. **E-mail address:** rose@hgllc.com. **World Wide Web address:** http://www.hgllc.com. **Description:** An executive search firm operating on a retainer basis. **Specializes in the areas of:** Information Technology. **Positions commonly filled include:** MIS Specialist. **Average salary range of placements:** More than $50,000. **Number of placements per year:** 100 - 199.

INFONET LLC
628 Hebron Avenue, Building 2, Suite 505, Glastonbury CT 06033. 860/652-8000. **Contact:** Manager. **E-mail address:** resources@netstaffer.com. **Description:** An executive search firm. **Specializes in the areas of:** Computer Programming; Computer Science/Software; Information Technology; Internet Development. **Other U.S. locations:** New York NY.

JOHNSON & COMPANY
184 Old Ridgefield Road, Wilton CT 06897. 203/761-1212. **Contact:** Manager. **Description:** An executive search firm.

A.T. KEARNEY EXECUTIVE SEARCH
One Landmark Square, Suite 426, Stamford CT 06901. 203/969-2222. **Contact:** Manager. **Description:** An executive search firm. **International locations:** Worldwide.

KILMAN ADVISORY GROUP
406 Farmington Avenue, Farmington CT 06032-1964. 860/676-7817. **Fax:** 860/676-7839. **Contact:** Paul Kilman, Principal. **Description:** An executive search firm operating on a retainer basis. **Specializes in the areas of:** Legal. **Positions commonly filled include:** Attorney. **Average salary range of placements:** More than $50,000. **Number of placements per year:** 1 - 49.

KORN/FERRY INTERNATIONAL
One Landmark Square, Stamford CT 06901. 203/359-3350. **Fax:** 203/327-2044. **Contact:** Manager. **World Wide Web address:** http://www.kornferry.com. **Description:** An executive search firm that places upper-level managers in a variety of industries. **Corporate headquarters location:** Los Angeles CA. **International locations:** Worldwide. **Average salary range of placements:** More than $50,000.

THE LA POINTE GROUP INC.
365 Highland Avenue, Suite 101, Cheshire CT 06410. 203/250-1900. **Contact:** Manager. **Description:** An executive search firm. **Specializes in the areas of:** Engineering; Health/Medical; Information Technology.

LUTZ ASSOCIATES
9 Stephen Street, Manchester CT 06040. 860/647-9338. **Fax:** 860/647-7918. **Contact:** Al Lutz, Owner. **Description:** An executive search firm. Founded in 1987. **Specializes in the areas of:** Automation/Robotics; Computer Science/Software; Engineering; Industrial; Manufacturing; Technical. **Positions commonly filled include:** Aerospace Engineer; Biomedical Engineer; Chemical Engineer; Chemist; Computer Programmer; Design Engineer; Designer; Engineer; MIS Specialist; Quality Control Supervisor; Science Technologist; Software Engineer; Systems Analyst; Technical Writer/Editor; Telecommunications Manager. **Average salary range of placements:** More than $50,000. **Number of placements per year:** 1 - 49.

MJF ASSOCIATES
P.O. Box 132, Wallingford CT 06492. 203/284-9878. **Fax:** 203/284-9871. **Contact:** Matt Furman, President. **E-mail address:** mjf@imcinternet.net. **World Wide Web address:** http://www.imcinternet.net/mjf. **Description:** An executive search firm operating on both retainer and contingency bases. The firm also offers some contract services. **Specializes in the areas of:** Engineering; General Management; Industrial; Manufacturing; Marketing; Sales; Technical. **Positions commonly filled include:** Account Manager; Account Representative; Aerospace Engineer; Applications Engineer; Branch Manager; Buyer; Chemical Engineer; Computer Programmer; Credit Manager; Customer Service Rep.; Database Manager; Design Engineer; Draftsperson; Electrical/Electronics Engineer; Electrician; Environmental Engineer; General Manager; Human Resources Manager; Industrial Engineer; Industrial Production Manager; Internet Services Manager; Manufacturing Engineer; Market Research Analyst; Marketing Manager; Marketing Specialist; Mechanical Engineer; Metallurgical Engineer; MIS Specialist; Operations Manager; Production Manager; Purchasing Agent/Manager; Quality Control Supervisor; Sales Engineer; Sales Executive; Sales Manager; Sales Rep.; Services Sales Representative; Software Engineer; Technical Writer/Editor; Telecommunications Manager; Vice President of Marketing; Vice President of Sales. **Corporate headquarters location:** This Location. **Average salary range of placements:** More than $50,000. **Number of placements per year:** 1 - 49.

MRG SEARCH & PLACEMENT INC.
2679 Whitney Avenue, Hamden CT 06518. 203/624-0161. **Contact:** Manager. **Description:** An executive search firm. **Specializes in the areas of:** Computer Programming; Health/Medical. **Positions commonly filled include:** Computer Programmer; Occupational Therapist; Physical Therapist; Physician; Speech-Language Pathologist.

MANAGEMENT RECRUITERS INTERNATIONAL
61 Cherry Street, Milford CT 06460. 203/876-8755. **Fax:** 203/877-1281. **Contact:** Sandra Campbell, Senior Partner. **Description:** An executive search firm that places executive management, middle management, and technical professionals. **Specializes in the areas of:** Biology; Biotechnology; Computer Science/Software; Engineering; Health/Medical; Industrial; Manufacturing; Pharmaceuticals; Sales; Technical. **Positions commonly filled include:** Biochemist; Biological Scientist; Biomedical Engineer; Chemical Engineer; Chemist; Clinical Lab Technician; Computer Programmer; Design Engineer; Environmental Engineer; Food Scientist/Technologist; Industrial Engineer; Materials Engineer; Mathematician; Mechanical Engineer; Quality Control Supervisor; Science Technologist; Software Engineer; Statistician. **Corporate headquarters location:** Cleveland OH. **Other U.S. locations:** Nationwide.

Average salary range of placements: More than $50,000. **Number of placements per year:** 1 - 49.

MANAGEMENT RECRUITERS INTERNATIONAL
2139 Silas Deane Highway, Rocky Hill CT 06067. 860/563-1268. **Contact:** Manager. **Description:** An executive search firm. **Specializes in the areas of:** Engineering; Finance. **Positions commonly filled include:** Electrical/Electronics Engineer; Mechanical Engineer; Systems Engineer. **Corporate headquarters location:** Cleveland OH. **Other U.S. locations:** Nationwide.

MANAGEMENT RECRUITERS INTERNATIONAL
154 West Street, Building 3, Unit C, Cromwell CT 06416. 860/635-0612. **Contact:** Manager. **Description:** An executive search firm. **Specializes in the areas of:** Sales. **Corporate headquarters location:** Cleveland OH. **Other U.S. locations:** Nationwide.

MANAGEMENT RECRUITERS OF NORWALK
396 Danbury Road, Wilton CT 06897-2024. 203/834-1111. **Contact:** Manager. **Description:** An executive search firm. **Specializes in the areas of:** Accounting/Auditing; Administration; Advertising; Architecture/Construction; Banking; Communications; Computer Science/Software; Construction; Electrical; Engineering; Finance; Food; General Management; Health/Medical; Insurance; Legal; Manufacturing; MIS/EDP; Operations Management; Personnel/Labor Relations; Procurement; Publishing; Retail; Sales; Technical; Textiles; Transportation. **Corporate headquarters location:** Cleveland OH. **Other U.S. locations:** Nationwide.

MANAGEMENT RECRUITERS OF WINSTED
P.O. Box 1017, Winsted CT 06098. 860/738-5035. **Fax:** 860/738-5039. **Contact:** Jack Bourque, President. **World Wide Web address:** http://www.wirelesscareers.com. **Description:** An executive search firm. **Specializes in the areas of:** Engineering; Manufacturing; Operations Management; Sales; Scientific; Technical. **Positions commonly filled include:** Chemical Engineer; Electrical/Electronics Engineer; General Manager; Mechanical Engineer; Metallurgical Engineer; Process Engineer; Sales and Marketing Representative. **Corporate headquarters location:** Cleveland OH. **Other U.S. locations:** Nationwide. **Number of placements per year:** 50 - 99.

MANAGEMENT SEARCH
50 Founders Plaza, Suite 304, East Hartford CT 06108. 860/289-1581. **Contact:** Manager. **Description:** An executive search firm. **Specializes in the areas of:** Accounting/Auditing; Engineering; Environmental; Information Systems; Manufacturing.

MATTHEWS & STEPHENS ASSOCIATES
1344 Silas Deane Highway, Suite 303, Rocky Hill CT 06067. 860/258-1995. **Contact:** Manager. **Description:** An executive search firm.

MAXWELL-MARCUS STAFFING CONSULTANTS
266 Broad Street, Milford CT 06460. 203/874-5424. **Fax:** 203/874-5571. **Contact:** Dan Regan, President. **E-mail address:** maxwell@interserv.com. **Description:** An executive search firm operating on a contingency basis. **Specializes in the areas of:** Computer Science/Software; Engineering; General Management; Sales; Technical. **Positions commonly filled include:** Administrative Manager; Applications Engineer; Architect; Biochemist; Biological Scientist; Biomedical Engineer; Broadcast Technician; Chemical Engineer; Chemist; Civil Engineer; Computer Operator; Computer Programmer; Database Manager; Design Engineer; Electrical/Electronics Engineer; Environmental Engineer; General Manager; Industrial Engineer; Industrial Production Manager; Internet Services Manager; Management Analyst/Consultant; Marketing Manager; Mechanical Engineer; Metallurgical Engineer; MIS Specialist; Multimedia Designer; Operations/Production Manager; Sales Executive; Sales Manager; Software Engineer; Statistician; Systems Analyst; Technical Writer/Editor;

Telecommunications Manager; Webmaster. **Average salary range of placements:** More than $50,000. **Number of placements per year:** 50 - 99.

C.A. McINNIS & ASSOCIATES
203 Broad Street, Suite 7, Milford CT 06460. 203/876-7110. **Fax:** 203/783-1230. **Contact:** Carol McInnis, President. **E-mail address:** carol@mcinnisinc.com. **Description:** An executive search firm operating on a retainer basis. **Specializes in the areas of:** Pharmaceuticals. **Positions commonly filled include:** Biological Scientist; Chemist; Database Manager; Market Research Analyst; Marketing Manager; Pharmacist; Physician; Project Manager; Registered Nurse; Sales Executive; Statistician. **Average salary range of placements:** More than $50,000. **Number of placements per year:** 50 - 99.

McINTYRE ASSOCIATES
3 Forest Park Drive, Farmington CT 06032. 860/284-1000. **Contact:** Manager. **Description:** An executive search firm. **Specializes in the areas of:** Computer Hardware/Software; Telecommunications.

THE McKNIGHT GROUP
4 Landmark Square, Suite 201, Stamford CT 06901. 203/357-1891. **Fax:** 203/425-2495. **Contact:** Richard F. McKnight, Managing Partner. **Description:** An executive search firm operating on both retainer and contingency bases. Client company pays fee. **Specializes in the areas of:** Accounting/Auditing; Banking; Clerical; Finance; Insurance; Marketing; Personnel/Labor Relations; Sales; Secretarial. **Positions commonly filled include:** Accountant; Administrative Assistant; Bank Manager; Bookkeeper; Buyer; Financial Analyst; General Manager; Legal Secretary; Marketing Specialist; Receptionist; Sales Rep.; Secretary; Underwriter. **Average salary range of placements:** $50,000 - $100,000. **Number of placements per year:** 50 - 99.

PRH MANAGEMENT, INC.
2777 Summer Street, Stamford CT 06905. 203/327-3900. **Fax:** 203/327-6324. **Contact:** Peter R. Hendelman, President. **Description:** An executive search firm. **Specializes in the areas of:** Accounting/Auditing; Advertising; Bookkeeping; Computer Science/Software; Engineering; Finance; General Management; Sales; Technical. **Positions commonly filled include:** Accountant/Auditor; Branch Manager; Software Engineer; Telecommunications Manager. **Average salary range of placements:** More than $50,000.

PASCALE & LAMORTE, LLC
500 Summer Street, Stamford CT 06901. 203/358-8155. **Fax:** 203/969-3990. **Contact:** Ron Pascale, Principal. **E-mail address:** pascale@earthlink.net. **World Wide Web address:** http://www.pascale-lamorte.com. **Description:** An executive search firm operating on a contingency basis. **Specializes in the areas of:** Accounting; Administration; Computer Science/Software; Finance; Information Technology; MIS/EDP. **Positions commonly filled include:** Accountant; Budget Analyst; CFO; Computer Programmer; Controller; Database Manager; Finance Director; Financial Analyst; Financial Consultant; Information Systems Consultant; Management Analyst/Consultant; MIS Specialist; Project Manager; Software Engineer; Systems Analyst; Systems Manager; Telecommunications Manager. **Average salary range of placements:** More than $50,000. **Number of placements per year:** 100 - 199.

BARRY PERSKY & CO.
256 Post Road East, Westport CT 06880. 203/454-4500. **Fax:** 203/454-3318. **Contact:** Barry Persky, President. **Description:** An executive search firm. **Specializes in the areas of:** Engineering; Finance; Food; General Management; Health/Medical; Industrial; Manufacturing; Personnel/Labor Relations; Sales; Technical; Transportation. **Positions commonly filled include:** Chemical Engineer; Civil Engineer; Editor; Environmental Engineer; General Manager; Human Resources Manager; Mechanical Engineer; MIS

Specialist; Operations Manager; Science Technologist; Structural Engineer; Technical Writer/Editor. **Average salary range of placements:** More than $50,000.

EDWARD J. POSPESIL & COMPANY
44 Long Hill Road, Guilford CT 06437. 203/458-6566. **Fax:** 203/458-6564. **Contact:** Ed Pospesil, Principal. **E-mail address:** ed@ejp.com. **World Wide Web address:** http://www.ejp.com. **Description:** An executive search firm. **Specializes in the areas of:** Administration; Computer Science/Software; Technical. **Positions commonly filled include:** Computer Programmer; Internet Services Manager; Management Analyst/Consultant; MIS Specialist; Software Engineer; Systems Analyst; Technical Writer/Editor; Telecommunications Manager. **Number of placements per year:** 1 - 49.

QUALITY CONTROL RECRUITERS
P.O. Box 1900, Bristol CT 06011-1900. 860/582-0003. **Fax:** 860/585-7395. **Contact:** Charles V. Urban, CPC/President. **Description:** An executive search firm operating on both retainer and contingency bases. **Specializes in the areas of:** Architecture/Construction; Banking; Biology; Chemicals; Cosmetics; Engineering; Food; Health/Medical; Industrial; Light Industrial; Manufacturing; Medical Devices; Printing; Quality Assurance; Scientific; Technical. **Positions commonly filled include:** Quality Assurance Engineer; Quality Control Supervisor; Regulatory Affairs Director; Statistician. **Corporate headquarters location:** This Location. **Other U.S. locations:** Nationwide. **Average salary range of placements:** More than $50,000. **Number of placements per year:** 50 - 99.

R/K INTERNATIONAL, INC.
1720 Post Road East-Post House, Suite 222, Westport CT 06880. 203/255-9490. **Fax:** 203/255-9633. **Contact:** Manager. **E-mail address:** info@rkinternational.com. **World Wide Web address:** http://rkinternational.com. **Description:** An executive search firm operating on a retainer basis. Founded in 1993. **Corporate headquarters location:** This Location.

RETAIL EXECUTIVES
265 Bic Drive, Milford CT 06460. 203/877-9293. **Contact:** Manager. **Description:** An executive search firm. **Specializes in the areas of:** Retail.

RETAIL RECRUITERS
2189 Silas Deane Highway, Rocky Hill CT 06067. 860/721-9550. **Contact:** Manager. **Description:** An executive search firm. **Specializes in the areas of:** Retail.

ROMAC INTERNATIONAL
One Corporate Drive, Suite 215, Shelton CT 06484. 203/944-9001. **Toll-free phone:** 800/851-0792. **Fax:** 203/926-1414. **Contact:** Manager. **Description:** An executive search firm.

ROMAC INTERNATIONAL
111 Founders Plaza, Suite 1501, East Hartford CT 06108. 860/528-0300. **Fax:** 860/291-9497. **Contact:** Manager. **Description:** An executive search firm. **Specializes in the areas of:** Accounting; Computer Hardware/Software; Finance; Information Technology.

RUSSO STAFFING INC.
2345 Flat Rock Turnpike, Fairfield CT 06432. 203/333-7761. **Contact:** Manager. **Description:** An executive search firm. **Specializes in the areas of:** Engineering; Technical.

SEDER ASSOCIATES
998 Farmington Avenue, Suite 201, West Hartford CT 06107. 860/236-7511. **Contact:** Manager. **Description:** An executive search firm. **Specializes in the areas of:** Legal.

SIGER & ASSOCIATES, LLC
966 Westover Road, Stamford CT 06902. 203/348-0976. **Fax:** 203/348-0698. **Contact:** Ray Milo, President. **E-**

mail address: siger@juno.com. Description: An executive search firm. Specializes in the areas of: Banking; Computer Science/Software; Consulting; Finance; Health/Medical. Average salary range of placements: More than $50,000. Number of placements per year: 1 - 49.

HOWARD W. SMITH ASSOCIATES
P.O. Box 230877, Hartford CT 06123. 860/549-2060. Fax: 860/246-7871. Contact: Howard Smith, Principal. Description: An executive search firm operating on a retainer basis. Specializes in the areas of: Accounting/Auditing; Banking; Finance; Health/Medical; Insurance; Personnel/Labor Relations. Positions commonly filled include: Accountant/Auditor; Actuary; Attorney; Economist; Health Services Manager; Investment Manager. Average salary range of placements: More than $50,000. Number of placements per year: 1 - 49.

SNYDER & COMPANY
35 Old Avon Village, Suite 185, Avon CT 06001-3822. 860/521-9760. Contact: James F. Snyder, President. Description: An executive search firm operating on a retainer basis. Specializes in the areas of: Banking; Food; Health/Medical. Positions commonly filled include: Bank Manager; Biochemist; Biological Scientist; Biomedical Engineer; Chemist; CFO; Controller; Dietician; Finance Director; Financial Analyst; Food Technologist; General Manager; Human Resources Manager; Management Analyst/Consultant; Market Research Analyst; Marketing Manager; Marketing Specialist; Mechanical Engineer; Physician; Production Manager; Public Relations Specialist; Quality Control Supervisor; Sales Executive; Sales Manager; Software Engineer. Corporate headquarters location: This Location. Other U.S. locations: Nationwide. Average salary range of placements: More than $50,000. Number of placements per year: 1 - 49.

STEWART ASSOCIATES
201 Ann Street, Hartford CT 06103. 860/548-1388. Contact: Manager. Description: An executive search firm. Specializes in the areas of: Engineering; Sales.

STRATEGIC EXECUTIVES, INC.
6 Landmark Square, 4th Floor, Stamford CT 06901. 203/359-5757. Contact: Manager. Description: An executive search firm. Specializes in the areas of: Finance; Marketing.

SUPER SYSTEMS, INC.
345 North Main Street, Suite 319, West Hartford CT 06117. 860/523-4246. Toll-free phone: 800/759-2487. Fax: 860/233-6943. Contact: Mary Ann Salas, CPC/President. E-mail address: staffing@supersystemsinc.com. World Wide Web address: http://www.supersystemsinc.com. Description: An executive search firm operating on a contingency basis. Client company pays fee. Specializes in the areas of: Computer Science/Software; Finance; Marketing; Sales. Positions commonly filled include: Account Manager; Accountant; AS400 Programmer Analyst; CFO; Computer Operator; Computer Programmer; Controller; Database Administrator; Database Manager; Finance Director; Financial Analyst; Market Research Analyst; Marketing Manager; Marketing Specialist; MIS Specialist; Network/Systems Administrator; Project Manager; Sales Engineer; Sales Executive; Sales Manager; Sales Rep.; Software Engineer; Systems Analyst; Systems Manager. Corporate headquarters location: This Location. Other U.S. locations: Atlanta GA. Average salary range of placements: $50,000 - $100,000. Number of placements per year: 50 - 99.

TMP WORLDWIDE
One Station Place, Metro Center, Stamford CT 06902-6800. 203/324-4445. Fax: 203/324-4031. Contact: Robert R. Stone, Partner. World Wide Web address: http://www.tmpw.com. Description: An executive search firm. Specializes in the areas of: Biotechnology; Consumer Products; Finance; Health/Medical; Industrial; Pharmaceuticals; Technical. Corporate headquarters

location: New York NY. Other area locations: West Hartford CT. Other U.S. locations: Nationwide.

TMP WORLDWIDE
998 Farmington Avenue, Suite 205, West Hartford CT 06107-2184. 860/523-7100. Fax: 860/523-8510. Contact: David J. Beed, Partner. World Wide Web address: http://www.tmpw.com. Description: An executive search firm. Specializes in the areas of: Biotechnology; Consumer Products; Finance; Health/Medical; Industrial; Pharmaceuticals; Technical. Corporate headquarters location: New York NY. Other area locations: Stamford CT. Other U.S. locations: Nationwide.

TSW ASSOCIATES, LLC
One Selleck Street, Suite 570, Norwalk CT 06855. 203/866-7300. Fax: 203/838-7390. Contact: Frank M. Wilkinson, Partner. E-mail address: tswassoc@aol.com. Description: An executive search firm operating on a retainer basis. Specializes in the areas of: Marketing; Sales. Positions commonly filled include: Fund Manager; Investment Manager; Portfolio Manager. Average salary range of placements: More than $50,000. Number of placements per year: 1 - 49.

TECHNICAL SEARCH
20 Richards Lane, Norwalk CT 06851. 203/846-9030. Contact: Manager. Description: An executive search firm. Specializes in the areas of: Computer Science/Software; Engineering. Positions commonly filled include: Electrical/Electronics Engineer; Software Developer; Software Engineer.

VEZAN ASSOCIATES
117 Garfield Road, West Hartford CT 06127-0753. 860/521-8848. Contact: Manager. Description: An executive search firm operating on a contingency basis. Specializes in the areas of: Health/Medical.

WALLACE ASSOCIATES
P.O. Box 11294, Waterbury CT 06703. 203/575-1311. Fax: 203/879-2407. Contact: Greg Gordon, Principal. Description: An executive search firm. Specializes in the areas of: Computer Hardware/Software; Engineering; General Management; Health/Medical; Manufacturing; Packaging; Physician Executive; Technical. Positions commonly filled include: Biological Scientist; Biomedical Engineer; Chemical Engineer; Chemist; Computer Programmer; EDP Specialist; Electrical/Electronics Engineer; Industrial Designer; Industrial Engineer; Manufacturing Engineer; Mechanical Engineer; Metallurgical Engineer; MIS Specialist; Operations Research Analyst; Quality Control Supervisor; Software Engineer. Number of placements per year: 1 - 49.

WARD LIEBELT & ASSOCIATES, INC.
19 Ludlow Road, Suite 302, Westport CT 06880. 203/454-0414. Fax: 203/454-2310. Contact: Manager. Description: An executive search firm. Specializes in the areas of: Manufacturing. Positions commonly filled include: Industrial Production Manager; Operations Manager. Number of placements per year: 1 - 49.

WEATHERBY HEALTH CARE
25 Van Zant Street, South Norwalk CT 06855-1786. Toll-free phone: 800/365-8900. Contact: Manager. Description: An executive search firm that only recruits physicians. Specializes in the areas of: Health/Medical.

WILLIAM WILLIS WORLDWIDE INC.
P.O. Box 4444, Greenwich CT 06831. 203/532-9292. Fax: 203/532-1919. Contact: Manager. Description: An executive search firm. Founded in 1965. Specializes in the areas of: Research and Development.

WITTLAN GROUP
181 Post Road West, Westport CT 06880. 203/227-2455. Contact: Manager. Description: An executive search

firm. **Specializes in the areas of:** Marketing; Sales Promotion.

BOB WRIGHT RECRUITING, INC.
56 DeForest Road, Wilton CT 06897. 203/762-9046. **Fax:** 203/762-5807. **Contact:** Bob Wright, President. **E-mail address:** jrobertwright@msn.com. **Description:** An executive search firm operating on a contingency basis. **Specializes in the areas of:** Advertising; Finance; Food; General Management; Printing; Publishing; Sales. **Positions commonly filled include:** Account Manager; Account Representative; Advertising Clerk; Database Manager; Marketing Specialist; Sales Executive; Sales

Manager; Sales Representative; Telecommunications Manager. **Number of placements per year:** 1 - 49.

YANKEE HOSPITALITY SEARCH
406 Farmington Avenue, Farmington CT 06032. 860/738-1900. **Toll-free phone:** 800/YANKEE1. **Fax:** 860/738-4972. **Contact:** Dan Tolman, President. **Description:** An executive search firm. **Specializes in the areas of:** Food; Hotel/Restaurant. **Positions commonly filled include:** Food Scientist/Technologist; Hotel Manager; Management Trainee; Restaurant/Food Service Manager. **Number of placements per year:** 50 - 99.

PERMANENT EMPLOYMENT AGENCIES

AVAILABILITY OF HARTFORD INC.
936 Silas Deane Highway, Suite 1T2, Wethersfield CT 06109-4202. 860/529-1688. **Fax:** 860/257-7829. **Contact:** David Roser, President. **Description:** A permanent employment agency specializing in the placement of engineering, middle management, and production management professionals in the precision metalworking and plastic injection molding industries. **Specializes in the areas of:** Engineering. **Positions commonly filled include:** Applications Engineer; Manufacturing Engineer; Manufacturing Manager. **Average salary range of placements:** $50,000 - $100,000. **Number of placements per year:** 1 - 49.

BA STAFFING, INC.
1208 Main Street, Branford CT 06405. 203/488-2504. **Contact:** Dean Troxell, President. **Description:** A permanent employment agency. **Specializes in the areas of:** Computer Science/Software. **Positions commonly filled include:** Computer Programmer; Customer Service Representative; Electrical/Electronics Engineer; MIS Specialist; Multimedia Designer; Software Engineer; Systems Analyst. **Average salary range of placements:** More than $50,000. **Number of placements per year:** 200 - 499.

BOHAN & BRADSTREET
34 Park Drive East, Branford CT 06405. 203/488-0068. **Fax:** 203/483-8338. **Contact:** Edward Bradstreet, CPC/President. **E-mail address:** ebb@bohan-bradstreet.com. **World Wide Web address:** http://www.bohan-bradstreet.com. **Description:** A permanent employment agency that also offers executive searches. **Specializes in the areas of:** Accounting/Auditing; Administration; Computer Science/Software; Data Processing; Engineering; Finance; General Management; Industrial; Personnel/Labor Relations; Sales. **Positions commonly filled include:** Account Manager; Accountant; Administrative Manager; Applications Engineer; Auditor; Budget Analyst; Chief Financial Officer; Computer Programmer; Controller; Credit Manager; Database Manager; Design Engineer; Distribution Manager; Electrical/Electronics Engineer; Environmental Engineer; Finance Director; Financial Analyst; General Manager; Human Resources Manager; Industrial Engineer; Industrial Production Manager; Internet Services Manager; Management Analyst/Consultant; Manufacturing Engineer; Market Research Analyst; Marketing Manager; Marketing Specialist; Mechanical Engineer; Metallurgical Engineer; MIS Specialist; Operations Manager; Production Manager; Project Manager; Purchasing Agent/Manager; Quality Control Supervisor; Sales Engineer; Sales Executive; Sales Manager; Software Engineer; Systems Analyst; Systems Manager; Vice President of Marketing; Webmaster.

THOMAS BYRNE ASSOCIATES
7 Melrose Drive, Farmington CT 06032. 860/676-2468. **Fax:** 860/676-0272. **Contact:** Tom Byrne, Owner. **E-mail address:** resumes@thomasbyrne.com. **Description:** A permanent employment agency. **Specializes in the areas of:** Accounting/Auditing; Finance; Insurance; Manufacturing. **Positions commonly filled include:**

Accountant/Auditor; MIS Specialist. **Average salary range of placements:** More than $50,000.

CHOICE PERSONNEL INC.
733 Summer Street, Suite 406, Stamford CT 06901. 203/324-4744. **Contact:** Manager. **Description:** A permanent employment agency. **Positions commonly filled include:** Administrative Assistant.

CORPORATE SOFTWARE SOLUTIONS
108 Barrack Hill Road, Ridgefield CT 06877. 203/431-7631. **Fax:** 203/431-8116. **Contact:** Rick Maiolo, Marketing Manager. **E-mail address:** maiolo@corp-soft.com. **Description:** A permanent employment agency that also provides contract consulting. **Specializes in the areas of:** Information Systems.

DATA PROS
340 Broad Street, Suite 105, Windsor CT 06095-3030. 860/688-0020. **Contact:** Len Collyer, President. **Description:** A permanent employment agency. **Specializes in the areas of:** Computer Science/Software; Engineering; Insurance. **Positions commonly filled include:** Computer Programmer; Electrician; Emergency Medical Technician; Engineer; Systems Analyst. **Number of placements per year:** 100 - 199.

DIVERSIFIED EMPLOYMENT SERVICES, INC.
531 Whalley Avenue, New Haven CT 06511. 203/397-2500. **Fax:** 203/387-5778. **Contact:** D. William DeRosa, Jr., President. **Description:** A permanent employment agency. Founded in 1970. **Specializes in the areas of:** Accounting/Auditing; Sales; Secretarial. **Positions commonly filled include:** Accountant/Auditor; Draftsperson; Typist/Word Processor. **Average salary range of placements:** $20,000 - $29,999. **Number of placements per year:** 50 - 99.

DIVERSIFIED EMPLOYMENT SERVICES, INC.
63 Center Street, Shelton CT 06484. 203/924-8364. **Contact:** Manager. **Description:** A permanent employment agency. **Specializes in the areas of:** Accounting/Auditing; Engineering; Manufacturing; Sales; Secretarial. **Positions commonly filled include:** Accountant/Auditor; Blue-Collar Worker Supervisor; Chemist; Clinical Lab Technician; Computer Programmer; Customer Service Rep.; Draftsperson; Paralegal; Services Sales Representative; Typist/Word Processor. **Number of placements per year:** 50 - 99.

DUNHILL OF NEW HAVEN
DUNHILL SEARCH INTERNATIONAL
59 Elm Street, Suite 520, New Haven CT 06510. 203/562-0511. **Fax:** 203/562-2637. **Contact:** Donald Kaiser, President. **E-mail address:** nhdunhill@aol.com. **World Wide Web address:** http://www.nhdunhill.com. **Description:** A permanent employment agency that also offers some temporary and contract placements. Dunhill Search International (also at this location) provides permanent placements internationally. This location also has a legal staffing division. Founded in 1978. **Specializes in the areas of:** Accounting/Auditing; Administration; Engineering; Finance; International Executives; Legal; Personnel/Labor Relations; Sales.

Positions commonly filled include: Account Rep.; Accountant; Administrative Assistant; Auditor; Branch Manager; Buyer; Chief Financial Officer; Computer Operator; Computer Programmer; Controller; Customer Service Rep.; Design Engineer; Electrical/Electronics Engineer; Financial Analyst; General Manager; Human Resources Manager; Manufacturing Engineer; Marketing Manager; Marketing Specialist; Mechanical Engineer; MIS Specialist; Paralegal; Purchasing Agent/Manager; Quality Control Supervisor; Sales Engineer; Sales Executive; Sales Manager; Sales Rep.; Software Engineer; Systems Analyst; Transportation/Traffic Specialist. **Benefits available to temporary workers:** Paid Holidays; Paid Vacation. **Average salary range of placements:** More than $50,000. **Number of placements per year:** 500 - 999.

EMPLOYMENT OPPORTUNITIES
57 North Street, Suite 320, Danbury CT 06810. 203/797-2653. **Fax:** 203/797-2657. **Contact:** Manager. **Description:** A permanent employment agency. **Specializes in the areas of:** Accounting/Auditing; Banking; Clerical; Computer Science/Software; Engineering; Food; Health/Medical; Manufacturing; MIS/EDP; Personnel/Labor Relations; Sales; Secretarial; Technical. **Positions commonly filled include:** Accountant/Auditor; Biochemist; Biological Scientist; Biomedical Engineer; Buyer; Chemist; Civil Engineer; Claim Rep.; Clerk; Computer Operator; Computer Programmer; Credit Manager; Customer Service Rep.; Data Entry Clerk; Draftsperson; Driver; EDP Specialist; Electrical/Electronics Engineer; Financial Analyst; Food Scientist/Technologist; Human Resources Manager; Industrial Engineer; Insurance Agent/Broker; Internet Services Manager; Legal Secretary; Marketing Specialist; Mechanical Engineer; Medical Secretary; Metallurgical Engineer; MIS Specialist; Operations/ Production Manager; Physicist; Purchasing Agent/ Manager; Quality Control Supervisor; Receptionist; Secretary; Systems Analyst; Typist/Word Processor. **Number of placements per year:** 1 - 49.

FAIRFIELD TEACHERS AGENCY, INC.
P.O. Box 1141, Fairfield CT 06432. 203/333-0611. **Fax:** 203/334-7224. **Contact:** Mr. Sandy Peterson, Placement Counselor. **Description:** A permanent employment agency that places professionals in educational systems in the New York and New England areas. Founded in 1965. **Positions commonly filled include:** Education Administrator; Librarian; Social Worker; Speech-Language Pathologist; Teacher/Professor. **Number of placements per year:** 200 - 499.

GOLDEN DOOR
111 East Avenue, Norwalk CT 06851. 203/853-9242. **Contact:** Manager. **Description:** A permanent employment agency.

J.G. HOOD ASSOCIATES
599 Riverside Avenue, Westport CT 06880. 203/226-1126. **Contact:** Joyce Hood, Owner/President. **E-mail address:** jghood@att.net. **Description:** A permanent employment agency. **Specializes in the areas of:** Administration; Computer Science/Software; Engineering; Industrial; Manufacturing; MIS/EDP; Personnel/Labor Relations. **Positions commonly filled include:** Buyer; Computer Programmer; Database Manager; Design Engineer; Electrical/Electronics Engineer; Human Resources Manager; Manufacturing Engineer; Market Research Analyst; Marketing Manager; Marketing Specialist; Mechanical Engineer; MIS Specialist; Operations Manager; Project Manager; Purchasing Agent/Manager; Quality Control Supervisor; Sales Engineer; Software Engineer; Systems Analyst; Telecommunications Manager; Transportation/Traffic Specialist. **Corporate headquarters location:** This Location. **Average salary range of placements:** More than $50,000. **Number of placements per year:** 1 - 49.

JAT, LTD.
P.O. Box 1146, Fairfield CT 06432. 203/371-5877. **Fax:** 203/374-6950. **Contact:** Lois Karni, Counselor.

Description: A permanent employment agency. **Specializes in the areas of:** Engineering; Manufacturing; Scientific; Technical. **Positions commonly filled include:** Aerospace Engineer; Aircraft Mechanic/Engine Specialist; Blue-Collar Worker Supervisor; Chemical Engineer; Civil Engineer; Design Engineer; Designer; Draftsperson; Electrical/Electronics Engineer; Environmental Engineer; Industrial Engineer; Industrial Production Manager; Mechanical Engineer; Quality Control Supervisor; Software Engineer; Structural Engineer; Systems Analyst. **Average salary range of placements:** More than $20,000. **Number of placements per year:** 1 - 49.

JOBSOURCE
Two Corporate Drive, Trumbull CT 06611. 203/268-9987. **Fax:** 203/261-2443. **Contact:** Deborah G. Palmieri, President. **Description:** A permanent employment agency. **Specializes in the areas of:** Accounting/Auditing; Administration; Sales; Secretarial. **Positions commonly filled include:** Accountant/Auditor; Administrative Assistant; Bookkeeper; Budget Analyst; Clerical Supervisor; Computer Programmer; Customer Service Representative; Financial Analyst; Management Trainee; Paralegal; Secretary; Systems Analyst. **Number of placements per year:** 50 - 99.

JUDLIND EMPLOYMENT SERVICES, INC.
One Bank Street, Suite 306, Stamford CT 06901-3016. 203/964-8116. **Fax:** 203/357-0671. **Contact:** Manager. **E-mail address:** jobs@judlind.com. **Description:** A permanent employment agency that also provides some temporary placements. Client company pays fee. **Specializes in the areas of:** Accounting; Administration; Finance; Secretarial. **Positions commonly filled include:** Accountant; Administrative Assistant; Auditor; Controller; Credit Manager; Financial Analyst; Human Resources Manager; Marketing Specialist; Paralegal; Secretary; Typist/Word Processor. **Corporate headquarters location:** This Location. **Average salary range of placements:** $30,000 - $49,999. **Number of placements per year:** 50 - 99.

W.R. LAWRY, INC.
12 Station Street, Simsbury CT 06070. 860/651-0281. **Contact:** Bill Lawry, Owner. **Description:** A permanent employment agency. **Specializes in the areas of:** Computer Science/Software; Engineering; General Management; Technical. **Positions commonly filled include:** Biological Scientist; Engineer; General Manager. **Number of placements per year:** 1 - 49.

LINEAL RECRUITING SERVICES
46 Copper Kettle Road, Trumbull CT 06611. 203/386-1091. **Fax:** 203/386-9788. **Contact:** Lisa Lineal, Owner. **Description:** A permanent employment agency specializing in the electromechanical industry. **Specializes in the areas of:** Engineering; Sales; Technical. **Positions commonly filled include:** Blue-Collar Worker Supervisor; Customer Service Representative; Design Engineer; Electrical/Electronics Engineer; Electrician; Industrial Production Manager; Mining Engineer; Services Sales Representative. **Number of placements per year:** 1 - 49.

MANAGEMENT SOLUTIONS
36 State Street, North Haven CT 06473. 203/239-7006. **Contact:** Manager. **Description:** A permanent employment agency that also offers contract services. **Specializes in the areas of:** Computer Programming.

MATRIX SEARCH INC.
495 Route 184, Suite 211, Groton CT 06340. 860/449-0860. **Fax:** 860/449-0898. **Contact:** Jerry Trotta. **E-mail address:** matrix@matrixsearch.com. **World Wide Web address:** http://www.matrixsearch.com. **Description:** A permanent employment agency. **Specializes in the areas of:** Electrical; Electronics; Engineering; Technical.

MERRY EMPLOYMENT GROUP INC.
433 South Main Street, Suite 216, West Hartford CT 06110. 860/678-8891. **Contact:** Manager. **Description:**

A permanent employment agency that also provides some executive searches. **Specializes in the areas of:** Finance; MIS/EDP.

NAPOLITANO & WULSTER, LLC
311 South Main Street, Cheshire CT 06410. 203/272-2820. **Fax:** 203/250-7207. **Contact:** Tony Napolitano, Owner. **E-mail address:** napwul@aol.com. **Description:** A permanent employment agency. **Specializes in the areas of:** Health/Medical. **Positions commonly filled include:** Technical Writer/Editor. **Number of placements per year:** 50 - 99.

NEW ENGLAND PERSONNEL, INC.
100 Wells Street, Hartford CT 06103. 860/525-8616. **Contact:** Manager. **Description:** A permanent employment agency. **Specializes in the areas of:** Administration; Computer Programming; Engineering; Health/Medical.

OFFICE SERVICES OF CONNECTICUT, INC.
940 White Plains Road, Professional Building, Trumbull CT 06611. 203/268-7084. **Fax:** 203/261-0502. **Contact:** Ms. Terry Gates, President. **Description:** A permanent employment agency that also offers some temporary placements. Founded in 1971. **Specializes in the areas of:** Accounting/Auditing; Administration; Advertising; Banking; Engineering; Finance; Food; General Management; Industrial; Insurance; Legal; Manufacturing; Sales; Secretarial. **Positions commonly filled include:** Accountant/Auditor; Actuary; Administrative Manager; Advertising Clerk; Architect; Chemist; Clinical Lab Technician; Computer Programmer; Customer Service Rep.; Environmental Engineer; Financial Analyst; Food Scientist/Technologist; Human Resources Specialist; Industrial Engineer; Manufacturer's/Wholesaler's Sales Rep.; Mechanical Engineer; MIS Specialist; Securities Sales Representative; Services Sales Representative; Software Engineer; Systems Analyst; Typist/Word Processor. **Average salary range of placements:** $30,000 - $50,000. **Number of placements per year:** 200 - 499.

PARAMOUNT RESOURCES
25 Sylvan Road South, Suite F, Westport CT 06880. 203/227-4101. **Contact:** Manager. **Description:** A permanent employment agency. **Specializes in the areas of:** Accounting/Auditing; Computer Graphics; Finance; Secretarial.

PROFESSIONAL EMPLOYMENT
20 South Anguilla Road, P.O. Box 12A, Pawcatuck CT 06379. 860/599-8430. **Fax:** 860/599-1779. **Contact:** Mary Cassidy, Personnel Consultant. **Description:** A permanent employment agency that also offers some temporary placements. **Positions commonly filled include:** Accountant/Auditor; Biochemist; Blue-Collar Worker Supervisor; Clerical Supervisor; Clinical Lab Technician; Customer Service Representative; Food Scientist/Technologist; Human Resources Specialist; Medical Records Technician; Paralegal; Secretary. **Average salary range of placements:** $20,000 - $29,999. **Number of placements per year:** 100 - 199.

Q.S.I.
P.O Box 185606, Hamden CT 06518. 203/287-8900. **Fax:** 203/248-0911. **Contact:** Technical Recruiter. **Description:** A permanent employment agency. **Specializes in the areas of:** Accounting/Auditing; Computer Science/Software; Finance; Legal. **Positions commonly filled include:** Accountant/Auditor; Attorney; Computer Programmer; Financial Analyst; MIS Specialist; Systems Analyst; Telecommunications Manager. **Average salary range of placements:** More than $50,000. **Number of placements per year:** 1 - 49.

RJS ASSOCIATES, INC.
10 Columbus Boulevard, Hartford CT 06106. 860/278-5840. **Fax:** 860/522-8313. **Contact:** Richard J. Stewart, President. **Description:** A permanent employment agency. **Positions commonly filled include:** Accountant/Auditor; Actuary; Administrative Manager; Aerospace Engineer; Bank Officer/Manager; Biological Scientist; Biomedical Engineer; Blue-Collar Worker Supervisor; Branch Manager; Budget Analyst; Buyer; Chemical Engineer; Chemist; Civil Engineer; Claim Rep.; Clerical Supervisor; Clinical Lab Technician; Cost Estimator; Credit Manager; Customer Service Representative; Dental Assistant/Dental Hygienist; Dental Lab Technician; Designer; Draftsperson; EEG Technologist; EKG Technician; Electrical/Electronics Engineer; Electrician; Financial Analyst; General Manager; Geologist/Geophysicist; Health Services Manager; Industrial Engineer; Industrial Production Manager; Insurance Agent/Broker; Licensed Practical Nurse; Manufacturer's/Wholesaler's Sales Rep.; Mechanical Engineer; Medical Records Technician; Metallurgical Engineer; Nuclear Engineer; Nuclear Medicine Technologist; Occupational Therapist; Physical Therapist; Purchasing Agent/Manager; Quality Control Supervisor; Radiological Technologist; Recreational Therapist; Respiratory Therapist; Science Technologist; Services Sales Rep.; Software Engineer; Structural Engineer; Systems Analyst; Technical Writer/Editor; Underwriter/Assistant Underwriter. **Number of placements per year:** 200 - 499.

RKS RESOURCES
22 Fifth Street, Stamford CT 06902. 203/359-9290. **Contact:** Manager. **Description:** A permanent employment agency.

RESOURCE ASSOCIATES
730 Hopmeadow Street, Simsbury CT 06070. 860/651-4918. **Fax:** 860/651-3137. **Contact:** Eric Grossman, President. **Description:** A permanent employment agency. **Specializes in the areas of:** Accounting/Auditing; Computer Science/Software; Finance. **Positions commonly filled include:** Accountant/Auditor; Computer Programmer; Financial Analyst; Software Engineer; Systems Analyst.

REYNOLDS TECHNICAL SERVICES INC.
3638 Main Street, Stratford CT 06614. 203/375-1953. **Contact:** Manager. **Description:** A permanent employment agency that also provides some temporary placements. **Specializes in the areas of:** Technical. **Positions commonly filled include:** Computer Programmer; Designer; Draftsperson; Technical Writer/Editor; Tool and Die Maker; Tool Engineer.

SENIOR EMPLOYMENT SERVICE
1642 Bedford Street, Suite 106, Stamford CT 06905. 203/327-4422. **Fax:** 203/327-4098. **Contact:** Karen Cornwell, Director. **Description:** A permanent employment agency. **Positions commonly filled include:** Bookkeeper; Clerk; Computer Operator; Customer Service Rep.; Data Entry Clerk; Driver; Executive Assistant; Legal Secretary; Medical Secretary; Receptionist; Sales Rep.; Secretary; Typist/Word Processor. **Number of placements per year:** 50 - 99.

SNELLING PERSONNEL SERVICES
One Hartfield Boulevard, East Windsor CT 06088. 860/292-5330. **Contact:** Manager. **Description:** A permanent employment agency that also offers some temporary placements.

TURNER ASSOCIATES
P.O. Box 2192, Manchester CT 06040. 860/645-7877. **Contact:** Ruby Banks, Assistant Director. **Description:** A permanent employment agency. **Positions commonly filled include:** Accountant/Auditor; Advertising Clerk; Blue-Collar Worker Supervisor; Buyer; Computer Programmer; Environmental Engineer; General Manager; Industrial Engineer; Industrial Production Manager; Licensed Practical Nurse; Management Trainee; Manufacturer's/Wholesaler's Sales Rep.; MIS Specialist; Purchasing Agent/Manager; Recreational Therapist; Registered Nurse; Respiratory Therapist; Services Sales Rep.; Software Engineer; Systems Analyst; Typist/Word Processor. **Average salary range of placements:** $30,000 - $50,000. **Number of placements per year:** 1 - 49.

J.R. VAUGHAN & ASSOCIATES
1177 Silas Deane Highway, Wethersfield CT 06109. 860/563-2555. **Contact:** Recruiter. **Description:** A permanent employment agency. **Specializes in the areas of:** Sales. **Positions commonly filled include:** Manufacturer's/Wholesaler's Sales Rep.; Services Sales Rep.. **Number of placements per year:** 100 - 199.

VELEN ASSOCIATES
One Bank Street, Stamford CT 06901. 203/324-5900. **Contact:** Manager. **Description:** A permanent placement agency. **Specializes in the areas of:** Accounting/Auditing; Bookkeeping; Finance.

WORKFORCE ONE
235 Interstate Lane, Waterbury CT 06705. 203/759-2180. **Fax:** 203/759-2182. **Contact:** Laura Sebach, Owner. **E-mail address:** info@workforceone.com. **World Wide Web address:** http://www.workforceone.com. **Description:** A permanent employment agency. **Specializes in the areas of:** Accounting; Computer Science/Software; Electronics; Finance; Manufacturing; Personnel/Labor Relations; Secretarial; Technical. **Positions commonly filled include:** Accountant; Administrative Manager; Aerospace Engineer; Aircraft Mechanic/Engine Specialist; Bank Officer/Manager; Blue-Collar Worker Supervisor; Branch Manager; Budget Analyst; Buyer; Chemical Engineer; Chemist; Civil Engineer; Clerical Supervisor; Clinical Lab Technician; Computer Programmer; Construction and Building Inspector; Construction Contractor; Cost Estimator; Credit Manager; Customer Service Rep.; Design Engineer; Designer; Draftsperson; Electrical/Electronics Engineer; Environmental Engineer; Financial Analyst; General Manager; Human Resources Specialist; Industrial Engineer; Industrial Production Manager; Management Analyst/Consultant; Mechanical Engineer; Medical Records Technician; MIS Specialist; Purchasing Agent/Manager; Quality Control Supervisor; Software Engineer; Stationary Engineer; Structural Engineer; Systems Analyst; Technical Writer/Editor; Typist/Word Processor. **Average salary range of placements:** $30,000 - $50,000. **Number of placements per year:** 1 - 49.

TEMPORARY EMPLOYMENT AGENCIES

ADMIRAL STAFFING SERVICES
69 Wall Street, Norwalk CT 06850. 203/855-8367. **Contact:** Jan Schneider, Personnel Manager. **Description:** A temporary agency. Founded in 1982. **Specializes in the areas of:** Accounting/Auditing; Art/Design; Banking; Education; Engineering; Finance; Food; General Management; Health/Medical; Industrial; Insurance; Legal; Manufacturing; Secretarial; Technical; Transportation. **Positions commonly filled include:** Advertising Clerk; Aircraft Mechanic/Engine Specialist; Bank Officer/Manager; Blue-Collar Worker Supervisor; Budget Analyst; Buyer; Claim Representative; Clerical Supervisor; Customer Service Representative; Design Engineer; Designer; Draftsperson; Electrical/Electronics Engineer; Electrician; Food Scientist/Technologist; Human Resources Specialist; Medical Records Technician; Quality Control Supervisor; Restaurant/Food Service Manager; Technical Writer/Editor; Typist/Word Processor. **Corporate headquarters location:** This Location. **Other area locations:** Bridgeport CT; Milford CT. **Number of placements per year:** 500 - 999.

ADVANCED PLACEMENT INC.
58 River Street, Milford CT 06460. 203/878-9392. **Toll-free phone:** 800/771-9392. **Fax:** 203/878-9936. **Contact:** Laurie Yontef, CPC. **Description:** A temporary agency that also provides some permanent placements. **Specializes in the areas of:** Finance; General Management; Personnel/Labor Relations; Sales; Secretarial. **Positions commonly filled include:** Administrative Assistant; Administrative Manager; Advertising Clerk; Budget Analyst; Buyer; Claim Rep.; Clerical Supervisor; Credit Manager; Customer Service Manager; Human Resources Manager; Human Resources Specialist; Management Analyst/Consultant; Market Research Analyst; Mechanical Engineer; Operations/Production Manager; Paralegal; Public Relations Specialist; Typist/Word Processor. **Average salary range of placements:** $30,000 - $50,000. **Number of placements per year:** 200 - 499.

AQUENT PARTNERS
2 Stamford Landing, 68 Southfield Avenue, Suite 150, Stamford CT 06902. 203/425-9600. **Toll-free phone:** 877/PARTNER. **Fax:** 203/425-9639. **Contact:** Allen Ripke, Manager. **E-mail address:** aripke@aquent.com. **World Wide Web address:** http://www.aquentpartners.com. **Description:** A temporary agency that places creative, Web, and technical professionals. Aquent Partners also provides some temp-to-perm, permanent, and contract placements. **Specializes in the areas of:** Administration; Art/Design; Computer Science/Software; Marketing. **Positions commonly filled include:** Computer Animator; Computer Engineer; Computer Operator; Computer Programmer; Computer Support Technician; Computer Technician; Content Developer; Database Administrator; Database Manager; Desktop Publishing Specialist; Editor; Editorial Assistant; Graphic Artist; Graphic Designer; Internet Services Manager; Managing Editor; MIS Specialist; Multimedia Designer; Network/Systems Administrator; Production Manager; Project Manager; Software Engineer; SQL Programmer; Systems Analyst; Systems Manager; Technical Writer/Editor; Webmaster. **Benefits available to temporary workers:** 401(k); Dental Insurance; Disability Coverage; Medical Insurance. **CEO:** John Chuang.

CPH STAFFING & CONSULTING, LLC
4 Forest Park Drive, Farmington CT 06032. 860/676-9532. **Fax:** 860/676-9535. **Contact:** Cheryl Hooper, Owner. **E-mail address:** cph@cphstaffing.com. **World Wide Web address:** http://www.cphstaffing.com. **Description:** A temporary agency that also offers some executive searches and permanent placements. Client company pays fee. **Specializes in the areas of:** Health/Medical; Human Resources. **Positions commonly filled include:** Administrative Assistant; Administrative Manager; Customer Service Rep.; Human Resources Manager; Medical Assistant; Nurse Practitioner; Project Manager; Registered Nurse; Secretary. **Corporate headquarters location:** This Location. **Average salary range of placements:** $50,000 - $100,000. **Number of placements per year:** 1 - 49.

COMPUTER GRAPHICS RESOURCES
2 Stamford Plaza, 281 Tresser Boulevard, Stamford CT 06901. 203/316-4642. **Fax:** 203/316-4680. **Contact:** Patricia Hanaway, Manager. **Description:** A temporary agency. **Specializes in the areas of:** Advertising; Art/Design; Computer Graphics; Publishing; Sales; Technical. **Positions commonly filled include:** Administrative Manager; Broadcast Technician; Computer Programmer; Customer Service Rep.; Designer; Internet Services Manager; MIS Specialist; Multimedia Designer; Technical Writer/Editor; Typist/Word Processor. **Corporate headquarters location:** This Location. **Other U.S. locations:** New York NY. **Average salary range of placements:** $30,000 - $50,000.

CORPORATE STAFFING SOLUTIONS
98 Mill Plain Road, Danbury CT 06811. 203/744-6020. **Contact:** Office Manager. **Description:** A temporary agency. **Specializes in the areas of:** Administration; Computer Science/Software; Electronics; General Management; Manufacturing; Personnel/Labor

Relations; Sales; Technical. **Corporate headquarters location:** Wallingford CT. **Number of placements per year:** 1000+.

CORPORATE STAFFING SOLUTIONS

433 South Main Street, Corporate Center West, Suite 108, West Hartford CT 06110. 860/561-1952. **Contact:** Tonya Borla, Branch Manager. **Description:** A temporary agency. **Specializes in the areas of:** Accounting; Administration; Advertising; Finance; Industrial; Insurance; Legal; Manufacturing; Personnel/Labor Relations; Sales; Secretarial. **Positions commonly filled include:** Accountant; Advertising Clerk; Branch Manager; Claim Rep.; Computer Programmer; Customer Service Rep.; Human Service Worker; Paralegal; Purchasing Agent/Manager; Restaurant/Food Service Manager; Services Sales Rep.; Systems Analyst; Telecommunications Manager; Typist/Word Processor. **Benefits available to temporary workers:** Medical Insurance; Paid Holidays; Paid Vacation. **Corporate headquarters location:** Wallingford CT. **Number of placements per year:** 1000+.

CREATIVE SEARCH & MANAGEMENT

208 Harbor Drive, Stamford CT 06902. 203/961-8811. **Contact:** Manager. **Description:** A temporary agency. Founded in 1988. **Specializes in the areas of:** Advertising; Publishing. **Positions commonly filled include:** Designer; Editor; Internet Services Manager; Multimedia Designer. **Number of placements per year:** 1 - 49.

FOX RIDGE SERVICES, INC.

624 Village Walk, Guilford CT 06437. 203/458-2000. **Fax:** 203/458-1313. **Contact:** Manager. **Description:** A temporary agency. **Specializes in the areas of:** Engineering; Manufacturing; Technical. **Positions commonly filled include:** Designer; Hardware Engineer; Manufacturing Engineer; Mechanical Engineer; Software Engineer; Technical Illustrator; Technical Writer/Editor. **Average salary range of placements:** More than $50,000. **Number of placements per year:** 1 - 49.

HIRE LOGIC

435 Buckland Road, South Windsor CT 06074. 860/644-8877. **Fax:** 860/644-8801. **Contact:** Suzanne Lingua, Member. **Description:** A temporary agency. **Specializes in the areas of:** Computer Science/Software; Engineering; Industrial; Manufacturing; Technical. **Positions commonly filled include:** Aerospace Engineer; Aircraft Mechanic/Engine Specialist; Biochemist; Biological Scientist; Biomedical Engineer; Broadcast Technician; Buyer; Chemical Engineer; Chemist; Computer Programmer; Cost Estimator; Design Engineer; Designer; Draftsperson; Electrical/Electronics Engineer; Financial Analyst; General Manager; Human Resources Specialist; Industrial Engineer; Industrial Production Manager; Mechanical Engineer; MIS Specialist; Quality Control Supervisor; Software Engineer; Structural Engineer; Systems Analyst; Technical Writer/Editor; Telecommunications Manager. **Average salary range of placements:** More than $50,000. **Number of placements per year:** 100 - 199.

IMPACT PERSONNEL, INC.

40 Richards Avenue, Norwalk CT 06854. 203/866-2444. **Toll-free phone:** 800/283-0087. **Fax:** 203/831-5501. **Contact:** Maryann Donovan, President. **Description:** A temporary agency that also provides some permanent placements. Founded in 1989. **Specializes in the areas of:** Accounting/Auditing; Administration; Advertising; Finance; Office Support; Personnel/Labor Relations; Sales; Secretarial. **Positions commonly filled include:** Human Resources Specialist; Typist/Word Processor. **Benefits available to temporary workers:** Medical Insurance; Paid Vacation. **Corporate headquarters location:** This Location. **Other area locations:** Fairfield CT.

INTERTEC PERSONNEL

235 Post Road West, Westport CT 06880. 203/222-0050. **Fax:** 203/222-7691. **Contact:** Susan Littman, Director of Personnel. **Description:** A temporary agency. **Specializes in the areas of:** Accounting/Auditing; Administration; Advertising; Architecture/Construction; Computer Science/Software; Finance; Health/Medical; Legal; Personnel/Labor Relations; Publishing; Sales; Secretarial. **Positions commonly filled include:** Administrative Manager; Clerical Supervisor; Computer Programmer; Services Sales Representative; Typist/Word Processor. **Corporate headquarters location:** Cherry Hill NJ. **Other U.S. locations:** CA; MI. **Average salary range of placements:** $20,000 - $29,999. **Number of placements per year:** 100 - 199.

MANPOWER, INC.

2247 East Main Street, Waterbury CT 06705. 203/756-8303. **Contact:** Manager. **Description:** A temporary agency. **Specializes in the areas of:** Accounting/Auditing; Clerical; Secretarial. **Positions commonly filled include:** Accountant/Auditor; Clerk; Construction Trade Worker; Customer Service Representative; Data Entry Clerk; Draftsperson; Secretary; Stenographer; Technical Writer/Editor; Technician; Typist/Word Processor. **Number of placements per year:** 1000+.

McINTYRE ASSOCIATES

1281 East Main Street, Stamford CT 06902. 203/324-0000. **Fax:** 203/324-1102. **Contact:** Diana Burns, Office Manager. **Description:** A temporary agency that also provides some permanent placements. Founded in 1986. **Specializes in the areas of:** Accounting/Auditing; Administration; Computer Science/Software; Finance; General Management; Legal; Personnel/Labor Relations; Sales; Secretarial. **Positions commonly filled include:** Account Manager; Account Rep.; Accountant; Administrative Assistant; Administrative Manager; Advertising Clerk; Chief Financial Officer; Computer Programmer; Consultant; Controller; Credit Manager; Customer Service Manager; Finance Director; Financial Analyst; Human Resources Manager; Internet Services Manager; Market Research Analyst; Marketing Manager; Marketing Specialist; MIS Specialist; Paralegal; Safety Engineer; Sales Executive; Sales Manager; Sales Rep.; Secretary; Systems Analyst; Systems Manager; Typist/Word Processor; Vice President of Finance. **Benefits available to temporary workers:** 401(k); Direct Deposit; Medical Insurance; Paid Vacation; Travel Allowance. **Corporate headquarters location:** This Location. **Other area locations:** Danbury CT; Shelton CT. **Average salary range of placements:** More than $50,000. **Number of placements per year:** 1000+.

McLAUGHLIN PERSONNEL

6 Main Street, Chester CT 06412. 860/526-9096. **Contact:** Sharon McLaughlin, Principal. **World Wide Web address:** http://www.sharmac.com. **Description:** A temporary agency. **Specializes in the areas of:** Computer Science/Software. **Positions commonly filled include:** Computer Programmer; MIS Specialist; Systems Analyst. **Other U.S. locations:** Simsbury CT. **Average salary range of placements:** $30,000 - $50,000. **Number of placements per year:** 1 - 49.

TECH/AID

21 New Britain Avenue, Rocky Hill CT 06067. 860/529-5710. **Contact:** Office Manager. **Description:** A temporary agency. **Specializes in the areas of:** Architecture/Construction; Computer Science/Software; Construction; Engineering; Manufacturing; Technical. **Positions commonly filled include:** Aerospace Engineer; Architectural Engineer; Buyer; Ceramics Engineer; Chemical Engineer; Civil Engineer; Draftsperson; Electrical/Electronics Engineer; Estimator; Industrial Designer; Mechanical Engineer; Metallurgical Engineer; Mining Engineer; Operations/Production Manager; Petroleum Engineer; Purchasing Agent/Manager; Quality Control Supervisor; Technical Writer/Editor; Technician. **Number of placements per year:** 1000+.

TECHNICAL STAFFING SOLUTIONS

919-2 Stratford Avenue, Stratford CT 06615. 203/381-9700. **Fax:** 203/381-9458. **Contact:** Manager. **E-mail**

address: tecstasol@aol.com. **Description:** A temporary agency that also offers some permanent placements. **Specializes in the areas of:** Engineering; Industrial; Manufacturing; Technical. **Positions commonly filled include:** Aerospace Engineer; Aircraft Mechanic/Engine Specialist; Biomedical Engineer; Budget Analyst; Buyer; Chemical Engineer; Chemist; Civil Engineer; Clinical Lab Technician; Computer Programmer; Design Engineer; Designer; Draftsperson; Electrical/Electronics Engineer; Environmental Engineer; Human Resources Specialist; Industrial Engineer; Materials Engineer; Mechanical Engineer; MIS Specialist; Physicist; Purchasing Agent/Manager; Quality Control Supervisor; Science Technologist; Software Engineer; Structural Engineer; Systems Analyst; Technical Writer/Editor. **Average salary range of placements:** $30,000 - $50,000. **Number of placements per year:** 100 - 199.

UNITED PERSONNEL SERVICES
99 Pratt Street, Hartford CT 06103-1614. 860/560-8009. **Fax:** 860/560-8099. **Contact:** Manager. **Description:** A temporary agency that also offers some temp-to-perm placements. **Specializes in the areas of:** Administration; Light Industrial; Sales.

WESTAFF
100 Constitution Plaza, Suite 400, Hartford CT 06103. 860/249-7721. **Contact:** Manager. **Description:** A temporary agency that also provides some permanent placements. **Specializes in the areas of:** Accounting/Auditing; Advertising; Banking; Clerical; Computer Science/Software; Engineering; Finance; Insurance; Legal; Manufacturing; MIS/EDP; Personnel/Labor Relations; Publishing; Sales; Technical. **Positions commonly filled include:** Accountant/Auditor; Actuary; Administrative Assistant; Advertising Clerk; Aerospace Engineer; Agricultural Engineer; Architect; Attorney; Bank Officer/Manager; Biological Scientist; Biomedical Engineer; Bookkeeper; Buyer; Ceramics Engineer; Chemist; Civil Engineer; Claim Rep.; Clerk; Commercial Artist; Computer Programmer; Credit Manager; Customer Service Rep.; Data Entry Clerk; Draftsperson; Economist; EDP Specialist; Electrical/Electronics Engineer; Financial Analyst; Food Scientist/Technologist; General Manager; Industrial Designer; Industrial Engineer; Insurance Agent/Broker; Legal Secretary; Marketing Specialist; Mechanical Engineer; Medical Secretary; Metallurgical Engineer; MIS Specialist; Purchasing Agent/Manager; Receptionist; Secretary; Stenographer; Systems Analyst; Technical Writer/Editor; Technician; Typist/Word Processor; Underwriter/Assistant Underwriter. **Corporate headquarters location:** Walnut Creek CA.

WESTAFF
14 Hayestown Avenue, Danbury CT 06811. 203/798-8367. **Fax:** 203/744-1878. **Contact:** Jean Palumbo, CPC/Manager. **Description:** A temporary agency. Founded in 1948. **Specializes in the areas of:** Accounting/Auditing; Administration; Banking; Engineering; Finance; General Management; Industrial; Insurance; Manufacturing; Personnel/Labor Relations; Secretarial; Technical. **Positions commonly filled include:** Bank Officer/Manager; Biochemist; Blue-Collar Worker Supervisor; Branch Manager; Budget Analyst; Chemical Engineer; Chemist; Claim Rep.; Clerical Supervisor; Computer Programmer; Design Engineer; Designer; Draftsperson; Electrical/Electronics Engineer; Environmental Engineer; Financial Analyst; Human Resources Specialist; Industrial Engineer; Mechanical Engineer; Medical Records Technician; Purchasing Agent/Manager; Quality Control Supervisor; Software Engineer; Structural Engineer; Systems Analyst; Technical Writer/Editor; Typist/Word Processor; Underwriter/Assistant Underwriter. **Corporate headquarters location:** Walnut Creek CA. **Number of placements per year:** 500 - 999.

CONTRACT SERVICES FIRMS

ADECCO/TAD TECHNICAL SERVICES
One Research Drive, Shelton CT 06464. **Toll-free phone:** 888/577-4392. **Contact:** Manager. **Description:** A contract services firm that also offers some temporary placements. **Specializes in the areas of:** Computer Science/Software; Engineering; Technical. **Positions commonly filled include:** Assembler; Software Engineer.

ADECCO/TAD TECHNICAL SERVICES
151 New Park Avenue, Hartford CT 06106. 860/586-2376. **Toll-free phone:** 800/303-0823. **Contact:** Manager. **Description:** A contract services firm that also offers some temporary and permanent placements.

EDP CONTRACT SERVICES
727 Post Road East, Westport CT 06880. 203/227-2088. **Contact:** Office Manager. **Description:** A contract services firm. **Specializes in the areas of:** Accounting/Auditing; Banking; Computer Science/Software; Engineering; Finance; Insurance; Manufacturing; MIS/EDP; Nonprofit; Personnel/Labor Relations; Publishing; Technical. **Positions commonly filled include:** Computer Operator; Computer Programmer; EDP Specialist; MIS Specialist; Systems Analyst; Technical Writer/Editor. **Number of placements per year:** 1000+.

HALL KINION
6527 Main Street, Trumbull CT 06611. 203/261-1166. **Fax:** 203/452-9153. **Contact:** Manager. **E-mail address:** ctresume@hallkinion.com. **World Wide Web address:** http://www.hallkinion.com. **Description:** A contract services firm that also provides some permanent placements. **Specializes in the areas of:** Information Systems; Information Technology; Internet Development; Network Administration; Quality Assurance; Systems Administration; Systems Design; Technical Writing.

H.L. YOH COMPANY
YOH INFORMATION TECHNOLOGY ASSOCIATES
161 East Avenue, Norwalk CT 06851. 203/299-0100. **Contact:** Manager. **Description:** A contract services firm. **Specializes in the areas of:** Information Technology; Pharmaceuticals; Scientific.

CAREER/OUTPLACEMENT COUNSELING FIRMS

A&R RESUME SERVICE OF WEST HAVEN
33 Donald Street, West Haven CT 06516. 203/934-7639. **Contact:** Branch Manager. **Description:** A&R Resume Service of West Haven is a resume and career counseling firm.

HIGHLANDS PROGRAM
769 Newfield Street, Middletown CT 06457. 860/635-6517. **Contact:** Nancy Johnson, Director. **World Wide Web address:** http://www.highlandsprogram.com. **Description:** Provides career counseling and training and development services.

◆ D E L A W A R E ◆

BUSINESS CONTROL SYSTEMS
1201 North Orange Street, Wilmington DE 19801. 302/661-1262. **Contact:** Manager. **Description:** An executive search firm.

ELLIOTT DAVIS & ASSOCIATES
1400 Delaware Avenue, Suite 3A, Wilmington DE 19806. 302/654-2070. **Fax:** 302/654-2080. **Contact:** Manager. **Description:** Elliot Davis & Associates is an executive search firm. **Specializes in the areas of:** Engineering; Finance; Restaurant; Sales; Sales Management.

EMPLOYMENT NETWORK
1601 Concord Pike, Suite 38A, Wilmington DE 19803. 302/654-0696. **Contact:** Manager. **Description:** An executive search firm.

FINANCIAL SEARCH & STAFFING, INC.
Plaza 273, Suite 212, 56 W. Main Street, Christiana DE 19702. 302/292-1767. **Fax:** 302/292-1467. **Contact:** Manager. **E-mail address:** bankstaf@delanet.com. **World Wide Web address:** http://www. bigonline.com/searchstaff. **Description:** Financial Search & Staffing is an executive search firm. **Specializes in the areas of:** Accounting.

F-O-R-T-U-N-E PERSONNEL CONSULTANTS
191 South Chapel Street, Newark DE 19711. 302/453-0404. **Fax:** 302/453-0405. **Contact:** Leonard Weston, President. **Description:** F-O-R-T-U-N-E Personnel Consultants is an executive search firm. **Specializes in the areas of:** Biotechnology; Engineering; General Management; Manufacturing; Petrochemical; Technical. **Positions commonly filled include:** Biochemist; Biological Scientist; Biomedical Engineer; Chemical Engineer; Clinical Lab Technician; Mechanical Engineer; Operations/Production Manager; Quality Control Supervisor; Science Technologist; Technical Writer/Editor. **Corporate headquarters location:** New York NY. **Other U.S. locations:** Nationwide. **Average salary range of placements:** More than $50,000. **Number of placements per year:** 1 - 49.

THE FRANKLIN COMPANY
3801 Kennett Pike, Building C, Suite 109, Wilmington DE 19807. 302/661-4100. **Contact:** Manager. **Description:** The Franklin Company is an executive search firm. **Specializes in the areas of:** Chemicals; Pharmaceuticals.

FRANKLIN CONSULTING GROUP
One Daylilly Court, Wilmington DE 19808. 302/998-3759. **Contact:** Manager. **Description:** Franklin Consulting Group is an executive search firm that focuses exclusively on higher education. **Specializes in the areas of:** Education.

J.B. GRONER EXECUTIVE SEARCH INC.
P.O. Box 101, Claymont DE 19703. 302/792-9228. **Fax:** 610/497-5500. **Contact:** James Groner, President. **Description:** An executive search firm that also provides some contract services for the computer and engineering fields. J.B. Groner Executive Search operates on both retainer and contingency bases. **Specializes in the areas of:** Accounting/Auditing; Administration; Banking; Computer Science/Software; Economics; Engineering; Finance; General Management; Health/Medical; Industrial; Insurance; Legal; Manufacturing; Nonprofit; Personnel/Labor Relations; Sales; Technical. **Positions commonly filled include:** Accountant/Auditor; Administrative Manager; Aerospace Engineer; Architect; Attorney; Biochemist; Biological Scientist; Biomedical Engineer; Branch Manager; Budget Analyst; Buyer; Chemical Engineer; Chemist; Civil Engineer; Claim Representative; Computer Programmer; Construction Manager; Counselor; Credit Manager; Customer Service Representative; Design Engineer; Economist; Editor; Education Administrator; Electrical/Electronics Engineer; Environmental Engineer; Financial Analyst; General Manager; Geologist/Geophysicist; Health Services Manager; Hotel Manager; Human Resources Manager; Industrial Engineer; Industrial Production Manager; Insurance Agent/Broker; Internet Services Manager; Landscape Architect; Librarian; Licensed Practical Nurse; Management Analyst/Consultant; Management Trainee; Manufacturer's/Wholesaler's Sales Rep.; Market Research Analyst; Mathematician; Mechanical Engineer; Medical Records Technician; Metallurgical Engineer; Mining Engineer; MIS Specialist; Multimedia Designer; Nuclear Engineer; Nuclear Medicine Technologist; Operations/Production Manager; Petroleum Engineer; Pharmacist; Physician; Physicist; Property and Real Estate Manager; Psychologist; Public Relations Specialist; Purchasing Agent/Manager; Quality Control Supervisor; Restaurant/Food Service Manager; Science Technologist; Securities Sales Representative; Services Sales Representative; Social Worker; Sociologist; Software Engineer; Speech-Language Pathologist; Stationary Engineer; Statistician; Strategic Relations Manager; Structural Engineer; Surgical Technician; Surveyor; Systems Analyst; Teacher/Professor; Technical Writer/ Editor; Telecommunications Manager; Underwriter/ Assistant Underwriter; Urban/Regional Planner. **Average salary range of placements:** More than $50,000. **Number of placements per year:** 1 - 49.

ROBERT HALF INTERNATIONAL ACCOUNTEMPS
200 Bellevue Parkway, Suite 140, Wilmington DE 19809. 302/798-2929. **Fax:** 302/791-0171. **Contact:** Branch Manager. **Description:** Robert Half International is an executive search firm. Accountemps (also at this location) provides temporary placements. **Specializes in the areas of:** Accounting/Auditing.

HEALTHCARE NETWORK
P.O. Box 304, New Castle DE 19720. 302/322-9396. **Toll-free phone:** 800/497-4551. **Fax:** 302/322-3586. **Contact:** Judith A. Smith, President. **Description:** Healthcare Network is an executive search firm. **Specializes in the areas of:** Health/Medical. **Positions commonly filled include:** Health Care Administrator; Physician. **Corporate headquarters location:** This Location. **Average salary range of placements:** More than $50,000. **Number of placements per year:** 1 - 49.

E.W. HODGES & ASSOCIATES
3 McCormick Drive, Hockessin DE 19707. 302/995-6022. **Contact:** Edward W. Hodges, President. **E-mail address:** ehodges@udel.edu. **Description:** E.W. Hodges & Associates is an executive search firm. **Specializes in the areas of:** Accounting/Auditing; Administration; Banking; Biology; Engineering; Finance; General Management; Industrial; Legal; Manufacturing; Personnel/Labor Relations; Technical. **Positions commonly filled include:** Accountant/Auditor; Actuary; Administrative Manager; Attorney; Bank Officer/ Manager; Biological Scientist; Branch Manager; Budget Analyst; Buyer; Chemist; Computer Programmer; Construction Contractor; Designer; Economist; Editor; Education Administrator; Engineer; Financial Analyst; General Manager; Health Services Manager; Hotel Manager; Human Resources Manager; Management Analyst/Consultant; Mathematician; Operations/ Production Manager; Paralegal; Psychologist; Public Relations Specialist; Purchasing Agent/Manager; Quality Control Supervisor; Systems Analyst; Teacher/Professor; Technical Writer/Editor; Transportation/Traffic Specialist. **Average salary range of placements:** More than $50,000. **Number of placements per year:** 1 - 49.

HORNBERGER MANAGEMENT COMPANY
1201 North Orange Street, Suite 747, Wilmington DE 19801-1119. 302/573-2541. **Fax:** 302/573-2507. **Contact:** Manager. **E-mail address:** hmc@hmc.com. **World Wide Web address:** http://www.hmc.com. **Description:** An executive search firm. **Specializes in the areas of:** Construction. **Corporate headquarters location:** This Location. **International locations:** Worldwide.

HUNTER ASSOCIATES
13 Gristmill Court, Wilmington DE 19803. 302/764-7887. **Contact:** Manager. **Description:** Hunter Associates is an executive search firm. **Specializes in the areas of:** Plastics.

INDEPENDENT NATIONAL SEARCH & ASSOCIATES (INS)
258 East Camden Avenue, Camden DE 19934. 302/698-1466. **Fax:** 302/698-0659. **Contact:** Wallace Collins, Manager. **E-mail address:** wcinsac@dmv.com. **Description:** Independent National Search & Associates is an executive search firm operating on both retainer and contingency bases. **Specializes in the areas of:** Accounting; Engineering; General Management; Personnel/Labor Relations; Scientific; Technical; Transportation. **Positions commonly filled include:** Accountant; AS400 Programmer Analyst; Auditor; Biochemist; Biomedical Engineer; Buyer; Chemical Engineer; Chemist; Computer Programmer; Controller; Credit Manager; Database Administrator; Financial Analyst; Human Resources Manager; Industrial Production Manager; Production Manager; Project Manager; Purchasing Agent/Manager; Quality Control Supervisor; Statistician. **Corporate headquarters location:** This Location. **Other U.S. locations:** Nationwide. **Average salary range of placements:** $50,000 - $100,000. **Number of placements per year:** 100 - 199.

JAGER PERSONNEL
1305 South Governors Avenue, Dover DE 19904. 302/659-3805. **Contact:** Manager. **Description:** An executive search firm.

NORRIS & ROBERTS LTD.
P.O. Box 8, Nassau DE 19969. 302/644-1224. **Fax:** 302/664-1224. **Contact:** Manager. **Description:** Norris & Roberts Ltd. is an executive search firm. **Specializes in the areas of:** Industrial; Industrial Sales and Marketing.

PROVIEW RESOURCES INCORPORATED
230 Benjamin Boulevard, Bear DE 19701. 302/834-0349. **Contact:** Manager. **Description:** An executive search firm. **Specializes in the areas of:** Computer Hardware/Software.

PERMANENT EMPLOYMENT AGENCIES

BARRETT BUSINESS SERVICES, INC.
540-B South Bedford Street, Georgetown DE 19947. 302/856-7308. **Contact:** Mary Kay Barna, Manager. **Description:** A permanent employment agency. **Specializes in the areas of:** Clerical. **Positions commonly filled include:** Accountant/Auditor; Administrative Assistant; Administrative Worker/Clerk; Bookkeeper; Clerk; Computer Operator; Computer Programmer; Construction Trade Worker; Customer Service Representative; Data Entry Clerk; Draftsperson; EDP Specialist; Factory Worker; Legal Secretary; Light Industrial Worker; Medical Secretary; Receptionist; Secretary; Stenographer; Typist/Word Processor. **Number of placements per year:** 100 - 199.

CALDWELL STAFFING SERVICES
405 Newark Shopping Center, Newark DE 19711. 302/731-1111. **Fax:** 302/731-5745. **Contact:** Office Manager/Technical Representative. **Description:** Caldwell Staffing Services is a permanent employment agency that also provides some temporary placements. **Specializes in the areas of:** Administration; Banking; Sales. **Positions commonly filled include:** Account Manager; Customer Service Representative; Sales Executive; Sales Representative. **Average salary range of placements:** $30,000 - $50,000. **Number of placements per year:** 50 - 99.

CALDWELL STAFFING SERVICES
3520 Silverside Road, Suite 30, The Commons, Wilmington DE 19810. 302/478-8700. **Fax:** 302/479-5418. **Contact:** Laurie Pysczynski, Branch Manager. **Description:** A permanent employment agency that also provides some temporary placements. **Specializes in the areas of:** Accounting/Auditing; Banking; Finance; Insurance; Legal; Sales; Secretarial. **Positions commonly filled include:** Accountant/Auditor; Administrative Assistant; Bookkeeper; Clerk; Credit Manager; Customer Service Representative; Data Entry Clerk; Legal Secretary; Light Industrial Worker; Medical Secretary; Receptionist; Sales Representative; Secretary; Typist/Word Processor. **Number of placements per year:** 50 - 99.

HRDIRECT INCORPORATED
100 Enterprise Place, Dover DE 19901. **Toll-free phone:** 800/346-1231. **Fax:** 302/678-4335. **Contact:** Manager. **Description:** A permanent employment agency. **Specializes in the areas of:** Human Resources.

PERSONAL PLACEMENTS INC.
1303 Delaware Avenue, Suite 12, Wilmington DE 19806. 302/656-0706. **Fax:** 302/656-0709. **Contact:** Manager. **Description:** Personal Placements Inc. is a permanent employment agency. **Specializes in the areas of:** Administration; Finance; Human Resources; Marketing.

PROFESSIONAL RECRUITING CONSULTANTS
3617 Silverside Road, Suite A, Wilmington DE 19810. 302/479-9550. **Contact:** Manager. **Description:** Professional Recruiting Consultants is a permanent employment agency. **Specializes in the areas of:** Information Technology.

PROGRESSIVE HUMAN RESOURCES MANAGEMENT INC.
4001 Kennett Pike, Suite 134, Wilmington DE 19807. 302/234-3300. **Contact:** Manager. **Description:** Progressive Human Resources Management is a permanent employment agency.

WILMINGTON SENIOR CENTER/ EMPLOYMENT SERVICES
1909 North Market Street, Wilmington DE 19802. 302/651-3440. **Contact:** Sandria L. Thompson, Director of Employment Services. **Description:** A permanent employment agency that focuses on helping people over 50 years of age to find full- and part-time positions. The agency also operates a federally-funded program that provides temporary placements for people over 50 who are facing economic difficulties. Other services provided include job search training, resume preparation, and career counseling. **Specializes in the areas of:** Banking; Elderly; Food; Secretarial. **Positions commonly filled include:** Accountant/Auditor; Administrative Worker/Clerk; Bookkeeper; Certified Nurses Aide; Clerk; Driver; Gardener; Management Trainee; Medical Records Technician; Receptionist; Repair Specialist; Sales Manager; Sales Representative; Secretary; Typist/Word Processor. **Corporate headquarters location:** This Location. **Average salary range of placements:** Less than $20,000. **Number of placements per year:** 200 - 499.

TEMPORARY EMPLOYMENT AGENCIES

NETWORK PERSONNEL
1700 Shallcross Avenue, Suite 1, Wilmington DE 19806. 302/656-5555. **Contact:** Manager. **Description:** A temporary agency that also provides some temp-to-perm placements. **Specializes in the areas of:** Customer Service.

THE PLACERS, INC.
111 Continental Drive, Suite 201, Newark DE 19713. 302/456-6800. **Contact:** Manager. **Description:** A temporary agency that also offers some temp-to-perm and permanent placements. Founded in 1972. **Specializes in the areas of:** Accounting/Auditing; Administration; Banking; Finance; Information Technology; Insurance; Legal; Personnel/Labor Relations; Secretarial. **Positions commonly filled include:** Accountant/Auditor; Administrative Manager; Bank Officer/Manager; Branch Manager; Budget Analyst; Clerical Supervisor; Computer Programmer; Credit Manager; Customer Service Representative; Financial Analyst; Human Resources Specialist; MIS Specialist; Paralegal; Software Engineer; Statistician; Systems Analyst; Typist/Word Processor; Underwriter/Assistant Underwriter. **Benefits available to temporary workers:** Paid Holidays; Paid Vacation. **Corporate headquarters location:** Wilmington DE. **Average salary range of placements:** $30,000 - $50,000. **Number of placements per year:** 100 - 199.

THE PLACERS, INC.
2000 Pennsylvania Avenue, Suite 201, Wilmington DE 19806. 302/571-8367. **Contact:** Manager. **Description:** A temporary agency that also provides some permanent placements. Founded in 1992. **Specializes in the areas of:** Accounting/Auditing; Banking; Food; General Management; Industrial; Manufacturing; Personnel/Labor Relations. **Positions commonly filled include:** Accountant/Auditor; Administrative Manager; Bank Officer/Manager; Blue-Collar Worker Supervisor; Branch Manager; Budget Analyst; Chemist; Civil Engineer; Claim Representative; Clerical Supervisor; Clinical Lab Technician; Computer Programmer; Construction Contractor; Cost Estimator; Credit Manager; Customer Service Representative; Draftsperson; Electrician; Insurance Agent/Broker; Management Trainee; Paralegal; Restaurant/Food Service Manager; Underwriter/Assistant Underwriter. **Benefits available to temporary workers:** Paid Holidays; Paid Vacation. **Corporate headquarters location:** This Location.

CONTRACT SERVICES FIRMS

DW TECHNOLOGIES
5700 Kennett Pike, Centreville DE 19807. 302/777-5559. **Fax:** 302/777-1696. **Contact:** Manager. **Description:** A contract services firm. **Specializes in the areas of:** Engineering; Finance; Information Systems; Information Technology; Pharmaceuticals; Telecommunications.

TAD STAFFING SERVICES
2 Read's Way, Suite 113, New Castle DE 19720. 302/324-8400. **Contact:** Manager. **Description:** A contract services firm that also provides some temporary placements.

H.L. YOH COMPANY
200 Continental Drive, Suite 201, Newark DE 19713. 302/368-6210. **Contact:** Manager. **Description:** A contract services firm. **Specializes in the areas of:** Computer Hardware/Software; Engineering. **Other U.S. locations:** Nationwide.

CAREER/OUTPLACEMENT COUNSELING FIRMS

HIGHLANDS PROGRAM
2601 Annand Drive, Suite 16, Wilmington DE 19808. 302/993-0800. **Contact:** Alfonse Mercatante, Counselor. **World Wide Web address:** http://www.highlandsprogram.com. **Description:** Provides career counseling to students and adults, and training and development services to corporations.

◆ DISTRICT OF COLUMBIA ◆

ACCOUNTANTS EXECUTIVE SEARCH
ACCOUNTANTS ON CALL
1150 17th Street NW, Suite 408, Washington DC 20006. 202/829-0003. **Contact:** Manager. **Description:** An executive search firm. Accountants on Call (also at this location) is a temporary agency. **Specializes in the areas of:** Accounting/Auditing; Finance.

ACSYS STAFFING
1020 19th Street NW, Suite 650, Washington DC 20036. 202/463-7210. **Fax:** 202/331-9743. **Contact:** Manager. **Description:** An executive search firm that also provides temporary placements, contract services, and career counseling. The firm operates on both retainer and contingency bases. **Specializes in the areas of:** Accounting; Administration; Architecture/Construction; Banking; Computer Science/Software; Finance; Marketing; Nonprofit; Printing; Publishing; Sales; Secretarial. **Positions commonly filled include:** Account Manager; Account Rep.; Accountant; Administrative Assistant; Auditor; Bank Officer/Manager; Budget Analyst; Chief Financial Officer; Controller; Credit Manager; Customer Service Rep.; Finance Director; Financial Analyst; Financial Consultant; Graphic Artist; Graphic Designer; Human Resources Manager; Management Analyst/Consultant; Sales Executive; Sales Manager; Sales Rep.; Secretary; Systems Analyst. **Benefits available to temporary workers:** Medical Insurance; Paid Vacation. **Corporate headquarters location:** This Location. **Other U.S. locations:** Tampa FL; Atlanta GA; Rockville MD; Charlotte NC; Philadelphia PA; McLean VA. **Average salary range of placements:** More than $50,000. **Number of placements per year:** 1000+.

BOYDEN
2445 M Street NW, Suite 250, Washington DC 20037-1435. 202/342-7200. **Contact:** Manager. **E-mail address:** boydendc@aol.com. **World Wide Web address:** http://www.boyden.com. **Description:** A generalist executive search firm. **Corporate headquarters location:** New York NY. **Other U.S. locations:** San Francisco CA; Chicago IL; Bloomfield Hills MI; Chesterfield MO; Morristown NJ; Hawthorne NY; New York NY; Pittsburgh PA; Houston TX. **International locations:** Worldwide.

BUCKNER & ASSOCIATES
1700 K Street NW, Suite 403, Washington DC 20006. 202/463-4088. **Contact:** Manager. **Description:** An executive search firm.

C ASSOCIATES
1707 H Street NW, Washington DC 20006. 202/518-8595. **Fax:** 202/387-7033. **Contact:** John Capozzi, Jr., President. **E-mail address:** classoc@aol.com. **World Wide Web address:** http://www.cassociates.com. **Description:** An executive search firm that operates on both retainer and contingency bases. **Specializes in the areas of:** Computer Science/Software. **Positions commonly filled include:** Computer Programmer; Software Engineer; Systems Analyst; Webmaster. **International locations:** Canada. **Average salary range of placements:** More than $50,000. **Number of placements per year:** 50 - 99.

CAPITOL SEARCH
1700 K Street NW, Suite 1003, Washington DC 20006. 202/296-8800. **Fax:** 202/296-8820. **Contact:** Manager. **Description:** An executive search firm.

DHR INTERNATIONAL INC.
1717 Pennsylvania Avenue, Suite 650, Washington DC 20006. 202/822-9555. **Fax:** 202/822-9525. **Contact:** Manager. **Description:** An executive search firm.

DEVELOPMENT RESOURCE GROUP, INC.
1629 K Street NW, Suite 802, Washington DC 20006. 202/223-6528. **Fax:** 202/775-7465. **Contact:** Manager. **Description:** A generalist executive search firm.

FRANKLIN ROSS AND ASSOCIATES
1701 16th Street NW, Washington DC 20009. 202/626-4464. **Contact:** Manager. **E-mail address:** frnklnross@aol.com. **Description:** An executive search firm. **Specializes in the areas of:** Legal.

GKA RESOURCES, LLC
1717 K Street NW, Suite 601, Washington DC 20036. 202/293-7020. **Fax:** 202/293-7267. **Contact:** Roberta Alexander, Director of Recruitment. **E-mail address:** searchgka@aol.com. **Description:** An executive search firm that operates on both retainer and contingency bases. Client company pays fee. **Specializes in the areas of:** Accounting; Banking; Computer Science/Software; Economics; Engineering; Finance; General Management; Insurance; Internet Development; Internet Marketing; Marketing; MIS/EDP; Sales. **Positions commonly filled include:** Account Manager; Account Representative; Accountant; Adjuster; Administrative Manager; Applications Engineer; Assistant Manager; Auditor; Bank Officer/Manager; Blue-Collar Worker Supervisor; Branch Manager; Budget Analyst; Chemical Engineer; Chief Financial Officer; Civil Engineer; Clerical Supervisor; Computer Technician; Content Developer; Controller; Cost Estimator; Credit Manager; Database Administrator; Database Manager; Design Engineer; Economist; Environmental Engineer; Finance Director; Financial Analyst; Fund Manager; General Manager; Human Resources Manager; Industrial Engineer; Industrial Production Manager; Insurance Agent/Broker; Internet Services Manager; Management Analyst/Consultant; Management Trainee; Manufacturing Engineer; Mechanical Engineer; MIS Specialist; Network/Systems Administrator; Operations Manager; Production Manager; Project Manager; Purchasing Agent/Manager; Quality Assurance Engineer; Quality Control Supervisor; Sales Executive; Sales Rep.; Software Engineer; SQL Programmer; Systems Analyst; Systems Manager; Technical Support Engineer; Underwriter/Assistant Underwriter; Webmaster. **Corporate headquarters location:** This Location. **Average salary range of placements:** $50,000 - $100,000. **Number of placements per year:** 50 - 99.

GOODWIN & COMPANY
1150 Connecticut Avenue NW, Suite 200, Washington DC 20036. 202/785-9292. **Fax:** 202/785-9297. **Contact:** James Dudney, Senior Associate. **World Wide Web address:** http://www.goodwinco.com. **Description:** An executive search firm that provides placements nationwide. **Specializes in the areas of:** Art/Design; Communications; Economics; Education; Environmental; Finance; Government; Health/Medical; Public Relations; Social Services.

HARTMAN, GREEN & WELLS
1025 Connecticut Avenue NW, Suite 1012, Washington DC 20036. 202/223-7644. **Contact:** Manager. **Description:** An executive search firm. **Positions commonly filled include:** Attorney.

HEIDRICK & STRUGGLES
1301 K Street NW, Suite 500E, Washington DC 20005. 202/289-4450. **Fax:** 202/289-4451. **Contact:** Manager. **Description:** An executive search firm.

KORN/FERRY INTERNATIONAL
900 19th Street NW, Suite 800, Washington DC 20006. 202/822-9444. **Fax:** 202/822-8127. **Contact:** Manager. **World Wide Web address:** http://www.kornferry.com. **Description:** An executive search firm. **Corporate headquarters location:** Los Angeles CA. **International**

locations: Worldwide. **Average salary range of placements:** More than $50,000.

MEE DERBY & COMPANY
1522 K Street NW, Suite 704, Washington DC 20005. 202/842-8442. **Toll-free phone:** 800/MEE-DERB. **Fax:** 202/842-1900. **Contact:** Robin Mee, President. **E-mail address:** robin@meederby.com. **Description:** An executive search firm that operates on a contingency basis. **Specializes in the areas of:** Sales. **Positions commonly filled include:** Account Manager; Account Representative; Customer Service Representative; Sales Executive; Sales Manager; Sales Representative. **Average salary range of placements:** $30,000 - $50,000. **Number of placements per year:** 50 - 99.

MORRISON ASSOCIATES
3907 Harrison Street NW, Washington DC 20015. 202/223-6523. **Fax:** 202/223-6522. **Contact:** Manager. **Description:** An executive search firm. **Specializes in the areas of:** Nonprofit.

NATIONWIDE ATTORNEY PLACEMENT
1010 Vermont Avenue NW, Suite 408, Washington DC 20005. 202/393-1550. **Contact:** Manager. **Description:** An executive search firm. **Specializes in the areas of:** Legal. **Positions commonly filled include:** Attorney.

NORTH BERMAN & BEEBE INC.
1111 14th Street NW, Washington DC 20005. 202/371-1100. **Fax:** 202/371-5527. **Contact:** Manager. **Description:** An executive search firm. **Positions commonly filled include:** Attorney.

PACE-CAREERS, INC.
1737 Connecticut Avenue NW, Suite 2, Washington DC 20009. 202/667-4992. **Fax:** 202/667-4980. **Contact:** Manager. **Description:** An executive search firm which also offers consulting and contracting services. **Specializes in the areas of:** Computer Hardware/Software; Engineering; High-Tech; Marketing; Network Administration; Sales.

R.H. PERRY & ASSOCIATES
2607 31st Street NW, Washington DC 20008. 202/965-6464. **Fax:** 202/338-3953. **Contact:** Manager. **Description:** An executive search firm that focuses on higher education. **Specializes in the areas of:** Education.

PIERCE & ASSOCIATES
Federal Bar Building, Suite 900, 1815 Pennsylvania Avenue NW, Washington DC 20006. 202/835-1776. **Contact:** Manager. **Description:** An executive search firm. **Specializes in the areas of:** Legal. **Positions commonly filled include:** Attorney. **Other U.S. locations:** Los Angeles CA.

PREFERRED PLACEMENTS INC.
2000 L Street NW, Suite 200, Washington DC 20036. 202/232-4800. **Fax:** 202/232-1208. **Contact:** Manager. **Description:** An executive search firm. **Specializes in the areas of:** Legal.

ROMAC INTERNATIONAL
1111 19th Street NW, Suite 620, Washington DC 20036. 202/223-6000. **Contact:** Manager. **Description:** An executive search firm that also provides some temporary placements.

RURAK & ASSOCIATES, INC.
1350 Connecticut Avenue NW, Suite 801, Washington DC 20036. 202/293-7603. **Contact:** Principal. **Description:** A generalist executive search firm operating on a retainer basis.

RUSSELL REYNOLDS ASSOCIATES, INC.
1700 Pennsylvania Avenue NW, Suite 850, Washington DC 20006. 202/628-2150. **Fax:** 202/331-9348. **Contact:** Manager. **Description:** A generalist executive search firm.

SAVOY PARTNERS LTD.
1620 L Street NW, Suite 801, Washington DC 20036. 202/887-0666. **Contact:** Manager. **Description:** An executive search firm. **Specializes in the areas of:** General Management; Sales; Telecommunications.

ROBERT SELLERY ASSOCIATES LIMITED
1155 Connecticut Avenue NW, 5th Floor, Washington DC 20036. 202/331-0090. **Fax:** 202/452-8654. **Contact:** Manager. **Description:** Robert Sellery Associates is an executive search firm.

SITCOV DIRECTOR
2000 L Street, Suite 200, Washington DC 20036. 202/416-1600. **Fax:** 202/416-1601. **Contact:** Manager. **Description:** An executive search firm.

SNELLING PERSONNEL SERVICES
1000 16th Street NW, Suite 805, Washington DC 20036. 202/223-3540. **Fax:** 202/872-1967. **Contact:** Richard Whitney, President. **World Wide Web address:** http://www.snellingdc.com. **Description:** An executive search firm operating on both retainer and contingency bases. Snelling Personnel Services also provides some temporary placements. Client company pays fee. **Specializes in the areas of:** Banking; Bookkeeping; Clerical; MIS/EDP; Office Support; Secretarial. **Positions commonly filled include:** Accountant; Adjuster; Administrative Assistant; Auditor; Bank Officer/Manager; Claim Representative; Desktop Publishing Specialist; Editor; Editorial Assistant; Graphic Artist; Graphic Designer; Managing Editor; Sales Representative; Secretary; Technical Writer/Editor; Typist/Word Processor. **Corporate headquarters location:** Dallas TX. **Average salary range of placements:** $30,000 - $49,999. **Number of placements per year:** 1 - 49.

TANGENT CORPORATION
1901 L Street NW, Suite 705, Washington DC 20036. 202/331-9484. **Fax:** 202/466-4059. **Contact:** Fran D'Ooge, President. **E-mail address:** info@tangentcorp.com. **World Wide Web address:** http://www.tangentcorp.com. **Description:** An executive search firm operating on a contingency basis. Client company pays fee. **NOTE:** This firm does not accept unsolicited resumes. Please only respond to advertised openings. **Specializes in the areas of:** Administration; General Management; Nonprofit; Secretarial. **Positions commonly filled include:** Accountant; Administrative Assistant; Administrative Manager; Assistant Manager; Clerical Supervisor; Database Administrator; Database Manager; Desktop Publishing Specialist; Editorial Assistant; Financial Analyst; Human Resources Manager; Internet Services Manager; Management Trainee; Marketing Specialist; Network/Systems Administrator; Public Relations Specialist; Secretary; Webmaster. **Corporate headquarters location:** This Location. **Other U.S. locations:** Denver CO; Vail CO. **Average salary range of placements:** $30,000 - $49,999. **Number of placements per year:** 100 - 199.

TRAVAILLE EXECUTIVE SEARCH
1730 Rhode Island Avenue NW, Suite 401, Washington DC 20036. 202/463-6342. **Contact:** Manager. **Description:** An executive search firm. **Specializes in the areas of:** Communications.

PERMANENT EMPLOYMENT AGENCIES

ACCUSTAFF
1212 New York Avenue NW, Suite 250, Washington DC 20005. 202/289-8970. **Fax:** 202/289-8938. **Contact:**

Account Executive. **Description:** A permanent employment agency that also provides some temporary and temp-to-perm placements, as well as resume/career outplacement counseling services. Client company pays fee. **Specializes in the areas of:** Accounting; Administration; Banking; Health/Medical; Legal; Secretarial. **Positions commonly filled include:** Accountant; Administrative Assistant; Administrative Manager; Computer Programmer; Computer Support Technician; Computer Technician; Customer Service Representative; Human Resources Manager; Licensed Practical Nurse; Medical Records Technician; MIS Specialist; Network/Systems Administrator; Nurse Practitioner; Operations Manager; Paralegal; Registered Nurse; Secretary; Systems Analyst; Systems Manager; Typist/Word Processor. **Benefits available to temporary workers:** 401(k); Direct Deposit; Medical Insurance; Paid Holidays; Paid Vacation; Referral Bonus Plan; Training. **Other U.S. locations:** Nationwide. **International locations:** Canada; the Netherlands; United Kingdom. **Average salary range of placements:** $20,000 - $49,999. **Number of placements per year:** 1000+.

CAREER BLAZERS PERSONNEL SERVICE
1025 Connecticut Avenue NW, Suite 210, Washington DC 20036. 202/467-4222. **Fax:** 202/467-0820. **Contact:** Jeffrey Oxman, Area Vice President. **World Wide Web address:** http://www.careerblazers.com. **Description:** A permanent employment agency that also provides some temporary placements. Founded in 1949. **Specializes in the areas of:** Administration; Finance; General Management; Personnel/Labor Relations; Sales; Secretarial. **Positions commonly filled include:** Accountant/Auditor; Administrative Manager; Advertising Clerk; Branch Manager; Claim Rep.; Customer Service Representative; Editor; Human Resources Manager; Human Service Worker; Management Trainee; Manufacturer's/Wholesaler's Sales Rep.; Paralegal; Services Sales Representative; Typist/Word Processor. **Corporate headquarters location:** New York NY. **Other U.S. locations:** Nationwide. **Average salary range of placements:** $30,000 - $50,000. **Number of placements per year:** 1000+.

FRIENDS & COMPANY
1101 Connecticut Avenue NW, Suite 1250, Washington DC 20036. 202/223-2020. **Fax:** 202/429-8717. **Contact:** Manager. **Description:** A permanent employment agency that also provides some temporary placements.

GRAHAM STAFFING SERVICES
1211 Connecticut Avenue NW, Suite 204, Washington DC 20036. 202/861-1260. **Fax:** 202/223-5805. **Contact:** Manager. **World Wide Web address:** http://www. grahaminc.com. **Description:** A permanent employment agency.

HIRE STANDARD STAFFING
1350 Connecticut Avenue, Suite 1050, Washington DC 20036. 202/496-0300. **Fax:** 202/496-0309. **Contact:** Helen Hopkins, President. **Description:** A permanent employment agency that also provides some temporary and contract placements. **Specializes in the areas of:** Accounting/Auditing; Legal Secretarial; Nonprofit; Office Support; Sales; Secretarial. **Positions commonly filled include:** Account Manager; Account Representative; Accountant; Administrative Assistant; Administrative Manager; Auditor; Controller; Customer Service Representative; Database Manager; Management Trainee; Operations Manager; Paralegal; Sales Executive; Sales Manager; Sales Representative; Secretary; Typist/Word Processor. **Benefits available to temporary workers:** Medical Insurance; Paid Holidays. **Corporate headquarters location:** This Location. **Other U.S. locations:** Fort Lauderdale FL; Bethesda MD; McLean VA. **Average salary range of placements:** $20,000 - $29,999. **Number of placements per year:** 100 - 199.

K.M.S. ASSOCIATES
1620 L Street NW, Suite 801, Washington DC 20036. 202/822-8383. **Fax:** 703/255-6560. **Contact:** Karen Sadowski, President. **Description:** A permanent

employment agency. **Specializes in the areas of:** Legal; Nonprofit. **Positions commonly filled include:** Administrative Assistant; Benefit Analyst; Executive Assistant; Human Resources Generalist; Legal Secretary; MIS Manager; Paralegal; Training Specialist. **Average salary range of placements:** $30,000 - $50,000. **Number of placements per year:** 50 - 99.

MAYFAIR ASSOCIATES
1828 L Street NW, Suite 720, Washington DC 20036. 202/872-0112. **Fax:** 202/457-0015. **Contact:** Manager. **Description:** A permanent employment agency.

MEDICAL PERSONNEL SERVICES, INC.
1707 L Street, Suite 250, Washington DC 20036. 202/466-2955. **Contact:** Janet Cline Patrick, President. **Description:** A permanent employment agency. **Specializes in the areas of:** Health/Medical. **Positions commonly filled include:** Medical Secretary; Nurse.

POSITIONS INC.
1730 K Street NW, Suite 907, Washington DC 20006. 202/659-9270. **Fax:** 202/659-9245. **Contact:** Ellen Andrews, Managing Partner. **Description:** A permanent employment agency. **Specializes in the areas of:** Administration; Office Support. **Positions commonly filled include:** Administrative Assistant; Executive Assistant; Receptionist; Secretary.

PRIME PLACEMENTS, INC.
PRIME TEMPS, INC.
1835 K Street NW, Suite 400, Washington DC 20006. 202/785-7800. **Fax:** 202/785-0840. **Contact:** Manager. **World Wide Web address:** http://www. primeplacements.com. **Description:** A permanent employment agency. Prime Temps, Inc. (also at this location) provides temporary placements. **Specializes in the areas of:** Legal Secretarial; Secretarial. **Positions commonly filled include:** Administrative Assistant; Executive Assistant; Legal Secretary; Office Manager. **Office hours:** Monday - Friday, 8:30 a.m. - 5:30 p.m.

TRAK STAFFING
1155 Connecticut Avenue NW, Suite 800, Washington DC 20036. 202/466-8850. **Fax:** 202/466-4499. **Contact:** Wendy Fishman, Branch Manager. **E-mail address:** wfishman@trakstaffing.com. **World Wide Web address:** http://www.trakstaffing.baweb.com. **Description:** A permanent employment agency that also provides some temporary and temp-to-perm placements. Client company pays fee. **Specializes in the areas of:** Administration; Legal; Marketing; Sales; Secretarial. **Positions commonly filled include:** Account Manager; Account Rep.; Administrative Assistant; Administrative Manager; Auditor; Customer Service Representative; Database Administrator; Desktop Publishing Specialist; Editor; Financial Analyst; Market Research Analyst; Marketing Specialist; Network/Systems Administrator; Operations Manager; Paralegal; Production Manager; Project Manager; Real Estate Agent; Sales Manager; Sales Representative; Secretary; Typist/Word Processor; Underwriter/Assistant Underwriter. **Office hours:** Monday - Friday, 8:00 a.m. - 5:00 p.m. **Corporate headquarters location:** This Location. **Average salary range of placements:** $30,000 - $49,999. **Number of placements per year:** 1000+.

TRIFAX CORPORATION
4121 Minnesota Avenue NE, Washington DC 20019. 202/388-6000. **Contact:** Manager. **Description:** A permanent employment agency. **Specializes in the areas of:** Health/Medical; Personnel/Labor Relations. **Positions commonly filled include:** Administrative Assistant; Clerk; Data Entry Clerk; Marketing Specialist; Medical Secretary; Nurse; Social Worker; Typist/Word Processor. **Number of placements per year:** 50 - 99.

WHITMAN ASSOCIATES INC.
1730 K Street NW, Suite 309, Washington DC 20006. 202/659-2111. **Contact:** Manager. **Description:** A permanent employment agency that also provides some temporary placements. **Specializes in the areas of:**

Secretarial. **Positions commonly filled include:** Administrative Assistant; Legal Secretary; Secretary.

WOODSIDE EMPLOYMENT CONSULTANTS, INC.
1225 I Street NW, Suite 401, Washington DC 20005. 202/789-3105. **Contact:** Manager. **Description:** A permanent employment agency that also provides some temporary placements. **Specializes in the areas of:** Accounting/Auditing; Office Support. **Positions commonly filled include:** Administrative Assistant; Executive Assistant; Legal Secretary; Office Manager; Paralegal; Receptionist.

TEMPORARY EMPLOYMENT AGENCIES

ADECCO
1300 Connecticut Avenue NW, Suite 750, Washington DC 20036. 202/857-0800. **Fax:** 202/659-0743. **Contact:** Office Supervisor. **Description:** A temporary agency. **Specializes in the areas of:** Light Industrial; Office Support; Retail; Sales; Secretarial. **Positions commonly filled include:** Customer Service Representative; Paralegal; Typist/Word Processor. **Benefits available to temporary workers:** Medical Insurance; Paid Holidays; Paid Vacation; Tuition Assistance. **Corporate headquarters location:** Redwood City CA. **Other area locations:** Baltimore MD; Laurel MD; Rockville MD; Towson MD. **Other U.S. locations:** Washington DC; Alexandria VA; Vienna VA. **International locations:** Worldwide. **Average salary range of placements:** $20,000 - $29,999.

AQUENT PARTNERS
1730 K Street NW, Suite 1350, Washington DC 20006-3817. 202/293-4987. **Toll-free phone:** 877/PARTNER. **Fax:** 202/293-9025. **Contact:** Blanche Woodbridge, Marketing Manager. **E-mail address:** blanchew@ aquent.com. **World Wide Web address:** http://www. aquent.com. **Description:** A temporary agency that provides placements for creative, Web, and technical professionals. Aquent Partners also provides some temp-to-perm, permanent, and contract placements. **Specializes in the areas of:** Administration; Art/Design; Computer Science/Software; Marketing. **Positions commonly filled include:** Computer Animator; Computer Engineer; Computer Operator; Computer Programmer; Computer Support Technician; Computer Technician; Content Developer; Database Administrator; Database Manager; Desktop Publishing Specialist; Editor; Editorial Assistant; Graphic Artist; Graphic Designer; Internet Services Manager; Managing Editor; MIS Specialist; Multimedia Designer; Network/Systems Administrator; Production Manager; Promotion Manager; Software Engineer; SQL Programmer; Systems Analyst; Systems Manager; Technical Writer/Editor; Webmaster. **Benefits available to temporary workers:** 401(k); Dental Insurance; Disability Coverage; Medical Insurance. **CEO:** John Chuang.

GRAPHIC MAC
1301 Connecticut Avenue NW, Lower Level, Washington DC 20036-1815. 202/785-1333. **Fax:** 202/785-5927. **Contact:** Kevin Toler, Operations Manager. **E-mail address:** info@graphicmac.com. **Description:** A temporary agency that also provides some permanent placements. **Specializes in the areas of:** Art/Design; Graphic Arts; Printing; Publishing. **Positions commonly filled include:** Art Director; Designer; Desktop Publishing Specialist; Graphic Designer; Multimedia Designer; Online Content Specialist; Production Manager. **Benefits available to temporary workers:** Health Benefits; Paid Vacation. **Corporate headquarters location:** This Location. **Average salary range of placements:** $20,000 - $50,000. **Number of placements per year:** 200 - 499.

HIREKNOWLEDGE
9 St. Matthew's Court NW, Washington DC 20036. 202/347-7890. **Toll-free phone:** 800/937-3622. **Fax:** 202/347-7896. **Contact:** Recruiter. **World Wide Web address:** http://www.hireknowledge.com. **Description:** A temporary agency placing creative and technical individuals. The agency also offers some permanent placements. Client company pays fee. **Specializes in the areas of:** Architecture/Construction; Art/Design; Computer Science/Software; Internet Development; Internet Marketing; MIS/EDP; Printing; Publishing. **Positions commonly filled include:** Applications Engineer; AS400 Programmer Analyst; Computer Animator; Computer Engineer; Computer Graphics Specialist; Computer Operator; Computer Programmer; Computer Scientist; Computer Support Technician; Computer Technician; Content Developer; Database Administrator; Database Manager; Editor; Editorial Assistant; Graphic Artist; Graphic Designer; Internet Services Manager; Managing Editor; MIS Specialist; Multimedia Designer; Network/Systems Administrator; Software Engineer; SQL Programmer; Systems Analyst; Systems Manager; Technical Writer/Editor; Webmaster. **Benefits available to temporary workers:** 401(k); Direct Deposit; Health Benefits; Vacation Pay. **Corporate headquarters location:** Providence RI. **Other U.S. locations:** Nationwide. **Average salary range of placements:** $30,000 - $49,999. **Number of placements per year:** 200 - 499.

LAWCORPS LEGAL STAFFING SERVICES
1819 L Street NW, Suite 900, Washington DC 20036. 202/785-5996. **Fax:** 202/785-1118. **Contact:** Ms. Lee E. Arrowood, Managing Director. **World Wide Web address:** http://www.lawcorps.com. **Description:** A temporary agency that also provides some temp-to-perm and permanent placements. Founded in 1988. **Specializes in the areas of:** Legal. **Positions commonly filled include:** Attorney; Paralegal. **Benefits available to temporary workers:** Bonus Award/Plan; Medical Insurance; Paid Vacation; Profit Sharing.

MANPOWER
1130 Connecticut Avenue NW, Suite 530, Washington DC 20036. 202/331-8300. **Fax:** 202/293-4882. **Contact:** Branch Manager. **Description:** A temporary agency. **Specializes in the areas of:** Industrial; Office Support; Telecommunications; Word Processing. **Positions commonly filled include:** Accountant/Auditor; Administrative Assistant; Assembly Worker; Biological Scientist; Bookkeeper; Chemist; Customer Service Representative; Designer; Desktop Publishing Specialist; Electrician; Inspector/Tester/Grader; Inventory Control Specialist; Librarian; Machine Operator; Order Clerk; Packaging/Processing Worker; Painter; Project Engineer; Proofreader; Receptionist; Research Assistant; Secretary; Software Engineer; Stenographer; Stock Clerk; Systems Analyst; Typist/Word Processor; Welder. **Benefits available to temporary workers:** Life Insurance; Medical Insurance; Paid Holidays; Paid Vacation. **Number of placements per year:** 1000+.

NRI LEGAL RESOURCES
NRI ACCOUNTING RESOURCES
734 15th Street NW, Suite 200, Washington DC 20005. 202/628-3060. **Fax:** 202/628-2838. **Contact:** Dori Konopka, General Manager. **E-mail address:** nri@nri-staffing.com. **World Wide Web address:** http://www. nri-staffing.com. **Description:** A temporary agency that also provides some temp-to-perm and permanent placements. NRI Accounting Resources (also at this location) places accounting professionals. **Specializes in the areas of:** Accounting; Administration; Finance; Legal. **Positions commonly filled include:** Accountant; Administrative Assistant; Attorney; Auditor; Budget Analyst; Chief Financial Officer; Controller; Financial Analyst; Human Resources Manager; MIS Specialist; Paralegal; Secretary; Typist/Word Processor. **Corporate headquarters location:** Washington DC. **Other U.S.**

locations: Rockville MD; Annandale VA; Reston VA. **Average salary range of placements:** $30,000 - $50,000. **Number of placements per year:** 500 - 999.

NRI STAFFING RESOURCES
1899 L Street NW, Suite 300, Washington DC 20036. 202/466-4670. **Fax:** 202/466-6593. **Contact:** Robert Mulberger, President. **E-mail address:** nri@nri-staffing.com. **World Wide Web address:** http://www. nri-staffing.com. **Description:** A temporary agency that also provides some temp-to-perm and permanent placements. **Specializes in the areas of:** Administration; General Management. **Positions commonly filled include:** Accountant/Auditor; Actuary; Administrative Manager; Advertising Clerk; Attorney; Financial Analyst; Health Services Manager; Medical Records Technician; Paralegal; Physical Therapist; Services Sales Representative; Technical Writer/Editor; Typist/Word Processor. **Corporate headquarters location:** This Location. **Other U.S. locations:** Rockville MD; Annandale VA; Reston VA. **Average salary range of placements:** $20,000 - $29,999. **Number of placements per year:** 500 - 999.

NORRELL SERVICES
4401 Connecticut Avenue NW, Suite 604, Washington DC 20008. 202/686-1199. **Fax:** 202/966-7291. **Contact:** Recruiter. **Description:** A temporary agency that also offers some contract placements. **Specializes in the areas of:** Accounting/Auditing; Administration; Banking; Computer Science/Software; Engineering; Finance; Industrial; Insurance; Secretarial; Technical. **Positions commonly filled include:** Accountant/Auditor; Advertising Clerk; Claim Representative; Computer Programmer; Customer Service Representative; Designer; Editor; Financial Analyst; Human Resources Manager; Management Analyst/Consultant; MIS Specialist; Operations/Production Manager; Paralegal; Public Relations Specialist; Quality Control Supervisor; Software Engineer; Typist/Word Processor. **Benefits available to temporary workers:** 401(k); Dental Insurance; Medical Insurance; Paid Holidays; Paid Vacation; Stock Purchase. **Average salary range of placements:** $20,000 - $29,999. **Number of placements per year:** 1000+.

SPECIAL COUNSEL
1800 K Street NW, Suite 1100, Washington DC 20006. 202/737-3436. **Fax:** 202/776-0084. **Contact:** Manager. **World Wide Web address:** http://www. specialcounsel.com. **Description:** A temporary agency that also provides some permanent placements. **Specializes in the areas of:** Legal. **Other U.S. locations:** Nationwide.

TEMPORARY STAFFING, INC. (TSI)
1150 17th Street NW, Suite 202, Washington DC 20036. 202/466-8230. **Fax:** 202/466-8234. **Contact:** Bernadette Gilson, Vice President. **Description:** A temporary agency that also provides some permanent placements. **Specializes in the areas of:** Administration; Clerical; Legal; Office Support; Secretarial. **Positions commonly filled include:** Administrative Assistant; Paralegal. **Benefits available to temporary workers:** Credit Union; Medical Insurance; Paid Holidays; Paid Vacation; Training. **Average salary range of placements:** $25,000 - $45,000. **Number of placements per year:** 1000+.

TEMPWORLD STAFFING SERVICES
1050 17th Street NW, Suite 750, Washington DC 20036. 202/296-7530. **Contact:** Barbara Smith, Staffing Manager. **E-mail address:** washingtondc@ tempworld.com. **Description:** A temporary agency. **Specializes in the areas of:** Accounting/Auditing; Administration; Sales; Secretarial. **Positions commonly filled include:** Administrative Assistant; Computer Operator; Customer Service Representative; Editorial Assistant; Sales Representative; Typist/Word Processor. **Benefits available to temporary workers:** Bonus Award/Plan; Medical Insurance; Paid Holidays; Paid Vacation. **Other U.S. locations:** Nationwide. **Average salary range of placements:** $30,000 - $50,000. **Number of placements per year:** 1000+.

CAREER/OUTPLACEMENT COUNSELING FIRMS

BLACKWELL CAREER MANAGEMENT
626 A Street SE, Capitol Hill, Washington DC 20003. 202/546-6835. **Fax:** 202/547-7308. **Contact:** Mary Ann Blackwell, Executive Director. **E-mail address:** mablack@citizen.infi.net. **World Wide Web address:** http://www.piedmontpress.com/blackwell. **Description:** An education and career management firm specializing in career transition and advanced marketing services. The firm offers lectures, seminars, workshops, career evaluations, and consultations. Jobseeker pays fee. **Corporate headquarters location:** This Location.

FORTY PLUS OF WASHINGTON, INC.
1718 P Street NW, Washington DC 20036. 202/387-1582. **Contact:** Manager. **Description:** Forty Plus of Washington, Inc. is a volunteer organization which offers a two-week seminar focused on teaching self-marketing, resume writing, and interviewing skills. Open-House meetings are held Mondays at 10:00 p.m. and are open to the public.

EXECUTIVE SEARCH FIRMS

ACCOUNTANTS EXECUTIVE SEARCH
ACCOUNTANTS ON CALL
1715 North Westshore Boulevard, Suite 460, Tampa FL 33607. 813/289-0051. **Fax:** 813/289-6004. **Contact:** Jeffrey Waldon, President. **Description:** An executive search firm. Accountants On Call (also at this location) is a temporary agency. **Corporate headquarters location:** Saddle Brook NJ.

ACCOUNTANTS EXECUTIVE SEARCH
ACCOUNTANTS ON CALL
2 Alhambra Plaza, Suite 640, Miami FL 33134. 305/443-9333. **Contact:** Katherine Audi, Manager. **Description:** An executive search firm. Accountants On Call (also at this location) is a temporary agency. **Corporate headquarters location:** Saddle Brook NJ.

ACCOUNTANTS EXECUTIVE SEARCH
ACCOUNTANTS ON CALL
1801 Lee Road, Suite 235, Winter Park FL 32789. 407/629-2999. **Contact:** Manager. **Description:** An executive search firm. Accountants On Call (also at this location) is a temporary agency. **Corporate headquarters location:** Saddle Brook NJ.

ACTIVE PROFESSIONALS
2572 Atlantic Boulevard, Jacksonville FL 32207. 904/396-7148. **Fax:** 904/396-6321. **Contact:** John Logan, Vice President. **Description:** An executive search firm. **Specializes in the areas of:** Accounting/Auditing; Architecture/Construction; Computer Hardware/Software; Engineering; Finance; General Management; Industrial; Insurance; Manufacturing; Personnel/Labor Relations; Sales; Secretarial. **Number of placements per year:** 100 - 199.

ACTIVE WIRELESS INC.
414 Canal Street, Victoria Building, New Smyrna Beach FL 32168. 904/409-8550. **Fax:** 904/409-5801. **Contact:** Manager. **World Wide Web address:** http://www.activewireless.com. **Description:** An executive search firm. **Specializes in the areas of:** Telecommunications; Wireless Communications.

AFFINITY EXECUTIVE SEARCH
17210 NE 11th Court, North Miami Beach FL 33162. 305/770-1177. **Fax:** 305/770-4010. **Contact:** Manager. **World Wide Web address:** http://www.affinitysearch.com. **Description:** An executive search firm. **Specializes in the areas of:** Electrical; Electronics.

AMERICAN RECRUITERS
3900 NW 79th Avenue, Suite 401, Miami FL 33166. 305/592-1455. **Contact:** Branch Manager. **World Wide Web address:** http://www.americanrecruiters.com. **Description:** An executive search firm. **Specializes in the areas of:** Administration; General Management; Sales. **Corporate headquarters location:** Fort Lauderdale FL. **Other U.S. locations:** San Diego CA.

AMERICAN RECRUITERS
800 West Cypress Creek Road, Suite 310, Fort Lauderdale FL 33309. 954/493-9200. **Toll-free phone:** 800/493-9201. **Fax:** 954/493-9582. **Contact:** Carl R. Carieri, Owner. **E-mail address:** ccarieri@arcimail.com. **World Wide Web address:** http://www.americanrecruiters.com. **Description:** An executive search firm operating on both retainer and contingency bases. The firm also provides some contract services. Client company pays fee. **Specializes in the areas of:** Engineering; Food; Health/Medical; High-Tech; Information Technology; Insurance; Manufacturing; Marketing; Sales. **Positions commonly filled include:** Account Manager; Account Rep.; Accountant; Adjuster; Administrative Assistant; Applications Engineer; Auditor; Branch Manager; Budget Analyst; Buyer; Chief Financial Officer; Claim Rep.; Clerical Supervisor; Computer Programmer; Electrical/Electronics Engineer; Finance Director; Financial Analyst; Food Scientist/Technologist; General Manager; Industrial Engineer; Industrial Production Manager; Insurance Agent/Broker; Management Analyst/Consultant; Manufacturing Engineer; Market Research Analyst; Marketing Manager; Marketing Specialist; Mechanical Engineer; MIS Specialist; Occupational Therapist; Operations Manager; Physical Therapist; Production Manager; Project Manager; Sales Engineer; Sales Exec.; Sales Manager; Sales Rep.; Secretary; Software Engineer; Systems Analyst; Systems Manager; Telecommunications Manager; Transportation/Traffic Specialist; Typist/Word Processor; Underwriter/Assistant Underwriter; Vice President of Sales; Webmaster. **Benefits available to temporary workers:** 401(k); Dental Insurance; Medical Insurance. **Corporate headquarters location:** This Location. **Other U.S. locations:** San Diego CA; Miami FL. **Average salary range of placements:** More than $50,000. **Number of placements per year:** 1000+.

ASH & ASSOCIATES EXECUTIVE SEARCH
P.O. Box 862, Pompano Beach FL 33061. **Fax:** 954/946-3531. **Contact:** Kim Stone, Executive Recruiter. **E-mail address:** hdhunter3@aol.com. **Description:** An executive search firm operating on both retainer and contingency bases. The firm also provides some contract services. Founded in 1992. **Specializes in the areas of:** Finance; Human Resources; Information Systems; Management; Pharmaceuticals; Telecommunications. **Positions commonly filled include:** Account Manager; Accountant; Applications Engineer; Biochemist; Biological Scientist; Biomedical Engineer; Budget Analyst; Chemical Engineer; Chemist; Chief Financial Officer; Computer Programmer; Controller; Database Manager; Design Engineer; Finance Director; Financial Analyst; Human Resources Manager; Industrial Engineer; Industrial Production Manager; Internet Services Manager; Management Analyst/Consultant; Manufacturing Engineer;. Mechanical Engineer; MIS Specialist; Operations Manager; Production Manager; Project Manager; Quality Control Supervisor; Sales Manager; Software Engineer; Systems Analyst; Systems Manager; Technical Writer/Editor; Telecommunications Manager; Vice President of Finance; Webmaster. **Corporate headquarters location:** This Location. **Other U.S. locations:** San Diego CA. **Average salary range of placements:** More than $50,000. **Number of placements per year:** 1 - 49.

ATLANTIC PROFESSIONAL RECRUITERS
3836 Arrow Lakes Drive South, Jacksonville FL 32257. 904/262-3939. **Contact:** Ed Landers, Owner. **Description:** An executive search firm. **Specializes in the areas of:** Engineering; Manufacturing.

AUSTER ASSOCIATES
283 North Northlake Boulevard, Suite 111, Altamonte Springs FL 32701. 407/831-2400. **Contact:** Manager. **Description:** An executive search firm.

BALCOR ASSOCIATES
P.O. Box 190877, Miami Beach FL 33119. 305/535-9798. **Contact:** Manager. **Description:** An executive search firm. **Specializes in the areas of:** Administration; Finance; Human Resources.

BALES-WAUGH GROUP
BALES SALES RECRUITERS, INC.
1301 Riverplace Tower, Suite 2016, Jacksonville FL 32207. 904/398-9080. **Fax:** 904/398-8121. **Contact:** Beau Bales, Account Manager. **Description:** An executive search firm that also offers funding and strategic alliance assistance. Bales Sales Recruiters, Inc. (also at this location) specializes in sales recruiting for the medical, consumer, business products, and industrial fields. **Specializes in the areas of:** Computer

Science/Software; General Management; Health/ Medical; Sales. **Positions commonly filled include:** Computer Programmer; EEG Technologist; EKG Technician; General Manager; Human Resources Manager; Manufacturer's/Wholesaler's Sales Rep.; MIS Specialist; Radiological Technologist; Registered Nurse; Respiratory Therapist; Surgical Technician; Systems Analyst. **Number of placements per year:** 100 - 199.

BEACH EXECUTIVE SEARCH
10100 West Sample Road, Suite 325, Coral Springs FL 33065. 954/340-7337. **Contact:** Manager. **Description:** An executive search firm.

BENSON & ASSOCIATES
660 Linton Boulevard, Suite 200, Delray Beach FL 33444. 561/278-8898. **Toll-free phone:** 800/275-1221. **Fax:** 561/278-8884. **Contact:** Lou Benson, President. **Description:** An executive search firm. **Specializes in the areas of:** Banking; Brokerage; Sales. **Positions commonly filled include:** Securities Sales Rep.; Services Sales Representative. **Average salary range of placements:** More than $50,000. **Number of placements per year:** 1 - 49.

THE BRAND COMPANY, INC.
181 Shores Drive, Vero Beach FL 32963. 561/231-1807. **Contact:** Mr. J.B. Spangenberg, President. **Description:** An executive search firm. **Specializes in the areas of:** Engineering; General Management; Industrial; Manufacturing; Personnel/Labor Relations; Sales. **Positions commonly filled include:** General Manager; Human Resources Manager; Operations Research Analyst; Quality Control Supervisor. **Number of placements per year:** 1 - 49.

BRICKELL PERSONNEL CONSULTANTS
1110 Brickell Avenue, Suite 430, Miami FL 33131. 305/371-6187. **Contact:** Nidia Torres, President. **Description:** An executive search firm that also provides temporary and temp-to-perm placements. **Specializes in the areas of:** Accounting/Auditing; Administration; Banking; Computer Science/Software; Finance; Legal. **Positions commonly filled include:** Accountant/Auditor; Bank Officer/Manager; Computer Programmer; Credit Manager; Customer Service Representative; Financial Analyst; Internet Services Manager; Management Analyst/Consultant; Management Trainee; MIS Specialist; Paralegal; Systems Analyst; Typist/Word Processor. **Number of placements per year:** 200 - 499.

BURLINGTON WELLS OF SOUTHERN FLORIDA
80 SW 8th Street, Miami FL 33130. 305/810-2792. **Contact:** Manager. **Description:** An executive search firm.

THE BUTLERS COMPANY INSURANCE RECRUITERS
2753 State Road 580, Suite 103, Clearwater FL 33761. 727/725-1065. **Fax:** 727/726-7125. **Contact:** Mr. Kirby B. Butler, CPC/President. **Description:** An executive search firm. **Specializes in the areas of:** Insurance; Risk Management; Safety. **Positions commonly filled include:** Accountant/Auditor; Actuary; Adjuster; Branch Manager; Chief Financial Officer; Claim Rep.; Computer Programmer; Controller; Customer Service Rep.; General Manager; Insurance Agent/Broker; Loss Prevention Specialist; Marketing Manager; Sales Executive; Systems Analyst; Underwriter/Assistant Underwriter. **Average salary range of placements:** More than $50,000. **Number of placements per year:** 1 - 49.

CANTRELL & ASSOCIATES
433 Harrison Avenue, Panama City FL 32401. 850/784-1680. **Contact:** Manager. **Description:** An executive search firm. **Specializes in the areas of:** Engineering.

CAPITAL DATA, INC.
P.O. Box 2244, Palm Harbor FL 34682-2244. 727/784-4100. **Toll-free phone:** 800/771-4100. **Fax:** 800/787-4172. **Contact:** Jack Logan, Manager. **E-mail address:** as400@capitaldata.net. **World Wide Web address:** http://www.capitaldata.net. **Description:** An executive search firm that also provides some permanent, temporary, and contract placements, as well as career/outplacement counseling services. **Specializes in the areas of:** Computer Science/Software; Technical. **Positions commonly filled include:** Computer Programmer; Software Engineer; Systems Analyst; Technical Writer/Editor; Telecommunications Manager. **Average salary range of placements:** More than $50,000. **Number of placements per year:** 100 - 199.

CARADYNE GROUP
752 Blanding Boulevard, Orange Park FL 32065. 904/298-1294. **Fax:** 904/298-1296. **Contact:** Tara Floyd, President. **E-mail address:** info@pcsjobs.com. **World Wide Web address:** http://www.pcsjobs.com. **Description:** An executive search firm. **Specializes in the areas of:** Engineering; Sales; Telecommunications; Wireless Communications.

CAREER CHOICE, INC.
One Purlieu Place, Suite 240, Winter Park FL 32792. 407/679-5150. **Fax:** 407/679-0998. **Contact:** C.M. Herrick, President. **Description:** An executive search firm. **Specializes in the areas of:** Food; Hotel/Restaurant; Sales. **Positions commonly filled include:** Accountant/Auditor; Budget Analyst; Buyer; Chef/Cook/Kitchen Worker; Dietician/Nutritionist; General Manager; Hotel Manager; Human Resources Manager; Insurance Agent/Broker; Physician; Purchasing Agent/Manager; Restaurant/Food Service Manager. **Average salary range of placements:** More than $50,000. **Number of placements per year:** 100 - 199.

CAREERS UNLIMITED, INC.
1515 University Drive, Suite 204B, Coral Springs FL 33071. 954/341-7100. **Toll-free phone:** 800/777-0957. **Fax:** 954/341-7104. **Contact:** John S. Barton, Manager. **E-mail address:** jbcareers@msn.com. **Description:** Careers Unlimited, Inc. is an executive search firm that operates on a contingency basis. **Specializes in the areas of:** Health/Medical; Insurance. **Corporate headquarters location:** This Location. **Other U.S. locations:** Hendersonville NC. **Average salary range of placements:** More than $50,000. **Number of placements per year:** 1 - 49.

CHASE-GARDNER EXECUTIVE SEARCH
36181 East Lake Road, Box A, Palm Harbor FL 34685. 727/934-7000. **Fax:** 727/934-2390. **Contact:** Manager. **World Wide Web address:** http://www. chasegardner.com. **Description:** An executive search firm. **Specializes in the areas of:** Engineering; Human Resources; Manufacturing; Technical.

COLLI ASSOCIATES OF TAMPA
P.O. Box 2865, Tampa FL 33601. 813/681-2145. **Fax:** 813/661-5217. **Contact:** Carolyn Colli, Manager. **E-mail address:** colli@gte.net. **Description:** Colli Associates of Tampa is an executive search firm. **Specializes in the areas of:** Computer Science/Software; Engineering; Industrial; Manufacturing. **Positions commonly filled include:** Aerospace Engineer; Biomedical Engineer; Buyer; Chemical Engineer; Designer; Electrical/ Electronics Engineer; Human Resources Manager; Industrial Engineer; Industrial Production Manager; Mechanical Engineer; Metallurgical Engineer; Nuclear Engineer; Operations/Production Manager; Purchasing Agent/Manager; Quality Control Supervisor; Software Engineer; Stationary Engineer; Structural Engineer. **Number of placements per year:** 1 - 49.

CONSTRUCTION RESOURCES GROUP, INC.
466 94th Avenue North, St. Petersburg FL 33702. 727/578-1962. **Fax:** 727/578-9982. **Contact:** Cheryl P. Harris, President. **Description:** An executive search firm. **Specializes in the areas of:** Architecture/Construction. **Positions commonly filled include:** Civil Engineer; Construction Contractor; Construction Manager; Cost Estimator. **Average salary range of placements:** More than $50,000. **Number of placements per year:** 1 - 49.

CORPORATE ADVISORS, INC.
250 NE 27th Street, Miami FL 33137. 305/573-7753. **Fax:** 305/573-7929. **Contact:** Manager. **World Wide Web address:** http://www.corporateadvisors.com. **Description:** An executive search firm. **Specializes in the areas of:** Banking; Finance; High-Tech; Manufacturing; Marketing.

CORPORATE CONSULTANTS OF AMERICA
2807 West Busch Boulevard, Suite 202, Tampa FL 33618. 813/932-8804. **Fax:** 813/932-8703. **Contact:** Dana Andrews, President. **Description:** An executive search firm. **Specializes in the areas of:** Restaurant. **Positions commonly filled include:** Restaurant/Food Service Manager. **Average salary range of placements:** $30,000 - $50,000. **Number of placements per year:** 100 - 199.

CORPORATE SEARCH CONSULTANTS
509 West Colonial Drive, Orlando FL 32804. 407/578-3888. **Fax:** 407/578-5153. **Contact:** Anthony Ciamitaro, President. **Description:** An executive search firm. **Specializes in the areas of:** Banking; Finance; Information Systems.

CRITERION EXECUTIVE SEARCH INC.
5420 Bay Center Drive, Suite 101, Tampa FL 33609. 813/286-2000. **Fax:** 813/287-1660. **Contact:** Richard James, President. **Description:** An executive search firm. **Specializes in the areas of:** Administration; Computer Science/Software; Engineering; Insurance; Legal; Manufacturing; Technical. **Positions commonly filled include:** Accountant/Auditor; Adjuster; Administrative Manager; Aerospace Engineer; Agricultural Engineer; Biological Scientist; Biomedical Engineer; Branch Manager; Chemical Engineer; Chemist; Civil Engineer; Electrical/Electronics Engineer; Human Resources Manager; Industrial Engineer; Industrial Production Manager; Insurance Agent/Broker; Manufacturer's/Wholesaler's Sales Rep.; Mechanical Engineer; Metallurgical Engineer; Mining Engineer; Nuclear Engineer; Nuclear Medicine Technologist; Operations/Production Manager; Petroleum Engineer; Purchasing Agent/Manager; Radiological Technologist; Software Engineer; Stationary Engineer; Structural Engineer; Underwriter/Assistant Underwriter. **Number of placements per year:** 100 - 199.

DGA PERSONNEL GROUP, INC.
2691 East Oakland Park Boulevard, Suite 201, Fort Lauderdale FL 33306. 954/561-1771. **Fax:** 954/561-1774. **Contact:** David Grant, President. **E-mail address:** dgagroup@aol.com. **Description:** An executive search firm operating on a contingency basis. **Specializes in the areas of:** Accounting/Auditing; Administration; Architecture/Construction; Banking; Clerical; Computer Hardware/Software; Design; Engineering; Finance; Health/Medical; Industrial; Legal; Manufacturing; Sales; Secretarial; Technical; Transportation. **Positions commonly filled include:** Accountant/Auditor; Adjuster; Administrative Manager; Aerospace Engineer; Architect; Bank Officer/Manager; Biological Scientist; Biomedical Engineer; Branch Manager; Budget Analyst; Buyer; Chemical Engineer; Civil Engineer; Claim Rep.; Clerical Supervisor; Design Engineer; Draftsperson; Electrical/Electronics Engineer; Financial Analyst; General Manager; Human Resources Manager; Industrial Engineer; Industrial Production Manager; Insurance Agent/Broker; Market Research Analyst; Mechanical Engineer; Metallurgical Engineer; Property and Real Estate Manager; Purchasing Agent/Manager; Quality Control Supervisor; Registered Nurse; Restaurant/Food Service Manager; Services Sales Rep.; Software Engineer; Strategic Relations Manager; Structural Engineer; Technical Writer/Editor; Telecommunications Manager; Transportation/Traffic Specialist; Typist/Word Processor; Underwriter/Assistant Underwriter. **Average salary range of placements:** $30,000 - $90,000.

DHR INTERNATIONAL INC.
2810 East Oakland Park Boulevard, Suite 104, Fort Lauderdale FL 33306. 954/564-6110. **Fax:** 954/564-

6119. **Contact:** Manager. **Description:** An executive search firm. **Specializes in the areas of:** Latin America.

DMG MAXIMUS, INC.
1949 Commonwealth Lane, Tallahassee FL 32303. **Toll-free phone:** 888/498-2679. **Contact:** Manager. **Description:** An executive search firm.

DATA SEARCH NETWORK (DSN)
21218 St. Andrew's Boulevard, Suite 611, Boca Raton FL 33433. 561/488-8788. **Contact:** Manager. **Description:** An executive search firm. **Specializes in the areas of:** Information Systems.

DELTA SEARCH
10014 North Dale Mabry Highway, Suite 101, Tampa FL 33618. 813/269-7822. **Fax:** 813/269-7742. **Contact:** Dave Smith, President. **Description:** An executive search firm.

STEVEN DOUGLAS ASSOCIATES
3040 Universal Boulevard, Suite 190, Weston FL 33331. 954/385-8595. **Contact:** Manager. **Description:** An executive search firm. **Specializes in the areas of:** Accounting/Auditing; Banking; Finance; Information Systems.

DUNHILL PROFESSIONAL SEARCH
4350 West Cypress Street, Suite 225, Tampa FL 33607. 813/872-8118. **Contact:** Administrative Assistant. **Description:** An executive search firm. **Specializes in the areas of:** Accounting/Auditing; Data Processing; Health/Medical. **Positions commonly filled include:** Accountant/Auditor; EEG Technologist; EKG Technician; Medical Records Technician; Network Administrator; Occupational Therapist; Physical Therapist; Registered Nurse; Respiratory Therapist; Surgical Technician.

DUNHILL PROFESSIONAL SEARCH
1915 East Bay Drive, Suite B3, Largo FL 33771. 727/585-0000. **Contact:** Richard Williams, Owner. **Description:** An executive search firm. **Specializes in the areas of:** Technical.

ENVIRONMENTAL HEALTH & SAFETY SEARCH ASSOCIATES (EH&S)
P.O. Box 1325, Palm Harbor FL 34682. 727/787-3225. **Fax:** 727/787-5599. **Contact:** Randy L. Williams, Principal. **Description:** An executive search firm. **Specializes in the areas of:** Environmental; Industrial; Safety. **Positions commonly filled include:** Environmental Scientist; Safety Specialist. **Average salary range of placements:** More than $50,000. **Number of placements per year:** 50 - 99.

ETHAN ALLEN PERSONNEL PLACEMENT
5070 Sweetwater Terrace, Cooper City FL 33330. 954/252-8544. **Fax:** 954/252-8728. **Contact:** Michael H. Houlihan, President. **Description:** An executive search firm. **Specializes in the areas of:** Accounting/Auditing; Administration; Banking; Computer Science/Software; Engineering; Finance; General Management; Industrial; Manufacturing; Personnel/Labor Relations; Sales; Technical. **Positions commonly filled include:** Accountant/Auditor; Aerospace Engineer; Agricultural Engineer; Bank Officer/Manager; Budget Analyst; Buyer; Chemical Engineer; Computer Programmer; Cost Estimator; Credit Manager; Design Engineer; Designer; Draftsperson; Electrical/Electronics Engineer; Environmental Engineer; Financial Analyst; General Manager; Human Resources Manager; Industrial Engineer; Industrial Production Manager; Internet Services Manager; Management Analyst/Consultant; Manufacturer's/Wholesaler's Sales Rep.; Market Research Analyst; Mechanical Engineer; Metallurgical Engineer; MIS Specialist; Nuclear Engineer; Operations/Production Manager; Purchasing Agent/Manager; Quality Control Supervisor; Software Engineer; Stationary Engineer; Structural Engineer; Systems Analyst; Technical Writer/Editor; Telecommunications

Manager; Transportation/Traffic Specialist. **Number of placements per year:** 100 - 199.

EXECUTIVE CAREER STRATEGIES
7900 North University Drive, Suite 201, Tamarac FL 33321. 954/720-9764. **Contact:** Manager. **Description:** An executive search firm. **Specializes in the areas of:** Insurance.

EXECUTIVE EMPLOYMENT SEARCH INC.
4370 South Tamiami Trail, Suite 162, Sarasota FL 34231. 941/921-4744. **Contact:** Manager. **Description:** An executive search firm. **Positions commonly filled include:** Management.

EXECUTIVE MANNING CORPORATION
3000 NE 30th Place, Suite 402, Fort Lauderdale FL 33306. 954/561-5100. **Contact:** Manager. **Description:** An executive search firm.

EXECUTIVE SEARCH INTERNATIONAL
733 North Magnolia Avenue, Orlando FL 32803. 407/425-6000. **Contact:** Manager. **Description:** An executive search firm. **Specializes in the areas of:** Hotel/Restaurant.

THE EYE GROUP
22828 Horseshoe Way, Boca Raton FL 33428. 561/852-0008. **Contact:** Manager. **Description:** An executive search firm. **Positions commonly filled include:** Ophthalmologist; Optometrist. **Specializes in the areas of:** Health/Medical.

FARWELL GROUP INC.
One Alhambra Plaza, Suite 1425, Coral Gables FL 33134. 305/529-4811. **Fax:** 305/529-4827. **Contact:** Sandra Farwell, President. **E-mail address:** sandraf@farwellgroup.com. **World Wide Web address:** http://www.farwellgroup.com. **Description:** An executive search firm operating on a contingency basis. Client company pays fee. **Specializes in the areas of:** Accounting; Banking; Computer Science/Software; Finance; MIS/EDP; Personnel/Labor Relations. **Positions commonly filled include:** Accountant; Administrative Manager; Applications Engineer; AS400 Programmer Analyst; Auditor; Bank Officer/Manager; Branch Manager; Budget Analyst; CFO; Computer Engineer; Computer Operator; Computer Programmer; Computer Support Technician; Computer Technician; Content Developer; Controller; Cost Estimator; Credit Manager; Database Administrator; Database Manager; Economist; Finance Director; Financial Analyst; Fund Manager; General Manager; Human Resources Manager; Management Trainee; MIS Specialist; Network/Systems Administrator; Operations Manager; Project Manager; Purchasing Agent/Manager; Software Engineer; Systems Analyst; Systems Manager. **Corporate headquarters location:** This Location. **Average salary range of placements:** $50,000 - $100,000. **Number of placements per year:** 100 - 199.

FIRST RECRUITERS GROUP INC.
5440 NW 33rd Avenue, Suite 106, Fort Lauderdale FL 33309. 954/735-5264. **Fax:** 954/735-6264. **Contact:** Manager. **E-mail address:** info@firstrecruiters.com. **World Wide Web address:** http://www.firstrecruiters.com. **Description:** An executive search firm operating on a contingency basis. The company focuses on the placement of mid- to senior-level executives. **Specializes in the areas of:** Finance; Human Resources; Information Technology; Management; Marketing; Sales. **Corporate headquarters location:** This Location. **Other U.S. locations:** Nationwide.

F-O-R-T-U-N-E PERSONNEL CONSULTANTS
98 Sarasota Center Boulevard, Unit C, Sarasota FL 34240. 941/378-5262. **Fax:** 941/379-9233. **Contact:** Arthur R. Grindlinger, President. **E-mail address:** recruit@fpcsarasota.com. **World Wide Web address:** http://www.fpcsarasota.com. **Description:** An executive search firm. **Specializes in the areas of:** Automotive; Consumer Package Goods; Electronics; Engineering;

Industrial; Manufacturing; Materials; Mechanical; Metals; Pharmaceuticals; Plastics; Quality Assurance; Transportation. **Positions commonly filled include:** Biomedical Engineer; Chemical Engineer; Electrical/Electronics Engineer; General Manager; Industrial Engineer; Industrial Production Manager; Mechanical Engineer; Metallurgical Engineer; Operations/Production Manager; Purchasing Agent/Manager; Quality Control Supervisor; Software Engineer; Transportation/Traffic Specialist. **Corporate headquarters location:** New York NY. **Other U.S. locations:** Nationwide. **Average salary range of placements:** More than $50,000. **Number of placements per year:** 50 - 99.

F-O-R-T-U-N-E PERSONNEL CONSULTANTS
923 Fourth Street West, Palmetto FL 34221. 941/729-3674. **Fax:** 941/729-7927. **Contact:** Manager. **Description:** An executive search firm. **Specializes in the areas of:** Computer Hardware/Software; Data Communications; Electronics; Engineering; General Management; Human Resources; Industrial; Manufacturing; Process Technology; Purchasing; Quality Assurance; Sales; Telecommunications. **Corporate headquarters location:** New York NY. **Other U.S. locations:** Nationwide.

F-O-R-T-U-N-E PERSONNEL CONSULTANTS
11211 Prosperity Farms Road, Suite B-205, Palm Beach Gardens FL 33410. 561/624-7550. **Fax:** 561/624-7551. **Contact:** Manager. **E-mail address:** resume@fpcpalmbeach.com. **World Wide Web address:** http://www.fpcpalmbeach.com. **Description:** An executive search firm. **Specializes in the areas of:** Automotive; Computer Hardware/Software; Data Processing; Design; Engineering; Industrial; Information Technology; Management; Manufacturing; Mechanical; MIS/EDP; Plastics; Quality Assurance; Rubber. **Corporate headquarters location:** New York NY. **Other U.S. locations:** Nationwide.

F-O-R-T-U-N-E PERSONNEL CONSULTANTS
2531 Landmark Drive, Suite 207, Clearwater FL 33761. 727/797-9577. **Fax:** 727/791-8128. **Contact:** Manager. **Description:** An executive search firm. **Specializes in the areas of:** Automotive; Computer Hardware/Software; Distribution; Electrical; Electronics; Engineering; Food; Industrial; Logistics; Manufacturing; Materials; Mechanical; Medical Devices; Pharmaceuticals; Plastics; Purchasing; Quality Assurance; Telecommunications; Transportation. **Corporate headquarters location:** New York NY. **Other U.S. locations:** Nationwide.

F-O-R-T-U-N-E PERSONNEL CONSULTANTS
2175 Tamiami Trail, Osprey FL 34229. 941/966-6441. **Fax:** 941/966-1912. **Contact:** Manager. **Description:** An executive search firm. **Specializes in the areas of:** Engineering; Food; Manufacturing; Marketing; Medical Devices; Medical Sales and Marketing; Operations Management; Pharmaceuticals; Quality Assurance; Regulatory Affairs; Research and Development. **Corporate headquarters location:** New York NY. **Other U.S. locations:** Nationwide.

F-O-R-T-U-N-E PERSONNEL CONSULTANTS OF JACKSONVILLE
3000-6 Hartley Road, Jacksonville FL 32257. 904/886-2471. **Fax:** 904/886-2472. **Contact:** Bob Pepple, President. **E-mail address:** careers@fpcjax.com. **World Wide Web address:** http://www.fpcjax.com. **Description:** An executive search firm. **Specializes in the areas of:** Engineering; Manufacturing; Quality Assurance. **Positions commonly filled include:** Biological Scientist; Biomedical Engineer; Chemist; Engineer; General Manager; Industrial Production Manager; Management Analyst/Consultant; Quality Control Supervisor; Statistician; Telecommunications Manager. **Corporate headquarters location:** New York NY. **Other U.S. locations:** Nationwide. **Number of placements per year:** 50 - 99.

F-O-R-T-U-N-E PERSONNEL CONSULTANTS OF ORLANDO
982 Douglas Avenue, Suite 104, Altamonte Springs FL 32714. 407/875-0833. **Fax:** 407/875-1975. **Contact:** Manager. **World Wide Web address:** http://www.fco.com. **Description:** An executive search firm. **Specializes in the areas of:** Communications; Computer Hardware/Software; General Management; Information Systems; Marketing. **Corporate headquarters location:** New York NY. **Other U.S. locations:** Nationwide.

GALLIN ASSOCIATES
P.O. Box 1065, Safety Harbor FL 34695. 727/724-8303. **Fax:** 727/724-8503. **Contact:** Office Manager. **Description:** An executive search firm. **Specializes in the areas of:** Chemicals; Computer Science/Software; Engineering; MIS/EDP; Personnel/Labor Relations. **Positions commonly filled include:** Chemical Engineer; Chemist; Computer Programmer; Design Engineer; Environmental Engineer; Human Resources Manager; Internet Services Manager; MIS Specialist; Systems Analyst. **Average salary range of placements:** More than $50,000. **Number of placements per year:** 1 - 49.

GIMBEL & ASSOCIATES
201 NE Second Street, Fort Lauderdale FL 33301. 954/525-7000. **Fax:** 954/525-7300. **Contact:** Michael S. Gimbel, President. **Description:** An executive search firm. Founded in 1980. **Specializes in the areas of:** Accounting/Auditing; Administration; Banking; Computer Science/Software; Consulting; Finance; Health/Medical; Legal. **Positions commonly filled include:** Accountant; Attorney; Bank Officer/Manager; Budget Analyst; Chief Financial Officer; Consultant; Controller; Finance Director; Financial Analyst; Management Analyst/Consultant; MIS Specialist; Physician; Project Manager; Systems Analyst; Systems Manager; Telecommunications Manager; Webmaster. **Average salary range of placements:** More than $50,000. **Number of placements per year:** 100 - 199.

GLOBAL TECHNICAL RESOURCES
14004 Roosevelt Boulevard, Suite 612, Clearwater FL 33763. 727/524-3777. **Contact:** Manager. **Description:** An executive search firm. **Specializes in the areas of:** Finance.

BOB GRAHAM & ASSOCIATES
5401 West Kennedy Boulevard, Suite 1070, Tampa FL 33609. 813/282-4623. **Contact:** Manager. **Description:** An executive search firm. **Specializes in the areas of:** Computer Hardware/Software; Engineering.

ANN GROGAN & ASSOCIATES INC.
370 Waymont Court, Suite 100, Lake Mary FL 32746. 407/324-3355. **Contact:** Manager. **Description:** An executive search firm. **Specializes in the areas of:** Sales.

GULF COAST ASSOCIATES (GCA)
998 14th Street NE, Winter Haven FL 33881. 941/401-2900. **Contact:** Mr. Chris Gordon, Proprietor. **Description:** An executive search firm. **Specializes in the areas of:** Engineering; Heating, Air Conditioning, and Refrigeration; Manufacturing. **Positions commonly filled include:** Electrical/Electronics Engineer; Industrial Engineer; Mechanical Engineer; Metallurgical Engineer; Technical Writer/Editor.

HR PROFESSIONAL CONSULTANTS, INC.
1975 East Sunrise Boulevard, Suite 604, Fort Lauderdale FL 33304. 954/485-6506. **Fax:** 954/523-6888. **Contact:** Placement Director. **E-mail address:** info@hr-pro.com. **World Wide Web address:** http://www.hr-pro.com. **Description:** An executive search firm operating on both retainer and contingency bases. **Specializes in the areas of:** Accounting/Auditing; Computer Science/Software; Engineering; Personnel/Labor Relations; Secretarial; Technical. **Positions commonly filled include:** Accountant; Biochemist; Biomedical Engineer; Chemical Engineer; Chemist; CFO; Computer Programmer; Electrical Engineer; Finance Director; Financial Analyst; Human Resources Manager; Industrial Engineer;

Industrial Production Manager; Manufacturing Engineer; Mechanical Engineer; Operations Manager; Purchasing Agent; Quality Control Supervisor; Scientist; Software Engineer; Statistician. **Average salary range of placements:** More than $50,000. **Number of placements per year:** 1 - 49.

ROBERT HALF INTERNATIONAL ACCOUNTEMPS
1401 Forum Way, Suite 200, West Palm Beach FL 33401. 561/684-8500. **Fax:** 561/684-9946. **Contact:** Manager. **World Wide Web address:** http://www.roberthalf.com. **Description:** Robert Half International is an executive search firm. Accountemps (also at this location) provides temporary placements. **Specializes in the areas of:** Accounting/Auditing; Finance; Information Systems. **Positions commonly filled include:** Accountant/Auditor; Budget Analyst; Financial Analyst; Market Research Analyst. **Benefits available to temporary workers:** Bonus Award/Plan; Dental Insurance; Medical Insurance; Paid Holidays. **Corporate headquarters location:** Menlo Park CA. **Other U.S. locations:** Nationwide. **Number of placements per year:** 200 - 499.

ROBERT HALF INTERNATIONAL ACCOUNTEMPS
200 East Las Olas Boulevard, Suite 1650, Fort Lauderdale FL 33301. 954/761-3811. **Contact:** Manager. **World Wide Web address:** http://www.roberthalf.com. **Description:** Robert Half International is an executive search firm. Accountemps (also at this location) provides temporary placements. **Specializes in the areas of:** Accounting/Auditing. **Corporate headquarters location:** Menlo Park CA. **Other U.S. locations:** Nationwide.

ROBERT HALF INTERNATIONAL ACCOUNTEMPS
315 East Robinson Street, Suite 550, Orlando FL 32801. 407/422-2275. **Contact:** Manager. **E-mail address:** orlando@roberthalf.com. **World Wide Web address:** http://www.roberthalf.com. **Description:** Robert Half International is an executive search firm. Accountemps (also at this location) provides temporary placements. **Specializes in the areas of:** Accounting/Auditing. **Corporate headquarters location:** Menlo Park CA. **Other U.S. locations:** Nationwide.

ROBERT HALF INTERNATIONAL ACCOUNTEMPS
500 North Westshore Boulevard, Suite 500, Tampa FL 33607. 813/636-5000. **Contact:** Manager. **World Wide Web address:** http://www.roberthalf.com. **Description:** Robert Half International is an executive search firm. Accountemps (also at this location) provides temporary placements. **Specializes in the areas of:** Accounting/Auditing. **Corporate headquarters location:** Menlo Park CA. **Other U.S. locations:** Nationwide.

ROBERT HALF INTERNATIONAL ACCOUNTEMPS
220 Alhambra Circle, Suite 300, Coral Gables FL 33134. 305/447-1757. **Contact:** Manager. **World Wide Web address:** http://www.roberthalf.com. **Description:** Robert Half International is an executive search firm. Accountemps (also at this location) provides temporary placements. **Specializes in the areas of:** Accounting/Auditing. **Corporate headquarters location:** Menlo Park CA. **Other U.S. locations:** Nationwide.

HEALTHCARE RECRUITERS OF CENTRAL FLORIDA
215 Lincoln Avenue South, Clearwater FL 33756. 727/467-9620. **Fax:** 727/467-9249. **Contact:** Tom Fleury, President. **E-mail address:** hcri-central-florida@prodigy.net. **Description:** An executive search firm. **Specializes in the areas of:** Health/Medical; Sales. **Positions commonly filled include:** Biological Scientist; Biomedical Engineer; Health Services Manager; Manufacturer's/Wholesaler's Sales Rep.; Occupational Therapist; Pharmacist; Physical Therapist; Respiratory

Therapist; Services Sales Representative. **Number of placements per year:** 1 - 49.

HEIDRICK & STRUGGLES
5301 Blue Lagoon Drive, Suite 590, Miami FL 33126. 305/262-2606. **Fax:** 305/262-6697. **Contact:** Manager. **Description:** An executive search firm.

HEIDRICK & STRUGGLES
76 South Laura Street, Suite 2110, Jacksonville FL 32202. 904/355-6674. **Fax:** 904/355-6841. **Contact:** Manager. **Description:** An executive search firm.

HOWARD/WILLIAMS ASSOCIATES
105 South Narcissus Avenue, Suite 806, West Palm Beach FL 33401-5524. 561/833-4888. **Contact:** John Williams, President. **Description:** An executive search firm. **Specializes in the areas of:** Legal. **Positions commonly filled include:** Attorney; Paralegal. **Average salary range of placements:** More than $50,000. **Number of placements per year:** 50 - 99.

INNOTECH GLOBAL RESOURCES
12968 SW 133 Court, Miami FL 33186. 305/232-3432. **Contact:** Manager. **Description:** An executive search firm. **Specializes in the areas of:** Computer Hardware/Software. **Positions commonly filled include:** Computer Programmer.

INTERIM FINANCIAL SOLUTIONS
6710 Main Street, Suite 234, Miami Lakes FL 33014. 305/558-1700. **Contact:** Manager. **Description:** An executive search firm. **Specializes in the areas of:** Accounting/Auditing; Human Resources.

INTERNATIONAL INSURANCE CONSULTANTS, INC.
1191 East Newport Center Drive, Suite 206, Deerfield Beach FL 33442. 954/421-0122. **Fax:** 954/421-5751. **Contact:** Glenn A. Wootton, CPC/President. **Description:** An executive search firm operating on both retainer and contingency bases. **Specializes in the areas of:** Insurance. **Positions commonly filled include:** Actuary; Branch Manager; Broker; Chief Financial Officer; Claim Rep.; Environmental Engineer; Finance Director; Financial Analyst; Insurance Agent/Broker; Sales Executive; Underwriter/Assistant Underwriter. **Average salary range of placements:** More than $50,000. **Number of placements per year:** 50 - 99.

JUST MANAGEMENT SERVICES
701 Enterprise Road East, Suite 805, Safety Harbor FL 34695-5342. 727/726-4000. **Fax:** 727/725-4966. **Contact:** Susan Just, President. **Description:** An executive search firm. **Specializes in the areas of:** Apparel; Engineering; Fashion; General Management; Manufacturing; Plastics; Sales; Technical; Textiles. **Positions commonly filled include:** Designer; Industrial Engineer; Quality Control Supervisor. **Average salary range of placements:** $30,000 - $50,000.

KAY CONCEPTS
P.O. Box 4825, Palm Harbor FL 34685. 813/786-3580. **Toll-free phone:** 800/879-5850. **Fax:** 813/786-3358. **Toll-free fax number:** 800-879-5828.**Contact:** Heidi Kay, Principal. **E-mail address:** kconcept@staffing.net. **Description:** An executive search firm. **Specializes in the areas of:** Computer Programming; Engineering; High-Tech; Marketing; Mechanical.

A.T. KEARNEY EXECUTIVE SEARCH
200 South Biscayne Boulevard, Suite 3500, Miami FL 33131. 305/577-0046. **Contact:** Manager. **Description:** An executive search firm.

KEYS EMPLOYMENT AGENCY
P.O. Box 1973, Big Pine Key FL 33043. 305/872-9692. **Contact:** Donna Glenn, Owner. **E-mail address:** DG305@aol.com. **Description:** An executive search firm. **Specializes in the areas of:** Computer Science/Software. **Positions commonly filled include:** Accountant/Auditor; Adjuster; Administrative Manager;

Advertising Clerk; Architect; Attorney; Bank Officer/Manager; Biological Scientist; Branch Manager; Broadcast Technician; Budget Analyst; Civil Engineer; Clerical Supervisor; Clinical Lab Technician; Computer Programmer; Construction and Building Inspector; Construction Contractor; Cost Estimator; Counselor; Credit Manager; Customer Service Rep.; Dental Assistant/Dental Hygienist; Dental Lab Technician; Designer; Dietician/Nutritionist; Draftsperson; Education Administrator; Electrical/Electronics Engineer; Electrician; Emergency Medical Technician; Financial Analyst; General Manager; Health Services Manager; Human Resources Manager; Human Service Worker; Landscape Architect; Librarian; Library Technician; Licensed Practical Nurse; Management Analyst/Consultant; Management Trainee; Mathematician; Medical Records Technician; Occupational Therapist; Operations/Production Manager; Paralegal; Pharmacist; Physical Therapist; Preschool Worker; Property and Real Estate Manager; Psychologist; Public Relations Specialist; Purchasing Agent/Manager; Quality Control Supervisor; Radio/TV Announcer/Broadcaster; Registered Nurse; Reporter; Respiratory Therapist; Restaurant/Food Service Manager; Securities Sales Rep.; Services Sales Rep.; Social Worker; Sociologist; Structural Engineer; Surveyor; Systems Analyst; Teacher/Professor; Technical Writer/Editor; Transportation/Traffic Specialist; Travel Agent; Urban/Regional Planner. **Average salary range of placements:** More than $50,000. **Number of placements per year:** 1 - 49.

KORN/FERRY INTERNATIONAL
200 South Biscayne Boulevard, Suite 2790, Miami FL 33131. 305/377-4121. **Fax:** 305/377-4428. **Contact:** Manager. **World Wide Web address:** http://www.kornferry.com. **Description:** An executive search firm. **Corporate headquarters location:** Los Angeles CA. **International locations:** Worldwide.

LaMORTE SEARCH ASSOCIATES, INC.
3003 Yamato Road, Suite 1073, Boca Raton FL 33434. 561/997-1100. **Fax:** 561/997-1103. **Contact:** William M. LaMorte, President. **E-mail address:** lamortesearch@aol.com. **Description:** An executive search firm operating on a contingency basis. **Specializes in the areas of:** Insurance. **Positions commonly filled include:** Claim Representative; Insurance Agent/Broker; Loss Prevention Specialist; Risk Manager; Underwriter/Assistant Underwriter. **Average salary range of placements:** More than $50,000. **Number of placements per year:** 50 - 99.

R.H. LARSEN & ASSOCIATES, INC.
3900 NE 21st Avenue, Fort Lauderdale FL 33308. 954/763-9000. **Fax:** 954/563-3805. **Contact:** Manager. **Description:** An executive search firm operating on a retainer basis. Founded in 1971. **Specializes in the areas of:** Accounting/Auditing; Administration; Architecture/Construction; Banking; Computer Science/Software; Finance; General Management; Manufacturing; Personnel/Labor Relations; Sales. **Average salary range of placements:** More than $75,000. **Number of placements per year:** 1 - 49.

LASHER ASSOCIATES
1200 South Pine Island Road, Suite 370, Fort Lauderdale FL 33324-4402. 954/472-5658. **Contact:** Manager. **Description:** An executive search firm. **Specializes in the areas of:** High-Tech.

LEAR & ASSOCIATES
505 North Park Avenue, Winter Park FL 32789-3268. 407/645-4611. **Fax:** 407/645-5735. **Contact:** Roger Lear, President. **E-mail address:** roger@learsearch.com. **World Wide Web address:** http://www.learsearch.com. **Description:** An executive search firm. **Specializes in the areas of:** Insurance. **Positions commonly filled include:** Actuary; Adjuster; Claim Rep.; Computer Programmer; Insurance Agent/Broker; Loss Prevention Specialist; Underwriter/Assistant Underwriter. **Other U.S. locations:** Nationwide. **Average salary range of**

placements: More than $50,000. **Number of placements per year:** 50 - 99.

F.P. LENNON ASSOCIATES
1701 West Hillsboro Boulevard, Suite 305, Deerfield Beach FL 33442. 954/418-9900. **Toll-free phone:** 888/234-9867. **Fax:** 954/418-0556. **Contact:** Manager. **E-mail address:** fplassoc@fplennon.com. **World Wide Web address:** http://www.fplennon.com. **Description:** An executive search firm. **Specializes in the areas of:** Computer Hardware/Software; Computer Programming; Consulting; Internet Marketing; Sales.

PAT LIPTON & ASSOCIATES, INC.
4425 Kensington Park Way, Lake Worth FL 33467. 561/966-4688. **Fax:** 561/966-3583. **Contact:** Pat Lipton, President. **Description:** An executive search firm. **Other U.S. locations:** Princeton NJ.

MH EXECUTIVE SEARCH GROUP
PMB 108, 35246 U.S. Highway 19 North, Palm Harbor FL 34684. 727/442-5545. **Contact:** Recruiter. **E-mail address:** pkgjobs@mhgroup.com. **World Wide Web address:** http://www.mhgroup.com. **Description:** An executive search firm. **Specializes in the areas of:** Packaging. **Corporate headquarters location:** This Location. **Other U.S. locations:** Plano TX.

MANAGEMENT RECRUITERS INTERNATIONAL
815 NW 57th Avenue, Suite 110, Miami FL 33126. 305/264-4212. **Fax:** 305/264-4251. **Contact:** Del Diaz, President. **Description:** An executive search firm. **Specializes in the areas of:** Accounting/Auditing; Administration; Architecture/Construction; Computer Science/Software; Engineering; Finance; Health/Medical; Industrial; Manufacturing; Personnel/Labor Relations; Sales. **Positions commonly filled include:** Accountant/Auditor; Administrative Manager; Aerospace Engineer; Agricultural Engineer; Biological Scientist; Biomedical Engineer; Branch Manager; Buyer; Ceramics Engineer; Chemical Engineer; Chemist; Civil Engineer; Clinical Lab Technician; Computer Programmer; Construction Contractor; Cost Estimator; Customer Service Rep.; Designer; EEG Technologist; EKG Technician; Electrical/Electronics Engineer; Financial Analyst; General Manager; Geologist/Geophysicist; Health Services Manager; Human Resources Manager; Industrial Engineer; Industrial Production Manager; Licensed Practical Nurse; Manufacturer's/Wholesaler's Sales Rep.; Materials Engineer; Mechanical Engineer; Medical Records Technician; Metallurgical Engineer; Mining Engineer; Nuclear Engineer; Nuclear Medicine Technologist; Occupational Therapist; Petroleum Engineer; Physical Therapist; Property and Real Estate Manager; Public Relations Specialist; Purchasing Agent/Manager; Quality Control Supervisor; Radiological Technologist; Recreational Therapist; Registered Nurse; Respiratory Therapist; Science Technologist; Services Sales Rep.; Software Engineer; Stationary Engineer; Structural Engineer; Surveyor; Systems Analyst; Technical Writer/Editor; Wholesale and Retail Buyer. **Corporate headquarters location:** Cleveland OH. **Other U.S. locations:** Nationwide. **Number of placements per year:** 50 - 99.

MANAGEMENT RECRUITERS INTERNATIONAL
3606 Evans Avenue, Fort Myers FL 33901. 941/939-2223. **Fax:** 941/939-2742. **Contact:** Calvin Beals, Manager. **Description:** An executive search firm. **Specializes in the areas of:** Banking; Engineering. **Positions commonly filled include:** Actuary; Bank Officer/Manager; Chemical Engineer; Civil Engineer; Electrical/Electronics Engineer; Financial Analyst; Industrial Engineer; Mechanical Engineer; Physical Therapist. **Corporate headquarters location:** Cleveland OH. **Other U.S. locations:** Nationwide. **Number of placements per year:** 50 - 99.

MANAGEMENT RECRUITERS INTERNATIONAL
498 Palm Springs Drive, Suite 100, Altamonte Springs FL 32701. 407/260-0039. **Fax:** 407/260-0255. **Description:** An executive search firm. **Specializes in**

the areas of: Administration; Computer Science/Software; Engineering; Insurance; Sales; Telecommunications. **Positions commonly filled include:** Computer Programmer; Electrical/Electronics Engineer; General Manager; Insurance Agent/Broker; MIS Manager; Software Engineer; Telecommunications Manager; Underwriter/Assistant Underwriter. **Corporate headquarters location:** Cleveland OH. **Other U.S. locations:** Nationwide. **Average salary range of placements:** $60,000 - $90,000. **Number of placements per year:** 1 - 49.

MANAGEMENT RECRUITERS INTERNATIONAL
P.O. Box 7711, Clearwater FL 33758. 727/791-3277. **Contact:** Helen Gleason, Manager. **Description:** An executive search firm. **Specializes in the areas of:** Health/Medical; Packaging; Sales. **Positions commonly filled include:** Accountant/Auditor; Computer Programmer; Designer; Dietician/Nutritionist; EEG Technologist; EKG Technician; Health Services Manager; Medical Records Technician; Nuclear Medicine Technologist; Occupational Therapist; Pharmacist; Quality Control Supervisor; Registered Nurse; Respiratory Therapist; Systems Analyst. **Corporate headquarters location:** Cleveland OH. **Other U.S. locations:** Nationwide. **Number of placements per year:** 50 - 99.

MANAGEMENT RECRUITERS INTERNATIONAL
1700 East Las Olas Boulevard, Fort Lauderdale FL 33301. 954/525-0355. **Fax:** 954/525-0353. **Contact:** Thomas K. Johasky, President. **E-mail address:** tjohasky@hotmail.com. **Description:** An executive search firm operating on both retainer and contingency bases. **Specializes in the areas of:** Medical Devices; Sales; Telecommunications. **Positions commonly filled include:** Biomedical Engineer; Design Engineer; General Manager; Human Resources Manager; Manufacturing Engineer; Mechanical Engineer; Operations/Production Manager; Product Development Engineer; Product Manager; Project Manager; Regional Manager; Telecommunications Manager; Vice President of Marketing; Vice President of Sales. **Corporate headquarters location:** Cleveland OH. **Other U.S. locations:** Nationwide. **Average salary range of placements:** More than $100,000. **Number of placements per year:** 200 - 499.

MANAGEMENT RECRUITERS INTERNATIONAL
996B Laguna Drive, Venice FL 34285. 941/484-3900. **Fax:** 941/485-5822. **Contact:** Manager. **Description:** An executive search firm. **Specializes in the areas of:** Information Technology. **Corporate headquarters location:** Cleveland OH. **Other U.S. locations:** Nationwide.

MANAGEMENT RECRUITERS INTERNATIONAL
9240 Bonita Beach Road, Suite 3307, Bonita Springs FL 34135. 941/495-7885. **Fax:** 941/495-7686. **Contact:** Gary F. Shearer, President. **World Wide Web address:** http://www.mriheadhunter.com. **Description:** An executive search firm. Client company pays fee. **Specializes in the areas of:** General Management; Management Consulting; Paper. **Positions commonly filled include:** Consultant; Development Officer; Engineer. **Corporate headquarters location:** Cleveland OH. **Other U.S. locations:** Nationwide. **Average salary range of placements:** More than $70,000. **Number of placements per year:** 50 - 99.

MANAGEMENT RECRUITERS OF BOCA RATON INC.
370 West Camino Garden Boulevard, Suite 200, Boca Raton FL 33432. **Toll-free phone:** 800/886-3991. **Fax:** 561/393-3992. **Contact:** Ernie Labadie, President. **E-mail address:** mrboca@worldnet.att.net. **Description:** An executive search firm operating on both retainer and contingency bases. **Specializes in the areas of:** Chemicals. **Positions commonly filled include:** Chemical Engineer; Chemist; Design Engineer; Electrical/Electronics Engineer; Environmental Engineer; General Manager; Human Resources Manager; Industrial

Production Manager; Manufacturing Engineer; Mechanical Engineer; Operations Manager; Production Manager; Project Manager. **Corporate headquarters location:** Cleveland OH. **Other U.S. locations:** Nationwide.

MANAGEMENT RECRUITERS OF JACKSONVILLE
12708 San Jose Boulevard, Suite 1A, Jacksonville FL 32223. 904/260-4444. **Fax:** 904/260-4666. **Contact:** Robert Lee, President. **World Wide Web address:** http://www.mrijax.com. **Description:** An executive search firm operating on a contingency basis. **NOTE:** The firm prefers to have resumes sent via e-mail. **Specializes in the areas of:** Engineering; Industrial; Packaging; Sales. **Positions commonly filled include:** Design Engineer; Electrical/Electronics Engineer; Manufacturer's/Wholesaler's Sales Rep.; Mechanical Engineer; Software Engineer. **Corporate headquarters location:** Cleveland OH. **Other U.S. locations:** Nationwide. **Average salary range of placements:** More than $50,000. **Number of placements per year:** 1 - 49.

MANAGEMENT RECRUITERS OF JENSEN BEACH, INC.
3332 NE Sugar Hill Avenue, Jensen Beach FL 34957. 561/334-8633. **Fax:** 561/334-4145. **Contact:** Douglas Lane, President. **E-mail address:** dwl1@adelphia.net. **World Wide Web address:** http://www. freeyellow.com/members2/mrjbeau. **Description:** An executive search firm. **Specializes in the areas of:** Information Technology; Marketing; Sales; Telecommunications. **Corporate headquarters location:** Cleveland OH. **Other U.S. locations:** Nationwide.

MANAGEMENT RECRUITERS OF LAKE COUNTY
1117 North Donnelley Street, Mount Dora FL 32757. 352/383-7101. **Toll-free phone:** 800/856-1941. **Fax:** 352/383-7103. **Contact:** Roger Holloway, President. **E-mail address:** mrilakeco@lcia.com. **Description:** An executive search firm operating on a contingency basis. Founded in 1980. Client company pays fee. **Specializes in the areas of:** Chemicals; Engineering; Food; General Management; Industrial; Light Industrial; Medical Devices; Metals; Plastics. **Positions commonly filled include:** Administrative Manager; Biomedical Engineer; Blue-Collar Worker Supervisor; Chemical Engineer; Chemist; Design Engineer; Electrical/Electronics Engineer; Food Scientist/Technologist; General Manager; Industrial Engineer; Industrial Production Manager; Management Trainee; Manufacturing Engineer; Mechanical Engineer; Operations Manager; Production Manager; Quality Assurance Engineer; Quality Control Supervisor; Vice President of Operations. **Corporate headquarters location:** Cleveland OH. **Other U.S. locations:** Nationwide. **Average salary range of placements:** $30,000 - $100,000. **Number of placements per year:** 50 - 99.

MANAGEMENT RECRUITERS OF MELBOURNE
134 Fifth Avenue, Suite 208, Indialantic FL 32903-3170. 407/951-7644. **Fax:** 407/951-4235. **Contact:** Lawrence Cinco, General Manager. **World Wide Web address:** http://mrirecruiter.com. **Description:** An executive search firm operating on a contingency basis. **Specializes in the areas of:** Computer Science/Software; Engineering; Manufacturing; Sales. **Positions commonly filled include:** Agricultural Engineer; Computer Programmer; Design Engineer; Designer; Electrical/ Electronics Engineer; Industrial Engineer; Mechanical Engineer; MIS Specialist; Systems Analyst. **Corporate headquarters location:** Cleveland OH. **Other U.S. locations:** Nationwide. **Average salary range of placements:** More than $50,000. **Number of placements per year:** 100 - 199.

MANAGEMENT RECRUITERS OF ORLANDO/WINTER PARK
230 South New York Avenue, Suite 200, Winter Park FL 32789. 407/629-2424. **Fax:** 407/629-6424. **Contact:**

Stacy L. Gulden, President/CEO. **E-mail address:** mrorlando@parkave.net. **World Wide Web address:** http://www.mrorlando.com. **Description:** An executive search firm operating on both retainer and contingency bases. **Specializes in the areas of:** Banking; Finance. **Corporate headquarters location:** Cleveland OH. **Other U.S. locations:** Nationwide.

MANAGEMENT RECRUITERS OF PENSACOLA
603-A East Government Street, Pensacola FL 32501. 850/434-6500. **Fax:** 850/434-9911. **Contact:** Ken Kirchgessner, President. **World Wide Web address:** http://www.mriplastics.com. **Description:** An executive search firm. **Specializes in the areas of:** Engineering; Industrial; Manufacturing; Packaging; Plastics. **Positions commonly filled include:** Chemical Engineer; Electrical/Electronics Engineer; General Manager; Industrial Engineer; Industrial Production Manager; Mechanical Engineer. **Corporate headquarters location:** Cleveland OH. **Other U.S. locations:** Nationwide. **Average salary range of placements:** More than $50,000. **Number of placements per year:** 1 - 49.

MANAGEMENT RECRUITERS OF PLANT CITY
117 West Alexander Street, Plant City FL 33567. 813/754-6340. **Fax:** 813/754-7557. **Contact:** Office Manager. **Description:** An executive search firm. **Specializes in the areas of:** Biology; Chemicals; Pharmaceuticals. **Positions commonly filled include:** Biochemist; Biological Scientist; Chemical Engineer; Chemist; Science Technologist. **Corporate headquarters location:** Cleveland OH. **Other U.S. locations:** Nationwide. **Average salary range of placements:** More than $50,000. **Number of placements per year:** 1 - 49.

MANAGEMENT RECRUITERS OF ROYAL PALM BEACH
685 Royal Palm Beach Boulevard, Suite 105, Royal Palm Beach FL 33411. 561/793-8400. **Fax:** 561/793-8471. **Contact:** Branch Manager. **World Wide Web address:** http://www.mricareercenter.com/telecomjob. **Description:** An executive search firm. **Specializes in the areas of:** Wireless Communications. **Corporate headquarters location:** Cleveland OH. **Other U.S. locations:** Nationwide.

MANAGEMENT RECRUITERS OF ST. PETERSBURG
9500 Koger Boulevard, Suite 203, St. Petersburg FL 33702. 727/577-2116. **Contact:** Manager. **Description:** An executive search firm. **Specializes in the areas of:** Engineering; Finance; Food; General Management; Health/Medical; Industrial; Insurance; Legal; Manufacturing; Operations Management; Sales. **Corporate headquarters location:** Cleveland OH. **Other U.S. locations:** Nationwide.

MANAGEMENT RECRUITERS OF TALLAHASSEE
1406 Hays Street, Suite 6, Tallahassee FL 32308. 850/656-8444. **Contact:** Kitte Carter, Manager. **World Wide Web address:** http://www. managementrecruiters.com. **Description:** An executive search firm. **Specializes in the areas of:** Accounting; Administration; Advertising; Architecture/Construction; Banking; Chemicals; Communications; Computer Hardware/Software; Construction; Design; Electrical; Engineering; Finance; Food; General Management; Health/Medical; Industrial; Insurance; Legal; Manufacturing; Operations Management; Personnel/ Labor Relations; Pharmaceuticals; Procurement; Publishing; Retail; Sales; Technical; Textiles; Transportation. **Corporate headquarters location:** Cleveland OH. **Other U.S. locations:** Nationwide.

MANCHESTER INC.
One Independence Drive, Suite 206, Jacksonville FL 32202. **Toll-free phone:** 800/220-1234. **Fax:** 610/617-9966. **Contact:** Manager. **Description:** An executive search firm. **Specializes in the areas of:** Advertising;

Apparel; Banking; Chemicals; Construction; Consumer Products; Electronics; Entertainment; Finance; Food; Government; Graphic Arts; Health/Medical; Heavy Equipment; Insurance; Metals; Packaging; Pharmaceuticals; Property Management; Real Estate; Retail; Telecommunications; Textiles; Transportation.

MANKUTA GALLAGHER & ASSOCIATES INC.
8333 West McNab Road, Suite 231, Fort Lauderdale FL 33321. 954/720-9645. **Toll-free phone:** 800/797-4276. **Fax:** 954/720-5813. **Contact:** Manager. **Description:** An executive search firm. **Specializes in the areas of:** Administration; Biology; Computer Science/Software; Engineering; Manufacturing. **Positions commonly filled include:** Biochemist; Biological Scientist; Biomedical Engineer; Chemical Engineer; Chemist; Civil Engineer; Computer Programmer; Design Engineer; Electrical/ Electronics Engineer; Industrial Engineer; Internet Services Manager; Management Analyst/Consultant; Mechanical Engineer; MIS Specialist; Occupational Therapist; Physical Therapist; Physician; Quality Control Supervisor; Registered Nurse; Science Technologist; Software Engineer; Speech-Language Pathologist; Systems Analyst. **Average salary range of placements:** More than $50,000. **Number of placements per year:** 50 - 99.

THE MARATHON GROUP, INC.
2320 South Third Street, Suite 8, Jacksonville Beach FL 32250. 904/270-2121. **Fax:** 904/270-2120. **Contact:** Manager. **E-mail address:** jobs@pslabels.com. **World Wide Web address:** http://www.pslabels.com. **Description:** An executive search firm. **Specializes in the areas of:** Packaging; Sales. **Corporate headquarters location:** This Location. **Other U.S. locations:** Atlanta GA. **Average salary range of placements:** More than $50,000. **Number of placements per year:** 1 - 49.

McMILLAN ASSOCIATES, INC.
4969 Alamanda Drive, Melbourne FL 32940. 407/254-4423. **Fax:** 407/254-4820. **Contact:** Manager. **World Wide Web address:** http://www.mcmillanassoc.com. **Description:** An executive search firm. Founded in 1968. **Specializes in the areas of:** Logistics; Materials; Purchasing.

MEADS & ASSOCIATES
6700 South Florida Avenue, Suite 4, Lakeland FL 33813. 941/644-0411. **Contact:** Manager. **Description:** An executive search firm. **Specializes in the areas of:** Advertising.

NPF ASSOCIATES LTD., INC.
1999 University Drive, Suite 405, Coral Springs FL 33071. 954/753-8560. **Contact:** Manager. **Description:** An executive search firm. **Specializes in the areas of:** Human Resources; Personnel/Labor Relations. **Number of placements per year:** 1 - 49.

NATIONAL MEDICAL RECRUITING & CONSULTING INC.
3655 Boca Ciega Drive, Suite 111, Naples FL 34112. 941/417-1848. **Toll-free phone:** 800/755-6954. **Fax:** 941/417-2994. **Contact:** Jackie Griffin, President/ National Medical Recruiter. **E-mail address:** nmrcinc@ aol.com. **Description:** An executive search firm operating on a contingency basis. Client company pays fee. **Specializes in the areas of:** Health/Medical. **Positions commonly filled include:** Administrative Manager; Certified Nurses Aide; Certified Occupational Therapy Assistant; Dietician/Nutritionist; EEG Technologist; EKG Technician; Emergency Medical Tech.; General Manager; Home Health Aide; Human Resources Manager; Licensed Practical Nurse; Management Analyst/Consultant; Medical Assistant; Medical Records Tech.; Nuclear Medicine Technologist; Occupational Therapist; Pharmacist; Physical Therapist; Physical Therapy Assistant; Physician; Registered Nurse; Respiratory Therapist; Speech-Language Pathologist. **Average salary range of placements:** More than $100,000. **Number of placements per year:** 100 - 199.

NATIONWIDE RECRUITERS
5327 Commercial Way, Suite C-111, Spring Hill FL 34606. 352/597-5950. **Contact:** Manager. **Description:** An executive search firm. **Specializes in the areas of:** Paper.

NORRELL TECHNICAL SERVICES
1801 Sarno Road, Suite One, Melbourne FL 32951. 407/259-8619. **Toll-free phone:** 800/689-8367. **Fax:** 407/255-2982. **Contact:** Renee O'Hara, Manager. **World Wide Web address:** http://www.norrelltech.com. **Description:** An executive search firm. **Specializes in the areas of:** Computer Science/Software; Engineering; Industrial; Manufacturing; Personnel/Labor Relations; Technical. **Positions commonly filled include:** Aerospace Engineer; Buyer; Chemical Engineer; Chemist; Civil Engineer; Computer Programmer; Cost Estimator; Design Engineer; Designer; Draftsperson; Electrical/Electronics Engineer; Food Scientist/ Technologist; Human Resources Manager; Industrial Engineer; Industrial Production Manager; Internet Services Manager; Mechanical Engineer; MIS Specialist; Multimedia Designer; Software Engineer; Systems Analyst; Technical Writer/Editor. **Benefits available to temporary workers:** 401(k); Dental Insurance; Life Insurance; Medical Insurance. **International locations:** Worldwide. **Average salary range of placements:** More than $50,000.

OMNIPARTNERS
861 SW 78th Avenue, Suite 200, Fort Lauderdale FL 33324. 954/748-9800. **Fax:** 954/747-1156. **Contact:** Marvin Cohen, President. **Description:** An executive search firm. **Specializes in the areas of:** Accounting; Engineering; Finance; General Management; Hotel/ Restaurant; Insurance; Retail; Sales; Technical; Transportation. **Positions commonly filled include:** Accountant; Applications Engineer; Auditor; Buyer; CFO; Civil Engineer; Computer Programmer; Electrical/ Electronics Engineer; General Manager; Project Manager; Quality Control Supervisor; Sales Manager; Software Engineer; Telecommunications Manager; Typist/Word Processor. **Average salary range of placements:** More than $50,000. **Number of placements per year:** 50 - 99.

OMNISEARCH INC.
3442 East Lake Road, Suite 308, Palm Harbor FL 34685. 727/789-4442. **Fax:** 727/787-7743. **Contact:** Manager. **E-mail address:** osiflorida@aol.com. **Description:** An executive search firm. **Specializes in the areas of:** Consumer Package Goods; Food; Marketing; Medical Sales and Marketing; Pharmaceuticals; Sales. **Average salary range of placements:** More than $50,000. **Number of placements per year:** 50 - 99.

PMR SEARCH CONSULTANTS
428-B Osceola Avenue, Jacksonville Beach FL 32250. 904/270-0505. **Contact:** Manager. **Description:** An executive search firm. **Specializes in the areas of:** Legal.

PEARCE & ASSOCIATES
9116 Cypress Green Drive, Suite 202, Jacksonville FL 32256. 904/739-1736. **Fax:** 904/739-1746. **Contact:** Frank Pearce, Owner. **E-mail address:** fpearce@ leading.net. **Description:** An executive search firm. **Specializes in the areas of:** Accounting/Auditing; Real Estate; Sales. **Positions commonly filled include:** Account Rep.; Branch Manager; Controller; Sales Executive; Sales Manager; Sales Rep.. **Average salary range of placements:** $30,000 - $50,000.

PERFECT SEARCH INC.
1801 Clint Moore Road, Suite 109, Boca Raton FL 33487. 561/995-7533. **Fax:** 561/995-7477. **Contact:** Ms. Robin Callicott, President. **Description:** An executive search firm. **Specializes in the areas of:** Health/Medical; Sales. **Positions commonly filled include:** Manufacturer's/Wholesaler's Sales Rep.; Medical Records Technician. **Number of placements per year:** 50 - 99.

PHYSICIAN EXECUTIVE MANAGEMENT CENTER
3403 West Fletcher Avenue, Tampa FL 33618. 813/963-1800. **Fax:** 813/264-2207. **Contact:** David R. Kirschman, President. **Description:** An executive search firm operating on a retainer basis. **Specializes in the areas of:** Health/Medical; Physician Executive. **Average salary range of placements:** More than $50,000. **Number of placements per year:** 1 - 49.

PRIORITY SEARCH
2600 Maitland Center Parkway, Suite 295, Maitland FL 32751. 407/660-0089. **Fax:** 407/660-2066. **Contact:** Terrie Goodman, Administrative Manager. **E-mail address:** frontdesk@prioritysearch.com. **World Wide Web address:** http://www.prioritysearch.com. **Description:** An executive search firm operating on both retainer and contingency bases. **Specializes in the areas of:** Accounting/Auditing; Engineering; Finance; Industrial; Insurance; Marketing; Publishing; Sales; Technical. **Positions commonly filled include:** Account Manager; Account Representative; Accountant/Auditor; Bank Officer/Manager; Chemical Engineer; Chemist; Chief Financial Officer; Controller; Design Engineer; Editor; Electrical/Electronics Engineer; Finance Director; Financial Analyst; Fund Manager; Human Resources Manager; Industrial Engineer; Industrial Production Manager; Managing Editor; Marketing Manager; Mechanical Engineer; Operations Manager; Production Manager; Project Manager; Purchasing Agent/Manager; Quality Control Supervisor; Sales Engineer; Sales Executive; Sales Representative; Telecommunications Manager. **Average salary range of placements:** More than $50,000. **Number of placements per year:** 100 - 199.

PRO-TEAM SERVICES, INC.
1211 North Westshore Boulevard, Suite 102, Tampa FL 33607-4601. 813/281-0118. **Fax:** 813/281-2310. **Contact:** Neal Reeves, President. **E-mail address:** jobs@pro-team.com. **World Wide Web address:** http://www.pro-team.com. **Description:** An executive search firm operating on a contingency basis. The firm also provides some temporary and contract placements. Client company pays fee. **NOTE:** This firm does not accept unsolicited resumes. Please respond only to advertised openings. **Specializes in the areas of:** Architecture/Construction; Biology; Computer Science/Software; Engineering; General Management; Industrial; Internet Development; MIS/EDP; Scientific; Technical. **Positions commonly filled include:** Administrative Manager; Applications Engineer; Architect; AS400 Programmer Analyst; Assistant Manager; Biochemist; Biological Scientist; Chemical Engineer; Chemist; Civil Engineer; Computer Animator; Computer Engineer; Computer Operator; Computer Programmer; Computer Scientist; Computer Support Technician; Computer Technician; Content Developer; Database Administrator; Database Manager; Design Engineer; Draftsperson; Electrical/Electronics Engineer; Electrician; Environmental Engineer; General Manager; Geologist/Geophysicist; Industrial Engineer; Industrial Production Manager; Internet Services Manager; Manufacturing Engineer; Mechanical Engineer; Metallurgical Engineer; MIS Specialist; Multimedia Designer; Network/Systems Administrator; Operations Manager; Production Manager; Project Manager; Quality Assurance Engineer; Quality Control Supervisor; Sales Engineer; Sales Manager; Sales Representative; Software Engineer; SQL Programmer; Systems Analyst; Systems Manager; Webmaster. **Benefits available to temporary workers:** Paid Holidays; Paid Vacation. **Average salary range of placements:** $30,000 - $49,999. **Number of placements per year:** 100 - 199.

PULP & PAPER INTERNATIONAL
P.O. Box 540929, Orlando FL 32854. 407/444-9960. **Fax:** 407/444-9964. **Contact:** Philip Riesling, President. **E-mail address:** pulppaper@aol.com. **Description:** An executive search firm. **Specializes in the areas of:** Accounting/Auditing; Engineering; Manufacturing; Paper; Technical. **Positions commonly filled include:** Accountant/Auditor; Biochemist; Biological Scientist; Buyer; Chemical Engineer; Computer Programmer; Design Engineer; Electrician; Forester/Conservation Scientist; General Manager; Human Resources Manager; Mechanical Engineer; Operations/Production Manager; Stationary Engineer; Systems Analyst. **Average salary range of placements:** More than $50,000. **Number of placements per year:** 1 - 49.

RETAIL EXECUTIVE SEARCH, INC. (RES)
4620 North State Road 7, Suite 212, Fort Lauderdale FL 33319. 954/731-2300. **Fax:** 954/733-0642. **Contact:** Manuel Kaye, President. **Description:** An executive search firm. **Specializes in the areas of:** Fashion; Retail. **Positions commonly filled include:** Branch Manager; Budget Analyst; Buyer; General Manager; Human Resources Manager; MIS Specialist; Retail Executive; Retail Manager; Retail Merchandiser. **Number of placements per year:** 200 - 499.

JACK RICHMAN & ASSOCIATES
P.O. Box 25412, Fort Lauderdale FL 33320. 954/389-9563. **Fax:** 954/389-9572. **Contact:** Jack Richman, President. **E-mail address:** jrafl@bellsouth.net. **Description:** An executive search firm operating on a contingency basis. **Specializes in the areas of:** Computer Science/Software; Scientific; Technical. **Positions commonly filled include:** Computer Programmer; Consultant; MIS Specialist; Software Engineer; Systems Analyst; Systems Manager; Technical Writer/Editor; Webmaster. **Average salary range of placements:** More than $50,000. **Number of placements per year:** 1 - 49.

ROBINSON & ASSOCIATES
4000 St. John's Avenue, Suite 35, Jacksonville FL 32205. 904/388-5111. **Contact:** Manager. **Description:** An executive search firm. **Specializes in the areas of:** Administration; Finance; Health/Medical; Information Systems.

GENE ROGERS ASSOCIATES, INC.
13211 SW 32nd Court, Davie FL 33330-4604. 954/476-0221. **Toll-free phone:** 888/333-4589. **Fax:** 954/476-8437. **Contact:** Gene Rogers, President. **E-mail address:** grogers190@aol.com. **Description:** An executive search firm. **Specializes in the areas of:** Banking; Investment. **Positions commonly filled include:** Bank Officer/Manager; Trust Officer. **Average salary range of placements:** More than $50,000. **Number of placements per year:** 1 - 49.

ROMAC INTERNATIONAL
500 West Cypress Creek Road, Suite 100, Fort Lauderdale FL 33309. 954/928-0800. **Fax:** 954/771-7649. **Contact:** Manager. **World Wide Web address:** http://www.romac.com. **Description:** An executive search firm. **Specializes in the areas of:** Accounting/Auditing; Computer Hardware/Software; Government. **Positions commonly filled include:** Accountant/Auditor; Computer Programmer; EDP Specialist; MIS Specialist; Systems Analyst. **Corporate headquarters location:** Tampa FL. **Other U.S. locations:** Nationwide.

ROMAC INTERNATIONAL
120 West Hyde Park Place, Suite 200, Tampa FL 33606. 813/258-8855. **Toll-free phone:** 800/395-5575. **Contact:** Manager. **World Wide Web address:** http://www. romac.com. **Description:** An executive search firm. **Specializes in the areas of:** Accounting/Auditing; Banking; Finance. **Corporate headquarters location:** This Location. **Other U.S. locations:** Nationwide.

ROMAC INTERNATIONAL
111 North Orange Avenue, Suite 1150, Orlando FL 32801. 407/843-0765. **Contact:** Manager. **World Wide Web address:** http://www.romac.com. **Description:** An executive search firm. **Specializes in the areas of:** Accounting/Auditing; Finance. **Corporate headquarters location:** Tampa FL. **Other U.S. locations:** Nationwide.

ROMAC INTERNATIONAL
15600 NW 67th Avenue, Suite 201, Miami Lakes FL 33014. 305/556-8000. **Fax:** 305/819-9544. **Contact:** Manager. **World Wide Web address:** http://www. romac.com. **Description:** An executive search firm. **Specializes in the areas of:** Accounting/Auditing; Computer Hardware/Software; Finance. **Corporate headquarters location:** Tampa FL. **Other U.S. locations:** Nationwide.

ROPES ASSOCIATES, INC.
333 North New River Drive, Third Floor, Fort Lauderdale FL 33301. 954/525-6600. **Fax:** 954/779-7279. **Contact:** Manager. **World Wide Web address:** http://www.ropesassociates.com. **Description:** An executive search firm. Founded in 1975. **Specializes in the areas of:** Finance; Real Estate.

ROTH YOUNG OF TAMPA BAY
5121 Ehrlich Road, Suite 104A, Tampa FL 33624. 813/269-9889. **Fax:** 813/269-9919. **Contact:** Barry Cushing, President. **Description:** An executive search firm. **Specializes in the areas of:** Engineering; Food; Health/Medical; Sales. **Positions commonly filled include:** Buyer; General Manager; Hotel Manager; Medical Doctor. **Number of placements per year:** 50 - 99.

THE RYAN CHARLES GROUP, INC.
2151 West Hillsboro Boulevard, Suite 203, Deerfield FL 33442. 954/421-9112. **Fax:** 954/428-4940. **Contact:** Norman St. Jean, President. **E-mail address:** ryanc@ gate.net. **World Wide Web address:** http://www. ryancharlesgroup.com. **Description:** An executive search firm. **Specializes in the areas of:** Accounting/Auditing; Administration; Advertising; Engineering; Finance; General Management; Industrial; Insurance; Manufacturing; Personnel/Labor Relations; Sales. **Positions commonly filled include:** Accountant/Auditor; Chemical Engineer; Credit Manager; Design Engineer; Electrical/Electronics Engineer; General Manager; Human Resources Manager; Industrial Engineer; Industrial Production Manager; Materials Engineer; Mechanical Engineer; MIS Manager; Production Manager; Purchasing Agent/Manager; Structural Engineer; Systems Analyst; Telecommunications Manager; Transportation/Traffic Specialist. **Corporate headquarters location:** This Location. **Other U.S. locations:** Oak Brook IL. **Average salary range of placements:** More than $50,000. **Number of placements per year:** 50 - 99.

SALES ADVANTAGE
BECKER PROFESSIONAL SERVICES
6301 NW Fifth Way, Suite 2100, Fort Lauderdale FL 33309. 954/351-9461. **Fax:** 954/776-5855. **Contact:** Manager. **E-mail address:** mail@salesadvantage.com. **World Wide Web address:** http://www. salesadvantage.com/sales.html. **Description:** An executive search firm. Becker Professional Services (also at this location) offers temporary and permanent placements in accounting, financial services, human resources, and information systems. **Specializes in the areas of:** Sales.

SALES CONSULTANTS OF CORAL SPRINGS
9900 West Sample Road, Suite 407, Coral Springs FL 33065. **Contact:** Manager. **Description:** An executive search firm operating on a contingency basis. **Specializes in the areas of:** Retail; Sales. **Positions commonly filled include:** Chemical Engineer; Manufacturer's/Wholesaler's Sales Rep. **Corporate headquarters location:** Cleveland OH. **Other U.S. locations:** Nationwide. **Average salary range of placements:** More than $50,000. **Number of placements per year:** 1 - 49.

SALES CONSULTANTS OF FORT LAUDERDALE
100 West Cypress Creek Road, Suite 880, Fort Lauderdale FL 33309. 954/772-5100. **Fax:** 954/772-0777. **Contact:** Jeff Taylor, Manager/General Partner. **E-mail address:** reshunter@aol.com. **World Wide Web**

address: http://www.mri-sc-usa.com. **Description:** An executive search firm. **Specializes in the areas of:** Accounting; Administration; Advertising; Architecture/Construction; Banking; Chemicals; Communications; Computer Hardware/Software; Construction; Design; Electrical; Engineering; Finance; Food; General Management; Health/Medical; Industrial; Insurance; Legal; Manufacturing; Operations Management; Personnel/Labor Relations; Procurement; Publishing; Retail; Sales; Technical; Textiles; Transportation. **Corporate headquarters location:** Cleveland OH. **Other U.S. locations:** Nationwide. **Average salary range of placements:** $40,000+. **Number of placements per year:** 100 - 199.

SALES CONSULTANTS OF JACKSONVILLE
9471 Baymeadows Road, Suite 204, Jacksonville FL 32256. 904/737-5770. **Fax:** 904/737-7927. **Contact:** Scott Sheridan, General Manager. **E-mail address:** scjacks@bellsouth.net. **World Wide Web address:** http://www.scjacks.com. **Description:** An executive search firm operating on both retainer and contingency bases. Client company pays fee. **Specializes in the areas of:** Engineering; Industrial. **Positions commonly filled include:** Account Manager; Applications Engineer; Buyer; Chemical Engineer; Civil Engineer; Design Engineer; Electrical/Electronics Engineer; Industrial Engineer; Mechanical Engineer; Metallurgical Engineer; Quality Assurance Engineer; Sales Engineer; Sales Manager; Sales Rep. **Corporate headquarters location:** Cleveland OH. **Other U.S. locations:** Nationwide.

SALES CONSULTANTS OF SARASOTA, INC.
1343 Main Street, Suite 600, Sarasota FL 34236. 941/365-5151. **Fax:** 941/365-1869. **Contact:** Janice Cascio, Administrative Assistant. **World Wide Web address:** http://www.scsarasota.com. **Description:** An executive search firm operating on both retainer and contingency bases. **Specializes in the areas of:** Computer Hardware/Software; Engineering; Health/Medical; Industrial; Insurance; Sales. **Positions commonly filled include:** Design Engineer; Industrial Engineer; Industrial Production Manager; Market Research Analyst; Marketing Manager; Mechanical Engineer; Production Manager; Purchasing Agent/Manager; Sales Engineer; Sales Executive; Sales Manager; Sales Rep. **Corporate headquarters location:** Cleveland OH. **Other U.S. locations:** Nationwide. **Average salary range of placements:** More than $50,000. **Number of placements per year:** 50 - 99.

SANFORD ROSE ASSOCIATES
3 West Garden Street, Suite 349, Pensacola FL 32501. 850/438-8178. **Fax:** 850/438-6592. **Contact:** Manager. **World Wide Web address:** http://www. sanfordrose.com. **Description:** An executive search firm. **Specializes in the areas of:** Administration; Auditing; Banking; Finance; Information Technology; Operations Management.

SANFORD ROSE ASSOCIATES
2623 McCormick Drive, Suite 104, Clearwater FL 33759. 727/796-2201. **Fax:** 727/669-2942. **Contact:** Manager. **World Wide Web address:** http://www. sanfordrose.com. **Description:** An executive search firm. **Specializes in the areas of:** General Management; Marketing.

SEA-CHANGE, INC.
333 Southern Boulevard, West Palm Beach FL 33405-2654. 561/833-8315. **Fax:** 561/833-8325. **Contact:** Diane McCabe, President. **Description:** An executive search firm. **Specializes in the areas of:** Health/Medical. **Positions commonly filled include:** Physician. **Average salary range of placements:** More than $50,000.

SEARCH ENTERPRISES SOUTH, INC.
12358 Wiles Road, Coral Springs FL 33076. 954/755-3121. **Fax:** 954/755-1094. **Contact:** Frank Polacek, President. **E-mail address:** sesi@searchenterprises.com. **World Wide Web address:** http://www. searchenterprises.com. **Description:** An executive search

firm. **Specializes in the areas of:** Engineering; Personnel/Labor Relations; Technical. **Positions commonly filled include:** Biomedical Engineer; Chemical Engineer; Electrical/Electronics Engineer; Human Resources Manager; Materials Engineer; Mechanical Engineer; Metallurgical Engineer. **Average salary range of placements:** More than $50,000. **Number of placements per year:** 100 - 199.

SEARCH MASTERS INTERNATIONAL
4598 Hamlets Grove, Sarasota FL 34235. 941/351-7307. **Contact:** Alex Stevenson, Executive Search Consultant/ Founder. **Description:** An executive search firm. **Specializes in the areas of:** Health/Medical; Sales. **Positions commonly filled include:** Production Manager; Sales and Marketing Manager. **Average salary range of placements:** More than $50,000. **Number of placements per year:** 1 - 49.

SEARCH SPECIALISTS
3319 Powerline Road, Lithia FL 33547. 813/689-1991. **Contact:** Manager. **Description:** An executive search firm. **Specializes in the areas of:** Engineering.

DOUG SEARS & ASSOCIATES (DS&A)
320 Corporate Way, Suite 100, Orange County FL 32073. 904/278-9998. **Toll-free phone:** 800/553-5361. **Fax:** 904/278-9995. **Contact:** Recruitment. **Description:** An executive search firm operating on both retainer and contingency bases. The firm also offers career counseling and resume services. **Specializes in the areas of:** Accounting/Auditing; Administration; Banking; Computer Science/Software; Engineering; Finance; General Management; Health/Medical; Industrial; Insurance; Legal; Manufacturing; Personnel/Labor Relations; Sales; Technical. **Positions commonly filled include:** Adjuster; Administrative Manager; Aerospace Engineer; Architect; Attorney; Bank Officer/Manager; Biomedical Engineer; Branch Manager; Chemical Engineer; Civil Engineer; Claim Rep.; Computer Programmer; Customer Service Rep.; Financial Analyst; Human Resources Specialist; Industrial Engineer; Insurance Agent/Broker; Internet Services Manager; Management Analyst/Consultant; Manufacturer's/ Wholesaler's Sales Representative; MIS Specialist; Occupational Therapist; Operations/Production Manager; Physical Therapist; Physician; Property and Real Estate Manager; Public Relations Specialist; Registered Nurse; Respiratory Therapist; Securities Sales Rep.; Services Sales Rep.; Software Engineer; Statistician; Surgical Technician; Systems Analyst; Technical Writer/Editor; Telecommunications Manager. **Corporate headquarters location:** This Location. **Average salary range of placements:** More than $50,000. **Number of placements per year:** 200 - 499.

SEDULOUS, INC.
4532 West Kennedy Boulevard, Suite 298, Tampa FL 33609. 813/254-8474. **Contact:** Manager. **World Wide Web address:** http://www.sedulous.com. **Description:** An executive search firm.

SNYDER EXECUTIVE SEARCH, INC.
8840 Southhampton Drive, Miramar FL 33025. 954/436-2803. **Toll-free phone:** 800/866-7169. **Fax:** 954/436-3465. **Contact:** Alfred Snyder, Vice President. **E-mail address:** snyder@csusa.net. **World Wide Web address:** http://www.asnyder.com. **Description:** An executive search firm operating on a contingency basis. Client company pays fee. **Specializes in the areas of:** Administration; Computer Science/Software; Marketing; Sales. **Positions commonly filled include:** Account Manager; Administrative Assistant; Administrative Manager; Assistant Manager; Computer Programmer; Computer Scientist; Computer Support Tech.; Customer Service Rep.; Database Administrator; Internet Services Manager; Sales Engineer; Sales Executive; Sales Manager; Sales Rep.; Secretary; Software Engineer; Systems Analyst; Telecommunications Manager. **Corporate headquarters location:** This Location. **Average salary range of placements:** $50,000 - $100,000. **Number of placements per year:** 50 - 99.

SOUTHERN RESEARCH SERVICES
5121 Ehrlich Road, Suite 107A, Tampa FL 33624. 813/269-9595. **Fax:** 813/264-6847. **Contact:** Manager. **Description:** An executive search firm. **Specializes in the areas of:** Technical.

SPECIALIZED SEARCH ASSOCIATES
15200 Jog Road, Suite 1156, Delray Beach FL 33446. 561/499-3711. **Contact:** Leonard Morris, President. **Description:** An executive search firm operating on a contingency basis. **Specializes in the areas of:** Construction; Engineering; Sales. **Positions commonly filled include:** Architect; Chemical Engineer; Civil Engineer; Construction and Building Inspector; Construction Contractor; Environmental Engineer; Marketing Manager; Mechanical Engineer; Operations Manager; Sales Engineer; Sales Executive; Sales Manager; Structural Engineer. **Average salary range of placements:** More than $50,000. **Number of placements per year:** 1 - 49.

STERLING CAREER CONSULTANTS, INC.
2240 Palm Beach Lakes Boulevard, Suite 330, West Palm Beach FL 33409. 561/689-8530. **Fax:** 561/689-4557. **Contact:** Yvonne Ellis, President. **Description:** An executive search firm operating on both retainer and contingency bases. The firm also offers temporary and temp-to-perm placements. **Specializes in the areas of:** Legal. **Positions commonly filled include:** Administrative Assistant; Attorney; Legal Assistant; Legal Secretary; Paralegal; Secretary; Typist/Word Processor. **Benefits available to temporary workers:** Flexible Schedule. **Average salary range of placements:** $30,000 - $50,000. **Number of placements per year:** 100 - 199.

STERLING-SHARPE, INC.
5420 Bay Center Drive, Suite 202, Tampa FL 33609. 813/289-2890. **Fax:** 813/288-9031. **Contact:** Recruiter. **World Wide Web address:** http://www.sterling-sharpe.com/project.htm. **Description:** A generalized executive search firm that also offers some outplacement services and temporary placements.

THE STEWART SEARCH GROUP, INC.
201 ATP Tour Boulevard, P.O. Box 2588, Ponte Vedra Beach FL 32004. 904/285-6622. **Fax:** 904/285-0076. **Contact:** James Stewart, President. **World Wide Web address:** http://www.stewartgroup.net. **Description:** An executive search firm operating on both retainer and contingency bases. **Specializes in the areas of:** Accounting; Administration; Advertising; Engineering; Finance; Food; General Management; Health/Medical; Hotel/Restaurant; Marketing; Pharmaceuticals; Sales; Telecommunications. **Positions commonly filled include:** CFO; Computer Programmer; Controller; Credit Manager; Database Manager; Design Engineer; Electrical/Electronics Engineer; Finance Director; Financial Analyst; General Manager; Human Resources Manager; Industrial Engineer; Insurance Agent/Broker; Licensed Practical Nurse; Manufacturing Engineer; Market Research Analyst; Mechanical Engineer; MIS Specialist; Pharmacist; Physician; Quality Control Supervisor; Registered Nurse; Respiratory Therapist; Sales Engineer; Sales Exec.; Sales Manager; Sales Rep.; Software Engineer; Systems Analyst; Systems Manager; Technical Writer/Editor; Telecommunications Manager. **Average salary range of placements:** More than $50,000. **Number of placements per year:** 100 - 199.

SUMMIT EXECUTIVE SEARCH CONSULTANTS
420 Lincoln Road, Suite 265, Miami Beach FL 33139. 305/672-5008. **Fax:** 305/672-5007. **Contact:** Manager. **E-mail address:** summitsearch@compuserve.com. **Description:** An executive search firm operating on a retainer basis. **Specializes in the areas of:** Engineering; Industrial; Manufacturing; Safety. **Positions commonly filled include:** Buyer; Civil Engineer; Design Engineer; Electrical/Electronics Engineer; Environmental Engineer; Human Resources Manager; Industrial Engineer; Industrial Production Manager; Mechanical Engineer; Metallurgical Engineer; Purchasing Agent/Manager;

Quality Control Supervisor; Structural Engineer. **Average salary range of placements:** More than $50,000. **Number of placements per year:** 1 - 49.

SUMMIT HEALTH CARE, INC.
7301 NW Fourth Street, Suite 107A, Plantation FL 33317. 954/583-9288. **Contact:** Manager. **Description:** An executive search firm. **Specializes in the areas of:** Health/Medical.

SUMMIT HEALTH CARE, INC.
6950 Phillips Highway, Suite 19, Jacksonville FL 32216. 904/296-6003. **Contact:** Manager. **Description:** An executive search firm. **Specializes in the areas of:** Dental; Health/Medical.

SUN PERSONNEL WEST
5444 Bay Center Drive, Suite 215, Tampa FL 33609-3400. 813/286-2009. **Contact:** Recruiter. **Description:** An executive search firm. **Specializes in the areas of:** Finance; General Management; Health/Medical; Industrial; Manufacturing; Sales. **Average salary range of placements:** $30,000 - $50,000. **Number of placements per year:** 200 - 499.

TMP WORLDWIDE
3903 Northdale Boulevard, Suite 200E, Tampa FL 33624. 813/961-7494. **Contact:** Manager. **Description:** A generalist executive search firm.

TOWER CONSULTANTS, LTD.
943 Central Parkway, Central Parkway Professional Plaza, Stuart FL 34994. 561/288-3590. **Fax:** 561/288-3540. **Contact:** Donna Friedman, President. **E-mail address:** friedman@towerconsultants.com. **Description:** An executive search firm operating on a retainer basis. **Specializes in the areas of:** Personnel/Labor Relations. **Positions commonly filled include:** Human Resources Manager. **Average salary range of placements:** More than $50,000. **Number of placements per year:** 50 - 99.

UNIQUEST INTERNATIONAL, INC.
4350 West Cypress Street, Suite 450, Tampa FL 33607. 813/387-1000. **Contact:** Tony Valone, President. **Description:** An executive search firm. **Specializes in the areas of:** Accounting; Administration; Finance; Health/Medical; Insurance; Legal; Telecommunications. **Average salary range of placements:** More than $50,000. **Number of placements per year:** 100 - 199.

UNIVERSAL SEARCH
1460 Brickell Avenue, Suite 204, Miami FL 33131. 305/374-1922. **Contact:** Manager. **Description:** An executive search firm.

WEATHERBY HEALTH CARE
5352 NW 21st Terrace, Fort Lauderdale FL 33309. 954/771-2501. **Contact:** Manager. **Description:** Weatherby Health Care is an executive search firm offering placements for physicians only. **Specializes in the areas of:** Health/Medical.

WEBER & COMPANY
MANAGEMENT RECRUITERS INTERNATIONAL
2121 Ponce de Leon Boulevard, Suite 940, Coral Gables FL 33134. 305/444-1200. **Toll-free phone:** 800/536-3840. **Fax:** 305/444-2266. **Contact:** Jim Weber, Owner. **E-mail address:** email@weberstaff.com. **World Wide Web address:** http://www.weberstaff.com. **Description:** An executive search firm operating on a retainer basis. Client company pays fee. **Specializes in the areas of:** Engineering; Health/Medical. **Positions commonly filled** include: Biomedical Engineer; General Manager; Industrial Engineer; Manufacturing Engineer; Mechanical Engineer; Operations Manager; Production Manager; Project Manager; Quality Assurance Engineer; Quality Control Supervisor; Sales Exec.; Sales Manager; Sales Rep.; Transportation Specialist; V.P.t of Project Development. **Corporate headquarters location:** Cleveland OH. **Other U.S. locations:** Nationwide. **Average salary range of placements:** $50,000 - $100,000. **Number of placements per year:** 1 - 49.

TERRY M. WEISS & ASSOCIATES
P.O. Box 915656, Longwood FL 32791-5656. 407/774-1212. **Fax:** 407/774-0084. **Contact:** Mr. Terry M. Weiss, Esq., President. **E-mail address:** lawhunter@aol.com. **Description:** An executive search firm. **Specializes in the areas of:** Accounting/Auditing; Legal; Tax. **Positions commonly filled include:** Accountant; Attorney. **Number of placements per year:** 1 - 49.

WILSON & ASSOCIATES INTERNATIONAL
P.O. Box 4220, Clearwater FL 33758. 727/796-4955. **Fax:** 727/796-4014. **Contact:** Wayne Wilson, President. **E-mail address:** ww@wilsonandassociates.com. **World Wide Web address:** http://www.wilsonandassociates. com. **Description:** An executive search firm. Founded in 1990. **Specializes in the areas of:** Apparel; Home Furnishings; Manufacturing; Sales; Textiles. **Corporate headquarters location:** This Location.

THE WITT GROUP
P.O. Box 521281, Longwood FL 32752. 407/324-4137. **Fax:** 407/322-5172. **Contact:** Jerry Witt, President. **Description:** The Witt Group is an executive search firm operating on both retainer and contingency bases. Client company pays fee. **Specializes in the areas of:** Chemicals; Scientific; Technical. **Positions commonly filled** include: Chemical Engineer; Chemist; Construction Contractor; Environmental Engineer; General Manager; Human Resources Manager; Marketing Manager; Marketing Specialist; Mechanical Engineer; Operations Manager; Product Manager; Project Manager; Quality Assurance Engineer; Quality Control Supervisor; Sales Engineer; Sales Representative; Vice President of Operations. **Average salary range of placements:** $50,000 - $100,000. **Number of placements per year:** 1 - 49.

ZACKRISON ASSOCIATES INC.
P.O. Box 1808, Dunnellon FL 34430. 352/489-2215. **Contact:** Manager. **Description:** Zackrison Associates is an executive search firm. **Specializes in the areas of:** Pharmaceuticals.

PERMANENT EMPLOYMENT AGENCIES

A CHOICE NANNY
1413 South Howard Avenue, Suite 201, Tampa FL 33606. 813/254-8687. **Contact:** Eleanor Nesbit, Owner/Manager. **Description:** A permanent employment agency that also provides some temporary placements. **Specializes in the areas of:** Nannies. **Number of placements per year:** 100 - 199.

AAA EMPLOYMENT
4035 South Florida Avenue, Suite 11, Lakeland FL 33813. 863/701-8675. **Fax:** 863/701-8926. **Contact:** Nikki Harrison, Franchise Owner. **Description:** A permanent employment agency. Founded in 1957. **Specializes in the areas of:** Finance; Health/Medical; Industrial; Insurance; Legal; Manufacturing; Personnel/ Labor Relations; Publishing; Retail; Sales; Secretarial; Technical; Transportation. **Positions commonly filled** include: Accountant/Auditor; Administrative Manager; Advertising Clerk; Bank Officer/Manager; Blue-Collar Worker Supervisor; Branch Manager; Brokerage Clerk; Budget Analyst; Buyer; Chemist; Civil Engineer; Claim Rep.; Clerical Supervisor; Clinical Lab Technician; Computer Programmer; Counselor; Credit Manager; Customer Service Rep.; Dental Assistant/Dental Hygienist; Draftsperson; General Manager; Geologist/ Geophysicist; Hotel Manager; Industrial Production Manager; Insurance Agent/Broker; Licensed Practical Nurse; Management Trainee; Manufacturer's/

Wholesaler's Sales Rep.; Mechanical Engineer; Operations/Production Manager; Paralegal; Property and Real Estate Manager; Purchasing Agent/Manager; Quality Control Supervisor; Registered Nurse; Restaurant/Food Service Manager; Services Sales Rep.; Software Engineer; Systems Analyst; Transportation/Traffic Specialist; Travel Agent; Typist/Word Processor; Underwriter/Assistant Underwriter; Wholesale and Retail Buyer. **Corporate headquarters location:** St. Petersburg FL. **Other U.S. locations:** GA; IN; MI; NC; SC; TN; VA; WV. **Average salary range of placements:** $20,000 - $29,999. **Number of placements per year:** 100 - 199.

AAA EMPLOYMENT
12995 South Cleveland Avenue, Suite 235A, Fort Myers FL 33907. 941/939-7200. **Contact:** V. Jane Kappler, Managing Partner. **Description:** A permanent employment agency. Founded in 1957. **Specializes in the areas of:** Accounting/Auditing; Computer Science/ Software; Finance; General Management; Health/ Medical; Insurance; Legal; Retail; Sales; Secretarial. **Positions commonly filled include:** Accountant/Auditor; Administrative Manager; Advertising Clerk; Blue-Collar Worker Supervisor; Branch Manager; Broadcast Technician; Brokerage Clerk; Clerical Supervisor; Computer Programmer; Construction Contractor; Cost Estimator; Credit Manager; Customer Service Rep.; Dental Assistant/Dental Hygienist; Draftsperson; Electrical/Electronics Engineer; Financial Analyst; General Manager; Health Services Manager; Hotel Manager; Human Resources Specialist; Human Service Worker; Industrial Agent/Broker; Internet Services Manager; Landscape Architect; Licensed Practical Nurse; Management Trainee; Manufacturer's/ Wholesaler's Sales Rep.; Medical Records Technician; MIS Specialist; Operations/Production Manager; Paralegal; Preschool Worker; Property and Real Estate Manager; Public Relations Specialist; Radio/TV Announcer/Broadcaster; Registered Nurse; Restaurant/ Food Service Manager; Securities Sales Rep.; Services Sales Representative; Surveyor; Systems Analyst; Telecommunications Manager; Travel Agent; Video Production Coordinator. **Corporate headquarters location:** St. Petersburg FL. **Other U.S. locations:** GA; IN; MI; NC; SC; TN; VA; WV. **Average salary range of placements:** $20,000 - $29,999.

AAA EMPLOYMENT
1311 North Westshore Boulevard, Suite 114, Tampa FL 33607. **Contact:** Manager. **Description:** A permanent employment agency. Founded in 1957. **Specializes in the areas of:** Accounting/Auditing; Administration; Art/Design; Banking; Biology; Engineering; Food; General Management; Health/Medical; Industrial; Insurance; Legal; Manufacturing; Nonprofit; Personnel/ Labor Relations; Publishing; Retail; Sales; Secretarial; Technical. **Positions commonly filled include:** Accountant/Auditor; Adjuster; Administrative Manager; Advertising Clerk; Aircraft Mechanic/Engine Specialist; Automotive Mechanic; Bank Officer/Manager; Biological Scientist; Biomedical Engineer; Blue-Collar Worker Supervisor; Branch Manager; Buyer; Chemist; Claim Rep.; Clerical Supervisor; Clinical Lab Technician; Computer Programmer; Construction Contractor; Cost Estimator; Credit Manager; Customer Service Rep.; Dental Assistant/Dental Hygienist; Design Engineer; Dietician/Nutritionist; Draftsperson; EEG Technologist; EKG Technician; Electrician; Environmental Engineer; Financial Analyst; General Manager; Geologist/Geophysicist; Health Services Manager; Hotel Manager; Human Resources Specialist; Human Service Worker; Industrial Production Manager; Insurance Agent/Broker; Landscape Architect; Licensed Practical Nurse; Management Analyst/Consultant; Management Trainee; Manufacturer's/Wholesaler's Sales Rep.; Mechanical Engineer; Medical Records Technician; Occupational Therapist; Operations/ Production Manager; Paralegal; Property and Real Estate Manager; Public Relations Specialist; Purchasing Agent/ Manager; Quality Control Supervisor; Real Estate Agent; Registered Nurse; Respiratory Therapist; Restaurant/

Food Service Manager; Science Technologist; Securities Sales Rep.; Services Sales Rep.; Social Worker; Surveyor; Systems Analyst; Technical Writer/Editor; Telecommunications Manager; Transportation/Traffic Specialist; Travel Agent; Typist/Word Processor; Underwriter/Assistant Underwriter. **Corporate headquarters location:** St. Petersburg FL. **Other U.S. locations:** GA; IN; MI; NC; SC; TN; VA; WV. **Average salary range of placements:** Less than $20,000. **Number of placements per year:** 100 - 199.

ATS HEALTH SERVICES
5161 Beach Boulevard, Suite 4, Jacksonville FL 32207. 904/398-9098. **Contact:** Manager. **Description:** A permanent employment agency. **Specializes in the areas of:** Health/Medical. **Positions commonly filled include:** Certified Nurses Aide; Licensed Practical Nurse.

ACCOUNTANTS EXPRESS
5200 NW 33rd Avenue, Suite 220, Fort Lauderdale FL 33309. 954/486-8585. **Fax:** 954/733-6444. **Contact:** Steven Sloane, President. **Description:** A permanent employment agency that also provides some temporary placements. **Specializes in the areas of:** Accounting/ Auditing; Finance. **Positions commonly filled include:** Accountant/Auditor; Budget Analyst; Chief Financial Officer; Controller; Credit Manager; Finance Director; Financial Analyst. **Average salary range of placements:** $30,000 - $50,000. **Number of placements per year:** 100 - 199.

AD HOC LAW ASSOCIATES
444 Brickell Avenue, Suite 611, Miami FL 33131. 305/381-9600. **Fax:** 305/381-9396. **Contact:** Suzanne Pallot, President. **E-mail address:** adhoc01@ mindspring.com. **Description:** A permanent employment agency. **Specializes in the areas of:** Legal. **Positions commonly filled include:** Attorney; Paralegal. **Average salary range of placements:** More than $50,000. **Number of placements per year:** 1 - 49.

ALPHA PERSONNEL
ALPHA TEMPS
10790 66th Street North, Suite B, Pinellas Park FL 33782. 727/548-9675. **Contact:** Director. **Description:** A permanent employment agency. Alpha Temps (also at this location) is a temporary agency. **Specializes in the areas of:** Accounting/Auditing; Banking; Computer Science/Software; Legal; Manufacturing; Nonprofit; Personnel/Labor Relations; Secretarial. **Positions commonly filled include:** Accountant; Administrative Assistant; Administrative Manager; Assistant Manager; Blue-Collar Worker Supervisor; Branch Manager; Chief Financial Officer; Claim Rep.; Clerical Supervisor; Computer Operator; Controller; Cost Estimator; Credit Manager; Customer Service Rep.; Draftsperson; Electrical/Electronics Engineer; Finance Director; Financial Analyst; Graphic Artist; Graphic Designer; Human Resources Manager; Management Trainee; Manufacturing Engineer; Marketing Specialist; Operations Manager; Production Manager; Project Manager; Purchasing Agent/Manager; Quality Control Supervisor; Sales Rep.; Secretary; Social Worker; Technical Writer/Editor; Typist/Word Processor. **Benefits available to temporary workers:** Dental Insurance; Disability Coverage; Health Benefits; Life Insurance; Paid Holidays; Paid Vacation. **Other U.S. locations:** Altamonte Springs FL; Lakeland FL; Tampa FL. **Average salary range of placements:** $20,000 - $29,999. **Number of placements per year:** 200 - 499.

AMBIANCE PERSONNEL INC.
7990 SW 117th Avenue, Suite 125, Miami FL 33183-3845. 305/274-7419. **Fax:** 305/598-8071. **Contact:** Eric S. Pollack, Vice President/General Manager. **E-mail address:** ambiance@netrunner.net. **Description:** A permanent employment agency that also offers some executive searches. **Specializes in the areas of:** Accounting; Logistics; Sales; Secretarial; Transportation. **Positions commonly filled include:** Accountant/Auditor; Branch Manager; Controller; Credit Manager; Customer Service Rep.; General Manager; Marketing Manager;

Sales Executive; Sales Manager; Sales Rep.; Secretary; Transportation/Traffic Specialist; Vice President. **Benefits available to temporary workers:** Medical Insurance; Paid Holidays; Paid Vacation. **Corporate headquarters location:** This Location. **Average salary range of placements:** $20,000 - $50,000. **Number of placements per year:** 200 - 499.

AVAILABILITY, INC.
5340 West Kennedy Boulevard, Suite 100, Tampa FL 33609. 813/286-8800. **Fax:** 813/286-0574. **Contact:** Manager. **Description:** A permanent employment agency that also offers temporary and contract placements. **Specializes in the areas of:** Accounting/ Auditing; Administration; Banking; Clerical; Computer Science/Software; Engineering; Finance; General Management; Health/Medical; Legal; Personnel/Labor Relations; Publishing; Secretarial. **Positions commonly filled include:** Accountant/Auditor; Administrative Manager; Advertising Clerk; Bank Officer/Manager; Branch Manager; Brokerage Clerk; Claim Rep.; Clerical Supervisor; Computer Programmer; Cost Estimator; Credit Manager; Customer Service Rep.; Dental Assistant/Dental Hygienist; Dentist; Editor; Education Administrator; Emergency Medical Tech.; Financial Analyst; General Manager; Health Services Manager; Human Resources Specialist; Human Service Worker; Internet Services Manager; Management Analyst/ Consultant; Management Trainee; Medical Records Tech.; Occupational Therapist; Operations/Production Manager; Paralegal; Public Relations Specialist; Recreational Therapist; Registered Nurse; Respiratory Therapist; Software Engineer; Systems Analyst; Technical Writer/Editor; Telecommunications Manager; Typist/Word Processor; Underwriter.

BELMONT TRAINING & EMPLOYMENT CENTER
17800 NW 27th Avenue, Opa-Locka FL 33056. 305/628-3838. **Fax:** 305/628-2331. **Contact:** Center Coordinator. **Description:** A permanent employment agency. **Specializes in the areas of:** Administration; Computer Science/Software; Education; General Management; Retail; Sales; Secretarial. **Positions commonly filled include:** Accountant/Auditor; Administrative Manager; Advertising Clerk; Automotive Mechanic; Blue-Collar Worker Supervisor; Clerical Supervisor; Customer Service Representative; Data Entry Clerk; EKG Technician; Financial Analyst; Human Resources Specialist; Management Trainee; Market Research Analyst; Paralegal; Registered Nurse; Restaurant/Food Service Manager; Teacher/Professor; Typist/Word Processor. **Number of placements per year:** 500 - 999.

BRADFORD ONE STOP CAREER CENTER
609 North Orange Street, Starke FL 32091. 904/964-8092. **Fax:** 904/964-3969. **Contact:** Supervisor. **Description:** A permanent employment agency. **Corporate headquarters location:** Tallahassee FL.

CTI GROUP
1535 SE 17th Street, Suite 206, Fort Lauderdale FL 33316. 954/728-9975. **Contact:** Manager. **Description:** A permanent employment agency. **Specializes in the areas of:** Maritime.

CAREER PLANNERS, INC.
5730 Corporate Way, Suite 100, West Palm Beach FL 33407. 561/683-8785. **Fax:** 561/683-4047. **Contact:** Deborah M. Finley, President. **E-mail address:** cpi@flinet.com. **Description:** A permanent employment agency that also offers some temporary placements. **Specializes in the areas of:** Accounting; Administration; Architecture/Construction; Banking; Computer Science/ Software; Engineering; Finance; Legal; Manufacturing; Personnel/Labor Relations; Sales; Secretarial. **Positions commonly filled include:** Accountant; Administrative Manager; Bank Officer/Manager; Branch Manager; Budget Analyst; Buyer; Civil Engineer; Computer Programmer; Cost Estimator; Credit Manager; Design Engineer; Draftsperson; Environmental Engineer; Financial Analyst; Management Trainee; Market Research Analyst; Mechanical Engineer; MIS Specialist;

Operations/Production Manager; Paralegal; Petroleum Engineer; Property and Real Estate Manager; Purchasing Agent/Manager; Quality Control Supervisor; Securities Sales Rep.; Services Sales Rep.; Systems Analyst; Technical Writer/Editor; Telecommunications Manager; Typist/Word Processor; Underwriter. **Average salary range of placements:** $30,000 - $50,000. **Number of placements per year:** 200 - 499.

CREW UNLIMITED INC.
2065 South Federal Highway, Fort Lauderdale FL 33316. 954/462-4624. **Fax:** 954/523-6712. **Contact:** Manager. **Description:** A permanent employment agency for the marine industry. The firm supplies crew members for yachts. **Positions commonly filled include:** Chef/ Cook/Kitchen Worker; Electrical/Electronics Engineer; Electrician; Mechanical Engineer; Registered Nurse; Restaurant/Food Service Manager; Ship's Captain; Ship's Mate. **Other U.S. locations:** Newport RI. **Average salary range of placements:** $30,000 - $50,000. **Number of placements per year:** 100 - 199.

DECISION CONSULTANTS INC.
8800 Grand Oak Circle, Suite 600, Tampa FL 33637. 813/977-8170. **Contact:** Technical Staffing Manager. **Description:** A permanent employment agency. **Specializes in the areas of:** Administration; Computer Hardware/Software.

EXECUTIVE DIRECTIONS INC.
450 North Park Road, Suite 302, Hollywood FL 33021. 954/962-9444. **Fax:** 954/963-4333. **Contact:** Bob Silverman, Director. **E-mail address:** jobs@edifla.com. **Description:** A permanent employment agency. **Specializes in the areas of:** Administration; Computer Science/Software. **Positions commonly filled include:** Computer Programmer; Management Analyst/ Consultant; Software Engineer; Systems Analyst; Telecommunications Manager. **Average salary range of placements:** $30,000 - $50,000. **Number of placements per year:** 100 - 199.

GANS, GANS & ASSOCIATES
4129 East Fowler Avenue, Tampa FL 33617. 813/971-6501. **Contact:** Manager. **Description:** A permanent employment agency. **Specializes in the areas of:** Insurance; Legal. **Positions commonly filled include:** Actuary; Attorney; Claim Rep.; Insurance Agent/Broker; Legal Secretary; Paralegal; Underwriter/Assistant Underwriter.

IMPACT PERSONNEL
1270 Rogers Street, Clearwater FL 33756. 727/447-2288. **Fax:** 727/461-1813. **Contact:** Sheila Sliter, Director. **E-mail address:** impactpersonnel@mindspring.com. **Description:** A permanent employment agency. **Specializes in the areas of:** Clerical.

JANUS CAREER SERVICES
157 East New England Avenue, Suite 240, Winter Park FL 32789. 407/628-1090. **Fax:** 407/628-5115. **Contact:** Jan Leach, President. **Description:** A permanent employment agency. **Specializes in the areas of:** Administration; Engineering; Finance; Food; General Management; Health/Medical; Personnel/Labor Relations; Sales. **Positions commonly filled include:** Accountant/Auditor; Administrative Manager; Aerospace Engineer; Architect; Attorney; Bank Officer/Manager; Branch Manager; Civil Engineer; Claim Rep.; Computer Programmer; Construction Contractor; Cost Estimator; Counselor; Credit Manager; Customer Service Rep.; Designer; Draftsperson; Economist; Editor; Electrical/ Electronics Engineer; Financial Analyst; General Manager; Hotel Manager; Human Resources Manager; Human Service Worker; Industrial Engineer; Industrial Production Manager; Insurance Agent/Broker; Management Analyst/Consultant; Management Trainee; Manufacturer's/Wholesaler's Sales Rep.; Mechanical Engineer; Metallurgical Engineer; Mining Engineer; Operations/Production Manager; Property and Real Estate Manager; Psychologist; Public Relations Specialist; Purchasing Agent/Manager; Quality Control

Supervisor; Reporter; Restaurant/Food Service Manager; Securities Sales Representative; Services Sales Representative; Software Engineer; Statistician; Structural Engineer; Systems Analyst; Teacher/Professor; Technical Writer/Editor; Transportation/Traffic Specialist; Urban/Regional Planner; Wholesale and Retail Buyer. **Number of placements per year:** 100 - 199.

THE JOB PLACE, INC.
428 Julia Street, Titusville FL 32796. 407/268-2250. **Fax:** 407/383-3147. **Contact:** Debra Shuler, President. **Description:** The Job Place, Inc. is a permanent employment agency that also provides some temporary placements. **Number of placements per year:** 50 - 99.

LEGAL-EASE, INC.
2002 East Robinson Street, Orlando FL 32803. 407/895-2565. **Fax:** 407/898-5931. **Contact:** Jeanna Juliano, Co-Owner. **Description:** Legal-Ease is a permanent employment agency that also provides some resume assistance and career counseling services. **Specializes in the areas of:** Legal; Secretarial. **Positions commonly filled include:** Attorney; Clerk; Paralegal; Receptionist; Secretary. **Average salary range of placements:** $20,000 - $29,999. **Number of placements per year:** 100 - 199.

MADISON TRAVEL CAREERS UNLIMITED
P.O. Box 331052, Miami FL 33233. 305/576-9917. **Fax:** 305/674-7872. **Contact:** Manager. **Description:** A permanent employment agency that also provides some career/outplacement counseling services. **Specializes in the areas of:** Travel. **Positions commonly filled include:** Reservationist; Sales and Marketing Representative; Travel Agent.

MANPOWER TECHNICAL SERVICES
5310 NW 33rd Avenue, Suite 108, Fort Lauderdale FL 33309. 954/677-0900. **Fax:** 954/677-0000. **Contact:** Paul Gilmore, Recruitment. **E-mail address:** mptech@earthlink.net. **World Wide Web address:** http://www.manpower.com. **Description:** A permanent employment agency. **Specializes in the areas of:** Engineering; Technical. **Positions commonly filled include:** Biological Scientist; Chemist; Computer Programmer; Electrical/Electronics Engineer; Sales and Marketing Rep.; Systems Analyst. **Corporate headquarters location:** Milwaukee WI. **Other U.S. locations:** Nationwide.

NANNIES 'N MORE, INC.
2700 West Oakland Park Boulevard, Suite 2750-D, Fort Lauderdale FL 33311. 954/735-0902. **Contact:** Marilyn Racow, Owner. **Description:** Nannies 'N More is a permanent employment agency. **Specializes in the areas of:** Domestic Help; Nannies. **Positions commonly filled include:** Chef/Cook/Kitchen Worker; Housekeeper; Nanny. **Average salary range of placements:** Less than $20,000. **Number of placements per year:** 200 - 499.

OFFICEMATES5 (OM5)
1900 West Commercial Boulevard, Fort Lauderdale FL 33309. 954/776-4477. **Fax:** 954/776-4488. **Contact:** Manager. **Description:** A permanent employment agency. **Specializes in the areas of:** Legal; Office Support; Secretarial. **Positions commonly filled include:** Advertising Clerk; Brokerage Clerk; Customer Service Representative; Paralegal; Typist/Word Processor. **Corporate headquarters location:** Cleveland OH. **Other U.S. locations:** Nationwide. **Average salary range of placements:** $20,000 - $29,999. **Number of placements per year:** 1000+.

ONE STOP JOBS ETCETERA
5729 Manatee Avenue West, Bradenton FL 34209. 941/714-7449. **Fax:** 941/714-7458. **Contact:** Susan R. Stubbs, Manager. **Description:** One Stop Jobs Etcetera is a permanent employment agency. **Positions commonly filled include:** Bookkeeper; Clerk; Computer Operator;

Construction Trade Worker; Data Entry Clerk; Driver; Factory Worker; Legal Secretary; Light Industrial Worker; Nurse; Receptionist; Secretary; Typist/Word Processor. **Corporate headquarters location:** Tallahassee FL. **Number of placements per year:** 1000+.

PMC&L ASSOCIATES, INC.
328 Banyan Boulevard, Suite K, West Palm Beach FL 33401. 561/659-4523. **Contact:** Manager. **Description:** PMC&L Associates is a permanent employment agency that also offers some temporary placements. PMC&L Associates also provides outplacement/career counseling services. **Specializes in the areas of:** Accounting/Auditing; Bookkeeping; Chef; Clerical; Data Processing; Engineering; General Management; Office Support; Professional. **Number of placements per year:** 100 - 199.

PASSPORT MARINE
3535 West Fairfield Drive, Pensacola FL 32505. 850/455-8833. **Fax:** 850/455-2700. **Contact:** Johnny M. Smith, President. **Description:** Passport Marine is a permanent employment agency. **Specializes in the areas of:** Maritime. **Positions commonly filled include:** Ship's Captain; Ship's Mate. **Other U.S. locations:** Mobile AL. **Average salary range of placements:** Less than $20,000. **Number of placements per year:** 200 - 499.

PERSONNEL CENTER
P.O. Box 1111, Gainesville FL 32602-1111. 352/372-6377. **Fax:** 352/376-6783. **Contact:** Marion Voyles, Manager. **Description:** Personnel Center is a permanent employment agency. **Specializes in the areas of:** Accounting/Auditing; Data Processing; Finance.

SHAVER EMPLOYMENT AGENCY
254 West Tampa Avenue, Venice FL 34285. 941/484-6821. **Fax:** 941/484-6822. **Contact:** Lee Shaver, Owner. **Description:** Shaver Employment Agency is a permanent employment agency. **Specializes in the areas of:** Accounting/Auditing; Administration; Architecture/Construction; Banking; Computer Science/Software; Food; General Management; Legal; Manufacturing; Retail; Sales. **Positions commonly filled include:** Accountant/Auditor; Administrative Manager; Architect; Attorney; Automotive Mechanic; Bank Officer/Manager; Blue-Collar Worker Supervisor; Branch Manager; Brokerage Clerk; Buyer; Civil Engineer; Computer Programmer; Construction Contractor; Cost Estimator; Counselor; Credit Manager; Customer Service Representative; Dental Assistant/Dental Hygienist; Draftsperson; Electrical/Electronics Engineer; Electrician; Financial Analyst; Food Scientist/Technologist; Health Services Manager; Hotel Manager; Human Resources Specialist; Insurance Agent/Broker; Landscape Architect; Licensed Practical Nurse; Management Trainee; Mechanical Engineer; Medical Records Technician; MIS Specialist; Operations/Production Manager; Paralegal; Property and Real Estate Manager; Purchasing Agent/Manager; Real Estate Agent; Registered Nurse; Restaurant/Food Service Manager; Securities Sales Representative; Services Sales Representative; Software Engineer; Systems Analyst; Technical Writer/Editor; Travel Agent; Typist/Word Processor. **Number of placements per year:** 200 - 499.

STAFFING SOLUTIONS BY PERSONNEL ONE
1895 West Commercial Boulevard, Suite 140, Fort Lauderdale FL 33309. 954/491-4100. **Fax:** 954/771-0700. **Contact:** Area Manager. **World Wide Web address:** http://www.ssbyp1.com. **Description:** A permanent employment agency. **Specializes in the areas of:** Administration; Legal; Personnel/Labor Relations; Sales; Secretarial. **Positions commonly filled include:** Accountant/Auditor; Administrative Manager; Administrative Worker/Clerk; Clerical Supervisor; Computer Programmer; Customer Service Rep.; Human Resources Manager; Paralegal; Services Sales Rep.; Systems Analyst; Technical Writer/Editor. **Other area**

locations: Boca Raton FL; Hollywood FL. **Number of placements per year:** 200 - 499.

STAFFING SOLUTIONS BY PERSONNEL ONE
6200 North Federal Highway, Boca Raton FL 33487. 561/994-4600. **Fax:** 561/994-9635. **Contact:** Recruiter. **World Wide Web address:** http://www.ssbyp1.com. **Description:** A permanent employment agency that also provides some outplacement counseling services. **Specializes in the areas of:** Computer Science/Software; Personnel/Labor Relations; Sales; Secretarial. **Positions commonly filled include:** Accountant/Auditor; Administrative Manager; Blue-Collar Worker Supervisor; Brokerage Clerk; Clerical Supervisor; Credit Manager; Customer Service Rep.; Human Resources Specialist; Management Trainee; Manufacturer's/Wholesaler's Sales Rep.; Services Sales Representative; Software Engineer. **Other area locations:** Fort Lauderdale FL; Hollywood FL. **Average salary range of placements:** $20,000 - $29,999. **Number of placements per year:** 1000+.

STAFFING SOLUTIONS BY PERSONNEL ONE
3475 Sheridan Street, Suite 103, Hollywood FL 33021. 954/983-4000. **Contact:** Manager. **World Wide Web address:** http://www.ssbyp1.com. **Description:** A permanent employment agency that also provides some temporary and temp-to-perm placements. **Positions commonly filled include:** Accountant/Auditor; Administrative Manager; Advertising Clerk; Aerospace Engineer; Agricultural Engineer; Biomedical Engineer; Blue-Collar Worker Supervisor; Brokerage Clerk; Chemical Engineer; Chemist; Civil Engineer; Claim Rep.; Clerical Supervisor; Computer Programmer; Cost Estimator; Counselor; Credit Manager; Customer Service Rep.; Design Engineer; Draftsperson; Electrical/Electronics Engineer; Electrician; Environmental Engineer; Financial Analyst; General Manager; Human Resources Specialist; Industrial Engineer; Industrial Production Manager; Management Analyst/Consultant; Management Trainee; Manufacturer's/Wholesaler's Sales Rep.; Medical Records Technician; MIS Specialist; Operations/Production Manager; Paralegal; Public Relations Specialist; Purchasing Agent/Manager; Software Engineer; Stationary Engineer; Systems Analyst; Typist/Word Processor; Underwriter. **Other area locations:** Boca Raton FL; Fort Lauderdale FL.

STRATEGY RESOURCES INC.
4190 Belfort Road, Suite 255, Jacksonville FL 32216. 904/296-1101. **Fax:** 904/296-1140. **Contact:** Janet Shuman, Manager. **E-mail address:** janet@strategyresources.com. **World Wide Web address:** http://www.strategyresources.com. **Description:** A permanent employment agency that also provides some executive searches and contract services. **Specializes in the areas of:** Computer Science/Software; Internet Development; Marketing; Sales. **Positions commonly filled include:** Account Manager; Applications Engineer; AS400 Programmer Analyst; Computer Animator; Computer Engineer; Computer Graphics Specialist; Computer Operator; Computer Programmer; Computer Scientist; Computer Support Technician; Content Developer; Database Administrator; Database Manager; Human Resources Manager; Internet Services Manager; MIS Specialist; Multimedia Designer; Network Administrator; Sales Executive; Sales Manager; Software Engineer; SQL Programmer; Systems Analyst; Webmaster. **Corporate headquarters location:** Bethesda MD. **Other U.S. locations:** Nationwide. **Average salary range of placements:** $50,000 - $100,000. **Number of placements per year:** 200 - 499.

SUNCOAST GROUP
3808 Gunn Highway, Suite 102, Tampa FL 33624. 813/961-1485. **Fax:** 813/961-2038. **Contact:** Michael Loos, Owner. **E-mail address:** suncoastgrp@ij.net. **Description:** A permanent employment agency serving recent college graduates and individuals changing careers. **Specializes in the areas of:** Entry-Level Management; Finance; General Management; Retail; Sales. **Positions commonly filled include:** Branch Manager; General Manager; Management Trainee; Services Sales Representative. **Average salary range of placements:** $20,000 - $29,999. **Number of placements per year:** 1 - 49.

VELKIN PERSONNEL SERVICES
6405 NW 36th Street, Suite 220, Miami FL 33166. 305/876-9800. **Contact:** Manager. **Description:** A permanent employment agency that also offers some temporary placements, executive searches, and career/outplacement counseling services. **Specializes in the areas of:** Personnel/Labor Relations. **Positions commonly filled include:** Accountant/Auditor; Adjuster; Administrative Assistant; Administrative Manager; Advertising Clerk; Bank Officer/Manager; Brokerage Clerk; Budget Analyst; Claim Rep.; Clerical Supervisor; Computer Programmer; Customer Service Rep.; General Manager; Health Services Manager; Hotel Manager; Human Resources Specialist; MIS Specialist; Multimedia Designer; Paralegal; Secretary; Services Sales Rep.; Systems Analyst; Typist/Word Processor. **Other area locations:** Sunrise FL. **Average salary range of placements:** $20,000 - $29,999. **Number of placements per year:** 200 - 499.

VICTORIA & ASSOCIATES PERSONNEL SERVICES
8181 NW 36th Street, Suite 22, Miami FL 33166. 305/477-2233. **Fax:** 305/477-2149. **Contact:** Odalys Rioseco, Operations Manager. **Description:** A permanent employment agency that also provides some temporary and temp-to-perm placements. Client company pays fee. **Specializes in the areas of:** Accounting/Auditing; Administration; Banking; Finance; Legal; Light Industrial; Sales; Secretarial. **Positions commonly filled include:** Accountant/Auditor; Administrative Assistant; Advertising Clerk; Computer Operator; Customer Service Representative; Human Resources Manager; MIS Specialist; Operations Manager; Sales Representative; Secretary. **Benefits available to temporary workers:** Medical Insurance; Paid Holidays; Paid Vacation. **Corporate headquarters location:** Miramar FL. **Average salary range of placements:** $20,000 - $29,999. **Number of placements per year:** 1000+.

TEMPORARY EMPLOYMENT AGENCIES

ABLEST STAFFING SERVICES
3101 Maguire Boulevard, Suite 265, Orlando FL 32803. 407/896-1912. **Fax:** 407/898-1015. **Contact:** Lori Layton, Manager. **Description:** A temporary agency specializing in administrative placements for jobseekers with Word or Excel backgrounds. **Specializes in the areas of:** Administration.

ACCUSTAFF INCORPORATED
1875 West Commercial Boulevard, Suite 165, Fort Lauderdale FL 33309. 954/928-0699. **Fax:** 954/772-8343. **Contact:** Branch Manager. **World Wide Web address:** http://www.accustaff.com. **Description:** A temporary agency. **Specializes in the areas of:** Clerical; Light Industrial; Marketing; Personnel/Labor Relations; Sales. **Positions commonly filled include:** Sales Representative; Secretary. **Benefits available to temporary workers:** 401(k); Paid Holidays; Paid Vacation. **Corporate headquarters location:** Jacksonville FL. **Other U.S. locations:** Nationwide. **Average salary range of placements:** $20,000 - $29,999. **Number of placements per year:** 1000+.

ADECCO
330 South Pineapple Avenue, Suite 101, Sarasota FL 34236. 941/365-5546. **Contact:** Recruiter. **Description:** A temporary agency. **Specializes in the areas of:** Accounting/Auditing; Administration; Banking; General

Management; Industrial; Manufacturing; Sales; Secretarial. **Positions commonly filled include:** Accountant/Auditor; Automotive Mechanic; Blue-Collar Worker Supervisor; Branch Manager; Customer Service Representative; Electrical/Electronics Engineer; Human Resources Specialist; Management Trainee; Public Relations Specialist; Typist/Word Processor. **Benefits available to temporary workers:** 401(k); Medical Insurance; Paid Holidays; Paid Vacation; Tuition Assistance. **Corporate headquarters location:** Redwood City CA. **Other U.S. locations:** Nationwide. **International locations:** Worldwide. **Average salary range of placements:** $20,000 - $29,999. **Number of placements per year:** 200 - 499.

ALL MEDICAL PERSONNEL
8700 West Flagler Street, Suite 260, Miami FL 33174. **Toll-free phone:** 800/706-2378. **Contact:** Regional Director. **Description:** A temporary agency that also provides some permanent placements. **Specializes in the areas of:** Health/Medical. **Corporate headquarters location:** Hollywood FL. **Other area locations:** Delray Beach FL; Merritt Island FL; Tampa FL. **Average salary range of placements:** $20,000 - $29,999.

ALL-WAYS LEGAL SECRETARIES, INC.
P.O. Box 21812, Fort Lauderdale FL 33335-1812. 954/565-6565. **Fax:** 954/522-4659. **Contact:** President. **Description:** A temporary agency that also provides some permanent placements. **Specializes in the areas of:** Legal. **Average salary range of placements:** $20,000 - $40,000. **Number of placements per year:** 200 - 499.

AQUENT PARTNERS
15280 NW 79th Court, Suite 250, Miami Lakes FL 33016. 305/819-3600. **Toll-free phone:** 877/PARTNER. **Fax:** 305/819-3311. **Contact:** Bill Sweeney, Manager. **E-mail address:** bsweeney@aquent.com. **World Wide Web address:** http://www.aquent.com. **Description:** A temporary agency that provides placements for creative, Web, and technical professionals. Aquent Partners also provides some temp-to-perm, permanent, and contract placements. **Specializes in the areas of:** Administration; Art/Design; Computer Science/Software; Marketing. **Positions commonly filled include:** Computer Animator; Computer Engineer; Computer Operator; Computer Programmer; Computer Support Technician; Computer Technician; Content Developer; Database Administrator; Database Manager; Desktop Publishing Specialist; Editor; Editorial Assistant; Graphic Artist; Graphic Designer; Internet Services Manager; Managing Editor; MIS Specialist; Multimedia Designer; Network/ Systems Administrator; Production Manager; Project Manager; Software Engineer; SQL Programmer; Systems Analyst; Systems Manager; Technical Writer/Editor; Webmaster. **Benefits available to temporary workers:** 401(k); Dental Insurance; Disability Coverage; Medical Insurance. **CEO:** John Chuang.

CAREERS USA
4400 North Federal Highway, Suite 124, Boca Raton FL 33431-5187. 561/362-4200. **Fax:** 561/362-9299. **Contact:** Robin Schwartz, Regional Director. **Description:** A temporary agency that also provides some temp-to-perm placements. **Specializes in the areas of:** Accounting/Auditing; Administration; Data Processing; Light Industrial; Secretarial; Telemarketing. **Benefits available to temporary workers:** Bonus Award/Plan; Medical Insurance; Retirement Plan. **Corporate headquarters location:** Philadelphia PA. **Other U.S. locations:** DC; GA; IL; MD; NJ. **Number of placements per year:** 1000+.

CAREERXCHANGE
10689 North Kendall Drive, Suite 209, Miami FL 33176. 305/595-3800. **Fax:** 305/279-8903. **Contact:** Sue Romanos, President. **Description:** A temporary agency that also provides some permanent placements and training services. **Specializes in the areas of:** Accounting/Auditing; General Management; Legal; Personnel/Labor Relations; Secretarial. **Positions commonly filled include:** Accountant/Auditor;

Administrative Manager; Administrator; Advertising Clerk; Blue-Collar Worker Supervisor; Branch Manager; Brokerage Clerk; Budget Analyst; Buyer; Claim Representative; Clerical Supervisor; Clerk; Construction and Building Inspector; Construction Contractor; Cost Estimator; Credit Manager; Customer Service Rep.; Financial Analyst; General Manager; Health Services Manager; Human Resources Specialist; Internet Services Manager; Management; Management Trainee; Medical Secretary; Paralegal; Property and Real Estate Manager; Purchasing Agent/Manager; Quality Control Supervisor; Real Estate Agent; Receptionist; Secretary; Technical Writer/Editor; Telecommunications Manager; Typist/ Word Processor. **Benefits available to temporary workers:** Medical Insurance; Paid Holidays; Paid Vacation. **Number of placements per year:** 200 - 499.

COMPUTER PLUS STAFFING SOLUTIONS, INC.
11300 Fourth Street North, Suite 115, St. Petersburg FL 33716. 727/578-1121. **Contact:** Marie Solages, Staffing Specialist. **Description:** A temporary agency. **Specializes in the areas of:** Administration; Computer Science/Software; Personnel/Labor Relations. **Positions commonly filled include:** Computer Support Technician; MIS Specialist; Network Support Technician; Operations Engineer; Technical Writer/ Editor; Telecommunications Analyst; Typist/Word Processor. **Benefits available to temporary workers:** 401(k); Medical Insurance; Paid Holidays; Paid Vacation. **Other area locations:** Orlando FL; Sarasota FL; Tampa FL. **Average salary range of placements:** $30,000 - $50,000. **Number of placements per year:** 200 - 499.

CONSULTIS INC.
1615 South Federal Highway, Suite 100, Boca Raton FL 33432. 561/750-8745. **Fax:** 561/750-9950. **Contact:** Kathy Gaffney, Resource Coordinator. **Description:** A temporary agency that also provides some temp-to-perm placements. **Specializes in the areas of:** Computer Science/Software; Technical.

CUSTOM STAFFING, INC.
485 North Keller Road, Maitland FL 32751. 407/667-8755. **Fax:** 407/667-8760. **Contact:** Don Langmo, President. **Description:** A temporary agency. **Specializes in the areas of:** Accounting/Auditing; Administration; Customer Service; Office Support; Secretarial; Telemarketing; Word Processing. **Other area locations:** Jacksonville FL; Orlando FL.

DENTAL FILLINS INC.
9520 Corkscrew Road, Estelo FL 33928. 941/992-6522. **Contact:** Jodi Bowers, President. **Description:** A temporary agency that also provides some permanent placements. **Specializes in the areas of:** Dental. **Positions commonly filled include:** Dental Assistant/Dental Hygienist.

DONBAR SERVICE CORPORATION
4319 West Kennedy Boulevard, Tampa FL 33609. 813/287-8925. **Fax:** 813/289-4839. **Contact:** Bill Patterson, Account Representative. **E-mail address:** dsc@donbar.com. **World Wide Web address:** http://www.donbar.com. **Description:** A temporary agency that also provides some contract services and permanent placements. **Specializes in the areas of:** Computer Science/Software; Engineering; Industrial; Manufacturing; Secretarial. **Positions commonly filled include:** Accountant/Auditor; Administrative Manager; Aerospace Engineer; Blue-Collar Worker Supervisor; Ceramics Engineer; Civil Engineer; Computer Programmer; Construction and Building Inspector; Construction Contractor; Customer Service Rep.; Design Engineer; Designer; Draftsperson; Electrical/Electronics Engineer; Electrician; Environmental Engineer; Industrial Engineer; Industrial Production Manager; Materials Engineer; Mechanical Engineer; Metallurgical Engineer; MIS Specialist; Operations/Production Manager; Purchasing Agent/Manager; Quality Control Supervisor; Software Engineer; Structural Engineer; Surveyor; Systems Analyst; Typist/Word Processor. **Other U.S.**

locations: Lakeland FL; Largo FL. **Number of placements per year:** 1000+.

EMPLOYERS' ASSISTANT, INC.
25 East Wright Street, Suite 2510, Pensacola FL 32501. 850/432-6311. **Fax:** 850/202-8704. **Contact:** Laura Maki, Placement Manager. **Description:** A temporary agency. **Specializes in the areas of:** Accounting/Auditing; Administration; Banking; Education; General Management; Health/Medical; Industrial; Personnel/Labor Relations; Retail; Sales; Secretarial. **Positions commonly filled include:** Accountant/Auditor; Branch Manager; Computer Programmer; Counselor; Health Services Manager; Human Resources Specialist; Medical Records Technician; Pharmacist; Travel Agent; Typist/Word Processor. **Benefits available to temporary workers:** Credit Union; Dental Insurance; Medical Insurance. **Number of placements per year:** 200 - 499.

FIVE STAR TEMPORARY INC.
2943 East Colonial Drive, Orlando FL 32803. 407/898-1125. **Fax:** 407/898-4940. **Contact:** Karen Randolph, Branch Manager. **Description:** A temporary agency. **Specializes in the areas of:** Administration; Banking; Food; General Management; Health/Medical; Industrial; Legal; Manufacturing; Personnel/Labor Relations; Retail; Sales; Secretarial; Technical. **Positions commonly filled include:** Accountant/Auditor; Administrative Manager; Blue-Collar Worker Supervisor; Branch Manager; Buyer; Claim Representative; Clerical Supervisor; Computer Programmer; Cost Estimator; Counselor; Credit Manager; Draftsperson; General Manager; Industrial Production Manager; Management Trainee; MIS Specialist; Public Relations Specialist; Typist/Word Processor; Underwriter/Assistant Underwriter. **Benefits available to temporary workers:** Medical Insurance; Paid Vacation. **Other area locations:** Longwood FL; Tampa FL. **Average salary range of placements:** $20,000 - $29,999. **Number of placements per year:** 1000+.

FUTURE FORCE PERSONNEL
15800 NW 57th Avenue, Miami Lakes FL 33014. **Contact:** Adela Gonzalez, President. **Description:** A temporary agency that also provides some permanent placements. **Specializes in the areas of:** Accounting/Auditing; Administration; Banking; Computer Science/Software; Food; Legal; Manufacturing; Personnel/Labor Relations; Publishing; Retail; Sales; Secretarial. **Benefits available to temporary workers:** Medical Insurance; Paid Holidays; Paid Vacation. **Average salary range of placements:** $20,000 - $29,999. **Number of placements per year:** 1000+.

HASTINGS & HASTINGS PERSONNEL CONSULTANTS
1001 Brickell Bay Drive, Suite 2902, Miami FL 33131. 305/374-7171. **Contact:** Tracy Kamen, Senior Temporary Coordinator. **Description:** A temporary agency that also provides some permanent placements. **Specializes in the areas of:** Accounting/Auditing; Administration; Advertising; Banking; Computer Science/Software; Economics; Finance; Insurance; Legal; Personnel/Labor Relations; Sales; Secretarial. **Positions commonly filled include:** Accountant/Auditor; Adjuster; Administrative Manager; Advertising Clerk; Bank Officer/Manager; Branch Manager; Brokerage Clerk; Budget Analyst; Buyer; Claim Representative; Clerical Supervisor; Computer Programmer; Cost Estimator; Credit Manager; Customer Service Representative; Economist; Editor; Financial Analyst; Human Resources Specialist; Insurance Agent/Broker; Internet Services Manager; Management Analyst/Consultant; Management Trainee; Manufacturer's/Wholesaler's Sales Rep.; Market Research Analyst; MIS Specialist; Multimedia Designer; Operations/Production Manager; Paralegal; Property and Real Estate Manager; Public Relations Specialist; Purchasing Agent/Manager; Quality Control Supervisor; Securities Sales Representative; Services Sales Representative; Systems Analyst; Technical Writer/Editor; Telecommunications

Manager; Transportation/Traffic Specialist; Travel Agent; Typist/Word Processor; Underwriter/Assistant Underwriter. **Benefits available to temporary workers:** Paid Vacation. **Average salary range of placements:** $30,000 - $50,000. **Number of placements per year:** 200 - 499.

INTERIM PERSONNEL
2551 Drew Street, Suite 102, Clearwater FL 33765. 727/797-2171. **Fax:** 727/726-4061. **Contact:** Client Service Supervisor. **World Wide Web address:** http://www.interim.com. **Description:** A temporary agency that also provides some permanent placements. **Specializes in the areas of:** Accounting/Auditing; Manufacturing; Sales; Secretarial. **Positions commonly filled include:** Accountant/Auditor; Clerical Supervisor; Customer Service Representative; Paralegal; Typist/Word Processor. **Corporate headquarters location:** Fort Lauderdale FL. **International locations:** Worldwide. **Average salary range of placements:** $20,000 - $29,999. **Number of placements per year:** 500 - 999.

KELLY SERVICES, INC.
3300 PGA Boulevard, Palm Beach Gardens FL 33410. 561/694-0116. **Contact:** Manager. **World Wide Web address:** http://www.kellyservices.com. **Description:** A temporary agency. **Specializes in the areas of:** Clerical; Manufacturing; Technical. **Corporate headquarters location:** Troy MI. **Other U.S. locations:** Nationwide.

KELLY SERVICES, INC.
15050 NW 79th Court, Suite 102, Miami Lakes FL 33016. 305/822-8210. **Fax:** 305/828-9312. **Contact:** Office Manager. **World Wide Web address:** http://www.kellyservices.com. **Description:** A temporary agency. **Specializes in the areas of:** Banking; Industrial; Light Industrial; Sales; Secretarial. **Positions commonly filled include:** Administrative Assistant; Customer Service Representative; Secretary; Typist/Word Processor. **Benefits available to temporary workers:** Medical Insurance; Paid Holidays; Paid Vacation. **Average salary range of placements:** $20,000 - $29,999. **Number of placements per year:** 1 - 49. **Corporate headquarters location:** Troy MI. **Other U.S. locations:** Nationwide.

KELLY SERVICES, INC.
4803 George Road, Suite 300, Tampa FL 33615. 813/243-8855. **Fax:** 813/243-9166. **Contact:** Bernadette M. Pello, Regional Service Operations Manager. **World Wide Web address:** http://www.kellyservices.com. **Description:** A temporary agency that also provides some permanent placements. **Specializes in the areas of:** Clerical; Industrial; Light Industrial; Manufacturing; Personnel/Labor Relations; Sales; Secretarial; Technical. **Positions commonly filled include:** Accountant/Auditor; Clerical Supervisor; Customer Service Representative; Human Resources Specialist; Typist/Word Processor. **Benefits available to temporary workers:** Medical Insurance; Paid Holidays; Paid Vacation. **Corporate headquarters location:** Troy MI. **Other U.S. locations:** Nationwide. **Number of placements per year:** 1000+.

KELLY SERVICES, INC.
211 North Ridgewood Avenue, Suite 202, Daytona Beach FL 32114. 904/255-1661. **Toll-free phone:** 800/775-2060. **Fax:** 904/258-9015. **Contact:** Denise Breneman, Area Branch Manager. **World Wide Web address:** http://www.kellyservices.com. **Description:** A temporary agency that also provides some temp-to-perm placements. **Specializes in the areas of:** Administration; Clerical; Office Support; Retail; Sales; Secretarial; Technical. **Benefits available to temporary workers:** Paid Holidays; Paid Vacation. **Corporate headquarters location:** Troy MI. **Other U.S. locations:** Nationwide. **Average salary range of placements:** Less than $20,000. **Number of placements per year:** 1 - 49.

MANPOWER TEMPORARY SERVICES
10750 North 56th Street, Temple Terrace FL 33617. 813/985-8184. **Contact:** Branch Manager. **World Wide

Web address: http://www.manpower.com. **Description:** A temporary agency. **Specializes in the areas of:** Clerical; Industrial; Personnel/Labor Relations. **Corporate headquarters location:** Milwaukee WI. **Other U.S. locations:** Nationwide.

MANPOWER TEMPORARY SERVICES
4450 West Eau Gallie Boulevard, Suite 104, Melbourne FL 32934. 407/242-2296. **Fax:** 407/242-2217. **Contact:** Jacqueline Cobb, Service Supervisor. **World Wide Web address:** http://www.manpower.com. **Description:** A temporary agency. **Specializes in the areas of:** Engineering; General Management; Publishing. **Positions commonly filled include:** Administrative Manager; Advertising Clerk; Blue-Collar Worker Supervisor; Branch Manager; Buyer; Chemical Engineer; Clerical Supervisor; Electrical/Electronics Engineer; Electrician; Human Resources Specialist; Industrial Engineer; Mechanical Engineer; Public Relations Specialist; Purchasing Agent/Manager; Services Sales Representative; Structural Engineer; Technical Writer/Editor; Typist/Word Processor. **Benefits available to temporary workers:** 401(k); Medical Insurance; Paid Vacation. **Corporate headquarters location:** Milwaukee WI. **Other U.S. locations:** Nationwide. **Average salary range of placements:** Less than $20,000. **Number of placements per year:** 200 - 499.

MANPOWER TEMPORARY SERVICES
5200 West Newberry Road, Suite D6, Gainesville FL 32607. 352/376-5388. **Contact:** Branch Manager. **World Wide Web address:** http://www.manpower.com. **Description:** A temporary agency. **Specializes in the areas of:** Data Processing; Light Industrial; Office Support; Technical; Telemarketing; Word Processing. **Positions commonly filled include:** Accountant/Auditor; Accounting Clerk; Administrative Assistant; Assembler; Biological Scientist; Bookkeeper; Chemist; Computer Operator; Customer Service Representative; Designer; Desktop Publishing Specialist; Electrician; Inspector/Tester/Grader; Inventory Control Specialist; Machine Operator; Material Control Specialist; Packaging/Processing Worker; Painter; Project Engineer; Proofreader; Receptionist; Records Manager; Research Assistant; Secretary; Software Engineer; Stenographer; Stock Clerk; Systems Analyst; Technical Writer/Editor; Technician; Telemarketer; Transcriptionist; Typist/Word Processor. **Benefits available to temporary workers:** Life Insurance; Medical Insurance; Paid Holidays; Paid Vacation. **Corporate headquarters location:** Milwaukee WI. **Other U.S. locations:** Nationwide. **Number of placements per year:** 1000+.

NORRELL SERVICES INC.
966 North Cocoa Boulevard, Suite 4, Cocoa FL 32922. 407/633-8028. **Fax:** 407/633-8038. **Contact:** Employee Service Specialist. **Description:** A temporary agency that also provides some temp-to-perm placements. **Specializes in the areas of:** Accounting/Auditing; Administration; Clerical; Industrial; Sales; Secretarial; Technical. **Positions commonly filled include:** Accountant/Auditor; Blue-Collar Worker Supervisor; Budget Analyst; Clerical Supervisor; Customer Service Representative; Electrician; Human Resources Specialist; Typist/Word Processor. **Benefits available to temporary workers:** Bonus Award/Plan; Daycare Assistance; Medical Insurance. **Corporate headquarters location:** Atlanta GA. **Other U.S. locations:** Nationwide. **Average salary range of placements:** Less than $20,000. **Number of placements per year:** 1000+.

OFFICE OURS
7000 West Palmetto Park Road, Boca Raton FL 33433. 561/392-0202. **Toll-free phone:** 800/925-2955. **Fax:** 561/392-6448. **Contact:** Manager. **Description:** A temporary agency that also provides some temp-to-perm placements. **Specializes in the areas of:** Accounting/ Auditing; Clerical; Legal; Secretarial. **Number of placements per year:** 500 - 999.

OFFICE SPECIALISTS
1270 South Pine Island Road, Plantation FL 33324. 954/437-5074. **Contact:** Recruiter. **Description:** A temporary agency. **Specializes in the areas of:** Accounting/Auditing; Clerical; Finance; Legal; Word Processing. **Other U.S. locations:** Nationwide.

OLSTEN FINANCIAL STAFFING
4890 West Kennedy Boulevard, Suite 810, Tampa FL 33609. 813/282-9050. **Toll-free phone:** 888/222-8693. **Fax:** 813/282-9130. **Contact:** Manager. **World Wide Web address:** http://www.olsten.com/ofs. **Description:** A temporary agency that also offers provides permanent placements and executive search services. Client company pays fee. **Specializes in the areas of:** Accounting; Banking; Finance. **Positions commonly filled include:** Accountant; Auditor; Budget Analyst; Chief Financial Officer; Controller; Credit Manager; Finance Director; Financial Analyst. **Corporate headquarters location:** Melville NY. **Other U.S. locations:** Nationwide. **Average salary range of placements:** $50,000 - $100,000. **Number of placements per year:** 200 - 499.

OLSTEN PROFESSIONAL STAFFING
One North Dale Mabry Highway, Suite 1005, Tampa FL 33609-1845. 813/354-0707. **Contact:** Branch Manager. **World Wide Web address:** http://www.olsten.com. **Description:** A temporary agency that also provides some permanent placements. **Specializes in the areas of:** Accounting/Auditing; Computer Science/Software. **Positions commonly filled include:** Accountant/Auditor; Computer Engineer; Computer Programmer; Multimedia Designer; Systems Analyst. **Benefits available to temporary workers:** Medical Insurance; Paid Vacation. **Corporate headquarters location:** Melville NY. **Other U.S. locations:** Nationwide. **Average salary range of placements:** $20,000 - $29,999.

OLSTEN STAFFING SERVICES
7200 NW 19th Street, Suite 111, Miami FL 33126. 305/358-5053. **Contact:** Recruiter. **World Wide Web address:** http://www.olsten.com. **Description:** A temporary agency. **Specializes in the areas of:** Accounting/Auditing; Banking; Broadcasting; Computer Science/Software; Finance; Health/Medical; Insurance; Legal; Personnel/Labor Relations. **Positions commonly filled include:** Accountant/Auditor; Clerical Supervisor; Computer Programmer; Customer Service Representative; Paralegal; Preschool Worker; Systems Analyst; Typist/Word Processor. **Corporate headquarters location:** Melville NY. **Other U.S. locations:** Nationwide. **Number of placements per year:** 200 - 499.

OLSTEN STAFFING SERVICES
380 North Wickham Road, Suite G, Melbourne FL 32935. 407/255-7777. **Fax:** 407/255-7772. **Contact:** Manager. **World Wide Web address:** http://www. olsten.com. **Description:** A temporary agency that also provides some temp-to-perm placements. **Specializes in the areas of:** Computer Science/Software; Engineering; Legal; Manufacturing; Personnel/Labor Relations; Secretarial; Technical. **Positions commonly filled include:** Administrative Manager; Aerospace Engineer; Brokerage Clerk; Buyer; Civil Engineer; Computer Programmer; Customer Service Representative; Design Engineer; Electrical/Electronics Engineer; Electrician; Human Resources Specialist; Industrial Engineer; Library Technician; MIS Specialist; Multimedia Designer; Operations/Production Manager; Paralegal; Purchasing Agent/Manager; Quality Control Supervisor; Structural Engineer; Systems Analyst; Technical Writer/Editor; Typist/Word Processor. **Benefits available to temporary workers:** Medical Insurance; Paid Vacation. **Corporate headquarters location:** Melville NY. **Other U.S. locations:** Nationwide. **Average salary range of placements:** Less than $20,000. **Number of placements per year:** 1000+.

OLSTEN STAFFING SERVICES
8380 Baymeadows Road, Suite 12, Jacksonville FL 32285. 904/737-2400. **Fax:** 904/636-8802. **Recorded jobline:** 904/355-1500x7266. **Contact:** Manager. **World Wide Web address:** http://www.olsten.com. **Description:** A temporary agency that also provides some permanent placements. **Specializes in the areas of:** Accounting/Auditing; Administration; Computer Science/Software; Finance; Light Industrial; Secretarial; Technical. **Positions commonly filled include:** Accountant/Auditor; Administrative Manager; Budget Analyst; Buyer; Computer Operator; Computer Programmer; Financial Analyst; Human Resources Manager; Paralegal; Systems Analyst. **Benefits available to temporary workers:** Bonus Award/Plan; Medical Insurance; Paid Vacation. **Corporate headquarters location:** Melville NY. **Other U.S. locations:** Nationwide. **Average salary range of placements:** $20,000 - $29,999. **Number of placements per year:** 1000+.

O'QUIN PERSONNEL
P.O. Box 2263, Lakeland FL 33806-2263. 941/687-2336. **Fax:** 941/687-7321. **Contact:** Manager. **Description:** A temporary agency. **Specializes in the areas of:** Accounting/Auditing; Computer Science/Software; Engineering; Marketing; Sales; Secretarial. **Positions commonly filled include:** Accountant/Auditor; Branch Manager; Clerical Supervisor; Clinical Lab Technician; Computer Operator; Computer Programmer; Controller; Customer Service Representative; Design Engineer; Draftsperson; General Manager; Human Resources Manager; Industrial Engineer; Manufacturing Engineer; Marketing Manager; Metallurgical Engineer; Production Manager; Quality Control Supervisor; Sales Manager; Sales Representative; Secretary; Typist/Word Processor. **Average salary range of placements:** Less than $20,000. **Number of placements per year:** 500 - 999.

PRO STAFF
1101 North Lake Destiny Drive, Suite 125, Maitland FL 32751. 407/875-1611. **Fax:** 407/875-1225. **Contact:** Pamie Miller, General Manager. **World Wide Web address:** http://www.prostaff.com. **Description:** A temporary agency that also provides some temp-to-perm placements. Client company pays fee. **Specializes in the areas of:** Accounting/Auditing; Administration; Light Industrial; Secretarial; Technical. **Positions commonly filled include:** Accounting Clerk; Assembler; Collections Agent; Customer Service Representative; Secretary. **Benefits available to temporary workers:** 401(k); Medical Insurance; Paid Holidays; Paid Vacation. **Corporate headquarters location:** Minneapolis MN. **Other U.S. locations:** Nationwide. **Average salary range of placements:** $15,000 - $30,000. **Number of placements per year:** 1000+.

THE RESERVES NETWORK
1813 East Colonial, Orlando FL 32803. 407/228-8080. **Fax:** 407/228-8082. **Contact:** Manager. **Description:** A temporary agency. **Specializes in the areas of:** Administration; Industrial; Secretarial. **Positions commonly filled include:** Accountant/Auditor; Automotive Mechanic; Blue-Collar Worker Supervisor; Buyer; Customer Service Representative; Electrical/Electronics Engineer; Quality Control Supervisor; Typist/Word Processor. **Benefits available to temporary workers:** 401(k); Medical Insurance; Paid Holidays; Paid Vacation. **Corporate headquarters location:** Cleveland OH. **Average salary range of placements:** Less than $20,000. **Number of placements per year:** 100 - 199.

LINDA ROBINS & ASSOCIATES INC.
10647 SW 88th Street, Suite 6C, Miami FL 33176. 305/598-8848. **Fax:** 305/598-9314. **Contact:** Linda Robins, President. **Description:** A temporary agency that also provides some permanent placements. **Specializes in the areas of:** Accounting/Auditing; Banking; Finance; Health/Medical; Insurance; Manufacturing; Secretarial. **Positions commonly filled include:** Administrative Assistant; Credit Manager; Financial Analyst; Human Resources Manager; Typist/Word Processor. **Benefits available to temporary workers:** 401(k); Credit Union; Medical Insurance; Paid Holidays; Paid Vacation. **Average salary range of placements:** $20,000 - $29,999. **Number of placements per year:** 1000+.

SECRETARIES UNLIMITED, INC.
9428 Baymeadows Road, Suite 120, Jacksonville FL 32256. 904/737-7756. **Fax:** 904/731-1856. **Contact:** Elaine Harris, President. **Description:** A temporary agency that also provides some permanent placements. **Specializes in the areas of:** Accounting/Auditing; Secretarial. **Positions commonly filled include:** Administrative Assistant; Computer Programmer; Secretary; Systems Analyst; Typist/Word Processor. **Average salary range of placements:** $20,000 - $50,000. **Number of placements per year:** 200 - 499.

SNELLING PERSONNEL SERVICES
6555 NW Ninth Avenue, Suite 203, Fort Lauderdale FL 33309. 954/771-0090. **Contact:** K. Jerry Philips, Manager/Owner. **World Wide Web address:** http://www.snelling.com. **Description:** A temporary agency. **Specializes in the areas of:** Administration; Sales. **Corporate headquarters location:** Dallas TX. **Other U.S. locations:** Nationwide. **International locations:** Worldwide.

SNELLING PERSONNEL SERVICES
9500 Koger Boulevard, Suite 102, St. Petersburg FL 33702. 727/577-9711. **Fax:** 727/577-1071. **Contact:** Manager. **World Wide Web address:** http://www.snelling.com. **Description:** A temporary agency that also provides some executive search services. **Specializes in the areas of:** Computer Science/Software; Engineering; Manufacturing. **Positions commonly filled include:** Aerospace Engineer; Agricultural Engineer; Aircraft Mechanic/Engine Specialist; Chemical Engineer; Civil Engineer; Computer Programmer; Design Engineer; Designer; Electrical/Electronics Engineer; Industrial Engineer; Industrial Production Manager; Mechanical Engineer; Nuclear Engineer; Software Engineer; Systems Analyst. **Corporate headquarters location:** Dallas TX. **Other U.S. locations:** Nationwide. **International locations:** Worldwide. **Average salary range of placements:** $30,000 - $100,000. **Number of placements per year:** 200 - 499.

SNELLING PERSONNEL SERVICES
2161 Palm Beach Lakes Boulevard, Suite 412, West Palm Beach FL 33409. 561/689-5400. **Fax:** 561/689-5055. **Contact:** Bill Powers, Manager. **World Wide Web address:** http://www.snelling.com. **Description:** A temporary agency. Client company pays fee. **Specializes in the areas of:** Engineering; Health/Medical; Insurance; Marketing; Sales. **Positions commonly filled include:** Account Rep.; Chemical Engineer; Customer Service Rep.; Industrial Engineer; Medical Records Technician; Radiological Technologist; Sales Engineer; Sales Rep.; Ultrasound Technologist; Underwriter/Assistant Underwriter. **Benefits available to temporary workers:** Paid Holidays; Paid Vacation. **Corporate headquarters location:** Dallas TX. **Other U.S. locations:** Nationwide. **International locations:** Worldwide. **Average salary range of placements:** $30,000 - $49,999. **Number of placements per year:** 100 - 199.

SPECIAL COUNSEL
One Independence Drive, Suite 215, Jacksonville FL 32202. 904/737-3436. **Fax:** 904/360-2350. **Contact:** Manager. **World Wide Web address:** http://www. specialcounsel.com. **Description:** A temporary agency that also provides some permanent placements. **Specializes in the areas of:** Legal.

STAFFING NOW
4786 West Commercial Boulevard, Fort Lauderdale FL 33319. 954/735-5392. **Contact:** Nancy Hollins, Manager. **Description:** A temporary agency. **Specializes in the areas of:** Clerical; Manufacturing; Secretarial. **Benefits available to temporary workers:** Medical

Insurance; Paid Holidays; Paid Vacation. **Corporate headquarters location:** Sarasota FL.

STAFFING NOW
4378 Park Boulevard, Pinellas Park FL 33781. 727/541-5704. **Contact:** Manager. **Description:** A temporary agency. **Specializes in the areas of:** Accounting/ Auditing; Personnel/Labor Relations; Secretarial. **Positions commonly filled include:** Clerical Supervisor; Customer Service Representative; Data Entry Clerk; Human Resources Specialist; Medical Records Technician; Receptionist; Typist/Word Processor. **Corporate headquarters location:** Sarasota FL. **Average salary range of placements:** Less than $20,000. **Number of placements per year:** 500 - 999.

STAFFING NOW
2002 North Lois Avenue, Suite 110, Tampa FL 33607. 813/870-3801. **Fax:** 813/870-3959. **Contact:** Jennifer Carter, Branch Manager. **Description:** A temporary agency that also provides some permanent placements. **Specializes in the areas of:** Accounting; Administration; Advertising; Banking; Clerical; Computer Science/ Software; Finance; General Management; Health/ Medical; Industrial; Insurance; Legal; Personnel/Labor Relations; Sales; Secretarial. **Positions commonly filled include:** Accountant/Auditor; Administrative Manager; Advertising Clerk; Bank Officer/Manager; Blue-Collar Worker Supervisor; Bookkeeper; Branch Manager; Brokerage Clerk; Budget Analyst; Buyer; Claim Rep.; Clerical Supervisor; Computer Programmer; Credit Manager; Customer Service Rep.; Education Administrator; Executive Assistant; General Manager; Hotel Manager; Human Resources Specialist; Internet Services Manager; Management Trainee; Manufacturer's/ Wholesaler's Sales Rep.; Medical Records Technician; MIS Specialist; Paralegal; Preschool Worker; Purchasing Agent/Manager; Services Sales Representative; Strategic Relations Manager; Systems Analyst; Typist/Word Processor. **Benefits available to temporary workers:** Bonus Award/Plan; Medical Insurance; Paid Vacation. **Corporate headquarters location:** Sarasota FL. **Number of placements per year:** 500 - 999.

TRC STAFFING SERVICES
9770 Baymeadows Road, Suite 123, Jacksonville FL 32256. 904/641-1665. **Fax:** 904/641-1662. **Contact:** Keith Fairchild, President. **E-mail address:** trcjax@aol.com. **Description:** A temporary agency that also provides some temp-to-perm and permanent placements. **Specializes in the areas of:** Accounting/Auditing; Administration; Architecture/ Construction; Clerical; Computer Science/Software; Engineering; General Management; Insurance; Manufacturing; Nonprofit; Personnel/Labor Relations; Secretarial. **Positions commonly filled include:** Accountant/Auditor; Administrative Manager; Architect; Biomedical Engineer; Blue-Collar Worker Supervisor; Branch Manager; Budget Analyst; Buyer; Civil Engineer; Claim Representative; Clerical Supervisor; Computer Programmer; Cost Estimator; Customer Service Representative; Design Engineer; Draftsperson; Financial Analyst; General Manager; Human Resources Specialist; Industrial Engineer; Landscape Architect;

Management Analyst/Consultant; Management Trainee; Mechanical Engineer; Medical Records Technician; MIS Specialist; Operations/Production Manager; Property and Real Estate Manager; Purchasing Agent/Manager; Quality Control Supervisor; Science Technologist; Software Engineer; Statistician; Systems Analyst; Technical Writer/Editor; Telecommunications Manager; Transportation/Traffic Specialist; Travel Agent; Typist/Word Processor; Underwriter/Assistant Underwriter. **Benefits available to temporary workers:** Medical Insurance; Paid Holidays; Paid Vacation. **Corporate headquarters location:** Atlanta GA. **Other U.S. locations:** Nationwide. **Average salary range of placements:** $20,000 - $29,999. **Number of placements per year:** 200 - 499.

TEMP-ART
P.O. Box 030398, Fort Lauderdale FL 33303-0398. 954/468-5550. **Contact:** Steven Cohen, Owner/ President. **E-mail address:** info@tempart.com. **World Wide Web address:** http://www.tempart.com. **Description:** A temporary agency. **Specializes in the areas of:** Advertising; Art/Design. **Positions commonly filled include:** Art Director; Computer Programmer; Designer; Layout Specialist; Multimedia Designer; Systems Analyst. **Average salary range of placements:** $30,000 - $50,000. **Number of placements per year:** 1000+.

TEMPSOLUTIONS, INC.
5118 North 56th Street, Suite 105, Tampa FL 33610. 813/628-4788. **Fax:** 813/628-4836. **Contact:** Sandy Lachs, President. **Description:** A temporary agency that also provides some temp-to-perm and permanent placements. **Specializes in the areas of:** Administration; Art/Design; Computer Science/Software; Publishing; Technical. **Positions commonly filled include:** Accountant/Auditor; Administrative Manager; Computer Programmer; Customer Service Representative; Draftsperson; Editor; Editorial Assistant; Graphic Artist; Graphic Designer; Human Resources Specialist; MIS Specialist; Multimedia Designer; Paralegal; Public Relations Specialist; Software Engineer; Systems Analyst; Technical Writer/Editor. **Corporate headquarters location:** This Location. **Average salary range of placements:** $30,000 - $50,000. **Number of placements per year:** 100 - 199.

TODAYS TEMPORARY
2300 Maitland Center Parkway, Suite 114, Maitland FL 32751. **Fax:** 407/660-5753. **Contact:** Lea Hampton, Operations Manager. **Description:** A temporary agency. **Specializes in the areas of:** Accounting/Auditing; Clerical; Finance; Insurance; Legal; Personnel/Labor Relations; Secretarial. **Positions commonly filled include:** Administrative Worker/Clerk; Claim Representative; Clerical Supervisor; Customer Service Representative; Medical Records Technician; Paralegal; Purchasing Agent/Manager; Typist/Word Processor. **Benefits available to temporary workers:** Paid Holidays; Paid Vacation. **Corporate headquarters location:** Dallas TX. **Other U.S. locations:** Nationwide. **Average salary range of placements:** Less than $20,000. **Number of placements per year:** 1000+.

CONTRACT SERVICES FIRMS

AR&D QUANTUM RESOURCES
6704-B Plantation Road, Pensacola FL 32504. 850/484-8662. **Fax:** 850/484-8775. **Contact:** Chris Luchsinger, Sales Manager. **E-mail address:** cluchsinger@quantum-res.com. **World Wide Web address:** http://www.quantum-res.com. **Description:** A contract services firm. **Corporate headquarters location:** Richmond VA.

ABLE BODY CORPORATE SERVICES, INC.
30750 US Highway 19 North, Palm Harbor FL 34684. 727/771-1111. **Fax:** 727/786-5835. **Contact:** Chris Mongelluzzi, Vice President. **Description:** A contract services firm. Able Body Corporate Services also

provides some temporary placements. **Specializes in the areas of:** Accounting/Auditing; Administration; Architecture/Construction; Banking; Computer Science/Software; Engineering; Finance; Food; General Labor; General Management; Industrial; Manufacturing; Personnel/Labor Relations; Publishing; Retail; Sales; Secretarial; Technical; Transportation. **Positions commonly filled include:** Administrative Manager; Advertising Clerk; Blue-Collar Worker Supervisor; Branch Manager; Construction Contractor; Construction Manager; Credit Manager; Customer Service Representative; Electrical/Electronics Engineer; General Manager; Hotel Manager; Human Resources Specialist;

Industrial Production Manager; Management Analyst/ Consultant; Management Trainee; Manufacturer's/ Wholesaler's Sales Rep.; Market Research Analyst; Operations/Production Manager; Purchasing Agent/ Manager; Quality Control Supervisor; Services Sales Representative; Typist/Word Processor. **Corporate headquarters location:** This Location. **Other U.S. locations:** AL; NC; TN. **Number of placements per year:** 1000+.

ACADEMY DESIGN & TECHNICAL SERVICES, INC.
1303 North State Road 7, Margate FL 33063. 954/973-7600. **Fax:** 954/973-4890. **Contact:** Roseanne Ambrico, Office Manager. **Description:** A contract services firm. **Specializes in the areas of:** Architecture/Construction; Computer Science/Software; Engineering; Industrial; Manufacturing; Technical. **Positions commonly filled include:** Aerospace Engineer; Architect; Buyer; Chemical Engineer; Civil Engineer; Clinical Lab Technician; Computer Programmer; Construction and Building Inspector; Cost Estimator; Design Engineer; Designer; Draftsperson; Electrical/Electronics Engineer; Environmental Engineer; Geologist/Geophysicist; Industrial Engineer; Industrial Production Manager; Mechanical Engineer; MIS Specialist; Quality Control Supervisor; Software Engineer; Structural Engineer; Surveyor; Systems Analyst; Telecommunications Manager; Transportation/Traffic Specialist. **Benefits available to temporary workers:** Paid Holidays. **Average salary range of placements:** $30,000 - $50,000. **Number of placements per year:** 200 - 499.

ARCUS STAFFING RESOURCES, INC.
777 South Harbour Island Boulevard, Suite 780, Tampa FL 33602. 813/273-9555. **Fax:** 813/273-6469. **Contact:** Ken Vreeland, Branch Manager. **Description:** A contract services firm. **Specializes in the areas of:** Computer Science/Software. **Positions commonly filled include:** Computer Programmer; Internet Services Manager; MIS Specialist; Operations/Production Manager; Software Engineer; Systems Analyst; Technical Writer/Editor; Telecommunications Manager. **Average salary range of placements:** $30,000 - $50,000. **Number of placements per year:** 100 - 199.

B2D TECHNICAL SERVICES
9455 Koger Boulevard, Suite 114, St. Petersburg FL 33702. 727/570-8008. **Fax:** 727/579-4299. **Contact:** Robert Castor, Account Executive. **Description:** A contract services firm. Founded in 1992. **Specializes in the areas of:** Administration; Computer Science/ Software; Design; Engineering; Technical. **Positions commonly filled include:** Aerospace Engineer; Biochemist; Biological Scientist; Biomedical Engineer; Chemical Engineer; Chemist; Civil Engineer; Computer Programmer; Cost Estimator; Design Engineer; Designer; Draftsperson; Editor; Electrical/Electronics Engineer; Industrial Engineer; Industrial Production Manager; Mechanical Engineer; Nuclear Engineer; Operations/ Production Manager; Quality Control Supervisor; Science Technologist; Software Engineer; Structural Engineer; Systems Analyst; Technical Writer/Editor. **Benefits available to temporary workers:** Paid Holidays; Paid Vacation. **Average salary range of placements:** $30,000 - $50,000. **Number of placements per year:** 50 - 99.

CDI CORPORATION
621 NW 53rd Street, Suite 240, Boca Raton FL 33487. 561/995-1443. **Fax:** 561/995-1442. **Contact:** Manager. **World Wide Web address:** http://www.cdicorp.com. **Description:** A contract services firm. **Specializes in the areas of:** Engineering; Technical. **Corporate headquarters location:** Philadelphia PA. **Other U.S. locations:** Nationwide. **International locations:** Worldwide.

COMFORCE
612 North Indiana Avenue, Englewood FL 34223. 941/475-6600. **Fax:** 941/475-5708. **Contact:** Bruce Anderson, President. **Description:** A contract services

and consulting firm. **Specializes in the areas of:** Telecommunications.

COMPUTER EXPRESS INTERNATIONAL
3201 West Commercial Boulevard, Suite 200, Fort Lauderdale FL 33309. 954/730-7500. **Fax:** 954/730-2224. **Contact:** Manager. **Description:** A contract services firm. **Specializes in the areas of:** Computer Science/Software.

CONTRACT HEALTH PROFESSIONALS
7108 Fairway Drive, Suite 290, Palm Beach Gardens FL 33418. 561/624-4334. **Fax:** 800/525-8419. **Contact:** Mort Fishman, Owner. **Description:** A contract services firm. **Specializes in the areas of:** Health/Medical; Pharmaceuticals.

EN-DATA CORPORATION
380 South State Road 434, Suite 1004-272, Altamonte Springs FL 32714. 407/522-6868. **Fax:** 407/522-0944. **Contact:** Virginia Smith, President. **Description:** A contract services firm. **Specializes in the areas of:** Accounting/Auditing; Computer Science/Software; Data Processing; Information Systems. **Positions commonly filled include:** Computer Operator; Computer Programmer; Database Manager; MIS Specialist; Project Manager; Software Engineer; Systems Analyst; Systems Manager. **Corporate headquarters location:** Orlando FL. **Average salary range of placements:** More than $50,000. **Number of placements per year:** 50 - 99.

ENTEGEE
One Independence Drive, Suite 215, Jacksonville FL 32202-5039. 904/396-4100. **Fax:** 904/360-2322. **Contact:** June Griffin, Senior Account Specialist. **E-mail address:** June.Griffin@Entegee.com. **Description:** A contract services firm that also provides some permanent placements. **Specializes in the areas of:** Engineering; Technical.

HALL KINION
3030 North Rocky Point Drive West, Suite 400, Tampa FL 33607. **Toll-free phone:** 800/441-5720. **Fax:** 813/207-0488. **Contact:** Manager. **E-mail address:** taresume@hallkinion.com. **World Wide Web address:** http://www.hallkinion.com. **Description:** A contract services firm that also provides some permanent placements. **Specializes in the areas of:** High-Tech; Information Systems; Information Technology; Internet Development; Quality Assurance; Systems Administration; Systems Design; Technical Writing.

HEADWAY CORPORATE STAFFING SERVICES
14750 NW 77th Court, Room 305, Miami Lakes FL 33016. 305/820-0531. **Fax:** 305/364-0228. **Contact:** Manager. **Description:** A contract services firm. **Average salary range of placements:** $20,000 - $29,999. **Number of placements per year:** 200 - 499.

NOVACARE EMPLOYEE SERVICES
402 43rd Street West, Bradenton FL 34209. 941/746-0004. **Contact:** Manager. **Description:** A contract services firm. **Specializes in the areas of:** Payroll.

STAFF LEASING GROUP
2403 Trade Center Way, Suite 1, Naples FL 34109. 941/513-9300. **Contact:** Richard Foster, Branch Manager. **Description:** A contract services firm. **Specializes in the areas of:** Accounting/Auditing; Sales. **Corporate headquarters location:** Bradenton FL. **Average salary range of placements:** $30,000 - $50,000. **Number of placements per year:** 1 - 49.

STRATEGIC STAFFING SOLUTIONS
5300 West Cypress Street, Suite 190, Tampa FL 33607. 813/288-0808. **Toll-free phone:** 888/695-TEAM. **Fax:** 813/282-1653. **Contact:** Craig Sanne, Recruiting Manager. **E-mail address:** s3tampa@strategicstaff.com. **World Wide Web address:** http://www. strategicstaff.com. **Description:** A contract services firm. **Specializes in the areas of:** Communications; Computer Science/Software; Engineering; Marketing. **Positions**

commonly filled include: Applications Engineer; Computer Animator; Computer Operator; Computer Programmer; Construction Contractor; Consultant; Customer Service Rep.; Internet Services Manager; MIS Specialist; Multimedia Designer; Online Content Specialist; Operations Manager; Project Manager; Quality Control Supervisor; Software Engineer; Systems Analyst; Systems Manager; Technical Writer/Editor; Telecommunications Manager; Webmaster. **Benefits available to temporary workers:** 401(k); Dental Insurance; Disability Coverage; Financial Planning Assistance; Flexible Schedule; Life Insurance; Savings Plan; Telecommuting; Tuition Assistance. **Corporate headquarters location:** Detroit MI.

SYSTEM ONE SERVICES
4902 Eisenhower Boulevard, Suite 370, Tampa FL 33634. 813/249-1757. **Contact:** Recruiter. **E-mail address:** corp@systemone.com. **World Wide Web address:** http://www.systemone.com. **Description:** A contract services firm that also provides temporary and permanent placements. Client company pays fee. **Specializes in the areas of:** Administration; Computer Science/Software; Engineering; Industrial; Information Technology; Technical. **Positions commonly filled include:** Architect; Biochemist; Biological Scientist; Biomedical Engineer; Budget Analyst; Buyer; Chemical Engineer; Chemist; Civil Engineer; Clinical Lab Tech.; Computer Operator; Computer Programmer; Database Manager; Design Engineer; Draftsperson; Electrical/Electronics Engineer; Electrician; Environmental Engineer; Geologist/Geophysicist; Graphic Designer; Human Resources Manager; Industrial Engineer; Industrial Production Manager; Internet Services Manager; Manufacturing Engineer; Market Research Analyst; Mechanical Engineer; Metallurgical Engineer; MIS Specialist; Multimedia Designer; Operations Manager; Pharmacist; Project Manager; Quality Control Supervisor; Sales Engineer; Software Engineer; Systems

Analyst; Systems Manager; Technical Writer/Editor; Telecommunications Manager; Webmaster. **Benefits available to temporary workers:** 401(k); Paid Vacation. **Corporate headquarters location:** This Location. **Other U.S. locations:** Boca Raton FL; Jacksonville FL; Orlando FL; Atlanta GA; Baltimore MD; Charlotte NC; Raleigh NC; Valley Forge PA; Dallas TX. **Average salary range of placements:** $30,000 - $50,000. **Number of placements per year:** 500 - 999.

TECHNISOURCE
1901 West Cypress Creek Road, Suite 202, Fort Lauderdale FL 33309. 954/493-8601. **Contact:** Manager. **Description:** A contract services firm. **Specializes in the areas of:** Technical.

TECHSTAFF
1100 North Florida Avenue, Tampa FL 33602. 813/221-1222. **Fax:** 813/221-6658. **Contact:** Sandy Barret, Recruiter. **World Wide Web address:** http://www.techstaff.com. **Description:** A contract services firm. **Specializes in the areas of:** Architecture/Construction; Computer Science/Software; Engineering; Manufacturing; Technical. **Positions commonly filled include:** Buyer; Ceramics Engineer; Civil Engineer; Computer Programmer; Design Engineer; Designer; Draftsperson; Electrical/Electronics Engineer; Electrician; Environmental Engineer; Industrial Engineer; Industrial Production Manager; Materials Engineer; Mechanical Engineer; Metallurgical Engineer; MIS Specialist; Purchasing Agent/Manager; Software Engineer; Structural Engineer; Systems Analyst; Technical Writer/Editor; Telecommunications Manager. **Benefits available to temporary workers:** Medical Insurance; Paid Holidays; Paid Vacation. **Corporate headquarters location:** Milwaukee WI. **Other U.S. locations:** CA; IA; IL; MI. **Number of placements per year:** 200 - 499.

CAREER/OUTPLACEMENT COUNSELING FIRMS

ADVANCE CAREER PLANNING (ACP)
101 Century 21 Drive, Jacksonville FL 32216. 904/725-3223. **Fax:** 904/725-0879. **Contact:** Libby Sewell, President. **Description:** Provides career counseling and specialized outplacement services.

ALLEN & ASSOCIATES
517 South Lake Destiny Drive, Orlando FL 32810. 407/660-8899. **Toll-free phone:** 800/253-JOBS. **Fax:** 407/661-1294. **Contact:** Branch Manager. **World Wide Web address:** http://www.allenandassociates.com. **Description:** A career/outplacement counseling firm. Founded in 1960. **Corporate headquarters location:** This Location. **Other U.S. locations:** Nationwide.

ALLEN & ASSOCIATES
800 West Cypress Creek Road, Suite 280, Fort Lauderdale FL 33309. 954/772-5600. **Toll-free phone:** 800/562-7705. **Fax:** 954/776-1101. **Contact:** Manager. **World Wide Web address:** http://www.allenandassociates.com. **Description:** A career/outplacement counseling firm. Founded in 1960. **Corporate headquarters location:** Orlando FL. **Other U.S. locations:** Nationwide.

CAREERPRO RESUME & CAREER DEVELOPMENT CENTER, INC.
201 North Federal Highway, Suite 108, Deerfield Beach FL 33441. 954/428-4935. **Fax:** 954/428-0965. **Contact:** G. William Amme, President. **Description:** A career/outplacement counseling and resume writing firm. CareerPro also offers interview skills training and job hunting workshops. **Corporate headquarters location:** This Location. **Other U.S. locations:** Nationwide.

CARRIER'S CAREER SERVICE, INC.
707 Chillingworth Drive, Suite 16, West Palm Beach FL 33409-4124. 561/686-0911. **Fax:** 561/686-7026. **Contact:** Robert Galt, President. **E-mail address:** rbtgalt@aol.com. **Description:** A career counseling and resume writing firm. **Specializes in the areas of:** Accounting/Auditing; Advertising; Banking; Finance; General Management; Health/Medical; Insurance; Marketing; Personnel/Labor Relations; Retail; Sales; Secretarial. **Positions commonly filled include:** Account Manager; Account Representative; Accountant/Auditor; Administrative Assistant; Advertising Executive; Applications Engineer; Bank Officer/Manager; Branch Manager; Budget Analyst; CFO; Counselor; Customer Service Representative; Database Manager; Emergency Medical Technician; Health Services Manager; Hotel Manager; Licensed Practical Nurse; Registered Nurse; Respiratory Therapist; Typist/Word Processor.

CENTER FOR CAREER DECISIONS
6100 Glades Road, Suite 210, Boca Raton FL 33434. 561/470-9333. **Fax:** 561/470-9335. **Contact:** Linda Friedman, M.A., Director. **Description:** A career/outplacement counseling firm. **Specializes in the areas of:** Executives; Professional.

ONE STOP CAREER CENTER
900 SE Central Parkway, Stuart FL 34994. 561/223-2653. **Contact:** Manager. **Description:** A career/outplacement counseling firm. **Number of placements per year:** 100 - 199.

P.H.F. CAREER SERVICES INC.
9900 West Sample Road, Suite 300, Coral Springs FL 33065. 954/344-0004. **Contact:** Paul H. Friedman,

Manager. **Description:** A career/outplacement counseling firm that also offers resume writing services.

PROFESSIONAL RESUME AND BUSINESS WRITING SERVICE
8306 Mills Drive, PMB 192, Miami FL 33183. 305/274-2813. **Fax:** 305/598-8067. **Contact:** Joseph P. Garbin, President. **E-mail address:** proresum@mindspring.com.

World Wide Web address: http://www.jobexchange.com/pr. **Description:** A career/outplacement counseling firm.

RESUMES & MORE
Park Place Offices, 12968 SW 133 Court, Miami FL 33186. 305/232-3432. **Contact:** Tony Molina, Vice President. **Description:** A resume writing firm.

A.D. & ASSOCIATES EXECUTIVE SEARCH INC.
5589 Woodsong Drive, Suite 100, Dunwoody GA
30338-2933. 770/393-0021. **Fax:** 770/393-9060.
Contact: A. Dwight Hawksworth, President. **E-mail
address:** hawks@mindspring.com. **Description:** An
executive search firm that operates on both retainer and
contingency bases. **Specializes in the areas of:**
Accounting/Auditing; Administration; Engineering;
Finance; General Management; Sales; Technical.
Positions commonly filled include: Account Manager;
Account Representative; Accountant; Attorney; Auditor;
Chief Financial Officer; Controller; Finance Director;
Financial Analyst; General Manager; Human Resources
Manager; Management Analyst/Consultant; Marketing
Manager; Sales Executive; Sales Manager; Sales
Representative; Systems Analyst; Telecommunications
Manager; Vice President. **Corporate headquarters
location:** This Location. **Average salary range of
placements:** More than $50,000. **Number of
placements per year:** 1 - 49.

ABLEST
3761 Venture Drive, Suite 170, Duluth GA 30136-5528.
770/418-1051. **Fax:** 770/476-2871. **Contact:** Manager.
Description: An executive search firm. **Specializes in
the areas of:** Computer Science/Software. **Positions
commonly filled include:** AS400 Programmer Analyst;
Computer Operator; Computer Programmer; Database
Administrator; Database Manager; MIS Specialist;
Network/Systems Administrator; Software Engineer;
SQL Programmer; Systems Analyst; Systems Manager;
Webmaster. **Benefits available to temporary workers:**
Medical Insurance. **Average salary range of
placements:** More than $50,000. **Number of
placements per year:** 100 - 199.

ACCOUNTANTS & BOOKKEEPERS PERSONNEL
1841 Montreal Road, Suite 212, Tucker GA 30084.
770/938-7730. **Contact:** Manager. **Description:** An
executive search firm. **Specializes in the areas of:**
Accounting/Auditing; Finance.

**ACCOUNTANTS EXECUTIVE SEARCH
ACCOUNTANTS ON CALL**
3355 Lenox Road, Suite 530, Atlanta GA 30326.
404/261-4800. **Contact:** Area Vice President.
Description: An executive search firm. Accountants On
Call (also at this location) is a temporary agency.
Specializes in the areas of: Accounting/Auditing;
Finance. **Positions commonly filled include:**
Accountant/Auditor; Budget Analyst; Credit Manager;
Financial Analyst. **Benefits available to temporary
workers:** Medical Insurance; Paid Vacation; Referral
Bonus Plan. **Corporate headquarters location:** Saddle
Brook NJ. **Other U.S. locations:** Nationwide. **Average
salary range of placements:** More than $50,000.
Number of placements per year: 100 - 199.

AGRI-ASSOCIATES
895-B McFarland Road, Alpharetta GA 30004. 770/475-
2201. **Fax:** 770/475-1136. **Contact:** Michael T. Deel,
Manager. **Description:** An executive search firm
operating on both retainer and contingency bases.
Specializes in the areas of: Agri-Business; Food.
Positions commonly filled include: Account Manager;
Account Rep.; Accountant; Administrative Assistant;
Administrative Manager; Advertising Executive;
Assistant Manager; Buyer; Chemical Engineer; Chief
Financial Officer; Controller; Credit Manager; Customer
Service Representative; Design Engineer; Editor;
Environmental Engineer; Food Scientist; General
Manager; Human Resources Manager; Managing Editor;
Marketing Manager; Marketing Specialist; Mechanical
Engineer; Operations Manager; Production Manager;
Project Manager; Purchasing Agent; Quality Assurance
Engineer; Quality Control Supervisor; Sales Engineer;

Sales Executive; Sales Manager; Sales Rep.; Technical
Writer Transportation/Traffic Specialist.

MICHAEL ALEXANDER GROUP, INC.
301 Millbrook Farm Court, Marietta GA 30068.
770/321-1600. **Contact:** Al Shulhan, President.
Description: An executive search firm operating on a
contingency basis. **Specializes in the areas of:**
Accounting/Auditing; Banking; Finance. **Positions
commonly filled include:** Accountant; Auditor; Budget
Analyst; Chief Financial Officer; Controller; Cost
Estimator; Credit Manager; Economist; Finance Director;
Financial Analyst; Fund Manager; General Manager;
Management Analyst; MIS Specialist; Systems Analyst.

ANDERSON INDUSTRIAL ASSOCIATES, INC.
P.O. Box 2266, Cumming GA 30040. 770/844-9027.
Fax: 770/844-9656. **Contact:** Greg Anderson, President.
E-mail address: aia@atl.mindspring.com. **Description:**
Anderson Industrial Associates, Inc. is an executive
search firm that also provides some temporary
placements. **Specializes in the areas of:** Engineering;
Industrial; Manufacturing; Technical. **Positions
commonly filled include:** Aerospace Engineer;
Biomedical Engineer; Chemical Engineer; Chemist; Civil
Engineer; Design Engineer; Draftsperson;
Electrical/Electronics Engineer; Environmental Engineer;
Industrial Engineer; Mechanical Engineer; Metallurgical
Engineer; Mining Engineer; Purchasing Agent/Manager;
Quality Control Supervisor; Structural Engineer.
Average salary range of placements: More than
$50,000. **Number of placements per year:** 1 - 49.

APEX SYSTEMS INC.
41 Perimeter Center East, Suite 399, Atlanta GA 30346.
770/481-0044. **Contact:** Manager. **Description:** An
executive search firm. **Specializes in the areas of:**
Computer Hardware/Software; Data Processing;
Technical.

ARJAY & ASSOCIATES
4546 Atlanta Highway, Suite 112, Loganville GA 30052.
770/554-2300. **Fax:** 770/985-7696. **Contact:** David L.
Hubert, Director of Operations. **Description:** An
executive search firm. **Specializes in the areas of:**
Computer Science/Software; Engineering; Industrial;
Manufacturing. **Positions commonly filled include:**
Applications Engineer; Computer Programmer; Design
Engineer; EKG Technician; Industrial Engineer;
Mechanical Engineer; Metallurgical Engineer; Mining
Engineer; Nuclear Engineer; Quality Control Supervisor;
Sales Engineer; Software Engineer; Systems Analyst.
Average salary range of placements: More than
$50,000. **Number of placements per year:** 1 - 49.

ASHFORD MANAGEMENT GROUP
2295 Parklake Drive NE, Suite 425, Atlanta GA 30345.
770/938-6260. **Contact:** Manager. **Description:** An
executive search firm. **Specializes in the areas of:**
Retail.

ASK GUY TUCKER
4990 High Point Road NE, Atlanta GA 30342. 404/303-
7177. **Fax:** 404/303-0136. **Contact:** Manager.
Description: An executive search firm.

B.A. ASSOCIATES INC.
5881 Glenridge Drive, Suite 100, Atlanta GA 30328.
404/843-2955. **Fax:** 404/843-0874. **Contact:** Bob Allen,
President. **Description:** An executive search firm.
Specializes in the areas of: Executives; High-Tech;
Industrial; Management.

BARRINGTON ASSOCIATES LIMITED
3949 Holcomb Bridge Road, Suite 202, Norcross GA
30092. 770/447-0100. **Contact:** Manager. **Description:**
An executive search firm.

BASILONE-OLIVER EXECUTIVE SEARCH
1080 Holcomb Bridge Road, Building 200, Suite 130, Roswell GA 30076. 770/649-0553. **Fax:** 770/649-0565. **Contact:** Manager. **World Wide Web address:** http://www.basilone-oliver.com. **Description:** An executive search firm. **Specializes in the areas of:** Accounting; Finance. **Other U.S. locations:** Pittsburgh PA.

BELL OAKS COMPANY
10 Glenlake Parkway, Suite 300, Atlanta GA 30328. 678/287-2000. **Fax:** 678/287-2001. **Contact:** Manager. **World Wide Web address:** http://www.belloaks.com. **Description:** An executive search firm. **Specializes in the areas of:** Accounting; Chemistry; Engineering; Executives; Finance; General Management; Human Resources; Information Technology; Manufacturing; Marketing; Operations Management; Purchasing; Quality Assurance; Sales; Telecommunications.

BLACKSHAW OLMSTEAD LYNCH KOENIG
3414 Peachtree Road NE, Suite 1010, Atlanta GA 30326. 404/261-7770. **Contact:** Manager. **Description:** An executive search firm.

BOREHAM INTERNATIONAL
275 Carpenter Drive, Suite 309, Atlanta GA 30328. 404/252-2199. **Fax:** 404/851-9157. **Contact:** Mili Boreham, President. **Description:** An executive search firm that places professionals in office support, middle management, and senior-level executive positions. **Specializes in the areas of:** Accounting/Auditing; Administration; Computer Science/Software; Food; General Management; Import/Export; International Executives; Personnel/Labor Relations; Retail; Sales; Secretarial; Transportation. **Positions commonly filled include:** Accountant/Auditor; Administrative Manager; Claim Rep.; Clerical Supervisor; Credit Manager; Customer Service Representative; General Manager; Human Resources Manager; Marketing Specialist; MIS Specialist; Services Sales Representative; Software Engineer; Transportation/Traffic Specialist; Typist/Word Processor. **Number of placements per year:** 1 - 49.

THE BOWERS GROUP, INC.
BRADSHAW & ASSOCIATES
1850 Parkway Place, Suite 420, Marietta GA 30067-4439. 770/421-1019. **Fax:** 770/509-1095. **Contact:** Brenda Bowers, President. **E-mail address:** jobs@bowersgroup.com. **World Wide Web address:** http://www.bowersgroup.com. **Description:** An executive search firm. Bradshaw & Associates (also at this location) is an executive search firm operating on both retainer and contingency bases. NOTE: Resumes for Bradshaw & Associates should be put to the attention of Rod Bradshaw, President. **Specializes in the areas of:** Accounting/Auditing; Biotechnology; Chemicals; Computer Hardware/Software; Computer Science/Software; Data Processing; Finance; MIS/EDP. **Positions commonly filled include:** Accountant/Auditor; Aerospace Engineer; Agricultural Engineer; Applications Engineer; Architect; AS400 Programmer Analyst; Bank Officer/Manager; Biochemist; Biological Scientist; Budget Analyst; Chemical Engineer; Chemist; Civil Engineer; Computer Programmer; Construction and Building Inspector; Construction Contractor; Design Engineer; Electrical/Electronics Engineer; Environmental Engineer; Financial Analyst; General Manager; Geographer; Geologist/Geophysicist; Health Services Manager; Human Resources Manager; Industrial Engineer; Internet Services Manager; Management Analyst/Consultant; Management Trainee; Manufacturer's/Wholesaler's Sales Rep.; Mathematician; Mechanical Engineer; Metallurgical Engineer; Mining Engineer; MIS Specialist; Nuclear Engineer; Operations/Production Manager; Petroleum Engineer; Pharmacist; Physical Therapist; Physician; Project Manager; Public Relations Specialist; Quality Control Supervisor; Registered Nurse; Respiratory Therapist; Securities Sales Representative; Services Sales Representative; Software Engineer; Statistician; Strategic Relations Manager; Structural Engineer; Surgical Technician; Systems Analyst; Systems Manager; Telecommunications Manager; Transportation/Traffic Specialist. **Average salary range of placements:** $50,000 - $100,000. **Number of placements per year:** 50 - 99.

THE BRADY GROUP, INC.
4129 Gregory Manor Circle, Smyrna GA 30082. 770/819-8532. **Contact:** Manager. **World Wide Web address:** http://www.bradygroup.net. **Description:** An executive search firm. **Specializes in the areas of:** High-Tech.

BRIDGERS & ASSOCIATES
100 River Hollow Court, Duluth GA 30097. 770/368-9835. **Fax:** 770/368-0822. **Contact:** President. **Description:** An executive search firm. **Specializes in the areas of:** Insurance. **Number of placements per year:** 1 - 49.

BROWARD-DOBBS INC.
1532 Dunwoody Village Parkway, Suite 200, Atlanta GA 30338. 770/399-0744. **Fax:** 770/395-6881. **Contact:** Luke Greene, President. **Description:** An executive search firm. **Specializes in the areas of:** Engineering. **Positions commonly filled include:** Architect; Chemical Engineer; Civil Engineer; Designer; Draftsperson; Electrical/Electronics Engineer; Industrial Engineer; Mechanical Engineer; Nuclear Engineer; Software Engineer; Stationary Engineer; Structural Engineer. **Average salary range of placements:** More than $50,000. **Number of placements per year:** 50 - 99.

CAMERON BROWN & ASSOCIATES
1254 Concord Road SE, Smyrna GA 30080. 770/437-8553. **Contact:** Manager. **Description:** An executive search firm.

CEO
6045 Atlantic Boulevard, Norcross GA 30071. 770/662-1560. **Contact:** Manager. **Description:** An executive search firm.

CMS PERSONNEL SERVICES
102 West Meadow Street, Vidalia GA 30474. 912/537-2825. **Fax:** 912/537-6945. **Contact:** Virginia Scott, Owner. **Description:** An executive search firm that also provides some temporary placements.

R.A. CLARK CONSULTING
5 Concourse Parkway, Suite 3100, Atlanta GA 30328. 404/982-0495. **Toll-free phone:** 800/251-0041. **Fax:** 404/982-0499. **Contact:** Richard Clark, President. **E-mail address:** raclarkhrs@aol.com. **World Wide Web address:** http://www.raclark.com. **Description:** An executive search firm. NOTE: This firm prefers faxed resumes. **Specializes in the areas of:** Human Resources; Personnel/Labor Relations. **Positions commonly filled include:** Human Resources Manager; Management Analyst/Consultant. **Average salary range of placements:** More than $50,000. **Number of placements per year:** 50 - 99.

COMFORCE BRANNON & TULLY
5445 Triangle Parkway, Suite 325, Norcross GA 30092. 770/447-8773. **Contact:** Manager. **Description:** An executive search firm. **Specializes in the areas of:** Information Technology.

COMMONWEALTH CONSULTANTS
5064 Roswell Road, Suite B-101, Atlanta GA 30342. 404/256-0000. **Contact:** Manager. **Description:** An executive search firm. **Specializes in the areas of:** Computer Science/Software; Sales.

COMPREHENSIVE SEARCH GROUP
316 South Lewis Street, LaGrange GA 30240. 706/884-3232. **Fax:** 706/884-4106. **Contact:** Ms. Merritt Shelton, Researcher/Database Manager. **E-mail address:** databank@comp-search.com. **Description:** An executive search firm. **Specializes in the areas of:** Administration; Advertising; Architecture/Construction; Art/Design;

Computer Science/Software; Industrial; Manufacturing; Retail; Sales. **Positions commonly filled include:** Administrative Manager; Architect; Computer Programmer; Construction and Building Inspector; Construction Contractor; Design Engineer; Designer; Draftsperson; Industrial Engineer; Industrial Production Manager; Internet Services Manager; Management Trainee; Manufacturer's/Wholesaler's Sales Rep.; MIS Specialist; Services Sales Representative; Software Engineer; Systems Analyst. **Corporate headquarters location:** Atlanta GA. **Other U.S. locations:** Brooklyn NY; New York NY. **Average salary range of placements:** More than $50,000. **Number of placements per year:** 50 - 99.

COMPUTER SEARCH ASSOCIATES

P.O. Box 8403, Atlanta GA 31106. 404/231-0965. **Contact:** Manager. **Description:** Computer Search Associates is an executive search firm. **Specializes in the areas of:** Computer Programming; Computer Science/Software.

COMPUTER TECHNOLOGY SEARCH

DATA MANAGEMENT & STAFF RECRUITERS

3490 Piedmont Road, Suite 310, Atlanta GA 30305. 404/233-6780. **Contact:** Manager. **E-mail address:** opportunities@ctscareers.com. **World Wide Web address:** http://www.ctscareers.com. **Description:** An executive search firm. Computer Technology Search is a division of MAGIC (Management Alliance Group of Independent Companies). Data Management & Staff Recruiters (also at this location, 404/233-0925, http://www.dmsr.com) is an executive search firm. **Specializes in the areas of:** Computer Science/Software; Information Technology. **Corporate headquarters location:** Dallas TX. **Other U.S. locations:** Los Angeles CA; Chicago IL; Kansas City KS.

CORPORATE IMAGE GROUP

P.O. Box 669516, Marietta GA 30066-0109. 770/924-9432. **Fax:** 770/728-8704. **Contact:** Manager. **World Wide Web address:** http://www.corpimg.com. **Description:** A full-service executive search firm. **Specializes in the areas of:** Accounting; Auditing; Distribution; Engineering; Finance; Health/Medical; Human Resources; Insurance; Manufacturing; Marketing; Sales. **Corporate headquarters location:** Memphis TN.

CORPORATE RESOURCES, INC.

11285 Elkins Road, Suite L-3, Roswell GA 30076. 770/442-1030. **Fax:** 770/442-1034. **Contact:** Branch Manager. **E-mail address:** corpresources@ mindspring.com. **Description:** Corporate Resources, Inc. is an executive search firm operating on both retainer and contingency bases. **Specializes in the areas of:** Telecommunications. **Positions commonly filled include:** Account Manager; Account Representative; Accountant; Advertising Executive; Branch Manager; Chief Financial Officer; Controller; Customer Service Representative; Economist; Finance Director; General Manager; Human Resources Manager; Management Analyst/Consultant; Market Research Analyst; Marketing Manager; Network/Systems Administrator; Purchasing Agent/Manager; Sales Engineer; Sales Executive; Sales Manager; Sales Representative. **Corporate headquarters location:** This Location. **Average salary range of placements:** $50,000 - $100,000. **Number of placements per year:** 100 - 199.

CORPORATE SEARCH CONSULTANTS

47 Perimeter Center East, Suite 260, Atlanta GA 30346-2001. 770/399-6205. **Fax:** 770/399-6416. **Contact:** Harriet Rothberg, President. **World Wide Web address:** http://www.rothberg.com. **Description:** An executive search firm operating on a retainer basis. **Specializes in the areas of:** Accounting/Auditing; Administration; Architecture/Construction; Computer Science/Software; Engineering; Finance; General Management; Health/Medical; Industrial; Manufacturing; Personnel/ Labor Relations; Sales; Secretarial; Technical. **Positions commonly filled include:** Accountant/Auditor; Administrative Manager; Architect; Blue-Collar Worker Supervisor; Branch Manager; Budget Analyst; Buyer; Civil Engineer; Clerical Supervisor; Clinical Lab Technician; Computer Programmer; Construction and Building Inspector; Construction Contractor; Cost Estimator; Credit Manager; Customer Service Representative; Design Engineer; Designer; Draftsperson; Electrical/Electronics Engineer; Environmental Engineer; Financial Analyst; General Manager; Health Services Manager; Landscape Architect; Librarian; Management Analyst/Consultant; Management Trainee; Manufacturer's/Wholesaler's Sales Rep.; Market Research Analyst; Mechanical Engineer; Medical Records Technician; Metallurgical Engineer; MIS Specialist; Multimedia Designer; Occupational Therapist; Operations/Production Manager; Physical Therapist; Physician; Physician Assistant; Purchasing Agent/Manager; Quality Control Supervisor; Respiratory Therapist; Services Sales Representative; Software Engineer; Speech-Language Pathologist; Structural Engineer; Systems Analyst; Technical Writer/Editor; Telecommunications Manager; Transportation/Traffic Specialist; Typist/Word Processor. **Average salary range of placements:** $30,000 - $50,000. **Number of placements per year:** 1000+.

CREATIVE HUMAN RESOURCES SOLUTIONS

P.O. Box 1966, Stone Mountain GA 30086. 404/508-2093. **Fax:** 404/508-3454. **Contact:** Manager. **Description:** Creative Human Resources Solutions is an executive search firm. **Positions commonly filled include:** IT Specialist. **Office hours:** Monday - Friday, 8:30 a.m. - 6:00 p.m.

CREATIVE SEARCH

887 West Marietta Street, Studio N-109, Atlanta GA 30318. 404/892-7475. **Contact:** Manager. **Description:** An executive search firm. **Specializes in the areas of:** Advertising.

DSA

501 Village Trace, Building 9, Marietta GA 30067. 770/850-0250. **Fax:** 770/850-9295. **Contact:** Manager. **E-mail address:** dsa@mindspring.com. **World Wide Web address:** http://www.mindspring.com/~dsa/. **Description:** An executive search firm. **Specializes in the areas of:** Food; Hotel/Restaurant. **Number of placements per year:** 100 - 199.

DATA PROCESSING SERVICES, INC.

5855 Jimmy Carter Boulevard, Suite 260, Norcross GA 30071. 770/368-1300. **Contact:** Manager. **Description:** Data Processing Services, Inc. Is an executive search firm. **Specializes in the areas of:** Data Processing; Technical.

DELTA RESOURCE GROUP

P.O. Box 672642, Marietta GA 30006. **Physical address:** 720 Old Town, Marietta GA 30068. 770/579-8702. **Fax:** 770/579-8816. **Contact:** Manager. **E-mail address:** theheadhunter@mindspring.com. **Description:** Delta Resource Group is an executive search firm. **Specializes in the areas of:** Data Communications; Information Technology; Telecommunications.

THE DIVERSIFIED SEARCH COMPANIES

3575 Piedmont Road, Suite 300, 15 Piedmont Center, Atlanta GA 30305. 404/262-1049. **Fax:** 404/262-1096. **Contact:** Manager. **World Wide Web address:** http://www.divsearch.com. **Description:** The Diversified Search Companies is an executive search firm. **Specializes in the areas of:** Consulting; Finance; Health/Medical; Nonprofit; Professional. **Corporate headquarters location:** Philadelphia PA. **Other U.S. locations:** Boston MA; Charlotte NC.

DUNHILL PROFESSIONAL SEARCH

3348 Peachtree Road NE, Suite 150, Atlanta GA 30326. 404/261-3751. **Fax:** 404/237-8361. **Contact:** Recruiter.

World Wide Web address: http://www.
dunhillstaff.com. **Description:** An executive search firm.
Specializes in the areas of: Accounting/Auditing;
Computer Hardware/Software; Finance; Health/Medical;
Marketing; Sales. **Positions commonly filled include:**
Accountant; Auditor; Chief Financial Officer; Controller;
Financial Analyst; Human Resources Manager; Sales
Executive; Sales Manager; Sales Representative.
Corporate headquarters location: Hauppauge NY.
Other U.S. locations: Nationwide. **Average salary
range of placements:** $30,000 - $50,000. **Number of
placements per year:** 50 - 99.

DUNHILL PROFESSIONAL SEARCH
2110 Powers Ferry Road, Suite 110, Atlanta GA 30339.
770/952-0009. **Fax:** 770/952-9422. **Contact:** Jon Harvill,
CPC/President. **E-mail address:** dswatlga@
mindspring.com. **World Wide Web address:**
http://www.dunhillstaff.com. **Description:** An executive
search firm operating on both retainer and contingency
bases. **Specializes in the areas of:** Engineering; Food;
Manufacturing; Personnel/Labor Relations; Technical;
Transportation. **Positions commonly filled include:**
Biomedical Engineer; Buyer; Chemical Engineer; Design
Engineer; Designer; Electrical/Electronics Engineer;
Environmental Engineer; Human Resources Manager;
Industrial Engineer; Industrial Production Manager;
Mechanical Engineer; Metallurgical Engineer;
Operations/Production Manager; Purchasing Agent/
Manager; Quality Control Supervisor; Statistician;
Transportation/Traffic Specialist. **Other U.S. locations:**
Nationwide. **Average salary range of placements:**
More than $50,000. **Number of placements per year:** 1
- 49.

EASTMAN & BEAUDINE, INC.
One Ravinia Drive, Suite 1110, Atlanta GA 30346.
770/390-0801. **Fax:** 770/390-0875. **Contact:** Branch
Manager. **E-mail address:** Beaudine@tripod.net. **World
Wide Web address:** http://members.tripod.
com/~Beaudine/index.html. **Description:** A senior-level,
generalist executive search firm that works on a retainer
basis.

BRUCE EIDE & ASSOCIATES INC.
256 Woods Edge Court, Marietta GA 30068. 770/977-
5800. **Contact:** Bruce Eide, President. **Description:** An
executive search firm.

ELITE MEDICAL SEARCH
100 Crescent Center Parkway, Suite 360, Tucker GA
30084-7039. **Toll-free phone:** 800/849-5502. **Fax:**
770/908-2203. **Contact:** David Alexander, President. **E-
mail address:** elite@elitesearch.com. **Description:** An
executive search firm that specializes in placing mid- to
upper-level hospital and biomedical personnel. Client
company pays fee. **Specializes in the areas of:**
Engineering; Health/Medical. **Positions commonly filled
include:** Biological Scientist; Biomedical Engineer;
Chemical Engineer; Chemist; Clinical Lab Technician;
Dietician/Nutritionist; Mechanical Engineer; Medical
Records Technician; Nuclear Medicine Technologist;
Occupational Therapist; Pharmacist; Physical Therapist;
Physician; Physician Assistant; Physicist; Psychologist;
Quality Control Supervisor; Radiological Technologist;
Recreational Therapist; Registered Nurse; Respiratory
Therapist; Surgical Technician. **Corporate
headquarters location:** This Location. **Other U.S.
locations:** Tallahassee FL. **Average salary range of
placements:** More than $50,000. **Number of
placements per year:** 200 - 499.

ELLIOT ASSOCIATES
131 Roswell Street, Suite B2-2, Alpharetta GA 30004.
770/664-5354. **Fax:** 770/664-0233. **Contact:** Joan Ray,
Senior Vice President. **E-mail address:**
jray@theelliotgroup.com. **World Wide Web address:**
http://www.elliotgroup.com. **Description:** An executive
search firm operating on both retainer and contingency
bases. **Specializes in the areas of:** Hotel/Restaurant.
Positions commonly filled include: Chief Financial
Officer; Controller; General Manager; Human Resources

Manager; Market Research Analyst; Marketing Manager;
Public Relations Specialist; Purchasing Agent/Manager;
Restaurant/Food Service Manager. **Corporate
headquarters location:** Tarrytown NY. **Other U.S.
locations:** AZ; OH; PA; TX. **Average salary range of
placements:** More than $50,000. **Number of
placements per year:** 50 - 99.

EMERGING TECHNOLOGY SEARCH, INC.
1080 Holcomb Bridge Road, Building 200, Suite 305,
Roswell GA 30076. 770/643-4994. **Toll-free phone:**
888/NOW4ETS. **Fax:** 770/643-4991. **Contact:** Manager.
World Wide Web address: http://www.emergingtech.
com. **Description:** An executive search firm. **Specializes
in the areas of:** Software Engineering. **Positions
commonly filled include:** Communications Engineer;
Database Specialist; Network Engineer; Software
Engineer.

EXECU SEARCH
4405 Mall Boulevard, Suite 330, Union City GA 30291.
770/969-8781. **Fax:** 770/969-1259. **Contact:** Manager.
Description: An executive search firm.

EXECUTIVE RESOURCE GROUP
127 Peachtree Street, Suite 922, Atlanta GA 30303.
404/522-0888. **Fax:** 404/522-1354. **Contact:** Robert
Pauley, Managing Director. **Description:** An executive
search firm operating on both retainer and contingency
bases. **Specializes in the areas of:** Finance;
Health/Medical; Insurance. **Positions commonly filled
include:** Chief Executive Officer; Chief Financial
Officer; Financial Analyst; Health Services Manager;
Management Analyst/Consultant; Marketing Manager;
Sales Executive; Sales Manager; Systems Manager.
Average salary range of placements: More than
$50,000. **Number of placements per year:** 50 - 99.

EXECUTIVE RESOURCE GROUP
2470 Windy Hill Road, Marietta GA 30067. 770/955-
1811. **Contact:** Dave Balunas, Manager. **Description:**
An executive search firm.

**EXECUTIVE SEARCH & PERSONNEL
STAFFING**
415 East Walnut Avenue, Dalton GA 30720. 706/272-
4103. **Fax:** 706/226-7785. **Contact:** Nancy Hampton,
President. **Description:** An executive search firm
operating on both retainer and contingency bases.
Specializes in the areas of: Textiles. **Positions
commonly filled include:** Accountant/Auditor;
Administrative Assistant; Administrative Manager; Chief
Financial Officer; Clerical Supervisor; Computer
Operator; Computer Programmer; Controller; Customer
Service Representative; Design Engineer; Draftsperson;
Electrical/Electronics Engineer; Finance Director;
Graphic Artist; Human Resources Manager; Industrial
Engineer; Manufacturing Engineer; Marketing Manager;
Production Manager; Quality Control Supervisor; Sales
Executive; Sales Representative; Typist/Word Processor.
Number of placements per year: 200 - 499.

EXECUTIVE SOURCE INTERNATIONAL
3340 Peachtree Road NE, Suite 790, Atlanta GA 30326.
404/262-2952. **Contact:** Manager. **Description:** An
executive search firm.

EXECUTIVE STRATEGIES, INC.
11205 Alpharetta Highway, Suite C-1, Roswell GA
30075. 770/552-3085. **Fax:** 770/552-1043. **Contact:**
Manager. **E-mail address:** esi@esisearch.com. **World
Wide Web address:** http://www.esisearch.com.
Description: An executive search firm. **Specializes in
the areas of:** Consulting; General Management;
Health/Medical; Human Resources; Information
Technology; Network Administration; Nuclear Power;
Retail; Systems Administration; Systems Programming;
Telecommunications; Travel.

FELLOWS STUDENTS ASSOCIATES (FSA, INC.)
707 Whitlock Avenue, Marietta GA 30064. 770/427-
8813. **Fax:** 770/427-8835. **Contact:** Recruiter. **World**

Wide Web address: http://www.fsasearch.com. **Description:** An executive search firm. **Specializes in the areas of:** Insurance. **Positions commonly filled include:** Actuary.

F-O-R-T-U-N-E PERSONNEL CONSULTANTS
7 East Congress Street, Suite 712, Savannah GA 31401. 912/233-4556. **Fax:** 912/233-8633. **Contact:** Manager. **E-mail address:** savannah@fpcweb.com. **Description:** An executive search firm. **Positions commonly filled include:** Human Resources Manager; Industrial Engineer; Maintenance Technician; Manufacturing Engineer; Manufacturing Manager; Materials Manager; Operations Manager; Plant Engineer; Purchasing Agent/Manager; Quality Assurance Engineer; Quality Control Supervisor. **Corporate headquarters location:** New York NY.

F-O-R-T-U-N-E PERSONNEL CONSULTANTS OF ATLANTA
ALTERNASTAFF
6525 The Corners Parkway, Suite 216, Norcross GA 30092. 770/246-9757. **Fax:** 770/246-0526. **Contact:** James M. Deavours, President. **E-mail address:** search@fpccareers.com. **World Wide Web address:** http://www.fpccareers.com. **Description:** An executive search firm operating nationwide on both retainer and contingency bases. Alternastaff (also at this location) is a contract services firm. Client company pays fee. **Specializes in the areas of:** Biology; Chemicals; Electronics; Engineering; Food; Industrial; Manufacturing; Medical Devices; Pharmaceuticals; Plastics; Quality Assurance; Regulatory Affairs; Research and Development. **Positions commonly filled include:** Applications Engineer; Biochemist; Biological Scientist; Biomedical Engineer; Ceramics Engineer; Chemical Engineer; Chemist; Civil Engineer; Design Engineer; Electrical/Electronics Engineer; Environmental Engineer; Food Scientist/Technologist; Industrial Designer; Industrial Engineer; Industrial Production Manager; Maintenance Supervisor; Manufacturing Engineer; Mechanical Engineer; Metallurgical Engineer; MIS Specialist; Operations Manager; Production Manager; Project Manager; Purchasing Agent/Manager; Quality Control Supervisor; Software Engineer; Statistician; Systems Analyst; Systems Manager; Telecommunications Manager. **Average salary range of placements:** More than $50,000. **Number of placements per year:** 50 - 99.

FOX-MORRIS ASSOCIATES
1140 Hammond Drive, Suite I-9250, Atlanta GA 30328. 770/399-4497. **Fax:** 770/399-4499. **Contact:** Robert Smith, Branch Manager. **Description:** An executive search firm. **Specializes in the areas of:** Accounting/Auditing; Computer Hardware/Software; Engineering; Finance; Manufacturing; MIS/EDP; Personnel/Labor Relations; Sales. **Number of placements per year:** 1000+.

THE GATEKEEPERS INTERNATIONAL
2964 Peachtree Road Northwest, Suite 400, Atlanta GA 30305. 800/273-7388. **Fax:** 800/218-7201. **Contact:** Manager. **E-mail address:** register@thegatekeepers.com. **World Wide Web address:** http://www.thegatekeepers.com. **Description:** An executive search firm. **Specializes in the areas of:** Information Technology.

H&A CONSULTING
420 Marketplace, Roswell GA 30075. 770/998-0099. **Fax:** 770/993-7406. **Contact:** Ellen Howie-Brown, President. **E-mail address:** howieinc@ik.netcom.com. **Description:** An executive search firm operating on a contingency basis. **Specializes in the areas of:** Computer Science/Software; Data Processing. **Positions commonly filled include:** Computer Programmer; Internet Services Manager; Software Engineer; Systems Analyst; Technical Writer/Editor; Telecommunications Manager. **Average salary range of placements:** More than $50,000. **Number of placements per year:** 100 - 199.

THE HR GROUP, INC.
P.O. Box 680634, Marietta GA 30068-0011. 770/993-9577. **Fax:** 770/993-9404. **Contact:** Manager. **Description:** An executive search firm that also provides some temporary placements. **Specializes in the areas of:** Engineering; Personnel/Labor Relations. **Positions commonly filled include:** Electrical Engineer; Human Resources Manager; Telecommunications Manager. **Number of placements per year:** 1 - 49.

WILLIAM HALDERSON ASSOCIATES
P.O. Box 566, Dahlonega GA 30533. 706/864-5800. **Contact:** Bill Halderson, President. **Description:** An executive search firm. **Specializes in the areas of:** Health/Medical. **Positions commonly filled include:** Marketing Specialist; Research Scientist; Sales and Marketing Manager; Sales Representative. **Number of placements per year:** 50 - 99.

ROBERT HALF INTERNATIONAL
ACCOUNTEMPS
3424 Peachtree Road, Suite 2000, Atlanta GA 30326. 770/392-0540. **Contact:** Manager. **World Wide Web address:** http://www.roberthalf.com. **Description:** An executive search firm. Accountemps (also at this location) provides temporary placements. **Corporate headquarters location:** Menlo Park CA. **Other U.S. locations:** Nationwide.

HALL MANAGEMENT GROUP
201-A Forrest Avenue NW, Gainesville GA 30501. 770/534-5568. **Fax:** 770/534-5572. **Contact:** Bill Lennon, President. **Description:** An executive search firm. **Specializes in the areas of:** Accounting/Auditing; Automotive; Computer Science/Software; Engineering; Manufacturing; Medical Devices; Personnel/Labor Relations; Plastics; Technical. **Positions commonly filled include:** Accountant/Auditor; Biomedical Engineer; Chemical Engineer; Electrical/Electronics Engineer; Financial Analyst; Human Resources Manager; Mechanical Engineer; Operations/Production Manager; Purchasing Agent/Manager; Systems Analyst. **Benefits available to temporary workers:** Life Insurance; Medical Insurance; Paid Vacation. **Average salary range of placements:** More than $50,000. **Number of placements per year:** 1 - 49.

W.L. HANDLER & ASSOCIATES
2255 Cumberland Parkway, Building 1500, Atlanta GA 30339. 770/805-5000. **Fax:** 770/805-5020. **Contact:** Manager. **E-mail address:** info@wlhandler.com. **World Wide Web address:** http://www.wlhandler.com. **Description:** An executive search firm operating on a retainer basis. Founded in 1977.

HEALTHCARE RECRUITERS INTERNATIONAL
800 Old Roswell Lake Parkway, Suite 160, Roswell GA 30076. 770/640-8681. **Contact:** Manager. **Description:** An executive search firm. **Specializes in the areas of:** Health/Medical.

HEIDRICK & STRUGGLES
303 Peachtree Street, Suite 3100, Atlanta GA 30308. 404/577-2410. **Fax:** 404/577-4048. **Contact:** Manager. **Description:** An executive search firm.

HIGH TECH PROFESSIONALS
2775 South Main, Suite G, Kennesaw GA 30144. 770/420-7440. **Fax:** 770/420-7126. **Contact:** Todd Porter, Senior Recruiter. **E-mail address:** inquiries@htprof.com. **World Wide Web address:** http://www.htprof.com. **Description:** An executive search firm specializing in data management and data warehousing.

HINES RECRUITING ASSOCIATION
18 Peachtree Avenue NE, Suite D-3, Atlanta GA 30305. 404/262-7131. **Fax:** 404/842-1815. **Contact:** Bill Harris, Recruiting. **Description:** An executive search firm. **Specializes in the areas of:** Engineering; Manufacturing. **Positions commonly filled include:** Chemical Engineer; Electrical/Electronics Engineer; Human Resources

Manager; Industrial Engineer; Mechanical Engineer. **Number of placements per year:** 1 - 49.

HYGUN GROUP, INC.
P.O. Box 70635, Marietta GA 30007. 770/973-0838. **Fax:** 770/973-0877. **Contact:** Manager. **E-mail address:** office@hygun.com. **World Wide Web address:** http://www.hygun.com. **Description:** An executive search firm. **Specializes in the areas of:** Engineering; Scientific. **Corporate headquarters location:** This Location. **Other U.S. locations:** Bellevue WA.

ISC OF ATLANTA
INTERNATIONAL CAREER CONTINUATION
4350 Georgetown Square, Suite 707, Atlanta GA 30338. 770/458-4180. **Fax:** 770/458-4131. **Contact:** A. Arthur Kwapisz, President. **Description:** An executive search firm. International Career Continuation (also at this location) offers career transition services, corporate and individual outplacement, and spousal assistance programs. **Specializes in the areas of:** Accounting/ Auditing; Architecture/Construction; Banking; Biology; Engineering; Finance; General Management; Health/ Medical; Industrial; Manufacturing; Personnel/Labor Relations; Publishing; Sales. **Positions commonly filled include:** Accountant; Administrative Manager; Aerospace Engineer; Bank Officer/Manager; Biochemist; Biological Scientist; Biomedical Engineer; Buyer; Chemical Engineer; Chemist; Civil Engineer; Construction and Building Inspector; Construction Contractor; Designer; Electrical Engineer; Environmental Engineer; General Manager; Health Services Manager; Human Resources Manager; Industrial Engineer; Industrial Production Manager; Manufacturer's/ Wholesaler's Sales Rep.; Mechanical Engineer; Operations Manager; Pharmacist; Purchasing Agent; Quality Control Supervisor; Restaurant/Food Service Manager; Services Sales Rep.; Telecommunications Manager. **Average salary range of placements:** More than $50,000. **Number of placements per year:** 50 - 99.

JJ&H LTD.
JACOBSON ASSOCIATES
1775 The Exchange, Suite 240, Atlanta GA 30339. 770/952-3877. **Contact:** Greg Jacobson, President. **E-mail address:** atlanta@jacobson-associates.com. **World Wide Web address:** http://www.jacobson-associates.com. **Description:** An executive search firm operating on both retainer and contingency bases. **Specializes in the areas of:** Health/Medical; Insurance. **Positions commonly filled include:** Account Manager; Account Representative; Accountant; Adjuster; Attorney; Chief Financial Officer; Claim Representative; Controller; General Manager; Human Resources Manager; Insurance Agent; Marketing Manager; Marketing Specialist; Occupational Therapist; Pharmacist; Physical Therapist; Physician; Sales Exec.; Sales Manager; Systems Manager; Underwriter/Assistant Underwriter. **Corporate headquarters location:** Chicago IL. **Other U.S. locations:** Philadelphia PA. **Average salary range of placements:** More than $50,000. **Number of placements per year:** 100 - 199.

JOB SHOP INC.
218-E Oak Street, Martinez GA 30907. 706/860-4820. **Fax:** 706/860-4871. **Contact:** President. **Description:** An executive search firm. Founded in 1979. **Specializes in the areas of:** Engineering; Industrial; Manufacturing; Personnel; Technical. **Positions commonly filled include:** Accountant; Blue-Collar Worker Supervisor; Chemical Engineer; Clerical Supervisor; Computer Programmer; Draftsperson; Electrical Engineer; Environmental Engineer; Human Resources Specialist; Industrial Engineer; Industrial Production Manager; Mechanical Engineer; Word Processor. **Average salary range of placements:** $30,000 - $50,000. **Number of placements per year:** 1000+.

CHRIS KAUFFMAN & ASSOCIATES
P.O. Box 53218, Atlanta GA 30355. 404/233-3530. **Fax:** 404/262-7960. **Contact:** Chris Kauffman, President. **Description:** An executive search firm.

A.T. KEARNEY EXECUTIVE SEARCH
3455 Peachtree Street NE, Suite 1600, Atlanta GA 30326. 770/393-9900. **Contact:** Manager. **Description:** A generalist executive search firm.

KENZER CORPORATION OF GEORGIA
1600 Parkwood Circle, Suite 310, Atlanta GA 30339. 770/955-7210. **Fax:** 770/955-6504. **Contact:** Marie Powell, Vice President. **Description:** An executive search firm. **Specializes in the areas of:** Accounting/Auditing; Advertising; Banking; Fashion; Food; General Management; Manufacturing; Personnel/Labor Relations; Retail; Sales. **Positions commonly filled include:** Buyer; General Manager; Human Resources Manager; MIS Specialist; Restaurant/Food Service Manager. **Corporate headquarters location:** New York NY. **Other U.S. locations:** Los Angeles CA; Chicago IL; Minneapolis MN; Dallas TX. **Average salary range of placements:** More than $50,000.

KORN/FERRY INTERNATIONAL
303 Peachtree Street NE, Suite 1600, Atlanta GA 30308. 404/577-7542. **Fax:** 404/584-9781. **Contact:** Manager. **World Wide Web address:** http://www.kornferry.com. **Description:** An executive search firm that places upper-level managers. **Corporate headquarters location:** Los Angeles CA. **International locations:** Worldwide. **Average salary range of placements:** More than $50,000.

KREISLER & ASSOCIATES
2575 Peachtree Road, Plaza Towers, Atlanta GA 30305. 404/262-0599. **Fax:** 404/262-0699. **Contact:** Debbi Kreisler, President. **Description:** An executive search firm providing middle- and upper-management placements. **Specializes in the areas of:** Art/Design; Engineering; Fashion; Manufacturing; Retail; Sales. **Positions commonly filled include:** Buyer; Designer; Industrial Engineer; Manufacturer's/Wholesaler's Sales Rep.; Operations/Production Manager; Quality Control Supervisor. **Average salary range of placements:** More than $50,000. **Number of placements per year:** 200 - 499.

LEADER INSTITUTE, INC.
2000 Riveredge Parkway, Suite 920, Atlanta GA 30328. 770/984-2700x100. **Fax:** 770/984-2990. **Contact:** Rick Zabor, President. **E-mail address:** rick@peoplestaff.com. **World Wide Web address:** http://www.peoplestaff.com. **Description:** An executive search firm. **Specializes in the areas of:** Computer Science/Software; Information Technology. **Positions commonly filled include:** Account Representative; Computer Programmer; Human Resources Manager; Information Systems Consultant; Internet Services Manager; Systems Analyst; Systems Manager. **Average salary range of placements:** More than $50,000. **Number of placements per year:** 50 - 99.

LEGAL PROFESSIONAL STAFFING
2 Ravinia Drive, Suite 1295, Atlanta GA 30346. 770/392-7181. **Fax:** 770/392-7175. **Contact:** Manager. **Description:** An executive search firm. **Specializes in the areas of:** Legal.

DOROTHY LONG SEARCH
6065 Roswell Road NE, Suite 416, Atlanta GA 30328. 404/252-3787. **Contact:** Manager. **Description:** An executive search firm. **Specializes in the areas of:** Property Management.

LOWDERMAN & ASSOCIATES
3939 Roswell Road NE, Suite 100, Marietta GA 30062. 770/977-3020. **Fax:** 770/977-6549. **Contact:** Search Consultant. **E-mail address:** lowderman1@aol.com. **Description:** An executive search firm operating on a retainer basis. The firm focuses on placing individuals in hospitals and integrated health care delivery systems. Client company pays fee. **Specializes in the areas of:** Accounting; Administration; Finance; General Management; Health/Medical; Personnel/Labor

Relations. **Positions commonly filled include:** Chief Financial Officer; Controller; Finance Director; Human Resources Manager. **Corporate headquarters location:** This Location. **Other U.S. locations:** Nationwide. **Average salary range of placements:** $50,000 - $100,000. **Number of placements per year:** 1 - 49.

LUCAS GROUP
3384 Peachtree Road NE, Suite 700, Atlanta GA 30326. 404/239-5635. **Fax:** 404/239-5692. **Contact:** Administrative Assistant. **World Wide Web address:** http://www.lucascareers.com. **Description:** An executive search firm that also provides some temporary and contract placements. **Specializes in the areas of:** Accounting/Auditing; Finance; Tax. **Positions commonly filled include:** Accountant/Auditor; Auditor; Bookkeeper; Budget Analyst; Chief Financial Officer; Controller; Financial Analyst; Purchasing Agent/Manager; Systems Analyst. **Benefits available to temporary workers:** Medical Insurance. **Other U.S. locations:** Irvine CA; Chicago IL; Dallas TX; Houston TX. **Average salary range of placements:** $30,000 - $50,000. **Number of placements per year:** 1 - 49.

LYNN SEARCH CONSULTANTS
5665 Highway 9 North, Suite 103, Alpharetta GA 30004. 770/667-9473. **Fax:** 770/667-9017. **Contact:** Manager. **Description:** An executive search firm.

MSI INTERNATIONAL
245 Peachtree Center Avenue, Suite 2500, Marquis One Tower, Atlanta GA 30303. 404/659-5050. **Toll-free phone:** 800/511-0383. **Fax:** 404/659-7139. **Contact:** Mike Giuseffi, Vice President. **World Wide Web address:** http://www.msi-intl.com. **Description:** An executive search firm. **Specializes in the areas of:** Banking; Engineering; General Management; Health/Medical.

MSI INTERNATIONAL
1050 Crown Pointe Parkway, Suite 100, Atlanta GA 30338. 770/394-2494. **Toll-free phone:** 800/659-2762. **Fax:** 770/394-2251. **Contact:** James T. Watson, Vice President. **E-mail address:** msimsp@mindspring.com. **Description:** An executive search firm operating on both retainer and contingency bases. **Specializes in the areas of:** Architecture/Construction; Banking; Engineering; General Management; Health/Medical; Industrial; Insurance; Sales; Technical. **Positions commonly filled include:** Account Manager; Accountant/Auditor; Administrative Assistant; Applications Engineer; Bank Officer/Manager; Branch Manager; Chemical Engineer; Chief Financial Officer; Civil Engineer; Construction Contractor; Cost Estimator; Design Engineer; Environmental Engineer; Financial Analyst; Fund Manager; Industrial Engineer; Mechanical Engineer; Metallurgical Engineer; Mining Engineer; Operations Manager; Purchasing Agent/Manager; Software Engineer; Structural Engineer; Underwriter/Assistant Underwriter. **Other U.S. locations:** CA; LA; TX; VA. **Average salary range of placements:** More than $50,000. **Number of placements per year:** 100 - 199.

BOB MADDOX ASSOCIATES
3134 West Roxboro Road NE, Suite 300, Atlanta GA 30324. 404/231-0558. **Contact:** Robert E. Maddox, President. **Description:** An executive search firm operating on a retainer basis. **Specializes in the areas of:** General Management; Nonprofit. **Positions commonly filled include:** Branch Manager; Chief Financial Officer; Development Officer; Executive Director; General Manager. **Other U.S. locations:** Charlotte NC. **Average salary range of placements:** More than $50,000. **Number of placements per year:** 1 - 49.

MANAGEMENT RECRUITERS INTERNATIONAL
3700 Crestwood Parkway NW, Suite 320, Duluth GA 30096. 770/925-2266. **Fax:** 770/925-1090. **Contact:** David Riggs, Manager. **E-mail address:** mri.atlanta@internetmci.com. **Description:** An executive search firm. **Specializes in the areas of:** Biology; Computer Science/Software; Finance; Sales; Technical.

Positions commonly filled include: Biochemist; Biological Scientist; Biomedical Engineer; Chemical Engineer; Credit Manager; Environmental Engineer; Financial Analyst; Market Research Analyst; Operations/Production Manager; Securities Sales Representative. **Corporate headquarters location:** Cleveland OH. **Other U.S. locations:** Nationwide. **International locations:** Worldwide. **Average salary range of placements:** More than $50,000. **Number of placements per year:** 200 - 499.

MANAGEMENT RECRUITERS INTERNATIONAL
21 North Main Street, Alpharetta GA 30004. 770/664-5512. **Fax:** 770/664-5046. **Contact:** John Harvey, President. **Description:** An executive search firm. **Specializes in the areas of:** Engineering; Food; General Management; Manufacturing; Sales; Technical. **Positions commonly filled include:** Design Engineer; Electrical/Electronics Engineer; Food Scientist/Technologist; Forester/Conservation Scientist; Human Resources Manager; Industrial Engineer; Industrial Production Manager; Management Analyst/Consultant; Mechanical Engineer; Operations/Production Manager; Science Technologist; Structural Engineer; Telecommunications Manager; Transportation/Traffic Specialist. **Corporate headquarters location:** Cleveland OH. **Other U.S. locations:** Nationwide. **Average salary range of placements:** More than $50,000. **Number of placements per year:** 1 - 49.

MANAGEMENT RECRUITERS INTERNATIONAL SALES CONSULTANTS OF COBB COUNTY
2840 Johnson Ferry Road, Suite 150, Marietta GA 30062. 770/643-9990. **Contact:** Larry Dougherty, General Manager. **E-mail address:** officemgr@mriatlanta.com. **Description:** An executive search firm that also provides video conferencing, interexecutive placement, and outplacement services. **Specializes in the areas of:** Computer Science/Software; Engineering; General Management; Logistics; Manufacturing; Technical; Transportation. **Positions commonly filled include:** Branch Manager; Budget Analyst; Computer Programmer; General Manager; Industrial Engineer; Management Analyst/Consultant; Manufacturer's/Wholesaler's Sales Rep.; Marketing/Public Relations Manager; MIS Specialist; Operations/Production Manager; Software Engineer; Systems Analyst; Telecommunications Manager; Transportation/Traffic Specialist. **Corporate headquarters location:** Cleveland OH. **Other U.S. locations:** Nationwide. **Average salary range of placements:** More than $50,000. **Number of placements per year:** 100 - 199.

MANAGEMENT RECRUITERS OF ATLANTA
230 Peachtree Street NW, Suite 1985, Atlanta GA 30303. 404/221-1021. **Contact:** Manager. **Description:** An executive search firm. **Specializes in the areas of:** Accounting/Auditing; Advertising; Banking; Health/Medical; Industrial; Insurance; Pharmaceuticals; Transportation. **Positions commonly filled include:** Industrial Engineer; Industrial Production Manager; Sales Manager; Sales Representative; Software Engineer; Transportation/Traffic Specialist; Underwriter/Assistant Underwriter. **Corporate headquarters location:** Cleveland OH. **Other U.S. locations:** Nationwide.

MANAGEMENT RECRUITERS OF ATLANTA (NORTH)
20 Perimeter Park Drive, Suite 101, Atlanta GA 30341. 770/455-1958. **Fax:** 770/455-6529. **Contact:** Art Katz, Manager. **E-mail address:** resumes@mrian.com. **Description:** An executive search firm. **Specializes in the areas of:** Accounting/Auditing; Administration; Advertising; Architecture/Construction; Banking; Chemicals; Communications; Computer Hardware/Software; Construction; Electrical; Engineering; Finance; Food; General Management; Health/Medical; Insurance; Legal; Manufacturing; Operations Management; Personnel/Labor Relations; Pharmaceuticals; Procurement; Publishing; Real Estate; Retail; Sales; Technical; Textiles; Transportation. **Corporate**

headquarters location: Cleveland OH. **Other U.S. locations:** Nationwide.

MANAGEMENT RECRUITERS OF ATLANTA (SOUTH)
406 Line Creek Drive, Suite B, Peachtree City GA 30269. 770/486-0603. **Fax:** 770/631-7684. **Contact:** Ron Wise, Owner. **Description:** An executive search firm. **Specializes in the areas of:** Chemicals; Electrical; Engineering; Food; General Management; Manufacturing; Operations Management; Personnel/ Labor Relations; Procurement; Sales; Technical; Textiles; Transportation. **Positions commonly filled include:** Branch Manager; Chemical Engineer; Engineer; Mathematician. **Corporate headquarters location:** Cleveland OH. **Other U.S. locations:** Nationwide. **Average salary range of placements:** More than $50,000. **Number of placements per year:** 50 - 99.

MANAGEMENT RECRUITERS OF ATLANTA (WEST)
4260 Bankhead Highway, Suite A, Lithia Springs GA 30122. 770/948-5560. **Contact:** Steven Kendall, Owner. **Description:** An executive search firm. **Specializes in the areas of:** Consumer Products; Packaging; Sales. **Positions commonly filled include:** General Manager; Manufacturer's/Wholesaler's Sales Rep.; Sales and Marketing Manager. **Corporate headquarters location:** Cleveland OH. **Other U.S. locations:** Nationwide. **Average salary range of placements:** More than $50,000. **Number of placements per year:** 50 - 99.

MANAGEMENT RECRUITERS OF COLUMBUS
233 12th Street, Suite 818A, Columbus GA 31901. 706/571-9611. **Fax:** 706/571-3288. **Contact:** Michael Silverstein, President. **E-mail address:** michael@ mricolumbusga.com. **World Wide Web address:** http://www.mricolumbusga.com. **Description:** An executive search firm operating on both retainer and contingency bases. **Specializes in the areas of:** Computer Science/Software; Engineering; Information Systems. **Positions commonly filled include:** Applications Engineer; Computer Programmer; Database Manager; Electrical/Electronics Engineer; Industrial Engineer; Manufacturing Engineer; Mechanical Engineer; MIS Specialist; Systems Analyst. **Corporate headquarters location:** Cleveland OH. **Other U.S. locations:** Nationwide. **Average salary range of placements:** More than $50,000.

MANAGEMENT RECRUITERS OF MARIETTA
274 North Marietta Parkway, Suite C, Marietta GA 30060. 770/423-1443. **Fax:** 770/423-1303. **Contact:** James E. Kirby, Managing Principal. **E-mail address:** jkirby@mindspring.com. **Description:** An executive search firm. **Specializes in the areas of:** Computer Science/Software; Engineering; Fashion; General Management; Industrial; Information Systems; Logistics; Manufacturing; Personnel/Labor Relations; Sales; Transportation. **Positions commonly filled include:** Accountant/Auditor; Aerospace Engineer; Biomedical Engineer; Chemical Engineer; Computer Programmer; Design Engineer; Electrical/Electronics Engineer; General Manager; Human Resources Manager; Industrial Engineer; Management Analyst/Consultant; Mechanical Engineer; MIS Specialist; Operations/Production Manager; Purchasing Agent/Manager; Quality Control Supervisor; Software Engineer; Systems Analyst; Transportation/Traffic Specialist. **Corporate headquarters location:** Cleveland OH. **Other U.S. locations:** Nationwide. **Average salary range of placements:** More than $50,000. **Number of placements per year:** 50 - 99.

MANAGEMENT RECRUITERS OF MIDDLE GEORGIA
P.O. Box 1455, Perry GA 31069. 912/988-4444. **Fax:** 912/988-4445. **Contact:** Terry Wentz, Manager. **E-mail address:** twentz@msn.com. **Description:** An executive search firm operating on both retainer and contingency bases. Client company pays fee. **Specializes in the areas of:** Apparel; Textiles. **Positions commonly filled**

include: Account Manager; Account Representative; Accountant; Chief Financial Officer; Computer Programmer; Controller; Designer; Financial Analyst; General Manager; Human Resources Manager; Industrial Engineer; Industrial Production Manager; Manufacturing Engineer; Marketing Manager; Mechanical Engineer; Purchasing Agent/Manager; Quality Control Supervisor; Sales Executive; Sales Manager; Sales Representative; Systems Manager; Vice President of Marketing and Sales; Vice President of Operations. **Other U.S. locations:** Nationwide. **Average salary range of placements:** Less than $20,000. **Number of placements per year:** 1 - 49.

MANAGEMENT RECRUITERS OF SAVANNAH
P.O. Box 22548, Savannah GA 31403. 912/232-0132. **Toll-free phone:** 800/886-0135. **Fax:** 912/232-0136. **Contact:** Ronald W. McElhaney, Managing Partner. **Description:** An executive search firm operating on both retainer and contingency bases. **Specializes in the areas of:** Chemicals; Engineering; Environmental; Industrial; Plastics; Safety. **Positions commonly filled include:** Chemical Engineer; Chemist; Electrical/Electronics Engineer; General Manager; Human Resources Manager; Industrial Engineer; Industrial Production Manager; Mechanical Engineer; Quality Control Supervisor; Regulatory Affairs Director; Software Engineer; Transportation/Traffic Specialist; Vice President of Operations. **Corporate headquarters location:** Cleveland OH. **Other U.S. locations:** Nationwide. **Average salary range of placements:** More than $50,000. **Number of placements per year:** 1 - 49.

MED PRO PERSONNEL
1955 Cliff Valley Way, Suite 116, Atlanta GA 30329. 404/633-8280. **Fax:** 404/633-9856. **Contact:** Manager. **Description:** An executive search firm. **Specializes in the areas of:** Health/Medical.

MEDICAL SEARCH OF AMERICA, INC.
P.O. Box 1716, Duluth GA 30096. 770/232-0530. **Toll-free phone:** 800/523-1351. **Fax:** 770/232-0610. **Contact:** Charles Sikes, President. **Description:** An executive search firm. **Specializes in the areas of:** Health/Medical. **Positions commonly filled include:** Administrative Manager; Computer Programmer; Counselor; Credit Manager; Dietician/Nutritionist; Education Administrator; Health Services Manager; MIS Specialist; Occupational Therapist; Pharmacist; Physical Therapist; Physician; Psychologist; Purchasing Agent/Manager; Quality Control Supervisor; Radiological Technologist; Registered Nurse; Respiratory Therapist; Social Worker; Speech-Language Pathologist. **Other U.S. locations:** Nationwide. **Number of placements per year:** 1 - 49.

THE MERCER GROUP, INC.
5579B Chamblee Dunwoody Road, Suite 511, Atlanta GA 30338. 770/551-0403. **Contact:** Manager. **World Wide Web address:** http://www.mercergroupinc.com. **Description:** An executive search firm.

NATIONAL PERSONNEL RECRUITERS
6151 Powers Ferry Road, Suite 605, Atlanta GA 30339. 770/955-4221. **Fax:** 770/859-0856. **Contact:** Manager. **Description:** An executive search firm. **Specializes in the areas of:** Management; Marketing; Sales.

NATIONAL RESTAURANT SEARCH INC.
555 Sun Valley Drive, Suite J-1, Roswell GA 30076. 770/650-1800. **Contact:** John Chitvanni, President. **Description:** An executive search firm operating on a retainer basis. **Specializes in the areas of:** Executives; Food; Restaurant. **Positions commonly filled include:** Hotel Manager; Restaurant/Food Service Manager. **Corporate headquarters location:** This Location. **Other U.S. locations:** Nationwide. **International locations:** Worldwide. **Average salary range of placements:** More than $50,000. **Number of placements per year:** 100 - 199.

OSI (OLIVER SEARCH, INC.)
P.O. Box 81092, Conyers GA 30013. 770/760-7661.
Fax: 770/760-7729. **Contact:** Tim Oliver, Owner.
Description: An executive search firm operating on both retainer and contingency bases. Client company pays fee.
Specializes in the areas of: Food. **Positions commonly filled include:** Account Manager; Buyer; Chemical Engineer; Design Engineer; Electrical/Electronics Engineer; Food Scientist/Technologist; General Manager; Human Resources Manager; Industrial Engineer; Industrial Production Manager; Manufacturing Engineer; Market Research Analyst; Marketing Manager; Mechanical Engineer; Operations Manager; Production Manager; Project Manager; Sales Manager; Sales Representative. **Corporate headquarters location:** This Location. **Other U.S. locations:** Raleigh NC. **Average salary range of placements:** $50,000 - $100,000. **Number of placements per year:** 1 - 49.

OMEGA EXECUTIVE SEARCH
2033 Monroe Drive, Atlanta GA 30324. 404/873-2000.
Contact: Manager. **Description:** An executive search firm. **Specializes in the areas of:** Hotel/Restaurant.

OMNI RECRUITING
1950 Spectrum Circle, Suite 400, Marietta GA 30067.
770/988-2788. **Fax:** 770/988-2789. **Contact:** Manager.
Description: An executive search firm. **Specializes in the areas of:** Sales.

PRI
INVESEARCH
620 Colonial Park Drive, Suite 101, Roswell GA 30075.
770/351-9546. **Fax:** 770/650-9219. **Contact:** Manager.
E-mail address: info@pri1.com. **Description:** An executive search firm. Invesearch (also at this location) is an executive search firm that focuses exclusively on placements in the accounting and finance industries.
Specializes in the areas of: Finance; Human Resources; Information Technology.

PARKER, McFADDEN ASSOCIATES
1581 Phoenix Boulevard, Suite 3, Atlanta GA 30349.
770/991-0873. **Fax:** 770/996-2455. **Contact:** Manager.
E-mail address: pma.info@parker-mcfadden.com.
World Wide Web address: http://www.parker-mcfadden.com. **Description:** An executive search firm.
Specializes in the areas of: Aerospace; Automotive; Engineering; Heavy Equipment; Industrial; Mechanical.
Positions commonly filled include: Buyer; Director; Finance Director; Human Resources Manager; Maintenance Supervisor; Management; Materials Manager; Planner; Purchasing Agent/Manager; Quality Control Supervisor; Vice President.

PERIMETER PLACEMENT
24 Perimeter Center East, Suite 2417, Atlanta GA 30346.
770/393-0000. **Contact:** Manager. **Description:** An executive search firm. **Specializes in the areas of:** Administration; Finance; Sales.

PERSONALIZED MANAGEMENT ASSOCIATES
1950 Spectrum Circle, Suite B-310, Marietta GA 30067-6059. 770/916-1668. **Toll-free phone:** 800/466-7822.
Fax: 770/916-1429. **Contact:** Bill Lins, CPC/Director of Operations. **E-mail address:** jobs@pmasearch.com.
Description: An executive search firm. **Specializes in the areas of:** Food; Restaurant; Retail; Sales. **Positions commonly filled include:** Human Resources Manager; Management Trainee; Restaurant/Food Service Manager.
Other U.S. locations: Phoenix AZ. **Average salary range of placements:** More than $50,000. **Number of placements per year:** 500 - 999.

PERSONNEL OPPORTUNITIES INC.
5064 Roswell Road, Suite D-301, Atlanta GA 30342.
404/252-9484. **Fax:** 404/252-9821. **Contact:** President.
Description: An executive search firm. Founded in 1966. **Specializes in the areas of:** Accounting/Auditing; Computer Hardware/Software; Engineering; Health/Medical; Insurance; Legal; Manufacturing; Sales.
Positions commonly filled include: Accountant/Auditor;

Chemical Engineer; Chemist; Claim Representative; Computer Programmer; Manufacturing Engineer; Mechanical Engineer; Nurse; Sales Representative; Software Engineer; Systems Analyst. **Number of placements per year:** 100 - 199.

PHOENIX PARTNERS
5607 Glenridge Drive, Suite 460, Atlanta GA 30342.
404/250-1133. **Contact:** Manager. **Description:** An executive search firm. **Specializes in the areas of:** High-Tech.

POWER INDUSTRY CONSULTANTS (PIC)
1165 Northchase Parkway, 4th Floor, Marietta GA 30067. 770/850-0100. **Fax:** 770/850-0102. **Contact:** Recruiter. **E-mail address:** executive@picworld.com.
World Wide Web address: http://www.picworld.com.
Description: An executive search firm.

PRO-TECH INC.
P.O. Box 141, Oakwood GA 30566. 770/532-9815. **Fax:** 770/535-6796. **Contact:** Ann Johnson, Plastics Recruiter/Co-Owner. **Description:** An executive search firm operating on a contingency basis. **Specializes in the areas of:** Engineering; Manufacturing; Plastics; Technical. **Positions commonly filled include:** Chemical Engineer; Chemist; Design Engineer; Designer; General Manager; Industrial Engineer; Mechanical Engineer; Quality Control Supervisor.
Average salary range of placements: More than $50,000. **Number of placements per year:** 1 - 49.

RIF (RESOURCES IN FOOD)
1720 Peachtree Street, Suite 629, North Tower, Atlanta GA 30309. 404/897-5535. **Fax:** 404/897-5454. **Contact:** Placement Specialist. **Description:** An executive search firm. **Specializes in the areas of:** Food; General Management. **Positions commonly filled include:** Branch Manager; Dietician/Nutritionist; General Manager; Hotel Manager; Management Trainee; Restaurant/Food Service Manager. **Corporate headquarters location:** St. Louis MO. **Average salary range of placements:** $30,000 - $50,000. **Number of placements per year:** 1000+.

RAY & BERNDTSON, INC.
191 Peachtree Street NE, Suite 3800, Atlanta GA 30303.
404/215-4600. **Fax:** 404/215-4620. **Contact:** Manager.
World Wide Web address: http://www.rayberndtson.com. **Description:** An executive search firm. **Positions commonly filled include:** Senior Management. **Benefits available to temporary workers:** Non-Smoking Environment. **International locations:** Worldwide.

P.J. REDA & ASSOCIATES, INC.
1955 Cliff Valley Way, Suite 117, Atlanta GA 30329.
404/325-8812. **Fax:** 404/325-8850. **Contact:** Pat Reda, President. **Description:** An executive search firm that also conducts interview skills workshops for supervisors and managers. **Specializes in the areas of:** Food; General Management; Health/Medical; Personnel/Labor Relations. **Positions commonly filled include:** General Manager; Health Services Manager; Management Trainee; Restaurant/Food Service Manager. **Number of placements per year:** 100 - 199.

REEDER & ASSOCIATES, LTD.
1095 Old Roswell Road, Roswell GA 30076. 770/649-7523. **Fax:** 770/649-7543. **Contact:** Manager. **World Wide Web address:** http://www.reederassoc.com.
Description: An executive search firm. **Specializes in the areas of:** Executives; Health/Medical; Managed Care. **Average salary range of placements:** More than $100,000.

DON RICHARD ASSOCIATES
3475 Lenox Road NE, Suite 210, Atlanta GA 30326.
404/231-3688. **Fax:** 404/364-0124. **Contact:** Ed Pease, Co-Owner. **Description:** An executive search firm.
Specializes in the areas of: Accounting/Auditing; Bookkeeping; Finance. **Positions commonly filled**

include: Accountant/Auditor; Budget Analyst; Credit Manager; Financial Analyst. **Average salary range of placements:** $30,000 - $50,000. **Number of placements per year:** 200 - 499.

RITA CORPORATION
679 Glen Spring Drive NW, Atlanta GA 30243. **Contact:** Manager. **Description:** An executive search firm. **Specializes in the areas of:** Computer Hardware/Software.

ROLLINS SEARCH GROUP
5345 Bells Ferry Road, Suite 114, Acworth GA 30102. 770/516-6042. **Contact:** Manager. **Description:** An executive search firm. **Specializes in the areas of:** Insurance; Technical. **Positions commonly filled include:** Actuary; Insurance Agent/Broker.

ROMAC INTERNATIONAL
3 Ravinia Drive, Suite 1460, Atlanta GA 30346. 770/604-3880. **Contact:** Manager. **Description:** An executive search firm. **Specializes in the areas of:** Accounting/Auditing; Finance; Information Technology.

ROWLAND, MOUNTAIN & ASSOCIATES
4-E Executive Park, Suite 100, Atlanta GA 30329. 404/325-2189. **Fax:** 404/321-1842. **Contact:** Russ Mountain, President. **Description:** An executive search firm operating on both retainer and contingency bases. **Specializes in the areas of:** Sales. **Positions commonly filled include:** Account Manager; Account Representative; Branch Manager; General Manager; Marketing Manager; Marketing Specialist; Sales Executive; Sales Manager; Sales Representative. **Average salary range of placements:** More than $50,000. **Number of placements per year:** 100 - 199.

RUSSELL REYNOLDS ASSOCIATES, INC.
50 Hurt Plaza, Suite 600, Atlanta GA 30303. 404/577-3000. **Fax:** 404/577-2832. **Contact:** Manager. **Description:** A generalist executive search firm.

SCI RECRUITERS
1874 Independence Square, Suite B, Dunwoody GA 30338. 770/396-7788. **Contact:** Manager. **World Wide Web address:** http://www.sciatlanta.com. **Description:** An executive search firm. **Specializes in the areas of:** Computer Hardware/Software; Computer Programming; Information Technology; Quality Assurance. **Positions commonly filled include:** Computer Programmer; Database Administrator; Quality Assurance Engineer; Software Developer; Systems Engineer.

SALES OPPORTUNITIES
6065 Roswell Road, Suite 518, Atlanta GA 30328. 404/256-9314. **Contact:** Manager. **Description:** An executive search firm. **Specializes in the areas of:** Computer Science/Software; Sales.

SANFORD ROSE ASSOCIATES
9650 Ventana Way, Suite 204, Alpharetta GA 30022. 770/232-9900. **Fax:** 770/232-1933. **Contact:** Mr. Don Patrick, President. **E-mail address:** sranorcross@mindspring.com. **World Wide Web address:** http://www.sanfordrose.com. **Description:** An executive search firm operating on both retainer and contingency bases. Client company pays fee. **Specializes in the areas of:** Computer Science/Software; General Management; Marketing; Sales; Technical; Wireless Communications. **Positions commonly filled include:** Account Manager; Branch Manager; Consultant - Computer; General Manager; Sales Executive; Sales Manager; Science Technologist; Software Engineer; Vice President of Marketing and Sales. **Average salary range of placements:** More than $50,000. **Number of placements per year:** 1 - 49.

SANFORD ROSE ASSOCIATES
2500 West Broad Street, Suite 106, Athens GA 30606. 706/548-3942. **Contact:** Manager. **World Wide Web address:** http://www.sanfordrose.com. **Description:** An executive search firm. **Specializes in the areas of:** Manufacturing.

SANFORD ROSE ASSOCIATES
3626 Chamblee-Tucker Road, Suite B, Atlanta GA 30341. 770/723-1115. **Fax:** 770/723-1198. **Contact:** Manager. **World Wide Web address:** http://www.sanfordrose.com. **Description:** An executive search firm. **Specializes in the areas of:** Banking; Finance.

SEARCH ATLANTA
3200 Windy Hill Road, Marietta GA 30067. 770/984-0880. **Contact:** Manager. **Description:** An executive search firm.

SELECTIVE SEARCH
7000 Peachtree-Dunwoody Road, Building 11, Suite 300, Atlanta GA 30338. 770/390-9666. **Contact:** Manager. **Description:** An executive search firm. **Specializes in the areas of:** Information Systems.

THE SHEPARD GROUP, INC.
999 Whitlock Avenue, Suite 5, Marietta GA 30064. 770/794-1117. **Contact:** Manager. **World Wide Web address:** http://www.shepardgroup.com. **Description:** An executive search firm. **Specializes in the areas of:** Construction; Engineering; Information Technology; Manufacturing.

SNELLING PERSONNEL SERVICES
1337 Canton Road, Suite D-3, Marietta GA 30066. 770/423-1177. **Fax:** 770/423-0558. **Contact:** Manager. **E-mail address:** snelling1@mindspring.com. **World Wide Web address:** http://www.snelling.com. **Description:** An executive search firm operating on a contingency basis. The firm also provides some temporary placements. Founded in 1986. **Specializes in the areas of:** Computer Science/Software; Engineering; Health/Medical; Information Systems; Sales; Secretarial. **Positions commonly filled include:** Chemical Engineer; Clerical Supervisor; Computer Programmer; Credit Manager; Customer Service Representative; Environmental Engineer; Manufacturer's/Wholesaler's Sales Rep.; Mechanical Engineer; Physical Therapist; Services Sales Representative; Software Engineer. **Corporate headquarters location:** Dallas TX. **Other U.S. locations:** Nationwide. **Average salary range of placements:** $30,000 - $50,000. **Number of placements per year:** 100 - 199.

SOFTWARE SEARCH
2163 Northlake Parkway, Suite 100, Tucker GA 30084. 770/934-5138. **Fax:** 770/939-6410. **Contact:** Larry Okeson, Vice President. **Description:** An executive search firm operating on a contingency basis. The firm also provides some contract services. **Specializes in the areas of:** Administration; Computer Science. **Positions commonly filled include:** Computer Programmer; Database Manager; Software Engineer; Systems Analyst; Systems Manager; Telecommunications Manager. **Other U.S. locations:** Minneapolis MN. **Average salary range of placements:** $30,000 - $50,000. **Number of placements per year:** 200 - 499.

SONDRA SEARCH
P.O. Box 101, Roswell GA 30077. 770/552-1910. **Fax:** 770/552-7340. **Contact:** Sondra Katnik, Vice President. **Description:** An executive search firm operating on a contingency basis. Client company pays fee. **Specializes in the areas of:** Food; Industrial; Information Technology; Management; Medical Sales and Marketing; Sales. **Positions commonly filled include:** Account Manager; Account Representative; Sales Engineer; Sales Executive; Sales Manager; Sales Representative. **Corporate headquarters location:** This Location. **Other U.S. locations:** Nationwide. **Average salary range of placements:** $50,000 - $100,000. **Number of placements per year:** 1 - 49.

SOUTHERN PROFESSIONAL RECRUITERS
5920 Roswell Road, Suite B107, Atlanta GA 30328. 404/851-9889. **Fax:** 404/843-2984. **Contact:** Manager.

Description: An executive search firm. **Specializes in the areas of:** Finance; Health/Medical.

STERLING LEGAL SEARCH
5180 Roswell Road, Suite 202 South, Atlanta GA 30342. 404/250-9766. **Contact:** Branch Manager. **Description:** Sterling Legal Search is an executive search firm. **Specializes in the areas of:** Legal.

STRATEGIC SEARCH CONSULTANTS
4405 International Boulevard, Suite B-117, Norcross GA 30093. 678/380-6005. **Toll-free phone:** 888/772-3932. **Fax:** 678/380-6006. **Contact:** Manager. **World Wide Web address:** http://www.corporatepartners.com. **Description:** Strategic Search Consultants is an executive search firm.

TMP WORLDWIDE
191 Peachtree Street NE, Suite 800, Atlanta GA 30303-1747. 404/688-0800. **Fax:** 404/688-0133. **Contact:** Executive VP/Managing Partner. **World Wide Web address:** http://www.tmpw.com. **Description:** TMP Worldwide is an executive search firm. **Specializes in the areas of:** Biotechnology; Consumer Products; Finance; Health/Medical; Industrial; Pharmaceuticals; Technical. **Corporate headquarters location:** New York NY. **Other U.S. locations:** Nationwide.

TAURION CORPORATION
P.O. Box 956716, Duluth GA 30095. 770/449-7155. **Fax:** 770/449-6421. **Contact:** John Puchis, Vice President. **Description:** Taurion Corporation is an executive search firm. **Specializes in the areas of:** Administration; Computer Science/Software; Data Processing. **Positions commonly filled include:** Computer Programmer; Director; Management; Software Engineer; Systems Analyst. **Number of placements per year:** 1 - 49.

TECHNICAL ALLIANCE GROUP
3500 Piedmont Road, Suite 500, Atlanta GA 30305. 404/816-9119. **Fax:** 404/231-2152. **Contact:** Shanon O'Toole, CPC. **E-mail address:** opportunities@technical-alliance.com. **World Wide Web address:** http://www.technical-alliance.com. **Description:** Technical Alliance Group is an executive search firm. **Specializes in the areas of:** I.T.. **Positions commonly filled include:** AS400 Programmer Analyst; Business Analyst; Database Administrator; Database Specialist; Internet Specialist; Network Administrator; Quality Assurance Engineer; Sales Rep.; Software Engineer; Technical Support Manager; Technical Writer; Telecommunications Analyst; UNIX System Administrator.

TENNANT & ASSOCIATES
11285 Elkins Road, Suite L-3B, Roswell GA 30076. 770/740-1609. **Contact:** Manager. **Description:** Tennant & Associates is an executive search firm. **Specializes in the areas of:** Computer Science/Software; Telecommunications.

THORNE CONSULTING
4067 Riverlook Parkway, Marietta GA 30067. 770/951-8075. **Toll-free phone:** 800/962-9763. **Fax:** 770/951-1823. **Contact:** Richard Thorne, Search Consultant. **E-mail address:** thorcon@mindspring.com. **Description:** An executive search firm operating on both retainer and contingency bases. **Specializes in the areas of:** Health/Medical. **Positions commonly filled include:** Biomedical Engineer; CFO; Controller; Dietician; Financial Analyst; Health Care Risk Consultant; Human Resources Manager; Management Analyst; Marketing Manager; Nurse Practitioner; Sales Manager; Sales Rep.

Average salary range of placements: $50,000 - $100,000. **Number of placements per year:** 1 - 49.

TOAR CONSULTING
1176 Grimes Bridge Road, Suite 300, Roswell GA 30075. 770/993-7663. **Fax:** 770/998-5853. **Contact:** Manager. **Description:** An executive search firm. **Specializes in the areas of:** Accounting; Banking; Engineering; Finance; Publishing. **Positions commonly filled include:** Accountant; Bank Officer; Chemical Engineer; Civil Engineer; Computer Programmer; Design Engineer; Electrician; Engineer; MIS Manager; Operations Manager; Q.C. Supervisor; Systems Analyst. **Average salary range of placements:** More than $50,000. **Number of placements per year:** 50 - 99.

TRITECH ASSOCIATES
3525 Piedmont Road, 7 Piedmont Center, Atlanta GA 30305. 404/261-7710. **Fax:** 404/261-7298. **Contact:** Manager. **E-mail address:** tritech@tritechpeople.com. **World Wide Web address:** http://www.tritechpeople.com. **Description:** An executive search firm. **Specializes in the areas of:** Administration; Executives; Finance; Information Technology; Marketing; Start-up Organizations; Web Development.

TYLER & COMPANY
1000 Abernathy Road NE, Suite 1400, Atlanta GA 30328. 770/396-3939. **Fax:** 770/396-6693. **Contact:** Manager. **Description:** An executive search firm. **Specializes in the areas of:** Health/Medical. **Positions commonly filled include:** Physician.

WARREN EXECUTIVE SERVICES
P.O. Box 1517, Lilburn GA 30048. 770/381-1175. **Fax:** 770/279-7865. **Contact:** Manager. **Description:** An executive search firm. **Specializes in the areas of:** Engineering; Manufacturing.

WHITTAKER & ASSOCIATES
2675 Cumberland Parkway, Suite 263, Atlanta GA 30339. 770/434-3779. **Fax:** 770/431-0213. **Contact:** Manager. **Description:** An executive search firm. **Specializes in the areas of:** Food. **Positions commonly filled include:** Branch Manager; Buyer; Chemist; Civil Engineer; Cost Estimator; Credit Manager; Customer Service Representative; Environmental Engineer; Financial Analyst; Food Scientist/Technologist; General Manager; Human Resources Manager; Industrial Engineer; Manufacturer's/Wholesaler's Sales Rep.; Market Research Analyst; Mechanical Engineer; Operations/Production Manager; Purchasing Agent/Manager; Quality Control Supervisor; Services Sales Rep.; Systems Analyst; Transportation/Traffic Specialist. **Average salary range of placements:** $30,000 - $50,000. **Number of placements per year:** 50 - 99.

WITT/KIEFFER, FORD, HADELMAN & LLOYD
3414 Peachtree Road, Suite 510, Atlanta GA 30326. 404/233-1370. **Fax:** 404/261-1371. **Contact:** Manager. **World Wide Web address:** http://www.wittkieffer.com. **Description:** Witt/Kieffer, Ford, Hadelman & Lloyd is an executive search firm. **Specializes in the areas of:** Health/Medical.

WORKMAN & ASSOCIATES
223 Brolley Woods Drive, Woodstock GA 30189. 770/926-8892. **Contact:** Jim Workman, Owner. **Description:** An executive search firm. **Specializes in the areas of:** Banking; Investment. **Positions commonly filled include:** Financial Services Sales Representative; Securities Sales Rep. **Number of placements per year:** 1 - 49.

PERMANENT EMPLOYMENT AGENCIES

A-OK PERSONNEL
P.O. Box 617, Gainesville GA 30503. 770/532-4002. **Physical address:** 200 Main Street, Gainesville GA.

Fax: 770/535-8367. **Contact:** John O'Kelley, Owner. **Description:** A permanent employment agency. **Specializes in the areas of:** Accounting/Auditing;

Administration; Finance; Health/Medical; Legal; Sales; Secretarial; Transportation. **Positions commonly filled include:** Accountant/Auditor; Clerical Supervisor; Computer Programmer; Dental Assistant/Dental Hygienist; General Manager; Management Trainee; Manufacturer's/Wholesaler's Sales Rep.; Paralegal; Services Sales Representative; Typist/Word Processor. **Average salary range of placements:** $20,000 - $29,999. **Number of placements per year:** 50 - 99.

ACCESS PERSONNEL SERVICES, INC.
200 Galleria Parkway, Suite 260, Atlanta GA 30339. 770/988-8484. **Fax:** 770/988-8522. **Contact:** Beverly Floyd, Recruiter. **Description:** A permanent employment agency. Founded in 1990. **Specializes in the areas of:** Accounting/Auditing; Administration; Banking; Clerical; Customer Service; Secretarial. **Positions commonly filled include:** Accountant/Auditor; Administrative Assistant; Customer Service Representative; Typist/Word Processor. **Benefits available to temporary workers:** Medical Insurance; Paid Holidays; Paid Vacation. **Corporate headquarters location:** This Location. **Average salary range of placements:** $21,000 - $30,000. **Number of placements per year:** 200 - 499.

ACCESS PERSONNEL SERVICES, INC.
1175 Peachtree Street, 100 Colony Square, Suite 1750, Atlanta GA 30361. 404/872-0888. **Fax:** 404/872-7790. **Contact:** Recruiter. **Description:** A permanent employment agency. Founded in 1990. **Specializes in the areas of:** Accounting/Auditing; Administration; Banking; Clerical; Customer Service; Secretarial. **Positions commonly filled include:** Accountant; Administrative Assistant; Customer Service Representative; Typist/Word Processor. **Benefits available to temporary workers:** Medical Insurance; Paid Holidays; Paid Vacation.

ACCOUNTANTS ONE
1870 Independence Square, Suite C, Atlanta GA 30338. 770/395-6969. **Contact:** Manager. **Description:** A permanent placement agency. **Specializes in the areas of:** Accounting.

ACTUARIAL SOURCE
1489 Mill Creek Court, Suite 100, Marietta GA 30008. 770/437-9292. **Contact:** Manager. **Description:** A permanent placement agency. **Positions commonly filled include:** Actuary.

AD OPTIONS INC.
P.O. Box 7778, Marietta GA 30065. 770/424-7778. **Fax:** 770/919-2254. **Contact:** Alex Wilson, President. **World Wide Web address:** http://www.ad-options.com. **Description:** A permanent employment agency that also provides some temporary placements. Founded in 1993. **Specializes in the areas of:** Advertising; Art/Design; Marketing. **Positions commonly filled include:** Account Manager; Advertising Executive; Art Director; Copywriter; Graphic Artist; Graphic Designer; Market Research Analyst; Marketing Manager; Marketing Specialist; Media Buyer; Media Specialist; Public Relations Specialist. **Average salary range of placements:** $30,000 - $50,000. **Number of placements per year:** 50 - 99.

AUGUSTA STAFFING ASSOCIATES
218 Oak Street, Suite E, Martinez GA 30907. 706/860-4820. **Fax:** 706/860-4871. **Contact:** Cynthia Kelly, President. **E-mail address:** asaoffice1@aol.com. **Description:** A permanent employment agency that also provides some temporary placements. Founded in 1992. **Specializes in the areas of:** Accounting/Auditing; Administration; Computer Hardware/Software; Engineering; General Management; Industrial; Manufacturing; Personnel/Labor Relations; Retail; Secretarial. **Positions commonly filled include:** Account Manager; Account Representative; Accountant; Administrative Assistant; Administrative Manager; Advertising Executive; Assistant Manager; Bank Officer/Manager; Blue-Collar Worker Supervisor;

Branch Manager; Buyer; Chemical Engineer; Chemist; Claim Representative; Computer Operator; Computer Programmer; Controller; Counselor; Credit Manager; Customer Service Representative; Database Manager; Draftsperson; Electrical/Electronics Engineer; Graphic Designer; Human Resources Manager; Industrial Engineer; Industrial Production Manager; Management Trainee; Manufacturing Engineer; Marketing Specialist; Mechanical Engineer; Production Manager; Public Relations Specialist; Purchasing Agent/Manager; Quality Control Supervisor; Sales Executive; Sales Manager; Sales Representative; Secretary; Software Engineer; Systems Analyst; Transportation/Traffic Specialist; Typist/Word Processor. **Corporate headquarters location:** This Location. **Average salary range of placements:** $20,000 - $29,999. **Number of placements per year:** 500 - 999.

BUSINESS PROFESSIONAL GROUP, INC.
3490 Piedmont Road, Suite 212, Atlanta GA 30305. 404/262-2577. **Fax:** 404/262-3463. **Contact:** Michelle Abel, CPC. **E-mail address:** BPGi@BPGi.com. **Description:** A permanent employment agency specializing in placing college graduates in entry-level career positions. **Specializes in the areas of:** Accounting/Auditing; Advertising; CIS; Computer Science/Software; Engineering; Entry-Level; Finance; Marketing; MIS/EDP; Sales; Technical. **Positions commonly filled include:** Account Manager; Editor; Electrical/Electronics Engineer; Financial Analyst; Industrial Engineer; Instructor/Trainer; Management; Marketing Specialist; Mechanical Engineer; Systems Analyst; Technical Support Representative; Underwriter/Assistant Underwriter. **Average salary range of placements:** $25,000 - $60,000. **Number of placements per year:** 100 - 199.

CAREER PLACEMENTS
Bank of America Plaza, Suite 204, 777 Gloucester Street, Brunswick GA 31520. 912/264-3401. **Contact:** President. **Description:** A permanent employment agency. **Specializes in the areas of:** Accounting/Auditing; Engineering; Sales. **Positions commonly filled include:** Accountant/Auditor; Actuary; Claim Representative; Dietician/Nutritionist; Electrical/Electronics Engineer; Financial Analyst; General Manager; Health Services Manager; Human Resources Manager; Industrial Engineer; Manufacturer's/Wholesaler's Sales Rep.; Mechanical Engineer; Registered Nurse; Software Engineer. **Number of placements per year:** 1 - 49.

CATALINA HUMAN RESOURCES, INC.
4470 Chamblee-Dunwoody Road, Suite 445, Atlanta GA 30338. 770/220-0770. **Fax:** 770/220-0767. **Contact:** Geri H. Frye, Branch Manager. **E-mail address:** geri@catalinaresources.com. **World Wide Web address:** http://www.catalinaresources.com. **Description:** A permanent employment agency. **Specializes in the areas of:** Accounting/Auditing; Administration; Banking; Computer Science/Software; Finance; Health/Medical; Sales; Technical. **Positions commonly filled include:** Accountant/Auditor; Administrative Manager; Bank Officer/Manager; Computer Programmer; Customer Service Representative; Financial Analyst; Financial Services Sales Representative; Internet Services Manager; Management Analyst/Consultant; MIS Specialist; Multimedia Designer; Securities Sales Representative; Systems Analyst; Technical Writer/Editor; Typist/Word Processor. **Corporate headquarters location:** Tampa FL. **Average salary range of placements:** $30,000 - $50,000. **Number of placements per year:** 100 - 199.

CLAREMONT-BRANAN, INC.
1298 Rockbridge Road, Suite B, Stone Mountain GA 30087. 770/925-2915. **Contact:** Phil Collins, President. **Description:** A permanent employment agency. **Specializes in the areas of:** Architecture/Construction; Design; Engineering. **Positions commonly filled include:** Architect; Civil Engineer; Electrical/Electronics

Engineer; Interior Designer; Mechanical Engineer. **Number of placements per year:** 50 - 99.

DDS STAFFING RESOURCES INC.
9755 Dogwood Road, Suite 200, Roswell GA 30075. 770/998-7779. **Contact:** Manager. **Description:** A permanent employment agency. **Specializes in the areas of:** Health/Medical. **Positions commonly filled include:** Claim Representative; Dental Assistant/Dental Hygienist; Dentist; Licensed Practical Nurse; Medical Records Technician; Registered Nurse; Social Worker. **Number of placements per year:** 500 - 999.

EXECUTIVE PLACEMENT SERVICES
5901-C Peachtree-Dunwoody Road, Suite 498, Atlanta GA 30328. 770/396-9114. **Fax:** 770/393-3040. **Contact:** John J. Weiss, President. **E-mail address:** execplac@mindspring.com. **World Wide Web address:** http://www.execplacement.com. **Description:** A permanent employment agency. Founded in 1986. **Specializes in the areas of:** Accounting; Casinos; Finance; Food; Hotel/Restaurant; Management; Marketing; Retail; Security. **Positions commonly filled include:** Buyer; EDP Specialist; Management; Security Manager.

EXPRESS PERSONNEL SERVICES
8 Amlajack Boulevard, Newnan GA 30265. 770/253-0133. **Fax:** 770/253-2827. **Contact:** Manager. **World Wide Web address:** http://www.expresspersonnel.com. **Description:** A permanent employment agency that also provides some temporary placements. **Specializes in the areas of:** Accounting/Auditing; Administration; Light Industrial; MIS/EDP; Sales; Secretarial; Technical. **Positions commonly filled include:** Administrative Assistant; Assembler; Draftsperson; Machine Operator; Machinist; MIS Specialist; Production Worker; Sales Executive; Sales Representative; Secretary; Warehouse/Distribution Worker; Welder. **Benefits available to temporary workers:** 401(k); Accident/ Emergency Insurance; Medical Insurance; Paid Holidays; Paid Vacation. **Corporate headquarters location:** Oklahoma City OK. **Other U.S. locations:** Nationwide. **International locations:** United Kingdom; Russia; Sweden. **Average salary range of placements:** Less than $20,000. **Number of placements per year:** 1000+.

EXPRESS PERSONNEL SERVICES
712 West Taylor Street, Griffin GA 30223. 770/227-9103. **Fax:** 770/227-1139. **Contact:** Phillip Purser, General Manager. **E-mail address:** jobs@griffinga.expresspersonnel.com. **World Wide Web address:** http://www.expresspersonnel.com. **Description:** Express Personnel Services is a permanent employment agency that also provides some temporary placements. **Specializes in the areas of:** Accounting/Auditing; Administration; Banking; Computer Science/Software; Engineering; Finance; General Management; Industrial; Manufacturing; Personnel/Labor Relations; Sales; Technical. **Positions commonly filled include:** Chemical Engineer; Clerical Supervisor; Computer Programmer; Credit Manager; Customer Service Representative; Electrical/Electronics Engineer; Electrician; Human Resources Manager; Industrial Engineer; Industrial Production Manager; Mechanical Engineer; MIS Specialist; Operations/ Production Manager; Systems Analyst; Typist/Word Processor. **Number of placements per year:** 1000+.

HORIZONS STAFFING
3354 Shamblee Tucker, Atlanta GA 30341. 770/457-6858. **Contact:** Manager. **Description:** Horizons Staffing is a permanent employment agency that also provides some temporary placements. **Specializes in the areas of:** Banking; Secretarial. **Positions commonly filled include:** Accountant; Administrative Assistant; Administrative Manager; Bank Officer/Manager; Claim Representative; Medical Records Technician; Paralegal; Sales Executive; Secretary; Typist/Word Processor. **Average salary range of placements:** $20,000 - $50,000.

INTERNATIONAL INSURANCE PERSONNEL
300 West Wieuca Road, Building 2, Suite 101, Atlanta GA 30342. 404/255-9710. **Fax:** 404/255-9864. **Contact:** Julie B. Dickerson, President. **Description:** A permanent employment agency. **Specializes in the areas of:** Insurance. **Positions commonly filled include:** Administrative Assistant; Claim Representative; Data Entry Clerk; Insurance Agent/Broker; Management Analyst/Consultant; Sales Representative; Secretary; Stenographer; Typist/Word Processor; Underwriter/ Assistant Underwriter. **Benefits available to temporary workers:** Medical Insurance; Paid Vacation. **Average salary range of placements:** $20,000 - $100,000. **Number of placements per year:** 1000+.

JES SEARCH FIRM, INC.
950 East Paces Ferry Road, Suite 2245, Atlanta GA 30326. 404/262-7222. **Fax:** 404/266-3533. **Contact:** Brenda Evers, President. **Description:** A permanent employment agency that also provides some contract placements. **Specializes in the areas of:** Computer Science/Software. **Positions commonly filled include:** Software Developer. **Number of placements per year:** 200 - 499.

MAU, INC.
501 Greene Street, Augusta GA 30901. 706/722-6806. **Contact:** Randy Hatcher, President. **Description:** A permanent employment agency. **Specializes in the areas of:** Engineering; Health/Medical; Manufacturing; MIS/EDP. **Positions commonly filled include:** EDP Specialist; Electrical/Electronics Engineer; Industrial Designer; Mechanical Engineer; Physician. **Number of placements per year:** 50 - 99.

THE MALCOLM GROUP, INC.
P.O. Box 178, Marble Hill GA 30148. 770/893-3485. **Fax:** 770/893-3489. **Contact:** Charles Malcolm, President/Owner. **Description:** A permanent employment agency. **Specializes in the areas of:** Insurance. **Positions commonly filled include:** Actuary; Claim Representative; Insurance Agent/Broker; Underwriter/Assistant Underwriter.

MARATHON CONSULTING
425 East Crossville Road, Suite 115, Roswell GA 30075. 770/640-1595. **Contact:** Manager. **Description:** A permanent employment agency. **Specializes in the areas of:** Nuclear Power.

MORE PERSONNEL SERVICES INC.
4501 Circle 75 Parkway, Suite A-1190, Atlanta GA 30339. 770/955-0885. **Fax:** 770/955-0767. **Contact:** Manager. **E-mail address:** morepers@mindspring.com. **World Wide Web address:** http://www.job-morepersonnel.com. **Description:** A permanent employment agency that provides placements to college graduates. Founded in 1988. **Specializes in the areas of:** Finance; General Management; Insurance; Sales. **Positions commonly filled include:** Account Representative; Accountant; Adjuster; Advertising Executive; Assistant Manager; Branch Manager; Claim Representative; Clerical Supervisor; Consultant; Controller; Counselor; Credit Manager; Customer Service Representative; Database Manager; Finance Director; Financial Analyst; General Manager; Human Resources Manager; Internet Services Manager; Management Analyst/Consultant; Management Trainee; Market Research Analyst; Marketing Manager; Marketing Specialist; Multimedia Designer; Operations Manager; Public Relations Specialist; Purchasing Agent/Manager; Sales Engineer; Sales Executive; Sales Manager; Sales Representative. **Corporate headquarters location:** This Location. **Average salary range of placements:** $30,000 - $50,000. **Number of placements per year:** 200 - 499.

NEW BOSTON SELECT
3391 Peachtree Road, Suite 270, Atlanta GA 30326. 404/266-1969. **Contact:** Manager. **Description:** A permanent employment agency. **Specializes in the areas of:** Accounting; Banking; Finance; Personnel/Labor

Relations; Secretarial. **Positions commonly filled include:** Accountant; Credit Manager; Customer Service Rep.; Human Resources Specialist; Word Processor; Underwriter. **Benefits available to temporary workers:** Medical Insurance; Paid Holidays; Paid Vacation. **Number of placements per year:** 500 - 999.

NORRED & ASSOCIATES INC.
3420 Norman Berry Drive, Suite 301, Atlanta GA 30354. 404/761-5058. **Fax:** 404/761-1152. **Contact:** Frank Ruggiero. **Description:** A permanent employment agency. Founded in 1981. **Specializes in the areas of:** Industrial; Security. **Positions commonly filled include:** Management Trainee; Security Officer. **Average salary range of placements:** Less than $20,000. **Number of placements per year:** 500 - 999.

OFFICEMATES5 (OM5)
DAYSTAR TEMPORARY SERVICES
1201 Peachtree Street, Suite 1001, Atlanta GA 30361. 404/892-1900. **Fax:** 404/892-4792. **Contact:** Kathleen Luck, Manager. **Description:** A permanent employment agency. DayStar Temporary Services (also at this location) is a temporary agency. **Specializes in the areas of:** Accounting/Auditing; Office Support; Secretarial. **Positions commonly filled include:** Administrative Manager; Advertising Clerk; Clerical Supervisor; Clerk; Customer Service Representative; Human Resources Specialist; Management Trainee; Typist/Word Processor. **Corporate headquarters location:** Cleveland OH. **Other U.S. locations:** Nationwide. **Average salary range of placements:** $20,000 - $29,999. **Number of placements per year:** 500 - 999.

OLSTEN PROFESSIONAL STAFFING
3424 Peachtree Road NE, Suite 125, Atlanta GA 30326. 404/467-2300. **Fax:** 404/364-6220. **Contact:** Recruiter. **World Wide Web address:** http://www.worknow.com. **Description:** A permanent employment agency that also provides some temporary placements. **Specializes in the areas of:** Computer Science; Engineering; Technical. **Positions commonly filled include:** Applications Engineer; Architect; Chemical Engineer; Civil Engineer; Computer Operator; Computer Programmer; Design Engineer; Draftsperson; Electricals Engineer; Industrial Engineer; Manufacturing Engineer; Mechanical Engineer; Metallurgical Engineer; MIS Specialist; Project Manager; Purchasing Agent; Quality Control Supervisor; Software Engineer; Structural Engineer; Systems Analyst; Technical Writer; Telecommunications Manager. **Corporate headquarters location:** Melville NY. **Average salary range of placements:** More than $50,000. **Number of placements per year:** 1000+.

PATHFINDERS, INC.
229 Peachtree Street NE, 1500 International Tower, Atlanta GA 30303. 404/688-5940. **Contact:** Diane Post, President. **Description:** A permanent employment agency. **Specializes in the areas of:** Secretarial. **Positions commonly filled include:** Administrative Assistant; Administrative Worker/Clerk; Legal Secretary; Secretary. **Number of placements per year:** 500 - 999.

QUEST SYSTEMS, INC.
3 Corporate Square, Suite 210, Atlanta GA 30329. 404/636-3000. **Contact:** Manager. **World Wide Web address:** http://www.questsyst.com. **Description:** A permanent employment agency. **Specializes in the areas of:** Computer Science. **Corporate headquarters location:** Bethesda MD.

SMITH AGENCY
2970 Peachtree Road NW, Suite 820, Atlanta GA 30305. 404/261-4257. **Contact:** Cynthia Adams, Personnel

Placement Consultant. **Description:** A permanent employment agency. **Specializes in the areas of:** Domestic Help; Nannies. **Positions commonly filled include:** Chauffeur; Chef/Cook/Kitchen Worker; Domestic Help; Housekeeper; Nanny. **Number of placements per year:** 100 - 199.

SOUTHERN EMPLOYMENT SERVICE
1233 54th Street, Columbus GA 31904. 706/327-6533. **Fax:** 706/323-7920. **Contact:** Manager. **Description:** A permanent employment agency. **Specializes in the areas of:** Accounting/Auditing; Administration; Banking; Computer Hardware/Software; General Management; Industrial; Manufacturing; Personnel/Labor Relations; Sales; Secretarial. **Positions commonly filled include:** Accountant; Administrative Assistant; Bookkeeper; Civil Engineer; Clerk; Computer Operator; Computer Programmer; Credit Manager; Customer Service Rep.; Data Entry Clerk; Manufacturing Engineer; Marketing Specialist; Mechanical Engineer; MIS Specialist; Operations Manager; Quality Control Supervisor; Receptionist; Sales Manager; Systems Analyst; Word Processor. **Number of placements per year:** 100 - 199.

STAFFING RESOURCES
4275 Shackleford Road, Suite 250, Norcross GA 30093. 770/638-8100. **Contact:** Operations Manager. **Description:** A permanent employment agency. **Specializes in the areas of:** Accounting; Administration; Advertising; Health/Medical; Insurance; Personnel/Labor Relations; Publishing; Sales; Secretarial. **Positions commonly filled include:** Accountant/Auditor; Advertising Clerk; Claim Rep.; Clerical Supervisor; Computer Programmer; Customer Service Representative; Human Resources Specialist; Medical Records Technician; Quality Control Supervisor; Services Sales Rep.; Word Processor. **Benefits available to temporary workers:** 401(k); Medical Insurance; Paid Holidays; Paid Vacation. **Other area locations:** Atlanta GA. **Average salary range of placements:** $20,000 - $29,999. **Number of placements per year:** 1000+.

TODAYS EMPLOYMENT SOLUTIONS
P.O. Box 68, Chatsworth GA 30705. 706/695-7951. **Contact:** Ms. Jamie Jones, President. **Description:** A permanent employment agency. **Specializes in the areas of:** Industrial; Personnel/Labor Relations. **Positions commonly filled include:** Accountant/Auditor; Blue-Collar Worker Supervisor; Computer Programmer; Credit Manager; Customer Service Representative; Electrician; Management Trainee; Quality Control Supervisor; Typist/Word Processor. **Average salary range of placements:** $20,000 - $29,999. **Number of placements per year:** 500 - 999.

TYLER TECHNICAL STAFFING
750 Hammond Drive, Building 9, Atlanta GA 30328. 404/250-9525. **Fax:** 404/250-0557. **Contact:** Manager. **Description:** A permanent employment agency that also provides some temporary and contract placements. **Specializes in the areas of:** Electronics; Engineering; Information Technology.

VAN ZANT RESOURCE GROUP
6700 Sugarloaf Parkway, Duluth GA 30097. 678/775-6789. **Fax:** 678/775-6790. **Contact:** Manager. **E-mail address:** vrg@vrg-inc.com. **World Wide Web address:** http://www.vrg-inc.com. **Description:** A permanent placement agencies that also offers contract placements. **Specializes in the areas of:** Cable TV; Information Technology; Software Training; Telecommunications. **Corporate headquarters location:** This Location.

TEMPORARY EMPLOYMENT AGENCIES

ACCOUNTANTS INC.
6 Concourse Parkway, Suite 300, Atlanta GA 30328. 770/393-2228. **Fax:** 770/393-8522. **Contact:** Manager.

E-mail address: atlanta@accountantsinc.com. **World Wide Web address:** http://www.accountantsinc.com. **Description:** A temporary employment agency that also offers some permanent placements. **Specializes in the areas of:** Accounting; Finance. **Corporate headquarters location:** Burlingame CA. **Other U.S. locations:** Nationwide.

ACCOUNTING RESOURCE TEMPORARIES
PMB 183, 12460 Crab Apple Road, Suite 202, Alpharetta GA 30004. 770/740-9833. **Contact:** Manager. **Description:** A temporary agency that also provides some temp-to-perm placements. **Specializes in the areas of:** Accounting/Auditing.

ALL-STAR TEMPORARY & EMPLOYMENT SERVICES
5848 Bankhead Highway, Suite K, Douglasville GA 30134. 770/942-0264. **Contact:** Marlene Van Camp, Owner. **Description:** A temporary agency. Founded in 1978. **Specializes in the areas of:** Industrial; Secretarial; Transportation. **Positions commonly filled include:** Accountant/Auditor; Blue-Collar Worker Supervisor; Computer Programmer; Quality Control Supervisor. **Benefits available to temporary workers:** Medical Insurance; Paid Holidays; Paid Vacation. **Other area locations:** Atlanta GA; Smyrna GA. **Average salary range of placements:** Less than $20,000. **Number of placements per year:** 1000+.

AQUENT PARTNERS
140 First Union Plaza, 999 Peachtree Street NE, Atlanta GA 30309-3964. 404/222-9600. **Toll-free phone:** 877/PARTNER. **Fax:** 404/874-9092. **Contact:** Audrie Eidson, Market Manager. **E-mail address:** aeidson@aquent.com. **World Wide Web address:** http://www.aquentpartners.com. **Description:** A temporary agency that provides placements for creative, Web, and technical professionals. Aquent Partners also provides some temp-to-perm, permanent, and contract placements. **Specializes in the areas of:** Administration; Art/Design; Communications; Computer Science/Software; Marketing. **Positions commonly filled include:** Computer Animator; Computer Engineer; Computer Operator; Computer Programmer; Computer Support Technician; Computer Technician; Content Developer; Database Administrator; Database Manager; Desktop Publishing Specialist; Editor; Editorial Assistant; Graphic Artist; Graphic Designer; Internet Services Manager; Managing Editor; MIS Specialist; Multimedia Designer; Network/Systems Administrator; Production Manager; Project Manager; Software Engineer; SQL Programmer; Systems Analyst; Systems Manager; Technical Writer/Editor; Webmaster. **Benefits available to temporary workers:** 401(k); Dental Insurance; Disability Coverage; Medical Insurance. **CEO:** John Chuang. **Average salary range of placements:** $30,000 - $40,000. **Number of placements per year:** 500 - 999.

COAST TO COAST
6015 Atlantic Boulevard, Suite A, Norcross GA 30071. 770/447-8708. **Toll-free phone:** 800/532-6278. **Fax:** 770/447-5197. **Contact:** Manager. **E-mail address:** atlanta@jobs-coast2coast.com. **Description:** A temporary agency that also provides contract services. Founded in 1994. **Specializes in the areas of:** Computer Science/Software; Engineering; Technical. **Positions commonly filled include:** Aerospace Engineer; Aircraft Mechanic/Engine Specialist; Architect; Biomedical Engineer; Buyer; Chemical Engineer; Chemist; Civil Engineer; Computer Programmer; Construction Contractor; Cost Estimator; Design Engineer; Designer; Draftsperson; Electrical/Electronics Engineer; Environmental Engineer; Geologist/Geophysicist; Industrial Engineer; Internet Services Manager; Landscape Architect; Mechanical Engineer; Metallurgical Engineer; Mining Engineer; MIS Specialist; Nuclear Engineer; Petroleum Engineer; Purchasing Agent/Manager; Quality Control Supervisor; Science Technologist; Software Engineer; Structural Engineer; Technical Writer/Editor; Urban/Regional Planner. **Benefits available to temporary workers:** Credit Union; Paid Holidays; Paid Vacation. **Average**

salary range of placements: More than $50,000. **Number of placements per year:** 1000+.

DURHAM STAFFING INC.
1343 Canton Road, Suite D2, Marietta GA 30066. 770/499-1665. **Fax:** 770/499-8407. **Contact:** Brian Durham, Co-Owner. **Description:** A temporary agency. **Specializes in the areas of:** Distribution; Manufacturing. **Positions commonly filled include:** Secretary; Typist/Word Processor. **Other U.S. locations:** Buffalo NY; Columbus OH; Chattanooga TN. **Number of placements per year:** 1000+.

DYNAMIC PEOPLE
260 Peachtree Street NW, Suite 800, Atlanta GA 30303. 404/688-1124. **Contact:** President. **Description:** A temporary agency. Founded in 1990. **Specializes in the areas of:** Personnel/Labor Relations; Secretarial. **Positions commonly filled include:** Administrative Assistant; Customer Service Representative; Secretary; Typist/Word Processor. **Number of placements per year:** 1000+.

ELITE STAFFING SERVICES
5881 Glenridge Drive, Suite 260, Atlanta GA 30328. 404/255-7737. **Fax:** 404/303-7736. **Contact:** Natasha Goff-Buckner. **E-mail address:** resume@elitestaff.com. **World Wide Web address:** http://www.elitestaff.com. **Description:** A temporary agency that also provides some permanent placements and resume and career counseling services. Client company pays fee. **Specializes in the areas of:** Accounting; Administration; Advertising; Banking; Broadcasting; Computer Science/Software; Finance; General Management; Health/Medical; Insurance; Internet Development; Internet Services; Legal; Light Industrial; Marketing; MIS/EDP; Nonprofit; Personnel/Labor Relations; Retail; Sales; Scientific; Secretarial; Technical. **Positions commonly filled include:** Account Manager; Account Representative; Accountant; Administrative Assistant; Administrative Manager; Advertising Clerk; Advertising Executive; Applications Engineer; AS400 Programmer Analyst; Assistant Manager; Attorney; Auditor; Bank Officer/Manager; Blue-Collar Worker Supervisor; Branch Manager; Budget Analyst; Buyer; Certified Nurses Aide; Chemist; Chief Financial Officer; Claim Representative; Clerical Supervisor; Clinical Lab Technician; Computer Programmer; Computer Support Technician; Controller; Credit Manager; Customer Service Representative; Database Administrator; Database Manager; Desktop Publishing Specialist; Dietician/Nutritionist; Editor; Editorial Assistant; Electrical/Electronics Engineer; Emergency Medical Technician; Financial Analyst; Fund Manager; General Manager; Graphic Artist; Graphic Designer; Home Health Aide; Human Resources Manager; Insurance Agent/Broker; Internet Services Manager; Licensed Practical Nurse; Management Analyst/Consultant; Management Trainee; Managing Editor; Manufacturing Engineer; Marketing Manager; Marketing Specialist; Mechanical Engineer; Network/Systems Administrator; Operations Manager; Paralegal; Pharmacist; Physical Therapist; Physical Therapy Assistant; Production Manager; Project Manager; Psychologist; Public Relations Specialist; Purchasing Agent/Manager; Quality Assurance Engineer; Quality Control Supervisor; Real Estate Agent; Registered Nurse; Sales Engineer; Sales Executive; Sales Manager; Sales Representative; Secretary; Social Worker; Software Engineer; Statistician; Systems Analyst; Systems Manager; Technical Writer/Editor; Telecommunications Manager; Transportation/Traffic Specialist; Typist/Word Processor; Underwriter/Assistant Underwriter. **Benefits available to temporary workers:** 401(k); Paid Holidays; Paid Vacation. **Corporate headquarters location:** This Location. **Other U.S. locations:** Phoenix AZ. **Average salary range of placements:** $30,000 - $49,999. **Number of placements per year:** 1000+.

FIRST PRO
3859 Peachtree Road, Atlanta GA 30319. 404/365-8367. **Contact:** Manager. **Description:** A temporary agency.

Specializes in the areas of: Administration; General Management; Sales; Secretarial. **Average salary range of placements:** $20,000 - $29,999. **Number of placements per year:** 50 - 99.

HEALTHCARE FINANCIAL STAFFING
LAB SUPPORT
2300 Northlake Center Drive, Suite 210, Tucker GA 30084. 770/492-0706. **Toll-free phone:** 800/726-2898. **Fax:** 770/491-0230. **Contact:** Adenika Smith, Certified Account Manager. **Description:** A temporary agency. Lab Support (also at this location, 770/621-0307, http://www.labsupport.com) is a temporary agency that provides placements for scientific professionals. **Specializes in the areas of:** Health/Medical. **Positions commonly filled include:** Billing Clerk; Collector; Medical Secretary. **Benefits available to temporary workers:** Dental Insurance; Life Insurance; Medical Insurance. **Corporate headquarters location:** Calabasas CA. **Average salary range of placements:** $20,000 - $29,999. **Number of placements per year:** 200 - 499.

HIRE INTELLECT INC.
2401 Lake Park Drive, Suite 260, Smyrna GA 30080. 770/435-2111. **Fax:** 770/435-2177. **Contact:** Resume Coordinator. **E-mail address:** resumes@hireintellect.com. **Description:** A temporary agency. Founded in 1992. **Specializes in the areas of:** Marketing. **Positions commonly filled include:** Advertising Executive; Editor; Graphic Artist; Graphic Designer; Internet Services Manager; Market Research Analyst; Marketing Manager; Marketing Specialist; Public Relations Specialist; Webmaster. **Benefits available to temporary workers:** Paid Holidays; Paid Vacation. **Average salary range of placements:** $30,000 - $50,000.

KELLY SCIENTIFIC RESOURCES
2302 Parklake Drive, Suite 370, Atlanta GA 30345. 770/270-1892. **Fax:** 770/493-9325. **Contact:** Branch Manager. **World Wide Web address:** http://www.kellyscientific.com. **Description:** A temporary agency. **Specializes in the areas of:** Biomedical; Biotechnology; Chemicals; Environmental; Food; Pharmaceuticals. **Corporate headquarters location:** Troy MI. **Other U.S. locations:** Nationwide.

KELLY SERVICES, INC.
590 Thornton Road, Suite D, Lithia Springs GA 30122. 770/739-1818. **Contact:** Manager. **Description:** A temporary agency. **Specializes in the areas of:** Accounting/Auditing; Clerical; Industrial; Light Industrial; Manufacturing. **Positions commonly filled include:** Blue-Collar Worker Supervisor; Buyer; Customer Service Representative. **Benefits available to temporary workers:** Paid Holidays; Paid Vacation. **Corporate headquarters location:** Troy MI. **Other U.S. locations:** Nationwide. **Number of placements per year:** 1000+.

KELLY SERVICES, INC.
211 Broad Street, Rome GA 30161. 706/235-9117. **Contact:** Manager. **Description:** A temporary agency. **Specializes in the areas of:** Personnel/Labor Relations; Secretarial; Technical. **Benefits available to temporary workers:** Medical Insurance; Paid Holidays; Paid Vacation. **Corporate headquarters location:** Troy MI. **Other U.S. locations:** Nationwide. **Average salary range of placements:** $20,000 - $29,999. **Number of placements per year:** 1 - 49.

MANPOWER TEMPORARY SERVICES
1355 Peachtree Street NE, Suite 108, Atlanta GA 30309. 404/724-0780. **Contact:** Branch Manager. **Description:** A temporary agency. **Specializes in the areas of:** Data Processing; Light Industrial; Office Support; Technical; Telemarketing. **Positions commonly filled include:** Accountant/Auditor; Accounting Clerk; Administrative Assistant; Assembly Worker; Biological Scientist; Bookkeeper; CADD Operator; Chemist; Computer Operator; Customer Service Representative; Desktop Publishing Specialist; Electrician; Inspector/Tester/

Grader; Inventory Control Specialist; Machine Operator; Material Control Specialist; Order Clerk; Packaging/Processing Worker; Painter; Project Engineer; Proofreader; Receptionist; Research Assistant; Secretary; Software Engineer; Stenographer; Stock Clerk; Systems Analyst; Technician; Telemarketer; Test Operator; Typist/Word Processor. **Benefits available to temporary workers:** Life Insurance; Medical Insurance; Paid Holidays; Paid Vacation. **Corporate headquarters location:** Milwaukee WI. **Other U.S. locations:** Nationwide. **Number of placements per year:** 1000+.

MANPOWER TEMPORARY SERVICES
187 Roberson Mill Road NE, Suite 202, Milledgeville GA 31061. 912/453-3600. **Contact:** Manager. **Description:** A temporary agency. **Specializes in the areas of:** Accounting/Auditing; Administration; Banking; Computer Hardware/Software; General Management; Manufacturing; Secretarial; Technical. **Positions commonly filled include:** Accountant/Auditor; Administrative Manager; Advertising Clerk; Bank Officer/Manager; Branch Manager; Buyer; Computer Programmer; Credit Manager; Customer Service Representative; Electrician; General Manager; Health Services Manager; Human Resources Specialist; Human Service Worker; Landscape Architect; Medical Records Technician; Paralegal; Public Relations Specialist; Restaurant/Food Service Manager; Services Sales Representative; Typist/Word Processor. **Benefits available to temporary workers:** Medical Insurance; Paid Holidays; Paid Vacation. **Corporate headquarters location:** Milwaukee WI. **Other U.S. locations:** Nationwide. **Average salary range of placements:** $20,000 - $29,999. **Number of placements per year:** 1000+.

MISSION CORPS INTERNATIONAL
HELPING HANDS TEMPORARY SERVICE
975 Memorial Drive, Atlanta GA 30316. 404/584-2304. **Contact:** Manager. **Description:** A temporary agency. Founded in 1993. **Specializes in the areas of:** Administration; Computer Science; Education; Nonprofit; Retail; Sales. **Positions commonly filled include:** Accountant/Auditor; Blue-Collar Worker Supervisor; Counselor; Education Administrator; Financial Analyst; Paralegal; Public Relations Specialist; Services Sales Rep. **Other U.S. locations:** TN; TX. **Average salary range of placements:** Less than $20,000. **Number of placements per year:** 100 - 199.

NORRELL CORPORATION
3535 Piedmont Road NE, Atlanta GA 30305. 404/262-2100. **Contact:** Manager. **World Wide Web address:** http://www.norrell.com. **Description:** A temporary agency. **Specializes in the areas of:** Banking; Clerical. **Positions commonly filled include:** Accountant/Auditor; Bookkeeper; Clerk; Computer Operator; Computer Programmer; Customer Service Representative; Data Entry Clerk; Driver; Factory Worker; Legal Secretary; Medical Secretary; Receptionist; Sales Rep.; Secretary; Typist/Word Processor. **Corporate headquarters location:** This Location. **Other U.S. locations:** Nationwide. **Number of placements per year:** 1000+.

NORRELL SERVICES INC.
1350 Spring Street, Suite 100, Atlanta GA 30309. 404/872-4330. **Contact:** Manager. **World Wide Web address:** http://www.norrell.com. **Description:** A temporary agency. **Specializes in the areas of:** Administration; Data Processing; Secretarial. **Benefits available to temporary workers:** Medical Insurance; Paid Holidays; Paid Vacation. **Other U.S. locations:** Nationwide. **Average salary range of placements:** Less than $20,000. **Number of placements per year:** 1000+.

OFFICE SPECIALISTS
3500 Piedmont Road NE, Suite 112, Atlanta GA 30305. 404/814-9865. **Fax:** 404/814-9866. **Contact:** Recruiting. **Description:** A temporary agency that also provides some permanent placements. **Specializes in the areas of:** Accounting/Auditing; Banking; Secretarial. **Positions commonly filled include:** Accountant/Auditor;

Customer Service Representative; Medical Records Technician; Typist/Word Processor. **Other U.S. locations:** Nationwide. **Average salary range of placements:** $20,000 - $29,999. **Number of placements per year:** 1000+.

OFFICE SPECIALISTS
1100 Circle 75 Parkway, Suite 125, Atlanta GA 30339. 770/984-6760. **Fax:** 770/984-6770. **Contact:** Ted Townsend, Team Leader. **Description:** A temporary agency. **Specializes in the areas of:** Administration; Technical. **Other U.S. locations:** Nationwide.

OLSTEN STAFFING SERVICES
2116 Henderson Mill Road, Atlanta GA 30345. 770/938-0212. **Contact:** Manager. **World Wide Web address:** http://www.worknow.com. **Description:** A temporary agency. **Specializes in the areas of:** Accounting/Auditing; Administration; Finance; Health/Medical; Secretarial; Technical. **Positions commonly filled include:** Accountant/Auditor; Clerical Supervisor; Customer Service Representative; Medical Records Technician; Paralegal; Typist/Word Processor. **Corporate headquarters location:** Melville NY. **Other U.S. locations:** Nationwide. **Average salary range of placements:** $20,000 - $29,999.

OLSTEN STAFFING SERVICES
2131 Pleasant Hill Road, Suite 108, Duluth GA 30096. 770/497-0045. **Fax:** 770/476-5696. **Contact:** Staffing Coordinator. **World Wide Web address:** http://www.worknow.com. **Description:** A temporary agency. Founded in 1950. **Specializes in the areas of:** Accounting/Auditing; Administration; Banking; Engineering; Finance; Health/Medical; Insurance; Legal; Nonprofit; Personnel/Labor Relations; Retail; Sales; Secretarial. **Positions commonly filled include:** Accountant/Auditor; Claim Representative; Customer Service Representative; Financial Analyst; Human Resources Specialist; Management Trainee; Medical Records Technician; Paralegal; Quality Control Supervisor; Software Engineer; Typist/Word Processor. **Benefits available to temporary workers:** Bonus Award/Plan; Medical Insurance. **Corporate headquarters location:** Melville NY. **Other U.S. locations:** Nationwide. **Average salary range of placements:** $20,000 - $29,999. **Number of placements per year:** 1000+.

PERSONNEL AT LAW, INC.
235 Peachtree Street NE, Suite 1707, Atlanta GA 30303. 404/222-9711. **Fax:** 404/222-9714. **Contact:** Judy Wells, President. **E-mail address:** smartpal@atlanta.com. **Description:** A temporary agency. Founded in 1978. **Specializes in the areas of:** Legal; Secretarial. **Positions commonly filled include:** Attorney; Clerical Supervisor; Paralegal; Typist/Word Processor. **Benefits available to temporary workers:** Medical Insurance; Paid Vacation. **Corporate headquarters location:** Southfield MI. **Other U.S. locations:** Nationwide. **Average salary range of placements:** $20,000 - $40,000. **Number of placements per year:** 100 - 199.

PRIORITY 1 STAFFING SERVICES
5805 State Bridge Road, Suite N, Duluth GA 30097. 770/813-1877. **Contact:** Staffing Services Manager. **Description:** A temporary agency. **Specializes in the areas of:** Accounting/Auditing; Banking; Computer Science/Software; Finance; Industrial; Insurance; Legal; Personnel/Labor Relations; Sales; Secretarial. **Positions commonly filled include:** Accountant/Auditor; Credit Manager; Customer Service Representative; Human Resources Specialist; Securities Sales Representative; Typist/Word Processor; Underwriter/Assistant Underwriter. **Benefits available to temporary workers:** Medical Insurance. **Corporate headquarters location:** Atlanta GA. **Other U.S. locations:** Baltimore MD. **Number of placements per year:** 1000+.

QUALITY EMPLOYMENT SERVICE
315 Fifth Avenue SE, Moultrie GA 31768. 912/891-3458. **Contact:** John E. Folds, Owner. **Description:** A temporary agency. **Specializes in the areas of:** Accounting/Auditing; Industrial; Manufacturing; Secretarial. **Positions commonly filled include:** Accountant/Auditor; Advertising Clerk; Automotive Mechanic; Blue-Collar Worker Supervisor; Brokerage Clerk; Buyer; Clerical Supervisor; Customer Service Representative; Draftsperson; Electrician; Human Service Worker; Licensed Practical Nurse; Operations/Production Manager; Purchasing Agent/Manager; Quality Control Supervisor; Registered Nurse; Typist/Word Processor. **Average salary range of placements:** Less than $20,000. **Number of placements per year:** 200 - 499.

RANDSTAD STAFFING SERVICES
1910 Highway 20 South, Suite 275, Conyers GA 30013. 770/922-2888. **Fax:** 770/922-5392. **Contact:** Branch Manager. **World Wide Web address:** http://www.randstadstaffing.com. **Description:** A temporary agency. **Specializes in the areas of:** Accounting/Auditing; Banking; Computer Science/Software; Engineering; Finance; Health/Medical; Industrial; Insurance; Manufacturing; Sales; Secretarial; Technical; Transportation. **Positions commonly filled include:** Accountant/Auditor; Administrative Manager; Blue-Collar Worker Supervisor; Branch Manager; Claim Representative; Computer Programmer; Credit Manager; Customer Service Representative; Draftsperson; Electrician; General Manager; Human Resources Specialist; Management Trainee; Manufacturer's/Wholesaler's Sales Rep.; Mechanical Engineer; Purchasing Agent/Manager; Quality Control Supervisor; Services Sales Representative; Transportation/Traffic Specialist. **Benefits available to temporary workers:** 401(k); Credit Union; Dental Insurance; Medical Insurance; Vision Insurance. **Corporate headquarters location:** Atlanta GA. **Other U.S. locations:** AL; FL; MS; SC; TN. **Average salary range of placements:** $20,000 - $29,999. **Number of placements per year:** 500 - 999.

RANDSTAD STAFFING SERVICES
P.O. Box 724198, Atlanta GA 30339. 770/937-7000. **Physical address:** 2015 South Park Place, Atlanta GA. **Contact:** Manager. **World Wide Web address:** http://www.randstadstaffing.com. **Description:** A temporary agency. **Specializes in the areas of:** Accounting/Auditing; Advertising; Banking; Computer Science/Software; Education; General Management; Industrial; Legal; Personnel/Labor Relations; Publishing; Retail; Sales; Secretarial; Technical; Transportation. **Positions commonly filled include:** Accountant/Auditor; Administrative Manager; Advertising Clerk; Brokerage Clerk; Budget Analyst; Buyer; Claim Representative; Computer Programmer; Cost Estimator; Counselor; Credit Manager; Customer Service Representative; Electrician; Financial Analyst; Human Resources Specialist; Industrial Engineer; Paralegal; Teacher/Professor; Travel Agent; Typist/Word Processor; Underwriter/Assistant Underwriter. **Benefits available to temporary workers:** 401(k); Dental Insurance; Disability Coverage; Life Insurance; Medical Insurance; Paid Holidays; Paid Vacation; Vision Plan. **Corporate headquarters location:** This Location. **Other U.S. locations:** AL; FL; MS; SC; TN. **Average salary range of placements:** Less than $20,000. **Number of placements per year:** 100 - 199.

RANDSTAD STAFFING SERVICES
420 Crosstown Drive, Peachtree City GA 30269-2915. 770/487-1446. **Fax:** 770/487-1398. **Contact:** Julie K. White, Branch Manager. **World Wide Web address:** http://www.randstadstaffing.com. **Description:** A temporary agency. **Specializes in the areas of:** Manufacturing; Personnel/Labor Relations; Retail; Secretarial. **Positions commonly filled include:** Customer Service Representative; Services Sales Representative; Typist/Word Processor. **Benefits available to temporary workers:** 401(k); Medical Insurance; Paid Holidays; Paid Vacation. **Corporate headquarters location:** Atlanta GA. **Other U.S. locations:** AL; FL; MS; SC; TN. **Average salary range**

of placements: Less than $20,000. Number of placements per year: 1000+.

RANDSTAD STAFFING SERVICES
196 Alps Road, Suite 1, Athens GA 30606. 706/548-9590. Contact: Manager. World Wide Web address: http://www.randstadstaffing.com. Description: A temporary agency. Specializes in the areas of: Accounting; Administration; Banking; Computer Science/Software; Light Industrial; Marketing; MIS/EDP; Sales; Secretarial. Positions commonly filled include: Administrative Assistant; Computer Operator; Customer Service Representative; Database Manager; MIS Specialist; Sales Representative; Secretary; Typist/Word Processor. Benefits available to temporary workers: 401(k); Credit Union; Dental Insurance; Disability Coverage; Life Insurance; Medical Insurance; Vacation Pay. Corporate headquarters location: Atlanta GA. Other U.S. locations: AL; FL; MS; SC; TN. Average salary range of placements: Less than $20,000. Number of placements per year: 1000+.

RANDSTAD STAFFING SERVICES
6681-E Roswell Road, Atlanta GA 30328. 404/250-1008. Fax: 404/252-0605. Contact: Branch Manager. World Wide Web address: http://www.randstadstaffing.com. Description: A temporary agency. Specializes in the areas of: Accounting/Auditing; Computer Science/Software; Industrial; Manufacturing; Personnel/Labor Relations; Technical. Positions commonly filled include: Accountant/Auditor; Administrative Manager; Advertising Clerk; Blue-Collar Worker Supervisor; Branch Manager; Claim Representative; Clerical Supervisor; Credit Manager; Customer Service Representative; Draftsperson; Financial Analyst; General Manager; Health Services Manager; Hotel Manager; Human Resources Specialist; Industrial Engineer; Internet Services Manager; Management Trainee; Market Research Analyst; Mechanical Engineer; MIS Specialist; Quality Control Supervisor; Software Engineer; Statistician; Telecommunications Manager; Typist/Word Processor. Benefits available to temporary workers: 401(k); Medical Insurance; Paid Holidays; Paid Vacation. Corporate headquarters location: 2015 South Park Place, Atlanta GA 30339. Other U.S. locations: AL; FL; MS; SC; TN. Average salary range of placements: $30,000 - $50,000. Number of placements per year: 1000+.

RIGHT CHOICE STAFFING
282 South Main Street, Suite A, Alpharetta GA 30004. 770/664-6909. Fax: 770/664-7649. Contact: Ray D. Martin, Vice President. E-mail address: rdmartin@rightchoicestaffing.com. Description: A temporary agency that also provides some temp-to-perm placements. Specializes in the areas of: Restaurant. Positions commonly filled include: Assistant Manager; Clerical Supervisor; Management Trainee. Average salary range of placements: $20,000 - $29,999. Number of placements per year: 100 - 199.

SPECIAL COUNSEL
100 Colony Square, Suite 840, Atlanta GA 30361. 404/872-6672. Contact: Manager. World Wide Web address: http://www.specialcounsel.com. Description: A temporary agency that also provides some permanent placements. Specializes in the areas of: Legal.

STAFFMARK
861 Holcomb Bridge Road, Suite 105, Roswell GA 30076. 770/998-8024. Fax: 770/998-0875. Contact: Coordinator. Description: A temporary agency. Founded in 1974. Specializes in the areas of: Accounting/Auditing; Personnel/Labor Relations; Secretarial. Positions commonly filled include: Accountant/Auditor; Chemist; Customer Service Representative; Typist/Word Processor. Benefits available to temporary workers: Bonus Award/Plan; Medical Insurance; Paid Holidays; Paid Vacation. Other U.S. locations: AR; IN; NC; SC. Average salary range

of placements: Less than $20,000. Number of placements per year: 500 - 999.

STAFFMARK
200 Galleria Parkway, Suite 905, Atlanta GA 30339. 770/955-1767. Fax: 770/955-0114. Contact: Donna Vassil, Vice President. Description: A temporary agency. Founded in 1974. Specializes in the areas of: Accounting/Auditing; Administration; Manufacturing; Personnel/Labor Relations; Sales; Secretarial; Technical. Positions commonly filled include: Accountant/Auditor; Administrative Manager; Blue-Collar Worker Supervisor; Branch Manager; Claim Representative; Clinical Lab Technician; Computer Programmer; Customer Service Representative; Electrical/Electronics Engineer; Human Resources Specialist; MIS Specialist; Services Sales Representative; Systems Analyst; Typist/Word Processor. Benefits available to temporary workers: Bonus Award/Plan; Medical Insurance; Paid Holidays; Paid Vacation. Other U.S. locations: AR; IN; NC; SC. Average salary range of placements: $20,000 - $29,999. Number of placements per year: 1000+.

TRC STAFFING SERVICES
7000 Central Parkway, Suite 260, Atlanta GA 30328. 770/399-3006. Contact: Manager. Description: A temporary agency. Founded in 1970. Specializes in the areas of: Administration; Banking; Engineering; Insurance; Personnel/Labor Relations; Sales; Secretarial. Positions commonly filled include: Administrative Manager; Advertising Clerk; Claim Representative; Clerical Supervisor; Customer Service Representative; Editor; Human Resources Specialist; Librarian; Market Research Analyst; Public Relations Specialist; Purchasing Agent/Manager; Services Sales Representative; Technical Writer/Editor; Typist/Word Processor; Underwriter/Assistant Underwriter. Benefits available to temporary workers: Paid Holidays; Paid Vacation. Average salary range of placements: $20,000 - $29,999. Number of placements per year: 500 - 999.

TRI STAFFING
34 Peachtree Street NW, Suite 1680, Atlanta GA 30303. 404/659-9400. Contact: Manager. Description: A temporary agency. Specializes in the areas of: Administration; Personnel/Labor Relations. Positions commonly filled include: Accountant/Auditor; Administrative Manager; General Manager; Human Resources Specialist; Telecommunications Manager. Average salary range of placements: Less than $20,000. Number of placements per year: 50 - 99.

TAC STAFFING SERVICES
900 Circle 75 Parkway, Suite 150, Atlanta GA 30339. 770/955-5340. Contact: Manager. Description: A temporary agency. Specializes in the areas of: Customer Service. Other U.S. locations: Nationwide.

TEMPORARY SPECIALTIES
7513 Roswell Road, Atlanta GA 30350. 404/303-8611. Fax: 678/443-9949. Contact: Stephanie Acey, Senior Recruiter. Description: A temporary agency. Founded in 1982. Specializes in the areas of: Accounting/Auditing; Insurance; Manufacturing; Personnel/Labor Relations; Publishing; Secretarial. Positions commonly filled include: Buyer; Clerical Supervisor; Customer Service Representative; Typist/Word Processor. Benefits available to temporary workers: Dental Insurance; Life Insurance; Medical Insurance; Paid Holidays; Paid Vacation. Corporate headquarters location: Jonesboro GA. Number of placements per year: 200 - 499.

TEMPWORLD STAFFING SERVICES
2140 Peachtree Road NW, Suite 325, Atlanta GA 30309. 404/351-2077. Contact: Branch Manager. Description: A temporary agency that also provides some permanent placements. Specializes in the areas of: Customer Service; Sales; Secretarial; Word Processing. Positions commonly filled include: Customer Service Representative; Secretary; Typist/Word Processor.

Benefits available to temporary workers: 401(k); Scholarship Program.

WPPS SOFTWARE STAFFING
1175 Peachtree Street NE, 100 Colony Square, Suite 760, Atlanta GA 30361. 404/815-0440. **Fax:** 404/815-6666. **Contact:** Manager. **Description:** A temporary agency. Founded in 1978. **Specializes in the areas of:** Administration; Advertising; Architecture/Construction; Banking; Computer Science/Software; Finance; Legal; Nonprofit; Personnel/Labor Relations; Publishing; Sales; Secretarial. **Positions commonly filled include:** Administrative Manager; Clerical Supervisor; Computer Programmer; Customer Service Representative; Designer; Editor; Human Resources Specialist; Human Service Worker; Paralegal; Software Engineer; Technical Writer/Editor; Typist/Word Processor. **Corporate headquarters location:** Charlotte NC. **Average salary range of placements:** $21,000 - $29,999. **Number of placements per year:** 1 - 49.

WESTAFF
6351-A Jonesboro Road, Morrow GA 30260. 770/960-8166. **Contact:** Manager. **Description:** A temporary agency. **Specializes in the areas of:** Accounting/Auditing; Computer Science/Software; Engineering; Personnel/Labor Relations. **Positions commonly filled include:** Accountant/Auditor; Buyer; Computer Programmer; Engineer; Financial Analyst; Human Resources Manager; Telecommunications Manager. **Corporate headquarters location:** Walnut Creek CA. **Other U.S. locations:** Nationwide. **Average**

salary range of placements: $30,000 - $50,000. **Number of placements per year:** 1 - 49.

WESTAFF
537 North Expressway, Griffin GA 30223. 770/229-2411. **Fax:** 770/229-2494. **Contact:** Manager. **Description:** A temporary agency that also provides some permanent placements. Founded in 1948. **Specializes in the areas of:** Accounting/Auditing; Finance; Industrial; Light Industrial; Manufacturing; Personnel/Labor Relations; Sales; Secretarial. **Positions commonly filled include:** Accountant/Auditor; Branch Manager; Customer Service Representative; Draftsperson; Electrician; Management Trainee; Purchasing Agent/Manager; Quality Control Supervisor. **Benefits available to temporary workers:** 401(k); Paid Holidays; Paid Vacation. **Corporate headquarters location:** Walnut Creek CA. **Other U.S. locations:** Nationwide. **Number of placements per year:** 1000+.

WESTAFF
2200 Century Parkway, Suite 3, Atlanta GA 30345. 404/888-0003. **Contact:** Area Manager. **Description:** A temporary agency. Founded in 1948. **Specializes in the areas of:** Accounting/Auditing; Advertising; Computer Science/Software; Industrial; Legal; Manufacturing; Publishing; Secretarial; Technical. **Benefits available to temporary workers:** 401(k); Daycare Assistance; Medical Insurance; Paid Holidays; Paid Vacation. **Corporate headquarters location:** Walnut Creek CA. **Other U.S. locations:** Nationwide. **Average salary range of placements:** $20,000 - $29,999. **Number of placements per year:** 1000+.

CONTRACT SERVICES FIRMS

ADECCO/TAD TECHNICAL SERVICES
3039 Premier Parkway, Suite 900, Duluth GA 30097. 678/584-8686. **Fax:** 678/584-2602. **Contact:** Manager. **Description:** A contract services firm. **Corporate headquarters location:** Redwood City CA. **Other U.S. locations:** Nationwide.

COMMS PEOPLE
2550 Northwinds Parkway, Suite 100, Alpharetta GA 30004. 678/297-3340. **Contact:** Manager. **Description:** A contract services firm. **Specializes in the areas of:** Information Technology.

RECRUITMENT SOLUTIONS INC.
2265 Roswell Road, Marietta GA 30062. 770/509-2224. **Contact:** Manager. **Description:** A contract services firm.

TECHNICAL ASSOCIATES
P.O. Box 2048, Albany GA 31702. 912/888-6632. **Physical address:** 2423 Westgate Drive, Albany GA 31707. **Fax:** 912/435-2826. **Contact:** Technical Services Manager. **Description:** A contract services firm. **Specializes in the areas of:** Engineering; Technical. **Positions commonly filled include:** Chemical Engineer; Chemist; Civil Engineer; Computer Programmer; Construction Contractor; Database Manager; Design Engineer; Designer; Draftsperson; Electrical Engineer; Environmental Engineer; Industrial Engineer; Manufacturing Engineer; Mechanical Engineer; MIS Specialist; Project Manager; Purchasing Agent; Software Engineer; Structural Engineer; Systems Analyst; Technical Writer; Telecommunications Manager. **Benefits available to temporary workers:** 401(k); Paid Holidays; Paid Vacation. **Corporate headquarters location:** This Location. **Other U.S. locations:** Atlanta

GA; Macon GA; Jackson TN; Memphis TN. **Average salary range of placements:** More than $50,000. **Number of placements per year:** 200 - 499.

THINK RESOURCES
9000 Central Park West, Suite 350, Atlanta GA 30328. 770/390-0963. **Fax:** 770/392-1342. **Contact:** Recruiting Manager. **World Wide Web address:** http://www.thinkjobs.com. **Description:** A contract services firm that also provides some temp-to-perm placements. Founded in 1988. **Specializes in the areas of:** Engineering; Information Technology; Technical; Telecommunications. **Positions commonly filled include:** Aerospace Engineer; Agricultural Engineer; Aircraft Mechanic/Engine Specialist; Architect; Biochemist; Biological Scientist; Biomedical Engineer; Clinical Lab Technician; Computer Programmer; Construction and Building Inspector; Construction Manager; Cost Estimator; Design Engineer; Designer; Draftsperson; Electrical/Electronics Engineer; Electrician; Geographer; Geologist/Geophysicist; Industrial Engineer; Industrial Production Manager; Internet Services Manager; Landscape Architect; Management Analyst/Consultant; Mechanical Engineer; Metallurgical Engineer; Mining Engineer; MIS Specialist; Multimedia Designer; Nuclear Engineer; Operations/Production Manager; Petroleum Engineer; Purchasing Agent/Manager; Quality Control Supervisor; Science Technologist; Software Engineer; Stationary Engineer; Structural Engineer; Surveyor; Technical Writer/Editor; Telecommunications Manager; Transportation/Traffic Specialist. **Benefits available to temporary workers:** Medical Insurance; Paid Holidays; Paid Vacation. **Average salary range of placements:** More than $50,000. **Number of placements per year:** 500 - 999.

CAREER/OUTPLACEMENT COUNSELING FIRMS

ADVANCED RESUMES
438 Shearwater Drive, Fortson GA 31808. 706/320-0546. **Toll-free phone:** 877/353-0025. **Fax:** 888/811-

3241. **Contact:** Gwen Harrison, President. **E-mail address:** questions@advancedresumes.com. **World Wide Web address:** http://www.advancedresumes.com.

Description: A career counseling service that offers free resume critiques and a free monthly on-line newsletter. **Specializes in the areas of:** Manufacturing. **Positions commonly filled include:** Purchasing Agent/Manager. **Corporate headquarters location:** This Location. **Average salary range of placements:** $50,000 - $100,000. **Number of placements per year:** 1 - 49.

ALLEN & ASSOCIATES
1100 Circle 75 Parkway, Suite 920, Atlanta GA 30339. 770/916-1999. **Toll-free phone:** 800/562-7404. **Fax:** 770/916-0755. **Contact:** Manager. **World Wide Web address:** http://www.allenandassociates.com. **Description:** A career/outplacement counseling firm.

Corporate headquarters location: Maitland FL. **Other U.S. locations:** Nationwide.

HIGHLANDS PROGRAM
999 Peachtree Street NE, Suite 1790, Atlanta GA 30309. 404/872-9974. **Contact:** Manager. **World Wide Web address:** http://www.highlandsprogram.com. **Description:** Provides career counseling to students and adults, and training and developments to corporations. **Corporate headquarters location:** This Location.

NATIONAL RESUME SERVICE
2660 Holcomb Bridge Road, Suite 224, Alpharetta GA 30022. 770/552-4334. **Contact:** Manager. **Description:** A resume and career/outplacement counseling firm.

◆ H A W A I I ◆

BENEFICIAL EMPLOYMENT SERVICE
841 Bishop Street, Suite 904, Honolulu HI 96813. 808/526-4121. **Contact:** Manager. **Description:** An executive search firm.

DUNHILL PROFESSIONAL STAFFING OF HAWAII
PMB 206, 1164 Bishop Street, Suite 124, Honolulu HI 96813. 808/524-2550. **Fax:** 808/533-2196. **Contact:** Nadine Stollenmaier, President. **E-mail address:** jobsrus@aloha.net. **World Wide Web address:** http://www.dunhillstaff.com. **Description:** An executive search firm. **Specializes in the areas of:** Accounting/Auditing; Administration; Architecture/ Construction; Banking; Computer Science/Software; Engineering; Finance; Food; General Management; Industrial; Manufacturing; Sales; Technical. **Positions commonly filled include:** Accountant/Auditor; Bank Officer/Manager; Computer Operator; Computer Programmer; Data Entry Clerk; Engineer; Insurance Agent/Broker; Secretary. **Other area locations:** 602 Kailua Road, Suite 124, Kailua HI 96734. **Average salary range of placements:** $30,000 - $50,000. **Number of placements per year:** 1 - 49.

EXECUTIVE SEARCH WORLD
700 Richards Street, Suite 2503, Honolulu HI 96813. 808/526-3812. **Fax:** 808/523-9356. **Contact:** James P. Ellis, President. **E-mail address:** ExecutiveSearchWorld@mail.com. **World Wide Web address:** http://www.executivesearchworld.com. **Description:** An executive search firm operating on a retainer basis. **Specializes in the areas of:** Accounting/Auditing; Administration; Architecture/Construction; Banking; Computer Science/Software; Engineering; Fashion; Finance; Food; General Management; Health/Medical; Insurance; Personnel/Labor Relations; Retail; Sales; Technical; Transportation. **Positions commonly filled include:** Advertising Executive; Bank Officer/Manager; Chief Financial Officer; Controller; Database Manager; Design Engineer; Finance Director; General Manager; Human Resources Manager; Internet Services Manager; Management Analyst/Consultant; Marketing Manager; MIS Specialist; Operations Manager; Project Manager; Sales Executive; Sales Manager; Software Engineer; Systems Manager; Telecommunications Manager; Webmaster. **Corporate headquarters location:** This Location. **Average salary range of placements:** More than $50,000. **Number of placements per year:** 100 - 199.

HR PACIFIC INC.
841 Bishop Street, Suite 1621, Honolulu HI 96813. 808/521-8941. **Fax:** 808/521-8943. **Contact:** Manager. **Description:** An executive search firm.

INKINEN & ASSOCIATES
1001 Bishop Street, Pau Ahi Tower, Suite 477, Honolulu HI 96813. 808/521-2331. **Fax:** 808/521-2380. **Contact:** Manager. **Description:** An executive search firm.

LAM ASSOCIATES PHYSICIAN SEARCH
444 Hobron Lane, Suite 207H, Department AM, Honolulu HI 96815. 808/947-9815. **Contact:** Pat Lam, General Manager/Owner. **Description:** An executive search firm. **Specializes in the areas of:** Health/Medical. **Positions commonly filled include:** Nurse Practitioner; Pharmacist; Physician; Registered Nurse. **Average salary range of placements:** More than $50,000. **Number of placements per year:** 50 - 99.

MANAGEMENT RECRUITERS
66-1735 Kawaihee Road, P.O. Box 2100, Kamuela HI 96743. 808/885-7503. **Fax:** 808/885-6338. **Contact:**

Manager. **Description:** An executive search firm that mainly provides placements in the continental U.S.

MANAGEMENT SEARCH & CONSULTING, INC.
1001 Bishop Street, Pacific Tower, Suite 1540, Honolulu HI 96813. 808/533-4423. **Fax:** 808/545-2435. **Contact:** Peter S. Glick, President. **E-mail address:** hdhunter@lava.net. **Description:** An executive search firm that places mid-, upper-, and senior-level managers. **Specializes in the areas of:** Accounting/Auditing; Finance; General Management; Health/Medical. **Positions commonly filled include:** Accountant/Auditor; Budget Analyst; Buyer; Chief Executive Officer; Chief Financial Officer; Electrical/Electronics Engineer; Finance Director; Financial Analyst; General Manager; Human Resources Manager; Marketing Manager; President; Project Manager; Systems Analyst; Systems Manager; Vice President of Finance; Vice President of Marketing; Wholesale and Retail Buyer. **Average salary range of placements:** More than $50,000. **Number of placements per year:** 1 - 49.

MARESCA AND ASSOCIATES
P.O. Box 235698, Honolulu HI 96823. 808/455-3097. **Fax:** 808/456-6088. **Contact:** Shannon Maresca, Owner/Manager. **E-mail address:** smaresca@worldnet. att.net. **Description:** An executive search firm operating on a contingency basis. **Specializes in the areas of:** Computer Science/Software; General Management; Health/Medical; Personnel/Labor Relations. **Positions commonly filled include:** Accountant/Auditor; Administrative Manager; Bank Officer/Manager; Branch Manager; Buyer; Chief Financial Officer; Civil Engineer; Computer Operator; Computer Programmer; Construction Manager; Controller; Cost Estimator; Education Administrator; Electrical/Electronics Engineer; Finance Director; Financial Analyst; General Manager; Health Services Manager; Hotel Manager; Human Resources Manager; Licensed Practical Nurse; Marketing Manager; Mechanical Engineer; MIS Manager; Paralegal; Physical Therapist; Physician; Registered Nurse; Restaurant/Food Service Manager; Software Engineer; Structural Engineer; Systems Analyst; Technical Writer/Editor; Telecommunications Manager. **Average salary range of placements:** More than $50,000. **Number of placements per year:** 1 - 49.

PROFESSIONAL SEARCH GROUP
841 Bishop Street, Suite 800, Honolulu HI 96813. 808/521-8941. **Contact:** Manager. **Description:** An executive search firm.

SALES CONSULTANTS OF HONOLULU
810 Richards Street, Suite 800, Honolulu HI 96813. 808/533-3282. **Fax:** 808/599-4760. **Contact:** Don Bishop, Recruiter. **E-mail address:** schon@lava.net. **World Wide Web address:** http://www.sacbiz.com/ sc.honolulu. **Description:** An executive search firm. Client company pays fee. **Specializes in the areas of:** Business Services; Construction; Health/Medical; Marketing; Pharmaceuticals; Sales. **Positions commonly filled include:** Account Manager; Account Representative; Computer Programmer; Computer Support Technician; Computer Technician; Heating/AC/ Refrigeration Technician; Sales Engineer; Sales Executive; Sales Manager; Sales Representative; Software Engineer. **Average salary range of placements:** $50,000 - $100,000. **Number of placements per year:** 50 - 99.

VIOS & ASSOCIATES
350 Ward Avenue, Suite 106, Honolulu HI 96814. 808/595-7199. **Contact:** Manager. **Description:** An executive search firm. **Specializes in the areas of:** Hotel/Restaurant.

PERMANENT EMPLOYMENT AGENCIES

ADECCO
1001 Bishop Street, Pacific Tower, Suite 2001, Honolulu HI 96813. 808/533-8889. **Fax:** 808/823-7506. **Contact:** Manager. **World Wide Web address:** http://www.jobs-hawaii.com. **Description:** A permanent employment agency that also provides some temporary placements. Client company pays fee. **Company slogan:** The employment people with aloha. **Positions commonly filled include:** Accountant; Administrator; Analytical Engineer; CADD Operator; Computer Operator; Computer Programmer; Customer Service Representative; IT Specialist; LAN/WAN Designer/Developer; Legal Assistant; Legal Secretary; Network Administrator; Project Manager; Secretary; Telemarketer. **Benefits available to temporary workers:** Bonus Award/Plan; Health Benefits; Paid Holidays; Referral Bonus Plan; Tuition Assistance. **International locations:** Worldwide.

EXECUTIVE SUPPORT HAWAII
PMB 316, 1164 Bishop Street, Suite 124, Honolulu HI 96813. 808/946-3410. **Fax:** 808/945-0076. **Contact:** Manager. **Description:** A permanent employment agency. **Specializes in the areas of:** Hotel/Restaurant; Legal; Telecommunications.

REMEDY INTELLIGENT STAFFING
1357 Kapiolani Boulevard, Honolulu HI 96814. 808/949-3669. **Fax:** 808/949-4022. **Contact:** Roxanne Wallace, Operations Manager. **Description:** A permanent employment agency. Founded in 1965. **Positions commonly filled include:** Accountant/Auditor; Administrative Manager; Bank Officer/Manager; Blue-Collar Worker Supervisor; Branch Manager; Brokerage Clerk; Budget Analyst; Chemical Engineer; Civil Engineer; Claim Representative; Computer Programmer; Design Engineer; Electrician; Human Resources Specialist; Management Trainee; Quality Control Supervisor; Services Sales Representative; Typist/Word Processor. **Benefits available to temporary workers:** Medical Insurance; Paid Holidays; Paid Vacation. **Other U.S. locations:** Nationwide. **Average salary range of placements:** Less than $20,000. **Number of placements per year:** 500 - 999.

REMEDY INTELLIGENT STAFFING
98-211 Pali Momi Street, Suite 102, Aiea HI 96701. 808/487-7787. **Fax:** 808/487-8847. **Contact:** Manager. **Description:** A permanent employment agency. **Benefits available to temporary workers:** Medical Insurance; Paid Holidays; Paid Vacation. **Average salary range of placements:** $20,000 - $29,999. **Number of placements per year:** 1000+.

TEMPORARY EMPLOYMENT AGENCIES

ALTRES STAFFING
711 Kapiolani Boulevard, Suite 120, Honolulu HI 96813. 808/591-4940. **Fax:** 808/591-8420. **Contact:** Manager. **Description:** A temporary agency that also provides some permanent placements and career/outplacement counseling. **Specializes in the areas of:** Accounting/Auditing; Administration; Architecture/Construction; Banking; Computer Science/Software; Health/Medical; Industrial; Legal; Light Industrial; MIS/EDP; Scientific; Secretarial; Technical. **Positions commonly filled include:** Accountant; Administrative Assistant; Bookkeeper; Claim Representative; Clerk; Computer Operator; Construction Trade Worker; Controller; Customer Service Representative; Data Entry Clerk; Driver; Factory Worker; Legal Secretary; Light Industrial Worker; Medical Secretary; MIS Specialist; Paralegal; Receptionist; Secretary; Stenographer; Typist/Word Processor. **Benefits available to temporary workers:** 401(k); Computer Training; Dental Insurance; Medical Insurance; Paid Vacation. **Corporate headquarters location:** This Location. **Average salary range of placements:** $20,000-$29,999. **Number of placements per year:** 1000+.

KELLY SERVICES, INC.
1100 Ward Avenue, Suite 1020, Honolulu HI 96814. 808/536-9343. **Fax:** 808/545-1506. **Contact:** Elizabeth Swanson, Branch Manager. **Description:** A temporary agency that also provides some permanent placements. Client company pays fee. **Specializes in the areas of:** Industrial; Sales; Secretarial. **Positions commonly filled include:** Accountant/Auditor; Blue-Collar Worker Supervisor; Computer Programmer; Systems Analyst; Typist/Word Processor. **Benefits available to temporary workers:** Computer Training; Medical Insurance; Paid Holidays; Paid Vacation. **Average salary range of placements:** $18,000 - $30,000. **Number of placements per year:** 1000+.

OLSTEN STAFFING SERVICES
900 Fort Street Mall, Suite 1202, Honolulu HI 96813. 808/523-3313. **Contact:** Signe Godfrey, President/Owner. **Description:** A temporary agency that also offers some temp-to-perm placements. Founded in 1987. **Specializes in the areas of:** Accounting/Auditing; Administration; Clerical; Food; Industrial; Legal; Light Industrial; Personnel/Labor Relations; Secretarial; Technical. **Positions commonly filled include:** Accountant/Auditor; Administrative Manager; Bookkeeper; Brokerage Clerk; Clerical Supervisor; Computer Technician; Draftsperson; Human Resources Specialist; Services Sales Representative; Software Engineer; Typist/Word Processor. **Benefits available to temporary workers:** Medical Insurance; Paid Holidays; Paid Vacation. **Corporate headquarters location:** Melville NY. **International locations:** Worldwide. **Average salary range of placements:** $20,000 - $29,999. **Number of placements per year:** 1000+.

SELECT STAFFING SERVICES, INC.
550 Paiea Street, Suite 222, Honolulu HI 96818. 808/839-2200. **Fax:** 808/839-4844. **Contact:** President. **Description:** A temporary agency. **Specializes in the areas of:** Accounting/Auditing; Advertising; Computer Hardware/Software. **Positions commonly filled include:** Accountant/Auditor; Administrative Assistant; Bookkeeper; Clerk; Construction Trade Worker; Data Entry Clerk; Driver; Factory Worker; Legal Secretary; Light Industrial Worker; Medical Secretary; Receptionist; Secretary; Stenographer; Typist/Word Processor. **Number of placements per year:** 1000+.

CONTRACT SERVICES FIRMS

ASAP EXPRESS
15 Kanoa Street, Hilo HI 96720. 808/935-2935. **Contact:** Manager. **Description:** A contract services firm. Client company pays fee. **Company slogan:** Do what you do best, let us do the rest. **Specializes in the areas of:** General Labor; Health/Medical; Industrial; Office

Support; Technical. **Office hours:** Monday - Friday, 8:00 a.m. - 5:30 p.m.

ASAP EXPRESS
Pines Plaza, 75-240 Nani Kailua Drive, Suite 10, Kailua-Kona HI 96739. 808/329-8367. **Contact:** Manager. **Description:** A contract services firm. Client company pays fee. **Specializes in the areas of:** General Labor; Health/Medical; Industrial; Office Support; Technical.

RIDERS PERSONNEL SERVICES, INC.
1314 South King Street, Suite 522, Honolulu HI 96814. 808/597-8866. **Contact:** Manager. **E-mail address:** riders@riderspersonnel.com. **World Wide Web address:** http://www.riderspersonnel.com. **Description:** A contract services firm. Founded in 1997. **Specializes in the areas of:** Accounting; Administration; Clerical; Health/Medical; Legal. **Positions commonly filled include:** Clerk; Custodian; Maintenance Technician; Receptionist; Warehouse/Distribution Worker. **Office hours:** Monday - Friday, 8:00 a.m. - 5:00 p.m.

CAREER/OUTPLACEMENT COUNSELING FIRMS

ALU LIKE INC.
Kauai Island Center, 3129 Peleke Street, Lihue HI 96766. 808/245-8545. **Contact:** Personnel. **Description:** A career/outplacement agency. **Specializes in the areas of:** Nonprofit. **Positions commonly filled include:** Accountant/Auditor; Bank Officer/Manager; Bookkeeper; Construction Trade Worker; Customer Service Representative; Data Entry Clerk; Driver; Factory Worker; Food and Beverage Service Worker; Hotel Manager; Legal Secretary; Light Industrial Worker; Medical Secretary; Nurse; Public Relations Specialist; Purchasing Agent/Manager; Receptionist; Sales Representative; Secretary; Typist/Word Processor.

◆ I D A H O ◆

DIVERSIFIED DATA SYSTEMS
3355 North Five Mile Road, Suite 202, Boise ID 83713. 208/884-3385. **Fax:** 208/884-4487. **Contact:** Manager. **World Wide Web address:** http://www.div-data.com. **Description:** An executive search firm that also provides some contract services. **Specializes in the areas of:** Computer Hardware/Software. **Positions commonly filled include:** AS400 Programmer Analyst. **Average salary range of placements:** More than $50,000.

F-O-R-T-U-N-E PERSONNEL CONSULTANTS
415 East Park Center, Suite 106, Boise ID 83706. 208/343-5190. **Fax:** 208/343-6067. **Contact:** Manager. **Description:** An executive search firm. **Specializes in the areas of:** Banking; Finance; Paper. **Corporate headquarters location:** New York NY. **Other U.S. locations:** Nationwide.

HORNE/BROWN INTERNATIONAL
101 South Capitol, Suite 1200, Boise ID 83702. 208/344-9004. **Fax:** 208/344-0681. **Contact:** Mr. Gene Horne, President. **Description:** An executive search firm. **Specializes in the areas of:** Accounting/Auditing; Administration; Banking; Engineering; Finance; Food; General Management; Health/Medical; Insurance; Manufacturing; Personnel/Labor Relations; Sales. **Positions commonly filled include:** Accountant; Bank Officer/Manager; Biomedical Engineer; Chemical Engineer; Civil Engineer; Electrical Engineer; Financial Analyst; Food Scientist/Technologist; General Manager; Health Services Manager; Human Resources Manager; Industrial Engineer; Mechanical Engineer; Metallurgical Engineer; Mining Engineer; Nuclear Engineer; Structural Engineer; Underwriter/Assistant Underwriter.

ROBERT WILLIAM JAMES & ASSOCIATES EXPRESS PERSONNEL SERVICES
1714 G Street, Lewiston ID 83501. 208/743-6507. **Contact:** Manager. **Description:** An executive search firm. Express Personnel (also at this location) provides temporary and temp-to-perm placements.

LOST DUTCHMAN SEARCH
261 A Street, Idaho Falls ID 83402. 208/528-9836. **Fax:** 208/528-9941. **Contact:** Manager. **Description:** An executive search firm. **Specializes in the areas of:** Business Systems Analysis; Computer Programming; Finance.

MANAGEMENT RECRUITERS OF BOISE, INC.
345 Bobwhite Court, Suite 215, Boise ID 83706. 208/336-6770. **Contact:** Craig Alexander, General Manager. **Description:** An executive search firm. **Specializes in the areas of:** Chemicals; Food; Industrial Sales and Marketing; Mining. **Positions commonly filled include:** Chemical Engineer; Chemist; Civil Engineer; Electrical/Electronics Engineer; Food Scientist/Technologist; Mechanical Engineer; Metallurgical Engineer; Mining Engineer; Production Manager; Quality Assurance Engineer. **Number of placements per year:** 50 - 99.

TROUVER.NET
221 South River Street, Hailey ID 83333. 208/578-1000. **Fax:** 208/578-0335. **Contact:** Manager. **World Wide Web address:** http://www.trouver.net. **Description:** An executive search firm with an online support network.

EXPRESS PERSONNEL SERVICES
5193 Overland, Boise ID 83706. 208/343-7552. **Contact:** Manager. **Description:** A permanent employment agency that also provides some temporary placements. **Other U.S. locations:** Nationwide.

EXPRESS PERSONNEL SERVICES
115 North Main, Pocatello ID 83204. 208/232-1040. **Contact:** Manager. **Description:** A permanent employment agency that also provides some temporary placements. **Other U.S. locations:** Nationwide.

IDAHO DEPARTMENT OF EMPLOYMENT JOBSERVICE
P.O. Box 1147, Lewiston ID 83501-1147. 208/799-5000. **Fax:** 208/799-5007. **Contact:** Pat Paasch, Consultant. **Description:** A permanent employment agency. **Specializes in the areas of:** General Management; Health/Medical; Insurance; Manufacturing; Retail; Sales. **Positions commonly filled include:** Claim Representative; Clerk; Computer Operator; Customer Service Representative; Data Entry Clerk; Factory Worker; Legal Secretary; Light Industrial Worker; Medical Secretary; Nurse; Receptionist; Sales Representative; Secretary; Technician; Typist/Word Processor. **Number of placements per year:** 1000+.

INTERMOUNTAIN STAFFING RESOURCES
770 Vista Avenue, Boise ID 83705. 208/345-8200. **Fax:** 208/345-8266. **Contact:** Manager. **Description:** A permanent employment agency. **Specializes in the areas of:** Industrial; Personnel/Labor Relations. **Positions commonly filled include:** Blue-Collar Worker Supervisor; Construction Contractor; Customer Service Representative; Draftsperson; Electrical/Electronics Engineer; Electrician; Quality Control Supervisor. **Corporate headquarters location:** Salt Lake City UT. **Number of placements per year:** 200 - 499.

SOS STAFFING SERVICES
663 Blue Lakes Boulevard North, Twin Falls ID 83301. 208/736-4473. **Contact:** Manager. **Description:** A permanent employment agency that also makes some temporary placements.

MANPOWER TEMPORARY SERVICES
8050 West Rifleman Drive, Suite 200, Boise ID 83704. 208/375-8040. **Fax:** 208/376-8635. **Contact:** Joe Tueller, Branch Manager. **Description:** A temporary agency. **Specializes in the areas of:** Administration; Architecture/Construction; Food; Legal; Light Industrial; Personnel/Labor Relations; Secretarial. **Positions commonly filled include:** Administrative Assistant; Customer Service Representative; Secretary. **Benefits available to temporary workers:** Medical Insurance; Paid Holidays; Paid Vacation. **Corporate headquarters location:** Milwaukee WI. **Other U.S. locations:** Nationwide. **International locations:** Worldwide. **Average salary range of placements:** Less than $20,000. **Number of placements per year:** 1000+.

SNELLING PERSONNEL SERVICES
308 North 15th Street, Boise ID 83702. 208/426-8367. **Contact:** Manager. **Description:** A temporary agency

that also provides some temp-to-perm placements. **Specializes in the areas of:** Clerical; Marketing; Sales; Technical. **Positions commonly filled include:** Office Manager. **Corporate headquarters location:** Dallas TX. **Other U.S. locations:** Nationwide.

CONTRACT SERVICES FIRMS

ADECCO/TAD TECHNICAL SERVICES
5440 Franklin Road, Suite 202, Boise ID 83705. 208/331-2100. **Contact:** Manager. **Description:** A contract services firm. **Other U.S. locations:** Nationwide.

VOLT TECHNICAL SERVICES
8100 West Emerald Drive, Suite 120, Boise ID 83704. **Toll-free phone:** 888/375-9930. **Contact:** Dan Tennant, Branch Manager. **World Wide Web address:** http://www.volt-nw.com. **Description:** A contract services firm. **Specializes in the areas of:** Clerical; Computer Programming; Engineering; Technical.

CAREER/OUTPLACEMENT COUNSELING FIRMS

MAGIC VALLEY REHABILITATION SERVICES, INC.
484 Eastland Drive South, Twin Falls ID 83301. 208/734-4112. **Fax:** 208/734-1514. **Contact:** John Bodden, Director of Rehabilitation. **Description:** A career/outplacement counseling and vocational rehabilitation firm. Founded in 1973. **Specializes in the** areas of: Education; Nonprofit. **Positions commonly filled include:** Clerical Supervisor; Counselor; General Manager; Human Resources Specialist; Human Service Worker; Operations/Production Manager; Public Relations Specialist; Typist/Word Processor. **Average salary range of placements:** Less than $20,000. **Number of placements per year:** 1 - 49.

ASI (ACCESS SEARCH INC.)
218 North Jefferson, Suite 200, Chicago IL 60661. 312/930-1063. **Contact:** John Brzowski, Senior Manager. **Description:** An executive search firm operating on both retainer and contingency bases. **Specializes in the areas of:** Accounting; Finance. **Positions commonly filled include:** Accountant; Auditor; Budget Analyst; Controller; Credit Manager; Financial Analyst; Tax Specialist; Treasurer. **Corporate headquarters location:** This Location. **Average salary range of placements:** More than $50,000. **Number of placements per year:** 100 - 199.

ABBOTT SMITH ASSOCIATES
2600 Lexington Street, Broadview IL 60153. 708/649-3310. **Fax:** 708/344-1912. **Contact:** Frank Calzaretta, Managing Partner. **World Wide Web address:** http://www.abbottsmith.com. **Description:** An executive search firm operating on both retainer and contingency bases. **Specializes in the areas of:** Accounting/Auditing; Banking; Computer Science/Software; Human Resources; Marketing; Personnel/Labor Relations; Sales. **Positions commonly filled include:** Account Manager; Accountant; Administrative Manager; Advertising Executive; Applications Engineer; Branch Manager; Chief Financial Officer; Controller; Credit Manager; Finance Director; Financial Analyst; Human Resources Manager; Intellectual Property Lawyer; Management Analyst/Consultant; Marketing Manager; Network Administrator; Purchasing Agent/Manager; Sales Executive; Sales Manager; Software Engineer; Systems Manager. **Other U.S. locations:** Millbrook NY. **Average salary range of placements:** $50,000 - $100,000. **Number of placements per year:** 200 - 499.

THE ABILITY GROUP
1011 East State Street, Rockford IL 61104. 815/964-0119. **Fax:** 815/964-9965. **Contact:** Al Weir, Vice President. **Description:** An executive search firm. **Specializes in the areas of:** Accounting/Auditing; Administration; Computer Science/Software; Engineering; Industrial; Manufacturing; Personnel/Labor Relations; Technical. **Positions commonly filled include:** Accountant/Auditor; Aerospace Engineer; Aircraft Mechanic/Engine Specialist; Automotive Mechanic; Biomedical Engineer; Blue-Collar Worker Supervisor; Buyer; Chemical Engineer; Civil Engineer; Clerical Supervisor; Computer Programmer; Customer Service Representative; Design Engineer; Designer; Draftsperson; Electrical/Electronics Engineer; Electrician; Environmental Engineer; Human Resources Manager; Industrial Engineer; Management Trainee; Mathematician; Mechanical Engineer; Metallurgical Engineer; MIS Specialist; Purchasing Agent/Manager; Software Engineer; Stationary Engineer; Statistician; Structural Engineer; Systems Analyst; Technical Writer/Editor. **Benefits available to temporary workers:** Medical Insurance; Paid Holidays. **Corporate headquarters location:** This Location. **Other U.S. locations:** Oregon IL; Beloit WI. **Average salary range of placements:** $30,000 - $50,000. **Number of placements per year:** 100 - 199.

B.J. ABRAMS & ASSOCIATES INC.
550 Frontage Road, Suite 3600, Northfield IL 60093. 847/446-2966. **Fax:** 847/446-2973. **Contact:** Burt Abrams, President. **Description:** An executive search firm operating on a contingency basis. **Specializes in the areas of:** Accounting/Auditing; Engineering; General Management; Health/Medical; Human Resources; Manufacturing; Publishing; Sales. **Positions commonly filled include:** Account Manager; Accountant; Auditor; Buyer; Chief Financial Officer; Controller; Customer Service Representative; Financial Analyst; General Manager; Human Resources Manager; Manufacturing Engineer; Mechanical Engineer; Production Manager; Purchasing Agent/Manager; Quality Control Supervisor;

Sales Manager; Technical Writer/Editor. **Average salary range of placements:** More than $50,000. **Number of placements per year:** 50 - 99.

ACCORD INC.
10301 West Roosevelt Road, Westchester IL 60154. 708/345-7900. **Contact:** Chester Dombrowski, Manager. **Description:** An executive search firm. **Specializes in the areas of:** Computer Science/Software; Engineering; Manufacturing; MIS/EDP; Technical. **Positions commonly filled include:** Computer Programmer; Customer Service Representative; Draftsperson; EDP Specialist; Electrical/Electronics Engineer; General Manager; Industrial Engineer; Industrial Production Manager; Mechanical Engineer; MIS Specialist; Quality Control Supervisor; Sales Representative; Software Engineer; Technical Writer/Editor; Technician. **Number of placements per year:** 50 - 99.

ACCOUNT PROS
20 South Clark Street, Suite 2400, Chicago IL 60603. 312/263-9300. **Fax:** 312/263-9103. **Contact:** Shirley Brown, Branch Manager. **Description:** An executive search firm. **Specializes in the areas of:** Accounting/Auditing; Banking; Finance. **Positions commonly filled include:** Accountant/Auditor; Budget Analyst; Credit Manager; Customer Service Representative; Financial Analyst. **Benefits available to temporary workers:** 401(k); Dental Insurance; Medical Insurance; Paid Holidays; Paid Vacation. **Corporate headquarters location:** Boston MA. **Other U.S. locations:** Los Angeles CA; Des Plaines IL; Burlington MA. **Average salary range of placements:** $30,000 - $50,000.

ACCOUNT PROS
1700 Higgins Road, Suite 430, Des Plaines IL 60018. 847/298-9400. **Contact:** Branch Manager. **Description:** An executive search firm. **Specializes in the areas of:** Accounting/Auditing; Banking; Finance; Insurance. **Positions commonly filled include:** Accountant/Auditor; Brokerage Clerk; Budget Analyst; Credit Manager; Customer Service Representative; Financial Analyst; Typist/Word Processor. **Corporate headquarters location:** Boston MA. **Other U.S. locations:** Los Angeles CA; Chicago IL; Burlington MA. **Average salary range of placements:** $20,000 - $29,999. **Number of placements per year:** 200 - 499.

ACCOUNTANTS EXECUTIVE SEARCH
ACCOUNTANTS ON CALL
200 North LaSalle Street, Suite 1745, Chicago IL 60601. 312/782-7711. **Fax:** 312/782-0171. **Contact:** Manager. **Description:** An executive search firm operating on a contingency basis. Accountants On Call (also at this location) is a temporary agency. **Specializes in the areas of:** Accounting/Auditing; Banking; Finance. **Corporate headquarters location:** Saddle Brook NJ. **International locations:** Worldwide.

ACCOUNTANTS EXECUTIVE SEARCH
ACCOUNTANTS ON CALL
3400 Dundee Road, Suite 260, Northbrook IL 60062. 847/205-0808. **Contact:** Manager. **Description:** An executive search firm. Accountants On Call (also at this location) is a temporary agency. **Specializes in the areas of:** Accounting/Auditing; Banking; Finance. **Corporate headquarters location:** Saddle Brook NJ. **International locations:** Worldwide.

ADAMS & ASSOCIATES INTERNATIONAL
463 West Ruffle Street, Suite D, Barrington IL 60010. 847/304-5300. **Contact:** Manager. **Description:** An executive search firm.

ADVANCED TECHNICAL SEARCH
7416 County Line Road, Suite C, Burr Ridge IL 60521. 708/387-7200. **Contact:** Manager. **Description:** An

executive search firm. **Specializes in the areas of:** Engineering; Manufacturing; Technical.

ADVANCEMENT INC.
721 Fair Links Way, Gurnee IL 60031. 847/247-2100. **Toll-free phone:** 888/220-2529. **Fax:** 847/247-2105. **Contact:** Manager. **E-mail address:** info@advancement.com. **World Wide Web address:** http://www.advancement.com. **Description:** An executive search firm. Founded in 1963. **Specializes in the areas of:** Computer Hardware/Software; Data Communications; Graphic Arts; High-Tech; Multimedia; Systems Administration; Telecommunications; Wireless Communications.

ADVANTAGE PERSONNEL INC.
1550 Northwest Highway, Suite 109-C, Park Ridge IL 60068-1458. 847/803-4422. **Fax:** 847/803-4423. **Contact:** Jim Harrison, Owner/Recruiter. **Description:** An executive search firm specializing in direct marketing placements. **Specializes in the areas of:** Administration; Direct Marketing; Sales. **Positions commonly filled include:** Client Services Representative. **Number of placements per year:** 1 - 49.

AGRA PLACEMENTS, LTD.
2200 North Kickapoo, Suite 2, Lincoln IL 62656. 217/735-4373. **Fax:** 217/732-2041. **Contact:** Perry M. Schneider, President. **E-mail address:** agrail@abelink.com. **World Wide Web address:** http://www.agraplacements.com. **Description:** An executive search firm operating on both retainer and contingency bases. **Specializes in the areas of:** Agri-Business; Agriculture; Food. **Positions commonly filled include:** Account Manager; Administrative Assistant; Assistant Manager; Auditor; Chemical Engineer; Civil Engineer; Computer Operator; Customer Service Representative; Database Manager; Design Engineer; Draftsperson; Finance Director; General Manager; Human Resources Manager; Industrial Production Manager; Manufacturing Engineer; MIS Specialist; Operations Manager; Production Manager; Quality Control Supervisor; Sales Engineer; Sales Representative; Systems Analyst; Systems Manager. **Corporate headquarters location:** West Des Moines IA. **Other U.S. locations:** Peru IN; Sioux Falls SD. **Average salary range of placements:** $30,000 - $50,000. **Number of placements per year:** 200 - 499.

AMERICAN ENGINEERING COMPANY
188 Industrial Drive, Suite 216, Elmhurst IL 60126. 630/941-7750. **Contact:** Anthony Davero, President. **Description:** An executive search firm operating on both retainer and contingency bases. **Specializes in the areas of:** Accounting/Auditing; Computer Science/Software; Engineering; Finance; Manufacturing; Sales; Secretarial; Technical. **Positions commonly filled include:** Accountant/Auditor; Administrative Manager; Attorney; Blue-Collar Worker Supervisor; Budget Analyst; Buyer; Clerical Supervisor; Computer Programmer; Cost Estimator; Counselor; Credit Manager; Customer Service Representative; Design Engineer; Designer; Draftsperson; Electrical/Electronics Engineer; Financial Analyst; Human Resources Manager; Industrial Engineer; Industrial Production Manager; Insurance Agent/Broker; Internet Services Manager; Management Analyst/Consultant; Manufacturer's/Wholesaler's Sales Rep.; Market Research Analyst; Mechanical Engineer; Metallurgical Engineer; MIS Specialist; Operations/Production Manager; Paralegal; Public Relations Specialist; Purchasing Agent/Manager; Quality Control Supervisor; Software Engineer; Stationary Engineer; Systems Analyst; Technical Writer/Editor; Telecommunications Manager; Typist/Word Processor; Underwriter/Assistant Underwriter. **Average salary range of placements:** More than $50,000. **Number of placements per year:** 200 - 499.

AMERICAN MEDICAL STAFFING
555 West Madison Street, Suite 371, Chicago IL 60661. 312/559-7878. **Contact:** Manager. **Description:** An executive search firm. **Positions commonly filled**

include: Occupational Therapist; Physical Therapist; Speech-Language Pathologist.

AMERICAN TECHNICAL SEARCH, INC.
2215 York Road, Suite 204, Oak Brook IL 60523. 630/990-1001. **Toll-free phone:** 800/899-7467. **Fax:** 630/990-1009. **Contact:** Raymond Landers, President. **Description:** An executive search firm. **Specializes in the areas of:** Engineering; Food; General Management; Industrial; Manufacturing; Technical. **Positions commonly filled include:** Aerospace Engineer; Agricultural Engineer; Draftsperson; Electrical/Electronics Engineer; Electrician; General Manager; Industrial Engineer; Industrial Production Manager; Mechanical Engineer; Metallurgical Engineer; Operations/Production Manager; Software Engineer; Technical Writer/Editor. **Corporate headquarters location:** This Location. **Average salary range of placements:** More than $50,000. **Number of placements per year:** 50 - 99.

ARMSTRONG-HAMILTON ASSOCIATES
203 North LaSalle Street, Suite 2100, Chicago IL 60601. 312/558-1461. **Fax:** 312/444-9463. **Contact:** Glenda Peters, President. **Description:** An executive search firm. **Specializes in the areas of:** Accounting/Auditing; Banking; Finance; General Management; Logistics; Office Support; Personnel/Labor Relations; Sales. **Positions commonly filled include:** Account Manager; Accountant; Administrative Assistant; Customer Service Representative; Financial Analyst; Financial Manager; Human Resources Manager; Marketing Specialist; Office Manager; Purchasing Agent/Manager; Quality Control Supervisor; Sales Manager; Systems Analyst; Systems Manager; Technical Writer/Editor. **Number of placements per year:** 50 - 99.

E.J. ASHTON & ASSOCIATES, LTD.
P.O. Box 1048, Lake Zurich IL 60047. 847/540-9922. **Contact:** Ed Lipinski, President. **Description:** An executive search firm. **Specializes in the areas of:** Accounting/Auditing; Administration; Computer Science/Software; Finance; Health/Medical; Insurance; Legal. **Positions commonly filled include:** Accountant/Auditor; Actuary; Adjuster; Attorney; Branch Manager; Budget Analyst; Claim Representative; Computer Programmer; Financial Analyst; Health Services Manager; Human Resources Manager; Insurance Agent/Broker; Internet Services Manager; Management Analyst/Consultant; MIS Specialist; Securities Sales Representative; Software Engineer; Statistician; Systems Analyst; Telecommunications Manager; Underwriter/Assistant Underwriter. **Average salary range of placements:** More than $50,000. **Number of placements per year:** 1 - 49.

B.D.G. SOFTWARE NETWORK
1785 Woodhaven Drive, Crystal Lake IL 60014. 815/477-2334. **Fax:** 815/477-2265. **Contact:** Barry D. Gruner, President. **Description:** An executive search firm operating on both retainer and contingency bases. **Specializes in the areas of:** Computer Science/Software. **Positions commonly filled include:** Computer Programmer; Management Analyst/Consultant; Market Research Analyst; MIS Specialist; Software Engineer; Systems Analyst; Telecommunications Manager. **Average salary range of placements:** More than $50,000. **Number of placements per year:** 1 - 49.

THE BANKERS GROUP
10 South Riverside Plaza, Suite 1424, Chicago IL 60606. 312/930-9456. **Contact:** Manager. **Description:** An executive search firm. **Specializes in the areas of:** Banking; Finance; Insurance.

BARCLAY CONSULTANTS, INC.
155 North Michigan Avenue, 6th Floor, Chicago IL 60601. 312/856-1545. **Contact:** Ms. Daryl Homer, President. **Description:** An executive search firm. **Specializes in the areas of:** Legal. **Positions commonly filled include:** Attorney; Paralegal. **Average salary range of placements:** More than $50,000. **Number of placements per year:** 1 - 49.

BARRETT PARTNERS
100 North LaSalle Street, Suite 1420, Chicago IL 60602. 312/443-8877. **Fax:** 312/443-8866. **Contact:** Joseph Thielman, CPC/President. **World Wide Web address:** http://www.barrettpartners.com. **Description:** An executive search firm. **Specializes in the areas of:** Accounting/Auditing; Banking; Engineering; Finance. **Positions commonly filled include:** Accountant/Auditor; Aerospace Engineer; Agricultural Engineer; Bank Officer/Manager; Biomedical Engineer; Budget Analyst; Chemical Engineer; Civil Engineer; Controller; Credit Manager; Electrical/Electronics Engineer; Financial Analyst; Industrial Engineer; Mechanical Engineer; Metallurgical Engineer; Mining Engineer; Nuclear Engineer; Petroleum Engineer; Software Engineer; Stationary Engineer; Structural Engineer. **Number of placements per year:** 50 - 99.

BATTALIA WINSTON INTERNATIONAL
150 South Wacker Drive, Suite 1220, Chicago IL 60606. 312/704-0050. **Contact:** Manager. **World Wide Web address:** http://www.battaliawinston.com. **Description:** An executive search firm. **Specializes in the areas of:** Consumer Products; Finance; Health/Medical; Industrial; Nonprofit; Professional; Technical. **Other U.S. locations:** Los Angeles CA; San Francisco CA; Boston MA; Edison NJ; New York NY.

C. BERGER GROUP, INC.
327 East Gunderson Drive, Carol Stream IL 60188. 630/653-1115. **Toll-free phone:** 800/382-4222. **Fax:** 630/653-1691. **Contact:** Carol Berger, President. **World Wide Web address:** http://www.cberger.com. **Description:** An executive search firm. **Specializes in the areas of:** Library Services. **Positions commonly filled include:** Librarian; Records Manager. **Number of placements per year:** 1 - 49.

BETA TECHNOLOGIES
566 West Adams, Suite 250, Chicago IL 60661. 312/627-1200. **Contact:** Manager. **Description:** An executive search firm. **Specializes in the areas of:** Information Technology.

BEVELLE & ASSOCIATES, INC.
180 North LaSalle Street, Suite 2010, Chicago IL 60601. 312/807-3852. **Fax:** 312/807-3840. **Contact:** Sadie Bevelle, President. **Description:** An executive search firm. **Specializes in the areas of:** Accounting/Auditing; Banking; Engineering; General Management; Legal; Personnel/Labor Relations; Secretarial; Transportation. **Positions commonly filled include:** Accountant/Auditor; Administrative Manager; Advertising Clerk; Attorney; Bank Officer/Manager; Blue-Collar Worker Supervisor; Branch Manager; Brokerage Clerk; Civil Engineer; Clerical Supervisor; Computer Programmer; Customer Service Representative; Electrical/Electronics Engineer; General Manager; Human Resources Manager; Mechanical Engineer; Paralegal; Purchasing Agent/Manager; Quality Control Supervisor; Travel Agent; Typist/Word Processor. **Number of placements per year:** 100 - 199.

BICKHAUS & ASSOCIATES
P.O. Box 5083, Bloomington IL 61702. 309/454-2323. **Contact:** Richard Bickhaus, President. **Description:** A generalist executive search firm.

WILLIAM J. BLENDER & ASSOCIATES
715 Sunset Drive, East Peoria IL 61611. 309/699-3864. **Contact:** William J. Blender, President. **E-mail address:** bblen@aol.com. **Description:** An executive search firm operating on a contingency basis. **Specializes in the areas of:** Computer Hardware/Software; Internet Development. **Positions commonly filled include:** Applications Engineer; AS400 Programmer Analyst; Computer Animator; Computer Engineer; Computer Programmer; Computer Scientist; Computer Support Technician; Content Developer; Database Administrator; Database Manager; Internet Services Manager; MIS Specialist; Multimedia Designer; Network Administrator;

Software Engineer; SQL Programmer; Systems Analyst; Systems Manager; Webmaster.

BLOOM, GROSS & ASSOCIATES, INC.
625 North Michigan Avenue, Suite 500, Chicago IL 60611. 312/751-3490. **Fax:** 312/915-0621. **Contact:** Karen Bloom, Principal. **E-mail address:** bloomgross@aol.com. **Description:** An executive search firm. **Specializes in the areas of:** Art/Design; Market Research; Marketing; Public Relations; Sales Promotion. **Average salary range of placements:** More than $50,000. **Number of placements per year:** 1 - 49.

BONNER & STRICKLIN & ASSOCIATES
8 South Michigan Avenue, Suite 3800, Chicago IL 60603. 312/629-9090. **Contact:** Manager. **Description:** An executive search firm. **Specializes in the areas of:** Telecommunications.

BOULEWARE & ASSOCIATES INC.
175 West Jackson, Suite 1841, Chicago IL 60604. 312/322-0088. **Contact:** Manager. **Description:** A generalist executive search firm.

BOYDEN
Two Prudential Plaza, 180 North Stetson Avenue, Suite 2500, Chicago IL 60601. 312/565-1300. **Contact:** Manager. **E-mail address:** ram@boydenchi.com. **World Wide Web address:** http://www.boyden.com. **Description:** A generalist executive search firm. **Corporate headquarters location:** New York NY. **Other U.S. locations:** San Francisco CA; Washington DC; Bloomfield Hills MI; Chesterfield MO; Hawthorne NY; Morristown PA; Pittsburgh PA; Houston TX. **International locations:** Worldwide.

BRATLAND & ASSOCIATES
5424 Brittany Drive, McHenry IL 60050. 815/344-4335. **Contact:** Manager. **Description:** An executive search firm. **Specializes in the areas of:** Information Systems; Telecommunications.

BRITANNIA
160 East Chicago Street, Elgin IL 60120. 847/697-4600. **Fax:** 847/697-4608. **Contact:** Mary Gedmin, Division Coordinator. **Description:** An executive search firm operating on a contingency basis. **Specializes in the areas of:** Computer Science/Software; Engineering; Industrial; Manufacturing; Sales; Secretarial; Technical. **Positions commonly filled include:** Architect; Biological Scientist; Civil Engineer; Computer Programmer; Customer Service Representative; Design Engineer; Draftsperson; Electrical/Electronics Engineer; Industrial Engineer; Industrial Production Manager; Mechanical Engineer; Operations/Production Manager; Purchasing Agent/Manager; Quality Control Supervisor; Software Engineer; Systems Analyst; Technical Writer/Editor; Telecommunications Manager. **Average salary range of placements:** $30,000 - $50,000. **Number of placements per year:** 50 - 99.

BROOKE CHASE ASSOCIATES, INC.
505 North Lake Shore Drive, Suite 5507, Chicago IL 60611. 312/744-0033. **Fax:** 312/822-0475. **Contact:** Joseph McElmeel, President. **Description:** An executive search firm. **Specializes in the areas of:** Sales. **Positions commonly filled include:** Market Research Analyst; Marketing Manager; Marketing Specialist; Sales Engineer; Sales Executive; Sales Manager; Sales Representative. **Number of placements per year:** 50 - 99.

BURLING GROUP LTD.
333 West Wacker Drive, Suite 680, Chicago IL 60606-1225. 312/346-0888x239. **Contact:** Ron Deitch, President. **E-mail address:** web@burlinggroup.com. **Description:** An executive search firm operating on a retainer basis. **Specializes in the areas of:** Accounting/Auditing; Finance; Food; General Management; Health/Medical; Industrial; Insurance; Manufacturing; Personnel/Labor Relations; Publishing; Technical. **Positions commonly filled include:**

Accountant/Auditor; Administrative Manager; Branch Manager; Counselor; Customer Service Representative; Financial Analyst; General Manager; Human Resources Manager; Industrial Production Manager; Management Analyst/Consultant; Operations/Production Manager; Quality Control Supervisor; Strategic Relations Manager. **Average salary range of placements:** More than $75,000. **Number of placements per year:** 1 - 49.

BURTON PLACEMENT SERVICES
3917 East Lincolnway, Sterling IL 61081. 815/626-8168. **Fax:** 815/625-6606. **Contact:** Catherine Sheets, Corporate Manager. **Description:** An executive search firm. **Positions commonly filled include:** Accountant/Auditor; Advertising Clerk; Automotive Mechanic; Bank Officer/Manager; Blue-Collar Worker Supervisor; Branch Manager; Buyer; Clerical Supervisor; Clinical Lab Technician; Computer Programmer; Counselor; Customer Service Representative; General Manager; Health Services Manager; Human Resources Manager; Human Service Worker; Management Trainee; Operations/Production Manager; Public Relations Specialist; Registered Nurse; Systems Analyst. **Benefits available to temporary workers:** Medical Insurance; Paid Vacation. **Corporate headquarters location:** This Location. **Other area locations:** Dixon IL; Oregon IL; Rochelle IL; Sycamore IL; West Chicago IL. **Other U.S. locations:** Clinton IA.

BURTON PLACEMENT SERVICES
122 May Mart Drive, Rochelle IL 61068. 815/562-5627. **Contact:** Michelle Quest, Staffing/Sales Representative. **Description:** An executive search firm. **Corporate headquarters location:** Sterling IL. **Other U.S. locations:** Clinton IA; Dixon IL; Oregon IL; Sycamore IL; West Chicago IL.

BUSINESS SYSTEMS OF AMERICA, INC.
200 West Adams Street, Suite 2015, Chicago IL 60606. 312/849-9222. **Toll-free phone:** 800/317-4744. **Fax:** 312/849-9260. **Contact:** Lou Costabile, Recruiter. **E-mail address:** recruiter@bussysam.com. **World Wide Web address:** http://www.bussysam.com. **Description:** An executive search firm placing consultants in the areas of LAN and PC technical support. The firm also provides some temporary placements. Founded in 1993. **Specializes in the areas of:** Computer Science/Software. **Positions commonly filled include:** Computer Programmer; MIS Specialist; Systems Analyst; Systems Manager; Telecommunications Manager; Webmaster. **Benefits available to temporary workers:** Medical Insurance; Public Transit Available. **Corporate headquarters location:** This Location. **Average salary range of placements:** $30,000 - $50,000. **Number of placements per year:** 50 - 99.

CCS GROUP
13522 West Chocktaw Trail, Lockport IL 60441. 708/645-0130. **Fax:** 708/645-0135. **Contact:** Victor Persico, President. **E-mail address:** ccsgroup@pop.net. **Description:** An executive search firm. **Specializes in the areas of:** Banking. **Positions commonly filled include:** Bank Officer/Manager; Commercial Lending Officer. **Number of placements per year:** 1 - 49.

CES ASSOCIATES
112 South Grant Street, Hinsdale IL 60521. 630/654-2596. **Fax:** 630/654-2713. **Contact:** James F. Baker, Ph.D./President. **E-mail address:** cesassoc@aol.com. **World Wide Web address:** http://www.cesassoc.com. **Description:** An executive search firm operating on a retainer basis. CES Associates also offers career planning services, training programs, and seminars. Founded in 1973. **Specializes in the areas of:** Administration; Computer Science/Software; Education; Health/Medical. **Positions commonly filled include:** Biomedical Engineer; Chemical Engineer; Computer Programmer; Education Administrator; Health Services Manager; MIS Specialist; Nuclear Engineer; Software Engineer. **Average salary range of placements:** $45,000 - $75,000. **Number of placements per year:** 1 - 49.

CFR EXECUTIVE SEARCH, INC.
175 West Jackson, Suite 1900, Chicago IL 60604. 312/435-0990. **Fax:** 312/435-1333. **Contact:** Joe Sexton, Vice President. **E-mail address:** cfrexecsearch@msn.com. **Description:** An executive search firm. **Specializes in the areas of:** Accounting/Auditing; Finance. **Positions commonly filled include:** Accountant/Auditor; Budget Analyst; Credit Manager. **Average salary range of placements:** More than $50,000.

C.R.T., INC.
301 East Main Street, Suite 100, Barrington IL 60010. 847/816-0610. **Fax:** 847/487-0195. **Contact:** William Mellor, Executive Recruiter. **Description:** An executive search firm. **Specializes in the areas of:** Computer Science/Software. **Positions commonly filled include:** Computer Programmer; Internet Specialist; LAN/WAN Designer/Developer; Operations/Production Manager; Software Engineer; Systems Analyst; Technical Writer/Editor. **Number of placements per year:** 1 - 49.

C.S. GLOBAL PARTNERS
101 West Grand Avenue, Chicago IL 60610. 312/587-9912. **Contact:** Christopher Melillo, President. **Description:** An executive search firm. **Specializes in the areas of:** Accounting/Auditing; Finance. **Positions commonly filled include:** Accountant/Auditor; Financial Analyst; Management Analyst/Consultant; MIS Specialist. **Number of placements per year:** 50 - 99.

CALLAN & ASSOCIATES
2021 Spring Road, Suite 175, Oak Brook IL 60523. 630/574-9300. **Contact:** Manager. **Description:** An executive search firm operating on a retainer basis.

CAPRIO & ASSOCIATES INC.
2 Mid America Plaza, Suite 800, Oak Brook Terrace IL 60181. 630/705-9101. **Fax:** 630/705-9102. **Contact:** Jerry A. Caprio, President. **Description:** An executive search firm operating on a retainer basis. Caprio & Associates focuses on placing senior-level management for the printing, publishing, packaging, and converting industries. Founded in 1975. **Specializes in the areas of:** Advertising; Packaging; Printing; Publishing. **Average salary range of placements:** More than $50,000. **Number of placements per year:** 1 - 49.

NEAL CARDEN ASSOCIATES INC.
345 Browning Court, Wheaton IL 60187. 630/665-3932. **Contact:** Manager. **Description:** An executive search firm.

CAREER PLACEMENTS, INC.
P.O. Box 327, Philo IL 61864. 217/684-2517. **Fax:** 217/684-2106. **Contact:** Manager. **World Wide Web address:** http://www.cpicareers.com. **Description:** An executive search firm. **Specializes in the areas of:** Information Systems; Information Technology.

CAREERLINK USA, INC.
2239 Charles Street, Rockford IL 61108. 815/227-5465. **Fax:** 815/227-5482. **Contact:** Ms. Mickey Tyler, President. **E-mail address:** hrlinks@aol.com. **World Wide Web address:** http://www.careerlinkusa.com. **Description:** An executive search firm that also provides human resources consulting and a confidential resume service. Client company pays fee. **Specializes in the areas of:** Accounting; Administration; Advertising; Banking; Computer Science/Software; Engineering; Finance; Food; General Management; Industrial; Insurance; Legal; Light Industrial; Manufacturing; Marketing; MIS/EDP; Nonprofit; Personnel/Labor Relations; Printing; Publishing; Sales; Scientific; Secretarial; Technical; Transportation. **Positions commonly filled include:** Account Manager; Account Representative; Accountant; Administrative Assistant; Administrative Manager; Advertising Executive; Applications Engineer; Assistant Manager; Auditor; Bank Officer/Manager; Budget Analyst; Buyer; Chief Financial Officer; Civil Engineer; Clerical Supervisor; Computer Operator; Computer Programmer; Controller;

Credit Manager; Customer Service Representative; Database Manager; Design Engineer; Draftsperson; Electrical/Electronics Engineer; Finance Director; Financial Analyst; General Manager; Human Resources Manager; Industrial Engineer; Industrial Production Manager; Insurance Agent/Broker; Management Trainee; Manufacturing Engineer; Marketing Manager; Marketing Specialist; Mechanical Engineer; MIS Specialist; Operations Manager; Pharmacist; Production Manager; Project Manager; Public Relations Specialist; Purchasing Agent/Manager; Quality Control Supervisor; Sales Engineer; Sales Executive; Sales Manager; Sales Representative; Secretary; Software Engineer; Systems Analyst; Systems Manager; Technical Writer/Editor; Telecommunications Manager; Transportation/Traffic Specialist; Typist/Word Processor. **Corporate headquarters location:** This Location. **Average salary range of placements:** $30,000 - $50,000. **Number of placements per year:** 50 - 99.

CARPENTER ASSOCIATES INC.
322 South Green Street, Suite 408, Chicago IL 60607. 312/243-1000. **Contact:** Manager. **Description:** An executive search firm. **Specializes in the areas of:** Direct Marketing.

CARRINGTON & CARRINGTON LTD.
39 South LaSalle Street, Chicago IL 60603. 312/606-0015. **Contact:** Manager. **Description:** An executive search firm operating on a retainer basis. **Positions commonly filled include:** Accountant/Auditor; Budget Analyst; Chief Financial Officer; Civil Engineer; Controller; Design Engineer; Finance Director; Financial Analyst; Marketing Manager; Marketing Specialist; Mechanical Engineer; Network Administrator; Public Relations Specialist; Purchasing Agent/Manager; Systems Analyst; Systems Manager.

CARTER ASSOCIATES
P.O. Box 310, Matteson IL 60443. 708/503-5020. **Fax:** 708/503-5024. **Contact:** Chuck Carter, President. **Description:** An executive search firm. **Specializes in the areas of:** Architecture/Construction; Engineering. **Positions commonly filled include:** Architect; Civil Engineer; Construction Contractor; Electrical/Electronics Engineer; Landscape Architect; Mechanical Engineer; Mining Engineer; Surveyor. **Average salary range of placements:** More than $50,000. **Number of placements per year:** 50 - 99.

CAST METALS PERSONNEL INC.
512 West Burlington Avenue, La Grange IL 60525. 708/354-0085. **Fax:** 708/354-2490. **Contact:** Chuck Lundeen, President. **Description:** An executive search firm operating on a contingency basis. Cast Metals Personnel focuses on placing individuals in the foundry, and diecasting industries. **Specializes in the areas of:** Engineering; General Management; Industrial. **Positions commonly filled include:** Blue-Collar Worker Supervisor; Electrical/Electronics Engineer; Environmental Engineer; General Manager; Human Resources Representative; Industrial Engineer; Industrial Production Manager; Maintenance Supervisor; Mechanical Engineer; Metallurgical Engineer; Operations Manager; Production Manager; Project Manager; Quality Control Supervisor; Sales Engineer; Sales Manager. **Average salary range of placements:** $35,000 - $75,000. **Number of placements per year:** 1 - 49.

CEMCO LTD.
20 South Clark Street, Suite 610, Chicago IL 60603. 312/855-1500. **Fax:** 312/855-1510. **Contact:** Manager. **Description:** An executive search firm. **Specializes in the areas of:** Accounting/Auditing; Banking; Finance; Health/Medical; Real Estate. **Positions commonly filled include:** Accountant/Auditor; Actuary; Financial Analyst; Health Services Manager; Property and Real Estate Manager; Registered Nurse; Respiratory Therapist; Speech-Language Pathologist. **Number of placements per year:** 50 - 99.

CEMCO SYSTEMS
2001 Spring Road, Suite 250, Oak Brook IL 60523. 630/573-5050. **Fax:** 630/573-5060. **Contact:** David Gordon, General Manager. **E-mail address:** info@cemcosystems.com. **World Wide Web address:** http://www.cemcosystems.com. **Description:** An executive search firm operating on a contingency basis. **Specializes in the areas of:** Computer Science/Software. **Positions commonly filled include:** Computer Programmer; Database Manager; Information Systems Consultant; Management Analyst/Consultant; MIS Specialist; Software Engineer; Systems Analyst; Systems Manager; Webmaster. **Average salary range of placements:** More than $50,000. **Number of placements per year:** 200 - 499.

CHATTERTON & ASSOCIATES
135 South Wheeling Road, Wheeling IL 60090. 847/537-3830. **Contact:** Manager. **Description:** An executive search firm. **Specializes in the areas of:** Health/Medical.

CHICAGO FINANCIAL SEARCH
200 South Wacker Drive, Suite 3100, Chicago IL 60606. 312/207-0400. **Contact:** Mike Kelly, Manager. **Description:** An executive search firm. **Specializes in the areas of:** Accounting/Auditing; Banking; Brokerage; Computer Science/Software; Finance. **Positions commonly filled include:** Accountant/Auditor; Computer Operator; Computer Programmer; MIS Specialist. **Number of placements per year:** 100 - 199.

CHICAGO LEGAL SEARCH, LTD.
33 North Dearborn Street, Suite 2302, Chicago IL 60602-3109. 312/251-2580. **Fax:** 312/251-0223. **Contact:** Gary A. D'Alessio, Esq., President. **E-mail address:** attorneys@chicagolegalsearch.com. **World Wide Web address:** http://www.chicagolegalsearch.com. **Description:** An executive search firm that operates on a contingency basis. Client company pays fee. **Specializes in the areas of:** Legal. **Positions commonly filled include:** Attorney; Intellectual Property Lawyer; Paralegal. **Average salary range of placements:** More than $100,000. **Number of placements per year:** 50 - 99.

CLAREY & ANDREWS INC.
1200 Shermer Road, Suite 108, Northbrook IL 60062. 847/498-2870. **Contact:** Manager. **Description:** An executive search firm operating on a retainer basis. **Positions commonly filled include:** General Manager. **Average salary range of placements:** More than $100,000.

D. CLESEN COMPANY
9239 Nagle, Morton Grove IL 60053. 847/965-1211. **Contact:** Donna M. Clesen, President. **Description:** An executive search firm operating on a contingency basis. **Specializes in the areas of:** Accounting/Auditing; Finance. **Positions commonly filled include:** Accountant/Auditor; Computer Programmer; Controller; Financial Analyst; Human Resources Manager; Systems Analyst. **Average salary range of placements:** More than $50,000. **Number of placements per year:** 1 - 49.

COFFOU PARTNERS, INC.
330 North Wabash Avenue, Suite 2111, Chicago IL 60611. 312/464-0894. **Contact:** Manager. **World Wide Web address:** http://www.coffou.com. **Description:** An executive search firm. **Specializes in the areas of:** Finance; Human Resources; Information Technology; Internet Marketing; Marketing; Sales.

COGAN PERSONNEL SERVICES, INC.
7004 North California Avenue, Chicago IL 60645. 773/761-1100. **Contact:** Manager. **Description:** An executive search firm. **Specializes in the areas of:** Banking; Finance; Insurance.

COMPUPRO
1117 South Milwaukee Avenue, Suite B9, Libertyville IL 60048. 847/549-8603. **Fax:** 847/549-7429. **Contact:** Doug Baniqued, Owner. **Description:** An executive

search firm operating on both retainer and contingency bases. Founded in 1971. **Specializes in the areas of:** Banking; Computer Science/Software; General Management; Internet Development; MIS/EDP; Sales. **Positions commonly filled include:** Account Manager; Account Representative; AS400 Programmer Analyst; Auditor; Chief Financial Officer; Computer Programmer; Computer Support Technician; Content Developer; Database Administrator; Financial Analyst; General Manager; Internet Services Manager; Management Analyst/Consultant; MIS Specialist; Network Administrator; Operations Manager; Project Manager; Quality Control Supervisor; Sales Engineer; SQL Programmer; Systems Analyst; Systems Manager; Telecommunications Manager; Webmaster. **Other U.S. locations:** Nationwide. **Average salary range of placements:** $50,000 - $100,000. **Number of placements per year:** 1 - 49.

COMPUTER FUTURES EXCHANGE, INC.
137 North Oak Park Avenue, Oak Park IL 60301. 708/445-8000. **Contact:** Corey D. Gimbel, President. **Description:** An executive search firm. **Specializes in the areas of:** Administration; Banking; Computer Science/Software; Economics; Finance. **Positions commonly filled include:** Computer Programmer; Economist; Mathematician; Securities Sales Representative; Software Engineer; Systems Analyst. **Other area locations:** Chicago IL. **Number of placements per year:** 50 - 99.

COMPUTER SEARCH GROUP
20 North Wacker Drive, Suite 2200, Chicago IL 60606. 312/269-9950. **Contact:** Manager. **Description:** An executive search firm. **Specializes in the areas of:** Computer Science/Software; Information Technology.

CONTEMPORARY SERVICES
1701 East Woodfield Road, Suite 1030, Schaumburg IL 60173. 847/619-4000. **Toll-free phone:** 800/474-9200. **Fax:** 847/619-1077. **Contact:** Manager. **World Wide Web address:** http://www.contempserv.com. **Description:** An executive search firm. **Specializes in the areas of:** Banking; Finance; Mortgage; Real Estate. **Positions commonly filled include:** Bank Officer/Manager; Branch Manager; Credit Manager; Customer Service Representative; Financial Analyst; Property and Real Estate Manager; Quality Control Supervisor; Securities Sales Representative; Underwriter/Assistant Underwriter. **Benefits available to temporary workers:** Paid Holidays; Paid Vacation. **Corporate headquarters location:** This Location. **Other U.S. locations:** Galena IL; Indianapolis IN; Troy MI. **Average salary range of placements:** $30,000 - $50,000. **Number of placements per year:** 200 - 499.

CONWAY & ASSOCIATES
1007 Church Street, Suite 408, Evanston IL 60201. 847/866-6832. **Contact:** Manager. **Description:** A generalist executive search firm.

COOK ASSOCIATES, INC.
212 West Kinzie Street, Chicago IL 60610. 312/329-0900. **Fax:** 312/329-1528. **Contact:** Arnie Kins, President. **E-mail address:** akins@cookassociates.com. **Description:** An executive search firm. **Specializes in the areas of:** Architecture/Construction; Banking; Chemicals; Food; General Management; Graphic Arts; Health/Medical; Industrial; Insurance; Legal; Manufacturing; Paper; Publishing; Retail. **Positions commonly filled include:** Executive Assistant; General Manager. **Average salary range of placements:** More than $50,000. **Number of placements per year:** 200 - 499.

CORPORATE CONSULTANTS
480 Central Avenue, Northfield IL 60093. 847/446-5627. **Fax:** 847/446-3536. **Contact:** Allen M. Arends, President. **E-mail address:** resumes@corpconsult.net. **Description:** An executive search firm operating on both retainer and contingency bases. **Specializes in the areas of:** Data Communications; Marketing; Sales;

Telecommunications. **Positions commonly filled include:** Account Manager; Account Representative; Sales Engineer; Sales Executive; Sales Manager; Sales Representative. **Average salary range of placements:** More than $50,000. **Number of placements per year:** 1 - 49.

CORPORATE ENVIRONMENT, LTD.
P.O. Box 798, Crystal Lake IL 60039-0798. 815/455-6070. **Fax:** 815/455-0124. **Contact:** Thomas P. McDermott, President. **Description:** An executive search firm. **Specializes in the areas of:** Architecture/Construction; Chemicals; Engineering; Environmental; Food; General Management; Industrial; Manufacturing; Operations Management; Pharmaceuticals; Sales; Technical. **Positions commonly filled include:** Chemical Engineer; Environmental Engineer; Management. **Number of placements per year:** 1 - 49.

CORPORATE SEARCH GROUP
2711 West 183rd Street, Homewood IL 60430. 708/957-4520. **Contact:** Manager. **Description:** An executive search firm that provides placements in the medical diagnostics industry.

CREDENTIA INC.
980 North Michigan Avenue, Suite 1400, Chicago IL 60611. 312/649-0522. **Contact:** Manager. **Description:** An executive search firm. **Specializes in the areas of:** Legal. **Positions commonly filled include:** Attorney.

CROSLY & ASSOCIATES
707 Skokie Boulevard, Suite 500, Northbrook IL 60062. 847/564-3800. **Contact:** Manager. **Description:** An executive search firm.

CUMBERLAND GROUP
608 South Washington Street, Suite 101, Naperville IL 60540. 630/416-9494. **Fax:** 630/416-3250. **Contact:** Jerry Vogus, Senior Partner. **Description:** An executive search firm. **Specializes in the areas of:** Engineering; Industrial; Sales. **Positions commonly filled include:** Mechanical Engineer; Metallurgical Engineer; Sales Manager; Sales Representative. **Average salary range of placements:** More than $50,000. **Number of placements per year:** 1 - 49.

DMG-MAXIMUS, INC.
630 Dundee Road, Suite 200, Northbrook IL 60062. 847/564-9270. **Contact:** Manager. **Description:** An executive search firm. **Corporate headquarters location:** This Location.

DRC & ASSOCIATES
6900 Main Street, Downers Grove IL 60516. 630/810-1411. **Contact:** Manager. **Description:** An executive search firm. **Specializes in the areas of:** Data Processing.

DATA CAREER CENTER, INC.
225 North Michigan Avenue, Suite 930, Chicago IL 60601. 312/565-1060. **Fax:** 312/565-0246. **Contact:** Larry Chaplik, President. **Description:** An executive search firm. **Specializes in the areas of:** Data Processing; Telecommunications. **Positions commonly filled include:** Administrator; Computer Programmer; Database Manager; LAN/WAN Designer/Developer; Management Analyst/Consultant; Software Engineer; Systems Analyst; Voice/Data Engineer. **Number of placements per year:** 1 - 49.

DATAQUEST INC.
7105 Virginia Road, Suite 2A, Crystal Lake IL 60014. 815/356-7500. **Fax:** 815/477-2359. **Contact:** Bob & Shirley Vincent, Co-owners. **E-mail address:** dataqst@mc.net. **Description:** An executive search firm operating on a contingency basis. **Specializes in the areas of:** Computer Science/Software. **Positions commonly filled include:** Computer Programmer; Software Engineer. **Average salary range of placements:** $30,000 - $50,000. **Number of placements per year:** 50 - 99.

T.A. DAVIS & ASSOCIATES, INC.
604 Green Bay Road, Kenilworth IL 60043. 847/256-8900. **Fax:** 847/256-8955. **Contact:** Lynn Robertson, Office Manager. **E-mail address:** lynn@tadavis.com. **Description:** An executive search firm operating on both retainer and contingency bases. **Specializes in the areas of:** Hotel/Restaurant. **Average salary range of placements:** More than $50,000. **Number of placements per year:** 1 - 49.

NED DICKEY & ASSOCIATES, INC.
DICKEY STAFFING SOLUTIONS
P.O. Box 15068, Loves Park IL 61132. 815/636-4480. **Fax:** 815/636-4486. **Contact:** Kurt Dickey, President. **Description:** An executive search firm. Dickey Staffing Solutions (also at this location) provides office support and industrial positions. **Specializes in the areas of:** Engineering; Manufacturing; Personnel/Labor Relations. **Positions commonly filled include:** Accountant/Auditor; Advertising Clerk; Aerospace Engineer; Architect; Bank Officer/Manager; Blue-Collar Worker Supervisor; Branch Manager; Buyer; Chemical Engineer; Chemist; Civil Engineer; Clerical Supervisor; Computer Programmer; Counselor; Customer Service Representative; Design Engineer; Designer; Draftsperson; Electrical/Electronics Engineer; Electrician; Environmental Engineer; General Manager; Human Resources Manager; Industrial Engineer; Industrial Production Manager; Management Analyst/Consultant; Management Trainee; Mechanical Engineer; Medical Records Technician; Metallurgical Engineer; Paralegal; Purchasing Agent/Manager; Quality Control Supervisor; Software Engineer; Strategic Relations Manager; Structural Engineer; Technical Writer/Editor; Transportation/Traffic Specialist; Typist/Word Processor. **Benefits available to temporary workers:** Credit Union; Paid Holidays; Paid Vacation.

DIECKMANN & ASSOCIATES
2 Prudential Plaza, Suite 5555, 180 North Stetson Avenue, Chicago IL 60601. 312/819-5900. **Contact:** Ralph Dieckmann, Owner. **Description:** A generalist executive search firm.

DIENER & ASSOCIATES INC.
P.O. Box 946, Northbrook IL 60065. 847/564-3160. **Contact:** Joel Diener, President. **Description:** An executive search firm operating on both retainer and contingency bases. **Specializes in the areas of:** Accounting; Administration; Advertising; Art/Design; Banking; Biology; Engineering; Finance; Food; General Management; Health/Medical; Industrial; Legal; Personnel/Labor Relations; Printing; Real Estate; Sales; Technical. **Positions commonly filled include:** Account Manager; Account Representative; Accountant; Architect; Auditor; Bank Officer/Manager; Biochemist; Biological Scientist; Biomedical Engineer; Buyer; Chemical Engineer; Chemist; Chief Financial Officer; Civil Engineer; Construction Contractor; Controller; Design Engineer; Electrical/Electronics Engineer; Finance Director; Financial Analyst; Food Scientist/Technologist; General Manager; Geologist/Geophysicist; Human Resources Manager; Industrial Engineer; Industrial Production Manager; Insurance Agent/Broker; Management Analyst/Consultant; Manufacturing Engineer; Marketing Manager; Marketing Specialist; Mechanical Engineer; Metallurgical Engineer; Operations Manager; Pharmacist; Physician; Production Manager; Project Manager; Purchasing Agent/Manager; Quality Assurance Engineer; Quality Control Supervisor; Registered Nurse; Sales Engineer; Sales Executive; Sales Manager; Sales Representative; Underwriter/Assistant Underwriter. **Other U.S. locations:** Nationwide. **Average salary range of placements:** $50,000 - $100,000. **Number of placements per year:** 1 - 49.

DONAHUE/BALES ASSOCIATES
303 West Madison, Suite 1150, Chicago IL 60606. 312/732-0999. **Fax:** 312/732-0990. **Contact:** Manager. **Description:** An executive search firm operating on a retainer basis. Client company pays fee. **Average salary range of placements:** More than $100,000. **Number of placements per year:** 1 - 49.

DUNHILL PROFESSIONAL SEARCH OF ROLLING MEADOWS
5005 Newport Drive, Suite 201, Rolling Meadows IL 60008. 847/398-3400. **Contact:** Russ Kunke, Consultant. **Description:** An executive search firm operating on a contingency basis. **Specializes in the areas of:** Computer Science/Software; MIS/EDP. **Positions commonly filled include:** Applications Engineer; AS400 Programmer Analyst; Computer Engineer; Computer Programmer; Computer Support Technician; Database Administrator; Database Manager; Internet Services Manager; MIS Specialist; Network Administrator; Project Manager; Software Engineer; SQL Programmer; Systems Analyst; Systems Manager; Webmaster. **Average salary range of placements:** $50,000 - $100,000. **Number of placements per year:** 1 - 49.

DYNAMIC SEARCH SYSTEMS, INC.
3800 North Wilke Road, Suite 485, Arlington Heights IL 60004. 847/259-3444. **Fax:** 847/259-3480. **Contact:** Michael J. Brindise, President. **Description:** An executive search firm. **Specializes in the areas of:** Administration; Computer Science/Software; MIS/EDP. **Positions commonly filled include:** Computer Animator; Computer Operator; Computer Programmer; Database Manager; Internet Services Manager; Management Analyst/Consultant; MIS Specialist; Project Manager; Software Engineer; Systems Analyst; Systems Manager; Technical Writer/Editor; Telecommunications Manager; Webmaster. **Corporate headquarters location:** This Location. **Average salary range of placements:** More than $50,000. **Number of placements per year:** 200 - 499.

EARLY COCHRAN & OLSON
401 North Michigan Avenue, Suite 515, Chicago IL 60611-4205. 312/595-4200. **Fax:** 312/595-4209. **Contact:** Corinne Cochran, Principal. **Description:** An executive search firm operating on a retainer basis. Early Cochran & Olson provides primarily senior-level placements. **Specializes in the areas of:** Legal. **Positions commonly filled include:** Attorney.

EASTMAN & ASSOCIATES
1717 North Naper Boulevard, Suite 104, Naperville IL 60563. 630/505-8855. **Fax:** 630/505-8860. **Contact:** Marilyn Wilcox, Recruiter. **Description:** An executive search firm operating on a retainer basis. **Specializes in the areas of:** Accounting/Auditing; Finance; Personnel/Labor Relations; Retail; Sales. **Positions commonly filled include:** Accountant/Auditor; Bank Officer/Manager; Customer Service Representative; Financial Analyst; Human Resources Manager; Industrial Engineer; Securities Sales Representative; Underwriter/Assistant Underwriter. **Corporate headquarters location:** This Location. **Other U.S. locations:** Nationwide. **Average salary range of placements:** $30,000 - $50,000.

THE EASTWOOD GROUP
900 Skokie Boulevard, Suite 116, Northbrook IL 60062. 847/291-8383. **Fax:** 847/291-9753. **Contact:** Bonnie Miller, President. **E-mail address:** eastwoodg@aol.com. **Description:** An executive search firm operating on a contingency basis. **Specializes in the areas of:** Advertising; Art/Design; Banking; Finance; Health/Medical; Sales. **Positions commonly filled include:** Designer; Editor; Financial Analyst; Market Research Analyst; Public Relations Manager; Technical Writer/Editor; Video Production Coordinator. **Average salary range of placements:** More than $50,000. **Number of placements per year:** 1 - 49.

EFFECTIVE SEARCH INC.
11718 North Main Street, Roscoe IL 61073. 815/623-7400. **Fax:** 815/623-6171. **Contact:** Manager. **Description:** An executive search firm. **Specializes in the areas of:** Engineering.

ELECTRONIC SEARCH INC.
3601 Algonquin Road, Suite 820, Rolling Meadows IL 60008. 847/506-0700. **Contact:** Manager. **Description:** An executive search firm. **Specializes in the areas of:** Technical. **Corporate headquarters location:** This Location.

ELSKO EXECUTIVE SEARCH
3601 Algonquin Road, Suite 130, Rolling Meadows IL 60008. 847/394-2400. **Contact:** Training Manager. **Description:** An executive search firm. **Specializes in the areas of:** Accounting/Auditing; Finance. **Number of placements per year:** 100 - 199.

EVERGREENE PARTNERS
635 Elmwood Drive, Wheaton IL 60187. 630/665-4850. **Contact:** Manager. **Description:** An executive search firm. **Specializes in the areas of:** Food. **Positions commonly filled include:** Chemical Engineer; Electrical/Electronics Engineer; Food Scientist/Technologist; Human Resources Manager; Industrial Engineer; Mechanical Engineer. **Number of placements per year:** 1 - 49.

EXECU SEARCH
1525 South Michigan Avenue, Suite 309, Chicago IL 60605. 312/935-1100. **Contact:** Manager. **Description:** An executive search firm.

EXECUTIVE CONCEPTS INC.
1000 Woodfield Road, Suite 235, Schaumburg IL 60173-4728. 847/605-8300. **Fax:** 847/605-8089. **Contact:** Tom Werle, President. **Description:** An executive search firm operating on both retainer and contingency bases. **Specializes in the areas of:** Computer Science/Software. **Positions commonly filled include:** Computer Programmer; Systems Analyst. **Average salary range of placements:** $40,000 - $150,000. **Number of placements per year:** 100 - 199.

EXECUTIVE DIRECTIONS
10 South Riverside Plaza, Suite 1424, Chicago IL 60606. 312/930-1106. **Contact:** Manager. **Description:** An executive search firm. **Specializes in the areas of:** Finance; Insurance.

EXECUTIVE FINANCIAL CONSULTANTS
6900 Main Street, Suite 52, Downers Grove IL 60516. 630/663-9010. **Contact:** Manager. **Description:** An executive search firm. **Specializes in the areas of:** Accounting/Auditing; Finance.

EXECUTIVE INTERVIEWERS
2000 North Racine, Chicago IL 60614. 773/929-3200. **Contact:** Manager. **Description:** A generalist executive search firm.

EXECUTIVE OPTIONS LTD.
8707 Skokie Boulevard, Suite 300, Skokie IL 60077. 847/933-8760. **Contact:** Manager. **Description:** An executive search firm that places mid- and upper-level management professionals. **Specializes in the areas of:** Finance; Marketing. **Positions commonly filled include:** Human Resources Manager.

EXECUTIVE OPTIONS LTD.
625 North Michigan Avenue, Suite 500, Chicago IL 60611. 312/751-5413. **Contact:** Manager. **Description:** An executive search firm.

EXECUTIVE PLACEMENT CONSULTANTS
2700 South River Road, Suite 107, Des Plaines IL 60018. 847/298-6445. **Contact:** Manager. **Description:** An executive search firm. **Specializes in the areas of:** Accounting/Auditing; Finance; Information Systems.

EXECUTIVE REFERRAL SERVICES, INC.
8770 West Bryn Mawr, Suite 110, Chicago IL 60631. 773/693-6622. **Fax:** 773/693-8466. **Contact:** Bruce Freier, President. **Description:** An executive search firm. **Specializes in the areas of:** Accounting/Auditing; Architecture/Construction; Fashion; Finance; Food; General Management; Health/Medical; Hotel/Restaurant;

Personnel/Labor Relations; Pharmaceuticals; Retail; Sales. **Positions commonly filled include:** Accountant; Branch Manager; Buyer; Chief Financial Officer; Construction Contractor; Controller; Finance Director; Financial Analyst; General Manager; Graphic Designer; Human Resources Manager; Marketing Manager; Pharmacist; Physical Therapist; Sales Executive; Sales Manager.

EXECUTIVE SEARCH CONSULTANTS
8 South Michigan Avenue, Suite 1205, Chicago IL 60603. 312/251-8400. **Contact:** Manager. **Description:** An executive search firm. **Specializes in the areas of:** Insurance.

EXECUTIVE SEARCH INTERNATIONAL
4300 North Brandywine Drive, Suite 104, Peoria IL 61614-5550. 309/685-6273. **Contact:** Robert Vaughan, President. **Description:** An executive search firm operating on both contingency and retainer bases. **Specializes in the areas of:** Advertising; Computer Science/Software; Engineering; Industrial; Sales. **Positions commonly filled include:** Account Manager; Account Representative; Accountant; Buyer; Computer Programmer; Controller; Customer Service Representative; Database Manager; Design Engineer; Electrical/Electronics Engineer; Financial Analyst; General Manager; Human Resources Manager; Industrial Engineer; Industrial Production Manager; Manufacturer's/Wholesaler's Sales Rep.; Manufacturing Engineer; Market Research Analyst; Marketing Specialist; Mechanical Engineer; MIS Specialist; Multimedia Designer; Production Manager; Purchasing Agent/Manager; Quality Control Supervisor; Sales Engineer; Sales Executive; Sales Manager; Software Engineer; Systems Analyst; Systems Manager; Technical Writer/Editor; Telecommunications Manager; Underwriter/Assistant Underwriter; Vice President. **Corporate headquarters location:** This Location. **Other U.S. locations:** Nationwide. **Average salary range of placements:** More than $50,000. **Number of placements per year:** 100 - 199.

EXECUTIVE SEARCH LINK, LTD.
P.O. Box 40, Seymour IL 61875. 217/687-2888. **Contact:** Manager. **Description:** An executive search firm. **Specializes in the areas of:** Engineering; Operations Management.

EXECUTIVE SEARCH NETWORK
500 North Lake Street, Suite 107, Mundelein IL 60060. 847/837-1460. **Contact:** Mike Tollefson, President. **Description:** An executive search firm. **Specializes in the areas of:** Computer Hardware/Software; Engineering; Technical. **Positions commonly filled include:** Aerospace Engineer; Buyer; Ceramics Engineer; Chemical Engineer; Computer Programmer; Electrical/Electronics Engineer; Industrial Engineer; Manufacturing Engineer; Marketing Specialist; Mechanical Engineer; Metallurgical Engineer; Purchasing Agent/Manager; Quality Control Supervisor; Software Engineer; Technical Representative; Technical Writer/Editor. **Number of placements per year:** 1 - 49.

FINANCIAL SEARCH CORPORATION
2720 Des Plaines Avenue, Suite 106, Des Plaines IL 60018. 847/297-4900. **Fax:** 847/297-0294. **Contact:** Robert Collins, President. **E-mail address:** admin@financial-search.com. **World Wide Web address:** http://www.financial-search.com. **Description:** An executive search firm. **Specializes in the areas of:** Accounting/Auditing; Banking; Finance; Insurance. **Positions commonly filled include:** Accountant; Auditor; Budget Analyst; Controller; Cost Estimator; Credit Manager; Finance Director; Financial Analyst. **Corporate headquarters location:** This Location. **Other area locations:** Chicago IL. **Average salary range of placements:** $30,000 - $50,000. **Number of placements per year:** 50 - 99.

FINANCIAL SEARCH CORPORATION
333 West Wacker Drive, Suite 700, Chicago IL 60606. 312/444-2019. **Contact:** Manager. **World Wide Web**

address: http://www.financial-search.com. **Description:** An executive search firm. **Specializes in the areas of:** Finance. **Corporate headquarters location:** Des Plaines IL.

FIRST ATTORNEY CONSULTANTS LTD.
P.O. Box 42751, Evergreen Park IL 60805. 708/425-5515. **Contact:** Manager. **Description:** An executive search firm. **Specializes in the areas of:** Legal. **Positions commonly filled include:** Attorney.

FIRST CHAIR TECHNOLOGIES, INC.
1910 West North Avenue, Suite 200, Chicago IL 60622. 773/235-0444. **Contact:** Manager. **Description:** An executive search firm. **Specializes in the areas of:** Computer Science/Software. **Other U.S. locations:** Oak Park IL.

FIRST SEARCH, INC.
6584 NW Highway, Chicago IL 60631. 773/774-0001. **Fax:** 773/774-5571. **Contact:** Al Katz, Vice President. **E-mail address:** resume@firstsearch.com. **Description:** An executive search firm. **Specializes in the areas of:** Computer Science/Software; Engineering; Sales; Technical; Telecommunications. **Positions commonly filled include:** Computer Operator; Computer Programmer; Consultant; Customer Service Representative; Database Manager; Design Engineer; Electrical/Electronics Engineer; Systems Analyst; Systems Manager; Telecommunications Manager; Vice President of Sales. **Benefits available to temporary workers:** 401(k); Life Insurance; Medical Insurance. **Corporate headquarters location:** This Location. **Average salary range of placements:** More than $50,000. **Number of placements per year:** 200 - 499.

F-O-R-T-U-N-E PERSONNEL CONSULTANTS
825 East Golf Road, Suite 1146, Arlington Heights IL 60005. 847/228-7205. **Fax:** 847/228-7206. **Contact:** Manager. **Description:** An executive search firm. **Specializes in the areas of:** Automotive; Insurance; Manufacturing; Quality Assurance. **Corporate headquarters location:** New York NY. **Other U.S. locations:** Nationwide.

F-O-R-T-U-N-E PERSONNEL CONSULTANTS
115 First Street, Suite 2E, Hinsdale IL 60521. 630/920-1952. **Fax:** 630/920-0793. **Contact:** Manager. **Description:** An executive search firm. **Specializes in the areas of:** Accounting; Finance. **Corporate headquarters location:** New York NY. **Other U.S. locations:** Nationwide.

GAINES INTERNATIONAL
650 North Dearborn Street, Suite 450, Chicago IL 60610. 312/654-2900. **Fax:** 312/654-2903. **Contact:** Manager. **Description:** An executive search firm.

GENERAL COUNSEL CORPORATION
980 North Michigan Avenue, Suite 1400, Chicago IL 60611. 312/649-1959. **Fax:** 312/642-8444. **Contact:** John C. Hoppe, President. **Description:** An executive search firm. **Specializes in the areas of:** Legal. **Positions commonly filled include:** Attorney. **Number of placements per year:** 1 - 49.

GIOVANNINI ASSOCIATES
4811 Emerson Avenue, Suite 101, Palatine IL 60067. 847/303-1199. **Contact:** Manager. **Description:** An executive search firm. **Specializes in the areas of:** Medical Sales and Marketing.

THE GLENWOOD GROUP
6428 Joliet Road, Suite 112, Countryside IL 60525. 708/482-3750. **Fax:** 708/482-0633. **Contact:** Frank Filippelli, President. **E-mail address:** glenwood@glenwoodgrp.com. **Description:** An executive search firm operating on a contingency basis. **Specializes in the areas of:** Engineering; Food. **Positions commonly filled include:** Design Engineer; Electrical/Electronics Engineer; Industrial Engineer; Manufacturing Engineer; Mechanical Engineer; Quality

Assurance Engineer. **Average salary range of placements:** $50,000 - $100,000. **Number of placements per year:** 1 - 49.

GNODDE ASSOCIATES
128 North Lincoln Street, Hinsdale IL 60521. 630/887-9510. **Fax:** 630/887-9531. **Contact:** Dirk Gnodde, Owner. **Description:** An executive search firm operating on a contingency basis. **Specializes in the areas of:** Banking; Finance. **Positions commonly filled include:** Accountant/Auditor; Bank Officer/Manager; Branch Manager; Budget Analyst; Credit Manager; Financial Analyst. **Average salary range of placements:** More than $50,000. **Number of placements per year:** 1 - 49.

GODFREY PERSONNEL INC.
300 West Adams Street, Suite 612, Chicago IL 60606. 312/236-4455. **Fax:** 312/580-6292. **Contact:** James Godfrey, President. **Description:** An executive search firm. **Specializes in the areas of:** Insurance. **Number of placements per year:** 200 - 499.

DAVID GOMEZ & ASSOCIATES, INC.
20 North Clark Street, Suite 3535, Chicago IL 60602. 312/346-5525. **Fax:** 312/346-1438. **Contact:** Consultant. **World Wide Web address:** http://www.dgai.com. **Description:** An executive search firm. **Specializes in the areas of:** Accounting/Auditing; Administration; Advertising; Art/Design; Banking; Computer Science/Software; Finance; General Management; Insurance; Manufacturing; Personnel/Labor Relations; Publishing; Sales; Secretarial. **Positions commonly filled include:** Accountant/Auditor; Administrative Manager; Advertising Clerk; Bank Officer/Manager; Branch Manager; Budget Analyst; Computer Programmer; Credit Manager; Customer Service Representative; Design Engineer; Designer; Financial Analyst; General Manager; Human Resources Manager; Librarian; Management Analyst/Consultant; Market Research Analyst; MIS Specialist; Operations/Production Manager; Software Engineer; Systems Analyst; Telecommunications Manager; Typist/Word Processor; Underwriter/Assistant Underwriter. **Average salary range of placements:** More than $50,000. **Number of placements per year:** 200 - 499.

GORDON & ASSOCIATES
980 North Michigan Avenue, Suite 1400, Chicago IL 60611. 312/943-2800. **Contact:** Manager. **Description:** A generalist executive search firm.

GRICE HOLDENER & ASSOCIATES INC.
39 South Barrington Road, South Barrington IL 60010. 847/382-2950. **Contact:** Manager. **Description:** An executive search firm. **Specializes in the areas of:** Computer Programming; Data Processing.

GROSSBERG & ASSOCIATES
1100 Jorie Boulevard, Suite 251, Oak Brook IL 60523. 630/574-0066. **Contact:** Robert Grossberg. **Description:** An executive search firm operating on a retainer basis.

HT ASSOCIATES
3030 Salt Creek Lane, Suite 121, Arlington Heights IL 60005. 847/577-0300. **Contact:** Manager. **Description:** An executive search firm. **Specializes in the areas of:** Technical.

HALE & ASSOCIATES
1010 Jorie Boulevard, Suite 102, Oak Brook IL 60523. 630/990-7750. **Contact:** Manager. **Description:** An executive search firm.

ROBERT HALF INTERNATIONAL ACCOUNTEMPS
One Northbrook Place, 5 Revere Drive, Suite 355, Northbrook IL 60062-1561. 847/480-1556. **Fax:** 847/480-1871. **Contact:** Recruiting Manager. **World Wide Web address:** http://www.roberthalf.com. **Description:** An executive search firm. Accountemps (also at this location) provides temporary placements. **Specializes in the areas of:** Accounting/Auditing;

Finance. **Positions commonly filled include:** Accountant/Auditor; Bookkeeper; Credit Manager; EDP Specialist. **Corporate headquarters location:** Menlo Park CA. **Other U.S. locations:** Nationwide. **Number of placements per year:** 1000+.

ROBERT HALF INTERNATIONAL ACCOUNTEMPS
2800 West Higgins Road, Suite 180, Hoffman Estates IL 60195. 847/882-7866. **Fax:** 847/885-6387. **Contact:** Branch Manager. **World Wide Web address:** http://www.roberthalf.com. **Description:** An executive search firm. Accountemps (also at this location) provides temporary placements. **Specializes in the areas of:** Accounting/Auditing; Finance. **Positions commonly filled include:** Accountant/Auditor; Bookkeeper; Credit Manager; EDP Specialist. **Corporate headquarters location:** Menlo Park CA. **Other U.S. locations:** Nationwide. **Number of placements per year:** 1000+.

ROBERT HALF INTERNATIONAL ACCOUNTEMPS
One Oakbrook Terrace, Suite 718, Oakbrook Terrace IL 60181. 630/261-3080. **Fax:** 630/261-3088. **Contact:** Staffing Manager. **E-mail address:** oakbrook_terrace@roberthalf.com. **World Wide Web address:** http://www.roberthalf.com. **Description:** An executive search firm. Accountemps (also at this location) provides temporary placements. **Specializes in the areas of:** Accounting/Auditing; Banking; Finance. **Positions commonly filled include:** Accountant/Auditor; Adjuster; Administrative Assistant; Bank Officer/Manager; Bookkeeper; Budget Analyst; Chief Financial Officer; Claim Representative; Clerk; Computer Operator; Computer Programmer; Controller; Cost Estimator; Credit Manager; Data Entry Clerk; Database Manager; EDP Specialist; Finance Director; Financial Analyst; Purchasing Agent/Manager; Receptionist; Software Engineer; Systems Analyst; Technical Writer/Editor; Typist/Word Processor. **Benefits available to temporary workers:** Computer Training; Dental Insurance; Medical Insurance; Paid Holidays; Tuition Assistance; Vision Insurance. **Corporate headquarters location:** Menlo Park CA. **Other U.S. locations:** Nationwide. **Average salary range of placements:** $30,000 - $50,000. **Number of placements per year:** 1000+.

ROBERT HALF INTERNATIONAL ACCOUNTEMPS
205 North Michigan Avenue, Suite 3301, Chicago IL 60601. 312/616-8200. **Fax:** 312/616-8560. **Contact:** Placement Manager. **World Wide Web address:** http://www.roberthalf.com. **Description:** An executive search firm. Accountemps (also at this location) provides temporary placements. **Specializes in the areas of:** Accounting/Auditing; Finance. **Positions commonly filled include:** Accountant/Auditor; Administrative Assistant; Bookkeeper; Credit Manager; EDP Specialist. **Corporate headquarters location:** Menlo Park CA. **Other U.S. locations:** Nationwide. **Number of placements per year:** 1000+.

HAMILTON GREY EXECUTIVE SEARCH, INC.
2803 Butterfield Road, Suite 340, Oak Brook IL 60523. 630/472-5400. **Contact:** Frank Baron, President. **Description:** An executive search firm operating on a contingency basis. Hamilton Grey Executive Search also provides contract services. **Specializes in the areas of:** Information Technology; MIS/EDP. **Positions commonly filled include:** MIS Specialist. **Average salary range of placements:** More than $50,000. **Number of placements per year:** 200 - 499.

HANOVER CROWN & ASSOCIATES
P.O. Box 1606, Oak Brook IL 60522-1606. 630/834-4250. **Contact:** Tony Bonner, President. **Description:** An executive search firm. **Specializes in the areas of:** Chemicals; Engineering; Food. **Positions commonly filled include:** Biological Scientist; Biomedical Engineer; Chemical Engineer; Chemist; Civil Engineer; Electrical/Electronics Engineer; Food Scientist/Technologist; Mechanical Engineer; Quality Control Supervisor;

Science Technologist; Software Engineer. **Average salary range of placements:** More than $50,000. **Number of placements per year:** 1 - 49.

RONALD B. HANSON & ASSOCIATES
22 East Dundee Road, Suite 7, Barrington IL 60010. 847/304-8882. **Fax:** 847/304-8892. **Contact:** Ron Hanson, Owner/President. **Description:** An executive search firm. **Specializes in the areas of:** Executives; Insurance. **Positions commonly filled include:** Actuary; Administrative Manager; General Manager; Insurance Agent/Broker; Management; Management Analyst/Consultant; Operations/Production Manager; Underwriter/Assistant Underwriter. **Corporate headquarters location:** This Location. **Other U.S. locations:** Nationwide. **Average salary range of placements:** More than $50,000. **Number of placements per year:** 1 - 49.

HEALTH PROFESSIONALS INTERNATIONAL
1601 Sherman Avenue, Suite 430, Evanston IL 60201. 847/328-5262. **Fax:** 847/328-5049. **Contact:** Recruiter. **Description:** An executive search firm that also provides some contract services. **Average salary range of placements:** $30,000 - $50,000. **Number of placements per year:** 200 - 499.

HEALTHCARE RECRUITERS INTERNATIONAL
850 North Milwaukee Avenue, Suite 204, Vernon Hills IL 60061. 847/549-5885. **Fax:** 847/549-1570. **Contact:** Joseph Scully, President. **Description:** An executive search firm. **Specializes in the areas of:** Engineering; Health/Medical; Sales. **Positions commonly filled include:** Biomedical Engineer; Chemical Engineer; Industrial Engineer; Manufacturer's/Wholesaler's Sales Rep.; MIS Specialist; Occupational Therapist; Pharmacist; Physical Therapist; Physician; Registered Nurse; Respiratory Therapist; Software Engineer.

HEIDRICK & STRUGGLES
233 South Wacker Drive, Suite 7000, Chicago IL 60606. 312/496-1000. **Fax:** 312/496-1046. **Contact:** Manager. **Description:** An executive search firm.

HELLER ASSOCIATES, LTD.
One Northfield Plaza, Suite 300, Northfield IL 60093. 847/441-2626. **Fax:** 847/441-2645. **Contact:** Gary A. Heller, Owner. **E-mail address:** info@hellerassociates.com. **World Wide Web address:** http://www.hellerassociates.com. **Description:** An executive search firm. Founded in 1990. **Corporate headquarters location:** This Location. **Other U.S. locations:** San Francisco CA; Atlanta GA; New York NY. **International locations:** Worldwide.

HERSHER & ASSOCIATES, LTD.
3000 Dundee Road, Suite 314, Northbrook IL 60062. 847/272-4050. **Fax:** 847/272-1998. **Contact:** Betsy Hersher, President. **E-mail address:** hersher@hersher.com. **Description:** An executive search firm operating on a retainer basis. Founded in 1980. **Specializes in the areas of:** Health/Medical; Information Systems; Insurance; MIS/EDP; Technical. **Positions commonly filled include:** Chief Financial Officer; Management Analyst/Consultant; Medical Records Technician; MIS Specialist; Network Administrator; Physician; Project Manager; Systems Analyst. **Average salary range of placements:** More than $100,000. **Number of placements per year:** 50 - 99.

HIGHLAND GROUP
1639 Highland Avenue, Wilmette IL 60091. 847/251-2900. **Contact:** Manager. **Description:** An executive search firm. **Specializes in the areas of:** Health/Medical.

HOLLINS GROUP INC.
225 West Wacker Drive, Suite 2125, Chicago IL 60606. 312/606-8000. **Contact:** Manager. **Description:** An executive search firm operating on a retainer basis.

E.A. HOOVER & ASSOCIATES
P.O. Box 37, Villa Park IL 60181. 630/833-2300. **Contact:** Manager. **Description:** An executive search

firm. **Specializes in the areas of:** Engineering. **Positions commonly filled include:** Electrical/Electronics Engineer.

E.J. HOWE & ASSOCIATES
645 North Michigan Avenue, Suite 800, Chicago IL 60611. 312/906-3700. **Fax:** 312/906-3747. **Contact:** Elizabeth Howe, Owner. **E-mail address:** contact@ejhowe.com. **World Wide Web address:** http://www.ejhowe.com. **Description:** An executive search firm operating on a contingency basis. E.J. Howe & Associates primarily places individuals with software companies and mid- to large-size MIS operations. Founded in 1991. **NOTE:** Candidates typically have backgrounds in sales/marketing, management, pre- and post-sales, or project management. **Specializes in the areas of:** Computer Science/Software. **Positions commonly filled include:** Account Manager; Account Representative; Applications Engineer; Computer Programmer; Consultant; Database Manager; Financial Analyst; Internet Services Manager; Management Analyst/Consultant; MIS Specialist; Project Manager; Sales Executive; Sales Manager; Services Sales Representative; Software Engineer; Systems Analyst; Systems Manager. **Corporate headquarters location:** This Location. **Other U.S. locations:** Los Angeles CA. **Average salary range of placements:** More than $50,000. **Number of placements per year:** 50 - 99.

HUFFORD ASSOCIATES
3 Pembrook Court, Bolingbrook IL 60440. 630/378-0005. **Contact:** Craig Hufford, President. **E-mail address:** craig@huffordassociates.com. **Description:** An executive search firm operating on both retainer and contingency bases. **Specializes in the areas of:** Marketing; Research and Development; Sales. **Positions commonly filled include:** Hardware Engineer; Product Manager; Software Developer. **Average salary range of placements:** More than $75,000. **Number of placements per year:** 1 - 49.

HUNTERSOFT.COM, INC.
645 North Michigan Avenue, Suite 800, Chicago IL 60611. 312/944-7563. **Contact:** Manager. **Description:** An executive search firm. **Specializes in the areas of:** Computer Hardware/Software.

CATHY HURLESS EXECUTIVE RECRUITING
333 West Wacker Drive, Suite 700, Chicago IL 60606. 312/444-2053. **Contact:** Manager. **Description:** An executive search firm. **Specializes in the areas of:** Advertising.

IZS EXECUTIVE SEARCH
20 North Wacker Drive, Suite 556, Chicago IL 60606. 312/346-6300. **Contact:** Manager. **Description:** An executive search firm. **Specializes in the areas of:** Accounting/Auditing; Finance.

JOHN IMBER ASSOCIATES, LTD.
3601 Algonquin Road, Suite 129, Rolling Meadows IL 60008. 847/506-1700. **Contact:** John Imber, Owner. **Description:** A generalist executive search firm.

INNOVATIVE SYSTEMS GROUP, INC.
799 Roosevelt Road, Building 4, Suite 109, Glen Ellyn IL 60137. 630/858-8500. **Fax:** 630/858-8532. **Contact:** Recruiter. **Description:** An executive search firm. **Specializes in the areas of:** Administration. **Positions commonly filled include:** Computer Programmer; Software Engineer; Systems Engineer. **Number of placements per year:** 50 - 99.

INTERIM FINANCIAL STAFFING
35 East Wacker Drive, Suite 1545, Chicago IL 60601. 312/460-0417. **Fax:** 312/460-0319. **Contact:** Tammy Mancl, Manager. **Description:** An executive search firm operating on a contingency basis. **Other U.S. locations:** Nationwide.

IRWIN & WAGNER, INC.
17720 67th Avenue, Tinley Park IL 60477. 708/532-2800. **Fax:** 708/532-2936. **Contact:** Mary Ellen Irwin,

President. **Description:** An executive search firm operating on a retainer basis. **Specializes in the areas of:** Food; General Management; Sales. **Positions commonly filled include:** General Manager; Human Resources Manager; Marketing Manager; Sales Executive; Vice President of Marketing; Vice President of Operations. **Average salary range of placements:** $50,000 - $100,000. **Number of placements per year:** 1 - 49.

ITEX EXECUTIVE SEARCH
2700 River Road, Suite 116, Des Plaines IL 60018. 847/299-2000. **Fax:** 847/299-8564. **Contact:** Manager. **Description:** An executive search firm operating on both retainer and contingency bases. Founded in 1975. **Specializes in the areas of:** Accounting/Auditing; Finance; Tax. **Positions commonly filled include:** Accountant; Auditor; Finance Director; Financial Analyst; Project Manager. **Average salary range of placements:** $50,000 - $100,000. **Number of placements per year:** 50 - 99.

JACOBSON ASSOCIATES INSURANCE STAFFERS
120 South LaSalle Street, Suite 1410, Chicago IL 60603. 312/726-1578. **Contact:** David Jacobson, President. **Description:** An executive search firm. Insurance Staffers (also at this location) is a temporary agency. **Specializes in the areas of:** Health/Medical; Insurance. **Number of placements per year:** 100 - 199.

JOHNSON PERSONNEL COMPANY
861 North Madison Street, Rockford IL 61107. 815/964-0840. **Fax:** 815/964-0855. **Contact:** Darrell Johnson, Owner. **Description:** An executive search firm. **Specializes in the areas of:** Accounting/Auditing; Computer Science/Software; Engineering; Manufacturing; Personnel/Labor Relations. **Positions commonly filled include:** Accountant/Auditor; Buyer; Ceramics Engineer; Computer Programmer; Electrical/Electronics Engineer; Financial Analyst; Human Resources Manager; Industrial Engineer; Materials Engineer; Mechanical Engineer; Metallurgical Engineer; Operations/Production Manager; Quality Control Supervisor; Software Engineer; Statistician; Systems Analyst. **Number of placements per year:** 1 - 49.

JERRY L. JUNG COMPANY, INC.
140 Iowa Avenue, Belleville IL 62220. 618/277-8881. **Contact:** Jerry L. Jung, Principal. **Description:** An executive search firm. **Specializes in the areas of:** Computer Science/Software; Engineering; Heating, Air Conditioning, and Refrigeration; Manufacturing. **Positions commonly filled include:** Aerospace Engineer; Agricultural Engineer; Computer Programmer; Design Engineer; Designer; Draftsperson; Electrical/Electronics Engineer; General Manager; Industrial Engineer; Industrial Production Manager; Mechanical Engineer; Metallurgical Engineer; Operations/Production Manager; Quality Assurance Engineer; Software Engineer. **Average salary range of placements:** More than $50,000. **Number of placements per year:** 1 - 49.

K-FORCE
3701 West Algonquin Road, Suite 380, Rolling Meadows IL 60008. 847/392-0244. **Fax:** 847/577-7693. **Contact:** Manager. **Description:** An executive search firm.

K-FORCE
150 South Wacker Drive, Suite 400, Chicago IL 60606. 312/346-7000. **Fax:** 312/372-2943. **Contact:** Manager. **Description:** An executive search firm. **Specializes in the areas of:** Information Technology.

RAYMOND KARSON ASSOCIATES
2340 River Road, Suite 414, Des Plaines IL 60018. 847/297-8000. **Contact:** Manager. **Description:** An executive search firm operating on a retainer basis. **Specializes in the areas of:** Accounting/Auditing; Administration; Computer Science/Software; Engineering; Finance; Food; General Management;

Health/Medical; Insurance; Manufacturing; Marketing; Personnel/Labor Relations; Publishing; Sales; Technical. **Positions commonly filled include:** Accountant/Auditor; Actuary; Aerospace Engineer; Agricultural Engineer; Biological Scientist; Biomedical Engineer; Blue-Collar Worker Supervisor; Budget Analyst; Buyer; Ceramics Engineer; Chemical Engineer; Chemist; Civil Engineer; Claim Representative; Computer Programmer; Credit Manager; Customer Service Representative; Electrical/Electronics Engineer; Financial Analyst; Food Scientist/Technologist; General Manager; Human Resources Manager; Industrial Engineer; Industrial Production Manager; Maitre d'Hotel; Materials Engineer; Mechanical Engineer; Metallurgical Engineer; Mining Engineer; Operations/Production Manager; Petroleum Engineer; Physical Therapist; Quality Control Supervisor; Software Engineer; Stationary Engineer; Statistician; Structural Engineer; Systems Analyst; Underwriter/Assistant Underwriter. **Average salary range of placements:** More than $50,000. **Number of placements per year:** 200 - 499.

KENNEDY & COMPANY
20 North Wacker Drive, Suite 1745, Chicago IL 60606. 312/372-0099. **Contact:** Manager. **Description:** An executive search firm. **Specializes in the areas of:** Banking; Finance.

KENNETH NICHOLAS & ASSOCIATES
7 Salt Creek Lane, Suite 205, Hinsdale IL 60521. 630/789-0097. **Fax:** 630/789-0543. **Contact:** Kenneth A. Gorski, President. **E-mail address:** knasearch@aol.com. **Description:** An executive search firm operating on both retainer and contingency bases. **Specializes in the areas of:** Accounting; Computer Science/Software; Finance; MIS/EDP; Personnel/Labor Relations; Sales. **Positions commonly filled include:** Accountant; AS400 Programmer Analyst; Auditor; Computer Programmer; Controller; Financial Analyst; Human Resources Manager; Management Analyst/Consultant; Marketing Manager; MIS Specialist; Sales Executive; Sales Manager; Sales Representative; SQL Programmer; Systems Analyst; Systems Manager. **Average salary range of placements:** $50,000 - $100,000. **Number of placements per year:** 50 - 99.

KENZER CORPORATION
625 North Michigan Avenue, Suite 1244, Chicago IL 60611. 312/266-0976. **Contact:** Manager. **Description:** Kenzer Corporationa is an executive search firm. **Specializes in the areas of:** Finance; Food; Manufacturing; Retail; Wholesaling.

KINDERIS & LOERCHER GROUP
9510 Turnberry Trail, Crystal Lake IL 60014. 815/459-6370. **Fax:** 815/459-6314. **Contact:** Paul Kinderis, President. **Description:** An executive search firm. Clients include reinsurance and mutual insurance companies, major brokers and agencies, risk management companies, and self-insured corporations. **Specializes in the areas of:** Insurance. **Positions commonly filled include:** Actuary; Adjuster; Claim Representative; Risk Manager; Underwriter/Assistant Underwriter. **Average salary range of placements:** More than $50,000.

KINGSTON/ZAK INC.
3158 Des Plaines Avenue, Suite 202, Des Plaines IL 60018-4211. 847/298-0404. **Fax:** 847/298-0408. **Contact:** Recruiter. **E-mail address:** info@kingstonzak.com. **World Wide Web address:** http://www.kingstonzak.com. **Description:** An executive search firm. **Specializes in the areas of:** Accounting; Banking; Distribution; Finance; Government; Health/Medical; Insurance; Manufacturing; Real Estate; Retail.

KORN/FERRY INTERNATIONAL
233 South Wacker Drive, Suite 3300, Chicago IL 60606. 312/466-1834. **Fax:** 312/466-0451. **Contact:** Manager. **World Wide Web address:** http://www.kornferry.com. **Description:** An executive search firm that places professionals in upper-level management positions.

Corporate headquarters location: Los Angeles CA. **Average salary range of placements:** More than $50,000. **International locations:** Worldwide.

EVIE KREISLER ASSOCIATES INC.
333 North Michigan Avenue, Suite 818, Chicago IL 60601. 312/251-0077. **Contact:** Manager. **Description:** Evie Kreisler Associates Inc. is an executive search firm. **Specializes in the areas of:** Manufacturing; Retail.

KUNZER ASSOCIATES, LTD.
1415 West 22nd Street, Suite 1180, Oak Brook IL 60523. 630/574-0010. **Contact:** William Kunzer, President. **Description:** An executive search firm specializing in mid- to senior-level placements. **Specializes in the areas of:** Accounting/Auditing; Administration; Advertising; Art/Design; Banking; Computer Science/Software; Engineering; Finance; Food; General Management; Health/Medical; Industrial; Manufacturing; Personnel/Labor Relations; Publishing; Retail; Sales; Technical. **Positions commonly filled include:** Administrative Manager; Attorney; Bank Officer/Manager; Buyer; Chemical Engineer; Chemist; Credit Manager; Design Engineer; Electrical/Electronics Engineer; General Manager; Health Services Manager; Human Resources Manager; Industrial Engineer; Mechanical Engineer; Metallurgical Engineer; MIS Specialist; Purchasing Agent/Manager; Quality Control Supervisor. **Average salary range of placements:** More than $50,000. **Number of placements per year:** 1 - 49.

LMB ASSOCIATES
1468 Sunnyside Avenue, Highland Park IL 60035. 847/831-5990. **Contact:** Lorena Blonsky, Owner. **Description:** An executive search firm.

THE LASO CORPORATION
220 West Huron, Suite 4001, Chicago IL 60610. 312/255-1110. **Contact:** Manager. **Description:** An executive search firm. **Specializes in the areas of:** MIS/EDP.

LAUER SBARBARO ASSOCIATES INC.
30 North LaSalle Street, Suite 4030, Chicago IL 60602. 312/372-7050. **Fax:** 312/704-4393. **Contact:** Manager. **Description:** A generalist executive search firm.

LE BEAU & ASSOCIATES
900 Jorie Boulevard, Oak Brook IL 60521. 630/990-2233. **Contact:** Carl Le Beau, Owner. **Description:** An executive search firm that places professionals in the rotating equipment field.

ARLENE LEFF & ASSOCIATES
203 North LaSalle Street, Suite 2100, Chicago IL 60601. 312/558-1350. **Fax:** 312/558-1346. **Contact:** Arlene Leff, Owner. **Description:** Arlene Leff & Associates is an executive search firm. **Specializes in the areas of:** Accounting/Auditing; Administration; Advertising; Computer Science/Software; Engineering; Fashion; Finance; General Management; Health/Medical; Industrial; Insurance; Publishing; Retail; Sales; Secretarial. **Positions commonly filled include:** Accountant/Auditor; Administrative Manager; Advertising Clerk; Bank Officer/Manager; Blue-Collar Worker Supervisor; Branch Manager; Buyer; Chemical Engineer; Computer Programmer; Construction Contractor; Cost Estimator; Credit Manager; Design Engineer; Electrical/Electronics Engineer; General Manager; Human Resources Manager; Industrial Engineer; Management Trainee; MIS Specialist; Purchasing Agent/Manager; Quality Control Supervisor; Services Sales Representative; Software Engineer; Systems Analyst; Technical Writer/Editor; Typist/Word Processor. **Number of placements per year:** 100 - 199.

LORD & RICHARDS GROUP
1420 Renaissance Drive, Park Ridge IL 60068. 847/298-9010. **Contact:** Manager. **Description:** A generalist executive search firm.

LYONS & ASSOCIATES
7815 Loch Glen Drive, Crystal Lake IL 60014-3317. 815/477-9292. **Fax:** 815/477-9296. **Contact:** Kent T. Lyons, President. **Description:** An executive search firm operating on a contingency basis. **Specializes in the areas of:** Direct Marketing; Engineering; Finance; General Management; Graphic Arts; Printing; Sales. **Positions commonly filled include:** Account Manager; Account Representative; Cost Estimator; Electrical/Electronics Engineer; General Manager; Human Resources Manager; Industrial Engineer; Industrial Production Manager; Mechanical Engineer; Operations/Production Manager; Sales Executive; Sales Manager; Sales Representative. **Average salary range of placements:** $50,000 - $100,000. **Number of placements per year:** 50 - 99.

THE MBP GROUP
3000 Dundee Road, Suite 411, Northbrook IL 60062. 847/272-3272. **Fax:** 847/272-7398. **Contact:** Alan Cohen, President. **Description:** An executive search firm operating on both retainer and contingency bases. Client company pays fee. **Specializes in the areas of:** Health/Medical. **Positions commonly filled include:** Administrative Manager; Chief Executive Officer; Chief Financial Officer; Consultant; General Manager; Management Analyst/Consultant; Operations Manager; Physician; Vice President. **Average salary range of placements:** $50,000 - $100,000. **Number of placements per year:** 50 - 99.

MACRO RESOURCES
68 East Wacker Drive, Suite 1600, Chicago IL 60601. 312/849-9100. **Fax:** 312/849-9120. **Contact:** Frank Roti, President. **E-mail address:** frank@macroresources.com. **World Wide Web address:** http://www.macroresources.com. **Description:** An executive search firm operating on both retainer and contingency bases. **Specializes in the areas of:** Internet Development. **Positions commonly filled include:** Applications Engineer; Computer Engineer; Computer Programmer; Computer Support Technician; Content Developer; Database Administrator; Database Manager; Internet Services Manager; MIS Specialist; Multimedia Designer; Network Administrator; Software Engineer; SQL Programmer; Systems Analyst; Webmaster. **Average salary range of placements:** More than $50,000. **Number of placements per year:** 1 - 49.

MAGNUM SEARCH
1000 East Golfhurst Avenue, Mount Prospect IL 60056. 847/577-0007. **Contact:** Arthur N. Kristufek, President. **Description:** An executive search firm operating on both retainer and contingency bases. **Specializes in the areas of:** Accounting/Auditing; Administration; Engineering; Finance; General Management; Industrial; Manufacturing; Metals; Personnel/Labor Relations; Technical. **Positions commonly filled include:** Accountant/Auditor; Administrative Manager; Buyer; Computer Programmer; Credit Manager; Customer Service Representative; Design Engineer; Designer; Draftsperson; Electrical/Electronics Engineer; Financial Analyst; General Manager; Human Resources Manager; Industrial Engineer; Industrial Production Manager; Management Trainee; Market Research Analyst; Mechanical Engineer; Metallurgical Engineer; MIS Specialist; Operations/Production Manager; Purchasing Agent/Manager; Quality Control Supervisor; Software Engineer; Systems Analyst; Technical Writer/Editor; Transportation/Traffic Specialist.

MAJOR HAGEN & AFRICA
35 East Wacker Drive, Suite 2150, Chicago IL 60601. 312/372-1010. **Contact:** Manager. **Description:** An executive search firm. **Specializes in the areas of:** Legal. **Positions commonly filled include:** Attorney.

MANAGEMENT RECRUITERS
SALES CONSULTANTS OF OAK BROOK
1415 West 22nd Street, Suite 725, Oak Brook IL 60523. 630/990-8233. **Fax:** 630/990-2973. **Contact:** Gary Miller, Manager. **Description:** An executive search firm. **Specializes in the areas of:** Accounting/Auditing; Administration; Advertising; Architecture/Construction; Banking; Chemicals; Communications; Computer Science/Software; Design; Finance; Food; General Management; Health/Medical; Industrial; Insurance; Legal; Manufacturing; Operations Management; Personnel/Labor Relations; Pharmaceuticals; Procurement; Publishing; Regulatory Affairs; Sales; Technical; Textiles; Transportation.

MANAGEMENT RECRUITERS INTERNATIONAL
2585 Brian Drive, Northbrook IL 60062. 847/564-3998. **Fax:** 847/564-7049. **Contact:** Manager. **Description:** Management Recruiters International is an executive search firm. **Specializes in the areas of:** Accounting/Auditing; Administration; Advertising; Architecture/Construction; Banking; Chemicals; Communications; Computer Science/Software; Design; Electrical; Engineering; Finance; Food; General Management; Health/Medical; Industrial; Insurance; Legal; Manufacturing; Operations Management; Personnel/Labor Relations; Pharmaceuticals; Procurement; Publishing; Retail; Sales; Technical; Textiles; Transportation. **Corporate headquarters location:** Cleveland OH. **Other U.S. locations:** Nationwide.

MANAGEMENT RECRUITERS INTERNATIONAL
211 Landmark Drive, Suite B5, Normal IL 61761. 309/452-1844. **Fax:** 309/452-0403. **Contact:** M. Allan Snedden, Owner/General Manager. **Description:** Management Recruiters International is an executive search firm. **Specializes in the areas of:** Accounting/Auditing; Administration; Computer Programming; Engineering; Finance; Health/Medical; Manufacturing; Personnel/Labor Relations. **Positions commonly filled include:** Accountant/Auditor; Computer Programmer; EDP Specialist; Human Resources Manager; Industrial Engineer; Manufacturing Engineer; MIS Specialist; Systems Analyst. **Corporate headquarters location:** Cleveland OH. **Other U.S. locations:** Nationwide. **Number of placements per year:** 50 - 99.

MANAGEMENT RECRUITERS INTERNATIONAL
406 North Hough Street, Barrington IL 60010. 847/382-5544. **Contact:** Manager. **Description:** An executive search firm. **Specializes in the areas of:** Heating, Air Conditioning, and Refrigeration. **Corporate headquarters location:** Cleveland OH. **Other U.S. locations:** Nationwide.

MANAGEMENT RECRUITERS OF ARLINGTON HEIGHTS
SALES CONSULTANTS
3415 North Arlington Heights Road, Arlington Heights IL 60004. 847/590-8880. **Fax:** 847/590-0847. **Contact:** Steve Briody, General Manager. **Description:** Management Recruiters of Arlington Heights is an executive search firm operating on a contingency basis. **Specializes in the areas of:** Food; Industrial; Management; Manufacturing; Marketing; Personnel/Labor Relations; Sales; Technical. **Positions commonly filled include:** Accountant/Auditor; Administrative Manager; Branch Manager; Customer Service Representative; Dietician/Nutritionist; Electrical/Electronics Engineer; Food Scientist/Technologist; General Manager; Human Resources Manager; Manufacturer's/Wholesaler's Sales Representative; Services Sales Representative. **Corporate headquarters location:** Cleveland OH. **Other U.S. locations:** Nationwide. **Average salary range of placements:** More than $50,000. **Number of placements per year:** 100 - 199.

MANAGEMENT RECRUITERS OF DES PLAINES, INC.
OFFICEMATES5 PERSONNEL
1400 East Touhy Avenue, Suite 160, Des Plaines IL 60018. 847/297-7102. **Fax:** 847/297-8477. **Contact:** Manager. **Description:** An executive search firm. OfficeMates5 (also at this location) is a permanent employment agency. **Specializes in the areas of:** Accounting/Auditing; Administration; Advertising; Banking; Communications; Computer Science/Software; Design; Electrical; Engineering; Finance; Food; General

Management; Health/Medical; Industrial; Manufacturing; Operations Management; Personnel/Labor Relations; Pharmaceuticals; Procurement. **Corporate headquarters location:** Cleveland OH. **Other U.S. locations:** Nationwide.

MANAGEMENT RECRUITERS OF ELGIN, INC.
OFFICEMATES5 PERSONNEL
472 North McLean Boulevard, Suite 202, Elgin IL 60123-3274. 847/697-2201. **Fax:** 847/697-0622. **Contact:** Ronald C. Reeves, President. **E-mail address:** ron@mrelgin.com. **World Wide Web address:** http://www.mrelgin.com. **Description:** An executive search firm operating on both retainer and contingency bases. **Specializes in the areas of:** Administration; Art/Design; Computer Science/Software; Engineering; Finance; Graphic Arts; Health/Medical; Industrial; Manufacturing; MIS/EDP; Printing; Publishing; Sales; Secretarial; Technical. **Positions commonly filled include:** Account Manager; Administrative Assistant; Applications Engineer; AS400 Programmer Analyst; Clerical Supervisor; Computer Programmer; Customer Service Representative; Database Administrator; Database Manager; Design Engineer; Finance Director; Financial Analyst; General Manager; Industrial Engineer; Manufacturing Engineer; Mechanical Engineer; MIS Specialist; Network Administrator; Operations Manager; Production Manager; Project Manager; Quality Control Supervisor; Sales Representative; Secretary; Systems Analyst; Systems Manager; Webmaster. **Corporate headquarters location:** Cleveland OH. **Other U.S. locations:** Nationwide. **Average salary range of placements:** $50,000 - $100,000. **Number of placements per year:** 50 - 99.

MANAGEMENT RECRUITERS OF MATTOON
P.O. Box 461, Mattoon IL 61938-9396. 217/235-9393. **Fax:** 217/235-9396. **Contact:** David Tolle, President. **Description:** An executive search firm specializing in the flavor and fragrance industries. **Specializes in the areas of:** Food. **Positions commonly filled include:** Chemical Engineer; Chemist; Food Scientist/Technologist; Mechanical Engineer. **Corporate headquarters location:** Cleveland OH. **Other U.S. locations:** Nationwide. **Average salary range of placements:** More than $50,000. **Number of placements per year:** 1 - 49.

MANAGEMENT RECRUITERS OF ROCKFORD, INC.
1463 South Bell School Road, Suite 3, Rockford IL 61108. 815/399-1942. **Fax:** 815/399-2750. **Contact:** D. Michael Carter, Manager. **Description:** An executive search firm. **Specializes in the areas of:** Accounting/Auditing; Administration; Advertising; Architecture/Construction; Banking; Chemicals; Communications; Computer Science/Software; Design; Electrical; Engineering; Film Production; Food; General Management; Health/Medical; Industrial; Insurance; Legal; Manufacturing; Operations Management; Personnel/Labor Relations; Pharmaceuticals; Procurement; Publishing; Retail; Sales; Technical; Textiles; Transportation. **Corporate headquarters location:** Cleveland OH. **Other U.S. locations:** Nationwide.

MANAGEMENT RECRUITERS OF ST. CHARLES, INC.
318 South Second Street, St. Charles IL 60174-2817. 630/377-6466. **Contact:** Dan Lasse, President. **Description:** An executive search firm operating on a contingency basis. **Specializes in the areas of:** Manufacturing; Personnel/Labor Relations; Sales. **Positions commonly filled include:** Accountant/Auditor; Biological Scientist; Human Resources Manager; Manufacturing Engineer; Mechanical Engineer; Technical Representative. **Corporate headquarters location:** Cleveland OH. **Other U.S. locations:** Nationwide. **Average salary range of placements:** More than $50,000. **Number of placements per year:** 50 - 99.

MANNING & ASSOCIATES
P.O. Box 666, Belvidere IL 61008. 815/544-0944. **Contact:** John Manning, Owner. **Description:** An executive search firm. **Specializes in the areas of:** Banking.

MANUFACTURING RESOURCES INC.
156 South Prairie Avenue, Bloomingdale IL 60108-1626. 630/529-6200. **Fax:** 630/529-6224. **Contact:** Larry Pemberton, General Manager. **Description:** An executive search firm. **Specializes in the areas of:** Engineering; Food; Industrial; Manufacturing. **Positions commonly filled include:** Blue-Collar Worker Supervisor; Chemical Engineer; Design Engineer; Designer; Draftsperson; Electrical/Electronics Engineer; Electrician; Food Scientist/Technologist; General Manager; Industrial Engineer; Mechanical Engineer; Quality Control Supervisor; Software Engineer. **Average salary range of placements:** $30,000 - $50,000. **Number of placements per year:** 100 - 199.

MANUFACTURING SEARCH COMPANY
175 Olde Half Day Road, Lincolnshire IL 60069. 847/634-5518. **Contact:** Manager. **Description:** An executive search firm. **Specializes in the areas of:** Manufacturing.

MANUFACTURING TECHNICAL SEARCH
One Westbrook, Corporate Center, Suite 330, Westchester IL 60154. 708/409-9999. **Fax:** 708/409-8485. **Contact:** Manager. **E-mail address:** info@topqualitypeople.com. **Description:** Manufacturing Technical Search is an executive search firm. **Specializes in the areas of:** Manufacturing.

MARGESON & ASSOCIATES
P.O. Box 668, West Dundee IL 60118. 847/428-5757. **Contact:** Manager. **Description:** An executive search firm operating on a retainer basis.

RICHARD MARKS & ASSOCIATES
2319 Hartzell Street, Evanston IL 60201. 847/475-7600. **Contact:** Richard Marks, Owner. **Description:** An executive search firm. **Specializes in the areas of:** Sales; Systems Design. **Positions commonly filled include:** Systems Engineer.

MARSTELLER WILCOX ASSOCIATES, LTD.
799 Roosevelt Road, Building 3, Suite 108, Glen Ellyn IL 60137. 630/790-4300. **Contact:** Mark A. Wilcox, President. **World Wide Web address:** http://www.mwaltd.com. **Description:** An executive search firm operating on both retainer and contingency bases. Marsteller Wilcox Associates also provides on-site recruiting and human resources support services. **Specializes in the areas of:** Engineering; Food; General Management; Industrial; Manufacturing; Personnel/Labor Relations; Sales; Technical. **Positions commonly filled include:** Account Representative; Accountant/Auditor; Aerospace Engineer; Agricultural Engineer; Applications Engineer; Branch Manager; Buyer; Chemical Engineer; Chemist; Chief Financial Officer; Civil Engineer; Computer Programmer; Controller; Design Engineer; Electrical/Electronics Engineer; Environmental Engineer; General Manager; Health Services Manager; Human Resources Manager; Industrial Engineer; Industrial Production Manager; Manufacturing Engineer; Marketing Manager; Mechanical Engineer; Metallurgical Engineer; Operations/Production Manager; Petroleum Engineer; Production Worker; Project Manager; Public Relations Specialist; Purchasing Agent/Manager; Quality Control Supervisor; Sales Executive; Sales Manager; Sales Representative; Software Engineer; Structural Engineer; Systems Analyst; Technical Writer/Editor; Transportation/Traffic Specialist; Vice President of Marketing and Sales. **Benefits available to temporary workers:** Dental Insurance; Medical Insurance; Paid Holidays; Paid Vacation. **Average salary range of placements:** More than $50,000. **Number of placements per year:** 200 - 499.

MARTIN PARTNERS LLC
224 South Michigan Avenue, Suite 620, Chicago IL 60604. 312/922-1800. **Fax:** 312/922-1813. **Contact:** Manager. **World Wide Web address:** http://www. martinptrs.com. **Description:** Martin Partners LLC is a generalist executive search firm that operates on a retainer basis.

MATHEY SERVICES
15170 Bethany Road, Sycamore IL 60178. 815/895-3846. **Fax:** 815/895-1046. **Contact:** Joyce Mathey, President. **Description:** An executive search firm. **Specializes in the areas of:** Chemicals; Engineering; Industrial; Manufacturing; Plastics; Technical. **Positions commonly filled include:** Chemical Engineer; Chemist; Electrical/Electronics Engineer; Industrial Engineer; Mechanical Engineer. **Average salary range of placements:** More than $50,000. **Number of placements per year:** 1 - 49.

PAUL MAY & ASSOCIATES (PMA)
8 South Michigan Avenue, Suite 2700, Chicago IL 60603. 312/782-0100. **Fax:** 312/782-7255. **Contact:** Paul May, President. **E-mail address:** pma4jobs@computer-jobs.com. **World Wide Web address:** http://www.computer-jobs.com. **Description:** An executive search firm operating on a contingency basis. Client company pays fee. **Specializes in the areas of:** Computer Science/Software; Internet Development; MIS/EDP; Scientific; Technical. **Positions commonly filled include:** Applications Engineer; AS400 Programmer Analyst; Computer Programmer; Computer Support Technician; Computer Technician; Content Developer; Database Administrator; Database Manager; Internet Services Manager; MIS Manager; Multimedia Designer; Network/Systems Administrator; Project Manager; Sales Engineer; Sales Manager; Sales Representative; Software Engineer; SQL Programmer; Systems Analyst; Systems Manager; Webmaster. **Corporate headquarters location:** This Location. **Average salary range of placements:** $30,000 - $150,000. **Number of placements per year:** 100 - 199.

M.W. McDONALD & ASSOCIATES, INC.
P.O. Box 541, Barrington IL 60011. 847/842-7400. **Fax:** 847/842-7410. **Contact:** Pamela Niedermeier, Director of Research and Operations. **E-mail address:** research@mwmsearch.com. **Description:** An executive search firm operating on a retainer basis. **Specializes in the areas of:** Computer Science/Software; Engineering; Sales; Technical. **Positions commonly filled include:** Computer Programmer; Design Engineer; Designer; Draftsperson; Electrical/Electronics Engineer; Industrial Engineer; Mechanical Engineer; Metallurgical Engineer; Multimedia Designer; Systems Analyst. **Corporate headquarters location:** This Location. **Other U.S. locations:** San Francisco CA. **Average salary range of placements:** More than $50,000. **Number of placements per year:** 50 - 99.

MEDICAL RECRUITERS
145 Locust Street, Carrollton IL 62016. 217/942-9034. **Contact:** Manager. **Description:** An executive search firm. **Specializes in the areas of:** Medical Sales and Marketing.

JUAN MENEFEE & ASSOCIATES
503 South Oak Park Avenue, Oak Park IL 60304. 708/848-7722. **Fax:** 708/848-6008. **Contact:** Juan Menefee, President. **E-mail address:** jmenefee@jmarecruiter.com. **World Wide Web address:** http://www.jmarecruiter.com. **Description:** An executive search firm operating on both retainer and contingency bases. **Specializes in the areas of:** Accounting/Auditing; Advertising; Engineering; Personnel/Labor Relations; Sales. **Positions commonly filled include:** Accountant/Auditor; Attorney; Computer Programmer; General Manager; Human Resources Manager; Market Research Analyst; Systems Analyst. **Average salary range of placements:** More than $50,000. **Number of placements per year:** 50 - 99.

R. MICHAELS & ASSOCIATES
P.O. Box 220, Coal Valley IL 61240. 309/234-5062. **Fax:** 309/234-5063. **Contact:** Managing Partner. **E-mail address:** rmainc@qconline.com. **Description:** An executive search firm operating on both retainer and contingency bases. **Specializes in the areas of:** Engineering; Industrial; Manufacturing; Technical. **Positions commonly filled include:** Architect; Chemical Engineer; Chemist; Chief Financial Officer; Civil Engineer; Controller; Design Engineer; Electrical/Electronics Engineer; Environmental Engineer; General Manager; Human Resources Generalist; Industrial Engineer; Industrial Production Manager; Manufacturing Engineer; Mechanical Engineer; Metallurgical Engineer; Operations Manager; Production Manager; Project Manager; Purchasing Agent/Manager; Quality Assurance Engineer; Quality Control Supervisor. **Average salary range of placements:** $50,000 - $100,000.

MICHAELS & MOERE, LTD.
P.O. Box 728, Roscoe IL 61073-0728. 815/623-6888. **Fax:** 815/623-3848. **Contact:** Manager. **E-mail address:** search@michaels-moere.com. **World Wide Web address:** http://www.michaels-moere.com. **Description:** An executive search firm operating on both retainer and contingency bases. **Specializes in the areas of:** Manufacturing.

MIDWEST CONSULTING CORPORATION
1110 Lake Cook Road, Suite 245, Buffalo Grove IL 60089. 847/229-1800. **Contact:** Greg Miller, President. **E-mail address:** gmiller@midwestco.com. **Description:** An executive search firm operating on a retainer basis. **Specializes in the areas of:** Engineering; Sales. **Positions commonly filled include:** Computer Programmer; Electrical/Electronics Engineer; Software Engineer; Systems Analyst; Telecommunications Manager. **Average salary range of placements:** More than $70,000. **Number of placements per year:** 50 - 99.

NATIONAL RESTAURANT SEARCH INC.
617 North Tyler Road, St. Charles IL 60174. 630/584-8448. **Fax:** 630/584-8597. **Contact:** Manager. **Description:** An executive search firm. **Specializes in the areas of:** Hotel/Restaurant.

NATIONAL SEARCH
850 South Lorraine Road, Suite 3M, Wheaton IL 60187. 630/665-8026. **Fax:** 630/665-2992. **Contact:** Walter Pierson III, President. **E-mail address:** ntlsrch@worldnet.att.net. **Description:** An executive search firm operating on both retainer and contingency bases. **Specializes in the areas of:** Administration; Computer Science/Software; Engineering; Finance; Food; General Management; Health/Medical; Industrial; Insurance; Marketing; Personnel/Labor Relations; Sales; Technical; Wireless Communications. **Positions commonly filled include:** Account Manager; Account Representative; Administrative Manager; Applications Engineer; Assistant Manager; Biomedical Engineer; Branch Manager; Chemical Engineer; Computer Operator; Computer Programmer; Counselor; Customer Service Representative; Electrical/Electronics Engineer; Financial Analyst; General Manager; Human Resources Manager; Industrial Engineer; Industrial Production Manager; Management Analyst/Consultant; Manufacturing Engineer; Marketing Manager; Marketing Specialist; Mechanical Engineer; MIS Specialist; Operations Manager; Production Manager; Project Manager; Sales Engineer; Sales Executive; Sales Manager; Sales Representative; Software Engineer; Systems Analyst; Systems Manager; Telecommunications Manager. **Corporate headquarters location:** This Location. **Other U.S. locations:** Nationwide. **Average salary range of placements:** $30,000 - $50,000. **Number of placements per year:** 1 - 49.

NETWORK SEARCH INC.
676 North St. Claire Street, Suite 2050, Chicago IL 60611. 312/397-8811. **Contact:** Manager. **Description:**

An executive search firm. **Specializes in the areas of:** Computer Hardware/Software.

NEW DIRECTIONS, INC.
P.O. Box 88, Wheaton IL 60189. 630/462-1840. **Contact:** Manager. **Description:** An executive search firm. **Specializes in the areas of:** Manufacturing.

NU-WAY SEARCH
P.O. Box 494, Lake Zurich IL 60047-0494. 847/726-8444. **Contact:** Steve Riess, Counselor. **Description:** An executive search firm operating on a contingency basis. **Specializes in the areas of:** Computer Science/Software. **Positions commonly filled include:** Computer Programmer; Internet Services Manager; Software Engineer; Statistician; Systems Analyst; Technical Writer/Editor; Telecommunications Manager. **Number of placements per year:** 50 - 99.

JOHN R. O'CONNOR & ASSOCIATES
111 West Jackson Boulevard, Suite 1300, Chicago IL 60604-3505. 312/939-1392. **Contact:** John O'Connor, Owner. **Description:** An executive search firm that focuses on the placement of architects, engineers, and environmental scientists. Placements are primarily made for infrastructure projects such as highways, bridges, rail/rapid transit, airports, treatment plants, and municipal engineering. **Specializes in the areas of:** Engineering; Transportation. **Positions commonly filled include:** Architect; Civil Engineer; Construction Engineer; Cost Estimator; Design Engineer; Electrical/Electronics Engineer; Environmental Engineer; Environmental Scientist; Mechanical Engineer; Structural Engineer; Surveyor. **Average salary range of placements:** More than $50,000. **Number of placements per year:** 1 - 49.

OMNI SEARCH LTD.
7400 North Waukegan Road, Suite I, Niles IL 60714. 847/647-7570. **Contact:** Andrew Kavathas, President. **Description:** An executive search firm. **Specializes in the areas of:** Engineering; Industrial; Manufacturing; Technical. **Positions commonly filled include:** Designer; Draftsperson; Electrical/Electronics Engineer; Industrial Engineer; Industrial Production Manager; Mechanical Engineer; Operations/Production Manager; Quality Control Supervisor; Stationary Engineer. **Number of placements per year:** 1 - 49.

JAMES C. PAPPAS & ASSOCIATES
3136 Doriann Drive, Northbrook IL 60062. 708/449-5400. **Fax:** 708/449-5405. **Contact:** Jim Pappas, President. **Description:** An executive search firm operating on both retainer and contingency bases. **Specializes in the areas of:** Design; Engineering; Food; General Management; Industrial; Logistics; Manufacturing; Technical. **Positions commonly filled include:** Chemical Engineer; Design Engineer; Draftsperson; Electrical/Electronics Engineer; Electrician; Environmental Engineer; Industrial Engineer; Industrial Production Manager; Management Analyst/Consultant; Manufacturing Engineer; Mechanical Engineer; Metallurgical Engineer; Operations Manager; Production Manager; Project Manager; Quality Assurance Engineer; Quality Control Supervisor. **Average salary range of placements:** $50,000 - $100,000.

PARKER CROMWELL & ASSOCIATES
122-B Calendar Court, La Grange IL 60525. 708/352-8350. **Fax:** 708/352-8355. **Contact:** Suzanne Bruce, General Manager. **Description:** A generalist executive search firm. **Specializes in the areas of:** Accounting/Auditing; Administration; Finance; Food; General Management; Industrial; Insurance; Light Industrial; Personnel/Labor Relations; Printing; Publishing; Retail; Sales; Secretarial; Transportation. **Positions commonly filled include:** Account Manager; Account Representative; Accountant; Administrative Assistant; Assistant Manager; Blue-Collar Worker Supervisor; Branch Manager; Chief Financial Officer; Clerical Supervisor; Controller; Credit Manager; Customer Service Representative; Desktop Publishing Specialist; Editor; Editorial Assistant; General Manager; Human Resources Manager; Management Trainee; Operations Manager; Paralegal; Production Manager; Project Manager; Purchasing Agent/Manager; Quality Control Supervisor; Sales Engineer; Sales Executive; Sales Manager; Sales Representative; Secretary; Technical Writer/Editor; Transportation/Traffic Specialist; Typist/Word Processor; Underwriter/Assistant Underwriter. **Average salary range of placements:** $20,000 - $100,000.

PELICHEM ASSOCIATES
928 Warren Avenue, Downers Grove IL 60515. 630/960-1940. **Fax:** 630/960-1942. **Contact:** Ken Pelczarski, Owner. **E-mail address:** pelichem@aol.com. **Description:** An executive search firm focusing on technical, sales/marketing, and operations positions in the chemical, mechanical, and lubrication industries. **Specializes in the areas of:** Biology; Engineering; General Management; Industrial; Manufacturing; Sales; Technical. **Positions commonly filled include:** Biological Scientist; Ceramics Engineer; Chemical Engineer; Chemist; Food Scientist/Technologist; General Manager; Industrial Production Manager; Manufacturer's/Wholesaler's Sales Rep.; Materials Engineer; Metallurgical Engineer; Operations/Production Manager; Petroleum Engineer; Purchasing Agent/Manager; Quality Control Supervisor; Science Technologist; Services Sales Representative. **Average salary range of placements:** $40,000 - $100,000. **Number of placements per year:** 1 - 49.

PATRICIA POCOCK & ASSOCIATES, INC.
P.O. Box 313, Wilmette IL 60091. 847/256-6730. **Fax:** 847/853-7457. **Contact:** Manager. **E-mail address:** resumes@ppassoc.com. **World Wide Web address:** http://www.ppassoc.com. **Description:** Patricia Pocock & Associates is an executive search firm. Founded in 1991. **Specializes in the areas of:** Management; Sales; Technical.

POLYTECHNICAL CONSULTANTS, INC.
7213 West Breen Street, Niles IL 60714. 847/470-9000. **Contact:** Manager. **Description:** Polytechnical Consultants is an executive search firm. **Specializes in the areas of:** Engineering.

THE PRAIRIE GROUP
One Westbrook Corporate Center, Suite 300, Westchester IL 60154. 708/449-7710. **Contact:** Manager. **Description:** An executive search firm.

PRATZER & PARTNERS
20 North Wacker Drive, Suite 3230, Chicago IL 60606. 312/977-1300. **Fax:** 312/977-1303. **Contact:** Manager. **Description:** An executive search firm. **Specializes in the areas of:** Communications; Finance; Information Systems; Information Technology; Real Estate; Start-up Organizations.

PRO-TECH SEARCH INC.
400 Chatham Road, Springfield IL 62704. 217/793-2790. **Contact:** Manager. **World Wide Web address:** http://www.pro-techsearch.com. **Description:** An executive search firm. **Specializes in the areas of:** Information Technology.

PROFESSIONAL RESEARCH SERVICES, INC.
1101 Perimeter Drive, Suite 610, Schaumburg IL 60173. 847/995-8800. **Fax:** 847/995-8812. **Contact:** Thomas DeBourcy, President. **E-mail address:** prs1@netwave.net. **World Wide Web address:** http://www.prs1.com. **Description:** An executive search firm. Professional Research Services provides recruiting lists, contacts, candidate generation, minority recruiting, and multiple position project hiring. **Specializes in the areas of:** Accounting/Auditing; Banking; Engineering; General Management; Insurance; Manufacturing; Personnel/Labor Relations; Retail; Sales. **Positions commonly filled include:** Accountant/Auditor; Aerospace Engineer; Agricultural Engineer; Attorney; Bank Officer/Manager; Biological Scientist; Biomedical

Engineer; Branch Manager; Budget Analyst; Buyer; Ceramics Engineer; Chemical Engineer; Chemist; Civil Engineer; Computer Programmer; Credit Manager; Customer Service Representative; Economist; Electrical/Electronics Engineer; Financial Analyst; General Manager; Human Resources Manager; Industrial Engineer; Management Analyst/Consultant; Management Trainee; Manufacturer's/Wholesaler's Sales Rep.; Mechanical Engineer; Metallurgical Engineer; Operations/Production Manager; Public Relations Specialist; Purchasing Agent/Manager; Quality Control Supervisor; Restaurant/Food Service Manager; Securities Sales Representative; Services Sales Representative; Software Engineer; Statistician; Structural Engineer; Systems Analyst; Transportation/Traffic Specialist; Underwriter/Assistant Underwriter; Wholesale and Retail Buyer. **Average salary range of placements:** More than $50,000. **Number of placements per year:** 100 - 199.

PROFESSIONAL SEARCH CENTER LIMITED
1450 East American Lane, Suite 1875, Schaumburg IL 60173-6046. 847/330-3250. **Fax:** 847/330-3255. **Contact:** Jerry Hirschel, CPC/President. **E-mail address:** jerryh@psc-usa.com. **Description:** An executive search firm operating on both retainer and contingency bases. **Specializes in the areas of:** Computer Science/Software; Information Technology. **Positions commonly filled include:** Administrator; Computer Programmer; Database Administrator; Systems Analyst; Webmaster.

PROSEARCH PLUS
555 East Butterfield Road, Lombard IL 60148. 630/515-0500. **Fax:** 630/515-0510. **Contact:** Manager. **Description:** An executive search firm operating on both retainer and contingency bases. **Specializes in the areas of:** Accounting/Auditing; Administration; Art/Design; Banking; Finance; Food; Personnel/Labor Relations; Retail; Sales; Secretarial. **Positions commonly filled include:** Accountant/Auditor; Bank Officer/Manager; Buyer; Clerical Supervisor; Computer Programmer; Credit Manager; Customer Service Representative; Financial Analyst; General Manager; Human Resources Manager; MIS Specialist; Services Sales Representative; Software Engineer; Systems Analyst; Technical Writer/Editor; Typist/Word Processor. **Average salary range of placements:** More than $50,000. **Number of placements per year:** 200 - 499.

QUANTUM PROFESSIONAL SEARCH
QUANTUM STAFFING SERVICES
100 West 22nd Street, Suite 115, Lombard IL 60148. 630/916-7300. **Fax:** 630/916-8338. **Contact:** Patrick Brady, President. **E-mail address:** info@quantumstaffing.com. **Description:** An executive search firm. **Specializes in the areas of:** Computer Hardware/Software; Industrial; Light Industrial; Sales; Secretarial. **Positions commonly filled include:** Account Manager; Account Representative; Administrative Assistant; Administrative Manager; Branch Manager; Clerical Supervisor; Consultant; Credit Manager; Customer Service Representative; General Manager; Industrial Engineer; Industrial Production Manager; Management Analyst/Consultant; Manufacturer's/Wholesaler's Sales Rep.; Manufacturing Engineer; Marketing Manager; Operations/Production Manager; Production Manager; Project Manager; Sales Engineer; Sales Executive; Sales Manager; Secretary; Services Sales Representative; Software Engineer; Typist/Word Processor; Vice President of Sales. **Corporate headquarters location:** This Location. **Average salary range of placements:** More than $50,000. **Number of placements per year:** 100 - 199.

QUEST ENTERPRISES, LTD.
112 West Liberty Drive, Wheaton IL 60187. 630/588-8400. **Fax:** 630/588-0675. **Contact:** Richard W. Honquest, Founder. **E-mail address:** admin@questent.com. **World Wide Web address:** http://www.questent.com. **Description:** An executive search firm. Founded in 1984. **Specializes in the areas of:** Information Technology.

VERA L. RAST PARTNERS, INC. (VLRPI)
One South Wacker Drive, Suite 3890, Chicago IL 60606. 312/629-0339. **Fax:** 312/629-0347. **Contact:** Vera Rast, President. **Description:** An executive search firm. **Specializes in the areas of:** Legal. **Positions commonly filled include:** Attorney. **Number of placements per year:** 1 - 49.

RAY & BERNDTSON, INC.
Sears Tower, 233 South Wacker Drive, Suite 4020, Chicago IL 60606. 312/876-0730. **Fax:** 312/876-6850. **Contact:** Manager. **World Wide Web address:** http://www.rayberndtson. **Description:** An executive search firm. **Positions commonly filled include:** Senior Management. **International locations:** Worldwide.

RECRUITMENT NETWORK
2720 River Road, Suite 238, Des Plaines IL 60018. 847/298-8830. **Fax:** 847/298-1652. **Contact:** Manager. **Description:** An executive search firm. **Specializes in the areas of:** Information Technology; Sales.

M. RECTOR & ASSOCIATES
40 South Prospect, Suite 200, Roselle IL 60172. 630/894-5060. **Fax:** 630/894-5607. **Contact:** Manager. **Description:** An executive search firm. **Specializes in the areas of:** Real Estate.

REDELL SEARCH, INC.
6101 Sheridan Road East, Suite 31A, Chicago IL 60660. 773/764-6100. **Fax:** 773/764-6111. **Contact:** John T. Redell, Jr., Managing Partner. **E-mail address:** redell@ix.netcom.com. **Description:** An executive search firm. **Specializes in the areas of:** Administration; Computer Science/Software. **Positions commonly filled include:** Applications Engineer; AS400 Programmer Analyst; Computer Animator; Computer Engineer; Computer Operator; Computer Programmer; Computer Support Technician; Computer Technician; Content Developer; Database Administrator; Database Manager; Internet Services Manager; MIS Specialist; Multimedia Designer; Network Administrator; Software Engineer; SQL Programmer; Systems Analyst; Systems Manager; Webmaster. **Average salary range of placements:** More than $100,000. **Number of placements per year:** 50 - 99.

RESPONSIVE SEARCH INC.
600 South Washington Street, Suite 303, Naperville IL 60540. 630/718-1300. **Fax:** 630/718-0059. **Contact:** Keith D. Hansel, President. **Description:** An executive search firm operating on both retainer and contingency bases. **Specializes in the areas of:** Computer Science/Software. **Positions commonly filled include:** Computer Programmer; Systems Analyst. **Average salary range of placements:** More than $50,000. **Number of placements per year:** 50 - 99.

RETAIL RECRUITERS
1400 East Touhy Road, Suite 410, Des Plaines IL 60018. 847/390-6100. **Contact:** Manager. **Description:** An executive search firm. **Specializes in the areas of:** Retail.

RETAIL STAFFERS, INC.
150 East Cook Avenue, Libertyville IL 60048. 847/362-6100. **Fax:** 847/362-1826. **Contact:** Liz Paris, Manager. **Description:** An executive search firm operating on a contingency basis. **Specializes in the areas of:** General Management; Human Resources; Loss Prevention; Retail; Sales. **Positions commonly filled include:** Assistant Manager; General Manager; Loss Prevention Specialist; Management Trainee. **Number of placements per year:** 100 - 199.

REYMAN & ASSOCIATES
20 North Michigan Avenue, Suite 520, Chicago IL 60602. 312/580-0808. **Contact:** Susan Reyman. **Description:** A generalist executive search firm.

RIDENOUR & ASSOCIATES
One East Wacker Drive, Suite 3500, Chicago IL 60601. 312/644-1888. **Contact:** Suzanne S. Ridenour, Principal.

World Wide Web address: http://www. ridenourassociates.com. **Description:** An executive search firm. **Specializes in the areas of:** Direct Marketing.

RITT-RITT AND ASSOCIATES
5105 Tollview Drive, Suite 110, Rolling Meadows IL 60008. 847/483-9330. **Fax:** 847/483-9331. **Contact:** Art Ritt, President. **Description:** Ritt-Ritt and Associates is an executive search firm operating on both retainer and contingency bases. **Specializes in the areas of:** Food; General Management; Hotel/Restaurant; Personnel/Labor Relations. **Positions commonly filled include:** Dietician/Nutritionist; Hotel Manager; Human Resources Manager; Restaurant/Food Service Manager; Sales Representative. **Average salary range of placements:** More than $50,000.

THE ROBINSON GROUP
800 East NW Highway, Suite 254, Palatine IL 60067. 847/359-0990. **Contact:** Donald Robinson, President. **Description:** An executive search firm. **Specializes in the areas of:** Accounting/Auditing; Consulting; General Management; Manufacturing; Sales; Tax. **Positions commonly filled include:** Auditor; Marketing Manager; Sales Manager; Tax Specialist. **Number of placements per year:** 1 - 49.

ROMAC INTERNATIONAL
20 North Wacker Drive, Suite 2850, Chicago IL 60606. 312/263-0902. **Fax:** 312/263-3023. **Contact:** Recruiter. **Description:** Romac International is an executive search firm. **Specializes in the areas of:** Accounting/Auditing; Banking; Finance. **Positions commonly filled include:** Accountant/Auditor; Administrative Manager; Bank Officer/Manager; Budget Analyst; Computer Programmer; Customer Service Representative; Financial Analyst; General Manager; Human Resources Manager; Internet Services Manager; MIS Specialist; Property and Real Estate Manager; Services Sales Representative; Software Engineer; Strategic Relations Manager; Technical Writer/Editor. **Benefits available to temporary workers:** Dental Insurance; Medical Insurance; Paid Holidays; Paid Vacation. **Corporate headquarters location:** Tampa FL. **Average salary range of placements:** $30,000 - $50,000. **Number of placements per year:** 1000+.

ROONEY ASSOCIATES, INC.
501 Pennsylvania Avenue, Glen Ellyn IL 60137. 630/469-7102. **Fax:** 630/469-0749. **Contact:** Joseph J. Rooney, Founder. **E-mail address:** info@exec-recruit.com. **World Wide Web address:** http://www. exec-recruit.com. **Description:** An executive search firm. Founded in 1986.

KEITH ROSS & ASSOCIATES, INC.
45 South Park Boulevard, Glen Ellyn IL 60137-6280. 630/858-1000. **Fax:** 630/858-9307. **Contact:** Keith Ross, President. **Description:** An executive search firm operating on both retainer and contingency bases. **Specializes in the areas of:** Legal. **Positions commonly filled include:** Attorney. **Average salary range of placements:** More than $50,000.

DAVID ROWE & ASSOCIATES INC.
9047 Monroe Avenue, Brookfield IL 60513. 708/387-1000. **Contact:** Manager. **Description:** David Rowe & Associates Inc. Is an executive search firm. **Specializes in the areas of:** Health/Medical.

RUSSELL REYNOLDS ASSOCIATES, INC.
200 South Wacker Drive, Suite 3600, Chicago IL 60606. 312/993-9696. **Fax:** 312/876-1919. **Contact:** Manager. **World Wide Web address:** http://www.russreyn.com. **Description:** An executive search firm operating on a retainer basis. Russell Reynolds Associates primarily places mid- and upper-level managers.

THE RYAN CHARLES GROUP, INC.
2021 Midwest Road, Suite 200, Oak Brook IL 60523. 773/233-9111. **Contact:** Manager. **Description:** An

executive search firm. **Specializes in the areas of:** Accounting/Auditing; Administration; Advertising; Engineering; Finance; General Management; Sales.

SC INTERNATIONAL
1430 Branding Lane, Suite 119, Downers Grove IL 60515. 630/963-3033. **Fax:** 630/963-3170. **Contact:** Scott Rollins, President. **Description:** SC International is an executive search firm. **Specializes in the areas of:** Insurance; Personnel/Labor Relations. **Positions commonly filled include:** Actuary; Human Resources Manager. **Average salary range of placements:** $30,000 - $50,000. **Number of placements per year:** 50 - 99.

SHS, INC.
205 West Wacker Drive, Suite 600, Chicago IL 60606. 312/419-0370. **Fax:** 312/419-8953. **Contact:** Ric Pantaleo, Vice President. **Description:** An executive search firm. Founded in 1988. **Specializes in the areas of:** Advertising; Broadcasting; General Management; Health/Medical; Sales; Telecommunications. **Positions commonly filled include:** Account Manager; Account Representative; Advertising Executive; Biochemist; Branch Manager; Broadcast Technician; Chief Financial Officer; Computer Programmer; Customer Service Representative; Design Engineer; Editor; Editorial Assistant; General Manager; Graphic Artist; Graphic Designer; Health Services Manager; Industrial Production Manager; Insurance Agent/Broker; Internet Services Manager; Managing Editor; Manufacturer's/Wholesaler's Sales Rep.; Marketing Manager; Marketing Specialist; Multimedia Designer; Nuclear Medicine Technologist; Operations/Production Manager; Sales Engineer; Sales Manager; Science Technologist; Services Sales Representative; Technical Writer/Editor; Telecommunications Manager; Vice President of Finance; Video Production Coordinator; Webmaster. **Average salary range of placements:** $30,000 - $50,000. **Number of placements per year:** 1 - 49.

SALES CONSULTANTS OF CHICAGO
6420 West 127th Street, Suite 209, Palos Heights IL 60463. 708/371-9677. **Fax:** 708/371-9678. **Contact:** Branch Manager. **E-mail address:** frontdesk@card-recruiter.com. **World Wide Web address:** http://www.card-recruiter.com. **Description:** Sales Consultants of Chicago is an executive search firm specializing in the payment services industry. **Specializes in the areas of:** Administration; Banking; Computer Hardware/Software; Sales; Telecommunications. **Positions commonly filled include:** Auditor; Bank Officer/Manager; Credit Manager; Database Manager; EDP Specialist; Electrical/Electronics Engineer; Financial Analyst; Marketing Manager; Marketing Specialist; MIS Specialist; Sales Manager; Sales Representative; Statistician; Systems Analyst; Systems Manager. **Average salary range of placements:** More than $50,000. **Number of placements per year:** 1 - 49.

SANFORD ROSE ASSOCIATES
44 North Virginia Street, Suite 2A, Crystal Lake IL 60014. 815/444-8382. **Fax:** 815/444-8390. **Contact:** Branch Manager. **World Wide Web address:** http://www.sanfordrose.com. **Description:** Sanford Rose Associates is an executive search firm. **Specializes in the areas of:** Chemicals; Engineering; General Management; Marketing; Operations Management; Research and Development; Sales. **Corporate headquarters location:** Akron OH. **Other U.S. locations:** Nationwide. **International locations:** Singapore.

SANFORD ROSE ASSOCIATES
655 Roackland Road, Lake Bluff IL 60044. 847/482-1210. **Fax:** 847/482-1213. **Contact:** Manager. **World Wide Web address:** http://www.sanfordrose.com. **Description:** Sanford Rose Associates is an executive search firm. **Specializes in the areas of:** General Management; Medical Devices; Medical Sales and Marketing. **Corporate headquarters location:** Akron

OH. **Other U.S. locations:** Nationwide. **International locations:** Singapore.

SANFORD ROSE ASSOCIATES
416 East State Street, Rockford IL 61104-1037. 815/964-4080. **Fax:** 815/964-3917. **Contact:** Dennis Wallace, Director. **E-mail address:** srarfi@aol.com. **World Wide Web address:** http://www.sanfordrose.com. **Description:** Sanford Rose Associates is an executive search firm. **Specializes in the areas of:** Automotive; Engineering. **Positions commonly filled include:** Design Engineer; Industrial Engineer; Manufacturing Engineer; Packaging Engineer; Tool Engineer. **Corporate headquarters location:** Akron OH. **Other U.S. locations:** Nationwide. **International locations:** Singapore. **Average salary range of placements:** More than $50,000. **Number of placements per year:** 50 - 99.

SANFORD ROSE ASSOCIATES
944 Adare Drive, Wheaton IL 60187. 630/690-5987. **Fax:** 630/690-4696. **Contact:** Branch Manager. **World Wide Web address:** http://www.sanfordrose.com. **Description:** An executive search firm. **Specializes in the areas of:** Banking; Finance; Real Estate. **Corporate headquarters location:** Akron OH. **Other U.S. locations:** Nationwide. **International locations:** Singapore.

SANFORD ROSE ASSOCIATES
444 South Willow, Suite 11, Effingham IL 62401. 217/342-3928. **Fax:** 217/347-7111. **Contact:** Branch Manager. **World Wide Web address:** http://www.sanfordrose.com. **Description:** An executive search firm. **Specializes in the areas of:** Printing. **Corporate headquarters location:** Akron OH. **Other U.S. locations:** Nationwide. **International locations:** Singapore.

SANFORD ROSE ASSOCIATES
233 East Erie, Suite 410, Chicago IL 60611. 312/787-7171. **Fax:** 312/787-7190. **Contact:** Branch Manager. **World Wide Web address:** http://www.sanfordrose.com. **Description:** Sanford Rose Associates is an executive search firm. **Specializes in the areas of:** Health/Medical; Medical Devices. **Corporate headquarters location:** Akron OH. **Other U.S. locations:** Nationwide. **International locations:** Singapore.

SANFORD ROSE ASSOCIATES
9405 West Bormet Drive, Suite 1, Mokena IL 60448. 708/479-4854. **Fax:** 708/479-4750. **Contact:** Branch Manager. **World Wide Web address:** http://www.sanfordrose.com. **Description:** An executive search firm. **Specializes in the areas of:** Distribution; Logistics. **Corporate headquarters location:** Akron OH. **Other U.S. locations:** Nationwide. **International locations:** Singapore.

DAVID SAXNER & ASSOCIATES
3 First National Plaza, Suite 1400, Chicago IL 60602. 312/214-3360. **Contact:** David Saxner, Owner. **Description:** An executive search firm. David Saxner & Associates also provides management consulting services to the commercial real estate market. **Specializes in the areas of:** Real Estate.

J.R. SCOTT & ASSOCIATES
One South Wacker Drive, Suite 1616, Chicago IL 60606. 312/795-4400. **Contact:** Managing Director. **Description:** J.R. Scott & Associates is an executive search firm operating on both retainer and contingency bases. **Specializes in the areas of:** Accounting; Banking; Brokerage; Finance; Insurance. **Positions commonly filled include:** Accountant; Bank Officer/Manager; Chief Financial Officer; Controller; Economist; Finance Director; Financial Analyst; Fund Manager; Research Technician; Risk Manager; Underwriter/Assistant Underwriter. **Average salary range of placements:** $50,000 - $100,000. **Number of placements per year:** 200 - 499.

SEARCH CONSULTING GROUP
1540 East Dundee Road, Suite 170, Palatine IL 60074. 847/991-4473. **Contact:** Manager. **Description:** Search Consulting Group is a generalist executive search firm.

SEARCH DYNAMICS INC.
19W 555 Lake Street, Addison IL 60101. 630/458-8700. **Fax:** 630/458-8703. **Contact:** George Apostle, President. **Description:** An executive search firm operating on both retainer and contingency bases. **Specializes in the areas of:** Computer Science/Software; Engineering; Manufacturing; Technical. **Positions commonly filled include:** Design Engineer; Designer; Draftsperson; Industrial Engineer; Industrial Production Manager; Metallurgical Engineer; Quality Control Supervisor; Software Engineer. **Number of placements per year:** 50 - 99.

SEARCH ENTERPRISES, INC.
1737 South Naperville Road, Suite 203, Wheaton IL 60187. 630/510-8400. **Fax:** 630/510-2922. **Contact:** Frank Polacek, President. **E-mail address:** sesi@searchenterprises.com. **World Wide Web address:** http://www.searchenterprises.com. **Description:** An executive search firm operating on a contingency basis. **Specializes in the areas of:** Engineering; Food; Technical. **Positions commonly filled include:** Biomedical Engineer; Chemical Engineer; Electrical/Electronics Engineer; Industrial Production Manager; Manufacturing Engineer; Mechanical Engineer; Metallurgical Engineer; Production Manager; Project Manager; Quality Control Supervisor. **Average salary range of placements:** More than $50,000. **Number of placements per year:** 100 - 199.

SEARCH SOURCE
2945 Madison Avenue, Granite City IL 62040. 618/876-6060. **Contact:** Manager. **Description:** Search Source is an executive search firm. **Specializes in the areas of:** Broadcasting; Telecommunications.

SELECT SEARCH INC.
3411 North Arlington Heights Road, Arlington Heights IL 60004. 847/368-8900. **Contact:** Manager. **Description:** Select Search Inc. Is an executive search firm. **Specializes in the areas of:** Data Processing; Engineering; Technical.

SEVCOR INTERNATIONAL, INC.
One Pierce Place, Suite 400E, Itasca IL 60143. 630/250-3088. **Fax:** 630/250-3089. **Contact:** J. Randy Severinsen, President. **Description:** An executive search firm. **Specializes in the areas of:** Computer Science/Software; Insurance; Technical. **Positions commonly filled include:** Actuary; Computer Programmer; Systems Analyst. **Number of placements per year:** 100 - 199.

SHORR GROUP
500 North Michigan Avenue, Suite 820, Chicago IL 60611. 312/644-5100. **Contact:** Manager. **Description:** Shorr Group is an executive search firm operating on a retainer basis. **Positions commonly filled include:** Accountant; Administrative Assistant; Bank Officer/Manager; Buyer; Chief Financial Officer; Controller; Credit Manager; Customer Service Representative; Finance Director; Financial Analyst; Graphic Designer; Human Resources Manager; Purchasing Agent/Manager. **Average salary range of placements:** $30,000 - $100,000.

D.W. SIMPSON & CO.
1800 West Larchmont Avenue, Chicago IL 60611. 312/654-5220. **Fax:** 312/951-8386. **Contact:** Beth Rave, Director of Operations. **E-mail address:** actuaries@dwsimpson.com. **Description:** D.W. Simpson & Co. Is an executive search firm. **Specializes in the areas of:** Insurance. **Positions commonly filled include:** Actuary. **Average salary range of placements:** More than $50,000. **Number of placements per year:** 100 - 199.

RALPH SMITH & ASSOCIATES
540 West Frontage Road, Suite 3335, Northfield IL
60093. 847/441-0900. **Fax:** 847/441-0902. **Contact:**
Ralph E. Smith, President. **Description:** Ralph Smith &
Associates is an executive search firm. **Specializes in the
areas of:** Food; General Management; Industrial;
Manufacturing; Personnel/Labor Relations; Sales.
Positions commonly filled include: Controller; General
Manager; Human Resources Manager; Marketing
Manager; Operations/Production Manager; Sales
Manager. **Average salary range of placements:**
More than $50,000. **Number of placements per year:** 1
- 49.

SMITH HANLEY ASSOCIATES, INC.
200 West Madison, Suite 2110, Chicago IL 60606.
312/629-2400. **Fax:** 312/629-0615. **Contact:** Linda
Burtch, General Manager. **World Wide Web address:**
http://www.smithhanley.com. **Description:** Smith
Hanley Associates, Inc. Is an executive search firm.
Specializes in the areas of: Banking; Finance; Food;
Health/Medical; Insurance; Market Research;
Quantitative Marketing. **Positions commonly filled
include:** Credit Manager; Database Manager; Market
Research Analyst; Marketing Manager; Statistician;
Systems Analyst. **Corporate headquarters location:**
New York NY. **Average salary range of placements:**
More than $50,000. **Number of placements per year:**
50 - 99.

SMITH SCOTT & ASSOCIATES
P.O. Box 941, Lake Forest IL 60045. 847/295-9517.
Fax: 847/295-9534. **Contact:** Gary J. Smith, Managing
Partner. **E-mail address:** gjsmith@smithscott.com.
World Wide Web address: http://www.smithscott.com.
Description: Smith Scott & Associates is an executive
search firm. **Specializes in the areas of:** Computer
Science/Software; Information Technology; Personnel/
Labor Relations. **Positions commonly filled include:**
Human Resources Manager; Systems Analyst. **Average
salary range of placements:** More than $50,000.
Number of placements per year: 1 - 49.

SNELLING SEARCH
100 North LaSalle Street, Suite 2005, Chicago IL 60602.
312/419-6100. **Fax:** 312/419-6646. **Contact:** Mark
Stevens, General Manager. **Description:** Snelling Search
is an executive search firm focusing on the recruitment of
sales professionals. **Specializes in the areas of:** Sales;
Secretarial. **Corporate headquarters location:** Dallas
TX. **Other U.S. locations:** Nationwide. **Average salary
range of placements:** $30,000 - $50,000. **Number of
placements per year:** 200 - 499.

SNELLING SEARCH
331 Fulton Street, Suite 322, Peoria IL 61602. 309/676-
5581. **Contact:** Sara Zoeller, Manager. **Description:**
Snelling Search is an executive search firm. **Specializes
in the areas of:** Accounting/Auditing; Engineering;
Finance; Sales. **Positions commonly filled include:**
Accountant/Auditor; Branch Manager; Budget Analyst;
Chemical Engineer; Computer Programmer; Design
Engineer; Electrical/Electronics Engineer; General
Manager; Hotel Manager; Management Trainee;
Manufacturer's/Wholesaler's Sales Representative;
Mechanical Engineer; MIS Specialist; Restaurant/Food
Service Manager; Services Sales Representative; Software
Engineer; Systems Analyst; Telecommunications
Manager. **Corporate headquarters location:** Dallas TX.
Other U.S. locations: Nationwide. **Average salary
range of placements:** $30,000 - $50,000. **Number of
placements per year:** 100 - 199.

THE STANTON GROUP, INC.
374 East Marseilles Street, Vernon Hills IL 60061.
847/540-1183. **Fax:** 847/540-1154. **Contact:** Recruiter.
World Wide Web address: http://www.stantongp.com.
Description: The Stanton Group is an executive search
firm. **Specializes in the areas of:** Automotive;
Health/Medical; Insurance; Software Development;
Telecommunications.

STERLING-GRANT
4433 West Touhy Avenue, Suite 301, Lincolnwood
IL 60712. 847/982-6860. **Contact:** Office
Manager. **Description:** Sterling-Grant is an executive
search firm.

**STERN PROFESSIONAL SEARCH &
CONSULTANTS, INC.**
680 North Lake Shore Drive, Suite 607, Lake Tower,
Chicago IL 60611. 312/587-7777. **Fax:** 312/587-8907.
Contact: Janet Grodsky, President. **Description:** Stern
Professional Search & Consultants, Inc. is an executive
search firm focusing on the contract furnishings and
interior design industries. **Specializes in the areas of:**
Sales. **Positions commonly filled include:** Account
Representative; Architect; Branch Manager; CADD
Operator; Interior Designer; Project Manager; Sales
Executive; Sales Manager; Sales Representative;
Vice President of Sales. **Other U.S. locations:**
Nationwide. **Average salary range of placements:**
$30,000 - $50,000. **Number of placements per year:**
100 - 199.

STONE ENTERPRISES, LTD.
645 North Michigan Avenue, Suite 800, Chicago IL
60611. 773/404-9300. **Fax:** 773/404-9388. **Contact:**
Susan L. Stone, President. **Description:** Stone
Enterprises, Ltd. Is an executive search firm that focuses
on providing placements in *Fortune* 1000 companies.
Specializes in the areas of: Accounting; Auditing;
Computer Hardware/Software; Distribution; Engineering;
Manufacturing; Sales Promotion; Tax;
Telecommunications.

STRATEGIC RESOURCES UNLIMITED
8410 West Bryn Mawr, Suite 400, Chicago IL 60631.
773/380-1250. **Fax:** 773/380-1358. **Contact:** Roberta A.
Gilna, President. **Description:** Strategic Resources
Unlimited is an executive search firm operating on
both retainer and contingency bases. **Specializes in the
areas of:** Accounting/Auditing; Architecture/
Construction; Finance; Food; General Management;
Personnel/Labor Relations; Sales. **Positions commonly
filled include:** Accountant; Auditor; Budget Analyst;
Buyer; Chief Financial Officer; Controller; Finance
Director; Financial Analyst; General Manager; Human
Resources Manager; Market Research Analyst;
Marketing Manager; Public Relations Specialist;
Purchasing Agent/Manager; Sales Executive. **Corporate
headquarters location:** This Location. **Average salary
range of placements:** More than $50,000. **Number of
placements per year:** 1 - 49.

STRATEGIC SEARCH CORPORATION
645 North Michigan Avenue, Suite 800, Chicago IL
60611. 312/944-4000. **Contact:** Branch Manager.
Description: Strategic Search Corporation is an
executive search firm.

RON SUNSHINE ASSOCIATES
20 North Wacker Drive, Suite 1731, Chicago IL 60606.
312/558-5502. **Fax:** 312/558-9770. **Contact:** Ron
Sunshine, Owner. **E-mail address:** rlsunshine@aol.com.
Description: Ron Sunshine Associates is an executive
search firm operating on both retainer and contingency
bases. **Specializes in the areas of:** Engineering; General
Management; Industrial; Manufacturing. **Positions
commonly filled include:** General Manager; Human
Resources Manager; Industrial Engineer; Industrial
Production Manager; Manufacturing Engineer;
Mechanical Engineer; Operations Manager; Production
Manager; Project Manager; Quality Assurance Engineer;
Quality Control Supervisor. **Average salary range of
placements:** $50,000 - $100,000. **Number of
placements per year:** 1 - 49.

SYNERGISTICS ASSOCIATES LTD.
400 North State Street, Suite 400, Chicago IL 60610.
312/467-5450. **Fax:** 312/822-0246. **Contact:** Alvin
Borenstine, President. **Description:** An executive search
firm operating on a retainer basis. Synergistics Associates
focuses on the placement of chief information officers and

computer technology professionals. **Specializes in the areas of:** Computer Science/Software. **Average salary range of placements:** More than $50,000. **Number of placements per year:** 1 - 49.

SYSTEMS ONE, LTD.
1700 East Golf Road, Schaumburg IL 60173. 847/619-9300. **Fax:** 847/619-0071. **Contact:** Branch Manager. **Description:** System One, Ltd. is an executive search firm operating on both retainer and contingency bases. **Specializes in the areas of:** Computer Science/Software. **Positions commonly filled include:** Computer Programmer; Management Analyst/Consultant; MIS Specialist; Software Engineer; Systems Analyst; Telecommunications Manager. **Average salary range of placements:** More than $50,000.

TSC MANAGEMENT SERVICES GROUP, INC.
P.O. Box 384, Barrington IL 60011. 847/381-0167. **Fax:** 847/381-2169. **Contact:** Robert G. Stanton, Sr., President. **E-mail address:** tscmgtserv@aol.com. **Description:** TSC Management Services Group, Inc. is an executive search firm operating on both retainer and contingency bases. **Specializes in the areas of:** Computer Science/Software; Engineering; Technical. **Positions commonly filled include:** Computer Programmer; Designer; Electrical/Electronics Engineer; Industrial Engineer; Mechanical Engineer; Quality Control Supervisor; Software Engineer; Statistician; Systems Analyst; Technical Writer/Editor. **Average salary range of placements:** $50,000 - $100,000. **Number of placements per year:** 50 - 99.

ROY TALMAN & ASSOCIATES
150 South Wacker Drive, Suite 2250, Chicago IL 60606-4103. 312/425-1300. **Fax:** 312/425-0100. **Contact:** Roy Talman, President. **E-mail address:** resume@roy-talman.com. **World Wide Web address:** http://www.roy-talman.com. **Description:** An executive search firm. **NOTE:** Please send resumes via e-mail with the subject Attention: Roy, and include the appropriate job number. **Specializes in the areas of:** Administration; Banking; Computer Science/Software; Engineering; Finance. **Positions commonly filled include:** Computer Programmer; EDP Specialist; Financial Analyst; Mathematician; MIS Specialist; Software Engineer; Systems Analyst. **Average salary range of placements:** $30,000 - $50,000. **Number of placements per year:** 100 - 199.

TECHNICAL RECRUITING CONSULTANTS
1100 West NW Highway, Suite 208, Mount Prospect IL 60056. 847/394-1101. **Contact:** Dick Latimer, President. **Description:** Technical Recruiting Consultants is an executive search firm. **Specializes in the areas of:** Administration; Computer Science/Software; Engineering; Manufacturing. **Positions commonly filled include:** Civil Engineer; Computer Programmer; EDP Specialist; Electrical/Electronics Engineer; Industrial Engineer; Manufacturing Engineer; Mechanical Engineer; MIS Specialist; Software Engineer; Systems Analyst. **Number of placements per year:** 50 - 99.

TECHNICAL SEARCH
450 East Devon Avenue, Suite 225, Itasca IL 60143-1261. 630/775-0700. **Contact:** Recruiter. **Description:** An executive search firm. **Specializes in the areas of:** Engineering; Food; Manufacturing. **Positions commonly filled include:** Design Engineer; Designer; Draftsperson; Electrical/Electronics Engineer; Mechanical Engineer; Software Engineer. **Average salary range of placements:** More than $50,000. **Number of placements per year:** 50 - 99.

TEXCEL, INC.
35 East Wacker Avenue, Suite 2800, Chicago IL 60601. 312/629-8803. **Fax:** 312/629-8817. **Contact:** Branch Manager. **E-mail address:** opportunities@texcelinc.com. **Description:** An executive search firm that also provides some contract services. Texcel is a division of MAGIC (Management Alliance Group of Independent Companies). **Specializes in the areas of:** Accounting;

Engineering; Finance; Information Technology; Manufacturing; Pharmaceuticals.

TUFT & ASSOCIATES
1209 North Astor Street, Chicago IL 60610. 312/642-8889. **Contact:** Branch Manager. **Description:** Tuft & Associates is an executive search firm whose primary focus is on providing placements in professional associations. **Specializes in the areas of:** Nonprofit.

TWIN OAKS TECHNICAL, INC.
12503 South 90th Street, Palos Park IL 60464. 708/923-6040. **Contact:** Manager. **Description:** Twin Oaks Technical is an executive search firm. **Specializes in the areas of:** Chemicals.

TWO DEGREES
101 West Grand Avenue, Suite 200, Chicago IL 60610. 312/422-9600. **Fax:** 312/670-6755. **Contact:** Nageen Shariff, Managing Director. **World Wide Web address:** http://www.twodegrees.com. **Description:** An executive search firm operating on a retainer basis that also provides some contract services. The agency only works with experienced accounting and finance professionals. Client company pays fee. **Specializes in the areas of:** Accounting; Finance; Tax. **Corporate headquarters location:** Seattle WA. **Other U.S. locations:** Englewood CO. **Average salary range of placements:** $50,000 - $100,000.

K. DAVID UMLAUF EXECUTIVE SEARCH CONSULTANTS
444 North Wells Street, Suite 203, Chicago IL 60610. 312/467-9630. **Contact:** K. David Umlauf, President. **Description:** K. David Umlauf Executive Search Consultants is an executive search firm operating on both retainer and contingency bases. The firm recruits administrative, investment, and business development executives for placement with bank trust departments. **Specializes in the areas of:** Banking. **Positions commonly filled include:** Bank Officer/Manager. **Average salary range of placements:** More than $50,000. **Number of placements per year:** 1 - 49.

VALENTINE & ASSOCIATES
One Woodfield Lake, Suite 117, Schaumburg IL 60173. 847/605-8090. **Contact:** Janice Book, Recruiter. **Description:** Valentine & Associates is an executive search firm focusing on the placement of material management professionals. **Specializes in the areas of:** Food; Manufacturing. **Positions commonly filled include:** Buyer; Customer Service Representative; Industrial Production Manager; Operations/Production Manager; Purchasing Agent/Manager; Systems Analyst. **Average salary range of placements:** $30,000 - $50,000.

VERDIN ASSOCIATES
25 East Washington Street, Suite 1500, Chicago IL 60602. 312/855-1055. **Contact:** Manager. **Description:** An executive search firm. **Specializes in the areas of:** Legal.

T. VINCENT & ASSOCIATES, LTD.
24362 Tanager Court, Barrington IL 60010. 847/540-8440. **Contact:** Tom LuBecky, Vice President. **Description:** T. Vincent & Associates is an executive search firm. **Specializes in the areas of:** Brokerage; Finance; Investment. **Positions commonly filled include:** Branch Manager; Broker; Brokerage Clerk; Management; Securities Sales Representative; Support Personnel. **Number of placements per year:** 1 - 49.

ANNE VIOLANTE & ASSOCIATES
770 North Halsted Street, Suite 206, Chicago IL 60622. 312/633-9067. **Contact:** Anne Violante, President. **Description:** Anne Violante & Associates is an executive search firm operating on both retainer and contingency bases. **Specializes in the areas of:** Legal.

Positions commonly filled include: Attorney. **Average salary range of placements:** More than $50,000. **Number of placements per year:** 1 - 49.

VOIGT ASSOCIATES
601 Skokie Boulevard, Northbrook IL 60062. 847/568-9801. **Contact:** Raymond Voigt, President. **Description:** Voigt Associates is an executive search firm operating on a retainer basis. **Specializes in the areas of:** Biotechnology; General Management; Pharmaceuticals; Scientific. **Positions commonly filled include:** Biochemist; Biological Scientist; General Manager; Microbiologist; Operations Manager; Production Manager; Quality Assurance Engineer; Quality Control Supervisor; Regulatory Affairs Director; Validation Scientist. **Average salary range of placements:** $50,000 - $100,000. **Number of placements per year:** 1 - 49.

WATERFORD EXECUTIVE GROUP
One North 141 County Farm Road, Winfield IL 60190. 630/690-0055. **Contact:** Office Manager. **Description:** Waterford Executive Group is an executive search firm. **Specializes in the areas of:** Insurance.

MICHAEL WAYNE RECRUITERS
59 St. Mary's Lane, Lindenhurst IL 60046. 847/245-7100. **Fax:** 847/245-7199. **Contact:** Irwin Goldman, President. **E-mail address:** mwrecruit@aol.com. **World Wide Web address:** http://www. michaelwaynerecruiters.com. **Description:** Michael Wayne Recruiters is an executive search firm operating on both retainer and contingency bases. **Specializes in the areas of:** Food. **Positions commonly filled include:** Architect; Buyer; Draftsperson; Food Scientist/Technologist; Human Resources Manager; Transportation/Traffic Specialist; Wholesale and Retail Buyer. **Average salary range of placements:** More than $50,000. **Number of placements per year:** 1 - 49.

RAY WHITE ASSOCIATES
875 North Michigan Avenue, Suite 3717, Chicago IL 60611. 312/266-0100. **Fax:** 312/266-9149. **Contact:** Ray White, President. **E-mail address:** raywhiteassoc@ worldnet.att.net. **Description:** Ray White Associates is an executive search firm that operates on both retainer and contingency bases and specializes in recruiting executives in the automotive parts industry. Clients are manufacturers of parts supplied to Ford, General Motors, and Transplants. **Specializes in the areas of:** Automotive; Engineering; Human Resources; Industrial; Manufacturing; Marketing; Quality Assurance; Sales. **Positions commonly filled include:** Account Manager; Account Representative; Accountant; Advertising Executive; Applications Engineer; Buyer; Controller; Design Engineer; Electrical/Electronics Engineer; General Manager; Human Resources Manager; Industrial Production Manager; Manufacturing Engineer; Market Research Analyst; Marketing Manager; Marketing Specialist; Mechanical Engineer; Metallurgical Engineer; Operations Manager; Production Manager; Project Manager; Purchasing Agent/Manager; Quality Assurance Engineer; Quality Control Supervisor; Sales Engineer; Sales Executive; Sales Manager; Sales Representative; Software Engineer; Vice

President of Marketing; Vice President of Sales. **Corporate headquarters location:** This Location. **Average salary range of placements:** More than $50,000.

ROBERT WHITFIELD ASSOCIATES
155 North Michigan Avenue, Suite 523, Chicago IL 60601. 312/938-9120. **Contact:** Robert Whitfield. **Description:** An executive search firm. **Specializes in the areas of:** Legal. **Positions commonly filled include:** Attorney.

WHITNEY CARLYSLE
625 North Michigan Avenue, Suite 2100, Chicago IL 60611. 312/587-3030. **Contact:** Office Manager. **Description:** Whitney Carlysle is an executive search firm.

PHILIP WIELAND & ASSOCIATES
1831D North Hudson Avenue, Chicago IL 60614. 847/256-8666. **Contact:** Philip J. Wieland, President. **Description:** Philip Wieland & Associates is an executive search firm. **Specializes in the areas of:** Legal.

WILSON-DOUGLAS-JORDAN
70 West Madison Street, Suite 1400, Chicago IL 60602-4205. 312/782-0286. **Fax:** 312/214-3424. **Contact:** John Wilson, President. **E-mail address:** wdjinc@aol.com. **Description:** Wilson-Douglas-Jordan is an executive search firm operating on a retainer basis. **Specializes in the areas of:** Computer Science/Software; Information Technology. **Positions commonly filled include:** Architect; Computer Programmer; Database Administrator; Management Analyst/Consultant; MIS Specialist; Project Manager; Software Engineer; Systems Analyst; Telecommunications Manager. **Number of placements per year:** 50 - 99.

WINSTON & GREEN
225 West Washington Street, Suite 525, Chicago IL 60606. 312/201-9777. **Fax:** 312/201-9781. **Contact:** David Winston, Recruiter. **Description:** Winston & Green is an executive search firm. **Positions commonly filled include:** Attorney. **Number of placements per year:** 1 - 49.

WITT/KIEFFER, FORD, HADELMAN & LLOYD
2015 Spring Road, Suite 510, Oak Brook IL 60521. 630/990-1370. **Fax:** 630/990-1382. **Contact:** Branch Manager. **World Wide Web address:** http://www.wittkieffer.com. **Description:** Witt/Kieffer, Ford, Hadelman & Lloyd is an executive search firm. **Specializes in the areas of:** Health/Medical. **Other U.S. locations:** Nationwide.

XAGAS & ASSOCIATES
1127 Fargo Boulevard, Geneva IL 60134. 630/232-7044. **Contact:** Steve Xagas, President. **Description:** Xagas & Associates is an executive search firm operating on a retainer basis. **Specializes in the areas of:** Engineering; Food; Industrial; Manufacturing; Technical. **Positions commonly filled include:** Operations/Production Manager; Quality Control Supervisor; Software Engineer; Software Manager. **Average salary range of placements:** More than $50,000. **Number of placements per year:** 1 - 49.

PERMANENT EMPLOYMENT AGENCIES

AARP FOUNDATION
SENIOR COMMUNITY SERVICE EMPLOYMENT PROGRAM
9 West Ferguson Avenue, Wood River IL 62095. 618/254-0195. **Contact:** Robert Clark Jr., Project Director. **Description:** AARP Foundation is a permanent employment agency that focuses on finding placements for senior citizens. **Specializes in the areas of:** Nonprofit.

A.B.A. PLACEMENTS
A.B.A. TEMPORARIES
1526 Miner Street, Des Plaines IL 60016. 847/297-3535. **Fax:** 847/297-4545. **Contact:** Vice President. **Description:** A permanent employment agency. A.B.A. Temporaries (also at this location) provides temporary placements. **Specializes in the areas of:** Accounting/Auditing; Administration; Banking; Food;

Industrial; Insurance; Legal; Light Industrial; Office Support; Personnel/Labor Relations; Printing; Retail; Sales; Secretarial. **Positions commonly filled include:** Account Manager; Account Representative; Accountant/Auditor; Administrative Assistant; Bank Officer/Manager; Blue-Collar Worker Supervisor; Branch Manager; Brokerage Clerk; Buyer; Claim Representative; Clerical Supervisor; Computer Operator; Counselor; Credit Manager; Customer Service Representative; Editorial Assistant; Human Resources Manager; Management Analyst/Consultant; Management Trainee; Operations Manager; Paralegal; Production Manager; Purchasing Agent/Manager; Quality Control Supervisor; Sales Executive; Sales Manager; Sales Representative; Secretary; Telecommunications Manager; Transportation/Traffic Specialist; Typist/Word Processor. **Benefits available to temporary workers:** Bonus Award/Plan; Medical Insurance; Paid Vacation. **Corporate headquarters location:** This Location. **Other U.S. locations:** Rolling Meadows IL; Wheeling IL. **Average salary range of placements:** $20,000 - $29,999. **Number of placements per year:** 500 - 999.

ASI STAFFING SERVICE, INC.
333 North Michigan Avenue, Suite 2106, Chicago IL 60601. 312/782-4690. **Contact:** Clarice Moore, Client Relations. **Description:** A permanent employment agency. **Specializes in the areas of:** Accounting/Auditing; Banking; General Management; Personnel/Labor Relations; Sales; Secretarial. **Positions commonly filled include:** Accountant/Auditor; Administrative Manager; Advertising Clerk; Bank Officer/Manager; Blue-Collar Worker Supervisor; Branch Manager; Claim Representative; Clerical Supervisor; Counselor; Customer Service Representative; General Manager; Hotel Manager; Human Resources Specialist; MIS Specialist; Public Relations Specialist; Services Sales Representative; Typist/Word Processor. **Corporate headquarters location:** This Location. **Number of placements per year:** 500 - 999.

ACCURATE PERSONNEL INC.
9 South Fairview Avenue, Park Ridge IL 60068. 847/692-6740. **Fax:** 847/692-6751. **Contact:** Manager. **Description:** A permanent employment agency. **Specializes in the areas of:** Accounting/Auditing; Banking; Industrial; Secretarial. **Positions commonly filled include:** Accountant/Auditor; Blue-Collar Worker Supervisor; Clerical Supervisor; Counselor; Human Resources Specialist; Management Trainee; Quality Control Supervisor; Services Sales Representative; Typist/Word Processor. **Average salary range of placements:** $20,000 - $29,999. **Number of placements per year:** 50 - 99.

ACCURATE RECRUITING INC.
200 West Adams, Suite 2007, Chicago IL 60606. 312/357-2500. **Fax:** 312/630-1165. **Contact:** Manager. **Description:** A permanent employment agency that also provides some temporary placements. **Specializes in the areas of:** Advertising; Economics; Personnel/Labor Relations; Publishing; Sales; Secretarial. **Positions commonly filled include:** Advertising Clerk; Brokerage Clerk; Clerical Supervisor; Customer Service Representative; Editor; General Manager; Human Resources Specialist; Management Trainee; Manufacturer's/Wholesaler's Sales Rep.; Public Relations Specialist; Securities Sales Representative; Services Sales Representative; Telecommunications Manager; Typist/Word Processor. **Average salary range of placements:** $20,000 - $29,999.

ADVANCED PERSONNEL, INC.
1020 Milwaukee Avenue, Suite 105, Deerfield IL 60015. 847/520-9111. **Fax:** 847/520-9489. **Contact:** Operations Manager. **Description:** A permanent employment agency that also provides some temporary placements. Advanced Personnel also provides career/outplacement counseling. Founded in 1987. **Specializes in the areas of:** Office Support. **Positions commonly filled include:** Administrative Assistant; Customer Service Representative; Data Entry Clerk. **Benefits available to temporary workers:** 401(k); Paid Vacation; Referral Bonus Plan. **Corporate headquarters location:** This

Location. **Other U.S. locations:** Chicago IL; Gurnee IL; Lombard IL; Rosemont IL; Schaumburg IL. **Average salary range of placements:** $20,000 - $29,999. **Number of placements per year:** 100 - 199.

ADVANCED PERSONNEL, INC.
225 West Washington Street, Suite 500, Chicago IL 60606. 312/422-9333. **Fax:** 312/422-9310. **Contact:** Manager. **Description:** A permanent employment agency. **Specializes in the areas of:** Finance. **Corporate headquarters location:** Deerfield IL. **Other area locations:** Gurnee IL; Lombard IL; Rosemont IL; Schaumburg IL.

AFFILIATED PERSONNEL CONSULTANTS, LTD.
750 West Lake Cook Road, Suite 110, Buffalo Grove IL 60089. 847/520-3200. **Fax:** 847/520-3455. **Contact:** Karen Chern, Owner. **Description:** A permanent employment agency that also provides some temporary placements. **Specializes in the areas of:** Accounting/Auditing; Computer Science/Software; Personnel/Labor Relations; Sales; Secretarial. **Positions commonly filled include:** Account Representative; Administrative Assistant; Clerical Supervisor; Computer Operator; Computer Programmer; Customer Service Representative; Human Resources Manager; Management Trainee; Marketing Specialist; Purchasing Agent/Manager; Sales Executive; Secretary; Typist/Word Processor. **Average salary range of placements:** $20,000 - $29,999.

AMERICAN MEDICAL PERSONNEL INC.
30 East Huron Street, Suite 4102, Chicago IL 60611-2722. 312/337-4221. **Contact:** Director. **Description:** A permanent employment agency. **Specializes in the areas of:** Health/Medical; Insurance. **Positions commonly filled include:** Clinical Lab Technician; EEG Technologist; EKG Technician; Health Services Manager; Medical Assistant; Medical Doctor; Nuclear Medicine Technologist; Occupational Therapist; Office Manager; Pharmacist; Physical Therapist; Physician; Radiological Technologist; Registered Nurse; Respiratory Therapist; Surgical Technician; Transcriptionist. **Number of placements per year:** 100 - 199.

AVAILABILITY, INC.
P.O. Box 562, Alton IL 62002. 618/465-6449. **Contact:** Lee J. Hamel, Owner. **Description:** A permanent employment agency. **Specializes in the areas of:** Accounting/Auditing; Administration; Banking; Clerical; Computer Hardware/Software; Engineering; Finance; Sales; Technical.

B-W AND ASSOCIATES, INC.
4415 West Harrison Street, Suite 444, Hillside IL 60162. 708/449-5400. **Fax:** 708/449-5405. **Contact:** Jim Burns, Manager. **Description:** A permanent employment agency. **Specializes in the areas of:** Architecture/Construction; Engineering; Food; Health/Medical; Manufacturing.

BANNER PERSONNEL SERVICE, INC.
122 South Michigan Avenue, Suite 1510, Chicago IL 60603. 312/704-6000. **Fax:** 312/580-2515. **Contact:** Laura Long, Vice President. **Description:** A permanent employment agency. Founded in 1970. **Specializes in the areas of:** Industrial; Personnel/Labor Relations; Sales; Secretarial. **Positions commonly filled include:** Blue-Collar Worker Supervisor; Clerical Supervisor; Computer Programmer; Customer Service Representative; Human Resources Specialist; Quality Control Supervisor; Typist/Word Processor. **Corporate headquarters location:** This Location. **Average salary range of placements:** $20,000 - $29,999. **Number of placements per year:** 200 - 499.

BANNER PERSONNEL SERVICE, INC.
2215 York Road, Suite 103, Oak Brook IL 60523. 630/574-9499. **Fax:** 630/574-2218. **Contact:** Manager. **Description:** A permanent employment agency. **Specializes in the areas of:** Accounting; General

Management; Industrial; Office Support; Sales; Secretarial. **Positions commonly filled include:** Accountant; Administrator; Bookkeeper; Data Entry Clerk; EDP Specialist; Management Trainee; Plant Manager; Quality Control Supervisor; Sales Representative; Secretary; Supervisor; Support Personnel. **Corporate headquarters location:** Chicago IL.

BANNER PERSONNEL SERVICE, INC.
1701 East Woodfield Road, Suite 611, Schaumburg IL 60173. 847/706-9180. **Fax:** 847/706-9187. **Contact:** Branch Manager. **Description:** A permanent employment agency. Founded in 1970. **Specializes in the areas of:** Accounting/Auditing; Clerical; Consulting; Engineering; Entry-Level Management; Finance; General Management; Industrial; Manufacturing; Office Support; Sales; Secretarial; Technical. **Positions commonly filled include:** Accountant/Auditor; Aerospace Engineer; Bookkeeper; Chemical Engineer; Civil Engineer; Computer Programmer; Consultant; Data Entry Clerk; EDP Specialist; Electrical/Electronics Engineer; Factory Worker; Financial Analyst; Industrial Engineer; Management Trainee; Manufacturing Engineer; Mechanical Engineer; Nuclear Engineer; Packaging Engineer; Plant Manager; Quality Control Supervisor; Safety Engineer; Sales Representative; Secretary; Software Engineer; Supervisor; Support Personnel; Systems Analyst; Tax Specialist; Water/Wastewater Engineer. **Corporate headquarters location:** Chicago IL.

BANNER PERSONNEL SERVICE, INC.
800 East Diehl Road, Suite 100, Naperville IL 60563. 630/505-8881. **Fax:** 630/505-4566. **Contact:** Jonnell Crawford, Recruiter. **Description:** A permanent employment agency that also provides some temporary placements. Founded in 1970. **Specializes in the areas of:** Accounting; Finance; Industrial. **Positions commonly filled include:** Administrative Assistant; Clerical Supervisor; Customer Service Representative; Electrical/Electronics Engineer; Human Resources Manager; Sales Representative; Secretary; Typist/Word Processor. **Benefits available to temporary workers:** Computer Training. **Corporate headquarters location:** Chicago IL. **Average salary range of placements:** $20,000 - $29,999. **Number of placements per year:** 1000+.

BANNER PERSONNEL SERVICE, INC.
1580 South Milwaukee Avenue, Suite 102, Libertyville IL 60048. 847/247-2200. **Fax:** 847/247-2202. **Contact:** Recruiter. **Description:** A permanent employment agency. Founded in 1970. **Specializes in the areas of:** Clerical; Office Support; Secretarial. **Corporate headquarters location:** Chicago IL.

BARRY PERSONNEL RESOURCES, INC.
53 West Jackson Boulevard, Suite 1505, Chicago IL 60604. 312/922-3300. **Fax:** 312/922-1212. **Contact:** Peg Barry, President. **E-mail address:** barryinc@ccm.net. **World Wide Web address:** http://www.barrypersonnel.com. **Description:** A permanent employment agency that also provides some temporary placements and resume/career counseling services. Client company pays fee. **Specializes in the areas of:** Administration; Human Resources; Information Technology. **Corporate headquarters location:** This Location.

BELL PERSONNEL INC.
5368 West 95th Street, Oak Lawn IL 60453. 708/636-3151. **Fax:** 708/636-9315. **Contact:** Manager. **Description:** A permanent employment agency. **Specializes in the areas of:** Accounting/Auditing; Administration; Advertising; Banking; Computer Science/Software; Finance; Insurance; Legal; Sales; Secretarial. **Positions commonly filled include:** Accountant/Auditor; Advertising Clerk; Buyer; Clerical Supervisor; Cost Estimator; Credit Manager; Customer Service Representative; General Manager; Human Resources Specialist; Management Trainee; Paralegal; Typist/Word Processor. **Average salary range of placements:** $30,000 - $50,000.

CASEY SERVICES, INC.
121 South Wilke Road, Suite 600, Arlington Heights IL 60005. 847/253-9030. **Fax:** 847/253-9545. **Recorded jobline:** 847/582-9068. **Contact:** Robert Casey, CEO. **Description:** A permanent employment agency that also provides some temporary placements. **Specializes in the areas of:** Accounting/Auditing; Banking; Finance; Information Systems. **Positions commonly filled include:** Accountant/Auditor; Accounting Clerk; Accounting Supervisor; Bookkeeper; Collector; Computer Operator; Computer Programmer; Credit Analyst; Data Entry Clerk; Financial Analyst; MIS Specialist; Network Engineer; Payroll Clerk; Systems Analyst. **Corporate headquarters location:** This Location. **Other U.S. locations:** Chicago IL.

CASEY SERVICES, INC.
180 North Michigan Avenue, Suite 1605, Chicago IL 60601. 312/332-8367. **Contact:** Manager. **Description:** A permanent employment agency that also provides some temporary placements. **Specializes in the areas of:** Accounting/Auditing; Finance. **Corporate headquarters location:** Arlington Heights IL.

CHAMPION STAFFING
5105 Tollview Drive, Suite 110, Rolling Meadows IL 60008. 847/394-5660. **Fax:** 847/394-5664. **Contact:** Pauline DeGrazia, Co-owner. **Description:** A permanent employment agency. **Specializes in the areas of:** Clerical; General Management; Office Support; Secretarial. **Positions commonly filled include:** Administrative Manager; Clerical Supervisor; Customer Service Representative; General Manager; Management Trainee; Typist/Word Processor.

CO-COUNSEL, INC.
10 South LaSalle Street, Suite 1310, Chicago IL 60603-1002. 312/201-8020. **Fax:** 312/201-8028. **Contact:** Ms. Callie Urban, Office Manager. **Description:** A permanent employment agency. **Positions commonly filled include:** Attorney; Litigation Support Consultant; Paralegal. **Corporate headquarters location:** Houston TX. **Other U.S. locations:** San Francisco CA; Washington DC; Fort Lauderdale FL; Miami FL; Tampa FL; Atlanta GA; Minneapolis MN; New York NY; Dallas TX.

CORPORATE RESOURCES, LTD.
C.R. TEMPORARIES
300 North Martingale Road, Suite 450, Schaumburg IL 60173. 847/619-1600. **Fax:** 847/619-1554. **Contact:** Ingrid Moore, Co-Owner. **Description:** A permanent employment agency. C.R. Temporaries (also at this location) is a temporary agency. **Specializes in the areas of:** Secretarial. **Positions commonly filled include:** Administrative Manager; Advertising Clerk; Customer Service Representative; Human Resources Specialist; Paralegal; Receptionist; Services Sales Representative; Typist/Word Processor. **Average salary range of placements:** $20,000 - $29,999. **Number of placements per year:** 500 - 999.

CORPORATE STAFFING, INC.
PROVEN PERFORMERS
3 First National Plaza, 70 West Madison Street, Suite 530, Chicago IL 60602. 312/917-1117. **Contact:** Collette Russell, President. **World Wide Web address:** http://www.greatchicagojobs.com. **Description:** A permanent employment agency that also provides career/outplacement counseling services. Proven Performers (also at this location, 312/917-1111, Fax: 312/917-0474) is a temporary agency that also provides some temp-to-perm placements and contract services. **NOTE:** Resumes for Proven Performers should be addressed to Robert Dyer, President. **Specializes in the areas of:** Accounting; Administration; Advertising; Health/Medical; Personnel/Labor Relations; Real Estate; Secretarial. **Positions commonly filled include:** Accountant; Administrative Assistant; Claim Representative; Clerical Supervisor; Customer Service Representative; Project Manager; Secretary; Typist/Word Processor. **Benefits available to temporary workers:**

Paid Holidays; Paid Vacation. **Corporate headquarters location:** This Location. **Average salary range of placements:** $20,000 - $49,999. **Number of placements per year:** 500 - 999.

CROWN PERSONNEL
325 West Prospect Avenue, Mount Prospect IL 60056. 847/392-5151. **Fax:** 847/392-0114. **Contact:** Dan Hyland, President. **Description:** A permanent employment agency. **Specializes in the areas of:** Banking; Engineering. **Positions commonly filled include:** Bank Officer/Manager; Electrical/Electronics Engineer; Mechanical Engineer; Typist/Word Processor. **Average salary range of placements:** $30,000 - $50,000. **Number of placements per year:** 1 - 49.

DANNEHL & ASSOCIATES
107 North Second Street, Cissna Park IL 60924. 815/457-2660. **Contact:** Manager. **Description:** A permanent employment agency. **Specializes in the areas of:** Restaurant.

DENTAL AUXILIARY PLACEMENT SERVICE, INC.
2 Talcott Road, Suite 32, Park Ridge IL 60068. 847/696-1988. **Fax:** 847/696-4371. **Contact:** Karen Anderson, Director. **Description:** A permanent employment agency that also provides some temporary placements. **Positions commonly filled include:** Dental Assistant/Dental Hygienist; Dentist. **Average salary range of placements:** $30,000 - $50,000. **Number of placements per year:** 1000+.

DESMOND SERVICES INC.
1648 East New York Street, Aurora IL 60505. 630/820-3300. **Contact:** Manager. **Description:** A permanent employment agency.

THE ESQUIRE STAFFING GROUP, LTD.
One South Wacker Drive, Suite 1616, Chicago IL 60606-4616. 312/795-4300. **Fax:** 312/795-4329. **Contact:** Scott J. Fischer, Executive Vice President. **Description:** A permanent employment agency that also provides some temporary placements. Founded in 1955. **Specializes in the areas of:** Accounting; Advertising; Banking; Brokerage; Data Entry; Finance; Health/Medical; Human Resources; Insurance; Legal; Office Support; Sales; Secretarial; Word Processing. **Positions commonly filled include:** Account Representative; Accountant; Adjuster; Administrative Assistant; Administrative Manager; Advertising Clerk; Auditor; Bank Officer/Manager; Branch Manager; Chief Financial Officer; Claim Representative; Clerical Supervisor; Computer Programmer; Controller; Credit Manager; Customer Service Representative; Graphic Designer; Human Resources Manager; Industrial Production Manager; Insurance Agent/Broker; Legal Secretary; Management Trainee; Market Research Analyst; Marketing Specialist; Paralegal; Purchasing Agent/Manager; Quality Control Supervisor; Sales Executive; Sales Manager; Sales Representative; Secretary; Telecommunications Manager; Typist/Word Processor. **Benefits available to temporary workers:** Medical Insurance; Pension Plan. **Corporate headquarters location:** This Location. **Other U.S. locations:** Nationwide. **Average salary range of placements:** $30,000 - $50,000. **Number of placements per year:** 500 - 999.

EVE RECRUITERS LTD.
203 North Wabash Avenue, Suite 305, Chicago IL 60601. 312/372-7445. **Fax:** 312/372-3182. **Contact:** Bob Schmidt, Manager. **E-mail address:** everecruiter@earthlink.net. **Description:** A permanent employment agency that places individuals in *Fortune* 500 companies. Eve Recruiters also provides resume and career counseling services. Client company pays fee. **Specializes in the areas of:** Accounting; Administration; Advertising; Finance; Legal; Printing; Publishing; Real Estate; Scientific; Secretarial; Technical. **Positions commonly filled include:** Administrative Assistant; Advertising Clerk; Advertising Executive; Applications Engineer; AS400 Programmer Analyst; Attorney; Bank Officer/Manager; Branch Manager; Civil Engineer; Claim Representative; Clerical Supervisor; Computer Animator; Computer Engineer; Computer Operator; Computer Programmer; Computer Scientist; Computer Support Technician; Computer Technician; Content Developer; Controller; Database Administrator; Database Manager; Desktop Publishing Specialist; Environmental Engineer; Finance Director; Financial Analyst; Graphic Artist; Graphic Designer; Human Resources Manager; Industrial Engineer; Intellectual Property Lawyer; Internet Services Manager; Management Analyst/Consultant; Market Research Analyst; Marketing Manager; Marketing Specialist; Mechanical Engineer; MIS Specialist; Multimedia Designer; Network/Systems Administrator; Paralegal; Public Relations Specialist; Secretary; Software Engineer; SQL Programmer; Systems Analyst; Systems Manager; Typist/Word Processor; Underwriter/Assistant Underwriter; Webmaster. **Corporate headquarters location:** This Location. **Average salary range of placements:** $30,000 - $49,999. **Number of placements per year:** 100 - 199.

EXCELL PERSONNEL
33 North Dearborn Street, Suite 400, Chicago IL 60602. 312/372-0014. **Contact:** Manager. **Description:** A permanent employment agency that also provides some temporary placements. **Specializes in the areas of:** Office Support.

GENERAL EMPLOYMENT ENTERPRISES, INC.
280 West Shuman Boulevard, Suite 185, Naperville IL 60563. 630/983-1233. **Fax:** 630/983-2993. **Contact:** Manager. **World Wide Web address:** http://www.genp.com. **Description:** A permanent employment agency. **Specializes in the areas of:** Accounting/Auditing; Administration; Computer Science/Software; Engineering; Finance; Technical. **Positions commonly filled include:** Accountant/Auditor; Budget Analyst; Chemical Engineer; Computer Programmer; Credit Manager; Customer Service Representative; Design Engineer; Designer; Draftsperson; Electrical/Electronics Engineer; Financial Analyst; Industrial Engineer; Industrial Production Manager; Mechanical Engineer; Metallurgical Engineer; MIS Specialist; Multimedia Designer; Purchasing Agent/Manager; Quality Control Supervisor; Software Engineer; Structural Engineer; Systems Analyst; Technical Writer/Editor; Telecommunications Manager. **Corporate headquarters location:** Oakbrook Terrace IL. **Other U.S. locations:** Nationwide. **Average salary range of placements:** More than $50,000. **Number of placements per year:** 1 - 49.

GENERAL EMPLOYMENT ENTERPRISES, INC. TRIAD PERSONNEL
1101 Perimeter Drive, Suite 735, Schaumburg IL 60173. 847/240-1233. **Fax:** 847/240-1671. **Contact:** Frank Anichini, Branch Manager. **E-mail address:** sch@genp.com. **World Wide Web address:** http://www.genp.com. **Description:** A permanent employment agency that also provides some contract services. Founded in 1893. **Specializes in the areas of:** Administration; Computer Hardware/Software. **Positions commonly filled include:** Computer Operator; Computer Programmer; Consultant; Customer Service Representative; Database Manager; Internet Services Manager; MIS Specialist; Software Engineer; Systems Analyst; Systems Manager; Telecommunications Manager; Webmaster. **Corporate headquarters location:** Oakbrook Terrace IL. **Other U.S. locations:** Nationwide. **Average salary range of placements:** $30,000 - $50,000. **Number of placements per year:** 200 - 499.

HKA MORTGAGE STAFFING & TRAINING
1500 Waukegan Road, Suite 221, Glenview IL 60025. 847/998-9300. **Toll-free phone:** 800/969-8930. **Fax:** 847/729-6941. **Contact:** Cynthia K. Espinosa, Staffing Consultant. **Description:** A permanent employment agency that also provides some temporary placements and contract services. **Specializes in the areas of:** Banking; Mortgage. **Positions commonly filled include:**

Accountant/Auditor; Bank Officer/Manager; Mortgage Banker. **Number of placements per year:** 100 - 199.

HR SEARCH
35 East Wacker Drive, Suite 1052, Chicago IL 60601. 312/658-1400x206. **Fax:** 312/658-1408. **Contact:** Nancy Campbell-Phillips, Manager. **Description:** A permanent employment agency. **Specializes in the areas of:** Legal; Personnel/Labor Relations; Secretarial. **Positions commonly filled include:** Account Representative; Administrative Assistant; Administrative Manager; Assistant Manager; Computer Operator; Controller; Financial Analyst; Human Resources Manager; Paralegal; Sales Executive; Secretary; Typist/Word Processor. **Other U.S. locations:** Dallas TX. **Average salary range of placements:** $30,000 - $50,000.

HALLMARK PERSONNEL INC.
3158 South River Road, Suite 220, Des Plaines IL 60018. 847/298-1900. **Contact:** Manager. **Description:** A permanent employment agency. **Specializes in the areas of:** Insurance.

HUMAN RESOURCE CONNECTION, INC.
1900 East Golf Road, Suite M100, Schaumburg IL 60173. 847/995-8090. **Fax:** 847/519-7080. **Contact:** Kim Dooley, Owner. **Description:** A permanent employment agency. **Specializes in the areas of:** Accounting/Auditing; Administration; Banking; Finance; General Management; Insurance; Legal; Manufacturing; Personnel/Labor Relations; Retail; Sales; Secretarial. **Positions commonly filled include:** Accountant/Auditor; Adjuster; Administrative Assistant; Administrative Manager; Branch Manager; Buyer; Clerical Supervisor; Credit Manager; Customer Service Representative; Financial Analyst; General Manager; Human Resources Manager; Management Trainee; Marketing Specialist; Paralegal; Receptionist; Services Sales Representative; Typist/Word Processor. **Number of placements per year:** 200 - 499.

INITIAL STAFFING
2 North LaSalle Street, Suite 950, Chicago IL 60602. 312/855-1390. **Contact:** Area Manager. **Description:** A permanent employment agency that also provides some temporary placements. **Specializes in the areas of:** Clerical.

INTERVIEWING CONSULTANTS INC.
19 South LaSalle Street, Suite 900, Chicago IL 60603. 312/263-1710. **Contact:** Ron (Gia) Giambarberee, Owner/Manager. **Description:** A permanent employment agency that also provides some temporary placements. **Specializes in the areas of:** Accounting/Auditing; Banking; Clerical; Computer Science/Software; Engineering; General Management; Insurance; Legal Secretarial; Office Support; Sales; Secretarial. **Positions commonly filled include:** Accountant/Auditor; Adjuster; Administrative Assistant; Advertising Clerk; Brokerage Clerk; Budget Analyst; Buyer; Claim Representative; Clerical Supervisor; Computer Programmer; Cost Estimator; Customer Service Representative; Electrical/Electronics Engineer; Financial Analyst; General Manager; Human Resources Manager; Legal Secretary; Management Analyst/Consultant; Management Trainee; Mechanical Engineer; Medical Records Technician; Paralegal; Property and Real Estate Manager; Receptionist; Securities Sales Representative; Services Sales Representative; Software Engineer; Systems Analyst; Typist/Word Processor; Underwriter/Assistant Underwriter. **Number of placements per year:** 200 - 499.

J.C.G. LIMITED, INC.
2300 Higgins Road, Elk Grove Village IL 60007. 847/439-1400. **Contact:** James Greene, President. **Description:** A permanent employment agency. **Specializes in the areas of:** Engineering; Manufacturing; Transportation.

KINGSLEY EMPLOYMENT SERVICE
208 South LaSalle Street, Suite 1877, Chicago IL 60604. 312/726-8190. **Contact:** Edward Friedman, Owner.

Description: A permanent employment agency. **Specializes in the areas of:** Banking; Finance.

KREZOWSKI & COMPANY
4811 Emerson Avenue, Suite 101, Palatine IL 60067. 847/303-0400. **Contact:** Manager. **Description:** A permanent employment agency. **Specializes in the areas of:** Medical Sales and Marketing.

MACINTYRE EMPLOYMENT SERVICE
15 North Arlington Heights Road, Suite 100, Arlington Heights IL 60004. 847/577-8860. **Fax:** 847/577-8863. **Contact:** Elizabeth E. MacIntyre, President. **Description:** A permanent employment agency. **Specializes in the areas of:** Art/Design; Secretarial. **Positions commonly filled include:** Clerical Supervisor; Customer Service Representative; Typist/Word Processor. **Average salary range of placements:** $20,000 - $29,999. **Number of placements per year:** 50 - 99.

MARAMAX PERSONNEL, INC.
5105 Tollview Drive, Suite 101, Rolling Meadows IL 60008. 847/253-0220. **Fax:** 847/253-0463. **Contact:** Maryellen Mackey, Manager. **E-mail address:** maramax@mindspring.com. **Description:** Specializing in only full-time, regular placements for office support and professional level staffing. Salaries are attached to level of position. All staffing inquiries are welcome. **Specializes in the areas of:** Accounting; Administration; Computer Science/Software; Customer Service; Human Resources; Marketing; MIS/EDP; Office Support; Sales; Secretarial.

MERIT PERSONNEL INC.
640 Pearson Street, Suite 301, Des Plaines IL 60016. 847/296-2040. **Fax:** 847/296-2051. **Contact:** Manager. **Description:** A permanent employment agency. **Specializes in the areas of:** Accounting/Auditing; Banking; Personnel/Labor Relations; Secretarial. **Positions commonly filled include:** Customer Service Representative. **Average salary range of placements:** $20,000 - $29,999. **Number of placements per year:** 100 - 199.

MICHAEL DAVID ASSOCIATES, INC.
180 North Michigan Avenue, Suite 1016, Chicago IL 60601. 312/236-4460. **Fax:** 312/236-5401. **Contact:** Director of Administrative Services. **Description:** A permanent employment agency. **Specializes in the areas of:** Accounting; Administration; Advertising; Banking; Finance; Legal; Personnel/Labor Relations; Secretarial. **Positions commonly filled include:** Accountant; Adjuster; Administrative Assistant; Administrative Manager; Advertising Clerk; Auditor; Bank Officer/Manager; Budget Analyst; Buyer; Chief Financial Officer; Claim Representative; Clerical Supervisor; Computer Operator; Computer Support Technician; Controller; Cost Estimator; Credit Manager; Customer Service Representative; Database Administrator; Desktop Publishing Specialist; Economist; Editorial Assistant; Finance Director; Financial Analyst; Fund Manager; Graphic Designer; Human Resources Manager; Internet Services Manager; Market Research Analyst; MIS Specialist; Multimedia Designer; Network Administrator; Paralegal; Public Relations Specialist; Sales Representative; Secretary; Systems Analyst; Typist/Word Processor; Underwriter/Assistant Underwriter; Webmaster. **Number of placements per year:** 200 - 499.

THE MORAN GROUP
274 Torino Drive, Cary IL 60013. 847/639-0770. **Fax:** 847/639-1771. **Contact:** Manager. **Description:** A permanent employment agency. **Specializes in the areas of:** Retail. **Positions commonly filled include:** Credit Manager. **Number of placements per year:** 1 - 49.

MULLINS & ASSOCIATES, INC.
522 South NW Highway, Barrington IL 60010. 847/382-1800. **Fax:** 847/382-1329. **Contact:** Ms. Terri Mullins, Vice President. **Description:** A permanent employment

agency. **Specializes in the areas of:** Computer Science/Software; Engineering. **Positions commonly filled include:** Chemical Engineer; Computer Programmer; Design Engineer; Designer; Draftsperson; Industrial Engineer; MIS Specialist; Software Engineer; Systems Analyst. **Number of placements per year:** 200 - 499.

THE MURPHY GROUP
150 East Cook Avenue, Libertyville IL 60048. 847/362-6100. **Fax:** 847/362-1826. **Contact:** Leah Kayle, President. **Description:** A permanent employment agency. **Specializes in the areas of:** Accounting/Auditing; Clerical; Personnel/Labor Relations; Retail; Sales; Secretarial. **Positions commonly filled include:** Clerical Supervisor; Customer Service Representative; Management Trainee; Services Sales Representative; Typist/Word Processor. **Corporate headquarters location:** Oak Brook IL. **Number of placements per year:** 100 - 199.

THE MURPHY GROUP
1211 West 22nd Street, Suite 221, Oak Brook IL 60523. 630/574-2840. **Contact:** James R. Bruno, Vice President. **Description:** A permanent employment agency. **Specializes in the areas of:** Accounting/Auditing; Advertising; Banking; Clerical; Computer Science/Software; Engineering; Finance; Food; Insurance; Manufacturing; MIS/EDP; Publishing; Sales; Secretarial; Technical. **Corporate headquarters location:** This Location.

THE MURPHY GROUP
133 Vine Avenue, Park Ridge IL 60068. 847/825-2136. **Fax:** 847/696-1662. **Contact:** Beth Parsch, Owner. **Description:** A permanent employment agency. **Specializes in the areas of:** Accounting/Auditing; Clerical; Finance; Office Support; Secretarial; Word Processing. **Positions commonly filled include:** Accountant/Auditor; Administrator; Bookkeeper; Budget Analyst; Clerical Supervisor; Clerk; Receptionist; Secretary. **Corporate headquarters location:** Oak Brook IL.

THE MURPHY GROUP
1555 Bond Street, Suite 131, Naperville IL 60563. 630/355-7030. **Fax:** 630/355-8670. **Contact:** Director. **World Wide Web address:** http://www.murphygroup.com. **Description:** A permanent employment agency. **Specializes in the areas of:** Administration; General Management; Office Support; Secretarial; Word Processing. **Positions commonly filled include:** Administrator; Clerk; Receptionist; Secretary; Support Personnel. **Corporate headquarters location:** Oak Brook IL. **Average salary range of placements:** $30,000 - $50,000.

NETWORK RESOURCE GROUP, INC.
920 South Spring Street, Springfield IL 62704. **Toll-free phone:** 800/519-1000. **Fax:** 800/519-2425. **Contact:** Martine Davis, Recruiter. **E-mail address:** nrg@nrgjobs.com. **World Wide Web address:** http://www.nrgjobs.com. **Description:** A permanent employment agency that also provides some contract services. **Specializes in the areas of:** Computer Science/Software; Internet Development; MIS/EDP. **Positions commonly filled include:** AS400 Programmer Analyst; Computer Engineer; Computer Programmer; Computer Support Technician; Database Administrator; Database Manager; Internet Services Manager; MIS Specialist; Network Administrator; Software Engineer; SQL Programmer; Systems Analyst; Systems Manager; Webmaster. **Average salary range of placements:** $50,000 - $100,000.

OFFICEMATES5 (OM5)
1400 East Lake Cook Road, Suite 115, Buffalo Grove IL 60089. 847/459-6160. **Fax:** 847/459-8195. **Contact:** Manager. **Description:** A permanent employment agency. **Specializes in the areas of:** Accounting/Auditing; Administration; Advertising; Architecture/Construction; Banking; Chemicals; Communications; Computer Science/Software; Electrical; Engineering; Finance; Food;

General Management; Health/Medical; Legal; Manufacturing; Operations Management; Pharmaceuticals; Procurement; Publishing; Retail; Sales; Technical; Textiles; Transportation.

OFFICEMATES5 (OM5)
DAYSTAR TEMPORARY SERVICES
191 Waukegan Road, Northfield IL 60093. 847/446-7737. **Fax:** 847/446-0090. **Contact:** Manager. **E-mail address:** resume@officemates5anddaystar.com. **Description:** A permanent employment agency. DayStar Temporaries (also at this location) provides temporary placements. **Specializes in the areas of:** Administration; Secretarial. **Positions commonly filled include:** Accounting Clerk; Administrative Assistant; Administrative Manager; Clerical Supervisor; Customer Service Representative; Editorial Assistant; Human Resources Manager; Secretary; Transportation/Traffic Specialist; Typist/Word Processor. **Benefits available to temporary workers:** Software Training. **Average salary range of placements:** $20,000 - $29,999. **Number of placements per year:** 200 - 499.

OFFICETEAM
One Oakbrook Terrace, Suite 718, Oakbrook Terrace IL 60181. 630/261-3086. **Fax:** 630/261-9699. **Contact:** Assignment Manager. **Description:** A permanent employment agency. **Specializes in the areas of:** Administration; Secretarial. **Positions commonly filled include:** Administrative Assistant; Claim Representative; Clerical Supervisor; Clerk; Computer Operator; Legal Secretary; Medical Secretary; Receptionist; Typist/Word Processor. **Number of placements per year:** 1000+.

OFFICETEAM
5 Revere Drive, Suite 355, Northbrook IL 60062. 847/480-2073. **Fax:** 847/480-1871. **Contact:** Assignment Manager. **Description:** A permanent employment agency. **Specializes in the areas of:** Administration; Office Support. **Positions commonly filled include:** Administrative Assistant; Customer Service Representative; Data Entry Clerk; Desktop Publishing Specialist; Executive Assistant; Receptionist. **Number of placements per year:** 1000+.

OFFICETEAM
2800 West Higgins Road, Suite 180, Hoffman Estates IL 60195. 847/885-6228. **Fax:** 847/885-6387. **Contact:** Staffing Manager. **Description:** A permanent employment agency. **Specializes in the areas of:** Administration; Secretarial. **Positions commonly filled include:** Administrative Assistant; Claim Representative; Clerical Supervisor; Clerk; Computer Operator; Customer Service Representative; Data Entry Clerk; Receptionist; Secretary; Typist/Word Processor. **Number of placements per year:** 1000+.

OFFICETEAM
205 North Michigan Avenue, Suite 3300, Chicago IL 60601. 312/616-8258. **Fax:** 312/616-1807. **Contact:** Assignment Manager. **Description:** A permanent employment agency. **Specializes in the areas of:** Administration; Secretarial. **Positions commonly filled include:** Administrative Assistant; Claim Representative; Clerical Supervisor; Clerk; Computer Operator; Legal Secretary; Medical Secretary; Receptionist; Secretary; Typist/Word Processor. **Number of placements per year:** 1000+.

OMNI ONE
2200 East Devon Avenue, Suite 246, Des Plaines IL 60018. 847/299-1400. **Fax:** 847/299-4926. **Contact:** Steve Leibovitz, Branch Manager. **E-mail address:** omnione@omnione.com. **World Wide Web address:** http://www.omnione.com. **Description:** A permanent employment agency. **Specializes in the areas of:** Computer Science/Software; Engineering; MIS/EDP; Technical.

THE OPPORTUNITIES GROUP
53 West Jackson Boulevard, Suite 215, Chicago IL 60604. 312/922-5400. **Fax:** 312/347-1206. **Contact:**

Manager. **Description:** A permanent employment agency that also provides some temporary placements. **Specializes in the areas of:** Personnel/Labor Relations; Secretarial. **Positions commonly filled include:** Typist/Word Processor. **Average salary range of placements:** $20,000 - $29,999.

PS INC.
70 West Madison Avenue, Suite 1400, Chicago IL 60602. 312/922-3222. **Fax:** 312/214-7299. **Contact:** Mary Parker, President. **Description:** A permanent employment agency that also provides some temporary placements. **Specializes in the areas of:** Accounting/Auditing; Administration; Computer Science/Software; Finance; Personnel/Labor Relations; Sales; Secretarial. **Positions commonly filled include:** Accountant/Auditor; Administrative Manager; Advertising Clerk; Computer Programmer; Customer Service Representative; Human Resources Specialist; Internet Services Manager; Market Research Analyst; MIS Specialist; Purchasing Agent/Manager; Software Engineer; Systems Analyst; Telecommunications Manager; Typist/Word Processor. **Number of placements per year:** 100 - 199.

PAIGE PERSONNEL SERVICES
5215 Old Orchard Road, Suite 500, Skokie IL 60077. 847/966-0700. **Contact:** Manager. **Description:** A permanent employment agency. **Specializes in the areas of:** Accounting; Administration; Finance; Personnel. **Corporate headquarters location:** This Location.

PAIGE PERSONNEL SERVICES
175 East Hawthorne Parkway, Suite 330, Vernon Hills IL 60061. 847/362-4696. **Fax:** 847/362-3977. **Contact:** Sharon Murphy, Personnel Manager. **Description:** A permanent employment agency. **Specializes in the areas of:** Secretarial. **Positions commonly filled include:** Administrative Assistant; Customer Service Representative; Human Resources Specialist; Management Trainee. **Corporate headquarters location:** Skokie IL. **Average salary range of placements:** $20,000 - $29,999. **Number of placements per year:** 50 - 99.

PEAK PROFESSIONAL HEALTH SERVICE
104 East Third Street, Rock Falls IL 61071. 815/625-1167. **Contact:** Manager. **Description:** A permanent employment agency that also provides some temporary placements, primarily in nursing homes. **Specializes in the areas of:** Health/Medical. **Positions commonly filled include:** Certified Nurses Aide.

PERSONNEL CONNECTIONS INC.
944 South Second Street, Suite E, Springfield IL 62704. 217/544-9092. **Fax:** 217/544-9042. **Contact:** Carla J. Oller, President. **Description:** A permanent employment agency. **Specializes in the areas of:** Accounting/Auditing; Administration; Banking; Computer Science/Software; General Management; Insurance; Personnel/Labor Relations; Sales; Secretarial. **Positions commonly filled include:** Accountant/Auditor; Branch Manager; Buyer; Claim Representative; Clerical Supervisor; Computer Programmer; Credit Manager; Customer Service Representative; Human Resources Manager; Industrial Engineer; Management Trainee; Mechanical Engineer; Medical Records Technician; Purchasing Agent/Manager; Systems Analyst; Underwriter/Assistant Underwriter; Wholesale and Retail Buyer.

PERSONNEL PLACEMENT CONSULTANTS
6841 West Cermak Road, Suite 7, Berwyn IL 60402. 708/795-9012. **Contact:** President. **Description:** A permanent employment agency. **Specializes in the areas of:** Accounting/Auditing; Banking; General Management; Legal; Nonprofit; Office Support; Personnel/Labor Relations; Secretarial. **Positions commonly filled include:** Accountant/Auditor; Bank Officer/Manager; Blue-Collar Worker Supervisor; Clerical Supervisor; Counselor; Credit Manager; Customer Service Representative; Dental

Assistant/Dental Hygienist; General Manager; Human Resources Specialist; Insurance Agent/Broker; Operations/Production Manager; Property and Real Estate Manager; Travel Agent; Typist/Word Processor; Underwriter/Assistant Underwriter.

PRESTIGE EMPLOYMENT SERVICES, INC.
19624 Governor's Highway, P.O. Box 160, Flossmoor IL 60422. 708/798-9010. **Fax:** 708/798-9099. **Contact:** Manager. **Description:** A permanent employment agency. **Specializes in the areas of:** Accounting/Auditing; Engineering; Manufacturing; Office Support; Sales; Secretarial; Word Processing. **Positions commonly filled include:** Administrator; Bookkeeper; Civil Engineer; Clerk; Electrical/Electronics Engineer; Factory Worker; Industrial Engineer; Manufacturing Engineer; Mechanical Engineer; Plant Manager; Quality Control Supervisor; Receptionist; Safety Engineer; Secretary; Services Sales Representative; Supervisor; Technician.

SALEM SERVICES, INC.
2 TransAm Plaza Drive, Suite 170, Oakbrook Terrace IL 60181. 630/932-7000. **Fax:** 630/932-7010. **Contact:** Dori Lorenz, President. **Description:** A permanent employment agency. **Specializes in the areas of:** Office Support.

SELECT STAFFING
8501 West Higgins Road, Suite 740, Chicago IL 60631. 847/699-1147. **Contact:** Dina Morgan, Manager. **Description:** A permanent employment agency. **Specializes in the areas of:** Accounting/Auditing; General Management; Personnel/Labor Relations; Secretarial. **Positions commonly filled include:** Accountant/Auditor; Advertising Clerk; Branch Manager; Brokerage Clerk; Budget Analyst; Claim Representative; Clerical Supervisor; Computer Programmer; Counselor; Credit Manager; Customer Service Representative; General Manager; Human Resources Specialist; Management Trainee; Manufacturer's/Wholesaler's Sales Rep.; Operations/Production Manager; Property and Real Estate Manager; Purchasing Agent/Manager; Quality Control Supervisor; Services Sales Representative; Systems Analyst; Telecommunications Manager; Typist/Word Processor; Underwriter/Assistant Underwriter. **Corporate headquarters location:** Schaumburg IL. **Average salary range of placements:** $20,000 - $45,000. **Number of placements per year:** 200 - 499.

SELECTABILITY, INC.
1011 East State Street, Rockford IL 61104. 815/964-9777. **Fax:** 815/964-6386. **Contact:** Al Weir, Manager. **Description:** A permanent employment agency. **Specializes in the areas of:** Engineering; General Management; Manufacturing; Technical. **Positions commonly filled include:** Aerospace Engineer; Human Resources Specialist; Industrial Engineer; Mechanical Engineer; Metallurgical Engineer; Software Engineer. **Other U.S. locations:** WI.

SNELLING PERSONNEL SERVICES
415 East Main, Belleville IL 62220. 618/277-1141. **Contact:** A.H. Harter, Jr., President. **Description:** A permanent employment agency. **Specializes in the areas of:** Accounting/Auditing; Administration; Advertising; Banking; Computer Hardware/Software; Engineering; Finance; Food; General Management; Industrial; Insurance; Legal; Manufacturing; Retail; Sales; Secretarial; Technical. **Positions commonly filled include:** Accountant/Auditor; Administrative Assistant; Aerospace Engineer; Architect; Attorney; Biological Scientist; Biomedical Engineer; Bookkeeper; Buyer; Ceramics Engineer; Chemical Engineer; Chemist; Civil Engineer; Claim Representative; Clerk; Computer Operator; Computer Programmer; Credit Manager; Customer Service Representative; Data Entry Clerk; Draftsperson; EDP Specialist; Electrical/Electronics Engineer; Hotel Manager; Industrial Designer; Industrial Engineer; Legal Secretary; Manufacturing Engineer; Marketing Specialist; Mechanical Engineer; Medical Secretary; Metallurgical Engineer; MIS Specialist;

Operations/Production Manager; Public Relations Specialist; Purchasing Agent/Manager; Quality Control Supervisor; Receptionist; Recruiter; Sales Representative; Secretary; Software Engineer; Systems Analyst; Systems Engineer; Technical Illustrator; Technical Writer/Editor; Technician; Typist/Word Processor; Underwriter/Assistant Underwriter. **Corporate headquarters location:** Dallas TX. **Number of placements per year:** 500 - 999.

SNELLING PERSONNEL SERVICES
2201 Fifth Avenue, Suite 5, Moline IL 61265. 309/797-1101. **Fax:** 309/797-7099. **Contact:** James Roeder, Vice President. **World Wide Web address:** http://www.snellingmoline.com. **Description:** A permanent employment agency. **Specializes in the areas of:** Accounting/Auditing; Administration; Computer Science/Software; Engineering; Personnel/Labor Relations; Sales. **Positions commonly filled include:** Agricultural Engineer; Buyer; Claim Representative; Computer Programmer; Design Engineer; Electrical/Electronics Engineer; Industrial Engineer; Industrial Production Manager; Internet Services Manager; Management Analyst/Consultant; Management Trainee; Manufacturer's/Wholesaler's Sales Rep.; Materials Engineer; Metallurgical Engineer; Multimedia Designer; Purchasing Agent/Manager; Services Sales Representative; Software Engineer; Systems Analyst. **Corporate headquarters location:** Dallas TX. **Average salary range of placements:** $30,000 - $50,000. **Number of placements per year:** 100 - 199.

STAFFING CONSULTANTS INC.
1701 Woodfield Road, Suite 903, Schaumburg IL 60173. 847/240-5300. **Toll-free phone:** 800/699-0825. **Fax:** 847/240-5310. **Contact:** Branch Manager. **Description:** A permanent employment agency that also provides some temporary placements. **Specializes in the areas of:** Banking; Industrial; Insurance; Light Industrial; Marketing; Nonprofit; Personnel/Labor Relations; Printing; Publishing; Retail; Sales; Secretarial. **Positions commonly filled include:** Account Representative; Administrative Assistant; Assistant Manager; Clerical Supervisor; Customer Service Representative; Human Resources Manager; Public Relations Specialist; Sales Executive; Sales Manager; Sales Representative; Secretary; Systems Analyst; Typist/Word Processor. **Benefits available to temporary workers:** Bonus Award/Plan; Dental Insurance; Medical Insurance. **Corporate headquarters location:** Chicago IL. **Other U.S. locations:** Bloomingdale IL; Crystal Lake IL; Naperville IL; Oak Brook IL. **Average salary range of placements:** $20,000 - $29,999. **Number of placements per year:** 100 - 199.

STRAND ASSOCIATES, INC.
2400 West Glenwood Avenue, Suite 226, Joliet IL 60435. 815/744-4200. **Fax:** 815/744-4215. **Contact:** Deirdre F. Egeland, Human Resources Coordinator. **E-mail address:** joliet@strand.com. **Description:** A permanent employment agency. **Specializes in the areas of:** Distribution; Engineering; Transportation. **Positions commonly filled include:** Civil Engineer; Consultant; Draftsperson. **Corporate headquarters location:** Madison WI. **Other U.S. locations:** Lexington KY; Louisville KY. **Average salary range of placements:** $30,000 - $50,000. **Number of placements per year:** 1 - 49.

SYSTEMS RESEARCH INC.
1250 Bank Drive, Schaumburg IL 60173. 847/330-1222. **Contact:** Bonnie Albrecht, Office Manager. **Description:** A permanent employment agency. **Specializes in the areas of:** Engineering; Manufacturing; Technical.

TEMPLETON & ASSOCIATES
One East Wacker Drive, Suite 3130, Chicago IL 60601. 312/644-8400. **Fax:** 312/644-8700. **Contact:** Shirley Campus, Manager. **Description:** A permanent employment agency that also provides some temporary placements. **Specializes in the areas of:** Legal. **Positions commonly filled include:** Attorney; Data Entry Clerk; Litigation Support Consultant; Paralegal. **Benefits**

available to temporary workers: Medical Insurance; Paid Holidays; Vacation Pay. **Corporate headquarters location:** Minneapolis MN. **Other U.S. locations:** Denver CO; Philadelphia PA. **Average salary range of placements:** $30,000 - $49,999. **Number of placements per year:** 1000+.

THIRTY THREE PERSONNEL CENTER
33 North Dearborn Street, Suite 1201, Chicago IL 60602. 312/236-2023. **Contact:** Peter Vanes, CPC/President. **Description:** A permanent employment agency that also provides some temporary placements. **Specializes in the areas of:** Entry-Level Management; Office Support; Personnel/Labor Relations; Word Processing. **Positions commonly filled include:** Administrator; Clerk; Human Resources Manager; Management Trainee; Receptionist; Secretary; Support Personnel.

U.S. MEDICAL PLACEMENTS INC.
325 West Huron Street, Suite 508, Chicago IL 60610. 312/440-2323. **Fax:** 312/440-3803. **Contact:** Bobbie Beser, Manager. **Description:** A permanent employment agency. **Specializes in the areas of:** Health/Medical.

VG & ASSOCIATES
9865 West Roosevelt Road, Westchester IL 60154. 708/343-0405. **Fax:** 708/343-1940. **Contact:** Mr. Val T. Grandys, Owner. **Description:** A permanent employment agency. **Specializes in the areas of:** Food; Insurance; Publishing; Sales. **Positions commonly filled include:** Insurance Agent/Broker; Management Trainee; Sales Representative; Services Sales Representative; Underwriter/Assistant Underwriter. **Corporate headquarters location:** This Location. **Average salary range of placements:** $20,000 - $29,999. **Number of placements per year:** 1 - 49.

LADONNA WALLACE & ASSOCIATES
6301 South Cass Avenue, Suite 200, Westmont IL 60559. 630/963-7733. **Contact:** Manager. **Description:** A permanent employment agency.

WALSH & COMPANY
731 South Durkin Drive, Springfield IL 62704. 217/793-0200. **Fax:** 217/793-9078. **Contact:** Jack Walsh, Owner. **Description:** A permanent employment agency. **Specializes in the areas of:** Computer Science/Software; Sales; Secretarial. **Positions commonly filled include:** Computer Programmer; Manufacturer's/Wholesaler's Sales Rep.; MIS Specialist; Software Engineer; Systems Analyst. **Average salary range of placements:** $30,000 - $50,000. **Number of placements per year:** 50 - 99.

J.A. WARD ASSOCIATES INC.
One North La Grange Road, La Grange IL 60525. 708/354-7035. **Contact:** Manager. **Description:** A permanent employment agency that also provides some temporary placements.

WATTERS & BYRD, INC.
2210 West Wabansia, Suite 309, Chicago IL 60647. 773/278-2525. **Contact:** Kenny Haas, Electrical/Electronics Industry Specialist. **Description:** A permanent employment agency. **Specializes in the areas of:** Industrial Sales and Marketing; Sales. **Positions commonly filled include:** Electrical/Electronics Engineer; Manufacturer's/Wholesaler's Sales Rep.; Technical Representative. **Number of placements per year:** 1 - 49.

WEST PERSONNEL SERVICE
1100 Lake Street, Suite 120, Oak Park IL 60301. 708/771-8210. **Contact:** Service Representative. **Description:** A permanent employment agency that also provides some temporary placements. **Specializes in the areas of:** Administration; Office Support; Sales; Secretarial; Word Processing. **Positions commonly filled include:** Administrative Assistant; Sales Representative; Secretary; Typist/Word Processor. **Benefits available to temporary workers:** 401(k); Dental Insurance; Medical Insurance; Paid Holidays; Paid Vacation; Referral Bonus Plan.

WEST PERSONNEL SERVICE
1750 East Golf Road, Suite 230, Schaumburg IL 60173. 847/605-0555. **Fax:** 847/605-0568. **Contact:** Pamela Turner, Area Manager. **Description:** A permanal employment agency that also provides some temporary placements. **Specializes in the areas of:** Accounting/Auditing; Administration; Computer Science/Software; General Management; Marketing; Sales. **Positions commonly filled include:** Account Manager; Account Representative; Accountant; Administrative Assistant; Administrative Manager; Assistant Manager; Auditor; Blue-Collar Worker Supervisor; Branch Manager; Budget Analyst; Buyer; Clerical Supervisor; Computer Programmer; Computer Technician; Controller; Cost Estimator; Credit Manager; Financial Analyst; General Manager; Human Resources Representative; Internet Services Manager; Management Analyst/Consultant; Management Trainee; Marketing Manager; Operations Manager; Paralegal; Production Manager; Project Manager; Public Relations Specialist; Purchasing Agent/Manager; Quality Control Supervisor; Sales Executive; Sales Manager; Sales Representative; Secretary; Systems Manager; Typist/Word Processor; Underwriter/Assistant Underwriter. **Benefits available to temporary workers:** Dental Insurance; Medical Insurance; Paid Holidays; Stock Purchase; Training. **Average salary range of placements:** $20,000 - $49,999. **Number of placements per year:** 200 - 499.

WEST PERSONNEL SERVICE
1301 West 22nd Street, Oak Brook IL 60523. 630/571-3800. **Contact:** Manager. **Description:** A permanent employment agency. **Specializes in the areas of:** Administration; Industrial; Office Support; Sales. **Positions commonly filled include:** Accountant/Auditor; Administrative Assistant; Buyer; Clerk; Customer Service Representative; Data Entry Clerk; Human Resources Specialist; Industrial Engineer; Management Trainee; Receptionist; Sales Representative. **Average salary range of placements:** $20,000 - $35,000. **Number of placements per year:** 200 - 499.

WILLS & COMPANY, INC.
222 East Wisconsin, Suite 100, Lake Forest IL 60045. 847/735-1622. **Fax:** 847/735-1633. **Contact:** Don Wills, President. **Description:** A permanent employment agency. **Specializes in the areas of:** Computer Hardware/Software; Data Processing.

WORLD EMPLOYMENT SERVICE
1403 Dundee Road, Plaza Verde, Buffalo Grove IL 60089. 847/870-0900. **Fax:** 847/870-0906. **Contact:** Manager. **Description:** A permanent employment agency. **Specializes in the areas of:** Accounting/Auditing; Administration; Advertising; Banking; Computer Science/Software; Engineering; Finance; Food; General Management; Health/Medical; Industrial; Insurance; Legal; Manufacturing; Personnel/Labor Relations; Retail; Sales; Technical. **Positions commonly filled include:** Accountant/Auditor; Adjuster; Administrative Manager; Advertising Clerk; Architect; Bank Officer/Manager; Brokerage Clerk; Budget Analyst; Buyer; Chemical Engineer; Claim Representative; Clerical Supervisor; Computer Programmer; Counselor; Credit Manager; Customer Service Representative; Design Engineer; Draftsperson; Electrical/Electronics Engineer; Financial Analyst; Health Services Manager; Hotel Manager; Human Resources Specialist; Industrial Engineer; Industrial Production Manager; Insurance Agent/Broker; Internet Services Manager; Management Analyst/Consultant; Management Trainee; Manufacturer's/Wholesaler's Sales Rep.; Market Research Analyst; Mechanical Engineer; Medical Records Technician; Metallurgical Engineer; MIS Specialist; Operations/Production Manager; Paralegal; Property and Real Estate Manager; Public Relations Specialist; Purchasing Agent/Manager; Restaurant/Food Service Manager; Services Sales Representative; Software Engineer; Statistician; Strategic Relations Manager; Systems Analyst; Technical Writer/Editor; Telecommunications Manager; Transportation/Traffic Specialist; Travel Agent; Typist/Word Processor; Underwriter/Assistant Underwriter. **Average salary range of placements:** $20,000 - $29,999. **Number of placements per year:** 100 - 199.

TEMPORARY EMPLOYMENT AGENCIES

ABLEST STAFFING SERVICES
611 East State Street, Geneva IL 60134. 630/232-1883. **Contact:** Carolyn Melka, Operations Manager. **Description:** A temporary agency that also provides some temp-to-perm placements. Founded in 1978. **Specializes in the areas of:** Customer Service; Industrial; Light Industrial; Secretarial. **Positions commonly filled include:** Administrative Assistant; Assembler; Computer Operator; Customer Service Representative; Machine Operator; Secretary; Typist/Word Processor; Warehouse/Distribution Worker. **Benefits available to temporary workers:** 401(k); Credit Union; Direct Deposit; Medical Insurance; Pension Plan; Referral Bonus Plan; Training; Tuition Assistance; Vacation Pay. **Corporate headquarters location:** Clearwater FL. **Other U.S. locations:** AL; MO; MS; NC; NY; TN. **Average salary range of placements:** Less than $20,000. **Number of placements per year:** 500 - 999.

ADECCO
266 Hawthorne Village Commons, Vernon Hills IL 60061. 847/247-1300. **Contact:** Athena Tarsinos, Office Supervisor. **World Wide Web address:** http://www.adecco.com. **Description:** A temporary agency that also provides some temp-to-perm placements. **Specializes in the areas of:** Accounting/Auditing; Industrial; Light Industrial; Manufacturing; Secretarial. **Positions commonly filled include:** Accountant; Administrative Assistant; Customer Service Representative; Secretary; Typist/Word Processor. **Benefits available to temporary workers:** 401(k); Dental Insurance; Direct Deposit; Medical Insurance; Paid Holidays; Paid Vacation; Referral Bonus Plan. **Corporate headquarters location:** Redwood City CA. **Other U.S. locations:** Nationwide.

International locations: Worldwide. **Average salary range of placements:** $20,000 - $29,999. **Number of placements per year:** 1 - 49.

ADECCO
6340 West 95th Street, Oak Lawn IL 60453. 708/430-5200. **Fax:** 708/430-5435. **Contact:** Branch Manager. **World Wide Web address:** http://www.adecco.com. **Description:** A temporary agency. **Specializes in the areas of:** Accounting/Auditing; Banking; Computer Science/Software; Legal; Manufacturing; Personnel/Labor Relations; Sales; Secretarial; Technical. **Positions commonly filled include:** Advertising Clerk; Bank Officer/Manager; Branch Manager; Brokerage Clerk; Clerical Supervisor; Computer Programmer; Credit Manager; Customer Service Representative; Draftsperson; Human Resources Specialist; Systems Analyst; Typist/Word Processor. **Corporate headquarters location:** Redwood City CA. **Other U.S. locations:** Nationwide. **International locations:** Worldwide. **Average salary range of placements:** $20,000 - $29,999. **Number of placements per year:** 1 - 49.

ADECCO
One Mid America Plaza, Suite 120, Oakbrook Terrace IL 60181. 630/368-0211. **Contact:** Michelle Salisbury, Branch Manager. **World Wide Web address:** http://www.adecco.com. **Description:** A temporary agency that also provides some permanent placements. **Specializes in the areas of:** Accounting/Auditing; Administration; Banking; Computer Science/Software; Legal; Manufacturing; Personnel/Labor Relations; Sales; Secretarial; Technical. **Positions commonly filled include:** Advertising Clerk; Bank Officer/Manager;

Branch Manager; Brokerage Clerk; Clerical Supervisor; Computer Programmer; Credit Manager; Customer Service Representative; Draftsperson; Human Resources Specialist; Systems Analyst; Typist/Word Processor. **Corporate headquarters location:** Redwood City CA. **Other U.S. locations:** Nationwide. **International locations:** Worldwide. **Average salary range of placements:** $20,000 - $29,999. **Number of placements per year:** 1 - 49.

ADECCO
178 East Golf Road, Schaumburg IL 60173. 847/310-8230. **Fax:** 847/310-8785. **Contact:** Manager. **World Wide Web address:** http://www.adecco.com. **Description:** A temporary agency. **Specializes in the areas of:** Accounting/Auditing; Administration; Banking; Computer Science/Software; Legal; Manufacturing; Personnel/Labor Relations; Sales; Secretarial; Technical. **Positions commonly filled include:** Advertising Clerk; Bank Officer/Manager; Branch Manager; Brokerage Clerk; Clerical Supervisor; Computer Programmer; Credit Manager; Customer Service Representative; Draftsperson; Human Resources Specialist; Systems Analyst; Typist/Word Processor. **Corporate headquarters location:** Redwood City CA. **Other U.S. locations:** Nationwide. **International locations:** Worldwide. **Average salary range of placements:** $20,000 - $29,999. **Number of placements per year:** 1 - 49.

ADECCO
200 West Madison Avenue, Suite 520, Chicago IL 60606. 312/372-6783. **Contact:** Dan Miller, Branch Manager. **World Wide Web address:** http://www.adecco.com. **Description:** A temporary agency. **Specializes in the areas of:** Accounting/Auditing; Administration; Banking; Computer Science/Software; Legal; Manufacturing; Personnel/Labor Relations; Sales; Secretarial; Technical. **Positions commonly filled include:** Advertising Clerk; Bank Officer/Manager; Branch Manager; Brokerage Clerk; Clerical Supervisor; Computer Programmer; Credit Manager; Customer Service Representative; Draftsperson; Human Resources Specialist; Systems Analyst; Typist/Word Processor. **Corporate headquarters location:** Redwood City CA. **Other U.S. locations:** Nationwide. **International locations:** Worldwide. **Average salary range of placements:** $20,000 - $29,999. **Number of placements per year:** 1 - 49.

ADECCO
1101 Lake Street, Oak Park IL 60301. 708/848-7800. **Fax:** 708/848-3288. **Contact:** Geri Dugin, Area Manager. **World Wide Web address:** http://www.adecco.com. **Description:** A temporary agency. **Specializes in the areas of:** Accounting/Auditing; Administration; Banking; Computer Science/Software; Legal; Manufacturing; Personnel/Labor Relations; Sales; Secretarial; Technical. **Positions commonly filled include:** Advertising Clerk; Bank Officer/Manager; Branch Manager; Brokerage Clerk; Clerical Supervisor; Credit Manager; Customer Service Representative; Draftsperson; Human Resources Specialist; Systems Analyst; Typist/Word Processor. **Benefits available to temporary workers:** 401(k); Dental Insurance; Medical Insurance; Paid Holidays; Referral Bonus Plan. **Corporate headquarters location:** Redwood City CA. **Other U.S. locations:** Nationwide. **International locations:** Worldwide. **Average salary range of placements:** $20,000 - $29,999. **Number of placements per year:** 1 - 49.

ADECCO
1560 Sherman Avenue, Evanston IL 60201. 847/328-8300. **Fax:** 847/328-1608. **Contact:** Branch Manager. **World Wide Web address:** http://www.adecco.com. **Description:** A temporary agency. **Specializes in the areas of:** Accounting/Auditing; Administration; Banking; Computer Science/Software; Legal; Manufacturing; Personnel/Labor Relations; Sales; Secretarial; Technical. **Positions commonly filled include:** Advertising Clerk; Bank Officer/Manager;

AQUENT PARTNERS
221 North LaSalle Street, Suite 1500, Chicago IL 60601. 312/332-6868. **Toll-free phone:** 877/PARTNER. **Fax:** 312/332-6865. **Contact:** Karen Desko, Manager. **World Wide Web address:** http://www.aquentpartners.com. **Description:** A temporary agency that provides placements for creative, Web, and technical professionals. Aquent Partners also provides some temp-to-perm, permanent, and contract placements. **Specializes in the areas of:** Administration; Art/Design; Communications; Computer Science/Software; Marketing. **Positions commonly filled include:** Computer Animator; Computer Engineer; Computer Operator; Computer Programmer; Computer Support Technician; Computer Technician; Content Developer; Database Administrator; Database Manager; Desktop Publishing Specialist; Editor; Editorial Assistant; Graphic Artist; Graphic Designer; Internet Services Manager; Managing Editor; MIS Specialist; Multimedia Designer; Network/Systems Administrator; Production Manager; Project Manager; Software Engineer; SQL Programmer; Systems Analyst; Systems Manager; Technical Writer/Editor; Webmaster. **Benefits available to temporary workers:** 401(k); Dental Insurance; Disability Coverage; Medical Insurance. **CEO:** John Chuang.

ASSURED STAFFING
651 West Terra Cotta, Suite 132, Crystal Lake IL 60014. 815/459-8367. **Fax:** 815/459-8450. **Contact:** Patti Conner, Division Manager. **Description:** A temporary agency. **Specializes in the areas of:** Administration; Industrial; Manufacturing; Personnel/Labor Relations; Secretarial. **Positions commonly filled include:** Account Manager; Account Representative; Accountant; Administrative Assistant; Administrative Manager; Advertising Clerk; Aircraft Mechanic/Engine Specialist; Applications Engineer; Assistant Manager; Automotive Mechanic; Bank Officer/Manager; Branch Manager; Claim Representative; Clerical Supervisor; Computer Operator; Credit Manager; Customer Service Representative; Database Manager; General Manager; Graphic Artist; Graphic Designer; Human Resources Specialist; Industrial Engineer; Industrial Production Manager; Management Trainee; Marketing Specialist; Purchasing Agent/Manager; Quality Control Supervisor; Sales Executive; Sales Representative; Secretary; Typist/Word Processor. **Benefits available to temporary workers:** Medical Insurance; Paid Holidays. **Corporate headquarters location:** Barrington IL. **Other area locations:** Marengo IL; Rockford IL; Wheaton IL. **Average salary range of placements:** $20,000 - $29,999. **Number of placements per year:** 500 - 999.

CONSULTIS INC.
566 West Adams Street, Suite 440, Chicago IL 60661. 312/669-0606. **Contact:** Manager. **Description:** A temporary agency that also provides some permanent placements. **Specializes in the areas of:** Computer Science/Software; Technical.

DAVIS STAFFING, INC.
21031 Governors Highway, Olympia Fields IL 60461. 708/747-6100. **Toll-free phone:** 888/61-DAVIS . **Fax:** 708/747-6189. **Contact:** Deborah Davis, Vice President. **E-mail address:** ddavis@davis-staffing.com. **Description:** A temporary agency that also provides some permanent placements. **Specializes in the areas of:** Administration; Banking; Clerical; Light Industrial. **Positions commonly filled include:** Accountant; Administrative Assistant; Administrative Manager;

Clerical Supervisor; Clerk; Customer Service Representative; Management Trainee; Operations Manager; Paralegal; Production Manager; Project Manager; Quality Control Supervisor; Secretary; Typist/Word Processor. **Other U.S. locations:** Oak Lawn IL; Munster IN. **Average salary range of placements:** Less than $20,000. **Number of placements per year:** 500 - 999.

DUNHILL STAFFING SERVICES OF CHICAGO
211 West Wacker Drive, Suite 1150, Chicago IL 60606. 312/346-0933. **Contact:** George Baker, Owner/President. **Description:** A temporary agency. **Specializes in the areas of:** Accounting/Auditing; Banking; Computer Science/Software; Finance; Sales.

DYNAMIC PEOPLE
570 Lake Cook Road, Suite 114, Deerfield IL 60015. 847/940-7040. **Fax:** 847/940-4500. **Contact:** Paul M. Duski, Owner. **E-mail address:** pduski@norrell.com. **Description:** A temporary agency that also provides some permanent placements. **Specializes in the areas of:** Accounting/Auditing; Health/Medical; Insurance; Legal; Personnel/Labor Relations; Sales; Secretarial. **Positions commonly filled include:** Accountant; Administrative Assistant; Claim Representative; Clerical Supervisor; Computer Operator; Credit Manager; Customer Service Representative; Financial Analyst; Graphic Artist; Human Resources Specialist; Medical Records Technician; Paralegal; Secretary. **Benefits available to temporary workers:** 401(k); Bonus Award/Plan; Daycare Assistance; Medical Insurance; Paid Holidays; Paid Vacation. **Corporate headquarters location:** Atlanta GA. **Other U.S. locations:** Nationwide. **Average salary range of placements:** $20,000 - $29,999. **Number of placements per year:** 500 - 999.

EXPRESS PERSONNEL SERVICES
977 Lakeview Parkway, Suite 190, Vernon Hills IL 60061. 847/816-8422. **Fax:** 847/816-0888. **Contact:** Cal Rich, Manager. **Description:** A temporary agency. **Specializes in the areas of:** Accounting/Auditing; Administration; Computer Science/Software; Engineering; Finance; General Management; Industrial; Manufacturing; Personnel/Labor Relations; Retail; Sales; Technical. **Positions commonly filled include:** Accountant/Auditor; Adjuster; Administrative Manager; Advertising Clerk; Aerospace Engineer; Automotive Mechanic; Bank Officer/Manager; Biochemist; Biological Scientist; Blue-Collar Worker Supervisor; Branch Manager; Brokerage Clerk; Budget Analyst; Buyer; Chemical Engineer; Chemist; Civil Engineer; Claim Representative; Clerical Supervisor; Computer Programmer; Credit Manager; Customer Service Representative; Design Engineer; Draftsperson; Editor; Electrical/Electronics Engineer; Environmental Engineer; Financial Analyst; General Manager; Hotel Manager; Human Resources Specialist; Industrial Engineer; Management Analyst/Consultant; Mechanical Engineer; Operations/Production Manager; Paralegal; Public Relations Specialist; Quality Control Supervisor; Restaurant/Food Service Manager; Securities Sales Representative; Software Engineer; Systems Analyst; Telecommunications Manager; Transportation/Traffic Specialist; Typist/Word Processor; Underwriter/Assistant Underwriter. **Average salary range of placements:** $20,000 - $29,999. **Number of placements per year:** 1000+.

FELLOWS PLACEMENT
1411 Opus Place, Executive Towers West, Suite 118, Downers Grove IL 60515. 630/968-2771. **Contact:** Manager. **Description:** A temporary agency that also provides some permanent placements. **Specializes in the areas of:** Accounting/Auditing; Administration; Banking; Clerical; Entry-Level Management; Finance; Insurance; Office Support; Sales; Secretarial. **Positions commonly filled include:** Accountant; Administrative Assistant; Advertising Clerk; Assistant Manager; Claim Representative; Clerical Supervisor; Computer Operator; Counselor; Credit Manager; Customer Service Representative; Graphic Designer; Management Trainee;

Sales Representative; Secretary; Typist/Word Processor. **Benefits available to temporary workers:** Bonus Award/Plan; Medical Insurance; Paid Holidays; Paid Vacation; Profit Sharing; Referral Bonus Plan. **Other U.S. locations:** Buffalo Grove IL; Rosemont IL; Schaumburg IL. **Average salary range of placements:** $30,000 - $50,000.

FELLOWS PLACEMENT
2150 East Lake Cook Road, Suite 180, Buffalo Grove IL 60089. 847/520-7300. **Contact:** Manager. **Description:** A temporary agency that also provides some permanent placements. **Specializes in the areas of:** Food; Health/Medical; Insurance; Manufacturing; Personnel/Labor Relations; Sales; Secretarial. **Positions commonly filled include:** Advertising Clerk; Clerical Supervisor; Customer Service Representative; Human Resources Specialist; Market Research Analyst; Services Sales Representative; Typist/Word Processor. **Average salary range of placements:** $20,000 - $29,999. **Number of placements per year:** 500 - 999.

FURST STAFFING SERVICES
P.O. Box 5863, Rockford IL 61125. 815/229-7815. **Contact:** Darlene Furst, President. **World Wide Web address:** http://www.furststaff.com. **Description:** A temporary agency. **Specializes in the areas of:** Accounting/Auditing; Banking; Clerical; Computer Science/Software; Engineering; Finance; Health/Medical; Insurance; Manufacturing; MIS/EDP; Secretarial. **Corporate headquarters location:** This Location.

HEALTHCARE TRAINING & PLACEMENT
260 East Chestnut Street, Chicago IL 60611. 312/787-9028. **Contact:** Phyllis Dobrin, Director. **Description:** A temporary agency that also provides some permanent placements. **Specializes in the areas of:** Dental; Health/Medical. **Positions commonly filled include:** Dental Assistant/Dental Hygienist; Dentist. **Average salary range of placements:** $20,000 - $29,999. **Number of placements per year:** 50 - 99.

INTERIM PERSONNEL
1515 West 22nd Street, Suite 750, Oak Brook IL 60523. **Toll-free phone:** 888/421-4686. **Fax:** 630/571-1629. **Contact:** Nicole Eckman, Manager. **E-mail address:** neckman@norrell.com. **World Wide Web address:** http://www.norrell.com. **Description:** Interim Personnel is a temporary agency that also provides some permanent placements.

INTERIM PERSONNEL
820 Broadway, Mattoon IL 61938. 217/235-2299. **Contact:** Wayne Meinhart, President. **Description:** A temporary agency that also provides some permanent placements. **Specializes in the areas of:** Personnel/Labor Relations. **Positions commonly filled include:** Accountant/Auditor; Advertising Clerk; Bank Officer/Manager; Blue-Collar Worker Supervisor; Claim Representative; Clerical Supervisor; Customer Service Representative; Draftsperson; Electrician; Financial Analyst; General Manager; Human Resources Specialist; Human Service Worker; Industrial Production Manager; Insurance Agent/Broker; Management Trainee; Services Sales Representative; Typist/Word Processor. **Other U.S. locations:** Nationwide. **Average salary range of placements:** Less than $20,000. **Number of placements per year:** 100 - 199.

INTERSTAFF
35 East Wacker Drive, Suite 2350, Chicago IL 60601. 312/551-0777. **Fax:** 312/551-1186. **Contact:** Denny Bennett, President. **E-mail address:** jobs@istaff.com. **World Wide Web address:** http://www.istaff.com. **Description:** A temporary agency. Through its Project Staff program, InterStaff places recent college graduates in internship-type temporary assignments. **Specializes in the areas of:** Accounting/Auditing; Administration; Advertising; Art/Design; Banking; Economics; Finance; General Management; Insurance; Legal; Nonprofit; Personnel/Labor Relations; Publishing; Sales; Secretarial. **Positions commonly filled include:** Account

Manager; Administrative Manager; Advertising Clerk; Bank Officer/Manager; Branch Manager; Brokerage Clerk; Budget Analyst; Cost Estimator; Customer Service Representative; Financial Analyst; General Manager; Human Resources Specialist; Management Trainee; Paralegal; Public Relations Specialist; Securities Sales Representative; Typist/Word Processor. **Other U.S. locations:** Indianapolis IN; Minneapolis MN; Milwaukee WI. **International locations:** Prague, Czech Republic. **Average salary range of placements:** $20,000 - $29,999. **Number of placements per year:** 500 - 999.

KELLY SCIENTIFIC RESOURCES
1101 West 31st Street, Suite 120, Downers Grove IL 60515. 630/964-0239. **Fax:** 630/964-0562. **Contact:** Branch Manager. **World Wide Web address:** http://www.kellyscientific.com. **Description:** A temporary agency. **Specializes in the areas of:** Biomedical; Chemicals; Pharmaceuticals; Scientific.

LAW CORPS LEGAL STAFFING
10 South Riverside Plaza, Suite 1800, Chicago IL 60606. 312/474-6060. **Contact:** Manager. **Description:** A temporary agency that also provides some temp-to-perm placements. **Specializes in the areas of:** Legal.

LOMACK AGENCY INC.
30 East Adams Street, Suite 401, Chicago IL 60603. 312/357-0117. **Fax:** 312/357-0119. **Contact:** Ms. Sterling, Vice President. **Description:** A temporary agency. **Specializes in the areas of:** Sales; Secretarial. **Positions commonly filled include:** Accountant/Auditor; Administrative Manager; Claim Representative; Clerical Supervisor; Human Resources Specialist; Licensed Practical Nurse; Management Trainee; Medical Records Technician; Typist/Word Processor. **Average salary range of placements:** $30,000 - $50,000. **Number of placements per year:** 50 - 99.

MACK & ASSOCIATES, LTD.
100 North LaSalle Street, Suite 2110, Chicago IL 60602. 312/368-0677. **Fax:** 312/368-1868. **Contact:** Charlene Gorzela, President. **E-mail address:** mail2mack@mackltd.com. **World Wide Web address:** http://www.mackltd.com. **Description:** A temporary agency that also provides some temp-to-perm and permanent placements. **Specializes in the areas of:** Administration; Personnel/Labor Relations; Real Estate; Secretarial. **Positions commonly filled include:** Account Manager; Account Representative; Accountant; Administrative Assistant; Administrative Manager; Assistant Manager; Clerical Supervisor; Customer Service Representative; Editorial Assistant; Human Resources Manager; Management Trainee; Purchasing Agent/Manager; Sales Representative; Secretary; Typist/Word Processor. **Average salary range of placements:** $30,000 - $49,999. **Number of placements per year:** 200 - 499.

MANPOWER TEMPORARY SERVICES
500 West Madison Street, Suite 2950, Chicago IL 60661. 312/648-4555. **Contact:** Branch Manager. **Description:** A temporary agency. **Specializes in the areas of:** Industrial; Office Support; Telecommunications; Word Processing. **Positions commonly filled include:** Accountant/Auditor; Administrative Assistant; Assembly Worker; Biological Scientist; Bookkeeper; Chemist; Computer Operator; Computer Support Technician; Designer; Desktop Publishing Specialist; Electrician; Inspector/Tester/Grader; Inventory Control Specialist; Machine Operator; Order Clerk; Painter; Proofreader; Secretary; Technical Writer/Editor; Typist/Word Processor; Welder. **Benefits available to temporary workers:** Life Insurance; Medical Insurance; Paid Holidays; Paid Vacation. **Corporate headquarters location:** Milwaukee WI. **Number of placements per year:** 1000+.

MANPOWER TEMPORARY SERVICES
1324 East Empire Street, Bloomington IL 61701. 309/663-1324. **Contact:** Manager. **Description:** A temporary agency. **Specializes in the areas of:** Accounting/Auditing; Banking; Engineering; Industrial; Insurance; Legal; Personnel/Labor Relations. **Positions commonly filled include:** Blue-Collar Worker Supervisor; Computer Programmer; Customer Service Representative; Human Resources Specialist; Market Research Analyst; Mechanical Engineer; Paralegal; Quality Control Supervisor; Systems Analyst. **Corporate headquarters location:** Milwaukee WI. **Number of placements per year:** 1000+.

MANPOWER TEMPORARY SERVICES
735 Main Street, Peoria IL 61602. 309/674-4163. **Fax:** 309/673-0940. **Contact:** John E. Vilberg, Owner. **Description:** A temporary agency. **Specializes in the areas of:** Engineering; Health/Medical; Personnel/Labor Relations. **Positions commonly filled include:** Administrative Manager; Advertising Clerk; Aerospace Engineer; Blue-Collar Worker Supervisor; Chemical Engineer; Civil Engineer; Clerical Supervisor; Customer Service Representative; Design Engineer; Designer; Draftsperson; Electrical/Electronics Engineer; Environmental Engineer; Industrial Engineer; Mechanical Engineer; Quality Control Supervisor; Structural Engineer; Typist/Word Processor. **Corporate headquarters location:** Milwaukee WI. **Average salary range of placements:** $20,000 - $29,999. **Number of placements per year:** 50 - 99.

McCULLUM ASSOCIATES INC.
36 South Wabash Avenue, Suite 714, Chicago IL 60603. 312/578-9849. **Contact:** Sylvia L. McCullum, President. **Description:** A temporary agency. **Specializes in the areas of:** Advertising; Architecture/Construction; Engineering; Publishing; Secretarial. **Positions commonly filled include:** Administrative Assistant; Architect; Civil Engineer; Computer Operator; Computer Programmer; Cost Estimator; Database Manager; Draftsperson; Electrical/Electronics Engineer; Graphic Designer; Mechanical Engineer; MIS Specialist; Paralegal; Secretary; Social Worker; Systems Analyst; Technical Writer/Editor; Typist/Word Processor. **Average salary range of placements:** $20,000 - $29,999. **Number of placements per year:** 200 - 499.

MEDIA STAFFING NETWORK
150 East Huron Street, Suite 825, Chicago IL 60611. 312/944-9194. **Fax:** 312/944-9195. **Contact:** Account Manager. **Description:** A temporary agency. **Specializes in the areas of:** Advertising; Advertising Sales; Broadcasting; Media Sales. **Corporate headquarters location:** This Location.

MEDICAL TECHNICAL PLACEMENTS, INC.
3166 North Lincoln Avenue, Suite 314, Chicago IL 60657. 773/528-6070. **Toll-free phone:** 800/570-4671. **Fax:** 773/528-1226. **Contact:** Manager. **Description:** A temporary agency. **Specializes in the areas of:** Health/Medical; Personnel/Labor Relations; Technical. **Positions commonly filled include:** EEG Technologist; EKG Technician; Licensed Practical Nurse; Medical Assistant; Medical Technologist; Radiological Technologist. **Average salary range of placements:** Less than $20,000.

NJW & ASSOCIATES, INC.
One East Wacker Drive, Suite 2120, Chicago IL 60601. 312/464-1999. **Fax:** 312/464-1777. **Contact:** Norma Williams, President/CEO. **Description:** A temporary agency. **Specializes in the areas of:** Accounting/Auditing; Administration; General Management; Legal; Personnel/Labor Relations; Sales; Secretarial. **Positions commonly filled include:** Customer Service Representative; Health Services Worker; Human Resources Manager; Operations/Production Manager; Paralegal; Services Sales Representative; Software Engineer; Systems Analyst; Technical Writer/Editor; Telecommunications Manager; Typist/Word Processor. **Other U.S. locations:** Skokie IL. **Average salary range of placements:** $30,000 - $50,000.

NORRELL SERVICES
11 South LaSalle Street, Suite 2155, Chicago IL 60603. 312/346-9276. **Contact:** Branch Manager. **Description:** A temporary agency that also provides contract services. **Specializes in the areas of:** Personnel/Labor Relations; Secretarial. **Positions commonly filled include:** Accountant/Auditor; Administrative Manager; Human Resources Specialist; Typist/Word Processor. **Corporate headquarters location:** Atlanta GA. **Other U.S. locations:** Nationwide. **Number of placements per year:** 1000+.

OLSTEN STAFFING SERVICES
16 West Ontario, Chicago IL 60610. 312/661-0490. **Fax:** 312/661-0491. **Contact:** Melissa Brown, Recruiting Coordinator. **E-mail address:** olsten@xnet.com. **World Wide Web address:** http://www.olsten-chicago.com. **Description:** A temporary agency. **Specializes in the areas of:** Accounting/Auditing; Banking; Computer Science/Software; Industrial; Insurance; Legal; Sales. **Positions commonly filled include:** Computer Programmer; MIS Specialist; Multimedia Designer; Software Engineer; Systems Analyst; Technical Writer/Editor. **Number of placements per year:** 1000+.

OLSTEN STAFFING SERVICES
880 West 75th Street, Willowbrook IL 60521. 630/794-9675. **Fax:** 630/794-9725. **Contact:** Monica Malte, Branch Manager. **Description:** A temporary agency. **Specializes in the areas of:** Accounting/Auditing; Administration; Computer Science/Software; Legal; Manufacturing; Personnel/Labor Relations. **Positions commonly filled include:** Accountant/Auditor; Administrative Manager; Attorney; Branch Manager; Clerical Supervisor; Computer Programmer; Credit Manager; Customer Service Rep.; Financial Analyst; Human Resources Specialist; Paralegal; Systems Analyst. **Average salary range of placements:** $20,000 - $29,999. **Number of placements per year:** 100 - 199.

PILLAR PERSONNEL
1111 Plaza Drive, Suite 530, Schaumburg IL 60173. 847/995-1200. **Fax:** 847/619-7255. **Contact:** Michelle Mouhelis, Staffing Coordinator. **Description:** A temporary agency. **Specializes in the areas of:** Accounting/Auditing; Administration; Clerical; Secretarial; Word Processing. **Positions commonly filled include:** Clerical Supervisor; Customer Service Representative; Typist/Word Processor. **Average salary range of placements:** $20,000 - $29,999. **Number of placements per year:** 200 - 499.

PRO STAFF PERSONNEL SERVICES
10 South Wacker Drive, Suite 2250, Chicago IL 60606. 312/575-2120. **Contact:** Manager. **World Wide Web address:** http://www.prostaff.com. **Description:** A temporary agency. **Specializes in the areas of:** Accounting/Auditing; Administration; Information Technology; Office Support.

PROFILE TEMPORARY SERVICE
222 North LaSalle Street, Suite 450, Chicago IL 60601. 312/541-4141. **Contact:** Manager. **Description:** A temporary agency. **Specializes in the areas of:** Accounting/Auditing; Banking; Finance; Insurance; Manufacturing. **Number of placements per year:** 500 - 999.

RPH ON THE GO, USA, INC.
3330 Old Glenview Road, Suite 9, Wilmette IL 60091. 847/251-9389. **Toll-free phone:** 800/553-7359. **Fax:** 847/251-9690. **Contact:** Manager. **World Wide Web address:** http://www.rphonthego.com. **Description:** A temporary agency focusing on the placement of pharmacy professionals. **Specializes in the areas of:** General Management; Health/Medical. **Positions commonly filled include:** Pharmacist. **Average salary range of placements:** More than $50,000.

RELIEF MEDICAL SERVICES, INC.
323 East Ontario, Chicago IL 60611. 312/266-1486. **Fax:** 312/266-0732. **Contact:** Director of Nursing.

Description: Relief Medical Services, Inc. is a temporary agency. **Specializes in the areas of:** Health/Medical. **Positions commonly filled include:** Licensed Practical Nurse; Medical Records Technician; Registered Nurse; Surgical Technician. **Other area locations:** Skokie IL. **Average salary range of placements:** $20,000 - $29,999. **Number of placements per year:** 1000+.

REMEDY INTELLIGENT STAFFING
6 North Michigan Avenue, Suite 1505, Chicago IL 60602. 312/630-9090. **Fax:** 312/630-9069. **Contact:** Vice President of Operations. **Description:** Remedy Intelligent Staffing is a temporary agency. **Specializes in the areas of:** Accounting/Auditing; Administration; Banking; Computer Science/Software; Finance; Food; General Management; Health/Medical; Industrial; Insurance; Legal; Manufacturing; Nonprofit; Personnel/Labor Relations; Publishing; Retail; Sales; Secretarial; Technical. **Positions commonly filled include:** Accountant/Auditor; Administrative Manager; Advertising Clerk; Bank Officer/Manager; Blue-Collar Worker Supervisor; Branch Manager; Brokerage Clerk; Claim Representative; Clerical Supervisor; Computer Programmer; Credit Manager; Customer Service Representative; Editor; General Manager; Health Services Manager; Hotel Manager; Human Resources Specialist; Industrial Production Manager; Librarian; Management Trainee; Manufacturer's/Wholesaler's Sales Representative; Market Research Analyst; Medical Records Technician; MIS Specialist; Operations/Production Manager; Paralegal; Public Relations Specialist; Purchasing Agent/Manager; Restaurant/Food Service Manager; Services Sales Representative; Surveyor; Systems Analyst; Technical Writer/Editor; Telecommunications Analyst; Typist/Word Processor; Underwriter/Assistant Underwriter. **Corporate headquarters location:** Aliso Viejo CA. **Other U.S. locations:** Nationwide.

RIGHT SERVICES INC.
3960 West 95th Street, Evergreen Park IL 60805. 708/636-6800. **Fax:** 708/636-1784. **Contact:** Branch Manager. **Description:** Right Services Inc. is a temporary agency. **Specializes in the areas of:** Accounting/Auditing; Administration; Banking; Computer Science/Software; Finance; Health/Medical; Insurance; Legal; Manufacturing; Nonprofit; Personnel/Labor Relations; Sales; Secretarial. **Positions commonly filled include:** Financial Analyst; Human Resources Specialist; Medical Records Technician; Public Relations Specialist; Purchasing Agent/Manager; Quality Control Supervisor; Statistician; Typist/Word Processor. **Average salary range of placements:** $20,000 - $29,999. **Number of placements per year:** 500 - 999.

RIGHT SERVICES INC.
53 West Jackson Boulevard, Suite 1315, Chicago IL 60604. 312/427-4352. **Fax:** 312/427-3145. **Contact:** Branch Manager. **Description:** Right Services Inc. is a temporary agency that also provides some permanent placements. **Specializes in the areas of:** Accounting/Auditing; Administration; Banking; Finance; General Management; Health/Medical; Nonprofit; Personnel/Labor Relations; Sales; Secretarial. **Positions commonly filled include:** Accountant/Auditor; Clerical Supervisor; Customer Service Representative; Financial Analyst; General Manager; Human Resources Specialist; Human Service Worker; Medical Records Technician; Multimedia Designer; Purchasing Agent/Manager; Typist/Word Processor.

RIGHT SERVICES INC.
477 East Butterfield Road, Suite 100, Lombard IL 60148. 630/969-7010. **Contact:** Sue Murphy, Office Manager. **Description:** A temporary agency. **Specializes in the areas of:** Accounting/Auditing; Banking; Finance; General Management; Health/Medical; Personnel/Labor Relations; Secretarial. **Positions commonly filled include:** Accountant/Auditor; Customer Service Representative; Human Resources Specialist; Paralegal;

Typist/Word Processor. **Average salary range of placements:** $20,000 - $29,999. **Number of placements per year:** 1000+.

SEVILLE TEMPORARY SERVICES
180 North Michigan Avenue, Suite 1510, Chicago IL 60601. 312/368-1144. **Fax:** 312/368-0207. **Contact:** Matt Bukovy, Operations Manager. **E-mail address:** sevilleinc@aol.com. **Description:** A temporary agency. **Specializes in the areas of:** Legal; Personnel/Labor Relations; Secretarial. **Positions commonly filled include:** Insurance Agent/Broker; Paralegal; Typist/Word Processor; Underwriter/Assistant Underwriter.

SHANNONWOOD STAFFERS, INC.
150 East Cook Avenue, Libertyville IL 60048. 847/362-6100. **Fax:** 847/362-1826. **Contact:** Manager. **Description:** A temporary agency. **Specializes in the areas of:** Computer Science/Software; Sales; Secretarial. **Positions commonly filled include:** Claim Representative; Clerical Supervisor; Customer Service Representative; Services Sales Representative; Typist/Word Processor. **Average salary range of placements:** $20,000 - $29,999. **Number of placements per year:** 1 - 49.

SNELLING PERSONNEL SERVICES
999 East Touhy Avenue, Suite 135, Des Plaines IL 60018. 847/296-1026. **Contact:** Manager. **Description:** A temporary agency. **Specializes in the areas of:** Clerical; Food; Sales. **Corporate headquarters location:** Dallas TX. **Other U.S. locations:** Nationwide.

SNELLING PERSONNEL SERVICES
2029 Ogden Avenue, Lisle IL 60532. 630/515-9088. **Fax:** 630/515-9616. **Contact:** Personnel Manager. **Description:** A temporary agency. **Specializes in the areas of:** Administration. **Positions commonly filled include:** Customer Service Representative; Light Industrial Worker. **Corporate headquarters location:** Dallas TX. **Other U.S. locations:** Nationwide.

SNYDER & ASSOCIATES INC.
111 North Sangamon Street, Suite 3, Lincoln IL 62656. 217/732-1108. **Contact:** Manager. **Description:** A temporary agency. **Specializes in the areas of:** Administration; Clerical; Industrial.

STAFFING TEAM INTERNATIONAL
1100 Jorie Boulevard, Suite 132, Oak Brook IL 60523. 630/573-8640. **Fax:** 630/573-8644. **Contact:** Christy Catalano-Penman, Employment Counselor. **Description:** A temporary agency. **Specializes in the areas of:** Office Support; Sales; Secretarial; Technical; Transportation. **Positions commonly filled include:** Accountant/Auditor; Administrative Manager; Blue-Collar Worker Supervisor; Branch Manager; Brokerage Clerk; Buyer; Claim Representative; Clerical Supervisor; Computer Programmer; Customer Service Representative; Designer; Draftsperson; Financial Analyst; General

Manager; Human Service Worker; Management Trainee; Market Research Analyst; MIS Specialist; Operations/Production Manager; Paralegal; Public Relations Specialist; Purchasing Agent/Manager; Services Sales Representative; Systems Analyst; Transportation/Traffic Specialist; Typist/Word Processor. **Average salary range of placements:** $20,000 - $29,999. **Number of placements per year:** 500 - 999.

STIVERS TEMPORARY PERSONNEL, INC.
1225 Corporate Boulevard, Suite 100, Aurora IL 60504. 630/851-9330. **Contact:** Manager. **Description:** A temporary agency. **Specializes in the areas of:** Accounting/Auditing; Banking; Clerical; Engineering; Finance; Health/Medical; Insurance; Legal; Manufacturing; MIS/EDP; Personnel/Labor Relations; Real Estate; Transportation.

TEMPFLEET
8 South Michigan Avenue, Suite 1306, Chicago IL 60603. 312/236-0155. **Fax:** 312/236-4629. **Contact:** President. **Description:** A temporary agency. **Specializes in the areas of:** Accounting/Auditing; Secretarial; Word Processing.

TEMPORARY ASSOCIATES
675 East Irving Park Road, Roselle IL 60172. 630/893-7336. **Contact:** Manager. **Description:** A temporary agency. **Specializes in the areas of:** Administration; Banking; Food; Industrial; Sales; Secretarial. **Positions commonly filled include:** Accountant/Auditor; Blue-Collar Worker Supervisor; Claim Representative; Clerical Supervisor; Customer Service Representative; Operations/Production Manager; Quality Control Supervisor; Services Sales Representative; Telecommunications Manager; Transportation/Traffic Specialist; Typist/Word Processor; Video Production Coordinator. **Average salary range of placements:** $20,000 - $29,999. **Number of placements per year:** 100 - 199.

WORKING WORLD INC.
P.O. Box 58, Richmond IL 60071. 815/678-2442. **Fax:** 815/678-2616. **Contact:** Branch Manager. **World Wide Web address:** http://www.work-world.com. **Description:** A temporary agency. **Specializes in the areas of:** Accounting/Auditing; Administration; Computer Science/Software; Finance; General Management; Industrial; Insurance; Legal; Manufacturing; Personnel/Labor Relations; Sales; Secretarial; Technical. **Positions commonly filled include:** Accountant/Auditor; Blue-Collar Worker Supervisor; Customer Service Representative; Industrial Production Manager; Management Trainee; Manufacturer's/Wholesaler's Sales Rep.; Medical Records Technician; MIS Specialist; Operations/Production Manager; Quality Control Supervisor; Typist/Word Processor; Underwriter/Assistant Underwriter. **Corporate headquarters location:** Crystal Lake IL. **Other area locations:** Woodstock IL. **Number of placements per year:** 200 - 499.

CONTRACT SERVICES FIRMS

ADECCO/TAD TECHNICAL SERVICES
1717 North Naper Boulevard, Suite 101, Naperville IL 60563. 630/505-1913. **Contact:** Manager. **Description:** A contract services firm.

ADVANCED CLINICAL
ADVANCED PERSONNEL
1300 East Woodfield Road, Suite 610, Schaumburg IL 60173. 847/995-9222. **Fax:** 847/995-9290. **Contact:** Kay Tracey, Branch Manager. **Description:** A contract services firm that focuses on placements in the biology and health/medical fields. Advanced Personnel (also at this location) is a temporary agency that places accounting, administrative, and customer service personnel. Founded in 1993. **NOTE:** Resumes should be sent to Dave Kihm, Internet Manager at 501 North Riverside, Suite 204, Gurnee IL 60031. **Specializes in**

the areas of: Health/Medical. **Positions commonly filled include:** Physician; Pharmacist; Registered Nurse; Emergency Medical Technician; Medical Records Technician; Respiratory Therapist.. **Benefits available to temporary workers:** 401(k). **Corporate headquarters location:** This Location. **Other U.S. locations:** San Francisco CA; Atlanta GA. **Average salary range of placements:** More than $50,000. **Number of placements per year:** 50 - 99.

ALTERNATIVE RESOURCES CORPORATION
222 South Riverside Plaza, Suite 830, Chicago IL 60606. 312/474-9200. **Contact:** Recruiter. **Description:** A contract services firm that focuses on placing mainframe and networking professionals. **Specializes in the areas of:** Computer Science/Software; Information Technology; Technical. **Positions commonly filled**

include: Computer Operator; Consultant; Database Manager; MIS Manager; Software Engineer; Systems Analyst; Systems Manager; Technical Writer/Editor; Telecommunications Manager; Vice President; Webmaster. **Corporate headquarters location:** Lincolnshire IL. **Other U.S. locations:** Nationwide.

AMERICAN CONTRACT SERVICES, INC.
2215 York Road, Suite 204, Oak Brook IL 60523. 630/571-4100. **Toll-free phone:** 800/899-7467. **Fax:** 630/990-1009. **Contact:** Manager. **Description:** A contract services firm. **Specializes in the areas of:** Architecture/Construction; Engineering; Food; Industrial; Technical. **Positions commonly filled include:** Architect; Chemical Engineer; Civil Engineer; Construction Contractor; Cost Estimator; Draftsperson; Environmental Engineer; Mining Engineer; Nuclear Engineer; Petroleum Engineer; Structural Engineer. **Average salary range of placements:** $30,000 - $50,000. **Number of placements per year:** 100 - 199.

CDI CORPORATION
2485 Federal Drive, Building 3, Decatur IL 62526. 217/875-0393. **Contact:** Manager. **World Wide Web address:** http://www.cdicorp.com. **Description:** A contract services firm. **Specializes in the areas of:** Engineering; Technical. **Corporate headquarters location:** Philadelphia PA. **Other U.S. locations:** Nationwide. **International locations:** Worldwide.

CARSON MANAGEMENT ASSOCIATES
456 Fulton, Suite 394, Peoria IL 61602. 309/637-7800. **Fax:** 309/637-7836. **Contact:** James Carson, Owner. **Description:** A contract services firm. **Specializes in the areas of:** Accounting/Auditing; Administration; Art/Design; Computer Science/Software; Engineering; Finance; General Management; Manufacturing; Personnel/Labor Relations; Publishing; Sales; Technical. **Positions commonly filled include:** Accountant/Auditor; Aerospace Engineer; Agricultural Engineer; Blue-Collar Worker Supervisor; Branch Manager; Chemical Engineer; Civil Engineer; Computer Programmer; Cost Estimator; Customer Service Representative; Design Engineer; Designer; Draftsperson; Electrical/Electronics Engineer; Electrician; Environmental Engineer; Financial Analyst; General Manager; Health Services Manager; Human Resources Manager; Industrial Engineer; Manufacturer's/Wholesaler's Sales Rep.; Mechanical Engineer; Metallurgical Engineer; MIS Specialist; Multimedia Designer; Operations/Production Manager; Purchasing Agent/Manager; Quality Control Supervisor; Software Engineer; Systems Analyst; Technical Writer/Editor; Transportation/Traffic Specialist. **Average salary range of placements:** $30,000 - $50,000. **Number of placements per year:** 1 - 49.

COMFORCE TELECOM, INC.
110 East Schiller Street, Suite 208, Elmhurst IL 60126. 630/279-9200. **Fax:** 630/279-9310. **Contact:** Manager. **Description:** A contract services firm that also provides some permanent placements. **Specializes in the areas of:** Telecommunications.

EDP CONTRACT SERVICES
2115 Butterfield Road, Suite 101, Oak Brook IL 60523. 630/620-7171. **Fax:** 630/620-6932. **Contact:** Manager. **Description:** A contract services firm. **Specializes in the areas of:** Computer Science/Software. **Positions commonly filled include:** Computer Programmer; Software Engineer; Systems Analyst; Technical Writer/Editor. **Number of placements per year:** 200 - 499.

HALL KINION
475 Martingale Road, Suite 450, Schaumburg IL 60173. 847/517-9500. **Fax:** 847/517-9400. **Contact:** Manager. **World Wide Web address:** http://www.hallkinion.com. **Description:** A contract services firm that also provides some permanent placements. **Specializes in the areas of:** Information Systems; Information Technology; Internet Development; Network Administration; Quality

Assurance; Systems Administration; Systems Design; Technical Writing.

HALL KINION
One Financial Place, 440 South La Salle Street, Suite 3904, Chicago IL 60605. **Toll-free phone:** 888/913-0111. **Fax:** 312/913-1180. **Contact:** Manager. **E-mail address:** chresume@hallkinion.com. **World Wide Web address:** http://www.hallkinion.com. **Description:** A contract services firm that also provides some permanent placements. **Specializes in the areas of:** Computer Hardware/Software; Information Systems; Information Technology; Internet Development; Network Administration; Quality Assurance; Systems Administration; Systems Design.

OMEGA TECHNICAL CORPORATION
15 Spinning Wheel Road, Suite 120, Hinsdale IL 60521. 630/986-8116. **Fax:** 630/986-0036. **Contact:** Jason Lentz, Senior Recruiter. **E-mail address:** chicago@omegajobs.com. **World Wide Web address:** http://www.omegatechnical.com. **Description:** A contract services firm. **Specializes in the areas of:** Architecture/Construction; Computer Science/Software; Engineering; Industrial; Technical. **Positions commonly filled include:** Administrative Assistant; Applications Engineer; Architect; AS400 Programmer Analyst; Biomedical Engineer; Chemical Engineer; Civil Engineer; Computer Animator; Computer Engineer; Computer Operator; Computer Programmer; Computer Support Technician; Database Administrator; Database Manager; Network Administrator; Sales Representative; Secretary; Software Engineer; SQL Programmer; Systems Analyst; Systems Manager; Technical Writer/Editor; Webmaster. **Benefits available to temporary workers:** 401(k); Dental Insurance; Medical Insurance; Paid Vacation. **Corporate headquarters location:** Brookfield WI. **Other U.S. locations:** Tampa FL; Chicago IL; Detroit MI; Columbus OH; Austin TX; Houston TX. **Average salary range of placements:** $30,000 - $49,999. **Number of placements per year:** 100 - 199.

THE POLLAK AND SKAN GROUP
25 NW Point Boulevard, Suite 900, Elk Grove Village IL 60007. 847/437-8888. **Toll-free phone:** 800/544-7817. **Fax:** 847/437-9073. **Contact:** Account Executive. **World Wide Web address:** http://www.pscts.com. **Description:** A contract services firm. **Specializes in the areas of:** Computer Science/Software; Engineering; Industrial; Manufacturing; Technical. **Positions commonly filled include:** Aerospace Engineer; Aircraft Mechanic/Engine Specialist; Architect; Biomedical Engineer; Chemical Engineer; Chemist; Civil Engineer; Clinical Lab Technician; Computer Programmer; Cost Estimator; Design Engineer; Designer; Draftsperson; Electrical/Electronics Engineer; Electrician; Environmental Engineer; Food Scientist/Technologist; Industrial Engineer; Mechanical Engineer; Metallurgical Engineer; MIS Specialist; Multimedia Designer; Nuclear Engineer; Petroleum Engineer; Quality Control Supervisor; Software Engineer; Stationary Engineer; Structural Engineer; Systems Analyst; Technical Writer/Editor. **Corporate headquarters location:** Chicago IL. **Other U.S. locations:** Nationwide.

TDF CORPORATION
1717 Park Street, Suite 301, Naperville IL 60563-8478. 630/355-1800. **Fax:** 630/355-1338. **Contact:** Steve Levenske, Commercial Operations. **E-mail address:** tdfcorp@aol.com. **Description:** A contract services firm that places professionals in systems integration, software services, technology deployment, application development, program management, management services, logistics, information engineering, strategic business and systems planning, migrations, and business process re-engineering. **Specializes in the areas of:** Administration; Computer Science/Software; Engineering. **Positions commonly filled include:** Computer Programmer; Design Engineer; Electrical/Electronics Engineer; Human Resources Manager; Management Analyst/Consultant; MIS

Specialist; Services Sales Representative; Software Engineer; Systems Analyst; Technical Writer/Editor. **Average salary range of placements:** $30,000 - $50,000. **Number of placements per year:** 1 - 49.

H.L. YOH COMPANY
1420 Kensington Road, Suite 116, Oak Brook IL 60523. 630/990-8800. **Contact:** Manager. **Description:** A contract services firm. **Specializes in the areas of:** Engineering; Scientific.

CAREER/OUTPLACEMENT COUNSELING FIRMS

A ADVANCED RESUME SERVICE, INC.
1900 East Golf Road, Suite M100, Schaumburg IL 60173. 847/517-1088. **Fax:** 847/517-1126. **Contact:** Steven Provenzano, President/CPRW. **E-mail address:** advresumes@aol.com. **World Wide Web address:** http://www.topsecretresumes.com. **Description:** A resume writing and career/outplacement counseling firm. The firm provides free resume analysis, writing, and printing as well as personal interviews with clients. A Advanced Resume Service also conducts career marketing seminars for large corporations. **Corporate headquarters location:** This Location.

A ADVANCED RESUME SERVICE, INC.
701 East Irving Park Road, Suite 201, Roselle IL 60172. 630/582-1088. **Contact:** Steven Provenzano, President/CPRW. **World Wide Web address:** http://www.topsecretresumes.com. **Description:** A resume writing and career/outplacement counseling firm. The firm provides free resume analysis, writing, and printing as well as personal interviews with clients. A Advanced Resume Service also conducts career marketing seminars for large corporations. **Corporate headquarters location:** Schaumburg IL.

ABSOLUTE CAREER SERVICES
1122 Westgate Street, Suite 201, Oak Park IL 60301. **Toll-free phone:** 800/747-2987. **Contact:** Robert Meier, Owner/Founder. **E-mail address:** wmmeier@aol.com. **World Wide Web address:** http://www.absolutecareer.com. **Description:** A career/resume counseling firm, focusing on strategic career planning, expert composition, and interview preparation. The firm also provides free digital formats for Web postings. **Corporate headquarters location:** Chicago IL. **Other area locations:** 333 North Michigan Avenue, Chicago IL 60601, 312/726-2350.

ABSOLUTE CAREER SERVICES
WILLIAM MEIER AND ASSOCIATES
333 North Michigan Avenue, Chicago IL 60601. 312/726-2350. **Toll-free phone:** 800/747-2987. **Fax:** 312/726-2790. **Contact:** Robert Meier, Owner/Founder. **E-mail address:** wmmeier@aol.com. **World Wide Web address:** http://www.absolutecareer.com. **Description:** A career/resume counseling firm, focusing on strategic career planning, expert composition, and interview preparation. William Meier and Associates (also at this location) provides outplacement counseling services. **Corporate headquarters location:** This Location.

ALL WRITE RESUMES, INC.
287 Peterson Road, Libertyville IL 60048. 847/816-1800. **Fax:** 847/816-1822. **Contact:** Alice Jorgensen, Chief Writer. **Description:** A career/outplacement counseling and resume writing firm.

CORPORATE ORGANIZING AND RESEARCH SERVICES, INC.
One Pierce Place, Suite 300 East, Itasca IL 60143. 630/250-8677. **Contact:** Manager. **Description:** A career/outplacement counseling firm.

SHEA ASSOCIATES
800 Enterprise Drive, Suite 128, Oak Brook IL 60523. 630/573-4266. **Contact:** Manager. **Description:** A career/outplacement counseling firm.

UNITED WORKFORCE DEVELOPMENT
700 East Oak Street, Canton IL 61520-3168. 309/647-5680. **Fax:** 309/647-5688. **Contact:** Karen Latimer, Manager. **Description:** A career counseling firm that also provides employment training.

EXECUTIVE SEARCH FIRMS

A.B.S.
8515 Cedar Place Drive, Suite 103B, Indianapolis IN 46240. 317/251-0125. **Fax:** 317/251-0127. **Contact:** Manager. **Description:** An executive search firm. **Specializes in the areas of:** Sales.

ACCOUNTANTS EXECUTIVE SEARCH
ACCOUNTANTS ON CALL
111 Monument Circle, Suite 3510, Indianapolis IN 46204. 317/686-0001. **Fax:** 317/686-0007. **Contact:** Manager. **Description:** An executive search firm. Accountants On Call (also at this location) is a temporary agency. **Specializes in the areas of:** Accounting/Auditing.

AGRA PLACEMENTS, LTD.
55 South Wabash, P.O. Box 4, Peru IN 46970. 765/472-1988. **Fax:** 765/472-7568. **Contact:** Dave Lawrence, Manager. **E-mail address:** agrain@netusa1.net. **World Wide Web address:** http://www.agraplacements.com. **Description:** An executive search firm. **Specializes in the areas of:** Agri-Business; Chemicals.

ALEXANDER & ASSOCIATES
527 Park Place Court, Suite 100, Mishawaka IN 46545. 219/271-0594. **Fax:** 219/272-7566. **Contact:** Manager. **Description:** An executive search firm. **Specializes in the areas of:** Manufacturing. **Positions commonly filled include:** General Manager; Human Resources Specialist; Product Engineer. **Average salary range of placements:** $30,000 - $50,000.

THE BENNETT GROUP
5640 Professional Circle, Indianapolis IN 46241. 317/247-1240. **Contact:** Manager. **Description:** An executive search firm. **Specializes in the areas of:** Electronics; Engineering; High-Tech.

CANIS MAJOR, INC.
HR QUEST
P.O. Box 742, Carmel IN 46032-0742. 317/581-8880. **Toll-free phone:** 800/536-4276. **Fax:** 317/581-8856. **Contact:** Carol Albright, President. **Description:** An executive search firm operating on a contingency basis. **Specializes in the areas of:** Administration; Computer Science/Software; Engineering; Health/Medical; Industrial; Insurance; Manufacturing; MIS/EDP; Personnel/Labor Relations; Safety. **Positions commonly filled include:** Adjuster; Claim Representative; Electrical/Electronics Engineer; Human Resources Manager; Industrial Engineer; Licensed Practical Nurse; Registered Nurse; Underwriter/Assistant Underwriter. **Average salary range of placements:** $30,000 - $50,000. **Number of placements per year:** 1 - 49.

CAREERS UNLIMITED INC.
1238 South Main Street, Elkhart IN 46516. 219/293-0659. **Fax:** 219/294-1254. **Contact:** Steve Berger, President/Owner. **Description:** An executive search firm operating on a contingency basis. The firm also provides some contract services. **Specializes in the areas of:** Computer Science/Software; Engineering; General Management; Industrial; Manufacturing. **Positions commonly filled include:** Computer Programmer; Electrical/Electronics Engineer; Industrial Engineer; Industrial Production Manager; Manufacturing Engineer; Mechanical Engineer; Production Manager; Systems Analyst. **Number of placements per year:** 1 - 49.

CHEVIGNY PERSONNEL AGENCY
P.O. Box 11342, Merrillville IN 46411. 219/663-7801. **Fax:** 219/663-7819. **Contact:** Jule Chevigny, President. **Description:** An executive search firm operating on a contingency basis. **Specializes in the areas of:** Engineering; Industrial; Manufacturing; MIS/EDP. **Positions commonly filled include:** Accountant/Auditor; Bank Officer/Manager; Chemical Engineer; Civil Engineer; Computer Programmer; Design Engineer; Electrical/Electronics Engineer; Environmental Engineer; Hotel Manager; Industrial Engineer; Industrial Production Manager; Mechanical Engineer; Metallurgical Engineer; MIS Specialist; Operations/Production Manager; Petroleum Engineer; Purchasing Agent/Manager; Quality Control Supervisor; Restaurant/Food Service Manager; Structural Engineer; Systems Analyst.

COMPUSEARCH
1657 Commerce Drive, Suite 15B, South Bend IN 46628. 219/239-2970. **Toll-free phone:** 800/692-2977. **Fax:** 219/239-2980. **Contact:** James H. Mead, CDP, Project Manager/System Administrator. **E-mail address:** compusearch@skyenet.net. **World Wide Web address:** http://www.compusearchsb.com. **Description:** An executive search firm operating on both retainer and contingency bases. Client company pays fee. **Specializes in the areas of:** Computer Science/Software. **Positions commonly filled include:** Applications Engineer; AS400 Programmer Analyst; Computer Engineer; Computer Programmer; Computer Scientist; Computer Support Technician; Computer Technician; Consultant; Database Administrator; Database Manager; Internet Services Manager; MIS Specialist; Network/Systems Administrator; Software Engineer; SQL Programmer; Systems Analyst; Systems Manager; Vice President; Webmaster. **Other U.S. locations:** Nationwide. **Number of placements per year:** 1 - 49.

THE CONSULTING FORUM, INC.
9200 Keystone Crossing, Indianapolis IN 46240. 317/580-4800. **Fax:** 317/580-4801. **Contact:** Don Kellner, President. **E-mail address:** dkellner@consultingforum.com. **Description:** An executive search firm operating on both retainer and contingency bases. **Specializes in the areas of:** Administration; Computer Science/Software; Information Systems. **Positions commonly filled include:** Computer Programmer; MIS Specialist; Software Engineer; Systems Analyst; Technical Writer/Editor. **Average salary range of placements:** $30,000 - $50,000. **Number of placements per year:** 100 - 199.

CREATIVE FINANCIAL STAFFING
340 Columbia Street, Suite 105, South Bend IN 46601. 219/236-7600. **Fax:** 219/239-7878. **Contact:** Manager. **Description:** An executive search firm. **Specializes in the areas of:** Accounting. **Positions commonly filled include:** Accountant; Auditor; Budget Analyst; Chief Financial Officer; Controller; Financial Analyst. **Average salary range of placements:** $50,000 - $100,000. **Number of placements per year:** 1 - 49.

THE CURARE GROUP, INC.
4627 East Morningside Drive, Bloomington IN 47408. 812/331-0645. **Fax:** 812/331-0659. **Contact:** David Witte, Senior Recruiter. **Description:** An executive search firm operating on a contingency basis. The firm recruits primary care physicians, in fields including family practice, internal medicine, pediatrics, and OB/GYN. Founded in 1991. **Specializes in the areas of:** Health/Medical. **Positions commonly filled include:** Physician. **Other U.S. locations:** New Orleans LA. **Average salary range of placements:** More than $50,000.

MONTE DENBO ASSOCIATES
127 North Front Street, Rising Sun IN 47040. 812/438-2400. **Fax:** 812/438-2567. **Contact:** Manager. **Description:** An executive search firm. **Specializes in the areas of:** Engineering.

THE DOBIAS GROUP
Merrill Lynch Plaza, 130 West Main Street, Fort Wayne IN 46802. 219/436-6570. **Fax:** 219/432-7396. **Contact:**

Manager. **Description:** An executive search firm. **Specializes in the areas of:** Hotel/Restaurant.

DUNHILL OF BROWN COUNTY
P.O. Box 1068, Nashville IN 47448. 812/988-1944. **Contact:** George W. Rogers, President. **Description:** An executive search firm. **Specializes in the areas of:** Engineering; Health/Medical; Industrial; Manufacturing; Personnel/Labor Relations; Technical. **Positions commonly filled include:** Aerospace Engineer; Agricultural Engineer; Biomedical Engineer; Chemical Engineer; Chemist; Civil Engineer; Designer; Electrical/Electronics Engineer; Health Services Manager; Industrial Engineer; Industrial Production Manager; Mechanical Engineer; Metallurgical Engineer. **Number of placements per year:** 100 - 199.

DUNHILL OF FORT WAYNE
9918 Coldwater Road, Fort Wayne IN 46825. 219/489-5966. **Fax:** 219/489-6120. **Contact:** Office Manager. **E-mail address:** dunftwin@aol.com. **Description:** An executive search firm operating on a contingency basis. **Specializes in the areas of:** Food. **Positions commonly filled include:** Chemical Engineer; Chemist; Design Engineer; General Manager; Industrial Engineer; Industrial Production Manager; Mechanical Engineer; Operations/Production Manager; Quality Control Supervisor; Statistician. **Other U.S. locations:** Nationwide. **Average salary range of placements:** $30,000 - $70,000.

EXCELLENCE IN SEARCH
186 Amy's Run Drive, Carmel IN 46032. 317/573-5222. **Fax:** 317/573-5223. **Contact:** Manager. **Description:** An executive search firm. **Specializes in the areas of:** Data Processing; Health/Medical.

EXECUSEARCH
105 East Jefferson Boulevard, Suite 800, South Bend IN 46601-1811. 219/233-9353. **Fax:** 219/236-4840. **Contact:** Manager. **Description:** An executive search firm. **Specializes in the areas of:** Accounting/Auditing; Administration; Advertising; Architecture/Construction; Banking; Chemicals; Communications; Computer Hardware/Software; Construction; Electrical; Engineering; Finance; Food; General Management; Health/Medical; Insurance; Legal; Manufacturing; Personnel/Labor Relations; Pharmaceuticals; Procurement; Publishing; Real Estate; Retail; Sales; Technical; Textiles; Transportation.

F-O-R-T-U-N-E PERSONNEL CONSULTANTS
347 West Berry Street, Suite 319, Fort Wayne IN 46802. 219/424-5159. **Fax:** 219/424-4201. **Contact:** Manager. **Description:** An executive search firm. **Specializes in the areas of:** Electronics; Plastics; Rubber. **Corporate headquarters location:** New York NY. **Other U.S. locations:** Nationwide.

F-O-R-T-U-N-E PERSONNEL CONSULTANTS
1904 South Elizabeth Street, Kokomo IN 46902. 765/868-2242. **Fax:** 765/868-2282. **Contact:** Manager. **E-mail address:** kokomo@fpcweb.com. **World Wide Web address:** http://fpckokomocareers.com. **Description:** An executive search firm. **Specializes in the areas of:** Aerospace; Automotive. **Positions commonly filled include:** Design Engineer; Engineer; Financial Manager; Operations Engineer; Project Engineer; Quality Assurance Engineer; Sales and Marketing Manager. **Corporate headquarters location:** New York NY.

F-O-R-T-U-N-E PERSONNEL CONSULTANTS
52303 Emmons Road, Suite 27, South Bend IN 46637. 219/273-3188. **Fax:** 219/273-3887. **Contact:** Branch Manager. **E-mail address:** southbend@fpcweb.com. **World Wide Web address:** http://business.michiana.org/fortune/index.htm. **Description:** An executive search firm. **Specializes in the areas of:** Automotive; Plastics. **Positions commonly filled include:** Design Engineer; Industrial Engineer; Manufacturing Engineer; Metallurgical Engineer; Plant Manager; Production

Engineer; Production Manager; Project Engineer; Research and Development Engineer; Test Engineer. **Corporate headquarters location:** New York NY.

F-O-R-T-U-N-E PERSONNEL CONSULTANTS
909 West 4th Street, Mount Vernon IN 47620. 812/838-6636. **Fax:** 812/838-6648. **Contact:** Manager. **Description:** An executive search firm. **Specializes in the areas of:** Automotive; Chemicals; Human Resources; Manufacturing; Plastics. **Positions commonly filled include:** Buyer; Chemist; Electrical/Electronics Engineer; Engineer; Environmental Engineer; Finance Director; Financial Manager; Inventory Control Specialist; Management; Materials Engineer; Purchasing Agent/Manager; Quality Assurance Engineer; Quality Control Supervisor; Safety Engineer; Technical Support Engineer; Tool and Die Maker. **Corporate headquarters location:** New York NY.

HMO EXECUTIVE SEARCH
8910 Purdue Road, Suite 200, Indianapolis IN 46268-1155. 317/872-1056. **Fax:** 317/879-1233. **Contact:** Dick Carroll, CPC/President. **Description:** An executive search firm. **Specializes in the areas of:** Health/Medical. **Positions commonly filled include:** Registered Nurse. **Number of placements per year:** 50 - 99.

ROBERT HALF INTERNATIONAL OFFICETEAM/ACCOUNTEMPS
135 North Pennsylvania Avenue, Suite 2300, Indianapolis IN 46204. 317/687-3270. **Contact:** Manager. **World Wide Web address:** http://www.roberthalf.com. **Description:** An executive search firm. OfficeTeam (also at this location) provides temporary and permanent administrative placements. Accountemps (also at this location) provides temporary placements. **Specializes in the areas of:** Accounting/Auditing. **Corporate headquarters location:** Menlo Park CA. **Other U.S. locations:** Nationwide.

THE HART LINE INC.
P.O. Box 39, Brazil IN 47834. 812/448-3490. **Fax:** 812/442-5227. **Contact:** Eric V. Stearley, CPC/President. **Description:** An executive search firm. **Specializes in the areas of:** Engineering; Manufacturing. **Positions commonly filled include:** Electrical/Electronics Engineer; Industrial Engineer; Mechanical Engineer; Software Engineer. **Average salary range of placements:** $50,000 - $100,000. **Number of placements per year:** 50 - 99.

KEITH HAYES & ASSOCIATES
8420 Galley Court, Indianapolis IN 46236. 317/823-7100. **Contact:** Manager. **Description:** An executive search firm. **Specializes in the areas of:** Health/Medical; Pharmaceuticals.

INSURANCE PEOPLE
P.O. Box 55171, Indianapolis IN 46205. 317/253-2128. **Contact:** Manager. **Description:** Insurance People is an executive search firm. **Specializes in the areas of:** Insurance.

JOHNSON BROWN ASSOCIATES
55 Monument Circle, Suite 1214, Indianapolis IN 46204. 317/237-4328. **Fax:** 317/237-4335. **Contact:** Dan Brown/Kim Johnson, Principals. **Description:** An executive search firm operating on both retainer and contingency bases. **Specializes in the areas of:** Accounting/Auditing; Engineering; Industrial; Information Technology; Investment; Personnel/Labor Relations; Sales. **Positions commonly filled include:** Account Manager; Account Representative; Accountant; Administrative Assistant; Applications Engineer; Architect; Auditor; Budget Analyst; Buyer; Chief Financial Officer; Controller; Customer Service Representative; Design Engineer; Education Administrator; Financial Analyst; Fund Manager; General Manager; Human Resources Manager; Industrial Engineer; Industrial Production Manager; Manufacturing Engineer; Market Research Analyst; Marketing Manager;

Marketing Specialist; Mechanical Engineer; Metallurgical Engineer; Operations Manager; Project Manager; Public Relations Specialist; Purchasing Agent/Manager; Quality Control Supervisor; Sales Engineer; Sales Executive; Sales Manager; Sales Representative; Systems Manager. **Corporate headquarters location:** This Location. **Average salary range of placements:** More than $50,000. **Number of placements per year:** 1 - 49.

KEY SALES PERSONNEL
312 NW Martin Luther King Boulevard, Suite 100, Evansville IN 47708. 812/426-2244. **Contact:** George Krauss, Vice President. **Description:** An executive search firm. **Specializes in the areas of:** Sales. **Positions commonly filled include:** Manufacturer's/Wholesaler's Sales Rep.; Sales Engineer; Services Sales Representative.

LANGE & ASSOCIATES, INC.
107 West Market Street, Wabash IN 46992. 219/563-7402. **Fax:** 219/563-3897. **Contact:** Jim Lange, President. **E-mail address:** langeassoc@ctlnet.com. **Description:** An executive search firm operating on a contingency basis. Client company pays fee. **Specializes in the areas of:** Engineering; Finance; General Management; Industrial; Marketing; Personnel/Labor Relations; Sales. **Positions commonly filled include:** Account Manager; Account Representative; Accountant; Blue-Collar Worker Supervisor; Buyer; Chemical Engineer; Chemist; Chief Financial Officer; Controller; Design Engineer; Electrical/Electronics Engineer; General Manager; Human Resources Manager; Industrial Engineer; Industrial Production Manager; Manufacturing Engineer; Mechanical Engineer; Operations Manager; Production Manager; Project Manager; Purchasing Agent/Manager; Quality Assurance Engineer; Quality Control Supervisor; Sales Engineer; Sales Executive; Sales Manager; Sales Representative. **Corporate headquarters location:** This Location. **Average salary range of placements:** $50,000 - $100,000. **Number of placements per year:** 1 - 49.

THE MALLARD GROUP
3322 Oak Borough, Fort Wayne IN 46804. 219/436-3970. **Fax:** 219/436-7012. **Contact:** Director. **Description:** An executive search firm operating on a contingency basis. **Specializes in the areas of:** Computer Science/Software; Engineering; Manufacturing; Sales. **Positions commonly filled include:** Design Engineer; Electrical/Electronics Engineer; Human Resources Manager; Industrial Engineer; Mechanical Engineer; Metallurgical Engineer; Purchasing Agent/Manager; Software Engineer. **Number of placements per year:** 1 - 49.

MANAGEMENT RECRUITERS INTERNATIONAL
99 Sputh Dan Jones Road, Suite 200, Avon IN 46123. 317/272-5454. **Fax:** 317/272-5440. **Contact:** Manager. **World Wide Web address:** http://www.recruiters-careers.com. **Description:** An executive search firm. **Specializes in the areas of:** Engineering; Finance; Information Technology; Manufacturing; Sales. **Corporate headquarters location:** Cleveland OH. **Other U.S. locations:** Nationwide.

MANAGEMENT RECRUITERS INTERNATIONAL SALES CONSULTANTS
8200 Haverstick Road, Suite 240, Indianapolis IN 46240. 317/257-5411. **Fax:** 317/259-6886. **Contact:** Manager. **Description:** An executive search firm. **Specializes in the areas of:** Marketing; Sales; Technical. **Corporate headquarters location:** Cleveland OH.

MANAGEMENT RECRUITERS INTERNATIONAL, INC. (MRI)
15209 Herriman Boulevard, Noblesville IN 46060. 317/773-4323. **Fax:** 317/773-9744. **Contact:** H. Peter Isenberg, President. **Description:** An executive search firm. **Specializes in the areas of:** Administration; Computer Science/Software; Engineering; General Management; Industrial; Manufacturing; Sales. **Positions commonly filled include:** Computer Programmer; Designer; Draftsperson; Electrical/Electronics Engineer; Food Scientist/Technologist; Industrial Engineer; Industrial Production Manager; Manufacturer's/Wholesaler's Sales Rep.; Mechanical Engineer; Metallurgical Engineer; Pharmacist; Software Engineer; Systems Analyst. **Corporate headquarters location:** Cleveland OH. **Average salary range of placements:** More than $50,000. **Number of placements per year:** 1 - 49.

MANAGEMENT RECRUITERS INTERNATIONAL, INC. (MRI)
P.O. Box 2234, Columbus IN 47202. 812/372-5500. **Fax:** 812/372-8292. **Contact:** Manager. **Description:** An executive search firm. **Specializes in the areas of:** Banking; Computer Programming; Engineering. **Corporate headquarters location:** Cleveland OH.

MANAGEMENT RECRUITERS OF RICHMOND
2519 East Main Street, Suite 101, Richmond IN 47374. 765/935-3356. **Contact:** Manager. **Description:** An executive search firm. **Specializes in the areas of:** Accounting/Auditing; Administration; Advertising; Architecture/Construction; Banking; Chemicals; Communications; Computer Hardware/Software; Construction; Electrical; Engineering; Finance; Food; General Management; Health/Medical; Insurance; Legal; Manufacturing; Operations Management; Personnel/Labor Relations; Pharmaceuticals; Procurement; Publishing; Real Estate; Retail; Sales; Technical; Textiles; Transportation. **Corporate headquarters location:** Cleveland OH.

MANAGEMENT SERVICES
P.O. Box 830, Middlebury IN 46540. 219/825-3909. **Fax:** 219/825-7115. **Contact:** Office Manager. **Description:** An executive search firm operating on a contingency basis. **Specializes in the areas of:** Administration; Computer Science/Software; Engineering; Manufacturing; Personnel/Labor Relations; Sales; Technical. **Positions commonly filled include:** Accountant/Auditor; Buyer; Chemical Engineer; Computer Programmer; Electrical/Electronics Engineer; Financial Analyst; General Manager; Human Resources Manager; Industrial Engineer; Industrial Production Manager; Landscape Architect; Mechanical Engineer; Metallurgical Engineer; MIS Specialist; Operations/Production Manager; Purchasing Agent/Manager; Quality Control Supervisor; Software Engineer; Systems Analyst; Transportation/Traffic Specialist. **Number of placements per year:** 1 - 49.

MANAGEMENT SUPPORT SERVICES
P.O. Box 3291, Munster IN 46321. 219/923-0190. **Contact:** Mark Hickey, Senior Partner. **Description:** An executive search firm. **Specializes in the areas of:** Engineering; Finance; General Management; Industrial; Legal; Personnel/Labor Relations; Sales; Technical. **Positions commonly filled include:** Accountant/Auditor; Aerospace Engineer; Attorney; Bank Officer/Manager; Blue-Collar Worker Supervisor; Chemical Engineer; Chemist; Civil Engineer; Designer; Electrical/Electronics Engineer; Electrician; Environmental Engineer; General Manager; Human Resources Manager; Industrial Engineer; Industrial Production Manager; Metallurgical Engineer; Mining Engineer; Nuclear Engineer; Operations/Production Manager; Petroleum Engineer; Purchasing Agent/Manager; Software Engineer; Structural Engineer; Transportation/Traffic Specialist. **Average salary range of placements:** More than $50,000. **Number of placements per year:** 100 - 199.

MAYHALL SEARCH GROUP INC.
4410 Executive Boulevard, Suite 1A, Fort Wayne IN 46808. 219/484-7770. **Fax:** 219/482-9397. **Contact:** Manager. **Description:** An executive search firm. **Specializes in the areas of:** Accounting/Auditing; Manufacturing; Sales.

MICHIANA PERSONNEL SERVICE
1441 Northside Boulevard, South Bend IN 46615. 219/232-3364. **Contact:** Manager. **Description:** An executive search firm.

MILLER PERSONNEL
931 East 86th Street, Suite 103, Indianapolis IN 46240. 317/251-5938. **Toll-free phone:** 800/851-5938. **Fax:** 317/251-5762. **Contact:** Mark Miller, Owner/Manager. **Description:** An executive search firm operating on a contingency basis. **Specializes in the areas of:** Engineering; Manufacturing. **Positions commonly filled include:** Applications Engineer; Design Engineer; Electrical/Electronics Engineer; Industrial Engineer; Industrial Production Manager; Manufacturing Engineer; Mechanical Engineer; Operations Manager; Production Manager; Purchasing Agent/Manager; Quality Control Supervisor; Sales Engineer; Software Engineer. **Other U.S. locations:** Nationwide. **Average salary range of placements:** More than $50,000. **Number of placements per year:** 50 - 99.

MORLEY GROUP
6201 Corporate Drive, Suite 200, Indianapolis IN 46278. 317/879-4770. **Fax:** 317/879-4787. **Contact:** Manager. **Description:** An executive search firm that also provides some contract and temporary placements. **Specializes in the areas of:** Banking; Clerical; Engineering; Finance; Health/Medical; Human Resources; Information Systems; Manufacturing.

NATIONAL RECRUITING SERVICE
P.O. Box 218, 1832 Hart Street, Dyer IN 46311. 219/865-2373. **Fax:** 219/865-2375. **Contact:** Stanley M. Hendricks II, Owner. **Description:** An executive search firm operating on both retainer and contingency bases. **Specializes in the areas of:** Metals; Plastics. **Positions commonly filled include:** General Manager; Industrial Engineer; Industrial Production Manager; Manufacturing Engineer; Marketing Manager; Mechanical Engineer; Metallurgical Engineer; Operations/Production Manager; Sales Engineer; Sales Executive; Sales Representative. **Average salary range of placements:** More than $50,000. **Number of placements per year:** 1 - 49.

OAKWOOD INTERNATIONAL INC.
3935 Lincoln Way East, Suite A, Mishawaka IN 46544. 219/255-9861. **Fax:** 219/257-8914. **Contact:** Scott Null, President. **E-mail address:** oakwood@mvillage.com. **World Wide Web address:** http://interact.withus.com/oakwood. **Description:** An executive search firm operating on a contingency basis. **Specializes in the areas of:** Administration; Computer Science/Software; Engineering; General Management; Manufacturing; Sales; Technical. **Positions commonly filled include:** Aerospace Engineer; Biomedical Engineer; Branch Manager; Chemical Engineer; Chemist; Civil Engineer; Computer Programmer; Design Engineer; Designer; Draftsperson; Electrical/Electronics Engineer; Industrial Engineer; Internet Services Manager; Mechanical Engineer; Metallurgical Engineer; MIS Specialist; Multimedia Designer; Quality Control Supervisor; Software Engineer; Structural Engineer; Systems Analyst; Technical Writer/Editor; Telecommunications Manager. **Average salary range of placements:** More than $50,000. **Number of placements per year:** 1 - 49.

OFFICEMATES5 (OM5)
DAYSTAR TEMPORARY SERVICES
251 North Illinois Street, Indianapolis IN 46204. 317/237-2787. **Fax:** 317/237-2786. **Contact:** Manager. **Description:** An executive search firm. DayStar Temporary Services (also at this location) provides temporary placements. **Specializes in the areas of:** Accounting/Auditing; Administration; Advertising; Architecture/Construction; Banking; Chemicals; Communications; Computer Hardware/Software; Construction; Electrical; Engineering; Finance; Food; General Management; Health/Medical; Insurance; Legal; Manufacturing; Personnel/Labor Relations; Pharmaceuticals; Procurement; Publishing; Real Estate; Retail; Sales; Technical; Textiles; Transportation.

P.R.C.
3077 East 98th Street, Suite 210, Indianapolis IN 46280. 317/580-5730. **Contact:** Manager. **Description:** An

executive search firm. **Specializes in the areas of:** Administration; Engineering.

PERSONNEL PLUS, INC.
300 West Jefferson Street, Plymouth IN 46563. 219/935-5727. **Fax:** 219/935-4521. **Contact:** Marcy Eckhoff, CPC/President. **Description:** An executive search firm focusing on placements in the automotive, HVAC, and engine cooling industries. The company operates on both retainer and contingency bases. Founded in 1976. **Specializes in the areas of:** Engineering; Technical; Transportation. **Positions commonly filled include:** Electrical/Electronics Engineer; Mechanical Engineer.

QUALITY SEARCH
1100 South Calumet Road, Suite One, Chesterton IN 46304. 219/926-8202. **Fax:** 219/926-3834. **Contact:** President. **E-mail address:** quality@staffing.net. **World Wide Web address:** http://www.niia.net/~quality. **Description:** An executive search firm. **Specializes in the areas of:** Engineering; Food; General Management; Packaging; Technical. **Positions commonly filled include:** Buyer; Chemical Engineer; Design Engineer; Designer; Industrial Engineer; Manufacturing Engineer; Mechanical Engineer; Production Manager; Purchasing Agent/Manager; Quality Control Supervisor. **Corporate headquarters location:** This Location. **Other U.S. locations:** Show Low AZ; Grand Rapids MI. **Average salary range of placements:** More than $50,000. **Number of placements per year:** 50 - 99.

REACH CONSULTING GROUP
401 East Colfax Avenue, Suite 207, South Bend IN 46617. 219/232-1818. **Fax:** 219/288-3838. **Contact:** Manager. **Description:** An executive search firm. **Specializes in the areas of:** Accounting/Auditing; Information Systems; Manufacturing; Marketing; Sales.

ROMAC INTERNATIONAL
111 Monument Circle, Suite 3930, Indianapolis IN 46204-5139. 317/631-2900. **Fax:** 317/682-6100. **Contact:** Manager. **Description:** An executive search firm. **Specializes in the areas of:** Accounting/Auditing; Computer Hardware/Software; Health/Medical; Information Technology.

SALES SEARCH
2420 North Coliseum Boulevard, Suite 220, Fort Wayne IN 46805. 219/485-0850. **Fax:** 219/484-7121. **Contact:** Manager. **Description:** An executive search. **Specializes in the areas of:** Sales.

SANFORD ROSE ASSOCIATES
P.O. Box 1106, Newburgh IN 47629. 812/853-9325. **Fax:** 812/853-1953. **Contact:** Ken Forbes, Director. **E-mail address:** kforbes@aol.com. **World Wide Web address:** http://www.sanfordrose.com. **Description:** An executive search firm operating on both retainer and contingency bases. **Positions commonly filled include:** Account Manager; Account Representative; Advertising Clerk; Advertising Executive; Graphic Artist; Graphic Designer; Human Resources Manager; Market Research Analyst; Marketing Manager; Marketing Specialist; Multimedia Designer; Operations Manager; Public Relations Specialist; Sales Executive; Sales Manager; Sales Representative. **Average salary range of placements:** $30,000 - $50,000. **Number of placements per year:** 1 - 49.

SANFORD ROSE ASSOCIATES
650 East Carmel Drive, Suite 450, Carmel IN 46032. 317/848-9987. **Fax:** 317/848-9979. **Contact:** Michael A. Nichpor, President. **World Wide Web address:** http://www.sanfordrose.com/carmel. **Description:** An executive search firm. **Specializes in the areas of:** Insurance.

SEARCH FORCE/DATA FORCE
626 North Park Avenue, Indianapolis IN 46202. 317/636-9900. **Toll-free phone:** 800/837-9902. **Fax:** 317/686-6384. **Contact:** Shawn Miller, President. **E-mail address:** smiller@searchforceinc.com. **World**

Wide Web address: http://www.searchforceinc.com. **Description:** An executive search firm operating on a contingency basis. Client company pays fee. **Specializes in the areas of:** Accounting; Computer Science/Software; Engineering; MIS/EDP. **Positions commonly filled include:** Accountant; Applications Engineer; AS400 Programmer Analyst; Auditor; Budget Analyst; Chief Financial Officer; Computer Animator; Computer Engineer; Computer Operator; Computer Programmer; Computer Scientist; Computer Support Technician; Computer Technician; Content Developer; Controller; Credit Manager; Database Administrator; Database Manager; Finance Director; Financial Analyst; Internet Services Manager; MIS Specialist; Multimedia Designer; Network/Systems Administrator; Software Engineer; SQL Programmer; Systems Analyst; Systems Manager; Webmaster. **Average salary range of placements:** $50,000 - $100,000. **Number of placements per year:** 100 - 199.

SMITH & SYBERG INC.
825 Washington Street, Suite 2A, Columbus IN 47201. 812/372-7254. **Contact:** Manager. **Description:** An executive search firm.

STRATEGIC RESOURCE MANAGEMENT
3500 DePauw Boulevard, Suite 1034, Indianapolis IN 46268. 317/872-8900. **Contact:** Manager. **Description:** An executive search firm. **Specializes in the areas of:**

Health/Medical. **Positions commonly filled include:** Certified Nurses Aide; Physical Therapist; Physician.

TOMLINSON-MILLER, INC.
301 South Adams Street, Suite 103, Marion IN 46952. 765/668-3213. **Fax:** 765/651-6616. **Contact:** Dan L. Tomlinson, Principal. **E-mail address:** tmi@tmi-careers.com. **World Wide Web address:** http://www.tmi-careers.com. **Description:** An executive search firm. **Specializes in the areas of:** Manufacturing.

UNIQUE, INC.
9850 North Michigan Road, Carmel IN 46032. 317/875-8281. **Fax:** 317/875-3127. **Contact:** Jennifer Flora, President. **Description:** An executive search firm. **Specializes in the areas of:** Computer Science/Software; Data Processing; Food; General Management; High-Tech; Legal; Office Support; Personnel/Labor Relations; Publishing; Sales; Secretarial; Telecommunications. **Positions commonly filled include:** Branch Manager; Clerical Supervisor; Computer Programmer; Customer Service Representative; General Manager; Hotel Manager; Human Resources Manager; Management Trainee; Paralegal; Restaurant/Food Service Manager; Services Sales Representative; Software Engineer; Systems Analyst; Telecommunications Manager; Typist/Word Processor. **Number of placements per year:** 500 - 999.

PERMANENT EMPLOYMENT AGENCIES

ADECCO
1417 Coliseum Boulevard West, Fort Wayne IN 46808. 219/482-2390. **Fax:** 219/482-1589. **Contact:** Branch Manager. **Description:** A permanent employment agency that also provides some temporary placements. **Specializes in the areas of:** Clerical.

ALPHA RAE PERSONNEL, INC.
127 West Berry Street, Suite 200, Fort Wayne IN 46802. 219/426-8227. **Fax:** 219/426-1152. **Contact:** Rae Pearson, President. **Description:** A permanent employment agency. **Specializes in the areas of:** Computer Science/Software; Data Processing; Engineering; Legal; Sales; Software Engineering.

AMERICA WORKS
2021 North Meridian Street, Indianapolis IN 46202. 317/923-3600. **Fax:** 317/921-6877. **Contact:** Office Manager. **Description:** A permanent employment agency.

ANGOLA PERSONNEL SERVICES, INC.
901 North Wayne Street, Angola IN 46703. 219/665-1162. **Fax:** 219/665-6997. **Contact:** Jeff Peters, President/Owner. **Description:** Angola Personnel Services, Inc. is a permanent employment agency. **Specializes in the areas of:** Clerical; Engineering; Industrial; Light Industrial; Manufacturing; Personnel/Labor Relations; Secretarial; Technical. **Positions commonly filled include:** Blue-Collar Worker Supervisor; Clerical Supervisor; Customer Service Representative; Design Engineer; Designer; General Manager; Human Resources Specialist; Industrial Engineer; Industrial Production Manager; Mechanical Engineer; Quality Control Supervisor. **Benefits available to temporary workers:** Paid Holidays; Paid Vacation. **Other area locations:** Auburn IN. **Other U.S. locations:** Archbold OH. **Average salary range of placements:** $20,000 - $29,999. **Number of placements per year:** 1000+.

BANE & ASSOCIATES
19 1/2 South Eighth Street, Richmond IN 47374. 765/966-5512. **Fax:** 765/966-2623. **Contact:** David Bane, Owner/CEO. **Description:** A permanent employment agency that also provides some executive searches. **Specializes in the areas of:** Industrial.

BARRISTER PERSONNEL
155 East Market Street, Suite 701, Indianapolis IN 46204. 317/637-0123. **Fax:** 317/637-0163. **Contact:** Manager. **Description:** A permanent employment agency that also provides some temporary placements. **Specializes in the areas of:** Legal Secretarial.

BONE PERSONNEL, INC.
6424 Lima Road, Fort Wayne IN 46818. 219/489-3350. **Fax:** 219/489-0556. **Contact:** Manager. **Description:** A permanent employment agency. **Positions commonly filled include:** Accountant; Administrative Manager; Advertising Clerk; Aerospace Engineer; Agricultural Scientist; Biomedical Engineer; Branch Manager; Budget Analyst; Buyer; Chemical Engineer; Chemist; Civil Engineer; Clerical Supervisor; Computer Programmer; Construction Contractor; Cost Estimator; Credit Manager; Designer; Draftsperson; Electrical Engineer; Electrician; Financial Analyst; General Manager; Health Services Manager; Hotel Manager; Industrial Engineer; Industrial Production Manager; Manufacturer's/Wholesaler's Sales Rep.; Mechanical Engineer; Metallurgical Engineer; Paralegal; Quality Control Supervisor; Restaurant/Food Service Manager; Science Technologist; Services Sales Rep.; Software Engineer; Stationary Engineer; Structural Engineer; Systems Analyst. **Number of placements per year:** 1000+.

BILL CALDWELL EMPLOYMENT SERVICE
123 Main Street, Suite 307, Evansville IN 47708. 812/423-8006. **Fax:** 812/423-8008. **Contact:** Manager. **Description:** A permanent employment agency. **Specializes in the areas of:** Accounting/Auditing; Banking; Computer Science/Software; Engineering; Finance; General Management; Health/Medical; Industrial; Manufacturing; Retail; Sales. **Positions commonly filled include:** Accountant/Auditor; Actuary; Adjuster; Administrative Manager; Advertising Clerk; Agricultural Engineer; Architect; Attorney; Automotive Mechanic; Bank Officer/Manager; Biochemist; Biological Scientist; Biomedical Engineer; Blue-Collar Worker Supervisor; Branch Manager; Broadcast Technician; Brokerage Clerk; Budget Analyst; Buyer; Chemical Engineer; Chemist; Civil Engineer; Claim Representative; Clerical Supervisor; Clinical Lab Technician; Computer Programmer; Construction Contractor; Cost Estimator; Customer Service Representative; Design Engineer; Designer;

Draftsperson; Economist; Editor; EEG Technologist; Electrical/Electronics Engineer; Electrician; Financial Analyst; Food Scientist/Technologist; General Manager; Health Services Manager; Human Resources Specialist; Industrial Engineer; Internet Services Manager; Librarian; Management Analyst/Consultant; Market Research Analyst; Materials Engineer; Mechanical Engineer; Metallurgical Engineer; Mining Engineer; Operations/Production Manager; Pharmacist; Physical Therapist; Public Relations Specialist; Quality Control Supervisor; Radio/TV Announcer/Broadcaster; Radiological Technologist; Real Estate Agent; Recreational Therapist; Restaurant/Food Service Manager; Services Sales Representative; Sociologist; Software Engineer; Statistician; Structural Engineer; Systems Analyst; Teacher/Professor; Telecommunications Manager; Typist/Word Processor; Underwriter/Assistant Underwriter.

CAREER CONSULTANTS, INC.
O.I. PARTNERS
107 North Pennsylvania Street, Suite 1008, Indianapolis IN 46204. 317/639-5601. **Fax:** 317/634-0277. **Contact:** Manager. **Description:** A permanent employment agency. **Specializes in the areas of:** Accounting/Auditing; Computer Science/Software; Engineering; Food; Industrial; Information Systems; Manufacturing; Technical. **Positions commonly filled include:** Accountant/Auditor; Computer Programmer; Electrical/Electronics Engineer; Financial Analyst; Human Resources Manager; Industrial Engineer; Industrial Production Manager; Mechanical Engineer; Metallurgical Engineer; Purchasing Agent/Manager; Quality Control Supervisor; Software Engineer; Statistician; Systems Analyst; Technical Writer/Editor. **Number of placements per year:** 50 - 99.

CENTURY PERSONNEL INC.
11590 North Meridian Street, Suite 500, Carmel IN 46032. 317/580-8500. **Fax:** 317/580-8535. **Contact:** Manager. **Description:** A permanent employment agency. **Specializes in the areas of:** Accounting/Auditing; Data Processing; Engineering; Health/Medical; Technical.

CROWE, CHIZEK AND COMPANY
330 East Jefferson Boulevard, P.O. Box 7, South Bend IN 46624-0007. 219/232-3992. **Fax:** 219/236-8692. **Contact:** Janet Racht, Senior Manager. **Description:** A permanent employment agency. **Specializes in the areas of:** Accounting/Auditing; Banking; Finance; Manufacturing.

DATA ACCESS GR
5445 Southeast Street, Indianapolis IN 46227. 317/545-5882. **Contact:** Manager. **Description:** A permanent employment agency. **Specializes in the areas of:** Clerical; Engineering.

PAT DAY PERSONNEL INC.
6100 North Keystone, Suite 222, Indianapolis IN 46220. 317/257-1411. **Fax:** 317/257-1305. **Contact:** Manager. **Description:** A permanent employment agency. **Specializes in the areas of:** Clerical; Office Support; Restaurant; Retail; Sales. **Positions commonly filled include:** Restaurant/Food Service Manager; Retail Manager; Sales Representative.

DENTAL MEDICAL POWER INC.
6249 Southeast Street, Suite B, Indianapolis IN 46227. 317/337-1312. **Fax:** 317/781-0112. **Contact:** Manager. **Description:** A permanent employment agency that also provides some temporary placements. **Specializes in the areas of:** Health/Medical.

EMPLOYMENT MART INC.
7002 North Graham Road, Suite 100, Indianapolis IN 46220. 317/842-8890. **Fax:** 317/842-8892. **Contact:** Manager. **Description:** A permanent employment agency. **Specializes in the areas of:** Engineering.

EMPLOYMENT RECRUITERS INC.
P.O. Box 1624, Elkhart IN 46515-1624. 219/262-2654. **Fax:** 219/262-0095. **Contact:** Suzanne Pedler, President.

Description: A permanent employment agency that provides placements with manufacturers throughout the Midwest. Founded in 1982. **Specializes in the areas of:** Computer Science/Software; Engineering; General Management; Industrial; Manufacturing; Sales. **Positions commonly filled include:** Chemical Engineer; Chemist; Computer Programmer; Credit Manager; Customer Service Manager; Customer Service Representative; Design Engineer; Designer; Draftsperson; Electrical/Electronics Engineer; Environmental Engineer; Food Scientist/Technologist; General Manager; Industrial Engineer; Industrial Production Manager; Manufacturer's/Wholesaler's Sales Rep.; Market Research Analyst; Mathematician; Metallurgical Engineer; Mining Engineer; MIS Specialist; Operations/Production Manager; Purchasing Agent/Manager; Quality Control Supervisor; Safety Engineer; Science Technologist; Software Engineer; Stationary Engineer; Statistician; Strategic Relations Manager; Structural Engineer; Systems Analyst; Technical Writer/Editor. **Average salary range of placements:** $30,000 - $50,000. **Number of placements per year:** 1 - 49.

JOB PLACEMENT SERVICE INC.
5404 North Calumet Avenue, Valparaiso IN 46383. 219/462-7894. **Contact:** Manager. **Description:** A permanent employment agency. **Specializes in the areas of:** Accounting/Auditing; Administration; Advertising; Architecture/Construction; Computer Science/Software; Engineering; Finance; General Management; Industrial; Insurance; Legal; Manufacturing; Nonprofit; Personnel/Labor Relations; Retail; Sales; Secretarial. **Positions commonly filled include:** Accountant/Auditor; Advertising Clerk; Architect; Automotive Mechanic; Blue-Collar Worker Supervisor; Branch Manager; Buyer; Chemist; Claim Representative; Clerical Supervisor; Clinical Lab Technician; Computer Programmer; Cost Estimator; Counselor; Credit Manager; Customer Service Representative; Design Engineer; Designer; Draftsperson; Economist; Editor; Electrical/Electronics Engineer; Electrician; Financial Analyst; General Manager; Hotel Manager; Human Resources Specialist; Industrial Engineer; Industrial Production Manager; Insurance Agent/Broker; Management Trainee; Operations/Production Manager; Paralegal; Services Sales Representative; Social Worker; Software Engineer; Systems Analyst; Typist/Word Processor. **Average salary range of placements:** Less than $20,000. **Number of placements per year:** 500 - 999.

KENDALL & DAVIS RESOURCES, INC.
415 East Cook Road, Suite 600, Fort Wayne IN 46825. 219/489-8014. **Fax:** 800/860-2982. **Contact:** Manager. **Description:** A permanent employment agency that also provides some contract services. **Specializes in the areas of:** Computer Science/Software. **Positions commonly filled include:** Computer Operator; Computer Programmer; MIS Specialist; Systems Analyst; Technical Writer/Editor; Telecommunications Manager. **Benefits available to temporary workers:** 401(k); Dental Insurance; Disability Coverage; Life Insurance; Medical Insurance; Profit Sharing. **Corporate headquarters location:** This Location. **Other U.S. locations:** Detroit MI. **Average salary range of placements:** More than $50,000. **Number of placements per year:** 200 - 499.

KRISE PROFESSIONAL PERSONNEL SERVICES
P.O. Box 53136, Indianapolis IN 46253. 317/299-3882. **Contact:** Randy Krise, CPC/Owner. **Description:** A permanent employment agency. **Specializes in the areas of:** Engineering; Manufacturing; Personnel/Labor Relations. **Positions commonly filled include:** Aerospace Engineer; Agricultural Engineer; Biomedical Engineer; Chemical Engineer; Civil Engineer; Electrical/Electronics Engineer; Human Resources Manager; Industrial Engineer; Industrial Production Manager; Mechanical Engineer; Metallurgical Engineer; Purchasing Agent/Manager; Quality Control Supervisor; Software Engineer; Stationary Engineer; Structural Engineer. **Average salary range of**

placements: $30,000 - $50,000. **Number of placements per year:** 1 - 49.

DAN LANE PERSONNEL
8395 Keystone Crossing Road, Suite 213, Indianapolis IN 46240. 317/255-9632. **Contact:** Manager. **Description:** A permanent employment agency.

LIFE EMPLOYMENT SERVICE
600 Life Building, 300 Main Street, Lafayette IN 47901. 765/742-0278. **Fax:** 765/742-0270. **Contact:** Charles A. Hoovler, Manager. **E-mail address:** charlie@life-employment.com. **Description:** A permanent employment agency. **Specializes in the areas of:** Accounting/Auditing; Banking; Fashion; Finance; Food; General Management; Retail; Sales; Secretarial. **Positions commonly filled include:** Branch Manager; Buyer; Clerical Supervisor; Credit Manager; General Manager; Hotel Manager; Management Trainee; Manufacturer's/Wholesaler's Sales Rep.; Purchasing Agent/Manager; Restaurant/Food Service Manager; Securities Sales Representative; Services Sales Representative; Typist/Word Processor. **Average salary range of placements:** $30,000 - $50,000. **Number of placements per year:** 100 - 199.

MAYS & ASSOCIATES INC.
941 East 86th Street, Indianapolis IN 46240. 317/253-9999. **Fax:** 317/569-0126. **Contact:** Roger R. Mays, President. **Description:** A permanent employment agency. **Specializes in the areas of:** Computer Science/Software; Engineering; Manufacturing. **Positions commonly filled include:** Aerospace Engineer; Biomedical Engineer; Chemical Engineer; Computer Programmer; Designer; Electrical/Electronics Engineer; General Manager; Human Resources Manager; Industrial Engineer; Mechanical Engineer; Metallurgical Engineer; Purchasing Agent/Manager; Quality Control Supervisor; Software Engineer; Structural Engineer; Systems Analyst. **Number of placements per year:** 50 - 99.

P.R. PERSONNEL
1925 Spy Run Avenue, Fort Wayne IN 46805. 219/422-4671. **Fax:** 219/422-4675. **Contact:** Manager. **Description:** A permanent employment agency.

PERRY PERSONNEL PLUS
200 West Pike Street, Goshen IN 46526. 219/533-7330. **Fax:** 219/533-1417. **Contact:** Manager. **Description:** A permanent employment agency. **Specializes in the areas of:** Accounting/Auditing; Banking; General Management; Industrial; Manufacturing; Personnel/Labor Relations; Sales; Secretarial. **Positions commonly filled include:** Accountant/Auditor; Bank Officer/Manager; Blue-Collar Worker Supervisor; Branch Manager; Buyer; Clerical Supervisor; Computer Programmer; Credit Manager; Customer Service Representative; General Manager; Human Resources Specialist; Industrial Engineer; Industrial Production Manager; Management Trainee; Mechanical Engineer; MIS Specialist; Operations/Production Manager; Purchasing Agent/Manager; Quality Control Supervisor; Systems Analyst. **Corporate headquarters location:** Sturgis MI. **Other U.S. locations:** Coldwater MI; Three Rivers MI.

PERSONNEL PARTNERS
828 East Jefferson Boulevard, Suite 200, South Bend IN 46617. 219/234-2115. **Fax:** 219/234-2834. **Contact:** Manager. **Description:** A permanent employment agency. **Specializes in the areas of:** Light Industrial.

PRO RESOURCES
1728 Spy Run Avenue, Fort Wayne IN 46805. 219/420-2117. **Fax:** 219/420-1925. **Contact:** Manager. **Description:** A permanent employment agency that also provides some temporary placements. **Specializes in the areas of:** Light Industrial.

PYRAMIDS PERSONNEL GROUP
3500 DePauw Boulevard, Suite 2050, Indianapolis IN 46268. 317/872-4960. **Fax:** 317/879-1233. **Contact:**

Manager. **Description:** A permanent employment agency. **Specializes in the areas of:** Clerical; Office Support.

QUIRING ASSOCIATES, INC.
7321 Shadeland Station Way, Suite 150, Indianapolis IN 46256-3935. 317/841-7575x4. **Fax:** 317/577-8240. **Contact:** Patti Quiring, CPC/President. **E-mail address:** quiring@iquest.net. **World Wide Web address:** http://web.iquest.net/quiring. **Description:** A permanent employment agency that also provides some temporary placements, and contract and career/outplacement services. **Specializes in the areas of:** Computer Science/Software; Engineering; Health/Medical; Nonprofit; Personnel/Labor Relations; Sales; Secretarial. **Positions commonly filled include:** Account Manager; Account Representative; Accountant; Administrative Assistant; Applications Engineer; Biomedical Engineer; Chemical Engineer; Computer Operator; Computer Programmer; Consultant; Controller; Cost Estimator; Customer Service Representative; Database Manager; Design Engineer; Electrical/Electronics Engineer; Financial Analyst; Human Resources Manager; Industrial Engineer; Licensed Practical Nurse; Manufacturing Engineer; Marketing Manager; MIS Specialist; Operations Manager; Physician; Purchasing Agent/Manager; Quality Control Supervisor; Sales Manager; Sales Representative; Software Engineer; Systems Analyst; Systems Manager; Typist/Word Processor. **Average salary range of placements:** More than $50,000. **Number of placements per year:** 50 - 99.

THE REGISTRY INC.
600 King Cole Building, 7 North Meridian Street, Indianapolis IN 46204-3033. 317/634-1200. **Fax:** 317/263-3845. **Contact:** Director of Operations. **Description:** A permanent employment agency. **Specializes in the areas of:** Accounting/Auditing; Administration; Bookkeeping; Clerical; Computer Science/Software; Health/Medical; Legal; Real Estate.

RELIABLE TECHNICAL SERVICES
2817 Oakwood Avenue, Muncie IN 47304. 765/282-6907. **Fax:** 765/282-6292. **Contact:** Manager. **Description:** A permanent employment agency. **Specializes in the areas of:** Technical.

SNELLING PERSONNEL SERVICES
1000 East 80th Place, Suite 207 South, Merrillville IN 46410-5644. 219/769-2922. **Fax:** 219/755-0557. **Contact:** Cheri K. Elser, General Manager. **Description:** A permanent employment agency. Founded in 1985. **Specializes in the areas of:** Accounting/Auditing; Sales; Secretarial. **Positions commonly filled include:** Bookkeeper; Restaurant/Food Service Manager; Secretary; Services Sales Representative. **Number of placements per year:** 100 - 199.

STAFFMARK ACCOUNTANTS
STAFFMARK TECHNICAL
11118 Coldwater Road, Fort Wayne IN 46845. 219/637-8881. **Contact:** Janet Hambrock, Branch Manager. **Description:** A permanent employment agency that also provides some temporary placements. Staffmark Technical (also at this location; 219/637-9564) is an executive search firm. Great Lakes Search (also at this location; 219/637-1436; http://www.fwi.com/greatlakes) is an executive search firm. **Specializes in the areas of:** Accounting/Auditing; Finance. **Positions commonly filled include:** Accountant; Auditor; Budget Analyst; Controller; Credit Manager; Finance Director; Financial Analyst. **Benefits available to temporary workers:** Paid Holidays; Paid Vacation; Referral Bonus Plan. **Other U.S. locations:** Nationwide. **Number of placements per year:** 100 - 199.

TIME SERVICES, INC.
1346 South Grandstaff Drive, Auburn IN 46706. 219/927-0323. **Toll-free phone:** 800/837-8463. **Fax:** 219/927-0424. **Contact:** Melissa Carpenter, Branch Manager. **Description:** A permanent employment agency. **Specializes in the areas of:** Clerical; Industrial;

Manufacturing; Secretarial; Technical. **Positions commonly filled include:** Data Entry Clerk. **Benefits available to temporary workers:** Medical Insurance; Paid Holidays; Paid Vacation. **Corporate headquarters location:** Fort Wayne IN. **Other area locations:** Ligonier IN. **Average salary range of placements:** Less than $20,000. **Number of placements per year:** 200 - 499.

TEMPORARY EMPLOYMENT AGENCIES

ADECCO
3500 West DePauw Boulevard, Suite 2041, Indianapolis IN 46268. 317/872-8091. **Fax:** 317/879-2388. **Contact:** Branch Manager. **Description:** A temporary agency that also provides some temp-to-perm placements. **Specializes in the areas of:** Administration; Secretarial; Word Processing.

ARTISAN STAFFING
3500 DePauw Boulevard, Suite 1076, Indianapolis IN 46268. 317/872-5153. **Fax:** 317/876-7029. **Contact:** Manager. **Description:** A temporary agency. **Specializes in the areas of:** Administration; Advertising; Art/Design; Computer Science/Software; Publishing. **Positions commonly filled include:** Designer; Draftsperson; Editor; Multimedia Designer; Technical Writer/Editor; Typist/Word Processor; Video Production Coordinator. **Number of placements per year:** 200 - 499.

CORPORATE STAFFING RESOURCES (CSR)
820 North Baldwin Avenue, Marion IN 46952. **Contact:** Debbie Weaver, Branch Manager. **World Wide Web address:** http://www.csronline.com. **Description:** A temporary agency. Founded in 1985. **Specializes in the areas of:** Personnel/Labor Relations. **Positions commonly filled include:** Blue-Collar Worker Supervisor; Branch Manager; Clerical Supervisor; Computer Programmer; Credit Manager; Customer Service Representative; Draftsperson; Financial Analyst; General Manager; Human Resources Manager; Human Service Worker; Industrial Engineer; Industrial Production Manager; Insurance Agent/Broker; Operations/Production Manager; Quality Control Supervisor; Securities Sales Representative; Systems Analyst; Typist/Word Processor; Underwriter/Assistant Underwriter. **Corporate headquarters location:** South Bend IN. **Average salary range of placements:** Less than $20,000. **Number of placements per year:** 200 - 499.

CORPORATE STAFFING RESOURCES (CSR)
130 South Main Street, Suite 120, South Bend IN 46601. 219/233-8209. **Fax:** 219/280-2660. **Contact:** Manager. **World Wide Web address:** http://www.csronline.com. **Description:** A temporary agency that also provides some contract technical placements. Founded in 1987. **Specializes in the areas of:** Accounting/Auditing; Administration; Computer Science/Software; Engineering; Industrial; Manufacturing; Technical. **Positions commonly filled include:** Accountant/Auditor; Administrative Manager; Architect; Biological Scientist; Buyer; Chemical Engineer; Chemist; Civil Engineer; Computer Programmer; Cost Estimator; Credit Manager; Customer Service Representative; Design Engineer; Designer; Draftsperson; Electrical/Electronics Engineer; Electrician; Environmental Engineer; Financial Analyst; Human Resources Manager; Industrial Engineer; Industrial Production Manager; Laboratory Technician; Mechanical Engineer; Metallurgical Engineer; MIS Specialist; Operations/Production Manager; Purchasing Agent/Manager; Quality Control Supervisor; Software Engineer; Structural Engineer; Systems Analyst; Technical Writer/Editor. **Corporate headquarters location:** This Location. **Other U.S. locations:** MI; MO; OH. **Number of placements per year:** 1000+.

CORPORATE STAFFING RESOURCES (CSR)
3552 Commerce Drive, Warsaw IN 46580. 219/269-2149. **Fax:** 219/269-3465. **Contact:** Christy Eldridge, Branch Manager. **World Wide Web address:** http://www.csronline.com. **Description:** A temporary agency that also provides some career/outplacement counseling. **Specializes in the areas of:** Administration; Computer Science/Software; Engineering; General Management; Industrial; Manufacturing; Sales; Technical. **Positions commonly filled include:** Agricultural Engineer; Biomedical Engineer; Blue-Collar Worker Supervisor; Buyer; Chemical Engineer; Chemist; Civil Engineer; Claim Representative; Clerical Supervisor; Computer Programmer; Customer Service Representative; Design Engineer; Draftsperson; Editor; Electrical/Electronics Engineer; Environmental Engineer; Financial Analyst; General Manager; Industrial Engineer; Industrial Production Manager; Mechanical Engineer; Metallurgical Engineer; Operations/Production Manager; Purchasing Agent/Manager; Quality Control Supervisor; Services Sales Representative; Software Engineer; Stationary Engineer; Systems Analyst; Technical Writer/Editor; Typist/Word Processor. **Corporate headquarters location:** South Bend IN. **Average salary range of placements:** Less than $20,000. **Number of placements per year:** 1000+.

CROWN TEMPORARY SERVICES OF INDIANAPOLIS
4503 West 16th Street, Indianapolis IN 46222. 317/243-1999. **Fax:** 317/243-9130. **Contact:** Manager. **Description:** A temporary agency. **Specializes in the areas of:** Accounting/Auditing; Banking; Clerical; Engineering; Finance; Insurance; Legal; Manufacturing; Personnel/Labor Relations. **Positions commonly filled include:** Accountant/Auditor; Administrative Assistant; Advertising Clerk; Bookkeeper; Claim Representative; Clerk; Computer Operator; Computer Programmer; Construction Trade Worker; Customer Service Representative; Data Entry Clerk; Driver; Factory Worker; Legal Secretary; Light Industrial Worker; Marketing Specialist; Medical Secretary; Receptionist; Sales Representative; Secretary; Typist/Word Processor. **Number of placements per year:** 1000+.

DUNHILL STAFFING SYSTEMS
5420 Southern Avenue, Suite 103, Indianapolis IN 46241. 317/247-1775. **Fax:** 317/241-4029. **Contact:** Manager. **Description:** A temporary agency that also provides some temp-to-perm placements. **Specializes in the areas of:** Clerical; Computer Science/Software; Industrial; Light Industrial; Manufacturing; Secretarial; Technical. **Positions commonly filled include:** Blue-Collar Worker Supervisor; Branch Manager; Claim Representative; Clerical Supervisor; Computer Programmer; Customer Service Representative; Mechanical Engineer; Medical Records Technician; Systems Analyst. **Number of placements per year:** 1000+.

EMPLOYMENT PLUS
4629 Morningside Drive, Bloomington IN 47408. 812/333-1070. **Fax:** 812/331-8017. **Contact:** Manager. **Description:** A temporary agency that also provides some temp-to-perm and permanent placements. **Specializes in the areas of:** Clerical; Light Industrial; Technical.

EXPRESS PERSONNEL
332 West U.S. Highway 30, Suite C, Valparaiso IN 46385. 219/465-1868. **Fax:** 219/477-5915. **Contact:** Manager. **Description:** A temporary agency. **Specializes in the areas of:** Accounting/Auditing; Clerical; Finance; Industrial.

INTERIM PERSONNEL
52 South Girls School Road, Indianapolis IN 46231. 317/273-4444. **Fax:** 317/273-4440. **Contact:** Manager. **Description:** A temporary agency. **Specializes in the**

areas of: Administration; Industrial; Office Support; Word Processing. **Corporate headquarters location:** Fort Lauderdale FL.

KELLY SERVICES, INC.
3413 North Briarwood Lane, Muncie IN 47304-5210. 765/284-0897. **Fax:** 765/284-0655. **Contact:** Supervisor. **Description:** A temporary agency. **Specializes in the areas of:** Secretarial; Technical. **Positions commonly filled include:** Customer Service Representative; Typist/Word Processor. **Corporate headquarters location:** Troy MI. **International locations:** Worldwide.

MANPOWER TECHNICAL SERVICES
300 North Meridian Street, Suite 900, Indianapolis IN 46204. 317/262-2020. **Toll-free phone:** 800/366-0557. **Fax:** 317/262-2451. **Contact:** Connie Whisner, Technical Services Manager. **Description:** A temporary agency. **Specializes in the areas of:** Computer Science/Software; Engineering; Technical. **Positions commonly filled include:** Chemical Engineer; Civil Engineer; Computer Programmer; Design Engineer; Electrical/Electronics Engineer; Industrial Engineer; Mechanical Engineer; Metallurgical Engineer; MIS Specialist; Quality Control Supervisor; Software Engineer; Structural Engineer; Systems Analyst. **Corporate headquarters location:** Milwaukee WI. **Average salary range of placements:** $30,000 - $50,000. **Number of placements per year:** 200 - 499.

NORRELL SERVICES, INC.
4770 Covert Avenue, Suite 211, Evansville IN 47714. 812/473-3838. **Fax:** 813/473-3939. **Contact:** Manager. **Description:** A temporary agency. **Specializes in the areas of:** Clerical; Manufacturing. **Positions commonly filled include:** Bookkeeper; Clerk; Computer Operator; Draftsperson; Factory Worker; Legal Secretary; Light Industrial Worker; Medical Secretary; Receptionist; Secretary; Stenographer; Typist/Word Processor. **Corporate headquarters location:** Atlanta GA. **Other U.S. locations:** Nationwide.

NORRELL STAFFING SERVICES
201 South Emerson Avenue, Suite 140, Greenwood IN 46143. 317/885-9599. **Fax:** 317/885-9899. **Contact:** Manager. **Description:** A temporary agency. **Specializes in the areas of:** Industrial; Manufacturing; Personnel/Labor Relations; Secretarial. **Positions commonly filled include:** Accountant/Auditor; Administrative Manager; Advertising Clerk; Blue-Collar Worker Supervisor; Claim Representative; Clerical Supervisor; Clinical Lab Technician; Customer Service Representative; Human Resources Specialist; Librarian; Manufacturer's/Wholesaler's Sales Rep.; Purchasing Agent/Manager; Systems Analyst; Typist/Word Processor. **Corporate headquarters location:** Atlanta GA. **Other U.S. locations:** Nationwide. **Average salary range of placements:** Less than $20,000. **Number of placements per year:** 1000+.

OLSTEN STAFFING SERVICES
3005 25th Street, Columbus IN 47203. 812/372-2722. **Fax:** 812/372-2999. **Contact:** Tammy Gillespie, Branch Manager. **Description:** A temporary agency. **Specializes in the areas of:** Accounting/Auditing; Industrial; Legal; Manufacturing; Personnel/Labor Relations; Secretarial. **Positions commonly filled include:** Accountant/Auditor; Administrative Manager; Advertising Clerk; Blue-Collar Worker Supervisor; Clerical Supervisor; Computer Programmer; Customer Service Representative; Industrial Production Manager; Paralegal; Quality Control Supervisor; Restaurant/Food Service Manager; Systems Analyst; Typist/Word Processor. **Corporate headquarters location:** Melville NY. **Average salary range of placements:** Less than $20,000. **Number of placements per year:** 1000+.

PERSONNEL MANAGEMENT, INC. (PMI)
P.O. Box 322, Jeffersonville IN 47131. 812/284-3223. **Fax:** 812/285-6506. **Contact:** Manager. **Description:** A temporary agency. **Specializes in the areas of:** Industrial; Light Industrial; Retail; Secretarial. **Positions**

commonly filled include: Account Representative; Administrative Assistant; Blue-Collar Worker Supervisor; Customer Service Representative; Secretary. **Benefits available to temporary workers:** 401(k); Life Insurance; Medical Insurance; Paid Holidays; Paid Vacation. **Corporate headquarters location:** Greenwood IN. **Other U.S. locations:** FL; GA; KY. **Average salary range of placements:** Less than $20,000. **Number of placements per year:** 1000+.

STAFFMARK MEDICAL STAFFING
6738 East State Boulevard, Suite E, Fort Wayne IN 46815. 219/749-7449. **Contact:** Manager. **Description:** A temporary agency that also provides some temp-to-perm and direct placements. **Specializes in the areas of:** Health/Medical.

STAR STAFFING
332 Third Avenue, Suite 5, Jasper IN 47546. 812/482-6836. **Toll-free phone:** 800/551-6823. **Fax:** 812/482-2490. **Contact:** Manager. **Description:** A temporary agency. Founded in 1961. **Specializes in the areas of:** Industrial; Manufacturing; Secretarial. **Positions commonly filled include:** Clerical Supervisor; Computer Programmer; Customer Service Representative; Management Trainee; MIS Specialist; Services Sales Representative; Software Engineer; Typist/Word Processor. **Benefits available to temporary workers:** Medical Insurance; Paid Holidays; Paid Vacation. **Corporate headquarters location:** South Bend IN. **Average salary range of placements:** Less than $20,000. **Number of placements per year:** 1000+.

TRY TEMPS INC.
P.O. Box 339, Chandler IN 47610. 812/925-3903. **Fax:** 812/925-3920. **Contact:** Manager. **Description:** A temporary agency that also provides some permanent placements. **Specializes in the areas of:** Engineering; Industrial; Technical. **Positions commonly filled include:** Applications Engineer; Architect; Biomedical Engineer; Buyer; Chemical Engineer; Chemist; Chief Financial Officer; Civil Engineer; Computer Operator; Computer Programmer; Controller; Design Engineer; Draftsperson; Electrical/Electronics Engineer; Food Scientist/Technologist; General Manager; Graphic Designer; Human Resources Manager; Industrial Engineer; Industrial Production Manager; Management Analyst/Consultant; Manufacturing Engineer; Marketing Manager; Mechanical Engineer; Metallurgical Engineer; MIS Specialist; Operations Manager; Physical Therapist; Physician; Product Manager; Project Manager; Public Relations Specialist; Purchasing Agent/Manager; Quality Control Supervisor; Sales Manager; Secretary; Software Engineer; Systems Analyst; Technical Writer/Editor. **Benefits available to temporary workers:** Medical Insurance; Paid Holidays; Paid Vacation. **Average salary range of placements:** $30,000 - $50,000. **Number of placements per year:** 1 - 49.

WESTAFF
512 Noble Drive, Fort Wayne IN 46825. 219/486-5649. **Fax:** 219/484-8877. **Contact:** Marcia Norris, Manager. **Description:** A temporary agency that also provides some permanent placements. **Specializes in the areas of:** Manufacturing; Secretarial. **Positions commonly filled include:** Accountant/Auditor; Blue-Collar Worker Supervisor; Clerical Supervisor; Computer Programmer; Customer Service Representative; Dental Assistant/Dental Hygienist; Electrical/Electronics Engineer; Mechanical Engineer; MIS Specialist; Paralegal; Systems Analyst; Typist/Word Processor. **Corporate headquarters location:** Walnut Creek CA. **Average salary range of placements:** Less than $20,000. **Number of placements per year:** 200 - 499.

WIMMER TEMPORARIES AND DIRECT PLACEMENT
1415 West Jeffras Avenue, Marion IN 46952. 765/664-9550. **Fax:** 765/664-9553. **Contact:** Bill Wimmer, President. **Description:** A temporary agency. **Specializes in the areas of:** Computer Science/Software; Engineering; General Management; Industrial; Manufacturing;

Personnel/Labor Relations; Technical. **Positions commonly filled include:** Accountant/Auditor; Administrative Manager; Agricultural Engineer; Blue-Collar Worker Supervisor; Buyer; Chemical Engineer; Clerical Supervisor; Customer Service Representative; Design Engineer; Draftsperson; Electrical/Electronics Engineer; Electrician; General Manager; Human Resources Manager; Industrial Engineer; Licensed Practical Nurse; Mechanical Engineer; Metallurgical Engineer; Operations/Production Manager; Paralegal; Purchasing Agent/Manager; Quality Control Supervisor; Registered Nurse; Typist/Word Processor. **Benefits available to temporary workers:** Life Insurance; Medical Insurance; Paid Holidays; Paid Vacation; Tuition Assistance. **Other area locations:** Highland IN. **Average salary range of placements:** $20,000 - $29,999. **Number of placements per year:** 200 - 499.

CONTRACT SERVICES FIRMS

ADECCO/TAD TECHNICAL SERVICES
7321 Shadeland Station Way, Suite 245, Indianapolis IN 46256. 317/842-2870. **Fax:** 317/842-3085. **Contact:** Jane Moore, Branch Manager. **World Wide Web address:** http://www.adeccotad.com. **Description:** A contract services firm. **Specializes in the areas of:** Administration; Architecture/Construction; Computer Science/Software; Engineering; Manufacturing; Technical. **Positions commonly filled include:** Aerospace Engineer; Architect; Biochemist; Biomedical Engineer; Blue-Collar Worker Supervisor; Buyer; Chemical Engineer; Chemist; Civil Engineer; Clinical Lab Technician; Computer Programmer; Design Engineer; Designer; Draftsperson; Electrical/Electronics Engineer; Industrial Engineer; Industrial Production Manager; Internet Services Manager; Mechanical Engineer; MIS Specialist; Multimedia Designer; Operations/Production Manager; Software Engineer; Structural Engineer; Systems Analyst; Technical Writer/Editor; Telecommunications Manager. **Average salary range of placements:** $30,000 - $50,000. **Number of placements per year:** 200 - 499.

ALLIANCE GROUP TECHNOLOGIES
8252 Virginia Street, Merrillville IN 46410. 219/736-3855. **Fax:** 219/736-3864. **Contact:** Manager. **Description:** A contract services firm. **Specializes in the areas of:** Engineering; Technical.

ALLIANCE GROUP TECHNOLOGIES
911 Broad Ripple Avenue, Indianapolis IN 46221. 317/254-8285. **Fax:** 317/254-8339. **Contact:** Manager. **Description:** A contract services firm that also provides some permanent placements. **Specializes in the areas of:** Engineering; Technical.

ALLIANCE GROUP TECHNOLOGIES
1830 South Plate Street, Kokomo IN 46902. 765/459-3931. **Fax:** 765/452-2091. **Contact:** Manager. **Description:** A contract services firm. **Specializes in the areas of:** Engineering; Technical.

BELCAN TECHNICAL SERVICES
8355 Rockville Road, Suite 100, Indianapolis IN 46234. 317/273-6700. **Fax:** 317/273-6707. **Contact:** Michael G. Tribul, Branch Manager. **E-mail address:** techind@tech.belcan.com. **World Wide Web address:** http://www.belcan.com. **Description:** A contract services firm. **Specializes in the areas of:** Engineering; Industrial; Technical. **Positions commonly filled include:** Chemical Engineer; Chemist; Civil Engineer; Computer Operator; Database Manager; Design Engineer; Draftsperson; Electrical/Electronics Engineer; Environmental Engineer; Geologist/Geophysicist; Industrial Engineer; Internet Services Manager; Manufacturing Engineer; Mechanical Engineer; Metallurgical Engineer; MIS Specialist; Production Manager; Purchasing Agent/Manager; Quality Control Supervisor; Registered Nurse; Software Engineer; Systems Analyst; Systems Manager; Technical Writer/Editor; Telecommunications

Manager. **Corporate headquarters location:** Cincinnati OH. **Other U.S. locations:** Nationwide. **Average salary range of placements:** $30,000 - $50,000. **Number of placements per year:** 200 - 499.

CMS MANAGEMENT SERVICES
5920 Castleway West Drive, Suite 120, Indianapolis IN 46250. 317/842-5777. **Fax:** 317/577-3077. **Contact:** Manager. **Description:** A contract services firm that also provides some permanent placements. **Specializes in the areas of:** Accounting/Auditing; Engineering; Finance.

QCI TECHNICAL STAFFING
4705 Illinois Road, Suite 113, Fort Wayne IN 46804. 219/436-9797. **Fax:** 219/436-6228. **Contact:** William E. Quackenbush, President. **World Wide Web address:** http://www.qcitechstaffing.com. **Description:** A contract services firm. **Specializes in the areas of:** Administration; Computer Science/Software; Engineering; Technical. **Positions commonly filled include:** Computer Programmer; Design Engineer; Draftsperson; Electrical/Electronics Engineer; Electrician; Industrial Engineer; Manufacturing Engineer; Mechanical Engineer; Metallurgical Engineer; MIS Specialist; Project Manager; Purchasing Agent/Manager; Quality Control Supervisor; Software Engineer; Systems Analyst. **Benefits available to temporary workers:** Holiday Bonus; Paid Vacation. **Average salary range of placements:** $30,000 - $50,000. **Number of placements per year:** 100 - 199.

TECHNETICS CORPORATION
8383 Craig Street, Suite 200, Indianapolis IN 46250. 317/842-5377. **Toll-free phone:** 800/467-8324. **Fax:** 317/842-6992. **Contact:** Recruiter. **Description:** A contract services firm. **Specializes in the areas of:** Architecture/Construction; Computer Science/Software; Engineering; Industrial; Manufacturing; Technical. **Positions commonly filled include:** Architect; Biomedical Engineer; Chemical Engineer; Civil Engineer; Computer Programmer; Design Engineer; Designer; Draftsperson; Editor; Electrical/Electronics Engineer; Electrician; Environmental Engineer; Industrial Engineer; Industrial Production Manager; Internet Services Manager; Mechanical Engineer; Metallurgical Engineer; MIS Specialist; Multimedia Designer; Operations/Production Manager; Purchasing Agent/Manager; Quality Control Supervisor; Science Technologist; Software Engineer; Structural Engineer; Systems Analyst; Technical Writer/Editor. **Average salary range of placements:** $30,000 - $50,000. **Number of placements per year:** 100 - 199.

H.L. YOH COMPANY
5420 West Southern Avenue, Indianapolis IN 46241. 317/381-7000. **Fax:** 317/244-3735. **Contact:** Manager. **Description:** A contract services firm that also provides some temporary and temp-to-perm placements. **Specializes in the areas of:** Administration; Computer Hardware/Software; Engineering; Technical.

CAREER/OUTPLACEMENT COUNSELING FIRMS

GREEN THUMB, INC.
P.O. Box 687, Seymour IN 47274. 812/522-7930. **Fax:** 812/522-7684. **Contact:** Manager. **Description:**

Provides job training and skills training to individuals 55 years of age and over.

JOB CORPS
504 Broadway, Gary IN 46402-1921. 219/882-2677. Fax: 219/882-6718. **Contact:** Counselor. **Description:** A career/outplacement counseling firm. **Positions commonly filled include:** Claim Representative; Clinical Lab Technician; Computer Programmer; Customer Service Representative; Dental Assistant/Dental Hygienist; Dietician/Nutritionist; Electrical/Electronics Engineer; Electrician; Hotel Manager; Licensed Practical Nurse; Medical Records Technician; Restaurant/Food Service Manager; Services Sales Representative; Typist/Word Processor. **Number of placements per year:** 1000+.

WARRICK COUNTY EMPLOYMENT & TRAINING CENTER
224 West Main Street, P.O. Box 377, Boonville IN 47601. 812/897-4700. **Fax:** 812/897-6352. **Contact:** Paul K. Wright, Executive Director. **Description:** A career/outplacement counseling and training center. **NOTE:** Clients must be JTPA (Job Training Partnership Act) eligible. **Specializes in the areas of:** Industrial; Manufacturing; Retail; Sales; Secretarial; Transportation. **Positions commonly filled include:** Draftsperson; Electrician; Maintenance Technician. **Average salary range of placements:** $20,000 - $29,999. **Number of placements per year:** 50 - 99.

◆ I O W A ◆

AGRA PLACEMENTS, LTD.
4949 Pleasant Street, Suite 1, West Des Moines IA 50266. 515/225-6562. **Fax:** 515/225-7733. **Contact:** Manager. **Description:** An executive search firm. **Specializes in the areas of:** Agri-Business; Chemicals; Engineering; Manufacturing.

ANDERSON & ASSOCIATES
30657 Deer Drive, Huxley IA 50124. 515/597-3642. **Contact:** Manager. **Description:** An executive search firm.

ATKINSON SEARCH & PLACEMENT INC.
P.O. Box 493, Fairfield IA 52556. 515/472-3666. **Fax:** 515/472-7270. **Contact:** Arthur Atkinson, President. **E-mail address:** asap@aatkinson.com. **World Wide Web address:** http://www.aatkinson.com. **Description:** An executive search firm. **Specializes in the areas of:** Computer Science/Software. **Positions commonly filled include:** Engineer; Marketing Specialist; Sales Representative; Software Engineer; Technical Writer/Editor. **Number of placements per year:** 1 - 49.

BURTON PLACEMENT SERVICES
1629 Lincolnway, Clinton IA 52732. 319/243-6791. **Fax:** 319/243-6895. **Contact:** Sales/Staffing Consultant. **Description:** An executive search firm. **Specializes in the areas of:** Accounting/Auditing; Administration; Banking; Computer Science/Software; Engineering; Finance; General Management; Industrial; Legal; Manufacturing; Personnel/Labor Relations; Publishing; Retail; Sales; Secretarial; Technical. **Positions commonly filled include:** Accountant/Auditor; Administrative Manager; Advertising Clerk; Aircraft Mechanic/Engine Specialist; Bank Officer/Manager; Claim Rep.; Clerical Supervisor; Computer Programmer; Counselor; Credit Manager; General Manager; Health Services Manager; Health Services Worker; Hotel Manager; Human Resources Manager; Industrial Engineer; Management Trainee; Medical Records Technician; Public Relations Specialist; Purchasing Agent/Manager; Quality Control Supervisor; Systems Analyst; Telecommunications Manager; Underwriter. **Corporate headquarters location:** Sterling IL. **Other U.S. locations:** Dixon IL; Oregon IL; Rochelle IL; Sycamore IL.

BYRNES & RUPKEY, INC.
3356 Kimball Avenue, Waterloo IA 50702. 319/234-6201. **Fax:** 319/234-6360. **Contact:** Lois Rupkey, Executive Vice President. **Description:** An executive search firm. **Specializes in the areas of:** Administration; Architecture/Construction; Banking; Computer Science/Software; Engineering; Finance; General Management; Health/Medical; Industrial; Insurance; Manufacturing; Personnel/Labor Relations; Retail; Sales; Secretarial; Technical. **Positions commonly filled include:** Civil Engineer; Computer Programmer; Draftsperson; Electrical/Electronics Engineer; Human Resources Manager; Manufacturer's/Wholesaler's Sales Rep.; Mechanical Engineer; Occupational Therapist; Petroleum Engineer; Physical Therapist; Physician; Restaurant/Food Service Manager; Software Engineer. **Other U.S. locations:** Warwick RI.

CSI EMPLOYMENT
319 North Main, Burlington IA 52601. 319/753-0223. **Toll-free phone:** 800/615-2850. **Fax:** 319/753-5268. **Contact:** Rhonda Kennedy, Staffing Specialist. **Description:** An executive search firm that also provides contract, permanent, and temporary placements. **NOTE:** Please address resumes for sales positions to Karen Fredrickson. All other resumes should be addressed to Rhonda Kennedy. **Specializes in the areas of:** Administration; Engineering; General Management; Industrial; Light Industrial; Personnel/Labor Relations; Secretarial. **Positions commonly filled include:** Account

Manager; Accountant; Administrative Assistant; Chemical Engineer; Chemist; Civil Engineer; Clerical Supervisor; Computer Operator; Computer Programmer; Customer Service Representative; Design Engineer; Draftsperson; Electrical/Electronics Engineer; Electrician; Environmental Engineer; Human Resources Manager; Industrial Engineer; Industrial Production Manager; Management Trainee; Manufacturing Engineer; Mechanical Engineer; Operations Manager; Production Manager; Project Manager; Purchasing Agent/Manager; Quality Control Supervisor; Sales and Marketing Representative; Secretary; Typist/Word Processor. **Benefits available to temporary workers:** Life Insurance; Medical Insurance; Paid Holidays; Paid Vacation. **Corporate headquarters location:** This Location. **Other area locations:** Fort Madison, IA; Mount Pleasant, IA. **Average salary range of placements:** Less than $20,000. **Number of placements per year:** 1000+.

CAREER SEARCH ASSOCIATES
Regency West One, 1501 50th Street, Suite 381, West Des Moines IA 50266. 515/224-2183. **Contact:** Manager. **Description:** An executive search firm. **Specializes in the areas of:** Accounting/Auditing; Administration; Engineering; Information Systems.

DRAKE-BRENNAN, INC.
dba SNELLING PERSONNEL
2423 Ingersoll, Des Moines IA 50312. 515/244-9999. **Contact:** Charles Drake, President. **Description:** An executive search firm that also provides some temporary placements. **Specializes in the areas of:** Engineering; Finance; Insurance; Sales; Technical. **Positions commonly filled include:** Accountant/Auditor; Actuary; Agricultural Engineer; Bank Officer/Manager; Chemical Engineer; Civil Engineer; Computer Programmer; Electrical/Electronics Engineer; Financial Analyst; Health Services Manager; Industrial Engineer; Insurance Agent/Broker; Mechanical Engineer; Operations/Production Manager; Securities Sales Representative; Software Engineer; Structural Engineer; Underwriter/Assistant Underwriter. **Benefits available to temporary workers:** 401(k); Paid Holidays; Paid Vacation. **Number of placements per year:** 200 - 499.

EXECUTIVE RESOURCES
3816 Ingersoll Avenue, Des Moines IA 57312. 515/287-6880. **Fax:** 515/255-9445. **Contact:** Ms. Gerry Mullane, President. **Description:** An executive search firm. Client company pays fee. **Specializes in the areas of:** Computer Hardware/Software; Data Processing; Insurance; Sales.

F-O-R-T-U-N-E PERSONNEL CONSULTANTS
208 Collins Road NE, Suite 204, Cedar Rapids IA 52402. 319/373-1163. **Fax:** 319/373-1696. **Contact:** Manager. **E-mail address:** cedarrapids@fpcweb.com. **Description:** An executive search firm. **Specializes in the areas of:** Aerospace; Electronics; Telecommunications. **Positions commonly filled include:** Customer Service Manager; Engineer; Operations Engineer; Sales and Marketing Manager.

FRANCIS & ASSOCIATES
6923 Vista Drive, West Des Moines IA 50266. 515/221-9800. **Contact:** Manager. **E-mail address:** fransearch@aol.com. **Description:** An executive search firm.

ROBERT HALF INTERNATIONAL
316 Sixth Avenue, Suite 700, Des Moines IA 50309. 515/244-4414. **Contact:** Manager. **World Wide Web address:** http://www.roberthalf.com. **Description:** An executive search firm. **Corporate headquarters location:** Menlo Park CA. **Other U.S. locations:** Nationwide.

**ROBERT HALF INTERNATIONAL
ACCOUNTEMPS**
1200 35th Street, Suite 600, West Des Moines IA 50266. 515/226-1700. **Contact:** Manager. **World Wide Web address:** http://www.roberthalf.com. **Description:** An executive search firm. Accountemps (also at this location) provides temporary placements. **Specializes in the areas of:** Accounting/Auditing. **Corporate headquarters location:** Menlo Park CA. **Other U.S. locations:** Nationwide.

THE HUMAN RESOURCE GROUP
808 Fifth Avenue, Des Moines IA 50309. 515/243-8855. **Fax:** 515/243-8866. **Contact:** Will Canine, President. **Description:** An executive search firm operating on a contingency basis. **Specializes in the areas of:** Architecture/Construction; Banking; Engineering; Finance; General Management. **Positions commonly filled include:** Civil Engineer; Construction Trade Worker; Electrical/Electronics Engineer; Mechanical Engineer; MIS Specialist. **Average salary range of placements:** $30,000 - $50,000. **Number of placements per year:** 1 - 49.

HUMBERT GROUP
P.O. Box 514, Marion IA 52303. 319/373-4434. **Fax:** 319/373-4435. **Contact:** Bill Humbert, Manager. **E-mail address:** recruiterguy@msn.com. **Description:** An executive search firm. **Specializes in the areas of:** Aerospace; Information Systems; Telecommunications.

MANAGEMENT RECRUITERS INTERNATIONAL
1312 Fourth Street SW, Suite 102, Mason City IA 50401. 515/424-1680. **Fax:** 515/424-6868. **Contact:** Cheryl Plagge, President. **E-mail address:** mrimc@willowtree.com. **Description:** An executive search firm. **Specializes in the areas of:** Administration; Computer Science/Software; Food; Information Systems; Insurance; Manufacturing; Technical. **Positions commonly filled include:** Computer Programmer; Management Analyst/Consultant; MIS Specialist; Software Engineer; Systems Analyst; Telecommunications Manager. **Corporate headquarters location:** Cleveland OH. **Other U.S. locations:** Nationwide. **Average salary range of placements:** More than $50,000. **Number of placements per year:** 1 - 49.

MANAGEMENT RECRUITERS INTERNATIONAL
150 First Avenue NE, Suite 400, Cedar Rapids IA 52401. 319/366-8441. **Fax:** 319/366-1103. **Contact:** Office Manager. **World Wide Web address:** http://www.mricr.com. **Description:** An executive search firm. **Specializes in the areas of:** Accounting/Auditing; Administration; Advertising; Architecture/Construction; Banking; Chemicals; Communications; Computer Hardware/Software; Design; Electrical; Engineering; Food; General Management; Insurance; Legal; Manufacturing; Operations Management; Personnel/Labor Relations; Procurement; Publishing; Retail; Sales; Technical; Transportation. **Corporate headquarters location:** Cleveland OH. **Other U.S. locations:** Nationwide.

MANAGEMENT RECRUITERS INTERNATIONAL
106 West Lowe, Fairfield IA 52556. 515/469-5811. **Fax:** 515/469-6012. **Contact:** Manager. **World Wide Web address:** http://www.mgmtrecruiters.com. **Description:** An executive search firm. **Specializes in the areas of:** Administration; Health/Medical; Human Resources; Information Technology. **Corporate headquarters location:** Cleveland OH. **Other U.S. locations:** Nationwide.

**MANAGEMENT RECRUITERS INTERNATIONAL
COMPUSEARCH**
Alpine Centre South, Penthouse, 2435 Kimberly Road, Bettendorf IA 52722. 319/359-3503. **Contact:** Jerry Herrmann, Manager. **Description:** An executive search firm. Compusearch (also at this location) is an executive search firm. **Specializes in the areas of:** Accounting/Auditing; Administration; Advertising;

Architecture/Construction; Banking; Communications; Computer Hardware/Software; Design; Electrical; Engineering; Food; General Management; Health/Medical; Insurance; Legal; Manufacturing; Operations Management; Personnel/Labor Relations; Procurement; Publishing; Retail; Sales; Technical; Textiles; Transportation. **Corporate headquarters location:** Cleveland OH. **Other U.S. locations:** Nationwide.

MANAGEMENT RECRUITERS OF DES MOINES
1801 25th Street, West Des Moines IA 50266. 515/224-9142. **Contact:** Manager. **Description:** An executive search firm. **Corporate headquarters location:** Cleveland OH. **Other U.S. locations:** Nationwide.

MANAGEMENT RECRUITERS OF SPENCER
P.O. Box 840, Arnolds Park IA 51331. 712/332-2011. **Fax:** 712/332-2051. **Contact:** Manager. **Description:** An executive search firm. **Specializes in the areas of:** Banking; Computer Hardware/Software; Engineering; Food; Manufacturing; Technical. **Corporate headquarters location:** Cleveland OH. **Other U.S. locations:** Nationwide.

McGLADREY SEARCH GROUP
400 Locust Street, Suite 640, Des Moines IA 50309. 515/281-9200. **Fax:** 515/284-1545. **Contact:** Thomas Hamilton, Manager. **Description:** An executive search firm operating on a retainer basis. **Specializes in the areas of:** Accounting/Auditing; Administration; Banking; Data Processing; Engineering; General Management; Manufacturing; Personnel/Labor Relations; Sales. **Positions commonly filled include:** Chief Financial Officer; Controller; Human Resources Manager; Industrial Production Manager; Manufacturing Engineer; Marketing Manager; Mechanical Engineer; MIS Specialist; Production Manager; Purchasing Agent/Manager; Sales Engineer; Sales Executive; Sales Manager; Sales Representative; Secretary. **Corporate headquarters location:** Minneapolis MN. **Other U.S. locations:** Nationwide. **Average salary range of placements:** More than $50,000. **Number of placements per year:** 50 - 99.

MID AMERICA SEARCH
6917 Vista Drive, West Des Moines IA 50266-9309. 515/225-1942. **Fax:** 515/225-3941. **Contact:** Manager. **Description:** An executive search firm. **Specializes in the areas of:** Insurance.

PERSONNEL, INC.
604 Locust Street, Suite 516, Des Moines IA 50309-3720. 515/243-7687. **Fax:** 515/243-3350. **Contact:** Diane Boatwright, Vice President. **Description:** An executive search firm that also offers some career/outplacement services, testing services, and temporary placements. **Specializes in the areas of:** Banking; Clerical; Computer Hardware/Software; Finance; Food; General Management; Legal; Sales; Secretarial; Technical. **Positions commonly filled include:** Bookkeeper; Data Entry Clerk; Legal Secretary; Medical Secretary; Receptionist; Sales Representative; Secretary; Typist/Word Processor. **Number of placements per year:** 100 - 199.

PREMIER SEARCH GROUP
417 First Avenue SE, Cedar Rapids IA 52401. 319/362-2300. **Fax:** 319/362-2333. **Contact:** Ronda Hill, Owner. **E-mail address:** psgroup@uswest.net. **World Wide Web address:** http://www.premiersearchgroup.com. **Description:** An executive search firm operating on a contingency basis. Client company pays fee. **Specializes in the areas of:** Accounting; Banking; Engineering; Finance; Health/Medical; Human Resources; Industrial; Insurance; Manufacturing; Marketing; Personnel/Labor Relations; Publishing; Sales; Technical. **Positions commonly filled include:** Account Manager; Accountant; Applications Engineer; Bank Officer/Manager; Chief Financial Officer; Controller; Credit Manager; Design Engineer; Electrical/Electronics Engineer; Finance Director; Financial Analyst; Fund Manager; Human Resources Manager; Industrial

Engineer; Industrial Production Manager; Insurance Agent/Broker; Manufacturing Engineer; Marketing Manager; Mechanical Engineer; Occupational Therapist; Operations Manager; Pharmacist; Physical Therapist; Production Manager; Purchasing Agent/Manager; Quality Control Supervisor; Registered Nurse; Respiratory Therapist; Sales Engineer; Sales Manager; Systems Analyst; Telecommunications Manager. **Corporate headquarters location:** This Location. **Average salary range of placements:** More than $50,000. **Number of placements per year:** 50 - 99.

QUALITY RECRUITERS INC.
P.O. Box 1075, Fort Dodge IA 50501. 515/573-2400. **Contact:** Manager. **Description:** An executive search firm. **Specializes in the areas of:** Automotive; Health/Medical.

SANFORD ROSE ASSOCIATES
3343 Southgate Court SW, Suite 205, Cedar Rapids IA 52404. 319/286-2969. **Fax:** 319/286-2971. **Contact:** Manager. **World Wide Web address:** http://www.sanfordrose.com. **Description:** An executive search firm. **Specializes in the areas of:** General Management; Transportation.

SEDONA STAFFING SERVICES, INC.
3392 Hillcrest Road, Dubuque IA 52002. 319/556-3040. **Toll-free phone:** 800/383-7641. **Contact:** James

Townsend, President. **Description:** An executive search firm that also provides some temporary placements. **Specializes in the areas of:** Accounting/Auditing; Banking; Clerical; Manufacturing; Secretarial. **Positions commonly filled include:** Accountant/Auditor; Administrative Assistant; Bank Officer/Manager; Bookkeeper; Claim Representative; Computer Programmer; Credit Manager; Customer Service Representative; Electrical/Electronics Engineer; Human Resources Manager; Legal Secretary; Marketing Specialist; Mechanical Engineer; Medical Secretary; Purchasing Agent/Manager; Receptionist; Sales Representative; Secretary; Stenographer; Systems Analyst; Typist/Word Processor. **Benefits available to temporary workers:** 401(k); Bonus Award/Plan; Medical Insurance. **Average salary range of placements:** $30,000 - $50,000. **Number of placements per year:** 1 - 49.

LEE SMITH & ASSOCIATES
7177 Hickman Road, Suite 10, Des Moines IA 50322. 515/270-2791. **Contact:** Manager. **Description:** An executive search firm.

TUCKER PERSONNEL CONSULTANTS
1728 34th Street NE, Cedar Rapids IA 52402. 319/362-2936. **Contact:** Manager. **Description:** An executive search firm. **Specializes in the areas of:** Engineering.

PERMANENT EMPLOYMENT AGENCIES

BREI & ASSOCIATES, INC.
P.O. Box 445, Marion IA 52302-0445. 319/377-9196. **Fax:** 319/377-9219. **Contact:** Randy Brei, President. **Description:** Brei & Associates is a permanent employment agency. **Specializes in the areas of:** Computer Science/Software; Engineering. **Positions commonly filled include:** Computer Programmer; Design Engineer; Electrical Engineer; Mechanical Engineer; Software Engineer; Systems Analyst; Technical Writer/Editor. **Average salary range of placements:** More than $50,000. **Number of placements per year:** 1 - 49.

BRYANT BUREAU
2435 Kimberly Road, Suite 110 North, Bettendorf IA 52722. 319/355-4411. **Toll-free phone:** 800/873-4411. **Fax:** 319/355-3635. **Contact:** Doug Ryan, CPC, President. **World Wide Web address:** http://www.bbureau.com. **Description:** A permanent employment agency. Client company pays fee. **Specializes in the areas of:** Sales. **Positions commonly filled include:** Account Manager; Account Representative; Insurance Agent/Broker; Marketing Manager; Sales Engineer; Sales Executive; Sales Manager; Sales Representative. **Corporate headquarters location:** This Location. **Other U.S. locations:** Nationwide. **Average salary range of placements:** $20,000 - $50,000. **Number of placements per year:** 50 - 99.

CAMBRIDGE CAREERS
610 32nd Avenue SW, Suite A, Cedar Rapids IA 52404-3910. 319/366-7771. **Contact:** Office Manager. **Description:** A permanent employment agency. **Specializes in the areas of:** Accounting/Auditing; Clerical; Computer Science/Software; Engineering; Health/Medical; Manufacturing; Sales; Secretarial. **Positions commonly filled include:** Accountant/Auditor; Aerospace Engineer; Architect; Bank Officer/Manager; Blue-Collar Worker Supervisor; Clerical Supervisor; Computer Programmer; Design Engineer; Human Resources Manager; Industrial Designer; Industrial Engineer; Mechanical Engineer; MIS Specialist; Physical Therapist; Physician; Purchasing Agent/Manager; Quality Control Supervisor; Respiratory Therapist; Sales Representative; Secretary; Typist/Word Processor. **Benefits available to temporary workers:** 401(k); Bonus Award/Plan; Dental Insurance; Medical

Insurance; Paid Holidays; Paid Vacation. **Corporate headquarters location:** This Location. **Other U.S. locations:** Nationwide. **Average salary range of placements:** More than $50,000. **Number of placements per year:** 100 - 199.

CAREER FINDERS
2936 104th Street, Urbandale IA 50322. 515/278-9467. **Contact:** Manager. **Description:** A permanent employment agency that also provides some temporary placements.

CAREERNET, INC.
2120 Grand Avenue, Des Moines IA 50312. 515/244-3902. **Fax:** 515/244-5119. **Contact:** Recruiter. **Description:** A permanent employment agency that also offers career/outplacement counseling. **Specializes in the areas of:** Office Support. **Positions commonly filled include:** Accountant/Auditor; Administrative Manager; Advertising Clerk; Brokerage Clerk; Claim Representative; Customer Service Representative; General Manager; Operations/Production Manager; Services Sales Representative; Technical Writer/Editor; Typist/Word Processor. **Average salary range of placements:** Less than $20,000. **Number of placements per year:** 100 - 199.

CITY & NATIONAL STAFFING/RECRUITING COMPANY
P.O. Box 83, Waterloo IA 50704. 319/232-6641. **Fax:** 319/232-5700. **Contact:** Michael C. Grillo, Manager of Engineering/Recruitment. **E-mail address:** michaelgrillo@wordnet.att.net. **Description:** A permanent employment agency. **Specializes in the areas of:** Data Processing; Engineering. **Positions commonly filled include:** Aerospace Engineer; Agricultural Engineer; Biomedical Engineer; Ceramics Engineer; Chemical Engineer; Civil Engineer; Electrical/Electronics Engineer; Manufacturing Engineer; Materials Engineer; Mechanical Engineer; Metallurgical Engineer; Software Engineer; Structural Engineer. **Number of placements per year:** 200 - 499.

IOWA WORKFORCE DEVELOPMENT CENTER
2700 First Avenue South, Fort Dodge IA 50501. 515/576-3131. **Fax:** 515/955-1420. **Contact:** Terry Augustus, Manager. **World Wide Web address:** http://www.state.ia.us/government/wd/index.htm.

Description: A permanent employment agency. **Specializes in the areas of:** Nonprofit. **Positions commonly filled include:** Accountant/Auditor; Administrative Assistant; Aerospace Engineer; Architect; Biological Scientist; Biomedical Engineer; Bookkeeper; Buyer; Ceramics Engineer; Chemical Engineer; Chemist; Civil Engineer; Claim Representative; Clerk; Commercial Artist; Computer Operator; Computer Programmer; Construction Trade Worker; Credit Manager; Customer Service Representative; Data Entry Clerk; Draftsperson; Driver; Editor; EDP Specialist; Electrical/Electronics Engineer; Factory Worker; Hotel Manager; Industrial Designer; Industrial Engineer; Legal Secretary; Light Industrial Worker; Manufacturing Engineer; Marketing Specialist; Mechanical Engineer; Medical Secretary; Metallurgical Engineer; MIS Specialist; Nurse; Operations/Production Manager; Public Relations Specialist; Purchasing Agent/Manager; Quality Control Supervisor; Receptionist; Sales Representative; Secretary; Software Engineer; Systems Analyst; Technical Writer/Editor; Technician; Typist/Word Processor. **Number of placements per year:** 1000+.

IOWA WORKFORCE DEVELOPMENT CENTER
524 Lawler Street, Iowa Falls IA 50126. 515/648-4781. **Contact:** Norman Bissell, Job Service Interviewer. **Description:** A permanent employment agency. **Positions commonly filled include:** Blue-Collar Worker Supervisor; Branch Manager; Clerical Supervisor; Construction Contractor; General Manager; Insurance Agent/Broker; Management Trainee; Registered Nurse. **Number of placements per year:** 200 - 499.

PRATT-YOUNGLOVE, INC.
504 Nebraska Street, Sioux City IA 51101. 712/255-7961. **Fax:** 712/277-3744. **Contact:** Rick Eberle, Manager of Recruiting. **Description:** A permanent employment agency that also provides some temporary placements, executive searches, and resume and career counseling services. Client company pays fee. **Specializes in the areas of:** Accounting; Administration; Banking; Computer Science/Software; Finance; General Management; Legal; Marketing; Sales; Secretarial. **Positions commonly filled include:** Account Manager; Account Representative; Accountant; Adjuster; Administrative Assistant; Administrative Manager; Advertising Clerk; Advertising Executive; Applications Engineer; Architect; AS400 Programmer Analyst; Assistant Manager; Auditor; Bank Officer/Manager;
Blue-Collar Worker Supervisor; Branch Manager; Broadcast Technician; Buyer; Chief Financial Officer; Claim Representative; Clerical Supervisor; Computer Engineer; Computer Operator; Computer Programmer; Computer Support Technician; Computer Technician; Content Developer; Controller; Cost Estimator; Credit Manager; Customer Service Representative; Database Administrator; Database Manager; Design Engineer; Draftsperson; Economist; Electrical/Electronics Engineer; Electrician; Finance Director; General Manager; Graphic Designer; Human Resources Manager; Industrial Engineer; Insurance Agent/Broker; Internet Services Manager; Management Analyst/Consultant; Management Trainee; Manufacturing Engineer; Market Research Analyst; Marketing Manager; Marketing Specialist; Mechanical Engineer; Medical Assistant; Medical Records Technician; Metallurgical Engineer; MIS Specialist; Multimedia Designer; Network/Systems Administrator; Paralegal; Production Manager; Public Relations Specialist; Purchasing Agent/Manager; Sales Executive; Sales Manager; Sales Representative; Secretary; Software Engineer; SQL Programmer; Systems Analyst; Systems Manager; Typist/Word Processor; Video Production Coordinator. **Corporate headquarters location:** This Location. **Average salary range of placements:** $20,000 - $75,000. **Number of placements per year:** 100 - 199.

DEE SPRINGER PERSONNEL
2435 Kimberly Road, Suite 140 South, Bettendorf IA 52722. 319/355-0241. **Contact:** Manager. **Description:** A permanent employment agency.

STAFFING EDGE
1001 Office Park Road, Suite 320, West Des Moines IA 50265. 515/224-0446. **Fax:** 515/224-6599. **Contact:** Manager. **Description:** A permanent employment agency. **Specializes in the areas of:** Accounting/Auditing; Data Processing; Engineering; Finance; Insurance; Personnel/Labor Relations; Sales; Software Engineering.

NATE VIALL & ASSOCIATES
P.O. Box 12238, Des Moines IA 50312. 515/274-1729. **Fax:** 515/274-5646. **Contact:** Nate Viall, President. **Description:** A permanent employment agency. **Specializes in the areas of:** Administration; Computer Science/Software. **Positions commonly filled include:** Computer Programmer; Systems Analyst.

TEMPORARY EMPLOYMENT AGENCIES

ENTEGEE
5309 Victoria Avenue, Davenport IA 52807-2989. 319/359-7042. **Fax:** 319/359-6331. **Contact:** Manager. **Description:** A temporary agency that also offers some contract services. **Specializes in the areas of:** Engineering. **Positions commonly filled include:** Chemical Engineer; Civil Engineer; Computer Programmer; Draftsperson; Electrical/Electronics Engineer; Electrician; Environmental Engineer; Industrial Engineer; Industrial Production Manager; Manufacturing Engineer; Mechanical Engineer; Mining Engineer; MIS Specialist; Production Manager; Project Manager; Software Engineer; Systems Analyst; Systems Manager; Technical Writer/Editor. **Benefits available to temporary workers:** 401(k); Medical Insurance. **Corporate headquarters location:** This Location. **Other U.S. locations:** Louisville KY. **Average salary range of placements:** $30,000 - $50,000. **Number of placements per year:** 200 - 499.

HELPING HANDS TEMPORARY SERVICE
27 North Center Street, Marshalltown IA 50158. 515/752-5040. **Fax:** 515/753-2165. **Contact:** Manager. **Description:** A temporary agency. **Specializes in the areas of:** Accounting/Auditing; Administration; Architecture/Construction; Banking; Computer Science/Software; Education; Engineering; Fashion;
Finance; Food; General Management; Health/Medical; Industrial; Insurance; Legal; Manufacturing; Nonprofit; Personnel/Labor Relations; Publishing; Retail; Sales; Secretarial. **Positions commonly filled include:** Administrative Manager; Advertising Clerk; Architect; Blue-Collar Worker Supervisor; Buyer; Claim Representative; Clerical Supervisor; Computer Programmer; Credit Manager; Customer Service Representative; Draftsperson; Human Service Worker; Paralegal; Systems Analyst; Typist/Word Processor. **Benefits available to temporary workers:** Medical Insurance; Paid Holidays; Paid Vacation. **Number of placements per year:** 500 - 999.

KELLY SERVICES, INC.
400 Locust Street, Suite 250, Des Moines IA 50309-2331. 515/282-0264. **Fax:** 515/243-6948. **Contact:** Reagen Petterson, Supervisor. **Description:** A temporary agency. Founded in 1946. **Specializes in the areas of:** Accounting/Auditing; Administration; Computer Science/Software; Light Industrial; Personnel/Labor Relations; Sales; Secretarial. **Positions commonly filled include:** Accountant/Auditor; Clerk; Computer Programmer; Customer Service Representative; MIS Specialist; Services Sales Representative; Systems Analyst; Typist/Word Processor. **Benefits available to temporary workers:** Medical Insurance; Paid Holidays;

Paid Vacation. **Corporate headquarters location:** Troy MI. **Average salary range of placements:** Less than $30,000. **Number of placements per year:** 1000+.

KELLY SERVICES, INC.
10101 University Avenue, Suite 201, Clive IA 50325. 515/223-6599. **Fax:** 515/222-0560. **Contact:** Manager. **Description:** A temporary agency. **Specializes in the areas of:** Sales; Secretarial. **Positions commonly filled include:** Claim Representative; Customer Service Representative; Typist/Word Processor. **Benefits available to temporary workers:** Medical Insurance; Paid Holidays; Paid Vacation. **Corporate headquarters location:** Troy MI. **Average salary range of placements:** Less than $20,000. **Number of placements per year:** 200 - 499.

SALEM MANAGEMENT INC.
dba RUDY SALEM STAFFING SERVICES
319 Grand Avenue, P.O. Box 701, Spencer IA 51301. 712/262-5990. **Toll-free phone:** 800/517-2536. **Fax:** 712/262-4383. **Contact:** Office Manager. **Description:** A temporary agency that also offers some permanent placements. Founded in 1994. **Specializes in the areas of:** Accounting/Auditing; Administration; Clerical; Industrial; Light Industrial; Manufacturing; Secretarial. **Positions commonly filled include:** Accountant/Auditor; Administrative Manager; Automotive Mechanic; Blue-Collar Worker Supervisor; Branch Manager; Brokerage Clerk; Buyer; Claim Representative; Clerical Supervisor; Clinical Lab Technician; Construction and Building Inspector; Counselor; Credit Manager; Customer Service Representative; Draftsperson; Editor; General Manager; Health Services Manager; Hotel Manager; Human Resources Specialist; Industrial Production Manager; Landscape Architect; Management Trainee; Manufacturer's/Wholesaler's Sales Rep.; MIS Specialist; Occupational Therapist; Operations/Production Manager; Paralegal; Property and Real Estate Manager; Public Relations Specialist; Purchasing Agent/Manager; Quality Control Supervisor; Reporter; Restaurant/Food Service Manager; Securities Sales Representative; Systems Analyst; Travel Agent; Typist/Word Processor; Underwriter/Assistant Underwriter. **Benefits available to temporary workers:** Paid Holidays; Referral Bonus Plan. **Corporate headquarters location:** Sioux City IA. **Average salary range of placements:** Less than $20,000. **Number of placements per year:** 100 - 199.

SALEM MANAGEMENT INC.
dba RUDY SALEM STAFFING SERVICES
701 Pierce, Suite 303, P.O. Box 3124, Sioux City IA 51102. 712/277-4204. **Fax:** 712/277-1512. **Contact:** Steve Salem, President. **Description:** A temporary agency that also provides some permanent placements and contract services. **Specializes in the areas of:** Accounting/Auditing; Clerical; Engineering; Finance; General Management; Industrial; Light Industrial; Personnel/Labor Relations; Sales; Secretarial. **Positions commonly filled include:** Account Manager; Account Representative; Accountant/Auditor; Adjuster; Administrative Assistant; Advertising Executive; Assistant Manager; Auditor; Bank Officer/Manager; Blue-Collar Worker Supervisor; Branch Manager; Buyer; Chemical Engineer; Chief Financial Officer; Civil Engineer; Claim Representative; Clerical Supervisor; Clinical Lab Technician; Computer Operator; Computer Programmer; Construction Contractor; Controller; Cost Estimator; Credit Manager; Customer Service Representative; Database Manager; Dietician/Nutritionist; Draftsperson; Editor; Editorial Assistant; Electrical/Electronics Engineer; Electrician; Environmental Engineer; ESL Teacher; Finance Director; Financial Analyst; General Manager; Graphic Artist; Graphic Designer; Health Services Manager; Human Resources Manager; Industrial Engineer; Industrial Production Manager; Insurance Agent/Broker; Management Analyst/Consultant; Management Trainee; Manufacturing Engineer; Marketing Manager; Marketing Specialist; Mechanical Engineer; Medical Records Technician; MIS Specialist; Operations/Production Manager; Paralegal; Pharmacist; Production Manager; Project Manager; Public Relations Specialist; Purchasing Agent/Manager; Quality Control Supervisor; Reporter; Sales Engineer; Sales Executive; Sales Manager; Sales Representative; Secretary; Systems Analyst; Technical Writer/Editor; Telecommunications Manager; Typist/Word Processor; Vice President; Webmaster. **Benefits available to temporary workers:** Medical Insurance; Paid Holidays. **Corporate headquarters location:** This Location. **Other area locations:** Spencer IA. **Average salary range of placements:** $20,000 - $29,999. **Number of placements per year:** 1000+.

TECHSTAFF, INC.
5115 Utica Ridge Road, Davenport IA 52807. 319/355-4400. **Fax:** 319/355-0694. **Contact:** Steven Nord, Sales Manager. **Description:** A temporary agency that also provides some permanent placements. **Specializes in the areas of:** Computer Science/Software; Engineering; Manufacturing; Technical. **Positions commonly filled include:** Aerospace Engineer; Agricultural Engineer; Architect; Biomedical Engineer; Buyer; Chemical Engineer; Chemist; Civil Engineer; Clinical Lab Technician; Computer Programmer; Design Engineer; Designer; Draftsperson; Electrical/Electronics Engineer; Electrician; Environmental Engineer; Food Scientist/Technologist; General Manager; Industrial Engineer; Mechanical Engineer; Mining Engineer; MIS Specialist; Operations/Production Manager; Purchasing Agent/Manager; Quality Control Supervisor; Software Engineer; Structural Engineer; Systems Analyst; Technical Writer/Editor. **Corporate headquarters location:** Milwaukee WI. **Other U.S. locations:** Oxnard CA; Tampa FL; Chicago IL; Grand Rapids MI; Green Bay WI. **Number of placements per year:** 100 - 199.

TRI-STATE NURSING ENTERPRISES, INC.
621 16th Street, Sioux City IA 51105-1237. 712/277-4442. **Toll-free phone:** 800/727-1912. **Contact:** Bridget Hoefling, President. **Description:** A temporary agency. **Specializes in the areas of:** Health/Medical. **Positions commonly filled include:** Certified Nurses Aide; Clinical Lab Technician; Dental Assistant/Dental Hygienist; Licensed Practical Nurse; Occupational Therapist; Physical Therapist; Recreational Therapist; Registered Nurse; Respiratory Therapist; Social Worker. **Average salary range of placements:** $20,000 - $60,000. **Number of placements per year:** 50 - 99.

CONTRACT SERVICES FIRMS

CDI CORPORATION
P.O. Box 854, Bettendorf IA 52722. 319/359-8233. **Fax:** 319/359-5817. **Contact:** Manager. **World Wide Web address:** http://www.cdicorp.com. **Description:** A contract services firm. **Specializes in the areas of:** Engineering; Technical. **Corporate headquarters location:** Philadelphia PA. **Other U.S. locations:** Nationwide. **International locations:** Worldwide.

MANPOWER PROFESSIONAL
845 A Avenue NE, Cedar Rapids IA 52402. 319/366-1660. **Fax:** 319/366-6536. **Contact:** Scott Fisher, Professional Supervisor. **Description:** A contract services firm. Founded in 1969. **Specializes in the areas of:** Computer Science/Software; Engineering. **Positions commonly filled include:** Aerospace Engineer; Agricultural Engineer; Aircraft Mechanic/Engine Specialist; Biochemist; Biological Scientist; Biomedical Engineer; Buyer; Chemical Engineer; Civil Engineer; Computer Programmer; Draftsperson; Electrical/Electronics Engineer; Industrial Engineer; Mechanical Engineer; MIS Specialist; Nuclear Engineer; Software Engineer; Systems Analyst; Technical Writer/Editor; Telecommunications Manager. **Benefits available to**

temporary workers: 401(k); Dental Insurance; Medical Insurance; Paid Vacation. **Number of placements per year:** 200 - 499.

NATIONJOB INC.
601 SW Ninth Street, Suite J, Des Moines IA 50309. **Toll-free phone:** 800/292-7731. **Fax:** 515/283-1223. **Contact:** Bob Levinstein, Vice President. **World Wide Web address:** http://www.nationjob.com. **Description:** A contract services firm.

PROFESSIONAL RESOURCES GROUP
1331 50th Street, Suite 102, West Des Moines IA 50266-1602. 515/222-0248. **Toll-free phone:** 800/944-8689. **Fax:** 515/222-5351. **Contact:** Tom Hildebrand, President. **Description:** A contract services firm. **Positions commonly filled include:** Accountant/Auditor; Clerical Supervisor; Human Resources Specialist; Paralegal; Technical Writer/Editor. **Average salary range of placements:** $30,000 - $50,000. **Number of placements per year:** 1 - 49.

STAFF MANAGEMENT, INC.
2712 Orchard Drive, Suite A, Cedar Falls IA 50613. 319/266-1320. **Fax:** 319/266-1616. **Contact:** Leah Gutknecht, Branch Manager. **Description:** A contract services firm. **Specializes in the areas of:** Accounting/Auditing; Administration; Computer Science/Software; Engineering; Health/Medical; Industrial; Insurance; Manufacturing; Personnel/Labor Relations; Secretarial; Technical. **Positions commonly filled include:** Accountant/Auditor; Buyer; Claim Representative; Computer Programmer; Design Engineer; Designer; Draftsperson; Human Resources Engineer; Designer; Draftsperson; Human Resources Specialist; Industrial Engineer; Licensed Practical Nurse; Mechanical Engineer; MIS Specialist; Purchasing Agent/Manager; Registered Nurse; Software Engineer; Systems Analyst; Technical Writer/Editor; Typist/Word Processor. **Benefits available to temporary workers:** 401(k); Dental Insurance; Life Insurance; Medical Insurance.

◆ KANSAS ◆

ABLE EMPLOYMENT INC.
10 East Cambridge Circle Drive, Kansas City KS 66103.
913/281-1600. **Fax:** 913/281-2468. **Contact:** Manager.
Description: An executive search firm.

ACCESS
4220 Shawnee Mission Parkway, Suite 101-B, Fairway
KS 66205. 913/722-4200. **Contact:** Manager. **Description:**
An executive search firm.

ACCOUNTING RESOURCES INC.
6800 College Boulevard, Suite 420, Overland Park KS
66211. 913/498-0600. **Contact:** Manager. **Description:**
An executive search firm.

AGRA PLACEMENTS, LTD.
603 East Lincoln Boulevard, Hesston KS 67062.
316/327-2128. **Fax:** 316/327-2177. **Contact:** Manager.
World Wide Web address:
http://www.agraplacements.com. **Description:** An
executive search firm. **Specializes in the areas of:** Agri-
Business; Chemicals; Food.

ANTHONY'S EXECUTIVE SEARCH
1301 Brady Street, Wichita KS 67204. 316/831-9744.
Contact: Manager. **Description:** An executive search
firm.

ARWOOD & ASSOCIATES
7304 West 130th Street, Shawnee Mission KS 66213.
913/685-1900. **Contact:** Manager. **E-mail address:**
arwood@qni.com. **World Wide Web address:**
http://www.arwoodassociates.com. **Description:** Arwood
& Associates is an executive search firm. **NOTE:**
Jobseekers should complete an online application.
Resumes should be sent via e-mail, and need to be in
Word format. **Specializes in the areas of:**
Administration; Insurance.

BLACKWELL ASSOCIATES
8105 West 142nd Terrace, Shawnee Mission KS 66223.
913/681-1848. **Contact:** Burman Blackwell, President.
Description: An executive search firm. **Specializes in
the areas of:** Information Technology; Insurance;
Marketing.

BRINKMAN & ASSOCIATES
P.O. Box 4424, Shawnee Mission KS 66204. 913/341-
8422. **Fax:** 913/381-2046. **Contact:** Manager.
Description: An executive search firm. Founded in 1979.
Specializes in the areas of: Biotechnology; Distribution;
Food; Health/Medical.

D.F. BRYANT & COMPANY
7600 West 110th Street, Suite 107, Overland Park KS
66210. 913/345-2806. **Contact:** Manager. **Description:**
An executive search firm.

BURGESS ASSOCIATES
15940 College Boulevard, Shawnee Mission KS 66219.
913/438-3662. **Fax:** 913/438-0846. **Contact:** C.M.
Burgess, President. **Description:** An executive search
firm operating on a retainer basis.

CAMBRIDGE GROUP
1155 Adams Street, Suite 130, Kansas City KS 66103.
913/342-1345. **Contact:** Manager. **Description:** An
executive search firm.

CAREERS UNLIMITED, INC.
P.O. Box 12111, Overland Park KS 66282-2111.
913/469-1709. **Fax:** 913/469-5568. **Contact:** Bud Burris,
President. **Description:** Careers Unlimited, Inc. is an
executive search firm. **Average salary range of
placements:** More than $75,000. **Number of
placements per year:** 100 - 199.

CENTURY
7096 West 105th Street, Overland Park KS 66212.
913/383-0001. **Contact:** Tim Thornton, Vice President.
Description: Century is an executive search firm.
Specializes in the areas of: Banking; Health/Medical.
Positions commonly filled include: Chief Financial
Officer; Laboratory Technician; Lender; Nurse;
Occupational Therapist; Physical Therapist; Trust
Officer.

THE CHASE GROUP
7300 West 110th Street, Suite 560, Overland Park KS
66210. 913/663-3100. **Fax:** 913/663-3131. **Contact:**
Manager. **Description:** An executive search firm.
Specializes in the areas of: Biotechnology;
Pharmaceuticals.

CORPORATE RESOURCES
10308 Metcalf Avenue, Suite 328, Overland Park KS
66212. 913/599-5445. **Fax:** 913/599-5455. **Contact:**
Manager. **Description:** Corporate Resources is an
executive search firm. **Specializes in the areas of:**
Electrical; Technical.

EFFECTIVE SEARCH INC.
301 North Main Street, Suite 1320, Wichita KS 67202.
316/267-9180. **Contact:** Manager. **Description:**
Effective Search Inc. is an executive search firm
operating on a retainer basis. The firm also provides some
permanent placements. **Specializes in the areas of:**
Information Systems. **Positions commonly filled include:**
AS400 Programmer Analyst; Computer Engineer;
Computer Programmer; Computer Support Technician;
Computer Technician; Database Administrator; Database
Manager; Internet Services Manager; MIS Specialist;
Multimedia Designer; Network/Systems Administrator;
Software Engineer; SQL Programmer; Systems Analyst;
Systems Manager; Webmaster.

EXECU-SEARCH INTERNATIONAL
250 North Rock Road, Suite 300, Wichita KS 67206.
316/683-3525. **Contact:** Manager. **Description:** An
executive search firm. **Specializes in the areas of:**
Manufacturing; Sales.

**ROBERT HALF INTERNATIONAL
ACCOUNTEMPS**
10955 Lowell Avenue, Suite 490, Overland Park KS
66210. 913/451-7600. **Contact:** Branch Manager.
Description: Robert Half International is an executive
search firm. Accountemps (also at this location) provides
temporary placements. **Corporate headquarters
location:** Menlo Park CA. **Other U.S. locations:**
Nationwide.

HEALTH SEARCH, INC.
600 South Washington Street, El Dorado KS 67042.
316/322-8077. **Fax:** 316/322-8290. **Contact:** Manager.
Description: An executive search firm. **Specializes in
the areas of:** Health/Medical.

HENSLER & ASSOCIATES
9900 West 109th Street, Building 70, Suite 380,
Overland Park KS 66210. 913/451-9460. **Contact:**
Manager. **Description:** Hensler & Associates is an
executive search firm. **Specializes in the areas of:** Data
Processing.

HOWARD GROUP
7600 West 110th Street, Suite 204, Overland Park KS
66210. 913/663-2323. **Fax:** 913/663-3424. **Contact:**
Manager. **Description:** An executive search firm.

ALEXANDER HOYT & ASSOCIATES
9200 Indian Creek Parkway, Shawnee Mission KS
66210. 913/663-1065. **Fax:** 913/663-1403. **Contact:**

Manager. Description: A generalist executive search firm.

BRACK HUNTER CORPORATION
12725 Maple Street, Overland Park KS 66209. 913/685-9991. **Contact:** Manager. **Description:** An executive search firm.

IDA GROUP
12565 West 82nd Terrace, Shawnee Mission KS 66215. 913/492-2358. **Fax:** 913/492-8954. **Contact:** Manager. **Description:** An executive search firm. **Specializes in the areas of:** Banking; Technical. **Positions commonly filled include:** Technician.

J&J CONSULTANTS LIMITED
10999 Metcalf Avenue, Suite 200, Overland Park KS 66210. 913/498-0010. **Contact:** Manager. **Description:** An executive search firm.

JAG & ASSOCIATES ATTORNEY SEARCH
7299 West 98th Terrace, Building 6, Overland Park KS 66212. 913/648-6627. **Toll-free phone:** 800/884-2115. **Contact:** Manager. **Description:** An executive search firm. **Specializes in the areas of:** Legal. **Positions commonly filled include:** Attorney.

LAWRENCE-LEITER & COMPANY
4400 Shawnee Mission Parkway, Suite 208, Fairway KS 66205. 913/677-5500. **Fax:** 913/677-1975. **Contact:** Manager. **Description:** An executive search firm.

LEGAL SEARCH ASSOCIATES
6701 West 64th Street, Suite 210, Overland Park KS 66202. 913/722-3500. **Fax:** 913/362-4864. **Contact:** Dr. Terry W. Basher. **E-mail address:** LSA@jdhunter.com. **World Wide Web address:** http://www.jdhunter.com. **Description:** An executive search firm operating on a contingency basis. Client company pays fee. **Specializes in the areas of:** Legal. **Positions commonly filled include:** Attorney. **Corporate headquarters location:** This Location. **Average salary range of placements:** $50,000 - $100,000. **Number of placements per year:** 1 - 49.

MANAGEMENT RECRUITERS INTERNATIONAL
8100 East 22nd Street North, Building 1500, Suite B, Wichita KS 67226. 316/682-8239. **Contact:** Manager. **Description:** An executive search firm. **Corporate headquarters location:** Cleveland OH. **Other U.S. locations:** Nationwide.

MANAGEMENT RECRUITERS OF FORT SCOTT
2401 Cooper Street, Fort Scott KS 66701. 316/223-3133. **Fax:** 316/223-3733. **Contact:** Branch Manager. **Description:** Management Recruiters of Fort Scott is an executive search firm. **Specializes in the areas of:** Printing. **Corporate headquarters location:** Cleveland OH. **Other U.S. locations:** Nationwide.

MANAGEMENT RECRUITERS OF OVERLAND PARK
SALES CONSULTANTS OF OVERLAND PARK/OFFICEMATES5
9401 Indian Creek Parkway, Suite 920, Overland Park KS 66210. 913/661-9300. **Fax:** 913/661-9030. **Contact:** Office Manager. **Description:** Management Recruiters of Overland Park is an executive search firm. **Specializes in the areas of:** Accounting/Auditing; Administration; Advertising; Architecture/Construction; Banking; Chemicals; Communications; Computer Hardware/Software; Design; Electrical; Engineering; Food; General Management; Health/Medical; Insurance; Legal; Manufacturing; Operations Management; Personnel/Labor Relations; Procurement; Publishing; Retail; Sales; Technical; Textiles; Transportation. **Corporate headquarters location:** Cleveland OH. **Other U.S. locations:** Nationwide.

MANAGEMENT RECRUITERS OF TOPEKA
3400 SW Van Buren, Topeka KS 66611. 785/267-5430. **Fax:** 785/267-0513. **Contact:** Matt McFarland, Owner.

Description: Management Recruiters of Topeka is an executive search firm operating on both contingency and retainer bases. **Specializes in the areas of:** Accounting/Auditing; Agriculture; Engineering; Finance; Health/Medical; Industrial. **Positions commonly filled include:** Accountant/Auditor; Administrative Assistant; Auditor; Chief Financial Officer; Civil Engineer; Clerical Supervisor; Clinical Laboratory Technician; Controller; EEG Technologist; EKG Technician; Electrical/Electronics Engineer; Finance Director; Financial Analyst; Industrial Engineer; Manufacturing Engineer; Occupational Therapist; Paralegal; Pharmacist; Physical Therapist; Registered Nurse; Respiratory Therapist; Secretary; Surgical Technician. **Corporate headquarters location:** Cleveland OH. **Other U.S. locations:** Nationwide. **Average salary range of placements:** More than $50,000. **Number of placements per year:** 50 - 99.

RON MAUPIN & ASSOCIATES
P.O. Box 13231, Shawnee Mission KS 66282. 913/888-2820. **Contact:** Manager. **Description:** An executive search firm. **Positions commonly filled include:** IT Specialist.

MIDWEST SEARCH GROUP
P.O. Box 26423, Shawnee Mission KS 66225. 913/681-8228. **Contact:** Office Manager. **Description:** Midwest Search Group is an executive search firm focusing on the accounting and finance industries. **Specializes in the areas of:** Accounting/Auditing; Finance.

MORGAN HUNTER CORPORATE SEARCH
6800 College Boulevard, Suite 550, Overland Park KS 66211. 913/491-3434. **Contact:** Jerry Hellebusch, President/Owner. **Description:** Morgan Hunter Corporate Search is an executive search firm. **Specializes in the areas of:** Accounting/Auditing; Administration; Computer Science/Software; Finance; Insurance; Secretarial. **Positions commonly filled include:** Accountant/Auditor; Administrative Manager; Budget Analyst; Claim Representative; Clerical Supervisor; Computer Programmer; Credit Manager; Customer Service Representative; Financial Analyst; Systems Analyst; Underwriter/Assistant Underwriter. **Number of placements per year:** 200 - 499.

NETWORK
8014 State Line Road, Suite 210, Leawood KS 66208. 913/383-3080. **Fax:** 913/383-1818. **Contact:** Manager. **Description:** An executive search firm. **Specializes in the areas of:** Medical Sales and Marketing; Pharmaceuticals. **Positions commonly filled include:** Sales Representative.

PETERSON GROUP
14351 West 81st Place, Shawnee Mission KS 66215. 913/599-4804. **Contact:** Office Manager. **Description:** Peterson Group is an executive search firm that only places physicians. **Specializes in the areas of:** Health/Medical.

SPENCER REED TECHNICAL GROUP
6900 College Boulevard, Suite 1, Overland Park KS 66211. 913/663-4400. **Contact:** Office Manager. **Description:** Spencer Reed Technical Group is an executive search firm. **Specializes in the areas of:** Engineering; Technical.

ROMAC INTERNATIONAL
10300 West 103rd Street, Suite 101, Overland Park KS 66214. 913/888-8885. **Contact:** Office Manager. **Description:** Romac International is an executive search firm. **Specializes in the areas of:** Computer Hardware/Software; Data Processing; Finance; Information Technology.

SALES CONSULTANTS
9401 Indian Creek Parkway, Suite 920, Overland Park KS 66210. 913/661-9200. **Fax:** 913/661-9030. **Contact:** Manager. **Description:** An executive search firm.

Specializes in the areas of: Management; Sales; Sales Management.

SEARCH CONSULTANTS, INC.
P.O. Box 780932, Wichita KS 67278. 316/684-0615. **Contact:** Manager. **Description:** Search Consultants, Inc. is an executive search firm. **Specializes in the areas of:** Data Processing.

SEARCH ONE INC.
7700 Shawnee Mission Parkway, Suite 304, Overland Park KS 66202. 913/451-2408. **Contact:** Manager. **Description:** Search One Inc. is an executive search firm. **Specializes in the areas of:** Information Technology.

SHERRIFF & ASSOCIATES
4200 Somerset, Suite 256, Prairie Village KS 66208. 913/451-2112. **Fax:** 913/341-2992. **Contact:** Julie A. Sherriff, President. **Description:** Sherriff & Associates is an executive search firm operating on both retainer and contingency bases. **Specializes in the areas of:** Health/Medical. **Positions commonly filled include:** Physician. **Average salary range of placements:** More than $50,000. **Number of placements per year:** 1 - 49.

MICHAEL SHIRLEY ASSOCIATES
10709 Barkley, Suite B, Overland Park KS 66211. 913/341-7655. **Contact:** Office Manager. **Description:** Michael Shirley Associates is a generalist executive search firm.

SLACK & ASSOCIATES
151 South Whittier Street, Suite 2200, Wichita KS 67207. 316/291-3588. **Fax:** 316/681-4449. **Contact:** Manager. **Description:** Slack & Associates is an executive search firm.

B.E. SMITH ASSOCIATES
10100 Santa Fe Drive, Suite 204, Overland Park KS 66212. 913/341-9116. **Contact:** Manager. **Description:** An executive search firm. **Specializes in the areas of:** Health/Medical.

SMITH, BROWN & JONES
P.O. Box 6513, Shawnee Mission KS 66206. 913/814-7770. **Fax:** 913/814-8440. **Contact:** Don Smith, President. **E-mail address:** dlsmith@streek.com. **World Wide Web address:** http://www.streek.com/sbj. **Description:** Smith, Brown & Jones is an executive search firm. **Specializes in the areas of:** Architecture/Construction; Banking; Biology; Engineering; Food; Manufacturing; Personnel/Labor Relations; Sales; Transportation. **Positions commonly filled include:** Accountant/Auditor; Agricultural Scientist; Bank Officer/Manager; Biological Scientist; Buyer; Chemist; Dietician/Nutritionist; Economist; Engineer; Food Scientist/Technologist; General Manager; Occupational Therapist; Pharmacist; Physical Therapist; Property and Real Estate Manager; Quality Control Supervisor; Transportation/Traffic Specialist; Veterinarian. **Other U.S. locations:** Naples FL. **Average salary range of placements:** More than $50,000. **Number of placements per year:** 50 - 99.

STONEBURNER ASSOCIATES, INC.
10000 West 75th Street, Suite 102, Shawnee Mission KS 66204. 913/432-0055. **Fax:** 913/432-0056. **Contact:** Dwight Stoneburner, Owner. **Description:** Stoneburner Associates is an executive search firm. **Specializes in the areas of:** Accounting/Auditing; Computer Science/Software; Data Processing; Engineering; Food; General Management; Health/Medical; Industrial; Manufacturing; Personnel/Labor Relations; Publishing; Sales; Technical. **Positions commonly filled include:** Biological Scientist; Biomedical Engineer; Buyer; Chemical Engineer; Chemist; Civil Engineer; Computer Programmer; Designer; Electrical/Electronics Engineer; Food Scientist/Technologist; Human Resources Manager; Industrial Engineer; Mechanical Engineer; Metallurgical Engineer; Operations/Production Manager;

Physical Therapist; Physician; Purchasing Agent/ Manager; Quality Control Supervisor; Software Engineer; Systems Analyst. **Average salary range of placements:** $30,000 - $50,000. **Number of placements per year:** 100 - 199.

UNI
4550 West 109th Street, Suite 312, Overland Park KS 66211. 913/498-3900. **Contact:** Office Manager. **Description:** UNI is an executive search firm operating on both retainer and contingency bases. **Specializes in the areas of:** Accounting; Finance. **Positions commonly filled include:** Accountant; Budget Analyst; Chief Financial Officer; Controller; Finance Director; Financial Analyst. **Corporate headquarters location:** This Location. **Average salary range of placements:** $50,000 - $100,000. **Number of placements per year:** 1 - 49.

U.S.A. BUSINESS SYSTEMS
5845 Horton Street, Suite 108, Mission KS 66202. 913/677-0200. **Fax:** 913/677-0760. **Contact:** Larry McWilliams, President. **Description:** U.S.A. Business Systems is an executive search firm. **Specializes in the areas of:** Computer Science/Software; Data Processing. **Positions commonly filled include:** Computer Operator; Computer Programmer; Database Manager; Operations Manager; Software Engineer; Systems Analyst; Systems Manager; Technical Writer/Editor; Telecommunications Manager; Webmaster. **Average salary range of placements:** More than $50,000. **Number of placements per year:** 50 - 99.

WESSYX
P.O. Box 390, Leavenworth KS 66048. 800/593-7832. **Fax:** 800/693-7832. **Contact:** Recruiter. **E-mail address:** careers@wessyx.com. **World Wide Web address:** http://www.wessyx.com. **Description:** Wessyx is an executive search firm that recruits management professionals in the AS/400 industry. Founded in 1991. **Specializes in the areas of:** Information Systems; Information Technology.

WHITE ASSOCIATES/TEMTECH, INC.
10000 West 75th Street, Suite 118, Shawnee Mission KS 66204. 913/831-1821. **Toll-free phone:** 800/880-1821. **Fax:** 913/831-1834. **Contact:** Carlene White, President. **Description:** An executive search firm that also provides some contract services and permanent placements. This firm operates on both retainer and contingency bases. **Specializes in the areas of:** Architecture/Construction; Art/Design; Computer Science/Software; Engineering; Food; General Management; Health/Medical; Manufacturing; Personnel/Labor Relations; Sales; Technical. **Positions commonly filled include:** Accountant/Auditor; Administrative Manager; Aerospace Engineer; Agricultural Engineer; Architect; Biomedical Engineer; Buyer; Chemical Engineer; Chemist; Civil Engineer; Design Engineer; Designer; Draftsperson; EEG Technologist; EKG Technician; Electrical/Electronics Engineer; Emergency Medical Technician; Environmental Engineer; Financial Analyst; General Manager; Geologist/Geophysicist; Human Resources Manager; Industrial Engineer; Industrial Production Manager; Landscape Architect; Mechanical Engineer; Metallurgical Engineer; Mining Engineer; MIS Specialist; Operations/Production Manager; Paralegal; Pharmacist; Physical Therapist; Purchasing Agent/Manager; Software Engineer; Structural Engineer; Systems Analyst; Technical Writer/Editor; Telecommunications Manager; Transportation/Traffic Specialist. **Benefits available to temporary workers:** Paid Holidays; Paid Vacation. **Average salary range of placements:** More than $40,000. **Number of placements per year:** 100 - 199.

WINN GROUP
501 Lawrence Avenue, Lawrence KS 66049. 913/842-7111. **Contact:** Manager. **Description:** An executive search firm. **Specializes in the areas of:** Insurance. **Positions commonly filled include:** Actuary.

PERMANENT EMPLOYMENT AGENCIES

BOSSLER-HIX FINANCIAL CAREERS
6405 Metcalf, Suite 418, Overland Park KS 66202.
913/262-8635. **Contact:** Jennifer Walston, Manager.
Description: Bossler-Hix Financial Careers is a
permanent employment agency that also provides some
temporary placements. **Specializes in the areas of:**
Banking. **Benefits available to temporary workers:**
Paid Holidays; Paid Vacation. **Average salary range of
placements:** Less than $30,000.

BOWMAN & MARSHALL
P.O. Box 25503, Overland Park KS 66225. 913/648-
3332. **Fax:** 913/341-9596. **Contact:** Peter O. Grassl,
President. **E-mail address:** bowmarsh@aol.com. **World
Wide Web address:** http://www.bowmarsh.com.
Description: Bowman & Marshall is a permanent
employment agency. **Specializes in the areas of:**
Accounting/Auditing; Finance. **Positions commonly
filled include:** Accountant; Auditor; Budget Analyst;
Controller; Finance Director; Financial Analyst.

BUSINESS SPECIALISTS
105 South Broadway Street, Suite 200, Wichita KS
67202-4217. 316/267-7375. **Fax:** 316/267-1085.
Contact: Vice President. **Description:** A permanent
employment agency. **Specializes in the areas of:**
Accounting/Auditing; Administration; Advertising;
Architecture/Construction; Banking; Computer
Science/Software; Engineering; Finance; Food; General
Management; Health/Medical; Industrial; Insurance;
Legal; Manufacturing; Nonprofit; Personnel/Labor
Relations; Publishing; Retail; Sales; Secretarial;
Technical. **Corporate headquarters location:** This
Location. **Other U.S. locations:** San Francisco CA;
Denver CO. **Number of placements per year:** 1000+.

DUNHILL OF WICHITA
1210 East First Street, Wichita KS 67214. 316/265-9541.
Contact: Recruiter. **Description:** A permanent
employment agency. **Specializes in the areas of:**
Accounting/Auditing; Banking; Computer
Hardware/Software; Engineering; Manufacturing;
Technical. **Positions commonly filled include:**
Accountant/Auditor; Bank Officer/Manager; Computer
Operator; Computer Programmer; General Manager;
Industrial Designer; Industrial Engineer; Purchasing
Agent/Manager; Technician.

FLAMING AND ASSOCIATES
120 West Sixth, Suite 120, Newton KS 67114. 316/283-
3851. **Contact:** Don Stucky, Owner. **Description:**
Flaming and Associates is a permanent employment
agency. **Specializes in the areas of:** Engineering;
Manufacturing.

MANPOWER TECHNICAL
7130 West Maple, Suite 250, Wichita KS 67209.
316/946-0088. **Fax:** 316/946-0151. **Contact:** Branch
Manager. **E-mail address:** info@wichitajobsource.com.
World Wide Web address: http://www.manpower.com.
Description: Manpower Technical is a permanent
placement firm. **Specializes in the areas of:** Information
Systems; Technical. **Corporate headquarters location:**
Milwaukee WI.

MEGAFORCE LTD.
7450 West 130th Street, Suite 110, Overland Park KS
66213. 913/491-6625x309. **Toll-free phone:** 800/676-
6625x309. **Fax:** 913/402-8454. **Contact:** Ryan
MacDonald, Director of Marketing. **E-mail address:**
rmac@megaforceusa.com. **World Wide Web address:**
http://www.megaforceusa.com. **Description:** A
permanent employment agency that focuses on computer
and information technology areas including mainframe,
client/server, and computer software. **Specializes in the
areas of:** Computer Science/Software; Information
Technology. **Positions commonly filled include:**

Computer Operator; Computer Programmer; Technical
Writer/Editor. **Benefits available to temporary
workers:** 401(k); Dental Insurance; Medical Insurance;
Tuition Assistance. **Corporate headquarters location:**
This Location. **Other U.S. locations:** Colorado Springs
CO; Springfield IL. **Average salary range of
placements:** More than $50,000. **Number of
placements per year:** 1000+.

J.T. NELSON & ASSOCIATES
7700 West 63rd Street, Suite 201, Overland Park KS
66202. 913/236-9433. **Fax:** 913/236-9491. **Contact:** J.T.
Nelson, President. **Description:** A permanent
employment agency. **Specializes in the areas of:**
Engineering; Manufacturing; Technical. **Positions
commonly filled include:** Chemical Engineer; Chemist;
Electrical/Electronics Engineer; Maintenance Supervisor;
Mechanical Engineer. **Number of placements per year:**
1 - 49.

PREFERRED MEDICAL PLACEMENT
125 South Clairborne Road, Olathe KS 66062. 913/780-
6845. **Contact:** Manager. **Description:** A permanent
employment agency. **Specializes in the areas of:**
Health/Medical.

ROLLHEISER & ASSOCIATES
9393 West 110th Street, Suite 500, Overland Park KS
66210. 913/681-8060. **Contact:** Manager. **Description:**
A permanent employment agency. **Specializes in the
areas of:** Computer Science/Software.

TALENT SCOUTS INC. (TSI)
115 South 18th Street, Suite 210, Parsons KS 67357.
316/423-3500. **Contact:** Manager. **Description:** Talent
Scouts is a permanent employment agency. **Specializes
in the areas of:** Accounting; Operations Management;
Sales.

TECHNICAL JOB SERVICE
6916 West Harry Street, Wichita KS 67209. 316/946-
0705. **Contact:** John M. Provorse. **Description:** A
permanent employment agency that also provides some
temporary placements. **Specializes in the areas of:**
Engineering. **Positions commonly filled include:**
Administrative Assistant; Design Engineer; Industrial
Engineer; Mechanical Engineer. **Corporate
headquarters location:** This Location. **Other U.S.
locations:** Anchorage AK. **Average salary range of
placements:** $30,000 - $49,999. **Number of placements
per year:** 1 - 49.

**WICHITA BAR ASSOCIATION LEGAL
PLACEMENT SERVICE**
301 North Main Street, Suite 700, Wichita KS 67202.
316/263-2251. **Fax:** 316/263-0629. **Contact:** Linda
Fuson, Placement Director. **Description:** A permanent
employment agency. **Specializes in the areas of:** Legal;
Secretarial. **Positions commonly filled include:** Legal
Assistant; Legal Secretary; Office Manager; Paralegal;
Receptionist; Secretary; Stenographer; Typist/Word
Processor. **Average salary range of placements:**
$20,000 - $29,999. **Number of placements per year:** 50
- 99.

WILLIAM LAWRENCE & ASSOCIATES
125 North Market Street, Suite 1250, Wichita KS 67202.
316/269-4010. **Contact:** Larry Coons, President.
Description: A permanent employment agency.
Positions commonly filled include: Accountant/Auditor;
Administrative Assistant; Advertising Executive; Bank
Officer/Manager; Bookkeeper; Claim Representative;
Computer Programmer; Credit Manager; Customer
Service Representative; Data Entry Clerk; EDP
Specialist; Electrical/Electronics Engineer; Financial
Analyst; General Manager; Hotel Manager; Human
Resources Manager; Industrial Designer; Industrial

Engineer; Insurance Agent/Broker; Interior Designer; Legal Secretary; Marketing Specialist; Mechanical Engineer; Medical Secretary; Nurse; Public Relations Specialist; Purchasing Agent/Manager; Receptionist; Sales Representative; Secretary; Statistician; Stenographer; Systems Analyst; Technical Writer/Editor; Technician; Typist/Word Processor; Underwriter/Assistant Underwriter. **Number of placements per year:** 500 - 999.

TEMPORARY EMPLOYMENT AGENCIES

DUNHILL STAFFING SYSTEMS
3706 SW Topeka Boulevard, Suite 201, Topeka KS 66609-1239. 785/267-2773. **Contact:** Bob Washatka, President/Owner. **Description:** A temporary agency that also provides some executive searches. **Specializes in the areas of:** Accounting/Auditing; Administration; Computer Hardware/Software; Finance; Office Support; Secretarial. **Positions commonly filled include:** Accountant; Administrative Assistant; Applications Engineer; Computer Programmer; Secretary. **Benefits available to temporary workers:** Paid Holidays; Paid Vacation. **Average salary range of placements:** $30,000 - $50,000. **Number of placements per year:** 50 - 99.

INTERIM PERSONNEL
10520 Barkley Street, Suite 9, Overland Park KS 66212. 913/381-3659. **Contact:** Manager. **Description:** A temporary agency. **Specializes in the areas of:** Personnel/Labor Relations. **Positions commonly filled include:** Administrative Assistant; Administrative Manager; Clerical Supervisor; Customer Service Representative; Typist/Word Processor. **Corporate headquarters location:** Fort Lauderdale FL. Client company pays fee. **Number of placements per year:** 200 - 499.

KANSAS WORKFORCE, INC.
P.O. Box 708, El Dorado KS 67042. 316/320-5288. **Fax:** 316/320-3525. **Contact:** Cyle Moon, Office Manager. **Description:** A temporary agency that also provides some permanent placements. **Specializes in the areas of:** Industrial; Manufacturing; Secretarial. **Positions commonly filled include:** Computer Operator; Secretary; Typist/Word Processor. **Average salary range of placements:** Less than $20,000. **Number of placements per year:** 200 - 499.

KELLY ASSISTED LIVING SERVICES
1047 SW Gage Boulevard, Topeka KS 66604-1780. **Contact:** Recruiter. **Description:** A temporary agency. **Specializes in the areas of:** Health/Medical. **Positions commonly filled include:** Branch Manager; Licensed Practical Nurse; Registered Nurse. **Benefits available to temporary workers:** Paid Holidays; Paid Vacation. **Corporate headquarters location:** Detroit MI. **Other U.S. locations:** Nationwide.

KEY STAFFING
2815 SW Wanamaker, Topeka KS 66614. 785/272-9999. **Contact:** President. **E-mail address:** keystaffing@keystaffing.com. **World Wide Web address:** http://www.keystaffing.com. **Description:** A temporary agency that also provides some permanent placements. **Specializes in the areas of:** Clerical; Computer Science/Software; Industrial; Light Industrial; Manufacturing; Nonprofit; Publishing; Retail; Sales; Secretarial. **Positions commonly filled include:** Accountant/Auditor; Blue-Collar Worker Supervisor; Branch Manager; Clerical Supervisor; Computer Operator; Computer Programmer; Credit Manager; Customer Service Representative; Human Resources Specialist; Industrial Production Manager; Management Trainee; Manufacturer's/Wholesaler's Sales Rep.; Operations/Production Manager; Purchasing Agent/Manager; Services

Sales Representative; Typist/Word Processor. **Average salary range of placements:** $30,000 - $50,000. **Number of placements per year:** 1000+.

LEGALTEMPS OF KANSAS, INC.
154 North Emporia Street, Suite 100, Wichita KS 67202-2515. 316/267-8677. **Fax:** 316/267-8069. **Contact:** Dana M. Milby, President. **Description:** A temporary agency that also provides some permanent placements. Founded in 1994. **Specializes in the areas of:** Legal. **Positions commonly filled include:** Attorney; Legal Secretary; Paralegal. **Benefits available to temporary workers:** Bonus Award/Plan; Medical Insurance; Paid Holidays. **Average salary range of placements:** $20,000 - $29,999.

MANPOWER TEMPORARY SERVICES
555 Poyntz Avenue, Suite 245, Manhattan KS 66502. 785/776-1094. **Contact:** Office Manager. **Description:** A temporary agency. **Specializes in the areas of:** Clerical; Computer Hardware/Software; Construction; Legal; Manufacturing; Personnel/Labor Relations. **Positions commonly filled include:** Administrative Assistant; Advertising Clerk; Bookkeeper; Buyer; Clerk; Computer Operator; Computer Programmer; Construction Trade Worker; Data Entry Clerk; Driver; Factory Worker; Legal Secretary; Light Industrial Worker; Medical Secretary; Public Relations Specialist; Receptionist; Secretary; Stenographer; Typist/Word Processor. **Corporate headquarters location:** Milwaukee WI. **Other U.S. locations:** Nationwide.

MANPOWER TEMPORARY SERVICES
335 North Washington Street, Suite 160, Hutchinson KS 67501. 316/665-5213. **Toll-free phone:** 800/962-5580. **Fax:** 316/665-6089. **Contact:** Charlotte Summers, Manager. **Description:** A temporary agency. Founded in 1947. **Specializes in the areas of:** Industrial; Technical. **Positions commonly filled include:** Accountant/Auditor; Administrative Manager; Aerospace Engineer; Clerical Supervisor; Electrician. **Benefits available to temporary workers:** Medical Insurance; Paid Holidays; Paid Vacation. **Corporate headquarters location:** Milwaukee WI. **Other U.S. locations:** Nationwide. **Average salary range of placements:** Less than $20,000. **Number of placements per year:** 200 - 499.

WESTAFF
1031 SW Gage Boulevard, Topeka KS 66604. 785/273-3939. **Fax:** 785/273-4078. **Contact:** Branch Manager. **Description:** A temporary agency that also provides some permanent placements. **Specializes in the areas of:** Accounting/Auditing; Finance; Industrial; Legal; Personnel/Labor Relations; Publishing; Secretarial. **Positions commonly filled include:** Accountant/Auditor; Administrative Manager; Architect; Blue-Collar Worker Supervisor; Computer Programmer; Customer Service Representative; Draftsperson; General Manager; Human Resources Specialist; Medical Records Technician; Paralegal; Services Sales Representative; Travel Agent; Typist/Word Processor. **Corporate headquarters location:** Walnut Creek CA. **Average salary range of placements:** $20,000 - $29,999. **Number of placements per year:** 1 - 49.

CONTRACT SERVICES FIRMS

CDI CORPORATION MIDWEST
505 South Broadway, Suite 222, Wichita KS 67202. 316/267-3434. **Contact:** Manager. **World Wide Web** address: http://www.cdicorp.com. **Description:** A contract services firm. **Specializes in the areas of:** Engineering; Technical. **Corporate headquarters**

location: Philadelphia PA. **Other U.S. locations:** Nationwide. **International locations:** Worldwide.

COMPUTER PROFESSIONALS
P.O. Box 2184, Shawnee Mission KS 66201. 913/384-3056. **Fax:** 913/384-9516. **Contact:** Norm Capps, Account Executive. **E-mail address:** norm@cpnotes.com. **World Wide Web address:** http://www.cpnotes.com. **Description:** A contract services firm that focuses on placing implementors of SAP, Baan, and PeopleSoft. **Specializes in the areas of:** Computer Science/Software. **Positions commonly filled include:** Computer Programmer; Project Manager; Software Engineer; Systems Analyst; Systems Manager; Telecommunications Manager. **Benefits available to temporary workers:** 401(k); Medical Insurance. **Corporate headquarters location:** This Location. **Average salary range of placements:** More than $50,000. **Number of placements per year:** 50 - 99.

FOSTER DESIGN COMPANY
P.O. Box 47280, Wichita KS 67201-7280. **Toll-free phone:** 800/345-3394. **Fax:** 316/832-9357. **Contact:** Barbara Taggart, Vice President of Contract Staffing. **Description:** A contract services firm. **Specializes in the areas of:** Computer Science/Software; Engineering; Industrial; Manufacturing; Technical. **Positions commonly filled include:** Aerospace Engineer; Aircraft Mechanic/Engine Specialist; Biochemist; Biological Scientist; Biomedical Engineer; Ceramics Engineer; Chemical Engineer; Chemist; Civil Engineer; Computer Programmer; Design Engineer; Designer; Draftsperson; Electrical/Electronics Engineer; Environmental Engineer; Geographer; Geologist/Geophysicist; Human Resources Specialist; Materials Engineer; Mechanical Engineer; Metallurgical Engineer; MIS Specialist; Nuclear Engineer; Operations/Production Manager; Quality Control Supervisor; Software Engineer; Structural Engineer; Systems Analyst; Technical Writer/Editor; Telecommunications Manager. **Benefits available to temporary workers:** 401(k); Paid Holidays; Paid Vacation. **Number of placements per year:** 200 - 499.

METRO INFORMATION SERVICES
5800 Foxridge Drive, Suite 304, Shawnee Mission KS 66202. 913/236-8288. **Contact:** Office Manager. **Description:** A contract services firm. **Specializes in the areas of:** Data Processing. **Positions commonly filled include:** Computer Operator; Computer Programmer; Customer Service Representative; Data Entry Clerk; EDP Specialist; Marketing Specialist; MIS Specialist; Systems Analyst; Technical Writer/Editor; Technician; Typist/Word Processor. **Number of placements per year:** 100 - 199.

WYATT & ASSOCIATES INC.
P.O. Box 72500, Wichita KS 67278. 316/682-6740. **Physical address:** 9235 East Harry Street, Building 100, Wichita KS 67207. **Contact:** Manager. **Description:** A contract services firm. **Specializes in the areas of:** Engineering.

H.L. YOH COMPANY
7133 West 95th Street, Suite 205, Overland Park KS 66212. 913/648-4004. **Contact:** Manager. **Description:** A contract services firm. **Specializes in the areas of:** Technical. **Other U.S. locations:** Nationwide.

EXECUTIVE SEARCH FIRMS

APA
519 East Warnock Street, Louisville KY 40217. 502/635-7721. **Contact:** Manager. **Description:** An executive search firm.

ACCOUNTANTS EXECUTIVE SEARCH
950 Breckenridge Lane, Suite 175, St. Matthews KY 40207. 502/895-0065. **Fax:** 502/893-5599. **Contact:** Manager. **Description:** An executive search firm. **Specializes in the areas of:** Accounting/Auditing.

ANGEL GROUP INTERNATIONAL
4360 Brownsboro Road, Suite 240, Louisville KY 40207. 502/897-0333. **Fax:** 502/897-0496. **Contact:** Leah Stone, Project Coordinator. **E-mail address:** info@angel-group.com. **World Wide Web address:** http://www.angel-group.com. **Description:** An executive search firm. **Specializes in the areas of:** Accounting/Auditing; Administration; Advertising; Architecture/Construction; Banking; Chemicals; Communications; Computer Hardware/Software; Design; Electrical; Engineering; Food; General Management; Health/Medical; Insurance; Legal; Manufacturing; Operations Management; Personnel/Labor Relations; Procurement; Publishing; Retail; Sales; Technical; Textiles; Transportation.

BELCAN STAFFING & PROFESSIONAL SERVICES
6895 Burlington Pike, Suite 300, Florence KY 41042. 606/525-3799. **Fax:** 606/282-3641. **Contact:** Mary Beth Puthoff, Manager. **E-mail address:** mbp@belcan.com. **World Wide Web address:** http://www.belcan.com. **Description:** An executive search firm operating on a contingency basis. Belcan Staffing & Professional Search also provides some temporary and permanent placements. Client company pays fee. **Specializes in the areas of:** Administration; Marketing; Sales; Secretarial. **Positions commonly filled include:** Account Manager; Account Representative; Accountant; Administrative Assistant; Administrative Manager; Assistant Manager; Attorney; Auditor; Branch Manager; Buyer; Claim Representative; Clerical Supervisor; Credit Manager; Customer Service Representative; Desktop Publishing Specialist; Fund Manager; Graphic Designer; Human Resources Manager; Industrial Production Manager; Management Trainee; Marketing Manager; Medical Assistant; Preschool Worker; Production Manager; Purchasing Agent/Manager; Sales Manager; Sales Representative; Secretary; Social Worker. **Benefits available to temporary workers:** 401(k); Health Benefits; Referral Bonus Plan; Training; Vacation Pay. **Corporate headquarters location:** This Location. **Average salary range of placements:** $20,000 - $29,999. **Number of placements per year:** 1000+.

BINDER HOSPITALITY GROUP
526 Silverbrook Drive, Danville KY 40422. 606/239-0096. **Fax:** 606/238-1256. **Contact:** Manager. **Description:** An executive search firm operating exclusively in placements in the hospitality field. **Specializes in the areas of:** Hotel/Restaurant. **Positions commonly filled include:** Assistant Kitchen Manager; Assistant Manager; Chef/Cook/Kitchen Worker; Hotel Manager; Management; Restaurant/Food Service Manager.

CAREER COUNSELING INC.
1401 Spring Bank Drive, Building C, Suite 4, Owensboro KY 42303. 270/686-7766. **Contact:** Manager. **Description:** An executive search firm operating on a contingency basis.

COMPTON & ASSOCIATES
881 Corporate Drive, Suite 204, Lexington KY 40503. 606/223-0880. **Fax:** 606/223-1073. **Contact:** Manager. **E-mail address:** execjobs1@aol.com. **Description:** An executive search firm. **Specializes in the areas of:**

Distribution; Engineering; Human Resources; Manufacturing; Purchasing.

ENGINEERING & EXECUTIVE SEARCH INC.
141 North Sherrin Avenue, Suite 221, Louisville KY 40207. 502/895-3055. **Fax:** 502/895-9810. **Contact:** Patrick A. Thomas, President. **Description:** An executive search firm. **Specializes in the areas of:** Banking; Communications; Finance; Food; Health/Medical. **Positions commonly filled include:** Accountant/Auditor; Attorney; Buyer; Computer Programmer; Cost Estimator; Electrical/Electronics Engineer; Financial Analyst; Food Scientist/Technologist; Human Resources Manager; Industrial Engineer; Industrial Production Manager; Mechanical Engineer; Metallurgical Engineer; Public Relations Specialist; Purchasing Agent/Manager; Quality Control Supervisor; Science Technologist; Structural Engineer; Systems Analyst. **Number of placements per year:** 1 - 49.

THE EXECUTIVE ADVANTAGE
P.O. Box 1176, Bowling Green KY 42102-1176. 270/781-0234. **Fax:** 270/842-9116. **Contact:** Manager. **Description:** An executive search firm. **Specializes in the areas of:** Customer Service; Direct Marketing; Industrial; Marketing; Sales. **Positions commonly filled include:** Accountant/Auditor; Bank Officer/Manager; Cost Estimator; Credit Manager; Electrical/Electronics Engineer; Environmental Engineer; Manufacturer's/Wholesaler's Sales Rep.; MIS Specialist; Operations/Production Manager; Services Sales Representative; Software Engineer; Systems Analyst. **Average salary range of placements:** $30,000 - $80,000. **Number of placements per year:** 1 - 49.

F.C.S.
1711 Ashley Circle, Suite 6, Bowling Green KY 42104. 270/782-9152. **Contact:** Bob Toth, President. **Description:** An executive search firm. **Specializes in the areas of:** Health/Medical. **Positions commonly filled include:** Physician.

F-O-R-T-U-N-E PERSONNEL CONSULTANTS
841 Corporate Drive, Suite 203, Lexington KY 40503. 606/296-2996. **Fax:** 606/296-2998. **Contact:** Manager. **Description:** An executive search firm. Client company pays fee. **Specializes in the areas of:** Aerospace; Automotive; Engineering; Manufacturing; Operations Management. **Other U.S. locations:** Nationwide. **Average salary range of placements:** More than $50,000. **Number of placements per year:** 1 - 49.

F-O-R-T-U-N-E PERSONNEL CONSULTANTS
1200 Envoy Circle, Suite 1203, Louisville KY 40299. 502/493-4113. **Fax:** 502/493-4810. **Contact:** Manager. **E-mail address:** louisville@fpcweb.com. **World Wide Web address:** http://www.fpclouisville.com. **Description:** An executive search firm. **Specializes in the areas of:** Automotive; Electronics; Plastics. **Positions commonly filled include:** Design Engineer; Electrical/Electronics Engineer; Industrial Engineer; Operations Manager; Plant Manager.

ROBERT HALF INTERNATIONAL ACCOUNTEMPS
220 Lexington Green Circle, Suite 510, Lexington KY 40503. 606/245-1800. **Contact:** Manager. **World Wide Web address:** http://www.roberthalf.com. **Description:** An executive search firm. Accountemps (also at this location) provides temporary placements. **Specializes in the areas of:** Accounting/Auditing. **Corporate headquarters location:** Menlo Park CA. **Other U.S. locations:** Nationwide.

ROBERT HALF INTERNATIONAL ACCOUNTEMPS
9300 Shelbyville Road, Suite 920, Louisville KY 40222. 502/394-0300. **Fax:** 502/394-9080. **Contact:** Manager.

World Wide Web address: http://www.roberthalf.com. **Description:** An executive search firm. Accountemps (also at this location) provides temporary placements. OfficeTeam (also at this location) provides temporary placements for high skilled administrators. **Specializes in the areas of:** Accounting/Auditing. **Corporate headquarters location:** Menlo Park CA. **Other U.S. locations:** Nationwide.

HEALTHCARE RECRUITERS INTERNATIONAL
101 North Seventh Street, Louisville KY 40202. 502/561-3484. **Contact:** Manager. **Description:** An executive search firm. **Specializes in the areas of:** Health/Medical.

THE HINDMAN COMPANY
Browenton Place, 2000 Warrington Way, Suite 110, Louisville KY 40222. 502/426-4040. **Contact:** Manager. **Description:** An executive search firm. **Specializes in the areas of:** High-Tech.

KESTLER & ASSOCIATES
P.O. Box 659, Burgin KY 40310. 606/748-9516. **Contact:** Manager. **Description:** An executive search firm. **Specializes in the areas of:** Manufacturing.

KOLOK ENTERPRISES
2104 Sheridan Place, Owensboro KY 42301. 270/685-3676. **Fax:** 270/683-8897. **Contact:** Joan Kolok, Personnel Consultant. **Description:** An executive search firm operating on a contingency basis. **Specializes in the areas of:** Engineering; Manufacturing. **Positions commonly filled include:** Chemical Engineer; Electrical/Electronics Engineer; Industrial Engineer; Mechanical Engineer; Metallurgical Engineer; MIS Specialist. **Average salary range of placements:** $30,000 - $50,000. **Number of placements per year:** 1 - 49.

KOVAC BERRINS AG INC.
257 Regency Circle, Lexington KY 40503. 606/278-0482. **Contact:** David Dryden, Managing Partner. **Description:** An executive search firm operating on both retainer and contingency bases. **Specializes in the areas of:** Engineering; General Management; Sales. **Positions commonly filled include:** Accountant/Auditor; Branch Manager; Buyer; Chemical Engineer; Chemist; Civil Engineer; Computer Programmer; Construction Contractor; Cost Estimator; General Manager; Industrial Engineer; Mechanical Engineer; Metallurgical Engineer; Mining Engineer; Software Engineer. **Average salary range of placements:** $30,000 - $50,000.

J.C. MALONE ASSOCIATES
1941 Bishop Lane, Suite 100, Louisville KY 40218. 502/456-2380. **Contact:** Manager. **Description:** An executive search firm.

MANAGEMENT RECRUITERS INTERNATIONAL
1999 Richmond Road, 2nd Floor, Lexington KY 40502. 606/269-7227. **Fax:** 606/269-6400. **Contact:** Manager. **Description:** An executive search firm. **Specializes in the areas of:** Engineering; Information Systems; Insurance; Manufacturing. **Corporate headquarters location:** Cleveland OH. **Other U.S. locations:** Nationwide.

MANAGEMENT RECRUITERS INTERNATIONAL
105 Citation Drive, Suite A, Danville KY 40422. 606/236-0505. **Contact:** Manager. **Description:** An executive search firm. **Specializes in the areas of:** Manufacturing. **Corporate headquarters location:** Cleveland OH. **Other U.S. locations:** Nationwide.

MANAGEMENT RECRUITERS OF RICHMOND
P.O. Box 263, Richmond KY 40476. 606/624-3535. **Fax:** 606/624-3539. **Contact:** Ron Lawson, General Manager. **Description:** An executive search firm. **Specializes in the areas of:** Engineering; General Management; Manufacturing. **Positions commonly filled include:** Chemical Engineer; Electrical/Electronics Engineer; Industrial Engineer; Mechanical Engineer; Quality Control Supervisor. **Corporate headquarters**

location: Cleveland OH. **Other U.S. locations:** Nationwide. **Number of placements per year:** 1 - 49.

MANUFACTURING ASSOCIATES LLC
P.O. Box 862, Versailles KY 40383. 606/873-0033. **Contact:** James R. Neessen, Owner/President. **Description:** An executive search firm. **Specializes in the areas of:** Accounting/Auditing; Engineering; General Management; Manufacturing; Personnel/Labor Relations. **Positions commonly filled include:** Applications Engineer; Buyer; Chief Financial Officer; Controller; Design Engineer; Electrical/Electronics Engineer; Human Resources Manager; Industrial Engineer; Industrial Production Manager; Manufacturing Engineer; Operations Manager; Production Manager; Project Manager; Purchasing Agent/Manager; Quality Control Supervisor. **Average salary range of placements:** $30,000 - $50,000. **Number of placements per year:** 1 - 49.

KAREN MARSHALL ASSOCIATES
6304 Deep Creek Drive, Prospect KY 40059. 502/228-0800. **Fax:** 502/228-0663. **Contact:** Karen Marshall, Systems Recruiter. **Description:** An executive search firm operating on a contingency basis. **Specializes in the areas of:** Administration; Computer Science/Software. **Positions commonly filled include:** Computer Programmer; Internet Services Manager; MIS Specialist; Software Engineer; Statistician; Systems Analyst; Telecommunications Manager. **Corporate headquarters location:** Louisville KY. **Average salary range of placements:** $50,000 - $100,000. **Number of placements per year:** 1 - 49.

POWER STAFFING INC.
833 West Main Street, Suite 102A, Louisville KY 40202. 502/568-2060. **Fax:** 502/568-8812. **Contact:** Manager. **Description:** An executive search firm which also provides some temporary placements.

PROFESSIONAL SEARCH
P.O. Box 22236, Louisville KY 40252. 502/222-1860. **Contact:** Barry R. Wilhelm, Principal Consultant. **Description:** An executive search firm. **Specializes in the areas of:** Engineering; Manufacturing; Personnel/Labor Relations; Technical. **Positions commonly filled include:** Chemical Engineer; Chemist; Civil Engineer; Electrical/Electronics Engineer; Human Resources Manager; Industrial Engineer; Industrial Production Manager; Mechanical Engineer; Metallurgical Engineer; Operations/Production Manager; Quality Control Supervisor; Science Technologist. **Average salary range of placements:** $30,000 - $50,000. **Number of placements per year:** 1 - 49.

PROFESSIONAL SEARCH CONSULTANTS
210 Meidinger Tower, Louisville KY 40202. 502/583-1530. **Fax:** 502/587-6960. **Contact:** Andrew Payton, President. **Description:** An executive search firm operating on both retainer and contingency bases. Client company pays fee. **Specializes in the areas of:** Accounting; Banking; Finance; Legal; Marketing; Personnel/Labor Relations; Sales. **Positions commonly filled include:** Attorney; Chief Financial Officer; Controller; Sales Executive; Sales Manager; Sales Representative. **Corporate headquarters location:** This Location. **Average salary range of placements:** $50,000 - $100,000.

ROMAC INTERNATIONAL
2850 National City Tower, Louisville KY 40202. 502/581-9900. **Contact:** Larry Childs, Business Unit Manager. **Description:** An executive search firm operating on both retainer and contingency bases. Romac International also provides some temporary and permanent placements, contract services, and resume and career/outplacement counseling. Client company pays fee. **Specializes in the areas of:** Accounting; Finance; General Management. **Corporate headquarters location:** Tampa FL. **Other U.S. locations:** Nationwide. **International locations:** Canada. **Average salary range of placements:** $30,000 - $100,000. **Number of placements per year:** 100 - 199.

location: Cleveland OH. **Other U.S. locations:** Nationwide. **Number of placements per year:** 1 - 49.

SALES CONSULTANTS
3138 Custer Drive, Suite 220, Lexington KY 40517. 606/245-8228. **Contact:** Manager. **Description:** An executive search firm. **Specializes in the areas of:** Sales.

WELLER-WOOLEY & ASSOCIATES
P.O. Box 892, Covington KY 41012. 606/491-1891. **Fax:** 606/655-2952. **Contact:** R. Vernon Weller, Partner.

Description: An executive search firm operating on a contingency basis. **Specializes in the areas of:** Engineering. **Positions commonly filled include:** Applications Engineer; Biomedical Engineer; Electrical Engineer; Mechanical Engineer; Metallurgical Engineer; Quality Control Supervisor. **Average salary range of placements:** $30,000 - $50,000. **Number of placements per year:** 1 - 49.

PERMANENT EMPLOYMENT AGENCIES

ACCESS COMPUTER CAREERS
404 Republic Building, Louisville KY 40202. 502/569-2810. **Contact:** Manager. **Description:** A permanent employment agency.

C.M. MANAGEMENT SERVICES
698 Perimeter Drive, Suite 200, Lexington KY 40517. 606/266-5000. **Contact:** Office Manager. **Description:** A permanent employment agency. **Specializes in the areas of:** Accounting; Banking; Clerical; Computer Science; Engineering; Food; Manufacturing; Sales; Secretarial; Technical. **Positions commonly filled include:** Accountant; Admin. Assistant; Bank Officer; Biologist; Bookkeeper; Computer Programmer; Customer Service Rep.; Draftsperson; EDP Specialist; Electrical Engineer; Financial Analyst; Human Resources Manager; Industrial Engineer; Legal Secretary; Marketing Specialist; Mechanical Engineer; Metallurgical Engineer; Receptionist; Sales Rep.; Stenographer; Systems Analyst; Word Processor. **Number of placements per year:** 50 - 99.

COMPUTER CAREER CONSULTANTS
P.O. Box 22426, Louisville KY 40252. 502/394-0388. **Fax:** 502/394-9443. **Contact:** Recruiter. **Description:** A permanent employment agency. **Positions commonly filled include:** Account Representative; Applications Engineer; AS400 Programmer; Computer Programmer; Computer Support Tech.; Database Admin.; Network Administrator; SQL Programmer; Systems Analyst; Webmaster.

CROWN PERSONNEL SERVICES
2100 Gardiner Lane, Suite 215, Louisville KY 40205. 502/454-5500. **Fax:** 502/473-0140. **Contact:** Jay Hodge, Manager. **Description:** A permanent employment agency. **Positions commonly filled include:** Blue-Collar Worker Supervisor; Claim Rep.; Clerical Supervisor; Computer Programmer; Construction Contractor; Credit Manager; Customer Service Rep.; Data Entry Clerk; Draftsperson; Electrician; Factory Worker; Human Resources Specialist; Legal Secretary; Management Trainee; Manufacturer's Sales Rep.; Marketing Specialist; Medical Secretary; Paralegal; Quality Control Supervisor; Receptionist; Word Processor. **Average salary range of placements:** Less than $20,000. **Number of placements per year:** 1000+.

GRAPHIC ARTS EMPLOYMENT SERVICE, INC.
P.O. Box 176127, Covington KY 41017. 606/331-6567. **Fax:** 606/331-6568. **Contact:** James Carlin, President. **Description:** Graphic Arts Employment Service, Inc. is a permanent employment agency. **Specializes in the areas of:** Packaging; Printing; Publishing. **Positions commonly filled include:** Cost Estimator; Customer Service; Electrical Engineer; Manager; Operations Mgr.; Printing Press Operator; Quality Control Supervisor; Sales Representative. **Average salary range of placements:** $30,000 - $90,000. **Number of placements per year:** 1 - 49.

HR AFFILIATES
4139 Cadillac Court, Suite 201, Louisville KY 40213. 502/485-1140. **Contact:** Manager. **Description:** A permanent employment agency.

HOUCK CAREER CONSULTANTS (HCC)
7404 Old Coach Road, Suite 110, Crestwood KY 40014-9787. 502/241-2882. **Fax:** 502/241-6411. **Contact:** Recruiter. **Description:** A permanent employment agency. **Specializes in the areas of:** Computer Hardware/Software. **Positions commonly filled include:** Computer Programmer; EDP Specialist; MIS Specialist; Software Engineer; Systems Analyst. **Number of placements per year:** 1 - 49.

NESSEN PROFESSIONAL SEARCH
2363 Chauvin Drive, Lexington KY 40517. 606/873-0033. **Contact:** Manager. **Description:** A permanent employment agency.

PRECISION STAFFING, INC.
113 Consumer Lane, Frankfort KY 40601-8489. 502/227-7000. **Fax:** 502/227-2929. **Contact:** Jana Grugin, Branch Manager. **Description:** A permanent employment agency. **Specializes in the areas of:** Accounting/Auditing; Administration; Banking; Clerical; Food; Health/Medical; Industrial; Insurance; Legal; Light Industrial; Manufacturing; Personnel/Labor Relations; Secretarial. **Benefits available to temporary workers:** Medical Insurance; Paid Holidays; Paid Vacation. **Corporate headquarters location:** Lexington KY. **Other area locations:** Shelbyville KY; Mount Sterling KY. **Average salary range of placements:** $20,000 - $29,999. **Number of placements per year:** 500 - 999.

PRECISION STAFFING, INC.
2350 Sterlington Drive, Lexington KY 40517. 606/272-2030. **Contact:** Manager. **Description:** A permanent employment agency that also provides some temporary placements. **Specializes in the areas of:** Clerical; Industrial; Technical.

SNELLING PERSONNEL SERVICES
4010 DuPont Circle, Suite 419, Louisville KY 40207. 502/895-9494. **Contact:** Steve Steinmetz, President. **Description:** A permanent employment agency that also provides some temporary placements. **Specializes in the areas of:** Administration; Computer Hardware/Software; Engineering; Manufacturing; Sales; Technical.

SUPERIOR OFFICE SUPPORT
3191 Nicholasville Road, Suite 200, Lexington KY 40502. 606/245-1975. **Toll-free phone:** 800/962-4606. **Fax:** 606/245-1088. **Contact:** Ken Harmon, President. **World Wide Web address:** lexsos@lex.infi.net. **Description:** A permanent employment agency. **Specializes in the areas of:** Accounting; Clerical; Information Systems.

TEMPORARY EMPLOYMENT AGENCIES

J.E.M. & ASSOCIATES, INC.
306 Preachersville Road, Stanford KY 40484. 606/365-2900. **Fax:** 606/365-1449. **Contact:** John Marcum, President. **Description:** A temporary agency. Founded in 1991. **Specializes in the areas of:** Accounting/Auditing; Engineering; Manufacturing; Personnel/Labor Relations.

Positions commonly filled include: Accountant/Auditor; Blue-Collar Worker Supervisor; Civil Engineer; Clerical Supervisor; Computer Programmer; Cost Estimator; Design Engineer; Designer; Draftsperson; Electrical/Electronics Engineer; Environmental Engineer; Financial Analyst; General Manager; Human Resources

Specialist; Industrial Engineer; Management Analyst/Consultant; Management Trainee; Mechanical Engineer; Operations/Production Manager; Purchasing Agent/Manager; Quality Control Supervisor; Structural Engineer; Systems Analyst; Technical Writer/Editor. **Benefits available to temporary workers:** Paid Holidays; Paid Vacation. **Average salary range of placements:** $15,000 - $29,999. **Number of placements per year:** 100 - 199.

THE LEGAL EDGE, INC.
THE PROFESSIONAL EDGE, INC.
1249 Starks Building, Louisville KY 40202. 502/581-9861. **Fax:** 502/581-0587. **Contact:** Donna Walters, Placement Specialist. **Description:** A temporary agency that also offers some permanent placements. The Legal Edge offers legal administrative support, while The Professional Edge offers general administrative support. **Specializes in the areas of:** Legal. **Positions commonly filled include:** Attorney; Legal Secretary; Paralegal; Receptionist; Typist/Word Processor. **Benefits available to temporary workers:** Medical Insurance; Paid Vacation. **Average salary range of placements:** $20,000 - $29,999. **Number of placements per year:** 200 - 499.

MANPOWER INC.
3280 Blazer Parkway, Suite 102, Lexington KY 40509. 606/268-1331. **Contact:** Area Manager. **E-mail address:** manprlex@mis.net. **World Wide Web address:** http://www.manpower.com. **Description:** A temporary agency. **Specializes in the areas of:** Accounting/Auditing; Administration; Computer Science/Software; Engineering; Industrial; Light Industrial; MIS/EDP; Scientific; Secretarial; Technical. **Positions commonly filled include:** Accountant/Auditor; Administrative Assistant; Buyer; Chemical Engineer; Chemist; Clinical Lab Technician; Computer Programmer; Database Manager; Design Engineer; Draftsperson; Electrical/Electronics Engineer; Environmental Engineer; Financial Analyst; Graphic Artist; Human Resources Manager; Industrial Engineer; Industrial Production Manager; Manufacturing Engineer;

Mechanical Engineer; MIS Specialist; Online Content Specialist; Operations/Production Manager; Project Manager; Quality Control Supervisor; Software Engineer; Systems Analyst; Technical Writer/Editor; Typist/Word Processor; Webmaster. **Benefits available to temporary workers:** 401(k); Franchise Program; Life Insurance; Medical Insurance; Paid Holidays; Paid Vacation; Referral Bonus Plan. **Corporate headquarters location:** Milwaukee WI. **Other U.S. locations:** Nationwide. **International locations:** Worldwide. **Number of placements per year:** 1000+.

STAFFING ALTERNATIVES
200 High Rise Drive, Suite 147, Louisville KY 40213. 502/962-4100. **Fax:** 502/962-4105. **Contact:** Robin Rose, Manager. **Description:** A temporary agency. **Specializes in the areas of:** Industrial; Light Industrial; Manufacturing. **Benefits available to temporary workers:** Medical Insurance; Paid Holidays; Paid Vacation; Referral Bonus Plan. **Average salary range of placements:** Less than $20,000. **Number of placements per year:** 1000+.

TEMPORARY PROFESSIONALS INC.
1402 East Fourth Street, Owensboro KY 42303. 270/685-2090. **Contact:** Gary Boswell, President. **Description:** A temporary agency. **Specializes in the areas of:** Accounting/Auditing; Clerical; Construction; Insurance. **Positions commonly filled include:** Accountant/Auditor; Administrative Worker/Clerk; Bookkeeper; Clerk; Computer Operator; Computer Programmer; Data Entry Clerk; Factory Worker; Legal Secretary; Medical Secretary; Nurse; Receptionist; Secretary; Stenographer; Typist/Word Processor. **Average salary range of placements:** Less than $20,000. **Number of placements per year:** 1000+.

TEMPS PLUS
819 Broadway Street, Paducah KY 42001-6807. 270/444-0030. **Fax:** 270/442-6679. **Contact:** Manager. **E-mail address:** tempsplus@sunsixinsi.net. **Description:** A temporary agency that also provides some permanent placements.

CONTRACT SERVICES FIRMS

BJM & ASSOCIATES, INC.
2365 Harrodsburg Road, Lexington KY 40504. 606/223-3036. **Fax:** 606/223-5456. **Contact:** Manager. **World Wide Web address:** http://www.gtesupersite.com/bjmstaffing. **Description:** A contract staffing and management services company. Founded in 1970. **Specializes in the areas of:** Accounting/Auditing; Assembly; Computer Graphics; Computer Programming; Engineering; Legal Secretarial; Manufacturing; Systems Programming; Word Processing. **Positions commonly filled include:** Data Entry Clerk; Machine Operator; Maintenance Technician; Receptionist; Warehouse/Distribution Worker. **President/CEO:** Janey Moores.

BJM & ASSOCIATES, INC.
193 Versailles Road, Frankfort KY 40601. 502/695-0087. **Fax:** 502/695-4672. **Contact:** Manager. **Description:** A contract staffing and management services company. Founded in 1970. **Specializes in the areas of:** Accounting; Assembly; Computer Graphics; Computer Programming; Engineering; Legal Secretarial; Manufacturing; Systems Programming; Word Processing. **Positions commonly filled include:** Data Entry Clerk; Machine Operator; Maintenance Technician; Receptionist; Warehouse/Distribution Worker. **President/CEO:** Janey Moores.

BJM & ASSOCIATES, INC.
122 Edwards Avenue, Georgetown KY 40843. 502/863-6234. **Fax:** 502/863-0429. **Contact:** Manager. **World Wide Web address:** http://www.gtesupersite.com/bjmstaffing. **Description:** A contract staffing and management services company. Founded in 1970. **Specializes in the areas of:** Accounting/Auditing; Assembly; Computer Graphics; Computer Programming; Engineering; Legal Secretarial; Manufacturing; Systems Programming; Word Processing. **Positions commonly filled include:** Data Entry Clerk; Machine Operator; Maintenance Technician; Receptionist; Warehouse/Distribution Worker. **President/CEO:** Janey Moores.

ROMAC INTERNATIONAL
4965 U.S. Highway 42, Suite 2900, Louisville KY 40222. 502/339-2900. **Toll-free phone:** 800/682-9784. **Fax:** 502/339-2888. **Contact:** Steven Friedman, Area Technical Manager. **Description:** A contract services firm. Client company pays fee. **Specializes in the areas of:** Computer Science/Software; MIS/EDP. **Positions commonly filled include:** Applications Engineer; AS400 Programmer Analyst; Computer Programmer; Computer Support Technician; Database Administrator; Database Manager; Internet Services Manager; MIS Specialist; Network/Systems Administrator; Software Engineer; SQL Programmer; Systems Analyst; Systems Manager. **Corporate headquarters location:** Tampa FL. **Other U.S. locations:** Nationwide. **Average salary range of placements:** $50,000 - $100,000. **Number of placements per year:** 200 - 499.

CAREER/OUTPLACEMENT COUNSELING FIRMS

RESUMES, ETC.
366 Waller Avenue, Lexington KY 40504. 606/273-7863. **Contact:** Owner. **Description:** Provides resume writing services. **Average salary range of placements:** $30,000 - $50,000. **Number of placements per year:** 1000+.

◆ L O U I S I A N A ◆

CAREER PERSONNEL CONSULTANTS
P.O. Box 19163, New Orleans LA 70179. **Contact:** Henry LaRoche, President. **Description:** An executive search firm operating on both retainer and contingency bases. **Specializes in the areas of:** Accounting/Auditing; Finance; Industrial; Manufacturing; Personnel/Labor Relations; Technical. **Positions commonly filled include:** Accountant/Auditor; Administrative Manager; Bank Officer/Manager; Chemical Engineer; Chemist; Civil Engineer; Design Engineer; Electrical/Electronics Engineer; Environmental Engineer; Financial Analyst; Human Resources Manager; Industrial Engineer; Management Analyst/Consultant; Mechanical Engineer; Metallurgical Engineer; Mining Engineer; Petroleum Engineer; Surveyor. **Average salary range of placements:** More than $50,000. **Number of placements per year:** 1 - 49.

CLERTECH GROUP, INC.
P.O. Box 19344, New Orleans LA 70179. 504/486-9733. **Fax:** 504/288-3856. **Contact:** George Dorko, Director of Technical Recruiting. **Description:** An executive search firm operating on both retainer and contingency bases. **Specializes in the areas of:** Computer Science/Software; Economics; Electrical; Engineering; Technical. **Positions commonly filled include:** Computer Programmer; Cost Estimator; Design Engineer; Economist; Electrical/Electronics Engineer; Mechanical Engineer; MIS Specialist; Nuclear Engineer; Operations/Production Manager; Software Engineer; Structural Engineer; Systems Analyst; Telecommunications Manager. **Average salary range of placements:** More than $50,000. **Number of placements per year:** 1 - 49.

DUNHILL OF BATON ROUGE
5723 Superior Drive, Suite B-4, Baton Rouge LA 70816. 225/291-0450. **Contact:** Mr. E.H. Falcon, Owner. **Description:** An executive search firm. **Specializes in the areas of:** Chemicals; Engineering; Paper; Petrochemical; Technical. **Number of placements per year:** 50 - 99.

DUNHILL PROFESSIONAL SEARCH
2920 Knight Street, Suite 140, Shreveport LA 71105-2412. 318/861-3576. **Contact:** Manager. **Description:** An executive search firm. **Specializes in the areas of:** Engineering; Information Technology; Technical.

FLEMING ASSOCIATES
3850 North Causeway Boulevard, Suite 770, Metairie LA 70002. 504/836-7090. **Contact:** Manager. **Description:** A generalist executive search firm.

FRANKLIN RECRUITERS
P.O. Box 3553, Baton Rouge LA 70821-3553. 225/383-1520. **Contact:** Manager. **Description:** An executive search firm.

FRAZEE RECRUITING CONSULTANTS, INC.
2332 Eastgate Drive, Suite E, Baton Rouge LA 70816. 225/295-1177. **Fax:** 225/291-9277. **Contact:** Marianne Frazee, Owner. **E-mail address:** info@frazeerecruit.com. **World Wide Web address:** http://www.frazeerecruit.com. **Description:** An executive search firm operating on a contingency basis. The firm also provides some temporary placements. Client company pays fee. **Specializes in the areas of:** Accounting/Auditing; Administration; Computer Science/Software; Engineering; Finance; General Management; Industrial; Light Industrial; Secretarial; Technical. **Positions commonly filled include:** Account Manager; Account Representative; Accountant; Administrative Assistant; Administrative Manager; Assistant Manager; Bank Officer/Manager; Branch Manager; Chemical Engineer; Chemist; Clerical Supervisor; Computer Engineer; Computer Operator;

Computer Programmer; Computer Support Technician; Computer Technician; Controller; Customer Service Representative; Draftsperson; Electrical/Electronics Engineer; Environmental Engineer; General Manager; Human Resources Manager; Management Trainee; Mechanical Engineer; MIS Specialist; Network/Systems Administrator; Operations Manager; Paralegal; Production Manager; Project Manager; Purchasing Agent/Manager; Quality Control Supervisor; Sales Executive; Sales Manager; Secretary; Software Engineer; Systems Analyst. **Corporate headquarters location:** This Location. **Average salary range of placements:** $50,000 - $100,000. **Number of placements per year:** 100 - 199.

GELPI & ASSOCIATES
P.O. Box 231187, Harahan LA 70183-1187. 504/737-6086. **Contact:** Manager. **Description:** An executive search firm. **Specializes in the areas of:** Insurance.

GRAHAM SEARCH GROUP
300 Washington Plaza, Suite 212, Monroe LA 71201. 318/361-2090. **Contact:** Manager. **Description:** An executive search firm. **Specializes in the areas of:** Health/Medical.

HALE & ASSOCIATES
P.O. Box 6941, New Orleans LA 70174. 504/394-2956. **Fax:** 504/391-3256. **Contact:** Manager. **Description:** An executive search firm. **Specializes in the areas of:** Health/Medical; Manufacturing. **Positions commonly filled include:** Chief Executive Officer; Chief Financial Officer; Pharmacist.

ROBERT HALF INTERNATIONAL
3117 22nd Street, Metairie LA 70002. 504/835-4296. **Contact:** Manager. **Description:** An executive search firm.

HEALTHCARE RECRUITERS INTERNATIONAL
3500 North Causeway Boulevard, Suite 1472, Metairie LA 70002. 504/838-8875. **Contact:** Manager. **Description:** Healthcare Recruiters International is an executive search firm. **Specializes in the areas of:** Health/Medical.

HOWARD ENTERPRISES
3925 North I-10 Service Road, Suite 201E, Metairie LA 70002. 504/830-2935. **Contact:** Manager. **Description:** An executive search firm.

MSI PHYSICIANS
One Shell Square, 701 Poydras Street, Suite 3880, New Orleans LA 70139. 504/522-6700. **Fax:** 504/522-1998. **Contact:** Manager. **E-mail address:** msi_mno@mindspring.com. **World Wide Web address:** http://www.msi-intl.com. **Description:** An executive search firm operating on both retainer and contingency bases. MSI Physicians also provides some contract services. Client company pays fee. **Specializes in the areas of:** Banking; Computer Science/Software; Finance; Health/Medical; MIS/EDP. **Positions commonly filled include:** Applications Engineer; AS400 Programmer Analyst; Bank Officer/Manager; Branch Manager; Budget Analyst; Chief Financial Officer; Computer Animator; Computer Engineer; Computer Operator; Computer Programmer; Computer Scientist; Computer Support Technician; Computer Technician; Content Developer; Controller; Cost Estimator; Credit Manager; Database Administrator; Database Manager; Finance Director; Fund Manager; Internet Services Manager; Medical Records Technician; MIS Specialist; Multimedia Designer; Network/Systems Administrator; Nuclear Medicine Technologist; Nurse Practitioner; Occupational Therapist; Pharmacist; Physical Therapist; Physical Therapy Assistant; Physician; Radiological

Technologist; Registered Nurse; Software Engineer; SQL Programmer; Systems Analyst; Systems Manager; Webmaster. **Other U.S. locations:** Nationwide. **International locations:** Worldwide. **Average salary range of placements:** More than $100,000. **Number of placements per year:** 100 - 199.

MANAGEMENT RECRUITERS INTERNATIONAL
3124 Kilpatrick Boulevard, Monroe LA 71201. 318/322-2200. **Contact:** Manager. **Description:** An executive search firm. **Specializes in the areas of:** Engineering.

MANAGEMENT RECRUITERS INTERNATIONAL
920 Pierremont Road, Suite 112, Shreveport LA 71106. 318/865-8411. **Contact:** Manager. **Description:** An executive search firm. **Specializes in the areas of:** Health/Medical; Information Systems; Manufacturing.

MANAGEMENT RECRUITERS OF BATON ROUGE
SALES CONSULTANTS OF BATON ROUGE
2237 South Acadian Thruway, Suite 707, Baton Rouge LA 70808. 225/928-2212. **Fax:** 225/928-1109. **Contact:** Manager. **Description:** An executive search firm. **Specializes in the areas of:** Health/Medical.

MANAGEMENT RECRUITERS OF METAIRIE
SALES CONSULTANTS OF METAIRIE
P.O. Box 6605, Metairie LA 70009. 504/831-7333. **Contact:** Office Manager. **Description:** An executive search firm. Another division of Management Recruiters, CompuSearch, also operates at this location. **Specializes in the areas of:** Accounting/Auditing; Administration; Advertising; Architecture/Construction; Banking; Chemicals; Communications; Computer Hardware/Software; Design; Electrical; Engineering; Food; General Management; Health/Medical; Insurance; Legal; Manufacturing; Operations Management; Personnel/Labor Relations; Procurement; Publishing; Retail; Sales; Technical; Textiles; Transportation. **Corporate headquarters location:** Cleveland OH. **Other U.S. locations:** Nationwide.

MANAGEMENT RECRUITERS OF ST. TAMMANY
202 Village Circle, Suite 3, Slidell LA 70458. 504/847-1900. **Fax:** 504/847-1984. **Contact:** Victoria Pecot, Internet Researcher. **E-mail address:** vpecot@jobscenter.com. **Description:** An executive search firm. **Specializes in the areas of:** Computer Science/Software; Internet Development; Marketing; MIS/EDP; Sales; Scientific; Technical. **Positions commonly filled include:** Account Manager; Account Representative; Applications Engineer; AS400 Programmer Analyst; Computer Engineer; Computer Operator; Computer Programmer; Computer Scientist; Computer Support Technician; Computer Technician; Content Developer; Database Administrator; Database Manager; Internet Services Manager; MIS Specialist; Multimedia Designer; Network/Systems Administrator; Operations Manager; Sales Engineer; Sales Executive; Sales Manager; Sales Representative; Software Engineer; SQL Programmer; Systems Analyst; Systems Manager; Technical Writer/Editor; Webmaster. **Corporate headquarters location:** Cleveland OH. **Other U.S. locations:** Nationwide.

PMR NETWORK
1220 Saint Andrew Street, New Orleans LA 70130-5122. 504/522-5444. **Contact:** Manager. **Description:** An executive search firm.

RHEMA EMPLOYMENT AGENCY
1304 Bertrand Drive, Building D7, Lafayette LA 70506. 318/234-8880. **Contact:** Manager. **Description:** An executive search firm. **Specializes in the areas of:** Maritime.

RIVER REGION PERSONNEL, INC.
1537 Metairie Road, Metairie LA 70005. 504/831-4746. **Fax:** 504/831-9916. **Contact:** Chuck Zamjahn, President. **E-mail address:** czamjahn@aol.com. **Description:** An executive search firm operating on both retainer and contingency bases. **Specializes in the areas of:** Engineering; Personnel/Labor Relations; Technical. **Positions commonly filled include:** Buyer; Chemical Engineer; Chemist; Civil Engineer; Electrical/Electronics Engineer; Geologist/Geophysicist; Human Resources Manager; Industrial Engineer; Mechanical Engineer; Metallurgical Engineer; Nuclear Engineer; Petroleum Engineer. **Average salary range of placements:** More than $50,000. **Number of placements per year:** 1 - 49.

SALES AND ENGINEERING RESOURCES
P.O. Box 73130, Metairie LA 70033-3130. 504/455-3771. **Fax:** 504/455-3776. **Contact:** Manager. **Description:** An executive search firm.

SALES CONSULTANTS OF ALEXANDRIA
1605 Murray Street, Alexandria LA 71301. 318/561-2882. **Contact:** Manager. **Description:** An executive search firm.

SANFORD ROSE ASSOCIATES
300 Mariners Plaza, Suite 321A, Mandeville LA 70433. 504/674-5050. **Contact:** Manager. **World Wide Web address:** http://www.sanfordrose.com. **Description:** An executive search firm. **Specializes in the areas of:** General Management; Medical Sales and Marketing.

SNELLING PERSONNEL SERVICES
1500 Louisville Avenue, Monroe LA 71201. 318/387-6090. **Fax:** 318/361-6097. **Contact:** Wayne Williamson, President. **Description:** An executive search firm. **Specializes in the areas of:** Accounting/Auditing; Administration; Banking; Computer Science/Software; Engineering; Health/Medical; Manufacturing; Personnel/Labor Relations; Sales. **Positions commonly filled include:** Accountant/Auditor; Bank Officer/Manager; Biological Scientist; Chemical Engineer; Chemist; Civil Engineer; Claim Representative; Computer Programmer; Construction Contractor; Draftsperson; Electrical/Electronics Engineer; Human Resources Manager; Industrial Engineer; Management Trainee; Mechanical Engineer; Occupational Therapist; Paralegal; Pharmacist; Physical Therapist; Physician; Quality Control Supervisor; Registered Nurse; Respiratory Therapist; Restaurant/Food Service Manager; Systems Analyst. **Number of placements per year:** 200 - 499.

SNELLING PERSONNEL SERVICES
7742 Office Park Boulevard, Suite C-1, Baton Rouge LA 70809. 225/927-0550. **Contact:** Office Manager. **Description:** An executive search firm. **Specializes in the areas of:** Accounting/Auditing; Banking; Computer Hardware/Software; Engineering; Sales. **Number of placements per year:** 50 - 99.

TALLEY & ASSOCIATES, INC.
TALLEY TEMPORARIES
1105 West Prien Lake Road, Suite D, Lake Charles LA 70601. 318/474-JOBS. **Fax:** 318/474-0885. **Contact:** Burt Bollotte, Manager. **Description:** An executive search firm. Talley Temporaries (also at this location) provides temporary placements. **Specializes in the areas of:** Accounting/Auditing; Administration; Advertising; Architecture/Construction; Banking; Biology; Computer Science/Software; Engineering; Fashion; Finance; Food; General Management; Health/Medical; Legal; Manufacturing; Personnel/Labor Relations; Publishing; Retail; Sales; Secretarial; Technical; Transportation. **Positions commonly filled include:** Accountant/Auditor; Adjuster; Administrative Manager; Advertising Clerk; Architect; Attorney; Bank Officer/Manager; Biochemist; Blue-Collar Worker Supervisor; Branch Manager; Broadcast Technician; Buyer; Chemical Engineer; Chemist; Civil Engineer; Claim Representative; Clerical Supervisor; Clinical Lab Technician; Computer Programmer; Construction Contractor; Cost Estimator; Credit Manager; Customer Service Representative; Dental Assistant/Dental Hygienist; Dentist; Design Engineer; Dietician/Nutritionist; Draftsperson; Electrical/Electronics Engineer; Environmental Engineer; Financial Analyst; General Manager; Geologist/

Geophysicist; Health Services Manager; Hotel Manager; Human Resources Manager; Human Service Worker; Industrial Engineer; Industrial Production Manager; Insurance Agent/Broker; Landscape Architect; Licensed Practical Nurse; Management Trainee; Manufacturer's/ Wholesaler's Sales Rep.; Mechanical Engineer; Medical Records Technician; MIS Specialist; Occupational Therapist; Operations/Production Manager; Paralegal; Petroleum Engineer; Pharmacist; Physical Therapist; Physician; Property and Real Estate Manager; Psychologist; Public Relations Specialist; Purchasing Agent/Manager; Quality Control Supervisor; Radio/ TV Announcer/Broadcaster; Radiological Technologist; Registered Nurse; Restaurant/Food Service Manager; Securities Sales Representative; Social Worker; Sociologist; Systems Analyst; Technical Writer/Editor; Telecommunications Manager; Transportation/Traffic Specialist; Travel Agent; Typist/Word Processor; Video Maintenance Engineer.

TECHNICAL & PROFESSIONAL SOURCES
14726 Avalon Avenue, Baton Rouge LA 70816. 225/273-4001. **Contact:** Dennis Harris, Process Industry Specialist. **Description:** An executive search firm operating on both retainer and contingency bases. **Specializes in the areas of:** Engineering; Industrial; Manufacturing; Sales. **Positions commonly filled include:** Aerospace Engineer; Chemical Engineer; Chemist; Electrical/Electronics Engineer; Industrial Engineer; Industrial Production Manager; Mechanical Engineer; Operations/Production Manager; Quality Control Supervisor; Services Sales Representative; Structural Engineer. **Average salary range of placements:** More than $50,000. **Number of placements per year:** 1 - 49.

PERMANENT EMPLOYMENT AGENCIES

ACCOUNTING PERSONNEL CONSULTANTS STAT RESOURCES
210 Baronne Street, Suite 922, New Orleans LA 70112. 504/581-7800. **Contact:** Manager. **Description:** A permanent employment agency. **Specializes in the areas of:** Accounting/Auditing; Engineering.

ADVANTAGE PERSONNEL INC.
11224 Boardwalk Drive, Baton Rouge LA 70816. 225/273-8900. **Contact:** Manager. **Description:** A permanent employment agency.

BADON'S EMPLOYMENT AGENCY
5422 Galeria Drive, Baton Rouge LA 70815. 225/295-1240. **Toll-free phone:** 800/769-7708. **Fax:** 225/295-3972. **Contact:** Manager. **Description:** A permanent placement agency.

CORPORATE CONNECTION INC.
433 Metairie Road, Suite 113, Metairie LA 70005. 504/828-2210. **Contact:** Manager. **Description:** A permanent employment agency that also provides some temporary placements.

DELTA PERSONNEL
616 Causeway Boulevard, Metairie LA 70001. 504/833-5200. **Fax:** 504/833-5296. **Contact:** David Lawrence, President. **Description:** A permanent employment agency. **Specializes in the areas of:** Engineering; General Management; Sales. **Positions commonly filled include:** Branch Manager; Chemical Engineer; Chemist; Civil Engineer; Customer Service Rep.; Draftsperson; Electrical/Electronics Engineer; General Manager; Human Resources Manager; Industrial Engineer; Industrial Production Manager; Management Trainee; Manufacturer's/Wholesaler's Sales Rep.; Mechanical Engineer; Operations/Production Manager; Petroleum Engineer; Restaurant/Food Service Manager; Securities Sales Representative; Services Sales Rep.; Structural Engineer. **Number of placements per year:** 1 - 49.

DRIGGERS & BLACKWELL PERSONNEL
1440 Goodwin Road, Ruston LA 71270. 318/251-0244. **Contact:** Manager. **Description:** A permanent employment agency.

LOUISIANA OFFICE OF EMPLOYMENT SECURITY
1510 Lee Street, Alexandria LA 71309. 318/487-5532. **Contact:** Office Manager. **Description:** A permanent employment agency. **Number of placements per year:** 1000+.

MEDFORCE
3409 North Hullen Street, Suite 201, Metairie LA 70002. 504/455-1322. **Fax:** 504/455-0411. **Contact:** Manager. **Description:** A permanent employment agency. **Specializes in the areas of:** Health/Medical. **Positions commonly filled include:** Physician. **Number of placements per year:** 50 - 99.

MEDI-LEND NURSING SERVICES, INC.
6305 Elysian Fields, New Orleans LA 70122. 504/283-3767. **Fax:** 504/283-6004. **Contact:** Manager. **Description:** A permanent employment agency that also provides some temporary placements and contract services. Client company pays fee. **Specializes in the areas of:** Health/Medical. **Positions commonly filled include:** Licensed Practical Nurse; Registered Nurse. **Corporate headquarters location:** This Location. **Other U.S. locations:** FL; TX. **Average salary range of placements:** $30,000 - $49,999. **Number of placements per year:** 100 - 199.

SHIELL PERSONNEL
2040 North Causeway Boulevard, Mandeville LA 70471. 504/674-1616. **Fax:** 504/674-1611. **Contact:** Donald M. Shiell, Owner. **Description:** A permanent employment agency. Shiell Personnel also provides some executive searches. **Specializes in the areas of:** Health/Medical; Medical Devices; Pharmaceuticals; Sales. **Positions commonly filled include:** Accountant/Auditor; Chemical Engineer; Chemist; Environmental Engineer; Human Resources Manager; Marketing Manager; Mechanical Engineer; Sales Executive; Sales Manager; Services Sales Representative. **Corporate headquarters location:** New Orleans LA. **Average salary range of placements:** More than $50,000. **Number of placements per year:** 200 - 499.

TEMPORARY EMPLOYMENT AGENCIES

ASCENT CONSULTING GROUP
650 Poydras Street, Suite 2010, New Orleans LA 70130. 504/522-6611. **Fax:** 504/524-5701. **Contact:** Manager. **E-mail address:** infotech@ascentconsulting.com. **Description:** A temporary agency. **Specializes in the areas of:** Accounting/Auditing; Administration; Computer Science/Software; Finance; Sales. **Positions commonly filled include:** Account Manager; Account Representative; Accountant; Administrative Assistant; Administrative Manager; Budget Analyst; Chief Financial Officer; Clerical Supervisor; Computer Operator; Computer Programmer; Controller; Cost Estimator; Credit Manager; Customer Service Representative; Database Manager; Finance Director; Financial Analyst; Human Resources Manager; Internet Services Manager; Management Analyst/Consultant; Market Research Analyst; MIS

Specialist; Systems Analyst; Systems Manager; Technical Writer/Editor; Webmaster. **Average salary range of placements:** $30,000 - $50,000. **Number of placements per year:** 100 - 199.

INTERIM PERSONNEL
9634 Airline Highway, Suite 1A, Baton Rouge LA 70815. 225/925-5686. **Contact:** Christine Doiron, Area Manager. **World Wide Web address:** http://www.interim.com. **Description:** A temporary agency. **Specializes in the areas of:** Clerical; Engineering; Industrial; Technical. **Positions commonly filled include:** Accountant/Auditor; Administrative Assistant; Advertising Clerk; Bookkeeper; Chemical Engineer; Chemist; Clerk; Computer Operator; Computer Programmer; Construction Trade Worker; Customer Service Representative; Data Entry Clerk; Draftsperson; Driver; EDP Specialist; Electrical/Electronics Engineer; Factory Worker; Food Scientist/Technologist; Industrial Designer; Industrial Engineer; Legal Secretary; Light Industrial Worker; Mechanical Engineer; Medical Secretary; Operations/Production Manager; Public Relations Specialist; Receptionist; Secretary; Statistician; Stenographer; Systems Analyst; Technician; Typist/Word Processor. **Number of placements per year:** 1000+.

KEENAN STAFFING INC.
2901 North Causeway Boulevard, Suite 201, Metairie LA 70002. 504/834-0511. **Fax:** 504/834-1301. **Contact:** Thomas Keenan, President. **Description:** A temporary agency. **Specializes in the areas of:** Accounting/Auditing; Art/Design; Banking; Finance; Health/Medical; Insurance; Personnel/Labor Relations; Sales; Secretarial. **Positions commonly filled include:** Accountant/Auditor; Administrative Manager; Advertising Clerk; Blue-Collar Worker Supervisor; Branch Manager; Brokerage Clerk; Budget Analyst; Buyer; Claim Representative; Clerical Supervisor; Credit Manager; Customer Service Representative; Draftsperson; Financial Analyst; Geographer; Human Resources Specialist; Insurance Agent/Broker; Librarian; Management Trainee; Manufacturer's/Wholesaler's Sales Rep.; Market Research Analyst; Medical Records Technician; Operations/Production Manager; Paralegal; Public Relations Specialist; Purchasing Agent/Manager; Services Sales Representative; Typist/Word Processor. **Average salary range of placements:** $20,000 - $29,999. **Number of placements per year:** 500 - 999.

MANPOWER, INC.
1000 Parkview Drive, Suite 30, New Iberia LA 70563. 318/367-7173. **Fax:** 318/367-7176. **Contact:** Janet Neil, Branch Manager. **Description:** A temporary agency. Computer training courses are offered. **Specializes in the areas of:** Clerical; Computer Science/Software; Industrial; Technical. **Benefits available to temporary workers:** Medical Insurance; Paid Vacation.

OLSTEN STAFFING SERVICES
BRIGGS LEGAL STAFFING
1555 Poydras Street, Suite 140, New Orleans LA 70112. 504/581-9401. **Contact:** Manager. **Description:** A temporary agency that also provides some permanent placements. Briggs Legal Staffing (also at this location) provides permanent placements for the legal industry. **Specializes in the areas of:** Industrial; Legal; Secretarial. **Positions commonly filled include:** Accountant/Auditor; Blue-Collar Worker Supervisor; Clerical Supervisor; Computer Programmer; Credit Manager; Customer Service Representative; Human Resources Specialist; Paralegal; Typist/Word Processor. **Benefits available to temporary workers:** 401(k); Paid Holidays; Paid Vacation. **Corporate headquarters location:** Melville NY. **Average salary range of placements:** $20,000 - $29,999. **Number of placements per year:** 100 - 199.

PREMIER STAFFING, INC.
P.O. Box 91107, Lafayette LA 70509. 318/896-4140. **Fax:** 318/896-9278. **Contact:** Manager. **Description:** A temporary agency that also provides some permanent placements. Founded in 1990. **Specializes in the areas**

of: Architecture/Construction; Health/Medical. **Positions commonly filled include:** Construction Contractor; Construction Manager; Electrician; Landscape Architect; Licensed Practical Nurse; Occupational Therapist; Physical Therapist; Registered Nurse. **Corporate headquarters location:** This Location. **Other area locations:** New Iberia LA. **Average salary range of placements:** $20,000 - $29,999. **Number of placements per year:** 1 - 49.

PROFESSIONAL TEMPORARIES
P.O. Box 50788, New Orleans LA 70150. 504/522-5665. **Fax:** 504/524-3248. **Contact:** Manager. **Description:** A temporary agency. **Specializes in the areas of:** Clerical; Light Industrial; Technical. **Positions commonly filled include:** Accountant/Auditor; Blue-Collar Worker Supervisor; Buyer; Customer Service Representative; Dental Assistant/Dental Hygienist; Draftsperson; Electrician; Landscape Architect; Management Trainee; Paralegal; Purchasing Agent/Manager; Services Sales Representative; Typist/Word Processor. **Average salary range of placements:** Less than $20,000. **Number of placements per year:** 200 - 499.

SPECIAL COUNSEL
1100 Poydras Street, Suite 1260, New Orleans LA 70163. 504/522-0133. **Fax:** 504/522-0195. **Contact:** Branch Manager. **World Wide Web address:** http://www. specialcounsel.com. **Description:** Special Counsel is a temporary agency. **Specializes in the areas of:** Legal.

TECH 2000 SERVICES & STAFFING, INC.
11715 Bricksome Avenue, Suite B2, Baton Rouge LA 70816. 225/293-9908. **Fax:** 225/293-9367. **Contact:** Julia J. Collins, Chief Operating Officer. **Description:** A temporary agency. Founded in 1994. **Specializes in the areas of:** Technical. **Positions commonly filled include:** Biochemist; Biological Scientist; Chemical Engineer; Chemist; Clinical Lab Technician; Design Engineer; Designer; Draftsperson; Environmental Engineer; Food Scientist/Technologist; Geologist/Geophysicist; Laboratory Technician; Mechanical Engineer; Quality Control Supervisor. **Benefits available to temporary workers:** Dental Insurance; Life Insurance; Medical Insurance; Paid Holidays; Vision Insurance. **Corporate headquarters location:** This Location. **Other U.S. locations:** Pasadena TX. **Average salary range of placements:** $30,000 - $50,000. **Number of placements per year:** 50 - 99.

WESTAFF
2015 Gus Kaplan Drive, Alexandria LA 71301. 318/487-0416. **Fax:** 318/443-5704. **Contact:** Kathy Littlepage, Recruiter. **World Wide Web address:** http://www.westaff.com. **Description:** A temporary agency. **Specializes in the areas of:** Clerical; Health/Medical; Light Industrial; Personnel/Labor Relations; Secretarial; Technical. **Positions commonly filled include:** Carpenter; Construction Contractor; Medical Records Technician; Operations/Production Manager; Paralegal; Typist/Word Processor. **Benefits available to temporary workers:** Medical Insurance. **Corporate headquarters location:** Walnut Creek CA. **Other U.S. locations:** Nationwide. **Average salary range of placements:** Less than $20,000. **Number of placements per year:** 200 - 499.

WESTAFF
601 Poydras Street, Suite 2425, New Orleans LA 70130. 504/529-2338. **Contact:** Allison Thomas, Manager. **Description:** A temporary agency. **Specializes in the areas of:** Accounting/Auditing; Administration; Computer Science/Software; Food; Insurance; Legal; Personnel/Labor Relations; Secretarial. **Positions commonly filled include:** Accountant/Auditor; Claim Representative; Clerical Supervisor; Computer Programmer; Customer Service Representative; Draftsperson; Human Resources Specialist; Management Trainee; Medical Records Technician; Paralegal; Services Sales Representative; Systems Analyst; Technical Writer/Editor; Typist/Word Processor.

Corporate headquarters location: Walnut Creek CA. **Other U.S. locations:** Nationwide. **Average salary range of placements:** $20,000 - $29,999.

X TECHS
4829 Prytania Street, Suite 102, New Orleans LA 70115. 504/895-8324. **Fax:** 504/895-8353. **Contact:** Patricia Hamilton, President. **Description:** A temporary agency.

Specializes in the areas of: Health/Medical. **Positions commonly filled include:** Clinical Lab Technician; Nuclear Medicine Technologist; Occupational Therapist; Physical Therapist; Radiological Technologist; Surgical Technician. **Average salary range of placements:** $30,000 - $50,000. **Number of placements per year:** 50 - 99.

CONTRACT SERVICES FIRMS

CDI ENGINEERING GROUP
P.O. Box 336, Welsh LA 70591. 318/439-1659. **Contact:** Manager. **World Wide Web address:** http://www.cdicorp.com. **Description:** A contract services firm. **Specializes in the areas of:** Engineering. **Corporate headquarters location:** Philadelphia PA. **Other U.S. locations:** Nationwide. **International locations:** Worldwide.

CONCRETE SOLUTIONS INC.
9151 Interline Avenue, Suite 5B, Baton Rouge LA 70809. 225/923-2026. **Contact:** Manager. **Description:** A contract services firm.

THE POLLAK AND SKAN GROUP
6400 Congress Avenue, Boca Raton LA 33487. 800/995-6858. **Contact:** Manager. **Description:** A contract services firm. **Specializes in the areas of:** Computer Hardware/Software; Engineering.

UNIVERSAL PERSONNEL
4949 Bullard Avenue, Suite 190, New Orleans LA 70128. 504/241-1724. **Fax:** 504/246-1815. **Contact:** Tim Horton, General Manager. **Description:** A contract

services firm that also provides some permanent placements. **Specializes in the areas of:** Engineering; Technical. **Positions commonly filled include:** Applications Engineer; Architect; Biomedical Engineer; Chemical Engineer; Chemist; Civil Engineer; Computer Animator; Computer Operator; Computer Programmer; Construction and Building Inspector; Cost Estimator; Database Manager; Design Engineer; Draftsperson; Electrical/Electronics Engineer; Environmental Engineer; Geographer; Geologist/Geophysicist; Industrial Engineer; Internet Services Manager; Licensed Practical Nurse; Mechanical Engineer; Occupational Therapist; Petroleum Engineer; Physical Therapist; Project Manager; Purchasing Agent/Manager; Quality Control Supervisor; Registered Nurse; Respiratory Therapist; Sales Engineer; Software Engineer; Structural Engineer; Systems Analyst; Technical Writer/Editor; Telecommunications Manager. **Benefits available to temporary workers:** 401(k); Life Insurance; Medical Insurance; Paid Holidays; Paid Vacation. **Corporate headquarters location:** This Location. **Other U.S. locations:** Fort Walton FL; Biloxi MS. **Average salary range of placements:** $30,000 - $50,000. **Number of placements per year:** 200 - 499.

CAREER/OUTPLACEMENT COUNSELING FIRMS

HIGHLANDS PROGRAM
910 Pierremont Road, Suite 214, Shreveport LA 71106. 318/869-1632. **Contact:** Karen Logan, Counselor. **World Wide Web address:** http://www. highlandsprogram.com. **Description:** Provides career counseling to students and adults, and training and development services to corporations.

PORT CITY ENTERPRISES
P.O. Box 113, Port Allen LA 70767. 225/344-1142. **Fax:** 225/344-1192. **Contact:** Christine Dunlevy, Executive Director. **Description:** A career/outplacement counseling

agency that provides supported employment and shelter employment to persons with severe disabilities. **Specializes in the areas of:** Nonprofit; Personnel/Labor Relations. **Positions commonly filled include:** Accountant/Auditor; Administrative Manager; Employment Interviewer. **Number of placements per year:** 1 - 49.

SUCCESS IMAGES
7330 Highland Road, Baton Rouge LA 70808. 225/769-2307. **Contact:** Manager. **Description:** A career/outplacement counseling agency.

◆ M A I N E ◆

ACORN FINANCIAL GROUP
62 Portland Street, Kennebunk ME 04083. 207/985-8776. **Contact:** Manager. **Description:** An executive search firm. **Specializes in the areas of:** Accounting/Auditing.

ALL STAFF PLACEMENT SERVICES
AMERICAN PERSONNEL
550 Forest Avenue, Suite 204, Portland ME 04101. 207/774-0114. **Contact:** Manager. **Description:** An executive search firm that also offers permanent placements. American Personnel (also at this location) is a contract services firm.

CAREER MANAGEMENT ASSOCIATES
72 Pine Street, Portland ME 04102. 207/780-1125. **Fax:** 207/780-1253. **Contact:** Mark Rajotte, President. **Description:** An executive search firm that also offers career development services. **Specializes in the areas of:** Accounting/Auditing; Administration; Advertising; Banking; Engineering; Finance; General Management; Health/Medical; Insurance; Manufacturing; Nonprofit; Publishing; Retail; Sales. **Positions commonly filled include:** Accountant/Auditor; Actuary; Adjuster; Budget Analyst; Buyer; Chemical Engineer; Civil Engineer; Claim Representative; Computer Programmer; Credit Manager; Customer Service Representative; Financial Analyst; MIS Specialist; Sales Manager; Services Sales Representative; Software Engineer; Systems Analyst; Underwriter/Assistant Underwriter. **Average salary range of placements:** $30,000 - $85,000. **Number of placements per year:** 1 - 49.

DIX CONSULTING GROUP
75 Pearl Street, Portland ME 04101. 207/775-0101. **Contact:** Manager. **Description:** An executive search firm.

EXECUTIVE SEARCH OF NEW ENGLAND
131 Ocean Street, South Portland ME 04106. 207/741-4100. **Fax:** 207/741-4110. **Contact:** Charles Kimball, Systems Specialist. **Description:** An executive search firm that also offers temporary placements. **Specializes in the areas of:** Accounting/Auditing; Administration; Banking; Computer Science/Software; Finance; General Management; Manufacturing; Personnel/Labor Relations; Sales. **Positions commonly filled include:** Accountant/Auditor; Adjuster; Bank Officer/Manager; Branch Manager; Budget Analyst; Buyer; Claim Representative; Computer Programmer; Credit Manager; General Manager; Human Resources Manager; Industrial Production Manager; Insurance Agent/Broker; Manufacturer's/Wholesaler's Sales Rep.; Mechanical Engineer; Physical Therapist; Physician; Registered Nurse; Systems Analyst; Travel Agent. **Average salary range of placements:** $30,000 - $50,000.

F-O-R-T-U-N-E PERSONNEL CONSULTANTS OF BANGOR
17 Elm Street, Skowhegan ME 04976. 207/474-6110. **Fax:** 207/474-5091. **Contact:** Manager. **E-mail address:** info@fpcbangor.com. **World Wide Web address:** http://www.fpcbangor.com. **Description:** An executive search firm. **Specializes in the areas of:** Chemicals; Distribution; Environmental; Manufacturing; Marketing; Operations Management; Packaging; Paper; Purchasing; Regulatory Affairs; Research and Development; Sales; Warehousing. **Corporate headquarters location:** New York NY.

GOODRICH CONSULTING
P.O. Box 4534, Portland ME 04112. 207/799-6192. **Contact:** Wayne Goodrich, President. **Description:** An executive search firm. **Specializes in the areas of:** Engineering; Industrial; Manufacturing; Personnel/Labor Relations; Sales. **Positions commonly filled include:** Accountant/Auditor; Buyer; Ceramics Engineer;

Electrical/Electronics Engineer; Industrial Engineer; Manufacturing Engineer; Mechanical Engineer; Metallurgical Engineer; Operations/Production Manager; Purchasing Agent/Manager; Sales Representative. **Number of placements per year:** 1 - 49.

GREAT MOOSE LAKE CORPORATION
605 U.S. Route 1, Scarborough ME 04074. 207/883-6561. **Toll-free phone:** 800/434-6561. **Fax:** 207/883-2964. **Contact:** Chris Griffith, President. **E-mail address:** chrisg@mainecareers.com. **World Wide Web address:** http://www.mainecareers.com. **Description:** An executive search firm. **Specializes in the areas of:** Information Technology. **Positions commonly filled include:** Computer Programmer; MIS Specialist; Multimedia Designer; Software Engineer; Systems Analyst; Technical Writer/Editor; Telecommunications Manager. **Average salary range of placements:** More than $50,000. **Number of placements per year:** 1 - 49.

ROSS GREEN & ASSOCIATES
P.O. Box 547, Cumberland ME 04021. 207/829-6595. **Contact:** Manager. **Description:** An executive search firm. **Specializes in the areas of:** Manufacturing.

THE HAYSTACK GROUP
15 High Street, P.O. Box 823, Vinalhaven ME 04863. 207/863-2793. **Fax:** 207/863-9916. **Contact:** Manager. **World Wide Web address:** http://www.haystack-group.com. **Description:** An executive search firm. **Specializes in the areas of:** Biotechnology; Marketing; Medical Devices; Pharmaceuticals; Quality Assurance; Regulatory Affairs; Research and Development.

LEIGH HUNT & ASSOCIATES
14 Maine Street, Suite 312, Brunswick ME 04011. 207/729-3840. **Fax:** 207/729-3888. **Contact:** Manager. **E-mail address:** LHunt@leighhunt.com. **World Wide Web address:** http://www.leighhunt.com. **Description:** An executive search firm specializing in the paints, coatings, and polyurethane industries.

MOUNTAIN LTD.
106 Lafayette Street, Yarmouth ME 04096. 207/846-1166. **Fax:** 207/846-6779. **Contact:** Joseph H. Hosmer, President. **E-mail address:** hosmer@mountainltd.com. **World Wide Web address:** http://www.mountainltd.com. **Description:** An executive search firm. Mountain Ltd. is a division of MAGIC (Management Alliance Group of Independent Companies). **Specializes in the areas of:** Telecommunications.

NORTHERN CONSULTANTS
P.O. Box 220, Hampden ME 04444. 207/862-2323. **Contact:** Alta L. Chase, President. **Description:** An executive search firm.

PEMBERTON & ASSOCIATES
75 Market Street, Suite 301, Portland ME 04101. 207/775-1772. **Contact:** Manager. **Description:** An executive search firm.

THE PORTER HAMEL GROUP, INC.
565 Congress, Suite 203, Portland ME 04101. 207/828-1134. **Contact:** Jeff Porter, President. **Description:** An executive search firm specializing in the placement of operations and technical professionals in the food manufacturing industry. This firm operates on both retainer and contingency bases. **Specializes in the areas of:** Engineering; Food; Manufacturing; Personnel/Labor Relations. **Positions commonly filled include:** Biological Scientist; Chemical Engineer; Electrical/Electronics Engineer; Electrician; Environmental Engineer; Food Scientist/Technologist; Human Resources Manager; Industrial Engineer; Mechanical Engineer; Operations/Production Manager; Purchasing

Agent/Manager; Quality Control Supervisor. **Corporate headquarters location:** This Location. **Other U.S. locations:** Lansdale PA. **Average salary range of placements:** More than $50,000. **Number of placements per year:** 1 - 49.

PRO SEARCH, INC.
P.O. Box 7489, Portland ME 04112. 207/775-7600. **Contact:** Manager. **Description:** An executive search firm. **Specializes in the areas of:** Accounting/Auditing; Customer Service; Information Systems; Sales.

RAND ASSOCIATES
204 Lafayette Center, Kennebunk ME 04043. 207/985-7700. **Contact:** Manager. **Description:** An executive

search firm. **Specializes in the areas of:** Finance; Manufacturing.

RECRUITING PROFESSIONALS
206 New Settlement Road, Hiram ME 04041. 207/625-7100. **Fax:** 207/625-7190. **Contact:** Manager. **World Wide Web address:** http://www.recpros.com. **Description:** An executive search firm. **Specializes in the areas of:** Engineering; Environmental.

WIN WIN SOLUTIONS
P.O. Box 626, Brunswick ME 04011. 207/833-6650. **Fax:** 207/833-0098. **Contact:** Manager. **Description:** An executive search firm. **Specializes in the areas of:** Information Systems; Information Technology.

PERMANENT EMPLOYMENT AGENCIES

AMES PERSONNEL SERVICE
P.O. Box 490, Brunswick ME 04011. 207/729-5158. **Toll-free phone:** 800/639-8802. **Fax:** 207/729-5246. **Contact:** Manager. **Description:** A permanent placement agency that also provides some temporary placements.

BONNEY STAFFING & TRAINING CENTERS
477 Congress Street, Portland ME 04101. 207/773-3829. **Fax:** 207/773-1864. **Contact:** Joel Gratwick, CPC/President. **E-mail address:** joelg@bonneystaffing.com. **World Wide Web address:** http://www.bonneystaffing.com. **Description:** A permanent employment agency that also offers some temporary and temp-to-perm placements, executive searches on a contingency basis, contract services, and career counseling services. Bonney Staffing Center (also at this location) focuses on temporary, temp-to-perm, and direct placements in office support and light industrial positions. Bonney Pro Center (also at this location) focuses on professional placement and contract services. Bonney Training Center (also at this location) focuses on computer training. Client company pays fee. **Specializes in the areas of:** Accounting; Administration; Computer Science/Software; Finance; General Management; Industrial; Light Industrial; Personnel/Labor Relations; Scientific; Secretarial; Technical. **Positions commonly filled include:** Account Manager; Account Rep.; Accountant; Administrative Assistant; Administrative Manager; Applications Engineer; AS400 Programmer Analyst; Assistant Manager; Auditor; Blue-Collar Worker Supervisor; Branch Manager; Budget Analyst; CFO; Claim Rep.; Clerical Supervisor; Computer Engineer; Computer Operator; Computer Programmer; Computer Support Tech.; Computer Tech.; Content Developer; Controller; Cost Estimator; Credit Manager; Customer Service Rep.; Database Administrator; Database Manager; ESL Teacher; Finance Director; Financial Analyst; Fund Manager; General Manager; Human Resources Manager; Industrial Production Manager; Internet Services Manager; Management Analyst/Consultant; Medical Records Technician; MIS Specialist; Network/Systems Administrator; Operations Manager; Paralegal; Production Manager; Project Manager; Purchasing Agent/Manager; Quality Control Supervisor; Sales Manager; Secretary; Software Engineer; SQL Programmer; Systems Analyst; Systems Manager; Teacher/Professor; Technical Writer/Editor; Telecommunications Manager; Typist/Word Processor; Vice President; Webmaster. **Corporate headquarters location:** This Location. **Average salary range of placements:** $20,000 - $49,999. **Number of placements per year:** 1000+.

BONNEY STAFFING & TRAINING CENTERS
37 Park Street, Lewiston ME 04240. 207/783-7000. **Contact:** Manager. **Description:** A permanent employment agency that also offers some temp-to-perm placements.

CREATIVE WORK SYSTEMS
168 Lisbon Street, Lewiston ME 04240. 207/795-6737. **Contact:** Manager. **Description:** A nonprofit, permanent

employment agency that provides placements for the disabled.

EMPLOYMENT TRUST INC. (ETI)
P.O. Box 11058, 2301 Congress Street, Portland ME 04104. 207/775-1924. **Contact:** Richard C. Petersen, President. **Description:** A permanent employment agency providing placements for disadvantaged workers.

EXPRESS PERSONNEL SERVICE
2063 Congress Street, Portland ME 04102. 207/761-9933. **Fax:** 297/761-9990. **Contact:** Manager. **Description:** A permanent employment agency. **Specializes in the areas of:** Clerical; Industrial; Office Support; Technical.

GOODWILL PROFESSIONAL SERVICES
347 Leighton Road, Augusta ME 04330. 207/626-0170. **Contact:** Manager. **Description:** A permanent employment agency.

INITIAL STAFFING SERVICES
11 Free Street, Portland ME 04101. 207/774-5300. **Contact:** Manager. **Description:** A permanent employment agency.

LEBEL PERSONNEL
99 Larrabee Road, Westbrook ME 04092. 207/854-2422. **Contact:** Manager. **Description:** A permanent employment agency.

PAGEMPLOYMENT
P.O. Box 910, Brewer ME 04412. 207/945-3301. **Contact:** Manager. **Description:** A permanent employment agency. Founded in 1945.

PAPER INDUSTRY RECRUITMENT (PIR)
36 Main Street, Gorham ME 04038. 207/839-2633. **Fax:** 207/839-2634. **Contact:** Maynard Charron, Owner. **E-mail address:** mc@pirecruitment.com. **World Wide Web address:** http://www.pirecruitment.com. **Description:** A permanent employment agency. **Specializes in the areas of:** Engineering; Industrial; Manufacturing; Paper. **Positions commonly filled include:** Chemical Engineer; Chemist; Designer; Electrical/Electronics Engineer; General Manager; Human Resources Manager; Mechanical Engineer; Quality Control Supervisor. **Number of placements per year:** 1 - 49.

PHOENIX EMPLOYMENT AND REHABILITATION
230 Bomarc Road, Bangor ME 04401. 207/941-2895. **Contact:** Manager. **Description:** A permanent employment agency that provides placements for the disabled.

RO-LAN ASSOCIATES, INC.
725 Sabattus Street, Lewiston ME 04240. 207/784-1010. **Fax:** 207/782-3446. **Contact:** Rolande L. LaPointe, President. **E-mail address:** rolanAI@aol.com. **Description:** A permanent employment agency that also offers temporary and temp-to-perm placements in all

fields. RO-LAN Associates also provides resume writing, career counseling, and contract services, and operates on a contingency basis.

SPRINGBORN STAFFING SERVICE
130 Middle Street, Portland ME 04101. 207/761-8367. **Contact:** Branch Manager. **Description:**

Springborn Staffing Service is a permanent employment agency.

TWIN CITY EMPLOYMENT SERVICES
159 State Street, Bangor ME 04401. 207/942-0977. **Contact:** Manager. **Description:** A permanent employment agency.

TEMPORARY EMPLOYMENT AGENCIES

ACCOMPLISHED PROFESSIONALS
P.O. Box 7040, Portland ME 04112. 207/773-4749. **Fax:** 207/773-2645. **Contact:** Mr. Louis LaPierre, President. **Description:** A temporary agency. **Specializes in the areas of:** Accounting/Auditing; Administration; Banking; Computer Science/Software; Finance; General Management; Insurance; Manufacturing; Personnel/Labor Relations; Secretarial. **Positions commonly filled include:** Accountant/Auditor; Actuary; Adjuster; Administrative Manager; Bank Officer/Manager; Branch Manager; Claim Representative; Computer Programmer; Cost Estimator; Credit Manager; Customer Service Representative; Economist; Financial Analyst; General Manager; Health Services Worker; Human Resources Specialist; Insurance Agent/Broker; MIS Specialist; Paralegal; Quality Control Supervisor; Real Estate Agent; Securities Sales Representative; Software Engineer; Systems Analyst; Technical Writer/Editor; Telecommunications Manager; Typist/Word Processor; Underwriter/Assistant Underwriter. **Average salary range of placements:** $30,000 - $50,000. **Number of placements per year:** 50 - 99.

AT WORK PERSONNEL SERVICE
43 Acme Road, Brewer ME 04412. 207/989-0824. **Toll-free phone:** 800/947-2166. **Contact:** Service Coordinator. **Description:** A temporary agency that also offers some temp-to-perm placements. **Specializes in the areas of:** Accounting/Auditing; Architecture/Construction; Education; Finance; Food; General Management; Health/Medical; Industrial; Insurance; Legal; Manufacturing; Retail; Sales; Secretarial; Transportation. **Positions commonly filled include:** Accountant/Auditor; Actuary; Adjuster; Administrative Manager; Advertising Clerk; Automotive Mechanic; Bank Officer/Manager; Blue-Collar Worker Supervisor; Branch Manager; Buyer; Claim Representative; Clerical Supervisor; Clinical Lab Technician; Computer Programmer; Construction and Building Inspector; Construction Contractor; Cost Estimator; Counselor; Credit Manager; Customer Service Representative; Dental Assistant/Dental Hygienist; Dietician/Nutritionist; Draftsperson; Editor; Education Administrator; EEG Technologist; EKG Technician; Electrician; Emergency Medical Technician; Financial Analyst; Food Scientist/Technologist; Forester/Conservation Scientist; General Manager; Health Services Manager; Hotel Manager; Human Resources Specialist; Human Service Worker; Industrial Production Manager; Insurance Agent/Broker; Internet Services Manager; Librarian; Licensed Practical Nurse; Management Analyst/Consultant; Management Trainee; Manufacturer's/Wholesaler's Sales Rep.; Medical Records Technician; MIS Specialist; Occupational

Therapist; Operations/Production Manager; Paralegal; Physical Therapist; Preschool Worker; Property and Real Estate Manager; Public Relations Specialist; Purchasing Agent/Manager; Quality Control Supervisor; Radio/TV Announcer/Broadcaster; Radiological Technologist; Real Estate Agent; Recreational Therapist; Registered Nurse; Reporter; Respiratory Therapist; Restaurant/Food Service Manager; Services Sales Rep.; Statistician; Systems Analyst; Teacher/Professor; Telecommunications Manager; Travel Agent; Typist/Word Processor; Video Production Coordinator. **Benefits available to temporary workers:** Medical Insurance. **Corporate headquarters location:** Brooks ME. **Average salary range of placements:** Less than $20,000. **Number of placements per year:** 200 - 499.

MAINE STAFFING SERVICES
71 Hospital Street, Augusta ME 04330-6617. 207/622-5352. **Toll-free phone:** 800/456-0660. **Fax:** 207/622-5987. **Contact:** Morrison Bump, Owner. **World Wide Web address:** http://www.mainestaff.com. **Description:** A temporary agency that also provides some permanent placements. Client company pays fee. **Specializes in the areas of:** Accounting; Administration; Architecture/Construction; Computer Science/Software; Engineering; Finance; Light Industrial; Personnel/Labor Relations; Secretarial. **Positions commonly filled include:** Accountant; Administrative Assistant; Chemist; Civil Engineer; Clerical Supervisor; Computer Support Tech.; Computer Tech.; Construction Contractor; Counselor; Customer Service Rep.; Database Administrator; Design Engineer; Draftsperson; Electrician; Financial Analyst; Insurance Agent/Broker; Mechanical Engineer; Network/Systems Administrator; Paralegal; Purchasing Agent/Manager; Sales Representative; Secretary; Social Worker; Systems Analyst; Systems Manager; Typist/Word Processor; Webmaster. **Benefits available to temporary workers:** EAP. **Corporate headquarters location:** This Location. **Other area locations:** Saco ME. **Average salary range of placements:** Less than $30,000. **Number of placements per year:** 100 - 199.

TEMPO EMPLOYMENT SERVICE
P.O. Box 31, Presque Isle ME 04769. 207/764-0772. **Fax:** 207/764-2620. **Contact:** Manager. **Description:** A temporary agency. **Specializes in the areas of:** Retail; Secretarial. **Positions commonly filled include:** Accountant/Auditor; Automotive Mechanic; Broadcast Technician; Budget Analyst; Construction and Building Inspector; Construction Contractor; Customer Service Representative; Health Services Manager; Human Resources Specialist; Typist/Word Processor. **Average salary range of placements:** Less than $20,000. **Number of placements per year:** 200 - 499.

CONTRACT SERVICES FIRMS

ADECCO/TAD TECHNICAL SERVICES
43 Silver Street, Portland ME 04101. 207/797-8600. **Contact:** Manager. **Description:** Adecco/TAD Technical Services is a contract services firm. **Specializes in the areas of:** Technical.

COMBINED MANAGEMENT INC.
67 Minot Avenue, Auburn ME 04210. 207/782-8246. **Contact:** Manager. **Description:** A contract services firm. **Specializes in the areas of:** Human Services.

GLOBAL ENGINEERS, INC.
P.O. Box 782, Bailey Island ME 04003. 207/833-2800.
Fax: 207/833-0021. **Contact:** Manager. **World Wide
Web address:** http://www.globalengineers.com.
Description: Global Engineers, Inc. is a contract
services firm that provides placements nationwide.
Specializes in the areas of: Engineering; Technical.

Positions commonly filled include: Aerospace
Engineer; Biomedical Engineer; Chemical Engineer;
Civil Engineer; Design Engineer; Draftsperson;
Electrical/Electronics Engineer; Environmental
Engineer; Industrial Engineer; Mechanical Engineer;
Metallurgical Engineer; Mining Engineer; Nuclear
Engineer; Petroleum Engineer; Software Engineer;

◆ MARYLAND ◆

ACCESS ASSOCIATES INC.
1107 Kenilworth Drive, Suite 307, Towson MD 21204. 410/821-7190. **Contact:** Manager. **Description:** An executive search firm.

ACCOUNTANTS EXECUTIVE SEARCH
ACCOUNTANTS ON CALL
201 North Charles Street, Suite 1106, Baltimore MD 21201. 410/685-5700. **Fax:** 410/685-5736. **Contact:** Manager. **Description:** An executive search firm. Accountants On Call (also at this location) is a temporary agency. **Specializes in the areas of:** Accounting/ Auditing; Banking; Finance.

AUTO CAREERS
11700 Rutledge Road, Timonium MD 21093-2021. 410/561-1818. **Contact:** John O'Hare, President. **Description:** An executive search firm operating on a retainer basis. **Specializes in the areas of:** Automotive; Sales. **Positions commonly filled include:** Accountant/ Auditor; Automotive Mechanic. **Average salary range of placements:** More than $50,000. **Number of placements per year:** 50 - 99.

BG AND ASSOCIATES
10112 Langhorne Court, Suite B, Bethesda MD 20817-1250. 301/365-4046. **Fax:** 301/365-0435. **Contact:** Manager. **Description:** An executive search firm that also provides contract placements and performs payroll services. **Specializes in the areas of:** Accounting; Finance; Human Resources; Information Technology.

ANN BOND ASSOCIATES
275 West Street, Suite 304, Annapolis MD 21401. 410/280-6002. **Fax:** 410/280-5442. **Contact:** Robert S. Bond, Vice President. **E-mail address:** annbondassociates@erols.com. **World Wide Web address:** http://www.annbondassociates.com. **Description:** Ann Bond Associates is an executive search firm. Client company pays fee. **Specializes in the areas of:** Food. **Positions commonly filled include:** Account Manager; Account Rep.; Marketing Manager; Sales Executive; Sales Manager; Sales Rep.; Vice President. **Corporate headquarters location:** This Location. **Average salary range of placements:** $50,000 - $100,000.

BRANDJES ASSOCIATES
16 South Calvert Street, Suite 500, Baltimore MD 21202. 410/547-6886. **Fax:** 410/727-2489. **Contact:** Michael Brandjes, President. **E-mail address:** mbrandjes@ msn.com. **Description:** An executive search firm. **Specializes in the areas of:** Banking. **Positions commonly filled include:** Bank Officer/Manager; Budget Analyst; Chief Financial Officer; Controller; Credit Manager; Economist; Finance Director; Financial Analyst; Fund Manager. **Average salary range of placements:** $50,000 - $100,000. **Number of placements per year:** 50 - 99.

BRINDISI SEARCH
10751 Falls Road, Suite 250, Lutherville MD 21093. 410/339-7673. **Fax:** 410/823-0146. **Contact:** Thomas J. Brindisi, President. **E-mail address:** tbrindisi@aol.com. **World Wide Web address:** http://www. brindisisearch.com. **Description:** Brindisi Search is an executive search firm operating on a retainer basis. Client company pays fee. **Specializes in the areas of:** General Management; Human Resources. **Positions commonly filled include:** General Manager; Human Resources Manager; Management Analyst/ Consultant; Vice President. **Corporate headquarters location:** This Location. **Average salary range of placements:** More than $100,000. **Number of placements per year:** 1 - 49.

BECKETT BROWN INTERNATIONAL
3 Church Circle, Suite 207, Annapolis MD 21401. 410/315-9077. **Fax:** 410/315-8882. **Contact:** Manager. **Description:** Beckett Brown International is an executive search firm.

CAPLAN/GROSS ASSOCIATES, INC.
28 Allegheny Avenue, Suite 600, Baltimore MD 21204. 410/821-9351. **Fax:** 410/583-1901. **Contact:** Robert Caplan, President. **Description:** Caplan/Gross Associates is an executive search firm. **Specializes in the areas of:** Accounting; Administration; Computer Science/Software; Finance; Food; General Management; Health/Medical; Legal; MIS/EDP; Nonprofit; Personnel/Labor Relations; Printing; Publishing; Sales; Technical. **Positions commonly filled include:** Accountant; Applications Engineer; Attorney; Auditor; Budget Analyst; Chief Financial Officer; Computer Engineer; Computer Programmer; Computer Scientist; Controller; Cost Estimator; Credit Manager; Database Administrator; Database Manager; Finance Director; Financial Analyst; General Manager; Human Resources Manager; Internet Services Manager; Management Analyst/Consultant; MIS Specialist; Network/Systems Administrator; Paralegal; Physical Therapist; Physician; Sales Engineer; Sales Manager; Software Engineer; SQL Programmer; Systems Analyst; Systems Manager. **Corporate headquarters location:** This location. **Average salary range of placements:** $50,000 - $100,000. **Number of placements per year:** 100 - 199.

CHARLES, PROPHET, AND HAMILTON
6106 Biltmore Avenue, Baltimore MD 21215. 410/358-4373. **Fax:** 410/358-5377. **Contact:** Manager. **Description:** An executive search firm.

CHESAPEAKE CONSULTING GROUP
10751 Falls Road, Suite 250, Lutherville MD 21093. 410/339-7670. **Contact:** President. **Description:** Chesapeake Consulting Group is an executive search firm. **Specializes in the areas of:** Engineering; General Management; Industrial; Manufacturing; Sales; Technical. **Positions commonly filled include:** Chemical Engineer; Chemist; Electrical/Electronics Engineer; Environmental Engineer; General Manager; Industrial Engineer; Mechanical Engineer; Plant Manager; Quality Control Supervisor. **Average salary range of placements:** More than $50,000. **Number of placements per year:** 1 - 49.

COLUMBIA CONSULTING
8323 Cherry Lane, Laurel MD 20707. 301/470-1555. **Contact:** Manager. **Description:** An executive search firm. **Specializes in the areas of:** Computer Hardware/Software; Information Systems; Information Technology.

COMPREHENSIVE SEARCH GROUP
201 West Padonia Road, Suite 101, Timonium MD 21093. 410/252-8911. **Toll-free phone:** 800/535-8466. **Fax:** 410/252-7289. **Contact:** Lawrence Beaudon, Certified Personnel Consultant. **E-mail address:** cscjobs@ix.netcom.com. **Description:** Comprehensive Search Group is an executive search firm operating on a contingency basis. Client company pays fee. **Specializes in the areas of:** Marketing; Sales. **Positions commonly filled include:** Account Manager; Account Representative; Sales Executive; Sales Manager; Sales Representative. **Corporate headquarters location:** This Location. **Average salary range of placements:** $50,000 - $100,000.

COMPUTER MANAGEMENT INC.
809 Glen Eagle Court, Suite 205, Towson MD 21286. 410/583-0050. **Fax:** 410/494-9410. **Contact:** Janet Miller, President. **Description:** An executive search firm. **Specializes in the areas of:** Computer Operations; Information Systems. **Positions commonly filled include:** Computer Programmer; Network Engineer; Software Engineer; Systems Analyst. **Number of placements per year:** 1 - 49.

COMPUTRADE, INC.
3020 Homewood Parkway, Suite 301, Kensington MD 20895. 301/309-6800. **Contact:** George Schnabel, Managing Director. **Description:** An executive search firm. **Specializes in the areas of:** Finance. **Positions commonly filled include:** Financial Analyst. **Average salary range of placements:** More than $50,000. **Number of placements per year:** 50 - 99.

CONTINENTAL SEARCH AND OUTPLACEMENT
4134 East Joppa Road, Suite 203, Baltimore MD 21236. 410/529-7000. **Contact:** Manager. **Description:** An executive search firm.

CORPORATE RESOURCES
110 North Potomac Street, Hagerstown MD 21740. 301/797-3434. **Fax:** 301/797-3331. **Contact:** Jane Stevens, President. **Description:** An executive search firm. **Specializes in the areas of:** Engineering; Heating, Air Conditioning, and Refrigeration; Manufacturing; Telecommunications.

CROSS COUNTRY CONSULTANTS, INC.
FALLSTAFF SEARCH
111 Warren Road, Suite 4B, Hunt Valley MD 21030. 410/666-1100. **Contact:** Robert Chertkof, President. **Description:** An executive search firm. Fallstaff Search (also at this location) is an executive search firm that specializes in health care, sales, and industrial positions. **Specializes in the areas of:** Accounting/Auditing; Engineering; Finance. **Number of placements per year:** 50 - 99.

DESAI ASSOCIATES
34 Trailridge Court, Potomac MD 20854. 301/424-6444. **Contact:** Manager. **Description:** An executive search firm.

C.A. DURAKIS & ASSOCIATES
5550 Sterrett Place, Suite 302, Columbia MD 21044. 410/740-5590. **Contact:** Manager. **Description:** A generalist executive search firm.

EMPLOYER EMPLOYEE EXCHANGE (EEE)
200 East Joppa Road, Suite 304, Towson MD 21286. 410/821-1900. **Toll-free phone:** 800/821-1902. **Fax:** 410/821-1904. **Contact:** Technical Recruiter. **E-mail address:** resumes@cybernerd.com. **World Wide Web address:** http://www.eeejobs.com. **Description:** An executive search firm. NOTE: Please include salary requirements when applying. **Specializes in the areas of:** Administration; Computer Science/Software; Engineering; Sales; Secretarial; Technical. **Positions commonly filled include:** Accountant/Auditor; Chemical Engineer; Chemist; Civil Engineer; Clerical Supervisor; Computer Programmer; Customer Service Rep.; Draftsperson; Electrical/Electronics Engineer; Industrial Engineer; Management Trainee; Manufacturer's/Wholesaler's Sales Rep.; MIS Specialist; Services Sales Rep.; Software Engineer; Structural Engineer; Systems Analyst; Technical Writer/Editor; Telecommunications Manager; Typist/Word Processor. **Benefits available to temporary workers:** Bonus Award/Plan; Medical Insurance; Paid Holidays; Paid Vacation. **Average salary range of placements:** $30,000 - $65,000. **Number of placements per year:** 100 - 199.

EXECUTIVE DYNAMICS, INC.
1107 Kenilworth Drive, Suite 208, Towson MD 21204. 410/494-1400. **Contact:** Manager. **Description:** An executive search firm operating on a contingency basis.

EXECUTIVE PLACEMENT ASSOCIATES
6001 Montrose Road, Suite 702, Rockville MD 20852. 301/231-8150. **Fax:** 301/881-2918. **Contact:** Mark Suss, President. **Description:** An executive search firm. **Specializes in the areas of:** Advertising; Retail. **Positions commonly filled include:** Branch Manager; Buyer; District Manager; General Manager; Human Resources Manager; Operations/Production Manager; Store Manager; Wholesale and Retail Buyer. **Number of placements per year:** 50 - 99.

EXECUTIVE RECRUITERS
7315 Wisconsin Avenue, Suite 333E, Bethesda MD 20814. 301/469-3100. **Contact:** Manager. **Description:** An executive search firm. **Specializes in the areas of:** Retail.

A.G. FISHKIN AND ASSOCIATES, INC.
P.O. Box 34413, Bethesda MD 20827. 301/983-0303. **Fax:** 301/983-0415. **Contact:** Anita Fishkin, President. **E-mail address:** afishkin@us.net. **Description:** An executive search firm operating on both retainer and contingency bases. **Specializes in the areas of:** Computer Hardware/Software; Data Communications; Information Technology; Sales; Technical; Telecommunications; Wireless Communications. **Positions commonly filled include:** Computer Programmer; Electrical/Electronics Engineer; Management Analyst/Consultant; Sales Representative; Systems Analyst. **Average salary range of placements:** More than $50,000. **Number of placements per year:** 1 - 49.

F-O-R-T-U-N-E PERSONNEL CONSULTANTS
838 Ritchie Highway, Suite 2, Severna Park MD 21146. 410/544-5151. **Fax:** 410/544-6788. **Contact:** Ray Williams, President. **Description:** An executive search firm. **Specializes in the areas of:** Paper; Petrochemical; Process Technology. **Corporate headquarters location:** New York NY.

F-O-R-T-U-N-E PERSONNEL CONSULTANTS
Fortune Center, 42 Idlewild Street, Bel Air MD 21014. 410/893-0450. **Fax:** 410/893-1121. **Contact:** Office Manager. **Description:** An executive search firm. **Specializes in the areas of:** Engineering; Manufacturing. **Positions commonly filled include:** Chemical Engineer; Electrical/Electronics Engineer; Environmental Engineer; Industrial Engineer; Mechanical Engineer. **Corporate headquarters location:** New York NY. **Other U.S. locations:** Nationwide. **Average salary range of placements:** More than $50,000. **Number of placements per year:** 50 - 99.

F-O-R-T-U-N-E PERSONNEL CONSULTANTS
10 Crossroads Drive, Suite 201, Owings Mills MD 21117. 410/581-0012. **Fax:** 410/581-2280. **Contact:** Manager. **Description:** An executive search firm. **Specializes in the areas of:** Biomedical; Biotechnology; Data Processing; Elderly; Electrical; Electronics; Health/Medical; Legal; Medical Devices; MIS/EDP; Pharmaceuticals; Research and Development; Scientific; Software Engineering; Telecommunications. **Corporate headquarters location:** New York NY.

GRANT MORGAN ASSOCIATES
7316 Wisconsin Avenue, Suite 350, Bethesda MD 20814. 301/718-8888. **Contact:** Manager. **Description:** An executive search firm. **Specializes in the areas of:** Finance.

GREEN-WAY ASSOCIATES INC.
714 Potomac Avenue, Hagerstown MD 21740. 301/790-0345. **Toll-free phone:** 800/296-0345. **Fax:** 301/790-0345. **Contact:** Manager. **Description:** A generalist executive search firm.

ROBERT HALF INTERNATIONAL
ACCOUNTEMPS
100 East Pratt Street, Suite 310, Baltimore MD 21202. 410/385-1600. **Contact:** Manager. **World Wide Web address:** http://www.roberthalf.com. **Description:** An

executive search firm. Accountemps (also at this location) provides temporary placements. **Corporate headquarters location:** Menlo Park CA. **Other U.S. locations:** Nationwide.

THE HANOVER GROUP
11707 Hunters Run Drive, Hunt Valley MD 21030. 410/785-1912. **Fax:** 410/785-1913. **Contact:** Tom Graff, President. **Description:** An executive search firm operating on a contingency basis. **Specializes in the areas of:** Banking; Finance. **Positions commonly filled include:** Bank Officer/Manager. **Corporate headquarters location:** This Location. **Other area locations:** Baltimore MD. **Average salary range of placements:** More than $50,000. **Number of placements per year:** 1 - 49.

HAYDDEN & ASSOCIATES
100 West Road, Suite 300, Towsen MD 21204. 410/337-7878. **Fax:** 410/339-5303. **Contact:** Manager. **Description:** An executive search firm.

HEALTHCARE RECRUITERS OF THE MID-ATLANTIC
4500 Black Rock Road, Suite 102, Hampstead MD 21074. 410/239-6464. **Contact:** Manager. **Description:** An executive search firm. **Specializes in the areas of:** Health/Medical.

HORTON INTERNATIONAL INC.
217 East Redwood Street, Suite 1470, Baltimore MD 21202-3316. 410/625-3800. **Contact:** Manager. **Description:** An executive search firm.

INTERIM FINANCIAL SOLUTIONS
120 East Baltimore Street, Suite 2220, Baltimore MD 21202. 410/752-5244. **Contact:** Manager. **E-mail address:** ifsbaltimore@interim.com. **World Wide Web address:** http://www.interim.com. **Description:** An executive search firm.

JDG ASSOCIATES LIMITED
1700 Research Boulevard, Rockville MD 20850. 301/340-2210. **Fax:** 301/762-3117. **Contact:** Joseph DeGioia, President. **E-mail address:** info@jdgsearch.com. **World Wide Web address:** http://www.jdgsearch.com. **Description:** An executive search firm operating on both retainer and contingency bases. **Specializes in the areas of:** Administration; Computer Science/Software; Economics; Engineering; Information Technology; Management; Management Consulting; Nonprofit. **Positions commonly filled include:** Budget Analyst; Computer Programmer; Economist; Electrical/Electronics Engineer; Financial Analyst; Industrial Engineer; Management Analyst/Consultant; Mathematician; MIS Specialist; Multimedia Designer; Science Technologist; Software Engineer; Statistician; Systems Analyst; Telecommunications Manager; Transportation/Traffic Specialist. **Average salary range of placements:** More than $50,000. **Number of placements per year:** 200 - 499.

KOSTMAYER ASSOCIATES
1410 Harbor House, Baltimore MD 21210. 410/435-2288. **Contact:** Roger Kostmayer, President. **Description:** An executive search firm.

KRAUTHAMER & ASSOCIATES
5530 Wisconsin Avenue, Suite 1202, Chevy Chase MD 20815. 301/654-7533. **Contact:** Manager. **Description:** A generalist executive search firm.

LARSON & LEE INC.
4915 Saint Elmo Avenue, Suite 504, Bethesda MD 20814. 301/718-4280. **Fax:** 301/718-9587. **Contact:** Manager. **Description:** An executive search firm.

KEN LEINER ASSOCIATES, INC.
11510 Georgia Avenue, Suite 105, Wheaton MD 20902. 301/933-8800. **Contact:** Manager. **Description:** An executive search firm. **Specializes in the areas of:** Information Technology; Sales; Technical.

MANAGEMENT RECRUITERS
5044 Dorsey Hall Drive, Suite 204, Ellicott City MD 21042. 410/884-1363. **Contact:** Manager. **Description:** An executive search firm. **Corporate headquarters location:** Cleveland OH. **Other U.S. locaitons:** Nationwide.

MANAGEMENT RECRUITERS INTERNATIONAL
132 East Main Street, Suite 300, Salisbury MD 21801. 410/548-4473. **Contact:** Manager. **Description:** An executive search firm. **Corporate headquarters location:** Cleveland OH. **Other U.S. locations:** Nationwide. **International locations:** Worldwide.

MANAGEMENT RECRUITERS INTERNATIONAL
5550 Sterrett Place, Suite 314, Columbia MD 21044. 410/715-1141. **Toll-free phone:** 800/267-1226. **Fax:** 410/715-1145. **Contact:** Renee Crespo, Manager. **E-mail address:** mricolum@erols.com. **World Wide Web address:** http://www.mriplastic-packaging.com. **Description:** An executive search firm. Client company pays fee. **Specializes in the areas of:** Engineering; Manufacturing; Plastics. **Positions commonly filled include:** Design Engineer; Manufacturing Engineer; Mechanical Engineer; Quality Assurance Engineer. **Corporate headquarters location:** Cleveland OH. **Other U.S. locations:** Nationwide. **International locations:** Worldwide.

MANAGEMENT RECRUITERS INTERNATIONAL OF BALTIMORE/TIMONIUM
SALES CONSULTANTS OF BALTIMORE
9515 Deereco Road, Suite 900, Timonium MD 21093. 410/252-6616. **Fax:** 410/252-7076. **Contact:** Linda Burton, Vice President. **Description:** An executive search firm operating on both retainer and contingency bases. **Specializes in the areas of:** Administration; Computer Science/Software; Engineering; Food; Marketing; MIS/EDP; Sales; Secretarial. **Positions commonly filled include:** Account Manager; Account Representative; Administrative Assistant; Administrative Manager; Applications Engineer; AS400 Programmer Analyst; Computer Animator; Computer Engineer; Computer Operator; Computer Programmer; Computer Support Tech.; Computer Tech.; Customer Service Rep.; Database Administrator; Database Manager; Design Engineer; Electrical/Electronics Engineer; Human Resources Manager; Industrial Engineer; Internet Services Manager; Manufacturing Engineer; Mechanical Engineer; MIS Specialist; Multimedia Designer; Network/Systems Administrator; Operations Manager; Paralegal; Production Manager; Project Manager; Quality Assurance Engineer; Quality Control Supervisor; Sales Engineer; Sales Executive; Sales Manager; Sales Rep.; Secretary; Software Engineer; SQL Programmer; Systems Analyst; Systems Manager; Typist/Word Processor; Webmaster. **Corporate headquarters location:** Cleveland OH. **Other U.S. locations:** Nationwide. **International locations:** Worldwide. **Average salary range of placements:** $50,000 - $100,000. **Number of placements per year:** 200 - 499.

MANAGEMENT RECRUITERS OF ANNAPOLIS
2083 West Street, Suite 5A, Annapolis MD 21401. 410/841-6600. **Contact:** John Czajkowski, Manager. **Description:** An executive search firm. **Specializes in the areas of:** Accounting/Auditing; Administration; Advertising; Architecture/Construction; Banking; Chemicals; Communications; Computer Hardware/Software; Design; Electrical; Engineering; Finance; Food; General Management; Health/Medical; Insurance; Legal; Manufacturing; Operations Management; Personnel/Labor Relations; Pharmaceuticals; Procurement; Publishing; Retail; Sales; Technical; Textiles; Transportation. **Corporate headquarters location:** Cleveland OH. **Other U.S. locations:** Nationwide. **International locations:** Worldwide.

MANAGEMENT RECRUITERS OF FREDERICK OFFICEMATES5
4 East Street, Frederick MD 21702. 301/663-0600. **Fax:** 301/663-0454. **Contact:** Ms. Pat Webb, Owner/Manager.

Description: An executive search firm. **Specializes in the areas of:** Accounting/Auditing; Administration; Advertising; Architecture/Construction; Banking; Chemicals; Communications; Computer Hardware/Software; Design; Electrical; Engineering; Finance; Food; General Management; Health/Medical; Insurance; Legal; Manufacturing; Operations Management; Personnel/Labor Relations; Pharmaceuticals; Procurement; Publishing; Retail; Sales; Technical; Textiles; Transportation. **Corporate headquarters location:** Cleveland OH. **Other U.S. locations:** Nationwide. **International locations:** Worldwide.

MANAGEMENT RECRUITERS OF ROCKVILLE
3750 University Boulevard West, Kensington MD 20895. 301/949-6226. **Contact:** Manager. **Description:** An executive search firm. **Corporate headquarters location:** Cleveland OH. **Other U.S. locations:** Nationwide.

MANAGEMENT RECRUITERS OF WASHINGTON, D.C.
1100 Wayne Avenue, Suite 1080, Silver Spring MD 20910. 301/589-5400. **Fax:** 301/589-3033. **Contact:** Manager. **Description:** An executive search firm. **Specializes in the areas of:** Accounting/Auditing; Computer Hardware/Software; Design; Finance; Health/Medical; Market Research. **Corporate headquarters location:** Cleveland OH. **Other U.S. locations:** Nationwide. **International locations:** Worldwide.

MARK HOFMEISTER & ASSOCIATES EXECUTIVE RECRUITERS
214 Washington Avenue, 1st Floor, Towson MD 21204. 410/823-4060. **Toll-free phone:** 800/595-7966. **Fax:** 410/823-4063. **Contact:** Mark Hofmeister, President. **E-mail address:** mdhof@aol.com. **Description:** An executive search firm. **Specializes in the areas of:** Health/Medical; Manufacturing; Technical.

McKENNA & ASSOCIATES
P.O. Box 3238, Gaithersburg MD 20885. 301/610-0665. **Contact:** Chuck McKenna, President. **Description:** An executive search firm.

NATIONS EXECUTIVE SEARCH GROUP
152 Overlook Avenue, Queenstown MD 21658. 410/827-0180. **Fax:** 410/827-0181. **Contact:** Manager. **Description:** An executive search firm. **Specializes in the areas of:** CIS; Computer Hardware/Software; Sales Management; Software Engineering. **Positions commonly filled include:** Information Specialist; IT Specialist.

NETWORK SEARCH INC.
14609 Settlers Landing Way, Gaithersburg MD 20878. 301/762-7960. **Contact:** Manager. **Description:** An executive search firm. **Specializes in the areas of:** Accounting/Auditing; Finance.

PLACEMENT ASSOCIATES
6001 Montrose Road, Suite 702, Rockville MD 20852. 301/231-8150. **Fax:** 301/881-2918. **Contact:** Manager. **Description:** An executive search firm. **Specializes in the areas of:** Advertising; Marketing; Retail.

PORTER GROUP INC.
10320 Little Patuxent Parkway, Suite 1100, Columbia MD 21044. 410/992-7776. **Fax:** 410/992-7796. **Contact:** Lynn Dobson, Administrator. **Description:** An executive search firm. **Specializes in the areas of:** Sales. **Average salary range of placements:** More than $50,000. **Number of placements per year:** 200 - 499.

PROFESSIONAL CAREER CONSULTANTS
537 Day View Drive, Lusby MD 20657. 410/394-1886. **Contact:** Christine Garber, General Manager. **Description:** An executive search firm. **Specializes in the areas of:** Insurance. **Positions commonly filled include:** Account Representative; Accountant; Adjuster; Administrative Assistant; Chief Financial Officer; Claim Representative; Consultant; Controller; Customer Service Representative; Finance Director; Human Resources Manager; Industrial Engineer; Insurance Agent/Broker; Marketing Manager; Marketing Specialist; Operations Manager; Paralegal; Sales Executive; Sales Manager; Sales Representative; Statistician; Underwriter/Assistant Underwriter. **Average salary range of placements:** $30,000 - $50,000. **Number of placements per year:** 1 - 49.

ROLPHCO INC.
4848 Flower Valley Drive, Rockville MD 20853. 301/929-1020. **Contact:** Manager. **Description:** An executive search firm.

ROMAC INTERNATIONAL
120 East Baltimore Street, Suite 1840, Baltimore MD 21202. 410/727-4050. **Fax:** 410/727-6808. **Contact:** Manager. **Description:** An executive search firm. **Specializes in the areas of:** Computer Hardware/Software; Finance. **Other U.S. locations:** Nationwide.

SALES CONSULTANTS OF BALTIMORE CITY
575 South Charles Street, Suite 401, Baltimore MD 21201. 410/727-5750. **Fax:** 410/727-1253. **Contact:** Steven Braun, President. **Description:** An executive search firm operating on both retainer and contingency bases. Client company pays fee. **Specializes in the areas of:** Advertising; Broadcasting; Computer Science/Software; Fashion; Food; General Management; Health/Medical; Internet Marketing; Marketing; MIS/EDP; Printing; Publishing; Sales; Scientific; Technical. **Positions commonly filled include:** Account Manager; Account Representative; Advertising Executive; Credit Manager; Customer Service Representative; Insurance Agent/Broker; Internet Services Manager; Management Analyst/Consultant; Management Trainee; MIS Specialist; Operations Manager; Public Relations Specialist; Sales Engineer; Sales Executive; Sales Manager; Sales Representative. **Other U.S. locations:** Nationwide. **International locations:** Worldwide. **Average salary range of placements:** $50,000 - $100,000. **Number of placements per year:** 1000+.

SALES CONSULTANTS OF COLUMBIA
10320 Little Patuxent Parkway, Suite 511, Columbia MD 21044. 410/992-4900. **Fax:** 410/992-4905. **Contact:** David Rubin, General Manager. **Description:** An executive search firm. **Specializes in the areas of:** Computer Hardware/Software; Data Communications; Engineering; Sales; Telecommunications. **Positions commonly filled include:** Sales Representative; Telecommunications Analyst. **Other U.S. locations:** Nationwide. **International locations:** Worldwide. **Number of placements per year:** 1 - 49.

SALES CONSULTANTS OF PRINCE GEORGES COUNTY
7515 Annapolis Road, Suite 304, Hyattsville MD 20784. 301/731-4201. **Contact:** Tom Hummel, Manager. **Description:** An executive search firm. **Specializes in the areas of:** Advertising; Chemicals; Electrical; Engineering; Finance; Health/Medical; Pharmaceuticals; Sales; Scientific; Technical. **Other U.S. locations:** Nationwide. **International locations:** Worldwide.

SALES CONSULTANTS OF ROCKVILLE
51 Monroe Street, Suite 1405, Rockville MD 20850. 301/610-7300. **Toll-free phone:** 800/875-9630. **Fax:** 301/610-0100. **Contact:** Brian Hoffman, General Manager. **E-mail address:** info@scisuccess.com. **World Wide Web address:** http://www.scisuccess.com. **Description:** An executive search firm operating on both retainer and contingency bases. **Specializes in the areas of:** Information Technology. **Positions commonly filled include:** Computer Programmer; Internet Services Manager; Online Content Specialist; Operations Manager; Project Manager; Sales Engineer; Sales Executive; Sales Representative; Software Engineer;

Systems Analyst; Systems Manager; Telecommunications Manager. **Other U.S. locations:** Nationwide. **International locations:** Worldwide. **Average salary range of placements:** More than $50,000. **Number of placements per year:** 200 - 499.

SANFORD ROSE ASSOCIATES
10630 Little Patuxent Parkway, Suite 309, Columbia MD 21044. 301/596-4000. **Toll-free phone:** 800/206-9192. **Fax:** 301/596-4001. **Contact:** Howard Gostin, President. **E-mail address:** sracolummd@aol.com. **World Wide Web address:** http://www.sanfordrose.com. **Description:** An executive search firm operating on both retainer and contingency bases. Client company pays fee. **Specializes in the areas of:** Biology; Engineering; Health/Medical; Scientific; Technical. **Positions commonly filled include:** Biochemist; Biological Scientist; Biomedical Engineer; Chemical Engineer; Chemist; General Manager; Industrial Production Manager; Manufacturing Engineer; Mechanical Engineer; Operations Manager; Production Manager; Project Manager; Quality Assurance Engineer; Quality Control Supervisor; Statistician; Vice President. **Other U.S. locations:** Nationwide. **Average salary range of placements:** $50,000 - $100,000. **Number of placements per year:** 1 - 49.

SANFORD ROSE ASSOCIATES
51 Monroe Street, Suite 1211, Rockville MD 20850. 301/570-1776. **Contact:** Manager. **World Wide Web address:** http://www.sanfordrose.com. **Description:** An executive search firm. **Specializes in the areas of:** Engineering; Food; Paper. **Other U.S. locations:** Nationwide.

SEARCH CONNECTION
10490 Little Patuxent Parkway, Suite 500, Columbia MD 21044. 410/715-0900. **Contact:** Manager. **E-mail address:** clientresp@searchconnection.com. **World Wide Web address:** http://www.searchconnection.com. **Description:** An executive search firm. Founded in 1993. **Specializes in the areas of:** Accounting; Finance; Health/Medical; Information Systems. **Positions commonly filled include:** Accountant; IT Specialist. **Other U.S. locations:** McLean VA.

THE SEARCH GROUP
9405 Hickory Limb, Columbia MD 21045. 410/381-3940. **Contact:** Manager. **Description:** An executive search firm. **Specializes in the areas of:** Insurance.

SEEK INTERNATIONAL, INC.
15 Stablemere Court, Baltimore MD 21209-1062. 410/653-9680. **Fax:** 410/653-9682. **Contact:** Manager. **E-mail address:** mail@seekinternational.com. **World Wide Web address:** http://www.seekinternational.com. **Description:** An executive search firm. **Specializes in the areas of:** Computer Science/Software; High-Tech; Sales. **Positions commonly filled include:** Account Manager; Account Representative; Sales Executive; Sales Manager; Sales Representative; Software Engineer; Systems Analyst. **Corporate headquarters location:** This Location. **Average salary range of placements:** More than $50,000. **Number of placements per year:** 1 - 49.

SEMPER PRIMUS
1201 Angora Drive, Suite 2A, Bel Air MD 21014. 410/420-0812. **Fax:** 410/420-0813. **Contact:** Mark Albe, Vice President. **Description:** An executive search firm. **Specializes in the areas of:** Plastics.

STANTON CHASE INTERNATIONAL
100 East Pratt Street, Suite 2530, Baltimore MD 21202. 410/528-8400. **Fax:** 410/528-8409. **Contact:** Manager. **Description:** An executive search firm.

SUDINA SEARCH INC.
375 West Padonia Road, Suite 235, Timonium MD 21093-2100. 410/252-6900. **Fax:** 410/252-8033. **Contact:** Chuck Sudina, President. **E-mail address:** sudina@sudinasearch.com. **World Wide Web address:**

http://www.sudinasearch.com. **Description:** An executive search firm. **Specializes in the areas of:** Accounting/Auditing; Computer Science/Software; Finance; Health/Medical. **Positions commonly filled include:** Accountant/Auditor; Computer Programmer; Financial Analyst; Health Services Manager; MIS Specialist; Multimedia Designer; Software Engineer; Systems Analyst; Telecommunications Manager. **Corporate headquarters location:** Baltimore MD. **Other U.S. locations:** Nationwide. **Average salary range of placements:** More than $50,000. **Number of placements per year:** 200 - 499.

TCM ENTERPRISES
57 West Timonium Road, Suite 310, Timonium MD 21093. 410/561-5244. **Fax:** 410/561-5248. **Contact:** Tom McPoyle, Director. **E-mail address:** tmcpoyle@erols.com. **Description:** An executive search firm. **Specializes in the areas of:** Computer Science/Software; Engineering; General Management; Sales; Technical. **Positions commonly filled include:** Aerospace Engineer; Biochemist; Biomedical Engineer; Chemical Engineer; Civil Engineer; Computer Programmer; Design Engineer; Electrical/Electronics Engineer; Environmental Engineer; General Manager; Geologist/Geophysicist; Human Resources Manager; Industrial Engineer; Industrial Production Manager; Mechanical Engineer; Metallurgical Engineer; Software Engineer; Structural Engineer; Systems Analyst; Telecommunications Manager; Transportation/Traffic Specialist. **Other U.S. locations:** Nationwide. **Average salary range of placements:** More than $50,000. **Number of placements per year:** 1 - 49.

UNIVERSAL HEALTHCARE PLACEMENTS
5602 Baltimore National Pike, Suite 508, Baltimore MD 21228. 410/719-7800. **Contact:** Manager. **Description:** Universal Healthcare Placements is an executive search firm with an emphasis on health care billing and practices. **Specializes in the areas of:** Health/Medical.

VEY MARK ASSOCIATES, INC.
P.O. Box 3598, Silver Spring MD 20918. 410/992-8422. **Fax:** 410/992-8934. **Contact:** Manager. **Description:** An executive search firm operating on both retainer and contingency bases. **Specializes in the areas of:** Computer Science/Software; Engineering. **Positions commonly filled include:** Computer Programmer; Electrical/Electronics Engineer; Mathematician; Software Engineer; Systems Analyst. **Average salary range of placements:** More than $50,000. **Number of placements per year:** 1 - 49.

WALLACH ASSOCIATES, INC.
6101 Executive Boulevard, Suite 380, Rockville MD 20852. 301/231-9000. **Contact:** Manager. **Description:** An executive search firm. **Specializes in the areas of:** Aerospace; Defense Industry; Electronics; Research and Development.

WINSTON SEARCH, INC.
2219 Dalewood Road, Timonium MD 21093. 410/560-1111. **Fax:** 410/560-0112. **Contact:** Tom Winston, President. **World Wide Web address:** http://www.winstonsearch.com. **Description:** An executive search firm operating on a retainer basis. Winston Search also offers career/outplacement counseling. **Specializes in the areas of:** Accounting/Auditing; Administration; Advertising; Engineering; Finance; General Management; Industrial; Manufacturing; Personnel/Labor Relations; Sales. **Positions commonly filled include:** Accountant/Auditor; Aerospace Engineer; Biomedical Engineer; Branch Manager; Chemical Engineer; Chemist; Civil Engineer; Design Engineer; Designer; Electrical/Electronics Engineer; Financial Analyst; General Manager; Human Resources Manager; Industrial Engineer; Industrial Production Manager; Management Analyst/Consultant; Manufacturer's/Wholesaler's Sales Rep.; Market Research Analyst; Mechanical Engineer; MIS Specialist; Nuclear Engineer; Operations/Production Manager; Software Engineer; Systems Analyst; Telecommunications Manager.

Average salary range of placements: More than $50,000. **Number of placements per year:** 100 - 199.

WITT/KIEFFER, FORD, HADELMAN & LLOYD
4550 Montgomery Avenue, Suite 615N, Bethesda MD 20814. 301/654-5070. **Fax:** 301/654-1318. **Contact:**

Manager. **World Wide Web address:** http://www. wittkieffer.com. **Description:** Witt/Kiefer, Ford, Hadelman & Lloyd is an executive search firm. **Specializes in the areas of:** Health/Medical. **Other U.S. locations:** Nationwide.

PERMANENT EMPLOYMENT AGENCIES

AAA EMPLOYMENT
1501 Edgemore Avenue, Suite A, Salisbury MD 21801. 410/546-5955. **Fax:** 410/548-5312. **Contact:** John Menzel, Owner. **E-mail address:** john@dmv.com. **Description:** A permanent employment agency that also offers some temporary placements. **Positions commonly filled include:** Accountant/Auditor; Administrative Manager; Advertising Clerk; Bank Officer/Manager; Blue-Collar Worker Supervisor; Chemist; Computer Programmer; Construction and Building Inspector; Cost Estimator; Counselor; Customer Service Representative; Designer; Draftsperson; Editor; Electrician; Food Scientist/Technologist; General Manager; Human Resources Manager; Industrial Designer; Industrial Engineer; Mechanical Engineer; MIS Specialist; Operations/Production Manager; Quality Control Supervisor; Registered Nurse; Restaurant/Food Service Manager; Securities Sales Representative. **Number of placements per year:** 100 - 199.

NANCY ADAMS PERSONNEL
10420 Little Patuxent Parkway, Suite 400, Columbia MD 21044. 410/730-5200. **Fax:** 410/730-1780. **Contact:** Manager. **Description:** A permanent employment agency that also provides some temporary placements.

ADMINISTRATION PERSONNEL SERVICES
1112 Wayne Avenue, Silver Spring MD 20910. 301/565-3900. **Fax:** 301/588-9044. **Contact:** Robert L. McDermott, Owner. **Description:** A permanent employment agency. **Specializes in the areas of:** Accounting/Auditing; Administration; Banking; Clerical; Computer Hardware/Software; Finance; Mortgage; Sales. **Positions commonly filled include:** Accountant/Auditor; Administrative Assistant; Administrative Worker/Clerk; Bank Officer/Manager; Bookkeeper; Clerk; Computer Operator; Computer Programmer; Credit Manager; Customer Service Representative; Data Entry Clerk; EDP Specialist; Legal Secretary; Medical Secretary; Receptionist; Sales Executive; Sales Representative; Secretary; Stenographer; Typist/Word Processor. **Other U.S. locations:** DC; VA. **Number of placements per year:** 1000+.

ATLAS PERSONNEL AGENCY
11820 Parklawn Drive, Suite 330, Rockville MD 20852. 301/984-8075. **Contact:** Manager. **Description:** A permanent employment agency. **Specializes in the areas of:** Accounting/Auditing; Banking; Computer Science/Software; Finance; Office Support. **Positions commonly filled include:** Accountant/Auditor; Administrative Assistant; Bookkeeper; Financial Analyst; Secretary. **Number of placements per year:** 200 - 499.

BETATECH INC.
10401 Connecticut Avenue, Suite 102, Kensington MD 20895. 301/942-7840. **Fax:** 301/942-7430. **Contact:** Manager. **World Wide Web address:** http://www. betatechinc.com. **Description:** A permanent employment agency that also provides search and placement services for the commercial software industry.

CAREERS III, INC.
9037 Shady Grove Court, Gaithersburg MD 20877. 301/977-7000. **Contact:** Ms. Pat Busbice, President. **Description:** A permanent employment agency. **Specializes in the areas of:** Clerical. **Positions commonly filled include:** Administrative Assistant; Bookkeeper; Clerk; Customer Service Representative; Data Entry Clerk; Legal Secretary; Medical Secretary;

Receptionist; Secretary; Stenographer; Technical Writer/Editor; Typist/Word Processor. **Number of placements per year:** 200 - 499.

CEMCON INTERNATIONAL INC.
1517 Reisterstown Road, Suite 205, Baltimore MD 21208. 410/653-9121. **Fax:** 410/653-8864. **Contact:** Mr. Lee Rudolph, General Manager. **Description:** A permanent employment agency serving the cement and concrete industry. **Specializes in the areas of:** Engineering; Manufacturing. **Positions commonly filled include:** Chemical Engineer; Civil Engineer; Electrical/Electronics Engineer; Mechanical Engineer; Mining Engineer. **Average salary range of placements:** More than $50,000. **Number of placements per year:** 50 - 99.

CHARTER BUSINESS SERVICES INC.
4367 Northview Drive, Bowie MD 20716. 301/464-5500. **Fax:** 301/805-6863. **Contact:** Manager. **E-mail address:** charterbusiness@erols.com. **Description:** A permanent employment agency. **Specializes in the areas of:** Business Services; Government; Legal; Technical. **Office hours:** Monday - Friday, 8 a.m. - 5:00 p.m.

DUNHILL OF ROCKVILLE, INC.
414 Hungerford Drive, Suite 252, Rockville MD 20850. 301/654-2115. **Contact:** Stuart Harper, Vice President. **Description:** A permanent employment agency. **Specializes in the areas of:** Accounting/Auditing; Banking; Clerical; Finance. **Positions commonly filled include:** Accountant/Auditor; Bank Officer/Manager; Bookkeeper; Financial Analyst; Legal Secretary; Medical Secretary; Purchasing Agent/Manager; Receptionist; Secretary; Statistician; Stenographer; Typist/Word Processor. **Number of placements per year:** 1 - 49.

GRAHAM STAFFING SERVICES
12300 Twinbrook Parkway, Rockville MD 20852. 301/770-4180. **Fax:** 301/770-9898. **Contact:** Manager. **Description:** A permanent employment agency. Founded in 1984. **Specializes in the areas of:** Accounting; Administration; Finance; Legal; Library Services; Technical. **Positions commonly filled include:** Account Representative; Administrative Assistant; Desktop Publishing Specialist; Executive Assistant; Legal Secretary; Librarian; Office Manager; Project Engineer; Public Relations Specialist; Receptionist; Research Assistant.

HOLLAND & ASSOCIATES, LTD.
2345 York Road, Suite 300, Timonium MD 21093. 410/557-0044. **Fax:** 410/557-8749. **Contact:** Ray Holland, President. **E-mail address:** ray@ hollandcpasearch.com. **World Wide Web address:** http://www.hollandcpasearch.com. **Description:** A permanent employment agency dealing exclusively with placements in financial and accounting positions. Founded in 1976. **Specializes in the areas of:** Accounting; Finance. **Positions commonly filled include:** Accountant/Auditor; Chief Financial Officer; Controller; CPA; Financial Analyst; Financial Consultant; Management. **Office hours:** Monday - Friday, 8:00 a.m. - 8:00 p.m.

J.R. ASSOCIATES
152 Rollins Avenue, Suite 200, Rockville MD 20852. 301/984-8885. **Contact:** Daniel Keller, President. **Description:** A permanent employment agency. **Specializes in the areas of:** Administration; Computer Hardware/Software; Engineering; Sales; Technical.

Positions commonly filled include: Computer Programmer; Data Analyst; EDP Specialist; Financial Analyst; Marketing Specialist; MIS Specialist; Sales Engineer; Sales Representative; Systems Analyst; Telecommunications Analyst. **Number of placements per year:** 50 - 99.

THE JONATHAN LADD COMPANY
14504 Greenview Drive, Suite 204, Laurel MD 20708. 301/470-4100. **Contact:** Candidate Sourcing Manager. **Description:** A permanent employment agency that also organizes sales recruitment fairs nationwide. **Specializes in the areas of:** Sales. **Positions commonly filled include:** Account Manager; Account Representative; Real Estate Agent; Registered Nurse; Sales Engineer; Sales Executive; Sales Manager; Sales Representative. **Corporate headquarters location:** This Location. **Other U.S. locations:** Atlanta GA. **Average salary range of placements:** $30,000 - $50,000. **Number of placements per year:** 500 - 999.

TOM McCALL & ASSOCIATES
10 North Calvert Street, Suite 506, Baltimore MD 21202. 410/539-0700. **Contact:** Charley Greene, Manager. **Description:** A permanent employment agency. Founded in 1948. **Specializes in the areas of:** General Management; Sales. **Positions commonly filled include:** Account Manager; General Manager; Management Trainee; Marketing Manager; Marketing Specialist; Sales Executive; Sales Representative. **Average salary range of placements:** $30,000 - $50,000. **Number of placements per year:** 100 - 199.

MERIT EMPLOYMENT AGENCY
6001 Montrose Road, Suite 703, Rockville MD 20852. 301/738-1600. **Fax:** 301/770-9717. **Contact:** Stephanie Godwin, CPC/President. **Description:** A permanent employment agency. **Specializes in the areas of:** Accounting/Auditing; Administration; Finance; Secretarial. **Positions commonly filled include:** Accountant/Auditor; Administrative Assistant; Administrative Manager; Chief Executive Officer; Clerical Supervisor; Computer Programmer; Controller; Customer Service Representative; Editor; Financial Analyst; Human Resources Manager; MIS Specialist; Secretary; Software Engineer; Systems Analyst; Typist/Word Processor. **Average salary range of placements:** $30,000 - $50,000. **Number of placements per year:** 1 - 49.

MOTHERS WORLD, INC.
P.O. Box 11066, Takoma Park MD 20913. 301/270-8804. **Contact:** Manager. **Description:** A permanent employment agency. **Positions commonly filled include:** Health Services Manager; Licensed Practical Nurse; Medical Records Technician; Nanny; Registered Nurse; Social Worker.

OPPORTUNITY SEARCH INC.
P.O. Box 751, Olney MD 20830. 301/924-4741. **Fax:** 301/924-1318. **Contact:** Marc Tappis, President. **Description:** A permanent employment agency that also provides some executive searches. **Specializes in the areas of:** Computer Science/Software. **Positions commonly filled include:** Computer Programmer; Electrical/Electronics Engineer; Systems Analyst. **Average salary range of placements:** More than $50,000. **Number of placements per year:** 1 - 49.

PROFESSIONAL PERSONNEL SERVICES
1420 East Joppa Road, Towson MD 21286. 410/823-5630. **Fax:** 410/821-9423. **Contact:** Neal Fisher, President. **Description:** A permanent employment agency that also provides some temporary placements. **Specializes in the areas of:** Computer Science/Software. **Positions commonly filled include:** Computer Operator; Computer Programmer; Database Manager; MIS Specialist; Operations Manager; Software Engineer; Systems Analyst; Systems Manager; Telecommunications Manager. **Benefits available to temporary workers:** Paid Holidays; Paid Vacation. **Number of placements per year:** 1 - 49.

QUEST SYSTEMS, INC.
4701 Sangamore Road, Suite 260N, Bethesda MD 20816. 301/229-4200. **Fax:** 301/229-0965. **Contact:** Tom Carter, Manager. **World Wide Web address:** http://www.questsyst.com. **Description:** A permanent employment agency. **Specializes in the areas of:** Computer Science/Software; MIS/EDP. **Positions commonly filled include:** Computer Programmer; MIS Specialist; Software Engineer; Systems Analyst. **Corporate headquarters location:** This Location. **Other area locations:** Hunt Valley MD. **Other U.S. locations:** Atlanta GA; Philadelphia PA. **Average salary range of placements:** $30,000 - $50,000. **Number of placements per year:** 1000+.

QUEST SYSTEMS, INC.
11350 McCormick Road, Executive Plaza One, Suite 408, Hunt Valley MD 21031. 410/771-6600. **Fax:** 410/771-1907. **Contact:** Susan Lindsay, Manager. **E-mail address:** questsyst@aol.com. **World Wide Web address:** http://www.questsyst.com. **Description:** A permanent employment agency. **Specializes in the areas of:** Administration; Computer Science/Software. **Positions commonly filled include:** Computer Programmer; MIS Specialist; Software Engineer; Systems Analyst. **Corporate headquarters location:** Bethesda MD. **Other area locations:** Baltimore MD. **Other U.S. locations:** Atlanta GA; Philadelphia PA. **Average salary range of placements:** $30,000 - $50,000. **Number of placements per year:** 1000+.

SIGMAN & SUMMERFIELD ASSOCIATES, INC.
One Investment Place, Baltimore MD 21204. 410/828-0777. **Fax:** 410/828-0958. **Contact:** Manager. **Description:** A permanent employment agency. **Specializes in the areas of:** Administration; Legal; Nonprofit; Personnel/Labor Relations; Secretarial. **Positions commonly filled include:** Administrative Assistant; Administrative Manager; Clerical Supervisor; Paralegal; Secretary. **Number of placements per year:** 1 - 49.

SNELLING PERSONNEL SERVICES
20 South Charles Street, 4th Floor, Baltimore MD 21201. 410/528-9400. **Contact:** Manager. **Description:** A permanent employment agency that also provides some temporary placements. **Positions commonly filled include:** Accountant/Auditor; Administrative Assistant; Aerospace Engineer; Architect; Bank Officer/Manager; Biomedical Engineer; Bookkeeper; Chemical Engineer; Claim Representative; Clerk; Credit Manager; Customer Service Representative; Data Entry Clerk; Electrical/Electronics Engineer; Electronics Technician; Financial Analyst; General Manager; Human Resources Manager; Industrial Engineer; Insurance Agent/Broker; Legal Secretary; Marketing Specialist; Mechanical Engineer; Medical Secretary; Operations/Production Manager; Quality Control Supervisor; Receptionist; Sales Manager; Sales Representative; Secretary; Technical Writer/Editor; Technician; Typist/Word Processor. **Number of placements per year:** 50 - 99.

TECHNICAL TALENT LOCATORS, LTD.
8830 Stanford Boulevard, Suite 404, Columbia MD 21045-4753. 410/995-6051. **Fax:** 410/995-6281. **Contact:** Stephen Horn, President. **Description:** A permanent employment agency. **Specializes in the areas of:** Computer Science/Software; Engineering; Technical. **Positions commonly filled include:** Computer Programmer; Design Engineer; Software Engineer; Systems Analyst. **Average salary range of placements:** More than $50,000. **Number of placements per year:** 50 - 99.

TRI-SERV INC.
22 West Padonia Road, Suite C-353, Timonium MD 21093. 410/561-1740. **Fax:** 410/252-7417. **Contact:** Walter J. Braczynski, President. **Description:** A permanent employment agency. **Specializes in the areas of:** Computer Hardware/Software; Engineering; Manufacturing; Technical. **Positions commonly filled include:** Aerospace Engineer; Ceramics Engineer;

Chemical Engineer; Chemist; Civil Engineer; Computer Operator; Computer Programmer; Draftsperson; Electrical/Electronics Engineer; Industrial Engineer; Mechanical Engineer; Operations/Production Manager; Quality Control Supervisor; Systems Analyst; Technical Writer/Editor; Technician. **Average salary range of placements:** $30,000 - $50,000. **Number of placements per year:** 200 - 499.

VIRTUAL STAFFING SERVICES
P.O. Box 757, Lexington Park MD 20653. 301/862-5388. **Physical address:** 21615 South Essex Drive, Suite 50, Lexington Park MD. **Toll-free phone:** 800/439-9402. **Fax:** 301/862-9189. **Contact:** Ann Gallagher, Database Administrator. **Description:** A permanent employment agency that also provides some temporary placements. **Specializes in the areas of:** Administration; Computer Science/Software; Engineering; Secretarial; Technical. **Positions commonly filled include:** Accountant/Auditor; Administrative Assistant; Administrative Manager; Budget Analyst; Clerical Supervisor; Computer

Operator; Computer Programmer; Cost Estimator; Customer Service Rep.; Dental Assistant/Dental Hygienist; Design Engineer; Draftsperson; Editor; Electrical/Electronics Engineer; Electrician; Environmental Engineer; Financial Analyst; General Manager; Health Services Manager; Human Service Worker; Insurance Agent/Broker; Management Analyst/Consultant; Management Trainee; Manufacturer's/Wholesaler's Sales Rep.; Mechanical Engineer; MIS Specialist; Multimedia Designer; Paralegal; Physical Therapist; Public Relations Specialist; Purchasing Agent/Manager; Quality Control Supervisor; Registered Nurse; Restaurant/Food Service Manager; Services Sales Rep.; Software Engineer; Structural Engineer; Systems Analyst; Technical Writer/Editor; Telecommunications Manager; Typist/Word Processor. **Benefits available to temporary workers:** Medical Insurance; Paid Holidays; Paid Vacation. **Corporate headquarters location:** Eatontown NJ. **Average salary range of placements:** $20,000 - $29,999. **Number of placements per year:** 500 - 999.

TEMPORARY EMPLOYMENT AGENCIES

ACCOUNTANTS INC.
201 International Circle, Suite 280, Hunt Valley MD 21031. 410/584-2662. **Fax:** 410/584-2699. **Contact:** Manager. **World Wide Web address:** http://www.accountantsinc.com. **Description:** A temporary employment agency that also offers some permanent placements. **Specializes in the areas of:** Accounting; Finance. **Corporate headquarters location:** Burlingame CA. **Other area locations:** Baltimore MD. **Other U.S. locations:** Nationwide.

ACCOUNTANTS INC.
250 West Pratt Street, Suite 990, Baltimore MD 21201. 410/752-1008. **Fax:** 410/752-0383. **Contact:** Manager. **World Wide Web address:** http://www.accountantsinc.com. **Description:** A temporary employment agency that also offers some permanent placements. **Specializes in the areas of:** Accounting; Finance. **Corporate headquarters location:** Burlingame MD. **Other area locations:** Hunt Valley MD. **Other U.S. locations:** Nationwide.

ADECCO
300 East Lombard Street, Suite 935, Baltimore MD 21202. 410/837-2444. **Contact:** Branch Manager. **Description:** A temporary agency. **Specializes in the areas of:** Accounting/Auditing; Communications; Data Processing; General Labor; Secretarial; Word Processing. **Corporate headquarters location:** Redwood City CA. **Other area locations:** Greenbelt MD; Laurel MD; Rockville MD; Towson MD. **Other U.S. locations:** Washington DC; Alexandria VA; Vienna VA. **International locations:** Worldwide.

ADECCO
8600 LaSalle Road, 515 York Building, Towson MD 21286. 410/821-0900. **Fax:** 410/821-7067. **Contact:** Manager. **Description:** A temporary agency. **Specializes in the areas of:** Administration; Secretarial. **Positions commonly filled include:** Administrative Assistant; Advertising Clerk; Claim Representative; Customer Service Representative; Secretary; Typist/Word Processor. **Corporate headquarters location:** Redwood City CA. **Other area locations:** Baltimore MD; Greenbelt MD; Laurel MD; Rockville MD. **Other U.S. locations:** Washington DC; Alexandria VA; Vienna VA. **International locations:** Worldwide.

ADECCO
1901 Research Boulevard, Suite 460, Rockville MD 20850. 301/330-8000. **Fax:** 301/330-6791. **Contact:** Helen Monica, Office Supervisor. **Description:** A temporary agency that also provides some temp-to-perm placements. Client company pays fee. **Specializes in the areas of:** Administration; Light Industrial. **Positions commonly filled include:** Administrative Assistant;

Administrative Manager; Clerical Supervisor; Customer Service Rep.; Human Resources Manager; Sales Rep.; Secretary; Typist/Word Processor. **Benefits available to temporary workers:** 401(k); Dental Insurance; Medical Insurance; Vision Insurance. **Corporate headquarters location:** Redwood City CA. **Other area locations:** Baltimore MD; Greenbelt MD; Laurel MD; Towson MD. **Other U.S. locations:** Washington DC; Alexandria VA; Vienna VA. **International locations:** Worldwide. **Number of placements per year:** 1000+.

COMPUTER TEMPORARIES
8100 Professional Place, Suite 200, Lanham MD 20785. 301/306-7600. **Contact:** Manager. **Description:** A temporary agency. **Specializes in the areas of:** Computer Programming; Computer Science/Software.

CONTEMPORARIES, INC.
1010 Wayne Avenue, Suite 1230, Silver Spring MD 20910-5600. 301/565-0445. **Fax:** 301/565-0452. **Contact:** Recruiter. **E-mail address:** contemps@erols.com. **World Wide Web address:** http://www.contemporariesinc.com. **Description:** A temporary agency. **Specializes in the areas of:** Administration; Secretarial. **Positions commonly filled include:** Accountant/Auditor; Administrative Manager; Paralegal. **Average salary range of placements:** Less than $20,000. **Number of placements per year:** 500 - 999.

MARGE FOX PERSONNEL SERVICES INC.
40 York Road, Suite 210, Baltimore MD 21204-5243. 410/296-5044. **Fax:** 410/339-7937. **Contact:** Thomas Fox, Vice President. **Description:** A temporary agency that also provides some permanent placements. Founded in 1974. **Specializes in the areas of:** Computer Science/Software; Secretarial. **Positions commonly filled include:** Computer Programmer; Customer Service Representative; Systems Analyst; Typist/Word Processor. **Benefits available to temporary workers:** Medical Insurance; Paid Holidays; Paid Vacation. **Average salary range of placements:** $20,000 - $29,999. **Number of placements per year:** 200 - 499.

HIREKNOWLEDGE
16 South Calvert Street, Suite 806, Baltimore MD 21202. 410/783-0411. **Toll-free phone:** 800/937-3622. **Fax:** 410/783-0676. **Contact:** Recruiter. **World Wide Web address:** http://www.hireknowledge.com. **Description:** A temporary agency placing creative and technical individuals. The agency also offers some permanent placements. Client company pays fee. **Specializes in the areas of:** Advertising; Art/Design; Computer Science/Software; Internet Development; Internet Marketing; MIS/EDP; Printing; Publishing. **Positions commonly filled include:** Applications Engineer; AS400 Programmer Analyst; Computer Animator; Computer

Engineer; Computer Graphics Specialist; Computer Operator; Computer Programmer; Computer Scientist; Computer Support Technician; Content Developer; Database Administrator; Database Manager; Editor; Editorial Assistant; Graphic Artist; Graphic Designer; Internet Services Manager; Managing Editor; MIS Specialist; Multimedia Designer; Network/Systems Administrator; Software Engineer; SQL Programmer; Systems Analyst; Systems Manager; Technical Writer/Editor; Webmaster. **Benefits available to temporary workers:** 401(k); Direct Deposit; Health Benefits; Vacation Pay. **Corporate headquarters location:** Providence RI. **Other U.S. locations:** Nationwide. **Average salary range of placements:** $30,000 - $49,999. **Number of placements per year:** 200 - 499.

INTERIM PERSONNEL
102 West Pennsylvania Avenue, Suite 204, Towson MD 21204. 410/828-8071. **Fax:** 410/828-6384. **Contact:** Nancy Cuellar, Branch Manager. **World Wide Web address:** http://www.interim.com. **Description:** A temporary agency that also provides some permanent placements and career/outplacement and consulting services. **Specializes in the areas of:** Administration; Food; Light Industrial; Personnel/Labor Relations; Retail; Secretarial. **Positions commonly filled include:** Assembly Worker; Bookkeeper; Clerk; Computer Operator; Customer Service Rep.; Data Entry Clerk; Draftsperson; Factory Worker; Legal Secretary; Light Industrial Worker; Medical Secretary; Receptionist; Secretary; Stenographer; Technician; Typist/Word Processor. **Corporate headquarters location:** Fort Lauderdale FL. **Other U.S. locations:** Nationwide. **Average salary range of placements:** $20,000 - $29,999. **Number of placements per year:** 1000+.

KELLY SCIENTIFIC RESOURCES
One Church Street, Suite 304, Rockville MD 20850. 301/424-6484. **Fax:** 301/424-6977. **Contact:** Branch Manager. **World Wide Web address:** http://www. kellyscientific.com. **Description:** A temporary agency. **Specializes in the areas of:** Biomedical; Biotechnology; Chemicals; Environmental; Food; Petrochemical.

NRI HEALTHCARE
11400 Rockville Pike, Suite 820, Rockville MD 20852. 301/230-0444. **Fax:** 301/230-0451. **Contact:** Wanda Smith, General Manager. **World Wide Web address:** http://www.nri-staffing.com. **Description:** A temporary agency that also offers some permanent placements. **Specializes in the areas of:** Health/Medical. **Positions commonly filled include:** Certified Nurses Aide; Licensed Practical Nurse; Pharmacist; Physical Therapist; Speech-Language Pathologist. **Average salary range of placements:** $30,000 - $50,000. **Number of placements per year:** 200 - 499.

SALSBURY & ASSOCIATES PERSONNEL, INC.
102 West Pennsylvania Avenue, Suite 301, Towson MD 21204. 410/321-8310. **Fax:** 410/321-8312. **Contact:** Marshall Salsbury, CPA/President. **Description:** A temporary agency that also provides some permanent placements. **Specializes in the areas of:** Accounting/Auditing; Bookkeeping. **Positions commonly filled include:** Accountant/Auditor; Bookkeeper; Controller; Credit Manager; Finance Director; Financial Analyst.

SPARKS PERSONNEL SERVICES
15825 Shady Grove Road, Suite 150, Rockville MD 20850. 301/926-7800. **Fax:** 301/948-5890. **Contact:** Meredith McClimon, Staffing Supervisor. **Description:** A temporary agency. **Specializes in the areas of:** Customer Service; Personnel/Labor Relations; Sales; Secretarial. **Positions commonly filled include:** Administrative Manager; Typist/Word Processor. **Benefits available to temporary workers:** Medical Insurance; Paid Holidays; Paid Vacation. **Number of placements per year:** 1000+.

SPECIAL COUNSEL
2 North Charles Street, Suite 960, Baltimore MD 21201. 410/385-5350. **Fax:** 410/385-5352. **Contact:** Vice President of Operations. **World Wide Web address:** http://www.specialcounsel.com. **Description:** A temporary agency that also provides some permanent placements. **Specializes in the areas of:** Legal. **Benefits available to temporary workers:** 401(k); Bonus Award/Plan; Paid Holidays; Paid Vacation. **Average salary range of placements:** $30,000 - $50,000. **Number of placements per year:** 500 - 999.

TAC ENGINEERING RESOURCES
7500 Greenway Center Drive, Suite 400, Greenbelt MD 20770. 301/474-9063. **Contact:** Manager. **Description:** A temporary agency. **Specializes in the areas of:** Administration; Computer Science/Software; Engineering; Technical. **Positions commonly filled include:** Communications Engineer; Computer Operator; Computer Programmer; Design Engineer; EDP Specialist; MIS Specialist; Software Engineer; Systems Analyst; Systems Engineer; Technical Writer/Editor. **Number of placements per year:** 1000+.

TAC STAFFING SERVICES
7500 Greenway Center Drive, Suite 330, Greenbelt MD 20770. 301/963-9590. **Contact:** Manager. **Description:** A temporary agency. **Specializes in the areas of:** Accounting/Auditing; Advertising; Banking; Clerical; Education; Finance; Health/Medical; Insurance; Legal; Manufacturing; Nonprofit; Personnel/Labor Relations; Publishing; Sales; Transportation. **Positions commonly filled include:** Bookkeeper; Clerk; Data Entry Clerk; Driver; Factory Worker; Legal Secretary; Light Industrial Worker; Medical Secretary; Receptionist; Secretary; Typist/Word Processor. **Other U.S. locations:** Nationwide. **Number of placements per year:** 1000+.

TECH/AID OF MARYLAND
7000 Security Boulevard, Suite 108, Baltimore MD 21244. 410/597-9550. **Contact:** Manager. **Description:** A temporary agency. **Specializes in the areas of:** Architecture/Construction; Cable TV; Computer Hardware/Software; Engineering; Manufacturing; Technical. **Positions commonly filled include:** Aerospace Engineer; Architect; Buyer; Ceramics Engineer; Chemical Engineer; Civil Engineer; Draftsperson; Electrical/Electronics Engineer; Estimator; Industrial Designer; Industrial Engineer; Mechanical Engineer; Metallurgical Engineer; Mining Engineer; Operations/Production Manager; Petroleum Engineer; Purchasing Agent/Manager; Quality Control Supervisor; Technical Writer/Editor; Technician. **Number of placements per year:** 1000+.

TEMPS & COMPANY
10320 Little Patuxent Parkway, Suite 101, Columbia MD 21044. 410/740-4311. **Fax:** 410/997-5030. **Contact:** Lisa Miller, Operations Manager. **Description:** A temporary agency. Founded in 1981. **Specializes in the areas of:** Administration; Secretarial. **Positions commonly filled include:** Administrative Manager; Brokerage Clerk; Clerical Supervisor; Customer Service Representative. **Benefits available to temporary workers:** Dental Insurance; Life Insurance; Medical Insurance. **Average salary range of placements:** $20,000 - $29,999. **Number of placements per year:** 100 - 199.

TODAYS TEMPORARY
130 Holiday Court, Suite 101, Annapolis MD 21401. 410/266-9191. **Fax:** 410/266-7806. **Contact:** Manager. **World Wide Web address:** http://www.todays.com. **Description:** A temporary agency. **Specializes in the areas of:** Administration; Secretarial. **Positions commonly filled include:** Accountant/Auditor; Administrative Assistant; Advertising Clerk; Computer Operator; Customer Service Rep.; Human Resources Specialist; Manufacturer's/Wholesaler's Sales Rep.; Multimedia Designer; Paralegal; Securities Sales Rep.; Services Sales Rep.; Technical Writer/Editor; Typist/Word Processor. **Corporate headquarters location:** Dallas TX. **Other U.S. locations:** Nationwide. **Average salary range of placements:** $20,000 - $29,999. **Number of placements per year:** 200 - 499.

CONTRACT SERVICES FIRMS

A CHOICE NANNY
5110 Ridgefield Road, Suite 403, Bethesda MD 20816. 301/652-2229. **Toll-free phone:** 888/MY-NANNY. **Fax:** 301/652-0069. **Contact:** Manager. **Description:** A contract services firm. **Specializes in the areas of:** Child Care, In-Home; Nannies. **Positions commonly filled include:** Nanny; Teacher/Professor. **Corporate headquarters location:** This Location. **Other area locations:** Baltimore MD. **Other U.S. locations:** Washington DC; Wilmington DE; Falls Church VA.

AMERICAN SERVICE TECHNOLOGY, INC.
26825 Point Lookout Road, Leonardtown MD 20650. 301/737-0010. **Fax:** 301/737-0011. **Contact:** John A. Mason, President. **Description:** A contract services firm. **Specializes in the areas of:** Education; Transportation. **Positions commonly filled include:** Marine Scientist; Teacher/Professor. **Average salary range of placements:** $30,000 - $50,000. **Number of placements per year:** 1 - 49.

DANSOURCES TECHNICAL SERVICES, INC.
1010 Rockville Pike, Suite 405, Rockville MD 20852-1419. 301/217-0425. **Fax:** 301/217-0508. **Contact:** Manager. **E-mail address:** resumes@dansources.com. **World Wide Web address:** http://www.dansources.com. **Description:** Dansources Technical Services is a contract services firm. **Specializes in the areas of:** Computer Science/Software; Technical. **Positions commonly filled include:** Computer Programmer; Internet Services Manager; Multimedia Designer; Software Engineer; Systems Analyst. **Benefits available to temporary workers:** Medical Insurance. **Average salary range of placements:** More than $50,000. **Number of placements per year:** 50 - 99.

ECHELON SERVICE COMPANY
7604 York Road, Suite 302, Towson MD 21204. 410/321-8254. **Fax:** 410/321-8385. **Contact:** Gordon Barclay, Personnel Manager. **E-mail address:** esc@echelonservice.com. **Description:** A contract services firm that also provides some permanent placements. Founded in 1982. **Specializes in the areas of:** Computer Science/Software; Engineering; Industrial; Manufacturing; Technical. **Positions commonly filled include:** Aerospace Engineer; Aircraft Mechanic/Engine Specialist; Biomedical Engineer; Buyer; Ceramics Engineer; Chemical Engineer; Computer Programmer; Design Engineer; Designer; Draftsperson; Editor; Electrical/Electronics Engineer; Environmental Engineer; Industrial Engineer; Industrial Production Manager; Materials Engineer; Mechanical Engineer; Metallurgical Engineer; MIS Specialist; Multimedia Designer; Software Engineer; Stationary Engineer; Structural Engineer; Systems Analyst; Technical Writer/Editor; Telecommunications Manager; Typist/Word Processor. **Benefits available to temporary workers:** 401(k); Bonus Award/Plan; Medical Insurance; Paid Holidays; Paid Vacation. **Average salary range of placements:** More than $50,000. **Number of placements per year:** 100 - 199.

INSURANCE OVERLOAD SYSTEMS (IOS)
401 East Pratt Street, Suite 1222, Baltimore MD 21202. 410/547-8484. **Toll-free phone:** 800/810-5778. **Fax:** 410/547-8487. **Contact:** Manager. **World Wide Web address:** http://www.insuranceoverload.com. **Description:** A contract services firm that places candidates exclusively in the insurance industry. **Specializes in the areas of:** Insurance. **Benefits available to temporary workers:** Credit Union; Health Benefits; Referral Bonus Plan; Section 125 Plan.

CAREER/OUTPLACEMENT COUNSELING FIRMS

SAM BLATE ASSOCIATES
10331 Watkins Mill Drive, Montgomery Village MD 20886. 301/840-2248. **Fax:** 301/990-0707. **Contact:** Sam Blate, President. **E-mail address:** samblate@bellatlantic.net. **World Wide Web address:** http://members.bellatlantic.net/~samblate. **Description:** A career counseling service that assists candidates with resume and cover letter development. **Average salary range of placements:** More than $50,000. **Number of placements per year:** 100 - 199.

CAREER & VOCATIONAL COUNSELING
7100 Baltimore Avenue, College Park MD 20740. 301/779-1917. **Contact:** Anne S. Headley, M.A., Owner. **Description:** A career/outplacement counseling firm.

CAREER CHANGERS & CO.
7315 Wisconsin Avenue, Suite 1300-W, Bethesda MD 20814. 301/654-5155. **Fax:** 301/907-8637. **Contact:**

Karen Kaye, Director. **Description:** A career counseling and resume service. Jobseeker pays fee. **Corporate headquarters location:** This Location. **Other area locations:** Silver Spring MD.

THE RESUME PLACE
2 Holmehurst Avenue, Baltimore MD 21228. 410/744-4324. **Contact:** Kathy Troutman, Owner. **Description:** A resume and career counseling service.

WHITE RIDGELY ASSOCIATES, INC.
2201 Old Court Road, Baltimore MD 21208. 410/296-1900. **Contact:** Manager. **Description:** A career/outplacement counseling firm. **Specializes in the areas of:** Accounting/Auditing; Administration; Banking; Finance; Health/Medical; Insurance; Personnel/Labor Relations; Sales. **Number of placements per year:** 50 - 99.

◆ MASSACHUSETTS ◆

EXECUTIVE SEARCH FIRMS

AKS ASSOCIATES LTD.
175 Derby Street, Suite 27, Hingham MA 02043.
781/740-1704. **Contact:** Manager. **Description:** An
executive search firm.

AARDVARK SYSTEMS & PROGRAMMING
129 South Street, Boston MA 02111. 617/367-8081.
Fax: 617/367-2334. **Contact:** Manager. **Description:** An
executive search firm. **Specializes in the areas of:**
Computer Science/Software; Consulting.

ABBOTT'S OF BOSTON, INC.
P.O. Box 588, Waltham MA 02454. 617/332-1100. **Fax:**
617/558-7771. **Contact:** Ivan Samuels, President.
Description: An executive search firm operating on a
contingency basis. **Specializes in the areas of:**
Computer Science/Software; Engineering; Health/
Medical; Industrial; Manufacturing; Personnel/Labor
Relations; Technical. **Positions commonly filled
include:** Biological Scientist; Biomedical Engineer;
Computer Programmer; Design Engineer; Electrical/
Electronics Engineer; Health Services Manager; Human
Resources Manager; Internet Services Manager;
Mechanical Engineer; MIS Specialist; Multimedia
Designer; Software Engineer; Statistician; Systems
Analyst. **Corporate headquarters location:** Newton
MA. **Average salary range of placements:** More than
$50,000. **Number of placements per year:** 1 - 49.

ABLE ASSOCIATES
1531 Pleasant Street, Fall River MA 02723. 508/999-
0212. **Contact:** Manager. **Description:** An executive
search firm.

ACCOUNTANTS EXECUTIVE SEARCH
ACCOUNTANTS ON CALL
121 High Street, 2nd Floor, Boston MA 02110. 617/345-
0440. **Fax:** 617/345-0423. **Contact:** Joanne Hogan,
Executive Search Manager. **Description:** An executive
search firm. Accountants On Call (also at this location) is
a temporary agency. **Specializes in the areas of:**
Accounting/Auditing. **Positions commonly filled
include:** Accountant/Auditor. **Other U.S. locations:**
Nationwide. **Average salary range of placements:**
$30,000 - $50,000. **Number of placements per year:** 50
- 99.

ACCOUNTPROS
8 New England Executive Park East, 3rd Floor,
Burlington MA 01803. 781/229-2288. **Fax:** 781/229-
6696. **Contact:** Manager. **E-mail address:** apbur@
ix.netcom.com. **World Wide Web address:** http://www.
accountpros.com. **Description:** An executive search firm
that also offers some temporary and contract placements.
Founded in 1989. Client company pays fee. **Specializes
in the areas of:** Accounting; Finance. **Positions
commonly filled include:** Accountant; Auditor; Bank
Officer/Manager; Budget Analyst; Chief Financial
Officer; Controller; Cost Estimator; Credit Manager;
Economist; Finance Director; Financial Analyst;
Financial Manager; Fund Manager; Purchasing Agent/
Manager; Vice President of Finance. **Benefits available
to temporary workers:** 401(k); Dental Insurance;
Flexible Benefits; Life Insurance; Medical Insurance.
Corporate headquarters location: Boston MA. **Other
U.S. locations:** Los Angeles CA; Chicago IL; New York
NY; Houston TX; Vienna VA. **Average salary range of
placements:** $30,000 - $100,000. **Number of
placements per year:** 1000+.

**AMERICAN INSURANCE EXECUTIVES
(AMINEX)**
148 State Street, Suite 405, Boston MA 02109. 617/248-
6883. **Fax:** 617/248-8650. **Contact:** Manager.
Description: An executive search firm. **Specializes in
the areas of:** Insurance.

ANSARA, BICKFORD, & FISKE
P.O. Box 6037, Plymouth MA 02362. 508/830-0079.
Fax: 508/830-1780. **Contact:** Manager. **Description:** An
executive search firm operating on both retained and
contingency bases. **Specializes in the areas of:**
Engineering. **Positions commonly filled include:**
Biomedical Engineer; Chemist; Civil Engineer;
Communications Engineer; Design Engineer; Electrical/
Electronics Engineer; Industrial Engineer; Manufacturing
Engineer; Mechanical Engineer; Metallurgical Engineer;
Sales Engineer; Software Engineer; Structural Engineer;
Systems Manager; Technical Writer/Editor. **Average
salary range of placements:** More than $50,000.
Number of placements per year: 100 - 199.

MICHAEL ANTHONY ASSOCIATES
42 Washington Street, Wellesley MA 02481. 781/237-
4950. **Contact:** Manager. **Description:** An executive
search firm. **Specializes in the areas of:** Environmental;
Health/Medical; Information Technology.

APPLIED RESOURCES INC.
P.O. Box 525, Medford MA 02155. 781/391-1202.
Contact: Manager. **Description:** An executive search
firm operating on a contingency basis. **Specializes in the
areas of:** Engineering.

ARCHITECHS
2 Electronics Avenue, Danvers MA 01923. 978/777-
8500. **Fax:** 978/774-5620. **Contact:** Bob Jones,
Principal. **E-mail address:** bjones@architechs.com.
Description: An executive search firm operating on both
retainer and contingency bases. **Specializes in the areas
of:** Computer Science/Software; Engineering;
Information Systems. **Positions commonly filled
include:** Computer Programmer; Internet Services
Manager; MIS Specialist; Multimedia Designer; Science
Technologist; Software Engineer; Systems Analyst.
Average salary range of placements: More than
$50,000. **Number of placements per year:** 100 - 199.

ARNOLD ASSOCIATES
10 Post Office Square, Suite 600 South, Boston MA
02109. 617/988-0403. **Contact:** Christopher J. Arnold,
Principal. **Description:** An executive search firm that
focuses on placing individuals in the mutual fund,
investment management, and financial services
industries. **Specializes in the areas of:** Finance.
Positions commonly filled include: Sales Executive.
Average salary range of placements: More than
$100,000. **Number of placements per year:** 50 - 99.

NANCY ATKINS ASSOCIATES
199 Sudbury Road, Concord MA 01742. 978/371-9794.
Contact: Manager. **Description:** An executive search
firm. **Specializes in the areas of:** Retail.

ATLANTIC SEARCH GROUP INC.
One Liberty Square, Boston MA 02109-4825. **Contact:**
Dan Jones, Manager. **Description:** An executive search
firm operating on a contingency basis. **Specializes in the
areas of:** Accounting; Finance. **Positions commonly
filled include:** Accountant/Auditor; Budget Analyst;
Controller; Cost Accountant; Credit Manager; Financial
Analyst; Financial Manager. **Average salary range of
placements:** $30,000 - $80,000. **Number of placements
per year:** 100 - 199.

AUBIN INTERNATIONAL INC.
30 Rowes Wharf, Boston MA 02110. 617/443-9922.
Fax: 617/443-9955. **Contact:** Manager. **World Wide
Web address:** http://www.aubin.com. **Description:** An
executive search firm.

AUERBACH ASSOCIATES
65 Franklin Street, Suite 400, Boston MA 02110.
617/451-0095. **Contact:** Manager. **Description:** An

executive search firm. **Specializes in the areas of:** Education; Health/Medical; Nonprofit.

NATHAN BARRY & ASSOCIATES
301 Union Wharf, Boston MA 02109. 617/227-6067. **Contact:** Manager. **Description:** An executive search firm. **Specializes in the areas of:** Biotechnology; Health/Medical.

BASKIND CONSULTING & PLACEMENT
1253 Worcester Road, Framingham MA 01701. 508/620-0610. **Contact:** Manager. **Description:** An executive search firm. **Specializes in the areas of:** Accounting/ Auditing; Finance.

BATTALIA WINSTON INTERNATIONAL
20 William Street, Suite 240, Wellesley Hills MA 02481. 781/239-1400. **Contact:** Manager. **World Wide Web address:** http://www.battaliawinston.com. **Description:** An executive search firm. **Specializes in the areas of:** Consumer Products; Finance; Health/Medical; Industrial; Nonprofit; Professional; Technical. **Other U.S. locations:** Los Angeles CA; San Francisco CA; Chicago IL; Edison NJ; New York NY.

BEACON SEARCH PROFESSIONALS
146 North Main Street, Leominster MA 01453. 978/534-8400. **Fax:** 978/534-4313. **Contact:** Gary Safer, President. **Description:** An executive search firm operating on both retainer and contingency bases. **Specializes in the areas of:** Food; Hotel/Restaurant. **Positions commonly filled include:** Hotel Manager; Human Resources Manager; Management Trainee; Restaurant/Food Service Manager. **Other U.S. locations:** Nationwide. **Average salary range of placements:** $30,000 - $50,000. **Number of placements per year:** 200 - 499.

BELL OAKS COMPANY
85 Main Street, Suite 200, Watertown MA 02472. 617/972-8585. **Fax:** 617/972-6149. **Contact:** Manager. **World Wide Web address:** http://www.belloaks.com. **Description:** An executive search firm. **Specializes in the areas of:** Accounting; Chemistry; Engineering; Executives; Finance; General Management; Human Resources; Information Technology; Manufacturing; Marketing; Operations Management; Purchasing; Quality Assurance; Sales; Telecommunications.

BENNET ASSOCIATES
335 Washington Street, Suite 12, Norwell MA 02061. 781/659-9950. **Contact:** Manager. **Description:** An executive search firm.

BLANEY EXECUTIVE SEARCH
Damon Mill Square, Concord MA 01742. 978/371-2192. **Contact:** Manager. **Description:** An executive search firm. **Specializes in the areas of:** Computer Hardware/Software; High-Tech.

BOSTON PROFESSIONAL SEARCH
20 Park Plaza, Suite 637, Boston MA 02116. 617/451-5900. **Fax:** 617/451-3825. **Contact:** Manager. **Description:** An executive search firm operating on a contingency basis. **Specializes in the areas of:** Accounting; Computer Science/Software; Finance; Legal; Marketing; Sales. **Positions commonly filled include:** Account Manager; Account Representative; Accountant; Attorney; Auditor; Branch Manager; Budget Analyst; Chief Financial Officer; Controller; Credit Manager; Finance Director; Financial Analyst; Paralegal; Sales Engineer; Sales Executive; Sales Manager; Sales Representative. **Corporate headquarters location:** This Location. **Number of placements per year:** 50 - 99.

BOSTON SEARCH GROUP
224 Clarendon Street, Suite 41, Boston MA 02116. 617/266-4333. **Fax:** 617/266-3130. **Contact:** Ralph Protsik, Co-Founder. **E-mail address:** rprotsik@ bsgweb.com. **World Wide Web address:** http://www. bsgweb.com. **Description:** An executive search firm.

Founded in 1997. **Specializes in the areas of:** Information Technology; New Media.

BOWDOIN GROUP
40 Williams Street, Suite G-90, Wellesley MA 02481. 781/239-9933. **Contact:** Manager. **Description:** An executive search firm. **Specializes in the areas of:** Data Communications; Health/Medical; Telecommunications.

BREITNER CLARK & HALL
63 South Main Street, Randolph MA 02368. 781/986-0011. **Contact:** Manager. **Description:** An executive search firm. **Specializes in the areas of:** Health/Medical. **Positions commonly filled include:** Physician; Physician Assistant.

CEC ASSOCIATES
52 Accord Park Drive, Norwell MA 02061. 781/982-0205. **Contact:** Manager. **Description:** An executive search firm. **Specializes in the areas of:** Health/Medical.

CAMPBELL ASSOCIATES
150 Federal Street, Boston MA 02110. 617/737-7277. **Contact:** Joan Campbell, President. **Description:** An executive search firm operating on a contingency basis. **Specializes in the areas of:** Administration; Advertising; Banking; Computer Science/Software; Finance; Marketing; Sales; Word Processing. **Positions commonly filled include:** Financial Analyst; Human Resources Manager; Market Research Analyst; Public Relations Specialist; Securities Sales Representative.

MICHAEL CANTOR ASSOCIATES
P.O. Box 977, Middleton MA 01949. 978/777-9855. **Contact:** Manager. **Description:** An executive search firm. **Specializes in the areas of:** Computer Science/Software.

CAREER SERVICES EXECUTIVE SEARCH, INC.
One West Street, Beverly Farms MA 01915. **Toll-free phone:** 800/335-3609. **Contact:** Manager. **Description:** An executive search firm. **Specializes in the areas of:** Insurance. **Positions commonly filled include:** Insurance Agent/Broker; Management; Transcriptionist.

CARNEY, SANDOE AND ASSOCIATES
136 Boylston Street, Boston MA 02116. 617/542-0260. **Toll-free phone:** 800/225-7986. **Fax:** 617/542-9400. **Contact:** Director of Recruitment. **World Wide Web address:** http://www.csa-teach.com. **Description:** An executive search firm that places teachers and education administrators in independent schools. The firm operates on a retainer basis. **Specializes in the areas of:** Education. **Positions commonly filled include:** Education Administrator; Teacher/Professor. **Number of placements per year:** 500 - 999.

CARTER/MACKAY OF FRAMINGHAM
111 Speen Street, Framingham MA 01701. 508/626-2240. **Fax:** 508/879-2327. **Contact:** Michael Rowell, Vice President. **E-mail address:** carmac@tiac.net. **Description:** An executive search firm operating on a contingency basis. **Specializes in the areas of:** Biotechnology; Computer Science/Software; Data Communications; Industrial; Medical Technology; Pharmaceuticals; Sales; Telecommunications. **Positions commonly filled include:** Product Manager; Sales and Marketing Manager; Technical Support Manager. **Corporate headquarters location:** This Location. **Other U.S. locations:** Cary NC; Hasbrouck Heights NJ; Great Neck NY. **Average salary range of placements:** More than $50,000.

CHALONER ASSOCIATES
36 Milford Street, Boston MA 02118. 617/451-5170. **Contact:** Manager. **Description:** An executive search firm. **Specializes in the areas of:** Communications; Public Relations.

CIAK ASSOCIATES
227 Gore Road, Webster MA 01570. 508/943-3126. **Fax:** 508/943-5351. **Contact:** Kenneth R. Ciak,

President. **Description:** An executive search firm. **Specializes in the areas of:** Administration; Computer Science/Software. **Positions commonly filled include:** Computer Programmer; Systems Analyst. **Number of placements per year:** 1 - 49.

CLAYMAN & COMPANY INC.
197 Commonwealth Avenue, Suite 3, Boston MA 02116. 617/578-9999. **Fax:** 617/578-9929. **Contact:** Mr. S.G. Clayman, President. **E-mail address:** clayco@ma.ultranet.com. **Description:** An executive search firm operating on a retainer basis. **Specializes in the areas of:** Sales. **Positions commonly filled include:** Public Relations Specialist. **Average salary range of placements:** More than $50,000. **Number of placements per year:** 50 - 99.

CLEAR POINT CONSULTANTS
900 Cummings Center, Suite 130T, Beverly MA 01915. 978/524-1900. **Fax:** 978/927-7015. **Contact:** Cynthia A. Thornton, Vice President. **E-mail address:** cthorn@clearpnt.com. **World Wide Web address:** http://www.clearpnt.com. **Description:** An executive search firm operating on a contingency basis. The firm also provides some contract placements. **Specializes in the areas of:** Computer Science/Software; Publishing; Technical Writing. **Positions commonly filled include:** Editor; Instructional Designer; Internet Services Manager; Multimedia Designer; Online Content Specialist; Technical Writer/Editor; Webmaster. **Average salary range of placements:** More than $50,000. **Number of placements per year:** 200 - 499.

COMMONWEALTH RESOURCES INC.
262 Washington Street, 8th Floor, Boston MA 02108. 617/250-1100. **Fax:** 617/250-1199. **Contact:** Tim Fraser, Executive Vice President. **World Wide Web address:** http://www.crijobs.com. **Description:** An executive search firm operating on a contingency basis. **Specializes in the areas of:** Architecture/Construction; Electrical; Mechanical. **Positions commonly filled include:** Architect; Chief Financial Officer; Civil Engineer; Controller; Cost Estimator; Design Engineer; Draftsperson; Electrician; Environmental Engineer; Mechanical Engineer; Project Manager; Purchasing Agent/Manager; Quality Control Supervisor. **Corporate headquarters location:** This Location. **Average salary range of placements:** More than $50,000. **Number of placements per year:** 100 - 199.

COMPUTER SECURITY PLACEMENT
P.O. Box 204-B, Northborough MA 01532. 508/393-7803. **Fax:** 508/393-6802. **Contact:** Cameron Carey, President. **Description:** An executive search firm operating on a contingency basis. The firm focuses on placing high-level professionals in the fields of data security and disaster recovery planning. **Specializes in the areas of:** Banking; Computer Science/Software; Data Security; Finance; Food; Insurance. **Positions commonly filled include:** Systems Analyst. **Average salary range of placements:** More than $50,000. **Number of placements per year:** 1 - 49.

CORPORATE GROWTH RESOURCES
550 Worcester Road, Framingham MA 01701. 508/879-8200. **Contact:** Manager. **Description:** An executive search firm. **Specializes in the areas of:** Technical.

CYR ASSOCIATES, INC.
177 Worcester Street, Suite 303, Wellesley Hills MA 02481. 781/235-5900. **Fax:** 781/239-0140. **Contact:** Maury N. Cyr, President. **World Wide Web address:** http://www.cyrassociates.com. **Description:** An executive search firm operating on both retainer and contingency bases. The firm focuses on consumer products and direct marketing placements. Founded in 1985. Client company pays fee. **Specializes in the areas of:** Art/Design; Fashion; Food; General Management; Logistics; Manufacturing; Marketing; Materials; Purchasing; Sales. **Positions commonly filled include:** Advertising Executive; Buyer; Graphic Artist; Graphic

Designer; Market Research Analyst; Marketing Manager; Production Manager; Quality Control Supervisor; Sales Executive; Sales Manager. **Average salary range of placements:** $50,000 - $100,000. **Number of placements per year:** 1 - 49.

DANA ASSOCIATES INC.
353 R. Huron Avenue, Cambridge MA 02138. 617/661-0779. **Contact:** Manager. **Description:** An executive search firm. **Specializes in the areas of:** Marketing; Sales.

ROBERT H. DAVIDSON ASSOCIATES, INC.
EXECUTIVE AND PROFESSIONAL RESUME SERVICE
1410 Providence Highway, Norwood MA 02062. 781/769-8350. **Fax:** 781/769-8391. **Contact:** Robert H. Davidson, President. **E-mail address:** rdjobs@gis.net. **World Wide Web address:** http://www.gis.net/~rdjobs. **Description:** An executive search firm that also provides consulting services. Executive and Professional Resume Service (also at this location) provides resume services. **Specializes in the areas of:** Accounting/Auditing; Automotive; Computer Science/Software; Electronics; Engineering; Environmental; Finance; Health/Medical; Manufacturing; Sales. **Positions commonly filled include:** Biological Scientist; Budget Analyst; Buyer; Chemist; Computer Programmer; Electrical/Electronics Engineer; Industrial Engineer; Mechanical Engineer; Metallurgical Engineer; Purchasing Agent/Manager; Software Engineer; Technical Writer/Editor. **Number of placements per year:** 1 - 49.

DELUCA & ASSOCIATES
80 Davis Street, Falmouth MA 02540. 508/457-1122. **Contact:** David Deluca, President. **Description:** An executive search firm. **Specializes in the areas of:** Health/Medical. **Positions commonly filled include:** Physician.

DEREK ASSOCIATES
P.O. Box 13, Mendon MA 01765. 508/883-2289. **Fax:** 508/883-2264. **Contact:** Joren Fishback, President. **E-mail address:** joren@kersur.net. **Description:** An executive search firm operating on a contingency basis. The firm also provides some contract placements. **Specializes in the areas of:** Computer Science/Software; Environmental; Transportation. **Positions commonly filled include:** Chemical Engineer; Civil Engineer; Computer Programmer; Database Manager; Design Engineer; Environmental Engineer; MIS Specialist; Software Engineer; Systems Analyst; Systems Manager; Transportation/Traffic Specialist; Webmaster. **Average salary range of placements:** More than $50,000. **Number of placements per year:** 1 - 49.

DIRECTIONS MEDICAL GROUP
1661 Worcester Road, Suite 207, Framingham MA 01701. 508/620-1300. **Contact:** Manager. **Description:** An executive search firm. **Specializes in the areas of:** Health/Medical.

DIVERSIFIED COMMUNICATIONS GROUP
A DIVISION OF QUINCY CONSULTING, INC.
50 Mall Road, Burlington MA 01824. 781/229-7777. **Fax:** 781/229-2533. **Contact:** Scott Long, Senior Consultant. **E-mail address:** divcom@tiac.net. **World Wide Web address:** http://www.diversifiedrecruiting.com. **Description:** An executive search firm operating on a contingency basis. Founded in 1987. **Specializes in the areas of:** Computer Hardware/Software; Consulting; Customer Service; Data Communications; Finance; Marketing; Medical Technology; Office Automation; Sales Management; Sales Promotion; Technical; Telemarketing. **Positions commonly filled include:** Engineer; Management; Marketing Specialist; Sales Representative. **Corporate headquarters location:** This Location. **Average salary range of placements:** $80,000 - $250,000. **Number of placements per year:** 1000+.

DIVERSIFIED MANAGEMENT RESOURCES
10 Post Office Square, Suite 600 South, Boston MA 02109. 617/338-3040. **Contact:** Manager. **Description:** An executive search firm. **Specializes in the areas of:** Investment.

THE DIVERSIFIED SEARCH COMPANIES
255 State Street, 5th Floor, Boston MA 02109. 617/523-6870. **Fax:** 617/737-9101. **Contact:** Manager. **World Wide Web address:** http://www.divsearch.com. **Description:** An executive search firm. **Specializes in the areas of:** Consulting; Finance; Health/Medical; Nonprofit; Professional. **Corporate headquarters location:** Philadelphia PA. **Other U.S. locations:** Atlanta GA; Charlotte NC.

DIVERSITY ASSOCIATES
281 Andover Street, North Andover MA 01845. 978/689-0036. **Fax:** 978/688-7310. **Contact:** Mary Mascola, President. **E-mail address:** diversity@mediaone.net. **World Wide Web address:** http://www.diversityassociates.com. **Description:** An executive search firm operating on both retainer and contingency bases. **Specializes in the areas of:** Computer Science/ Software; Engineering; Manufacturing; Sales; Scientific; Technical. **Positions commonly filled include:** Account Manager; Aerospace Engineer; Database Manager; Design Engineer; Electrical/Electronics Engineer; Industrial Engineer; Mechanical Engineer; Sales Engineer; Software Engineer. **Average salary range of placements:** More than $50,000. **Number of placements per year:** 1 - 49.

DIVERSITY SEARCH SPECIALISTS
10 Winthrop Square, 4th Floor, Boston MA 02110. 617/426-5110. **Fax:** 617/426-2298. **Contact:** Manager. **Description:** An executive search firm. **Specializes in the areas of:** Accounting/Auditing; Administration; Engineering; Legal; Personnel/Labor Relations; Technical. **Average salary range of placements:** More than $50,000.

DOUGLAS ALLEN, INC.
1500 Main Street, Suite 2408, Springfield MA 01115. 413/739-0900. **Contact:** Manager. **Description:** An executive search firm. **Specializes in the areas of:** Finance.

EM HEATH & COMPANY
Paragon Towers, 233 Needham Street, Third Floor, Newton MA 02464. 617/527-8839. **Fax:** 617/527-0116. **Contact:** Manager. **E-mail address:** mheath@emheath.com. **World Wide Web address:** http://emheath.com. **Description:** An executive search firm. **Specializes in the areas of:** Engineering; Marketing; MIS/EDP; Sales Management; Systems Design; Systems Programming.

EASTWOOD PERSONNEL ASSOCIATES, INC.
P.O. Box 462, Franklin MA 02038. 508/528-8111. **Fax:** 508/528-1221. **Contact:** Rick Hohenberger, President. **Description:** An executive search firm operating on both retainer and contingency basis. Client company pays fee. **Specializes in the areas of:** Banking; Finance. **Positions commonly filled include:** Accountant; Auditor; Bank Officer/Manager; Computer Programmer; Credit Manager; Financial Analyst; MIS Specialist; Network/Systems Administrator; Systems Analyst. **Average salary range of placements:** $50,000 - $100,000. **Number of placements per year:** 1 - 49.

EDUCATIONAL MANAGEMENT NETWORK (EMN)
98 Old South Road, Nantucket MA 02554. 508/228-6700. **Contact:** Manager. **Description:** An executive search firm. **Specializes in the areas of:** Education; Nonprofit.

HENRY ELLIOTT & COMPANY INC.
One Washington Street, Suite 208, Wellesley MA 02481. **Toll-free phone:** 800/417-7000. **Contact:** Manager.

Description: An executive search firm. **Specializes in the areas of:** Computer Programming.

ENGINUITY SEARCH INCORPORATED
76 Bedford Street, Suite 30, Lexington MA 02420. 781/862-6300. **Contact:** Manager. **Description:** An executive search firm. **Specializes in the areas of:** Computer Hardware/Software; Engineering.

EXECUTIVE SEARCH INTERNATIONAL
60 Walnut Street, Wellesley MA 02481. 781/239-0303. **Contact:** Meg Piccione, Manager. **Description:** A generalist executive search firm.

EXECUTIVE SEARCH NORTHEAST, INC.
800 Hingham Street, Suite 204-S, Rockland MA 02370. 781/871-6010. **Fax:** 781/871-6030. **Contact:** Michael A. Arieta, President/CEO. **E-mail address:** michael_arieta@executivesearch-boston.com. **World Wide Web address:** http://www.executivesearch-boston.com. **Description:** An executive search firm operating on a retainer basis. Client company pays fee. **Specializes in the areas of:** Construction; Environmental. **Positions commonly filled include:** Civil Engineer; Construction and Building Inspector; Construction Contractor; Cost Estimator. **Corporate headquarters location:** This Location. **Average salary range of placements:** More than $50,000. **Number of placements per year:** 1 - 49.

FINANCIAL SEARCH GROUP
P.O. Box 266, North Andover MA 01845. 978/682-4123. **Fax:** 978/688-0516. **Contact:** Manager. **Description:** An executive search firm. **Specializes in the areas of:** Finance.

FITZGERALD ASSOCIATES
21 Muzzey Street, Lexington MA 02173. 781/863-1945. **Contact:** Manager. **Description:** An executive search firm operating on a retainer basis. **Specializes in the areas of:** Health/Medical; Insurance; Managed Care. **Positions commonly filled include:** Marketing Specialist; MIS Specialist; Physician; Registered Nurse; Sales Executive; Software Engineer. **Other U.S. locations:** Nationwide. **Average salary range of placements:** More than $50,000. **Number of placements per year:** 1 - 49.

FORD & FORD EXECUTIVE SEARCH
105 Chestnut Street, Suite 34, Needham MA 02492. 781/449-8200. **Fax:** 781/444-7335. **Contact:** Bernard Ford, Principal. **E-mail address:** seek@staffing.net. **Description:** An executive search firm operating on both retainer and contingency bases. **Specializes in the areas of:** Accounting/Auditing; Administration; Advertising; Art/Design; Computer Science/Software; Fashion; Personnel/Labor Relations; Publishing; Retail; Sales. **Positions commonly filled include:** Branch Manager; Environmental Engineer; General Manager; Human Resources Manager; Internet Services Manager; Market Research Analyst; MIS Specialist; Multimedia Designer; Public Relations Specialist; Technical Writer/Editor.

F-O-R-T-U-N-E PERSONNEL CONSULTANTS
288 Littleton Road, Suite 4, Westford MA 01886. 978/692-3500. **Fax:** 978/692-4500. **Contact:** Manager. **Description:** An executive search firm. **Specializes in the areas of:** Biotechnology; Pharmaceuticals. **Positions commonly filled include:** Chemical Engineer; Chemist; Product Development Engineer; Quality Control Supervisor; Research and Development Engineer; Scientist. **Corporate headquarters location:** New York NY.

F-O-R-T-U-N-E PERSONNEL CONSULTANTS
100 Corporate Place, Suite 200, Peabody MA 01960. 978/535-9920. **Fax:** 978/535-4482. **Contact:** Manager. **Description:** An executive search firm. **Specializes in the areas of:** Biotechnology; Pharmaceuticals. **Corporate headquarters location:** New York NY. **Other U.S. locations:** Nationwide.

F-O-R-T-U-N-E PERSONNEL CONSULTANTS
180 Denslow Road, Suite 4, East Longmeadow MA
01028. 413/525-3800. **Fax:** 413/525-2971. **Contact:**
Manager. **Description:** An executive search firm.
Specializes in the areas of: Health/Medical; Medical
Technology; Pharmaceuticals. **Corporate headquarters
location:** New York NY. **Other U.S. locations:**
Nationwide.

F-O-R-T-U-N-E PERSONNEL CONSULTANTS
54 Main Street, Suite 3, Leominster MA 01453. 978/466-
6800. **Contact:** Manager. **E-mail address:**
rcp@frontiernet.net. **World Wide Web address:**
http://www.frontiernet.net/~rcp. **Description:** An
executive search firm. **Specializes in the areas of:**
Computer Hardware/Software; Network Administration;
Quality Assurance; Systems Design.

**F-O-R-T-U-N-E PERSONNEL CONSULTANTS OF
TOPSFIELD**
458 Boston Street, Topsfield MA 01983. 978/887-2032.
Fax: 978/887-2336. **Contact:** James E. Slate, President.
E-mail address: plastics@topsfpc.com. **World Wide
Web address:** http://www.topsfpc.com. **Description:** An
executive search firm operating on both retainer and
contingency bases. **Specializes in the areas of:**
Engineering; General Management; Manufacturing;
Plastics; Sales. **Positions commonly filled include:**
Chemical Engineer; Electrical/Electronics Engineer;
Industrial Engineer; Industrial Production Manager;
Mechanical Engineer; Plastics Engineer. **Corporate
headquarters location:** New York NY. **Other U.S.
locations:** Nationwide. **Average salary range of
placements:** More than $50,000. **Number of
placements per year:** 1 - 49.

FRANKLIN INTERNATIONAL SEARCH, INC.
4 Franklin Commons, Framingham MA 01702. 508/872-
1133. **Contact:** Manager. **Description:** An executive
search firm. **Specializes in the areas of:**
Communications; Data Communications;
Telecommunications.

GATTI & ASSOCIATES
266 Main Street, Suite 21, Medfield MA 02052.
508/359-4153. **Fax:** 508/359-5902. **Contact:** Mike
Fitzgerald, Associate. **Description:** An executive search
firm operating on both retainer and contingency bases.
Specializes in the areas of: Human Resources;
Personnel/Labor Relations. **Positions commonly filled
include:** Human Resources Manager. **Average salary
range of placements:** More than $50,000. **Number of
placements per year:** 100 - 199.

DELORES F. GEORGE, CPC
269 Hamilton Street, Suite 1, Worcester MA 01604.
508/754-3451. **Fax:** 508/754-1367. **Contact:** Delores F.
George, Employment Specialist. **E-mail address:**
deloresg@ma.ultranet.com. **Description:** An executive
search firm that also provides some temporary
placements. **Specializes in the areas of:** Information
Technology. **Positions commonly filled include:**
Chemical Engineer; Computer Operator; Computer
Programmer; Consultant; Database Manager; Design
Engineer; Electrical/Electronics Engineer; Internet
Services Manager; Manufacturing Engineer; MIS
Specialist; Software Engineer; Systems Analyst; Systems
Manager; Telecommunications Manager; Webmaster.
Corporate headquarters location: This Location.
Other U.S. locations: Nationwide. **International
locations:** Worldwide. **Average salary range of
placements:** More than $50,000. **Number of
placements per year:** 50 - 99.

GILREATH WEATHERBY INC.
P.O. Box 1483, Manchester MA 01944. 978/526-8771.
Contact: Jim Gilreath, President. **Description:** An
executive search firm operating on a retainer basis.
Specializes in the areas of: Accounting/Auditing;
Consumer Package Goods; Engineering; General
Management; Industrial; Manufacturing; Personnel/
Labor Relations; Quality Assurance; Sales. **Positions**

commonly filled include: General Manager. **Average
salary range of placements:** More than $50,000.
Number of placements per year: 1 - 49.

GLOU INTERNATIONAL
687 Highland Avenue, Needham MA 02494. 781/449-
3310. **Contact:** Alan Glou, President. **Description:** An
executive search firm operating on a retainer basis.
Founded in 1960.

MARTIN GRANT ASSOCIATES, INC.
65 Franklin Street, Boston MA 02110. 617/357-5380.
Fax: 617/482-6581. **Contact:** Barry Davis, Manager.
Description: An executive search firm operating on both
retainer and contingency bases. **Specializes in the areas
of:** Insurance. **Positions commonly filled include:**
Account Manager; Account Rep.; Adjuster; Claim Rep.;
Insurance Agent/Broker; Marketing Specialist; Sales
Rep.; Underwriter/Assistant Underwriter. **Number of
placements per year:** 1 - 49.

GREENE & COMPANY
5 Powderhouse Lane, P.O. Box 1025, Sherborn MA
01770. 508/655-1210. **Contact:** Timothy G. Greene,
President. **Description:** An executive search firm
operating on a retainer basis. The firm focuses on placing
professionals in senior-level management positions.
Specializes in the areas of: Banking; Finance. **Positions
commonly filled include:** Bank Officer/Manager;
Branch Manager; Credit Manager; Financial Analyst;
Market Research Analyst. **Average salary range of
placements:** More than $50,000. **Number of
placements per year:** 1 - 49.

A. GREENSTEIN & COMPANY
20 Vernon Street, Norwood MA 02062. 781/769-4966.
Fax: 781/769-9269. **Contact:** Arlene C. Greenstein,
President. **Description:** An executive search firm
operating on a retainer basis. **Specializes in the areas of:**
Engineering; High-Tech; Management; Sales. **Average
salary range of placements:** $80,000 - $150,000.
Number of placements per year: 100 - 199.

GUSTIN PARTNERS LTD.
Ware Mill, 2276 Washington Street, Newton Lower Falls
MA 02462. 617/332-0800. **Contact:** Manager.
Description: An executive search firm. **Specializes in
the areas of:** High-Tech; Information Technology.

HM ASSOCIATES
2 Electronics Avenue, Danvers MA 01923. 978/762-
7474. **Fax:** 978/739-9071. **Contact:** Hugh MacKenzie,
CPC/President. **E-mail address:** hmackenzie@
hmassc.com. **Description:** An executive search firm
operating on a contingency basis. **Specializes in the
areas of:** Computer Science/Software; Engineering; IT;
Technical; Telecommunications. **Positions commonly
filled include:** Design Engineer; Electrical/Electronics
Engineer; Manufacturing Engineer; Marketing Manager;
Mechanical Engineer; MIS Specialist; Online Content
Specialist; Sales Manager; Software Engineer; Systems
Manager; Telecommunications Manager. **Average
salary range of placements:** More than $50,000.
Number of placements per year: 1 - 49.

**ROBERT HALF INTERNATIONAL
ACCOUNTEMPS**
222 Rosewood Drive, Suite 740, Danvers MA 01923.
978/774-8110. **Contact:** Manager. **World Wide Web
address:** http://www.roberthalf.com. **Description:** An
executive search firm. Accountemps (also at this
location) provides temporary placements. **Specializes in
the areas of:** Accounting/Auditing. **Corporate
headquarters location:** Menlo Park CA. **Other U.S.
locations:** Nationwide.

**ROBERT HALF INTERNATIONAL
ACCOUNTEMPS**
101 Arch Street, Suite 2000, Boston MA 02110.
617/951-4000. **Contact:** Manager. **World Wide Web
address:** http://www.roberthalf.com. **Description:** An
executive search firm. Accountemps (also at this

location) provides temporary placements. The Creative Group (also at this location; 617/526-8899) is a permanent employment agency that also provides some temporary placements. **Specializes in the areas of:** Accounting/Auditing. **Corporate headquarters location:** Menlo Park CA. **Other U.S. locations:** Nationwide.

ROBERT HALF INTERNATIONAL ACCOUNTEMPS
One Monarch Place, Springfield MA 01144. 413/734-7752. **Contact:** Manager. **World Wide Web address:** http://www.roberthalf.com. **Description:** An executive search firm. Accountemps (also at this location) provides temporary placements. **Specializes in the areas of:** Accounting/Auditing. **Corporate headquarters location:** Menlo Park CA. **Other U.S. locations:** Nationwide.

ROBERT HALF INTERNATIONAL ACCOUNTEMPS
2 Westborough Business Park, 200 Friberg Parkway, Suite 4003, Westborough MA 01581. 508/898-0900. **Contact:** Manager. **World Wide Web address:** http://www.roberthalf.com. **Description:** An executive search firm. Accountemps (also at this location) provides temporary placements. Office Team (also at this location; 508/836-4141) is a temporary agency that provides administrative placements. **Specializes in the areas of:** Accounting/Auditing. **Corporate headquarters location:** Menlo Park CA. **Other U.S. locations:** Nationwide.

HAMBLIN GROUP
526 Boston Post Road, Wayland MA 01778. 508/358-0191. **Fax:** 508/358-0193. **Contact:** Karen Curley, President. **Description:** An executive search firm operating on a contingency basis. **Specializes in the areas of:** Marketing; Sales. **Average salary range of placements:** More than $50,000. **Number of placements per year:** 50 - 99.

HEALTHCARE RECRUITERS INTERNATIONAL
100 Corporate Place, Suite 401, Peabody MA 01960. 978/535-3302. **Contact:** Manager. **Description:** An executive search firm. **Specializes in the areas of:** Health/Medical.

HEIDRICK & STRUGGLES/FENWICK PARTNERS
57 Bedford Street, Suite 101, Lexington MA 02420. 781/862-3370. **Contact:** Manager. **Description:** An executive search firm. **Specializes in the areas of:** High-Tech.

HIGH TECH VENTURES
18 Hurley Street, Cambridge MA 02141. 617/520-2138. **Contact:** Manager. **Description:** An executive search firm. **Specializes in the areas of:** Computer Science/Software.

HOFFMAN RECRUITERS
841 Main Street, Suite 1, Walpole MA 02081. 508/660-2220. **Toll-free phone:** 888/5-RECRUIT. **Fax:** 508/668-5460. **Contact:** Manager. **E-mail address:** resume@HoffmanRecruiters.com. **World Wide Web address:** http://www.HoffmanRecruiters.com. **Description:** A technical recruiting firm. **Specializes in the areas of:** Information Systems; Information Technology; Software Development; Technical.

HOSPITALITY EXECUTIVE SEARCH
729 Boylston Street, Boston MA 02116-2639. 617/266-7000. **Fax:** 617/267-2033. **Contact:** Jonathan M. Spatt, President. **Description:** An executive search firm operating on a retainer basis. Founded in 1976. Client company pays fee. **Specializes in the areas of:** Food; Hotel/Restaurant. **Positions commonly filled include:** Hotel Manager; Restaurant/Food Service Manager. **Corporate headquarters location:** This Location. **Average salary range of placements:** More than $100,000. **Number of placements per year:** 100 - 199.

INTELLIMARK
One Cranberry Hill, Lexington MA 02421. 781/861-1020. **Contact:** Manager. **Description:** A permanent employment agency. **Specializes in the areas of:** Software Engineering.

JNB ASSOCIATES, INC.
990 Washington Street, Suite 200, Dedham MA 02026. 617/451-0355. **Contact:** Manager. **Description:** An executive search firm. **Specializes in the areas of:** Banking; Finance.

KM ASSOCIATES
30 Colpitts Road, Weston MA 02193. 617/899-6655. **Fax:** 617/899-6444. **Contact:** Manager. **E-mail address:** kma@shore.net. **World Wide Web address:** http://www.kmasearch.com. **Description:** An executive search firm. **Specializes in the areas of:** Software Development.

A.T. KEARNEY EXECUTIVE SEARCH
One Memorial Drive, Cambridge MA 02142. 617/374-2600. **Contact:** Manager. **Description:** An executive search firm.

S.D. KELLY & ASSOCIATES
990 Washington Street, Suite 314 South, Dedham MA 02026. 781/326-8038. **Fax:** 781/326-6123. **Contact:** Susan Kelly, President. **World Wide Web address:** http://www.sdkelly.com. **Description:** An executive search firm operating on a retainer basis. **Specializes in the areas of:** Engineering; Marketing; Sales. **Positions commonly filled include:** Account Manager; Applications Engineer; Design Engineer; Designer; Electrical/Electronics Engineer; Environmental Engineer; General Manager; Industrial Engineer; Industrial Production Manager; Manufacturer's/Wholesaler's Sales Rep.; Manufacturing Engineer; Market Research Analyst; Marketing Manager; Mechanical Engineer; Metallurgical Engineer; Project Manager; Sales Engineer; Sales Representative. **Average salary range of placements:** More than $50,000. **Number of placements per year:** 100 - 199.

KINGSBURY WAX BOVA
60 Hamilton Street, Cambridge MA 02139. 617/868-6166. **Fax:** 617/868-0817. **Contact:** Robert M. Wax, President. **Description:** An executive search firm operating on a retainer basis. Client company pays fee. **Specializes in the areas of:** Accounting/Auditing; Publishing. **Positions commonly filled include:** Account Representative; Auditor; Budget Analyst; Chief Financial Officer; Controller; Counselor; Finance Director; Financial Analyst; Marketing Manager; Operations Manager; Sales Executive; Sales Manager; Sales Representative. **Corporate headquarters location:** This Location. **Other U.S. locations:** New York NY. **Average salary range of placements:** More than $50,000. **Number of placements per year:** 50 - 99.

THE KINLIN COMPANY
749 Main Street, Osterville MA 02655. 508/420-1165. **Contact:** Manager. **Description:** An executive search firm. **Specializes in the areas of:** Finance.

KORN/FERRY INTERNATIONAL
One International Place, 11th Floor, Boston MA 02110. 617/345-0200. **Fax:** 617/345-0544. **Contact:** Manager. **World Wide Web address:** http://www.kornferry.com. **Description:** An executive search firm that places upper-level managers in a variety of industries. **Corporate headquarters location:** Los Angeles CA. **International locations:** Worldwide. **Average salary range of placements:** More than $50,000.

THE KOTEEN ASSOCIATES
70 Walnut Street, Wellesley MA 02481. 781/239-0011. **Fax:** 781/239-0607. **Contact:** Anne Koteen, President. **E-mail address:** recruit@koteenassoc.com. **Description:** An executive search firm. **Specializes in the areas of:** Computer Science/Software. **Positions commonly filled include:** Computer Programmer; Development Manager;

Internet Services Manager; Management Analyst/ Consultant; MIS Specialist; Software Engineer; Systems Analyst; Telecommunications Manager. **Average salary range of placements:** More than $50,000. **Number of placements per year:** 50 - 99.

LAKE CONSULTANTS
4 Evergreen Lane, Hopedale MA 01747. 508/473-6955. **Contact:** Audrey Lake, Partner. **Description:** An executive search firm. **Specializes in the areas of:** Advertising; Computer Hardware/Software; Engineering; General Management; Publishing; Sales; Technical. **Positions commonly filled include:** Commercial Artist; Computer Programmer; Editor; Electrical/Electronics Engineer; Industrial Designer; Marketing Specialist; Operations/Production Manager; Public Relations Specialist; Reporter; Sales Representative; Software Engineer; Systems Analyst; Technical Illustrator; Technical Writer/Editor; Typist/Word Processor.

ALAN LEVINE ASSOCIATES
275 Turnpike Street, Suite 202, Canton MA 02021. 781/821-1133. **Contact:** Manager. **Description:** An executive search firm. **Specializes in the areas of:** Retail.

THE LITTLETON GROUP
136 Main Street, Acton MA 01720. 978/263-7221. **Fax:** 978/263-7740. **Contact:** Carl Tomforde, President. **E-mail address:** jobs@littletongroup.com. **World Wide Web address:** http://www.littletongroup.com. **Description:** An executive search firm operating on a contingency basis. **Specializes in the areas of:** Accounting; Computer Hardware/Software; Engineering; General Management; High-Tech; Manufacturing; Personnel/Labor Relations; Sales; Technical. **Positions commonly filled include:** Accountant; Buyer; Computer Programmer; Draftsperson; Electrical/Electronics Engineer; Industrial Engineer; Manufacturing Engineer; Marketing Specialist; Mechanical Engineer; Operations/ Production Manager; Purchasing Agent/Manager; Quality Control Supervisor; Sales Rep.; Software Engineer. **Average salary range of placements:** More than $50,000. **Number of placements per year:** 1 - 49.

LOCKE ASSOCIATES ENGINEERING RECRUITERS
Tower Square, 500 East Washington Street, North Attleboro MA 02760. 508/643-0444. **Fax:** 508/643-1443. **Contact:** John A. Locke, President. **Description:** An executive search firm operating on a contingency basis. **Specializes in the areas of:** Computer Science/Software; Engineering; Environmental. **Positions commonly filled include:** Architect; Attorney; Chemical Engineer; Civil Engineer; Computer Programmer; Consultant; Database Manager; Electrical Engineer; Environmental Engineer; Geologist; MIS Specialist; Sales Engineer; Software Engineer; Systems Analyst; Transportation/Traffic Specialist. **Corporate headquarters location:** This Location. **Other U.S. locations:** Charlotte NC. **Average salary range of placements:** More than $50,000. **Number of placements per year:** 1 - 49.

MADISON GROUP
92 Hayden Avenue, Lexington MA 02421. 781/862-7717. **Contact:** Manager. **Description:** A generalist executive search firm.

MANAGEMENT DEVELOPERS INC. (MDI)
687 Highland Avenue, Needham MA 02194. 781/449-8400. **Contact:** Dale Boch, Owner. **Description:** An executive search firm operating on both retainer and contingency bases. The firm also provides consulting services and short-term financing for small businesses. **Specializes in the areas of:** Automotive. **Positions commonly filled include:** Automotive Mechanic; Financial Analyst; Human Resources Manager. **Average salary range of placements:** $30,000 - $50,000. **Number of placements per year:** 50 - 99.

MANAGEMENT RECRUITERS INTERNATIONAL
607 Boylston Street, Suite 700, Boston MA 02116. 617/262-5050. **Contact:** Jack Nehiley, General Manager.

Description: An executive search firm. **Specializes in the areas of:** Accounting; Administration; Advertising; Architecture/Construction; Banking; Communications; Computer Hardware/Software; Construction; Electrical; Engineering; Finance; Food; General Management; Health/Medical; Industrial; Insurance; Manufacturing; MIS/EDP; Operations Management; Personnel/Labor Relations; Pharmaceuticals; Procurement; Publishing; Retail; Sales; Technical; Transportation.

MANAGEMENT RECRUITERS INTERNATIONAL OF BRAINTREE
639 Granite Street, Braintree MA 02184. 781/848-1666. **Contact:** Calvin Seitler, Manager. **Description:** An executive search firm. **Specializes in the areas of:** Accounting/Auditing; Administration; Advertising; Architecture/Construction; Banking; Communications; Computer Hardware/Software; Construction; Electrical; Engineering; Finance; Food; General Management; Health/Medical; Insurance; Legal; Manufacturing; Operations Management; Personnel/Labor Relations; Pharmaceuticals; Procurement; Publishing; Retail; Sales; Technical; Textiles; Transportation.

MANAGEMENT RECRUITERS INTERNATIONAL OF SPRINGFIELD
1500 Main Street, Suite 1822, Springfield MA 01115. 413/781-1550. **Contact:** Manager. **Description:** An executive search firm. **Specializes in the areas of:** Accounting/Auditing; Administration; Advertising; Architecture/Construction; Banking; Communications; Computer Hardware/Software; Electrical; Engineering; Finance; Food; General Management; Health/Medical; Personnel/Labor Relations; Pharmaceuticals; Procurement; Publishing; Sales; Technical; Textiles; Transportation.

MANAGEMENT RECRUITERS INTERNATIONAL OF WESTBOROUGH
Westborough Office Park, 2000 West Park Drive, Westborough MA 01581. 508/366-9900. **Contact:** Irene Garrity, Manager. **Description:** An executive search firm. **Specializes in the areas of:** Accounting/Auditing; Administration; Advertising; Architecture/Construction; Banking; Communications; Computer Hardware/ Software; Construction; Electrical; Engineering; Finance; Food; General Management; Health/Medical; Insurance; Legal; Personnel/Labor Relations; Pharmaceuticals; Procurement; Retail; Sales; Technical; Textiles; Transportation.

MANAGEMENT SEARCH, INC.
201 Park Avenue, West Springfield MA 01089. 413/732-2384. **Contact:** Manager. **Description:** An executive search firm. **Specializes in the areas of:** Engineering; Finance; Information Systems.

MASTER SEARCH
531 Pleasant Street, Southbridge MA 01550. 508/765-2633. **Contact:** George R. Downing, Technical Services Manager. **Description:** An executive search firm. **Specializes in the areas of:** Engineering; General Management; Industrial; Manufacturing; Plastics; Technical. **Positions commonly filled include:** Designer; Draftsperson; Electrician; Engineer; Food Scientist/Technologist; Industrial Production Manager; Operations/Production Manager; Pharmacist; Purchasing Agent/Manager; Quality Control Supervisor. **Number of placements per year:** 1 - 49.

McCORMICK GROUP
20 Walnut Street, Suite 308, Wellesley Hills MA 02481. **Contact:** Manager. **Description:** An executive search firm. **Specializes in the areas of:** Engineering; Information Systems; Insurance; Legal. **Positions commonly filled include:** Attorney; Environmental Engineer.

McDEVITT ASSOCIATES
90 Madison Street, Suite 200B, Worcester MA 01608. 508/752-5226. **Fax:** 508/755-2940. **Contact:** Larry McDevitt, Executive Recruiter. **E-mail address:**

mcdassoc@ultranet.com. **Description:** An executive search firm that also provides some contract placements. **Specializes in the areas of:** Accounting; Administration; Computer Science/Software; Engineering; Finance; General Management; Insurance; Manufacturing; Personnel/Labor Relations; Sales. **Positions commonly filled include:** Accountant/Auditor; Claim Rep.; Computer Programmer; Customer Service Rep.; Design Engineer; Draftsperson; Human Resources Manager; Internet Services Manager; MIS Specialist; Quality Control Supervisor; Systems Analyst; Telecommunications Manager; Underwriter. **Average salary range of placements:** $30,000 - $50,000. **Number of placements per year:** 50 - 99.

MEDICAL BUREAU
101 Tremont Street, Boston MA 02108. 617/482-2400. **Contact:** Manager. **Description:** An executive search firm operating on both retainer and contingency bases. **Specializes in the areas of:** Health/Medical. **Positions commonly filled include:** Biological Scientist; Biomedical Engineer; Clinical Lab Technician; Dental Assistant/Dental Hygienist; Dentist; Dietician/ Nutritionist; EEG Technologist; EKG Technician; Health Services Manager; Medical Records Technician; Occupational Therapist; Pharmacist; Physical Therapist; Physician; Recreational Therapist; Registered Nurse; Respiratory Therapist; Stationary Engineer. **Number of placements per year:** 100 - 199.

ANTHONY MICHAEL & COMPANY
800 Hingham Street, Suite 200 North, Rockland MA 02370. 781/871-9600. **Contact:** Manager. **Description:** An executive search firm. **Specializes in the areas of:** Banking; Finance.

MICRO-COMM EXECUTIVE SEARCH
800 Turnpike Street, Suite 102, North Andover MA 01845. 978/685-2272. **Contact:** Manager. **Description:** An executive search firm. **Specializes in the areas of:** Communications; Technical.

MINUTEMAN TECHNICAL SERVICES
P.O. Box 193, Lexington MA 02420. 781/861-7493. **Contact:** Manager. **Description:** An executive search firm.

MORENCY ASSOCIATES
301 Newbury Street, Suite 242, Danvers MA 01923. 978/750-4460. **Fax:** 978/750-4465. **Contact:** Marcia Morency, President. **E-mail address:** mmorency@ aol.com. **Description:** An executive search firm operating on a contingency basis. Client company pays fee. **Specializes in the areas of:** Accounting; Administration; Internet Development; Marketing; Printing; Publishing; Sales. **Positions commonly filled include:** Account Manager; Account Rep.; Accountant; Administrative Assistant; Computer Support Tech.; Computer Tech.; Content Developer; Credit Manager; Customer Service Rep.; Database Administrator; Database Manager; Desktop Publishing Specialist; Financial Analyst; Internet Services Manager; Market Research Analyst; Marketing Manager; Marketing Specialist; Network/Systems Administrator; Public Relations Specialist; Sales Engineer; Sales Exec.; Sales Manager; Sales Rep.; Transportation/Traffic Specialist. **Average salary range of placements:** $50,000 - $100,000. **Number of placements per year:** 1 - 49.

MORGAN & ASSOCIATES
P.O. Box 379, Granby MA 01033. 413/467-9156. **Fax:** 413/467-3003. **Contact:** Diane R. Morgan, Owner. **E-mail address:** morgan.assoc@the-spa.com. **Description:** An executive search firm operating on both retainer and contingency bases. **Specializes in the areas of:** Automation/Robotics; Computer Science/Software; Engineering; Manufacturing. **Positions commonly filled include:** Aerospace Engineer; Computer Programmer; Design Engineer; Electrical/Electronics Engineer; Engineer; Mechanical Engineer; Metallurgical Engineer; Operations/Production Manager; Physical Therapist; Software Engineer; Systems Analyst. **Average salary**

range of placements: $30,000 - $50,000. **Number of placements per year:** 50 - 99.

MURPHY ASSOCIATES
160 Speen Street, Suite 307, Framingham MA 01701. 508/460-0336. **Contact:** Manager. **Description:** An executive search firm. **Specializes in the areas of:** Sales.

NACHMAN BIOMEDICAL
50 Church Street, Cambridge MA 02138. 617/492-8911. **Contact:** Manager. **Description:** An executive search firm. **Specializes in the areas of:** Biomedical.

NAGLER, ROBINS AND POE
65 William Street, Wellesley MA 02481. 781/431-1330. **Contact:** Jim Poe, Managing Director. **Description:** An executive search firm. **Number of placements per year:** 1 - 49.

NAVIN GROUP
80 Washington Street, Norwell MA 02061. 781/871-6770. **Fax:** 781/878-8703. **Contact:** Jim Navin, President. **E-mail address:** search@navingroup.com. **World Wide Web address:** http://www. navingroup.com. **Description:** An executive search firm operating on both retainer and contingency bases. Navin Group focuses on placing mid- and upper-level information technology and clinical management personnel. **Specializes in the areas of:** Accounting; Administration; Computer Science/Software; Health/ Medical; Information Technology. **Positions commonly filled include:** Applications Engineer; CFO; Controller; Database Manager; Pharmacist; Physician; Registered Nurse; Systems Analyst; Systems Manager. **Average salary range of placements:** $50,000 - $100,000. **Number of placements per year:** 100 - 199.

NELSON ASSOCIATES
P.O. Box 2763, Worcester MA 01613-2763. 508/835-2500. **Contact:** Manager. **Description:** An executive search firm. **Specializes in the areas of:** Insurance.

NEW AMERICAN SEARCH
P.O. Box 451, Hingham MA 02043. 781/740-8141. **Contact:** Manager. **Description:** An executive search firm. **Specializes in the areas of:** Hotel/Restaurant.

NEW DIMENSIONS IN TECHNOLOGY, INC.
74 Atlantic Avenue, Suite 101, Marblehead MA 01945. 781/639-0866. **Fax:** 781/639-0863. **Contact:** Beverly A. Kahn, President. **E-mail address:** jobs@ndt.com. **World Wide Web address:** http://www.ndt.com. **Description:** An executive search firm operating on both retainer and contingency bases. The firm focuses on providing senior-level placements. **Specializes in the areas of:** Computer Hardware/Software; Computer Science/Software; Consulting; Electronics; Engineering; Finance; General Management; Information Technology; Insurance; Marketing; Multimedia; Network Administration; Software Engineering; Start-up Organizations; Telecommunications. **Positions commonly filled include:** Computer Programmer; Consultant; Electrical/ Electronics Engineer; Financial Analyst; Information Systems Consultant; Management Analyst/Consultant; Software Engineer; Systems Analyst. **Corporate headquarters location:** This Location. **Other U.S. locations:** Seattle WA. **Average salary range of placements:** More than $50,000. **Number of placements per year:** 500 - 999.

NEW ENGLAND LEGAL SEARCH
280 Commonwealth Avenue, Suite 304, Boston MA 02116. 617/266-6068. **Fax:** 617/266-8510. **Contact:** Dee B. McMeekan, Esq., President. **Description:** An executive search firm operating on a contingency basis. **Specializes in the areas of:** Legal. **Positions commonly filled include:** Attorney. **Average salary range of placements:** More than $50,000.

NEW ENGLAND RECRUITERS
809 Turnpike Street, Suite 204, North Andover MA 01845. 978/681-5627. **Fax:** 978/681-6442. **Contact:**

Manager. **Description:** An executive search firm. **Specializes in the areas of:** Accounting/Auditing; Engineering; Manufacturing; Sales.

NEW ENGLAND SEARCH, INC.
P.O. Box 1248, Webster MA 01570. 508/943-3000. **Fax:** 508/943-9958. **Contact:** Maureen V. Duso, CPC/President. **E-mail address:** nesars@ziplink.net. **Description:** An executive search firm operating on both retainer and contingency bases. **Specializes in the areas of:** Accounting/Auditing; Administration; Computer Science/Software; Engineering; Finance; General Management; Industrial; Marketing; Personnel/Labor Relations; Sales. **Positions commonly filled include:** Accountant; Applications Engineer; Auditor; Blue-Collar Worker Supervisor; Budget Analyst; Buyer; Chemical Engineer; Chief Financial Officer; Civil Engineer; Computer Programmer; Controller; Credit Manager; Customer Service Rep.; Database Manager; Design Engineer; Draftsperson; Electrical/Electronics Engineer; Finance Director; Financial Analyst; Graphic Designer; Human Resources Manager; Industrial Engineer; Industrial Production Manager; Internet Services Manager; Manufacturing Engineer; Marketing Manager; Mechanical Engineer; MIS Specialist; Operations Manager; Production Manager; Project Manager; Quality Assurance Engineer; Sales Engineer; Sales Executive; Sales Manager; Sales Rep.; Software Engineer; Systems Analyst; Systems Manager; Telecommunications Manager; Webmaster. **Corporate headquarters location:** This Location. **Average salary range of placements:** More than $50,000. **Number of placements per year:** 50 - 99.

OLSTEN FINANCIAL STAFFING
100 Summer Street, Suite 3210, Boston MA 02210. 617/542-1480. **Toll-free phone:** 888/222-8693. **Fax:** 617/542-1484. **Contact:** Jason Gasdick, Manager. **E-mail address:** ofs.hq@olsten.com. **World Wide Web address:** http://www.olsten.com/ofs. **Description:** An executive search firm operating on both retainer and contingency bases. **Specializes in the areas of:** Accounting/Auditing; Administration; Banking; Economics; Finance; Personnel/Labor Relations. **Positions commonly filled include:** Accountant/Auditor; Adjuster; Administrative Manager; Bank Officer/Manager; Budget Analyst; Buyer; Clerical Supervisor; Cost Estimator; Customer Service Rep.; Economist; Financial Analyst; General Manager; Management Analyst/Consultant; Operations/Production Manager; Purchasing Agent/Manager; Secretary; Statistician; Transportation/Traffic Specialist; Underwriter/Assistant Underwriter. **Corporate headquarters location:** Melville NY. **Other U.S. locations:** Nationwide. **Average salary range of placements:** $50,000 - $100,000. **Number of placements per year:** 200 - 499.

THE ONSTOTT GROUP
60 William Street, Wellesley MA 02181. 781/235-3050. **Fax:** 781/235-8653. **Contact:** Joseph E. Onstott, Managing Director. **E-mail address:** info@onstott.com. **World Wide Web address:** http://www.onstott.com. **Description:** An executive search firm that operates on a retainer basis. Founded in 1987. **Specializes in the areas of:** Consumer Products; Finance; High-Tech; Management; Manufacturing.

ORGANIZATION RESOURCES INC.
63 Atlantic Avenue, Boston MA 02110. 617/742-8970. **Contact:** Manager. **Description:** An executive search firm.

OXFORD GLOBAL RESOURCES, INC.
4 Centennial Drive, Peabody MA 01960. 978/977-0727. **Fax:** 978/977-0732. **Contact:** Manager. **World Wide Web address:** http://www.oxfordcorp.com. **Description:** An executive search firm. **Specializes in the areas of:** High-Tech.

P.A.R. ASSOCIATES INC.
60 State Street, Suite 1040, Boston MA 02109. 617/367-0320. **Contact:** Peter A. Rabinowitz, President.

Description: An executive search firm. **Specializes in the areas of:** Health/Medical. **Number of placements per year:** 50 - 99.

D.P. PARKER & ASSOCIATES INC.
372 Washington Street, Wellesley MA 02181. 781/237-1220. **Fax:** 781/237-4702. **Contact:** Dr. David P. Parker, President. **E-mail address:** information@dpparker.com. **World Wide Web address:** http://www.dpparker.com. **Description:** An executive search firm operating on a retainer basis. **Specializes in the areas of:** Engineering; General Management; Manufacturing. **Positions commonly filled include:** Biological Scientist; Chemical Engineer; Chemist; Electrical/Electronics Engineer; General Manager; Mechanical Engineer; Metallurgical Engineer; Nuclear Engineer; Operations/Production Manager. **Average salary range of placements:** More than $50,000.

PARTRIDGE ASSOCIATES, INC.
1200 Providence Highway, Sharon MA 02067. 781/784-4144. **Contact:** Manager. **Description:** An executive search firm. **Specializes in the areas of:** Hotel/Restaurant.

PENDLETON JAMES ASSOCIATES, INC.
One International Place, Suite 2350, Boston MA 02110. 617/261-9696. **Fax:** 617/261-9697. **Contact:** Manager. **World Wide Web address:** http://penjames.com. **Description:** An executive search firm. **Specializes in the areas of:** Communications; Finance; General Labor; Health/Medical; Industrial; Nonprofit; Retail; Technical.

PHILLIPS & ASSOCIATES
62 Derby Street, Hingham MA 02043. 781/740-9699. **Contact:** Manager. **Description:** An executive search firm operating on a retainer basis. **Specializes in the areas of:** Health/Medical. **Positions commonly filled include:** Auditor; Chief Financial Officer; Controller; Finance Director; Human Resources Manager; Nurse Practitioner; Pharmacist; Sales Exec.; Sales Manager. **Corporate headquarters location:** This Location. **Average salary range of placements:** $50,000 - $100,000. **Number of placements per year:** 100 - 199.

THE PICKWICK GROUP, INC.
36 Washington Street, Suite 240, Wellesley MA 02481. 781/235-6222. **Contact:** Cecile J. Klavens, President. **Description:** An executive search firm operating on a contingency basis. The firm also provides some contract services. **Specializes in the areas of:** Accounting/Auditing; Computer Science/Software; Finance; Health/Medical; Nonprofit; Personnel/Labor Relations. **Positions commonly filled include:** Account Manager; Accountant/Auditor; Budget Analyst; Chief Financial Officer; Controller; Credit Manager; Finance Director; Financial Analyst; Graphic Designer; Human Resources Manager; Internet Services Manager; Management Analyst/Consultant; Market Research Analyst; Project Manager; Public Relations Specialist; Sales Manager; Software Engineer; Systems Analyst; Systems Manager; Technical Writer/Editor; Telecommunications Manager; Webmaster. **Benefits available to temporary workers:** Medical Insurance. **Average salary range of placements:** More than $50,000. **Number of placements per year:** 50 - 99.

PILE AND COMPANY
535 Boylston Street, Boston MA 02116. 617/267-5000. **Fax:** 617/421-1899. **Contact:** Manager. **Description:** An executive search and management consulting firm. **Specializes in the areas of:** Advertising. **Average salary range of placements:** More than $50,000. **Number of placements per year:** 100 - 199.

NORMAN POWERS ASSOCIATES INC.
P.O. Box 3221, Framingham MA 01705. 508/877-2025. **Fax:** 508/877-0541. **Contact:** Manager. **Description:** An executive search firm operating on both retainer and contingency bases. The firm focuses on the placement of professionals in the commercial and military electronics industry. **Specializes in the areas of:** Computer Science/

Software; Engineering; Manufacturing. **Positions commonly filled include:** Computer Programmer; Design Engineer; Electrical/Electronics Engineer; Mechanical Engineer; Software Engineer; Systems Analyst.

PRESTONWOOD ASSOCIATES
266 Main Street, Suite 12A, Old Medfield Square, Medfield MA 02052. 508/359-7100. **Contact:** Manager. **Description:** An executive search firm. **Specializes in the areas of:** Marketing; Sales.

PROFESSIONAL PLACEMENT CONSULTING GROUP (PPCG)
P.O. Box 462, Whitinsville MA 01588. 508/234-6674. **Contact:** Manager. **Description:** An executive search firm. **Specializes in the areas of:** Computer Science/Software; High-Tech; Telecommunications.

PROGRESSIVE SEARCH ASSOCIATES, INC.
465 Auburn Street, Auburndale MA 02466. 617/244-1250. **Contact:** David J. Abrams, President. **E-mail address:** djab@ix.netcom.com. **Description:** An executive search firm operating on both retainer and contingency bases. **Specializes in the areas of:** Computer Science/Software; Sales; Technical. **Positions commonly filled include:** Internet Services Manager; MIS Specialist; Software Engineer; Technical Writer/Editor; Telecommunications Manager. **Average salary range of placements:** More than $50,000. **Number of placements per year:** 50 - 99.

PROSEARCH, INC.
50 Salem Street, Building B, Lynnfield MA 01940. 781/224-1025. **Fax:** 781/224-4252. **Contact:** Manager. **E-mail address:** search@share.net. **Description:** An executive search firm operating on a contingency basis. **Specializes in the areas of:** Administration; Computer Science/Software; Finance. **Positions commonly filled include:** Computer Programmer; Internet Services Manager; MIS Specialist; Systems Analyst. **Average salary range of placements:** More than $50,000. **Number of placements per year:** 1 - 49.

QUALITY SEARCH
314 Liberty Square, Danvers MA 01923. 978/777-0220. **Fax:** 978/777-9110. **Contact:** Manager. **Description:** An executive search firm. **Specializes in the areas of:** Software Quality Assurance.

BRUCE RAFEY ASSOCIATES
140 Union Street, Lynn MA 01905. 781/581-3373. **Toll-free phone:** 800/44-RAFEY. **Fax:** 781/599-6849. **Contact:** Bruce Rafey, President. **Description:** An executive search firm. **Specializes in the areas of:** Electronics.

J.E. RANTA ASSOCIATES
112 Washington Street, Marblehead MA 01945. 781/639-0788. **Fax:** 781/631-9828. **Contact:** Ed Ranta, Owner/President. **Description:** An executive search firm operating on both retainer and contingency bases. Founded in 1985. **Specializes in the areas of:** Administration; Computer Science/Software; Data Processing; Finance; MIS/EDP; Technical. **Positions commonly filled include:** Computer Programmer; Internet Services Manager; Management Analyst/Consultant; MIS Specialist; Systems Analyst; Telecommunications Manager. **Average salary range of placements:** More than $50,000. **Number of placements per year:** 1 - 49.

RAYMOND KARSAN ASSOCIATES
18 Commerce Way, 7th Floor, Woburn MA 01801. 781/932-0400. **Contact:** Angelo Buono, Principal. **Description:** An executive search firm operating on a retainer basis. **Positions commonly filled include:** Biomedical Engineer; Design Engineer; Electrical/Electronics Engineer; General Manager; Human Resources Manager; Mechanical Engineer; MIS Specialist; Multimedia Designer; Quality Control Supervisor; Software Engineer; Telecommunications

Manager. **Average salary range of placements:** More than $50,000. **Number of placements per year:** 50 - 99.

RECRUITING SPECIALISTS
P.O. Box 572, Dedham MA 02027-0572. 781/329-5850. **Fax:** 781/329-5840. **Contact:** Cindy Laughlin, President. **Description:** An executive search firm operating on a contingency basis. **Specializes in the areas of:** Food; Retail. **Other U.S. locations:** Nationwide. **Average salary range of placements:** $30,000 - $50,000. **Number of placements per year:** 100 - 199.

THE RENAISSANCE NETWORK
2 Oliver Street, Boston MA 02109. 617/946-2222. **Fax:** 617/946-2220. **Contact:** John Pompeii, Business Administrator. **E-mail address:** recruiting@ren-network.com. **World Wide Web address:** http://www.ren-network.com. **Description:** An executive search firm operating on a contingency basis. Client company pays fee. **Specializes in the areas of:** Computer Science/Software; Internet Development. **Positions commonly filled include:** Applications Engineer; AS400 Programmer Analyst; Computer Engineer; Computer Programmer; Computer Support Tech.; Computer Tech.; Content Developer; Database Administrator; Database Manager; Internet Services Manager; MIS Specialist; Software Engineer; SQL Programmer; Systems Analyst; Webmaster. **Average salary range of placements:** $50,000 - $100,000.

RESOURCES OBJECTIVES INC.
33 Broad Street, Boston MA 02109. 617/523-7788. **Fax:** 617/523-7939. **Contact:** Director. **E-mail address:** mtemp@tiac.net. **Description:** An executive search firm operating on a retainer basis. **Specializes in the areas of:** Banking; Computer Science/Software; Legal; Sales. **Positions commonly filled include:** Attorney; Bank Officer/Manager; Branch Manager; Physician; Software Engineer; Technical Writer/Editor. **Other U.S. locations:** Nationwide. **Number of placements per year:** 50 - 99.

THE RETAIL NETWORK
161 Forbes Road, Suite 104, Braintree MA 02184. 781/380-8830. **Fax:** 781/380-7656. **Contact:** Gary Belastock, Vice President. **Description:** An executive search firm operating on both retainer and contingency bases. **Specializes in the areas of:** Retail. **Positions commonly filled include:** Buyer; Retail Executive; Retail Manager; Retail Merchandiser; Wholesale and Retail Buyer. **Corporate headquarters location:** Boynton Beach FL. **Other U.S. locations:** Nationwide. **Average salary range of placements:** $30,000 - $50,000. **Number of placements per year:** 100 - 199.

RETAIL SEARCH OF NEW ENGLAND
194 Forbes Road, Braintree MA 02184. 781/849-9909. **Fax:** 781/849-9908. **Contact:** Manager. **E-mail address:** retail_search@msn.com. **Description:** An executive search firm operating on a contingency basis. Client company pays fee. **Specializes in the areas of:** Retail.

RUSSELL REYNOLDS ASSOCIATES, INC.
45 School Street, Boston MA 02108-3296. 617/523-1111. **Contact:** Manager. **Description:** An executive search firm. **Specializes in the areas of:** Finance; Health/Medical; High-Tech; Industrial.

ROBSHAM & ASSOCIATES
Faneuil Hall Marketplace, 4 South Market, Boston MA 02109. 617/742-2944. **Contact:** Manager. **Description:** An executive search firm. **Specializes in the areas of:** Finance; Marketing.

ROMAC INTERNATIONAL
20 Mall Road, Suite 400, Burlington MA 01803. 781/272-5000. **Fax:** 781/273-4969. **Contact:** Peter Woolford, Manager. **Description:** An executive search firm. **Specializes in the areas of:** Accounting/Auditing; Computer Hardware/Software; Engineering.

ROMAC INTERNATIONAL
1500 West Park Drive, Westborough MA 01581. 508/366-2600. **Fax:** 508/898-0115. **Contact:** Manager. **Description:** An executive search firm. **Specializes in the areas of:** Computer Hardware/Software; Engineering; Information Technology.

ROSTIE & ASSOCIATES
20 Park Plaza, Suite 628, Boston MA 02116. 617/350-6350. **Fax:** 617/350-6354. **Contact:** Manager. **Description:** An executive search firm. **Specializes in the areas of:** Computer Operations.

LOUIS RUDZINSKY ASSOCIATES, INC.
394 Lowell Street, P.O. Box 640, Lexington MA 02420. 781/862-6727. **Contact:** Howard Rudzinsky, Vice President. **Description:** An executive search firm. **Specializes in the areas of:** Computer Hardware/Software; Engineering; Sales; Technical. **Number of placements per year:** 50 - 99.

SALES & MARKETING SEARCH INC.
100 Cummings Center, Suite 453-H, Beverly MA 01915. 978/921-8282. **Fax:** 978/921-8283. **Contact:** Russell Smith, Managing Partner. **E-mail address:** russ@smsearch.com. **World Wide Web address:** http://www.smsearch.com. **Description:** An executive search firm operating on both retainer and contingency bases. **Specializes in the areas of:** Computer Hardware/Software; Computer Science/Software; Data Communications; Marketing; Sales; Telecommunications. **Positions commonly filled include:** Marketing Manager; Sales Manager; Sales Rep. **Average salary range of placements:** More than $50,000. **Number of placements per year:** 50 - 99.

SALES CONSULTANTS OF CAPE COD
P.O. Box 420, Sagamore Beach MA 02562. 508/888-8704. **Contact:** Ed Cahan. **Description:** An executive search firm. **Specializes in the areas of:** Accounting/Auditing; Administration; Advertising; Architecture/Construction; Banking; Communications; Computer Hardware/Software; Construction; Electrical; Engineering; Finance; Food; General Management; Health/Medical; Operations Management; Personnel/Labor Relations; Pharmaceuticals; Procurement; Publishing; Real Estate; Retail; Sales; Technical; Textiles; Transportation. **Corporate headquarters location:** Cleveland OH. **Other U.S. locations:** Nationwide.

SALES CONSULTANTS OF MANSFIELD
272 Chauncy Street, Mansfield MA 02048. 508/339-1924. **Contact:** James L. Noyes, Manager. **Description:** An executive search firm operating on a contingency basis. The firm places marketing, sales, management, and technical support personnel nationally and works with suppliers of chemicals and materials used in the electronics industry. **Specializes in the areas of:** General Management; Operations Management; Sales; Technical. **Positions commonly filled include:** General Manager; Market Research Analyst; Services Sales Representative. **Corporate headquarters location:** Cleveland OH. **Other U.S. locations:** Nationwide. **Average salary range of placements:** More than $50,000. **Number of placements per year:** 1 - 49.

SALES CONSULTANTS OF PLYMOUTH COUNTY
567 Pleasant Street, Suite 8, Brockton MA 02301. 508/587-2030. **Fax:** 508/587-9261. **Contact:** Milt Feinson, President. **Description:** An executive search firm. **Specializes in the areas of:** Accounting/Auditing; Administration; Advertising; Architecture/Construction; Banking; Communications; Computer Hardware/Software; Electrical; Engineering; Finance; Food; General Management; Health/Medical; Insurance; Legal; Manufacturing; Operations Management; Personnel/Labor Relations; Pharmaceuticals; Procurement; Publishing; Retail; Sales; Technical; Textiles; Transportation. **Corporate headquarters location:** Cleveland OH. **Average salary range of placements:** $30,000 - $50,000.

SALES CONSULTANTS OF WELLESLEY
888 Worcester Street, Suite 95, Wellesley MA 02482. 781/235-7700. **Fax:** 781/237-7207. **Contact:** General Manager. **Description:** An executive search firm. **Specializes in the areas of:** Accounting/Auditing; Administration; Advertising; Architecture/Construction; Banking; Communications; Computer Hardware/Software; Construction; Electrical; Engineering; Finance; Food; General Management; Health/Medical; Insurance; Legal; Manufacturing; Operations Management; Personnel/Labor Relations; Pharmaceuticals; Procurement; Publishing; Retail; Sales; Technical; Textiles; Transportation. **Corporate headquarters location:** Cleveland OH.

SCIENTIFIC RESOURCES
214 Garden Street, Needham MA 02492. 781/449-8760. **Contact:** Manager. **Description:** An executive search firm. **Specializes in the areas of:** Biotechnology; Medical Technology; Pharmaceuticals.

J. ROBERT SCOTT
255 State Street, Boston MA 02109. 617/563-2770. **Fax:** 617/723-1282. **Contact:** Manager. **E-mail address:** resumes@j-robert-scott.com. **World Wide Web address:** http://www.j-robert-scott.com. **Description:** An executive search firm that operates on a retainer basis. **Specializes in the areas of:** Biomedical; Finance; Pharmaceuticals; Technical.

SEARCH INTERNATIONAL
P.O. Box 81, Newburyport MA 01950. 978/465-4000. **Fax:** 978/465-4069. **Contact:** Brian E. Eagar, President. **Description:** An executive search firm operating on a retainer basis. Client company pays fee. **Specializes in the areas of:** Administration; Food; General Management; MIS/EDP. **Positions commonly filled include:** CFO; Controller; Food Scientist/Technologist; General Manager; MIS Specialist; Sales Executive; Sales Manager; Software Engineer; Vice President. **Other U.S. locations:** Phoenix AZ; Framingham MA; Hyde Park NY. **International locations:** Nassau, Bahamas. **Average salary range of placements:** More than $50,000. **Number of placements per year:** 50 - 99.

SEARCH PROFESSIONALS
P.O. Box 1900, Sandwich MA 02563. 508/833-6161. **Fax:** 508/833-6106. **Contact:** Richard Barzelay, President. **Description:** An executive search firm. **Specializes in the areas of:** Personnel/Labor Relations; Retail. **Positions commonly filled include:** Accountant/Auditor; Architect; Budget Analyst; Buyer; General Manager; Human Resources Manager; Property and Real Estate Manager; Purchasing Agent/Manager; Wholesale and Retail Buyer. **Number of placements per year:** 100 - 199.

SELECTED EXECUTIVES INC.
76 Winn Street, Woburn MA 01801. 781/933-1500. **Toll-free phone:** 800/811-1609. **Fax:** 781/933-4145. **Contact:** Mr. Lee R. Sanborn, Jr., President. **Description:** An executive search firm operating on both retainer and contingency bases. Founded in 1970. **Specializes in the areas of:** Accounting; Banking; Computer Science/Software; Engineering; Finance; Industrial; Marketing; MIS/EDP; Personnel/Labor Relations; Sales; Scientific; Technical. **Positions commonly filled include:** Account Rep.; Accountant; Advertising Exec.; Applications Engineer; Auditor; Bank Officer/Manager; Biochemist; Biomedical Engineer; Budget Analyst; Buyer; Chemical Engineer; Chemist; Chief Financial Officer; Computer Engineer; Computer Programmer; Computer Scientist; Controller; Database Administrator; Database Manager; Design Engineer; Electrical/Electronics Engineer; Electrician; Environmental Engineer; Financial Analyst; Food Scientist/Technologist; General Manager; Human Resources Manager; Industrial Engineer; Internet Services Manager; Manufacturing Engineer; Market Research Analyst; Marketing Manager; Marketing Specialist; Mechanical Engineer; Metallurgical Engineer; Microbiologist; MIS Specialist; Network/Systems

Administrator; Nuclear Engineer; Operations Manager; Packaging Engineer; Production Manager; Purchasing Agent/Manager; Quality Assurance Engineer; Quality Control Supervisor; Sales Engineer; Sales Exec.; Sales Manager; Sales Rep.; Software Engineer; SQL Programmer; Statistician; Systems Analyst; Systems Manager. **Corporate headquarters location:** This Location. **Average salary range of placements:** $50,000 - $100,000. **Number of placements per year:** 200 - 499.

SETFORD-SHAW-NAJARIAN ASSOCIATES
10 High Street, 6th Floor, Suite 650, Boston MA 02110. 617/422-0441. **Fax:** 617/422-0487. **Contact:** Matthew Malvese, Manager. **E-mail address:** mmalvese@ tisny.com. **Description:** An executive search firm that also offers some contract placements. **Specializes in the areas of:** Information Technology. **Positions commonly filled include:** Computer Operator; Computer Programmer; Database Manager; Human Resources Manager; Management Analyst/Consultant; MIS Specialist; Software Engineer; Systems Analyst; Systems Manager; Webmaster. **Corporate headquarters location:** New York NY. **Other U.S. locations:** NJ; PA; TX. **Number of placements per year:** 100 - 199.

L.A. SILVER ASSOCIATES
463 Worcester Road, Framingham MA 01701. 508/879-2603. **Fax:** 508/879-8425. **Contact:** Mr. Lee Silver, President. **Description:** An executive search firm operating on a retainer basis. **Specializes in the areas of:** Computer Science/Software; Telecommunications. **Corporate headquarters location:** This Location. **Average salary range of placements:** More than $50,000. **Number of placements per year:** 100 - 199.

CHRISTOPHER SMALLHORN EXECUTIVE RECRUITING
One Boston Place, 18th Floor, Boston MA 02108. 617/723-8180. **Contact:** Manager. **Description:** An executive search firm.

SNELLING PERSONNEL
65 James Street, Worcester MA 01603. 508/792-4545. **Contact:** Manager. **Description:** An executive search firm operating on a contingency basis. **Specializes in the areas of:** Accounting/Auditing; Administration; Banking; Biology; Computer Science/Software; Engineering; Finance; General Management; Health/ Medical; Insurance; Legal; Secretarial; Technical. **Positions commonly filled include:** Accountant/Auditor; Aerospace Engineer; Attorney; Bank Officer/Manager; Biological Scientist; Biomedical Engineer; Budget Analyst; Buyer; Claim Rep.; Clinical Lab Technician; Computer Programmer; Dental Assistant/Dental Hygienist; Dentist; Design Engineer; Designer; Dietician/Nutritionist; Draftsperson; EEG Technologist; EKG Technician; Electrical/Electronics Engineer; Environmental Engineer; Financial Analyst; General Manager; Health Services Manager; Human Resources Manager; Industrial Engineer; Industrial Production Manager; Internet Services Manager; Licensed Practical Nurse; Mechanical Engineer; Medical Records Technician; Metallurgical Engineer; MIS Specialist; Multimedia Designer; Nuclear Medicine Technologist; Occupational Therapist; Operations/Production Manager; Paralegal; Pharmacist; Physical Therapist; Purchasing Agent/Manager; Quality Control Supervisor; Registered Nurse; Respiratory Therapist; Science Technologist; Services Sales Rep.; Software Engineer; Structural Engineer; Surgical Technician; Technical Writer/Editor; Typist/Word Processor; Underwriter/Assistant Underwriter. **Other U.S. locations:** Nationwide. **Average salary range of placements:** $30,000 - $50,000. **Number of placements per year:** 1000+.

SNELLING PERSONNEL SERVICES
545 Boylston Street, Boston MA 02116. 617/262-5151. **Fax:** 617/267-9789. **Contact:** Ed Diamond, President. **Description:** An executive search firm operating on a contingency basis.

STEPHEN M. SONIS ASSOCIATES
275 Turnpike Street, Suite 202, Canton MA 02021. 781/821-0303. **Contact:** Manager. **Description:** An executive search firm. **Specializes in the areas of:** Retail.

STONE & YOUNGBLOOD
304 Newbury Street, Boston MA 02115. 781/647-0070. **Fax:** 781/647-0460. **Contact:** Stephen Sarkis, Vice President. **Description:** An executive search firm operating on both retainer and contingency bases. **Specializes in the areas of:** Advertising; Architecture/ Construction; Art/Design; Broadcasting; Computer Science/Software; Finance; Food; General Management; Health/Medical; Insurance; Publishing; Retail; Sales. **Positions commonly filled include:** Account Manager; Account Rep.; Advertising Exec.; Assistant Manager; Broadcast Technician; Buyer; Chief Financial Officer; Controller; Editor; Food Scientist/Technologist; General Manager; Graphic Artist; Graphic Designer; Human Resources Manager; Insurance Agent/Broker; Internet Services Manager; Managing Editor; Marketing Manager; Marketing Specialist; Online Content Specialist; Operations Engineer; Production Manager; Public Relations Specialist; Radio/TV Announcer/ Broadcaster; Real Estate Agent; Reporter; Sales Engineer; Sales Executive; Sales Rep.; Telecommunications Manager; Vice President of Marketing; Vice President of Operations. **Average salary range of placements:** More than $50,000.

STONE CONSULTING GROUP & LEGAL SEARCH SPECIALISTS
10 Winthrop Square, 4th Floor, Boston MA 02110. 617/426-2992. **Fax:** 617/426-2298. **Contact:** Jonathan Stone, Principal. **Description:** An executive search firm operating on a retainer basis. **Specializes in the areas of:** Administration; Biology; Computer Science/Software; Engineering; Personnel/Labor Relations; Technical. **Positions commonly filled include:** Attorney; Bank Officer/Manager; Biological Scientist; Biomedical Engineer; Chief Financial Officer; Client Services Rep.; Computer Programmer; Controller; Economist; Fundraising Specialist; Human Resources Manager; Intellectual Property Lawyer; MIS Specialist; Paralegal.

STONE GROUP INC.
715 Boylston Street, Boston MA 02116. 617/262-2700. **Contact:** President. **Description:** An executive search firm operating on both retainer and contingency bases. **Specializes in the areas of:** Insurance. **Positions commonly filled include:** Insurance Agent/Broker; Underwriter/Assistant Underwriter. **Average salary range of placements:** More than $50,000.

MARK STRANBERG AND ASSOCIATES
4 Wadsworth Road, Sudbury MA 01776. 978/440-8800. **Fax:** 978/440-8354. **Contact:** Mark Stranberg, Managing Director. **Description:** An executive search firm operating on a retainer basis. **Specializes in the areas of:** Investment. **Positions commonly filled include:** Economist; Fund Manager; Marketing Manager; Sales Manager; Vice President. **International locations:** Worldwide. **Average salary range of placements:** More than $50,000. **Number of placements per year:** 1 - 49.

STRAUBE ASSOCIATES
855 Turnpike Street, North Andover MA 01845. 978/687-1993. **Fax:** 978/687-1886. **Contact:** Stanley H. Straube, President. **Description:** An executive search firm. **Specializes in the areas of:** Banking; Computer Science/Software; Engineering; General Management; Health/Medical; Manufacturing; Personnel/Labor Relations; Sales; Technical. **Number of placements per year:** 1 - 49.

SULLIVAN ASSOCIATES
175 Derby Street, Suite 7, Hingham MA 02043. 781/749-2242. **Contact:** Manager. **Description:** An executive search firm. **Specializes in the areas of:** Finance; High-Tech; Manufacturing; Sales.

TMP WORLDWIDE
99 High Street, 27th Floor, Boston MA 02110-2320. 617/292-6242. **Fax:** 617/292-6247. **Contact:** Walter E. Williams, Partner. **World Wide Web address:** http://www.tmpw.com. **Description:** An executive search firm. **Specializes in the areas of:** Biotechnology; Consumer Products; Finance; Health/Medical; Industrial; Pharmaceuticals; Technical. **Corporate headquarters location:** New York NY. **Other U.S. locations:** Nationwide.

TASA INTERNATIONAL
101 Federal Street, Suite 1900, Boston MA 02110. 617/342-7441. **Contact:** Manager. **Description:** An executive search firm. **Specializes in the areas of:** Consumer Products; Fashion; Finance; Health/Medical; Industrial; Information Technology; Manufacturing; Pharmaceuticals; Retail; Telecommunications. **Corporate headquarters location:** New York NY. **International locations:** Worldwide.

THE TOWER GROUP
8 Hunton Circle, Attleboro MA 02703. 508/226-6735. **Contact:** Jim Tower, President. **Description:** An executive search firm operating on both retainer and contingency bases. **Specializes in the areas of:** Marketing; Sales.

UNITED PROFESSIONAL PLACEMENT
3 East Mountain Street, Worcester MA 01606. 508/853-9000. **Fax:** 508/853-0311. **Contact:** Mr. Patrick Kelley, President. **Description:** An executive search firm operating on both retainer and contingency bases. **Specializes in the areas of:** Communications; Engineering; Food; Industrial; Manufacturing; Plastics; Sales. **Positions commonly filled include:** Accountant/Auditor; Branch Manager; Customer Service Rep.; Design Engineer; Draftsperson; Electrical/Electronics Engineer; Industrial Engineer; Management Trainee; Mechanical Engineer; Restaurant/Food Service Manager. **Number of placements per year:** 100 - 199.

VAN/GRACE ASSOCIATES, INC.
276 West Main Street, Northborough MA 01532. 508/393-1700. **Fax:** 508/393-1780. **Contact:** Stephen J. Morris, President. **E-mail address:** vangrace@vangrace.com. **Description:** An executive search firm. Van/Grace Associates focuses on the plastic, rubber, polymer, coating, converting, biomedical, and adhesive industries. Founded in 1962. **Specializes in the areas of:** Chemicals; Engineering; Manufacturing; Marketing; Sales. **Positions commonly filled include:** Design Engineer; Environmental Engineer; Facilities Engineer; General Manager; Manufacturing Engineer; Marketing Specialist; Operations Manager; Plant Engineer; Plant Manager; Process Engineer; Product Development Engineer; Product Manager; Project Engineer; Quality Control Supervisor; Technical Support Engineer. **Average salary range of placements:** More than $50,000. **Number of placements per year:** 50 - 99.

VANGUARD EXECUTIVE SERVICES
512 West Main Street, Shrewsbury MA 01545. 508/842-5600. **Fax:** 508/842-4959. **Contact:** Irene Maloney,

Office Manager. **Description:** An executive search firm operating on a retainer basis. **Specializes in the areas of:** Engineering; Manufacturing.

VERSION 2.0 CORPORATION
60 State Street, Suite 700, Boston MA 02109. 617/742-3802. **Fax:** 617/742-3805. **Contact:** Manager. **Description:** An executive search firm. **Specializes in the areas of:** Technical. **Positions commonly filled include:** Computer Programmer; Network Engineer; Project Manager; Software Engineer.

THE WARD GROUP
8 Cedar Street, Woburn MA 01801. 781/938-4000. **Fax:** 781/938-4100. **Contact:** Jim Ward, President. **Description:** An executive search firm operating on a retainer basis. **Specializes in the areas of:** Advertising; Communications; Marketing; Public Relations; Sales. **Average salary range of placements:** More than $50,000. **Number of placements per year:** 50 - 99.

S.B. WEBSTER & ASSOCIATES, INC.
P.O. Box 1007, Duxbury MA 02331. 781/934-6603. **Contact:** William L. Webster, President. **Description:** An executive search firm operating on a retainer basis. **Specializes in the areas of:** Administration; Computer Science/Software; General Management; Manufacturing. **Positions commonly filled include:** Management Trainee; MIS Specialist; Operations/Production Manager; Software Engineer; Telecommunications Manager. **Average salary range of placements:** More than $50,000. **Number of placements per year:** 1 - 49.

WINFIELD ASSOCIATES
53 Winter Street, Weymouth MA 02188. 781/337-1010. **Fax:** 781/335-0089. **Contact:** Carl W. Siegel, Principal. **Description:** An executive search firm operating on a contingency basis. **Specializes in the areas of:** Biology; Engineering; Health/Medical; Information Technology. **Positions commonly filled include:** Biological Scientist; Biomedical Engineer; Chemist; Designer; Electrical/Electronics Engineer; Market Research Analyst; Mechanical Engineer; Metallurgical Engineer; Statistician. **Number of placements per year:** 1 - 49.

WITT/KIEFFER, FORD, HADELMAN & LLOYD
25 Burlington Mall Road, 6th Floor, Burlington MA 01803. 781/272-8899. **Fax:** 781/272-6677. **Contact:** Manager. **World Wide Web address:** http://www.wittkieffer.com. **Description:** An executive search firm. **Specializes in the areas of:** Health/Medical.

WRIGHT ASSOCIATES
929 Main Street, Millis MA 02054. 508/376-0000. **Contact:** Manager. **Description:** An executive search firm. **Specializes in the areas of:** Administration.

XAVIER ASSOCIATES, INC.
1350 Belmont Street, Brockton MA 02301. 508/584-9414. **Contact:** Manager. **Description:** An executive search firm. **Specializes in the areas of:** Consumer Products; Finance; High-Tech.

PERMANENT EMPLOYMENT AGENCIES

AARP FOUNDATION
SENIOR EMPLOYMENT PROGRAM
P.O. Box 2065, Danvers MA 01923. 978/777-7582. **Contact:** Harold O'Connell, Project Director. **Description:** A permanent employment agency that provides placements for senior citizens.

AARP FOUNDATION
SENIOR EMPLOYMENT PROGRAM
27 Water Street, Suite 104, Wakefield MA 01880. 781/246-5307. **Fax:** 781/246-5355. **Contact:** Liane H.

Gould, Project Director. **Description:** A permanent employment agency that provides placements for senior citizens. **Average salary range of placements:** $20,000 - $29,999. **Number of placements per year:** 1 - 49.

ABBOT PERSONNEL CONSULTING SERVICES
4 Faneuil Hall Marketplace, South Market, 4th Floor, Boston MA 02109. 617/423-0202. **Fax:** 617/227-7915. **Contact:** Manager. **Description:** A permanent employment agency. **Specializes in the areas of:** Administration; Clerical; Office Support; Personnel/Labor Relations.

ABILITY SEARCH OF NEW ENGLAND
P.O. Box 883, Framingham MA 01701. 508/872-2060. **Contact:** Jerry Vengrow, President. **Description:** A permanent employment agency. **Specializes in the areas of:** Accounting; Administration; Biology; Computer Science/Software; Engineering; Finance; General Management; Industrial; Legal; Manufacturing; Personnel/Labor Relations; Publishing; Sales; Secretarial; Technical. **Positions commonly filled include:** Accountant; Aerospace Engineer; Agricultural Engineer; Architect; Attorney; Biological Scientist; Biomedical Engineer; Blue-Collar Worker Supervisor; Budget Analyst; Buyer; Chemical Engineer; Chemist; Civil Engineer; Clerical Supervisor; Clinical Lab Tech.; Computer Engineer; Computer Programmer; Credit Manager; Customer Service Rep.; Dental Assistant/ Dental Hygienist; Dental Lab Technician; Designer; Draftsperson; Economist; EEG Technologist; EKG Technician; Electrical/Electronics Engineer; Electrician; Financial Analyst; Geologist/Geophysicist; Human Resources Manager; Industrial Engineer; Industrial Production Manager; Management Analyst/Consultant; Mathematician; Mechanical Engineer; Medical Records Technician; Metallurgical Engineer; Nuclear Engineer; Nuclear Medicine Technologist; Operations/Production Manager; Paralegal; Physician; Physicist; Purchasing Agent/Manager; Quality Control Supervisor; Radiological Technologist; Science Technologist; Software Engineer; Statistician; Structural Engineer; Systems Analyst; Technical Writer/Editor; Transportation/Traffic Specialist. **Number of placements per year:** 50 - 99.

ACCURATE STAFFING SERVICES INC.
390 Main Street, Suite 830, Worcester MA 01608. 508/799-9599. **Toll-free phone:** 800/640-9599. **Fax:** 508/798-2731. **Contact:** Christine D. Gervais, Branch Manager. **E-mail address:** astaff@accurate-staffing.com. **World Wide Web address:** http://www.accurate-staffing.com. **Description:** A permanent employment agency that also offers some contract services and resume consulting. Client company pays fee. **Specializes in the areas of:** Accounting; Administration; Banking; Computer Science/Software; Finance; Health/Medical; Marketing; MIS/EDP; Personnel/Labor Relations; Sales; Secretarial. **Positions commonly filled include:** Account Manager; Account Rep.; Accountant; Adjuster; Administrative Assistant; Applications Engineer; AS400 Programmer Analyst; Auditor; Bank Officer/Manager; Branch Manager; Budget Analyst; Buyer; Claim Rep.; Clerical Supervisor; Computer Engineer; Computer Operator; Computer Programmer; Computer Support Tech.; Computer Tech.; Controller; Cost Estimator; Credit Manager; Customer Service Rep.; Database Administrator; Database Manager; Finance Director; Financial Analyst; Human Resources Manager; Human Resources Representative; Internet Services Manager; Market Research Analyst; Marketing Manager; Marketing Specialist; MIS Specialist; Network/Systems Administrator; Operations Manager; Public Relations Specialist; Purchasing Agent/ Manager; Sales Engineer; Sales Exec.; Sales Manager; Sales Rep.; Secretary; Software Engineer; SQL Programmer; Systems Analyst; Systems Manager; Technical Writer/Editor; Typist/Word Processor. **Benefits available to temporary workers:** Paid Holidays; Training. **Corporate headquarters location:** This Location. **Average salary range of placements:** $30,000 - $49,999.

ACTIVE EMPLOYMENT SERVICE
108 Grove Street, Worcester MA 01605. 508/756-6550. **Contact:** Recruiter. **Description:** A permanent employment agency that also provides some resume writing services and temporary placements.

ALL PRO PERSONNEL
18 Tremont Street, Suite 308, Boston MA 02108. 617/742-5585. **Contact:** Manager. **Description:** A permanent employment agency that also provides some temp-to-perm placements.

AMERICAN NANNY COMPANY
NEWTONVILLE BRANCH
P.O. Box 765, Boston MA 02460. 617/244-5154. **Contact:** Manager. **Description:** A permanent employment agency. **Specializes in the areas of:** Child Care, In-Home. **Positions commonly filled include:** Nanny. **Average salary range of placements:** Less than $20,000. **Number of placements per year:** 100 - 199.

AMERICAN PERSONNEL SERVICE
185 Devonshire Street, Boston MA 02110. 617/350-0080. **Contact:** Manager. **Description:** A permanent employment agency.

ARTHUR-BLAIR ASSOCIATES INC.
One Court Street, Suite 500, Boston MA 02108. 617/723-8135. **Fax:** 617/723-8140. **Contact:** Tom Phinney, Owner. **Description:** A permanent employment agency that also provides some temporary placements. **Specializes in the areas of:** Banking; Finance; Mortgage; Personnel/Labor Relations; Secretarial. **Positions commonly filled include:** Branch Manager; Brokerage Clerk; Clerical Supervisor; Underwriter/ Assistant Underwriter. **Number of placements per year:** 100 - 199.

ASSOCIATED CAREER NETWORK
355 Union Street, New Bedford MA 02740. 508/990-1118. **Contact:** Manager. **Description:** A permanent employment agency that also provides some temporary placements. **Specializes in the areas of:** Manufacturing.

BOSTONIAN PERSONNEL COMPANY
P.O. Box 95, South Weymouth MA 02190. 781/340-3300. **Fax:** 781/340-0812. **Contact:** Jim Perfetuo, Manager. **E-mail address:** jim_perfetuo@bostonianpers.com. **World Wide Web address:** http://www.bostonianpers.com. **Description:** A permanent employment agency. **Specializes in the areas of:** Legal.

BRADY EMPLOYMENT SERVICE
44 Bromfield Street, Room 405, Boston MA 02108. 617/422-0488. **Fax:** 617/422-0490. **Contact:** George J. Brady, Owner/Manager. **Description:** A permanent employment agency. **Specializes in the areas of:** Electrical; Engineering; General Management; Industrial; Manufacturing; Personnel/Labor Relations. **Positions commonly filled include:** Blue-Collar Worker Supervisor; Buyer; Chemical Engineer; Designer; Draftsperson; Electrical/Electronics Engineer; Electrician; General Manager; Human Resources Manager; Industrial Engineer; Industrial Production Manager; Manufacturing Engineer; Mechanical Engineer; Metallurgical Engineer; Operations/Production Manager; Purchasing Agent/Manager; Quality Control Supervisor; Transportation/Traffic Specialist.

BUCKINGHAM PERSONNEL SERVICE
470 Washington Street, Suite 23, Norwood MA 02062. 781/762-7888. **Contact:** Gregg Buckingham, Manager. **E-mail address:** bps@buckinghampersonnel.com. **World Wide Web address:** http://www.buckinghampersonnel.com. **Description:** A permanent employment agency that also provides some temporary placements.

CQ PERSONNEL
76 Canal Street, Boston MA 02114. 617/248-8688. **Contact:** Manager. **Description:** A permanent employment agency that also provides some temporary placements.

CENTOR PERSONNEL
185 New Boston Road, Woburn MA 01801. 978/808-4954. **Contact:** Paulette Centor, President. **E-mail address:** pcentor@tiac.net. **Description:** A permanent employment agency. **Specializes in the areas of:** Computer Science/Software; Sales. **Positions commonly filled include:** Account Manager; Account Rep.; Marketing Manager; Marketing Specialist; Sales Executive; Sales Manager; Sales Representative.

Average salary range of placements: More than $50,000. **Number of placements per year:** 1 - 49.

CLEARY CONSULTANTS INC.
21 Merchants Row, Boston MA 02109. 617/367-7189. **Fax:** 617/367-3202. **Contact:** Mary Cleary, President. **Description:** A permanent employment agency. **Specializes in the areas of:** Accounting/Auditing; Administration; Advertising; Banking; Computer Science/Software; Finance; Health/Medical; Legal; Personnel/Labor Relations; Sales; Secretarial. **Positions commonly filled include:** Accountant/Auditor; Actuary; Administrative Manager; Advertising Clerk; Attorney; Bank Officer/Manager; Branch Manager; Brokerage Clerk; Clerical Supervisor; Customer Service Rep.; Financial Analyst; Health Services Manager; Human Resources Manager; Licensed Practical Nurse; Medical Records Technician; Paralegal; Pharmacist; Physician; Quality Control Supervisor; Registered Nurse; Services Sales Rep.; Software Engineer; Systems Analyst; Travel Agent. **Number of placements per year:** 500 - 999.

CONSTRUCTION DIRECTORY
850 Bridge Road, Eastham MA 02642. 508/255-9082. **Fax:** 508/255-9107. **Contact:** Dave Toms, President. **Description:** A permanent employment agency. **Specializes in the areas of:** Construction; Engineering. **Positions commonly filled include:** Civil Engineer; Construction Contractor; Surveyor. **Number of placements per year:** 1 - 49.

DERBY ASSOCIATES INC.
420 Washington Street, Braintree MA 02184-4755. 781/848-6969. **Fax:** 781/848-6984. **Contact:** Kelly Hillary, Assistant Manager. **Description:** A permanent employment agency. **Specializes in the areas of:** Accounting; Administration; Advertising; Architecture/Construction; Art/Design; Banking; Computer Science/Software; Engineering; Finance; Sales. **Positions commonly filled include:** Accountant; Administrative Assistant; Administrative Manager; Advertising Clerk; Bank Officer/Manager; Branch Manager; Brokerage Clerk; Budget Analyst; Clerical Supervisor; Computer Programmer; Credit Manager; Customer Service Rep.; Paralegal; Purchasing Agent/Manager; Travel Agent; Typist/Word Processor. **Average salary range of placements:** $30,000 - $50,000. **Number of placements per year:** 500 - 999.

DISCOVERY PERSONNEL INC.
P.O. Box 2862, Framingham MA 01703. 508/872-5100. **Fax:** 508/875-5818. **Contact:** Janet Brouthers, Manager. **Description:** A permanent employment agency. Client company pays fee. **Specializes in the areas of:** Accounting; Administration; Banking; Marketing; Personnel/Labor Relations; Sales; Secretarial. **Positions commonly filled include:** Account Manager; Accountant; Administrative Assistant; Advertising Clerk; Bank Officer/Manager; Branch Manager; Buyer; Clerical Supervisor; Computer Operator; Customer Service Representative; Database Administrator; Human Resources Manager; Marketing Specialist; Paralegal; Purchasing Agent/Manager; Sales Representative; Secretary; Typist/Word Processor. **Corporate headquarters location:** This Location. **Average salary range of placements:** $30,000 - $49,999. **Number of placements per year:** 100 - 199.

ENTEGEE
150 Bear Hill Road, Waltham MA 02451. 781/522-0400. **Contact:** Office Manager. **Description:** A permanent employment agency. **Specializes in the areas of:** Computer Hardware/Software; Engineering; Manufacturing; MIS/EDP; Technical. **Positions commonly filled include:** Aerospace Engineer; Civil Engineer; Computer Programmer; Draftsperson; Electrical/Electronics Engineer; Industrial Engineer; Mechanical Engineer; MIS Specialist; Purchasing Agent/Manager; Quality Control Supervisor; Sales Representative; Secretary; Systems Analyst; Technical Writer/Editor; Technician. **Number of placements per year:** 500 - 999.

FANNING PERSONNEL
20 Park Plaza, Suite 1409, Boston MA 02116. 617/728-4100. **Toll-free phone:** 877/FANNING. **Fax:** 617/728-4115. **Contact:** Ms. Chris Flynn, Recruiter. **World Wide Web address:** http://www.fanning-boston.com. **Description:** A permanent employment agency. Founded in 1968. Client company pays fee. **Specializes in the areas of:** Accounting; Administration; Advertising; Architecture/Construction; Economics; Finance; Insurance; Internet Development; Internet Marketing; Investment; Legal; New Media; Nonprofit; Real Estate; Secretarial. **Positions commonly filled include:** Account Manager; Accountant; Administrative Assistant; Advertising Clerk; Advertising Exec.; Art Director; Content Developer; Customer Service Rep.; Desktop Publishing Specialist; Editor; Financial Analyst; Fund Manager; Graphic Artist; Graphic Designer; Internet Services Manager; Market Research Analyst; Marketing Manager; Marketing Specialist; Multimedia Designer; Paralegal; Production Manager; Project Manager; Public Relations Specialist; Secretary; Technical Writer/Editor; Typist/Word Processor; Webmaster. **Corporate headquarters location:** New York NY. **Average salary range of placements:** $30,000 - $100,000. **Number of placements per year:** 500 - 999.

FRANKLIN-PIERCE ASSOCIATES
One Liberty Square, Boston MA 02109-4825. 617/695-1700. **Fax:** 617/695-0683. **Contact:** Edward A. Blum, Vice President/General Manager. **Description:** A permanent employment agency. **Specializes in the areas of:** Office Support; Secretarial. **Positions commonly filled include:** Administrative Assistant; Customer Service Rep.; Human Resources Specialist; Secretary; Typist/Word Processor. **Number of placements per year:** 500 - 999.

GILLARD ASSOCIATES
75 McNeil Road, Dedham MA 02026. 781/329-4731. **Fax:** 781/329-1357. **Contact:** Elizabeth Gillard, President. **E-mail address:** gillardlgl@aol.com. **Description:** A permanent employment agency. **Specializes in the areas of:** Legal. **Positions commonly filled include:** Attorney; Legal Secretary; Paralegal. **Number of placements per year:** 1 - 49.

HUMAN RESOURCE CONSULTANTS
1252 Elm Street, West Springfield MA 01089. 413/737-7563. **Fax:** 413/731-9897. **Contact:** John M. Turner, President. **Description:** A permanent employment agency. **Specializes in the areas of:** Biology; Computer Science/Software; Engineering; Health/Medical. **Positions commonly filled include:** Biomedical Engineer; Computer Programmer; Industrial Engineer; Mechanical Engineer; Physical Therapist; Respiratory Therapist; Software Engineer; Systems Analyst. **Number of placements per year:** 50 - 99.

HUNTER ASSOCIATES
181 Park Avenue, West Springfield MA 01089-3365. 413/737-6560. **Fax:** 413/785-1295. **Contact:** Daniel M. Shooshan, Principal. **E-mail address:** hunter@hunterworldwide.com. **World Wide Web address:** http://www.hunterworldwide.com. **Description:** A permanent employment agency. **Specializes in the areas of:** Engineering; Manufacturing. **Positions commonly filled include:** Buyer; Design Engineer; Electrical/Electronics Engineer; General Manager; Industrial Engineer; Mechanical Engineer; Software Engineer. **Average salary range of placements:** $50,000 - $90,000. **Number of placements per year:** 1 - 49.

IT RESOURCES
P.O. Box 305, Lexington MA 02420. 781/863-2661. **Fax:** 781/863-2686. **Contact:** Ken Loomis, President. **E-mail address:** mailbox@it-resources.com. **World Wide Web address:** http://www.it-resources.com. **Description:** A permanent employment agency. Client company pays fee. **Specializes in the areas of:** Computer Science/Software; MIS/EDP. **Positions commonly filled include:** Computer Programmer;

Computer Support Tech.; Database Administrator; Database Manager; Internet Services Manager; MIS Specialist; Network/Systems Administrator; Software Engineer; SQL Programmer; Systems Analyst; Systems Manager; Webmaster. **Corporate headquarters location:** This Location. **Average salary range of placements:** $50,000 - $100,000. **Number of placements per year:** 50 - 99.

IN SEARCH OF NANNY INC.
5 Cherry Hill Drive, Danvers MA 01923-2500. 978/777-9891. **Contact:** Betty Davis, President. **Description:** A permanent employment agency. **Specializes in the areas of:** Education; Nannies; Social Services. **Number of placements per year:** 200 - 499.

INSURANCE PERSONNEL RECRUITERS
20 Pulsifer Street, Newtonville MA 02460. 617/969-2192. **Fax:** 617/969-2192. **Contact:** Robert P. Whitten, President. **E-mail address:** ipr1@gis.net. **World Wide Web address:** http://www.gis.net/~ipr1. **Description:** A permanent employment agency. **Specializes in the areas of:** Insurance. **Positions commonly filled include:** Accountant/Auditor; Actuary; Adjuster; Administrative Manager; Attorney; Claim Rep.; Claims Investigator; Customer Service Rep.; Insurance Agent/Broker; Underwriter/Assistant Underwriter. **Number of placements per year:** 1 - 49.

THE INSURANCE STAFFING GROUP
50 Salem Street, Building B, Lynnfield MA 01940. 781/246-6786. **Toll-free phone:** 800/601-1113. **Fax:** 781/246-6788. **Contact:** Ms. Annis Legrow, Placement Manager. **E-mail address:** jobs@insurancestaffing.com. **Description:** A permanent employment agency that also provides temporary placements. **Specializes in the areas of:** Insurance. **Positions commonly filled include:** Adjuster; Brokerage Clerk; Claim Rep.; Clerical Supervisor; Customer Service Rep.; Insurance Agent/Broker; Operations/Production Manager; Underwriter/Assistant Underwriter. **Average salary range of placements:** $30,000 - $50,000. **Number of placements per year:** 50 - 99.

INTERACTIVE SOFTWARE PLACEMENT, INC.
465 Auburn Street, Auburndale MA 02166. 617/527-2700. **Fax:** 617/965-7998. **Contact:** Sean Leary, President. **Description:** A permanent employment agency. **Specializes in the areas of:** Software Development; Software Engineering; Software Quality Assurance.

WILLIAM JAMES ASSOCIATES
800 Turnpike Street, Suite 300, North Andover MA 01845-6156. 978/685-0700. **Fax:** 978/685-7113. **Contact:** Bill Josephson, President. **Description:** A permanent employment agency. **Specializes in the areas of:** Computer Science/Software. **Positions commonly filled include:** Computer Programmer; Software Engineer; Systems Analyst.

KNF&T INC.
133 Federal Street, 3rd Floor, Boston MA 02169. 617/574-8200. **Fax:** 617/574-8223. **Contact:** Personnel Consultant. **World Wide Web address:** http://www.knft.com. **Description:** A permanent employment agency that also offers temporary placements. Founded in 1983. **Specializes in the areas of:** Administration. **Positions commonly filled include:** Account Manager; Administrative Assistant; Administrative Manager; Bookkeeper; Clerical Supervisor; Customer Service Rep.; Data Entry Clerk; Editorial Assistant; Graphic Designer; Receptionist; Sales Rep.; Telemarketer; Typist/Word Processor; Webmaster. **Benefits available to temporary workers:** Medical Insurance; Paid Holidays; Paid Vacation; Transportation Pass. **Average salary range of placements:** $30,000 - $50,000. **Number of placements per year:** 1000+.

KINGSTON-DWIGHT ASSOCIATES
100 Franklin Street, Suite 300, Boston MA 02110. 617/350-8811. **Fax:** 617/350-8816. **Contact:** Joseph J.

Hyde, Jr., Partner. **Description:** A permanent employment agency. **Specializes in the areas of:** Accounting/Auditing; Banking; Finance. **Positions commonly filled include:** Account Rep.; Bookkeeper; Controller; Credit Manager; EDP Specialist; Financial Analyst. **Number of placements per year:** 100 - 199.

LANE EMPLOYMENT SERVICE, INC.
5 Mount Royal Avenue, Marlborough MA 01752. 508/757-5678. **Contact:** Manager. **Description:** A permanent employment agency. **Specializes in the areas of:** Accounting/Auditing; Banking; Clerical; Computer Hardware/Software; Engineering; Finance; Insurance; Manufacturing; MIS/EDP; Secretarial. **Positions commonly filled include:** Accountant/Auditor; Actuary; Administrative Assistant; Bank Officer/Manager; Biological Scientist; Bookkeeper; Claim Rep.; Clerk; Computer Programmer; Credit Manager; Data Entry Clerk; EDP Specialist; Electrical/Electronics Engineer; Financial Analyst; General Manager; Human Resources Manager; Industrial Designer; Industrial Engineer; Legal Secretary; Marketing Specialist; Mechanical Engineer; Medical Secretary; Metallurgical Engineer; Purchasing Agent/Manager; Receptionist; Secretary; Stenographer; Systems Analyst; Typist/Word Processor.

JOHN LEONARD PERSONNEL ASSOCIATES
75 Federal Street, 11th Floor, Boston MA 02110. 617/423-6800. **Fax:** 617/451-0384. **Contact:** Linda J. Poldoian, President. **Description:** A permanent employment agency that offers temporary placements. **Specializes in the areas of:** Advertising; Architecture/Construction; Biotechnology; Engineering; Finance; Health/Medical; Legal; Personnel/Labor Relations; Secretarial. **Positions commonly filled include:** Administrative Assistant; Bookkeeper; Clerk; Computer Operator; Customer Service Rep.; Data Entry Clerk; Human Resources Specialist; Internet Services Manager; Legal Secretary; Management Trainee; Medical Secretary; MIS Specialist; Paralegal; Sales Rep.; Telecommunications Manager; Typist/Word Processor. **Corporate headquarters location:** This Location. **Other U.S. locations:** Cambridge MA; Wellesley MA; Westborough MA. **Number of placements per year:** 500 - 999.

JOHN LEONARD PERSONNEL ASSOCIATES
20 Walnut Street, Suite 213, Wellesley MA 02481. 781/235-6400. **Contact:** Manager. **Description:** A permanent employment agency that also offers temporary placements. **Specializes in the areas of:** Advertising; Architecture/Construction; Banking; Biotechnology; Computer Hardware/Software; Engineering; Finance; Health/Medical; Legal; Personnel/Labor Relations; Secretarial. **Positions commonly filled include:** Administrative Assistant; Bookkeeper; Clerk; Computer Operator; Customer Service Rep.; Data Entry Clerk; Legal Secretary; Medical Secretary; Typist/Word Processor. **Corporate headquarters location:** Boston MA. **Other area locations:** Cambridge MA; Westborough MA.

JOHN LEONARD PERSONNEL ASSOCIATES
50 Church Street, Cambridge MA 02138. 617/864-7200. **Contact:** Manager. **Description:** A permanent employment agency that also provides some temporary placements. **Specializes in the areas of:** Administration. **Corporate headquarters location:** Boston MA. **Other U.S. locations:** Wellesley MA; Westborough MA.

NATIONWIDE BUSINESS SERVICE
P.O. Box 457, Westfield MA 01086. 413/568-9568. **Fax:** 413/568-9607. **Contact:** Alan Cheika, President/Technical Recruiter. **E-mail address:** alcheika@searchnw.com. **World Wide Web address:** http://www.searchnw.com. **Description:** A permanent employment agency that also provides some temporary and contract placements. Client company pays fee. **Specializes in the areas of:** Computer Science/Software; Engineering; Industrial; Internet Development; Marketing; MIS/EDP; Sales; Scientific; Technical. **Positions commonly filled include:** Applications Engineer; AS400 Programmer

Analyst; Chemical Engineer; Chemist; Clinical Lab Technician; Computer Animator; Computer Engineer; Computer Programmer; Computer Scientist; Computer Support Tech.; Computer Tech.; Database Manager; Design Engineer; Draftsperson; Electrical/Electronics Engineer; Environmental Engineer; Industrial Engineer; Internet Services Manager; Manufacturing Engineer; Marketing Manager; Mechanical Engineer; Metallurgical Engineer; Quality Assurance Engineer; SQL Programmer; Systems Analyst; Systems Manager; Webmaster. **Average salary range of placements:** $30,000 - $49,999. **Number of placements per year:** 1 - 49.

NEW ENGLAND PERSONNEL, INC.
2 Oliver Street, 9th Floor, Boston MA 02109. 617/542-3500. **Fax:** 617/542-3501. **Contact:** Kim Gonsalves, President. **Description:** A permanent employment agency that also provides some temporary placements. **Specializes in the areas of:** Administration; Industrial; Legal; Personnel/Labor Relations; Sales; Secretarial. **Positions commonly filled include:** Administrative Manager; Clerical Supervisor; Customer Service Rep.; Paralegal; Services Sales Representative; Typist/Word Processor. **Number of placements per year:** 50 - 99.

OPEN SYSTEMS TECHNOLOGIES INC.
155 Massachusetts Avenue, Suite 301, Boston MA 02115. 617/424-8880. **Fax:** 617/424-8881. **Contact:** Michael Ryan, Vice President. **E-mail address:** ost@boston.opensyst.com. **World Wide Web address:** http://www.opensyst.com. **Description:** A permanent employment agency that also provides some temporary and contract placements. **Specializes in the areas of:** Banking; Computer Science/Software; Finance; Scientific; Technical. **Positions commonly filled include:** Computer Operator; Computer Programmer; Consultant; Database Manager; MIS Specialist; Software Engineer; Systems Analyst; Systems Manager; Technical Writer/Editor; Vice President; Webmaster. **Benefits available to temporary workers:** 401(k); Dental Insurance; Medical Insurance. **Average salary range of placements:** More than $50,000. **Number of placements per year:** 100 - 199.

THE ORIGINAL NANNY SERVICE
172 Institute Road, Worcester MA 01602-2136. 508/755-9284. **Contact:** Judy Flynn, President. **Description:** A permanent employment agency. **Specializes in the areas of:** Child Care, In-Home; Nannies. **Positions commonly filled include:** Nanny. **Average salary range of placements:** Less than $20,000.

PARENTS IN A PINCH
45 Bartlett Crescent, Brookline MA 02446-2208. 617/739-5437. **Fax:** 617/739-1939. **Contact:** Joy Manon, Recruitment Specialist. **Description:** A permanent employment agency that also provides some temporary placements. **Specializes in the areas of:** Child Care, In-Home. **Average salary range of placements:** Less than $20,000. **Number of placements per year:** 1000+.

PRESTIGE PLACEMENT CONSULTANTS
25 Storey Avenue, Suite 330, Newburyport MA 01950-1869. 978/462-5037. **Contact:** Jill Healey, President. **Description:** A permanent employment agency. **Specializes in the areas of:** Insurance. **Positions commonly filled include:** Claim Rep.; Customer Service Rep.; Insurance Services Manager; Sales Rep.

PROFESSIONAL STAFFING GROUP
85 Devonshire Street, 2nd Floor, Boston MA 02109. 617/250-1000. **Fax:** 617/250-1099. **Contact:** Janine Galanti, President. **E-mail address:** staffing@tiac.net. **World Wide Web address:** http://www.prof-staf.com. **Description:** A permanent employment agency that also provides some temporary placements. Founded in 1992. **Specializes in the areas of:** Advertising; Architecture/Construction; Finance; Health/Medical; Human Resources; Legal; Marketing; Printing; Public Relations; Publishing; Real Estate; Sales. **Positions commonly filled include:** Administrative Assistant; Receptionist;

Secretary. **Benefits available to temporary workers:** 401(k); Bonus Award/Plan; Computer Training. **Corporate headquarters location:** This Location. **Average salary range of placements:** $20,000 - $29,999. **Number of placements per year:** 100 - 199.

PROPOS ASSOCIATES, INC.
South End Bridge Circle, Agawam MA 01001. 413/789-3750. **Fax:** 413/789-3755. **Contact:** David Anable, President. **Description:** A permanent employment agency that also provides some temporary placements. **Specializes in the areas of:** Engineering; Insurance; Secretarial; Technical. **Positions commonly filled include:** Bookkeeper; Claim Rep.; Customer Service Rep.; Data Entry Clerk; Electrical/Electronics Engineer; Factory Worker; Legal Secretary; Light Industrial Worker; Manufacturing Engineer; Mechanical Engineer; Medical Secretary; Receptionist; Secretary; Technician; Typist/Word Processor. **Number of placements per year:** 1 - 49.

QUALITY PERSONNEL INC.
QUALITY TEMPS
623 Pleasant Street, Brockton MA 02301. 508/588-0500. **Contact:** Recruiter. **Description:** A permanent employment agency that also provides some temporary placements. **Specializes in the areas of:** General Management; Light Industrial; Personnel/Labor Relations; Secretarial. **Positions commonly filled include:** General Manager; Human Resources Specialist; MIS Specialist; Services Sales Rep.; Typist/Word Processor. **Office hours:** Monday - Friday, 8:00 a.m. - 5:00 p.m. **Average salary range of placements:** $20,000 - $29,999. **Number of placements per year:** 100 - 199.

E.S. RANDO ASSOCIATES, INC.
P.O. Box 654, Wilmington MA 01887. 978/657-4730. **Fax:** 978/658-4650. **Contact:** Recruiter. **E-mail address:** jobs@rando.com. **World Wide Web address:** http://www.rando.com. **Description:** A permanent employment agency that also provides some temporary and contract placements. Founded in 1970. **Specializes in the areas of:** Computer Hardware/Software; Health/Medical; Information Systems; MIS/EDP; Software Engineering. **Positions commonly filled include:** Computer Programmer; Database Manager; EDP Specialist; Finance Director; Financial Analyst; Management Analyst/Consultant; MIS Specialist; Project Manager; Software Engineer; Statistician; Systems Analyst. **Average salary range of placements:** More than $50,000. **Number of placements per year:** 50 - 99.

REARDON ASSOCIATES, INC.
990 Washington Street, Dedham MA 02026. 781/329-2660. **Fax:** 781/329-9918. **Contact:** Donald B. Tule, President. **World Wide Web address:** http://www.reardonassoc.com. **Description:** A permanent employment agency. **Specializes in the areas of:** Accounting/Auditing; Administration; Finance; Manufacturing; Personnel/Labor Relations; Secretarial. **Positions commonly filled include:** Accountant/Auditor; Budget Analyst; Buyer; Computer Programmer; Credit Manager; Financial Analyst; Human Resources Manager; Industrial Engineer; Purchasing Agent/Manager; Quality Control Supervisor; Systems Analyst. **Corporate headquarters location:** This Location. **Number of placements per year:** 200 - 499.

REARDON ASSOCIATES, INC.
27 Cambridge Street, Burlington MA 01803. 781/270-4400. **Fax:** 781/229-6814. **Contact:** Lisa McCarthy, Division Manager. **E-mail address:** reardon@tiac.net. **World Wide Web address:** http://www.reardonassoc.com. **Description:** A permanent employment agency. **Specializes in the areas of:** Accounting/Auditing; Computer Science/Software; Finance; Human Resources; Manufacturing; MIS/EDP; Operations Management; Personnel/Labor Relations; Secretarial. **Positions commonly filled include:** Accountant/Auditor; Administrative Assistant; Bookkeeper; Clerk; Customer Service Representative;

Human Resources Specialist; MIS Specialist; Operations/ Production Manager; Purchasing Agent/Manager; Receptionist; Secretary; Typist/Word Processor. **Benefits available to temporary workers:** Medical Insurance; Paid Holidays; Paid Vacation. **Corporate headquarters location:** Dedham MA. **Average salary range of placements:** $30,000 - $50,000. **Number of placements per year:** 500 - 999.

THE RESOURCE PARTNERSHIP

251 West Central Street, Suite 31, Natick MA 01760. 508/647-1722. **Fax:** 508/647-9622. **Contact:** Kathleen Petkauskos, President. **Description:** A permanent employment agency. **Specializes in the areas of:** Disabled Applicants. **Number of placements per year:** 200 - 499.

ROMAC INTERNATIONAL

155 Federal Street, 10th Floor, Boston MA 02110. 617/482-8211. **Fax:** 617/482-9084. **Contact:** Steve McMahan, Regional Vice President. **World Wide Web address:** http://www.romac.com. **Description:** A permanent employment agency that also provides some temporary and contract placements. **Specializes in the areas of:** Accounting; Banking; Computer Science/ Software; Engineering; Finance; MIS/EDP. **Positions commonly filled include:** Accountant; Applications Engineer; AS400 Programmer Analyst; Auditor; Budget Analyst; Chief Financial Officer; Computer Programmer; Computer Scientist; Computer Support Technician; Controller; Cost Estimator; Credit Manager; Database Administrator; Database Manager; Finance Director; Financial Analyst; Internet Services Manager; MIS Specialist; Network/Systems Administrator; Software Engineer; SQL Programmer; Systems Analyst; Webmaster. **Corporate headquarters location:** Tampa FL. **Other U.S. locations:** Nationwide. **Number of placements per year:** 1000+.

ROUTHIER PLACEMENT SPECIALISTS

160 State Street, 3rd Floor, Boston MA 02109. 617/742-2747. **Fax:** 617/742-3374. **Contact:** Tom Routhier, President. **Description:** A permanent employment agency that also provides some temporary placements. **Specializes in the areas of:** Administration; Legal; Secretarial. **Positions commonly filled include:** Administrative Assistant; Data Entry Clerk; Secretary; Typist/Word Processor. **Average salary range of placements:** $30,000 - $50,000. **Number of placements per year:** 100 - 199.

GEORGE D. SANDEL ASSOCIATES

P.O. Box 588, Waltham MA 02454. 617/558-7770. **Contact:** Ivan Samuels, President. **E-mail address:** irsxgdsa@erols.com. **Description:** A permanent employment agency. **Specializes in the areas of:** Administration; Computer Science/Software; Engineering; Health/Medical; Industrial; Manufacturing; Personnel/Labor Relations; Sales; Technical. **Positions commonly filled include:** Aerospace Engineer; Biological Scientist; Biomedical Engineer; Computer Programmer; Electrical/Electronics Engineer; Health Services Manager; Human Resources Manager; Industrial Engineer; Mechanical Engineer; Physical Therapist; Physicist; Registered Nurse; Software Engineer; Systems Analyst. **Number of placements per year:** 1 - 49.

SCOTT-WAYNE ASSOCIATES, INC.

425 Boylston Street, 4th Floor, Boston MA 02116. 617/587-3000. **Fax:** 617/587-3030. **Contact:** R. Steven Dow, Executive Vice President. **E-mail address:** swa@gte.net. **Description:** A permanent employment agency. **Specializes in the areas of:** Accounting; Banking; Finance. **Positions commonly filled include:** Account Manager; Accountant; Auditor; Budget Analyst; Chief Financial Officer; Controller; Cost Estimator; Credit Manager; Finance Director; Financial Analyst; Fund Manager; Purchasing Agent/Manager; Underwriter/ Assistant Underwriter; Vice President of Finance. **Corporate headquarters location:** Topsfield MA.

Average salary range of placements: More than $50,000. **Number of placements per year:** 50 - 99.

SELECTIVE OFFICE STAFFING

218 Boston Street, Suite 107, Topsfield MA 01983-2200. 978/887-0200. **Toll-free phone:** 800/427-0204. **Fax:** 978/887-0286. **Contact:** Sheila Burke, President. **Description:** A permanent employment agency that also provides some temporary placements. **Specializes in the areas of:** Accounting/Auditing; Personnel/Labor Relations; Sales; Secretarial. **Positions commonly filled include:** Accountant/Auditor; Administrative Manager; Buyer; Clerical Supervisor; Computer Programmer; Credit Manager; Customer Service Rep.; Electrical/ Electronics Engineer; Financial Analyst; Human Resources Specialist; MIS Specialist; Operations/ Production Manager; Paralegal; Sales Executive; Sales Manager; Sales Rep.; Software Engineer; Systems Analyst; Systems Manager; Technical Writer/Editor; Telecommunications Manager; Typist/Word Processor. **Average salary range of placements:** More than $25,000. **Number of placements per year:** 50 - 99.

THE SKILL BUREAU, INC.

129 Tremont Street, Boston MA 02108. 617/423-2986. **Fax:** 617/423-9183. **Contact:** Sandy Poritzky, Vice President. **E-mail address:** tsb@skillbureau.com. **World Wide Web address:** http://www.skillbureau.com. **Description:** A permanent employment agency that also provides some temporary placements. Founded in 1966. **Specializes in the areas of:** Secretarial; Word Processing. **Positions commonly filled include:** Administrative Assistant; Administrative Manager; Clerical Supervisor; Computer Operator; Customer Service Representative; Secretary; Typist/Word Processor. **Benefits available to temporary workers:** Medical Insurance; Paid Holidays; Paid Vacation; Profit Sharing; Referral Bonus Plan. **Corporate headquarters location:** This Location. **Average salary range of placements:** $30,000 - $50,000.

SNELLING PERSONNEL SERVICES

3 Courthouse Lane, Suite 2, Chelmsford MA 01824. 978/970-3434. **Fax:** 978/970-3637. **Contact:** Manager. **Description:** A permanent employment agency that also provides some temporary placements. **Specializes in the areas of:** Accounting; Administration; Advertising; Computer Science/Software; Manufacturing; Personnel/ Labor Relations; Publishing; Sales; Secretarial. **Positions commonly filled include:** Accountant/Auditor; Adjuster; Administrative Manager; Blue-Collar Worker Supervisor; Buyer; Chemist; Claim Rep.; Clerical Supervisor; Clinical Lab Technician; Computer Programmer; Cost Estimator; Counselor; Credit Manager; Customer Service Rep.; Designer; Draftsperson; Electrician; Human Resources Manager; Insurance Agent/Broker; Management Trainee; Manufacturer's/Wholesaler's Sales Rep.; Paralegal; Property and Real Estate Manager; Public Relations Specialist; Purchasing Agent/Manager; Quality Control Supervisor; Services Sales Rep.; Software Engineer; Systems Analyst. **Corporate headquarters location:** Dallas TX. **Number of placements per year:** 200 - 499.

SPECTRA PROFESSIONAL SEARCH
SPECTRA TEMPS

Faneuil Hall Marketplace, 2 South Building, 4th Floor, Boston MA 02109. 617/720-0010. **Fax:** 617/720-1483. **Contact:** Dorothy Matanes, Director of Temporary Services. **Description:** A permanent employment agency. Spectra Temps (also at this location) provides temporary placements. **Specializes in the areas of:** Advertising; Banking; Finance; Legal; Office Support; Secretarial. **Positions commonly filled include:** Administrative Assistant; Administrative Worker/Clerk; Paralegal; Secretary. **Benefits available to temporary workers:** Dental Insurance; Medical Insurance. **Average salary range of placements:** $20,000 - $29,999. **Number of placements per year:** 100 - 199.

TECHNICAL PERSONNEL SERVICES INC.
1060 Osgood Street, P.O. Box 355, North Andover MA 01845. 978/794-3347. **Toll-free phone:** 800/567-3493. **Fax:** 978/794-9291. **Contact:** Paul Donatio, General Manager. **E-mail address:** techpers@tpsjobs.com. **World Wide Web address:** http://www.tpsjobs.com. **Description:** A permanent employment agency that also provides some temporary placements. **Specializes in the areas of:** Architecture/Construction; Banking; Computer Science/Software; Engineering; Industrial; Scientific; Technical. **Positions commonly filled include:** Architect; Buyer; Chemical Engineer; Civil Engineer; Computer Operator; Computer Programmer; Consultant; Controller; Design Engineer; Draftsperson; Editor; Electrical/Electronics Engineer; Electrician; Environmental Engineer; Graphic Designer; Industrial Engineer; Internet Services Manager; Manufacturing Engineer; Mechanical Engineer; MIS Specialist; Multimedia Designer; Operations Manager; Production Manager; Project Manager; Purchasing Agent/Manager; Quality Assurance Engineer; Sales Engineer; Systems Analyst; Technical Writer/Editor; Webmaster. **Corporate headquarters location:** This Location. **Average salary range of placements:** $30,000 - $50,000. **Number of placements per year:** 100 - 199.

TESMER ALLEN ASSOCIATES
P.O. Box 1491, Westborough MA 01581. 508/366-1160. **Fax:** 508/366-6419. **Contact:** John B. Allen, Vice President. **E-mail address:** jballen@tiac.net. **Description:** A permanent employment agency. **Specializes in the areas of:** Computer Hardware/Software; Engineering; MIS/EDP. **Positions commonly filled include:** Applications Engineer; Biomedical Engineer; Chemical Engineer; Computer Programmer; Design Engineer; Draftsperson; Electrical/Electronics Engineer; Environmental Engineer; Internet Services Manager; Manufacturing Engineer; Mechanical Engineer; Metallurgical Engineer; MIS Specialist; Sales Engineer; Software Engineer; Systems Analyst; Systems Manager; Telecommunications Manager; Webmaster. **Other U.S. locations:** Nationwide. **Average salary range of placements:** $30,000 - $50,000. **Number of placements per year:** 50 - 99.

TOTAL TECHNICAL SERVICES, INC. (TTS)
167 Pleasant Street, Attleboro MA 02703. 508/226-3880. **Fax:** 508/226-4363. **Contact:** Rebecca Simmons, Recruiter. **Description:** A permanent employment agency. **Specializes in the areas of:** Administration; Computer Science/Software; Engineering; Industrial; Manufacturing; Personnel/Labor Relations; Secretarial; Technical. **Positions commonly filled include:** Administrative Manager; Bank Officer/Manager; Blue-Collar Worker Supervisor; Buyer; Chemical Engineer; Civil Engineer; Clerical Supervisor; Computer

Programmer; Credit Manager; Design Engineer; Designer; Draftsperson; Electrical/Electronics Engineer; Electrician; Environmental Engineer; Human Resources Specialist; Industrial Engineer; Mechanical Engineer; MIS Specialist; Multimedia Designer; Nuclear Engineer; Paralegal; Petroleum Engineer; Purchasing Agent/Manager; Quality Control Supervisor; Software Engineer; Statistician; Structural Engineer; Systems Analyst; Technical Writer/Editor; Typist/Word Processor; Urban/Regional Planner. **Benefits available to temporary workers:** Medical Insurance; Paid Vacation. **Corporate headquarters location:** Waltham MA. **Other U.S. locations:** Atlanta GA; Boston MA; Dallas TX. **Average salary range of placements:** $20,000 - $29,999. **Number of placements per year:** 200 - 499.

TRAVEL CAREER NETWORK, LTD.
44 School Street, Suite 705, Boston MA 02108. 617/722-0079. **Fax:** 617/722-4063. **Contact:** Kelvin Powell, Office Manager. **E-mail address:** kelvin@travelcareernetwork.com. **Description:** A permanent employment agency that also provides some temporary placements and resume and career counseling services. Client company pays fee. **Specializes in the areas of:** Travel. **Positions commonly filled include:** Account Manager; Account Rep.; Accountant/Auditor; Administrative Assistant; Buyer; Consultant; Customer Service Representative; General Manager; MIS Specialist; Network/Systems Administrator; Operations Manager; Project Manager; Sales Representative; Travel Agent. **Corporate headquarters location:** This Location. **Average salary range of placements:** $30,000 - $49,999. **Number of placements per year:** 100 - 199.

TRAVEL INDUSTRY CONSULTANTS
404 East Street, Hingham MA 02043. 781/749-8344. **Toll-free phone:** 800/343-5350. **Fax:** 781/749-7080. **Contact:** Cheryl M. Cormier, President. **E-mail address:** sabrejobs@aol.com. **Description:** Travel Industry Consultants is a permanent employment agency that also provides some temporary placements. **Specializes in the areas of:** Travel. **Positions commonly filled include:** Travel Agent.

WILLMOTT & ASSOCIATES
922 Waltham Street, Suite 103, Lexington MA 02421-8019. 781/863-5400. **Fax:** 781/863-8000. **Contact:** Clark Willmott, President. **E-mail address:** willmott@willmott.com. **World Wide Web address:** http://www.willmott.com. **Description:** A permanent employment agency that also provides some contract placements. **Specializes in the areas of:** Human Resources; Personnel/Labor Relations. **Positions commonly filled include:** Human Resources Manager.

TEMPORARY EMPLOYMENT AGENCIES

ABA PERSONNEL, INC.
25 Pleasant Street, Newburyport MA 01950. 978/462-4600. **Fax:** 978/462-4622. **Contact:** Sharon Bedford, Vice President. **Description:** A temporary agency that also provides some temp-to-perm placements. **Specializes in the areas of:** Accounting; Administration; Computer Science/Software; Engineering; General Management; Industrial; Light Industrial; Marketing; Sales; Scientific; Secretarial; Technical. **Positions commonly filled include:** Account Manager; Account Rep.; Accountant; Adjuster; Administrative Assistant; Administrative Manager; Applications Engineer; Auditor; Bank Officer/Manager; Biochemist; Biological Scientist; Biomedical Engineer; Branch Manager; Chemical Engineer; Chemist; Clerical Supervisor; Clinical Lab Technician; Computer Animator; Controller; Cost Estimator; Customer Service Rep.; Database Manager; Design Engineer; Dietician/Nutritionist; Draftsperson; EEG Technologist; EKG Technician; Electrical/Electronics Engineer; Finance Director; Financial Analyst; General Manager; Graphic

Artist; Graphic Designer; Industrial Engineer; Industrial Production Manager; Manufacturing Engineer; Marketing Manager; Mechanical Engineer; MIS Specialist; Operations Manager; Production Manager; Project Manager; Quality Control Supervisor; Sales Engineer; Sales Exec.; Sales Manager; Sales Rep.; Secretary; Software Engineer; Systems Analyst; Systems Manager; Technical Writer/Editor; Typist/Word Processor. **Corporate headquarters location:** This Location. **Number of placements per year:** 500 - 999.

A.S.I. TEMPS (ALTERNATIVE SOLUTIONS INC.)
MICHAEL WARD ASSOCIATES
P.O. Box 740, Boston MA 02117-0740. 617/262-4900. **Physical address:** 396 Commonwealth Avenue, Boston MA. **Fax:** 617/262-6217. **Contact:** Keith D. Alter, President. **World Wide Web address:** http://www.podi.com/asi. **Description:** A.S.I. Temps is a temporary agency. Michael Ward Associates (also at this location, 617/965-7333) is a permanent employment agency. **Specializes in the areas of:** Health/Medical; Insurance;

Legal. **Positions commonly filled include:** Insurance Agent/Broker; Medical Records Technician; Physical Therapist. **Benefits available to temporary workers:** Dental Insurance; Medical Insurance; Paid Vacation. **Other area locations:** Springfield MA. **Other U.S. locations:** Hartford CT. **Number of placements per year:** 1 - 49.

ALDEN AND CLARK, INC.
P.O. Box 180177, Boston MA 02118. 617/247-1147. **Contact:** Alden Thatcher, Vice President of Recruitment. **Description:** A temporary agency. **Specializes in the areas of:** Advertising; Art/Design; Publishing. **Positions commonly filled include:** Artist; Graphic Artist; Mechanical Artist. **Number of placements per year:** 200 - 499.

THE ALPHA GROUP
P.O. Box J, 175 Mansfield Avenue, Norton MA 02766. 508/285-8500. **Fax:** 508/285-4000. **Contact:** Olivia Cahill, Public Relations Manager. **E-mail address:** alphagrp@ix.netcom.com. **World Wide Web address:** http://www.the-alpha-group.com. **Description:** A temporary agency that also offers some permanent placements and resume/career counseling services. Client company pays fee. **Specializes in the areas of:** Administration; General Management; Light Industrial; Secretarial. **Positions commonly filled include:** Accountant; Administrative Assistant; Administrative Manager; Assistant Manager; Bank Officer/Manager; Blue-Collar Worker Supervisor; Branch Manager; Clerical Supervisor; Construction Contractor; Consultant; Customer Service Representative; Electrician; General Manager; Human Resources Manager; Management Analyst/Consultant; Operations Manager. **Corporate headquarters location:** This Location. **Average salary range of placements:** Less than $20,000. **Number of placements per year:** 500 - 999.

ANODYNE CORPORATION
1515 Hancock Street, Quincy MA 02169. **Contact:** Recruiter. **Description:** A temporary agency. Anodyne Corporation is a member of the Massachusetts Association of Temporary Help Services and the National Association of Temporary Help Services. Founded in 1972. **Specializes in the areas of:** Clerical; Health/Medical; Industrial. **Positions commonly filled include:** Bookkeeper; Clerk; Computer Programmer; Data Entry Clerk; Executive Assistant; Home Health Aide; Industrial Nurse; Licensed Practical Nurse; Light Industrial Worker; Nursing Aide; Product Specialist; Receptionist; Registered Nurse; Secretary; Shipping and Receiving Clerk; Telemarketer; Typist/Word Processor. **Office hours:** Monday - Friday, 7:00 a.m. - 5:00 p.m.; Saturday - Sunday, 8:00 a.m. - 4:00 p.m. **Other U.S. locations:** Waltham MA.

AQUENT PARTNERS
711 Boylston Street, Boston MA 02116. 617/535-6000. **Toll-free phone:** 877/PARTNER. **Fax:** 617/535-6001. **Contact:** David Daganhardt, Manager. **E-mail address:** ddaganhardt@aquent.com. **World Wide Web address:** http://www.aquentpartner.com. **Description:** A temporary agency that provides placements for creative, Web, and technical professionals. Aquent Partners also provides some temp-to-perm, permanent, and contract placements. **Specializes in the areas of:** Administration; Art/Design; Communications; Computer Science/Software; Marketing. **Positions commonly filled include:** Computer Animator; Computer Engineer; Computer Operator; Computer Programmer; Computer Support Tech.; Computer Tech.; Content Developer; Database Administrator; Database Manager; Desktop Publishing Specialist; Editor; Editorial Assistant; Graphic Artist; Graphic Designer; Internet Services Manager; Managing Editor; MIS Specialist; Multimedia Designer; Network/Systems Administrator; Production Manager; Project Manager; Software Engineer; SQL Programmer; Systems Analyst; Systems Manager; Technical Writer/Editor; Webmaster. **Benefits available to temporary workers:** 401(k); Dental Insurance; Disability Coverage; Medical Insurance. **CEO:** John Chuang.

ARBOR ASSOCIATES
15 Court Square, Suite 1050, Boston MA 02108. 617/227-8829. **Contact:** Mary Jo Welch, Director of Child Care. **Description:** A temporary agency that places behavioral health, human services, and child care professionals in residential, hospital, and daycare center settings. Arbor Associates also provides some contract services. **Specializes in the areas of:** Eldercare, In-Home; Human Services. **Positions commonly filled include:** Counselor; Daycare Teacher; Social Worker; Teacher Aide. **Other U.S. locations:** Framingham MA; Lawrence MA; Worcester MA; Providence RI. **Number of placements per year:** 1000+.

ATTORNEY SPECIAL ASSIGNMENT PLACEMENT PARALEGAL RESOURCE CENTER, INC.
4 Faneuil Hall Market Place, 4th Floor, Boston MA 02109-1647. 617/742-0112. **Fax:** 617/742-1417. **Contact:** Shelley Widoff, President. **Description:** A temporary agency that also provides some permanent placements. Paralegal Resource Center, Inc. (also at this location; 617/742-1939; http://www.paralegalboston.com) is a permanent employment agency that also provides some temporary placements. Client company pays fee. **Specializes in the areas of:** Finance; Legal; Real Estate. **Positions commonly filled include:** Attorney; Contract/Grant Administrator; Paralegal. **Corporate headquarters location:** This Location. **Average salary range of placements:** $30,000 - $100,000. **Number of placements per year:** 200 - 499.

B&M ASSOCIATES
18 Commerce Way, Suite 5000, Woburn MA 01801. 781/938-9120. **Fax:** 781/932-3930. **Contact:** Staffing Services. **World Wide Web address:** http://www.bmanet.com. **Description:** A temporary agency that also provides some permanent placements. **Specializes in the areas of:** Computer Science/Software; Engineering; Scientific; Technical. **Positions commonly filled include:** Aerospace Engineer; Applications Engineer; Buyer; Chemical Engineer; Civil Engineer; Computer Operator; Computer Programmer; Cost Estimator; Database Manager; Design Engineer; Draftsperson; Editor; Electrical/Electronics Engineer; Industrial Engineer; Manufacturing Engineer; Mechanical Engineer; MIS Specialist; Multimedia Designer; Purchasing Agent/Manager; Quality Control Supervisor; Software Engineer; Systems Analyst; Technical Writer/Editor. **Benefits available to temporary workers:** 401(k); Dental Insurance; Medical Insurance; Section 125 Plan; Vacation Pay. **Corporate headquarters location:** This Location. **Other U.S. locations:** San Diego CA; Santa Ana CA; Manchester NH; Dallas TX; Falls Church VA. **Average salary range of placements:** $30,000 - $50,000. **Number of placements per year:** 500 - 999.

BRATTLE TEMPS
50 Congress Street, Suite 935, Boston MA 02109. 617/523-4600. **Contact:** Recruiter. **Description:** A temporary agency. **Specializes in the areas of:** Advertising; Architecture/Construction; Education; Health/Medical; Nonprofit; Publishing; Secretarial. **Positions commonly filled include:** Administrative Assistant; Customer Service Rep.; Editor; Education Administrator; Human Resources Specialist; Human Service Worker; Librarian; Typist/Word Processor. **Average salary range of placements:** $20,000 - $29,999. **Number of placements per year:** 1000+.

CORPORATE STAFFING SOLUTIONS
180 Westfield Street, West Springfield MA 01089. 413/739-4100. **Fax:** 413/739-5584. **Contact:** Jeffrey N. Schneider, Vice President. **Description:** A temporary agency. **Specializes in the areas of:** Accounting/Auditing; Administration; Advertising; Finance; Industrial; Insurance; Legal; Manufacturing; Marketing; MIS/EDP; Personnel/Labor Relations; Sales; Secretarial. **Positions commonly filled include:** Accountant; Advertising Clerk; Auditor; Branch Manager; Claim Rep.; Computer Programmer; Customer Service Rep.; Human Service Worker; Paralegal; Purchasing

Agent/Manager; Restaurant/Food Service Manager; Services Sales Representative; Systems Analyst; Telecommunications Manager; Typist/Word Processor. **Benefits available to temporary workers:** Medical Insurance; Paid Holidays; Paid Vacation. **Corporate headquarters location:** Wallingford CT. **Number of placements per year:** 1000+.

DAVIS COMPANIES
33 Boston Post Road West, Marlborough MA 01752. 508/480-9500. **Fax:** 508/481-8519. **Contact:** Andrea Pion, Vice President. **Description:** A temporary agency that also offers some permanent placements. **Specializes in the areas of:** Accounting/Auditing; Banking; Finance; Insurance. **Positions commonly filled include:** Bank Officer/Manager; Branch Manager; Brokerage Clerk; Budget Analyst; Cost Estimator; Credit Manager; Financial Analyst; Insurance Agent/Broker; Securities Sales Representative. **Average salary range of placements:** $30,000 - $50,000. **Number of placements per year:** 1000+.

DUNHILL STAFFING SYSTEMS
138 Memorial Avenue, West Springfield MA 01089. 413/733-5147. **Contact:** Manager. **Description:** A temporary agency. **Specializes in the areas of:** Accounting/Auditing; Administration; Computer Science/Software; Engineering; Health/Medical; Industrial; Legal; Manufacturing; Personnel/Labor Relations; Sales; Secretarial. **Positions commonly filled include:** Accountant/Auditor; Administrative Manager; Advertising Clerk; Automotive Mechanic; Bank Officer/Manager; Biochemist; Biological Scientist; Biomedical Engineer; Blue-Collar Worker Supervisor; Branch Manager; Buyer; Chemical Engineer; Civil Engineer; Claim Rep.; Clerical Supervisor; Computer Programmer; Counselor; Customer Service Rep.; Design Engineer; Draftsperson; Electrical/Electronics Engineer; Environmental Engineer; General Manager; Human Resources Specialist; Industrial Engineer; Industrial Production Manager; Management Trainee; Manufacturer's/Wholesaler's Sales Rep.; Market Research Analyst; Medical Records Technician; MIS Specialist; Nuclear Engineer; Operations/Production Manager; Paralegal; Property and Real Estate Manager; Public Relations Specialist; Services Sales Representative; Software Engineer; Systems Analyst; Telecommunications Manager; Typist/Word Processor; Underwriter/Assistant Underwriter. **Benefits available to temporary workers:** Medical Insurance; Paid Holidays; Paid Vacation. **Corporate headquarters location:** Long Island NY. **Other U.S. locations:** Nationwide. **Average salary range of placements:** $20,000 - $29,999. **Number of placements per year:** 100 - 199.

ENDICOTT & COLBY PLACEMENT COMPANY
7 Faneuil Hall, Boston MA 02109. 617/723-2351. **Contact:** Manager. **Description:** A temporary agency that also provides some permanent and contract placements. Placement Company (also at this location) is a permanent employment agency specializing in providing placements in accounting and finance. **Specializes in the areas of:** Administration; Distribution; Manufacturing; Warehousing; Word Processing. **Corporate headquarters location:** This Location.

ENGINEERING MANAGEMENT SUPPORT, INC.
P.O. Box 5043, 330 Boston Road, Billerica MA 01821. 978/667-0896. **Toll-free phone:** 800/661-8268. **Fax:** 978/667-1630. **Contact:** Valerie Wrenn, Recruiter. **E-mail address:** emsi@tiac.net. **World Wide Web address:** http://www.tiac.net/users/emsi. **Description:** A temporary agency that also provides some permanent placements. **Specializes in the areas of:** Engineering; High-Tech; Industrial; Manufacturing; Technical. **Positions commonly filled include:** Administrative Assistant; Computer Programmer; Design Engineer; Designer; Electrical/Electronics Engineer; Electrician; Industrial Engineer; Mechanical Engineer; MIS Specialist; Purchasing Agent/Manager; Secretary;

Software Engineer; Systems Analyst; Transportation/Traffic Specialist. **Average salary range of placements:** $20,000 - $29,999. **Number of placements per year:** 100 - 199.

GENERAL COMPUTER RESOURCES (GCR)
24 Ray Avenue, Suite 105, Burlington MA 01803. 781/270-7020. **Contact:** Manager. **Description:** A temporary agency. **Specializes in the areas of:** Computer Hardware/Software; Computer Programming; Computer Science/Software.

HIREKNOWLEDGE
100 Boylston Street, Suite 1070, Boston MA 02116. 617/350-3033. **Toll-free phone:** 800/937-3622. **Fax:** 617/350-3076. **Contact:** Recruiter. **World Wide Web address:** http://www.hireknowledge.com. **Description:** A temporary agency placing creative and technical individuals. The agency also offers some temp-to-perm and permanent placements. Client company pays fee. **Specializes in the areas of:** Advertising; Art/Design; Computer Science/Software; Internet Development; Internet Marketing; MIS/EDP; Printing; Publishing. **Positions commonly filled include:** Applications Engineer; AS400 Programmer Analyst; Computer Animator; Computer Engineer; Computer Operator; Computer Programmer; Computer Scientist; Computer Support Tech.; Content Developer; Database Administrator; Database Manager; Editor; Editorial Assistant; Graphic Artist; Graphic Designer; Internet Services Manager; Managing Editor; MIS Specialist; Multimedia Designer; Network Administrator; Software Engineer; SQL Programmer; Systems Analyst; Systems Manager; Technical Writer/Editor; Webmaster. **Benefits available to temporary workers:** 401(k); Direct Deposit; Health Benefits; Vacation Pay. **Corporate headquarters location:** Providence RI. **Other U.S. locations:** Nationwide. **Average salary range of placements:** $30,000 - $49,999. **Number of placements per year:** 200 - 499.

INTERIM PERSONNEL
One State Street, Suite 550, Boston MA 02109. 617/248-8855. **Fax:** 617/248-1991. **Contact:** Branch Manager. **Description:** A temporary agency. **Specializes in the areas of:** Accounting/Auditing; Legal; Sales; Secretarial. **Positions commonly filled include:** Accountant/Auditor; Claim Rep.; Customer Service Representative; Paralegal; Typist/Word Processor. **Corporate headquarters location:** Fort Lauderdale FL. **Other U.S. locations:** Nationwide. **Number of placements per year:** 1000+.

INTERIM PERSONNEL
68 Westfield Street, West Springfield MA 01089. 413/781-4120. **Fax:** 413/747-9347. **Contact:** David Stickles, Manager. **Description:** A temporary agency. **Specializes in the areas of:** Accounting/Auditing; Industrial; Secretarial. **Positions commonly filled include:** Accountant/Auditor; Administrative Manager; Blue-Collar Worker Supervisor; Branch Manager; Claim Rep.; Clerical Supervisor; Customer Service Rep.; Hotel Manager; Management Trainee; Restaurant/Food Service Manager; Services Sales Rep.; Systems Analyst; Typist/Word Processor. **Benefits available to temporary workers:** Medical Insurance; Paid Vacation. **Corporate headquarters location:** Fort Lauderdale FL. **Other U.S. locations:** Nationwide. **Average salary range of placements:** $20,000 - $29,999. **Number of placements per year:** 1000+.

JOHNSON & HILL STAFFING SERVICE
95 State Street, Suite 501, Springfield MA 01103. 413/746-3535. **Contact:** Andrea Hill, Vice President of Operations. **Description:** A temporary agency that also offers some permanent placements. **Specializes in the areas of:** Banking; Education; Finance; General Management; Health/Medical; Industrial; Insurance; Legal; Manufacturing; Personnel/Labor Relations; Secretarial. **Positions commonly filled include:** Accountant/Auditor; Computer Programmer; Customer Service Rep.; Human Resources Specialist; Market Research Analyst; Paralegal; Purchasing Agent/Manager;

Quality Control Supervisor; Technical Writer/Editor; Typist/Word Processor. **Benefits available to temporary workers:** Medical Insurance; Paid Holidays; Paid Vacation. **Other U.S. locations:** Northampton MA. **Average salary range of placements:** $20,000 - $29,999. **Number of placements per year:** 500 - 999.

KELLY SERVICES, INC.
250 Commercial Street, Worcester MA 01608. 508/753-2954. **Contact:** Office Manager. **Description:** A temporary agency. **Specializes in the areas of:** Clerical; Industrial; Sales; Technical. **Positions commonly filled include:** Administrative Assistant; Bookkeeper; Clerk; Factory Worker; Legal Secretary; Light Industrial Worker; Receptionist; Secretary; Typist/Word Processor. **Corporate headquarters location:** Troy MI. **International locations:** Worldwide. **Number of placements per year:** 1000+.

KELLY SERVICES, INC.
75 South Church Street, 3rd Floor, Pittsfield MA 01201-6132. 413/445-4528. **Contact:** Christine MacNew, Supervisor/Account Representative. **Description:** A temporary agency. **Specializes in the areas of:** Accounting/Auditing; Personnel/Labor Relations; Secretarial; Technical. **Positions commonly filled include:** Accountant/Auditor; Medical Records Tech.; Secretary; Typist/Word Processor. **Corporate headquarters location:** Troy MI. **Other U.S. locations:** Nationwide. **International locations:** Worldwide. **Average salary range of placements:** Less than $20,000. **Number of placements per year:** 500 - 999.

KELLY SERVICES, INC.
295 Devonshire Street, Boston MA 02110. 617/482-8833. **Fax:** 617/482-2730. **Contact:** Technical Coordinator. **World Wide Web address:** http://www.kellyservices.com. **Description:** A temporary agency. **Specializes in the areas of:** Computer Science/Software; Education; Finance; Health/Medical; Insurance; Legal; Light Industrial; Marketing; Nonprofit; Sales; Scientific; Secretarial; Technical. **Positions commonly filled include:** Administrative Assistant; Budget Analyst; Buyer; Clerical Supervisor; Computer Operator; Computer Programmer; Customer Service Rep.; Database Manager; Design Engineer; Draftsperson; Editor; Electrical/Electronics Engineer; Financial Analyst; Fund Manager; Graphic Artist; Graphic Designer; Industrial Engineer; Manufacturing Engineer; Mechanical Engineer; MIS Specialist; Quality Control Supervisor; Secretary; Software Engineer; Systems Analyst; Technical Writer/Editor; Typist/Word Processor. **Benefits available to temporary workers:** Health Benefits; Paid Holidays; Vacation Pay. **Corporate headquarters location:** Troy MI. **Other U.S. locations:** Nationwide. **International locations:** Worldwide. **Number of placements per year:** 1000+.

KENNISON & ASSOCIATES, INC.
21 Custom House Street, Boston MA 02110. 617/478-2888. **Fax:** 617/478-2887. **Contact:** Recruiter. **Description:** A temporary agency that also provides some permanent placements. **Specializes in the areas of:** Finance; Legal; Secretarial. **Positions commonly filled include:** Administrative Manager; Brokerage Clerk; Budget Analyst; Clerical Supervisor; Customer Service Rep.; Financial Analyst; Human Resources Specialist; Technical Writer/Editor; Telecommunications Manager; Typist/Word Processor. **Benefits available to temporary workers:** Paid Holidays. **Average salary range of placements:** $30,000 - $50,000. **Number of placements per year:** 200 - 499.

L&L ASSOCIATES & TEMPORARIES
101 Tremont Street, Suite 515, Boston MA 02108-5004. 617/423-4455. **Fax:** 617/423-4955. **Contact:** Susan Yerdon, Director. **Description:** A temporary agency that also provides some permanent placements. **Specializes in the areas of:** Accounting/Auditing; Banking; Health/Medical; Industrial; Insurance; Legal; Light Industrial; Manufacturing; Secretarial. **Positions commonly filled include:** Accountant; Administrative Assistant; Advertising Clerk; Blue-Collar Worker Supervisor; Buyer; Computer Operator; Controller; Credit Manager; Customer Service Rep.; Medical Records Technician; Paralegal; Purchasing Agent/Manager; Secretary; Typist/Word Processor. **Benefits available to temporary workers:** Medical Insurance; Paid Holidays; Paid Vacation. **Corporate headquarters location:** This Location. **Average salary range of placements:** $20,000 - $29,999. **Number of placements per year:** 50 - 99.

LAB SUPPORT INC.
One New England Executive Park, Burlington MA 01803. 781/229-2505. **Fax:** 781/229-1902. **Contact:** Account Manager. **Description:** A temporary agency. **Specializes in the areas of:** Biology; Chemicals; Food; Manufacturing. **Positions commonly filled include:** Biochemist; Biological Scientist; Chemical Engineer; Chemist; Clinical Lab Technician; Food Scientist/Technologist; Quality Control Supervisor; Science Technologist. **Benefits available to temporary workers:** 401(k); Medical Insurance. **Other U.S. locations:** Nationwide. **Average salary range of placements:** $20,000 - $29,999. **Number of placements per year:** 200 - 499.

MANPOWER TEMPORARY SERVICES
10 New England Business Center, Andover MA 01810. 978/685-7778. **Fax:** 978/682-0470. **Contact:** Greg Feddersen, Manager. **Description:** A temporary agency that also provides some permanent placements. **Specializes in the areas of:** Accounting/Auditing; Administration; Banking; Computer Science/Software; Fashion; Finance; Food; Health/Medical; Industrial; Insurance; Manufacturing; Secretarial. **Positions commonly filled include:** Accountant/Auditor; Advertising Clerk; Blue-Collar Worker Supervisor; Buyer; Claim Rep.; Clerical Supervisor; Computer Operator; Computer Programmer; Customer Service Rep.; Database Manager; Human Resources Specialist; Human Service Worker; Insurance Agent/Broker; Medical Records Technician; Secretary; Services Sales Rep.; Software Engineer; Systems Analyst; Typist/Word Processor. **Benefits available to temporary workers:** 401(k); Medical Insurance. **Corporate headquarters location:** Milwaukee WI. **International locations:** Worldwide. **Number of placements per year:** 1000+.

MANPOWER TEMPORARY SERVICES
7 Essex Green Drive, Peabody MA 01960-2920. 978/977-9000. **Fax:** 978/977-9868. **Contact:** Service Representative. **Description:** A temporary agency. **Specializes in the areas of:** Administration; Health/Medical; Industrial; Insurance; Legal; Manufacturing; Personnel/Labor Relations; Sales; Secretarial. **Positions commonly filled include:** Accountant/Auditor; Blue-Collar Worker Supervisor; Buyer; Claim Rep.; Computer Programmer; Customer Service Rep.; Human Resources Specialist; Operations/Production Manager; Paralegal; Quality Control Supervisor; Systems Analyst; Technical Writer/Editor; Typist/Word Processor; Video Production Coordinator. **Benefits available to temporary workers:** Life Insurance; Medical Insurance; Paid Holidays; Paid Vacation. **Corporate headquarters location:** Milwaukee WI. **Other U.S. locations:** Nationwide. **International locations:** Worldwide. **Number of placements per year:** 1000+.

MANPOWER TEMPORARY SERVICES
110 Turnpike Road, Suite 212, Westborough MA 01581-2864. 508/870-0900. **Fax:** 508/870-0707. **Contact:** Ms. Simone Butler, Branch Supervisor. **Description:** A temporary agency that focuses on office and light industrial placements. **Specializes in the areas of:** Industrial; Light Industrial; Manufacturing; Secretarial. **Corporate headquarters location:** Milwaukee WI. **Other U.S. locations:** Nationwide. **International locations:** Worldwide. **Average salary range of placements:** Less than $20,000.

MANPOWER TEMPORARY SERVICES
15 Midstate Drive, Suite 210, Auburn MA 01501-1856. 508/832-8760. **Fax:** 508/832-8763. **Contact:** Michelle McCarthy, Service Representative. **Description:** A temporary agency. **Specializes in the areas of:** Banking; Industrial; Sales. **Positions commonly filled include:** Accountant/Auditor; Customer Service Representative; Receptionist; Typist/Word Processor. **Benefits available to temporary workers:** Bonus Award/Plan; Medical Insurance; Paid Vacation. **Corporate headquarters location:** Milwaukee WI. **Other U.S. locations:** Nationwide. **International locations:** Worldwide. **Average salary range of placements:** Less than $20,000. **Number of placements per year:** 500 - 999.

MANPOWER TEMPORARY SERVICES
101 Federal Street, 21st Floor, Boston MA 02110. 617/443-4100. **Contact:** Branch Manager. **Description:** A temporary agency. **Specializes in the areas of:** Light Industrial; Office Support; Technical; Telemarketing; Word Processing. **Positions commonly filled include:** Accountant; Accounting Clerk; Administrative Assistant; Assembler; Biological Scientist; Bookkeeper; Chemist; Computer Operator; Customer Service Rep.; Designer; Desktop Publishing Specialist; Electrician; Machine Operator; Material Control Specialist; Order Clerk; Packaging/Processing Worker; Painter; Project Engineer; Proofreader; Receptionist; Research Assistant; Secretary; Software Engineer; Systems Analyst; Technical Writer/ Editor; Typist/Word Processor. **Benefits available to temporary workers:** Life Insurance; Medical Insurance; Paid Holidays; Paid Vacation. **Corporate headquarters location:** Milwaukee WI. **International locations:** Worldwide. **Number of placements per year:** 1000+.

MASS TEMPS INC.
P.O. Box 6111, Haverhill MA 01831. 978/469-9004. **Fax:** 978/469-9006. **Contact:** Manager. **Description:** A temporary agency. **Specializes in the areas of:** Industrial; Manufacturing; Nonprofit; Publishing; Retail; Secretarial. **Positions commonly filled include:** Accountant/Auditor; Typist/Word Processor. **Average salary range of placements:** Less than $20,000. **Number of placements per year:** 200 - 499.

MICRO TECH CONSULTANTS INC.
42 Weston Street, Waltham MA 02453. 781/891-4870. **Contact:** Manager. **Description:** A temporary agency that also provides some permanent placements. **Specializes in the areas of:** Engineering; Manufacturing. **Positions commonly filled include:** Buyer; Design Engineer; Designer; Editor; Electrical/Electronics Engineer; Industrial Engineer; Mechanical Engineer; Purchasing Agent/Manager; Quality Control Supervisor; Technical Writer/Editor. **Number of placements per year:** 1000+.

MICRO TECH PROFESSIONALS, INC.
P.O. Box 496, Waltham MA 02451. 781/890-6444. **Fax:** 781/890-3355. **Contact:** Denise Dunne, President. **Description:** A temporary agency. **Specializes in the areas of:** Computer Science/Software; Engineering. **Positions commonly filled include:** MIS Specialist; Multimedia Designer; Software Engineer; Technical Writer/Editor. **Benefits available to temporary workers:** 401(k). **Number of placements per year:** 200 - 499.

MOLARI, INC.
80 Center Street, Pittsfield MA 01201. 413/499-4546. **Toll-free phone:** 800/649-4562. **Fax:** 413/442-6519. **Contact:** Bobby Boll, Director of Personnel. **World Wide Web address:** http://www.molaripeople.com. **Description:** A temporary agency that also provides some permanent placements. **Specializes in the areas of:** Clerical; Health/Medical; Industrial; Office Support. **Positions commonly filled include:** Accountant/Auditor; Administrative Assistant; Blue-Collar Worker Supervisor; Buyer; Certified Nurses Aide; Claim Rep.; Clerical Supervisor; Computer Operator; Computer

Programmer; Customer Service Rep.; Licensed Practical Nurse; Market Research Analyst; Marketing Specialist; MIS Specialist; Physical Therapist; Purchasing Agent/ Manager; Quality Control Supervisor; Recreational Therapist; Registered Nurse; Secretary; Systems Analyst; Technical Writer/Editor; Typist/Word Processor. **Benefits available to temporary workers:** Paid Holidays; Paid Vacation. **Average salary range of placements:** Less than $20,000. **Number of placements per year:** 500 - 999.

NATIONAL ENGINEERING SERVICE
10 Cedar Street, Suite 27, Woburn MA 01801. 781/938-4747. **Contact:** Recruiter. **Description:** A temporary agency. Client company pays fee. **Specializes in the areas of:** Art/Design; Engineering; Scientific; Technical. **Positions commonly filled include:** Design Engineer; Draftsperson; Electrical/Electronics Engineer; Industrial Engineer; Manufacturing Engineer; Mechanical Engineer; Purchasing Agent/Manager; Quality Assurance Engineer. **Number of placements per year:** 500 - 999.

NEED PERSONNEL PLACEMENT
151 Providence Highway, Norwood MA 02062. 781/769-4390. **Fax:** 781/769-1245. **Contact:** Larry Cedrone, Vice President. **E-mail address:** needjobs@ needjobs.com. **World Wide Web address:** http://www. needjobs.com. **Description:** A temporary agency that also provides permanent placements. **Specializes in the areas of:** Accounting; Administration; Architecture/ Construction; Art/Design; Biology; Computer Science/ Software; Economics; Engineering; General Management; Industrial; Manufacturing; Personnel/ Labor Relations; Publishing; Sales; Secretarial; Technical. **Positions commonly filled include:** Accountant; Administrative Assistant; Applications Engineer; Architect; Biochemist; Biological Scientist; Biomedical Engineer; Blue-Collar Worker Supervisor; Broadcast Technician; Buyer; Chemical Engineer; Chemist; CFO; Civil Engineer; Claim Rep.; Clerical Supervisor; Clinical Lab Tech.; Computer Animator; Computer Operator; Computer Programmer; Construction Contractor; Consultant; Controller; Cost Estimator; Credit Manager; Customer Service Rep.; Database Manager; Design Engineer; Draftsperson; Economist; Editor; Editorial Assistant; Electrical/ Electronics Engineer; Electrician; Environmental Engineer; Finance Director; Financial Analyst; General Manager; Geologist/Geophysicist; Health Services Manager; Human Resources Specialist; Industrial Engineer; Industrial Production Manager; Internet Services Manager; Management Analyst/Consultant; Manufacturing Engineer; Market Research Analyst; Marketing Manager; Marketing Specialist; Mechanical Engineer; Medical Records Tech.; Metallurgical Engineer; MIS Specialist; Multimedia Designer; Operations Manager; Paralegal; Production Manager; Project Manager; Purchasing Agent/Manager; Quality Control Supervisor; Sales Engineer; Sales Exec.; Sales Manager; Sales Rep.; Secretary; Software Engineer; Statistician; Surgical Technician; Systems Analyst; Systems Manager; Technical Writer/Editor; Telecommunications Manager; Typist/Word Processor; Underwriter/Assistant Underwriter; Video Production Coordinator; Webmaster. **Number of placements per year:** 500 - 999.

NEW BOSTON SELECT STAFFING
152 Bowdoin Street, Boston MA 02108. 617/720-0990. **Toll-free phone:** 800/833-9080. **Fax:** 617/723-8822. **Contact:** Elizabeth Nolan, Director of Sales and Training. **Description:** A temporary agency that also provides permanent placements. **Specializes in the areas of:** Sales; Secretarial. **Positions commonly filled include:** Administrative Assistant; Bookkeeper; Clerk; Customer Service Rep.; Data Entry Clerk; Legal Secretary; Medical Secretary; Receptionist; Sales Rep.; Secretary; Typist/Word Processor. **Corporate headquarters location:** Woburn MA. **Other area locations:** Braintree MA. **Other U.S. locations:** Atlanta GA. **Number of placements per year:** 500 - 999.

NEW BOSTON SELECT STAFFING
300 Granite Street, Suite 401, Braintree MA 02184. 781/848-2211. **Fax:** 781/356-8105. **Contact:** Manager. **Description:** A temporary agency that also provides some temp-to-perm placements. **Specializes in the areas of:** Administration; Clerical; Light Industrial; Office Support. **Corporate headquarters location:** Woburn MA. **Other area locations:** Boston MA.

NEW PERSPECTIVES PERSONNEL
600 West Cummings Park, Woburn MA 01801. 781/938-8247. **Fax:** 781/932-8622. **Contact:** Marsha Stelman, President. **Description:** A temporary agency that also provides permanent placements. **Specializes in the areas of:** Accounting/Auditing; Clerical; Personnel/Labor Relations; Secretarial. **Positions commonly filled include:** Account Representative; Administrative Assistant; Customer Service Representative; Secretary; Typist/Word Processor. **Benefits available to temporary workers:** Bonus Award/Plan; Dental Insurance; Medical Insurance; Paid Vacation; Referral Bonus Plan. **Corporate headquarters location:** Beverly MA. **Average salary range of placements:** $20,000 - $29,999. **Number of placements per year:** 100 - 199.

OFFICE SPECIALISTS
1256 Park Street, Stoughton MA 02072. 781/341-6070. **Fax:** 781/341-6072. **Contact:** Manager. **World Wide Web address:** http://www.officespec.com. **Description:** A temporary agency that also provides some temp-to-perm placements. Founded in 1963. **Specializes in the areas of:** Accounting/Auditing; Clerical; Office Support; Secretarial; Word Processing. **Positions commonly filled include:** Customer Service Representative; Desktop Publishing Specialist; Typist/Word Processor. **Benefits available to temporary workers:** Medical Insurance; Paid Vacation. **Corporate headquarters location:** Peabody MA. **Other U.S. locations:** Nationwide. **Average salary range of placements:** Less than $20,000. **Number of placements per year:** 1000+.

OFFICE SPECIALISTS
1253 Worcester Road, Suite 102, Framingham MA 01701-5250. 508/879-6332. **Toll-free phone:** 800/472-4949. **Contact:** Staffing Manager. **World Wide Web address:** http://www.officespec.com. **Description:** A temporary agency. Founded in 1963. **Specializes in the areas of:** Accounting/Auditing; Secretarial. **Positions commonly filled include:** Accounting Clerk; Administrative Assistant; Bookkeeper; Customer Service Representative; Data Entry Clerk; Receptionist; Secretary. **Corporate headquarters location:** Peabody MA. **Other U.S. locations:** Nationwide. **Average salary range of placements:** $20,000 - $29,999. **Number of placements per year:** 1000+.

OFFICE SPECIALISTS
800 Hingham Street, Suite 103N, Rockland MA 02370. **Fax:** 781/871-0453. **Contact:** Karen Valicenti, Branch Manager. **World Wide Web address:** http://www. officespec.com. **Description:** A temporary agency that also provides some temp-to-perm placements, project management services, and resident management services. Founded in 1963. **Specializes in the areas of:** Accounting; Clerical; Credit and Collection; Office Automation; Office Support; Secretarial. **Positions commonly filled include:** Accountant; Accounting Clerk; Administrative Assistant; Bilingual Secretary; Bookkeeper; Claim Rep.; Copy Center Operator; Cost Accountant; Customer Service Rep.; Data Entry Clerk; Database Specialist; Desktop Illustrator; Desktop Publishing Specialist; Executive Assistant; Facsimile Operator; Legal Secretary; Loan Processor; Medical Secretary; Message Center Operator; Payroll Clerk; Presentation Specialist; Receptionist; Researcher; Secretary; Spreadsheet Specialist; Staff Accountant; Switchboard Operator; Tax Specialist; Telemarketer; Typist/Word Processor. **Benefits available to temporary workers:** Career Development Program; Computer Training; Life Insurance; Medical Insurance; Paid Holidays; Paid Vacation. **Corporate headquarters**

location: Peabody MA. **Other U.S. locations:** Nationwide.

OFFICETEAM
ACCOUNTEMPS
10 Forbes Road West, Braintree MA 02184. 781/356-0104. **Fax:** 781/848-9866. **Contact:** Jennifer Sweeney, Division Director. **E-mail address:** braintree@officeteam.com. **World Wide Web address:** http://www.officeteam.com. **Description:** A temporary agency. Accountemps (also at this location) provides temporary placements for accounting professionals. **Specializes in the areas of:** Administration; Office Support. **Positions commonly filled include:** Administrative Assistant; Data Entry Clerk; Executive Assistant; Office Manager; Receptionist; Secretary; Switchboard Operator; Typist/Word Processor. **Corporate headquarters location:** Menlo Park CA. **Other U.S. locations:** Nationwide. **International locations:** Canada.

OFFICETEAM
ROBERT HALF INTERNATIONAL
14 Story Street, Cambridge MA 02138. 617/876-9000. **Fax:** 617/354-7025. **Contact:** Jill Pappalardo, Area Manager. **World Wide Web address:** http://www. officeteam.com. **Description:** A temporary agency. **Specializes in the areas of:** Administration; Data Processing; Secretarial. **Positions commonly filled include:** Advertising Clerk; Clerical Supervisor. **Benefits available to temporary workers:** Medical Insurance; Referral Bonus Plan. **Corporate headquarters location:** Menlo Park CA. **Other U.S. locations:** Nationwide. **International locations:** Canada. **Average salary range of placements:** $20,000 - $29,999. **Number of placements per year:** 1000+.

OLSTEN STAFFING SERVICES
600 West Cummings Park, Suite 1800, Woburn MA 01801. **Toll-free phone:** 800/964-9490. **Fax:** 781/938-9929. **Contact:** Branch Manager. **World Wide Web address:** http://www.worknow.com. **Description:** A temporary agency. **Specializes in the areas of:** Administration; Manufacturing; Personnel/Labor Relations; Secretarial. **Positions commonly filled include:** Administrative Manager; Clerical Supervisor; Customer Service Rep.; Quality Control Supervisor; Typist/Word Processor. **Benefits available to temporary workers:** Medical Insurance; Paid Vacation. **Corporate headquarters location:** Melville NY. **Other U.S. locations:** Nationwide. **International locations:** Worldwide. **Average salary range of placements:** $20,000 - $29,999. **Number of placements per year:** 500 - 999.

OLSTEN STAFFING SERVICES
111 Speen Street, Suite 304, Framingham MA 01701. 508/875-1970. **Fax:** 508/875-7779. **Contact:** Amy Dunklee, Personnel Supervisor. **World Wide Web address:** http://www.worknow.com. **Description:** A temporary agency. Founded in 1950. **Specializes in the areas of:** Customer Service; Secretarial. **Positions commonly filled include:** Administrative Assistant; Clerical Supervisor; Customer Service Representative; Secretary; Typist/Word Processor. **Benefits available to temporary workers:** Medical Insurance; Paid Vacation. **Corporate headquarters location:** Melville NY. **Other U.S. locations:** Nationwide. **International locations:** Worldwide. **Average salary range of placements:** $20,000 - $29,999. **Number of placements per year:** 1000+.

POMERANTZ STAFFING SERVICES
Merchant's Row Mall, 2053 Washington Street, Hanover MA 02339. **Contact:** Manager. **Description:** A temporary agency that also provides some permanent placements and outsourcing services. Founded in 1974. **Specializes in the areas of:** Accounting; Administration; Clerical; Finance; Light Industrial; Manufacturing; Office Automation; Office Support; Production; Sales; Secretarial; Technical. **Positions commonly filled include:** Accountant; Laboratory Technician;

Merchandiser; Secretary. **Benefits available to temporary workers:** 401(k); Credit Union; Direct Deposit; Life Insurance; Medical Insurance; Mortgage Program; Paid Vacation; Placement Assistance; Psychological Counseling; Referral Bonus Plan; Software Training. **Corporate headquarters location:** Watchung NJ. **Other U.S. locations:** Nationwide.

PRO STAFF
790 Boston Road, Billerica MA 01821. 978/663-5378. **Fax:** 978/670-2103. **Contact:** Manager. **Description:** A temporary agency that also provides temp-to-perm placements. **Specializes in the areas of:** Accounting/ Auditing; Administration; Advertising; Computer Science/Software; General Management; Health/ Medical; Industrial; Personnel/Labor Relations; Publishing; Retail; Sales; Secretarial; Technical. **Positions commonly filled include:** Accountant/Auditor; Administrative Assistant; Bank Officer/Manager; Bookkeeper; Buyer; Clerk; Customer Service Rep.; Draftsperson; Editor; EDP Specialist; Factory Worker; Legal Secretary; Light Industrial Worker; Marketing Specialist; Medical Secretary; Nurse; Operations/ Production Manager; Purchasing Agent/Manager; Quality Control Supervisor; Receptionist; Reporter; Sales Rep.; Secretary; Technical Illustrator; Technical Rep.; Technical Writer/Editor; Technician; Typist/Word Processor. **Benefits available to temporary workers:** 401(k); Medical Insurance; Paid Holidays; Paid Vacation. **Other U.S. locations:** Nationwide. **Average salary range of placements:** $20,000 - $29,999. **Number of placements per year:** 200 - 499.

PRO STAFF
1661 Worcester Road, Suite 101, Framingham MA 01701. 508/879-9251. **Contact:** Manager. **Description:** A temporary agency. **Specializes in the areas of:** Accounting; Finance; Human Services; Manufacturing; Office Support. **Positions commonly filled include:** Accountant; Administrative Assistant; Bookkeeper; Buyer; Clerk; Customer Service Rep.; Data Entry Clerk; Factory Worker; Legal Secretary; Medical Secretary; Quality Control Supervisor; Receptionist; Sales Rep.; Secretary; Technical Writer/Editor; Typist/Word Processor; Warehouse/Distribution Worker.

PRO STAFF
7 Alfred Street, Woburn MA 01801. 781/937-0111. **Contact:** Manager. **Description:** A temporary agency that also provides some permanent placements. **Specializes in the areas of:** Graphic Arts; Multimedia.

PRO STAFF
535 Boylston Street, 11th Floor, Boston MA 02116. 617/357-0330. **Fax:** 617/351-2611. **Contact:** Manager. **Description:** A temporary agency. **Specializes in the areas of:** Accounting/Auditing.

RELIEF RESOURCES INC.
P.O. Box 538, Hadley MA 01035-0538. 413/584-7667. **Toll-free phone:** 800/639-5094. **Contact:** Dale Jones, Recruiter. **Description:** A temporary agency. **Specializes in the areas of:** Nonprofit. **Positions commonly filled include:** Counselor; Human Service Worker; Preschool Worker; Special Education Teacher; Teacher Aide; Teacher/Professor. **Benefits available to temporary workers:** Paid Vacation. **Other area locations:** Cambridge MA; Worcester MA. **Other U.S. locations:** Hartford CT; Providence RI. **Average salary range of placements:** Less than $20,000. **Number of placements per year:** 1000+.

REMEDY INTELLIGENT STAFFING
1250 Hancock Street, President's Place, Suite 105 North, Quincy MA 02169. 617/471-9675. **Fax:** 617/471-3796. **Contact:** Bill Bacigalupo, Owner. **E-mail address:** remquin@cre8v.com. **World Wide Web address:** http://www.remedystaff.com. **Description:** A temporary agency that also provides some temp-to-perm and permanent placements. **NOTE:** This location focuses on placing individuals in office, accounting, and managerial positions. Jobseekers interested in positions in light

industrial, technical, and logistics should forward their resumes to Remedy Intelligent Staffing, 14 Allenyne Street, Quincy MA 02169; 617/774-1775. **Specializes in the areas of:** Accounting; Administration; Banking; Finance; Marketing; Nonprofit; Retail; Sales; Secretarial. **Positions commonly filled include:** Account Manager; Account Rep.; Accountant; Adjuster; Administrative Assistant; Administrative Manager; Advertising Clerk; Applications Engineer; Architect; AS400 Programmer Analyst; Assistant Manager; Auditor; Bank Officer/ Manager; Blue-Collar Worker Supervisor; Branch Manager; Budget Analyst; Buyer; Chemical Engineer; CFO; Civil Engineer; Claim Rep.; Clerical Supervisor; Clinical Lab Tech.; Computer Engineer; Computer Operator; Computer Programmer; Computer Support Tech.; Computer Tech.; Construction Contractor; Controller; Cost Estimator; Credit Manager; Customer Service Rep.; Database Administrator; Design Engineer; Draftsperson; Electrical/Electronics Engineer; Environmental Engineer; Finance Director; Financial Analyst; Fund Manager; General Manager; Human Resources Manager; Industrial Engineer; Industrial Production Manager; Internet Services Manager; Management Analyst/Consultant; Management Trainee; Manufacturing Engineer; Market Research Analyst; Marketing Specialist; Mechanical Engineer; Medical Assistant; Metallurgical Engineer; MIS Specialist; Network/Systems Administrator; Operations Manager; Paralegal; Production Manager; Project Manager; Public Relations Specialist; Purchasing Agent/Manager; Quality Assurance Engineer; Real Estate Agent; Sales Engineer; Sales Exec.; Sales Manager; Sales Rep.; Secretary; Software Engineer; Transportation/Traffic Specialist; Typist/Word Processor; Underwriter/Assistant Underwriter; Vice President of Finance; Webmaster. **Benefits available to temporary workers:** 401(k); Dental Insurance; Medical Insurance. **Office hours:** Monday - Friday, 8:00 a.m. - 6:00 p.m. **Corporate headquarters location:** Aliso Viejo CA. **Other U.S. locations:** Nationwide. **Average salary range of placements:** $30,000 - $49,999. **Number of placements per year:** 1000+.

REMEDY INTELLIGENT STAFFING
14 Alleyne Street, Quincy MA 02169. 617/774-1775. **Contact:** Bill Bacigalupo, Owner. **World Wide Web address:** http://www.remedystaff.com. **Description:** A temporary agency that also provides some permanent and temp-to-perm placements. **NOTE:** This location focuses on placing individuals in light industrial, technical, and logistics positions. Jobseekers interested in office, accounting, and managerial positions should forward their resumes to Remedy Intelligent Staffing, 1250 Hancock Street, President's Place, Suite 105 North, Quincy MA 02169; 617/471-9675. **Specializes in the areas of:** Architecture/Construction; Computer Science/Software; Engineering; Industrial; Internet Development; Light Industrial; Marketing; Nonprofit; Retail; Sales; Scientific; Technical. **Positions commonly filled include:** Account Manager; Account Rep.; Accountant; Adjuster; Administrative Assistant; Administrative Manager; Advertising Clerk; Applications Engineer; Architect; AS400 Programmer Analyst; Assistant Manager; Auditor; Bank Officer/ Manager; Blue-Collar Worker Supervisor; Branch Manager; Budget Analyst; Buyer; CFO; Civil Engineer; Claim Rep.; Clinical Lab Tech.; Computer Engineer; Computer Operator; Computer Programmer; Computer Support Tech.; Computer Tech.; Construction Contractor; Controller; Cost Estimator; Credit Manager; Customer Service Rep.; Database Administrator; Design Engineer; Draftsperson; Electrical/Electronics Engineer; Environmental Engineer; Finance Director; Financial Analyst; Fund Manager; Human Resources Manager; Industrial Engineer; Industrial Production Manager; Internet Services Manager; Management Analyst/ Consultant; Management Trainee; Manufacturing Engineer; Market Research Analyst; Marketing Specialist; Mechanical Engineer; Medical Assistant; Metallurgical Engineer; MIS Specialist; Network/ Systems Administrator; Operations Manager; Paralegal; Production Manager; Project Manager; Public Relations

Specialist; Purchasing Agent/Manager; Quality Assurance Engineer; Quality Control Supervisor; Real Estate Agent; Sales Engineer; Sales Exec.; Sales Manager; Sales Rep.; Secretary; Software Engineer; Transportation/Traffic Specialist; Typist/Word Processor; Underwriter/Assistant Underwriter; Vice President of Finance; Webmaster. **Benefits available to temporary workers:** 401(k); Dental Insurance; Medical Insurance. **Corporate headquarters location:** Aliso Viejo CA. **Other U.S. locations:** Nationwide. **Average salary range of placements:** $30,000 - $49,999. **Number of placements per year:** 1000+.

SALES TEMPS INC.
49 Winchester Street, Newton MA 02461. 617/964-8828. **Fax:** 617/332-0365. **Contact:** Ed Katzenberg, President. **E-mail address:** katzed@salestemps.com. **World Wide Web address:** http://www.salestemps.com. **Description:** A temporary agency. **Specializes in the areas of:** Sales. **Positions commonly filled include:** Account Manager; Account Rep.; Applications Engineer; Customer Service Rep.; Manufacturer's/Wholesaler's Sales Rep.; Market Research Analyst; Marketing Manager; Sales Engineer; Sales Exec.; Sales Manager; Sales Rep.; Securities Sales Rep.; Services Sales Rep.; Vice President of Marketing and Sales. **Average salary range of placements:** $30,000 - $50,000. **Number of placements per year:** 50 - 99.

SELECTEMPS
50 Franklin Street, Worcester MA 01608-1914. 508/792-1212. **Fax:** 508/792-5944. **Contact:** Branch Manager. **Description:** A temporary agency. **Specializes in the areas of:** Advertising; Architecture/Construction; Banking; Biology; Broadcasting; Computer Science/Software; Electronics; Industrial; Insurance; Legal; Light Industrial; Publishing; Sales; Secretarial; Technical. **Positions commonly filled include:** Typist/Word Processor. **Benefits available to temporary workers:** Bonus Award/Plan; Paid Vacation. **Corporate headquarters location:** Framingham MA. **Average salary range of placements:** $20,000 - $29,999. **Number of placements per year:** 1000+.

SPECIAL COUNSEL
40 Broad Street, 2nd Floor, Boston MA 02109. 617/338-7700. **Fax:** 617/338-1777. **Contact:** Manager. **World Wide Web address:** http://www.specialcounsel.com. **Description:** A temporary agency that also provides permanent placements. **Specializes in the areas of:** Legal.

SUMMIT TECHNICAL SERVICES INC.
50 Braintree Hill Park, Suite 201, Braintree MA 02184. 781/848-4321. **Fax:** 781/848-2306. **Contact:** Recruiting Manager. **World Wide Web address:** http://www.summit-technical.com. **Description:** A temporary agency that also provides some permanent placements. **Specializes in the areas of:** Architecture/Construction; Art/Design; Computer Science/Software; Engineering; Manufacturing. **Positions commonly filled include:** Buyer; Chemical Engineer; Chemist; Computer Programmer; Design Engineer; Designer; Draftsperson; Electrician; Graphic Artist; Graphic Designer; Industrial Engineer; Manufacturing Engineer; Materials Engineer; Mechanical Engineer; Purchasing Agent/Manager; Quality Control Supervisor; Software Engineer; Technical Writer/Editor; Webmaster. **Benefits available to temporary workers:** 401(k); Direct Deposit; Medical Insurance. **Corporate headquarters location:** Warwick RI. **Other U.S. locations:** Nationwide. **Average salary range of placements:** $30,000 - $50,000. **Number of placements per year:** 200 - 499.

TAC STAFFING SERVICES
980 Washington Street, Suite 218, Dedham MA 02026. 781/326-9056. **Fax:** 781/326-1958. **Contact:** Manager. **Description:** A temporary agency. **Specializes in the areas of:** Advertising; Education; Insurance; Nonprofit; Personnel/Labor Relations; Publishing; Secretarial. **Corporate headquarters location:** Newton MA. **Other U.S. locations:** Nationwide.

TAC STAFFING SERVICES
291 Main Street, Milford MA 01757. 508/478-5851. **Fax:** 508/478-5856. **Contact:** Personnel Recruiter. **Description:** A temporary agency. **Specializes in the areas of:** Accounting/Auditing; Secretarial. **Positions commonly filled include:** Assembler; Customer Service Representative; Receptionist; Secretary; Typist/Word Processor. **Benefits available to temporary workers:** Bonus Award/Plan; Computer Training; Medical Insurance. **Corporate headquarters location:** Newton MA. **Other U.S. locations:** Nationwide. **Number of placements per year:** 1000+.

TAD STAFFING SERVICES
221 Chelmsford Street, Chelmsford MA 01824. 978/256-5244. **Contact:** Manager. **Description:** A temporary agency. **Specializes in the areas of:** Accounting/Auditing; Clerical; Computer Hardware/Software; Engineering; Finance; Food; Health/Medical; Insurance; Manufacturing; Personnel/Labor Relations; Publishing. **Positions commonly filled include:** Accountant/Auditor; Administrative Assistant; Bookkeeper; Clerk; Computer Operator; Customer Service Representative; Data Entry Clerk; Driver; Factory Worker; Financial Analyst; Legal Secretary; Light Industrial Worker; Purchasing Agent/Manager; Receptionist; Secretary; Stenographer; Technician; Typist/Word Processor. **Other U.S. locations:** Nationwide. **Number of placements per year:** 1000+.

TAD STAFFING SERVICES
1250 Hancock Street, Quincy MA 02169. 617/472-2600. **Fax:** 617/770-3624. **Contact:** Parra Curry, Area Manager. **World Wide Web address:** http://www.adecco.com. **Description:** A temporary agency that also provides permanent placements. **Specializes in the areas of:** Administration; Banking; Fashion; Light Industrial; Retail; Secretarial. **Positions commonly filled include:** Administrative Assistant; Clerical Supervisor; Secretary; Typist/Word Processor. **Benefits available to temporary workers:** 401(k); Dental Insurance; Medical Insurance; Paid Holidays; Paid Vacation; Tuition Assistance. **Other U.S. locations:** Nationwide. **Average salary range of placements:** $20,000 - $29,999. **Number of placements per year:** 500 - 999.

TRAVCORPS
40 Eastern Avenue, Malden MA 02148. 781/322-2600. **Toll-free phone:** 800/343-3270. **Fax:** 781/397-0879. **Contact:** Recruiting & Sourcing Division. **World Wide Web address:** http://www.travcorps.com. **Description:** A temporary agency that also offers some permanent placements. Client company pays fee. **Specializes in the areas of:** Health/Medical. **Positions commonly filled include:** Certified Occupational Therapy Assistant; Nurse Practitioner; Occupational Therapist; Physical Therapist; Physical Therapy Assistant; Speech-Language Pathologist; Surgical Technician. **Benefits available to temporary workers:** 401(k); Bonus Award/Plan; Dental Insurance; Housing Allowance; Life Insurance; Medical Insurance. **Corporate headquarters location:** This Location. **Other U.S. locations:** Nationwide.

TRICOR ASSOCIATES
50 North Street, Medfield MA 02052-1624. 508/359-4455. **Fax:** 508/359-7965. **Contact:** Dotti Cohen, Partner. **Description:** A temporary agency that also provides some permanent placements. **Specializes in the areas of:** Accounting/Auditing; Administration; Advertising; Sales; Secretarial. **Positions commonly filled include:** Accountant/Auditor; Administrative Manager; Advertising Clerk; Buyer; Claim Rep.; Customer Service Rep.; Medical Records Technician.

UNLIMITED OPPORTUNITIES OF NEW ENGLAND
209 West Central Street, Suite 107, Natick MA 01760-3716. 508/650-3612. **Fax:** 508/652-0748. **Contact:** Recruiter. **Description:** A temporary agency that also provides permanent placements. **Specializes in the areas of:** Sales; Secretarial. **Positions commonly filled include:** Account Manager; Account Rep.; Accountant; Administrative Assistant; Administrative Manager;

Advertising Clerk; Customer Service Rep.; Human Resources Manager; Marketing Manager; Marketing Specialist; Sales Manager; Sales Representative; Secretary; Typist/Word Processor. **Benefits available to temporary workers:** Bonus Award/Plan; Paid Holidays. **Corporate headquarters location:** This Location. **Average salary range of placements:** $30,000 - $50,000. **Number of placements per year:** 1000+.

VOLT SERVICES GROUP
400 West Cummings Park, Suite 1800, Woburn MA 01801. 781/938-6969. **Fax:** 781/932-9298. **Contact:** Kelly Neal, Branch Manager. **Description:** A temporary agency. **Specializes in the areas of:** Administration; General Management; Industrial; Legal; Light Industrial; MIS/EDP; Office Support; Personnel/Labor Relations; Sales; Secretarial. **Positions commonly filled include:** Administrative Assistant; Administrative Manager; Blue-Collar Worker Supervisor; Buyer; Claim Rep.; Clerical Supervisor; Computer Operator; Customer Service Rep.; Human Resources Manager; Manufacturing Engineer; Marketing Manager; Marketing Specialist; Medical

Records Technician; Operations Manager; Paralegal; Production Manager; Project Manager; Purchasing Agent/Manager; Quality Control Supervisor; Sales Executive; Sales Manager; Sales Rep.; Secretary; Telecommunications Manager; Typist/Word Processor. **Benefits available to temporary workers:** Daycare Assistance; Dental Insurance; Medical Insurance; Paid Holidays; Paid Vacation. **Corporate headquarters location:** Orange CA. **Average salary range of placements:** $30,000-$50,000. **Number of placements per year:** 1000+.

THE WALLACE LAW REGISTRY
31 St. James Avenue, Suite 910, Boston MA 02116. 617/482-8052. **Toll-free phone:** 800/248-4529. **Fax:** 617/482-8054. **Contact:** Kathleen O'Donohue, Managing Director. **Description:** A temporary agency. **Specializes in the areas of:** Legal. **Positions commonly filled include:** Attorney; Paralegal. **Corporate headquarters location:** Hartford CA. **Average salary range of placements:** More than $50,000. **Number of placements per year:** 100 - 199.

CONTRACT SERVICES FIRMS

AEROTEK, INC.
20 Burlington Mall Road, Suite 100, Burlington MA 01803. 781/505-4100. **Contact:** Manager. **World Wide Web address:** http://www.aerotek.com. **Description:** A contract services firm. **Specializes in the areas of:** Accounting; Administration; Banking; Biology; Chemistry; Engineering; Human Resources; Management; Marketing; Purchasing; Research and Development; Software Development; Technical; Telecommunications. **Corporate headquarters location:** Hanover MD.

AMBIT TECHNOLOGY
4 Faneuil Hall Marketplace, 4th. Floor, Boston MA 02116. 617/367-2990. **Contact:** Manager. **Description:** A contract services firm that provides placements for professionals with AS400 or LAN/WAN experience. **Specializes in the areas of:** Computer Hardware/Software. **Positions commonly filled include:** LAN/WAN Designer/Developer.

CDI CORPORATION
492 Old Connecticut Path, Framingham MA 01701. 508/628-1700. **Fax:** 508/628-1711. **Contact:** Manager. **World Wide Web address:** http://www.cdicorp.com. **Description:** A contract services firm. **Specializes in the areas of:** Design; Engineering; Information Systems; Manufacturing; Technical. **Corporate headquarters location:** Philadelphia PA. **Other U.S. locations:** Nationwide. **International locations:** Worldwide.

COMPUTER EXPRESS INTERNATIONAL
301 North Avenue, Wakefield MA 01880. 781/246-4477. **Contact:** Manager. **Description:** A contract services firm. **Specializes in the areas of:** Computer Operations; Computer Science/Software.

DIGITAL ARTS GROUP
279 Cambridge Street, Burlington MA 01803. 781/273-2780. **Fax:** 781/273-5592. **Contact:** Robert Melillo, President. **Description:** A contract services firm. **Specializes in the areas of:** Computer Science/Software; Consulting; Engineering; Technical. **Positions commonly filled include:** Computer Programmer; Customer Service Rep.; Design Engineer; Designer; Draftsperson; Editor; Electrical/Electronics Engineer; Financial Analyst; Internet Services Manager; Mechanical Engineer; MIS Specialist; Multimedia Designer; Software Engineer; Statistician; Systems Analyst; Technical Writer/Editor; Telecommunications Manager. **Number of placements per year:** 200 - 499.

EDI SPECIALISTS, INC.
P.O. Box 116, Raynham MA 02767-1799. **Toll-free phone:** 800/821-4644. **Contact:** Joe Gilbody, President.

E-mail address: jgilbody@edispecialists.com. **World Wide Web address:** http://www.edispecialists.com. **Description:** A contract services firm. **Specializes in the areas of:** Computer Science/Software. **Positions commonly filled include:** Computer Programmer; Management Analyst/Consultant; MIS Specialist; Software Engineer; Strategic Relations Manager; Systems Analyst; Telecommunications Manager. **Other U.S. locations:** Nationwide. **Average salary range of placements:** More than $50,000. **Number of placements per year:** 200 - 499.

THE ENVIRONMENTAL CAREERS ORGANIZATION
179 South Street, Boston MA 02111. 617/426-4375. **Fax:** 617/423-0998. **Contact:** Manager. **World Wide Web address:** http://www.eco.org. **Description:** A contract services firm. **Specializes in the areas of:** Biology; Computer Science/Software; Engineering; Technical. **Positions commonly filled include:** Biological Scientist; Chemical Engineer; Chemist; Civil Engineer; Computer Programmer; Environmental Engineer; Forester/Conservation Scientist; Geographer; Geologist/Geophysicist; Science Technologist; Surveyor; Systems Analyst; Technical Writer/Editor. **Corporate headquarters location:** This Location. **Average salary range of placements:** $20,000 - $29,999. **Number of placements per year:** 500 - 999.

HALL KINION
10 Burlington Mall Road, Suite 250, Burlington MA 01803. **Toll-free phone:** 800/955-4254. **Fax:** 781/229-7772. **Contact:** Manager. **E-mail address:** boresume@hallkinion.com. **World Wide Web address:** http://www.hallkinion.com. **Description:** A contract services firm that also provides permanent placements. **Specializes in the areas of:** Computer Hardware/Software; Information Systems; Information Technology; Internet Development; Network Administration; Quality Assurance; Systems Administration; Systems Design; Technical Writing.

INTERIM TECHNOLOGY
31 St. James Avenue, Suite 210, Boston MA 02116. 617/542-1700. **Fax:** 617/956-4088. **Contact:** Staffing Specialist. **E-mail address:** itssg-boston@interim.com. **World Wide Web address:** http://www.interim.com. **Description:** A contract services firm. **Specializes in the areas of:** Technical. **Positions commonly filled include:** Computer Operator; Database Manager; MIS Specialist; Systems Analyst; Systems Manager; Technical Support Rep.; Technician. **Benefits available to temporary workers:** 401(k); Dental Insurance; Flexible Schedule; Medical Insurance; Stock Purchase. **Average salary range of placements:** $30,000 - $50,000. **Number of placements per year:** 50 - 99.

LYNX INC.
420 Bedford Street, Suite 200, Lexington MA 02420. 781/274-6400. **Fax:** 781/274-6300. **Contact:** Philip J. Hurd, President. **E-mail address:** discover@lynxinc.com. **World Wide Web address:** http://www.lynxinc.com. **Description:** A contract services firm. **Specializes in the areas of:** Accounting/Auditing; Administration; Computer Science/Software; Finance; MIS/EDP; Scientific; Software Engineering; Technical. **Positions commonly filled include:** Accountant; Applications Engineer; Auditor; Budget Analyst; CFO; Computer Animator; Computer Programmer; Controller; Cost Estimator; Credit Manager; Database Manager; Finance Director; Financial Analyst; Internet Services Manager; MIS Specialist; Multimedia Designer; Online Content Specialist; Software Engineer; Systems Analyst; Systems Manager; Telecommunications Manager; Vice President; Webmaster. **Average salary range of placements:** $30,000 - $50,000. **Number of placements per year:** 200 - 499.

NORRELL STAFFING SERVICES
18 Tremont Street, Boston MA 02108. 978/688-2007. **Contact:** General Manager. **World Wide Web address:** http://www.norrell.com. **Description:** A contract services firm. **Specializes in the areas of:** Administration; Computer Science/Software; Industrial; Manufacturing; Personnel/Labor Relations; Sales; Secretarial; Technical. **Positions commonly filled include:** Accountant/Auditor; Administrative Manager; Advertising Clerk; Blue-Collar Worker Supervisor; Clerical Supervisor; Construction Contractor; Customer Service Rep.; Human Resources Specialist; Manufacturer's/Wholesaler's Sales Rep.; Services Sales Rep.; Software Engineer; Typist/Word Processor. **Benefits available to temporary workers:** 401(k); Medical Insurance; Paid Holidays; Paid Vacation. **Average salary range of placements:** $20,000 - $29,999. **Number of placements per year:** 1000+.

RANDOLPH ASSOCIATES, INC.
950 Massachusetts Avenue, Suite 105, Cambridge MA 02139. 617/441-8777. **Fax:** 617/441-8778. **Contact:** Manager. **Description:** A contract services firm that also provides some permanent placements. Founded in 1984. Client company pays fee. **Positions commonly filled include:** Desktop Publishing Specialist; Editor; Graphic Designer; Instructional Designer; Instructor/Trainer; Online Content Specialist; Proofreader; Technical Illustrator; Technical Writer/Editor; Webmaster.

RESOURCE MANAGEMENT INTERNATIONAL
281 Main Street, Fitchburg MA 01420. 978/343-0048. **Contact:** Manager. **Description:** A contract services firm. **Specializes in the areas of:** Human Resources; Personnel/Labor Relations. **Positions commonly filled include:** Accountant; Human Resources Specialist.

SEARCHNET
P.O. Box 252, Stow MA 01775. 978/897-3855. **Fax:** 978/897-3455. **Contact:** Linda Rogers, Proprietor. **E-mail address:** searchnet@compuserve.com. **Description:** A contract services firm. **Specializes in the areas of:** Fashion; Marketing; Retail; Sales. **Positions commonly filled include:** Advertising Executive; Architect; Buyer; Controller; Database Manager; Finance Director; General Manager; Graphic Artist; Graphic Designer; Human Resources Manager; Marketing Manager; Project Manager; Public Relations Specialist; Retail Executive; Sales Manager; Systems Manager; Transportation/Traffic Specialist; Vice President. **Average salary range of placements:** More than $100,000. **Number of placements per year:** 50 - 99.

TECH RESOURCE INC.
639 Washington Street, Norwood MA 02062. 781/769-2115. **Contact:** Recruiter. **Description:** A contract services firm. **Specializes in the areas of:** Administration; Computer Science/Software; Secretarial; Technical. **Positions commonly filled include:** Advertising Clerk; Claim Repr.; Clerical Supervisor; Computer Programmer; Electrical/Electronics Engineer; Management Analyst/Consultant; Medical Records Technician; MIS Specialist; Services Sales Rep.; Software Engineer; Statistician; Structural Engineer; Systems Analyst; Typist/Word Processor. **Benefits available to temporary workers:** Paid Holidays; Paid Vacation. **Number of placements per year:** 200 - 499.

TECH/AID
295 Weston Street, Waltham MA 02454. 781/891-0800. **Contact:** Manager. **Description:** A contract services firm. **Specializes in the areas of:** Architecture/Construction; Cable TV; Computer Hardware/Software; Construction; Engineering; Manufacturing; Technical. **Positions commonly filled include:** Aerospace Engineer; Architect; Buyer; Ceramics Engineer; Chemical Engineer; Civil Engineer; Draftsperson; Electrical/Electronics Engineer; Estimator; Industrial Designer; Industrial Engineer; Mechanical Engineer; Metallurgical Engineer; Mining Engineer; Operations/Production Manager; Petroleum Engineer; Purchasing Agent/Manager; Quality Control Supervisor. **Corporate headquarters location:** Upper Newton Falls MA. **Number of placements per year:** 1000+.

TECH/AID
400 Grove Street, Worcester MA 01605. 508/792-6255. **Toll-free phone:** 800/645-0045. **Fax:** 508/792-2903. **Contact:** Office Manager. **World Wide Web address:** http://www.techaid.com. **Description:** A contract services firm that also provides temporary placements. **Specializes in the areas of:** Engineering; Industrial; Manufacturing; Personnel/Labor Relations; Scientific; Technical. **Positions commonly filled include:** Aerospace Engineer; Architect; Buyer; Ceramics Engineer; Chemical Engineer; Civil Engineer; Draftsperson; Electrical/Electronics Engineer; Estimator; Factory Worker; Industrial Designer; Industrial Engineer; Mechanical Engineer; Metallurgical Engineer; Mining Engineer; Operations/Production Manager; Petroleum Engineer; Purchasing Agent/Manager; Quality Control Supervisor; Technical Writer/Editor; Technician. **Corporate headquarters location:** Upper Newton Falls MA. **Number of placements per year:** 1000+.

H.L. YOH COMPANY
135 Beaver Street, Waltham MA 02154. 781/273-5151. **Contact:** Matt Glubiak, New England District Manager. **Description:** A contract services firm. **Specializes in the areas of:** Computer Hardware/Software; Engineering; Manufacturing; MIS/EDP; Technical. **Positions commonly filled include:** Aerospace Engineer; Architect; Buyer; Chemical Engineer; Chemist; Civil Engineer; Commercial Artist; Computer Operator; Computer Programmer; Data Entry Clerk; Draftsperson; Driver; Editor; EDP Specialist; Electrical/Electronics Engineer; Human Resources Manager; Industrial Designer; Industrial Engineer; Laboratory Technician; Manufacturing Engineer; Mechanical Engineer; Metallurgical Engineer; MIS Specialist; Operations/Production Manager; Purchasing Agent/Manager; Quality Control Supervisor; Reporter; Software Engineer; Systems Analyst; Technical Illustrator; Technical Writer/Editor; Technician; Typist/Word Processor. **Number of placements per year:** 100 - 199.

CAREER/OUTPLACEMENT COUNSELING FIRMS

BERKE & PRICE ASSOCIATES
6 Newtown Way, Chelmsford MA 01824. 978/256-0482. **Toll-free phone:** 800/552-3753. **Fax:** 978/250-0787. **Contact:** Judit E. Price, Principal. **E-mail address:** salprice@aol.com. **Description:** A career/outplacement counseling firm that also offers resume writing and interview preparation services. Founded in 1980.

THE BOSTON CAREER LINK
281 Huntington Avenue, Boston MA 02115. 617/536-1888. **Contact:** Manager. **Description:** A career/outplacement counseling firm.

THE CAREER PLACE
100 Sylvan Road, Woburn MA 01801. 781/932-5500. **Toll-free phone:** 888/273-WORK. **Fax:** 781/932-5566. **Contact:** Employer Services. **Description:** A nonprofit career counseling agency. The Career Place offers services to the general public including an online service and on-site listings of job openings; re-employment services; professional development opportunities; employment workshops; recruiting services; staffing services; and self-assessment services. **Positions commonly filled include:** Account Manager; Account Rep.; Accountant; Counselor; Librarian; Secretary; Systems Manager; Typist/Word Processor.

CAREER POINT
850 High Street, Holyoke MA 01040. 413/532-4900. **Contact:** Employee Services. **Description:** A career/outplacement counseling firm.

CAREER SOURCE
185 Alewife Brook Parkway, Cambridge MA 02138. 617/661-7867. **Toll-free phone:** 888/454-9675. **Contact:** Manager. **Description:** A career/outplacement counseling firm.

CAREER VENTURES COUNSELING SERVICES
70 Washington Street, Suite 322, Salem MA 01970. 978/744-1012. **Fax:** 978/745-2956. **Contact:** Andrew S. Brown, Principal. **Description:** A career/outplacement counseling firm offering career counseling, testing and assessment, pre-retirement planning, resume development, interview preparation, and job search assistance. Founded in 1993. **Other area locations:** Boston MA.

CAREER VENTURES COUNSELING SERVICES
3 School Street, Boston MA 02108. 617/263-7744. **Contact:** Andrew S. Brown, Principal. **Description:** A career/outplacement counseling firm that also provides career and personality testing for individuals and companies.

CAREERPRO CAREER DEVELOPMENT CENTER
50 Beacon Street, Boston MA 02108. 617/523-7660. **Fax:** 617/523-8622. **Contact:** Lynn G. Lieberman, Manager. **Description:** Provides career management, outplacement, employment counseling, job search assistance, and resume development services.

CAREERPRO CAREER DEVELOPMENT CENTER
950 Watertown Street, Suite 9, West Newton MA 02465. 617/965-7760. **Fax:** 617/964-2323. **Contact:** Michael Kaye, Manager. **Description:** Provides career management, outplacement, employment counseling, job search assistance, and resume development services.

CAREERPRO CAREER DEVELOPMENT CENTER
6 Pleasant Street, Suite 602, Malden MA 02148. 781/324-7890. **Contact:** Steve Dionne, Manager. **Description:** Provides career management, outplacement, employment counseling, job search assistance, and resume development services.

CENTER FOR PROFESSIONAL DEVELOPMENT IN THE LAW
6 Sevinor Road, Marblehead MA 01945. 617/868-6669. **Contact:** Ronald W. Fox, Managing Partner. **World Wide Web address:** http://www.shore.net/~cpdl. **Description:** A career counseling firm that works with law students and lawyers in transition. **Specializes in the areas of:** Legal.

THE COMPETITIVE EDGE
P.O. Box 311, Woburn MA 01801. 781/932-3232. **Contact:** Anne Savas, Principal. **E-mail address:** asavas@ix.netcom.com. **Description:** A career/outplacement counseling firm that also provides resume writing services.

FUTUREWORKS
One Federal Street, Building 103-3, Springfield MA 01105. 413/858-2800. **Contact:** Manager. **Description:** A career/outplacement counseling firm.

JEWISH VOCATIONAL SERVICE (JVS)
105 Chauncy Street, 6th Floor, Boston MA 02111. 617/451-8147. **Fax:** 617/451-9973. **Contact:** George Zeller, Employment Specialist. **E-mail address:** jvs@tiac.net. **World Wide Web address:** http://www.jvs.org. **Description:** A career/outplacement counseling agency that also provides resume writing services. Jobseeker pays fee. **Positions commonly filled include:** Account Representative; Accountant; Administrative Assistant; Administrative Manager; Assistant Manager; Counselor; Customer Service Representative; Editorial Assistant; Education Administrator; Electrical/Electronics Engineer; ESL Teacher; Financial Analyst; Graphic Artist; Human Resources Specialist; Human Service Worker; Manufacturing Engineer; Marketing Specialist; Public Relations Specialist; Sales Executive; Sales Representative; Services Sales Representative; Software Engineer; Systems Analyst. **Number of placements per year:** 100 - 199.

JEWISH VOCATIONAL SERVICE (JVS)
26 West Street, 3rd Floor, Boston MA 02111. 617/542-1993. **Fax:** 617/423-8711. **Contact:** Margaret Raisty, Project Coordinator. **World Wide Web address:** http://www.jvs.org. **Description:** A career/outplacement counseling firm.

JOBNET
210 South Street, Boston MA 02111. 617/338-0809. **Toll-free phone:** 800/5-JOBNET. **Contact:** Manager. **Description:** A career/outplacement counseling firm.

THE ORIGINAL RESUME COMPANY
ORIGINAL RESUME RECRUITING & MARKETING COMPANY
1105 Lakeview Avenue, Dracut MA 01826. 978/957-6600. **Fax:** 978/957-6605. **Contact:** Thomas P. Gove, President. **E-mail address:** origresume@aol.com. **World Wide Web address:** http://www.originalresume.com. **Description:** A career counseling company which offers resume and cover letter writing services, resume evaluations, and mass mailings to recruiters and companies worldwide. Original Resume Recruiting & Marketing Company (also at this location) is an executive search firm. **Average salary range of placements:** $30,000 - $50,000. **Number of placements per year:** 200 - 499.

THE RESUME WRITER
9 Carolyn Circle, Marshfield MA 02050. **Contact:** Sue McCarthy, Owner. **Description:** Provides resume writing services.

THE WORK PLACE
101 Federal Street, 3rd Floor, Boston MA 02110. 617/737-0093. **Toll-free phone:** 800/436-WORK. **Fax:** 617/428-0380. **Contact:** Eugene Ferraro, Assistant Director. **World Wide Web address:** http://www.masscareers.state.ma.us. **Description:** A career/outplacement counseling firm that also offers a career resource library, job listings, and workshops. **Specializes in the areas of:** Accounting/Auditing; Administration; Food; Light Industrial; Nonprofit; Secretarial. **Positions commonly filled include:** Administrative Assistant; Administrative Manager; Certified Nurses Aide; Computer Operator; Computer Programmer; Customer Service Rep.; Database Manager; Electrical/Electronics Engineer; Human Resources Manager; Sales Rep.; Typist/Word Processor. **Number of placements per year:** 200 - 499.

◆ M I C H I G A N ◆

AJM PROFESSIONAL SERVICES
803 West Big Beaver Road, Suite 357, Troy MI 48084. 248/244-2222. **Fax:** 248/244-2233. **Contact:** Principal. **World Wide Web address:** http://www.ajmps.com. **Description:** An executive search firm. **Specializes in the areas of:** Administration; Computer Science/ Software; Information Systems. **Positions commonly filled include:** Computer Programmer; Management Analyst/Consultant; MIS Specialist; Software Engineer; Systems Analyst. **Average salary range of placements:** More than $50,000. **Number of placements per year:** 100 - 199.

ABILITY SEARCH GROUP
30400 Telegraph Road, Suite 474, Bingham Farms MI 48025. 248/594-2100. **Fax:** 248/594-2121. **Contact:** Manager. **Description:** An executive search firm that provides data processing placements.

ACCENT ON ACHIEVEMENT
3190 Rochester Road, Suite 104, Troy MI 48083. 248/528-1390. **Toll-free phone:** 800/828-5340. **Fax:** 248/528-9335. **Contact:** Charlene Brown, CPA/ President. **Description:** An executive search firm that also provides some temporary placements. **Specializes in the areas of:** Accounting/Auditing; Finance. **Positions commonly filled include:** Accountant/Auditor; Actuary; Budget Analyst; Controller; Finance Director; Financial Analyst. **Benefits available to temporary workers:** Paid Holidays; Paid Vacation. **Other area locations:** Southfield MI. **Average salary range of placements:** More than $50,000. **Number of placements per year:** 50 - 99.

ACCOUNTANTS CONNECTION INC.
32540 Schoolcraft Road, Suite 100, Livonia MI 48150. 734/513-7800. **Contact:** Manager. **Description:** An executive search firm. **Specializes in the areas of:** Accounting/Auditing; Bookkeeping.

ACCOUNTANTS EXECUTIVE SEARCH ACCOUNTANTS ON CALL
28411 Northwestern Highway, Suite 910, Southfield MI 48034. 248/356-6999. **Contact:** Manager. **Description:** An executive search firm. Accountants On Call (also at this location) is a temporary agency. **Specializes in the areas of:** Accounting/Auditing; Finance.

ACTON SELL ASSOCIATES
24333 Southfield Road, Suite 201, Southfield MI 48075. 248/569-5460. **Contact:** Manager. **Description:** An executive search firm. **Specializes in the areas of:** Health/Medical. **Positions commonly filled include:** Physician.

ADVANCE ASSOCIATES
3680 Edgemont Drive, Troy MI 48084. 248/649-2456. **Contact:** Bruce Duncan, Owner. **Description:** An executive search firm. **Specializes in the areas of:** Engineering; Manufacturing; Technical.

ADVANCE EMPLOYMENT
1711 North West Avenue, Jackson MI 49202. 517/787-3333. **Fax:** 517/787-3380. **Contact:** Recruiter. **World Wide Web address:** http://www.advanceteam.com. **Description:** An executive search firm. **Specializes in the areas of:** Accounting/Auditing; Administration; Banking; Clerical; Computer Science/Software; Engineering; Light Industrial; Personnel/Labor Relations; Publishing; Sales; Technical. **Positions commonly filled include:** Accountant/Auditor; Adjuster; Automotive Mechanic; Branch Manager; Buyer; Chemical Engineer; Computer Programmer; Human Resources Specialist; Industrial Engineer; Internet Services Manager; Management Analyst/Consultant; Management Trainee; Mechanical Engineer; Public Relations Specialist; Typist/Word Processor. **Benefits available to** temporary workers: Paid Holidays; Paid Vacation; Tuition Assistance. **Number of placements per year:** 100 - 199.

ADVANCE PERSONNEL OF MICHIGAN
251 106th Avenue, Plainwell MI 49080-9302. 616/685-8505. **Fax:** 616/685-5857. **Contact:** Arthur Flanders, Owner. **Description:** An executive search firm. **Specializes in the areas of:** Engineering; Personnel/ Labor Relations. **Positions commonly filled include:** Accountant; Blue-Collar Worker Supervisor; Controller; Design Engineer; Draftsperson; Electrical/Electronics Engineer; Electrician; Graphic Artist; Graphic Designer; Human Resources Manager; Manufacturing Engineer; Mechanical Engineer; Metallurgical Engineer; MIS Specialist; Operations Manager; Production Manager; Public Relations Manager; Purchasing Agent/Manager; Quality Control Supervisor; Sales Engineer; Sales Manager; Sales Representative; Software Engineer. **Corporate headquarters location:** This Location. **Average salary range of placements:** More than $50,000. **Number of placements per year:** 100 - 199.

ADVANCED EXECUTIVE RESOURCES
3040 Charlevoix Drive SE, Grand Rapids MI 49546. 616/942-4030. **Fax:** 616/942-9950. **Contact:** Manager. **Description:** An executive search firm.

THE ADVANTAGE GROUP
2690 Crooks Road, Suite 414, Troy MI 48084. 248/362-1500. **Toll-free phone:** 888/362-1500. **Fax:** 248/362-2880. **Contact:** Anthony C. Fontana, CPA, Senior Partner. **E-mail address:** advntgrp@aol.com. **World Wide Web address:** http://www.advantagegrp.com. **Description:** An executive search firm operating on a contingency basis. The Advantage Group also provides some permanent and contract placements. Client company pays fee. **Specializes in the areas of:** Accounting; Administration; Banking; Finance. **Positions commonly filled include:** Accountant; Administrative Assistant; Auditor; Budget Analyst; Chief Financial Officer; Controller; Cost Estimator; Credit Manager; Finance Director; Financial Analyst; Network/Systems Administrator; Systems Analyst. **Corporate headquarters location:** This Location. **Average salary range of placements:** $30,000 - $100,000. **Number of placements per year:** 1 - 49.

AEGIS GROUP
23875 Novi Road, Novi MI 48375-3243. 248/344-1450. **Fax:** 248/347-2231. **Contact:** Tim Ignash, President. **E-mail address:** resume@aegis-group.com. **Description:** An executive search firm focusing on the recruitment of health care executives and physicians for health care systems, insurer groups, managed care organizations, and hospitals. **Specializes in the areas of:** Health/Medical. **Positions commonly filled include:** Accountant/Auditor; Financial Analyst; General Manager; Health Services Manager; Human Resources Manager; Medical Records Technician; MIS Specialist; Occupational Therapist; Physical Therapist; Registered Nurse; Respiratory Therapist; Surgical Technician. **Other U.S. locations:** Nationwide. **Average salary range of placements:** More than $50,000. **Number of placements per year:** 1 - 49.

ALLEGHENY SEARCH ASSOCIATES
846 Dahlia Lane, Rochester Hills MI 48307. 248/651-9550. **Contact:** Manager. **Description:** An executive search firm. **Specializes in the areas of:** Engineering.

ALLIANCE INDUSTRIES
33117 Hamilton Court, Suite 125, Farmington Hills MI 48334-3355. 248/489-9100. **Fax:** 248/489-9196. **Contact:** Manager. **Description:** An executive search firm. **Specializes in the areas of:** Automotive.

AMERICAN COMPUTER SERVICE
29777 Telegraph Road, Suite 2205, Southfield MI 48034-1303. 248/827-1200. **Fax:** 248/827-4644. **Contact:** Dan Corp, President. **Description:** An executive search firm operating on a contingency basis. **Specializes in the areas of:** Computer Science/Software; Sales. **Positions commonly filled include:** Sales Manager; Sales Representative; Software Engineer. **Average salary range of placements:** More than $50,000. **Number of placements per year:** 50 - 99.

ASSOCIATES
222 Franklin Street, Grand Haven MI 49417. 616/842-8596. **Contact:** Bob Clark, President. **Description:** An executive search firm. **Specializes in the areas of:** Automotive; Engineering; General Management; Manufacturing; Transportation. **Positions commonly filled include:** Account Rep.; Applications Engineer; Chemical Engineer; Design Engineer; Environmental Engineer; General Manager; Human Resources Manager; Industrial Engineer; Manufacturing Engineer; Mechanical Engineer; Operations Manager; Production Manager; Project Manager; Quality Control Supervisor; Sales Engineer; Sales Manager; Vice President of Operations. **Average salary range of placements:** More than $50,000. **Number of placements per year:** 1 - 49.

AUCON LLC
1982 Forest Glen Drive, Muskegon MI 49441. 231/798-4883. **Fax:** 231/798-4087. **Contact:** Janet Audo, President. **Description:** An executive search firm operating on both retainer and contingency bases. **Specializes in the areas of:** Accounting; Computer Science/Software; Engineering; Finance; General Management; Industrial; Marketing; Sales; Scientific; Technical. **Positions commonly filled include:** Account Manager; Accountant; Applications Engineer; AS400 Programmer Analyst; Auditor; Chemist; Computer Engineer; Computer Programmer; Computer Scientist; Controller; Database Administrator; Database Manager; Design Engineer; Electrical/Electronics Engineer; Finance Director; General Manager; Industrial Engineer; Manufacturing Engineer; Marketing Manager; Marketing Specialist; Mechanical Engineer; Metallurgical Engineer; MIS Specialist; Operations Manager; Production Manager; Project Manager; Purchasing Agent/Manager; Quality Control Supervisor; Research and Development Engineer; Sales Engineer; Sales Executive; Sales Manager; Software Engineer; Systems Analyst; Systems Manager; Vice President of Operations. **Corporate headquarters location:** This Location. **President:** Janet E. Audo. **Average salary range of placements:** $50,000 - $100,000. **Number of placements per year:** 1 - 49.

AUTOMOTIVE CAREERS
2130 Wealthy SE, Grand Rapids MI 49506. 616/942-5700. **Fax:** 616/942-5214. **Contact:** C. Thomas Conrad, President. **Description:** An executive search firm. **Specializes in the areas of:** Accounting/Auditing; Finance; Retail; Sales. **Positions commonly filled include:** Accountant/Auditor; General Manager; Manufacturer's/Wholesaler's Sales Rep. **Number of placements per year:** 1 - 49.

BEACON SERVICES INC.
4595 Broadmoor Avenue SE, Suite 180, Grand Rapids MI 49512. 616/698-7979. **Fax:** 616/698-0838. **Contact:** Division Manager. **World Wide Web address:** http://www.beaconweb.com. **Description:** An executive search firm that also provides some temporary placements. **Specializes in the areas of:** Administration; Engineering; General Management; Industrial; Manufacturing; Transportation. **Positions commonly filled include:** Design Engineer; Designer; Electrical/ Electronics Engineer; Industrial Engineer; Mechanical Engineer; MIS Specialist; Operations/Production Manager; Quality Control Supervisor. **Average salary range of placements:** More than $50,000.

BEACON SERVICES INC.
42 West 10th Street, Holland MI 49423. 616/639-1332. **Contact:** Manager. **World Wide Web address:**

http://www.beaconweb.com. **Description:** An executive search firm that also provides some temporary placements. **Specializes in the areas of:** Clerical; Health/Medical; Industrial; Legal.

BENFORD & ASSOCIATES
3000 Town Center, Suite 1333, Southfield MI 48075. 248/351-0250. **Fax:** 248/351-8698. **Contact:** Edward Benford, Manager. **Description:** An executive search firm operating on both retainer and contingency bases. **Specializes in the areas of:** Accounting/Auditing; Banking; Engineering; Food; Industrial; Manufacturing; Personnel/Labor Relations. **Positions commonly filled include:** Automotive Mechanic; Bank Officer/Manager; Budget Analyst; Buyer; Chemical Engineer; Financial Analyst; Human Resources Manager; Industrial Engineer; Mechanical Engineer; Metallurgical Engineer; Operations/Production Manager; Purchasing Agent/ Manager; Quality Control Supervisor. **Average salary range of placements:** More than $50,000. **Number of placements per year:** 50 - 99.

BOYDEN GLOBAL EXECUTIVE SEARCH
300 East Long Lake, Suite 375, Bloomfield Hills MI 48304. 248/647-4201. **Contact:** Manager. **E-mail address:** boyden@mich.com. **World Wide Web address:** http://www.boyden.com. **Description:** A generalist executive search firm. **Corporate headquarters location:** New York NY. **Other U.S. locations:** San Francisco CA; Washington DC; Chicago IL; Chesterfield MO; Morristown NJ; Hawthorne NY; Pittsburgh PA; Houston TX. **International locations:** Worldwide.

BROOKSIDE CONSULTING GROUP
6689 Orchard Lake Road, Suite PMB358, West Bloomfield MI 48322. 248/968-3210. **Fax:** 248/968-2908. **Contact:** Martin Rosenfeld, President. **Description:** An executive search firm operating on both retainer and contingency bases. **Specializes in the areas of:** Legal. **Positions commonly filled include:** Attorney; Finance Director; Intellectual Property Lawyer; Operations Manager. **Average salary range of placements:** More than $50,000. **Number of placements per year:** 1 - 49.

CAREER INTRODUCTIONS CORPORATION
30800 Telegraph Street, Suite 1850, Franklin MI 48025. 248/203-0000. **Toll-free phone:** 888/200-3033. **Fax:** 248/203-0047. **Contact:** Manager. **Description:** An executive search firm.

CAREER SEARCH INC.
33117 Hamilton Court, Suite 200, Farmington Hills MI 48334. 248/553-8200. **Contact:** Manager. **Description:** An executive search firm. **Specializes in the areas of:** Computer Hardware/Software.

CARMAC EXECUTIVE RECRUITING
32401 West Eight Mile Road, Livonia MI 48152. 248/478-5550. **Fax:** 248/478-5552. **Contact:** Thomas McInnes, Owner. **Description:** An executive search firm. **Specializes in the areas of:** Automotive; Engineering; Manufacturing; Sales. **Positions commonly filled include:** Account Manager; Account Representative; Design Engineer; General Manager; Human Resources Manager; Industrial Engineer; Marketing Manager; Mechanical Engineer; Metallurgical Engineer; Project Manager; Sales Engineer; Sales Executive; Sales Manager; Sales Representative; Vice President of Marketing; Vice President of Sales. **Number of placements per year:** 1 - 49.

CASE & COMPANY
15008 Kercheval Street, Grosse Pointe Park MI 48230. 313/331-6095. **Contact:** President. **Description:** An executive search firm operating on a contingency basis. **Specializes in the areas of:** Automotive; Engineering; General Management; Manufacturing. **Positions commonly filled include:** Buyer; Design Engineer; Designer; Human Resources Manager; Industrial Engineer; Industrial Production Manager; Manufacturing

Engineer; Mechanical Engineer; Metallurgical Engineer; Production Manager; Purchasing Agent/Manager; Quality Control Supervisor; Sales Engineer. **Number of placements per year:** 1 - 49.

CATALYST HEALTH CARE GROUP
2052 South Dye Road, Flint MI 48532. 810/762-6900. **Contact:** Manager. **Description:** An executive search firm that places experienced personnel in medical centers and hospitals. **Specializes in the areas of:** Health/Medical.

CHRISTOPHER ASSOCIATES
292 South Main Street, Plymouth MI 48170. 734/453-5656. **Contact:** Manager. **Description:** An executive search firm that focuses on providing placements in the automotive supply industry. **Specializes in the areas of:** Operations Management; Technical.

CIRCLEWOOD SEARCH GROUP, INC.
3307 East Kilgore, Suite 2, Kalamazoo MI 49001. 616/383-9520. **Fax:** 616/383-9530. **Contact:** Melissa Webb, President. **E-mail address:** circlewd@net-link.net. **World Wide Web address:** http://www.circlewood.com. **Description:** An executive search firm that places medical professionals in hospitals, health care systems, and private practices nationwide. **Specializes in the areas of:** Health/Medical. **Positions commonly filled include:** Health Care Administrator; Nurse Practitioner; Occupational Therapist; Physical Therapist; Physician; Physician Assistant; Registered Nurse. **Average salary range of placements:** More than $50,000. **Number of placements per year:** 50 - 99.

COASTAL DEVELOPMENT, INC.
44201 Ford Road, Suite 201, Canton MI 48187. 734/459-6564. **Contact:** Sam Banks, President. **E-mail address:** samcoastal@aol.com. **Description:** An executive search firm operating on a contingency basis. Client company pays fee. **Specializes in the areas of:** Automotive; Electronics; Engineering; Finance; General Management; Marketing; Sales. **Positions commonly filled include:** Account Manager; Account Representative; Chief Financial Officer; Design Engineer; Electrical/Electronics Engineer; Finance Director; Financial Analyst; General Manager; Industrial Production Manager; Manufacturing Engineer; Marketing Manager; Mechanical Engineer; Operations Manager; Project Manager; Purchasing Agent/Manager; Sales Engineer; Sales Executive; Sales Manager; Sales Representative; Vice President of Sales. **Corporate headquarters location:** This Location. **Other U.S. locations:** Ontario CA. **Average salary range of placements:** More than $50,000.

COLE'S PAPER INDUSTRY RECRUITERS, INC.
3419 Winter Wheat Road, Kalamazoo MI 49004. 616/341-4495. **Fax:** 616/341-4598. **Contact:** Manager. **E-mail address:** jcole@staffing.net. **World Wide Web address:** http://www.topechelon.com/mi43. **Description:** An executive search firm operating on both retained and contingency bases. **Specializes in the areas of:** General Management; Paper.

COMPASS GROUP LTD.
401 South Old Woodward Avenue, Suite 460, Birmingham MI 48009. 248/540-9110. **Fax:** 248/540-2944. **Contact:** Manager. **Description:** A generalist executive search firm.

CORPORATE AMERICA PERSONNEL CONSULTANTS
5310 Hertford Drive, Troy MI 48098. 248/879-1804. **Contact:** Manager. **Description:** An executive search firm.

CORPORATE BUSINESS SERVICES LTD.
913 West Holmes Road, Suite 100, Lansing MI 48910-0411. 517/394-1800. **Fax:** 517/394-2033. **Contact:** Michael Keen, President/General Manager. **Description:** An executive search firm operating on both retainer and contingency bases. Founded in 1974. **Specializes in the**

areas of: Computer Science/Software; Engineering; Food; General Management; Marketing; Sales. **Positions commonly filled include:** Branch Manager; Computer Programmer; Customer Service Rep.; Database Manager; General Manager; Human Resources Manager; Industrial Engineer; Management Trainee; Manufacturing Engineer; Market Research Analyst; Marketing Manager; Mechanical Engineer; MIS Specialist; Sales Engineer; Sales Executive; Sales Manager; Sales Representative; Software Engineer; Systems Analyst; Systems Manager. **Corporate headquarters location:** This Location. **Other U.S. locations:** Nationwide. **Average salary range of placements:** More than $30,000. **Number of placements per year:** 200 - 499.

CORPORATE SOLUTIONS
3155 West Big Beaver Road, Suite 123, Troy MI 48084. 248/649-7188. **Fax:** 248/649-7151. **Contact:** Jim Bryant, President. **Description:** An executive search firm that places data processing professionals and also offers some contract placements. **NOTE:** Data processing applicants should have at least one year of experience. **Specializes in the areas of:** Computer Science/Software. **Positions commonly filled include:** Computer Programmer; Project Manager; Systems Analyst. **Average salary range of placements:** $30,000 - $50,000. **Number of placements per year:** 1 - 49.

DAVIDSON, LAIRD & ASSOCIATES
29260 Franklin Road, Suite 110, Southfield MI 48034. 248/358-2160. **Fax:** 248/358-1225. **Contact:** Meri Laird, President. **E-mail address:** mlaird@rust.net. **Description:** An executive search firm. **Specializes in the areas of:** Accounting/Auditing; Administration; Automotive; Engineering; Manufacturing; Personnel/ Labor Relations; Plastics; Secretarial. **Positions commonly filled include:** Buyer; Chemical Engineer; Cost Estimator; Design Engineer; Designer; Electrical/Electronics Engineer; Industrial Engineer; Industrial Production Manager; Mechanical Engineer; Metallurgical Engineer; Typist/Word Processor. **Average salary range of placements:** $30,000 - $50,000. **Number of placements per year:** 50 - 99.

DICKSON ASSOCIATES INC.
3001 West Big Beaver Road, Suite 210, Troy MI 48084. 248/643-9480. **Contact:** Manager. **Description:** An executive search firm. **Specializes in the areas of:** Accounting/Auditing; Engineering; Finance; Information Systems.

DURHAM ASSOCIATES INC.
11678 Doane Road, South Lyon MI 48178. 248/486-3888. **Fax:** 248/486-5753. **Contact:** Manager. **Description:** An executive search firm. **Specializes in the areas of:** Chemicals.

G.L. DYKSTRA ASSOCIATES
P.O. Box 8035, Holland MI 49422. 616/786-9419. **Contact:** Manager. **Description:** An executive search firm.

GENE ELLEFSON & ASSOCIATES INC.
330 Town Center Drive, Suite 304, Dearborn MI 48126. 313/982-6000. **Fax:** 313/982-1277. **Contact:** Gene Ellefson, President. **E-mail address:** gellefson@ advdata.net. **Description:** An executive search firm that focuses on placing sales and engineering personnel with automotive manufacturers and suppliers. **Specializes in the areas of:** Accounting/Auditing; Automotive; Engineering; Manufacturing; Sales. **Positions commonly filled include:** Account Manager; Account Rep.; Accountant; Controller; Cost Estimator; Design Engineer; Electrical/Electronics Engineer; Finance Director; Industrial Engineer; Mechanical Engineer; Sales Engineer; Sales Executive; Sales Manager. **Average salary range of placements:** More than $50,000. **Number of placements per year:** 1 - 49.

ELWELL & ASSOCIATES
3100 West Liberty, Suite E, Ann Arbor MI 48103. 734/662-8775. **Contact:** Manager. **Description:** An

executive search firm. **Specializes in the areas of:** Manufacturing.

EMPLEX CORPORATION
25160 Lahser Road, Southfield MI 48034. 248/352-2361. **Contact:** Manager. **Description:** An executive search firm for mid-sized manufacturers and distributors. **Positions commonly filled include:** Accountant/Auditor; Design Engineer; General Manager; Industrial Production Manager; Mechanical Engineer; Metallurgical Engineer; MIS Specialist; Purchasing Agent/Manager; Sales Manager. **Average salary range of placements:** More than $50,000. **Number of placements per year:** 1 - 49.

EXECUQUEST, INC.
2050 Breton Road SE, Suite 103, Grand Rapids MI 49546. 616/949-1800. **Fax:** 616/949-0561. **Contact:** President. **E-mail address:** execuquest@aol.com. **Description:** An executive search firm that focuses on providing mid-level and senior-level management positions. The firm operates on a retainer basis. **Specializes in the areas of:** Accounting/Auditing; Banking; Finance; General Management; Manufacturing; Marketing; Personnel/Labor Relations; Sales. **Positions commonly filled include:** Accountant/Auditor; Bank Officer/Manager; Chief Financial Officer; Controller; Financial Analyst; Human Resources Manager. **Corporate headquarters location:** This Location. **Average salary range of placements:** More than $50,000. **Number of placements per year:** 1 - 49.

EXECUTECH, INC.
2002 Hogback Road, Suite 9, Ann Arbor MI 48105-9732. 734/483-8454. **Fax:** 734/483-0740. **Contact:** Donald Frederick, CEO. **E-mail address:** exiinc@mediaone.net. **Description:** An executive search firm operating on both retainer and contingency bases. Executech also provides career/outplacement counseling services. **Specializes in the areas of:** Administration; Computer Science/Software; Engineering; MIS/EDP; Personnel/Labor Relations; Scientific; Technical. **Positions commonly filled include:** Computer Programmer; Database Manager; Design Engineer; Electrical/Electronics Engineer; Human Resources Manager; Internet Services Manager; MIS Specialist; Multimedia Designer; Online Content Specialist; Software Engineer; Statistician; Systems Analyst; Systems Manager; Telecommunications Manager; Webmaster. **Corporate headquarters location:** This Location. **Average salary range of placements:** More than $50,000. **Number of placements per year:** 1 - 49.

EXECUTIVE & MEDICAL RECRUITERS
21751 West Nine Mile Road, Suite 202, Southfield MI 48075. 248/357-5373. **Contact:** Manager. **Description:** An executive search firm. **Specializes in the areas of:** Automotive; Computer Science/Software; Electronics; Engineering; Medical Sales and Marketing.

EXECUTIVE & TECHNICAL PERSONNEL
5409 Kelly Road, Flint MI 48504. 810/732-8390. **Fax:** 810/732-7463. **Contact:** John Lutz, President/Owner. **Description:** An executive search firm. **Specializes in the areas of:** Engineering; General Management; Industrial; Manufacturing; Technical. **Positions commonly filled include:** Biochemist; Buyer; Chemical Engineer; Chemist; Chief Financial Officer; Controller; Design Engineer; Finance Director; General Manager; Industrial Engineer; Manufacturing Engineer; Mechanical Engineer; Operations Manager; Production Manager; Project Manager; Purchasing Agent/Manager; Quality Control Supervisor; Sales Engineer. **Corporate headquarters location:** This Location. **Average salary range of placements:** $40,000 - $150,000. **Number of placements per year:** 1 - 49.

EXECUTIVE GOLF SEARCH, INC.
699 Westchester Road, Saginaw MI 48603. 517/797-0677. **Contact:** Manager. **Description:** An executive search firm.

EXECUTIVE RECRUITERS INTERNATIONAL
P.O. Box 365, Trenton MI 48183. 734/671-6200. **Fax:** 734/671-8714. **Contact:** Manager. **Description:** An executive search firm. **Specializes in the areas of:** Administration; Architecture/Construction; Automotive; Computer Science/Software; Engineering; Environmental; General Management; Industrial; Manufacturing; Personnel/Labor Relations; Publishing; Real Estate; Sales; Technical; Transportation. **Positions commonly filled include:** Accountant/Auditor; Administrative Manager; Architect; Automotive Mechanic; Biological Scientist; Biomedical Engineer; Blue-Collar Worker Supervisor; Buyer; Chemical Engineer; Chemist; Civil Engineer; Computer Programmer; Construction and Building Inspector; Construction Contractor; Cost Estimator; Customer Service Representative; Designer; Draftsperson; Economist; Electrical/Electronics Engineer; Electrician; Environmental Engineer; General Manager; Geologist/Geophysicist; Human Resources Manager; Industrial Engineer; Industrial Production Manager; Landscape Architect; Management Analyst/Consultant; Management Trainee; Manufacturer's/Wholesaler's Sales Rep.; Mechanical Engineer; Metallurgical Engineer; Mining Engineer; Nuclear Engineer; Operations/Production Manager; Petroleum Engineer; Public Relations Specialist; Purchasing Agent/Manager; Quality Control Supervisor; Services Sales Representative; Software Engineer; Stationary Engineer; Structural Engineer; Surveyor; Systems Analyst; Technical Writer/Editor; Transportation/Traffic Specialist; Urban/Regional Planner; Water Transportation Specialist. **International locations:** Worldwide. **President:** Kathleen A. Sinclair. **Number of placements per year:** 1 - 49.

EXECUTIVE SEARCH TEAM
32255 Northwestern Highway, Suite 190, Farmington Hills MI 48334. 248/932-9770. **Fax:** 248/932-9777. **Contact:** Phil Levin, Chairman. **E-mail address:** staffmatters@msn.com. **Description:** An executive search firm operating on a contingency basis. Client company pays fee. **Positions commonly filled include:** Account Manager; Accountant; Administrative Assistant; Administrative Manager; Applications Engineer; Auditor; Chief Financial Officer; Controller; Finance Director; Financial Analyst; General Manager; Human Resources Manager; Marketing Manager; Marketing Specialist; MIS Specialist; Network/Systems Administrator; Purchasing Agent/Manager; Secretary; Software Engineer; Systems Analyst; Vice President. **Corporate headquarters location:** This Location. **Average salary range of placements:** $50,000 - $100,000. **Number of placements per year:** 50 - 99.

F-O-R-T-U-N-E PERSONNEL CONSULTANTS
560 Kirts Boulevard, Suite 102, Troy MI 48084. 248/244-9646. **Fax:** 248/244-8568. **Contact:** Michael Dubeck, President. **Description:** An executive search firm that focuses on placing physician and healthcare executives. The firm operates on both retainer and contingency bases. **Specializes in the areas of:** Health/Medical. **Positions commonly filled include:** Administrative Manager; Biomedical Engineer; Chief Financial Officer; Finance Director; General Manager; Health Services Manager; Human Resources Manager; Occupational Therapist; Physical Therapist; Physician; Registered Nurse; Vice President of Finance; Vice President of Operations. **Corporate headquarters location:** New York NY. **Other U.S. locations:** Nationwide. **Average salary range of placements:** More than $50,000. **Number of placements per year:** 1 - 49.

F-O-R-T-U-N-E PERSONNEL CONSULTANTS
33045 Hamilton Court, Suite 105, Farmington Hills MI 48334-1664. 248/324-3700. **Fax:** 248/324-1602. **Contact:** Gary Snyder, President. **Description:** An executive search firm operating on both retainer and contingency bases. **Specializes in the areas of:** Accounting/Auditing; Engineering. **Positions commonly filled include:** Biomedical Engineer; Chemical Engineer;

Design Engineer; Mechanical Engineer; MIS Specialist; Physician; Software Engineer. **Corporate headquarters location:** New York NY. **Other U.S. locations:** Nationwide. **Average salary range of placements:** More than $50,000. **Number of placements per year:** 1 - 49.

F-O-R-T-U-N-E PERSONNEL CONSULTANTS
800 West Long Lake Road, Suite 200, Bloomfield Hills MI 48302-2056. 248/642-9383. **Fax:** 248/642-9575. **Contact:** Karl Zimmermann, President. **Description:** An executive search firm. **Specializes in the areas of:** General Management; Materials; Purchasing; Quality Assurance. **Positions commonly filled include:** General Manager; Materials Manager; Purchasing Agent/ Manager; Quality Control Supervisor. **Corporate headquarters location:** New York NY. **Other U.S. locations:** Nationwide. **Average salary range of placements:** More than $50,000. **Number of placements per year:** 1 - 49.

F-O-R-T-U-N-E PERSONNEL CONSULTANTS
17515 West Nine Mile Road, Suite 770, Southfield MI 48075. 248/557-7250. **Fax:** 248/557-7260. **Contact:** Manager. **E-mail address:** detroit@fpcweb.com. **Description:** An executive search firm. **Specializes in the areas of:** Legal. **Corporate headquarters location:** New York NY.

F-O-R-T-U-N-E PERSONNEL CONSULTANTS
1300 Hilton Street, Suite 5, Ferndale MI 48220. 248/548-4821. **Fax:** 248/548-4959. **Contact:** Manager. **Description:** An executive search firm. **Specializes in the areas of:** Automotive; Plastics; Quality Assurance.

GBL RESOURCES INC.
6966 Crooks Road, Suite 20, Troy MI 48098-1798. 248/813-9595. **Contact:** Manager. **Description:** An executive search firm. **Specializes in the areas of:** Engineering.

GENESYS HEALTH PERSONNEL
3915 Beecher Road, Flint MI 48532. 810/762-4700. **Contact:** Manager. **Description:** An executive search firm operating on a contingency basis. **Specializes in the areas of:** Health/Medical. **Positions commonly filled include:** Certified Nurses Aide; Home Health Aide; Medical Assistant; Medical Secretary; Registered Nurse.

GIACOMIN GROUP INC.
3000 Town Center, Suite 2237, Southfield MI 48075. 248/352-1470. **Fax:** 248/358-4499. **Contact:** Manager. **Description:** An executive search firm operating on both retainer and contingency bases. **Specializes in the areas of:** Engineering; General Management; Manufacturing; Sales. **Positions commonly filled include:** Electrical/ Electronics Engineer; Mechanical Engineer. **Average salary range of placements:** More than $50,000.

JOSEPH GOLDRING & ASSOCIATES
31500 West Thirteen Mile Road, Suite 200, Farmington Hills MI 48334. 248/539-2660. **Fax:** 248/539-2667. **Contact:** Joe Goldring, President. **Description:** An executive search firm. **Specializes in the areas of:** Accounting/Auditing; Administration; Computer Science/Software; Engineering; Finance; General Management; Health/Medical; Industrial; Manufacturing; Personnel/Labor Relations; Sales. **Positions commonly filled include:** Account Manager; Actuary; Aerospace Engineer; Attorney; Budget Analyst; Buyer; Chemical Engineer; Civil Engineer; Computer Programmer; Cost Estimator; Design Engineer; EEG Technologist; EKG Technician; Electrical/Electronics Engineer; Environmental Engineer; Financial Analyst; Health Services Manager; Human Resources Specialist; Industrial Engineer; Manufacturer's/Wholesaler's Sales Rep.; Mechanical Engineer; Medical Records Technician; Metallurgical Engineer; MIS Specialist; Occupational Therapist; Paralegal; Physical Therapist; Physician; Purchasing Agent/Manager; Registered Nurse; Respiratory Therapist; Software Engineer; Speech-Language Pathologist; Surgical Technician;

Systems Analyst. **Average salary range of placements:** $30,000 - $80,000. **Number of placements per year:** 50 - 99.

GRAPHIC ARTS MARKETING ASSOCIATES
3533 Deepwood Drive, Lambertville MI 48144. 734/854-5225. **Fax:** 734/854-5224. **Contact:** Jacqueline Crawford, President. **E-mail address:** graphicama@ aol.com. **Description:** An executive search firm. **Specializes in the areas of:** Advertising; Art/Design; Broadcasting; Market Research; Marketing; Printing. **Positions commonly filled include:** Account Rep.; Copywriter; Customer Service Representative; Designer; Graphic Artist; Multimedia Designer; Public Relations Specialist; Sales Representative; Technical Writer/Editor; Video Production Coordinator. **Number of placements per year:** 50 - 99.

GUIDARELLI ASSOCIATES, INC.
2933 West John Beers Road, Stevensville MI 49127. 616/429-7001. **Fax:** 616/429-7003. **Contact:** Shelly Guidarelli, President/Owner. **Description:** An executive search firm. **Specializes in the areas of:** Personnel/Labor Relations; Sales. **Positions commonly filled include:** Human Resources Manager. **Average salary range of placements:** More than $50,000. **Number of placements per year:** 1 - 49.

ROBERT HALF INTERNATIONAL ACCOUNTEMPS
One Towne Square, Suite 1050, Southfield MI 48076. 248/524-3100. **Fax:** 248/368-6456. **Contact:** Division Director. **World Wide Web address:** http://www. roberthalf.com. **Description:** An executive search firm. Accountemps (also at this location) provides temporary placements. The World Wide Web address for Accountemps is http://www.accountemps.com. **Specializes in the areas of:** Accounting/Auditing; Administration; Banking; Computer Science/Software; Finance. **Positions commonly filled include:** Accountant/Auditor; Bank Officer/Manager; Budget Analyst; Computer Programmer; Cost Estimator; Credit Manager; Financial Analyst; Internet Services Manager; Management Analyst/Consultant; MIS Specialist; Software Engineer; Systems Analyst; Technical Writer/Editor. **Corporate headquarters location:** Menlo Park CA. **Other U.S. locations:** Nationwide. **International locations:** Worldwide. **Average salary range of placements:** $30,000 - $50,000. **Number of placements per year:** 500 - 999.

ROBERT HALF INTERNATIONAL ACCOUNTEMPS
333 Bridge Street NW, Suite 500, Grand Rapids MI 49504. 616/454-9444. **Contact:** Manager. **World Wide Web address:** http://www.roberthalf.com. **Description:** An executive search firm. Accountemps (also at this location) provides temporary placements in finance. The World Wide Web address for Accountemps is http://www.accountemps.com. **Specializes in the areas of:** Accounting; Banking; Finance. **Corporate headquarters location:** Menlo Park CA. **Other U.S. locations:** Nationwide.

THE HALLMAN GROUP INC.
4528 West KL Avenue, Kalamazoo MI 49006. 616/353-6835. **Fax:** 616/353-6845. **Contact:** Ken Killman, Owner. **Description:** An executive search firm. **Specializes in the areas of:** Administration; Computer Science/Software; Engineering; Manufacturing. **Positions commonly filled include:** Accountant/Auditor; Chemical Engineer; Computer Programmer; Design Engineer; Electrical/Electronics Engineer; Industrial Engineer; Mechanical Engineer; Metallurgical Engineer; MIS Specialist; Software Engineer; Systems Analyst. **Average salary range of placements:** $30,000 - $50,000. **Number of placements per year:** 50 - 99.

HARPER ASSOCIATES
29870 Middlebelt Road, Farmington Hills MI 48334. 248/932-1170. **Fax:** 248/932-1214. **Contact:** Ben Schwartz, President. **World Wide Web address:**

http://www.harper-jobs.com. **Description:** An executive search firm operating on both retainer and contingency bases. Founded in 1969. Client company pays fee. **Specializes in the areas of:** Administration; Computer Science/Software; Food; Health/Medical; Hotel/ Restaurant; Marketing; MIS/EDP; Retail; Sales; Secretarial. **Positions commonly filled include:** Account Manager; Administrative Assistant; Administrative Manager; Assistant Manager; Clerical Supervisor; Computer Programmer; Controller; Customer Service Representative; Database Manager; Dietician/ Nutritionist; General Manager; Human Resources Manager; Internet Services Manager; Licensed Practical Nurse; Management Trainee; MIS Specialist; Physician; Registered Nurse; Sales Engineer; Systems Analyst; Systems Manager; Webmaster. **Corporate headquarters location:** This Location. **Average salary range of placements:** $30,000 - $50,000. **Number of placements per year:** 200 - 499.

HEALTHCARE RECRUITERS INTERNATIONAL
10327 East Grand River, Suite 409, Brighton MI 48116. 810/227-7055. **Fax:** 810/227-7307. **Contact:** Gayle Amlie, President. **Description:** An executive search firm. **Specializes in the areas of:** Administration; Biology; Computer Science/Software; Engineering; Finance; Health/Medical; Manufacturing; Sales. **Positions commonly filled include:** Accountant/Auditor; Administrative Manager; Attorney; Biological Scientist; Biomedical Engineer; Branch Manager; Budget Analyst; Buyer; Chemical Engineer; Chemist; Claim Rep.; Clinical Lab Technician; Computer Programmer; Computer Scientist; Customer Service Representative; Design Engineer; Dietician/Nutritionist; EEG Technologist; EKG Technician; Electrical/Electronics Engineer; Financial Analyst; General Manager; Health Services Manager; Industrial Engineer; Industrial Production Manager; Management Analyst/Consultant; Manufacturer's/Wholesaler's Sales Rep.; Market Research Analyst; Mechanical Engineer; Medical Records Technician; MIS Specialist; Nuclear Medicine Technologist; Occupational Therapist; Operations Engineer; Pharmacist; Physical Therapist; Physician; Registered Nurse; Respiratory Therapist; Science Technologist; Services Sales Representative; Software Engineer; Speech-Language Pathologist; Technical Writer/Editor; Telecommunications Manager. **Other U.S. locations:** Nationwide. **Average salary range of placements:** $60,000 - $85,000. **Number of placements per year:** 50 - 99.

HARVEY HOHAUSER & ASSOCIATES
5600 New King Street, Suite 355, Troy MI 48098-2652. **Contact:** Harvey Hohauser, President. **Description:** An executive search firm operating on a retainer basis. **Specializes in the areas of:** Administration; Banking; Engineering; Finance; Manufacturing. **Positions commonly filled include:** Management. **Average salary range of placements:** More than $50,000. **Number of placements per year:** 50 - 99.

IBA SEARCH
8300 Thornapple River Drive SE, Caledonia MI 49316. 616/891-2160. **Fax:** 616/891-1180. **Contact:** Certified Personnel Consultant. **Description:** An executive search firm operating on a contingency basis. **Specializes in the areas of:** Computer Science/Software; Engineering; Manufacturing; Technical. **Positions commonly filled include:** Aerospace Engineer; Agricultural Engineer; Biological Scientist; Biomedical Engineer; Chemical Engineer; Chemist; Civil Engineer; Computer Programmer; Designer; Draftsperson; Electrical/ Electronics Engineer; General Manager; Industrial Engineer; Industrial Production Manager; Mechanical Engineer; Metallurgical Engineer; Nuclear Engineer; Operations/Production Manager; Quality Control Supervisor; Science Technologist; Software Engineer; Stationary Engineer; Structural Engineer; Systems Analyst; Technical Writer/Editor; Telecommunications Manager. **Average salary range of placements:** $30,000 - $50,000. **Number of placements per year:** 1 - 49.

INFORMATION SYSTEMS EXECUTIVE RECRUITERS
600 South Adams, Suite 210, Birmingham MI 48009. 248/647-0850. **Contact:** Manager. **Description:** An executive search firm. **Specializes in the areas of:** Information Systems.

A.T. KEARNEY EXECUTIVE SEARCH
2000 Town Center, Suite 1600, Southfield MI 48075. 248/354-2226. **Contact:** Manager. **Description:** An executive search firm. **International locations:** Worldwide.

LAKE ASSOCIATES
105 South Cochran Avenue, Charlotte MI 48813. 517/543-1340. **Fax:** 517/543-1343. **Contact:** Richard Dowling, Owner. **Description:** An executive search firm operating on both retainer and contingency bases. **Specializes in the areas of:** Hotel/Restaurant; Sales. **Positions commonly filled include:** Controller; Food Service Manager; General Manager; Hotel Manager. **Average salary range of placements:** $30,000 - $50,000. **Number of placements per year:** 1 - 49.

LAMBERT INTERNATIONAL
P.O. Box 867, Jenison MI 49429. 616/261-0753. **Contact:** Manager. **Description:** An executive search firm. **Specializes in the areas of:** General Management; Technical.

JOHN LAWRENCE GROUP
26111 West 14 Mile Road, Suite LL-1, Franklin MI 48025. 248/932-7770. **Fax:** 248/932-7774. **Contact:** Manager. **E-mail address:** jlgcareer@aol.com. **World Wide Web address:** http://www. johnlawrencegroup.com. **Description:** An executive search firm focusing on the placement of individuals in a variety of printing/publishing fields. **Specializes in the areas of:** Publishing. **Positions commonly filled include:** Chief Financial Officer; Controller; Cost Estimator; Customer Service Representative; Financial Manager; General Manager; Multimedia Designer; Operations Manager; President; Production Manager; Sales Executive; Sales Manager; Sales Representative. **Average salary range of placements:** More than $50,000. **Number of placements per year:** 1 - 49.

LEGAL SEARCH & MANAGEMENT
22821 Violet Street, Suite 100, Farmington MI 48336. 248/471-3443. **Contact:** Manager. **Description:** An executive search firm. **Specializes in the areas of:** Legal.

DAVID LINDEMER ASSOCIATES
206 South Fifth Avenue, Suite 250, Ann Arbor MI 48104. 734/761-3999. **Fax:** 734/761-3010. **Contact:** David Lindemer, President. **World Wide Web address:** http://www.lindemer.com. **Description:** An executive search firm operating on both retainer and contingency bases. **Specializes in the areas of:** Information Technology. **Positions commonly filled include:** Client Services Representative; Product Manager; Vice President of Marketing and Sales. **Average salary range of placements:** More than $50,000. **Number of placements per year:** 1 - 49.

MANAGEMENT RECRUITERS INTERNATIONAL
10751 South Saginaw Street, Grand Blanc MI 48439. 810/695-0120. **Fax:** 810/695-0522. **Contact:** Rick Reed, Co-Owner. **Description:** An executive search firm operating on both contingency and retainer bases. **Specializes in the areas of:** Accounting/Auditing; Administration; Architecture/Construction; Chemicals; Communications; Computer Hardware/Software; Computer Science/Software; Design; Electrical; Engineering; Food; General Management; Health/Medical; Industrial; Insurance; Legal; Light Industrial; Manufacturing; Operations Management; Personnel/Labor Relations; Procurement; Retail; Sales; Scientific; Technical; Textiles; Transportation. **Positions commonly filled include:** Applications Engineer; Blue-Collar Worker Supervisor; Buyer; Chemical Engineer;

Civil Engineer; Computer Programmer; Cost Estimator; Database Manager; Design Engineer; Designer; Draftsperson; Electrical/Electronics Engineer; Electrician; Industrial Engineer; Industrial Production Manager; Manufacturing Engineer; Mechanical Engineer; Metallurgical Engineer; MIS Specialist; Operations Manager; Production Manager; Project Manager; Purchasing Agent/Manager; Quality Control Supervisor; Sales Engineer; Software Engineer; Systems Analyst; Systems Manager. **Corporate headquarters location:** Cleveland OH. **Other U.S. locations:** Nationwide. **Average salary range of placements:** $30,000 - $50,000. **Number of placements per year:** 50 - 99.

MANAGEMENT RECRUITERS INTERNATIONAL 755 West Big Beaver Road, Suite 101, Troy MI 48084. 248/764-4200. **Contact:** Ed Moeller, Manager. **Description:** An executive search firm. **Specializes in the areas of:** Automotive; Engineering; Industrial; Quality Assurance; Sales. **Corporate headquarters location:** Cleveland OH. **Other U.S. locations:** Nationwide.

MANAGEMENT RECRUITERS INTERNATIONAL 34405 W 12 Mile Road, Suite 115, Farmington Hills MI 48331. 313/568-4300. **Contact:** Manager. **Description:** An executive search firm. **Corporate headquarters location:** Cleveland OH. **Other U.S. locations:** Nationwide.

MANAGEMENT RECRUITERS INTERNATIONAL 400 North 136th Avenue, Suite 206, Holland MI 49424. 616/396-2620. **Contact:** Manager. **Description:** An executive search firm. **Specializes in the areas of:** Manufacturing; Technical. **Corporate headquarters location:** Cleveland OH. **Other U.S. locations:** Nationwide.

MANAGEMENT RECRUITERS OF ANN ARBOR 3600 Green Court, Suite 100, Ann Arbor MI 48105. 734/769-1720. **Contact:** Manager. **Description:** An executive search firm. **Specializes in the areas of:** Accounting/Auditing; Banking; Data Processing; Insurance. **Corporate headquarters location:** Cleveland OH. **Other U.S. locations:** Nationwide.

MANAGEMENT RECRUITERS OF BATTLE CREEK 590 W Columbia Avenue, Suite H, Battle Creek MI 49015. 616/968-5959. **Contact:** Manager. **Description:** An executive search firm. **Specializes in the areas of:** Accounting/Auditing; Administration; Advertising; Computer Science/Software; Engineering; Finance; Health/Medical; Industrial; Manufacturing. **Positions commonly filled include:** Buyer; Chemical Engineer; Computer Programmer; Cost Estimator; Design Engineer; Designer; Financial Analyst; Health Services Manager; Industrial Engineer; Industrial Production Manager; Mechanical Engineer; Medical Records Technician; Metallurgical Engineer; MIS Specialist; Operations/Production Manager; Quality Control Supervisor; Software Engineer; Systems Analyst. **Corporate headquarters location:** Cleveland OH. **Other U.S. locations:** Nationwide. **Average salary range of placements:** $30,000 - $50,000. **Number of placements per year:** 100 - 199.

MANAGEMENT RECRUITERS OF BIRMINGHAM 30700 Telegraph Road, Suite 3650, Bingham Farms MI 48025. 248/647-2828. **Contact:** Manager. **Description:** An executive search firm. **Specializes in the areas of:** Accounting/Auditing; Administration; Advertising; Architecture/Construction; Banking; Chemicals; Communications; Computer Hardware/Software; Design; Electrical; Engineering; Food; General Management; Health/Medical; Insurance; Legal; Manufacturing; Operations Management; Personnel/Labor Relations; Procurement; Publishing; Real Estate; Retail; Sales; Technical; Textiles; Transportation. **Corporate headquarters location:** Cleveland OH. **Other U.S. locations:** Nationwide.

MANAGEMENT RECRUITERS OF DEARBORN Parklane Towers West, Suite 1224, 3 Parklane Boulevard, Dearborn MI 48126-2591. 313/336-6650. **Contact:** Elaine Kozlowski, Manager. **Description:** An executive search firm. **Specializes in the areas of:** Accounting/Auditing; Administration; Architecture/Construction; Banking; Chemicals; Communications; Computer Hardware/Software; Design; Electrical; Engineering; Food; General Management; Health/Medical; Insurance; Manufacturing; Operations Management; Personnel/Labor Relations; Procurement; Publishing; Sales; Technical; Transportation. **Corporate headquarters location:** Cleveland OH. **Other U.S. locations:** Nationwide.

MANAGEMENT RECRUITERS OF GRAND RAPIDS 146 Monroe Center, Suite 1126, Grand Rapids MI 49503. 616/336-8484. **Contact:** Manager. **Description:** An executive search firm. **Specializes in the areas of:** Banking; Chemicals; Finance; Health/Medical; Metals; Sales. **Corporate headquarters location:** Cleveland OH. **Other U.S. locations:** Nationwide.

MANAGEMENT RECRUITERS OF GROSSE POINTE 15450 East Jefferson Avenue, Suite 150, Grosse Pointe MI 48230. 313/822-6770. **Toll-free phone:** 800/801-2295. **Fax:** 313/822-6775. **Contact:** Lowell D. Johnson, President. **E-mail address:** recruitco@earthlink.net. **World Wide Web address:** http://www.recruitco.com. **Description:** An executive search firm operating on both retainer and contingency bases. Client company pays fee. **Specializes in the areas of:** Accounting; Banking; Engineering; Finance; MIS/EDP; Transportation. **Positions commonly filled include:** Accountant; AS400 Programmer Analyst; Auditor; Bank Officer/Manager; Budget Analyst; CFO; Computer Programmer; Controller; Electrical/Electronics Engineer; Finance Director; Financial Analyst; Human Resources Manager; Management Analyst/Consultant; Manufacturing Engineer; Mechanical Engineer; MIS Specialist; Production Manager; Purchasing Agent/Manager; Systems Analyst; Vice President of Finance. **Corporate headquarters location:** Cleveland OH. **Average salary range of placements:** $50,000 - $100,000. **Number of placements per year:** 50 - 99.

MANAGEMENT RECRUITERS OF KALAMAZOO 4021 West Main Street, Suite 200, Kalamazoo MI 49006. 616/381-1153. **Fax:** 616/381-8031. **Contact:** Manager. **Description:** An executive search firm. **Specializes in the areas of:** Accounting/Auditing; Administration; Advertising; Architecture/Construction; Banking; Chemicals; Communications; Computer Hardware/Software; Design; Electrical; Engineering; Food; General Management; Health/Medical; Insurance; Legal; Manufacturing; Operations Management; Personnel/Labor Relations; Procurement; Publishing; Retail; Sales; Technical; Textiles; Transportation. **Corporate headquarters location:** Cleveland OH. **Other U.S. locations:** Nationwide.

MANAGEMENT RECRUITERS OF LANSING 2491 Cedar Park Drive, Holt MI 48842. 517/694-1153. **Contact:** John Peterson, Manager. **Description:** An executive search firm. **Specializes in the areas of:** Accounting/Auditing; Administration; Advertising; Architecture/Construction; Banking; Chemicals; Communications; Computer Hardware/Software; Design; Electrical; Engineering; Food; General Management; Health/Medical; Insurance; Legal; Manufacturing; Operations Management; Personnel/Labor Relations; Procurement; Publishing; Retail; Sales; Technical; Textiles; Transportation. **Corporate headquarters location:** Cleveland OH. **Other U.S. locations:** Nationwide.

MANAGEMENT RECRUITERS OF LIVONIA 37677 Professional Center Drive, Suite 100-C, Livonia MI 48154-1138. 734/953-9590. **Fax:** 734/953-0566. **Contact:** Don Eden, President. **Description:** An executive search firm operating on a contingency basis.

Specializes in the areas of: Accounting/Auditing; Administration; Engineering; Finance; General Management; Industrial; Sales. Positions commonly filled include: Accountant/Auditor; Branch Manager; Buyer; Chemical Engineer; Customer Service Representative; Designer; Electrical/Electronics Engineer; Electrician; Financial Analyst; General Manager; Industrial Engineer; Industrial Production Manager; Manufacturer's/Wholesaler's Sales Rep.; Mechanical Engineer; Metallurgical Engineer; Purchasing Agent/Manager; Quality Control Supervisor; Transportation/Traffic Specialist; Wholesale and Retail Buyer. Corporate headquarters location: Cleveland OH. Other U.S. locations: Nationwide. Average salary range of placements: $30,000 - $50,000. Number of placements per year: 1 - 49.

MANAGEMENT RECRUITERS OF MUSKEGON
919 W Norton Avenue, Suite 101, Muskegon MI 49441. 231/830-8400. Fax: 231/830-8500. Contact: Manager. Description: An executive search firm. Specializes in the areas of: Accounting/Auditing; Administration; Advertising; Architecture/Construction; Banking; Chemicals; Communications; Computer Hardware/Software; Design; Electrical; Engineering; Food; General Management; Health/Medical; Insurance; Legal; Manufacturing; Operations Management; Personnel/Labor Relations; Procurement; Publishing; Retail; Sales; Technical; Textiles; Transportation. Corporate headquarters location: Cleveland OH. Other U.S. locations: Nationwide.

MANAGEMENT RECRUITERS OF NORTH OAKLAND COUNTY
2530 South Rochester Road, Rochester Hills MI 48307. 248/299-1900. Fax: 248/299-5681. Contact: Manager. Description: An executive search firm operating on both retainer and contingency bases. Specializes in the areas of: Accounting; Administration; Banking; Computer Science/Software; Engineering; Finance; General Management; Health/Medical; Marketing; MIS/EDP; Nonprofit; Personnel/Labor Relations; Retail; Sales; Scientific; Technical. Positions commonly filled include: Account Manager; Accountant; Administrative Manager; Applications Engineer; Assistant Manager; Auditor; Bank Officer/Manager; Budget Analyst; Chemical Engineer; Chief Financial Officer; Clinical Lab Technician; Computer Animator; Computer Operator; Computer Programmer; Controller; Credit Manager; Customer Service Representative; Database Manager; Design Engineer; EEG Technologist; EKG Technician; Electrical/Electronics Engineer; Environmental Engineer; Finance Director; Financial Analyst; Food Scientist/Technologist; General Manager; Human Resources Manager; Industrial Engineer; Industrial Production Manager; Management Analyst/Consultant; Manufacturing Engineer; Marketing Manager; Marketing Specialist; MIS Specialist; Pharmacist; Physical Therapist; Physician; Production Manager; Project Manager; Purchasing Agent/Manager; Quality Control Supervisor; Respiratory Therapist; Software Engineer; Statistician; Systems Analyst; Systems Manager; Technical Writer/Editor; Telecommunications Manager. Corporate headquarters location: Cleveland OH. Other U.S. locations: Nationwide. International locations: Worldwide. Average salary range of placements: More than $50,000. Number of placements per year: 100 - 199.

MANAGEMENT RECRUITERS OF SOUTHEASTERN MICHIGAN
P.O. Box 3, Blissfield MI 49228-0003. 517/486-2167. Fax: 517/486-2324. Contact: Mary W. Snellbaker, Owner/Manager. Description: An executive search firm. Specializes in the areas of: Accounting/Auditing; Engineering; General Management; Industrial; Manufacturing; Personnel/Labor Relations; Technical. Positions commonly filled include: Design Engineer; Environmental Engineer; General Manager; Human Resources Manager; Industrial Engineer; Industrial Production Manager; Mechanical Engineer; Metallurgical Engineer; Purchasing Agent/Manager;

Quality Control Supervisor; Stationary Engineer. Corporate headquarters location: Cleveland OH. Other U.S. locations: Nationwide. Number of placements per year: 1 - 49.

MANAGEMENT RECRUITERS OF TRAVERSE CITY
124 North Division Street, Traverse City MI 49684. 231/947-8000. Fax: 231/922-9481. Contact: Manager. E-mail address: mrtc@traverse.com. World Wide Web address: http://www.traverse.com/mri/. Description: An executive search firm. Specializes in the areas of: Automotive; Information Technology; Manufacturing. Corporate headquarters location: Cleveland OH. Other U.S. locations: Nationwide.

MEDMATCH
441 South Livernois Road, Suite 175, Rochester Hills MI 48307. 248/651-0652. Fax: 248/651-2748. Contact: Manager. Description: An executive search firm. Specializes in the areas of: Health/Medical.

METROSTAFF
28637 Northwestern Highway, Southfield MI 48034. 248/350-2290. Fax: 248/350-2530. Contact: Michael Callaway, President. Description: An executive search firm that also offers some temporary placements. Specializes in the areas of: Computer Science/Software; Engineering; Health/Medical; Industrial; Secretarial; Transportation. Positions commonly filled include: Computer Programmer; Design Engineer; EEG Technologist; EKG Technician; Electrical/Electronics Engineer; Industrial Engineer; Industrial Production Manager; Licensed Practical Nurse; Mechanical Engineer; MIS Specialist; Occupational Therapist; Operations/Production Manager; Physical Therapist; Quality Control Supervisor; Registered Nurse; Software Engineer; Systems Analyst; Technical Writer/Editor; Typist/Word Processor. Number of placements per year: 1000+.

LOU MICHAELS ASSOCIATES, INC.
1230 East Columbia Avenue, Battle Creek MI 49014. 616/965-1486. Fax: 616/965-2232. Contact: Manager. Description: An executive search firm. Specializes in the areas of: Engineering; Industrial; Management.

MIDWEST DIRECT PERSONNEL
3319 Greenfield, Dearborn MI 48120. Toll-free phone: 888/611-2144. Fax: 888/611-2145. Contact: Manager. World Wide Web address: http://www.midwestdirectpersonnel.com. Description: A generalist executive search firm.

DARNELL MITCHELL & ASSOCIATES
25330 Telegraph Road, Suite 220, Southfield MI 48034. 248/357-5300. Contact: Manager. Description: An executive search firm operating on both retainer and contingency bases. Darnell Mitchell & Associates also provides some temporary and contract placements and resume and career/outplacement counseling. Client company pays fee. Specializes in the areas of: Engineering; Finance; Industrial; Marketing; Sales. Positions commonly filled include: Accountant; Computer Engineer; Design Engineer; Electrical/Electronics Engineer; Human Resources Manager; Manufacturing Engineer; Mechanical Engineer; MIS Specialist; Purchasing Agent/Manager; Quality Assurance Engineer; Quality Control Supervisor; Software Engineer; Systems Analyst. Average salary range of placements: $50,000 - $100,000. Number of placements per year: 100 - 199.

OFFICE STAFFING RECRUITING
4234 Cascade Road, Grand Rapids MI 49546. 616/949-2525. Fax: 616/949-2982. Contact: Manager. Description: An executive search firm. Specializes in the areas of: Accounting/Auditing; Administration; Banking; Computer Science/Software; Engineering; Finance; General Management; Industrial; Insurance; Manufacturing; Personnel/Labor Relations; Sales; Secretarial. Positions commonly filled include: Accountant/Auditor; Administrative Manager; Branch

Manager; Brokerage Clerk; Buyer; Claim Rep.; Clerical Supervisor; Computer Programmer; Design Engineer; General Manager; Human Resources Specialist; Human Service Worker; Industrial Production Manager; Insurance Agent/Broker; Manufacturer's/Wholesaler's Sales Rep.; Mechanical Engineer; Operations/Production Manager; Purchasing Agent/Manager; Quality Control Supervisor; Securities Sales Rep.; Software Engineer; Systems Analyst; Telecommunications Manager; Underwriter/Assistant Underwriter. **Average salary range of placements:** $30,000 - $50,000. **Number of placements per year:** 50 - 99.

OPEN PAGE SEARCH SERVICES
OPEN PAGE INSURANCE SEARCH
1354 Ardmoor Avenue, Ann Arbor MI 48103-5348. 734/761-3556. **Fax:** 734/761-1554. **Contact:** Frederick Page, Principal. **Description:** An executive search firm. Open Page Insurance Search (also at this location) is an executive search firm that focuses on actuarial and insurance executive placements. **Specializes in the areas of:** Administration; Computer Science/Software; Insurance. **Positions commonly filled include:** Actuary; Computer Programmer; Financial Analyst; Management Analyst/Consultant; Mathematician; MIS Specialist; Securities Sales Representative; Software Engineer; Systems Analyst; Underwriter/Assistant Underwriter. **Number of placements per year:** 1 - 49.

PARR SEARCH
385 Bay Pointe Road, Lake Orion MI 48362. **Contact:** Mauro Nobili, President. **Description:** An executive search firm operating on both retainer and contingency bases. **Specializes in the areas of:** Engineering; Industrial; Manufacturing; Technical. **Positions commonly filled include:** Chemical Engineer; Cost Estimator; Design Engineer; Designer; Electrical/Electronics Engineer; Environmental Engineer; General Manager; Human Resources Manager; Industrial Engineer; Industrial Production Manager; Mechanical Engineer; Metallurgical Engineer; Operations/Production Manager; Purchasing Agent/Manager; Stationary Engineer; Structural Engineer; Technical Writer/Editor. **Average salary range of placements:** More than $50,000. **Number of placements per year:** 1 - 49.

PREMIER HEALTHCARE RECRUITERS
5 Woodbury Lane, Dearborn MI 48120. 313/441-6450. **Fax:** 313/441-6460. **Contact:** Diana L. Watson, CPC, President. **E-mail address:** dianalynn4@aol.com. **Description:** An executive search firm operating on a contingency basis. Premier Healthcare Recruiters places physicians in both clinical and administrative positions. **Specializes in the areas of:** Health/Medical. **Positions commonly filled include:** Physician. **Average salary range of placements:** More than $50,000. **Number of placements per year:** 1 - 49.

PROFESSIONAL ADVANCEMENT INSTITUTE
28422 Tavistock Trail, Southfield MI 48034. 248/356-6660. **Fax:** 248/356-6662. **Contact:** Erwin Posner, President. **Description:** Professional Advancement Institute is an executive search firm focusing on placing professionals with SAS or COBOL programming experience. **Specializes in the areas of:** Biology; Engineering; Health/Medical; Pharmaceuticals. **Positions commonly filled include:** Biochemist; Biological Scientist; Chemical Engineer; Chemist; Computer Programmer; Health Services Manager; Industrial Engineer; Mechanical Engineer; Occupational Therapist; Pharmacist; Physical Therapist; Physician. **Average salary range of placements:** More than $50,000. **Number of placements per year:** 100 - 199.

PROFESSIONAL CAREER SEARCH (PCS)
4350 Plainfield NE, Grand Rapids MI 49525. 616/447-3110. **Fax:** 616/447-3111. **Contact:** Manager. **Description:** An executive search firm. **Specializes in the areas of:** Administration; Sales; Technical. **Other area locations:** Kalamazoo MI.

PROFESSIONAL CAREER SEARCH (PCS)
5464 Holiday Terrace, Kalamazoo MI 49009. 616/372-3339. **Fax:** 616/372-3363. **Contact:** Manager. **Description:** An executive search firm. **Specializes in the areas of:** Administration; Sales; Technical. **Other area locations:** Grand Rapids MI.

PROFESSIONAL PERSONNEL CONSULTANTS INTERNATIONAL
28200 Orchard Lake Road, Farmington Hills MI 48334. 248/737-1750. **Fax:** 248/737-5886. **Contact:** Dan Mistura, President. **Description:** An executive search firm. **Specializes in the areas of:** Accounting/Auditing; Administration; Computer Science/Software; Engineering; Finance; Health/Medical; Manufacturing; Personnel/Labor Relations; Sales; Secretarial; Technical. **Positions commonly filled include:** Accountant/Auditor; Budget Analyst; Buyer; Chemist; Computer Programmer; Credit Manager; Designer; Electrical/Electronics Engineer; Financial Analyst; General Manager; Human Resources Manager; Industrial Engineer; Mechanical Engineer; Metallurgical Engineer; Nuclear Engineer; Occupational Therapist; Pharmacist; Physical Therapist; Physician; Purchasing Agent/Manager; Quality Control Supervisor; Software Engineer; Structural Engineer; Systems Analyst. **Other U.S. locations:** Nationwide. **Average salary range of placements:** More than $50,000. **Number of placements per year:** 200 - 499.

PROSEARCH, INC.
34405 West Twelve Mile Road, Suite 196, Farmington Hills MI 48331. 248/488-3330. **Contact:** Vice President. **Description:** An executive search firm operating on both retainer and contingency bases. ProSearch, Inc. also provides contract and temp-to-perm placements and outsourcing services. Founded in 1991. **Specializes in the areas of:** Accounting/Auditing; Administration; Banking; Computer Science/Software; Finance; Manufacturing. **Positions commonly filled include:** Accountant/Auditor; Bank Officer/Manager; Budget Analyst; Computer Programmer; Credit Manager; Financial Analyst; MIS Specialist; Software Engineer; Systems Analyst. **Corporate headquarters location:** This Location.

ROONEY PERSONNEL COMPANY
149 Pierce Street, Birmingham MI 48009. 248/258-5533. **Toll-free phone:** 800/755-5888. **Fax:** 248/258-5671. **Contact:** Michael Rooney, President. **Description:** An executive search firm operating on a contingency basis. **Specializes in the areas of:** Hotel/Restaurant; Retail. **Positions commonly filled include:** Restaurant/Food Service Manager. **Average salary range of placements:** $30,000 - $50,000. **Number of placements per year:** 100 - 199.

ROTH YOUNG PERSONNEL SERVICES OF DETROIT, INC.
31275 Northwestern Highway, Suite 116, Farmington Hills MI 48334. 248/626-6033. **Fax:** 248/626-7079. **Contact:** Sam Skeegan, President. **Description:** An executive search firm. **Specializes in the areas of:** Advertising; Engineering; Food; Health/Medical; Manufacturing; Pharmaceuticals; Retail; Sales. **Positions commonly filled include:** Biological Scientist; Biomedical Engineer; Chemical Engineer; Chemist; Hotel Manager; Industrial Designer; Industrial Engineer; Marketing Specialist; Nurse; Quality Control Supervisor; Sales Rep. **Corporate headquarters location:** New York NY. **Other U.S. locations:** Nationwide. **Average salary range of placements:** More than $50,000. **Number of placements per year:** 100 - 199.

SALES CONSULTANTS OF AUBURN HILLS
2701 University Drive, Suite 205, Auburn Hills MI 48326. 248/373-7177. **Toll-free phone:** 800/699-7446. **Fax:** 248/373-7759. **Contact:** Boe Embrey, Owner/President. **Description:** An executive search firm operating on both retainer and contingency bases. Sales

Consultants of Auburn Hills also provides interim placement, videoconferencing, and compatibility assessment services. **Specializes in the areas of:** Computer Science/Software; General Management; Health/Medical; Marketing; Sales. **Positions commonly filled include:** Applications Engineer; Branch Manager; Respiratory Therapist; Sales Engineer; Sales Executive; Sales Manager; Sales Representative; Vice President of Marketing and Sales. **Corporate headquarters location:** Cleveland OH. **Other U.S. locations:** Nationwide. **Average salary range of placements:** More than $50,000. **Number of placements per year:** 100 - 199.

SALES CONSULTANTS OF DETROIT
29777 Telegraph Road, Suite 2260, Southfield MI 48034. 248/352-9200. **Fax:** 248/352-9374. **Contact:** Thomas Hoy, Manager. **E-mail address:** info@scjob.com. **World Wide Web address:** http://www.scjob.com. **Description:** An executive search firm operating on both retainer and contingency bases. Client company pays fee. **Specializes in the areas of:** Automotive; Chemicals; Electrical; Engineering; Management; Marketing; Plastics; Sales; Scientific; Technical. **Positions commonly filled include:** Account Manager; Account Representative; Chemical Engineer; Chemist; Marketing Manager; Sales Engineer; Sales Executive; Sales Manager; Sales Representative; Technical Representative. **Corporate headquarters location:** Cleveland OH. **Other U.S. locations:** Nationwide. **Average salary range of placements:** $50,000 - $100,000. **Number of placements per year:** 50 - 99.

SALES CONSULTANTS OF FARMINGTON HILLS
30445 Northwestern Highway, Suite 360, Farmington Hills MI 48334. 248/626-6600. **Toll-free phone:** 800/704-8772. **Fax:** 248/626-7542. **Contact:** Harvey Gersin, President. **E-mail address:** salcon@careers-usa.com. **World Wide Web address:** http://www.careers-usa.com. **Description:** An executive search firm operating on both retainer and contingency bases. **Specializes in the areas of:** Communications; Computer Hardware/Software; Engineering; Factory Automation; Health/Medical; Industrial; Marketing; Materials; Sales; Technical; Telecommunications. **Positions commonly filled include:** Account Manager; Account Representative; Applications Engineer; Branch Manager; Certified Nurses Aide; Computer Programmer; Design Engineer; Electrical/Electronics Engineer; General Manager; Industrial Engineer; Industrial Production Manager; Internet Services Manager; Marketing Manager; Marketing Specialist; Mechanical Engineer; Production Manager; Project Manager; Sales Engineer; Sales Executive; Sales Manager; Sales Representative; Software Engineer; Systems Analyst; Systems Manager; Telecommunications Manager; Vice President of Marketing; Vice President of Operations; Vice President of Sales. **Corporate headquarters location:** Cleveland OH. **Other U.S. locations:** Nationwide. **International locations:** Worldwide. **Average salary range of placements:** More than $50,000. **Number of placements per year:** 200 - 499.

SANFORD ROSE ASSOCIATES
416 St. Joseph Street, P.O. Box 156, Suttons Bay MI 49682. 231/271-6100. **Contact:** Manager. **World Wide Web address:** http://www.sanfordrose.com. **Description:** An executive search firm.

SANFORD ROSE ASSOCIATES
1000 West University Drive, Suite 203, Rochester MI 48307. 248/608-9005. **Fax:** 248/608-9010. **Contact:** Manager. **World Wide Web address:** http://www.sanfordrose.com. **Description:** An executive search firm. **Specializes in the areas of:** Engineering; General Management; Logistics.

SEARCH PLUS INTERNATIONAL
25882 Orchard Lake Road, Suite 207, Farmington Hills MI 48336. 248/471-6110. **Contact:** Christine Greeneisen, President. **Description:** An executive search firm. **Specializes in the areas of:** Administration;

Computer Science/Software; Engineering; Finance; General Management; Industrial; Manufacturing; Personnel/Labor Relations; Sales; Secretarial. **Positions commonly filled include:** Automotive Engineer; Biomedical Engineer; Blue-Collar Worker Supervisor; Buyer; Chemical Engineer; Chemist; Computer Programmer; Cost Estimator; Design Engineer; Designer; Draftsperson; Electrical/Electronics Engineer; Electrician; Environmental Engineer; Financial Analyst; Food Scientist/Technologist; General Manager; Human Resources Manager; Industrial Engineer; Industrial Production Manager; Manufacturer's/Wholesaler's Sales Rep.; Mechanical Engineer; Metallurgical Engineer; MIS Specialist; Operations/Production Manager; Paralegal; Purchasing Agent/Manager; Quality Control Supervisor; Science Technologist; Software Engineer; Systems Analyst; Transportation/Traffic Specialist. **Number of placements per year:** 50 - 99.

SEARCH SOLUTIONS
P.O. Box 125, Three Oaks MI 49128. 616/756-6830. **Contact:** Manager. **Description:** An executive search firm. **Specializes in the areas of:** Consumer Package Goods.

SELECTIVE RECRUITING ASSOCIATES, INC.
P.O. Box 130287, Ann Arbor MI 48113-0287. 734/994-5632. **Fax:** 734/996-8181. **Contact:** David Calhoun, CEO. **E-mail address:** recruiter@selective.com. **World Wide Web address:** http://www.selective.com. **Description:** An executive search firm. Selective Recruiting Associates, Inc. also offers some contract services. **Specializes in the areas of:** Automotive; Engineering; Industrial; Manufacturing; Technical. **Positions commonly filled include:** Chemical Engineer; Design Engineer; Designer; Electrical/Electronics Engineer; Industrial Engineer; Manufacturer's/Wholesaler's Sales Rep.; Operations/Production Manager; Purchasing Agent/Manager; Quality Control Supervisor; Software Engineer. **Other U.S. locations:** Nationwide. **Average salary range of placements:** More than $50,000. **Number of placements per year:** 50 - 99.

SHARROW & ASSOCIATES INC.
24735 Van Dyke Avenue, Center Line MI 48015. 810/759-6910. **Fax:** 810/759-6914. **Contact:** Beth Sharrow, President. **E-mail address:** sharrow@rust.net. **Description:** An executive search firm. **Specializes in the areas of:** Architecture/Construction; Computer Science/Software; Engineering; Health/Medical; Legal; Property Management. **Positions commonly filled include:** Chemical Engineer; Chemist; Computer Programmer; Construction and Building Inspector; Construction Contractor; Electrical/Electronics Engineer; Industrial Engineer; Mechanical Engineer; Occupational Therapist; Physical Therapist; Property and Real Estate Manager; Systems Analyst. **Other U.S. locations:** Angola IN; Florence KY. **Average salary range of placements:** More than $50,000. **Number of placements per year:** 50 - 99.

SMITH PROFESSIONAL SEARCH
600 South Adams Street, Suite 210, Birmingham MI 48009. 248/540-8580. **Contact:** Manager. **Description:** An executive search firm. **Specializes in the areas of:** Accounting/Auditing; Human Resources.

SOURCE TECHNOLOGY LLC
1965 Research Drive, Suite 200, Troy MI 48083. 248/816-8484. **Fax:** 248/816-3111. **Contact:** Greg Stephens, President. **Description:** An executive search firm. **Specializes in the areas of:** Computer Science/Software; Engineering; General Management; Industrial; Technical. **Positions commonly filled include:** Account Manager; Administrative Assistant; Applications Engineer; Computer Programmer; Controller; Cost Estimator; Design Engineer; Draftsperson; Electrician; Graphic Designer; Industrial Engineer; Mechanical Engineer; Operations Manager; Production Manager; Purchasing Agent/Manager; Quality Control Supervisor; Sales Engineer; Sales

Manager; Secretary; Systems Analyst; Typist/Word Processor. **Corporate headquarters location:** This Location. **Average salary range of placements:** More than $30,000. **Number of placements per year:** 100 - 199.

STERLING FIELD ASSOCIATES, INC.
697 Bridge Park Drive, Troy MI 48098. 248/879-7490. **Fax:** 248/879-2530. **Contact:** Steve Walmsley, President. **Description:** An executive search firm. **Specializes in the areas of:** Computer Science/Software; Finance; Health/Medical. **Positions commonly filled include:** Accountant/Auditor; Computer Programmer; Health Services Manager; Management Analyst/ Consultant; Medical Records Technician; MIS Specialist; Physical Therapist; Physician; Registered Nurse; Software Engineer; Systems Analyst. **Other U.S. locations:** Nationwide. **Average salary range of placements:** More than $50,000. **Number of placements per year:** 1 - 49.

SULLIVAN & ASSOCIATES
344 North Old Woodward, Suite 304, Birmingham MI 48009. 248/258-0616. **Fax:** 248/258-2823. **Contact:** Manager. **World Wide Web address:** http://www.sullivanassociates.com. **Description:** An executive search firm. **Specializes in the areas of:** Accounting; Consulting; Distribution; Education; Finance; Health/Medical; Information Systems; Insurance; Manufacturing; Metals; Nonprofit; Publishing; Real Estate; Research and Development; Retail; Software Development; Software Engineering; Telecommunications.

T.M.S. ASSOCIATES
3964 Old Creek Road, Troy MI 48084. 248/244-9406. **Contact:** Thomas Spada, President. **Description:** An executive search firm. **Specializes in the areas of:** Legal. **Positions commonly filled include:** Attorney; Legal Assistant. **Number of placements per year:** 1 - 49.

THOMAS & ASSOCIATES OF MICHIGAN
P.O. Box 366, Union Pier MI 49129. 616/469-5760. **Fax:** 616/469-5774. **Contact:** Thomas Zonka, President. **E-mail address:** tzonka@harborcountry.com. **Description:** An executive search firm that also provides some contract and temp-to-perm placements. **Specializes in the areas of:** Computer Science/Software; Engineering; General Management; Industrial; Manufacturing; Personnel/Labor Relations; Sales; Transportation. **Positions commonly filled include:** Buyer; Chemical Engineer; Computer Programmer; Designer; Electrical/Electronics Engineer; General Manager; Human Resources Manager; Industrial Engineer; Industrial Production Manager; Manufacturer's/ Wholesaler's Sales Rep.; Mechanical Engineer; Metallurgical Engineer; Operations/Production Manager; Purchasing Agent/Manager; Quality Control Supervisor; Software Engineer; Structural Engineer; Systems Analyst; Transportation/Traffic Specialist. **Average salary range of placements:** More than $50,000. **Number of placements per year:** 200 - 499.

TOTAL RECRUITMENT SERVICES
3680 44th Street SE, Grand Rapids MI 49512. 616/554-3344. **Contact:** Rich Gotch, General Manager.

Description: Total Recruitment Services is an executive search firm. **Specializes in the areas of:** Sales. **Positions commonly filled include:** Computer Programmer; Systems Analyst. **Number of placements per year:** 1 - 49.

WELIVER & ASSOCIATES
P.O. Box 15-135, Ann Arbor MI 48106. 734/913-0070. **Fax:** 734/913-0079. **Contact:** Billie Weliver, President. **Description:** An executive search firm. **Specializes in the areas of:** Engineering; Human Resources; MIS/EDP. **Positions commonly filled include:** Engineer; Human Resources Manager; Human Resources Specialist; MIS Manager; MIS Specialist. **Average salary range of placements:** $30,000 - $50,000. **Number of placements per year:** 50 - 99.

HENRY WELKER & ASSOCIATES
P.O. Box 530846, Livonia MI 48153-0846. 734/953-4900. **Fax:** 734/953-5918. **Contact:** Henry Welker, President. **E-mail address:** welker@aol.com. **Description:** An executive search firm operating on both retainer and contingency bases. **Specializes in the areas of:** Computer Science/Software; Engineering; General Management; Information Technology; Sales. **Positions commonly filled include:** Account Manager; Applications Engineer; Buyer; Computer Programmer; Database Manager; Design Engineer; Electrical/Electronics Engineer; General Manager; Industrial Engineer; Internet Services Manager; Manufacturing Engineer; Marketing Specialist; Mechanical Engineer; Metallurgical Engineer; MIS Specialist; Online Content Specialist; Operations Manager; Production Manager; Project Manager; Purchasing Agent/Manager; Quality Control Supervisor; Sales Engineer; Sales Executive; Sales Manager; Software Engineer; Statistician; Systems Analyst; Systems Manager; Vice President of Sales; Webmaster. **Corporate headquarters location:** This Location. **Average salary range of placements:** More than $50,000. **Number of placements per year:** 1 - 49.

WING TIPS AND PUMPS, INC.
P.O. Box 99580, Troy MI 48099. 248/641-0980. **Fax:** 248/641-0895. **Contact:** Mr. Verba L. Edwards, CEO. **Description:** An executive search firm operating on both retainer and contingency bases. **Specializes in the areas of:** Accounting/Auditing; Banking; Computer Science/Software; Engineering; Finance; Health/Medical; Insurance; Legal; Manufacturing; Personnel/Labor Relations; Sales; Technical. **Positions commonly filled include:** Accountant/Auditor; Aerospace Engineer; Attorney; Automotive Mechanic; Buyer; Chemical Engineer; Computer Programmer; Cost Estimator; Design Engineer; Designer; Electrical/Electronics Engineer; Electrician; Environmental Engineer; General Manager; Health Services Manager; Hotel Manager; Human Resources Manager; Industrial Engineer; Insurance Agent/Broker; Licensed Practical Nurse; Mechanical Engineer; Metallurgical Engineer; MIS Specialist; Physician; Quality Control Supervisor; Registered Nurse; Software Engineer; Systems Analyst; Underwriter/Assistant Underwriter. **Other U.S. locations:** Nationwide. **Average salary range of placements:** More than $50,000. **Number of placements per year:** 1 - 49.

PERMANENT EMPLOYMENT AGENCIES

A NANNY NETWORK INC.
P.O. Box 182192, Shelby Township MI 48318. 810/739-2100. **Fax:** 810/739-4217. **Contact:** Linda Guastella, President/CEO. **Description:** A permanent employment agency that also offers some temporary placements. **Specializes in the areas of:** Child Care, In-Home; Eldercare, In-Home; Nannies. **Positions commonly filled include:** Daycare Worker; Housekeeper; Nanny;

Preschool Worker. **Corporate headquarters location:** This Location. **Average salary range of placements:** $20,000 - $29,999. **Number of placements per year:** 200 - 499.

AE EMPLOYMENT SERVICES
1359 Northlawn NE, Grand Rapids MI 49505. 616/831-5323. **Fax:** 616/831-5324. **Contact:** Deb Laakso,

President. **Description:** A permanent employment agency. **Specializes in the areas of:** Architecture/Construction; Art/Design; Computer Science/Software; Engineering. **Positions commonly filled include:** Architect; Chemical Engineer; Civil Engineer; Computer Programmer; Construction and Building Inspector; Design Engineer; Designer; Draftsperson; Electrical/Electronics Engineer; Environmental Engineer; Geologist/Geophysicist; Landscape Architect; Mechanical Engineer; MIS Specialist; Multimedia Designer; Software Engineer; Structural Engineer; Surveyor; Systems Analyst; Transportation/Traffic Specialist. **Benefits available to temporary workers:** Medical Insurance; Paid Holidays. **Average salary range of placements:** $30,000 - $50,000. **Number of placements per year:** 1 - 49.

ACCOUNT ABILITY NOW
P.O. Box 1149, Grand Rapids MI 49501. 616/235-1149. **Fax:** 616/235-1148. **Contact:** Manager. **Description:** Account Ability Now is a permanent employment agency. **Specializes in the areas of:** Accounting/Auditing; Information Systems.

ACCOUNTANTS ONE INC.
24901 Northwestern Highway, Suite 516, Southfield MI 48075-2598. 248/354-2410. **Contact:** Richard Freimuth, President. **Description:** A permanent employment agency. **Specializes in the areas of:** Accounting/Auditing; Banking; Finance. **Positions commonly filled include:** Accountant/Auditor; Bookkeeper; Credit Manager; Data Entry Clerk; Financial Analyst. **Number of placements per year:** 1 - 49.

ACTION ASSOCIATES
100 Summit Street, P.O. Box 570, Brighton MI 48116. 810/227-4868. **Contact:** Manager. **Description:** A permanent employment agency.

ACTION MANAGEMENT CORPORATION
915 South Grand Traverse Street, Flint MI 48502. 810/234-2828. **Fax:** 810/234-5159. **Contact:** Paul Opsommer, Executive Search Coordinator. **E-mail address:** info@actionmanagement.com. **World Wide Web address:** http://www.actionmanagement.com. **Description:** A permanent employment agency. **Specializes in the areas of:** Computer Science/Software; Engineering; General Management; Personnel/Labor Relations; Sales; Technical. **Positions commonly filled include:** Account Representative; Advertising Executive; Blue-Collar Worker Supervisor; Branch Manager; Claim Rep.; Clerical Supervisor; Computer Programmer; Counselor; Customer Service Rep.; Draftsperson; Education Administrator; Electrical/Electronics Engineer; Financial Analyst; General Manager; Hotel Manager; Human Resources Manager; Human Resources Specialist; Human Service Worker; Industrial Engineer; Management Trainee; Manufacturer's/Wholesaler's Sales Representative; Manufacturing Engineer; Marketing Specialist; Mechanical Engineer; MIS Specialist; Production Manager; Public Relations Specialist; Quality Control Supervisor; Restaurant/Food Service Manager; Sales Engineer; Sales Executive; Services Sales Representative; Social Worker; Sociologist; Software Engineer; Systems Analyst; Telecommunications Manager; Typist/Word Processor. **Corporate headquarters location:** This Location. **Other area locations:** Detroit MI. **Other U.S. locations:** Arlington VA. **Average salary range of placements:** $30,000 - $70,000. **Number of placements per year:** 100 - 199.

ARKAY, INC.
23651 Goddard Street, Taylor MI 48180. 734/374-2929. **Fax:** 734/374-2453. **Contact:** Eric Esau, Business Manager. **Description:** A permanent employment agency. **Specializes in the areas of:** Nonprofit. **Positions commonly filled include:** Job Coach/Developer. **Number of placements per year:** 1 - 49.

BUSINESS TRENDS, INC.
5455 Corporate Drive, Suite 210, Troy MI 48098. 248/952-0070. **Fax:** 248/952-0089. **Contact:** Brad

Carson, Vice President. **Description:** A permanent employment agency that also provides contract, consulting, and outsourcing services. **Specializes in the areas of:** Information Technology; Telecommunications.

CALVERT ASSOCIATES INC.
1607 East Stadium Street, Ann Arbor MI 48104. 734/769-5413. **Contact:** Peter Calvert Cokinos, President. **Description:** A permanent employment agency focusing on sales, editorial, and management positions in college publishing. **Specializes in the areas of:** Publishing; Sales. **Positions commonly filled include:** Editor; Manufacturer's/Wholesaler's Sales Rep.; Sales Manager; Technical Writer/Editor. **Average salary range of placements:** $30,000 - $50,000. **Number of placements per year:** 1 - 49.

CAREER ASSOCIATES INC.
25160 Lahser Road, Suite 201, Southfield MI 48034. 248/208-0098. **Contact:** Jon Levy, Manager of Technical Services. **Description:** A permanent employment agency that also provides some temporary placements and contract services. **Specializes in the areas of:** Computer Science/Software; Engineering; Industrial; Manufacturing; Technical. **Positions commonly filled include:** Automotive Mechanic; Buyer; Ceramics Engineer; Chemist; Computer Programmer; Design Engineer; Designer; Draftsperson; Electrical/Electronics Engineer; Electrician; Environmental Engineer; Industrial Engineer; Industrial Production Manager; Materials Engineer; Mechanical Engineer; Metallurgical Engineer; Purchasing Agent/Manager; Quality Control Supervisor; Software Engineer; Systems Analyst; Technical Writer/Editor. **Benefits available to temporary workers:** Paid Holidays; Paid Vacation; Retirement Plan. **Number of placements per year:** 50 - 99.

CAREER QUEST, INC.
1760 East Grand River Avenue, East Lansing MI 48823. 517/318-3330. **Fax:** 517/318-3331. **Contact:** Manager. **Description:** A permanent employment agency that also provides career/outplacement counseling. **Specializes in the areas of:** Accounting/Auditing; Administration; Art/Design; Banking; Computer Science/Software; Economics; Finance; General Management; Insurance; Manufacturing; Sales; Secretarial. **Positions commonly filled include:** Accountant/Auditor; Administrative Manager; Bank Officer/Manager; Blue-Collar Worker Supervisor; Branch Manager; Brokerage Clerk; Budget Analyst; Buyer; Claim Rep.; Clerical Supervisor; Clinical Lab Tech.; Computer Programmer; Customer Service Rep.; Design Engineer; Designer; Draftsperson; Electrical/Electronics Engineer; Electrician; Financial Analyst; General Manager; Health Services Manager; Human Resources Specialist; Insurance Agent/Broker; Management Analyst/Consultant; Management Trainee; MIS Specialist; Property and Real Estate Manager; Public Relations Specialist; Quality Control Supervisor; Real Estate Agent; Services Sales Representative; Software Engineer; Systems Analyst; Typist/Word Processor. **Benefits available to temporary workers:** Bonus Award/Plan; Paid Vacation. **Corporate headquarters location:** Lansing MI. **Average salary range of placements:** $20,000 - $29,999. **Number of placements per year:** 50 - 99.

CLARK & HARTMAN PROFESSIONAL SEARCH
1829 West Stadium Boulevard, Suite 100, Ann Arbor MI 48103. 734/996-3100. **Fax:** 734/662-8550. **Contact:** Lewis Clark, President. **E-mail address:** chpsi@msn.com. **Description:** A permanent employment agency. Client company pays fee. **Specializes in the areas of:** Computer Science/Software; Internet Development; MIS/EDP. **Positions commonly filled include:** Applications Engineer; AS400 Programmer Analyst; Computer Engineer; Computer Operator; Computer Programmer; Computer Scientist; Computer Support Technician; Database Administrator; Database Manager; Internet Services Manager; MIS Specialist; Network/Systems Administrator; Software Engineer; SQL Programmer; Systems Analyst; Systems Manager;

Webmaster. **Corporate headquarters location:** This Location.

COLLINS & ASSOCIATES
10188 West H Avenue, Kalamazoo MI 49009-8506. 616/372-4300. **Fax:** 616/372-3921. **Contact:** Phil Collins, Principal. **E-mail address:** pcollins@collins-associates.com. **World Wide Web address:** http://www.collins-associates.com. **Description:** A permanent employment agency. **Specializes in the areas of:** Computer Science/Software; MIS/EDP. **Positions commonly filled include:** Applications Engineer; AS400 Programmer Analyst; Computer Engineer; Computer Programmer; Computer Scientist; Computer Support Technician; Content Developer; Database Administrator; Database Manager; Internet Services Manager; MIS Specialist; Multimedia Designer; Network/Systems Administrator; Software Engineer; SQL Programmer; Systems Analyst; Systems Manager; Webmaster. **Average salary range of placements:** $50,000 - $100,000. **Number of placements per year:** 1 - 49.

CONTRACT PROFESSIONALS, INC.
4141 West Walton Boulevard, Waterford MI 48329. 248/673-3800. **Toll-free phone:** 800/228-4803. **Fax:** 248/673-5992. **Contact:** Tina York, Technical Recruiter. **E-mail address:** cpi@cpijobs.com. **Description:** A permanent employment agency. **Specializes in the areas of:** Data Processing; Engineering. **Positions commonly filled include:** Aerospace Engineer; Ceramics Engineer; Chemical Engineer; Civil Engineer; Computer Programmer; Design Engineer; Draftsperson; EDP Specialist; Electrical/Electronics Engineer; Financial Analyst; Industrial Designer; Industrial Engineer; Interior Designer; Mechanical Engineer; Metallurgical Engineer; Mining Engineer; Petroleum Engineer; Services Sales Representative; Software Engineer; Structural Engineer; Systems Analyst; Technical Writer/Editor; Technician; Telecommunications Manager. **Benefits available to temporary workers:** 401(k); Dental Insurance; Life Insurance; Medical Insurance. **Other area locations:** Dearborn MI. **Other U.S. locations:** Cleveland OH. **Average salary range of placements:** More than $50,000. **Number of placements per year:** 500 - 999.

CORPORATE STAFFING RESOURCES
815 Main Street, Suite 5A, St. Joseph MI 49085. 616/983-5803. **Fax:** 616/983-5827. **Contact:** Linda McGlothlen, Branch Manager. **Description:** A permanent employment agency. **Specializes in the areas of:** Accounting; Administration; Computer Science/ Software; Engineering; General Management; Manufacturing; Personnel/Labor Relations; Sales; Technical. **Positions commonly filled include:** Accountant; Administrative Manager; Advertising Clerk; Aerospace Engineer; Agricultural Engineer; Aircraft Mechanic/Engine Specialist; Biochemist; Biological Scientist; Biomedical Engineer; Blue-Collar Worker Supervisor; Branch Manager; Chemical Engineer; Chemist; Civil Engineer; Clerical Supervisor; Computer Programmer; Cost Estimator; Credit Manager; Customer Service Rep.; Design Engineer; Designer; Draftsperson; Electrical/Electronics Engineer; Environmental Engineer; Financial Analyst; General Manager; Health Services Manager; Human Resources Specialist; Industrial Engineer; Industrial Production Manager; Internet Services Manager; Management Analyst/Consultant; Market Research Analyst; MIS Specialist; Multimedia Designer; Operations/Production Manager; Science Technologist; Software Engineer; Statistician; Structural Engineer; Systems Analyst; Technical Writer/Editor; Telecommunications Manager; Typist/Word Processor. **Corporate headquarters location:** South Bend IN. **Other U.S. locations:** Nationwide. **Number of placements per year:** 500 - 999.

DAVIS-SMITH MEDICAL EMPLOYMENT SERVICE INC.
27656 Franklin Road, Southfield MI 48034. 248/354-4100. **Contact:** Charles C. Corbert, CPC, President.

Description: A permanent employment agency. **Specializes in the areas of:** Clerical. **Positions commonly filled include:** Administrative Worker/Clerk; Bookkeeper; Medical Secretary; Nurse; Receptionist; Secretary; Technician; Typist/Word Processor. **Number of placements per year:** 50 - 99.

DAY PERSONNEL, INC.
3001 West Big Beaver Road, Suite 119, Troy MI 48084. 248/649-6797. **Fax:** 248/649-2496. **Contact:** Manager. **Description:** A permanent employment agency that also provides some temporary placements. Founded in 1953. **Specializes in the areas of:** Retail; Sales; Secretarial; Technical; Transportation. **Positions commonly filled include:** Accountant/Auditor; Adjuster; Administrative Manager; Advertising Clerk; Branch Manager; Chemical Engineer; Civil Engineer; Clerical Supervisor; Computer Programmer; Cost Estimator; Counselor; Credit Manager; Customer Service Representative; Design Engineer; Systems Analyst. **Corporate headquarters location:** This Location. **Number of placements per year:** 50 - 99.

DAY PERSONNEL, INC.
17199 Laurel Park Drive North, Suite 300, Livonia MI 48152. 313/591-6700. **Toll-free phone:** 888/LIVONIA. **Contact:** Manager. **E-mail address:** dayinc@aol.com. **World Wide Web address:** http://www. daypersonnel.com. **Description:** A permanent employment agency that also provides some temporary placements. Client company pays fee. **Specializes in the areas of:** Accounting; Administration; Bookkeeping; Engineering; Management; Sales; Secretarial; Technical. **Positions commonly filled include:** Administrative Assistant; Clerical Supervisor; Computer Operator; Computer Support Technician; Customer Service Rep.; Database Administrator; Network/Systems Administrator; Sales Manager; Sales Representative; Typist/Word Processor. **Corporate headquarters location:** Troy MI. **Average salary range of placements:** $20,000 - $100,000. **Number of placements per year:** 200 - 499.

DIVERSIFIED RECRUITERS
27400 Meadowbrook Road, Novi MI 48377. 248/344-6700. **Contact:** Manager. **Description:** A permanent employment agency. **Specializes in the areas of:** Clerical; Engineering; Office Support; Technical.

ELECTRONIC SYSTEMS PERSONNEL
3 Parklane Boulevard, Suite 106 West, Dearborn MI 48126. 313/336-3400. **Contact:** Manager. **Description:** A permanent employment agency that also provides contract services. **Specializes in the areas of:** Data Processing.

ENGINEERING PROFESSIONALS INC.
38869 Plumbrook Drive, Farmington Hills MI 48331. 248/489-9598. **Contact:** Manager. **Description:** A permanent employment agency that also provides contract services. **Specializes in the areas of:** Engineering.

EXECUSEARCH OF SOUTHWEST MICHIGAN
5205 Hitching Post Road, Kalamazoo MI 49009. 616/353-3600. **Fax:** 616/353-5310. **Contact:** John Compere, Owner. **Description:** A permanent employment agency. **Specializes in the areas of:** Engineering; Industrial; Manufacturing; Personnel/Labor Relations. **Positions commonly filled include:** Civil Engineer; Electrical/Electronics Engineer; Human Resources Manager; Industrial Production Manager; Mechanical Engineer; Metallurgical Engineer; Purchasing Agent/Manager.

EXECUTECH RESOURCE CONSULTANTS
5700 Crooks Road, Suite 105, Troy MI 48098. 248/828-3000. **Fax:** 248/828-3333. **Contact:** Jeff Bagnasco, Office Manager. **Description:** A permanent employment agency. **Specializes in the areas of:** Automotive;

Computer Programming; Office Support; Plastics; Sales. **Positions commonly filled include:** Administrative Worker/Clerk; Automotive Engineer; Computer Programmer; Manufacturing Engineer; Plastics Engineer.

STEVEN J. GREENE & ASSOCIATES
15900 10 Mile Road, Suite 205, Southfield MI 48075. 248/473-7210. **Fax:** 248/473-4548. **Contact:** Steven Greene, Owner/Manager. **Description:** A permanent employment agency. **Specializes in the areas of:** Industrial; Manufacturing; Office Support; Sales. **Positions commonly filled include:** Account Manager; Account Representative; Administrative Assistant; Management Trainee; Manufacturer's/Wholesaler's Sales Rep.; Quality Control Supervisor; Sales Engineer; Sales Manager; Sales Representative; Services Sales Representative. **Average salary range of placements:** $30,000 - $50,000. **Number of placements per year:** 100 - 199.

HEALTH CARE PROFESSIONALS
25899 West Twelve Mile Road, Suite 250, Southfield MI 48034-8343. 248/357-7080. **Fax:** 248/357-4606. **Contact:** Don Dezenski, Vice President. **Description:** A permanent employment agency that places personnel in health care facilities and health insurance organizations. **Specializes in the areas of:** Health/Medical. **Positions commonly filled include:** Clinical Lab Technician; Data Entry Clerk; EEG Technologist; EKG Technician; Medical Assistant; Medical Records Technician; Nuclear Medicine Technologist; Radiological Technologist; Receptionist; Registered Nurse; Respiratory Therapist; Surgical Technician. **Number of placements per year:** 200 - 499.

HUMAN RESOURCES EMPLOYMENT SERVICES
31 Oakland Avenue, Lower Level, Suite A, Pontiac MI 48342. 248/338-8880. **Fax:** 248/338-9434. **Contact:** Cherie Hunter, Accounts Coordinator. **Description:** A permanent employment agency. **Specializes in the areas of:** General Management; Industrial; Manufacturing; Personnel/Labor Relations; Sales; Secretarial. **Positions commonly filled include:** Blue-Collar Worker Supervisor; Clerical Supervisor; Customer Service Representative; Draftsperson; Human Resources Specialist; Industrial Production Manager; Quality Control Supervisor; Services Sales Representative; Typist/Word Processor. **Average salary range of placements:** $20,000 - $29,999. **Number of placements per year:** 1000+.

JOB FAIR NETWORK OF MICHIGAN
10823 Melbourne Street, Allen Park MI 48101. 313/381-0093. **Fax:** 313/381-0099. **Contact:** Chuck Vincent, President. **Description:** A permanent employment agency that also organizes technical and multi-industry job fairs. **Specializes in the areas of:** Administration; Architecture/Construction; Computer Science/Software; Engineering; Industrial; Manufacturing; Personnel/Labor Relations; Technical; Transportation. **Positions commonly filled include:** Aerospace Engineer; Agricultural Engineer; Aircraft Mechanic/Engine Specialist; Architect; Automotive Mechanic; Biochemist; Biological Scientist; Biomedical Engineer; Broadcast Technician; Budget Analyst; Chemical Engineer; Chemist; Civil Engineer; Computer Programmer; Construction Contractor; Construction Manager; Cost Estimator; Design Engineer; Designer; Draftsperson; Electrical/Electronics Engineer; Electrician; Environmental Engineer; Financial Analyst; Food Scientist/Technologist; Food Service Manager; Geologist/Geophysicist; Human Resources Manager; Industrial Engineer; Industrial Production Manager; Internet Services Manager; Landscape Architect; Management Analyst/Consultant; Market Research Analyst; Mathematician; Mechanical Engineer; Metallurgical Engineer; Mining Engineer; MIS Specialist; Multimedia Designer; Nuclear Engineer; Operations/Production Manager; Petroleum Engineer; Purchasing Agent/Manager; Quality Control Supervisor;

Software Engineer; Stationary Engineer; Statistician; Structural Engineer; Systems Analyst; Technical Writer/Editor; Telecommunications Manager. **Average salary range of placements:** $30,000 - $50,000. **Number of placements per year:** 500 - 999.

JOB LINE
660 Cascade West Parkway SE, Suite 55, Grand Rapids MI 49546. 616/949-2424. **Fax:** 616/949-4112. **Contact:** Rudy Sterrett, President. **Description:** A permanent employment agency. **Positions commonly filled include:** Accountant/Auditor; Adjuster; Administrative Manager; Advertising Clerk; Agricultural Engineer; Aircraft Mechanic/Engine Specialist; Architect; Automotive Mechanic; Bank Officer/Manager; Biochemist; Biological Scientist; Blue-Collar Worker Supervisor; Branch Manager; Budget Analyst; Chemical Engineer; Computer Programmer; Draftsperson; Electrician; Financial Analyst; General Manager; Human Resources Specialist; Industrial Production Manager; Management Analyst/Consultant; Occupational Therapist; Public Relations Specialist; Quality Control Supervisor; Real Estate Agent; Restaurant/Food Service Manager; Social Worker; Software Engineer; Systems Analyst; Technical Writer/Editor; Telecommunications Manager; Underwriter/Assistant Underwriter. **Average salary range of placements:** $20,000 - $50,000. **Number of placements per year:** 500 - 999.

KEY PERSONNEL
570 East 16th Street, Suite 1, Holland MI 49423. 616/396-7575. **Fax:** 616/396-3327. **Contact:** Manager. **Description:** A permanent employment agency. **Specializes in the areas of:** Accounting/Auditing; Administration; Art/Design; Computer Science/Software; Engineering; Industrial; Manufacturing; Personnel/Labor Relations. **Positions commonly filled include:** Accountant/Auditor; Administrative Manager; Designer; Draftsperson; Electrical/Electronics Engineer; Human Resources Manager; Industrial Engineer; Purchasing Agent/Manager; Quality Control Supervisor; Software Engineer. **Number of placements per year:** 500 - 999.

LUDOT PERSONNEL
6056 North Sheldon Road, Canton MI 48187. 248/353-9720. **Contact:** Michael Morton, Vice President. **Description:** A permanent employment agency. **Specializes in the areas of:** Automotive; Computer Hardware/Software; Engineering; Manufacturing; MIS/EDP. **Positions commonly filled include:** Accountant/Auditor; Aerospace Engineer; Economist; Electrical/Electronics Engineer; Industrial Engineer; Mechanical Engineer; Metallurgical Engineer; MIS Specialist; Quality Control Supervisor; Systems Analyst. **Number of placements per year:** 50 - 99.

MASTERSON PERSONNEL OF MICHIGAN, INC.
3800 Packard Road, Suite 110, Ann Arbor MI 48108. 734/677-2600. **Fax:** 734/677-4730. **Contact:** Staffing Supervisor. **Description:** A permanent employment agency. **Positions commonly filled include:** Administrative Assistant; Assembly Worker; Clerical Supervisor; Customer Service Representative; Maintenance Technician; Receptionist; Shipping and Receiving Clerk; Typist/Word Processor. **Benefits available to temporary workers:** 401(k); Medical Insurance. **Corporate headquarters location:** Minneapolis MN. **Other U.S. locations:** Edina MN; St. Paul MN. **Average salary range of placements:** Less than $20,000.

MICHIGAN INDIAN EMPLOYMENT AND TRAINING SERVICES
325 East Lake Street, Petoskey MI 49770. 231/347-9330. **Fax:** 231/347-9339. **Contact:** Tricia Naganasha, Regional Manager. **Description:** A permanent agency for Native Americans that also provides resume assistance, job referrals, and support services. **Specializes in the areas of:** Education. **Positions commonly filled include:** Assembly Worker;

Bookkeeper; Carpenter; Clerk; Construction Trade Worker; Light Industrial Worker; Receptionist; Reporter; Secretary; Typist/Word Processor. **Corporate headquarters location:** Lansing MI. **Other area locations:** Ann Arbor MI; Flint MI; Iron Mountain MI; Mount Pleasant MI; Portage MI. **Average salary range of placements:** Less than $20,000. **Number of placements per year:** 1 - 49.

MICHIGAN UNEMPLOYMENT AGENCY
3391 Plainfield NE, Grand Rapids MI 49525. 616/361-3200. **Fax:** 616/361-3229. **Contact:** Office Manager. **Description:** A permanent employment agency.

MICHIGAN WORKS SERVICE CENTER
304 Harriet Street, Ypsilanti MI 48197. 734/481-2517. **Contact:** Training Coordinator. **Description:** A federally-funded permanent employment agency. The agency also participates in Michigan's Welfare to Work program. **Positions commonly filled include:** Advertising Clerk; Automotive Mechanic; Bank Officer/Manager; Blue-Collar Worker Supervisor; Branch Manager; Buyer; Claim Representative; Clerical Supervisor; Computer Programmer; Customer Service Representative; Dental Assistant/Dental Hygienist; EKG Technician; Electrician; Emergency Medical Technician; Human Service Worker; Industrial Production Manager; Licensed Practical Nurse; Management Trainee; Medical Records Technician; MIS Specialist; Operations/Production Manager; Paralegal; Physical Therapist; Preschool Worker; Respiratory Therapist; Restaurant/Food Service Manager; Services Sales Representative; Social Worker; Travel Agent. **Average salary range of placements:** Less than $20,000. **Number of placements per year:** 500 - 999.

NANNY ATTACHMENT SERVICE
P.O. Box 382, Whitehall MI 49461. 231/893-6908. **Toll-free phone:** 800/528-2498. **Contact:** Teresa Grey, Owner/President. **Description:** A permanent employment agency. **Specializes in the areas of:** Child Care, In-Home; Nannies. **Average salary range of placements:** Less than $20,000. **Number of placements per year:** 50 - 99.

NATIONWIDE CAREER NETWORK
5445 Corporate Drive, Suite 160, Troy MI 48098-2683. 248/641-7779. **Fax:** 248/641-7778. **Contact:** Carol Peters, President. **Description:** A permanent employment agency that also offers some temporary placements. **Specializes in the areas of:** Computer Science/Software; Engineering; Finance; Health/Medical; Sales; Secretarial; Technical. **Positions commonly filled include:** Applications Engineer; Biomedical Engineer; Certified Nurses Aide; Chemical Engineer; Chemist; Civil Engineer; Clerical Supervisor; Clinical Lab Technician; Computer Operator; Computer Programmer; Cost Estimator; Customer Service Representative; Database Manager; Design Engineer; EKG Technician; Industrial Engineer; Industrial Production Manager; Licensed Practical Nurse; Management Analyst/Consultant; MIS Specialist; Physical Therapist; Physician; Purchasing Agent/Manager; Registered Nurse; Sales Engineer; Sales Manager; Sales Representative; Secretary; Software Engineer; Surgical Technician; Systems Analyst; Systems Manager; Technical Writer/Editor; Typist/Word Processor. **Average salary range of placements:** $30,000 - $50,000. **Number of placements per year:** 500 - 999.

OAKLAND RESOURCES
27600 Northwest Highway, Suite 240, Southfield MI 48034. 248/799-3022. **Fax:** 248/799-3023. **Contact:** General Manager. **Description:** A permanent employment agency. **Positions commonly filled include:** Computer Programmer; Management Analyst/Consultant; Systems Analyst. **Number of placements per year:** 1 - 49.

PERMANENT STAFF COMPANY
850 Stephenson Highway, Suite 303, Troy MI 48083. 248/585-2720. **Contact:** Recruiter. **Description:** A

permanent employment agency that also provides some temporary placements. **Specializes in the areas of:** Secretarial. **Positions commonly filled include:** Administrative Assistant; Administrative Manager; Advertising Clerk; Customer Service Representative; Human Resources Specialist; Management Trainee; Paralegal; Receptionist; Secretary; Services Sales Representative. **Average salary range of placements:** $20,000 - $29,999. **Number of placements per year:** 100 - 199.

PREFERRED EMPLOYMENT PLANNING
G-1479 West Bristol Road, Flint MI 48507. 810/233-7200. **Fax:** 810/233-3095. **Contact:** Dan LePard, Manager. **Description:** A permanent employment agency. **Specializes in the areas of:** Administration; Computer Science/Software; Engineering; Finance; Food; General Management; Industrial; Manufacturing; Personnel/Labor Relations; Retail; Sales; Secretarial; Technical. **Positions commonly filled include:** Accountant/Auditor; Administrative Manager; Advertising Clerk; Blue-Collar Worker Supervisor; Branch Manager; Ceramics Engineer; Chemical Engineer; Clerical Supervisor; Computer Programmer; Counselor; Credit Manager; Customer Service Representative; Design Engineer; Electrical/Electronics Engineer; Environmental Engineer; General Manager; Hotel Manager; Human Resources Specialist; Human Service Worker; Industrial Engineer; Industrial Production Manager; Management Trainee; Manufacturer's/Wholesaler's Sales Rep.; Materials Engineer; Mechanical Engineer; Metallurgical Engineer; MIS Specialist; Operations/Production Manager; Pharmacist; Property and Real Estate Manager; Purchasing Agent/Manager; Quality Control Supervisor; Radio/TV Announcer/Broadcaster; Reporter; Restaurant/Food Service Manager; Securities Sales Representative; Services Sales Representative; Social Worker; Software Engineer; Speech-Language Pathologist; Systems Analyst; Technical Writer/Editor; Typist/Word Processor. **Average salary range of placements:** $20,000 - $100,000. **Number of placements per year:** 100 - 199.

RESOURCE TECHNOLOGIES CORPORATION
P.O. Box 3201, Troy MI 48007. 248/585-4750. **Contact:** Manager. **Description:** A permanent employment agency. **Specializes in the areas of:** Computer Science/Software; Design; Engineering.

ROMAC INTERNATIONAL
2000 Town Center, Suite 850, Southfield MI 48075. 248/352-6520. **Fax:** 248/352-7514. **Contact:** Manager. **Description:** A permanent employment agency. **Specializes in the areas of:** Administration; Computer Science/Software. **Positions commonly filled include:** Computer Programmer; Software Engineer; Systems Analyst; Technical Writer/Editor. **Corporate headquarters location:** Tampa FL. **Number of placements per year:** 100 - 199.

ROMAC INTERNATIONAL
161 Ottawa NW, Suite 409-D, Grand Rapids MI 49503. 616/459-3600. **Fax:** 616/459-3670. **Contact:** Director. **Description:** A permanent employment agency. **Specializes in the areas of:** Accounting/Auditing; Computer Science/Software; Engineering; Finance; Manufacturing. **Positions commonly filled include:** Accountant/Auditor; Budget Analyst; Computer Programmer; Financial Analyst; MIS Specialist; Software Engineer; Systems Analyst. **Benefits available to temporary workers:** Medical Insurance. **Corporate headquarters location:** Tampa FL. **Other U.S. locations:** Nationwide. **Average salary range of placements:** $30,000 - $50,000. **Number of placements per year:** 200 - 499.

SALES EXECUTIVES INC.
755 West Big Beaver Road, Suite 2107, Troy MI 48084. 248/362-1900. **Fax:** 248/362-0253. **Contact:** Mr. Dale Statson, President. **Description:** A permanent employment agency. **Specializes in the areas of:**

Chemicals; Computer Hardware/Software; Finance; General Management; Health/Medical; Plastics; Sales. **Positions commonly filled include:** Marketing Specialist; Sales Manager; Sales Representative. **Number of placements per year:** 200 - 499.

SNELLING PERSONNEL SERVICES
3711 South Westnedge, Kalamazoo MI 49008. 616/343-8282. **Fax:** 616/343-0836. **Contact:** Vice President of Operations. **Description:** A permanent employment agency that also provides some temporary and temp-to-perm placements. **Specializes in the areas of:** Light Industrial; Secretarial. **Corporate headquarters location:** Dallas TX. **Other U.S. locations:** Nationwide. **Number of placements per year:** 1000+.

SNELLING PERSONNEL SERVICES BRYANT BUREAU
18600 Florence Street, Roseville MI 48066. 810/772-6760. **Contact:** Ron Daiza, Manager. **Description:** A permanent employment agency that also offers some temporary placements. Bryant Bureau (also at this location) is an executive search firm operating on both retainer and contingency bases. **NOTE:** Resumes for Bryant Bureau should be addressed to Jacqueline Nabat, Director of Engineering and Recruitment. **Specializes in the areas of:** Legal; Publishing; Secretarial. **Positions commonly filled include:** Administrative Worker/Clerk; Bookkeeper; Brokerage Clerk; Paralegal; Receptionist; Secretary; Typist/Word Processor. **Corporate headquarters location:** Dallas TX. **Number of placements per year:** 100 - 199.

SNELLING SEARCH
30100 Telegraph Road, Suite 474, Bingham Farms MI 48025. 248/644-4600. **Fax:** 248/644-4739. **Contact:** Jacqueline Dombroski, President. **Description:** A permanent employment agency. **Specializes in the areas of:** Engineering; Health/Medical; Manufacturing; Secretarial. **Positions commonly filled include:** Administrative Assistant; Bookkeeper; Chemical Engineer; Chemist; Clerk; Data Entry Clerk; Electrical/Electronics Engineer; Manufacturing Engineer; Mechanical Engineer; Quality Control Supervisor; Receptionist; Secretary; Typist/Word Processor. **Benefits available to temporary workers:** 401(k). **Corporate headquarters location:** Dallas TX. **Other area locations:** Roseville MI; Kalamazoo MI. **Average salary range of placements:** More than $50,000. **Number of placements per year:** 200 - 499.

TEA INC.
161 Ottawa Avenue NW, Suite 309H, Grand Rapids MI 49503-2704. 616/451-9891. **Contact:** Larry Wesholski, President. **Description:** A permanent employment agency that also offers some temporary and contract placements. **Specializes in the areas of:** Accounting/Auditing; Banking; Manufacturing; Secretarial. **Positions commonly filled include:** Accountant/Auditor; Administrative Manager; Attorney; Bank Officer/Manager; Blue-Collar Worker Supervisor; Branch Manager; Clerical Supervisor; Computer Programmer; Credit Manager; Electrical/Electronics Engineer; Human Resources Manager; Industrial Engineer; Industrial Production Manager; MIS Specialist; Paralegal; Quality Control Supervisor; Systems Analyst; Typist/Word Processor; Underwriter/Assistant Underwriter. **Average salary range of placements:** $30,000 - $50,000. **Number of placements per year:** 1 - 49.

TECHNICAL PROFESSIONAL SERVICE INC.
1405 South Yankee Springs Road, Middleville MI 49333. 616/891-9261. **Toll-free phone:** 888/228-3600. **Fax:** 616/891-9263. **Contact:** Arnaldo R. Rodriguez, President. **E-mail address:** info@tpsincorporated.com. **World Wide Web address:** http://www.tpsincorporated.com. **Description:** A permanent employment agency. **Specializes in the areas of:** Architecture/Construction; Art/Design; Computer Science/Software; Engineering; General Management;

Industrial; Manufacturing; MIS/EDP; Personnel/Labor Relations; Technical. **Positions commonly filled include:** Administrative Assistant; Administrative Manager; Applications Engineer; Architect; Biochemist; Biological Scientist; Biomedical Engineer; Blue-Collar Worker Supervisor; Broadcast Technician; Chemical Engineer; Chemist; Chief Financial Officer; Civil Engineer; Clinical Lab Technician; Computer Animator; Computer Operator; Computer Programmer; Cost Estimator; Database Manager; Design Engineer; Draftsperson; Electrical/Electronics Engineer; Electrician; Environmental Engineer; Finance Director; Financial Analyst; General Manager; Graphic Artist; Graphic Designer; Human Resources Manager; Industrial Engineer; Industrial Production Manager; Internet Services Manager; Management Analyst/Consultant; Manufacturing Engineer; Mechanical Engineer; Metallurgical Engineer; MIS Specialist; Online Content Specialist; Operations Manager; Production Manager; Project Manager; Purchasing Agent/Manager; Quality Control Supervisor; Sales Engineer; Secretary; Software Engineer; Statistician; Systems Analyst; Systems Manager; Technical Writer/Editor; Telecommunications Manager; Transportation/Traffic Specialist; Typist/Word Processor; Webmaster. **Benefits available to temporary workers:** Medical Insurance; Paid Holidays; Paid Vacation. **Corporate headquarters location:** This Location. **Average salary range of placements:** More than $50,000. **Number of placements per year:** 100 - 199.

VECTECH PHARMACEUTICALS CONSULTANTS
24543 Indoplex Circle, Farmington Hills MI 48335-2529. 248/442-2960. **Fax:** 248/442-0060. **Contact:** Elaine Douglass, Human Resources Manager. **Description:** A permanent employment agency. **Specializes in the areas of:** Engineering; Health/Medical; Pharmaceuticals. **Positions commonly filled include:** Biochemist; Biological Scientist; Biomedical Engineer; Chemical Engineer; Chemist; Computer Programmer; Construction Contractor; Cost Estimator; Design Engineer; Draftsperson; Electrical/Electronics Engineer; Environmental Engineer; Mechanical Engineer; MIS Specialist; Pharmacist; Software Engineer; Systems Analyst. **Average salary range of placements:** $30,000 - $40,000. **Number of placements per year:** 1 - 49.

WISE PERSONNEL SERVICES, INC.
200 Admiral Avenue, Portage MI 49002-3503. 616/323-2300. **Toll-free phone:** 800/842-2136. **Fax:** 616/323-8588. **Contact:** Manager. **Description:** A permanent employment agency. **Specializes in the areas of:** Accounting/Auditing; Administration; Computer Science/Software; Engineering; Sales; Technical. **Positions commonly filled include:** Accountant/Auditor; Administrative Manager; Architect; Blue-Collar Worker Supervisor; Branch Manager; Buyer; Chemical Engineer; Clerical Supervisor; Computer Programmer; Customer Service Rep.; Design Engineer; Designer; Draftsperson; Electrical/Electronics Engineer; Electrician; Geologist/Geophysicist; Human Resources Manager; Industrial Engineer; Industrial Production Manager; Internet Services Manager; Mechanical Engineer; Quality Control Supervisor; Services Sales Representative; Software Engineer; Surveyor; Systems Analyst. **Benefits available to temporary workers:** Dental Insurance; Medical Insurance; Paid Holidays; Paid Vacation. **Number of placements per year:** 50 - 99.

WOOD PERSONNEL SERVICES WOOD TEMPORARY STAFFING
P.O. Box 8670, Benton Harbor MI 49023. 616/925-6767. **Fax:** 616/925-6090. **Contact:** Recruiter. **Description:** A permanent employment agency. Wood Temporary Staffing (also at this location) is a temporary agency that provides clerical, light industrial, and technical placements. **Specializes in the areas of:** Accounting/Auditing; Agriculture; Computer Science/Software; Engineering; Industrial; Manufacturing;

Personnel/Labor Relations. **Positions commonly filled include:** Advertising Clerk; Agricultural Engineer; Buyer; Computer Programmer; Credit Manager; Design Engineer; Draftsperson; Electrical/Electronics Engineer; Environmental Engineer; Financial Analyst; General

Manager; Industrial Engineer; Mechanical Engineer; MIS Specialist; Quality Control Supervisor; Systems Analyst. **Average salary range of placements:** $30,000 - $50,000. **Number of placements per year:** 50 - 99.

TEMPORARY EMPLOYMENT AGENCIES

ACCOUNTANTS SUPPORT SERVICE CORP.
Grand Rapids MI 49506. 616/356-1383. **Fax:** 616/324-7492. **Contact:** Manager. **E-mail address:** account@gte.net. **World Wide Web address:** http://www.gtesupersite.com/accountstss. **Description:** A temporary agency. **Specializes in the areas of:** Accounting/Auditing; Bookkeeping; Office Support; Tax. **Positions commonly filled include:** Account Manager; Account Representative; Accountant; Administrative Assistant; Bookkeeper; Collection Manager; Controller; Credit Manager; Customer Service Representative; Executive Assistant; Legal Secretary; Medical Secretary; Receptionist; Tax Specialist. **Other area locations:** Portage MI; St. Joseph MI.

ACCOUNTEMPS
OFFICETEAM
305 West Big Beaver Road, Suite 201, Troy MI 48084. 248/524-9050. **Toll-free phone:** 800/803-8367. **Fax:** 248/524-3115. **Contact:** Manager. **Description:** A temporary agency. OfficeTeam (also at this location) is a temporary agency that also provides some permanent placements to office and administrative professionals. **Specializes in the areas of:** Accounting/Auditing; Administration; Banking; Finance; Secretarial. **Positions commonly filled include:** Accountant/Auditor; Administrative Manager; Advertising Clerk; Bank Officer/Manager; Budget Analyst; Claim Representative; Clerical Supervisor; Cost Estimator; Credit Manager; Financial Analyst; Services Sales Representative; Typist/Word Processor. **Benefits available to temporary workers:** Medical Insurance; Paid Holidays; Paid Vacation; Tuition Assistance. **Corporate headquarters location:** Menlo Park CA. **Other U.S. locations:** Nationwide. **Number of placements per year:** 1000+.

AQUENT PARTNERS
300 Galleria Officentre, Suite 111, Southfield MI 48034-7469. 248/353-1333. **Toll-free phone:** 877/PARTNER. **Fax:** 248/353-1336. **Contact:** Kelly Collins, Manager. **E-mail address:** kcollins@aquent.com. **World Wide Web address:** http://www.aquentpartners.com. **Description:** A temporary agency that provides placements for creative, Web, and technical professionals. Aquent Partners also provides some temp-to-perm, permanent, and contract placements. **Specializes in the areas of:** Administration; Art/Design; Computer Science/Software; Marketing. **Positions commonly filled include:** Computer Animator; Computer Engineer; Computer Operator; Computer Programmer; Computer Support Technician; Computer Technician; Content Developer; Database Administrator; Database Manager; Desktop Publishing Specialist; Editor; Editorial Assistant; Graphic Artist; Graphic Designer; Internet Services Manager; Managing Editor; MIS Specialist; Multimedia Designer; Network/Systems Administrator; Production Manager; Project Manager; Software Engineer; SQL Programmer; Systems Analyst; Systems Manager; Technical Writer/Editor; Webmaster. **Benefits available to temporary workers:** 401(k); Dental Insurance; Disability Coverage; Medical Insurance. **CEO:** John Chuang.

BARMAN STAFFING SOLUTIONS
255 28th Street SE, Grand Rapids MI 49508. 616/245-3300. **Fax:** 616/245-3353. **Contact:** Paul Baareman, President. **Description:** A temporary employment agency. **Specializes in the areas of:** Accounting; Computer Science/Software; Engineering; General Management; Industrial; Light Industrial; Marketing; Sales. **Positions commonly filled include:** Account

Representative; Accountant; Administrative Assistant; Buyer; Controller; Customer Service Representative; Electrical/Electronics Engineer; Environmental Engineer; General Manager; Graphic Designer; Human Resources Manager; Industrial Engineer; Manufacturing Engineer; Mechanical Engineer; Operations Manager; Production Manager; Quality Control Supervisor; Sales Engineer; Sales Executive; Sales Manager; Sales Representative; Secretary; Systems Analyst; Technical Writer/Editor; Telecommunications Manager; Typist/Word Processor. **Benefits available to temporary workers:** Bonus Award/Plan; Dental Insurance; Medical Insurance; Paid Holidays; Paid Vacation. **Corporate headquarters location:** This Location. **Average salary range of placements:** $30,000 - $50,000. **Number of placements per year:** 1 - 49.

DESIGN & ENGINEERING SERVICE
53305 Woodbridge Drive, Shelby Township MI 48316. 248/656-9302. **Contact:** Manager. **Description:** A temporary agency that also provides some temp-to-perm placements. **Specializes in the areas of:** Design; Engineering.

DYNAMIC PEOPLE
3011 West Grand Boulevard, Suite 418, Detroit MI 48202. 313/875-1455. **Fax:** 313/875-3808. **Contact:** Mary Fayerweather, Owner. **Description:** A temporary agency that also provides some contract services. **Specializes in the areas of:** Accounting/Auditing; Administration; Secretarial. **Positions commonly filled include:** Advertising Clerk; Claim Representative; Customer Service Representative; Human Resources Manager; Market Research Analyst; Systems Analyst; Typist/Word Processor. **Corporate headquarters location:** Atlanta GA. **Other U.S. locations:** Nationwide. **Number of placements per year:** 500 - 999.

ENTECH PERSONNEL SERVICES
363 West Big Beaver Road, Troy MI 48084. 248/528-1444. **Toll-free phone:** 800/33-ENTECH. **Fax:** 248/528-6981. **Contact:** Georgette Wyseaver, Corporate Marketing. **E-mail address:** entech@entechpersonnel.com. **World Wide Web address:** http://www.entechpersonnel.com. **Description:** A temporary agency. Client company pays fee. **Specializes in the areas of:** Administration; Architecture/Construction; Art/Design; Banking; Computer Science/Software; Engineering; Finance; General Management; Health/Medical; Light Industrial; Marketing; MIS/EDP; Personnel/Labor Relations; Sales; Scientific; Secretarial; Technical. **Positions commonly filled include:** Account Manager; Account Representative; Accountant; Administrative Assistant; Administrative Manager; Applications Engineer; Architect; AS400 Programmer Analyst; Assistant Manager; Bank Officer/Manager; Branch Manager; Budget Analyst; Buyer; Certified Nurses Aide; Certified Occupational Therapy Assistant; Chemical Engineer; Chief Financial Officer; Civil Engineer; Clerical Supervisor; Computer Animator; Computer Engineer; Computer Operator; Computer Programmer; Computer Scientist; Computer Support Technician; Computer Technician; Construction Contractor; Content Developer; Controller; Customer Service Representative; Database Administrator; Database Manager; Design Engineer; Desktop Publishing Specialist; Dietician/Nutritionist; Draftsperson; EEG Technologist; EKG Technician; Electrical/Electronics Engineer; Electrician; Emergency Medical Technician; Environmental Engineer; Finance Director; General Manager; Graphic Artist; Graphic

Designer; Home Health Aide; Human Resources Manager; Industrial Engineer; Industrial Production Manager; Internet Services Manager; Licensed Practical Nurse; Management Analyst/Consultant; Management Trainee; Manufacturing Engineer; Mechanical Engineer; Medical Assistant; Medical Records Technician; Metallurgical Engineer; MIS Specialist; Multimedia Designer; Network/Systems Administrator; Nuclear Medicine Technologist; Nurse Practitioner; Occupational Therapist; Operations Manager; Paralegal; Pharmacist; Physical Therapist; Physical Therapy Assistant; Physician; Production Manager; Project Manager; Purchasing Agent/Manager; Quality Assurance Engineer; Quality Control Supervisor; Radiological Technologist; Registered Nurse; Respiratory Therapist; Sales Engineer; Sales Executive; Sales Manager; Sales Representative; Secretary; Software Engineer; Speech-Language Pathologist; SQL Programmer; Surgical Technician; Systems Analyst; Systems Manager; Technical Writer/Editor; Typist/Word Processor; Underwriter/ Assistant Underwriter; Webmaster. **Benefits available to temporary workers:** 401(k); Dental Insurance; Life Insurance; Medical Insurance; Paid Holidays; Tuition Assistance; Vacation Pay. **Corporate headquarters location:** This Location. **Other area locations:** Auburn Hills MI; Detroit MI; Grand Blanc MI; Southfield MI. **Average salary range of placements:** $20,000 - $29,999. **Number of placements per year:** 1000+.

EXPRESS PERSONNEL SERVICES
1707 West Big Beaver Road, Suite 150, Troy MI 48084. 248/643-8590. **Fax:** 248/643-4362. **Contact:** Manager. **Description:** A temporary agency. Founded in 1983. **Specializes in the areas of:** Accounting/Auditing; Banking; Engineering; Food; Industrial; Insurance; Legal; Manufacturing; Personnel/Labor Relations; Publishing; Retail; Secretarial. **Positions commonly filled include:** Accountant/Auditor; Advertising Clerk; Blue-Collar Worker Supervisor; Clerical Supervisor; Customer Service Representative; Human Resources Manager; Management Trainee; Mechanical Engineer; Operations/Production Manager; Paralegal; Purchasing Agent/Manager; Quality Control Supervisor; Restaurant/Food Service Manager; Software Engineer; Technical Writer/Editor; Typist/Word Processor. **Benefits available to temporary workers:** Life Insurance; Medical Insurance; Paid Holidays; Paid Vacation; Scholarship Program. **Corporate headquarters location:** Oklahoma City OK. **Number of placements per year:** 200 - 499.

EXPRESS PERSONNEL SERVICES
38215 West Ten Mile Road, Farmington Hills MI 48335. 248/474-5000. **Fax:** 248/474-6833. **Contact:** Manager. **Description:** A temporary agency that also provides some contract placements. **Specializes in the areas of:** Accounting/Auditing; Banking; Food; Industrial; Insurance; Legal; Manufacturing; Personnel/Labor Relations; Publishing; Retail; Secretarial. **Positions commonly filled include:** Accountant/Auditor; Blue-Collar Worker Supervisor; Clerical Supervisor; Customer Service Representative; Human Resources Specialist; Management Trainee; Mechanical Engineer; Operations/ Production Manager; Paralegal; Purchasing Agent/ Manager; Quality Control Supervisor; Restaurant/Food Service Manager; Software Engineer; Technical Writer/Editor; Typist/Word Processor. **Benefits available to temporary workers:** 401(k); Life Insurance; Medical Insurance. **Corporate headquarters location:** Oklahoma City OK. **Average salary range of placements:** $30,000 - $50,000.

EXPRESS PERSONNEL SERVICES
3061 Walton Boulevard, Auburn Hills MI 48326. 248/373-0080. **Fax:** 248/373-7192. **Contact:** Manager. **Description:** A temporary agency that also provides some contract placements. **Specializes in the areas of:** Accounting/Auditing; Advertising; Banking; Food; Health/Medical; Industrial; Insurance; Manufacturing; Personnel/Labor Relations; Publishing; Retail; Secretarial. **Positions commonly filled include:** Accountant/Auditor; Blue-Collar Worker Supervisor;

Clerical Supervisor; Customer Service Representative; Human Resources Specialist; Management Trainee; Market Research Analyst; Operations/Production Manager; Paralegal; Purchasing Agent/Manager; Quality Control Supervisor; Services Sales Representative; Surveyor; Technical Writer/Editor; Typist/Word Processor; Underwriter/Assistant Underwriter. **Benefits available to temporary workers:** Life Insurance; Medical Insurance; Paid Holidays; Paid Vacation; Scholarship Program. **Corporate headquarters location:** Oklahoma City OK.

EXPRESS PERSONNEL SERVICES
16250 East Thirteen Mile Road, Roseville MI 48066-1524. 810/779-5090. **Fax:** 810/779-5453. **Contact:** Manager. **Description:** A temporary agency. **Specializes in the areas of:** Accounting/Auditing; Engineering; General Management; Industrial; Manufacturing; Personnel/Labor Relations; Sales; Secretarial. **Positions commonly filled include:** Accountant/Auditor; Adjuster; Administrative Manager; Advertising Clerk; Blue-Collar Worker Supervisor; Branch Manager; Buyer; Claim Representative; Clerical Supervisor; Computer Programmer; Customer Service Representative; Electrical/Electronics Engineer; Electrician; General Manager; Human Resources Specialist; Industrial Engineer; Industrial Production Manager; Management Trainee; Manufacturer's/Wholesaler's Sales Rep.; Mechanical Engineer; Operations/Production Manager; Quality Control Supervisor; Services Sales Representative; Software Engineer; Systems Analyst. **Corporate headquarters location:** Oklahoma City OK. **Number of placements per year:** 50 - 99.

INTERIM PERSONNEL
131 Columbia Avenue East, Suite 202, Battle Creek MI 49015. 616/963-6768. **Fax:** 616/963-6860. **Contact:** Kelly Witt, Customer Service Assistant. **Description:** A temporary agency. **Specializes in the areas of:** Industrial; Manufacturing; Personnel/Labor Relations; Secretarial. **Positions commonly filled include:** Blue-Collar Worker Supervisor; Draftsperson; Human Resources Specialist; Typist/Word Processor. **Other U.S. locations:** Nationwide.

KELLY SCIENTIFIC RESOURCES
33533 West 12 Mile Road, Suite 140, Farmington Hills MI 48331. 248/848-9360. **Fax:** 248/848-9315. **Contact:** Branch Manager. **World Wide Web address:** http://www.kellyscientific.com. **Description:** A temporary agency for scientific professionals. **Specializes in the areas of:** Automotive; Biotechnology; Chemicals; Environmental; Food; Pharmaceuticals.

KELLY SERVICES, INC.
3200 Greenfield Road, Suite 303, Dearborn MI 48120. 313/271-5300. **Fax:** 313/336-3115. **Contact:** Branch Manager. **Description:** A temporary agency. **Specializes in the areas of:** Personnel/Labor Relations; Sales; Secretarial. **Positions commonly filled include:** Administrative Manager; Human Resources Specialist. **Corporate headquarters location:** Troy MI. **Number of placements per year:** 1000+.

MANPOWER, INC.
3011 West Grand Boulevard, Suite 412, Detroit MI 48202. 313/871-1010. **Contact:** Manager. **Description:** A temporary agency. **Specializes in the areas of:** Clerical; Light Industrial; Office Support; Technical; Telemarketing; Word Processing. **Positions commonly filled include:** Accountant/Auditor; Accounting Clerk; Administrative Assistant; Assembler; Biological Scientist; Bookkeeper; Chemist; Computer Operator; Customer Service Representative; Design Engineer; Desktop Publishing Specialist; Electrician; Machine Operator; Material Control Specialist; Order Clerk; Packaging/Processing Worker; Painter; Project Engineer; Proofreader; Receptionist; Records Manager; Research Assistant; Secretary; Software Engineer; Stenographer; Systems Analyst; Technical Writer/Editor; Technician; Transcriptionist; Typist/Word Processor; Welder. **Benefits available to temporary workers:** 401(k); Life

Insurance; Medical Insurance; Paid Holidays; Paid Vacation. **Corporate headquarters location:** Milwaukee WI. **Other U.S. locations:** Nationwide. **Average salary range of placements:** Less than $20,000. **Number of placements per year:** 1000+.

MANPOWER, INC.
2341 Stone Bridge Drive, Building F, Flint MI 48532. 810/733-1520. **Fax:** 810/733-0240. **Contact:** District Manager. **Description:** A temporary agency. **Specializes in the areas of:** Personnel/Labor Relations. **Positions commonly filled include:** Accountant/Auditor; Blue-Collar Worker Supervisor; Clerical Supervisor; Medical Records Technician; Paralegal; Typist/Word Processor. **Benefits available to temporary workers:** Dental Insurance; Life Insurance; Medical Insurance. **Corporate headquarters location:** Milwaukee WI. **Other U.S. locations:** Nationwide. **Average salary range of placements:** Less than $20,000. **Number of placements per year:** 1000+.

NUSTAR TEMPORARY SERVICES
332 South Stephenson Avenue, Suite 2, Iron Mountain MI 49801. 906/779-1512. **Fax:** 906/779-2910. **Contact:** Jerry Robarge, President. **Description:** A temporary agency that also provides some permanent home health care placements. **Specializes in the areas of:** Health/Medical; Manufacturing; Secretarial; Transportation. **Positions commonly filled include:** Blue-Collar Worker Supervisor; Buyer; Cost Estimator; Customer Service Rep.; Dental Assistant/Dental Hygienist; Draftsperson; Electrician; Health Services Manager; Licensed Practical Nurse; Management Trainee; MIS Specialist; Recreational Therapist; Registered Nurse; Technical Writer/Editor; Typist/Word Processor. **Benefits available to temporary workers:** Life Insurance; Medical Insurance. **Other area locations:** Houghton MI; Jackson MI. **Average salary range of placements:** $20,000 - $29,999. **Number of placements per year:** 100 - 199.

OLSTEN PROFESSIONAL STAFFING
2935 Buchanan SW, Grand Rapids MI 49548. 616/247-0004. **Fax:** 616/452-7207. **Contact:** Placement Specialist. **Description:** A temporary agency that also provides permanent placements. **Specializes in the areas of:** Accounting/Auditing; Banking; Finance; Health/Medical; Manufacturing. **Positions commonly filled include:** Accountant/Auditor; Bank Officer/Manager; Brokerage Clerk; Budget Analyst; Buyer; Cost Estimator; Credit Manager; Financial Analyst; Securities Sales Rep. **Corporate headquarters location:** Melville NY. **Number of placements per year:** 500 - 999.

PERSONNEL AT LAW, INC.
3000 Town Center, Suite 2030, Southfield MI 48075. 248/358-0060. **Toll-free phone:** 888/THE-TEMP. **Fax:** 248/358-0235. **Contact:** Judy Wells, President. **Description:** A temporary agency that also provides some permanent placements. The company's two divisions, Secretaries EtCetera and Net Staffing also operate at this location. **Specializes in the areas of:** Information Technology; Legal; Secretarial. **Positions commonly filled include:** Attorney; Clerical Supervisor; Paralegal; Typist/Word Processor. **Benefits available to temporary workers:** Bonus Award/Plan; Medical Insurance; Paid Vacation. **Corporate headquarters location:** This Location. **Other U.S. locations:** Atlanta GA. **Average salary range of placements:** $20,000 - $29,999. **Number of placements per year:** 1000+.

SYGNETICS INC.
570 Kirts Boulevard, Suite 237, Troy MI 48084. 248/244-9595. **Fax:** 248/244-9720. **Contact:** President. **E-mail address:** eagle@mich.com. **Description:** A temporary agency that also provides some permanent placements. **Specializes in the areas of:** Computer Science/Software; Engineering; Manufacturing; Secretarial. **Positions commonly filled include:** Buyer; Computer Programmer; Customer Service Rep.; Design Engineer; Designer; Electrical/Electronics Engineer; MIS Specialist; Software Engineer; Systems Analyst;

Typist/Word Processor. **Benefits available to temporary workers:** Medical Insurance; Paid Holidays; Paid Vacation. **Average salary range of placements:** $30,000 - $50,000. **Number of placements per year:** 200 - 499.

TRC STAFFING SERVICES
2110 Fifteen Mile Road, Sterling Heights MI 48310-4806. 810/939-3210. **Fax:** 810/978-0572. **Contact:** Delores Patouhas, Vice President. **Description:** A temporary agency. Founded in 1980. **Specializes in the areas of:** Sales; Secretarial. **Positions commonly filled include:** Customer Service Representative; Human Resources Specialist; Services Sales Representative; Typist/Word Processor. **Benefits available to temporary workers:** Paid Holidays; Paid Vacation; Referral Bonus Plan. **Corporate headquarters location:** Atlanta GA. **Other U.S. locations:** Nationwide. **Number of placements per year:** 1000+.

TEMPORARY TECHNICAL SERVICES, INC.
2921 Wildwood Avenue, Jackson MI 49202. 517/784-7006. **Fax:** 517/784-5082. **Contact:** Nicole Watson, Recruiter. **Description:** A temporary agency that also provides some contract services. Founded in 1994. **Specializes in the areas of:** Engineering; Industrial; Manufacturing; Personnel/Labor Relations; Technical. **Positions commonly filled include:** Architect; Chemical Engineer; Chemist; Civil Engineer; Computer Programmer; Construction Contractor; Cost Estimator; Design Engineer; Designer; Draftsperson; Electrical/Electronics Engineer; Environmental Engineer; Food Scientist/Technologist; General Manager; Industrial Engineer; Industrial Production Manager; Mechanical Engineer; Metallurgical Engineer; Mining Engineer; Operations/Production Manager; Petroleum Engineer; Quality Control Supervisor; Science Technologist; Structural Engineer; Systems Analyst; Technical Writer/Editor. **Benefits available to temporary workers:** 401(k); Medical Insurance; Paid Holidays; Paid Vacation. **Other area locations:** Southfield MI. **Average salary range of placements:** $30,000 - $50,000. **Number of placements per year:** 50 - 99.

TOTAL EMPLOYEE MANAGEMENT
25600 Woodward Avenue, Suite 201, Royal Oak MI 48067. 248/548-5923. **Contact:** Office Manager. **Description:** A temporary agency that also provides some permanent placements and career counseling services. **Specializes in the areas of:** Insurance; Personnel/Labor Relations; Secretarial. **Positions commonly filled include:** Accountant/Auditor; Administrative Manager; Clerical Supervisor; Computer Programmer; Financial Analyst; Insurance Agent/Broker; Public Relations Specialist; Service Manager; Systems Analyst. **Benefits available to temporary workers:** Life Insurance; Medical Insurance. **Average salary range of placements:** $30,000 - $50,000. **Number of placements per year:** 200 - 499.

TRILLIUM STAFFING
2222 South Linden Road, Suite I, Flint MI 48532. 810/733-7180. **Fax:** 810/733-2560. **Contact:** Anne Magalski, Area Manager. **Description:** A temporary agency. **Specializes in the areas of:** Accounting/Auditing; Administration; Banking; Computer Science/Software; Engineering; General Management; Industrial; Manufacturing; Personnel/Labor Relations; Sales; Secretarial; Technical. **Positions commonly filled include:** Accountant/Auditor; Administrative Manager; Blue-Collar Worker Supervisor; Bookkeeper; Branch Manager; Clerical Supervisor; Computer Operator; Customer Service Representative; Data Entry Clerk; Design Engineer; Draftsperson; Factory Worker; General Manager; Human Resources Specialist; Industrial Engineer; Industrial Production Manager; Light Industrial Worker; Medical Secretary; MIS Specialist; Operations/Production Manager; Purchasing Agent/Manager; Quality Control Supervisor; Receptionist; Secretary; Services Sales Representative; Stenographer; Systems Analyst; Technician; Typist/Word Processor. **Benefits available to temporary workers:** 401(k);

Medical Insurance; Paid Holidays; Paid Vacation. **Corporate headquarters location:** Kalamazoo MI. **Other U.S. locations:** IN; WI. **Average salary range of placements:** $20,000 - $29,999. **Number of placements per year:** 500 - 999.

TRILLIUM STAFFING
4800 Fashion Square Boulevard, Suite 120, Saginaw MI 48604. 517/799-5960. **Fax:** 517/799-8570. **Contact:** Yvette M. Serrato, Area Manager. **Description:** A temporary agency. **Specializes in the areas of:** Accounting/Auditing; Architecture/Construction; Computer Science/Software; Engineering; General Management; Sales; Secretarial. **Positions commonly filled include:** Bank Officer/Manager; Bookkeeper; Branch Manager; Clerk; Computer Operator; Customer Service Representative; Data Entry Clerk; Draftsperson; Electronics Technician; Factory Worker; Human Resources Manager; Industrial Engineer; Legal Secretary; Light Industrial Worker; Mechanical Engineer; Medical Secretary; MIS Specialist; Purchasing Agent/Manager; Receptionist; Secretary; Services Sales Representative; Stenographer; Technician; Typist/Word Processor. **Corporate headquarters location:** Kalamazoo MI. **Other U.S. locations:** IN; WI. **Number of placements per year:** 1000+.

TRILLIUM STAFFING
836 East Bay Street, East Tawas MI 48730-0504. 517/362-3452. **Fax:** 517/362-6444. **Contact:** Bob Lee, Branch Manager. **Description:** A temporary agency that also provides some permanent placements, on-site management, testing, and training. Founded in 1984. **Specializes in the areas of:** Accounting/Auditing; Administration; Banking; Computer Science/Software; Engineering; Finance; Food; General Management; Industrial; Legal; Manufacturing; Personnel/Labor Relations; Publishing; Retail; Sales; Secretarial; Technical. **Positions commonly filled include:** Accountant/Auditor; Adjuster; Administrative Manager; Automotive Mechanic; Bank Officer/Manager; Blue-Collar Worker Supervisor; Branch Manager; Brokerage

Clerk; Budget Analyst; Buyer; Chemical Engineer; Chemist; Claim Representative; Clerical Supervisor; Computer Programmer; Construction Contractor; Credit Manager; Customer Service Manager; Designer; Draftsperson; Electrical/Electronics Engineer; Electrician; Financial Analyst; General Manager; Hotel Manager; Human Resources Manager; Industrial Engineer; Industrial Production Manager; Market Research Analyst; Mechanical Engineer; Medical Records Technician; MIS Specialist; Operations/Production Manager; Paralegal; Property and Real Estate Manager; Public Relations Specialist; Purchasing Agent/Manager; Quality Control Supervisor; Restaurant/Food Service Manager; Services Sales Representative; Software Engineer; Statistician; Structural Engineer; Systems Analyst; Technical Writer/Editor; Transportation/Traffic Specialist; Travel Agent; Typist/Word Processor. **Benefits available to temporary workers:** 401(k); Paid Holidays; Paid Vacation. **Corporate headquarters location:** Kalamazoo MI. **Other U.S. locations:** IN; WI. **Number of placements per year:** 200 - 499.

WORKFORCE, INC.
197 South Broadway, Lake Orion MI 48362. 248/693-3232. **Fax:** 248/693-3234. **Contact:** Pamela Boyd, President. **Description:** A temporary agency. **Specializes in the areas of:** Accounting/Auditing; Computer Science/Software; Engineering; General Management; Industrial; Insurance; Manufacturing; Nonprofit; Publishing; Sales; Secretarial. **Positions commonly filled include:** Accountant/Auditor; Adjuster; Administrative Manager; Buyer; Claim Representative; Clerical Supervisor; Customer Service Representative; Draftsperson; Manufacturer's/Wholesaler's Sales Rep.; Purchasing Agent/Manager; Services Sales Representative; Software Engineer; Systems Analyst; Travel Agent; Typist/Word Processor. **Benefits available to temporary workers:** Medical Insurance; Paid Vacation. **Other area locations:** Chesterfield MI. **Number of placements per year:** 500 - 999.

CONTRACT SERVICES FIRMS

ACRO ASI
17187 North Laurel Park Drive, Suite 165, Livonia MI 48152-2600. 734/591-1100. **Toll-free phone:** 800/844-2276. **Fax:** 734/591-1217. **Contact:** Dave Gaspard, Recruiting Manager. **E-mail address:** acro@oeonline. **Description:** A contract services firm. **Specializes in the areas of:** Computer Science/Software; Engineering. **Positions commonly filled include:** Aerospace Engineer; Chemical Engineer; Chemist; Civil Engineer; Computer Programmer; Cost Estimator; Design Engineer; Designer; Electrical/Electronics Engineer; Industrial Engineer; Internet Services Manager; Mechanical Engineer; MIS Specialist; Software Engineer; Structural Engineer; Systems Analyst; Technical Writer/Editor. **Average salary range of placements:** $20,000 - $29,999. **Number of placements per year:** 500 - 999.

ADECCO/TAD TECHNICAL SERVICES
3200 James Savage Road, Midland MI 48642. 517/496-9377. **Fax:** 517/496-2649. **Contact:** Branch Manager. **World Wide Web address:** http://www.adeccotad.com. **Description:** A contract services firm. **Specializes in the areas of:** Computer Science/Software; Engineering; Industrial; Scientific; Technical. **Positions commonly filled include:** Applications Engineer; Biochemist; Buyer; Chemical Engineer; Chemist; Civil Engineer; Clinical Lab Technician; Computer Operator; Computer Programmer; Cost Estimator; Customer Service Representative; Design Engineer; Draftsperson; Electrical/Electronics Engineer; Graphic Artist; Graphic Designer; Human Resources Manager; Industrial Engineer; Manufacturing Engineer; Mechanical Engineer; Metallurgical Engineer; MIS Specialist;

Purchasing Agent/Manager; Software Engineer; Systems Analyst; Systems Manager.

ADVANCED RESOURCES OF MICHIGAN, INC.
32300 Northwestern Highway, Suite 225, Farmington Hills MI 48334. 248/539-2280. **Fax:** 248/539-2288. **Contact:** Recruiter. **Description:** A contract services firm. Founded in 1985. **Specializes in the areas of:** Administration; Computer Science/Software; Telecommunications. **Positions commonly filled include:** Applications Engineer; Auditor; Computer Engineer; Computer Programmer; Computer Support Technician; Computer Technician; Database Administrator; Database Manager; Financial Analyst; MIS Specialist; Network/Systems Administrator; Software Engineer; SQL Programmer; Systems Analyst; Systems Manager. **Benefits available to temporary workers:** Life Insurance; Paid Vacation; Tuition Assistance. **Other U.S. locations:** Chicago IL. **Average salary range of placements:** $40,000 - $60,000. **Number of placements per year:** 1 - 49.

ALTERNATIVE STAFF, INC.
1000 John R. Road, Suite 102, Troy MI 48083. 248/589-3830. **Fax:** 248/589-3239. **Contact:** Sara Osman, President. **Description:** A contract services firm that also provides some temporary and permanent placements. **Specializes in the areas of:** Accounting; Administration; Computer Science/Software; Finance; General Management; Industrial; Light Industrial; Marketing; MIS/EDP; Sales; Secretarial; Technical. **Positions commonly filled include:** Administrative Assistant; Blue-Collar Worker Supervisor; Budget Analyst; Clerical Supervisor; Computer Operator; Controller; Customer Service Representative; Draftsperson; Financial Analyst;

General Manager; Human Resources Manager; Marketing Manager; Marketing Specialist; Operations Manager; Purchasing Agent/Manager; Quality Control Supervisor; Sales Executive; Sales Manager; Sales Representative; Secretary; Typist/Word Processor. **Benefits available to temporary workers:** Dental Insurance; Life Insurance; Medical Insurance; Paid Holidays; Paid Vacation; Pension Plan; Vision Insurance. **Corporate headquarters location:** This Location. **Average salary range of placements:** $20,000 - $50,000. **Number of placements per year:** 200 - 499.

APPNET
650 Avis Drive, Suite 100, Ann Arbor MI 48108. 734/996-3636. **Toll-free phone:** 800/448-1568. **Fax:** 734/669-2330. **Contact:** Director of Technical Recruiting. **World Wide Web address:** http://www. appnet.com. **Description:** A contract services firm. **Specializes in the areas of:** Computer Hardware/ Software; Engineering; Manufacturing; MIS/EDP; Technical. **Positions commonly filled include:** Computer Programmer; Database Manager; EDP Specialist; Electrical/Electronics Engineer; Industrial Engineer; Internet Services Manager; Mechanical Engineer; MIS Specialist; Project Manager; Software Engineer; Systems Analyst; Technical Writer/Editor; Telecommunications Manager; Webmaster. **Benefits available to temporary workers:** 401(k); Dental Insurance; Medical Insurance; Paid Holidays; Paid Vacation; Sick Days; STD/LTD Coverage; Tuition Assistance; Vision Insurance. **Number of placements per year:** 100 - 199.

ARGUS & ASSOCIATES
28064 Center Oak Court, Suite B, Wixom MI 48393. 248/344-8700. **Contact:** Manager. **Description:** A contract services firm that also provides some temporary and permanent placements. Client company pays fee. **Specializes in the areas of:** Computer Science/Software; Engineering; Industrial; Scientific; Technical. **Positions commonly filled include:** Applications Engineer; Civil Engineer; Computer Engineer; Computer Programmer; Database Administrator; Design Engineer; Draftsperson; Electrical/Electronics Engineer; Electrician; Environmental Engineer; Industrial Engineer; Manufacturing Engineer; Mechanical Engineer; Metallurgical Engineer; MIS Specialist; Network/ Systems Administrator; Quality Assurance Engineer; Software Engineer; SQL Programmer; Systems Analyst; Systems Manager. **Benefits available to temporary workers:** 401(k); Dental Insurance; Life Insurance; Medical Insurance; Paid Holidays; Paid Vacation. **Corporate headquarters location:** This Location. **Average salary range of placements:** $50,000 - $100,000. **Number of placements per year:** 50 - 99.

CDI CORPORATION
2627 East Beltline SE, Grand Rapids MI 49546. 616/942-0604. **Fax:** 616/942-7889. **Contact:** Manager. **World Wide Web address:** http://www.cdicorp.com. **Description:** A contract services firm. **Specializes in the areas of:** Engineering; Technical. **Corporate headquarters location:** Philadelphia PA. **Other U.S. locations:** Nationwide. **International locations:** Worldwide.

DYNAMIC PERSONNEL
2565 Van Omen Drive, Holland MI 49424-8208. 616/399-5220. **Contact:** Manager. **Description:** A contract services firm. **Specializes in the areas of:** Accounting/Auditing; Art/Design; Computer Science/ Software; Engineering; Industrial; Manufacturing; Personnel/Labor Relations. **Positions commonly filled include:** Accountant/Auditor; Bank Officer/Manager; Budget Analyst; Buyer; Ceramics Engineer; Civil Engineer; Computer Programmer; Design Engineer; Electrical/Electronics Engineer; Human Resources Specialist; Industrial Engineer; Materials Engineer; Metallurgical Engineer; Quality Control Supervisor; Systems Analyst; Technical Writer/Editor. **Number of placements per year:** 200 - 499.

WILLIAM HOWARD AGENCY
38701 Seven Mile Road, Suite 445, Livonia MI 48152. 734/464-6777. **Fax:** 734/464-7720. **Contact:** Christina Fortucci, Administrator. **E-mail address:** wha@ wmha.com. **World Wide Web address:** http://www. wmha.com. **Description:** A contract services firm that also provides career marketing services. Founded in 1967. **Specializes in the areas of:** Accounting/Auditing; Advertising; Architecture/Construction; Banking; Computer Hardware/Software; Construction; Design; Education; Engineering; Food; Health/Medical; Insurance; Legal; Manufacturing; MIS/EDP; Nonprofit; Publishing; Real Estate; Sales; Secretarial; Technical; Transportation. **Positions commonly filled include:** Accountant/Auditor; Actuary; Administrative Assistant; Advertising Executive; Aerospace Engineer; Agricultural Engineer; Architect; Attorney; Bank Officer/Manager; Biological Scientist; Biomedical Engineer; Bookkeeper; Ceramics Engineer; Civil Engineer; Claim Rep.; Clerk; Commercial Artist; Computer Programmer; Credit Manager; Customer Service Representative; Data Entry Clerk; Dietician/Nutritionist; Draftsperson; Economist; EDP Specialist; Electrical/Electronics Engineer; Financial Analyst; General Manager; Hotel Manager; Human Resources Manager; Industrial Designer; Industrial Engineer; Insurance Agent/Broker; Interior Designer; Legal Secretary; Management Analyst/ Consultant; Marketing Specialist; Mechanical Engineer; Medical Secretary; Metallurgical Engineer; Mining Engineer; Nurse; Petroleum Engineer; Physicist; Public Relations Specialist; Purchasing Agent/Manager; Receptionist; Secretary; Statistician; Stenographer; Systems Analyst; Technical Writer/Editor; Technician; Typist/Word Processor; Underwriter/Assistant Underwriter. **Corporate headquarters location:** This Location. **Number of placements per year:** 100 - 199.

KELLY TECHNICAL SERVICES
4400 South Saginaw Street, Suite 1335, Flint MI 48507. 810/232-2585. **Toll-free phone:** 800/728-7338. **Fax:** 810/232-2521. **Contact:** Jackie Smith, Recruiting Manager. **E-mail address:** smitjac@kellyservices.com. **World Wide Web address:** http://www. kellyservices.com. **Description:** A contract services firm. Client company pays fee. **Specializes in the areas of:** Accounting; Administration; Architecture/ Construction; Art/Design; Computer Science/Software; Engineering; Finance; General Management; Internet Development; Personnel/Labor Relations; Scientific; Technical. **Positions commonly filled include:** Account Manager; Accountant; Applications Engineer; Architect; AS400 Programmer Analyst; Auditor; Biochemist; Blue-Collar Worker Supervisor; Budget Analyst; Buyer; Chemical Engineer; Chemist; Chief Financial Officer; Civil Engineer; Computer Engineer; Computer Operator; Computer Programmer; Computer Scientist; Computer Support Technician; Computer Technician; Controller; Cost Estimator; Database Administrator; Database Manager; Design Engineer; Desktop Publishing Specialist; Draftsperson; Electrical/Electronics Engineer; Electrician; Environmental Engineer; Finance Director; Financial Analyst; General Manager; Graphic Artist; Graphic Designer; Human Resources Manager; Industrial Engineer; Industrial Production Manager; Internet Services Manager; Manufacturing Engineer; Market Research Analyst; Marketing Manager; Marketing Specialist; Mechanical Engineer; Metallurgical Engineer; MIS Specialist; Network/Systems Administrator; Operations Manager; Paralegal; Production Manager; Project Manager; Purchasing Agent/Manager; Quality Assurance Engineer; Quality Control Supervisor; Software Engineer; SQL Programmer; Systems Analyst; Systems Manager; Technical Writer/Editor; Telecommunications Manager; Webmaster. **Benefits available to temporary workers:** 401(k); Dental Insurance; Disability Coverage; Life Insurance; Medical Insurance; Paid Holidays; Paid Vacation; Tuition Assistance. **Corporate headquarters location:** Troy MI. **Other U.S. locations:** Nationwide. **Average salary range of placements:** $30,000 - $49,999. **Number of placements per year:** 100 - 199.

MANPOWER TECHNICAL SERVICES
25300 Telegraph Road, Suite 250, Southfield MI 48034. 248/351-0416. **Fax:** 248/351-9443. **Contact:** Mark Bourget, Manager. **E-mail address:** manpwrs@ globalbiz.net. **Description:** A contract services firm focusing on technical placements. **Specializes in the areas of:** Accounting; Computer Science/Software; Engineering; Finance; Technical. **Positions commonly filled include:** Accountant; Auditor; Budget Analyst; Computer Support Technician; Computer Technician; Controller; Database Administrator; Design Engineer; Electrical/Electronics Engineer; Financial Analyst; Mechanical Engineer; Network/Systems Administrator; Quality Assurance Engineer; Software Engineer; Systems Analyst; Webmaster. **Corporate headquarters location:** Milwaukee WI. **Other U.S. locations:** Nationwide. **International locations:** Worldwide. **Average salary range of placements:** $30,000 - $49,999. **Number of placements per year:** 200 - 499.

MODERN ENGINEERING
2401 West Big Beaver Road, Suite 400, Troy MI 48084. 248/458-6000. **Contact:** Tim D. Potter, Manager. **Description:** A contract services firm. **Specializes in the areas of:** Automotive. **Positions commonly filled include:** Automotive Engineer; Computer Programmer; Designer; Draftsperson; Electrical/Electronics Engineer; Industrial Engineer; Industrial Production Manager; Mechanical Engineer; Systems Analyst; Technical Writer/Editor. **Corporate headquarters location:** This Location.

PROFESSIONAL RESOURCE ASSOCIATES, INC.
201 Broadway, Marine City MI 48039. 810/765-1181. **Fax:** 810/765-1182. **Contact:** Jim Petitpren, Vice President. **E-mail address:** jim@pra-usa.com. **World Wide Web address:** http://www.pra-usa.com. **Description:** A contract services firm that also provides some permanent placements. **Specializes in the areas of:** Administration; Computer Science/Software; Engineering; Industrial; Manufacturing; Technical. **Positions commonly filled include:** Administrative Assistant; Chemical Engineer; Computer Programmer; Database Manager; Design Engineer; Draftsperson; Editor; Electrical/Electronics Engineer; Industrial Engineer; Manufacturing Engineer; Mechanical Engineer; Metallurgical Engineer; MIS Specialist; Project Manager; Quality Control Supervisor; Sales Engineer; Software Engineer; Systems Analyst; Systems Manager; Technical Writer/Editor. **Benefits available to temporary workers:** 401(k); Cafeteria; Medical Insurance; Paid Holidays; Paid Vacation. **Average salary range of placements:** $30,000 - $50,000. **Number of placements per year:** 50 - 99.

RC ENGINEERING AND MANAGEMENT SERVICES, INC.
10801 South Saginaw Street, Suite E, Grand Blanc MI 48439. 810/695-3381. **Toll-free phone:** 800/525-4118. **Fax:** 810/695-7904. **Contact:** Technical Recruiter. **World Wide Web address:** http://www. rcengineering.com. **Description:** A contract services firm. **Specializes in the areas of:** Engineering. **Positions commonly filled include:** Administrative Assistant; Civil Engineer; Design Engineer; Draftsperson; Industrial Engineer; Manufacturing Engineer; Mechanical Engineer; Software Engineer; Technical Writer/Editor. **Number of placements per year:** 1 - 49.

RCM TECHNOLOGIES
921 South Beechtree, Suite 5, Grand Haven MI 49417. 517/832-3300. **Contact:** Manager. **Description:** A contract services firm. **Specializes in the areas of:** Biology; Engineering. **Positions commonly filled include:** Buyer; Ceramics Engineer; Chemist; Civil Engineer; Construction and Building Inspector; Construction Contractor; Cost Estimator; Design Engineer; Designer; Draftsperson; Electrical/Electronics Engineer; Environmental Engineer; Industrial Engineer;

Materials Engineer; Mechanical Engineer; Metallurgical Engineer. **Number of placements per year:** 50 - 99.

TAC AUTOMOTIVE GROUP
500 Town Center Drive, Suite 100, Dearborn MI 48126. 313/271-3600. **Contact:** Manager. **Description:** A contract services firm. **Specializes in the areas of:** Computer Hardware/Software; Engineering; Information Technology.

TROY TECH SERVICES
1000 Three Mile Road NW, Grand Rapids MI 49544. 616/784-9100. **Toll-free phone:** 800/345-5710. **Fax:** 616/784-9705. **Contact:** Manager. **Description:** A contract services firm. **Specializes in the areas of:** Accounting; Administration; Computer Science/ Software; Engineering; Information Systems; Internet Development; Personnel/Labor Relations; Secretarial. **Positions commonly filled include:** Accountant; Administrative Assistant; Administrative Manager; Applications Engineer; AS400 Programmer Analyst; Blue-Collar Worker Supervisor; Clerical Supervisor; Computer Animator; Computer Engineer; Computer Operator; Computer Programmer; Computer Scientist; Computer Support Tech.; Computer Tech.; Content Developer; Controller; Cost Estimator; Database Administrator; Database Manager; Design Engineer; Draftsperson; Electrical/Electronics Engineer; Human Resources Manager; Industrial Engineer; Internet Services Manager; Manufacturing Engineer; Metallurgical Engineer; MIS Specialist; Multimedia Designer; Network/Systems Administrator; Quality Assurance Engineer; Quality Control Supervisor; Software Engineer; SQL Programmer; Systems Analyst; Systems Manager; Typist/Word Processor. **Corporate headquarters location:** This Location. **Other U.S. locations:** Nationwide. **Average salary range of placements:** $50,000 - $100,000. **Number of placements per year:** 1000+.

UNLIMITED STAFFING SOLUTIONS, INC.
22 West Huron Street, Pontiac MI 48342. 248/253-1505. **Fax:** 248/253-1512. **Contact:** Caleene Jones, President. **E-mail address:** ussi1@flash.net. **World Wide Web address:** http://www.unlimitedstaffing.com. **Description:** A contract services firm that also provides some temporary and permanent placements. **Specializes in the areas of:** Accounting; Administration; Computer Science/Software; Engineering; Finance; MIS/EDP; Personnel/Labor Relations; Printing; Publishing; Scientific; Secretarial; Technical; Transportation. **Positions commonly filled include:** Administrative Assistant; Applications Engineer; Auditor; Branch Manager; Buyer; Chief Financial Officer; Civil Engineer; Claim Rep.; Clerical Supervisor; Computer Animator; Computer Operator; Computer Programmer; Controller; Credit Manager; Customer Service Representative; Database Manager; Design Engineer; Draftsperson; Electrical/Electronics Engineer; Finance Director; General Manager; Graphic Artist; Graphic Designer; Industrial Engineer; Internet Services Manager; Manufacturing Engineer; Mechanical Engineer; Metallurgical Engineer; MIS Specialist; Operations Manager; Production Manager; Project Manager; Purchasing Agent/Manager; Quality Control Supervisor; Sales Engineer; Sales Executive; Sales Manager; Sales Representative; Software Engineer; Systems Analyst; Technical Writer/Editor; Telecommunications Manager; Typist/Word Processor; Webmaster. **Benefits available to temporary workers:** 401(k); Dental Insurance; Medical Insurance; Paid Holidays; Paid Vacation. **Corporate headquarters location:** This Location. **Average salary range of placements:** $30,000 - $50,000. **Number of placements per year:** 200 - 499.

H.L. YOH COMPANY
1767 West Big Beaver Road, Troy MI 48084. 248/822-0099. **Contact:** Manager. **Description:** A contract services firm. **Specializes in the areas of:** Automotive; Computer Science/Software; Information Technology; Technical.

CAREER/OUTPLACEMENT COUNSELING FIRMS

CAREER DIRECTIONS
101 North Main, Suite 850, Ann Arbor MI 48104.
734/663-0677. **Fax:** 734/663-8728. **Contact:** David
Gruner, Principal. **Description:** A career/outplacement
counseling service that offers hiring/promotion
evaluations, performance coaching, career development,
and outplacement services.

HIGHLANDS PROGRAM
2025 East Beltline, Suite 104, Grand Rapids MI 49546.
616/957-2442. **Contact:** David MacRae, Ph.D./
Counselor. **World Wide Web address:** http://www.
highlandsprogram.com. **Description:** Provides career
counseling to students and adults, and training and
development services to corporations.

THE LETTER WRITER
9437 Hagerty Road, Plymouth MI 48170. 734/455-8892.
Contact: Ginny Eades, Owner. **Description:** A
career/outplacement counseling service.

◆ M I N N E S O T A ◆

ACCOUNTANTS EXCHANGE, INC.
Roseville Professional Center, 2233 Hamline Avenue North, Suite 509, Roseville MN 55113. 651/636-5490. **Contact:** Chuck McBride, President. **Description:** An executive search firm. **Specializes in the areas of:** Accounting/Auditing; Finance. **Number of placements per year:** 1 - 49.

ACCOUNTANTS EXECUTIVE SEARCH
ACCOUNTANTS ON CALL
45 South Seventh Street, Suite 3004, Minneapolis MN 55402. 612/341-9900. **Contact:** Manager. **Description:** An executive search firm. Accountants On Call (also at this location) is a temporary agency. **Specializes in the areas of:** Accounting/Auditing; Finance. **Corporate headquarters location:** Saddle Brook NJ. **International locations:** Worldwide.

ACCOUNTANTS PLACEMENT REGISTRY, INC.
1705 Cope Avenue, Suite A, Maplewood MN 55109. 651/773-9018. **Fax:** 651/770-8071. **Recorded jobline:** 651/773-0648. **Contact:** Robert S. Culver, President. **Description:** An executive search firm. **Specializes in the areas of:** Accounting/Auditing; Finance. **Positions commonly filled include:** Accountant/Auditor; Bank Officer/Manager; Budget Analyst; Cost Estimator; Credit Manager; Financial Analyst. **Average salary range of placements:** $30,000 - $50,000. **Number of placements per year:** 50 - 99.

ADD ON STAFFING SOLUTIONS
255 East Roselawn Avenue, Suite 50, St. Paul MN 55117. 651/488-1000. **Toll-free phone:** 800/305-7761. **Fax:** 651/488-9585. **Contact:** Sharon Murphy, CEO. **Description:** An executive search firm. **Specializes in the areas of:** Telecommunications. **Positions commonly filled include:** Customer Service Representative; Sales Executive; Sales Manager; Sales Representative; Software Engineer; Telecommunications Manager. **Average salary range of placements:** $30,000 - $50,000. **Number of placements per year:** 1 - 49.

ADVANCE PERSONNEL RESOURCES
715 Florida Avenue South, Suite 301, Golden Valley MN 55426-1729. 612/546-6779. **Contact:** Larry Happe, CPC, Owner. **Description:** An executive search firm. **Specializes in the areas of:** Accounting/Auditing; Finance; General Management; Manufacturing; Personnel/Labor Relations; Publishing; Sales; Transportation. **Positions commonly filled include:** Accountant/Auditor; Attorney; Human Resources Specialist; Management Analyst/Consultant; Manufacturer's/Wholesaler's Sales Rep.; Market Research Analyst; Operations/Production Manager; Quality Control Supervisor; Services Sales Rep.; Strategic Relations Manager; Telecommunications Manager. **Average salary range of placements:** $30,000 - $80,000. **Number of placements per year:** 1 - 49.

ADVANTAGE INTERNATIONAL
15226 West Freeway Drive, Suite 200, Forest Lake MN 55025. 651/464-6677. **Fax:** 651/464-1716. **Contact:** Carl Braun, General Manager. **E-mail address:** Confidential@advantageintl.net. **World Wide Web address:** http://www.advantageintl.net. **Description:** An executive search firm operating on a retainer basis. **Specializes in the areas of:** Engineering; Finance; Human Resources; Information Technology; Manufacturing; Marketing; Sales. **Corporate headquarters location:** Minneapolis/St. Paul MN.

AGRA PLACEMENTS, LTD.
710 North Broadway, New Ulm MN 56073. 507/354-4900. **Fax:** 507/354-4909. **Contact:** Manager. **E-mail address:** agramn@newulmtel.net. **World Wide Web address:** http://www.agraplacements.com. **Description:** An executive search firm. **Specializes in the areas of:** Agri-Business; Chemicals; Food.

AGRI-BUSINESS SERVICES, INC.
P.O. Box 1237, Lakeville MN 55044. 612/469-6767. **Fax:** 612/469-6768. **Contact:** George White, President. **Description:** An executive search firm operating on a contingency basis. **Specializes in the areas of:** Agri-Business; Biology; Engineering; Food; General Management; Manufacturing; Sales; Technical. **Positions commonly filled include:** Biochemist; Biological Scientist; Blue-Collar Worker Supervisor; Branch Manager; Chemical Engineer; Chemist; Civil Engineer; Customer Service Rep.; Design Engineer; Dietician/Nutritionist; Food Scientist/Technologist; Forester/Conservation Scientist; General Manager; Manufacturer's/Wholesaler's Sales Rep.; Quality Control Supervisor; Services Sales Representative; Veterinarian.

ARCHAMBAULT GROUP
5831 Cedar Lake Road South, St. Louis Park MN 55416. 612/545-6296. **Contact:** Manager. **Description:** An executive search firm. **Specializes in the areas of:** Finance.

BOYLE & ASSOCIATES
238 Chester Avenue, Suite 200, St. Paul MN 55107. 651/223-5050. **Fax:** 651/297-6286. **Contact:** Manager. **Description:** An executive search firm.

BRADLEY & ASSOCIATES
5341 River Bluff Curve, Suite 116, Bloomington MN 55437. 612/884-2607. **Fax:** 612/884-2019. **Contact:** John Bradley, President. **Description:** An executive search firm. **Specializes in the areas of:** Accounting/Auditing; Engineering; Food; Manufacturing. **Positions commonly filled include:** Account Manager; Biological Scientist; Chemical Engineer; Controller; Electrical/Electronics Engineer; Mechanical Engineer.

BRIGHT SEARCH/PROFESSIONAL STAFFING
8120 Penn Avenue South, Suite 167, Bloomington MN 55431-1326. 612/884-8111. **Fax:** 612/881-9197. **Contact:** Leo Bright, Owner/President. **Description:** An executive search firm operating on both retainer and contingency bases. **Specializes in the areas of:** Consulting; Engineering; General Management; Health/Medical; Industrial; Legal; Manufacturing; Personnel/Labor Relations; Sales; Technical. **Positions commonly filled include:** Attorney; Chemical Engineer; Design Engineer; Electrical/Electronics Engineer; General Manager; Human Resources Specialist; Industrial Engineer; Industrial Production Manager; Management Analyst/Consultant; Mechanical Engineer; Metallurgical Engineer; Purchasing Agent/Manager; Quality Control Supervisor; Services Sales Rep.; Software Engineer; Systems Analyst; Technical Writer/Editor; Transportation/Traffic Specialist.

CERTIFIED ACCOUNTING PROS
5755 Wayzata Boulevard, Suite 700, Minneapolis MN 55416. 612/545-0952. **Contact:** Manager. **Description:** An executive search firm. **Specializes in the areas of:** Accounting/Auditing.

COMPUTER EMPLOYMENT
5151 Edina Industrial Boulevard, Suite 299, Edina MN 55439. 612/831-4566. **Fax:** 612/831-4684. **Contact:** Marty Koepp, Owner. **E-mail address:** mkoepp@computeremployment.com. **World Wide Web address:** http://www.computeremployment.com. **Description:** An executive search firm operating on a contingency basis. **Specializes in the areas of:** Administration; Computer Science/Software. **Positions commonly filled include:** Computer Programmer; Management Analyst/Consultant; MIS Specialist; Software Engineer; Systems Analyst; Telecommunications Manager. **Average salary**

range of placements: $50,000 - $75,000. **Number of placements per year:** 50 - 99.

COMPUTER PERSONNEL
5353 Wayzata Boulevard, Suite 604, Minneapolis MN 55416. 612/542-8053. **Contact:** Manager. **Description:** An executive search firm. **Specializes in the areas of:** Computer Science/Software.

CUSTOM SEARCH INC.
9800 Shelard Parkway, Suite 104, Plymouth MN 55441. 612/591-6111. **Contact:** Manager. **Description:** An executive search firm. **Specializes in the areas of:** Software Engineering; Technical.

CHARLES DAHL ASSOCIATES
77 13th Avenue NE, Minneapolis MN 55143-1001. 612/331-7777. **Contact:** Manager. **Description:** An executive search firm. **Specializes in the areas of:** Engineering; Finance; Information Technology.

DEVELOPMENT SEARCH SPECIALISTS
W-3072 First National Bank Building, 332 Minnesota Street, St. Paul MN 55101. 651/224-3750. **Contact:** Fred J. Lauerman, Principal. **Description:** An executive search firm. **Specializes in the areas of:** Nonprofit. **Positions commonly filled include:** Fundraising Specialist; General Manager; Public Relations Specialist. **Number of placements per year:** 1 - 49.

DIETRICH & ASSOCIATES
5775 Wayzata Boulevard, Suite 700, Minneapolis MN 55416. 612/525-2205. **Fax:** 612/545-0856. **Contact:** Marilyn Dietrich, Owner. **Description:** An executive search firm. **Specializes in the areas of:** Engineering; Manufacturing. **Positions commonly filled include:** Design Engineer; Electrical/Electronics Engineer; Industrial Engineer; Industrial Production Manager; Mechanical Engineer; Operations/Production Manager; Purchasing Agent/Manager; Quality Control Supervisor; Transportation/Traffic Specialist. **Average salary range of placements:** More than $50,000. **Number of placements per year:** 1 - 49.

DISCOVERY PERSONNEL, INC. (DPI)
P.O. Box 1228, Burnsville MN 55337. 612/431-2500. **Fax:** 612/431-2512. **Contact:** Manager. **Description:** An executive search firm. **Specializes in the areas of:** Automation/Robotics; Design; Engineering; Management; Manufacturing; Plastics.

EHS & ASSOCIATES, INC.
1005 West Franklin Avenue, Suite 2, Minneapolis MN 55408. 612/870-1337. **Contact:** Brian Hirt, Vice President. **Description:** An executive search firm. **Specializes in the areas of:** Hotel/Restaurant. **Positions commonly filled include:** Hotel Manager; Restaurant/ Food Service Manager. **Number of placements per year:** 200 - 499.

ESP SYSTEMS PROFESSIONALS
701 Fourth Avenue South, Suite 1800, Minneapolis MN 55415. 612/337-3000. **Fax:** 612/337-9199. **Contact:** Robert R. Hildreth, President. **E-mail address:** careers@ esp.com. **World Wide Web address:** http://www. esp.com. **Description:** An executive search firm. **Specializes in the areas of:** Information Systems. **Positions commonly filled include:** Computer Programmer; Internet Services Manager; MIS Specialist; Software Engineer; Systems Analyst. **Average salary range of placements:** $35,000 - $60,000. **Number of placements per year:** 500 - 999.

EMERGING TECHNOLOGY SERVICES
1600 Arboretum Boulevard, Suite 209, P.O. Box 215, Victoria MN 55386-0215. 612/443-4141. **Contact:** Manager. **Description:** An executive search firm. **Specializes in the areas of:** Information Systems.

ENTERPRISE SEARCH SERVICES
3639 Admiral Lane, Brooklyn Center MN 55429. 612/537-7310. **Contact:** Manager. **Description:** An

executive search firm. **Specializes in the areas of:** Computer Science/Software.

ERSPAMER ASSOCIATES
4010 West 65th Street, Suite 100, Edina MN 55435. 612/925-3747. **Fax:** 612/925-4022. **Contact:** Roy C. Erspamer, Principal. **Description:** An executive search firm. **Specializes in the areas of:** Health/Medical; Medical Technology. **Positions commonly filled include:** Biochemist; Biomedical Engineer; Chemical Engineer; Chemist; Design Engineer; Electrical/ Electronics Engineer; Manufacturing Engineer; Mechanical Engineer; Metallurgical Engineer; Project Manager; Quality Control Supervisor; Regulatory Affairs Director; Software Engineer; Statistician. **Number of placements per year:** 1 - 49.

THE ESQUIRE GROUP
501 Marquette Avenue South, Suite 1800, Minneapolis MN 55402. 612/340-9068. **Fax:** 612/340-1218. **Contact:** Patricia A. Comeford, President. **Description:** An executive search firm. **Specializes in the areas of:** Legal. **Positions commonly filled include:** Attorney.

EXECU-TECH SEARCH INC.
3500 West 80th Street, Suite 20, Bloomington MN 55431. 612/893-6915. **Contact:** Manager. **Description:** An executive search firm specializing in the placement of chemical, electrical, and mechanical engineering professionals. **Specializes in the areas of:** Engineering.

EXECUTIVE SEARCH INC.
5401 Gamble Drive, Suite 275, Minneapolis MN 55416. 612/541-9153. **Contact:** Manager. **Description:** An executive search firm.

FAIRFAX GROUP
9800 Shelard Parkway, Suite 110, Plymouth MN 55441. 612/541-9898. **Fax:** 612/541-9124. **Contact:** Manager. **Description:** An executive search firm. **Specializes in the areas of:** Information Systems; Logistics; Manufacturing.

FALLS MEDICAL SEARCH
34 Forest Dale Road, Minneapolis MN 55410. 612/922-0207. **Contact:** Manager. **Description:** An executive search firm that places physicians. **Specializes in the areas of:** Health/Medical. **Positions commonly filled include:** Physician.

FOCUS EXECUTIVE SEARCH
2852 Anthony Lane South, St. Anthony MN 55418. 612/706-4444. **Contact:** Tim McLafferty, President. **Description:** An executive search firm. **Specializes in the areas of:** Food. **Positions commonly filled include:** Agricultural Engineer; Biological Scientist; Chemical Engineer; Food Scientist/Technologist; Human Resources Manager; Plant Manager; Quality Control Supervisor; Sales Manager. **Average salary range of placements:** More than $50,000. **Number of placements per year:** 100 - 199.

FOGARTY & ASSOCIATES
6600 France Avenue, Suite 210, Edina MN 55435. 612/831-2828. **Contact:** Manager. **Description:** An executive search firm. **Specializes in the areas of:** Health/Medical.

GATEWAY SEARCH INC.
15500 Wayzata Boulevard, Building 604, Suite 221, Wayzata MN 55391-1438. 612/473-3137. **Fax:** 612/473-3276. **Contact:** James Bortolussi, President. **Description:** An executive search firm operating on a contingency basis. **Specializes in the areas of:** Computer Science/Software. **Positions commonly filled include:** Client/Server Specialist; Computer Programmer; Database Manager; Network Administrator; Software Engineer; Systems Analyst; UNIX System Administrator. **Average salary range of placements:** More than $50,000. **Number of placements per year:** 1 - 49.

GERDES SINGER & ASSOCIATES INC.
120 South Sixth Street, Suite 2480, Minneapolis MN 55402. 612/335-3553. **Contact:** Richard Gerdes. **Description:** An executive search firm. **Specializes in the areas of:** Advertising.

ROGER G. GILMER AND ASSOCIATES
14581 Grand Avenue South, Burnsville MN 55306. 612/469-3652. **Contact:** Roger Gilmer, Owner. **Description:** An executive search firm. **Specializes in the areas of:** Engineering; Manufacturing. **Positions commonly filled include:** Biomedical Engineer; Electrical/Electronics Engineer; Mechanical Engineer; Quality Control Supervisor. **Number of placements per year:** 1 - 49.

GLEASON DALE KEENE & ASSOCIATES, INC.
7401 Metro Boulevard, Suite 460, Minneapolis MN 55439. 612/844-0121. **Toll-free phone:** 800/927-5752. **Fax:** 612/844-0264. **Contact:** Manager. **World Wide Web address:** http://www.gleasondale.com. **Description:** An executive search firm operating on both retainer and contingency bases. The firm also provides some temporary placements. Client company pays fee. **Specializes in the areas of:** Accounting; Finance; General Management. **Positions commonly filled include:** Accountant; Administrative Assistant; Auditor; Budget Analyst; Certified Occupational Therapy Assistant; Chief Financial Officer; Claim Representative; Controller; Cost Estimator; Credit Manager; Customer Service Representative; Financial Analyst; Licensed Practical Nurse; Nurse Practitioner; Pharmacist; Registered Nurse; Secretary. **Average salary range of placements:** $50,000 - $100,000. **Number of placements per year:** 50 - 99.

HR SERVICES OF PLYMOUTH
P.O. Box 564, Rockford MN 55373. 612/477-6595. **Fax:** 612/477-6609. **Contact:** Manager. **Description:** An executive search firm. **Specializes in the areas of:** Architecture/Construction; Engineering; Food; Industrial; Manufacturing; Personnel/Labor Relations. **Positions commonly filled include:** Blue-Collar Worker Supervisor; Ceramics Engineer; Chemical Engineer; Chemist; Civil Engineer; Construction Trade Worker; Electrical/Electronics Engineer; Industrial Engineer; Manufacturing Engineer; Mechanical Engineer; Metallurgical Engineer; Operations/Production Manager; Purchasing Agent/Manager; Quality Control Supervisor; Structural Engineer; Technical Illustrator. **Average salary range of placements:** $30,000 - $50,000. **Number of placements per year:** 50 - 99.

ROBERT HALF INTERNATIONAL ACCOUNTEMPS
80 South Eighth Street, Suite 2850, Minneapolis MN 55402. 612/339-9001. **Contact:** Manager. **World Wide Web address:** http://www.roberthalf.com. **Description:** An executive search firm. Accountemps (also at this location) provides temporary placements. **Specializes in the areas of:** Accounting/Auditing. **Corporate headquarters location:** Menlo Park CA. **Other U.S. locations:** Nationwide.

ROBERT HALF INTERNATIONAL ACCOUNTEMPS
10405 Sixth Avenue North, Suite 220, Plymouth MN 55441. 612/545-0911. **Contact:** Manager. **World Wide Web address:** http://www.roberthalf.com. **Description:** An executive search firm. Accountemps (also at this location) provides temporary placements. **Specializes in the areas of:** Accounting/Auditing. **Corporate headquarters location:** Menlo Park CA. **Other U.S. locations:** Nationwide.

HAYDEN & ASSOCIATES
7825 Washington Avenue South, Suite 120, Bloomington MN 55439. 612/941-6300. **Contact:** Manager. **Description:** An executive search firm. **Specializes in the areas of:** Advertising; Data Processing; Finance; Marketing; Sales.

HAYDEN SEARCH GROUP
505 North Highway 169, Suite 275, Plymouth MN 55441. 612/593-2400. **Contact:** Todd Hayden, President. **Description:** An executive search firm. **Specializes in the areas of:** Accounting/Auditing; Finance. **Positions commonly filled include:** Accountant/Auditor; Accounting Supervisor; Administrative Manager; Budget Analyst; Cost Estimator; Credit Manager; Finance Director; Financial Analyst. **Number of placements per year:** 50 - 99.

HEALTHCARE RECRUITERS OF MINNESOTA
6442 City West Parkway, Suite 303, Eden Prairie MN 55344. 612/942-5424. **Fax:** 612/942-5452. **Contact:** Steven J. Yungner, President. **Description:** An executive search firm that places sales, sales management, marketing, and executive professionals in the health care industry. **Specializes in the areas of:** Health/Medical; Medical Sales and Marketing. **Positions commonly filled include:** Branch Manager; General Manager; Health Services Manager; Marketing Manager; Medical Sales; Pharmacist; Physical Therapist; Physician; Product Manager; Regulatory Affairs Director; Sales Manager; Sales Representative. **Other U.S. locations:** Nationwide. **Average salary range of placements:** $30,000 - $50,000. **Number of placements per year:** 50 - 99.

HEINZE & ASSOCIATES
6125 Blue Circle Drive, Suite 218, Minnetonka MN 55343. 612/938-2828. **Contact:** Manager. **Description:** An executive search firm. **Specializes in the areas of:** General Management. **Average salary range of placements:** More than $100,000.

HILLEREN & ASSOCIATES
3800 West 80th Street, Suite 880, Bloomington MN 55431. 612/956-9090. **Fax:** 612/956-9009. **Contact:** Jerry Hilleren, Owner. **Description:** An executive search firm. **Specializes in the areas of:** Health/Medical; Marketing; Pharmaceuticals; Sales. **Positions commonly filled include:** Sales Manager; Sales Representative; Vice President of Sales. **Average salary range of placements:** More than $50,000. **Number of placements per year:** 100 - 199.

T.H. HUNTER, INC.
815 Nicollet Mall, Suite 210, Minneapolis MN 55402. 612/339-0530. **Fax:** 612/338-4757. **Contact:** Martin Conroy, Executive Recruiter. **Description:** An executive search firm. **Specializes in the areas of:** Accounting/Auditing; Administration; Advertising; Banking; Biology; Computer Science/Software; Economics; Engineering; Finance; Food; Health/Medical; Insurance; Legal; Manufacturing; Nonprofit; Personnel/Labor Relations; Publishing; Retail; Sales; Technical. **Positions commonly filled include:** Accountant/Auditor; Actuary; Attorney; Bank Officer/Manager; Biomedical Engineer; Branch Manager; Budget Analyst; Buyer; Computer Programmer; Credit Manager; Economist; Electrical/Electronics Engineer; Financial Analyst; General Manager; Health Services Manager; Human Resources Manager; Internet Services Manager; Licensed Practical Nurse; Management Analyst/Consultant; Manufacturer's/Wholesaler's Sales Rep.; Mechanical Engineer; Mortgage Banker; Occupational Therapist; Physical Therapist; Physician; Quality Control Supervisor; Registered Nurse; Science Technologist; Software Engineer; Speech-Language Pathologist; Systems Analyst; Technical Writer/Editor; Telecommunications Manager; Urban/Regional Planner. **Average salary range of placements:** More than $50,000. **Number of placements per year:** 50 - 99.

JFK SEARCH
10 South Fifth Street, Suite 700, Minneapolis MN 55402. 612/332-8082. **Contact:** Manager. **Description:** An executive search firm. **Specializes in the areas of:** Advertising.

JACKLEY SEARCH CONSULTANTS
14581 Grand Avenue South, Burnsville MN 55306. 612/831-2344. **Contact:** Manager. **Description:** An

executive search firm. **Specializes in the areas of:** Engineering; High-Tech.

A.T. KEARNEY EXECUTIVE SEARCH
8500 Normandale Lake Boulevard, Suite 1630, Minneapolis MN 55437. 612/921-8436. **Contact:** Manager. **Description:** An executive search firm. **International locations:** Worldwide.

ERIC KERCHEVAL & ASSOCIATES
15 South First Street, Suite A4, Minneapolis MN 55401. 612/338-7944. **Contact:** Manager. **Description:** An executive search firm. **Specializes in the areas of:** Advertising; Hotel/Restaurant.

KORN/FERRY INTERNATIONAL
4816 IDS Center, Minneapolis MN 55402. 612/333-1834. **Fax:** 612/333-8971. **Contact:** Manager. **World Wide Web address:** http://www.kornferry.com. **Description:** An executive search firm. **Corporate headquarters location:** Los Angeles CA. **International locations:** Worldwide. **Average salary range of placements:** More than $50,000.

LABREE & ASSOCIATES
5211 Winnetka Avenue North, New Hope MN 55428. 612/535-5191. **Contact:** Manager. **Description:** An executive search firm. **Specializes in the areas of:** Construction; Finance; Insurance.

SUSAN LEE & ASSOCIATES
6100 Green Valley Drive, Suite 150, Bloomington MN 55438. 612/897-1170. **Fax:** 612/897-1314. **Contact:** Susan Lee, President. **E-mail address:** susan@susanlee.com. **World Wide Web address:** http://www.susanlee.com. **Description:** An executive search firm operating on a contingency basis. Client company pays fee. **Specializes in the areas of:** Marketing; Printing; Publishing; Sales. **Positions commonly filled include:** Desktop Publishing Specialist; General Manager; Graphic Artist; Graphic Designer; Operations Manager; Product Manager; Technical Writer/Editor. **Average salary range of placements:** $50,000 - $100,000. **Number of placements per year:** 50 - 99.

HOWARD LIEBERMAN & ASSOCIATES INC.
311 First Avenue North, Suite 503, Minneapolis MN 55401. 612/338-2432. **Fax:** 612/332-8860. **Contact:** Howard Lieberman, President. **Description:** An executive search firm. **Specializes in the areas of:** Legal. **Positions commonly filled include:** Attorney. **Number of placements per year:** 1 - 49.

MANAGEMENT RECRUITERS OF MINNEAPOLIS SALES CONSULTANTS OF MINNEAPOLIS
4700 West 77th Street, Suite 110, Edina MN 55435. 612/830-1420. **Contact:** Manager. **Description:** An executive search firm operating on a contingency basis. **Specializes in the areas of:** Accounting/Auditing; Administration; Advertising; Architecture/Construction; Banking; Chemicals; Communications; Computer Hardware/Software; Construction; Design; Electrical; Engineering; Finance; Food; General Management; Health/Medical; Industrial; Insurance; Legal; Manufacturing; Operations Management; Personnel/Labor Relations; Pharmaceuticals; Procurement; Publishing; Real Estate; Retail; Sales; Technical; Textiles; Transportation. **Corporate headquarters location:** Cleveland OH. **Other U.S. locations:** Nationwide.

MANAGEMENT RECRUITERS OF ROCHESTER
1652 Greenview Drive SW, Suite 600, Rochester MN 55902. 507/282-2400. **Fax:** 507/282-1308. **Contact:** Nona Vierkant, Chief Financial Officer. **E-mail address:** mrrocmn@ismidwest.com. **World Wide Web address:** http://www.ismidwest.com. **Description:** An executive search firm operating on a contingency basis. Client company pays fee. **Specializes in the areas of:** MIS/EDP; Quality Assurance. **Positions commonly filled include:** Applications Engineer; AS400 Programmer Analyst; Computer Operator; Computer Programmer; Computer Scientist; Computer Support Technician; Computer Technician; Database Administrator; Database Manager; Internet Services Manager; MIS Specialist; Network/Systems Administrator; Software Engineer; SQL Programmer; Systems Analyst; Systems Manager; Webmaster. **Corporate headquarters location:** Cleveland OH. **Other U.S. locations:** Nationwide. **Average salary range of placements:** $50,000 - $100,000. **Number of placements per year:** 50 - 99.

LEE MARSH & ASSOCIATES
1469 Highview Avenue, Eagan MN 55121. 651/452-5412. **Contact:** Lee Marsh, Owner. **Description:** An executive search firm. **Specializes in the areas of:** Software Engineering; Technical. **Positions commonly filled include:** Computer Programmer; Design Engineer; Electrical/Electronics Engineer; Sales Representative; Software Engineer; Systems Analyst. **Number of placements per year:** 50 - 99.

BRAD MARTIN & ASSOCIATES
5353 Wayzata Boulevard, Suite 403, Minneapolis MN 55416. 612/544-4130. **Contact:** Manager. **Description:** An executive search firm. **Specializes in the areas of:** Manufacturing.

MARY L. MAYER, LTD.
P.O. Box 250, Hamel MN 55340-0250. 612/473-7700. **Fax:** 612/449-0772. **Contact:** Mary Mayer, President. **Description:** An executive search firm focusing on the property/casualty insurance industry. **Specializes in the areas of:** Insurance; Sales. **Positions commonly filled include:** Actuary; Adjuster; Administrative Manager; Branch Manager; Claim Representative; Clerical Supervisor; Customer Service Representative; General Manager; Human Resources Specialist; Insurance Agent/Broker; MIS Specialist; Systems Analyst; Underwriter/Assistant Underwriter. **Average salary range of placements:** More than $50,000. **Number of placements per year:** 1 - 49.

MEDSEARCH CORPORATION
6545 France Avenue South, Edina MN 55435. 612/926-6584. **Contact:** Manager. **Description:** An executive search firm. **Specializes in the areas of:** Health/Medical. **Positions commonly filled include:** Physician.

C.A. MOORE & ASSOCIATES, INC.
15500 Wayzata Boulevard, Suite 803C, Wayzata MN 55391. 612/473-0990. **Contact:** Connie Moore, President. **E-mail address:** camoore@uswest.net. **Description:** An executive search firm operating on both retainer and contingency bases. **Specializes in the areas of:** Accounting/Auditing; Direct Marketing; Finance; Insurance; Legal; Risk Management. **Positions commonly filled include:** Accountant/Auditor; Adjuster; Administrative Worker/Clerk; Attorney; Controller; Finance Director; Financial Analyst; General Manager; Human Resources Manager; Insurance Agent/Broker; Operations/Production Manager; Sales Executive; Sales Manager; Sales Representative; Underwriter/Assistant Underwriter. **Number of placements per year:** 1 - 49.

NER, INC. (NATIONAL ENGINEERING RESOURCES)
6200 Shingle Creek Parkway, Suite 160, Brooklyn Center MN 55430. 612/561-7610. **Toll-free phone:** 800/665-7610. **Fax:** 612/561-7675. **Contact:** Technical Recruiter. **E-mail address:** info@nerinc.com. **World Wide Web address:** http://www.ner.com. **Description:** An executive search firm. **Specializes in the areas of:** Administration; Clerical; Computer Hardware/Software; Engineering; Industrial; Medical Technology; Oil and Gas; Petrochemical; Publishing; Scientific; Technical. **Positions commonly filled include:** Administrative Manager; Agricultural Engineer; Aircraft Mechanic/Engine Specialist; Ceramics Engineer; Computer Programmer; Materials Engineer; Medical Assistant; Metallurgical Engineer; Nuclear Engineer; Quality Control Supervisor; Software Engineer; Structural Engineer; Systems Analyst. **Number of placements per year:** 1 - 49.

NESS GROUP INC.
52 East Pleasant Lake Road, St. Paul MN 55127-2117. 651/482-8004. **Fax:** 651/482-0993. **Contact:** Manager. **Description:** An executive search firm.

G.J. NIENHAUS & ASSOCIATES
2800 East Cliff Road, Suite 260, Burnsville MN 55337. 612/890-5702. **Fax:** 612/895-8345. **Contact:** Skip Nienhaus, President. **Description:** An executive search firm operating on a contingency basis. Client company pays fee. **Specializes in the areas of:** Printing. **Positions commonly filled include:** Account Manager; Customer Service Rep.; Desktop Publishing Specialist; Graphic Designer; Product Manager; Sales Manager; Sales Rep. **Average salary range of placements:** $50,000 - $100,000. **Number of placements per year:** 1 - 49.

NORTHLAND EMPLOYMENT SERVICES INC.
10801 Wayzata Boulevard, Suite 325, Minnetonka MN 55305. 612/541-1060. **Fax:** 612/595-9878. **Contact:** David Gavin, President. **World Wide Web address:** http://www.jobsmn.com. **Description:** An executive search firm operating on both retainer and contingency bases. **Specializes in the areas of:** Architecture/Construction; Biology; Computer Science/Software; Engineering; Technical. **Positions commonly filled include:** Biochemist; Biological Scientist; Biomedical Engineer; Chemical Engineer; Chemist; Civil Engineer; Computer Animator; Computer Operator; Construction Contractor; Database Manager; Design Engineer; Electrical/Electronics Engineer; Environmental Engineer; Geologist/Geophysicist; Industrial Engineer; Manufacturing Engineer; Mechanical Engineer; MIS Specialist; Project Manager; Quality Control Supervisor; Software Engineer; Systems Analyst; Systems Manager; Webmaster. **Average salary range of placements:** More than $50,000. **Number of placements per year:** 200 - 499.

NYCOR SEARCH INC.
4930 West 77th Street, Suite 300, Minneapolis MN 55435-4809. 612/831-6444. **Fax:** 612/835-2883. **Contact:** Manager. **E-mail address:** jobs@nycor.com. **World Wide Web address:** http://www.nycor.com. **Description:** An executive search firm. **Specializes in the areas of:** Architecture/Construction; Computer Science/Software; Engineering; General Management; Industrial; Manufacturing; Technical. **Positions commonly filled include:** Biomedical Engineer; Chemical Engineer; Chemist; Civil Engineer; Clinical Lab Technician; Computer Programmer; Design Engineer; Designer; Draftsperson; Electrical/Electronics Engineer; Food Scientist/Technologist; General Manager; Industrial Engineer; Internet Services Manager; Materials Engineer; Mathematician; Mechanical Engineer; Metallurgical Engineer; MIS Specialist; Multimedia Designer; Operations/Production Manager; Petroleum Engineer; Purchasing Agent/Manager; Quality Control Supervisor; Science Technologist; Software Engineer; Systems Analyst; Technical Writer/Editor; Telecommunications Manager. **Benefits available to temporary workers:** Medical Insurance; Paid Holidays; Paid Vacation. **Average salary range of placements:** More than $50,000. **Number of placements per year:** 200 - 499.

PERSONNEL ASSISTANCE CORPORATION
1242 Homestead Trail, Long Lake MN 55356. 612/476-0674. **Contact:** Donald E. Pearson, President. **Description:** An executive search firm operating on a contingency basis. **Specializes in the areas of:** Engineering; Industrial; Manufacturing; Technical. **Positions commonly filled include:** Agricultural Engineer; Design Engineer; Designer; General Manager; Industrial Production Manager; Mechanical Engineer; Operations/Production Manager. **Average salary range of placements:** $30,000 - $100,000. **Number of placements per year:** 1 - 49.

PIONEER SEARCH, INC.
P.O. Box 277, Center City MN 55012. 651/257-3957. **Contact:** Manager. **Description:** An executive search

firm. **Specializes in the areas of:** Computer Hardware/Software; Engineering.

PROFESSIONAL RECRUITERS, INC.
17641 Kettering Trail, Lakeville MN 55044-9344. 612/892-3700. **Fax:** 612/892-3711. **Contact:** Robert Reinitz, Principal. **E-mail address:** headhunt@primenet.com. **World Wide Web address:** http://professionalrecruiters.com. **Description:** An executive search firm operating on both retainer and contingency bases. **Specializes in the areas of:** Electrical; Electronics; High-Tech; Industrial; Management; Marketing; Sales. **Positions commonly filled include:** Account Representative; Applications Engineer; Marketing Manager; Product Manager; Sales Engineer; Sales Manager; Vice President of Marketing; Vice President of Sales. **Average salary range of placements:** More than $50,000. **Number of placements per year:** 1 - 49.

QUANTUM CONSULTING & PLACEMENT
6600 City West Parkway, Suite 310, Eden Prairie MN 55344. 612/829-5950. **Fax:** 612/829-5988. **Contact:** Jeff Northrup, Director of Marketing. **World Wide Web address:** http://www.qconsult.com. **Description:** An executive search firm. **Specializes in the areas of:** Computer Science/Software. **Positions commonly filled include:** Computer Programmer; Systems Analyst. **Number of placements per year:** 1 - 49.

RCM TECHNOLOGIES
7701 France Avenue South, Suite 100, Edina MN 55435. 612/841-1188. **Contact:** Vince Freese, Vice President of Recruiting. **Description:** An executive search firm. **Specializes in the areas of:** Biotechnology; Computer Science/Software; Data Processing; Engineering; Industrial; Information Technology; Manufacturing; Technical. **Positions commonly filled include:** Aerospace Engineer; Biological Scientist; Biomedical Engineer; Chemical Engineer; Computer Programmer; Design Engineer; Electrical/Electronics Engineer; Industrial Designer; Mechanical Engineer; Metallurgical Engineer; MIS Specialist; Operations/Production Manager; Physicist; Purchasing Agent/Manager; Quality Control Supervisor; Software Engineer; Systems Analyst; Technical Writer/Editor; Telecommunications Manager. **Corporate headquarters location:** Minneapolis MN. **Average salary range of placements:** More than $50,000. **Number of placements per year:** 50 - 99.

RAUENHORST RECRUITING COMPANY
7600 Parklawn Avenue, Suite 215, Edina MN 55435. 612/897-1420. **Contact:** Manager. **Description:** A generalist executive search firm.

REGENCY RECRUITERS, INC.
7101 York Avenue South, Suite 308, Edina MN 55435-4450. 612/921-3377. **Contact:** David Tetzloff, President. **Description:** An executive search firm focusing on engineering positions. **Specializes in the areas of:** Computer Science/Software; Electrical; Engineering; Industrial; Manufacturing; Mechanical; Technical. **Positions commonly filled include:** Aerospace Engineer; Biomedical Engineer; Chemical Engineer; Computer Programmer; Draftsperson; Electrical/Electronics Engineer; Mechanical Engineer; Metallurgical Engineer; Quality Control Supervisor; Software Engineer. **Average salary range of placements:** More than $50,000.

RESOURCE SEARCH
8301 Golden Valley Road, Suite 240, Golden Valley MN 55427. 612/546-0099. **Fax:** 612/546-4102. **Contact:** John Breczinski, President. **Description:** An executive search firm. **Specializes in the areas of:** Advertising; Art/Design; Engineering; Food; General Management; Health/Medical; Industrial; Manufacturing; Sales. **Positions commonly filled include:** Design Engineer; Designer; Electrical/Electronics Engineer; General Manager; Manufacturer's/Wholesaler's Sales Rep.; Market Research Analyst; Mechanical Engineer; Operations/Production Manager; Public Relations

Specialist; Services Sales Representative. **Average salary range of placements:** More than $50,000. **Number of placements per year:** 1 - 49.

ROMAC INTERNATIONAL
8500 Normandale Lake Boulevard, Suite 1590, Bloomington MN 55437-3833. 612/835-5100. **Fax:** 612/835-1548. **Contact:** Recruiter. **World Wide Web address:** http://www.romac.com. **Description:** An executive search firm that also provides some temporary placements. **Specializes in the areas of:** Accounting/ Auditing; Computer Science/Software; Secretarial. **Positions commonly filled include:** Accountant/Auditor; Budget Analyst; Computer Programmer; Financial Analyst; MIS Specialist; Software Engineer; Systems Analyst; Telecommunications Manager; Typist/Word Processor. **Benefits available to temporary workers:** Medical Insurance; Paid Vacation; Profit Sharing. **Corporate headquarters location:** Dallas TX. **Other U.S. locations:** Nationwide. **Average salary range of placements:** $30,000 - $50,000. **Number of placements per year:** 200 - 499.

ROMAC INTERNATIONAL
Pillsbury Center South, 220 South Sixth Street, Suite 810, Minneapolis MN 55402. 612/332-6460. **Contact:** Manager. **World Wide Web address:** http://www. romac.com. **Description:** Romac International is an executive search firm. **Specializes in the areas of:** Accounting/Auditing; Computer Hardware/Software; Information Technology.

ROTH YOUNG EXECUTIVE RECRUITERS
4620 West 77th Street, Suite 290, Edina MN 55435-4924. 612/831-6655. **Fax:** 612/831-7413. **Contact:** Donald Spahr, President. **Description:** Roth Young Executive Recruiters is an executive search firm. **Specializes in the areas of:** Fashion; Food; Health/ Medical; Hotel/Restaurant; Personnel/Labor Relations; Retail; Sales. **Positions commonly filled include:** Buyer; Food Scientist/Technologist; Hotel Manager; Human Resources Manager; Manufacturer's/Wholesaler's Sales Rep.; Occupational Therapist; Physical Therapist; Quality Control Supervisor; Recreational Therapist; Restaurant/Food Service Manager; Retail Manager; Sales Rep.; Speech-Language Pathologist. **Number of placements per year:** 50 - 99.

RUSSELL REYNOLDS ASSOCIATES, INC.
90 South Seventh Street, Suite 3050, Minneapolis MN 55402. 612/332-6966. **Fax:** 612/332-2629. **Contact:** Manager. **Description:** A generalist executive search firm.

SATHE & ASSOCIATES EXECUTIVE SEARCH
5821 Cedar Lake Road, St. Louis Park MN 55416. 612/546-2100. **Fax:** 612/546-6930. **Contact:** Mark Sathe, President. **Description:** An executive search firm. **Specializes in the areas of:** Accounting/Auditing; Administration; Architecture/Construction; Banking; Engineering; Finance; Food; General Management; Industrial; Manufacturing; Nonprofit; Personnel/Labor Relations; Sales. **Positions commonly filled include:** Accountant/Auditor; Bank Officer/Manager; Buyer; Electrical/Electronics Engineer; Hotel Manager; Industrial Engineer; Mechanical Engineer; Purchasing Agent/Manager; Quality Control Supervisor. **Number of placements per year:** 1 - 49.

SCHALEKAMP & ASSOCIATES, INC.
2608 West 102nd Street, Minneapolis MN 55431-3346. 612/948-1948. **Fax:** 612/948-9677. **Contact:** Paul D. Schalekamp, President. **Description:** Schalekamp & Associates is an executive search firm focusing on providing placements in the property casualty insurance industry. **Specializes in the areas of:** Insurance. **Positions commonly filled include:** Adjuster; Claim Representative; Insurance Agent/Broker; Loss Prevention Specialist; MIS Specialist; Risk Manager. **Average salary range of placements:** More than $50,000. **Number of placements per year:** 1 - 49.

SEARCH SPECIALISTS
2655 North Shore Drive, Wayzata MN 55391. 612/449-8990. **Fax:** 612/449-0369. **Contact:** Tim Lindell, Vice President of Administration. **World Wide Web address:** http://www.cities-online.com/search. **Description:** An executive search firm. Client company pays fee. **Specializes in the areas of:** Architecture/Construction; Computer Science/Software; Data Processing; Engineering; Marketing; Sales; Software Development. **Positions commonly filled include:** Architect; Civil Engineer; Design Engineer; Draftsperson; Electrical/ Electronics Engineer; Landscape Architect; Mechanical Engineer; MIS Specialist; Software Engineer; Structural Engineer. **Average salary range of placements:** $50,000 - $100,000. **Number of placements per year:** 1 - 49.

SEARCHTEK
4900 North Highway 169, Suite 309, Minneapolis MN 55428. 612/531-0766. **Contact:** Gerald Otten, President. **World Wide Web address:** http://www.searchtek.com. **Description:** An executive search firm operating on both retainer and contingency bases. **Specializes in the areas of:** Engineering; High-Tech. **Positions commonly filled include:** Biomedical Engineer; Computer Programmer; Electrical/Electronics Engineer; Industrial Engineer; Industrial Production Manager; Manufacturing Engineer; Mechanical Engineer; Metallurgical Engineer; Production Manager; Quality Control Supervisor; Software Engineer. **Corporate headquarters location:** This Location. **Other U.S. locations:** Nationwide. **International locations:** Worldwide. **Average salary range of placements:** More than $50,000. **Number of placements per year:** 1 - 49.

STAFF CONNECTION, INC.
15500 Wayzata Boulevard, Suite 821, Wayzata MN 55391. 612/475-1554. **Contact:** Craig Lyon, Secretary/ Treasurer. **Description:** An executive search firm operating on a contingency basis. **Specializes in the areas of:** Computer Science/Software; Engineering; Technical. **Positions commonly filled include:** Computer Programmer; Internet Services Manager; MIS Specialist; Software Engineer; Systems Analyst. **Corporate headquarters location:** Minneapolis MN. **Other U.S. locations:** Phoenix AZ; Las Vegas NV. **Average salary range of placements:** $30,000 - $90,000.

SYSTEMS SEARCH, INC.
P.O. Box 600, Anoka MN 55303. 612/323-9690. **Contact:** Mike Fitzpatrick, President. **Description:** An executive search firm. **Specializes in the areas of:** Administration; Computer Science/Software. **Positions commonly filled include:** Computer Programmer; Internet Services Manager; Management Analyst/ Consultant; MIS Specialist; Multimedia Designer; Software Engineer; Systems Analyst; Telecommunications Manager. **Average salary range of placements:** $30,000 - $50,000. **Number of placements per year:** 1 - 49.

THE BRIMEYER GROUP
50 South Ninth Avenue, Suite 101, Hopkins MN 55343. 612/945-0246. **Contact:** Manager. **Description:** An executive search firm.

RICHARD THOMPSON ASSOCIATES
701 Fourth Avenue South, Suite 500, Minneapolis MN 55415. 612/339-6060. **Contact:** Manager. **Description:** An executive search firm.

TOTAL SEARCH
1541 Berne Road, Fridley MN 55421. 612/571-0247. **Contact:** Tom Harrington, President. **Description:** An executive search firm operating on a contingency basis. **Specializes in the areas of:** Computer Science/Software; Food; Retail. **Positions commonly filled include:** Computer Programmer; Restaurant/Food Service Manager; Retail Manager; Systems Analyst. **Number of placements per year:** 50 - 99.

TWIN CITY SEARCH
3989 Central Avenue North, Suite 215, Minneapolis MN 55421. 612/789-4537. **Contact:** Manager. **Description:** An executive search firm. **Specializes in the areas of:** Computer Hardware/Software; Technical.

WILLIAMS EXECUTIVE SEARCH
4200 Norwest Center, 90 South Seventh Street, Minneapolis MN 55402. 612/339-2900. **Contact:** Manager. **Description:** An executive search firm.

PERMANENT EMPLOYMENT AGENCIES

ADVANTAGE PERSONNEL INC.
408 West 65th Street, Richfield MN 55423-1402. 612/861-9930. **Fax:** 612/861-9543. **Contact:** W. John Knopf II, General Manager. **Description:** A permanent employment agency. **Specializes in the areas of:** Industrial; Light Industrial. **Average salary range of placements:** Less than $20,000. **Number of placements per year:** 50 - 99.

AGRO QUALITY SEARCH INC.
7260 University Avenue NE, Suite 305, Fridley MN 55432-3129. 612/572-3737. **Fax:** 612/572-3738. **Contact:** Jerry L. Olson, President. **Description:** A permanent employment agency. **Specializes in the areas of:** Agriculture; Food; Sales; Technical. **Positions commonly filled include:** Agricultural Engineer; Design Engineer; Food Scientist/Technologist; General Manager; Human Resources Specialist; Industrial Engineer; Manufacturer's/Wholesaler's Sales Rep.; Mechanical Engineer; Purchasing Agent/Manager; Transportation/Traffic Specialist. **Average salary range of placements:** $30,000 - $50,000. **Number of placements per year:** 1 - 49.

ALTERNATIVE STAFFING, INC.
8120 Penn Avenue South, Suite 570, Bloomington MN 55431-1326. 612/888-6077. **Contact:** Kim Howard, President. **Description:** A permanent employment agency. **Specializes in the areas of:** Accounting/Auditing; Clerical; Computer Hardware/Software; Legal; Manufacturing; Publishing; Sales; Secretarial. **Positions commonly filled include:** Accountant/Auditor; Administrative Assistant; Bookkeeper; Claim Rep.; Clerk; Computer Programmer; Credit Manager; Customer Service Representative; Data Entry Clerk; Draftsperson; Factory Worker; Financial Analyst; Human Resources Manager; Legal Secretary; Light Industrial Worker; Marketing Specialist; Medical Secretary; Purchasing Agent/Manager; Receptionist; Sales Representative; Secretary; Stenographer; Typist/Word Processor. **Number of placements per year:** 1000+.

BARTZ ROGERS & PARTNERS
6465 Wayzata Boulevard, Minneapolis MN 55426. 612/936-0657. **Fax:** 612/936-0142. **Contact:** Douglas Bartz, Partner. **Description:** A permanent employment agency. **Specializes in the areas of:** Computer Science/Software. **Positions commonly filled include:** Computer Programmer; Systems Analyst. **Number of placements per year:** 100 - 199.

DIVERSIFIED EMPLOYMENT INC.
1710 Douglas Drive, Suite 200, Golden Valley MN 55422. 612/546-8255. **Fax:** 612/546-4106. **Contact:** Dan Kelly, Account Manager. **E-mail address:** dei@fishnet.com. **Description:** A permanent employment agency. Client company pays fee. **Specializes in the areas of:** Accounting/Auditing; Administration; Advertising; Art/Design; Engineering; General Management; Industrial; Manufacturing; Publishing; Sales; Secretarial; Technical. **Positions commonly filled include:** Account Manager; Account Representative; Accountant; Adjuster; Administrative Assistant; Administrative Manager; Advertising Clerk; Advertising Executive; Architect; Assistant Manager; Attorney; Auditor; Bank Officer/Manager; Biochemist; Biological Scientist; Biomedical Engineer; Blue-Collar Worker Supervisor; Branch Manager; Broadcast Technician; Budget Analyst; Buyer; Chemical Engineer; Chemist; Chief Financial Officer; Civil Engineer; Claim Representative; Clerical Supervisor; Clinical Lab Technician; Computer Animator; Computer Programmer; Computer Support Technician; Computer Technician; Construction Contractor; Consultant; Controller; Cost Estimator; Counselor; Credit Manager; Customer Service Rep.; Database Administrator; Database Manager; Design Engineer; Desktop Publishing Specialist; Draftsperson; Economist; Editor; Editorial Assistant; Electrical/Electronics Engineer; Electrician; Environmental Engineer; Finance Director; Financial Analyst; Food Scientist/Technologist; Fund Manager; General Manager; Geographer; Geologist/Geophysicist; Graphic Artist; Graphic Designer; Human Resources Manager; Industrial Engineer; Industrial Production Manager; Instructional Technologist; Insurance Agent/Broker; Intellectual Property Lawyer; Management Analyst/Consultant; Management Trainee; Managing Editor; Manufacturing Engineer; Market Research Analyst; Marketing Manager; Marketing Specialist; Mechanical Engineer; Medical Assistant; Metallurgical Engineer; Multimedia Designer; Operations Manager; Paralegal; Production Manager; Project Manager; Psychologist; Public Relations Specialist; Purchasing Agent/Manager; Quality Assurance Engineer; Quality Control Supervisor; Radio/TV Announcer/Broadcaster; Radiological Technologist; Real Estate Agent; Reporter; Sales Engineer; Sales Executive; Sales Manager; Sales Representative; Secretary; Social Worker; Speech-Language Pathologist; Statistician; Teacher/Professor; Technical Writer/Editor; Telecommunications Manager; Transportation/Traffic Specialist; Typist/Word Processor; Underwriter/Assistant Underwriter; Vice President; Video Production Coordinator; Webmaster. **Corporate headquarters location:** This Location. **Average salary range of placements:** $20,000 - $90,000. **Number of placements per year:** 500 - 999.

EMPLOYMENT ADVISORS
6600 France Avenue South, Suite 515, Edina MN 55435. 612/925-3666. **Toll-free phone:** 800/488-8634. **Fax:** 612/924-0111. **Contact:** Manager. **Description:** A permanent employment agency. **Specializes in the areas of:** Banking; Customer Service; General Management; Sales. **Number of placements per year:** 500 - 999.

EMPLOYMENT ADVISORS
STAFF IT PERSONNEL SERVICES
900 Nicollet Mall, Suite 602, Minneapolis MN 55402-1008. 612/339-0521. **Toll-free phone:** 800/959-0521. **Fax:** 612/338-4757. **Contact:** Vicky Sherman, General Manager. **Description:** A permanent employment agency that places college graduates in entry- and mid-level business positions. Staff It Personnel Services (also at this location) provides temporary and temp-to-perm placements. **Specializes in the areas of:** Customer Service; Finance; General Management; Retail; Sales. **Positions commonly filled include:** Credit Manager; Customer Service Representative; Management Trainee; Public Relations Specialist; Restaurant/Food Service Manager; Sales Representative. **Average salary range of placements:** $20,000 - $29,999. **Number of placements per year:** 200 - 499.

EXPRESS PERSONNEL SERVICES
7101 France Avenue South, Edina MN 55435. 612/915-2000. **Contact:** Jim Johnson, Owner. **Description:** A permanent employment agency that also provides some temporary placements. **Specializes in the areas of:** Industrial; Manufacturing; Personnel/Labor Relations; Secretarial. **Positions commonly filled include:** Accountant/Auditor; Administrative Manager; Blue-Collar Worker Supervisor; Branch Manager; Brokerage

Clerk; Buyer; Claim Representative; Clerical Supervisor; Credit Manager; Customer Service Representative; General Manager; Human Resources Manager; MIS Specialist; Purchasing Agent/Manager; Quality Control Supervisor; Services Sales Representative; Technical Writer/Editor; Typist/Word Processor. **Benefits available to temporary workers:** Paid Holidays; Paid Vacation. **Corporate headquarters location:** Oklahoma City OK. **Average salary range of placements:** $20,000 - $29,999.

FINANCIAL STAFF RECRUITERS
1600 West 82nd Street, Suite 170, Bloomington MN 55431. 612/885-3040. **Contact:** Manager. **Description:** Financial Staff Recruiters is a permanent employment agency. **Specializes in the areas of:** Accounting/Auditing; Finance.

HUMAN RESOURCES PERSONNEL SERVICES
6800 France Avenue South, Suite 173, Edina MN 55435-2007. 612/929-3000. **Fax:** 612/927-4313. **Contact:** Susan Miller, Owner. **E-mail address:** hrps@hrsearch.com. **World Wide Web address:** http://www.hrsearch.com. **Description:** A permanent employment agency that also provides some temporary placements. **Specializes in the areas of:** Human Resources; Personnel/Labor Relations. **Positions commonly filled include:** Human Resources Manager.

KAPOSIA, INC.
380 East Lafayette Frontage Road South, St. Paul MN 55107-1216. 651/224-6974. **Fax:** 651/224-7249. **Contact:** Peg Ring, Human Resources/Administrative Assistant. **Description:** A permanent employment agency for individuals with developmental disabilities. **Specializes in the areas of:** Human Services; Nonprofit; Social Services. **Positions commonly filled include:** Accountant/Auditor; Counselor; Human Service Worker; Services Sales Representative. **Benefits available to temporary workers:** Paid Vacation. **Number of placements per year:** 1 - 49.

METRO HOSPITALITY CONSULTANTS
9448 Lyndale Avenue South, Suite 223, Bloomington MN 55420. 612/884-4299. **Contact:** Debra K.W. Kiefat, CPC, President. **Description:** A permanent employment agency operating on a contingency basis. The firm also provides some resume writing and interview coaching services. **Specializes in the areas of:** Food; General Management; Hotel/Restaurant; Marketing; Sales. **Positions commonly filled include:** Account Manager; Assistant Manager; General Manager; Human Resources Manager; Operations Manager; Sales Executive; Sales Manager. **Corporate headquarters location:** Minneapolis MN. **Average salary range of placements:** $30,000 - $49,999. **Number of placements per year:** 1 - 49.

PALESCH & ASSOCIATES, INC.
530 Kristen Lane, Maple Plain MN 55359. 612/955-3390. **Contact:** Tom Palesch, President. **Description:** A permanent employment agency. **Specializes in the areas of:** Metals. **Positions commonly filled include:** Operations/Production Manager. **Number of placements per year:** 50 - 99.

SECRETARY & ACCOUNTING SERVICES
50 West Second Street, Winona MN 55987-3440. 507/454-5804. **Fax:** 507/454-5804. **Contact:** Lucia Bartsh, Owner. **Description:** A permanent employment agency that also provides some temporary placements. **Specializes in the areas of:** Accounting/Auditing; Secretarial. **Positions commonly filled include:** Accountant/Auditor; Administrative Manager; Clerical Supervisor; Computer Programmer; Draftsperson; General Manager; Human Resources Manager; Management Trainee; Medical Records Technician; MIS Specialist; Paralegal; Purchasing Agent/Manager; Software Engineer; Systems Analyst; Technical Writer/Editor; Typist/Word Processor. **Average salary range of placements:** $20,000 - $29,999. **Number of placements per year:** 50 - 99.

ULTIMATE SEARCH UNLIMITED
TEMPS UNLIMITED
2233 University Avenue West, St. Paul MN 55114-1629. 651/649-3131. **Fax:** 651/649-3041. **Contact:** Robert H. Draack, Vice President/General Manager. **Description:** A permanent employment agency. Temps Unlimited (also at this location) provides temporary placements. **Specializes in the areas of:** Administration; Banking; Engineering; Finance; Food; General Management; Health/Medical; Legal; MIS/EDP; Sales; Secretarial. **Positions commonly filled include:** Account Manager; Account Rep.; Administrative Manager; Attorney; Bank Officer/Manager; Branch Manager; Certified Nurses Aide; Chief Financial Officer; Claim Rep.; Clerical Supervisor; Computer Operator; Computer Programmer; Credit Manager; Customer Service Rep.; Database Manager; Design Engineer; EEG Technologist; EKG Tech.; Electrical/Electronics Engineer; Emergency Medical Tech.; Finance Director; Financial Analyst; General Manager; Human Resources Manager; Industrial Engineer; Industrial Production Manager; Insurance Agent/Broker; Licensed Practical Nurse; Management Trainee; Marketing Manager; Medical Records Tech.; Occupational Therapist; Operations Manager; Paralegal; Pharmacist; Physical Therapist; Physician; Production Manager; Quality Control Supervisor; Registered Nurse; Respiratory Therapist; Sales Engineer; Sales Executive; Sales Rep.; Secretary; Services Sales Rep.; Software Engineer; Speech-Language Pathologist; Surgical Tech.; Telecommunications Manager; Transportation/Traffic Specialist; Typist/Word Processor. **Benefits available to temporary workers:** Paid Holidays; Paid Vacation. **Average salary range of placements:** $30,000 - $50,000. **Number of placements per year:** 200 - 499.

WORKING RELATIONSHIPS INC.
6468 City West Parkway, Eden Prairie MN 55344. 612/546-2999. **Fax:** 612/941-4334. **Contact:** Manager. **World Wide Web address:** http://www.workingrelationships.com. **Description:** A permanent employment agency. **Specializes in the areas of:** Accounting/Auditing; Administration; General Management; Sales; Secretarial. **Positions commonly filled include:** Administrative Assistant; Buyer; Customer Service Representative; Operations/Production Manager; Project Manager; Sales Representative; Secretary; Typist/Word Processor. **Average salary range of placements:** $20,000 - $29,999. **Number of placements per year:** 100 - 199.

TEMPORARY EMPLOYMENT AGENCIES

ABBY BLU INC.
821 Marquette Avenue, Suite 515, Minneapolis MN 55402. 612/338-3200. **Fax:** 612/349-2983. **Contact:** Manager. **Description:** A temporary agency that also provides some permanent placements. **Specializes in the areas of:** Accounting/Auditing; Advertising; Architecture/Construction; Banking; Computer Science/Software; General Management; Insurance; Legal; Manufacturing; Nonprofit; Personnel/Labor Relations; Secretarial. **Positions commonly filled include:** Accountant/Auditor; Claim Representative; Clerical Supervisor; Credit Manager; Customer Service Representative; Financial Analyst; Human Resources Specialist; Market Research Analyst; Medical Records Technician; Paralegal; Typist/Word Processor. **Benefits available to temporary workers:** 401(k); Paid Holidays; Paid Vacation. **Number of placements per year:** 1000+.

ANSWER PERSONNEL SERVICE, INC.
220 Robert Street South, Suite 208, St. Paul MN 55107-1626. 651/293-1887. **Contact:** Bruce Labelle,

Coordinator. **Description:** A temporary agency. **Specializes in the areas of:** Engineering; Food; Industrial; Manufacturing. **Positions commonly filled include:** Clerical Supervisor; Computer Programmer. **Average salary range of placements:** $20,000 - $29,999. **Number of placements per year:** 500 - 999.

AQUENT PARTNERS
43 Main Street SE, Suite 413, Minneapolis MN 55414-1029. 612/378-4930. **Toll-free phone:** 877/PARTNER. **Fax:** 612/378-2520. **Contact:** Ken Marshall, Manager. **E-mail address:** kmarshall@aquent.com. **World Wide Web address:** http://www.aquent.com. **Description:** A temporary agency that provides placements for creative, Web, and technical professionals. Aquent Partners also provides some temp-to-perm, permanent, and contract placements. **Specializes in the areas of:** Administration; Art/Design; Computer Science/Software; Marketing. **Positions commonly filled include:** Computer Animator; Computer Engineer; Computer Operator; Computer Programmer; Computer Support Technician; Computer Technician; Content Developer; Database Administrator; Database Manager; Desktop Publishing Specialist; Editor; Editorial Assistant; Graphic Artist; Graphic Designer; Internet Services Manager; Managing Editor; MIS Specialist; Multimedia Designer; Network/Systems Administrator; Production Manager; Project Manager; Software Engineer; SQL Programmer; Systems Analyst; Systems Manager; Technical Writer/Editor; Webmaster. **Benefits available to temporary workers:** 401(k); Dental Insurance; Disability Coverage; Medical Insurance. **CEO:** John Chuang.

DESIGN PERSONNEL RESOURCES INC.
3585 North Lexington Avenue, Suite 180, St. Paul MN 55126. 651/482-0075. **Contact:** Manager. **Description:** Design Personnel Resources Inc. is a temporary agency that also provides some permanent placements. **Specializes in the areas of:** Architecture/Construction; Design.

ENVIROSTAFF, INC.
4500 Park Glen Road, Suite 140, St. Louis Park MN 55416. 612/925-8655. **Toll-free phone:** 800/313-0685. **Fax:** 612/925-8632. **Contact:** Manager. **Description:** A temporary agency. Client company pays fee. **NOTE:** Interested jobseekers should call to speak with a placement specialist before sending a resume. **Specializes in the areas of:** Environmental. **Positions commonly filled include:** Environmental Protection Specialist. **Benefits available to temporary workers:** Dental Insurance; Life Insurance; Medical Insurance; Paid Holidays; Stock Option. **Average salary range of placements:** $20,000 - $49,999. **Number of placements per year:** 100 - 199.

GRAPHIC STAFFING INC.
1710 Douglas Drive, Suite 202, Golden Valley MN 55422. 612/546-1292. **Fax:** 612/546-7822. **Contact:** Dick Haines, Graphics Manager. **E-mail address:** DHainesGS@aol.com. **World Wide Web address:** http://www.graphicstaffing.com. **Description:** Graphic Staffing is a temporary agency that also provides some permanent placements. **Specializes in the areas of:** Advertising; Art/Design; Publishing. **Positions commonly filled include:** Art Director; Computer Animator; Copy Editor; Desktop Publishing Specialist; Graphic Artist; Graphic Designer; Layout Specialist; Multimedia Designer; Proofreader; Technical Illustrator; Video Production Coordinator; Webmaster. **Other U.S. locations:** Chicago IL. **Average salary range of placements:** $30,000 - $50,000. **Number of placements per year:** 100 - 199.

HEALTH PERSONNEL OPTIONS CORPORATION
2550 University Avenue West, Suite 315 North, St. Paul MN 55114. 651/647-1160. **Fax:** 651/647-1903. **Contact:** Martin Kieffer, President. **Description:** Health Personnel Options Corporation is a temporary agency. **Specializes in the areas of:** Health/Medical. **Positions commonly filled include:** Dental Assistant/Dental Hygienist;

Dentist; EEG Technologist; EKG Technician; Health Services Manager; Licensed Practical Nurse; Medical Records Technician; Nuclear Medicine Technologist; Occupational Therapist; Physical Therapist; Physician; Radiological Technologist; Registered Nurse; Respiratory Therapist; Social Worker; Speech-Language Pathologist; Surgical Technician. **Other U.S. locations:** Nationwide. **Number of placements per year:** 100 - 199.

INTERIM LEGAL PROFESSIONALS
80 South Eighth Street, Suite 3630, Minneapolis MN 55402. 612/339-7663. **Fax:** 612/339-9274. **Contact:** Holly Bilderback, Branch Manager. **World Wide Web address:** http://www.interim.com/legal. **Description:** Interim Legal Professionals is a temporary agency. **Specializes in the areas of:** Legal. **Positions commonly filled include:** Attorney; Paralegal. **Benefits available to temporary workers:** Dental Insurance; Medical Insurance; Vision Insurance. **Corporate headquarters location:** Fort Lauderdale FL. **Average salary range of placements:** $30,000 - $50,000. **Number of placements per year:** 500 - 999.

JOHNSON ASSOCIATES
1396 White Bear Avenue North, Suite A, St. Paul MN 55106. 651/774-5843. **Contact:** Dana Johnson, Director. **Description:** A temporary agency. **Specializes in the areas of:** Health/Medical. **Positions commonly filled include:** Counselor; Human Service Worker; Psychologist; Recreational Therapist; Registered Nurse; Social Worker. **Average salary range of placements:** $20,000 - $29,999. **Number of placements per year:** 200 - 499.

KELLY SCIENTIFIC RESOURCES
6465 Wayzata Boulevard, Suite 155, St. Louis Park MN 55426. 612/797-0500. **Fax:** 612/797-0611. **Contact:** Branch Manager. **World Wide Web address:** http://www.kellyscientific.com. **Description:** A temporary agency for scientific professionals. **Specializes in the areas of:** Biomedical; Chemicals; Food; Pharmaceuticals.

LYNN TEMPORARY
1821 University Avenue West, Suite 106 South, St. Paul MN 55104-2801. 651/645-9233. **Contact:** Carol Glewwe, President. **Description:** A temporary agency. **Specializes in the areas of:** Clerical; Computer Science/Software; Engineering; Nonprofit; Personnel/Labor Relations; Publishing; Secretarial; Technical. **Positions commonly filled include:** Accountant/Auditor; Administrative Manager; Architect; Biomedical Engineer; Buyer; Chemical Engineer; Clerical Supervisor; Computer Programmer; Customer Service Rep.; Design Engineer; Designer; Draftsperson; Editor; Electrical/Electronics Engineer; Landscape Architect; Library Technician; Mathematician; Mechanical Engineer; Medical Records Technician; MIS Specialist; Purchasing Agent/Manager; Science Technologist; Services Sales Representative; Software Engineer; Systems Analyst; Technical Writer/Editor; Typist/Word Processor; Video Production Coordinator. **Average salary range of placements:** $20,000 - $29,999. **Number of placements per year:** 200 - 499.

MANPOWER TEMPORARY SERVICES
150 South Fifth Street, Suite 336, Minneapolis MN 55402. 612/375-9200. **Contact:** Branch Manager. **Description:** A temporary agency. **Specializes in the areas of:** Data Processing; Industrial; Secretarial; Technical; Telephone Technical Support; Word Processing. **Positions commonly filled include:** Accountant/Auditor; Accounting Clerk; Administrative Assistant; Assembly Worker; Biological Scientist; Bookkeeper; Chemist; Computer Operator; Customer Service Manager; Designer; Desktop Publishing Specialist; Electrician; Inspector/Tester/Grader; Inventory Control Specialist; Machine Operator; Packaging/Processing Worker; Painter; Project Engineer; Proofreader; Receptionist; Research Assistant; Secretary; Software Engineer; Stenographer; Systems Analyst;

Technical Writer/Editor; Technician; Telemarketer; Transcriptionist; Typist/Word Processor; Welder. **Benefits available to temporary workers:** Life Insurance; Medical Insurance; Paid Holidays; Paid Vacation. **Other U.S. locations:** Nationwide.

MIDWEST STAFFING SERVICES
1145 Canterbury Road, Shakopee MN 55379. 612/896-2055. **Fax:** 612/896-2059. **Contact:** Director of Operations. **Description:** A temporary agency. **Specializes in the areas of:** Accounting/Auditing; Legal; Manufacturing; Personnel/Labor Relations; Secretarial. **Positions commonly filled include:** Blue-Collar Worker Supervisor; Claim Representative; Clerical Supervisor; Credit Manager; Customer Service Representative; General Manager; Human Resources Manager; Librarian; Library Technician; Medical Records Technician; Paralegal; Public Relations Specialist; Typist/Word Processor. **Average salary range of placements:** $20,000 - $29,999.

THOMAS MOORE INC.
608 Second Avenue South, Suite 465, Minneapolis MN 55402-1907. 612/338-4884. **Contact:** Manager. **Description:** A temporary agency. **Specializes in the areas of:** Accounting/Auditing; Banking; Finance. **Positions commonly filled include:** Accountant/Auditor; Budget Analyst; Credit Manager; Financial Analyst. **Benefits available to temporary workers:** Paid Holidays; Paid Vacation.

OLSTEN STAFFING SERVICES
7701 France Avenue South, Suite 110, Edina MN 55435. 612/837-8030. **Contact:** Tami Pulkrabek, General Manager. **Description:** Olsten Staffing Services is a temporary agency. **Specializes in the areas of:** Architecture/Construction; Consulting; Engineering; Manufacturing; Materials; Publishing; Technical. **Positions commonly filled include:** Architect; Architectural Engineer; Civil Engineer; Designer; Draftsperson; Electrical/Electronics Engineer; Industrial Engineer; Manufacturing Engineer; Mechanical Engineer; Production Manager; Purchasing Agent/Manager; Quality Control Supervisor; Software Engineer; Structural Engineer; Technical Illustrator; Technical Writer/Editor; Technician. **Number of placements per year:** 500 - 999.

TEMP FORCE
6550 York Avenue South, Suite 640, Edina MN 55435. 612/920-9119. **Contact:** Manager. **Description:** A temporary agency. **Specializes in the areas of:** Industrial; Secretarial; Technical.

JEANE THORNE INC.
336 North Robert Street, Suite 100, St. Paul MN 55101. 651/298-0400. **Toll-free phone:** 800/848-0402. **Fax:** 651/298-0448. **Contact:** Patricia Meier, Director of Corporate Development. **World Wide Web address:** http://www.jeane-thorne.com. **Description:** Jeane Thorne Inc. is a temporary agency. Jeane Thorne also provides employee training. **Specializes in the areas of:** Accounting/Auditing; Banking; Office Support; Secretarial. **Positions commonly filled include:** Accountant/Auditor; Administrative Assistant; Customer Service Representative; Data Entry Clerk; Executive Assistant; Legal Assistant; Receptionist. **Benefits available to temporary workers:** Dental Insurance; Life Insurance; Medical Insurance; Referral Bonus Plan. **Other area locations:** Arden Hills MN; Crystal MN; Eagan MN; Eden Prairie MN; Mankato MN; Midway MN; Minneapolis MN; St. Louis Park MN; Woodbury MN. **Other U.S. locations:** Fargo ND.

WHITNEY PROFESSIONAL STAFFING
616 Kinnard Financial Center, 920 Second Avenue South, Minneapolis MN 55402-4035. 612/337-5100. **Fax:** 612/336-4499. **Contact:** David L. Whitney, President. **E-mail address:** TemporaryStaffing@WhitneyInc.com. **World Wide Web address:** http://www.whitneyinc.com. **Description:** Whitney Professional Staffing is a temporary and temp-to-perm employment agency specializing in the placement of accounting professionals with four-year degrees. **Specializes in the areas of:** Accounting; Bookkeeping; Finance; Tax. **Positions commonly filled include:** Accountant; Accounting Clerk; Auditor; Bookkeeper; Budget Analyst; Chief Financial Officer; Controller; CPA; Finance Director; Financial Analyst; Financial Consultant; Tax Specialist; Treasurer. **Average salary range of placements:** $30,000 - $125,000. **Number of placements per year:** 200 - 499.

YOUTH EMPLOYMENT PROJECT, INC.
300 11th Avenue NW, Suite 120, Rochester MN 55901. 507/529-2709. **Contact:** Dawn Roush, Executive Director. **Description:** Youth Employment Project, Inc. is a temporary employment agency for youth between the ages of 13 and 19. **Specializes in the areas of:** Agri-Business; Child Care, In-Home; Hotel/Restaurant; Office Support; Retail. **Positions commonly filled include:** Daycare Worker; Retail Sales Worker. **Average salary range of placements:** Less than $20,000. **Number of placements per year:** 500 - 999.

CONTRACT SERVICES FIRMS

CDI CORPORATION
510 First Avenue North, Suite 600, Minneapolis MN 55403. 612/541-9967. **Fax:** 612/541-9605. **Contact:** Manager. **World Wide Web address:** http://www.cdicorp.com. **Description:** A contract services firm. **Specializes in the areas of:** Technical. **Corporate headquarters location:** Philadelphia PA. **Other U.S. locations:** Nationwide. **International locations:** Worldwide.

CDI CORPORATION
1915 Highway 52 North, Suite 222-B, Rochester MN 55901. **Toll-free phone:** 888/686-8979. **Contact:** Manager. **World Wide Web address:** http://www.cdicorp.com. **Description:** A contract services firm. **Specializes in the areas of:** Engineering; Technical. **Corporate headquarters location:** Philadelphia PA. **Other U.S. locations:** Nationwide. **International locations:** Worldwide.

CONSULTIS INC.
8500 Normandale Lake Boulevard, Suite 1670, Bloomington MN 55437. 612/921-8866. **Contact:** Manager. **Description:** Consultis Inc. is a contract services firm. **Specializes in the areas of:** Information Technology.

HALL KINION
1000 Shelard Parkway, Suite 360, Minneapolis MN 55426. 612/417-1630. **Fax:** 612/513-9681. **Contact:** Manager. **E-mail address:** mnresume@hallkinion.com. **World Wide Web address:** http://www.hallkinion.com. **Description:** A contract services firm that also provides some permanent placements. **Specializes in the areas of:** Information Systems; Information Technology; Internet Development; Network Administration; Quality Assurance; Systems Administration; Systems Design; Technical Writing.

GEORGE KONIK ASSOCIATES INC.
7242 Metro Boulevard, Edina MN 55439. 612/835-5550. **Fax:** 612/835-7294. **Contact:** Tom Goettl, Recruiter. **E-mail address:** gka@minn.net. **World Wide Web address:** http://www.georgekonik.com. **Description:** George Konik Associates is a contract services firm that also offers some temporary placements. Client company pays fee. **Specializes in the areas of:** Engineering; Personnel/Labor Relations. **Positions commonly filled**

include: Applications Engineer; AS400 Programmer Analyst; Chemical Engineer; Chemist; Civil Engineer; Computer Operator; Computer Programmer; Computer Technician; Design Engineer; Draftsperson; Electrical/Electronics Engineer; Human Resources Manager; Industrial Engineer; Manufacturing Engineer; Mechanical Engineer; Metallurgical Engineer; MIS Specialist; Quality Assurance Engineer; SQL Programmer; Webmaster. **Benefits available to temporary workers:** 401(k); Dental Insurance; Medical Insurance; Vacation Pay. **Average salary range of placements:** $30,000 - $49,999. **Number of placements per year:** 50 - 99.

MANPOWER TECHNICAL
3800 West 80th Street, Suite 260, Bloomington MN 55431. 612/820-0365. **Fax:** 612/820-0350. **Contact:** Branch Manager. **Description:** Manpower Technical is a contract services firm. **Specializes in the areas of:** Administration; Computer Science/Software; Engineering; Finance; Industrial; Manufacturing; Personnel/Labor Relations; Publishing; Technical. **Positions commonly filled include:** Accountant/Auditor; Administrative Manager; Aerospace Engineer; Aircraft Mechanic/Engine Specialist; Bank Officer/Manager; Biochemist; Biological Scientist; Biomedical Engineer; Blue-Collar Worker Supervisor; Branch Manager; Broadcast Technician; Chemical Engineer; Computer Programmer; Credit Manager; Customer Service Rep.; Design Engineer; Designer; Draftsperson; Editor; Electrical/Electronics Engineer; Environmental Engineer; Financial Analyst; Food Scientist/Technologist; General Manager; Geologist/Geophysicist; Human Resources Specialist; Industrial Engineer; Industrial Production Manager; Insurance Agent/Broker; Internet Services Manager; Library Technician; Management Analyst/Consultant; Management Trainee; Manufacturer's/Wholesaler's Sales Representative; Market Research Analyst; Materials Engineer; Mathematician; Mechanical Engineer; Metallurgical Engineer; MIS Specialist; Multimedia Designer; Nuclear Engineer; Operations/Production Manager; Paralegal; Physicist; Purchasing Agent/Manager; Quality Control Supervisor; Science Technologist; Securities Sales Representative; Services Sales Representative; Software Engineer; Structural Engineer; Systems Analyst; Technical Writer/Editor; Telecommunications Manager; Typist/Word Processor; Underwriter/Assistant Underwriter; Video Production Coordinator. **Benefits available to temporary workers:** 401(k); Medical Insurance. **Corporate headquarters location:** Milwaukee WI. **Other U.S. locations:** Nationwide. **Average salary range of placements:** More than $50,000. **Number of placements per year:** 500 - 999.

PRECISION DESIGN, INC.
15 10th Avenue South, Suite 102, Hopkins MN 55343-7561. 612/933-6550. **Fax:** 612/933-0344. **Contact:** Larry Helgerson, President. **E-mail address:** recruiter@precisionjobs.com. **World Wide Web address:** http://www.precisionjobs.com. **Description:** Precision Design, Inc. is a contract services firm. **Specializes in the areas of:** Engineering. **Positions commonly filled include:** Design Engineer; Draftsperson; Electrical/Electronics Engineer; Industrial Engineer; Manufacturing Engineer; Mechanical Engineer; Software Engineer; Technical Writer/Editor. **Benefits available to temporary workers:** 401(k); Medical Insurance; Paid Holidays; Paid Vacation. **Average salary range of placements:** More than $50,000. **Number of placements per year:** 100 - 199.

PROFESSIONAL ALTERNATIVES
926 Twelve Oaks Center, 15500 Wayzata Boulevard, Minneapolis MN 55391. 612/404-2600. **Fax:** 612/404-2602. **Contact:** Bobette Berno, Marketing Director. **E-mail address:** info@pro-alt.com. **World Wide Web address:** http://www.pro-alt.com. **Description:** Professional Alternatives is a contract services firm that also offers contract-to-hire placements and direct hire contingency search services. **Specializes in the**

areas of: Personnel/Labor Relations. **Positions commonly filled include:** Consultant; Human Resources Manager. **Corporate headquarters location:** This Location. **Average salary range of placements:** $50,000 - $100,000. **Number of placements per year:** 100 - 199.

THE RESOURCE GROUP, INC.
LABORATORY RESOURCES INC.
7700 Equitable Drive, Suite 101, Eden Prairie MN 55344. 612/974-9225. **Toll-free phone:** 800/298-5627. **Contact:** Manager. **E-mail address:** lri@rsgi.com. **World Wide Web address:** http://www.rsgi.com. **Description:** A contract services firm. **Specializes in the areas of:** Biology; Technical. **Positions commonly filled include:** Biological Scientist; Biomedical Engineer; Chemical Engineer; Chemist; Clinical Lab Technician; Food Scientist/Technologist; Forester/Conservation Scientist; Geologist/Geophysicist; Quality Control Supervisor; Science Technologist. **Benefits available to temporary workers:** 401(k); Dental Insurance; Medical Insurance; Paid Holidays; Paid Vacation. **Average salary range of placements:** $30,000 - $50,000. **Number of placements per year:** 50 - 99.

STROM AVIATION
10501 Wayzata Boulevard, Minnetonka MN 55305. 612/544-3611. **Toll-free phone:** 800/743-8988. **Fax:** 612/544-3948. **Contact:** Manager. **World Wide Web address:** http://www.stromaviation.com. **Description:** A contract services firm. **Positions commonly filled include:** Aircraft Mechanic/Engine Specialist. **Corporate headquarters location:** Minneapolis MN. **Other U.S. locations:** Tempe AZ; Dallas TX.

SYSDYNE CORPORATION
1660 South Highway 100, Suite 424, Minneapolis MN 55416-1533. 612/541-9889. **Toll-free phone:** 888/797-3963. **Fax:** 612/541-9887. **Contact:** Manager. **E-mail address:** techjobs@sysdyne.com. **World Wide Web address:** http://www.sysdyne.com. **Description:** Sysdyne Corporation is a contract services firm. **Specializes in the areas of:** Computer Science/Software; Engineering; Technical. **Positions commonly filled include:** Biomedical Engineer; Computer Programmer; Design Engineer; Draftsperson; Electrical/Electronics Engineer; Mechanical Engineer; MIS Specialist; Sales Engineer; Software Engineer; Technical Writer/Editor. **Benefits available to temporary workers:** 401(k); Cafeteria; Savings Plan. **Average salary range of placements:** $30,000 - $50,000. **Number of placements per year:** 50 - 99.

H.L. YOH COMPANY
2626 East 82nd Street, Suite 355, Bloomington MN 55425. 612/854-2400. **Toll-free phone:** 888/243-3557. **Fax:** 612/854-0512. **Contact:** Linda Eisenzimmer, Technical Recruiter. **Description:** H.L. Yoh Company is a contract services firm. **Specializes in the areas of:** Computer Science/Software; Engineering; Industrial; Technical. **Positions commonly filled include:** Administrative Assistant; Buyer; Chemical Engineer; Chemist; Computer Operator; Computer Programmer; Database Manager; Design Engineer; Draftsperson; Electrical/Electronics Engineer; Environmental Engineer; Graphic Artist; Graphic Designer; Industrial Engineer; Industrial Production Manager; Manufacturing Engineer; Mechanical Engineer; Metallurgical Engineer; Operations Manager; Project Manager; Purchasing Agent/Manager; Quality Control Supervisor; Secretary; Software Engineer; Systems Analyst; Systems Manager; Technical Writer/Editor; Typist/Word Processor. **Benefits available to temporary workers:** 401(k); Credit Union; Disability Coverage; Medical Insurance. **Corporate headquarters location:** Philadelphia PA. **Other U.S. locations:** Nationwide. **International locations:** China. **Average salary range of placements:** $30,000 - $50,000. **Number of placements per year:** 200 - 499.

CAREER/OUTPLACEMENT COUNSELING FIRMS

ALLEN AND ASSOCIATES
6600 France Avenue South, Suite 615, Minneapolis MN 55435. 612/925-9646. **Toll-free phone:** 800/562-7925. **Fax:** 612/925-9662. **Contact:** Manager. **E-mail address:** minneapolis@allenandassociates.com. **World Wide Web address:** http://www.allenandassociates.com. **Description:** Allen and Associates is a career/outplacement counseling firm, providing both corporate and private outplacement services. **Corporate headquarters location:** Orlando FL. **Other U.S. locations:** Nationwide.

QUALITY OFFICE SERVICES
12710 Falcon Court North, White Bear Lake MN 55110. 651/426-2516. **Contact:** Lois M. Rather, Owner. **Description:** A resume writing service.

WORKING OPPORTUNITIES FOR WOMEN
1295 Bandana Boulevard North, Suite 110, St. Paul MN 55108. 651/647-9961. **Contact:** Yvette Oldendorf, President. **Description:** A career/outplacement counseling firm that provides career development and planning services to women.

◆ M I S S I S S I P P I ◆

EXECUTIVE SEARCH FIRMS

AAA EMPLOYMENT
P.O. Box 2482, Tupelo MS 38803. 662/844-8448. **Contact:** Manager. **Description:** An executive search firm that also provides some temporary and permanent placements. **Specializes in the areas of:** Clerical; Engineering; Management; Manufacturing; Secretarial.

BUZHARDT ASSOCIATES
1385 Narrow Gauge Road, Bolton MS 39041. 601/852-8042. **Contact:** Joe Buzhardt, President. **Description:** An executive search firm.

THE CPI GROUP
112 Fifth Street North, Columbus MS 39903. 601/328-1042. **Fax:** 601/329-1017. **Contact:** Manager. **World Wide Web address:** http://www.cpi-group.com. **Description:** An executive search firm. Founded in 1983. **Specializes in the areas of:** Accounting; Chemicals; Civil Engineering; Computer Hardware/ Software; Construction; Electrical; Environmental; Finance; Human Resources; Industrial; Information Technology; Management; Manufacturing; Marketing; Mechanical; Network Administration; Production; Quality Assurance; Sales; Transportation; Warehousing.

COMPASS GROUP, INC.
1208 Antler, Suite A, Tupelo MS 38801. 601/844-1471. **Fax:** 601/844-3992. **Contact:** Manager. **World Wide Web address:** http://compassjobs.com. **Description:** An executive search firm. **Specializes in the areas of:** Health/Medical; Software Development; Technical.

DELKEN GROUP
403 Towne Center Boulevard, Suite 101, Ridgeland MS 39157. 601/952-0020. **Fax:** 601/952-0071. **Contact:** Manager. **Description:** An executive search firm.

DUNHILL OF MADISON
P.O. Box 1218, Madison MS 39130. 601/856-4095. **Contact:** Manager. **Description:** An executive search firm.

MANAGEMENT RECRUITERS INTERNATIONAL
1755 Lelia Drive, Suite 102, Jackson MS 39216. 601/366-4488. **Contact:** Manager. **Description:** An executive search firm. **Specializes in the areas of:** Accounting/Auditing; Data Processing; Engineering. **Corporate headquarters location:** Cleveland OH.

MANAGEMENT RECRUITERS OF RANKIN COUNTY
2506 Lakeland Drive, Suite 408, Jackson MS 39208. 601/936-7900. **Fax:** 601/936-9004. **Contact:** Michael Van Wick, President. **Description:** An executive search firm. **Specializes in the areas of:** Food. **Positions commonly filled include:** Chemical Engineer; Controller; Electrical/Electronics Engineer; Food Scientist/Technologist; General Manager; Human Resources Manager; Industrial Engineer; Manufacturing Engineer; Mechanical Engineer; Production Manager; Project Manager; Quality Control Supervisor. **Corporate headquarters location:** Cleveland OH. **Average salary range of placements:** More than $50,000. **Number of placements per year:** 50 - 99.

NEW CENTURY MANAGEMENT CONSULTANTS
1600 Second Street, Gulfport MS 39501. 228/864-3999. **Contact:** Manager. **Description:** An executive search firm.

PERSONNEL UNLIMITED
P.O. Box 686, Amory MS 38821-0686. 662/256-1462. **Contact:** Manager. **Description:** An executive search firm. **Specializes in the areas of:** Accounting/Auditing; Engineering; Industrial; Manufacturing; Personnel/Labor Relations. **Positions commonly filled include:** Accountant/Auditor; Clerical Supervisor; Clinical Lab Technician; Computer Programmer; Credit Manager; Customer Service Representative; Design Engineer; Draftsperson; Environmental Engineer; Human Resources Specialist; Industrial Engineer; Industrial Production Manager; Mechanical Engineer; Metallurgical Engineer; Purchasing Agent/Manager; Software Engineer; Systems Analyst; Typist/Word Processor. **Average salary range of placements:** $30,000 - $50,000. **Number of placements per year:** 50 - 99.

QUARLES KELLY ASSOCIATES
7040 Swinnea Road, Southhaven MS 38671. 662/349-4202. **Contact:** Manager. **Description:** An executive search firm that also provides some temp-to-perm placements.

JIM WOODSON & ASSOCIATES
1080 River Oaks Drive, Suite B-102, Jackson MS 39208. 601/936-4037. **Fax:** 601/936-4041. **Contact:** Jim Woodson, President. **E-mail address:** jwood0335@aol.com. **Description:** An executive search firm operating on a contingency basis. Client company pays fee. **Specializes in the areas of:** Accounting/Auditing; Engineering; Industrial; Scientific; Technical. **Positions commonly filled include:** Controller; Design Engineer; Electrical/Electronics Engineer; General Manager; Human Resources Manager; Industrial Engineer; Industrial Production Manager; Mechanical Engineer; Operations Manager; Production Manager; Project Manager; Quality Assurance Engineer; Quality Control Supervisor. **Number of placements per year:** 1 - 49.

PERMANENT EMPLOYMENT AGENCIES

CAPITOL STAFFING SOLUTIONS
460 Briarwood Drive, Suite 110, Jackson MS 39206. 601/957-1755. **Fax:** 601/957-3880. **Contact:** Carolyn Harrison, Certified Personnel Consultant. **Description:** A permanent employment agency that also offers some temporary and temp-to-perm placements. **Specializes in the areas of:** Accounting/Auditing; Clerical; Insurance; Legal; Office Support; Sales; Secretarial. **Positions commonly filled include:** Accountant/Auditor; Administrative Assistant; Bank Officer/Manager; Bookkeeper; Claim Representative; Clerk; Computer Programmer; Credit Manager; Customer Service Representative; Data Entry Clerk; General Manager; Human Resources Manager; Legal Secretary; Marketing Specialist; Medical Secretary; Paralegal; Public Relations Specialist; Purchasing Agent/Manager; Secretary; Stenographer; Systems Analyst; Technical Writer/Editor; Typist/Word Processor; Underwriter/Assistant Underwriter. **Average salary range of placements:** Less than $20,000. **Number of placements per year:** 200 - 499.

COATS & COATS PERSONNEL
2217 Sixth Street, Meridian MS 39302. 601/693-2991. **Fax:** 601/693-9983. **Contact:** Tom Coats, Owner. **Description:** A permanent employment agency. Founded in 1968. **Specializes in the areas of:** Accounting/Auditing; Aerospace; Computer Science/Software; Engineering; Food; General Management; Industrial; Manufacturing; Personnel/Labor Relations; Retail; Sales; Secretarial; Technical. **Positions commonly filled include:** Accountant/Auditor; Aerospace Engineer; Blue-Collar Worker Supervisor; Branch Manager; Chemical

Engineer; Civil Engineer; Computer Programmer; Counselor; Credit Manager; Design Engineer; Draftsperson; Electrical/Electronics Engineer; Environmental Engineer; General Manager; Human Resources Specialist; Industrial Engineer; Industrial Production Manager; Internet Services Manager; Management Trainee; Manufacturer's/Wholesaler's Sales Rep.; Mechanical Engineer; Medical Records Technician; MIS Specialist; Paralegal; Registered Nurse; Restaurant/Food Service Manager; Software Engineer; Speech-Language Pathologist; Typist/Word Processor. **Average salary range of placements:** Over $25,000. **Number of placements per year:** 500 - 999.

EXPRESS PERSONNEL SERVICE
1425 Lakeland Drive, Suite 110B, Jackson MS 39216. 601/366-8585. **Fax:** 601/981-0028. **Contact:** Manager. **Description:** A permanent placement agency that also does temporary and temp-to-perm placements. **Specializes in the areas of:** Clerical; Industrial; Professional.

IMPACT PERSONNEL
212 Haddon Circle, P.O. Box 4081, Brandon MS 39047. 601/992-1591. **Fax:** 601/992-5037. **Contact:** Office Manager. **World Wide Web address:** http://www.impactjobs.com. **Description:** Impact Personnel is a permanent placement agency that also provides some contract and temporary placements. Impact Personnel provides both national and international placements. Founded in 1990. **Specializes in the areas of:** Engineering; Industrial; Information Technology; Manufacturing.

LABORCHEX COMPANIES
3900 Lakeland Drive, Suite 300, Jackson MS 39208. 601/664-6760. **Fax:** 800/844-2722. **Contact:** Steven J. Austin, Director of Communications. **Description:** A permanent employment agency. Founded in 1985. **Specializes in the areas of:** Manufacturing; Secretarial. **Positions commonly filled include:** Administrative Manager; Credit Manager; Customer Service Representative; General Manager; Human Resources Specialist; Industrial Production Manager; Purchasing Agent/Manager; Quality Control Supervisor; Restaurant/Food Service Manager; Typist/Word Processor. **Average salary range of placements:** $20,000 - $29,999. **Number of placements per year:** 200 - 499.

MISSISSIPPI STATE EMPLOYMENT SERVICES
P.O. Box 640, Clarksdale MS 38614-0640. 662/627-1842. **Physical address:** 620 South State Street, Clarksdale MS. **Contact:** Alfred Jones, Office Manager. **Description:** A permanent employment agency that operates the state and federal job program. **Specializes in the areas of:** Advertising; Education; Nonprofit; Personnel/Labor Relations. **Positions commonly filled include:** Blue-Collar Worker Supervisor; Certified Nurses Aide; Claim Representative; Computer Operator; Construction Contractor; Counselor; Daycare Worker; Early Childhood Teacher; Electrician; Emergency Medical Technician; Finance Director; Human Resources Manager; Industrial Production Manager; Insurance Agent/Broker; Licensed Practical Nurse; Management Trainee; Medical Records Technician; Production Manager; Public Relations Specialist; Quality Control Supervisor; Real Estate Agent; Registered Nurse; Respiratory Therapist; Sales Manager; Secretary; Social Worker; Teacher/Professor. **Corporate headquarters location:** Jackson MS. **Average salary range of placements:** $20,000 - $29,999. **Number of placements per year:** 1000+.

OPPORTUNITIES UNLIMITED
P.O. Box 1518, Pascagoula MS 39568. 228/762-8068. **Physical address:** 3903 Market Street, Pascagoula MS. **Contact:** Bob Dubose, Manager. **Description:** A permanent employment agency. **Specializes in the areas of:** Accounting/Auditing; Clerical; Computer Hardware/Software; Engineering; Finance;

Manufacturing; Technical. **Positions commonly filled include:** Aerospace Engineer; Buyer; Chemical Engineer; Civil Engineer; Computer Programmer; EDP Specialist; Electrical/Electronics Engineer; Financial Analyst; Human Resources Manager; Industrial Engineer; Legal Secretary; Mechanical Engineer; Metallurgical Engineer; MIS Specialist; Nurse; Occupational Therapist; Petroleum Engineer; Physician; Physicist; Quality Control Supervisor; Receptionist; Secretary; Systems Analyst; Technical Writer/Editor; Typist/Word Processor. **Number of placements per year:** 50 - 99.

RECRUITMENT & TRAINING PROGRAMS OF MISSISSIPPI, INC.
P.O. Box 1461, Columbus MS 39703. 662/328-8037. **Fax:** 662/328-9459. **Contact:** Jeannette Harris, President. **Description:** A permanent employment agency. Founded in 1988. **Specializes in the areas of:** Administration; Broadcasting; Education; General Management; Health/Medical; Legal; Manufacturing; Nonprofit; Personnel/Labor Relations; Retail; Sales; Secretarial; Technical; Transportation. **Positions commonly filled include:** Administrative Manager; Broadcast Technician; Claim Representative; Clerical Supervisor; Computer Programmer; Customer Service Representative; Education Administrator; Electrician; Financial Analyst; Food Scientist/Technologist; General Manager; Health Services Manager; Hotel Manager; Human Resources Specialist; Human Service Worker; Librarian; Management Trainee; Occupational Therapist; Paralegal; Physical Therapist; Purchasing Agent/Manager; Services Sales Representative; Social Worker; Systems Analyst; Teacher/Professor; Technical Writer/Editor; Telecommunications Manager; Transportation/Traffic Specialist; Typist/Word Processor. **Average salary range of placements:** Less than $20,000. **Number of placements per year:** 100 - 199.

SERVICE SPECIALISTS LTD.
500 Greymont Avenue, Suite A, Jackson MS 39202-3446. 601/948-8980. **Fax:** 601/948-8983. **Contact:** Manager. **Description:** A permanent employment agency that also provides some temporary and temp-to-perm placements and career/outplacement counseling. **Specializes in the areas of:** Accounting/Auditing; Administration; Banking; Computer Science/Software; Engineering; Finance; Industrial; Manufacturing; Personnel/Labor Relations; Sales; Secretarial. **Positions commonly filled include:** Accountant/Auditor; Adjuster; Administrative Manager; Blue-Collar Worker Supervisor; Buyer; Chemical Engineer; Computer Programmer; Design Engineer; Draftsperson; Environmental Engineer; Financial Analyst; Human Resources Specialist; Industrial Engineer; Industrial Production Manager; Management Trainee; Mechanical Engineer; Purchasing Agent/Manager; Services Sales Representative; Typist/Word Processor. **Average salary range of placements:** $30,000 - $50,000. **Number of placements per year:** 100 - 199.

SNELLING PERSONNEL SERVICE
2224 25th Avenue, Gulfport MS 39501. 228/822-2225. **Contact:** Manager. **Description:** A permanent employment agency.

SNELLING PERSONNEL SERVICE
2480 South Frontage Road, Vicksburg MS 39180. 601/630-9011. **Fax:** 601/638-1725. **Contact:** Manager. **Description:** A permanent employment agency that also provides some temporary placements.

SNELLING PERSONNEL SERVICE
2009 Hardy Street, Suite 2B, Hattiesburg MS 39401. 601/544-0821. **Fax:** 601/544-0823. **Contact:** Manager. **Description:** A permanent employment agency.

SNELLING PERSONNEL SERVICE
407 Briarwood Drive, Suite 209, Jackson MS 39206. 601/956-5552. **Fax:** 601/956-5282. **Contact:** Manager. **Description:** A permanent employment agency.

TEMPORARY EMPLOYMENT AGENCIES

COLUMBUS PERSONNEL INC.
P.O. Box 828, Columbus MS 39701. 662/328-1042. **Physical address:** 112 Fifth Street North, Columbus MS 39701-4551. **Contact:** Mark A. Smith, Vice President. **Description:** A temporary agency that also provides some temp-to-perm and permanent placements. **Specializes in the areas of:** Industrial; Manufacturing; Secretarial. **Positions commonly filled include:** Blue-Collar Worker Supervisor; Customer Service Representative; Typist/Word Processor. **Benefits available to temporary workers:** Life Insurance; Medical Insurance; Paid Holidays; Paid Vacation. **Average salary range of placements:** $20,000 - $29,999. **Number of placements per year:** 1000+.

EPSCO PERSONNEL SERVICE, INC.
P.O. Box 5172, Columbus MS 39704. 662/327-2505. **Contact:** Cora Perkins, Manager. **Description:** A temporary agency that also provides some temp-to-perm and permanent placements. Founded in 1987. **Specializes in the areas of:** Accounting/Auditing; Banking; Computer Science/Software; Engineering; Food; Industrial; Legal; Light Industrial; Manufacturing; Personnel/Labor Relations; Sales; Secretarial; Technical. **Positions commonly filled include:** Accountant/Auditor; Blue-Collar Worker Supervisor; Customer Service Representative; Electrician; Human Resources Specialist; Industrial Engineer; Industrial Production Manager; Operations/Production Manager; Quality Control Supervisor; Restaurant/Food Service Manager; Services Sales Representative; Surveyor; Transportation/Traffic Specialist; Typist/Word Processor. **Benefits available to temporary workers:** Medical Insurance. **Corporate headquarters location:** Tupelo MS. **Other U.S. locations:** AL; AR; GA; TN. **Average salary range of placements:** Less than $20,000. **Number of placements per year:** 500 - 999.

EPSCO PERSONNEL SERVICE, INC.
2944 Terry Road, Jackson MS 39212-3055. 601/372-3787. **Contact:** Linda Mangum, Manager. **Description:** A temporary agency. Founded in 1987. **Specializes in the areas of:** Accounting/Auditing; Engineering; General Management; Industrial; Manufacturing; Personnel/Labor Relations; Sales; Secretarial. **Positions commonly filled include:** Accountant/Auditor; Administrative Manager; Blue-Collar Worker Supervisor; Branch Manager; Buyer; Chemical Engineer; Computer Programmer; Customer Service Representative; Electrical/Electronics Engineer; Financial Analyst; General Manager; Hotel Manager; Human Resources Specialist; Industrial Engineer; Industrial Production Manager; Management Analyst/Consultant; Management Trainee; Mechanical Engineer; Operations/Production Manager; Purchasing Agent/Manager; Quality Control Supervisor;

Restaurant/Food Service Manager; Typist/Word Processor. **Benefits available to temporary workers:** 401(k); Dental Insurance; Medical Insurance; Paid Holidays; Paid Vacation. **Corporate headquarters location:** Tupelo MS. **Other U.S. locations:** AL; AR; GA; TN. **Number of placements per year:** 100 - 199.

EPSCO PERSONNEL SERVICE, INC.
806-B East Waldron Street, Corinth MS 38834. 662/286-8066. **Fax:** 662/286-8042. **Contact:** Peggy Davis, Manager. **Description:** A temporary agency that also provides some temp-to-perm and permanent placements. Founded in 1987. **Specializes in the areas of:** Accounting; Advertising; Banking; Computer Science/Software; Food; General Management; Health/Medical; Industrial; Legal; Light Industrial; MIS/EDP; Nonprofit; Personnel/Labor Relations; Printing; Publishing; Retail; Sales; Secretarial; Technical; Transportation. **Positions commonly filled include:** Account Manager; Account Representative; Accountant; Administrative Assistant; Administrative Manager; Advertising Executive; Applications Engineer; Assistant Manager; Bank Officer/Manager; Blue-Collar Worker Supervisor; Buyer; Certified Nurses Aide; Chemical Engineer; Claim Representative; Clerical Supervisor; Computer Operator; Computer Programmer; Controller; Credit Manager; Customer Service Representative; Database Manager; Design Engineer; Electrical/Electronics Engineer; Electrician; Finance Director; Financial Analyst; Food Scientist/Technologist; General Manager; Human Resources Manager; Industrial Engineer; Industrial Production Manager; Licensed Practical Nurse; Mechanical Engineer; Medical Records Technician; Operations Manager; Paralegal; Production Manager; Project Manager; Purchasing Agent/Manager; Quality Control Supervisor; Registered Nurse; Secretary; Software Engineer; Typist/Word Processor. **Corporate headquarters location:** Tupelo MS. **Other U.S. locations:** AL; AR; GA; TN. **Average salary range of placements:** Less than $20,000. **Number of placements per year:** 200 - 499.

NORRELL STAFFING SERVICES
8912 Mid South Avenue, Olive Branch MS 38654. 662/895-5500. **Fax:** 662/895-8443. **Contact:** Customer Service Manager. **Description:** A temporary agency. **Specializes in the areas of:** Accounting/Auditing; Distribution; Manufacturing; Personnel/Labor Relations. **Benefits available to temporary workers:** Medical Insurance; Paid Holidays; Paid Vacation. **Corporate headquarters location:** Atlanta GA. **Other U.S. locations:** Nationwide. **Average salary range of placements:** Less than $20,000. **Number of placements per year:** 1000+.

AARON CONSULTING, INC.
P.O. Box 4757, St. Louis MO 63108. 314/367-2627. **Fax:** 314/367-2919. **Contact:** Aaron Williams, CPC/President. **World Wide Web address:** http://www.aaronlaw.com. **Description:** An executive search firm operating on a contingency basis. The firm places attorneys only. **Specializes in the areas of:** Legal. **Positions commonly filled include:** Attorney. **Average salary range of placements:** More than $50,000. **Number of placements per year:** 1 - 49.

ACCOUNTANTS EXECUTIVE SEARCH
ACCOUNTANTS ON CALL
911 Main Street, Suite 701, Kansas City MO 64105. 816/421-7774. **Contact:** Manager. **Description:** An executive search firm. Accountants On Call (also at this location) is a temporary agency. **Corporate headquarters location:** Saddle Brook NJ. **Other U.S. locations:** Nationwide.

ACCOUNTANTS EXECUTIVE SEARCH
ACCOUNTANTS ON CALL
One City Center, 515 North Sixth Street, Suite 1340, St. Louis MO 63101. 314/436-0500. **Contact:** Manager. **Description:** An executive search firm. Accountants On Call (also at this location) is a temporary agency. **Specializes in the areas of:** Accounting/Auditing; Finance.

ACCOUNTANTS EXECUTIVE SEARCH
ACCOUNTANTS ON CALL
111 Westport Plaza Drive, Suite 512, St. Louis MO 63146. 314/576-0006. **Contact:** Manager. **Description:** An executive search firm. Accountants On Call (also at this location) is a temporary agency. **Specializes in the areas of:** Accounting/Auditing; Finance.

ACCOUNTING CAREER CONSULTANTS
1001 Craig Road, Suite 429, St. Louis MO 63146. 314/569-9898. **Contact:** Manager. **Description:** An executive search firm. **Specializes in the areas of:** Accounting/Auditing; Finance.

ADVANCED CAREERS OF KANSAS CITY, INC.
6528 Raytown Road, Kansas City MO 64133. 816/358-3553. **Fax:** 816/358-3566. **Contact:** Hal Willis, Vice President. **Description:** An executive search firm operating on a contingency basis. **Specializes in the areas of:** Accounting/Auditing; Engineering; Finance; General Management; Manufacturing; Personnel/Labor Relations; Sales; Technical. **Positions commonly filled include:** Account Manager; Accountant/Auditor; Applications Engineer; Branch Manager; Budget Analyst; Buyer; Chemical Engineer; Chief Financial Officer; Electrical/Electronics Engineer; Environmental Engineer; Finance Director; Financial Analyst; General Manager; Human Resources Manager; Industrial Engineer; Industrial Production Manager; Manufacturing Engineer; Operations Manager; Project Manager; Purchasing Agent/Manager; Sales Engineer; Sales Manager; Sales Representative. **Number of placements per year:** 1 - 49.

AGRI-ASSOCIATES
2 Brush Creek Boulevard, Suite 130, Kansas City MO 64112. 816/531-7980. **Contact:** Manager. **Description:** An executive search firm. **Specializes in the areas of:** Agriculture.

AGRI-TECH PERSONNEL, INC.
3113 Northeast 69th Street, Kansas City MO 64119. 816/453-7200. **Fax:** 816/453-6001. **Contact:** Dale Pickering, President. **Description:** An executive search firm operating on a contingency basis. **Specializes in the areas of:** Agriculture; Engineering; Food; Manufacturing; Personnel/Labor Relations; Technical; Transportation. **Positions commonly filled include:** Agricultural Engineer; Buyer; Chemical Engineer; Chemist; Credit Manager; Design Engineer; Draftsperson; Electrical/Electronics Engineer; Environmental Engineer; Food Scientist/Technologist; General Manager; Human Resources Specialist; Industrial Engineer; Mechanical Engineer; Operations/Production Manager; Purchasing Agent/Manager; Quality Control Supervisor; Structural Engineer; Transportation/Traffic Specialist; Veterinarian.

ALLAN-JAMES ASSOCIATES
P.O. Box 11370, Springfield MO 65808-1370. 417/881-6767. **Fax:** 417/881-0366. **Contact:** Roger A. Aistrup, President. **E-mail address:** aja@jobsinplastics.com. **World Wide Web address:** http://www.jobsinplastics. com. **Description:** An executive search firm that focuses on the recruitment of management, engineering, administrative, and technical personnel for the plastics industry. **Specializes in the areas of:** Plastics. **Positions commonly filled include:** Applications Engineer; Biomedical Engineer; Buyer; Chemical Engineer; Chemist; Chief Financial Officer; Computer Programmer; Controller; Design Engineer; General Manager; Human Resources Manager; Industrial Engineer; Industrial Production Manager; Manufacturing Engineer; MIS Specialist; Operations Manager; Production Manager; Project Manager; Purchasing Agent/Manager; Quality Control Supervisor; Software Engineer; Systems Analyst. **Average salary range of placements:** $40,000 - $80,000. **Number of placements per year:** 1 - 49.

AMERICAN AUTOMOTIVE PERSONNEL CONSULTANTS, INC.
P.O. Box 1957, Maryland Heights MO 63043. **Contact:** A. H. (Buzz) Burling, President. **Description:** An executive search firm operating on both retainer and contingency bases. **Specializes in the areas of:** Automotive; Manufacturing; Retail; Sales. **Positions commonly filled include:** Accountant/Auditor; Automotive Engineer; Automotive Mechanic; Customer Service Representative; Design Engineer; Designer; Financial Analyst; General Manager; Industrial Engineer; Industrial Production Manager; Management Analyst/Consultant; Manufacturer's/Wholesaler's Sales Rep.; Mechanical Engineer; Operations/Production Manager; Quality Control Supervisor; Sales Manager; Service Manager; Services Sales Representative; Technical Writer/Editor. **Number of placements per year:** 50 - 99.

BOYDEN
1390 Timberlake Manor Parkway, Suite 260, Chesterfield MO 63017. 636/519-7400. **Contact:** Manager. **World Wide Web address:** http://www.boyden.com. **Description:** A generalist executive search firm. **Corporate headquarters location:** New York NY. **Other U.S. locations:** San Francisco CA; Washington DC; Chicago IL; Bloomfield Hills MI; Morristown NJ; Hawthorne NY; New York NY; Pittsburgh PA; Houston TX. **International locations:** Worldwide.

KEN BROWN & COMPANY
1036 West Battlefield, Springfield MO 65807. 417/883-9444. **Fax:** 417/883-9947. **Contact:** Ken Brown, President. **E-mail address:** bbrown@kenbrown.com. **World Wide Web address:** http://www.kenbrown.com. **Description:** An executive search firm operating on both retainer and contingency bases. **Specializes in the areas of:** Engineering; Food; Manufacturing. **Positions commonly filled include:** Chemical Engineer; Electrical/Electronics Engineer; Food Scientist/Technologist; Human Resources Manager; Industrial Engineer; Industrial Production Manager; Manufacturing Engineer; Mechanical Engineer; Operations Manager; Project Manager; Quality Control

Supervisor; Transportation/Traffic Specialist. **Average salary range of placements:** More than $50,000. **Number of placements per year:** 50 - 99.

BURNS EMPLOYMENT SERVICE
9229 Ward Parkway, Suite 285, Kansas City MO 64114. 816/361-6444. **Fax:** 816/361-7747. **Contact:** Kevin Burns, President. **E-mail address:** burns28s@aol.com. **Description:** An executive search firm operating on a contingency basis. Client company pays fee. **Specializes in the areas of:** Accounting; Administration; Biology; Computer Science/Software; Education; Engineering; Finance; Food; Health/Medical; Industrial; Insurance; Marketing; MIS/EDP; Sales; Scientific; Technical. **Positions commonly filled include:** Account Manager; Account Representative; Accountant; Adjuster; Administrative Manager; Applications Engineer; AS400 Programmer Analyst; Auditor; Biological Scientist; Buyer; Chemical Engineer; Chemist; Civil Engineer; Claim Representative; Computer Programmer; Computer Support Technician; Computer Technician; Content Developer; Cost Estimator; Customer Service Representative; Database Administrator; Database Manager; Design Engineer; Education Administrator; Electrical/Electronics Engineer; Electrician; Environmental Engineer; Financial Analyst; Food Scientist/Technologist; Industrial Engineer; Industrial Production Manager; Internet Services Manager; Licensed Practical Nurse; Manufacturing Engineer; Market Research Analyst; Marketing Manager; Marketing Specialist; Mechanical Engineer; Metallurgical Engineer; MIS Specialist; Network/Systems Administrator; Occupational Therapist; Operations Manager; Physical Therapist; Production Manager; Project Manager; Purchasing Agent/Manager; Quality Assurance Engineer; Quality Control Supervisor; Registered Nurse; Safety Engineer; Sales Executive; Sales Manager; Sales Representative; Software Engineer; SQL Programmer; Statistician; Systems Analyst; Systems Manager; Technical Writer/Editor; Telecommunications Manager; Transportation/Traffic Specialist; Underwriter/Assistant Underwriter. **Corporate headquarters location:** This Location. **Average salary range of placements:** $50,000 - $100,000. **Number of placements per year:** 50 - 99.

CAREER SERVICES, INC.
3447 South Campbell, Springfield MO 65807. 417/881-3554. **Contact:** Lynne Haggerman, President. **Description:** An executive search firm. **Positions commonly filled include:** Accountant/Auditor; Actuary; Administrative Manager; Advertising Clerk; Bank Officer/Manager; Blue-Collar Worker Supervisor; Branch Manager; Brokerage Clerk; Budget Analyst; Buyer; Claim Representative; Clerical Supervisor; Clinical Lab Technician; Computer Programmer; Construction and Building Inspector; Construction Contractor; Cost Estimator; Counselor; Credit Manager; Customer Service Representative; Dental Assistant/Dental Hygienist; Designer; Dietician/Nutritionist; Draftsperson; Editor; Education Administrator; EEG Technologist; EKG Technician; Electrician; Emergency Medical Technician; Financial Analyst; General Manager; Health Services Worker; Hotel Manager; Human Resources Specialist; Human Service Worker; Industrial Production Manager; Insurance Agent/Broker; Librarian; Licensed Practical Nurse; Management Analyst/Consultant; Management Trainee; Manufacturer's/Wholesaler's Sales Rep.; Market Research Analyst; Mathematician; Medical Records Technician; MIS Specialist; Nuclear Medicine Technologist; Occupational Therapist; Operations/Production Manager; Paralegal; Pharmacist; Physical Therapist; Preschool Worker; Psychologist; Public Relations Specialist; Quality Control Supervisor; Radio/TV Announcer/Broadcaster; Radiological Technologist; Real Estate Agent; Recreational Therapist; Registered Nurse; Reporter; Respiratory Therapist; Restaurant/Food Service Manager; Securities Sales Representative; Social Worker; Speech-Language

Pathologist; Surgical Technician; Surveyor; Teacher/Professor; Technical Writer/Editor; Telecommunications Manager; Transportation/Traffic Specialist; Travel Agent; Underwriter/Assistant Underwriter; Video Production Coordinator. **Number of placements per year:** 1 - 49.

THE CHRISTIANSEN GROUP
2101 West Chesterfield Boulevard, Suite B202, Springfield MO 65807. 417/889-9696. **Fax:** 417/889-8960. **Contact:** Scott Christiansen, Principal. **E-mail address:** cgroup1@aol.com. **Description:** An executive search firm that places manufacturing personnel in the food, beverage, and dairy industries. **Specializes in the areas of:** Engineering; Food; Industrial; Manufacturing; Technical; Transportation. **Positions commonly filled include:** Agricultural Engineer; Biochemist; Buyer; Chemical Engineer; Chemist; Clinical Lab Technician; Design Engineer; Electrical/Electronics Engineer; Environmental Engineer; Food Scientist/Technologist; General Manager; Human Resources Specialist; Industrial Engineer; Industrial Production Manager; Management Trainee; Mechanical Engineer; Operations/Production Manager; Quality Control Supervisor; Stationary Engineer; Transportation/Traffic Specialist. **Average salary range of placements:** More than $50,000. **Number of placements per year:** 1 - 49.

GRANT COOPER & ASSOCIATES
9900 Clayton Road, St. Louis MO 63124-4697. 314/567-4690. **Fax:** 314/567-4697. **Contact:** Manager. **Description:** An executive search firm.

CORPORATE PERSONNEL & ASSOCIATES
851 NW 45th Street, Gladstone MO 64116-4612. 816/454-4080. **Contact:** Recruiter. **Description:** An executive search firm. **Specializes in the areas of:** Sales. **Positions commonly filled include:** Branch Manager; Computer Programmer; General Manager; Management Trainee; Manufacturer's/Wholesaler's Sales Rep.; Services Sales Representative; Systems Analyst. **Number of placements per year:** 100 - 199.

JIM CRUMPLEY & ASSOCIATES
1200 East Woodhurst Drive, Suite B-400, Springfield MO 65804. 417/882-7555. **Fax:** 417/882-8555. **Contact:** Jim Crumpley, Owner. **E-mail address:** recruiter@crumpleyjobs.com. **World Wide Web address:** http://www.crumpleyjobs.com. **Description:** An executive search firm operating on a contingency basis. Client company pays fee. **Specializes in the areas of:** Architecture/Construction; Biology; Biotechnology; Engineering; General Management; Pharmaceuticals. **Positions commonly filled include:** Architect; Biochemist; Biological Scientist; Biomedical Engineer; Chemical Engineer; Chemist; Design Engineer; Electrical/Electronics Engineer; Industrial Engineer; Manufacturing Engineer; Mechanical Engineer; Metallurgical Engineer; Pharmacist; Quality Assurance Engineer; Statistician. **Corporate headquarters location:** This Location. **Average salary range of placements:** $50,000 - $100,000. **Number of placements per year:** 1 - 49.

DEBBON RECRUITING GROUP
P.O. Box 510323, St. Louis MO 63151. 314/846-9101. **Contact:** John Zipfel, President. **Description:** An executive search firm operating on both retainer and contingency bases. **Specializes in the areas of:** Engineering; Food; General Management; Personnel/Labor Relations; Pharmaceuticals. **Positions commonly filled include:** Biochemist; Biological Scientist; Chemical Engineer; Chemist; Food Scientist/Technologist; Human Resources Manager; Industrial Engineer; Industrial Production Manager; Mechanical Engineer; Operations/Production Manager; Plant Engineer; Production Manager; Project Manager; Quality Control Supervisor. **Other U.S. locations:** Nationwide. **Average salary range of placements:** $30,000 - $50,000. **Number of placements per year:** 1 - 49.

DUNHILL PERSONNEL SYSTEM OF MISSOURI
1350 Rustic View Drive, Ballwin MO 63011. 636/394-0602. **Fax:** 636/394-2802. **Contact:** Don Vogel, Manager. **Description:** An executive search firm operating on a contingency basis. **Specializes in the areas of:** Engineering; Industrial; Metals. **Positions commonly filled include:** Accountant/Auditor; Electrical/Electronics Engineer; Environmental Engineer; General Manager; Human Resources Manager; Industrial Engineer; Industrial Production Manager; Manufacturing Engineer; Mechanical Engineer; Metallurgical Engineer; MIS Specialist; Operations Manager; Production Manager; Project Manager; Purchasing Agent/Manager; Quality Control Supervisor; Sales Manager; Sales Representative. **Number of placements per year:** 1 - 49.

EMPLOYER ADVANTAGE
705 Illinois Avenue, Suite 7, Joplin MO 64801. 417/782-3909. **Toll-free phone:** 800/467-3909. **Fax:** 417/782-3802. **Contact:** Dr. Lee Allphin, President. **Description:** An executive search firm. **Specializes in the areas of:** Accounting/Auditing; Administration; Architecture/Construction; Banking; Computer Science/Software; Education; Engineering; Finance; General Management; Health/Medical; Industrial; Insurance; Manufacturing; Nonprofit; Personnel/Labor Relations; Publishing; Sales; Secretarial; Technical; Transportation. **Positions commonly filled include:** Accountant/Auditor; Administrative Manager; Bank Officer/Manager; Blue-Collar Worker Supervisor; Chemist; Clerical Supervisor; Computer Programmer; Construction and Building Inspector; Construction Contractor; Cost Estimator; Counselor; Credit Manager; Customer Service Manager; Dental Assistant/Dental Hygienist; Dentist; Draftsperson; Education Administrator; Electrical/Electronics Engineer; Electrician; Emergency Medical Technician; Environmental Engineer; Financial Analyst; General Manager; Health Services Manager; Hotel Manager; Human Resources Specialist; Human Service Worker; Industrial Engineer; Industrial Production Manager; Insurance Agent/Broker; Internet Services Manager; Landscape Architect; Librarian; Licensed Practical Nurse; Management Analyst/Consultant; Manufacturer's/Wholesaler's Sales Rep.; Market Research Analyst; Mechanical Engineer; Medical Records Technician; Metallurgical Engineer; MIS Specialist; Multimedia Designer; Occupational Therapist; Operations/Production Manager; Paralegal; Petroleum Engineer; Physical Therapist; Physician; Preschool Worker; Property and Real Estate Manager; Psychologist; Public Relations Specialist; Purchasing Agent/Manager; Quality Control Supervisor; Recreational Therapist; Registered Nurse; Respiratory Therapist; Restaurant/Food Service Manager; Sales Representative; Science Technologist; Securities Sales Representative; Social Worker; Sociologist; Software Engineer; Stationary Engineer; Surveyor; Systems Analyst; Teacher/Professor; Technical Writer/Editor; Telecommunications Manager; Transportation/Traffic Specialist; Typist/Word Processor; Underwriter/Assistant Underwriter; Veterinarian; Video Production Coordinator. **Other U.S. locations:** Phoenix AZ; Atlanta GA. **Average salary range of placements:** $20,000 - $29,999. **Number of placements per year:** 200 - 499.

EXECUSEARCH, INC.
12977 North 40 Drive, Suite 315, St. Louis MO 63141. 314/878-2090. **Fax:** 314/878-1337. **Contact:** Ronald G. Theby, CPA/President. **Description:** An executive search firm operating on a contingency basis. **Specializes in the areas of:** Accounting/Auditing; Finance. **Positions commonly filled include:** Accountant/Auditor; Budget Analyst; Financial Analyst. **Average salary range of placements:** $30,000 - $50,000. **Number of placements per year:** 100 - 199.

EXECUTARIES BY GRAY
12400 Olive Boulevard, Suite 555, St. Louis MO 63141. 314/275-4415. **Fax:** 314/523-4523. **Contact:** Annie Gray, CEO. **E-mail address:** aag@anniegray.com. **Description:** An executive search firm operating on a retainer basis. **Specializes in the areas of:** Secretarial. **Positions commonly filled include:** Administrative Assistant. **Benefits available to temporary workers:** Accident/Emergency Insurance. **Corporate headquarters location:** This Location. **Average salary range of placements:** $30,000 - $49,999. **Number of placements per year:** 1 - 49.

EXECUTIVE CAREER CONSULTANTS, INC.
2258 Schuetz Road, Suite 201, St. Louis MO 63146. 314/994-3737. **Fax:** 314/994-3742. **Contact:** Bruce Bauer, President. **Description:** An executive search firm. **Positions commonly filled include:** Accountant/Auditor; Computer Programmer; Systems Analyst. **Other U.S. locations:** Nationwide. **Average salary range of placements:** $30,000 - $50,000. **Number of placements per year:** 50 - 99.

FIRST PLACE EXECUTIVE SEARCH/DECK & DECKER PERSONNEL
715 West McCarty, Jefferson City MO 65109. 417/883-7353. **Toll-free phone:** 800/264-6737. **Fax:** 417/883-0421. **Contact:** Alice Pollock, Manager. **E-mail address:** cpcalice@aol.com. **Description:** An executive search firm operating on both retainer and contingency bases. This firm also provides some contract services. Client company pays fee. **Specializes in the areas of:** Accounting; Computer Science/Software; Engineering; Personnel/Labor Relations; Scientific; Technical. **Positions commonly filled include:** Accountant; AS400 Programmer Analyst; Auditor; Chief Financial Officer; Computer Programmer; Controller; Design Engineer; Financial Analyst; General Manager; Human Resources Manager; Industrial Engineer; Industrial Production Manager; Manufacturing Engineer; Mechanical Engineer; Operations Manager; Production Manager; Project Manager; Purchasing Agent/Manager; Quality Assurance Engineer; Quality Control Supervisor; Systems Analyst. **Corporate headquarters location:** This Location. **Average salary range of placements:** $30,000 - $100,000. **Number of placements per year:** 50 - 99.

F-O-R-T-U-N-E PERSONNEL CONSULTANTS
5309 South Golden, Springfield MO 65810. 417/887-6737. **Fax:** 417/887-6955. **Contact:** Manager. **Description:** An executive search firm operating on both retainer and contingency bases. **Specializes in the areas of:** Accounting/Auditing; Engineering; General Management; Industrial; Manufacturing; Publishing. **Positions commonly filled include:** Accountant/Auditor; Agricultural Engineer; Designer; Electrical/Electronics Engineer; Environmental Engineer; General Manager; Industrial Engineer; Industrial Production Manager; Mechanical Engineer; Metallurgical Engineer; Operations/Production Manager; Purchasing Agent/Manager; Quality Control Supervisor; Software Engineer; Structural Engineer. **Corporate headquarters location:** New York NY. **Other U.S. locations:** Nationwide. **Average salary range of placements:** More than $50,000. **Number of placements per year:** 1 - 49.

GIBSON & ASSOCIATES
2345 East Grand Avenue, Springfield MO 65804. 417/886-3534. **Fax:** 417/886-6963. **Contact:** Gary Gibson, President/Owner. **Description:** An executive search firm operating on a contingency basis. The firm also provides some career/outplacement counseling. **Specializes in the areas of:** Food; Industrial; Personnel/Labor Relations; Technical. **Positions commonly filled include:** Accountant/Auditor; Attorney; Bank Officer/Manager; Biological Scientist; Blue-Collar Worker Supervisor; Buyer; Chemist; Computer Programmer; Construction Contractor; Customer Service Representative; Designer; Draftsperson; Electrical/Electronics Engineer; Electrician; Financial Analyst; Food Scientist/Technologist; General Manager; Human Resources Manager; Human Service Worker; Industrial Engineer; Licensed Practical Nurse; Manufacturer's/Wholesaler's Sales Rep.; Mechanical Engineer; Operations/Production Manager; Physician;

Public Relations Specialist; Purchasing Agent/Manager; Quality Control Supervisor; Registered Nurse; Securities Sales Representative; Systems Analyst; Transportation/Traffic Specialist. **Number of placements per year:** 1 - 49.

GRUEN & ASSOCIATES, INC.
9467 Dilman Rock Island Drive, St. Louis MO 63132. 314/567-1478. **Fax:** 314/567-0567. **Contact:** Brian Gruen, Director of Recruitment. **E-mail address:** bgruen@aol.com. **Description:** An executive search firm operating on both retainer and contingency bases. **Specializes in the areas of:** Computer Science/Software; Information Systems; Market Research. **Positions commonly filled include:** Account Manager; Computer Programmer; Database Manager; Internet Services Manager; Market Research Analyst; MIS Manager; MIS Specialist; Software Engineer; Statistician; Systems Analyst; Systems Manager; Webmaster. **Corporate headquarters location:** Medora IL. **Other U.S. locations:** Nationwide. **Average salary range of placements:** More than $50,000. **Number of placements per year:** 50 - 99.

ROBERT HALF INTERNATIONAL ACCOUNTEMPS
One Metropolitan Square, Suite 2130, St. Louis MO 63102. 314/621-0500. **Contact:** Staffing Manager. **World Wide Web address:** http://www.roberthalf.com. **Description:** An executive search firm. Accountemps (also at this location) provides temporary placements. **Specializes in the areas of:** Accounting/Auditing; Finance. **Positions commonly filled include:** Accountant; Auditor; Budget Analyst; Credit Manager; Financial Analyst. **Benefits available to temporary workers:** Life Insurance; Medical Insurance; Paid Holidays; Paid Vacation. **Corporate headquarters location:** Menlo Park CA. **Other U.S. locations:** Nationwide. **Number of placements per year:** 1000+.

ROBERT HALF INTERNATIONAL ACCOUNTEMPS
12400 Olive Boulevard, Suite 100, Creve Coeur MO 63141. 314/205-1850. **Contact:** Manager. **World Wide Web address:** http://www.roberthalf.com. **Description:** An executive search firm. Accountemps (also at this location) provides temporary placements. **Specializes in the areas of:** Accounting/Auditing. **Corporate headquarters location:** Menlo Park CA. **Other U.S. locations:** Nationwide.

HEALTHCARE RECRUITERS INTERNATIONAL
15400 South Outer 40 Road, Suite 100, Chesterfield MO 63017. 636/530-1030. **Fax:** 636/530-1039. **Contact:** Manager. **Description:** An executive search firm. Specializes in the areas of: Health/Medical; Sales.

HUEY ENTERPRISES
273 Clarkson Executive Park, Ellisville MO 63011. 636/394-9393. **Fax:** 636/394-2569. **Contact:** Arthur T. Huey, President. **Description:** An executive search firm. **Specializes in the areas of:** Accounting/Auditing; Advertising; Architecture/Construction; Food; General Management; Legal; Sales. **Positions commonly filled include:** Account Manager; Advertising Executive; Architect; Attorney; Civil Engineer; Construction Contractor; Controller; Market Research Analyst; Mechanical Engineer; Planner; Property and Real Estate Manager; Real Estate Agent; Sales Executive; Sales Manager. **Average salary range of placements:** More than $50,000. **Number of placements per year:** 50 - 99.

HUNTRESS REAL ESTATE EXECUTIVE SEARCH
P.O. Box 8667, Kansas City MO 64114. 913/383-8180. **Fax:** 913/383-8184. **Contact:** Stan Stanton, President. **E-mail address:** info@huntress.net. **World Wide Web address:** http://www.huntress.net. **Description:** An executive search firm operating on a retainer basis. Client company pays fee. **Specializes in the areas of:** Architecture/Construction; Banking; Engineering; Finance; Industrial; Legal; Light Industrial; Real Estate;

Retail. **Positions commonly filled include:** Architect; Attorney; Chief Financial Officer; Construction Contractor; Design Engineer; Project Manager; Real Estate Agent; Vice President. **Corporate headquarters location:** This Location. **Average salary range of placements:** $50,000 - $100,000.

INDUSTRIAL RESOURCE GROUP
P.O. Box 66, Chesterfield MO 63006. 636/536-3737. **Fax:** 636/536-3740. **Contact:** Manager. **World Wide Web address:** http://www.employsearch.com. **Description:** An executive search firm. **Specializes in the areas of:** Engineering; Industrial; Manufacturing.

INFORMATION SYSTEMS CONSULTING CORPORATION
1100 Main Street, Suite 1650, Kansas City MO 64105. 816/701-3000. **Toll-free phone:** 800/242-3021. **Fax:** 816/221-3564. **Contact:** Gary Fox, Manager. **E-mail address:** opportunities@iscc.com. **World Wide Web address:** http://www.iscc.com. **Description:** An executive search firm. Information Systems Consulting Corporation is a division of MAGIC (Management Alliance Group of Independent Companies). **Specializes in the areas of:** Accounting; Computer Hardware/Software; Food; Investment; Telecommunications; Transportation. **Other U.S. locations:** Denver CO; Dallas TX; Reston VA.

J.M. GROUP
P.O. Box 724, Bridgeton MO 63044. 314/738-0022. **Contact:** Manager. **Description:** An executive search firm. **Specializes in the areas of:** Engineering.

JRL EXECUTIVE RECRUITERS
2700 Rockcreek Parkway, Suite 303, North Kansas City MO 64068. 816/471-4022. **Fax:** 816/471-8634. **Contact:** Larry E. Eason, President. **Description:** An executive search firm operating on retainer and contingency bases. This firm also provides some temporary placements and contract services. **Specializes in the areas of:** Architecture/Construction; Computer Science/Software; Engineering; Food; Industrial; Personnel/Labor Relations; Scientific; Technical. **Positions commonly filled include:** Architect; Biomedical Engineer; Chemical Engineer; Chemist; Chief Financial Officer; Civil Engineer; Clinical Lab Technician; Computer Engineer; Computer Programmer; Computer Scientist; Computer Technician; Database Administrator; Database Manager; Design Engineer; Draftsperson; Electrical/Electronics Engineer; Electrician; Environmental Engineer; Food Scientist/Technologist; General Manager; Graphic Designer; Human Resources Manager; Industrial Engineer; Industrial Production Manager; Manufacturing Engineer; Mechanical Engineer; Metallurgical Engineer; MIS Specialist; Network/Systems Administrator; Operations Manager; Production Manager; Project Manager; Purchasing Agent/Manager; Quality Assurance Engineer; Quality Control Supervisor; Sales Engineer; Software Engineer; SQL Programmer; Systems Analyst; Systems Manager; Telecommunications Manager; Vice President. **Corporate headquarters location:** This Location. **Other U.S. locations:** Atlanta GA. **Average salary range of placements:** More than $50,000. **Number of placements per year:** 100 - 199.

KENNISON & ASSOCIATES, INC.
3101 Broadway, Suite 280, Kansas City MO 64111. 816/753-4401. **Toll-free phone:** 800/496-7860. **Fax:** 816/753-3430. **Contact:** Gary S. Fawkes, Managing Partner. **E-mail address:** careerkc@kennison.com. **World Wide Web address:** http://www.kennison.com. **Description:** An executive search firm operating on a contingency basis. Client company pays fee. **Specializes in the areas of:** MIS/EDP. **Positions commonly filled include:** Applications Engineer; Computer Operator; Computer Programmer; Computer Support Technician; Computer Technician; Database Administrator; Database Manager; Internet Services Manager; MIS Specialist; Multimedia Designer; Network/Systems Administrator; Software Engineer; SQL Programmer; Systems Analyst;

Systems Manager; Webmaster. **Corporate headquarters location:** This Location. **Average salary range of placements:** $50,000 - $100,000. **Number of placements per year:** 1 - 49.

KEYSTONE PARTNERSHIP
200 South Hanley, St. Louis MO 63105. 314/721-7200. **Contact:** Manager. **Description:** An executive search firm.

J.B. LINDE & ASSOCIATES
1415 Elbridge Payne Road, Suite 148, Chesterfield MO 63017. 636/532-8040. **Contact:** Manager. **Description:** An executive search firm. **Specializes in the areas of:** Manufacturing.

LLOYD, MARTIN & ASSOCIATES
2258 Schuetz Road, Suite 108, St. Louis MO 63146. 314/991-8500. **Fax:** 314/991-8055. **Contact:** Fred Lloyd, Owner. **Description:** An executive search firm operating on a contingency basis. **Specializes in the areas of:** Administration; Computer Science/Software; Information Systems. **Positions commonly filled include:** Computer Programmer; Internet Services Manager; Management Analyst/Consultant; MIS Specialist; Multimedia Designer; Software Engineer; Systems Analyst; Technical Writer/Editor; Telecommunications Manager. **Average salary range of placements:** More than $50,000. **Number of placements per year:** 50 - 99.

CHARLES LUNTZ & ASSOCIATES, INC.
14323 South Outer 40 Road, Suite 400 South, Chesterfield MO 63017. 314/275-7992. **Fax:** 314/275-7063. **Contact:** Charles Luntz, President. **Description:** An executive search firm. **Specializes in the areas of:** Advertising; Architecture/Construction; Banking; General Management; Manufacturing; Personnel/Labor Relations; Publishing; Sales; Technical. **Positions commonly filled include:** Accountant/Auditor; Administrative Manager; Architect; Attorney; Bank Officer/Manager; Biological Scientist; Branch Manager; Chemist; Clinical Lab Technician; Construction Contractor; Credit Manager; Customer Service Representative; Designer; Engineer; Food Scientist/Technologist; General Manager; Health Services Manager; Human Resources Manager; Industrial Production Manager; Licensed Practical Nurse; Occupational Therapist; Operations/Production Manager; Pharmacist; Physical Therapist; Physician; Physicist; President; Public Relations Specialist; Quality Control Supervisor; Recreational Therapist; Registered Nurse; Respiratory Therapist; Securities Sales Representative; Vice President.

MANAGEMENT RECRUITERS INTERNATIONAL
P.O. Box 1197, Camdenton MO 65020. 573/346-4833. **Contact:** Manager. **Description:** An executive search firm. **Specializes in the areas of:** Computer Science/Software; Health/Medical. **Corporate headquarters location:** Cleveland OH.

MANAGEMENT RECRUITERS OF KANSAS CITY
712 Broadway, Suite 500, Kansas City MO 64105. 816/221-2377. **Contact:** Steve Orr, Manager. **Description:** An executive search firm. **Specializes in the areas of:** Accounting/Auditing; Administration; Advertising; Architecture/Construction; Banking; Chemicals; Communications; Computer Hardware/Software; Design; Electrical; Engineering; Finance; Food; General Management; Health/Medical; Industrial; Insurance; Legal; Manufacturing; Operations Management; Personnel/Labor Relations; Pharmaceuticals; Procurement; Publishing; Real Estate; Retail; Sales; Technical; Textiles; Transportation.

MANAGEMENT RECRUITERS OF SPRINGFIELD
1807 East Edgewood, Suite B, Springfield MO 65804. 417/882-6220. **Contact:** Manager. **Description:** An executive search firm. **Specializes in the areas of:** Accounting/Auditing; Administration; Advertising; Architecture/Construction; Banking; Chemicals; Communications; Computer Hardware/Software; Design;

Electrical; Engineering; Finance; Food; General Management; Health/Medical; Industrial; Insurance; Legal; Manufacturing; Operations Management; Personnel/Labor Relations; Pharmaceuticals; Procurement; Publishing; Real Estate; Retail; Sales; Technical; Textiles; Transportation.

MANAGEMENT RECRUITERS OF ST. LOUIS SALES CONSULTANTS
3301 Rider Trail South, Suite 100, St. Louis MO 63045. 314/344-0959. **Fax:** 314/298-7706. **Contact:** Patrick Hoene, Manager. **Description:** An executive search firm. **Specializes in the areas of:** Accounting/Auditing; Banking; Engineering; Finance; Industrial; Sales; Transportation. **Positions commonly filled include:** Account Manager; Accountant/Auditor; Chief Financial Officer; Computer Programmer; Controller; Database Manager; Financial Analyst; Industrial Engineer; Management Analyst/Consultant; MIS Specialist; Sales Executive; Sales Manager; Software Engineer; Systems Analyst. **Corporate headquarters location:** Cleveland OH. **Average salary range of placements:** More than $50,000. **Number of placements per year:** 50 - 99.

MANAGEMENT RECRUITERS OF ST. LOUIS (CLAYTON)
11701 Borman Drive, Suite 250, St. Louis MO 63146. 314/991-4355. **Contact:** Phil Bertsch, General Manager. **Description:** An executive search firm. **Specializes in the areas of:** Accounting/Auditing; Administration; Advertising; Architecture/Construction; Banking; Chemicals; Communications; Computer Hardware/Software; Design; Electrical; Engineering; Finance; Food; General Management; Health/Medical; Industrial; Insurance; Legal; Manufacturing; Operations Management; Personnel/Labor Relations; Pharmaceuticals; Procurement; Publishing; Real Estate; Retail; Sales; Technical; Textiles; Transportation.

MANAGEMENT RECRUITERS OF ST. LOUIS (WEST COUNTY)
200 Fabricator Drive, Fenton MO 63026. 636/349-4455. **Contact:** J. Edward Travis, General Manager. **Description:** An executive search firm. **Specializes in the areas of:** Accounting/Auditing; Administration; Advertising; Architecture/Construction; Banking; Chemicals; Communications; Computer Hardware/Software; Design; Electrical; Engineering; Finance; Food; General Management; Health/Medical; Industrial; Insurance; Legal; Manufacturing; Operations Management; Personnel/Labor Relations; Pharmaceuticals; Procurement; Publishing; Real Estate; Sales; Technical; Textiles; Transportation.

MEDICAL RESOURCES & ASSOCIATES
9523 East 32nd Street, Independence MO 64052. 816/461-1960. **Fax:** 816/461-1936. **Contact:** Sheri Scott, CPC/Recruiter. **Description:** An executive search firm operating on both retainer and contingency bases. **Specializes in the areas of:** Health/Medical. **Positions commonly filled include:** Administrative Manager; Dental Lab Technician; Dentist; Dietician/Nutritionist; Emergency Medical Technician; Health Services Manager; Licensed Practical Nurse; Management Analyst/Consultant; Medical Records Technician; Occupational Therapist; Pharmacist; Physical Therapist; Physician; Registered Nurse; Respiratory Therapist; Social Worker; Speech-Language Pathologist; Strategic Relations Manager; Surgical Technician; Systems Analyst. **Average salary range of placements:** More than $50,000. **Number of placements per year:** 1 - 49.

MIDWEST FINANCIAL SERVICES CO.
285 Country Pointe Court, Suite 100, Wentzville MO 63385. 636/332-8877. **Fax:** 636/639-9001. **Contact:** Paul G. Krienke, President. **E-mail address:** pkrienke@inlink.com. **Description:** An executive search firm operating on a contingency basis. **Specializes in the areas of:** Banking. **Positions commonly filled include:** Bank Officer/Manager; Branch Manager; Financial Analyst. **Average salary range of placements:** $30,000 - $50,000. **Number of placements per year:** 1 - 49.

J. MILES PERSONNEL SERVICES
3029 East Sunshine Street, Suite A, Springfield MO 65804. 417/882-5585. **Fax:** 417/882-0656. **Contact:** Jean Miles, Owner. **Description:** An executive search firm operating on a contingency basis. **Specializes in the areas of:** Engineering; Food; Industrial; Manufacturing; Personnel/Labor Relations; Transportation. **Positions commonly filled include:** Accountant/Auditor; Agricultural Engineer; Buyer; Chemical Engineer; Chemist; Design Engineer; Electrical/Electronics Engineer; Environmental Engineer; Food Scientist/Technologist; General Manager; Human Resources Specialist; Industrial Engineer; Industrial Production Manager; Mechanical Engineer; Operations/Production Manager; Purchasing Agent/Manager; Quality Control Supervisor; Transportation/Traffic Specialist. **Number of placements per year:** 1 - 49.

NATIONAL PHYSICIAN PLACEMENT SERVICES
1515 North Warson Road, St. Louis MO 63132. 314/426-6777. **Fax:** 314/426-0707. **Contact:** Michael J. Brenner, President. **Description:** An executive search firm operating on both retainer and contingency bases. The firm focuses on the placement of physicians. National Personnel Placement Services (also at this location) is a permanent and contract placement firm specializing in the print, chemicals, packaging, and financial industries. National Temporaries (also at this location) is a temporary placement agency for the banking, credit, finance, and insurance industries. **Specializes in the areas of:** Banking; Finance; Health/Medical; Industrial; Insurance; Publishing; Sales; Secretarial. **Positions commonly filled include:** Actuary; Adjuster; Bank Officer/Manager; Biochemist; Branch Manager; Budget Analyst; Chemical Engineer; Chemist; Claim Representative; Credit Manager; Customer Service Representative; Electrical/Electronics Engineer; Environmental Engineer; General Manager; Health Services Manager; Industrial Engineer; Manufacturer's/Wholesaler's Sales Rep.; Operations/Production Manager; Physician; Quality Control Supervisor; Securities Sales Representative; Services Sales Representative; Typist/Word Processor. **Other U.S. locations:** Nationwide. **Number of placements per year:** 50 - 99.

OFFICEMATES5 (OM5)
211 North Broadway, Suite 2360, St. Louis MO 63102. 314/241-5866. **Contact:** Carol Zagarri, General Manager. **Description:** An executive search firm. **Specializes in the areas of:** Accounting/Auditing; Administration; Advertising; Architecture/Construction; Banking; Chemicals; Communications; Computer Hardware/Software; Design; Electrical; Engineering; Finance; Food; General Management; Health/Medical; Industrial; Insurance; Legal; Manufacturing; Operations Management; Personnel/Labor Relations; Procurement; Publishing; Real Estate; Sales; Technical; Textiles; Transportation.

OLDFIELD GROUP
701 Emerson Road, Suite 475, St. Louis MO 63141. 314/569-2000. **Contact:** Manager. **Description:** An executive search firm. **Specializes in the areas of:** Engineering.

PINNACLE EXECUTIVE GROUP
705 NE Lake Point Drive, Lees Summit MO 64064. 816/350-7028. **Contact:** Managing Partner. **E-mail address:** pinnacle@pinnaclexec.com. **Description:** An executive search firm operating on both retainer and contingency bases. The firm focuses on the gas and electric utilities industries. **Specializes in the areas of:** Computer Science/Software; Finance; Information Systems; Scientific; Technical. **Positions commonly filled include:** Computer Programmer; Database Manager; Electrical/Electronics Engineer; Financial Analyst; Internet Services Manager; MIS Specialist; Systems Analyst; Systems Manager; Telecommunications Manager. **Average salary range of placements:** More than $50,000. **Number of placements per year:** 50 - 99.

RAICHE & ASSOCIATES, INC.
11027 Natural Bridge Road, Bridgeton MO 63044-2317. 314/895-4554. **Contact:** Donald L. Raiche, President. **Description:** An executive search firm. **Specializes in the areas of:** Computer Hardware/Software. **Positions commonly filled include:** Computer Programmer; MIS Manager; Program Manager; Project Manager; Systems Analyst; Systems Manager; Technical Support Manager. **Number of placements per year:** 1 - 49.

THE RIVERBEND GROUP
36 Four Seasons Shopping Center, Suite 343, Chesterfield MO 63017. 314/579-9729. **Fax:** 314/469-8592. **Contact:** John M. Sroka, Managing Partner. **E-mail address:** partner@trgonline.com. **World Wide Web address:** http://www.trgonline.com. **Description:** The Riverbend Group is an executive search firm operating on both retainer and contingency bases. Client company pays fee. **Specializes in the areas of:** Computer Science/Software. **Positions commonly filled include:** Applications Engineer; AS400 Programmer Analyst; Computer Animator; Computer Engineer; Computer Operator; Computer Programmer; Computer Scientist; Computer Support Technician; Computer Technician; Content Developer; Database Administrator; Database Manager; Internet Services Manager; MIS Specialist; Multimedia Designer; Network/Systems Administrator; Software Engineer; SQL Programmer; Systems Analyst; Systems Manager; Webmaster. **Corporate headquarters location:** St. Louis MO. **Other U.S. locations:** Nationwide. **Average salary range of placements:** $50,000 - $100,000. **Number of placements per year:** 50 - 99.

ROMAC INTERNATIONAL
2 City Place Drive, Suite 100, St. Louis MO 63141. 314/432-4500. **Fax:** 314/995-5311. **Contact:** Recruiter. **World Wide Web address:** http://www.sourceslm.com. **Description:** An executive search firm. **Specializes in the areas of:** Accounting/Auditing; Administration; Computer Science/Software; Finance; Technical. **Positions commonly filled include:** Accountant; Administrative Assistant; Administrative Manager; Auditor; Bank Officer/Manager; Budget Analyst; Buyer; Chief Financial Officer; Clerical Supervisor; Computer Operator; Computer Programmer; Controller; Cost Estimator; Credit Manager; Customer Service Representative; Database Manager; Finance Director; Financial Analyst; Human Resources Manager; Internet Services Manager; Management Analyst/Consultant; MIS Specialist; Operations Manager; Project Manager; Secretary; Software Engineer; Systems Analyst; Systems Manager; Technical Writer/Editor; Telecommunications Manager; Typist/Word Processor. **Benefits available to temporary workers:** Medical Insurance; Paid Vacation. **Other U.S. locations:** Nationwide. **Average salary range of placements:** $30,000 - $50,000. **Number of placements per year:** 200 - 499.

SALES RECRUITERS, INC.
P.O. Box 326, Grandview MO 64030-0326. 816/767-9229. **Fax:** 816/761-8399. **Contact:** Bill King, Executive Recruiter. **Description:** An executive search firm operating on both retainer and contingency bases. The firm also provides some contract services. Client company pays fee. **Specializes in the areas of:** Accounting; Computer Science/Software; Engineering; Finance; Marketing; Sales. **Positions commonly filled include:** Account Manager; Account Representative; Administrative Assistant; Administrative Manager; Applications Engineer; AS400 Programmer Analyst; Assistant Manager; Attorney; Bank Officer/Manager; Biomedical Engineer; Chemical Engineer; Chief Financial Officer; Civil Engineer; Computer Engineer; Computer Programmer; Credit Manager; Customer Service Representative; Database Administrator; Database Manager; Design Engineer; Electrical/Electronics Engineer; Environmental Engineer; Finance Director; Fund Manager; General Manager; Geologist/Geophysicist; Human Resources Manager; Industrial Engineer; Industrial Production Manager; Manufacturing Engineer; Marketing Manager; Marketing

Specialist; Mechanical Engineer; Metallurgical Engineer; Operations Manager; Quality Assurance Engineer; Sales Engineer; Sales Executive; Sales Manager; Sales Representative; Secretary; Systems Manager; Typist/Word Processor. **Corporate headquarters location:** This Location. **Other U.S. locations:** Nationwide. **International locations:** Worldwide. **Average salary range of placements:** $50,000 - $100,000. **Number of placements per year:** 1 - 49.

SANFORD ROSE ASSOCIATES
1000 Lake St. Louis Boulevard, Suite 213, Lake St. Louis MO 63367. **Toll-free phone:** 888/258-9082. **Fax:** 636/625-6034. **Contact:** Manager. **World Wide Web address:** http://www.sanfordrose.com. **Description:** An executive search firm. **Specializes in the areas of:** Marketing; Sales Management; Telecommunications.

SEARCH PROFESSIONALS
2055 Craigshire Road, Suite 300, St. Louis MO 63146. 314/434-0230. **Fax:** 314/434-0890. **Contact:** Ronald S. Silverstein, President. **Description:** An executive search firm. **Specializes in the areas of:** Accounting/Auditing; Finance. **Positions commonly filled include:** Accountant/Auditor; Budget Analyst; Credit Manager; Financial Analyst. **Average salary range of placements:** $30,000 - $50,000. **Number of placements per year:** 1 - 49.

GORDON A. SMITH & ASSOCIATES
330 South Sixth Street, St. Charles MO 63301-2637. 636/947-3019. **Fax:** 636/723-7226. **Contact:** Recruiter. **Description:** An executive search firm. **Specializes in the areas of:** Engineering; Manufacturing; Technical. **Positions commonly filled include:** Aerospace Engineer; Agricultural Engineer; Chemical Engineer; Chemist; Civil Engineer; Designer; Electrical/Electronics Engineer; General Manager; Industrial Engineer; Mechanical Engineer; Metallurgical Engineer; Mining Engineer; Software Engineer; Telecommunications Manager. **Other U.S. locations:** Nationwide. **Number of placements per year:** 1 - 49.

WITT/KIEFFER, FORD, HADELMAN & LLOYD
8000 Maryland Avenue, Suite 1080, St. Louis MO 63105. 314/862-1370. **Fax:** 314/727-5662. **Contact:** Manager. **World Wide Web address:** http://www.wittkieffer.com. **Description:** An executive search firm. **Specializes in the areas of:** Health/Medical. **Other U.S. locations:** Nationwide.

J.E. WOTTOWA & ASSOCIATES
326 South 21st Street, Suite 300, St. Louis MO 63103. 314/621-4900. **Contact:** Manager. **Description:** An executive search firm.

PERMANENT EMPLOYMENT AGENCIES

ABC EMPLOYMENT SERVICE
7730 Carondelet Avenue, Suite 116, Clayton MO 63105-3325. 314/725-3140. **Contact:** General Manager. **Description:** A permanent employment agency. **Specializes in the areas of:** Accounting/Auditing; Architecture/Construction; Biology; Engineering; Finance; General Management; Industrial; Manufacturing; Mining; Personnel/Labor Relations; Sales; Technical. **Positions commonly filled include:** Accountant/Auditor; Applications Engineer; Architect; Biochemist; Biological Scientist; Biomedical Engineer; Budget Analyst; Buyer; Chemical Engineer; Chemist; Chief Financial Officer; Civil Engineer; Computer Programmer; Credit Manager; Design Engineer; Draftsperson; Electrical/Electronics Engineer; Environmental Engineer; Financial Analyst; General Manager; Geologist/Geophysicist; Human Resources Manager; Industrial Engineer; Industrial Production Manager; Manufacturing Engineer; Marketing Specialist; Mechanical Engineer; Metallurgical Engineer; Operations/Production Manager; Production Manager; Purchasing Agent/Manager; Quality Control Supervisor; Software Engineer; Strategic Relations Manager; Structural Engineer; Technician.

JAY ALEXANDER & ASSOCIATES
dba KIRDONN GROUP
106 West 11th Street, Suite 1520, Kansas City MO 64106. 816/474-0700. **Fax:** 816/474-0702. **Contact:** Jim Panus, President. **Description:** A permanent employment agency that focuses on sales recruitment. **Specializes in the areas of:** Advertising; Broadcasting; Computer Science/Software; Food; Industrial; Manufacturing; Publishing; Sales. **Positions commonly filled include:** Management Trainee; Manufacturer's/Wholesaler's Sales Rep.; Sales Manager; Securities Sales Representative; Services Sales Representative. **Number of placements per year:** 200 - 499.

BESTEMPS INC.
3675 South Noland Road, Suite 125, Independence MO 64055. 816/254-8844. **Fax:** 816/254-4225. **Contact:** Recruiter. **E-mail address:** contact@bestemps.com. **World Wide Web address:** http://www.bestemps.com. **Description:** A permanent employment agency that also provides some temporary placements. **Specializes in the areas of:** Accounting/Auditing; Industrial; Secretarial. **Positions commonly filled include:** Blue-Collar Worker Supervisor; Buyer; Clerical Supervisor; Computer

Operator; Computer Programmer; Human Resources Manager; Production Manager; Project Manager; Secretary; Typist/Word Processor. **Benefits available to temporary workers:** Paid Holidays; Paid Vacation; Profit Sharing.

BRADFORD & GALT CONSULTING SERVICES
12400 Olive Boulevard, Suite 430, St. Louis MO 63141. 314/434-9200. **Fax:** 314/434-9266. **Contact:** Staff Manager. **Description:** A permanent employment agency. **Specializes in the areas of:** Computer Science/Software; Information Technology. **Positions commonly filled include:** Computer Programmer; Systems Analyst. **Other U.S. locations:** Chicago IL; Peoria IL; Kansas City KS; Dallas TX. **Number of placements per year:** 200 - 499.

CRIDER & ASSOCIATES
699 West Woodbine Avenue, St. Louis MO 63122. 314/965-6665. **Fax:** 314/965-2701. **Contact:** Patrick Crider, President. **Description:** A permanent employment agency. **Specializes in the areas of:** Engineering; Industrial; Manufacturing; Personnel/Labor Relations. **Positions commonly filled include:** Electrical/Electronics Engineer; Human Resources Manager; Industrial Engineer; Mechanical Engineer; Metallurgical Engineer; Purchasing Agent/Manager; Quality Control Supervisor. **Number of placements per year:** 50 - 99.

DECK & DECKER EMPLOYMENT SERVICE
1900 North Providence Road, Suite 207, Columbia MO 65202-3710. 573/449-0876. **Toll-free phone:** 888/562-4625. **Fax:** 573/449-0878. **Recorded jobline:** 573/449-0890. **Contact:** Jack W. Rogers, MA Ed., President. **E-mail address:** deckerjobs@aol.com. **World Wide Web address:** http://www.deckerjobs.com. **Description:** A permanent employment agency that also provides some contract and career counseling services. **Specializes in the areas of:** Accounting/Auditing; Administration; Computer Science/Software; Engineering; Finance; Food; General Management; Health/Medical; Hotel/Restaurant; Industrial; Light Industrial; Manufacturing; Personnel/Labor Relations; Retail; Sales; Technical. **Positions commonly filled include:** Account Manager; Account Representative; Adjuster; Administrative Assistant; Administrative Manager; Applications Engineer; Assistant Manager; Auditor; Bank Officer/Manager; Branch Manager; Budget

Analyst; Buyer; Chemical Engineer; Chief Financial Officer; Civil Engineer; Claim Representative; Clerical Supervisor; Computer Programmer; Controller; Cost Estimator; Credit Manager; Customer Service Representative; Database Manager; Design Engineer; Draftsperson; Environmental Engineer; Finance Director; Financial Analyst; Fund Manager; General Manager; Human Resources Manager; Industrial Engineer; Industrial Production Manager; Internet Services Manager; Licensed Practical Nurse; Management Trainee; Managing Editor; Manufacturing Engineer; Market Research Analyst; Marketing Manager; Marketing Specialist; Mechanical Engineer; Medical Records Technician; MIS Specialist; Online Content Specialist; Operations Manager; Production Manager; Project Manager; Purchasing Agent/Manager; Quality Control Supervisor; Registered Nurse; Sales Engineer; Sales Executive; Sales Manager; Sales Representative; Secretary; Software Engineer; Surgical Technician; Systems Analyst; Systems Manager; Telecommunications Manager; Transportation/Traffic Specialist; Typist/Word Processor; Webmaster. **Corporate headquarters location:** This Location. **Other U.S. locations:** Nationwide. **International locations:** Worldwide. **Average salary range of placements:** $30,000 - $50,000. **Number of placements per year:** 100 - 199.

DESIGN ALTERNATIVES
15 South Florissant Road, Ferguson MO 63135. 314/521-9988. **Toll-free phone:** 800/678-7194. **Fax:** 314/521-1088. **Contact:** Charles Henson, President. **Description:** A permanent employment agency that also provides some temporary placements. **Specializes in the areas of:** Architecture/Construction; Engineering; Technical. **Positions commonly filled include:** Architect; Biochemist; Chemical Engineer; Chemist; Civil Engineer; Computer Operator; Computer Programmer; Design Engineer; Draftsperson; Electrical/Electronics Engineer; Environmental Engineer; Graphic Artist; Graphic Designer; Industrial Engineer; Mechanical Engineer; MIS Specialist; Software Engineer; Technical Writer/Editor. **Benefits available to temporary workers:** Medical Insurance; Paid Vacation. **Average salary range of placements:** $30,000 - $50,000. **Number of placements per year:** 100 - 199.

EDUCATIONAL PLACEMENT SERVICE
1001 Craig Road, Suite 170, St. Louis MO 63146. 314/991-5855. **Fax:** 314/991-5295. **Contact:** Gary Loup, CTC/Placement Director. **Description:** A permanent employment agency focusing on education placements in public, private, and parochial schools. **Specializes in the areas of:** Education. **Positions commonly filled include:** Counselor; Education Administrator; Librarian; Registered Nurse; Speech-Language Pathologist; Teacher/Professor. **Average salary range of placements:** $20,000 - $29,999. **Number of placements per year:** 50 - 99.

JMROSS & ASSOCIATES, INC.
9417 Lackland Road, Overland MO 63114. 314/429-7677. **Toll-free phone:** 888/429-7677. **Fax:** 314/429-7600. **Contact:** Manager. **World Wide Web address:** http://www.jmross.com/. **Description:** A permanent

placement agency that also provides some temporary placements. **Specializes in the areas of:** Data Processing.

LANDAJOB
8117 Wornall, Kansas City MO 64114. 816/523-1881. **Contact:** Manager. **Description:** A permanent employment agency. **Specializes in the areas of:** Advertising; Clerical; Insurance; Publishing; Secretarial. **Positions commonly filled include:** Accountant/Auditor; Administrative Assistant; Advertising Executive; Bookkeeper; Commercial Artist; Factory Worker; Marketing Specialist; Public Relations Specialist; Receptionist; Sales Representative; Secretary; Technical Writer/Editor; Typist/Word Processor. **Number of placements per year:** 50 - 99.

LINDE GROUP
220 North Fourth Street, Suite 302, St. Louis MO 63102. 314/621-2950. **Contact:** Manager. **Description:** A permanent employment agency that also provides some temporary placements. **Specializes in the areas of:** Accounting/Auditing; Administration; Office Support. **Other area locations:** Kansas City MO.

PREFERRED RESOURCES
701 Emerson Road, Suite 475, St. Louis MO 63141. 314/567-7600. **Contact:** Michael Honer, Partner. **Description:** A permanent employment agency. **Specializes in the areas of:** MIS/EDP.

PROFESSIONAL RECRUITERS INC.
625 North Euclid Avenue, St. Louis MO 63108. 314/367-0052. **Contact:** Manager. **Description:** A permanent employment agency that also provides temporary placements.

ST. PATRICK EMPLOYMENT SERVICE
711 North 11th Street, St. Louis MO 63101. 314/421-4013. **Contact:** Employment Counselor. **Description:** A permanent employment agency. **Specializes in the areas of:** Nonprofit. **Positions commonly filled include:** Clerk; Computer Operator; Custodian; Customer Service Representative; Data Entry Clerk; Driver; Factory Worker; Housekeeper; Light Industrial Worker; Receptionist; Secretary; Typist/Word Processor.

TLC CAREGIVERS
8080 World Parkway, Suite 104, Kansas City MO 64114. 816/444-6400. **Toll-free phone:** 800/707-4852. **Fax:** 816/444-6499. **Contact:** President. **Description:** A permanent employment agency that also provides some temporary placements. **Specializes in the areas of:** Child Care, In-Home. **Positions commonly filled include:** Daycare Teacher; Nanny. **Number of placements per year:** 1000+.

THE TOBERSON GROUP
884 Woods Mill Road, Suite 101, Ballwin MO 63011. 636/891-9774. **Fax:** 636/891-9784. **Contact:** James C. Anderson, CEO. **E-mail address:** toberson@fclass.net. **Description:** A permanent employment agency. **Specializes in the areas of:** Food; Health/Medical; Hotel/Restaurant; Retail; Sales. **Number of placements per year:** 50 - 99.

TEMPORARY EMPLOYMENT AGENCIES

ADECCO
2639 East 32nd Street, Suite W, Joplin MO 64804. 417/624-1911. **Fax:** 417/624-2120. **Contact:** Karol Bowman, Branch Manager. **Description:** A temporary agency. **Specializes in the areas of:** Manufacturing; Retail; Sales; Secretarial. **Positions commonly filled include:** Buyer; Claim Representative; Customer Service Representative; Dental Assistant/Dental Hygienist; Electrician; Human Resources Specialist; Manufacturer's/Wholesaler's Sales Representative; Word Processor. **Benefits available to temporary workers:** Life Insurance; Medical Insurance. **Corporate**

headquarters location: Redwood City CA. **Other U.S. locations:** Nationwide. **International locations:** Worldwide. **Average salary range of placements:** Less than $20,000. **Number of placements per year:** 500 - 999.

ANESTEMPS, INC.
4096 Fox Island Drive, Florissant MO 63034-2014. 314/839-8004. **Toll-free phone:** 800/344-2882. **Fax:** 314/839-2345. **Contact:** President. **Description:** A temporary agency that focuses on providing

anesthesiology placements. **Specializes in the areas of:** Health/Medical.

AUSTIN NICHOLS/RCM
1100 Main Street, Suite 1560, Kansas City MO 64105. 816/471-5575. **Fax:** 816/471-6690. **Contact:** Lori Thompson, Staffing Manager. **Description:** Austin Nichols/RCM is a temporary agency that also provides some permanent placements and contract services. Client company pays fee. **Specializes in the areas of:** Computer Science/Software; Engineering; Information Technology; Internet Development; Manufacturing; Scientific; Technical. **Positions commonly filled include:** Applications Engineer; Architect; AS400 Programmer Analyst; Business Analyst; Civil Engineer; Computer Engineer; Computer Operator; Computer Programmer; Computer Scientist; Computer Support Technician; Computer Technician; Construction Contractor; Content Developer; Database Administrator; Database Manager; Design Engineer; Draftsperson; Electrical/Electronics Engineer; Electrician; Environmental Engineer; Industrial Engineer; Instructor/Trainer; Internet Services Manager; LAN/WAN Designer/Developer; Manufacturing Engineer; Mechanical Engineer; Metallurgical Engineer; MIS Specialist; Multimedia Designer; Network/Systems Administrator; Quality Assurance Engineer; Software Developer; Software Engineer; SQL Programmer; Systems Analyst; Systems Manager; Webmaster. **Benefits available to temporary workers:** Paid Holidays; Paid Vacation. **Corporate headquarters location:** Pennsauken NJ. **Other U.S. locations:** Nationwide. **Average salary range of placements:** $30,000 - $100,000. **Number of placements per year:** 100 - 199.

BUSINESS PERSONNEL SERVICES, INC.
7604 East 87th Street, Kansas City MO 64138. 816/356-7666. **Fax:** 816/356-0904. **Contact:** Office Manager. **Description:** Business Personnel Services, Inc. is a temporary agency that also provides some permanent and contract placements. **Specializes in the areas of:** Accounting/Auditing; Administration; Advertising; Banking; Clerical; Computer Science/Software; Data Processing; Education; Engineering; Finance; Food; General Management; Health/Medical; Industrial; Insurance; Legal; Manufacturing; Office Support; Personnel/Labor Relations; Publishing; Sales; Secretarial; Transportation. **Number of placements per year:** 200 - 499.

CROWN SERVICES, INC.
9666 Olive Boulevard, Suite 100, Olivette MO 63132. 314/993-5333. **Contact:** Branch Manager. **Description:** Crown Services, Inc. is a temporary agency. **Specializes in the areas of:** Accounting/Auditing; Banking; Clerical; Engineering; Insurance; Legal; Manufacturing; Personnel/Labor Relations. **Positions commonly filled include:** Accountant/Auditor; Administrative Assistant; Advertising Clerk; Bookkeeper; Claim Representative; Clerk; Computer Operator; Computer Programmer; Construction Trade Worker; Customer Service Representative; Data Entry Clerk; Driver; Factory Worker; Legal Secretary; Light Industrial Worker; Marketing Specialist; Medical Secretary; Receptionist; Sales Representative; Secretary; Typist/Word Processor. **Corporate headquarters location:** Columbus OH. **Number of placements per year:** 1000+.

CROWN SERVICES, INC.
3316 Broadway Street, Kansas City MO 64111-2402. 816/931-3222. **Fax:** 816/931-3380. **Contact:** Judy Mertz, Branch Manager. **Description:** Crown Services, Inc. is a temporary agency. **Specializes in the areas of:** Industrial; Manufacturing. **Benefits available to temporary workers:** Medical Insurance; Paid Vacation. **Corporate headquarters location:** Columbus OH. **Average salary range of placements:** Less than $20,000. **Number of placements per year:** 200 - 499.

EXECUTEMPS, INC.
307 East 63rd Street, Kansas City MO 64113. 816/363-8367. **Fax:** 816/523-0905. **Contact:** Michael Jack, President. **Description:** A temporary agency that also provides some permanent placements. **Specializes in the areas of:** Accounting/Auditing; Computer Science/Software; Finance; Legal; Secretarial. **Positions commonly filled include:** Accountant/Auditor; Administrative Assistant; Attorney; Chief Financial Officer; Clerical Supervisor; Computer Operator; Computer Programmer; Finance Director; Internet Services Manager; MIS Specialist; Paralegal; Secretary; Software Engineer; Systems Analyst; Typist/Word Processor.

ROBERT HALF OF KANSAS CITY, INC.
ACCOUNTEMPS
127 West 10th Street, Suite 956, Kansas City MO 64105. 816/474-4583. **Fax:** 816/474-1422. **Contact:** Michelle Hersh, Vice President. **E-mail address:** careers@ roberthalfkc.com. **World Wide Web address:** http://www.roberthalfkc.com. **Description:** A temporary agency that also provides some permanent placements. Client company pays fee. **Specializes in the areas of:** Accounting; Banking; Computer Science/Software; Finance; Marketing; MIS/EDP; Sales. **Positions commonly filled include:** Account Manager; Account Representative; Accountant/Auditor; Adjuster; Administrative Assistant; Administrative Manager; Applications Engineer; AS400 Programmer Analyst; Auditor; Bank Officer/Manager; Budget Analyst; Chief Financial Officer; Clerical Supervisor; Computer Engineer; Computer Operator; Computer Programmer; Computer Support Technician; Computer Technician; Consultant; Controller; Cost Estimator; Credit Manager; Customer Service Representative; Database Administrator; Database Manager; Desktop Publishing Specialist; Economist; Finance Director; Financial Analyst; Internet Services Manager; MIS Specialist; Network/Systems Administrator; Purchasing Agent/Manager; Receptionist; Sales Executive; Sales Manager; Sales Representative; Secretary; Software Engineer; SQL Programmer; Systems Analyst; Systems Manager; Typist/Word Processor; Vice President; Webmaster. **Benefits available to temporary workers:** Full Benefits Package; Non-Smoking Environment. **Other U.S. locations:** Nationwide. **International locations:** Worldwide.

HIREKNOWLEDGE
8000 Bonhomme Avenue, Suite 211, St. Louis MO 63105. 314/862-6227. **Toll-free phone:** 800/937-3622. **Fax:** 314/862-4994. **Contact:** Recruiter. **World Wide Web address:** http://www.hireknowledge.com. **Description:** A temporary agency placing creative and technical individuals. The agency also offers some permanent placements. Client company pays fee. **Specializes in the areas of:** Advertising; Art/Design; Computer Science/Software; Internet Development; Internet Marketing; MIS/EDP; Printing; Publishing. **Positions commonly filled include:** Applications Engineer; AS400 Programmer Analyst; Computer Animator; Computer Engineer; Computer Graphics Specialist; Computer Operator; Computer Programmer; Computer Scientist; Computer Support Technician; Computer Technician; Content Developer; Database Administrator; Database Manager; Editor; Editorial Assistant; Graphic Artist; Graphic Designer; Internet Services Manager; Managing Editor; MIS Specialist; Multimedia Designer; Network/Systems Administrator; Software Engineer; SQL Programmer; Systems Analyst; Systems Manager; Technical Writer/Editor; Webmaster. **Benefits available to temporary workers:** 401(k); Direct Deposit; Health Benefits; Vacation Pay. **Corporate headquarters location:** Providence RI. **Other U.S. locations:** Nationwide. **Average salary range of placements:** $30,000 - $49,999. **Number of placements per year:** 200 - 499.

INSURANCE OVERLOAD SYSTEMS
1807 Park 270 Drive, Building 1, Suite 470, St. Louis MO 63146. 314/434-0909. **Toll-free phone:** 800/822-

5848. Fax: 314/434-8820. **Contact:** Assistant Vice President. **World Wide Web address:** http://www.iostemps.com. **Description:** A temporary agency that also provides some contract services. **Specializes in the areas of:** Health/Medical; Insurance. **Positions commonly filled include:** Account Representative; Adjuster; Administrative Assistant; Auditor; Claim Representative; Customer Service Representative; Insurance Agent/Broker; Licensed Practical Nurse; Paralegal; Registered Nurse; Typist/Word Processor; Underwriter/Assistant Underwriter. **Benefits available to temporary workers:** Credit Union; Dental Insurance; Life Insurance; Medical Insurance; Vision Insurance. **Corporate headquarters location:** Dallas TX. **Other U.S. locations:** Nationwide. **Average salary range of placements:** $30,000 - $50,000. **Number of placements per year:** 200 - 499.

INTERIM PERSONNEL
2103 Zumbhel Road, St. Charles MO 63303. 636/949-6666. **Fax:** 636/947-4880. **Contact:** Manager. **Description:** A temporary employment agency. **Specializes in the areas of:** Manufacturing; Secretarial; Technical. **Positions commonly filled include:** Clinical Lab Technician; Typist/Word Processor. **Benefits available to temporary workers:** 401(k); Medical Insurance; Paid Holidays; Paid Vacation. **Average salary range of placements:** Less than $20,000. **Number of placements per year:** 200 - 499.

JODOC ENTERPRISES
655 East Springfield Avenue, Sullivan MO 63080. 573/468-5269. **Fax:** 573/468-5270. **Contact:** Damon D. Berti, President. **Description:** A temporary agency that also provides some permanent placements. **Specializes in the areas of:** Accounting/Auditing; Administration; Engineering; Food; General Management; Industrial; Legal; Light Industrial; Manufacturing; Personnel/Labor Relations; Retail; Secretarial. **Positions commonly filled include:** Accountant/Auditor; Blue-Collar Worker Supervisor; Buyer; Computer Programmer; Customer Service Representative; Design Engineer; Designer; Draftsperson; Electrician; Forester/Conservation Scientist; Human Resources Specialist; Licensed Practical Nurse; Medical Records Technician; Purchasing Agent/Manager; Typist/Word Processor. **Benefits available to temporary workers:** Medical Insurance; Paid Holidays; Paid Vacation. **Other area locations:** Sunrise Beach MO. **Average salary range of placements:** $20,000 - $29,999. **Number of placements per year:** 500 - 999.

KELLY SCIENTIFIC RESOURCES
55 West Port Plaza Drive, Suite 412, St. Louis MO 63146. 314/514-0179. **Fax:** 314/514-1589. **Contact:** Manager. **World Wide Web address:** http://www.kellyscientific.com. **Description:** A temporary agency. **Specializes in the areas of:** Chemicals; Environmental; Food; Health/Medical; Pharmaceuticals.

B. LOEHR TEMPORARIES
P.O. Box 21530, St. Louis MO 63132. 314/567-6500. **Contact:** John Hayes, President. **Description:** A temporary agency. **Specializes in the areas of:** Clerical; Industrial; Technical. **Positions commonly filled include:** Administrative Assistant; Bookkeeper; Chemist; Clerk; Data Entry Clerk; Draftsperson; Factory Worker; Legal Secretary; Light Industrial Worker; Medical Secretary; Receptionist; Secretary; Statistician; Stenographer; Technician; Typist/Word Processor.

MANPOWER TEMPORARY SERVICES
4473 Forest Park Boulevard, St. Louis MO 63108. 314/534-5211. **Contact:** Branch Manager. **Description:** A temporary agency. **Specializes in the areas of:** Light Industrial; Office Support; Technical; Word Processing. **Positions commonly filled include:** Accountant/Auditor; Accounting Clerk; Administrative Assistant; Assembler; Biological Scientist; Bookkeeper; Chemist; Computer Operator; Customer Service Representative; Designer; Desktop Publishing Specialist; Electrician; Inspector/Tester/Grader; Inventory Control Specialist;

Librarian; Machine Operator; Material Control Specialist; Order Clerk; Packaging/Processing Worker; Painter; Project Engineer; Proofreader; Receptionist; Research Technician; Software Engineer; Systems Analyst; Technical Writer/Editor; Telemarketer; Typist/Word Processor. **Benefits available to temporary workers:** Life Insurance; Medical Insurance; Paid Holidays; Paid Vacation. **Corporate headquarters location:** Milwaukee WI. **Other U.S. locations:** Nationwide. **Number of placements per year:** 1000+.

MANPOWER TEMPORARY SERVICES
422 North Main, Suite A, Sikeston MO 63801. 573/472-3800. **Toll-free phone:** 800/889-1827. **Fax:** 573/472-4669. **Contact:** Manager. **Description:** A temporary agency. **Specializes in the areas of:** Computer Science/Software; Industrial; Personnel/Labor Relations; Sales; Secretarial. **Positions commonly filled include:** Blue-Collar Worker Supervisor; Clerical Supervisor; Machine Operator; Secretary. **Benefits available to temporary workers:** Medical Insurance; Paid Holidays; Paid Vacation. **Corporate headquarters location:** Milwaukee WI. **Other U.S. locations:** Nationwide. **Average salary range of placements:** Less than $20,000. **Number of placements per year:** 200 - 499.

MANPOWER TEMPORARY SERVICES
3630 South Geyer Road, Suite 114, St. Louis MO 63127. 314/966-5747. **Fax:** 314/966-5819. **Contact:** Branch Manager. **Description:** A temporary agency that also provides some career/outplacement counseling. **Specializes in the areas of:** Accounting/Auditing; Banking; Computer Science/Software; Engineering; Finance; General Management; Industrial; Insurance; Legal; Manufacturing; Nonprofit; Personnel/Labor Relations; Publishing; Retail; Secretarial; Technical; Transportation. **Positions commonly filled include:** Accountant/Auditor; Chemical Engineer; Chemist; Claim Representative; Clerical Supervisor; Computer Programmer; Credit Manager; Customer Service Representative; Draftsperson; Electrical/Electronics Engineer; Electrician; Financial Analyst; Health Services Manager; Human Resources Specialist; Industrial Engineer; Management Trainee; Mechanical Engineer; Mining Engineer; MIS Specialist; Systems Analyst. **Benefits available to temporary workers:** Life Insurance; Medical Insurance; Paid Vacation. **Corporate headquarters location:** Milwaukee WI. **Other U.S. locations:** Nationwide. **Number of placements per year:** 1000+.

OLSTEN STAFFING SERVICES
1201 East 15th Street, Joplin MO 64804. 417/623-1212. **Fax:** 417/623-8966. **Contact:** Area Representative. **Description:** A temporary agency. **Specializes in the areas of:** General Management; Industrial; Personnel/Labor Relations; Secretarial; Technical. **Positions commonly filled include:** Accountant/Auditor; Advertising Clerk; Blue-Collar Worker Supervisor; Clerical Supervisor; Clinical Lab Technician; Customer Service Representative; Human Resources Specialist; Human Service Worker; Industrial Production Manager; Management Trainee; Manufacturer's/Wholesaler's Sales Rep.; MIS Specialist; Paralegal; Purchasing Agent/Manager; Typist/Word Processor. **Corporate headquarters location:** Melville NY. **Other U.S. locations:** Nationwide. **Average salary range of placements:** $20,000 - $29,999. **Number of placements per year:** 500 - 999.

SNELLING PERSONNEL SERVICES
11719 Old Ballas Road, Suite D, Creve Coeur MO 63141. 314/993-7800. **Contact:** Steve Golden, Owner. **Description:** A temporary agency that also provides some temp-to-perm placements and career counseling services. **Specializes in the areas of:** Administration; Secretarial. **Number of placements per year:** 1 - 49.

WORKFORCE, INC.
3 North Henry Street, Farmington MO 63640. 573/756-6700. **Contact:** Manager. **Description:** A temporary agency. **Specializes in the areas of:** Industrial;

Manufacturing; Secretarial. **Positions commonly filled include:** Accountant/Auditor; Administrative Manager; Blue-Collar Worker Supervisor; Chemical Engineer; Clerical Supervisor; Customer Service Representative; Electrician; Human Resources Specialist; Industrial Production Manager; Management Trainee;

Manufacturer's/Wholesaler's Sales Rep.; Mining Engineer; Operations/Production Manager; Quality Control Supervisor; Typist/Word Processor. **Benefits available to temporary workers:** Paid Vacation. **Average salary range of placements:** Less than $20,000. **Number of placements per year:** 1000+.

CONTRACT SERVICES FIRMS

BOTTOM LINE PROFESSIONAL SERVICES
320 Brookes Drive, Suite 211, Hazelwood MO 63042. 314/367-5691. **Fax:** 314/895-5925. **Contact:** Bob Frank, COO. **Description:** A contract services firm. **Specializes in the areas of:** Accounting; Administration; Biology; Computer Science/Software; Engineering; Finance; General Management; Legal; Personnel/Labor Relations; Technical. **Positions commonly filled include:** Accountant/Auditor; Aerospace Engineer; Architect; Attorney; Bank Officer/Manager; Biochemist; Biological Scientist; Biomedical Engineer; Budget Analyst; Buyer; Chemical Engineer; Chemist; Civil Engineer; Clinical Lab Technician; Computer Programmer; Construction Contractor; Cost Estimator; Customer Service Representative; Dentist; Design Engineer; Designer; Electrical/Electronics Engineer; Environmental Engineer; Financial Analyst; Forester/Conservation Scientist; General Manager; Health Services Manager; Human Resources Specialist; Industrial Engineer; Library Technician; Management Analyst/Consultant; Mathematician; Mechanical Engineer; Mining Engineer; MIS Specialist; Nuclear Engineer; Petroleum Engineer; Purchasing Agent/Manager; Registered Nurse; Social Worker; Software Engineer; Stationary Engineer; Structural Engineer; Systems Analyst; Telecommunications Manager; Veterinarian. **Average salary range of placements:** More than $50,000. **Number of placements per year:** 100 - 199.

CDI CORPORATION
800 West 47th Street, Suite 403, Kansas City MO 64112. 816/960-0450. **Contact:** Manager. **World Wide Web address:** http://www.cdicorp.com. **Description:** A contract services firm. **Specializes in the areas of:** Engineering; Technical. **Corporate headquarters location:** Philadelphia PA. **Other U.S. locations:** Nationwide. **International locations:** Worldwide.

KENDALL & DAVIS COMPANY
11325 Concord Village Avenue, St. Louis MO 63123. 314/843-8838. **Toll-free phone:** 800/950-1551. **Fax:** 314/843-2262. **Contact:** Judi Phillips, Administrative Assistant. **E-mail address:** kendall@theonramp.net. **World Wide Web address:** http://www.kendallanddavis.com. **Description:** A contract services firm. **Specializes in the areas of:** Health/Medical. **Positions commonly filled include:** Physician. **Number of placements per year:** 1 - 49.

KNOCHE EDP CONNECTION
621 Duncan Road, Blue Springs MO 64014. 816/224-3600. **Contact:** Jim Knoche, Consultant. **E-mail address:** knoche@qni.com. **Description:** A contract services firm that also provides some permanent placements. **Specializes in the areas of:** Computer Science/Software. **Positions commonly filled include:** Computer Programmer; Operations/Production Manager; Systems Analyst; Telecommunications Manager. **Average salary range of placements:** $30,000 - $50,000. **Number of placements per year:** 50 - 99.

REHABCARE GROUP
7733 Forsyth Boulevard, Suite 1700, St. Louis MO 63105. 314/863-7422. **Toll-free phone:** 800/677-1238. **Fax:** 314/863-0769. **Contact:** Ms. Sean Maloney, Vice President of Recruiting. **Description:** A contract services firm. RehabCare Group is a leading provider of acute rehabilitation, subacute, outpatient, and temporary therapist services placement. **Specializes in the areas of:** Health/Medical. **Positions commonly filled include:** Occupational Therapist; Physical Therapist; Recreational Therapist; Social Worker; Speech-Language Pathologist. **Benefits available to temporary workers:** 401(k); Dental Insurance; Life Insurance; Medical Insurance; Tuition Assistance. **Corporate headquarters location:** This Location. **Other U.S. locations:** Nationwide.

REHABWORKS
869 Mallard Woods Drive, St. Louis MO 63021. 636/405-1550. **Contact:** Manager. **Description:** RehabWorks is one of two contract rehabilitation companies owned by Horizon Healthcare Corporation. Together, Community Rehabilitation Center and RehabWorks provide occupational, speech, and physical therapy services to patients in nursing homes and geriatric units at hospitals through 276 contracts, covering approximately 31,000 beds. **Specializes in the areas of:** Health/Medical.

TEAM INTERNATIONAL INC.
P.O. Box 18157, Kansas City MO 64133. **Toll-free phone:** 800/786-7140. **Fax:** 816/737-1451. **Contact:** Account Executive. **Description:** A contract services firm. **Specializes in the areas of:** Engineering. **Positions commonly filled include:** Chemical Engineer; Civil Engineer; Design Engineer; Designer; Draftsperson; Industrial Engineer; Petroleum Engineer; Structural Engineer. **Benefits available to temporary workers:** Paid Holidays; Paid Vacation. **Corporate headquarters location:** Kansas City MO. **Average salary range of placements:** $30,000 - $50,000. **Number of placements per year:** 200 - 499.

WESTAFF
763 South New Ballas Road, Suite 300, St. Louis MO 63141. 314/994-3950. **Fax:** 314/994-3940. **Contact:** Greg Hill, Vice President. **Description:** A contract services firm. **Specializes in the areas of:** Accounting; Architecture/Construction; Biology; Computer Science/Software; Engineering; Food; Technical. **Positions commonly filled include:** Accountant/Auditor; Architect; Biochemist; Chemist; Computer Programmer; Draftsperson; Environmental Engineer; Industrial Engineer; Mechanical Engineer; MIS Specialist; Systems Analyst. **Average salary range of placements:** $20,000 - $29,999. **Number of placements per year:** 1000+.

H.L. YOH COMPANY
14323 South Outer 40 Road, Suite 484 South, Chesterfield MO 63017. 314/878-0666. **Contact:** Manager. **Description:** A contract services firm. **Specializes in the areas of:** Engineering; High-Tech.

CAREER/OUTPLACEMENT COUNSELING FIRMS

A-1 RESUME CO.
12025 Bruno Street, Suite 80-G, St. Louis MO 63131. 314/821-1171. **Contact:** Counselor. **Description:** Provides resume counseling services.

THOMAS E. BROWN CAREER PLANNING
225 South Meramec Avenue, Suite 728, St. Louis MO 63105. 314/725-8122. **Contact:** Thomas E. Brown, LPC,

Owner. **E-mail address:** tbrown10@ix.netcom.com. **Description:** A career/outplacement counseling firm.

BERNARD HALDANE ASSOCIATES
680 Craig Road, Suite 400, St. Louis MO 63141. 314/991-5444. **Toll-free phone:** 800/264-8898.

Fax: 314/991-5207. **Contact:** President. **E-mail address:** careers@haldanestl.com. **Description:** A career/outplacement counseling firm. **Number of placements per year:** 200 - 499.

◆ M O N T A N A ◆

CARIA RESOURCES, INC.
7580 Priest Pass Road, Helena MT 59601. 406/449-4854. Fax: 406/449-5117. Contact: Manager. E-mail address: caria@caria.com. World Wide Web address: http://www.caria.com. Description: An executive search firm. Specializes in the areas of: Consulting; Engineering; Information Systems; Internet Development; Management; Procurement; Sales; Software Development; Telecommunications.

FINN'S EMPLOYMENT
P.O. Box 30356, Billings MT 59107. 406/259-1548. Contact: Jim Finnerty, President. Description: An executive search firm operating on a contingency basis. Specializes in the areas of: Health/Medical. Positions commonly filled include: Nurse Practitioner; Occupational Therapist; Pharmacist; Physical Therapist; Physician; Physician Assistant; Registered Nurse. Number of placements per year: 1 - 49.

F-O-R-T-U-N-E PERSONNEL CONSULTANTS
104 East Main Street, Suite 302, Bozeman MT 59715. 406/585-1332. Fax: 406/585-2255. Contact: Manager. Description: An executive search firm. Specializes in the areas of: Biology; Biotechnology; Engineering; Medical Technology; Pharmaceuticals. Positions commonly filled include: Agricultural Scientist; Biological Scientist; Biomedical Engineer; Chemical Engineer; Chemist; Clinical Lab Technician; Mechanical Engineer; Quality Control Supervisor; Statistician. Corporate headquarters location: New York NY.

Other U.S. locations: Nationwide. Number of placements per year: 1 - 49.

ROBERT WILLIAM JAMES AND ASSOCIATES
3709 Brooks Street, Missoula MT 59801. 406/542-0324. Contact: Manager. Description: An executive search firm.

W.R. KNAPP AND ASSOCIATES, INC.
4290 Wild Fox, Suite 200, Missoula MT 59802. 406/721-2221. Fax: 406/721-2227. Contact: Bob Knapp, Principal. E-mail address: wrknapp@montana.com. Description: An executive search firm. NOTE: This firm specializes in placing structural and geotechnical engineers, and clients seeking employment in the transportation planning field. Specializes in the areas of: Engineering; Technical. Positions commonly filled include: Branch Manager; Civil Engineer; Engineer; Environmental Engineer; General Manager; Geologist/Geophysicist; Project Manager; Transportation/Traffic Specialist. Corporate headquarters location: This Location. Average salary range of placements: More than $50,000. Number of placements per year: 1 - 49.

NELSON-McKAY AND ASSOCIATES
NELSON PERSONNEL
3700 South Russell Street, Suite B110, Missoula MT 59801. 406/542-4700. Contact: Manager. Description: An executive search firm. Nelson Personnel (also at this location) is a temporary agency that also provides some temp-to-perm placements.

A WORKING SOLUTION
1801 South Third Street West, Missoula MT 59801. 406/721-4950. Contact: Manager. Description: A generalist permanent employment agency that also provides temporary and temp-to-hire placements.

BILLINGS EMPLOYMENT CENTER
2310 Broadwater Avenue, Billings MT 59102. 406/652-4990. Contact: Manager. Description: A permanent employment agency.

DAVID S. BURT ASSOCIATES
991 Dixon Circle, Billings MT 59105. 406/245-9500. Fax: 406/245-9570. Contact: David S. Burt, President. Description: A permanent employment agency. Specializes in the areas of: Chemicals; Paper.

CAREER CONCEPTS, INC.
220 East Center Street, Kalispell MT 59901. 406/755-0533. Contact: Manager. Description: A permanent placement agency.

CAREER QUEST EMPLOYMENT SERVICE
TEMP TRACK TEMPORARY PERSONNEL
724 First Avenue South, Great Falls MT 59401. 406/452-6423. Contact: Manager. Description: Career Quest Employment Service is a permanent employment agency. Temp Track Temporary Personnel (also at this location) is a temp agency.

EXECUTIVE GROUP
1645 Parkhill Drive #4, Billings MT 59102. 406/252-7770. Contact: Bill Crago, President. Description: A permanent employment agency. Specializes in the areas of: Banking.

EXPRESS PERSONNEL SERVICES
3709 Brooks, Missoula MT 59801. 406/542-0323. Contact: Jay Olson, Owner. Description: A permanent employment agency. Specializes in the areas of: Accounting/Auditing; Banking; Clerical; Engineering; Health/Medical; Legal; Sales; Secretarial. Positions commonly filled include: Accountant/Auditor; Architect; Bank Officer/Manager; Bookkeeper; Ceramics Engineer; Civil Engineer; Clerk; Computer Programmer; Construction Trade Worker; Credit Manager; Customer Service Representative; Data Entry Clerk; Dietician/Nutritionist; Draftsperson; Driver; Electrical/Electronics Engineer; General Manager; Hotel Manager; Human Resources Manager; Legal Secretary; Light Industrial Worker; Marketing Specialist; Mechanical Engineer; Medical Secretary; Mining Engineer; Public Relations Specialist; Receptionist; Sales Representative; Secretary; Typist/Word Processor; Underwriter/Assistant Underwriter. Number of placements per year: 200 - 499.

LC STAFFING SERVICE
2920 Garfield, Suite 102, Missoula MT 59801. 406/542-3377. Fax: 406/542-6203. Contact: Mike Guild, Manager. Description: A permanent employment agency that also provides some temporary placements. Client company pays fee. Specializes in the areas of: Accounting; Architecture/Construction; Art/Design; Banking; Computer Science/Software; General Management; Industrial; Light Industrial; Marketing; Personnel/Labor Relations; Retail; Sales; Secretarial; Technical. Positions commonly filled include: Account Manager; Administrative Assistant; Assistant Manager; Bank Officer/Manager; Blue-Collar Worker Supervisor; Branch Manager; Clerical Supervisor; Controller; Credit Manager; Customer Service Representative; Electrician; General Manager; Graphic Artist; Graphic Designer; Internet Services Manager; Medical Records Technician; Paralegal; Project Manager; Sales Representative; Secretary; Typist/Word Processor. Corporate headquarters location: Kalispell MT. Other area locations: Bozeman MT. Average salary range of placements: Less than $20,000. Number of placements per year: 500 - 999.

NANNIES PREFERRED
1313 Second West Hill Drive, Great Falls MT 59404-3029. 406/727-9897. **Contact:** Sandra Goff, President. **Description:** A permanent employment agency. Nannies Preferred works with other agencies around the United States in a referral capacity. Founded in 1986.

Specializes in the areas of: Child Care, In-Home. **Positions commonly filled include:** Nanny. **Average salary range of placements:** Less than $20,000. **Number of placements per year:** 1 - 49.

TEMPORARY EMPLOYMENT AGENCIES

KELLY SERVICES, INC.
2070 Overland Avenue, Suite 102, Billings MT 59102. 406/652-2070. **Fax:** 406/652-3468. **Contact:** Manager. **Description:** A temporary agency that also provides some permanent placements. **Specializes in the areas of:** Health/Medical; Insurance; Legal; Light Industrial; Sales; Secretarial. **Positions commonly filled include:** Blue-Collar Worker Supervisor; Clerical Supervisor; Computer Operator; Computer Programmer; Marketing Specialist; Medical Records Technician; Paralegal; Secretary; Typist/Word Processor. **Benefits available to temporary workers:** Health Club Discount; Training; Vacation Pay. **Average salary range of placements:** $20,000 - $29,999. **Number of placements per year:** 1 - 49.

LC STAFFING SERVICE
275 Corporate Drive, Suite J, Kalispell MT 59903. 406/752-0191. **Toll-free phone:** 800/477-2718. **Fax:**
406/752-4708. **Contact:** Manager. **Description:** A temporary agency that also offers temp-to-hire placements. Founded in 1985. **Specializes in the areas of:** Engineering; Manufacturing; Personnel/Labor Relations; Sales. **Benefits available to temporary workers:** Paid Vacation. **Corporate headquarters location:** This Location. **Other area locations:** Bozeman MT; Missoula MT. **Number of placements per year:** 1000+.

MANPOWER TEMPORARY SERVICES
2101 Overland Avenue, Suite 101, Billings MT 59102. 406/652-9401. **Fax:** 406/652-6763. **Contact:** Branch Manager. **Description:** A temporary agency. **Specializes in the areas of:** Clerical; Light Industrial; Technical. **Corporate headquarters location:** Milwaukee WI. **Other U.S. locations:** Nationwide. **International locations:** Worldwide.

CONTRACT SERVICES FIRMS

HEARTLAND NANNIES & COMPANIONS
HEARTLAND CAREGIVERS
P.O. Box 16623, Missoula MT 59808. 406/542-0241. **Fax:** 406/549-7304. **Contact:** Karen Ryan, Owner.

Description: A contract services firm. Client company pays fee. **Specializes in the areas of:** Domestic Help; Eldercare, In-Home; Nannies. **Number of placements per year:** 200 - 499.

◆ NEBRASKA ◆

ADAMS, INC.
13906 Gold Circle, Suite 101, Omaha NE 68144-2336. 402/333-3009. **Fax:** 402/333-3448. **Contact:** Jay B. Adams, President. **Description:** An executive search firm. **Specializes in the areas of:** Banking. **Positions commonly filled include:** Loan Officer; Trust Officer. **Number of placements per year:** 50 - 99.

APEX SYSTEMS INC.
1820 Hillcrest Drive, Suite F, Bellevue NE 68005. 402/291-1200. **Contact:** Manager. **Description:** An executive search firm. **Specializes in the areas of:** Data Processing.

AUREUS MEDICAL GROUP
11825 Q Street, Omaha NE 68137-3503. 402/891-1118. **Toll-free phone:** 800/456-5857. **Fax:** 402/895-7812. **Contact:** Craig Wolf, Division Manager. **E-mail address:** aureusmed@aureusgroup.com. **Description:** An executive search firm operating on both retainer and contingency bases. The firm also provides some temporary placements. **Specializes in the areas of:** Health/Medical. **Positions commonly filled include:** Chief Financial Officer; Controller; Dietician/Nutritionist; EEG Technologist; EKG Technician; Financial Analyst; Medical Records Technician; Nuclear Medicine Technologist; Occupational Therapist; Pharmacist; Physical Therapist; Physician; Radiological Technologist; Registered Nurse; Respiratory Therapist; Social Worker; Surgical Technician; Vice President. **Corporate headquarters location:** This Location. **Other U.S. locations:** Nationwide. **Average salary range of placements:** $30,000 - $50,000. **Number of placements per year:** 100 - 199.

COMPUSEARCH OF LINCOLN
210 Gateway, Suite 434, Lincoln NE 68505-2438. 402/467-5549. **Fax:** 402/467-1150. **Contact:** Bill Elam, Manager. **Description:** An executive search firm. **Specializes in the areas of:** Accounting/Auditing; Administration; Advertising; Architecture/Construction; Banking; Chemicals; Communications; Computer Hardware/Software; Design; Electrical; Engineering; Food; General Management; Health/Medical; Insurance; Legal; Manufacturing; Operations Management; Personnel/Labor Relations; Procurement; Publishing; Real Estate; Retail; Sales; Technical; Textiles; Transportation.

CORPORATE RECRUITERS, LTD.
HEALTH SERVICE PROFESSIONALS
12515 Crawford Road, Omaha NE 68144. 402/896-3881. **Contact:** Linda Malerbi, Vice President. **Description:** An executive search firm. **Specializes in the areas of:** Accounting/Auditing; Administration; Banking; Computer Science/Software; Food; General Management; Health/Medical; Industrial; Legal; Manufacturing; Personnel/Labor Relations; Sales; Secretarial; Transportation. **Number of placements per year:** 50 - 99.

DHR INTERNATIONAL INC.
5000 Central Park Drive, Suite 204, Lincoln NE 68504. 402/464-0566. **Contact:** Manager. **Description:** A generalist executive search firm.

EXPRESS PERSONNEL
1308 South 119th Street, Omaha NE 68144-1606. 402/333-5353. **Contact:** John Devrise, Owner. **Description:** An executive search firm that also provides some temporary and permanent placements. **Specializes in the areas of:** Administration; Computer Science/Software; Engineering; Finance; Food; General Management; Industrial; Insurance; Manufacturing;

Personnel/Labor Relations; Sales; Secretarial; Technical; Transportation. **Positions commonly filled include:** Administrative Manager; Agricultural Engineer; Attorney; Bank Officer/Manager; Branch Manager; Buyer; Computer Programmer; Credit Manager; Dietician/Nutritionist; Electrical/Electronics Engineer; Environmental Engineer; Financial Analyst; General Manager; Human Resources Specialist; Management Trainee; MIS Specialist; Multimedia Designer; Operations/Production Manager; Public Relations Specialist; Purchasing Agent/Manager; Quality Control Supervisor; Restaurant/Food Service Manager; Software Engineer; Systems Analyst; Telecommunications Manager; Transportation/Traffic Specialist; Travel Agent; Underwriter/Assistant Underwriter; Urban/Regional Planner; Video Production Coordinator. **Average salary range of placements:** $30,000 - $50,000. **Number of placements per year:** 100 - 199.

HAHN TECHNICAL STAFFING
170401 County Road 22, Gering NE 69341. 308/436-4792. **Contact:** Gary Hahn, President. **Description:** An executive search firm. **Specializes in the areas of:** Engineering; Manufacturing.

ROBERT HALF INTERNATIONAL
ACCOUNTEMPS
1125 South 103rd Street, Suite 100, Omaha NE 68124. 402/397-8107. **Contact:** Manager. **World Wide Web address:** http://www.roberthalf.com. **Description:** An executive search firm. Accountemps (also at this location) provides temporary placements. **Specializes in the areas of:** Accounting/Auditing. **Corporate headquarters location:** Menlo Park CA. **Other U.S. locations:** Nationwide.

HANSEN EMPLOYMENT SERVICE
P.O. Box 1172, Grand Island NE 68802. 308/382-7350. **Fax:** 308/382-7427. **Contact:** Jack Hansen, Owner. **E-mail address:** hansenag@kdsi.net. **Description:** An executive search firm operating on both retainer and contingency bases. **Specializes in the areas of:** Accounting; Administration; Biology; Computer Science/Software; Economics; Engineering; Finance; Food; General Management; Heavy Equipment; Industrial; Light Industrial; Marketing; MIS/EDP; Personnel/Labor Relations; Sales; Scientific; Technical; Transportation. **Positions commonly filled include:** Account Manager; Account Representative; Accountant; Administrative Manager; Advertising Executive; Applications Engineer; Architect; Assistant Manager; Attorney; Auditor; Biochemist; Biological Scientist; Biomedical Engineer; Branch Manager; Budget Analyst; Buyer; Chemical Engineer; Chemist; Chief Financial Officer; Civil Engineer; Clinical Lab Technician; Computer Programmer; Construction Contractor; Consultant; Controller; Cost Estimator; Credit Manager; Customer Service Representative; Database Manager; Design Engineer; Dietician/Nutritionist; Draftsperson; Economist; EEG Technologist; EKG Technician; Electrical/Electronics Engineer; Electrician; Emergency Medical Technician; Engineer; Environmental Engineer; Finance Director; Financial Analyst; Food Scientist/Technologist; General Manager; Graphic Artist; Graphic Designer; Human Resources Manager; Industrial Engineer; Industrial Production Manager; Internet Services Manager; Manufacturing Engineer; Market Research Analyst; Marketing Manager; Marketing Specialist; Mechanical Engineer; Metallurgical Engineer; MIS Specialist; Nuclear Medicine Technologist; Operations Manager; Pharmacist; Physical Therapist; Physician; Production Manager; Project Manager; Purchasing Agent/Manager; Quality Control Supervisor; Radiological Technologist; Registered Nurse; Sales Engineer; Sales Executive; Sales Manager; Sales

Representative; Software Engineer; Speech-Language Pathologist; Statistician; Systems Analyst; Systems Manager; Technical Writer/Editor; Telecommunications Manager; Transportation/Traffic Specialist; Underwriter/Assistant Underwriter; Veterinarian; Vice President of Sales; Webmaster. **Corporate headquarters location:** This Location. **International locations:** Worldwide. **Average salary range of placements:** $20,000 - $29,999. **Number of placements per year:** 1000+.

HARRISON MOORE INC.
16009 Orchard Circle, Omaha NE 68135. 402/391-5494. **Contact:** Manager. **Description:** An executive search firm. **Specializes in the areas of:** Metals.

HUMAN RESOURCES INNOVATIONS
6200 South 58th Street, Lincoln NE 68516. 402/434-2660. **Contact:** Manager. **Description:** An executive search firm.

LINCOLN GROUP INC.
P.O. Box 5208, Lincoln NE 68505. 402/434-5919. **Contact:** Manager. **Description:** An executive search firm. **Specializes in the areas of:** Food; Home Furnishings; Pharmaceuticals; Plastics.

MANAGEMENT RECRUITERS INTERNATIONAL
210 Gateway, Suite 434, Lincoln NE 68505. 402/467-5534. **Contact:** Bill J. Elam, Manager. **Description:** An executive search firm. **Specializes in the areas of:** Biotechnology; Engineering; Finance; Health/Medical; Information Technology; Insurance. **Corporate headquarters location:** Cleveland OH. **Other U.S. locations:** Nationwide.

MANAGEMENT RECRUITERS OF OMAHA OFFICEMATES5 OF OMAHA
7171 Mercy Road, Suite 252, Omaha NE 68106. 402/397-8320. **Fax:** 402/397-6322. **Contact:** Les Zanotti, Manager. **Description:** An executive search firm. Officemates5 (also at this location) is a permanent employment agency. **Specializes in the areas of:** Accounting/Auditing; Administration; Advertising; Architecture/Construction; Banking; Chemicals; Communications; Computer Hardware/Software; Design; Electrical; Engineering; Food; General Management; Health/Medical; Insurance; Legal; Manufacturing; Operations Management; Personnel/Labor Relations; Procurement; Publishing; Retail; Sales; Technical; Textiles; Transportation.

MID-AMERICA PLACEMENT SERVICE
1941 South 42nd Street, Suite 520, Omaha NE 68105. 402/341-3338. **Contact:** Manager. **Description:** An executive search firm. **Specializes in the areas of:** Sales.

NOLL HUMAN RESOURCE SERVICES
12905 West Dodge Road, Omaha NE 68154. 402/391-7736. **Toll-free phone:** 800/798-7736. **Fax:** 402/334-7333. **Contact:** Recruiter. **Description:** An executive search firm. **Specializes in the areas of:** Administration; Banking; Computer Science/Software; General Management; Health/Medical; Secretarial; Transportation. **Positions commonly filled include:** Actuary; Bank Officer/Manager; Clerical Supervisor; Computer Programmer; Financial Analyst; General Manager; Health Services Manager; Licensed Practical Nurse; Management Analyst/Consultant; Occupational Therapist; Operations/Production Manager; Paralegal; Physical Therapist; Physician; Radiological Technologist; Registered Nurse; Respiratory Therapist; Surgical Technician; Transportation/Traffic Specialist. **Other U.S. locations:** Dallas TX. **Number of placements per year:** 200 - 499.

ODYSSEY GROUP
1104 South 76th Avenue, Suite B, Omaha NE 68124. 402/391-2065. **Contact:** Manager. **Description:**

A generalist executive search firm. **Specializes in the areas of:** Clerical.

POWER BROKERS, LLC
12635 Izard Street, Omaha NE 68154. 402/498-8981. **Contact:** Earl Fisher, President. **E-mail address:** efisher@pwrbrokers.com. **World Wide Web address:** http://www.pwrbrokers.com. **Description:** An executive search firm that operates on contingency and retainer bases. **Specializes in the areas of:** Electrical; Oil and Gas; Sales.

PROBE INTERNATIONAL INC.
5808 South 176th Street, Omaha NE 68135. 402/896-9300. **Contact:** Manager. **Description:** An executive search firm. **Specializes in the areas of:** Data Processing.

PROFESSIONS
708 Cary Street, Papillion NE 68046. 402/968-0980. **Contact:** Dave Hawkins, Manager. **World Wide Web address:** http://www.jobsarus.com. **Description:** An executive search firm.

R.E.B. AND ASSOCIATES
256 North 115th Street, Suite 7B, Omaha NE 68154. 402/333-8248. **Contact:** Manager. **E-mail address:** headhunter@bankexecsearch.com. **Description:** An executive search firm. **Specializes in the areas of:** Banking.

RECRUITERS INTERNATIONAL, INC.
11330 Q Street, Suite 218, Omaha NE 68137. 402/339-9839. **Fax:** 402/339-4024. **Contact:** Kenneth H. Mertins, President. **Description:** An executive search firm. **Specializes in the areas of:** Sales. **Corporate headquarters location:** This Location. **Average salary range of placements:** More than $20,000.

THE REGENCY GROUP, LTD.
256 North 115th Street, Suite 1, Omaha NE 68154-2521. 402/334-7255. **Fax:** 402/334-7148. **Contact:** Dan J. Barrow, CPC, General Manager. **E-mail address:** info@regencygroup.com. **World Wide Web address:** http://www.regencygroup.com. **Description:** An executive search firm operating on a contingency basis. **Specializes in the areas of:** Computer Science/Software; MIS/EDP. **Positions commonly filled include:** Applications Engineer; Computer Operator; Computer Programmer; Database Manager; Design Engineer; Internet Services Manager; MIS Specialist; Software Developer; Systems Manager; Telecommunications Manager. **Average salary range of placements:** More than $50,000. **Number of placements per year:** 50 - 99.

RELIABLE NATIONAL PERSONNEL CONSULTANTS
11318 Davenport Street, Omaha NE 68154. 402/330-2814. **Fax:** 402/330-8164. **Contact:** Harlan Rohmberg, CPC, President. **Description:** An executive search firm that also provides some permanent placement services. **Specializes in the areas of:** Architecture/Construction; Computer Hardware/Software; Executives; Finance. **Positions commonly filled include:** Accountant/Auditor; Administrator; Architect; Data Processor; Engineer; Management. **Number of placements per year:** 50 - 99.

SALES CONSULTANTS OF OMAHA
3568 Dodge Street, Omaha NE 68131. **Contact:** Manager. **Description:** An executive search firm. **Specializes in the areas of:** Agriculture; Banking; Finance; Health/Medical; Industrial; Publishing; Sales; Telecommunications; Transportation. **Positions commonly filled include:** Accountant/Auditor; Actuary; Agricultural Engineer; Bank Officer/Manager; Branch Manager; Clerical Supervisor; Computer Programmer; Credit Manager; Dietician/Nutritionist; EKG Technician; Emergency Medical Technician; General Manager; Health Services Manager; Licensed Practical Nurse; Pharmacist; Physician; Recreational Therapist;

Registered Nurse; Respiratory Therapist; Telecommunications Manager; Transportation/Traffic Specialist; Travel Agent. **Number of placements per year:** 1 - 49.

VANTAGEPOINT INC.
10040 Regency Circle, Suite 250, Omaha NE 68114. 402/391-2128. **Contact:** Manager. **Description:** An executive search firm.

PERMANENT EMPLOYMENT AGENCIES

ACCOUNTING RESOURCES INC.
770 North Cotner Boulevard, Suite 325, Lincoln NE 68505. 402/464-4488. **Contact:** Manager. **Description:** A permanent employment agency that also provides some temporary placements. **Specializes in the areas of:** Accounting/Auditing.

AGRI-ASSOCIATES
P.O. Box 24046, Omaha NE 68124. 402/397-4410. **Contact:** Richard W. Robertson, President. **Description:** A permanent employment agency. **Specializes in the areas of:** Agri-Business; Agriculture.

AMERI SEARCH INC.
3710 Central Avenue, Suite 13, Kearney NE 68847. 308/237-2422. **Contact:** Manager. **Description:** A permanent employment agency that also provides some temporary placements and executive searches. **Specializes in the areas of:** Clerical; Data Processing; Sales.

ARCADIA HEALTH CARE
111 North 56th Street, Suite 100, Lincoln NE 68504. 402/464-2220. **Contact:** Manager. **Description:** A permanent employment agency. Arcadia Health Care provides skilled and unskilled nursing placements for both in-home patients and health care facilities. **Specializes in the areas of:** Health/Medical.

BUSINESS PROFESSIONS, INC.
11128 John Galt Boulevard, Suite 595, Omaha NE 68137. 402/593-0404. **Fax:** 402/593-0505. **Contact:** John Howard, Executive Recruiter. **E-mail address:** bpinc@radiks.net. **Description:** A permanent employment agency. Founded in 1994. **Specializes in the areas of:** General Management. **Positions commonly filled include:** Bank Officer/Manager; Hotel Manager; Restaurant/Food Service Manager; Retail Manager.

CONNECTING LINK
1001 South 70th Street, Suite 103, Lincoln NE 68510. 402/441-3085. **Contact:** Manager. **Description:** A generalist permanent employment agency.

EGGERS COMPANY
Eggers Plaza, 11272 Elm Street, Omaha NE 68144. 402/333-3480. **Fax:** 402/333-9759. **Contact:** Recruiter. **Description:** Eggers Company is a permanent employment agency. **NOTE:** Interested jobseekers should call this location before sending a resume. **Specializes in the areas of:** Accounting/Auditing; Banking; Computer Science/Software; Insurance; Manufacturing; Retail; Sales.

GREEN THUMB, INC.
P.O. Box 22060, Lincoln NE 68542. 402/465-5545. **Contact:** Manager. **Description:** A permanent

employment agency that provides placements for senior citizens. Most permanent positions are part-time.

DON PARISET & ASSOCIATES
1525 South 106th Street, Omaha NE 68124. 402/397-7092. **Fax:** 402/397-7092. **Contact:** Don Pariset, Owner. **Description:** A permanent employment agency. Client company pays fee. **Specializes in the areas of:** Engineering. **Positions commonly filled include:** Design Engineer; Draftsperson; Electrical/Electronics Engineer; Industrial Engineer; Manufacturing Engineer; Mechanical Engineer; Metallurgical Engineer; Quality Assurance Engineer. **Average salary range of placements:** $30,000 - $100,000.

PETERS PERSONNEL
11218 John Galt Boulevard, Suite 103, Omaha NE 68137. 402/593-9939. **Contact:** Manager. **Description:** A permanent employment agency.

PROFESSIONAL PERSONNEL SERVICE
3201 Pioneers Boulevard, Suite 222, Lincoln NE 68502. 402/483-7821. **Contact:** Manager. **Description:** A permanent placement agency. **Specializes in the areas of:** Administration; Technical.

PROFESSIONAL RECRUITERS INC.
P.O. Box 24227, 6790 Grover Street, Omaha NE 68106. 402/397-2885. **Fax:** 402/397-7357. **Contact:** President. **Description:** A permanent employment agency. **Specializes in the areas of:** Computer Science/Software; Engineering; Manufacturing; Personnel/Labor Relations. **Positions commonly filled include:** Agricultural Engineer; Ceramics Engineer; Chemical Engineer; Computer Programmer; Electrical/Electronics Engineer; Human Resources Manager; Industrial Engineer; Industrial Production Manager; Materials Engineer; Mechanical Engineer; Metallurgical Engineer; Purchasing Agent/Manager; Quality Control Supervisor; Software Engineer; Statistician; Systems Analyst. **Number of placements per year:** 200 - 499.

PROFESSIONAL RESOURCES MANAGEMENT
5101 Central Park Drive, Lincoln NE 68504. 402/465-4502. **Contact:** Manager. **Description:** A permanent placement agency.

STAFFING SERVICES
4828 Saint Paul Avenue, Lincoln NE 68504. 402/465-9060. **Contact:** Manager. **Description:** A permanent employment agency. **Specializes in the areas of:** Construction; Production.

WORKFORCE
525 North 48th Street, Suite 201, Lincoln NE 68504. 402/464-2900. **Contact:** Manager. **Description:** A permanent employment agency.

TEMPORARY EMPLOYMENT AGENCIES

ADECCO
1941 South 42nd Street, Suite 304, Omaha NE 68105. 402/346-7500. **Contact:** Mindy Smith. **Description:** A temporary agency that also provides some temp-to-permanent and permanent placements. Founded in 1957. **Specializes in the areas of:** Accounting/Auditing; Industrial; Secretarial; Technical. **Positions commonly filled include:** Customer Service Representative; Human

Resources Specialist; Medical Records Technician; Paralegal. **Benefits available to temporary workers:** 401(k); Dental Insurance; Medical Insurance; Paid Holidays; Paid Vacation. **Corporate headquarters location:** Redwood City CA. **Other U.S. locations:** Nationwide. **Average salary range of placements:** Less than $20,000. **Number of placements per year:** 200 - 499.

KELLY SERVICES, INC.
9140 West Dodge Road, Suite 230, Omaha NE 68114. 402/393-5000. **Contact:** Ms. Dee Felici, Branch Manager. **Description:** A temporary agency. Founded in 1946. **Specializes in the areas of:** Accounting/Auditing; Banking; Clerical; Health/Medical; Industrial; Manufacturing; Personnel/Labor Relations; Retail; Sales; Secretarial. **Positions commonly filled include:** Administrative Manager; Advertising Clerk; Bank Officer/Manager; Blue-Collar Worker Supervisor; Branch Manager; Clerical Supervisor; Computer Programmer; Credit Manager; Customer Service Representative; Food Scientist/Technologist; Human Resources Specialist; Human Service Worker; Management Trainee; Medical Records Technician; Quality Control Supervisor; Services Sales Representative; Telecommunications Manager; Typist/Word Processor. **Benefits available to temporary workers:** Paid Holidays; Paid Vacation. **Corporate headquarters location:** Troy MI. **Other U.S. locations:** Nationwide. **Average salary range of placements:** $20,000 - $29,999. **Number of placements per year:** 1000+.

OUTSOURCE II, INC.
11016 Mockingbird Drive, Omaha NE 68137. 402/331-7300. **Toll-free phone:** 800/259-7269. **Contact:** Manager. **Description:** A temporary agency that also provides some contract services. **Specializes in the areas of:** Computer Science/Software; Finance; General Management; Personnel/Labor Relations; Sales; Secretarial. **Positions commonly filled include:** Accountant/Auditor; Administrative Manager; Advertising Clerk; Bank Officer/Manager; Blue-Collar Worker Supervisor; Buyer; Claim Representative; Clerical Supervisor; Computer Programmer; Construction Contractor; Cost Estimator; Counselor; Credit Manager; Customer Service Representative; Draftsperson; Editor; Environmental Engineer; Financial Analyst; General Manager; Human Resources Specialist; Industrial Production Manager; Insurance Agent/Broker; Internet Services Manager; Management Analyst/Consultant; Management Trainee; Manufacturer's/Wholesaler's Sales Rep.; Market Research Analyst; MIS Specialist; Multimedia Designer; Operations/Production Manager; Paralegal; Public Relations Specialist; Quality Control Supervisor; Real Estate Agent; Securities Sales Representative; Services Sales Representative; Technical Writer/Editor; Telecommunications Manager; Transportation/Traffic Specialist; Typist/Word Processor; Underwriter/Assistant Underwriter; Video Production Coordinator.

CONTRACT SERVICES FIRMS

DONNA'S OFFICE SERVICE
221 South Jeffers Street, Suite 1, North Platte NE 69101-5371. 308/532-9236. **Contact:** Donna Fair, Owner. **Description:** A contract services firm. Founded in 1994. **Specializes in the areas of:** Accounting/Auditing; Clerical; Legal; Personnel/Labor Relations; Retail; Secretarial. **Positions commonly filled include:** Accountant/Auditor; Customer Service Representative; Human Service Worker; Legal Secretary; Typist/Word Processor. **Average salary range of placements:** $20,000 - $29,999. **Number of placements per year:** 1 - 49.

◆ N E V A D A ◆

EXECUTIVE SEARCH FIRMS

PAUL BODNER AND ASSOCIATES INC.
501 South Rancho Drive, Suite I62, Las Vegas NV
89119. 702/386-9007. **Contact:** Paul Bodner, President.
Description: An executive search firm. **Specializes in
the areas of:** Health/Medical.

CGS PERSONNEL
1380 Greg Street, Suite 212, Sparks NV 89431. 775/331-
5227. **Contact:** Manager. **Description:** An executive
search firm that also provides some temporary and
permanent placements. **Specializes in the areas of:**
Engineering.

CAREER DEVELOPMENT ASSOCIATES
6290 Harrison Drive, Suite 4, Las Vegas NV 89120.
702/798-0744. **Contact:** Manager. **Description:** An
executive search firm. **Specializes in the areas of:**
Casinos; Hotel/Restaurant.

COVENANT RECRUITERS
P.O. Box 1229, Zephyr Cove NV 89448. 775/588-5600.
Contact: Manager. **Description:** An executive search
firm. **Specializes in the areas of:** High-Tech;
Information Technology.

MICHAEL DENNIS ASSOCIATES
P.O. Box 12296, Zephyr Cove NV 89448. 775/588-5995.
Contact: Manager. **Description:** An executive search
firm. **Specializes in the areas of:** Insurance.

EXECUTEC SEARCH AGENCY INC.
2860 East Flamingo Road, Suite J, Las Vegas NV 89121.
702/892-8008. **Contact:** Mark Moyer, President.
Description: An executive search firm that operates on
both contingency and retainer bases. **Specializes in the
areas of:** Biotechnology.

EXECUTIVE RECRUITERS INTERNATIONAL
1325 Airmotive Way, Suite 175, Reno NV 89502.
775/322-3431. **Contact:** Ray Waggoner, Manager.
Description: An executive search firm. **Specializes in
the areas of:** Mining.

FLOWERS EXECUTIVE SEARCH GROUP
1565 Vassar Street, Reno NV 89502. 775/322-5004.
Fax: 775/322-8110. **Contact:** Robert Flowers, Owner.
Description: An executive search firm operating on both
retainer and contingency bases. Client company pays fee.
Specializes in the areas of: Accounting; Administration;
Art/Design; Computer Science/Software; Engineering;
Finance; General Management; Health/Medical;
Industrial; Insurance; Legal; Light Industrial; MIS/EDP;
Personnel/Labor Relations; Printing; Publishing;
Scientific; Technical; Transportation. **Positions
commonly filled include:** Account Manager;
Accountant; Administrative Assistant; Administrative
Manager; Advertising Executive; Applications Engineer;
Assistant Manager; Attorney; Auditor; Biomedical
Engineer; Blue-Collar Worker Supervisor; Branch
Manager; Budget Analyst; Chemical Engineer; Chemist;
Chief Financial Officer; Civil Engineer; Claim
Representative; Clerical Supervisor; Clinical Lab
Technician; Computer Engineer; Computer Operator;
Computer Programmer; Computer Support Technician;
Computer Technician; Construction Contractor;
Controller; Cost Estimator; Credit Manager; Customer
Service Representative; Database Administrator;
Database Manager; Design Engineer; Desktop Publishing
Specialist; Draftsperson; Electrical/Electronics Engineer;
Environmental Engineer; Finance Director; Financial
Analyst; General Manager; Geologist/Geophysicist;
Graphic Artist; Graphic Designer; Human Resources
Manager; Industrial Engineer; Industrial Production
Manager; Management Trainee; Manufacturing
Engineer; Marketing Manager; Marketing Specialist;
Mechanical Engineer; Metallurgical Engineer; MIS
Specialist; Operations Manager; Paralegal; Production

Manager; Project Manager; Purchasing Agent/Manager;
Quality Assurance Engineer; Quality Control Supervisor;
Sales Executive; Sales Manager; Sales Representative;
Secretary; Software Engineer; Systems Analyst; Systems
Manager; Technical Writer/Editor; Transportation/Traffic
Specialist; Typist/Word Processor; Underwriter/Assistant
Underwriter; Vice President. **Corporate headquarters
location:** This Location. **Average salary range of
placements:** $20,000 - $100,000. **Number of
placements per year:** 1 - 49.

**ROBERT HALF INTERNATIONAL
ACCOUNTEMPS/OFFICETEAM**
3980 Howard Hughes Parkway, Suite 380, Las Vegas
NV 89109. 702/739-9797. **Contact:** Manager.
Description: An executive search firm. Accountemps
(also at this location) provides temporary placements.
OfficeTeam (also at this location) provides temporary
clerical and office support placements. **Specializes in the
areas of:** Accounting/Auditing. **Corporate
headquarters location:** Menlo Park CA. **Other U.S.
locations:** Nationwide.

MANAGEMENT RECRUITERS INTERNATIONAL
4530 Southeastern Avenue, Suite A12, Las Vegas NV
89119. 702/733-1818. **Contact:** Manager. **Description:**
An executive search firm. **Specializes in the areas of:**
Construction; Engineering. **Corporate headquarters
location:** Cleveland OH. **Other U.S. locations:**
Nationwide.

**MANAGEMENT RECRUITERS OF LAKE TAHOE,
NV**
P.O. Box 4766, Stateline NV 89449. 775/588-7388.
Contact: Jim Cargill, Owner. **Description:** An executive
search firm. **Specializes in the areas of:** Logistics;
Transportation. **Corporate headquarters location:**
Cleveland OH.

MANAGEMENT RECRUITERS OF RENO
1025 Ridgeview Drive, Suite 100, Reno NV 89509.
775/826-5243. **Contact:** Ed Trapp, Manager.
Description: An executive search firm. **Corporate
headquarters location:** Cleveland OH. **Other U.S.
locations:** Nationwide.

NTR
3355 Lost Hills Drive, Las Vegas NV 89122. 702/898-
1077. **Contact:** Manager. **Description:** An executive
search firm. **Specializes in the areas of:** Advertising.

OMNI PARTNERS
8689 West Sahara Avenue, Las Vegas NV 89117.
702/968-9800. **Contact:** Manager. **Description:** An
executive search firm.

THE RESOURCE NETWORK
4535 West Sahara Avenue, Suite 217, Las Vegas NV
89102. 702/796-0111. **Contact:** Manager. **Description:**
An executive search firm. **Specializes in the areas of:**
Engineering; Finance; Information Technology;
Operations Management.

STAFFMARK
501 South Rancho Drive, Suite G46, Las Vegas NV
89106. 702/598-0070. **Contact:** Manager. **Description:**
An executive search firm. **Specializes in the areas of:**
Business Services; Clerical; Engineering; Human
Resources; Industrial; MIS/EDP; Mortgage.

DOUG STUMPF ASSOCIATES
2301 East Sunset Road, Box 8115, Las Vegas NV
89119. 702/597-2554. **Toll-free phone:** 800/405-8077.
Fax: 702/597-1160. **Contact:** Doug Stumpf, Manager.
Description: An executive search firm operating on a
contingency basis. Client company pays fee. **Specializes
in the areas of:** Fire Protection Engineering; Safety.

Positions commonly filled include: Assistant Manager; Branch Manager; Computer Operator; Computer Technician; Construction Contractor; Cost Estimator; Design Engineer; Designer; Draftsperson; Electrical/Electronics Engineer; Electrician; Fire Science/Protection Engineer; General Manager; Operations Manager; Project Manager; Safety Engineer; Sales Engineer; Sales Executive; Sales Manager; Sales Representative; Services Sales Representative. **Corporate headquarters location:** This Location. **Other U.S. locations:** Nationwide. **Average salary range of placements:** $40,000 - $80,000.

PERMANENT EMPLOYMENT AGENCIES

ADECCO
2909 West Charleston Boulevard, Las Vegas NV 89102. 702/877-6775. **Fax:** 702/878-9297. **Contact:** Lynn Murray, Owner. **Description:** A permanent employment agency that also provides some temporary placements. **Specializes in the areas of:** Accounting/Auditing; Computer Hardware/Software.

THE EASTRIDGE GROUP
4220 South Maryland Parkway, Suite 205, Las Vegas NV 89119. 702/732-8855. **Contact:** Manager. **Description:** A permanent placement agency that also provides some temporary placements.

EXPRESS PERSONNEL SERVICES
1955 East Tropicana, Las Vegas NV 89119. 702/434-3900. **Contact:** Manager. **Description:** A permanent employment agency that also offers some temporary placements. **Other U.S. locations:** Nationwide.

EXPRESS PERSONNEL SERVICES
3973 South McCarran Boulevard, Reno NV 89502. 775/826-4442. **Contact:** Manager. **Description:** A permanent employment agency that also offers some temporary placements. **Other U.S. locations:** Nationwide.

INITIAL STAFFING SERVICES
2920 South Jones Boulevard, Suite 220, Las Vegas NV 89146. 702/362-8600. **Fax:** 702/362-3724. **Contact:** Ms. Janice Wesen, President. **Description:** A permanent employment agency that also provides some temporary placements. **Specializes in the areas of:** Accounting/Auditing; Administration; Advertising; Banking; Education; Engineering; Finance; Insurance; Legal; Manufacturing; Personnel/Labor Relations; Publishing; Secretarial. **Positions commonly filled include:** Customer Service Representative; MIS Specialist; Paralegal; Typist/Word Processor. **Benefits available to temporary workers:** 401(k); Dental Insurance; Medical Insurance. **Corporate headquarters location:** Houston TX. **Other U.S. locations:** Nationwide. **Average salary range of placements:** $20,000 - $29,999. **Number of placements per year:** 1000+.

KIDS CARE CONNECTION
2441 Tech Center Court, Suite 112, Las Vegas NV 89128. 702/255-0003. **Fax:** 702/255-0779. **Recorded jobline:** 702/226-5538. **Contact:** David McManaway, President. **E-mail address:** dmcman@aol.com. **Description:** A permanent employment agency. Kids Care Connection provides live-in and live-out placements. **Specializes in the areas of:** Child Care, In-Home; Nannies. **Positions commonly filled include:** Nanny; Teacher/Professor. **Average salary range of placements:** Less than $20,000. **Number of placements per year:** 100 - 199.

NANNY SERVICES OF NEVADA
P.O. Box 33580, Reno NV 89533. 775/334-4725. **Contact:** Manager. **Description:** A permanent employment agency. **NOTE:** Nannies must be at least 21 years of age. U.S. citizenship or a work permit is necessary. References and criminal, credit, and driving reports are also required. **Specializes in the areas of:** Child Care, In-Home; Nannies. **Positions commonly filled include:** Nanny. **Average salary range of placements:** Less than $20,000. **Number of placements per year:** 1 - 49.

SALES STAFFING SPECIALISTS
4220 South Maryland Parkway, Suite 221, Las Vegas NV 89119. 702/257-3835. **Fax:** 702/732-3578. **Contact:** Susan Daum, Manager. **Description:** A permanent employment agency that also provides some executive searches. **Specializes in the areas of:** Advertising; Architecture/Construction; Chemicals; Computer Science/Software; Electronics; Finance; Health/Medical; Retail; Sales; Telecommunications. **Positions commonly filled include:** Sales Engineer; Sales Executive; Sales Manager; Sales Representative. **Corporate headquarters location:** San Diego CA. **Average salary range of placements:** $30,000 - $50,000. **Number of placements per year:** 200 - 499.

TEMPORARY EMPLOYMENT AGENCIES

ACCOUNTANTS INC.
5250 South Virginia, Suite 261, Reno NV 89502. 775/823-4411. **Fax:** 775/823-4400. **Contact:** Manager. **World Wide Web address:** http://www.accountantsincnv.com. **Description:** A temporary employment agency that also offers some permanent placements. **Specializes in the areas of:** Accounting; Finance. **Corporate headquarters location:** Burlingame CA. **Other U.S. locations:** Nationwide.

ACCOUNTANTS INC.
3770 Howard Hughes Parkway, Suite 205, Las Vegas NV 89109. 702/734-1110. **Fax:** 702/491-9411. **Contact:** Manager. **World Wide Web address:** http://www.accountantsincnv.com. **Description:** A temporary employment agency that also offers some permanent placements. **Specializes in the areas of:** Accounting; Finance. **Corporate headquarters location:** Burlingame CA. **Other U.S. locations:** Nationwide.

LABOR FINDERS
P.O. Box 20292, Carson City NV 89721. 775/884-4645. **Physical address:** 933 Woodside, Carson City NV. **Fax:** 775/884-2989. **Contact:** Manager. **Description:** A temporary agency. **Specializes in the areas of:** Construction; Food; Heavy Equipment; Industrial; Publishing. **Positions commonly filled include:** Blue-Collar Worker Supervisor; Electrical/Electronics Engineer; Electrician; Production Worker; Truck Driver. **Corporate headquarters location:** Palm Beach Gardens FL. **Other U.S. locations:** Nationwide. **Average salary range of placements:** $20,000 - $29,999. **Number of placements per year:** 50 - 99.

MANPOWER TEMPORARY SERVICES
1755 Vassar Street, Reno NV 89502. 775/322-2000. **Contact:** Branch Manager. **Description:** A temporary agency. **Specializes in the areas of:** Clerical; Computer Hardware/Software; Construction; Engineering; Secretarial; Technical. **Positions commonly filled include:** Accountant/Auditor; Aerospace Engineer; Agricultural Engineer; Biomedical Engineer; Bookkeeper; Civil Engineer; Clerk; Computer Programmer; Construction Trade Worker; Customer Service Representative; Data Entry Clerk; Draftsperson; Driver; Electrical/Electronics Engineer; Financial

Analyst; Industrial Designer; Industrial Engineer; Legal Secretary; Light Industrial Worker; Medical Secretary; Metallurgical Engineer; Receptionist; Secretary; Statistician; Stenographer; Technical Writer/Editor; Technician; Typist/Word Processor. **Corporate headquarters location:** Milwaukee WI. **Other U.S. locations:** Nationwide. **Number of placements per year:** 200 - 499.

MANPOWER TEMPORARY SERVICES
314 Las Vegas Boulevard North, Las Vegas NV 89101. 702/384-3168. **Contact:** Branch Manager. **Description:** A temporary agency. **Specializes in the areas of:** Data Processing; Industrial; Office Support; Professional; Technical; Word Processing. **Positions commonly filled include:** Accountant/Auditor; Accounting Supervisor; Administrative Assistant; Assembly Worker; Bookkeeper; Chemist; Computer Operator; Customer Service Representative; Desktop Publishing Specialist; Electrician; Inspector/Tester/Grader; Machine Operator; Packaging/Processing Worker; Painter; Project Engineer; Proofreader; Receptionist; Research Assistant; Secretary; Software Engineer; Stenographer; Systems Analyst; Technical Writer/Editor; Technician; Typist/Word Processor; Welder. **Benefits available to temporary workers:** Life Insurance; Medical Insurance; Paid Holidays; Paid Vacation. **Corporate headquarters location:** Milwaukee WI. **Other U.S. locations:** Nationwide. **Number of placements per year:** 1000+.

CAREER/OUTPLACEMENT COUNSELING FIRMS

NEVADA BUSINESS SERVICES (NBS)
940 West Owens, Las Vegas NV 89106. 702/646-7675. **Fax:** 702/646-7812. **Contact:** Bill Murphy, Program Manager. **Description:** A federally funded employment/training program available to eligible individuals. NBS offers career counseling, employment workshops, and classroom training in a wide variety of areas to increase job skills. NBS also arranges on-the-job training and job placement with employers. **Specializes in the areas of:** Administration; Clerical; Education; General Management; Nonprofit.

NEVADA BUSINESS SERVICES (NBS)
109 Military Circle, Tonopah NV 89049. 775/482-6038. **Contact:** Manager. **Description:** A federally funded employment/training program available to eligible individuals. NBS offers career counseling, employment workshops, and classroom training in a wide variety of areas to increase job skills. NBS also arranges on-the-job training and job placement with employers. **Specializes in the areas of:** Administration; Education; General Management; Nonprofit; Secretarial.

EXECUTIVE SEARCH FIRMS

ABLE 1 STAFFING
126 Daniel Street, Portsmouth NH 03801. 603/436-1151. **Fax:** 603/436-0285. **Contact:** Laura Montville, President. **E-mail address:** staffing@able1.com. **World Wide Web address:** http://www.able1.com. **Description:** An executive search firm. **Specializes in the areas of:** Accounting/Auditing; Banking; Clerical; Computer Hardware/Software; Engineering; Finance; Health/Medical; Insurance; Legal; Publishing; Sales; Secretarial; Technical; Transportation. **Positions commonly filled include:** Accountant/Auditor; Actuary; Administrative Assistant; Aerospace Engineer; Agricultural Engineer; Attorney; Bank Officer/Manager; Biological Scientist; Biomedical Engineer; Bookkeeper; Ceramics Engineer; Civil Engineer; Claim Representative; Clerk; Commercial Artist; Computer Programmer; Credit Manager; Customer Service Representative; Data Entry Clerk; Draftsperson; Economist; EDP Specialist; Electrical/Electronics Engineer; Financial Analyst; General Manager; Human Resources Manager; Industrial Designer; Industrial Engineer; Insurance Agent/Broker; Legal Secretary; Light Industrial Worker; Management Analyst/Consultant; Marketing Specialist; Mechanical Engineer; Medical Secretary; Metallurgical Engineer; Mining Engineer; Nurse; Physicist; Purchasing Agent/Manager; Receptionist; Secretary; Statistician; Stenographer; Systems Analyst; Technical Writer/Editor; Technician; Typist/Word Processor; Underwriter/Assistant Underwriter. **Number of placements per year:** 1 - 49.

ACCESS DATA PERSONNEL, INC.
649 Second Street, Manchester NH 03102. 603/641-6300. **Fax:** 603/641-8987. **Contact:** Manager. **Description:** An executive search firm. **Specializes in the areas of:** Information Systems; Information Technology.

ADVANCED RECRUITING & CONSULTING
75 Gilcreast Road, Londonderry NH 03053. 603/425-2488. **Contact:** Manager. **Description:** An executive search firm operating on a contingency basis. **Specializes in the areas of:** Accounting/Auditing; Finance. **Positions commonly filled include:** Accountant/Auditor; Budget Analyst; Chief Financial Officer; Financial Analyst. **Other U.S. locations:** Boston MA. **Number of placements per year:** 50 - 99.

SHAWN ALEXANDER ASSOCIATES
P.O. Box 417, Amherst NH 03031. 603/672-6116. **Contact:** Manager. **Description:** An executive search firm. **Specializes in the areas of:** High-Tech.

ASSOCIATED EXECUTIVE MANAGEMENT ASSOCIATED PERSONNEL
2456 Lafayette Road, Portsmouth NH 03801. 603/430-7537. **Contact:** Manager. **Description:** An executive search firm.

BAEDER KALINSKI INTERNATIONAL GROUP
40 South River Road, Unit 64, Bedford NH 03110. 603/669-1570. **Contact:** Manager. **Description:** An executive search firm.

BAER ASSOCIATES
4 High Street, Hampton NH 03842. 603/929-3544. **Contact:** Manager. **Description:** An executive search firm.

BARCLAY PERSONNEL SYSTEMS, INC.
One Executive Park Drive, Bedford NH 03110. 603/669-2011. **Contact:** Manager. **Description:** An executive search firm operating on a contingency basis. Barclay also provides some temporary placements. **Specializes in the areas of:** Accounting/Auditing; Engineering; Food; Industrial; Insurance; Legal; Marketing; Retail; Sales; Secretarial; Technical. **Positions commonly filled include:** Account Manager; Account Representative; Adjuster; Administrative Assistant; Buyer; Claim Representative; Controller; Cost Estimator; Credit Manager; Customer Service Representative; Design Engineer; Draftsperson; Finance Director; Fund Manager; General Manager; Manufacturing Engineer; Marketing Manager; Production Manager; Purchasing Agent/Manager; Sales Engineer; Sales Executive; Sales Representative; Secretary. **Average salary range of placements:** $30,000 - $50,000. **Number of placements per year:** 200 - 499.

BARRETT & COMPANY
59 Stiles Road, Suite 105, Salem NH 03079. 603/890-1111. **Fax:** 603/890-1118. **Contact:** LeeAnne Martino, Office Manager. **E-mail address:** resume@barrettcompany.com. **World Wide Web address:** http://www.barrettcompany.com. **Description:** An executive search firm. **Specializes in the areas of:** Advertising; Engineering; General Management; Health/Medical; Sales. **Positions commonly filled include:** Account Representative; Advertising Executive; Chief Executive Officer; Chief Financial Officer; General Manager; Human Resources Manager; Operations Manager; President; Sales Executive; Sales Manager; Sales Representative. **Corporate headquarters location:** This Location. **International locations:** Worldwide. **Number of placements per year:** 50 - 99.

BARTHOLDI & COMPANY
14 Douglas Way, Exeter NH 03833. 603/772-4228. **Contact:** Manager. **Description:** An executive search firm. **Specializes in the areas of:** High-Tech.

BELL QUEST ASSOCIATES
34 Franklin Street, Nashua NH 03060. 603/578-5550. **Contact:** Manager. **Description:** An executive search firm. **Specializes in the areas of:** Software Development.

CAREER PROFILES
P.O. Box 4430, Portsmouth NH 03802. 603/433-3355. **Fax:** 603/433-8678. **Contact:** Norm Gray, Owner. **E-mail address:** normgray@careerprofiles.net. **World Wide Web address:** http://www.careerprofiles.net. **Description:** An executive search firm operating on a contingency basis. **Specializes in the areas of:** Health/Medical; Publishing; Sales. **Positions commonly filled include:** Licensed Practical Nurse; Physical Therapist; Physician; Registered Nurse.

CHAUCER GROUP
55 Morrill Road, Canterbury NH 03224. 603/783-9500. **Fax:** 603/783-9229. **Contact:** Robert J. Thomason, CPC/President. **E-mail address:** info@chaucer.com. **World Wide Web address:** http://www.chaucer.com. **Description:** An executive search firm operating on both retainer and contingency bases. Chaucer Group also provides some permanent placements. **Specializes in the areas of:** Computer Science/Software; Engineering; Industrial; Manufacturing; Marketing; Sales; Technical. **Positions commonly filled include:** Applications Engineer; Biochemist; Biomedical Engineer; Buyer; Chemical Engineer; Chemist; Database Manager; Design Engineer; Draftsperson; Electrical/Electronics Engineer; General Manager; Industrial Engineer; Industrial Production Manager; Internet Services Manager; Management Analyst/Consultant; Manufacturing Engineer; Mechanical Engineer; Metallurgical Engineer; Online Content Specialist; Operations Manager; Project Manager; Public Relations Specialist; Quality Control Supervisor; Sales Engineer; Sales Executive; Sales Representative; Software Engineer; Systems Analyst; Technical Writer/Editor; Telecommunications Manager. **Corporate headquarters location:** This Location.

Other area locations: Jaffrey NH; Londonderry NH; Manchester NH; Windham NH. **Average salary range of placements:** $20,000 - $29,999. **Number of placements per year:** 100 - 199.

CLAYMAN MANAGEMENT SERVICE
500 North Commercial Street, Manchester NH 03101. 603/644-7800. **Fax:** 603/644-5560. **Contact:** Stan Clayman, President. **Description:** An executive search firm. **Specializes in the areas of:** Fashion; Footwear; Health/Medical; Sporting Goods. **Positions commonly filled include:** Chief Executive Officer; Chief Financial Officer; Designer; Emergency Medical Technician; Health Services Manager; Human Resources Specialist; Industrial Engineer; Licensed Practical Nurse; Market Research Analyst; Marketing Manager; Medical Records Technician; MIS Specialist; Occupational Therapist; Operations/Production Manager; Physical Therapist; Physician; Purchasing Agent/Manager; Quality Control Supervisor; Registered Nurse; Respiratory Therapist; Sales Executive; Sales Manager; Surgical Technician. **Number of placements per year:** 50 - 99.

CURTIS ASSOCIATES
P.O. Box 1543, Portsmouth NH 03802. 603/749-9700. **Contact:** Steve Curtis, Manager. **Description:** An executive search firm. **Specializes in the areas of:** Accounting/Auditing. **Other U.S. locations:** Boston MA; Portland ME.

DUBOIS & COMPANY
14 Birch Drive, Newmarket NH 03857. 603/659-6001. **Contact:** Paulette Dubois, Principal/Owner. **Description:** An executive search firm operating on both retainer and contingency bases. **Specializes in the areas of:** Accounting/Auditing; Administration; Banking; Biology; Computer Science/Software; Engineering; General Management; Health/Medical; Manufacturing; Personnel/Labor Relations; Publishing; Retail; Sales; Technical. **Positions commonly filled include:** Accountant/Auditor; Administrative Manager; Aerospace Engineer; Architect; Bank Officer/Manager; Biochemist; Biological Scientist; Biomedical Engineer; Budget Analyst; Buyer; Chemical Engineer; Chemist; Civil Engineer; Clerical Supervisor; Clinical Lab Technician; Computer Programmer; Credit Manager; Customer Service Representative; Design Engineer; Designer; Economist; Education Administrator; Electrical/ Electronics Engineer; Electrician; Emergency Medical Technician; Environmental Engineer; Financial Analyst; Food Scientist/Technologist; General Manager; Health Services Manager; Hotel Manager; Human Resources Specialist; Industrial Engineer; Industrial Production Manager; Internet Services Manager; Manufacturer's/ Wholesaler's Sales Rep.; Market Research Analyst; Mathematician; Mechanical Engineer; Medical Records Technician; Metallurgical Engineer; MIS Specialist; Multimedia Designer; Nuclear Engineer; Operations/ Production Manager; Public Relations Specialist; Purchasing Agent/Manager; Quality Control Supervisor; Science Technologist; Securities Sales Representative; Services Sales Representative; Software Engineer; Stationary Engineer; Statistician; Strategic Relations Manager; Structural Engineer; Systems Analyst; Telecommunications Manager; Transportation/Traffic Specialist. **Average salary range of placements:** More than $50,000. **Number of placements per year:** 1 - 49.

ENTERPRISE TECHNOLOGIES
130 Main Street, Suite 201, Salem NH 03079. 603/890-3700. **Fax:** 603/890-8701. **Contact:** Linda Bonvie, Executive Director. **E-mail address:** ent@ent-tech.com. **Description:** An executive search firm. **Specializes in the areas of:** Computer Science/Software; Engineering; Manufacturing; Personnel/Labor Relations; Technical. **Positions commonly filled include:** Computer Programmer; Design Engineer; Electrical/Electronics Engineer; MIS Specialist; Quality Control Supervisor; Software Engineer; Systems Analyst; Technical Writer/Editor; Telecommunications Manager. **Average salary range of placements:** More than $50,000. **Number of placements per year:** 1 - 49.

F-O-R-T-U-N-E PERSONNEL CONSULTANTS
505 West Hollis Street, Nashua NH 03062. 603/880-4900. **Contact:** Norman J. Oppenheim, President. **Description:** An executive search firm operating on a contingency basis. **Specializes in the areas of:** Biomedical; Biotechnology; Medical Technology; Pharmaceuticals. **Corporate headquarters location:** New York NY. **Other U.S. locations:** Nationwide. **Average salary range of placements:** More than $50,000. **Number of placements per year:** 50 - 99.

FUTURES, INC.
One Hampton Road, Suite 301, Exeter NH 03833. 603/775-7800. **Fax:** 603/775-7900. **Contact:** Thomas P. Colacchio, President. **Description:** An executive search firm that also provides some contract placements. **Specializes in the areas of:** Food; Sales; Transportation. **Positions commonly filled include:** Account Manager; Account Representative; Assistant Manager; Buyer; Food and Beverage Service Worker; General Manager; Human Resources Manager; Sales and Marketing Representative; Sales Executive; Sales Manager; Sales Representative; Transportation/Traffic Specialist. **Corporate headquarters location:** This Location. **Average salary range of placements:** More than $50,000. **Number of placements per year:** 100 - 199.

ROBERT HALF INTERNATIONAL ACCOUNTEMPS
1155 Elm Street, 8th Floor, Manchester NH 03101. 603/641-9400. **Contact:** Manager. **Description:** An executive search firm. Accountemps (also at this location) provides temporary placements. **Corporate headquarters location:** Menlo Park CA. **Other U.S. locations:** Nationwide.

HANOVER ASSOCIATES
P.O. Box 6661, Portsmouth NH 03802. 603/436-8778. **Contact:** Manager. **Description:** An executive search firm.

HIGH TECH OPPORTUNITIES INC.
264B North Broadway, Suite 206, Salem NH 03079. 603/893-9486. **Fax:** 603/893-9492. **Contact:** Manager. **Description:** An executive search firm operating on both retainer and contingency bases. The firm focuses on providing placements in the semiconductor, computer hardware and software, and satellite and communications fields. **Specializes in the areas of:** Engineering. **Positions commonly filled include:** Broadcast Technician; Design Engineer; Electrical/Electronics Engineer. **Average salary range of placements:** More than $50,000. **Number of placements per year:** 1 - 49.

MAINSTAY STAFFING
22 Greeley Street, Suite 7, Merrimack NH 03054. 603/424-0020. **Fax:** 603/424-8207. **Contact:** President. **Description:** An executive search firm operating on both retainer and contingency bases. **Specializes in the areas of:** Computer Science/Software; Manufacturing; Personnel/Labor Relations; Sales; Technical. **Positions commonly filled include:** Biochemist; Biological Scientist; Biomedical Engineer; Customer Service Representative; General Manager; Human Resources Specialist; Internet Services Manager; Operations/ Production Manager; Public Relations Specialist; Quality Control Supervisor; Services Sales Representative; Software Engineer; Systems Analyst. **Other U.S. locations:** NJ; NY. **Average salary range of placements:** More than $50,000. **Number of placements per year:** 50 - 99.

MANAGEMENT RECRUITERS INTERNATIONAL OF BEDFORD
Cold Stream Office Park, 116-C South River Road, Bedford NH 03110. 603/669-9800. **Fax:** 603/623-8609. **Contact:** Mike Bacon, Senior Vice President. **Description:** An executive search firm. **Specializes in the areas of:** Accounting/Auditing; Administration; Advertising; Banking; Communications; Computer Hardware/Software; Construction; Electrical; Engineering; Finance; Food; General Management;

Health/Medical; Insurance; Legal; Manufacturing; Operations Management; Personnel/Labor Relations; Procurement; Publishing; Sales; Technical; Transportation. **Corporate headquarters location:** Cleveland OH.

PAMELA L. MULLIGAN INC.
36 Country Club Road, Guilford NH 03246. 603/226-2262. **Contact:** Pamela L. Mulligan, President. **Description:** An executive search firm operating on a retainer basis. **Specializes in the areas of:** Health/Medical. **Positions commonly filled include:** CEO; CFO; Claim Rep.; Information Specialist; Marketing Specialist; Registered Nurse; Sales and Marketing Rep. **Number of placements per year:** 1 - 49.

PMG INC.
128 South River Road, Bedford NH 03110. 603/624-5900. **Contact:** Manager. **Description:** An executive search and recruiting firm.

POWER SEARCH INC.
472 State Route 111, Unit G-2, Hampstead NH 03841. 603/329-1144. **Contact:** Edward Murphy, President. **Description:** An executive search firm.

PREFERRED RESOURCE GROUP
P.O. Box 6370, Nashua NH 03063. 603/889-0112. **Fax:** 603/598-4915. **Contact:** Thomas Shiber, Principal. **E-mail address:** tshiber@aol.com. **Description:** An executive search firm operating on both retainer and contingency bases. **Specializes in the areas of:** Administration; Computer Science/Software; Engineering; General Management; Industrial; Manufacturing; Technical. **Positions commonly filled include:** Buyer; Chemical Engineer; Chemist; Computer Programmer; Design Engineer; Electrical/Electronics Engineer; General Manager; Industrial Engineer; Industrial Production Manager; Internet Services Manager; Mechanical Engineer; Metallurgical Engineer; MIS Specialist; Multimedia Designer; Operations/Production Manager; Purchasing Agent/Manager; Quality Control Supervisor; Software Engineer; Structural Engineer; Systems Analyst; Technical Writer/Editor; Telecommunications Manager. **Average salary range of placements:** More than $50,000. **Number of placements per year:** 1 - 49.

R.G.T. ASSOCIATES, INC.
2 Green Leaf Woods Drive, Suite 101, Portsmouth NH 03801. 603/431-9500. **Fax:** 603/431-6984. **Contact:** Bob Thiboutot, CPC, President. **Description:** An executive search firm. **Specializes in the areas of:** Accounting/Auditing; Administration; Banking; Clerical; Computer Hardware/Software; Engineering; Finance; Manufacturing; Sales; Technical. **Positions commonly filled include:** Accountant/Auditor; Administrative Assistant; Aerospace Engineer; Bank Officer/Manager; Bookkeeper; Computer Operator; Computer Programmer; Credit Manager; Customer Service Representative; Data Entry Clerk; Draftsperson; EDP Specialist; Electrical/Electronics Engineer; Financial Analyst; General Manager; Industrial Engineer; Legal Secretary; Marketing Specialist; Mechanical Engineer; Medical Secretary; MIS Specialist; Operations/Production Manager; Purchasing Agent/Manager; Quality Control Supervisor; Receptionist; Sales Representative; Secretary; Systems Analyst; Typist/Word Processor. **Average salary range of placements:** More than $50,000. **Number of placements per year:** 1 - 49.

RAYMOND KARSON ASSOCIATES
27 Lowell Street, Suite 502, Manchester NH 03101. 603/666-9600. **Contact:** Manager. **Description:** An executive search firm that also provides contract services.

REID AND COMPANY
500 Market Street, Suite 15, Portsmouth NH 03801. 603/433-6222. **Contact:** Manager. **Description:** An executive search firm. **Specializes in the areas of:** Apparel.

RETAIL RECRUITERS OF NEW HAMPSHIRE, INC.
Northbridge Business Center, Unit 33, 76 Northeastern Boulevard, Nashua NH 03062. 603/883-1900. **Toll-free phone:** 800/639-1919. **Fax:** 603/883-0482. **Contact:** Manager. **Description:** An executive search firm operating on a contingency basis. **Average salary range of placements:** $30,000 - $50,000. **Number of placements per year:** 50 - 99.

ROMAC INTERNATIONAL
71 Spit Brook Road, Suite 305, Nashua NH 03060. 603/888-1700. **Fax:** 603/888-7826. **Contact:** Manager. **Description:** An executive search firm. **Specializes in the areas of:** Engineering.

SALES CONSULTANTS
1106 Hooksett Road, Hooksett NH 03106. 603/626-8400. **Contact:** Manager. **Description:** An executive search firm operating on both retainer and contingency bases. **Specializes in the areas of:** Advertising; Art/Design; Fashion; Food; General Management; Health/Medical; Sales. **Positions commonly filled include:** Customer Service Representative; Design Engineer; Designer; Food Scientist/Technologist; General Manager; Management Analyst/Consultant; Market Research Analyst; Occupational Therapist; Physical Therapist; Physician. **Average salary range of placements:** More than $50,000. **Number of placements per year:** 1 - 49.

SALES CONSULTANTS OF NASHUA-MANCHESTER
6 Medallion Center, Merrimack NH 03054. 603/424-3282. **Fax:** 603/424-3286. **Contact:** Sheldon Baron, Manager/Owner. **Description:** An executive search firm. **Specializes in the areas of:** Advertising; Banking; Biology; Computer Science/Software; Engineering; Fashion; Finance; Health/Medical; Industrial; Insurance; Operations Management; Procurement; Retail; Sales; Technical. **Positions commonly filled include:** Bank Officer/Manager; Biological Scientist; Branch Manager; Chemical Engineer; Chemist; Design Engineer; Dietician/Nutritionist; Electrical/Electronics Engineer; Environmental Engineer; Financial Analyst; Health Services Manager; Industrial Engineer; Industrial Production Manager; Insurance Agent/Broker; Mechanical Engineer; Pharmacist; Physical Therapist; Physician; Registered Nurse; Respiratory Therapist; Science Technologist; Software Engineer; Telecommunications Manager. **Average salary range of placements:** $30,000 - $50,000. **Number of placements per year:** 50 - 99.

SALES RECRUITERS INC.
85 Stiles Road, Suite 104, Salem NH 03079. 603/888-3700. **Contact:** Henry Glickel, President. **Description:** An executive search firm operating on a contingency basis. **Specializes in the areas of:** Marketing; Sales. **Positions commonly filled include:** Account Manager; Account Representative; Management Trainee; Sales Engineer; Sales Executive; Sales Manager; Sales Representative. **Average salary range of placements:** More than $50,000. **Number of placements per year:** 50 - 99.

SELIG EXECUTIVE SEARCH
P.O. Box 160, Laconia NH 03247. 603/527-0111. **Contact:** Manager. **Description:** An executive search firm.

SNOWDEN ASSOCIATES
400 The Hill, Portsmouth NH 03801. 603/431-1553. **Fax:** 603/431-3809. **Contact:** Al Egan, Vice President. **E-mail address:** snowden44@aol.com. **Description:** A generalist executive search firm operating on a retainer basis. The firm focuses on placements in Northern New England, and also provides permanent placements and resume/career counseling services. Client company pays fee. **Positions commonly filled include:** Account Manager; Accountant; Administrative Manager; Bank Officer/Manager; Chief Financial Officer; Controller;

Design Engineer; Electrical/Electronics Engineer; Finance Director; Financial Analyst; General Manager; Human Resources Manager; Industrial Engineer; Industrial Production Manager; Manufacturing Engineer; Marketing Manager; Mechanical Engineer; Metallurgical Engineer; Operations Manager; Production Manager; Project Manager; Purchasing Agent/Manager; Quality Assurance Engineer; Quality Control Supervisor; Sales Engineer; Sales Executive; Sales Manager; Vice President of Operations. **Corporate headquarters location:** This Location. **Other area locations:** Bedford NH. **Average salary range of placements:** More than $30,000. **Number of placements per year:** 1 - 49.

SNOWDEN ASSOCIATES
116 South River Road, Bedford NH 03110. 603/626-6777. **Contact:** Al Egan, Vice President. **Description:** A generalist executive search firm operating on a retainer basis. The firm focuses on placements in Northern New England, and also provides permanent placements and resume/career counseling services.

SPROUT/STANDISH, INC.
82 Palomino Lane, Suite 503, Bedford NH 03110. 603/622-0700. **Fax:** 603/622-4172. **Contact:** David A. Clark, President. **E-mail address:** ssi@printquest.com. **World Wide Web address:** http://www.printquest.com. **Description:** An executive search firm. **Specializes in the areas of:** Electronics; Packaging; Publishing. **Number of placements per year:** 50 - 99.

STAT SEARCH
PMD 204, 7 Colby Court, Unit 4, Bedford NH 03110. 603/666-5500. **Fax:** 603/623-5322. **Contact:** Dale Pouklemba, President. **Description:** An executive search firm operating on both retainer and contingency bases. **Specializes in the areas of:** Finance; Health/Medical; Managed Care; Sales. **Positions commonly filled include:** General Manager; Sales Manager; Vice President. **Corporate headquarters location:** This Location. **Other U.S. locations:** Nationwide. **Average salary range of placements:** More than $50,000. **Number of placements per year:** 1 - 49.

LINFORD E. STILES ASSOCIATES, L.L.C.
45 Newport Road, Suite 210, New London NH 03257. 603/526-6566. **Fax:** 603/526-6185. **Contact:** Manager. **E-mail address:** lstiles@lesasearch.com. **World Wide Web address:** http://www.lesasearch.com. **Description:** An executive search firm. Founded in 1991. **Specializes in the areas of:** Aerospace; Automotive; Consumer Products; Electronics; High-Tech; Manufacturing; Telecommunications.

TECHNICAL NEEDS
18 Pelham Road, Salem NH 03079. 603/893-3033. **Fax:** 603/893-7154. **Contact:** Stephen Gudek, Jr., President.

Description: An executive search firm. **Specializes in the areas of:** Engineering; Manufacturing; Technical. **Positions commonly filled include:** Buyer; Design Engineer; Designer; Draftsperson; Electrical/Electronics Engineer; Industrial Engineer; Mechanical Engineer; MIS Specialist; Purchasing Agent/Manager; Quality Control Supervisor; Software Engineer; Technical Writer/Editor. **Number of placements per year:** 100 - 199.

TRINGALI AND ASSOCIATES
501 Islington Street, Portsmouth NH 03801. 603/436-6665. **Contact:** Manager. **Description:** An executive search firm.

VENTURE PROFILES CORP.
75 Gilcreast Road, Suite 305, Londonderry NH 03053. 603/437-3300x211. **Toll-free phone:** 888/942-7552. **Fax:** 603/432-2533. **Contact:** John Peterson, Principal. **E-mail address:** venturesus@aol.com. **Description:** An executive search firm operating on both retainer and contingency bases. The firm also provides some temporary and permanent placements. **Specializes in the areas of:** Accounting; Finance. **Positions commonly filled include:** Accountant; Auditor; Budget Analyst; Chief Financial Officer; Controller; Economist; Finance Director; Financial Analyst. **Corporate headquarters location:** This Location. **Other U.S. locations:** 8 Faneuil Hall Marketplace, Third Floor, Boston MA 02109. **Average salary range of placements:** $30,000 - $100,000. **Number of placements per year:** 1 - 49.

WARREN, MORRIS & MADISON, LTD.
132 Chapel Street, Portsmouth NH 03801. 603/431-7929. **Fax:** 603/431-3460. **Contact:** Manager. **World Wide Web address:** http://www.wmmltd.com. **Description:** An executive search firm. **Specializes in the areas of:** High-Tech; Telecommunications. **Corporate headquarters location:** Del Mar CA. **Other U.S. locations:** Del Mar CA; Durham NH; Virginia Beach VA.

WARREN, MORRIS & MADISON, LTD.
44 Newmarket Road, Durham NH 03824. 603/868-6200. **Fax:** 603/868-5061. **Contact:** Branch Manager. **World Wide Web address:** http://www.wmmltd.com. **Description:** An executive search firm. **Specializes in the areas of:** Telecommunications. **Corporate headquarters location:** Del Mar CA. **Other U.S. locations:** Del Mar CA; Portsmouth NH; Virginia Beach VA.

ZYMAC INC.
EDA PLUS
46B Nashua Road, Suite 8B, Londonderry NH 03053. 603/537-0400. **Contact:** Manager. **Description:** An executive search firm. **Specializes in the areas of:** Software Development.

PERMANENT EMPLOYMENT AGENCIES

ALLSTAFF
P.O. Box 385, North Hampton NH 03862. 603/964-1780. **Toll-free phone:** 800/854-4290. **Contact:** Kris Day, Office Manager. **Description:** A permanent employment agency that also provides some temporary placements. **Specializes in the areas of:** Accounting/Auditing; Administration; Art/Design; Biology; Clerical; Computer Science/Software; Education; Engineering; Finance; Food; General Management; Health/Medical; Legal; Light Industrial; Personnel/Labor Relations; Sales; Technical. **Positions commonly filled include:** Accountant/Auditor; Budget Analyst; Claim Representative; Clerical Supervisor; Computer Programmer; Customer Service Representative; Design Engineer; Electrical/Electronics Engineer; Environmental Engineer; Financial Analyst; Hotel Manager; Human Resources Specialist; Industrial Engineer; Industrial Production Manager; Internet Services Manager; Management Analyst/Consultant; Mechanical Engineer; Medical Records Technician; MIS Specialist;

Operations/Production Manager; Property and Real Estate Manager; Public Relations Specialist; Purchasing Agent/Manager; Quality Control Supervisor; Restaurant/Food Service Manager; Software Engineer; Systems Analyst; Teacher/Professor; Technical Writer/Editor; Telecommunications Manager; Typist/Word Processor. **Other U.S. locations:** Portland ME.

BARROS ASSOCIATES
16 Route 111, Unit 4, Derry NH 03038. 603/894-0055. **Fax:** 603/894-0066. **Contact:** Daniel Barros, President. **Description:** A permanent employment agency. **Specializes in the areas of:** Communications; Computer Science/Software; Network Administration. **Positions commonly filled include:** Software Engineer. **Number of placements per year:** 1 - 49.

CCSI INC.
402 Amherst Street, Nashua NH 03063. **Toll-free phone:** 800/598-0255. **Fax:** 603/598-0055. **Contact:**

Manager. **E-mail address:** admin@ccsiinc.com. **World Wide Web address:** http://www.ccsiinc.com. **Description:** A permanent employment agency that also provides some temporary placements and contract services. Client company pays fee. **Specializes in the areas of:** Computer Science/Software; Engineering; General Management; Internet Development; Scientific; Technical. **Positions commonly filled include:** Accountant; Applications Engineer; AS400 Programmer Analyst; Biochemist; Biological Scientist; Biomedical Engineer; Buyer; Civil Engineer; Computer Animator; Computer Engineer; Computer Operator; Computer Programmer; Computer Scientist; Computer Support Technician; Computer Technician; Construction Contractor; Content Developer; Controller; Credit Manager; Database Administrator; Database Manager; Design Engineer; Draftsperson; Electrical/Electronics Engineer; Electrician; Environmental Engineer; Human Resources Manager; Industrial Engineer; Industrial Production Manager; Internet Services Manager; Management Analyst/Consultant; Management Trainee; Manufacturing Engineer; Marketing Manager; Marketing Specialist; Mechanical Engineer; Metallurgical Engineer; MIS Specialist; Multimedia Designer; Network/Systems Administrator; Operations Manager; Production Manager; Project Manager; Quality Assurance Engineer; Quality Control Supervisor; Software Engineer; SQL Programmer; Systems Analyst; Systems Manager; Telecommunications Manager; Vice President; Webmaster. **Other area locations:** 41 Bunker Hill Avenue, Stratham NH 03885. **Average salary range of placements:** $50,000 - $100,000. **Number of placements per year:** 200 - 499.

CAREER CONNECTIONS, INC.
74 Northeastern Boulevard, Unit 17, Nashua NH 03062. 603/880-7184. **Fax:** 603/880-5460. **Contact:** Linda Piper, CPC/President. **E-mail address:** jobs4u@ careerconnectionsnh.com. **World Wide Web address:** http://www.careerconnectionsnh.com. **Description:** A permanent employment agency. **Specializes in the areas of:** Accounting/Auditing; Legal; Marketing; Personnel/Labor Relations; Sales; Secretarial. **Positions commonly filled include:** Account Representative; Accountant; Administrative Assistant; Human Resources Manager; Sales Manager; Sales Representative; Secretary; Typist/Word Processor; Underwriter/Assistant Underwriter.

CENTRAL NEW HAMPSHIRE EMPLOYMENT SERVICES
25 Beacon Street East, Suite 201, Laconia NH 03246. 603/528-2828. **Toll-free phone:** 800/256-2482. **Fax:** 603/528-6625. **Contact:** Christine St. Cyr, Vice President. **Description:** A permanent employment agency that also provides some temporary placements. **Specializes in the areas of:** Accounting/Auditing; Administration; Banking; Computer Science/Software; Engineering; Finance; Health/Medical; Insurance; Legal; Manufacturing; Personnel/Labor Relations; Sales; Secretarial. **Positions commonly filled include:** Accountant/Auditor; Aerospace Engineer; Architect; Bank Officer/Manager; Bookkeeper; Civil Engineer; Clerk; Computer Programmer; Credit Manager; Customer Service Representative; Data Entry Clerk; Draftsperson; EDP Specialist; Electrical/Electronics Engineer; Hotel Manager; Human Resources Manager; Industrial Designer; Legal Secretary; Mechanical Engineer; Medical Secretary; Metallurgical Engineer; Receptionist; Sales Representative; Secretary; Systems Analyst; Typist/Word Processor; Underwriter/Assistant Underwriter. **Other area locations:** Concord NH. **Average salary range of placements:** $20,000 - $29,999. **Number of placements per year:** 500 - 999.

EMERALD LEGAL SEARCH
22 Eastman Avenue, Bedford NH 03110. 603/623-5300. **Contact:** Manager. **Description:** A permanent employment agency. **Specializes in the areas of:** Legal.

EXETER 2100
Computer Park, P.O. Box 2120, Hampton NH 03843. 603/926-6712. **Fax:** 603/926-0536. **Contact:** Bruce Montville, Managing Partner. **Description:** A permanent

employment agency. **Specializes in the areas of:** Computer Science/Software; Information Systems. **Positions commonly filled include:** Computer Programmer; EDP Specialist; Software Engineer.

HITCHCOCK STAFFING
One Middle Street, Portsmouth NH 03801. 603/566-5628. **Toll-free phone:** 800/867-9188. **Fax:** 603/566-5627. **Contact:** Office Manager. **E-mail address:** jobs@hitchcockstaffing.com. **World Wide Web address:** http://www.hitchcockstaffing.com. **Description:** A permanent employment agency that also provides some temporary and contract placements. Client company pays fee. **Specializes in the areas of:** Administration; Computer Science/Software; MIS/EDP; Scientific; Technical. **Positions commonly filled include:** Account Manager; Administrative Assistant; Administrative Manager; Applications Engineer; AS400 Programmer Analyst; Branch Manager; Computer Engineer; Computer Programmer; Computer Support Technician; Computer Technician; Database Administrator; Database Manager; Desktop Publishing Specialist; Electrical/Electronics Engineer; General Manager; Human Resources Manager; Marketing Manager; Mechanical Engineer; MIS Specialist; Network/Systems Administrator; Operations Manager; Production Manager; Project Manager; Quality Assurance Engineer; Quality Control Supervisor; Sales Executive; Sales Manager; Sales Representative; Software Engineer; SQL Programmer; Systems Analyst; Technical Writer/Editor. **Average salary range of placements:** $30,000 - $49,999. **Number of placements per year:** 1 - 49.

INDIVIDUAL EMPLOYMENT SERVICES (IES)
P.O. Box 917, Dover NH 03821. 603/742-5616. **Contact:** Manager. **Description:** A permanent placement agency that also provides some career counseling, testing, and resume writing services. **Specializes in the areas of:** Administration; Business Services; Computer Programming; Payroll; Sales.

KENDA SYSTEMS
One Stiles Road, Suite 106, Salem NH 03079. 603/898-7884. **Contact:** Manager. **Description:** A permanent employment agency that also provides some temporary placements. **Specializes in the areas of:** Computer Science/Software. **Positions commonly filled include:** Consultant; Software Engineer. **Corporate headquarters location:** This Location.

KEY PARTNERS, INC.
216 Lafayette Road, North Hampton NH 03862. 603/964-9495. **Fax:** 603/964-4219. **Contact:** Manager. **E-mail address:** info@keypartnersinc.com. **World Wide Web address:** http://www.keypartnersinc.com. **Description:** A permanent employment agency that also provides some temporary placements. **Specializes in the areas of:** Accounting/Auditing; Administration; Computer Science/Software; Secretarial; Technical. **Positions commonly filled include:** Account Manager; Account Representative; Accountant; Administrative Assistant; Administrative Manager; Applications Engineer; Assistant Manager; Branch Manager; Budget Analyst; Buyer; Chemical Engineer; Chemist; Chief Financial Officer; Claim Representative; Clerical Supervisor; Clinical Lab Technician; Computer Operator; Computer Programmer; Controller; Credit Manager; Customer Service Representative; Database Manager; Project Manager; Secretary; Software Engineer; Systems Analyst; Systems Manager; Typist/Word Processor. **Benefits available to temporary workers:** Computer Training; Medical Insurance; Paid Holidays; Paid Vacation; Retirement Plan.

KOGEN PERSONNEL
P.O. Box 10154, Bedford NH 03110. 603/472-3303. **Contact:** Office Manager. **Description:** Kogen Personnel is a permanent employment agency. **Specializes in the areas of:** Accounting; Insurance; Legal.

ROGER MACON AND ASSOCIATES
11 North Mast Road, Goffstown NH 03045. 603/497-2704. **Contact:** Manager. **Description:** A permanent employment agency. **Specializes in the areas of:** Plastics; Technical.

NATIONAL EMPLOYMENT SERVICE CORPORATION
95 Albany Street, Suite 3, Portsmouth NH 03801. 603/427-0125. **Toll-free phone:** 800/367-5696x368. **Fax:** 603/427-1411. **Contact:** Contract Manager. **World Wide Web address:** http://www.nationalemployment.com. **Description:** A permanent employment agency. Founded in 1992. **Specializes in the areas of:** Accounting/Auditing; Administration; Architecture/Construction; Banking; Computer Science/Software; Economics; Engineering; Finance; Food; General Management; Health/Medical; Industrial; Manufacturing; Personnel/Labor Relations; Retail; Sales; Transportation. **Corporate headquarters location:** This Location. **Other U.S. locations:** Nashua NH. **Average salary range of placements:** $30,000 - $50,000. **Number of placements per year:** 1000+.

PERSONNEL CONNECTION
24 Airport Road, Unit 15, West Lebanon NH 03784. 603/298-5558. **Contact:** Manager. **Description:** A permanent employment agency that also provides some temporary placements.

PROFESSIONAL RECRUITERS INC.
40 South River Road, Unit 51, Bedford NH 03110. 603/644-0909. **Fax:** 603/644-0993. **Contact:** Timothy E. Moran, CPC/CEO. **Description:** A permanent employment agency. **Specializes in the areas of:** Accounting/Auditing; Banking; Computer Science/Software; Network Administration; Personnel/Labor Relations; Technical. **Positions commonly filled include:** Accountant/Auditor; Bank Officer/Manager; Branch Manager; Budget Analyst; Computer Programmer; Credit Manager; Financial Analyst; Software Engineer; Systems Analyst. **Average salary range of placements:** More than $50,000. **Number of placements per year:** 1000+.

REARDON ASSOCIATES
22 Greeley Street, Suite 8A, Merrimack NH 03054. 603/429-1777. **Contact:** Manager. **Description:** A permanent employment agency.

RESOURCE RECRUITING CONTEMPORARY ACCOUNTANTS
547 Amherst Street, Nashua NH 03063. 603/595-2822. **Fax:** 603/886-1822. **Contact:** Robert C. Harrington, Executive Vice President. **Description:** A permanent employment agency. **Specializes in the areas of:** Accounting/Auditing; Administration; Banking; Computer Science/Software; Legal; Manufacturing; Operations Management; Sales; Secretarial. **Positions commonly filled include:** Accountant/Auditor; Bookkeeper; Chief Financial Officer; Clerk; Collections Agent; Controller; Credit Manager; Manager of

Information Systems; Payroll Clerk; Secretary. **Average salary range of placements:** $30,000 - $50,000. **Number of placements per year:** 50 - 99.

SOFTWARE NETWORKS INC.
125 Main Street, Suite A, Newmarket NH 03857. 603/659-1000. **Fax:** 603/359-1005. **Contact:** Dan Craig, President. **Description:** A permanent employment agency. Founded in 1990. **Specializes in the areas of:** Communications; Computer Science/Software. **Positions commonly filled include:** Computer Programmer; Design Engineer; Electrical/Electronics Engineer; Software Engineer. **Average salary range of placements:** More than $50,000. **Number of placements per year:** 50 - 99.

TECH/AID OF NEW HAMPSHIRE
71 Spit Brook Road, Suite 102, Nashua NH 03060. 603/891-4100. **Contact:** Recruiter. **Description:** A permanent employment agency. **Specializes in the areas of:** Architecture/Construction; Cable TV; Computer Hardware/Software; Construction; Engineering; Manufacturing; Technical. **Positions commonly filled include:** Aerospace Engineer; Architectural Engineer; Buyer; Ceramics Engineer; Chemical Engineer; Civil Engineer; Draftsperson; Electrical/Electronics Engineer; Estimator; Industrial Designer; Mechanical Engineer; Metallurgical Engineer; Mining Engineer; Operations/Production Manager; Petroleum Engineer; Purchasing Agent/Manager; Quality Control Supervisor; Technical Writer/Editor; Technician. **Number of placements per year:** 1000+.

TECHNICAL DIRECTIONS, INC. (TDI)
78 Northeastern Boulevard, Suite 2B, Nashua NH 03062. 603/880-6720. **Fax:** 603/880-7859. **Contact:** Jeff Barsanti, Recruiter. **E-mail address:** jeff@tditech.com. **Description:** A permanent employment agency. **Specializes in the areas of:** Administration; Computer Hardware/Software; Engineering; Sales; Technical. **Positions commonly filled include:** Aerospace Engineer; Biomedical Engineer; Computer Programmer; EDP Specialist; Electrical/Electronics Engineer; Industrial Engineer; Marketing Specialist; Mechanical Engineer; Metallurgical Engineer; MIS Specialist; Systems Analyst; Technical Writer/Editor.

THOMAS & KAVANAUGH
277 Harmony Road, Northwood NH 03261. 603/942-5800. **Fax:** 603/225-5516. **Contact:** Robert Thomas, President. **Description:** A permanent employment agency. **Specializes in the areas of:** Accounting/Auditing; Banking. **Positions commonly filled include:** Account Representative; Construction Contractor; Structural Engineer. **Number of placements per year:** 1 - 49.

VISIONS PERSONNEL
33 Main Street, Suite 400, Nashua NH 03060. 603/883-5897. **Contact:** Manager. **Description:** A permanent placement agency. **Specializes in the areas of:** Hotel/Restaurant; Management.

TEMPORARY EMPLOYMENT AGENCIES

BENETEMPS INC.
59 Stiles Road, Suite 204, Salem NH 03079. 603/893-7472. **Contact:** Robert Spiegelman, President/Owner. **Description:** A temporary agency. **Specializes in the areas of:** Consulting; Personnel/Labor Relations. **Positions commonly filled include:** Actuary; Human Resources Specialist. **Benefits available to temporary workers:** 401(k); Life Insurance; Medical Insurance. **Average salary range of placements:** $30,000 - $100,000. **Number of placements per year:** 50 - 99.

CDI CORPORATION
Northridge Business Center, 74 Northeastern Boulevard, Suite 21A, Nashua NH 03062. 603/883-0705. **Fax:** 603/883-9973. **Contact:** Manager. **World Wide Web**

address: http://www.cdicorp.com. **Description:** A temporary agency that also provides contract services. **Specializes in the areas of:** Engineering; Scientific; Technical. **Positions commonly filled include:** Architect; Chemical Engineer; Civil Engineer; Design Engineer; Desktop Publishing Specialist; Draftsperson; Editor; Electrical/Electronics Engineer; Electrician; Environmental Engineer; Graphic Artist; Graphic Designer; Industrial Engineer; Manufacturing Engineer; Mechanical Engineer; Purchasing Agent/Manager; Quality Assurance Engineer; Technical Writer/Editor; Telecommunications Manager. **Benefits available to temporary workers:** 401(k); Dental Insurance; Health Benefits; Vision Plan. **Corporate headquarters location:** Philadelphia PA. **Other U.S. locations:**

Nationwide. **Average salary range of placements:** $30,000 - $100,000. **Number of placements per year:** 100 - 199.

CHESHIRE EMPLOYMENT SERVICE
800 Park Avenue, Keene NH 03431. 603/357-3400. **Fax:** 603/357-3406. **Contact:** Office Manager. **Description:** A temporary agency that also provides some permanent placements. **Specializes in the areas of:** Accounting/ Auditing; Administration; Advertising; Banking; Computer Science/Software; Engineering; Finance; General Management; Manufacturing; Personnel/Labor Relations; Publishing; Secretarial. **Average salary range of placements:** $20,000 - $29,999. **Number of placements per year:** 50 - 99.

GFI PROFESSIONAL STAFFING SERVICES
127 Washington Street, Keene NH 03431. 603/357-3116. **Fax:** 603/357-7818. **Contact:** Manager. **Description:** A temporary employment agency that also provides temp-to-hire and permanent placements. **Specializes in the areas of:** Administration; Data Processing; Marketing; Office Support; Purchasing.

KELLY SERVICES, INC.
6 Bedford Farms, Bedford NH 03110. 603/625-6457. **Contact:** Supervisor. **Description:** A temporary agency. **Specializes in the areas of:** Clerical; Industrial; Sales; Technical.

KELLY SERVICES, INC.
385 East Dunstable Road, Nashua NH 03062. 603/888-8180. **Toll-free phone:** 888/785-3559. **Fax:** 603/891-2575. **Contact:** Mercedes Cernuda, Supervisor. **Description:** A temporary agency. **Specializes in the areas of:** Accounting; Banking; Computer Science/ Software; Finance; General Management; Health/ Medical; Industrial; Insurance; Light Industrial; Personnel/Labor Relations; Secretarial. **Positions commonly filled include:** Administrative Assistant; Customer Service Representative; Secretary; Typist/Word Processor. **Benefits available to temporary workers:** Computer Training; Paid Holidays; Referral Bonus Plan; Vacation Pay.

MANPOWER TEMPORARY SERVICES
410 Amherst Street, Suite 349, Nashua NH 03063. 603/882-0015. **Contact:** Rosemary Gelinas, Manager. **Description:** A temporary agency. **Specializes in the areas of:** Accounting/Auditing; Banking; Food; General Management; Industrial; Insurance; Legal; Light Industrial; Marketing; Nonprofit; Retail; Sales; Secretarial; Technical. **Positions commonly filled include:** Administrative Assistant; Clerical Supervisor; Computer Operator; Customer Service Representative; Graphic Artist; Secretary; Typist/Word Processor. **Benefits available to temporary workers:** Life Insurance; Medical Insurance; Paid Holidays; Paid Vacation. **Corporate headquarters location:** Milwaukee WI.

MANPOWER TEMPORARY SERVICES
18 North Main Street, Concord NH 03301. 603/224-7115. **Contact:** Branch Manager. **Description:** A temporary agency. **Specializes in the areas of:** Data Processing; Light Industrial; Office Support; Technical; Word Processing. **Positions commonly filled include:** Accountant/Auditor; Accounting Clerk; Administrative Assistant; Assembler; Biological Scientist; Bookkeeper; Chemist; Computer Operator; Customer Service Representative; Designer; Desktop Publishing Specialist; Electrician; Inspector/Tester/Grader; Inventory Control Specialist; Machine Operator; Material Control Specialist; Packaging/Processing Worker; Painter;

Project Engineer; Proofreader; Receptionist; Records Manager; Research Assistant; Secretary; Software Engineer; Stenographer; Systems Analyst; Technical Writer/Editor; Technician; Telemarketer; Typist/Word Processor. **Benefits available to temporary workers:** Life Insurance; Medical Insurance; Paid Holidays; Paid Vacation. **Corporate headquarters location:** Milwaukee WI. **Number of placements per year:** 1000+.

OLSTEN STAFFING SERVICES
1750 Elm Street, Suite 502, Manchester NH 03104. 603/668-3334. **Toll-free phone:** 800/355-3334. **Fax:** 603/668-5785. **Contact:** Manager. **Description:** A temporary agency. **Specializes in the areas of:** Administration; Light Industrial; Office Support. **Positions commonly filled include:** Buyer; Human Resources Specialist; Paralegal; Purchasing Agent/Manager; Quality Control Supervisor; Typist/Word Processor. **Benefits available to temporary workers:** Paid Vacation. **Corporate headquarters location:** Melville NY. **Other U.S. locations:** Nationwide. **Average salary range of placements:** Less than $20,000. **Number of placements per year:** 1000+.

PELHAM PROFESSIONAL GROUP, INC.
339 Main Street, Nashua NH 03060. 603/882-6433. **Fax:** 603/882-5045. **Contact:** Office Manager. **Description:** A temporary agency. **Specializes in the areas of:** Administration; Food; Manufacturing; Retail; Secretarial; Technical. **Positions commonly filled include:** Clerical Supervisor; Customer Service Representative; Draftsperson; Electrical/Electronics Engineer; Industrial Production Manager; Mechanical Engineer; Purchasing Agent/Manager; Quality Control Supervisor; Typist/Word Processor. **Corporate headquarters location:** North Andover MA. **Number of placements per year:** 500 - 999.

TAC STAFFING SERVICES
One Trafalgar Square, Nashua NH 03063. 603/882-4200. **Fax:** 603/889-3572. **Contact:** Jim O'Neill, Office Manager. **Description:** A temporary agency. **Specializes in the areas of:** Accounting/Auditing; Banking; Clerical; Finance; Insurance; Light Industrial; Manufacturing; Retail; Sales; Secretarial; Transportation. **Positions commonly filled include:** Accountant; Administrative Assistant; Blue-Collar Worker Supervisor; Buyer; Claim Representative; Clerical Supervisor; Computer Operator; Customer Service Representative; Management Trainee; Purchasing Agent/Manager; Quality Control Supervisor; Sales Representative; Secretary; Telecommunications Manager; Typist/Word Processor; Underwriter/Assistant Underwriter. **Benefits available to temporary workers:** Computer Training. **Corporate headquarters location:** Newton MA. **Other U.S. locations:** Nationwide. **Average salary range of placements:** $20,000 - $29,999. **Number of placements per year:** 1000+.

TRI-STATE PROFESSIONALS
53 Marlboro Street, Keene NH 03431. 603/352-4155. **Toll-free phone:** 800/227-3577. **Fax:** 603/357-7701. **Contact:** Recruiter. **E-mail address:** tristateprofess@monad.net. **Description:** A temporary agency. Founded in 1987. **Specializes in the areas of:** Engineering; Technical. **Positions commonly filled include:** Certified Nurses Aide; Design Engineer; Draftsperson; Electrical/Electronics Engineer; Electrician; Industrial Engineer; Licensed Practical Nurse; Mechanical Engineer; Registered Nurse; Secretary; Technical Writer/Editor; Typist/Word Processor.

CONTRACT SERVICES FIRMS

AFFORDABLE SOLUTIONS
114 Perimeter Road, Suite D, Nashua NH 03063-1301. 603/880-4300. **Fax:** 603/880-0639. **Contact:** Thomas M.

Tate, Vice President. **Description:** A contract services firm. **Specializes in the areas of:** Engineering; Industrial; Manufacturing; Sales. **Positions commonly**

filled include: Buyer; Computer Programmer; Design Engineer; Designer; Draftsperson; Electrical/Electronics Engineer; Electrician; Mechanical Engineer; Purchasing Agent/Manager; Quality Control Supervisor; Software Engineer; Structural Engineer; Technical Writer/Editor; Telecommunications Manager. **Number of placements per year:** 200 - 499.

AMBIT TECHNOLOGY
2 Keewaydin Drive, Salem NH 03079. 603/893-6776. **Fax:** 603/893-4208. **Contact:** Recruiter. **Description:** A contract services firm. **Specializes in the areas of:** Computer Science/Software; Engineering; Information Technology. **Positions commonly filled include:** Computer Programmer; Internet Services Manager; Mining Engineer; MIS Specialist; Multimedia Designer; Nuclear Engineer; Quality Control Supervisor; Software Engineer; Systems Analyst; Technical Writer/Editor; Telecommunications Manager. **Other U.S. locations:** Boston MA; Rye NH; Cincinnati OH. **Number of placements per year:** 1000+.

AVAILABILITY CONTRACT SERVICE
169 South River Road, Suite 11-12, Nashua NH 03060. 603/669-4440. **Contact:** Manager. **Description:** A contract services firm that also offers some permanent placement services. Founded in 1968. **Specializes in the areas of:** Engineering; Manufacturing.

CUSTOM SOFTWARE SERVICES, INC.
P.O. Box 7587, Nashua NH 03060-7587. 603/888-8861. **Contact:** Manager. **Description:** A contract services firm. **Positions commonly filled include:** Computer Programmer; Electrical/Electronics Engineer; Systems Analyst. **Average salary range of placements:** $30,000 - $50,000. **Number of placements per year:** 1 - 49.

NORRELL SERVICES
630 Sheffield Road, Manchester NH 03103. 603/624-4220. **Fax:** 603/625-2980. **Contact:** Customer Service Specialist. **Description:** A contract services firm that also provides some temporary placements. **Benefits available to temporary workers:** Dental Insurance; Medical Insurance; Paid Holidays; Paid Vacation. **Corporate headquarters location:** Atlanta GA. **Other U.S. locations:** Nationwide. **Average salary range of placements:** Less than $20,000. **Number of placements per year:** 200 - 499.

SURGE RESOURCES INC.
136 Harvey Road, Londonderry NH 03053-7401. 603/623-0007. **Toll-free phone:** 800/SURGEUSA . **Fax:** 603/624-7007. **Contact:** Recruiter. **Description:** A contract services firm that also provides some temporary and permanent job placements. **Specializes in the areas of:** Accounting/Auditing; Administration; Architecture/Construction; Art/Design; Computer Science/Software; Economics; Education; Engineering; Finance; General Management; Industrial; Manufacturing; Nonprofit; Personnel/Labor Relations; Retail; Sales. **Positions commonly filled include:** Accountant/Auditor; Aerospace Engineer; Architect; Bank Officer/Manager; Blue-Collar Worker Supervisor; Civil Engineer; Clerical Supervisor; Computer Programmer; Construction and Building Inspector; Cost Estimator; Customer Service Representative; Design Engineer; Editor; Insurance Agent/Broker; Mechanical Engineer; MIS Specialist; Paralegal; Purchasing Agent/Manager; Quality Control Supervisor; Services Sales Representative; Software Engineer; Systems Analyst; Telecommunications Manager; Typist/Word Processor. **Benefits available to temporary workers:** 401(k); Dental Insurance; Medical Insurance. **Average salary range of placements:** $30,000 - $50,000. **Number of placements per year:** 1000+.

TECHNICAL EMPLOYMENT SERVICES INC.
127 Main Street, Suite 16, Nashua NH 03060. 603/881-8622. **Contact:** Dan Duncanson, President. **Description:** A contract services firm. Founded in 1992. **Specializes in the areas of:** Design; Engineering. **Positions commonly filled include:** Aerospace Engineer; Blue-Collar Worker Supervisor; Chemical Engineer; Civil Engineer; Computer Programmer; Design Engineer; Designer; Draftsperson; Electrical/Electronics Engineer; Environmental Engineer; Industrial Engineer; Industrial Production Manager; Internet Services Manager; Machinist; Mechanical Engineer; MIS Specialist; Operations/Production Manager; Petroleum Engineer; Science Technologist; Software Engineer; Structural Engineer; Systems Analyst; Technical Writer/Editor; Telecommunications Manager. **Benefits available to temporary workers:** Medical Insurance; Paid Holidays. **Average salary range of placements:** $30,000 - $50,000. **Number of placements per year:** 100 - 199.

CAREER/OUTPLACEMENT COUNSELING FIRMS

CAREERPRO
76 Jenkins Road, Bedford NH 03110. 603/471-1222. **Contact:** Office Manager. **Description:** A career/outplacement counseling service.

AES ASSOCIATES
One Kalisa Way, Suite 103, Paramus NJ 07652. 201/261-1600. **Toll-free phone:** 800/545-4518. **Fax:** 201/261-4343. **Contact:** Manager. **E-mail address:** aesnj@aol.com. **World Wide Web address:** http://aesrecruiting.com. **Description:** An executive search firm. **Specializes in the areas of:** Accounting; Administration; Architecture/Construction; Art/Design; Banking; Biology; Computer Science/Software; Engineering; Finance; Health/Medical; Information Systems; Information Technology; Insurance; Marketing; Sales. **Positions commonly filled include:** Account Manager; Account Representative; Accountant; Adjuster; Administrative Assistant; Applications Engineer; AS400 Programmer Analyst; Attorney; Auditor; Bank Officer/ Manager; Biochemist; Biological Scientist; Biomedical Engineer; Budget Analyst; Certified Occupational Therapy Assistant; Chemical Engineer; Chemist; Chief Financial Officer; Civil Engineer; Claim Representative; Clinical Lab Technician; Computer Animator; Computer Engineer; Computer Operator; Computer Programmer; Computer Scientist; Computer Support Technician; Computer Technician; Content Developer; Controller; Cost Estimator; Credit Manager; Database Administrator; Database Manager; Design Engineer; Draftsperson; Economist; Education Administrator; Electrical/Electronics Engineer; Environmental Engineer; ESL Teacher; Finance Director; Financial Analyst; Food Scientist/Technologist; Fund Manager; General Manager; Graphic Artist; Human Resources Manager; Industrial Engineer; Industrial Production Manager; Instructional Technologist; Insurance Agent/Broker; Internet Services Manager; Librarian; Management Analyst/Consultant; Management Trainee; Manufacturing Engineer; Mechanical Engineer; Metallurgical Engineer; MIS Manager; Multimedia Designer; Network/Systems Administrator; Occupational Therapist; Operations Manager; Physical Therapist; Physical Therapy Assistant; Physician; Preschool Worker; Production Manager; Project Manager; Purchasing Agent/Manager; Quality Assurance Engineer; Quality Control Supervisor; Sales Engineer; Sales Executive; Sales Manager; Sales Representative; Secretary; Social Worker; Software Engineer; Special Education Teacher; Speech-Language Pathologist; SQL Programmer; Systems Analyst; Systems Engineer; Teacher/Professor; Underwriter/ Assistant Underwriter; Webmaster.

ALS GROUP
104 Mount Joy Road, Milford NJ 08848. 908/995-9500. **Fax:** 908/995-7032. **Contact:** Scott Lysenko, President. **E-mail address:** alsgroup@webspan.net. **Description:** An executive search firm. **Specializes in the areas of:** Banking; Finance.

AUX TECHNOLOGY INC.
One Exchange Place, Suite 713, Jersey City NJ 07302. 201/332-6500. **Contact:** Manager. **Description:** An executive search firm. **NOTE:** This firm does not accept unsolicited resumes. Please only respond to advertised openings. **Specializes in the areas of:** Information Technology.

AV SEARCH CONSULTANTS
674 Route 202/206, Bridgewater NJ 08807. 908/429-7800. **Contact:** Manager. **Description:** An executive search firm. **Specializes in the areas of:** Legal.

ABBOTT ASSOCIATES INC.
1099 Wall Street West, Suite 214, Lyndhurst NJ 07071. 201/804-8100. **Contact:** Manager. **Description:** An executive search firm. **Specializes in the areas of:** Accounting/Auditing; Finance.

ABLE CAREERS
240 West Passaic Street, Maywood NJ 07607. 201/845-7771. **Fax:** 201/845-7954. **Contact:** Manager. **Description:** An executive search firm.

ACCESS SYSTEMS
101 Gibraltar Drive, Suite 2F, Morris Plains NJ 07950-1287. 973/984-7960. **Fax:** 973/984-7963. **Contact:** Joanne Palzer, President. **Description:** An executive search firm operating on a contingency basis. Access Systems focuses on the placement of high-level sales and technical sales support professionals. **Specializes in the areas of:** Computer Science/Software; Data Communications; Sales. **Positions commonly filled include:** Manufacturer's/Wholesaler's Sales Rep.; Services Sales Representative. **Average salary range of placements:** More than $50,000. **Number of placements per year:** 1 - 49.

ACCOUNTANTS EXECUTIVE SEARCH
Princeton Forrestal Village, 125 Village Boulevard, Princeton NJ 08540. 609/452-7117. **Fax:** 609/987-0681. **Contact:** Manager. **Description:** An executive search firm. **Specializes in the areas of:** Accounting.

ACCOUNTANTS EXECUTIVE SEARCH
30 Montgomery Street, Suite 620, Jersey City NJ 07302. 201/333-4227. **Fax:** 201/333-4248. **Contact:** Manager. **Description:** An executive search firm. **Specializes in the areas of:** Accounting.

ACCOUNTANTS EXECUTIVE SEARCH
ACCOUNTANTS ON CALL
80 Route 4 East, Suite 230, Paramus NJ 07652. 201/368-9200. **Contact:** Manager. **Description:** An executive search firm. Accountants On Call (also at this location) offers temporary placements. **Specializes in the areas of:** Accounting/Auditing; Banking; Finance.

ACCOUNTANTS EXECUTIVE SEARCH
ACCOUNTANTS ON CALL
379 Thornall Street, Edison NJ 08837. 732/906-1100. **Contact:** Manager. **Description:** An executive search firm. Accountants On Call (also at this location) provides temporary placements. **Specializes in the areas of:** Accounting/Auditing.

ACCOUNTANTS EXECUTIVE SEARCH
ACCOUNTANTS ON CALL
72 Eagle Rock Avenue, East Hanover NJ 07936. 973/533-0600. **Fax:** 973/781-0658. **Contact:** Manager. **Description:** An executive search firm. Accountants On Call (also at this location) provides temporary placements. **Specializes in the areas of:** Accounting/Auditing; Finance.

ACCOUNTANTS PROFESSIONAL SEARCH
114 Essex Street, Rochelle Park NJ 07662. 201/288-2888. **Contact:** Manager. **Description:** An executive search firm. **Specializes in the areas of:** Accounting/Auditing.

ADECCO/TAD TECHNICAL SERVICES
100 Menlo Park, Suite 302, Edison NJ 08837. 732/452-0438. **Fax:** 732/452-0512. **Contact:** Manager. **Description:** An executive search firm. **Specializes in the areas of:** Technical.

ADEL-LAWRENCE ASSOCIATES
1208 Highway 34, Suite 18, Aberdeen NJ 07747. 732/566-4914. **Fax:** 732/566-9326. **Contact:** Larry Radzely, President. **E-mail address:** info@adel-lawrence.com. **World Wide Web address:** http://www.adel-lawrence.com. **Description:** An executive search firm. Client company pays fee. **Specializes in the areas of:** Computer Science/Software; Engineering; Health/Medical; Technical. **Positions commonly filled include:** Biomedical Engineer; Computer Engineer; Computer Support Technician; Computer Technician; Design Engineer; Electrical/Electronics Engineer; Manufacturing Engineer; Mechanical Engineer; MIS Specialist; Software

Engineer; Systems Analyst; Telecommunications Manager. **Average salary range of placements:** $50,000 - $100,000. **Number of placements per year:** 200 - 499.

ADVANCE POSITIONS INC.
P.O. Box 346, Marlboro NJ 07746. 732/577-1122. **Contact:** President. **Description:** An executive search firm. **Specializes in the areas of:** Food; General Management; Logistics; Retail; Transportation. **Positions commonly filled include:** Buyer; Distribution Manager; Industrial Engineer; Logistics Manager; Operations/Production Manager; Purchasing Agent/Manager; Transportation/Traffic Specialist. **Number of placements per year:** 1 - 49.

ADVANCED TECHNOLOGY SEARCH
414 Eagle Rock Avenue, Suites 302 & 306, West Orange NJ 07052. 973/669-0400. **Contact:** Manager. **Description:** An executive search firm. **Specializes in the areas of:** Wireless Communications.

ALLEN ASSOCIATES, INC.
128 Elliot Place, South Plainfield NJ 07080. 908/753-3751. **Contact:** Manager. **Description:** An executive search firm.

ALLEN THOMAS ASSOCIATES
518 Prospect Avenue, Little Silver NJ 07739. 732/219-5353. **Fax:** 732/219-5805. **Contact:** Tom Benoit, President. **E-mail address:** recruit@allenthomas.com. **World Wide Web address:** http://www.allenthomas.com. **Description:** An executive search firm operating on a contingency basis. **Specializes in the areas of:** Health/Medical. **Positions commonly filled include:** Pharmacist; Physician; Sales Manager. **Average salary range of placements:** More than $50,000.

ALTA ASSOCIATES
8 Bartles Corner Road, Suite 021, Flemington NJ 08822. 908/806-8442. **Fax:** 908/806-8443. **Contact:** Joyce Brocaglia, Vice President. **E-mail address:** search@altaassociates.com. **World Wide Web address:** http://www.altaassociates.com. **Description:** An executive search firm specializing in information security, cryptography, and electronic business. Alta Associates also offers some consulting services. **Specializes in the areas of:** Computer Hardware/Software. **Positions commonly filled include:** Computer Programmer; Database Manager; EDP Specialist; MIS Specialist. **Number of placements per year:** 50 - 99.

ANDERSON WRIGHT ASSOCIATES
375 Johnson Avenue Annex, Englewood NJ 07631. 201/567-8080. **Contact:** Manager. **Description:** An executive search firm operating on both retainer and contingency bases. **Specializes in the areas of:** Banking; Finance; Pharmaceuticals; Research and Development.

ANDOS ASSOCIATES INC.
2 Stone House Road, Mendham NJ 07945. 201/934-7766. **Contact:** Manager. **Description:** An executive search firm. **Specializes in the areas of:** Pharmaceuticals.

R.W. APPLE & ASSOCIATES
P.O. Box 200, Manasquan NJ 08736. 732/223-4305. **Fax:** 732/223-4325. **Contact:** Richard Apple, Owner. **Description:** An executive search firm operating on a retainer basis. **Specializes in the areas of:** Engineering; Environmental. **Positions commonly filled include:** Chemical Engineer; Civil Engineer; Environmental Engineer; Geologist/Geophysicist. **Average salary range of placements:** More than $50,000. **Number of placements per year:** 1 - 49.

THE ASCHER GROUP
7 Becker Farm Road, Roseland NJ 07068. 973/597-1900. **Contact:** Personnel. **Description:** An executive search firm that also provides some temporary placements. **Specializes in the areas of:** Accounting/Auditing;

Finance; Personnel/Labor Relations; Secretarial. **Positions commonly filled include:** Accountant/Auditor; Bank Officer/Manager; Budget Analyst; Credit Manager; EKG Technician; Financial Analyst; Human Resources Specialist; Purchasing Agent/Manager; Typist/Word Processor. **Number of placements per year:** 1000+.

ASSURANCE GROUP
P.O. Box 465, Morris Plains NJ 07950. 973/538-7594. **Contact:** Manager. **Description:** An executive search firm. **Specializes in the areas of:** Health/Medical.

ASSURANCE GROUP
ASSURANCE HEALTH CARE SERVICES
25 East Spring Valley Avenue, Maywood NJ 07607. 201/845-4461. **Contact:** Manager. **Description:** An executive search firm. Assurance Health Care Services (also at this location) places home health care professionals. **Specializes in the areas of:** Health/Medical.

BAKER SCOTT & COMPANY
1259 U.S. Highway 46, Suite 1, Parsippany NJ 07054. 973/263-3355. **Fax:** 973/263-9255. **Contact:** Judy Bouer, Principal. **Description:** An executive search firm. **Specializes in the areas of:** Cable TV; Telecommunications.

BARCLAY CONSULTANTS
201 Union Lane, Brielle NJ 08730. 732/223-1131. **Contact:** Manager. **Description:** An executive search firm that specializes in placing computer sales professionals. **Specializes in the areas of:** Sales.

R.P. BARONE ASSOCIATES
3121 Atlantic Avenue, P.O. Box 706, Allenwood NJ 08720. 732/292-0900. **Contact:** L. Donald Rizzo, President. **Description:** An executive search firm operating on both retainer and contingency bases. **Specializes in the areas of:** Engineering; Manufacturing; Marketing. **Positions commonly filled include:** Architect; Biochemist; Biomedical Engineer; Chemical Engineer; Chemist; Civil Engineer; Construction and Building Inspector; Cost Estimator; Design Engineer; Draftsperson; Electrical/Electronics Engineer; Environmental Engineer; Food Scientist/Technologist; General Manager; Industrial Engineer; Industrial Production Manager; Market Research Analyst; Mechanical Engineer; Metallurgical Engineer; Operations/Production Manager; Purchasing Agent/Manager; Science Technologist; Structural Engineer. **Average salary range of placements:** More than $50,000. **Number of placements per year:** 1 - 49.

BATTALIA WINSTON INTERNATIONAL
379 Thornall Street, 10th Floor, Edison NJ 08837. 732/549-2002. **Fax:** 732/549-8443. **Contact:** Recruiter. **World Wide Web address:** http://www.battaliawinston.com. **Description:** An executive search firm. **Specializes in the areas of:** Consumer Products; Finance; Health/Medical; Industrial; Nonprofit; Professional; Technical. **Other U.S. locations:** Los Angeles CA; San Francisco CA; Chicago IL; Boston MA; New York NY.

GARY S. BELL ASSOCIATES, INC.
55 Harristown Road, Glen Rock NJ 07452. 201/670-4900. **Fax:** 201/670-4940. **Contact:** Gary S. Bell, President. **E-mail address:** gsbassoc@aol.com. **Description:** An executive search firm. **Specializes in the areas of:** Biology; Biotechnology; Chemicals; Clinical Research; Engineering; Environmental; General Management; Health/Medical; Manufacturing; Pharmaceuticals. **Positions commonly filled include:** Biochemist; Biological Scientist; Biomedical Engineer; Chemical Engineer; Chemist; Computer Programmer; Design Engineer; Electrical/Electronics Engineer; Licensed Practical Nurse; Market Research Analyst; Mechanical Engineer; MIS Specialist; Pharmacist; Physician; Purchasing Agent/Manager; Quality Control Supervisor; Registered Nurse; Respiratory Therapist; Software Engineer; Statistician; Systems Analyst.

Average salary range of placements: More than $50,000. **Number of placements per year:** 50 - 99.

BESEN ASSOCIATES
115 Route 46 West, Suite C-21, Mountain Lakes NJ 07046. 973/334-5533. **Contact:** Manager. **Description:** An executive search firm. **Specializes in the areas of:** Pharmaceuticals.

BLAIR ASSOCIATES
210 Summit Avenue, Montvale NJ 07645. 201/573-0900. **Contact:** Manager. **Description:** An executive search firm.

BLAKE & ASSOCIATES EXECUTIVE SEARCH
P.O. Box 1425, Pleasantville NJ 08232-6425. 609/645-3330. **Fax:** 609/383-0320. **Contact:** Ed Blake, President. **Description:** An executive search firm. **Specializes in the areas of:** Accounting/Auditing; Administration; Advertising; Architecture/Construction; Art/Design; Banking; Biology; Computer Science/Software; Economics; Engineering; Finance; Food; General Management; Health/Medical; Industrial; Insurance; Legal; Manufacturing; Personnel/Labor Relations; Publishing; Retail; Sales; Secretarial. **Positions commonly filled include:** Accountant/Auditor; Actuary; Adjuster; Administrative Manager; Agricultural Engineer; Agricultural Scientist; Architect; Attorney; Bank Officer/Manager; Biological Scientist; Biomedical Engineer; Branch Manager; Brokerage Clerk; Budget Analyst; Buyer; Chemical Engineer; Chemist; Civil Engineer; Claim Representative; Clerical Supervisor; Collector; Computer Programmer; Construction and Building Inspector; Construction Contractor; Cost Estimator; Credit Manager; Customer Service Representative; Dental Lab Technician; Dentist; Dietician/Nutritionist; Draftsperson; EEG Technologist; EKG Technician; Electrical/Electronics Engineer; Electrician; Financial Analyst; Food Scientist/Technologist; General Manager; Geologist/Geophysicist; Health Services Manager; Human Resources Manager; Industrial Engineer; Industrial Production Manager; Insurance Agent/Broker; Investigator; Landscape Architect; Management Trainee; Manufacturer's/Wholesaler's Sales Rep.; Materials Engineer; Mechanical Engineer; Medical Records Technician; Metallurgical Engineer; Mining Engineer; Nuclear Engineer; Nuclear Medicine Technologist; Occupational Therapist; Paralegal; Petroleum Engineer; Physical Therapist; Property and Real Estate Manager; Public Relations Specialist; Purchasing Agent/Manager; Quality Control Supervisor; Radiological Technologist; Recreational Therapist; Respiratory Therapist; Restaurant/Food Service Manager; Science Technologist; Securities Sales Representative; Services Sales Representative; Software Engineer; Speech-Language Pathologist; Stationary Engineer; Statistician; Structural Engineer; Surgical Technician; Surveyor; Systems Analyst; Technical Writer/Editor; Transportation/Traffic Specialist; Underwriter/Assistant Underwriter; Urban/Regional Planner; Wholesale and Retail Buyer. **Number of placements per year:** 50 - 99.

BLAU MANCINO & ASSOCIATES
12 Roszel Road, Suite C101, Princeton NJ 08540. 609/520-8400. **Fax:** 609/520-8993. **Contact:** Eugene Mancino, President. **Description:** An executive search firm. **Specializes in the areas of:** Biotechnology; Pharmaceuticals.

BONIFIELD ASSOCIATES
One Eves Drive, Suite 115, Marlton NJ 08053. 856/596-3300. **Fax:** 856/596-8866. **Contact:** Richard Tyson, President. **E-mail address:** info@bonifield.com. **World Wide Web address:** http://www.bonifield.com. **Description:** An executive search firm operating on a contingency basis. **Specializes in the areas of:** Banking; Insurance. **Positions commonly filled include:** Accountant/Auditor; Actuary; Attorney; Bank Officer/Manager; Claim Representative; Insurance Agent/Broker; Underwriter/Assistant Underwriter. **Average salary range of placements:** More than $50,000. **Number of placements per year:** 50 - 99.

THE BONNER GROUP
59 East Mill Road, Box 15, Long Valley NJ 07853. 908/876-5200. **Fax:** 908/876-9275. **Contact:** Manager. **Description:** An executive search firm. **Specializes in the areas of:** Biotechnology; Pharmaceuticals.

BOSLAND GRAY ASSOCIATES
2001 Route 46, Suite 310, Parsippany NJ 07054. 973/267-4007. **Fax:** 973/402-4965. **Contact:** Andy Gray, Manager. **Description:** An executive search firm.

BOVE ASSOCIATES INC.
560 Fellowship Road, Suite 108, Mt. Laurel NJ 08054. 856/231-4422. **Fax:** 856/231-7704. **Contact:** Manager. **Description:** A generalist executive search firm.

BOWMAN & COMPANY LLP
601 White Horse Road, Voorhees NJ 08043. 856/782-2891. **Fax:** 856/435-0440. **Contact:** Steven M. Packer, CPA/Manager. **E-mail address:** bhrc@bowmanllp.com. **World Wide Web address:** http://www.bowmanllp.com. **Description:** An executive search firm that also provides some contract services. Founded in 1997. **Specializes in the areas of:** Accounting/Auditing; Finance. **Positions commonly filled include:** Accountant; Auditor; Budget Analyst; Chief Financial Officer; Computer Operator; Computer Programmer; Consultant; Controller; Finance Director; Financial Analyst; Fund Manager; MIS Specialist; Systems Analyst; Systems Manager; Vice President of Finance. **Benefits available to temporary workers:** 401(k); Disability Coverage; Flexible Schedule; Life Insurance; Medical Insurance. **Corporate headquarters location:** This Location.

BOYDEN
55 Madison Avenue, Suite 400, Morristown NJ 07960. 973/267-0980. **Fax:** 973/267-6172. **Contact:** Manager. **E-mail address:** boydennj@aol.com. **World Wide Web address:** http://www.boyden.com. **Description:** A generalist executive search firm. **Corporate headquarters location:** New York NY. **Other U.S. locations:** San Francisco CA; Washington DC; Chicago IL; Bloomfield Hills MI; Chesterfield MO; Hawthorne NY; New York NY; Pittsburgh PA; Houston TX. **International locations:** Worldwide.

BRADIN SEARCH GROUP
One Madison Avenue, Morristown NJ 07960. 973/267-0080. **Fax:** 973/267-3384. **Contact:** Lori Bradin, President. **Description:** An executive search firm. **Specializes in the areas of:** Pharmaceuticals; Sales.

THE BRENTWOOD GROUP
170 Kinnelon Road, Suite 29B, Kinnelon NJ 07405. 973/283-1000. **Fax:** 973/283-1220. **Contact:** Doris Osenni, President. **Description:** A generalist executive search firm.

BRETT ASSOCIATES
2184 Morris Avenue, Union NJ 07083. 908/687-7772. **Contact:** Manager. **Description:** An executive search firm. **Specializes in the areas of:** Manufacturing.

BRISSENDEN, McFARLAND, FUCCELLA & REYNOLDS, INC.
1130 Route 202, Suite E7, Raritan NJ 08869. 908/704-9100. **Fax:** 908/704-9126. **Contact:** Manager. **E-mail address:** inquiry@bmfr.com. **World Wide Web address:** http://www.bmfr.com. **Description:** An executive search firm. **Specializes in the areas of:** Biotechnology; Health/Medical; Nuclear Power; Pharmaceuticals.

BROAD WAVERLY & ASSOCIATES
P.O. Box 741, 200 Broad Street, Red Bank NJ 07701. 732/747-4400. **Contact:** Manager. **Description:** An executive search firm. **Specializes in the areas of:** Accounting/Auditing; Insurance; Light Industrial; Technical.

BROOKDALE SEARCH ASSOCIATES
P.O. Box 1293, Bloomfield NJ 07003. 973/338-0515. **Fax:** 973/338-1242. **Contact:** Manager. **Description:** An executive search firm. **Specializes in the areas of:** Electrical; Electronics; Heating, Air Conditioning, and Refrigeration; Technical.

BUCKLEY GROUP
140 South Broadway, Suite 4, Pitman NJ 08071. 856/256-1844. **Fax:** 856/256-1855. **Contact:** Doug Webster, President. **Description:** An executive search firm. **Specializes in the areas of:** High-Tech; Marketing; Sales.

BUTTERFASS PEPE & McCALLAN
P.O. Box 721, Mahwah NJ 07430. 201/512-3330. **Contact:** Manager. **Description:** An executive search firm. **Specializes in the areas of:** Investment.

CEO SERVICES
305 Route 130 South, Cinnaminson NJ 08077. 609/786-3334. **Contact:** Gail Duncan, President. **Description:** An executive search firm. **NOTE:** This firm does not accept unsolicited resumes. Please only respond to advertised openings. **Specializes in the areas of:** Computer Programming; Information Technology; Technical.

CKR ASSOCIATES
440 South Main Street, Milltown NJ 08850. 732/238-4610. **Fax:** 732/238-8988. **Contact:** Manager. **Description:** A generalist executive search firm.

CSA ASSOCIATES
407 Main Street, Suite 204, Metuchen NJ 08840. 732/321-0088. **Fax:** 732/321-0394. **Contact:** Manager. **Description:** An executive search firm. **Specializes in the areas of:** Pharmaceuticals.

CAPITAL FINANCE RECRUITING
321 Commercial Avenue, Suite 220, Palisades Park NJ 07650. 201/585-8444. **Contact:** Manager. **Description:** An executive search firm. **Specializes in the areas of:** Administration; Data Processing.

CAPSTONE ASSOCIATES
33 Wood Avenue South, 5th Floor, Iselin NJ 08830. 732/906-1300. **Contact:** Manager. **Description:** An executive search firm. **Specializes in the areas of:** Computer Hardware/Software.

CAREER MANAGEMENT GROUP, LLC
434 Ridgedale Avenue, PNB 11-165, East Hanover NJ 07936. 973/428-5239. **Fax:** 973/428-5084. **Contact:** Toni Donofrio, Managing Member. **E-mail address:** careermanage@msn.com. **World Wide Web address:** http://www.careermgtgroup.com. **Description:** An executive search firm. **Specializes in the areas of:** Accounting; Administration; Computer Science/ Software; Engineering; Finance; General Management; Marketing; Personnel/Labor Relations; Sales; Secretarial. **Positions commonly filled include:** Account Manager; Accountant; Administrative Assistant; Administrative Manager; Applications Engineer; Auditor; Budget Analyst; Chemical Engineer; Computer Operator; Computer Programmer; Customer Service Representative; Database Manager; Design Engineer; Electrical/Electronics Engineer; Environmental Engineer; Financial Analyst; General Manager; Human Resources Manager; Industrial Engineer; Management Trainee; Manufacturing Engineer; Marketing Manager; Mechanical Engineer; MIS Specialist; Operations Manager; Purchasing Agent/Manager; Sales Engineer; Sales Executive; Sales Manager; Sales Representative; Secretary; Software Engineer; Systems Analyst; Technical Writer/Editor; Telecommunications Manager; Transportation/Traffic Specialist. **Corporate headquarters location:** This Location. **Average salary range of placements:** More than $50,000. **Number of placements per year:** 50 - 99.

CAREER MANAGEMENT INTERNATIONAL
197 Route 18, Suite 102, East Brunswick NJ 08816. 732/937-4800. **Fax:** 732/937-4770. **Contact:** Debbie Brower, Assistant to the President. **Description:** An executive search firm operating on a retainer basis. **Specializes in the areas of:** Fashion; Finance; General Management; Personnel/Labor Relations; Retail; Sales. **Positions commonly filled include:** Administrative Manager; Buyer; Credit Manager; Designer; Human Resources Manager; Management Analyst/Consultant; MIS Specialist; Operations/Production Manager. **Average salary range of placements:** More than $50,000. **Number of placements per year:** 50 - 99.

CAREERS ON TRACK
P.O. Box 222, Tenafly NJ 07670. 201/894-0600. **Fax:** 201/894-0563. **Contact:** Gary Tabor, Owner. **E-mail address:** tabortrak@aol.com. **Description:** An executive search firm. **Specializes in the areas of:** Sales. **Positions commonly filled include:** General Manager; Management Analyst/Consultant; Marketing Manager. **Average salary range of placements:** More than $50,000. **Number of placements per year:** 1 - 49.

CAREERWORKS
520 Main Street, Suite 302, Fort Lee NJ 07024-4501. 201/592-1460. **Contact:** Mark Raskin, President. **E-mail address:** careerw@aol.com. **Description:** An executive search firm operating on a contingency basis. **Specializes in the areas of:** Accounting/Auditing; Administration; Engineering; Finance; General Management; Manufacturing; Personnel/Labor Relations; Sales. **Positions commonly filled include:** Accountant/Auditor; Financial Analyst; General Manager; Hotel Manager; Operations/Production Manager; Restaurant/Food Service Manager; Transportation/Traffic Specialist. **Number of placements per year:** 50 - 99.

CARNEGIE ASSOCIATES
50 Cherry Hill Road, Parsippany NJ 07054. 973/334-9090. **Fax:** 973/334-7878. **Contact:** Larry Wagner, CPC/Manager. **World Wide Web address:** http://www.carnegieassociates.com. **Description:** An executive search firm. **Specializes in the areas of:** Information Systems; Information Technology.

CARNEGIE EXECUTIVE SEARCH
2 Carnegie Road, Lawrenceville NJ 08648. 609/883-8900. **Fax:** 609/883-6644. **Contact:** Bill Arguest, Recruiter. **Description:** An executive search firm. **Specializes in the areas of:** Communications.

CARTER McKENZIE INC.
300 Executive Drive, Suite 250, West Orange NJ 07052-3303. 973/736-7100. **Fax:** 973/736-9416. **Contact:** John Capo, Vice President. **E-mail address:** jcapo@carter-mckenzie.com. **World Wide Web address:** http://www.carter-mckenzie.com. **Description:** An executive search firm operating on both retainer and contingency bases. **Specializes in the areas of:** Administration; Computer Science/Software. **Positions commonly filled include:** Computer Programmer; MIS Specialist; Software Engineer; Systems Analyst; Telecommunications Manager. **Average salary range of placements:** More than $50,000. **Number of placements per year:** 100 - 199.

CARTER/MACKAY PERSONNEL INC.
777 Terrace Avenue, Hasbrouck Heights NJ 07604. 201/288-5100. **Fax:** 201/288-2660. **Contact:** Bruce Green, Vice President. **Description:** An executive search firm. **Specializes in the areas of:** Computer Hardware/Software; Computer Science/Software; Data Communications; Health/Medical; Pharmaceuticals; Sales; Technical. **Positions commonly filled include:** General Manager; Manufacturer's/Wholesaler's Sales Rep.; Marketing Manager; Sales Manager; Systems Analyst. **Other U.S. locations:** Framingham MA; Cary NC; Great Neck NY. **Average salary range of placements:** More than $50,000.

L. CAVALIERE & ASSOCIATES
2300 Route 27, North Brunswick NJ 08902. 732/940-3100. **Fax:** 732/940-2266. **Contact:** Louis Cavaliere, Managing Director. **Description:** An executive search

firm operating on both retainer and contingency bases. **Specializes in the areas of:** MIS/EDP. **Positions commonly filled include:** Computer Programmer; Management Analyst/Consultant; Software Engineer; Systems Analyst. **Average salary range of placements:** More than $50,000. **Number of placements per year:** 1 - 49.

CERTIFIED PERSONNEL CORPORATION

P.O. Box 36, Berkeley Heights NJ 07922. 908/322-0404. **Fax:** 908/322-1738. **Contact:** Peter Gilbert, Managing Partner. **E-mail address:** pgilbert@certifiedpersonnel.com. **World Wide Web address:** http://www.certifiedpersonnel.com. **Description:** An executive search firm operating on a contingency basis. Certified Personnel Corporation focuses on the placement of Lotus Notes developers and administrators. **Positions commonly filled include:** Computer Programmer; MIS Specialist; Systems Analyst. **Average salary range of placements:** More than $50,000.

CHRISTENSON HUTCHISON & McDOWELL

466 Southern Boulevard, Chatham NJ 07928. 973/966-1600. **Contact:** Manager. **Description:** An executive search firm.

CHURCHILL & HARRIMAN, INC.

244 Wall Street, Princeton NJ 08540. 609/921-3551. **Fax:** 609/921-1061. **Contact:** Kenneth J. Peterson, Principal. **Description:** An executive search firm that also provides some information technology consulting services on a per diem basis. **Specializes in the areas of:** Administration; Computer Science/Software. **Positions commonly filled include:** Computer Programmer; Systems Analyst. **Average salary range of placements:** More than $50,000. **Number of placements per year:** 50 - 99.

KEN CLARK INTERNATIONAL

5 Independence Way, Suite 210, Princeton NJ 08540. 609/514-2600. **Fax:** 609/514-2700. **Contact:** Ken Clark, President/CEO. **Description:** An executive search firm. **Specializes in the areas of:** Pharmaceuticals. **Corporate headquarters location:** This Location.

CLINFORCE

7 Headquarters Plaza, Morristown NJ 07960-3976. 973/538-1900. **Fax:** 973/538-1976. **Contact:** Ellen Maynard, Managing Director. **Description:** An executive search firm. **Specializes in the areas of:** Clinical Research; Pharmaceuticals.

COMMON AGENDA

617 Highway 71, Brielle NJ 08730. 732/223-7114. **Fax:** 732/223-7116. **Contact:** Manager. **Description:** An executive search firm. **Specializes in the areas of:** Data Communications; Telecommunications.

COMPUTER EASE

1301 Monmouth Avenue, Lakewood NJ 08701. 732/370-7148. **Contact:** Manager. **Description:** An executive search firm. **Positions commonly filled include:** Computer Programmer; Systems Analyst.

CORPORATE INFORMATION SYSTEMS INC.

71 Union Avenue, Rutherford NJ 07070. 201/896-0600. **Contact:** Manager. **Description:** An executive search firm. **Specializes in the areas of:** Information Technology.

CORPORATE SEARCH

35 Airport Road, Morristown NJ 07960. 973/540-0850. **Fax:** 973/984-8875. **Contact:** Manager. **Description:** An executive search firm. **Specializes in the areas of:** Data Processing; Information Technology.

COX DARROW & OWENS, INC.

6 East Clementon Road, Suite E4, Gibbsboro NJ 08026-1199. 856/782-1300. **Fax:** 856/782-7277. **Contact:** Bob Darrow, Vice President/Partner. **E-mail address:** cdo@snip.net. **Description:** An executive search firm operating on a contingency basis. **Specializes in the areas of:** Banking; Engineering; Industrial; Manufacturing; Mortgage; Personnel/Labor Relations; Sales; Technical. **Positions commonly filled include:** Chemical Engineer; Chemist; Computer Engineer; Electrical/Electronics Engineer; Human Resources Manager; Mechanical Engineer; Purchasing Agent/Manager; Quality Control Supervisor; Telecommunications Manager. **Other U.S. locations:** Nationwide. **Average salary range of placements:** $30,000 - $100,000. **Number of placements per year:** 50 - 99.

DHR INTERNATIONAL INC.

560 Valley Road, Montclair NJ 07043. 973/746-2100. **Fax:** 973/746-8716. **Contact:** Manager. **Description:** A generalist executive search firm.

D'ANDREA ASSOCIATES INC.

296 Amboy Avenue, Metuchen NJ 08840. 732/906-0110. **Fax:** 732/906-0116. **Contact:** Nick D'Andrea, President. **Description:** An executive search firm. **Specializes in the areas of:** Banking; General Management. **Positions commonly filled include:** Bank Officer/Manager; Financial Analyst; Fund Manager; General Manager; Human Resources Manager; Sales Executive; Sales Manager; Sales Representative. **Average salary range of placements:** More than $50,000. **Number of placements per year:** 1 - 49.

DATA HUNTERS, INC.

P.O. Box 884, Ramsey NJ 07446-0884. 201/825-1368. **Fax:** 201/327-4234. **Contact:** Bette Rosenfeld, President. **E-mail address:** datahunt@nis.net. **Description:** An executive search firm. **Specializes in the areas of:** Computer Science/Software; Data Processing. **Positions commonly filled include:** Computer Programmer; Internet Services Manager; MIS Specialist; Software Engineer; Systems Analyst; Telecommunications Manager. **Number of placements per year:** 1 - 49.

DATA SEARCH NETWORK

P.O. Box 305, Emerson NJ 07630. 201/967-8600. **Contact:** Manager. **Description:** An executive search firm. **Specializes in the areas of:** Information Systems.

THE DATAFINDERS GROUP, INC.

25 East Spring Valley Avenue, Maywood NJ 07607. 201/845-7700. **Fax:** 201/845-7365. **Contact:** Thomas J. Credidio, Vice President. **E-mail address:** postmaster@data-finders.com. **World Wide Web address:** http://www.data-finders.com. **Description:** An executive search firm. **Specializes in the areas of:** Computer Science/Software; MIS/EDP; Sales. **Positions commonly filled include:** Computer Programmer; EDP Specialist; Manufacturer's/Wholesaler's Sales Rep.; Services Sales Representative; Software Engineer; Systems Analyst. **Number of placements per year:** 200 - 499.

DAVID ALLEN ASSOCIATES

P.O. Box 56, Haddonfield NJ 08033. 856/795-6470. **Fax:** 856/795-0175. **Contact:** David Ritchings, Partner. **Description:** An executive search firm operating on both retainer and contingency bases. Founded in 1980. **Specializes in the areas of:** Banking; Food; General Management. **Positions commonly filled include:** Account Manager; Account Representative; Bank Officer/Manager; Budget Analyst; Chemical Engineer; Chief Financial Officer; Controller; Credit Manager; Economist; Finance Director; Financial Analyst; Fund Manager; General Manager; Human Resources Manager; Management Analyst/Consultant; Market Research Analyst; Marketing Manager; Marketing Specialist; Sales Representative; Securities Sales Representative. **Corporate headquarters location:** This Location. **Other U.S. locations:** Nationwide. **Average salary range of placements:** More than $50,000. **Number of placements per year:** 50 - 99.

CLARK DAVIS ASSOCIATES

5 Century Drive, Parsippany NJ 07054. 973/267-5511. **Contact:** Manager. **Description:** An executive search

firm. **Specializes in the areas of:** Accounting/Auditing; Engineering; Information Systems.

A. DAVIS GRANT & COMPANY
295 Pierson Avenue, Edison NJ 08837. 732/494-2266. **Fax:** 732/494-3626. **Contact:** Alan Grossman, Senior Partner. **E-mail address:** info@adg.net. **World Wide Web address:** http://www.adg.net. **Description:** An executive search firm operating on a retainer basis. **Specializes in the areas of:** Information Systems; Information Technology; Management.

DEAN-WHARTON ASSOCIATES
P.O. Box 279, Somerville NJ 08876. 908/231-1818. **Fax:** 908/231-1469. **Contact:** Manager. **Description:** An executive search firm. **Specializes in the areas of:** Human Resources.

DEVIN SCOTT ASSOCIATES, INC.
2125 Center Avenue, Suite 402, Fort Lee NJ 07024. 201/346-0331. **Fax:** 201/346-0338. **Contact:** Rocco Fedele, President. **Description:** An executive search firm. **Specializes in the areas of:** Hotel/Restaurant.

M.T. DONALDSON ASSOCIATES, INC.
4400 Route 9 South, Suite 1000, Freehold NJ 07728. 732/303-7890. **Fax:** 732/303-6440. **Contact:** Sol Premisler, President. **Description:** An executive search firm. **Specializes in the areas of:** Engineering; Food; Health/Medical; Industrial; Manufacturing; Personnel/Labor Relations. **Positions commonly filled include:** Chemical Engineer; Chemist; Food Scientist/Technologist; Industrial Engineer; Industrial Production Manager; Mechanical Engineer; Pharmacist; Purchasing Agent/Manager; Quality Control Supervisor. **Average salary range of placements:** More than $50,000. **Number of placements per year:** 1 - 49.

DOUGLAS ASSOCIATES INC.
158 Linwood Plaza, Suite 214, Fort Lee NJ 07024. 201/363-6500. **Fax:** 201/363-6550. **Contact:** Ms. Tobey Klein, President. **Description:** An executive search firm. **Specializes in the areas of:** Retail. **Positions commonly filled include:** Buyer; Human Resources Specialist. **Average salary range of placements:** $30,000 - $50,000. **Number of placements per year:** 50 - 99.

DOW-TECH
1700 Route 23 North, Suite 100, Wayne NJ 07470. 973/696-8000. **Fax:** 973/696-1964. **Contact:** Chris Dowling, President. **E-mail address:** dow@dow-tech.com. **World Wide Web address:** http://www.dow-tech.com. **Description:** An executive search firm operating on both retainer and contingency bases. The firm provides placements for the HVAC, energy, and water/wastewater industries. Dow-Tech also provides some contract services. **Positions commonly filled include:** Account Manager; Account Representative; Design Engineer; Electrical/Electronics Engineer; Environmental Engineer; General Manager; Operations Manager; Project Manager; Sales Engineer; Sales Executive; Sales Manager; Sales Representative. **Corporate headquarters location:** This Location. **Other U.S. locations:** Nationwide. **Average salary range of placements:** $50,000 - $100,000. **Number of placements per year:** 50 - 99.

THE DOWD GROUP
60 Grange Avenue, Fair Haven NJ 07704. 732/747-8100. **Fax:** 732/842-0597. **Contact:** Charlie Dowd. **Description:** An executive search firm. **Specializes in the areas of:** Information Systems; Marketing; Sales; Telecommunications.

DREIER CONSULTING
P.O. Box 356, Ramsey NJ 07446. 201/327-1113. **Fax:** 201/327-0816. **Contact:** Jennifer Hernandez, Administrative Assistant. **E-mail address:** jennifer@dreierconsulting.com. **World Wide Web address:** http://www.dreierconsulting.com. **Description:** An executive search firm operating on a contingency basis. **Specializes in the areas of:** Computer

Science/Software; Engineering; Manufacturing; Medical Technology; Sales; Telecommunications. **Positions commonly filled include:** Biomedical Engineer; Design Engineer; Electrical/Electronics Engineer; General Manager; Graphic Designer; Industrial Engineer; Manufacturing Engineer; Marketing Manager; Marketing Specialist; Mechanical Engineer; MIS Specialist; Operations Manager; Production Manager; Project Manager; Sales Engineer; Sales Executive; Software Engineer; Systems Analyst; Systems Manager; Telecommunications Manager; Vice President of Marketing; Vice President of Sales. **Corporate headquarters location:** This Location. **Average salary range of placements:** More than $50,000. **Number of placements per year:** 1 - 49.

DREW ASSOCIATES
25 Pompton Avenue, Suite 305, Verona NJ 07044. 973/571-9735. **Fax:** 973/571-9747. **Contact:** Manager. **Description:** An executive search firm. **Specializes in the areas of:** Health/Medical.

ROBERT DREXLER ASSOCIATES
210 River Street, Suite 30, Hackensack NJ 07601. 201/342-0200. **Fax:** 201/342-9062. **Contact:** Robert Drexler, President. **E-mail address:** drexler@engineeringemployment.com. **World Wide Web address:** http://www.engineeringemployment.com. **Description:** An executive search firm operating on a retainer basis. Founded in 1980. **Specializes in the areas of:** Chemicals; Engineering; Environmental; Insurance; Management; Petrochemical; Pharmaceuticals; Sales; Technical; Transportation. **Average salary range of placements:** More than $70,000.

DUNHILL PERSONNEL OF CHERRY HILL, INC.
1040 Kings Highway North, Suite 400, Cherry Hill NJ 08034. 856/667-9180. **Fax:** 856/667-0064. **Contact:** Bill Emerson, President. **World Wide Web address:** http://www.dunhillstaff.com. **Description:** An executive search firm operating on a contingency basis. Dunhill Personnel also provides some temporary placements. **Specializes in the areas of:** Marketing; Sales. **Positions commonly filled include:** Account Manager; Account Representative; Accountant; Adjuster; Administrative Assistant; Applications Engineer; AS400 Programmer Analyst; Auditor; Bank Officer/Manager; Budget Analyst; Buyer; Chief Financial Officer; Computer Animator; Computer Engineer; Computer Operator; Computer Programmer; Computer Scientist; Computer Support Technician; Computer Technician; Content Developer; Controller; Cost Estimator; Credit Manager; Customer Service Representative; Database Administrator; Database Manager; Economist; Finance Director; Financial Analyst; Fund Manager; Internet Services Manager; MIS Specialist; Multimedia Designer; Network/Systems Administrator; Real Estate Agent; Sales Engineer; Sales Executive; Sales Manager; Sales Representative; Secretary; Software Engineer; SQL Programmer; Systems Analyst; Systems Manager; Typist/Word Processor; Webmaster.

DUNHILL PROFESSIONAL SEARCH
303 West Main Street, Freehold NJ 07728. **Toll-free phone:** 888/431-2700. **Fax:** 732/431-0329. **Contact:** Rich Hanson, President. **Description:** An executive search firm. **Specializes in the areas of:** Accounting/Auditing; Banking; Finance; Secretarial. **Positions commonly filled include:** Accountant/Auditor; Administrative Assistant; Bookkeeper; Budget Analyst; Economist; EDP Specialist; Executive Assistant; Financial Analyst; Legal Secretary; Receptionist; Secretary; Typist/Word Processor. **Number of placements per year:** 1 - 49.

DUNHILL PROFESSIONAL SEARCH
393 Ramapo Valley Road, Oakland NJ 07436. 201/337-2200. **Fax:** 201/337-3445. **Contact:** Roger Lippincott, President. **Description:** An executive search firm. **Specializes in the areas of:** Personnel/Labor Relations; Sales. **Positions commonly filled include:** Human Resources Specialist; Manufacturer's/Wholesaler's Sales

Rep.; Sales Representative; Training Manager. **Average salary range of placements:** More than $50,000. **Number of placements per year:** 50 - 99.

DYNAMIC QUALITY SEARCH INC.
1312 Allenhurst Avenue, Ocean NJ 07712. 732/517-8841. **Fax:** 732/517-0985. **Contact:** Manager. **Description:** An executive search firm. **Specializes in the areas of:** Transportation.

DYNAMIC RECRUITERS INC.
59 East Mill Road, Box 16, Long Valley NJ 07853. 908/876-8420. **Contact:** Manager. **Description:** An executive search firm. **Specializes in the areas of:** Aerospace; Industrial; Pharmaceuticals; Plastics. **Benefits available to temporary workers:** Accident/Emergency Insurance.

E&A ASSOCIATES
1070 E Highway 34, Suite 194, Matawan NJ 07747. 732/739-6222. **Fax:** 732/739-5389. **Contact:** Allan M. Adelson. **E-mail address:** ea@ea-associates.com. **World Wide Web address:** http://www.ea-associates.com. **Description:** An executive search firm. **Specializes in the areas of:** Technical; Telecommunications.

E&A RECRUITERS
15 Roanoke Court, Bordentown NJ 08505. 609/324-1500. **Fax:** 609/324-1300. **Contact:** Angelo G. Angeledes, Partner. **Description:** An executive search firm. **Specializes in the areas of:** Biotechnology; Pharmaceuticals.

EAGLE RESEARCH INC.
373-D Route 46 West, Fairfield NJ 07004. 973/244-0992. **Fax:** 973/244-1239. **Contact:** Annette S. Baron, PA/President. **E-mail address:** asbaron@aol.com. **Description:** An executive search firm operating on both retainer and contingency bases. **Specializes in the areas of:** Biotechnology; Pharmaceuticals. **Positions commonly filled include:** Physician. **Other U.S. locations:** Nationwide. **Average salary range of placements:** More than $50,000.

ELECTRONIC SEARCH INC.
69 Main Avenue, Ocean Grove NJ 07756. 732/775-5017. **Fax:** 732/775-5035. **Contact:** Tom Manni, Regional Manager. **E-mail address:** tmanni@electronicsearch.com. **World Wide Web address:** http://www.electronicsearch.com. **Description:** An executive search firm operating on both retainer and contingency bases. **Specializes in the areas of:** Engineering; Wireless Communications. **Positions commonly filled include:** Applications Engineer; Electrical/Electronics Engineer; Sales Engineer; Software Engineer; Telecommunications Manager. **Corporate headquarters location:** Rolling Meadows IL. **Other U.S. locations:** Solona Beach CA. **Average salary range of placements:** More than $50,000. **Number of placements per year:** 100 - 199.

ELIAS ASSOCIATES INC.
P.O. Box 396, East Brunswick NJ 08816. 732/390. **Fax:** 732/390-9769. **Contact:** Bill Elias, President. **Description:** An executive search firm. **Specializes in the areas of:** Engineering.

ELIOT & CARR ASSOCIATES, INC.
Harmon Cove Tower 3, Suite 4A, A/L Level, Secaucus NJ 07094. 201/223-1700. **Fax:** 201/223-1818. **Contact:** Manager. **E-mail address:** eliotcarr@bigplanet.com. **World Wide Web address:** http://www.eliotcarr.com. **Description:** An executive search firm. **Specializes in the areas of:** Biotechnology; Chemicals; Marketing; Plastics; Sales.

ELLIS CAREER CONSULTANTS/CAREER SEARCH ASSOCIATES
1090 Broadway, West Long Branch NJ 07764. 732/222-5333. **Fax:** 732/222-2332. **Contact:** Lisa Shapiro, President. **Description:** An executive search firm.

Specializes in the areas of: Accounting/Auditing; Advertising; Distribution; Engineering; Finance; Food; General Management; Industrial; Manufacturing; Personnel/Labor Relations; Retail; Sales; Transportation. **Positions commonly filled include:** Accountant/Auditor; Branch Manager; Buyer; Computer Programmer; Credit Manager; Customer Service Representative; Engineer; Financial Analyst; General Manager; Manufacturer's/Wholesaler's Sales Rep.; Restaurant/Food Service Manager; Retail Manager; Systems Analyst; Transportation/Traffic Specialist; Wholesale and Retail Buyer. **Number of placements per year:** 50 - 99.

EVERGREEN PERSONNEL SERVICE
215 East Ridgewood Avenue, Ridgewood NJ 07450. 201/444-3997. **Fax:** 201/444-0511. **Contact:** Manager. **Description:** An executive search firm. **Specializes in the areas of:** Biotechnology; Clinical Research; Pharmaceuticals. **Positions commonly filled include:** Biological Scientist; Clinical Lab Technician.

EXECUTIVE EXCHANGE CORPORATION
2517 Highway 35, Suite G-103, Manasquan NJ 08736. 732/223-6655. **Fax:** 732/223-1162. **Contact:** Elizabeth B. Glosser, Owner. **Description:** An executive search firm operating on a contingency basis. The firm places computer-related sales professionals. Executive Exchange Corporation is also a member of Nationwide Interchange, a national job search network of recruiters. **Specializes in the areas of:** Sales. **Positions commonly filled include:** Account Manager; Marketing Manager; Recruiter; Services Sales Representative. **Average salary range of placements:** $30,000 - $50,000. **Number of placements per year:** 100 - 199.

EXECUTIVE RECRUITERS, INC.
P.O. Box 43396, Upper Montclair NJ 07043. 973/471-7878. **Contact:** Manager. **Description:** An executive search firm. **Specializes in the areas of:** Insurance.

EXECUTIVE REGISTRY INC.
12 Route 17 North, Paramus NJ 07652. 201/587-1010. **Contact:** Manager. **Description:** An executive search firm. **Specializes in the areas of:** Information Systems; Retail.

EXECUTIVE SEARCH, INC.
48 Headquarters Plaza, Morristown NJ 07960. 973/538-2300. **Contact:** Recruitment Coordinator. **Description:** An executive search firm. **Specializes in the areas of:** Accounting/Auditing; Administration; Banking; Finance; General Management; Insurance; Legal; Personnel/Labor Relations; Sales; Secretarial. **Positions commonly filled include:** Accountant/Auditor; Administrative Manager; Attorney; Bank Officer/Manager; Branch Manager; Claim Representative; Clerical Supervisor; Credit Manager; Customer Service Representative; Editor; Financial Analyst; General Manager; Health Services Manager; Human Resources Manager; Insurance Agent/Broker; Management Analyst/Consultant; Management Trainee; Manufacturer's/Wholesaler's Sales Rep.; Operations/Production Manager; Paralegal; Property and Real Estate Manager; Psychologist; Public Relations Specialist; Purchasing Agent/Manager; Securities Sales Representative; Services Sales Representative; Technical Writer/Editor; Underwriter/Assistant Underwriter; Wholesale and Retail Buyer.

FALLON & COMPANY
1115 Bloomfield Street, Hoboken NJ 07030. 201/792-7777. **Contact:** Michael Fallon, President. **Description:** An executive search firm.

FINANCIAL ACCOUNTING & MANAGEMENT
One Exchange Place, Jersey City NJ 07302. 201/333-8787. **Fax:** 201/333-6222. **Contact:** Jack Braunstein, President. **Description:** An executive search firm. **Specializes in the areas of:** Finance.

FOLEY PROCTOR YOSKOWITZ
One Cattano Avenue, Morristown NJ 07960. 973/605-1000. **Fax:** 973/605-1020. **Contact:** Richard W. Proctor,

Partner. **Description:** An executive search firm. **Specializes in the areas of:** Health/Medical. **Positions commonly filled include:** Administrator; Chief Executive Officer; Physician; Physician Assistant. **Other U.S. locations:** New York NY. **Average salary range of placements:** More than $50,000. **Number of placements per year:** 50 - 99.

F-O-R-T-U-N-E PERSONNEL CONSULTANTS
350 West Passaic Street, Rochelle Park NJ 07662. 201/843-7621. **Fax:** 201/843-8189. **Contact:** Manager. **Description:** An executive search firm operating on both retainer and contingency bases. **Specializes in the areas of:** Biotechnology; General Management; Materials; Medical Technology; Pharmaceuticals. **Corporate headquarters location:** New York NY.

F-O-R-T-U-N-E PERSONNEL CONSULTANTS
41 Vreeland Avenue, Totowa NJ 07512. 973/812-9819. **Fax:** 973/812-9821. **Contact:** Stan Goldberg, President. **Description:** An executive search firm. **Specializes in the areas of:** Management; Materials; Purchasing. **Corporate headquarters location:** New York NY.

F-O-R-T-U-N-E PERSONNEL CONSULTANTS OF MENLO PARK
16 Bridge Street, Metuchen NJ 08840. 732/494-6266. **Fax:** 732/494-5669. **Contact:** Peter Provda, President. **Description:** An executive search firm. **Specializes in the areas of:** Engineering; Food; Manufacturing; Personnel/Labor Relations; Technical. **Positions commonly filled include:** Biochemist; Biological Scientist; Biomedical Engineer; Buyer; Chemical Engineer; Chemist; Computer Programmer; Designer; Electrical/Electronics Engineer; Food Scientist/ Technologist; Human Resources Manager; Industrial Engineer; Mechanical Engineer; Operations/ Production Manager; Purchasing Agent/Manager; Quality Control Supervisor; Science Technologist; Software Engineer; Systems Analyst; Transportation/ Traffic Specialist. **Corporate headquarters location:** New York NY. **Number of placements per year:** 1 - 49.

FOSTER ASSOCIATES
The Livery, 209 Cooper Avenue, Upper Montclair NJ 07043. 973/746-2800. **Contact:** Manager. **Description:** An executive search firm. **Specializes in the areas of:** Accounting/Auditing; Consulting; Finance; Legal.

THE FOSTER McKAY GROUP
30 Vreeland Road, Florham Park NJ 07932. 973/966-0909. **Fax:** 973/966-6925. **Contact:** Allen Galorenzo, Partner. **Description:** An executive search firm operating on both retainer and contingency bases. **Specializes in the areas of:** Accounting/Auditing; Finance. **Positions commonly filled include:** Accountant/Auditor; Budget Analyst; Chief Financial Officer; Controller; Finance Director; Financial Analyst. **Average salary range of placements:** More than $50,000. **Number of placements per year:** 100 - 199.

FOX-MORRIS ASSOCIATES
1050 Wall Street West, Suite 310, Lyndhurst NJ 07071. 201/933-8900. **Contact:** Manager. **Description:** An executive search firm. **Specializes in the areas of:** Human Resources.

FRANK ALLEN & ASSOCIATES
15 James Street, Florham Park NJ 07932. 973/966-1606. **Contact:** Manager. **Description:** An executive search firm. **Specializes in the areas of:** Human Resources.

FREEMAN ENTERPRISES
748 Newman Springs Road, Lincroft NJ 07738. 732/933-4296. **Fax:** 732/933-4295. **Contact:** Lynn Freeman, President. **Description:** An executive search firm.

W.N. GARBARINI & ASSOCIATES
961 Cherokee Court, Westfield NJ 07090. 908/232-2737. **Fax:** 908/232-2326. **Contact:** William N. Garbarini, President. **Description:** An executive search firm.

Specializes in the areas of: Health/Medical; Pharmaceuticals.

GARRETT GROUP
342 Parsippany Road, Parsippany NJ 07054. 973/884-0711. **Fax:** 973/884-1307. **Contact:** Recruiting. **Description:** An executive search firm. **Specializes in the areas of:** Electronics; Engineering; Marketing. **Average salary range of placements:** More than $50,000.

GENDASON COOPER ASSOCIATES
177 Main Street, Suite 107, Fort Lee NJ 07024. 201/947-5171. **Fax:** 201/947-5306. **Contact:** Micheal Cooper, Partner. **Description:** An executive search firm. **Specializes in the areas of:** Retail.

GENESYS CONSULTING
1128 Route 31 North, Echo Hill Plaza, Suite 2, Lebanon NJ 08833. 908/735-6444. **Fax:** 908/735-6902. **Contact:** Deborah Marrero, Managing Principal. **Description:** An executive search firm.

GIBSON MARTIN CONSULTING
694 Route 15 South, Suite 207, Lake Hopatcong NJ 07849. 973/663-3300. **Fax:** 973/663-3316. **Contact:** Robert Lee, Principal. **E-mail address:** boblee@careergoals.com. **World Wide Web address:** http://www.careergoals.com. **Description:** An executive search firm. **Specializes in the areas of:** Accounting/Auditing; Administration; Computer Science/Software; Finance. **Positions commonly filled include:** Accountant/Auditor; Architect; Budget Analyst; Chemist; Computer Programmer; Financial Analyst; Systems Analyst.

GILBERT & VAN CAMPEN INTERNATIONAL
99 Lake Shore Drive, Belvidere NJ 07823. 908/475-2222. **Contact:** Manager. **Description:** An executive search firm. **Other area locations:** 420 Lexington Avenue, New York NY 10170.

LAWRENCE GLASER ASSOCIATES INC.
505 South Lenola Road, Moorestown NJ 08057. 856/778-9500. **Fax:** 856/778-4390. **Contact:** Lawrence Glaser, President. **Description:** An executive search firm. **Specializes in the areas of:** Food; Sales. **Average salary range of placements:** More than $50,000. **Number of placements per year:** 50 - 99.

GLOBAL RESOURCES GROUP, LLC
340 Marine Avenue, Haddonfield NJ 08033. 856/616-9700. **Fax:** 856/616-9291. **Contact:** Shari Rohlfing, Principal. **E-mail address:** srohlfing@globalresourcescorp.com. **World Wide Web address:** http://www.globalresourcescorp.com. **Description:** An executive search firm operating on both retainer and contingency bases. Global Resources Group also offers some temporary placements. Client company pays fee. **Specializes in the areas of:** Computer Science/Software; Information Technology; Internet Development; Marketing; MIS/EDP; Sales; Scientific; Technical. **Positions commonly filled include:** Account Manager; Account Representative; Applications Engineer; AS400 Programmer Analyst; Computer Animator; Computer Engineer; Computer Operator; Computer Programmer; Computer Scientist; Computer Support Technician; Computer Technician; Content Developer; Database Administrator; Database Manager; Internet Services Manager; MIS Specialist; Multimedia Designer; Network/Systems Administrator; Sales Engineer; Sales Executive; Sales Manager; Sales Representative; Software Engineer; SQL Programmer; Systems Analyst; Systems Manager; Vice President. **Corporate headquarters location:** This Location. **Average salary range of placements:** More than $100,000. **Number of placements per year:** 50 - 99.

GLOBAL SEARCH, INC.
8 Wood Hollow Road, Parsippany NJ 07054. 973/781-1900. **Fax:** 973/781-1999. **Contact:** Manager. **E-mail address:** jobs@gsearch.com. **World Wide Web**

122

_29

address: http://www.gsearch.com. **Description:** An executive search firm. **Specializes in the areas of:** Information Systems.

L.J. GONZER ASSOCIATES
1225 Raymond Boulevard, Newark NJ 07102. 973/624-5600. **Contact:** Manager. **Description:** An executive search firm.

GOODRICH & SHERWOOD ASSOCIATES, INC.
One Independence Way, Princeton NJ 08540. 609/452-0202. **Contact:** Manager. **World Wide Web address:** http://www.goodrichsherwood.com. **Description:** An executive search firm that also provides outplacement/career transition counseling, and executive coaching. **Specializes in the areas of:** Human Resources. **Corporate headquarters location:** New York NY. **Other area locations:** Parsippany NJ. **Other U.S. locations:** Norwalk CT; Shelton CT; Rochester NY.

GOODRICH & SHERWOOD ASSOCIATES, INC.
6 Century Drive, Parsippany NJ 07054. 973/455-7100. **Fax:** 973/455-1194. **Contact:** Manager. **World Wide Web address:** http://www.goodrichsherwood.com. **Description:** An executive search firm that also offers outplacement/career transition counseling, executive coaching, and Human Resources consulting. **Specializes in the areas of:** Human Resources. **Corporate headquarters location:** New York NY. **Other area locations:** Princeton NJ. **Other U.S. locations:** Norwalk CT; Shelton CT; Rochester NY.

GRAHAM & COMPANY
34 Sycamore Avenue, Building 2 South, Little Silver NJ 07739. 732/747-8000. **Fax:** 732/576-1676. **Contact:** Harold Scott, President. **Description:** An executive search firm. **Specializes in the areas of:** Chemicals; Rubber. **Average salary range of placements:** $75,000 - $100,000.

GRANT FRANKS & ASSOCIATES
929 North Kings Highway, Cherry Hill NJ 08034. 856/779-8844. **Fax:** 856/779-0898. **Contact:** Lou Franks, Owner. **Description:** An executive search firm operating on a contingency basis. **Specializes in the areas of:** Accounting/Auditing; Engineering; Manufacturing. **Positions commonly filled include:** Accountant/Auditor; Biomedical Engineer; Chemical Engineer; Chemist; Claim Representative; Credit Manager; Customer Service Representative; Electrical/Electronics Engineer; Financial Analyst; Food Scientist/Technologist; Human Resources Manager; Mechanical Engineer; Operations/Production Manager; Petroleum Engineer; Physical Therapist; Quality Control Supervisor; Underwriter/Assistant Underwriter.

HRD CONSULTANTS, INC.
60 Walnut Avenue, Clark NJ 07066. 732/815-7825. **Contact:** Manager. **World Wide Web address:** http://www.hrdconsultants.com. **Description:** An executive search firm that operates on a retainer basis. HRD Consultants recruits exclusively for executive level human resources positions. **Specializes in the areas of:** Human Resources. **Positions commonly filled include:** Human Resources Manager.

HADLEY ASSOCIATES
147 Columbia Turnpike, Suite 104, Florham Park NJ 07932. 973/377-9177. **Fax:** 973/377-9223. **Contact:** Thomas Hadley, President. **Description:** An executive search firm operating on both retainer and contingency bases. **Specializes in the areas of:** Health/Medical. **Positions commonly filled include:** Biological Scientist; Biomedical Engineer; Chemical Engineer; Chemist; Clinical Lab Technician; Environmental Engineer; Pharmacist; Quality Control Supervisor; Radiological Technologist; Statistician. **Average salary range of placements:** More than $50,000.

HALEY STUART, INC.
1605 John Street, Fort Lee NJ 07024. 201/944-7777. **Fax:** 201/944-3139. **Contact:** Manager. **E-mail address:** lawjobs@haleystuart.com. **Description:** An executive search firm that also provides some temporary placements. **Specializes in the areas of:** Legal.

ROBERT HALF INTERNATIONAL ACCOUNTEMPS
581 Main Street, 6th Floor, Woodbridge NJ 07095. 732/634-7200. **Contact:** Manager. **Description:** An executive search firm. Accountemps (also at this location) provides temporary placements. **Specializes in the areas of:** Accounting/Auditing. **Corporate headquarters location:** Menlo Park CA. **Other U.S. locations:** Nationwide.

ROBERT HALF INTERNATIONAL, INC. ACCOUNTEMPS
61 South Paramus Road, Paramus NJ 07652. 201/843-3799. **Fax:** 201/843-3977. **Contact:** Manager. **Description:** An executive search firm. Accountemps (also at this location) provides temporary placements. **Specializes in the areas of:** Accounting; Finance. **Corporate headquarters location:** Menlo Park CA. **Other U.S. locations:** Nationwide.

ROBERT HALF INTERNATIONAL ACCOUNTEMPS
959 Route 46 East, 4th Floor, Parsippany NJ 07054. 973/455-7300. **Fax:** 973/257-1322. **Contact:** Al Saverino, Branch Manager. **Description:** An executive search firm. Accountemps (also at this location) provides temporary placements. **Specializes in the areas of:** Accounting/Auditing. **Corporate headquarters location:** Menlo Park CA. **Other U.S. locations:** Nationwide.

HARRIS EXECUTIVE SEARCH
1800 Fairlawn Avenue, Fairlawn NJ 07410. 201/703-1414. **Contact:** Manager. **Description:** An executive search firm. **Specializes in the areas of:** Engineering; Manufacturing.

THE HARRISON GROUP
P.O. Box 743, Milltown NJ 08850. 732/249-6777. **Fax:** 732/249-9108. **Contact:** Scott Szur, Recruiter. **Description:** An executive search firm. **Specializes in the areas of:** Pharmaceuticals; Research and Development.

HEADHUNTERS EXECUTIVE SEARCH
96 Princeton Street, Nutley NJ 07110. 973/667-2799. **Fax:** 973/667-3609. **Contact:** Elaine Jones, Vice President. **Description:** An executive search firm. **Specializes in the areas of:** Health/Medical; Sales. **Number of placements per year:** 200 - 499.

HEALTHCARE RECRUITERS
3 Eves Drive, Suite 303, Marlton NJ 08053. 856/596-7179. **Fax:** 856/596-6895. **Contact:** Diane Rosamelea, General Manager. **Description:** An executive search firm. **Specializes in the areas of:** Health/Medical. **Positions commonly filled include:** Biological Scientist; Biomedical Engineer; Marketing Manager; MIS Specialist; Recruiter; Software Engineer. **Other U.S. locations:** Dallas TX. **Average salary range of placements:** $30,000 - $50,000. **Number of placements per year:** 50 - 99.

HEALTHCARE RECRUITERS
55 Harristown Road, Glen Rock NJ 07452. 201/670-9800. **Contact:** Manager. **Description:** An executive search firm. **Specializes in the areas of:** Health/Medical.

HILLSIDE GROUP
One Tenafly Court, Tenafly NJ 07670. 201/816-1005. **Fax:** 201/816-1501. **Contact:** Manager. **Description:** An executive search firm.

HINCKLEY ASSOCIATES
43 West Front, Red Bank NJ 07701. 732/747-0066. **Fax:** 732/747-6999. **Contact:** Jim Hinckley, President. **Description:** An executive search firm. **Specializes in the areas of:** Finance.

HOLM PERSONNEL CONSULTANTS
333-B Route 46 West, Suite 202, Fairfield NJ 07004. 973/808-1933. **Contact:** Manager. **Description:** An executive search firm. **Specializes in the areas of:** Accounting/Auditing; Administration; Computer Science/Software; General Management; Personnel/Labor Relations; Sales; Secretarial. **Positions commonly filled include:** Accountant/Auditor; Administrative Manager; Budget Analyst; Buyer; Computer Programmer; Credit Manager; Financial Analyst; Human Resources Specialist; Management Trainee; MIS Specialist; Purchasing Agent/Manager; Software Engineer; Systems Analyst; Telecommunications Manager; Transportation/Traffic Specialist. **Average salary range of placements:** $30,000 - $50,000. **Number of placements per year:** 50 - 99.

THE HOWARD GROUP, LTD.
522 Highway 9 North, Suite 101, Manalapan NJ 07726. 732/536-0345. **Fax:** 732/536-4559. **Contact:** Howard Engel, CEO. **E-mail address:** info@thg-ltd.com. **World Wide Web address:** http://www.thg-ltd.com. **Description:** An executive search firm operating on a contingency basis. **Specializes in the areas of:** Accounting; Banking; Computer Science/Software; Finance; Internet Development; Marketing; MIS/EDP; Sales. **Positions commonly filled include:** Account Manager; Account Representative; Accountant; Applications Engineer; AS400 Programmer Analyst; Chief Financial Officer; Computer Engineer; Computer Operator; Computer Programmer; Computer Support Technician; Computer Technician; Controller; Database Administrator; Database Manager; Desktop Publishing Specialist; Finance Director; Financial Analyst; Human Resources Manager; Internet Services Manager; MIS Specialist; Network/Systems Administrator; Project Manager; Sales Executive; Sales Manager; Sales Representative; Software Engineer; SQL Programmer; Systems Analyst; Systems Manager; Technical Writer/Editor; Telecommunications Manager; Webmaster. **Corporate headquarters location:** This Location. **Average salary range of placements:** $50,000 - $100,000. **Number of placements per year:** 100 - 199.

HRESHKO CONSULTING GROUP
850 U.S. Route 1 North, North Brunswick NJ 08902. 732/545-9000. **Fax:** 732/545-0080. **Contact:** Frank Hreshko, President. **Description:** An executive search firm. **Specializes in the areas of:** Accounting; Finance; Information Systems; Information Technology; Management Consulting; Manufacturing; Marketing; Sales.

HUFF ASSOCIATES
95 Reef Drive, Ocean City NJ 08226. 609/399-2867. **Contact:** W.Z. Huff, President. **Description:** An executive search firm. **Specializes in the areas of:** Biotechnology; Casinos; Communications; Computer Operations; Construction; Electronics; Engineering; Environmental; Health/Medical; High-Tech; Insurance; Manufacturing; Packaging; Pharmaceuticals; Telecommunications. **Positions commonly filled include:** Administrator; Engineer; Management; Physician. **Number of placements per year:** 1 - 49.

INSEARCH INC.
231 South White Horse Pike, Audubon NJ 08106. 856/546-6500. **Fax:** 856/546-6228. **Contact:** Charles Marcantonio, President. **Description:** An executive search firm operating on a contingency basis. **Specializes in the areas of:** Accounting; Administration; Computer Science/Software; Engineering; Finance; Insurance; MIS/EDP; Sales; Scientific; Technical. **Positions commonly filled include:** Account Manager; Account Representative; Accountant; Adjuster; Administrative Assistant; Administrative Manager; Advertising Executive; Applications Engineer; Assistant Manager; Auditor; Biological Scientist; Chief Financial Officer; Claim Representative; Clerical Supervisor; Computer Programmer; Consultant; Controller; Customer Service

Representative; Database Manager; Finance Director; Financial Analyst; Human Resources Manager; Insurance Agent/Broker; Market Research Analyst; Marketing Manager; Marketing Specialist; MIS Specialist; Operations Manager; Sales Executive; Sales Manager; Sales Representative; Software Engineer; Statistician; Systems Analyst; Systems Manager; Underwriter/Assistant Underwriter; Vice President. **Other U.S. locations:** Nationwide. **Number of placements per year:** 200 - 499.

INTELLIGENT STAFFING
991 U.S. Highway 22, Suite 200, Bridgewater NJ 08807. 908/218-4015. **Fax:** 908/218-9270. **Contact:** Manager. **World Wide Web address:** http://www.intelstaf.com. **Description:** Intelligent Staffing is an executive search firm. **Specializes in the areas of:** Information Technology.

INTER-REGIONAL EXECUTIVE SEARCH, INC.
191 Hamburg Turnpike, Pompton Lakes NJ 07442-2332. 973/616-8800. **Contact:** Frank Risalvato, Managing Partner. **E-mail address:** ires@erols.com. **Description:** An executive search firm operating on a contingency basis. **Specializes in the areas of:** Accounting/Auditing; Engineering; Finance; Insurance; Sales. **Positions commonly filled include:** Accountant/Auditor; Administrative Manager; Bank Officer/Manager; Biochemist; Biological Scientist; Biomedical Engineer; Budget Analyst; Chemical Engineer; Chemist; Claim Representative; Credit Manager; Customer Service Representative; Design Engineer; Designer; Economist; Financial Analyst; Industrial Engineer; Industrial Production Manager; Insurance Agent/Broker; Market Research Analyst; Mechanical Engineer; MIS Specialist; Nuclear Engineer; Pharmacist; Purchasing Agent/Manager; Telecommunications Manager; Underwriter/Assistant Underwriter. **Average salary range of placements:** $50,000 - $100,000. **Number of placements per year:** 100 - 199.

J.M. JOSEPH ASSOCIATES
P.O. Box 104, High Bridge NJ 08829-0104. 908/638-6877. **Fax:** 908/638-8220. **Contact:** C. Russell Ditzel, Managing Director. **E-mail address:** research@jmjoseph.com. **World Wide Web address:** http://www.jmjoseph.com. **Description:** An executive search firm. **Specializes in the areas of:** Administration; Computer Science/Software; Engineering; Food; Health/Medical; Manufacturing; Personnel/Labor Relations; Sales; Technical. **Positions commonly filled include:** Financial Analyst; Food Scientist/Technologist; Human Resources Specialist; Industrial Engineer; Industrial Production Manager; MIS Specialist; Operations/Production Manager; Strategic Relations Manager. **Average salary range of placements:** More than $50,000. **Number of placements per year:** 1 - 49.

KDC GROUP
114 Main Street, Kingston NJ 08528. 609/252-9060. **Fax:** 609/252-1871. **Contact:** K. David Cadieu, Owner. **Description:** An executive search firm. **Specializes in the areas of:** Pharmaceuticals.

KAMA CONSULTING INC.
Office Court of Ramsey, 300 Lake Street, Suite H, Ramsey NJ 07446. 201/934-7888. **Fax:** 201/934-7166. **Contact:** Rod McFadden, Vice President - Recruiting. **E-mail address:** kamaco@aol.com. **World Wide Web address:** http://www.kamaco.com. **Description:** An executive search firm. **Specializes in the areas of:** Computer Programming; Consulting.

KANE ASSOCIATES
41 Vreeland Avenue, Totowa NJ 07512. 973/890-9110. **Contact:** Manager. **Description:** An executive search firm operating on a contingency basis.

KARRAS PERSONNEL INC.
2 Central Avenue, Madison NJ 07940. 973/966-6800. **Contact:** Bill Karras, Recruiter. **Description:** An executive search firm. **Specializes in the areas of:**

Human Resources. **Positions commonly filled include:** Human Resources Specialist. **Average salary range of placements:** More than $50,000.

KAZAN INTERNATIONAL
5 Cold Hill Road, Suite 26, Mendham NJ 07945. 973/543-0300. **Fax:** 973/543-4235. **Contact:** Neil Kazan, President. **Description:** An executive search firm. **Specializes in the areas of:** Health/Medical.

KEY EMPLOYMENT
1014 Livingston Avenue, North Brunswick NJ 08902. 732/249-2454. **Fax:** 732/249-2521. **Contact:** Gary Silberger, President. **Description:** An executive search firm. **Specializes in the areas of:** Administration; Engineering; Marketing; Sales; Technical. **Positions commonly filled include:** Chemical Engineer; Chemist; Civil Engineer; Computer Programmer; Construction Contractor; Design Engineer; Designer; Electrical/Electronics Engineer; Environmental Engineer; Financial Analyst; General Manager; Industrial Engineer; Industrial Production Manager; Market Research Analyst; Mechanical Engineer; Metallurgical Engineer; MIS Specialist; Nuclear Engineer; Purchasing Agent/Manager; Software Engineer; Stationary Engineer; Structural Engineer; Systems Analyst; Telecommunications Manager. **Average salary range of placements:** More than $50,000. **Number of placements per year:** 1 - 49.

KILEY, OWEN & McGOVERN, INC.
P.O. Box 68, Blackwood NJ 08012. 856/227-5332. **Fax:** 856/227-5530. **Contact:** Ms. Sheila McGovern, President. **Description:** An executive search firm. **Specializes in the areas of:** Engineering; Information Technology; Manufacturing; Marketing; Sales; Technical; Telecommunications.

THE KLEINSTEIN GROUP
33 Wood Avenue South, Iselin NJ 08830. 732/494-7500. **Fax:** 732/494-7579. **Contact:** Jonathan Kleinstein, President. **Description:** A generalist executive search firm.

T.J. KOELLHOFFER & ASSOCIATES
250 Route 28, Suite 206, Bridgewater NJ 08807. 908/526-6880. **Fax:** 908/725-2653. **Contact:** Tom Koellhoffer, Principal. **E-mail address:** tkoell@aol.com. **Description:** An executive search firm operating on a retainer basis. Client company pays fee. **Specializes in the areas of:** Biotechnology; Broadcasting; Computer Science/Software; Engineering; Technical. **Positions commonly filled include:** Applications Engineer; Biochemist; Biological Scientist; Biomedical Engineer; Chief Financial Officer; Computer Animator; Computer Engineer; Computer Programmer; Computer Scientist; MIS Specialist; Multimedia Designer; Software Engineer; Telecommunications Manager; Vice President of Operations; Video Production Coordinator. **Corporate headquarters location:** This Location. **Average salary range of placements:** More than $100,000. **Number of placements per year:** 50 - 99.

KORN/FERRY INTERNATIONAL
7 Roszel Road, 5th Floor, Princeton NJ 08540. 609/452-8848. **Fax:** 609/452-9699. **Contact:** Manager. **World Wide Web address:** http://www.kornferry.com. **Description:** An executive search firm. **Corporate headquarters location:** Los Angeles CA. **International locations:** Worldwide. **Average salary range of placements:** More than $50,000.

PAUL KULL & COMPANY
18 Meadowbrook Road, Randolph NJ 07869. 973/361-7440. **Contact:** Paul Kull, Owner. **Description:** An executive search firm. **Specializes in the areas of:** Computer Hardware/Software; Engineering; General Management; Manufacturing; Sales; Technical. **Positions commonly filled include:** Aerospace Engineer; Biochemist; Biomedical Engineer; Chemical Engineer; Computer Programmer; Electrical/Electronics Engineer; Industrial Engineer; Manufacturing Engineer;

Marketing Specialist; Mechanical Engineer; Software Engineer. **Number of placements per year:** 1 - 49.

L&K ASSOCIATES
P.O. Box 202, Salem NJ 08079. 856/935-3070. **Contact:** Gene Lank, President. **Description:** An executive search firm operating on both retainer and contingency bases. **Specializes in the areas of:** Computer Science/Software; Legal; Technical; Telecommunications. **Positions commonly filled include:** Attorney; Computer Programmer; MIS Specialist; Systems Analyst; Telecommunications Manager. **Average salary range of placements:** More than $50,000. **Number of placements per year:** 1 - 49.

LANCASTER ASSOCIATES
THE SWAN GROUP
94 Grove Street, Somerville NJ 08876. 908/526-5440. **Fax:** 908/526-1992. **Contact:** Ray Lancaster, President. **E-mail address:** rfl@eclipse.net. **Description:** An executive search firm operating on both retainer and contingency bases. The Swan Group (also at this location) is an executive search firm. **Specializes in the areas of:** Internet Development; MIS/EDP. **Positions commonly filled include:** Applications Engineer; AS400 Programmer Analyst; Computer Programmer; Computer Support Technician; Database Administrator; Database Manager; Internet Services Manager; MIS Specialist; Network/Systems Administrator; Software Engineer; SQL Programmer; Systems Analyst; Systems Manager; Webmaster. **Average salary range of placements:** More than $50,000. **Number of placements per year:** 1 - 49.

LAW PROS LEGAL PLACEMENT SERVICES, INC.
511 Millburn Avenue, Short Hills NJ 07078. 973/912-8400. **Fax:** 973/912-8558. **Contact:** Beth Richmond, Principal. **Description:** An executive search firm. **Specializes in the areas of:** Legal. **Positions commonly filled include:** Attorney; Paralegal. **Average salary range of placements:** $30,000 - $50,000. **Number of placements per year:** 100 - 199.

ALAN LERNER ASSOCIATES
146 Lakeview Drive South, Gibbsboro NJ 08026. 856/435-1600. **Contact:** Manager. **Description:** An executive search firm.

LOGIC ASSOCIATES
9 Auer Court, East Brunswick NJ 08816. 732/238-5500. **Contact:** Manager. **Description:** An executive search firm. **Specializes in the areas of:** Insurance. **Corporate headquarters location:** New York NY.

AL LONDINO & ASSOCIATES
621 Shrewsbury Avenue, Shrewsbury NJ 07702. 732/219-8889. **Fax:** 732/219-9117. **Contact:** Al Londino, Manager/Owner. **Description:** An executive search firm. **Specializes in the areas of:** Printing.

MJE RECRUITERS, INC.
123 Columbia Turnpike, Suite 204A, Florham Park NJ 07932. 973/765-9400. **Fax:** 973/765-0881. **Contact:** Barry Emen, President. **E-mail address:** mjerecru@aol.com. **Description:** An executive search firm. **Specializes in the areas of:** Accounting/Auditing; Banking; Finance; Insurance; Investment. **Positions commonly filled include:** Accountant/Auditor; Bank Officer/Manager; Budget Analyst; Finance Director; Financial Analyst; Fund Manager. **Number of placements per year:** 50 - 99.

M.R. GROUP, INC.
1068 Oakland Avenue, Plainfield NJ 07060. 908/754-4713. **Fax:** 908/757-3987. **Contact:** Ted Prehodka, President. **E-mail address:** mrgroup@ix.netcom.com. **World Wide Web address:** http://www.careerenhancement.com. **Description:** An executive search firm. **Specializes in the areas of:** Banking; Information Systems; Information Technology; Marketing; Sales; Technical; Telecommunications. **Positions commonly filled include:** Database

Administrator; Information Specialist; Sales and Marketing Manager; UNIX System Administrator.

MADISON EXECUTIVE SEARCH, INC.
4 Birch Parkway, Sparta NJ 07871. 973/729-5520. **Contact:** Manager. **Description:** An executive search firm. **Specializes in the areas of:** Telecommunications.

MAJOR CONSULTANTS
500 North Franklin Turnpike, Suite 17, Ramsey NJ 07446. 201/934-9666. **Fax:** 201/818-0339. **Contact:** Consultant. **E-mail address:** recruiter@majorinc.com. **World Wide Web address:** http://www.majorinc.com. **Description:** An executive search firm operating on both retainer and contingency bases. **Specializes in the areas of:** Banking; Computer Science/Software; Engineering; Finance; General Management; Insurance; Personnel/Labor Relations; Sales; Scientific; Technical. **Positions commonly filled include:** Account Manager; Accountant/Auditor; Bank Officer/Manager; Branch Manager; Credit Manager; Design Engineer; Electrical/Electronics Engineer; General Manager; Human Resources Specialist; Mechanical Engineer; Operations/Production Manager; Software Engineer; Systems Analyst; Telecommunications Manager.

MANAGEMENT CATALYSTS
P.O. Box 70, Ship Bottom NJ 08008. 609/597-0079. **Fax:** 609/597-2860. **Contact:** Dr. J.R. Stockton, Principal. **Description:** An executive search firm. **Specializes in the areas of:** Food; Research and Development; Technical. **Positions commonly filled include:** Agricultural Engineer; Agricultural Scientist; Biochemist; Biological Scientist; Biomedical Engineer; Chemical Engineer; Chemist; Clinical Lab Technician; Dietician/Nutritionist; Environmental Engineer; Food Scientist/Technologist; Quality Control Supervisor; Science Technologist. **Average salary range of placements:** More than $50,000. **Number of placements per year:** 1 - 49.

MANAGEMENT GROUP OF AMERICA, INC.
250 Passaic Avenue, Suite 210, Fairfield NJ 07004. 973/808-3300. **Fax:** 973/882-9284. **Contact:** James W. Byrne, President. **Description:** An executive search firm operating on a contingency basis. The firm also provides some temporary and contract placements. **Specializes in the areas of:** Insurance. **Positions commonly filled include:** Customer Service Representative; Insurance Agent/Broker; Sales Representative. **Average salary range of placements:** $30,000 - $50,000. **Number of placements per year:** 100 - 199.

MANAGEMENT RECRUITERS
121 State Highway 36, Suite 180, West Long Branch NJ 07764. 732/222-6686. **Fax:** 732/222-5339. **Contact:** Amy Anson, Head Administrator. **E-mail address:** mrlongbranch@netlabs.net. **World Wide Web address:** http://www.mrienergy.com. **Description:** An executive search firm that recruits for the energy industry. **Corporate headquarters location:** Cleveland OH. **Other U.S. locations:** Nationwide.

MANAGEMENT RECRUITERS
OFFICEMATES5 OF UNION COUNTY
1104 Springfield Avenue, Mountainside NJ 07092. 908/789-9400. **Fax:** 908/789-8845. **Contact:** Anita Newhall, Internet Researcher. **E-mail address:** mriunion@aol.com. **World Wide Web address:** http://www.mriunion.com. **Description:** An executive search firm operating on a contingency basis. Client company pays fee. **Specializes in the areas of:** Accounting; Administration; Advertising; Banking; Finance; Industrial; Internet Marketing; Marketing; Personnel/Labor Relations; Sales; Secretarial. **Positions commonly filled include:** Account Manager; Account Representative; Accountant; Administrative Assistant; Administrative Manager; Advertising Executive; Auditor; Budget Analyst; Buyer; Chief Financial Officer; Clerical Supervisor; Controller; Customer Service Representative; Database Manager; Editor; Finance Director; Financial Analyst; Graphic Artist; Graphic Designer; Human Resources Manager; Management Trainee; Market Research Analyst; Marketing Manager; Marketing Specialist; Multimedia Designer; Operations Manager; Paralegal; Project Manager; Public Relations Specialist; Purchasing Agent/Manager; Sales Executive; Sales Manager; Sales Representative; Secretary; Technical Writer/Editor; Telecommunications Manager; Typist/Word Processor. **Corporate headquarters location:** Cleveland OH. **Other U.S. locations:** Nationwide.

MANAGEMENT RECRUITERS INTERNATIONAL
19 Tanner Street, Haddonfield NJ 08033. 856/428-2233. **Contact:** Manager. **Description:** An executive search firm. **Specializes in the areas of:** High-Tech; Sales. **Corporate headquarters location:** Cleveland OH. **Other U.S. locations:** Nationwide.

MANAGEMENT RECRUITERS INTERNATIONAL
P.O. Box 244, Hope NJ 07844. 908/459-5798. **Contact:** Manager. **E-mail address:** mrinw@planet.net. **Description:** An executive search firm operating on both retainer and contingency bases. Client company pays fee. **Specializes in the areas of:** Engineering; Personnel/Labor Relations. **Positions commonly filled include:** Human Resources Manager; Industrial Engineer; Manufacturing Engineer; Mechanical Engineer; Quality Assurance Engineer. **Corporate headquarters location:** Cleveland OH. **Other U.S. locations:** Nationwide.

MANAGEMENT RECRUITERS INTERNATIONAL
4 Waterloo Road, Stanhope NJ 07874. 973/691-2020. **Contact:** Manager. **Description:** An executive search firm. **Specializes in the areas of:** Computer Hardware/Software. **Corporate headquarters location:** Cleveland OH. **Other U.S. locations:** Nationwide.

MANAGEMENT RECRUITERS INTERNATIONAL
440 County Road 513, Califon NJ 07830. 908/832-6455. **Contact:** Manager. **Description:** An executive search firm. **Specializes in the areas of:** Insurance. **Corporate headquarters location:** Cleveland OH. **Other U.S. locations:** Nationwide.

MANAGEMENT RECRUITERS INTERNATIONAL SALES CONSULTANTS
1230 Parkway Avenue, Suite 102, West Trenton NJ 08628. 609/882-8388. **Fax:** 609/882-4862. **Contact:** Robert J. Bodnar, President. **Description:** An executive search firm. **Specializes in the areas of:** Engineering. **Corporate headquarters location:** Cleveland OH. **Other U.S. locations:** Nationwide.

MANAGEMENT RECRUITERS INTERNATIONAL
276 Main Street, Metuchen NJ 08840. 732/767-1025. **Fax:** 732/767-1218. **Contact:** Marge Noorani, Office Manager. **Description:** An executive search firm. **Specializes in the areas of:** Engineering. **Corporate headquarters location:** Cleveland OH. **Other U.S. locations:** Nationwide.

MANAGEMENT RECRUITERS INTERNATIONAL
186 Princeton Heightstown Road, Suite 3B, Princeton Junction NJ 08550. 609/897-0055. **Fax:** 609/897-0099. **Contact:** Robert Walling, President. **Description:** An executive search firm. **Specializes in the areas of:** Direct Marketing; Retail. **Corporate headquarters location:** Cleveland OH. **Other U.S. locations:** Nationwide.

MANAGEMENT RECRUITERS INTERNATIONAL COMPUSEARCH
10 Anderson Road, Suite 7, Bernardsville NJ 07924. 908/204-0070. **Contact:** Manager. **Description:** An executive search firm. **Specializes in the areas of:** Computer Hardware/Software. **Corporate headquarters location:** Cleveland OH.

MANAGEMENT RECRUITERS INTERNATIONAL OF MORRIS COUNTY
17 Hanover Road, Suite 450, Florham Park NJ 07932. 973/593-0400. **Contact:** Sue Young, General Manager.

E-mail address: sue@mrimc.com. World Wide Web address: http://www.mrimc.com. Description: An executive search firm. Specializes in the areas of: Computer Science/Software; Data Communications; Marketing; Public Relations; Sales; Sales Management; Telecommunications; Wireless Communications. Corporate headquarters location: Cleveland OH. Other U.S. locations: Nationwide.

MANAGEMENT RECRUITERS OF BAY HEAD
106 Bridge Avenue, Bay Head NJ 08742. 732/714-1300. Fax: 732/714-1311. Contact: Bob Ceresi, General Manager. E-mail address: bob@mrielectrical.com. World Wide Web address: http://www.mrielectrical.com. Description: An executive search firm operating on a contingency basis. Specializes in the areas of: Computer Science/Software; Engineering; Industrial; Light Industrial; Manufacturing; Marketing; Sales; Scientific; Technical. Positions commonly filled include: Account Manager; Account Representative; Branch Manager; Computer Programmer; Design Engineer; Electrical/Electronics Engineer; General Manager; Industrial Engineer; Manufacturing Engineer; Market Research Analyst; Marketing Manager; Marketing Specialist; Mechanical Engineer; Operations Manager; Production Manager; Purchasing Agent/Manager; Quality Control Supervisor; Sales Engineer; Sales Executive; Sales Manager; Sales Representative; Software Engineer. Corporate headquarters location: Cleveland OH. Other U.S. locations: Nationwide. International locations: Worldwide. Average salary range of placements: More than $50,000. Number of placements per year: 50 - 99.

MANAGEMENT RECRUITERS OF BRIDGEWATER
1170 U.S. Highway 22 East, Bridgewater NJ 08807. 908/725-2595. Fax: 908/725-0439. Contact: Jennifer Lebron, Account Executive. Description: An executive search firm operating on both retainer and contingency bases. Specializes in the areas of: Banking; Finance; Insurance; Sales; Transportation. Positions commonly filled include: Accountant/Auditor; Bank Officer/Manager; Buyer; Claim Representative; Credit Manager; Customer Service Representative; Financial Analyst; Health Services Manager; Insurance Agent/Broker; Manufacturer's/Wholesaler's Sales Rep.; Services Sales Representative; Transportation/Traffic Specialist; Underwriter/Assistant Underwriter. Corporate headquarters location: Cleveland OH. Other U.S. locations: Nationwide. Average salary range of placements: More than $50,000. Number of placements per year: 100 - 199.

MANAGEMENT RECRUITERS OF MEDFORD
30 Jackson Road, Suite C4, Medford NJ 08055. 609/654-9109. Contact: Norman Talbot, President. E-mail address: resumes@pharmabiosearch.com. World Wide Web address: http://www.pharmabiosearch.com. Description: An executive search firm. Specializes in the areas of: Architecture/Construction; Biotechnology; Chemicals; Electronics; Engineering; Food; General Management; Industrial; Manufacturing; Paper; Petrochemical; Pharmaceuticals; Sales; Technical. Positions commonly filled include: Aerospace Engineer; Biological Scientist; Biomedical Engineer; Chemical Engineer; Chemist; Civil Engineer; Draftsperson; Electrical/Electronics Engineer; Industrial Engineer; Industrial Hygienist; Manufacturing Engineer; Mechanical Engineer; Metallurgical Engineer; Quality Control Supervisor; Safety Engineer; Software Engineer; Systems Analyst. Corporate headquarters location: Cleveland OH. Other U.S. locations: Nationwide. Average salary range of placements: More than $50,000. Number of placements per year: 50 - 99.

MANAGEMENT RECRUITERS OF NEW PROVIDENCE
150 Floral Avenue, New Providence NJ 07974. 908/771-0600. Contact: Manager. Description: An executive search firm. Specializes in the areas of: Information

Systems; Sales. Corporate headquarters location: Cleveland OH. Other U.S. locations: Nationwide.

MANAGEMENT RECRUITERS OF PASSAIC COUNTY
750 Hamburg Turnpike, Suite 203, Pompton Lakes NJ 07442. 973/831-7778. Contact: David Zawicki, Manager. Description: An executive search firm. Specializes in the areas of: Accounting/Auditing; Administration; Advertising; Architecture/Construction; Banking; Communications; Computer Science/Software; Construction; Electrical; Engineering; Finance; Food; General Management; Health/Medical; Personnel/Labor Relations; Procurement; Publishing; Real Estate; Retail; Sales; Technical; Textiles; Transportation. Corporate headquarters location: Cleveland OH. Other U.S. locations: Nationwide.

MANAGEMENT RECRUITERS OF SHORT HILLS
181 Millburn Avenue, Millburn NJ 07041. 973/379-4020. Contact: Manager. Description: An executive search firm. Specializes in the areas of: Computer Hardware/Software; Computer Programming; Engineering; Sales. Corporate headquarters location: Cleveland OH. Other U.S. locations: Nationwide.

MANAGEMENT RECRUITERS OF SPARTA
191 Woodport Road, Suite 201, Sparta NJ 07871. 973/729-1888. Toll-free phone: 800/875-1896. Fax: 973/729-1620. Contact: Lance Incitti, President. E-mail address: recruiter@retailplacement.com. World Wide Web address: http://www.retailplacement.com. Description: An executive search firm. Specializes in the areas of: Accounting/Auditing; Finance; Retail. Positions commonly filled include: Auditor; Buyer; Controller; Financial Analyst; Human Resources Manager; Management Analyst/Consultant; Operations Manager. Corporate headquarters location: Cleveland OH. Other U.S. locations: Nationwide. Average salary range of placements: $30,000 - $50,000. Number of placements per year: 50 - 99.

MARTIN PERSONNEL SERVICE INC.
858 U.S. Highway 1 North, Edison NJ 08817. 732/287-3311. Fax: 732/287-3585. Contact: Martin Bell, President. Description: An executive search firm. Specializes in the areas of: Accounting.

McDERMOTT RESOURCES INC.
74 South Powder Mill Road, Morris Plains NJ 07950. 973/285-0066. Fax: 973/285-5463. Contact: Maureen McDermott, President. Description: An executive search firm operating on a contingency basis. Specializes in the areas of: Banking; Secretarial. Positions commonly filled include: Accountant/Auditor; Bank Officer/Manager; Credit Manager; Financial Analyst; Human Resources Specialist. Number of placements per year: 50 - 99.

McMAHON ASSOCIATES
26 Westover Avenue, Caldwell NJ 07006. 973/226-3888. Contact: Bob McMahon, President. Description: An executive search firm. NOTE: This firm does not accept unsolicited resumes. Please only respond to advertised openings. Specializes in the areas of: Engineering; Finance.

THE MELVILLE GROUP, INC.
7700 River Road, North Bergen NJ 07047. 201/295-1200. Contact: Ginny Pepper, President. Description: An executive search firm. Specializes in the areas of: Banking; Finance; Health/Medical. Positions commonly filled include: Bank Officer/Manager; Case Manager; Health Services Manager; Registered Nurse; Trust Officer.

MERLIN INTERNATIONAL INC.
600 East Crescent Avenue, Suite 303, Upper Saddle River NJ 07458. 201/825-7220. Fax: 201/825-1043. Contact: Jim Cinquina, President. Description: An executive search firm. Specializes in the areas of:

Pharmaceuticals. **Average salary range of placements:** $70,000 - $250,000.

RICHARD MEYERS & ASSOCIATES, INC.
15 James Street, Florham Park NJ 07932. 973/765-9000. **Fax:** 973/765-9009. **Contact:** Richard Meyers, President. **Description:** An executive search firm. **Specializes in the areas of:** Insurance; Risk Management. **Positions commonly filled include:** Insurance Agent/Broker; Underwriter/Assistant Underwriter. **Number of placements per year:** 100 - 199.

MIDDLEBROOK ASSOCIATES
6 Commerce Drive, Suite 2000, Cranford NJ 07016. 908/709-0707. **Fax:** 908/272-6297. **Contact:** Rita Richards, Manager of Scientific Recruiting. **Description:** An executive search firm. **Specializes in the areas of:** Biology; Engineering; Food; Technical. **Positions commonly filled include:** Biochemist; Biological Scientist; Biomedical Engineer; Chemical Engineer; Chemist; Design Engineer; Environmental Engineer; Food Scientist/Technologist; Industrial Engineer; Pharmacist; Science Technologist; Statistician. **Number of placements per year:** 1 - 49.

MILROD ASSOCIATES EXECUTIVE SEARCH
22 Riverside Drive, Princeton NJ 08540. 609/683-8787. **Fax:** 609/683-8221. **Contact:** Manager. **E-mail address:** milrodsearch@worldnet.att.net. **Description:** An executive search firm. **Specializes in the areas of:** Direct Marketing.

DIEDRE MOIRE CORPORATION, INC.
510 Horizon Center, Robbinsville NJ 08691. 609/584-9000x203. **Fax:** 609/584-9575. **Contact:** Manager. **World Wide Web address:** http://www.diedremoire1.com. **Description:** An executive search firm. **Specializes in the areas of:** Computer Hardware/Software; Engineering; Finance; Information Technology; Operations Management; Research and Development; Scientific; Systems Design; Technical.

MUFSON ASSOCIATES
580 Sylvan Avenue, Englewood Cliffs NJ 07632. 201/541-7700. **Fax:** 201/541-7674. **Contact:** John Mufson, President. **Description:** An executive search firm. **Specializes in the areas of:** Pharmaceuticals.

NORMYLE/ERSTLING HEALTH SEARCH GROUP
350 West Passaic Street, Rochelle Park NJ 07662. 201/843-6009. **Fax:** 201/843-2060. **Contact:** Charles D. Kreps, Managing Partner. **Description:** An executive search firm operating on a contingency basis. **Specializes in the areas of:** Biology; General Management; Health/Medical; Insurance; Marketing; Sales; Technical. **Positions commonly filled include:** Account Manager; Account Representative; Administrative Manager; Biochemist; Biomedical Engineer; Clinical Lab Technician; Marketing Manager; Marketing Specialist; Registered Nurse; Respiratory Therapist; Sales Engineer; Sales Executive; Sales Manager; Sales Representative; Vice President of Marketing and Sales. **Corporate headquarters location:** This Location. **Other U.S. locations:** Nationwide. **Average salary range of placements:** More than $50,000. **Number of placements per year:** 100 - 199.

NORTHEASTERN FINANCIAL CONSULTANTS
1163 Inman Avenue, Edison NJ 08820. 908/769-8888. **Fax:** 908/756-4043. **Contact:** Kerry Reilly, Vice President. **Description:** An executive search firm. **Specializes in the areas of:** Finance; Human Resources; Marketing; Mortgage; Technical.

ON TARGET SEARCH
21 Madison Plaza, Suite 154, Madison NJ 07940. 973/301-4001. **Toll-free phone:** 888/306-5035. **Fax:** 973/301-4005. **Contact:** Recruiter. **E-mail address:** jobs@ontargetsearch.com. **Description:** An executive search firm. On Target Search also offers some management consulting services. **Specializes in the areas of:** Information Systems.

ONLINE CAREER SEARCH, INC.
750 Routh 73 South, Suite 109, Marlton NJ 08053. 856/985-0110. **Fax:** 856/985-9394. **Contact:** Manager. **E-mail address:** info@onlinecareer.com. **World Wide Web address:** http://www.onlinecareer.com. **Description:** An executive search firm. **Specializes in the areas of:** Information Technology.

ORION CONSULTING, INC.
115 U.S. Highway 46, Suite 13-14, Mountain Lakes NJ 07046. 973/402-8866. **Fax:** 973/402-9258. **Contact:** James Dromsky, CEO. **E-mail address:** oci@orionconsultinginc.com. **World Wide Web address:** http://www.orionconsultinginc.com. **Description:** An executive search firm. **Specializes in the areas of:** Accounting/Auditing; Administration; Advertising; Chemicals; Communications; Design; Engineering; Finance; Food; General Management; Health/Medical; Industrial; Legal; Manufacturing; Military; Operations Management; Personnel/Labor Relations; Pharmaceuticals; Procurement; Sales; Technical; Transportation. **Number of placements per year:** 50 - 99.

PLC ASSOCIATES
7004 Boulevard East, Guttenberg NJ 07093. 201/854-4004. **Fax:** 201/869-8611. **Contact:** Peggy L. Cave, President. **Description:** An executive search firm. **Specializes in the areas of:** Finance; Information Technology; Marketing; Research and Development.

PR MANAGEMENT CONSULTANTS
601 Ewing Street, Suite C5, Princeton NJ 08540. 609/921-6565. **Contact:** Jerry Koenig, President. **Description:** An executive search firm. **Specializes in the areas of:** Engineering; General Management; Sales. **Positions commonly filled include:** Biochemist; Biomedical Engineer; Chemical Engineer; Design Engineer; Mechanical Engineer; Software Engineer; Statistician. **Average salary range of placements:** More than $50,000. **Number of placements per year:** 1 - 49.

SOLOMON PAGE GROUP, INC.
499 Thornall Street, Edison NJ 08837. 732/452-0212. **Fax:** 732/452-1101. **Contact:** Recruiter. **Description:** An executive search firm. **Specializes in the areas of:** Accounting; Fashion; Finance; Health/Medical; Information Technology; Legal.

FLORENCE PAPE LEGAL SEARCH, INC.
1208 Washington Street, Hoboken NJ 07030. 201/798-0200. **Toll-free phone:** 800/762-0096. **Fax:** 201/798-9088. **Contact:** Florence Pape, President. **E-mail address:** fpape@fpls.com. **Description:** An executive search firm operating on a contingency basis. **Specializes in the areas of:** Legal. **Positions commonly filled include:** Attorney. **Average salary range of placements:** $50,000 - $100,000+. **Number of placements per year:** 1 - 49.

RICK PASCAL & ASSOCIATES INC.
P.O. Box 543, Fair Lawn NJ 07410. 201/791-9541. **Fax:** 201/791-1861. **Contact:** Rick Pascal, CPC/President. **Description:** An executive search firm. **Specializes in the areas of:** Packaging. **Positions commonly filled include:** Designer; Management; Packaging Engineer; Packaging/Processing Worker.

PENNINGTON CONSULTING GROUP
65 South Main Street, Building B, Pennington NJ 08534. 609/737-8500. **Fax:** 609/737-8576. **Contact:** Robert B. White, President. **E-mail address:** rbw5725@aol.com. **World Wide Web address:** http://www.penningtonconsulting.com. **Description:** An executive search firm operating on both retainer and contingency bases. **Specializes in the areas of:** Wireless Communications. **Other U.S. locations:** Richmond VA.

Average salary range of placements: More than $50,000. Number of placements per year: 1 - 49.

THE PENNMOR GROUP
25 Chestnut Street, Suite 107, Haddonfield NJ 08033. 856/354-1414. **Fax:** 856/354-7660. **Contact:** Anthony Trasatti, President. **E-mail address:** ttrasatti@pennmor.com. **World Wide Web address:** http://www.pennmor.com. **Description:** An executive search firm. **Specializes in the areas of:** Accounting; Banking; Finance; Personnel/Labor Relations. **Positions commonly filled include:** Accountant; Auditor; Bank Officer/Manager; Chief Financial Officer; Controller; Finance Director; Financial Analyst; Human Resources Manager; Operations Manager. **Average salary range of placements:** $50,000 - $100,000. **Number of placements per year:** 1 - 49.

PERSONNEL ASSOCIATES INC.
239 U.S. Highway 22, Green Brook NJ 08812. 732/968-8866. **Fax:** 732/968-9437. **Contact:** Thomas C. Wood, President. **Description:** An executive search firm operating on a contingency basis. **Specializes in the areas of:** Administration; Computer Science/Software. **Positions commonly filled include:** Computer Programmer; Internet Services Manager; MIS Specialist; Project Manager; Systems Analyst. **Other U.S. locations:** Nationwide. **Number of placements per year:** 50 - 99.

PETRUZZI ASSOCIATES
P.O. Box 141, Scotch Plains NJ 07076. 908/754-1940. **Contact:** Manager. **Description:** An executive search firm. **Specializes in the areas of:** Chemicals; Health/Medical.

PHILADELPHIA SEARCH GROUP, INC.
One Cherry Hill, Suite 510, Cherry Hill NJ 08002. 856/667-2300. **Contact:** Manager. **Description:** An executive search firm operating on a contingency basis. **Specializes in the areas of:** Health/Medical; Sales. **Positions commonly filled include:** Sales Manager; Sales Representative. **Average salary range of placements:** More than $50,000. **Number of placements per year:** 50 - 99.

PHOENIX BIOSEARCH, INC.
P.O. Box 6157, West Caldwell NJ 07007-6157. 973/812-2666. **Fax:** 973/812-2727. **Contact:** Lee Stephenson, President. **Description:** An executive search firm operating on both retainer and contingency bases. **Specializes in the areas of:** Biology. **Positions commonly filled include:** Biochemist; Biological Scientist; Marketing Manager. **Average salary range of placements:** More than $50,000. **Number of placements per year:** 1 - 49.

PRICE BAKER SEARCH
139 Oxford Avenue, Boonton NJ 07005. 973/316-8877. **Fax:** 973/316-6888. **Contact:** Lou Baker, Owner. **Description:** An executive search firm. **Specializes in the areas of:** Manufacturing.

PRINCETON EXECUTIVE SEARCH
2667 Nottingham Way, Hamilton NJ 08619. 609/584-1100. **Fax:** 609/584-1141. **Contact:** Andrew B. Barkocy, CPC/President. **Description:** An executive search firm operating on both retainer and contingency bases. Client company pays fee. **Specializes in the areas of:** Accounting; Administration; Computer Science/Software; Engineering; Personnel/Labor Relations. **Positions commonly filled include:** Accountant/Auditor; Aerospace Engineer; AS400 Programmer Analyst; Bank Officer/Manager; Biomedical Engineer; Budget Analyst; Chemical Engineer; Chemist; Civil Engineer; Computer Programmer; Controller; Credit Manager; Electrical/Electronics Engineer; Financial Analyst; General Manager; Human Resources Manager; Industrial Engineer; Mechanical Engineer; Nuclear Engineer; Petroleum Engineer; Purchasing Agent/Manager; Software Engineer; SQL Programmer; Systems Analyst; Systems Manager. **Corporate headquarters location:**

This Location. **Other U.S. locations:** Nationwide. **Average salary range of placements:** $50,000 - $100,000. **Number of placements per year:** 1 - 49.

PRINCETON SEARCH PARTNERS, INC.
475 Wall Street, Princeton NJ 08540. 609/430-9600. **Fax:** 609/924-8270. **Contact:** Manager. **Description:** An executive search firm. **Specializes in the areas of:** Finance.

RCE ASSOCIATES
39 Tamarack Circle, Skillman NJ 08558. 609/688-1190. **Fax:** 609/688-1192. **Contact:** John W. Guarniere, President. **E-mail address:** jwg@plasticsearch.com. **World Wide Web address:** http://www.plasticsearch.com. **Description:** An executive search firm operating on a retainer basis. Client company pays fee. **Specializes in the areas of:** Engineering; Manufacturing; Plastics. **Positions commonly filled include:** Account Manager; Administrative Manager; Controller; Database Manager; Design Engineer; Electrical/Electronics Engineer; General Manager; Manufacturing Engineer; Marketing Manager; Mechanical Engineer; Metallurgical Engineer; Operations Manager; Production Manager; Sales Engineer; Sales Manager. **Corporate headquarters location:** This Location. **International locations:** 14 Back Street, Horsham St. Faith, Norwich NR103JP, United Kingdom. 011-441-304-813-857. Please address inquiries to Mr. Patrick Leonard. **Average salary range of placements:** More than $75,000. **Number of placements per year:** 1 - 49.

RAMMING & ASSOCIATES, INC.
3 Thackery Lane, Cherry Hill NJ 08003-1925. 856/428-7172. **Fax:** 856/428-7173. **Contact:** George Ramming, Owner. **E-mail address:** georger@dvnc.net. **Description:** An executive search firm. **Specializes in the areas of:** Engineering; General Management; Health/Medical; Manufacturing. **Positions commonly filled include:** Chemical Engineer; Design Engineer; Electrical/Electronics Engineer; General Manager; Mechanical Engineer; Software Engineer; Telecommunications Manager. **Average salary range of placements:** More than $50,000. **Number of placements per year:** 1 - 49.

RETAIL CONNECTION INC.
271 U.S. Highway 46 West, Suite D-105, Fairfield NJ 07004. 973/882-6662. **Toll-free phone:** 800/770-4945. **Fax:** 973/575-5858. **Contact:** Carole Thaller, President. **Description:** An executive search firm operating on a contingency basis. **Specializes in the areas of:** Retail. **Positions commonly filled include:** Chief Financial Officer; Sales Manager. **Number of placements per year:** 50 - 99.

JEFF RICH ASSOCIATES
67 Walnut Avenue, Suite 303, Clark NJ 07066. 732/574-3888. **Contact:** Manager. **Description:** An executive search firm. **Specializes in the areas of:** Accounting/Auditing; Finance.

RIDGEWOOD INTERMEDIARIES
51 South Broad Street, Ridgewood NJ 07450. 201/521-8111. **Fax:** 201/652-8996. **Contact:** Manager. **Description:** An executive search firm. **Specializes in the areas of:** Medical Sales and Marketing.

JAMES F. ROBINSON PROFESSIONAL RECRUITER
231 South White Horse Pike, Audubon NJ 08106. 856/547-5800. **Contact:** James F. Robinson, Owner. **Description:** An executive search firm. **Specializes in the areas of:** Legal. **Positions commonly filled include:** Attorney.

ROCHESTER SYSTEMS INC.
227 East Bergen Place, Red Bank NJ 07701. 732/747-7474. **Fax:** 732/747-7055. **Contact:** Manager. **Description:** An executive search firm. **Specializes in the areas of:** Accounting/Auditing; Computer

Science/Software; Logistics; Manufacturing; MIS/EDP. **Positions commonly filled include:** Computer Programmer; Financial Analyst; Industrial Production Manager; Management Analyst/Consultant; Manager of Information Systems; Operations/Production Manager; Software Engineer; Systems Analyst. **Number of placements per year:** 50 - 99.

ROMAC INTERNATIONAL
45 Eisenhower Drive, 4th Floor, Paramus NJ 07652. 201/843-2020. **Fax:** 201/843-7705. **Contact:** Branch Manager. **Description:** An executive search firm. **Specializes in the areas of:** Accounting/Auditing; Administration; Banking; Computer Science/Software; Engineering; Finance; Health/Medical; Legal; Manufacturing. **Positions commonly filled include:** Accountant/Auditor; Attorney; Budget Analyst; Computer Programmer; Credit Manager; Financial Analyst; Licensed Practical Nurse; MIS Specialist; Registered Nurse; Software Engineer. **Benefits available to temporary workers:** Profit Sharing. **Corporate headquarters location:** Tampa FL. **Other U.S. locations:** Nationwide. **Number of placements per year:** 1000+.

ROMAC INTERNATIONAL
100 Woodbridge Center Drive, Suite 101, Woodbridge NJ 07095. 732/283-9510. **Fax:** 732/283-0704. **Contact:** Manager. **Description:** An executive search firm. **Specializes in the areas of:** Computer Hardware/Software; Finance; Information Technology. **Corporate headquarters location:** Tampa FL.

ROMAC INTERNATIONAL
3 Independence Way, Suite 204, Princeton NJ 08540. 609/452-7277. **Fax:** 609/520-1742. **Contact:** Manager. **Description:** An executive search firm. **Specializes in the areas of:** Computer Hardware/Software; Information Technology. **Corporate headquarters location:** Tampa FL.

ROMAC INTERNATIONAL
One Gatehall Drive, 3rd Floor, Parsippany NJ 07054. 973/267-3222. **Fax:** 973/267-2741. **Contact:** Manager. **Description:** An executive search firm. **Specializes in the areas of:** Accounting/Auditing; Computer Hardware/Software; Information Technology. **Corporate headquarters location:** Tampa FL.

KEN ROSE ASSOCIATES
218 Route 17 North, Rochelle Park NJ 07662. 201/587-9611. **Fax:** 201/587-8609. **Contact:** Ken Rose, President. **Description:** An executive search firm. **Specializes in the areas of:** Fashion. **Average salary range of placements:** More than $50,000.

ROSENTHAL ASSOCIATES INTERNATIONAL (RAI)
60 Canterbury Road, Chatham NJ 07928. 973/701-9700. **Fax:** 973/701-9619. **Contact:** Abbe Rosenthal, Partner. **E-mail address:** abbe@raisearch.com. **World Wide Web address:** http://www.raisearch.com. **Description:** A global executive search and recruiting firm that also provides management support and executive coaching services. **Specializes in the areas of:** Accounting; Aerospace; Automotive; Biotechnology; Chemicals; Clinical Research; Communications; Consumer Package Goods; Consumer Products; Engineering; Environmental; Finance; High-Tech; Human Resources; Management; Management Consulting; Manufacturing; Marketing; Multimedia; Pharmaceuticals; Plastics; Public Relations; Quality Assurance; Sales; Telecommunications. **Other U.S. locations:** New York NY.

RUDERFER & COMPANY
908 Pompton Avenue, Cedar Grove NJ 07009. 973/857-2400. **Fax:** 973/857-4343. **Contact:** Irwin Ruderfer, President/CPC. **E-mail address:** search@ruderfer.com. **World Wide Web address:** http://www.ruderfer.com. **Description:** An executive search firm operating on both

retainer and contingency bases. Founded in 1993. **Specializes in the areas of:** Pharmaceuticals.

THE RUSSELL GROUP INC.
23 North Avenue East, Cranford NJ 07016. 908/709-1188. **Fax:** 908/709-0959. **Contact:** William Russell, President. **Description:** An executive search firm. **Specializes in the areas of:** Sales. **Average salary range of placements:** More than $50,000. **Number of placements per year:** 100 - 199.

ANTHONY RYAN ASSOCIATES
140 Route 17 North, Suite 309, Paramus NJ 07652. 201/967-7000. **Contact:** Marnie Livak, Manager. **Description:** An executive search firm. **Specializes in the areas of:** Computer Hardware/Software.

RYLAN FORBES CONSULTING GROUP
379 Thornall Street, 6th Floor, West Tower, Edison NJ 08837. 732/205-1900. **Fax:** 732/205-1901. **Contact:** Joe Stauffer, Vice President. **Description:** An executive search firm that also provides some temporary placements. **Specializes in the areas of:** Accounting/Auditing; Finance; Manufacturing; Retail. **Positions commonly filled include:** Accountant/Auditor; Budget Analyst; Financial Analyst. **Number of placements per year:** 50 - 99.

SK ASSOCIATES
CAREER CONSULTANTS
1767 Morris Avenue, Union NJ 07083. 908/687-7350. **Fax:** 908/688-5912. **Contact:** Manager. **Description:** An executive search firm. Career Consultants (also at this location) is a career/outplacement counseling firm. **Specializes in the areas of:** Apparel; Fashion.

R.S. SADOW ASSOCIATES
24 Heather Drive, Somerset NJ 08873. 732/545-4550. **Fax:** 732/545-0797. **Contact:** Ray Sadow, President. **Description:** An executive search firm operating on a contingency basis. **Specializes in the areas of:** Accounting/Auditing; Administration; Banking; Computer Science/Software; Engineering; Finance; Industrial; Manufacturing; Publishing; Scientific; Technical. **Positions commonly filled include:** Accountant/Auditor; Aerospace Engineer; Agricultural Engineer; Bank Officer/Manager; Biological Scientist; Biomedical Engineer; Budget Analyst; Ceramics Engineer; Chemical Engineer; Chemist; Civil Engineer; Clerical Supervisor; Computer Programmer; Controller; Credit Manager; Customer Service Representative; Draftsperson; Editor; Electrical/Electronics Engineer; Financial Analyst; Industrial Engineer; Industrial Production Manager; Materials Engineer; Mechanical Engineer; Metallurgical Engineer; Mining Engineer; Nuclear Engineer; Petroleum Engineer; Purchasing Agent/Manager; Quality Control Supervisor; Software Engineer; Stationary Engineer; Structural Engineer; Systems Analyst; Technical Writer/Editor. **Average salary range of placements:** More than $50,000. **Number of placements per year:** 1 - 49.

SALEM ASSOCIATES
1501 Paterson Hamburg Turnpike, Wayne NJ 07470. 973/305-6667. **Contact:** Recruiter. **Description:** An executive search firm. **Specializes in the areas of:** Advertising; Banking; Finance; Internet Marketing; Pharmaceuticals; Sales. **Corporate headquarters location:** New York NY.

SALES CONSULTANTS
800 Kings Highway North, Suite 402, Cherry Hill NJ 08034. 856/779-9100. **Fax:** 856/779-9193. **Contact:** General Manager. **Description:** An executive search firm. **Specializes in the areas of:** Food; General Management; Industrial; Information Technology; Manufacturing; Publishing; Retail; Sales. **Positions commonly filled include:** Buyer; Customer Service Representative; Financial Analyst; General Manager; Insurance Agent/Broker; Management Trainee; Market Research Analyst; Purchasing Agent/Manager; Restaurant/Food Service Manager; Telecommunications

Manager; Travel Agent. **Other U.S. locations:** Nationwide. **Number of placements per year:** 100 - 199.

SALES CONSULTANTS OF HUDSON COUNTY, INC.
2 Hudson Place, Hoboken NJ 07030. 201/659-5205. **Fax:** 201/659-5009. **Contact:** Rick Sinay, Manager. **Description:** An executive search firm operating on both retainer and contingency bases. Client company pays fee. **Specializes in the areas of:** Engineering; Food; Industrial; Marketing; Sales; Scientific; Technical. **Positions commonly filled include:** Account Manager; Account Representative; Applications Engineer; Design Engineer; Electrical/Electronics Engineer; Industrial Engineer; Manufacturing Engineer; Market Research Analyst; Marketing Manager; Marketing Specialist; Mechanical Engineer; Metallurgical Engineer; Sales Manager; Sales Representative. **Other U.S. locations:** Nationwide. **Average salary range of placements:** $50,000 - $100,000. **Number of placements per year:** 100 - 199.

SALES CONSULTANTS OF LIVINGSTON
355 Eisenhower Parkway, Suite 212, Livingston NJ 07039. 973/597-1870. **Fax:** 973/597-1871. **Contact:** Recruiter. **Description:** An executive search firm. **Specializes in the areas of:** Technical. **Other U.S. locations:** Nationwide.

SALES CONSULTANTS OF MIDDLESEX
242 Old New Brunswick Road, Suite 340, Piscataway NJ 08854. 732/981-8008. **Fax:** 732/981-1187. **Contact:** Recruiter. **Description:** An executive search firm. **Specializes in the areas of:** Packaging. **Other U.S. locations:** Nationwide.

SALES CONSULTANTS OF MIDDLETOWN
One Bethany Road, Suite 20, Hazlet NJ 07730. 732/739-4334. **Fax:** 732/739-2990. **Contact:** Recruiter. **Description:** An executive search firm. **Specializes in the areas of:** Food; Sales. **Other U.S. locations:** Nationwide.

SALES CONSULTANTS OF MORRIS COUNTY
364 Parsippany Road, Parsippany NJ 07054. 973/887-3838. **Fax:** 973/887-2304. **Contact:** Ernest Bivona, Manager. **E-mail address:** scmorris@marketing-sales.com. **World Wide Web address:** http://www.marketing-sales.com. **Description:** An executive search firm operating on a contingency basis. **Specializes in the areas of:** Computer Science/Software; Engineering; Finance; Food; General Management; Health/Medical; Industrial; Insurance; Publishing; Sales; Technical. **Positions commonly filled include:** Bank Officer/Manager; Biological Scientist; Biomedical Engineer; Chemical Engineer; Civil Engineer; Mechanical Engineer; Metallurgical Engineer; Sales Representative; Software Engineer; Telecommunications Manager. **Other U.S. locations:** Nationwide. **Number of placements per year:** 50 - 99.

SALES CONSULTANTS OF OCEAN, INC.
2516 Highway 35, Manasquan NJ 08736. 732/223-0300. **Fax:** 732/223-0450. **Contact:** Mark Daly, Manager. **Description:** An executive search firm. **Specializes in the areas of:** Electronics; Environmental; Marketing; Packaging; Publishing; Sales. **Positions commonly filled include:** Marketing Specialist; Sales Representative. **Other U.S. locations:** Nationwide. **Average salary range of placements:** More than $50,000. **Number of placements per year:** 100 - 199.

SALES CONSULTANTS OF SPARTA
376 Route 15, Suite 200, Sparta NJ 07871. 973/579-5555. **Fax:** 973/579-2220. **Contact:** Harvey Bass, Manager. **Description:** An executive search firm. **Specializes in the areas of:** Accounting/Auditing; Administration; Advertising; Architecture/Construction; Banking; Communications; Computer Science/Software; Design; Electrical; Engineering; Finance; Food; General Management; Health/Medical; Industrial; Insurance;

Legal; Manufacturing; Operations Management; Procurement; Publishing; Real Estate; Retail; Sales; Technical; Textiles; Transportation. **Other U.S. locations:** Nationwide.

SANFORD ROSE ASSOCIATES
12 Minneakoning Road, Suite 4, Flemington NJ 08809. 908/788-1788. **Toll-free phone:** 800/945-7697. **Fax:** 908/788-7847. **Contact:** Manager. **E-mail address:** sraflem@aol.com. **World Wide Web address:** http://www.sraflem.com. **Description:** An executive search firm. Client company pays fee. **Specializes in the areas of:** Accounting; Banking; Biology; Engineering; Finance; Legal. **Positions commonly filled include:** Accountant; Attorney; Auditor; Bank Officer/Manager; Budget Analyst; Chief Financial Officer; Controller; Design Engineer; Draftsperson; Electrical/Electronics Engineer; Electrician; Environmental Engineer; Human Resources Manager; Industrial Engineer; Manufacturing Engineer; Mechanical Engineer; Metallurgical Engineer; Paralegal; Purchasing Agent/Manager; Quality Assurance Engineer. **Corporate headquarters location:** This Location. **Other U.S. locations:** Nationwide. **Average salary range of placements:** $50,000 - $100,000. **Number of placements per year:** 1 - 49.

ROBERT SCOTT ASSOCIATES
P.O. Box 486, Rancocas NJ 08073-0486. 609/835-2224. **Fax:** 609/835-1933. **Contact:** Bob Scott, President. **Description:** An executive search firm. **Specializes in the areas of:** Chemicals; Engineering; Industrial; Manufacturing; Paper; Personnel/Labor Relations; Scientific; Technical. **Positions commonly filled include:** Biological Scientist; Biomedical Engineer; Ceramics Engineer; Chemical Engineer; Chemist; Civil Engineer; Electrical/Electronics Engineer; Human Resources Manager; Industrial Engineer; Manufacturing Engineer; Mechanical Engineer; Metallurgical Engineer; Operations Manager. **Average salary range of placements:** More than $50,000.

SCOVILLE GROUP
12 Broad Street, Red Bank NJ 07701. 732/345-9600. **Fax:** 732/345-0806. **Contact:** Recruiter. **Description:** An executive search firm. **Specializes in the areas of:** Food.

SEARCH CONSULTANTS, INC.
P.O. Box 402, Paramus NJ 07653-0402. 201/444-1770. **Contact:** Walter Perog, Executive Recruiter. **Description:** An executive search firm. **Specializes in the areas of:** Personnel/Labor Relations. **Positions commonly filled include:** Human Resources Specialist. **Average salary range of placements:** More than $50,000. **Number of placements per year:** 1 - 49.

SEARCH EDP INC.
150 River Road, Building C, Suite 3, Montville NJ 07045. 973/335-6600. **Fax:** 973/335-8053. **Contact:** Joe Hauser, President. **E-mail address:** info@searchedp.com. **World Wide Web address:** http://www.searchedp.com. **Description:** An executive search firm. **Specializes in the areas of:** Computer Science/Software; Information Technology; Internet Development; Technical. **Positions commonly filled include:** Applications Engineer; AS400 Programmer Analyst; Computer Animator; Computer Engineer; Computer Operator; Computer Programmer; Computer Scientist; Computer Support Technician; Computer Technician; Content Developer; Database Administrator; Database Manager; Internet Services Manager; MIS Specialist; Multimedia Designer; Network/Systems Administrator; Software Engineer; SQL Programmer; Systems Analyst; Systems Manager; Webmaster. **Average salary range of placements:** $50,000 - $100,000. **Number of placements per year:** 200 - 499.

SEARCHPRO INCORPORATED
280 Clinton Place, Hackensack NJ 07601. 201/489-0908. **Fax:** 201/342-3229. **Contact:** Recruiter. **Description:** An executive search firm. **Specializes in the areas of:** Hotel/Restaurant.

SHERBROOKE ASSOCIATES, INC.
727 Raritan Road, Suite 202B, Clark NJ 07066. 732/382-5505. **Contact:** Recruiter. **Description:** A generalist executive search firm.

SHIFRIN-FISCHER GROUP, INC.
409 North Avenue East, Cranford NJ 07016. 908/931-1000. **Fax:** 908/931-1009. **Contact:** Recruiter. **Description:** An executive search firm. **Specializes in the areas of:** Biotechnology; Marketing; Pharmaceuticals; Sales; Software Development; Telecommunications.

SILVER SCOTT GROUP
550 North Maple Avenue, Suite 2, Ridgewood NJ 07450. 201/493-1500. **Fax:** 201/493-1502. **Contact:** Recruiter. **Description:** An executive search firm. **Specializes in the areas of:** Computer Operations; Technical.

SKOTT/EDWARDS CONSULTANTS
1776 On the Green, Morristown NJ 07960. 972/644-0900. **Fax:** 972/644-0991. **Contact:** Skott B. Burkland, President. **E-mail address:** search@skottedwards.com. **World Wide Web address:** http://www.skottedwards.com. **Description:** An executive search firm operating on a retainer basis. Skott/Edwards Consultants also offers some outplacement services. Founded in 1974. **Specializes in the areas of:** Biotechnology; Health/Medical; Information Technology; Management. **Corporate headquarters location:** This Location. **Other U.S. locations:** San Francisco CA; Chicago IL.

SKUPPSEARCH, INC.
580 Sylvan Avenue, Englewood Cliffs NJ 07632. 201/894-1824. **Fax:** 201/894-1324. **Contact:** Holly Skupp, President. **Description:** An executive search firm. **Specializes in the areas of:** Banking; Communications; Computer Science/Software; Finance; Insurance; Technical. **Positions commonly filled include:** Editor; Multimedia Designer; Technical Writer/Editor; Training Specialist; Webmaster. **Average salary range of placements:** $30,000 - $50,000. **Number of placements per year:** 1 - 49.

SNELLINGSEARCH
80 Scenic Drive, Freehold NJ 07728. 732/431-2600. **Fax:** 732/431-2811. **Contact:** Manager. **E-mail address:** info@snellingsearch.com. **World Wide Web address:** http://www.snellingsearch.com. **Description:** An executive search firm. **Specializes in the areas of:** Computer Programming; Network Administration; Systems Administration; Telecommunications.

SOFTRIX, INC.
P.O. Box 937, Dayton NJ 08810. 732/274-0073. **Fax:** 732/274-0162. **Contact:** Manager. **E-mail address:** career@softrix.com. **World Wide Web address:** http://www.softrix.com. **Description:** An executive search firm. **Specializes in the areas of:** Computer Operations; Data Communications; Information Technology; Telecommunications.

SOFTSEARCH EXECUTIVE RECRUITERS
P.O. Box 8416, Turnersville NJ 08012. 856/218-1000. **Fax:** 856/218-9600. **Contact:** Recruiter. **E-mail address:** info@jobpros.com. **World Wide Web address:** http://www.jobpros.com. **Description:** An executive search firm that also provides consulting services. **Specializes in the areas of:** Information Systems; Information Technology. **Positions commonly filled include:** Business Analyst; Computer Operator; Computer Programmer; Database Administrator; Information Systems Consultant; LAN/WAN Designer/Developer; Management Analyst/Consultant; Network Engineer; Project Manager; Software Engineer; Systems Analyst; Technical Writer/Editor; Webmaster.

PHYLLIS SOLOMON EXECUTIVE SEARCH
120 Sylvan Avenue, Englewood Cliffs NJ 07632. 201/947-8600. **Contact:** Phyllis Solomon, President. **Description:** An executive search firm. **Specializes in** the areas of: Pharmaceuticals. **Positions commonly filled include:** Account Representative; Marketing Manager; Product Manager.

SONIMAX CORPORATION
P.O. Box 1519, Wayne NJ 07474-1519. 973/694-7185. **Fax:** 973/694-7001. **Contact:** Manager. **E-mail address:** sales@sonimax.com. **World Wide Web address:** http://www.sonimax.com. **Description:** An executive search firm that also provides computer consulting, training, and mentoring services. **Specializes in the areas of:** Computer Operations; Software Development. **Positions commonly filled include:** Software Engineer.

SPARTA GROUP
3 Deer Run, Andover NJ 07821. 973/786-6896. **Fax:** 973/786-7576. **Contact:** Manager. **Description:** An executive search firm. **Specializes in the areas of:** Transportation.

SPECTRUM SCIENTIFIC RECRUITERS
666 Plainsboro Road, Suite 220, Plainsboro NJ 08536. 609/936-8850. **Fax:** 609/936-9344. **Contact:** Scott Nagrod, Senior Recruiter/President. **Description:** An executive search firm. **Specializes in the areas of:** Pharmaceuticals.

THE STAFFING GROUP
37 Vreeland Avenue, Livingston NJ 07512. 973/785-4600. **Fax:** 973/785-9740. **Contact:** Frank Minutolo, Managing Partner. **E-mail address:** thestafgrp@aol.com. **World Wide Web address:** http://www.thestaffinggroup.com. **Description:** An executive search firm. **Specializes in the areas of:** Engineering; Finance; Information Technology.

THE STELTON GROUP, INC.
904 Oak Tree Road, Suite A, South Plainfield NJ 07080. 908/757-9888. **Contact:** Manager. **World Wide Web address:** http://steltongroup.com. **Description:** An executive search firm. **Specializes in the areas of:** Accounting; Automotive; Chemicals; Computer Hardware/Software; Cosmetics; Data Processing; Electronics; Engineering; Food; Human Resources; Manufacturing; Marketing; Medical Devices; Packaging; Plastics; Quality Assurance; Sales; Scientific; Telecommunications.

STEWART/LAURENCE ASSOCIATES, INC.
P.O. Box 1156, Atrium Executive Park, Englishtown NJ 07726. 732/972-3000. **Fax:** 732/972-8003. **Contact:** Manager. **E-mail address:** info@stewartlaurence.com. **World Wide Web address:** http://www.stewartlaurence.com. **Description:** An executive search firm. Founded in 1969. **Specializes in the areas of:** Biotechnology; Computer Hardware/Software; Finance; Health/Medical; High-Tech; Internet Development; Marketing; Pharmaceuticals; Sales; Software Development. **Corporate headquarters location:** This Location. **Other U.S. locations:** Mountain View CA.

JANET STOAKES ASSOCIATES INC.
150 West End Avenue, Somerville NJ 08876. 908/722-3636. **Fax:** 908/722-2111. **Contact:** Janet Stoakes, President. **Description:** An executive search firm. **Specializes in the areas of:** Pharmaceuticals.

HUNTER STONE INC.
28 Farview Terrace, Paramus NJ 07652. 201/845-0610. **Fax:** 201/845-4511. **Contact:** Sanford E. Berger, Vice President. **Description:** An executive search firm. **Specializes in the areas of:** Market Research.

SUMMIT GROUP, INC.
64 Lambert Drive, Sparta NJ 07871. 973/726-0800. **Contact:** Gary Pezzuti, General Partner. **Description:** An executive search firm. **Specializes in the areas of:** Engineering; Food; Health/Medical; Industrial; Manufacturing; Materials; Transportation. **Positions commonly filled include:** Buyer; General Manager; Industrial Engineer; Industrial Production Manager;

Manufacturing Engineer; Marketing Specialist; Mechanical Engineer; Metallurgical Engineer; Operations/Production Manager; Production Manager; Purchasing Agent/Manager; Quality Control Supervisor; Transportation/Traffic Specialist; Vice President. **Average salary range of placements:** More than $50,000. **Number of placements per year:** 50 - 99.

SYSTEM BUILDERS CORPORATION
3 Wing Drive, Suite 225, Cedar Knolls NJ 07927. 973/538-2121. **Fax:** 973/538-0188. **Contact:** Manager. **Description:** An executive search firm that also provides some consulting services. **Specializes in the areas of:** Computer Operations; Consulting.

TARGET PROS, INC.
80 Main Street, West Orange NJ 07052. 973/324-0900. **Fax:** 973/324-0901. **Contact:** Manager. **Description:** An executive search firm. **Specializes in the areas of:** Biotechnology; Health/Medical; Pharmaceuticals.

TATE & ASSOCIATES
1020 Springfield Avenue, Suite 201, Westfield NJ 07090. 908/232-2443. **Contact:** Manager. **Description:** An executive search firm.

TECHNICAL PATHWORKS CORPORATION (TPC)
1403 State Route 23, Route D3, Butler NJ 07405. 973/838-1200. **Fax:** 973/838-1065. **Contact:** Manager. **Description:** An executive search firm. **Specializes in the areas of:** Information Technology.

TECHNOLOGY SYSTEMS, INC.
27 East Main Street, Little Falls NJ 07424. 973/256-1772. **Fax:** 973/812-1761. **Contact:** John Beddes, President. **Description:** An executive search firm. **Specializes in the areas of:** Engineering. **Positions commonly filled include:** Design Engineer; Electrical/Electronics Engineer; Manufacturing Engineer; Mechanical Engineer; Sales Engineer; Software Engineer. **Corporate headquarters location:** This Location. **Average salary range of placements:** More than $50,000. **Number of placements per year:** 1 - 49.

TELEQUEST COMMUNICATIONS, INC.
P.O. Box 94, Mahwah NJ 07430. 914/357-2212. **Fax:** 914/369-8724. **Contact:** Tom Bartchak, President. **E-mail address:** mail@telequestcom.com. **World Wide Web address:** http://www.telequestcom.com. **Description:** An executive search firm operating on a contingency basis. **Specializes in the areas of:** Telecommunications. **Positions commonly filled include:** Telecommunications Analyst; Telecommunications Manager. **Number of placements per year:** 1 - 49.

THOMAS & ASSOCIATES
66 Elm Street, Westfield NJ 07090. 908/232-0400. **Contact:** Manager. **Description:** An executive search firm. **Specializes in the areas of:** Finance; Health/Medical; Pharmaceuticals.

TOPAZ ATTORNEY SEARCH
383 Northfield Avenue, West Orange NJ 07052. 973/669-7300. **Fax:** 973/669-9811. **Contact:** Stewart Michaels, Chairman. **Description:** An executive search firm operating on both retainer and contingency bases. **Specializes in the areas of:** Legal. **Positions commonly filled include:** Attorney. **Average salary range of placements:** More than $50,000. **Number of placements per year:** 100 - 199.

TROUT ASSOCIATES, INC.
31 South Street, Morristown NJ 07960. 973/984-9030. **Fax:** 973/984-9032. **Contact:** Manager. **Description:** An executive search firm. **Specializes in the areas of:** Advertising; Engineering; Finance; Marketing.

TSCHUDIN INC.
215 River Vale Road, River Vale NJ 07675. 201/666-3456. **Fax:** 201/666-8470. **Contact:** Manager. **E-mail address:** accessusa@tschudin.com. **World Wide Web address:** http://www.tschudin.com. **Description:** An

executive search firm. **Specializes in the areas of:** Marketing; Sales.

TUCKER ASSOCIATES
1015 Mercer Road, Princeton NJ 08540. 609/921-0800. **Fax:** 609/921-1293. **Contact:** Manager. **Description:** An executive search firm. **Specializes in the areas of:** Finance.

J. VINCENT ASSOCIATES
29 Valley Road, Succasunna NJ 07876. 973/334-5900. **Fax:** 973/584-7541. **Contact:** Dennis Caporusso, President. **Description:** An executive search firm. **Specializes in the areas of:** Accounting; Finance; Information Systems.

J. WHITE & COMPANY
1010 Haddonfield Berlin Road, Suite 300, Voorhees NJ 08043. 856/784-7777. **Fax:** 856/784-9060. **Contact:** Jim White, President. **Description:** J. White & Company is an executive search firm operating on a retainer basis. **Specializes in the areas of:** Finance; Insurance; Investment.

WILL-COX ASSOCIATES
P.O. Box 804, Marlton NJ 08053. 609/757-1511. **Fax:** 609/757-1513. **Contact:** Recruiter. **World Wide Web address:** http://www.willcox-assoc.com. **Description:** Will-Cox Associates is an executive search firm. **Specializes in the areas of:** Chemicals; Electronics; Engineering; Environmental; Manufacturing; Metals; Plastics.

WILLIAM BELL ASSOCIATES
605 Candlewood Commons, Howell NJ 07731. 732/901-6000. **Fax:** 732/901-2299. **Contact:** William Bell, President. **Description:** An executive search firm. **Specializes in the areas of:** Cosmetics.

WORKSOURCE 2000, INC.
14 Stirling Lane, Wayne NJ 07470. 973/628-2951. **Fax:** 973/628-2953. **Contact:** Manager. **Description:** Worksource 2000 is an executive search firm. **Specializes in the areas of:** Biotechnology; Health/Medical; Pharmaceuticals.

WORLCO COMPUTER RESOURCES, INC.
901 Route 38, Cherry Hill NJ 08002. 856/665-4700. **Fax:** 856/665-8142. **Contact:** Bob Hughes, Managing Partner. **Description:** An executive search firm. **Specializes in the areas of:** Administration; Computer Hardware/Software; Sales. **Positions commonly filled include:** Computer Programmer; Internet Services Manager; Marketing Specialist; MIS Specialist; Sales Representative; Systems Analyst; Technical Writer/Editor; Telecommunications Manager. **Number of placements per year:** 100 - 199.

WORLD HEALTH RESOURCES, INC.
7000 Boulevard East, Guttenberg NJ 07093. 201/662-8906. **Contact:** Manager. **Description:** World Health Resources is an executive search firm. **Specializes in the areas of:** Health/Medical. **Positions commonly filled include:** Certified Nurses Aide; Nurse; Physical Therapist.

ZACCARIA INTERNATIONAL, INC.
2130 Highway 35, Suite A121, Sea Girt NJ 08750. 732/282-1203. **Fax:** 732/282-1204. **Contact:** Recruiter. **Description:** An executive search firm. **Specializes in the areas of:** Retail.

MICHAEL D. ZINN & ASSOCIATES, INC.
601 Ewing Street, Suite C-11, Princeton NJ 08540. 609/921-8755. **Contact:** Michael Zinn, President. **World Wide Web address:** http://www.zinnassociates.com. **Description:** Michael D. Zinn & Associates is an executive search firm. **Specializes in the areas of:** Consumer Package Goods; Finance; Health/Medical; Industrial; Management; Pharmaceuticals; Technical. **Other U.S. locations:** New York NY.

ZWICKER ASSOCIATES
579 Franklin Turnpike, Suite 9, Ridgewood NJ 07450. 201/251-8300. **Contact: Manager. Description:** An executive search firm. **Specializes in the areas of:** Food; Market Research.

PERMANENT EMPLOYMENT AGENCIES

A CHOICE NANNY
637 Wyckoff Avenue, Wyckoff NJ 07481-1442. 201/891-2273. **Fax:** 201/891-1722. **Contact:** Sue Vigil, General Manager. **Description:** A permanent employment agency. **Specializes in the areas of:** Child Care, In-Home; Nannies. **Positions commonly filled include:** Nanny. **Average salary range of placements:** Less than $25,000. **Number of placements per year:** 100 - 199.

A CHOICE NANNY
248 Columbia Turnpike, Building One, Florham Park NJ 07932. 973/593-9090. **Contact: Owner. Description:** A permanent employment agency. **Specializes in the areas of:** Child Care, In-Home; Nannies. **Positions commonly filled include:** Nanny. **Average salary range of placements:** Less than $25,000. **Number of placements per year:** 100 - 199.

A CHOICE NANNY
27 Mountain Boulevard, Suite 9-B, Warren NJ 07059. 908/754-9090. **Contact:** General Manager. **Description:** A permanent employment agency. **Specializes in the areas of:** Child Care, In-Home; Nannies. **Positions commonly filled include:** Nanny. **Average salary range of placements:** Less than $25,000. **Number of placements per year:** 100 - 199.

A+ PERSONNEL PLACEMENT
1017 Broadway, Bayonne NJ 07002. 201/437-5594. **Fax:** 201/437-2914. **Contact:** Jill G. Rowland, Vice President. **Description:** A permanent employment agency that also provides some temporary placements. **Specializes in the areas of:** Accounting/Auditing; Administration; Computer Science/Software; Finance; Legal; Manufacturing; Personnel/Labor Relations; Secretarial. **Positions commonly filled include:** Accountant/Auditor; Advertising Clerk; Bank Officer/Manager; Blue-Collar Worker Supervisor; Brokerage Clerk; Budget Analyst; Buyer; Chemical Engineer; Civil Engineer; Claim Representative; Clerical Supervisor; Computer Programmer; Credit Manager; Customer Service Representative; Financial Analyst; General Manager; Human Resources Manager; Industrial Engineer; Industrial Production Manager; Insurance Agent/Broker; Management Analyst/Consultant; Management Trainee; Mechanical Engineer; Operations/Production Manager; Paralegal; Public Relations Specialist; Purchasing Agent/Manager; Quality Control Supervisor; Restaurant/Food Service Manager; Securities Sales Representative; Software Engineer; Systems Analyst; Travel Agent; Underwriter/Assistant Underwriter; Wholesale and Retail Buyer. **Number of placements per year:** 50 - 99.

ABC NATIONWIDE EMPLOYMENT
241 Main Street, Hackensack NJ 07601. 201/487-5515. **Fax:** 201/487-5591. **Contact:** Recruiter. **Description:** A permanent employment agency. **Specializes in the areas of:** Engineering; Finance; Legal; Manufacturing; Personnel/Labor Relations; Secretarial. **Positions commonly filled include:** Accountant/Auditor; Civil Engineer; Clerical Supervisor; Credit Manager; Customer Service Representative; Electrical/Electronics Engineer; Human Resources Manager; Industrial Engineer; Mechanical Engineer; Purchasing Agent/Manager.

ADVANCED PERSONNEL SERVICE
1341 Hamburg Turnpike, Suite 1, Wayne NJ 07470-4042. 973/694-0303. **Fax:** 973/696-3291. **Contact:** Vice President. **Description:** A permanent employment agency that also provides some temporary placements. **Specializes in the areas of:** Accounting/Auditing; Administration; Advertising; Banking; Economics;

Finance; Food; General Management; Industrial; Insurance; Legal; Manufacturing; Personnel/Labor Relations; Sales; Secretarial. **Positions commonly filled include:** Accountant/Auditor; Administrative Manager; Advertising Clerk; Bank Officer/Manager; Branch Manager; Budget Analyst; Claim Representative; Clerical Supervisor; Credit Manager; Customer Service Representative; Economist; Editor; Financial Analyst; General Manager; Human Resources Specialist; Insurance Agent/Broker; Management Trainee; Manufacturer's/Wholesaler's Sales Rep.; Operations/Production Manager; Public Relations Specialist; Purchasing Agent/Manager; Securities Sales Representative; Services Sales Representative; Technical Writer/Editor; Telecommunications Manager; Transportation/Traffic Specialist; Travel Agent; Typist/Word Processor; Underwriter/Assistant Underwriter. **Benefits available to temporary workers:** Bonus Award/Plan; Paid Holidays; Paid Vacation. **Number of placements per year:** 200 - 499.

RAYMOND ALEXANDER ASSOCIATES
97 Lackawanna Avenue, Suite 102, Totowa NJ 07512. **Contact:** Ray Jezierski, Recruiting Manager. **Description:** A permanent employment agency. **Specializes in the areas of:** Accounting; Finance. **Positions commonly filled include:** Accountant/Auditor; Financial Analyst. **Average salary range of placements:** $30,000 - $50,000. **Number of placements per year:** 100 - 199.

ALLEN ASSOCIATES, INC.
33 Wood Avenue South, Suite 600, Iselin NJ 08830. 732/549-7555. **Fax:** 732/549-7550. **Contact:** Amy Regan, President. **Description:** A permanent employment agency. **Specializes in the areas of:** Finance; Office Support; Personnel/Labor Relations; Secretarial. **Positions commonly filled include:** Accountant/Auditor; Administrative Manager; Clerical Supervisor; Credit Manager; Customer Service Representative; Human Resources Specialist; Management Trainee; Secretary; Transportation/Traffic Specialist; Typist/Word Processor. **Average salary range of placements:** $20,000 - $40,000. **Number of placements per year:** 50 - 99.

ALLSTAFF RESOURCES, INC.
929 North Kings Highway, Cherry Hill NJ 08034. 856/779-9030. **Fax:** 856/779-0898. **Contact:** Manager. **Description:** A permanent employment agency. Client company pays fee. **Specializes in the areas of:** Accounting; Administration; Engineering; Finance; Health/Medical; Industrial; Insurance; Personnel/Labor Relations; Printing; Publishing; Scientific; Secretarial; Technical. **Positions commonly filled include:** Account Manager; Account Representative; Accountant; Administrative Assistant; Auditor; Buyer; Credit Manager; Customer Service Representative; Design Engineer; Financial Analyst; Human Resources Manager; Industrial Engineer; Insurance Agent/Broker; Manufacturing Engineer; Mechanical Engineer; Operations Manager; Production Manager; Project Manager; Purchasing Agent/Manager; Sales Engineer; Sales Representative; Secretary; Underwriter/Assistant Underwriter. **Corporate headquarters location:** This Location. **Average salary range of placements:** $30,000 - $49,999.

AMERICAN STAFFING RESOURCES
Lawrenceville Office Park, Suite 2, 168 Franklin Corner Road, Lawrenceville NJ 08648. 609/219-1011. **Fax:** 609/219-1411. **Contact:** Branch Supervisor. **Description:** A permanent employment agency that also provides some temporary placements. **Specializes in the

areas of: Accounting; Administration; Industrial; Information Technology; Light Industrial; MIS/EDP; Office Support; Scientific; Secretarial; Technical. **Positions commonly filled include:** Accountant; Administrative Assistant; Blue-Collar Worker Supervisor; Chief Financial Officer; Computer Operator; Computer Programmer; Controller; Cost Estimator; Customer Service Representative; Editorial Assistant; Human Resources Manager; Secretary; Typist/Word Processor. **Benefits available to temporary workers:** Bonus Award/Plan; Legal Services; Medical Insurance; Paid Holidays; Tuition Assistance; Vacation Pay. **Corporate headquarters location:** Feasterville PA. **Other U.S. locations:** Fairless Hills PA; Philadelphia PA; Willow Grove PA. **Average salary range of placements:** $20,000 - $29,999. **Number of placements per year:** 500 - 999.

BAI PERSONNEL SOLUTIONS, INC.
110 Stanhope Street, Princeton NJ 08540. 609/734-9631. **Fax:** 609/734-9637. **Contact:** Leigh Clayton, President. **Description:** A permanent employment agency that also provides some contingency-based executive searches, as well as some temporary and contract placements. Client company pays fee. **Specializes in the areas of:** Accounting; Administration; Banking; Computer Science/Software; Economics; Finance; General Management; Health/Medical; Insurance; Internet Development; Internet Marketing; Legal; Marketing; MIS/EDP; Nonprofit; Personnel/Labor Relations; Sales; Secretarial. **Positions commonly filled include:** Account Manager; Account Representative; Accountant; Administrative Assistant; Administrative Manager; Applications Engineer; AS400 Programmer Analyst; Assistant Manager; Auditor; Branch Manager; Budget Analyst; Chief Financial Officer; Claim Representative; Clerical Supervisor; Computer Engineer; Computer Operator; Computer Programmer; Computer Support Technician; Computer Technician; Controller; Credit Manager; Customer Service Representative; Database Administrator; Database Manager; Finance Director; Financial Analyst; General Manager; Human Resources Manager; Insurance Agent/Broker; Internet Services Manager; Management Analyst/Consultant; Management Trainee; Market Research Analyst; Marketing Specialist; MIS Specialist; Network/Systems Administrator; Operations Manager; Paralegal; Public Relations Specialist; Purchasing Agent/Manager; Sales Executive; Sales Manager; Sales Representative; Secretary; Software Engineer; SQL Programmer; Systems Analyst; Systems Manager; Typist/Word Processor; Underwriter/Assistant Underwriter; Webmaster. **Corporate headquarters location:** This Location. **Number of placements per year:** 200 - 499.

BERMAN & LARSON
12 Route 17 North, Suite 209, Paramus NJ 07652. 201/262-9200. **Toll-free phone:** 800/640-0126. **Fax:** 201/262-7060. **Contact:** Bob Larson, CPC/President. **E-mail address:** jobs@jobsbl.com. **World Wide Web address:** http://www.jobsbl.com. **Description:** A permanent employment agency. **Specializes in the areas of:** Computer Science/Software; Industrial; Information Systems. **Positions commonly filled include:** Computer Programmer; Internet Services Manager; MIS Specialist; Software Engineer; Systems Analyst; Technical Writer/Editor. **Benefits available to temporary workers:** 401(k); Medical Insurance. **Number of placements per year:** 200 - 499.

CPS TECHNICAL PLACEMENTS
10 North Gaston Avenue, Somerville NJ 08876. 908/704-1770. **Fax:** 908/704-1554. **Contact:** Robert Fisher, Technical Employment Specialist. **World Wide Web address:** http://www.completepersonnel.com. **Description:** A permanent employment agency that also provides some temporary placements. **Specializes in the areas of:** Biology; Engineering; Food; Pharmaceuticals. **Positions commonly filled include:** Biochemist; Biological Scientist; Biomedical Engineer; Chemical Engineer; Chemist; Clinical Lab Technician; Computer Operator; Computer Programmer; Electrician; Food

Scientist/Technologist; MIS Specialist; Pharmacist; Quality Control Supervisor; Technical Writer/Editor. **Number of placements per year:** 50 - 99.

CAPITOL SEARCH
215 East Ridgewood Avenue, Ridgewood NJ 07450. 201/444-6666. **Fax:** 201/444-4121. **Contact:** Bob Sanders, Owner. **Description:** A permanent employment agency. **Specializes in the areas of:** Child Care, In-Home; Domestic Help; Eldercare, In-Home; Nannies. **Positions commonly filled include:** Computer Graphics Specialist; Domestic Help. **Number of placements per year:** 100 - 199.

CAREER CENTER, INC.
P.O. Box 1036, Hackensack NJ 07601. 201/342-1777. **Toll-free phone:** 800/227-3379. **Fax:** 201/342-1776. **Contact:** Sandra Franzino, CIS/Vice President. **Description:** A permanent employment agency that also provides some temporary placements. **Specializes in the areas of:** Accounting/Auditing; Administration; Advertising; Banking; Clerical; Communications; Computer Science/Software; Engineering; Fashion; Finance; Insurance; Manufacturing; Personnel/Labor Relations; Sales; Technical. **Positions commonly filled include:** Accountant/Auditor; Administrative Manager; Bank Officer/Manager; Customer Service Representative; Data Entry Clerk; Draftsperson; EDP Specialist; Electrical/Electronics Engineer; Financial Analyst; Human Resources Manager; Industrial Designer; Industrial Engineer; Legal Secretary; Marketing Specialist; Mechanical Engineer; Medical Secretary; Metallurgical Engineer; Mining Engineer; MIS Specialist; Operations/Production Manager; Petroleum Engineer; Purchasing Agent/Manager; Quality Control Supervisor; Receptionist; Sales Representative; Secretary; Stenographer; Systems Analyst; Technician; Typist/Word Processor; Underwriter/Assistant Underwriter. **Benefits available to temporary workers:** 401(k); Medical Insurance; Paid Holidays; Paid Vacation. **Number of placements per year:** 1000+.

CAREERS FIRST, INC.
305 U.S. Route 130, Cinnaminson NJ 08077. 856/786-0004. **Contact:** Gail Duncan, President. **Description:** A permanent employment agency. **Specializes in the areas of:** Administration; Computer Hardware/Software; Technical.

CAREERS, INC.
814 Perry Lane, Teaneck NJ 07666. 201/837-6612. **Fax:** 201/837-3783. **Contact:** Manager. **Description:** A permanent employment agency that places librarians with backgrounds in chemistry, biology, and engineering. **Specializes in the areas of:** Library Services. **Positions commonly filled include:** Librarian; Library Technician.

CAREERS 2000
515 Highway 70, Suite 209, Brick NJ 08723. 732/920-5555. **Fax:** 732/477-9327. **Contact:** Manager. **E-mail address:** jobs@careers2k.com. **World Wide Web address:** http://www.careers2k.com. **Description:** A permanent employment agency. **Specializes in the areas of:** Office Support; Technical.

CAREERS USA
533 North Evergreen Avenue, Woodbury NJ 08096. 856/384-1600. **Fax:** 856/384-1310. **Contact:** Carla Janoff, President/Owner. **Description:** A permanent employment agency. **Specializes in the areas of:** Accounting/Auditing; Administration; Computer Science/Software; General Management; Industrial; Manufacturing; Personnel/Labor Relations; Secretarial; Technical. **Positions commonly filled include:** Administrative Manager; Blue-Collar Worker Supervisor; Claim Representative; Clerical Supervisor; Customer Service Representative; Draftsperson; Editor; Financial Analyst; Human Resources Specialist; Industrial Production Manager; MIS Specialist; Operations/Production Manager; Paralegal; Purchasing Agent/Manager; Quality Control Supervisor; Typist/Word Processor. **Benefits available to**

temporary workers: Paid Holidays; Paid Vacation. **Average salary range of placements:** $20,000 - $29,999.

CASTLE CAREERS INC.
141 South Avenue, Fanwood NJ 07023. 908/322-9140. **Contact:** Manager. **Description:** A permanent employment agency. **Specializes in the areas of:** Office Support.

CENTRAL TECHNICAL SERVICE INC.
389 Main Street, Hackensack NJ 07605. 201/342-0055. **Contact:** Manager. **Description:** A permanent employment agency. **Specializes in the areas of:** Engineering; Technical.

CITIZENS EMPLOYMENT SERVICES, INC.
One Magnolia Avenue, Montvale NJ 07645. 201/391-5144. **Fax:** 201/391-4477. **Contact:** Elaine Larfier, Manager. **Description:** A permanent employment agency. **Specializes in the areas of:** Banking; Clerical; Computer Science/Software; Industrial; Insurance; Manufacturing; Retail; Sales. **Positions commonly filled include:** Accountant/Auditor; Actuary; Bank Officer/Manager; Bookkeeper; Chemical Engineer; Claim Representative; Computer Operator; Computer Programmer; Credit Manager; Customer Service Representative; Data Entry Clerk; Draftsperson; EDP Specialist; Electrical/Electronics Engineer; Industrial Production Manager; Insurance Agent/Broker; Legal Secretary; Mechanical Engineer; Operations/Production Manager; Purchasing Agent/Manager; Quality Control Supervisor; Sales Representative; Secretary; Stenographer; Systems Analyst; Technician; Travel Agent; Typist/Word Processor; Underwriter/Assistant Underwriter. **Other area locations:** Parsippany NJ. **Average salary range of placements:** $30,000 - $50,000. **Number of placements per year:** 1000+.

GLENN DAVIS ASSOCIATES
P.O. Box 1, Ironian NJ 07845. 973/895-4242. **Contact:** Glenn Davis, Manager. **Description:** A permanent employment agency. **Specializes in the areas of:** Computer Science/Software. **Positions commonly filled include:** MIS Specialist. **Number of placements per year:** 50 - 99.

EXECUTIVE SOFTWARE PLUS
24 Lyons Place, Westwood NJ 07675. 201/666-5484. **Fax:** 201/664-0693. **Contact:** Claire Monte, Vice President. **E-mail address:** esprecruit@aol.com. **Description:** A permanent employment agency. **Specializes in the areas of:** Computer Science/Software. **Positions commonly filled include:** Computer Programmer; Systems Analyst.

EXPRESS PERSONNEL SERVICES
2569 State Route 10, Morris Plains NJ 07950. 973/898-1001. **Fax:** 973/898-1005. **Contact:** Marianne Kemp, Operations Manager. **Description:** A permanent employment agency that also provides some temporary placements. **Specializes in the areas of:** Accounting/Auditing; Administration; Advertising; Computer Hardware/Software; Engineering; General Management; Industrial; Legal; Manufacturing; Publishing; Sales; Secretarial; Technical. **Positions commonly filled include:** Accountant/Auditor; Administrative Manager; Advertising Clerk; Blue-Collar Worker Supervisor; Claim Representative; Clerical Supervisor; Computer Programmer; Customer Service Representative; Design Engineer; Designer; Draftsperson; Editor; Electrical/Electronics Engineer; Electrician; General Manager; Human Resources Specialist; Management Trainee; Manufacturer's/Wholesaler's Sales Rep.; MIS Specialist; Paralegal; Quality Control Supervisor; Software Engineer; Typist/Word Processor. **Benefits available to temporary workers:** Medical Insurance; Paid Vacation. **Corporate headquarters location:** Oklahoma City OK. **Average salary range of placements:** $20,000 - $29,999. **Number of placements per year:** 500 - 999.

FLEXTIME SOLUTIONS, INC.
515 Summit Avenue, Maplewood NJ 07040. 973/763-6603. **Fax:** 973/763-2486. **Contact:** Kathleen Shelby, President. **E-mail address:** info@flextimesolutions.com. **World Wide Web address:** http://www.flextimesolutions.com. **Description:** A permanent employment agency that primarily places candidates in full-time positions with flex hours, telecommuting, and compressed workweeks. Flextime Solutions also offers long and short-term temporary assignments and temp-to-perm positions. **Specializes in the areas of:** Advertising; Communications; Finance; Health/Medical; Internet Marketing; Public Relations; Publishing; Sales. **Average salary range of placements:** $30,000 - $100,000. **Number of placements per year:** 1 - 49.

G.A. AGENCY
524 South Avenue East, Cranford NJ 07016. 908/272-2080. **Fax:** 908/272-2962. **Contact:** Mrs. Randy Ring, Manager. **Description:** A permanent employment agency. **Specializes in the areas of:** Education. **Positions commonly filled include:** Education Administrator; Teacher/Professor. **Other U.S. locations:** Nationwide. **Average salary range of placements:** $30,000 - $50,000. **Number of placements per year:** 200 - 499.

GLOBE EMPLOYMENT AGENCY
77 Ridge Road, North Arlington NJ 07031. 201/997-4251. **Fax:** 201/997-9877. **Contact:** Michele Ruvo, Office Manager. **Description:** A permanent employment agency that also provides some temporary placements and executive searches. **Specializes in the areas of:** Accounting; Office Support; Secretarial.

HALLMARK PERSONNEL INC.
140 Route 17 North, Suite 302, Paramus NJ 07652. 201/261-9010. **Contact:** Manager. **Description:** A permanent employment agency.

HORIZON GRAPHICS PERSONNEL
110 Cornelia Street, Boonton NJ 07005. 973/263-2126. **Fax:** 973/263-4601. **Contact:** John DeSalvo, Vice President. **Description:** A permanent employment agency that also provides some temporary placements. **Specializes in the areas of:** Advertising; Art/Design; Fashion; Health/Medical; Publishing; Retail. **Positions commonly filled include:** Advertising Executive; Computer Animator; Desktop Publishing Specialist; Draftsperson; Editor; Editorial Assistant; Graphic Artist; Graphic Designer; Librarian; Multimedia Designer; Proofreader; Technical Writer/Editor; Video Production Coordinator; Webmaster; Writer. **Benefits available to temporary workers:** Paid Holidays; Paid Vacation. **Corporate headquarters location:** This Location. **Average salary range of placements:** $30,000 - $50,000. **Number of placements per year:** 100 - 199.

HUGHES & PODESLA PERSONNEL INC.
281 East Main Street, Somerville NJ 08876. 908/231-0880. **Contact:** Paul Podesla, President. **Description:** A permanent employment agency. **Specializes in the areas of:** Accounting/Auditing; Engineering; Finance; General Management; Industrial; Manufacturing; Personnel/Labor Relations; Sales; Technical. **Positions commonly filled include:** Accountant/Auditor; Biomedical Engineer; Budget Analyst; Buyer; Credit Manager; Customer Service Representative; Design Engineer; Draftsperson; Electrical/Electronics Engineer; Financial Analyst; General Manager; Human Resources Manager; Industrial Engineer; Industrial Production Manager; Mechanical Engineer; Operations/Production Manager; Purchasing Agent/Manager; Quality Control Supervisor; Transportation/Traffic Specialist. **Number of placements per year:** 1 - 49.

HUNT, LTD.
1050 Wall Street West, Suite 330, Lyndhurst NJ 07071. 201/438-8200. **Fax:** 201/438-8372. **Contact:** Alex Metz, President. **World Wide Web address:** http://www.huntltd.com. **Description:** A permanent

employment agency that also provides some temporary placements. Founded in 1965. **Specializes in the areas of:** Distribution; Logistics. **Positions commonly filled include:** Industrial Engineer; Logistics Manager; Logistics Support Worker; Management Analyst/Consultant; Transportation/Traffic Specialist; Warehouse Manager. **Corporate headquarters location:** This Location. **Other U.S. locations:** Nationwide. **Average salary range of placements:** More than $50,000. **Number of placements per year:** 100 - 199.

IMPACT PERSONNEL, INC.
1901 North Olden Avenue, Suite 26A, Ewing NJ 08618. 609/406-1200. **Contact:** Manager. **Description:** A permanent employment agency. **Specializes in the areas of:** Accounting/Auditing; Administration; Advertising; Banking; Computer Hardware/Software; Engineering; Fashion; Finance; Food; General Management; Health/Medical; Industrial; Insurance; Legal; Manufacturing; Publishing; Retail; Sales; Secretarial; Technical. **Positions commonly filled include:** Accountant/Auditor; Administrative Assistant; Bookkeeper; Chemical Engineer; Claim Representative; Clerk; Commercial Artist; Computer Operator; Computer Programmer; Customer Service Representative; Data Entry Clerk; Driver; Electrical/Electronics Engineer; Factory Worker; Hotel Manager; Industrial Designer; Industrial Engineer; Legal Secretary; Light Industrial Worker; Mechanical Engineer; Medical Secretary; Quality Control Supervisor; Receptionist; Recruiter; Sales Representative; Secretary; Software Engineer; Technician; Typist/Word Processor. **Number of placements per year:** 500 - 999.

INFOSYSTEMS PLACEMENT SERVICES
17 Holmes Lane, Marlton NJ 08053. 856/596-7770. **Fax:** 856/596-7772. **Contact:** Joe Dougherty, Owner. **Description:** A permanent employment agency. **Specializes in the areas of:** Administration; Computer Science/Software. **Positions commonly filled include:** Computer Operator; Computer Programmer; Database Manager; Internet Services Manager; MIS Specialist; Project Manager; Software Engineer; Systems Analyst; Systems Manager; Telecommunications Manager. **Average salary range of placements:** More than $50,000. **Number of placements per year:** 1 - 49.

JOSEPH KEYES ASSOCIATES
275 Forest Avenue, Paramus NJ 07653. 201/261-7400. **Fax:** 201/261-4836. **Contact:** Ed Michaels, Vice President. **Description:** A permanent employment agency that also provides some temporary placements and career/outplacement counseling. **Specializes in the areas of:** Accounting/Auditing; Engineering; Finance; Industrial; Manufacturing; Publishing. **Positions commonly filled include:** Accountant/Auditor; Administrative Manager; Blue-Collar Worker Supervisor; Broadcast Technician; Budget Analyst; Buyer; Ceramics Engineer; Claim Representative; Clerical Supervisor; Credit Manager; Customer Service Representative; Design Engineer; Designer; Draftsperson; Electrical/Electronics Engineer; Environmental Engineer; Financial Analyst; Human Resources Specialist; Industrial Engineer; Industrial Production Manager; Materials Engineer; Mechanical Engineer; Metallurgical Engineer; Purchasing Agent/Manager; Quality Control Supervisor; Services Sales Representative; Software Engineer; Technical Writer/Editor; Transportation/Traffic Specialist. **Average salary range of placements:** $30,000 - $50,000. **Number of placements per year:** 50 - 99.

JOAN LESLIE PERSONNEL, INC.
100 Menlo Park, Edison NJ 08837. 732/494-6650. **Fax:** 732/549-8508. **Contact:** Manager. **E-mail address:** joanleslie@compuserve.com. **World Wide Web address:** http://www.joanleslie.baweb.com. **Description:** A permanent employment agency that also offers some temporary placements. Founded in 1981. **Specializes in the areas of:** Office Support; Technical.

MAYFAIR SERVICES
372 Buffalo Avenue, Paterson NJ 07503. 973/742-0990. **Fax:** 973/742-0991. **Contact:** Merry Costello, Owner. **Description:** A permanent employment agency that also provides some temporary placements. **Specializes in the areas of:** Administration; Art/Design; Biology; Computer Hardware/Software; Engineering; General Management; Health/Medical; Industrial; Manufacturing; Personnel/Labor Relations; Publishing; Technical; Transportation. **Positions commonly filled include:** Aerospace Engineer; Agricultural Engineer; Aircraft Mechanic/Engine Specialist; Architect; Biochemist; Biological Scientist; Biomedical Engineer; Blue-Collar Worker Supervisor; Buyer; Chemical Engineer; Chemist; Civil Engineer; Clinical Lab Technician; Construction and Building Inspector; Customer Service Representative; Design Engineer; Designer; Draftsperson; Electrical/Electronics Engineer; Electrician; Environmental Engineer; General Manager; Health Services Manager; Human Resources Specialist; Industrial Engineer; Industrial Production Manager; Library Technician; Management Trainee; Mathematician; Mechanical Engineer; Medical Records Technician; Metallurgical Engineer; MIS Specialist; Multimedia Designer; Nuclear Engineer; Nuclear Medicine Technologist; Occupational Therapist; Operations/Production Manager; Pharmacist; Quality Control Supervisor; Science Technologist; Software Engineer; Stationary Engineer; Structural Engineer; Typist/Word Processor; Veterinarian. **Average salary range of placements:** $20,000 - $29,999. **Number of placements per year:** 200 - 499.

MILLER RESOURCES
720 U.S. Highway 1, North Brunswick NJ 08902. 732/247-5600. **Fax:** 732/247-9022. **Contact:** Shelly Schwartz, Office Manager. **Description:** A permanent employment agency that also provides temporary placements. **Specializes in the areas of:** Accounting; Administration; Clerical; Secretarial.

NANNIES PLUS
520 Speedwell Avenue, Suite 114, Morris Plains NJ 07950-2132. **Toll-free phone:** 800/752-0078. **Fax:** 973/285-5055. **Contact:** Consultant. **Description:** A permanent employment agency. **Specializes in the areas of:** Child Care, In-Home. **Positions commonly filled include:** Nanny. **Average salary range of placements:** Less than $20,000. **Number of placements per year:** 200 - 499.

NEIGHBORHOOD NANNIES
5 Haddon Avenue, Haddonfield NJ 08033. 856/795-5833. **Contact:** Celia Sarajian, Executive Director. **Description:** A permanent employment agency that also provides some career/outplacement counseling services. **Specializes in the areas of:** Child Care, In-Home; Eldercare, In-Home; Nannies. **Positions commonly filled include:** Nanny. **Number of placements per year:** 50 - 99.

OFFICEMATES5 (OM5)
DAYSTAR TEMPORARY SERVICES
560 Sylvan Avenue, Englewood Cliffs NJ 07632. 201/871-2203. **Fax:** 201/871-1116. **Contact:** Alice Eckstein, President. **Description:** A permanent employment agency. DayStar Temporary Services (also at this location) provides temporary placements. **Specializes in the areas of:** Accounting/Auditing; Administration; Advertising; Banking; Computer Science/Software; Economics; Finance; General Management; Insurance; Legal; Personnel/Labor Relations; Publishing; Sales; Secretarial; Transportation. **Positions commonly filled include:** Accountant/Auditor; Administrative Manager; Advertising Clerk; Bank Officer/Manager; Branch Manager; Brokerage Clerk; Budget Analyst; Buyer; Claim Representative; Clerical Supervisor; Computer Programmer; Cost Estimator; Credit Manager; Customer Service Representative; Financial Analyst; General Manager; Hotel Manager; Human Resources Specialist; Human Service Worker; Management Analyst/Consultant; Market Research

Analyst; MIS Specialist; Paralegal; Public Relations Specialist; Purchasing Agent/Manager; Quality Control Supervisor; Securities Sales Representative; Services Sales Representative; Systems Analyst; Typist/Word Processor; Underwriter/Assistant Underwriter; Video Production Coordinator. **Number of placements per year:** 50 - 99.

PARK AVENUE PERSONNEL
394 Windsor Road, Suite E, Wood-Ridge NJ 07075. 201/939-1911. **Fax:** 201/939-3555. **Contact:** Mary Falzarano, President/Owner. **Description:** A permanent employment agency. **Specializes in the areas of:** Accounting/Auditing; Banking; Finance; Personnel/Labor Relations; Sales; Secretarial. **Positions commonly filled include:** Accountant/Auditor; Administrative Manager; Clerical Supervisor; Financial Analyst; Human Resources Manager. **Average salary range of placements:** $30,000 - $50,000. **Number of placements per year:** 1 - 49.

THE PERSONNEL GROUP
ARTHUR JAMES & ASSOCIATES INC.
P.O. Box 4582, Warren NJ 07059. 908/754-6000. **Contact:** Manager. **Description:** A permanent employment agency. Arthur James & Associates (also at this location) specializes in placing personnel in the field of solid waste management.

PERSONNEL PLUS
TEMPS PLUS
500 State Route 17 South, Hasbrouck Heights NJ 07604-3121. 201/288-7800. **Fax:** 201/288-7995. **Contact:** Placement Consultant. **Description:** A permanent employment agency. Temps Plus (also at this location) provides temporary placements. **Specializes in the areas of:** Accounting/Auditing; Clerical; Marketing; Personnel/Labor Relations; Sales. **Positions commonly filled include:** Account Representative; Accountant/Auditor; Administrative Assistant; Administrative Manager; Advertising Clerk; Clerical Supervisor; Controller; Credit Manager; Customer Service Representative; Financial Analyst; Human Resources Manager; Human Resources Specialist; Paralegal; Purchasing Agent/Manager; Sales Executive; Sales Manager; Sales Representative; Secretary; Services Sales Representative; Transportation/Traffic Specialist; Typist/Word Processor. **Average salary range of placements:** $30,000 - $50,000. **Number of placements per year:** 200 - 499.

POMERANTZ STAFFING SERVICES
1375 Plainfield Avenue, Watchung NJ 07060. 908/757-5300. **Toll-free phone:** 800/754-7000. **Fax:** 908/757-0144. **Contact:** Keith Grade, Corporate Director. **World Wide Web address:** http://www.pomerantzstaffing.com. **Description:** A permanent employment agency. **Specializes in the areas of:** Accounting/Auditing; Administration; Banking; Computer Hardware/Software; Food; General Management; Industrial; Light Industrial; Personnel/Labor Relations; Retail; Sales; Secretarial. **Positions commonly filled include:** Account Manager; Account Representative; Administrative Assistant; Advertising Clerk; Assistant Manager; Blue-Collar Worker Supervisor; Branch Manager; Buyer; Chemical Engineer; Chemist; Chief Financial Officer; Claim Representative; Clerical Supervisor; Credit Manager; Customer Service Representative; Database Manager; Design Engineer; Draftsperson; Editorial Assistant; Electrical/Electronics Engineer; Electrician; Finance Director; Financial Analyst; Food Scientist/Technologist; General Manager; Graphic Artist; Human Resources Manager; Industrial Engineer; Internet Services Manager; Management Analyst/Consultant; Management Trainee; Manufacturing Engineer; Marketing Manager; Mechanical Engineer; MIS Specialist; Operations Manager; Paralegal; Production Manager; Project Manager; Public Relations Manager; Purchasing Agent/Manager; Quality Control Supervisor; Sales Executive; Sales Manager; Sales Representative; Secretary; Software Engineer; Systems Analyst; Systems Manager; Technical Writer/Editor; Typist/Word

Processor. **Corporate headquarters location:** This Location. **Other U.S. locations:** Nationwide. **Average salary range of placements:** $20,000 - $50,000. **Number of placements per year:** 200 - 499.

PREMIER PERSONNEL GROUP, INC.
10 Woodbridge Center Drive, Woodbridge NJ 07095. 732/750-5600. **Fax:** 732/750-9787. **Contact:** Recruiter. **Description:** A permanent employment agency. **Specializes in the areas of:** Accounting/Auditing; Advertising; Banking; Finance; Legal; Marketing; Personnel/Labor Relations; Sales; Secretarial. **Positions commonly filled include:** Account Representative; Accountant; Administrative Assistant; Claim Representative; Computer Operator; Database Manager; Human Resources Manager; Sales Engineer; Sales Representative; Secretary. **Corporate headquarters location:** This Location. **Average salary range of placements:** $20,000 - $29,999. **Number of placements per year:** 200 - 499.

QUALITY DOMESTICS, INC.
484 Bloomfield Avenue, 2nd Floor, Suite 7, Montclair NJ 07042-3417. 973/509-7376. **Contact:** Lewis Ross, President. **Description:** A permanent employment agency. **Positions commonly filled include:** Child Care Worker; Home Health Aide; Housekeeper. **Average salary range of placements:** Less than $20,000. **Number of placements per year:** 100 - 199.

RSVP SERVICES
P.O. Box 8369, Cherry Hill NJ 08002-0369. 856/667-4488. **Toll-free phone:** 800/222-0153. **Contact:** Howard Levin, Director. **E-mail address:** hl@rsvpjobs.com. **World Wide Web address:** http://www.rsvpjobs.com. **Description:** A permanent employment agency. **Specializes in the areas of:** Aerospace; Communications; Electrical; Electronics.

READY PERSONNEL/READY TEMPS
Harborside Financial Center, 145 Plaza 2, Jersey City NJ 07311. 201/434-1800. **Fax:** 201/434-0900. **Contact:** Denise Arthur, Owner. **Description:** A permanent employment agency. **Specializes in the areas of:** Accounting/Auditing; Finance.

RECRUITMENT ALTERNATIVES, INC.
York House East, P.O. Box 554, Moorestown NJ 08057. 856/273-1066. **Contact:** Thomas J. Jaskel, Senior Vice President. **Description:** A permanent employment agency. **Specializes in the areas of:** Personnel/Labor Relations. **Positions commonly filled include:** Human Resources Manager; Recruiter. **Number of placements per year:** 1 - 49.

S-H-S OF CHERRY HILL
929 North Kings Highway, Cherry Hill NJ 08034. 856/779-9030. **Fax:** 856/779-0898. **Contact:** Lee Grant, Manager. **Description:** A permanent employment agency. **Specializes in the areas of:** Accounting/Auditing; Administration; Engineering; Human Resources; Insurance; Manufacturing; Office Support; Sales. **Positions commonly filled include:** Accountant/Auditor; Biomedical Engineer; Chemical Engineer; Chemist; Credit Manager; Electrical/Electronics Engineer; Financial Analyst; Human Resources Manager; Mechanical Engineer; Petroleum Engineer; Physical Therapist; Underwriter/Assistant Underwriter. **Corporate headquarters location:** This Location. **Average salary range of placements:** $20,000 - $100,000.

SCIENTIFIC SEARCH, INC.
560 Fellowship Road, Suite 309, Mount Laurel NJ 08054. 856/866-0200. **Fax:** 856/722-5307. **Contact:** Robert I. Greenberg, President. **Description:** A permanent employment agency. **Specializes in the areas of:** Computer Science/Software; Health/Medical. **Positions commonly filled include:** AS400 Programmer Analyst; Computer Programmer; Computer Support Technician; Database Administrator; Database Manager; Health Services Manager; Internet Services Manager;

MIS Specialist; Network/Systems Administrator; Software Engineer; SQL Programmer; Systems Analyst. **Average salary range of placements:** $50,000 - $100,000. **Number of placements per year:** 100 - 199.

SELECTIVE PERSONNEL
1200 Tices Lane, East Brunswick NJ 08816. 732/432-9500. **Contact:** Manager. **Description:** A permanent employment agency. **Specializes in the areas of:** Accounting/Auditing; Administration; Banking; Clerical; Computer Hardware/Software; Engineering; Finance; Health/Medical; Insurance; Legal; Manufacturing; Personnel/Labor Relations; Sales; Technical.

ARLINE SIMPSON ASSOCIATES, INC.
114 Essex Street, Rochelle Park NJ 07662. 201/843-1414. **Toll-free phone:** 800/843-1691. **Fax:** 201/843-6483. **Contact:** Arline Simpson, President. **Description:** A permanent employment agency that also provides some temporary placements. **Specializes in the areas of:** Accounting/Auditing; Administration; Advertising; Banking; Computer Science/Software; Engineering; Finance; Insurance; Legal; Publishing; Retail; Sales; Secretarial; Technical. **Positions commonly filled include:** Accountant/Auditor; Administrative Assistant; Bookkeeper; Buyer; Chemist; Computer Programmer; Credit Manager; Customer Service Representative; Designer; Draftsperson; Food Scientist/Technologist; Industrial Engineer; Legal Secretary; Manufacturer's/Wholesaler's Sales Rep.; Manufacturing Engineer; Mechanical Engineer; MIS Specialist; Paralegal; Receptionist; Sales Representative; Securities Sales Representative; Systems Analyst; Typist/Word Processor. **Average salary range of placements:** $20,000 - $29,999. **Number of placements per year:** 200 - 499.

SNELLING PERSONNEL SERVICES
5425 Route 70, Pennsauken NJ 08109. 856/662-5424. **Contact:** Chris Deegler, Owner/Manager. **Description:** A permanent employment agency. **Specializes in the areas of:** Accounting/Auditing; Banking; Clerical; Finance; Food; Health/Medical; Personnel/Labor Relations; Sales.

SNELLING PERSONNEL SERVICES
142 Highway 35, Eatontown NJ 07724. 732/389-0300. **Fax:** 732/460-2582. **Contact:** Frank Wyckoff, Owner/President. **Description:** A permanent employment agency that also provides some temporary placements. **Specializes in the areas of:** High-Tech; Sales. **Positions commonly filled include:** Administrative Manager; Branch Manager; Claim Representative; Clerical Supervisor; Computer Programmer; Design Engineer; Draftsperson; Financial Analyst; General Manager; Health Services Manager; Hotel Manager; Human Resources Manager; Industrial Engineer; Industrial Production Manager; Management Trainee; Paralegal; Pharmacist; Software Engineer; Systems Analyst; Telecommunications Manager; Typist/Word Processor. **Average salary range of placements:** More than $50,000. **Number of placements per year:** 1000+.

SNELLING PERSONNEL SERVICES
47 River Road, Summit NJ 07901. 908/273-6500. **Fax:** 908/273-4379. **Contact:** Marilyn Richards, Vice President. **Description:** A permanent employment agency that also provides some temporary placements. **Specializes in the areas of:** Administration; Clerical; Finance; Legal; Personnel/Labor Relations; Sales; Secretarial. **Positions commonly filled include:** Administrative Manager; Brokerage Clerk; Claim Representative; Clerical Supervisor; Customer Service Representative; Dental Assistant/Dental Hygienist; Human Resources Specialist; Management Trainee; Medical Records Technician; MIS Specialist; Paralegal; Receptionist; Securities Sales Representative; Services Sales Representative; Transportation/Traffic Specialist; Typist/Word Processor. **Benefits available to temporary workers:** 401(k); Paid Holidays. **Average**

salary range of placements: $20,000 - $29,999. **Number of placements per year:** 500 - 999.

SOURCE ONE PERSONNEL
133 Franklin Corner Road, Lawrenceville NJ 08648. 609/895-0895. **Fax:** 609/895-0574. **Contact:** Manager. **Description:** A permanent employment agency. **Specializes in the areas of:** Accounting/Auditing; Information Technology; Retail; Sales. **Positions commonly filled include:** Accountant/Auditor; Budget Analyst; Computer Programmer; Customer Service Representative; Internet Services Manager; MIS Specialist; Paralegal; Services Sales Representative; Software Engineer; Typist/Word Processor. **Benefits available to temporary workers:** Paid Holidays; Paid Vacation. **Average salary range of placements:** $20,000 - $29,999. **Number of placements per year:** 200 - 499.

SOURCE ONE PERSONNEL
2490 Brunswick Pike, Suite 202, Lawrenceville NJ 08648. 609/883-3000. **Fax:** 609/883-8344. **Contact:** Linda Vallyo, Branch Manager. **Description:** A permanent employment agency. **Specializes in the areas of:** Accounting/Auditing; Retail; Sales. **Positions commonly filled include:** Accountant/Auditor; Budget Analyst; Computer Programmer; Customer Service Representative; Internet Services Manager; MIS Specialist; Paralegal; Services Sales Representative; Software Engineer; Typist/Word Processor. **Benefits available to temporary workers:** Paid Holidays; Paid Vacation. **Average salary range of placements:** $20,000 - $29,999. **Number of placements per year:** 200 - 499.

ULTIMATE SOLUTIONS, INC.
151 West Passaic Street, Rochelle Park NJ 07662. 201/909-3717. **Fax:** 201/587-0772. **Contact:** Owner. **E-mail address:** jobs@ultimatesolutions.com. **World Wide Web address:** http://www.ultimatesolutions.com. **Description:** A permanent employment agency. **Specializes in the areas of:** Computer Science/Software; Scientific; Technical. **Positions commonly filled include:** Computer Programmer; Database Manager; MIS Specialist; Systems Analyst; Systems Manager; Telecommunications Manager. **Corporate headquarters location:** This Location. **Average salary range of placements:** More than $50,000. **Number of placements per year:** 200 - 499.

DON WALDRON & ASSOCIATES
220 North Centre Street, Merchantville NJ 08109. 856/663-5151. **Contact:** Manager. **Description:** A permanent employment agency. **Specializes in the areas of:** Sales.

WINTERS & ROSS
442 Main Street, Fort Lee NJ 07024. 201/947-8400. **Fax:** 201/947-1035. **Contact:** Marilyn Winters, Vice President. **Description:** A permanent employment agency. **Specializes in the areas of:** Accounting/Auditing; Bilingual; Clerical; Finance; Legal; Office Support; Personnel/Labor Relations; Secretarial. **Positions commonly filled include:** Accountant/Auditor; Administrative Assistant; Bookkeeper; Clerical Supervisor; Computer Programmer; Credit Manager; Customer Service Representative; Data Entry Clerk; EDP Specialist; Financial Analyst; Human Resources Specialist; Legal Secretary; Management Trainee; Receptionist; Secretary; Stenographer; Typist/Word Processor. **Average salary range of placements:** $20,000 - $29,999. **Number of placements per year:** 100 - 199.

CLAIRE WRIGHT ASSOCIATES
1280 U.S. Highway 46, Parsippany NJ 07054-4911. 973/402-8400. **Fax:** 973/402-8519. **Contact:** K. Kelley, Counselor. **Description:** A permanent employment agency. **Specializes in the areas of:** Accounting/Auditing; Administration; Advertising; Computer Hardware/Software; Engineering; Finance; Insurance; Legal; Manufacturing; Sales; Technical. **Positions commonly filled include:** Accountant/Auditor;

Advertising Clerk; Chemical Engineer; Claim Representative; Computer Programmer; Draftsperson; Electrical/Electronics Engineer; Environmental Engineer; Financial Analyst; Human Resources Specialist; Industrial Engineer; Insurance Agent/Broker; Internet Services Manager; Market Research Analyst; Mechanical Engineer; Metallurgical Engineer; MIS Specialist; Nuclear Engineer; Paralegal; Property and Real Estate Manager; Purchasing Agent/Manager; Securities Sales Representative; Software Engineer; Technical Writer/Editor; Telecommunications Manager; Typist/Word Processor; Underwriter/Assistant Underwriter. **Average salary range of placements:** $30,000 - $50,000. **Number of placements per year:** 1 - 49.

YOH SCIENTIFIC
30 Columbia Turnpike, Florham Park NJ 07932. 973/377-8634. **Fax:** 973/377-0261. **Contact:** Molly Calvert, Recruiting Specialist. **E-mail address:** Florham_Park@yoh.com. **World Wide Web address:** http://www.hlyoh.com. **Description:** Yoh Scientific is a permanent employment agency that also provides some temporary and temp-to-perm placements for laboratory and clinical personnel. **Specializes in the areas of:** Chemicals; Cosmetics; Health/Medical; Pharmaceuticals; Scientific.

YOURS IN TRAVEL PERSONNEL AGENCY, INC.
301 Route 17 North, Suite 800, Rutherford NJ 07070. 201/438-3500. **Contact:** Robyn Hering, Vice President. **Description:** A permanent employment agency. **Specializes in the areas of:** Travel. **Positions commonly filled include:** Travel Agent.

TEMPORARY EMPLOYMENT AGENCIES

ACCOUNTANTS ON CALL
Park 80 West, Plaza II, 9th Floor, Saddle Brook NJ 07663. 201/843-0006. **Fax:** 201/712-1033. **Contact:** Manager. **World Wide Web address:** http://www.aocnet.com. **Description:** A temporary agency that also provides some temp-to-perm placements. **Specializes in the areas of:** Accounting.

ANGELORD INC.
930 Stuyvesant Avenue, Suite 11, Union NJ 07083-6940. 908/687-5442. **Fax:** 908/688-5482. **Contact:** President. **Description:** A temporary agency. **Specializes in the areas of:** Sales; Secretarial. **Positions commonly filled include:** Accountant/Auditor; Services Sales Representative; Typist/Word Processor. **Average salary range of placements:** $20,000 - $29,999. **Number of placements per year:** 50 - 99.

ARC MEDICAL AND PROFESSIONAL PERSONNEL, INC.
36 State Route 10 West, Suite D, East Hanover NJ 07936. 973/428-0101. **Fax:** 973/428-8257. **Contact:** Roslyn Durkin, Assistant Director. **Description:** A temporary agency that also provides some permanent placements. **Specializes in the areas of:** Health/Medical; Pharmaceuticals. **Positions commonly filled include:** Biochemist; Biological Scientist; Chemist; Clinical Lab Technician; Medical Records Technician; Pharmacist; Physician; Registered Nurse; Scientist; Typist/Word Processor. **Number of placements per year:** 1 - 49.

ENRICHED LIVING
18 Davenport Street, Somerville NJ 08876. 908/707-9779. **Fax:** 908/707-4668. **Contact:** Lisa Blake, Nursing Coordinator. **Description:** A temporary agency. **Specializes in the areas of:** Health/Medical. **Positions commonly filled include:** Dietician/Nutritionist; Licensed Practical Nurse; Physical Therapist; Registered Nurse; Social Worker. **Number of placements per year:** 1 - 49.

ITC PERSONNEL SERVICES INC.
232 Boulevard, Suite 5, Hasbrouck Heights NJ 07604. 201/462-0264. **Fax:** 973/345-1229. **Contact:** Manager. **Description:** A temporary agency that also provides some contract services. **Specializes in the areas of:** Personnel/Labor Relations; Secretarial. **Positions commonly filled include:** Customer Service Representative; Human Resources Specialist; Typist/ Word Processor. **Benefits available to temporary workers:** Bonus Award/Plan; Medical Insurance; Paid Vacation. **Average salary range of placements:** $30,000 - $50,000. **Number of placements per year:** 1 - 49.

INTEGRO STAFFING SERVICES
One Gatehall Drive, Parsippany NJ 07054. 973/267-6363. **Fax:** 973/267-2158. **Contact:** Manager. **Description:** A temporary agency. **Specializes in the areas of:** Accounting/Auditing; Banking; Biology; Computer Science/Software; Finance; Legal; Secretarial; Technical. **Positions commonly filled include:** Accountant/Auditor; Administrative Manager; Biochemist; Biological Scientist; Brokerage Clerk; Chemical Engineer; Chemist; Clinical Lab Technician; Computer Programmer; Paralegal; Typist/Word Processor. **Benefits available to temporary workers:** Bonus Award/Plan; Paid Holidays; Paid Vacation. **Other area locations:** Bridgewater NJ; Cherry Hill NJ; Iselan NJ; Lawrenceville NJ; Mount Olive NJ; Paramus NJ. **Number of placements per year:** 1000+.

KAYE PERSONNEL INC.
1868 Route 70 East, Cherry Hill NJ 08003. 856/489-1200. **Fax:** 856/489-1010. **Contact:** Staffing Coordinator. **Description:** A temporary agency. **Specializes in the areas of:** Industrial; Manufacturing; Personnel/Labor Relations; Publishing; Secretarial; Technical. **Positions commonly filled include:** Customer Service Representative; Secretary; Typist/Word Processor. **Other U.S. locations:** Nationwide. **Number of placements per year:** 1000+.

KELLY SCIENTIFIC RESOURCES
140 Route 17 North, Suite 271, Paramus NJ 07652. 201/599-5959. **Fax:** 201/599-8470. **Contact:** Diane R. Long, District Manager. **World Wide Web address:** http://www.kellyscientific.com. **Description:** A temporary agency. Client company pays fee. **Specializes in the areas of:** Biology; Food; Scientific; Technical. **Positions commonly filled include:** Biochemist; Biological Scientist; Biomedical Engineer; Certified Nurses Aide; Certified Occupational Therapy Assistant; Chemical Engineer; Chemist; Clinical Lab Technician; Dietician/Nutritionist; EEG Technologist; EKG Technician; Emergency Medical Technician; Environmental Engineer; Food Scientist/Technologist; Geographer; Geologist/Geophysicist; Home Health Aide; Licensed Practical Nurse; Medical Assistant; Medical Records Technician; Nuclear Medicine Technologist; Nurse Practitioner; Occupational Therapist; Pharmacist; Physical Therapist; Physical Therapy Assistant; Physician; Radiological Technologist; Registered Nurse; Respiratory Therapist; Statistician; Surgical Technician; Veterinarian. **Corporate headquarters location:** Troy MI. **Average salary range of placements:** $30,000 - $49,999. **Number of placements per year:** 1000+.

KELLY SCIENTIFIC RESOURCES
242 Old New Brunswick Road, Suite 140, Piscataway NJ 08854. 732/981-1399. **Contact:** Branch Manager. **World Wide Web address:** http://www.kellyscientific.com. **Description:** A temporary agency. **Specializes in the areas of:** Biomedical; Biotechnology; Chemicals; Environmental; Food; Petrochemical; Pharmaceuticals. **Corporate headquarters location:** Troy MI.

KELLY SERVICES, INC.
70 South Orange Avenue, Suite 107, Livingston NJ 07039. 973/540-1800. **Fax:** 973/992-6511. **Contact:**

Branch Manager. **World Wide Web address:** http://www.kellyservices.com. **Description:** A temporary agency. **Specializes in the areas of:** Accounting/Auditing; Advertising; Engineering; Finance; Secretarial. **Positions commonly filled include:** Biochemist; Biological Scientist; Biomedical Engineer; Blue-Collar Worker Supervisor; Chemical Engineer; Chemist; Civil Engineer; Claim Representative; Clerical Supervisor; Clinical Lab Technician; Computer Programmer; Customer Service Representative; Human Resources Specialist; Industrial Engineer; MIS Specialist; Multimedia Designer; Paralegal; Pharmacist; Purchasing Agent/Manager; Quality Assurance Engineer; Software Engineer; Typist/Word Processor. **Benefits available to temporary workers:** Paid Holidays; Paid Vacation. **Corporate headquarters location:** Troy MI. **Number of placements per year:** 1000+.

KELLY SERVICES, INC.
313 Courtyard, Somerville NJ 08876. 908/526-6225. **Fax:** 908/526-1625. **Contact:** Office Manager. **World Wide Web address:** http://www.kellyservices.com. **Description:** A temporary agency. **Specializes in the areas of:** Accounting/Auditing; Administration; Engineering; Finance; Secretarial. **Positions commonly filled include:** Biochemist; Biological Scientist; Biomedical Engineer; Chemical Engineer; Chemist; Civil Engineer; Claim Representative; Clerical Supervisor; Clinical Lab Technician; Computer Programmer; Human Resources Specialist; Industrial Production Manager; Mechanical Engineer; MIS Specialist; Multimedia Designer; Paralegal; Purchasing Agent/Manager; Quality Assurance Engineer; Software Engineer; Typist/Word Processor. **Benefits available to temporary workers:** Paid Holidays; Paid Vacation. **Corporate headquarters location:** Troy MI. **Number of placements per year:** 1000+.

LAB SUPPORT INC.
475 Market Street, 1st Floor, Elmwood Park NJ 07407. 201/794-8077. **Contact:** Account Manager. **World Wide Web address:** http://www.labsupport.com. **Description:** A temporary agency. **Specializes in the areas of:** Biology; Food; Manufacturing; Technical. **Positions commonly filled include:** Biochemist; Biological Scientist; Chemist; Food Scientist/Technologist; Science Technologist; Scientist. **Benefits available to temporary workers:** 401(k); Medical Insurance; Paid Holidays; Paid Vacation. **Other U.S. locations:** Nationwide. **Average salary range of placements:** $30,000 - $50,000. **Number of placements per year:** 200 - 499.

NORRELL SERVICES
197 Route 18 South, Suite 110, East Brunswick NJ 08816. 732/828-9111. **Toll-free phone:** 800/848-JOBS. **Fax:** 732/828-7766. **Contact:** Corrie Kirklen, Office Manager. **Description:** A temporary agency. Client company pays fee. **Specializes in the areas of:** Accounting; Administration; Finance; General Management; Insurance; Light Industrial; Secretarial. **Positions commonly filled include:** Administrative Assistant; Customer Service Representative; Secretary. **Corporate headquarters location:** Atlanta GA. **Average salary range of placements:** $20,000 - $49,999. **Number of placements per year:** 200 - 499.

OLSTEN STAFFING SERVICES
200 Cottontail Lane, Building A, Somerset NJ 08873. 732/563-1660. **Fax:** 732/563-1665. **Contact:** Manager. **Description:** A temporary agency. **Specializes in the areas of:** Accounting/Auditing; Sales. **Positions commonly filled include:** Accountant/Auditor; Advertising Clerk; Biochemist; Biological Scientist; Blue-Collar Worker Supervisor; Brokerage Clerk; Budget Analyst; Chemist; Clinical Lab Technician; Computer Programmer; Customer Service Representative; Industrial Production Manager; Operations/Production Manager; Paralegal; Systems Analyst; Technical Writer/Editor; Typist/Word Processor. **Benefits available to temporary workers:** Medical Insurance; Paid Vacation. **Corporate headquarters location:** Melville NY. **Other U.S.** locations: Nationwide. **Average salary range of placements:** $20,000 - $29,999. **Number of placements per year:** 1000+.

OMNE STAFFING SERVICES, INC.
15 Bleeker Street, Millburn NJ 07041. 973/379-4900. **Toll-free phone:** 800/321-OMNE. **Fax:** 973/379-9119. **Contact:** Manager. **E-mail address:** info@omne-staffing.com. **World Wide Web address:** http://www.omne-staffing.com. **Description:** A temporary agency that also provides some permanent placements. Client company pays fee. **Specializes in the areas of:** Administration; Industrial; Light Industrial; Personnel/Labor Relations; Scientific; Secretarial; Technical. **Positions commonly filled include:** Accountant; Adjuster; Administrative Assistant; Advertising Clerk; Advertising Executive; Budget Analyst; Chief Financial Officer; Claim Representative; Computer Programmer; Controller; Credit Manager; Customer Service Representative; General Manager; Human Resources Manager; Industrial Production Manager; Market Research Analyst; Marketing Manager; Marketing Specialist; Paralegal; Public Relations Specialist; Secretary; Typist/Word Processor. **Corporate headquarters location:** This Location. **Other U.S. locations:** Nationwide. **Average salary range of placements:** $20,000 - $29,999. **Number of placements per year:** 1000+.

PAT'S SECRETARIAL SERVICE
50 South 21st Street, Kenilworth NJ 07033. 908/276-6366. **Contact:** Recruiter. **Description:** A temporary agency. **Specializes in the areas of:** Engineering; Legal; Secretarial. **Positions commonly filled include:** Clerical Supervisor; Clinical Lab Technician; Typist/Word Processor.

PROTOCALL BUSINESS STAFFING SERVICES
426 High Street, Burlington NJ 08016. 609/387-0300. **Fax:** 856/779-7471. **Contact:** Vince Moore, Regional Recruitment Coordinator. **Description:** A temporary agency. **Specializes in the areas of:** Accounting/Auditing; Computer Science/Software; Health/Medical; Industrial; Manufacturing; Secretarial. **Positions commonly filled include:** Accountant/Auditor; Claim Representative; Clinical Lab Technician; Computer Programmer; Customer Service Representative; Electrical/Electronics Engineer; Human Service Worker; Licensed Practical Nurse; Management Trainee; Medical Records Technician; MIS Specialist; Physical Therapist; Purchasing Agent/Manager; Quality Control Supervisor; Registered Nurse; Respiratory Therapist; Systems Analyst; Typist/Word Processor; Underwriter/Assistant Underwriter. **Corporate headquarters location:** Voorhees NJ. **Average salary range of placements:** $20,000 - $29,000. **Number of placements per year:** 1000+.

REMEDY INTELLIGENT STAFFING
1930 Route 70 East, Executive Mews, Suite W111, Cherry Hill NJ 08003. 856/751-1900. **Toll-free phone:** 888/751-1900. **Fax:** 856/751-1361. **Contact:** Tom Jenkins, President. **World Wide Web address:** http://www.remedystaff.com. **Description:** A temporary agency. **Specializes in the areas of:** Administration; Banking; Finance; Secretarial. **Positions commonly filled include:** Clerical Supervisor; Customer Service Representative; Human Resources Specialist; Management Trainee; Services Sales Representative; Typist/Word Processor. **Benefits available to temporary workers:** Medical Insurance. **Other U.S. locations:** Nationwide. **Average salary range of placements:** $20,000 - $29,999. **Number of placements per year:** 500 - 999.

SUPPORTIVE CARE, INC.
383 North Kings Highway, Suite 213, Cherry Hill NJ 08034. 856/482-6630. **Fax:** 856/482-6632. **Contact:** Debbie Kramer, Manager. **Description:** A temporary agency. **Specializes in the areas of:** Health/Medical. **Positions commonly filled include:** Certified Nurses Aide; Home Health Aide; Licensed Practical Nurse;

Registered Nurse. **Average salary range of placements:** Less than $20,000. **Number of placements per year:** 1 - 49.

TRS STAFFING SOLUTIONS, INC.
P.O. Box 566, Marlton NJ 08053. 856/985-9721. **Toll-free phone:** 800/535-8374. **Fax:** 856/985-6772. **Contact:** Joanne Becmer, Staffing Consultant. **Description:** A temporary agency. **Specializes in the areas of:** Administration; Computer Science/Software; Engineering; Manufacturing; Personnel/Labor Relations; Secretarial; Technical. **Positions commonly filled include:** Architect; Chemical Engineer; Chemist; Civil Engineer; Clerical Supervisor; Computer Programmer; Construction and Building Inspector; Cost Estimator; Draftsperson; Electrical/Electronics Engineer; Environmental Engineer; Internet Services Manager; Mechanical Engineer; Metallurgical Engineer; Mining Engineer; MIS Specialist; Multimedia Designer; Petroleum Engineer; Software Engineer; Structural Engineer; Surveyor; Systems Analyst; Telecommunications Manager. **Benefits available to temporary workers:** 401(k); Medical Insurance.

TEMPORARY CLAIM PROFESSIONAL (TCP)
The Pavillions, 12000 Lincoln Drive West, Suite 401, Marlton NJ 08053-3213. 856/988-0099. **Contact:** Patricia Winstein, Manager. **Description:** A temporary agency. **NOTE:** Resumes should be sent to P.O. Box 36, Mount Laurel NJ 08054. **Specializes in the areas of:** Insurance. **Positions commonly filled include:** Adjuster; Claim Representative; Underwriter/Assistant Underwriter. **Benefits available to temporary workers:** Bonus Award/Plan; Medical Insurance. **Other U.S. locations:** Bel Air MD. **Average salary range of placements:** $30,000 - $50,000. **Number of placements per year:** 50 - 99.

TEMPORARY EXCELLENCE INC.
P.O. Box 726, Paramus NJ 07653-0726. 201/599-1010. **Physical address:** 205 Robin Road, Suite 200, Paramus NJ. **Fax:** 201/599-1122. **Contact:** President. **Description:** A temporary agency. **Specializes in the areas of:** Accounting/Auditing; Fashion; Finance; Health/Medical; Personnel/Labor Relations; Retail; Sales; Secretarial. **Positions commonly filled include:** Accountant/Auditor; Clerical Supervisor; Credit Manager; Customer Service Representative; Human Resources Specialist; Typist/Word Processor. **Benefits available to temporary workers:** Medical Insurance; Paid Vacation. **Average salary range of placements:** $30,000 - $50,000. **Number of placements per year:** 1000+.

UNITEMP TEMPORARY PERSONNEL
95 Route 17 South, Paramus NJ 07652. 201/845-7444. **Toll-free phone:** 800/UNITEMP. **Fax:** 201/845-7451. **Contact:** Molly Kissel, Vice President. **Description:** A temporary agency. Founded in 1969. **Specializes in the areas of:** Administration; Computer Science/Software; Legal; Secretarial. **Positions commonly filled include:** Administrative Assistant; Computer Operator; Computer Programmer; Paralegal; Secretary; Systems Analyst; Typist/Word Processor. **Benefits available to temporary workers:** Bonus Award/Plan; Paid Vacation. **Corporate headquarters location:** This Location.

Other area locations: Secaucus NJ; Woodcliff Lake NJ. **Number of placements per year:** 1000+.

UNITEMP TEMPORARY PERSONNEL
50 Tice Boulevard, Woodcliff Lake NJ 07675. 201/391-3800. **Fax:** 201/391-9219. **Contact:** Office Manager. **E-mail address:** UNITEMP@aol.com. **Description:** A temporary agency. Client company pays fee. **Specializes in the areas of:** Accounting; Administration; Finance; Personnel/Labor Relations; Scientific; Secretarial; Technical. **Positions commonly filled include:** Accountant; Adjuster; Administrative Assistant; Advertising Clerk; Applications Engineer; AS400 Programmer Analyst; Auditor; Budget Analyst; Chief Financial Officer; Clerical Supervisor; Computer Animator; Computer Engineer; Computer Operator; Computer Programmer; Computer Scientist; Computer Support Technician; Computer Technician; Content Developer; Controller; Cost Estimator; Credit Manager; Customer Service Representative; Database Administrator; Database Manager; Desktop Publishing Specialist; Finance Director; Financial Analyst; Graphic Artist; Graphic Designer; Human Resources Manager; Internet Services Manager; Marketing Manager; Marketing Specialist; Medical Records Technician; MIS Specialist; Multimedia Designer; Network/Systems Administrator; Paralegal; Purchasing Agent/Manager; Secretary; Software Engineer; SQL Programmer; Systems Analyst; Systems Manager; Typist/Word Processor; Webmaster. **Benefits available to temporary workers:** Bonus Award/Plan; Paid Vacation; Training. **Corporate headquarters location:** Paramus NJ. **Other area locations:** Secaucus NJ. **Number of placements per year:** 500 - 999.

WINSTON STAFFING SERVICES
301 Route 17 North, Rutherford NJ 07070. 201/460-9200. **Contact:** Michael A. Gallo, Vice President. **Description:** A temporary agency. **Specializes in the areas of:** Accounting/Auditing; Advertising; Banking; Computer Science/Software; Fashion; Finance; General Management; Health/Medical; Legal; Personnel/Labor Relations; Sales; Secretarial. **Positions commonly filled include:** Accountant/Auditor; Administrator; Advertising Clerk; Attorney; Blue-Collar Worker Supervisor; Brokerage Clerk; Budget Analyst; Buyer; Claim Representative; Clerical Supervisor; Clinical Lab Technician; Computer Programmer; Counselor; Credit Manager; Customer Service Representative; Dental Assistant/Dental Hygienist; Dietician/Nutritionist; EEG Technologist; EKG Technician; Emergency Medical Technician; Health Services Manager; Human Resources Specialist; Licensed Practical Nurse; Management Trainee; Manufacturer's/Wholesaler's Sales Rep.; Market Research Analyst; Medical Records Technician; MIS Specialist; Multimedia Designer; Occupational Therapist; Paralegal; Pharmacist; Physical Therapist; Physician; Public Relations Specialist; Purchasing Agent/Manager; Quality Control Supervisor; Radiological Technologist; Recreational Therapist; Registered Nurse; Respiratory Therapist; Securities Sales Representative; Software Engineer; Statistician; Systems Analyst; Telecommunications Manager; Typist/Word Processor. **Benefits available to temporary workers:** Paid Vacation. **Number of placements per year:** 1000+.

CONTRACT SERVICES FIRMS

BUTLER INTERNATIONAL, INC.
110 Summit Avenue, Montvale NJ 07645. 201/573-8000. **Contact:** Manager. **World Wide Web address:** http://www.butlerintl.com. **Description:** A contract services firm. **Corporate headquarters location:** This Location.

CDI CORPORATION
899 Mountain Avenue, Springfield NJ 07081. 973/379-9790. **Contact:** Manager. **World Wide Web address:** http://www.cdicorp.com. **Description:** A contract services firm. **Specializes in the areas of:** Technical. **Corporate headquarters location:** Philadelphia PA. **International locations:** Worldwide.

HALL KINION
517 Route One South, Suite 3055, Iselin NJ 08830. **Toll-free phone:** 888/333-6083. **Fax:** 732/283-4052. **Contact:** Manager. **E-mail address:** njresume@hallkinion.com. **World Wide Web address:** http://www.hallkinion.com. **Description:** A contract services firm that also provides some permanent

placements. **Specializes in the areas of:** Information Systems; Information Technology; Internet Development; Network Administration; Quality Assurance; Systems Administration; Systems Design; Technical Writing.

INTERIM TECHNOLOGY
9 Polito Avenue, 9th Floor, Lyndhurst NJ 07071. 201/392-0800. **Contact:** Manager. **World Wide Web address:** http://www.interimtechnology.com. **Description:** A contract services firm.

JOULE INDUSTRIAL CONTRACTORS
429 East Broad Street, Gibbstown NJ 08027. 856/423-7500. **Toll-free phone:** 800/445-6853. **Fax:** 856/423-3209. **Contact:** Manager. **Description:** A contract services firm. **Specializes in the areas of:** Food; Light Industrial. **Positions commonly filled include:** Millwright; Pipe Fitter; Welder. **Benefits available to temporary workers:** 401(k); Dental Insurance; Life Insurance; Medical Insurance. **Corporate headquarters location:** Edison NJ. **Average salary range of placements:** $20,000 - $29,999. **Number of placements per year:** 100 - 199.

JOULE STAFFING SERVICES
2333 Whitehorse-Mercerville Road, Trenton NJ 08619. 609/588-5900. **Fax:** 609/588-9642. **Contact:** Manager. **Description:** A contract services firm. **Specializes in the areas of:** Accounting/Auditing; Education; Engineering; Industrial; Legal; Manufacturing; Personnel/Labor Relations; Secretarial; Technical. **Positions commonly filled include:** Accountant/Auditor; Administrative Manager; Blue-Collar Worker Supervisor; Claim Representative; Clerical Supervisor; Computer Programmer; Counselor; Customer Service Representative; Human Resources Specialist; Management Trainee; Typist/Word Processor. **Benefits available to temporary workers:** Incentive Plan; Medical Insurance; Paid Holidays; Paid Vacation. **Corporate headquarters location:** Edison NJ. **Other U.S. locations:** Nationwide. **Average salary range of placements:** $20,000 - $29,999. **Number of placements per year:** 1000+.

JOULE TECHNICAL STAFFING
1235 Route 1 South, Edison NJ 08837. 732/494-8880. **Toll-free phone:** 800/382-0382. **Fax:** 732/494-6790. **Contact:** Manager. **World Wide Web address:** http://www.jouleinc.com. **Description:** A contract services firm. Founded in 1965. **Specializes in the areas of:** Administration; Chemicals; Engineering. **Positions commonly filled include:** Branch Manager; Chemical Engineer; Chemist; Civil Engineer; Designer; Draftsperson; Electrical/Electronics Engineer; Electrician; Industrial Engineer; Mechanical Engineer; Services Sales Representative; Stationary Engineer. **Corporate headquarters location:** This Location. **Number of placements per year:** 200 - 499.

MANPOWER TECHNICAL SERVICES
51 Haddonfield Road, Suite 325, Cherry Hill NJ 08002. 856/665-8177. **Fax:** 856/665-8249. **Contact:** Manager. **Description:** A contract services firm. Founded in 1948. **Specializes in the areas of:** Accounting/Auditing; Administration; Biology; Computer Hardware/Software; Engineering; Finance; Manufacturing; Technical. **Positions commonly filled include:** Accountant/Auditor; Actuary; Aerospace Engineer; Biochemist; Biological Scientist; Buyer; Chemical Engineer; Chemist; Civil Engineer; Clinical Lab Technician; Computer Programmer; Credit Manager; Design Engineer; Designer; Dietician/Nutritionist; Draftsperson; Economist; Electrical/Electronics Engineer; Environmental Engineer; Geologist/Geophysicist; Industrial Engineer; Internet Services Manager; Mechanical Engineer; Metallurgical Engineer; Multimedia Designer; Nuclear Engineer; Petroleum Engineer; Purchasing Agent/Manager; Quality Control Supervisor; Science Technologist; Software Engineer; Stationary Engineer; Structural Engineer; Technical Writer/Editor. **Benefits available to temporary workers:** 401(k); Dental Insurance; Life Insurance; Medical Insurance; Paid Holidays; Paid Vacation.

Corporate headquarters location: Milwaukee WI. **Average salary range of placements:** $40,000 - $70,000. **Number of placements per year:** 100 - 199.

ROTATOR STAFFING SERVICES INC.
557 Cranbury Road, P.O. Box 366, East Brunswick NJ 08816. 732/238-6050. **Fax:** 732/238-2152. **Contact:** Dan Klein, Senior Staffing Specialist. **E-mail address:** dan@rotator.net. **World Wide Web address:** http://www.rotator.net. **Description:** A contract services firm that also provides temporary and permanent placements. Client company pays fee. **Specializes in the areas of:** Accounting; Administration; Architecture/Construction; Computer Science/Software; Engineering; Health/Medical; Industrial; Secretarial; Technical. **Positions commonly filled include:** Account Representative; Accountant; Administrative Assistant; Architect; Biochemist; Biological Scientist; Buyer; Chemist; Civil Engineer; Clinical Lab Technician; Computer Operator; Computer Programmer; Computer Support Technician; Computer Technician; Customer Service Representative; Database Administrator; Design Engineer; Dietician/Nutritionist; Draftsperson; EEG Technologist; EKG Technician; Electrical/Electronics Engineer; Graphic Artist; Human Resources Manager; Mechanical Engineer; Medical Records Technician; Network/Systems Administrator; Nuclear Medicine Technologist; Occupational Therapist; Physical Therapist; Physical Therapy Assistant; Physician; Quality Assurance Engineer; Registered Nurse; Sales Representative; Secretary; Statistician; Systems Manager; Telecommunications Analyst; Telecommunications Manager; Typist/Word Processor. **Benefits available to temporary workers:** 401(k); Medical Insurance. **Average salary range of placements:** $50,000 - $100,000. **Number of placements per year:** 500 - 999.

SCIENTIFIC STAFFING
51 West Prospect Street, East Brunswick NJ 08816. 732/651-1200. **Fax:** 732/651-5968. **Contact:** Branch Manager. **Description:** A contract services firm that also provides some temporary, temp-to-perm, and permanent placements. Founded in 1986. Client company pays fee. **Specializes in the areas of:** Food; Scientific; Technical. **Positions commonly filled include:** Biochemist; Biological Scientist; Biomedical Engineer; Chemical Engineer; Chemist; Clinical Lab Technician; Food Scientist/Technologist; Pharmacist; Statistician. **Benefits available to temporary workers:** 401(k); Direct Deposit; Medical Insurance; Paid Holidays; Paid Vacation. **Corporate headquarters location:** Stuart FL. **Other U.S. locations:** Nationwide. **Average salary range of placements:** $30,000 - $49,999.

SHARP TECHNICAL SERVICES, INC.
875 Kings Highway, Woodbury NJ 08096. 856/853-5752. **Fax:** 856/853-0780. **Contact:** Manager. **E-mail address:** resume@sharptechnical.com. **World Wide Web address:** http://www.sharptechnical.com. **Description:** A contract services firm. **Specializes in the areas of:** Design; Engineering. **Positions commonly filled include:** Biochemist; Buyer; Chemical Engineer; Civil Engineer; Computer Programmer; Construction and Building Inspector; Cost Estimator; Design Engineer; Designer; Draftsperson; Electrical/Electronics Engineer; Environmental Engineer; Industrial Engineer; Mechanical Engineer; MIS Specialist; Purchasing Agent/Manager; Software Engineer; Structural Engineer; Systems Analyst; Technical Writer/Editor; Telecommunications Manager. **Benefits available to temporary workers:** 401(k); Credit Union; Medical Insurance; Paid Holidays; Paid Vacation. **Other area locations:** Eatontown NJ. **Average salary range of placements:** $30,000 - $50,000. **Number of placements per year:** 200 - 499.

YOH SCIENTIFIC
H.L. YOH COMPANY
5 Independence Way, 1st Floor, Princeton NJ 08540. 609/514-1210. **Contact:** Manager. **World Wide Web address:** http://www.hlyoh.com. **Description:** A contract services firm. **Specializes in the areas of:** Pharmaceuticals; Scientific.

CAREER/OUTPLACEMENT COUNSELING FIRMS

A PROFESSIONAL EDGE
248 Columbia Turnpike, Florham Park NJ 07932-1210. 973/966-6963x14. **Fax:** 973/966-6539. **Contact:** Martin P. Murphy, Executive Vice President. **Description:** A career/outplacement counseling firm. **Specializes in the areas of:** Accounting/Auditing; Administration; Advertising; Banking; Computer Science/Software; Economics; Fashion; Finance; General Management; Insurance; Personnel/Labor Relations; Retail; Sales; Secretarial; Technical. **Positions commonly filled include:** Accountant/Auditor; Administrative Manager; Bank Officer/Manager; Branch Manager; Brokerage Clerk; Computer Programmer; Counselor; Customer Service Representative; Financial Analyst; Human Resources Specialist; Insurance Agent/Broker; Management Analyst/Consultant; Management Trainee; MIS Specialist; Operations/Production Manager; Public Relations Specialist; Securities Sales Representative; Services Sales Representative; Software Engineer; Systems Analyst; Telecommunications Manager; Typist/ Word Processor. **Average salary range of placements:** $20,000 - $100,000. **Number of placements per year:** 200 - 499.

AARON CAREER SERVICES
520 Main Street, Suite 302, Fort Lee NJ 07024. 201/592-0593. **Contact:** Manager. **Description:** A resume writing service that also provides executive searches and career counseling.

CAREER RESUME ADVANTAGE INC.
959 Route 46 East, Suite 101, Parsippany NJ 07054. 973/402-8777. **Toll-free phone:** 800/RESUME911. **Fax:** 973/402-6434. **Contact:** John Thorn, President. **E-mail address:** john@resume911.com. **World Wide Web address:** http://www.resume911.com. **Description:** A resume writing and career counseling service. **Other U.S. locations:** Hackensack NJ.

EXECUTIVE RESUME
1040 North Kings Highway, Suite 600, Cherry Hill NJ 08034. 856/875-3008. **Toll-free phone:** 800/563-6359. **Fax:** 856/875-8618. **Contact:** Sam Collins, President. **E-mail address:** jobcoach@juno.com. **World Wide Web address:** http://www.executiveresume.com. **Description:** Provides resume writing services. Founded in 1991.

SANDRA GRUNDFEST, ED.D.
601 Ewing Street, Suite C-1, Princeton NJ 08540. 609/921-8401. **Fax:** 609/921-9430. **Contact:** Dr. Sandra Grundfest, Principal. **E-mail address:** grundfest@worldnet.att.net. **Description:** Provides career management counseling services. Founded in 1984. **Specializes in the areas of:** Art/Design; Business Services; Education; Finance; Health/Medical; Legal; Nonprofit; Scientific. **Corporate headquarters location:** This Location. **Other U.S. locations:** Somerset NJ.

SANDRA GRUNDFEST, ED.D.
11 Clyde Road, Suite 103, Somerset NJ 08873. 732/873-1212. **Fax:** 732/873-2584. **Contact:** Dr. Sandra Grundfest. **E-mail address:** grundfest@worldnet.att.net. **Description:** Provides career management counseling services. **Corporate headquarters location:** Princeton NJ.

METRO CAREER SERVICES
784 Morris Turnpike, Suite 203, Short Hills NJ 07078. 973/912-0106. **Fax:** 973/379-5489. **Contact:** Judy Scherer, President. **E-mail address:** metcareer@aol.com. **Description:** A career/outplacement counseling firm.

PERMIAN INTERNATIONAL, INC.
227 Route 206, Flanders NJ 07836-9114. 973/927-7373. **Fax:** 973/927-7172. **Contact:** Don Marletta, President. **Description:** A career/outplacement counseling service. **Number of placements per year:** 1 - 49.

EXECUTIVE SEARCH FIRMS

COLUCCI-CORRIGAN ASSOCIATES
11000 Candelaria Road Northeast, Albuquerque NM 87112. 505/275-3031. **Contact:** Manager. **Description:** An executive search firm.

CREATIVE FINANCIAL STAFFING
707 Broadway Boulevard Northeast, Suite 400, Albuquerque NM 87102. 505/224-2575. **Contact:** Manager. **Description:** An executive search firm. **Specializes in the areas of:** Finance.

EXECUTIVE SEARCH
7901-B Mountain Road NE, Albuquerque NM 87110. 505/268-3100. **Fax:** 505/268-3572. **Contact:** Peter Dunlap, Manager. **Description:** An executive search firm.

ROBERT HALF INTERNATIONAL ACCOUNTEMPS
6501 Americas Parkway NE, Suite 675, Albuquerque NM 87110. 505/884-4557. **Contact:** Manager. **World Wide Web address:** http://www.roberthalf.com. **Description:** An executive search firm. Accountemps (also at this location) provides temporary placements. **Specializes in the areas of:** Accounting/Auditing. **Corporate headquarters location:** Menlo Park CA. **Other U.S. locations:** Nationwide.

HENDERSON BLACK AND COMPANY
6605 Uptown Boulevard NE, Suite 370, Albuquerque NM 87110. 505/830-2500. **Contact:** Manager. **Description:** An executive search firm. **Specializes in the areas of:** Accounting; Engineering; Health/Medical; Software Development.

MANAGEMENT RECRUITERS - SANTA FE
1850 Old Pecos Trail, Suite H, Santa Fe NM 87505. 505/982-5445. **Contact:** Bill Miller, President. **Description:** An executive search firm. **Specializes in the areas of:** Electronics; Engineering; Technical. **Corporate headquarters location:** Cleveland OH.

MANAGEMENT RECRUITERS INTERNATIONAL
2500 Louisiana Boulevard NE, Suite 506, Albuquerque NM 87110. 505/875-0920. **Contact:** Manager. **Description:** Management Recruiters International is an executive search firm. **Corporate headquarters location:** Cleveland OH.

MANAGEMENT RESOURCE CONSULTING
11200 Montgomery Boulevard NE, Suite 8, Albuquerque NM 87111. 505/275-1234. **Fax:** 505/275-1235. **Contact:** Robert Schultz, President. **Description:** An executive search firm focusing on human resource management and mining management primarily in base metals, as well as industrial minerals and coal. **Specializes in the areas of:** Human Resources; Mining. **Positions commonly filled include:** Human Resources Specialist; Mining Engineer. **Average salary range of placements:** More than $50,000. **Number of placements per year:** 50 - 99.

MERCER GROUP
551 West Cordova Road, Suite 726, Santa Fe NM 87501. 505/466-9500. **Contact:** Manager. **Description:** An executive search firm. **Specializes in the areas of:** Government.

MIERA CONSULTANTS INTERNATIONAL
2403 San Mateo Boulevard NE, Albuquerque NM 87110. 505/889-0456. **Contact:** Manager. **Description:** An executive search firm. **Specializes in the areas of:** Health/Medical.

NEW MEXICO HEALTH RESOURCES, INC.
300 San Mateo Boulevard NE, Suite 905, Albuquerque NM 87108. 505/260-0993. **Toll-free phone:** 800/288-6930. **Fax:** 505/260-1919. **Contact:** Office Manager. **E-mail address:** nmhealth@nmhr.org. **World Wide Web address:** http://www.rt66.com/nmhealth. **Description:** An executive search firm with an emphasis on the recruitment of health professionals for designated rural and underserved populations in New Mexico. **Specializes in the areas of:** Health/Medical; Nonprofit. **Positions commonly filled include:** Dental Assistant/Dental Hygienist; Dentist; Emergency Medical Technician; Nurse Practitioner; Occupational Therapist; Physical Therapist; Physician; Physician Assistant; Recreational Therapist; Registered Nurse; Respiratory Therapist. **Average salary range of placements:** More than $50,000. **Number of placements per year:** 1 - 49.

MARCIA OWEN ASSOCIATES
110 North Guadalupe, Suite 12, Santa Fe NM 87501. 505/983-7775. **Contact:** Manager. **Description:** An executive search firm. **Specializes in the areas of:** Administration.

RLR RESOURCES
56 Calle Conejo, Corrales NM 87048. 505/897-1201. **Contact:** Manager. **Description:** An executive search firm. **Specializes in the areas of:** Oil and Gas.

ROADRUNNER PERSONNEL, INC.
4015 Carlisle Boulevard NE, Suite C, Albuquerque NM 87107. 505/881-1994. **Fax:** 505/881-8749. **Contact:** Doug Elliott, Owner. **E-mail address:** delliott@exec-recruiter.com. **World Wide Web address:** http://www.exec-recruiter.com. **Description:** An executive search firm operating on a contingency basis. **Specializes in the areas of:** Marketing; Sales. **Positions commonly filled include:** Account Manager; Account Representative; Marketing Manager; Marketing Specialist; Sales Engineer; Sales Executive; Sales Representative. **Average salary range of placements:** More than $50,000. **Number of placements per year:** 50 - 99.

S.O.S. STAFFING SERVICE
5021 Indian School Road Northeast, Suite 500, Albuquerque NM 87110. 505/266-6722. **Contact:** Manager. **Description:** An executive search firm.

THE SCHROEDER ASSOCIATES
4800 Juan Tabo Boulevard NE, Suite C, Albuquerque NM 87111. 505/271-0702. **Contact:** Steven Schroeder, President. **Description:** An executive search firm. **Specializes in the areas of:** Health/Medical.

SNELLING SEARCH
2601 Wyoming Boulevard NE, Suite 106, Albuquerque NM 87112. 505/293-7800. **Fax:** 505/298-7408. **Contact:** Sue Lane, Manager. **E-mail address:** snelling@sandia.net. **Description:** An executive search firm operating on a contingency basis. **Specializes in the areas of:** Accounting; Finance; General Management; Health/Medical; Sales; Secretarial. **Positions commonly filled include:** Account Manager; Account Representative; Accountant; Adjuster; Administrative Manager; Branch Manager; Clerical Supervisor; Credit Manager; Customer Service Representative; Electrical/Electronics Engineer; General Manager; Human Resources Manager; Mechanical Engineer; Paralegal; Purchasing Agent/Manager; Sales Representative; Typist/Word Processor; Underwriter/Assistant Underwriter. **Corporate headquarters location:** Dallas TX. **International locations:** Worldwide. **Average salary range of placements:** $30,000 - $50,000. **Number of placements per year:** 50 - 99.

WEIRICH AND ASSOCIATES INC.
1650 University Boulevard Northeast, Suite 235, Albuquerque NM 87102. 505/242-2055. **Contact:** Manager. **Description:** An executive search firm.

PERMANENT EMPLOYMENT AGENCIES

ALBUQUERQUE PERSONNEL, INC.
5555 Montgomery Road NE, Suite 8, Albuquerque NM 87109. 505/888-3555. **Contact:** Manager. **Description:** A permanent employment agency. **Specializes in the areas of:** Accounting/Auditing; Administration; Advertising; Architecture/Construction; Banking; Broadcasting; Computer Science/Software; Engineering; Finance; Food; General Management; Health/Medical; Industrial; Legal; Manufacturing; Personnel/Labor Relations; Publishing; Retail; Sales; Secretarial; Technical; Transportation. **Positions commonly filled include:** Accountant/Auditor; Adjuster; Administrative Manager; Advertising Clerk; Automotive Mechanic; Bank Officer/Manager; Blue-Collar Worker Supervisor; Branch Manager; Budget Analyst; Buyer; Civil Engineer; Claim Representative; Clerical Supervisor; Computer Programmer; Construction and Building Inspector; Construction Contractor; Cost Estimator; Counselor; Credit Manager; Customer Service Representative; Dental Assistant/Dental Hygienist; Designer; Draftsperson; Economist; Electrician; Emergency Medical Technician; Financial Analyst; General Manager; Health Services Manager; Hotel Manager; Human Resources Manager; Industrial Engineer; Industrial Production Manager; Insurance Agent/Broker; Management Analyst/Consultant; Management Trainee; Manufacturer's/Wholesaler's Sales Rep.; Mechanical Engineer; Operations/Production Manager; Paralegal; Property and Real Estate Manager; Public Relations Specialist; Purchasing Agent/Manager; Quality Control Supervisor; Radio/TV Announcer/Broadcaster; Real Estate Agent; Restaurant/Food Service Manager; Services Sales Representative; Software Engineer; Systems Analyst; Technical Writer/Editor; Transportation/Traffic Specialist; Travel Agent; Urban/Regional Planner; Veterinarian; Wholesale and Retail Buyer. **Number of placements per year:** 50 - 99.

EXCEL STAFFING COMPANIES
1700 Louisiana Boulevard NE, Suite 210, Albuquerque NM 87110-7014. 505/262-1871. **Fax:** 505/268-4954. **Contact:** Office Manager. **E-mail address:** excelab@excelalb.com. **World Wide Web address:** http://www.excelalb.com. **Description:** A permanent employment agency that also provides some temporary placements. **Specializes in the areas of:** Accounting; Administration; Banking; Computer Science/Software; Engineering; Finance; Insurance; Internet Development; Legal; Light Industrial; Personnel/Labor Relations; Secretarial. **Positions commonly filled include:** Accountant; Adjuster; Administrative Assistant; Applications Engineer; AS400 Programmer Analyst;

Auditor; Budget Analyst; Chief Financial Officer; Claim Representative; Computer Animator; Computer Engineer; Computer Operator; Computer Programmer; Computer Scientist; Computer Support Technician; Computer Technician; Content Developer; Controller; Cost Estimator; Credit Manager; Customer Service Representative; Database Administrator; Database Manager; Design Engineer; Desktop Publishing Specialist; Electrical/Electronics Engineer; Financial Analyst; Internet Services Manager; MIS Specialist; Network/Systems Administrator; Paralegal; Purchasing Agent/Manager; Secretary; Software Engineer; SQL Programmer; Systems Analyst; Systems Manager; Technical Writer/Editor; Typist/Word Processor; Webmaster. **Corporate headquarters location:** This Location. **Average salary range of placements:** Less than $20,000. **Number of placements per year:** 1000+.

SANDERSON EMPLOYMENT SERVICE INC.
500 Chama Boulevard NE, Albuquerque NM 87108. 505/265-8827. **Fax:** 505/268-5536. **Contact:** Bill Sanderson, President. **Description:** A permanent employment agency. **Specializes in the areas of:** Accounting/Auditing; Clerical; Computer Hardware/Software; Engineering; Sales; Secretarial; Technical. **Positions commonly filled include:** Accountant/Auditor; Aerospace Engineer; Bookkeeper; Civil Engineer; Computer Programmer; Data Entry Clerk; EDP Specialist; Electrical/Electronics Engineer; Legal Secretary; Mechanical Engineer; Medical Secretary; Physicist; Receptionist; Sales Representative; Secretary; Stenographer; Systems Analyst; Typist/Word Processor. **Number of placements per year:** 100 - 199.

TRAMBLEY THE RECRUITER
5353 Wyoming Boulevard NE, Suite 8, Albuquerque NM 87109-3132. 505/821-5440. **Fax:** 505/821-8509. **Contact:** J. Brian Trambley, CPC. **Description:** A permanent employment agency. **Specializes in the areas of:** Heavy Equipment; Industrial; Technical. **Positions commonly filled include:** Agricultural Engineer; Design Engineer; Designer; Electrical/Electronics Engineer; Industrial Engineer; Mechanical Engineer; Metallurgical Engineer; Quality Control Supervisor; Software Engineer; Structural Engineer. **Number of placements per year:** 50 - 99.

SUE WILSON PERSONNEL SERVICE
1717 Louisiana Boulevard Northeast, Suite 101, Albuquerque NM 87110. 505/268-1905. **Contact:** Manager. **Description:** A permanent employment agency.

TEMPORARY EMPLOYMENT AGENCIES

MANPOWER, INC.
580 North Telshor, Las Cruces NM 88011. 505/522-6028. **Contact:** Branch Manager. **Description:** A temporary agency. **Specializes in the areas of:** Industrial; Office Support; Technical; Telecommunications; Word Processing. **Positions commonly filled include:** Accountant/Auditor; Accounting Clerk; Administrative Assistant; Assembly Worker; Biological Scientist; Bookkeeper; CADD Operator; Chemist; Computer Operator; Customer Service Manager; Desktop Publishing Specialist; Electrician; Inspector/Tester/Grader; Inventory Control Specialist; Machine Operator; Material Control Specialist; Order Clerk; Packaging/Processing Worker; Painter; Project Engineer; Proofreader; Receptionist; Records Manager; Research Assistant; Secretary; Software Engineer; Stenographer; Stock Clerk; Systems Analyst; Technical Writer/Editor; Technician; Telemarketer; Test Operator; Transcriptionist; Typist/Word Processor; Welder. **Benefits available to** temporary workers: Life Insurance; Medical Insurance; Paid Holidays; Paid Vacation. **Number of placements per year:** 1000+.

NORRELL STAFFING SERVICES
3737 Princeton Drive NE, Suite 150, Albuquerque NM 87107. 505/888-0330. **Fax:** 505/888-5840. **Contact:** Staffing Coordinator. **World Wide Web address:** http://www.norrell.com. **Description:** A temporary agency. **Specializes in the areas of:** Clerical; Light Industrial; Manufacturing; Office Support. **Positions commonly filled include:** Administrative Assistant; Customer Service Representative; Typist/Word Processor; Warehouse/Distribution Worker. **Benefits available to temporary workers:** 401(k); Dental Insurance; Medical Insurance; Vacation Pay. **Corporate headquarters location:** Atlanta GA. **Average salary range of placements:** Less than $20,000. **Number of placements per year:** 1000+.

SANTA FE SERVICES
142 Lincoln Avenue, Suite 205, Santa Fe NM 87501. 505/984-8511. **Fax:** 505/986-8122. **Contact:** Don Woodin, President. **Description:** A temporary agency that also provides some permanent placements. Founded in 1981. **Specializes in the areas of:** Accounting/ Auditing; Advertising; General Management; Legal; Secretarial. **Positions commonly filled include:** Accountant/Auditor; Administrative Manager; Bank Officer/Manager; Clerical Supervisor; General Manager; Hotel Manager; Management Trainee; Operations/ Production Manager; Paralegal; Property and Real Estate Manager; Purchasing Agent/Manager; Typist/Word Processor. **Average salary range of placements:** $20,000 - $29,999. **Number of placements per year:** 100 - 199.

SCIENTEMPS, INC.
P.O. Box 82035, Albuquerque NM 87198. 505/323-1600. **Fax:** 505/323-1670. **Contact:** Judi Richardson, President. **E-mail address:** judi@scientemps.com. **World Wide Web address:** http://www.scientemps.

com. **Description:** A temporary agency that also provides temp-to-perm and permanent positions. Founded in 1991. **Specializes in the areas of:** Biology; Computer Science/Software; Engineering; Food; Health/Medical; Technical. **Positions commonly filled** include: Biochemist; Biological Scientist; Biomedical Engineer; Broadcast Technician; Certified Nurses Aide; Chemical Engineer; Chemist; Civil Engineer; Clinical Lab Technician; Design Engineer; Draftsperson; EEG Technologist; EKG Technician; Electrical/Electronics Engineer; Environmental Engineer; Food Scientist/Technologist; Geologist/Geophysicist; Graphic Artist; Graphic Designer; Industrial Engineer; Licensed Practical Nurse; Mechanical Engineer; Metallurgical Engineer; MIS Specialist; Nuclear Medicine Technologist; Quality Control Supervisor; Registered Nurse; Software Engineer; Statistician; Surgical Technician; Technical Writer/Editor. **Benefits available to temporary workers:** Health Club Discount; Paid Holidays. **Average salary range of placements:** $30,000 - 50,000. **Number of placements per year:** 100 - 199.

CONTRACT SERVICES FIRMS

BUTLER SERVICE GROUP
2201 San Pedro Boulevard NE, Building 3, Suite 230, Albuquerque NM 87110. 505/883-2700. **Fax:** 505/881-8735. **Contact:** Steve Garcia, Senior Recruiter. **Description:** A contract services firm. **Specializes in the areas of:** Computer Science/Software; Engineering; Environmental; Manufacturing; Technical. **Positions commonly filled include:** Biological Scientist; Budget Analyst; Chemist; Computer Programmer; Design Engineer; Designer; Draftsperson; Electrical/Electronics Engineer; Environmental Engineer; Librarian; Library Technician; Mechanical Engineer; MIS Specialist; Nuclear Engineer; Software Engineer; Structural Engineer; Systems Analyst. **Benefits available to temporary workers:** 401(k); Medical Insurance; Paid Holidays. **Corporate headquarters location:** Montvale NJ. **International locations:** Worldwide. **Average salary range of placements:** $30,000 - $50,000. **Number of placements per year:** 100 - 199.

CDI TECHNICAL SERVICES
2730 San Pedro Drive NE, Suite A1, Albuquerque NM 87110. 505/888-4544. **Toll-free phone:** 800/975-6564. **Fax:** 505/888-3233. **Contact:** Shawn Murphy, Technical Manager. **E-mail address:** sgmurphy@cdicorp.com. **World Wide Web address:** http://www.cdicorp.com. **Description:** A contract services firm. Founded in 1945. **Specializes in the areas of:** Art/Design; Banking; Biology; Computer Science/Software; Engineering; Finance; Food; General Management; Health/Medical; Industrial; Light Industrial; MIS/EDP; Personnel/Labor Relations; Secretarial; Technical; Transportation. **Positions commonly filled include:** Account Manager; Account Representative; Accountant; Adjuster; Administrative Assistant; Applications Engineer; Architect; Assistant Manager; Bank Officer/Manager; Biochemist; Biological Scientist; Biomedical Engineer; Blue-Collar Worker Supervisor; Branch Manager; Broadcast Technician; Budget Analyst; Buyer; Chemical Engineer; Chemist; Chief Financial Officer; Civil Engineer; Claim Representative; Clerical Supervisor;

Computer Animator; Computer Programmer; Construction Contractor; Controller; Customer Service Representative; Design Engineer; Draftsperson; Economist; Editor; Editorial Assistant; Education Administrator; Electrical/Electronics Engineer; Electrician; Environmental Engineer; Finance Director; Financial Analyst; Food Scientist/Technologist; Fund Manager; General Manager; Geographer; Geologist/ Geophysicist; Graphic Artist; Graphic Designer; Human Resources Manager; Industrial Engineer; Industrial Production Manager; Insurance Agent/Broker; Internet Services Manager; Management Analyst/Consultant; Manufacturing Engineer; Market Research Analyst; Marketing Manager; Marketing Specialist; Mechanical Engineer; Medical Records Technician; Metallurgical Engineer; MIS Specialist; Multimedia Designer; Nuclear Medicine Technologist; Online Content Specialist; Operations/Production Manager; Preschool Worker; Production Engineer; Project Manager; Public Relations Specialist; Purchasing Agent/Manager; Quality Control Supervisor; Sales Engineer; Sales Executive; Sales Manager; Sales Representative; Secretary; Software Engineer; Statistician; Systems Analyst; Systems Manager; Teacher/Professor; Technical Writer/Editor; Telecommunications Manager; Transportation/Traffic Specialist; Typist/Word Processor; Video Production Coordinator; Webmaster. **Benefits available to temporary workers:** 401(k); Dental Insurance; Direct Deposit; Medical Insurance; Vacation Pay. **Corporate headquarters location:** Philadelphia PA. **Other U.S. locations:** Nationwide. **International locations:** Worldwide. **Average salary range of placements:** $50,000 - $80,000. **Number of placements per year:** 1000+.

COMFORCE TECHNICAL SERVICES, INC.
6400 Uptown Boulevard NE, Suite 460W, Albuquerque NM 87110. 505/889-3535. **Fax:** 505/889-3331. **Contact:** Manager. **Description:** A contract services firm. **Specializes in the areas of:** Technical.

EXECUTIVE SEARCH FIRMS

A-L ASSOCIATES, INC.
546 Fifth Avenue, New York NY 10036. 212/878-9000. **Fax:** 212/878-9096. **Contact:** Manager. **E-mail address:** webmaster@alassoc.com. **World Wide Web address:** http://www.alassoc.com. **Description:** An executive search firm. **Specializes in the areas of:** Accounting; Finance; Legal; Risk Management; Technical.

AJC SEARCH
119 North Park Avenue, Suite 403, Rockville Centre NY 11570. 516/766-1699. **Fax:** 516/766-3889. **Contact:** Jay Cohen, Principal. **Description:** An executive search firm. **Specializes in the areas of:** Accounting/Auditing; Computer Science; Economics; Finance; Health/Medical; Insurance; Legal; Sales. **Positions commonly filled include:** Accountant; Actuary; Attorney; Computer Programmer; Consultant; Dental Assistant/Dental Hygienist; Dentist; Dietician/Nutritionist; Financial Analyst; Insurance Agent; Mathematician; Paralegal; Pharmacist; Physical Therapist; Physician; Registered Nurse; Securities Sales Representative; Statistician; Systems Analyst; Underwriter/Assistant Underwriter. **Average salary range of placements:** More than $50,000. **Number of placements per year:** 1 - 49.

APA SEARCH
721 West Boston Post Road, Mamaroneck NY 10601. 914/698-2800. **Contact:** Howard Kesten, President. **Description:** An executive search firm. Client company pays fee. **Specializes in the areas of:** Automotive; General Management; Manufacturing; Retail; Sales; Transportation. **Positions commonly filled include:** Chief Financial Officer; General Manager; Operations Manager; Sales Manager. **Corporate headquarters location:** This Location. **Other U.S. locations:** Delray Beach FL. **Average salary range of placements:** More than $100,000.

AZR INC.
245 Fifth Avenue, Suite 2205, New York NY 10016. 212/545-7842. **Contact:** Richard Silverman, President. **Description:** An executive search firm operating on both retainer and contingency bases. Client company pays fee. **Specializes in the areas of:** Computer Science/Software; Internet Development. **Positions commonly filled include:** Account Manager; Account Representative; Applications Engineer; Computer Engineer; Computer Programmer; Computer Support Technician; Consultant; Content Developer; Database Administrator; Database Manager; Internet Services Manager; Management Analyst/Consultant; MIS Specialist; Multimedia Designer; Network/Systems Administrator; Sales Engineer; Sales Manager; Sales Representative; Software Engineer; SQL Programmer; Systems Analyst; Systems Manager; Webmaster. **Corporate headquarters location:** This Location. **Average salary range of placements:** More than $50,000. **Number of placements per year:** 50 - 99.

ACCOUNTANTS CHOICE PERSONNEL
50 Charles Lindbergh Boulevard, Suite 400, Uniondale NY 11553. 212/643-4400. **Contact:** Manager. **Description:** An executive search firm. **Specializes in the areas of:** Accounting/Auditing.

ACCOUNTANTS EXECUTIVE SEARCH
ACCOUNTANTS ON CALL
500 North Broadway, Suite 237, Jericho NY 11753. 516/935-0050. **Contact:** Manager. **Description:** An executive search firm. Accountants On Call (also at this location) is a temporary agency. **Specializes in the areas of:** Accounting/Auditing; Finance.

ACCOUNTANTS EXECUTIVE SEARCH
ACCOUNTANTS ON CALL
535 Fifth Avenue, Suite 1200, New York NY 10017. 212/682-5900. **Contact:** Manager. **Description:** An executive search firm. Accountants On Call (also at this location) is a temporary agency. **Specializes in the areas of:** Accounting/Auditing; Finance.

ACTUARIAL CAREERS, INC.
Westchester Financial Center, 50 Main Street, Suite 375, White Plains NY 10606. 914/285-5100. **Toll-free phone:** 800/766-0070. **Fax:** 914/285-9375. **Contact:** Aimee Kaye, President. **E-mail address:** AimeeKaye@actuarialcareers.com. **World Wide Web address:** http://www.actuarialcareers.com. **Description:** An executive search firm. **Specializes in the areas of:** Insurance. **Positions commonly filled include:** Actuary; Chief Financial Officer.

ADEPT TECH RECRUITING
219 Glendale Road, Scarsdale NY 10583. 914/725-8583. **Contact:** Director. **Description:** An executive search firm operating on both retainer and contingency bases. Client company pays fee. **Specializes in the areas of:** Advertising; Computer Science/Software; Internet Development; Internet Marketing; MIS/EDP. **Positions commonly filled include:** Advertising Clerk; Advertising Executive; Applications Engineer; AS400 Programmer Analyst; Computer Animator; Computer Engineer; Computer Operator; Computer Programmer; Computer Support Technician; Computer Technician; Content Developer; Database Administrator; Database Manager; Internet Services Manager; Market Research Analyst; Marketing Manager; Marketing Specialist; MIS Specialist; Multimedia Designer; Network/Systems Administrator; Software Engineer; SQL Programmer; Systems Analyst; Systems Manager; Webmaster. **Corporate headquarters location:** This Location. **Average salary range of placements:** $50,000 - $100,000. **Number of placements per year:** 1 - 49.

ADVICE PERSONNEL
230 Park Avenue, Suite 903, New York NY 10169-0005. 212/682-4400. **Fax:** 212/697-0343. **Contact:** Alan Schwartz, Principal. **Description:** An executive search firm operating on a contingency basis. **Specializes in the areas of:** Accounting/Auditing; Finance; Secretarial; Tax. **Positions commonly filled include:** Accountant/Auditor; Budget Analyst; Chief Financial Officer; Computer Operator; Controller; Credit Manager; Customer Service Representative; Finance Director; Financial Analyst; Secretary; Typist/Word Processor. **Average salary range of placements:** More than $50,000. **Number of placements per year:** 500 - 999.

ADVISORS' SEARCH GROUP
370 Lexington Avenue, New York NY 10017. 212/557-7533. **Contact:** Manager. **Description:** An executive search firm. **Specializes in the areas of:** Investment.

ALFUS GROUP
353 Lexington Avenue, New York NY 10016-0941. 212/599-1000. **Fax:** 212/599-1523. **Contact:** Phillip Alfus, President. **E-mail address:** mail@thealfusgroup.com. **Description:** An executive search firm focusing on the leisure and hospitality industries. Alfus Group operates on a retainer basis. Client company pays fee. **Specializes in the areas of:** Food; Hotel/Restaurant. **Positions commonly filled include:** General Manager; Sales Executive. **Corporate headquarters location:** This Location. **Other U.S. locations:** San Francisco CA. **International locations:** Rome, Italy. **Average salary range of placements:** More than $100,000. **Number of placements per year:** 50 - 99.

ALITE ASSOCIATES, INC.
150 Broadway, Suite 1515, New York NY 10038. 212/822-4300. **Contact:** Maria Alite, President. **Description:** An executive search firm operating on a

contingency basis. **Specializes in the areas of:** Accounting/Auditing; Banking; Brokerage; Finance. **Positions commonly filled include:** Telecommunications Manager.

FRANKLIN ALLEN CONSULTANTS LTD.
1205 Franklin Avenue, Garden City NY 11530. 516/248-4511. **Fax:** 516/294-6646. **Contact:** Howard Roher, Recruiter. **E-mail address:** frnklnalln@aol.com. **Description:** Frank Allen Consultants Ltd. is an executive search firm. **Specializes in the areas of:** Accounting/Auditing; Administration; Banking; Computer Science/Software; Finance; Food; General Management; Health/Medical; Marketing; MIS/EDP; Personnel/Labor Relations; Retail; Sales; Scientific; Technical. **Positions commonly filled include:** Accountant/Auditor; Biochemist; Biological Scientist; Cable TV Installer; Chief Financial Officer; Controller; EEG Technologist; EKG Technician; Finance Director; Financial Analyst; General Manager; Human Resources Manager; Industrial Engineer; Marketing Manager; MIS Specialist; Occupational Therapist; Physical Therapist; Physician; Purchasing Agent/Manager; Quality Control Supervisor; Respiratory Therapist; Sales Executive; Sales Manager; Speech-Language Pathologist; Statistician; Surgical Technician; Systems Analyst; Vice President. **Average salary range of placements:** $30,000 - $50,000. **Number of placements per year:** 50 - 99.

ALPHA HEALTH SERVICES CORPORATION
200 East 82nd Street, New York NY 10028. 212/517-8110. **Contact:** President. **Description:** Alpha Health Services Corporation is an executive search firm that provides placements for nurses and other health care professionals and paraprofessionals. Founded in 1981. Client company pays fee. **Specializes in the areas of:** Health/Medical; Internet Development; Internet Marketing. **Positions commonly filled include:** Certified Nurses Aide; Certified Occupational Therapy Assistant; Counselor; Dietician/Nutritionist; EEG Technologist; EKG Technician; Emergency Medical Technician; Home Health Aide; Licensed Practical Nurse; Medical Assistant; Medical Records Technician; Nuclear Medicine Technologist; Nurse Practitioner; Occupational Therapist; Pharmacist; Physical Therapist; Physical Therapy Assistant; Physician; Psychologist; Radiological Technologist; Social Worker; Speech-Language Pathologist; Surgical Technician; Veterinarian. **Corporate headquarters location:** This Location. **Average salary range of placements:** $30,000 - $100,000. **Number of placements per year:** 1 - 49.

AMERICAN MEDICAL PERSONNEL SERVICES, INC.
913 Old Liverpool Road, Liverpool NY 13088. 315/451-8585. **Toll-free phone:** 800/724-2443. **Fax:** 315/451-8999. **Contact:** Joseph F. Papa, President. **E-mail address:** papajoe@servtech.com. **Description:** American Medical Personnel Services is an executive search firm that also provides some temporary placements. **Specializes in the areas of:** Health/Medical. **Positions commonly filled include:** Medical Records Technician; Nuclear Medicine Technologist; Occupational Therapist; Pharmacist; Physical Therapist; Physician; Registered Nurse; Respiratory Therapist; Speech-Language Pathologist; Surgical Technician.

AMES O'NEILL ASSOCIATES INC.
330 Vanderbilt Motor Parkway, Hauppauge NY 11788. 516/582-4800. **Fax:** 516/234-6094. **Contact:** George C. Ames, President. **Description:** An executive search firm operating on a contingency basis. **Specializes in the areas of:** Computer Science/Software; Engineering; Marketing; Sales. **Positions commonly filled include:** Applications Engineer; Design Engineer; Electrical Engineer; Industrial Engineer; Manufacturing Engineer; Marketing Manager; Mechanical Engineer; MIS Specialist; Sales Engineer; Sales Manager; Software Engineer; Systems Analyst; Systems Manager; Technical Writer/Editor. **Average salary range of placements:**

More than $50,000. **Number of placements per year:** 1 - 49.

AMESGROUP
928 Broadway, Suite 1101-B, New York NY 10010-6008. 212/475-5900. **Fax:** 212/674-2401. **Contact:** Max Sabrin, Managing Partner. **E-mail address:** amesgroup@aol.com. **World Wide Web address:** http://www.amesgroup.qpg.com. **Description:** An executive search firm operating on a contingency basis. AMESgroup also provides temp-to-perm and permanent placements as well as consulting. Founded in 1979. Client company pays fee. **Specializes in the areas of:** Accounting; Administration; Advertising; Banking; Computer Science/Software; Finance; Health/Medical; MIS/EDP; Printing; Publishing; Scientific; Secretarial; Technical. **Positions commonly filled include:** Account Manager; Account Representative; Accountant; Administrative Assistant; Applications Engineer; Auditor; Budget Analyst; Computer Operator; Computer Programmer; Controller; Customer Service Representative; Database Administrator; Database Manager; Desktop Publishing Specialist; Financial Analyst; Graphic Artist; Graphic Designer; Human Resources Manager; Information Systems Consultant; LAN/WAN Designer/Developer; MIS Specialist; Multimedia Designer; Online Content Specialist; Production Manager; Project Manager; Quality Assurance Engineer; Quality Control Supervisor; Sales Engineer; Sales Executive; Sales Representative; Secretary; Software Engineer; Systems Analyst; Systems Manager; Technical Support Engineer; Technical Writer/Editor; Telecommunications Manager. **Corporate headquarters location:** This Location. **Average salary range of placements:** More than $50,000. **Number of placements per year:** 50 - 99.

ANALYTIC RECRUITING INC.
12 East 41st Street, 9th Floor, New York NY 10017. 212/545-8511. **Fax:** 212/545-8520. **Contact:** Rita Raz, Principal. **E-mail address:** rita@analyticrecruiting.com. **World Wide Web address:** http://www. analyticrecruiting.com. **Description:** An executive search firm. Client company pays fee. **Specializes in the areas of:** Advertising; Banking; Computer Science/Software; Economics; Finance; Internet Marketing. **Positions commonly filled include:** Computer Programmer; Computer Scientist; Database Administrator; Economist; Financial Analyst; Management Analyst; Market Research Analyst; MIS Specialist; Software Engineer; SQL Programmer; Statistician; Systems Analyst; Systems Manager. **Corporate headquarters location:** This Location. **Average salary range of placements:** $50,000 - $100,000. **Number of placements per year:** 100 - 199.

APRIL INTERNATIONAL
200 North Avenue, Suite 6, New Rochelle NY 10801. 914/632-2333. **Fax:** 914/632-3582. **Contact:** Kevin J. Collins, Vice President. **E-mail address:** kevin@aprilinternational.com. **Description:** An executive search firm operating on both retainer and contingency bases. April International focuses on providing placements for professionals in major financial institutions throughout New York, Boston, Chicago, San Francisco, Hong Kong, Tokyo, Singapore, Australia, and London. Client company pays fee. **Specializes in the areas of:** Accounting; Computer Science/Software; Japanese Bilingual; MIS/EDP. **Positions commonly filled include:** Accountant; Applications Engineer; Auditor; Chief Financial Officer; Controller; Credit Manager; Database Administrator; Database Manager; Economist; Financial Analyst; Internet Services Manager; Webmaster. **Average salary range of placements:** $50,000 - $100,000. **Number of placements per year:** 100 - 199.

ARIEL ASSOCIATES
410 West 53rd Street, Suite 126, New York NY 10019. 212/765-8300. **Fax:** 212/765-3450. **Contact:** Manager. **E-mail address:** info@arielassociates.com. **World Wide Web address:** http://www.arielassociates.com.

Description: An executive search firm. **Specializes in the areas of:** Media Sales; Publishing.

ASTER SEARCH GROUP
555 Madison Avenue, Suite 2300, New York NY 10022. 212/888-6182. **Contact:** Manager. **Description:** An executive search firm. **Specializes in the areas of:** Health/Medical.

AUDIT DATA SEARCH LTD.
535 Broadhollow Road, Melville NY 11747. 516/454-6666. **Fax:** 516/454-1595. **Contact:** Jack Rose, President. **Description:** An executive search firm. **Specializes in the areas of:** Information Systems. **Positions commonly filled include:** Information Systems Consultant. **Number of placements per year:** 50 - 99.

AVALON HEALTH GROUP
245 East 54th Street, Suite 3T, New York NY 10022. 212/758-3786. **Fax:** 212/758-5304. **Contact:** Manager. **Description:** An executive search firm. **Specializes in the areas of:** Health/Medical.

D. BACAL & ASSOCIATES
10 East 39th Street, New York NY 10016. 212/953-7200. **Contact:** Dorothea Bacal, Owner. **Description:** An executive search firm. **Specializes in the areas of:** Legal. **Positions commonly filled include:** Attorney.

BADER LEGAL SEARCH
110 East 42nd Street, Suite 1614, New York NY 10017. 212/682-4750. **Contact:** Manager. **Description:** An executive search firm. **NOTE:** Attorneys must have a minimum of two years post-law school legal experience. **Specializes in the areas of:** Legal. **Positions commonly filled include:** Attorney. **Average salary range of placements:** More than $50,000.

BARTL & EVINS
422 Jericho Turnpike, Jericho NY 11753-2007. 516/433-3333. **Fax:** 516/433-2692. **Contact:** Frank Bartl, Vice President. **E-mail address:** bartl@ibm.net. **World Wide Web address:** http://www.bartlandevins.com. **Description:** An executive search firm operating on both retainer and contingency bases. **Specializes in the areas of:** Accounting/Auditing; Administration; Finance. **Positions commonly filled include:** Accountant/Auditor; Financial Analyst; General Manager; Systems Analyst. **Average salary range of placements:** More than $50,000. **Number of placements per year:** 200 - 499.

BASELINE RECRUITERS NETWORK
230 Park Avenue, Suite 665, New York NY 10169. 212/697-7575. **Contact:** Manager. **Description:** An executive search firm. **Specializes in the areas of:** Legal. **Positions commonly filled include:** Attorney; Paralegal. **Average salary range of placements:** $30,000 - $50,000. **Number of placements per year:** 50 - 99.

BATTALIA WINSTON INTERNATIONAL
300 Park Avenue, New York NY 10022. 212/308-8080. **Contact:** Recruiter. **World Wide Web address:** http://www.battaliawinston.com. **Description:** An executive search firm. Founded in 1963. **Specializes in the areas of:** Consumer Products; Finance; Health/Medical; Industrial; Nonprofit; Professional; Technical. **Other U.S. locations:** Los Angeles CA; San Francisco CA; Chicago IL; Boston MA; Edison NJ.

NEAIL BEHRINGER CONSULTANTS, INC.
24 East 38th Street, Suite 4B, New York NY 10016. 212/689-7555. **Fax:** 212/689-6868. **Contact:** Neail Behringer, President. **Description:** An executive search firm operating on a retainer basis. **Specializes in the areas of:** Fashion; Health/Medical; Retail. **Positions commonly filled include:** Buyer; Chief Financial Officer; Controller; General Manager; Marketing Manager; Marketing Specialist; MIS Specialist; Operations Manager; Production Manager; Quality Control Supervisor; Sales Executive; Sales Manager;

Vice President of Operations; Vice President of Sales. **Other U.S. locations:** Nationwide. **Average salary range of placements:** More than $50,000. **Number of placements per year:** 1 - 49.

BEISHLINE EXECUTIVE SEARCH
451 Evergreen Drive, Tonawanda NY 14150. 716/694-5154. **Contact:** John R. Beishline, President. **Description:** An executive search firm. **Specializes in the areas of:** Architecture/Construction; Engineering; Food; General Management; Industrial; Personnel/Labor Relations; Sales. **Positions commonly filled include:** Aerospace Engineer; Agricultural Scientist; Architect; Biomedical Engineer; Buyer; Chemical Engineer; Chemist; Civil Engineer; Construction Contractor; Designer; Draftsperson; Electrical/Electronics Engineer; Food Scientist/Technologist; Geologist/Geophysicist; Human Resources Manager; Industrial Engineer; Industrial Production Manager; Mechanical Engineer; Metallurgical Engineer; Mining Engineer; Nuclear Engineer; Purchasing Agent/Manager; Quality Control Supervisor; Services Sales Representative; Structural Engineer. **Number of placements per year:** 1 - 49.

ROSA BENNETT ENTERPRISES INC.
235 North Main Street, Stonehedge Plaza, Suite 2, Spring Valley NY 10977. 914/425-4727. **Fax:** 914/425-7193. **Contact:** Rosa Bennett, President. **Description:** An executive search firm. **Positions commonly filled include:** Computer Programmer; Human Resources Specialist; Systems Analyst; Technical Writer/Editor; Telecommunications Manager. **Other U.S. locations:** New York NY.

BENSON ASSOCIATES
280 Madison Avenue, New York NY 10016. 212/683-5962. **Fax:** 212/679-2724. **Contact:** Irwin Cohen, Partner. **Description:** An executive search firm. **Specializes in the areas of:** Accounting/Auditing; Advertising; Broadcasting; Finance; Sales. **Positions commonly filled include:** Financial Analyst; Human Resources Manager. **Average salary range of placements:** $30,000 - $50,000. **Number of placements per year:** 50 - 99.

BERARDI & ASSOCIATES
1140 Avenue of the Americas, 8th Floor, New York NY 10036. 212/382-1616. **Contact:** Manager. **Description:** An executive search firm. **Specializes in the areas of:** Publishing.

BERKEL ASSOCIATES, INC.
477 Madison Avenue, Suite 707, New York NY 10022-4503. 212/826-3000. **Fax:** 212/826-3006. **Contact:** Carol Bernstein, President. **Description:** An executive search firm operating on a contingency basis. **Specializes in the areas of:** Administration; Computer Science/Software; Legal; Personnel/Labor Relations; Secretarial. **Positions commonly filled include:** Accountant/Auditor; Administrative Manager; Attorney; Clerical Supervisor; Computer Programmer; Counselor; Human Resources Specialist; Internet Services Manager; Legal Secretary; Library Technician; MIS Specialist; Paralegal; Typist/Word Processor.

MICHAEL BLITZER ASSOCIATES INC.
120 East 56th Street, Suite 1520, New York NY 10022. 212/935-9177. **Contact:** Michael Blitzer, Owner. **Description:** An executive search firm. **Specializes in the areas of:** High-Tech.

BORNHOLDT SHIVAS & FRIENDS
400 East 87th Street, Basement Suite, New York NY 10128-6533. 212/557-5252. **Fax:** 212/557-5704. **Contact:** John Bornholdt, President. **E-mail address:** bsandf@aol.com. **World Wide Web address:** http://members.aol.com/bsandf. **Description:** An executive search firm. Founded in 1982. **Specializes in the areas of:** Advertising; Art/Design; Food; General Management; Manufacturing; Personnel/Labor Relations; Publishing; Retail; Sales. **Positions commonly filled include:** Administrative Manager;

Advertising Clerk; Advertising Executive; Branch Manager; Budget Analyst; Computer Programmer; Customer Service Representative; Designer; Economist; Editor; Electrical/Electronics Engineer; Financial Analyst; Food Scientist/Technologist; General Manager; Human Resources Manager; Management Analyst/ Consultant; Management Trainee; Manufacturer's/ Wholesaler's Sales Rep.; Market Research Analyst; Operations/Production Manager; Paralegal; Physical Therapist; Production Manager; Public Relations Specialist; Services Sales Representative; Statistician; Systems Analyst; Technical Writer/Editor. **Number of placements per year:** 100 - 199.

BOS BUSINESS CONSULTANTS

4211 North Buffalo Street, Orchard Park NY 14127. 716/662-0800. **Fax:** 716/662-0623. **Contact:** Manager. **Description:** An executive search firm operating on both contingency and retainer bases. **Specializes in the areas of:** Computer Science/Software; Engineering; Industrial; Manufacturing; Marketing; Scientific. **Positions commonly filled include:** Aerospace Engineer; Biomedical Engineer; Chemical Engineer; Chemist; Computer Programmer; Design Engineer; Designer; Electrical/Electronics Engineer; Financial Analyst; Food Scientist/Technologist; Human Resources Manager; Industrial Engineer; Mechanical Engineer; Metallurgical Engineer; MIS Specialist; Operations/Production Manager; Quality Control Supervisor; Software Engineer; Systems Analyst. **Average salary range of placements:** More than $50,000. **Number of placements per year:** 1 - 49.

BOYDEN

100 Park Avenue, New York NY 10017. 212/843-0200. **Contact:** Manager. **E-mail address:** pobox@ boyden.com. **World Wide Web address:** http://www.boyden.com. **Description:** A generalist executive search firm. **Corporate headquarters location:** This Location. **Other area locations:** Hawthorne NY. **Other U.S. locations:** San Francisco CA; Washington DC; Chicago IL; Bloomfield Hills MI; Chesterfield MO; Morristown NJ; Pittsburgh PA; Houston TX. **International locations:** Worldwide.

BOYDEN

364 Elwood Avenue, Hawthorne NY 10532-1239. 914/747-0093. **Contact:** Manager. **E-mail address:** pobox@boyden.com. **World Wide Web address:** http://www.boyden.com. **Description:** A generalist executive search firm. **Corporate headquarters location:** New York NY. **Other U.S. locations:** San Francisco CA; Washington DC; Chicago IL; Bloomfield Hills MI; Chesterfield MO; Morristown NJ; Pittsburgh PA; Houston TX. **International locations:** Worldwide.

BRANTHOVER ASSOCIATES

360 Lexington Avenue, Suite 1300, New York NY 10017. 212/949-9400. **Fax:** 212/949-5905. **Contact:** Jeanne Branthover, President. **E-mail address:** branthover@aol.com. **Description:** An executive search firm. **Specializes in the areas of:** Accounting/Auditing; Administration; Advertising; Banking; Computer Science/Software; Finance; General Management; Manufacturing; Personnel/Labor Relations; Publishing; Sales. **Positions commonly filled include:** Bank Officer/Manager; Budget Analyst; Computer Programmer; Consultant; Controller; Finance Director; Industrial Engineer; Internet Services Manager; Management Analyst/Consultant; Marketing Manager; Operations Manager; Public Relations Specialist; Purchasing Agent/Manager; Sales Manager; Software Engineer; Systems Analyst; Systems Manager. **Number of placements per year:** 50 - 99.

BRIAN ASSOCIATES, INC. (BAI)

2152 81st Street, Suite 2, Brooklyn NY 11214-2508. 717/232-4500. **Contact:** Manager. **E-mail address:** brianassoc@aol.com. **World Wide Web address:** http://www.brianassociates.com. **Description:** An executive search firm operating on both retainer and contingency bases. **Specializes in the areas of:**

Chemicals; Electronics; Information Systems; Management; Marketing; Sales.

NORMAN BROADBENT INTERNATIONAL

200 Park Avenue, 20th Floor, New York NY 10166. 212/953-6990. **Fax:** 212/599-3673. **Contact:** Manager. **E-mail address:** info@nbisearch.com. **World Wide Web address:** http://www.nbisearch.com. **Description:** An executive search firm. **Specializes in the areas of:** Entertainment; Finance; New Media; Technical; Telecommunications. **Other U.S. locations:** San Francisco CA; Atlanta GA; Chicago IL; Reston VA.

C.C. BURKE, LTD.

60 East 42nd Street, Suite 911, New York NY 10165-0999. 212/286-0092. **Fax:** 212/286-0396. **Contact:** Charlene Burke, President. **E-mail address:** ccburke@mindspring.com. **Description:** An executive search firm. Client company pays fee. **Specializes in the areas of:** Computer Science/Software; Fashion; Internet Development; Internet Marketing; Marketing; Sales; Scientific; Technical. **Positions commonly filled include:** Account Manager; Account Representative; Assistant Manager; Computer Programmer; Computer Support Technician; Desktop Publishing Specialist; Graphic Artist; Graphic Designer; Internet Services Manager; Market Research Analyst; Marketing Manager; Marketing Specialist; MIS Specialist; Production Manager; Project Manager; Public Relations Manager; Sales Representative; Systems Analyst; Technical Writer/Editor; Telecommunications Manager. **Corporate headquarters location:** This Location. **Average salary range of placements:** $30,000 - $100,000. **Number of placements per year:** 50 - 99.

BURNS PERSONNEL

3300 Monroe Avenue, Rochester NY 14618. 716/385-6300. **Contact:** Jackie Tedesco, President. **World Wide Web address:** http://www.burnspersonnel.com. **Description:** An executive search firm that also provides some temporary placements. **Specializes in the areas of:** Computer Science/Software; Engineering; Industrial; Manufacturing; Personnel/Labor Relations; Secretarial; Technical. **Positions commonly filled include:** Biochemist; Biological Scientist; Biomedical Engineer; Chemical Engineer; Chemist; Computer Programmer; Draftsperson; EKG Technician; Electrical/Electronics Engineer; Emergency Medical Technician; Human Resources Specialist; Industrial Engineer; Materials Engineer; Mechanical Engineer; MIS Specialist; Software Engineer; Systems Analyst; Typist/Word Processor. **Average salary range of placements:** $20,000 - $29,999. **Number of placements per year:** 500 - 999.

CFI RESOURCES INC.

7 Clover Drive, Great Neck NY 11021-1817. 516/466-1221. **Fax:** 516/487-1774. **Contact:** Leo Cohen, Principal. **E-mail address:** careers@cfires.com. **World Wide Web address:** http://www.cfires.com. **Description:** An executive search firm operating on a contingency basis. **Specializes in the areas of:** Engineering; Marketing; Sales; Scientific; Technical. **Positions commonly filled include:** Account Manager; Account Representative; Applications Engineer; Branch Manager; Computer Programmer; Design Engineer; Electrical/Electronics Engineer; General Manager; Industrial Engineer; Marketing Manager; Mechanical Engineer; MIS Specialist; Sales Executive; Sales Manager; Sales Representative; Software Engineer. **Other U.S. locations:** Boca Raton FL. **Average salary range of placements:** More than $50,000. **Number of placements per year:** 50 - 99.

CK RESOURCES

420 Lexington Avenue, Suite 2024, New York NY 10170. 212/986-5929. **Fax:** 212/986-3718. **Contact:** Cindy Karp, President. **E-mail address:** cksearch@att.net. **Description:** An executive search firm. **Specializes in the areas of:** Accounting/Auditing; Banking; Finance; Human Resources; Personnel/Labor Relations; Purchasing; Telecommunications. **Positions**

commonly filled include: Financial Analyst; Human Resources Manager; Purchasing Agent/Manager; Telecommunications Manager. **Average salary range of placements:** $35,000 - $80,000.

CT GROUP
264 North Elm Street, North Massapequa NY 11758-2525. 516/797-3642. **Fax:** 516/795-4350. **Contact:** Camille Coppola, Managing Director. **Description:** An executive search firm. **Specializes in the areas of:** Health/Medical; Insurance. **Positions commonly filled include:** Branch Manager; General Manager; Health Services Manager; Home Health Aide; Nurse; Pharmacist; Registered Nurse; Services Sales Rep. **Number of placements per year:** 50 - 99.

CANNY, BOWEN INC.
521 Fifth Avenue, 19th Floor, New York NY 10175. 212/949-6611. **Fax:** 212/949-5191. **Contact:** Manager. **E-mail address:** cannybowen@aol.com. **World Wide Web address:** http://www.cannybowen.com. **Description:** An executive search firm. Founded in 1954. **Specializes in the areas of:** Chemicals; Engineering; General Management; Human Resources; Legal; Marketing; Paper; Publishing; Sales; Transportation. **Average salary range of placements:** More than $100,000.

J.P. CANON ASSOCIATES
225 Broadway, Suite 3602, New York NY 10007. 212/233-3131. **Fax:** 212/233-0457. **Contact:** James E. Rohan, Senior Partner. **World Wide Web address:** http://www.jpcanon.com. **Description:** An executive search firm operating on a contingency basis. The firm focuses on providing placements in the materials management, logistics, purchasing, and systems professions. **Positions commonly filled include:** Buyer; Consultant; Customer Service Representative; Database Manager; Industrial Engineer; Industrial Production Manager; Logistics Manager; Management Analyst/Consultant; Materials Manager; Operations Manager; Project Manager; Purchasing Agent/Manager; Systems Analyst; Systems Manager; Transportation/Traffic Specialist; Vice President. **Average salary range of placements:** More than $50,000. **Number of placements per year:** 100 - 199.

CANTOR CONCERN
330 West 58th Street, Suite 216, New York NY 10019-1827. 212/333-3000. **Fax:** 212/245-1012. **Contact:** Marie Raperto, President. **World Wide Web address:** http://www.cantorconcern.com. **Description:** An executive search firm operating on a retainer basis. Cantor Concern focuses on providing placements in public relations, corporate communications, and investor relations. **Specializes in the areas of:** Public Relations. **Positions commonly filled include:** Editor; Public Relations Specialist; Vice President. **Average salary range of placements:** More than $50,000. **Number of placements per year:** 50 - 99.

CARTER/MACKAY
1981 Marcus Avenue, Suite 201, Lake Success NY 11042. 516/616-7700. **Fax:** 516/616-4842. **Contact:** Manager. **Description:** An executive search firm. **Specializes in the areas of:** Sales. **Other U.S. locations:** Framingham MA; Cary NJ; Hasbrouck Heights NJ.

CARY HART ASSOCIATES
401 East 80th Street, New York NY 10021. 212/988-6700. **Fax:** 212/988-6975. **Contact:** David Cary Hart, President/CEO. **E-mail address:** davidhart@caryhart.com. **World Wide Web address:** http://www.caryhart.com. **Description:** An executive search firm operating on contingency and retainer bases. Cary Hart Associates also offers some consulting services. Founded in 1986. **Positions commonly filled include:** Senior Management; Training Manager.

CASALE MANAGEMENT SERVICES, INC.
The Jericho Atrium, 500 North Broadway, Suite 141, Jericho NY 11753. 516/938-1900. **Contact:** Frank Casale, President. **Description:** An executive search firm. **Specializes in the areas of:** MIS/EDP. **Positions commonly filled include:** Computer Programmer; MIS Specialist; Multimedia Designer; Systems Analyst; Technical Writer/Editor; Telecommunications Manager. **Average salary range of placements:** More than $50,000. **Number of placements per year:** 50 - 99.

CASTLEREA ASSOCIATES
30 Glenn Street, White Plains NY 10603. 914/946-1383. **Fax:** 914/946-2019. **Contact:** Frank DeLigio, President. **Description:** An executive search firm. **Specializes in the areas of:** Consulting; General Management. **Positions commonly filled include:** Account Manager; Account Representative; Branch Manager; Chief Financial Officer; Consultant; Controller; Customer Service Representative; Management Analyst/Consultant; Marketing Manager; Operations Manager; Sales Executive; Sales Manager; Sales Representative; Vice President of Marketing. **Average salary range of placements:** More than $50,000. **Number of placements per year:** 1 - 49.

CAVAN SYSTEMS, LTD.
10 Cuttermill Road, Suite 403A, Great Neck NY 11021. 516/487-7777. **Fax:** 516/487-7857. **Contact:** Chris O'Brien, President. **E-mail address:** cavangc@aol.com. **Description:** An executive search firm. **Specializes in the areas of:** Computer Science/Software; Information Systems; Multimedia. **Positions commonly filled include:** Communications Engineer; Computer Programmer; Internet Services Manager; Media Specialist; MIS Specialist; Network Engineer; Online Content Specialist; Software Engineer; Systems Analyst; Systems Manager; Telecommunications Analyst; Webmaster. **Average salary range of placements:** More than $50,000. **Number of placements per year:** 50 - 99.

CENTENNIAL/CENTERPOINT
4 Tobey Village Office Park, Pittsford NY 14534. 716/248-9090. **Contact:** Manager. **Description:** An executive search firm. **Specializes in the areas of:** Computer Science/Software; Engineering.

CHRISS CAREERS LTD.
220 White Plains Road, Tarrytown NY 10591. 914/631-3334. **Contact:** Judy Chriss, President. **Description:** An executive search firm operating on a contingency basis. **Specializes in the areas of:** Accounting; Finance; Human Resources; Information Technology; Office Support. **Positions commonly filled include:** Accountant; Administrative Assistant; Computer Technician. **Average salary range of placements:** $35,000 - $100,000. **Number of placements per year:** 200 - 499.

TOBY CLARK ASSOCIATES, INC.
405 East 54th Street, Suite 6C, New York NY 10022-5123. 212/752-5670. **Contact:** Mrs. Toby Clark, President. **Description:** An executive search firm. **Specializes in the areas of:** Communications; Marketing; Public Relations. **Positions commonly filled include:** Advertising Executive; Marketing Manager; Public Relations Manager. **Average salary range of placements:** More than $50,000.

COLTON PARTNERSHIP
39 Broadway, Suite 710, New York NY 10006. 212/248-9700. **Contact:** Scott Colton, President. **Description:** An executive search firm operating on a retainer basis. **Specializes in the areas of:** Banking; Computer Science/Software; Engineering; General Management; Insurance; Investment; Manufacturing; Personnel/Labor Relations; Technical. **Positions commonly filled include:** Bank Officer/Manager; Computer Programmer; Design Engineer; Designer; Electrical/Electronics Engineer; Financial Analyst; Human Resources Manager; Internet Services Manager; Management Analyst/Consultant; MIS Specialist; Multimedia Designer; Quality Control Supervisor; Science Technologist; Securities Sales Representative; Software

Engineer. **Other U.S. locations:** Nationwide. **Number of placements per year:** 1 - 49.

COLUMBIA CONSULTING GROUP
767 Third Avenue, 29th Floor, New York NY 10017-2023. 212/832-2525. **Fax:** 212/832-7722. **Contact:** William H. Johnson, Managing Principal. **E-mail address:** billjohnson1@mindspring.com. **Description:** A generalist executive search firm.

COMPASS SEARCH
P.O. Box 734, Schenectady NY 12301-0734. 518/383-1600. **Contact:** Manager. **Description:** An executive search firm. **Specializes in the areas of:** Construction. **Positions commonly filled include:** Controller; Estimator; President; Project Manager; Supervisor; Vice President.

COMPU-TECH PERSONNEL INC.
775 Park Avenue, Suite 118, Huntington NY 11743. 516/673-6944. **Contact:** Freda Frankel, President. **Description:** An executive search firm operating on a contingency basis. **Specializes in the areas of:** Accounting/Auditing; Administration; Computer Science/Software; Finance. **Positions commonly filled include:** Accountant/Auditor; Budget Analyst; Computer Programmer; Credit Manager; Financial Analyst; Systems Analyst. **Average salary range of placements:** $30,000 - $50,000. **Number of placements per year:** 50 - 99.

COMPUTECH CAREER SEARCH
P.O. Box 642, Mount Vision NY 13810. 607/433-5272. **Contact:** Manager. **Description:** An executive search firm. **Specializes in the areas of:** Business Services; Engineering; Information Technology.

COMPUTER PLACEMENTS UNLIMITED, INC.
102 Palo Alto Drive, Plainview NY 11803. 516/933-7707. **Contact:** Manager. **Description:** An executive search firm. **Specializes in the areas of:** Computer Science/Software; Data Processing; Information Technology.

COMPUTER RESOURCES CORPORATION
25 West 43rd Street, Suite 1502, New York NY 10036. 212/575-0817. **Contact:** Manager. **Description:** An executive search firm. **Specializes in the areas of:** Computer Science/Software; Information Systems; Information Technology.

CONCEPTS IN STAFFING, INC.
9 East 37th Street, 2nd Floor, New York NY 10016. 212/293-4325. **Fax:** 212/652-0805. **Contact:** Manager. **World Wide Web address:** http://www.cisnysearch.com. **Description:** Concepts In Staffing is an executive search firm. **Specializes in the areas of:** Information Technology.

CONSPECTUS INC.
222 Purchase Street, Rye NY 10580-2101. 914/698-8300. **Contact:** Eric Stieglitz, Managing Director. **Description:** An executive search firm operating on both retainer and contingency bases. **Specializes in the areas of:** Banking; Finance. **Positions commonly filled include:** Economist; Financial Analyst; Securities Sales Representative. **Average salary range of placements:** More than $100,000.

THE CORNELL GROUP
One Corwin Court, Suite 200, Newburgh NY 12550. 914/565-8905. **Fax:** 914/565-5688. **Contact:** Alan Guarino, CEO. **Description:** An executive search firm. **Specializes in the areas of:** Accounting/Auditing; Banking; Finance. **Positions commonly filled include:** Bank Officer/Manager; Financial Analyst; Securities Sales Representative. **Number of placements per year:** 50 - 99.

CORPORATE CAREERS, INC.
30 Glenn Street, White Plains NY 10603. 914/946-2003. **Fax:** 914/946-2019. **Contact:** Richard Birnbaum,

President. **Description:** An executive search firm operating on both retainer and contingency bases. **Specializes in the areas of:** Accounting/Auditing; Computer Science/Software; Economics; Engineering; Finance; Food; General Management; Industrial; Manufacturing; Personnel/Labor Relations; Publishing; Sales; Technical. **Positions commonly filled include:** Accountant; Applications Engineer; Biochemist; Biological Scientist; Biomedical Engineer; Chemical Engineer; Chemist; Chief Financial Officer; Computer Programmer; Controller; Credit Manager; Database Manager; Design Engineer; Economist; Electrical/Electronics Engineer; Environmental Engineer; Finance Director; Financial Analyst; Food Scientist/Technologist; Human Resources Manager; Industrial Engineer; Industrial Production Manager; Manufacturing Engineer; Market Research Analyst; Marketing Manager; Marketing Specialist; Mechanical Engineer; MIS Specialist; Operations Manager; Production Manager; Project Manager; Public Relations Specialist; Purchasing Agent/Manager; Quality Control Supervisor; Sales Engineer; Sales Executive; Sales Manager; Software Engineer; Systems Analyst; Systems Manager; Technical Writer/Editor; Telecommunications Manager. **Benefits available to temporary workers:** 401(k); Paid Holidays; Paid Vacation. **Corporate headquarters location:** This Location. **Average salary range of placements:** More than $50,000. **Number of placements per year:** 200 - 499.

CORPORATE MOVES, INC.
P.O. Box 1638, Williamsville NY 14231-1638. 716/633-0234. **Fax:** 716/626-9147. **Contact:** Office Manager. **E-mail address:** corpmoves@aol.com. **Description:** An executive search firm operating on both retainer and contingency bases. Client company pays fee. **Specializes in the areas of:** Health/Medical; Industrial; Internet Marketing; Marketing; Sales. **Positions commonly filled include:** Account Manager; Account Representative; Branch Manager; General Manager; Management Analyst/Consultant; Management Trainee; Marketing Manager; Marketing Specialist; Project Manager; Public Relations Specialist; Sales Engineer; Sales Executive; Sales Manager; Sales Representative; Vice President of Marketing and Sales. **Average salary range of placements:** $50,000 - $100,000. **Number of placements per year:** 50 - 99.

CORPORATE SEARCH INC.
6800 Jericho Turnpike, Suite 203W, Syosett NY 11791-4401. 516/496-3200. **Fax:** 516/496-3165. **Contact:** Claire Zukerman, President. **E-mail address:** clairez@corporatesearch.com. **World Wide Web address:** http://www.corporatesearch.com. **Description:** An executive search firm operating on a contingency basis. **Specializes in the areas of:** Accounting/Auditing; Finance; Manufacturing; Personnel/Labor Relations; Sales; Secretarial; Tax. **Positions commonly filled include:** Accountant/Auditor; Administrative Manager; Budget Analyst; Buyer; Credit Manager; Customer Service Representative; Financial Analyst; Human Resources Specialist; Management Trainee; Paralegal; Purchasing Agent/Manager; Services Sales Representative; Transportation/Traffic Specialist; Typist/Word Processor. **Number of placements per year:** 100 - 199.

COWIN ASSOCIATES
One Old Country Road, Carle Place NY 11514-1801. 516/741-3020. **Fax:** 516/741-4953. **Contact:** David M. Cowin, President. **E-mail address:** cowinone@aol.com. **Description:** An executive search firm operating on both retainer and contingency bases that focuses on the placement of high-level professionals in the aerospace and related high-technology industries. **Specializes in the areas of:** Aerospace; Engineering. **Positions commonly filled include:** Aerospace Engineer; Design Engineer; Electrical/Electronics Engineer; Mechanical Engineer; MIS Specialist; Systems Analyst; Telecommunications Manager. **Average salary range of placements:** More than $50,000. **Number of placements per year:** 50 - 99.

CRANDALL ASSOCIATES, INC.
114 East 32nd Street, New York NY 10016. 212/213-1700. **Fax:** 212/696-1287. **Contact:** Recruiter. **World Wide Web address:** http://www.crandallassociates.com. **Description:** An executive search firm. Founded in 1973. **Specializes in the areas of:** Customer Service; Direct Marketing; Telemarketing. **Corporate headquarters location:** This Location. **Other U.S. locations:** CA; IL. **Average salary range of placements:** $40,000 - $250,000.

CROMWELL PARTNERS INC.
441 Lexington Avenue, 7th Floor, New York NY 10017. 212/953-3220. **Contact:** Manager. **Description:** An executive search firm. **Specializes in the areas of:** Finance.

CROSS HILL PARTNERS L.L.C.
20 Cross Hill Road, Eastchester NY 10707. 914/395-1125. **Fax:** 914/395-1346. **Contact:** Diane Shea, Partner. **E-mail address:** info@crosshillpartners.com. **World Wide Web address:** http://www.crosshillpartners.com. **Description:** An executive search firm operating on a retainer basis. Founded in 1999. **Specializes in the areas of:** Banking; Information Technology; Insurance; Management; Media Sales; Publishing.

FRANK CUOMO & ASSOCIATES INC.
111 Brook Street, Scarsdale NY 10583. 914/723-8001. **Contact:** Frank Cuomo, President. **Description:** An executive search firm that operates on both contingency and retainer bases. **Specializes in the areas of:** Engineering; General Management; Industrial; Manufacturing; Sales. **Positions commonly filled include:** Chemical Engineer; Chemist; Civil Engineer; Construction Contractor; Cost Estimator; Design Engineer; Electrical/Electronics Engineer; Environmental Engineer; General Manager; Industrial Engineer; Industrial Production Manager; Manufacturer's/ Wholesaler's Sales Rep.; Market Research Analyst; Mechanical Engineer; Metallurgical Engineer; Petroleum Engineer; Product Manager; Services Sales Representative; Structural Engineer. **Average salary range of placements:** More than $50,000.

D&L ASSOCIATES, INC.
60 East 42nd Street, Suite 535, New York NY 10165. 212/687-7111. **Fax:** 212/687-0541. **Contact:** David Werner, CEO. **E-mail address:** dlinc@msn.com. **World Wide Web address:** http://www.dlassociates.com. **Description:** An executive search firm operating on a contingency basis. D&L Associates's clients are primarily *Fortune* 500 companies. Founded in 1993. **Specializes in the areas of:** Accounting/Auditing; Finance; Information Systems. **Positions commonly filled include:** Accountant; Billing Analyst; Bookkeeper; Budget Analyst; Business Analyst; Chief Financial Officer; Collection Manager; Cost Accountant; Credit Manager; Financial Analyst; MIS Manager; Network/Systems Administrator; Software Engineer; Systems Analyst. **Average salary range of placements:** More than $50,000. **Number of placements per year:** 500 - 999.

DAPEXS CONSULTANTS INC.
5320 West Genesee Street, Camillus NY 13031-2203. 315/484-9300. **Fax:** 315/484-9330. **Contact:** Peter J. Leofsky, President. **E-mail address:** dapexs@servtech.com. **World Wide Web address:** http://www.servtech.com/~dapexs. **Description:** An executive search firm operating on both retainer and contingency bases. **Specializes in the areas of:** Accounting/Auditing; Administration; Computer Science/Software; Finance. **Positions commonly filled include:** Computer Programmer; Internet Services Manager; Management Analyst; MIS Specialist; Software Engineer; Systems Analyst; Technical Writer/Editor; Telecommunications Manager.

THE DARTMOUTH GROUP
1200 Broadway, Suite 7D, New York NY 10001. 212/689-2713. **Fax:** 212/532-6519. **Contact:** Senior Associate. **Description:** An executive search firm operating on a retainer basis. **Specializes in the areas of:** Cosmetics; Engineering; Manufacturing; Packaging; Pharmaceuticals; Sales; Technical. **Positions commonly filled include:** General Manager; Manufacturer's/ Wholesaler's Sales Rep.; Quality Control Supervisor.

DATACOM PLACEMENTS INC.
309 Syosset Woodbury Road, Woodbury NY 11797. 516/496-9893. **Contact:** Manager. **Description:** An executive search firm. **Specializes in the areas of:** Computer Programming.

DATAMARK ASSOCIATES INC.
145 West 45th Street, Suite 401, New York NY 10036. 212/354-7800. **Contact:** Manager. **Description:** An executive search firm. **Specializes in the areas of:** Data Processing.

CAROLYN DAVIS ASSOCIATES INC.
701 Westchester Avenue, White Plains NY 10604. 914/682-7040. **Fax:** 914/682-8361. **Contact:** Carolyn Davis, President. **Description:** An executive search firm. **Specializes in the areas of:** Insurance. **Positions commonly filled include:** Accountant; Actuary; Broker; Claim Rep.; Financial Analyst; Insurance Agent/Broker; Marketing Specialist; Underwriter/Assistant Underwriter. **Number of placements per year:** 50 - 99.

BERT DAVIS EXECUTIVE SEARCH
425 Madison Avenue, Suite 14, New York NY 10017. 212/838-4000. **Contact:** Manager. **Description:** An executive search firm. **Specializes in the areas of:** Publishing.

THE DENISON GROUP
122 East 42nd Street, 46th Floor, New York NY 10168. 212/949-6594. **Fax:** 212/697-1820. **Contact:** Robert V. Long. **Description:** An executive search firm operating on a contingency basis. Client company pays fee. **Specializes in the areas of:** Finance. **Positions commonly filled include:** Economist; Financial Analyst; Fund Manager; Software Engineer. **Average salary range of placements:** More than $100,000.

THE DEVELOPMENT RESOURCE GROUP
104 East 40th Street, Suite 304, New York NY 10016. 212/983-1600. **Fax:** 212/983-1687. **Contact:** Manager. **Description:** An executive search firm that works exclusively with nonprofit organizations. **Specializes in the areas of:** Nonprofit. **Positions commonly filled include:** Chief Executive Officer; Director of Development; President. **Other U.S. locations:** Washington DC. **Average salary range of placements:** More than $50,000. **Number of placements per year:** 50 - 99.

SETH DIAMOND ASSOCIATES INC.
45 West 45th Street, Suite 801, New York NY 10036. 212/944-6190. **Fax:** 212/944-6197. **Contact:** Seth Diamond, CPC/President. **E-mail address:** sdiam85572 @aol.com. **Description:** An executive search firm. **Specializes in the areas of:** Accounting/Auditing; Administration; Advertising; Architecture/Construction; Banking; Computer Science/Software; Fashion; Finance; General Management; Health/Medical; Legal; Manufacturing; Marketing; MIS/EDP; Personnel/Labor Relations; Publishing; Retail; Sales; Secretarial. **Positions commonly filled include:** Accountant/Auditor; Administrative Assistant; Administrative Manager; Advertising Clerk; Advertising Executive; Bank Officer/ Manager; Budget Analyst; Buyer; Chief Financial Officer; Clerical Supervisor; Computer Animator; Computer Operator; Computer Programmer; Controller; Credit Manager; Customer Service Representative; Economist; Editor; Editorial Assistant; Finance Director; Financial Analyst; General Manager; Human Resources Manager; Internet Services Manager; Market Research Analyst; Marketing Manager; Marketing Specialist; Online Content Specialist; Paralegal; Sales Executive; Sales Manager; Sales Representative; Software Engineer; Statistician; Systems Analyst; Systems Manager;

Technical Writer/Editor; Telecommunications Manager; Typist/Word Processor. **Average salary range of placements:** $30,000 - $50,000. **Number of placements per year:** 200 - 499.

DIXON HEALTHCARE EMPLOYMENT
130 William Street, New York NY 10038. 212/766-3932. **Contact:** Manager. **Description:** An executive search firm. **Specializes in the areas of:** Health/Medical.

DONAHUE & MOORE ASSOCIATES LTD.
295 Madison Avenue, Suite 924, New York NY 10017. 212/683-8255. **Contact:** Manager. **Description:** An executive search firm. **Specializes in the areas of:** Data Processing.

DRUMMOND ASSOCIATES, INC.
50 Broadway, Suite 1201, New York NY 10004. 212/248-1120. **Contact:** Chester Fienberg, President. **Description:** An executive search firm. **Specializes in the areas of:** Banking; Finance. **Number of placements per year:** 1 - 49.

DURHAM MEDICAL STAFFING
6300 Transit Road, P.O. Box 478, Depew NY 14043. 716/681-7402. **Fax:** 716/681-7408. **Contact:** Manager. **Description:** An executive search firm. **Specializes in the areas of:** Health/Medical. **Positions commonly filled include:** Nurse Practitioner; Physician.

DYMANEX SEARCH INC.
P.O. Drawer 800, Hamburg NY 14075. 716/648-7800. **Contact:** Manager. **Description:** An executive search firm. **Specializes in the areas of:** Engineering; Manufacturing; Technical.

ETC SEARCH, INC.
226 East 54th Street, Suite 308, New York NY 10022. 212/371-3880. **Fax:** 212/754-4877. **Contact:** Marlene Eskenazie, Managing Director. **Description:** An executive search firm. Client company pays fee. **Specializes in the areas of:** Computer Science/Software; Information Technology; Systems Programming. **Positions commonly filled include:** Applications Engineer; Computer Engineer; Computer Operator; Computer Programmer; Computer Support Technician; Computer Technician; Database Administrator; Database Manager; Internet Services Manager; MIS Specialist; Network/Systems Administrator; Software Engineer; SQL Programmer; Systems Analyst; Systems Manager; Webmaster. **Corporate headquarters location:** This Location. **Average salary range of placements:** $50,000 - $100,000. **Number of placements per year:** 100 - 199.

ETR TECHNOLOGY CENTER
180 Oser Avenue, Suite 0400, Hauppauge NY 11788. 516/952-1300. **Fax:** 516/952-1248. **Contact:** Valerie Vecchio, Corporate Marketing Manager. **E-mail address:** jobs@etrtechcenter.com. **World Wide Web address:** http://www.etrtechcenter.com. **Description:** An executive search firm operating on a contingency basis. The company specializes in object-oriented technology placements. ETR Technology Center also provides contract services. Client company pays fee. **Specializes in the areas of:** Computer Science/Software; Finance. **Positions commonly filled include:** Applications Engineer; Biomedical Engineer; Chief Financial Officer; Computer Animator; Computer Engineer; Computer Programmer; Computer Scientist; Computer Support Technician; Computer Technician; Database Administrator; Database Manager; Electrical/Electronics Engineer; Financial Analyst; Internet Services Manager; Multimedia Designer; Network/Systems Administrator; Project Manager; Sales Engineer; Software Engineer; SQL Programmer; Systems Analyst; Systems Manager; Technical Writer/Editor; Vice President of Finance; Webmaster. **Corporate headquarters location:** This Location. **Average salary range of placements:** $50,000 - $100,000. **Number of placements per year:** 200 - 499.

IRWIN EDWARDS RECRUITERS INC.
420 Jericho Turnpike, Suite 321, Jericho NY 11753. 516/454-4850. **Fax:** 516/719-0966. **Contact:** Mitch Levy, President. **Description:** An executive search firm operating on a contingency basis. **Specializes in the areas of:** Banking; Finance; Insurance; Internet Marketing. **Positions commonly filled include:** Accountant/Auditor; Actuary; Bank Officer/Manager; Budget Analyst; Claim Representative; Credit Manager; Financial Analyst; Technical Writer/Editor; Underwriter/Assistant Underwriter. **Average salary range of placements:** $50,000 - $100,000. **Number of placements per year:** 200 - 499.

ALEXANDER EDWARDS INTERNATIONAL
2 World Trade Center, Suite 2112, New York NY 10048. 212/432-4100. **Fax:** 212/432-0475. **Contact:** Manager. **World Wide Web address:** http://alexanderedwards.com. **Description:** An executive search firm. **Specializes in the areas of:** Accounting; Administration; Advertising; Architecture/Construction; Education; Engineering; Executives; Finance; Government; Health/Medical; Information Technology; Legal; Management; Marketing; Retail; Sales.

EFCO CONSULTANTS, INC.
3 The Balsams, Roslyn Estates NY 11576. 516/829-9200. **Fax:** 516/484-7387. **Contact:** Norman Fells, President. **Description:** An executive search firm that focuses on MIS sales, marketing, and management placements. Efco Consultants operates on both retainer and contingency bases. **Specializes in the areas of:** Computer Science/Software; Sales. **Positions commonly filled include:** Management Analyst/Consultant; MIS Specialist; Software Engineer; Systems Analyst. **Average salary range of placements:** More than $50,000. **Number of placements per year:** 50 - 99.

ELLIOT ASSOCIATES INC.
104 South Broadway, Tarrytown NY 10591. 914/631-4904. **Fax:** 914/631-6481. **Contact:** Bernadette Kane, Vice President of Administration. **World Wide Web address:** http://www.elliotassociates.com. **Description:** An executive search firm operating on a retainer basis. **Specializes in the areas of:** Food; Retail. **Positions commonly filled include:** Chief Financial Officer; Food Scientist/Technologist; Hotel Manager; Human Resources Specialist. **Corporate headquarters location:** This Location. **Other U.S. locations:** Nationwide. **Average salary range of placements:** More than $50,000. **Number of placements per year:** 200 - 499.

DAVID M. ELLNER ASSOCIATES
2 Penn Plaza, Suite 1500, New York NY 10121. 212/279-0665. **Contact:** David Ellner, CEO. **Description:** An executive search firm. **Specializes in the areas of:** Computer Science/Software. **Positions commonly filled include:** Aerospace Engineer; Attorney; Computer Programmer; Editor; Electrical/Electronics Engineer; Systems Analyst. **Average salary range of placements:** More than $50,000.

MARK ELZWEIG COMPANY, LTD.
101 Fifth Avenue, Suite 10A, New York NY 10003. 212/243-0639. **Fax:** 212/243-0566. **Contact:** Mark Elzweig, President. **E-mail address:** elzweig@aol.com. **World Wide Web address:** http://www.elzweig.com. **Description:** An executive search firm. Founded in 1985. **Specializes in the areas of:** Finance.

THE EMPLOYMENT STORE
TES TECHNICAL
333 Andrews Street, Rochester NY 14604. 716/232-5402. **Fax:** 716/232-2147. **Contact:** Manager. **E-mail address:** inquiry@employmentstore.com. **World Wide Web address:** http://www.employmentstore.com. **Description:** An executive search firm that also provides some temporary and contract placements. **Specializes in the areas of:** Computer Science/Software; Engineering; Finance; General Management; Health/Medical; Sales;

Scientific; Secretarial; Technical. **Positions commonly filled include:** Administrative Assistant; Applications Engineer; Architect; Buyer; Chemical Engineer; Chief Financial Officer; Civil Engineer; Computer Animator; Computer Programmer; Controller; Cost Estimator; Credit Manager; Customer Service Representative; Database Manager; Design Engineer; Draftsperson; Editorial Assistant; Electrical/Electronics Engineer; Environmental Engineer; Finance Director; Financial Analyst; Graphic Designer; Human Resources Manager; Industrial Engineer; Industrial Production Manager; Metallurgical Engineer; MIS Specialist; Operations Manager; Production Manager; Project Manager; Purchasing Agent/Manager; Quality Control Supervisor; Sales Engineer; Sales Executive; Sales Manager; Sales Representative; Secretary; Software Engineer; Statistician; Systems Analyst; Systems Manager; Technical Writer/Editor; Typist/Word Processor. **Benefits available to temporary workers:** Paid Holidays; Paid Vacation. **Corporate headquarters location:** This Location. **Average salary range of placements:** $30,000 - $50,000. **Number of placements per year:** 50 - 99.

EQUATE EXECUTIVE SEARCH
12 West 37th Street, 7th Floor, New York NY 10018. 212/736-0606. **Contact:** Manager. **Description:** An executive search firm. **Specializes in the areas of:** Computer Science/Software; High-Tech.

ERIC ROBERT ASSOCIATES
350 Seventh Avenue, New York NY 10001-5013. 212/695-5900. **Fax:** 212/695-5809. **Contact:** Eric Silverman, President. **E-mail address:** ericrob@nyc.pipeline.com. **Description:** An executive search firm. Clients include *Fortune* 1000 companies. **Specializes in the areas of:** Computer Science/Software; High-Tech. **Positions commonly filled include:** Computer Programmer; Internet Services Manager; MIS Specialist; Technical Writer/Editor; Telecommunications Manager. **Average salary range of placements:** More than $50,000. **Number of placements per year:** 100 - 199.

ETHAN ALLEN MEDICAL SEARCH
404 Troy Schenectady Road, Latham NY 12110-3217. 518/785-7555. **Fax:** 518/785-8034. **Contact:** M. James Roarke, President. **Description:** An executive search firm operating on both contingency and retainer bases. **Specializes in the areas of:** Health/Medical. **Positions commonly filled include:** Occupational Therapist; Physical Therapist; Speech-Language Pathologist. **Average salary range of placements:** $30,000 - $50,000. **Number of placements per year:** 50 - 99.

EXECU/SEARCH GROUP
675 Third Avenue, New York NY 10017-5704. 212/922-1001. **Fax:** 212/922-0033. **Contact:** Ignacio Mardones, Website Editor. **E-mail address:** info@execu-search.com. **World Wide Web address:** http://www.execu-search.com. **Description:** An executive search firm operating on a contingency basis. The agency also offers some temporary placements. Client company pays fee. **Specializes in the areas of:** Accounting/Auditing; Administration; Banking; Finance; General Management; Internet Development; Scientific; Secretarial; Technical. **Positions commonly filled include:** Accountant; Adjuster; Administrative Assistant; Administrative Manager; AS400 Programmer Analyst; Assistant Manager; Auditor; Bank Officer/Manager; Blue-Collar Worker Supervisor; Branch Manager; Budget Analyst; Chief Financial Officer; Clerical Supervisor; Computer Animator; Computer Scientist; Computer Support Technician; Content Developer; Controller; Cost Estimator; Credit Manager; Customer Service Representative; Database Administrator; Economist; Finance Director; Financial Analyst; Fund Manager; Human Resources Manager; Industrial Production Manager; Intellectual Property Lawyer; Management Analyst/Consultant; Management Trainee; Multimedia Designer; Operations Manager; Production Manager; Project Manager; Purchasing Agent/Manager; Quality Control Supervisor; Secretary; Software Engineer; Typist/Word Processor; Webmaster. **Benefits available to temporary workers:** Bonus Award/Plan; Health Benefits; Stock Option. **Corporate headquarters location:** This Location. **Average salary range of placements:** $50,000 - $100,000. **Number of placements per year:** 500 - 999.

EXECUTIVE CONNECTIONS, INC.
575 North Street, White Plains NY 10605. 914/949-1923. **Toll-free phone:** 800/969-3932. **Fax:** 914/949-5324. **Contact:** Bob Friscia, President. **Description:** An executive search firm. **Positions commonly filled include:** Account Manager; Applications Engineer; Chemist; Marketing Manager; Marketing Specialist; Operations Manager; Sales Engineer; Sales Executive; Sales Manager.

EXECUTIVE DIRECTIONS INC.
450 Seventh Avenue, Suite 1509, New York NY 10123. 212/594-5775. **Fax:** 212/594-4183. **Contact:** Gus Oakes, CPC/President. **Description:** An executive search firm. **Specializes in the areas of:** Administration; Computer Science/Software. **Positions commonly filled include:** Computer Programmer; Management Analyst/Consultant; Systems Analyst. **Number of placements per year:** 100 - 199.

EXECUTIVE EXCHANGE
450 Seventh Avenue, 9th Floor, New York NY 10123. 212/736-2350. **Fax:** 212/736-3790. **Contact:** Manager. **Description:** An executive search firm. **Specializes in the areas of:** Telecommunications.

EXECUTIVE IMAGE
330 Third Avenue, Suite 11G, New York NY 10010. 212/532-8565. **Contact:** Manager. **Description:** An executive search firm. **Specializes in the areas of:** Accounting/Auditing; Finance.

EXECUTIVE LINK
8 West 38th Street, Suite 1208, New York NY 10018. 212/840-7270. **Fax:** 212/840-7815. **Contact:** Manager. **Description:** An executive search firm. **Specializes in the areas of:** Hotel/Restaurant.

EXECUTIVE PLACEMENT CORPORATION
1010 Sibley Tower, Rochester NY 14604. 716/454-1424. **Contact:** Manager. **Description:** An executive search firm.

EXECUTIVE RESOURCES LTD.
200 East 66th Street, New York NY 10021. 212/593-2819. **Contact:** Manager. **Description:** An executive search firm. **Specializes in the areas of:** Banking; Finance. **Positions commonly filled include:** Branch Manager; Broker; Financial Analyst.

EXECUTIVE SEARCH ASSOCIATES
300 Hempstead Turnpike, Suite 216, West Hempstead NY 11552. 516/292-9700. **Contact:** Manager. **Description:** An executive search firm. **Specializes in the areas of:** Information Technology.

EXECUTIVE SEARCH CONSULTANTS INTERNATIONAL
350 Fifth Avenue, Suite 5501, New York NY 10118. 212/330-1900. **Contact:** Manager. **Description:** An executive search firm. **Specializes in the areas of:** Consumer Sales and Marketing; Direct Marketing; Finance.

EXECUTIVE SEARCH GROUP
116 West 32nd Street, New York NY 10011. 212/594-1448. **Contact:** Manager. **Description:** An executive search firm.

EXECUTIVE SYSTEMS
One Penn Plaza, Suite 3306, New York NY 10119. 212/967-0505. **Contact:** Manager. **Description:** An executive search firm.

EXEK RECRUITERS LTD.
35 Flatt Road, Rochester NY 14623. 716/292-0550. **Fax:** 716/292-5645. **Contact:** Art Ploscowe, Owner. **E-mail address:** exek@rpa.net. **Description:** An executive search firm operating on a contingency basis. Client company pays fee. **Specializes in the areas of:** Accounting; Computer Science/Software; Engineering; General Management; Industrial; Legal; MIS/EDP; Scientific; Technical. **Positions commonly filled include:** Account Manager; Account Rep.; Accountant; Applications Engineer; Attorney; Buyer; Chemical Engineer; Chief Financial Officer; Controller; Cost Estimator; Database Administrator; Database Manager; Design Engineer; Electrical Engineer; Environmental Engineer; General Manager; Human Resources Manager; Industrial Engineer; Industrial Production Manager; Manufacturing Engineer; Mechanical Engineer; Metallurgical Engineer; MIS Specialist; Network Administrator; Operations Manager; Production Manager; Project Manager; Purchasing Agent/Manager; Quality Assurance Engineer; Quality Control Supervisor; Sales Engineer; Sales Exec.; Sales Manager; Software Engineer; Systems Analyst; Systems Manager. **Corporate headquarters location:** This Location. **Average salary range of placements:** $50,000 - $100,000. **Number of placements per year:** 1 - 49.

FANNING PERSONNEL
507 Fifth Avenue, 8th Floor, New York NY 10017-4906. 212/867-1725. **Fax:** 212/867-1338. **Contact:** Dave Cowen, President. **E-mail address:** resume@fanning.com. **World Wide Web address:** http://www.fanning.com. **Description:** An executive search firm operating on a contingency basis. **Specializes in the areas of:** Administration; Banking; Broadcasting; Computer Science/Software; Entertainment; Fashion; Finance; Personnel/Labor Relations; Secretarial. **Positions commonly filled include:** Computer Programmer; Human Resources Specialist; Internet Services Manager; MIS Specialist; Systems Analyst; Typist/Word Processor. **Average salary range of placements:** $30,000 - $50,000. **Number of placements per year:** 100 - 199.

FEDERAL PLACEMENT SERVICES
35 Park Avenue, Suite 6M, Suffern NY 10901. 914/357-4577. **Fax:** 914/357-5945. **Contact:** Joan Bialkin, President. **E-mail address:** fepl@aol.com. **Description:** An executive search firm operating on a contingency basis. **Specializes in the areas of:** Banking. **Positions commonly filled include:** Accountant/Auditor; Bank Officer/Manager; Branch Manager; Budget Analyst; Credit Manager; Financial Analyst; Human Resources Specialist; Property and Real Estate Manager. **Average salary range of placements:** More than $50,000. **Number of placements per year:** 1 - 49.

FIFTH AVENUE EXECUTIVE STAFFING
507 Fifth Avenue, 3rd Floor, New York NY 10017. 212/692-0800. **Contact:** Michael W. Huffman, President. **E-mail address:** resumes@executive-staffing.com. **World Wide Web address:** http://www.executive-staffing.com. **Description:** An executive search firm operating on both retainer and contingency bases. **Specializes in the areas of:** Computer Science/Software; Internet Development; MIS/EDP. **Positions commonly filled include:** Applications Engineer; AS400 Programmer Analyst; Computer Engineer; Computer Operator; Computer Programmer; Computer Scientist; Computer Support Technician; Computer Technician; Content Developer; Database Administrator; Database Manager; Internet Services Manager; MIS Specialist; Network/Systems Administrator; Software Engineer; SQL Programmer; Systems Analyst; Systems Manager; Webmaster. **Corporate headquarters location:** This Location. **Average salary range of placements:** More than $50,000. **Number of placements per year:** 500 - 999.

FIND NETWORK, INC.
1133 Broadway, Suite 812, New York NY 10010. 212/929-2000. **Fax:** 212/647-9842. **Contact:** Recruiter.

E-mail address: comments@findnetwork.com. **World Wide Web address:** http://www.findnetwork.com. **Description:** An executive search firm. **Specializes in the areas of:** New Media. **Other U.S. locations:** Los Angeles CA.

C.R. FLETCHER ASSOCIATES
108 East Washington Street, Syracuse NY 13202-1618. 315/471-1000. **Fax:** 315/471-6500. **Contact:** Carol R. Fletcher, President. **Description:** A nationwide executive search firm operating on both retainer and contingency bases. **Specializes in the areas of:** Accounting/Auditing; Administration; Finance; Personnel/Labor Relations; Sales. **Positions commonly filled include:** Accountant/Auditor; Budget Analyst; Computer Programmer; Financial Analyst; Human Resources Manager; Manufacturer's/Wholesaler's Sales Rep.; MIS Specialist; Pharmacist; Physical Therapist; Physician; Recreational Therapist; Services Sales Representative; Systems Analyst; Telecommunications Manager. **Average salary range of placements:** More than $50,000. **Number of placements per year:** 50 - 99.

FOCUS CAPITAL MARKETS
71 Vanderbilt Avenue, Suite 200, New York NY 10017. 212/986-3344. **Fax:** 212/986-3370. **Contact:** Scott Gerson, President. **E-mail address:** focuscapital@msn.com. **World Wide Web address:** http://www.focuscapital.com. **Description:** An executive search firm. **Specializes in the areas of:** Computer Science/Software. **Positions commonly filled include:** Computer Programmer; Consultant; Database Manager; EDP Specialist; Mathematician; MIS Specialist; Multimedia Designer; Software Engineer; Systems Analyst; Systems Manager. **Average salary range of placements:** More than $50,000. **Number of placements per year:** 100 - 199.

FOLEY PROCTOR YOSKOWITZ
24 East 39th Street, New York NY 10016. 212/928-1110. **Contact:** Manager. **Description:** An executive search firm. **Specializes in the areas of:** Health/Medical; Physician Executive. **Other U.S. locations:** Morristown NJ.

FORRAY ASSOCIATES, INC.
950 Third Avenue, 16th Floor, New York NY 10022. 212/279-0404. **Contact:** Manager. **Description:** An executive search firm. **Specializes in the areas of:** Finance; Marketing; Sales.

F-O-R-T-U-N-E PERSONNEL CONSULTANTS
71 East Eckerson Road, Suite A, Spring Valley NY 10977-3014. 914/426-3200. **Fax:** 914/426-3814. **Contact:** Mark Axelrod, President. **Description:** A search firm that provides middle-management and executive-level placements. **Specializes in the areas of:** Engineering; Manufacturing. **Positions commonly filled include:** Manufacturing Manager; Mechanical Engineer; Metallurgical Engineer; Quality Assurance Engineer; Quality Control Supervisor. **Other U.S. locations:** Nationwide. **Average salary range of placements:** More than $50,000. **Number of placements per year:** 1 - 49.

FRANKLIN SEARCH RESOURCES, INC.
225 West 34th Street, Suite 806, New York NY 10122. 212/465-0600. **Fax:** 212/629-8470. **Contact:** Peter Franklin, CPC/President. **E-mail address:** franklinsearch@erols.com. **Description:** An executive search firm operating on both retainer and contingency bases. **Specializes in the areas of:** Accounting/Auditing; General Management. **Positions commonly filled include:** Accountant/Auditor; Controller; Director; Finance Director; Financial Analyst; Tax Specialist; Vice President of Finance. **Average salary range of placements:** More than $50,000. **Number of placements per year:** 50 - 99.

FRONTRUNNER SEARCH, LTD.
P.O. Box 349, Baldwin NY 11510-0349. 516/223-5627. **Fax:** 516/867-6681. **Contact:** Daniel J. Ahrens,

President. **Description:** An executive search firm. **NOTE:** The company accepts applications from experienced personnel only. **Specializes in the areas of:** Banking; Mortgage. **Number of placements per year:** 50 - 99.

THE FRY GROUP INC.
369 Lexington Avenue, New York NY 10017. 212/557-0011. **Contact:** John Fry, President. **Description:** An executive search firm operating on both retainer and contingency bases. **Specializes in the areas of:** Communications; Public Relations. **Positions commonly filled include:** Public Relations Specialist. **Other U.S. locations:** Nationwide. **Average salary range of placements:** More than $50,000. **Number of placements per year:** 50 - 99.

GT SOLUTIONS, INC.
124 East 40th Street, 8th Floor, New York NY 10016. 212/922-1000. **Fax:** 212/922-3560. **Contact:** Recruiter. **E-mail address:** info@headhunting.com. **World Wide Web address:** http://www.headhunting.com. **Description:** An executive search firm. **Specializes in the areas of:** Computer Programming; Finance.

RONNIE GALE PERSONNEL CORPORATION
12-49 150th Street, Whitestone NY 11357. 718/767-1135. **Contact:** Gail Landres, President. **Description:** An executive search firm. **Specializes in the areas of:** Accounting/Auditing; Administration; Sales; Secretarial. **Positions commonly filled include:** Accountant/Auditor; Administrative Assistant; Administrative Manager; Advertising Clerk; Clerical Supervisor; Computer Programmer; Counselor; Credit Manager; Customer Service Representative; Radio/TV Announcer/ Broadcaster; Secretary; Systems Analyst; Typist/Word Processor. **Average salary range of placements:** $25,000 - $60,000. **Number of placements per year:** 200 - 499.

GARDINER, TOWNSEND & ASSOCIATES
101 East 52nd Street, New York NY 10022. 212/230-1889. **Fax:** 212/838-0424. **Contact:** Manager. **World Wide Web address:** http://www.gardinertownsend.com. **Description:** An executive search firm. **Specializes in the areas of:** Banking; Chemicals; Communications; Electrical; Finance; Human Resources; International Executives; MIS/EDP; Nuclear Power; Pharmaceuticals; Technical; Telecommunications; Transportation.

GATEWAY SEARCH INC.
1120 Avenue of the Americas, 4th Floor, New York NY 10036. 212/626-6714. **Contact:** Manager. **Description:** An executive search firm. **Specializes in the areas of:** Computer Hardware/Software.

GILBERT & VAN CAMPEN INTERNATIONAL NETWORK, INC.
420 Lexington Avenue, New York NY 10170. 212/661-2122. **Contact:** Manager. **Description:** A worldwide executive search firm that places high-level executives in a variety of industries. **Average salary range of placements:** More than $150,000.

GLOBAL MEDICAL SEARCH, INC.
135 Delaware Avenue, Buffalo NY 14202. 716/856-4811. **Toll-free phone:** 800/973-5223. **Fax:** 716/856-2176. **Contact:** Manager. **E-mail address:** gmsinfo@global-medicalsearch.com. **World Wide Web address:** http://www.global-medicalsearch.com. **Description:** An executive search firm. **Specializes in the areas of:** Health/Medical.

GLOBAL RECRUITING INC.
87 George Road, Old Chatham NY 12136. 518/392-2429. **Fax:** 518/392-2894. **Contact:** Tage Andersson, President. **E-mail address:** global_recruiting@taconic.net. **Description:** An executive search firm that places manufacturers, suppliers, and consultants in the chemical and paper industries.

THE GOLDMAN GROUP, INC.
GOLDMAN + BELL, LLC
381 Park Avenue South, Suite 1520, New York NY 10016. 212/685-9311. **Fax:** 212/532-2740. **Contact:** Elaine Goldman/Peter Bell, Presidents. **Description:** An executive search firm operating on a retainer basis. Goldman + Bell (also at this location) is an executive search firm operating on a contingency basis. Goldman + Bell also provides some temporary placements. **Specializes in the areas of:** Communications; Investment; Public Relations. **Positions commonly filled include:** Marketing Specialist; Public Relations Specialist. **Corporate headquarters location:** This Location. **Average salary range of placements:** More than $50,000. **Number of placements per year:** 1 - 49.

GOODRICH & SHERWOOD ASSOCIATES, INC.
400 Andrews Street, Rochester NY 14604. 716/262-4277. **Fax:** 716/362-3254. **Contact:** Manager. **World Wide Web address:** http://www.goodrichsherwood.com. **Description:** An executive search firm that also offers outplacement/career transition counseling, executive coaching, and Human Resources consulting. **Specializes in the areas of:** Human Resources. **Corporate headquarters location:** New York NY. **Other area locations:** New York NY. **Other U.S. locations:** Norwalk CT; Shelton CT; Parsippany NJ; Princeton NJ.

GOODRICH & SHERWOOD ASSOCIATES, INC.
521 Fifth Avenue, 19th Floor, New York NY 10175. 212/697-4131. **Fax:** 212/983-7499. **Contact:** Manager. **World Wide Web address:** http://www.goodrichsherwood.com. **Description:** An executive search firm that also offers outplacement/career transition counseling, executive coaching, and Human Resources consulting. **Specializes in the areas of:** Human Resources. **Corporate headquarters location:** This Location. **Other area locations:** Rochester NY. **Other U.S. locations:** Norwalk CT; Shelton CT; Parsippany NJ; Princeton NJ.

GOSSAGE REGAN ASSOCIATES, INC
25 West 43rd Street, Suite 812, New York NY 10036. 212/869-3348. **Fax:** 212/997-1127. **Contact:** Manager. **Description:** An executive search firm that specializes in the placement of library management personnel in corporations, academic institutions, and various library-related organizations. Gossage Regan Associates also provides some temporary placements. **Specializes in the areas of:** Library Services. **Positions commonly filled include:** Librarian; Library Technician.

GOULD, McCOY & CHADICK, INC.
300 Park Avenue, New York NY 10022. 212/688-8671. **Contact:** Manager. **World Wide Web address:** http://gouldmccoychadick.com. **Description:** A generalist executive search firm. Founded in 1977.

GRUEN RESOURCES, INC.
321 Clocktower Commons, Brewster NY 10509. 914/279-8827. **Fax:** 914/279-8845. **Contact:** Connie Gruen, President. **E-mail address:** cmgruen@aol.com. **Description:** An executive search firm that recruits commercial real estate and financial services personnel. The firm operates on both retainer and contingency bases. **Specializes in the areas of:** Banking; Computer Science/Software; Finance; Real Estate. **Positions commonly filled include:** Financial Analyst; Management Analyst/Consultant; MIS Specialist; Property and Real Estate Manager. **Average salary range of placements:** More than $50,000. **Number of placements per year:** 1 - 49.

GUNDERSEN PARTNERS L.L.C.
230 West 17th Street, 6th Floor, New York NY 10011. 212/675-2300. **Fax:** 212/675-6965. **Contact:** Steven G. Gundersen, President. **E-mail address:** sgg@gpllc.com. **World Wide Web address:** http://www.marketingalumni.com. **Description:** An executive search firm that also offers consulting and business planning services. Founded in 1984. **Specializes in the areas of:** Advertising; Finance; Human Resources; Marketing;

New Media; Sales. **Corporate headquarters location:** This Location. **Other U.S. locations:** Bloomfield Hills MI; Cary NC.

HBC GROUP
370 Lexington Avenue, Suite 2200, New York NY 10017. 212/661-8300. **Contact:** Norman Gershgorn, President. **Description:** An executive search firm that also provides some contract services and career counseling. **Specializes in the areas of:** Accounting/Auditing; Banking. **Positions commonly filled include:** Bank Officer/Manager; Financial Analyst; Financial Consultant; Financial Manager. **Average salary range of placements:** More than $50,000. **Number of placements per year:** 50 - 99.

THE HAAS ASSOCIATES, INC.
443 West 24th Street, New York NY 10011. 212/741-2457. **Contact:** Margaret Haas, President. **E-mail address:** mhaas@pipeline.com. **Description:** An executive search firm. **Specializes in the areas of:** Banking; Computer Science/Software; Engineering; Finance; Industrial; Manufacturing. **Average salary range of placements:** More than $50,000. **Number of placements per year:** 1 - 49.

STEPHEN M. HAAS LEGAL INC.
60 East 42nd Street, Room 1501, New York NY 10017. 212/661-5555. **Fax:** 212/972-1279. **Contact:** Marilyn Wallberg, President. **Description:** An executive search firm operating on a contingency basis. **Specializes in the areas of:** Legal. **Positions commonly filled include:** Attorney. **Number of placements per year:** 1 - 49.

ROBERT HALF INTERNATIONAL ACCOUNTEMPS
One HSBC Center, Suite 3560, Buffalo NY 14203. 716/833-5322. **Contact:** Manager. **Description:** An executive search firm. Accountemps (also at this location) provides temporary placements. **Corporate headquarters location:** Menlo Park CA. **Other U.S. locations:** Nationwide.

THE HAMPTON GROUP
33 Flying Point Road, Southampton NY 11968. 516/287-3330. **Fax:** 516/287-5610. **Contact:** Belle Lareau, Partner. **Description:** An executive search firm that focuses on placing middle and senior management professionals. **Specializes in the areas of:** Biology; Biotechnology; Health/Medical; Pharmaceuticals. **Positions commonly filled include:** Biological Scientist; Biomedical Engineer; Chemist; Pharmacist; Surgical Technician. **Other U.S. locations:** Nationwide. **Average salary range of placements:** More than $50,000. **Number of placements per year:** 1 - 49.

HART-MERRELL PERSONNEL
P.O. Box 92340, Rochester NY 14692. 716/359-3060. **Fax:** 716/359-2295. **Contact:** George W. Merrell, President. **E-mail address:** careers@hart-merrell.com. **Description:** A temporary agency. Founded in 1980. **Specializes in the areas of:** Accounting; Computer Science/Software; Engineering; General Management; Industrial; Light Industrial; Printing; Sales; Secretarial. **Positions commonly filled include:** Account Manager; Account Representative; Accountant; Administrative Assistant; Advertising Clerk; Applications Engineer; Assistant Manager; Biochemist; Biomedical Engineer; Blue-Collar Worker Supervisor; Buyer; Chemical Engineer; Chemist; Civil Engineer; Clerical Supervisor; Computer Operator; Computer Programmer; Construction Contractor; Consultant; Controller; Cost Estimator; Customer Service Representative; Database Manager; Design Engineer; Draftsperson; Electrical/Electronics Engineer; Electrician; General Manager; Graphic Artist; Graphic Designer; Human Resources Manager; Industrial Engineer; Industrial Production Manager; Internet Services Manager; Machinist; Management Trainee; Manufacturing Engineer; MIS Specialist; Production Manager; Project Manager; Purchasing Agent/Manager; Quality Control Supervisor; Sales Engineer; Sales Executive; Sales

Manager; Sales Representative; Secretary; Software Engineer; Statistician; Systems Analyst; Systems Manager; Technical Writer/Editor; Telecommunications Manager; Typist/Word Processor. **Corporate headquarters location:** This Location. **Other U.S. locations:** Avon NY. **Average salary range of placements:** $30,000 - $50,000. **Number of placements per year:** 100 - 199.

HAWKES-PEERS & COMPANY, INC.
224 Fifth Avenue, 6th Floor, New York NY 10001. 212/624-4070. **Contact:** Ted King, President. **Description:** An executive search firm. **Specializes in the areas of:** Banking; Sales. **Number of placements per year:** 100 - 199.

HEALTHCARE RECRUITERS OF NEW YORK
445 Electronics Parkway, Suite 208, Liverpool NY 13088. 315/453-4080. **Fax:** 315/453-9525. **Contact:** Dean McNitt, President. **E-mail address:** dean.mcnitt@hcrnetwork.com. **World Wide Web address:** http://www.healthcarerecruiters.com. **Description:** An executive search firm. **Specializes in the areas of:** Health/Medical. **Positions commonly filled include:** Biological Scientist; Biomedical Engineer; Chemical Engineer; Chemist; Clinical Lab Technician; Computer Programmer; Dental Assistant/Dental Hygienist; Dentist; Dietician/ Nutritionist; EKG Technician. **Corporate headquarters location:** Dallas TX. **Number of placements per year:** 100 - 199.

HEALTHSEARCH GROUP
109 Croton Avenue, Ossining NY 10562. 914/941-6107. **Fax:** 914/941-1748. **Contact:** Alan Gordon, President. **Description:** An executive search firm operating on both retainer and contingency bases. **Specializes in the areas of:** Health/Medical; Nonprofit; Personnel/Labor Relations. **Positions commonly filled include:** Branch Manager; Clinical Lab Technician; Dietician/Nutritionist; EEG Technologist; EKG Technician; Food Scientist/Technologist; Health Services Manager; Human Resources Specialist; Medical Records Technician; Nuclear Medicine Technologist; Occupational Therapist; Pharmacist; Physical Therapist; Physician; Psychologist; Radiological Technologist; Recreational Therapist; Registered Nurse; Respiratory Therapist; Social Worker; Speech-Language Pathologist. **Other U.S. locations:** Nationwide. **Average salary range of placements:** More than $50,000. **Number of placements per year:** 500 - 999.

F.P. HEALY & COMPANY INC.
307 East 44th Street, Suite E, New York NY 10017. **Toll-free phone:** 800/374-3259. **Contact:** Frank P. Healy, President. **Description:** An executive search firm operating on a retainer basis. **Specializes in the areas of:** Administration; Banking; Computer Science/Software; Engineering; General Management; Manufacturing; Sales. **Positions commonly filled include:** Accountant/Auditor; Actuary; Aerospace Engineer; Electrical Engineer; General Manager; Science Technologist; Software Engineer; Systems Analyst. **Average salary range of placements:** More than $50,000. **Number of placements per year:** 100 - 199.

HEIDRICK & STRUGGLES
245 Park Avenue, 43rd Floor, New York NY 10167. 212/867-9876. **Fax:** 212/370-9035. **Contact:** Manager. **Description:** An executive search firm.

HEIDRICK & STRUGGLES
40 Wall Street, 48th Floor, New York NY 10005. 212/699-3000. **Fax:** 212/699-3100. **Contact:** Manager. **Description:** An executive search firm.

STANLEY HERZ & CO.
Mill Pond Office Complex, Suite 103, Somers NY 10589. 914/277-7500. **Fax:** 914/277-7749. **Contact:** Stanley Herz, Principal. **World Wide Web address:** http://www.stanleyherz.com. **Description:** An executive search firm operating on a retainer basis. **Specializes in the areas of:** General Management. **Average salary**

range of placements: More than $50,000. Number of placements per year: 1 - 49.

HESSEL ASSOCIATES, INC.
420 Lexington Avenue, Suite 300, New York NY 10170. 212/297-6105. **Fax:** 212/682-1029. **Contact:** Jeffrey Hessel, President. **E-mail address:** haisearch@aol.com. **World Wide Web address:** http://www.haisearch.com. **Description:** An executive search firm operating on both retainer and contingency bases. Founded in 1982. **Specializes in the areas of:** Accounting/Auditing; Banking; Computer Science/Software; Consulting; Finance. **Average salary range of placements:** More than $50,000.

HEYMAN ASSOCIATES, INC.
11 Penn Plaza, Suite 1105, New York NY 10001. 212/784-2717. **Fax:** 212/244-9648. **Contact:** Manager. **E-mail address:** hai@heymanassociates.com. **World Wide Web address:** http://www.heymanassociates.com. **Description:** An executive search firm.

RUTH HIRSCH ASSOCIATES
201 East 66th Street, Suite 7C, New York NY 10021. 212/396-0200. **Contact:** Office Manager. **Description:** An executive search firm. **Specializes in the areas of:** Advertising; Architecture/Construction; Art/Design; Engineering.

J.B. HOMER ASSOCIATES
420 Lexington Avenue, Suite 2328, New York NY 10170-0002. 212/697-3300. **Fax:** 212/986-5086. **Contact:** Judy Homer, President. **E-mail address:** JHomer@JBHomer.com. **World Wide Web address:** http://www.jbhomer.com. **Description:** An executive search firm operating on a retained basis. Founded in 1982. **Specializes in the areas of:** Information Technology.

THE HORIZON GROUP
2001 Marcus Avenue, Suite E240, Lake Success NY 11042. 516/358-4141. **Fax:** 516/358-7133. **Contact:** Manager. **World Wide Web address:** http://www. horizong.com. **Description:** An executive search firm. Founded in 1990. **Specializes in the areas of:** Accounting; Computer Science/Software; Finance; Information Technology. **Corporate headquarters location:** This Location. **Other U.S. locations:** New York NY.

THE HORIZON GROUP
104 Fifth Avenue, 8th Floor, New York NY 10011. 212/324-9700. **Fax:** 212/791-7445. **Contact:** Branch Manager. **World Wide Web address:** http://www.horizong.com. **Description:** The Horizon Group is an executive search firm. **Specializes in the areas of:** Accounting; Computer Science/Software; Finance; Information Technology. **Corporate headquarters location:** Lake Success NY.

HOSPITALITY INTERNATIONAL
P.O. Box 5008, Cortland NY 13045. 607/756-8550. **Fax:** 607/756-8620. **Contact:** Susan Stafford, Vice President. **Description:** An executive search firm. **Specializes in the areas of:** Hotel/Restaurant.

HOWARD-SLOAN-KOLLER GROUP
353 Lexington Avenue, 11th Floor, New York NY 10016. 212/661-5250. **Contact:** Manager. **World Wide Web address:** http://www.hsksearch.com. **Description:** An executive search firm. **Specializes in the areas of:** Publishing.

HOWE-LEWIS INTERNATIONAL
521 Fifth Avenue, 36th Floor, New York NY 10175-3699. 212/697-5000. **Contact:** Esther Rosenberg, Co-Managing Director. **Description:** An executive search firm operating on a retainer basis. **Specializes in the areas of:** Health/Medical; Nonprofit. **Positions commonly filled include:** Education Administrator; Health Services Manager; Human Resources Manager;

Physician. **Average salary range of placements:** More than $50,000. **Number of placements per year:** 1 - 49.

ARNOLD HUBERMAN ASSOCIATES, INC.
51 East 25th Street, Suite 501, New York NY 10010. 212/545-9033. **Contact:** Manager. **Description:** An executive search firm. **Specializes in the areas of:** Public Relations.

HUDSON SEARCH CONSULTANTS INC.
271 Madison Avenue, Suite 1103, New York NY 10016. 212/949-9111. **Contact:** Manager. **Description:** An executive search firm. **Specializes in the areas of:** Finance.

HUNTER PLACEMENT INC.
656 Elmwood Avenue, Buffalo NY 14222. 716/884-9242. **Contact:** Gina Collora, President. **Description:** An executive search firm operating on a contingency basis. **Specializes in the areas of:** Accounting/Auditing; Administration; Finance; Health/Medical; Legal; Personnel/Labor Relations; Secretarial. **Positions commonly filled include:** Accountant/Auditor; Administrative Manager; Attorney; Budget Analyst; Buyer; Claim Representative; Clerical Supervisor; Construction Contractor; Credit Manager; Customer Service Representative; Financial Analyst; General Manager; Health Services Manager; Human Resources Manager; Licensed Practical Nurse; Medical Records Technician; Operations/Production Manager; Paralegal; Strategic Relations Manager; Typist/Word Processor. **Number of placements per year:** 100 - 199.

HUNTINGTON PERSONNEL CONSULTANTS, INC.
P.O. Box 1077, Huntington NY 11743-0640. 516/549-8888. **Fax:** 516/549-3012. **Contact:** Jeannette A. Henry, President. **E-mail address:** jahenry@i-2000.com. **Description:** An executive search firm. **Specializes in the areas of:** Administration; Business Systems Analysis; Computer Operations; Computer Programming; Consulting; Data Communications; Data Security; Information Technology; Network Administration; Software Development; Software Documentation; Software Engineering; Software Quality Assurance; Software Training; Systems Administration; Systems Design; Systems Programming; Technical Writing; Telecommunications; Telephone Technical Support. **Positions commonly filled include:** Computer Programmer; Software Engineer; Systems Analyst; Technical Writer/Editor.

INFORMATION SYSTEMS RESOURCES
747 Third Avenue, 31st Floor, New York NY 10017. 212/319-3700. **Contact:** Manager. **Description:** An executive search firm that focuses on the placement of PC and LAN support professionals. **Specializes in the areas of:** Computer Hardware/Software; Technical.

INTERNATIONAL MEDICAL PLACEMENT
100 Sylvan Parkway, Suite 200, Amherst NY 14228. 716/689-6000. **Contact:** Manager. **Description:** An executive search firm that places physicians. **Specializes in the areas of:** Health/Medical. **Positions commonly filled include:** Physician.

INTERSPACE INTERACTIVE INC.
50 East 42nd Street, Suite 2400, New York NY 10017. 212/867-6661. **Fax:** 212/867-6682. **Contact:** Bill Ellis, President. **Description:** An executive search firm. **Specializes in the areas of:** Accounting/Auditing; Computer Science/Software; Engineering; Finance; General Management; Personnel/Labor Relations; Sales. **Positions commonly filled include:** Accountant/Auditor; Manufacturer's/Wholesaler's Sales Rep.; Marketing Specialist; Public Relations Specialist; Services Sales Representative; Software Engineer; Systems Analyst. **Number of placements per year:** 100 - 199.

ANN ISRAEL & ASSOCIATES
730 Fifth Avenue, 9th Floor, New York NY 10019. 212/333-8730. **Contact:** Manager. **Description:** An

executive search firm. **Specializes in the areas of:** Legal.

IVANA LEGAL SERVICES, INC.
420 Lexington Avenue, Suite 2545, New York NY 10170. 212/286-9560. **Fax:** 212/490-2074. **Contact:** Manager. **Description:** An executive search firm. **Specializes in the areas of:** Finance; Legal. **Positions commonly filled include:** Paralegal; Typist/Word Processor. **Average salary range of placements:** $30,000 - $50,000. **Number of placements per year:** 1 - 49.

R.I. JAMES INC.
325 Riverside Drive, New York NY 10025-4156. 212/662-0203. **Fax:** 212/864-9602. **Contact:** Rhoda Isaacs, President. **Description:** An executive search firm operating on both retainer and contingency bases. **Specializes in the areas of:** Logistics; Transportation. **Positions commonly filled include:** Industrial Engineer; Logistics Manager; Management Analyst/Consultant; Operations Manager; Purchasing Agent/Manager; Transportation/Traffic Specialist; Vice President of Operations. **Average salary range of placements:** More than $50,000. **Number of placements per year:** 100 - 199.

JOSEPH ASSOCIATES INC.
229 Main Street, Huntington NY 11743-6955. 516/351-5805. **Fax:** 516/421-4123. **Contact:** Joe Nakelski, President. **E-mail address:** joeassoc@aol.com. **World Wide Web address:** http://www.josephassociates.com. **Description:** An executive search firm operating on both retainer and contingency bases. The firm also offers consulting services to client companies. **Specializes in the areas of:** Administration; Computer Hardware/Software. **Positions commonly filled include:** Computer Programmer; Database Manager; Economist; Human Resources Manager; Internet Services Manager; MIS Specialist; Software Engineer; Statistician; Systems Analyst; Systems Manager; Technical Writer/Editor; Telecommunications Manager; Webmaster. **Benefits available to temporary workers:** Disability Coverage; Medical Insurance; Workers' Compensation Plan. **Corporate headquarters location:** This Location. **Other U.S. locations:** Nationwide. **Average salary range of placements:** More than $50,000. **Number of placements per year:** 50 - 99.

KPA STAFFING GROUP, INC.
150 Broadway, Suite 1900, New York NY 10038. 212/964-3640. **Toll-free phone:** 800/BANKTEMP. **Fax:** 212/964-6959. **Contact:** Len Adams, President. **E-mail address:** lenadams@pipeline.com. **Description:** An executive search firm operating on both retainer and contingency bases. KPA Staffing Group also offers temporary and contract placements. **Specializes in the areas of:** Accounting/Auditing; Administration; Banking; Finance; Marketing; MIS/EDP; Personnel/Labor Relations; Sales; Secretarial. **Positions commonly filled include:** Account Manager; Account Representative; Accountant; Administrative Assistant; Auditor; Bank Officer/Manager; Branch Manager; Chief Financial Officer; Computer Operator; Controller; Database Manager; General Manager; Human Resources Manager; Management Analyst/Consultant; Marketing Manager; Sales Executive; Sales Manager; Sales Representative; Secretary; Systems Analyst. **Benefits available to temporary workers:** Paid Holidays; Paid Vacation. **Corporate headquarters location:** This Location. **Other U.S. locations:** Nationwide. **Average salary range of placements:** $30,000 - $50,000. **Number of placements per year:** 200 - 499.

IRENE KANE PERSONNEL
27 West Neck Road, Huntington NY 11743. 516/351-1800. **Fax:** 516/351-1626. **Contact:** Ellen West, Owner/Manager. **Description:** An executive search firm operating on a contingency basis. **Specializes in the areas of:** Computer Science/Software; Engineering; Technical. **Positions commonly filled include:** Computer Programmer; Design Engineer;

Electrical/Electronics Engineer; MIS Specialist; Network/Systems Administrator; Software Engineer; Systems Analyst; Technical Writer/Editor. **Average salary range of placements:** $50,000 - $100,000. **Number of placements per year:** 50 - 99.

KAUFMAN ASSOCIATES LTD.
450 Seventh Avenue, 9th Floor, New York NY 10123. 212/643-0625. **Fax:** 212/643-8598. **Contact:** Eugene A. Kaufman, CPC/President. **Description:** An executive search firm. **Specializes in the areas of:** Apparel; Fashion; Home Furnishings; Textiles. **Positions commonly filled include:** Designer; Merchandiser.

THE KAY GROUP OF FIFTH AVENUE
350 Fifth Avenue, Suite 2205, New York NY 10118. 212/947-4646. **Fax:** 212/947-3472. **Contact:** Joseph H. Kay, President. **Description:** An executive search firm operating on a contingency basis. **Specializes in the areas of:** Accounting/Auditing; Administration; Advertising; Communications; Food; General Management; Health/Medical; Industrial Sales and Marketing; Personnel/Labor Relations. **Average salary range of placements:** More than $50,000. **Number of placements per year:** 50 - 99.

A.T. KEARNEY INC.
153 East 53rd Street, New York NY 10022. 212/705-1311. **Contact:** Manager. **Description:** An executive search firm. **Specializes in the areas of:** Finance.

KENSINGTON GROUP, INC.
One Maiden Lane, 10th Floor, New York NY 10038-4015. 212/227-0099. **Contact:** Ken DeMott, President. **Description:** An executive search firm operating on both retainer and contingency bases. **Specializes in the areas of:** Banking; Brokerage. **Positions commonly filled include:** Bank Officer/Manager; Chief Financial Officer; Economist; Editor; Editorial Assistant; Finance Director; Financial Analyst; Fund Manager; Human Resources Manager; Managing Editor; Marketing Manager; Marketing Specialist; Operations Manager; Project Manager; Purchasing Agent/Manager; Sales Executive; Sales Manager; Sales Representative; Technical Writer/Editor; Telecommunications Manager. **Corporate headquarters location:** This Location. **Average salary range of placements:** More than $50,000. **Number of placements per year:** 1 - 49.

KINGSBURY WAX BOVA
230 Park Avenue, Suite 1000, New York NY 10169. 212/297-0300. **Contact:** Manager. **Description:** An executive search firm operating on a retainer basis. **Specializes in the areas of:** Finance.

FRED KOFFLER ASSOCIATES
942 Greenfield Road, Woodmere NY 11598. 516/569-6582. **Contact:** Fred Koffler, President. **Description:** An executive search firm operating on a retainer basis. **Specializes in the areas of:** Accounting/Auditing; Administration; Advertising; Computer Science/Software; Economics; Engineering; Finance; General Management; Industrial; Legal; Manufacturing; MIS/EDP; Sales; Technical. **Positions commonly filled include:** Account Manager; Account Representative; Administrative Manager; Advertising Executive; Attorney; Bank Officer/Manager; Branch Manager; Buyer; Chief Financial Officer; Computer Engineer; Computer Scientist; Controller; Design Engineer; Electrical/Electronics Engineer; Environmental Engineer; Finance Director; Financial Analyst; General Manager; Graphic Designer; Human Resources Manager; Industrial Engineer; Intellectual Property Lawyer; Management Analyst/Consultant; Manufacturing Engineer; Market Research Analyst; Marketing Manager; Marketing Specialist; Mechanical Engineer; MIS Specialist; Operations Manager; Production Manager; Project Manager; Public Relations Specialist; Purchasing Agent/Manager; Quality Assurance Engineer; Sales Engineer; Sales Executive; Sales Manager; Transportation/Traffic Specialist. **Average salary range**

of placements: More than $70,000. **Number of placements per year:** 1 - 49.

KOLTNOW & COMPANY
62 West 45th Street, 4th Floor, New York NY 10036. 212/921-8885. **Contact:** Emily Koltnow, President. **Description:** An executive search firm. **Specializes in the areas of:** Fashion. **Positions commonly filled include:** Designer; Sales Manager. **Number of placements per year:** 1 - 49.

KORN/FERRY INTERNATIONAL
200 Park Avenue, 37th Floor, New York NY 10017. 212/687-1834. **Fax:** 212/986-5684. **Contact: ranch Manager. World Wide Web address:** http://www.kornferry.com. **Description:** Korn/Ferry International is an executive search firm that places upper-level managers in a variety of industries. **Corporate headquarters location:** Los Angeles CA. **International locations:** Worldwide. **Average salary range of placements:** More than $50,000.

KRAMER EXECUTIVE RESOURCES
110 East 59th Street, Suite 2500, New York NY 10022. 212/832-1122. **Contact:** Manager. **Description:** An executive search firm. **Specializes in the areas of:** Accounting/Auditing; Finance.

EVIE KREISLER & ASSOCIATES
One West 34th Street, Suite 201, New York NY 10001. 212/279-8999. **Contact:** Kathy Gross, Vice President. **Description:** An executive search firm. The company operates on both retainer and contingency bases. **Specializes in the areas of:** Retail. **Positions commonly filled include:** Buyer; Human Resources Manager; MIS Specialist; Operations/Production Manager; Quality Control Supervisor. **Corporate headquarters location:** Los Angeles CA. **Average salary range of placements:** More than $50,000.

LAKE ASSOCIATES
453 Kinns Road, Clifton Park NY 12065. 518/877-3071. **Fax:** 518/877-3072. **Contact:** Ernest Steinmann, Director. **Description:** An executive search firm. **Specializes in the areas of:** Accounting/Auditing; Administration; Biology; Biotechnology; Computer Science/Software; Electronics; Engineering; Finance; Industrial; Manufacturing; Personnel/Labor Relations; Pharmaceuticals; Sales; Technical. **Positions commonly filled include:** Aerospace Engineer; Biochemist; Biological Scientist; Chemical Engineer; Chemist; Electrical/Electronics Engineer; Environmental Engineer; Food Scientist/Technologist; General Manager; Industrial Engineer; Mathematician; Mechanical Engineer; Metallurgical Engineer; MIS Specialist; Nuclear Engineer; Operations/Production Manager; Petroleum Engineer; Pharmacist; Purchasing Agent/Manager; Quality Control Supervisor; Science Technologist; Software Engineer; Structural Engineer; Technical Writer/Editor; Telecommunications Manager. **Average salary range of placements:** More than $50,000. **Number of placements per year:** 1 - 49.

LANDOVER ASSOCIATES, INC.
654 Madison Avenue, New York NY 10021. 212/759-6400. **Toll-free phone:** 800/759-0577. **Fax:** 212/980-4523. **Contact:** Manager. **E-mail address:** landover@landover.com. **World Wide Web address:** http://www.landover.com. **Description:** An executive search firm. **Specializes in the areas of:** Finance; Interactive Entertainment; Internet Development; Software Engineering; Technical.

JOHN LAWRENCE & ASSOCIATES, INC.
P.O. Box 398, Huntington NY 11743. 516/938-3636. **Contact:** Manager. **Description:** An executive search firm operating on both retainer and contingency bases. John Lawrence & Associates also provides career/outplacement services. **Specializes in the areas of:** Accounting/Auditing; Administration; Advertising; Banking; Education; Engineering; Finance; Food; General Management; Health/Medical; Industrial;

Insurance; Legal; Manufacturing; Personnel/Labor Relations; Retail; Sales. **Positions commonly filled include:** Accountant/Auditor; Actuary; Adjuster; Administrative Manager; Attorney; Bank Officer/Manager; Branch Manager; Chemical Engineer; Civil Engineer; Claim Representative; Counselor; Education Administrator; Environmental Engineer; Financial Analyst; General Manager; Health Services Manager; Hotel Manager; Human Resources Specialist; Industrial Engineer; Insurance Agent/Broker; Licensed Practical Nurse; Management Analyst/Consultant; Mechanical Engineer; MIS Specialist; Occupational Therapist; Operations/Production Manager; Paralegal; Physician; Property and Real Estate Manager; Psychologist; Public Relations Specialist; Quality Control Supervisor; Registered Nurse; Restaurant/Food Service Manager; Securities Sales Representative; Services Sales Representative; Social Worker; Software Engineer; Strategic Relations Manager; Telecommunications Manager; Typist/Word Processor; Underwriter/Assistant Underwriter; Urban/Regional Planner. **Average salary range of placements:** More than $50,000. **Number of placements per year:** 1 - 49.

DAVID LAWRENCE ASSOCIATES
120 East 42nd Street, New York NY 10017. 212/883-1100. **Fax:** 212/883-0838. **Contact:** Larry Rheingold, President. **Description:** An executive search firm. **Specializes in the areas of:** Computer Hardware/Software. **Positions commonly filled include:** Computer Programmer; MIS Specialist; Software Engineer; Technician.

LEGAL SEARCH LTD.
35 East 35th Street, New York NY 10016. 212/725-1704. **Contact:** Manager. **Description:** An executive search firm. **Specializes in the areas of:** Legal.

LEVINE HIRSHORN & ASSOCIATES
1065 Avenue of the Americas, 4th Floor, Suite 408A, New York NY 10018. 212/730-1388. **Fax:** 212/730-3909. **Contact:** Fashion Director. **Description:** An executive search firm operating on a retainer basis. **Specializes in the areas of:** Apparel; Cosmetics; Manufacturing; Retail. **Positions commonly filled include:** Associate Buyer; Buyer; Designer; Merchandiser; Production Manager; Public Relations Specialist.

LEVY-KERSON
399 Park Avenue, New York NY 10022. 212/421-1133. **Fax:** 212/421-8151. **Contact:** Robert E. Kerson, Chairman. **E-mail address:** rkerson@levykerson.com. **World Wide Web address:** http://www.levykerson.com. **Description:** An executive search firm. Levy-Kerson also publishes *THE e-tail REPORTER*, which covers the Internet retail economy. **Specializes in the areas of:** Retail.

LOGIC ASSOCIATES
67 Wall Street, Suite 2411, New York NY 10005. 212/227-8000. **Fax:** 212/766-0188. **Contact:** Bill Perry, President. **Description:** An executive search firm. **Specializes in the areas of:** Insurance. **Corporate headquarters location:** This Location.

WILLIAM K. LONG ASSOCIATES INC.
11 John Street, Room 300, New York NY 10038-4009. 212/571-0960. **Fax:** 212/732-0540. **Contact:** Maureen Cahill, President. **Description:** An executive search firm operating on both retainer and contingency bases. **Specializes in the areas of:** Insurance. **Average salary range of placements:** More than $50,000. **Number of placements per year:** 1 - 49.

M.B. INC. EXECUTIVE SEARCH
505 Fifth Avenue, 8th Floor, New York NY 10017. 212/661-4937. **Fax:** 212/661-4937. **Contact:** Alan Levine, President. **E-mail address:** info@mbincexec.com. **World Wide Web address:** http://www.mbincexec.com. **Description:** An executive search firm that specializes in providing senior-level

marketing, sales, financial, and general management placements. **Specializes in the areas of:** Finance; General Management; Marketing; Sales. **Positions commonly filled include:** Vice President of Marketing and Sales. **Average salary range of placements:** More than $75,000.

THE MVP GROUP
150 Broadway, Suite 2101, New York NY 10038. 212/571-1833. **Contact:** Manager. **Description:** An executive search firm. **Specializes in the areas of:** Administration; Banking; Computer Science/Software; Finance; Personnel/Labor Relations. **Positions commonly filled include:** Accountant/Auditor; Financial Analyst; Human Resources Manager; Securities Sales Representative. **Other U.S. locations:** Boston MA. **Number of placements per year:** 500 - 999.

MACINNIS, WARD & ASSOCIATES, INC.
551 Fifth Avenue, Suite 3300, New York NY 10176. 212/808-8080. **Fax:** 212/808-8088. **Contact:** Mary A. Ward, President. **Description:** An executive search firm. **Specializes in the areas of:** Banking; Real Estate. **Positions commonly filled include:** Accountant/Auditor; Attorney; Bank Officer/Manager; Budget Analyst; Civil Engineer; Construction Contractor; Economist; Electrical/Electronics Engineer; Financial Analyst; General Manager; Management Analyst/Consultant; Mechanical Engineer; Operations/Production Manager; Property and Real Estate Manager; Purchasing Agent/Manager; Real Estate Agent; Structural Engineer; Underwriter/Assistant Underwriter. **Number of placements per year:** 100 - 199.

IVAN A. MACK ASSOCIATES, INC.
420 Lexington Avenue, Suite 300, New York NY 10170. 212/297-6123. **Fax:** 212/682-8479. **Contact:** Ivan Mack, President. **Description:** An executive search firm operating on a contingency basis. **Specializes in the areas of:** Accounting. **Positions commonly filled include:** Accountant; Bookkeeper; Chief Financial Officer; Controller. **Average salary range of placements:** $50,000 - $100,000. **Number of placements per year:** 200 - 499.

MAGILL ASSOCIATES, INC.
3601 Hempstead Turnpike, Levittown NY 11756. 516/579-4100. **Fax:** 516/579-4998. **Contact:** Joel Hamroff, President. **World Wide Web address:** http://www.magillstaff.com. **Description:** An executive search firm. **Specializes in the areas of:** Accounting/Auditing; Administration; Banking; Computer Science/Software; Finance; Legal; Personnel/Labor Relations; Sales; Secretarial; Technical. **Positions commonly filled include:** Accountant/Auditor; Bank Officer/Manager; Chemist; Claim Representative; Clerical Supervisor; Clinical Lab Technician; Computer Programmer; Credit Manager; Customer Service Representative; Financial Analyst; Human Resources Specialist; MIS Specialist; Paralegal; Software Engineer; Systems Analyst; Typist/Word Processor. **Average salary range of placements:** $30,000 - $100,000. **Number of placements per year:** 200 - 499.

MANAGEMENT RECRUITERS INTERNATIONAL
1650 Broadway, Suite 410, New York NY 10019. 212/974-7676. **Fax:** 212/974-8585. **Contact:** Manager. **World Wide Web address:** http://www.mrusa.com. **Description:** An executive search firm. **Specializes in the areas of:** Finance; Marketing. **Corporate headquarters location:** Cleveland OH. **Other U.S. locations:** Nationwide.

MANAGEMENT RECRUITERS INTERNATIONAL
P.O. Box 386, Stone Ridge NY 12484. 914/339-1300. **Contact:** Manager. **Description:** An executive search firm. **Specializes in the areas of:** Chemicals; Sales. **Corporate headquarters location:** Cleveland OH.

MANAGEMENT RECRUITERS INTERNATIONAL
435 New Karner Road, Suite 201, Albany NY 12205. 518/464-1461. **Contact:** Manager. **Description:** An

executive search firm. **Specializes in the areas of:** Marketing. **Corporate headquarters location:** Cleveland OH.

MANAGEMENT RECRUITERS INTERNATIONAL
16 West Main Street, Suite 225, Rochester NY 14614. 716/454-2440. **Contact:** Manager. **Description:** An executive search firm. **Specializes in the areas of:** Data Processing; Engineering; Sales. **Corporate headquarters location:** Cleveland OH.

MANAGEMENT RECRUITERS OF GRAMERCY
200 Park Avenue South, Suite 1510, New York NY 10003. 212/505-5530. **Fax:** 212/505-6240. **Contact:** Steve Schwartz, Owner/Manager. **Description:** An executive search firm operating on both retainer and contingency bases. **Specializes in the areas of:** Advertising; Health/Medical; Market Research; Publishing; Sales; Sales Promotion. **Positions commonly filled include:** Market Research Analyst; Services Sales Representative; Technical Writer/Editor. **Corporate headquarters location:** Cleveland OH. **Average salary range of placements:** More than $50,000. **Number of placements per year:** 1 - 49.

MANAGEMENT RECRUITERS OF NASSAU INC.
2303 Grand Avenue, Baldwin NY 11510. 516/771-1200. **Contact:** Thomas Wielder, Executive Vice President. **Description:** An executive search firm. **Specializes in the areas of:** Banking; Engineering; Finance; General Management; Manufacturing; Sales; Technical. **Positions commonly filled include:** Accountant/Auditor; Bank Officer/Manager; Chemical Engineer; Environmental Engineer; Financial Analyst; Financial Services Sales Representative; Mechanical Engineer; Securities Sales Representative; Structural Engineer. **Corporate headquarters location:** Cleveland OH. **International locations:** Worldwide. **Average salary range of placements:** More than $50,000.

MANAGEMENT RECRUITERS OF ORANGE COUNTY
P.O. Box 1530, Greenwood Lake NY 10925. 914/477-9509. **Fax:** 914/477-3016. **Contact:** Carolyn Chermak, President. **Description:** An executive search firm. **Specializes in the areas of:** Administration; Architecture/Construction; Biology; Computer Science/Software; Engineering; Food; General Management; Industrial; Legal; Manufacturing; Nonprofit; Retail; Sales; Transportation. **Corporate headquarters location:** Cleveland OH. **Other U.S. locations:** Nationwide. **Average salary range of placements:** More than $50,000. **Number of placements per year:** 1 - 49.

MANAGEMENT RECRUITERS OF ST. LAWRENCE COUNTY
P.O. Box 218, Madrid NY 13660. 315/322-0222. **Fax:** 315/322-0220. **Contact:** Nicole Scott, Owner/Manager. **E-mail address:** mrslc@northweb.com. **World Wide Web address:** http://www.mrinet.com. **Description:** An executive search firm operating on both retainer and contingency bases. **Specializes in the areas of:** Engineering; Industrial. **Positions commonly filled include:** Account Manager; Buyer; Chemical Engineer; Customer Service Representative; Design Engineer; Electrical/Electronics Engineer; General Manager; Industrial Engineer; Manufacturing Engineer; Marketing Manager; Marketing Specialist; Mechanical Engineer; Metallurgical Engineer; Operations Manager; Production Manager; Project Manager; Purchasing Agent/Manager; Quality Control Supervisor; Sales Engineer; Sales Executive; Sales Manager; Sales Representative; Software Engineer; Vice President. **Corporate headquarters location:** Cleveland OH. **Other U.S. locations:** Nationwide. **Average salary range of placements:** More than $50,000. **Number of placements per year:** 1 - 49.

MANAGEMENT RECRUITERS OF SUFFOLK
225 Main Street, Suite 204, Northport NY 11768. 516/261-0400. **Contact:** Manager. **Description:** An

executive search firm. **Specializes in the areas of:** Industrial. **Corporate headquarters location:** Cleveland OH.

MANAGEMENT RECRUITERS OF UPPER WESTCHESTER, INC.
118 North Bedford Road, Suite 103, Mount Kisco NY 10549-9998. 914/241-2788. **Fax:** 914/241-2783. **Contact:** Vern Nepple, Managing Partner. **Description:** An executive search firm. **Specializes in the areas of:** Food; Sales; Sales Management. **Corporate headquarters location:** Cleveland OH.

MANAGEMENT RECRUITERS OF UTICA/ROME
1721 Black River Boulevard, Executive Building, Suite 205, Rome NY 13440-2425. 315/339-6342. **Fax:** 315/339-6415. **Contact:** Manager. **Description:** An executive search firm focusing on the placement and recruitment of technical and health care professionals. **Specializes in the areas of:** Engineering; Health/Medical; Manufacturing; Sales. **Positions commonly filled include:** Customer Service Representative; Design Engineer; Electrical/Electronics Engineer; Mechanical Engineer; Occupational Therapist; Operations/Production Manager; Pharmacist; Physical Therapist; Physician; Purchasing Agent/Manager; Quality Control Supervisor; Registered Nurse; Speech-Language Pathologist. **Corporate headquarters location:** Cleveland OH. **Other U.S. locations:** Nationwide. **Number of placements per year:** 1 - 49.

MANAGEMENT RECRUITERS OF WOODBURY COMPUSEARCH
100 Crossways Park West, Suite 208, Woodbury NY 11797. 516/364-9290. **Fax:** 516/364-4478. **Contact:** William Jose, Manager. **E-mail address:** mrcareers@mrcareers.com. **World Wide Web address:** http://www.mrcareers.com. **Description:** An executive search firm. **Specializes in the areas of:** Consumer Products; Information Technology; Medical Devices; Pharmaceuticals. **Corporate headquarters location:** Cleveland OH.

MAR-EL EMPLOYMENT AGENCY
3000 Hempstead Turnpike, Levittown NY 11756. 516/579-7777. **Fax:** 516/579-7765. **Contact:** Scott Harvey, Executive Recruiter. **Description:** An executive search firm operating on a contingency basis. **Specializes in the areas of:** Accounting/Auditing; Bookkeeping; Finance; Office Support; Secretarial; Technical. **Positions commonly filled include:** Accountant/Auditor; Administrative Worker/Clerk; Bookkeeper; Data Entry Clerk; Legal Secretary; Medical Secretary; Receptionist; Secretary; Technician; Typist/Word Processor. **Average salary range of placements:** $20,000 - $90,000. **Number of placements per year:** 200 - 499.

MARCUS & ASSOCIATES
501 Fifth Avenue, Suite 2014, New York NY 10017-3610. 212/856-9888. **Fax:** 212/856-0826. **Contact:** Ellen Marcus, President. **E-mail address:** jobs@marcusandassociates.com. **Description:** An executive search firm operating on a contingency basis. Client company pays fee. **Specializes in the areas of:** Accounting; Banking; Finance. **Positions commonly filled include:** Accountant; Auditor; Budget Analyst; Chief Financial Officer; Controller; Credit Manager; Database Administrator; Finance Director; Financial Analyst; Fund Manager; Human Resources Manager; Risk Manager; Systems Analyst; Treasurer. **Average salary range of placements:** $50,000 - $150,000. **Number of placements per year:** 100 - 199.

MARSHALL CONSULTANTS, INC.
360 East 65th Street, Penthouse B, New York NY 10021. 212/628-8400. **Fax:** 212/628-8449. **Contact:** Larry Marshall, President/CEO. **E-mail address:** MarshallCn@aol.com. **World Wide Web address:** http://www.marshallconsultants.com. **Description:** An executive search firm. **Specializes in the areas of:** Communications. **Corporate headquarters location:** This Location. **Other U.S. locations:** Los Angeles CA.

MARSHALL-ALAN ASSOCIATES, INC.
5 West 37th Street, 8th Floor, New York NY 10018. 212/382-2440. **Fax:** 212/764-5411. **Contact:** Alan Massarsky, President. **Description:** An executive search firm. **Specializes in the areas of:** Food. **Positions commonly filled include:** Caterer; Chef/Cook/Kitchen Worker; Food and Beverage Service Worker; Hotel Manager; Restaurant/Food Service Manager. **Number of placements per year:** 200 - 499.

MAXIMUM MANAGEMENT CORPORATION
230 Park Avenue, Suite 635, New York NY 10169. 212/867-4646. **Fax:** 212/682-4882. **Contact:** Melissa Brophy, President. **Description:** An executive search firm. **Specializes in the areas of:** Banking; Finance.

McLAUGHLIN RESOURCES
11 Penn Plaza, 5th Floor, New York NY 10001. 212/764-2120. **Fax:** 212/946-2746. **Contact:** Brian McLaughlin, President. **Description:** An executive search firm. **Specializes in the areas of:** Accounting/Auditing; Finance; Health/Medical; Insurance. **Positions commonly filled include:** Accountant/Auditor; Controller; Financial Analyst; Management Trainee; Mathematician; Mechanical Engineer; Physicist. **Average salary range of placements:** More than $50,000. **Number of placements per year:** 50 - 99.

MENTORTECH
462 Seventh Avenue, 4th Floor, New York NY 10018. 212/736-5870x212. **Fax:** 212/736-9046. **Contact:** Manager. **Description:** An executive search firm. **Specializes in the areas of:** Administration; Computer Science/Software; Personnel/Labor Relations; Sales. **Positions commonly filled include:** Human Resources Specialist; Internet Services Manager; MIS Specialist; Multimedia Designer; Services Sales Representative; Software Engineer; Technical Writer/Editor; Telecommunications Manager. **Number of placements per year:** 50 - 99.

METROPOLITAN PERSONNEL SYSTEMS
49 Court Street, Binghamton NY 13901. 607/722-1666. **Fax:** 607/722-0449. **Contact:** Technical Division Manager. **Description:** An executive search firm. **Specializes in the areas of:** Accounting/Auditing; Administration; Computer Science/Software; Education; Engineering; Food; General Management; Industrial; Manufacturing; Personnel/Labor Relations; Retail; Sales; Secretarial; Technical; Transportation. **Positions commonly filled include:** Accountant/Auditor; Administrative Manager; Advertising Clerk; Aerospace Engineer; Agricultural Engineer; Bank Officer/Manager; Biochemist; Biomedical Engineer; Blue-Collar Worker Supervisor; Branch Manager; Budget Analyst; Buyer; Chemical Engineer; Civil Engineer; Claim Representative; Clerical Supervisor; Computer Programmer; Construction and Building Inspector; Construction Contractor; Cost Estimator; Counselor; Credit Manager; Customer Service Representative; Design Engineer; Designer; Draftsperson; Education Administrator; Electrical/Electronics Engineer; Electrician; Environmental Engineer; Financial Analyst; Food Scientist/Technologist; General Manager; Hotel Manager; Human Resources Specialist; Human Service Worker; Industrial Engineer; Industrial Production Manager; Insurance Agent/Broker; Landscape Architect; Management Analyst/Consultant; Management Trainee; Manufacturer's/Wholesaler's Sales Rep.; Market Research Analyst; Mechanical Engineer; MIS Specialist; Multimedia Designer; Nuclear Engineer; Operations/Production Manager; Paralegal; Petroleum Engineer; Preschool Worker; Property and Real Estate Manager; Public Relations Specialist; Purchasing Agent/Manager; Quality Control Supervisor; Real Estate Agent; Reporter; Restaurant/Food Service Manager; Science Technologist; Securities Sales Representative; Services Sales Representative; Social Worker; Software Engineer; Speech-Language Pathologist; Stationary Engineer; Strategic Relations Manager; Structural Engineer; Surgical Technician; Systems Analyst;

Teacher/Professor; Technical Writer/Editor; Telecommunications Manager; Transportation/Traffic Specialist; Typist/Word Processor; Underwriter/Assistant Underwriter; Urban/Regional Planner; Video Production Coordinator. **Benefits available to temporary workers:** 401(k); Life Insurance; Paid Holidays; Paid Vacation. **Other area locations:** Cortland NY; Elmira NY; Ithaca NY; Syracuse NY. **Average salary range of placements:** $30,000 - $50,000. **Number of placements per year:** 1000+.

MICKLER ASSOCIATES INC.
P.O. Box 118, Buffalo NY 14209. 716/881-2222. **Contact:** Manager. **Description:** An executive search firm operating on both retainer and contingency bases. Mickler Associates focuses on providing sales and marketing with an emphasis on food and consumer products. **Specializes in the areas of:** Engineering; Food; Manufacturing; Sales. **Positions commonly filled include:** Buyer; Chemical Engineer; Chemist; Electrical/Electronics Engineer; Food Scientist/ Technologist; General Manager; Industrial Production Manager; Manufacturer's/Wholesaler's Sales Rep.; Market Research Analyst; Operations/Production Manager; Purchasing Agent/Manager; Quality Control Supervisor; Restaurant/Food Service Manager; Services Sales Representative. **Number of placements per year:** 1 - 49.

HERBERT MINES ASSOCIATES
375 Park Avenue, Suite 301, New York NY 10152. 212/355-0909. **Contact:** Manager. **Description:** An executive search firm. **Specializes in the areas of:** Retail.

THE MITCHELL GROUP
4 Woodhaven Drive, New City NY 10956. **Toll-free phone:** 800/648-2435. **Contact:** Ken Mitchell, Proprietor. **Description:** An executive search firm operating on both retainer and contingency bases. **Specializes in the areas of:** Insurance. **Positions commonly filled include:** Actuary. **Number of placements per year:** 1 - 49.

MOLLOY PARTNERS
340 Broadway, Sarasota Springs NY 12866. 518/581-2532. **Contact:** Manager. **Description:** An executive search firm that focuses on placing professionals in administrative positions within colleges and universities.

NATEK CORPORATION
27 Summerfield Lane, Saratoga Springs NY 12866. 518/583-0456. **Fax:** 518/583-0558. **Contact:** Mark Dillon, President. **E-mail address:** mdillon@natek.com. **World Wide Web address:** http://www.natek.com. **Description:** An executive search firm operating on both retainer and contingency bases. **Specializes in the areas of:** Engineering; Marketing; Sales; Scientific; Technical. **Positions commonly filled include:** Account Representative; Applications Engineer; Chemical Engineer; Construction Contractor; Design Engineer; Electrical/Electronics Engineer; Industrial Engineer; Manufacturing Engineer; Project Manager; Sales Executive; Sales Manager; Sales Representative. **Other U.S. locations:** Nationwide. **Average salary range of placements:** More than $50,000. **Number of placements per year:** 50 - 99.

NATIONAL ENGINEERING SEARCH
806 Linden Avenue, Rochester NY 14625. 716/248-3160. **Contact:** Manager. **Description:** An executive search firm. **Specializes in the areas of:** Computer Hardware/Software.

NEAL MANAGEMENT, INC.
152 Madison Avenue, Suite 605, New York NY 10016. 212/686-1686. **Fax:** 212/686-1590. **Contact:** Peter Tannenbaum, President. **Description:** An executive search firm. **Specializes in the areas of:** Accounting/Auditing; Banking; Finance. **Positions commonly filled include:** Accountant/Auditor; Bank Officer/Manager; Computer Programmer; Credit

Manager; Economist; Systems Analyst. **Number of placements per year:** 1 - 49.

THE NEIL MICHAEL GROUP
350 Fifth Avenue, Suite 2711, New York NY 10118. 212/631-0999. **Fax:** 212/631-0011. **Contact:** Dr. Neil M. Solomon, Founder. **E-mail address:** neils1@msn.com. **World Wide Web address:** http://www. neilmichaelgroup.com. **Description:** An executive search firm. Founded in 1983. **Specializes in the areas of:** Biotechnology; Health/Medical; Pharmaceuticals.

NETWORK DYNAMICS
200 West 57th Street, Suite 1104, New York NY 10019. 212/258-2600. **Fax:** 212/258-2236. **Contact:** Manager. **E-mail address:** jgrogan@networkdynamics.com. **World Wide Web address:** http://www. networkdynamics.com. **Description:** An executive search firm that also offers computer consulting services and systems integration. Founded in 1986. **Specializes in the areas of:** Sales; Software Development; Technical.

NOBLE & ASSOCIATES
420 Madison Avenue, New York NY 10017. 212/838-7020. **Fax:** 212/838-7344. **Contact:** Donald Noble, Principal. **Description:** An executive search firm operating on both retainer and contingency bases. **Specializes in the areas of:** Advertising; Personnel/Labor Relations; Retail; Sales. **Positions commonly filled include:** General Manager; Human Resources Manager; Public Relations Specialist. **Other U.S. locations:** San Francisco CA. **Average salary range of placements:** More than $50,000. **Number of placements per year:** 50 - 99.

OPTIMAL RESOURCES
18 East 48th Street, Suite 902, New York NY 10017. 212/486-7713. **Fax:** 212/486-8042. **Contact:** Manager. **Description:** An executive search firm operating on a contingency basis. Optimal Resources also provides some temporary placements. **Specializes in the areas of:** Administration; Advertising; Banking; Computer Science/Software; Fashion; Finance; Personnel/Labor Relations; Sales; Secretarial. **Positions commonly filled include:** Brokerage Clerk; Financial Analyst; Human Resources Specialist; Management Trainee; Paralegal; Public Relations Specialist; Securities Sales Representative; Services Sales Representative. **Average salary range of placements:** $30,000 - $50,000. **Number of placements per year:** 200 - 499.

LYNNE PALMER EXECUTIVE RECRUITMENT, INC.
342 Madison Avenue, Suite 1430, New York NY 10173. 212/883-0203. **Fax:** 212/883-0149. **Contact:** Elena Bourgoin, Office Manager. **Description:** An executive search firm operating on both retainer and contingency bases. **Specializes in the areas of:** Publishing.

ARTHUR PANN ASSOCIATES
701 Westchester Avenue, Suite 3A1, White Plains NY 10604. 914/686-0700. **Fax:** 914/946-2019. **Contact:** Art Pann, CPC, President. **Description:** An executive search firm operating on both retainer and contingency bases. **Specializes in the areas of:** Accounting/Auditing; Administration; Engineering. **Positions commonly filled include:** Applications Engineer; Architect; Chief Financial Officer; Computer Programmer; Controller; Database Manager; Design Engineer; Finance Director; Financial Analyst; Human Resources Manager; Manufacturing Engineer; Multimedia Designer; Software Engineer; Systems Analyst; Systems Manager; Telecommunications Manager; Webmaster. **Average salary range of placements:** More than $50,000. **Number of placements per year:** 50 - 99.

PARKER CLARK EXECUTIVE RECRUITMENT
370 Lexington Avenue, Suite 1804, New York NY 10017. 212/983-5950. **Contact:** Manager. **Description:** An executive search firm. **Specializes in the areas of:** Accounting/Auditing; Finance.

THE PARKS GROUP INC.
230 Park Avenue, Suite 450, New York NY 10169. 212/286-0777. **Fax:** 212/286-1973. **Contact:** Marie Parks, CPC/President. **E-mail address:** marie@gaparks.com. **World Wide Web address:** http://www.gaparks.com. **Description:** An executive search firm operating on a contingency basis. **Specializes in the areas of:** Finance; Human Resources; Investment; Legal. **Positions commonly filled include:** Accountant/Auditor; Attorney; Human Resources Manager; Legal Secretary; MIS Specialist; Paralegal. **Other U.S. locations:** Nationwide. **Average salary range of placements:** $40,000 - $125,000. **Number of placements per year:** 100 - 199.

PATHWAY EXECUTIVE SEARCH, INC.
60 East 42nd Street, Lincoln Building, Suite 405, New York NY 10165. 212/557-2650. **Fax:** 212/682-1743. **Contact:** Jay Berger, President. **Description:** An executive search firm. **Specializes in the areas of:** Banking; Computer Science/Software; Finance; Technical. **Positions commonly filled include:** Computer Programmer; Economist; Management Analyst/Consultant; Mathematician; Science Technologist; Securities Sales Representative; Software Engineer; Systems Analyst. **Number of placements per year:** 50 - 99.

PAXTON RESOURCES INC.
50 Main Street, Suite 1000, White Plains NY 10606. 914/682-2088. **Fax:** 914/682-2192. **Contact:** Barbara Paxton, President. **Description:** An executive search firm operating on a contingency basis. **Specializes in the areas of:** Human Resources; Public Relations. **Positions commonly filled include:** Human Resources Manager; Public Relations Specialist; Training Specialist. **Average salary range of placements:** More than $50,000. **Number of placements per year:** 1 - 49.

PEAK SEARCH INC.
25 West 31st Street, 12th Floor, New York NY 10001. 212/947-6600. **Fax:** 212/947-6780. **Contact:** Richard Eichenberg, President. **Description:** An executive search firm. **Specializes in the areas of:** Accounting; Banking; Finance; Legal. **Positions commonly filled include:** Accountant; Attorney; Auditor; Bank Officer/Manager; Budget Analyst; Chief Financial Officer; Controller; Credit Manager; Finance Director; Financial Analyst; Fund Manager; Paralegal; Vice President of Finance. **Average salary range of placements:** More than $50,000. **Number of placements per year:** 200 - 499.

PENCOM SYSTEMS INCORPORATED
40 Fulton Street, New York NY 10038-1850. 212/513-7777. **Fax:** 212/227-1854. **Contact:** Recruiter. **E-mail address:** ny-jobs@pencom.com. **World Wide Web address:** http://www.pencom.com. **Description:** An executive search firm that also provides some contract services and systems administration outsourcing. Founded in 1973. **Specializes in the areas of:** Technical. **Corporate headquarters location:** This Location. **Other U.S. locations:** Los Angeles CA; San Jose CA; Washington DC; Atlanta GA; Chicago IL; Boston MA; Austin TX.

PENDLETON JAMES ASSOCIATES, INC.
200 Park Avenue, Suite 1600, New York NY 10166. 212/557-1599. **Fax:** 212/697-5718. **Contact:** Manager. **World Wide Web address:** http://www.penjames.com. **Description:** An executive search firm. **Specializes in the areas of:** Communications; Finance; General Labor; Health/Medical; Industrial; Nonprofit; Retail; Technical.

PERSONNEL ASSOCIATES INC.
731 James Street, Suite 209, Syracuse NY 13203. 315/422-0070. **Fax:** 315/474-7293. **Contact:** Peter J. Baskin, CPC/President. **E-mail address:** pjbaskin@concentric.net. **Description:** An executive search firm operating on both retainer and contingency bases. **Specializes in the areas of:** Insurance. **Number of placements per year:** 1 - 49.

PERSONNEL CONSULTING ASSOCIATES
7600 Jericho Turnpike, Suite 304, Woodbury NY 11797. 212/269-8508. **Contact:** Joseph Slater, President. **Description:** An executive search firm. **Specializes in the areas of:** Banking; Finance; Investment; Personnel/Labor Relations.

PERSONNEL SERVICES CENTER
315 West 57th Street, Suite 7D, New York NY 10019. 212/247-2043. **Contact:** Michael R. Morano, Ph.D., President. **Description:** An executive search firm that also provides career/outplacement counseling. **Specializes in the areas of:** Accounting/Auditing; Administration; General Management; Retail; Sales; Secretarial. **Positions commonly filled include:** Account Manager; Accountant/Auditor; Administrative Assistant; Administrative Manager; Advertising Clerk; Advertising Executive; Applications Engineer; Branch Manager; Buyer; Clerical Supervisor; Computer Operator; Financial Analyst; General Manager; Management Analyst/Consultant; Management Trainee; Operations Manager; Production Manager; Project Manager; Sales Engineer; Sales Executive; Sales Manager; Sales Representative; Secretary; Social Worker; Systems Analyst; Systems Manager; Vice President. **Average salary range of placements:** More than $50,000. **Number of placements per year:** 1 - 49.

PHARMACEUTICAL RECRUITERS INC.
271 Madison Avenue, Suite 1200, New York NY 10016. 212/557-5627. **Fax:** 212/557-5866. **Contact:** Manager. **Description:** An executive search firm. **Specializes in the areas of:** Pharmaceuticals.

PHOENIX SEARCH GROUP
350 Fifth Avenue, Suite 2714, New York NY 10118. 212/564-3456. **Fax:** 212/695-8258. **Contact:** Recruitment Manager. **Description:** An executive search firm. Client company pays fee. **Specializes in the areas of:** Computer Science/Software; Internet Development; Internet Marketing. **Positions commonly filled include:** AS400 Programmer Analyst; Computer Engineer; Computer Operator; Computer Programmer; Database Administrator; Internet Services Manager; Multimedia Designer; Network/Systems Administrator; Software Engineer; SQL Programmer; Systems Analyst; Webmaster. **Corporate headquarters location:** This Location.

PIPT&HOCAPS
Gramercy House, 235 East 22nd Street, New York NY 10010-4630. 212/448-9300. **Toll-free phone:** 877/448-9300. **Fax:** 212/448-9305. **Contact:** Recruiter. **E-mail address:** execsearch@pipt-hocaps.com. **World Wide Web address:** http://www.pipt-hocaps.com. **Description:** An executive search firm that also offers Human Resources consulting services. Founded in 1976. **Specializes in the areas of:** Hotel/Restaurant. **Corporate headquarters location:** London. **International locations:** Cairo, Egypt; London, England.

P.G. PRAGER SEARCH ASSOCIATES, LTD.
1461 Franklin Avenue, Garden City NY 11530. 516/294-4400. **Fax:** 516/294-4443. **Contact:** Michael B. Prager, President. **Description:** An executive search firm operating on a contingency basis. **Specializes in the areas of:** Accounting/Auditing; Administration; Banking; Computer Science/Software; Finance; Insurance; Legal; Marketing; MIS/EDP; Office Support; Personnel/Labor Relations; Sales; Secretarial. **Positions commonly filled include:** Accountant/Auditor; Attorney; Bank Officer/Manager; Budget Analyst; Buyer; Credit Manager; Customer Service Representative; General Manager; Human Resources Manager; Industrial Production Manager; Insurance Agent/Broker; Management Analyst/Consultant; Manufacturer's/Wholesaler's Sales Rep.; Paralegal; Property and Real Estate Manager; Public Relations Specialist; Purchasing Agent/Manager; Quality Control Supervisor; Statistician; Systems Analyst; Underwriter/Assistant Underwriter. **Average salary range of placements:** More than $50,000. **Number of placements per year:** 1 - 49.

PRO SEARCH ASSOCIATES, INC.
15 North Mill Street, Nyack NY 10960. 914/353-2260.
Fax: 914/353-2366. **Contact:** Edwin Kahn, Principal.
Description: An executive search firm operating on both retainer and contingency bases. **Specializes in the areas of:** Administration; Computer Science/Software; Finance; Information Systems. **Positions commonly filled include:** Computer Programmer; Financial Analyst; Internet Services Manager; Systems Analyst; Telecommunications Manager. **Average salary range of placements:** More than $50,000. **Number of placements per year:** 1 - 49.

PRO/TECH NATIONWIDE STAFFING, INC.
271 Madison Avenue, Suite 1407, New York NY 10016.
212/685-1400. **Fax:** 212/685-4340. **Contact:** Manager.
Description: An executive search firm. **Specializes in the areas of:** Biotechnology; Consumer Products; Engineering; Logistics; Manufacturing; Materials; Pharmaceuticals; Purchasing; Quality Assurance.

PROFESSIONAL CORPORATE SEARCH INC.
234 Fifth Avenue, New York NY 10001. 212/213-3434.
Fax: 212/213-3433. **Contact:** Recruiter. **E-mail address:** jobs@procorpsearch.com. **World Wide Web address:** http://www.procorpsearch.com. **Description:** An executive search firm. Client company pays fee. **Specializes in the areas of:** Marketing; Sales.

PROFESSIONAL PLACEMENT ASSOCIATES INC.
14 Rye Ridge Plaza, Rye Brook NY 10573. 914/251-1000. **Fax:** 914/251-1055. **Contact:** Laura J. Schacter, President. **Description:** An executive search firm. **Specializes in the areas of:** Health/Medical. **Positions commonly filled include:** Biomedical Engineer; Chief Financial Officer; Controller; Dietician/Nutritionist; EEG Technologist; EKG Technician; Finance Director; Human Resources Manager; MIS Specialist; Occupational Therapist; Pharmacist; Physical Therapist; Physician; Registered Nurse; Respiratory Therapist; Speech-Language Pathologist. **Average salary range of placements:** More than $50,000. **Number of placements per year:** 200 - 499.

PROFESSIONAL SUPPORT INC.
501 John James Audubon Parkway, Amherst NY 14228-1143. 716/688-0235. **Toll-free phone:** 800/444-6760.
Fax: 716/688-0239. **Contact:** Greg Eastmer, Vice President. **Description:** An executive search firm. **Specializes in the areas of:** Accounting/Auditing; Administration; MIS/EDP; Personnel/Labor Relations. **Positions commonly filled include:** Accountant/Auditor; Computer Programmer; Financial Analyst; Human Resources Manager; Management Analyst/Consultant; MIS Specialist; Quality Control Supervisor; Software Engineer; Systems Analyst. **Benefits available to temporary workers:** 401(k); Life Insurance; Medical Insurance; Paid Holidays; Paid Vacation; Sick Days. **Other U.S. locations:** Rochester NY; Cleveland OH. **Average salary range of placements:** $30,000 - $50,000. **Number of placements per year:** 100 - 199.

PRYOR PERSONNEL AGENCY, INC.
147 Old Country Road, Hicksville NY 11801-4007.
516/935-0100. **Fax:** 516/931-7842. **Contact:** Patricia Pryor Bonica, President. **E-mail address:** ppryor1575@aol.com. **World Wide Web address:** http://www.pryor.com. **Description:** An executive search firm operating on both retainer and contingency bases. **Specializes in the areas of:** Insurance. **Positions commonly filled include:** Accountant/Auditor; Actuary; Adjuster; Claim Representative; Financial Analyst; Human Resources Manager; Insurance Agent/Broker; Systems Analyst; Underwriter/Assistant Underwriter. **Average salary range of placements:** More than $50,000. **Number of placements per year:** 500 - 999.

QUANTUM PERSONNEL AGENCY INC.
342 Madison Avenue, Suite 1223, New York NY 10173.
212/286-0111. **Fax:** 212/808-5279. **Contact:** Stu Howard, Manager. **E-mail address:** qdpjobs@aol.com.

Description: An executive search firm operating on a contingency basis. **Specializes in the areas of:** Computer Science/Software; Internet Development; MIS/EDP. **Positions commonly filled include:** Applications Engineer; AS400 Programmer Analyst; Computer Engineer; Computer Operator; Computer Programmer; Computer Scientist; Computer Support Technician; Computer Technician; Database Administrator; Database Manager; Internet Services Manager; LAN/WAN Designer/Developer; MIS Specialist; Network/Systems Administrator; Software Engineer; SQL Programmer; Systems Analyst; Systems Manager; Webmaster. **Number of placements per year:** 500 - 999.

QUEST ORGANIZATION
11 Penn Plaza, Suite 935, New York NY 10001.
212/971-0033. **Fax:** 212/971-6256. **Contact:** Michael F. Rosenblatt, President. **E-mail address:** questorg@ aol.com. **Description:** An executive search firm. **Specializes in the areas of:** Accounting/Auditing; Administration; Banking; Fashion; Finance; Personnel/Labor Relations. **Positions commonly filled include:** Accountant/Auditor; Budget Analyst; Chief Financial Officer; Consultant; Controller; EDP Specialist; Finance Director; Financial Analyst; Fund Manager; Human Resources Manager; Management Analyst/Consultant; Market Research Analyst. **Other U.S. locations:** Washington DC; Philadelphia PA. **Average salary range of placements:** More than $50,000. **Number of placements per year:** 100 - 199.

RHI CONSULTING
245 Park Avenue, New York NY 10167. 212/290-2700.
Fax: 212/290-8100. **Contact:** Director. **Description:** An executive search firm. **Specializes in the areas of:** Computer Science/Software; Information Technology; Technical. **Positions commonly filled include:** Computer Programmer; Financial Analyst; Management; Science Technologist; Software Engineer; Statistician; Systems Analyst; Technical Writer/Editor. **Corporate headquarters location:** Menlo Park CA. **International locations:** Worldwide. **Number of placements per year:** 200 - 499.

RJ ASSOCIATES
30 Glenn Street, White Plains NY 10603. 914/946-0278.
Fax: 914/946-2019. **Contact:** Manager. **E-mail address:** rjainfo@rjsearch.com. **World Wide Web address:** http://rjsearch.com/index.html. **Description:** An executive search firm. **Specializes in the areas of:** Accounting; Finance; Information Technology.

ROI ASSOCIATES INC.
P.O. Box 136, Massapequa Park NY 11762. 516/541-3800. **Fax:** 516/795-2300. **Contact:** Peter Portanova, Partner. **E-mail address:** pportanova@compuserve.com. **Description:** An executive search firm. **Specializes in the areas of:** Distribution; Finance; General Management; Manufacturing; Materials. **Positions commonly filled include:** General Manager; Operations/Production Manager; Purchasing Agent/ Manager. **Number of placements per year:** 1 - 49.

RAINES INTERNATIONAL, INC.
1120 Avenue of the Americas, 21st Floor, New York NY 10036. 212/997-1100. **Fax:** 212/944-7585. **Contact:** Manager. **Description:** An executive search firm that operates on a retainer basis.

RAND THOMPSON CONSULTANTS
MERLIN TEMPS
261 Madison Avenue, 27th Floor, New York NY 10016.
212/972-0090. **Toll-free phone:** 800/572-0292. **Fax:** 212/370-0047. **Contact:** John Kelly, President. **E-mail address:** rtconsult@aol.com. **Description:** An executive search firm operating on both retainer and contingency bases. Merlin Temps (also at this location) is a temporary agency. Client company pays fee. **Specializes in the areas of:** Accounting; Banking; Computer Science/Software; Finance; Insurance; MIS/EDP; Sales; Secretarial. **Positions commonly filled**

include: Accountant; Administrative Assistant; Architect; Auditor; Chief Financial Officer; Computer Programmer; Controller; Credit Manager; Database Manager; Finance Director; Financial Analyst; Fund Manager; General Manager; Graphic Designer; Human Resources Manager; Industrial Agent/Broker; Management Analyst/Consultant; Marketing Manager; Marketing Specialist; MIS Specialist; Network/Systems Administrator; Purchasing Agent/Manager; Sales Executive; Sales Manager; Secretary; Systems Analyst; Systems Manager; Underwriter/Assistant Underwriter. **Corporate headquarters location:** This Location. **Number of placements per year:** 200 - 499.

JOANNE E. RATNER SEARCH
10 East 39th Street, Suite 514, New York NY 10016. 212/683-1975. **Fax:** 212/683-4682. **Contact:** Joanne Ratner, Managing Director. **E-mail address:** ratner@ix.netcom.com. **World Wide Web address:** http://www.jrsearch.com. **Description:** An executive search firm operating on both retainer and contingency bases. Client company pays fee. **Specializes in the areas of:** Accounting; Finance; General Management; Internet Marketing. **Positions commonly filled include:** Accountant; Auditor; Budget Analyst; Chief Financial Officer; Controller; Credit Manager; Finance Director; Financial Analyst; General Manager; Management Analyst/Consultant; Market Research Analyst; Marketing Manager. **Corporate headquarters location:** This Location. **Average salary range of placements:** $50,000 - $100,000. **Number of placements per year:** 1 - 49.

RAY & BERNDTSON, INC.
245 Park Avenue, 33rd Floor, New York NY 10167. 212/370-1316. **Fax:** 212/370-1462. **Contact:** Manager. **World Wide Web address:** http://www. rayberndtson.com. **Description:** An executive search firm. **Positions commonly filled include:** Senior Management. **International locations:** Worldwide.

RECRUITMENT GROUP
P.O. Box 410, Williamsville NY 14231. 716/631-8960. **Contact:** Manager. **Description:** An executive search firm. **Specializes in the areas of:** Engineering; Sales.

RECRUITMENT INTERNATIONAL GROUP
298 Fifth Avenue, New York NY 10001. 212/868-1854. **Contact:** Ted R. Zupa, Managing Director. **Description:** An executive search firm operating on both retainer and contingency bases. Recruitment International also offers career/outplacement counseling. **Specializes in the areas of:** Accounting; Administration; Banking; Computer Science/Software; Fashion; Finance; General Management; Industrial; Marketing; MIS/EDP; Personnel/Labor Relations; Sales; Technical. **Positions commonly filled include:** Accountant; Administrative Manager; Applications Engineer; Attorney; Bank Officer/Manager; Controller; Finance Director; Financial Analyst; Human Resources Manager; Industrial Engineer; Industrial Production Manager; Internet Services Manager; Management Analyst/Consultant; Market Research Analyst; Marketing Manager; Operations Manager; Sales Engineer; Sales Executive; Sales Manager; Software Engineer; Statistician; Systems Analyst; Systems Manager; Teacher/Professor; Technical Writer/Editor; Telecommunications Manager; Typist/Word Processor. **Corporate headquarters location:** This Location. **Other U.S. locations:** Palm Beach FL. **Average salary range of placements:** More than $30,000. **Number of placements per year:** 200 - 499.

REDSTONE AFFILIATES
50 Main Street, White Plains NY 10606. 914/945-0735. **Contact:** Manager. **Description:** An executive search firm. **Specializes in the areas of:** Banking; Finance; Investment.

REDWOOD PARTNERS
152 Madison Avenue, 16th Floor, New York NY 10016. 212/843-8585. **Fax:** 212/843-9043. **Contact:**

Marcelo Wainberg, Senior Consultant. **E-mail address:** redwood@redwoodpartners.com. **World Wide Web address:** http://www.redwoodpartners.com. **Description:** An executive search firm. **Specializes in the areas of:** Advertising; Sales. **Positions commonly filled include:** Account Manager; Account Representative; Computer Animator; Computer Programmer; Consultant; Graphic Artist; Graphic Designer; Internet Services Manager; Management Analyst/Consultant; Market Research Analyst; Marketing Manager; Marketing Specialist; Online Content Specialist; Sales Executive; Sales Manager; Sales Representative; Vice President of Marketing. **Average salary range of placements:** More than $50,000. **Number of placements per year:** 100 - 199.

DANIEL F. REILLY AND ASSOCIATES INC.
481 Main Street, Mezzanine Level, New Rochelle NY 10801. 914/636-6542. **Fax:** 914/636-0221. **Contact:** Daniel Reilly, President. **E-mail address:** dfreilly@aol.com. **World Wide Web address:** http://crm21.com/dfreilly/dfreilly.html. **Description:** An executive search firm operating on a retainer basis. Client company pays fee. **Specializes in the areas of:** Software Engineering. **Positions commonly filled include:** Computer Programmer; Computer Scientist; Software Engineer. **Corporate headquarters location:** This Location. **Average salary range of placements:** More than $50,000. **Number of placements per year:** 50 - 99.

RESOURCE SERVICES, INC.
20 Crossways Park North, 3rd Floor, Woodbury NY 11797. 516/496-4100. **Fax:** 516/496-4110. **Contact:** Joseph Trainor, President. **Description:** An executive search firm operating on a contingency basis. **Specializes in the areas of:** Computer Science/Software; Telecommunications. **Positions commonly filled include:** MIS Specialist. **Average salary range of placements:** More than $50,000. **Number of placements per year:** 200 - 499.

RESPONSE STAFFING SERVICES
23 East 39th Street, New York NY 10016. 212/983-8870. **Fax:** 212/376-7492. **Contact:** Allen Gutterman, President. **Description:** An executive search firm operating on both retainer and contingency bases. **Specializes in the areas of:** Accounting/Auditing; Architecture/Construction; Banking; Computer Hardware/Software; Finance; Health/Medical; Insurance; Secretarial. **Positions commonly filled include:** Accountant/Auditor; Actuary; Bank Officer/Manager; Biological Scientist; Biomedical Engineer; Branch Manager; Brokerage Clerk; Budget Analyst; Claim Representative; Clinical Lab Technician; Computer Programmer; Construction and Building Inspector; Credit Manager; Customer Service Representative; EEG Technologist; EKG Technician; Emergency Medical Technician; Financial Analyst; Health Services Manager; Insurance Agent/Broker; Licensed Practical Nurse; Medical Records Technician; Nuclear Medicine Technologist; Occupational Therapist; Paralegal; Pharmacist; Physical Therapist; Physician; Property and Real Estate Manager; Recreational Therapist; Registered Nurse; Respiratory Therapist; Securities Sales Representative; Software Engineer; Surgical Technician; Systems Analyst; Underwriter/Assistant Underwriter. **Average salary range of placements:** $30,000 - $50,000. **Number of placements per year:** 200 - 499.

RETAIL RECRUITERS INC.
225 West 34th Street, Suite 1316, New York NY 10122. 212/714-0313. **Contact:** Manager. **Description:** An executive search firm. **Specializes in the areas of:** Retail.

E.J. RHODES EXECUTIVE SEARCH
555 Fifth Avenue, 6th Floor, New York NY 10017. 212/983-2000. **Fax:** 212/983-8333. **Contact:** Manager. **Description:** An executive search firm. **Specializes in the areas of:** Banking; Finance; Real Estate.

RITTA PROFESSIONAL SEARCH, INC.
6 Automation Lane, Albany NY 12205-1604. 518/458-7340. **Fax:** 518/458-7017. **Contact:** Arthur E. Hansen, President. **Description:** An executive search firm that focuses on the placement of research and development engineers and scientists in various electrical, mechanical, materials, and electronic fields. Founded in 1974. **Specializes in the areas of:** Computer Science/Software; Engineering. **Positions commonly filled include:** Aerospace Engineer; Computer Programmer; Design Engineer; Electrical Engineer; Environmental Engineer; Mechanical Engineer; Metallurgical Engineer; Software Engineer; Systems Analyst; Telecommunications Manager. **Average salary range of placements:** More than $50,000.

ROMAC INTERNATIONAL
60 East 42nd Street, 27th Floor, New York NY 10165. 212/868-5100. **Fax:** 212/868-5115. **Contact:** Phillip D. Bank, CPA/Managing Partner. **World Wide Web address:** http://www.experienceondemand.com. **Description:** An executive search firm operating on a contingency basis. **Specializes in the areas of:** Accounting/Auditing; Banking; Finance. **Positions commonly filled include:** Accountant/Auditor; Bank Officer/Manager; Budget Analyst; Credit Manager; Financial Analyst; Management Analyst/Consultant. **Benefits available to temporary workers:** Stock Purchase. **Corporate headquarters location:** Tampa FL. **Other U.S. locations:** Nationwide. **Average salary range of placements:** More than $50,000. **Number of placements per year:** 100 - 199.

ROMAC INTERNATIONAL
3 Gennett Drive, Suite 316, White Plains NY 10604. 914/251-9500. **Fax:** 914/251-9565. **Contact:** Manager. **Description:** An executive search firm. **Specializes in the areas of:** Computer Hardware/Software; Finance; Information Technology. **Corporate headquarters location:** Tampa FL.

ROSENTHAL ASSOCIATES INTERNATIONAL
230 Park Avenue, Suite 1000, New York NY 10169. 212/268-6300. **Contact:** Recruiter. **E-mail address:** info@raisearch.com. **World Wide Web address:** http://www.raisearch.com. **Description:** A global executive search and recruiting firm that also provides management support and executive coaching services. **Specializes in the areas of:** Accounting; Aerospace; Automotive; Biotechnology; Chemicals; Clinical Research; Communications; Consumer Package Goods; Consumer Products; Engineering; Environmental; Finance; High-Tech; Human Resources; Management; Management Consulting; Marketing; Multimedia; Pharmaceuticals; Plastics; Quality Assurance; Sales; Telecommunications. **Other U.S. locations:** Chatham NJ.

BOB ROSS EXECUTIVE SEARCH CORPORATION
150 West 51st Street, Suite 1811, New York NY 10019. 212/969-9030. **Fax:** 212/969-9067. **Contact:** Bob Ross, President. **E-mail address:** bobross7@ix.netcom.com. **Description:** An executive search firm operating on both retainer and contingency bases. **Specializes in the areas of:** Computer Operations; Software Quality Assurance. **Positions commonly filled include:** Computer Operator; Computer Programmer. **Other U.S. locations:** Nationwide. **Average salary range of placements:** More than $50,000. **Number of placements per year:** 200 - 499.

ROTH YOUNG OF LONG ISLAND
P.O. Box 7365, Hicksville NY 11801-7365. 516/822-6000. **Fax:** 516/822-6018. **Contact:** George T. Jung, President. **Description:** An executive search firm. **Specializes in the areas of:** Accounting/Auditing; Finance; Food; Hotel/Restaurant; Human Resources; Retail; Sales. **Positions commonly filled include:** Accountant/Auditor; Bank Officer/Manager; Buyer; Computer Programmer; Credit Manager; Dietician/Nutritionist; Financial Analyst; Food Scientist/Technologist; Health Services Manager; Human Resources Manager; Manufacturer's/Wholesaler's Sales Rep.; Occupational Therapist; Physical Therapist; Registered Nurse; Restaurant/Food Service Manager; Science Technologist; Store Manager; Systems Analyst. **Number of placements per year:** 200 - 499.

RUSSELL REYNOLDS ASSOCIATES, INC.
200 Park Avenue, 23rd Floor, New York NY 10166. 212/351-2000. **Fax:** 212/370-0896. **Contact:** Manager. **Description:** A generalist executive search firm.

SDC COMPUTER SERVICES
290 Elwood Davis Road, Suite 106, Liverpool NY 13088. 315/457-6560. **Fax:** 315/451-5243. **Contact:** Manager. **Description:** An executive search firm that focuses on placing computer programmers and analysts. **Specializes in the areas of:** Computer Science/Software.

S.W. MANAGEMENT
170 Broadway, Suite 608, New York NY 10038. 212/962-6310. **Fax:** 212/962-7733. **Contact:** Shirley Whelan, President. **Description:** An executive search firm. **Specializes in the areas of:** Accounting/Auditing; Administration; Banking; Economics; Finance; Insurance; Legal; Personnel/Labor Relations; Secretarial. **Positions commonly filled include:** Accountant/Auditor; Administrative Assistant; Assistant Manager; Bank Officer/Manager; Branch Manager; Budget Analyst; Claim Representative; Clerical Supervisor; Computer Programmer; Credit Manager; Customer Service Representative; Financial Analyst; Human Resources Manager; Insurance Agent/Broker; Librarian; Management Trainee; MIS Specialist; Operations Manager; Purchasing Agent/Manager; Secretary; Systems Analyst; Typist/Word Processor; Underwriter/Assistant Underwriter. **Number of placements per year:** 200 - 499.

SALEM ASSOCIATES
292 Madison Avenue, 17th Floor, New York NY 10017. 212/213-2600. **Fax:** 212/213-2728. **Contact:** Joseph Skaff, President. **Description:** An executive search firm. **Specializes in the areas of:** Advertising; Banking; Finance; Internet Marketing; Pharmaceuticals; Sales. **Corporate headquarters location:** This Location. **Other U.S. locations:** Wayne NJ.

SALES CAREERS
P.O. Box 1075, One Wolfs Lane, Pelham NY 10803. 914/632-8800. **Fax:** 914/632-9355. **Contact:** John Donahoe, President. **Description:** An executive search firm operating on a contingency basis. **Specializes in the areas of:** Sales. **Positions commonly filled include:** Sales Manager; Sales Representative. **Average salary range of placements:** More than $50,000. **Number of placements per year:** 100 - 199.

SALES CONSULTANTS OF WESTCHESTER
11 Twin Lakes Road, South Salem NY 10590. 914/592-1290. **Contact:** Bob Penney, Manager. **Description:** An executive search firm. **Specializes in the areas of:** Communications; Computer Science/Software; Food; General Management; Health/Medical; Publishing; Sales; Telecommunications. **Positions commonly filled include:** Marketing Manager; Sales Engineer; Sales Executive; Sales Manager; Sales Representative; Telecommunications Manager. **Average salary range of placements:** More than $50,000. **Number of placements per year:** 100 - 199.

SALES RECRUITERS INTERNATIONAL LTD.
660 White Plains Road, 5th Floor, Tarrytown NY 10591. 914/631-0090. **Fax:** 914/631-1089. **Contact:** Richard J. Harris, President. **Description:** An executive search firm. Client company pays fee. **Specializes in the areas of:** Marketing; Sales. **Positions commonly filled include:** Account Manager; Account Representative; Administrative Assistant; Customer Service Representative; Financial Analyst; Marketing Manager; Sales Executive; Sales Manager; Sales Representative; Secretary. **Corporate headquarters location:** This Location. **Other U.S. locations:** Nationwide. **Average**

salary range of placements: $30,000 - $100,000.
Number of placements per year: 100 - 199.

SALES SEARCH, LTD.
EXECUTIVE RESUME SERVICE
48 Burd Street, Suite 202, Nyack NY 10960. 914/353-2040. **Fax:** 914/353-2633. **Contact:** John Ratcliff, CPC, President. **Description:** An executive search firm. Executive Resume Service (also at this location) provides resume writing services. **Specializes in the areas of:** Engineering; Industrial; Light Industrial; Marketing; Sales; Scientific; Technical. **Positions commonly filled include:** Account Manager; Account Representative; Applications Engineer; Branch Manager; Chemical Engineer; Customer Service Representative; Electrical/Electronics Engineer; Management Trainee; Marketing Manager; Metallurgical Engineer; Sales Engineer; Sales Executive; Sales Manager; Sales Representative. **Average salary range of placements:** $30,000 - $50,000. **Number of placements per year:** 1 - 49.

SEARCH MASTERS INC.
60 East 42nd Street, Suite 453, New York NY 10165. 212/867-9494. **Contact:** Manager. **Description:** An executive search firm. **Specializes in the areas of:** Accounting/Auditing.

SEARCHAMERICA INC.
86 Kathleen Drive, Syosset NY 11791. 516/921-3120. **Contact:** Jonathan S. Messer, Chairman and CEO. **Description:** An executive search firm operating on both retainer and contingency bases. SearchAmerica also provides some contract placements and career counseling. Client company pays fee. **Specializes in the areas of:** Accounting; Administration; Advertising; Banking; Broadcasting; Computer Science/Software; Economics; Engineering; Finance; General Management; Government; Industrial; Information Systems; Information Technology; Insurance; Legal; Marketing; MIS/EDP; Personnel/Labor Relations; Sales. **Positions commonly filled include:** Account Manager; Account Representative; Accountant; Administrative Assistant; Administrative Manager; Advertising Executive; Applications Engineer; Architect; AS400 Programmer Analyst; Assistant Manager; Attorney; Auditor; Bank Officer/Manager; Branch Manager; Broker; Budget Analyst; Chief Financial Officer; Computer Animator; Computer Engineer; Computer Programmer; Computer Scientist; Content Developer; Controller; Customer Service Representative; Database Administrator; Database Manager; Design Engineer; Economist; Editor; Electrical/Electronics Engineer; Finance Director; Financial Analyst; Financial Consultant; Fund Manager; General Manager; Human Resources Manager; Industrial Engineer; Insurance Agent/Broker; Internet Services Manager; Management Analyst/Consultant; Managing Editor; Manufacturing Engineer; Market Research Analyst; Marketing Manager; Marketing Specialist; Mechanical Engineer; MIS Specialist; Multimedia Designer; Network/Systems Administrator; Operations Manager; Paralegal; Physician; Production Manager; Public Relations Specialist; Quality Assurance Engineer; Radio/TV Announcer/Broadcaster; Reporter; Sales Engineer; Sales Executive; Sales Manager; Sales Representative; Securities Sales Representative; Software Engineer; SQL Programmer; Strategic Relations Manager; Systems Analyst; Systems Manager; Technical Writer/Editor; Telecommunications Manager; Underwriter/Assistant Underwriter; Vice President of Finance. **Corporate headquarters location:** This Location. **Other U.S. locations:** San Francisco CA; Washington DC. **International locations:** London. **Average salary range of placements:** More than $50,000. **Number of placements per year:** 50 - 99.

SETFORD-SHAW-NAJARIAN ASSOCIATES
115 Broadway, 20th Floor, New York NY 10006. 212/962-1500. **Fax:** 212/962-1543. **Contact:** Consultant. **World Wide Web address:** http://www.tisny.com/current/consult/frm_consult_frm.html. **Description:** An executive search firm. **Specializes in the areas of:** Data Processing; Information Systems. **Positions commonly filled include:** Bank Officer/Manager; Computer Programmer; Financial Analyst; Software Engineer; Systems Analyst. **Number of placements per year:** 200 - 499.

SHARP PLACEMENT PROFESSIONALS
55 Post Avenue, Suite 202, Westbury NY 11590. 516/876-9222. **Fax:** 516/876-9080. **Contact:** Donald Levine, CPC/President. **E-mail address:** don@sharpsearch.com. **World Wide Web address:** http://www.sharpsearch.com. **Description:** An executive search firm. **Specializes in the areas of:** Computer Science/Software; Engineering; Personnel/Labor Relations; Sales; Technical. **Positions commonly filled include:** Account Manager; Account Representative; Chief Financial Officer; Computer Programmer; Construction Contractor; Database Manager; Design Engineer; Financial Consultant; General Manager; Human Resources Manager; Internet Services Manager; Management Analyst/Consultant; Manufacturing Engineer; Marketing Manager; Multimedia Designer; Online Content Specialist; Operations Manager; Project Manager; Public Relations Specialist; Sales Engineer; Sales Executive; Sales Representative; Software Engineer; Systems Analyst; Systems Manager; Telecommunications Manager; Webmaster. **Benefits available to temporary workers:** Medical Insurance. **Corporate headquarters location:** This Location. **Other U.S. locations:** Nationwide. **Average salary range of placements:** More than $50,000. **Number of placements per year:** 1 - 49.

SILICON ALLEY CONNECTIONS, L.L.C.
90 John Street, Suite 312, New York NY 10038. 212/328-3011. **Fax:** 201/328-3017. **Contact:** Alex Santic, Co-founder/Executive Manager. **E-mail address:** info@salley.com. **World Wide Web address:** http://www.salley.com. **Description:** An executive search firm. Founded in 1994. **Specializes in the areas of:** New Media.

MARINA SIRRAS & ASSOCIATES
420 Lexington Avenue, Suite 2545, New York NY 10170. 212/490-0333. **Fax:** 212/490-2074. **Contact:** Marina Sirras, Principal. **Description:** An executive search firm. **Specializes in the areas of:** Legal. **Positions commonly filled include:** Attorney; Paralegal.

SMYTH ASSOCIATES
630 Third Avenue, 15th Floor, New York NY 10017. 212/682-9300. **Contact:** Manager. **Description:** An executive search firm. **Specializes in the areas of:** Finance.

MITCHELL SPITZ EXECUTIVE SEARCH
575 Lexington Avenue, Suite 410, New York NY 10022. 212/572-8300. **Contact:** Manager. **Description:** An executive search firm that focuses on the placement of investment bankers.

TOBY SPITZ ASSOCIATES INC.
110 East 59th Street, 29th Floor, New York NY 10022. 212/909-0480. **Fax:** 212/909-0479. **Contact:** Manager. **Description:** An executive search firm. **Specializes in the areas of:** Legal.

SPORN GROUP INC.
11 Broadway, Suite 854, New York NY 10004. 212/344-5050. **Contact:** David Sporn, President. **Description:** An executive search firm. **Specializes in the areas of:** Accounting/Auditing; Finance; Legal; Personnel/Labor Relations; Sales. **Positions commonly filled include:** Accountant/Auditor; Attorney; Computer Programmer; Financial Analyst; Human Resources Manager; Management Analyst/Consultant; Systems Analyst. **Number of placements per year:** 50 - 99.

SPRING ASSOCIATES, INC.
10 East 23rd Street, New York NY 10010. 212/473-0013. **Fax:** 212/477-JOBS. **Contact:** Dennis Spring, President. **E-mail address:** thehiringline@msn.com.

World Wide Web address: http://www. springassociates.com. **Description:** An executive search firm operating on both retainer and contingency bases. Spring Associates also provides some temporary and contract placements. Client company pays fee. **Specializes in the areas of:** High-Tech; Marketing; Public Relations. **Positions commonly filled include:** Applications Engineer; AS400 Programmer Analyst; Computer Animator; Computer Engineer; Computer Operator; Computer Programmer; Computer Scientist; Computer Support Technician; Computer Technician; Content Developer; Database Administrator; Database Manager; Internet Services Manager; MIS Specialist; Multimedia Designer; Network/Systems Administrator; Public Relations Specialist; Software Engineer; SQL Programmer; Systems Analyst; Systems Manager; Webmaster. **Average salary range of placements:** $30,000 - $100,000+. **Number of placements per year:** 100 - 199.

STAFFING SERVICES
660 White Plains Road, Suite 400, Tarrytown NY 10591. 914/332-6660. **Fax:** 914/332-5178. **Contact:** Debra Pohl, Professional Recruiter. **Description:** An executive search firm operating on both retainer and contingency bases. **Specializes in the areas of:** Banking; Finance; General Management; Legal; Manufacturing; Personnel/Labor Relations; Pharmaceuticals; Real Estate; Sales. **Positions commonly filled include:** Accountant/Auditor; Actuary; Administrative Manager; Bank Officer/Manager; Biological Scientist; Budget Analyst; Chemist; Computer Programmer; Construction and Building Inspector; Construction Contractor; Cost Estimator; Credit Manager; Customer Service Representative; Financial Analyst; General Manager; Human Resources Manager; Market Research Analyst; MIS Specialist; Paralegal; Pharmacist; Property and Real Estate Manager; Public Relations Specialist; Quality Assurance Engineer; Systems Analyst; Technical Writer/Editor; Underwriter/Assistant Underwriter. **Corporate headquarters location:** Millburn NJ. **Number of placements per year:** 50 - 99.

STRATEGIC RECRUITING
450 Seventh Avenue, Suite 2102, New York NY 10123. 212/465-8300. **Contact:** Manager. **E-mail address:** stratrecru@aol.com. **Description:** An executive search firm operating on a contingency basis. **Specializes in the areas of:** Administration; Computer Science/Software; Information Technology; Public Relations; Secretarial. **Positions commonly filled include:** Administrative Assistant; Chief Financial Officer; Controller; Human Resources Manager; MIS Specialist; Public Relations Specialist; Secretary; Systems Analyst. **Corporate headquarters location:** Binghampton NY. **Average salary range of placements:** $30,000 - $50,000. **Number of placements per year:** 200 - 499.

STRATFORDGROUP
350 Park Avenue, 22nd Floor, New York NY 10022. 212/319-3810. **Toll-free phone:** 800/536-4384. **Fax:** 212/753-2086. **Contact:** Recruiter. **E-mail address:** corriemates@stratfordgroup.com. **World Wide Web address:** http://www.stratfordgroup.com. **Description:** An executive search firm operating on a retainer basis. Founded in 1997. **Specializes in the areas of:** Automotive; Consumer Products; Engineering; Entertainment; Finance; Health/Medical; Human Resources; Information Technology; Manufacturing; Nonprofit; Professional; Retail; Telecommunications; Transportation. **Corporate headquarters location:** Cleveland OH. **Other U.S. locations:** San Francisco CA; San Diego CA; Denver CO; Washington DC; Charlotte NC; Research Triangle Park NC; Cleveland OH; Dayton OH; Toledo OH; Philadelphia PA; Houston TX; Vienna VA; Bellevue WA.

SULLIVAN & COMPANY
40 Wall Street, New York NY 10005. 212/699-3000. **Fax:** 212/699-3100. **Contact:** Manager. **World Wide Web address:** http://www.sullivanco.com. **Description:** An executive search firm. Founded in 1988. **Specializes**

in the areas of: Finance; Insurance. **Positions commonly filled include:** Chief Executive Officer; Chief Financial Officer; General Manager; Investment Manager; Management; Senior Management; Trader. **Parent company:** Heidrick & Struggles.

SUNNY BATES ASSOCIATES
104 West 27th Street, Suite 11C, New York NY 10001. 212/691-5252. **Fax:** 212/691-3133. **Contact:** Sunny Bates, President. **E-mail address:** info@ sunnybates.com. **World Wide Web address:** http://www.sunnybates.com. **Description:** An executive search firm. **Specializes in the areas of:** Broadcasting; New Media; Printing.

SUTTON STAFFING
170 Broadway, Suite 201, New York NY 10038. 212/566-3800. **Fax:** 212/566-3504. **Contact:** Recruiter. **E-mail address:** inquiries@suttonstaffing.com. **World Wide Web address:** http://www.suttonstaffing.com. **Description:** An executive search firm. **Specializes in the areas of:** Finance; Technical.

SYNERGY PARTNERS INC.
275 Madison Avenue, 21st Floor, New York NY 10016. 212/922-2800. **Fax:** 212/922-2807. **Contact:** Marcy Becker, Principal. **E-mail address:** synergypart@ msn.com. **Description:** An executive search firm operating on a contingency basis. **Specializes in the areas of:** Accounting/Auditing; Banking; Finance. **Positions commonly filled include:** Accountant/Auditor; Budget Analyst; Financial Analyst. **Average salary range of placements:** More than $50,000. **Number of placements per year:** 100 - 199.

TMP WORLDWIDE
200 Park Avenue, Suite 3100, New York NY 10016. 212/953-7900. **Fax:** 212/953-7907. **Contact:** Roderick C. Gow, Executive Vice President/Managing Partner. **World Wide Web address:** http://www.tmpw.com. **Description:** An executive search firm. **Specializes in the areas of:** Biotechnology; Consumer Products; Finance; Health/Medical; Industrial; Pharmaceuticals; Technical. **Corporate headquarters location:** This Location. **Other U.S. locations:** Nationwide.

TAYLOR JORDAN ASSOCIATES, INC.
108-18 Queens Boulevard, Forest Hills NY 11375. 718/793-4400. **Contact:** Manager. **Description:** An executive search firm operating on a contingency basis. **Specializes in the areas of:** Accounting/Auditing; Computer Science/Software; General Management; Manufacturing. **Positions commonly filled include:** Accountant/Auditor; Human Resources Manager; Industrial Engineer; Industrial Production Manager; MIS Specialist; Operations/Production Manager. **Average salary range of placements:** More than $50,000.

TAYLOR SEARCH ASSOCIATES
550 Cross Keys Office Park, Fairport NY 14450. 716/425-4500. **Contact:** Manager. **Description:** An executive search firm. **Specializes in the areas of:** Sales.

TECH OPTIONS, INC.
P.O. Box 386, Lenox Hill Station NY 10021. 212/988-3067. **Contact:** Stacy Goldin, President. **Description:** An executive search firm focusing on the placement of client/server and computer systems experts. **Specializes in the areas of:** Computer Science/Software; Finance. **Positions commonly filled include:** Computer Programmer; MIS Specialist; Software Engineer; Systems Analyst. **Average salary range of placements:** More than $50,000. **Number of placements per year:** 1 - 49.

TECHNO-TRAC SYSTEMS, INC.
251 Central Park West, New York NY 10024. 212/769-TRAC. **Fax:** 212/873-1596. **Contact:** Mort Trachtenberg, President. **E-mail address:** technomt@bigfoot.com. **Description:** An executive search firm. **Specializes in the areas of:** Administration; Banking; Computer Science/Software; Finance;

Information Technology; Research and Development. **Positions commonly filled include:** Budget Analyst; Computer Operator; Computer Programmer; Database Manager; Financial Analyst; Management Analyst/Consultant; MIS Specialist; Software Engineer; Systems Analyst; Systems Manager. **Average salary range of placements:** More than $50,000. **Number of placements per year:** 1 - 49.

TELEMANAGEMENT SEARCH
114 East 32nd Street, New York NY 10016. 212/213-1818. **Contact:** Manager. **Description:** An executive search firm. **Specializes in the areas of:** Customer Service; Telemarketing.

PHILLIP THOMAS PERSONNEL, INC.
535 Fifth Avenue, Suite 606, New York NY 10017. 212/867-0860. **Fax:** 212/490-0315. **Contact:** Tina Carberry, President. **Description:** An executive search firm operating on a contingency basis. **Specializes in the areas of:** Accounting/Auditing; Banking; Finance. **Positions commonly filled include:** Accountant/Auditor; Administrative Assistant; Human Resources Specialist; MIS Specialist; Portfolio Securities Specialist; Securities Sales Representative. **Average salary range of placements:** $30,000 - $50,000. **Number of placements per year:** 50 - 99.

THORSEN ASSOCIATES, INC.
2020 Grand Avenue, Baldwin NY 11510. 516/868-6500. **Fax:** 516/868-7842. **Contact:** Peter T. Thorsen, President. **E-mail address:** thorsen@concentric.net. **Description:** An executive search firm. **Specializes in the areas of:** Engineering; Industrial; Manufacturing. **Positions commonly filled include:** Blue-Collar Worker Supervisor; Chemical Engineer; Chemist; Design Engineer; Draftsperson; Electrical/Electronics Engineer; Industrial Engineer; Industrial Production Manager; Materials Engineer; Mechanical Engineer; Operations/Production Manager; Purchasing Agent/Manager; Quality Control Supervisor; Stationary Engineer. **Average salary range of placements:** More than $50,000. **Number of placements per year:** 1 - 49.

TODD ARRO, INC.
P.O. Box 172, Kenmore NY 14217-0172. 716/871-0993. **Contact:** Joseph Todaro, President. **Description:** An executive search firm operating on a contingency basis. **Specializes in the areas of:** Engineering; Health/Medical; Industrial; Sales. **Positions commonly filled include:** Chemical Engineer; Electrical/Electronics Engineer; Manufacturer's/Wholesaler's Sales Rep.; Mechanical Engineer; Sales Executive; Sales Manager; Services Sales Representative. **Number of placements per year:** 1 - 49.

TOTAL COMPUTER PEOPLE INC.
70-40 137th Street, Kew Gardens Hills NY 11367. 718/268-7126. **Fax:** 718/263-1259. **Contact:** Manager. **E-mail address:** info@tcpcorp.com. **World Wide Web address:** http://www.tcpcorp.com. **Description:** An executive search firm. **Specializes in the areas of:** Computer Programming; Web Development.

TREBOR, WELDON, LAWRENCE, LEVINE
355 Lexington Avenue, 11th Floor, New York NY 10017. 212/867-0066. **Fax:** 212/867-2784. **Contact:** Lawrence Levine, Partner. **Description:** An executive search firm providing placements in marketing services, marketing research, and promotional marketing disciplines. The firm operates on a retainer basis. **Specializes in the areas of:** Advertising; Food; Sales. **Positions commonly filled include:** Marketing Manager. **Average salary range of placements:** More than $70,000.

KAREN TRIPI ASSOCIATES
60 East 42nd Street, Suite 2140, New York NY 10165. 212/972-5258. **Contact:** Manager. **Description:** An executive search firm. **Specializes in the areas of:** Direct Marketing.

TYLER SEARCH CONSULTANTS
42 West 38th Street, Suite 1200, New York NY 10018. 212/719-2200. **Fax:** 212/719-2898. **Contact:** William P. Conroy, President. **E-mail address:** tylersc@ibm.net. **Description:** An executive search firm. **Specializes in the areas of:** Banking; Brokerage; Communications; Finance; Import/Export; Transportation. **Positions commonly filled include:** Account Manager; Branch Manager; Controller; Credit Analyst; Credit Manager; Financial Analyst; Logistics Manager; Marketing Specialist; Operations/Production Manager; Project Manager; Sales Manager; Systems Specialist; Vice President.

VENTURE RESOURCES
11 Penn Plaza, Suite 1009, New York NY 10001. 212/273-7700. **Fax:** 212/273-7777. **Contact:** Corry Prohens, President. **World Wide Web address:** http://www.venre.com. **Description:** An executive search firm operating on both retainer and contingency bases. **Specializes in the areas of:** Banking; Computer Science/Software; Finance; MIS/EDP; Technical. **Positions commonly filled include:** Computer Operator; Computer Programmer; Database Manager; Financial Analyst; Internet Services Manager; MIS Specialist; Online Content Specialist; Operations Manager; Production Manager; Project Manager; Systems Analyst; Systems Manager. **Average salary range of placements:** More than $50,000. **Number of placements per year:** 100 - 199.

VINTAGE RESOURCES, INC.
11 East 44th Street, Suite 708, New York NY 10017. 212/867-1001. **Fax:** 212/490-9277. **Contact:** Perry Fishman, Vice President. **Description:** An executive search firm operating on a contingency basis. **Specializes in the areas of:** Advertising; Direct Marketing; Marketing; Sales. **Positions commonly filled include:** Account Manager; Advertising Clerk; Advertising Executive; Database Manager; Marketing Manager; Marketing Specialist; Production Manager. **Average salary range of placements:** $30,000 - $50,000. **Number of placements per year:** 200 - 499.

WALLACE LAW REGISTRY
11 East 44th Street, 3rd Floor, New York NY 10017. 212/972-3500. **Fax:** 212/972-3519. **Contact:** Placement Director. **Description:** An executive search firm operating on a contingency basis. The firm also provides some temporary placements in law firms. **Specializes in the areas of:** Legal. **Positions commonly filled include:** Attorney. **Other U.S. locations:** Nationwide. **Average salary range of placements:** More than $50,000. **Number of placements per year:** 500 - 999.

ROBERT WALTERS
1500 Broadway, Suite 1801, New York NY 10036. 212/704-9900. **Fax:** 212/704-4312. **Contact:** Manager. **World Wide Web address:** http://www.robertwalters.com. **Description:** An executive search firm. **Specializes in the areas of:** Quantitative Marketing; Risk Management.

CHARLES WANNER ASSOCIATES LTD.
60 East 42nd Street, Room 1401, New York NY 10165-1401. 212/557-2000. **Contact:** Manager. **Description:** Charles Wanner Associates is an executive search firm operating on both retainer and contingency bases. **Specializes in the areas of:** Accounting/Auditing; Administration; Banking; Finance; General Management; Legal; Technical. **Positions commonly filled include:** Accountant/Auditor; Bank Officer/Manager; Computer Programmer; Credit Manager; Financial Analyst; Human Resources Specialist; Librarian; Management Analyst/Consultant; MIS Specialist; Paralegal; Systems Analyst. **Average salary range of placements:** More than $50,000. **Number of placements per year:** 50 - 99.

WAYNE GROUP LTD.
84 Williams Street, New York NY 10038. 212/668-1414.
Contact: Manager. **Description:** An executive search firm. **Specializes in the areas of:** Technical.

WEBER MANAGEMENT CONSULTANTS
205 East Main Street, Suite 2-3A, Huntington NY 11743.
516/673-4700. **Fax:** 516/673-4885. **Contact:** Ronald Weber, President. **Description:** An executive search firm. **Specializes in the areas of:** Administration; Engineering; Food; General Management; Industrial; Manufacturing; Marketing; Personnel/Labor Relations; Sales. **Positions commonly filled include:** General Manager; Human Resources Manager; Industrial Production Manager; Management Analyst/Consultant; Purchasing Agent/Manager. **Number of placements per year:** 50 - 99.

WEHN ASSOCIATES, INC.
321 West 13th Street, Suite 1A, New York NY 10014.
212/675-3224. **Fax:** 212/633-2682. **Contact:** Manager.
Description: An executive search firm. **Specializes in the areas of:** Administration; Computer Science/Software. **Positions commonly filled include:** Architect; Computer Programmer; Designer; Software Engineer; Systems Analyst; Technical Writer/Editor. **Number of placements per year:** 50 - 99.

WERBIN ASSOCIATES EXECUTIVE SEARCH, INC.
140 Riverside Drive, Suite 10N, New York NY 10024.
212/799-6111. **Contact:** Susan Werbin, President.
Description: An executive search firm. Werbin Associates focuses on placing data processing professionals in both technical and managerial positions. The firm also places quantitative researchers and analysts for investment modeling, decision systems, and market research. Founded in 1978. **Specializes in the areas of:** Accounting/Auditing; Administration; Advertising; Banking; Computer Science/Software; Economics; Finance; Insurance; Manufacturing. **Positions commonly filled include:** Computer Programmer; Economist; Electrical/Electronics Engineer; Financial Analyst; Management Analyst/Consultant; Mathematician; Physicist; Researcher; Science Technologist; Software Engineer; Statistician; Systems Analyst; Technical Writer/Editor. **Average salary range of placements:** More than $50,000. **Number of placements per year:** 1 - 49.

WERT & COMPANY
222 Fifth Avenue, 5th Floor, New York NY 10001.
212/684-2796. **Contact:** Recruiter. **World Wide Web address:** http://www.wertco.com. **Description:** An executive search firm.

WESTFIELD ASSOCIATES, INC.
One North Broadway, White Plains NY 10601. 914/761-4333. **Fax:** 914/761-4341. **Contact:** Manager.
Description: An executive search firm. **Specializes in the areas of:** Accounting/Auditing; Personnel/Labor Relations; Secretarial. **Positions commonly filled include:** Accountant/Auditor; Credit Manager; Customer Service Rep.; Human Resources Manager; Paralegal; Purchasing Agent; Systems Analyst; Transportation Specialist. **Number of placements per year:** 100 - 199.

WINSTON STAFFING SERVICES
1400 Old Country Road, Westbury NY 11590. 516/333-3222. **Fax:** 516/333-5099. **Contact:** Manager.
Description: An executive search firm. **Specializes in the areas of:** Accounting/Auditing; Administration; Banking; Computer Science/Software; Fashion; Finance; General Management; Health/Medical; Legal; Marketing; MIS/EDP; Office Support; Personnel/Labor Relations. **Positions commonly filled include:** Accountant/Auditor; Advertising Clerk; Bank Officer/Manager; Brokerage Clerk; Budget Analyst; Claim Representative; Clerical Supervisor; Clinical Lab Technician; Computer Programmer; Customer Service Representative; Dietician/Nutritionist; EEG Technologist; EKG Technician; Financial Analyst; Health Services Manager; Human Resources Specialist; Internet Services Manager; Licensed Practical Nurse; Management Analyst/Consultant; Management Trainee; MIS Specialist; Nuclear Medicine Technologist; Occupational Therapist; Pharmacist; Radiological Technologist; Registered Nurse; Respiratory Therapist; Speech-Language Pathologist; Systems Analyst; Telecommunications Manager. **Corporate headquarters location:** New York NY. **Average salary range of placements:** $30,000 - $50,000. **Number of placements per year:** 200 - 499.

WITT/KIEFFER, FORD, HADELMAN & LLOYD
3 Park Avenue, 29th Floor, New York NY 10016.
212/686-2676. **Fax:** 212/686-2527. **Contact:** Manager.
World Wide Web address: http://www.wittkieffer.com.
Description: An executive search firm. **Specializes in the areas of:** Health/Medical. **Other U.S. locations:** Nationwide.

S.R. WOLMAN ASSOCIATES, INC.
133 East 35th Street, New York NY 10016. 212/685-2692. **Fax:** 212/889-4379. **Contact:** Steve Wolman, President. **Description:** An executive search firm operating on a retainer basis. **Specializes in the areas of:** Advertising; Art/Design; Fashion; Finance; General Management; Marketing; Personnel/Labor Relations; Retail; Sales. **Positions commonly filled include:** Account Manager; Account Representative; Accountant/Auditor; Advertising Clerk; Budget Analyst; Chemist; Chief Financial Officer; Finance Director; Financial Analyst; General Manager; Graphic Artist; Human Resources Manager; Market Research Analyst; Marketing Manager; Marketing Specialist; Production Manager; Public Relations Manager; Purchasing Agent/Manager; Quality Control Supervisor; Sales Executive; Sales Manager; Sales Representative. **Average salary range of placements:** More than $50,000. **Number of placements per year:** 50 - 99.

MICHAEL D. ZINN & ASSOCIATES, INC.
1120 Avenue of the Americas, 4th Floor, New York NY 10036. 212/391-0070. **Contact:** Manager. **World Wide Web address:** http://www.zinnassociates.com.
Description: An executive search firm. **Specializes in the areas of:** Consumer Package Goods; Finance; Health/Medical; Industrial; Management; Pharmaceuticals; Technical. **Other U.S. locations:** Princeton NJ.

PERMANENT EMPLOYMENT AGENCIES

AARP FOUNDATION
SENIOR EMPLOYMENT PROGRAM
331 Main Mall, Suite 103, Poughkeepsie NY 12601.
914/485-8030. **Fax:** 914/485-8031. **Contact:** Joseph F. Dirac, Project Director. **Description:** A permanent employment agency. **Specializes in the areas of:** Education; Food; Industrial; Personnel/Labor Relations; Secretarial. **Positions commonly filled include:** Accountant/Auditor; Administrative Manager; Clerical Supervisor; Library Technician; Teacher/Professor.
Number of placements per year: 1 - 49.

ACCOUNTING & COMPUTER PERSONNEL
200 Salina Meadows Parkway, Suite 180, Syracuse NY 13212. 315/457-8000. **Fax:** 315/457-0029. **Contact:** William E. Winnewisser, President. **E-mail address:** wew@a-c-p.com. **World Wide Web address:** http://www.a-c-p.com. **Description:** A permanent employment agency that also offers some contract services. **Specializes in the areas of:** Accounting/Auditing; Administration; Advertising; Architecture/Construction; Art/Design; Banking; Biology; Broadcasting; Computer Science/Software;

Economics; Engineering; Finance; Food; General Management; Health/Medical; Industrial; Insurance; Legal; Manufacturing; Nonprofit; Personnel/Labor Relations; Publishing; Retail; Sales; Technical. **Positions commonly filled include:** Account Manager; Accountant/Auditor; Bank Officer/Manager; Budget Analyst; Computer Programmer; Controller; Cost Estimator; Credit Manager; Financial Analyst; Project Manager; Software Engineer; Systems Analyst; Technical Writer/Editor; Vice President. **Number of placements per year:** 50 - 99.

ACCREDITED CARE, INC.
106 West Third Street, Suite 707, Jamestown NY 14701. 716/484-7101. **Contact:** Lisa Crandall, Placement Director. **Description:** A permanent employment agency. Client company pays fee. **Positions commonly filled include:** Administrative Assistant; Administrative Manager; Assistant Manager; Blue-Collar Worker Supervisor; Branch Manager; Certified Nurses Aide; Certified Occupational Therapy Assistant; Claim Representative; Clerical Supervisor; Counselor; Customer Service Representative; Dietician/Nutritionist; Home Health Aide; Human Resources Manager; Licensed Practical Nurse; Management Trainee; Medical Assistant; Nurse Practitioner; Occupational Therapist; Physical Therapist; Physical Therapy Assistant; Registered Nurse; Respiratory Therapist; Secretary; Social Worker; Speech-Language Pathologist. **Average salary range of placements:** $20,000 - $29,999. **Number of placements per year:** 50 - 99.

ADAM PERSONNEL, INC.
11 East 44th Street, New York NY 10017. 212/557-9150. **Fax:** 212/557-9348. **Contact:** Jill Barry, Vice President. **Description:** A permanent employment agency that also provides some temporary placements. **Specializes in the areas of:** Accounting/Auditing; Banking; Fashion; Legal; Nonprofit; Secretarial. **Positions commonly filled include:** Administrative Assistant; Clerical Supervisor; Controller; Credit Manager; Customer Service Representative; Editorial Assistant; Financial Analyst; Management Trainee; Secretary. **Corporate headquarters location:** This Location. **Average salary range of placements:** $20,000 - $29,999. **Number of placements per year:** 200 - 499.

ALL HOME SERVICES AGENCY, LTD.
2121 Broadway, New York NY 10023. 212/799-9360. **Contact:** Ms. Nedra J. Kleinman, President. **Description:** A permanent employment agency. **Specializes in the areas of:** Domestic Help; Eldercare, In-Home; Health/Medical. **Positions commonly filled include:** Chauffeur; Chef/Cook/Kitchen Worker; Housekeeper; Nanny; Nursing Aide. **Number of placements per year:** 200 - 499.

ALLEGHENY TRAVEL SERVICES
6 East 39th Street, New York NY 10016. 212/532-1300x223. **Fax:** 212/779-8344. **Contact:** Gary Seaman, Director. **E-mail address:** travel@alleghenypersonnel. com. **World Wide Web address:** http://www. alleghenytravel.com. **Description:** A permanent employment agency that also offers some temporary placements. **Specializes in the areas of:** Travel.

AMHERST PERSONNEL GROUP, INC.
550 West Old Country Road, Hicksville NY 11801. 516/433-7610. **Fax:** 516/433-7848. **Contact:** Recruiter. **Description:** A permanent employment agency. **Specializes in the areas of:** Retail; Sales.

ANTES ASSOCIATES
80 Ridgeview Drive, Pleasantville NY 10570. 914/773-1400. **Fax:** 914/773-0114. **Contact:** Barbara Antes, President. **Description:** A permanent employment agency. **Specializes in the areas of:** Health/Medical. **Positions commonly filled include:** Dietician/Nutritionist; Pharmacist; Registered Nurse; Social Worker. **Corporate headquarters location:** This Location. **Other U.S. locations:** CT; NJ. **Average salary range of placements:** More than $30,000. **Number of placements per year:** 1 - 49.

APRIL TECHNICAL RECRUITING
P.O. Box 40303, Rochester NY 14604-0803. 716/325-5220. **Fax:** 716/546-4870. **Contact:** Technical Recruiter. **Description:** A permanent employment agency. **Specializes in the areas of:** Administration; Computer Science/Software; Engineering; Manufacturing; Technical. **Positions commonly filled include:** Accountant/Auditor; Chemical Engineer; Civil Engineer; Computer Programmer; Cost Estimator; Design Engineer; Draftsperson; Electrical/Electronics Engineer; Environmental Engineer; Industrial Engineer; Industrial Production Manager; Mechanical Engineer; MIS Specialist; Quality Control Supervisor; Software Engineer; Structural Engineer; Systems Analyst. **Average salary range of placements:** $30,000 - $50,000.

ARROW EMPLOYMENT AGENCY, INC.
150 Route 110, Melville NY 11747. 516/271-3700. **Contact:** Don Becker, President. **Description:** A permanent employment agency that places experienced professionals, technical and skilled industrial personnel, and office support staff. **NOTE:** Applicants should include minimum salary requirements and maximum commuting distances with resumes. **Specializes in the areas of:** Computer Science/Software; Engineering; Industrial; Manufacturing; Secretarial; Technical. **Positions commonly filled include:** Bookkeeper; Chemist; Clerk; Computer Operator; Computer Programmer; Customer Service Representative; Data Entry Clerk; Draftsperson; Factory Worker; Industrial Engineer; Legal Secretary; Manufacturing Engineer; Mechanical Engineer; Medical Secretary; Operations/Production Manager; Quality Control Supervisor; Receptionist; Sales Executive; Secretary; Software Engineer; Systems Analyst; Technician. **Number of placements per year:** 50 - 99.

ARROW EMPLOYMENT AGENCY, INC.
320 North Broadway, Hicksville NY 11801-2910. 516/931-4200. **Fax:** 516/931-4298. **Contact:** Norman Shapp, Operations Manager. **Description:** A permanent employment agency. **Specializes in the areas of:** Industrial; Sales; Technical. **Positions commonly filled include:** Accountant/Auditor; Aerospace Engineer; Biomedical Engineer; Branch Manager; Budget Analyst; Chemical Engineer; Computer Programmer; Editor; Electrical/Electronics Engineer; Geological Engineer; Health Services Manager; Human Resources Manager; Industrial Engineer; Management Analyst/Consultant; Paralegal; Public Relations Specialist; Restaurant/Food Service Manager; Telecommunications Manager. **Average salary range of placements:** $30,000 - $50,000. **Number of placements per year:** 200 - 499.

ASHER PERSONNEL CONSULTANTS
507 Fifth Avenue, 3rd Floor, New York NY 10017-4906. 212/972-5627. **Contact:** David Glickman, President. **Description:** A permanent employment agency. Founded in 1985. **Specializes in the areas of:** Accounting/Auditing; Advertising; Banking; Consumer Package Goods; Cosmetics; Fashion; Finance; Insurance; Legal; Office Support; Personnel/Labor Relations; Retail; Sales; Secretarial. **Positions commonly filled include:** Accountant/Auditor; Administrative Assistant; Advertising Clerk; Budget Analyst; Buyer; Clerical Supervisor; Credit Manager; Financial Analyst; Human Resources Specialist; Paralegal; Typist/Word Processor. **Average salary range of placements:** $30,000 - $60,000.

AUTO CAREERS
P.O. Box 3004, Schenectady NY 12303-3004. 518/356-5090. **Fax:** 518/356-5091. **Contact:** Tom Anderson, President. **Description:** A permanent employment agency. **Specializes in the areas of:** Accounting/Auditing; Automotive; Finance; General Management; Sales; Secretarial; Technical. **Positions commonly filled include:** Automotive Mechanic.

Average salary range of placements: $30,000 - $50,000. Number of placements per year: 100 - 199.

BEAVER PERSONNEL, INC.
265 West 14th Street, Suite 1103, New York NY 10011-7103. 212/243-5540. Fax: 212/243-1266. Contact: John Klein, Manager. Description: A permanent employment agency that also provides some temporary placements. Specializes in the areas of: Graphic Arts; Printing. Positions commonly filled include: Cost Estimator; Customer Service Rep.; Desktop Publishing Specialist; Operations Manager; Press Operator; Purchasing Agent.

BEST DOMESTIC SERVICES AGENCY, INC.
2 West 45th Street, Suite 1000, New York NY 10036. 212/685-0351. Fax: 212/685-2067. Contact: Deborah Dickenson, Manager. Description: A permanent employment agency. Specializes in the areas of: Domestic Help; Nannies. Positions commonly filled include: Housekeeper; Nanny. Number of placements per year: 200 - 499.

BEVAN RESOURCES
50 Main Street, Suite 1000, White Plains NY 10606. 914/682-2060. Fax: 914/682-2194. Contact: Cathy Bevan, President. Description: A permanent employment agency. Client company pays fee. Specializes in the areas of: Accounting; Administration; Finance; Secretarial. Positions commonly filled include: Accountant; Administrative Assistant; Administrative Manager; Clerical Supervisor; Customer Service Representative; Financial Analyst; Human Resources Manager; Paralegal; Secretary. Corporate headquarters location: This Location. Average salary range of placements: $30,000 - $49,999. Number of placements per year: 50 - 99.

BEVLIN PERSONNEL INC.
110 Mamaroneck Avenue, White Plains NY 10601. 914/683-0880. Fax: 914/683-8625. Contact: Beverly Borwick, President. Description: A permanent employment agency with clients ranging from *Fortune* 500 corporations to small firms. Specializes in the areas of: Accounting/Auditing; Administration; Finance; Personnel/Labor Relations; Secretarial. Positions commonly filled include: Accountant; Administrative Assistant; Brokerage Clerk; Clerical Supervisor; Human Resources Manager; Marketing Specialist. Number of placements per year: 200 - 499.

THE BRITISH CONNECTION
120 East 56th Street, Suite 1110, 11th Floor, New York NY 10022-3607. 212/223-2510. Fax: 212/755-3238. Contact: Sally Dwek, President. E-mail address: britishconn@aol.com. Description: A permanent employment agency. Specializes in the areas of: Secretarial. Positions commonly filled include: Administrative Assistant; Receptionist; Secretary. Average salary range of placements: $30,000 - $50,000. Number of placements per year: 50 - 99.

E.E. BROOKE INC.
420 Lexington Avenue, Suite 2560, New York NY 10170-2599. 212/687-8400. Fax: 212/687-0118. Contact: John Kerr, President. Description: A permanent employment agency. Founded in 1923. Specializes in the areas of: Accounting/Auditing; Administration; Finance; General Management; Personnel/Labor Relations; Publishing. Positions commonly filled include: Accountant/Auditor; Budget Analyst; Credit Manager; Customer Service Representative; Editor; Financial Analyst; General Manager; Hotel Manager; Human Resources Manager; Management Trainee; MIS Specialist; Purchasing Agent/Manager; Services Sales Representative; Systems Analyst; Technical Writer/Editor; Transportation/Traffic Specialist; Travel Agent; Typist/Word Processor. Number of placements per year: 500 - 999.

BROOKVILLE STAFFING SERVICES, INC.
555 Broadhollow Road, Suite 102, Melville NY 11747. 516/694-6161. Toll-free phone: 800/474-8465. Fax:

516/694-1388. Contact: President. E-mail address: brookmis@aol.com. World Wide Web address: http://www.brookvillestaffing.com. Description: A permanent employment agency. Specializes in the areas of: Accounting/Auditing; Administration; Computer Science/Software; Finance; Legal; MIS/EDP; Personnel/Labor Relations; Secretarial. Positions commonly filled include: Accountant/Auditor; Administrative Assistant; Budget Analyst; Chief Financial Officer; Controller; Customer Service Representative; Financial Analyst; Human Resources Manager; Management Analyst/Consultant; Software Engineer; Systems Analyst; Systems Manager; Typist/Word Processor. Average salary range of placements: More than $50,000. Number of placements per year: 100 - 199.

CAREER BLAZERS PERSONNEL SERVICE
445 Broadhollow Road, Suite 19, Melville NY 11747. 516/756-2400. Fax: 516/756-2426. Contact: Barbara Gebhardt, President. World Wide Web address: http://www.cblazers.com. Description: A permanent employment agency that also provides some temporary placements. Founded in 1949. Specializes in the areas of: Accounting; Finance; Information Technology; Legal; Marketing; Office Support; Sales; Secretarial. Positions commonly filled include: Administrative Assistant; Customer Service Representative; Database Manager; Graphic Artist; Human Resources Manager; Management Trainee; MIS Specialist; Paralegal; Quality Control Supervisor; Sales Executive; Sales Manager; Sales Representative; Secretary; Software Engineer; Systems Analyst; Systems Manager; Typist/Word Processor. Corporate headquarters location: New York NY. Other U.S. locations: Nationwide. Average salary range of placements: More than $20,000. Number of placements per year: 500 - 999.

CAREER BLAZERS PERSONNEL SERVICE
590 Fifth Avenue, New York NY 10036. 212/719-3232. Contact: Office Manager. World Wide Web address: http://www.cblazers.com. Description: A permanent employment agency. Positions commonly filled include: Accountant/Auditor; Administrative Assistant; Advertising Clerk; Bookkeeper; Clerk; Commercial Artist; Computer Operator; Credit Manager; Customer Service Representative; Data Entry Clerk; Driver; Factory Worker; Human Resources Manager; Legal Secretary; Medical Secretary; Public Relations Specialist; Receptionist; Sales Representative; Stenographer; Technical Writer/Editor. Corporate headquarters location: This Location. Other U.S. locations: Nationwide. Number of placements per year: 1000+.

CAREER BLAZERS PERSONNEL SERVICE
202 Mamaroneck Avenue, White Plains NY 10601. 914/949-1166. Contact: Robert Miller, President. World Wide Web address: http://www.cblazers.com. Description: A permanent employment agency. Specializes in the areas of: Accounting/Auditing; Banking; Finance; Legal; Sales; Secretarial. Positions commonly filled include: Accountant/Auditor; Administrative Assistant; Bookkeeper; Clerk; Credit Manager; Customer Service Representative; Data Entry Clerk; Human Resources Manager; Legal Secretary; Medical Secretary; Receptionist; Sales Representative; Stenographer; Typist/Word Processor. Corporate headquarters location: New York NY. Other U.S. locations: Nationwide. Number of placements per year: 1000+.

CAREER CONCEPTS, INC.
25 West 43rd Street, Suite 708, New York NY 10036. 212/790-2600. Fax: 212/869-5598. Contact: Steven A. Sandler, President. Description: A permanent employment agency. Specializes in the areas of: Accounting/Auditing; Banking; Brokerage; Finance; Personnel/Labor Relations. Positions commonly filled include: Accountant/Auditor; Bank Officer/Manager; Budget Analyst; Chief Financial Officer; Controller; Finance Director; Financial Analyst; Human Resources

Manager; Operations Manager. **Corporate headquarters location:** This Location. **Average salary range of placements:** $30,000 - $50,000. **Number of placements per year:** 200 - 499.

CARLILE PERSONNEL AGENCY INC.
3 Ellinwood Court, Suite 202, New Hartford NY 13413. 315/736-3083. **Fax:** 315/736-5340. **Contact:** Doug Manning, Owner. **Description:** A permanent employment agency. **Specializes in the areas of:** Accounting/Auditing; Administration; Computer Science/Software; Engineering; Finance; Industrial; Manufacturing; Personnel/Labor Relations; Sales; Technical. **Positions commonly filled include:** Accountant/Auditor; Chemical Engineer; Civil Engineer; Computer Programmer; Designer; Draftsperson; Electrical/Electronics Engineer; Human Resources Manager; Industrial Engineer; Industrial Production Manager; Management Analyst/Consultant; Manufacturer's/Wholesaler's Sales Rep.; Mechanical Engineer; Metallurgical Engineer; Operations/Production Manager; Purchasing Agent/Manager; Quality Control Supervisor; Software Engineer; Structural Engineer; Systems Analyst. **Number of placements per year:** 1 - 49.

CONCORDE SEARCH
One North Broadway, Suite 400, White Plains NY 10601. 914/428-0700. **Fax:** 914/428-4865. **Contact:** Richard Greenwald, President. **Description:** A permanent employment agency. **Specializes in the areas of:** Accounting/Auditing; Finance; Personnel/Labor Relations; Sales. **Positions commonly filled include:** Accountant/Auditor; Bank Officer/Manager; Brokerage Clerk; Computer Programmer; Customer Service Representative; Financial Analyst; Mathematician; Securities Sales Representative; Underwriter/Assistant Underwriter.

CROSS STAFFING
150 Broadway, Suite 902, New York NY 10038. 212/227-6705. **Contact:** James Zamparelli, President. **Description:** A permanent employment agency. **Specializes in the areas of:** Banking; Brokerage; Clerical. **Positions commonly filled include:** Administrative Assistant; Bookkeeper; Brokerage Clerk; Data Entry Clerk; Receptionist; Secretary; Stenographer; Typist/Word Processor. **Number of placements per year:** 1000+.

MAGGI DOLAN PLACEMENT, INC.
5360 Genesee Street, P.O. Box 54, Bowmansville NY 14026-1044. 716/683-5360. **Fax:** 716/683-0203. **Contact:** Maggi Dolan, President. **E-mail address:** maggidolan@pcom.net. **World Wide Web address:** http://www.maggidolan.com. **Description:** A permanent employment agency that also provides some temporary placements. **Specializes in the areas of:** Advertising; Art/Design; Health/Medical; Insurance; Legal; Publishing; Secretarial; Technical. **Positions commonly filled include:** Advertising Clerk; Architect; Chemist; Claim Representative; Customer Service Representative; Dental Assistant/Dental Hygienist; Design Engineer; Designer; Draftsperson; Editor; EEG Technologist; EKG Technician; Emergency Medical Technician; Medical Records Technician; Multimedia Designer; Nuclear Medicine Technologist; Paralegal; Physical Therapist; Physician; Public Relations Specialist; Radiological Technologist; Registered Nurse; Surgical Technician; Technical Writer/Editor; Typist/Word Processor; Video Production Coordinator. **Average salary range of placements:** $30,000 - $90,000. **Number of placements per year:** 200 - 499.

EDEN STAFFING
280 Madison Avenue, New York NY 10016. 212/685-8600. **Contact:** Recruiter. **Description:** A permanent employment agency. **Specializes in the areas of:** Accounting/Auditing; Administration; Advertising; Computer Hardware/Software; Fashion; Finance; Food; Health/Medical; Industrial; Legal; Nonprofit; Personnel/Labor Relations; Retail; Secretarial. **Positions**

commonly filled include: Administrative Assistant; Clerk; Computer Operator; Data Entry Clerk; Legal Secretary; Light Industrial Worker; Medical Secretary; Nurse; Receptionist; Secretary; Stenographer; Typist/Word Processor.

EMPLOYMENT RECRUITERS AGENCY
118-21 Queens Boulevard, Suite 609, Forest Hills NY 11375. 718/263-2300. **Fax:** 718/263-9668. **Contact:** Brian Moran, President. **Description:** A permanent employment agency. **Specializes in the areas of:** Accounting/Auditing; Administration; Advertising; Architecture/Construction; Banking; Computer Science/Software; Fashion; Finance; General Management; Health/Medical; Insurance; Legal; Manufacturing; Personnel/Labor Relations; Secretarial. **Positions commonly filled include:** Accountant/Auditor; Administrative Manager; Clerical Supervisor; Credit Manager; Customer Service Representative; Financial Analyst; General Manager; Human Resources Manager; Management Analyst/Consultant; Management Trainee; Paralegal. **Number of placements per year:** 200 - 499.

ES VEE EDP PLACEMENT AGENCY
421 Seventh Avenue, Suite 1006, New York NY 10001. 212/947-7730. **Fax:** 212/629-4192. **Contact:** Steven Vanchel, General Manager. **Description:** A permanent employment agency. **Specializes in the areas of:** Data Processing. **Positions commonly filled include:** Computer Programmer; Software Engineer; Systems Analyst. **Average salary range of placements:** $30,000 - $80,000.

EXECUTIVE CORPORATE STAFFING
295 Madison Avenue, Suite 1830, New York NY 10017. 212/972-0350. **Contact:** Manager. **Description:** A permanent employment agency that also provides some temporary placements.

FILCRO PERSONNEL
342 Madison Avenue, Suite 706, New York NY 10017. 212/599-0909. **Fax:** 212/599-1024. **Contact:** Jana Evans, Manager of Recruitment. **Description:** A permanent employment agency. **Specializes in the areas of:** Communications; Finance; Legal; Secretarial; Word Processing. **Positions commonly filled include:** Administrative Assistant; Paralegal; Secretary; Typist/Word Processor. **Number of placements per year:** 200 - 499.

FINEST EMPLOYMENT AGENCY
50 East 42nd Street, Room 1305, New York NY 10017-5405. **Contact:** Richard Friedman, President. **Description:** A permanent employment agency that focuses on placement of office support personnel, primarily legal and medical. The agency also provides some temporary placements. **Specializes in the areas of:** Health/Medical; Legal; Secretarial. **Positions commonly filled include:** Customer Service Representative; Dental Assistant/Dental Hygienist; Health Services Manager; Legal Secretary; Medical Secretary; Paralegal; Typist/Word Processor. **Average salary range of placements:** $30,000 - $50,000. **Number of placements per year:** 200 - 499.

FRIEDMAN EMPLOYMENT AGENCY, INC.
45 West 34th Street, New York NY 10001. 212/695-4750. **Fax:** 212/239-4942. **Contact:** George Friedman, President. **Description:** A permanent employment agency. **Specializes in the areas of:** Legal; Secretarial. **Positions commonly filled include:** Accountant; Administrative Assistant; Attorney; Computer Operator; Paralegal; Secretary; Typist/Word Processor. **Number of placements per year:** 1000+.

GAMBRILL & ASSOCIATES
SOUND TEMPORARIES
130 North Main Street, Port Chester NY 10573. 914/939-1919. **Toll-free phone:** 800/783-2384. **Contact:** Manager. **Description:** A permanent employment agency. Sound Temporaries (also at this location) provides temporary placements in office support

positions. Founded in 1983. **Corporate headquarters location:** Port Chester NY.

GRAPHICS FOR HIRE, INC.
62 Bowman Avenue, Rye Brook NY 10573-2818. 914/937-9646. **Fax:** 914/937-0558. **Contact:** Patricia Simone, Creative Placement Director. **Description:** A permanent employment agency that focuses on placing experienced computer graphics professionals, designers, copywriters, proofreaders, and creative directors. **Specializes in the areas of:** Advertising; Art/Design; Publishing. **Number of placements per year:** 1 - 49.

GROUP AGENCY, INC.
1427 Coney Island Avenue, Brooklyn NY 11230. 718/258-9202. **Fax:** 718/258-9200. **Contact:** Counselor. **Description:** A permanent employment agency. **Specializes in the areas of:** Light Industrial; Office Support. **Positions commonly filled include:** Accountant/Auditor; Administrative Assistant; Assistant Manager; Blue-Collar Worker Supervisor; Bookkeeper; Clerk; Commercial Artist; Construction Contractor; Credit Manager; Customer Service Representative; Data Entry Clerk; Draftsperson; Driver; Electrician; Factory Worker; Human Resources Manager; Insurance Agent/Broker; Legal Secretary; Medical Secretary; Receptionist; Sales Representative; Secretary; Stenographer; Typist/Word Processor. **Number of placements per year:** 500 - 999.

HAMPSHIRE ASSOCIATES, INC.
71 West 23rd Street, Suite 509, New York NY 10010-4102. 212/924-3999. **Contact:** Charles A. Winston, President. **Description:** A permanent employment agency. Hampshire Associates has client companies in the fields of defense and aerospace, communications, computers, and electro-optics. **Specializes in the areas of:** Electronics; Engineering; Technical. **Positions commonly filled include:** Aerospace Engineer; Biomedical Engineer; Electrical/Electronics Engineer; Industrial Engineer; Manufacturing Engineer; Marketing Specialist; Mechanical Engineer; Software Engineer; Systems Analyst. **Average salary range of placements:** More than $50,000. **Number of placements per year:** 100 - 199.

HARBROWE, INC.
222 Mamaroneck Avenue, White Plains NY 10605. 914/949-6400. **Fax:** 914/949-6924. **Contact:** Valerie Gehn, Vice President. **Description:** A permanent employment agency. **Specializes in the areas of:** Accounting/Auditing; Industrial Sales and Marketing; Medical Sales and Marketing; Office Support; Sales; Secretarial. **Positions commonly filled include:** Accountant; Administrative Assistant; Buyer; Claim Representative; Clerical Supervisor; Computer Operator; Computer Programmer; Controller; Credit Manager; Human Resources Manager; Paralegal; Purchasing Agent/Manager; Sales Engineer; Sales Executive; Sales Manager; Sales Representative; Secretary; Typist/Word Processor; Underwriter/Assistant Underwriter. **Average salary range of placements:** $30,000 - $50,000. **Number of placements per year:** 100 - 199.

HEADWAY CORPORATE STAFFING
317 Madison Avenue, 3rd Floor, New York NY 10017. 212/672-6610. **Fax:** 212/672-6619. **Contact:** Diane Cohen, Executive Vice President. **E-mail address:** joblady@aol.com. **Description:** A permanent employment agency that also provides some temporary placements. Client company pays fee. **Specializes in the areas of:** Accounting; Administration; Finance; Legal; Personnel/Labor Relations; Secretarial. **Positions commonly filled include:** Accountant; Administrative Assistant; Administrative Manager; Advertising Clerk; Auditor; Budget Analyst; Chief Financial Officer; Clerical Supervisor; Customer Service Representative; Desktop Publishing Specialist; Editorial Assistant; Financial Analyst; Human Resources Manager; Paralegal; Typist/Word Processor. **Corporate headquarters location:** This Location. **Average salary**

range of placements: $30,000 - $49,999. **Number of placements per year:** 500 - 999.

HEALTHPRO PLACEMENT SERVICE
33 Park Drive, Putnam Valley NY 10579. 914/528-5300. **Fax:** 914/528-5303. **Contact:** Recruiter. **Description:** A permanent employment agency. **Specializes in the areas of:** Dental; Health/Medical. **Positions commonly filled include:** Dental Assistant/Dental Hygienist; Dental Lab Technician; Dentist; Licensed Practical Nurse; Respiratory Therapist.

HELLER & ASSOCIATES
2 West 45th Street, New York NY 10036. 212/819-1919. **Fax:** 212/819-9196. **Contact:** Charles Heller, President. **World Wide Web address:** http://www.hellerandassociates.com. **Description:** A permanent employment agency. **Specializes in the areas of:** Library Services. **Positions commonly filled include:** Librarian; Library Technician. **Number of placements per year:** 200 - 499.

HUNTER MAC & ASSOCIATES
139 Fulton Street, New York NY 10038. 212/267-2790. **Fax:** 212/962-2339. **Contact:** Patrick McKeown, Vice President. **Description:** A permanent employment agency. **Specializes in the areas of:** Accounting/Auditing; Administration; Banking; Computer Science/Software; Finance; Insurance; Personnel/Labor Relations; Secretarial. **Positions commonly filled include:** Accountant/Auditor; Administrative Manager; Brokerage Clerk; Computer Programmer; Financial Analyst; Human Resources Manager; Librarian; Management Trainee; Securities Sales Representative; Systems Analyst. **Number of placements per year:** 200 - 499.

IDEAL PERSONNEL
420 Jericho Turnpike, Suite 333, Jericho NY 11753. 516/433-3333. **Contact:** Nancy Young, Manager/Vice President. **Description:** A permanent employment agency. **Specializes in the areas of:** Secretarial. **Positions commonly filled include:** Administrative Assistant; Administrative Manager; Secretary. **Average salary range of placements:** $20,000 - $45,000. **Number of placements per year:** 200 - 499.

INITIAL STAFFING SERVICES
342 Madison Avenue, Suite 1207, New York NY 10173. 914/428-2020. **Contact:** Staffing Consultant. **Description:** A permanent employment agency that also provides some temporary placements. **Specializes in the areas of:** Clerical; Light Industrial; Word Processing. **Positions commonly filled include:** Blue-Collar Worker Supervisor; Customer Service Representative; Typist/Word Processor. **Benefits available to temporary workers:** 401(k); Dental Insurance; Vision Plan. **Corporate headquarters location:** Houston TX. **Other U.S. locations:** Nationwide. **Number of placements per year:** 1000+.

INNOVATIONS ASSOCIATES
627 Field Street, Johnson City NY 13790-1057. 607/798-9376. **Fax:** 607/797-3485. **Contact:** Gene P. George, Director of Personnel Services. **Description:** A permanent employment agency. **Specializes in the areas of:** Accounting/Auditing; Administration; Advertising; Art/Design; Computer Science/Software; Engineering; Sales. **Positions commonly filled include:** Accountant/Auditor; Advertising Clerk; Civil Engineer; Clerical Supervisor; Computer Programmer; Customer Service Representative; Draftsperson; Electrical/Electronics Engineer; Industrial Engineer; Library Technician; Market Research Analyst; Mechanical Engineer; MIS Specialist; Multimedia Designer; Public Relations Specialist; Quality Control Supervisor; Software Engineer; Structural Engineer; Surveyor; Systems Analyst; Technical Writer/Editor; Telecommunications Manager. **Benefits available to temporary workers:** 401(k); Medical Insurance.

ISLAND SEARCH GROUP INC.
20 Crossways Park North, Woodbury NY 11797. 516/677-0015. **Fax:** 516/677-6099. **Contact:** Illene Glasser, President. **E-mail address:** islandsearch@worldnet.att.net. **Description:** A permanent employment agency that also provides some temporary placements. Founded in 1991. Client company pays fee. **Specializes in the areas of:** Accounting; Administration; Advertising; Broadcasting; Health/Medical; Legal; Marketing; Personnel/Labor Relations; Real Estate; Sales; Secretarial. **Positions commonly filled include:** Administrative Assistant; Advertising Clerk; Customer Service Representative; Database Administrator; Human Resources Manager; Management Trainee; Market Research Analyst; Medical Assistant; Paralegal; Sales Representative; Secretary; Typist/Word Processor. **Benefits available to temporary workers:** Paid Holidays; Paid Vacation; Profit Sharing. **Corporate headquarters location:** This Location. **Average salary range of placements:** $30,000 - $49,999. **Number of placements per year:** 200 - 499.

JDC ASSOCIATES
300 Wheeler Road, Suite 104, Hauppauge NY 11788. 516/231-8581. **Fax:** 516/231-8011. **Contact:** Lori Boyle, President. **Description:** A permanent employment agency. **Specializes in the areas of:** Accounting/Auditing; Computer Science/Software; Health/Medical; Sales; Secretarial. **Positions commonly filled include:** Accountant/Auditor; Administrative Assistant; Clerical Supervisor; Computer Programmer; Customer Service Representative; Pharmacist; Physical Therapist; Sales Representative; Secretary.

JOSEF GROUP PERSONNEL
P.O. Box 14464, Albany NY 12212. 518/869-3388. **Fax:** 518/869-9950. **Contact:** Debora Peda, President. **E-mail address:** josefjobs@aol.com. **Description:** A permanent employment agency. Founded in 1992. Client company pays fee. **Specializes in the areas of:** Computer Science/Software; Health/Medical; Legal; Secretarial. **Positions commonly filled include:** Accountant; Administrative Assistant; AS400 Programmer Analyst; Attorney; Computer Operator; Computer Programmer; Database Administrator; Human Resources Manager; Intellectual Property Lawyer; Network/Systems Administrator; Paralegal; Secretary. **Corporate headquarters location:** This Location. **Average salary range of placements:** $20,000 - $29,999. **Number of placements per year:** 100 - 199.

KLK PERSONNEL
507 Fifth Avenue, Suite 900, New York NY 10017. 212/986-9200. **Fax:** 212/986-0197. **Contact:** President. **Description:** A permanent employment agency. **Specializes in the areas of:** Accounting/Auditing; Administration; Advertising; Banking; Broadcasting; Fashion; Finance; Insurance; Legal; Personnel/Labor Relations. **Positions commonly filled include:** Accountant/Auditor; Administrative Assistant; Bookkeeper; Buyer; Computer Operator; Computer Programmer; Customer Service Representative; Data Entry Clerk; Legal Secretary; MIS Specialist; Purchasing Agent/Manager; Sales Representative; Secretary; Systems Analyst; Typist/Word Processor. **Number of placements per year:** 500 - 999.

LISA KALUS & ASSOCIATES
26 Broadway, Suite 400, New York NY 10004-1701. 212/837-7889. **Contact:** Lisa Kalus, President. **Description:** A permanent employment agency that provides placements for managerial-level construction personnel and engineering professionals with expertise related to construction industries. **Specializes in the areas of:** Architecture/Construction; Engineering. **Positions commonly filled include:** Civil Engineer; Construction Contractor; Cost Estimator; Electrical/Electronics Engineer; Mechanical Engineer; Structural Engineer. **Average salary range of placements:** More than $50,000. **Number of placements per year:** 50 - 99.

KTECH SYSTEMS GROUP, INC.
One Silicon Alley Plaza, 90 William Street, Suite 302, New York NY 10038. 212/324-1444. **Toll-free phone:** 888/355-3133. **Fax:** 212/324-1451. **Contact:** Dick Lewis, CEO. **E-mail address:** info@ktechsys.com. **World Wide Web address:** http://www.ktechsys.com. **Description:** A permanent employment agency that also provides some contract services. **Specializes in the areas of:** Administration; Computer Science/Software; Finance; Information Systems; Technical. **Positions commonly filled include:** Applications Engineer; Computer Programmer; Database Manager; Internet Services Manager; MIS Specialist; Project Manager; Software Engineer; Systems Analyst; Systems Manager; Technical Writer/Editor; Telecommunications Manager; Webmaster. **Benefits available to temporary workers:** Medical Insurance. **Average salary range of placements:** More than $50,000. **Number of placements per year:** 500 - 999.

TINA LANE PERSONNEL, INC.
317 Madison Avenue, Suite 605, New York NY 10017. 212/682-1333. **Fax:** 212/682-1499. **Contact:** Helene G. Cohen, Executive Vice President. **Description:** A permanent employment agency. **Specializes in the areas of:** Accounting; Banking; Consumer Products; Finance; Real Estate. **Positions commonly filled include:** Accountant; Administrative Assistant; Financial Analyst; Human Resources Specialist; Property and Real Estate Manager; Systems Analyst; Typist/Word Processor. **Average salary range of placements:** $30,000 - $80,000. **Number of placements per year:** 200 - 499.

LLOYD STAFFING
445 Broadhollow Road, Suite 119, Melville NY 11747. 516/777-7600. **Fax:** 516/777-7626. **Contact:** Manager. **Description:** A permanent employment agency that also provides some temporary placements. **Specializes in the areas of:** Art/Design; Banking; Biology; Brokerage; Computer Science/Software; Food; Health/Medical; Mortgage; Publishing; Real Estate; Sales. **Positions commonly filled include:** Bank Officer/Manager; Biological Scientist; Computer Programmer; Credit Manager; Hotel Manager; Medical Records Technician; Occupational Therapist; Physical Therapist; Physician; Property and Real Estate Manager; Restaurant/Food Service Manager; Systems Analyst. **Number of placements per year:** 200 - 499.

JOSEPH T. MALONEY AND ASSOCIATES, INC.
51 East 42nd Street, Suite 1508, New York NY 10017. 212/377-0100. **Contact:** Betty Lopez, Manager. **Description:** A permanent employment agency. **Specializes in the areas of:** Accounting/Auditing; Banking; Clerical; Finance; Insurance; Legal; Personnel/Labor Relations; Sales. **Positions commonly filled include:** Accountant/Auditor; Administrative Assistant; Attorney; Bank Officer/Manager; Bookkeeper; Brokerage Clerk; Claim Representative; Clerk; Computer Operator; Computer Programmer; Customer Service Representative; Data Entry Clerk; Economist; EDP Specialist; Financial Analyst; Human Resources Manager; Legal Secretary; Marketing Specialist; MIS Specialist; Office Manager; Receptionist; Sales Representative; Secretary; Stenographer; Typist/Word Processor. **Number of placements per year:** 500 - 999.

LYNN MARSHALL PERSONNEL AGENCY, INC.
91-31 Queens Boulevard, Rego Park NY 11373. 718/446-5200. **Fax:** 718/446-5202. **Contact:** Lynn Marshall, Owner/President. **Description:** A permanent employment agency. **Specializes in the areas of:** Accounting/Auditing; Legal; Secretarial. **Positions commonly filled include:** Administrative Assistant; Bookkeeper; Clerical Supervisor; Computer Programmer; Credit Manager; Customer Service Representative; Human Resources Manager; Management Trainee; Services Sales Representative; Systems Analyst; Typist/Word Processor. **Number of placements per year:** 50 - 99.

MEDICAL STAFFERS

292 Madison Avenue, 17th Floor, New York NY 10017. 212/213-5632. **Fax:** 212/213-2728. **Contact:** Executive Director. **Description:** A permanent employment agency. **Specializes in the areas of:** Health/Medical. **Positions commonly filled include:** Chemist; Clinical Lab Technician; Dental Assistant/Dental Hygienist; Dentist; Dietician/Nutritionist; EEG Technologist; EKG Technician; Licensed Practical Nurse; Medical Records Technician; Nuclear Medicine Technologist; Nurse; Occupational Therapist; Pharmacist; Physical Therapist; Physician; Physician Assistant; Recreational Therapist; Registered Nurse; Respiratory Therapist; Science Technologist; Social Worker; Speech-Language Pathologist; Surgical Technician. **Number of placements per year:** 200 - 499.

METRO SUPPORT GROUP

370 Lexington Avenue, Suite 1508, New York NY 10017. 212/818-1177. **Fax:** 212/818-0291. **Contact:** Renee Chandler, President. **Description:** A permanent employment agency. Clients include brokerage firms, banks, advertising agencies, entertainment corporations, and legal firms. **Specializes in the areas of:** Communications; Personnel/Labor Relations; Secretarial. **Positions commonly filled include:** Administrative Assistant; Advertising Clerk; Brokerage Clerk; Clerical Supervisor; Human Resources Manager; Secretary. **Average salary range of placements:** $30,000 - $50,000. **Number of placements per year:** 200 - 499.

MILAZZO ASSOCIATES, INC.

17 Battery Place, Suite 626, New York NY 10004. 212/344-2334. **Fax:** 212/344-1910. **Contact:** Peter Milazzo, President. **Description:** A permanent employment agency. **Specializes in the areas of:** Accounting/Auditing; Administration; Banking; Computer Science/Software; Economics; Finance; Legal; Personnel/Labor Relations; Sales; Secretarial; Technical. **Positions commonly filled include:** Accountant/Auditor; Administrative Manager; Bank Officer/Manager; Brokerage Clerk; Credit Manager; Customer Service Representative; Economist; Financial Analyst; Human Resources Manager; Management Analyst/Consultant; Operations/Production Manager; Paralegal; Public Relations Specialist; Purchasing Agent/Manager; Securities Sales Representative; Services Sales Representative; Statistician; Strategic Relations Manager; Systems Analyst; Technical Writer/Editor; Telecommunications Manager; Typist/Word Processor. **Other U.S. locations:** Nationwide. **Number of placements per year:** 50 - 99.

MORTGAGE PERSONNEL OF AMERICA

170 East Post Road, White Plains NY 10601. 914/761-8900. **Contact:** Edward Aloe, President. **Description:** A permanent employment agency that places residential mortgage loan originators nationwide. **Specializes in the areas of:** Mortgage.

NATIONAL FIELD SERVICE CORPORATION

162 Orange Avenue, Suffern NY 10901. 914/368-1600. **Toll-free phone:** 800/368-1602. **Fax:** 914/368-1989. **Contact:** Margaret Forman, Vice President. **E-mail address:** nfsco@aol.com. **World Wide Web address:** http://www.nfsco.com. **Description:** A permanent employment agency that also provides some temporary and contract placements. **Specializes in the areas of:** Computer Science/Software; Engineering; Information Technology; MIS/EDP; Telecommunications. **Positions commonly filled include:** Administrative Assistant; Applications Engineer; AS400 Programmer Analyst; Computer Engineer; Computer Operator; Computer Programmer; Computer Support Technician; Computer Technician; Database Administrator; Database Manager; Internet Services Manager; MIS Specialist; Network/Systems Administrator; Software Engineer; SQL Programmer; Systems Analyst; Systems Manager; Webmaster. **Benefits available to temporary workers:** 401(k); Health Benefits. **Corporate headquarters location:** This Location.

NATIONWIDE PERSONNEL GROUP

474 Elmwood Avenue, P.O. Box 26, Buffalo NY 14222. 716/881-2144. **Fax:** 716/881-0711. **Contact:** Mark Gademsky, CPC/President. **E-mail address:** gademsky@localnet.com. **Description:** A permanent employment agency. **Specializes in the areas of:** Administration; Computer Science/Software; Engineering. **Positions commonly filled include:** Computer Programmer; Design Engineer; Electrical/Electronics Engineer; Internet Services Manager; Mathematician; Mechanical Engineer; MIS Specialist; Software Engineer; Systems Analyst; Telecommunications Manager. **Average salary range of placements:** $35,000 - $120,000. **Number of placements per year:** 50 - 99.

THE NEW YORK NANNY CENTER, INC.

31 South Bayles Avenue, Port Washington NY 11050. 516/767-5136. **Fax:** 516/767-5166. **Contact:** Carol Solomon, Director. **Description:** A permanent employment agency. **Specializes in the areas of:** Child Care, In-Home. **Positions commonly filled include:** Nanny. **Number of placements per year:** 100 - 199.

NEW YORK-NEW YORK PERSONNEL

170 Broadway, Suite 906, New York NY 10038. 212/267-3500. **Fax:** 212/791-3746. **Contact:** Personnel. **Description:** A permanent employment agency. **Specializes in the areas of:** Banking; Finance; Insurance; Legal; Secretarial. **Positions commonly filled include:** Administrative Assistant; Computer Operator; Legal Secretary; Paralegal; Secretary; Typist/Word Processor; Underwriter/Assistant Underwriter. **Corporate headquarters location:** This Location. **Average salary range of placements:** $30,000 - $50,000.

NOAH ASSOCIATES

P.O. Box 606, Amawalk NY 10501. 914/737-1819. **Fax:** 914/737-1853. **Contact:** Norman Houle, President. **Description:** A permanent employment agency. **Specializes in the areas of:** Accounting/Auditing; Administration; Biology; Computer Science/Software; Engineering; Finance; General Management; Industrial; Manufacturing; Personnel/Labor Relations; Sales; Technical; Transportation. **Positions commonly filled include:** Accountant/Auditor; Aerospace Engineer; Biological Scientist; Biomedical Engineer; Buyer; Ceramics Engineer; Chemical Engineer; Chemist; Civil Engineer; Compliance Analyst; Computer Programmer; Customer Service Representative; Electrical/Electronics Engineer; Human Resources Manager; Industrial Designer; Industrial Engineer; Manufacturing Engineer; Marketing Specialist; Mechanical Engineer; Metallurgical Engineer; MIS Specialist; Purchasing Agent/Manager; Quality Control Supervisor; Sales Representative; Software Engineer; Systems Analyst. **Number of placements per year:** 1 - 49.

NORRIS EMPLOYMENT CONSULTANTS

P.O. Box 2460, Liverpool NY 13089-2460. 315/695-4999. **Fax:** 315/695-4030. **Contact:** Donald W. Norris Jr., President. **Description:** A permanent employment agency. **Specializes in the areas of:** Engineering; Manufacturing; Personnel/Labor Relations. **Positions commonly filled include:** Electrical/Electronics Engineer; General Manager; Human Resources Manager; Industrial Engineer; Industrial Production Manager; Mechanical Engineer. **Number of placements per year:** 1 - 49.

K.A. NOWACK CAREER SPECIALISTS

170 Broadway, New York NY 10038. 212/732-1919. **Fax:** 212/233-1040. **Contact:** Kathleen Nowack, President. **Description:** A permanent employment agency. **Specializes in the areas of:** Accounting/Auditing; Art/Design; Banking; Economics; Finance; Insurance; Legal; Personnel/Labor Relations; Sales; Secretarial; Technical. **Positions commonly filled include:** Accountant/Auditor; Aerospace Engineer; Budget Analyst; Claim Representative; Computer Programmer; Customer Service Representative; Financial

Analyst; Management Trainee; Operations/Production Manager; Paralegal; Securities Sales Representative; Telecommunications Manager; Typist/Word Processor; Underwriter/Assistant Underwriter. **Number of placements per year:** 50 - 99.

OTEC INC.
24 West 40th Street, 11th Floor, New York NY 10018-3904. 212/768-0600. **Fax:** 212/768-8309. **Contact:** Ben Carroccio, President. **E-mail address:** jobs@otec.com. **World Wide Web address:** http://www.otec.com. **Description:** A permanent employment agency that also provides some contract services. **Specializes in the areas of:** Computer Science/Software; Engineering; Finance; Personnel/Labor Relations. **Positions commonly filled include:** Computer Animator; Computer Operator; Computer Programmer; Design Engineer; Internet Services Manager; Systems Analyst; Systems Manager; Webmaster. **Benefits available to temporary workers:** Medical Insurance. **Corporate headquarters location:** This Location. **Other U.S. locations:** San Francisco CA. **Average salary range of placements:** More than $50,000. **Number of placements per year:** 200 - 499.

PARSONS, ANDERSON AND GEE, INC.
44 Georgetown Lane, Fairport NY 14450-3334. 716/223-3770. **Toll-free phone:** 888/586-8679. **Fax:** 716/223-8536. **Contact:** Art Fandel, General Manager. **World Wide Web address:** http://www.parandge.com. **Description:** A permanent employment agency. **Specializes in the areas of:** Accounting/Auditing; Administration; Computer Science/Software; Engineering; Finance; Food; General Management; Industrial; Insurance; Manufacturing; Personnel/Labor Relations; Publishing; Sales; Technical. **Positions commonly filled include:** Accountant/Auditor; Biomedical Engineer; Buyer; Chemical Engineer; Computer Programmer; Designer; Electrical/Electronics Engineer; General Manager; Human Resources Manager; Industrial Engineer; Industrial Production Manager; Manufacturer's/Wholesaler's Sales Rep.; Mechanical Engineer; Metallurgical Engineer; Purchasing Agent/Manager; Quality Control Supervisor; Securities Sales Representative; Software Engineer; Stationary Engineer; Structural Engineer; Systems Analyst; Technical Writer/Editor. **Number of placements per year:** 1 - 49.

PHOENIX EMPLOYMENT AGENCY
205 West 14th Street, New York NY 10011-7114. 212/255-3436. **Fax:** 212/255-8308. **Contact:** Steve Blecher, Owner. **Description:** A permanent employment agency. **Specializes in the areas of:** Food; Industrial; Manufacturing. **Positions commonly filled include:** Blue-Collar Worker Supervisor; Electrician; Electronics Technician; Industrial Production Manager; Operations/Production Manager; Restaurant/Food Service Manager; Warehouse Manager. **Number of placements per year:** 100 - 199.

ADELE POSTON AGENCY
16 East 79th Street, New York NY 10021-0150. 212/879-7474. **Fax:** 212/988-7191. **Contact:** Mr. Jerry Bohne, Director. **Description:** A permanent employment agency. **Specializes in the areas of:** Domestic Help; Health/Medical; Nannies; Secretarial. **Positions commonly filled include:** Domestic Help; EEG Technologist; EKG Technician; Health Services Manager; Licensed Practical Nurse; Medical Records Technician; Nanny; Nuclear Medicine Technologist; Occupational Therapist; Pharmacist; Physical Therapist; Physician; Recreational Therapist; Registered Nurse; Respiratory Therapist; Social Worker; Speech-Language Pathologist. **Average salary range of placements:** $30,000 - $50,000. **Number of placements per year:** 500 - 999.

PRESTIGE PERSONNEL
32-30 58th Street, Woodside NY 11377. 718/721-2200. **Contact:** Office Manager. **Description:** A permanent employment agency. **Positions commonly filled**

include: Bookkeeper; Legal Secretary; Real Estate Agent. **Number of placements per year:** 500 - 999.

QUALITY CARE ASSOCIATES
68 Purchase Street, Rye NY 10580. 914/967-8254. **Fax:** 914/967-1854. **Contact:** Sue Felder, Owner. **E-mail address:** quality@newdirection.com. **Description:** A permanent employment agency focusing on providing placements for in-home child care providers. **Positions commonly filled include:** Child Care Center Director. **Corporate headquarters location:** Westchester NY. **Average salary range of placements:** $20,000 - $29,999. **Number of placements per year:** 50 - 99.

QUALITY HEALTHCARE STAFFING INC.
2298 Nostrand Avenue, Brooklyn NY 11210. 718/338-8500. **Fax:** 718/338-8838. **Contact:** Malca Fass, Administrator. **Description:** A permanent employment agency that focuses on placing health care professionals in the nursing home, hospital, and home care positions. **Specializes in the areas of:** Health/Medical. **Positions commonly filled include:** Certified Nurses Aide; Home Health Aide; Licensed Practical Nurse; Registered Nurse. **Number of placements per year:** 100 - 199.

RCM TECHNOLOGIES, INC.
1156 Avenue of the Americas, 4th Floor, New York NY 10036. 212/221-1544. **Fax:** 212/764-6848. **Contact:** Marilyn Oxenburg, Office Manager. **E-mail address:** nyjobs@rcmt.com. **World Wide Web address:** http://www.rcmt.com. **Description:** A permanent employment agency. RCM Technologies also provides consulting services. Client company pays fee. **Specializes in the areas of:** Computer Science/Software; Finance; Health/Medical; Internet Development; Legal; MIS/EDP; Tax; Technical. **Positions commonly filled include:** Applications Engineer; AS400 Programmer Analyst; Certified Occupational Therapy Assistant; Computer Engineer; Computer Programmer; Computer Support Technician; Computer Technician; Database Administrator; Database Manager; Internet Services Manager; MIS Specialist; Network/Systems Administrator; Occupational Therapist; Physical Therapist; Physical Therapy Assistant; Physician; Registered Nurse; Respiratory Therapist; Software Engineer; Speech-Language Pathologist; SQL Programmer; Systems Analyst; Systems Manager; Tax Specialist; Webmaster. **Corporate headquarters location:** Pennsauken NJ. **Other U.S. locations:** Nationwide. **Average salary range of placements:** $50,000 - $100,000. **Number of placements per year:** 200 - 499.

REM RESOURCES, INC.
507 Fifth Avenue, Suite 1106, New York NY 10017. 212/661-0090. **Fax:** 212/661-0107. **Contact:** Gabrielle Rem, President. **E-mail address:** reminc1@aol.com. **Description:** A permanent employment agency that also provides some temporary placements. **Specializes in the areas of:** Accounting/Auditing; Administration; Advertising; Broadcasting; Computer Science/Software; Fashion; Finance; Insurance; Legal; Nonprofit; Personnel/Labor Relations; Publishing; Sales; Secretarial. **Positions commonly filled include:** Accountant/Auditor; Administrative Assistant; Branch Manager; Brokerage Clerk; Budget Analyst; Business Analyst; Computer Operator; Computer Programmer; Customer Service Representative; Database Manager; Editorial Assistant; Executive Assistant; Finance Director; Financial Analyst; Fund Manager; Health Services Manager; Human Resources Manager; Internet Specialist; Market Research Analyst; Office Manager; Operations/Production Manager; Purchasing Agent/Manager; Receptionist; Systems Analyst. **Other U.S. locations:** Nationwide. **Number of placements per year:** 200 - 499.

REPUBLIC EMPLOYMENT AGENCY
198 Broadway, Suite 1205, New York NY 10038. 212/964-0640. **Fax:** 212/267-0032. **Contact:** Tony Freddo, Manager. **Description:** A permanent employment agency. **Specializes in the areas of:** Dental;

Health/Medical; Secretarial. **Positions commonly filled include:** Dental Assistant/Dental Hygienist; Dentist; Health Services Manager; Medical Records Technician; Registered Nurse. **Average salary range of placements:** $20,000 - $29,999. **Number of placements per year:** 200 - 499.

RIBOLOW ASSOCIATES
19 West 44th Street, New York NY 10036. 212/808-0580. **Fax:** 212/573-6050. **Contact:** Adele Ribolow, President. **Description:** A permanent employment agency that focuses on providing placements in publishing, nonprofit and corporate communications, and market research industries. **Specializes in the areas of:** Advertising; Nonprofit; Public Relations; Publishing; Secretarial. **Positions commonly filled include:** Editor; Editorial Assistant; Managing Editor; Market Research Analyst; Production Manager; Public Relations Specialist; Sales Executive; Secretary. **Corporate headquarters location:** This Location. **Number of placements per year:** 100 - 199.

BETH RICHMAN ASSOCIATES
535 Fifth Avenue, New York NY 10017-3610. 212/986-5169. **Fax:** 212/557-7148. **Contact:** Beth Richman, President. **E-mail address:** bethannny@aol.com. **Description:** A permanent employment agency. **Specializes in the areas of:** Accounting/Auditing; Banking; Computer Science/Software; Finance; Sales; Secretarial. **Positions commonly filled include:** Accountant/Auditor; Administrative Assistant; Bank Officer/Manager; Branch Manager; Brokerage Clerk; Budget Analyst; Computer Programmer; Financial Analyst; Human Resources Manager; Investment Manager; Management Trainee; MIS Specialist; Research Assistant; Securities Sales Representative. **Average salary range of placements:** $30,000 - $50,000. **Number of placements per year:** 50 - 99.

FRAN ROGERS PERSONNEL
One Huntington Quadrangle, Suite 2S09, Melville NY 11747. 516/752-8888. **Contact:** Fran Rogers, President. **Description:** A permanent employment agency. **Specializes in the areas of:** Accounting/Auditing; Administration; Banking; Computer Science/Software; Finance; Technical. **Positions commonly filled include:** Accountant/Auditor; Administrative Assistant; Bookkeeper; Credit Analyst; Financial Analyst; MIS Specialist; Receptionist; Secretary; Systems Analyst; Typist/Word Processor. **Number of placements per year:** 200 - 499.

ALEXANDER ROSS ASSOCIATES, INC.
21 East 40th Street, Suite 1802, New York NY 10016. 212/889-9333. **Contact:** Ben Lichtenstein, President. **Description:** A permanent employment agency. **Specializes in the areas of:** Change Management; Human Resources; Organization Development. **Number of placements per year:** 1 - 49.

SENIOR RESOURCES
60 East 42nd Street, Room 731, New York NY 10165. 212/986-8017. **Contact:** Thomas S. Lyons, Vice President. **Description:** A permanent employment agency. **Positions commonly filled include:** Bookkeeper; Clerk; Customer Service Representative; Data Entry Clerk; Receptionist; Typist/Word Processor. **Number of placements per year:** 100 - 199.

SIGMA STAFFING
535 Broadhollow Road, Melville NY 11747. 516/694-7707. **Fax:** 516/694-7709. **Contact:** Thea Linker, President. **Description:** A permanent employment agency that also offers some temporary placements. **Specializes in the areas of:** Accounting; Administration; General Management; Light Industrial; Secretarial. **Positions commonly filled include:** Account Representative; Accountant; Administrative Assistant; Auditor; Chemist; Clerical Supervisor; Clinical Lab Technician; Consultant; Controller; Credit Manager; Customer Service Representative; Human Resources Manager; Management Trainee; Purchasing

Agent/Manager; Quality Control Supervisor; Secretary; Typist/Word Processor. **Corporate headquarters location:** This Location. **Average salary range of placements:** $30,000 - $49,999. **Number of placements per year:** 100 - 199.

SLOAN STAFFING SERVICES
317 Madison Avenue, 21st Floor, New York NY 10017. 212/949-7200. **Fax:** 212/949-8599. **Contact:** Office Manager. **Description:** A permanent employment agency. **Specializes in the areas of:** Clerical; Office Support; Secretarial. **Positions commonly filled include:** Administrative Assistant; Bookkeeper; Clerk; Customer Service Representative; Data Entry Clerk; Legal Secretary; Medical Secretary; Receptionist; Secretary; Stenographer; Typist/Word Processor. **Number of placements per year:** 200 - 499.

SNELLING PERSONNEL SERVICES
1717 Central Avenue, Albany NY 12205-4756. 518/869-9575. **Fax:** 518/869-9256. **Contact:** Ms. Kristi Nastars, President. **Description:** A permanent employment agency. Founded in 1951. **Specializes in the areas of:** Accounting/Auditing; Administration; Engineering; Finance; Sales; Secretarial; Technical. **Positions commonly filled include:** Accountant/Auditor; Bank Officer/Manager; Chemical Engineer; Chemist; Civil Engineer; Computer Programmer; Customer Service Representative; Design Engineer; Electrical/Electronics Engineer; Environmental Engineer; Financial Analyst; Industrial Engineer; Mechanical Engineer; MIS Specialist; Software Engineer; Structural Engineer; Systems Analyst; Technical Writer/Editor. **Corporate headquarters location:** Dallas TX. **Other U.S. locations:** Nationwide. **Average salary range of placements:** $30,000 - $50,000. **Number of placements per year:** 50 - 99.

STAFF BY MANNING, LTD.
38 East 57th Street, Suite 7R, New York NY 10022-2512. 212/753-8080. **Fax:** 212/753-8079. **Contact:** Recruiter. **Description:** A permanent employment agency. **Specializes in the areas of:** Administration; Operations Management; Personnel/Labor Relations; Secretarial. **Positions commonly filled include:** Administrative Assistant; Administrative Manager; Clerical Supervisor; Office Manager. **Number of placements per year:** 1 - 49.

STAMM PERSONNEL AGENCY, INC.
27 Whitehall Street, New York NY 10004. 212/509-6600. **Fax:** 212/509-3773. **Contact:** Corey Barrett, Office Manager. **E-mail address:** pstamm1@compuserve.com. **Description:** A permanent employment agency. Stamm Personnel Agency also provides career counseling. **Specializes in the areas of:** Accounting; Administration; Finance; Operations Management; Research and Development; Sales; Secretarial. **Positions commonly filled include:** Administrative Assistant; Broker; Chief Financial Officer; Controller; Executive Assistant; Investment Manager; Operations Manager; Researcher; Sales Representative; Trader. **Number of placements per year:** 100 - 199.

HILLARY TAYLOR PERSONNEL
2 John Street, 2nd Floor, New York NY 10038. 212/619-8200. **Fax:** 212/385-0454. **Contact:** Hillary Taylor, President. **Description:** A permanent employment agency. **Specializes in the areas of:** Accounting/Auditing; Advertising; Banking; Fashion; Finance; Legal; Secretarial. **Positions commonly filled include:** Accountant; Administrative Assistant; Customer Service Representative; Financial Analyst; Paralegal; Secretary; Typist/Word Processor. **Average salary range of placements:** $30,000 - $50,000. **Number of placements per year:** 50 - 99.

TEMPO SERVICES, INC.
1400 Old Country Road, Suite 211, Westbury NY 11590. 516/333-2323. **Contact:** Office Manager. **Description:** A permanent employment agency that also offers some

temporary placements. **Positions commonly filled include:** Accountant/Auditor; Bookkeeper; Clerk; Computer Programmer; Credit Manager; Data Entry Clerk; Draftsperson; Driver; EDP Specialist; Factory Worker; Financial Analyst; Legal Secretary; Marketing Specialist; Medical Secretary; Nurse; Purchasing Agent/Manager; Receptionist; Secretary; Stenographer; Systems Analyst; Typist/Word Processor. **Corporate headquarters location:** Woodbury NY. **Number of placements per year:** 1000+.

TEMPO SERVICES, INC.
287 Northern Boulevard, Great Neck NY 11021. 516/466-4664. **Fax:** 516/466-7001. **Contact:** Branch Manager. **Description:** A permanent employment agency. **Specializes in the areas of:** Accounting/Auditing; Banking; Personnel/Labor Relations; Sales; Secretarial. **Positions commonly filled include:** Administrative Manager; Customer Service Representative; General Manager; Human Resources Manager; Market Research Analyst; Typist/Word Processor. **Benefits available to temporary workers:** 401(k); Paid Vacation; Referral Bonus Plan. **Corporate headquarters location:** Woodbury NY. **Average salary range of placements:** $20,000 - $29,999. **Number of placements per year:** 1000+.

UNITED PERSONNEL AGENCY, INC.
51 East 42nd Street, Suite 1410, New York NY 10017. 212/490-2197. **Fax:** 212/338-9677. **Contact:** Michael P. Williams, President. **E-mail address:** upagency@ ix.netcom.com. **Description:** A permanent employment agency that also provides some temporary placements. **Specializes in the areas of:** Accounting/ Auditing; Advertising; Banking; Broadcasting; Computer Science/Software; Legal; Nonprofit; Personnel/Labor Relations; Publishing; Secretarial; Word Processing. **Positions commonly filled include:** Accountant/Auditor; Budget Analyst; Claim Representative; Paralegal; Software Engineer; Systems Analyst. **Number of placements per year:** 1000+.

VANCE PERSONNEL
505 Fifth Avenue, Suite 1703, New York NY 10017. 212/661-8860. **Contact:** Larry Stevens, President. **Description:** A permanent employment agency. **Specializes in the areas of:** Brokerage; Finance; Secretarial. **Positions commonly filled include:** Accountant/Auditor; Advertising Clerk; Bookkeeper; Clerk; Computer Operator; Credit Manager; Customer Service Representative; Data Entry Clerk; General Manager; Human Resources Manager; Legal Secretary; Medical Secretary; Public Relations Specialist; Receptionist; Secretary; Stenographer; Typist/Word Processor. **Number of placements per year:** 200 - 499.

DON WALDRON & ASSOCIATES
450 Seventh Avenue, Suite 507A, New York NY 10123. 212/239-9110. **Fax:** 212/239-9114. **Contact:** Don Waldron, President. **Description:** A permanent employment agency. **Specializes in the areas of:** Advertising.

WEHINGER SERVICES
375 North Broadway, Suite 105, Jericho NY 11753. 516/938-7944. **Fax:** 516/938-3625. **Contact:** Chuck Copt, Vice President. **Description:** A permanent employment agency. **Specializes in the areas of:** Banking; Insurance; Retail. **Positions commonly filled include:** Actuary; Adjuster; Bank Officer/Manager; Branch Manager; Claim Representative; Customer Service Representative; Insurance Agent/Broker; Management Trainee; Underwriter/Assistant Underwriter; Wholesale and Retail Buyer. **Number of placements per year:** 100 - 199.

WESTCHESTER EMPLOYMENT AGENCY
109 Croton Avenue, Ossining NY 10562. 914/941-8150. **Fax:** 914/941-1748. **Contact:** Alan Gordon, President. **Description:** A permanent employment agency. Founded in 1962. **Specializes in the areas of:** Accounting/Auditing; Administration; Engineering; Finance; General Management; Industrial; Insurance; Legal; Manufacturing; Personnel/Labor Relations; Retail; Sales; Technical. **Positions commonly filled include:** Accountant/Auditor; Administrative Manager; Bookkeeper; Claim Representative; Clerk; Computer Operator; Customer Service Representative; Data Entry Clerk; Marketing Specialist; Medical Secretary; Operations/Production Manager; Public Relations Specialist; Purchasing Agent/Manager; Software Engineer; Technical Writer/Editor. **Number of placements per year:** 200 - 499.

WOODBURY PERSONNEL
375 North Broadway, Suite 105, Jericho NY 11753-2008. 516/938-7910. **Toll-free phone:** 800/641-0060. **Fax:** 516/938-7370. **Contact:** Chuck Copt, President. **World Wide Web address:** http://www. woodburypersonnel.com. **Description:** A permanent employment agency. **Specializes in the areas of:** Banking; Finance; Insurance; Legal; Personnel/Labor Relations; Retail. **Positions commonly filled include:** Accountant/Auditor; Adjuster; Attorney; Branch Manager; Buyer; Claim Representative; Human Resources Manager; Insurance Agent/Broker; Management Trainee; Paralegal; Underwriter/Assistant Underwriter. **Average salary range of placements:** $30,000 - $50,000. **Number of placements per year:** 200 - 499.

YOURS IN TRAVEL PERSONNEL AGENCY, INC.
12 West 37th Street, 5th Floor, New York NY 10018. 212/697-7855. **Contact:** Jason King, President. **World Wide Web address:** http://www.yoursintravel.com. **Description:** A permanent employment agency that provides placements ranging from entry-level to senior executives. **NOTE:** Candidates must have experience in the travel industry. All inquiries, applications, and resumes must be sent to this location or to the company Website. Founded in 1972. Client company pays fee. **Specializes in the areas of:** Hotel/Restaurant; Tourism; Transportation; Travel. **Positions commonly filled include:** Travel Agent. **Corporate headquarters location:** This Location. **Other U.S. locations:** Nationwide.

TEMPORARY EMPLOYMENT AGENCIES

AM & PM TEMPS INC.
619 Roanoke Avenue, Riverhead NY 11901-2727. 516/369-5980. **Toll-free phone:** 800/424-5059. **Fax:** 516/360-2333. **Contact:** Manager. **E-mail address:** ampmtemps@juno.com. **Description:** A temporary agency. **Specializes in the areas of:** General Management; Legal; Secretarial. **Positions commonly filled include:** Account Representative; Administrative Assistant; Light Industrial Worker; Sales Representative. **Corporate headquarters location:** This Location. **Other U.S. locations:** Nationwide. **Average salary range of placements:** $20,000 - $29,999. **Number of placements per year:** 100 - 199.

AADAMS PERSONNEL AGENCY
3915 Main Street, Suite 301, Flushing NY 11354. 718/359-0800. **Contact:** Manager. **Description:** A permanent employment agency that also provides some temporary placements. **Specializes in the areas of:** Sales; Secretarial; Technical. **Positions commonly filled include:** Accountant/Auditor; Aircraft Mechanic/Engine Specialist; Architect; Automotive Mechanic; Buyer; Chemical Engineer; Chemist; Civil Engineer; Clerical Supervisor; Clinical Lab Technician; Electrical/ Electronics Engineer; Electrician; Financial Analyst; General Manager; Human Resources Specialist; Industrial Engineer; MIS Specialist; Physical Therapist; Recreational Therapist; Systems Analyst. **Average**

salary range of placements: $20,000 - $29,999. **Number of placements per year:** 50 - 99.

ACCUSTAFF INCORPORATED
290 Broadhollow Road, 1st Floor, East Wing, Melville NY 11747. 516/293-7050. **Fax:** 516/293-7057. **Contact:** Marketing/Sales Department. **World Wide Web address:** http://www.accustaff.com. **Description:** A temporary agency. **Specializes in the areas of:** Office Support; Telemarketing. **Positions commonly filled include:** Accountant/Auditor; Bookkeeper; Claim Representative; Clerk; Customer Service Representative; Data Entry Clerk; Factory Worker; Legal Secretary; Medical Secretary; MIS Specialist; Quality Control Supervisor; Receptionist; Secretary; Typist/Word Processor. **Benefits available to temporary workers:** 401(k). **Corporate headquarters location:** Woodbury NY. **Other U.S. locations:** Nationwide. **Number of placements per year:** 1000+.

ACCUSTAFF INCORPORATED
180 Broadway, Suite 1101, New York NY 10038. 212/267-8367. **Fax:** 212/267-8412. **Contact:** Cynthia Peck, Office Manager. **World Wide Web address:** http://www.accustaff.com. **Description:** A temporary agency. Client company pays fee. **Specializes in the areas of:** Accounting; Administration; Advertising; Banking; Computer Science/Software; Finance; General Management; Insurance; Legal; Light Industrial; Retail; Secretarial. **Positions commonly filled include:** Accountant; Administrative Assistant; Bookkeeper; Clerk; Computer Operator; Computer Programmer; Customer Service Representative; Data Entry Clerk; Desktop Publishing Specialist; Factory Worker; Legal Secretary; Medical Secretary; Paralegal; Purchasing Agent/Manager; Receptionist; Secretary; Statistician; Stenographer; Typist/Word Processor. **Benefits available to temporary workers:** 401(k); Medical Insurance; Paid Vacation. **Corporate headquarters location:** Woodbury NY. **Other U.S. locations:** Nationwide. **Average salary range of placements:** $30,000 - $49,999. **Number of placements per year:** 1000+.

ACCUSTAFF INCORPORATED
1975 Hempstead Turnpike, East Meadow NY 11554. 516/227-2700. **Fax:** 516/795-2534. **Contact:** Branch Manager. **World Wide Web address:** http://www.accustaff.com. **Description:** A temporary agency that also provides some temp-to-hire and permanent placements. **Specializes in the areas of:** Banking; Publishing; Secretarial. **Positions commonly filled include:** Customer Service Representative; Typist/Word Processor. **Benefits available to temporary workers:** Paid Holidays; Paid Vacation; Referral Bonus Plan. **Corporate headquarters location:** Woodbury NY. **Other U.S. locations:** Nationwide. **Number of placements per year:** 500 - 999.

ACCUSTAFF INCORPORATED
466 Main Street, New Rochelle NY 10801. 914/654-9400. **Fax:** 914/654-9480. **Contact:** Patricia Longo, CPC/Manager. **World Wide Web address:** http://www.accustaff.com. **Description:** A temporary agency that also provides some temp-to-perm placements. **Specializes in the areas of:** Accounting/Auditing; Administration; General Management; Light Industrial; Personnel/Labor Relations; Sales; Secretarial. **Positions commonly filled include:** Account Manager; Account Representative; Administrative Assistant; Administrative Manager; Clerical Supervisor; Computer Operator; Credit Manager; Customer Service Representative; Database Manager; Human Resources Manager; Marketing Manager; Purchasing Agent/Manager; Sales Executive; Sales Manager; Sales Representative; Secretary; Typist/Word Processor. **Corporate headquarters location:** Woodbury NY. **Average salary range of placements:** $20,000 - $29,999. **Number of placements per year:** 100 - 199.

ADECCO
551 Fifth Avenue, Suite 501, New York NY 10017. 212/682-3438. **Contact:** Office Supervisor. **Description:** A temporary agency. **Specializes in the areas of:** Accounting/Auditing; Advertising; Banking; Broadcasting; Clerical; Communications; Fashion; Finance; Food; Insurance; Nonprofit; Personnel/Labor Relations; Public Relations; Publishing; Retail; Textiles. **Positions commonly filled include:** Accountant/Auditor; Administrative Assistant; Assistant Manager; Bookkeeper; Clerk; Computer Operator; Customer Service Representative; Data Entry Clerk; EDP Specialist; Factory Worker; Legal Secretary; Medical Secretary; Receptionist; Stenographer; Typist/Word Processor. **Corporate headquarters location:** Redwood City CA. **Other U.S. locations:** Nationwide. **Number of placements per year:** 1000+.

ADECCO
500 Old Country Road, Suite 110, Garden City NY 11530-1921. 516/741-4949. **Fax:** 516/741-5094. **Contact:** Manager. **Description:** A temporary agency that also provides some temp-to-perm and permanent placements. **Specializes in the areas of:** Accounting/Auditing; Administration; Advertising; Banking; Finance; Insurance; Manufacturing; Personnel/Labor Relations; Retail; Sales; Secretarial. **Positions commonly filled include:** Administrative Manager; Brokerage Clerk; Budget Analyst; Claim Representative; Clerical Supervisor; Clinical Lab Technician; Computer Programmer; Credit Manager; Customer Service Representative; Electrician; Financial Analyst; General Manager; Health Services Manager; Human Resources Specialist; Industrial Engineer; Industrial Production Manager; Internet Services Manager; Management Trainee; Market Research Analyst; Medical Records Technician; Property and Real Estate Manager; Statistician; Systems Analyst; Telecommunications Manager; Typist/Word Processor; Underwriter/Assistant Underwriter. **Benefits available to temporary workers:** Medical Insurance; Paid Holidays; Paid Vacation. **Corporate headquarters location:** Redwood City CA. **Other U.S. locations:** Nationwide. **Average salary range of placements:** $20,000 - $39,999. **Number of placements per year:** 50 - 99.

ADECCO HEALTH SERVICES
30 North Union Street, Suite 102, Rochester NY 14607. 716/454-5511. **Contact:** Manager. **Description:** A temporary agency that also provides some temp-to-perm placements. **Specializes in the areas of:** Health/Medical. **Positions commonly filled include:** Certified Nurses Aide; Certified Occupational Therapy Assistant; EKG Technician; Emergency Medical Technician; Licensed Practical Nurse; Medical Assistant; Medical Records Technician; Nurse Practitioner; Occupational Therapist; Physical Therapist; Physical Therapy Assistant; Radiological Technologist; Registered Nurse; Respiratory Therapist; Speech-Language Pathologist; Surgical Technician. **Corporate headquarters location:** Redwood City CA.

AQUENT PARTNERS
71 West 23rd Street, Suite 1608, New York NY 10010-4102. 212/228-7300. **Toll-free phone:** 877/PARTNER. **Fax:** 212/228-8002. **Contact:** Michael Krey, Manager. **E-mail address:** mkrey@aquent.com. **World Wide Web address:** http://www.aquentpartners.com. **Description:** A temporary agency that provides placements for creative, Web, and technical professionals. Aquent Partners also provides some temp-to-perm, permanent, and contract placements. **Specializes in the areas of:** Administration; Art/Design; Computer Science/Software; Marketing. **Positions commonly filled include:** Computer Animator; Computer Engineer; Computer Operator; Computer Programmer; Computer Support Technician; Computer Technician; Content Developer; Database Administrator; Database Manager; Desktop Publishing Specialist; Editor; Editorial Assistant; Graphic Artist; Graphic Designer; Internet Services Manager; Managing Editor; MIS Specialist; Multimedia Designer; Network/Systems Administrator; Production Manager; Project Manager; Software Engineer; SQL Programmer; Systems Analyst; Systems Manager; Technical Writer/Editor; Webmaster.

Benefits available to temporary workers: 401(k); Dental Insurance; Disability Coverage; Medical Insurance. **President/CEO/Owner:** John Chuang, CEO.

BESTEMP TEMPORARY SERVICES, INC.
49 South Main Street, Gloversville NY 12078. 518/725-1459. `Fax:` 518/725-1473. **Contact:** Mr. Jody Eschler, President. **Description:** A temporary agency. **Specializes in the areas of:** Industrial; Manufacturing; Sales; Secretarial. **Positions commonly filled include:** Blue-Collar Worker Supervisor; Customer Service Representative; Manufacturer's/Wholesaler's Sales Rep.; Typist/Word Processor. **Benefits available to temporary workers:** Paid Holidays; Paid Vacation. **Other U.S. locations:** Albany NY. **Average salary range of placements:** Less than $20,000. **Number of placements per year:** 200 - 499.

CGR STAFFING SERVICES
21 West 38th, New York NY 10018. 212/764-3434. **Fax:** 212/997-5072. **Contact:** Manager. **Description:** A temporary agency. **Specializes in the areas of:** Advertising; Art/Design; Publishing; Sales; Technical. **Positions commonly filled include:** Administrative Manager; Broadcast Technician; Computer Programmer; Customer Service Representative; Designer; Internet Services Manager; MIS Specialist; Multimedia Designer; Technical Writer/Editor; Typist/Word Processor. **Corporate headquarters location:** Stamford CT. **Average salary range of placements:** $30,000 - $50,000.

CAREER OBJECTIVES PERSONNEL
103 South Bedford Road, Suite 207, Mount Kisco NY 10549. 914/666-8318. **Fax:** 914/666-0296. **Contact:** Lynn Robins, President. **Description:** A temporary agency that also provides some permanent placements to office personnel. **Specializes in the areas of:** Accounting/Auditing; Administration; Computer Science/Software; Insurance; Legal; Nonprofit; Personnel/Labor Relations; Publishing; Secretarial. **Positions commonly filled include:** Accountant/Auditor; Administrative Manager; Advertising Clerk; Brokerage Clerk; Clerical Supervisor; Computer Programmer; Credit Manager; Customer Service Representative; Financial Analyst; Human Resources Manager; Paralegal; Public Relations Specialist; Purchasing Agent/Manager; Quality Control Supervisor; Typist/Word Processor. **Average salary range of placements:** $20,000 - $29,999. **Number of placements per year:** 200 - 499.

DENTAFORCE DENTAL PLACEMENTS
3097 Steinway Street, Long Island City NY 11103-3820. 718/728-5454. **Contact:** Recruiter. **Description:** A temporary agency that also provides some permanent placements. **Specializes in the areas of:** Health/Medical. **Positions commonly filled include:** Dental Assistant/Dental Hygienist; Dentist. **Average salary range of placements:** $20,000 - $29,999. **Number of placements per year:** 500 - 999.

DENTAL PLACEMENT PLUS
76 East Main Street, Suite 4, Huntington NY 11743. 516/423-8888. **Contact:** President. **Description:** A temporary agency that also provides some permanent placements. **Specializes in the areas of:** Dental; Health/Medical; Personnel/Labor Relations. **Positions commonly filled include:** Dental Assistant/Dental Hygienist; Dentist. **Average salary range of placements:** $20,000 - $29,999. **Number of placements per year:** 1 - 49.

DUNHILL STAFFING SYSTEMS OF BUFFALO
584 Delaware Avenue, Buffalo NY 14202-1207. 716/885-0245. **Contact:** Jeanne Ptak, Manager. **E-mail address:** dunbuf@aol.com. **World Wide Web address:** http://www.dunhillstaff.com. **Description:** A temporary agency. **Specializes in the areas of:** Accounting/Auditing; Administration; Health/Medical; Legal; Secretarial. **Positions commonly filled include:** Account Manager; Accountant; Administrative Assistant;

Clerical Supervisor; Human Resources Manager; Marketing Specialist; Medical Records Technician; Paralegal; Secretary; Typist/Word Processor. **Corporate headquarters location:** Hauppage NJ. **Average salary range of placements:** $30,000 - $50,000. **Number of placements per year:** 100 - 199.

EUROMONDE, INC.
370 Lexington Avenue, Suite 1003, New York NY 10017. 212/661-5577. **Fax:** 212/661-5841. **Contact:** Manager. **Description:** A temporary agency that provides placements for bilingual personnel. **Specializes in the areas of:** Administration; Advertising; Banking; Fashion; Finance; Insurance; Nonprofit; Personnel/Labor Relations; Publishing; Secretarial. **Positions commonly filled include:** Accountant/Auditor; Administrative Manager; Bank Officer/Manager; Computer Programmer; Customer Service Representative; Financial Analyst; Human Resources Specialist; MIS Specialist; Operations/Production Manager; Transportation/Traffic Specialist; Typist/Word Processor. **Other U.S. locations:** CT; NJ.

EXTRA HELP EMPLOYMENT SERVICE
478 Delaware Avenue, Buffalo NY 14202. 716/885-1004. **Fax:** 716/885-1719. **Contact:** Judy Millard, Branch Manager. **E-mail address:** jam.buf@extra-help.com. **Description:** A temporary agency that also provides some temp-to-perm and permanent placements. Client company pays fee. **Specializes in the areas of:** Administration; Banking; Manufacturing. **Positions commonly filled include:** Account Manager; Account Representative; Accountant; Adjuster; Administrative Assistant; Auditor; Bank Officer/Manager; Customer Service Representative; General Manager; Human Resources Manager; Industrial Engineer; Industrial Production Manager; Manufacturing Engineer; Mechanical Engineer; Metallurgical Engineer; Production Manager; Quality Assurance Engineer; Quality Control Supervisor; Secretary; Typist/Word Processor. **Benefits available to temporary workers:** 401(k); Paid Holidays. **Corporate headquarters location:** Rochester NY. **Number of placements per year:** 200 - 499.

EXTRA HELP EMPLOYMENT SERVICES
950 New Loudon Road, Latham NY 12110. 518/782-1200. **Fax:** 518/782-1273. **Contact:** Claire Linnan, Manager. **Description:** A temporary agency that also provides some permanent placement. **Specializes in the areas of:** Accounting/Auditing; Computer Science/Software; Engineering; General Management; Industrial; Legal. **Positions commonly filled include:** Administrative Manager; Clerical Supervisor; Computer Programmer; Customer Service Representative; Draftsperson; General Manager; Industrial Engineer; Insurance Agent/Broker; Manufacturer's/Wholesaler's Sales Rep.; Mechanical Engineer; Paralegal. **Corporate headquarters location:** Rochester NY. **Average salary range of placements:** $30,000 - $50,000. **Number of placements per year:** 500 - 999.

FORUM TEMPORARY SERVICES
342 Madison Avenue, Suite 404, New York NY 10017. 212/687-7200. **Fax:** 212/687-8302. **Contact:** Mary Beth Schmid, Vice President/Placement Counselor. **E-mail address:** temp@forumper.com. **World Wide Web address:** http://www.forumpersonnel.com. **Description:** A temporary agency that also provides some permanent placements. Client company pays fee. **Specializes in the areas of:** Accounting; Administration; Banking; Finance; Legal; Secretarial. **Positions commonly filled include:** Accountant; Administrative Assistant; Broker; Budget Analyst; Chief Financial Officer; Controller; Credit Manager; Customer Service Representative; Financial Analyst; Human Resources Manager; Paralegal; Proofreader; Receptionist; Records Manager; Sales Representative; Secretary; Securities Sales Representative; Typist/Word Processor. **Benefits available to temporary workers:** Paid Holidays. **Corporate headquarters location:** This Location. **Number of placements per year:** 1000+.

FREELANCE ADVANCERS, INC.
420 Lexington Avenue, Suite 2007, New York NY 10170. 212/661-0900. **Fax:** 212/661-1883. **Contact:** Manager. **Description:** A temporary agency focusing on the placement of desktop publishing and multimedia professionals including graphic designers, Web designers, art directors, illustrators, proofreaders, and production/trafficking personnel. **Specializes in the areas of:** Advertising; Art/Design; Publishing. **Positions commonly filled include:** Designer; Graphic Designer; Multimedia Designer. **Average salary range of placements:** $30,000 - $50,000. **Number of placements per year:** 50 - 99.

GRAPHIC TECHNIQUES, INC.
268 Central Avenue, Albany NY 12206. 518/449-3066. **Contact:** Richard L. Koza, General Manager. **Description:** A temporary agency. **Specializes in the areas of:** Administration; Architecture/Construction; Engineering; Industrial; Manufacturing; Secretarial; Technical. **Positions commonly filled include:** Ceramics Engineer; Chemical Engineer; Chemist; Civil Engineer; Computer Programmer; Customer Service Representative; Design Engineer; Designer; Draftsperson; Electrical/Electronics Engineer; Environmental Engineer; Industrial Engineer; Materials Engineer; Mechanical Engineer; Metallurgical Engineer; Paralegal; Software Engineer; Structural Engineer; Systems Analyst; Typist/Word Processor. **Benefits available to temporary workers:** Paid Holidays; Paid Vacation. **Number of placements per year:** 100 - 199.

HAESLOOP AND HEGARTY
342 Madison Avenue, New York NY 10173-0002. 212/370-4020. **Contact:** SueAnn Haesloop, President. **Description:** A temporary employment agency. **Specializes in the areas of:** Accounting/Auditing; Banking; Finance; Personnel/Labor Relations; Secretarial. **Positions commonly filled include:** Accountant/Auditor; Brokerage Clerk; Financial Analyst; Human Resources Manager; Management Trainee; Typist/Word Processor. **Average salary range of placements:** $30,000 - $50,000. **Number of placements per year:** 100 - 199.

HIREKNOWLEDGE
19 West 21st Street, Suite 604, New York NY 10010. 212/924-3979. **Toll-free phone:** 800/937-3622. **Fax:** 212/924-3791. **Contact:** Recruiter. **World Wide Web address:** http://www.hireknowledge.com. **Description:** A temporary agency placing creative and technical individuals. The agency also offers some permanent placements. Client company pays fee. **Specializes in the areas of:** Advertising; Art/Design; Computer Science/Software; Internet Development; Internet Marketing; MIS/EDP; Printing; Publishing. **Positions commonly filled include:** Applications Engineer; AS400 Programmer Analyst; Computer Animator; Computer Engineer; Computer Graphics Specialist; Computer Operator; Computer Programmer; Computer Scientist; Computer Support Technician; Content Developer; Database Administrator; Database Manager; Editor; Editorial Assistant; Graphic Artist; Graphic Designer; Internet Services Manager; Managing Editor; MIS Specialist; Multimedia Designer; Network/Systems Administrator; Software Engineer; SQL Programmer; Systems Analyst; Systems Manager; Technical Writer/Editor; Webmaster. **Benefits available to temporary workers:** 401(k); Direct Deposit; Health Benefits; Vacation Pay. **Corporate headquarters location:** Providence RI. **Other U.S. locations:** Nationwide. **Average salary range of placements:** $30,000 - $49,999. **Number of placements per year:** 200 - 499.

HOT BEAR/DE BELLA PRODUCTIONS AND EDITORIAL TEMPS
303 East 83rd Street, New York NY 10028. 212/988-8189. **Fax:** 212/988-8189. **Contact:** Rosalynd Carol Friedman, Copywriter/President. **Description:** A temporary agency. **Specializes in the areas of:** Advertising; Art/Design; Publishing. **Positions commonly filled include:** Advertising Clerk; Copy Editor; Editor; Proofreader; Writer. **Average salary range of placements:** $30,000 - $65,000. **Number of placements per year:** 1 - 49.

INSURANCE OVERLOAD SYSTEMS
35 Pinelawn Road, Suite 114E, Melville NY 11747. **Toll-free phone:** 800/221-5430. **Contact:** Branch Manager. **Description:** A temporary agency. **Specializes in the areas of:** Insurance. **Positions commonly filled include:** Adjuster; Claim Representative; Underwriter/Assistant Underwriter. **Corporate headquarters location:** Dallas TX. **Number of placements per year:** 100 - 199.

INTERIM PERSONNEL
259 Monroe Avenue, Rochester NY 14607. 716/454-3200. **Fax:** 716/454-6258. **Contact:** Daniel McGuinn, Manager/Owner. **Description:** A temporary agency that also provides some temp-to-perm and permanent placements. **Specializes in the areas of:** Computer Science/Software; Industrial; Secretarial. **Positions commonly filled include:** Accountant/Auditor; Clerical Supervisor; Credit Manager; Customer Service Representative; Industrial Production Manager; Typist/Word Processor. **Benefits available to temporary workers:** Direct Deposit; Medical Insurance; Paid Holidays; Paid Vacation.

KELLY SERVICES, INC.
7-11 South Broadway, Suite 408, White Plains NY 10601-3531. 914/761-5885. **Fax:** 914/761-5443. **Contact:** Office Manager. **Description:** A temporary agency. **Specializes in the areas of:** Accounting/Auditing; Administration; Secretarial. **Positions commonly filled include:** Accountant/Auditor; Administrative Manager; Customer Service Representative; Typist/Word Processor. **Benefits available to temporary workers:** Paid Holidays; Paid Vacation. **Corporate headquarters location:** Troy MI. **Other U.S. locations:** Nationwide. **Number of placements per year:** 1000+.

KELLY SERVICES, INC.
125 Wolf Road, Suite 403, Albany NY 12205. 518/489-6060. **Fax:** 518/489-6187. **Contact:** Staffing Coordinator. **Description:** A temporary agency. Founded in 1946. **Specializes in the areas of:** Clerical; Light Industrial; Manufacturing; Marketing; Personnel/Labor Relations; Sales; Secretarial; Technical. **Positions commonly filled include:** Accountant/Auditor; Blue-Collar Worker Supervisor; Chemical Engineer; Claim Representative; Clerical Supervisor; Computer Programmer; Customer Service Representative; Draftsperson; Electrical/Electronics Engineer; Human Resources Specialist; Management Trainee; Mechanical Engineer; Systems Analyst; Technical Writer/Editor; Typist/Word Processor. **Benefits available to temporary workers:** Medical Insurance; Paid Holidays; Paid Vacation. **Corporate headquarters location:** Troy MI. **Average salary range of placements:** Less than $20,000. **Number of placements per year:** 500 - 999.

LAB SUPPORT INC.
One Water Street, White Plains NY 10601-1009. 914/683-5700. **Contact:** Recruiter. **Description:** A temporary agency that focuses on placing professionals in industrial laboratories. **Specializes in the areas of:** Biology; Food; Industrial; Manufacturing; Personnel/Labor Relations; Technical. **Positions commonly filled include:** Biochemist; Biological Scientist; Chemical Engineer; Chemist; Food Scientist/Technologist; Science Technologist. **Benefits available to temporary workers:** Medical Insurance; Paid Holidays; Paid Vacation. **Corporate headquarters location:** Calabasas CA. **Average salary range of placements:** $30,000 - $50,000. **Number of placements per year:** 200 - 499.

MANPOWER TECHNICAL SERVICES
5 Penn Plaza, New York NY 10001-1810. 212/563-7080. **Fax:** 212/562-8393. **Contact:** Technical Recruiter.

Description: A temporary agency that also provides some contract services. **Specializes in the areas of:** Computer Science/Software; Engineering; Technical. **Positions commonly filled include:** Computer Programmer; Design Engineer; Industrial Engineer; Mechanical Engineer; Systems Analyst; Technical Writer/Editor; Telecommunications Manager. **Benefits available to temporary workers:** Life Insurance; Medical Insurance; Paid Vacation; Referral Bonus Plan; Stock Purchase. **Corporate headquarters location:** Milwaukee WI. **Other U.S. locations:** Nationwide. **Average salary range of placements:** $50,000. **Number of placements per year:** 200 - 499.

MANPOWER TEMPORARY SERVICES
720 Fifth Avenue, 10th Floor, New York NY 10019. 212/307-1008. **Contact:** Office Manager. **Description:** A temporary agency. **Specializes in the areas of:** Banking; Clerical; Fashion; Nonprofit; Publishing. **Positions commonly filled include:** Bookkeeper; Clerk; Data Entry Clerk; Receptionist; Secretary; Statistician; Stenographer; Typist/Word Processor. **Corporate headquarters location:** Milwaukee WI. **Other U.S. locations:** Nationwide. **Number of placements per year:** 1000+.

MANPOWER TEMPORARY SERVICES
111 Broadway, 5th Floor, New York NY 10006. 212/366-6005. **Contact:** Branch Manager. **Description:** A temporary agency. **Specializes in the areas of:** Clerical; Data Processing; Industrial; Professional; Technical; Telecommunications; Word Processing. **Positions commonly filled include:** Accountant/Auditor; Accounting Clerk; Administrative Assistant; Assembly Worker; Biological Scientist; Bookkeeper; Chemist; Computer Operator; Customer Service Manager; Designer; Desktop Publishing Specialist; Electrician; Inventory Control Specialist; Library Technician; Machine Operator; Materials Engineer; Order Clerk; Packaging/Processing Worker; Painter; Project Engineer; Proofreader; Receptionist; Secretary; Software Engineer; Stenographer; Stock Clerk; Systems Analyst; Technical Writer/Editor; Telemarketer; Transcriptionist; Typesetter; Welder. **Corporate headquarters location:** Milwaukee WI. **Other U.S. locations:** Nationwide. **Number of placements per year:** 1000+.

MANPOWER TEMPORARY SERVICES
350 Motor Parkway, Room 201, Hauppauge NY 11788-5101. 516/434-1405. **Contact:** Branch Manager. **Description:** A temporary agency. **Specializes in the areas of:** Accounting/Auditing; Banking; Industrial; Secretarial; Telemarketing; Word Processing. **Positions commonly filled include:** Accountant/Auditor; Administrative Assistant; Clerk; Telemarketer; Typist/Word Processor. **Benefits available to temporary workers:** Medical Insurance; Paid Holidays; Paid Vacation. **Corporate headquarters location:** Milwaukee WI. **Other U.S. locations:** Nationwide.

MANPOWER TEMPORARY SERVICES
7550 South State Street, Lowville Commons, Lowville NY 13367. 315/376-6899. **Contact:** Branch Supervisor. **Description:** A temporary agency. **Specializes in the areas of:** Accounting/Auditing; Banking; Clerical; Computer Science/Software; Industrial; Manufacturing; Personnel/Labor Relations; Sales; Secretarial; Technical. **Positions commonly filled include:** Automotive Mechanic; Blue-Collar Worker Supervisor; Customer Service Representative; Mechanical Engineer; Paralegal; Typist/Word Processor. **Benefits available to temporary workers:** Life Insurance; Medical Insurance; Paid Holidays; Paid Vacation. **Corporate headquarters location:** Milwaukee WI. **Number of placements per year:** 100 - 199.

MANPOWER TEMPORARY SERVICES
5790 Widewaters Parkway, De Witt NY 13214. 315/446-1000. **Contact:** Branch Manager. **Description:** A temporary agency. **Specializes in the areas of:** Light Industrial; Office Support; Technical; Telemarketing; Word Processing. **Positions commonly filled include:** Accountant/Auditor; Accounting Clerk; Administrative Assistant; Assembler; Biological Scientist; Bookkeeper; Chemist; Computer Operator; Customer Service Representative; Designer; Desktop Publishing Specialist; Electrician; Inventory Control Specialist; Machine Operator; Materials Manager; Packaging/Processing Worker; Painter; Project Engineer; Receptionist; Records Manager; Research Assistant; Secretary; Software Engineer; Systems Analyst; Technical Writer/Editor; Technician; Telemarketer; Typist/Word Processor; Welder. **Benefits available to temporary workers:** Life Insurance; Medical Insurance; Paid Holidays; Paid Vacation. **Number of placements per year:** 1000+.

MANPOWER TEMPORARY SERVICES
125 Park Avenue, 3rd Floor, New York NY 10017. 212/557-9110. **Fax:** 212/557-9111. **Contact:** Branch Manager. **Description:** A temporary agency. **Specializes in the areas of:** Accounting; Advertising; Banking; Finance; Insurance; Legal; Publishing; Secretarial. **Positions commonly filled include:** Administrative Assistant; Computer Programmer; Customer Service Representative; Financial Analyst; Graphic Artist; Sales Representative; Secretary; Technical Writer/Editor; Typist/Word Processor. **Benefits available to temporary workers:** Medical Insurance; Paid Holidays; Paid Vacation; Referral Bonus Plan; Stock Purchase. **Corporate headquarters location:** Milwaukee WI. **Other U.S. locations:** Nationwide. **International locations:** Worldwide. **Average salary range of placements:** $20,000 - $29,999. **Number of placements per year:** 500 - 999.

MED-SCRIBE, INC.
215 Alexander Street, Rochester NY 14607. 716/262-3668. **Fax:** 716/262-3694. **Contact:** Bobbie Reif, Administrator. **E-mail address:** medjobs@medscribe.com. **Description:** A temporary agency that also provides some permanent placements for medical and dental office personnel. **Specializes in the areas of:** Health/Medical. **Positions commonly filled include:** Health Services Manager; Medical Records Technician; Secretary. **Benefits available to temporary workers:** Medical Insurance; Paid Holidays. **Average salary range of placements:** Less than $20,000. **Number of placements per year:** 1 - 49.

MEDIA STAFFING NETWORK
100 Park Avenue, New York NY 10017. 212/818-8955. **Fax:** 212/818-8956. **Contact:** David Sexter, Account Manager. **Description:** A temporary agency that focuses on providing placements in television, radio, cable, and print media companies. **Specializes in the areas of:** Advertising; Broadcasting; Personnel/Labor Relations; Sales. **Corporate headquarters location:** Chicago IL. **Other U.S. locations:** Nationwide.

METRO RESOURCES OF ROCHESTER INC.
1825 Buffalo Road, Rochester NY 14624-1501. 716/426-8060. **Fax:** 716/426-7720. **Contact:** James Pisaturo, President. **Description:** A temporary agency. **Specializes in the areas of:** Accounting/Auditing; Banking; Computer Science/Software; Engineering; Industrial; Manufacturing; Personnel/Labor Relations; Secretarial; Technical. **Positions commonly filled include:** Accountant/Auditor; Administrative Manager; Advertising Clerk; Architect; Automotive Mechanic; Blue-Collar Worker Supervisor; Buyer; Chemical Engineer; Civil Engineer; Claim Representative; Clerical Supervisor; Clinical Lab Technician; Computer Programmer; Construction and Building Inspector; Construction Contractor; Cost Estimator; Credit Manager; Customer Service Representative; Design Engineer; Designer; Draftsperson; Editor; Electrical/Electronics Engineer; Electrician; Environmental Engineer; Financial Analyst; Human Resources Manager; Human Service Worker; Industrial Engineer; Industrial Production Manager; Management Trainee; Mechanical Engineer; Multimedia Designer; Services Sales Representative; Software Engineer; Statistician; Structural Engineer; Surveyor; Systems Analyst; Technical Writer/Editor; Typist/Word

Processor. **Benefits available to temporary workers:** Paid Holidays; Paid Vacation. **Average salary range of placements:** $20,000 - $29,999.

MORGAN-MURRAY PERSONNEL
M&M TOP TEMPS
1461 Lakeland Avenue, Suite 6, Bohemia NY 11716. 516/567-7474. **Fax:** 516/567-9483. **Contact:** Barbara Murray, President. **Description:** A temporary agency that also provides some permanent placements. **Specializes in the areas of:** Accounting/Auditing; Advertising; Art/Design; Banking; Broadcasting; Economics; Engineering; Finance; Food; General Management; Health/Medical; Industrial; Insurance; Legal; Manufacturing; Personnel/Labor Relations; Retail; Sales; Secretarial; Technical. **Positions commonly filled include:** Accountant/Auditor; Adjuster; Administrative Manager; Advertising Clerk; Bank Officer/Manager; Biochemist; Blue-Collar Worker Supervisor; Branch Manager; Buyer; Chemical Engineer; Chemist; Claim Representative; Clerical Supervisor; Credit Manager; Customer Service Representative; Draftsperson; Environmental Engineer; General Manager; Hotel Manager; Human Resources Specialist; Industrial Production Manager; Insurance Agent/Broker; Management Trainee; Paralegal; Property and Real Estate Manager; Purchasing Agent/Manager; Quality Control Supervisor; Restaurant/Food Service Manager; Telecommunications Manager; Typist/Word Processor. **Number of placements per year:** 50 - 99.

NESCO SERVICE COMPANY
740 Driving Park Avenue, Rochester NY 14613. 716/458-5550. **Fax:** 716/458-1013. **Contact:** Recruiter. **Description:** A temporary agency. **Specializes in the areas of:** Clerical; Light Industrial; Technical.

NORRELL STAFFING SERVICES
120 Broadway, 17th Floor, New York NY 10271. 212/227-5000. **Contact:** Kelly Storm, Recruiter. **Description:** A temporary employment agency. **Specializes in the areas of:** Accounting/Auditing; Administration; Computer Science/Software; Finance; Personnel/Labor Relations; Sales; Secretarial; Technical. **Positions commonly filled include:** Administrative Assistant; Clerical Supervisor; Data Entry Clerk; Receptionist; Secretary; Typist/Word Processor. **Benefits available to temporary workers:** Dental Insurance; Medical Insurance; Paid Holidays; Paid Vacation; Stock Purchase. **Corporate headquarters location:** Atlanta GA. **Other U.S. locations:** Nationwide. **Average salary range of placements:** $25,000 - $40,000. **Number of placements per year:** 1000+.

OLSTEN FINANCIAL STAFFING
1140 Avenue of the Americas, 19th Floor, New York NY 10038. 212/730-8814. **Fax:** 212/730-8825. **Contact:** Manager. **E-mail address:** olsten@worldnet.att.net. **World Wide Web address:** http://www.olsten.com. **Description:** A temporary agency that also provides some permanent and contract placements. Client company pays fee. **Specializes in the areas of:** Accounting; Advertising; Banking; Finance; Food; Industrial; Insurance; Internet Development; Legal; Nonprofit; Printing; Publishing; Retail. **Positions commonly filled include:** Accountant; Auditor; Bank Officer/Manager; Budget Analyst; Chief Financial Officer; Controller; Cost Estimator; Credit Manager; Finance Director; Financial Analyst; Fund Manager. **Corporate headquarters location:** Melville NY. **Other U.S. locations:** Nationwide.

OLSTEN STAFFING SERVICES
35 Pinelawn Road, Melville NY 11747. 516/752-8851. **Toll-free phone:** 800/WORKNOW. **Contact:** Manager. **World Wide Web address:** http://www.worknow.com. **Description:** A temporary agency. Founded in 1950. **Specializes in the areas of:** Accounting/Auditing; Banking; Finance; Industrial; Legal; Technical. **Positions commonly filled include:** Accountant/Auditor; Attorney; Customer Service Representative; Draftsperson; Financial Analyst; Paralegal; Typist/Word Processor.

Benefits available to temporary workers: Bonus Award/Plan. **Corporate headquarters location:** This Location. **Other U.S. locations:** Nationwide. **Number of placements per year:** 1000+.

OLSTEN STAFFING SERVICES
36 West Main Street, Rochester NY 14614. 716/232-4070. **Fax:** 716/232-6926. **Contact:** Evelyn Reed, Customer Service Manager. **Description:** A temporary agency. Founded in 1950. **Specializes in the areas of:** Accounting/Auditing; Administration; Banking; Data Entry; Engineering; Finance; Industrial; Legal; Light Industrial; Manufacturing; Marketing; Office Support; Personnel/Labor Relations; Publishing; Retail; Sales; Secretarial; Technical; Telemarketing. **Positions commonly filled include:** Administrative Assistant; Administrative Manager; Bank Officer/Manager; Blue-Collar Worker Supervisor; Branch Manager; Brokerage Clerk; Budget Analyst; Buyer; Civil Engineer; Claim Representative; Clerical Supervisor; Clinical Lab Technician; Computer Programmer; Construction and Building Inspector; Construction Contractor; Cost Estimator; Credit Manager; Customer Service Representative; Design Engineer; Designer; Draftsperson; Electrical/Electronics Engineer; Financial Analyst; Hotel Manager; Human Resources Specialist; Human Service Worker; Industrial Engineer; Industrial Production Manager; Internet Services Manager; Management Trainee; Market Research Analyst; Medical Records Technician; MIS Specialist; Operations/Production Manager; Paralegal; Restaurant/Food Service Manager; Sales Representative; Secretary; Software Engineer; Stationary Engineer; Statistician; Strategic Relations Manager; Systems Analyst; Technical Writer/Editor; Telecommunications Manager; Typist/Word Processor; Underwriter/Assistant Underwriter. **Benefits available to temporary workers:** Daycare Assistance; Medical Insurance; Paid Holidays; Paid Vacation. **Corporate headquarters location:** Melville NY. **Other U.S. locations:** Nationwide.

PAYWISE INC.
122 East 42nd Street, Suite 520, New York NY 10168. 212/953-1287. **Contact:** Manager. **Description:** A temporary agency. **Specializes in the areas of:** Accounting/Auditing; Banking; Computer Science/Software; Finance; General Management; Secretarial. **Positions commonly filled include:** Accountant/Auditor; Administrative Manager; Blue-Collar Worker Supervisor; Branch Manager; Brokerage Clerk; Claim Representative; Clerical Supervisor; Computer Programmer; Credit Manager; Customer Service Representative; Management Trainee; MIS Specialist; Services Sales Representative; Systems Analyst; Typist/Word Processor. **Average salary range of placements:** $20,000 - $29,999. **Number of placements per year:** 500 - 999.

PREFERRED PROFESSIONALS
777 Third Avenue, New York NY 10017. 212/688-6347. **Contact:** Debbie Pazanski, General Manager. **Description:** A temporary agency that focuses on providing office support placements for the advertising industry. **Specializes in the areas of:** Advertising; Secretarial. **Positions commonly filled include:** Accountant/Auditor; Advertising Clerk; Receptionist; Typist/Word Processor. **Other U.S. locations:** Nationwide. **Number of placements per year:** 1000+.

REMEDY INTELLIGENT STAFFING
570 Taxter Road, Elmsford NY 10523. 914/592-5444. **Fax:** 914/592-2737. **Contact:** Manager. **Description:** A temporary agency. **Specializes in the areas of:** Accounting/Auditing; Architecture/Construction; Banking; Finance; Food; Health/Medical; Industrial; Legal; Manufacturing; Personnel/Labor Relations; Publishing; Secretarial. **Positions commonly filled include:** Customer Service Representative. **Benefits available to temporary workers:** Dental Insurance; Life Insurance; Medical Insurance. **Corporate headquarters location:** San Juan Capistrano CA. **Other U.S. locations:** Nationwide. **Average salary range of**

placements: $20,000 - $29,999. **Number of placements per year:** 500 - 999.

SHARP NURSES INC.
215 Park Avenue South, Suite 1304, New York NY 10003. 212/780-0044. **Fax:** 212/780-0046. **Contact:** Ms. Ruth Rama Witt, Vice President/General Manager. **Description:** A temporary agency that places nurses within institutional settings only. **Specializes in the areas of:** Health/Medical. **Positions commonly filled include:** Certified Nurses Aide; Home Health Aide; Licensed Practical Nurse; Registered Nurse. **Corporate headquarters location:** Los Angeles CA. **Other U.S. locations:** Nationwide. **Number of placements per year:** 1000+.

SPECIAL COUNSEL
360 West 31st Street, Suite 1510, New York NY 10001. 212/245-5599. **Fax:** 212/245-6010. **Contact:** Manager. **World Wide Web address:** http://www. specialcounsel.com. **Description:** A temporary agency that also provides some permanent placements. **Specializes in the areas of:** Legal.

STAFF MANAGERS
77 Jericho Turnpike, Suite 201, Mineola NY 11501. 516/294-7214. **Fax:** 516/294-1431. **Contact:** Ruth Stuart, President. **Description:** A temporary agency that also provides some permanent placements. **Specializes in the areas of:** Accounting/Auditing; Administration; Banking; Computer Science/Software; Engineering; Finance; General Management; Industrial; Insurance; Manufacturing; Personnel/Labor Relations; Sales; Secretarial; Technical. **Positions commonly filled include:** Accountant/Auditor; Adjuster; Aerospace Engineer; Bank Officer/Manager; Blue-Collar Worker Supervisor; Branch Manager; Buyer; Chemical Engineer; Claim Representative; Clerical Supervisor; Computer Programmer; Credit Manager; Customer Service Representative; Design Engineer; Draftsperson; Electrical/Electronics Engineer; Environmental Engineer; Financial Analyst; General Manager; Human Resources Specialist; Industrial Engineer; Industrial Production Manager; Insurance Agent/Broker; Internet Services Manager; Management Trainee; MIS Specialist; Operations/Production Manager; Purchasing Agent/Manager; Quality Control Supervisor; Software Engineer; Systems Analyst; Technical Writer/Editor; Telecommunications Manager; Typist/Word Processor. **Benefits available to temporary workers:** Bonus Award/Plan; Medical Insurance; Paid Holidays. **Number of placements per year:** 100 - 199.

STAFFING SOLUTIONS USA, INC.
370 Lexington Avenue, Suite 2110, New York NY 10017. 212/972-5100. **Fax:** 212/972-1377. **Contact:** Cliff Shaw, President. **World Wide Web address:** http://www.staffingsolutionsusa.com. **Description:** A temporary agency that also provides some permanent placements. Client company pays fee. **Specializes in the areas of:** MIS/EDP; Scientific; Technical. **Positions commonly filled include:** Applications Engineer; Computer Engineer; Computer Operator; Computer Programmer; Computer Support Technician; Computer Technician; Content Developer; Database Administrator; Database Manager; Internet Services Manager; MIS Specialist; Network/Systems Administrator; Operations Manager; Project Manager; Software Engineer; SQL Programmer; Systems Analyst; Systems Manager; Webmaster. **Corporate headquarters location:** This Location. **Number of placements per year:** 200 - 499.

STAFKINGS HEALTH CARE SYSTEMS
66 Hawley Street, Binghamton NY 13902. 607/772-8080. **Contact:** Manager. **Description:** A temporary employment agency focusing on the placement of home health aides, CNAs, LPNs, and some RNs. Positions typically begin as temporary and may become permanent. Please contact Stafkings Health Care Systems for more details. **Specializes in the areas of:** Health/Medical. **Corporate headquarters location:** This Location.

STAFKINGS HEALTH CARE SYSTEMS
221 West Church Street, Elmira NY 14901. 607/734-3646. **Contact:** Manager. **Description:** A temporary employment agency focusing on the placement of home health aides, CNAs, LPNs, and some RNs. Positions typically begin as temporary and may become permanent. Please contact Stafkings Health Care Systems for more details. **Specializes in the areas of:** Health/Medical. **Corporate headquarters location:** Binghamton NY.

STAFKINGS HEALTH CARE SYSTEMS
100 Genesee Street, Suite C, Auburn NY 13021. 315/252-3441. **Contact:** Manager. **Description:** A temporary employment agency focusing on the placement of home health aides, CNAs, LPNs, and some RNs. Positions typically begin as temporary and may become permanent. Please contact Stafkings Health Care Systems for more details. **Specializes in the areas of:** Health/Medical. **Corporate headquarters location:** Binghamton NY. **Other U.S. locations:** Elmira NY.

STAFKINGS PERSONNEL SYSTEMS
224 South Fulton Street, Ithaca NY 14850-3306. 607/273-5335. **Fax:** 607/273-1054. **Contact:** Branch Manager. **Description:** A temporary agency. **Specializes in the areas of:** Food; Health/Medical; Industrial. **Positions commonly filled include:** Accountant/Auditor; Clerical Supervisor; Clinical Lab Technician; Customer Service Representative; Food Scientist/Technologist; Human Resources Specialist; Licensed Practical Nurse; Medical Records Technician; MIS Specialist; Registered Nurse; Systems Analyst; Travel Agent; Typist/Word Processor. **Corporate headquarters location:** Binghamton NY. **Average salary range of placements:** Less than $20,000.

SWING SHIFT
One Horatio Street, New York NY 10014-1618. 212/206-1222. **Fax:** 212/727-9754. **Contact:** Harriet Livathinos, President. **Description:** A temporary agency focusing on the placement of office support and desktop publishing production personnel. Backgrounds sought include graphics, page layout, and presentation software. **Specializes in the areas of:** Advertising; Computer Science/Software; Secretarial. **Positions commonly filled include:** Desktop Publishing Specialist; Proofreader; Typist/Word Processor. **Average salary range of placements:** $20,000 - $49,999. **Number of placements per year:** 1000+.

TAC STAFFING SERVICES
505 Fifth Avenue, Suite 1000, New York NY 10017. 212/687-5213. **Contact:** Manager. **Description:** A temporary agency. **Specializes in the areas of:** Clerical; Data Processing; Office Support. **Other U.S. locations:** Nationwide.

TEMPORARY RESOURCE CENTER
18 East 48th Street, Suite 902, New York NY 10017. 212/486-7884. **Toll-free phone:** 888/693-8367. **Fax:** 212/486-8042. **Contact:** Andrew Greenberg, President. **Description:** A temporary agency. **Specializes in the areas of:** Accounting/Auditing; Banking; Finance; Personnel/Labor Relations; Secretarial. **Positions commonly filled include:** Advertising Clerk; Brokerage Clerk; Computer Programmer; Customer Service Representative; Financial Analyst; Human Resources Specialist; Internet Services Manager; Systems Analyst; Typist/Word Processor.

TEMPOSITIONS, INC.
420 Lexington Avenue, Suite 2100, New York NY 10170. 212/490-7400. **Fax:** 212/867-1759. **Contact:** Anne Marie Karash, Director of Operations. **Description:** A temporary agency. **Specializes in the areas of:** Advertising; Communications; Computer Science/Software; Legal; Office Support; Personnel/Labor Relations; Secretarial. **Positions commonly filled include:** Accountant/Auditor; Administrative Assistant; Customer Service Representative; Data Entry Clerk; Desktop Publishing

Specialist; Licensed Practical Nurse; MIS Specialist; Paralegal; Registered Nurse; Secretary; Social Worker; Technician; Telemarketer; Therapist; Typist/Word Processor. **Benefits available to temporary workers:** Daycare Assistance; Paid Holidays; Paid Vacation; Referral Bonus Plan. **Other area locations:** Melville NY; White Plains NY. **Other U.S. locations:** San Francisco CA. **Average salary range of placements:** $20,000 - $29,999. **Number of placements per year:** 1000+.

UNIQUE SUPPORT SERVICES, INC.
160 Broadway, Suite 905, New York NY 10038. 212/406-0062. **Toll-free phone:** 800/232-4303. **Fax:** 212/406-5882. **Contact:** Professional Staffing Manager. **Description:** A temporary agency that also provides some permanent placements. **Specializes in the areas of:** Computer Science/Software; General Management; Secretarial. **Positions commonly filled include:** Typist/Word Processor. **Other U.S. locations:** Washington DC; Morristown NJ; Newark NJ; Wyomissing PA. **Average salary range of placements:** $20,000 - $29,999. **Number of placements per year:** 200 - 499.

UNITED STAFFING SYSTEMS
16 East 40th Street, 4th Floor, New York NY 10016-0113. 212/743-0300. **Fax:** 212/576-2427. **Contact:** Manager. **E-mail address:** recruiters@unitedstaffing.com. **World Wide Web address:** http://www.unitedstaffing.com. **Description:** A temporary agency that also provides some temp-to-perm and permanent placements. Client company pays fee. **Specializes in the areas of:** Accounting; Administration; Banking; Computer Science/Software; Fashion; Finance; General Management; Health/Medical; Insurance; Legal; Secretarial. **Positions commonly filled include:** Accountant; Adjuster; Administrative Assistant; Administrative Manager; Advertising Clerk; Advertising Executive; Applications Engineer; AS400 Programmer Analyst; Assistant Manager; Attorney; Auditor; Bank Officer/Manager; Blue-Collar Worker Supervisor; Broadcast Technician; Budget Analyst; Certified Nurses Aide; Certified Occupational Therapy Assistant; Chief Financial Officer; Claim Representative; Clerical Supervisor; Clinical Lab Technician; Computer Animator; Computer Engineer; Computer Operator; Computer Programmer; Computer Scientist; Computer Support Technician; Computer Technician; Content Developer; Controller; Cost Estimator; Counselor; Credit Manager; Customer Service Representative; Database Administrator; Database Manager; Desktop Publishing Specialist; Dietician/Nutritionist; Economist; Editor; Editorial Assistant; EEG Technologist; EKG Technician; Finance Director; Financial Analyst; Fund Manager; General Manager; Graphic Artist; Graphic Designer; Home Health Aide; Human Resources Manager; Insurance Agent/Broker; Internet Services Manager; Licensed Practical Nurse; Managing Editor; Market Research Analyst; Marketing Manager; Marketing Specialist; Medical Assistant; Medical Records Technician; MIS Specialist; Multimedia Designer; Network/Systems Administrator; Nuclear Medicine Technologist; Nurse Practitioner; Occupational Therapist; Operations Manager; Paralegal; Pharmacist; Physical Therapist; Physical Therapy Assistant; Physician; Production Manager; Project Manager; Psychologist; Public Relations Specialist; Purchasing Agent/Manager; Radio/TV Announcer/Broadcaster; Radiological Technologist; Registered Nurse; Reporter; Respiratory Therapist; Secretary; Social Worker;

Software Engineer; Speech-Language Pathologist; SQL Programmer; Surgical Technician; Systems Analyst; Systems Manager; Technical Writer/Editor; Telecommunications Manager; Typist/Word Processor; Underwriter/Assistant Underwriter; Veterinarian; Video Production Coordinator; Webmaster. **Other U.S. locations:** Newark NJ; Long Island NY; Westchester NY. **Average salary range of placements:** $30,000 - $49,999. **Number of placements per year:** 1000+.

VANTAGE STAFFING SERVICES
180 East Post Road, White Plains NY 10601. 914/761-1120. **Fax:** 914/997-8319. **Contact:** Kathy O'Connor, President. **Description:** A temporary agency that also provides some permanent placements. **Specializes in the areas of:** Accounting/Auditing; Banking; Finance; Legal; Personnel/Labor Relations; Secretarial. **Positions commonly filled include:** Accountant/Auditor; Administrative Manager; Bank Officer/Manager; Brokerage Clerk; Clerical Supervisor; Credit Manager; Customer Service Representative; Financial Analyst; Human Resources Specialist; Paralegal; Typist/Word Processor. **Benefits available to temporary workers:** Dental Insurance; Paid Holidays; Paid Vacation. **Other U.S. locations:** Stamford CT. **Average salary range of placements:** $30,000 - $50,000. **Number of placements per year:** 100 - 199.

WESTAFF
7525 Morgan Road, Liverpool NY 13090-3938. 315/453-5533. **Fax:** 315/453-3958. **Contact:** Michele Washburn, Office Manager. **World Wide Web address:** http://www.westaff.com. **Description:** A temporary agency that also provides some permanent placements. **Specializes in the areas of:** Accounting/Auditing; Administration; General Management; Industrial; Light Industrial; Personnel/Labor Relations; Secretarial. **Positions commonly filled include:** Administrative Manager; Blue-Collar Worker Supervisor; Claim Representative; Clerical Supervisor; Customer Service Representative; Electrical/Electronics Engineer; General Manager; Human Resources Specialist; Industrial Production Manager; Purchasing Agent/Manager; Quality Control Supervisor; Services Sales Representative; Typist/Word Processor. **Benefits available to temporary workers:** 401(k); Paid Holidays; Paid Vacation. **Number of placements per year:** 1000+.

WESTAFF
3 Ellinwood Court, Suite 202, New Hartford NY 13413. 315/736-3884. **Fax:** 315/736-5340. **Contact:** Jack Altdoerffer, Vice President of Marketing. **Description:** A temporary agency that also provides some permanent placements. **Specializes in the areas of:** Banking; Broadcasting; Engineering; Finance; Food; General Management; Industrial; Personnel/Labor Relations; Retail; Sales; Secretarial; Technical. **Positions commonly filled include:** Accountant/Auditor; Administrative Manager; Bank Officer/Manager; Blue-Collar Worker Supervisor; Branch Manager; Claim Representative; Clerical Supervisor; Computer Programmer; Cost Estimator; Design Engineer; Designer; Electrical/Electronics Engineer; Electrician; Human Resources Specialist; Human Service Worker; Industrial Engineer; Library Technician; Management Trainee; Services Sales Representative; Technical Writer/Editor; Telecommunications Manager; Transportation/Traffic Specialist; Travel Agent; Typist/Word Processor. **Other U.S. locations:** Nationwide.

CONTRACT SERVICES FIRMS

ATS RELIANCE, INC.
250 Mill Street, 5th Floor, Rochester NY 14614-1026. 716/777-4090. **Fax:** 716/777-4058. **Contact:** Chris Bell, Manager. **Description:** A contract services firm. **Specializes in the areas of:** Computer Science/Software; Engineering; Industrial; Manufacturing; Technical.

Positions commonly filled include: Aerospace Engineer; Agricultural Engineer; Aircraft Mechanic/Engine Specialist; Biochemist; Biological Scientist; Buyer; Ceramics Engineer; Chemical Engineer; Chemist; Civil Engineer; Computer Programmer; Construction and Building Inspector; Construction

Contractor; Cost Estimator; Design Engineer; Designer; Draftsperson; Electrical/Electronics Engineer; Environmental Engineer; Industrial Engineer; Industrial Production Manager; Internet Services Manager; Landscape Architect; Materials Engineer; Mechanical Engineer; Metallurgical Engineer; Mining Engineer; MIS Specialist; Nuclear Engineer; Petroleum Engineer; Purchasing Agent/Manager; Quality Control Supervisor; Science Technologist; Software Engineer; Stationary Engineer; Structural Engineer; Systems Analyst; Technical Writer/Editor; Telecommunications Manager; Transportation/Traffic Specialist; Urban/Regional Planner.

ADECCO/TAD TECHNICAL SERVICES
1040B University Avenue, Rochester NY 14607. 716/242-5320. **Toll-free phone:** 800/836-1411. **Fax:** 716/242-5323. **Contact:** Recruiter. **World Wide Web address:** http://www.adeccotad.com. **Description:** A contract services firm that also provides some temporary and permanent placements. Client company pays fee. **Specializes in the areas of:** Computer Science/Software; Engineering; Industrial; Internet Development; Scientific; Technical. **Positions commonly filled include:** Applications Engineer; Architect; AS400 Programmer Analyst; Buyer; Chemical Engineer; Chemist; Civil Engineer; Computer Animator; Computer Engineer; Computer Operator; Computer Programmer; Computer Scientist; Computer Support Technician; Computer Technician; Construction Contractor; Content Developer; Database Administrator; Database Manager; Design Engineer; Draftsperson; Electrical/Electronics Engineer; Environmental Engineer; Graphic Artist; Graphic Designer; Industrial Engineer; Internet Services Manager; Manufacturing Engineer; Mechanical Engineer; Metallurgical Engineer; MIS Specialist; Multimedia Designer; Network/Systems Administrator; Quality Assurance Engineer; Sales Engineer; Software Engineer; SQL Programmer; Statistician; Systems Analyst; Systems Manager; Technical Writer/Editor; Webmaster. **Corporate headquarters location:** Redwood City CA. **Other U.S. locations:** Nationwide. **International locations:** Worldwide.

ADVANCED CONSULTANCY GROUP INTERNATIONAL, INC.
60 East 42nd Street, Suite 2810, New York NY 10016. 212/883-1010. **Fax:** 212/883-1174. **Contact:** Doug Klares, Director of Sales/Recruiting. **Description:** A contract services firm. **Positions commonly filled include:** Applications Engineer; AS400 Programmer Analyst; Computer Operator; Computer Programmer; Computer Support Technician; Database Administrator; Database Manager; Network/Systems Administrator; Quality Assurance Engineer; SQL Programmer; Systems Analyst; Systems Manager. **Benefits available to temporary workers:** Health Benefits. **Number of placements per year:** 50 - 99.

CDI CORPORATION
2060 Fairport Nine Mile Point Road, Suite 400, Penfield NY 14526. 716/377-3310. **Toll-free phone:** 800/207-3140. **Fax:** 716/377-5225. **Contact:** Beverly Haynes, Recruiting Manager. **E-mail address:** penfield@cdicorp.com. **World Wide Web address:** http://www.cdicorp.com. **Description:** A contract services firm providing placements for supplemental engineering, technical, and information services personnel. **Specializes in the areas of:** Advertising; Computer Science/Software; Engineering; Manufacturing; Technical. **Positions commonly filled include:** Buyer; Chemist; Computer Programmer; Customer Service Representative; Design Engineer; Designer; Draftsperson; Electrical/Electronics Engineer; Financial Analyst; Industrial Engineer; Industrial Production Manager; Mechanical Engineer; MIS Specialist; Purchasing Agent/Manager; Quality Control Supervisor; Software Engineer; Systems Analyst; Technical Writer/Editor; Telecommunications Manager. **Corporate headquarters location:** Philadelphia PA. **Other U.S. locations:** Nationwide. **International**

locations: Worldwide. **Number of placements per year:** 200 - 499.

CDI CORPORATION
1811 Route 52, Suite G, Hopewell Junction NY 12533. 914/226-1066. **Contact:** Recruiting. **World Wide Web address:** http://www.cdicorp.com. **Description:** A contract services firm. Client company pays fee. **Specializes in the areas of:** Information Systems. **Positions commonly filled include:** Applications Engineer; AS400 Programmer Analyst; Computer Animator; Computer Engineer; Computer Operator; Computer Programmer; Computer Scientist; Computer Support Technician; Computer Technician; Content Developer; Database Administrator; Database Manager; Internet Services Manager; MIS Specialist; Multimedia Designer; Network/Systems Administrator; Software Engineer; SQL Programmer; Systems Analyst; Systems Manager; Webmaster. **Corporate headquarters location:** Philadelphia PA. **Other U.S. locations:** Nationwide. **International locations:** Worldwide.

COMFORCE INFORMATION TECHNOLOGIES, INC.
6780 Pittsford-Palmyra Road, Suite 16, Fairport NY 14450. 716/223-2300. **Toll-free phone:** 800/724-1223. **Fax:** 716/223-3484. **Contact:** Janet Longtin, Recruiter. **E-mail address:** staffing@comforce.com. **World Wide Web address:** http://www.comforce.com. **Description:** A contract services firm. **Specializes in the areas of:** Computer Science/Software. **Positions commonly filled include:** Computer Programmer; Consultant; Database Manager; Design Engineer; Graphic Designer; MIS Specialist; Multimedia Designer; Project Manager; Software Engineer; Systems Analyst; Systems Manager; Technical Writer/Editor. **Benefits available to temporary workers:** 401(k); Life Insurance; Medical Insurance; Paid Holidays; Paid Vacation; Referral Bonus Plan; Tuition Assistance. **Corporate headquarters location:** Woodbury NY. **Other U.S. locations:** Nationwide. **Average salary range of placements:** More than $50,000. **Number of placements per year:** 50 - 99.

COMFORCE INFORMATION TECHNOLOGIES, INC.
5788 Widewaters Parkway, De Witt NY 13214. 315/445-5550. **Contact:** Manager. **World Wide Web address:** http://www.comforce.com. **Description:** A contract services firm. **Specializes in the areas of:** Computer Science/Software. **Corporate headquarters location:** Woodbury NY.

COMFORCE TELECOM, INC.
2001 Marcus Avenue, Suite S160, Lake Success NY 11042-1011. 516/352-3200. **Fax:** 516/352-3362. **Contact:** Manager. **E-mail address:** contact@comforce.com. **World Wide Web address:** http://www.comforce.com. **Description:** A contract services firm. **Specializes in the areas of:** Computer Science/Software; Telecommunications. **Positions commonly filled include:** Computer Programmer; Electrical/Electronics Engineer; MIS Specialist; Software Engineer; Systems Analyst; Telecommunications Manager. **Benefits available to temporary workers:** Medical Insurance; Paid Holidays; Paid Vacation. **Average salary range of placements:** $30,000 - $50,000. **Number of placements per year:** 500 - 999.

COMFORCE TELECOM, INC.
P.O. Box 1009, Highland Mills NY 10930. 914/928-3634. **Physical address:** 583 Route 32, Highland Mills NY. **Fax:** 914/928-6108. **Contact:** Manager. **World Wide Web address:** http://www.comforce.com. **Description:** A contract services firm. **Specializes in the areas of:** Telecommunications.

CONTRACT SPECIALTIES GROUP
755 Waverly Avenue, Suite 305, Holtsville NY 11742. 516/475-7900. **Toll-free phone:** 800/755-1524. **Fax:** 516/475-7920. **Contact:** Dan DeFini, President. **E-mail address:** defini@csgjobs.com. **World Wide Web**

address: http://www.csgjobs.com. **Description:** A contract services firm that also provides some permanent placements. Client company pays fee. **Specializes in the areas of:** Engineering; Light Industrial; Technical. **Positions commonly filled include:** Applications Engineer; Architect; Buyer; Chemical Engineer; Civil Engineer; Computer Programmer; Computer Support Technician; Computer Technician; Construction Contractor; Design Engineer; Draftsperson; Electrical/Electronics Engineer; Environmental Engineer; Industrial Production Manager; Manufacturing Engineer; Mechanical Engineer; Metallurgical Engineer; MIS Specialist; Production Manager; Project Manager; Quality Assurance Engineer; Quality Control Supervisor; Software Engineer; Systems Analyst; Systems Manager; Technical Writer/Editor. **Benefits available to temporary workers:** Paid Holidays; Paid Vacation. **Corporate headquarters location:** This Location. **Other U.S. locations:** Nationwide. **Average salary range of placements:** $30,000 - $100,000. **Number of placements per year:** 200 - 499.

EDP CONTRACT SERVICES, INC.
505 Fifth Avenue, Suite 1000, New York NY 10017. 212/947-6033. **Contact:** Douglas Heppner, Manager. **Description:** A contract services firm. **Specializes in the areas of:** Accounting/Auditing; Banking; Computer Science/Software; Engineering; Finance; Insurance; Manufacturing; MIS/EDP; Nonprofit; Personnel/Labor Relations; Publishing; Technical. **Positions commonly filled include:** Computer Operator; EDP Specialist; MIS Specialist; Systems Analyst; Technical Writer/Editor. **Number of placements per year:** 1000+.

ELITE TECHNICAL SERVICES, INC.
898 Veterans Memorial Highway, Suite 340, Hauppauge NY 11788. 516/366-2345. **Toll-free phone:** 800/ELITE50. **Contact:** Manager. **E-mail address:** elite500@aol.com. **Description:** A contract services firm. **Positions commonly filled include:** Electrical/Electronics Engineer; Software Engineer.

HALL KINION
590 Fifth Avenue, 18th Floor, New York NY 10036. **Toll-free phone:** 800/963-8326. **Fax:** 212/575-2640. **Contact:** Manager. **E-mail address:** nyresume@hallkinion.com. **World Wide Web address:** http://www.hallkinion.com. **Description:** A contract services firm that also provides some permanent placements. **Specializes in the areas of:** Information Systems; Information Technology; Internet Development; Network Administration; Quality Assurance; Systems Administration; Systems Design; Technical Writing.

INFORMATION SYSTEMS STAFFING, INC.
5730 Commons Park Drive, East Syracuse NY 13057. 315/449-1838. **Toll-free phone:** 800/466-1939. **Fax:** 315/449-1939. **Contact:** Manager. **E-mail address:** office@issi-syr.com. **World Wide Web address:** http://www.issi-syr.com. **Description:** A contract services firm. **Specializes in the areas of:** Administration; Computer Science/Software; MIS/EDP. **Positions commonly filled include:** Computer Programmer; Database Administrator; Project Manager; Software Engineer; Systems Analyst; Systems Manager; Vice President. **Average salary range of placements:** $40,000 - $70,000. **Number of placements per year:** 50 - 99.

KIRK-MAYER
535 Broadhollow Road, Suite A16-A, Melville NY 11747. 516/694-8800. **Fax:** 516/694-8804. **Contact:** Branch Manager. **Description:** A contract services firm. **Specializes in the areas of:** Computer Science/Software; Engineering; Industrial; Manufacturing; Transportation. **Positions commonly filled include:** Aerospace Engineer; Aircraft Mechanic/Engine Specialist; Biomedical Engineer; Buyer; Ceramics Engineer; Chemical Engineer; Civil Engineer; Computer Programmer; Construction and Building Inspector; Construction Contractor; Cost Estimator; Design

Engineer; Designer; Draftsperson; Electrical/Electronics Engineer; Environmental Engineer; Industrial Engineer; Materials Engineer; Mechanical Engineer; MIS Specialist; Nuclear Engineer; Operations/Production Manager; Purchasing Agent/Manager; Quality Control Supervisor; Software Engineer; Structural Engineer; Systems Analyst; Technical Writer/Editor; Telecommunications Manager. **Corporate headquarters location:** Cambridge MA. **Average salary range of placements:** More than $50,000. **Number of placements per year:** 50 - 99.

PLATINUM IT CONSULTING
535 Fifth Avenue, Suite 1004, New York NY 10017. 212/661-8355. **Fax:** 212/687-4347. **Contact:** Recruiter. **E-mail address:** platinum@haven.ios.com. **Description:** A contract services firm. **Specializes in the areas of:** Computer Science/Software. **Positions commonly filled include:** Computer Operator; Computer Programmer; Database Manager; Internet Services Manager; MIS Specialist; Project Manager; Systems Analyst; Technical Writer/Editor. **Benefits available to temporary workers:** Medical Insurance. **Other U.S. locations:** Madison NJ.

SUPERIOR CONCEPTS
21 Front Street, Schenectady NY 12305-1301. 518/393-4425. **Fax:** 518/370-0103. **Contact:** Gayle C. Belden, President/Program Director. **Description:** A contract services firm that also provides some contract-to-permanent placements. Superior Concepts focuses on providing international placements. **Specializes in the areas of:** Accounting/Auditing; Administration; Architecture/Construction; Banking; Computer Science/Software; Education; Engineering; Finance; Food; Health/Medical; Industrial; Manufacturing; Personnel/Labor Relations; Sales; Technical. **Positions commonly filled include:** Accountant/Auditor; Administrative Manager; Aerospace Engineer; Aircraft Mechanic/Engine Specialist; Architect; Attorney; Bank Officer/Manager; Biomedical Engineer; Chemical Engineer; Computer Programmer; Construction and Building Inspector; Dental Assistant/Dental Hygienist; Design Engineer; Education Administrator; EEG Technologist; Electrical/Electronics Engineer; Financial Analyst; Food Scientist/Technologist; Health Services Manager; Human Resources Specialist; Industrial Engineer; Internet Services Manager; Landscape Architect; Manufacturer's/Wholesaler's Sales Rep.; Market Research Analyst; Mechanical Engineer; MIS Specialist; Multimedia Designer; Occupational Therapist; Operations/Production Manager; Petroleum Engineer; Pharmacist; Physician; Property and Real Estate Manager; Quality Control Supervisor; Registered Nurse; Restaurant/Food Service Manager; Securities Sales Representative; Software Engineer; Stationary Engineer; Structural Engineer; Systems Analyst; Technical Writer/Editor; Telecommunications Manager; Transportation/Traffic Specialist; Urban/Regional Planner. **Number of placements per year:** 50 - 99.

VOLT SERVICES GROUP
1212 Avenue of the Americas, New York NY 10036. 212/719-7841. **Toll-free phone:** 800/367-8658. **Fax:** 212/719-7850. **Contact:** John Sexton, Branch Manager. **World Wide Web address:** http://www.volteast.com. **Description:** A contract services firm. **Specializes in the areas of:** Banking; Broadcasting; Computer Science/Software; Engineering; Industrial; Insurance. **Positions commonly filled include:** Account Manager; Account Representative; Administrative Assistant; Architect; Buyer; Computer Animator; Computer Operator; Computer Programmer; Database Manager; Design Engineer; Human Resources Manager; Manufacturing Engineer; MIS Specialist; Project Manager; Purchasing Agent/Manager; Software Engineer; Stationary Engineer; Systems Analyst; Technical Writer/Editor; Telecommunications Manager. **Benefits available to temporary workers:** Medical Insurance; Paid Holidays; Paid Vacation. **Corporate headquarters location:** This Location. **Other U.S. locations:** Nationwide. **Average salary range of**

placements: More than $50,000. **Number of placements per year:** 1000+.

H.L. YOH COMPANY
301 Exchange Boulevard, Rochester NY 14608. 716/454-5400. **Toll-free phone:** 800/841-3709. **Fax:** 716/454-2105. **Contact:** Alisa Lama, Technical Recruiter. **E-mail address:** hlyoh@netacc.net. **Description:** A contract services firm. Founded in 1942. **Specializes in the areas of:** Computer Science/Software; Engineering; Information Technology; Light Industrial; Manufacturing; Secretarial; Technical. **Positions commonly filled include:** Administrative Assistant; Applications Engineer; Blue-Collar Worker Supervisor; Buyer; Chemical Engineer; Civil Engineer; Computer Operator; Computer Programmer; Customer Service

Representative; Database Manager; Design Engineer; Electrical/Electronics Engineer; Environmental Engineer; Financial Analyst; Industrial Engineer; Internet Services Manager; Manufacturing Engineer; Mechanical Engineer; MIS Manager; Multimedia Designer; Operations Manager; Project Manager; Secretary; Software Engineer; Systems Analyst; Systems Manager; Technical Writer/Editor; Typist/Word Processor; Webmaster. **Benefits available to temporary workers:** Medical Insurance; Paid Holidays; Paid Vacation. **Corporate headquarters location:** Philadelphia PA. **Other U.S. locations:** Nationwide. **International locations:** Toronto. **Average salary range of placements:** $30,000 - $50,000. **Number of placements per year:** 200 - 499.

CAREER/OUTPLACEMENT COUNSELING FIRMS

MERRILL ADAMS ASSOCIATES
30 Rockefeller Plaza, Suite 2835, New York NY 10112. 212/332-7888. **Fax:** 212/332-7887. **Contact:** Arthur Schill, Executive Vice President. **Description:** A career/outplacement counseling firm. **Specializes in the areas of:** Accounting/Auditing; Administration; Advertising; Banking; Computer Science/Software; Economics; Education; Engineering; Finance; Food; General Management; Health/Medical; Industrial; Insurance; Legal; Manufacturing; Personnel/Labor Relations; Publishing; Retail; Sales; Technical. **Positions commonly filled include:** Accountant/Auditor; Administrative Manager; Aerospace Engineer; Architect; Attorney; Bank Officer/Manager; Biochemist; Biological Scientist; Branch Manager; Broadcast Technician; Budget Analyst; Buyer; Chemical Engineer; Chemist; Chief Executive Officer; Chief Financial Officer; Civil Engineer; Computer Programmer; Construction Contractor; Credit Manager; Customer Service Representative; Design Engineer; Designer; Dietician/Nutritionist; Draftsperson; Economist; Editor; Education Administrator; Electrical/Electronics Engineer; Environmental Engineer; Financial Analyst; Food Scientist/Technologist; General Manager; Health Services Manager; Hotel Manager; Human Resources Specialist; Industrial Engineer; Industrial Production Manager; Insurance Agent/Broker; Internet Services Manager; Librarian; Management Analyst/Consultant; Management Trainee; Manufacturer's/Wholesaler's Sales Rep.; Market Research Analyst; Mathematician; Mechanical Engineer; Medical Records Technician; MIS Specialist; Multimedia Designer; Nuclear Engineer; Occupational Therapist; Operations/Production Manager; Petroleum Engineer; Pharmacist; Physician; Property and Real Estate Manager; Psychologist; Public Relations Specialist; Quality Control Supervisor; Real Estate Agent; Recreational Therapist; Restaurant/Food Service Manager; Services Sales Representative; Social Worker; Software Engineer; Strategic Relations Manager; Structural Engineer; Systems Analyst; Technical Writer/Editor; Telecommunications Manager; Travel Agent; Underwriter/Assistant Underwriter; Vice President. **Corporate headquarters location:** Parsippany NJ. **Other U.S. locations:** Princeton NJ. **Number of placements per year:** 1 - 49.

ADVANTAGE RESUMES OF NEW YORK
77 Buffalo Avenue, Medford NY 11763. 631/475-8513. **Toll-free phone:** 888/272-8899. **Fax:** 631/475-8513. **Contact:** Deborah Wile-Dib, President. **E-mail address:** gethired@advantageresumes.com. **World Wide Web address:** http://www.advantageresumes.com. **Description:** A global, internet-based resume and career counseling firm. Jobseeker pays fee. **Specializes in the areas of:** Banking; Computer Science/Software; Engineering; Executives; Finance; General Management; Internet Development; Internet Marketing; Marketing; Sales; Scientific; Technical. **Corporate headquarters location:** This Location.

CAREER CIRCUIT
730 Fifth Avenue, 9th Floor, New York NY 10019. 212/879-2401. **Toll-free phone:** 800/753-4112. **Fax:** 212/879-2395. **Contact:** Manager. **E-mail address:** mail@careercircuit.com. **World Wide Web address:** http://www.careercircuit.com. **Description:** A career counseling firm that also provides some placement services. **Specializes in the areas of:** Technical.

CAREER DEVELOPMENT SERVICES
706 East Avenue, Rochester NY 14607-2105. 716/244-0750. **Fax:** 716/244-7115. **Contact:** Ellie Cope, Director of Community Services. **E-mail address:** info@careerdev.org. **World Wide Web address:** http://www.careerdev.org. **Description:** A career/outplacement counseling firm providing corporate training, in-house career resource library services, career coaching, employee career centers, and national client services. Founded in 1975. **Positions commonly filled include:** Administrative Assistant; Chemical Engineer; Chemist; Commercial Artist; Customer Service Representative; Draftsperson; EDP Specialist; Factory Worker; Manufacturing Engineer; Marketing Specialist; Medical Secretary; Nurse; Public Relations Specialist; Receptionist; Secretary; Software Engineer; Technical Writer/Editor. **Number of placements per year:** 200 - 499.

RLS CAREER CENTER
3049 East Genesee Street, Syracuse NY 13224. 315/446-0566. **Fax:** 315/446-5869. **Contact:** Rebecca A. Livingood, Executive Director. **Description:** A career/outplacement counseling firm.

EXECUTIVE SEARCH FIRMS

A FIRST RESOURCE
P.O. Box 15451, Winston-Salem NC 27113. 336/784-5898. **Fax:** 336/784-6702. **Contact:** Karen L. Siburt, CPC/President. **Description:** An executive search firm operating on a retainer basis. Client company pays fee. **Specializes in the areas of:** Computer Science/Software; Engineering; Furniture; General Management; Health/Medical; Industrial; MIS/EDP; Personnel/Labor Relations; Scientific; Technical; Textiles. **Positions commonly filled include:** AS400 Programmer Analyst; Biochemist; Biological Scientist; Biomedical Engineer; Chemical Engineer; Chemist; Clinical Lab Technician; Computer Programmer; Computer Technician; Database Administrator; Database Manager; Electrical/Electronics Engineer; Environmental Engineer; Food Scientist/Technologist; General Manager; Human Resources Manager; Industrial Engineer; Industrial Production Manager; Manufacturing Engineer; Mechanical Engineer; MIS Specialist; Operations Manager; Production Manager; Project Manager; Quality Assurance Engineer; Quality Control Supervisor; Systems Analyst. **Corporate headquarters location:** This Location. **Average salary range of placements:** $30,000 - $100,000. **Number of placements per year:** 50 - 99.

A&B PERSONNEL SERVICE
1201 South 16th Street, Wilmington NC 28401. 910/251-0505. **Fax:** 910/251-0901. **Contact:** Doreen Snyder, Recruiter. **Description:** A generalized executive search firm.

ACCOUNTANTS EXECUTIVE SEARCH
ACCOUNTANTS ON CALL
227 West Trade Street, Suite 1810, Charlotte NC 28202. 704/376-0006. **Fax:** 704/376-4787. **Contact:** Manager. **World Wide Web address:** http://www.aocnet.com. **Description:** An executive search firm. Accountants On Call (also at this location) is a temporary agency. **Specializes in the areas of:** Accounting/Auditing; Banking; Finance; Manufacturing.

ACCOUNTANTS EXECUTIVE SEARCH
ACCOUNTANTS ON CALL
5565 Center View Drive, Suite 214, Raleigh NC 27606. 919/859-5550. **Contact:** Manager. **World Wide Web address:** http://www.aocnet.com. **Description:** An executive search firm. Accountants On Call (also at this location) is a temporary agency. **Specializes in the areas of:** Accounting/Auditing; Finance.

ACCOUNTANTS EXECUTIVE SEARCH
ACCOUNTANTS ON CALL
1801 Stanley Road, Suite 206, Greensboro NC 27407. 336/292-3800. **Contact:** Manager. **World Wide Web address:** http://www.aocnet.com. **Description:** An executive search firm. Accountants On Call (also at this location) is a temporary agency. **Specializes in the areas of:** Accounting/Auditing; Finance.

ACCOUNTING PERSONNEL
4400 Silas Creek Parkway, Suite 200, Winston-Salem NC 27104. 336/768-8188. **Fax:** 336/768-1768. **Contact:** Dawson Nesbitt, Owner. **Description:** An executive search firm. **Specializes in the areas of:** Accounting.

ACCURATE STAFFING CONSULTANTS, INC.
1328-D Starbrook Drive, Charlotte NC 28210. 704/554-9675. **Fax:** 704/554-5914. **Contact:** Catherine Wall, President. **Description:** An executive search firm. **Specializes in the areas of:** Accounting/Auditing; Administration; Banking; Computer Science/Software; Engineering; Industrial; Manufacturing; Personnel/Labor Relations; Secretarial; Technical. **Average salary range of placements:** $30,000 - $50,000. **Number of placements per year:** 50 - 99.

ACTIVE SEARCH RECRUITERS, LLC
5838 Faringdon Place, Suite 1, Raleigh NC 27609. 919/876-0660. **Fax:** 919/876-0355. **Contact:** Robert J. Helfenbein, Sr., President. **Description:** An executive search firm operating on a contingency basis. **Specializes in the areas of:** Computer Science/Software; Engineering; Industrial; Manufacturing; Sales. **Positions commonly filled include:** Branch Manager; Design Engineer; Electrical/Electronics Engineer; Industrial Engineer; Manufacturer's/Wholesaler's Sales Rep.; Mechanical Engineer; Medical Sales; Network Engineer; Sales Representative; Software Engineer. **Average salary range of placements:** $30,000 - $150,000. **Number of placements per year:** 50 - 99.

ADKINS & ASSOCIATES
P.O. Box 16062, Greensboro NC 27416. 336/378-1261. **Contact:** Manager. **Description:** An executive search firm. **Specializes in the areas of:** Apparel; Textiles.

ADVANCED PERSONNEL RESOURCES (APR)
701 Green Valley Road, Suite 310, Greensboro NC 27408. 336/272-7720. **Fax:** 336/272-7729. **Contact:** Diane Z. Gaines, President. **E-mail address:** aprinc@greensboro.com **Description:** An executive search firm. **Specializes in the areas of:** Accounting/Auditing; Administration; Computer Science/Software; Finance; General Management; Insurance; Legal; Manufacturing; Personnel/Labor Relations; Publishing; Sales; Secretarial.

ADVANCED PROFESSIONAL RESOURCES (APR)
3653 Sweeten Creek Road, Arden NC 28704. 828/684-1960. **Fax:** 828/684-3779. **Contact:** Alan Medlock, Owner. **Description:** An executive search firm. **Specializes in the areas of:** Engineering; Management; Manufacturing; Metals; Plastics.

ALPHA OMEGA EXECUTIVE SEARCH
7522 LaSater Road, Clemmons NC 27012. 336/778-1271. **Fax:** 336/778-1274. **Contact:** Tracy Barnes, President. **Description:** An executive search firm operating on both retainer and contingency bases. **Specializes in the areas of:** Accounting/Auditing; Engineering; Industrial; Personnel/Labor Relations; Technical. **Positions commonly filled include:** Accountant; Applications Engineer; Budget Analyst; Buyer; Chief Financial Officer; Controller; Cost Estimator; Design Engineer; Draftsperson; Electrical/Electronics Engineer; Electrician; Environmental Engineer; Finance Director; Financial Analyst; Graphic Designer; Human Resources Manager; Industrial Engineer; Industrial Production Manager; Manufacturing Engineer; Mechanical Engineer; Metallurgical Engineer; MIS Specialist; Operations Manager; Production Manager; Project Manager; Purchasing Agent/Manager; Quality Control Supervisor; Sales Engineer; Sales Executive; Software Engineer; Technical Writer/Editor. **Average salary range of placements:** More than $50,000. **Number of placements per year:** 1 - 49.

AMCELL ASSOCIATES
5970 Fairview Road, Suite 512, Charlotte NC 28210. 704/643-1247. **Contact:** Manager. **Description:** An executive search firm. **Specializes in the areas of:** Banking; Finance; Manufacturing; Paper; Pharmaceuticals; Publishing; Textiles.

AMERICAN QUALITY STAFFING, INC.
4205 Timberwood Drive, Raleigh NC 27612. 919/785-5000. **Contact:** Nancy Callihan, President. **Description:** An executive search firm operating on a contingency basis. **Specializes in the areas of:** Computer Science/Software; Engineering; Technical. **Positions commonly filled include:** Draftsperson; Electrical/Electronics Engineer; MIS Specialist; Software

Engineer. Other U.S. locations: Nationwide. **Average salary range of placements:** $30,000 - $50,000. **Number of placements per year:** 100 - 199.

AMERIPRO SEARCH, INC.
119 Yacht Cove Lane, Mooresville NC 28117. 704/660-0991. **Contact:** Elaine C. Brauninger, President/Owner. **World Wide Web address:** http://www.ameriprosearch.com. **Description:** An executive search firm. **Specializes in the areas of:** Accounting/Auditing; Administration; Computer Science/Software; Data Processing; Engineering; Finance; General Management; Industrial; Manufacturing; MIS/EDP; Personnel/Labor Relations; Sales; Technical. **Positions commonly filled include:** Accountant/Auditor; Administrative Manager; Advertising Clerk; Aerospace Engineer; Biochemist; Biological Scientist; Branch Manager; Designer; Engineer; Financial Analyst; General Manager; Industrial Production Manager; Internet Services Manager; MIS Specialist; Operations Research Analyst; Science Technologist; Scientist; Software Engineer; Technical Writer/Editor; Telecommunications Manager. **Average salary range of placements:** More than $50,000. **Number of placements per year:** 100 - 199.

AMOS & ASSOCIATES
633-B Chapel Hill Road, Burlington NC 27215. 336/222-0231. **Fax:** 336/222-1214. **Contact:** Diane Amos, President. **E-mail address:** diane@amosassociates.com. **World Wide Web address:** http://www.amosassociates.com. **Description:** An executive search firm. **Specializes in the areas of:** Computer Science/Software. **Positions commonly filled include:** Computer Programmer; MIS Specialist; Operations Manager; Software Engineer; Systems Analyst; Systems Manager. **Average salary range of placements:** More than $50,000. **Number of placements per year:** 50 - 99.

ANDERSON & ASSOCIATES
112 South Tryon Street, Suite 800, Charlotte NC 28284. 704/347-0090. **Contact:** Manager. **Description:** An executive search firm.

ANDERSON RESOURCES
3523 St. Francis Drive, Wilmington NC 28409. 910/799-9493. **Fax:** 910/392-6937. **Contact:** Wanda Anderson, President. **Description:** An executive search firm. **Specializes in the areas of:** Accounting; Banking.

ANDREWS & ASSOCIATES, INC.
6100 Fairview Road, Suite 1205, Charlotte NC 28210. 704/556-0088. **Contact:** Dwight L. Andrews, Principal. **Description:** An executive search firm. **Specializes in the areas of:** Accounting/Auditing; Administration; Finance. **Positions commonly filled include:** Accountant/Auditor; Bookkeeper. **Number of placements per year:** 1 - 49.

ARIAIL & ASSOCIATES
210 West Friendly Avenue, Suite 200, Greensboro NC 27401. 336/275-2906. **Contact:** Randolph Ariail, President. **Description:** An executive search firm. **NOTE:** This firm does not accept unsolicited resumes. Please only respond to advertised openings. **Specializes in the areas of:** Home Furnishings.

ARJAY & ASSOCIATES
875 Walnut Street, Suite 150, Cary NC 27511. 919/469-5540. **Contact:** Manager. **Description:** An executive search firm. **Specializes in the areas of:** Engineering; Technical.

ATCHISON & ASSOCIATES, INC.
612 Pasteur Drive, Suite 209, Greensboro NC 27403. 336/855-5943. **Contact:** Bill Atchison, President. **Description:** An executive search firm operating on both retainer and contingency bases. **Specializes in the areas of:** Accounting/Auditing; Engineering; Industrial; Manufacturing; Technical. **Positions commonly filled include:** Accountant/Auditor; Chemical Engineer; Chemist; Credit Manager; Electrical/Electronics

Engineer; Environmental Engineer; Financial Analyst; Industrial Engineer; Manufacturing Engineer; Mechanical Engineer; Metallurgical Engineer; Operations/Production Manager; Purchasing Agent/Manager; Quality Control Supervisor; Software Engineer. **Average salary range of placements:** $30,000 - $50,000. **Number of placements per year:** 1 - 49.

AYERS & ASSOCIATES, INC.
P.O. Box 16065, Greensboro NC 27416. 336/378-1761. **Fax:** 336/275-8232. **Contact:** Dick Ayers, Account Manager. **E-mail address:** ayersSearch@msn.com. **Description:** An executive search firm operating on a contingency basis. **Specializes in the areas of:** Engineering; General Management; Industrial; Manufacturing; Personnel/Labor Relations; Textiles. **Positions commonly filled include:** Accountant/Auditor; Buyer; Chemical Engineer; Chemist; Credit Manager; Electrical/Electronics Engineer; Industrial Engineer; Industrial Production Manager; Management Analyst/Consultant; Management Trainee; Mechanical Engineer; Operations/Production Manager; Quality Control Supervisor; Systems Analyst; Textile Manager; Transportation/Traffic Specialist. **Average salary range of placements:** $30,000 - $75,000. **Number of placements per year:** 1 - 49.

BANK SEARCH
P.O. Box 491, Ayden NC 28513. 252/355-8282. **Contact:** David Melvin, Owner. **Description:** An executive search firm. **Specializes in the areas of:** Banking. **Positions commonly filled include:** Bank Officer/Manager; Branch Manager. **Average salary range of placements:** $30,000 - $50,000. **Number of placements per year:** 1 - 49.

FRED BARNETTE & ASSOCIATES
1213 Culbreth Drive, Wilmington NC 28405. 910/256-0883. **Fax:** 910/256-1183. **Contact:** Fred Barnette, President. **Description:** An executive search firm. **Specializes in the areas of:** Health/Medical.

JIM BEATTY & ASSOCIATES
6525 Morrison Boulevard, Suite 121, Charlotte NC 28211. **Contact:** Jim Beatty, Manager. **Description:** An executive search firm. **Positions commonly filled include:** Bank Officer/Manager; Construction Contractor; Education Administrator; Health Services Manager; Human Resources Specialist; Internet Services Manager; MIS Specialist; Physician; Property and Real Estate Manager; Quality Control Supervisor; Securities Sales Representative; Software Engineer.

BENNETT ALLEN & ASSOCIATES
7422 Carmel Executive Park, Charlotte NC 28226. 704/541-5891. **Contact:** Ben Liebstein, President. **Description:** An executive search firm. **Specializes in the areas of:** Engineering. **Positions commonly filled include:** Agricultural Engineer; Electrical/Electronics Engineer; Mechanical Engineer; Mining Engineer; Structural Engineer.

BETA CONSULTING SERVICE
1495 Rymco Drive, Suite 102, Winston-Salem NC 27103. 336/774-8778. **Fax:** 336/774-8776. **Contact:** Greig Burdick, Owner. **Description:** An executive search firm. **Specializes in the areas of:** Printing.

BRYANT & COMPANY
936 West Fourth Street, Winston-Salem NC 27101. 336/723-7007. **Fax:** 336/723-7078. **Contact:** David Bryant, President. **Description:** An executive search firm. **Specializes in the areas of:** Information Technology.

BULLINGTON ASSOCIATES
3700 National Drive, Suite 214, Raleigh NC 27612. 919/781-1350. **Fax:** 919/781-5947. **Contact:** Hal Keyser, Manager. **E-mail address:** hkeyser@aol.com. **Description:** An executive search firm operating on a contingency basis. Client company pays fee. **Specializes**

in the areas of: Marketing; Sales. **Positions commonly filled include:** Account Manager; Account Representative; Sales Engineer; Sales Executive; Sales Manager; Sales Representative. **Corporate headquarters location:** This Location. **Other U.S. locations:** Nationwide. **Average salary range of placements:** $50,000 - $100,000. **Number of placements per year:** 50 - 99.

BUTLER-McCALL GROUP, LTD.
131 Providence Road, Charlotte NC 28207. 704/358-9006. **Fax:** 704/358-0001. **Contact:** Manager. **Description:** An executive search firm operating on a retainer basis.

CARDINAL PERSONNEL CONSULTING
602 North Church Street, Mount Olive NC 28365. 919/658-0621. **Fax:** 919/658-0623. **Contact:** Sue Stoudt, Owner. **Description:** An executive search firm. **Specializes in the areas of:** Paper.

CAREER SEARCH INC.
P.O. Box 97007, Raleigh NC 27624. 919/878-7900. **Fax:** 919/878-1865. **Contact:** Ron Burton, President. **Description:** An executive search firm. **Specializes in the areas of:** Engineering; General Management; Manufacturing; Materials; Personnel/Labor Relations; Purchasing. **Positions commonly filled include:** Buyer; Chemical Engineer; Electrical/Electronics Engineer; Environmental Engineer; General Manager; Human Resources Specialist; Industrial Engineer; Industrial Production Manager; Materials Engineer; Mechanical Engineer; Operations/Production Manager; Purchasing Agent/Manager; Quality Control Supervisor. **Average salary range of placements:** More than $50,000. **Number of placements per year:** 1 - 49.

CARTER/MACKAY OF CARY
2000 Regency Parkway, Suite 460, Cary NC 27511. 919/380-1200. **Fax:** 919/380-1267. **Contact:** Al Hertz, Vice President. **Description:** An executive search firm. **Specializes in the areas of:** Sales; Sales Management. **Other U.S. locations:** Framingham MA; Hasbrouck Heights NJ; Great Neck NY.

CHRISTOPHER GROUP
P.O. Box 4887, Cary NC 27519. 919/319-3123. **Fax:** 919/319-3183. **Contact:** Manager. **E-mail address:** chrisgroup@ibm.net. **World Wide Web address:** http://www.christophergroup.net. **Description:** An executive search firm operating on a contingency basis. Christopher Group specializes in the placement of experienced real estate and mortgage professionals with financial institutions, corporate real estate entities, developers, valuation/consulting firms, and brokerage/management organizations. Founded in 1985. **Specializes in the areas of:** Banking; Finance; Real Estate. **Positions commonly filled include:** Bank Officer/Manager; Real Estate Agent; Underwriter/Assistant Underwriter. **Average salary range of placements:** More than $50,000. **Number of placements per year:** 1 - 49.

CLARKS & ASSOCIATES
2536 Reynolda Road, Winston-Salem NC 27106. 336/765-7377. **Contact:** Manager. **Description:** An executive search firm.

CLINE, JOBE & ASSOCIATES
812 Salem Woods Drive, Suite 201, Raleigh NC 27615. 919/870-9333. **Fax:** 919/870-9444. **Contact:** Manager. **Description:** An executive search firm operating on a retainer basis. **Specializes in the areas of:** Manufacturing.

COLEMAN, LEW & ASSOCIATES, INC.
P.O. Box 36489, Charlotte NC 28236. 704/377-0362. **Fax:** 704/377-0424. **Contact:** Manager. **E-mail address:** mail@colemanlew.com. **World Wide Web address:** http://www.colemanlew.com. **Description:** An executive search firm.

S.L. COLLINS ASSOCIATES
P.O. Box 472181, Charlotte NC 28247-2181. 704/759-8500. **Fax:** 704/759-8501. **Contact:** Steve Collins, President/Owner. **E-mail address:** collins@slcollins.com. **World Wide Web address:** http://www.slcollins.com. **Description:** An executive search firm. **Specializes in the areas of:** Biotechnology; Pharmaceuticals. **Positions commonly filled include:** Biological Scientist; Chemical Engineer; Chemist; Industrial Engineer; Manufacturing Engineer; Operations Manager; Production Manager; Project Manager. **Number of placements per year:** 50 - 99.

CREATIVE RESOURCE SYSTEMS, INC.
200 Centreport Drive, Suite 160, Greensboro NC 27409. 336/665-0203. **Fax:** 336/665-0312. **Contact:** Manager. **Description:** An executive search firm. **Specializes in the areas of:** Computer Graphics; Technical; Technical Writing.

DLG ASSOCIATES, INC.
1515 Mockingbird Lane, Suite 560, Charlotte NC 28209. 704/522-9993. **Fax:** 704/522-7730. **Contact:** Manager. **Description:** An executive search firm. **Specializes in the areas of:** Finance.

DATA MANAGEMENT AND STAFF RECRUITERS
111 Corning Road, Suite 130, Cary NC 27511. 919/233-0684. **Contact:** Janet Turnure, Manager. **E-mail address:** jturnure@dmsrnc.com. **World Wide Web address:** http://www.dmsrnc.com. **Description:** An executive search firm that also provides some contract services and temporary placements. Data Management and Staff Recruiters is a division of MAGIC (Management Alliance Group of Independent Companies).

PAUL DAY & ASSOCIATES
5020 Celbridge Place, Raleigh NC 27613. 919/845-3307. **Fax:** 919/846-8782. **Contact:** Manager. **E-mail address:** donpaul@earthlink.net. **World Wide Web address:** http://paulday-associates.2kweb.net/corpinfo. **Description:** An executive search firm. **Specializes in the areas of:** Aerospace; Electrical; Engineering; High-Tech; Telecommunications.

DIRECT MARKETING RESOURCES
2915 Providence Road, Charlotte NC 28211. 704/365-5890. **Fax:** 704/365-5892. **Contact:** Dan Sullivan, President. **Description:** An executive search firm. **Specializes in the areas of:** Direct Marketing.

THE DIVERSIFIED SEARCH COMPANIES
128 South Tryon Street, Suite 1570, Charlotte NC 28202. 704/331-0006. **Fax:** 704/376-5988. **Contact:** Manager. **World Wide Web address:** http://www.divsearch.com. **Description:** An executive search firm. **Specializes in the areas of:** Consulting; Finance; Health/Medical; Nonprofit; Professional. **Corporate headquarters location:** Philadelphia PA. **Other U.S. locations:** Atlanta GA; Boston MA.

DUNHILL PROFESSIONAL SEARCH
200 East Arlington Boulevard, Suite D, Greenville NC 27858. 252/355-3808. **Contact:** Manager. **Description:** An executive search firm. **Corporate headquarters location:** Woodbury NY. **Other U.S. locations:** Nationwide.

EASTERN SEARCH GROUP
P.O. Box 4655, Wilmington NC 28406. 910/799-7700. **Fax:** 910/392-6266. **Contact:** Fred Wells, President. **E-mail address:** eastsrch@wilmington.net. **Description:** An executive search firm. **Specializes in the areas of:** Computer Science/Software; Engineering; Industrial; Scientific; Technical. **Positions commonly filled include:** Chemical Engineer; Computer Programmer; Electrical/Electronics Engineer; Industrial Engineer; Mechanical Engineer; MIS Specialist; Production Manager; Quality Control Supervisor; Software Engineer; Statistician; Systems Analyst. **Average salary**

range of placements: More than $50,000. **Number of placements per year:** 50 - 99.

BRUCE EDWARDS & ASSOCIATES INC.
P.O. Box 13546, Research Triangle Park NC 27709. 919/481-4112. **Contact:** Manager. **Description:** An executive search firm.

ELIN VAR
3200 Beechleaf Court, Suite 409, Raleigh NC 27604. 919/878-4454. **Contact:** Manager. **Description:** An executive search firm. **Specializes in the areas of:** Accounting/Auditing; Finance.

ELLIS ASSOCIATES, INC.
2030 Eastwood Road, Suite 5, Wilmington NC 28403. 910/256-9810. **Fax:** 910/256-9887. **Contact:** Phil Ellis, President. **Description:** An executive search firm operating on both retainer and contingency bases. **Specializes in the areas of:** Biology; Manufacturing; Pharmaceuticals; Technical. **Positions commonly filled include:** Biochemist; Biological Scientist; Biomedical Engineer; Chemical Engineer; Chemist; Electrical/Electronics Engineer; Environmental Engineer; General Manager; Industrial Engineer; Industrial Production Manager; Mechanical Engineer; Metallurgical Engineer; Operations/Production Manager; Pharmacist; Quality Control Supervisor; Science Technologist. **Average salary range of placements:** More than $50,000. **Number of placements per year:** 50 - 99.

ENGINEERING MANAGEMENT STAFF RECRUITERS
111 Corning Drive, Suite 230, Cary NC 27511. 919/859-2242. **Fax:** 919/859-9320. **Contact:** Craig Arledge, Manager. **E-mail address:** opportunities@emsr.com. **World Wide Web address:** http://www.emsr.com. **Description:** An executive search firm. Engineering Management Staff Recruiters is a division of MAGIC (Management Alliance Group of Independent Companies). **Specializes in the areas of:** Engineering. **Other U.S. locations:** Dallas TX.

ENVIRONMENTAL RECRUITING SERVICES
21514 Gulfstar Court, Cornelius NC 28031. 704/896-3336. **Fax:** 704/896-3337. **Contact:** Brian MacLamroc, President. **Description:** An executive search firm operating on both retainer and contingency bases. **Specializes in the areas of:** Civil Engineering; Environmental. **Positions commonly filled include:** Chemical Engineer; Civil Engineer; Construction Contractor; Cost Estimator; Structural Engineer; Transportation/Traffic Specialist. **Average salary range of placements:** More than $50,000. **Number of placements per year:** 50 - 99.

EXECUTIVE CONNECTIONS
P.O. Box 1853, Lexington NC 27293. 336/249-0031. **Fax:** 336/249-0036. **Contact:** Manager. **E-mail address:** execconnace@lexcom.net. **Description:** An executive search firm. **Specializes in the areas of:** Engineering; Human Resources; Information Technology; Manufacturing.

EXECUTIVE RECRUITMENT SPECIALISTS
6407 Idlewild Road, Building 1, Suite 103, Charlotte NC 28212. 704/536-8830. **Fax:** 704/536-8893. **Contact:** Eric Sklut, President. **Description:** An executive search firm. **Specializes in the areas of:** Computer Science/Software; Engineering; Finance; General Management; Government; Health/Medical; Manufacturing. **Positions commonly filled include:** Accountant/Auditor; Biomedical Engineer; Electrical/Electronics Engineer; General Manager; Health Services Manager; Licensed Practical Nurse; Mechanical Engineer; Medical Records Technician; Nuclear Medicine Technologist; Occupational Therapist; Physical Therapist; Quality Control Supervisor; Radiological Technologist; Recreational Therapist; Registered Nurse; Respiratory Therapist; Software Engineer; Speech-Language Pathologist. **Number of placements per year:** 50 - 99.

EXECUTIVE STAFFING GROUP
4101 Lake Boone Trail, Suite 112, Raleigh NC 27607-7506. 919/783-6695. **Recorded jobline:** 919/990-2455. **Contact:** Brenda Savage, Recruiting Specialist. **Description:** An executive search firm. **Specializes in the areas of:** Accounting/Auditing; Art/Design; Computer Science/Software; Electronics; Engineering; Industrial; Manufacturing; Personnel/Labor Relations; Sales; Secretarial; Technical. **Positions commonly filled include:** Administrative Manager; Advertising Clerk; Buyer; Computer Programmer; Customer Service Representative; Designer; Draftsperson; Electrical/Electronics Engineer; Human Resources Specialist; Medical Records Technician; Purchasing Agent/Manager; Quality Control Supervisor; Technical Writer/Editor; Telecommunications Manager; Typist/Word Processor. **Benefits available to temporary workers:** Medical Insurance; Paid Holidays; Paid Vacation. **Corporate headquarters location:** Cary NC. **Other U.S. locations:** Greensboro NC; Winston-Salem NC; Columbia SC. **Number of placements per year:** 1000+.

D.D. FAYLING ASSOCIATES, INC.
P.O. Box 2011, Pinehurst NC 28370. 910/295-4901. **Contact:** Manager. **Description:** An executive search firm. **Specializes in the areas of:** Accounting/Auditing; Engineering; General Management; Manufacturing; Personnel/Labor Relations; Sales. **Positions commonly filled include:** Accountant/Auditor; Attorney; Branch Manager; Buyer; Customer Service Representative; Design Engineer; Electrical/Electronics Engineer; General Manager; Human Resources Specialist; Industrial Engineer; Industrial Production Manager; Purchasing Agent/Manager; Quality Control Supervisor. **Average salary range of placements:** More than $50,000. **Number of placements per year:** 1 - 49.

F-O-R-T-U-N-E PERSONNEL CONSULTANTS
3831 West Market Street, Greensboro NC 27407. 336/852-4455. **Fax:** 336/852-3429. **Contact:** Rhonda Stone, Manager. **E-mail address:** fpc@fpcgboro.com. **World Wide Web address:** http://www.fpcgboro.com. **Description:** An executive search firm operating on both retainer and contingency bases. Client company pays fee. **Specializes in the areas of:** Engineering; General Management; Industrial; Logistics; Manufacturing; MIS/EDP; Personnel/Labor Relations; Transportation. **Positions commonly filled include:** Chief Financial Officer; Design Engineer; Electrical/Electronics Engineer; General Manager; Human Resources Manager; Industrial Engineer; Manufacturing Engineer; Mechanical Engineer; MIS Specialist; Operations Manager; Production Manager; Purchasing Agent/Manager; Quality Assurance Engineer; Quality Control Supervisor; Systems Analyst; Systems Manager; Vice President. **Corporate headquarters location:** New York NY. **Other U.S. locations:** Nationwide. **International locations:** Worldwide. **Average salary range of placements:** $50,000 - $100,000.

F-O-R-T-U-N-E PERSONNEL CONSULTANTS OF CHARLOTTE
P.O. Box 460, 315 Main Street, Suite C, Pineville NC 28134-0460. 704/889-1100. **Toll-free phone:** 800/210-8121. **Fax:** 704/889-1109. **Contact:** David Griffith, Owner. **E-mail address:** ftnchar@ix.netcom.com. **World Wide Web address:** http://www.ftnchar.com. **Description:** An executive search firm operating on both retainer and contingency bases. **Specializes in the areas of:** Accounting; Biology; Engineering; Finance; General Management; Light Industrial; Marketing; Scientific; Technical. **Positions commonly filled include:** Biomedical Engineer; Chemical Engineer; Chemist; Chief Financial Officer; Controller; Cost Estimator; Credit Manager; Design Engineer; Electrical/Electronics Engineer; Finance Director; General Manager; Manufacturing Engineer; Mechanical Engineer; Metallurgical Engineer; Operations Manager; Production Manager; Project Manager; Purchasing Agent/Manager; Quality Assurance Engineer; Quality Control Supervisor; Statistician. **Corporate headquarters location:** New

York NY. **Other U.S. locations:** Nationwide. **International locations:** Worldwide. **Average salary range of placements:** $50,000 - $100,000. **Number of placements per year:** 1 - 49.

FOX-MORRIS ASSOCIATES
9140 Arrow Point Boulevard, Suite 380, Charlotte NC 28273. 704/522-8244. **Fax:** 704/529-1465. **Contact:** Tonia Sanders, Researcher. **Description:** An executive search firm. **Specializes in the areas of:** Accounting; Consumer Products; Human Resources; Information Technology; Manufacturing; Sales.

THE FURNITURE AGENCY INC.
P.O. Box 53, High Point NC 27261. 336/841-3221. **Toll-free phone:** 800/833-3261. **Fax:** 336/841-5651. **Contact:** Brady Stern, President. **Description:** An executive search firm. **Specializes in the areas of:** Design; Engineering; Furniture; Industrial; Manufacturing. **Positions commonly filled include:** Engineer; General Manager; Plant Manager; Superintendent. **Average salary range of placements:** More than $50,000.

GLOVIER & ASSOCIATES
4732 Lebanon Road, Charlotte NC 28227. 704/545-0877. **Contact:** Jim Glovier, Owner. **Description:** An executive search firm. **Specializes in the areas of:** Engineering; General Management; Manufacturing; Sales. **Positions commonly filled include:** Accountant/Auditor; Chemist; Cost Estimator; Credit Manager; Designer; Draftsperson; Environmental Engineer; Forester/Conservation Scientist; General Manager; Industrial Engineer; Mechanical Engineer; Operations/Production Manager; Quality Control Supervisor. **Average salary range of placements:** More than $50,000. **Number of placements per year:** 1 - 49.

ROBERT HALF INTERNATIONAL ACCOUNTEMPS
101 Centerport Drive, Suite 240, Greensboro NC 27409. 336/668-2996. **Fax:** 336/668-7079. **Contact:** Placement Manager. **Description:** An executive search firm. Accountemps (also at this location) provides temporary placements. **Specializes in the areas of:** Accounting/Auditing; Administration; Banking; Computer Hardware/Software; Finance. **Positions commonly filled include:** Accountant/Auditor; Bookkeeper; Clerk; Computer Operator; Computer Programmer; CPA; Credit Manager; Data Entry Clerk; EDP Specialist; Software Engineer; Systems Analyst. **Corporate headquarters location:** Menlo Park CA. **Other U.S. locations:** Nationwide. **International locations:** Worldwide.

ROBERT HALF INTERNATIONAL ACCOUNTEMPS
3605 Glenwood Avenue, Suite 390, Raleigh NC 27612. 919/682-3944. **Contact:** Manager. **Description:** An executive search firm. Accountemps (also at this location) provides temporary placements. **Corporate headquarters location:** Menlo Park CA. **Other U.S. locations:** Nationwide. **International locations:** Worldwide.

ROBERT HALF INTERNATIONAL ACCOUNTEMPS
201 South College Street, Suite 2200, Charlotte NC 28244. 704/548-8447. **Contact:** Manager. **Description:** An executive search firm. Accountemps (also at this location) provides temporary placements. **Corporate headquarters location:** Menlo Park CA. **Other U.S. locations:** Nationwide. **International locations:** Worldwide.

ROBERT HALF INTERNATIONAL ACCOUNTEMPS
11440 Carmel Commons Boulevard, Suite 106, Charlotte NC 28226. 704/553-7100. **Contact:** Manager. **Description:** An executive search firm. Accountemps (also at this location) provides temporary placements. **Corporate headquarters location:** Menlo Park CA.

Other U.S. locations: Nationwide. **International locations:** Worldwide.

HEIDRICK & STRUGGLES
227 West Trade Street, Suite 1600, Charlotte NC 28202. 704/333-1953. **Fax:** 704/335-7274. **Contact:** Manager. **Description:** An executive search firm.

HIGHLANDER SEARCH
210 West Friendly Avenue, Suite 200, Greensboro NC 27401. 336/333-9886. **Contact:** Jeffrey Penley, CPC/President. **Description:** An executive search firm. **Specializes in the areas of:** Accounting/Auditing; Engineering; Manufacturing. **Positions commonly filled include:** Controller. **Average salary range of placements:** More than $50,000. **Number of placements per year:** 1 - 49.

HUNKLER MEDICAL ASSOCIATES
8800 Sweetwater Place, Suite 204, Weddington NC 28173. 704/814-9683. **Fax:** 704/814-9685. **Contact:** Manager. **Description:** An executive search firm. **Specializes in the areas of:** Medical Sales and Marketing.

INFORMATION SYSTEMS PROFESSIONALS, INC.
5904 Castlebrook Drive, Raleigh NC 27604. 919/954-9100. **Toll-free phone:** 800/951-9100. **Fax:** 919/954-1947. **Contact:** Brad Moses, Principal. **E-mail address:** ispros@staffing.net. **World Wide Web address:** http://www.citysearch.com/rdu/ispros. **Description:** An executive search firm. **Specializes in the areas of:** Computer Science/Software; Scientific; Technical. **Positions commonly filled include:** Computer Animator; Computer Operator; Computer Programmer; Database Manager; Electrical/Electronics Engineer; Internet Services Manager; Management Analyst/Consultant; Operations Manager; Project Manager; Software Engineer; Systems Analyst; Systems Manager; Technical Writer/Editor; Telecommunications Manager; Webmaster. **Average salary range of placements:** More than $50,000. **Number of placements per year:** 1 - 49.

INSURANCE PROFESSIONAL SEARCH
2101 Rexford Road, Suite 300E, Charlotte NC 28211. 704/362-5638. **Contact:** Susan Belton, Owner. **Description:** An executive search firm. **Specializes in the areas of:** Insurance. **Positions commonly filled include:** Accountant/Auditor; Actuary; Adjuster; Claim Representative; Collector; Insurance Agent/Broker; Investigator; Underwriter/Assistant Underwriter. **Average salary range of placements:** More than $50,000. **Number of placements per year:** 1 - 49.

S.N. JONES & ASSOCIATES
406 Southway Gardens, Arden NC 28704. 828/687-1510. **Contact:** Sandra Jones, Principal. **Description:** An executive search firm. **Specializes in the areas of:** Accounting/Auditing; Health/Medical. **Positions commonly filled include:** Health Services Manager; Medical Records Technician; Physical Therapist; Registered Nurse. **Average salary range of placements:** $30,000 - $50,000. **Number of placements per year:** 1 - 49.

KILGO & COMPANY
8126 Lake Providence Drive, Matthews NC 28104. 704/708-4483. **Contact:** Don Kilgo, Owner. **Description:** An executive search firm. **NOTE:** The firm places experienced technical personnel only. **Specializes in the areas of:** Computer Science/Software. **Positions commonly filled include:** Sales and Marketing Representative; Sales Manager. **Number of placements per year:** 1 - 49.

LaVALLEE & ASSOCIATES
4176 Sulgrave Court, Winston-Salem NC 27104. 336/760-1911. **Contact:** Michael J. LaVallee, Managing Partner. **Description:** An executive search firm. **Positions commonly filled include:** Computer

Programmer; Systems Analyst. **Number of placements per year:** 1 - 49.

LEGAL PLACEMENT SPECIALISTS
606 Wade Avenue, Suite 100, Raleigh NC 27605. 919/829-2550. **Contact:** Manager. **Description:** An executive search firm. **Specializes in the areas of:** Legal.

LINDEN GROUP INC.
6408 Honegger Drive, Suite B, Charlotte NC 28211. 704/367-0309. **Contact:** Manager. **Description:** An executive search firm. **Specializes in the areas of:** Automotive; Food.

MF BRANCH ASSOCIATES, INC.
P.O. Box 18105, Asheville NC 28814. 828/658-0055. **Fax:** 828/645-9866. **Contact:** Manager. **E-mail address:** mfbranch@aol.com. **World Wide Web address:** http://www.mfbranch.com. **Description:** An executive search firm. Founded in 1982. **Specializes in the areas of:** Telecommunications; Wireless Communications.

MANAGEMENT ADVISORS INTERNATIONAL, INC. (MAI)
100 Main Avenue NW, Hickory NC 28601. 828/324-5772. **Fax:** 828/324-4831. **Contact:** William J. Castell, Jr., President/CEO. **World Wide Web address:** http://www.maisearch.com. **Description:** An executive search firm operating on both retainer and contingency bases. Founded in 1982. **Specializes in the areas of:** Accounting; Banking; Finance; Health/Medical; Operations Management. **Other area locations:** Charlotte NC.

MANAGEMENT ADVISORS INTERNATIONAL, INC. (MAI)
4600 Park Road, Suite 400, Charlotte NC 28209. 704/521-9595. **Fax:** 704/527-6616. **Contact:** William J. Castell, Jr., President/CEO. **World Wide Web address:** http://www.maisearch.com. **Description:** An executive search firm operating on both retainer and contingency bases. Founded in 1982. **Specializes in the areas of:** Accounting; Banking; Finance; Health/Medical; Operations Management. **Other area locations:** Hickory NC.

MANAGEMENT RECRUITERS INTERNATIONAL
103 Commerce Center Drive, Suite 102, Huntersville NC 28078. 704/947-0660. **Fax:** 704/947-0705. **Contact:** Manager. **World Wide Web address:** http://www.mrcn.com. **Description:** An executive search firm. **Specializes in the areas of:** Human Resources; Information Systems. **Corporate headquarters location:** Cleveland OH. **Other U.S. locations:** Nationwide. **International locations:** Worldwide.

MANAGEMENT RECRUITERS INTERNATIONAL
835 Highland Avenue SE, Hickory NC 28602. 828/324-2020. **Contact:** Manager. **Description:** An executive search firm. **Specializes in the areas of:** Accounting/Auditing; Administration; Advertising; Architecture/Construction; Banking; Communications; Computer Hardware/Software; Design; Electrical; Engineering; Food; General Management; Health/Medical; Insurance; Legal; Manufacturing; Operations Management; Personnel/Labor Relations; Procurement; Publishing; Technical; Textiles; Transportation. **Corporate headquarters location:** Cleveland OH. **Other U.S. locations:** Nationwide. **International locations:** Worldwide.

MANAGEMENT RECRUITERS INTERNATIONAL
120 North Franklin, Building J, P.O. Box 4139, Rocky Mount NC 27803. 252/442-8000. **Fax:** 252/442-9000. **Contact:** Bob Manning, Manager. **E-mail address:** mri@web-point.com. **Description:** An executive search firm. **Specializes in the areas of:** Accounting/Auditing; Administration; Advertising; Architecture/Construction; Banking; Communications; Computer Hardware/Software; Design; Electrical; Engineering; Food; General Management; Health/Medical; Insurance; Legal;

Manufacturing; Operations Management; Personnel/Labor Relations; Procurement; Publishing; Retail; Sales; Technical; Textiles; Transportation. **Corporate headquarters location:** Cleveland OH. **Other U.S. locations:** Nationwide. **International locations:** Worldwide.

MANAGEMENT RECRUITERS INTERNATIONAL
P.O. Box 1354, Roxboro NC 27573. 336/597-4000. **Contact:** Don Buckner, Manager. **Description:** An executive search firm operating on a contingency basis. **Specializes in the areas of:** Engineering; Home Furnishings; Industrial; Manufacturing; Personnel/Labor Relations; Sales. **Positions commonly filled include:** Accountant/Auditor; Blue-Collar Worker Supervisor; General Manager; Industrial Engineer; Plant Manager; Quality Control Supervisor. **Corporate headquarters location:** Cleveland OH. **Other U.S. locations:** Nationwide. **International locations:** Worldwide. **Average salary range of placements:** $30,000 - $50,000. **Number of placements per year:** 1 - 49.

MANAGEMENT RECRUITERS INTERNATIONAL
P.O. Box 395, Cove City NC 28523. 252/633-1900. **Fax:** 252/633-3121. **Contact:** Fred Eatman, Owner/Manager. **Description:** An executive search firm operating on a retainer basis. The firm also provides some career/outplacement counseling services. **Specializes in the areas of:** Engineering; Food; General Management; Manufacturing. **Positions commonly filled include:** Accountant/Auditor; Agricultural Engineer; Biomedical Engineer; Blue-Collar Worker Supervisor; Ceramics Engineer; Chemical Engineer; Civil Engineer; Electrical/Electronics Engineer; Environmental Engineer; General Manager; Human Resources Specialist; Industrial Engineer; Industrial Production Manager; Manufacturing Engineer; Materials Engineer; Mechanical Engineer; Purchasing Agent/Manager; Telecommunications Manager. **Corporate headquarters location:** Cleveland OH. **Other U.S. locations:** Nationwide. **International locations:** Worldwide. **Average salary range of placements:** $30,000 - $50,000. **Number of placements per year:** 50 - 99.

MANAGEMENT RECRUITERS INTERNATIONAL
19501 Highway 73 West, Suite 20, Cornelius NC 28031. 704/896-1916. **Contact:** Manager. **Description:** An executive search firm. **Specializes in the areas of:** Data Processing. **Corporate headquarters location:** Cleveland OH. **Other U.S. locations:** Nationwide. **International locations:** Worldwide.

MANAGEMENT RECRUITERS INTERNATIONAL
111 NW Railroad Street, Enfield NC 27823. 252/445-4251. **Contact:** Manager. **Description:** An executive search firm. **Specializes in the areas of:** Paper; Plastics. **Corporate headquarters location:** Cleveland OH. **Other U.S. locations:** Nationwide. **International locations:** Worldwide.

MANAGEMENT RECRUITERS INTERNATIONAL
117 South Center Street, Statesville NC 28677. 704/871-9890. **Fax:** 704/873-2143. **Contact:** Neil Coleman, General Manager. **Description:** An executive search firm. **Specializes in the areas of:** Plastics. **Corporate headquarters location:** Cleveland OH. **Other U.S. locations:** Nationwide. **International locations:** Worldwide.

MANAGEMENT RECRUITERS INTERNATIONAL SALES CONSULTANTS
5955 Carnegie Boulevard, Suite 300, Charlotte NC 28209. 704/525-9270. **Fax:** 704/527-0070. **Contact:** Dave Camp, General Manager. **Description:** An executive search firm. **Specializes in the areas of:** Art/Design; Computer Science/Software; Engineering; Finance; Food; General Management; Health/Medical; Industrial; Insurance; Manufacturing; Personnel/Labor Relations; Publishing; Sales; Technical; Transportation. **Positions commonly filled include:** Administrative Manager; Bank Officer/Manager; Biomedical Engineer; Branch Manager; Buyer; Chemical Engineer;

Chiropractor; Computer Programmer; Construction Contractor; Customer Service Representative; Dentist; Designer; EEG Technologist; EKG Technician; Financial Analyst; General Manager; Health Services Manager; Industrial Engineer; Industrial Production Manager; Management Analyst/Consultant; Manufacturer's/ Wholesaler's Sales Rep.; Occupational Therapist; Operations/Production Manager; Pharmacist; Physical Therapist; Physician; Purchasing Agent/Manager; Quality Control Supervisor; Recreational Therapist; Registered Nurse; Respiratory Therapist; Securities Sales Representative; Software Engineer; Surveyor; Systems Analyst; Transportation/Traffic Specialist; Underwriter/Assistant Underwriter; Veterinarian. **Corporate headquarters location:** Cleveland OH. **Other U.S. locations:** Nationwide. **International locations:** Worldwide. **Number of placements per year:** 200 - 499.

MANAGEMENT RECRUITERS INTERNATIONAL SALES CONSULTANTS
107 Edinburgh South, Suite 213, Cary NC 27511. 919/460-9595. **Fax:** 919/460-0642. **Contact:** Rose Hays, Manager. **Description:** An executive search firm. **Specializes in the areas of:** Administration; Advertising; Banking; Communications; Computer Hardware/Software; Computer Science/Software; Design; Electrical; Engineering; General Management; Health/Medical; Industrial; Insurance; Legal; Manufacturing; Marketing; Operations Management; Publishing; Sales; Scientific; Technical; Textiles; Transportation. **Positions commonly filled include:** Account Representative; Aerospace Engineer; Branch Manager; Chemical Engineer; Claim Representative; Consultant; Design Engineer; Electrical/Electronics Engineer; General Manager; Marketing Manager; Marketing Specialist; Mechanical Engineer; Sales Engineer; Sales Executive; Sales Manager; Sales Representative; Software Engineer; Systems Analyst; Telecommunications Manager; Vice President of Marketing and Sales. **Corporate headquarters location:** Cleveland OH. **Other U.S. locations:** Nationwide. **International locations:** Worldwide. **Average salary range of placements:** More than $50,000. **Number of placements per year:** 100 - 199.

MANAGEMENT RECRUITERS OF ASHEVILLE
53 Arlington Street, Asheville NC 28801. 828/258-9646. **Fax:** 828/252-0866. **Contact:** Paul Rumson, President. **Description:** An executive search firm operating on both retainer and contingency bases. **Specializes in the areas of:** Computer Science/Software; Engineering; Industrial; Manufacturing. **Positions commonly filled include:** Chemical Engineer; Chemist; Computer Programmer; Designer; Draftsperson; Electrical/Electronics Engineer; Industrial Engineer; Industrial Production Manager; Materials Engineer; Mechanical Engineer; Mining Engineer; Purchasing Agent/Manager; Quality Control Supervisor; Software Engineer; Structural Engineer. **Corporate headquarters location:** Cleveland OH. **Other U.S. locations:** Nationwide. **International locations:** Worldwide. **Average salary range of placements:** More than $50,000. **Number of placements per year:** 1 - 49.

MANAGEMENT RECRUITERS OF BURLINGTON
336 Holly Hill Lane, Burlington NC 27215. 336/584-1444. **Fax:** 336/584-9754. **Contact:** Dick Pike, Owner. **E-mail address:** mgmtrec@netpath.net. **Description:** An executive search firm. **Specializes in the areas of:** Engineering; Industrial; Manufacturing; Publishing; Sales; Technical. **Positions commonly filled include:** Chemical Engineer; Chemist; Design Engineer; Industrial Engineer; Industrial Production Manager; Manufacturer's/Wholesaler's Sales Rep.; Mechanical Engineer; Quality Control Supervisor; Science Technologist. **Corporate headquarters location:** Cleveland OH. **Other U.S. locations:** Nationwide. **International locations:** Worldwide. **Average salary range of placements:** More than $50,000. **Number of placements per year:** 1 - 49.

MANAGEMENT RECRUITERS OF DURHAM
5102 Durham-Chapel Hill Boulevard, Durham NC 27707. 919/489-6521. **Contact:** Steve Knauss, Manager. **Description:** An executive search firm. **Specializes in the areas of:** Accounting/Auditing; Administration; Advertising; Architecture/Construction; Banking; Communications; Computer Hardware/Software; Design; Electrical; Engineering; Food; General Management; Health/Medical; Insurance; Legal; Manufacturing; Operations Management; Personnel/Labor Relations; Procurement; Publishing; Retail; Sales; Technical; Textiles; Transportation. **Corporate headquarters location:** Cleveland OH. **Other U.S. locations:** Nationwide. **International locations:** Worldwide.

MANAGEMENT RECRUITERS OF FAYETTEVILLE
951 South McPherson Church Road, Suite 105, Fayetteville NC 28303. 910/483-2555. **Fax:** 910/483-6524. **Contact:** John Semmes, Manager. **E-mail address:** mrifaync@worldnet.att.net. **World Wide Web address:** http://home.att.net/~mrifaync/. **Description:** An executive search firm. **Specializes in the areas of:** Engineering; General Management; Scientific; Technical. **Positions commonly filled include:** Applications Engineer; Design Engineer; Electrical/Electronics Engineer; Human Resources Manager; Industrial Engineer; Manufacturing Engineer; Mechanical Engineer; Operations Manager; Production Manager; Project Manager; Quality Control Supervisor. **Corporate headquarters location:** Cleveland OH. **Other U.S. locations:** Nationwide. **International locations:** Worldwide. **Average salary range of placements:** $30,000-$50,000. **Number of placements per year:** 50 - 99.

MANAGEMENT RECRUITERS OF GREENSBORO
324 West Wendover Avenue, Suite 230, Greensboro NC 27408. 336/378-1818. **Fax:** 336/378-0129. **Contact:** Manager. **Description:** An executive search firm that also provides some contract services and career counseling. **Specializes in the areas of:** Apparel; Engineering; General Management; Pharmaceuticals; Textiles. **Positions commonly filled include:** Accountant/Auditor; Biochemist; Biological Scientist; Biomedical Engineer; Buyer; Chemical Engineer; Chemist; Civil Engineer; Computer Programmer; Design Engineer; Designer; Electrical/Electronics Engineer; Environmental Engineer; Financial Analyst; Food Scientist/Technologist; General Manager; Industrial Engineer; Industrial Production Manager; Management Analyst/Consultant; Market Research Analyst; Mechanical Engineer; Metallurgical Engineer; MIS Specialist; Purchasing Agent/Manager; Quality Control Supervisor; Services Sales Representative; Statistician; Telecommunications Manager. **Corporate headquarters location:** Cleveland OH. **Other U.S. locations:** Nationwide. **International locations:** Worldwide. **Average salary range of placements:** More than $50,000. **Number of placements per year:** 100 - 199.

MANAGEMENT RECRUITERS OF HIGH POINT
110 Scott Avenue, High Point NC 27262. 336/869-1200. **Fax:** 336/869-1566. **Contact:** Manager. **Description:** An executive search firm. Client company pays fee. **Specializes in the areas of:** Agriculture. **Positions commonly filled include:** Cost Estimator. **Corporate headquarters location:** Cleveland OH. **Other U.S. locations:** Nationwide. **International locations:** Worldwide.

MANAGEMENT RECRUITERS OF KANNAPOLIS
305 South Main Street, Kannapolis NC 28081. 704/938-6144. **Fax:** 704/938-3480. **Contact:** Tom Whitley, President. **Description:** An executive search firm operating on a contingency basis. **Specializes in the areas of:** Computer Science/Software; Information Systems. **Positions commonly filled include:** Computer Programmer; Database Manager; MIS Specialist; Software Engineer; Systems Analyst; Systems Manager; Telecommunications Manager. **Corporate headquarters location:** Cleveland OH. **Other U.S. locations:**

Nationwide. **International locations:** Worldwide. **Number of placements per year:** 50 - 99.

MANAGEMENT RECRUITERS OF KINSTON
P.O. Box 219, Kinston NC 28502. 252/527-9191. **Fax:** 252/527-3625. **Contact:** Allan Turner, President/Owner. **E-mail address:** mrkinston@esn.net. **World Wide Web address:** http://www.esn.net/mrkinston. **Description:** An executive search firm operating on both contingency and retainer bases. **Specializes in the areas of:** Engineering; Food; General Management; Health/Medical; Industrial; Light Industrial; Manufacturing; Paper; Scientific; Technical. **Positions commonly filled include:** Electrical/Electronics Engineer; Environmental Engineer; Human Resources Manager; Industrial Engineer; Industrial Production Manager; Manufacturing Engineer; Mechanical Engineer; Metallurgical Engineer; Nuclear Medicine Technologist; Occupational Therapist; Operations Manager; Physical Therapist; Physician; Production Manager; Purchasing Agent/Manager; Quality Control Supervisor; Registered Nurse; Respiratory Therapist; Sales Engineer; Surgical Technician. **Corporate headquarters location:** Cleveland OH. **Other U.S. locations:** Nationwide. **International locations:** Worldwide. **Average salary range of placements:** More than $50,000. **Number of placements per year:** 100 - 199.

MANAGEMENT RECRUITERS OF LOUISBURG
P.O. Box 8, Louisburg NC 27549. 919/496-2153. **Fax:** 919/496-1417. **Contact:** Darrell Perry, Owner. **Description:** An executive search firm. **Specializes in the areas of:** Administration; Engineering. **Positions commonly filled include:** Chemical Engineer; Design Engineer; Electrical/Electronics Engineer; Environmental Engineer; Industrial Engineer; Mechanical Engineer; Quality Control Supervisor; Transportation/Traffic Specialist. **Corporate headquarters location:** Cleveland OH. **Other U.S. locations:** Nationwide. **International locations:** Worldwide. **Average salary range of placements:** More than $50,000. **Number of placements per year:** 50 - 99.

MANAGEMENT RECRUITERS OF RALEIGH
5171 Glenwood Avenue, Suite 350, Raleigh NC 27612. 919/781-0400. **Fax:** 919/881-0117. **Contact:** Phillip Stanley, Manager. **E-mail address:** mrraleigh@horizons.net. **World Wide Web address:** http://www.mriraleigh.com. **Description:** An executive search firm operating on a contingency basis. **Specializes in the areas of:** Accounting; Administration; Biology; Computer Science/Software; Economics; Engineering; Finance; Food; General Management; Industrial; Insurance; Manufacturing; Marketing; Personnel/Labor Relations; Printing; Publishing; Retail; Sales; Scientific; Technical; Transportation. **Positions commonly filled include:** Account Manager; Account Rep.; Accountant; Applications Engineer; Auditor; Biochemist; Biological Scientist; Biomedical Engineer; Buyer; Chemical Engineer; Chemist; Civil Engineer; Controller; Cost Estimator; Customer Service Rep.; Design Engineer; Electrical/Electronics Engineer; Financial Analyst; General Manager; Human Resources Manager; Industrial Engineer; Industrial Production Manager; Manufacturing Engineer; Marketing Manager; Mechanical Engineer; Metallurgical Engineer; MIS Specialist; Operations Manager; Production Manager; Project Manager; Quality Control Supervisor; Sales Engineer; Sales Executive; Sales Manager; Sales Representative; Software Engineer; Statistician; Systems Manager; Technical Writer/Editor; Telecommunications Manager; Transportation/Traffic Specialist; Underwriter/Assistant Underwriter. **Corporate headquarters location:** Cleveland OH. **Other U.S. locations:** Nationwide. **International locations:** Worldwide. **Average salary range of placements:** More than $50,000. **Number of placements per year:** 100 - 199.

MANAGEMENT RECRUITERS OF WINSTON-SALEM
P.O. Box 17054, Winston-Salem NC 27116. 336/723-0484. **Fax:** 336/723-0841. **Contact:** Mike Jones, Manager. **E-mail address:** mriwinsal@aol.com. **Description:** An executive search firm. **Specializes in the areas of:** Accounting/Auditing; Administration; Advertising; Architecture/Construction; Banking; Communications; Computer Hardware/Software; Design; Electrical; Engineering; Food; General Management; Health/Medical; Insurance; Legal; Manufacturing; Operations Management; Personnel/Labor Relations; Procurement; Publishing; Retail; Sales; Technical; Textiles; Transportation. **Corporate headquarters location:** Cleveland OH. **Other U.S. locations:** Nationwide. **International locations:** Worldwide.

MARK III PERSONNEL INC.
4801 East Independence Boulevard, Suite 604, Charlotte NC 28212. 704/535-5883. **Contact:** President. **Description:** An executive search firm. **Specializes in the areas of:** Engineering; Environmental; Personnel/Labor Relations; Technical. **Positions commonly filled include:** Chemical Engineer; Chemist; Electrical/Electronics Engineer; Environmental Engineer; Logistics Manager; Materials Engineer; Mechanical Engineer. **Average salary range of placements:** More than $50,000. **Number of placements per year:** 1 - 49.

MEDICAL PROFESSIONALS (MED PRO)
P.O. Box 837, Wrightsville Beach NC 28480. 910/256-8115. **Fax:** 910/256-6961. **Contact:** Donna Paap, President. **E-mail address:** donna@medpro-search.com. **World Wide Web address:** http://www.medpro-search.com. **Description:** An executive search firm. **Specializes in the areas of:** Health/Medical. **Positions commonly filled include:** Physician; Physician Assistant. **Average salary range of placements:** More than $50,000. **Number of placements per year:** 1 - 49.

MERRICK & MOORE
P.O. Box 8816, Asheville NC 28814. 828/258-1831. **Contact:** M.B. Parker, President. **Description:** An executive search firm operating on a retainer basis. **Specializes in the areas of:** Banking; Engineering; Health/Medical; Manufacturing; Technical. **Positions commonly filled include:** Accountant/Auditor; Aerospace Engineer; Attorney; Bank Officer/Manager; Biological Scientist; Chemist; EDP Specialist; Electrical/Electronics Engineer; Financial Analyst; Health Services Worker; Industrial Engineer; Mechanical Engineer; Systems Analyst. **Number of placements per year:** 1 - 49.

MOFFITT INTERNATIONAL, INC.
Park Terrace Center, Suite 1316A, Asheville NC 28806. 828/251-4550. **Fax:** 828/251-4555. **Contact:** Tim Moffitt, President. **Description:** An executive search firm operating on a retainer basis. **Specializes in the areas of:** Accounting/Auditing; Administration; Architecture/Construction; Banking; Computer Science/Software; Engineering; General Management; Health/Medical; Legal; Marketing; Personnel/Labor Relations; Pharmaceuticals; Sales; Scientific; Technical. **Positions commonly filled include:** Accountant; Architect; Attorney; Auditor; Bank Officer/Manager; Branch Manager; Budget Analyst; Chief Financial Officer; Civil Engineer; Computer Operator; Construction Contractor; Controller; Cost Estimator; Database Manager; Design Engineer; Draftsperson; Electrical/Electronics Engineer; Environmental Engineer; Finance Director; Financial Analyst; Fund Manager; Human Resources Manager; Internet Services Manager; Management Analyst/Consultant; Marketing Manager; Marketing Specialist; Mechanical Engineer; MIS Specialist; Operations Manager; Physical Therapist; Physician; Project Manager; Sales Engineer; Sales Executive; Sales Manager; Sales Representative; Software Engineer; Statistician; Systems Analyst; Systems Manager; Technical Writer/Editor; Telecommunications Manager; Transportation/Traffic Specialist. **Corporate headquarters location:** This Location. **Other U.S. locations:** Nationwide. **International locations:** Worldwide. **Average salary range of placements:** More than $50,000. **Number of placements per year:** 500 - 999.

MORGAN GROUP
P.O. Box 470488, Charlotte NC 28247. 704/541-0040.
Fax: 704/541-0810. **Contact:** John Chaplin, President.
E-mail address: jchaplin@mindspring.com.
Description: An executive search firm. **Specializes in
the areas of:** Computer Hardware/Software;
Engineering. **Positions commonly filled include:**
Electrical/Electronics Engineer; Environmental Engineer;
General Manager; Industrial Engineer; Quality Control
Supervisor; Software Engineer. **Average salary range of
placements:** More than $50,000. **Number of
placements per year: 50 - 99.**

NAGEL EXECUTIVE SEARCH INC.
376 John S. Mosby Drive, Wilmington NC 28402.
910/392-0797. **Contact:** Manager. **Description:** An
executive search firm. **Specializes in the areas of:**
Apparel.

NATIONWIDE RECRUITERS
7523 Little Avenue, Suite 208, Charlotte NC 28226.
704/541-2595. **Contact:** Manager. **Description:** An
executive search firm. **Specializes in the areas of:**
Packaging; Paper; Publishing.

THE NOLAN GROUP, INC.
16415 A Northcross Drive, Huntersville NC 28078.
704/944-7700. **Fax:** 704/944-7744. **Contact:** Manager.
Description: An executive search firm. Founded in
1982. **Specializes in the areas of:** Biotechnology;
Computer Hardware/Software; Data Communications;
New Media; Start-up Organizations.

OLSTEN FINANCIAL STAFFING
227 West Trade Street, Suite 310, Charlotte NC 28202.
704/358-1990. **Toll-free phone:** 888/222-8693. **Fax:**
704/358-1996. **Contact:** Manager. **E-mail address:**
ofs.hq@olsten.com. **World Wide Web address:**
http://www.olsten.com/ofs. **Description:** An executive
search firm operating on a contingency basis. The firm
also provides some temporary placements. **Specializes in
the areas of:** Accounting; Banking; Finance. **Positions
commonly filled include:** Accountant; Auditor; Budget
Analyst; Chief Financial Officer; Controller; Credit
Manager; Finance Director; Financial Analyst.
Corporate headquarters location: Melville NY. **Other
U.S. locations:** Nationwide. **Average salary range of
placements:** $50,000 - $100,000. **Number of
placements per year: 200 - 499.**

PARENICA & COMPANY
19250 Stableford Lane, Cornelius NC 28031. 704/896-
0060. **Fax:** 704/896-0240. **Contact:** James Parenica,
President. **Description:** An executive search firm.
Specializes in the areas of: Banking; Computer
Science/Software; General Management; Personnel/
Labor Relations. **Positions commonly filled include:**
General Manager; Human Resources Specialist; MIS
Specialist. **Average salary range of placements:** More
than $50,000. **Number of placements per year: 1 - 49.**

THE PERKINS GROUP
7621 Little Avenue, Suite 216, Charlotte NC 28226.
704/543-1111. **Fax:** 704/543-0945. **Contact:** R. Patrick
Perkins, President. **E-mail address:** perk@vnet.net.
World Wide Web address: http://www.
perkinsgroup.com. **Description:** An executive search
firm. **Specializes in the areas of:** Accounting/Auditing;
Engineering; Finance; Industrial; Manufacturing;
Marketing; Personnel/Labor Relations; Sales. **Positions
commonly filled include:** Accountant/Auditor; Chemical
Engineer; Chief Financial Officer; Controller; Credit
Manager; Design Engineer; EDP Specialist;
Electrical/Electronics Engineer; Financial Analyst;
General Manager; Human Resources Manager; Industrial
Engineer; Industrial Production Manager; Manufacturing
Engineer; Marketing Manager; Mechanical Engineer;
Metallurgical Engineer; MIS Specialist; Operations
Manager; Product Manager; Purchasing Agent/Manager;
Sales Engineer; Sales Executive; Sales Manager.
Average salary range of placements: More than
$50,000. **Number of placements per year: 100 - 199.**

ROMAC INTERNATIONAL
201 North Tryon Street, Suite 2660, Charlotte NC 28202.
704/333-8311. **Toll-free phone:** 800/334-3617. **Fax:**
704/334-6006. **Contact:** Manager. **Description:** An
executive search firm that also provides some temporary
placements. **Specializes in the areas of:**
Accounting/Auditing; Administration; Banking;
Computer Science/Software; Finance; Technical.
Positions commonly filled include: Accountant/Auditor;
Bank Officer/Manager; Branch Manager; Budget
Analyst; Computer Programmer; Credit Manager;
Financial Analyst; Human Resources Specialist; MIS
Manager; Systems Analyst; Technical Writer/Editor.
Average salary range of placements: More than
$50,000. **Number of placements per year: 100 - 199.**

SGI (SPORTS GROUP INTERNATIONAL)
804 Salem Woods Drive, Suite 103, Raleigh NC 27615.
919/846-1860. **Fax:** 919/848-0236. **Contact:** Lesley
White, Manager. **E-mail address:** sgisearch@aol.com.
World Wide Web address: http://www.sgisearch.com.
Description: An executive search firm operating on a
retainer basis. SGI focuses on placing individuals in the
sporting goods and consumer products industries.
Specializes in the areas of: Marketing; Sales. **Positions
commonly filled include:** General Manager; Marketing
Manager; Public Relations Specialist; Sales Executive;
Sales Manager. **Corporate headquarters location:** This
Location. **Average salary range of placements:**
$50,000 - $100,000. **Number of placements per year: 1
- 49.**

SALES CONSULTANTS OF CONCORD, INC.
254 Church Street, Concord NC 28025. 704/786-0700.
Fax: 704/782-1356. **Contact:** Anna Lee Pearson,
President. **Description:** An executive search firm.
Specializes in the areas of: Computer Science/Software;
General Management; Health/Medical; Sales; Technical;
Telecommunications. **Positions commonly filled
include:** Branch Manager; Customer Service
Representative; Economist; Electrical/Electronics
Engineer; General Manager; Health Services Manager;
Management Analyst/Consultant; Manufacturer's/
Wholesaler's Sales Rep.; Marketing Manager; Physical
Therapist; Physician; Product Manager; Psychologist;
Sales Manager; Services Sales Representative; Software
Engineer. **Number of placements per year: 1 - 49.**

SALES CONSULTANTS OF HIGH POINT
2411 Penny Road, Suite 101, High Point NC 27265.
336/883-4433. **Contact:** Manager. **Description:** An
executive search firm. **Specializes in the areas of:**
Accounting/Auditing; Administration; Advertising;
Architecture/Construction; Banking; Communications;
Computer Hardware/Software; Design; Electrical;
Engineering; Food; General Management;
Health/Medical; Insurance; Legal; Manufacturing;
Operations Management; Personnel/Labor Relations;
Procurement; Publishing; Retail; Sales; Technical;
Textiles; Transportation.

SANFORD ROSE ASSOCIATES - BURLINGTON
P.O. Box 831, 4736 Pleasant Garden Road, Pleasant
Garden NC 27313. 336/676-9300. **Fax:** 336/676-9397.
Contact: Ronald R. Roach, President. **E-mail address:**
sraburlnc@aol.com. **World Wide Web address:**
http://www.sanfordrose.com. **Description:** An executive
search firm operating on both retainer and contingency
bases. Client company pays fee. **Specializes in the areas
of:** Engineering; General Management; Industrial;
Manufacturing. **Positions commonly filled include:**
Account Manager; Account Representative; Buyer;
Chemical Engineer; Controller; Design Engineer;
Electrical/Electronics Engineer; Environmental Engineer;
Financial Analyst; General Manager; Human Resources
Manager; Industrial Engineer; Industrial Production
Manager; Manufacturing Engineer; Mechanical
Engineer; MIS Specialist; Operations Manager;
Production Manager; Project Manager; Purchasing
Agent/Manager; Quality Assurance Engineer; Quality
Control Supervisor; Sales Engineer; Sales Executive;
Sales Manager; Sales Representative; Vice President of

Operations. **Corporate headquarters location:** Akron OH. **Average salary range of placements:** $50,000 - $100,000. **Number of placements per year:** 1 - 49.

SANFORD ROSE ASSOCIATES - CHARLOTTE
PMB 374, 338 South Sharon Amity Road, Charlotte NC 28270. 704/366-0730. **Toll-free phone:** 800/272-8760. **Fax:** 704/365-0620. **Contact:** James L. Downs, CEO. **E-mail address:** jdownssra@aol.com. **World Wide Web address:** http://www.sra-charlotte.com. **Description:** An executive search firm operating on a contingency basis. The firm also provides some contract services. **Specializes in the areas of:** Administration; Computer Science/Software. **Positions commonly filled include:** Account Manager; Account Representative; Computer Operator; Computer Programmer; Database Manager; General Manager; Human Resources Manager; Internet Services Manager; Management Analyst/Consultant; MIS Specialist; Online Content Specialist; Operations Manager; Sales Executive; Sales Manager; Software Engineer; Systems Analyst; Systems Manager; Technical Writer/Editor; Telecommunications Manager. **Corporate headquarters location:** Akron OH. **Average salary range of placements:** More than $50,000. **Number of placements per year:** 50 - 99.

SANFORD ROSE ASSOCIATES - GASTONIA
3816-21 South New Hope Road, Gastonia NC 28056-8439. 704/824-0895. **Toll-free phone:** 800/373-0790. **Fax:** 704/824-0995. **Contact:** Frederick D. Halek, President/Director. **World Wide Web address:** http://www.sanfordrose.com/gastonia. **Description:** An executive search firm operating on both retainer and contingency bases. Client company pays fee. **Specializes in the areas of:** Architecture/Construction; Engineering; General Management; Marketing; Sales. **Positions commonly filled include:** Accountant; Architect; Chief Financial Officer; Civil Engineer; Construction Contractor; Customer Service Representative; Design Engineer; Draftsperson; General Manager; Human Resources Manager; Industrial Engineer; Manufacturing Engineer; Mechanical Engineer; Metallurgical Engineer; Operations Manager; Production Manager; Project Manager; Quality Assurance Engineer; Quality Control Supervisor; Sales Engineer; Sales Executive; Sales Manager; Sales Representative; Vice President of Operations. **Corporate headquarters location:** Akron OH. **Average salary range of placements:** $50,000 - $100,000. **Number of placements per year:** 1 - 49.

SANFORD ROSE ASSOCIATES - GREENSBORO
3405-H West Wendover Avenue, Greensboro NC 27407. 336/852-3003. **Fax:** 336/852-3039. **Contact:** Manager. **World Wide Web address:** http://www.sanfordrose.com. **Description:** An executive search firm. **Specializes in the areas of:** Publishing. **Corporate headquarters location:** Akron OH.

SEARCH CONSULTANTS WORLDWIDE INC.
8929 St. Croix Lane, Charlotte NC 28277. 704/814-0977. **Contact:** Gordon Graybiel, Managing Principal. **Description:** An executive search firm operating on a contingency basis. **Specializes in the areas of:** Engineering; General Management; Industrial. **Positions commonly filled include:** Electrical/Electronics Engineer; Environmental Engineer; Geologist/Geophysicist; Industrial Engineer; Mechanical Engineer. **Number of placements per year:** 1 - 49.

SEARCHPRO, INC.
8206 Providence Road, BMP 1200-400, Charlotte NC 28277. 704/849-5690. **Fax:** 704/849-9095. **Contact:** Manager. **World Wide Web address:** http://searchpro.com. **Description:** An executive search firm. **Specializes in the areas of:** Banking; Finance.

SICKENBERGER ASSOCIATES
612 Pasteur Drive, Suite 300, Greensboro NC 27403. 336/852-4220. **Contact:** Manager. **Description:** An executive search firm. **Specializes in the areas of:** Engineering; Fashion; Sales.

SOCKWELL & ASSOCIATES
227 West Trade Street, Suite 1930, Charlotte NC 28202. 704/372-1865. **Fax:** 704/372-8960. **Contact:** Manager. **E-mail address:** email@sockwell.com. **World Wide Web address:** http://www.sockwell.com. **Description:** An executive search firm operating on a retainer basis. **Specializes in the areas of:** Banking; Education; Electrical; Finance; Health/Medical; High-Tech; Hotel/Restaurant; Investment; Nonprofit; Real Estate; Technical. **Positions commonly filled include:** Chief Executive Officer; Chief Financial Officer; Human Resources Manager; Information Specialist; Operations Manager; Sales and Marketing Manager.

SPARKS PERSONNEL SERVICES
1400 Battleground Avenue, Greensboro NC 27408. 336/851-2500. **Contact:** Manager. **Description:** An executive search firm. **Specializes in the areas of:** Accounting/Auditing; Administration; Advertising; Banking; Computer Science/Software; Engineering; Finance; General Management; Industrial; Manufacturing; Personnel/Labor Relations; Sales; Secretarial; Textiles. **Positions commonly filled include:** Accountant/Auditor; Bank Officer/Manager; Blue-Collar Worker Supervisor; Branch Manager; Buyer; Claim Representative; Computer Programmer; Credit Manager; Customer Service Representative; Electrical/Electronics Engineer; Financial Analyst; General Manager; Human Resources Specialist; Industrial Engineer; Industrial Production Manager; Insurance Agent/Broker; Management Analyst/Consultant; Management Trainee; Mechanical Engineer; MIS Specialist; Purchasing Agent/Manager; Securities Sales Representative; Software Engineer; Systems Analyst; Travel Agent. **Other area locations:** Charlotte NC; Raleigh NC; Wilmington NC. **Average salary range of placements:** $30,000 - $50,000. **Number of placements per year:** 50 - 99.

STAFF ACCOUNTANTS
5109 Monroe Road, Charlotte NC 28205. 704/563-2996. **Fax:** 704/563-5551. **Contact:** Manager. **Description:** An executive search firm. **Specializes in the areas of:** Accounting/Auditing. **Positions commonly filled include:** Accountant/Auditor; Tax Specialist. **Average salary range of placements:** $30,000 - $50,000. **Number of placements per year:** 1 - 49.

STEWART GREENE & COMPANY/THE TRIAD
P.O. Box 625, Pleasant Garden NC 27313. 336/674-5345. **Physical address:** 5504 Stonebridge Road, Pleasant Garden NC. **Fax:** 336/674-5937. **Contact:** Bill Greene, President. **Description:** An executive search firm. **Specializes in the areas of:** Architecture/Construction; Engineering; Furniture; General Management; Manufacturing; Sales. **Positions commonly filled include:** Buyer; Credit Manager; Design Engineer; Designer; Engineer; General Manager; Human Resources Specialist; Industrial Designer; Industrial Production Manager; Mechanical Engineer; Purchasing Agent/Manager; Quality Control Supervisor. **Number of placements per year:** 50 - 99.

STRATFORDGROUP
4825 Creekstone Drive, Suite 100, Research Triangle Park NC 27703. 919/572-6400. **Toll-free phone:** 800/536-4384. **Fax:** 919/572-9190. **Contact:** Recruiter. **E-mail address:** corriemates@stratfordgroup.com. **World Wide Web address:** http://www.stratfordgroup.com. **Description:** An executive search firm operating on a retainer basis. Founded in 1997. **Specializes in the areas of:** Automotive; Consumer Products; Engineering; Entertainment; Finance; Health/Medical; Human Resources; Information Technology; Manufacturing; Nonprofit; Professional; Retail; Telecommunications; Transportation. **Corporate headquarters location:** Cleveland OH. **Other area locations:** Charlotte NC. **Other U.S. locations:** San Diego CA; San Francisco CA; Denver CO; Washington DC; New York NY; Cleveland OH; Dayton OH; Toledo OH; Philadelphia PA; Houston TX; Vienna VA; Bellevue WA.

STRATFORDGROUP
6000 Fairview Road, Suite 550, Charlotte NC 28210. 704/969-8103. **Toll-free phone:** 800/536-4384. **Fax:** 704/643-7078. **Contact:** Recruiter. **E-mail address:** corriemates@stratfordgroup.com. **World Wide Web address:** http://www.stratfordgroup.com. **Description:** An executive search firm operating on a retainer basis. Founded in 1997. **Specializes in the areas of:** Automotive; Consumer Products; Engineering; Entertainment; Finance; Health/Medical; Human Resources; Information Technology; Manufacturing; Nonprofit; Professional; Retail; Telecommunications; Transportation. **Corporate headquarters location:** Cleveland OH. **Other area locations:** Research Triangle Park NC. **Other U.S. locations:** San Francisco CA; San Diego CA; Denver CO; Washington DC; New York NY; Cleveland OH; Dayton OH; Toledo OH; Philadelphia PA; Houston TX; Vienna VA; Bellevue WA.

SUMMIT OCCUPATIONAL STAFFING
523 Summit Street, Winston-Salem NC 27101. 336/777-1978. **Toll-free phone:** 800/568-2575. **Fax:** 336/777-0706. **Contact:** James L. Salkeld, National Placement Director. **Description:** An executive search firm operating on a contingency basis. The firm also provides some temporary and temp-to-perm placements. **Specializes in the areas of:** Health/Medical; Legal; Nonprofit; Personnel/Labor Relations; Secretarial. **Positions commonly filled include:** Administrative Assistant; Administrative Manager; Biomedical Engineer; Certified Nurses Aide; Chief Financial Officer; Clerical Supervisor; Clinical Lab Technician; Counselor; Credit Manager; Customer Service Representative; Emergency Medical Technician; Finance Director; General Manager; Human Resources Manager; Licensed Practical Nurse; Medical Records Technician; Nuclear Medicine Technologist; Occupational Therapist; Paralegal; Pharmacist; Physical Therapist; Physician; Psychologist; Purchasing Agent/Manager; Radiological Technologist; Registered Nurse; Respiratory Therapist; Secretary; Speech-Language Pathologist; Surgical Technician; Typist/Word Processor. **Benefits available to temporary workers:** Workers' Compensation Plan. **Average salary range of placements:** $30,000 - $50,000. **Number of placements per year:** 50 - 99.

TECHNICAL ASSOCIATES
347 North Caswell Road, Charlotte NC 28204. 704/333-9011. **Contact:** Ron Kretel, Manager. **Description:** An executive search firm. **Specializes in the areas of:** Engineering.

WADDY R. THOMSON ASSOCIATES
233 South Sharon Amity Road, Charlotte NC 28211. 704/366-1956. **Contact:** Waddy R. Thomson, Principal. **Description:** An executive search firm operating on a contingency basis. **Specializes in the areas of:** Food; Industrial; Insurance; Manufacturing; Retail; Transportation. **Positions commonly filled include:** Environmental Engineer; Environmental Scientist; Safety Engineer. **Average salary range of placements:** More than $50,000. **Number of placements per year:** 1 - 49.

RANDY WALLEY ASSOCIATES
P.O. Box 2701, High Point NC 27261. 336/885-0644. **Contact:** Manager. **Description:** An executive search firm. **Specializes in the areas of:** Apparel.

DAVID WEINFELD GROUP
6512 Six Forks Road, Suite 603B, Raleigh NC 27615. 919/676-7828. **Fax:** 919/676-7399. **Contact:** David Weinfeld, President. **E-mail address:** email@weinfeldgroup.com. **World Wide Web address:** http://www.weinfeldgroup.com. **Description:** An executive search firm. **Specializes in the areas of:** Computer Science/Software; Engineering; Information Technology; Sales; Telecommunications. **Positions commonly filled include:** Computer Programmer; Design Engineer; Electrical Engineer; Management Analyst/Consultant; Marketing Manager; Project Manager; Services Sales Representative; Software Engineer; Systems Analyst; Telecommunications Manager. **Average salary range of placements:** More than $50,000. **Number of placements per year:** 50 - 99.

WILSON PERSONNEL INC.
134 Montford Avenue, Asheville NC 28801. 828/258-3900. **Fax:** 828/258-3902. **Contact:** Ken Schapira, Executive Vice President. **Description:** An executive search firm operating on a contingency basis. **Specializes in the areas of:** Engineering; Management; Manufacturing; Technical.

PERMANENT EMPLOYMENT AGENCIES

ACSYS
2650 One First Union Center, 301 South College Street, Suite 2650, Charlotte NC 28202. 704/377-6447. **Fax:** 704/377-2410. **Contact:** Edward K. Turner, President. **Description:** A permanent employment agency. **Specializes in the areas of:** Accounting; Administration; Banking; Finance; Information Technology.

ALEXIUS PERSONNEL ASSOCIATES INC.
3807 Wrightsville Avenue, Suite 24, Wilmington NC 28403. 910/799-6700. **Contact:** Manager. **Description:** A permanent employment agency that also provides some temporary placements.

ANDERSON & DANIEL PERSONNEL ASSOCIATES
P.O. Box 5157, Wilmington NC 28403. 910/799-8500. **Physical address:** 4900 Randall Parkway, Suite F, Wilmington NC. **Fax:** 910/791-0706. **Contact:** Mike Halpern, Owner. **Description:** A permanent employment agency that also provides some temporary and temp-to-perm placements. **Specializes in the areas of:** Accounting/Auditing; Administration; Computer Science/Software; Engineering; Legal; Personnel/Labor Relations; Secretarial; Technical; Transportation. **Positions commonly filled include:** Account Representative; Accountant; Accountant/Auditor; Adjuster; Administrative Assistant; Administrative Manager; Applications Engineer; Auditor; Blue-Collar Worker Supervisor; Budget Analyst; Buyer; Chemical Engineer; Chemist; Chief Financial Officer; Civil Engineer; Claim Representative; Clerical Supervisor;

Computer Operator; Computer Programmer; Controller; Cost Estimator; Credit Manager; Customer Service Representative; Database Manager; Design Engineer; Draftsperson; Electrical/Electronics Engineer; Financial Analyst; Graphic Artist; Graphic Designer; Human Resources Manager; Industrial Engineer; Industrial Production Manager; Manufacturing Engineer; Mechanical Engineer; Medical Records Technician; MIS Specialist; Paralegal; Production Manager; Purchasing Agent/Manager; Quality Control Supervisor; Sales Representative; Secretary; Software Engineer; Statistician; Systems Analyst; Systems Manager; Technical Writer/Editor; Transportation/Traffic Specialist; Typist/Word Processor. **Benefits available to temporary workers:** Paid Holidays. **Corporate headquarters location:** This Location. **Average salary range of placements:** $30,000 - $50,000. **Number of placements per year:** 100 - 199.

ASSOCIATES EMPLOYMENT INC.
5200 Park Road, Suite 226, Charlotte NC 28209. 704/525-4344. **Contact:** Manager. **Description:** A permanent employment agency. **Specializes in the areas of:** Legal.

CALDWELL PERSONNEL SERVICES
P.O. Box 1561, Taylorsville NC 28681. 828/632-4995. **Physical address:** 214 South Center Street, Taylorsville NC. **Fax:** 828/635-1264. **Contact:** Cara Kelso, Office Manager. **Description:** A permanent employment agency. **Specializes in the areas of:** Industrial; Light

Industrial; Secretarial. **Positions commonly filled include:** Accountant; Blue-Collar Worker Supervisor; Clerical Supervisor; Computer Operator; Customer Service Representative; Electrician; Paralegal; Sales Representative; Secretary. **Benefits available to temporary workers:** Medical Insurance. **Corporate headquarters location:** Lenoir NC. **Other area locations:** Hickory NC; Morganton NC; North Wilkesboro NC; Statesville NC. **Average salary range of placements:** Less than $20,000. **Number of placements per year:** 100 - 199.

DATAMASTERS
P.O. Box 14548, Greensboro NC 27415-4548. **Toll-free phone:** 800/328-2627. **Fax:** 336/373-1501. **Contact:** Manager. **E-mail address:** email@datamasters.com. **World Wide Web address:** http://www. datamasters.com/dm. **Description:** A permanent employment agency. **Specializes in the areas of:** Computer Science/Software. **Positions commonly filled include:** Computer Programmer; Science Technologist; Systems Analyst. **Average salary range of placements:** $30,000 - $100,000. **Number of placements per year:** 100 - 199.

DURHAM JOB SERVICE OFFICE
1105 South Briggs Avenue, Durham NC 27703. 919/560-6880. **Contact:** Manager. **Description:** A permanent employment agency. **Positions commonly filled include:** Accountant/Auditor; Actuary; Administrative Assistant; Advertising Clerk; Aerospace Engineer; Agricultural Engineer; Architect; Attorney; Bank Officer/Manager; Biological Scientist; Biomedical Engineer; Bookkeeper; Buyer; Ceramics Engineer; Chemical Engineer; Chemist; Civil Engineer; Claim Representative; Clerk; Commercial Artist; Computer Operator; Computer Programmer; Construction Trade Worker; Credit Manager; Customer Service Representative; Data Entry Clerk; Dietician/Nutritionist; Draftsperson; Driver; Economist; EDP Specialist; Electrical/Electronics Engineer; Factory Worker; Financial Analyst; Food Scientist/Technologist; General Manager; Hotel Manager; Human Resources Manager; Industrial Designer; Industrial Engineer; Insurance Agent/Broker; Legal Secretary; Light Industrial Worker; Marketing Specialist; Mechanical Engineer; Medical Secretary; Metallurgical Engineer; Mining Engineer; MIS Specialist; Nurse; Operations/Production Manager; Petroleum Engineer; Physicist; Public Relations Specialist; Purchasing Agent/Manager; Quality Control Supervisor; Receptionist; Reporter; Sales Representative; Secretary; Statistician; Stenographer; Systems Analyst; Technical Writer/Editor; Technician; Typist/Word Processor; Underwriter/Assistant Underwriter. **Number of placements per year:** 1000+.

F-O-R-T-U-N-E PERSONNEL CONSULTANTS OF RALEIGH, INC.
7521 Morning Dove Road, Suite 101, Raleigh NC 27615. 919/848-9929. **Fax:** 919/848-1062. **Contact:** Rick Deckelbaum, President. **Description:** A permanent employment agency. **Specializes in the areas of:** Accounting/Auditing; Banking; Computer Science/Software; Engineering; Finance; Food; Manufacturing; Personnel/Labor Relations. **Positions commonly filled include:** Accountant/Auditor; Aerospace Engineer; Biomedical Engineer; Ceramics Engineer; Chemical Engineer; Chemist; Civil Engineer; Computer Programmer; Electrical/Electronics Engineer; Financial Analyst; General Manager; Human Resources Manager; Industrial Engineer; Materials Engineer; Mechanical Engineer; Metallurgical Engineer; Petroleum Engineer; Software Engineer; Statistician; Systems Analyst. **Number of placements per year:** 200 - 499.

FRIDAY STAFFING
1944 Hendersonville Road, Asheville NC 28803. 828/684-1788. **Contact:** Manager. **Description:** A permanent employment agency. **Positions commonly filled include:** Accountant/Auditor; Administrative Assistant; Bookkeeper; Customer Service Representative; Data Entry Clerk; Draftsperson; Factory Worker; Light Industrial Worker; Medical Secretary; Receptionist; Secretary; Typist/Word Processor. **Other area locations:** Hendersonville NC.

FRIDAY STAFFING
227 Duncan Hill Road, Hendersonville NC 28792. 828/697-1507. **Contact:** Manager. **Description:** A permanent employment agency. **Positions commonly filled include:** Accountant/Auditor; Administrative Assistant; Bookkeeper; Customer Service Representative; Data Entry Clerk; Draftsperson; Factory Worker; Light Industrial Worker; Medical Secretary; Receptionist; Secretary; Typist/Word Processor. **Other area locations:** Asheville NC.

GRAHAM & ASSOCIATES
2100-J West Cornwallis Drive, Greensboro NC 27408. 336/288-9330. **Contact:** Gary Graham, CPC/President. **Description:** A permanent employment agency. **Specializes in the areas of:** Accounting/Auditing; Banking; Clerical; Computer Hardware/Software; Engineering; Legal; Manufacturing; MIS/EDP; Personnel/Labor Relations; Technical. **Positions commonly filled include:** Accountant/Auditor; Administrative Assistant; Aerospace Engineer; Agricultural Engineer; Attorney; Bank Officer/Manager; Bookkeeper; Buyer; Ceramics Engineer; Chemical Engineer; Chemist; Civil Engineer; Clerk; Computer Operator; Computer Programmer; Credit Manager; Customer Service Representative; Data Entry Clerk; Draftsperson; Economist; EDP Specialist; Electrical/Electronics Engineer; Factory Worker; Financial Analyst; General Manager; Human Resources Manager; Industrial Designer; Industrial Engineer; Legal Secretary; Light Industrial Worker; Marketing Specialist; Mechanical Engineer; Medical Secretary; Metallurgical Engineer; Mining Engineer; Operations/Production Manager; Petroleum Engineer; Physicist; Purchasing Agent/Manager; Quality Control Supervisor; Receptionist; Secretary; Stenographer; Systems Analyst; Technical Writer/Editor; Technician; Typist/Word Processor. **Number of placements per year:** 200 - 499.

GRANITE PERSONNEL SERVICE
5955 Dunbar Road, Granite Falls NC 28630. 828/396-2369. **Contact:** Manager. **Description:** A permanent employment agency. **Specializes in the areas of:** Administration; Clerical; Sales; Technical. **Number of placements per year:** 50 - 99.

THE GREER GROUP
3109 Charles B. Root Wind, Raleigh NC 27612. 919/571-0051. **Fax:** 919/571-7450. **Contact:** Deborah G. Greer, President/Owner. **Description:** A permanent employment agency. **Specializes in the areas of:** Accounting/Auditing; Bookkeeping; Clerical; Engineering; Finance; Legal; Office Support.

INITIAL STAFFING SERVICES
6000 Fairview Road, Suite 275, Charlotte NC 28210. 704/553-1111. **Fax:** 704/554-0524. **Contact:** Zina Lyons, Service Manager. **Description:** A permanent employment agency that also provides some temporary placements. **Other U.S. locations:** Nationwide.

THE JOBS MARKET, INC.
902 Greensboro Road, High Point NC 27260. 336/889-3777. **Fax:** 336/889-7795. **Contact:** David Phillips, President. **World Wide Web address:** http://www.jobsmarket.com. **Description:** A permanent employment agency that also provides some temporary placements. **Corporate headquarters location:** This Location. **Number of placements per year:** 1 - 49.

THE JOBS MARKET, INC.
237 SW Main Street, Lenoir NC 28645-5418. 828/758-9519. **Contact:** Manager. **World Wide Web address:** http://www.jobsmarket.com. **Description:** A permanent employment agency. **Specializes in the areas of:** Architecture/Construction; General Management; Industrial; Manufacturing; Personnel/Labor Relations; Sales; Secretarial; Transportation. **Positions commonly**

filled include: Architect; Automotive Mechanic; Blue-Collar Worker Supervisor; Claim Representative; Clerical Supervisor; Computer Programmer; Construction Contractor; Customer Service Representative; Dental Assistant/Dental Hygienist; Dietician/Nutritionist; Electrician; Forester/Conservation Scientist; General Manager; Health Services Manager; Industrial Production Manager; Landscape Architect; Management Trainee; Manufacturer's/Wholesaler's Sales Rep.; Operations/Production Manager; Paralegal; Pharmacist; Preschool Worker; Public Relations Specialist; Restaurant/Food Service Manager; Securities Sales Representative; Structural Engineer; Surveyor; Typist/Word Processor. **Corporate headquarters location:** High Point NC. **Average salary range of placements:** $20,000 - $29,999. **Number of placements per year:** 500 - 999.

LEGAL PERSONNEL SERVICES
P.O. Drawer 1368, Raleigh NC 27602. 919/787-0049. **Contact:** Manager. **Description:** A permanent employment agency that also provides some temporary placements. **Specializes in the areas of:** Legal. **Positions commonly filled include:** Legal Secretary; Paralegal.

MEGA FORCE
P.O. Box 8994, Rocky Mount NC 27804. 252/972-2914. **Contact:** Manager. **Description:** A permanent employment agency. **Specializes in the areas of:** Clerical; Office Support.

MYERS & ASSOCIATES
13420 Reese Boulevard West, Huntersville NC 28078. 704/875-8300. **Fax:** 704/875-8891. **Contact:** Joseph N. Myers, Sr., President. **Description:** A permanent employment agency operating on a contingency basis. **Specializes in the areas of:** Accounting/Auditing; Engineering; Industrial; Manufacturing; Textiles. **Positions commonly filled include:** Accountant/Auditor; Auditor; Buyer; Chemical Engineer; Computer Programmer; Electrical/Electronics Engineer; Financial Analyst; Industrial Engineer; Industrial Production Manager; Mechanical Engineer; Metallurgical Engineer; Occupational Therapist; Physical Therapist; Respiratory Therapist; Software Engineer; Systems Analyst; Textile Technologist. **Corporate headquarters location:** This Location. **Average salary range of placements:** More than $50,000. **Number of placements per year:** 1 - 49.

NEASE PERSONNEL SERVICES
1706 East Arlington Boulevard, Suite B, Greenville NC 27858. 252/756-5820. **Fax:** 252/756-0697. **Contact:** Lori D. Nease, CPC/President. **Description:** A permanent employment agency.

OPPORTUNITY PLUS
P.O. Box 35481, Charlotte NC 28235. 704/376-4735. **Fax:** 704/376-4738. **Contact:** Manager. **E-mail address:** info@opportunity-plus.org. **World Wide Web address:** http://www.opportunity-plus.org. **Description:** A permanent employment agency. The agency also provides some temporary placements and career/outplacement counseling services to people with physical disabilities. **Number of placements per year:** 200 - 499.

PRO STAFF PERSONNEL SERVICES
212 South Tryon Street, Suite 1300, Charlotte NC 28246. 704/376-8367. **Fax:** 704/376-8355. **Contact:** Vicki Sweginnis, Staffing Manager. **World Wide Web address:** http://www.prostaff-carolinas.com. **Description:** A permanent employment agency. Founded in 1982. **Specializes in the areas of:** Administration; Banking; Secretarial. **Positions commonly filled include:** Accountant/Auditor; Administrative Manager; Bank Officer/Manager; Customer Service Representative; Typist/Word Processor. **Corporate headquarters location:** Minneapolis MN. **Number of placements per year:** 1000+.

PROFESSIONAL PERSONNEL ASSOCIATES INC.
7520 East Independence Boulevard, Suite 160, Charlotte NC 28227. 704/532-2599. **Toll-free phone:** 888/771-6248. **Fax:** 704/536-8192. **Contact:** Gregory Whitt, President/Owner. **E-mail address:** ppajobs@worldnet.att.net. **World Wide Web address:** http://www.ppajobs.com. **Description:** A permanent employment agency that also provides some contract services. **Specializes in the areas of:** Computer Science/Software; Engineering; Industrial; Manufacturing; Personnel/Labor Relations. **Positions commonly filled include:** Aerospace Engineer; Buyer; Chemical Engineer; Chemist; Civil Engineer; Computer Programmer; Design Engineer; Designer; Electrical/Electronics Engineer; Environmental Engineer; Human Resources Specialist; Industrial Engineer; Industrial Production Manager; Mechanical Engineer; Metallurgical Engineer; MIS Specialist; Nuclear Engineer; Purchasing Agent/Manager; Quality Control Supervisor; Software Engineer; Structural Engineer. **Average salary range of placements:** $40,000 - $60,000. **Number of placements per year:** 50 - 99.

REP & ASSOCIATES
P.O. Box 55, Washington NC 27889. 252/946-6643. **Fax:** 252/974-0668. **Contact:** Richard Phelan, Recruiter. **E-mail address:** dick_rep@computerplacement.com. **Description:** A permanent employment agency. **Specializes in the areas of:** Computer Science/Software. **Positions commonly filled include:** MIS Specialist; Systems Analyst; Systems Manager. **Corporate headquarters location:** This Location. **Average salary range of placements:** More than $50,000.

REMEDY INTELLIGENT STAFFING
4421 Stuart Andrew Boulevard, Suite 102, Charlotte NC 28217. 704/521-9818. **Fax:** 704/525-7736. **Contact:** Staffing Coordinator. **Description:** A permanent employment agency. **Specializes in the areas of:** Sales; Secretarial. **Positions commonly filled include:** Accountant/Auditor; Administrative Manager; Clerical Supervisor; Customer Service Representative; Human Resources Specialist; Industrial Production Manager; Management Trainee; MIS Specialist; Operations/Production Manager; Paralegal; Services Sales Representative; Typist/Word Processor. **Benefits available to temporary workers:** 401(k); Daycare Assistance; Dental Insurance; Medical Insurance; Paid Holidays. **Corporate headquarters location:** San Juan Capistrano CA. **Other U.S. locations:** Nationwide. **Average salary range of placements:** $20,000 - $29,999. **Number of placements per year:** 1000+.

SNELLING PERSONNEL SERVICES
1911 Hillandale Road, Suite 1210, Durham NC 27705. 919/383-2575. **Fax:** 919/383-5706. **Contact:** Manager. **Description:** A permanent employment agency.

SNELLING PERSONNEL SERVICES
P.O. Box 5879, Asheville NC 28813-5879. 828/654-0310. **Fax:** 828/654-0051. **Contact:** Larry R. Davis, Owner. **E-mail address:** snelling@ioa.com. **World Wide Web address:** http://www.snelling.com/asheville. **Description:** A permanent employment agency that also provides some temporary placements. **Specializes in the areas of:** Accounting/Auditing; Administration; Computer Science/Software; Engineering; Industrial; Manufacturing; Sales; Secretarial; Technical. **Positions commonly filled include:** Accountant/Auditor; Biomedical Engineer; Blue-Collar Worker Supervisor; Chemical Engineer; Chemist; Civil Engineer; Clerical Supervisor; Computer Programmer; Customer Service Representative; Design Engineer; Designer; Draftsperson; Electrical/Electronics Engineer; Financial Analyst; Industrial Engineer; Industrial Production Manager; Management Trainee; Manufacturer's/Wholesaler's Sales Rep.; Mechanical Engineer; MIS Specialist; Quality Control Supervisor; Restaurant/Food Service Manager; Services Sales Representative; Software Engineer; Structural Engineer; Surveyor; Systems Analyst; Technical Writer/Editor; Typist/Word Processor. **Benefits available to temporary workers:** 401(k); Medical Insurance; Paid Holidays; Paid Vacation. **Average salary range of**

placements: $30,000 - $50,000. **Number of placements per year:** 1000+.

SNELLING PERSONNEL SERVICES
5970 Fairview Road, Suite 220, Charlotte NC 28210. 704/553-0050. **Contact:** Manager. **Description:** A permanent employment agency that also provides some temporary placements. **Specializes in the areas of:** Office Support.

THE UNDERWOOD GROUP
2840 Plaza Place, Suite 211, Raleigh NC 27612. 919/782-3024. **Fax:** 919/783-0492. **Contact:** Manager. **E-mail address:** tug@underwoodgroup.com. **Description:** A permanent employment agency that also provides some contract services. **Specializes in the areas of:** Administration; Computer Science/Software; Data Processing; Engineering. **Positions commonly filled include:** Computer Programmer; Database Manager; Design Engineer; Electrical/Electronics Engineer; MIS Specialist; Software Engineer; Systems Analyst. **Benefits available to temporary workers:** 401(k); Dental Insurance; Medical Insurance; Reimbursement Accounts. **Average salary range of placements:** $30,000 - $50,000. **Number of placements per year:** 1 - 49.

USA STAFFING
25 Victoria Road, Asheville NC 28801. 828/252-0708. **Toll-free phone:** 800/645-0708. **Fax:** 828/252-0788. **Contact:** Sherry West, Manager. **Description:** A permanent employment agency. Employer pays half of the fee. **Specializes in the areas of:** Accounting/Auditing; Administration; Banking; Computer Science/Software; Engineering; Fashion; Finance; Food; General Management; Health/Medical; Industrial; Insurance; Legal; Light Industrial; Nonprofit; Personnel/Labor Relations; Printing; Publishing; Retail; Sales; Scientific; Secretarial; Technical; Transportation. **Positions commonly filled include:** Account Representative; Accountant/Auditor; Administrative Assistant; Assistant Manager; Attorney; Auditor; Bank Officer/Manager; Branch Manager; Chemical Engineer; Chemist; Civil Engineer; Claim Representative; Clerical Supervisor; Clinical Lab Technician; Computer Programmer; Controller; Credit Manager; Customer Service Representative; Database Manager; Draftsperson; Electrical/Electronics Engineer; Electrician; Financial Analyst; General Manager; Human Resources Manager; Industrial Engineer; Industrial Production Manager; Mechanical Engineer; Medical Records Technician; MIS Specialist; Sales Engineer; Sales Executive; Sales Manager; Sales Representative; Secretary; Social Worker; Typist/Word Processor; Underwriter/Assistant Underwriter. **Average salary range of placements:** $20,000 - $29,999. **Number of placements per year:** 100 - 199.

WESTAFF
800 Clanton Road, Suite W, Charlotte NC 28217. 704/525-8400. **Fax:** 704/525-8682. **Contact:** Manager.

Description: A permanent employment agency. **Specializes in the areas of:** Light Industrial; Secretarial.

WOODS-HOYLE, INC.
P.O. Box 9902, Greensboro NC 27429. 336/273-4557. **Fax:** 336/275-4945. **Contact:** Anne Marie Woods, President. **World Wide Web address:** http://www.woodshoyle.com. **Description:** A permanent employment agency. **Specializes in the areas of:** Computer Science/Software. **Positions commonly filled include:** Computer Programmer; Database Manager; MIS Specialist; Systems Analyst; Systems Manager; Telecommunications Manager. **Average salary range of placements:** $30,000 - $50,000. **Number of placements per year:** 50 - 99.

YOUNGBLOOD STAFFING
117 West Main Street, Whiteville NC 28472. 910/640-2341. **Fax:** 910/640-2126. **Contact:** Melissa Reeves, Resource Specialist. **Description:** A permanent employment agency. **Specializes in the areas of:** Industrial; Secretarial. **Positions commonly filled include:** Administrative Manager; Automotive Mechanic; Clerical Supervisor; Customer Service Representative; Human Resources Specialist; Quality Control Supervisor; Services Sales Representative; Typist/Word Processor. **Other area locations:** Elizabethtown NC; Wilmington NC. **Average salary range of placements:** Less than $20,000. **Number of placements per year:** 500 - 999.

YOUNGBLOOD STAFFING
4024 Oleander Drive, Suite A, Wilmington NC 28403-6814. 910/799-0103. **Fax:** 910/791-1503. **Contact:** Traci A. Roberts, CFO. **Description:** A permanent employment agency. **Specializes in the areas of:** Accounting/Auditing; Administration; Banking; Finance; General Management; Industrial; Manufacturing; Personnel/Labor Relations; Sales; Secretarial. **Positions commonly filled include:** Accountant/Auditor; Administrative Manager; Advertising Clerk; Bank Officer/Manager; Blue-Collar Worker Supervisor; Branch Manager; Brokerage Clerk; Chemical Engineer; Claim Representative; Clerical Supervisor; Clinical Lab Technician; Computer Programmer; Credit Manager; Customer Service Representative; Electrical/Electronics Engineer; Financial Analyst; Food Scientist/Technologist; General Manager; Human Resources Specialist; Industrial Production Manager; Management Analyst/Consultant; Management Trainee; Manufacturer's/Wholesaler's Sales Rep.; Medical Records Technician; Operations/Production Manager; Paralegal; Property and Real Estate Manager; Purchasing Agent/Manager; Quality Control Supervisor; Services Sales Representative; Technical Writer/Editor; Typist/Word Processor; Underwriter/Assistant Underwriter. **Other area locations:** Elizabethtown NC; Whiteville NC. **Average salary range of placements:** Less than $20,000. **Number of placements per year:** 1000+.

TEMPORARY EMPLOYMENT AGENCIES

ATS HEALTH SERVICES
601 South Kings Drive, Suite HH, Charlotte NC 28204. 704/342-2710. **Contact:** Manager. **Description:** A temporary agency. **Specializes in the areas of:** Health/Medical. **Positions commonly filled include:** Certified Nurses Aide; Licensed Practical Nurse.

ACCOUNTANTS INC.
128 South Tryon Street, Suite 850, Charlotte NC 28202. 704/334-1117. **Fax:** 704/334-7673. **Contact:** Pete Nash, Owner. **E-mail address:** charlotte@accountantsinc.com. **World Wide Web address:** http://www.accountantsinc.com. **Description:** A temporary agency that also provides some permanent placements. **Specializes in the areas of:** Accounting; Finance. **Corporate headquarters location:** Burlingame CA. **Other U.S. locations:** Nationwide.

ACCOUNTANTS INC.
The Summit, 4101 Lake Boone Trail, Suite 502, Raleigh NC 27607. 919/783-0002. **Fax:** 919/783-0110. **Contact:** Manager. **E-mail address:** raleigh@accountantsinc.com. **World Wide Web address:** http://www.accountantsinc.com. **Description:** A temporary agency that also provides some permanent placements. **Specializes in the areas of:** Accounting; Finance. **Corporate headquarters location:** Burlingame CA. **Other area locations:** Charlotte NC. **Other U.S. locations:** Nationwide.

ACTION STAFFING GROUP
214A East Arlington Boulevard, Greenville NC 27858. 252/353-1000. **Fax:** 252/353-1414. **Contact:** Manager. **Description:** A temporary agency. **Specializes in the areas of:** Accounting/Auditing; Administration;

Computer Science/Software; Engineering; Industrial; Manufacturing; Personnel/Labor Relations; Secretarial; Technical. **Positions commonly filled include:** Accountant/Auditor; Administrative Manager; Aerospace Engineer; Agricultural Engineer; Aircraft Mechanic/Engine Specialist; Bank Officer/Manager; Blue-Collar Worker Supervisor; Buyer; Chemical Engineer; Chemist; Draftsperson; Electrical/Electronics Engineer; Financial Analyst; Human Resources Specialist; Industrial Engineer; Industrial Production Manager; MIS Specialist; Operations/Production Manager; Paralegal; Pharmacist; Purchasing Agent/Manager; Quality Control Supervisor; Securities Sales Representative; Surveyor; Technical Writer/Editor; Telecommunications Manager; Typist/Word Processor. **Benefits available to temporary workers:** 401(k); Paid Vacation. **Average salary range of placements:** $30,000 - $50,000. **Number of placements per year:** 50 - 99.

ACTION STAFFMASTERS
805 Spring Forest Road, Suite 800, Raleigh NC 27609. 919/873-0567. **Fax:** 919/873-9454. **Contact:** Branch Manager. **World Wide Web address:** http://www.citysearch.com/rdu/actionstaff. **Description:** A temporary agency that also offers some permanent placements and contract services. **Specializes in the areas of:** Light Industrial; Printing; Publishing; Secretarial. **Positions commonly filled include:** Administrative Assistant; AS400 Programmer Analyst; Computer Support Technician; Customer Service Representative; Database Administrator; Graphic Artist; Graphic Designer; MIS Specialist; Project Manager; Quality Control Supervisor; Secretary; SQL Programmer; Systems Analyst. **Benefits available to temporary workers:** Paid Holidays. **Average salary range of placements:** Less than $20,000. **Number of placements per year:** 1000+.

BARRETT BUSINESS SERVICES
P.O. Box 2789, Gastonia NC 28053. 704/854-5011. **Fax:** 704/854-5009. **Contact:** Randy Vincent, Branch Manager. **Description:** A temporary agency that also provides some contract services. **Specializes in the areas of:** Industrial; Manufacturing; Secretarial. **Positions commonly filled include:** Administrative Assistant; Blue-Collar Worker Supervisor; Branch Manager; Chemical Engineer; Clerical Supervisor; Clerk; Computer Programmer; Customer Service Representative; Draftsperson; Electrician; Engineer; Factory Worker; General Manager; Human Resources Specialist; Industrial Designer; Industrial Production Manager; Light Industrial Worker; Management Trainee; Mechanical Engineer; Metallurgical Engineer; MIS Specialist; Secretary; Typist/Word Processor. **Benefits available to temporary workers:** Bonus Award/Plan; Medical Insurance. **Other area locations:** Charlotte NC; Hendersonville NC; Hickory NC; Lenoir NC; Lincolnton NC; Mount Holly NC; Shelby NC. **Number of placements per year:** 200 - 499.

EXPRESS PERSONNEL SERVICES
1100 South Mint Street, Suite 104, Charlotte NC 28203. 704/347-5077. **Contact:** Jane Childrey, Vice President. **Description:** A temporary agency that also provides some permanent placements. **Specializes in the areas of:** Administration; Architecture/Construction; Electronics; Engineering; Sales; Secretarial; Technical. **Positions commonly filled include:** Architect; Civil Engineer; Computer Programmer; Draftsperson; Services Sales Representative; Software Engineer; Systems Analyst; Typist/Word Processor. **Benefits available to temporary workers:** Computer Training; Medical Insurance; Paid Holidays; Paid Vacation. **Average salary range of placements:** $20,000 - $29,999. **Number of placements per year:** 1 - 49.

FIVE STAR STAFFING, INC.
5404 Hillsboro Street, Raleigh NC 27606. 919/854-4488. **Contact:** Janice Hill, Operations Manager. **E-mail address:** fivestarstaffing@mindspring.com. **Description:** A temporary agency that also provides some permanent

placements. Client company pays fee. **Specializes in the areas of:** Accounting; Administration. **Positions commonly filled include:** Administrative Assistant; Claim Representative; Customer Service Representative; Human Resources Manager; Secretary; Typist/Word Processor. **Corporate headquarters location:** This Location. **Average salary range of placements:** $20,000 - $49,999. **Number of placements per year:** 200 - 499.

FORBES TEMPORARY STAFFING
6401 Carmel Road, Suite 107, Charlotte NC 28226. 704/542-0312. **Contact:** Frieda Smith, President. **Description:** A temporary agency. **Specializes in the areas of:** Apparel; Computer Hardware/Software; Food; Health/Medical; Hotel/Restaurant; Office Support; Technical; Textiles.

INTERIM PERSONNEL, INC.
4300 Six Forks Road, Suite 100, Raleigh NC 27609. 919/420-0026. **Contact:** Manager. **Description:** A temporary agency. **Specializes in the areas of:** Administration; Clerical; Domestic Help; Food. **Positions commonly filled include:** Administrative Worker/Clerk; Construction Trade Worker; Data Entry Clerk; Draftsperson; Driver; Factory Worker; Legal Secretary; Light Industrial Worker; Marketing Specialist; Medical Secretary; Nurse; Purchasing Agent/Manager; Quality Control Supervisor; Receptionist; Secretary; Statistician; Stenographer; Technical Writer/Editor; Technician; Typist/Word Processor; Underwriter/Assistant Underwriter. **Corporate headquarters location:** Fort Lauderdale FL. **Other U.S. locations:** Nationwide. **Number of placements per year:** 500 - 999.

INTERIM PERSONNEL, INC.
4101-C Stuart Andrews Boulevard, Charlotte NC 28217. 704/521-9491. **Fax:** 704/521-9549. **Contact:** Manager. **Description:** A temporary agency. **Specializes in the areas of:** Administration; Banking; Clerical; Industrial; Light Industrial; Manufacturing; Personnel/Labor Relations; Secretarial; Technical; Transportation. **Positions commonly filled include:** Blue-Collar Worker Supervisor; Branch Manager; Claim Representative; Clerical Supervisor; Customer Service Representative; Draftsperson; Electrician; Human Resources Specialist; Operations/Production Manager; Quality Control Supervisor; Typist/Word Processor. **Corporate headquarters location:** Fort Lauderdale FL. **Other U.S. locations:** Nationwide. **Average salary range of placements:** $20,000 - $29,999. **Number of placements per year:** 1000+.

KELLY SERVICES, INC.
620 Green Valley Road, Suite 206, Greensboro NC 27408. 336/292-4371. **Fax:** 336/852-6822. **Contact:** District Manager. **Description:** A temporary agency. **Specializes in the areas of:** Accounting/Auditing; Administration; Advertising; Banking; Computer Science/Software; Engineering; Finance; General Management; Industrial; Insurance; Legal; Manufacturing; Personnel/Labor Relations; Publishing; Sales; Secretarial; Technical. **Positions commonly filled include:** Accountant/Auditor; Administrative Assistant; Bookkeeper; Clerk; Computer Operator; Computer Programmer; Customer Service Representative; Data Entry Clerk; Designer; Human Resources Manager; Insurance Agent/Broker; Legal Secretary; Light Industrial Worker; Marketing Specialist; MIS Specialist; Purchasing Agent/Manager; Receptionist; Records Manager; Secretary; Technical Writer/Editor; Typist/Word Processor. **Number of placements per year:** 1000+.

KELLY SERVICES, INC.
2701 Coltsgate Road, Suite 102, Charlotte NC 28211. 704/364-4790. **Fax:** 704/364-6616. **Contact:** Office Manager. **Description:** A temporary agency. **Specializes in the areas of:** Accounting/Auditing; Administration; Advertising; Banking; Computer Science/Software; Engineering; Finance; General Management; Industrial;

Insurance; Legal; Manufacturing; Personnel/Labor Relations; Publishing; Sales; Secretarial; Technical. **Positions commonly filled include:** Accountant/Auditor; Administrative Assistant; Bookkeeper; Clerk; Computer Operator; Computer Programmer; Customer Service Representative; Data Entry Clerk; Designer; Human Resources Manager; Insurance Agent/Broker; Legal Secretary; Light Industrial Worker; Marketing Specialist; MIS Specialist; Purchasing Agent/Manager; Receptionist; Records Manager; Secretary; Technical Writer/Editor; Typist/Word Processor. **Number of placements per year:** 1000+.

MANPOWER, INC.
351 Walnut Street, Waynesville NC 28786-3219. 828/452-1494. **Fax:** 828/452-7392. **Contact:** Traci Burrell, Branch Manager. **Description:** A temporary agency. **Specializes in the areas of:** Finance; Manufacturing; Sales; Secretarial. **Positions commonly filled include:** Claim Representative; Credit Manager; Customer Service Representative; Financial Analyst; Paralegal; Services Sales Representative; Typist/Word Processor. **Benefits available to temporary workers:** 401(k); Paid Holidays; Paid Vacation; Stock Option. **Corporate headquarters location:** Milwaukee WI. **Other U.S. locations:** Nationwide. **Average salary range of placements:** $20,000 - $29,999. **Number of placements per year:** 100 - 199.

MANPOWER, INC.
5033-E South Boulevard, Charlotte NC 28217. 704/522-9288. **Contact:** Branch Manager. **Description:** A temporary agency. **Specializes in the areas of:** Data Processing; Light Industrial; Office Support. **Corporate headquarters location:** Milwaukee WI. **Other U.S. locations:** Nationwide. **Number of placements per year:** 1000+.

McCAIN EMPLOYMENT SERVICE
P.O. Box 2522, Kinston NC 28502-2522. 252/527-8367. **Fax:** 252/527-0250. **Contact:** Patricia McCain, President. **Description:** A temporary agency that also provides some permanent placements. **Specializes in the areas of:** Accounting/Auditing; Banking; Finance; Industrial; Manufacturing; Personnel/Labor Relations; Sales; Secretarial. **Positions commonly filled include:** Accountant/Auditor; Administrative Manager; Blue-Collar Worker Supervisor; Claim Representative; Computer Programmer; Counselor; Customer Service Representative; Electrician; General Manager; Industrial Production Manager; Management Trainee; Manufacturer's/Wholesaler's Sales Rep.; Medical Records Technician; Paralegal; Purchasing Agent/Manager; Quality Control Supervisor; Typist/Word Processor; Video Production Coordinator. **Benefits available to temporary workers:** Medical Insurance; Paid Holidays; Paid Vacation; Vision Insurance. **Average salary range of placements:** Less than $20,000. **Number of placements per year:** 500 - 999.

NORRELL SERVICES
3200 Beechleaf Court, Suite 301, Raleigh NC 27604. 919/850-0588. **Contact:** Manager. **Description:** A temporary agency. **Specializes in the areas of:** Administration; Clerical; Light Industrial; Office Support; Secretarial. **Positions commonly filled include:** Administrative Assistant; Assembler; Customer Service Representative; Telemarketer; Typist/Word Processor; Warehouse/Distribution Worker. **Benefits available to temporary workers:** Dental Insurance; Medical Insurance; Vision Insurance. **Corporate headquarters location:** Atlanta GA. **Other U.S. locations:** Nationwide.

OFFICE SPECIALISTS
1100 Crescent Green, Suite 120, Cary NC 27511-4587. 919/233-8383. **Contact:** Manager. **Description:** A temporary agency. **Specializes in the areas of:** Chemicals; Computer Science/Software; Pharmaceuticals; Secretarial. **Positions commonly filled include:** Customer Service Representative; Data Entry Clerk; Typist/Word Processor. **Benefits available to temporary workers:** Medical Insurance; Paid Vacation. **Corporate headquarters location:** Peabody MA. **Average salary range of placements:** Less than $20,000. **Number of placements per year:** 1000+.

OLSTEN STAFFING SERVICES
1216D Bridford Parkway, Greensboro NC 27407. 336/852-0500. **Contact:** Heather Sutton, Personnel Supervisor. **Description:** A temporary agency. **Specializes in the areas of:** Clerical; Manufacturing. **Positions commonly filled include:** Accountant/Auditor; Administrative Assistant; Bank Officer/Manager; Bookkeeper; Clerk; Computer Operator; Computer Programmer; Construction Trade Worker; Customer Service Representative; Data Entry Clerk; Draftsperson; Driver; EDP Specialist; Factory Worker; General Manager; Human Resources Manager; Legal Secretary; Light Industrial Worker; Medical Secretary; MIS Specialist; Operations/Production Manager; Public Relations Specialist; Purchasing Agent/Manager; Quality Control Supervisor; Receptionist; Sales Representative; Secretary; Stenographer; Systems Analyst; Technician; Typist/Word Processor. **Corporate headquarters location:** Melville NY. **Other U.S. locations:** Nationwide. **Number of placements per year:** 1000+.

OLSTEN STAFFING SERVICES
P.O. Box 12877, Research Triangle Park NC 27709. 919/549-8383. **Fax:** 919/541-2059. **Contact:** Cynthia S. Heath, Vice President. **Description:** A temporary agency. **Specializes in the areas of:** Accounting/Auditing; Administration; Advertising; Banking; Computer Science/Software; Data Processing; Economics; Engineering; Finance; General Management; Industrial; Insurance; Legal; Manufacturing; Nonprofit; Personnel/Labor Relations; Publishing; Sales; Secretarial; Technical; Transportation. **Positions commonly filled include:** Accountant/Auditor; Administrative Manager; Advertising Clerk; Attorney; Blue-Collar Worker Supervisor; Budget Analyst; Buyer; Chemical Engineer; Chemist; Claim Representative; Clerical Supervisor; Clinical Lab Technician; Customer Service Representative; Design Engineer; Designer; Draftsperson; Electrical/Electronics Engineer; Human Resources Specialist; Industrial Engineer; Industrial Production Manager; Librarian; Mechanical Engineer; Medical Records Technician; Paralegal; Purchasing Agent/Manager; Quality Control Supervisor; Reporter; Software Engineer; Statistician; Structural Engineer; Technical Writer/Editor; Typist/Word Processor. **Benefits available to temporary workers:** 401(k); Medical Insurance; Paid Vacation. **Corporate headquarters location:** Melville NY. **Other U.S. locations:** Nationwide. **Average salary range of placements:** $16,000 - $29,999. **Number of placements per year:** 1000+.

PERSONNEL SERVICES UNLIMITED, INC.
824 South DeKalb Street, Shelby NC 28150. 704/484-0344. **Contact:** Tim Blackwell, President. **Description:** A temporary agency. **Specializes in the areas of:** Clerical; Insurance; Legal; Manufacturing. **Positions commonly filled include:** Administrative Assistant; Bookkeeper; Clerk; Computer Operator; Customer Service Representative; Data Entry Clerk; Factory Worker; Legal Secretary; Light Industrial Worker; Receptionist; Secretary; Typist/Word Processor.

PRO STAFF ACCOUNTING SERVICES
212 South Tryon Street, Suite 410, Charlotte NC 28246. 704/370-0075. **Contact:** Manager. **World Wide Web address:** http://www.prostaff-carolinas.com. **Description:** A temporary agency. **Specializes in the areas of:** Accounting/Auditing. **Benefits available to temporary workers:** 401(k); Direct Deposit; Paid Holidays; Paid Vacation; Referral Bonus Plan. **Corporate headquarters location:** Minneapolis MN.

QUALITY TEMPORARY SERVICES
934 Durham Road, Suite E, Wake Forest NC 27587-9033. 919/556-1201. **Fax:** 919/556-1447. **Contact:**

Manager. **Description:** A temporary agency that also provides some temp-to-perm placements. **Specializes in the areas of:** Accounting/Auditing; Industrial; Manufacturing; Personnel/Labor Relations; Secretarial; Technical. **Positions commonly filled include:** Accountant/Auditor; Biochemist; Chemist; Computer Programmer; Credit Manager; Customer Service Representative; Electrician; Human Resources Specialist; Mechanical Engineer; Medical Records Technician; Purchasing Agent/Manager; Quality Control Supervisor; Typist/Word Processor. **Benefits available to temporary workers:** Paid Holidays; Paid Vacation. **Corporate headquarters location:** Flint MI. **Other area locations:** Rocky Mount NC; Tarboro NC. **Other U.S. locations:** SC. **Number of placements per year:** 200 - 499.

QUALITY TEMPORARY SERVICES
3031 Zebulon Road, Rocky Mount NC 27804. 252/443-4001. **Fax:** 252/443-3831. **Contact:** Sandy Godwin, Administrative Assistant. **Description:** A temporary agency. **Specializes in the areas of:** Administration; Industrial; Manufacturing; Personnel/Labor Relations; Retail; Sales; Secretarial; Technical. **Positions commonly filled include:** Accountant/Auditor; Administrative Manager; Blue-Collar Worker Supervisor; Claim Representative; Clerical Supervisor; Customer Service Representative; Electrician; Human Resources Specialist; Landscape Architect; Management Trainee; Manufacturer's/Wholesaler's Sales Rep.; Medical Records Technician; MIS Specialist; Operations/Production Manager; Paralegal; Quality Control Supervisor; Services Sales Representative; Typist/Word Processor. **Benefits available to temporary workers:** Medical Insurance; Paid Holidays; Paid Vacation. **Corporate headquarters location:** Flint MI. **Other area locations:** Tarboro NC; Wake Forest NC. **Other U.S. locations:** SC. **Number of placements per year:** 100 - 199.

SPECIAL COUNSEL
5600 77 Center Drive, Suite 170, Charlotte NC 28217. 704/529-5590. **Fax:** 704/529-5639. **Contact:** Manager. **World Wide Web address:** http://www.specialcounsel.com. **Description:** A temporary agency that also provides some permanent placements. **Specializes in the areas of:** Legal.

STAFFMARK
220 Dabney Drive, Henderson NC 27536. 252/438-3888. **Toll-free phone:** 800/211-1169. **Fax:** 252/438-2619. **Contact:** Office Manager. **Description:** A temporary agency that also provides some temp-to-perm placements. **Specializes in the areas of:** General Labor;

Personnel/Labor Relations; Secretarial; Technical. **Positions commonly filled include:** Advertising Clerk; Blue-Collar Worker Supervisor; Customer Service Representative; Draftsperson; Human Resources Specialist; Human Service Worker; Management Trainee; Paralegal; Preschool Worker; Public Relations Specialist; Reporter. **Benefits available to temporary workers:** Paid Holidays; Paid Vacation. **Average salary range of placements:** Less than $20,000. **Number of placements per year:** 1000+.

TOTAL CARE OF THE CAROLINAS
1200 East Morehead Street, Suite 120, Charlotte NC 28204. 704/332-8545. **Contact:** Recruiter. **Description:** A temporary agency. Founded in 1984. **Specializes in the areas of:** Health/Medical. **Positions commonly filled include:** Licensed Practical Nurse; Occupational Therapist; Physical Therapist; Registered Nurse. **Average salary range of placements:** Less than $20,000. **Number of placements per year:** 200 - 499.

WILL/STAFF PERSONNEL SERVICES
221-F East Exmore Street, Charlotte NC 28217. 704/529-6222. **Fax:** 704/525-4790. **Contact:** Pam VanRiper, Office Manager. **Description:** A temporary agency. **Specializes in the areas of:** Engineering; Secretarial. **Positions commonly filled include:** Accountant/Auditor; Administrative Manager; Automotive Mechanic; Bank Officer/Manager; Branch Manager; Buyer; Clerical Supervisor; Computer Programmer; Cost Estimator; Dental Assistant/Dental Hygienist; Draftsperson; Electrician; Industrial Engineer; Industrial Production Manager; Mechanical Engineer; MIS Specialist; Paralegal; Purchasing Agent/Manager; Restaurant/Food Service Manager; Systems Analyst; Typist/Word Processor. **Benefits available to temporary workers:** Medical Insurance; Paid Vacation. **Corporate headquarters location:** Greenville SC. **Other U.S. locations:** Atlanta GA; Columbia SC; Spartanburg SC. **Average salary range of placements:** $20,000 - $29,999. **Number of placements per year:** 100 - 199.

WINSTON PERSONNEL GROUP
253 Executive Park Boulevard, Winston-Salem NC 27103. 336/760-9300. **Fax:** 336/765-0630. **Contact:** Manager. **Description:** A temporary agency. **Specializes in the areas of:** Food; Industrial; Manufacturing. **Positions commonly filled include:** Blue-Collar Worker Supervisor; Electrician; Quality Control Supervisor; Restaurant/Food Service Manager. **Benefits available to temporary workers:** Dental Insurance; Medical Insurance. **Average salary range of placements:** Less than $20,000. **Number of placements per year:** 200 - 499.

CONTRACT SERVICES FIRMS

CDI IT SERVICES
301 McCullough Drive, Suite 100, Charlotte NC 28262. 704/510-1090. **Contact:** Manager. **E-mail address:** charlotte@cdicorp.com. **World Wide Web address:** http://www.cdicorp.com. **Description:** A contract services firm. **Specializes in the areas of:** Engineering; Technical. **Corporate headquarters location:** Philadelphia PA. **Other U.S. locations:** Nationwide. **International locations:** Worldwide.

CDI TECHNICAL SERVICES
8001 Aerial Center Parkway, Suite 100, Morrisville NC 27560. 919/481-9043. **Fax:** 919/467-7653. **Contact:** Manager. **World Wide Web address:** http://www.cdicorp.com. **Description:** A contract services firm. **Specializes in the areas of:** Computer Science/Software. **Corporate headquarters location:** Philadelphia PA. **Other U.S. locations:** Nationwide. **International locations:** Worldwide.

COMFORCE TECHNICAL SERVICES, INC.
2221 Edge Lake Drive, Suite 160, Charlotte NC 28217. 704/357-3030. **Fax:** 704/357-3134. **Contact:** Colleen

LeGrand, Office Manager. **Description:** A contract services firm. **Specializes in the areas of:** Administration; Banking; Computer Science/Software; Finance; Information Technology; Technical. **Positions commonly filled include:** Bank Officer/Manager; Computer Programmer; Human Service Worker; Internet Services Manager; Management Analyst/Consultant; MIS Specialist; Software Engineer; Systems Analyst; Technical Writer/Editor; Telecommunications Manager. **Average salary range of placements:** $30,000 - $50,000. **Number of placements per year:** 200 - 499.

COMFORCE TELECOM, INC.
5410 Highway 55, Suite AJ, Durham NC 27713. 919/484-1147. **Fax:** 919/484-1226. **Contact:** Manager. **Description:** A contract services firm. **Specializes in the areas of:** Telecommunications.

EMPLOYMENT NETWORK
4401 Colwick Road, Suite 406, Charlotte NC 28211. 704/365-8294. **Fax:** 704/365-2581. **Contact:** Manager. **Description:** A contract services firm.

HALL KINION
2525 Research Triangle Park, Suite 280, Durham NC 27713. **Toll-free phone:** 800/365-3031. **Fax:** 919/527-6550. **Contact:** Manager. **E-mail address:** ncresume@hallkinion.com. **World Wide Web address:** http://www.hallkinion.com. **Description:** A contract services firm that also provides some permanent placements. **Specializes in the areas of:** Information Systems; Information Technology; Internet Development; Network Administration; Quality Assurance; Systems Administration; Technical Writing.

MKR PERSONNEL SOLUTIONS INC.
P.O. Box 52071, Raleigh NC 27612. 919/783-6571. **Physical address:** 5540 McNeely Drive, Suite 303, Raleigh NC. **Toll-free phone:** 800/489-6571. **Fax:** 919/783-0207. **Contact:** Mike Kidwell, President. **E-mail address:** mkidwell@mindspring.com. **Description:** A contract services firm. **Specializes in the areas of:** Administration; Computer Science/Software; Data Communications; Telecommunications. **Positions commonly filled include:** MIS Specialist; Software Engineer; Systems Analyst; Telecommunications Manager. **Benefits available to temporary workers:** Medical Insurance; Paid Vacation. **Average salary range of placements:** More than $50,000.

PCS (PERSONAL COMMUNICATIONS SERVICE)
P.O. Box 12311, Research Triangle Park NC 27709. 919/544-4575. **Fax:** 919/544-3725. **Contact:** Manager. **Description:** A contract services firm. **Specializes in the areas of:** Art/Design; Computer Science/Software; Publishing; Technical. **Positions commonly filled include:** Civil Engineer; Computer Programmer; Customer Service Representative; Design Engineer; Designer; Editor; Environmental Engineer; Internet Services Manager; Market Research Analyst; MIS Specialist; Multimedia Designer; Software Engineer; Systems Analyst; Technical / Writer/Editor; Telecommunications Manager. **Other U.S. locations:** CA; CO; GA; MA; NJ; OH; TX. **Average salary range of placements:** $30,000 - $50,000.

SENC TECHNICAL SERVICES INC.
3142 Wrightsville Avenue, Wilmington NC 28403-4112. 910/251-1925. **Fax:** 910/251-0225. **Contact:** Recruiter. **Description:** A contract services firm. **Specializes in the areas of:** Engineering; Technical. **Positions commonly filled include:** Architect; Biochemist; Biological Scientist; Chemical Engineer; Chemist; Civil Engineer; Clinical Lab Technician; Computer Programmer; Construction and Building Inspector; Cost Estimator; Design Engineer; Designer; Draftsperson; Electrical/Electronics Engineer; Electrician; Environmental Engineer; Financial Analyst; Industrial Engineer; Industrial Production Manager; Mechanical Engineer; MIS Specialist; Quality Control Supervisor; Software Engineer; Structural Engineer; Surveyor; Systems Analyst; Technical Writer/Editor. **Average salary range of placements:** $20,000 - $29,999. **Number of placements per year:** 100 - 199.

VOLT TECHNICAL SERVICES
3733 National Drive, Suite 203, Raleigh NC 27612. 919/782-7440. **Toll-free phone:** 800/595-8658. **Fax:** 919/782-5549. **Contact:** Manager. **E-mail address:** voltral@volt.com. **World Wide Web address:** http://www.volt.com. **Description:** A contract services firm. **Specializes in the areas of:** Computer Programming; Engineering; Manufacturing; Technical. **Positions commonly filled include:** Biological Scientist; Biomedical Engineer; Ceramics Engineer; Chemical Engineer; Civil Engineer; Clinical Lab Technician; Computer Programmer; Design Engineer; Designer; Draftsperson; Electrical/Electronics Engineer; Environmental Engineer; Materials Engineer; Mechanical Engineer; Metallurgical Engineer; MIS Specialist; Multimedia Designer; Nuclear Engineer; Operations/Production Manager; Petroleum Engineer; Software Engineer; Structural Engineer; Systems Analyst; Technical Writer/Editor; Telecommunications Manager. **Corporate headquarters location:** New York NY. **Other U.S. locations:** Nationwide. **Number of placements per year:** 100 - 199.

H.L. YOH COMPANY
717 South Torrence, Suite 300, Charlotte NC 28204. 704/332-1020. **Contact:** Manager. **Description:** A contract services firm. **Specializes in the areas of:** Engineering; High-Tech.

H.L. YOH COMPANY
16 East Rowan Street, Suite 308, Raleigh NC 27609. 919/781-1380. **Contact:** Manager. **Description:** A contract services firm that also provides some temporary and permanent placements. **Specializes in the areas of:** Computer Science/Software; Engineering; Information Technology; Scientific.

CAREER/OUTPLACEMENT COUNSELING FIRMS

CP RESUMES, INC.
1727-8B Sardis Road North, Charlotte NC 28270. 704/849-2333. **Fax:** 704/849-2322. **Contact:** Vasant K. Patel, Senior Consultant. **Description:** A resume writing and job search consulting firm.

HIGHLANDS PROGRAM
716 East Boulevard, Charlotte NC 28203. 704/370-0101. **Contact:** Dick Blackwell, Ph.D/Clinical Supervisor. **World Wide Web address:** http://www. highlandsprogram.com. **Description:** Provides career counseling to students and adults, and training and development services to corporations.

KING CAREER CONSULTANTS
2915 Providence Road, Suite 300, Charlotte NC 28211-2750. 704/366-1685. **Fax:** 704/364-9678. **Contact:** Jerry King, President. **Description:** A career/outplacement counseling firm. **Specializes in the areas of:** Executives; General Management. **Number of placements per year:** 50 - 99.

◆ N O R T H   D A K O T A ◆

CAREER CONNECTION
1621 South University Drive, Suite 215, Fargo ND 58103. 701/232-4614. **Fax:** 701/241-9822. **Contact:** Recruiter. **E-mail address:** jobs@careerconnection.net. **Description:** An executive search firm operating on a contingency basis. **Specializes in the areas of:** Administration; Computer Science/Software; Engineering; Industrial; Manufacturing; Personnel/Labor Relations; Technical. **Positions commonly filled include:** Accountant/Auditor; Agricultural Engineer; Civil Engineer; Computer Programmer; Design Engineer; Designer; Draftsperson; Electrical/Electronics Engineer; Environmental Engineer; Manufacturer's/Wholesaler's Sales Rep.; Mechanical Engineer; MIS Specialist; Operations/Production Manager; Purchasing Agent/Manager; Quality Control Supervisor; Services Sales Representative; Software Engineer; Structural Engineer; Surveyor; Systems Analyst; Technical Writer/Editor; Telecommunications Manager. **Average salary range of placements:** $30,000 - $50,000. **Number of placements per year:** 100 - 199.

DUNHILL PROFESSIONAL SEARCH
118 Broadway, Suite 212, Fargo ND 58102. 701/235-3719. **Toll-free phone:** 800/473-2512. **Fax:** 701/235-7092. **Contact:** Kent Hochgraber, President. **E-mail address:** dsfargo@mail.rrnet.com. **Description:** An executive search firm. **Specializes in the areas of:** Accounting/Auditing; Computer Science/Software; Engineering; Health/Medical. **Corporate headquarters location:** Hauppauge NY. **Average salary range of placements:** More than $50,000. **Number of placements per year:** 1 - 49.

GREAT PLAINS BENEFIT GROUP INC.
523 East Bismarck Expressway, Suite 1, Bismarck ND 58504. 701/258-0039. **Fax:** 701/258-4207. **Contact:** Roger Krueger, President. **Description:** An executive search firm. **Specializes in the areas of:** Banking; Insurance; Nursing Administration.

SNELLING PERSONNEL SERVICES
609 1/2 First Avenue North, Suite 200, Fargo ND 58102. 701/237-0600. **Fax:** 701/241-9998. **Contact:** Debbie Almeida, Owner/Manager. **E-mail address:** snelling@fargocity.com. **World Wide Web address:** http://www.snelling.com. **Description:** An executive search firm that also provides some permanent placements. Client company pays fee. **Specializes in the areas of:** Accounting; Computer Science/Software; Finance; Marketing; Sales. **Positions commonly filled include:** Account Manager; Account Representative; Accountant; AS400 Programmer Analyst; Branch Manager; Chief Financial Officer; Computer Programmer; Computer Technician; Controller; General Manager; Human Resources Manager; Management Trainee; Operations Manager; Production Manager; Project Manager; Sales Manager; Sales Representative; Systems Analyst. **Corporate headquarters location:** Dallas TX. **Other U.S. locations:** Nationwide. **International locations:** Worldwide. **Number of placements per year:** 1 - 49.

EXPRESS PERSONNEL SERVICES
2650 32nd Avenue South, Suite K, Grand Forks ND 58201. 701/787-5655. **Contact:** Manager. **Description:** A permanent employment agency that also provides some temporary placements.

INTERIM PERSONNEL
1450 25th Street South, Fargo ND 58103. 701/298-8300. **Contact:** Manager. **Description:** A permanent employment agency that also provides some temporary placements. **Specializes in the areas of:** Clerical; Light Industrial.

PREFERENCE PERSONNEL EMPLOYMENT
2600 Ninth Avenue Southwest, Fargo ND 58103. 701/293-6905. **Contact:** Manager. **E-mail address:** prefjobs@rrnet.com. **World Wide Web address:** http://www.preferencepersonnel.com. **Description:** A permanent employment agency that also provides some temporary placements.

STAFF SEARCH
1323 23rd Street South, Suite C, Fargo ND 58103. 701/235-7551. **Contact:** Manager. **Description:** A permanent employment agency that also provides some temporary placements.

OLSTEN STAFFING SERVICES
EXPRESSWAY PERSONNEL
P.O. Box 105, Bismarck ND 58502-0105. 701/222-0071. **Fax:** 701/222-8481. **Contact:** Al Kramer, President. **Description:** A temporary agency. Expressway Personnel (also at this location) is a permanent employment agency that also provides some temporary placements. Full benefits are available. Founded in 1950. **Specializes in the areas of:** Accounting/Auditing; Administration; Advertising; Architecture/Construction; Art/Design; Banking; Computer Science/Software; Economics; Education; Engineering; Fashion; Finance; Food; General Management; Industrial; Insurance; Legal; Manufacturing; Nonprofit; Personnel/Labor Relations; Publishing; Retail; Sales; Secretarial; Technical; Transportation. **Positions commonly filled include:** Accountant/Auditor; Adjuster; Administrative Manager; Advertising Clerk; Agricultural Engineer; Architect; Attorney; Bank Officer/Manager; Biochemist; Blue-Collar Worker Supervisor; Branch Manager; Broadcast Technician; Brokerage Clerk; Budget Analyst; Buyer; Civil Engineer; Claim Representative; Clerical Supervisor; Clinical Lab Technician; Computer Programmer; Construction and Building Inspector; Construction Contractor; Cost Estimator; Counselor; Credit Manager; Customer Service Representative; Dental Assistant/Dental Hygienist; Design Engineer; Designer; Dietician/Nutritionist; Draftsperson; Economist; Editor; Education Administrator; Electrical/Electronics Engineer; Electrician; Emergency Medical Technician; Environmental Engineer; Financial Analyst; General Manager; Health Services Manager; Human Resources Specialist; Industrial Engineer; Librarian; Licensed Practical Nurse; Management Analyst/Consultant; Management Trainee; Manufacturer's/Wholesaler's Sales Rep.; Market Research Analyst; Mechanical Engineer; Medical Records Technician; Mining Engineer; Occupational Therapist; Paralegal; Public Relations Specialist; Quality Control Supervisor; Real Estate Agent; Restaurant/Food

Service Manager; Services Sales Representative; Software Engineer; Systems Analyst; Teacher/Professor; Technical Writer/Editor; Telecommunications Manager; Typist/Word Processor; Underwriter/Assistant Underwriter. **International locations:** Worldwide. **Number of placements per year:** 1000+.

CAREER/OUTPLACEMENT COUNSELING FIRMS

AAA RESUMES & EMPLOYMENT
701 10th Street North, Fargo ND 58102. 701/232-7115. **Contact:** Counselor. **Description:** Provides resume counseling services.

CURTIS & ASSOCIATES
600 South Second Street, Suite 6A, Bismarck ND 58504. 701/258-8212. **Contact:** Counselor. **Description:** Provides resume and career/outplacement counseling services.

GREEN THUMB, INC.
2206 East Broadway, Bismarck ND 58501. 701/258-8879. **Fax:** 701/258-8874. **Contact:** Project Director. **Description:** A career/outplacement counseling firm that also serves as an employment agency. Green Thumb also operates the Senior Community Service Program. **Specializes in the areas of:** Education; Nonprofit; Personnel/Labor Relations; Retail. **Positions commonly filled include:** Clerk; Daycare Worker; Typist/Word Processor. **Corporate headquarters location:** Arlington VA. **Number of placements per year:** 200 - 499.

EXECUTIVE SEARCH FIRMS

ACCOUNTANTS EXECUTIVE SEARCH ACCOUNTANTS ON CALL
250 East Fifth Street, Suite 1630, Cincinnati OH 45202. 513/381-4545. **Fax:** 513/381-4672. **Contact:** Joseph Vitale, Branch Manager. **E-mail address:** jsvitale@mindspring.com. **World Wide Web address:** http://www.aocnet.com. **Description:** An executive search firm operating on a contingency basis. Accountants On Call (also at this location) is a temporary agency. **Specializes in the areas of:** Accounting/Auditing; Finance. **Positions commonly filled include:** Accountant/Auditor; Chief Financial Officer; Controller; Finance Director; Financial Analyst; Vice President of Finance. **Benefits available to temporary workers:** Medical Insurance; Paid Vacation. **Corporate headquarters location:** Saddle Brook NJ. **Other U.S. locations:** Nationwide. **Average salary range of placements:** $30,000 - $50,000.

ACCOUNTANTS EXECUTIVE SEARCH ACCOUNTANTS ON CALL
700 Ackerman Road, Suite 390, Columbus OH 43202. 614/267-7200. **Fax:** 614/267-7595. **Contact:** Frank Bishop, President. **E-mail address:** fbishop@aoc-aes.com. **Description:** An executive search firm operating on both retainer and contingency bases. Accountants On Call (also at this location) is a temporary agency. **Specializes in the areas of:** Accounting/Auditing; Administration; Banking; Computer Science/Software; Finance. **Positions commonly filled include:** Accountant/Auditor; Budget Analyst; Computer Programmer; Credit Manager; Financial Analyst; Internet Services Manager; Management Analyst/Consultant; MIS Specialist; Systems Analyst; Telecommunications Manager. **Corporate headquarters location:** Saddle Brook NJ. **Other U.S. locations:** Nationwide. **Number of placements per year:** 200 - 499.

ACCOUNTANTS EXECUTIVE SEARCH ACCOUNTANTS ON CALL
Rockside Square 2, 6133 Rockside Road, Suite 206, Independence OH 44131. 216/328-0888. **Contact:** Manager. **Description:** An executive search firm. Accountants On Call (also at this location) is a temporary agency. **Specializes in the areas of:** Accounting/Auditing; Finance. **Corporate headquarters location:** Saddle Brook NJ. **Other U.S. locations:** Nationwide.

ACCOUNTANTS SELECT
P.O. Box 16366, Cleveland OH 44116. 440/333-5122. **Contact:** Manager. **Description:** An executive search firm. **Specializes in the areas of:** Accounting/Auditing; Finance.

ALLTECH RESOURCES, INC.
6060 Rockside Woods Boulevard, Suite 115, Cleveland OH 44131. 216/642-5689. **Fax:** 216/642-9419. **Contact:** Manager. **E-mail address:** recruiting@alltech-inc.com. **World Wide Web address:** http://www.alltech-inc.com. **Description:** An executive search firm that also provides contract placements. **Specializes in the areas of:** Administration; Architecture/Construction; Banking; Computer Science/Software; Finance; Health/Medical; Insurance; Marketing; Sales; Technical. **Positions commonly filled include:** Computer Operator; Computer Programmer; Draftsperson; Management Analyst/Consultant; MIS Specialist; Science Technologist; Software Engineer; Systems Analyst; Technical Writer/Editor; Telecommunications Manager. **Benefits available to temporary workers:** Dental Insurance; Medical Insurance; Paid Holidays; Paid Vacation. **Corporate headquarters location:** Chicago IL. **Average salary range of placements:** More than $50,000. **Number of placements per year:** 200 - 499.

DAVE ARNOLD & ASSOCIATES, INC.
P.O. Box 182, Aurora OH 44202-0182. 440/543-8551. **Fax:** 440/543-8551. **Contact:** Dave Arnold, President. **E-mail address:** arnold@now-online.com. **Description:** An executive search firm operating on both retainer and contingency bases. **Specializes in the areas of:** Chemicals; Graphic Arts; Industrial; Manufacturing; Printing; Publishing; Sales; Technical. **Positions commonly filled include:** Ceramics Engineer; Chemical Engineer; Chemist; Industrial Engineer; Manufacturing Engineer; Marketing Specialist; Mechanical Engineer; Metallurgical Engineer; Sales Representative. **Number of placements per year:** 50 - 99.

AUTOMOTIVE CAREERS
77 West Elmwood Drive, Suite 205, Centerville OH 45459. 937/438-8090. **Fax:** 937/433-1758. **Contact:** President. **Description:** An executive search firm. **Specializes in the areas of:** Automotive; Automotive Retailing.

BALDWIN & ASSOCIATES
3975 Erie Avenue, Cincinnati OH 45208. 513/272-2400. **Contact:** W. Keith Baldwin, President. **World Wide Web address:** http://www.baldwin-assoc.com. **Description:** An executive search firm. **Specializes in the areas of:** Engineering; Manufacturing; Technical. **Positions commonly filled include:** Aerospace Engineer; Bank Officer/Manager; Biomedical Engineer; Ceramics Engineer; Civil Engineer; Electrical/Electronics Engineer; General Manager; Industrial Engineer; Marketing Specialist; Mechanical Engineer; Metallurgical Engineer; Purchasing Agent/Manager; Quality Control Supervisor; Systems Analyst. **Number of placements per year:** 50 - 99.

J.W. BARLEYCORN & ASSOCIATES
1614 Lancaster Avenue, Reynoldsburg OH 43068. 614/861-4400. **Contact:** Manager. **Description:** An executive search firm.

BASON ASSOCIATES INC.
11311 Cornell Park Drive, Suite 200, Cincinnati OH 45242. 513/469-9881. **Fax:** 513/469-9691. **Contact:** Manager. **E-mail address:** execsearch@bason.com. **World Wide Web address:** http://www.bason.com. **Description:** An executive search firm providing placements both locally and worldwide. **Specializes in the areas of:** Finance; Health/Medical; Manufacturing; Professional; Retail.

BOWDEN & COMPANY
P.O. Box 467, Medina OH 44258. 330/722-1722. **Fax:** 330/722-1755. **Contact:** Manager. **E-mail address:** bowdenandco@bowdenandco.com. **World Wide Web address:** http://www.bowdenandco.com. **Description:** An executive search firm. Founded in 1972. **Specializes in the areas of:** Banking; Finance; Information Technology; Insurance; Manufacturing.

J.W. BRANDENBURG & ASSOCIATES
1362 Snowmass Road, Suite 101, Columbus OH 43235. 614/785-9630. **Contact:** Jack Brandenburg, Manager. **Description:** An executive search firm.

J.B. BROWN & ASSOCIATES
820 Terminal Tower, Cleveland OH 44113. 216/696-2525. **Fax:** 216/696-5825. **Contact:** Jeffrey B. Brown, President. **Description:** An executive search firm that also provides contract services. **Specializes in the areas of:** Accounting/Auditing; Administration; Advertising; Banking; Computer Science/Software; Engineering; Finance; Insurance; Manufacturing; Personnel/Labor Relations; Sales. **Positions commonly filled include:** Accountant/Auditor; Actuary; Attorney; Bank Officer/Manager; Budget Analyst; Buyer; Chemical Engineer; Computer Programmer; Credit Manager;

Design Engineer; Designer; Electrical/Electronics Engineer; Environmental Engineer; Financial Analyst; General Manager; Human Resources Specialist; Industrial Engineer; Industrial Production Manager; Insurance Agent/Broker; Management Trainee; Market Research Analyst; Mechanical Engineer; MIS Specialist; Pharmacist; Purchasing Agent/Manager; Software Engineer; Structural Engineer; Telecommunications Manager; Underwriter/Assistant Underwriter. **Average salary range of placements:** $30,000 - $50,000. **Number of placements per year:** 200 - 499.

BUCKMAN-ENOCHS & ASSOCIATES INC.
590 Enterprise Drive, Lewis Center OH 43035. 614/825-6215. **Fax:** 614/825-6242. **Contact:** Manager. **Description:** An executive search firm. **Specializes in the areas of:** Sales.

CAREER ENTERPRISES
5 East Main Street, Hudson OH 44236. 330/656-1700. **Fax:** 330/656-1234. **Contact:** Stuart Taylor, President. **World Wide Web address:** http://www.careerenterprises.com. **Description:** An executive search firm. **Specializes in the areas of:** Information Systems; Scientific; Technical. **Positions commonly filled include:** Database Manager; General Manager; Internet Services Manager; Project Manager; Software Engineer; Telecommunications Manager; Webmaster. **Average salary range of placements:** More than $50,000. **Number of placements per year:** 50 - 99.

CAREER SPECIALISTS INC.
P.O. Box 371, Delphos OH 45833. 419/695-1234. **Contact:** Jerry Backus, Recruiter. **Description:** An executive search firm. **Specializes in the areas of:** Accounting/Auditing; Engineering; General Management; Manufacturing; Personnel/Labor Relations. **Positions commonly filled include:** Accountant/Auditor; Buyer; Ceramics Engineer; Chemical Engineer; Chemist; Computer Programmer; Customer Service Representative; Draftsperson; Electrical/Electronics Engineer; Industrial Designer; Industrial Engineer; Manufacturing Engineer; Mechanical Engineer; Metallurgical Engineer; Operations/Production Manager; Purchasing Agent/Manager; Quality Control Supervisor; Software Engineer; Technical Illustrator; Technical Writer/Editor. **Number of placements per year:** 50 - 99.

CASCADE GROUP
136 East Main Street, Kent OH 44240. 330/677-1118. **Contact:** Manager. **Description:** An executive search firm.

CENTRAL EXECUTIVE SEARCH, INC.
6151 Wilson Mills Road, Suite 240, Highland Heights OH 44143. 440/461-5400. **Contact:** Manager. **Description:** An executive search firm. **Specializes in the areas of:** Packaging; Paper.

CHOICE PERSONNEL
LaGRANGE & ASSOCIATES
4115 Edwards Road, Suite 7, Cincinnati OH 45209. 513/333-2500. **Fax:** 513/333-2504. **Contact:** Robert LaGrange, President. **Description:** An executive search firm operating on a contingency basis. LaGrange & Associates (also at this location) is an executive search firm operating on a contingency basis and specializing in the hospitality field. **Specializes in the areas of:** Food; Insurance; Printing; Sales; Transportation. **Positions commonly filled include:** Account Manager; Account Representative; Accountant; Assistant Manager; Buyer; Claim Representative; Computer Programmer; Customer Service Representative; Human Resources Manager; Industrial Engineer; Industrial Production Manager; Management Trainee; Manufacturing Engineer; Mechanical Engineer; MIS Specialist; Production Manager; Purchasing Agent/Manager; Sales Executive; Sales Manager; Sales Representative; Transportation/Traffic Specialist. **Corporate headquarters location:** This Location. **Other U.S. locations:** Nationwide. **Average salary range of placements:** $30,000 - $50,000. **Number of placements per year:** 100 - 199.

COMBINED RESOURCES INC.
25300 Lorain Road, Suite 2C, North Olmsted OH 44070. 440/716-2244. **Contact:** Gil Sherman, President. **Description:** An executive search firm. **Specializes in the areas of:** Administration; Advertising; Art/Design; Computer Science/Software; Economics; Engineering; General Management; Industrial; Manufacturing; Personnel/Labor Relations; Retail; Sales. **Positions commonly filled include:** Administrative Manager; Branch Manager; Buyer; Computer Programmer; Credit Manager; Customer Service Representative; Designer; Economist; Electrical/Electronics Engineer; Financial Analyst; General Manager; Human Resources Manager; Industrial Engineer; Management Analyst/Consultant; Manufacturer's/Wholesaler's Sales Rep.; Mechanical Engineer; Operations/Production Manager; Purchasing Agent/Manager; Services Sales Representative; Software Engineer; Systems Analyst; Transportation/Traffic Specialist; Wholesale and Retail Buyer.

CONTINENTAL SEARCH ASSOCIATES
P.O. Box 14, Pickerington OH 43147. 614/868-8100. **Fax:** 614/868-5344. **Contact:** James Allen, Principal. **Description:** An executive search firm. **Specializes in the areas of:** Computer Science/Software; Engineering; Food; General Management; Industrial; Manufacturing; Personnel/Labor Relations; Sales. **Positions commonly filled include:** Chemical Engineer; Computer Programmer; Electrical/Electronics Engineer; Environmental Engineer; General Manager; Human Service Worker; Industrial Engineer; Industrial Production Manager; Internet Services Manager; Materials Engineer; Mechanical Engineer; Metallurgical Engineer; Purchasing Agent/Manager; Quality Control Supervisor; Restaurant/Food Service Manager; Software Engineer; Systems Analyst. **Average salary range of placements:** More than $50,000. **Number of placements per year:** 1 - 49.

CORPORATE RESEARCH
3540 Secor Road, Suite 300, Toledo OH 43606. 419/535-1941. **Contact:** Manager. **Description:** An executive search firm.

CORPORATE RESEARCH CONSULTING GROUP INC.
2545 Farmers Drive, Suite 270, Columbus OH 43235. 614/760-1833. **Contact:** Manager. **Description:** An executive search firm. **Specializes in the areas of:** Computer Science/Software; Finance; General Management; Sales.

J.D. COTTER SEARCH, INC.
2999 East Dublin-Granville Road, Suite 301, Columbus OH 43231. 614/895-2065. **Fax:** 614/895-3071. **Contact:** Joseph Cotter, Manager. **Description:** An executive search firm. **Specializes in the areas of:** Accounting/Auditing; Administration; Engineering; Food; General Management; Manufacturing; Personnel/Labor Relations; Sales. **Positions commonly filled include:** Accountant/Auditor; Biomedical Engineer; Budget Analyst; Buyer; Chemical Engineer; Chemist; Civil Engineer; Credit Manager; Electrical/Electronics Engineer; Financial Analyst; General Manager; Geologist/Geophysicist; Human Resources Manager; Industrial Engineer; Management Analyst/Consultant; Mechanical Engineer; Purchasing Agent/Manager; Quality Control Supervisor; Software Engineer; Structural Engineer; Systems Analyst; Transportation/Traffic Specialist. **Average salary range of placements:** More than $50,000. **Number of placements per year:** 200 - 499.

CROSS-JORDAN CORPORATION
4986 Gateway Drive, Suite B, Medina OH 44256. 330/723-7203. **Fax:** 330/722-7436. **Contact:** President. **Description:** An executive search firm operating on both retainer and contingency bases. Cross-Jordan Corporation is a member of the Nationwide Interchange Service (NIS), one of the world's largest independent recruiter networks. **Specializes in the areas of:** Engineering; General Management; Technical. **Positions**

commonly filled include: Buyer; Chemical Engineer; Draftsperson; Electrical/Electronics Engineer; Industrial Engineer; Industrial Production Manager; Mechanical Engineer; Metallurgical Engineer; Operations/Production Manager; Purchasing Agent/Manager; Quality Control Supervisor; Software Engineer; Structural Engineer; Technical Writer/Editor; Telecommunications Manager. **Number of placements per year:** 1 - 49.

DANKOWSKI AND ASSOCIATES, INC.
P.O. Box 39478, North Ridgeville OH 44039-0478. 440/327-8717. **Fax:** 440/327-1853. **Contact:** Thomas A. Dankowski, President. **E-mail address:** dankowski@aol.com. **Description:** A generalist executive search firm operating on both retainer and contingency bases. Client company pays fee. **Specializes in the areas of:** Personnel/Labor Relations. **Positions commonly filled include:** Human Resources Generalist; Human Resources Manager; Human Resources Representative; Human Resources Specialist; Vice President. **Corporate headquarters location:** Elyria OH. **Average salary range of placements:** $50,000 - $100,000. **Number of placements per year:** 1 - 49.

DATA BANK CORPORATION
927 Avondale Avenue, Cincinnati OH 45203. 513/559-9300. **Toll-free phone:** 800/733-0020. **Fax:** 425/732-9683. **Contact:** Wayne Ivey, President. **E-mail address:** jobs@databankcorp.com. **World Wide Web address:** http://www.databankcorp.com. **Description:** An executive search firm operating on both retainer and contingency bases. **Specializes in the areas of:** Administration; Computer Science/Software; Information Systems; Scientific; Technical. **Positions commonly filled include:** Computer Programmer; Database Manager; Information Systems Consultant; Internet Services Manager; MIS Specialist; Project Manager; Software Engineer; Systems Analyst; Systems Manager; Technical Writer/Editor; Telecommunications Manager; Webmaster. **Corporate headquarters location:** This Location. **Other U.S. locations:** Dayton OH. **Average salary range of placements:** More than $50,000. **Number of placements per year:** 200 - 499.

TONIA DEAL CONSULTANTS
P.O. Box 746, Hudson OH 44236. 330/463-3610. **Contact:** Recruiting Manager. **E-mail address:** tdc@gwis.com. **Description:** An executive search firm. **Specializes in the areas of:** Engineering; General Management; Purchasing; Technical; Transportation. **Positions commonly filled include:** Buyer; Chemical Engineer; Chemist; Cost Estimator; Industrial Engineer; Industrial Production Manager; Mechanical Engineer; Purchasing Agent/Manager; Quality Control Supervisor; Transportation/Traffic Specialist. **Number of placements per year:** 1 - 49.

DEFFET GROUP INC.
7801 Marysville Road, Ostrander OH 43061. 740/666-7600. **Fax:** 740/666-7610. **Contact:** Daniel Deffet, Managing Partner. **Description:** An executive search firm. **Specializes in the areas of:** Health/Medical. **Positions commonly filled include:** Health Services Manager; Physical Therapist; Respiratory Therapist; Speech-Language Pathologist. **Number of placements per year:** 50 - 99.

DELTA MEDICAL SEARCH ASSOCIATES
615 Rome-Hilliard Road, Columbus OH 43228. 614/878-0550. **Contact:** Connie Fox, Administrative Assistant. **E-mail address:** associates@deltasearch.com. **World Wide Web address:** http://www. deltasearch.com. **Description:** An executive search firm operating on both retainer and contingency bases. The firm focuses on the placement of health care professionals in clinical, administrative, technical, and management positions nationwide. Clients are primarily hospitals, clinics, and physician practices. **NOTE:** Please address all resumes to Connie Fox, Administrative Assistant. All other inquiries should be addressed to Marilyn Wallace, CPC-PRC/President. Client company pays fee. **Specializes in the areas of:** Health/Medical.

Positions commonly filled include: Nurse Practitioner; Physician; Registered Nurse. **Average salary range of placements:** $50,000 - $100,000. **Number of placements per year:** 1 - 49.

PETE DELUKE & ASSOCIATES, INC.
113 North Ohio Avenue, Suite 204, Sidney OH 45365. 937/497-1515. **Contact:** Pete Deluke, Owner/President. **E-mail address:** pdajob4u@bright.net. **Description:** An executive search firm operating on both retainer and contingency bases. The firm also provides some contract placements. Client company pays fee. **Specializes in the areas of:** Accounting; Engineering; General Management; Human Resources. **Positions commonly filled include:** Engineer; Human Resources Manager; Plant Manager. **Average salary range of placements:** $50,000 - $100,000.

DOWNING & DOWNING
7757 Auburn Road, Unit 9, Concord OH 44077. 440/357-1996. **Contact:** Gus Downing, President. **Description:** An executive search firm. **Specializes in the areas of:** Security. **Positions commonly filled include:** Investigator; Loss Prevention Specialist; Security Manager.

DUNHILL PROFESSIONAL SEARCH OF COLUMBUS
1200 West Fifth Avenue, Suite 106, Columbus OH 43212. 614/486-2716. **Contact:** John Salzman, Owner. **Description:** An executive search firm. **Specializes in the areas of:** Computer Hardware/Software; Sales.

ELITE RESOURCES GROUP
71 Baker Boulevard, Akron OH 44333. 330/867-9412. **Fax:** 330/867-0468. **Contact:** Gary Suhay, President. **Description:** An executive search firm operating on a retainer basis. **Specializes in the areas of:** Engineering; General Management; Industrial; Technical; Transportation. **Positions commonly filled include:** Buyer; Chemical Engineer; Chemist; Design Engineer; Designer; Electrical/Electronics Engineer; Environmental Engineer; Industrial Engineer; Industrial Production Manager; Mathematician; Mechanical Engineer; Metallurgical Engineer; Statistician; Transportation/Traffic Specialist. **Average salary range of placements:** More than $50,000. **Number of placements per year:** 1 - 49.

EMPLOYMENT SOLUTIONS GROUP, INC.
7801 Laurel Avenue, Cincinnati OH 45243. 513/561-4040. **Fax:** 513/561-4095. **Contact:** Christopher Albrecht, President. **E-mail address:** chris@esgsearch.com. **World Wide Web address:** http://www.esgsearch.com. **Description:** An executive search firm. **Specializes in the areas of:** Architecture/Construction; Design; Retail. **Positions commonly filled include:** Architect; Buyer; General Manager; Project Manager. **Average salary range of placements:** More than $50,000. **Number of placements per year:** 1 - 49.

EXECUTECH
P.O. Box 707, Kent OH 44240. 330/677-0010. **Fax:** 330/677-0148. **Contact:** Mark Seaholts, President. **Description:** An executive search firm that also provides contract services. The firm provides senior- and mid-level management placements. **Specializes in the areas of:** Accounting/Auditing; Administration; Chemicals; Engineering; General Management; Industrial; Manufacturing; Personnel/Labor Relations; Publishing; Sales; Technical. **Positions commonly filled include:** Administrative Manager; Chemical Engineer; Chemist; Design Engineer; Electrical/Electronics Engineer; General Manager; Human Resources Specialist; Industrial Engineer; Industrial Production Manager; Mechanical Engineer; MIS Specialist; Operations/Production Manager; Physician. **Other U.S. locations:** Tampa FL; Raleigh NC. **Average salary range of placements:** More than $50,000. **Number of placements per year:** 50 - 99.

EXECUTIVE CONNECTION
8221 Brecksville Road, Building 3, Suite 2, Brecksville OH 44141. 440/838-5657. **Fax:** 440/838-5668. **Contact:** Mr. Steven Brandvold, President. **E-mail address:** econnect@staffing.net. **Description:** An executive search firm operating on both retainer and contingency bases. **Specializes in the areas of:** Engineering; Food; General Management; Industrial; Manufacturing. **Positions commonly filled include:** Account Manager; Applications Engineer; Buyer; Chemical Engineer; Chemist; Controller; Design Engineer; Electrical/Electronics Engineer; Human Resources Manager; Industrial Engineer; Industrial Production Manager; Manufacturing Engineer; Mechanical Engineer; Operations Manager; Production Manager; Project Manager; Quality Control Supervisor. **Corporate headquarters location:** This Location. **Average salary range of placements:** More than $50,000. **Number of placements per year:** 1 - 49.

EXECUTIVE DIRECTIONS
9701 Cleveland Avenue NW, North Canton OH 44720. 330/499-1001. **Contact:** R. Glenn Richards, Vice President. **Description:** An executive search firm. **Specializes in the areas of:** Automotive; Engineering; General Management; Packaging; Publishing; Sales; Technical. **Positions commonly filled include:** Biological Scientist; Chemical Engineer; Chemist; General Manager; Human Resources Manager; Industrial Production Manager; Mechanical Engineer; Operations/Production Manager; Purchasing Agent/Manager; Quality Control Supervisor. **Number of placements per year:** 1 - 49.

EXECUTIVE RESOURCES, INC.
P.O. Box 32, Dayton OH 45401. 937/274-4500. **Contact:** Manager. **Description:** An executive search firm. **Specializes in the areas of:** Data Processing; Food; Management; Pharmaceuticals; Retail; Sales.

EXECUTIVE SEARCH LTD.
4834 Interstate Drive, Cincinnati OH 45246-1114. 513/874-6901. **Fax:** 513/874-6901. **Contact:** Jim Cimino, Vice President. **E-mail address:** execsrch@concentric.net. **World Wide Web address:** http://www.executivesearch.net. **Description:** An executive search firm operating on both retainer and contingency bases. **Specializes in the areas of:** Accounting; Computer Science/Software; Engineering; Finance; General Management; Industrial; Information Systems; Information Technology; Manufacturing; Personnel/Labor Relations; Technical. **Positions commonly filled include:** Account Manager; Accountant; Applications Engineer; Auditor; Biomedical Engineer; Budget Analyst; Buyer; Chemical Engineer; Chemist; Chief Executive Officer; Chief Financial Officer; Civil Engineer; Computer Animator; Computer Programmer; Controller; Cost Estimator; Credit Manager; Database Manager; Design Engineer; Electrical/Electronics Engineer; Environmental Engineer; Finance Director; Financial Analyst; General Manager; Graphic Designer; Health Services Manager; Human Resources Manager; Industrial Engineer; Industrial Production Manager; Internet Services Manager; Manufacturer's/Wholesaler's Sales Rep.; Manufacturing Engineer; Market Research Analyst; Marketing Manager; Mechanical Engineer; Metallurgical Engineer; Mining Engineer; MIS Specialist; Multimedia Designer; Nuclear Engineer; Operations Manager; Physician; Production Manager; Project Manager; Public Relations Specialist; Purchasing Agent/Manager; Quality Control Supervisor; Sales Engineer; Sales Executive; Sales Manager; Sales Representative; Software Engineer; Stationary Engineer; Structural Engineer; Systems Analyst; Systems Manager; Technical Writer/Editor; Telecommunications Manager; Transportation/Traffic Specialist; Vice President of Finance; Vice President of Operations; Video Production Coordinator. **Corporate headquarters location:** This Location. **Average salary range of placements:** More than $50,000. **Number of placements per year:** 200 - 499.

F.L.A.G.
625 East County Line Road, Springfield OH 45502. 937/342-0200. **Fax:** 603/737-0702. **Contact:** Tom Warren, Manager. **Description:** An executive search firm focusing on the placement of technical and sales professionals nationwide in the fuel, lubricants, and greases industries. The firm operates on both retainer and contingency bases. **Specializes in the areas of:** Industrial; Sales; Technical. **Positions commonly filled include:** Chemist. **Average salary range of placements:** More than $50,000. **Number of placements per year:** 1 - 49.

FENZEL MILAR ASSOCIATES
602 Quincy Street, Ironton OH 45638. 740/532-6409. **Fax:** 740/533-0813. **Contact:** John Milar, Owner. **Description:** An executive search firm operating on a contingency basis. **Specializes in the areas of:** Administration; Computer Science/Software; Engineering; Manufacturing. **Positions commonly filled include:** Chemical Engineer; Electrical/Electronics Engineer; Industrial Engineer; Materials Engineer; Mechanical Engineer; Metallurgical Engineer; MIS Specialist; Software Engineer; Systems Analyst. **Average salary range of placements:** $30,000 - $60,000. **Number of placements per year:** 1 - 49.

FITZPATRICK & ASSOCIATES
6187 Sorrento Avenue NW, Canton OH 44718. 330/497-8994. **Fax:** 330/497-8993. **Contact:** James L. Fitzpatrick, Manager. **E-mail address:** fitzpat@ix.netcom.com. **Description:** An executive search firm operating on a contingency basis. The firm also provides some contract placements. Client company pays fee. **Specializes in the areas of:** Computer Science/Software; Data Communications; Engineering; Scientific; Technical; Telecommunications. **Positions commonly filled include:** Computer Engineer; Computer Programmer; Computer Scientist; Software Engineer. **Corporate headquarters location:** This Location. **Average salary range of placements:** $50,000 - $100,000. **Number of placements per year:** 50 - 99.

F-O-R-T-U-N-E PERSONNEL CONSULTANTS
8170 Corporate Park Drive, Suite 304, Cincinnati OH 45242. 513/891-6996. **Fax:** 513/891-7382. **Contact:** James Boule, President. **Description:** An executive search firm operating on both retainer and contingency bases. Client company pays fee. **Specializes in the areas of:** Engineering; General Management; Industrial; Printing; Publishing. **Positions commonly filled include:** Account Manager; Design Engineer; Electrical/Electronics Engineer; General Manager; Manufacturing Engineer; Marketing Manager; Mechanical Engineer; Metallurgical Engineer; Operations Manager; Production Manager; Project Manager; Quality Assurance Engineer; Quality Control Supervisor; Sales Executive; Sales Manager; Vice President of Operations. **Corporate headquarters location:** New York NY. **Other U.S. locations:** Nationwide. **Average salary range of placements:** $50,000 - $100,000. **Number of placements per year:** 1 - 49.

FREDERICK-LEHMANN & ASSOCIATES
TEMPORARILY YOURS
7750 Reynolds Road, Mentor OH 44060. 440/951-6306. **Contact:** Manager. **Description:** An executive search firm. Temporarily Yours (also at this location) is a temporary agency that places personnel in clerical and industrial positions. Tech Force (also at this location) provides placements for people in the technical and computer industries. **Specializes in the areas of:** Computer Science/Software; Industrial; Technical.

FRISTOE & CARLETON
77 Milford Drive, Hudson OH 44236. 330/655-3535. **Fax:** 330/655-3585. **Contact:** Jack Fristoe, President. **Description:** An executive search firm. **Specializes in the areas of:** Advertising; Sales. **Positions commonly**

filled include: Advertising Executive; Public Relations Specialist. **Number of placements per year:** 1 - 49.

GAMMILL GROUP
8425 Pulsar Place, Suite 410, Columbus OH 43240. 614/848-7726. **Contact:** Manager. **Description:** An executive search firm. **Specializes in the areas of:** Information Technology.

GAYHART & ASSOCIATES
1250 Old River Road, 2nd Floor, Cleveland OH 44113. 216/861-7010. **Contact:** Richard F. Albertini, President. **Description:** An executive search firm. **Specializes in the areas of:** Architecture/Construction; Computer Science/Software; Engineering; General Management; Industrial; Manufacturing; Personnel/Labor Relations; Technical. **Positions commonly filled include:** Aerospace Engineer; Aircraft Mechanic/Engine Specialist; Architect; Biological Scientist; Biomedical Engineer; Buyer; Ceramics Engineer; Chemical Engineer; Chemist; Civil Engineer; Computer Programmer; Construction and Building Inspector; Construction Contractor; Cost Estimator; Designer; Draftsperson; Electrical/Electronics Engineer; Food Scientist/Technologist; General Manager; Geologist/Geophysicist; Industrial Engineer; Landscape Architect; Materials Engineer; Mechanical Engineer; Metallurgical Engineer; Mining Engineer; Nuclear Engineer; Petroleum Engineer; Quality Control Supervisor; Software Engineer; Stationary Engineer; Structural Engineer; Systems Analyst; Technical Writer/Editor. **Number of placements per year:** 100 - 199.

H.L. GOEHRING & ASSOCIATES, INC.
3200 Wrenford Street, Dayton OH 45409. 937/294-8854. **Contact:** Hal Goehring, President. **Description:** An executive search firm. **Specializes in the areas of:** Engineering; General Management; Industrial; Manufacturing; Personnel/Labor Relations; Publishing; Sales. **Positions commonly filled include:** Buyer; Electrical/Electronics Engineer; Financial Analyst; General Manager; Human Resources Manager; Industrial Engineer; Mechanical Engineer; Purchasing Agent/Manager; Quality Control Supervisor. **Average salary range of placements:** More than $50,000. **Number of placements per year:** 1 - 49.

R. GREEN & ASSOCIATES
One South St. Clair Street, Toledo OH 43602. 419/249-2800. **Fax:** 419/249-2083. **Contact:** Manager. **Description:** An executive search firm. **Specializes in the areas of:** Automotive; Consumer Products; Manufacturing.

GRIFFITHS & ASSOCIATES
P.O. Box 13854, Fairlawn OH 44334. 330/865-9660. **Fax:** 330/865-9483. **Contact:** Bob Griffiths, President. **Description:** An executive search firm. **Specializes in the areas of:** Accounting/Auditing; Engineering; Food; General Management; Industrial; Manufacturing; Personnel/Labor Relations; Sales; Technical. **Positions commonly filled include:** Accountant/Auditor; Aerospace Engineer; Biological Scientist; Biomedical Engineer; Buyer; Ceramics Engineer; Chemical Engineer; Chemist; Electrical/Electronics Engineer; Environmental Engineer; Industrial Designer; Industrial Engineer; Manufacturing Engineer; Marketing Specialist; Mechanical Engineer; Metallurgical Engineer; Operations/Production Manager; Purchasing Agent/Manager; Quality Control Supervisor; Safety Engineer; Software Engineer. **Number of placements per year:** 1 - 49.

GEORGE GUM & ASSOCIATES
24400 Highland Road, Suite 30, Richmond Heights OH 44143. 216/531-1888. **Contact:** Manager. **Description:** An executive search firm. **Specializes in the areas of:** Retail.

GUTHOFF & ASSOCIATES
659-A Park Meadow Road, Westerville OH 43081. 614/794-9950. **Contact:** Manager. **Description:** An

executive search firm. **Specializes in the areas of:** Banking; Engineering; Human Resources; Manufacturing; Telecommunications.

RUSS HADICK & ASSOCIATES
7100 Corporate Way, Suite B, Centerville OH 45459. 937/439-7700. **Fax:** 937/439-7705. **Contact:** Russ Hadick, President. **World Wide Web address:** http://www.rharecruiters.com. **Description:** An executive search firm. **Specializes in the areas of:** Accounting; Administration; Computer Hardware/Software; Engineering; Finance; Manufacturing; Personnel/Labor Relations; Technical. **Positions commonly filled include:** Accountant/Auditor; Aerospace Engineer; Agricultural Engineer; Attorney; Buyer; Chemical Engineer; Chemist; Civil Engineer; Computer Programmer; Credit Manager; Draftsperson; Economist; EDP Specialist; Electrical/Electronics Engineer; Financial Analyst; General Manager; Human Resources Manager; Industrial Engineer; Marketing Specialist; Mechanical Engineer; Metallurgical Engineer; MIS Specialist; Purchasing Agent/Manager; Quality Control Supervisor; Sales Representative; Systems Analyst; Technical Writer/Editor; Technician. **Number of placements per year:** 50 - 99.

HAHN & ASSOCIATES, INC.
P.O. Box 41009, Dayton OH 45441-0009. 937/436-3141. **Fax:** 937/436-3252. **Contact:** Kenneth R. Hahn, President/Owner. **Description:** An executive search firm operating on a contingency basis that places professionals in manufacturing environments. **Specializes in the areas of:** Administration; Engineering; General Management; Materials; Personnel/Labor Relations. **Positions commonly filled include:** Accountant; Buyer; Controller; Design Engineer; General Manager; Human Resources Manager; Industrial Engineer; Mechanical Engineer; Metallurgical Engineer; Operations Manager; Production Manager; Project Manager; Purchasing Agent/Manager; Quality Control Supervisor; Sales Engineer; Software Engineer; Systems Analyst; Systems Manager. **Corporate headquarters location:** This Location.

ROBERT HALF INTERNATIONAL ACCOUNTEMPS
140 East Town Street, Suite 1150, Columbus OH 43215. 614/221-9300. **Contact:** Manager. **Description:** An executive search firm. Accountemps (also at this location) provides temporary placements. **Corporate headquarters location:** Menlo Park CA. **International locations:** Worldwide.

HAMMANN & ASSOCIATES
3540 Blue Rock Road, Cincinnati OH 45239. 513/385-2528. **Fax:** 513/741-2692. **Contact:** Ed Hammann, Owner. **E-mail address:** ehammann@cssweb.com. **Description:** An executive search firm operating on a contingency basis. **Specializes in the areas of:** Administration; Computer Science/Software. **Positions commonly filled include:** Computer Operator; Computer Programmer; Database Manager; Internet Services Manager; Management Analyst/Consultant; MIS Specialist; Multimedia Designer; Project Manager; Software Engineer; Systems Analyst; Systems Manager; Technical Writer/Editor; Telecommunications Manager; Webmaster. **Average salary range of placements:** $30,000 - $50,000. **Number of placements per year:** 1 - 49.

HEALTH CARE ADVANTAGE
3373 Wilkinson Drive, Fairlawn OH 44333. 330/666-0552. **Fax:** 330/666-8122. **Contact:** Lucy J. Randles, President/Owner. **E-mail address:** HCAlucy@aol.com. **Description:** An executive search firm focusing exclusively on the health care industry. Client employers include academic institutions, research and development organizations, hospitals, clinics, nursing homes, managed care companies, and medical supply companies. The firm operates on both retainer and contingency bases. **Specializes in the areas of:** Biology; Health/Medical; Technical. **Positions commonly filled include:**

Biochemist; Biological Scientist; Biomedical Engineer; Chemical Engineer; Chemist; Clinical Lab Technician; Dental Lab Technician; Dietician/Nutritionist; EEG Technologist; EKG Technician; Emergency Medical Technician; Environmental Engineer; Health Services Manager; Human Resources Manager; Human Service Worker; Management Analyst/Consultant; Medical Records Technician; Nuclear Engineer; Nuclear Medicine Technologist; Occupational Therapist; Pharmacist; Physical Therapist; Radiological Technologist; Recreational Therapist; Registered Nurse; Respiratory Therapist; Sales Manager; Sales Representative; Science Technologist; Social Worker; Speech-Language Pathologist; Surgical Technician; Teacher/Professor; Technical Writer/Editor. **Corporate headquarters location:** This Location. **Average salary range of placements:** $30,000 - $50,000. **Number of placements per year:** 1 - 49.

HEALTHCARE RECRUITERS INTERNATIONAL
10 North Locust Street, Suite C1, Oxford OH 45056-1182. 513/523-8004. **Fax:** 513/523-9004. **Contact:** Manager. **Description:** An executive search firm focusing exclusively on the health care industry. The firm also offers career and outplacement counseling. **Specializes in the areas of:** Health/Medical. **Positions commonly filled include:** Attorney; Biomedical Engineer; Branch Manager; Computer Programmer; Dental Assistant/Dental Hygienist; Dentist; Dietician/Nutritionist; Economist; Electrical/Electronics Engineer; Financial Analyst; General Manager; Health Services Manager; Human Resources Specialist; Management Analyst/Consultant; Market Research Analyst; MIS Specialist; Occupational Therapist; Operations/Production Manager; Pharmacist; Physical Therapist; Physician; Psychologist; Recreational Therapist; Registered Nurse; Respiratory Therapist; Services Sales Rep.; Social Worker; Sociologist; Software Engineer; Speech-Language Pathologist; Surgical Technician; Systems Analyst; Veterinarian. **Average salary range of placements:** More than $50,000. **Number of placements per year:** 1 - 49.

HEIDRICK & STRUGGLES
600 Superior Avenue East, Suite 2500, Cleveland OH 44114. 216/241-7410. **Fax:** 216/241-2217. **Contact:** Manager. **Description:** An executive search firm.

J.D. HERSEY & ASSOCIATES
1695 Old Henderson Road, Columbus OH 43220. 614/459-4555. **Fax:** 614/459-4544. **Contact:** Jeff Hersey, President. **E-mail address:** jdhersey@earthlink.net. **World Wide Web address:** http://www.jdhersey.com. **Description:** An executive search firm operating on both retainer and contingency bases. **Specializes in the areas of:** Architecture/Construction; Computer Science/Software; General Management; Marketing; Real Estate; Sales. **Positions commonly filled include:** Buyer; Chief Financial Officer; Computer Operator; Cost Estimator; General Manager; Human Resources Manager; Internet Services Manager; Manufacturer's/Wholesaler's Sales Rep.; Marketing Manager; MIS Specialist; Real Estate Agent; Sales Executive; Sales Manager; Sales Representative; Telecommunications Manager. **Average salary range of placements:** More than $50,000. **Number of placements per year:** 50 - 99.

HIGGINS & ASSOCIATES
P.O. Box 375, Kent OH 44240. 330/673-2245. **Contact:** Manager. **Description:** An executive search firm.

W.A. HILL & ASSOCIATES
632 Vine Street, Suite 800, Cincinnati OH 45202. 513/241-1255. **Contact:** Manager. **Description:** An executive search firm. **Specializes in the areas of:** Information Systems.

HITE EXECUTIVE SEARCH
HITE MANAGEMENT CONSULTANTS, INC.
P.O. Box 43217, Cleveland OH 44143-0217. 440/461-1600. **Contact:** William A. Hite, III, President. **World**

Wide Web address: http://www.hite-mgmt.com. **Description:** An executive search firm operating on a retainer basis. **Specializes in the areas of:** Accounting/Auditing; Administration; Advertising; Architecture/Construction; Banking; Computer Hardware/Software; Engineering; Finance; General Management; Health/Medical; Legal; Manufacturing; Nonprofit; Personnel/Labor Relations; Sales; Technical. **Corporate headquarters location:** This Location. **Other U.S. locations:** Nationwide. **Average salary range of placements:** More than $50,000. **Number of placements per year:** 50 - 99.

HOSPITALITY PROSERVICES
8803 Brecksville Road, Suite 7-104, Brecksville OH 44141. 440/582-9580. **Fax:** 440/582-9581. **Contact:** Frank Vento, Owner. **E-mail address:** FAVento@aol.com. **World Wide Web address:** http://www.hospitality-pro.com. **Description:** An executive search firm. **Specializes in the areas of:** Hotel/Restaurant.

R.W. HUNT GROUP
10999 Reed Hartman Highway, Suite 333, Cincinnati OH 45242. 513/792-4255. **Contact:** Rick Ramsay, President. **E-mail address:** rwhunt@aol.com. **Description:** An executive search firm operating on both retainer and contingency bases. **Positions commonly filled include:** Chemical Engineer; Design Engineer; Designer; Electrical/Electronics Engineer; Environmental Engineer; Industrial Engineer; Industrial Production Manager; Mechanical Engineer; Metallurgical Engineer; Operations/Production Manager; Quality Control Supervisor; Software Engineer; Stationary Engineer. **Average salary range of placements:** $30,000 - $50,000. **Number of placements per year:** 1 - 49.

ITS TECHNICAL STAFFING
313 Jefferson Avenue, Toledo OH 43604. 419/259-3656. **Fax:** 419/255-0519. **Contact:** Roger Radelhoff, President. **Description:** An executive search firm operating on a contingency basis. The company also offers permanent employment consulting services. **Specializes in the areas of:** Computer Science/Software; Engineering; Industrial; Manufacturing; Personnel/Labor Relations; Technical. **Positions commonly filled include:** Chemical Engineer; Civil Engineer; Computer Programmer; Construction and Building Inspector; Construction Contractor; Cost Estimator; Design Engineer; Designer; Draftsperson; Electrical/Electronics Engineer; Electrician; Environmental Engineer; Human Resources Specialist; Industrial Engineer; Industrial Production Manager; Mechanical Engineer; Petroleum Engineer; Software Engineer; Strategic Relations Manager; Structural Engineer; Surveyor; Technical Writer/Editor. **Other area locations:** Cleveland OH; Columbus OH. **Other U.S. locations:** Fort Wayne IN; Flint MI. **Average salary range of placements:** $30,000 - $50,000. **Number of placements per year:** 100 - 199.

ITS TECHNICAL STAFFING
4111 Executive Parkway, Suite 201, Westerville OH 43081. 614/841-7799. **Contact:** Manager. **Description:** An executive search firm. **Specializes in the areas of:** Computer Science/Software; Engineering; Information Systems; Technical.

INDUSTRIAL PERSONNEL
14701 Detroit Avenue, Suite 430, Lakewood OH 44107. 216/226-7958. **Fax:** 216/226-7987. **Contact:** Kevin Roche. **World Wide Web address:** http://www.industrialpersonnel.com. **Description:** An executive search firm operating on both retainer and contingency bases. The firm recruits engineers and industrial management personnel. **Specializes in the areas of:** Engineering. **Positions commonly filled include:** Account Manager; Branch Manager; Chemical Engineer; Controller; Design Engineer; Draftsperson; Electrical/Electronics Engineer; Environmental Engineer; Finance Director; General Manager; Industrial Engineer; Industrial Production Manager; Manufacturing Engineer; Mechanical Engineer; Metallurgical Engineer; Operations Manager; Production Manager; Quality

Assurance Engineer; Sales Engineer; Sales Executive; Sales Manager; Sales Representative. **Corporate headquarters location:** This Location. **Average salary range of placements:** $50,000 - $100,000. **Number of placements per year:** 50 - 99.

INTERIM EXECUTIVE RECRUITING
1760 Manley Road, Maumee OH 43537. 419/893-2400. **Fax:** 419/893-2491. **Contact:** Jeff DePerro, President. **Description:** Interim Executive Recruiting is an executive search firm. **Positions commonly filled include:** Accountant; Auditor; Computer Programmer; Designer; Draftsperson; Employment Interviewer; Engineer; Financial Manager; Human Resources Manager; Industrial Production Manager; Machinist; Millwright; Purchasing Agent/Manager; Quality Control Supervisor; Systems Analyst; Tool and Die Maker; Welder. **Number of placements per year:** 500 - 999.

IVES & ASSOCIATES, INC.
471 East Broad Street, Suite 2010, Columbus OH 43215. 614/228-0202. **Contact:** Phyllis E. Ives, President. **Description:** An executive search firm. **Specializes in the areas of:** Accounting/Auditing; Advertising; Communications; Distribution; Food; General Management; Legal; Manufacturing; Operations Management; Personnel/Labor Relations; Sales; Transportation.

J. JOSEPH & ASSOCIATES
PMB 322, 3766 Fishcreek Road, Stow OH 44224. 330/676-0522. **Contact:** Manager. **Description:** J. Joseph & Associates is an executive search firm. **Specializes in the areas of:** Medical Sales and Marketing; Sales.

KBK MANAGEMENT ASSOCIATES
5500 Market Street, Suite 92, Youngstown OH 44512. 330/788-6508. **Toll-free phone:** 800/875-6546. **Fax:** 330/788-0645. **Contact:** Joanne Malys, Recruiting Specialist. **E-mail address:** jamalys@aol.com. **Description:** An executive search firm operating on a contingency basis. **Specializes in the areas of:** Accounting; Administration; Computer Science/Software; Engineering; Finance; Industrial; Metals; Personnel/Labor Relations; Scientific; Technical. **Positions commonly filled include:** Accountant; Applications Engineer; Auditor; Blue-Collar Worker Supervisor; Budget Analyst; Buyer; Chemical Engineer; Chemist; Computer Programmer; Controller; Cost Estimator; Database Manager; Design Engineer; Draftsperson; Electrical/Electronics Engineer; Electrician; Environmental Engineer; Finance Director; Financial Analyst; Food Scientist/Technologist; Human Resources Manager; Industrial Engineer; Information Systems Consultant; Internet Services Manager; Management Analyst/Consultant; Manufacturing Engineer; Marketing Manager; Marketing Specialist; Mechanical Engineer; Metallurgical Engineer; MIS Specialist; Production Manager; Project Manager; Purchasing Agent/Manager; Quality Control Supervisor; Sales Engineer; Sales Manager; Sales Representative; Software Engineer; Statistician; Systems Analyst; Systems Manager; Technical Writer/Editor; Telecommunications Manager; Transportation/Traffic Specialist; Webmaster. **Corporate headquarters location:** This Location. **Other U.S. locations:** Nationwide. **Average salary range of placements:** More than $30,000. **Number of placements per year:** 50 - 99.

RICHARD KADER & ASSOCIATES
7850 Freeway Circle, Suite 201, Cleveland OH 44130. 440/891-1700. **Contact:** Richard Kader, President. **Description:** Richard Kader & Associates is an executive search firm. **Specializes in the areas of:** Sales.

A.T. KEARNEY EXECUTIVE SEARCH
1200 Bank One Center, 600 Superior Avenue East, Cleveland OH 44114. 216/241-6880. **Contact:** David Lauderback, Managing Director. **Description:** A.T. Kearney Executive Search is an executive search firm operating on a retainer basis. **Specializes in the areas of:** Finance; High-Tech; Industrial; Nonprofit. **Corporate headquarters location:** Chicago IL. **International locations:** Worldwide.

LAUGHLIN & ASSOCIATES
110 Boggs Lane, Suite 151, Cincinnati OH 45246. 513/772-1082. **Contact:** Manager. **Description:** Laughlin & Associates is an executive search firm. **Specializes in the areas of:** Sales.

LEITH & ASSOCIATES
24500 Center Ridge Road, Suite 325, Westlake OH 44145. 216/808-1130. **Contact:** Manager. **Description:** Leith & Associates is an executive search firm. Client company pays fee. **Specializes in the areas of:** Marketing; Sales; Transportation. **Positions commonly filled include:** Account Manager; Account Representative; Branch Manager; Computer Programmer; General Manager; Human Resources Manager; Industrial Production Manager; Manufacturing Engineer; Operations Manager; Production Manager; Project Manager; Quality Control Supervisor; Sales Engineer; Sales Executive; Sales Manager; Sales Representative; Transportation/Traffic Specialist. **Corporate headquarters location:** This Location. **Average salary range of placements:** $30,000 - $100,000.

LOPRESTI & ASSOCIATES
12 Westerville Square, Suite 216, Westerville OH 43081. 614/794-9494. **Contact:** Manager. **Description:** Lopresti & Associates is an executive search firm. **Specializes in the areas of:** Banking; Finance.

MANAGEMENT RECRUITERS INTERNATIONAL
3450 West Central Avenue, Suite 360, Toledo OH 43606. 419/537-1100. **Fax:** 419/537-8730. **Contact:** Branch Manager. **Description:** Management Recruiters International is an executive search firm. **Specializes in the areas of:** Computer Science/Software; Engineering; General Management; Industrial; Manufacturing; Personnel/Labor Relations; Sales. **Positions commonly filled include:** Chemical Engineer; Computer Programmer; Electrical/Electronics Engineer; General Manager; Human Resources Manager; Industrial Engineer; Industrial Production Manager; Mechanical Engineer; Metallurgical Engineer; Operations/Production Manager; Purchasing Agent/Manager; Quality Control Supervisor; Systems Analyst. **Corporate headquarters location:** Cleveland OH. **Other U.S. locations:** Nationwide. **Number of placements per year:** 50 - 99.

MANAGEMENT RECRUITERS INTERNATIONAL
2300 East Dublin-Granville Road, Suite 110B, Columbus OH 43229. 614/794-3200. **Fax:** 614/794-3233. **Contact:** Dick Stoltz, President. **Description:** Management Recruiters International is an executive search firm. **Specializes in the areas of:** Administration; Architecture/Construction; Computer Science/Software; Engineering; Food; General Management; Industrial; Information Technology; Logistics; Manufacturing; Personnel/Labor Relations; Transportation. **Positions commonly filled include:** Agricultural Engineer; Biochemist; Buyer; Chemical Engineer; Computer Programmer; Construction Manager; Cost Estimator; Credit Manager; Customer Service Representative; Electrical/Electronics Engineer; Environmental Engineer; Food Scientist/Technologist; General Manager; Human Resources Specialist; Industrial Engineer; Industrial Production Manager; Internet Services Manager; Metallurgical Engineer; MIS Specialist; Multimedia Designer; Operations/Production Manager; Purchasing Agent/Manager; Quality Control Supervisor; Software Engineer; Systems Analyst; Telecommunications Manager. **Corporate headquarters location:** Cleveland OH. **Other U.S. locations:** Nationwide. **Number of placements per year:** 200 - 499.

MANAGEMENT RECRUITERS INTERNATIONAL
6690 Beta Drive, Suite 100, Mayfield Village OH 44143. 440/684-6150. **Contact:** Terry Wesley, Manager. **Description:** Management Recruiters International is an executive search firm. **Specializes in the areas of:** Accounting/Auditing; Administration; Advertising; Architecture/Construction; Banking; Communications; Computer Hardware/Software; Construction; Electrical; Engineering; Finance; Food; General Management; Health/Medical; Industrial; Insurance; Legal; Manufacturing; Operations Management; Procurement; Publishing; Real Estate; Retail; Sales; Technical; Textiles; Transportation. **Corporate headquarters location:** Cleveland OH. **Other U.S. locations:** Nationwide.

MANAGEMENT RECRUITERS INTERNATIONAL
20600 Chagrin Boulevard, Suite 703, Cleveland OH 44122. 216/561-6776. **Fax:** 216/561-2393. **Contact:** Manager. **Description:** An executive search firm. **Specializes in the areas of:** Finance; Food; Health/Medical; Industrial; Insurance; Manufacturing; Personnel/Labor Relations; Publishing; Sales. **Positions commonly filled include:** Actuary; Administrative Manager; Branch Manager; General Manager; Health Services Manager; Human Resources Manager; Manufacturer's/Wholesaler's Sales Rep.; Occupational Therapist; Operations/Production Manager; Physical Therapist; Physician; Purchasing Agent/Manager; Telecommunications Manager. **Corporate headquarters location:** 7530 Lucerne Drive, Suite 303, Cleveland OH 44130. **Other U.S. locations:** Nationwide. **Average salary range of placements:** More than $50,000. **Number of placements per year:** 200 - 499.

MANAGEMENT RECRUITERS INTERNATIONAL COMPUSEARCH OF YOUNGSTOWN
8090 Market Street, Youngstown OH 44512. 330/726-6656. **Fax:** 330/726-0199. **Contact:** Donald A. Somers, President. **Description:** Management Recruiters International is an executive search firm operating on both retainer and contingency bases. **Positions commonly filled include:** Bank Officer/Manager; Computer Programmer; MIS Specialist; Software Engineer; Systems Analyst; Technical Writer/Editor; Telecommunications Manager. **Corporate headquarters location:** Cleveland OH. **Other U.S. locations:** Nationwide. **Average salary range of placements:** More than $50,000. **Number of placements per year:** 100 - 199.

MANAGEMENT RECRUITERS OF AKRON
1900 West Market Street, Akron OH 44313-6927. 330/867-2900. **Contact:** Tom Gerst, Manager. **Description:** An executive search firm. **Specializes in the areas of:** Plastics; Professional. **Corporate headquarters location:** Cleveland OH. **Other U.S. locations:** Nationwide.

MANAGEMENT RECRUITERS OF CINCINNATI
36 East Fourth Street, Suite 800, Cincinnati OH 45202. 513/651-5500. **Fax:** 513/651-3298. **Contact:** Joe McCullough, Co-Owner/Manager. **World Wide Web address:** http://www.mricincy.com. **Description:** Management Recruiters of Cincinnati is an executive search firm. **Specializes in the areas of:** Accounting/Auditing; Administration; Advertising; Architecture/Construction; Banking; Communications; Computer Hardware/Software; Construction; Design; Electrical; Engineering; Finance; Food; General Management; Health/Medical; Industrial; Insurance; Legal; Manufacturing; Operations Management; Personnel/Labor Relations; Procurement; Publishing; Real Estate; Retail; Sales; Technical; Textiles; Transportation. **Corporate headquarters location:** Cleveland OH. **Other U.S. locations:** Nationwide.

MANAGEMENT RECRUITERS OF CLEVELAND
812 Huron Road East, Suite 550, Cleveland OH 44115. 216/436-2436. **Fax:** 216/436-2441. **Contact:** Gary Gardiner, President. **E-mail address:** mricleveland@compuserve.com. **Description:** An executive search firm. **Specializes in the areas of:** Heating, Air Conditioning, and Refrigeration. **Positions commonly filled include:** Applications Engineer; Construction Contractor; Environmental Engineer; Industrial Engineer; Project Manager; Sales Executive; Sales Manager; Sales Representative. **Corporate headquarters location:** 7530 Lucerne Drive, Suite 303, Cleveland OH 44130. **Other U.S. locations:** Nationwide. **Average salary range of placements:** $50,000 - $70,000. **Number of placements per year:** 50 - 99.

MANAGEMENT RECRUITERS OF CLEVELAND (DOWNTOWN)
7530 Lucerne Drive, Suite 303, Cleveland OH 44130. 440/243-5151. **Fax:** 440/243-4868. **Contact:** Jeff DiPaolo, Manager. **Description:** An executive search firm operating on a contingency basis. **Specializes in the areas of:** Accounting; Administration; Architecture/Construction; Biology; Communications; Data Processing; Engineering; Industrial; Legal; Manufacturing; Operations Management; Personnel/Labor Relations; Sales. **Positions commonly filled include:** Aerospace Engineer; Agricultural Engineer; Aircraft Mechanic; Architect; Attorney; Biochemist; Biological Scientist; Biomedical Engineer; Chemical Engineer; Design Engineer; Draftsperson; Electrical Engineer; Environmental Engineer; Human Resources Specialist; Industrial Engineer; Internet Services Manager; Mechanical Engineer; MIS Specialist; Operations/Production Manager; Paralegal; Quality Control Supervisor; Software Engineer; Structural Engineer; Technical Writer/Editor; Telecommunications Manager. **Corporate headquarters location:** This Location. **Other U.S. locations:** Nationwide. **Number of placements per year:** 100 - 199.

MANAGEMENT RECRUITERS OF CLEVELAND (NORTHEAST)
8039 Broadmoor Road, Suite 20, Mentor OH 44060. 440/946-2355. **Contact:** General Manager. **Description:** An executive search firm. **Specializes in the areas of:** Banking. **Corporate headquarters location:** 7530 Lucerne Drive, Suite 303, Cleveland OH 44130. **Other U.S. locations:** Nationwide.

MANAGEMENT RECRUITERS OF CLEVELAND (SOUTH)
9700 Rockside Road, Suite 100, Cleveland OH 44125-6264. 216/642-5788. **Fax:** 216/642-5933. **Contact:** Paul Montigny, Owner. **Description:** An executive search firm. **Specializes in the areas of:** Accounting/Auditing; Administration; Advertising; Architecture/Construction; Banking; Communications; Computer Hardware/Software; Construction; Design; Electrical; Engineering; Finance; Food; General Management; Health/Medical; Legal; Manufacturing; Operations Management; Personnel/Labor Relations; Procurement; Publishing; Real Estate; Retail; Sales; Technical; Textiles; Transportation. **Corporate headquarters location:** 7530 Lucerne Drive, Suite 303, Cleveland OH 44130. **Other U.S. locations:** Nationwide.

MANAGEMENT RECRUITERS OF CLEVELAND (SOUTHWEST)
P.O. Box 178, Brunswick OH 44212-0178. 330/273-4300. **Fax:** 330/273-2862. **Contact:** Bob Boal, Manager. **Description:** An executive search firm. **Specializes in the areas of:** Accounting; Administration; Advertising; Architecture/Construction; Banking; Communications; Computer Hardware/Software; Construction; Design; Electrical; Engineering; Finance; Food; General Management; Health/Medical; Industrial; Insurance; Legal; Manufacturing; Operations Management; Personnel; Procurement; Publishing; Real Estate; Retail; Sales; Technical; Textiles; Transportation. **Corporate headquarters location:** 7530 Lucerne Drive, Cleveland OH 44130. **Other U.S. locations:** Nationwide.

MANAGEMENT RECRUITERS OF COLUMBUS (WEST)
555 South Front Street, Suite 100, Columbus OH 43215. 614/252-6200. **Contact:** Office Manager. **Description:**

An executive search firm. **Specializes in the areas of:** Accounting/Auditing; Administration; Advertising; Architecture/Construction; Banking; Communications; Computer Hardware/Software; Construction; Design; Electrical; Engineering; Finance; Food; General Management; Health/Medical; Industrial; Insurance; Legal; Manufacturing; Operations Management; Personnel/Labor Relations; Procurement; Publishing; Real Estate; Retail; Sales; Technical; Textiles; Transportation. **Corporate headquarters location:** Cleveland OH. **Other U.S. locations:** Nationwide.

MANAGEMENT RECRUITERS OF DAYTON
333 West First Street, Suite 515, Dayton OH 45402-1831. 937/228-8271. **Fax:** 937/228-2620. **Contact:** Manager. **Description:** An executive search firm. **Specializes in the areas of:** Accounting/Auditing; Administration; Advertising; Architecture/Construction; Banking; Communications; Computer Hardware/Software; Construction; Design; Electrical; Engineering; Finance; Food; General Management; Health/Medical; Industrial; Insurance; Legal; Manufacturing; Operations Management; Personnel/Labor Relations; Procurement; Publishing; Real Estate; Retail; Sales; Technical; Textiles; Transportation. **Corporate headquarters location:** Cleveland OH. **Other U.S. locations:** Nationwide.

MANAGEMENT RECRUITERS OF NORTH CANTON
7300 Whipple Avenue, P.O. Box 2970, North Canton OH 44720. 330/497-0122. **Fax:** 330/497-9730. **Contact:** Shirley Bascom, President. **E-mail address:** mrnc@raex.com. **World Wide Web address:** http://www.mrnc.com. **Description:** An executive search firm operating on both retainer and contingency bases. **Specializes in the areas of:** Computer Science/Software; Information Technology; Internet Development; MIS/EDP. **Positions commonly filled include:** Applications Engineer; AS400 Programmer Analyst; Computer Animator; Computer Engineer; Computer Operator; Computer Programmer; Computer Scientist; Computer Support Technician; Computer Technician; Content Developer; Database Administrator; Database Manager; Internet Services Manager; MIS Specialist; Multimedia Designer; Network/Systems Administrator; Software Engineer; SQL Programmer; Systems Analyst; Systems Manager; Webmaster. **Corporate headquarters location:** Cleveland OH. **Other U.S. locations:** Nationwide. **Average salary range of placements:** $50,000 - $100,000. **Number of placements per year:** 50 - 99.

BENNY MARTINEZ EXECUTIVE SEARCH
1215 Rosedale, Maumee OH 43537. 419/893-2933. **Contact:** Manager. **Description:** An executive search firm. **Specializes in the areas of:** Consumer Package Goods. **Positions commonly filled include:** Marketing Specialist; Sales Executive.

MARVEL CONSULTANTS INC.
28601 Chagrin Boulevard, Suite 470, Cleveland OH 44122. 216/292-2855. **Fax:** 216/292-7207. **Contact:** Marvin B. Basil, President. **Description:** An executive search firm operating on both retainer and contingency bases. Founded in 1973. **Specializes in the areas of:** Accounting/Auditing; Administration; Banking; Computer Science/Software; Engineering; Finance; General Management; Health/Medical; Industrial; Legal; Marketing; Personnel/Labor Relations; Sales; Transportation. **Positions commonly filled include:** Account Manager; Account Representative; Accountant; Applications Engineer; Attorney; Auditor; Bank Officer/Manager; Blue-Collar Worker Supervisor; Branch Manager; Budget Analyst; Buyer; Chemical Engineer; Chief Financial Officer; Computer Operator; Computer Programmer; Controller; Cost Estimator; Credit Manager; Database Manager; Design Engineer; Draftsperson; Electrical/Electronics Engineer; Finance Director; Financial Analyst; Fund Manager; General Manager; Industrial Engineer; Industrial Production Manager; Intellectual Property Lawyer; Management

Analyst/Consultant; Manufacturing Engineer; Marketing Manager; Mechanical Engineer; Metallurgical Engineer; MIS Specialist; Occupational Therapist; Operations Manager; Pharmacist; Physical Therapist; Physician; Production Manager; Quality Control Supervisor; Sales Engineer; Sales Executive; Sales Manager; Sales Representative; Software Engineer; Systems Analyst; Systems Manager. **Corporate headquarters location:** This Location. **Other U.S. locations:** Nationwide. **Average salary range of placements:** $30,000 - $50,000. **Number of placements per year:** 200 - 499.

MESSINA MANAGEMENT SYSTEMS
4770 Duke Drive, Suite 140, Mason OH 45040. 513/398-3331. **Fax:** 513/398-0496. **Contact:** Vincent Messina, President. **Description:** An executive search firm that also provides some temporary placements. **Specializes in the areas of:** Accounting/Auditing; Administration; Computer Science/Software; Engineering; Finance; Industrial; Manufacturing; Sales; Scientific; Secretarial. **Average salary range of placements:** $30,000 - $50,000. **Number of placements per year:** 100 - 199.

MIAMI PROFESSIONAL SEARCH
1341 Stratford Drive, Piqua OH 45356. 937/778-9797. **Fax:** 937/773-2142. **Contact:** Lloyd E. Shoemaker, Owner. **Description:** An executive search firm. **Specializes in the areas of:** Accounting/Auditing; Banking; Engineering; Finance; General Management; Industrial; Manufacturing; Personnel/Labor Relations; Sales. **Positions commonly filled include:** Accountant/Auditor; Bank Officer/Manager; Branch Manager; Budget Analyst; Buyer; Chemical Engineer; Computer Programmer; Credit Manager; Draftsperson; Electrical/Electronics Engineer; Financial Analyst; General Manager; Human Resources Manager; Industrial Engineer; Industrial Production Manager; Management Trainee; Mechanical Engineer; Operations/Production Manager; Purchasing Agent/Manager; Quality Control Supervisor; Systems Analyst; Telecommunications Manager; Transportation/Traffic Specialist. **Average salary range of placements:** $30,000 - $50,000. **Number of placements per year:** 1 - 49.

MIDLAND CONSULTANTS
4311 Ridge Road, Brooklyn OH 44144. 216/398-9330. **Fax:** 216/398-0879. **Contact:** Manager. **E-mail address:** midland@bright.net. **Description:** An executive search firm. **Specializes in the areas of:** Computer Science/Software; Engineering; General Management; Industrial; Manufacturing; Plastics; Publishing; Rubber; Sales. **Positions commonly filled include:** Chemist; Computer Programmer; Design Engineer; Designer; Draftsperson; Electrical/Electronics Engineer; Environmental Engineer; General Manager; Human Resources Specialist; Industrial Engineer; Mechanical Engineer; MIS Manager; Operations/Production Manager; Software Engineer; Systems Analyst. **Average salary range of placements:** $30,000 - $150,000. **Number of placements per year:** 200 - 499.

MILLION & ASSOCIATES
441 Vine Street, 1831 Carew Tower, Cincinnati OH 45202. 513/579-8770. **Contact:** Ken Million, President. **Description:** An executive search firm operating on a retainer basis. **Specializes in the areas of:** Banking; Health/Medical; Manufacturing. **Other U.S. locations:** Chantilly VA. **Average salary range of placements:** More than $50,000.

MINORITY EXECUTIVE SEARCH
P.O. Box 18063, Cleveland OH 44118. 216/932-2022. **Contact:** Eral Burks, Managing Director. **Description:** An executive search firm that provides job placements for women and minorities. **Specializes in the areas of:** Accounting/Auditing; Banking; Engineering; Finance; Legal; Manufacturing; Personnel/Labor Relations; Sales; Technical; Transportation. **Positions commonly filled include:** Accountant/Auditor; Aircraft Mechanic/Engine Specialist; Bank Officer/Manager; Biomedical Engineer; Branch Manager; Buyer; Chemical Engineer; Chemist; Computer Programmer; Credit Manager; Customer

Service Representative; Design Engineer; Electrical/Electronics Engineer; Environmental Engineer; Financial Analyst; Human Resources Specialist; Industrial Engineer; Mechanical Engineer; Metallurgical Engineer; MIS Specialist; Operations/Production Manager; Public Relations Specialist; Purchasing Agent/Manager; Services Sales Representative; Software Engineer; Systems Analyst; Technical Writer/Editor; Telecommunications Manager. **Average salary range of placements:** More than $50,000. **Number of placements per year:** 200 - 499.

MYERS & ASSOCIATES
4571 Stephen Circle, Canton OH 44718. 330/494-3274. **Fax:** 330/489-0790. **Contact:** George Myers, President. **Description:** An executive search firm operating on a contingency basis. **Specializes in the areas of:** Computer Science; Engineering; Manufacturing. **Positions commonly filled include:** Accountant/Auditor; Attorney; Computer Programmer; Design Engineer; Designer; Draftsperson; Electrical/Electronics Engineer; Electrician; Industrial Engineer; Industrial Production Manager; Mechanical Engineer; Metallurgical Engineer; Systems Analyst. **Average salary range of placements:** Less than $20,000. **Number of placements per year:** 1 - 49.

NATIONAL REGISTER OF AKRON
3050 Ridgewood Road, Akron OH 44333. 330/665-3720. **Fax:** 330/665-3780. **Contact:** Michael Hamilton, CPC/Manager. **Description:** An executive search firm operating on both retainer and contingency bases. **Specializes in the areas of:** Sales; Transportation. **Positions commonly filled include:** Manufacturer's/Wholesaler's Sales Rep.; Sales Engineer; Sales Executive; Sales Manager; Sales Rep.; Transportation Specialist. **Other U.S. locations:** Nationwide. **Average salary range of placements:** $30,000 - $50,000. **Number of placements per year:** 100 - 199.

NATIONAL REGISTER OF COLUMBUS
2700 East Dublin-Granville Road, Suite 555, Columbus OH 43231. 614/890-1200. **Fax:** 614/890-1259. **Contact:** Dave Molnar, President. **Description:** An executive search firm. **Specializes in the areas of:** Sales. **Positions commonly filled include:** Account Manager; Sales Manager; Sales Representative. **Other U.S. locations:** Nationwide. **Number of placements per year:** 200 - 499.

NATIONAL REGISTER OF TOLEDO
8245-B Farnsworth Road, Waterville OH 43566. 419/878-9810. **Fax:** 419/878-9402. **Contact:** Randy Seidletz, General Manager. **Description:** An executive search firm operating on both retainer and contingency bases. **Specializes in the areas of:** Sales; Transportation. **Positions commonly filled include:** Account Manager; Account Representative; Branch Manager; Customer Service Representative; Distribution Manager; Marketing Manager; Marketing Specialist; Operations Manager; Sales Engineer; Sales Executive; Sales Representative; Transportation/Traffic Specialist; Warehouse Manager. **Other U.S. locations:** Nationwide. **Average salary range of placements:** $30,000 - $50,000. **Number of placements per year:** 100 - 199.

NEWCOMB-DESMOND & ASSOCIATES
P.O. Box 201, Milford OH 45150. 513/831-9522. **Fax:** 513/831-9557. **Contact:** Michael J. Desmond, Chief Operating Officer. **E-mail address:** mdesmond@ fuse.net. **Description:** An executive search firm operating on both retainer and contingency bases. The company also provides contract services and career/outplacement counseling. Founded in 1979. **Specializes in the areas of:** Computer Science/Software; Engineering; Industrial; Insurance; Manufacturing; Personnel/Labor Relations. **Positions commonly filled include:** Applications Engineer; Auditor; Claim Representative; Computer Operator; Computer Programmer; Customer Service Representative; Database Manager; Electrical/Electronics Engineer; Finance Director; Human Resources Manager; Insurance

Agent/Broker; Manufacturing Engineer; MIS Specialist; Sales Engineer; Sales Executive; Sales Manager; Software Engineer; Systems Analyst; Systems Manager; Technical Writer/Editor; Underwriter/Assistant Underwriter. **Benefits available to temporary workers:** Paid Holidays; Paid Vacation. **Corporate headquarters location:** This Location. **Average salary range of placements:** $30,000 - $50,000. **Number of placements per year:** 200 - 499.

NORTH PEAK GROUP
812 Huron Road, Suite 315, Cleveland OH 44115. 216/621-1070. **Fax:** 216/621-0825. **Contact:** Matthew Bruns, President. **E-mail address:** mbruns6108@aol.com. **Description:** An executive search firm. **Specializes in the areas of:** Computer Science/Software; Environmental; Information Systems; MIS/EDP. **Positions commonly filled include:** Computer Operator; Computer Programmer; Database Manager; Environmental Engineer; Internet Services Manager; MIS Specialist; Software Engineer; Systems Analyst; Systems Manager; Telecommunications Manager. **Corporate headquarters location:** This Location. **Other U.S. locations:** Nationwide. **Average salary range of placements:** More than $50,000. **Number of placements per year:** 50 - 99.

NORTHCOAST PERSONNEL
1250 Old River Road, Cleveland OH 44113. 216/861-2200. **Contact:** Recruiter. **Description:** An executive search firm. **Specializes in the areas of:** Administration; Engineering; Industrial; Manufacturing. **Positions commonly filled include:** Accountant/Auditor; Architect; Buyer; Ceramics Engineer; Chemical Engineer; Chemist; Civil Engineer; Computer Programmer; Cost Estimator; Design Engineer; Designer; Draftsperson; Electrical/Electronics Engineer; Environmental Engineer; Industrial Engineer; Industrial Production Manager; Landscape Architect; Materials Engineer; Mechanical Engineer; Metallurgical Engineer; Structural Engineer; Systems Analyst. **Number of placements per year:** 100 - 199.

O'BRIEN & ROOF COMPANY
6812 Caine Road, Columbus OH 43235. 614/766-8500. **Fax:** 614/766-8505. **Contact:** Lindy O'Brien, President. **E-mail address:** mail@obrienroof.com. **World Wide Web address:** http://www.obrienroof.com. **Description:** An executive search firm. **Positions commonly filled include:** Accountant; Controller; Cost Estimator; Credit Manager; Financial Analyst; Market Research Analyst; Marketing Manager; Purchasing Agent/Manager. **Average salary range of placements:** $30,000 - $50,000. **Number of placements per year:** 50 - 99.

OLSTEN FINANCIAL STAFFING
Ohio Savings Plaza, 1801 East Ninth Street, Suite 1040, Cleveland OH 44114. 216/241-7100. **Toll-free phone:** 888/222-8693. **Fax:** 216/241-7170. **Contact:** Mary Jo Lake, Region Vice President. **E-mail address:** ofs.hq@olsten.com. **World Wide Web address:** http://www.olsten.com/ofs. **Description:** An executive search firm that also provides temporary and temp-to-perm financial placements. **Specializes in the areas of:** Accounting/Auditing; Banking; Finance. **Positions commonly filled include:** Accountant; Auditor; Budget Analyst; Chief Financial Officer; Controller; Credit Manager; Finance Director; Financial Analyst. **Corporate headquarters location:** Melville NY. **Other U.S. locations:** Nationwide. **Average salary range of placements:** $50,000 - $100,000. **Number of placements per year:** 200 - 499.

OLSTEN PROFESSIONAL STAFFING SERVICES
4520 Cooper Road, Suite 100, Cincinnati OH 45242. 513/985-9605. **Fax:** 513/936-5627. **Contact:** Manager. **E-mail address:** professional@olstencincinnati.com. **Description:** An executive search firm that also provides some contract services. **Specializes in the areas of:** Accounting/Auditing; Administration; Art/Design; Banking; Computer Science/Software; Engineering; Finance; General Management; Manufacturing;

Personnel/Labor Relations; Publishing; Sales; Technical. **Positions commonly filled include:** Accountant; Bank Officer/Manager; Branch Manager; Budget Analyst; Ceramics Engineer; Chemical Engineer; Civil Engineer; Claim Representative; Clinical Lab Technician; Computer Programmer; Customer Service Rep.; Draftsperson; Electrical Engineer; Environmental Engineer; Financial Analyst; Human Resources Specialist; Industrial Engineer; Industrial Production Manager; Internet Services Manager; Manufacturer's/Wholesaler's Sales Rep.; Market Research Analyst; Materials Engineer; Mechanical Engineer; Metallurgical Engineer; MIS Specialist; Operations/Production Manager; Quality Control Supervisor; Securities Sales Representative; Services Sales Representative; Software Engineer; Stationary Engineer; Structural Engineer; Surveyor; Systems Analyst; Technical Writer/Editor; Telecommunications Manager; Typist/Word Processor. **Benefits available to temporary workers:** Bonus Award/Plan; Medical Insurance; Paid Vacation. **Average salary range of placements:** More than $50,000.

PARAGON RECRUITING OFFICIALS
2000 West Henderson Road, Suite 350, Columbus OH 43220. 614/442-8900. **Contact:** Vince Procopio, President. **Description:** An executive search firm. **Specializes in the areas of:** Computer Science/Software; Data Processing. **Positions commonly filled include:** Computer Programmer; MIS Specialist; Systems Analyst. **Number of placements per year:** 1 - 49.

PATTERSON PERSONNEL
P.O. Box 101, Millersburg OH 44654. 330/674-4040. **Fax:** 330/674-3765. **Contact:** Manager. **Description:** An executive search firm operating on a contingency basis. **Specializes in the areas of:** Engineering. **Positions commonly filled include:** Applications Engineer; Ceramics Engineer; Chemical Engineer; Chemist; Chief Financial Officer; Controller; Design Engineer; Electrical Engineer; Financial Analyst; General Manager; Human Resources Manager; Industrial Engineer; Manufacturing Engineer; Marketing Manager; Marketing Specialist; Materials Engineer; Mechanical Engineer; Metallurgical Engineer; Plant Engineer; Production Manager; Purchasing Agent/Manager; Quality Control Supervisor; Sales Engineer; Sales Executive; Sales Manager; Sales Rep; Technical Writer/Editor. **Average salary range of placements:** $30,000 - $70,000. **Number of placements per year:** 50 - 99.

PERSONALIZED PLACEMENT
6641 Suffield Road, Mayfield Heights OH 44124. 440/449-3380. **Fax:** 440/449-3381. **Contact:** Ronald Kemelhar, Employment Specialist. **Description:** An executive search firm. **Specializes in the areas of:** Automotive; Health/Medical; Light Industrial; Marketing; Sales; Scientific; Technical. **Positions commonly filled include:** Account Manager; Account Representative; Applications Engineer; Branch Manager; Chemical Engineer; Civil Engineer; Environmental Engineer; Industrial Engineer; Management Trainee; Mechanical Engineer; Metallurgical Engineer; Sales Engineer; Sales Executive; Sales Manager; Sales Representative; Software Engineer; Vice President of Sales. **Average salary range of placements:** $30,000 - $50,000. **Number of placements per year:** 1 - 49.

K.J. PHILLIPS ASSOCIATES
10671 Tech Woods Circle, Cincinnati OH 45242. 513/733-5562. **Contact:** Manager. **Description:** An executive search firm. **Specializes in the areas of:** Information Systems.

PREMIUM SEARCH
1200 West Fifth Avenue, Suite 106, Columbus OH 43212. 614/487-2975. **Contact:** Manager. **Description:** An executive search firm. **Specializes in the areas of:** Insurance.

PROFESSIONAL DYNAMICS, INC.
1799 Akron-Peninsula Road, Suite 311, Akron OH 44313. 330/922-4244. **Fax:** 330/922-4258. **Contact:**

Manager. **World Wide Web address:** http://www.pdijobs.com. **Description:** An executive search firm. **Specializes in the areas of:** Automotive; Manufacturing.

PROVIDENCE PERSONNEL CONSULTANTS
2404 Fourth Street, Suite 1, Cuyahoga Falls OH 44221-2659. 330/929-6431. **Toll-free phone:** 800/968-5717. **Fax:** 330/929-4335. **Contact:** Donna Early, President. **E-mail address:** ppcconsult@aol.com. **Description:** An executive search firm operating on a contingency basis. Providence Personnel Consultants also provides career/outplacement counseling services. **Specializes in the areas of:** Accounting/Auditing; Administration; Advertising; Banking; Construction; Engineering; Finance; Health/Medical; Industrial; Management; Manufacturing; Personnel/Labor Relations; Professional; Sales; Technical; Transportation. **Positions commonly filled include:** Account Manager; Account Representative; Accountant/Auditor; Administrative Assistant; Administrative Manager; Advertising Clerk; Advertising Executive; Aerospace Engineer; Agricultural Engineer; Applications Engineer; Assistant Manager; Auditor; Bank Officer/Manager; Blue-Collar Worker Supervisor; Branch Manager; Budget Analyst; Buyer; Ceramics Engineer; Chemical Engineer; Chemist; Chief Financial Officer; Civil Engineer; Clerical Supervisor; Computer Operator; Computer Programmer; Controller; Cost Estimator; Credit Manager; Customer Service Representative; Database Manager; Design Engineer; Draftsperson; Electrical/Electronics Engineer; Environmental Engineer; Finance Director; Financial Analyst; Food Scientist/Technologist; General Manager; Graphic Artist; Graphic Designer; Human Resources Manager; Industrial Engineer; Industrial Production Manager; Internet Services Manager; Manufacturing Engineer; Market Research Analyst; Marketing Manager; Marketing Specialist; Mechanical Engineer; Medical Records Technician; Metallurgical Engineer; MIS Specialist; Operations Manager; Paralegal; Pharmacist; Physical Therapist; Production Manager; Project Manager; Purchasing Agent/Manager; Quality Control Supervisor; Registered Nurse; Sales Engineer; Sales Executive; Sales Manager; Sales Representative; Secretary; Software Engineer; Systems Analyst; Systems Manager; Typist/Word Processor. **Corporate headquarters location:** This Location. **Average salary range of placements:** More than $50,000. **Number of placements per year:** 200 - 499.

QUALITY PLUS
9930 Johnny Cake Ridge Road, Suite 2C, Mentor OH 44060. 440/350-1666. **Fax:** 440/354-4111. **Contact:** Manager. **Description:** An executive search firm operating on a contingency basis. **Specializes in the areas of:** Accounting/Auditing; Engineering; General Management; Manufacturing; Personnel/Labor Relations; Secretarial; Technical; Transportation. **Positions commonly filled include:** Accountant/Auditor; Buyer; Cost Estimator; Design Engineer; Designer; Draftsperson; Electrical/Electronics Engineer; Industrial Engineer; Metallurgical Engineer; Purchasing Agent/Manager; Quality Control Supervisor. **Number of placements per year:** 200 - 499.

QUALITY SOURCE, INC.
14650 Detroit Avenue, Suite 321, Cleveland OH 44107. 216/529-9911. **Contact:** President. **E-mail address:** qeagle@aol.com. **Description:** An executive search firm. **Specializes in the areas of:** Legal; Personnel/Labor Relations; Secretarial. **Positions commonly filled include:** Administrative Manager; Clerical Supervisor; Customer Service Representative; Editor; Human Resources Specialist; Librarian; Paralegal. **Number of placements per year:** 50 - 99.

BILL REBER & ASSOCIATES, INC.
P.O. Box 41690, Dayton OH 45441. 937/433-5400. **Physical address:** 77 West Elmwood Drive, Suite 205, Dayton OH. **Fax:** 937/433-1758. **Contact:** Bill Reber, CPC/President. **E-mail address:** billreber@usa.net. **World Wide Web address:** http://www.billreber.com.

Description: An executive search firm. **Specializes in the areas of:** Accounting/Auditing; Engineering; Manufacturing; Materials; Personnel/Labor Relations; Sales. **Positions commonly filled include:** Human Resources Manager; Inventory Control Specialist; Materials Engineer; Planner; Plant Manager; Purchasing Agent/Manager; Quality Control Supervisor; Safety Engineer.

RECRUITING SERVICES INC.
2367 Auburn Avenue, Cincinnati OH 45219. 513/721-3030. **Contact:** Vice President. **Description:** An executive search firm operating on a contingency basis. **Specializes in the areas of:** Computer Science/Software; Electronics; Network Administration. **Positions commonly filled include:** Computer Programmer; Design Engineer; Software Engineer; Systems Analyst. **Number of placements per year:** 100 - 199.

RECRUITMASTERS OF CINCINNATI
5237 Traverse Court, West Chester OH 45069. 513/860-1717. **Fax:** 513/860-1717. **Contact:** Frank J. Watson, President. **Description:** An executive search firm operating on a contingency basis. **Specializes in the areas of:** Computer Science/Software; Personnel/Labor Relations; Sales. **Positions commonly filled include:** Accountant/Auditor; Computer Programmer; Sales Representative; Systems Analyst. **Average salary range of placements:** $30,000 - $50,000. **Number of placements per year:** 1 - 49.

RESOURCE TECHNE GROUP
9991 Walnutridge Court, Cincinnati OH 45242. 513/793-3121. **Contact:** Cathy Landers, Manager. **Description:** An executive search firm. **Specializes in the areas of:** Engineering; Industrial; Manufacturing; Personnel/Labor Relations. **Positions commonly filled include:** Chemical Engineer; Chemist; Design Engineer; Electrical/Electronics Engineer; Human Resources Specialist; Materials Engineer; Mechanical Engineer; MIS Specialist; Software Engineer; Systems Analyst. **Average salary range of placements:** $30,000 - $50,000.

REVERE ASSOCIATES
P.O. Box 498, Bath OH 44210. 330/666-6442. **Contact:** Manager. **Description:** An executive search firm. **Specializes in the areas of:** Industrial.

ROMAC INTERNATIONAL
525 Vine Street, Suite 2250, Cincinnati OH 45202. 513/651-4044. **Fax:** 513/651-9643. **Contact:** Managing Director. **Description:** An executive search firm operating on a contingency basis. **Specializes in the areas of:** Accounting; Administration; Computer Science/Software; Finance; Health/Medical. **Positions commonly filled include:** Accountant/Auditor; Bank Officer/Manager; Budget Analyst; Clerical Supervisor; Computer Programmer; Cost Estimator; Credit Manager; Customer Service Representative; Financial Analyst; Internet Services Manager; Licensed Practical Nurse; Management Analyst/Consultant; Market Research Analyst; MIS Specialist; Purchasing Agent/Manager; Registered Nurse; Software Engineer; Systems Analyst. **Corporate headquarters location:** Tampa FL. **Other U.S. locations:** Nationwide. **Average salary range of placements:** More than $50,000. **Number of placements per year:** 200 - 499.

ROMAC INTERNATIONAL
3 Summit Park Drive, Suite 550, Independence OH 44131. 216/328-5900. **Fax:** 216/328-5909. **Contact:** Manager. **Description:** An executive search firm. **Specializes in the areas of:** Accounting/Auditing; Computer Hardware/Software; Finance; Information Technology.

ROMAC INTERNATIONAL
1105 Schrock Road, Suite 510, Columbus OH 43229. 614/846-3311. **Fax:** 614/846-4439. **Contact:** Manager. **Description:** An executive search firm. **Specializes in the areas of:** Accounting/Auditing; Computer Hardware/Software; Finance; Information Technology.

ROMAC INTERNATIONAL
One South Main Street, Suite 1440, Dayton OH 45402. 937/461-4660. **Fax:** 937/461-5848. **Contact:** Manager. **Description:** An executive search firm. **Specializes in the areas of:** Accounting/Auditing; Computer Hardware/Software; Finance; Information Technology; Manufacturing.

SJR & ASSOCIATES
24300 Chagrin Boulevard, Suite 214, Cleveland OH 44122. 216/831-5228. **Fax:** 216/991-8436. **Contact:** Scott Riffle, CPC/Owner. **Description:** An executive search firm operating on a contingency basis. **Specializes in the areas of:** Engineering; Manufacturing. **Positions commonly filled include:** Buyer; Ceramics Engineer; Chemical Engineer; Design Engineer; Electrical/Electronics Engineer; General Manager; Industrial Engineer; Materials Engineer; Mechanical Engineer; Metallurgical Engineer; Operations/Production Manager; Purchasing Agent/Manager; Quality Control Supervisor. **Average salary range of placements:** More than $50,000. **Number of placements per year:** 50 - 99.

SACHS ASSOCIATES
509 Liberty Drive, Suite B, Huron OH 44839. 419/433-3837. **Contact:** Scott Sachs, President. **E-mail address:** greatscott@nwonline.net. **Description:** An executive search firm operating on both retainer and contingency bases. **Specializes in the areas of:** Information Technology. **Positions commonly filled include:** Aerospace Engineer; Computer Programmer; Design Engineer; Electrical/Electronics Engineer; Internet Services Manager; Management Analyst/Consultant; MIS Specialist; Sales Executive; Software Engineer; Systems Analyst. **Average salary range of placements:** $30,000 - $50,000. **Number of placements per year:** 1 - 49.

SALES CONSULTANTS OF CINCINNATI
625 Eden Park Drive, Suite 1175, Cincinnati OH 45202. 513/639-3000. **Toll-free phone:** 800/808-0804. **Fax:** 513/639-3001. **Contact:** Rick Phillips, General Manager. **Description:** An executive search firm. **Specializes in the areas of:** Accounting/Auditing; Administration; Advertising; Architecture/Construction; Banking; Communications; Computer Hardware/Software; Construction; Design; Electrical; Engineering; Finance; Food; General Management; Health/Medical; Industrial; Insurance; Manufacturing; Operations Management; Personnel/Labor Relations; Procurement; Publishing; Retail; Sales; Technical; Textiles; Transportation. **Corporate headquarters location:** Cleveland OH. **Other U.S. locations:** Nationwide. **International locations:** Worldwide.

SANFORD ROSE ASSOCIATES
545 North Broad Street, Suite 2, Canfield OH 44406-9204. 330/533-9270. **Fax:** 330/533-9272. **Contact:** Richard H. Ellison, CPC/President. **E-mail address:** ellisor@aol.com. **World Wide Web address:** http://www.sanfordrose.com. **Description:** An executive search firm. Founded in 1970. **Specializes in the areas of:** Administration; Computer Science/Software; Information Systems. **Positions commonly filled include:** Computer Programmer; Internet Services Manager; MIS Specialist; Multimedia Designer; Software Engineer; Systems Analyst; Telecommunications Manager. **Other U.S. locations:** Nationwide. **Average salary range of placements:** More than $50,000. **Number of placements per year:** 50 - 99.

SANFORD ROSE ASSOCIATES
26250 Euclid Avenue, Suite 211, Cleveland OH 44132. 216/731-0005. **Fax:** 216/731-0007. **Contact:** Ralph Orkin, Owner. **World Wide Web address:** http://www.sanfordrose.com. **Description:** An executive search firm operating on a contingency basis. **Specializes in the areas of:** Administration; Computer

Science/Software; Information Systems. **Positions commonly filled include:** Computer Programmer; MIS Specialist; Software Engineer; Systems Analyst. **Other U.S. locations:** Nationwide. **Average salary range of placements:** $30,000 - $50,000. **Number of placements per year:** 1 - 49.

SANFORD ROSE ASSOCIATES
130 Weatherby Lane, Westerville OH 43081. 614/523-1663. **Fax:** 614/523-1689. **Contact:** Bill Earhart, Owner/President. **E-mail address:** bill@sracols.com. **World Wide Web address:** http://www.sracols.com. **Description:** An executive search firm. **Specializes in the areas of:** Administration; Computer Science/Software; Data Processing; Engineering. **Positions commonly filled include:** Computer Programmer; MIS Specialist; Software Engineer; Systems Analyst; Telecommunications Manager. **Other U.S. locations:** Nationwide. **Average salary range of placements:** More than $50,000. **Number of placements per year:** 1 - 49.

SANFORD ROSE ASSOCIATES
265 South Main Street, Akron OH 44308. 330/762-6211. **Fax:** 330/762-6161. **Contact:** Manager. **World Wide Web address:** http://www.sanfordrose.com. **Description:** An executive search firm. **Specializes in the areas of:** Aerospace; Chemicals.

SANFORD ROSE ASSOCIATES
4450 Belden Village Street NW, Suite 209, Canton OH 44718. 330/649-9100. **Contact:** Manager. **World Wide Web address:** http://www.sanfordrose.com. **Description:** An executive search firm. **Specializes in the areas of:** Engineering; General Management; Sales. **Other U.S. locations:** Nationwide.

SANFORD ROSE ASSOCIATES
3040 West Market Street, Fairlawn OH 44333. 330/865-4545. **Contact:** Manager. **World Wide Web address:** http://www.sanfordrose.com. **Description:** An executive search firm. **Specializes in the areas of:** Chemicals; General Management; Marketing; Plastics; Rubber; Sales; Technical. **Other U.S. locations:** Nationwide.

SANFORD ROSE ASSOCIATES
P.O. Box 963, Hudson OH 44236. 330/653-3325. **Contact:** Manager. **World Wide Web address:** http://www.sanfordrose.com. **Description:** An executive search firm. **Specializes in the areas of:** Engineering. **Other U.S. locations:** Nationwide.

SEARCH TECHNOLOGY
P.O. Box 48, Powell OH 43065. 614/761-3383. **Fax:** 614/761-0122. **Contact:** Dennis T. Caron, Principal. **E-mail address:** dcaronmail@aol.com. **Description:** An executive search firm. **NOTE:** The firm requires that candidates have two or more years experience related to large-scale process industries and a degree in engineering. **Specializes in the areas of:** Engineering; Manufacturing. **Positions commonly filled include:** Chemical Engineer; Controls Engineer; Electrical/Electronics Engineer; Instrument Engineer; Process Engineer; Software Engineer. **Average salary range of placements:** More than $50,000. **Number of placements per year:** 1 - 49.

SEARCHMARK MEDICAL
4 Triangle Park Drive, Suite 403, Cincinnati OH 45246. 513/772-7720. **Contact:** Manager. **Description:** An executive search firm that focuses on sales, marketing, and management positions in the health care industry. **Specializes in the areas of:** Health/Medical. **Corporate headquarters location:** This Location. **Other area locations:** Cleveland OH.

SEARCHMARK MEDICAL
7050 Engle Road, Suite 101, Cleveland OH 44130. 440/816-7600. **Contact:** Manager. **Description:** An executive search firm that focuses on sales, marketing, and management positions in the health care industry.

Specializes in the areas of: Health/Medical. **Corporate headquarters location:** Cincinnati OH.

SELECTIVE SEARCH
659 Park Meadow Road, Westerville OH 43081. 614/899-0575. **Contact:** Manager. **Description:** An executive search firm. **Specializes in the areas of:** Plastics; Rubber.

SHAFER JONES ASSOCIATES
P.O. Box 405, Troy OH 45373. 937/335-1885. **Fax:** 937/335-2237. **Contact:** Paul Jones, Owner. **Description:** An executive search firm operating on a contingency basis. Founded in 1992. **Specializes in the areas of:** Accounting/Auditing; Computer Science/Software; Engineering; Finance; Health/Medical; Manufacturing; Personnel/Labor Relations. **Positions commonly filled include:** Accountant/Auditor; Buyer; Computer Programmer; Design Engineer; Electrical/Electronics Engineer; Financial Analyst; Human Resources Specialist; Mechanical Engineer; MIS Specialist; Pharmacist; Purchasing Agent/Manager; Quality Control Supervisor; Software Engineer; Technical Writer/Editor. **Average salary range of placements:** More than $50,000.

SNIDER & ASSOCIATES INC.
6929 West 130th Street, Suite 307, Parma Heights OH 44130. 440/884-1656. **Contact:** Manager. **Description:** An executive search firm. **Specializes in the areas of:** Legal.

SPEER & ASSOCIATES
9624 Cincinnati Columbus Road, Suite 312, Cincinnati OH 45241. 513/777-0200. **Contact:** Manager. **Description:** An executive search firm. **Specializes in the areas of:** Transportation.

STEPHENS ASSOCIATES LTD.
P.O. Box 151114, Columbus OH 43215. 614/469-9990. **Physical address:** 480 South Third Street, 2nd Floor, Columbus OH. **Contact:** Manager. **Description:** A generalist executive search firm.

STERLING PERSONNEL RESOURCES
1129 West Miamisburg Centerville Road, Suite 307, Dayton OH 45449. 937/384-0190. **Contact:** Manager. **Description:** An executive search firm. **Specializes in the areas of:** Accounting/Auditing; Administration; Engineering; Information Systems; Manufacturing.

STRATFORDGROUP
6120 Parkland Boulevard, Cleveland OH 44124. 440/460-3232. **Toll-free phone:** 800/536-4384. **Fax:** 440/460-3230. **Contact:** Recruiter. **E-mail address:** corriemates@stratfordgroup.com. **World Wide Web address:** http://www.stratfordgroup.com. **Description:** An executive search firm operating on a retainer basis. Founded in 1997. **Specializes in the areas of:** Automotive; Consumer Products; Engineering; Entertainment; Finance; Health/Medical; Information Technology; Manufacturing; Nonprofit; Professional; Retail; Telecommunications; Transportation. **Corporate headquarters location:** This Location. **Other area locations:** Dayton OH; Toledo OH. **Other U.S. locations:** San Francisco CA; San Diego CA; Denver CO; Washington DC; Charlotte NC; Research Triangle Park NC; New York NY; Philadelphia PA; Houston TX; Vienna VA; Bellevue WA.

STRATFORDGROUP
445 Byers Road, Dayton OH 45342. 937/859-6797. **Toll-free phone:** 800/536-4384. **Fax:** 937/859-1767. **Contact:** Recruiter. **E-mail address:** corriemates@stratfordgroup.com. **World Wide Web address:** http://www.stratfordgroup.com. **Description:** An executive search firm operating on a retainer basis. **Specializes in the areas of:** Automotive; Consumer Products; Engineering; Entertainment; Finance; Human Resources; Information Technology; Manufacturing; Nonprofit; Professional; Retail; Telecommunications; Transportation. **Corporate headquarters location:**

Cleveland OH. **Other area locations:** Cleveland OH; Toledo OH. **Other U.S. locations:** San Francisco CA; San Diego CA; Denver CO; Washington DC; Charlotte NC; Research Triangle Park NC; New York NY; Philadelphia PA; Houston TX; Vienna VA; Bellevue WA.

STRATFORDGROUP
1760 Manley Road, Toledo OH 43537. 419/893-2400. **Toll-free phone:** 800/536-4384. **Fax:** 419/893-2491. **Contact:** Recruiter. **E-mail address:** corriemates@stratfordgroup.com. **World Wide Web address:** http://www.stratfordgroup.com. **Description:** An executive search firm operating on a retainer basis. Founded in 1997. **Specializes in the areas of:** Automotive; Consumer Products; Engineering; Entertainment; Finance; Health/Medical; Human Resources; Information Technology; Manufacturing; Nonprofit; Professional; Retail; Telecommunications; Transportation. **Corporate headquarters location:** Cleveland OH. **Other area locations:** Cleveland OH; Dayton OH. **Other U.S. locations:** San Francisco CA; San Diego CA; Denver CO; Washington DC; Charlotte NC; Research Triangle Park NC; New York NY; Philadelphia PA; Houston TX; Vienna VA; Bellevue WA.

SUCCESS PERSONNEL
6120 McNaughtan Centre, Columbus OH 43232. 614/221-5125. **Contact:** Manager. **Description:** An executive search firm.

SUTTON ASSOCIATES
1200 Stephens Road, Sidney OH 45365. 937/497-1700. **Contact:** Tom Sutton, Owner. **Description:** An executive search firm operating on a retainer basis. The firm places mid- to upper-level managers.

TABB & ASSOCIATES
1460 West Lane Avenue, Suite 250, Columbus OH 43221. 614/486-8888. **Fax:** 614/486-3950. **Contact:** Roosevelt Tabb, President. **E-mail address:** tabrus@msn.com. **World Wide Web address:** http://www.tabbandassociates.com. **Description:** An executive search firm. **Specializes in the areas of:** Computer Science/Software; Engineering; Food; General Management; Industrial; Insurance; Light Industrial; Marketing; Sales; Scientific; Technical. **Positions commonly filled include:** Applications Engineer; Auditor; Branch Manager; Chemical Engineer; Chief Financial Officer; Computer Programmer; Controller; Database Manager; Finance Director; Financial Analyst; Human Resources Manager; Manufacturing Engineer; Marketing Manager; Mechanical Engineer; Metallurgical Engineer; MIS Specialist; Operations Manager; Project Manager; Quality Control Supervisor; Sales Engineer; Sales Executive; Sales Manager; Software Engineer; Systems Analyst; Systems Manager. **Average salary range of placements:** More than $50,000. **Number of placements per year:** 1 - 49.

TALENT RESEARCH CORPORATION
P.O. Box 36214, Cincinnati OH 45236. 513/242-4100. **Fax:** 513/641-0204. **Contact:** Robert Wick, President. **Description:** An executive search firm operating on a contingency basis. Founded in 1962. **Specializes in the areas of:** Engineering; Manufacturing; Technical. **Positions commonly filled include:** Aerospace Engineer; Agricultural Engineer; Ceramics Engineer; Chemical Engineer; Computer Programmer; Design Engineer; Electrical/Electronics Engineer; Industrial Engineer; Materials Engineer; Mechanical Engineer; MIS Specialist; Petroleum Engineer; Quality Control Supervisor; Software Engineer; Systems Analyst. **Average salary range of placements:** $30,000 - $50,000. **Number of placements per year:** 50 - 99.

TECHNICAL RECRUITING SERVICES
9769 Chaucer Court, Pickerington OH 43147. 614/837-6556. **Contact:** President. **Description:** An executive search firm. **Specializes in the areas of:** Engineering; General Management; Industrial; Manufacturing;

Technical. **Positions commonly filled include:** Electrical/Electronics Engineer; Industrial Engineer; Manufacturer's/Wholesaler's Sales Rep.; Mechanical Engineer. **Number of placements per year:** 50 - 99.

TECHNICAL SEARCH ASSOCIATES
20325 Center Ridge Road, Suite 622, Cleveland OH 44116. 440/356-0880. **Fax:** 440/356-9036. **Contact:** Director. **Description:** Technical Search Associates is an executive search firm. **Specializes in the areas of:** Engineering; Manufacturing. **Positions commonly filled include:** Aerospace Engineer; Electrical/Electronics Engineer; Mechanical Engineer; Software Engineer; Structural Engineer. **Number of placements per year:** 1 - 49.

TEKNON EMPLOYMENT RESOURCES, INC.
17 South St. Clair Street, Suite 300, Dayton OH 45402-2137. 937/222-5300. **Fax:** 937/222-6311. **Contact:** Bill Gaffney, Vice President of Recruiting. **Description:** An executive search firm operating on both retainer and contingency bases. **Specializes in the areas of:** Computer Science/Software; Data Communications; Engineering; Telecommunications. **Positions commonly filled include:** Branch Manager; Design Engineer; Electrical/Electronics Engineer; General Manager; Mechanical Engineer; Product Manager; Sales Engineer; Sales Executive. **Corporate headquarters location:** This Location. **Average salary range of placements:** More than $50,000. **Number of placements per year:** 50 - 99.

FRED C. TIPPEL AND ASSOCIATES
105 Shawnee Drive, Marietta OH 45750. 740/374-3288. **Fax:** 740/374-3294. **Contact:** Fred C. Tippel, Owner/Director. **E-mail address:** tipcruit@wirefire.com. **Description:** An executive search firm operating on both contingency and retainer bases. **Specializes in the areas of:** Engineering; General Management; Manufacturing; Plastics; Technical. **Positions commonly filled include:** Chemical Engineer; Chemist; Design Engineer; Electrical/Electronics Engineer; Environmental Engineer; General Manager; Industrial Engineer; Operations/Production Manager. **Number of placements per year:** 1 - 49.

TRUE NORTH CONSULTANTS
35590 Center Ridge Road, Suite 206, North Ridgeville OH 44039. 440/353-3050. **Fax:** 440/353-3171. **Contact:** Recruiter. **E-mail address:** info@truenorthconsultants.com. **World Wide Web address:** http://www.truenorthconsultants.com. **Description:** True North Consultants is an executive search firm. **Specializes in the areas of:** Information Systems; Information Technology.

TULLY WOODMANSEE INTERNATIONAL
7720 Rivers Edge Drive, Columbus OH 43235. 614/844-5480. **Contact:** Manager. **Description:** A generalist executive search firm for upper-level professionals. **Average salary range of placements:** More than $50,000.

WRS, LTD.
6329 Montgomery Road, Cincinnati OH 45213. 513/631-9888. **Fax:** 513/631-4443. **Contact:** Manager. **Description:** An executive search firm operating on a contingency basis. **Specializes in the areas of:** Computer Science/Software; Information Technology. **Positions commonly filled include:** Computer Programmer; Internet Services Manager; Systems Analyst. **Average salary range of placements:** $30,000 - $50,000. **Number of placements per year:** 50 - 99.

J.P. WALTON & ASSOCIATES
9601 Dorothy Avenue, Cleveland OH 44125. 216/883-4141. **Fax:** 216/883-5717. **Contact:** Patrick Walton, Owner. **Description:** An executive search firm that focuses on providing placements in the corrugated containers and folding carton industries. **Specializes in the areas of:** Accounting/Auditing; Administration; Art/Design; Engineering; General Management;

Industrial; Manufacturing; Sales. **Positions commonly filled include:** Accountant/Auditor; Administrative Manager; Blue-Collar Worker Supervisor; Computer Programmer; Customer Service Representative; General Manager; Industrial Engineer; Industrial Production Manager; Management Trainee; Manufacturer's/Wholesaler's Sales Rep.; Mechanical Engineer; MIS Specialist; Purchasing Agent/Manager; Quality Control Supervisor; Services Sales Representative; Systems Analyst. **Number of placements per year:** 1 - 49.

R. WEGESIN & ASSOCIATES
P.O. Box 721, Dublin OH 43017. 614/798-0431. **Contact:** Manager. **Description:** An executive search firm. **Specializes in the areas of:** Manufacturing.

WORLD SEARCH
4130 Linden Avenue, Claypool Building, Suite 125, Dayton OH 45432. 937/254-9071. **Fax:** 937/254-0229. **Contact:** Manager. **Description:** An executive search firm. **Specializes in the areas of:** Engineering.

PERMANENT EMPLOYMENT AGENCIES

ALL STAR PERSONNEL, INC.
21625 Chagrin Boulevard, Suite 260, Beachwood OH 44122. 216/991-7827. **Fax:** 216/991-3704. **Contact:** Joyce Goodman, CPC/President. **E-mail address:** info@a1jobs.com. **World Wide Web address:** http://www.a1jobs.com. **Description:** A permanent employment agency that also provides some temporary placements. **Specializes in the areas of:** Accounting; Administration; Computer Science/Software. **Positions commonly filled include:** Accounting Clerk; Administrative Assistant; Computer Programmer; CPA; Customer Service Representative; Financial Analyst; MIS Specialist; Network Administrator; Receptionist; Secretary; Securities Sales Representative; Staff Accountant; Systems Analyst; Typist/Word Processor. **Number of placements per year:** 50 - 99.

AMERICAN BUSINESS PERSONNEL SERVICES, INC.
11499 Chester Road, Suite 701, Cincinnati OH 45246. 513/772-1200. **Fax:** 513/326-2278. **Contact:** Bruce Menefield, Office Manager. **Description:** A permanent employment agency. **Specializes in the areas of:** Computer Hardware/Software; Computer Programming; Computer Science/Software; Engineering. **Positions commonly filled include:** Computer Programmer; Engineer; Systems Analyst; Technical Support Representative. **Average salary range of placements:** $30,000 - $50,000. **Number of placements per year:** 1000+.

RICHARD L. BENCIN & ASSOCIATES
8553 Timber Trail, Brecksville OH 44141. 440/526-6726. **Contact:** Richard Bencin, President. **Description:** A permanent employment agency that places personnel in call centers. **Specializes in the areas of:** Direct Marketing; Telemarketing.

N.L. BENKE & ASSOCIATES, INC.
1422 Euclid Avenue, Suite 956, Cleveland OH 44115. 216/771-6822. **Contact:** Norman L. Benke, President. **Description:** A permanent employment agency. **Specializes in the areas of:** Accounting/Auditing; Banking; Computer Science/Software; Finance; Insurance; Personnel/Labor Relations. **Positions commonly filled include:** Accountant/Auditor; Adjuster; Administrative Manager; Attorney; Bank Officer/Manager; Branch Manager; Budget Analyst; Buyer; Chief Financial Officer; Clerical Supervisor; Computer Programmer; Controller; Credit Manager; Customer Service Representative; Database Manager; Economist; Finance Director; Financial Analyst; General Manager; Human Resources Manager; Internet Services Manager; Management Analyst/Consultant; Management Trainee; MIS Specialist; Property and Real Estate Manager; Purchasing Agent/Manager; Quality Control Supervisor; Securities Sales Representative; Software Engineer; Systems Analyst; Underwriter/Assistant Underwriter. **Number of placements per year:** 200 - 499.

BRADLEY-PIERCE PERSONNEL
1392 Warren Road, Cleveland OH 44107. 216/521-0032. **Fax:** 216/521-0032. **Contact:** Recruiter. **Description:** A permanent employment agency. **Specializes in the areas of:** Accounting/Auditing; Banking; Engineering; Finance; Manufacturing; Personnel/Labor Relations.

Positions commonly filled include: Accountant/Auditor; Administrative Manager; Bank Officer/Manager; Branch Manager; Chemical Engineer; Chemist; Credit Manager; Customer Service Representative; Electrical/Electronics Engineer; General Manager; Human Resources Specialist; Industrial Engineer; Management Trainee; Manufacturer's/Wholesaler's Sales Rep.; Mechanical Engineer.

CBS PERSONNEL SERVICES
435 Elm Street, Suite 300, Cincinnati OH 45202. 513/651-1111. **Fax:** 513/651-3052. **Contact:** Manager. **Description:** A permanent employment agency that also provides some temporary and contract placements and career/outplacement counseling. **Specializes in the areas of:** Accounting/Auditing; Administration; Banking; Bookkeeping; Clerical; Computer Science/Software; Engineering; Finance; General Management; Health/Medical; Industrial; Manufacturing; Personnel/Labor Relations; Retail; Sales; Secretarial; Technical; Transportation. **Positions commonly filled include:** Accountant/Auditor; Actuary; Adjuster; Administrative Manager; Advertising Clerk; Bank Officer/Manager; Blue-Collar Worker Supervisor; Branch Manager; Budget Analyst; Chemical Engineer; Civil Engineer; Claim Representative; Clerical Supervisor; Clinical Lab Technician; Computer Programmer; Counselor; Credit Manager; Customer Service Representative; Dental Assistant/Dental Hygienist; Design Engineer; Designer; Dietician/Nutritionist; Draftsperson; Economist; EEG Technologist; EKG Technician; Electrical/Electronics Engineer; Emergency Medical Technician; Financial Analyst; Food Scientist/Technologist; General Manager; Health Services Manager; Human Resources Specialist; Industrial Engineer; Industrial Production Manager; Internet Services Manager; Licensed Practical Nurse; Management Analyst/Consultant; Management Trainee; Manufacturer's/Wholesaler's Sales Rep.; Market Research Analyst; Mechanical Engineer; Medical Records Technician; MIS Specialist; Multimedia Designer; Occupational Therapist; Operations/Production Manager; Physical Therapist; Property and Real Estate Manager; Public Relations Specialist; Purchasing Agent/Manager; Quality Control Supervisor; Radiological Technologist; Recreational Therapist; Registered Nurse; Respiratory Therapist; Science Technologist; Securities Sales Representative; Services Sales Representative; Software Engineer; Strategic Relations Manager; Structural Engineer; Surgical Technician; Systems Analyst; Technical Writer/Editor; Telecommunications Manager; Typist/Word Processor. **Benefits available to temporary workers:** Medical Insurance. **Other U.S. locations:** IN; KY.

CBS PERSONNEL SERVICES
130 West Second Street, Suite 1910, Dayton OH 45402. 937/222-2525. **Contact:** Robert L. Brown, CPC/President. **Description:** A permanent employment agency. **Specializes in the areas of:** Clerical; Computer Science/Software; Finance; Office Support.

CHAMPION PERSONNEL SYSTEM, INC.
668 Euclid Avenue, Suite 300A, Cleveland OH 44114. 216/781-5900. **Fax:** 216/781-8786. **Contact:** Robert Schepens, President. **E-mail address:** employu@aol.com. **Description:** A permanent employment agency that also provides some temporary placements.

Specializes in the areas of: Accounting/Auditing; Administration; Advertising; Bookkeeping; Broadcasting; Clerical; Finance; Health/Medical; Personnel/Labor Relations; Publishing; Secretarial; Word Processing. **Positions commonly filled include:** Accountant/Auditor; Bookkeeper; Budget Analyst; Clerical Supervisor; Credit Manager; Customer Service Representative; Financial Analyst; Human Resources Specialist; Office Manager; Tax Specialist; Typist/Word Processor. **Benefits available to temporary workers:** Bonus Award/Plan; Paid Vacation. **Other area locations:** Beachwood OH. **Number of placements per year:** 1000+.

CLOPTON'S PLACEMENT SERVICE
23241 Shurmer Drive, Cleveland OH 44128-4927. 216/292-4830. **Fax:** 216/292-4830. **Contact:** Fred Clopton, President. **Description:** A permanent employment agency. **Specializes in the areas of:** Computer Science/Software; Engineering; Technical. **Positions commonly filled include:** Biomedical Engineer; Electrical/Electronics Engineer; Mechanical Engineer; Quality Control Supervisor; Software Engineer; Systems Analyst; Technical Writer/Editor. **Number of placements per year:** 1 - 49.

CORELL ASSOCIATES
5017 Cooper Road, Cincinnati OH 45242. 513/793-9808. **Fax:** 513/793-9304. **Contact:** Ed Corell, Owner. **Description:** A permanent employment agency. **Specializes in the areas of:** Accounting/Auditing; Engineering; Industrial; Manufacturing; Technical. **Positions commonly filled include:** Accountant/Auditor; Actuary; Adjuster; Aerospace Engineer; Agricultural Engineer; Biological Scientist; Biomedical Engineer; Blue-Collar Worker Supervisor; Buyer; Ceramics Engineer; Chemical Engineer; Chemist; Civil Engineer; Collector; Computer Programmer; Designer; Draftsperson; Electrical/Electronics Engineer; Financial Analyst; Human Resources Manager; Industrial Engineer; Industrial Production Manager; Investigator; Management Trainee; Materials Engineer; Mechanical Engineer; Metallurgical Engineer; Mining Engineer; Nuclear Engineer; Petroleum Engineer; Purchasing Agent/Manager; Quality Control Supervisor; Science Technologist; Software Engineer; Stationary Engineer; Structural Engineer; Systems Analyst; Travel Agent. **Number of placements per year:** 1 - 49.

CORPORATE DIRECTIONS GROUP
P.O. Box 2051, Sheffield Lake OH 44054. 440/949-1503. **Fax:** 440/949-1504. **Contact:** Connie Dobrow, Senior Partner. **Description:** A permanent employment agency. **Specializes in the areas of:** Sales. **Number of placements per year:** 50 - 99.

ALAN N. DAUM & ASSOCIATES
6241 Riverside Drive, Dublin OH 43017. 614/793-1200. **Contact:** Alan N. Daum, President. **E-mail address:** al@adaum.com. **Description:** A permanent employment agency. The firm places process control engineers primarily in the process industries. **Specializes in the areas of:** Computer Hardware/Software; Engineering; Food; Manufacturing; Technical. **Positions commonly filled include:** Computer Programmer; Electrical/Electronics Engineer; Software Engineer. **Number of placements per year:** 1 - 49.

DENTAL PERSONNEL PLACEMENT SERVICE
4857 Westerville Run Drive, Columbus OH 43230. 614/471-1220. **Contact:** Tracy Brown, Owner. **E-mail address:** tbrown@netset.com. **Description:** A permanent employment agency that also provides temporary placements for dental assistants, dentists, hygienists, and front desk personnel. **Average salary range of placements:** $30,000 - $50,000. **Number of placements per year:** 200 - 499.

EASTERN PERSONNEL SERVICES INC.
326 West Fourth Street, Cincinnati OH 45202. 513/421-4666. **Contact:** Angelita M. Jones, Manager. **Description:** A permanent employment agency that also

provides some temporary and contract placements. **Specializes in the areas of:** Accounting/Auditing; Administration; Advertising; Architecture/Construction; Banking; Computer Science/Software; Engineering; Finance; Food; Industrial; Insurance; Manufacturing; Nonprofit; Personnel/Labor Relations; Retail; Sales; Secretarial; Technical; Transportation. **Positions commonly filled include:** Accountant/Auditor; Administrative Manager; Advertising Clerk; Architect; Bank Officer/Manager; Blue-Collar Worker Supervisor; Buyer; Civil Engineer; Clerical Supervisor; Clinical Lab Technician; Computer Programmer; Counselor; Credit Manager; Customer Service Representative; Design Engineer; Designer; Electrical/Electronics Engineer; Electrician; Environmental Engineer; Financial Analyst; General Manager; Human Resources Specialist; Human Service Worker; Industrial Engineer; Industrial Production Manager; Mechanical Engineer; MIS Specialist; Operations/Production Manager; Purchasing Agent/Manager; Quality Control Supervisor; Restaurant/Food Service Manager; Social Worker; Software Engineer; Stationary Engineer; Structural Engineer; Systems Analyst; Telecommunications Manager; Typist/Word Processor. **Average salary range of placements:** $20,000 - $75,000. **Number of placements per year:** 200 - 499.

ELITE PERSONNEL AGENCY
940 Terminal Tower, Cleveland OH 44113. 216/771-7810. **Fax:** 216/348-7085. **Contact:** Recruiter. **Description:** A permanent employment agency. **Specializes in the areas of:** Legal; Secretarial. **Average salary range of placements:** $20,000 - $29,999. **Number of placements per year:** 100 - 199.

ENTERPRISE SEARCH ASSOCIATES
77 West Elmwood Drive, Suite 117, Dayton OH 45459. 937/438-8774. **Contact:** Jeff Linck, Owner. **Description:** A permanent employment agency. **Specializes in the areas of:** Administration; Computer Hardware/Software. **Positions commonly filled include:** Computer Programmer; EDP Specialist; MIS Specialist; Software Engineer; Systems Analyst.

EXACT PERSONNEL SPECIALISTS
Terminal Tower, Suite 820, Cleveland OH 44113. 216/736-4800. **Fax:** 216/696-5825. **Contact:** Linda Stevens, CPC/Executive Director. **Description:** A permanent employment agency focusing on the placement of office support personnel in corporate and legal communities. **Specializes in the areas of:** Accounting/Auditing; Legal; Secretarial. **Positions commonly filled include:** Administrative Assistant; Attorney; Executive Assistant; Human Resources Specialist; Legal Secretary; Management Trainee; Paralegal; Typist/Word Processor. **Average salary range of placements:** $20,000 - $29,999. **Number of placements per year:** 200 - 499.

FWC CONSULTANTS
5755 Grainger Road, Suite 760, Independence OH 44131. 216/351-3930. **Fax:** 216/351-0504. **Contact:** Manager. **Description:** A permanent employment agency that also offers contract placements. **Specializes in the areas of:** Software Development.

GRADUATE CONSULTANTS
16600 Sprague Road, Suite 380, Middleburg Heights OH 44130. 440/891-6800. **Contact:** Bob Satullo, Owner. **Description:** A permanent employment agency focusing on the placement of recent college graduates. **Specializes in the areas of:** Banking; Finance; Food; Retail. **Positions commonly filled include:** Bank Officer/Manager; Branch Manager; Claim Representative; Management Trainee; Restaurant/Food Service Manager. **Average salary range of placements:** $20,000 - $29,999. **Number of placements per year:** 100 - 199.

DONALD A. HECKAMAN & ASSOCIATES INC.
23210 Chagrin Boulevard, Suite 201, Beachwood OH 44122. 216/591-1400. **Contact:** Manager. **Description:**

A permanent employment agency that provides placements ranging from entry-level to mid-management.

RICHARD JOHNS CAREER CONSULTANTS
26949 Chagrin Boulevard, Suite 202, Cleveland OH 44122. 216/464-2912. **Fax:** 216/464-0927. **Contact:** Richard Johns, CPC/President. **Description:** A permanent employment agency. **Specializes in the areas of:** Accounting/Auditing; Banking; Film Production; Hotel/Restaurant; Retail.

ANNE JONES STAFFING, INC.
571 High Street, Worthington OH 43085-4132. 614/848-6033. **Toll-free phone:** 800/WIL-WORK. **Fax:** 614/848-6016. **Contact:** Sheila A. Jones, President. **Description:** A permanent employment agency that also provides some temporary placements. **Specializes in the areas of:** Health/Medical; Industrial; Secretarial. **Positions commonly filled include:** Administrative Assistant; Bookkeeper; Clerk; Customer Service Representative; Dietician/Nutritionist; Medical Secretary; Nurse; Office Manager; Receptionist; Secretary; Typist/Word Processor.

R.E. LOWE ASSOCIATES, INC.
8080 Ravines Edge Court, Worthington OH 43235. 614/436-6650. **Fax:** 614/848-8033. **Contact:** Dave Deringer, Recruiter. **Description:** A permanent employment agency. **Specializes in the areas of:** Accounting/Auditing; Computer Science/Software; Engineering; Finance; Health/Medical; Insurance. **Positions commonly filled include:** Accountant/Auditor; Budget Analyst; Chemical Engineer; Claim Representative; Consultant; Credit Manager; Data Analyst; EDP Specialist; Electrical/Electronics Engineer; Environmental Engineer; Financial Analyst; Industrial Engineer; Manufacturing Engineer; Nurse; Packaging Engineer; Physician; Tax Specialist; Underwriter/Assistant Underwriter; Water/Wastewater Engineer. **Number of placements per year:** 200 - 499.

MASTERSON PERSONNEL, INC.
MASTERSON TEMPORARY SERVICES
705 Central Avenue, Suite 340, Cincinnati OH 45202. 513/381-3400. **Fax:** 513/381-3401. **Contact:** Liz Timmeras, Branch Manager. **Description:** A permanent employment agency. Masterson Temporary Services (also at this location) provides temporary placements. Founded in 1969. **Specializes in the areas of:** Accounting; Administration; General Management; Industrial; Legal; Light Industrial; Secretarial. **Positions commonly filled include:** Account Manager; Account Representative; Administrative Assistant; Administrative Manager; Assistant Manager; Branch Manager; Customer Service Representative; Database Manager; Human Resources Manager; Production Manager; Secretary; Typist/Word Processor. **Average salary range of placements:** $20,000 - $29,999. **Number of placements per year:** 200 - 499.

MEDSEARCH STAFFING SERVICES INC.
7271 Engle Road, Corporate Suite 115, Middleburg Heights OH 44130. 440/243-6363. **Contact:** Ralph E. Steeber, CPC/President. **E-mail address:** rsteeber@medstaffing.com. **World Wide Web address:** http://www.medstaffing.com. **Description:** A permanent employment agency. **Specializes in the areas of:** Health/Medical. **Positions commonly filled include:** Marketing Specialist; Medical Secretary; Occupational Therapist; Pharmacist; Physical Therapist; Physician; Psychologist; Respiratory Therapist; Sales Manager; Sales Representative; Surgical Technician. **Number of placements per year:** 100 - 199.

OHIO BUREAU OF EMPLOYMENT SERVICES
P.O. Box 398, Marysville OH 43040-0398. 937/644-9195. **Fax:** 937/642-1129. **Contact:** Karen Jordan, Manager. **Description:** A permanent employment agency and state unemployment office. **Positions commonly filled include:** Administrative Assistant; Bookkeeper; Clerk; Construction Trade Worker; Customer Service Representative; Data Entry Clerk; Electrical/Electronics Engineer; Factory Worker; Legal Secretary; Light Industrial Worker; Mechanical Engineer; Medical Secretary; Purchasing Agent/Manager; Quality Control Supervisor; Receptionist; Secretary; Typist/Word Processor. **Number of placements per year:** 500 - 999.

OPRANDI STAFFING
15 West Locust Street, Newark OH 43055. 740/345-9783. **Contact:** Manager. **Description:** A permanent employment agency that also provides temporary placements and executive searches.

JERRY PAUL ASSOCIATES
1662 State Road, Cuyahoga Falls OH 44223. 330/923-2345. **Contact:** Jerry Paul, President. **Description:** A permanent employment agency. **Specializes in the areas of:** Administration; Banking; Computer Hardware/Software; Hotel/Restaurant; Sales. **Positions commonly filled include:** Hotel Manager; Restaurant/Food Service Manager; Sales Representative. **Number of placements per year:** 50 - 99.

PROFESSIONAL DOMESTIC SERVICES
6660 Doubletree Avenue, Suite 10, Columbus OH 43229. **Contact:** Gay Metz. **World Wide Web address:** http://www.professionaldomestics.com. **Description:** A permanent employment agency that places household professionals including butlers, chefs, personal assistants, nannies, and household managers. Client company pays fee. **Positions commonly filled include:** Chef/Cook/Kitchen Worker; Nanny; Teacher/Professor. **Average salary range of placements:** $20,000 - $70,000.

PROFESSIONAL EMPLOYMENT SERVICES
3975 Everhard Road NW, Canton OH 44709. 330/966-2277. **Fax:** 330/966-2419. **Contact:** Audrey H. Stull, Vice President/Owner. **Description:** A permanent employment agency. Founded in 1992. **Specializes in the areas of:** Health/Medical; Industrial; Legal; Manufacturing; Marketing; Non-Specialized; Sales; Scientific; Technical. **Positions commonly filled include:** Accountant/Auditor; Blue-Collar Worker Supervisor; Clinical Lab Technician; Computer Programmer; Dental Assistant/Dental Hygienist; Draftsperson; General Manager; Industrial Production Manager; Management Trainee; Typist/Word Processor. **Benefits available to temporary workers:** Paid Holidays; Paid Vacation. **Corporate headquarters location:** Akron OH. **Other area locations:** Barberton OH; Streetsboro OH. **Number of placements per year:** 1000+.

PROFESSIONAL RESTAFFING OF OHIO, INC.
373 North Washington Street, Tiffin OH 44883. 419/447-3465. **Contact:** Recruiter. **Description:** A permanent employment agency. **Specializes in the areas of:** Accounting/Auditing; Engineering; Food; Industrial; Manufacturing; Personnel/Labor Relations; Sales; Secretarial. **Positions commonly filled include:** Accountant/Auditor; Administrative Manager; Blue-Collar Worker Supervisor; Clerical Supervisor; Computer Programmer; Customer Service Representative; Design Engineer; Draftsperson; Occupational Therapist; Paralegal; Physical Therapist; Services Sales Representative; Systems Analyst; Typist/Word Processor. **Benefits available to temporary workers:** Paid Vacation. **Number of placements per year:** 200 - 499.

QUALITY ASSOCIATES INC.
4921 Para Drive, Cincinnati OH 45237. 513/242-4477. **Contact:** Manager. **Description:** A permanent employment agency.

THE RESERVES NETWORK
2525 Maple Avenue, Zanesville OH 43701. 740/453-0326. **Contact:** Manager. **Description:** A permanent employment agency. **Specializes in the areas of:** Manufacturing; Mining. **Positions commonly filled include:** Accountant/Auditor; Bookkeeper; Buyer;

Ceramics Engineer; Chemical Engineer; Chemist; Civil Engineer; Clerk; Computer Operator; Computer Programmer; Data Entry Clerk; Draftsperson; EDP Specialist; Electrical/Electronics Engineer; Industrial Engineer; Legal Secretary; Mechanical Engineer; Medical Secretary; Metallurgical Engineer; Mining Engineer; Office Manager; Operations/Production Manager; Purchasing Agent/Manager; Quality Control Supervisor; Receptionist; Sales Representative; Secretary; Stenographer; Systems Analyst; Technical Writer/Editor; Technician; Typist/Word Processor. **Number of placements per year:** 50 - 99.

SELECTIVE SEARCH ASSOCIATES
1206 North Main Street, Suite 112, North Canton OH 44720. 330/494-5584. **Fax:** 330/494-8911. **Contact:** Michael E. Ziarko, President. **Description:** A permanent employment agency. **Specializes in the areas of:** Computer Science/Software; Engineering. **Positions commonly filled include:** Computer Programmer; Electrical/Electronics Engineer; Mechanical Engineer; Software Engineer; Systems Analyst. **Number of placements per year:** 1 - 49.

TECH/AID OF OHIO
34600 Chardon Road, Willoughby Hills OH 44094. 440/944-9672. **Contact:** Manager. **Description:** A permanent employment agency. **Specializes in the areas of:** Accounting/Auditing; Banking; Computer Hardware/Software; Engineering; Finance; Insurance; Manufacturing; MIS/EDP; Nonprofit; Personnel/Labor Relations; Publishing; Technical. **Positions commonly filled include:** Computer Operator; Computer Programmer; EDP Specialist; MIS Specialist; Systems Analyst; Technical Writer/Editor. **Number of placements per year:** 1000+.

TECHNICAL/MANAGEMENT RESOURCES
P.O. Box 467, Pickerington OH 43147. 614/837-8888. **Fax:** 614/837-9718. **Contact:** President. **E-mail address:** techmgmtr@sprintmail.com. **Description:** A permanent employment agency. **Specializes in the areas of:** Engineering; Industrial. **Positions commonly filled**

include: Electrical/Electronics Engineer; General Manager; Industrial Engineer; Manufacturing Engineer; Mechanical Engineer; Operations Manager; Production Manager; Project Manager. **Average salary range of placements:** More than $50,000. **Number of placements per year:** 1 - 49.

VECTOR TECHNICAL INC.
7911 Enterprise Drive, 2nd Floor, Mentor OH 44060. 440/946-8800. **Fax:** 440/946-8808. **Contact:** Manager. **E-mail address:** vectortech@buckeyeweb.com. **World Wide Web address:** http://www.vectortechnicalinc.com. **Description:** A permanent employment agency that also offers temporary and contract placements. **Specializes in the areas of:** Biology; Computer Science/Software; Engineering; Industrial; Manufacturing; Technical. **Positions commonly filled include:** Aerospace Engineer; Agricultural Engineer; Architect; Biological Scientist; Biomedical Engineer; Blue-Collar Worker Supervisor; Ceramics Engineer; Chemical Engineer; Chemist; Civil Engineer; Computer Programmer; Cost Estimator; Designer; Draftsperson; Electrical/Electronics Engineer; Electrician; Industrial Engineer; Industrial Production Manager; Materials Engineer; Mechanical Engineer; Metallurgical Engineer; Mining Engineer; Nuclear Engineer; Operations/Production Manager; Petroleum Engineer; Software Engineer; Stationary Engineer; Structural Engineer; Systems Analyst. **Number of placements per year:** 200 - 499.

WARNER & ASSOCIATES, INC.
101 East College Avenue, Westerville OH 43081. 614/891-9003. **Fax:** 614/890-8405. **Contact:** Tom Warner, President. **Description:** A permanent employment agency. **Specializes in the areas of:** Engineering; Manufacturing; Materials. **Positions commonly filled include:** Chemical Engineer; Civil Engineer; Electrical/Electronics Engineer; Environmental Engineer; Industrial Engineer; Inventory Control Specialist; Manufacturing Engineer; Mechanical Engineer; Nuclear Engineer; Packaging Engineer; Plant Manager; Purchasing Agent/Manager; Quality Control Supervisor; Water/Wastewater Engineer.

TEMPORARY EMPLOYMENT AGENCIES

ACCUSTAFF
1014 Vine Street, Suite 1650, Cincinnati OH 45202. 513/241-4222. **Fax:** 513/241-5294. **Contact:** Manager. **Description:** A temporary agency. **Specializes in the areas of:** Administration; Banking; Computer Science/Software; Industrial; Legal; Manufacturing; Personnel/Labor Relations; Publishing; Secretarial. **Positions commonly filled include:** Attorney; Bank Officer/Manager; Blue-Collar Worker Supervisor; Branch Manager; Claim Representative; Clerical Supervisor; Computer Programmer; Credit Manager; Customer Service Representative; Dietician/Nutritionist; Draftsperson; Editor; Financial Analyst; General Manager; Human Resources Specialist; Human Service Worker; Management Trainee; Manufacturer's/Wholesaler's Sales Rep.; MIS Specialist; Operations/Production Manager; Paralegal; Pharmacist; Property and Real Estate Manager; Public Relations Manager; Purchasing Agent/Manager; Quality Control Supervisor; Restaurant/Food Service Manager; Services Sales Representative; Systems Analyst; Typist/Word Processor; Underwriter/Assistant Underwriter. **Average salary range of placements:** $20,000 - $29,999. **Number of placements per year:** 1 - 49.

ADECCO
3655 Soldano Boulevard, Columbus OH 43228. 614/279-6614. **Contact:** Manager. **Description:** A temporary agency. **Specializes in the areas of:** Clerical; Construction; Food; Personnel. **Positions commonly filled include:** Computer Operator; Computer Programmer; Construction Trade Worker; Data Entry Clerk; Draftsperson; Driver; Factory Worker; Food Scientist; Food Service Manager; Light Industrial

Worker; Office Manager; Operations Manager; Quality Control Supervisor; Receptionist; Typist/Word Processor. **Number of placements per year:** 500 - 999.

ADECCO
580 Walnut Street, Plaza Level, Cincinnati OH 45202-3110. 513/241-2342. **Contact:** Vonda Baldwin, Service Manager. **Description:** A temporary agency that also provides some permanent placements. **Specializes in the areas of:** Administration; Advertising; Banking; Data Processing; Finance; General Management; Insurance; Legal; Manufacturing; Nonprofit; Personnel/Labor Relations; Sales; Secretarial; Transportation. **Positions commonly filled include:** Accountant/Auditor; Administrative Assistant; Administrative Manager; Advertising Clerk; Bank Officer/Manager; Branch Manager; Brokerage Clerk; Budget Analyst; Buyer; Claim Rep.; Clerical Supervisor; Cost Estimator; Counselor; Credit Manager; Customer Service Rep.; Data Entry Clerk; Editor; General Manager; Health Services Manager; Human Resources Specialist; Management Trainee; Market Research Analyst; Operations/Production Manager; Paralegal; Public Relations Specialist; Purchasing Agent/Manager; Quality Control Supervisor; Secretary; Strategic Relations Manager; Telecommunications Manager; Transportation/Traffic Specialist; Typist/Word Processor; Underwriter. **Benefits available to temporary workers:** Medical Insurance; Paid Holidays; Paid Vacation; Referral Bonus Plan. **Other U.S. locations:** Nationwide.

AQUENT PARTNERS
2 Summit Park Drive, Suite 615, Independence OH 44131-2553. 216/642-9909. **Toll-free phone:**

877/PARTNER. Fax: 216/642-5530. **Contact:** Sue English, Manager. **E-mail address:** senglish@aquent.com. **World Wide Web address:** http://www.aquentpartners.com. **Description:** A temporary agency that provides placements for creative, Web, and technical professionals. Aquent Partners also provides some temp-to-perm, permanent, and contract placements. **Specializes in the areas of:** Administration; Art/Design; Computer Science/Software; Marketing. **Positions commonly filled include:** Computer Animator; Computer Engineer; Computer Operator; Computer Programmer; Computer Support Technician; Computer Technician; Content Developer; Database Administrator; Database Manager; Desktop Publishing Specialist; Editor; Editorial Assistant; Graphic Artist; Graphic Designer; Internet Services Manager; Managing Editor; MIS Specialist; Multimedia Designer; Network/Systems Administrator; Production Manager; Project Manager; Software Engineer; SQL Programmer; Systems Analyst; Systems Manager; Technical Writer/Editor; Webmaster. **Benefits available to temporary workers:** 401(k); Dental Insurance; Disability Coverage; Medical Insurance. **CEO:** John Chuang.

BELCAN STAFFING SERVICES
425 Walnut Street, Suite 200, Cincinnati OH 45202. 513/241-8367. **Contact:** Recruiter. **Description:** A temporary agency that also provides some temp-to-perm placements. **Specializes in the areas of:** Clerical; Data Processing; General Labor; Health/Medical; Light Industrial; Professional; Secretarial; Word Processing. **Positions commonly filled include:** Accountant/Auditor; Blue-Collar Worker Supervisor; Claim Representative; Credit Manager; Customer Service Representative; Financial Analyst; Health Services Manager; Human Resources Specialist; Management Trainee; Medical Records Technician; Services Sales Representative. **Benefits available to temporary workers:** 401(k); Medical Insurance; Paid Holidays; Paid Vacation; Referral Bonus Plan. **Other area locations:** Fairfield OH; Kenwood OH. **Other U.S. locations:** Florence KY; Raleigh NC. **Average salary range of placements:** Less than $20,000. **Number of placements per year:** 1000+.

CAREER CONNECTIONS, INC.
35 Elliott Street, Athens OH 45701. 740/594-4941. **Fax:** 740/592-6289. **Contact:** Valerie Kinnard, General Manager. **E-mail address:** careerconnections@compuserve.com. **Description:** A temporary agency that also provides some permanent placements. **Specializes in the areas of:** General Management; Light Industrial; Secretarial. **Positions commonly filled include:** Administrative Assistant; Computer Operator; Customer Service Representative; Database Manager; Graphic Designer; Secretary; Technical Writer/Editor; Typist/Word Processor. **Corporate headquarters location:** This Location. **Average salary range of placements:** Less than $20,000. **Number of placements per year:** 200 - 499.

CENTRAL STAR
1164 Lexington Avenue, Mansfield OH 44907. 419/756-9449. **Fax:** 419/756-4550. **Contact:** Jennifer Smith, Recruiter. **Description:** A temporary agency. **Specializes in the areas of:** Health/Medical. **Positions commonly filled include:** Certified Nurses Aide; Nurse. **Corporate headquarters location:** New York NY. **Average salary range of placements:** $20,000 - $29,999. **Number of placements per year:** 1 - 49.

CROWN TEMPORARY SERVICES OF CINCINNATI
289C Northland Boulevard, Cincinnati OH 45246. 513/772-7242. **Contact:** Dick Diana, Manager. **Description:** A temporary agency. **Specializes in the areas of:** Accounting; Banking; Clerical; Engineering; Finance; Insurance; Legal; Manufacturing; Personnel. **Positions commonly filled include:** Accountant/Auditor; Administrative Assistant; Advertising Clerk; Bookkeeper; Claim Representative; Clerk; Computer Operator; Computer Programmer; Construction Trade Worker. **Number of placements per year:** 1000+.

CUSTOM STAFFING, INC.
712 West North Street, Lima OH 45801. 419/221-3097. **Toll-free phone:** 800/860-3072. **Fax:** 419/221-2564. **Contact:** D. Roche Simmons, Manager. **Description:** A temporary agency. **Specializes in the areas of:** Accounting/Auditing; Industrial; Manufacturing; Secretarial; Technical. **Positions commonly filled include:** Accountant/Auditor; Automotive Mechanic; Blue-Collar Worker Supervisor; Broadcast Technician; Clerical Supervisor; Clinical Lab Technician; Computer Programmer; Customer Service Representative; Draftsperson; Electrician; Landscape Architect; Licensed Practical Nurse; Medical Records Technician; Registered Nurse. **Other area locations:** Columbus OH; Findlay OH; Marysville OH. **Average salary range of placements:** Less than $20,000. **Number of placements per year:** 200 - 499.

INITIAL STAFFING SERVICES
17 South High Street, Suite 1060, Columbus OH 43215. 614/280-9800. **Fax:** 614/280-0787. **Contact:** Manager. **Description:** A temporary agency. **Specializes in the areas of:** Accounting/Auditing; Finance; Health/Medical; Sales; Secretarial. **Positions commonly filled include:** Account Representative; Administrative Assistant; Advertising Clerk; Claim Representative; Clerical Supervisor; Customer Service Representative; Sales Representative; Secretary; Typist/Word Processor. **Benefits available to temporary workers:** 401(k); Medical Insurance; Paid Vacation; Referral Bonus Plan. **Other U.S. locations:** Nationwide. **Average salary range of placements:** $20,000 - $29,999.

INTERIM PERSONNEL
6924 Spring Valley Drive, Suite 240, Holland OH 43528. 419/865-3017. **Contact:** Manager. **Description:** A temporary agency that also provides permanent placements. **Specializes in the areas of:** Engineering; Industrial; Manufacturing; Personnel/Labor Relations; Technical. **Positions commonly filled include:** Blue-Collar Worker Supervisor; Bookkeeper; Chemical Engineer; Clerk; Computer Programmer; Credit Manager; Customer Service Representative; Data Entry Clerk; Design Engineer; Draftsperson; Electrical/Electronics Engineer; Factory Worker; General Manager; Human Resources Specialist; Industrial Engineer; Legal Secretary; Light Industrial Worker; Mechanical Engineer; Medical Secretary; MIS Specialist; Office Manager; Paralegal; Purchasing Agent/Manager; Quality Control Supervisor; Receptionist; Science Technologist; Secretary; Systems Analyst; Technician; Typist/Word Processor. **Benefits available to temporary workers:** Medical Insurance; Paid Holidays; Paid Vacation. **Corporate headquarters location:** Fort Lauderdale FL. **Other U.S. locations:** Nationwide. **Number of placements per year:** 1000+.

KELLY SERVICES, INC.
6430 East Main Street, Reynoldsburg OH 43068. 614/863-0020. **Fax:** 614/863-6620. **Contact:** Connee Kennedy, District Manager. **Description:** A temporary agency. Kelly Services also provides permanent placements in the areas of office services, marketing, technical, light industrial, and outsourcing. **Specializes in the areas of:** Accounting/Auditing; Banking; Computer Science/Software; Finance; Industrial; Insurance; Legal; Manufacturing; Personnel/Labor Relations; Secretarial. **Positions commonly filled include:** Accountant/Auditor; Administrative Manager; Blue-Collar Worker Supervisor; Claim Rep.; Clerical Supervisor; Clinical Lab Technician; Computer Programmer; Credit Manager; Draftsperson; Human Resources Specialist; Paralegal; Typist/Word Processor; Underwriter. **Benefits available to temporary workers:** Medical Insurance; Paid Holidays; Paid Vacation. **Corporate headquarters location:** Troy MI. **Other U.S. locations:** Nationwide. **Average salary range of placements:** Less than $20,000. **Number of placements per year:** 500 - 999.

MANPOWER TEMPORARY SERVICES
1275 North Fairfield Road, Beaver Creek OH 45432. 937/426-2668. **Fax:** 937/426-1762. **Contact:** Branch

Manager. **Description:** A temporary agency. **Specializes in the areas of:** Industrial; Sales; Secretarial. **Positions commonly filled include:** Claim Representative; Clerical Supervisor; Customer Service Representative; Paralegal; Property and Real Estate Manager; Public Relations Specialist; Purchasing Agent/Manager; Services Sales Representative; Typist/Word Processor. **Corporate headquarters location:** Milwaukee WI. **Other U.S. locations:** Nationwide. **Average salary range of placements:** Less than $20,000. **Number of placements per year:** 200 - 499.

MANPOWER TEMPORARY SERVICES
70 Fairway Drive, Unit 3, Wilmington OH 45177. 937/382-4900. **Fax:** 937/383-1414. **Contact:** Branch Manager. **Description:** A temporary agency. Founded in 1948. **Specializes in the areas of:** Clerical; Computer Science/Software; Industrial; Manufacturing; Personnel/Labor Relations; Secretarial; Technical. **Positions commonly filled include:** Accountant/Auditor; Customer Service Representative. **Benefits available to temporary workers:** 401(k); Medical Insurance; Paid Holidays; Paid Vacation; Stock Purchase. **Corporate headquarters location:** Milwaukee WI. **Other U.S. locations:** Nationwide. **Average salary range of placements:** Less than $20,000.

MANPOWER TEMPORARY SERVICES
One Cleveland Center, 1375 East Ninth Street, Cleveland OH 44114. 216/771-5474. **Contact:** Branch Manager. **Description:** A temporary agency. **Specializes in the areas of:** Data Processing; Light Industrial; Office Support; Professional; Technical; Telemarketing; Word Processing. **Positions commonly filled include:** Accountant/Auditor; Accounting Clerk; Administrative Assistant; Assembler; Biological Scientist; Bookkeeper; Chemist; Computer Operator; Customer Service Representative; Designer; Desktop Publishing Specialist; Electrician; Inspector/Tester/Grader; Inventory Control Specialist; Machine Operator; Material Control Specialist; Order Clerk; Packaging/Processing Worker; Painter; Project Engineer; Proofreader; Receptionist; Records Manager; Research Assistant; Secretary; Software Engineer; Stock Clerk; Systems Analyst; Technical Writer/Editor; Technician; Telemarketer; Typist/Word Processor. **Benefits available to temporary workers:** Life Insurance; Medical Insurance; Paid Holidays; Paid Vacation. **Corporate headquarters location:** Milwaukee WI. **Other U.S. locations:** Nationwide. **Number of placements per year:** 1000+.

MANPOWER TEMPORARY SERVICES
3 Centennial Plaza, Suite 101, 895 Central Avenue, Cincinnati OH 45202-1961. 513/621-7250. **Contact:** Branch Manager. **Description:** A temporary agency. **Specializes in the areas of:** Data Processing; Light Industrial; Office Support; Professional; Technical; Telemarketing; Word Processing. **Positions commonly filled include:** Accountant/Auditor; Accounting Clerk; Administrative Assistant; Assembler; Biological Scientist; Bookkeeper; Chemist; Computer Operator; Customer Service Representative; Designer; Desktop Publishing Specialist; Electrician; Inspector/Tester/ Grader; Inventory Control Specialist; Machine Operator; Material Control Specialist; Order Clerk; Packaging/Processing Worker; Painter; Project Engineer; Proofreader; Receptionist; Records Manager; Research Assistant; Secretary; Software Engineer; Systems Analyst; Technical Writer/Editor; Technician; Telemarketer; Transcriptionist; Typist/Word Processor; Welder. **Benefits available to temporary workers:** Life Insurance; Medical Insurance; Paid Holidays; Paid Vacation. **Corporate headquarters location:** Milwaukee WI. **Other U.S. locations:** Nationwide. **Number of placements per year:** 1000+.

NESCO SERVICE COMPANY
1115 Lyons Road, Dayton OH 45458-1856. 937/435-2700. **Fax:** 937/435-2716. **Contact:** Duane Golden, District Manager. **Description:** A temporary agency. **Specializes in the areas of:** Industrial; Manufacturing. **Positions commonly filled include:** Draftsperson;

Industrial Production Manager; Mechanical Engineer. **Benefits available to temporary workers:** 401(k); Medical Insurance; Paid Vacation. **Number of placements per year:** 500 - 999.

NORRELL SERVICES, INC.
5151 Monroe Street, Suite 110, Toledo OH 43623. 419/842-0111. **Contact:** Branch Manager. **Description:** A temporary agency. **Specializes in the areas of:** Banking; Clerical; Personnel/Labor Relations. **Positions commonly filled include:** Accountant/Auditor; Bookkeeper; Clerk; Computer Programmer; Data Entry Clerk; General Manager; Legal Secretary; Light Industrial Worker; Receptionist; Secretary; Stenographer; Typist/Word Processor. **Number of placements per year:** 1000+.

NORTH AMERICAN TECHNICAL SERVICES
3951 Erie Street, Suite 214, Willoughby OH 44094. 440/975-0400. **Toll-free phone:** 800/330-9680. **Fax:** 440/975-1211. **Contact:** Recruiter. **Description:** A temporary agency. **Specializes in the areas of:** Engineering; Sales; Transportation. **Positions commonly filled include:** Ceramics Engineer; Chemical Engineer; Civil Engineer; Design Engineer; Draftsperson; Electrical/Electronics Engineer; Environmental Engineer; Industrial Engineer; Materials Engineer; Mechanical Engineer; Metallurgical Engineer; Mining Engineer; Nuclear Engineer; Operations/Production Manager; Petroleum Engineer; Software Engineer; Structural Engineer; Technical Writer/Editor.

OLSTEN STAFFING SERVICES
2052 Front Street, Cuyahoga Falls OH 44221. 330/922-8367. **Contact:** Branch Manager. **Description:** A temporary agency. **Specializes in the areas of:** Clerical; Manufacturing. **Positions commonly filled include:** Bookkeeper; Clerk; Computer Operator; Customer Service Representative; Data Entry Clerk; Draftsperson; Driver; Factory Worker; Human Resources Manager; Legal Secretary; Light Industrial Worker; Medical Secretary; Nurse; Office Manager; Public Relations Specialist; Receptionist; Secretary; Statistician; Stenographer; Typist/Word Processor. **Corporate headquarters location:** Melville NY. **Other U.S. locations:** Nationwide. **International locations:** Worldwide. **Number of placements per year:** 1000+.

OLSTEN STAFFING SERVICES
314 Wilson Road, Great Western Shopping Plaza, Columbus OH 43204. 614/276-4200. **Fax:** 614/276-0574. **Contact:** Recruiter. **Description:** A temporary agency. **Specializes in the areas of:** Accounting; Administration; Computer Science/Software; Light Industrial. **Positions commonly filled include:** Customer Service Representative; Typist/Word Processor. **Benefits available to temporary workers:** Medical Insurance; Paid Vacation. **Corporate headquarters location:** Melville NY. **Other U.S. locations:** Nationwide. **International locations:** Worldwide. **Average salary range of placements:** Less than $20,000. **Number of placements per year:** 1000+.

PALMER TEMPS
THE PALMER GROUP
4302 Roosevelt Boulevard, Middletown OH 45044-6625. 513/422-1126. **Toll-free phone:** 800/860-8367. **Fax:** 513/422-1503. **Contact:** Manager. **E-mail address:** palmer@palmergroup.com. **World Wide Web address:** http://www.palmergroup.com. **Description:** A temporary agency that also provides permanent placements and career/outplacement counseling. **Specializes in the areas of:** Accounting/Auditing; Computer Science/Software; Insurance; Personnel/Labor Relations; Sales; Secretarial. **Positions commonly filled include:** Accountant/Auditor; Advertising Clerk; Credit Manager; Draftsperson; Human Resources Specialist; Technical Writer/Editor; Typist/Word Processor. **Benefits available to temporary workers:** Computer Training; Paid Holidays; Paid Vacation. **Average salary range of placements:** $20,000 - $29,999. **Number of placements per year:** 1000+.

PHARMACY RELIEF NETWORK
P.O. Box 659, Lima OH 45802-0659. 419/222-7070. **Toll-free phone:** 888/727-2007. **Fax:** 419/227-6108. **Contact:** Helen Hooks, Operations Coordinator. **Description:** A temporary agency that also provides permanent placements. The agency places medical professionals in hospital, retail, and institutional settings. **Specializes in the areas of:** Health/Medical. **Positions commonly filled include:** Dental Assistant/Dental Hygienist; Licensed Practical Nurse; Pharmacist; Pharmacy Technician; Registered Nurse. **Average salary range of placements:** More than $50,000. **Number of placements per year:** 200 - 499.

SANKER & ASSOCIATES
7522 Redcoat Drive, Indian Springs OH 45011. 513/887-8000. **Contact:** Patricia Sanker, President. **Description:** A temporary agency. **Specializes in the areas of:** Advertising; Art/Design; Publishing. **Positions commonly filled include:** Designer; Desktop Publishing Specialist; Graphic Designer; Technical Writer/Editor. **Corporate headquarters location:** Cincinnati OH. **Average salary range of placements:** $20,000 - $29,999. **Number of placements per year:** 1 - 49.

SNELLING PERSONNEL SERVICES
3460 South Dixie Drive, Suite 200, Dayton OH 45439. 937/297-2300. **Fax:** 937/297-2305. **Contact:** Doug Wales, President. **E-mail address:** snelling@erinet.com. **World Wide Web address:** http://www.snelling. com/dayton. **Description:** A temporary agency that also provides some temp-to-perm placements. **Specializes in the areas of:** Health/Medical; Office Support.

SPECIAL COUNSEL
1000 Terminal Tower Building, 50 Public Square, Cleveland OH 44113. 216/622-2100. **Fax:** 216/622-2110. **Contact:** Manager. **World Wide Web address:** http://www.specialcounsel.com. **Description:** A temporary agency that also provides some permanent placements. **Specializes in the areas of:** Legal.

TANDEM STAFFING
787 North Main Street, Akron OH 44310. 330/253-0088. **Fax:** 330/253-9818. **Contact:** Howard W. Ryder, President. **Description:** A temporary agency. **Specializes in the areas of:** Light Industrial; Manufacturing. **Positions commonly filled include:** Blue-Collar Worker Supervisor; Industrial Production Manager. **Average salary range of placements:** $20,000 - $29,999. **Number of placements per year:** 100 - 199.

THE TARGET HUMAN RESOURCE COMPANIES, INC.
14650 Detroit Avenue, Suite 430, Cleveland OH 44107. **Toll-free phone:** 800/244-1779. **Fax:** 216/226-5708. **Contact:** Mary Kaye Wirkner, President. **E-mail address:** tthrc@aol.com. **Description:** A temporary agency that also provides permanent placements and human resource consulting. Founded in 1987. **Specializes in the areas of:** Accounting/Auditing; Food; Industrial; Manufacturing; Personnel/Labor Relations; Sales; Secretarial; Technical. **Positions commonly filled include:** Accountant/Auditor; Automotive Mechanic; Blue-Collar Worker Supervisor; Customer Service Representative; Electrician; Human Resources Specialist; Industrial Production Manager; Quality Control Supervisor; Restaurant/Food Service Manager; Services Sales Representative; Typist/Word Processor. **Benefits available to temporary workers:** Bonus Award/Plan; Life Insurance; Medical Insurance. **Corporate headquarters location:** This Location. **Other area locations:** Brunswick OH; Columbus OH; Elyria OH. **Average salary range of placements:** $20,000 - $29,999. **Number of placements per year:** 500 - 999.

TEMPORARILY YOURS PLACEMENT
4630 Richmond Road, Suite 265, Cleveland OH 44128. **Contact:** Recruiter. **Description:** A temporary agency. **Specializes in the areas of:** Accounting/Auditing; Food; Health/Medical; Industrial; Personnel/Labor Relations; Publishing; Retail; Sales; Secretarial; Technical. **Positions commonly filled include:** Blue-Collar Worker Supervisor; Clerical Supervisor; Counselor; Electrician; Human Resources Specialist; Landscape Architect; Paralegal; Services Sales Representative; Typist/Word Processor. **Benefits available to temporary workers:** Paid Vacation. **Corporate headquarters location:** Mentor OH. **Other area locations:** Warrensville Heights OH. **Average salary range of placements:** Less than $20,000. **Number of placements per year:** 200 - 499.

CONTRACT SERVICES FIRMS

ADECCO/TAD TECHNICAL SERVICES
6555 Busch Boulevard, Suite 240, Columbus OH 43229. **Toll-free phone:** 800/260-8007. **Fax:** 614/431-1614. **Contact:** John Graves, Branch Manager. **Description:** A contract services firm. **Specializes in the areas of:** Administration; Architecture/Construction; Automotive; Computer Hardware/Software; Engineering; Food; Health/Medical; Industrial; Light Industrial; Manufacturing; Publishing; Technical; Transportation. **Positions commonly filled include:** Account Representative; Administrative Assistant; Administrative Manager; Applications Engineer; Architect; Assistant Manager; Biochemist; Biomedical Engineer; Buyer; Chemical Engineer; Clerical Supervisor; Computer Operator; Computer Programmer; Customer Service Representative; Design Engineer; Draftsperson; Electrical/Electronics Engineer; Electrician; Food Scientist/Technologist; Geologist/Geophysicist; Human Resources Specialist; Management Analyst/Consultant; Manufacturing Engineer; Mechanical Engineer; Medical Records Technician; MIS Specialist; Operations Manager; Production Manager; Project Manager; Quality Control Supervisor; Sales Engineer; Secretary; Statistician; Surgical Technician; Systems Analyst; Systems Manager; Telecommunications Manager; Transportation/Traffic Specialist; Typist/Word Processor. **Benefits available to temporary workers:** 401(k); Dental Insurance; Medical Insurance; Paid Holidays; Paid Vacation. **Corporate headquarters location:** Redwood City CA. **Other U.S. locations:** Nationwide. **Number of placements per year:** 1000+.

ADVANCEMENT LLC
32200 Solon Road, Solon OH 44139-3535. 440/248-8550. **Fax:** 440/248-0740. **Contact:** Patrick Gallagher, Account Executive. **Description:** A contract services firm. **Specializes in the areas of:** Computer Science/Software; Engineering; Information Technology; Scientific; Technical. **Positions commonly filled include:** Applications Engineer; Chemical Engineer; Civil Engineer; Computer Operator; Computer Programmer; Database Manager; Design Engineer; Draftsperson; Electrical/Electronics Engineer; Industrial Engineer; Internet Services Manager; Manufacturing Engineer; Mechanical Engineer; Metallurgical Engineer; MIS Specialist; Production Manager; Project Manager; Software Engineer; Systems Analyst; Systems Manager; Technical Writer/Editor; Telecommunications Manager; Webmaster. **Benefits available to temporary workers:** Dental Insurance; Life Insurance; Medical Insurance; Paid Holidays; Paid Vacation; Vision Insurance. **Corporate headquarters location:** This Location. **Average salary range of placements:** More than $50,000. **Number of placements per year:** 200 - 499.

ALLIANCE TECHNICAL SERVICES
5045 North Main Street, Suite 330, Dayton OH 45415-3637. 937/277-6117. **Fax:** 937/277-1979. **Contact:** Ken Overholser, Regional Manager. **Description:** A contract services firm. **Specializes in the areas of:** Computer Science/Software; Engineering; Industrial; Manufacturing; Technical. **Positions commonly filled include:** Ceramics Engineer; Civil Engineer; Clinical

Lab Technician; Computer Programmer; Design Engineer; Designer; Draftsperson; Electrical/Electronics Engineer; Electrician; Industrial Engineer; Industrial Production Manager; Materials Engineer; Mechanical Engineer; Metallurgical Engineer; Operations/Production Manager; Quality Control Supervisor; Software Engineer; Structural Engineer; Systems Analyst; Technical Writer/Editor. **Corporate headquarters location:** Alliance OH. **Other area locations:** Columbus OH; Warren OH. **Other U.S. locations:** Bingham Farms MI; Greenville SC. **Average salary range of placements:** $30,000 - $50,000.

BELCAN TECHNICAL SERVICES
11591 Goldcoast Drive, Cincinnati OH 45249. **Toll-free phone:** 800/945-1900. **Fax:** 513/489-0830. **Contact:** Rob Russell, Recruiter. **E-mail address:** tech@tech.belcan.com. **World Wide Web address:** http://www.belcan.com. **Description:** A contract services firm. **Specializes in the areas of:** Architecture/Construction; Computer Science/Software; Engineering; Industrial; Manufacturing; Real Estate; Scientific; Technical. **Positions commonly filled include:** Accountant/Auditor; Aerospace Engineer; Agricultural Engineer; Aircraft Mechanic/Engine Specialist; Applications Engineer; Architect; Biological Scientist; Biomedical Engineer; Buyer; Chemical Engineer; Chemist; Civil Engineer; Clinical Lab Technician; Computer Operator; Computer Programmer; Construction Contractor; Cost Estimator; Database Manager; Design Engineer; Designer; Draftsperson; Editor; Electrical/Electronics Engineer; Financial Analyst; Food Scientist/Technologist; Geographer; Geologist/Geophysicist; Health Services Manager; Human Resources Manager; Industrial Engineer; Industrial Production Manager; Mathematician; Mechanical Engineer; Metallurgical Engineer; Mining Engineer; Online Content Specialist; Purchasing Agent/Manager; Quality Control Supervisor; Radiological Technologist; Software Engineer; Stationary Engineer; Structural Engineer; Surveyor; Systems Analyst; Technical Writer/Editor; Wholesale and Retail Buyer. **Benefits available to temporary workers:** 401(k); Paid Holidays; Paid Vacation. **Corporate headquarters location:** This Location. **Other area locations:** Cleveland OH; Dayton OH. **Other U.S. locations:** St. Louis MO; Raleigh NC. **Average salary range of placements:** $30,000 - $50,000. **Number of placements per year:** 1000+.

BELCAN TECHNICAL SERVICES
2494 Technical Drive, Miamisburg OH 45342. 937/859-8880. **Contact:** Manager. **Description:** A contract services firm. **Specializes in the areas of:** Computer Science/Software; Engineering.

DLD TECHNICAL SERVICES
24050 Commerce Park, Suite 203, Cleveland OH 44122. 216/360-9595. **Fax:** 216/360-9599. **Contact:** Recruiter. **Description:** A contract services firm. **Specializes in the areas of:** Computer Science/Software; Engineering; Industrial; Technical. **Positions commonly filled include:** Aerospace Engineer; Buyer; Ceramics Engineer; Chemical Engineer; Civil Engineer; Computer Programmer; Design Engineer; Designer; Draftsperson; Electrical/Electronics Engineer; Industrial Engineer; Materials Engineer; Mechanical Engineer; Metallurgical Engineer; Nuclear Engineer; Purchasing Agent/Manager; Quality Control Supervisor; Radiological Technologist; Software Engineer; Structural Engineer; Systems Analyst; Technical Writer/Editor. **Benefits available to temporary workers:** Paid Holidays; Paid Vacation. **Average salary range of placements:** More than $50,000. **Number of placements per year:** 50 - 99.

FLEX-TECH PROFESSIONAL SERVICES
413 Columbus Avenue, Suite 300, Sandusky OH 44870. 419/625-3974. **Fax:** 419/625-7417. **Contact:** Cecil Weatherspoon, President. **Description:** A contract services firm. **Specializes in the areas of:** Banking; Computer Hardware/Software; Engineering; General Management; Industrial; Manufacturing; Personnel;

Sales. **Positions commonly filled include:** Administrative Assistant; Aerospace Engineer; Architect; Biological Scientist; Budget Analyst; Buyer; Ceramics Engineer; Chemical Engineer; Chemist; Computer Operator; Computer Programmer; Customer Service Representative; Draftsperson; EDP Specialist; Electrical/Electronics Engineer; Industrial Designer; Industrial Engineer; Manufacturing Engineer; Marketing Specialist; Mechanical Engineer; Metallurgical Engineer; MIS Specialist; Operations/ Production Manager; Purchasing Agent/Manager; Quality Control Supervisor; Secretary; Software Engineer; Systems Analyst; Technical Writer/Editor. **Benefits available to temporary workers:** Bonus Award/Plan; Paid Vacation. **Other area locations:** Cleveland OH. **Other U.S. locations:** Phoenix AZ; Detroit MI. **Average salary range of placements:** $30,000 - $50,000. **Number of placements per year:** 100 - 199.

GLOBAL RESOURCES GROUP
3974 Reed Road, Columbus OH 43220. 614/451-3208. **Contact:** Peadar Lynch, President/CEO. **Description:** A contract services firm focusing on the placement of human resources personnel. **Specializes in the areas of:** Engineering; Health/Medical; Industrial; Manufacturing; Personnel/Labor Relations; Technical. **Positions commonly filled include:** Accountant/Auditor; Administrative Manager; Attorney; Blue-Collar Worker Supervisor; Buyer; Chemical Engineer; Clerical Supervisor; Computer Programmer; Design Engineer; Designer; Draftsperson; Electrical/Electronics Engineer; Environmental Engineer; Financial Analyst; General Manager; Human Resources Specialist; Industrial Engineer; Internet Services Manager; Licensed Practical Nurse; Management Analyst/Consultant; Mechanical Engineer; MIS Specialist; Operations/Production Manager; Paralegal; Purchasing Agent/Manager; Quality Control Supervisor; Registered Nurse; Science Technologist; Software Engineer; Systems Analyst.

HEALTH CARE PERSONNEL
6240 East Livingston Avenue, Reynoldsburg OH 43068. 614/864-9292. **Fax:** 614/575-3468. **Contact:** Staffing Coordinator. **E-mail address:** hcpcorp@aol.com. **Description:** A contract services firm. **Specializes in the areas of:** Health/Medical. **Positions commonly filled include:** Certified Nurses Aide; Dietician/Nutritionist; EEG Technologist; EKG Technician; Licensed Practical Nurse; Medical Records Technician; Pharmacist; Physical Therapist; Physician; Psychologist; Registered Nurse; Social Worker; Surgical Technician.

NORTH STAR RESOURCES
29170 Euclid Avenue, Wickliffe OH 44092-2473. 440/944-8484. **Toll-free phone:** 800/875-9562. **Fax:** 440/944-8909. **Contact:** Joyce McLean, President. **Description:** A contract services firm that also provides permanent placements. **Specializes in the areas of:** Architecture/Construction; Chemicals; Computer Science/Software; Electronics; Engineering; Manufacturing; Technical. **Positions commonly filled include:** Aerospace Engineer; Architect; Buyer; Ceramics Engineer; Chemical Engineer; Chemist; Civil Engineer; Computer Programmer; Cost Estimator; Design Engineer; Designer; Draftsperson; Electrical/Electronics Engineer; Environmental Engineer; Industrial Engineer; Materials Engineer; Mechanical Engineer; Metallurgical Engineer; MIS Specialist; Operations/Production Manager; Purchasing Agent/Manager; Quality Control Supervisor; Software Engineer; Structural Engineer; Surveyor; Systems Analyst; Technical Writer/Editor. **Benefits available to temporary workers:** Paid Holidays. **Average salary range of placements:** $30,000 - $50,000. **Number of placements per year:** 1 - 49.

PAK/TEEM TECHNICAL SERVICES, INC.
11500 Rockfield Court, Cincinnati OH 45241. 513/772-1515. **Fax:** 513/772-6381. **Contact:** Denise DeMoss, General Manager. **E-mail address:** pakteem-tech@pakteem.com. **World Wide Web address:** http://www.pakteem.com. **Description:** A contract

services firm that also provides some temp-to-perm and permanent placements. **Specializes in the areas of:** Engineering; Light Industrial. **Positions commonly filled include:** Design Engineer; Draftsperson; Electrical/Electronics Engineer; Industrial Engineer; Manufacturing Engineer; Mechanical Engineer. **Benefits available to temporary workers:** Credit Union; Dental Insurance; Medical Insurance; Paid Holidays; Paid Vacation. **Corporate headquarters location:** This Location. **Average salary range of placements:** $30,000 - $50,000. **Number of placements per year:** 1 - 49.

PROFESSIONAL STAFF MANAGEMENT
120 East Fourth Street, Suite 700, Cincinnati OH 45202. 513/721-7880. **Contact:** Manager. **Description:** A contract services firm.

RDS, INC.
P.O. Box 24389, Dayton OH 45424-0389. 937/236-8602. **Toll-free phone:** 800/876-8602. **Fax:** 937/237-3835. **Contact:** In-Client Services Manager. **E-mail address:** rapiddsgn@aol.com. **Description:** A contract services firm. RDS focuses on engineering and design services and project engineering management services. Founded in 1946. **Specializes in the areas of:** Design; Engineering; Industrial; Manufacturing; Technical. **Positions commonly filled include:** Ceramics Engineer; Chemical Engineer; Design Engineer; Designer; Draftsperson; Electrical/Electronics Engineer; Industrial Engineer; Industrial Production Manager; Materials Engineer; Mechanical Engineer; Metallurgical Engineer; Operations/Production Manager; Quality Control Supervisor; Technical Writer/Editor. **Benefits available to temporary workers:** Medical Insurance; Paid Holidays; Paid Vacation. **Other U.S. locations:** Nationwide. **Average salary range of placements:** $30,000 - $50,000. **Number of placements per year:** 200 - 499.

S&P SOLUTIONS
35000 Chardon Road, Suite 200, Willoughby Hills OH 44094. 440/646-9111. **Toll-free phone:** 800/978-9113. **Fax:** 440/646-1429. **Contact:** Suzanne Nebe, Recruiter. **E-mail address:** suzanne_n@sps-solutions.com. **World Wide Web address:** http://www.sps-solutions.com. **Description:** A contract services firm. **Specializes in the areas of:** Computer Science/Software; Scientific; Technical. **Positions commonly filled include:** Computer Programmer; Consultant; Database Manager; MIS Specialist; Software Engineer; Systems Analyst. **Number of placements per year:** 100 - 199.

TEAMWORK U.S.A.
27801 Euclid Avenue, Suite 550, Euclid OH 44132. 216/261-5151. **Toll-free phone:** 888/550-TEAM. **Fax:** 216/261-7248. **Contact:** Michael Freshwater, General Manager. **Description:** A contract services firm. **Specializes in the areas of:** Computer Science/Software; Engineering; Industrial; Manufacturing; Personnel/Labor Relations; Technical. **Positions commonly filled include:** Administrative Manager; Aerospace Engineer; Agricultural Engineer; Aircraft Mechanic/Engine

Specialist; Biomedical Engineer; Blue-Collar Worker Supervisor; Branch Manager; Budget Analyst; Buyer; Ceramics Engineer; Chemical Engineer; Chemist; Civil Engineer; Clinical Lab Technician; Computer Programmer; Construction and Building Inspector; Construction Contractor; Cost Estimator; Customer Service Representative; Design Engineer; Designer; Draftsperson; EEG Technologist; EKG Technician; Electrical/Electronics Engineer; Electrician; Environmental Engineer; Human Resources Specialist; Human Service Worker; Industrial Engineer; Industrial Production Manager; Materials Engineer; Mechanical Engineer; Mining Engineer; Nuclear Engineer; Nuclear Medicine Technologist; Petroleum Engineer; Public Relations Specialist; Services Sales Representative; Software Engineer; Structural Engineer; Systems Analyst. **Average salary range of placements:** $20,000 - $29,999. **Number of placements per year:** 200 - 499.

TRADESMAN INTERNATIONAL
1549 Boettler Road, Unit D, Uniontown OH 44685-7766. 330/896-0420. **Toll-free phone:** 800/896-4062. **Fax:** 330/896-1183. **Contact:** Gary Price, Recruiter. **Description:** A contract services firm that pairs skilled labor with industrial manufacturers. **Specializes in the areas of:** Construction; Industrial; Manufacturing; Personnel/Labor Relations. **Positions commonly filled include:** Blue-Collar Worker Supervisor; Construction Contractor; Electrician. **Corporate headquarters location:** Solon OH. **Other area locations:** Cincinnati OH; Cleveland OH; Columbus OH; Dayton OH. **Other U.S. locations:** Washington DC; Indianapolis IN; Lexington KY; Louisville KY; Baltimore MD; Charlotte NC; Greenville NC; Raleigh NC; Greensboro SC; Memphis TN; Nashville TN; Dallas TX; Fort Worth TX; San Antonio TX; Norfolk VA; Richmond VA; Milwaukee WI. **Average salary range of placements:** $20,000 - $29,999. **Number of placements per year:** 1000+.

H.L. YOH COMPANY
11311 Cornell Park Drive, Suite 402, Cincinnati OH 45242. 513/469-6202. **Toll-free phone:** 800/696-6488. **Fax:** 513/469-6205. **Contact:** Mike Brogan, Account Representative. **World Wide Web address:** http://www.hlyoh.com. **Description:** A contract services firm. **Specializes in the areas of:** Computer Operations; Computer Programming; Electrical; Engineering. **Positions commonly filled include:** Buyer; Chemical Engineer; Computer Operator; Computer Programmer; Construction Contractor; Cost Estimator; Database Manager; Design Engineer; Draftsperson; Electrical/ Electronics Engineer; Environmental Engineer; Manufacturing Engineer; Mechanical Engineer; MIS Specialist; Systems Analyst; Systems Manager; Technical Writer/Editor; Webmaster. **Benefits available to temporary workers:** 401(k); Medical Insurance; Paid Holidays; Paid Vacation. **Corporate headquarters location:** Philadelphia PA. **Other U.S. locations:** Nationwide. **Average salary range of placements:** $30,000 - $50,000. **Number of placements per year:** 100 - 199.

CAREER/OUTPLACEMENT COUNSELING FIRMS

A BETTER RESUME
409 Red Haw Road, Dayton OH 45405. 937/278-3242. **Contact:** Stephen Coleman, President. **E-mail address:** steveco85@aol.com. **Description:** A resume writing service.

A+ RESUME AND TYPING SERVICE
P.O. Box 328, Englewood OH 45322. 937/264-3025. **Fax:** 937/264-9930. **Contact:** Teena Rose, CPRW/Manager. **E-mail address:** APlusSvc00@aol.com. **World Wide Web address:** http://www.aplusresumeandtyping.com. **Description:** Specializes in

assisting back to work parents and those leaving the military. Services offered include interview preparation and assistance with writing resumes, cover letters, reference sheets, and thank you letters.

ALLEN & ASSOCIATES
25825 Science Park Drive, Suite 260, Beachwood OH 44122. 216/765-8220. **Toll-free phone:** 800/562-7911. **Fax:** 216/765-8309. **Contact:** Manager. **World Wide Web address:** http://www.allenandassociates.com. **Description:** A career/outplacement counseling firm. **Corporate headquarters location:** Maitland FL. **Other U.S. locations:** Nationwide.

40 PLUS OF CENTRAL OHIO
1100 King Avenue, Columbus OH 43212. 614/297-0040.
Contact: President. **Description:** A career/outplacement
counseling firm.

JOB TRAINING PARTNERSHIP
300 Market Avenue North, Canton OH 44702. 330/455-
7121. **Contact:** Industrial Training Coordinator.
Description: A career/outplacement counseling firm.
Specializes in the areas of: Nonprofit. **Positions
commonly filled include:** Case Manager. **Number of
placements per year:** 1 - 49.

MORAN & ASSOCIATES
126 West John Street, Maumee OH 43537. 419/893-
9707. **Contact:** Weston Moran, Owner. **Description:** A
resume writing and counseling service.

DAVID G. ROBERTS GROUP
29525 Chagrin Boulevard, Suite 214, Pepper Pike OH
44122. 216/595-8200. **Fax:** 216/595-8208. **Contact:**
David G. Roberts, Human Resources. **Description:** A
career/outplacement counseling firm.

R.L. STEVENS & ASSOCIATES
5005 Rockside Road, Suite 900, Independence OH
44131. 216/642-1933. **Contact:** Manager. **Description:**
A career counseling firm.

ACCOUNTING PRINCIPALS
4860 South Lewis Avenue, Suite 102, Tulsa OK 74105. 918/744-9900. **Fax:** 918/744-9994. **Contact:** Lynn Flinn, Branch Manager. **Description:** An executive search firm that also offers contract and permanent placements. **Specializes in the areas of:** Accounting.

ADVANCED RECRUITING INC.
7300 NW Expressway, Suite 183, Oklahoma City OK 73132. 405/720-9445. **Fax:** 405/720-9133. **Contact:** Manager. **E-mail address:** advrec@icon.net. **World Wide Web address:** http://www.adrec.com. **Description:** An executive search firm. **Specializes in the areas of:** Information Systems. **Positions commonly filled include:** MIS Specialist.

AMERI RESOURCE
2525 NW Expressway, Suite 532, Oklahoma City OK 73112. 405/842-5900. **Toll-free phone:** 800/583-7823. **Fax:** 405/843-9879. **Contact:** Manager. **Description:** An executive search firm operating on a contingency basis. **Specializes in the areas of:** Administration; Banking; Computer Science/Software; Engineering; Finance; Food; General Management; Health/Medical; Industrial; Manufacturing; Personnel/Labor Relations; Publishing; Secretarial; Technical. **Positions commonly filled include:** Accountant/Auditor; Actuary; Administrative Manager; Aerospace Engineer; Agricultural Engineer; Aircraft Mechanic/Engine Specialist; Architect; Automotive Mechanic; Bank Officer/Manager; Blue-Collar Worker Supervisor; Branch Manager; Civil Engineer; Clerical Supervisor; Computer Programmer; Construction and Building Inspector; Construction Contractor; Cost Estimator; Credit Manager; Customer Service Representative; Dental Assistant/Dental Hygienist; Design Engineer; Designer; Draftsperson; Electrical/Electronics Engineer; Electrician; Financial Analyst; General Manager; Geographer; Geologist/Geophysicist; Human Resources Specialist; Industrial Engineer; Industrial Production Manager; Internet Services Manager; Licensed Practical Nurse; Management Analyst/Consultant; Management Trainee; Manufacturer's/Wholesaler's Sales Rep.; Market Research Analyst; Mechanical Engineer; MIS Specialist; Multimedia Designer; Nuclear Engineer; Operations/Production Manager; Petroleum Engineer; Purchasing Agent/Manager; Quality Control Supervisor; Software Engineer; Structural Engineer; Systems Analyst; Technical Writer/Editor; Telecommunications Manager; Typist/Word Processor. **Corporate headquarters location:** This Location. **Other area locations:** Tulsa OK. **Average salary range of placements:** $20,000 - $29,999. **Number of placements per year:** 1000+.

ANDREWS & ASSOCIATES INC.
2720 North Hemlock Court, Suite 100, Broken Arrow OK 74012. 918/251-8839. **Fax:** 918/258-1843. **Contact:** Jeffrey L. Andrews, President. **Description:** An executive search firm. **Specializes in the areas of:** Accounting/Auditing. **Positions commonly filled include:** Tax Specialist.

BANCSEARCH, INC.
P.O. Box 700516, Tulsa OK 74170. 918/496-9477. **Fax:** 918/494-2003. **Contact:** Don Cunningham, President. **E-mail address:** bancsearch@aol.com. **World Wide Web address:** http://www.bancsearch.com. **Description:** An executive search firm operating on both retainer and contingency bases. **Specializes in the areas of:** Banking; Finance. **Positions commonly filled include:** Bank Officer/Manager; Credit Manager; Financial Analyst; Mortgage Banker; Trust Officer. **Average salary range of placements:** More than $50,000. **Number of placements per year:** 1 - 49.

BANKER PERSONNEL SERVICE
2211 Westpark Drive, Norman OK 73069. 405/364-4322. **Contact:** Manager. **Description:** An executive search firm. **Specializes in the areas of:** Banking.

BRADLEY GROUP
1401 Pecan Avenue, Norman OK 73072. 405/447-9200. **Fax:** 405/447-9206. **Contact:** Manager. **Description:** An executive search firm. **Specializes in the areas of:** Computer Science/Software.

BULLOCK & COMPANY
221 East 45th Place, Tulsa OK 74105. 918/742-6170. **Fax:** 918/742-0430. **Contact:** Manager. **E-mail address:** bullock@oklahoma.net. **World Wide Web address:** http://www.oklahoma.net/~bullock. **Description:** An executive search firm. **Specializes in the areas of:** Accounting; Information Technology.

CAREER CONCEPTS
5601 NW 72nd Street, Suite 312, Oklahoma City OK 73132. 405/721-7542. **Fax:** 405/721-7555. **Contact:** David Ferguson, President. **E-mail address:** ccna@icon.net. **Description:** An executive search firm. **Specializes in the areas of:** Computer Programming; Engineering.

DUNHILL PERSONNEL OF NORTHEAST TULSA, INC.
10159 East 11th Street, Suite 370, Tulsa OK 74128. 918/832-8857. **Toll-free phone:** 800/466-8857. **Fax:** 918/832-8859. **Contact:** Joy M. Porrello, President. **Description:** An executive search firm operating on a contingency basis. **Specializes in the areas of:** Credit and Collection. **Average salary range of placements:** More than $50,000. **Number of placements per year:** 1 - 49.

EXECUTIVE RESOURCES GROUP, INC.
2601 West Wilshire Boulevard, Oklahoma City OK 73116. 405/843-8344. **Fax:** 405/879-0393. **Contact:** George Orr, President. **Description:** An executive search firm. **Specializes in the areas of:** Engineering; Manufacturing. **Positions commonly filled include:** Accountant/Auditor; Biomedical Engineer; Chemical Engineer; Civil Engineer; Electrical/Electronics Engineer; Industrial Engineer; Manufacturing Engineer; Mechanical Engineer; Purchasing Agent/Manager; Quality Control Supervisor; Software Engineer. **Number of placements per year:** 1 - 49.

EXPRESS PERSONNEL SERVICES
6300 NW Expressway, Oklahoma City OK 73132. 405/840-5000. **Fax:** 405/720-9390. **Contact:** Harvey (H.H.) Homsey, Research & Development Manager. **Description:** An executive search firm. **Specializes in the areas of:** Accounting/Auditing; Advertising; Computer Science/Software; Food; General Management; Industrial; Insurance; Legal; Manufacturing; Personnel/Labor Relations; Publishing; Sales; Secretarial; Technical. **Positions commonly filled include:** Administrative Manager; Advertising Clerk; Architect; Automotive Mechanic; Blue-Collar Worker Supervisor; Branch Manager; Buyer; Claim Representative; Computer Programmer; Customer Service Representative; Dental Assistant/Dental Hygienist; Designer; Dietician/Nutritionist; Draftsperson; Editor; Education Administrator; EEG Technologist; EKG Technician; Electrical/Electronics Engineer; Electrician; Emergency Medical Technician; Food Scientist/Technologist; General Manager; Human Resources Specialist; Human Service Worker; Librarian; Manufacturer's/Wholesaler's Sales Rep.; Market Research Analyst; Medical Records Technician; Multimedia Designer; Paralegal; Public Relations Specialist; Quality Control Supervisor; Restaurant/Food Service Manager; Services Sales Representative;

Software Engineer; Systems Analyst; Technical Writer/Editor; Travel Agent. **Average salary range of placements:** $30,000 - $50,000. **Number of placements per year:** 1000+.

JAMES FARRIS ASSOCIATES
4101 North Classen, Suite E, Oklahoma City OK 73118. 405/848-0535. **Contact:** Manager. **Description:** An executive search firm.

FARRIS PERSONNEL INC.
700 Eastern Drive, Hulbert OK 74441. 918/772-2683. **Fax:** 918/772-2685. **Contact:** Ray Farris, Owner. **Description:** An executive search firm. **Specializes in the areas of:** Manufacturing.

FOOD MANUFACTURING CONSULTANTS
5929 North May Avenue, Suite 506, Oklahoma City OK 73112. 405/840-3632. **Contact:** Larry Toth, President. **Description:** An executive search firm operating on both retainer and contingency bases. **Specializes in the areas of:** Food; Manufacturing; Sales. **Positions commonly filled include:** Food Scientist/Technologist; Industrial Engineer; Industrial Production Manager; Operations/Production Manager; Quality Control Supervisor. **Average salary range of placements:** More than $50,000. **Number of placements per year:** 100 - 199.

BERNARD HALDANE ASSOCIATES
3030 NW Expressway, Suite 727, Oklahoma City OK 73112. 405/948-7668. **Toll-free phone:** 800/646-8333. **Fax:** 405/948-7869. **Contact:** Henry Dumas, Vice President. **Description:** A generalized executive search firm.

ROBERT HALF INTERNATIONAL ACCOUNTEMPS
6120 South Yale Avenue, Suite 420, Tulsa OK 74136. 918/493-3393. **Contact:** Manager. **World Wide Web address:** http://www.roberthalf.com. **Description:** An executive search firm. Accountemps (also at this location) provides temporary placements in the accounting industry. **NOTE:** Accountemps can be reached at 918/493-5775. **Specializes in the areas of:** Accounting/Auditing; Finance. **Corporate headquarters location:** Menlo Park CA. **Other U.S. locations:** Nationwide. **International locations:** Worldwide.

ROBERT HALF INTERNATIONAL ACCOUNTEMPS
211 North Robinson, Suite 310, Oklahoma City OK 73102. 405/236-0880. **Fax:** 405/236-0279. **Contact:** Branch Manager. **World Wide Web address:** http://www.roberthalf.com. **Description:** An executive search firm operating on a contingency basis. Accountemps (also at this location) provides temporary placements in the accounting industry. **Specializes in the areas of:** Accounting/Auditing; Administration; Banking; Finance; Secretarial. **Positions commonly filled include:** Accountant/Auditor; Bank Officer/Manager; Budget Analyst; Computer Programmer; Credit Manager; Customer Service Representative; Financial Analyst; Human Resources Specialist; Management Analyst/Consultant; MIS Specialist; Purchasing Agent/Manager; Systems Analyst; Typist/Word Processor; Underwriter/Assistant Underwriter. **Corporate headquarters location:** Menlo Park CA. **Other U.S. locations:** Nationwide. **International locations:** Worldwide. **Average salary range of placements:** $20,000 - $29,999. **Number of placements per year:** 500 - 999.

HEALTHCARE RESOURCES GROUP
3945 SE 15th Street, Oklahoma City OK 73115. 405/677-7872. **Contact:** Manager. **Description:** An executive search firm. **Specializes in the areas of:** Health/Medical; Marketing; Sales.

HI-TECH STAFFING
6834 South Trenton, Suite 210, Tulsa OK 74136. 918/448-8997. **Contact:** Recruiter. **World Wide Web address:** http://www.jobstogo.com. **Description:** An executive search firm that also provides some contract placements and consulting services. **Specializes in the areas of:** High-Tech; Information Technology.

HIGH TECH RESOURCES
6120 South Yale Avenue, Suite 100, Tulsa OK 74136. 918/481-8822. **Contact:** Manager. **Description:** An executive search firm. **Specializes in the areas of:** High-Tech.

HOLBROOK ASSOCIATES
2 East 11, Suite 115, Edmond OK 73034. 405/341-9559. **Fax:** 405/340-1418. **Contact:** Manager. **Description:** An executive search firm. **Specializes in the areas of:** Engineering; Environmental; Manufacturing; Quality Assurance.

HUDDLESTON ASSOCIATES
4007 East 37th Street, Tulsa OK 74135. 918/742-5166. **Fax:** 918/744-0206. **Contact:** Manager. **World Wide Web address:** http://members.aol.com/lkhudd/index.html. **Description:** An executive search firm. **Specializes in the areas of:** Executives; Management; Technical.

IRON MOUNTAIN SEARCH, INC.
60599 East 100th Road, Miami OK 74354. **Toll-free phone:** 800/542-8066. **Contact:** Manager. **Description:** An executive search firm. **Specializes in the areas of:** Computer Programming.

JDL & ASSOCIATES
6613 NW 131st Street, Oklahoma City OK 73142. 405/722-2288. **Fax:** 405/722-7332. **Contact:** Jan Latimer, President. **E-mail address:** jdl@nstar.net. **Description:** An executive search firm. **Specializes in the areas of:** Distribution; Engineering; Manufacturing.

ROBERT WILLIAM JAMES & ASSOCIATES
5909 NW Expressway, Suite 110, Oklahoma City OK 73132. 405/720-4616. **Fax:** 405/717-8392. **Contact:** Manager. **Description:** A generalist executive search firm.

JOY REED BELT & ASSOCIATES
P.O. Box 18446, Oklahoma City OK 73154. 405/842-6336. **Fax:** 405/842-6357. **Contact:** Manager. **Description:** An executive search firm. **Specializes in the areas of:** Health/Medical.

MANAGEMENT CONSULTANTS
5929 North May Avenue, Oklahoma City OK 73112. 405/848-6858. **Fax:** 405/840-3632. **Contact:** Manager. **Description:** An executive search firm. **Specializes in the areas of:** Sales.

MANAGEMENT RECRUITERS INTERNATIONAL
1320 East Ninth Street, Suite 3, Edmond OK 73034. 405/348-5550. **Fax:** 405/348-8808. **Contact:** Manager. **Description:** An executive search firm. **Specializes in the areas of:** Health/Medical; Telecommunications.

MANAGEMENT RECRUITERS INTERNATIONAL
5801 East 41st Street, Suite 440, Tulsa OK 74135. 918/663-6744. **Contact:** Manager. **Description:** An executive search firm. **Specializes in the areas of:** Administration; Engineering; Sales.

MANAGEMENT RECRUITERS INTERNATIONAL
3441 West Memorial Road, Suite 4, Oklahoma City OK 73134. 405/752-8848. **Fax:** 405/752-8783. **Contact:** Gary Roy, Manager. **Description:** Management Recruiters International is an executive search firm. **Specializes in the areas of:** Accounting/Auditing; Administration; Advertising; Architecture/Construction; Banking; Communications; Computer Hardware/Software; Finance; Food; General Management; Health/Medical; Insurance; Legal; Manufacturing; Publishing; Real Estate; Retail; Sales; Technical; Textiles; Transportation.

MANAGEMENT SEARCH, INC.
6051 North Brookline, Suite 125, Oklahoma City OK 73112. 405/842-3173. **Fax:** 405/842-8360. **Contact:** David Orwig, President. **Description:** An executive search firm. **Specializes in the areas of:** Agri-Business. **Positions commonly filled include:** Agricultural Engineer; Agricultural Scientist; Biological Scientist; Veterinarian. **Number of placements per year:** 1 - 49.

MONTANYE GROUP
3761 East 81st Place, Tulsa OK 74137. 918/488-8305. **Fax:** 918/488-8311. **Contact:** Mike Montanye, President. **Description:** An executive search firm. **Specializes in the areas of:** High-Tech.

NATIONAL RECRUITERS
720 North Commerce, Suite 345, Ardmore OK 73401. 580/561-6500. **Fax:** 580/561-6600. **Contact:** Manager. **E-mail address:** national@natrec.com. **World Wide Web address:** http://www.natrec.com. **Description:** An executive search firm. **Specializes in the areas of:** Human Resources.

PHILLIPS & ASSOCIATES
6202 South Lewis Avenue, Suite C, Tulsa OK 74136. 918/747-9486. **Fax:** 918/747-9488. **Contact:** Jim Phillips, President. **Description:** An executive search firm. **Specializes in the areas of:** Construction; Engineering.

PROFESSIONAL RESOURCES GROUP
7030 South Yale Avenue, Suite 300, Tulsa OK 74136. 918/481-0088. **Contact:** Manager. **Description:** An executive search firm.

PROSPECTIVE PERSONNEL SERVICE, INC.
P.O. Box 4727, Tulsa OK 74159. 918/584-5000. **Contact:** Linda Kinney, President. **E-mail address:** bankrcrtr@aol.com. **Description:** An executive search firm operating on a contingency basis. Founded in 1981. **Specializes in the areas of:** Banking. **Positions commonly filled include:** Auditor; Bank Officer/Manager. **Number of placements per year:** 1 - 49.

THE REALITY GROUP
P.O. Box 2675, Broken Arrow OK 74013-2675. 918/451-4057. **Fax:** 918/451-4743. **Contact:** Manager. **Description:** An executive search firm operating on a contingency basis. **Specializes in the areas of:** Chemicals; Engineering. **Positions commonly filled include:** Chemical Engineer; Environmental Engineer; Mechanical Engineer; Safety Engineer.

SALES CONSULTANTS OF OKLAHOMA CITY, INC.
6525 North Meridian Avenue, Suite 212, Oklahoma City OK 73116. 405/721-6400. **Toll-free phone:** 888/876-1908. **Fax:** 405/728-6716. **Contact:** Darla Salisbury, Owner. **E-mail address:** scoklacity@aol.com. **Description:** An executive search firm operating on a contingency basis. **Specializes in the areas of:** Marketing; Sales. **Positions commonly filled include:** Sales Engineer; Sales Executive; Sales Manager; Sales

Representative. **Average salary range of placements:** $30,000 - $49,999.

SALES RECRUITERS INC.
6803 South Western, Suite 305, Oklahoma City OK 73139. 405/848-1536. **Fax:** 405/636-1561. **Contact:** J.R. Rimele, President. **E-mail address:** salesrec@telepath.com. **World Wide Web address:** http://www.telepath.com/salesrec. **Description:** An executive search firm. **Specializes in the areas of:** Health/Medical; Sales. **Positions commonly filled include:** Account Representative; Marketing Manager; Safety Engineer; Sales Manager; Sales Representative. **Average salary range of placements:** $30,000 - $50,000. **Number of placements per year:** 1 - 49.

SUNDANCE GROUP
7030 South Yale Avenue, Suite 103, Tulsa OK 74136. 918/494-9992. **Fax:** 918/492-7182. **Contact:** Jeff Baldwin, President. **Description:** An executive search firm. **Specializes in the areas of:** Computer Science/Software.

TAXSEARCH INCORPORATED
7050 South Yale Avenue, Suite 310, Tulsa OK 74136. 918/252-3100. **Fax:** 918/252-3063. **Contact:** Manager. **E-mail address:** taxsearch@taxsearchinc.com. **World Wide Web address:** http://www.taxsearchinc.com. **Description:** An executive search firm focusing on placing tax professionals. **Specializes in the areas of:** Tax.

U.S. GAS SEARCH
P.O. Box 701048, Tulsa OK 74170. 918/492-6668. **Physical address:** 5215 East 71st Street, Suite 1500, Tulsa, OK. **Fax:** 918/492-6674. **Contact:** Keith Louderback, President. **E-mail address:** keithl@ionet.net. **Description:** An executive search firm focusing on the placement of marketing, supply, trading, transportation, and risk management professionals in the natural gas and gas processing industries. **Specializes in the areas of:** Oil and Gas. **Positions commonly filled include:** Marketing Manager; Marketing Specialist. **Average salary range of placements:** More than $50,000. **Number of placements per year:** 1 - 49.

VILLAREAL & ASSOCIATES
427 South Boston Avenue, Suite 215, Tulsa OK 74103. 918/584-0808. **Fax:** 918/584-6281. **Contact:** Morey Villareal, President. **E-mail address:** villareal@webzone.net. **Description:** An executive search firm operating on a retainer basis. Client company pays fee. **Positions commonly filled include:** Applications Engineer; Chief Financial Officer; Controller; Financial Analyst; General Manager; Operations Manager; Project Manager; Sales Manager; Vice President. **Average salary range of placements:** $50,000 - $100,000. **Number of placements per year:** 1 - 49.

JOHN WYLIE ASSOCIATES, INC.
1727 East 71st Street, Tulsa OK 74136. 918/496-2100. **Contact:** John L. Wylie, President. **Description:** An executive search firm. **Specializes in the areas of:** Computer Hardware; Engineering; Manufacturing; Technical. **Number of placements per year:** 1 - 49.

PERMANENT EMPLOYMENT AGENCIES

AC PERSONNEL SERVICES, INC.
P.O. Box 271052, Oklahoma City OK 73137. 405/728-3503. **Fax:** 405/681-7070. **Contact:** Delores Lantz, President. **Description:** A permanent employment agency. **Positions commonly filled include:** Computer Programmer; General Manager; Management Trainee; Services Sales Representative; Systems Analyst. **Number of placements per year:** 100 - 199.

MANPOWER TECHNICAL SERVICES
5727 South Lewis, Suite 575, Tulsa OK 74105. 918/712-8700. **Contact:** Manager. **Description:** A permanent

employment agency. **Positions commonly filled include:** Buyer; Computer Programmer; Designer; Draftsperson; Editor; Engineer; Purchasing Agent/Manager; Systems Analyst; Technical Writer/Editor; Technician. **Other U.S. locations:** Nationwide.

SOONER PLACEMENT SERVICE
4001 North Classen Boulevard, Suite 210, Oklahoma City OK 73118. 405/528-2501. **Fax:** 405/524-8046. **Contact:** Louis Borgman, Owner. **Description:** A

permanent employment agency. **Specializes in the areas of:** Accounting/Auditing; Engineering; Legal; Oil and Gas; Sales; Secretarial. **Positions commonly filled include:** Accountant/Auditor; Paralegal; Petroleum Engineer. **Number of placements per year:** 50 - 99.

TEMPORARY EMPLOYMENT AGENCIES

CHEROKEE TEMPS, INC.
1728 South Fourth Street, Chickasha OK 73018. 405/224-1482. **Contact:** Manager. **Description:** A temporary agency. **Specializes in the areas of:** Administration; Industrial; Manufacturing; Personnel/Labor Relations; Sales; Secretarial. **Positions commonly filled include:** Automotive Mechanic; Clerical Supervisor; Construction Contractor; Customer Service Representative; Management Trainee; Manufacturer's/Wholesaler's Sales Rep.; Medical Records Technician; Typist/Word Processor. **Benefits available to temporary workers:** 401(k); Dental Insurance; Medical Insurance. **Corporate headquarters location:** Muskegee OK.

DOW PERSONNEL INC.
4833 South Sheridan Road, Suite 418, Tulsa OK 74145. 918/664-6811. **Contact:** Paul McKinney, President. **Description:** A temporary agency. **Specializes in the areas of:** Light Industrial; Nonprofit; Secretarial. **Positions commonly filled include:** Customer Service Representative; Management Trainee; Secretary; Typist/Word Processor. **Average salary range of placements:** Less than $20,000. **Number of placements per year:** 1 - 49.

EXPRESS PERSONNEL SERVICES
RWJ & ASSOCIATES
7321 South Western, Oklahoma City OK 73139. 405/634-6600. **Contact:** Ms. P.J. Jackson, Regional Manager. **Description:** A temporary agency. RWJ & Associates (also at this location) is an executive search firm. **Specializes in the areas of:** Accounting/Auditing; Computer Science/Software; Engineering; Health/Medical; Industrial; Legal. **Positions commonly filled include:** Accountant/Auditor; Administrative Manager; Advertising Clerk; Automotive Mechanic; Blue-Collar Worker Supervisor; Branch Manager; Clerical Supervisor; Computer Programmer; Customer Service Representative; Draftsperson; General Manager; Human Resources Specialist; Industrial Production Manager; Registered Nurse; Typist/Word Processor. **Other U.S. locations:** Nationwide. **Average salary range of placements:** Less than $20,000.

INTERIM PERSONNEL
5319 South Lewis Avenue, Suite 111, Tulsa OK 74105. 918/742-1121. **Fax:** 918/742-1578. **Contact:** Manager. **World Wide Web address:** http://www.interim.com. **Description:** A temporary agency. **Specializes in the areas of:** Accounting/Auditing; Personnel/Labor Relations; Secretarial. **Positions commonly filled include:** Accountant; Administrative Assistant; Administrative Manager; Auditor; Budget Analyst; Buyer; Claim Representative; Clerical Supervisor; Controller; Credit Manager; Customer Service Representative; Database Manager; Finance Director; Financial Analyst; Human Resources Manager; Secretary; Underwriter/Assistant Underwriter. **Benefits available to temporary workers:** Bonus Award/Plan; Medical Insurance; Paid Holidays; Paid Vacation. **Corporate headquarters location:** Fort Lauderdale FL. **Other U.S. locations:** Nationwide. **International locations:** Europe. **Average salary range of placements:** $20,000 - $29,999. **Number of placements per year:** 500 - 999.

KEY TEMPORARY PERSONNEL
5272 South Lewis Avenue, Tulsa OK 74105. 918/747-0000. **Fax:** 918/747-0140. **Recorded jobline:** 918/748-3333. **Contact:** Recruiting and Training Specialist. **World Wide Web address:** http://www.keyjobs.com. **Description:** A temporary agency. **Specializes in the areas of:** Administration; Advertising; Banking; Engineering; Finance; Health/Medical; Industrial; Legal; Light Industrial; Manufacturing; Personnel/Labor Relations; Secretarial; Technical. **Positions commonly filled include:** Accountant/Auditor; Administrative Manager; Advertising Clerk; Attorney; Blue-Collar Worker Supervisor; Branch Manager; Buyer; Chemical Engineer; Chemist; Clerical Supervisor; Computer Programmer; Cost Estimator; Credit Manager; Customer Service Representative; Design Engineer; Designer; Draftsperson; Electrical/Electronics Engineer; Financial Analyst; Health Services Manager; Human Resources Specialist; Industrial Engineer; Mechanical Engineer; Medical Records Technician; MIS Specialist; Paralegal; Quality Control Supervisor; Systems Analyst; Technical Writer/Editor; Typist/Word Processor. **Benefits available to temporary workers:** 401(k); Medical Insurance; Paid Vacation; Performance Bonus; Referral Bonus Plan. **Average salary range of placements:** $20,000 - $29,999. **Number of placements per year:** 1000+.

MANPOWER TEMPORARY SERVICES
3030 NW Expressway, Suite 702, Oklahoma City OK 73112. 405/942-5111. **Contact:** Dave Keith, Regional Vice President. **Description:** A temporary agency. **Specializes in the areas of:** Accounting/Auditing; Banking; Clerical; Computer Hardware/Software; Construction; Finance; Insurance; Legal; Manufacturing. **Positions commonly filled include:** Accountant/Auditor; Administrative Assistant; Bookkeeper; Clerk; Computer Operator; Computer Programmer; Construction Trade Worker; Data Entry Clerk; Draftsperson; EDP Specialist; Factory Worker; Legal Secretary; Light Industrial Worker; Medical Secretary; Receptionist; Secretary; Stenographer; Systems Analyst; Technician; Typist/Word Processor. **Number of placements per year:** 1000+.

TERRY NEESE PERSONNEL AGENCY
2709 West I-44 Service Road, Oklahoma City OK 73112. 405/942-8551. **Fax:** 405/942-2840. **Contact:** Manager. **Description:** A temporary agency that also provides some permanent placements and executive searches. **Specializes in the areas of:** Accounting/Auditing; Administration; Banking; Computer Science/Software; Engineering; Finance; General Management; Health/Medical; Legal; Light Industrial; Personnel/Labor Relations; Sales; Secretarial. **Positions commonly filled include:** Account Representative; Accountant; Administrative Assistant; Advertising Clerk; Applications Engineer; Assistant Manager; Auditor; Bank Officer/Manager; Blue-Collar Worker Supervisor; Branch Manager; Chemical Engineer; Civil Engineer; Clerical Supervisor; Clinical Lab Technician; Computer Operator; Computer Programmer; Construction Contractor; Controller; Credit Manager; Customer Service Representative; Database Manager; Design Engineer; Environmental Engineer; Finance Director; Financial Analyst; General Manager; Human Resources Manager; Industrial Engineer; Management Trainee; Manufacturing Engineer; Marketing Manager; Mechanical Engineer; MIS Manager; Operations Manager; Paralegal; Production Manager; Project Manager; Public Relations Specialist; Purchasing Agent/Manager; Sales Engineer; Sales Executive; Sales Manager; Sales Representative; Secretary; Software Engineer; Systems Analyst; Systems Manager; Telecommunications Manager; Typist/Word Processor; Underwriter/Assistant Underwriter. **Benefits available to temporary workers:** Life Insurance; Medical Insurance; Paid Vacation; Sick Days. **Corporate headquarters location:** This Location. **Average salary range of placements:** $20,000 - $29,999. **Number of placements per year:** 200 - 499.

STAFFMARK
4775 South Harvard Avenue, Tulsa OK 74135. 918/744-8367. **Fax:** 918/744-1232. **Contact:** Division Manager. **Description:** A temporary agency that also provides some temp-to-perm placements. **Specializes in the areas of:** General Labor; Industrial; Light Industrial; Manufacturing. **Positions commonly filled include:** Aircraft Mechanic/Engine Specialist; Automotive Mechanic; Blue-Collar Worker Supervisor; Construction and Building Inspector; Cost Estimator; Draftsperson; Electrician; General Manager; Industrial Production Manager; Machinist. **Benefits available to temporary workers:** 401(k); Medical Insurance; Paid Holidays; Paid Vacation. **Average salary range of placements:** Less than $20,000. **Number of placements per year:** 500 - 999.

STAFFMARK
201 South Main Street, Bristow OK 74010. **Contact:** Recruiter. **Description:** A temporary agency that also provides some contract services. **Specializes in the areas of:** Industrial; Manufacturing; Secretarial. **Positions commonly filled include:** Claim Representative; Clerical Supervisor; Customer Service Representative; Typist/Word Processor. **Benefits available to temporary workers:** 401(k); Medical Insurance; Paid Holidays; Paid Vacation. **Corporate headquarters location:** Tulsa OK. **Average salary range of placements:** Less than $20,000. **Number of placements per year:** 200 - 499.

STAFFMARK
6349 South Memorial Avenue, Tulsa OK 74133. 918/252-9696. **Fax:** 918/461-1083. **Contact:** Branch Manager. **Description:** A temporary agency that also provides some temp-to-perm placements. **Specializes in the areas of:** Accounting/Auditing; Administration; Advertising; Banking; Finance; Insurance; Legal; Personnel/Labor Relations; Publishing; Sales; Secretarial. **Positions commonly filled include:** Administrative Manager; Advertising Clerk; Brokerage Clerk; Claim Representative; Clerical Supervisor; Computer Programmer; Credit Manager; Customer Service Representative; Human Resources Specialist; Paralegal; Systems Analyst; Typist/Word Processor. **Benefits available to temporary workers:** 401(k); Medical Insurance; Paid Holidays; Paid Vacation. **Number of placements per year:** 1000+.

STAFFMARK MEDICAL STAFFING
2140 South Harvard, Suite 100, Tulsa OK 74114. 918/743-5900. **Fax:** 918/742-3773. **Contact:** Cindy Woodward, Division Manager. **Description:** A temporary agency that also provides some temp-to-perm placements. **Specializes in the areas of:** Health/Medical. **Positions commonly filled include:** Claim Representative; Clinical Lab Technician; EEG Technologist; EKG Technician; Emergency Medical Technician; Licensed Practical Nurse; Medical Assistant; Medical Records Technician; Operations Manager; Pharmacist; Radiological Technologist; Registered Nurse; Respiratory Therapist; Surgical Technician. **Benefits available to temporary workers:** 401(k); Medical Insurance; Paid Holidays; Paid Vacation. **Average salary range of placements:** $20,000 - $29,999. **Number of placements per year:** 1000+.

CAREER/OUTPLACEMENT COUNSELING FIRMS

PAB PERSONNEL AGENCY, INC.
121 South Santa Fe, Suite A, Norman OK 73069. 405/329-1933. **Contact:** Manager. **Description:** A career/outplacement counseling firm.

RESUME WRITER'S INK
5601 NW 72nd Street, Suite 312, Oklahoma City OK 73132. 405/721-7542. **Contact:** Counselor. **Description:** Provides resume counseling services.

◆ O R E G O N ◆

APA EMPLOYMENT AGENCY INC.
700 NE Multnomah Street, Suite 274, Portland OR 97232. 503/233-1200. **Fax:** 503/233-0071. **Contact:** Manager. **Description:** An executive search firm. **Specializes in the areas of:** Administration; Industrial; Management; Marketing; Professional; Sales; Technical.

ACCOUNTANTS EXECUTIVE SEARCH
ACCOUNTANTS ON CALL
222 SW Columbia Street, Suite 1115, Portland OR 97201. 503/228-0300. **Contact:** Manager. **Description:** An executive search firm. Accountants On Call (also at this location) is a temporary agency. **Specializes in the areas of:** Accounting/Auditing; Finance.

ACCOUNTANTS NORTHWEST
522 SW Fifth Avenue, Suite 625, Portland OR 97204. 503/242-3528. **Contact:** Manager. **Description:** An executive search firm. **Specializes in the areas of:** Accounting/Auditing.

ACCOUNTING QUEST
101 SW Main Street, Suite 370, Portland OR 97204. 503/221-9800. **Fax:** 503/221-1595. **Contact:** Erin Leonard, Director. **E-mail address:** erinl@ accountingquest.com. **World Wide Web address:** http://www.accountingquest.com. **Description:** An executive search firm operating on a contingency basis. Accounting Quest also provides some temporary, permanent, and contract placements. Client company pays fee. **Specializes in the areas of:** Accounting; Finance; Tax. **Other U.S. locations:** Phoenix AZ; Denver CO; Seattle WA. **Average salary range of placements:** $30,000 - $49,999. **Number of placements per year:** 100 - 199.

ANDREW ASSOCIATES EXECUTIVE SEARCH
4000 Kruse Way Place, Suite 2-225, Lake Oswego OR 97035. 503/635-7222. **Contact:** Manager. **E-mail address:** andy@andysrch.com. **Description:** An executive search firm. **Specializes in the areas of:** Finance; Information Technology; Management.

AUGUSTON & ASSOCIATES
173 NE Ridgetown Road, River Suite 4, Portland OR 97211. 503/299-6298. **Contact:** Manager. **Description:** An executive search firm. **Specializes in the areas of:** Health/Medical.

THE BRENTWOOD GROUP LIMITED
9 Monroe Parkway, Suite 230, Lake Oswego OR 97035. 503/697-8136. **Fax:** 503/697-8161. **Contact:** Manager. **E-mail address:** brentwood@transport.com. **Description:** An executive search firm that operates on a retainer basis. **Specializes in the areas of:** Computer Science/Software; High-Tech; Insurance. **Positions commonly filled include:** Adjuster; Chief Executive Officer; Claim Representative; Underwriter/Assistant Underwriter. **Average salary range of placements:** More than $50,000. **Number of placements per year:** 50 - 99.

D. BROWN & ASSOCIATES, INC.
610 SW Alder Street, Suite 1111, Portland OR 97205. 503/224-6860. **Fax:** 503/241-8855. **Contact:** Manager. **World Wide Web address:** http://www. dbrown.net/dbaintro.html. **Description:** An executive search firm. Founded in 1968. **Specializes in the areas of:** Accounting/Auditing; Computer Science/Software; Health/Medical; Information Systems; Information Technology. **Positions commonly filled include:** Accountant/Auditor; Database Manager; Hardware Engineer; MIS Specialist; Software Engineer; Systems Analyst. **Office hours:** Monday - Thursday, 8:00 a.m. - 5:00 p.m.; Friday, 8:00 a.m. - 4:30 p.m. **Average salary range of placements:** More than $50,000. **Number of placements per year:** 50 - 99.

JOHN M. CLARKE & ASSOCIATES
13625 SW 32nd Street, Beaverton OR 97008. 503/627-0820. **Contact:** John Clarke, Manager/Owner. **Description:** An executive search firm that specializes in recruiting and consulting services for the trust industry.

COMPUTER RECRUITERS
CREATIVE DATA CORPORATION
Denney Square, 6700 SW 105th Avenue, Suite 311, Beaverton OR 97008. 503/643-2464. **Fax:** 503/646-1118. **Contact:** Manager. **Description:** An executive search firm. Creative Data Corporation (also at this location) is a contract services firm. **Specializes in the areas of:** Computer Hardware/Software; Information Systems.

CORPORATE BUILDERS, INC.
P.O. Box 4343, Portland OR 97208. 503/223-4344. **Fax:** 503/221-7778. **Contact:** William C. Meysing, CEO. **Description:** An executive search firm. Founded in 1981. **Specializes in the areas of:** Architecture/ Construction; Engineering. **Positions commonly filled include:** Civil Engineer; Construction Contractor; Cost Estimator; Design Engineer; Electrical/Electronics Engineer; Environmental Engineer; Mechanical Engineer; Mining Engineer; Operations Manager; Project Manager; Structural Engineer.

E.D.P. MARKETS, INC.
E.D.P. CONSULTANTS, INC.
4905 SW Butternut Place, Suite A, Aloha OR 97007. 503/356-8899. **Fax:** 503/356-8898. **Contact:** Manager. **E-mail address:** jobs@edpmarkets.com. **World Wide Web address:** http://www. edpmarkets.com. **Description:** An executive search firm and permanent placement agency. E.D.P. Consultants, Inc. (also at this location) provides contract services. **Specializes in the areas of:** High-Tech.

THE EMERALD GROUP, INC.
10300 SW Greenburg Road, Suite 485, Portland OR 97223. 503/684-8881. **Fax:** 503/224-4197. **Contact:** Recruiter. **E-mail address:** executives@emerald-staffing.com. **World Wide Web address:** http://www. emerald-staffing.com. **Description:** An executive search firm that also offers some temporary placements. Founded in 1978.

EXECUTIVES WORLDWIDE, INC.
158 NE Greenwood, Suite 4, Bend OR 97701. 541/385-5405. **Fax:** 541/385-5407. **Contact:** K.L. Erickson, Owner. **E-mail address:** eworldwide@eworldwide.com. **World Wide Web address:** http://www. eworldwide.com. **Description:** An executive search firm that operates on both retainer and contingency bases. **Specializes in the areas of:** Administration; Biology; Computer Science/Software; Engineering; Health/ Medical; High-Tech; Industrial; Legal; Personnel/Labor Relations; Scientific; Technical. **Positions commonly filled include:** Attorney; Biomedical Engineer; Computer Animator; Computer Operator; Computer Programmer; Electrical/Electronics Engineer; General Manager; Human Resources Manager; Intellectual Property Lawyer; Internet Services Manager; MIS Specialist; Multimedia Designer; Online Content Specialist; Operations/Production Manager; Paralegal; Pharmacist; Radiological Technologist; Sales Executive; Sales Manager; Software Engineer; Systems Analyst; Systems Manager; Technical Writer/Editor; Telecommunications Manager. **Number of placements per year:** 50 - 99.

EXPRESS PERSONNEL SERVICES
621 SW Morrison Street, Suite 500, Portland OR 97205-3808. 503/224-5500. **Fax:** 503/242-1527. **Contact:** Recruiting Coordinator. **Description:** An executive search firm that also provides some temporary and

contract placements. **Specializes in the areas of:** Accounting/Auditing; Administration; Banking; Clerical; Computer Science/Software; Engineering; Finance; Food; General Management; Industrial; Insurance; Light Industrial; Manufacturing; Nonprofit; Personnel/Labor Relations; Sales; Secretarial; Technical. **Positions commonly filled include:** Accountant/Auditor; Administrative Manager; Advertising Clerk; Automotive Mechanic; Bank Officer/Manager; Blue-Collar Worker Supervisor; Branch Manager; Buyer; Chemical Engineer; Clerical Supervisor; Computer Programmer; Credit Manager; Customer Service Rep.; Design Engineer; Draftsperson; Electrical/Electronics Engineer; Electrician; Environmental Engineer; Financial Analyst; Food Scientist/Technologist; General Manager; Human Resources Specialist; Industrial Engineer; Internet Services Manager; Management Analyst/Consultant; Manufacturer's/Wholesaler's Sales Rep.; Market Research Analyst; Mechanical Engineer; MIS Specialist; Operations/Production Manager; Purchasing Agent/Manager; Quality Control Supervisor; Science Technologist; Securities Sales Rep.; Software Engineer; Systems Analyst; Technical Writer/Editor; Typist/Word Processor. **Benefits available to temporary workers:** 401(k); Medical Insurance; Paid Holidays; Paid Vacation; Referral Bonus Plan. **Corporate headquarters location:** Oklahoma City OK. **Average salary range of placements:** $30,000 - $50,000. **Number of placements per year:** 500 - 999.

F-O-R-T-U-N-E PERSONNEL CONSULTANTS
Executive Centre, 12725 SW 66th Avenue, Suite 100, Portland OR 97223-2500. 503/670-9541. **Fax:** 503/670-1594. **Contact:** Mark Vague, President. **Description:** An executive search firm. **Specializes in the areas of:** Automotive; Medical Devices; Pharmaceuticals; Plastics. **Corporate headquarters location:** New York NY. **Other U.S. locations:** Nationwide.

GLOBAL RECRUITMENT SERVICES, INC.
P.O. Box 82592, Portland OR 97282. 503/230-2521. **Contact:** Recruiter. **Description:** An executive search firm. **Positions commonly filled include:** Energy Engineer; Environmental Engineer; Utilities Director. **Average salary range of placements:** More than $50,000. **Number of placements per year:** 1 - 49.

HACKENSCHMIDT, WEAVER & FOX, INC.
13747 SW Farmington Road, Beaverton OR 97005-2603. 503/644-7744. **Fax:** 503/644-8730. **Contact:** Bob Weaver, Senior Recruiter. **Description:** An executive search firm operating on both retainer and contingency bases. Founded in 1980. **Specializes in the areas of:** Computer Science/Software; Engineering; General Management; Industrial; Personnel/Labor Relations. **Positions commonly filled include:** Applications Engineer; Chemical Engineer; Chemist; Chief Financial Officer; Computer Programmer; Controller; Design Engineer; General Manager; Human Resources Manager; Industrial Engineer; Industrial Production Manager; Manufacturing Engineer; Mechanical Engineer; Metallurgical Engineer; Production Manager; Project Manager; Purchasing Agent/Manager; Quality Control Supervisor; Sales Engineer; Software Engineer; Systems Analyst; Systems Manager. **Average salary range of placements:** More than $50,000. **Number of placements per year:** 1 - 49.

ROBERT HALF INTERNATIONAL ACCOUNTEMPS
222 SW Columbia Street, Suite 800, Portland OR 97201. 503/222-9778. **Fax:** 503/224-0190. **Contact:** Manager. **World Wide Web address:** http://www.roberthalf.com. **Description:** An executive search firm. Accountemps (also at this location) provides temporary accounting placements. **Specializes in the areas of:** Accounting/Auditing; Finance. **Corporate headquarters location:** Menlo Park CA. **International locations:** Worldwide.

HEARTBEAT MEDICAL
260 SW Madison Avenue, Suite 106, Corvallis OR 97333. 541/752-5557. **Fax:** 541/752-5559. **Contact:** Manager. **Description:** An executive search firm. **Specializes in the areas of:** Medical Devices.

HIGH TECH STAFFING GROUP
1020 SW Taylor Street, Suite 720, Portland OR 97205. 503/227-2565. **Fax:** 503/227-2413. **Contact:** Frank Odia, Recruiter. **E-mail address:** jobs@htsg.com. **World Wide Web address:** http://www.htsg.com. **Description:** An executive search firm. **Specializes in the areas of:** High-Tech.

ROBERT WILLIAM JAMES & ASSOCIATES
7401 SW Washoe Court, Suite 200, Tualatin OR 97062. 503/612-1414. **Fax:** 503/612-1410. **Contact:** Manager. **Description:** An executive search firm. **Specializes in the areas of:** Accounting; Engineering; Finance; Information Technology; Manufacturing; Marketing; Sales.

ROBERT WILLIAM JAMES & ASSOCIATES
977 Garfield Street, Suite 6, Eugene OR 97402. 541/686-0003. **Contact:** Manager. **Description:** An executive search firm. **NOTE:** This firm does not accept unsolicited resumes. Please only respond to advertised openings. **Specializes in the areas of:** Accounting; Finance; Information Technology.

THE KDS GROUP
4380 SW Macadam Avenue, Suite 200, Portland OR 97201. 503/229-4457. **Fax:** 503/229-4454. **Contact:** Manager. **Description:** An executive search firm. **Specializes in the areas of:** Management; Sales.

MADUELL ASSOCIATES
10250 SW Greenburg Road, Suite 102, Portland OR 97223. 503/245-7588. **Contact:** Paul Maduell, Manager/Owner. **Description:** An executive search firm.

MANAGEMENT RECRUITERS OF PORTLAND
Lloyd Center, Suite 2020, Portland OR 97232. 503/287-7918. **Fax:** 503/282-4380. **Contact:** Recruiter. **E-mail address:** manager@mri.pdx.com. **World Wide Web address:** http://www.mrportland.com. **Description:** An executive search firm. **Corporate headquarters location:** Cleveland OH.

MANAGEMENT SOLUTIONS
One SW Columbia Street, Suite 1100, Portland OR 97258-2013. 503/222-6600. **Fax:** 503/228-3310. **Contact:** Manager. **Description:** An executive search firm. **Specializes in the areas of:** High-Tech.

MESA INTERNATIONAL
679 East Harbor Drive, Warrenton OR 97146. 503/861-9878. **Fax:** 503/861-9893. **Contact:** Bruce Ericksen, Senior Partner. **Description:** An executive search firm. **Specializes in the areas of:** Entertainment; Retail.

PAUL MILLIUS ASSOCIATES
3115 NE Broadway Street, Portland OR 97232. 503/287-6754. **Fax:** 503/287-3828. **Contact:** Paul Millius, Manager/Owner. **E-mail address:** pmillius@aol.com. **Description:** An executive search firm.

NATIONAL ENGINEERING SEARCH
158 NE Greenwood Avenue, Suite 4, Bend OR 97701. 541/317-4150. **Fax:** 541/385-5407. **Contact:** Manager. **Description:** An executive search firm. **Specializes in the areas of:** Engineering. **Positions commonly filled include:** Engineer.

NATIONWIDE PERSONNEL RECRUITING & CONSULTING INC. (NPRC)
20834 SW Martinazzi Avenue, Tualatin OR 97062-9327. 503/692-4925. **Fax:** 503/692-6764. **Contact:** Barbara Bodle, President. **Description:** An executive search firm. **Specializes in the areas of:** Architecture/Construction; Computer Science/Software; Engineering; General Management; Industrial; Manufacturing; Sales; Technical. **Positions commonly filled include:** Ceramics Engineer; Chemical Engineer; Civil Engineer; Design Engineer; Electrical/Electronics Engineer; Environmental

Engineer; Financial Analyst; General Manager; Industrial Engineer; Industrial Production Manager; Manufacturer's/Wholesaler's Sales Rep.; Mechanical Engineer; MIS Specialist; Nuclear Engineer; Operations/ Production Manager; Quality Control Supervisor; Services Sales Rep.; Software Engineer; Stationary Engineer; Structural Engineer. **Average salary range of placements:** More than $50,000. **Number of placements per year:** 100 - 199.

NORTHWEST LEGAL SEARCH
2701 NW Vaughn, Suite 450, Portland OR 97210. 503/224-9601. **Contact:** Linda Green, Manager. **E-mail address:** lindagreen@aol.com. **World Wide Web address:** http://www.nwlegalsearch.com. **Description:** An executive search firm that also offers outplacement counseling services. **Specializes in the areas of:** Legal. **Positions commonly filled include:** Attorney.

PACIFIC COAST RECRUITERS
65 W1 Division Avenue, PMB 144, Eugene OR 97404. 541/345-6866. **Fax:** 541/345-0547. **Contact:** David Watson, Executive Director. **Description:** An executive search firm, operating on both retainer and contingency bases, that specializes in all facets of the property/ casualty insurance market including underwriting, claims, loss control, risk management, sales and marketing, and worker's compensation. Founded in 1984. **Specializes in the areas of:** Insurance. **Positions commonly filled include:** Branch Manager; Claim Rep.; Customer Service Rep.; Financial Analyst; Human Resources Manager; Insurance Agent/Broker; Marketing Manager; Sales Manager; Sales Rep.; Underwriter/ Assistant Underwriter. **Average salary range of placements:** More than $50,000. **Number of placements per year:** 1 - 49.

ROBERT E. PFAENDLER & ASSOCIATES INC.
P.O. Box 23025, Tigard OR 97281. 503/968-7777. **Fax:** 503/620-8881. **Contact:** Manager. **Description:** An executive search firm. **Specializes in the areas of:** Banking; Finance.

PROVIDER MANAGEMENT
11501 SW Pacific Highway, Suite 201, Portland OR 97223. 503/452-3790. **Fax:** 503/452-3793. **Contact:** Stan Smith, Owner. **Description:** An executive search firm. **Specializes in the areas of:** Health/Medical.

DOUGLAS REITER COMPANY INC.
P.O. Box 947, Lake Oswego OR 97034. 503/228-6916. **Fax:** 503/699-3577. **Contact:** Douglas Reiter, Manager/ Owner. **Description:** An executive search firm operating on a retainer basis.

ROMAC INTERNATIONAL
10220 SW Greenburg Road, Suite 625, Portland OR 97223. 503/768-4546. **Contact:** Manager. **Description:** An executive search firm. **Specializes in the areas of:** Computer Hardware/Software; Finance. **Corporate headquarters location:** Tampa FL.

SANFORD ROSE ASSOCIATES
10200 SW Eastridge Street, Suite 200, Portland OR 97225. 503/297-9191. **Fax:** 503/297-3528. **Contact:** Director. **World Wide Web address:** http://www. sanfordrose.com. **Description:** An executive search firm. **Specializes in the areas of:** Electronics; Engineering; Food. **Positions commonly filled include:** Controller; Electrical/Electronics Engineer; Food Scientist/ Technologist.

SEARCH & RECRUITING SPECIALIST
2435 SW Fifth Avenue, Redmond OR 97756. 541/923-2334. **Fax:** 541/923-2319. **Contact:** Manager. **Description:** An executive search and recruiting firm. **Specializes in the areas of:** Health/Medical; High-Tech.

SEARCH NORTH AMERICA
P.O. Box 3577, Sunriver OR 97707. 503/222-6461. **Contact:** Manager. **Description:** An executive search firm. **Specializes in the areas of:** Paper.

SEARCH NORTHWEST ASSOCIATES (SNA)
10117 SE Sunnyside Road, Suite F-727, Clackamas OR 97015. 503/654-1487. **Fax:** 503/654-9110. **Contact:** Douglas L. Jansen, CPC/President. **Description:** An executive search firm. Founded in 1977. **Specializes in the areas of:** Chemicals; Computer Science/Software; Engineering; General Management; High-Tech; Manufacturing; Metals. **Positions commonly filled include:** Biomedical Engineer; Ceramics Engineer; Chemical Engineer; Civil Engineer; Electrical/ Electronics Engineer; Environmental Engineer; General Manager; Industrial Engineer; Materials Engineer; Mechanical Engineer; Metallurgical Engineer; Mining Engineer; Petroleum Engineer; Purchasing Agent/ Manager; Quality Control Supervisor; Software Engineer. **Average salary range of placements:** More than $50,000. **Number of placements per year:** 100 - 199.

WALTER SHIPP GROUP
P.O. Box 387, Lake Oswego OR 97034. 503/243-2222. **Fax:** 503/655-5087. **Contact:** Pete Shipp, Managing Principal. **Description:** A generalist executive search firm.

SHULER & ASSOCIATES
510 Alternate Highway 101, Warrenton OR 97146. 503/861-3992. **Fax:** 503/861-2725. **Contact:** Billie Cokley, Executive Recruiter. **Description:** An executive search firm. **Specializes in the areas of:** Advertising.

SMITH & LAUE
4370 NE Halsey Street, Portland OR 97213. 503/460-9181. **Fax:** 503/460-9182. **Contact:** Chuck Smith, Recruiter. **Description:** An executive search firm. **Specializes in the areas of:** Food.

SPECIALIZED SEARCH COMPANY
3804 SW Council Crest Drive, Portland OR 97201. 503/274-2250. **Fax:** 503/274-2350. **Contact:** Manager. **Description:** An executive search firm. **Specializes in the areas of:** Chemicals; Industrial; Manufacturing.

STEPHENSON & STEPHENSON
1840 Tabor Street, Eugene OR 97401. 541/349-0808. **Fax:** 541/349-0809. **Contact:** Mark Stephenson, Owner/Manager. **Description:** An executive search firm. **Specializes in the areas of:** Electronics; Engineering; Information Technology; Manufacturing.

VANDERHOUWEN & ASSOCIATES
Harbor Square SW, 5520 SW Macadam, Suite 112, Portland OR 97201. 503/299-6811. **Fax:** 503/224-6181. **Contact:** Cynthia Phoenix, Technical Recruiter. **E-mail address:** TE@vanderhouwen.com. **World Wide Web address:** http://www.vanderhouwen.com. **Description:** An executive search firm. **Specializes in the areas of:** Data Processing; Software Engineering.

WOLF ENVIRONMENTAL GROUP
25 NW 23rd Place, PMB 116, Portland OR 97210. 503/241-0881. **Fax:** 503/241-0976. **Contact:** Judy Stockton, Owner. **E-mail address:** judywolf@aol.com. **Description:** An executive search firm specializing in the placement of mid- to senior-level environmental and health safety professionals. Founded in 1991. **Specializes in the areas of:** Engineering; Environmental. **Positions commonly filled include:** Biological Scientist; Branch Manager; Chemical Engineer; Chemist; Civil Engineer; Design Engineer; Environmental Engineer; Geologist/Geophysicist; Marketing Manager; Project Manager; Sales Engineer; Sales Executive; Sales Manager; Technical Writer/Editor. **Corporate headquarters location:** This Location. **International locations:** Vancouver, Canada. **Average salary range of placements:** More than $50,000. **Number of placements per year:** 1 - 49.

WOODWORTH INTERNATIONAL GROUP
620 SW Fifth Avenue, Suite 1225, Portland OR 97204-1426. 503/225-5000. **Fax:** 503/225-5005. **Contact:** Gail Woodworth, President. **Description:** An executive

search firm operating on a retainer basis. The firm also provides management consulting services to companies. **Specializes in the areas of:** Accounting/Auditing; Administration; Advertising; Computer Science/ Software; Engineering; Finance; General Management; Health/Medical; Marketing; Personnel/Labor Relations; Sales; Scientific; Technical; Transportation. **Positions commonly filled include:** Account Manager; Applications Engineer; Biomedical Engineer; Chief Financial Officer; Controller; Credit Manager; Database Manager; Design Engineer; Electrical/Electronics Engineer; Finance Director; Financial Analyst; General Manager; Human Resources Manager; Internet Services Manager; Manufacturing Engineer; Marketing Manager;

Operations Manager; Production Manager; Project Manager; Purchasing Agent/Manager; Quality Control Supervisor; Sales Executive; Software Engineer; Systems Manager; Telecommunications Manager. **Corporate headquarters location:** This Location. **Other U.S. locations:** San Diego CA. **Average salary range of placements:** More than $50,000. **Number of placements per year:** 100 - 199.

WORLD CLASS MANAGEMENT INC.
5550 SW Macadam Avenue, Suite 100, Portland OR 97201. 503/225-9128. **Fax:** 503/225-1848. **Contact:** Lynette Evans, Researcher. **Description:** A generalist executive search firm.

PERMANENT EMPLOYMENT AGENCIES

AARP SENIOR EMPLOYMENT PROGRAM
4610 SE Belmont, Suite 104, Portland OR 97215. 503/231-8078. **Contact:** Director. **Description:** A permanent employment agency that places people aged 55 and over in minimum wage positions of 20 hours a week. AARP Senior Employment Program also offers a training program.

API EMPLOYMENT AGENCY
5022 Commercial Street SE, Salem OR 97302. 503/585-9572. **Fax:** 503/364-3722. **Contact:** Recruiter. **Description:** A permanent employment agency. **Specializes in the areas of:** Automotive; Computer Science/Software; Industrial; Manufacturing. **Positions commonly filled include:** Accountant/Auditor; Automotive Mechanic; Clerical Supervisor; Customer Service Representative; Electrical/Electronics Engineer; General Manager. **Average salary range of placements:** $30,000 - $50,000. **Number of placements per year:** 50 - 99.

ADAMS & ASSOCIATES PERSONNEL, INC.
121 SW Morrison Street, Suite 430, Portland OR 97204. 503/224-5870. **Contact:** Office Manager. **Description:** A permanent employment agency. **Specializes in the areas of:** Clerical. **Positions commonly filled include:** Administrative Assistant; Advertising Clerk; Bookkeeper; Claim Rep.; Clerk; Computer Operator; Customer Service Representative; Data Entry Clerk; Legal Secretary; Medical Secretary; Public Relations Specialist; Purchasing Agent/Manager; Receptionist; Sales Rep.; Secretary; Stenographer; Typist/Word Processor. **Number of placements per year:** 500 - 999.

ADVANCE PERSONNEL SERVICES
441 Union Street NE, Salem OR 97301. 503/581-8906. **Contact:** Phil Lackaff, Manager. **Description:** A permanent employment agency. **Positions commonly filled include:** Accountant/Auditor; Administrative Assistant; Bank Officer/Manager; Bookkeeper; Buyer; Claim Rep.; Clerk; Commercial Artist; Computer Operator; Computer Programmer; Credit Manager; Customer Service Rep.; Data Entry Clerk; Draftsperson; Driver; General Manager; Human Resources Manager; Legal Secretary; Purchasing Agent/Manager; Receptionist; Sales Rep.; Secretary; Stenographer; Typist/Word Processor; Underwriter. **Number of placements per year:** 200 - 499.

AUNTIE FAY DOMESTIC AGENCY
10725 SW Barbur Boulevard, Suite 60, Portland OR 97219. 503/293-6252. **Contact:** Loyce Swayze, Owner. **Description:** A permanent employment agency that also provides some temporary placements. **Specializes in the areas of:** Child Care, In-Home; Eldercare, In-Home; Health/Medical. **Positions commonly filled include:** Certified Nurses Aide; Cook; Domestic Help; Housekeeper; Licensed Practical Nurse; Nanny; Preschool Worker; Registered Nurse.

FIRST CHOICE PERSONNEL
11330 SW Ambiance Place, Tigard OR 97223. 503/620-0717. **Fax:** 503/244-1544. **Contact:** Randall B. Carrier,

CPC/President. **Description:** A permanent employment agency. **Specializes in the areas of:** Computer Science/Software. **Positions commonly filled include:** Computer Programmer; Software Engineer; Systems Analyst. **Number of placements per year:** 1 - 49.

INITIAL STAFFING SERVICES
One Center Point Drive, Lake Oswego OR 97035. 503/603-9040. **Contact:** Manager. **Description:** A permanent employment agency that also provides some temporary placements. Founded in 1976. **Specializes in the areas of:** Accounting/Auditing; Administration; Banking; Computer Science/Software; Finance; Health/ Medical; Manufacturing; Personnel/Labor Relations; Retail; Sales; Secretarial; Technical. **Positions commonly filled include:** Accountant/Auditor; Administrative Manager; Bank Officer/Manager; Branch Manager; Claim Representative; Clerical Supervisor; Customer Service Representative; Human Resources Specialist; Operations/Production Manager; Public Relations Specialist; Purchasing Agent/Manager; Quality Control Supervisor; Services Sales Representative. **Benefits available to temporary workers:** Bonus Award/Plan; Dental Insurance; Medical Insurance; Referral Bonus Plan. **Number of placements per year:** 1000+.

INITIAL STAFFING SERVICES
700 NE Multnomah, Suite 1125, Portland OR 97232. 503/233-9121. **Contact:** Manager. **Description:** A permanent employment agency that also provides some temporary placements. **Specializes in the areas of:** Administration; Finance; Marketing; Sales; Technical. **Positions commonly filled include:** Accountant; Collections Agent; Customer Service Representative; Financial Analyst; Loan Processor; Network Administrator. **Benefits available to temporary workers:** Bonus Award/Plan; Medical Insurance; Paid Vacation. **Corporate headquarters location:** Houston TX. **Other U.S. locations:** Nationwide.

LEGAL NORTHWEST
522 SW Fifth Avenue, Suite 625, Portland OR 97204. 503/242-2514. **Contact:** Manager. **Description:** A permanent employment agency that also provides some temporary placements. **Specializes in the areas of:** Legal.

OFFICE CAREERS INC.
dba CORPORATE CAREERS INC.
1001 SW Fifth Avenue, Suite 1210, Portland OR 97204-1128. 503/242-2323. **Contact:** Manager. **Description:** A permanent agency. Founded in 1972. **Specializes in the areas of:** Accounting/Auditing; Administration; General Management; Personnel/Labor Relations; Sales; Secretarial. **Positions commonly filled include:** Accountant/Auditor; Administrative Manager; Advertising Clerk; Clerical Supervisor; Customer Service Rep.; Financial Analyst; Human Resources Manager; Human Service Worker; Paralegal; Public Relations Specialist; Services Sales Representative; Typist/Word Processor.

NANCY L. SABIN EMPLOYMENT AGENCY
1717 Avalon Street, Klamath Falls OR 97603. 541/882-5872. **Fax:** 541/882-5468. **Contact:** Manager. **Description:** A permanent employment agency. **Positions commonly filled include:** Accountant/Auditor; Administrative Manager; Advertising Clerk; Automotive Mechanic; Bank Officer/Manager; Blue-Collar Worker Supervisor; Branch Manager; Claim Representative; Clerical Supervisor; Computer Programmer; Construction and Building Inspector; Credit Manager; Draftsperson; Forester/Conservation Scientist; General Manager; Health Services Manager; Hotel Manager; Industrial Production Manager; Insurance Agent/Broker; Landscape Architect; Licensed Practical Nurse; Manufacturer's/Wholesaler's Sales Rep.; Market Research Analyst; Medical Records Technician; Occupational Therapist; Physical Therapist; Preschool Worker; Property and Real Estate Manager; Radiological Technologist; Real Estate Agent; Registered Nurse; Securities Sales Representative; Services Sales Representative; Social Worker; Stationary Engineer; Surveyor; Systems Analyst; Telecommunications Manager; Transportation/Traffic Specialist; Typist/Word Processor; Veterinarian.

TRIAD TECHNOLOGY GROUP
Lincoln Center Five, 10260 SW Greenburg Road, Suite 560, Portland OR 97223. 503/293-9545. **Fax:** 503/293-9546. **Contact:** Bruno Amicci, President. **E-mail address:** triadjob@triadtechnology.com. **World Wide Web address:** http://www.triadtechnology.com. **Description:** A permanent employment agency that also provides some contract placements. **Specializes in the areas of:** Administration; Engineering; Information Technology. **Positions commonly filled include:** Computer Programmer; Database Manager; Internet Services Manager; MIS Specialist; Project Manager; Software Engineer; Systems Analyst; Systems Manager; Technical Writer/Editor; Telecommunications Manager. **Average salary range of placements:** More than $50,000. **Number of placements per year:** 50 - 99.

TEMPORARY EMPLOYMENT AGENCIES

ACCOUNTANTS INC.
4949 SW Meadows Road, Suite 400, Lake Oswego OR 97035. 503/635-0073. **Fax:** 503/635-0128. **Contact:** Manager. **E-mail address:** accountantsinc@teleport.com. **World Wide Web address:** http://www.accountantsinc.com. **Description:** A temporary agency that also offers some permanent placements. **Specializes in the areas of:** Accounting; Finance. **Corporate headquarters location:** Burlingame CA. **Other area locations:** Portland OR. **Other U.S. locations:** Nationwide.

ACCOUNTANTS INC.
121 SW Morrison Street, Suite 825, Portland OR 97204. 503/248-4123. **Fax:** 503/248-4163. **Contact:** Manager. **World Wide Web address:** http://www.accountantsinc.com. **Description:** A temporary agency that also offers some permanent placements. **Specializes in the areas of:** Accounting; Finance. **Corporate headquarters location:** Burlingame CA. **Other area locations:** Lake Oswego OR. **Other U.S. locations:** Nationwide.

ADAMS TEMPORARIES
7567 SW Mohawk Street, Tualatin OR 97062. 503/692-6106. **Contact:** Manager. **Description:** A temporary agency. **Specializes in the areas of:** Administration; Clerical; Light Industrial; Office Support; Telemarketing.

AQUENT PARTNERS
124 SW Yamhill Street, 2nd Floor, Portland OR 97204-3007. 503/220-1820. **Toll-free phone:** 877/PARTNER. **Fax:** 503/220-1821. **Contact:** Kerry Muir, Manager. **E-mail address:** kmuir@aquent.com. **World Wide Web address:** http://www.aquentpartners.com. **Description:** A temporary agency that provides placements for creative, Web, and technical professionals. Aquent Partners also provides some temp-to-perm, permanent, and contract placements. **Specializes in the areas of:** Administration; Art/Design; Computer Science/Software; Marketing. **Positions commonly filled include:** Computer Animator; Computer Engineer; Computer Operator; Computer Programmer; Computer Support Technician; Computer Technician; Content Developer; Database Administrator; Database Manager; Desktop Publishing Specialist; Editor; Editorial Assistant; Graphic Artist; Graphic Designer; Internet Services Manager; Managing Editor; MIS Specialist; Multimedia Designer; Network/Systems Administrator; Production Manager; Project Manager; Software Engineer; SQL Programmer; Systems Analyst; Systems Manager; Technical Writer/Editor; Webmaster. **Benefits available to temporary workers:** 401(k); Dental Insurance; Disability Coverage; Medical Insurance. **CEO:** John Chuang.

BARRETT BUSINESS SERVICES, INC.
2401 NE Cornell Road, Suite K, Hillsboro OR 97124. 503/648-5053. **Contact:** Manager. **Description:** A temporary agency. Founded in 1951. **Specializes in the areas of:** Architecture/Construction; Engineering; Industrial; Personnel/Labor Relations; Secretarial. **Positions commonly filled include:** Blue-Collar Worker Supervisor; Civil Engineer; Clerical Supervisor; Computer Programmer; Construction and Building Inspector; Construction Contractor; Cost Estimator; Customer Service Rep.; Design Engineer; Designer; Draftsperson; Electrical/Electronics Engineer; Electrician; Human Resources Specialist; Industrial Engineer; Industrial Production Manager; Mechanical Engineer; Purchasing Agent/Manager; Quality Control Supervisor; Software Engineer; Structural Engineer; Systems Analyst; Typist/Word Processor. **Benefits available to temporary workers:** Medical Insurance; Paid Holidays; Paid Vacation. **Corporate headquarters location:** Portland OR. **Average salary range of placements:** $20,000 - $29,999. **Number of placements per year:** 1000+.

BARRETT BUSINESS SERVICES, INC.
1100 East Marina Way, Suite 221, Hood River OR 97031. 541/386-4407. **Fax:** 541/386-4414. **Contact:** Judy Dutcher, Manager. **E-mail address:** jobworks@gorge.net. **World Wide Web address:** http://www.barrettbusiness.com. **Description:** A temporary agency that also provides some permanent placements. Client company pays fee. **Specializes in the areas of:** Accounting; Administration; Construction; Light Industrial; Secretarial. **Positions commonly filled include:** Account Rep.; Accountant; Administrative Assistant; Administrative Manager; Assistant Manager; Clerical Supervisor; Computer Support Tech.; Customer Service Rep.; Database Administrator; Draftsperson; Graphic Designer; Human Resources Manager; Production Manager; Project Manager; Public Relations Specialist; Sales Representative; Secretary; Typist/Word Processor. **Benefits available to temporary workers:** 401(k). **Corporate headquarters location:** Portland OR. **Average salary range of placements:** $20,000 - $29,999. **Number of placements per year:** 50 - 99.

BARRETT BUSINESS SERVICES, INC.
700 North Hayden Island Drive, Suite 360, Tigard OR 97217. 503/285-1349. **Contact:** Manager. **Description:** A temporary agency. **Specializes in the areas of:** Transportation. **Positions commonly filled include:** Truck Driver. **Corporate headquarters location:** Portland OR.

CREATIVE ASSETS
400 SW Sixth Avenue, Suite 600, Portland OR 97204. **Contact:** Manager. **World Wide Web address:**

http://www.creativeassets.com. **Description:** A temporary agency. **Specializes in the areas of:** Digital Arts; Graphic Arts. **Office hours:** Monday - Friday, 8:00 a.m. - 5:30 p.m. **Other U.S. locations:** Los Angeles CA; San Francisco CA; Seattle WA.

EMPLOYMENT TRENDS, LLC
4800 SW Griffith Drive, Suite 104, Beaverton OR 97005. 503/350-2300. **Fax:** 503/644-7087. **Contact:** Heather Vanderwater, Operations Manager. **E-mail address:** hq@employmenttrends.com. **World Wide Web address:** http://www.employmenttrends.com. **Description:** A temporary agency. Founded in 1993. **Specializes in the areas of:** Clerical; Industrial; Light Industrial; Personnel/Labor Relations; Secretarial. **Positions commonly filled include:** Administrative Assistant; Assembler; Clerical Supervisor; Customer Service Rep.; Secretary; Typist/Word Processor; Warehouse/Distribution Worker. **Benefits available to temporary workers:** Bonus Award/Plan; Paid Holidays. **Other area locations:** 720 SW Washington Street, Suite 710, Portland OR 97205; 7931 NE Halsey, Suite 210, Portland OR 97213. **Average salary range of placements:** Less than $20,000. **Number of placements per year:** 1000+.

KELLY SERVICES, INC.
581 NE Third Street, McMinnville OR 97128. 503/434-4337. **Fax:** 503/472-0969. **Contact:** Recruiter/Trainer. **Description:** A temporary agency. Founded in 1946. **Specializes in the areas of:** Accounting/Auditing; Administration; Data Processing; Industrial; Manufacturing; Personnel/Labor Relations; Sales; Secretarial; Technical. **Positions commonly filled include:** Accountant/Auditor; Clerical Supervisor; Customer Service Rep.; Typist/Word Processor. **Benefits available to temporary workers:** Paid Holidays; Paid Vacation. **Corporate headquarters location:** Troy MI. **Average salary range of placements:** $20,000 - $29,999. **Number of placements per year:** 500 - 999.

KELLY SERVICES, INC.
8285 SW Nimbus Avenue, Suite 130, Beaverton OR 97008. 503/643-1614. **Fax:** 503/641-9086. **Contact:** Recruiter/Trainer. **Description:** A temporary agency. Founded in 1946. **Specializes in the areas of:** Administration; Industrial; Light Industrial; Manufacturing; Personnel/Labor Relations; Sales; Secretarial; Technical. **Positions commonly filled include:** Accountant/Auditor; Clerical Supervisor; Customer Service Rep.; Typist/Word Processor. **Benefits available to temporary workers:** Paid Holidays; Paid Vacation. **Corporate headquarters location:** Troy MI. **Average salary range of placements:** $20,000 - $29,999. **Number of placements per year:** 500 - 999.

KELLY SERVICES, INC.
456 State Street, Suite 100, Salem OR 97301. 503/364-3591. **Fax:** 503/588-1965. **Contact:** Recruiter/Trainer. **Description:** A temporary agency. Founded in 1946. **Specializes in the areas of:** Administration; Industrial; Light Industrial; Manufacturing; Personnel/Labor Relations; Sales; Secretarial; Technical. **Positions commonly filled include:** Accountant/Auditor; Clerical Supervisor; Customer Service Rep.; Typist/Word Processor. **Benefits available to temporary workers:** Paid Holidays; Paid Vacation. **Corporate headquarters location:** Troy MI. **Average salary range of placements:** $20,000 - $29,999. **Number of placements per year:** 500 - 999.

KELLY SERVICES, INC.
1823 14th Avenue SE, Albany OR 97321. 541/967-8858. **Fax:** 541/967-7152. **Contact:** Recruiter/Trainer. **Description:** A temporary agency. Founded in 1946. **Specializes in the areas of:** Administration; Industrial; Light Industrial; Manufacturing; Personnel/Labor Relations; Sales; Secretarial; Technical. **Positions commonly filled include:** Accountant/Auditor; Clerical Supervisor; Customer Service Representative; Typist/Word Processor. **Benefits available to temporary workers:** Paid Holidays; Paid Vacation. **Corporate**

headquarters location: Troy MI. **Average salary range of placements:** $20,000 - $29,999. **Number of placements per year:** 500 - 999.

KELLY SERVICES, INC.
700 NE Multnomah, Suite 350, Portland OR 97232. 503/230-2221. **Contact:** Recruiter/Trainer. **Description:** A temporary agency. Founded in 1946. **Specializes in the areas of:** Administration; Industrial; Light Industrial; Manufacturing; Personnel/Labor Relations; Sales; Secretarial; Technical. **Positions commonly filled include:** Accountant/Auditor; Clerical Supervisor; Customer Service Representative; Human Service Worker; Typist/Word Processor. **Benefits available to temporary workers:** Paid Holidays; Paid Vacation. **Corporate headquarters location:** Troy MI. **Average salary range of placements:** $20,000 - $29,999. **Number of placements per year:** 500 - 999.

MANPOWER TEMPORARY SERVICES
1000 SW Broadway, Suite 1550, Portland OR 97205. 503/226-6281. **Contact:** Branch Manager. **Description:** A temporary agency. **Specializes in the areas of:** Data Processing; Industrial; Office Support; Technical; Word Processing. **Positions commonly filled include:** Accountant/Auditor; Accounting Clerk; Administrative Assistant; Assembly Worker; Biological Scientist; Bookkeeper; Chemist; Computer Operator; Customer Service Representative; Desktop Publishing Specialist; Electrician; Inspector/Tester/Grader; Inventory Control Specialist; Machine Operator; Packaging/Processing Worker; Painter; Project Engineer; Proofreader; Receptionist; Research Assistant; Secretary; Software Engineer; Stenographer; Systems Analyst; Technical Writer/Editor; Technician; Typist/Word Processor; Welder. **Benefits available to temporary workers:** Life Insurance; Medical Insurance; Paid Holidays; Paid Vacation. **Number of placements per year:** 1000+.

NORTHWEST TEMPORARY & STAFFING SERVICES
522 SW Fifth Avenue, Suite 825, Portland OR 97204. 503/242-0611. **Fax:** 503/323-9137. **Contact:** Peggy A. Pollem, Recruiter. **E-mail address:** ppollem@ntss.com. **World Wide Web address:** http://www.ntss.com. **Description:** A temporary agency. Founded in 1985. **Specializes in the areas of:** Accounting; Administration; Computer Science/Software; Finance; Health/Medical; Industrial; Insurance; Legal; Light Industrial; Secretarial. **Positions commonly filled include:** Accountant; Administrative Assistant; Auditor; Budget Analyst; Clerical Supervisor; Controller; Customer Service Representative; Desktop Publishing Specialist; Financial Analyst; Paralegal; Secretary; Technical Writer/Editor; Typist/Word Processor. **Benefits available to temporary workers:** 401(k); Medical Insurance; Paid Holidays; Paid Vacation. **Corporate headquarters location:** This Location. **Other U.S. locations:** CA; ID; WA. **Number of placements per year:** 1000+.

PROTEM PROFESSIONAL STAFFING SERVICES
1001 SW Fifth Avenue, Suite 1225, Portland OR 97204. 503/228-1177. **Contact:** Office Manager. **Description:** A temporary agency that also provides some permanent placements. **Specializes in the areas of:** Personnel/Labor Relations. **Positions commonly filled include:** Accountant/Auditor; Clerk; Computer Operator; Computer Programmer; Data Entry Clerk; Draftsperson; Electrical/Electronics Engineer; Financial Analyst; Legal Secretary; Receptionist; Secretary; Stenographer; Systems Analyst; Technical Writer/Editor; Technician; Typist/Word Processor. **Number of placements per year:** 1000+.

QUEST TEMPORARY SERVICES
9150 SW Pioneer Court, Suite Q, Wilsonville OR 97070. 503/682-9292. **Fax:** 503/682-4912. **Contact:** B.J. Shrock, Owner. **Description:** A temporary agency that also provides career/outplacement counseling. Founded in 1995. **Specializes in the areas of:** Industrial; Manufacturing; Personnel/Labor Relations; Publishing; Secretarial. **Positions commonly filled include:** Administrative Manager; Blue-Collar Worker

Supervisor; Clerical Supervisor; Computer Programmer; Credit Manager; Customer Service Representative; Draftsperson; Human Resources Specialist; Industrial Production Manager; Management Trainee; Medical Records Technician; Operations/Production Manager; Paralegal; Purchasing Agent/Manager; Quality Control Supervisor; Technical Writer/Editor; Typist/Word Processor; Underwriter/Assistant Underwriter. **Benefits available to temporary workers:** Paid Holidays; Paid Vacation. **Corporate headquarters location:** This Location. **Other area locations:** Tigard OR. **Average salary range of placements:** Less than $20,000. **Number of placements per year:** 1000+.

UNIFORCE STAFFING SERVICES
10121 SE Sunnyside Road, Suite 235, Clackamas OR 97015-9749. 503/652-2543. **Fax:** 503/659-0257. **Contact:** Manager. **E-mail address:** uniforc4@

ix.netcom.com. **Description:** A temporary agency. **Specializes in the areas of:** Accounting/Auditing; Light Industrial; Printing; Publishing; Retail; Secretarial. **Positions commonly filled include:** Administrative Manager; Biological Scientist; Biomedical Engineer; Chemical Engineer; Chemist; Civil Engineer; Computer Programmer; Customer Service Representative; Design Engineer; Designer; Draftsperson; Electrical/Electronics Engineer; Environmental Engineer; Food Scientist/ Technologist; Industrial Engineer; Mechanical Engineer; Metallurgical Engineer; MIS Specialist; Software Engineer; Stationary Engineer; Structural Engineer; Systems Analyst; Technical Writer/Editor. **Benefits available to temporary workers:** 401(k); Dental Insurance; Health Club Discount; Medical Insurance; Vision Plan. **Corporate headquarters location:** New York NY. **Number of placements per year:** 1000+.

CONTRACT SERVICES FIRMS

CDI TECHNICAL SERVICES
15250 NW Greenbriar Parkway, Beaverton OR 97006. 503/533-2200. **Contact:** Manager. **World Wide Web address:** http://www.cdicorp.com. **Description:** A contract services firm. **Specializes in the areas of:** Engineering; Technical. **Corporate headquarters location:** Philadelphia PA. **Other U.S. locations:** Nationwide. **International locations:** Worldwide.

HALL KINION
10260 SW Greenburg Road, Suite 810, Portland OR 97223. **Toll-free phone:** 888/302-2700. **Fax:** 503/244-6522. **Contact:** Manager. **E-mail address:** orresume@ hallkinion.com. **World Wide Web address:** http://www. hallkinion.com. **Description:** A contract services firm that also provides some permanent placements. **Specializes in the areas of:** Information Systems; Information Technology; Internet Development; Network Administration; Quality Assurance; Systems Administration; Systems Design; Technical Writing.

UNIFORCE STAFFING SERVICES
7320 SW Hunziker Road, Suite 103, Tigard OR 97223. 503/968-1311. **Fax:** 503/968-1088. **Contact:** Vice

President. **Description:** A contract services firm. **Specializes in the areas of:** Computer Science/Software; Engineering; Industrial; Scientific; Technical. **Positions commonly filled include:** Applications Engineer; Biochemist; Biological Scientist; Biomedical Engineer; Chemical Engineer; Chemist; Civil Engineer; Clinical Lab Technician; Computer Operator; Computer Programmer; Database Manager; Design Engineer; Draftsperson; Electrical/Electronics Engineer; Environmental Engineer; Geologist/Geophysicist; Graphic Artist; Graphic Designer; Industrial Engineer; Internet Services Manager; Manufacturing Engineer; Mechanical Engineer; Metallurgical Engineer; Sales Engineer; Software Engineer; Systems Analyst; Systems Manager; Technical Writer/Editor; Webmaster. **Corporate headquarters location:** New York NY. **Other U.S. locations:** Nationwide. **Number of placements per year:** 1000+.

VOLT SERVICES GROUP
6443 SW Beaverton Hillsdale Highway, Suite 102, Portland OR 97221. 503/292-7525. **Contact:** Manager. **Description:** A contract services firm. **Specializes in the areas of:** Technical.

CAREER/OUTPLACEMENT COUNSELING FIRMS

BERNARD HALDANE ASSOCIATES
1221 SW Yamhill, Suite 124, Portland OR 97205. 503/295-5926. **Contact:** Manager. **Description:** Bernard Haldane Associates is a career/outplacement consulting firm.

HIGHLANDS PROGRAM
635 Church Street NE, Salem OR 97301. 503/588-2362. **Contact:** David Sweet, Ph.D., Counselor. **World Wide Web address:** http://www.highlandsprogram.com. **Description:** Provides career counseling to students and adults, and training and development to corporations.

EXECUTIVE SEARCH FIRMS

ACCOUNTANTS EXECUTIVE SEARCH ACCOUNTANTS ON CALL
2005 Market Street, Suite 520, Philadelphia PA 19103. 215/568-5600. **Contact:** Mark S. Libes, President. **Description:** An executive search firm. Accountants On Call (also at this location) provides temporary placements. **Specializes in the areas of:** Accounting/Auditing; Banking; Finance.

ACCOUNTANTS EXECUTIVE SEARCH ACCOUNTANTS ON CALL
437 Grant Street, Suite 1615, Pittsburgh PA 15219. 412/391-0900. **Fax:** 412/391-8288. **Contact:** Manager. **E-mail address:** pittsburgh@aocnet.com. **World Wide Web address:** http://www.aocnet.com. **Description:** An executive search firm operating on a contingency basis. Accountants On Call (also at this location) provides temporary placements. Founded in 1979. Client company pays fee. **Specializes in the areas of:** Accounting; Finance. **Positions commonly filled include:** Accountant; Auditor; Budget Analyst; Chief Financial Officer; Controller; Cost Estimator; Finance Director; Financial Analyst. **Corporate headquarters location:** Saddle Brook NJ. **Other U.S. locations:** Nationwide. **International locations:** Australia; Canada; United Kingdom.

J.N. ADAMS & ASSOCIATES INC.
301 South Allen Street, State College PA 16801. 814/234-0670. **Fax:** 814/234-4361. **Contact:** Eric M. Berg, President. **E-mail address:** jnadams@naccess.net. **World Wide Web address:** http://www. statecollege.net/jnadams. **Description:** An executive search firm. **Specializes in the areas of:** Engineering; Manufacturing; Quality Assurance. **Positions commonly filled include:** Chemical Engineer; Design Engineer; Manufacturing Engineer; Metallurgical Engineer; Quality Assurance Engineer; Statistician. **Corporate headquarters location:** This Location. **Average salary range of placements:** More than $50,000. **Number of placements per year:** 50 - 99.

ADVANCE RECRUITING SERVICES
1250 Wall Avenue, Clairton PA 15025. 412/233-8808. **Fax:** 412/233-8814. **Contact:** Joe Giansante, Owner. **Description:** An executive search firm operating on a contingency basis. The firm also provides some temporary placements and contract services. **Specializes in the areas of:** Computer Science/Software; Sales; Telephone Technical Support. **Positions commonly filled include:** MIS Specialist; Multimedia Designer; Services Sales Representative; Software Engineer; Technical Writer/Editor; Telecommunications Manager; Video Production Coordinator. **Benefits available to temporary workers:** Medical Insurance. **Average salary range of placements:** $30,000 - $50,000. **Number of placements per year:** 1 - 49.

ADVANCED TECHNOLOGY RESOURCES
Advanced Technology Center, 350 Saxonburg Road, Suite 100, Butler PA 16002-3621. 724/282-3333. **Fax:** 724/282-3345. **Contact:** Bernie Flynn, Principal. **E-mail address:** bflynn@atrinc.com. **World Wide Web address:** http://www.industry.net/advanced.tech. **Description:** An executive search firm operating on both retainer and contingency bases. Advanced Technology Resources also provides contract services. **Specializes in the areas of:** Engineering; Information Technology; Software Engineering; Telecommunications. **Other area locations:** Pittsburgh PA.

ADVENT ASSOCIATES
350 Carogin Drive, State College PA 16803. 814/235-1401. **Fax:** 814/235-1405. **Contact:** Howie Shultz, President. **Description:** An executive search firm. **Specializes in the areas of:** Health/Medical; Information Systems.

ALEXANDER PERSONNEL ASSOCIATES
P.O. Box 456, Langhorne PA 19047. 215/757-4935. **Contact:** Tom Sliwinski, Manager. **Description:** An executive search firm operating on a contingency basis. **Specializes in the areas of:** Accounting/Auditing; Engineering; General Management; Industrial; Manufacturing; Office Support; Sales; Secretarial; Technical.

AMATO & ASSOCIATES INSURANCE RECRUITERS
1313 Medford Road, Suite 100, Wynnewood PA 19096-2418. 610/642-9696. **Fax:** 610/642-9797. **Contact:** Ms. Bobbi Amato, President. **Description:** An executive search firm operating on both retainer and contingency bases. Client company pays fee. **Specializes in the areas of:** Insurance. **Positions commonly filled include:** Account Representative; Branch Manager; Insurance Agent/Broker; Loss Prevention Specialist; Underwriter/Assistant Underwriter. **Corporate headquarters location:** This Location. **Average salary range of placements:** More than $50,000. **Number of placements per year:** 1 - 49.

AMERICAN SEARCH ASSOCIATES
3801 Kings Arms Lane, York PA 17402-5125. 717/757-2033. **Fax:** 717/757-2422. **Contact:** Bill Willson, President. **Description:** An executive search firm operating on both retainer and contingency bases. **Specializes in the areas of:** Accounting/Auditing; Engineering; Food; General Management; Industrial; Manufacturing; Personnel/Labor Relations; Publishing. **Positions commonly filled include:** Accountant/Auditor; Aerospace Engineer; Architect; Attorney; Biological Scientist; Buyer; Chemical Engineer; Chemist; Civil Engineer; Computer Programmer; Customer Service Rep.; Design Engineer; Designer; Draftsperson; Electrical/Electronics Engineer; Electrician; Environmental Engineer; General Manager; Human Resources Manager; Industrial Engineer; Industrial Production Manager; Manufacturer's/Wholesaler's Sales Rep.; Materials Engineer; Mechanical Engineer; Mining Engineer; MIS Specialist; Nuclear Engineer; Operations/Production Manager; Petroleum Engineer; Purchasing Agent/Manager; Quality Control Supervisor; Services Sales Rep.; Software Engineer; Stationary Engineer; Structural Engineer; Systems Analyst. **Other U.S. locations:** Nationwide. **Average salary range of placements:** $30,000 - $50,000. **Number of placements per year:** 50 - 99.

ANDRE GROUP, INC.
500 North Gulph Road, Suite 210, King of Prussia PA 19406. 610/337-0600. **Fax:** 610/337-1333. **Contact:** Richard Andre, President. **Description:** An executive search firm. **Specializes in the areas of:** Human Resources. **Average salary range of placements:** More than $50,000. **Number of placements per year:** 200 - 499.

ANITA'S CAREERS, INC.
The Colonade, 100 Old York Road, Suite E-714, Jenkintown PA 19046. 215/517-8089. **Fax:** 215/517-8556. **Contact:** Anita Klein, President. **E-mail address:** careers2k@aol.com. **World Wide Web address:** http://members.aol.com/careers2k. **Description:** An executive search firm operating on a contingency basis. The agency also provides some contract and career/outplacement counseling services. **Specializes in the areas of:** Accounting; Administration; Engineering; Finance; General Management; Insurance; MIS/EDP; Printing; Publishing; Sales; Secretarial. **Positions commonly filled include:** Account Manager; Account Rep.; Accountant; Adjuster; Administrative Assistant; Administrative Manager; Ad Clerk; Ad Exec.; Applications Engineer; Assistant Manager; Auditor; Branch Manager; Buyer; Chemist; CFO; Civil Engineer; Claim Rep.; Clerical Supervisor; Clinical Lab Tech.;

Computer Operator; Computer Programmer; Consultant; Controller; Cost Estimator; Credit Manager; Customer Service Rep.; Editor; Editorial Assistant; Electrical/Electronics Engineer; Finance Director; Financial Analyst; General Manager; Graphic Artist; Human Resources Manager; Industrial Engineer; Industrial Production Manager; Management Analyst/Consultant; Management Trainee; Managing Editor; Market Research Analyst; Marketing Manager; Marketing Specialist; Medical Records Technician; Metallurgical Engineer; MIS Specialist; Multimedia Designer; Operations Manager; Paralegal; Production Manager; Project Manager; Public Relations Specialist; Purchasing Agent/Manager; Quality Control Supervisor; Sales Engineer; Sales Exec.; Sales Manager; Sales Rep.; Secretary; Software Engineer; Systems Analyst; Systems Manager; Technical Writer/Editor; Telecommunications Manager; Transportation/Traffic Specialist; Typist/Word Processor; Underwriter/Assistant Underwriter; Vice President of Operations. **Corporate headquarters location:** This Location. **Other U.S. locations:** Nationwide. **Average salary range of placements:** More than $50,000. **Number of placements per year:** 100 - 199.

ARROW SEARCH CONSULTANTS
736 Louis Drive, Warminster PA 18974. 215/957-9750. **Fax:** 215/441-4094. **Contact:** Manager. **Description:** An executive search firm. **Specializes in the areas of:** Engineering; Manufacturing; Marketing; Sales.

ASHLEY SEARCH CONSULTANTS
One Neshaming Plaza, Suite 221, Bensalem PA 19020. 215/245-5200. **Fax:** 215/245-5779. **Contact:** Craig Belnick, President. **E-mail address:** ashleysc@erols.com. **Description:** An executive search firm operating on a contingency basis. **Specializes in the areas of:** Accounting/Auditing; Administration; Engineering; Fashion; General Management; Personnel/Labor Relations; Retail. **Positions commonly filled include:** Accountant/Auditor; Chief Financial Officer; Computer Programmer; Controller; Design Engineer; Finance Director; Human Resources Manager; Management Trainee; MIS Specialist; Purchasing Agent/Manager; Software Engineer; Systems Analyst; Systems Manager. **Average salary range of placements:** $30,000 - $50,000. **Number of placements per year:** 50 - 99.

ATOMIC PERSONNEL, INC.
P.O. Box 11244, Elkins Park PA 19027-0244. 215/885-4223. **Fax:** 215/885-4225. **Contact:** Arthur L. Krasnow, President. **Description:** An executive search firm operating on a contingency basis. Founded in 1959. **Specializes in the areas of:** Construction; Engineering; Food; Industrial; Marketing; Sales; Scientific; Technical. **Positions commonly filled include:** Applications Engineer; Biochemist; Biomedical Engineer; Buyer; Chemical Engineer; Civil Engineer; Construction Engineer; Design Engineer; Electrical/Electronics Engineer; Environmental Engineer; Food Scientist/Technologist; Geologist/Geophysicist; Industrial Engineer; Industrial Production Manager; Manufacturing Engineer; Marketing Manager; Marketing Specialist; Mechanical Engineer; Metallurgical Engineer; Production Manager; Project Manager; Purchasing Agent/Manager; Quality Assurance Engineer; Sales Engineer; Sales Manager; Statistician. **Corporate headquarters location:** This Location.

BARR ASSOCIATES
93 South Westend Boulevard, Suite 105B, Quakertown PA 18951. 215/538-9411. **Fax:** 215/538-9466. **Contact:** Sharon Barr, Owner/Director. **E-mail address:** barr@pipeline.com. **Description:** An executive search firm. **Specializes in the areas of:** Electronics; Engineering; High-Tech. **Positions commonly filled include:** Design Engineer; Electrical/Electronics Engineer; Human Resources Manager; Market Research Analyst; Operations/Production Manager; Quality Control Supervisor; Software Engineer; Technical Writer/Editor;

Telecommunications Manager. **Number of placements per year:** 50 - 99.

BARTON PERSONNEL SYSTEMS, INC.
121 North Cedar Crest Boulevard, Allentown PA 18104-4664. 610/439-8751. **Fax:** 610/439-1207. **Contact:** Malcolm Singerman, Manager. **Description:** An executive search firm operating on a retainer basis. **Specializes in the areas of:** Accounting/Auditing; Engineering; Finance; Health/Medical; Information Technology; Sales. **Positions commonly filled include:** Accountant/Auditor; Buyer; Computer Programmer; Electrical/Electronics Engineer; Human Resources Manager; Management Analyst/Consultant; MIS Specialist; Physical Therapist; Software Engineer; Systems Analyst. **Average salary range of placements:** More than $50,000. **Number of placements per year:** 200 - 499.

BASILONE-OLIVER EXECUTIVE SEARCH
4840 McKnight Road, Suite 101, Pittsburgh PA 15237. 412/931-9501. **Fax:** 412/931-9741. **Contact:** Larry S. Basilone, Partner/Owner. **World Wide Web address:** http://www.basilone-oliver.com. **Description:** An executive search firm operating on a contingency basis. **Specializes in the areas of:** Accounting/Auditing; Banking; Computer Science/Software; Economics; Finance; Industrial; Manufacturing; Personnel/Labor Relations; Retail. **Positions commonly filled include:** Accountant/Auditor; Chief Financial Officer; Controller; Financial Analyst; Human Resources Manager; Manufacturing Manager; Market Research Analyst; President; Statistician. **Other U.S. locations:** Atlanta GA. **Average salary range of placements:** More than $50,000. **Number of placements per year:** 50 - 99.

BENDER & ASSOCIATES INTERNATIONAL INC.
Penn Center West, Building 3, Suite 221, Pittsburgh PA 15276. 412/787-8550. **Contact:** Manager. **Description:** An executive search firm. **Specializes in the areas of:** Computer Hardware/Software; Engineering.

T.W. BORIS ASSOCIATES
375 Warner Road, Wayne PA 19087. 610/687-8165. **Fax:** 610/687-5830. **Contact:** Theodore Boris, President. **Description:** An executive search firm operating on both retainer and contingency bases. Founded in 1977. Client company pays fee. **Specializes in the areas of:** Administration; Computer Science/Software; Engineering; Information Technology; MIS/EDP; Sales; Technical. **Positions commonly filled include:** Account Manager; Account Representative; Applications Engineer; AS400 Programmer Analyst; Branch Manager; Chemical Engineer; Chemist; Civil Engineer; Computer Operator; Computer Programmer; Consultant; Cost Estimator; Database Administrator; Database Manager; Design Engineer; Draftsperson; Electrical/Electronics Engineer; Environmental Engineer; General Manager; Geologist/Geophysicist; Internet Services Manager; Manufacturing Engineer; Marketing Manager; Marketing Specialist; Mechanical Engineer; MIS Specialist; Multimedia Designer; Network/Systems Administrator; Operations Manager; Project Manager; Sales Engineer; Sales Executive; Sales Manager; Software Engineer; SQL Programmer; Systems Analyst; Systems Manager; Technical Writer/Editor; Telecommunications Manager; Transportation/Traffic Specialist; Vice President. **Corporate headquarters location:** This Location. **Average salary range of placements:** More than $50,000. **Number of placements per year:** 50 - 99.

BOYDEN
625 Stanwix Street, Suite 2405, Pittsburgh PA 15222. 412/391-3020. **Contact:** Manager. **E-mail address:** boydenpgh@aol.com. **World Wide Web address:** http://www.boyden.com. **Description:** A generalist executive search firm. **Corporate headquarters location:** New York NY. **Other U.S. locations:** San Francisco CA; Washington DC; Chicago IL; Bloomfield Hills MI; Chesterfield MO; Morristown NJ; Hawthorne NY; Houston TX. **International locations:** Worldwide.

BRACKIN & SAYERS ASSOCIATES
1000 McKnight Park Drive, Pittsburgh PA 15237. 412/367-4644. **Contact:** Manager. **Description:** An executive search firm. **Specializes in the areas of:** Accounting/Auditing; Finance; Human Resources; Manufacturing; Materials; Public Relations.

CMIS
24 Hagerty Boulevard, Suite 9, West Chester PA 19380. 610/430-0013. **Fax:** 610/696-5430. **Contact:** Peter DiNicola, President. **E-mail address:** cmis@erols.com. **Description:** An executive search firm. **Specializes in the areas of:** Computer Science/Software; Sales. **Positions commonly filled include:** Computer Programmer; Software Engineer; Systems Analyst; Telecommunications Manager. **Average salary range of placements:** More than $50,000. **Number of placements per year:** 1 - 49.

CALIBER ASSOCIATES
125 Strafford Avenue, Suite 112, Wayne PA 19087. 610/971-1880. **Fax:** 610/971-1887. **Contact:** Steven P. Hochberg, President. **Description:** An executive search firm. **Specializes in the areas of:** Biology; Food; General Management; Health/Medical. **Positions commonly filled include:** Biological Scientist; Chemist; Health Services Manager; Pharmacist. **Number of placements per year:** 1 - 49.

CAREER CONCEPTS STAFFING SERVICES
4504 Peach Street, Erie PA 16509. 814/868-2333. **Fax:** 814/868-3238. **Contact:** Joseph A. DiGiorgio, Vice President. **Description:** An executive search firm. **Specializes in the areas of:** Accounting; Administration; Computer Science/Software; Engineering; Finance; Food; General Management; Industrial; Manufacturing; Personnel/Labor Relations; Plastics; Sales; Technical. **Positions commonly filled include:** Accountant/Auditor; Aerospace Engineer; Agricultural Engineer; Biological Scientist; Biomedical Engineer; Buyer; Chemical Engineer; Chemist; Civil Engineer; Electrical/Electronics Engineer; General Manager; Health Services Manager; Human Resources Manager; Industrial Engineer; Industrial Production Manager; Mechanical Engineer; Purchasing Agent/Manager; Quality Control Supervisor; Science Technologist; Technical Writer/Editor. **Number of placements per year:** 50 - 99.

CAREER QUEST CONFIDENTIAL, INC.
355 Fifth Avenue, Park Building, Suite 1021, Pittsburgh PA 15222. 412/471-9577. **Fax:** 412/471-9580. **Contact:** Thomas Geibel, President. **Description:** An executive search firm. **Specializes in the areas of:** Administration; Computer Science/Software; Engineering; Finance; Health/Medical; Legal; Manufacturing; Secretarial; Technical. **Positions commonly filled include:** Accountant; Brokerage Clerk; Chemical Engineer; Civil Engineer; Clerical Supervisor; Computer Programmer; Credit Manager; Dental Assistant/Dental Hygienist; Design Engineer; Designer; Draftsperson; Electrical/Electronics Engineer; Environmental Engineer; Financial Analyst; General Manager; Human Resources Manager; Industrial Engineer; Industrial Production Manager; Legal Secretary; Mechanical Engineer; Medical Records Technician; Metallurgical Engineer; Mining Engineer; Nuclear Engineer; Operations/Production Manager; Paralegal; Petroleum Engineer; Registered Nurse; Software Engineer; Stationary Engineer; Structural Engineer; Surveyor; Systems Analyst; Technical Writer/Editor; Typist/Word Processor. **Average salary range of placements:** $20,000 - $29,999. **Number of placements per year:** 1 - 49.

CAWLEY ASSOCIATES
670 Louis Drive, Warminster PA 18974. 215/957-9162. **Fax:** 215/957-6090. **Contact:** Manager. **Description:** An executive search firm. **Specializes in the areas of:** Accounting.

CENTURY ASSOCIATES
1420 Walnut Street, Philadelphia PA 19102. 215/732-4311. **Fax:** 215/735-1804. **Contact:** Manager. **E-mail address:** questions@centuryassociates.com. **World Wide Web address:** http://www.centuryassociates.com. **Description:** An executive search firm. **Specializes in the areas of:** Information Technology; Marketing; Medical Sales and Marketing; Sales; Technical.

A.D. CHECK & ASSOCIATES, INC.
204 South Franklin, Wilkes-Barre PA 18701. 570/829-5066. **Contact:** Manager. **Description:** An executive search firm. **Specializes in the areas of:** Manufacturing.

R. CHRISTINE ASSOCIATES
Front & Orange Streets, Media PA 19063. 610/565-3310. **Fax:** 610/565-3313. **Contact:** Richard Christine, Owner. **Description:** An executive search firm. **Specializes in the areas of:** Engineering; Manufacturing; Sales; Technical. **Positions commonly filled include:** Chemical Engineer; Electrical/Electronics Engineer; Industrial Engineer; Mechanical Engineer. **Number of placements per year:** 1 - 49.

CHURCHILL & AFFILIATES
1200 Bustleton Pike, Suite 3, Feasterville PA 19053-4118. 215/364-8070. **Contact:** Harvey Wasserman, President. **Description:** An executive search firm operating on a retainer basis. **Specializes in the areas of:** Sales. **Positions commonly filled include:** Internet Services Manager; Market Research Analyst; Multimedia Designer; Public Relations Specialist; Strategic Relations Manager. **Average salary range of placements:** More than $50,000. **Number of placements per year:** 50 - 99.

COMPUTER PROFESSIONALS, INC.
175 Strafford Avenue, Suite 310, Wayne PA 19087. 610/687-7732. **Fax:** 610/687-7885. **Contact:** Manager. **E-mail address:** admin@cpicpi.com. **World Wide Web address:** http://www.cpicpi.com. **Description:** An executive search firm. **Specializes in the areas of:** Computer Hardware/Software; Computer Operations; Computer Programming; Network Administration; Web Development.

JOSEPH CONAHAN EXECUTIVE RECRUITERS
251 South 24th Street, 3rd Floor, Philadelphia PA 19103. 215/545-3337. **Fax:** 215/545-6555. **Contact:** Manager. **Description:** An executive search firm. **Specializes in the areas of:** Accounting/Auditing; Finance.

CONSEARCH
911 Poplar Street, Erie PA 16502. 814/459-5588. **Fax:** 814/459-5582. **Contact:** Jim Lyons, President/Owner. **Description:** An executive search firm. **Specializes in the areas of:** Engineering; Manufacturing. **Positions commonly filled include:** Accountant; Aerospace Engineer; Bank Officer/Manager; Buyer; Ceramics Engineer; Computer Programmer; Electrical/Electronics Engineer; Human Resources Manager; Industrial Engineer; Industrial Production Manager; Materials Engineer; Mechanical Engineer; Metallurgical Engineer; Occupational Therapist; Operations/Production Manager; Purchasing Agent/Manager; Quality Control Supervisor; Software Engineer; Systems Analyst. **Number of placements per year:** 1 - 49.

CORPORATE MANAGEMENT SERVICES
P.O. Box 16271, Pittsburgh PA 15220. 412/279-1180. **Contact:** Manager. **Description:** An executive search firm. **Specializes in the areas of:** Engineering; Manufacturing.

COURTRIGHT & ASSOCIATES
P.O. Box 503, Clarks Summit PA 18411. 570/586-0735. **Contact:** Robert Courtright, President. **Description:** An executive search firm. **Specializes in the areas of:** Biotechnology. **Average salary range of placements:** $50,000 - $100,000. **Number of placements per year:** 1 - 49.

DPSI MEDICAL
5105 Clinton Street, Erie PA 16509. 814/868-0961. **Contact:** Ron Spero, CPC/President/Owner.

Description: An executive search firm operating on both retainer and contingency bases. **Specializes in the areas of:** Health/Medical. **Positions commonly filled include:** Physical Therapist; Physician.

P. ROBERT DANN
1601 Market Street, Suite 600, Philadelphia PA 19103. 215/563-8008. **Fax:** 215/563-4456. **Contact:** Robert Schneiderman, President. **Description:** An executive search firm. **Specializes in the areas of:** Accounting/ Auditing; Administration; General Management; Health/ Medical; Legal. **Positions commonly filled include:** Accountant/Auditor; Attorney; Branch Manager; Computer Programmer; Customer Service Rep.; Dietician/Nutritionist; General Manager; Health Services Manager; Hotel Manager; Human Resources Manager; MIS Specialist; Occupational Therapist; Paralegal; Physical Therapist; Physician; Restaurant/Food Service Manager; Securities Sales Representative; Services Sales Representative; Systems Analyst; Travel Agent. **Average salary range of placements:** $20,000 - $29,999. **Number of placements per year:** 200 - 499.

D'ELIA & ASSOCIATES, INC.
One First Avenue, Conshohocken PA 19428. 610/940-1463. **Fax:** 610/834-8470. **Contact:** Manager. **E-mail address:** info@deliassoc.com. **World Wide Web address:** http://www.deliassoc.com. **Description:** An executive search firm. **Specializes in the areas of:** Consulting; Finance; Human Resources; Information Technology; Management; Marketing; Telecommunications.

DELTA PROSEARCH
P.O. Box 267, Delta PA 17314. 717/456-7172. **Toll-free phone:** 800/753-6693. **Contact:** John Banister, President. **Description:** An executive search firm. **Specializes in the areas of:** Health/Medical; Pharmaceuticals. **Positions commonly filled include:** Medical Technologist; Pharmacist; Physical Therapist. **Number of placements per year:** 1 - 49.

ROBERT J. DePAUL & ASSOCIATES INC.
71 McMurray Road, Brookside Office Park, Suite 208, Pittsburgh PA 15241. 412/561-0417. **Contact:** David J. Schopt, Placement Counselor. **World Wide Web address:** http://www.rjdepaul.com. **Description:** An executive search firm specializing in information management. The firm also provides some permanent, temporary and contract placements, and management consulting services. Consulting services include the fields of third generation programming languages (COBOL, CICS, C); database design (IMS, Oracle, Rdb, DB2); PC support and training services; microcomputer-based languages (DBase, Clipper, Paradox); and networking and client-server technology (Novell). **Specializes in the areas of:** Administration; Banking; Computer Science/Software; Health/Medical; Retail. **Positions commonly filled include:** Computer Programmer; Network Engineer; Systems Analyst; Telecommunications Manager. **Benefits available to temporary workers:** Dental Insurance; Medical Insurance. **Average salary range of placements:** $30,000 - $60,000.

DiCENZO PERSONNEL SPECIALISTS
428 Forbes Avenue, Suite 110, Pittsburgh PA 15219. 412/281-6207. **Fax:** 412/281-9326. **Contact:** Carmela DiCenzo, Owner. **Description:** An executive search firm operating on both retainer and contingency bases. **Specializes in the areas of:** Engineering; Marketing; Sales; Secretarial. **Positions commonly filled include:** Account Manager; Account Representative; Accountant; Administrative Assistant; Advertising Clerk; Applications Engineer; Auditor; Biomedical Engineer; Buyer; Chemical Engineer; Chemist; Civil Engineer; Computer Operator; Computer Programmer; Cost Estimator; Database Manager; Design Engineer; Electrical/Electronics Engineer; Environmental Engineer; Human Resources Manager; Management Trainee; Manufacturing Engineer; Marketing Manager; Marketing Specialist; Mechanical Engineer; Metallurgical Engineer;

Occupational Therapist; Project Manager; Purchasing Agent/Manager; Quality Control Supervisor; Sales Engineer; Sales Executive; Sales Manager; Sales Rep.; Secretary; Software Engineer; Speech-Language Pathologist; Systems Analyst; Systems Manager; Technical Writer/Editor; Telecommunications Manager; Typist/Word Processor; Vice President of Sales. **Benefits available to temporary workers:** Health Benefits; Paid Holidays; Vacation Pay. **Corporate headquarters location:** This Location.

THE DIVERSIFIED SEARCH COMPANIES
2005 Market Street, Suite 3300, Philadelphia PA 19103. 215/732-6666. **Fax:** 215/568-8399. **Contact:** Leslie Mazza, Manager. **World Wide Web address:** http://www.divsearch.com. **Description:** An executive search firm. Founded in 1973. **Specializes in the areas of:** Consulting; Finance; Health/Medical; Nonprofit; Professional. **Corporate headquarters location:** This Location. **Other U.S. locations:** Atlanta GA; Boston MA; Charlotte NC.

DUNHILL PROFESSIONAL SEARCH
801 West Street Road, Feasterville PA 19053. 215/357-6591. **Fax:** 215/953-1612. **Contact:** Branch Manager. **Description:** An executive search firm. **Specializes in the areas of:** Accounting/Auditing; Finance; Information Systems; Sales; Secretarial. **Positions commonly filled include:** Accountant/Auditor; Customer Service Rep.; EDP Specialist; Financial Analyst; Typist/Word Processor. **Number of placements per year:** 100 - 199.

DUNN ASSOCIATES
229 Limberline Drive, Greensburg PA 15601. 724/832-9822. **Fax:** 724/832-9836. **Contact:** Margaret Dunn, President. **Description:** An executive search firm operating on a retainer basis. **Specializes in the areas of:** Accounting/Auditing; Administration; Engineering; Finance; General Management; Home Furnishings; Industrial; Manufacturing; Personnel/Labor Relations; Sales. **Positions commonly filled include:** Human Resources Manager; Manufacturing Engineer; Manufacturing Manager; Plant Manager; Vice President. **Average salary range of placements:** More than $50,000. **Number of placements per year:** 1 - 49.

ECLECTIC INTERNATIONAL
1400 Morris Drive, Suite 102, Wayne PA 19087. 610/722-5101. **Fax:** 610/722-5105. **Contact:** Manager. **E-mail address:** info@eclectic.nl. **World Wide Web address:** http://www.eclectic-usa.com. **Description:** An executive search firm. **Specializes in the areas of:** Computer Hardware/Software; High-Tech; Telecommunications. **International locations:** The Netherlands.

EDEN & ASSOCIATES, INC.
794 North Valley Road, Paoli PA 19301. 610/889-9993. **Fax:** 610/889-9660. **Contact:** Brooks D. Eden, President. **World Wide Web address:** http://www.edenandassociates.com. **Description:** An executive search firm. **Specializes in the areas of:** Accounting; Administration; Advertising; Architecture/Construction; Engineering; Fashion; Finance; Food; General Management; Personnel/Labor Relations; Retail; Sales; Transportation. **Positions commonly filled include:** Accountant/Auditor; Architect; Buyer; Chief Financial Officer; Controller; Draftsperson; General Manager; Human Resources Manager; Industrial Engineer; Market Research Analyst; Marketing Manager; MIS Specialist; Pharmacist; Production Manager; Sales Executive; Sales Manager; Sales Rep.; Systems Analyst; Transportation/ Traffic Specialist. **Average salary range of placements:** More than $50,000. **Number of placements per year:** 100 - 199.

EXECU-SEARCH
4232 Northern Pike, Commerce Building, Suite 201, Monroeville PA 15146. 412/374-9904. **Contact:** Recruiter. **Description:** An executive search firm. **Specializes in the areas of:** Administration; Management; Marketing; Sales.

EXECUTIVE AVAIL-A-SEARCH
2938 Columbia Avenue, Suite 1502, Lancaster PA 17603. 717/291-1871. **Contact:** Anthony Spinelli, President. **Description:** An executive search firm. **Specializes in the areas of:** Accounting/Auditing; Administration; Clerical; Engineering; Finance; Legal; Manufacturing; Sales; Technical.

EXECUTIVE CAREER RESOURCE GROUP
1235 West Lakes Drive, Suite 280, Berwyn PA 19312. 610/640-2020. **Contact:** Manager. **Description:** An executive search firm.

THE FINANCIAL SEARCH GROUP
1100 Bank Tower, Fourth Avenue at Wood Street, Pittsburgh PA 15222. 412/288-0505. **Contact:** Manager. **Description:** An executive search firm. **Specializes in the areas of:** Finance.

HOWARD FISCHER ASSOCIATES, INC.
1800 JFK Boulevard, 7th Floor, Philadelphia PA 19103. 215/568-8363. **Contact:** Manager. **Description:** An executive search firm.

FOCUS PERSONNEL ASSOCIATES, INC.
550 Pinetown Road, Suite 230, Fort Washington PA 19034. 215/654-7000. **Fax:** 215/654-7925. **Contact:** Gail C. Welkes, President. **E-mail address:** gail@ focuspersonnel.com. **Description:** An executive search firm. **Specializes in the areas of:** Sales. **Positions commonly filled include:** Account Manager; Account Rep.; Branch Manager; Management Trainee; Manufacturer's/Wholesaler's Sales Rep.; Sales Engineer; Sales Exec.; Sales Manager; Sales Rep.; Services Sales Rep. **Average salary range of placements:** $30,000 - $100,000. **Number of placements per year:** 100 - 199.

F-O-R-T-U-N-E PERSONNEL CONSULTANTS
3644 Route 378, Unit C, Bethlehem PA 18015. 610/866-1300. **Contact:** Manager. **Description:** An executive search firm. **Specializes in the areas of:** Computer Science/Software; Manufacturing. **Corporate headquarters location:** New York NY. **Other U.S. locations:** Nationwide.

F-O-R-T-U-N-E PERSONNEL CONSULTANTS
455 Pennsylvania Avenue, Suite 105, Fort Washington PA 19034. 215/542-9800. **Contact:** Manager. **Description:** An executive search firm. **Specializes in the areas of:** Finance; Insurance; Legal. **Corporate headquarters location:** New York NY. **Other U.S. locations:** Nationwide.

FOX-MORRIS ASSOCIATES
One Gateway Center, North Wing, 18th Floor, Pittsburgh PA 15222. 412/232-0410. **Fax:** 412/232-3055. **Contact:** Murray S. Leety, Branch Manager. **Description:** An executive search firm operating on both retainer and contingency bases. The firm also offers career/ outplacement services. **Specializes in the areas of:** Accounting/Auditing; Engineering; Finance; General Management; Industrial; Manufacturing; Personnel/ Labor Relations; Technical. **Positions commonly filled include:** Chemical Engineer; Chemist; Civil Engineer; Computer Programmer; Design Engineer; Electrical/ Electronics Engineer; Environmental Engineer; Financial Analyst; General Manager; Human Resources Specialist; Industrial Engineer; Industrial Production Manager; Mechanical Engineer; Metallurgical Engineer; MIS Specialist; Property and Real Estate Manager; Purchasing Agent/Manager; Software Engineer; Systems Analyst; Transportation/Traffic Specialist. **Corporate headquarters location:** Philadelphia PA. **Other U.S. locations:** Nationwide. **Average salary range of placements:** More than $50,000. **Number of placements per year:** 50 - 99.

FOX-MORRIS ASSOCIATES
1617 JFK Boulevard, Suite 1850, Philadelphia PA 19103. 215/561-6300. **Contact:** Manager. **Description:** An executive search firm. **Specializes in the areas of:** Banking; Engineering; Finance; Human Resources;

Information Systems. **Corporate headquarters location:** This Location. **Other U.S. locations:** Nationwide.

THE GMW GROUP, INC.
900 Fifth Avenue, Pittsburgh PA 15219. 412/281-6057. **Contact:** Shelley Millen, President. **Description:** An executive search firm that also provides career/ outplacement services. **Specializes in the areas of:** Engineering; Sales. **Positions commonly filled include:** Chemical Engineer; Civil Engineer; Computer Programmer; Customer Service Representative; Human Resources Manager; Mechanical Engineer; Metallurgical Engineer; Mining Engineer; MIS Specialist; Public Relations Specialist; Securities Sales Representative; Services Sales Representative; Software Engineer; Systems Analyst; Telecommunications Manager. **Average salary range of placements:** More than $50,000. **Number of placements per year:** 100 - 199.

GATEWAY RESOURCES INC.
21 Yost Boulevard, Suite 302, Pittsburgh PA 15221. 412/824-9470. **Contact:** Manager. **Description:** An executive search firm. **Specializes in the areas of:** Computer Hardware/Software; Engineering.

D. GILLESPIE & ASSOCIATES
450 North Sproul Road, Broomall PA 19008. 610/355-2383. **Contact:** D. Gillespie, Manager. **Description:** An executive search firm operating on both retainer and contingency bases. **Specializes in the areas of:** Finance; Information Technology; Marketing; Sales.

J.H. GLASS & ASSOCIATES
P.O. Box 1015, Bala-Cynwyd PA 19004. 215/877-0101. **Contact:** J.H. Glass, President. **Description:** An executive search firm. **Specializes in the areas of:** Computer Science/Software; Engineering; General Management; Manufacturing; Sales; Technical. **Positions commonly filled include:** Accountant/Auditor; Computer Programmer; Design Engineer; Engineer; General Manager; Industrial Production Manager; Internet Services Manager; Management Analyst/ Consultant; Manufacturer's/Wholesaler's Sales Rep.; MIS Specialist; Multimedia Designer; Operations/Production Manager; Physical Therapist; Purchasing Agent/ Manager; Quality Control Supervisor; Systems Analyst. **Average salary range of placements:** More than $50,000. **Number of placements per year:** 200 - 499.

GLEN ALAN & ASSOCIATES INC.
5421 Downs Run, Suite B, Pipersville PA 18947-1155. 215/766-0376. **Contact:** Glenn Marad, President. **Description:** An executive search firm. **Specializes in the areas of:** Marketing; Sales. **Number of placements per year:** 200 - 499.

HRS/TND ASSOCIATES, INC.
506 Park Road North, Wyomissing PA 19610. 610/371-9505. **Fax:** 610/373-8618. **Contact:** Thomas N. Dondore, President. **E-mail address:** tomhrs@1usa.com. **World Wide Web address:** http://www. hrstndassociates.com. **Description:** An executive search firm. The firm also provides some Human Resources consulting, training and development, and contract recruiting services. **Specializes in the areas of:** Accounting/Auditing; Administration; Banking; Computer Science/Software; Engineering; Fashion; Finance; Food; General Management; Industrial; Insurance; Manufacturing; Personnel/Labor Relations; Retail; Sales; Technical. **Positions commonly filled include:** Accountant/Auditor; Administrative Manager; Aerospace Engineer; Agricultural Engineer; Attorney; Bank Officer/Manager; Biological Scientist; Biomedical Engineer; Branch Manager; Budget Analyst; Buyer; Chemical Engineer; Chemist; Civil Engineer; Computer Programmer; Credit Manager; Design Engineer; Designer; Economist; Editor; Electrical/Electronics Engineer; Environmental Engineer; Financial Analyst; General Manager; Health Services Manager; Human Resources Manager; Industrial Engineer; Industrial Production Manager; Management Analyst/Consultant;

Management Trainee; Manufacturer's/Wholesaler's Sales Representative; Market Research Analyst; Materials Engineer; Mechanical Engineer; MIS Specialist; Multimedia Designer; Nuclear Engineer; Petroleum Engineer; Purchasing Agent/Manager; Quality Control Supervisor; Science Technologist; Securities Sales Rep.; Services Sales Rep.; Software Engineer; Stationary Engineer; Strategic Relations Manager; Structural Engineer; Systems Analyst; Telecommunications Manager; Transportation/Traffic Specialist.

ROBERT HALF INTERNATIONAL ACCOUNTEMPS
2000 Market Street, 18th Floor, Philadelphia PA 19103. 215/568-4580. **Fax:** 215/564-1968. **Contact:** Manager. **Description:** An executive search firm. **Corporate headquarters location:** Menlo Park CA. **International locations:** Worldwide.

ROBERT HALF INTERNATIONAL ACCOUNTEMPS
120 Fifth Avenue, Suite 2690, Fifth Avenue Place, Pittsburgh PA 15222. 412/471-5946. **Contact:** Manager. **Description:** An executive search firm. **Specializes in the areas of:** Accounting/Auditing; Finance. **Corporate headquarters location:** Menlo Park CA. **International locations:** Worldwide.

GARRICK HALL & ASSOCIATES
301 Lindenwood Drive, Suite 1, Malvern PA 19355. 610/640-3134. **Fax:** 610/640-0454. **Contact:** William J. Yamarick, President. **Description:** An executive search firm. **Specializes in the areas of:** Computer Science/Software; Health/Medical; Industrial; Manufacturing; Sales. **Positions commonly filled include:** Management Trainee; Services Sales Rep. **Number of placements per year:** 100 - 199.

THE HASTINGS GROUP
P.O. Box 36, Palm PA 18070-0036. 215/541-0303. **Fax:** 215/541-0305. **Contact:** Frank Hastings, President/ Owner. **Description:** An executive search firm. **Specializes in the areas of:** Accounting/Auditing; Administration; Banking; Economics; Engineering; Finance; Food; General Management; Health/Medical; Industrial; Manufacturing; Personnel/Labor Relations; Sales. **Positions commonly filled include:** Accountant/ Auditor; Administrative Manager; Attorney; Bank Officer/Manager; Branch Manager; Budget Analyst; Buyer; Clerical Supervisor; Cost Estimator; Credit Manager; Customer Service Rep.; Economist; Facilities Engineer; Food Scientist/Technologist; General Manager; Health Services Manager; Human Resources Specialist; Industrial Engineer; Industrial Production Manager; Management Analyst/Consultant; Market Research Analyst; Mechanical Engineer; Medical Records Tech.; MIS Specialist; Occupational Therapist; Operations/Production Manager; Paralegal; Pharmacist; Physical Therapist; Purchasing Agent/Manager; Quality Control Supervisor; Registered Nurse; Respiratory Therapist; Services Sales Rep.; Statistician; Systems Analyst; Telecommunications Manager. **Average salary range of placements:** More than $50,000. **Number of placements per year:** 50 - 99.

HAYES ASSOCIATES
522 Lanfair Road, Elkins Park PA 19027. 215/735-3079. **Contact:** Manager. **Description:** An executive search firm. **Specializes in the areas of:** Computer Science/Software.

HEALTHCARE RECRUITERS INTERNATIONAL
428 Forbes Avenue, Suite 600, Pittsburgh PA 15219. 412/261-2244. **Fax:** 412/261-3577. **Contact:** Manager. **Description:** An executive search firm. **Specializes in the areas of:** Health/Medical.

HEIDRICK & STRUGGLES
One Logan Square, 18th & Cherry Streets, Suite 3075, Philadelphia PA 19103. 215/988-1000. **Fax:** 215/988-9496. **Contact:** Manager. **Description:** An executive search firm.

KAY HENRY INCORPORATED
1200 Bustleton Pike, Suite 5, Feasterville PA 19053. 215/355-1600. **Fax:** 215/355-4395. **Contact:** Kay Henry, President. **E-mail address:** khinc@axs2000.net. **Description:** An executive search firm operating on a contingency basis. **Specializes in the areas of:** Advertising; Art/Design; Marketing; Public Relations. **Positions commonly filled include:** Advertising Clerk; Advertising Executive; Desktop Publishing Specialist; Editor; Editorial Assistant; Graphic Artist; Graphic Designer; Market Research Analyst; Marketing Manager; Marketing Specialist; Public Relations Specialist; Technical Writer/Editor; Webmaster. **Corporate headquarters location:** This Location. **Average salary range of placements:** $50,000 - $100,000. **Number of placements per year:** 1 - 49.

HIRE SOLUTIONS
Station Square One, Suite 204, Paoli PA 19301. 610/889-2000. **Fax:** 610/889-2424. **Contact:** Manager. **E-mail address:** solutions@hire-solutions.com. **Description:** An executive search firm operating on a contingency basis. **Specializes in the areas of:** Food. **Positions commonly filled include:** Dietician/Nutritionist; General Manager; Operations Manager; Project Manager; Sales Executive; Sales Manager. **Other U.S. locations:** Nationwide. **Average salary range of placements:** $50,000 - $100,000. **Number of placements per year:** 50 - 99.

HOSKINS HAINS ASSOCIATES
3835 Walnut Street, Harrisburg PA 17109. 717/657-8444. **Fax:** 717/657-8459. **Contact:** Patricia Hoskins, Owner. **Description:** An executive search firm operating on both retainer and contingency bases. **Specializes in the areas of:** Accounting; Computer Hardware/Software; Engineering; Finance; Manufacturing; Personnel/Labor Relations. **Positions commonly filled include:** Accountant; Budget Analyst; Chemical Engineer; Chief Financial Officer; Computer Animator; Computer Operator; Computer Programmer; Controller; Database Manager; Design Engineer; Draftsperson; Electrical/ Electronics Engineer; Finance Director; Financial Analyst; Human Resources Manager; Industrial Engineer; Industrial Production Manager; Internet Services Manager; Manufacturing Engineer; Mechanical Engineer; Metallurgical Engineer; MIS Specialist; Operations Manager; Production Manager; Project Manager; Purchasing Agent/Manager; Quality Control Supervisor; Sales Engineer; Software Engineer; Systems Analyst; Systems Manager; Technical Writer/Editor; Telecommunications Manager; Webmaster. **Corporate headquarters location:** This Location. **Average salary range of placements:** $30,000 - $50,000. **Number of placements per year:** 50 - 99.

I/S COMPUTER SERVICES, INC.
P.O. Box 187, Richboro PA 18954. 215/355-5380. **Contact:** Manager. **Description:** An executive search firm. **Specializes in the areas of:** Computer Operations; Computer Programming; Management; Network Administration.

IMPACT SEARCH & STRATEGY
161 Leverington Avenue, Suite 102, Philadelphia PA 19127. 215/482-6881. **Fax:** 215/482-7518. **Contact:** Recruiter. **World Wide Web address:** http://www. impactsearch.com. **Description:** An executive search firm. **Specializes in the areas of:** Administration; Information Technology; Legal; Marketing; Pharmaceuticals.

INTERACTIVE SEARCH ASSOCIATES
2949 West Germantown Pike, Norristown PA 19403. 610/630-3670. **Fax:** 610/630-3678. **Contact:** John P. Zerkle, Manager. **E-mail address:** isa@jobswitch.com. **World Wide Web address:** http://www.jobswitch.com. **Description:** An executive search firm operating on both retainer and contingency bases. **Specializes in the areas of:** Architecture/Construction; Computer Science/ Software; Engineering; General Management; Health/ Medical; Insurance; Internet Marketing; Marketing; MIS/EDP; Personnel/Labor Relations; Retail; Sales.

Positions commonly filled include: Account Manager; Applications Engineer; Architect; Biochemist; Biomedical Engineer; Certified Occupational Therapy Assistant; Chemical Engineer; Chemist; Civil Engineer; Computer Engineer; Controller; Customer Service Rep.; Database Manager; Electrical/Electronics Engineer; Emergency Medical Technician; Finance Director; General Manager; Human Resources Manager; Manufacturing Engineer; MIS Specialist; Network/ Systems Administrator; Occupational Therapist; Pharmacist; Physical Therapist; Physician; Purchasing Agent/Manager; Respiratory Therapist; Safety Engineer; Sales Engineer; Sales Executive; Sales Manager; Sales Representative; Systems Analyst; Systems Manager; Underwriter/Assistant Underwriter. **Average salary range of placements:** $50,000 - $100,000. **Number of placements per year:** 100 - 199.

INTERCONTINENTAL EXECUTIVE GROUP
674 Louis Drive, The Vogel Building, Warminster PA 18974. 215/957-9012. **Contact:** Manager. **Description:** An executive search firm.

J-RAND SEARCH
P.O. Box B, Bethlehem PA 18015. 610/867-4649. **Fax:** 610/867-9750. **Contact:** Michael P. Watts, President. **Description:** An executive search firm. **Specializes in the areas of:** Accounting/Auditing; Administration; Banking; Biology; Computer Science/Software; Engineering; Finance; Food; General Management; Health/Medical; Industrial; Manufacturing; Personnel/Labor Relations; Technical; Transportation. **Positions commonly filled include:** Accountant/Auditor; Aerospace Engineer; Agricultural Engineer; Biological Scientist; Biomedical Engineer; Ceramics Engineer; Chemical Engineer; Chemist; Civil Engineer; Computer Programmer; Cost Estimator; Designer; Electrical/ Electronics Engineer; Financial Analyst; Food Scientist/ Technologist; General Manager; Industrial Engineer; Industrial Production Manager; Materials Engineer; Mechanical Engineer; Metallurgical Engineer; Meteorologist; Mining Engineer; Operations/Production Manager; Petroleum Engineer; Pharmacist; Physician; Purchasing Agent/Manager; Quality Control Supervisor; Software Engineer; Stationary Engineer; Statistician; Structural Engineer; Systems Analyst. **Number of placements per year:** 50 - 99.

JK RESOURCES
1056 Jeter Avenue, Bethlehem PA 18015-2552. 610/867-5997. **Fax:** 610/867-5946. **Contact:** Jane Kauffman, Owner. **Description:** An executive search firm. **Specializes in the areas of:** Engineering; Environmental; Industrial; Insurance; Manufacturing; Personnel/Labor Relations; Safety; Technical. **Positions commonly filled include:** Chemical Engineer; Civil Engineer; Environmental Engineer; Human Resources Manager. **Number of placements per year:** 1 - 49.

NANCY JACKSON INC.
343 North Washington Avenue, Scranton PA 18503. 570/346-8711. **Fax:** 570/346-9940. **Contact:** Nancy Jackson, President. **Description:** An executive search firm operating on a contingency basis. **Specializes in the areas of:** Accounting/Auditing; Administration; Banking; Computer Science/Software; Engineering; Finance; General Management; Health/Medical; Manufacturing; Personnel/Labor Relations; Publishing; Sales; Secretarial. **Positions commonly filled include:** Accountant/Auditor; Administrative Manager; Bank Officer/Manager; Biomedical Engineer; Buyer; Ceramics Engineer; Chemical Engineer; Chemist; Civil Engineer; Claim Rep.; Clerical Supervisor; Computer Programmer; Credit Manager; Customer Service Rep.; Dental Assistant/Dental Hygienist; Draftsperson; Economist; Electrical/Electronics Engineer; Financial Analyst; General Manager; Health Services Manager; Human Resources Manager; Industrial Engineer; Industrial Production Manager; Management Analyst/Consultant; Materials Engineer; Mechanical Engineer; Metallurgical Engineer; Occupational Therapist; Operations/Production Manager; Paralegal; Physical Therapist; Public Relations Specialist; Purchasing Agent/Manager; Quality Control Supervisor; Software Engineer. **Number of placements per year:** 100 - 199.

KENNETH JAMES ASSOCIATES, INC.
506 Lakeside Park, Southampton PA 18966. 215/322-5080. **Contact:** Manager. **Description:** An executive search firm. **Specializes in the areas of:** Accounting; Administration; Banking; Clerical; Finance; Human Resources; Management; Marketing; Sales; Secretarial.

JEFFERSON-ROSS ASSOCIATES, INC.
2 Penn Center, Suite 312, Philadelphia PA 19102. 215/564-5322. **Fax:** 215/587-0766. **Contact:** Craig Zander, Vice President of Operations. **Description:** An executive search firm. **Specializes in the areas of:** Accounting/Auditing; Administration; Banking; Computer Science/Software; Finance; General Management; Health/Medical; Insurance; Marketing; Sales. **Positions commonly filled include:** Account Manager; Administrative Manager; Branch Manager; Computer Operator; Computer Programmer; Consultant; Controller; Credit Manager; Database Manager; Finance Director; General Manager; Human Resources Manager; Information Systems Consultant; Insurance Agent/ Broker; Market Research Analyst; Marketing Manager; Marketing Specialist; MIS Specialist; Operations Manager; Project Manager; Sales Executive; Sales Manager; Sales Representative; Software Engineer; Systems Manager; Telecommunications Manager. **Average salary range of placements:** More than $50,000. **Number of placements per year:** 100 - 199.

CLIFTON JOHNSON ASSOCIATES INC.
One Monroeville Center, Suite 725, Monroeville PA 15146. 412/856-8000. **Fax:** 412/856-8026. **Contact:** Clifton Johnson, President. **E-mail address:** clifton@ nb.net. **Description:** An executive search firm. Founded in 1969. **Specializes in the areas of:** Computer Science/Software; Engineering; Industrial; Manufacturing. **Positions commonly filled include:** Aerospace Engineer; Chemical Engineer; Civil Engineer; Computer Programmer; Design Engineer; Electrical/Electronics Engineer; Environmental Engineer; Food Scientist/Technologist; Geologist/Geophysicist; Industrial Engineer; Industrial Production Manager; Mechanical Engineer; Metallurgical Engineer; Mining Engineer; Petroleum Engineer; Quality Control Supervisor; Software Engineer; Structural Engineer; Systems Analyst; Telecommunications Manager. **Average salary range of placements:** $30,000 - $80,000.

KATRON INC.
1865 New Hope Street, Norristown PA 19401. 610/239-4286. **Contact:** Manager. **Description:** An executive search firm. **Specializes in the areas of:** Engineering.

BLAIR KERSHAW ASSOCIATES, INC.
1903 West Eighth Street, PMB 302, Erie PA 16505. 814/454-5872. **Contact:** Blair Kershaw, President. **Description:** An executive search firm operating on both contingency and retainer bases. **Specializes in the areas of:** Accounting/Auditing; Engineering; Manufacturing; Technical. **Positions commonly filled include:** Accountant/Auditor; Chemical Engineer; Chemist; Design Engineer; Electrical/Electronics Engineer; Food Scientist/Technologist; General Manager; Mechanical Engineer; Physical Therapist. **Average salary range of placements:** More than $50,000.

KORN/FERRY INTERNATIONAL
2 Logan Square, Suite 2530, Philadelphia PA 19103. 215/496-6666. **Fax:** 215/568-9911. **Contact:** Manager. **World Wide Web address:** http://www.kornferry.com. **Description:** An executive search firm. **Corporate headquarters location:** Los Angeles CA. **International locations:** Worldwide.

LAWRENCE PERSONNEL
1000 Valley Forge Circle, Suite 110, King of Prussia PA 19406. 610/783-5400. **Contact:** Larry Goldberg,

CPC/General Manager. **Description:** An executive search firm operating on both retainer and contingency bases. **Specializes in the areas of:** Computer Science/Software; Data Communications; Engineering; Telecommunications. **Positions commonly filled include:** Broadcast Technician; Designer; Electrical/ Electronics Engineer; Internet Services Manager; Mechanical Engineer; MIS Specialist; Software Engineer; Systems Analyst; Technical Writer/Editor; Telecommunications Manager. **Number of placements per year:** 1 - 49.

F.P. LENNON ASSOCIATES
300 Berwyn Park, Suite 202, Berwyn PA 19312. 610/407-0300. **Toll-free phone:** 888/LENNON-7. **Fax:** 610/407-0533. **Contact:** Manager. **E-mail address:** fplassoc@fplennon.com. **World Wide Web address:** http://www.fplennon.com. **Description:** An executive search firm. **Specializes in the areas of:** Computer Hardware/Software; Computer Programming; Consulting; Network Administration; Sales.

J. WRIGHT LEONARD
1500 Walnut Street, Suite 506, Philadelphia PA 19102. 215/732-6677. **Fax:** 215/735-4022. **Contact:** Manager. **Description:** An executive search firm.

ROBERT LOHRKE ASSOCIATES
4318 Northern Pike, Suite 202, Monroeville PA 15146. 412/261-2601. **Fax:** 412/856-3678. **Contact:** Manager. **Description:** An executive search firm. **Specializes in the areas of:** Engineering; Technical.

M.K. & ASSOCIATES
309 East Brady Street, Butler PA 16001. 724/285-7474. **Fax:** 724/285-8339. **Contact:** John Mossman, Partner. **Description:** An executive search firm operating on a contingency basis. **Specializes in the areas of:** Food. **Positions commonly filled include:** Chemical Engineer; Food Scientist/Technologist; Mechanical Engineer; Operations/Production Manager; Quality Control Supervisor; Science Technologist.

MANAGEMENT RECRUITERS INTERNATIONAL NEWTOWN CONSULTING GROUP, INC.
301 South State Street, Newtown PA 18940. 215/579-2450. **Fax:** 215/579-2458. **Contact:** Jim Plappert, Owner. **E-mail address:** mrinewtown@ mrinewtown.com. **World Wide Web address:** http://www.mrinewtown.com. **Description:** An executive search firm focusing on the placement of management personnel in the life, health, and pension insurance industries. Founded in 1989. **Specializes in the areas of:** Insurance; Sales. **Positions commonly filled include:** Account Manager; Account Representative; Customer Service Representative; Insurance Agent/ Broker; Marketing Manager; Sales Representative; Underwriter/Assistant Underwriter. **Corporate headquarters location:** Cleveland OH. **Other U.S. locations:** Nationwide. **Number of placements per year:** 50 - 99.

MANAGEMENT RECRUITERS INTERNATIONAL
115 Hidden Valley Road, McMurray PA 15317. 724/942-4100. **Fax:** 724/942-4111. **Contact:** Manager. **E-mail address:** resume@chemicaljobs.com. **World Wide Web address:** http://www.chemicaljobs.com. **Description:** An executive search firm operating on both retainer and contingency bases. Client company pays fee. **Specializes in the areas of:** Chemicals; Engineering. **Positions commonly filled include:** Chemical Engineer; Chemist. **Corporate headquarters location:** Cleveland OH. **Other U.S. locations:** Nationwide. **Average salary range of placements:** $50,000 - $100,000.

MANAGEMENT RECRUITERS INTERNATIONAL
2 Chatham Center, Suite 1400, Pittsburgh PA 15219. 412/566-2100. **Fax:** 412/566-2229. **Contact:** Manager. **World Wide Web address:** http://www.mrinet.com. **Description:** An executive search firm. **Specializes in the areas of:** Computer Hardware/Software; Information Technology; Telecommunications. **Corporate**

headquarters location: Cleveland OH. **Other U.S. locations:** Nationwide.

MANAGEMENT RECRUITERS INTERNATIONAL
2654 Cedarvue Drive, Upper St. Clair PA 15241. 412/851-9996. **Contact:** Manager. **World Wide Web address:** http://www.mrinet.com. **Description:** An executive search firm. **Specializes in the areas of:** Engineering; Information Technology; Manufacturing. **Corporate headquarters location:** Cleveland OH. **Other U.S. locations:** Nationwide.

MANAGEMENT RECRUITERS INTERNATIONAL
3925 Reed Boulevard, Suite 200, Murrysville PA 15668. 724/325-4011. **Contact:** Manager. **E-mail address:** mriwc@mriwc.com. **World Wide Web address:** http://www.mriwc.com. **Description:** An executive search firm. **Specializes in the areas of:** Chemicals; Health/Medical. **Corporate headquarters location:** Cleveland OH. **Other U.S. locations:** Nationwide.

MANAGEMENT RECRUITERS INTERNATIONAL
300 Weyman Plaza, Suite 200, Pittsburgh PA 15236. 412/885-5222. **Contact:** Manager. **World Wide Web address:** http://www.mrinet.com. **Description:** An executive search firm. **Specializes in the areas of:** Information Systems. **Corporate headquarters location:** Cleveland OH. **Other U.S. locations:** Nationwide.

MANAGEMENT RECRUITERS OF BUCKS COUNTY
678 Louis Drive, Warminster PA 18974. 215/675-6440. **Contact:** Michael Mashack, Manager. **World Wide Web address:** http://www.mrinet.com. **Description:** An executive search firm. **Specializes in the areas of:** Construction; Health/Medical; Real Estate. **Positions commonly filled include:** Administrator; Estimator; Information Systems Consultant; Leasing Specialist/ Consultant; Nurse; Project Manager; Property and Real Estate Manager. **Corporate headquarters location:** Cleveland OH. **Other U.S. locations:** Nationwide.

MANAGEMENT RECRUITERS OF DELAWARE COUNTY COMPUSEARCH
3614 Chapel Road, Newtown Square PA 19073. 610/356-8360. **Fax:** 610/356-8731. **Contact:** Sandy Bishop, Manager. **World Wide Web address:** http://www.mrinet.com. **Description:** An executive search firm. **Specializes in the areas of:** Accounting/ Auditing; Administration; Advertising; Architecture/ Construction; Banking; Communications; Computer Hardware/Software; Design; Electrical; Engineering; Finance; Food; General Management; Health/Medical; Insurance; Legal; Manufacturing; Operations Management; Personnel/Labor Relations; Procurement; Publishing; Retail; Sales; Technical; Textiles; Transportation. **Corporate headquarters location:** Cleveland OH. **Other U.S. locations:** Nationwide.

MANAGEMENT RECRUITERS OF LEHIGH VALLEY COMPUSEARCH
3895 Adler Place, Suite 150A, Bethlehem PA 18017. 610/974-9770. **Fax:** 610/974-9775. **Contact:** Fred Meyer, Manager. **World Wide Web address:** http://www.mrinet.com. **Description:** An executive search firm. **Specializes in the areas of:** Accounting/ Auditing; Administration; Advertising; Architecture/ Construction; Banking; Communications; Computer Hardware/Software; Design; Electrical; Engineering; Finance; Food; General Management; Health/Medical; Insurance; Legal; Manufacturing; Operations Management; Personnel/Labor Relations; Procurement; Publishing; Retail; Sales; Technical; Textiles; Transportation. **Corporate headquarters location:** Cleveland OH. **Other U.S. locations:** Nationwide.

MANAGEMENT RECRUITERS OF PHILADELPHIA COMPUSEARCH
325 Chestnut Street, Constitution Place, Suite 1106, Philadelphia PA 19106. 215/829-1900. **Contact:**

Manager. **World Wide Web address:** http://www. mrinet.com. **Description:** An executive search firm. **Specializes in the areas of:** Accounting/Auditing; Administration; Advertising; Architecture/Construction; Banking; Communications; Computer Hardware/ Software; Design; Electrical; Engineering; Finance; Food; General Management; Health/Medical; Insurance; Legal; Manufacturing; Operations Management; Personnel/Labor Relations; Procurement; Publishing; Retail; Sales; Technical; Textiles; Transportation. **Corporate headquarters location:** Cleveland OH. **Other U.S. locations:** Nationwide.

MANAGEMENT RECRUITERS OF PITTSBURGH-NORTH
435 Broad Street, Sewickley PA 15143. 412/741-5805. **Fax:** 412/741-3801. **Contact:** Recruiter. **E-mail address:** mri@city-net.com. **World Wide Web address:** http://www.mri-pitt.com. **Description:** An executive search firm. **Specializes in the areas of:** Biotechnology; Health/Medical; Information Technology; Insurance; Medical Devices. **Corporate headquarters location:** Cleveland OH. **Other U.S. locations:** Nationwide.

MANAGEMENT RECRUITERS OF READING CAREER SENTINEL, INC.
4 Park Plaza, Wyomissing PA 19610. 610/375-1500. **Fax:** 610/375-1504. **Contact:** Manager. **E-mail address:** mrireading@mrireading.com. **World Wide Web address:** http://www.mrireading.com. **Description:** An executive search firm. **Specializes in the areas of:** Accounting; Engineering; Finance; Human Resources; Information Technology; Logistics; Manufacturing; Marketing; Medical Devices; Pharmaceuticals; Sales; Transportation.

MANAGEMENT RECRUITERS OF WEST CHESTER.
129 Willowbrook Lane, West Chester PA 19382-5571. 610/436-6556. **Contact:** Robert Meitz, President. **World Wide Web address:** http://www.mrinet.com. **Description:** An executive search firm operating on both retainer and contingency bases. **Specializes in the areas of:** Chemicals; Engineering; Food; Petrochemical. **Positions commonly filled include:** Account Manager; Account Representative; Accountant; Biochemist; Biological Scientist; Buyer; Chemical Engineer; Chemist; Controller; Electrical/Electronics Engineer; Financial Analyst; Food Scientist/Technologist; General Manager; Human Resources Manager; Industrial Engineer; Marketing Manager; Marketing Specialist; Sales Engineer; Sales Executive; Sales Manager; Sales Representative. **Corporate headquarters location:** Cleveland OH. **Other U.S. locations:** Nationwide. **Average salary range of placements:** More than $50,000. **Number of placements per year:** 1 - 49.

GEORGE R. MARTIN EXECUTIVE SEARCH
P.O. Box 673, Doylestown PA 18901. 215/348-8146. **Contact:** George R. Martin, Owner/Manager. **Description:** An executive search firm. **Specializes in the areas of:** Chemicals; Engineering; Manufacturing; Personnel/Labor Relations; Pharmaceuticals; Plastics; Sales; Technical.

MASTERSEARCH
200 Barr Harbor Drive, Suite 400, West Conshohocken PA 19428. 610/415-0888. **Fax:** 610/415-0814. **Contact:** Manager. **Description:** An executive search firm. **Specializes in the areas of:** Accounting; Administration; Biomedical; Biotechnology; Clerical; Executives; Finance; Health/Medical; Management; Pharmaceuticals; Sales.

K. MAXIN & ASSOCIATES
Allegheny Center, Building 10, Suite 421, Pittsburgh PA 15212. 412/322-2595. **Toll-free phone:** 800/867-8447. **Fax:** 412/322-7027. **Contact:** Keith A. Maxin, President. **Description:** An executive search firm operating on a retainer basis. **Specializes in the areas of:** Construction; Real Estate. **Positions commonly filled include:** Branch Manager; Construction and Building Inspector; Cost Estimator; Electrical/Electronics Engineer; General

Manager; Human Resources Manager; Mechanical Engineer; Property and Real Estate Manager; Purchasing Agent/Manager. **Average salary range of placements:** More than $50,000. **Number of placements per year:** 1 - 49.

McANNEY, ESPOSITO & KRAYBILL ASSOCIATES
5 Widgeon Drive, Pittsburgh PA 15238. 412/288-0825. **Contact:** Manager. **Description:** An executive search firm. **Specializes in the areas of:** Legal.

ROBERT McCLURE LTD.
P.O. Box 497, Beaver PA 15009. 724/775-1525. **Fax:** 724/775-9633. **Contact:** Manager. **Description:** An executive search firm operating on both retainer and contingency bases. **Specializes in the areas of:** Computer Science/Software; Engineering; Industrial; Manufacturing; Personnel/Labor Relations; Sales; Technical. **Positions commonly filled include:** Civil Engineer; Computer Programmer; Cost Estimator; Design Engineer; Electrical/Electronics Engineer; Environmental Engineer; Geologist/Geophysicist; Human Resources Specialist; Industrial Engineer; Industrial Production Manager; Mechanical Engineer; Metallurgical Engineer; MIS Specialist; Multimedia Designer; Quality Control Supervisor; Software Engineer; Structural Engineer; Systems Analyst; Technical Writer/Editor. **Other U.S. locations:** Nationwide.

McNICHOL & ASSOCIATES
8419 Germantown Avenue, Philadelphia PA 19118. 215/922-4142. **Contact:** Manager. **Description:** An executive search firm. **Specializes in the areas of:** Architecture/Construction; Engineering.

THE MEDICAL CONNECTION
P.O. Box 57175, Philadelphia PA 19111-7175. 215/663-1705. **Fax:** 215/663-1706. **Contact:** Paul R. Stevens, CPC/President. **E-mail address:** stevens025@aol.com. **World Wide Web address:** http://www. nvo.com/medconnection. **Description:** An executive search firm. **Positions commonly filled include:** Biomedical Engineer; Medical Sales; Medical Technologist. **Average salary range of placements:** $30,000 - $50,000. **Number of placements per year:** 50 - 99.

B. PAUL MICKEY & ASSOCIATES
1001 Liberty Center, Suite 500, Pittsburgh PA 15222. 412/261-5858. **Fax:** 412/471-0263. **Contact:** B. Paul Mickey, President/Owner. **Description:** An executive search firm operating on a retainer basis. **Specializes in the areas of:** Engineering; General Management; Industrial; Manufacturing. **Positions commonly filled include:** Chemical Engineer; Electrical/Electronics Engineer; Mechanical Engineer; Metallurgical Engineer. **Average salary range of placements:** More than $50,000. **Number of placements per year:** 1 - 49.

THE MORRIS GROUP
P.O. Box 188, Bryn Mawr PA 19010-0188. 610/520-0100. **Fax:** 610/520-0814. **Contact:** Peter J. Mays, Manager of Sales Recruitment. **Description:** An executive search firm operating on a contingency basis. **Specializes in the areas of:** Accounting/Auditing; Architecture/Construction; Finance; General Management; Industrial; Insurance; Manufacturing; Personnel/Labor Relations; Sales; Technical. **Positions commonly filled include:** Budget Analyst; Chemical Engineer; Civil Engineer; Design Engineer; Financial Analyst; Human Resources Manager; Insurance Agent/Broker; Manufacturer's/Wholesaler's Sales Rep.; Market Research Analyst; Securities Sales Representative; Services Sales Representative; Strategic Relations Manager; Underwriter/Assistant Underwriter. **Number of placements per year:** 200 - 499.

JOHN MORROW & ASSOCIATES
320 Main Street, Irwin PA 15642. 724/864-9512. **Fax:** 724/864-9654. **Contact:** John Morrow, Owner. **Description:** An executive search firm operating on a

retainer basis. **Specializes in the areas of:** Architecture/Construction; Engineering; Finance. **Positions commonly filled include:** Construction Contractor; Financial Analyst; General Manager; Landscape Architect; Management Analyst/Consultant; Market Research Analyst; Property and Real Estate Manager; Stationary Engineer. **Corporate headquarters location:** Pittsburgh PA. **Average salary range of placements:** More than $50,000. **Number of placements per year:** 1 - 49.

NATIONAL COMPUTERIZED EMPLOYMENT SERVICE INC.
2014 West Eighth Street, Erie PA 16505. 814/454-3874. **Fax:** 814/454-8097. **Contact:** Joseph W. Beck, CPC/ President. **World Wide Web address:** http://www. ncesinc.com. **Description:** An executive search firm operating on a contingency basis. The firm also provides some contract services. Client company pays fee. **Specializes in the areas of:** Accounting; Computer Science/Software; Engineering; Finance; Industrial; Personnel/Labor Relations; Plastics; Scientific; Technical. **Positions commonly filled include:** Chemical Engineer; Computer Programmer; Controller; Cost Estimator; Financial Analyst; General Manager; Human Resources Manager; Operations Manager; Project Manager; Quality Control Supervisor; Software Engineer. **Corporate headquarters location:** This Location. **Other U.S. locations:** Nationwide. **Average salary range of placements:** $50,000 - $100,000. **Number of placements per year:** 50 - 99.

NORCON ASSOCIATES, INC.
P.O. Box 405, Newtown Square PA 19073-0405. 610/359-1707. **Fax:** 610/359-0965. **Contact:** Joseph J. Conlin, President. **E-mail address:** norcon@icdc.com. **World Wide Web address:** http://www. norconsearch.com. **Description:** An executive search firm operating on a contingency basis. Client company pays fee. **Specializes in the areas of:** Chemicals; Consumer Products; Food; Health/Medical; Industrial; Medical Devices; Pharmaceuticals.

ORION DELTA GROUP LTD.
2100 Smallman Street, Pittsburgh PA 15222. 412/281-9800. **Contact:** Manager. **Description:** An executive search firm. **Specializes in the areas of:** Health/Medical.

LaMONTE OWENS, INC.
P.O. Box 27742, Philadelphia PA 19118. 215/248-0500. **Fax:** 215/233-3737. **Contact:** LaMonte Owens, President/Owner. **Description:** An executive search firm. **Specializes in the areas of:** Accounting/Auditing; Administration; Architecture/Construction; Banking; Biology; Computer Science/Software; Engineering; Finance; Health/Medical; Personnel/Labor Relations; Sales; Technical. **Positions commonly filled include:** Accountant/Auditor; Administrative Manager; Aerospace Engineer; Architect; Bank Officer/Manager; Biological Scientist; Biomedical Engineer; Branch Manager; Budget Analyst; Buyer; Ceramics Engineer; Chemical Engineer; Chemist; Civil Engineer; Clerical Supervisor; Computer Programmer; Credit Manager; Economist; Electrical/ Electronics Engineer; Financial Analyst; Health Services Manager; Human Resources Manager; Industrial Engineer; Management Analyst/Consultant; Materials Engineer; Mechanical Engineer; Metallurgical Engineer; Nuclear Engineer; Purchasing Agent/Manager; Registered Nurse; Securities Sales Representative; Software Engineer; Statistician; Systems Analyst. **Number of placements per year:** 1 - 49.

PENN ASSOCIATES
2 Penn Center, Suite 200, Philadelphia PA 19102. 215/854-6336. **Contact:** Joseph A. Dickerson, Principal. **Description:** An executive search firm. **Specializes in the areas of:** Personnel/Labor Relations. **Positions commonly filled include:** Human Resources Manager; Management Analyst/Consultant; Psychologist. **Average salary range of placements:** More than $50,000. **Number of placements per year:** 1 - 49.

PENN SEARCH
997 Old Eagle School Road, Suite 202, Wayne PA 19087. 610/964-8820. **Fax:** 610/964-8916. **Contact:** Charlie DiGiovanni, President. **E-mail address:** pennsear@erols.com. **Description:** An executive search firm. **Specializes in the areas of:** Accounting/Auditing; Finance. **Positions commonly filled include:** Accountant; Auditor; Budget Analyst; Chief Financial Officer; Controller; Credit Manager; Finance Director; Financial Analyst; Management Analyst/Consultant. **Average salary range of placements:** More than $50,000.

PERSONNEL RESOURCES ORGANIZATION
121 South Broad Street, Suite 1030, Philadelphia PA 19107. 215/735-7500. **Fax:** 215/735-5426. **Contact:** Larry Cesare, President. **Description:** An executive search firm. **Specializes in the areas of:** Legal. **Positions commonly filled include:** Attorney. **Average salary range of placements:** More than $50,000.

PRESTIGE PERSONNEL
999 Old Eagle School Road, Suite 106, Wayne PA 19087. 610/995-1066. **Fax:** 610/995-1080. **Contact:** Chris Hooven, Owner. **Description:** An executive search firm. **Specializes in the areas of:** Engineering; Manufacturing; Technical. **Positions commonly filled include:** Chemical Engineer; Design Engineer; Designer; Industrial Engineer; Mechanical Engineer; Metallurgical Engineer; Mining Engineer; Operations/Production Manager; Quality Control Supervisor; Software Engineer. **Average salary range of placements:** $30,000 - $50,000.

PROBE TECHNOLOGY
293 Bernard Drive, King of Prussia PA 19406. 610/337-8544. **Fax:** 610/337-8068. **Contact:** Tom Belletieri, Owner. **Description:** An executive search firm. **Specializes in the areas of:** Biology; Engineering; General Management; Health/Medical; Industrial; Manufacturing; Research and Development; Sales; Technical. **Positions commonly filled include:** Biomedical Engineer; Buyer; Ceramics Engineer; Chemical Engineer; Chief Executive Officer; Electrical/ Electronics Engineer; General Manager; Industrial Engineer; Industrial Production Manager; Materials Engineer; Mechanical Engineer; Metallurgical Engineer; Operations Manager; Production Manager; Purchasing Agent/Manager; Quality Control Supervisor; Sales Manager; Services Sales Representative; Vice President. **Average salary range of placements:** More than $50,000. **Number of placements per year:** 1 - 49.

PROFESSIONAL RECRUITERS INC.
P.O. Box 4, Bala-Cynwyd PA 19004. 610/667-9355. **Contact:** Manager. **Description:** An executive search firm.

PROSEARCH, INC.
400 Baldwin Road, Pittsburgh PA 15205. 412/276-4200. **Contact:** Manager. **Description:** An executive search firm. **Specializes in the areas of:** Engineering; Finance; Human Resources.

QUESTOR CONSULTANTS, INC.
2515 North Broad Street, Colmar PA 18915. 215/997-9262. **Fax:** 215/997-9226. **Contact:** Sal Bevivino, President. **E-mail address:** qtor@cynet.net. **World Wide Web address:** http://www.qtor.com. **Description:** An executive search firm. **Specializes in the areas of:** Insurance; Legal. **Positions commonly filled include:** Adjuster; Attorney; Claim Representative; Underwriter/ Assistant Underwriter. **Average salary range of placements:** More than $50,000. **Number of placements per year:** 1 - 49.

RCM TECHNOLOGIES
724 West Lancaster Avenue, One Devon Square, Suite 206, Wayne PA 19087. 610/293-9110. **Contact:** Manager. **Description:** An executive search firm. **Specializes in the areas of:** Computer Hardware/Software.

R.H.A. EXECUTIVE PERSONNEL SERVICES
33 West Lancaster Avenue, Ardmore PA 19003. 610/642-3092x33. **Contact:** Manager. **Description:** An executive search firm operating on a retainer basis. R.H.A. Executive Personnel Services also offers some career/outplacement counseling services. **Specializes in the areas of:** Food; General Management; Legal; Manufacturing; Personnel/Labor Relations; Retail; Sales; Secretarial; Technical; Transportation. **Positions commonly filled include:** Administrative Manager; Agricultural Engineer; Attorney; Automotive Mechanic; Biological Scientist; Blue-Collar Worker Supervisor; Budget Analyst; Buyer; Chemist; Claim Representative; Clerical Supervisor; Clinical Lab Technician; Electrician; Food Scientist/Technologist; Health Services Manager; Hotel Manager; Human Resources Manager; Market Research Analyst; Public Relations Specialist; Purchasing Agent/Manager; Quality Control Supervisor; Restaurant/Food Service Manager; Systems Analyst; Typist/Word Processor. **Number of placements per year:** 100 - 199.

ALAN RAEBURN CONSULTANTS
5471 Pocusset Street, Pittsburgh PA 15217. 412/422-6110. **Fax:** 412/422-6112. **Contact:** Recruiter. **E-mail address:** alan@hdhunter.com. **Description:** An executive search firm operating on both retainer and contingency bases. Founded in 1988. **Specializes in the areas of:** Distribution; Engineering; High-Tech; Marketing; Sales. **Positions commonly filled include:** Branch Manager; General Manager; Human Resources Manager; Industrial Engineer; Manufacturer's/Wholesaler's Sales Rep.; Sales Engineer; Technical Support Engineer. **Other U.S. locations:** Nationwide. **Average salary range of placements:** More than $50,000. **Number of placements per year:** 1 - 49.

RICE COHEN INTERNATIONAL
301 Oxford Valley Road, Suite 1506-A, Yardley PA 19067. 215/321-4100. **Fax:** 215/321-6370. **Contact:** Gene Rice, Managing Partner. **World Wide Web address:** http://www.ricecohen.com. **Description:** An executive search firm operating on both retainer and contingency bases. **Specializes in the areas of:** Accounting; Computer Science/Software; Finance; Food; Health/Medical. **Positions commonly filled include:** Account Manager; Account Representative; Chief Financial Officer; Computer Operator; Computer Programmer; Consultant; Electrical/Electronics Engineer; General Manager; Graphic Artist; Human Resources Manager; Internet Services Manager; Management Analyst/Consultant; Manufacturing Engineer; Marketing Manager; Marketing Specialist; Mechanical Engineer; Multimedia Designer; Project Manager; Sales Engineer; Sales Executive; Sales Representative; Vice President of Marketing and Sales. **Corporate headquarters location:** This Location. **Average salary range of placements:** More than $50,000. **Number of placements per year:** 200 - 499.

RITTENHOUSE EXECUTIVE SEARCH
1700 Benjamin Franklin Parkway, The Windsor, Penthouse Suite, Philadelphia PA 19103. 215/564-6007. **Fax:** 215/564-6051. **Contact:** Manager. **E-mail address:** recruiter@ritsearch.com. **World Wide Web address:** http://www.ritsearch.com. **Description:** An executive search firm. **Specializes in the areas of:** Accounting; Finance; Legal.

JASON ROBERTS ASSOCIATES INC.
200 Monument Road, Suite 5, Bala-Cynwyd PA 19004. 610/667-1440. **Fax:** 610/667-1573. **Contact:** Robert Kirschner, President. **Description:** An executive search firm operating on both retainer and contingency bases. The firm provides placements exclusively in the SAP (System-Application-Program) and technology resources fields. **Average salary range of placements:** $30,000 - $50,000. **Number of placements per year:** 100 - 199.

ROMAC INTERNATIONAL
150 South Warner Road, Suite 238, King of Prussia PA 19406. 610/341-1960. **Contact:** Manager. **World Wide Web address:** http://www.romac.com. **Description:** An executive search firm. **Specializes in the areas of:** Administration; Computer Hardware/Software; Technical.

ROMAC INTERNATIONAL
2 Gateway Center, Suite 1799, 603 Stanwix Street, Pittsburgh PA 15222. 412/209-2400. **Contact:** Manager. **World Wide Web address:** http://www.romac.com. **Description:** An executive search firm. **Specializes in the areas of:** Accounting/Auditing; Information Systems.

ROMAC INTERNATIONAL
4 Glenhardie Corporate Center, 1255 Drummers Lane, Suite 103, Wayne PA 19087. 610/989-3680. **Contact:** Manager. **Description:** An executive search firm that also provides some temporary placements. **Specializes in the areas of:** Accounting/Auditing; Finance; Human Resources; Information Technology.

ROMAC INTERNATIONAL
1760 Market Street, 12th Floor, Philadelphia PA 19103. 215/665-1717. **Fax:** 215/665-2894. **Contact:** Manager. **World Wide Web address:** http://www.romac.com. **Description:** An executive search firm. **Specializes in the areas of:** Accounting/Auditing; Computer Hardware/Software; Finance; Information Technology.

ROTH YOUNG PERSONNEL SERVICES
3087 Carson Avenue, Murrysville PA 15668. 724/733-5900. **Contact:** Manager. **Description:** An executive search firm. **Specializes in the areas of:** Health/Medical; Hotel/Restaurant; Retail.

SHS ASSOCIATES, INC.
P.O. Box 472, Newtown Square PA 19072. 610/240-1800. **Fax:** 610/240-0700. **Contact:** Skip W. Schneider, Managing Partner. **Description:** An executive search firm providing mid- to senior-level placements. Founded in 1964. **Specializes in the areas of:** Accounting/Auditing; Finance; Marketing; Personnel/Labor Relations. **Positions commonly filled include:** Chief Financial Officer; Controller; Finance Director; Human Resources Manager. **Other U.S. locations:** Nationwide. **Average salary range of placements:** More than $65,000. **Number of placements per year:** 1 - 49.

SHS INTERNATIONAL
15 Paoli Plaza, Paoli PA 19301. 610/408-8351. **Fax:** 610/408-8353. **Contact:** Paul Reitman, General Manager. **Description:** An executive search firm. **Specializes in the areas of:** Accounting/Auditing; Banking; Computer Science/Software; Engineering; Finance; Insurance; Legal; Sales; Secretarial; Technical. **Positions commonly filled include:** Accountant/Auditor; Actuary; Adjuster; Administrative Manager; Architect; Attorney; Bank Officer/Manager; Biochemist; Biological Scientist; Biomedical Engineer; Branch Manager; Buyer; Chemical Engineer; Chemist; Civil Engineer; Claim Rep.; Clerical Supervisor; Computer Programmer; Customer Service Rep.; Dental Assistant/Dental Hygienist; Design Engineer; Draftsperson; Editor; EKG Technician; Electrical/Electronics Engineer; Emergency Medical Tech.; Environmental Engineer; Financial Analyst; Food Scientist/Technologist; Industrial Engineer; Insurance Agent/Broker; Internet Services Manager; Management Analyst/Consultant; Management Trainee; Market Research Analyst; Mechanical Engineer; Medical Records Tech.; Metallurgical Engineer; MIS Specialist; Multimedia Designer; Nuclear Engineer; Occupational Therapist; Operations/Production Manager; Paralegal; Pharmacist; Physical Therapist; Physician; Purchasing Agent/Manager; Quality Control Supervisor; Radiological Technologist; Registered Nurse; Respiratory Therapist; Science Technologist; Securities Sales Rep.; Services Sales Rep.; Software Engineer; Statistician; Structural Engineer; Technical Writer/Editor; Telecommunications Manager; Travel Agent; Typist/

Word Processor; Underwriter/Assistant Underwriter. **Number of placements per year:** 50 - 99.

SHS INTERNATIONAL
P.O. Box 1204, Wilkes-Barre PA 18703-1204. 570/825-3411. **Fax:** 570/825-7790. **Contact:** Chris Hackett, Search Consultant. **E-mail address:** contact@shstechstaffing.com. **Description:** An executive search firm. Founded in 1968. **Specializes in the areas of:** Accounting/Auditing; Banking; Computer Science/Software; Engineering; Finance; Personnel/Labor Relations; Publishing. **Positions commonly filled include:** Accountant/Auditor; Aerospace Engineer; Biological Scientist; Budget Analyst; Ceramics Engineer; Chemical Engineer; Chemist; Civil Engineer; Clinical Lab Technician; Computer Programmer; Credit Manager; Designer; Draftsperson; Editor; Financial Analyst; Human Resources Manager; Industrial Engineer; Landscape Architect; Materials Engineer; Mechanical Engineer; Medical Records Technician; Metallurgical Engineer; Occupational Therapist; Physical Therapist; Purchasing Agent/Manager; Software Engineer; Systems Analyst; Technical Writer/Editor. **Average salary range of placements:** $30,000 - $50,000. **Number of placements per year:** 50 - 99.

SHS OF ALLENTOWN
4327 Route 309, Schnecksville PA 18078. 610/799-2131. **Fax:** 610/799-2141. **Contact:** David Mostow, President. **Description:** An executive search firm that specializes in the placement of professionals in the minerals processing, battery, explosives, and chemical industries. **Positions commonly filled include:** Chemist; Construction Contractor; Designer; Engineer; General Manager; Mining Engineer; Operations/Production Manager; Quality Control Supervisor. **Average salary range of placements:** More than $50,000. **Number of placements per year:** 50 - 99.

SPC F-O-R-T-U-N-E
1410 West Street Road, Suite C, Warminster PA 18974. 215/675-3100. **Fax:** 215/675-3080. **Contact:** Michael G. Strand, President. **Description:** An executive search firm. **Specializes in the areas of:** Architecture/Construction; Computer Hardware/Software; Health/Medical; Marketing; Sales; Scientific; Technical. **Positions commonly filled include:** Architect; Attorney; Biomedical Engineer; Buyer; Chemical Engineer; Civil Engineer; Database Manager; Design Engineer; Electrical/Electronics Engineer; Environmental Engineer; Manufacturing Engineer; Marketing Manager; Mechanical Engineer; MIS Specialist; Operations Manager; Physician; Production Manager; Project Manager; Purchasing Agent/Manager; Quality Control Supervisor; Sales Engineer; Sales Executive; Software Engineer; Statistician; Telecommunications Manager. **Corporate headquarters location:** New York NY. **Other U.S. locations:** Nationwide. **Average salary range of placements:** $80,000 - $250,000.

SANFORD ROSE ASSOCIATES
3500 Brooktree Center, Suite 220, Wexford PA 15090. 724/934-2261. **Contact:** Manager. **World Wide Web address:** http://www.sanfordrose.com. **Description:** An executive search firm. **Specializes in the areas of:** Finance; Manufacturing.

SANFORD ROSE ASSOCIATES
130 Almshouse Road, Suite 107A, Richboro PA 18954. 215/953-7433. **Fax:** 215/953-7449. **Contact:** Branch Manager. **World Wide Web address:** http://www.sanfordrose.com. **Description:** An executive search firm. **Specializes in the areas of:** Computer Hardware/Software; Graphic Arts; Management; Marketing; MIS/EDP; Printing; Technical.

SANFORD ROSE ASSOCIATES
P.O. Box 1017, Buckingham PA 18912. 215/794-5570. **Fax:** 215/794-5672. **Contact:** Branch Manager. **World Wide Web address:** http://www.sanfordrose.com.

Description: An executive search firm. **Specializes in the areas of:** Engineering; Manufacturing; Marketing.

SCHULER CONSULTANTS, INC.
1030 Irving Street, Philadelphia PA 19107. 215/925-9935. **Fax:** 215/592-8473. **Contact:** Adam D. Diomedo, Consultant. **Description:** An executive search firm. **Specializes in the areas of:** Computer Programming.

SNELLING PERSONNEL SERVICES
111 Presidential Boulevard, Bala-Cynwyd PA 19004. 610/667-4222. **Contact:** Office Manager. **Description:** An executive search firm. **Specializes in the areas of:** Engineering; Finance; General Management; Sales.

SPECIALTY CONSULTANTS INC.
2710 Gateway Towers, Pittsburg PA 15222. 412/355-8200. **Fax:** 412/355-0498. **Contact:** Manager. **World Wide Web address:** http://www.specon.com. **Description:** An executive search firm. Founded in 1970. **Specializes in the areas of:** Construction; Real Estate. **Positions commonly filled include:** Director; Finance Director; Management; Marketing Specialist; Vice President.

SPECTRUM CONSULTANTS, INC.
RETAIL RECRUITERS
111 Presidential Boulevard, Suite 105, Bala-Cynwyd PA 19004-1008. 610/667-6565. **Fax:** 610/667-5323. **Contact:** Shirlee Berman, President. **Description:** An executive search firm. Founded in 1978. **Specializes in the areas of:** Accounting/Auditing; Administration; Advertising; Architecture/Construction; Food; Health/Medical; Manufacturing; Marketing; Personnel/Labor Relations; Retail; Sales. **Positions commonly filled include:** Accountant; Advertising Executive; Assistant Manager; Auditor; Buyer; Chief Financial Officer; Consultant; Controller; Designer; Dietician/Nutritionist; Finance Director; Financial Analyst; Graphic Artist; Graphic Designer; Human Resources Manager; Industrial Engineer; Management Analyst/Consultant; Market Research Analyst; Marketing Manager; MIS Specialist; Occupational Therapist; Operations Manager; Pharmacist; Physical Therapist; Production Manager; Project Manager; Quality Control Supervisor; Registered Nurse; Respiratory Therapist; Sales Executive; Sales Manager; Speech-Language Pathologist; Systems Analyst; Systems Manager; Telecommunications Manager; Transportation/Traffic Specialist. **Average salary range of placements:** More than $50,000. **Number of placements per year:** 100 - 199.

KENN SPINRAD INC.
P.O. Box 4095, Reading PA 19606. 610/779-0944. **Fax:** 610/779-8338. **Contact:** Manager. **E-mail address:** kspinrad@ptd.net. **World Wide Web address:** http://www.elecsp.com/kspin/kspin.htm. **Description:** An executive search firm operating on both retainer and contingency bases. **Specializes in the areas of:** Engineering; Fashion; Industrial; Textiles. **Positions commonly filled include:** Buyer; Chemical Engineer; Chemist; Chief Financial Officer; Computer Programmer; Industrial Engineer; Industrial Production Manager; Manufacturing Engineer; Market Research Analyst; Mechanical Engineer; Metallurgical Engineer; Operations/Production Manager; Purchasing Agent/Manager; Quality Control Supervisor; Software Engineer; Systems Analyst. **Average salary range of placements:** More than $50,000. **Number of placements per year:** 100 - 199.

STAFFING ALLIANCE
P.O. Box 3165, West Chester PA 19381. 610/430-7430. **Contact:** Jeannine Jubeck, Owner. **World Wide Web address:** http://www.staffalliance.com. **Description:** An executive search firm. **Specializes in the areas of:** Personnel/Labor Relations.

DANIEL STERN & ASSOCIATES
211 North Whitfield Street, Pittsburgh PA 15206. 412/363-9700. **Contact:** Manager. **Description:** An

executive search firm. **Specializes in the areas of:** Health/Medical.

STEWART ASSOCIATES
245 Butler Avenue, Lancaster PA 17601. 717/299-9242. **Fax:** 717/299-4879. **Contact:** Walter S. Poyck, Owner. **Description:** An executive search firm operating on a contingency basis. Client company pays fee. **Specializes in the areas of:** Engineering. **Positions commonly filled include:** Auditor; Biochemist; Blue-Collar Worker Supervisor; Chemical Engineer; Chemist; Controller; Design Engineer; Electrical/Electronics Engineer; Environmental Engineer; Financial Analyst; General Manager; Human Resources Manager; Industrial Engineer; Industrial Production Manager; Management Trainee; Mechanical Engineer; Metallurgical Engineer; Quality Control Supervisor; Sales Engineer; Sales Manager. **Corporate headquarters location:** This Location. **Number of placements per year:** 1 - 49.

STRATFORDGROUP
610 West Germantown Pike, Suite 150, Plymouth Meeting PA 19462. 610/828-0713. **Toll-free phone:** 800/536-4384. **Fax:** 610/825-5890. **Contact:** Recruiter. **World Wide Web address:** http://www. stratfordgroup.com. **Description:** An executive search firm operating on a retainer basis. Founded in 1997. **Specializes in the areas of:** Automotive; Consumer Products; Engineering; Entertainment; Finance; Health/Medical; Human Resources; Information Technology; Manufacturing; Nonprofit; Professional; Retail; Telecommunications; Transportation. **Corporate headquarters location:** Cleveland OH. **Other U.S. locations:** San Diego CA; San Francisco CA; Denver CO; Washington DC; Charlotte NC; Research Triangle Park NC; New York NY; Cleveland OH; Dayton OH; Toledo OH; Houston TX; Vienna VA; Bellevue WA.

SPENCER STUART & ASSOCIATES
2005 Market Street, Suite 2350, Philadelphia PA 19103. 215/814-1600. **Toll-free phone:** 800/258-9288. **Fax:** 215/814-1681. **Contact:** Manager. **Description:** An executive search firm.

SUBER & McAULEY TECHNICAL SEARCH
One Parkway Center, Suite 200, Pittsburgh PA 15220. 412/922-3336. **Fax:** 412/922-5716. **Contact:** John C. Suber, Partner/Recruiter. **E-mail address:** smts@ aol.com. **Description:** An executive search firm operating on both contingency and retainer bases. Founded in 1991. **Specializes in the areas of:** Engineering; Manufacturing; Technical. **Positions commonly filled include:** Chemical Engineer; Design Engineer; Electrical/Electronics Engineer; General Manager; Industrial Engineer; Industrial Production Manager; Market Research Analyst; Mechanical Engineer; Metallurgical Engineer; Operations/Production Manager; Purchasing Agent/Manager; Quality Control Supervisor; Science Technologist; Software Engineer; Telecommunications Manager; Video Production Coordinator. **Average salary range of placements:** More than $50,000. **Number of placements per year:** 100 - 199.

SUBURBAN PLACEMENT SERVICE
21 North York Road, Willow Grove PA 19090-3420. 215/657-6262. **Fax:** 215/657-6431. **Contact:** Ed Fort, Manager. **Description:** An executive search firm. Founded in 1971. **Specializes in the areas of:** Computer Science/Software. **Positions commonly filled include:** Aerospace Engineer; Computer Programmer; Customer Service Representative; Electrical/Electronics Engineer; MIS Specialist; Software Engineer; Systems Analyst; Telecommunications Analyst. **Number of placements per year:** 50 - 99.

SYSTEMS PERSONNEL INC.
115 West State Street, Media PA 19063. 610/565-8880. **Fax:** 610/565-1482. **Contact:** Manager. **Description:** An executive search firm operating on both retainer and contingency bases. Founded in 1974. **Specializes in the areas of:** Computer Science/Software; MIS/EDP;

Technical. **Positions commonly filled include:** Applications Engineer; AS400 Programmer Analyst; Computer Programmer; Computer Scientist; Computer Support Technician; Content Developer; Database Administrator; Database Manager; Internet Services Manager; MIS Specialist; Network/Systems Administrator; Project Manager; Software Engineer; SQL Programmer; Statistician; Systems Analyst; Systems Manager; Telecommunications Manager; Webmaster. **Average salary range of placements:** $50,000 - $100,000. **Number of placements per year:** 100 - 199.

TERRY TAYLOR & ASSOCIATES
459 Bechman Street, Springdale PA 15144. 724/274-5627. **Contact:** Terry Taylor, Principal. **Description:** An executive search firm operating on both retainer and contingency bases. Founded in 1975. **Specializes in the areas of:** Administration; Consulting; Finance; Health/Medical; Human Resources; Information Systems; Information Technology; Telecommunications. **Positions commonly filled include:** Accountant/Auditor; Economist; Financial Analyst; Internet Services Manager; Management Analyst/Consultant; Mathematician; Securities Sales Rep.; Systems Analyst; Telecommunications Manager. **Average salary range of placements:** More than $50,000. **Number of placements per year:** 1 - 49.

TECHNICAL SEARCH SERVICES
401 Walnut Street, Norristown PA 19401-5024. 610/275-5024. **Fax:** 610/275-5370. **Contact:** Fred Giuffrida, Owner/Manager. **Description:** An executive search firm. **Specializes in the areas of:** Information Systems.

TELL/COM RECRUITERS
807 Floral Vale Boulevard, Yardley PA 19087. 215/860-4100. **Fax:** 215/968-6680. **Contact:** Dennis F. Young, President. **Description:** An executive search firm. Founded in 1983. **Specializes in the areas of:** Engineering; Management; Sales; Telecommunications. **Positions commonly filled include:** Telecommunications Manager. **Number of placements per year:** 200 - 499.

TEMPLETON & ASSOCIATES
1518 Walnut Street, Suite 1210, Philadelphia PA 19102. 215/772-0555. **Contact:** Manager. **Description:** An executive search firm. **Specializes in the areas of:** Legal.

TEXCEL, INC.
5170 Campus Drive, Plymouth Meeting PA 19462. 610/825-3850. **Fax:** 610/828-1095. **Contact:** Manager. **Description:** An executive search firm. **Specializes in the areas of:** Technical.

TOWER CONSULTANTS, LTD.
621B Swedesford Road, Malvern PA 19355. 610/722-9300. **Contact:** Donna DeHart, Vice President. **E-mail address:** dehart@towerconsultants.com. **Description:** An executive search firm operating on a retainer basis. Founded in 1988. **Specializes in the areas of:** Personnel/Labor Relations. **Positions commonly filled include:** Human Resources Manager. **Number of placements per year:** 50 - 99.

W.G. TUCKER & ASSOCIATES
2908 McKelvey Road, Suite 2, Pittsburgh PA 15221-4569. 412/244-9309. **Fax:** 412/244-9195. **Contact:** Weida G. Tucker, President. **Description:** An executive search firm operating on a retainer basis. **Specializes in the areas of:** Accounting/Auditing; Administration; Banking; General Management; Marketing; MIS/EDP; Personnel/Labor Relations; Sales; Transportation. **Positions commonly filled include:** Account Manager; Advertising Exec.; Attorney; CFO; Controller; Customer Service Rep.; Environmental Engineer; Financial Analyst; Geologist/Geophysicist; Human Resources Manager; Industrial Production Manager; Intellectual Property Lawyer; Marketing Manager; MIS Manager; Operations Manager; Project Manager; Sales Engineer;

Sales Executive; Sales Manager; Systems Manager; Telecommunications Manager; Transportation/Traffic Specialist; Vice President. **Corporate headquarters location:** This Location. **Average salary range of placements:** More than $50,000.

VOGUE PERSONNEL INC.
1515 Market Street, Suite 702, Philadelphia PA 19102. 215/564-0720. **Fax:** 215/564-0722. **Contact:** Ronald Sacks, President. **Description:** An executive search firm. **Specializes in the areas of:** Accounting; Administration; Advertising; Banking; Finance; Health/Medical; Insurance; International Executives; Legal; Marketing; MIS/EDP; Personnel/Labor Relations; Sales; Secretarial. **Positions commonly filled include:** Accountant/Auditor; Advertising Clerk; Clerical Supervisor; Customer Service Rep.; Human Resources Manager; Management Trainee; Medical Records Technician; Paralegal; Public Relations Specialist; Secretary. **Average salary range of placements:** $30,000 - $50,000. **Number of placements per year:** 50 - 99.

GORDON WAHLS EXECUTIVE SEARCH
P.O. Box 386, Broomall PA 19008. **Toll-free phone:** 800/523-7112. **Fax:** 610/359-8803. **Contact:** Manager. **World Wide Web address:** http://www.gwahls.com. **Description:** An executive search firm. **Specializes in the areas of:** Packaging; Printing; Publishing.

C.D. WARNER & ASSOCIATES
12 Davenport Drive, Downington PA 19335. 610/458-8335. **Fax:** 610/458-0498. **Contact:** C. Douglas Warner, President. **E-mail address:** doug@cdwarner.com. **World Wide Web address:** http://www.cdwarner.com. **Description:** An executive search firm operating on both retainer and contingency bases. The firm places only senior executive management personnel. Client company pays fee. **Specializes in the areas of:** Computer Science/Software; Engineering; High-Tech; Information Technology; Marketing; Sales. **Positions commonly filled include:** Account Manager; Account Rep.; Branch Manager; Marketing Manager; Sales Engineer; Sales Executive; Sales Manager; Sales Rep.; Software Engineer. **Corporate headquarters location:** This Location. **Other U.S. locations:** Forest Hill MD. **Average salary range of placements:** More than $50,000. **Number of placements per year:** 50 - 99.

WHITTLESEY & ASSOCIATES, INC.
300 South High Street, West Chester PA 19382. 610/436-6500. **Fax:** 610/344-0018. **Contact:** Toni J.

Ritchey, Director of Research. **Description:** Whittlesey & Associates is an executive search firm operating on a retainer basis. **Specializes in the areas of:** Engineering; Food; General Management; Health/Medical; Industrial; Light Industrial; Personnel/Labor Relations; Sales; Technical. **Positions commonly filled include:** Account Manager; Chemical Engineer; Controller; Electrical/Electronics Engineer; General Manager; Human Resources Manager; Industrial Engineer; Manufacturer's/Wholesaler's Sales Rep.; Marketing Manager; Production Manager; Project Manager; Sales Executive; Sales Manager. **Average salary range of placements:** More than $50,000. **Number of placements per year:** 1 - 49.

WITTHAUER ASSOCIATES LTD.
P.O. Box 40, Chalfont PA 18914. 215/822-6411. **Contact:** Manager. **Description:** An executive search firm. **Specializes in the areas of:** Computer Hardware/Software; Technical.

WOLDOFF ASSOCIATES
301 Oxford Valley Road, Suite 1106 B, Yardley PA 19067. 215/321-6619. **Fax:** 215/493-8086. **Contact:** Manager. **World Wide Web address:** http://www.woldoff.com. **Description:** An executive search firm. **Specializes in the areas of:** Accounting; Finance.

YORKTOWNE PERSONNEL
103 East Market Street, York PA 17401. 717/843-0079. **Fax:** 717/843-5792. **Contact:** Roger M. Geiger, President. **Description:** Yorktowne Personnel is an executive search firm operating on both retainer and contingency bases. **Specializes in the areas of:** Accounting/Auditing; Engineering; Food; General Management; Industrial; Personnel/Labor Relations; Technical. **Positions commonly filled include:** Account Manager; Accountant/Auditor; Budget Analyst; Buyer; Chemical Engineer; Chief Financial Officer; Civil Engineer; Controller; Credit Manager; Design Engineer; Electrical/Electronics Engineer; Environmental Engineer; Financial Analyst; Human Resources Manager; Industrial Designer; Industrial Engineer; Industrial Production Manager; Manufacturing Engineer; Mechanical Engineer; Metallurgical Engineer; Operations/Production Manager; Production Manager; Purchasing Agent/Manager; Quality Control Supervisor; Sales Engineer; Software Engineer; Transportation/Traffic Specialist. **Number of placements per year:** 50 - 99.

PERMANENT EMPLOYMENT AGENCIES

ACSYS RESOURCES
1700 Market Street, Suite 3110, Philadelphia PA 19103. 215/568-6810. **Contact:** Manager. **Description:** Acsys Resources is a permanent employment agency. **Specializes in the areas of:** Accounting/Auditing; Consulting; Finance; Sales.

ACTION PERSONNEL SERVICES
1622 Main Street, Dickson City PA 18447. 570/383-0243. **Fax:** 570/383-2565. **Contact:** Nick Swatkowski, President. **Description:** Action Personnel Services is a permanent employment agency. **Specializes in the areas of:** Accounting/Auditing; Engineering; General Management; Industrial; Manufacturing; Personnel/Labor Relations. **Positions commonly filled include:** Accountant/Auditor; Buyer; Ceramics Engineer; Chemical Engineer; Civil Engineer; Computer Programmer; Draftsperson; Electrical/Electronics Engineer; Industrial Engineer; Industrial Production Manager; Manufacturing Engineer; Materials Engineer; Mechanical Engineer; Metallurgical Engineer; Occupational Therapist; Petroleum Engineer; Physical Therapist; Sales Executive; Sales Manager; Software Engineer; Systems Analyst; Telecommunications Manager. **Number of placements per year:** 1 - 49.

ADVANCE PERSONNEL
P.O. Box 8383, Reading PA 19603. 610/374-4089. **Contact:** Manager. **Description:** A permanent employment agency. **Positions commonly filled include:** Administrative Assistant; Bookkeeper; Claim Representative; Clerk; Customer Service Representative; Data Entry Clerk; Legal Secretary; Medical Secretary; Receptionist; Secretary; Stenographer; Typist/Word Processor. **Number of placements per year:** 200 - 499.

ALL STAFFING INC.
P.O. Box 219, Lansford PA 18232. 570/645-5000. **Fax:** 570/645-5255. **Contact:** Stan Costello, Jr., President. **Description:** A permanent employment agency. **Specializes in the areas of:** Accounting/Auditing; Administration; Advertising; Computer Science/Software; Finance; Health/Medical; Industrial; Manufacturing; Personnel/Labor Relations; Retail; Sales; Secretarial. **Positions commonly filled include:** Accountant/Auditor; Computer Programmer; Dental Assistant/Dental Hygienist; Dental Lab Technician; Dentist; Draftsperson; Economist; EEG Technologist; EKG Technician; Financial Analyst; General Manager; Health Services Manager; Human Resources Manager; Insurance Agent/Broker; Management Trainee; Manufacturer's/Wholesaler's Sales Rep.; Medical

Records Technician; Nuclear Medicine Technologist; Occupational Therapist; Pharmacist; Physical Therapist; Physician; Physicist; Psychologist; Radiological Technologist; Registered Nurse; Respiratory Therapist; Services Sales Representative; Surgical Technician; Systems Analyst; Wholesale and Retail Buyer. **Number of placements per year:** 50 - 99.

BECKER PERSONNEL
P.O. Box 2471, Bala-Cynwyd PA 19004. 610/667-3010. **Contact:** Manager. **Description:** A permanent employment agency that also provides some temporary placements. **Specializes in the areas of:** Insurance; Marketing; Secretarial. **Positions commonly filled include:** Accountant; Administrative Assistant; Administrative Manager; Branch Manager; Clerical Supervisor; Computer Operator; Controller; Credit Manager; Customer Service Rep.; Draftsperson; Financial Analyst; General Manager; Graphic Artist; Graphic Designer; Management Trainee; Managing Editor; Paralegal; Production Manager; Sales Exec.; Sales Rep.; Salon Manager; Secretary; Typist/Word Processor. **Benefits available to temporary workers:** Paid Holidays; Vacation Pay. **Corporate headquarters location:** This Location. **Average salary range of placements:** $30,000 - $50,000. **Number of placements per year:** 100 - 199.

BRADLEY PROFESSIONAL SERVICES
440 East Swedesford Road, Suite 1070, Wayne PA 19087. 610/254-9995. **Fax:** 610/971-9480. **Contact:** Manager. **Description:** A permanent employment agency. **Specializes in the areas of:** Accounting/Auditing; Biology; Computer Science/Software; Engineering; Health/Medical; Personnel/Labor Relations; Technical. **Positions commonly filled include:** Accountant/Auditor; Aerospace Engineer; Agricultural Scientist; Architect; Biological Scientist; Biomedical Engineer; Buyer; Ceramics Engineer; Chemical Engineer; Chemist; Civil Engineer; Clinical Lab Technician; Computer Programmer; Designer; Draftsperson; Electrical/Electronics Engineer; Human Resources Manager; Industrial Engineer; Management Analyst/Consultant; Materials Engineer; Mechanical Engineer; Metallurgical Engineer; Mining Engineer; Nuclear Engineer; Petroleum Engineer; Pharmacist; Physician; Science Technologist; Software Engineer; Stationary Engineer; Statistician; Structural Engineer; Systems Analyst; Technical Writer/Editor. **Number of placements per year:** 100 - 199.

CAREERS USA
1825 JFK Boulevard, Philadelphia PA 19103. 215/561-3800. **Contact:** Manager. **Description:** A permanent employment agency.

CLIFFORD ASSOCIATES INC.
306 Corporate Drive East, Langhorne PA 19047. 215/968-1980. **Fax:** 215/860-4109. **Contact:** Cliff Milles, Owner. **E-mail address:** cai@voicenet.com. **Description:** A permanent employment agency. **Specializes in the areas of:** Computer Hardware/Software; Information Technology. **Positions commonly filled include:** Computer Programmer; MIS Specialist; Systems Analyst; Systems Manager. **Number of placements per year:** 1 - 49.

COMPUTER PROFESSIONALS UNLIMITED
5000 McKnight Road, Suite 302, Pittsburgh PA 15237. 412/367-4191. **Fax:** 412/367-1152. **Contact:** Personnel Manager. **Description:** A permanent employment agency. **Specializes in the areas of:** Banking; Computer Science/Software. **Positions commonly filled include:** Bank Officer/Manager; Computer Programmer; Human Resources Manager; Software Engineer; Systems Analyst. **Number of placements per year:** 100 - 199.

J. CROYLE & ASSOCIATES, INC.
3244 USX Tower, 32nd Floor, Pittsburgh PA 15219. 412/281-4080. **Fax:** 412/281-8308. **Contact:** Joan Croyle, President. **Description:** A permanent employment agency. **Specializes in the areas of:**

Administration; Clerical; Fashion; Finance; Food; General Management; Legal; Retail; Secretarial. **Positions commonly filled include:** Clerical Supervisor; Customer Service Rep.; Hotel Manager; Management Trainee; Restaurant/Food Service Manager; Services Sales Rep.; Typist/Word Processor. **Average salary range of placements:** $20,000 - $29,999. **Number of placements per year:** 100 - 199.

DENTAL POWER OF DELAWARE VALLEY, INC.
1528 Walnut Street, Suite 1802, Philadelphia PA 19102. 215/735-6929. **Contact:** Manager. **Description:** A permanent employment agency that also provides some temporary placements. Founded in 1975. **Specializes in the areas of:** Dental.

DOUGHERTY & ASSOCIATES, INC.
1730 Walton Road, Suite 207, Blue Bell PA 19422. 610/825-2131. **Contact:** George J. Dougherty, President. **Description:** A permanent employment agency.

EMPLOYMENT CORPORATION OF AMERICA
2250 Hickory Road, Plymouth Meeting PA 19462. 610/941-0800. **Fax:** 610/941-0810. **Contact:** Recruiter. **Description:** A permanent employment agency specializing in making placements within *Fortune* 500 companies. **Specializes in the areas of:** Sales. **Average salary range of placements:** $30,000 - $50,000.

EXPRESS PERSONNEL SERVICE
260 South Broad Street, 14th Floor, Philadelphia PA 19102. 215/893-1200. **Contact:** Office Manager. **Description:** A permanent employment agency.

FINANCIAL INDUSTRY STAFFING COMPANY
831 DeKalb Pike, Blue Bell PA 19422. 610/277-4997. **Fax:** 610/277-0220. **Contact:** Manager. **Description:** A permanent employment agency. Founded in 1986. **Specializes in the areas of:** Accounting Administration; Banking; Computer Science/Software; Finance; General Management. **Positions commonly filled include:** Accountant; Actuary; Adjuster; Bank Officer/Manager; Branch Manager; Brokerage Clerk; Budget Analyst; Claim Rep.; Clerical Supervisor; Computer Programmer; Cost Estimator; Credit Manager; Customer Service Rep.; Economist; Financial Analyst; General Manager; Human Resources Specialist; Management Analyst/Consultant; Management Trainee; Manufacturer's/Wholesaler's Sales Rep.; Market Research Analyst; MIS Specialist; Operations/Production Manager; Purchasing Agent/Manager; Quality Control Supervisor; Securities Sales Rep.; Services Sales Rep.; Systems Analyst; Technical Writer/Editor; Telecommunications Manager; Typist/Word Processor; Underwriter/Assistant Underwriter. **Benefits available to temporary workers:** Life Insurance; Medical Insurance; Referral Bonus Plan. **Corporate headquarters location:** Boston MA. **Number of placements per year:** 200 - 499.

GENERAL EMPLOYMENT
TRIAD PERSONNEL
1617 JFK Boulevard, Suite 930, Philadelphia PA 19103. 215/569-3226. **Fax:** 215/569-8164. **Contact:** Donna Nusslein, Branch Manager. **Description:** A permanent employment agency. **Specializes in the areas of:** Computer Science/Software. **Positions commonly filled include:** Applications Engineer; Computer Engineer; Computer Operator; Computer Programmer; Computer Support Technician; Computer Technician; Database Administrator; Database Manager; Internet Services Manager; MIS Specialist; Multimedia Designer; Network/Systems Administrator; Safety Engineer; Software Engineer; SQL Programmer; Systems Analyst; Systems Manager; Webmaster. **Corporate headquarters location:** Oak Brook IL. **Other U.S. locations:** Nationwide. **Average salary range of placements:** $50,000 - $100,000. **Number of placements per year:** 100 - 199.

JERRY GOLDBERG & ASSOCIATES INC.
1404 East Market Street, York PA 17403. 717/843-0041. **Fax:** 717/843-8883. **Contact:** Jerry Goldberg, President.

Description: A permanent employment agency. **Specializes in the areas of:** Engineering; Environmental; Industrial; Manufacturing; Personnel/Labor Relations; Safety; Technical. **Positions commonly filled include:** Accountant/Auditor; Agricultural Engineer; Biomedical Engineer; Buyer; Chemical Engineer; Computer Programmer; Designer; Electrical/Electronics Engineer; Financial Analyst; Human Resources Manager; Industrial Engineer; Industrial Production Manager; Mechanical Engineer; Operations/Production Manager; Purchasing Agent/Manager; Quality Control Supervisor; Software Engineer; Structural Engineer; Systems Analyst.

MERRILL GRUMER ASSOCIATES, INC.
1500 Walnut Street, Suite 307, Philadelphia PA 19102. 215/875-8100. **Fax:** 215/875-8200. **Contact:** Merrill Grumer, President. **Description:** A permanent employment agency. **Specializes in the areas of:** Administration; Legal; MIS/EDP; Secretarial. **Positions commonly filled include:** Administrative Assistant; Administrative Manager; Branch Manager; Clerical Supervisor; Controller; Database Manager; Finance Director; Human Resources Manager; Librarian; Marketing Manager; MIS Specialist; Operations Manager; Paralegal; Secretary; Systems Manager; Typist/Word Processor. **Average salary range of placements:** $30,000 - $50,000. **Number of placements per year:** 50 - 99.

HALLMARK PERSONNEL INC.
ABEL TEMPS
1845 Market Street, Camp Hill PA 17011. 717/761-8111. **Fax:** 717/761-8862. **Contact:** Manager. **Description:** A permanent employment agency. Abel Temps (also at this location) provides temporary placements. **Specializes in the areas of:** General Management; Health/Medical; Legal; Sales; Secretarial. **Positions commonly filled include:** Accountant/Auditor; Administrative Manager; Bank Officer/Manager; Branch Manager; Brokerage Clerk; Budget Analyst; Claim Rep.; Credit Manager; Customer Service Representative; General Manager; Hotel Manager; Human Resources Specialist; Insurance Agent/Broker; Management Trainee; Manufacturer's/Wholesaler's Sales Rep.; Market Research Analyst; Medical Records Technician; Paralegal; Purchasing Agent/Manager; Quality Control Supervisor; Securities Sales Representative; Services Sales Representative; Technical Writer/Editor; Typist/Word Processor; Underwriter/Assistant Underwriter. **Average salary range of placements:** $20,000 - $29,999. **Number of placements per year:** 100 - 199.

THE HOBART WEST GROUP
1608 Walnut Street, Suite 1702, Philadelphia PA 19103. 215/735-9450. **Fax:** 215/735-9430. **Contact:** Larry Atken, General Manager. **Description:** A permanent employment agency. Founded in 1984. Client company pays fee. **Specializes in the areas of:** Administration; Computer Science/Software; Health/Medical; Marketing; Personnel/Labor Relations; Sales; Secretarial. **Positions commonly filled include:** Actuary; Administrative Assistant; Administrative Manager; AS400 Programmer Analyst; Claim Rep.; Clerical Supervisor; Computer Programmer; Customer Service Representative; Health Services Manager; Human Resources Manager; Management Trainee; Medical Records Technician; Network/Systems Administrator; Operations/Production Manager; Registered Nurse; Sales Manager; Sales Representative; Secretary; Services Sales Representative; SQL Programmer; Systems Analyst; Systems Manager; Technical Writer/Editor; Telecommunications Manager; Transportation/Traffic Specialist; Typist/Word Processor. **Average salary range of placements:** $30,000 - $49,999. **Number of placements per year:** 100 - 199.

HOSPITALITY SERVICES
P.O. Box 597, Blue Bell PA 19422. 215/643-9040. **Fax:** 215/283-2504. **Contact:** Ron Miles, Partner. **Description:** A permanent employment agency. **Specializes in the areas of:** Food; General Management; Personnel/Labor Relations. **Positions commonly filled include:** Accountant/Auditor; Construction Contractor;

Dietician/Nutritionist; Food Scientist/Technologist; Hotel Manager; Restaurant/Food Service Manager. **Number of placements per year:** 50 - 99.

INTERIM HEALTHCARE
2255 Paxton Church Road, Suite 301, Harrisburg PA 17110. 717/526-4355. **Contact:** Manager. **Description:** A permanent employment agency that also provides some temporary placements. **Specializes in the areas of:** Health/Medical.

INTERIM LEGAL PROFESSIONALS, INC.
1617 JFK Boulevard, Suite 1020, Philadelphia PA 19103. 215/568-5899. **Fax:** 215/568-5810. **Contact:** Don Jeffries, Managing Director. **Description:** A permanent employment agency. **Specializes in the areas of:** Legal. **Positions commonly filled include:** Attorney; Legal Secretary; Paralegal. **Average salary range of placements:** $30,000 - $50,000. **Number of placements per year:** 100 - 199.

JEWISH EMPLOYMENT & VOCATIONAL SERVICE
1845 Walnut Street, 7th Floor, Philadelphia PA 19103. 215/854-1800. **Contact:** Manager. **Description:** A permanent employment agency.

MARK JOSEPH ASSOCIATES
1521 Cedar Cliff Drive, Camp Hill PA 17011. 717/975-3505. **Fax:** 717/975-3565. **Contact:** Manager. **Description:** A permanent employment agency. **Specializes in the areas of:** Accounting/Auditing; Finance.

KATHY KARR PERSONNEL, INC.
2512 West Main Street, Jeffersonville PA 19403. 610/630-0760. **Fax:** 610/630-9155. **Contact:** Kathy Karr, President. **Description:** A permanent employment agency. **Specializes in the areas of:** Accounting/Auditing; Administration; Architecture/Construction; Banking; Clerical; Engineering; Finance; General Management; Industrial; Legal; Manufacturing; Sales; Secretarial; Transportation. **Positions commonly filled include:** Accountant/Auditor; Administrative Manager; Advertising Clerk; Aerospace Engineer; Agricultural Engineer; Architect; Bank Officer/Manager; Biochemist; Biological Scientist; Biomedical Engineer; Blue-Collar Worker Supervisor; Branch Manager; Brokerage Clerk; Budget Analyst; Buyer; Ceramics Engineer; Chemical Engineer; Chemist; Civil Engineer; Claim Representative; Clerical Supervisor; Computer Programmer; Construction and Building Inspector; Construction Contractor; Cost Estimator; Credit Manager; Customer Service Representative; Dental Assistant/Dental Hygienist; Design Engineer; Designer; Draftsperson; Economist; Editor; Electrical/Electronics Engineer; Electrician; Environmental Engineer; Financial Analyst; General Manager; Health Services Manager; Human Resources Specialist; Industrial Engineer; Industrial Production Manager; Landscape Architect; Library Technician; Management Analyst/Consultant; Management Trainee; Manufacturer's/Wholesaler's Sales Rep.; Market Research Analyst; Materials Engineer; Mathematician; Mechanical Engineer; Metallurgical Engineer; MIS Specialist; Operations/Production Manager; Paralegal; Property and Real Estate Manager; Public Relations Specialist; Purchasing Agent/Manager; Quality Control Supervisor; Services Sales Rep.; Software Engineer; Strategic Relations Manager; Systems Analyst; Technical Writer/Editor; Telecommunications Manager; Travel Agent; Typist/Word Processor; Underwriter/Assistant Underwriter. **Number of placements per year:** 200 - 499.

EVERETT KELLEY ASSOCIATES, INC.
1601 Market Street, Suite 325, Philadelphia PA 19103. 215/981-0800. **Contact:** Manager. **Description:** A permanent employment agency.

LAW SKIL
429 Forbes Avenue, Suite 1200, Pittsburgh PA 15219. 412/471-7944. **Fax:** 412/471-1922. **Contact:** Joan Csaszar, President. **Description:** A permanent

employment agency that also provides some temporary placements. **Specializes in the areas of:** Legal. **Positions commonly filled include:** Attorney; Paralegal; Secretary; Typist/Word Processor. **Benefits available to temporary workers:** Paid Vacation. **Corporate headquarters location:** This Location. **Number of placements per year:** 200 - 499.

LONDON PERSONNEL SERVICES
3 Garrett Road, Upper Darby PA 19082. 610/734-3223. **Fax:** 610/734-3226. **Contact:** Manager. **Description:** A permanent employment agency. **Specializes in the areas of:** Administration; Industrial; Light Industrial; MIS/EDP; Scientific; Secretarial; Technical. **Positions commonly filled include:** Administrative Assistant; Blue-Collar Worker Supervisor; Secretary; Typist/Word Processor; Warehouse/Distribution Worker. **Average salary range of placements:** Less than $20,000. **Number of placements per year:** 1000+.

MAIN LINE PERSONNEL SERVICE
100 Presidential Boulevard North, P.O. Drawer 448, Bala-Cynwyd PA 19004. 610/667-1820. **Fax:** 610/668-5000. **Contact:** Bart Marshall, Vice President. **Description:** A permanent employment agency. **Specializes in the areas of:** Computer Science/Software; Engineering; Personnel/Labor Relations; Technical. **Positions commonly filled include:** Aerospace Engineer; Agricultural Scientist; Biological Scientist; Biomedical Engineer; Ceramics Engineer; Chemical Engineer; Civil Engineer; Computer Programmer; Electrical/Electronics Engineer; Geologist/Geophysicist; Human Resources Manager; Industrial Engineer; Materials Engineer; Mechanical Engineer; Metallurgical Engineer; Mining Engineer; Nuclear Engineer; Petroleum Engineer; Software Engineer; Stationary Engineer; Structural Engineer; Systems Analyst. **Number of placements per year:** 1000+.

J. McMANUS ASSOCIATES
237 West Lancaster Avenue, Devon PA 19333. 610/688-2006. **Contact:** Jeanne McManus, Owner. **Description:** A permanent employment agency. **Specializes in the areas of:** Administration; Computer Science/Software; Insurance; Legal; Secretarial. **Positions commonly filled include:** Computer Programmer; Customer Service Representative; MIS Specialist; Systems Analyst; Typist/Word Processor; Underwriter/Assistant Underwriter. **Average salary range of placements:** $20,000 - $29,999. **Number of placements per year:** 1 - 49.

NORTHEAST AGRI EMPLOYMENT SERVICE
P.O. Box 233, Roaring Spring PA 16673. 814/224-4542. **Contact:** Russell F. Brown, Owner. **Description:** A permanent employment agency. **Specializes in the areas of:** Agri-Business; Sales. **Positions commonly filled include:** Agricultural Scientist; Dietician/Nutritionist; Sales Manager. **Average salary range of placements:** $30,000 - $50,000. **Number of placements per year:** 50 - 99.

PRN CONSULTANTS
941 Durham Road, Langhorne PA 19047. 215/750-6161. **Contact:** Placement Recruiter. **Description:** A permanent employment agency. **Specializes in the areas of:** Health/Medical.

THE PHILADELPHIA NANNY NETWORK
76 Writtenhouse Place, Suite 201, Ardmore PA 19003. 610/645-6550. **Toll-free phone:** 800/765-6269. **Fax:** 610/645-6540. **Contact:** Director. **Description:** A permanent employment agency providing placements throughout Pennsylvania, Delaware, New Jersey, New York, and Connecticut. **Specializes in the areas of:** Nannies. **Number of placements per year:** 100 - 199.

PHYSICIAN BILLING SOLUTIONS, INC. (PBSI)
1265 Drummers Lane, Suite 207, Wayne PA 19087-1570. 610/341-0902. **Fax:** 610/341-0907. **Contact:** Manager. **Description:** A permanent employment agency that also provides some temporary placements. **Specializes in the areas of:** Health/Medical; Insurance.

Positions commonly filled include: Collector; Customer Service Representative; Financial Analyst; Medical Records Technician. **Benefits available to temporary workers:** Medical Insurance. **Corporate headquarters location:** This Location. **Other area locations:** Pittsburgh PA. **Other U.S. locations:** Baltimore MD. **Average salary range of placements:** $20,000 - $29,999. **Number of placements per year:** 100 - 199.

PITTSBURGH PLACEMENT SERVICE
356 Locust Avenue, Washington PA 15301. 724/225-8100. **Toll-free phone:** 888/809-2133. **Fax:** 724/225-8827. **Contact:** Jerome T. Cypher, President. **Description:** A permanent employment agency. **Specializes in the areas of:** Food. **Positions commonly filled include:** Hotel Manager; Human Resources Specialist; Management Trainee; Restaurant/Food Service Manager. **Average salary range of placements:** $20,000 - $29,999. **Number of placements per year:** 200 - 499.

POWERS PERSONNEL
1530 Chestnut Street, Suite 310, Philadelphia PA 19102. 215/563-5520. **Contact:** Manager. **Description:** A permanent employment agency that also provides some temporary placements. **Specializes in the areas of:** Clerical; Legal; Secretarial.

QUEST SYSTEMS, INC.
1150 First Avenue, Suite 330, King of Prussia PA 19406. 610/265-8100. **Toll-free phone:** 800/368-2900. **Fax:** 610/265-6974. **Contact:** Charles Lagana, Manager. **E-mail address:** questsyst@aol.com. **World Wide Web address:** http://www.questsyst.com. **Description:** A permanent employment agency. **Specializes in the areas of:** Administration; Computer Science/Software; Scientific; Technical. **Positions commonly filled include:** Computer Programmer; Database Manager; Electrical/Electronics Engineer; Financial Analyst; Internet Services Manager; MIS Specialist; Multimedia Designer; Software Engineer; Systems Analyst; Systems Manager; Technical Writer/Editor; Telecommunications Manager; Vice President; Webmaster. **Corporate headquarters location:** Bethesda MD. **Other U.S. locations:** Atlanta GA; Baltimore MD. **Average salary range of placements:** More than $50,000. **Number of placements per year:** 200 - 499.

ELAYNE SCOTT ASSOCIATES
1601 Market Street, Suite 1595, Philadelphia PA 19103. 215/561-0088. **Contact:** Manager. **Description:** A permanent employment agency. **Specializes in the areas of:** Legal.

SELECT PERSONNEL, INC.
3070 Bristol Pike, Building 2, Suite 205, Bensalem PA 19020. 215/245-4800. **Fax:** 215/245-4990. **Contact:** Marjorie Stilwell, President. **E-mail address:** selectpersonnel@jobnet.com. **Description:** A permanent employment agency. **Specializes in the areas of:** Administration; Computer Science/Software; Engineering; Industrial; MIS/EDP; Personnel/Labor Relations; Sales. **Positions commonly filled include:** Accountant; Auditor; Broadcast Engineer; Chemist; Computer Operator; Computer Programmer; Controller; Customer Service Rep.; Database Manager; Design Engineer; Electrical/Electronics Engineer; Electrician; Environmental Engineer; Financial Analyst; Human Resources Manager; Industrial Engineer; Internet Services Manager; Manufacturing Engineer; Marketing Manager; Mechanical Engineer; Metallurgical Engineer; MIS Specialist; Online Content Specialist; Purchasing Agent/Manager; Quality Control Supervisor; Sales Engineer; Sales Exec,; Sales Manager; Sales Rep,; Software Engineer; Systems Analyst; Systems Manager; Technical Writer/Editor; Telecommunications Manager; Webmaster. **Corporate headquarters location:** This Location. **Number of placements per year:** 200 - 499.

SINGMASTER PERSONNEL SERVICES
P.O. Box 708, Devon PA 19333. 610/687-4970. **Physical address:** 406 Devon State Road, Devon PA. **Fax:**

610/687-4927. **Contact:** Alan Singmaster, Owner. **Description:** A permanent employment agency that focuses on placing management and engineering professionals in heavy manufacturing positions. Founded in 1980. **Specializes in the areas of:** Engineering; General Management; Manufacturing; Metals. **Positions commonly filled include:** Ceramics Engineer; Design Engineer; Electrical/Electronics Engineer; Mechanical Engineer; Metallurgical Engineer; Purchasing Agent/Manager; Quality Control Supervisor. **Average salary range of placements:** More than $50,000. **Number of placements per year:** 1 - 49.

STRAUSS PERSONNEL SERVICE
239 Fourth Avenue, Suite 1105, Pittsburgh PA 15222. 412/281-8235. **Toll-free phone:** 888/457-4777. **Fax:** 412/281-9417. **Contact:** T. Jeff McGraw, Vice President/General Manager. **Description:** A permanent employment agency. Founded in 1952. **Specializes in the areas of:** Accounting/Auditing; Banking; Finance; Sales; Secretarial. **Positions commonly filled include:** Accountant/Auditor; Administrative Assistant; Bank Officer/Manager; Branch Manager; Budget Analyst; Chief Financial Officer; Controller; Customer Service Representative; Financial Analyst; Internet Services Manager; Management Analyst/Consultant; Paralegal; Sales Executive; Sales Manager; Sales Representative; Secretary; Typist/Word Processor. **Number of placements per year:** 50 - 99.

STRONGIN TECHNICAL ENTERPRISES OF PENNSYLVANIA, INC.
958 Town Center, New Britain PA 18901. 215/230-8530. **Contact:** Kenneth Strongin, President. **Description:** A permanent employment agency. Founded in 1993. **Specializes in the areas of:** Architecture/Construction; Engineering; Manufacturing; Technical. **Positions commonly filled include:** Chemical Engineer; Chemist; Civil Engineer; Draftsperson; Electrical/Electronics Engineer; Environmental Engineer; Industrial Engineer; Mechanical Engineer; Pharmacist. **Average salary range of placements:** $30,000 - $50,000. **Number of placements per year:** 50 - 99.

TOD STAFFING INC.
332 Fifth Avenue, Warner Center, 6th Floor, Pittsburgh PA 15222. 412/391-7500. **Fax:** 412/391-9488. **Contact:** Manager. **Description:** A permanent employment agency. **Specializes in the areas of:** Legal. **Positions commonly filled include:** Accountant/Auditor;

Administrative Manager; Advertising Clerk; Branch Manager; Budget Analyst; Buyer; Claim Representative; Clerical Supervisor; Computer Programmer; Cost Estimator; Credit Manager; Customer Service Representative; Financial Analyst; Management Trainee; Paralegal; Purchasing Agent/Manager; Services Sales Representative; Statistician; Systems Analyst; Technical Writer/Editor. **Number of placements per year:** 500 - 999.

TODAYS STAFF
5415 North Fifth Street, Philadelphia PA 19120. 215/924-1985. **Contact:** Manager. **Description:** A permanent employment agency.

TRIANGLE ASSOCIATES INTERNATIONAL
P.O. Box 506, Warrington PA 18976. 215/343-3702. **Fax:** 215/343-3703. **Contact:** Mr. S.R. Ostroff, President. **Description:** A permanent employment agency. **Specializes in the areas of:** Chemicals; Engineering; Pharmaceuticals; Plastics. **Positions commonly filled include:** Ceramics Engineer; Chemical Engineer; Chemist; Electrical/Electronics Engineer; Materials Engineer; Mechanical Engineer; Metallurgical Engineer.

UNITED EMPLOYMENT
2030 Tilgman Street, Suite 201, Allentown PA 18104. 610/437-5040. **Fax:** 610/437-9650. **Contact:** Manager. **Description:** A permanent employment agency. **Specializes in the areas of:** Economics; Engineering; Food; Industrial; Manufacturing; Personnel/Labor Relations; Sales. **Positions commonly filled include:** Agricultural Engineer; Biological Scientist; Chemical Engineer; Chemist; Civil Engineer; Construction Contractor; Cost Estimator; Design Engineer; Draftsperson; Environmental Engineer; General Manager; Geologist/Geophysicist; Human Resources Manager; Industrial Engineer; Mechanical Engineer; Metallurgical Engineer; Nuclear Engineer; Physicist; Science Technologist; Structural Engineer. **Number of placements per year:** 100 - 199.

YOUR OTHER HANDS, INC.
714-B South Colorado Street, Philadelphia PA 19146. 215/790-0990. **Fax:** 215/545-5237. **Contact:** Manager. **Description:** A permanent employment agency. **Specializes in the areas of:** Child Care, In-Home; Nannies. **Positions commonly filled include:** Preschool Worker. **Number of placements per year:** 100 - 199.

TEMPORARY EMPLOYMENT AGENCIES

AAP INC.
6154 Steubenville Pike, McKees Rocks PA 15136. 412/788-1511. **Fax:** 412/788-4430. **Contact:** Barbara Cost, President/Owner. **E-mail address:** aap@pgh.net. **World Wide Web address:** http://www.aap-employ.com. **Description:** A temporary agency that also offers some temp-to-perm, permanent, and executive search services. The Office Support Division fills administrative, clerical, and legal positions. The Medical Division fills nursing positions for hospitals and private homes. Founded in 1995. **Specializes in the areas of:** Administration; Clerical; Health/Medical; Legal; Office Support. **Benefits available to temporary workers:** Medical Insurance; Referral Bonus Plan; Temp-of-the-Year; Vacation Pay. **Corporate headquarters location:** This Location.

ADECCO
150 South Warner Road, Walnut Hill Plaza, Suite 132, King of Prussia PA 19406. 610/341-9050. **Fax:** 610/341-9057. **Contact:** Manager. **Description:** A temporary agency. **Specializes in the areas of:** Accounting/Auditing; Administration; Clerical; General Management; Personnel/Labor Relations; Sales; Secretarial. **Positions commonly filled include:** Accountant/Auditor; Adjuster; Administrative Manager; Branch Manager; Claim Representative; Clerical

Supervisor; Clinical Lab Technician; Collector; Counselor; Customer Service Representative; General Manager; Human Resources Manager; Investigator; Management Trainee; Manufacturer's/Wholesaler's Sales Rep.; Medical Records Technician; Public Relations Specialist; Quality Control Supervisor; Securities Sales Representative; Services Sales Representative. **Number of placements per year:** 100 - 199.

ALLEGHENY PERSONNEL SERVICES
1009 Beaver Grade Road, Edgetown Commons, Suite 110, Moon Township PA 15108. 412/264-7733. **Fax:** 412/264-8883. **Contact:** Ron Alvarado, Branch Manager. **Description:** A temporary agency that also provides some permanent placements. **Specializes in the areas of:** Accounting/Auditing; Administration; Banking; Finance; General Management; Health/Medical; Industrial; Insurance; Legal; Personnel/Labor Relations; Sales; Secretarial. **Positions commonly filled include:** Accountant/Auditor; Administrative Manager; Customer Service Representative; Typist/Word Processor. **Benefits available to temporary workers:** Computer Training; Medical Insurance; Paid Vacation; Referral Bonus Plan. **Corporate headquarters location:** Pittsburgh PA. **Other area locations:** Monroeville PA; North Hills PA.

AMERICAN STAFFING RESOURCES
255 East Street Road, Feasterville PA 19053. 215/364-3838. **Toll-free phone:** 800/AMSTAFF. **Fax:** 215/364-5381. **Contact:** Carolyn Anderson, Vice President of Operations. **Description:** A temporary agency that also provides some permanent placements. **Specializes in the areas of:** Accounting; Finance; Information Technology; Light Industrial; Technical. **Positions commonly filled include:** Accountant; Administrative Assistant; Computer Programmer; Customer Service Rep.; Light Industrial Worker; Secretary; Software Engineer; Typist/Word Processor. **Benefits available to temporary workers:** Medical Insurance; Paid Holidays; Vacation Pay. **Corporate headquarters location:** This Location.

AQUENT PARTNERS
One North Presidential Boulevard, Suite 200, Bala-Cynwyd PA 19004-1001. 610/667-9900. **Toll-free phone:** 877/PARTNER. **Fax:** 610/667-9903. **Contact:** Kim Schaefer, Manager. **E-mail address:** kschaefer@aquent.com. **World Wide Web address:** http://www.aquentpartners.com. **Description:** A temporary agency that provides placements for creative, Web, and technical professionals. Aquent Partners also provides some temp-to-perm, permanent, and contract placements. **Specializes in the areas of:** Administration; Art/Design; Computer Science/Software; Marketing. **Positions commonly filled include:** Computer Animator; Computer Engineer; Computer Operator; Computer Programmer; Computer Support Technician; Computer Technician; Content Developer; Database Administrator; Database Manager; Desktop Publishing Specialist; Editor; Editorial Assistant; Graphic Artist; Graphic Designer; Internet Services Manager; Managing Editor; MIS Specialist; Multimedia Designer; Network/Systems Administrator; Production Manager; Project Manager; Software Engineer; SQL Programmer; Systems Analyst; Systems Manager; Technical Writer/Editor; Webmaster. **Benefits available to temporary workers:** 401(k); Dental Insurance; Disability Coverage; Medical Insurance. **CEO:** John Chuang.

AQUENT PARTNERS
800 Vinial Street, Suite B-304, Pittsburgh PA 15212-5128. 412/322-4940. **Toll-free phone:** 877/PARTNER. **Fax:** 412/322-4950. **Contact:** Joani Kostley, Recruiter. **E-mail address:** jkostley@aquent.com. **World Wide Web address:** http://www.aquentpartners.com. **Description:** A temporary agency that provides placements for creative, Web, and technical professionals. Aquent Partners also provides some temp-to-perm, permanent, and contract placements. **Specializes in the areas of:** Administration; Art/Design; Computer Science/Software; Marketing. **Positions commonly filled include:** Computer Animator; Computer Engineer; Computer Operator; Computer Programmer; Computer Support Technician; Computer Technician; Content Developer; Database Administrator; Database Manager; Desktop Publishing Specialist; Editor; Editorial Assistant; Graphic Artist; Graphic Designer; Internet Services Manager; Managing Editor; MIS Specialist; Multimedia Designer; Network/Systems Administrator; Production Manager; Project Manager; Software Engineer; SQL Programmer; Systems Analyst; Systems Manager; Technical Writer/Editor; Webmaster. **Benefits available to temporary workers:** 401(k); Dental Insurance; Disability Coverage; Medical Insurance. **CEO:** John Chuang.

BON TEMPS STAFFING SERVICES
801 West Street Road, Feasterville PA 19053. 215/357-6590. **Fax:** 215/953-1612. **Contact:** David Bontempo, Vice President. **E-mail address:** dbon@integra-net.com. **Description:** A temporary agency that also provides some permanent placements. Client company pays fee. **Specializes in the areas of:** Accounting; Administration; Finance; Light Industrial; Marketing; Sales. **Positions commonly filled include:** Account Manager; Account Representative; Accountant; Administrative Assistant; Auditor; Chief Financial Officer; Customer Service Representative; Sales Representative; Secretary.

Average salary range of placements: $30,000 - $49,999. **Number of placements per year:** 100 - 199.

CAPITAL AREA TEMPORARY SERVICES
839 Market Street, P.O. Box 32, Lemoyne PA 17043. 717/761-0133. **Contact:** Paul V. Gaughan, President. **Description:** A temporary agency. **Specializes in the areas of:** Clerical; Manufacturing. **Positions commonly filled include:** Administrative Worker/Clerk; Bookkeeper; Clerk; Factory Worker; Legal Secretary; Light Industrial Worker; Receptionist; Secretary; Stenographer; Typist/Word Processor.

CHARLEY'S PERSONNEL STAFFING INC.
2 Poplar Street, P.O. Box 747, Conshohocken PA 19428. 610/834-7608. **Fax:** 610/834-7665. **Contact:** Barbara Bass, Director of Recruitment. **Description:** A temporary agency that also provides some permanent placements. **Specializes in the areas of:** Accounting/Auditing; Administration; Advertising; Banking; Computer Science/Software; Engineering; Food; Health/Medical; Sales; Secretarial. **Positions commonly filled include:** Administrative Manager; Advertising Clerk; Clerical Supervisor; Clinical Lab Technician; Credit Manager; Customer Service Representative; Financial Analyst; General Manager; Hotel Manager; Human Service Worker; Market Research Analyst; Medical Records Technician; Paralegal; Preschool Worker; Restaurant/Food Service Manager; Typist/Word Processor. **Number of placements per year:** 1 - 49.

CORESTAFF INC.
P.O. Box 15444, Philadelphia PA 19149-0444. **Physical address:** Sterling Commerce Center, Suite 303, 1819 JFK Boulevard, Philadelphia PA 19103. **Toll-free phone:** 800/564-1755. **Fax:** 215/563-6329. **Contact:** Joan Valk, Manager. **Description:** A temporary agency. **Specializes in the areas of:** Accounting; Administration; Advertising; Architecture/Construction; Art/Design; Banking; Biology; Computer Science/Software; Education; Engineering; Fashion; Finance; Food; General Management; Health/Medical; Industrial; Insurance; Legal; Light Industrial; Nonprofit; Personnel/Labor Relations; Printing; Publishing; Retail; Sales; Scientific; Secretarial; Technical; Transportation. **Positions commonly filled include:** Accountant; Administrative Assistant; Administrative Manager; Advertising Clerk; Applications Engineer; Architect; Auditor; Biochemist; Biological Scientist; Biomedical Engineer; Blue-Collar Worker Supervisor; Branch Manager; Budget Analyst; Chemical Engineer; Chemist; Civil Engineer; Clerical Supervisor; Clinical Lab Technician; Computer Operator; Computer Programmer; Construction Contractor; Controller; Cost Estimator; Customer Service Rep.; Database Manager; Design Engineer; Dietician/Nutritionist; Draftsperson; Editorial Assistant; EEG Technologist; EKG Technician; Electrical/Electronics Engineer; Electrician; Environmental Engineer; General Manager; Graphic Artist; Graphic Designer; Human Resources Manager; Industrial Engineer; Industrial Production Manager; Librarian; Management Trainee; Manufacturing Engineer; Marketing Manager; Mechanical Engineer; Medical Records Technician; Metallurgical Engineer; MIS Manager; Operations Manager; Paralegal; Pharmacist; Production Manager; Project Manager; Purchasing Agent/Manager; Quality Control Supervisor; Sales Representative; Secretary; Software Engineer; Statistician; Systems Analyst; Systems Manager; Transportation/Traffic Specialist; Typist/Word Processor. **Benefits available to temporary workers:** Medical Insurance; Paid Holidays; Paid Vacation. **Corporate headquarters location:** This Location. **Other U.S. locations:** NJ. **Average salary range of placements:** $30,000 - $50,000. **Number of placements per year:** 1000+.

HIREKNOWLEDGE
1420 Walnut Street, Suite 600, Philadelphia PA 19102. 215/985-9100. **Toll-free phone:** 800/937-3622. **Fax:** 215/985-9300. **Contact:** Recruiter. **World Wide Web address:** http://www.hireknowledge.com. **Description:** A temporary agency that also provides some permanent

placements. Client company pays fee. **Specializes in the areas of:** Advertising; Art/Design; Computer Science/ Software; Internet Development; Internet Marketing; MIS/EDP; Printing; Publishing. **Positions commonly filled include:** Applications Engineer; AS400 Programmer Analyst; Computer Animator; Computer Engineer; Computer Operator; Computer Programmer; Computer Scientist; Computer Support Technician; Content Developer; Database Administrator; Database Manager; Editor; Editorial Assistant; Graphic Artist; Graphic Designer; Internet Services Manager; Managing Editor; MIS Specialist; Multimedia Designer; Network/ Systems Administrator; Software Engineer; SQL Programmer; Systems Analyst; Systems Manager; Technical Writer/Editor; Webmaster. **Benefits available to temporary workers:** 401(k); Direct Deposit; Health Benefits; Paid Vacation. **Corporate headquarters location:** Providence RI. **Other U.S. locations:** Nationwide. **Average salary range of placements:** $30,000 - $49,999. **Number of placements per year:** 200 - 499.

HOBBIE PERSONNEL SERVICES
349 York Road, 2nd Floor, Willow Grove PA 19090. 215/658-0100. **Contact:** Staffing Specialist. **Description:** A temporary agency that also provides some permanent placements. **Specializes in the areas of:** Industrial; Secretarial; Technical. **Positions commonly filled include:** Customer Service Rep.; Industrial Engineer; Receptionist; Typist/Word Processor. **Corporate headquarters location:** Allentown PA. **Other area locations:** Lansdale PA; Quakertown PA. **Average salary range of placements:** Less than $20,000. **Number of placements per year:** 500 - 999.

HUMAN ASSETS INC.
4 Park Plaza, Wyomissing PA 19610. 610/375-2773. **Fax:** 610/375-2844. **Contact:** Kerry S. Seward, President. **World Wide Web address:** http://www.human-assets.com. **Description:** A temporary agency that also provides some permanent placements. **Specializes in the areas of:** Accounting; Administration; Advertising; Banking; Finance; Marketing; Retail; Sales; Secretarial. **Positions commonly filled include:** Account Manager; Account Representative; Administrative Assistant; Administrative Manager; AS400 Programmer Analyst; Assistant Manager; Blue-Collar Worker Supervisor; Branch Manager; Buyer; Clerical Supervisor; Computer Programmer; Computer Support Technician; Consultant; Customer Service Rep.; Electrician; General Manager; Human Resources Manager; Industrial Production Manager; Management Analyst/Consultant; Management Trainee; Network/Systems Administrator; Operations Manager; Production Manager; Project Manager; Quality Control Supervisor; Sales Executive; Sales Manager; Sales Representative; Secretary; Transportation/Traffic Specialist; Typist/Word Processor; Vice President. **Average salary range of placements:** Less than $20,000. **Number of placements per year:** 50 - 99.

INTERIM PERSONNEL
1040-3 Benner Pike, State College PA 16801. 814/238-4244. **Contact:** General Manager. **World Wide Web address:** http://www.interim.com. **Description:** A temporary agency that also provides some permanent placements. **Specializes in the areas of:** Administration; Industrial; Manufacturing; Sales; Secretarial; Technical. **Positions commonly filled include:** Administrative Manager; Aircraft Mechanic/Engine Specialist; Automotive Mechanic; Blue-Collar Worker Supervisor; Claim Representative; Clerical Supervisor; Computer Programmer; Customer Service Rep.; Draftsperson; Management Trainee; Operations/Production Manager; Quality Control Supervisor; Services Sales Rep.; Travel Agent; Typist/Word Processor. **Benefits available to temporary workers:** Dental Insurance; Medical Insurance; Paid Vacation; Referral Bonus Plan. **Corporate headquarters location:** Fort Lauderdale FL. **Other U.S. locations:** Nationwide. **Average salary range of placements:** $20,000 - $29,999.

INTERIM PERSONNEL OF LEHIGH VALLEY PA
1045 South Cedar Crest Boulevard, Allentown PA 18103-5443. 610/432-7500. **Fax:** 610/435-3114. **Contact:** Tina I. Hamilton, President/Owner. **World Wide Web address:** http://www.interim.com. **Description:** A temporary agency that also provides some permanent placements. **Specializes in the areas of:** Computer Science/Software; Industrial; Light Industrial; Marketing; Sales; Scientific; Secretarial; Technical. **Positions commonly filled include:** Account Representative; Administrative Assistant; Administrative Manager; Advertising Clerk; Applications Engineer; Blue-Collar Worker Supervisor; Claim Representative; Clerical Supervisor; Computer Operator; Computer Programmer; Construction Contractor; Customer Service Representative; Database Manager; Electrical/Electronics Engineer; Food Scientist/Technologist; Industrial Engineer; Sales Executive; Sales Representative; Secretary; Typist/Word Processor. **Benefits available to temporary workers:** Bonus Award/Plan; Dental Insurance; Medical Insurance; Paid Vacation; Prescription Drugs; Scholarship Program; Vision Insurance. **Corporate headquarters location:** Fort Lauderdale FL. **Other U.S. locations:** Nationwide. **Average salary range of placements:** $20,000 - $29,999. **Number of placements per year:** 500 - 999.

KELLY SERVICES, INC.
200 East State Street, Suite 106, Media PA 19063. 610/565-7030. **Fax:** 610/892-9308. **Contact:** Branch Manager. **Description:** A temporary agency. **Specializes in the areas of:** Secretarial; Technical. **Positions commonly filled include:** Attorney; Computer Programmer; Systems Analyst; Typist/Word Processor. **Corporate headquarters location:** Troy MI. **Other U.S. locations:** Nationwide. **Average salary range of placements:** $20,000 - $29,999. **Number of placements per year:** 1000+.

KEYNOTE SYSTEMS INC.
500 Standard Life Building, 345 Fourth Avenue, Pittsburgh PA 15222. 412/261-0187. **Fax:** 412/261-1073. **Contact:** Manager. **Description:** A temporary agency. **Specializes in the areas of:** Computer Science/Software; Government; Health/Medical. **Positions commonly filled include:** Claim Representative; Computer Operator; Customer Service Representative; Data Entry Clerk; Human Service Worker; Licensed Practical Nurse; Medical Records Technician; Registered Nurse; Systems Analyst. **Benefits available to temporary workers:** Bonus Award/Plan; Paid Vacation. **Average salary range of placements:** $30,000 - $50,000. **Number of placements per year:** 50 - 99.

LAB SUPPORT INC.
Foster Plaza, Building 5, 651 Holiday Drive, Suite 300, Pittsburgh PA 15220. 412/364-6240. **Contact:** Manager. **Description:** A temporary agency. **Specializes in the areas of:** Biology; Chemicals; Technical. **Corporate headquarters location:** Calabasas CA. **Other U.S. locations:** Nationwide.

MARSETTA LANE TEMPORARY SERVICES
355 Fifth Avenue, Suite 1104, Pittsburgh PA 15222-2407. 412/261-6076. **Contact:** Placement Coordinator. **Description:** A temporary agency that also provides some permanent placements. **Specializes in the areas of:** Accounting/Auditing; Office Support; Secretarial; Word Processing. **Positions commonly filled include:** Accountant/Auditor; Customer Service Representative; Data Entry Clerk; Legal Secretary; Medical Secretary; Receptionist; Secretary; Typist/Word Processor. **Number of placements per year:** 1000+.

LEGAL SEARCH
1515 Market Street, Philadelphia PA 19103. 215/568-7191. **Fax:** 215/568-7194. **Contact:** Mark Rocco, President. **Description:** A temporary agency that also provides some permanent placements. **Specializes in the areas of:** Legal; Secretarial. **Positions commonly filled include:** Administrative Assistant; Legal Secretary; Paralegal. **Average salary range of placements:**

$20,000 - $40,000. **Number of placements per year:** 200 - 499.

MANPOWER TEMPORARY SERVICES
555 Grant Street, Suite 300, Pittsburgh PA 15219. 412/434-6507. **Contact:** Branch Manager. **Description:** A temporary agency. **Specializes in the areas of:** Industrial; Office Support; Technical; Telecommunications; Word Processing. **Positions commonly filled include:** Accountant/Auditor; Accounting Clerk; Administrative Assistant; Assembly Worker; Biological Scientist; Bookkeeper; CADD Operator; Chemist; Computer Operator; Customer Service Representative; Desktop Publishing Specialist; Electrician; Inspector/Tester/Grader; Inventory Control Specialist; Machine Operator; Material Control Specialist; Order Clerk; Packaging/Processing Worker; Painter; Project Engineer; Proofreader; Receptionist; Records Manager; Research Assistant; Secretary; Software Engineer; Stenographer; Stock Clerk; Systems Analyst; Technical Writer/Editor; Telemarketer; Test Operator; Transcriptionist; Typist/Word Processor; Welder. **Benefits available to temporary workers:** Computer Training; Life Insurance; Medical Insurance; Paid Holidays; Paid Vacation. **Corporate headquarters location:** Milwaukee WI. **Number of placements per year:** 1000+.

MANPOWER TEMPORARY SERVICES
10 Penn Center, Suite 615, 1801 Market Street, Philadelphia PA 19103. 215/568-4050. **Fax:** 215/569-1421. **Contact:** Branch Manager. **Description:** A temporary agency. **Specializes in the areas of:** Data Processing; Light Industrial; Office Support; Professional; Technical; Telemarketing; Word Processing. **Positions commonly filled include:** Accountant/Auditor; Accounting Clerk; Administrative Assistant; Assembler; Biological Scientist; Bookkeeper; Chemist; Computer Operator; Customer Service Representative; Designer; Desktop Publishing Specialist; Electrician; Inspector/Tester/Grader; Inventory Control Specialist; Machine Operator; Material Control Specialist; Order Clerk; Packaging/Processing Worker; Painter; Project Engineer; Proofreader; Receptionist; Research Assistant; Secretary; Software Engineer; Systems Analyst; Technical Writer/Editor; Technician; Telemarketer; Typist/Word Processor; Welder. **Benefits available to temporary workers:** Computer Training; Life Insurance; Medical Insurance; Paid Holidays; Paid Vacation. **Corporate headquarters location:** Milwaukee WI. **Number of placements per year:** 1000+.

METROPOLITAN PERSONNEL, INC.
P.O. Box 641, Valley Forge PA 19482. 610/933-4000. **Fax:** 610/933-4670. **Contact:** Lawrence J. LaBoon, President. **E-mail address:** staffing@metpersnl.com. **Description:** A temporary agency that also provides some temp-to-perm and permanent placements. **Specializes in the areas of:** Accounting/Auditing; Administration; Computer Science/Software; General Management; Light Industrial; Marketing; Personnel/Labor Relations; Sales; Secretarial. **Positions commonly filled include:** Accountant; Administrative Assistant; Administrative Manager; Blue-Collar Worker Supervisor; Branch Manager; Clerical Supervisor; Customer Service Representative; Database Manager; Editor; Editorial Assistant; Human Resources Manager; Management Trainee; Paralegal; Sales Manager; Sales Representative; Secretary; Technical Writer/Editor; Typist/Word Processor. **Benefits available to temporary workers:** Paid Holidays; Referral Bonus Plan; Vacation Pay. **Corporate headquarters location:** This Location. **Average salary range of placements:** $20,000 - $29,999. **Number of placements per year:** 100 - 199.

NORRELL SERVICES
330 Grand Street, Suite 103, Pittsburgh PA 15219. 412/201-3101. **Fax:** 412/201-5838. **Contact:** Manager. **Description:** A temporary agency that also offers some temp-to-perm placements, outsourcing, and project management services. Founded in 1960. **Specializes in the areas of:** Industrial; Light Industrial; Secretarial; Technical. **Positions commonly filled include:** Accounting Clerk; Administrative Assistant; Advertising Clerk; Customer Service Representative; Receptionist; Secretary; Services Sales Representative; Typist/Word Processor. **Benefits available to temporary workers:** 401(k); Dental Insurance; Medical Insurance; Stock Purchase; Vision Plan. **Corporate headquarters location:** Atlanta GA. **Other U.S. locations:** Nationwide. **Average salary range of placements:** Less than $20,000. **Number of placements per year:** 100 - 199.

NORRELL SERVICES
70-10 East Swedesford Road, Malvern PA 19355. 610/296-9103. **Contact:** Branch Manager. **Description:** A temporary agency. **Specializes in the areas of:** Accounting/Auditing; Personnel/Labor Relations; Secretarial. **Positions commonly filled include:** Accountant/Auditor; Customer Service Representative; Typist/Word Processor. **Benefits available to temporary workers:** Medical Insurance; Paid Holidays; Paid Vacation. **Corporate headquarters location:** Atlanta GA. **Other U.S. locations:** Nationwide. **Average salary range of placements:** $20,000 - $29,999. **Number of placements per year:** 500 - 999.

OFFICETEAM
630 Freedom Business Center, Suite 116, King of Prussia PA 19406. 610/337-5848. **Toll-free phone:** 800/804-8367. **Fax:** 610/337-7038. **Contact:** Sandi Nush, Division Director. **Description:** A temporary agency. **Specializes in the areas of:** Administration; Personnel/Labor Relations. **Positions commonly filled include:** Administrative Manager; Advertising Clerk; Clerical Supervisor; Customer Service Representative; Typist/Word Processor.

OLSTEN FINANCIAL STAFFING
1617 JFK Boulevard, Suite 425, Philadelphia PA 19103. 215/568-1740. **Toll-free phone:** 888/222-8693. **Fax:** 215/569-3172. **Contact:** Manager. **E-mail address:** ofs.hq@olsten.com. **World Wide Web address:** http://www.olsten.com/ofs. **Description:** A temporary agency that also provides some permanent placements. Client company pays fee. **Specializes in the areas of:** Accounting; Banking; Finance. **Positions commonly filled include:** Accountant; Auditor; Budget Analyst; Chief Financial Officer; Controller; Credit Manager; Finance Director; Financial Analyst. **Corporate headquarters location:** Melville NY. **Other U.S. locations:** Nationwide. **Average salary range of placements:** $50,000 - $100,000. **Number of placements per year:** 200 - 499.

OLSTEN STAFFING SERVICES
1503 North Cedarcrest Boulevard, Suite 318, Allentown PA 18104. 610/435-0553. **Contact:** Manager. **World Wide Web address:** http://www.olsten.com. **Description:** A temporary agency that also provides some permanent placements. Client company pays fee. **Specializes in the areas of:** Accounting; Administration; Computer Science/Software; Industrial; Light Industrial; MIS/EDP; Scientific; Secretarial; Technical. **Positions commonly filled include:** Account Representative; Accountant; Adjuster; Administrative Assistant; AS400 Programmer Analyst; Auditor; Blue-Collar Worker Supervisor; Chemical Engineer; Chemist; Computer Programmer; Customer Service Rep.; Draftsperson; Electrical/Electronics Engineer; Mechanical Engineer; Production Manager; Sales Representative; Secretary; Systems Analyst; Systems Manager; Typist/Word Processor. **Corporate headquarters location:** Melville NY. **Other U.S. locations:** Nationwide.

OLSTEN STAFFING SERVICES
4720 Carlisle Pike, Suite 300, Mechanicsburg PA 17055. 717/731-6100. **Contact:** Branch Manager. **World Wide Web address:** http://www.olsten.com. **Description:** A temporary agency. **Specializes in the areas of:** Accounting/Auditing; Advertising; Architecture/

Construction; Clerical; Computer Hardware/Software; Design; Food; Insurance; Legal; Manufacturing; Nonprofit; Publishing; Sales; Secretarial; Technical. **Positions commonly filled include:** Accountant/Auditor; Administrative Assistant; Bookkeeper; Claim Rep.; Computer Programmer; Customer Service Rep.; Data Entry Clerk; Designer; Draftsperson; EDP Specialist; Factory Worker; Financial Analyst; Insurance Agent/Broker; Legal Secretary; Light Industrial Worker; Mechanical Engineer; Medical Secretary; Purchasing Agent/Manager; Receptionist; Records Manager; Sales Representative; Secretary; Statistician; Stenographer; Systems Analyst; Technical Writer/Editor; Technician; Typist/Word Processor. **Corporate headquarters location:** Melville NY. **Other U.S. locations:** Nationwide. **Number of placements per year:** 1000+.

OLSTEN STAFFING SERVICES
4 Gateway Center, Suite 205, Pittsburgh PA 15222. 412/261-7200. **Fax:** 412/261-5647. **Contact:** Cindy Cheran, Operations Manager. **World Wide Web address:** http://www.olsten.com. **Description:** A temporary agency. **Specializes in the areas of:** Accounting/Auditing; Engineering; Office Support; Secretarial. **Positions commonly filled include:** Administrative Assistant; Attorney; Secretary. **Benefits available to temporary workers:** Medical Insurance; Paid Holidays; Paid Vacation. **Corporate headquarters location:** Melville NY. **Other U.S. locations:** Nationwide. **Average salary range of placements:** $20,000 - $29,999. **Number of placements per year:** 1000+.

OLSTEN STAFFING SERVICES
1023 East Baltimore Pike, Suite 220, Media PA 19063-5126. 610/565-7510. **Fax:** 610/565-7516. **Contact:** Chris Leady, Personnel Supervisor. **World Wide Web address:** http://www.olsten.com. **Description:** A temporary agency. **Specializes in the areas of:** Administration; Industrial; Legal; Manufacturing; Personnel/Labor Relations; Secretarial; Technical. **Positions commonly filled include:** Claim Rep.; Computer Programmer; Customer Service Rep.; Electrical/Electronics Engineer; Human Resources Specialist; MIS Specialist; Paralegal; Services Sales Representative; Typist/Word Processor. **Benefits available to temporary workers:** Bonus Award/Plan; Paid Vacation. **Corporate headquarters location:** Melville NY. **Other U.S. locations:** Nationwide.

PANCOAST TEMPORARY SERVICES, INC.
100 Fifth Avenue Building, Suite 609, Pittsburgh PA 15222. 412/261-4820. **Contact:** Scott Senott, President. **Description:** A temporary agency. **Specializes in the areas of:** Accounting/Auditing; Administration; Banking; Computer Science/Software; Finance; Insurance; Nonprofit; Personnel/Labor Relations; Sales; Secretarial. **Positions commonly filled include:** Accountant/Auditor; Actuary; Administrative Manager; Bank Officer/Manager; Blue-Collar Worker Supervisor; Branch Manager; Brokerage Clerk; Budget Analyst; Buyer; Claim Rep.; Customer Service Representative; Financial Analyst; General Manager; Human Resources Manager; Librarian; Library Technician; Services Sales Rep.; Technical Writer/Editor; Telecommunications Manager; Typist/Word Processor; Underwriter/Assistant Underwriter. **Benefits available to temporary workers:** Paid Vacation; Referral Bonus Plan. **Number of placements per year:** 1000+.

THE PLACERS, INC.
311 East Street Road, Feasterville PA 19053. 215/364-5627. **Fax:** 215/364-5638. **Contact:** Rick Dunlop, Office Manager. **Description:** A temporary agency that also provides permanent placements. **Specializes in the areas of:** Manufacturing; Secretarial. **Positions commonly filled include:** Customer Service Representative; Human Resources Specialist; Operations/Production Manager; Typist/Word Processor. **Benefits available to temporary workers:** Bonus Award/Plan; Paid Holidays; Paid Vacation. **Average salary range of placements:**

$30,000 - $50,000. **Number of placements per year:** 1 - 49.

PRATT PERSONNEL SERVICES (EAST)
7434 Frankford Avenue, Philadelphia PA 19136-3826. 215/537-1212. **Fax:** 215/537-1223. **Contact:** Cyndi Russelle, Branch Manager. **Description:** A temporary agency. **Specializes in the areas of:** Accounting/Auditing; Clerical; Engineering; Light Industrial; Manufacturing; Publishing; Secretarial. **Positions commonly filled include:** Accountant/Auditor; Blue-Collar Worker Supervisor; Chemical Engineer; Chemist; Customer Service Representative; Electrical/Electronics Engineer; Industrial Engineer; Mechanical Engineer; Purchasing Agent/Manager; Structural Engineer; Typist/Word Processor. **Average salary range of placements:** Less than $20,000. **Number of placements per year:** 200 - 499.

PRATT PERSONNEL SERVICES (WEST)
218 South Easton Road, Glenside PA 19038. 215/542-8367. **Fax:** 215/572-7818. **Contact:** Manager. **Description:** A temporary agency. **Specializes in the areas of:** Accounting/Auditing; Clerical; Light Industrial; Manufacturing; Publishing; Secretarial. **Positions commonly filled include:** Blue-Collar Worker Supervisor; Claim Representative; Customer Service Representative; Typist/Word Processor. **Average salary range of placements:** Less than $20,000. **Number of placements per year:** 500 - 999.

PROTOCALL BUSINESS STAFFING
400 Market Street, Suite 810, Philadelphia PA 19106. 215/592-7111. **Contact:** Branch Manager. **Description:** A temporary agency. **Specializes in the areas of:** Business Services; Health/Medical; Industrial; Manufacturing; Personnel/Labor Relations. **Positions commonly filled include:** Accountant/Auditor; Administrative Assistant; Administrative Manager; Administrative Worker/Clerk; Bookkeeper; Clerk; Computer Operator; Computer Programmer; Customer Service Representative; Data Entry Clerk; Draftsperson; Driver; EDP Specialist; Factory Worker; Health Services Worker; Legal Secretary; Light Industrial Worker; Medical Records Technician; Medical Secretary; Nurse; Receptionist; Sales Rep.; Secretary; Stenographer; Technician; Typist/Word Processor. **Corporate headquarters location:** Voorhees NJ. **Other U.S. locations:** DE. **Number of placements per year:** 1000+.

SNELLING PERSONNEL SERVICES
160 North Pointe Boulevard, Suite 101, Lancaster PA 17601. 717/560-1110. **Fax:** 717/560-2828. **Contact:** Daniel Birk, Manager. **World Wide Web address:** http://www.snelling.com/lancaster. **Description:** A temporary agency that also provides some permanent placements. Client company pays fee. **Specializes in the areas of:** Accounting; Administration; Computer Science/Software; Engineering; Finance; General Management; Light Industrial; Marketing; Sales. **Positions commonly filled include:** Account Manager; Account Representative; Accountant; Adjuster; Administrative Assistant; Administrative Manager; Advertising Clerk; Advertising Executive; Applications Engineer; Architect; AS400 Programmer Analyst; Assistant Manager; Auditor; Bank Officer/Manager; Blue-Collar Worker Supervisor; Branch Manager; Budget Analyst; Buyer; Chemical Engineer; Chemist; Chief Financial Officer; Civil Engineer; Claim Representative; Clerical Supervisor; Clinical Lab Technician; Computer Animator; Computer Engineer; Computer Operator; Computer Programmer; Computer Scientist; Computer Support Technician; Computer Technician; Construction Contractor; Consultant; Content Developer; Controller; Cost Estimator; Credit Manager; Customer Service Representative; Database Administrator; Database Manager; Design Engineer; Desktop Publishing Specialist; Draftsperson; Economist; Electrical/Electronics Engineer; Environmental Engineer; Finance Director; Financial Analyst; Fund Manager; General Manager; Graphic Artist; Graphic Designer; Human Resources Manager; Industrial Engineer;

Industrial Production Manager; Internet Services Manager; Management Analyst/Consultant; Management Trainee; Manufacturing Engineer; Market Research Analyst; Marketing Manager; Marketing Specialist; Mechanical Engineer; Metallurgical Engineer; MIS Specialist; Multimedia Designer; Network/Systems Administrator; Operations Manager; Production Manager; Project Manager; Public Relations Specialist; Purchasing Agent/Manager; Quality Assurance Engineer; Quality Control Supervisor; Sales Engineer; Sales Executive; Sales Manager; Sales Representative; Secretary; Software Engineer; SQL Programmer; Systems Analyst; Systems Manager; Typist/Word Processor; Vice President; Webmaster. **Benefits available to temporary workers:** 401(k); Medical Insurance; Paid Holidays; Paid Vacation. **Corporate headquarters location:** Dallas TX. **Average salary range of placements:** $20,000 - $29,999. **Number of placements per year:** 50 - 99.

SPECIAL COUNSEL
One Penn Center, 1617 JFK Boulevard, Suite 810, Philadelphia PA 19103. 215/569-0999. **Fax:** 215/569-0299. **Contact:** Branch Manager. **World Wide Web address:** http://www.specialcounsel.com. **Description:** Special Counsel is a temporary agency that also provides some permanent placements. **Specializes in the areas of:** Legal.

TRC STAFFING SERVICES
2018 East Old Lincoln Highway, Langhorne PA 19047. 215/752-3502. **Fax:** 215/752-3501. **Contact:** Manager. **Description:** A temporary agency. **Specializes in the areas of:** Accounting/Auditing; Administration; Advertising; Architecture/Construction; Computer Science/Software; Food; General Management; Health/Medical; Industrial; Insurance; Legal; Manufacturing; Personnel/Labor Relations; Sales; Secretarial. **Positions commonly filled include:** Accountant/Auditor; Administrative Manager; Claim Representative; Clerical Supervisor; Computer Programmer; Credit Manager; Customer Service Representative; Human Resources Specialist; Landscape Architect; MIS Specialist; Paralegal; Typist/Word Processor; Underwriter/Assistant Underwriter. **Benefits available to temporary workers:** Medical Insurance; Paid Holidays; Paid Vacation. **Average salary range of placements:** Less than $20,000. **Number of placements per year:** 1000+.

TAC STAFFING SERVICES, INC.
One Radnor Corporate Center, Suite 290, Radnor PA 19087. 610/225-0565. **Contact:** Office Manager. **World Wide Web address:** http://www.tacstaffing.com. **Description:** A temporary agency. **Specializes in the areas of:** Accounting/Auditing; Advertising; Banking; Clerical; Education; Finance; Health/Medical; Insurance; Legal; Manufacturing; Nonprofit; Personnel/Labor Relations; Publishing; Sales; Transportation. **Corporate headquarters location:** Newton Upper Falls MA. **Other U.S. locations:** Nationwide. **International locations:** Worldwide.

TAC STAFFING SERVICES, INC.
1617 JFK Boulevard, Suite 326, Philadelphia PA 19103. 215/568-4466. **Fax:** 215/568-3096. **Contact:** Branch Manager. **World Wide Web address:** http://www.tacstaffing.com. **Description:** A temporary agency. **Specializes in the areas of:** Accounting/Auditing; Advertising; Banking; Clerical; Education; Finance; Health/Medical; Insurance; Legal; Nonprofit; Personnel/Labor Relations; Publishing; Sales; Secretarial; Transportation. **Positions commonly filled include:** Administrative Assistant; Clerical Supervisor; Customer Service Representative; Daycare Worker; Medical Records Technician; Secretary. **Benefits available to temporary workers:** Medical Insurance; Paid Vacation. **Corporate headquarters location:** Newton Upper Falls MA. **Other U.S. locations:** Nationwide. **International locations:** Worldwide. **Average salary range of placements:** $20,000 - $29,999. **Number of placements per year:** 500 - 999.

TODAYS TEMPORARY
Glenhardie 4, 1255 Drummers Lane, Suite 101, Wayne PA 19087. **Fax:** 610/995-2530. **Contact:** Branch Manager. **World Wide Web address:** http://www.todays.com. **Description:** A temporary agency. **Specializes in the areas of:** Marketing; Sales; Secretarial. **Positions commonly filled include:** Administrative Assistant; Claim Representative; Customer Service Representative; Data Entry Clerk; Human Resources Manager; Marketing Manager; Receptionist; Sales Representative; Secretary; Switchboard Operator; Telemarketer; Typist/Word Processor. **Benefits available to temporary workers:** Computer Training; Life Insurance; Medical Insurance; Paid Holidays; Paid Vacation; Prescription Drugs; Vision Insurance. **Corporate headquarters location:** Dallas TX. **Other U.S. locations:** Nationwide. **Average salary range of placements:** $20,000 - $29,999. **Number of placements per year:** 100 - 199.

TOPS TEMPORARIES INC.
11900 Frankstown Road, Suite 100, Pittsburgh PA 15235. 412/798-0779. **Fax:** 412/798-0796. **Contact:** J. David Cepicka, Sales Manager. **Description:** A temporary agency. Founded in 1987. **Specializes in the areas of:** Engineering; Secretarial. **Positions commonly filled include:** Accountant/Auditor; Aerospace Engineer; Architect; Buyer; Chemical Engineer; Civil Engineer; Computer Programmer; Design Engineer; Designer; Draftsperson; Electrical/Electronics Engineer; Industrial Engineer; Mechanical Engineer; Metallurgical Engineer; Nuclear Engineer; Purchasing Agent/Manager; Quality Control Supervisor; Software Engineer; Technical Writer/Editor; Typist/Word Processor. **Benefits available to temporary workers:** Paid Holidays; Paid Vacation. **Corporate headquarters location:** This Location. **Other area locations:** Murrysville PA; New Stanton PA; Warrendale PA. **Average salary range of placements:** Less than $20,000. **Number of placements per year:** 1000+.

UNI-TEMP TEMPORARY SERVICE
1709 East Chocolate Avenue, Hershey PA 17033. 717/533-8367. **Contact:** Patricia Finan, Manager. **Description:** A temporary agency that also offers some career/outplacement counseling services. **Specializes in the areas of:** Accounting/Auditing; Administration; Advertising; Finance; Food; Health/Medical; Industrial; Insurance; Legal; Manufacturing; Publishing; Secretarial; Technical. **Positions commonly filled include:** Accountant/Auditor; Administrative Manager; Advertising Clerk; Automotive Mechanic; Buyer; Claim Representative; Clerical Supervisor; Clinical Lab Technician; Computer Programmer; Credit Manager; Customer Service Representative; Draftsperson; Electrician; Manufacturer's/Wholesaler's Sales Rep.; Medical Records Technician; MIS Specialist; Paralegal; Purchasing Agent/Manager; Quality Control Supervisor; Systems Analyst; Typist/Word Processor. **Benefits available to temporary workers:** Medical Insurance; Paid Holidays; Paid Vacation. **Corporate headquarters location:** Lebanon PA. **Average salary range of placements:** $20,000 - $29,999. **Number of placements per year:** 1 - 49.

UNITED STAFFING SERVICES
2901 Cheltenham Avenue, 2nd Floor, Philadelphia PA 19150. 215/881-6820. **Contact:** Manager. **Description:** A temporary agency that focuses on placements in the mental health field. **Specializes in the areas of:** Health/Medical; Nonprofit. **Positions commonly filled include:** Counselor; Human Service Worker; Psychologist; Recreational Therapist; Social Worker; Sociologist. **Benefits available to temporary workers:** Medical Insurance.

VIRTUAL WORKPLACE, INC. (VWI)
400 Penn Center Boulevard, Suite 600, Pittsburgh PA 15235. 412/829-9552. **Toll-free phone:** 800/999-2VWI. **Contact:** Leslie Twigger, Recruiter. **E-mail address:** ltwigger@crouse.com. **Description:** A temporary agency that provides placements with environmental consulting

firms. Virtual Workplace, Inc. (VWI) is affiliated with Crouse Enterprises, Inc., an environmental engineering, consulting, and remediation group. VWI's ISO Division provides consulting services in the ISO 9000, QA 9000, and the initial introduction of a new 14000 series of certifications for design and production industries. VWI also offers permanent placements. Founded in 1994. **Specializes in the areas of:** Architecture/Construction; Biology; Engineering; Environmental; Industrial; Technical. **Positions commonly filled include:** Chemical Engineer; Chemist; Civil Engineer; Construction and Building Inspector; Cost Estimator; Design Engineer; Designer; Draftsperson; Environmental Engineer; Forester/Conservation Scientist; Geologist/ Geophysicist; Industrial Engineer; Mechanical Engineer; Metallurgical Engineer; Mining Engineer; Petroleum Engineer. **Benefits available to temporary workers:** 401(k); Medical Insurance; Paid Holidays; Paid Vacation. **Corporate headquarters location:** This Location. **Other U.S. locations:** Anchorage AK.

Average salary range of placements: $20,000 - $29,999. **Number of placements per year:** 50 - 99.

WILLIFORD & ASSOCIATES
WILLIFORD LEGAL SUPPORT SERVICES
1616 Walnut Street, Suite 1908, Philadelphia PA 19103. 215/893-1148. **Fax:** 215/893-1149. **Contact:** Darece Williford, Principal. **Description:** A temporary agency that also provides some permanent placements, resume services, and a legal secretarial training program. **Specializes in the areas of:** Legal; Secretarial. **Positions commonly filled include:** Administrative Assistant; Clerical Supervisor; Computer Operator; Customer Service Representative; Legal Secretary; Paralegal; Secretary; Typist/Word Processor. **Benefits available to temporary workers:** Bonus Award/Plan; Medical Insurance. **Average salary range of placements:** $20,000 - $29,999. **Number of placements per year:** 200 - 499.

CONTRACT SERVICES FIRMS

AA STAFFING SOLUTIONS, INC.
667 Union Boulevard, Allentown PA 18103. 610/770-8880. **Fax:** 610/770-8882. **Contact:** Chris Oncidi, Owner. **Description:** A contract services firm. **Specializes in the areas of:** Computer Science/Software; Engineering; Industrial; Manufacturing; Personnel/Labor Relations; Secretarial; Technical. **Positions commonly filled include:** Blue-Collar Worker Supervisor; Claim Representative; Clerical Supervisor; Computer Programmer; Construction and Building Inspector; Construction Contractor; Cost Estimator; Customer Service Representative; Draftsperson; Electrical/ Electronics Engineer; Electrician; General Manager; Geographer; Industrial Engineer; Landscape Architect; MIS Specialist; Quality Control Supervisor; Services Sales Representative; Software Engineer; Surveyor; Systems Analyst; Technical Writer/Editor; Typist/Word Processor. **Benefits available to temporary workers:** Medical Insurance; Paid Holidays; Paid Vacation. **Average salary range of placements:** $20,000 - $29,999. **Number of placements per year:** 500 - 999.

CDI CORPORATION
1717 Arch Street, 35th Floor, Philadelphia PA 19103. 215/569-2200. **Contact:** Recruiter. **Description:** A contract services firm. **Specializes in the areas of:** Aerospace; Design; Electronics; Engineering; Industrial; Technical; Transportation. **Positions commonly filled include:** Assembly Worker; Buyer; Data Processor; Designer; Engineer; Inspector/Tester/Grader; Machinist; Software Engineer; Systems Analyst; Technical Illustrator; Technical Writer/Editor; Technician. **Corporate headquarters location:** This Location. **Other U.S. locations:** Nationwide. **International locations:** Worldwide.

CDI INFORMATION SERVICES
8 Parkway Center, Suite 320, Pittsburgh PA 15220. 412/922-5660. **Fax:** 412/922-5703. **Contact:** Manager. **World Wide Web address:** http://www.cdicorp.com. **Description:** A contract services firm. **Specializes in the areas of:** Administration; Computer Science/Software; Engineering. **Positions commonly filled include:** Computer Programmer; Design Engineer; Draftsperson; Electrical/Electronics Engineer; Mechanical Engineer; Nuclear Engineer; Software Engineer; Systems Analyst; Technical Writer/Editor. **Corporate headquarters location:** Philadelphia PA. **Other U.S. locations:** Nationwide. **International locations:** Worldwide.

EDP CONTRACT SERVICES
P.O. Box 2598, Bala-Cynwyd PA 19004. 610/667-2990. **Contact:** Manager. **Description:** A contract services firm. **Specializes in the areas of:** Accounting/Auditing; Administration; Banking; Computer Hardware/Software; Engineering; Finance; Insurance; Manufacturing; Nonprofit; Personnel/Labor Relations; Publishing; Technical.

H-TECH INC.
ALTERNATIVE STAFFING, INC.
P.O. Box 436, Bridgeville PA 15017. 412/221-5920. **Fax:** 412/221-2193. **Contact:** Victor Paolicelli, Recruiter. **Description:** A contract services firm. Alternative Staffing, Inc. (also at this location, 412/221-4541) provides contract services for the personnel/labor relations field. **NOTE:** Jobseekers should send resumes for Alternative Staffing, Inc. to P.O. Box 394, Bridgeville PA 15017. **Specializes in the areas of:** Engineering. **Positions commonly filled include:** Chemical Engineer; Design Engineer; Designer; Draftsperson; Electrical/Electronics Engineer; Mechanical Engineer. **Benefits available to temporary workers:** 401(k); Medical Insurance; Paid Holidays; Paid Vacation. **Average salary range of placements:** $30,000 - $50,000. **Number of placements per year:** 50 - 99.

IMC INTERNATIONAL, INC.
P.O. Box 46, Murrysville PA 15668. 412/372-7808. **Fax:** 412/372-1314. **Contact:** E. Niles Morgan, President. **Description:** A contract services firm. **Specializes in the areas of:** Computer Science/Software; Engineering; General Management; Industrial; Personnel/Labor Relations; Technical; Transportation. **Positions commonly filled include:** Buyer; Chemical Engineer; Civil Engineer; Construction and Building Inspector; Construction Contractor; Cost Estimator; Design Engineer; Designer; Draftsperson; Electrical/Electronics Engineer; Electrician; Emergency Medical Technician; Environmental Engineer; Human Resources Manager; Industrial Engineer; Mechanical Engineer; Metallurgical Engineer; Mining Engineer; MIS Specialist; Nuclear Engineer; Petroleum Engineer; Purchasing Agent/Manager; Quality Control Supervisor; Services Sales Representative; Software Engineer; Structural Engineer; Surveyor; Technical Writer/Editor; Telecommunications Manager; Transportation/Traffic Specialist. **Average salary range of placements:** $30,000 - $50,000. **Number of placements per year:** 500 - 999.

PROFESSIONAL RESOURCE GROUP, INC.
4076 Market Street, Suite 213, Camp Hill PA 17011. 717/612-9800. **Fax:** 717/730-6088. **Contact:** General Manager. **Description:** A contract services firm that focuses on providing placements for MIS professionals. **Specializes in the areas of:** Computer Programming; Computer Science/Software. **Positions commonly filled include:** Computer Programmer; Software Engineer; Systems Analyst; Technical Writer/Editor; Telecommunications Manager. **Average salary range of**

placements: $30,000 - $50,000. **Number of placements per year:** 1 - 49.

RHI CONSULTING
630 Freedom Business Center, King of Prussia PA 19406. 610/337-3650. **Toll-free phone:** 800/803-8367. **Fax:** 610/337-8595. **Contact:** Jacqueline K. Lloyd, Division Director. **E-mail address:** rhickop@aol.com. **World Wide Web address:** http://www.rhic.com. **Description:** A contract services firm. **Specializes in the areas of:** Computer Science/Software; Information Technology. **Positions commonly filled include:** Computer Operator; Computer Programmer; Consultant; Database Manager; Internet Services Manager; Online Content Specialist; Systems Analyst; Systems Manager; Technical Writer; Telecomm. Manager; Webmaster. **Benefits available to temporary workers:** Health Benefits. **Corporate headquarters location:** Menlo Park CA. **Number of placements per year:** 200 - 499.

TECH/AID OF PENNSYLVANIA
630 West Germantown Pike, Suite 361, Plymouth Meeting PA 19462. 610/834-7340. **Toll-free phone:** 800/642-6881. **Fax:** 610/834-7531. **Contact:** Branch Manager. **E-mail address:** plymouthmtg@techaid.com. **World Wide Web address:** http://www.techaid.com. **Description:** A contract services firm. **Specializes in the areas of:** Computer Science/Software; Engineering; Scientific; Technical. **Positions commonly filled include:** Architect; Buyer; Chemical Engineer; Civil Engineer; Design Engineer; Draftsperson; Electrical/Electronics Engineer; Environmental Engineer; Industrial Engineer; Industrial Production Manager; Manufacturing Engineer; Mechanical Engineer; Production Manager; Quality Control Supervisor;

Technical Writer/Editor. **Benefits available to temporary workers:** 401(k); Paid Holidays; Vacation Pay. **Corporate headquarters location:** Newton Upper Falls MA. **Other U.S. locations:** Nationwide. **International locations:** United Kingdom. **Average salary range of placements:** $30,000 - $50,000. **Number of placements per year:** 1000+.

H.L. YOH COMPANY
1259 South Cedarcrest Boulevard, Suite 225, Allentown PA 18103. 610/434-6446. **Contact:** John F. Pavlick, Manager. **World Wide Web address:** http://www. hlyoh.com. **Description:** A contract services firm. **Other U.S. locations:** Nationwide.

H.L. YOH COMPANY
5500 Allentown Boulevard, 2nd Floor, Harrisburg PA 17112. 717/657-3106. **Contact:** Manager. **World Wide Web address:** http://www.hlyoh.com. **Description:** A contract services firm. **Other U.S. locations:** Nationwide.

H.L. YOH COMPANY
1121 Snyder Road, Reading PA 19609. 610/678-5882. **Contact:** Manager. **World Wide Web address:** http://www.hlyoh.com. **Description:** A contract services firm. **Other U.S. locations:** Nationwide.

H.L. YOH COMPANY
1818 Market Street, 20th Floor, Philadelphia PA 19103. 215/656-2650. **Contact:** Manager. **World Wide Web address:** http://www.hlyoh.com. **Description:** A contract services firm. **Specializes in the areas of:** Engineering; Information Technology. **Other U.S. locations:** Nationwide.

CAREER/OUTPLACEMENT COUNSELING FIRMS

R. DAVENPORT & ASSOCIATES
1910 Cochran Road, Suite 740, Pittsburgh PA 15220. 412/561-4003. **Contact:** Manager. **Description:** A career management and counseling firm.

BERNARD HALDANE ASSOCIATES
401 Liberty Avenue, Suite 18 East, Pittsburgh PA 15222. 412/263-5627. **Contact:** Manager. **Description:** A career/outplacement counseling firm.

MANCHESTER INC.
1735 Market Street, 43rd Floor, Philadelphia PA 19103. **Toll-free phone:** 800/220-1234. **Fax:** 610/617-9966. **Contact:** Manager. **E-mail address:** info@ manchesterus.com. **World Wide Web address:** http://www.manchesterus.com. **Description:** A career/outplacement counseling firm focused on career management, performance improvement, and executive training. **Specializes in the areas of:** Advertising; Apparel; Architecture/Construction; Banking; Chemicals; Electronics; Entertainment; Food; Government; Graphic Arts; Health/Medical; Insurance; Metals; Nonprofit; Packaging; Pharmaceuticals; Printing; Real Estate; Retail; Telecommunications; Textiles; Transportation. **Other U.S. locations:** Nationwide. **International locations:** Worldwide.

THE RAPHAEL GROUP, INC.
925 Harvest Drive, Suite 250, Blue Bell PA 19522. 215/540-9998. **Fax:** 215/628-4286. **Contact:** Manager. **E-mail address:** careers@raphaelgroup.com. **World Wide Web address:** http://www.raphaelgroup.com. **Description:** Provides resume and career counseling services. The agency also specializes in high-performance management and executive/leadership development. **Specializes in the areas of:** Accounting; Advertising; Architecture/Construction; Banking; Biology; Computer Science; Economics; Education; Engineering; Fashion; Finance; Food; General Management; Health/Medical; Industrial; Insurance;

Internet Dev.; Internet Marketing; Legal; Light Industrial; Marketing; MIS/EDP; Nonprofit; Personnel; Printing; Publishing; Real Estate; Retail; Sales; Scientific; Secretarial; Technical; Transportation. **Positions commonly filled include:** Account Manager; Account Rep.; Accountant; Adjuster; Admin. Manager; Advertising Executive; Applications Engineer; Architect; Attorney; Auditor; Bank Officer/Manager; Biochemist; Biological Scientist; Biomedical Engineer; Blue Collar Worker/Supervisor; Branch Manager; Budget Analyst; Buyer; Chemical Engineer; Chemist; Chief Financial Officer; Civil Engineer; Computer Engineer; Computer Programmer; Construction Contractor; Content Developer; Controller; Cost Estimator; Counselor; Credit Manager; Database Manager; Design Engineer; Dietitian/Nutritionist; Economist; Editor; Electrical Engineer; Environmental Manager; Finance Director; Financial Consultant; Fund Manager; General Manager; Graphic Artist; Graphic Designer; Human Resources Manager; Industrial Engineer; Industrial Production Manager; Insurance Agent/Broker; Intellectual Property Lawyer; Internet Services Manager; Librarian; Licensed Practical Nurse; Management Consultant; Management Trainee; Manufacturing Engineer; Marketing Manager; Marketing Specialist; Mechanical Engineer; Metallurgical Engineer; MIS Specialist; Nurse Practitioner; Occupational Therapist; Operations Manager; Paralegal; Pharmacist; Physical Therapist; Physician; Production Manager; Project Manager; Psychologist; Public Relations Specialist; Purchasing Agent/Manager; Quality Assurance Engineer; Quality Control Supervisor; Real Estate Manager; Registered Nurse; Respiratory Therapist; Sales Engineer; Sales Executive; Sales Manager; Sales Representative; Social Worker; Software Engineer; Special Education Teacher; Speech Language Pathologist; Systems Analyst; Systems Manager; Teacher/Professor; Telecommunications Manager; Transportation Specialist; Underwriter. **Corporate headquarters location:** This Location.

EXECUTIVE SEARCH FIRMS

ACCOUNTANTS EXECUTIVE SEARCH ACCOUNTANTS ON CALL
10 Weybosset Street, Suite 201, Providence RI 02903. 401/277-9944. **Fax:** 401/277-0660. **Contact:** Manager. **Description:** Accountants Executive Search is an executive search firm for accounting professionals. Accountants On Call (also at this location) is a temporary agency that primarily places clerical workers. **Specializes in the areas of:** Accounting; Clerical. **Average salary range of placements:** 30,000 and up.

ACCOUNTING RESOURCES INC.
155 Westminster Street, Suite 1250, Providence RI 02903. 401/272-1200. 401/272-1201. **Contact:** Manager. **Description:** An executive search firm. **Specializes in the areas of:** Accounting/Auditing; Finance. **Positions commonly filled include:** Accountant/Auditor; Bank Officer/Manager; Budget Analyst; Computer Programmer; Cost Estimator; Credit Manager; Financial Analyst; Human Resources Manager; MIS Specialist; Systems Analyst. **Average salary range of placements:** $30,000 - $50,000. **Number of placements per year:** 100 - 199.

BAY SEARCH GROUP
26 Bosworth Street, Unit 6, Barrington RI 02806. 401/245-3100. **Fax:** 401/245-3117. **Contact:** Manager. **Description:** An executive search firm. **Specializes in the areas of:** Computer Operations.

BEDFORD GROUP
154 Quicksand Pond Road, Little Compton RI 02837. 401/635-4646. **Contact:** Manager. **Description:** An executive search firm. **Specializes in the areas of:** Communications; Electronics; Health/Medical; Medical Devices; Telecommunications. **Average salary range of placements:** $50,000 - $100,000.

CAREER CONSULTANTS
One Jackson Walkway, Providence RI 02903. 401/273-8910. **Fax:** 401/273-5435. **Contact:** Manager. **Description:** An executive search firm. **Specializes in the areas of:** Marketing; Sales.

CENTRAL 2000 EMPLOYMENT AGENCY
1246 Chalkstone Avenue, Providence RI 02908. 401/273-9150. **Contact:** Manager. **Description:** An executive search firm that also provides temp-to-perm placements. **Specializes in the areas of:** Light Industrial.

CREATIVE INPUT, INC.
P.O. Box 1725, East Greenwich RI 02818. 401/885-3254. **Contact:** Richard Brien, Manager. **Description:** An executive search firm. **Specializes in the areas of:** Textiles.

DHR INTERNATIONAL INC.
2843 South County Trail, East Greenwich RI 02818. 401/884-1695. **Fax:** 401/884-2394. **Contact:** Manager. **Description:** An executive search firm. **Corporate headquarters location:** Chicago IL.

DALEY & ASSOCIATES INC.
P.O. Box 41088, Providence RI 02904. 401/725-1390. **Contact:** Manager. **Description:** An executive search firm. **Specializes in the areas of:** Accounting; Engineering; Insurance; MIS/EDP.

DORRA SEARCH INC.
One Richmond Square, Providence RI 02906. 401/453-1555. **Fax:** 401/453-1566. **Contact:** Bethany Gold, Managing Director. **Description:** An executive search firm. **Specializes in the areas of:** Accounting/Auditing; Administration; Computer Science/Software. **Positions commonly filled include:** Accountant/Auditor; Computer Programmer; MIS Specialist; Systems

Analyst. **Average salary range of placements:** More than $50,000. **Number of placements per year:** 1 - 49.

EXECUTIVE RESOURCES
155 Westminster Street, Suite 1250, Providence RI 02903. 401/861-8620. **Contact:** Maurice Paradis, President. **Description:** An executive search firm.

EXECUTIVE'S SILENT PARTNER
400 Reservoir Avenue, Providence RI 02907. 401/461-5170. **Contact:** Manager. **Description:** An executive search firm focusing on placing individuals in the jewelry industry. **Specializes in the areas of:** Manufacturing.

FURLONG PROFESSIONAL SERVICES
227 James Trail, West Kingston RI 02892. 401/539-9011. **Fax:** 401/539-7482. **Contact:** Manager. **Description:** An executive search firm. **Specializes in the areas of:** Information Systems.

ROBERT GRAHAM ASSOCIATES
P.O. Box 1320, Portsmouth RI 02871-1320. 401/682-2277. **Contact:** Robert W. Graham, Owner. **Description:** An executive search firm. **Specializes in the areas of:** Finance.

GREENE PERSONNEL CONSULTANTS
1925 Broad Street, Cranston RI 02905. 401/461-9700. **Contact:** Manager. **Description:** An executive search firm. **Specializes in the areas of:** Advertising; Consumer Package Goods; Finance; Marketing; Public Relations.

ROBERT HALF INTERNATIONAL ACCOUNTEMPS
275 Promenade Street, Suite 140, Providence RI 02908. 401/274-8700. **Contact:** Manager. **World Wide Web address:** http://www.roberthalf.com. **Description:** An executive search firm. Accountemps (also at this location) provides temporary accounting placements. OfficeTeam (also at this location) provides temporary placements in office support. **Corporate headquarters location:** Menlo Park CA. **Other U.S. locations:** Nationwide. **International locations:** Worldwide.

HIGHLAND EMPLOYMENT AGENCY
368 Cranston Street, Providence RI 02907. 401/751-5520. **Fax:** 401/751-4999. **Contact:** Manager. **Description:** An executive search firm.

JEFFREY & ASSOCIATES SEARCH CONSULTANTS
Centerville Commons, Building 2, 875 Centerville Road, Unit 2, Warwick RI 02886-4382. 401/821-2525. **Fax:** 401/821-4343. **Contact:** William F. Jeffrey, President. **Description:** An executive search firm. **Specializes in the areas of:** Human Resources.

KENNEDY PERSONNEL SERVICES
438 East Main Road, Suite 203, Middletown RI 02842. 401/846-2190. **Contact:** Manager. **Description:** An executive search firm. **Specializes in the areas of:** Office Support.

ALBERT G. LEE & ASSOCIATES
106 Greenwood Avenue, Rumford RI 02916. 401/434-7614. **Contact:** Albert G. Lee, CEO. **Description:** An executive search firm. **Specializes in the areas of:** Accounting/Auditing; Administration; Advertising; Biology; Engineering; Finance; Food; General Management; Health/Medical; High-Tech; Industrial; Legal; Manufacturing; Personnel/Labor Relations; Pharmaceuticals; Retail; Sales; Technical. **Positions commonly filled include:** Accountant/Auditor; Advertising Executive; Bank Officer/Manager; Biological Scientist; Computer Programmer; Computer Scientist; Design Engineer; Human Resources Manager; Manufacturing Engineer; Sales and Marketing Manager.

Average salary range of placements: More than $50,000. Number of placements per year: 1 - 49.

LOFLIN GROUP INC.
24 Hemingway Drive, East Providence RI 02915. 401/438-4949. Fax: 401/434-9424. Contact: Kevin Loflin, President. Description: An executive search firm operating on a contingency basis. Positions commonly filled include: Accountant/Auditor; Computer Programmer; Controller; Financial Analyst; Systems Analyst. Average salary range of placements: More than $50,000. Number of placements per year: 100 - 199.

LYBROOK ASSOCIATES, INC.
P.O. Box 572, Newport RI 02840. 401/683-6990. Fax: 401/683-6355. Contact: Karen Lybrook, President. E-mail address: recruiter@lybrook.com. World Wide Web address: http://www.lybrook.com. Description: An executive search firm operating on both retainer and contingency bases. Client company pays fee. Specializes in the areas of: Biology; Engineering; Food; Pharmaceuticals; Plastics; Scientific; Technical. Positions commonly filled include: Biochemist; Biological Scientist; Biomedical Engineer; Chemical Engineer; Chemist; Food Scientist/Technologist; Quality Assurance Engineer; Sales Engineer. Corporate headquarters location: This Location. Other U.S. locations: Nationwide. Average salary range of placements: $50,000 - $100,000. Number of placements per year: 50 - 99.

MANAGEMENT RECRUITERS INTERNATIONAL
101 Dyer Street, Providence RI 02903. 401/274-2810. Contact: Manager. Description: An executive search firm. Specializes in the areas of: Accounting/Auditing; Administration; Advertising; Architecture/Construction; Banking; Communications; Computer Hardware/Software; Design; Electrical; Engineering; Food; General Management; Health/Medical; Insurance; Legal; Manufacturing; Operations Management; Personnel/Labor Relations; Procurement; Publishing; Retail; Sales; Technical; Textiles; Transportation. Corporate headquarters location: Cleveland OH. Other U.S. locations: Nationwide.

MANAGEMENT SEARCH INC.
One State Street, Suite 501, Providence RI 02908. 401/273-5511. Contact: Manager. Description: An executive search firm placing professionals in a wide range of industries.

NUGENT ASSOCIATES
200 Centerville Road, Suite 11, Warwick RI 02886. 401/739-9918. Contact: Manager. Description: An executive search firm. Specializes in the areas of: Technical.

PKS ASSOCIATES, INC.
P.O. Box 5021, Greene RI 02827. 401/397-6154. Fax: 401/397-6722. Contact: Paul Spremulli, Operations Manager. Description: An executive search firm operating on a contingency basis. Specializes in the areas of: Computer Science/Software; Engineering; General Management; Industrial; Manufacturing; Personnel/Labor Relations; Technical. Positions commonly filled include: Accountant/Auditor; Attorney; Blue-Collar Worker Supervisor; Computer Programmer; Dental Assistant/Dental Hygienist; Dentist; Design Engineer; Designer; Draftsperson; Electrical/Electronics Engineer; Environmental Engineer; General Manager; Human Resources Specialist; Industrial Engineer; Industrial Production Manager; Licensed Practical Nurse; Mechanical Engineer; MIS Specialist; Occupational Therapist; Operations/Production Manager; Physical Therapist; Quality Control Supervisor; Recreational Therapist; Registered Nurse; Respiratory Therapist; Software Engineer; Structural Engineer; Systems Analyst. Corporate headquarters location: This Location. Other U.S. locations: Warwick RI. Average salary range of placements: $30,000 - $50,000. Number of placements per year: 200 - 499.

ALAN J. PRICE ASSOCIATES
300 Front Street, Suite 507, Pawtucket RI 02860. 401/728-8499. Contact: Manager. Description: An executive search firm. Specializes in the areas of: Engineering.

PRO-SEARCH, INC.
3960 Post Road, Warwick RI 02886. 401/885-9595. Contact: Manager. Description: An executive search firm. Specializes in the areas of: Banking; Sales; Telecommunications.

LOU RICCI ASSOCIATES
3 Regency Plaza, Providence RI 02903. 401/273-8910. Fax: 401/273-5435. Contact: Lou Ricci, President. Description: An executive search firm operating on both retainer and contingency bases. Client company pays fee. Specializes in the areas of: Marketing; Sales. Positions commonly filled include: Account Manager; Account Representative; Branch Manager; Customer Service Representative; General Manager; Management Analyst/Consultant; Sales Engineer; Sales Executive; Sales Manager; Sales Representative; Vice President of Sales. Average salary range of placements: $50,000 - $100,000.

SALES CONSULTANTS OF RHODE ISLAND
349 Centerville Road, Warwick RI 02886-4324. 401/737-3200. Contact: Manager. World Wide Web address: http://www.mrinet.com. Description: An executive search firm operating on both retainer and contingency bases. Specializes in the areas of: Marketing; Sales. Positions commonly filled include: Account Manager; Account Representative; Customer Service Representative; General Manager; Management Analyst/Consultant; Management Trainee; Market Research Analyst; Marketing Manager; Marketing Specialist; Sales Engineer; Sales Executive; Sales Manager; Sales Representative. Corporate headquarters location: Cleveland OH. Average salary range of placements: More than $50,000. Number of placements per year: 1 - 49.

THE SCHATTLE GROUP
1130 Ten Rod Road, North Kingstown RI 02852. 401/739-0500. Contact: Manager. Description: An executive search firm. Specializes in the areas of: Management; MIS/EDP; Sales.

SEARCH PARTNERS LIMITED
3 Regency Plaza, Providence RI 02903. 401/455-7777. Contact: Manager. Description: An executive search firm.

SEARCH PERSONNEL, INC.
5 Mechanic Street, Hope Valley RI 02832. 401/539-7600. Fax: 401/539-6040. Contact: Manager. Description: An executive search firm.

SPECTRUM BUSINESS ASSOCIATES LTD.
P.O. Box 95, Newport RI 02840. 401/849-6560. Contact: Manager. Description: An executive search firm. Specializes in the areas of: Maritime.

SULLIVAN & COGLIANO
100 Jefferson Boulevard, Warwick RI 02888. 401/463-3811. Contact: Manager. Description: An executive search firm. Specializes in the areas of: Construction; Engineering; Health/Medical; Information Technology; Logistics; Marketing; Sales; Transportation.

SYLVESTRO ASSOCIATES
5586 Post Road, Suite 208, East Greenwich RI 02818. 401/885-0855. Contact: Manager. Description: An executive search firm.

WESTMINSTER GROUP
40 Westminster Street, Providence RI 02903. 401/273-9300. Contact: Manager. Description: An executive search firm. Specializes in the areas of: Health/Medical; Sales.

PERMANENT EMPLOYMENT AGENCIES

AQUIDNECK EMPLOYMENT SERVICE
170 Aquidneck Avenue, Middletown RI 02842-7600.
Contact: Kenneth Quirk, Recruiter. **Description:** A
permanent employment agency that also provides
temporary placements. **Specializes in the areas of:**
Banking; Legal; Manufacturing; Sales; Secretarial.
Positions commonly filled include: Customer Service
Representative; Typist/Word Processor. **Average salary
range of placements:** Less than $20,000.

THE BARRETT GROUP
300 Centerville Road, Summit South, Suite 115,
Warwick RI 02886. 401/736-8788. **Fax:** 401/736-8796.
Contact: Kevin Tetler, Vice President. **Description:** A
permanent employment agency that also provides
career/outplacement counseling. Founded in 1989.
Number of placements per year: 200 - 499.

CAREERS UNLIMITED
560 Jefferson Boulevard, Suite 205, Warwick RI 02886.
401/736-8880. **Contact:** Arlette Dumais, President.
Description: A permanent employment agency that also
provides contract services. **Specializes in the areas of:**
Information Systems; Insurance. **Positions commonly
filled include:** Database Administrator; Insurance Agent/
Broker; Network Administrator; Underwriter. **Number
of placements per year:** 100 - 199.

CASS & COMPANY
One Richmond Square, Providence RI 02906. 401/453-
2277. **Contact:** Manager. **Description:** A permanent
employment agency. **Specializes in the areas of:**
Nannies.

INITIAL STAFFING SERVICES
26 Ship Street, Providence RI 02903. 401/421-0488.
Toll-free phone: 800/839-5595. **Fax:** 401/454-6818.
Contact: Manager. **World Wide Web address:**
http://www.initial.com. **Description:** A permanent
employment agency that also provides some temporary
placements and resume/career outplacement counseling.
Specializes in the areas of: Administration; Clerical;
Light Industrial. **Positions commonly filled include:**
Administrative Assistant; Claim Rep.; Customer Service
Rep.; Secretary; Typist/Word Processor. **Average salary
range of placements:** $20,000 - $29,999. **Number of
placements per year:** 200 - 499.

JOB CONNECTION, LTD.
189 Governor Street, Suite 202, Providence RI 02906.
401/274-4450. **Fax:** 401/274-4451. **Contact:** Laurie
Robinson, Human Resources Coordinator. **E-mail
address:** jobconnection@compuserve.com. **World Wide
Web address:** http://ourworld.compuserve.com/
homepages/jobconnection. **Description:** A permanent
employment agency that focuses on providing human
service agencies with professional staff. Founded in
1986. **Specializes in the areas of:** Human Services.
Positions commonly filled include: Counselor; Human
Service Worker; Occupational Therapist; Physical
Therapist; Registered Nurse; Social Worker; Speech-
Language Pathologist; Teacher/Professor. **Other U.S.
locations:** Natick MA. **Average salary range of**

placements: $20,000 - $29,999. **Number of placements
per year:** 50 - 99.

JOHNSON & TREGAR ASSOCIATES
321 Turks Head Building, Providence RI 02903.
401/831-5550. **Fax:** 401/831-5558. **Contact:** Jack
Tregar, Owner. **Description:** A permanent employment
agency. Placements are primarily made at manufacturing
companies. **Specializes in the areas of:** Engineering;
General Management; Industrial; Manufacturing;
Personnel/Labor Relations. **Positions commonly filled
include:** Biological Scientist; Biomedical Engineer;
Buyer; Chemical Engineer; Chemist; Design Engineer;
Electrical/Electronics Engineer; Environmental Engineer;
General Manager; Human Resources Specialist;
Industrial Engineer; Industrial Production Manager;
Mechanical Engineer; Metallurgical Engineer;
Operations/Production Manager; Purchasing Agent/
Manager; Quality Control Supervisor; Software
Engineer; Stationary Engineer; Statistician;
Transportation/Traffic Specialist.

KAF STAFFING SERVICES
1742 Lonsdale Avenue, Lincoln RI 02865. 401/723-
1600. **Contact:** Manager. **Description:** A permanent
employment agency.

OCCUPATIONS UNLIMITED, INC.
560 Jefferson Boulevard, Suite 204, Warwick RI 02886.
401/732-9377. **Toll-free phone:** 800/575-9675. **Fax:**
401/732-9666. **Contact:** Manny Rivas, Office Manager.
Description: A permanent employment agency that also
provides some temporary and temp-to-hire placements.
Founded in 1992. **Specializes in the areas of:**
Personnel/Labor Relations; Secretarial; Technical.
Positions commonly filled include: Administrative
Manager; Blue-Collar Worker Supervisor; Claim Rep.;
Clerical Supervisor; Computer Programmer;
Construction Contractor; Customer Service Rep.;
Electrical/Electronics Engineer; Financial Analyst;
General Manager; Human Resources Specialist;
Industrial Engineer; Mechanical Engineer; MIS
Specialist; Operations/Production Manager; Purchasing
Agent/Manager; Transportation/Traffic Specialist.
Average salary range of placements: $20,000 -
$29,999. **Number of placements per year:** 1000+.

PERSONNEL PEOPLE, INC.
203 Turks Head Building, Providence RI 02903.
401/275-2500. **Contact:** Manager. **Description:** A
permanent employment agency that also provides some
temporary placements. **Specializes in the areas of:**
Administration; Clerical. **Positions commonly filled
include:** Administrative Assistant; Customer Service
Rep.; Secretary; Typist/Word Processor. **Average salary
range of placements:** $20,000 - $29,999.

PROJECTS WITH INDUSTRY
40 Fountain Street, 2nd Floor, Providence RI 02903.
401/861-4460. **Contact:** Manager. **Description:** A
federally funded permanent employment agency that
provides placements for people with physical and mental
disabilities. **Other U.S. locations:** Wakefield RI.

TEMPORARY EMPLOYMENT AGENCIES

BLUE COLLAR STAFFING
389 Main Street, Pawtucket RI 02860. 401/728-2234.
Contact: Manager. **Description:** A temporary agency.
Specializes in the areas of: Manufacturing.

CAPITOL PERSONNEL INC.
850 Waterman Avenue, East Providence RI 02914.
401/438-6067. **Fax:** 401/438-6099. **Contact:** Elaine
White, Owner. **Description:** A temporary agency that

also provides some permanent placements. Client
company pays fee. **Specializes in the areas of:**
Administration; Industrial; Legal; Light Industrial;
Secretarial. **Positions commonly filled include:**
Accountant; Administrative Assistant; Administrative
Manager; AS400 Programmer Analyst; Assistant
Manager; Attorney; Clerical Supervisor; Computer
Operator; Computer Programmer; Graphic Artist; Human
Resources Manager; Intellectual Property Lawyer;

Medical Assistant; Medical Records Technician; MIS Specialist; Paralegal; Quality Control Supervisor; Secretary; Technical Writer/Editor; Typist/Word Processor; Underwriter/Assistant Underwriter. **Number of placements per year:** 1000+.

COLONY PERSONNEL ASSOCIATES INC.
2845 Post Road, Warwick RI 02886-3145. 401/739-0670. **Fax:** 401/738-5523. **Contact:** Elaine Atturio, President. **Description:** A temporary agency that also provides temp-to-perm and contract placements. Founded in 1989. **Specializes in the areas of:** Accounting/Auditing; Administration; Engineering; Finance; General Management; Manufacturing; Retail; Sales; Secretarial; Technical. **Positions commonly filled include:** Accountant/Auditor; Adjuster; Administrative Manager; Bank Officer/Manager; Blue-Collar Worker Supervisor; Branch Manager; Chemical Engineer; Chemist; Civil Engineer; Claim Rep.; Clerical Supervisor; Computer Programmer; Cost Estimator; Credit Manager; Customer Service Rep.; Design Engineer; Designer; Electrical/Electronics Engineer; Electrician; Environmental Engineer; General Manager; Health Services Manager; Industrial Engineer; Management Analyst/Consultant; Management Trainee; Manufacturer's/Wholesaler's Sales Rep.; Mechanical Engineer; Metallurgical Engineer; MIS Specialist; Purchasing Agent/Manager; Quality Control Supervisor; Software Engineer; Statistician; Structural Engineer; Systems Analyst; Typist/Word Processor. **Number of placements per year:** 100 - 199.

KELLY SERVICES, INC.
100 Jefferson Boulevard, Warwick RI 02888. 401/463-8767. **Fax:** 401/467-3530. **Contact:** Donna Dugas, Senior Supervisor. **World Wide Web address:** http://www.kellyservices.com. **Description:** A temporary agency. **Specializes in the areas of:** Accounting/Auditing; Administration; Clerical; Computer Science/Software; Engineering; Finance; General Management; Health/Medical; Industrial; Manufacturing; Marketing; Office Support; Personnel/Labor Relations; Sales; Secretarial; Technical. **Positions commonly filled include:** Accountant/Auditor; Biomedical Engineer; Blue-Collar Worker Supervisor; Buyer; Claim Representative; Clerical Supervisor; Clerk; Clinical Lab Technician; Computer Operator; Computer Programmer; Construction Trade Worker; Customer Service Representative; Data Entry Clerk; Design Engineer; Draftsperson; Driver; Electrical/Electronics Engineer; Factory Worker; Financial Analyst; Food Scientist/Technologist; Human Resources Specialist; Legal Secretary; Light Industrial Worker; Management Trainee; Mechanical Engineer; Medical Records Technician; Medical Secretary; MIS Specialist; Purchasing Agent/Manager; Quality Control Supervisor; Sales Representative; Secretary; Software Engineer; Stenographer; Systems Analyst; Typist/Word Processor. **Benefits available to temporary workers:** 401(k); Medical Insurance; Paid Holidays; Paid Vacation. **Corporate headquarters location:** Troy MI. **Other U.S. locations:** Nationwide. **Average salary range of placements:** $30,000 - $50,000. **Number of placements per year:** 500 - 999.

NORRELL SERVICES
855 Waterman Avenue, East Providence RI 02914. 401/434-0851. **Contact:** Lora Bernier, Manager. **Description:** A temporary agency that also provides permanent placements. **Specializes in the areas of:** Accounting/Auditing; Administration; Banking; Computer Science/Software; Economics; Engineering; Finance; Food; General Management; Industrial; Insurance; Legal; Manufacturing; Nonprofit; Personnel/Labor Relations; Publishing; Retail; Sales; Secretarial; Technical; Transportation. **Positions commonly filled include:** Accountant/Auditor; Administrative Manager; Aerospace Engineer; Bank Officer/Manager; Biomedical Engineer; Branch Manager; Budget Analyst; Buyer; Chemical Engineer; Chemist; Civil Engineer; Claim Rep.; Clerical Supervisor; Computer Programmer; Cost Estimator; Credit Manager; Customer Service Rep.; Design Engineer; Designer; Dietician/Nutritionist;

Draftsperson; Electrical/Electronics Engineer; Environmental Engineer; Financial Analyst; Food Scientist/Technologist; General Manager; Hotel Manager; Human Resources Specialist; Industrial Engineer; Industrial Production Manager; Management Analyst/Consultant; Management Trainee; Market Research Analyst; Mechanical Engineer; Metallurgical Engineer; MIS Specialist; Nuclear Engineer; Operations/Production Manager; Paralegal; Public Relations Specialist; Purchasing Agent/Manager; Quality Control Supervisor; Restaurant/Food Service Manager; Services Sales Representative; Software Engineer; Stationary Engineer; Strategic Relations Manager; Structural Engineer; Systems Analyst; Technical Writer/Editor; Telecommunications Manager; Typist/Word Processor. **Benefits available to temporary workers:** 401(k); Medical Insurance; Paid Holidays; Paid Vacation. **Corporate headquarters location:** Atlanta GA. **Other U.S. locations:** Nationwide. **Average salary range of placements:** $20,000 - $29,999. **Number of placements per year:** 50 - 99.

OFFICE SPECIALISTS
235 Promenade Street, Suite 419, Providence RI 02908. 401/831-1234. **Contact:** Manager. **Description:** A temporary agency that also provides some temp-to-perm and direct hire placements. **Specializes in the areas of:** Office Support.

ON LINE STAFF INC.
One Richmond Square, Providence RI 02906. 401/274-1500. **Fax:** 401/274-1803. **Contact:** Susan Reid, Owner. **Description:** A temporary agency that provides some permanent placements. **Specializes in the areas of:** Computer Science/Software; Engineering; Personnel/Labor Relations; Technical. **Positions commonly filled include:** Biochemist; Biological Scientist; Chemist; Computer Programmer; Design Engineer; Designer; Draftsperson; Editor; Engineer; Internet Services Manager; Mathematician; MIS Specialist; Multimedia Designer; Science Technologist; Systems Analyst; Technical Writer/Editor; Telecommunications Manager. **Number of placements per year:** 100 - 199.

PRO STAFF PERSONNEL SERVICES
115 Cedar Street, Providence RI 02903. 401/351-0720. **Contact:** Manager. **World Wide Web address:** http://www.prostaff.com. **Description:** A temporary agency that also provides some permanent placements. **Specializes in the areas of:** Administration; Clerical; Light Industrial.

QUALIFIED RESOURCES
175 Main Street, Pawtucket RI 02860. 401/729-5848. **Fax:** 401/729-5851. **Contact:** Manager. **Description:** A temporary agency that also provides some permanent placements. **Specializes in the areas of:** Accounting; Administration; Finance; Light Industrial; Secretarial. **Positions commonly filled include:** Accountant; Administrative Assistant; Administrative Manager; Assistant Manager; Auditor; Bank Officer/Manager; Blue-Collar Worker Supervisor; Branch Manager; Budget Analyst; Chief Financial Officer; Claim Rep.; Clerical Supervisor; Controller; Cost Estimator; Credit Manager; Customer Service Rep.; Finance Director; Financial Analyst; General Manager; Human Resources Manager; Operations Manager; Production Manager; Quality Control Supervisor; Secretary; Transportation/Traffic Specialist; Typist/Word Processor. **Benefits available to temporary workers:** Health Benefits; Incentive Plan. **Corporate headquarters location:** Cranston RI. **Average salary range of placements:** $30,000 - $49,999. **Number of placements per year:** 1000+.

SPECTRA TEMPS/TRACEY ASSOCIATES
260 West Exchange Street, Suite 207, Providence RI 02903. 401/521-4400. **Fax:** 401/521-3992. **Contact:** Kerry Tracey, President. **Description:** A temporary agency that also provides permanent placements and some management-level searches. **Specializes in the areas of:** Accounting; Legal; Personnel/Labor Relations;

Secretarial. **Positions commonly filled include:** Clerical Supervisor; Human Resources Specialist; Paralegal; Typist/Word Processor. **Benefits available to temporary workers:** Paid Vacation. **Average salary range of placements:** $20,000 - $29,999. **Number of placements per year:** 1 - 49.

TAC STAFFING SERVICES
55 Dorrance Street, Providence RI 02903. 401/272-5410. **Fax:** 401/272-9138. **Contact:** Office Manager. **Description:** TAC Staffing Services is a temporary agency. **Specializes in the areas of:** Accounting/ Auditing; Advertising; Banking; Clerical; Education; Health/Medical; Insurance; Legal; Manufacturing; Nonprofit; Personnel/Labor Relations; Publishing; Sales; Transportation. **Positions commonly filled include:** Administrative Worker/Clerk; Bookkeeper; Clerk; Data Entry Clerk; Driver; Factory Worker; Legal Secretary; Light Industrial Worker; Medical Secretary; Receptionist; Secretary; Typist/Word Processor. **Number of placements per year:** 1000+.

CONTRACT SERVICES FIRMS

ADECCO/TAD TECHNICAL SERVICES
2 Richmond Square, Providence RI 02906. 401/273-2300. **Contact:** Manager. **Description:** A contract services firm.

SUMMIT TECHNICAL SERVICES
349 Centerville Road, Warwick RI 02886. 401/738-9097. **Toll-free phone:** 800/556-0742. **Fax:** 401/738-5242. **Contact:** Karen Medeiros, Branch Manager. **E-mail address:** warwick@summit-technical.com. **World Wide Web address:** http://www.summit-technical.com. **Description:** Summit Technical Services is a contract services firm. Client company pays fee. **Specializes in the areas of:** Art/Design; Engineering; Sales; Technical. **Positions commonly filled include:** Biochemist; Biomedical Engineer; Buyer; Chemical Engineer; Chemist; Civil Engineer; Clinical Lab Technician; Design Engineer; Desktop Publishing Specialist; Draftsperson; Electrical/Electronics Engineer; Electrician; Environmental Engineer; Graphic Designer; Industrial Engineer; Industrial Production Manager; Manufacturing Engineer; Mechanical Engineer; Metallurgical Engineer; Production Manager; Quality Assurance Engineer; Quality Control Supervisor; Technical Writer/Editor. **Benefits available to temporary workers:** 401(k); Bonus Award/Plan; Direct Deposit; Health Benefits. **Corporate headquarters location:** This Location. **Average salary range of placements:** $30,000 - $49,999. **Number of placements per year:** 200 - 499.

TECH/AID OF RHODE ISLAND
240 Chestnut Street, Warwick RI 02888. 401/467-7560. **Toll-free phone:** 800/525-7555. **Fax:** 401/461-4880. **Contact:** Kevin Garvey, Manager. **Description:** A contract services firm. Client company pays fee. **Specializes in the areas of:** Architecture/Construction; Art/Design; Biology; Engineering. **Positions commonly filled include:** Architect; Biochemist; Biological Scientist; Biomedical Engineer; Buyer; Chemical Engineer; Chemist; Civil Engineer; Clinical Lab Tech.; Construction Contractor; Design Engineer; Desktop Publishing Specialist; Draftsperson; Electrical/ Electronics Engineer; Electrician; Environmental Engineer; Food Scientist/Technologist; Geographer; Geologist/Geophysicist; Graphic Artist; Graphic Designer; Human Resources Manager; Industrial Engineer; Internet Services Manager; Manufacturing Engineer; Mechanical Engineer; Metallurgical Engineer; MIS Specialist; Production Manager; Project Manager; Quality Assurance Engineer; Quality Control Supervisor; Sales Engineer; Technical Writer/Editor. **Benefits available to temporary workers:** 401(k); Medical Insurance; Paid Holidays. **Corporate headquarters location:** Newton MA. **Other U.S. locations:** Nationwide. **Number of placements per year:** 1000+.

UNIFIED MANAGEMENT CORPORATION
1420 Mineral Spring Avenue, North Providence RI 02904. 401/354-8600. **Contact:** Manager. **Description:** A contract services firm. **Specializes in the areas of:** Payroll.

◆ SOUTH CAROLINA ◆

A-PLUS STAFFING
1527 Sam Rittenberg Boulevard, Suite 203, Charleston SC 29407. 843/556-1800. **Fax:** 843/556-7690. **Contact:** Gloria Purcell, Owner. **Description:** An executive search firm. **Specializes in the areas of:** Legal; Manufacturing.

DAVID ANTHONY CONSULTANTS
114 Main Street, Fort Mill SC 29715. 803/547-2006. **Fax:** 803/547-2030. **Contact:** Michael D. Gutowski, President. **E-mail address:** mikeg@worldrecruiters.com. **Description:** An executive search firm. **Specializes in the areas of:** Engineering.

BOCK & ASSOCIATES
2375 East Main Street, Suite A105, Spartanburg SC 29307. 864/579-7396. **Contact:** Kevin Bock, Owner/President. **Description:** An executive search firm that provides placements for professionals who work with polymer-based materials used primarily in the manufacturing of medical devices. **Specializes in the areas of:** Engineering; Industrial; Manufacturing; Personnel/Labor Relations; Technical. **Positions commonly filled include:** Biological Scientist; Biomedical Engineer; Chemical Engineer; Chemist; Human Resources Manager; Mechanical Engineer. **Average salary range of placements:** More than $50,000. **Number of placements per year:** 1 - 49.

THE BOSTIC GROUP, INC.
348 Feaster Road, Suite E, Greenville SC 29615. 864/284-0070. **Fax:** 864/284-0071. **Contact:** Manager. **World Wide Web address:** http://www. bosticgroup.com. **Description:** An executive search firm. **Specializes in the areas of:** Information Technology.

COLUMBIA HEALTH CARE SERVICES
530 Howell Road, Suite 203, Greenville SC 29615. 864/322-7122. **Contact:** Manager. **NOTE:** The first 90 days are spent under the employment of Columbia Health Care, after which time workers may become full-time employees of the client company and receive benefits. Please contact Columbia Health Care Services for more details. **Specializes in the areas of:** Health/Medical. **Positions commonly filled include:** Licensed Practical Nurse; Registered Nurse.

COLUMBIA HEALTH CARE SERVICES
P.O. Box 8386, Columbia SC 29202. 803/782-2000. **Contact:** Manager. **Description:** This location houses the corporate offices, as well as the company's legal staffing branch. Overall, Columbia Health Care Services is an executive search firm focusing on the placement of medical receptionists, medical assistants, nurses, LPNs, and some health insurance personnel. **Specializes in the areas of:** Health/Medical.

COLUMBUS INTERNATIONAL GROUP
180 Meeting Place, Charleston SC 29401. 843/973-3500. **Fax:** 843/973-3513. **Contact:** Recruiter. **E-mail address:** recruiter@columbusgroup.net. **World Wide Web address:** http://www.columbusgroup.net. **Description:** An executive search firm that also offers some Human Resources consulting services. **Specializes in the areas of:** Health/Medical; Information Technology; Telecommunications.

CORPORATE SOLUTIONS
P.O. Box 1974, Simpsonville SC 29681-1974. 864/228-9508. **Contact:** Manager. **Description:** An executive search firm. **Specializes in the areas of:** Engineering; Finance; Information Systems; Manufacturing.

THOMAS J. DOUGHERTY & ASSOCIATES
1215 Schirmer Avenue, Mount Pleasant SC 29464. 843/881-9898. **Fax:** 843/881-1598. **Contact:** Manager.

Description: An executive search firm. **Specializes in the areas of:** Automotive; Manufacturing; Plastics.

DUNHILL PROFESSIONAL SEARCH
6 Village Square, 231F Hampton Street, Greenwood SC 29646. 864/229-5251. **Contact:** Hal Freese, President. **Description:** An executive search firm. **Specializes in the areas of:** Accounting/Auditing; Computer Hardware/Software; Engineering; Manufacturing.

EDMONDS PERSONNEL INC.
P.O. Box 26313, Greenville SC 29616. 864/288-4848. **Fax:** 864/288-2114. **Contact:** Dave Edmonds, Owner. **E-mail address:** edmonds@edmondspersonnel.com. **World Wide Web address:** http://www. edmondspersonnel.com. **Description:** An executive search firm. **Specializes in the areas of:** Engineering; Manufacturing. **Positions commonly filled include:** Aerospace Engineer; Buyer; Design Engineer; Designer; Electrical/Electronics Engineer; Electrician; Human Resources Specialist; Industrial Engineer; Industrial Production Manager; Mechanical Engineer; Metallurgical Engineer; Quality Control Supervisor; Science Technologist; Technical Writer/Editor; Telecommunications Manager. **Average salary range of placements:** $30,000 - $50,000. **Number of placements per year:** 1 - 49.

ENGINEERING PERSONNEL NETWORK
P.O. Box 1246, Irmo SC 29063. 803/781-2087. **Contact:** Manager. **Description:** An executive search firm. **Specializes in the areas of:** Engineering; Environmental; Industrial; Public Administration.

EVERS PERSONNEL SEARCH
6236 St. Andrews Road, Suite 9, Columbia SC 29212. 803/772-0451. **Contact:** Jim Evers, Owner. **Description:** An executive search firm. Founded in 1991. **Specializes in the areas of:** Sales. **Positions commonly filled include:** Branch Manager; Manufacturer's/Wholesaler's Sales Rep.; Sales Representative. **Average salary range of placements:** $30,000 - $50,000. **Number of placements per year:** 50 - 99.

EXECUTIVE PLACEMENT
P.O. Box 5663, Hilton Head Island SC 29938. 843/785-2705. **Contact:** Manager. **Description:** An executive search firm.

FINANCIAL SEARCH ASSOCIATES
312 Wilton Street, Greenville SC 29609. 864/370-9872. **Fax:** 864/370-0516. **Contact:** Manager. **Description:** An executive search firm. **Specializes in the areas of:** Accounting/Auditing; Finance.

FORD & ASSOCIATES
P.O. Box 3648, Myrtle Beach SC 29578. 843/497-5350. **Fax:** 843/497-5351. **Contact:** Travis Ford, President. **E-mail address:** tford@fordsearch.com. **World Wide Web address:** http://www.fordsearch.com. **Description:** An executive search firm operating on a contingency basis. The firm also provides some contract services. **Specializes in the areas of:** Accounting/Auditing; Chemical Engineering; Data Processing; Engineering; Industrial; Logistics; Manufacturing; Personnel/Labor Relations; Quality Assurance. **Positions commonly filled include:** Accountant/Auditor; Chemical Engineer; Computer Programmer; Environmental Engineer; Human Resources Manager; Industrial Engineer; Industrial Production Manager; Manufacturing Engineer; Mechanical Engineer; Operations/Production Manager; Quality Assurance Engineer. **Number of placements per year:** 50 - 99.

F-O-R-T-U-N-E PERSONNEL CONSULTANTS
25 Woods Lake Road, Suite 410, Greenville SC 29607. 864/241-7700. **Fax:** 864/241-7704. **Contact:** Recruiter.

E-mail address: fpcgrev@mindspring.com. **Description:** An executive search firm. **Specializes in the areas of:** Health/Medical; Manufacturing. **Positions commonly filled include:** Biochemist; Biological Scientist; Biomedical Engineer; Chemical Engineer; Chemist; Clinical Lab Technician; Design Engineer; Environmental Engineer; Industrial Engineer; Industrial Production Manager; Mechanical Engineer; MIS Specialist; Operations/Production Manager; Pharmacist; Quality Control Supervisor; Veterinarian. **Corporate headquarters location:** New York NY. **Other U.S. locations:** Nationwide. **Average salary range of placements:** More than $50,000. **Number of placements per year:** 1 - 49.

F-O-R-T-U-N-E PERSONNEL CONSULTANTS
100 Miracle Mile Drive, Suite F, Anderson SC 29621. 864/226-5322. **Fax:** 864/225-6767. **Contact:** Manager. **Description:** An executive search firm. **Specializes in the areas of:** Biotechnology; Health/Medical; Pharmaceuticals. **Corporate headquarters location:** New York NY. **Other U.S. locations:** Nationwide.

F-O-R-T-U-N-E PERSONNEL CONSULTANTS OF CHARLESTON
410 Mill Street, Suite 106, Mount Pleasant SC 29464. 843/884-0505. **Fax:** 843/849-9522. **Contact:** Robert Spears, President. **E-mail address:** fpc_chas@ ix.netcom.com. **Description:** An executive search firm operating on both retainer and contingency bases. Client company pays fee. **Specializes in the areas of:** Engineering; Transportation. **Positions commonly filled include:** Design Engineer; Electrical/Electronics Engineer; General Manager; Industrial Engineer; Industrial Production Manager; Manufacturing Engineer; Mechanical Engineer; Metallurgical Engineer; Operations Manager; Production Manager; Quality Assurance Engineer; Quality Control Supervisor. **Corporate headquarters location:** New York NY. **Other U.S. locations:** Nationwide. **Average salary range of placements:** $50,000 - $100,000. **Number of placements per year:** 100 - 199.

F-O-R-T-U-N-E PERSONNEL CONSULTANTS OF COLUMBIA
108 Columbia Northeast Drive, Suite H, Columbia SC 29223. 803/788-8877. **Fax:** 803/788-1509. **Contact:** Robert Thompson, General Manager. **E-mail address:** fortune@conterra.com. **World Wide Web address:** http://www.conterra.com/fortune. **Description:** An executive search firm. Founded in 1980. **Specializes in the areas of:** Accounting/Auditing; Administration; Engineering; Finance; General Management; Industrial; Manufacturing; Quality Assurance; Sales; Technical; Transportation. **Positions commonly filled include:** Account Manager; Accountant/Auditor; Buyer; Chief Financial Officer; Controller; Design Engineer; Electrical/Electronics Engineer; Finance Director; Financial Analyst; General Manager; Human Resources Manager; Industrial Engineer; Industrial Production Manager; Management Analyst/Consultant; Manufacturer's/Wholesaler's Sales Rep.; Manufacturing Engineer; Marketing Manager; Mechanical Engineer; Metallurgical Engineer; Operations/Production Manager; Purchasing Agent/Manager; Quality Control Supervisor; Sales Engineer; Software Engineer; Systems Manager; Transportation/Traffic Specialist. **Corporate headquarters location:** New York NY. **Other U.S. locations:** Nationwide. **Average salary range of placements:** More than $50,000. **Number of placements per year:** 200 - 499.

GODSHALL STAFFING
P.O. Box 1984, Greenville SC 29602. 864/242-3491. **Fax:** 864/232-5658. **Contact:** Manager. **Description:** A generalist executive search firm.

ROBERT HALF INTERNATIONAL ACCOUNTEMPS
75 Beattie Place, Suite 930, Greenville SC 29601. 864/232-4253. **Contact:** Manager. **Description:** An executive search firm. Accountemps (also at this location) provides temporary placements. **Corporate headquarters location:** Menlo Park CA. **Other U.S. locations:** Nationwide.

HALLMARK RECRUITERS
3073 Hickory Hill Circle, Conway SC 29526. 843/347-9067. **Fax:** 843/347-9070. **Contact:** Linda Boyette, President. **E-mail address:** boyette@sccoast.net. **Description:** An executive search firm. **Specializes in the areas of:** Manufacturing. **Positions commonly filled include:** Biochemist; Chemical Engineer; Chemist; Hotel Manager; Materials Engineer; Purchasing Agent/ Manager; Quality Control Supervisor. **Average salary range of placements:** More than $50,000. **Number of placements per year:** 100 - 199.

THE HARRINGTON GROUP
2811 Reidville Road, Suite 16, Spartanburg SC 29301. 864/587-1045. **Fax:** 864/587-1048. **Contact:** Manager. **Description:** An executive search firm. **Specializes in the areas of:** Computer Operations.

HEALTH CARE SEARCH ASSOCIATES
P.O. Box 17334, Greenville SC 29606-8334. 864/242-1999. **Contact:** Manager. **Description:** An executive search firm. **Specializes in the areas of:** Finance; Health/Medical; Quality Assurance. **Positions commonly filled include:** Medical Records Technician; Registered Nurse. **Number of placements per year:** 1 - 49.

HOSPITALITY RECRUITERS
P.O. Box 1089, Lugoff SC 29078. 803/438-1104. **Contact:** Manager. **Description:** An executive search firm. **Specializes in the areas of:** Hotel/Restaurant.

JOB SHOP
950 Millbrook Avenue, Suite B, Aiken SC 29803. 803/649-3435. **Fax:** 803/649-0195. **Contact:** Manager. **Description:** A generalist executive search firm.

KAPP & ASSOCIATES
P.O. Box 103, Greenville SC 29602. 864/250-0123. **Fax:** 864/250-0127. **Contact:** Donald Kapp, President. **Description:** An executive search firm. **Specializes in the areas of:** Manufacturing. **Positions commonly filled include:** Executive Director; Management.

MBI FINANCIAL STAFFING
1201 Main Street, Suite 1980, Columbia SC 29201. 803/252-4646. **Fax:** 803/252-1414. **Contact:** Manager. **Description:** An executive search firm. **Specializes in the areas of:** Finance.

MBI FINANCIAL STAFFING
7 North Laurens Street, Suite 506, Greenville SC 29601. 864/232-5650. **Fax:** 864/232-7675. **Contact:** Manager. **Description:** An executive search firm. **Specializes in the areas of:** Finance.

MANAGEMENT RECRUITERS INTERNATIONAL
2800 Bush River Road, Suite 4, Columbia SC 29210. 803/772-0300. **Fax:** 803/772-4600. **Contact:** Manager. **Description:** An executive search firm. **Corporate headquarters location:** Cleveland OH. **Other U.S. locations:** Nationwide.

MANAGEMENT RECRUITERS INTERNATIONAL
113 Court Street, Pickens SC 29671. 864/878-1113. **Contact:** Manager. **Description:** An executive search firm. **Specializes in the areas of:** Automotive; Consumer Products; Manufacturing. **Corporate headquarters location:** Cleveland OH. **Other U.S. locations:** Nationwide.

MANAGEMENT RECRUITERS INTERNATIONAL
P.O. Box 639, Travelers Rest SC 29690-0639. 864/834-0643. **Contact:** Manager. **Description:** An executive search firm. **Specializes in the areas of:** Manufacturing.

Corporate headquarters location: Cleveland OH. Other U.S. locations: Nationwide.

MANAGEMENT RECRUITERS OF AIKEN
P.O. Box 730, Aiken SC 29802. 803/648-1361. Fax: 803/642-5114. Contact: Manager. Description: An executive search firm. Specializes in the areas of: Apparel; Computer Hardware/Software; Electronics; Health/Medical; Medical Software; Metals; Plastics; Textiles. Corporate headquarters location: Cleveland OH. Other U.S. locations: Nationwide. Number of placements per year: 500 - 999.

MANAGEMENT RECRUITERS OF ANDERSON
P.O. Box 2874, Anderson SC 29622. 864/225-1258. Fax: 864/225-2332. Contact: Rod Pagan, Owner. Description: An executive search firm. Specializes in the areas of: Automotive; Computer Science/Software; Data Processing; Health/Medical; Pharmaceuticals. Positions commonly filled include: Accountant/Auditor; Biological Scientist; Biomedical Engineer; Buyer; Chemical Engineer; Chemist; Computer Programmer; Electrical/Electronics Engineer; General Manager; Human Resources Manager; Industrial Engineer; Mechanical Engineer; Purchasing Agent/Manager; Systems Analyst. Corporate headquarters location: Cleveland OH. Other U.S. locations: Nationwide. Number of placements per year: 50 - 99.

MANAGEMENT RECRUITERS OF COLUMBIA
1201 Hampton Street, Suite 3B, Columbia SC 29201. 803/254-1334. Fax: 803/254-1527. Contact: Bob Keen, Manager. Description: An executive search firm. Specializes in the areas of: Accounting/Auditing; Administration; Advertising; Architecture/Construction; Banking; Communications; Computer Hardware/Software; Design; Electrical; Engineering; Food; General Management; Health/Medical; Insurance; Legal; Manufacturing; Operations Management; Personnel/Labor Relations; Procurement; Publishing; Retail; Sales; Technical; Textiles; Transportation. Corporate headquarters location: Cleveland OH. Other U.S. locations: Nationwide.

MANAGEMENT RECRUITERS OF FLORENCE
1224 West Evans Street, Florence SC 29501. 843/664-1112. Contact: Manager. Description: An executive search firm. Specializes in the areas of: Manufacturing. Corporate headquarters location: Cleveland OH. Other U.S. locations: Nationwide.

MANAGEMENT RECRUITERS OF FORREST ACRES
2711 Middleburg Drive, Columbia SC 29204. 803/758-5920. Fax: 803/758-5921. Contact: Manager. Description: An executive search firm. Corporate headquarters location: Cleveland OH. Other U.S. locations: Nationwide.

MANAGEMENT RECRUITERS OF GREENVILLE SALES CONSULTANTS
330 Pelham Road, Suite 109B, Greenville SC 29615. 864/370-1341. Contact: Dick Brennecke, President. E-mail address: dick@mrigreenvillesc.com. World Wide Web address: http://www.mrigreenvillesc.com. Description: An executive search firm. Client company pays fee. Specializes in the areas of: Computer Science/Software; Marketing; Sales. Positions commonly filled include: Account Manager; Account Representative; AS400 Programmer Analyst; Manufacturing Engineer; MIS Specialist; Network/Systems Administrator; Sales Engineer; Sales Executive; Sales Manager; Sales Representative. Corporate headquarters location: Cleveland OH. Other U.S. locations: Nationwide. Average salary range of placements: $30,000 - $49,999. Number of placements per year: 50 - 99.

MANAGEMENT RECRUITERS OF NORTH CHARLESTON
4975 Lacross Road, Suite 311, North Charleston SC 29406. 843/744-5888. Contact: Manager. Description: An executive recruiting firm. Corporate headquarters location: Cleveland OH. Other U.S. locations: Nationwide.

MANAGEMENT RECRUITERS OF ORANGEBURG
2037 St. Matthews Road, Orangeburg SC 29118. 803/531-4101. Fax: 803/536-3714. Contact: Ed Chewning, Manager. World Wide Web address: http://www.oburg.net/mri/index.html. Description: An executive search firm operating on both retainer and contingency bases. Specializes in the areas of: Computer Science/Software; Engineering; Industrial; Personnel/Labor Relations; Scientific; Technical. Positions commonly filled include: Applications Engineer; Auditor; Chemical Engineer; Computer Programmer; Electrical/Electronics Engineer; General Manager; Human Resources Manager; Industrial Engineer; Industrial Production Manager; Manufacturing Engineer; Marketing Manager; Mechanical Engineer; Metallurgical Engineer; MIS Specialist; Operations Manager; Production Manager; Project Manager; Purchasing Agent/Manager; Quality Control Supervisor; Sales Engineer; Software Engineer; Systems Analyst; Systems Manager; Transportation/Traffic Specialist. Corporate headquarters location: Cleveland OH. Other U.S. locations: Nationwide. Average salary range of placements: $30,000 - $50,000. Number of placements per year: 50 - 99.

MANAGEMENT RECRUITERS OF ROCK HILL
P.O. Box 36788, Rock Hill SC 29732. 803/324-5181. Contact: Herman Smith, Manager. Description: An executive search firm. Specializes in the areas of: Accounting/Auditing; Administration; Advertising; Architecture/Construction; Banking; Communications; Computer Hardware/Software; Design; Electrical; Engineering; Food; General Management; Health/Medical; Insurance; Legal; Manufacturing; Operations Management; Personnel/Labor Relations; Procurement; Publishing; Retail; Sales; Technical; Textiles; Transportation. Corporate headquarters location: Cleveland OH. Other U.S. locations: Nationwide.

MANAGEMENT RECRUITERS OF SUMMERVILLE
1675 North Main Street, Summerville SC 29483. 843/821-1119. Fax: 843/821-1117. Contact: Manager. Description: An executive search firm. Corporate headquarters location: Cleveland OH. Other U.S. locations: Nationwide.

McCORMICK ASSOCIATES
304 Pine Bark Road, Anderson SC 29625. 864/225-1468. Contact: Manager. Description: An executive search firm.

MILLER & ASSOCIATES
1852 Wallace School Road, Suite E, Charleston SC 29407. 843/571-6630. Fax: 843/571-0230. Contact: Al E. Miller Jr., Owner/Manager. Description: An executive search firm. Specializes in the areas of: Accounting; Administration; Computer Science/Software; Engineering; Finance; Industrial; Manufacturing; Personnel/Labor Relations; Sales; Technical. Positions commonly filled include: Accountant; Ceramics Engineer; Civil Engineer; Design Engineer; Designer; Draftsperson; Electrical/Electronics Engineer; Environmental Engineer; Financial Analyst; General Manager; Human Resources Specialist; Industrial Engineer; Industrial Production Manager; Manufacturing Engineer; Materials Engineer; Mechanical Engineer; Metallurgical Engineer; MIS Specialist; Purchasing Agent/Manager; Quality Control Supervisor; Software Engineer; Systems Analyst. Average salary range of placements: More than $50,000. Number of placements per year: 1 - 49.

NATIONWIDE PHYSICIAN RECRUITERS
6569 East Shore Road, Columbia SC 29206. Toll-free phone: 800/533-6799. Fax: 803/787-6441. Contact: Jerry Roberts, Physician Recruiter. Description:

Nationwide Physician Recruiters is an executive search firm operating on a contingency basis. Founded in 1984. **Positions commonly filled include:** Physician. **Average salary range of placements:** More than $50,000. **Number of placements per year:** 1 - 49.

PALACE PERSONNEL SERVICES
1900 Broad River Road, Columbia SC 29210. 803/798-3533. **Fax:** 803/750-3113. **Contact:** Dick Powlas, President. **Description:** An executive search firm that also provides some temporary placements. Founded in 1984. **Specializes in the areas of:** Industrial; Light Industrial; Production. **Positions commonly filled include:** Accountant/Auditor; Blue-Collar Worker Supervisor; Branch Manager; Buyer; Chemist; Civil Engineer; Clerical Supervisor; Computer Programmer; Customer Service Representative; Design Engineer; Designer; Draftsperson; Electrician; Environmental Engineer; General Manager; Human Resources Specialist; Industrial Engineer; Industrial Production Manager; Manufacturer's/Wholesaler's Sales Rep.; Mechanical Engineer; MIS Specialist; Software Engineer. **Benefits available to temporary workers:** Medical Insurance; Paid Holidays; Paid Vacation. **Average salary range of placements:** $30,000 - $50,000. **Number of placements per year:** 100 - 199.

PENN HILL ASSOCIATES
P.O. Box 1367, Pawleys Island SC 29585. 843/237-8988. **Fax:** 843/237-9220. **Contact:** Manager. **Description:** An executive search firm. **Specializes in the areas of:** Consumer Finance.

PHILLIPS RESOURCE GROUP
P.O. Box 5664, Greenville SC 29606. 864/271-6350. **Fax:** 864/271-8499. **Contact:** Mr. A.M. Hicks, President. **World Wide Web address:** http://www.sbphillips.com. **Description:** An executive search firm. **Specializes in the areas of:** Administration; Engineering; Manufacturing; Personnel/Labor Relations; Sales; Technical. **Positions commonly filled include:** Accountant/Auditor; Chemical Engineer; Chemist; Computer Programmer; EDP Specialist; Electrical/Electronics Engineer; Industrial Engineer; Manufacturing Engineer; Marketing Specialist; Mechanical Engineer; Metallurgical Engineer; MIS Specialist. **Corporate headquarters location:** This Location. **Other U.S. locations:** Charlotte NC; Charleston SC. **Average salary range of placements:** More than $50,000. **Number of placements per year:** 50 - 99.

PROQUEST, INC.
505 Pettigru Street, Greenville SC 29601. 864/239-0237. **Fax:** 864/239-0293. **Contact:** Manager. **Description:** An executive search firm.

RAND COMPANY
890 Johnnie Dodds Boulevard, Suite 2C, Mount Pleasant SC 29464. 843/849-1980. **Fax:** 843/884-4081. **Contact:** Manager. **Description:** An executive search firm. **Specializes in the areas of:** Engineering.

RENEGAR CHRISTIAN CORPORATE
P.O. Box 682, Mount Pleasant SC 29465-0682. 843/849-0333. **Fax:** 843/971-1028. **Contact:** Manager.

Description: An executive search firm. **Specializes in the areas of:** Computer Operations; Finance.

SALES CONSULTANTS
402 Old Trolley Road, Suite 207, Summerville SC 29483. 843/851-7773. **Fax:** 843/851-7774. **Contact:** Manager. **Description:** An executive search firm. **Specializes in the areas of:** Marketing; Sales.

SALES CONSULTANTS OF MOUNT PLEASANT
1203 Two Island Court, Suite 103, Mount Pleasant SC 29466. 843/849-8080. **Contact:** Manager. **Description:** An executive search firm. **Specializes in the areas of:** Chemicals; High-Tech; Insurance.

SANFORD ROSE ASSOCIATES
211 Century Drive, Suite 106D, Greenville SC 29607. 864/233-6100. **Fax:** 864/233-3837. **Contact:** Manager. **E-mail address:** rrwsrai@aol.com. **World Wide Web address:** http://www.sanfordrose.com. **Description:** An executive search firm. **Specializes in the areas of:** Management; Manufacturing; Operations Management; Quality Assurance; Technical.

JOHN SHELL ASSOCIATES, INC.
P.O. Box 23291, Columbia SC 29224. 803/788-6619. **Physical address:** 115 Atrium Way, Suite 122, Columbia SC. **Fax:** 803/788-1758. **Contact:** John C. Shell III, CPA/President. **E-mail address:** shellacc@aol.com. **Description:** An executive search firm. **Specializes in the areas of:** Accounting/Auditing; Finance. **Positions commonly filled include:** Accountant/Auditor; Credit Manager; Financial Analyst. **Average salary range of placements:** $30,000 - $50,000. **Number of placements per year:** 50 - 99.

SOUTHERN RECRUITERS & CONSULTANTS
P.O. Box 2745, Aiken SC 29802-2745. 803/648-7834. **Fax:** 803/642-2770. **Contact:** Ray Fehrenbach, President. **World Wide Web address:** http://www.southernrecruiters.com. **Description:** An executive search firm. **Specializes in the areas of:** Accounting/Auditing; Administration; Computer Science/Software; Engineering; General Management; Health/Medical; Manufacturing; MIS/EDP; Personnel/Labor Relations; Technical. **Positions commonly filled include:** Accountant/Auditor; Bank Officer/Manager; Biochemist; Biomedical Engineer; Buyer; Civil Engineer; Computer Programmer; Design Engineer; Designer; Draftsperson; Electrical/Electronics Engineer; Environmental Engineer; General Manager; Human Resources Manager; Industrial Engineer; Mechanical Engineer; Metallurgical Engineer; MIS Specialist; Purchasing Agent/Manager; Quality Control Supervisor; Software Engineer; Structural Engineer; Systems Analyst. **Average salary range of placements:** $30,000 - $50,000. **Number of placements per year:** 100 - 199.

TCG SEARCH
2935 Seabrook Island Road, Johns Island SC 29455. 843/768-4050. **Toll-free phone:** 800/494-3373. **Fax:** 843/768-0310. **Contact:** Manager. **E-mail address:** TCGSearch@mindspring.com. **Description:** An executive search firm. **Specializes in the areas of:** Design; Management; Manufacturing; Technical.

PERMANENT EMPLOYMENT AGENCIES

ASAP SEARCH & RECRUITERS
16 Berryhill Road, Suite 120, Columbia SC 29210. 803/772-6751. **Contact:** Manager. **Description:** ASAP Search & Recruiters is a permanent employment agency. **Specializes in the areas of:** Engineering; Industrial; Manufacturing; Sales; Textiles. **Positions commonly filled include:** Accountant/Auditor; Aerospace Engineer; Computer Programmer; Electrical/Electronics Engineer; Human Resources Manager; Industrial Engineer; Industrial Production Manager; Manufacturer's/Wholesaler's Sales Rep.; Materials Engineer; Mechanical

Engineer; Meteorologist; Operations/Production Manager; Quality Control Supervisor; Software Engineer; Systems Analyst. **Number of placements per year:** 50 - 99.

ACCUSTAFF
201 Columbia Mall Boulevard, Suite 239, Columbia SC 29223. 803/699-3373. **Contact:** Branch Manager. **Description:** A permanent employment agency. **Other area locations:** 612 Saint Andrews Road, Suite 5, Columbia SC 29210. 803/772-1211.

ACCUSTAFF
612 Saint Andrews Road, Suite 5, Columbia SC 29210. 803/772-1211. **Fax:** 803/772-1244. **Contact:** Branch Manager. **Description:** A permanent employment agency. **Other area locations:** 201 Columbia Mall Boulevard, Suite 239, Columbia SC 29223. 803/699-3373.

AUTOMOTIVE CAREERS AND TRAINING, INC.
P.O. Box 88, Mountain Rest SC 29664. 864/718-7100. **Fax:** 864/718-7118. **Contact:** David Freeborn, President. **Description:** A permanent employment agency that also provides contract services. **Corporate headquarters location:** This Location. **Average salary range of placements:** $30,000 - $50,000.

BELCHER STAFFING SERVICES, INC.
989 Knox Abbott Drive, Cayce SC 29033. 843/572-9901. **Contact:** Manager. **Description:** A permanent employment agency.

COMPANION EMPLOYMENT SERVICES
P.O. Box 969, Columbia SC 29205. 803/771-6454. **Physical address:** 2511 Devine Street, Columbia SC. **Contact:** Personnel Consultant. **Description:** A permanent employment agency. **Specializes in the areas of:** Computer Science/Software; Data Processing.

CRAIN SEARCH
P.O. Box 17606, Greenville SC 29606. 864/271-4555. **Contact:** Manager. **Description:** A permanent employment agency.

EMPLOYMENT STAFFING
122 Trinity Street, Abbeville SC 29620. 864/459-2346. **Contact:** Manager. **Description:** A permanent employment agency that also provides some temporary placements. **Corporate headquarters location:** Shelby NC. **Other area locations:** Columbia SC. **Other U.S. locations:** Marion NC. **Average salary range of placements:** $20,000 - $29,999. **Number of placements per year:** 1000+.

HARVEY PERSONNEL, INC.
P.O. Box 1931, Spartanburg SC 29304. 864/582-5616. **Fax:** 864/582-3588. **Contact:** Howard L. Harvey, CPC/President. **Description:** A permanent employment agency. **Specializes in the areas of:** Accounting; Administration; Computer Hardware/Software; Engineering; General Management; Industrial; Manufacturing; Personnel/Labor Relations; Technical. **Positions commonly filled include:** Accountant; Biological Scientist; Biomedical Engineer; Buyer; Ceramics Engineer; Chemical Engineer; Chemist; Civil Engineer; EDP Specialist; Electrical/Electronics Engineer; Industrial Engineer; Manufacturing Engineer; Manufacturing Manager; Mechanical Engineer; Metallurgical Engineer; MIS Specialist; Operations/Production Manager; Plastics Engineer; Purchasing Agent/Manager; Quality Control Supervisor; Software Engineer; Systems Analyst. **Number of placements per year:** 1 - 49.

INITIAL STAFFING
45 South Pleasantburg Drive, Greenville SC 29607. 864/233-4301. **Contact:** Branch Manager. **Description:** A permanent employment agency that also provides some temporary placements. **Positions commonly filled include:** Administrative Worker/Clerk; Clerk; Computer Operator; Construction Trade Worker; Data Entry Clerk; Driver; Factory Worker; Light Industrial Worker; Receptionist; Typist/Word Processor. **Number of placements per year:** 1000+.

PRL & ASSOCIATES, INC.
P.O. Box 340, Lexington SC 29071. 803/957-3222. **Contact:** Perrin R. Love, President. **Description:** A permanent employment agency. **Specializes in the areas of:** Accounting; Administration; Banking; Computer Science/Software; Engineering; Finance; General Management; Manufacturing; Personnel/Labor Relations. **Positions commonly filled include:** Accountant;

Administrative Manager; Bank Officer/Manager; Biomedical Engineer; Branch Manager; Buyer; Chemical Engineer; Civil Engineer; Computer Programmer; Electrical/Electronics Engineer; Environmental Engineer; Financial Analyst; General Manager; Human Resources Manager; Industrial Engineer; Mechanical Engineer; Metallurgical Engineer; MIS Specialist; Operations/Production Manager; Purchasing Agent/Manager; Quality Control Supervisor; Software Engineer; Systems Analyst. **Average salary range of placements:** $50,000 - $100,000. **Number of placements per year:** 1 - 49.

PHELPS PERSONNEL
P.O. Box 4177, Greenville SC 29608. 864/232-8139. **Fax:** 864/271-1426. **Contact:** Ronald A. Phelps, President. **Description:** A permanent employment agency. Founded in 1976. **Specializes in the areas of:** Engineering; Manufacturing. **Positions commonly filled include:** Design Engineer; Electrical/Electronics Engineer; Industrial Engineer; Manufacturing Engineer; Mechanical Engineer; Quality Assurance Engineer. **Average salary range of placements:** $30,000 - $50,000. **Number of placements per year:** 1 - 49.

SNELLING PERSONNEL SERVICES
P.O. Box 1800, Lexington SC 29071. 803/359-7644. **Physical address:** 114 Haygood Avenue, Lexington SC. **Fax:** 803/359-3008. **Contact:** Gina A. McCuen, CPC/Owner. **Description:** A permanent employment agency that also offers temporary and temp-to-perm placements. **Specializes in the areas of:** Accounting; Administration; Computer Science/Software; Finance. **Positions commonly filled include:** Accountant; Administrative Assistant; Applications Engineer; Assistant Manager; Auditor; Bank Officer/Manager; Budget Analyst; Chief Financial Officer; Computer Operator; Controller; Customer Service Rep.; Database Manager; Electrical/Electronics Engineer; Electrician; Finance Director; Financial Analyst; General Manager; Human Resources Manager; MIS Specialist; Sales Rep.; Secretary; Software Engineer; Systems Analyst; Systems Manager; Technical Writer/Editor. **Benefits available to temporary workers:** Paid Vacation; Referral Bonus Plan; Tuition Assistance; Workers' Compensation Plan. **Corporate headquarters location:** Dallas TX. **Average salary range of placements:** More than $50,000. **Number of placements per year:** 500 - 999.

SNELLING PERSONNEL SERVICES
2704 East North Street, Greenville SC 29615-1715. 864/268-9300. **Fax:** 864/268-7676. **Contact:** Sharon Hill, Manager. **Description:** A permanent employment agency that also provides some temporary placements. **Specializes in the areas of:** Accounting/Auditing; Administration; Engineering; Industrial; Light Industrial; Manufacturing; Secretarial; Transportation. **Positions commonly filled include:** Accountant; Administrative Assistant; Administrative Manager; Applications Engineer; Blue-Collar Worker Supervisor; Buyer; Chemical Engineer; Clerical Supervisor; Computer Operator; Computer Programmer; Electrical/Electronics Engineer; Environmental Engineer; Human Resources Manager; Industrial Engineer; Manufacturing Engineer; Mechanical Engineer; MIS Specialist; Production Manager; Purchasing Agent/Manager; Secretary; Software Engineer; Typist/Word Processor. **Benefits available to temporary workers:** Bonus Award/Plan; Paid Holidays. **Corporate headquarters location:** Dallas TX. **Average salary range of placements:** $30,000 - $50,000. **Number of placements per year:** 100 - 199.

THE STROMAN COMPANY
P.O. Box 701, Mauldin SC 29662. 864/297-4387. **Fax:** 864/297-7182. **Contact:** Michael Stroman, President. **E-mail address:** mstroman@mindspring.com. **Description:** A permanent employment agency. **Specializes in the areas of:** Apparel; Engineering; Fashion; Finance; General Management; Industrial. **Positions commonly filled include:** CFO; Civil Engineer; Computer Programmer; Controller; Design Engineer; Electrical/Electronics Engineer; Financial

Analyst; General Manager; Industrial Engineer; Manufacturing Engineer; Mechanical Engineer; Operations Manager; Production Manager; Quality Control Supervisor. **Corporate headquarters location:** This Location. **International locations:** Mexico. **Average salary range of placements:** More than $50,000. **Number of placements per year:** 100 - 199.

TEMPORARY EMPLOYMENT AGENCIES

ACCEL TEMPORARY SERVICES
600 Pettigru Street, Greenville SC 29601. 864/271-8638. **Contact:** Donald Coker, Manager. **Description:** A temporary agency. **Specializes in the areas of:** Accounting; Computer Science/Software; Engineering; Food; General Management; Industrial; Legal; Light Industrial; Scientific; Secretarial; Technical. **Positions commonly filled include:** Accountant; Administrative Assistant; Assistant Manager; Auditor; Computer Operator; Design Engineer; Draftsperson; Human Resources Manager; Industrial Engineer; Industrial Production Manager; Paralegal; Production Manager; Secretary; Typist/Word Processor. **Number of placements per year:** 50 - 99.

CAROLINA PERSONNEL SERVICES
600 Columbia Avenue, Lexington SC 29072. 803/356-7004. **Contact:** Manager. **Description:** A temporary agency that also provides some permanent placements and executive searches. **Specializes in the areas of:** Accounting; Clerical; Light Industrial; Secretarial. **Positions commonly filled include:** Secretary.

DUNHILL STAFFING
96 Villa Road, Greenville SC 29615. 864/242-9870. **Fax:** 864/271-7181. **Contact:** Duke Haynie, President. **Description:** A temporary agency. **Specializes in the areas of:** Human Resources. **Positions commonly filled include:** Human Resources Manager. **Average salary range of placements:** More than $50,000. **Number of placements per year:** 1 - 49.

CHARLES FOSTER STAFFING, INC.
7301 Rivers Avenue, Suite 240, North Charleston SC 29406. 843/572-8100. **Contact:** Dottie Karst, President. **E-mail address:** cfstaff@ix.netcom.com. **Description:** A temporary agency that also provides permanent placements. **Specializes in the areas of:** Sales; Secretarial; Technical. **Positions commonly filled include:** Accountant/Auditor; Administrative Manager; Advertising Clerk; Attorney; Bank Officer/Manager; Biochemist; Biological Scientist; Biomedical Engineer; Branch Manager; Budget Analyst; Buyer; Chemical Engineer; Civil Engineer; Clerical Supervisor; Clinical Lab Tech.; Computer Programmer; Cost Estimator; Credit Manager; Customer Service Rep.; Design Engineer; Designer; Draftsperson; Electrical/Electronics Engineer; Environmental Engineer; Financial Analyst; Health Services Manager; Human Resources Specialist; Industrial Engineer; Manufacturer's/Wholesaler's Sales Rep.; MIS Specialist; Paralegal; Purchasing Agent/Manager; Quality Control Supervisor; Software Engineer; Systems Analyst; Technical Writer/Editor; Typist/Word Processor. **Benefits available to temporary workers:** Paid Holidays; Paid Vacation. **Average salary range of placements:** $30,000 - $50,000. **Number of placements per year:** 50 - 99.

HEALTH FORCE
681 Orleans Road, Charleston SC 29407. 843/556-2784. **Contact:** Manager. **Description:** A temporary agency. **Specializes in the areas of:** Health/Medical.

JERMAN PERSONNEL SERVICES, INC.
455 St. Andrews Road, Suite C4, Columbia SC 29210. 803/798-0556. **Contact:** Tony Cashion, Vice President. **Description:** A temporary agency that also provides permanent placements. **Specializes in the areas of:** Banking; Legal; Publishing; Sales; Secretarial. **Positions commonly filled include:** Customer Service Rep.; Manufacturer's/Wholesaler's Sales Rep.; Medical Records Tech.; Paralegal; Typist/Word Processor.

SMITH TEMPS
SMITH PERSONNEL, INC.
P.O. Box 5815, Hilton Head Island SC 29938. 843/785-4604. **Fax:** 843/785-4639. **Contact:** Joni Drayton, Operations Manager. **E-mail address:** smthper@sprynet.com. **Description:** A temporary agency. Smith Temps is a division of Smith Personnel, Inc. (also at this location), which provides permanent placements. **Specializes in the areas of:** Accounting/Auditing; Administration; Architecture/Construction; Computer Science/Software; Food; General Management; Insurance; Legal; Marketing; Sales; Secretarial. **Positions commonly filled include:** Account Rep.; Accountant; Accountant; Administrative Assistant; Administrative Manager; Architect; Assistant Manager; Bank Officer/Manager; Branch Manager; Chief Financial Officer; Clerical Supervisor; Computer Operator; Controller; Credit Manager; Customer Service Rep.; Database Manager; Draftsperson; Economist; Finance Director; Financial Analyst; Human Resources Manager; Insurance Agent/Broker; Management Analyst/Consultant; Management Trainee; Marketing Manager; Operations Manager; Paralegal; Preschool Worker; Production Manager; Project Manager; Public Relations Specialist; Purchasing Agent/Manager; Sales Manager; Sales Representative; Secretary; Typist/Word Processor.

STAFFINGSOLUTIONS
2000 Centerpoint Drive, Suite 2250, Columbia SC 29210. 803/798-1700. **Contact:** Larry Howell, Branch Manager. **Description:** A temporary agency that also provides some permanent placements. **Specializes in the areas of:** Accounting/Auditing; Health/Medical; Industrial; Sales; Secretarial. **Positions commonly filled include:** Administrative Manager; Claim Representative; Clerical Supervisor; Customer Service Representative; EKG Technician; Licensed Practical Nurse; Management Trainee; Registered Nurse. **Corporate headquarters location:** Dallas TX. **Other U.S. locations:** Nationwide. **Average salary range of placements:** Less than $20,000. **Number of placements per year:** 1000+.

STAFFMARK
P.O. Box 2952, Spartanburg SC 29304. 864/585-6562. **Fax:** 864/573-5047. **Contact:** General Manager. **Description:** A temporary agency that also provides some permanent placements. **Specializes in the areas of:** Industrial; Manufacturing; Secretarial; Technical. **Positions commonly filled include:** Administrative Assistant; Blue-Collar Worker Supervisor; Bookkeeper; Clerical Supervisor; Clerk; Computer Programmer; Construction Trade Worker; Customer Service Representative; Data Entry Clerk; Draftsperson; Electrical/Electronics Engineer; Environmental Engineer; Factory Worker; General Manager; Human Resources Specialist; Industrial Engineer; Industrial Production Manager; Legal Secretary; Light Industrial Worker; Operations/Production Manager; Paralegal; Purchasing Agent/Manager; Receptionist; Restaurant/Food Service Manager; Secretary; Software Engineer; Stenographer; Surveyor; Transportation/Traffic Specialist; Typist/Word Processor. **Benefits available to temporary workers:** Medical Insurance; Paid Holidays; Paid Vacation. **Average salary range of placements:** Less than $20,000. **Number of placements per year:** 200 - 499.

TECHNICAL SOUTH INC.
100 Executive Center Drive, Greenville SC 29615. 864/288-8105. **Contact:** Manager. **Description:** A temporary agency. **Specializes in the areas of:** Engineering; Industrial; Manufacturing. **Positions commonly filled include:** Buyer; Ceramics Engineer; Chemical Engineer; Civil Engineer; Computer

Programmer; Construction Contractor; Cost Estimator; Design Engineer; Designer; Draftsperson; Electrical/ Electronics Engineer; Environmental Engineer; Industrial Engineer; Materials Engineer; Mechanical Engineer; Metallurgical Engineer; Purchasing Agent/Manager; Software Engineer; Structural Engineer; Surveyor; Technical Writer/Editor.

CONTRACT SERVICES FIRMS

AIDE INC. DESIGN SERVICES
P.O. Box 6226, Greenville SC 29606. 864/244-6123. **Toll-free phone:** 800/968-8971. **Fax:** 864/322-1040. **Contact:** Recruiter. **E-mail address:** recruit@aide.com. **World Wide Web address:** http://www.aide.com. **Description:** A contract services firm that also provides some permanent placements. **Specializes in the areas of:** Computer Science/Software; Engineering; Information Technology; Manufacturing. **Positions commonly filled include:** Architect; Ceramics Engineer; Chemical Engineer; Civil Engineer; Computer Programmer; Design Engineer; Designer; Draftsperson; Electrical/Electronics Engineer; Environmental Engineer; Industrial Engineer; Materials Engineer; Mechanical Engineer; Metallurgical Engineer; MIS Specialist; Software Engineer; Structural Engineer; Systems Analyst. **Benefits available to temporary workers:** 401(k); Dental Insurance; Life Insurance; Medical Insurance; Paid Holidays; Paid Vacation. **Number of placements per year:** 200 - 499.

CDI CORPORATION
2800 Bush River Road, Suite 5-B, Columbia SC 29210. 803/798-9180. **Contact:** Manager. **World Wide Web address:** http://www.cdicorp.com. **Description:** A contract services firm. **Specializes in the areas of:** Engineering; Technical. **Corporate headquarters location:** Philadelphia PA. **Other U.S. locations:** Nationwide. **International locations:** Worldwide.

CDI IT SERVICES
1517 Gregg Street, Columbia SC 29201. 803/988-0012. **Fax:** 803/988-0096. **Contact:** Manager. **World Wide Web address:** http://www.cdicorp.com. **Description:** CDI IT Services is a contract services firm. **Specializes in the areas of:** Computer Science/Software. **Corporate headquarters location:** Philadelphia PA. **Other U.S. locations:** Nationwide. **International locations:** Worldwide.

CAREER/OUTPLACEMENT COUNSELING FIRMS

HIGHLANDS PROGRAM
7 North Laurens Street, Suite 305, Greenville SC 29601. 864/233-3277. **Contact:** Berkeley Little, Counselor. **World Wide Web address:** http://www. highlandsprogram.com. **Description:** Provides career counseling to students and adults, and training and development services to corporations.

◆ S O U T H   D A K O T A ◆

AGRA PLACEMENTS, LTD.
6009 West 41st Street, Suite 1A, Sioux Falls SD 57106. 605/362-9883. **Fax:** 605/362-9150. **Contact:** Manager. **E-mail address:** agrasd@iw.net. **World Wide Web address:** http://www.agraplacements.com. **Description:** An executive search firm. **Specializes in the areas of:** Agri-Business; Chemicals; Food.

MANAGEMENT RECRUITERS OF SIOUX FALLS
2600 South Minnesota Avenue, Suite 202, Sioux Falls SD 57105. 605/334-9291. **Fax:** 605/334-9826. **Contact:** Manager. **Description:** An executive search firm. **Specializes in the areas of:** Accounting; Agriculture; Banking; Computer Science/Software; Construction; Engineering; Finance; Food; Insurance.

MIDWEST RECRUITERS (MIR)
1018 South Garfield, Suite 101, Lennox SD 57039. 605/647-5447. **Contact:** Recruiter. **Description:** An executive search firm. **Specializes in the areas of:** Banking; Insurance.

REGENCY RECRUITING, INC.
P.O. Box 77, North Sioux City SD 57049. 605/232-3205. **Fax:** 605/232-3159. **Contact:** Brad Moore, CPC/President. **E-mail address:** rgncyrctg@aol.com. **World Wide Web address:** http://www.regencyrecruiting.com. **Description:** An executive search firm focusing on the placement of computer and computer management personnel in the Midwest. **Specializes in the areas of:** Computer Science/Software. **Positions commonly filled include:** Computer Programmer; Management Analyst/Consultant; MIS Specialist; Systems Analyst. **Number of placements per year:** 50 - 99.

STAFF SEARCH
312 Ninth Avenue SE, Suite C, Watertown SD 57201. 605/882-3406. **Fax:** 605/882-4490. **Contact:** Branch Manager. **Description:** Staff Search is an executive search firm. **Specializes in the areas of:** Computer Science/Software.

ALTERNATIVE HUMAN RESOURCES DEVELOPMENT
2116 South Minnesota Avenue, Suite 5, Sioux Falls SD 57105. 605/335-8198. **Fax:** 605/335-4423. **Contact:** Manager. **Description:** A permanent employment agency that also provides some recruiting and career counseling services. **Specializes in the areas of:** Accounting; Office Support. **Positions commonly filled include:** Accountant; Bookkeeper; Management; Office Manager.

ALTERNATIVE STAFFING
3800 West Technology Circle, Suite 201, Sioux Falls SD 57105. 605/361-6465. **Fax:** 605/361-6691. **Contact:** Manager. **Description:** A permanent employment agency that also provides some temporary and temp-to-hire placements.

CAREERS UNLIMITED
3905 Southwestern Avenue, Suite 201, Sioux Falls SD 57105. 605/336-9800. **Fax:** 605/336-9890. **Contact:** Carol Dane, Owner/Manager. **Description:** A permanent employment agency that also provides some temporary and temp-to-hire placements, as well as contract services. Careers Unlimited also networks with several executive search firms. Founded in 1986. **Specializes in the areas of:** Accounting/Auditing; Banking; Finance; Food; General Management; Sales. **Positions commonly filled include:** Accountant/Auditor; Administrative Manager; Bank Officer/Manager; Blue-Collar Worker Supervisor; Branch Manager; Claim Representative; Clerical Supervisor; Computer Programmer; Cost Estimator; Credit Manager; Customer Service Representative; Draftsperson; Electrical/Electronics Engineer; Financial Analyst; General Manager; Health Services Manager; Hotel Manager; Industrial Engineer; Management Trainee; Manufacturer's/Wholesaler's Sales Rep.; Mechanical Engineer; Medical Records Technician; MIS Specialist; Paralegal; Public Relations Specialist; Purchasing Agent/Manager; Restaurant/Food Service Manager; Services Sales Representative; Software Engineer; Telecommunications Manager; Typist/Word Processor; Underwriter/Assistant Underwriter. **Average salary range of placements:** $20,000 - $29,999. **Number of placements per year:** 50 - 99.

EXPRESS PERSONNEL SERVICES
221 6th Avenue Southeast, Aberdeen SD 57401. 605/225-9222. **Contact:** Manager. **Description:** A permanent employment agency that also provides some temporary placements. **Other U.S. locations:** Nationwide.

EXPRESS PERSONNEL SERVICES
P.O. Box 90059, Sioux Falls SD 57109. 605/338-3551. **Contact:** Manager. **Description:** Express Personnel Services is a permanent employment agency that also provides some temporary placements. **Other U.S. locations:** Nationwide.

METRO PERSONNEL SERVICE
3700 South Kiwanis Avenue, Suite 3, Sioux Falls SD 57105. 605/334-1000. **Fax:** 605/334-0159. **Contact:** Jan Kaufman, Owner. **Description:** A permanent employment agency that also provides executive search services. **Specializes in the areas of:** Banking; Manufacturing.

SNELLING PERSONNEL SERVICE
2720 West 12th Street, Suite 200, Sioux Falls SD 57104. 605/334-1434. **Contact:** Staffing Specialist. **Description:** A permanent employment agency. **Specializes in the areas of:** Accounting/Auditing; Banking; Engineering; Hotel/Restaurant; Sales; Secretarial.

SNELLING PERSONNEL SERVICE
1508 Mountain View Road, Suite 101, Rapid City SD 57702. 605/341-4111. **Fax:** 605/341-0641. **Contact:** Evan L. Hutchings, Owner. **World Wide Web address:** http://www.snelling.com. **Description:** A permanent employment agency. **Other U.S. locations:** Nationwide.

UNITED SIOUX TRIBES DEVELOPMENT CORPORATION
401 East Sioux Avenue, Pierre SD 57501. 605/224-8864. **Fax:** 605/224-0069. **Contact:** Office Manager. **Description:** The United Sioux Tribes Development Corporation is a permanent employment agency that also provides some temporary placements and other general employment assistance services. **Specializes in the areas of:** Nonprofit. **Corporate headquarters location:** This Location. **Other area locations:** Rapid City SD.

UNITED SIOUX TRIBES DEVELOPMENT CORPORATION
P.O. Box 2187, Rapid City SD 57709. 605/343-1100. **Fax:** 605/343-4474. **Contact:** Manager. **Description:** A

permanent employment agency that also provides some temporary placements and general employment assistance. **Specializes in the areas of:** Nonprofit. **Corporate headquarters location:** Pierre SD.

TEMPORARY EMPLOYMENT AGENCIES

AVAILABILITY EMPLOYMENT SERVICES
2701 South Minnesota Avenue, Suite 6, Sioux Falls SD 57105. 605/336-0353. **Fax:** 605/336-0310. **Contact:** Manager. **Description:** A temporary agency that also provides some permanent placements, contract services, and resume and career counseling. Client company pays fee. **Specializes in the areas of:** Administration; Computer Science/Software; Marketing; Sales. **Positions commonly filled include:** Account Manager; Account Representative; Accountant; Administrative Assistant; Advertising Clerk; Advertising Executive; AS400 Programmer Analyst; Auditor; Bank Officer/Manager; Broadcast Technician; Chief Financial Officer; Claim Representative; Computer Operator; Computer Programmer; Computer Support Technician; Computer Technician; Controller; Credit Manager; Customer Service Representative; Database Administrator; Desktop Publishing Specialist; Finance Director; Graphic Artist; Graphic Designer; Human Resources Manager; Insurance Agent/Broker; Management Trainee; Manufacturing Engineer; Marketing Manager; Marketing Specialist; Mechanical Engineer; MIS Specialist; Network/Systems Administrator; Pharmacist; Production Manager; Purchasing Agent/Manager; Quality Assurance Engineer; Quality Control Supervisor; Sales Engineer; Sales Executive; Sales Manager; Sales Representative; Secretary; Systems Analyst; Telecommunications Manager; Typist/Word Processor; Underwriter/Assistant Underwriter; Webmaster. **Average salary range of placements:** $30,000 - $49,999.

KEY STAFFING
500 North Western Avenue, Sioux Falls SD 57104. 605/333-9999. **Fax:** 605/333-9887. **Contact:** Rachel Walpole, Recruiter. **Description:** A temporary agency that also provides some permanent placements. Client company pays fee. **Specializes in the areas of:**

Accounting; Administration; Computer Science/Software; Engineering; General Management; Industrial; Light Industrial; Marketing; MIS/EDP; Sales; Secretarial. **Positions commonly filled include:** Account Manager; Account Representative; Accountant; Administrative Assistant; AS400 Programmer Analyst; Computer Operator; Computer Programmer; Controller; Customer Service Representative; Database Administrator; Database Manager; Draftsperson; Environmental Engineer; Financial Analyst; General Manager; Graphic Artist; Human Resources Manager; Industrial Engineer; Insurance Agent/Broker; Management Trainee; Manufacturing Engineer; Marketing Manager; Marketing Specialist; Mechanical Engineer; MIS Specialist; Network/Systems Administrator; Operations Manager; Paralegal; Production Manager; Purchasing Agent/Manager; Quality Control Supervisor; Sales Executive; Sales Manager; Sales Representative; Secretary; Systems Analyst; Systems Manager; Typist/Word Processor. **Average salary range of placements:** $20,000 - $49,999. **Number of placements per year:** 1000+.

OLSTEN STAFFING SERVICES
209 East St. Joseph Street, Rapid City SD 57701. 605/348-8010. **Fax:** 605/348-8050. **Contact:** Alice Pullins, Personnel Supervisor. **Description:** A temporary agency that also provides some permanent placements. **Specializes in the areas of:** Accounting/Auditing; Banking; Clerical; Health/Medical; Insurance; Sales. **Positions commonly filled include:** Accountant/Auditor; Administrative Worker/Clerk; Claim Representative; Clerk; Computer Operator; Construction Trade Worker; Credit Manager; Customer Service Representative; Data Processor; Insurance Agent/Broker; Marketing Specialist; Nurse; Public Relations Specialist; Receptionist; Sales Representative; Secretary; Stenographer; Typist/Word Processor.

CONTRACT SERVICES FIRMS

INTERIM HEALTHCARE
2520 West 41st Street, Sioux Falls SD 57105. 605/332-3939. **Fax:** 605/332-2118. **Contact:** Manager. **Description:** A contract services firm that also provides temporary placements. **Specializes in the areas of:** Health/Medical. **Positions commonly filled include:**

Dental Assistant/Dental Hygienist; Dental Lab Technician; Dietician/Nutritionist; Health Care Administrator; Home Health Aide; Medical Assistant; Nurse; Physician; Physician Assistant; Registered Nurse.

CAREER/OUTPLACEMENT COUNSELING FIRMS

CAREER PLANNING CENTER
P.O. Box 4730, Aberdeen SD 57401. 605/626-2298. **Fax:** 605/626-3154. **Contact:** Jeff Mitchell, Director. **Description:** A career/outplacement counseling firm. Founded in 1985. **Positions commonly filled include:** Accountant/Auditor; Automotive Mechanic; Blue-Collar Worker Supervisor; Clinical Lab Technician; Counselor;

Electrician; Emergency Medical Technician; General Manager; Human Service Worker; Management Trainee; Preschool Worker; Services Sales Representative; Social Worker; Typist/Word Processor. **Average salary range of placements:** Less than $20,000. **Number of placements per year:** 100 - 199.

◆ T E N N E S S E E ◆

ACCOUNTANTS & BOOKKEEPERS
P.O. Box 38304, Cordova TN 38183. 901/755-6444. **Contact:** Office Manager. **Description:** An executive search firm. **Specializes in the areas of:** Accounting/ Auditing; Bookkeeping.

ACCOUNTANTS EXECUTIVE SEARCH ACCOUNTANTS ON CALL
1101 Kermit Drive, Suite 600, Nashville TN 37217-5110. 615/399-0200. **Fax:** 615/399-2285. **Contact:** Milton Ellis, President. **World Wide Web address:** http://www.aocnet.com. **Description:** An executive search firm. Accountants On Call (also at this location) is a temporary agency. **Specializes in the areas of:** Accounting/Auditing; Finance. **Positions commonly filled include:** Accountant/Auditor; Actuary; Chief Financial Officer; Controller; Cost Estimator; Credit Manager; Finance Director; Financial Analyst. **Other U.S. locations:** Nationwide. **Average salary range of placements:** $20,000 - $29,999. **Number of placements per year:** 1000+.

ANDERSON McINTYRE PERSONNEL SERVICES
6148 Lee Highway, Suite 100, Chattanooga TN 37421. 423/894-9571. **Fax:** 423/892-7413. **Contact:** Maureen McIntyre, Owner. **Description:** An executive search firm that also provides some permanent placements and career counseling and contract services. **Specializes in the areas of:** Administration; Advertising; Architecture/ Construction; Computer Science/Software; Finance; General Management; Health/Medical; Legal; Manufacturing; Sales; Secretarial. **Positions commonly filled include:** Accountant/Auditor; Administrative Manager; Advertising Clerk; Branch Manager; Claim Rep.; Clerical Supervisor; Computer Programmer; Credit Manager; Draftsperson; Management Trainee; Medical Records Technician; Paralegal; Physical Therapist; Physician; Systems Analyst; Travel Agent; Typist/Word Processor. **Average salary range of placements:** $25,000 - $50,000. **Number of placements per year:** 200 - 499.

AUSTIN-ALLEN COMPANY
8127 Walnut Grove Road, Cordova TN 38018. 901/756-0900. **Fax:** 901/756-0933. **Contact:** Mr. C.A. Cupp, General Manager. **Description:** An executive search firm operating on a contingency basis. **Specializes in the areas of:** Accounting/Auditing; Engineering; Personnel/ Labor Relations. **Positions commonly filled include:** Accountant/Auditor; Chemical Engineer; Electrical/ Electronics Engineer; Industrial Engineer; Industrial Production Manager; Manufacturing Engineer; Materials Engineer; Mechanical Engineer; Metallurgical Engineer; Personnel Manager; Purchasing Agent/Manager; Quality Control Supervisor. **Number of placements per year:** 100 - 199.

BAKER & BAKER EMPLOYMENT SERVICE
P.O. Box 160087, Nashville TN 37216. 615/228-3018. **Fax:** 615/262-1982. **Contact:** Owner. **Description:** An executive search firm operating on a contingency basis. **Specializes in the areas of:** Engineering; Industrial; Manufacturing. **Positions commonly filled include:** Accountant/Auditor; Ceramics Engineer; Chemical Engineer; Civil Engineer; Design Engineer; Electrical/ Electronics Engineer; Environmental Engineer; Industrial Engineer; Management Trainee; Materials Engineer; Mechanical Engineer; Metallurgical Engineer; Occupational Therapist; Personnel Specialist; Physical Therapist; Quality Control Supervisor; Technical Writer. **Average salary range of placements:** $30,000 - $50,000. **Number of placements per year:** 50 - 99.

GREG BEATTY & ASSOCIATES
394 Main Street, Nashville TN 37201. 615/826-4904. **Fax:** 615/826-9000. **Contact:** Greg Beatty, President. **Description:** An executive search firm.

BISHOP PLACEMENT SERVICE
1321 Murfreesboro Pike, Suite 600, Nashville TN 37217. 615/367-6177. **Fax:** 615/399-2009. **Contact:** Otis Bishop, President. **Description:** An executive search firm operating on a contingency basis. **Specializes in the areas of:** Restaurant; Retail; Sales.

BISSONETTE & ASSOCIATES
1233 Courtfield Road, Knoxville TN 37922. 423/691-2700. **Fax:** 423/694-6282. **Contact:** William T. Bissonette Sr., President. **Description:** An executive search firm. **Specializes in the areas of:** Sales. **Positions commonly filled include:** Sales Representative. **Number of placements per year:** 1 - 49.

CAREER PROFESSIONALS, INC.
P.O. Box 1216, Morristown TN 37816. 423/587-4363. **Toll-free phone:** 800/476-0111. **Fax:** 423/587-0143. **Contact:** Jim Beelaert, President. **E-mail address:** cpisearch@usit.net. **World Wide Web address:** http://www.cpisearch.com. **Description:** An executive search firm operating on a contingency basis. The firm deals with Southeastern U.S. manufacturing sites. The majority of successful placements have technical degrees and range from product designers to automation experts to production and quality managers. Some permanent placements are also provided. Client company pays fee. **Specializes in the areas of:** Accounting; Engineering; Industrial; Personnel/Labor Relations. **Positions commonly filled include:** Accountant; AS400 Programmer Analyst; Chemical Engineer; Chemist; Controller; Design Engineer; Environmental Engineer; Human Resources Manager; Industrial Engineer; Industrial Production Manager; Manufacturing Engineer; Mechanical Engineer; Metallurgical Engineer; Network/ Systems Administrator; Operations Manager; Production Manager; Project Manager; Purchasing Agent/Manager; Quality Assurance Engineer; Quality Control Supervisor; Software Engineer; Statistician; Systems Analyst. **Corporate headquarters location:** This Location. **Average salary range of placements:** $50,000 - $100,000. **Number of placements per year:** 50 - 99.

CARROLL & ASSOCIATES
4646 Poplar Avenue, Suite 418, Memphis TN 38117. 901/683-1332. **Contact:** Manager. **Description:** An executive search firm. **Specializes in the areas of:** Accounting/Auditing; Administration.

COOK ASSOCIATES INTERNATIONAL, INC.
P.O. Box 962, Brentwood TN 37024-0962. 615/373-8264. **Fax:** 615/371-8215. **Contact:** Stephen G. Cook, General Manager. **E-mail address:** cai@bellsouth.net. **Description:** Cook Associates International is an executive search firm operating on both retainer and contingency bases. **Specializes in the areas of:** Accounting/Auditing; Administration; Computer Science/Software; Engineering; Health/Medical; Industrial; Insurance; Legal; Manufacturing; Personnel/ Labor Relations; Publishing. **Positions commonly filled include:** Accountant/Auditor; Actuary; Attorney; Biomedical Engineer; Budget Analyst; Buyer; Chemical Engineer; Computer Programmer; Cost Estimator; Design Engineer; Dietician/Nutritionist; Electrical/ Electronics Engineer; Electrician; Environmental Engineer; Financial Analyst; General Manager; Health Services Manager; Hotel Manager; Human Resources Specialist; Industrial Engineer; Mathematician; Mechanical Engineer; MIS Specialist; Occupational Therapist; Paralegal; Physical Therapist; Quality Control Supervisor; Registered Nurse; Software Engineer; Stationary Engineer; Statistician; Systems Analyst. **Corporate headquarters location:** This Location. **Other U.S. locations:** Hopkinsville KY; Greenville SC. **Number of placements per year:** 100 - 199.

CORPORATE IMAGE GROUP
3145 Hickory Hill, Suite 204, Memphis TN 38115. 901/360-8091. **Toll-free phone:** 800/823-5100. **Fax:** 901/360-0813. **Contact:** Manager. **World Wide Web address:** http://www.corpimg.com. **Description:** A full-service executive search firm. **Specializes in the areas of:** Accounting; Auditing; Distribution; Engineering; Finance; Health/Medical; Human Resources; Insurance; Manufacturing; Marketing; Sales. **Corporate headquarters location:** This Location. **Other U.S. locations:** Marietta GA.

CRAIG SERVICES
P.O. Box 1202, Morristown TN 37815. 423/587-3189. **Contact:** Manager. **Description:** An executive search firm.

ELITE RECRUITING & SEARCH
1321 Murfreesboro Pike, Suite 601, Nashville TN 37217. 615/360-7773. **Fax:** 615/360-9018. **Contact:** Manager. **Description:** A generalist executive search firm.

EXEC-U-TECH RECRUITING SERVICES
7221 Highway 70 South, Suite 423, Nashville TN 37221. 615/673-2292. **Fax:** 615/673-6794. **Contact:** Roxanne Mead, CPC, Manager. **World Wide Web address:** http://www.exec-u-tech.com. **Description:** An executive search firm. **Specializes in the areas of:** Computer Operations; Information Technology; Software Development.

F-O-R-T-U-N-E PERSONNEL CONSULTANTS
5726 Marlin Road, Franklin Building, Suite 212, Chattanooga TN 37411. 423/855-0444. **Fax:** 423/892-0083. **Contact:** Brenda Hayes, President. **Description:** An executive search firm operating on both retainer and contingency bases. **Specializes in the areas of:** Accounting/Auditing; Administration; Engineering; Manufacturing; Personnel/Labor Relations. **Positions commonly filled include:** Accountant/Auditor; Buyer; Chemical Engineer; Chemist; Civil Engineer; Computer Programmer; Design Engineer; Electrical/Electronics Engineer; Environmental Engineer; Financial Analyst; General Manager; Human Resources Specialist; Industrial Engineer; Industrial Production Manager; Mechanical Engineer; Metallurgical Engineer; Purchasing Agent/Manager; Quality Control Supervisor; Systems Analyst; Transportation/Traffic Specialist. **Corporate headquarters location:** New York NY. **Other U.S. locations:** Nationwide. **Average salary range of placements:** $30,000 - $50,000.

F-O-R-T-U-N-E PERSONNEL CONSULTANTS
52 Timber Creek Drive, Cordova TN 38018. 901/757-5031. **Fax:** 901/757-5048. **Contact:** Gordon Taylor, President. **Description:** An executive search firm. **Specializes in the areas of:** Manufacturing. **Corporate headquarters location:** New York NY. **Other U.S. locations:** Nationwide.

F-O-R-T-U-N-E PERSONNEL CONSULTANTS OF NASHVILLE
406 North Main Street, Kingston Springs TN 37082. 615/952-9310. **Contact:** Tom Oglesby, President. **Description:** An executive search firm. **Specializes in the areas of:** Manufacturing. **Positions commonly filled include:** Design Engineer; Electrical/Electronics Engineer; General Manager; Human Resources Manager; Industrial Engineer; Mechanical Engineer; Purchasing Agent/Manager; Quality Control Supervisor. **Corporate headquarters location:** New York NY.

F-O-R-T-U-N-E PERSONNEL OF KNOXVILLE
111 Center Park Drive, Suite 1004, Knoxville TN 37922. 423/769-9444. **Fax:** 423/769-9449. **Contact:** Manager. **Description:** An executive search firm. **Corporate headquarters location:** New York NY. **Other U.S. locations:** Nationwide.

FRYE/JOURE & ASSOCIATES, INC.
4515 Poplar Avenue, Suite 215, Memphis TN 38117. 901/683-7792. **Fax:** 901/682-9636. **Contact:** Gloria Cathey, Recruiter. **Description:** An executive search firm that operates on both contingency and retainer bases. **Specializes in the areas of:** Biotechnology; Manufacturing; Petrochemical; Pharmaceuticals; Sales. **Average salary range of placements:** $40,000 - $100,000.

GRANT & ASSOCIATES INC.
2 Northgate Park, Suite 418, Chattanooga TN 37213. 423/877-4561. **Fax:** 423/870-9222. **Contact:** Manager. **Description:** An executive search firm operating on a retainer basis. **Specializes in the areas of:** Human Resources; Management.

GROS PLASTICS RECRUITERS
155 Franklin Road, Suite 181, Brentwood TN 37027-4646. 615/661-4568. **Toll-free phone:** 800/283-5643. **Fax:** 615/370-8512. **Contact:** Dennis Gros, President. **E-mail address:** careers@plasticsjobs.com. **World Wide Web address:** http://www.plasticsjobs.com. **Description:** An executive search firm operating on both retainer and contingency bases. The firm focuses on placements in blowmolding, injection molding, extrusion, thermoforming, and plastics processing machinery. Client company pays fee. **Specializes in the areas of:** Plastics. **Corporate headquarters location:** This Location. **Other U.S. locations:** Nationwide. **Average salary range of placements:** $50,000 - $100,000.

H R GROUP
404 James Robertson Parkway, Suite 1215, Nashville TN 37219. 615/244-8484. **Fax:** 615/782-4225. **Contact:** Manager. **Description:** An executive search firm. **Specializes in the areas of:** Architecture/Construction; Health/Medical; Management; Manufacturing.

ROBERT HALF INTERNATIONAL ACCOUNTEMPS
7405 Shallowford Road, Suite 320, Chattanooga TN 37421. 423/894-6088. **Contact:** Manager. **World Wide Web address:** http://www.roberthalf.com. **Description:** An executive search firm. Accountemps (also at this location) is a temporary agency that specializes in accounting and financial services. **Corporate headquarters location:** Menlo Park CA. **Other U.S. locations:** Nationwide.

ROBERT HALF INTERNATIONAL ACCOUNTEMPS
402 BNA Drive, Building 100, Suite 410, Nashville TN 37217. 615/360-7900. **Contact:** Manager. **E-mail address:** rhicbna@aol.com. **Description:** An executive search firm. Accountemps (also at this location) is a temporary agency. Management Resources (also at this location) provides temporary business consulting placements. **Specializes in the areas of:** Administration; Computer Science/Software. **Positions commonly filled include:** Computer Programmer; Internet Services Manager; MIS Specialist; Multimedia Designer; Operations Manager; Software Engineer; Systems Analyst; Technical Writer/Editor; Telecommunications Manager. **Corporate headquarters location:** Menlo Park CA. **Other U.S. locations:** Nationwide. **Average salary range of placements:** $30,000 - $50,000. **Number of placements per year:** 1 - 49.

ROBERT HALF INTERNATIONAL ACCOUNTEMPS
6750 Poplar Avenue, Suite 701, Memphis TN 38138. 901/753-7600. **Contact:** Manager. **Description:** An executive search firm. Accountemps (also at this location) provides temporary placements. Management Resources (also at this location) provides temporary business consulting placements. **Corporate headquarters location:** Menlo Park CA. **Other U.S. locations:** Nationwide.

ROBERT HALF INTERNATIONAL ACCOUNTEMPS
1111 Northshore Drive, Suite N525, Knoxville TN 37919. 423/588-6500. **Contact:** Manager. **World Wide**

Web address: http://www.roberthalf.com. **Description:** An executive search firm. Accountemps (also at this location) provides temporary placements. **Specializes in the areas of:** Accounting/Auditing. **Corporate headquarters location:** Menlo Park CA. **Other U.S. locations:** Nationwide.

HEALTHCARE RECRUITERS OF THE MID SOUTH
356 New Byhalia Road, Suite 2, Collierville TN 38017. 901/853-0900. **Fax:** 901/853-6500. **Contact:** Manager. **Description:** An executive search firm. **Specializes in the areas of:** Health/Medical.

HESTER & ASSOCIATES
P.O. Box 4331, Chattanooga TN 37405. 423/265-0148. **Fax:** 423/265-6418. **Contact:** Mike Schoonover, President. **E-mail address:** mschoon500@aol.com. **Description:** An executive search firm operating on a retainer basis. The firm concentrates on industrial/manufacturing environments. Founded in 1984. **Specializes in the areas of:** Computer Science/Software; Engineering; Finance; General Management; Industrial; Manufacturing; Personnel/Labor Relations; Sales; Technical. **Positions commonly filled include:** Aerospace Engineer; Chemical Engineer; Computer Programmer; Credit Manager; Design Engineer; Engineer; General Manager; Human Resources Manager; Industrial Production Manager; Operations/Production Manager; Purchasing Agent/Manager; Quality Control Supervisor; Systems Analyst; Telecommunications Manager. **Average salary range of placements:** More than $50,000. **Number of placements per year:** 50 - 99.

RANDALL HOWARD & ASSOCIATES, INC.
P.O. Box 382397, Memphis TN 38183-2397. 901/754-3333. **Fax:** 901/758-5578. **Contact:** Randall C. Howard, CPC, President. **Description:** An executive search firm that focuses on senior management positions. **Specializes in the areas of:** Accounting; Management; Technical. **Average salary range of placements:** More than $50,000. **Number of placements per year:** 1 - 49.

J&D RESOURCES (JDR)
6555 Quince Road, Suite 425, Memphis TN 38119. 901/753-0500. **Fax:** 901/753-0550. **Contact:** Jill T. Herrin, President. **Description:** An executive search firm. J&D Resources (JDR) provides permanent and contract information systems positions. Founded in 1987. **Specializes in the areas of:** Administration; Computer Science/Software. **Positions commonly filled include:** Computer Programmer; MIS Specialist; Software Engineer; Systems Analyst. **Average salary range of placements:** $30,000 - $50,000. **Number of placements per year:** 50 - 99.

DOROTHY JOHNSON'S CAREER CONSULTANTS
315 Deaderick Street, Suite 2120, Nashville TN 37238. 615/244-4060. **Fax:** 615/255-1074. **Contact:** Manager. **Description:** An executive search firm. **Specializes in the areas of:** Accounting; Administration; Management.

JUST MANAGEMENT SERVICE
1121 North Chucky Pike, Jefferson City TN 37760. 423/475-1188. **Fax:** 423/471-5155. **Contact:** Manager. **Description:** An executive search firm. **Specializes in the areas of:** Management.

KOERNER & ASSOCIATES, INC.
P.O. Box 2126, Brentwood TN 37024. 615/371-6162. **Contact:** Pam L. Koerner, President. **Description:** An executive search firm that handles attorney placement at all levels and for all practice areas, including corporate in-house, management, and financial institutions. Founded in 1989. **Specializes in the areas of:** Legal. **Positions commonly filled include:** Attorney. **Average salary range of placements:** More than $50,000.

LEEDS AND LEEDS
116 Wilson Pike, Suite 205, Brentwood TN 37027. 615/371-1119. **Toll-free phone:** 800/829-9755. **Fax:** 615/371-1225. **Contact:** Manager. **E-mail address:** info@leedsandleeds.com. **World Wide Web address:**
http://www.leedsandleeds.com. **Description:** Leeds and Leeds is an executive search firm. **Specializes in the areas of:** Insurance. **Positions commonly filled include:** Insurance Agent/Broker; Insurance Services Manager.

THE LYNN GROUP, HLF INC.
P.O. Box 158793, Nashville TN 37215-8793. 615/340-0800. **Fax:** 615/340-0974. **Contact:** Heather Lynn Fike, President. **E-mail address:** heather@thelynngroup.com. **World Wide Web address:** http://www.thelynngroup.com. **Description:** An executive search firm. **Specializes in the areas of:** Architecture/Construction; Design; Engineering.

MANAGEMENT RECRUITERS
1117 Trotwood Avenue, Columbia TN 38401. 931/388-5586. **Fax:** 931/380-0615. **Contact:** Office Manager. **Description:** An executive search firm. **Specializes in the areas of:** Automotive. **Corporate headquarters location:** Cleveland OH. **Other U.S. locations:** Nationwide.

MANAGEMENT RECRUITERS
131 Heritage Park Drive, Suite 2, Murfreesboro TN 37129. 615/890-7623. **Fax:** 615/890-9511. **Contact:** Manager. **Description:** An executive search firm. **Specializes in the areas of:** Manufacturing. **Corporate headquarters location:** Cleveland OH. **Other U.S. locations:** Nationwide.

MANAGEMENT RECRUITERS INTERNATIONAL
5495 Winchester Road, Suite 5, Memphis TN 38115. 901/794-3130. **Fax:** 901/794-5671. **Contact:** Wally Watson, General Manager. **Description:** An executive search firm that focuses on logistics management and warehouse/distribution management. **Specializes in the areas of:** Accounting/Auditing; Engineering; Finance; General Management; Industrial; Logistics; Manufacturing; Personnel/Labor Relations; Sales. **Positions commonly filled include:** Accountant/Auditor; Chemical Engineer; Electrical/Electronics Engineer; Financial Analyst; General Manager; Human Resources Manager; Industrial Engineer; Mechanical Engineer; Operations/Production Manager; Quality Control Supervisor; Transportation/Traffic Specialist. **Number of placements per year:** 1 - 49.

MANAGEMENT RECRUITERS OF BRENTWOOD
SALES CONSULTANTS OF BRENTWOOD
7003 Chadwick Drive, Suite 331, Brentwood TN 37027. 615/373-1111. **Fax:** 615/373-0988. **Contact:** Branch Manager. **Description:** An executive search firm. Sales Consultants of Brentwood (also at this location) is a division of Management Recruiters. **Specializes in the areas of:** Accounting/Auditing; Administration; Advertising; Architecture/Construction; Banking; Communications; Computer Hardware/Software; Electrical; Engineering; Finance; Food; General Management; Health/Medical; Insurance; Legal; Manufacturing; Operations Management; Personnel/Labor Relations; Publishing; Retail; Sales; Technical; Textiles; Transportation.

MANAGEMENT RECRUITERS OF CHATTANOOGA NORTH
4808 Hixson Pike, Hixson TN 37343. 423/877-4040. **Fax:** 423/877-4466. **Contact:** Mr. C. E. Ensminger, President. **Description:** An executive search firm operating on a contingency basis. **Specializes in the areas of:** Accounting/Auditing; Administration; Computer Science/Software; Engineering; Finance; Industrial; Manufacturing; Marketing; Personnel/Labor Relations; Sales. **Positions commonly filled include:** Accountant/Auditor; Branch Manager; Budget Analyst; Buyer; Ceramics Engineer; Chemical Engineer; Chemist; Computer Programmer; Design Engineer; Draftsperson; Financial Analyst; General Manager; Human Resources Specialist; Industrial Engineer; Materials Engineer; Mechanical Engineer; Metallurgical Engineer; MIS Specialist; Operations/Production Manager; Purchasing Agent/Manager; Quality Control Supervisor; Software Engineer; Telecommunications Manager. **Other U.S.**

locations: Nationwide. **Average salary range of placements:** $30,000 - $90,000. **Number of placements per year:** 100 - 199.

MANAGEMENT RECRUITERS OF CHATTANOOGA-BRAINERD
SALES CONSULTANTS OF CHATTANOOGA
7010 Lee Highway, Suite 216, Chattanooga TN 37421. 423/894-5500. **Fax:** 423/894-1177. **Contact:** Bill Cooper, General Manager. **Description:** An executive search firm operating on a contingency basis. Sales Consultants (also at this location) provides temporary placements. A third division, CompuSearch, also has an office based at this location. Founded in 1980. **Specializes in the areas of:** Administration; Computer Science/Software; Engineering; General Management; Health/Medical; Manufacturing; Marketing; Pharmaceuticals; Sales; Software Development; Technical; Telecommunications. **Positions commonly filled include:** Chemical Engineer; Chemist; Computer Programmer; Design Engineer; Environmental Engineer; General Manager; Industrial Engineer; Information Systems Consultant; Internet Services Manager; Manufacturer's/Wholesaler's Sales Rep.; Mechanical Engineer; MIS Specialist; Quality Control Supervisor; Services Sales Representative; Software Engineer; Systems Analyst. **Corporate headquarters location:** Cleveland OH. **Other U.S. locations:** Nationwide. **Average salary range of placements:** $40,000 - $110,000. **Number of placements per year:** 100 - 199.

MANAGEMENT RECRUITERS OF CORDOVA
780 Walnut Knoll Lane, Cordova TN 38018. 901/432-1674. **Fax:** 901/432-2674. **Contact:** Eddy Hatcher, Owner/President. **Description:** An executive search firm. **Specializes in the areas of:** Administration; Management; Technical. **Corporate headquarters location:** Cleveland OH. **Other U.S. locations:** Nationwide.

MANAGEMENT RECRUITERS OF FRANKLIN
236 Public Square, Suite 201, Franklin TN 37064-2520. 615/791-4391. **Fax:** 615/791-4769. **Contact:** Roger H. Marriott, President. **Description:** An executive search firm operating on a contingency basis. Founded in 1989. **Specializes in the areas of:** Printing; Publishing. **Positions commonly filled include:** Cost Estimator; Customer Service Representative; General Manager; Operations Manager; Production Manager; Purchasing Agent/Manager; Quality Control Supervisor; Sales Executive; Sales Manager; Sales Representative; Systems Manager; Transportation/Traffic Specialist; Vice President of Sales. **Corporate headquarters location:** Cleveland OH. **Other U.S. locations:** Nationwide. **Average salary range of placements:** More than $50,000. **Number of placements per year:** 1 - 49.

MANAGEMENT RECRUITERS OF JOHNSON CITY
904 Sunset Drive, Suite 9B, Johnson City TN 37604. 423/952-0900. **Contact:** Manager. **Description:** An executive search firm. **Specializes in the areas of:** Management.

MANAGEMENT RECRUITERS OF KNOXVILLE
9050B Executive Park Drive, Suite 16, Knoxville TN 37923. 423/694-1628. **Contact:** Manager. **Description:** An executive search firm. **Specializes in the areas of:** Accounting/Auditing; Administration; Advertising; Architecture/Construction; Banking; Communications; Computer Hardware/Software; Finance; Food; General Management; Health/Medical; Insurance; Legal; Manufacturing; Personnel/Labor Relations; Publishing; Retail; Technical; Textiles; Transportation.

MANAGEMENT RECRUITERS OF LENOIR CITY
530 Highway 321 North, Suite 303, Lenoir City TN 37771. 423/986-3000. **Contact:** Mr. R.S. Strobo, Branch Manager. **Description:** An executive search firm operating on a contingency basis. **Specializes in the areas of:** Engineering; Industrial; Light Industrial; Manufacturing. **Positions commonly filled include:**

Applications Engineer; Design Engineer; Electrical/Electronics Engineer; Industrial Engineer; Industrial Production Manager; Manufacturing Engineer; Mechanical Engineer; Production Manager; Quality Control Supervisor; Sales Engineer.

W.R. McLEOD & ASSOCIATES
201 Thompson Lane, Suite 8A, Nashville TN 37211. 615/333-2969. **Fax:** 615/331-3139. **Contact:** Manager. **Description:** An executive search firm. **Specializes in the areas of:** Computer Science/Software; Food; General Management; Health/Medical; Publishing; Retail; Sales; Secretarial. **Positions commonly filled include:** Computer Programmer; General Manager; Hotel Manager; Management Analyst/Consultant; Management Trainee; Restaurant/Food Service Manager; Services Sales Representative; Systems Analyst. **Average salary range of placements:** $30,000 - $50,000. **Number of placements per year:** 100 - 199.

MEDICAL & DENTAL RESOURCES
1916 Patterson Street, Suite 403, Nashville TN 37203. 615/329-2033. **Contact:** Manager. **Description:** An executive search firm. **Specializes in the areas of:** Dental; Health/Medical.

MEMPHIS LEGAL PERSONNEL SERVICE
One Commerce Square, Suite 1050, Memphis TN 38103. 901/527-3573. **Contact:** Manager. **Description:** An executive search firm. **Specializes in the areas of:** Legal.

RUSSELL MONTGOMERY OI PARTNERS
101 Continental Place, Suite 105, Brentwood TN 37027. 615/377-9603. **Fax:** 615/370-5768. **Contact:** Dennis Russell, Managing Partner. **Description:** A generalist executive search firm.

THE MORGAN GROUP
P.O. Box 121153, Nashville TN 37212. 615/297-5272. **Fax:** 615/297-6945. **Contact:** E. Allen Morgan, Managing Partner. **Description:** An executive search firm. Founded in 1978. **Specializes in the areas of:** Accounting/Auditing; Administration; Finance; General Management; Industrial; Manufacturing. **Positions commonly filled include:** Accountant/Auditor; Bank Officer/Manager; Branch Manager; Budget Analyst; Cost Estimator; Financial Analyst; Financial Services Sales Representative; General Manager; Management Analyst/Consultant; Systems Analyst. **Average salary range of placements:** $30,000 - $50,000. **Number of placements per year:** 1 - 49.

PIRC
1028 Cresthaven Road, Suite 202, Memphis TN 38119. 901/685-2042. **Fax:** 901/685-2729. **Contact:** James Murrell, President. **Description:** An executive search firm. **Specializes in the areas of:** Managed Care.

PERSONNEL LINK
3935 Summer Avenue, Memphis TN 38122. 901/327-9182. **Fax:** 901/324-7603. **Contact:** Mrs. Leonell Klank, Recruiter. **Description:** An executive search firm operating on a contingency basis. Founded in 1993. **Specializes in the areas of:** Accounting/Auditing; Advertising; Engineering; Food; Health/Medical; Insurance; Legal; Manufacturing; Personnel/Labor Relations; Sales; Secretarial; Transportation. **Positions commonly filled include:** Accountant/Auditor; Adjuster; Administrative Manager; Advertising Clerk; Biological Scientist; Blue-Collar Worker Supervisor; Branch Manager; Broadcast Technician; Brokerage Clerk; Budget Analyst; Buyer; Chemist; Chiropractor; Claim Representative; Clerical Supervisor; Clinical Lab Technician; Computer Programmer; Counselor; Credit Manager; Customer Service Representative; Dental Assistant/Dental Hygienist; Dental Lab Technician; Draftsperson; EEG Technologist; EKG Technician; Electrician; Engineer; Financial Analyst; Food Scientist/Technologist; General Manager; Health Services Manager; Hotel Manager; Human Resources Manager; Human Service Worker; Industrial Production

Manager; Insurance Agent/Broker; Landscape Architect; Librarian; Licensed Practical Nurse; Management Trainee; Manufacturer's/Wholesaler's Sales Rep.; Medical Records Technician; Operations/Production Manager; Paralegal; Physical Therapist; Property and Real Estate Manager; Public Relations Specialist; Purchasing Agent/Manager; Quality Control Supervisor; Radiological Technologist; Recreational Therapist; Reporter; Respiratory Therapist; Restaurant/Food Service Manager; Securities Sales Rep.; Services Sales Rep.; Social Worker; Statistician; Surgical Technician; Surveyor; Systems Analyst; Transportation/Traffic Specialist; Travel Agent; Underwriter; Water Transportation Specialist; Wholesale and Retail Buyer. **Average salary range of placements:** $20,000 - $29,999. **Number of placements per year:** 100 - 199.

PHOENIX CONSULTING GROUP
P.O. Box 21060, Chattanooga TN 37424. 423/892-3897. **Fax:** 706/965-3897. **Contact:** Manager. **Description:** An executive search firm that recruits for midwestern automotive firms. **Specializes in the areas of:** Automotive; Rubber.

PHYSICIAN PLACEMENT SERVICE OF AMERICA
906 Loggers Run Trail, Suite B, Franklin TN 37069. 615/662-5435. **Toll-free phone:** 800/359-7421. **Contact:** Dennis Bottomley, Executive Director. **E-mail address:** ppsadb@aol.com. **World Wide Web address:** http://www.physician-placement.com. **Description:** An executive search firm. Founded in 1989. Specializes in the areas of: Health/Medical. **Positions commonly filled include:** Physician. **Corporate headquarters location:** This Location. **Other U.S. locations:** Escondido CA; Acworth GA. **Average salary range of placements:** More than $50,000. **Number of placements per year:** 1 - 49.

PITTMAN GROUP
P.O. Box 1244, Collierville TN 38027. 901/854-6828. **Contact:** Manager. **Description:** An executive search firm. Specializes in the areas of: Information Systems.

QUARLES KELLY ASSOCIATES
813 Ridge Lake Boulevard, Suite 440, Memphis TN 38120. 901/682-5352. **Contact:** Manager. **Description:** An executive search firm that also provides temporary and temp-to-perm placements. **Specializes in the areas of:** Administration; Legal Secretarial; Office Support. **Other U.S. locations:** Southhaven MS.

QUEST INTERNATIONAL
123 Lake Haven Lane, Hendersonville TN 37075. 615/824-8900. **Fax:** 615/264-3333. **Contact:** Bill Griffin, President. **Description:** An executive search firm operating on both retained and contingency bases. **Specializes in the areas of:** Food; Hotel/Restaurant. **Positions commonly filled include:** Controller; General Manager; Hotel Manager; Human Resources Specialist; Marketing Manager; MIS Specialist; Restaurant/Food Service Manager; Sales Executive; Sales Manager. **Corporate headquarters location:** This Location. **Number of placements per year:** 1 - 49.

QUESTAR PARTNERS INC.
100 Winners Circle, Suite 160, Brentwood TN 37027. 615/371-8800. **Fax:** 615/371-8804. **Contact:** Manager. **Description:** An executive search firm that also provides temp-to-perm placements. **Specializes in the areas of:** Accounting; Administration; Computer Operations; Marketing; Office Support; Sales.

RMA SEARCH
1355 Lynnfield Road, Suite 184, Memphis TN 38119. 901/681-0488. **Fax:** 901/763-1828. **Contact:** Manager. **Description:** An executive search firm.

SALES CONSULTANTS
P.O. Box 38328, Memphis TN 38183. 901/751-1995. **Contact:** Wayne Williams, Managing Principal. **E-mail address:** info@saleshunter.com. **World Wide Web address:** http://www.saleshunter.com. **Description:** An

executive search firm operating on a contingency basis. **Specializes in the areas of:** Sales. **Positions commonly filled include:** Account Manager; Account Representative; Sales Engineer; Sales Executive; Sales Manager; Sales Representative. **Average salary range of placements:** More than $50,000. **Number of placements per year:** 50 - 99.

SALES SEARCH INTERNATIONAL
7003 Chadwick Drive, Suite 331, Brentwood TN 37027. 615/373-1111. **Fax:** 615/373-0988. **Contact:** Manager. **Description:** An executive search firm. **Specializes in the areas of:** Sales.

SANFORD ROSE ASSOCIATES - NASHVILLE
9000 Church Street East, Suite 100, Brentwood TN 37027. 615/346-3000. **Fax:** 615/346-3003. **Contact:** Manager. **World Wide Web address:** http://www.sanfordrose.com. **Description:** An executive search firm. **Specializes in the areas of:** Direct Marketing; Graphic Arts; Market Research; Paper; Printing.

SHAW ASSOCIATES, INC.
315 West Main Street, Suite 32, Hendersonville TN 37075. 615/826-6001. **Fax:** 615/826-6002. **Contact:** Manager. **World Wide Web address:** http://www.shawassociates.com. **Description:** An executive search firm. Founded in 1995. **Specializes in the areas of:** Biotechnology; Medical Devices; Pharmaceuticals. **Corporate headquarters location:** Richardson TX.

SOFTWARE RESOURCE CONSULTANTS INC.
P.O. Box 38118, Memphis TN 38183. 901/759-7225. **Fax:** 901/759-1721. **Contact:** Manager. **E-mail address:** src1@bellsouth.net. **Description:** Software Resource Consultants is an executive search firm operating on a contingency basis. **Specializes in the areas of:** Computer Science/Software; Engineering; Information Technology; Technical; Telecommunications; Wireless Communications. **Positions commonly filled include:** Computer Programmer; Database Manager; Design Engineer; Development Manager; Project Manager; Software Engineer; Systems Analyst; Systems Manager; Telecommunications Manager. **Other U.S. locations:** Washington DC. **Average salary range of placements:** More than $50,000. **Number of placements per year:** 1 - 49.

STAFFMARK
5110 Maryland Way, Suite 190, Brentwood TN 37027. 615/371-1400. **Fax:** 615/376-4604. **Contact:** Manager. **Description:** An executive search firm. **Specializes in the areas of:** Accounting; Human Resources; Management; Marketing; Sales.

STEWART & ASSOCIATES INC.
P.O. Box 6004, Kingsport TN 37663. 423/239-7995. **Contact:** Manager. **Description:** A generalist executive search firm.

SUMMERFIELD ASSOCIATES
6555 Quince Road, Suite 311, Memphis TN 38119. 901/753-7068. **Fax:** 901/753-8947. **Contact:** Dottie Summerfield, President. **Description:** An executive search firm.

TECHNICAL RESOURCE ASSOCIATES (TRA)
1127 Sunset Drive, Gallatin TN 37066. 615/824-1444. **Fax:** 615/824-7696. **Contact:** Richard D. Holtz, President. **Description:** An executive search firm operating on both retained and contingency bases. The firm focuses on high-tech, advanced materials industries as well as environmental, safety, and health industries. Founded in 1978. **Specializes in the areas of:** Engineering; General Management; Industrial; Manufacturing; Sales; Technical. **Positions commonly filled include:** Aerospace Engineer; Ceramics Engineer; Chemical Engineer; Chemist; Civil Engineer; Design Engineer; Electrical/Electronics Engineer; Environmental Engineer; General Manager; Industrial Engineer; Industrial Production Manager; Manufacturing Engineer; Materials Engineer; Mechanical Engineer; Metallurgical

Engineer; Operations/Production Manager; Project Manager; Quality Control Supervisor; Science Technologist; Statistician; Structural Engineer. **Average salary range of placements:** More than $30,000. **Number of placements per year:** 1 - 49.

ROBERT WALKER PERSONNEL INC.
P.O. Box 166, Old Hickory TN 37138. 615/847-2311. **Fax:** 615/847-2315. **Contact:** Manager. **Description:** An executive search firm. **Specializes in the areas of:** Manufacturing.

PERMANENT EMPLOYMENT AGENCIES

AAA EMPLOYMENT
5700 Building, Eastgate Center, Suite 102, Chattanooga TN 37411. 423/855-0583. **Contact:** Office Manager. **Description:** A permanent employment agency.

ADVANCED COMPUTER CAREERS
5115 Maryland Way, Brentwood TN 37027. 615/385-3778. **Toll-free phone:** 800/457-5802. **Fax:** 615/292-1661. **Contact:** Edina Frohman, Recruiter. **E-mail address:** accjobs@mindspring.com. **World Wide Web address:** http://www.mindspring.com/~accjobs. **Description:** A permanent employment agency. Client company pays fee. **Specializes in the areas of:** MIS/EDP. **Positions commonly filled include:** Computer Programmer; Computer Technician; Database Administrator; Database Manager; Internet Services Manager; MIS Specialist; Network/Systems Administrator; Software Engineer; SQL Programmer; Systems Analyst; Systems Manager. **Corporate headquarters location:** This Location. **Number of placements per year:** 1 - 49.

ADVANTAGE PERSONNEL INC.
P.O. Box 9878, Chattanooga TN 37412. 423/499-9397. **Contact:** Manager. **Description:** A permanent placement agency.

ARVIE PERSONNEL SERVICES, LLC
1719 West End Avenue, Suite 116 West, Nashville TN 37203. 615/321-9577. **Fax:** 615/321-4949. **Contact:** Warren A. Sawyers, Executive Vice President/General Manager. **Description:** A permanent employment agency that also provides some temporary placements. **Specializes in the areas of:** Accounting; Clerical; Legal; Secretarial. **Positions commonly filled include:** Administrative Assistant; Computer Programmer; Customer Service Representative; Electrical/Electronics Engineer; Paralegal; Sales Executive; Sales Rep.; Secretary; Typist/Word Processor. **Benefits available to temporary workers:** Paid Holidays; Paid Vacation; Training. **Average salary range of placements:** $20,000 - $29,999. **Number of placements per year:** 500 - 999.

CORNERSTONE EMPLOYMENT SERVICES
702 Inverness Avenue, Nashville TN 37204. 615/297-0298. **Contact:** Manager. **Description:** A permanent employment agency. **Specializes in the areas of:** Retail. **Positions commonly filled include:** Retail Manager.

DUNHILL OF MEMPHIS, INC.
5120 Stage Road, Suite 2, Memphis TN 38134. 901/386-2500. **Contact:** Manager. **Description:** A permanent employment agency. **Specializes in the areas of:** Distribution; Engineering; Manufacturing.

EAGLE SYSTEMS
6060 Primacy Parkway, Memphis TN 38119. 901/683-7851. **Contact:** Benny Dix, Recruiter. **Description:** A permanent employment agency. **Specializes in the areas of:** Computer Programming; Computer Science/Software.

ENGINEER ONE, INC.
P.O. Box 23037, Knoxville TN 37933. 423/675-1221. **Toll-free phone:** 800/251-9847. **Contact:** Manager. **Description:** A permanent employment agency that focuses primarily on the placement of engineers and professionals in the chemical processing, electrical/electronic, and mechanical manufacturing industries. **Specializes in the areas of:** Computer Science/Software; Engineering; Food; Industrial; Manufacturing; Sales; Technical. **Positions commonly filled include:** Aerospace Engineer; Agricultural Engineer; Biochemist; Ceramics Engineer; Chemical Engineer; Civil Engineer; Computer Programmer; Electrical/Electronics Engineer; General Manager; Geologist/Geophysicist; Industrial Engineer; Mechanical Engineer; MIS Specialist; Nuclear Engineer; Operations/Production Manager; Petroleum Engineer; Purchasing Agent/Manager; Quality Control Supervisor; Software Engineer; Structural Engineer; Systems Engineer. **Other U.S. locations:** TX. **Average salary range of placements:** More than $50,000. **Number of placements per year:** 100 - 199.

EXPRESS PERSONNEL SERVICES, INC.
8807 Kingston Pike, Suite B, Knoxville TN 37923. 423/531-1720. **Fax:** 423/531-3267. **Contact:** Celia Spinner, Owner. **Description:** A permanent employment agency. **Specializes in the areas of:** Computer Science/Software; Engineering; General Management; Industrial; Manufacturing; Personnel/Labor Relations; Sales; Technical; Transportation. **Positions commonly filled include:** Administrative Manager; Biomedical Engineer; Branch Manager; Chemical Engineer; Clerical Supervisor; Computer Programmer; Construction Contractor; Customer Service Representative; Electrical/Electronics Engineer; Emergency Medical Technician; General Manager; Human Resources Manager; Industrial Engineer; Industrial Production Manager; Management Analyst/Consultant; Mechanical Engineer; Metallurgical Engineer; Operations/Production Manager; Purchasing Agent/Manager; Quality Control Supervisor; Sociologist; Software Engineer; Systems Analyst; Technical Writer/Editor; Transportation/Traffic Specialist. **Number of placements per year:** 1 - 49.

FREIDA JAMES PERSONNEL
3343 Perimeter Hill Drive, Suite 222, Nashville TN 37221. 615/781-4800. **Fax:** 615/781-2853. **Contact:** Freida James, President. **Description:** A permanent employment agency.

MADISON PERSONNEL
1864 Poplar Crest Cove, Memphis TN 38119. 901/761-2660. **Fax:** 901/761-3339. **Contact:** David White, Owner/Manager. **Description:** A permanent employment agency. **Specializes in the areas of:** Accounting/Auditing; Clerical; Computer Science/Software; Engineering; Manufacturing. **Positions commonly filled include:** Accountant/Auditor; Administrative Assistant; Bookkeeper; Chemical Engineer; Credit Manager; Design Engineer; Electrical/Electronics Engineer; Financial Analyst; Industrial Engineer; Legal Secretary; Mechanical Engineer; Medical Secretary; Quality Control Supervisor; Secretary; Stenographer; Systems Analyst. **Average salary range of placements:** More than $50,000. **Number of placements per year:** 50 - 99.

PIERCY EMPLOYMENT SERVICES
386-D Carriage House Drive, Jackson TN 38305. 901/664-4400. **Contact:** Placement Consultant. **Description:** Piercy Employment Services is a permanent employment agency. **Specializes in the areas of:** Administration; Clerical; Data Processing; Industrial; Secretarial; Technical. **Number of placements per year:** 1 - 49.

RASMUSSEN & ASSOCIATES, INC.
P.O. Box 5037, Kingsport TN 37663. 423/239-6664. **Fax:** 423/239-4832. **Contact:** Manager. **Description:** A permanent employment agency that also provides some executive searches on a contingency basis. **Specializes in the areas of:** Accounting/Auditing; Engineering; Finance; General Management; Manufacturing;

Personnel/Labor Relations; Publishing. **Positions commonly filled include:** Accountant/Auditor; Budget Analyst; Buyer; Chemist; Designer; Electrical/ Electronics Engineer; Financial Analyst; General Manager; Human Resources Manager; Industrial Engineer; Mechanical Engineer; Metallurgical Engineer; Nuclear Engineer; Purchasing Agent/Manager; Quality Control Supervisor; Software Engineer. **Number of placements per year:** 1 - 49.

SHILOH CAREERS INTERNATIONAL, INC.
7105 Peach Court, Brentwood TN 37027. 615/373-3090. **Fax:** 615/373-3480. **Contact:** President. **Description:** A permanent employment agency serving the property and casualty insurance industry. **Specializes in the areas of:** Insurance. **Number of placements per year:** 1 - 49.

SNELLING PERSONNEL SERVICES
5721 Marlin Road, Building 6100, Suite 3300, Chattanooga TN 37411. 423/894-1500. **Fax:** 423/894-1507. **Contact:** Mark Spencer, Sales Manager. **Description:** A permanent employment agency that also provides some temporary placements. **Specializes in the areas of:** Accounting/Auditing; Administration; Banking; Computer Science/Software; Engineering; Finance; General Management; Health/Medical; Industrial; Insurance; Manufacturing; Personnel/Labor Relations. **Positions commonly filled include:** Accountant/Auditor; Architect; Bank Officer/Manager; Chemical Engineer; Chemist; Civil Engineer; Computer Programmer; Credit Manager; Customer Service Representative; Design Engineer; Designer; Draftsperson; Education Administrator; Electrical/

Electronics Engineer; Environmental Engineer; Industrial Engineer; Management Analyst/Consultant; Management Trainee; Manufacturer's/Wholesaler's Sales Rep.; Mechanical Engineer; MIS Specialist; Operations/ Production Manager; Personnel Specialist; Physician; Purchasing Agent/Manager; Quality Control Supervisor; Restaurant/Food Service Manager; Software Engineer; Structural Engineer; Systems Analyst; Technical Writer/Editor; Telecommunications Manager; Typist/ Word Processor; Underwriter/Assistant Underwriter. **Corporate headquarters location:** Dallas TX. **Other U.S. locations:** Nationwide. **Average salary range of placements:** $30,000 - $50,000. **Number of placements per year:** 50 - 99.

STAFFINGSOLUTIONS
1801 Downtown West Boulevard, Knoxville TN 37919. 423/690-2311. **Contact:** Manager. **Description:** A permanent employment agency. **Specializes in the areas of:** Accounting/Auditing; Banking; Computer Science/ Software; Finance; Office Support; Technical. **Positions commonly filled include:** Accountant/Auditor; Administrative Assistant; Computer Operator; Computer Programmer; Data Entry Clerk; Engineer; Industrial Designer.

WOOD PERSONNEL SERVICES
1321 Murfreesboro Road, Suite 140, Nashville TN 37217. 615/399-0019. **Contact:** Manager. **Description:** A permanent employment agency. **Specializes in the areas of:** Accounting; Engineering; Information Systems; Information Technology; Manufacturing.

TEMPORARY EMPLOYMENT AGENCIES

A-1 STAFFING & PERSONNEL
10368 Wallace Alley Street, Suite 18, Kingsport TN 37663. 423/279-0788. **Fax:** 423/279-0575. **Contact:** Janice Wininger, Operations Director. **Description:** A temporary agency that also provides some temp-to-perm and permanent placements. The agency places entry-through executive-level positions. **Specializes in the areas of:** Administration; Computer Science/Software; Engineering; Finance; Food; General Management; Health/Medical; Insurance; Legal; Personnel/Labor Relations; Printing; Retail; Sales; Secretarial; Technical. **Positions commonly filled include:** Accountant; Administrative Assistant; Assistant Manager; Clerical Supervisor; Computer Programmer; Controller; Credit Manager; Customer Service Representative; Draftsperson; Electrical/Electronics Engineer; Finance Director; Financial Analyst; General Manager; Human Resources Manager; Management Trainee; Manufacturing Engineer; Mechanical Engineer; Medical Records Technician; MIS Specialist; Paralegal; Production Manager; Project Manager; Secretary; Systems Analyst; Typist/Word Processor. **Benefits available to temporary workers:** Medical Insurance; Paid Vacation. **Corporate headquarters location:** This Location. **Other U.S. locations:** Asheville NC. **Average salary range of placements:** $20,000 - $29,999. **Number of placements per year:** 100 - 199.

ACCOUNTING SOLUTIONS
115 Suburban Road, Knoxville TN 37923. 423/690-0055. **Toll-free phone:** 888/531-9344. **Fax:** 423/690-0055. **Contact:** Carolyn Keziah, Branch Manager. **Description:** A temporary agency that also provides some permanent placements. Client company pays fee. **Specializes in the areas of:** Accounting; Finance. **Positions commonly filled include:** Accountant; Accounting Clerk; Budget Analyst; Credit Manager. **Benefits available to temporary workers:** 401(k); Medical Insurance; Vacation Pay. **Corporate headquarters location:** Denver CO. **Other U.S. locations:** Nationwide. **Average salary range of placements:** $30,000 - $49,999.

AMENITY STAFFING
119 Fourth Street, Lawrenceburg TN 38464. 931/762-0803. **Contact:** Manager. **Description:** A temporary agency. **Specializes in the areas of:** Banking; Construction; Engineering; Food; Industrial; Manufacturing; Secretarial. **Positions commonly filled include:** Electrician; Licensed Practical Nurse; Typist/ Word Processor. **Average salary range of placements:** Less than $20,000. **Number of placements per year:** 200 - 499.

ANGEL MEDICAL PERSONNEL POOL
1326 Eighth Avenue North, Nashville TN 37208. 615/726-0308. **Contact:** Manager. **Description:** A temporary agency. **Specializes in the areas of:** Health/Medical.

COMFORCE SERVICES
302 Wesley Street, Suite 2, Johnson City TN 37601. 423/283-7774. **Contact:** Beth Begley, Account Manager. **Description:** A temporary agency. **Specializes in the areas of:** Technical. **Positions commonly filled include:** Biochemist; Biological Scientist; Ceramics Engineer; Chemist; Food Scientist/Technologist; Materials Engineer; Metallurgical Engineer; Science Technologist. **Benefits available to temporary workers:** 401(k); Medical Insurance; Paid Vacation. **Corporate headquarters location:** New Hyde Park NY. **Other U.S. locations:** Nationwide. **Average salary range of placements:** $20,000 - $29,999. **Number of placements per year:** 100 - 199.

GATEWAY GROUP PERSONNEL, LLC
1770 Kirby Parkway, Suite 216, Memphis TN 38138-7405. 901/756-6050. **Fax:** 901/756-8445. **Contact:** Darlene Murphy, Agency President. **E-mail address:** gateway@gatewaypersonnel.com. **World Wide Web address:** http://www.gatewaypersonnel.com. **Description:** A temporary agency that also provides permanent placements. Client company pays fee. **Specializes in the areas of:** Accounting; Banking; Finance; Health/Medical; MIS/EDP; Secretarial. **Positions commonly filled include:** Accountant; Accounting Supervisor; Administrative Assistant;

Attorney; Auditor; Bank Officer/Manager; Bookkeeper; Budget Analyst; Chief Financial Officer; Commercial Lending Officer; Controller; Cost Estimator; Credit Analyst; Credit Manager; Customer Service Rep.; Employee Benefits Administrator; Finance Director; Financial Analyst; Human Resources Manager; Inventory Control Specialist; Management; Mortgage Banker; Secretary; Tax Specialist. **Benefits available to temporary workers:** Dental Insurance; Medical Insurance. **Corporate headquarters location:** This Location. **Average salary range of placements:** $20,000 - $49,999. **Number of placements per year:** 200 - 499.

HAMILTON-RYKER COMPANY
947 Main Street, Martin TN 38237. 901/587-3161. **Fax:** 901/588-0810. **Contact:** Professional Staffing Manager. **Description:** A temporary agency that also provides some executive searches. **Specializes in the areas of:** Accounting/Auditing; Administration; Architecture/Construction; Computer Science/Software; Engineering; General Management; Industrial; Manufacturing; Personnel/Labor Relations; Technical. **Positions commonly filled include:** Accountant/Auditor; Architect; Budget Analyst; Buyer; Chemical Engineer; Civil Engineer; Computer Programmer; Cost Estimator; Credit Manager; Design Engineer; Designer; Draftsperson; Electrical/Electronics Engineer; Environmental Engineer; Financial Analyst; General Manager; Human Resources Specialist; Industrial Engineer; Industrial Production Manager; Management Analyst/Consultant; Management Trainee; Market Research Analyst; Mechanical Engineer; Metallurgical Engineer; Mining Engineer; MIS Specialist; Operations/Production Manager; Purchasing Agent/Manager; Quality Control Supervisor; Software Engineer; Structural Engineer; Systems Analyst. **Corporate headquarters location:** This Location. **Other area locations:** Memphis TN; Nashville TN; Cleveland TN.

HEALTH STAFF
5100 Poplar Avenue, Suite 117, Memphis TN 38137. 901/761-4878. **Contact:** Manager. **Description:** A temporary and temp-to-perm agency. **Specializes in the areas of:** Health/Medical; Pharmaceuticals.

KELLY SERVICES, INC.
404 BNA Drive, Suite 200, Nashville TN 37217. 615/367-1940. **Fax:** 615/399-2031. **Contact:** Manager. **Description:** A temporary agency that also provides some permanent placements. **Specializes in the areas of:** Accounting; Administration; Computer Science/Software; Marketing; Sales; Secretarial. **Positions commonly filled include:** Accountant; Administrative Assistant; Administrative Manager; Cashier; Claim Representative; Customer Service Representative; Data Entry Clerk; Database Manager; Driver; Medical Records Technician; Paralegal; Secretary; Typist/Word Processor. **Benefits available to temporary workers:** Medical Insurance; Paid Holidays; Paid Vacation. **Corporate headquarters location:** Troy MI. **Other U.S. locations:** Nationwide. **International locations:** Worldwide. **Average salary range of placements:** $20,000 - $29,999. **Number of placements per year:** 1000+.

MANPOWER, INC.
121 Henslee Drive, Suite H, Dickson TN 37055. 615/446-4483. **Fax:** 615/446-4881. **Contact:** Branch Manager. **Description:** A temporary agency. **Specializes in the areas of:** Accounting/Auditing; Administration; Computer Science/Software; Engineering; Food; General Management; Health/Medical; Legal; Manufacturing; Personnel/Labor Relations; Secretarial. **Positions commonly filled include:** Accountant/Auditor; Adjuster; Advertising Clerk; Blue-Collar Worker Supervisor; Branch Manager; Customer Service Representative; Draftsperson; Electrician; Health Services Manager; Human Resources Specialist; Industrial Engineer; Insurance Agent/Broker; Landscape Architect; Management Analyst/Consultant; Management Trainee;

Manufacturer's/Wholesaler's Sales Rep.; Mechanical Engineer; Medical Records Technician; Metallurgical Engineer; Multimedia Designer; Paralegal; Public Relations Specialist; Purchasing Agent/Manager; Quality Control Supervisor; Reporter; Securities Sales Rep.; Software Engineer; Typist/Word Processor. **Benefits available to temporary workers:** Life Insurance; Medical Insurance; Paid Holidays; Paid Vacation; Referral Bonus Plan; Stock Purchase. **Corporate headquarters location:** Milwaukee WI. **Other U.S. locations:** Nationwide. **Number of placements per year:** 500 - 999.

MANPOWER, INC.
1875 Highway 51 Bypass, Suite B, Dyersburg TN 38024. 901/285-3124. **Contact:** Lana Wood, Branch Manager. **Description:** A temporary agency. **Specializes in the areas of:** Accounting/Auditing; Computer Science/Software; Engineering; Industrial; Manufacturing; Personnel/Labor Relations; Sales; Secretarial; Technical. **Positions commonly filled include:** Accountant/Auditor; Administrative Manager; Architect; Bank Officer/Manager; Blue-Collar Worker Supervisor; Budget Analyst; Claim Representative; Clerical Supervisor; Computer Programmer; Credit Manager; Customer Service Rep.; Draftsperson; Electrical/Electronics Engineer; Electrician; General Manager; Hotel Manager; Human Resources Specialist; Industrial Engineer; Library Technician; Mechanical Engineer; Medical Records Technician; MIS Specialist; Public Relations Specialist; Purchasing Agent/Manager; Securities Sales Representative; Services Sales Representative; Typist/Word Processor. **Benefits available to temporary workers:** Paid Holidays; Paid Vacation. **Corporate headquarters location:** Milwaukee WI. **Other U.S. locations:** Nationwide. **Number of placements per year:** 200 - 499.

MANPOWER, INC.
1801 West End Avenue, Suite 100, Nashville TN 37203. 615/327-9922. **Contact:** Branch Manager. **Description:** A temporary agency. **Specializes in the areas of:** Data Processing; Light Industrial; Office Support; Professional; Technical; Telemarketing; Word Processing. **Positions commonly filled include:** Accountant/Auditor; Accounting Clerk; Administrative Assistant; Biological Scientist; Bookkeeper; Chemist; Computer Operator; Customer Service Representative; Designer; Desktop Publishing Specialist; Electrician; Inspector/Tester/Grader; Machine Operator; Material Control Specialist; Order Clerk; Packaging/Processing Worker; Painter; Project Engineer; Proofreader; Receptionist; Research Assistant; Secretary; Software Engineer; Systems Analyst; Technical Writer/Editor; Telemarketer; Typist/Word Processor; Welder. **Benefits available to temporary workers:** Life Insurance; Medical Insurance; Paid Holidays; Paid Vacation. **Corporate headquarters location:** Milwaukee WI. **Other U.S. locations:** Nationwide. **Number of placements per year:** 1000+.

NORRELL SERVICES
1770 Kirby Parkway, Suite 330, Memphis TN 38138. 901/751-0501. **Contact:** Branch Manager. **Description:** A temporary agency. **Specializes in the areas of:** Banking; Clerical; Finance; Insurance; Secretarial. **Positions commonly filled include:** Administrative Assistant; Customer Service Representative; Data Entry Clerk; Receptionist; Secretary; Stenographer. **Number of placements per year:** 1000+.

OLSTEN STAFFING SERVICES
7417 Kingston Pike, Suite 103, Knoxville TN 37919. 423/583-0013. **Toll-free phone:** 800/WORKNOW. **Fax:** 423/583-0448. **Contact:** Larry Marion, Branch Manager. **Description:** A temporary agency. **Specializes in the areas of:** Accounting/Auditing; Administration; Engineering; General Management; Industrial; Legal; Manufacturing; Personnel/Labor Relations; Secretarial; Technical. **Positions commonly filled include:** Accountant/Auditor; Actuary; Administrative Assistant; Administrative Manager; Biomedical Engineer; Blue-

Collar Worker Supervisor; Bookkeeper; Branch Manager; Broadcast Technician; Budget Analyst; Ceramics Engineer; Chemical Engineer; Civil Engineer; Claim Representative; Clerical Supervisor; Clerk; Computer Programmer; Customer Service Rep.; Design Engineer; Draftsperson; Electrical/Electronics Engineer; Environmental Engineer; Factory Worker; General Manager; Human Resources Specialist; Industrial Engineer; Industrial Production Manager; Internet Services Manager; Legal Secretary; Light Industrial Worker; Manufacturer's/Wholesaler's Sales Rep.; Market Research Analyst; Materials Engineer; Mechanical Engineer; Medical Secretary; Metallurgical Engineer; MIS Specialist; Paralegal; Quality Control Supervisor; Receptionist; Secretary; Software Engineer; Stenographer; Structural Engineer; Systems Analyst; Technical Writer/Editor; Typist/Word Processor. **Benefits available to temporary workers:** Life Insurance; Medical Insurance; Paid Vacation. **Corporate headquarters location:** Melville NY. **Other U.S. locations:** Nationwide. **Number of placements per year:** 1000+.

SPECIAL COUNSEL
AMICUS LEGAL STAFFING INC.
1900 Church Street, Suite 425, Signature Center, Nashville TN 37203. 615/320-7700. **Contact:** Manager. **Description:** A temporary agency that also provides some permanent placements and executive searches. **Specializes in the areas of:** Legal.

CONTRACT SERVICES FIRMS

ADECCO/TAD TECHNICAL SERVICES
3900 New Covington Pike, Suite 112, Memphis TN 38128. 901/385-1127. **Contact:** Manager. **Description:** A contract services firm. **Specializes in the areas of:** Technical.

AMERICAN TECHNICAL ASSOCIATES, INC.
P.O. Box 10844, Knoxville TN 37918. 423/588-5751. **Toll-free phone:** 877/ATA-JOBS. **Fax:** 423/584-4138. **Contact:** Allen A. McGill, Manager of Technical Recruiting. **E-mail address:** atajobs@atatech.com. **World Wide Web address:** http://www.atatech.com. **Description:** A contract services firm that also provides some temporary and permanent placements. Founded in 1963. Client company pays fee. **Specializes in the areas of:** Computer Science/Software; Engineering; Industrial. **Positions commonly filled include:** Architect; AS400 Programmer Analyst; Chemical Engineer; Civil Engineer; Computer Engineer; Computer Operator; Computer Programmer; Computer Support Technician; Computer Technician; Database Administrator; Design Engineer; Draftsperson; Electrical/Electronics Engineer; Electrician; Environmental Engineer; Industrial Engineer; Manufacturing Engineer; Mechanical Engineer; Network Administrator; Quality Assurance Engineer; Software Engineer; Systems Analyst. **Benefits available to temporary workers:** 401(k); Paid Holidays. **Corporate**

headquarters location: This Location. **Number of placements per year:** 200 - 499.

CDI INFORMATION SYSTEMS
2 Union Square, Suite 610, Chattanooga TN 37402. 423/266-9720. **Fax:** 423/266-9737. **Contact:** Manager. **Description:** A contract services firm. **Specializes in the areas of:** Technical. **Corporate headquarters location:** Philadelphia PA. **Other U.S. locations:** Nationwide. **International locations:** Worldwide.

C.J. STAFFING SERVICES
7010 Lee Highway, Suite 214, Chattanooga TN 37421. 423/899-0866. **Toll-free phone:** 800/264-5519. **Fax:** 423/894-3819. **Contact:** Manager. **Description:** A contract services firm. This is the personnel placement division of C.J. Enterprises, Inc., which provides consulting, administrative management, and technical services. **Specializes in the areas of:** Health/Medical; Personnel/Labor Relations. **Positions commonly filled include:** Blue-Collar Worker Supervisor; Customer Service Rep.; Draftsperson; Human Resources Specialist; Management Analyst/Consultant; Management Trainee; Pharmacist; Physician; Radio/TV Announcer; Registered Nurse; Systems Analyst. **Benefits available to temporary workers:** 401(k); Paid Holidays; Paid Vacation. **Number of placements per year:** 200 - 499.

CAREER/OUTPLACEMENT COUNSELING FIRMS

BRADEN RESUME SOLUTIONS
108 La Plaza Drive, Hendersonville TN 37075. 615/822-3317. **Fax:** 615/826-9611. **Contact:** Carolyn S. Braden, CPRW, Owner. **E-mail address:** bradenres@aol.com. **Description:** A firm that provides resume development and secretarial services. Braden Resume & Secretarial provides writing, editing, design, and typesetting of professional job search materials for entry-level to senior management candidates, skilled trades and services, career transitions, and recent college graduates.

COCHRAN ADVERTISING RESUME SERVICE
1430 Madison Street, Clarksville TN 37040. 931/551-4074. **Contact:** Jim Watson, Resume Writer. **Description:** A resume writing service that focuses on developing resumes to highlight skills and experience. Cochran Advertising Resume Service utilizes in-depth interviews to identify job skills and ascertain goals and objectives. The company is professionally certified to

create resumes, and its resume package includes data on interview preparation and an ongoing resume updating service.

MS. SECRETARY
131 Third Avenue North, Franklin TN 37064. 615/794-3223. **Contact:** Manager. **Description:** Ms. Secretary provides resume and secretarial services. Assistance in the development and writing of resumes is provided by a Certified Professional Resume Writer.

PENCIL FOUNDATION
421 Great Circle Road, Suite 100, Nashville TN 37228. 615/242-3167. **Fax:** 615/254-6748. **Contact:** Program Director. **Description:** A career/outplacement counseling service. PENCIL (Public Education and Nashville Citizens Involved in Leadership) also provides skills training. **Number of placements per year:** 200 - 499.

EXECUTIVE SEARCH FIRMS

ABA EXECUTIVE SEARCH
P.O. Box 35806, Houston TX 77235. 713/661-9909.
Fax: 713/661-5246. **Contact:** Allan Butler, Owner.
Description: An executive search firm. **Specializes in the areas of:** General Management; Oil and Gas; Sales.

ACCOUNTANTS EXECUTIVE SEARCH ACCOUNTANTS ON CALL
1990 Post Oak Boulevard, Suite 720, Houston TX 77056. 713/961-5603. **Fax:** 713/961-3256. **Contact:** Rich Thompson, Branch Manager. **Description:** An executive search firm. Accountants On Call (also at this location) is a temporary agency. **Specializes in the areas of:** Accounting/Auditing; Finance. **Corporate headquarters location:** Saddle Brook NJ. **International locations:** Worldwide.
Other U.S. locations:
- 2828 Routh Street, Suite 690, Dallas TX 75201. 214/979-9001.
- 5550 LBJ Freeway, Suite 310, Dallas TX 75240. 972/980-4184.
- 1612 Summit Avenue, Suite 420, Fort Worth TX 76102. 817/870-1800.

ACCUSEARCH TECHNIFIND
5959 Gateway West, Suite 601, El Paso TX 79925. 915/778-9312. **Fax:** 915/778-9314. **Contact:** Manager. **Description:** An executive search firm. Technifind (also at this location) is an executive search firm specializing in high-tech placements. **Specializes in the areas of:** Manufacturing.

ACKERMAN JOHNSON INC.
333 North Sam Houston Parkway East, Suite 1210, Houston TX 77060-2417. 281/999-8879. **Fax:** 281/999-7570. **Contact:** Frederick W. Stang, President. **E-mail address:** jobs@ackermanjohnson.com. **World Wide Web address:** http://www.ackermanjohnson.com. **Description:** An executive search firm. Founded in 1981. **Specializes in the areas of:** Advertising; Computer Science/Software; Engineering; Food; General Management; Industrial; Manufacturing; Personnel/Labor Relations; Sales. **Positions commonly filled include:** Aerospace Engineer; Biochemist; Branch Manager; Chemical Engineer; Chemist; Civil Engineer; Computer Programmer; Customer Service Rep.; Design Engineer; Electrical/Electronics Engineer; Environmental Engineer; General Manager; Industrial Engineer; Management Analyst/Consultant; Management Trainee; Manufacturer's/Wholesaler's Sales Rep.; Mechanical Engineer; Petroleum Engineer; Public Relations Specialist; Restaurant/Food Service Manager; Services Sales Representative; Software Engineer; Stationary Engineer; Structural Engineer; Systems Analyst; Telecommunications Manager. **Average salary range of placements:** More than $50,000. **Number of placements per year:** 100 - 199.

ACTION RECRUITING SERVICES
2525 North Loop West, Suite 480, Houston TX 77008. 713/629-9740. **Contact:** M. Ken Smith III, President. **Description:** An executive search firm. **Specializes in the areas of:** Restaurant. **Positions commonly filled include:** Restaurant/Food Service Manager. **Average salary range of placements:** $30,000 - $50,000. **Number of placements per year:** 100 - 199.

ADVANCED SYSTEMS CONSULTING
12801 North Central Expressway, Suite 460, Dallas TX 75243. 972/726-9664. **Fax:** 972/726-9881. **Contact:** Manager. **E-mail address:** opportunities@asccareers.com. **World Wide Web address:** http://www.asccareers.com. **Description:** An executive search firm that also provides contract and contract-to-hire services. Advanced Systems Consulting is a division of MAGIC (Management Alliance Group of Independent Companies). **Specializes**

in the areas of: Information Technology; Management. **Other area locations:** Austin TX.

AGRI-ASSOCIATES
131 Degan Street, Suite 203, Lewisville TX 75057. 972/221-7568. **Fax:** 972/221-1409. **Contact:** Lawrence W. Keeley, Owner/Manager. **Description:** An executive search firm. **Specializes in the areas of:** Accounting/Auditing; Administration; Advertising; Agriculture; Biology; Engineering; Finance; Food; General Management; Manufacturing; Personnel/Labor Relations; Sales. **Positions commonly filled include:** Accountant/Auditor; Administrative Manager; Agricultural Engineer; Bank Officer/Manager; Biochemist; Biological Scientist; Blue-Collar Worker Supervisor; Branch Manager; Budget Analyst; Buyer; Chemical Engineer; Chemist; Civil Engineer; Computer Programmer; Construction Contractor; Credit Manager; Customer Service Rep.; Design Engineer; Editor; Environmental Engineer; Financial Analyst; Food Scientist/Technologist; Forester/Conservation Scientist; General Manager; Human Resources Specialist; Industrial Engineer; Landscape Architect; Licensed Practical Nurse; Management Trainee; Mechanical Engineer; MIS Specialist; Purchasing Agent/Manager; Quality Control Supervisor; Restaurant/Food Service Manager; Systems Analyst; Transportation/Traffic Specialist; Underwriter/Assistant Underwriter; Veterinarian. **Corporate headquarters location:** Kansas City KS. **Average salary range of placements:** $30,000 - $50,000. **Number of placements per year:** 1 - 49.

ALBRECHT & ASSOCIATES EXECUTIVE SEARCH
10700 Richmond Avenue, Suite 217, Houston TX 77042. 713/784-7444. **Fax:** 713/784-5049. **Contact:** Mrs. Franke M. Albrecht, President. **E-mail address:** albrecht@albrecht-assoc.com. **World Wide Web address:** http://www.albrecht-assoc.com. **Description:** An executive search firm operating on both retainer and contingency bases. **Specializes in the areas of:** Administration; Biology; Computer Science/Software; Engineering; Health/Medical; Technical. **Positions commonly filled include:** Biochemist; Biological Scientist; Biomedical Engineer; Chemical Engineer; Chemist; Civil Engineer; Clinical Lab Tech.; Geologist/Geophysicist; Management Analyst/Consultant; Mechanical Engineer; MIS Specialist; Operations/Production Manager; Petroleum Engineer; Pharmacist; Structural Engineer; Systems Analyst. **Corporate headquarters location:** Cleveland OH. **Average salary range of placements:** More than $50,000. **Number of placements per year:** 100 - 199.

ALEXANDER & COMPANY
8308 Barber Oak Drive, Plano TX 75025. 214/495-8998. **Toll-free phone:** 877/495-8300. **Fax:** 214/495-8999. **Contact:** Penny Alexander, Principal. **E-mail address:** penny@dhc.net. **Description:** An executive search firm. **Specializes in the areas of:** Advertising; Computer Hardware/Software; Marketing; Multimedia; Public Relations. **Positions commonly filled include:** Internet Services Manager; Multimedia Designer; Public Relations Specialist; Strategic Relations Manager; Technical Writer/Editor. **Number of placements per year:** 1 - 49.

ALPHA RESOURCE GROUP
1916 Brabant Drive, Plano TX 75025. 972/527-1616. **Contact:** Manager. **Description:** An executive search firm. **Specializes in the areas of:** Hotel/Restaurant.

AMERICAN RESOURCES
4420 FM 1960 West, Suite 129, Houston TX 77068. 281/444-6515. **Fax:** 281/580-7838. **Contact:** Terri Sanford, General Manager. **E-mail address:** terris31@aol.com. **Description:** An executive search firm operating on a

contingency basis. Client company pays fee. **Specializes in the areas of:** Accounting; Architecture/Construction; Banking; Computer Science/Software; Engineering; Finance; Food; General Management; Industrial; Marketing; MIS/EDP; Personnel/Labor Relations; Sales; Transportation. **Positions commonly filled include:** Account Manager; Account Rep.; Accountant; Bank Officer/Manager; Buyer; Chemical Engineer; Chemist; Chief Financial Officer; Computer Engineer; Computer Programmer; Computer Support Technician; Construction Contractor; Controller; Cost Estimator; Credit Manager; Database Administrator; Database Manager; Design Engineer; Electrical/Electronics Engineer; Environmental Engineer; Finance Director; Financial Analyst; Geologist/Geophysicist; Human Resources Manager; Industrial Engineer; Industrial Production Manager; Manufacturing Engineer; Marketing Manager; Mechanical Engineer; Metallurgical Engineer; MIS Specialist; Network/Systems Administrator; Operations Manager; Production Manager; Project Manager; Purchasing Agent/Manager; Quality Assurance Engineer; Quality Control Supervisor; Sales Engineer; Sales Executive; Sales Manager; Sales Representative. **Corporate headquarters location:** This Location. **Average salary range of placements:** $50,000 - $100,000. **Number of placements per year:** 1 - 49.

APEX COMPUTER PLACEMENTS INC.
616 North Bell Avenue, Denton TX 76201. 940/565-0658. **Contact:** Manager. **Description:** An executive search firm. **Specializes in the areas of:** Computer Hardware/Software.

AREND & ASSOCIATES, INC.
P.O. Box 821311, Houston TX 77282-1311. 713/827-7800. **Contact:** Lewis Arend, President. **Description:** An executive search firm.

ATWOOD PROFESSIONAL SEARCH
P.O. Box 58411, Houston TX 77258. 281/333-1061. **Contact:** Dan Atwood, President. **Description:** An executive search firm. **Specializes in the areas of:** Engineering; Oil and Gas.

AUDIT PROFESSIONALS INTERNATIONAL
3312 Woodford Drive, Suite 400, Arlington TX 76013-1139. 817/277-0888. **Contact:** Keith Malcolm, CPA/Vice President. **Description:** Audit Professionals International is an executive search firm that also provides contract services. Founded in 1987. **Specializes in the areas of:** Accounting/Auditing; Administration; Finance; Information Systems. **Positions commonly filled include:** Accountant/Auditor; Actuary; Internet Services Manager; Telecommunications Manager. **Average salary range of placements:** More than $50,000. **Number of placements per year:** 50 - 99.

MARILYN AUSTIN & ASSOCIATES PERSONNEL SERVICES
11999 Katy Freeway, Suite 290, Houston TX 77079. 281/493-5706. **Fax:** 281/759-7676. **Contact:** Marilyn Austin, Owner. **Description:** An executive search firm. **Specializes in the areas of:** Banking; Finance; Health/Medical.

AUSTIN GROUP
11511 Katy Freeway, Suite 290, Houston TX 77079. 281/497-8595. **Fax:** 281/597-0099. **Contact:** Manager. **Description:** An executive search firm. **Specializes in the areas of:** Accounting/Auditing; Chemicals; Economics; Electronics; Engineering; Tax.

AUSTIN McGREGOR INTERNATIONAL
12005 Ford Road, Suite 540, Dallas TX 75234-7247. 972/488-0500. **Fax:** 972/488-0535. **Contact:** Chip McCreary, President. **E-mail address:** jobs@amidallas.com. **World Wide Web address:** http://www.amidallas.com. **Description:** An executive search firm operating on a retainer basis. Founded in 1987. **Specializes in the areas of:** Consumer Products; Industrial; Technical. **Other U.S. locations:** San Diego CA; St. Louis MO.

B.G.A. & ASSOCIATES
100 Congress Avenue, 18th Floor, Austin TX 78704. 512/912-1900. **Fax:** 512/916-0436. **Contact:** Manager. **E-mail address:** bgaassoc@pop.mindspring.com. **World Wide Web address:** http://www.bgaassoc.com. **Description:** An executive search firm that also offers some temporary and temp-to-perm placements. Founded in 1990. **Specializes in the areas of:** Finance. **Other U.S. locations:** Santa Monica CA.

BALDWIN & COMPANY
5858 Westheimer Boulevard, Suite 100, Houston TX 77057. 713/977-2300. **Fax:** 713/977-2381. **Contact:** Manager. **Description:** An executive search firm. **Specializes in the areas of:** Accounting/Auditing; Finance.

KAYE BASSMAN INTERNATIONAL CORP.
18333 Preston Road, Suite 500, Dallas TX 75252. 972/931-5242. **Fax:** 972/931-9683. **Contact:** Manager. **World Wide Web address:** http://www.kbic.com. **Description:** An executive search firm. **Specializes in the areas of:** Health/Medical; Information Technology.

R. GAINES BATY ASSOCIATES, INC.
12750 Merritt Drive, Suite 990, Lockbox 199, Dallas TX 75251. 972/386-7900. **Fax:** 972/387-2224. **Contact:** R. Gaines Baty, President. **E-mail address:** rgba@rgba.com. **Description:** An executive search firm offering MIS management and information technology consulting positions, as well as bilingual accounting and auditing positions. **Specializes in the areas of:** Computer Science/Software; Finance; MIS/EDP. **Positions commonly filled include:** Accountant/Auditor; Management Analyst/Consultant; MIS Specialist; Systems Analyst; Telecommunications Manager. **Average salary range of placements:** More than $50,000. **Number of placements per year:** 1 - 49.

BENCHMARK PROFESSIONALS
P.O. Box 1212, Leander TX 78646. 512/259-5666. **Fax:** 512/259-5670. **Contact:** Mr. J.B. Pearson, Owner. **Description:** An executive search firm. **Specializes in the areas of:** Engineering; Health/Medical; Manufacturing; Technical. **Positions commonly filled include:** Biological Scientist; Biomedical Engineer; Chemical Engineer; Chemist; Electrical/Electronics Engineer; General Manager; Health Services Manager; Industrial Engineer; Mechanical Engineer; Operations/Production Manager; Physician; Quality Control Supervisor; Registered Nurse.

BEST/WORLD ASSOCIATES
505 West Abram Street, Arlington TX 76010. 817/861-0000. **Toll-free phone:** 800/749-2846. **Fax:** 817/459-2378. **Contact:** G. Tim Best, President. **E-mail address:** jobbank@bestworld.com. **World Wide Web address:** http://www.bestworld.com. **Description:** An executive search firm operating on a retainer basis. **Specializes in the areas of:** Banking; Computer Science/Software; Engineering; Finance; Food; Manufacturing; Personnel/Labor Relations; Sales. **Positions commonly filled include:** Accountant/Auditor; Chemical Engineer; Economist; Electrical/Electronics Engineer; Environmental Engineer; Financial Analyst; Food Scientist/Technologist; Human Resources Specialist; Management Analyst/Consultant; Market Research Analyst; Mechanical Engineer; MIS Specialist; Quality Control Supervisor; Software Engineer; Statistician; Systems Analyst. **Corporate headquarters location:** This Location. **Other U.S. locations:** AZ. **Average salary range of placements:** More than $100,000. **Number of placements per year:** 50 - 99.

BILSON & HAZEL INTERNATIONAL HAZEL STAFFING
5800 East Campus Circle, Suite 12A, Irving TX 75063. 972/753-1193. **Fax:** 972/753-0969. **Contact:** Frederick Sagoe, President. **Description:** An executive search firm that also offers temporary and contract services. Hazel Staffing (also at this location) provides temp-to-perm administrative staffing services. **Specializes in the areas**

of: Computer Science/Software; Personnel/Labor Relations; Sales. **Positions commonly filled include:** Administrative Manager; Branch Manager; Claim Representative; Computer Programmer; Design Engineer; Electrical/Electronics Engineer; Human Resources Specialist; Manufacturer's/Wholesaler's Sales Rep.; Market Research Analyst; MIS Specialist; Software Engineer; Technical Writer/Editor; Telecommunications Manager. **Benefits available to temporary workers:** Dental Insurance; Medical Insurance. **Average salary range of placements:** More than $50,000. **Number of placements per year:** 50 - 99.

BIOSOURCE INTERNATIONAL
1878 Hilltop Drive, Suite 100, Lewisville TX 75077-2114. 972/317-7060. **Fax:** 972/317-0500. **Contact:** Ric J. Favors, Principal. **E-mail address:** mail@biosourceinternational.com. **World Wide Web address:** http://www.biosourceinternational.com. **Description:** An executive search firm. **Specializes in the areas of:** Biotechnology; Health/Medical; Pharmaceuticals; Scientific; Technical. **Positions commonly filled include:** Biochemist; Biological Scientist; Biomedical Engineer; Chemical Engineer; Chemist; Chief Executive Officer; Compliance Analyst; Computer Programmer; Electrical/Electronics Engineer; General Manager; Management Analyst/Consultant; Mechanical Engineer; MIS Specialist; Multimedia Designer; Physician; President; Production Manager; Quality Assurance Engineer; Quality Control Supervisor; Science Technologist; Software Engineer; Statistician; Systems Analyst; Technical Writer/Editor. **Corporate headquarters location:** This Location. **Other U.S. locations:** Carlsbad CA; Sarasota FL; Greensboro NC. **Average salary range of placements:** More than $50,000. **Number of placements per year:** 1 - 49.

MARTIN BIRNBACH & ASSOCIATES
15150 Preston Road, Suite 300, Dallas TX 75248. 972/490-5627. **Contact:** Manager. **Description:** An executive search firm. **Specializes in the areas of:** Sales.

THE HOWARD C. BLOOM CO.
INTERIM LEGAL PROFESSIONALS
5000 Quorum Drive, Suite 550, Dallas TX 75240. 972/385-6455. **Fax:** 972/385-1006. **Contact:** Howard Bloom, President. **Description:** An executive search firm. Interim Legal Professionals (also at this location) provides permanent placements. **Specializes in the areas of:** Legal. **Positions commonly filled include:** Attorney. **Number of placements per year:** 1 - 49.

BOLES & ASSOCIATES
1701 North Collins Boulevard, Suite 200, Richardson TX 75080. 972/480-0660. **Fax:** 972/480-9886. **Contact:** Terry C. Boles, Managing Partner. **E-mail address:** bolesassoc@aol.com. **Description:** An executive search firm operating on a retainer basis. **Specializes in the areas of:** Administration; Engineering; General Management; Human Resources; Sales. **Positions commonly filled include:** Telecommunications Manager. **Average salary range of placements:** More than $50,000. **Number of placements per year:** 1 - 49.

BOND & ASSOCIATES
8509 Fair Haven Court, Fort Worth TX 76179. 817/236-3549. **Contact:** Manager. **Description:** An executive search firm. **Specializes in the areas of:** Engineering; Health/Medical; Information Technology.

BORCHERT ASSOCIATES
17430 Campbell Road, Suite 111, Dallas TX 75252. 972/818-2801. **Toll-free phone:** 888/818-2801. **Fax:** 972/818-2777. **Contact:** Gregory Borchert, President. **E-mail address:** greg@glborchert.com. **World Wide Web address:** http://www.glborchert.com. **Description:** An executive search firm. Founded in 1987. **Specializes in the areas of:** Manufacturing; Metals.

BORREL PERSONNEL
P.O. Box 31900-386, Houston TX 77231-1900. 713/541-1328. **Contact:** Manager. **Description:** An executive

search firm. **Specializes in the areas of:** Accounting/Auditing; Finance; Health/Medical; Real Estate; Software Development.

BRIDGE PERSONNEL
6510 Abrams Road, Comerica Bank Building, Suite 540, Dallas TX 75231. 214/340-7055. **Contact:** Jim Peeler, CPA/Owner. **Description:** An executive search firm operating on both retainer and contingency bases. **Specializes in the areas of:** Accounting/Auditing; Administration; Computer Science/Software; Finance; Information Systems. **Positions commonly filled include:** Accountant/Auditor; Computer Programmer; Financial Analyst; Software Engineer; Systems Analyst; Telecommunications Manager.

BROOKLEA & ASSOCIATES, INC.
12200 Ford Road, Suite 108, Dallas TX 75234. 972/484-9400. **Contact:** Recruiter. **Description:** An executive search firm operating on a contingency basis. **Specializes in the areas of:** Accounting/Auditing; Architecture; Construction; Art/Design; Finance; Health/Medical; Sales; Secretarial. **Positions commonly filled include:** Accountant/Auditor; Architect; Draftsperson; Emergency Medical Technician; Health Services Manager; Landscape Architect; Licensed Practical Nurse; Medical Records Technician; Occupational Therapist; Physical Therapist; Physician; Recreational Therapist; Registered Nurse; Respiratory Therapist; Services Sales Rep.; Surgical Technician; Surveyor; Veterinarian. **Number of placements per year:** 100 - 199.

D. BRUSH & ASSOCIATES
11811 Charles Street, Houston TX 77041. 713/849-9800. **Contact:** Ms. D. Brush, Owner. **Description:** An executive search firm. **Specializes in the areas of:** Computer Hardware/Software.

BUCKLEY GROUP
15851 Dallas Parkway, Suite 675, Dallas TX 75248. 972/490-1722. **Contact:** Manager. **Description:** An executive search firm. **Specializes in the areas of:** High-Tech; Marketing; Sales.

BUNDY-STEWART ASSOCIATES, INC.
13601 Preston Road, Suite 107W, Dallas TX 75240. 972/458-0626. **Fax:** 972/661-2670. **Contact:** Carolyn Stewart, Owner. **Description:** An executive search firm operating on a contingency basis. **Specializes in the areas of:** Accounting/Auditing; Administration; Computer Science/Software; Engineering; Industrial; Insurance; Manufacturing; Personnel/Labor Relations; Real Estate; Sales; Telecommunications. **Positions commonly filled include:** Accountant/Auditor; Aircraft Mechanic/Engine Specialist; Attorney; Buyer; Computer Programmer; Credit Manager; Customer Service Rep.; Design Engineer; Draftsperson; Electrical/Electronics Engineer; Human Resources Specialist; Industrial Engineer; Industrial Production Manager; Market Research Analyst; Mechanical Engineer; MIS Specialist; Operations/Production Manager; Purchasing Agent/Manager; Quality Control Supervisor; Securities Sales Representative; Software Engineer; Systems Analyst; Telecommunications Manager.

BURGESON HOSPITALITY SEARCH
13300 Old Blanco Road, Suite 201, San Antonio TX 78216. 210/493-1237. **Fax:** 210/492-9921. **Contact:** Tom Burgeson, President. **Description:** An executive search firm. Founded in 1979. **Specializes in the areas of:** Hotel/Restaurant. **Positions commonly filled include:** Hotel Manager. **Number of placements per year:** 50 - 99.

C.G. & COMPANY
5050 East University, Suite 9B, Odessa TX 79762. 915/362-7681. **Fax:** 915/362-3578. **Contact:** Cathy George, CPC/Owner. **Description:** An executive search firm operating on both retainer and contingency bases. **Specializes in the areas of:** Computer Science/Software; Engineering; Manufacturing; Technical. **Positions commonly filled include:** Accountant/Auditor;

Administrative Manager; Advertising Clerk; Aerospace Engineer; Agricultural Engineer; Aircraft Mechanic/ Engine Specialist; Architect; Attorney; Bank Officer/ Manager; Blue-Collar Worker Supervisor; Branch Manager; Brokerage Clerk; Budget Analyst; Buyer; Chemical Engineer; Chemist; Civil Engineer; Clerical Supervisor; Computer Programmer; Construction Contractor; Cost Estimator; Counselor; Credit Manager; Customer Service Representative; Design Engineer; Designer; Draftsperson; Electrical/Electronics Engineer; Electrician; Environmental Engineer; Financial Analyst; General Manager; Geologist/Geophysicist; Human Resources Specialist; Industrial Engineer; Industrial Production Manager; Management Analyst/Consultant; Management Trainee; Manufacturer's/Wholesaler's Sales Rep.; Market Research Analyst; Mechanical Engineer; Medical Records Technician; Metallurgical Engineer; Mining Engineer; MIS Specialist; Multimedia Designer; Occupational Therapist; Operations/Production Manager; Paralegal; Petroleum Engineer; Physical Therapist; Physician; Public Relations Specialist; Purchasing Agent/ Manager; Quality Control Supervisor; Radio/TV Announcer/Broadcaster; Radiological Technologist; Recreational Therapist; Registered Nurse; Respiratory Therapist; Restaurant/Food Service Manager; Securities Sales Rep.; Services Sales Representative; Software Engineer; Speech-Language Pathologist; Systems Analyst; Technical Writer/Editor; Telecommunications Manager; Travel Agent; Typist/Word Processor. **Average salary range of placements:** More than $50,000. **Number of placements per year:** 100 - 199.

CAD TECHNOLOGY, INC.
1111 Wilcrest Green, Suite 450, Houston TX 77042. 713/785-2411. **Fax:** 713/785-1625. **Contact:** Marlene Flores, Staffing Coordinator. **Description:** An executive search firm operating on a contingency basis. **Specializes in the areas of:** Architecture/Construction; Computer Science/Software; Engineering. **Positions commonly filled include:** Architect; Buyer; Chemical Engineer; Civil Engineer; Computer Programmer; Construction and Building Inspector; Cost Estimator; Design Engineer; Designer; Draftsperson; Electrical/Electronics Engineer; Environmental Engineer; Geologist/Geophysicist; Industrial Engineer; Mechanical Engineer; Mining Engineer; MIS Specialist; Operations/Production Manager; Petroleum Engineer; Quality Control Supervisor; Software Engineer; Structural Engineer; Systems Analyst; Technical Writer/Editor; Telecommunications Manager; Transportation/Traffic Specialist. **Number of placements per year:** 100 - 199.

CAP ASSOCIATES
15303 Dallas Parkway, Suite 230, Dallas TX 75248. 972/458-4700. **Toll-free phone:** 800/893-1550x2027. **Fax:** 972/458-4711. **Contact:** Recruiter. **E-mail address:** capassoc@ix.netcom.com. **World Wide Web address:** http://www.capassociates.com. **Description:** An executive search firm. **Specializes in the areas of:** Health/Medical; Information Technology.

CARPENTER & ASSOCIATES
11551 Forest Central Drive, Suite 305, Dallas TX 75243. 214/691-6585. **Fax:** 214/691-6838. **Contact:** Elsie Carpenter, President. **Description:** An executive search firm. **Specializes in the areas of:** Advertising; Fashion; Personnel/Labor Relations; Retail. **Positions commonly filled include:** Buyer; Retail Manager; Retail Merchandiser. **Number of placements per year:** 1 - 49.

CHAMPION PERSONNEL SERVICE
8326 Wind Willow Drive, Houston TX 77040-1447. 713/937-6160. **Fax:** 713/896-0543. **Contact:** Dee Jones, Consultant. **E-mail address:** djones1052@aol.com. **Description:** An executive search firm operating on a contingency basis. Client company pays fee. **Specializes in the areas of:** Accounting; Administration; Architecture/Construction; Construction; Engineering; General Management; Industrial. **Positions commonly filled include:** Accountant; Administrative Assistant; Administrative Manager; Assistant Manager; Biochemist; Biological Scientist; Biomedical Engineer;

Branch Manager; Chemical Engineer; Chemist; Chief Financial Officer; Civil Engineer; Clerical Supervisor; Construction Contractor; Controller; Cost Estimator; Customer Service Rep.; Design Engineer; Electrical/ Electronics Engineer; Environmental Engineer; General Manager; Human Resources Manager; Industrial Engineer; Industrial Production Manager; Manufacturing Engineer; Marketing Manager; Mechanical Engineer; Metallurgical Engineer; MIS Specialist; Operations Manager; Production Manager; Project Manager; Purchasing Agent/Manager; Quality Assurance Engineer; Quality Control Supervisor; Secretary; Typist/Word Processor; Vice President. **Average salary range of placements:** $50,000 - $100,000. **Number of placements per year:** 1 - 49.

COMPUTER PROFESSIONALS UNLIMITED
13612 Midway Road, Suite 333, Dallas TX 75244. 972/233-1773. **Fax:** 972/233-9619. **Contact:** V.J. Zapotocky, Owner/President. **E-mail address:** zipzap@onramp.net. **Description:** An executive search firm that also provides contract services. Founded in 1978. **Specializes in the areas of:** Computer Science/Software; Engineering; Information Technology. **Positions commonly filled include:** Computer Programmer; Electrical/Electronics Engineer; Internet Services Manager; MIS Specialist; Software Engineer; Systems Analyst; Technical Writer/Editor; Telecommunications Manager. **Average salary range of placements:** More than $50,000. **Number of placements per year:** 50 - 99.

CORPORATE SEARCH INC.
3028 Lubbock Avenue, Fort Worth TX 76109. 817/926-0320. **Toll-free phone:** 800/429-1763. **Fax:** 817/926-1610. **Contact:** John S. Gramentine, President. **Description:** An executive search firm. **Specializes in the areas of:** Computer Science/Software; Food; Personnel/Labor Relations; Retail; Sales. **Positions commonly filled include:** Branch Manager; General Manager; Human Resources Specialist; Management Trainee; Public Relations Specialist; Services Sales Representative; Software Engineer; Systems Analyst; Telecommunications Manager. **Average salary range of placements:** More than $50,000. **Number of placements per year:** 200 - 499.

CRAIG SEARCH
901 Waterfall Way, Suite 107, Richardson TX 75080. 972/644-3264. **Fax:** 972/644-4065. **Contact:** Edward C. Nemec, President. **Description:** An executive search firm. **Specializes in the areas of:** Food. **Positions commonly filled include:** Branch Manager; Buyer; General Manager. **Number of placements per year:** 50 - 99.

DDR, INC.
4925 Greenville Avenue, Suite 660, Dallas TX 75206-4014. 214/361-4608. **Contact:** Account Executive. **E-mail address:** ddrdal@gte.net. **Description:** An executive search firm. **Specializes in the areas of:** Technical. **Positions commonly filled include:** Computer Animator; Computer Operator; Computer Programmer; Database Manager; Financial Analyst; Hardware Engineer; Operations Manager; Project Manager; Software Engineer; Systems Analyst; Technical Writer/Editor. **Benefits available to temporary workers:** Dental Insurance; Life Insurance; Medical Insurance.

DFM & ASSOCIATES
14001 Dallas Parkway, Suite 1200, Dallas TX 75240. 972/934-6504. **Fax:** 972/934-6505. **Contact:** Denise M. Frost, President. **Description:** An executive search firm. **Specializes in the areas of:** Legal. **Positions commonly filled include:** Attorney; Legal Secretary; Paralegal. **Number of placements per year:** 100 - 199.

DKS & ASSOCIATES
P.O. Box 69, Katy TX 77492. 281/395-6300. **Fax:** 800/398-3113. **Contact:** Manager. **Description:** An executive search firm. **Specializes in the areas of:** Food.

DAHER & ASSOCIATES INSURANCE SEARCH SPECIALISTS, INC.
5311 Kirby Drive, Suite 200, Houston TX 77005. 713/520-8261. **Toll-free phone:** 800/458-9176. **Fax:** 713/520-0526. **Contact:** Liz Daher, President. **E-mail address:** daherinc@aol.com. **Description:** An executive search firm operating on both retainer and contingency bases. Client company pays fee. **Specializes in the areas of:** Insurance; Risk Management. **Positions commonly filled include:** Account Rep.; Accountant; Branch Manager; Chief Financial Officer; Claim Representative; Consultant; Controller; Financial Analyst; Fund Manager; Insurance Agent/Broker; Loss Prevention Specialist; Marketing Specialist; MIS Specialist; Technical Support Representative; Underwriter/Assistant Underwriter. **Corporate headquarters location:** This Location. **Other U.S. locations:** Nationwide. **Average salary range of placements:** More than $50,000. **Number of placements per year:** 200 - 499.

DAMON & ASSOCIATES, INC.
333 West Campbell Road, Richardson TX 75080. 214/696-6990. **Fax:** 214/696-6993. **Contact:** Dick Damon, President. **Description:** An executive search firm. Founded in 1978. **Specializes in the areas of:** Sales. **Average salary range of placements:** $30,000 - $50,000. **Number of placements per year:** 50 - 99.

THE DANBROOK GROUP
4100 Spring Valley Road, Suite 700, Dallas TX 75244. 972/392-0057. **Contact:** Anne Kennedy, Senior Partner. **Description:** An executive search firm operating on a contingency basis. **Specializes in the areas of:** Accounting/Auditing; Banking; Finance; General Management; Insurance. **Positions commonly filled include:** Accountant/Auditor; Adjuster; Bookkeeper; Chief Financial Officer; Claim Representative; Credit Manager; Customer Service Representative; Finance Director; Financial Analyst; Insurance Agent/Broker; Sales Representative; Underwriter/Assistant Underwriter. **Average salary range of placements:** More than $50,000. **Number of placements per year:** 100 - 199.

DENSON & ASSOCIATES
3100 Wesleyan, Suite 300, Houston TX 77027. 713/993-9191. **Fax:** 713/993-9911. **Contact:** Manager. **Description:** An executive search firm. **Specializes in the areas of:** Oil and Gas. **Positions commonly filled include:** Petroleum Engineer.

DILWORTH & WOOLRIDGE INC.
12 Greenway Plaza, Suite 1100, Houston TX 77046. 713/521-2800. **Contact:** Manager. **Description:** An executive search firm. **Specializes in the areas of:** Legal.

C. MICHAEL DIXON ASSOCIATES, INC.
P.O. Box 293371, Lewisville TX 75029. 972/317-0608. **Fax:** 972/317-0349. **Contact:** Mike Dixon, President. **E-mail address:** cmdixon@flash.net. **Description:** An executive search firm. **Specializes in the areas of:** Chemicals; Engineering; Manufacturing; Petrochemical; Technical. **Positions commonly filled include:** Chemical Engineer; Electrical/Electronics Engineer; Industrial Engineer; Mechanical Engineer; Systems Analyst. **Average salary range of placements:** More than $50,000. **Number of placements per year:** 1 - 49.

DMARK GROUP
6205 Turtle Point Drive, Austin TX 78746. 512/328-9808. **Fax:** 214/853-5283. **Contact:** Manager. **World Wide Web address:** http://www.dmarkgroup.com. **Description:** An executive search firm. **Specializes in the areas of:** Computer Programming; High-Tech.

JOHN A. DOMINO & ASSOCIATES
2121 East Broadway Street, Suite F, Pearland TX 77581. 281/485-2595. **Fax:** 281/485-3239. **Contact:** Manager. **E-mail address:** jadomino@argohouston.com. **World Wide Web address:** http://www.johnadomino.com. **Description:** An executive search firm. **Specializes in the areas of:** Health/Medical.

DUNHILL PROFESSIONAL SEARCH
P.O. Box 3114, McAllen TX 78502-3114. 956/687-9531. **Contact:** Lloyd Steele, President. **E-mail address:** lfsteele@juno.com. **Description:** An executive search firm operating on a contingency basis. **Specializes in the areas of:** Engineering; Food; Industrial; Manufacturing; Technical. **Positions commonly filled include:** Applications Engineer; Buyer; Chemical Engineer; Controller; Design Engineer; Electrical/Electronics Engineer; Environmental Engineer; Human Resources Manager; Industrial Engineer; Industrial Production Manager; Manufacturing Engineer; Mechanical Engineer; Production Manager; Purchasing Agent/Manager; Quality Control Supervisor. **Corporate headquarters location:** Hauppauge NY. **Other area locations:** 10303 Northwest Freeway, Suite 520, Houston TX 77092. 713/956-1146; 1301 South Bowen Road, Suite 370, Arlington TX 76013. 817/265-2291.. **Other U.S. locations:** Nationwide. **Average salary range of placements:** $30,000 - $50,000. **Number of placements per year:** 1 - 49.

E*ONLINE LEARNING RECRUITERS
14232 Marsh Lane, PMB 406, Addison TX 75001. 972/490-9171. **Contact:** Manager. **Description:** An executive search firm. **Specializes in the areas of:** Internet Development; Internet Marketing.

EAI HEALTHCARE STAFFING SOLUTIONS
3120 Southwest Freeway, Suite 215, Houston TX 77098. 713/529-1001. **Fax:** 713/529-9589. **Contact:** Manager. **Description:** An executive search firm. **Specializes in the areas of:** Health/Medical.

EDP COMPUTER SERVICES
4600 Post Oak Place, Suite 203, Houston TX 77027. 713/960-1717. **Fax:** 713/960-0607. **Contact:** Manager. **Description:** An executive search firm. **Specializes in the areas of:** Computer Science/Software; Information Systems; Information Technology.

EISSLER & ASSOCIATES
26214 Oak Ridge Drive, The Woodlands TX 77380. 281/367-1052. **Fax:** 281/292-6489. **Contact:** Manager. **Description:** An executive search firm. **Specializes in the areas of:** Plastics; Sales; Telecommunications.

ELLIOT ASSOCIATES INC.
5025 Burnet Road, Suite 202, Austin TX 78756. 512/454-0477. **Contact:** Manager. **Description:** An executive search firm. **Specializes in the areas of:** Hotel/Restaurant.

THE ELSWORTH GROUP
12910 Queens Forest, San Antonio TX 78230. 210/493-7211. **Contact:** Manager. **Description:** An executive search firm. **Specializes in the areas of:** Computer Science/Software; Engineering; General Management; Industrial; Manufacturing; Sales; Technical; Transportation. **Positions commonly filled include:** Aerospace Engineer; Aircraft Mechanic/Engine Specialist; Biomedical Engineer; Chemical Engineer; Civil Engineer; Computer Programmer; Cost Estimator; Designer; Draftsperson; Electrical/Electronics Engineer; General Manager; Industrial Engineer; Management Analyst/Consultant; Manufacturer's/Wholesaler's Sales Rep.; Mechanical Engineer; Metallurgical Engineer; Nuclear Engineer; Operations/Production Manager; Petroleum Engineer; Physicist; Production Manager; Purchasing Agent/Manager; Quality Control Supervisor; Software Engineer; Structural Engineer; Systems Analyst; Technical Writer/Editor. **Number of placements per year:** 1 - 49.

THE ENERGISTS
10260 Westheimer Boulevard, Suite 300, Houston TX 77042. 713/781-6881. **Fax:** 713/781-2998. **Contact:** Alex Preston, President. **E-mail address:** search@energists.com. **World Wide Web address:** http://www.energists.com. **Description:** An executive search firm. **Specializes in the areas of:** Engineering; Management; Oil and Gas. **Positions commonly filled include:**

Geologist/Geophysicist; Petroleum Engineer; Senior Management. **Number of placements per year:** 50 - 99.

ENERGY PERSONNEL
P.O. Box 52200, Houston TX 77027. 713/621-2580. **Toll-free phone:** 888/228-2580. **Fax:** 888/229-2580. **Contact:** Recruiter. **World Wide Web address:** http://www.energypersonnel.com. **Description:** An executive search firm. Founded in 1978. **Specializes in the areas of:** Electrical; Oil and Gas.

ENGINEERING MANAGEMENT STAFF RECRUITERS
12801 North Central Expressway, Suite 470, Dallas TX 75243. 972/239-6572. **Fax:** 972/239-6590. **Contact:** Scott Higby, Manager. **E-mail address:** opportunities@emsr.com. **World Wide Web address:** http://www.emsr.com. **Description:** An executive search firm. Engineering Management Staff Recruiters is a division of MAGIC (Management Alliance Group of Independent Companies). **Specializes in the areas of:** Engineering. **Other U.S. locations:** Raleigh NC.

EPPA, INC.
1953 Branch Hollow, Carrollton TX 75007. 972/394-9668. **Contact:** Manager. **E-mail address:** eppa@eppainc.com. **World Wide Web address:** http://www.eppainc.com. **Description:** An executive search firm. **NOTE:** This firm does not accept unsolicited resumes. Please only respond to advertised openings. **Specializes in the areas of:** Printing.

EXECUTEAM
5858 Westheimer Boulevard, Suite 600, Houston TX 77057. 713/952-6760. **Fax:** 713/952-0755. **Contact:** Laura Bowen, Operations Manager. **Description:** An executive search firm. **Specializes in the areas of:** Accounting/Auditing; Clerical; Executives; Legal; Office Support; Secretarial.

THE EXECUTIVE CONSULTING GROUP
701 North Post Oak Road, Suite 610, Houston TX 77024. 713/686-9500. **Fax:** 713/686-9599. **Contact:** Manager. **Description:** An executive search firm operating on a contingency basis. **Specializes in the areas of:** Banking; Finance. **Positions commonly filled include:** Accountant/Auditor; Bank Officer/Manager; Budget Analyst; Financial Analyst; Management Analyst/Consultant.

EXECUTIVE RESTAURANT SEARCH PINNACLE SEARCH GROUP
2925 LBJ Freeway, Suite 253, Dallas TX 75234. 972/484-8600. **Contact:** Brian Blocker, Partner. **Description:** An executive search firm. Pinnacle Search Group (also at this location) is the agency's food sales division. **Specializes in the areas of:** Restaurant.

EXECUTIVE SEARCH INTERNATIONAL
1700 Alma Drive, Suite 370, Plano TX 75075. 972/424-4714. **Fax:** 972/424-5314. **Contact:** Ed Nalley, Owner. **E-mail address:** mail@esihbc.com. **World Wide Web address:** http://www.esihbc.com. **Description:** An executive search firm operating on both retainer and contingency bases. Client company pays fee. **Specializes in the areas of:** Consumer Products; Food; Marketing; Sales. **Positions commonly filled include:** Account Manager; Market Research Analyst; Marketing Manager; Sales Executive; Sales Manager. **Corporate headquarters location:** This Location. **Average salary range of placements:** $50,000 - $100,000. **Number of placements per year:** 50 - 99.

EXECUTIVE SOURCE INTERNATIONAL
16500 San Pedro Avenue, Suite 295, San Antonio TX 78232. 210/494-0103. **Contact:** Warren Cook, Owner. **Description:** An executive search firm operating on both retainer and contingency bases. **Specializes in the areas of:** Biotechnology; Pharmaceuticals. **Positions commonly filled include:** Chemical Engineer; Civil Engineer; Clinical Lab Technician; Electrical/Electronics Engineer; Environmental Engineer; Industrial Engineer;

Mechanical Engineer; Operations/Production Manager; Quality Assurance Engineer; Quality Control Supervisor; Regulatory Affairs Director. **Average salary range of placements:** More than $50,000. **Number of placements per year:** 1 - 49.

OTIS FAULKNER & ASSOCIATES INC.
2628 Windsor Place, Plano TX 75075. 972/423-1712. **Contact:** Manager. **Description:** An executive search firm. **Specializes in the areas of:** Medical Sales and Marketing.

FINANCIAL SEARCH CONSULTANTS
5599 San Felipe Road, Suite 850, Houston TX 77056. 713/877-1396. **Fax:** 713/621-0862. **Contact:** Manager. **E-mail address:** opportunities@fscjobs.com. **World Wide Web address:** http://www.fscjobs.com. **Description:** An executive search firm that also provides some temporary and contract placements. Financial Search Consultants is a division of MAGIC (Management Alliance Group of Independent Companies). **Specializes in the areas of:** Accounting/Auditing; Finance. **Positions commonly filled include:** Accountant; Auditor; Controller; Cost Accountant; Credit Analyst; Financial Analyst; Financial Consultant; Tax Specialist. **Other area locations:** Dallas TX.

CLAIRE FONTAINE & ASSOCIATES
701 Brazos Street, Suite 495, Austin TX 78701. 512/320-1400. **Contact:** Manager. **Description:** An executive search firm. **Specializes in the areas of:** Administration; Clerical.

FOODPRO RECRUITERS, INC.
14526 Jones-Maltsberger, Suite 210, San Antonio TX 78247. 210/494-9272. **Fax:** 210/494-9662. **Contact:** Richard W. King, Executive Recruiter. **E-mail address:** kingrh@txdirect.net. **Description:** An executive search firm operating on both retainer and contingency bases. Client company pays fee. **Specializes in the areas of:** Distribution; Engineering; Food; Pharmaceuticals; Production; Purchasing; Research and Development; Warehousing. **Positions commonly filled include:** Account Manager; Chemical Engineer; Controller; Electrical/Electronics Engineer; Financial Analyst; Food Scientist/Technologist; Industrial Engineer; Manufacturing Engineer; Marketing Manager; Marketing Specialist; Mechanical Engineer; Quality Assurance Engineer; Systems Manager. **Average salary range of placements:** $30,000 - $100,000. **Number of placements per year:** 50 - 99.

F-O-R-T-U-N-E PERSONNEL CONSULTANTS
5403 Everhart Road, Suite 54 PMB, Corpus Christi TX 78411. 361/852-3836. **Contact:** Manager. **Description:** An executive search firm operating on a contingency basis. **Specializes in the areas of:** Engineering; Manufacturing. **Positions commonly filled include:** Aerospace Engineer; Chemical Engineer; Chemist; Design Engineer; Electrical/Electronics Engineer; Mechanical Engineer. **Corporate headquarters location:** New York NY. **Average salary range of placements:** $30,000 - $50,000. **Number of placements per year:** 1 - 49.

F-O-R-T-U-N-E PERSONNEL CONSULTANTS OF SAN ANTONIO
10924 Vance Jackson Road, Suite 303, San Antonio TX 78230. 210/690-9797. **Fax:** 210/696-6909. **Contact:** Jim Morrisey, CPC/President. **E-mail address:** fpcsat@fpcsat.com. **World Wide Web address:** http://www.fpcsat.com. **Description:** An executive search firm operating on both contingency and retainer bases. **Specializes in the areas of:** Engineering; Industrial; Information Technology; Manufacturing; MIS/EDP; Quality Assurance. **Positions commonly filled include:** Design Engineer; Electrical/Electronics Engineer; Industrial Engineer; Mechanical Engineer; Software Engineer. **Corporate headquarters location:** New York NY. **Other U.S. locations:** Nationwide. **Average salary range of placements:** More than $50,000. **Number of placements per year:** 50 - 99.

FOX-MORRIS ASSOCIATES
5400 LBJ Freeway, Suite 1445, Dallas TX 75240. 972/404-8044. **Contact:** Manager. **Description:** An executive search firm that places upper-level managers. **Specializes in the areas of:** Human Resources; Sales.

ABEL M. GONZALEZ & ASSOCIATES
P.O. Box 681845, San Antonio TX 78268. 210/695-5555. **Fax:** 210/695-8955. **Contact:** Abel Gonzalez, General Manager. **Description:** An executive search firm operating on both retainer and contingency bases. **Specializes in the areas of:** Advertising; Banking; Food; General Management; Industrial; Manufacturing; Personnel/Labor Relations; Sales. **Positions commonly filled include:** Account Manager; Account Rep.; Accountant; Advertising Executive; Auditor; Bank Officer/Manager; Branch Manager; Chemical Engineer; Chemist; Civil Engineer; Computer Programmer; Environmental Engineer; Finance Director; Financial Analyst; Food Scientist/Technologist; General Manager; Human Resources Manager; Industrial Engineer; Industrial Production Manager; Manufacturing Engineer; Marketing Manager; Mechanical Engineer; Operations Manager; Production Manager; Public Relations Specialist; Sales Engineer; Sales Executive; Sales Rep.; Systems Analyst; Transportation/Traffic Specialist; Vice President. **Corporate headquarters location:** This Location. **Average salary range of placements:** More than $50,000. **Number of placements per year:** 1 - 49.

GRIFFIN ANDERSON & ASSOCIATES
1631 Dorchester Drive, Suite 104-A, Plano TX 75075. 972/612-0188. **Contact:** Manager. **Description:** An executive search firm. **Specializes in the areas of:** Sales.

H.P.R. HEALTH STAFF
1600 East Pioneer Parkway, Suite 340, Arlington TX 76010-6562. 817/261-3355. **Fax:** 817/543-3155. **Contact:** Vera E. Harris, CPC/Owner. **E-mail address:** vharris@iamerica.net. **Description:** An executive search firm. H.P.R. Health Staff operates on a contingency basis. **Specializes in the areas of:** Health/Medical. **Positions commonly filled include:** Chief Financial Officer; Clinical Lab Technician; Controller; Dental Assistant/Dental Hygienist; Dentist; Dietician/Nutritionist; EEG Technologist; EKG Technician; Environmental Engineer; Health Services Manager; Human Resources Manager; Licensed Practical Nurse; Medical Records Tech.; Nuclear Medicine Technologist; Occupational Therapist; Pharmacist; Physical Therapist; Physician; Psychologist; Radiological Technologist; Registered Nurse; Respiratory Therapist; Speech-Language Pathologist; Surgical Technician. **Average salary range of placements:** $30,000 - $50,000.

HR SEARCH
12801 North Central Expressway, Suite 220, Dallas TX 75243. 972/458-8077. **Fax:** 972/458-0143. **Contact:** Manager. **E-mail address:** opportunities@hr-jobs.com. **World Wide Web address:** http://www.hr-jobs.com. **Description:** An executive search firm. HR Search is a division of MAGIC (Management Alliance Group of Independent Companies). **Specializes in the areas of:** Customer Service; Human Resources; Office Support.

ROBERT HALF INTERNATIONAL
RHI MANAGEMENT RESOURCES
1300 Post Oak Boulevard, Suite 300, Houston TX 77056. 713/623-4700. **Fax:** 713/623-6782. **Recorded jobline:** 713/993-2504. **Contact:** Manager. **E-mail address:** rhishou@aol.com. **Description:** An executive search firm. RHI Management Resources (also at this location) is a permanent employment agency. **Specializes in the areas of:** Accounting/Auditing; Administration; Banking; Computer Science/Software; Finance; Secretarial. **Positions commonly filled include:** Accountant/Auditor; Bank Officer/Manager; Budget Analyst; Clerical Supervisor; Computer Programmer; Credit Manager; Customer Service Rep.; Financial Analyst; Internet Services Manager; Management Analyst/Consultant; Market Research Analyst; MIS Specialist; Systems Analyst; Typist/Word Processor.

Benefits available to temporary workers: Holiday Bonus; Medical Insurance; Paid Vacation; Vision Plan. **Corporate headquarters location:** Menlo Park CA. **Other U.S. locations:** Nationwide. **Average salary range of placements:** $30,000 - $50,000. **Number of placements per year:** 500 - 999.

HARAGAN ASSOCIATES
4925 Greenville Avenue, Suite 1105, Dallas TX 75206. 214/363-3634. **Contact:** Mr. Pat W. Haragan, Principal/Owner. **Description:** An executive search firm operating on a retainer basis. **Specializes in the areas of:** Biology; General Management; Health/Medical; Manufacturing; Sales; Technical. **Positions commonly filled include:** Biochemist; Biological Scientist; Biomedical Engineer; Chemist; Clinical Lab Technician; Food Scientist/Technologist; General Manager; Health Services Manager; Human Resources Specialist; Nuclear Medicine Technologist; Occupational Therapist; Pharmacist; Physical Therapist; Physician; Quality Control Supervisor; Registered Nurse; Veterinarian. **Average salary range of placements:** More than $50,000. **Number of placements per year:** 1 - 49.

HEALTH NETWORK USA
5902 Smoke Glass Trail, Dallas TX 75252. **Toll-free phone:** 800/872-0212. **Fax:** 972/818-9395. **Contact:** David J. Elliott, President. **E-mail address:** hninfo@hnusa.com. **Description:** An executive search firm. **Specializes in the areas of:** Health/Medical. **Positions commonly filled include:** Clinical Lab Technician; Dental Assistant/Dental Hygienist; Dental Lab Technician; Dentist; Dietician/Nutritionist; EEG Technologist; EKG Technician; Health Services Manager; Human Resources Manager; Licensed Practical Nurse; Medical Records Technician; Nuclear Medicine Technologist; Occupational Therapist; Pharmacist; Physical Therapist; Physician; Psychologist; Public Relations Specialist; Purchasing Agent/Manager; Radiological Technologist; Recreational Therapist; Registered Nurse; Respiratory Therapist; Social Worker; Speech-Language Pathologist; Surgical Technician. **Number of placements per year:** 50 - 99.

HEALTH PROFESSIONALS OF AMERICA
P.O. Box 34829, Houston TX 77234. 281/481-9923. **Fax:** 281/481-9922. **Contact:** Joseph Balesky, CEO. **Description:** An executive search firm operating on a contingency basis. **Specializes in the areas of:** Health/Medical. **Positions commonly filled include:** Accountant/Auditor; Biomedical Engineer; Claim Rep.; Clerical Supervisor; Clinical Lab Technician; Computer Programmer; Dietician/Nutritionist; Education Administrator; EEG Technologist; EKG Technician; Financial Analyst; Health Services Manager; Licensed Practical Nurse; Medical Records Technician; MIS Specialist; Nuclear Medicine Technologist; Occupational Therapist; Pharmacist; Physical Therapist; Physician; Psychologist; Public Relations Specialist; Registered Nurse; Respiratory Therapist; Restaurant/Food Service Manager; Speech-Language Pathologist; Surgical Technician; Systems Analyst; Typist/Word Processor. **Average salary range of placements:** More than $50,000. **Number of placements per year:** 1 - 49.

HEALTHCARE RECRUITERS OF HOUSTON
14015 Southwest Freeway, Building 3, Sugarland TX 77478. 281/340-2700. **Fax:** 281/340-2720. **Contact:** James Tipton, President. **Description:** An executive search firm. **Specializes in the areas of:** Health/Medical; Sales. **Positions commonly filled include:** Biological Scientist; Branch Manager; Chemist; Dentist; Dietician/Nutritionist; General Manager; Health Services Manager; Licensed Practical Nurse; Medical Records Technician; Occupational Therapist; Pharmacist; Physical Therapist; Physician; Registered Nurse; Respiratory Therapist; Social Worker; Veterinarian. **Number of placements per year:** 100 - 199.

HEDMAN & ASSOCIATES
3312 Woodford, Suite 200-400, Arlington TX 76013-1139. 817/277-0888. **Contact:** Kent R. Hedman, Owner.

Description: An executive search firm. **Specializes in the areas of:** Accounting/Auditing; Finance; MIS/EDP.

HERNDON & ASSOCIATES
5100 Westheimer Road, Suite 200, Houston TX 77056. 713/968-6577. **Contact:** Manager. **Description:** An executive search firm. **Specializes in the areas of:** Finance; Legal; Technical.

KEN HERST HOTEL EXECUTIVE SEARCH AND CONSULTING
6750 West Loop South, Suite 940, Bellaire TX 77401. 713/660-0008. **Fax:** 713/660-0009. **Contact:** Ken Herst, Owner. **Description:** An executive search firm. Client company pays fee. **Specializes in the areas of:** Hotel/Restaurant. **Positions commonly filled include:** Accountant; General Manager; Hotel Manager; Human Resources Manager; Property and Real Estate Manager. **Average salary range of placements:** $30,000 - $90,000. **Number of placements per year:** 1 - 49.

HORN & ASSOCIATES
P.O. Box 151944, Arlington TX 76015. 817/465-3463. **Contact:** Brian Horn, Owner. **Description:** An executive search firm. **Specializes in the areas of:** Health/Medical.

HOUSTON CREATIVE CONNECTIONS
7026 Old Katy Road, Suite 300, Houston TX 77024. 713/861-1780. **Toll-free phone:** 800/361-6152. **Contact:** Manager. **World Wide Web address:** http://www. houstoncreative.com. **Description:** An executive search firm that also provides temporary, temp-to-perm, and contract placements. Founded in 1985. **Specializes in the areas of:** Advertising; Art/Design; Engineering; Printing; Publishing; Technical. **Positions commonly filled include:** Advertising Clerk; Civil Engineer; Computer Animator; Computer Operator; Computer Programmer; Database Manager; Draftsperson; Graphic Artist; Graphic Designer; Internet Services Manager; MIS Specialist; Multimedia Designer; Software Engineer; Systems Analyst; Systems Manager; Tech. Writer/Editor. **Corporate headquarters location:** This Location. **Average salary range of placements:** $30,000 - $50,000. **Number of placements per year:** 50 - 99.

THE HUMAN ELEMENT OF BUSINESS, INC.
307 Texas Avenue, El Paso TX 79901. 915/544-5698. **Fax:** 915/534-7738. **Contact:** Pam Fishell, Search Manager. **E-mail address:** humanele@swbell.net. **Description:** An executive search firm operating on both retainer and contingency bases. The firm also offers resume and career counseling services. Client company pays fee. **Positions commonly filled include:** Account Manager; Account Rep.; Accountant; Administrative Assistant; AS400 Programmer Analyst; Assistant Manager; Attorney; Auditor; Bank Officer/Manager; Branch Manager; Budget Analyst; Buyer; Chief Financial Officer; Clerical Supervisor; Computer Operator; Computer Programmer; Computer Support Technician; Controller; Counselor; Customer Service Rep.; Database Administrator; Database Manager; Finance Director; Financial Analyst; General Manager; Graphic Artist; Graphic Designer; Human Resources Manager; Industrial Engineer; Industrial Production Manager; Licensed Practical Nurse; Manufacturing Engineer; Marketing Manager; Marketing Specialist; Mechanical Engineer; Medical Records Technician; MIS Specialist; Network/Systems Administrator; Nurse Practitioner; Occupational Therapist; Operations Manager; Pharmacist; Physical Therapist; Production Manager; Project Manager; Purchasing Agent/Manager; Quality Assurance Engineer; Quality Control Supervisor; Registered Nurse; Respiratory Therapist; Sales Executive; Sales Manager; Sales Representative; Secretary; Social Worker; Speech-Language Pathologist; SQL Programmer; Systems Analyst; Systems Manager; Technical Writer/Editor; Telecommunications Manager; Transportation/Traffic Specialist. **Corporate headquarters location:** This Location. **Other U.S. locations:** Austin TX. **Average salary range of placements:** $30,000 - $49,999. **Number of placements per year:** 1 - 49.

HUNTER & MICHAELS
7502 Greenville Avenue, Suite 500, Dallas TX 75231. 214/750-4666. **Fax:** 214/750-4476. **Contact:** President. **Description:** An executive search firm operating on both retainer and contingency bases. Client company pays fee. **Specializes in the areas of:** Marketing; Sales. **Positions commonly filled include:** Market Research Analyst; Marketing Manager; Sales Executive; Sales Manager. **Corporate headquarters location:** This Location. **Other U.S. locations:** Nationwide. **Average salary range of placements:** $50,000 - $100,000. **Number of placements per year:** 1 - 49.

HYMAN & ASSOCIATES
P.O. Box 8943, The Woodlands TX 77387-8943. 281/292-1969. **Contact:** Manager. **Description:** An executive search firm. **Specializes in the areas of:** Human Resources; Operations Management; Sales.

INFORMATION SYSTEMS CONSULTING CORP.
North Central Plaza III, 12801 North Central Expressway, Suite 250, Dallas TX 75243-1712. 972/490-1881. **Toll-free phone:** 800/877-1881. **Fax:** 972/490-4429. **Contact:** Jim Henry, Recruiter. **E-mail address:** opportunities@iscc.com. **World Wide Web address:** http://www.iscc.com. **Description:** An executive search firm. Information Systems Consulting Corporation is a division of MAGIC (Management Alliance Group of Independent Companies). **Specializes in the areas of:** Accounting; Computer Hardware/Software; Food; Telecommunications; Transportation. **Other U.S. locations:** Denver CO; Kansas City MO; Reston VA.

INNOVATIVE STAFF SEARCH
425 Soledad Street, Suite 200, San Antonio TX 78205. 210/472-1636. **Fax:** 210/472-1686. **Contact:** Manager. **Description:** An executive search firm. **Specializes in the areas of:** Health/Medical. **Positions commonly filled include:** Nurse Practitioner; Pharmacist; Physician Assistant. **Average salary range of placements:** More than $50,000. **Number of placements per year:** 100 - 199.

INSIDE TRACK
504 Hilltop Drive, Weatherford TX 76086-5724. 817/599-7094. **Fax:** 817/596-0807. **Contact:** Matthew DiLorenzo, Senior Technical Recruiter. **E-mail address:** trak1@airmail.net. **Description:** An executive search firm. **Specializes in the areas of:** Administration; Computer Science/Software; Engineering; High-Tech; Industrial; Manufacturing; Sales; Telecommunications. **Positions commonly filled include:** Computer Programmer; Design Engineer; Electrical/Electronics Engineer; General Manager; Marketing Manager; Materials Engineer; Mechanical Engineer; MIS Specialist; Operations Manager; Quality Control Supervisor; Sales Manager; Software Engineer; Systems Analyst; Telecommunications Manager. **Average salary range of placements:** More than $50,000. **Number of placements per year:** 1 - 49.

INSURANCE SEARCH
P.O. Box 7354, The Woodlands TX 77387. 281/367-0137. **Fax:** 281/367-3842. **Contact:** Bert Dionne, President. **Description:** An executive search firm. Founded in 1979. **Specializes in the areas of:** Insurance. **Positions commonly filled include:** Accountant/Auditor; Actuary; Administrative Manager; Attorney; Claim Rep.; Computer Programmer; Construction and Building Inspector; Insurance Agent/Broker; Sales Representative; Systems Analyst; Underwriter/Assistant Underwriter. **Average salary range of placements:** $30,000 - $50,000. **Number of placements per year:** 100 - 199.

INTERNATIONAL DATA SEARCH
9420 Research Boulevard, Echelon III, Suite 250, Austin TX 78759. 512/349-9904. **Fax:** 512/342-7034. **Contact:** Manager. **E-mail address:** opportunities@idscareers.com. **World Wide Web address:** http://www.idscareers.com. **Description:** An executive search firm. International Data Search is a division of MAGIC (Management Alliance Group of Independent Companies). **Specializes**

in the areas of: Accounting; Engineering; Finance; Information Technology; Management; Marketing; Sales; Technical.

INTRATECH RESOURCE GROUP, INC.
6565 West Loop South, Suite 540, Bellaire TX 77401. 713/669-1733. **Fax:** 713/667-5507. **Contact:** James B. Lewis, President. **Description:** An executive search firm. **Specializes in the areas of:** Computer Science/Software. **Positions commonly filled include:** Computer Programmer; Management Analyst/Consultant; Software Engineer; Systems Analyst. **Number of placements per year:** 50 - 99.

JORDAN-SITTER ASSOCIATES
23995 Bat Cave Road, Suite 200, San Antonio TX 78266. 210/651-5561. **Fax:** 210/651-5562. **Contact:** William P. Sitter, Owner. **E-mail address:** info@jordan-sitter.com. **World Wide Web address:** http://www.jordan-sitter.com. **Description:** An executive search firm operating on a retainer basis. Founded in 1978. **Specializes in the areas of:** Distribution; Manufacturing.

JOSEPH CHRIS PARTNERS
900 Rockmead Drive, Suite 101, Kingwood TX 77339. 281/359-0060x257. **Toll-free phone:** 800/877-4930. **Fax:** 281/359-0154. **Contact:** Joe C. Ramirez. **E-mail address:** jramirez@josephchris.com. **World Wide Web address:** http://www.josephchris.com. **Description:** An executive search firm operating on both retainer and contingency bases. Client company pays fee. **Specializes in the areas of:** Architecture/Construction; Engineering; General Management; Real Estate. **Positions commonly filled include:** Architect; Blue-Collar Worker Supervisor; Chief Financial Officer; Civil Engineer; Construction Contractor; Controller; Cost Estimator; Design Engineer; Draftsperson; Electrical/Electronics Engineer; Electrician; Environmental Engineer; Financial Analyst; Industrial Engineer; Manufacturing Engineer; Marketing Specialist; Mechanical Engineer; Metallurgical Engineer; MIS Specialist; Project Manager; Quality Assurance Engineer; Underwriter/Assistant Underwriter. **Corporate headquarters location:** This Location. **Other U.S. locations:** AZ; CA; FL; GA; IL; KS; MA; PA; VA. **Average salary range of placements:** $50,000 - $100,000. **Number of placements per year:** 200 - 499.

KAHN RICHARDS & ASSOCIATES
22618 Elsinore Drive, Katy TX 77450. 281/392-8488. **Contact:** Manager. **Description:** An executive search firm. **Specializes in the areas of:** Computer Science/Software.

KANE & ASSOCIATES, INC.
2825 Wilcrest, Suite 675, Houston TX 77042. 713/977-3600. **Fax:** 713/430-5512. **Contact:** Bernie Kane, President. **E-mail address:** bkane@jobmenu.com. **World Wide Web address:** http://www.jobmenu.com. **Description:** An executive search firm that also offers some outplacement services. **Specializes in the areas of:** Accounting; Auditing; Finance; Human Resources; Tax.

KAWA STIEWIG & EDWARDS INC. (KS&E)
KSE TEMPORARIES
12880 Hillcrest Road, Suite 232, Dallas TX 75230. 972/385-7757. **Contact:** Manager. **Description:** An executive search firm. KSE Temporaries (also at this location) provides temporary placements. **Specializes in the areas of:** Automotive.

KENZER CORPORATION
3030 LBJ Freeway, Suite 1430, Dallas TX 75234. 972/620-7776. **Fax:** 972/243-7570. **Contact:** Dawn Jones, Vice President. **Description:** An executive search firm operating on a retainer basis. Founded in 1973. **Specializes in the areas of:** Fashion; Food; General Management; Retail; Sales. **Positions commonly filled include:** Accountant/Auditor; Branch Manager; Financial Analyst; Hotel Manager; Human Resources Specialist; Management Trainee; Manufacturer's/Wholesaler's Sales Rep.; Operations/Production Manager; Public Relations Specialist; Restaurant/Food Service Manager; Services Sales Representative. **Corporate headquarters location:** New York NY. **Average salary range of placements:** More than $50,000. **Number of placements per year:** 200 - 499.

KEY PEOPLE INC.
520 Post Oak Boulevard, Suite 830, Houston TX 77027. 713/877-1427. **Fax:** 713/877-1826. **Contact:** Betty Thompson, President. **Description:** An executive search firm. **Specializes in the areas of:** Accounting; Computer Science/Software; Secretarial. **Positions commonly filled include:** Accountant/Auditor; Administrative Assistant; Bookkeeper; Clerk; Computer Programmer; EDP Specialist; Systems Analyst. **Benefits available to temporary workers:** Paid Holidays; Paid Vacation. **Average salary range of placements:** $30,000 - $50,000. **Number of placements per year:** 1 - 49.

KEY PEOPLE INC.
P.O. Box 24773, Fort Worth TX 76124-1773. 817/457-6108. **Contact:** Don (Petro) Petrusaitis, President. **Description:** An executive search firm operating on a contingency basis. **Specializes in the areas of:** Graphic Arts; Publishing. **Positions commonly filled include:** Administrative Manager; Blue-Collar Worker Supervisor; Buyer; Chemist; Clerical Supervisor; Computer Programmer; Customer Service Rep.; Electrical/Electronics Engineer; General Manager; Human Resources Specialist; Industrial Engineer; Industrial Production Manager; Management Trainee; Mechanical Engineer; MIS Specialist; Operations/Production Manager; Quality Control Supervisor; Transportation/Traffic Specialist. **Average salary range of placements:** More than $50,000.

KORN/FERRY INTERNATIONAL
1100 Louisiana, Suite 2850, Houston TX 77002. 713/651-1834. **Fax:** 713/651-0848. **Contact:** Manager. **World Wide Web address:** http://www.kornferry.com. **Description:** An executive search firm. **Specializes in the areas of:** Health/Medical; Oil and Gas. **Corporate headquarters location:** Los Angeles CA. **International locations:** Worldwide. **Average salary range of placements:** More than $50,000.
Other U.S. locations:
- 500 North Akard Street, Suite 3232, Dallas TX 75201. 214/954-1834.
- 111 Congress Avenue, Suite 2230, Austin TX 78701. 512/236-1834.

EVIE KREISLER & ASSOCIATES
2720 Stemmons Freeway, Suite 711, Dallas TX 75207. 214/631-8994. **Contact:** Manager. **Description:** An executive search firm. **Specializes in the areas of:** Distribution; Manufacturing; Retail.

KRISTAN INTERNATIONAL EXECUTIVE SEARCH
12 Greenway Plaza, Suite 1100, Houston TX 77046. 713/961-3040. **Fax:** 713/961-3626. **Contact:** Robert P. Kristan, President. **World Wide Web address:** http://www.kristan.com. **Description:** An executive search firm operating on a retainer basis. **Specializes in the areas of:** Architecture/Construction; Computer Science/Software; General Management; Home Furnishings; Sales. **Positions commonly filled include:** Account Manager; Architect; General Manager; Human Resources Specialist; Manufacturing Engineer; Marketing Manager; Sales Executive; Sales Manager; Vice President of Sales. **Corporate headquarters location:** This Location. **Average salary range of placements:** More than $50,000. **Number of placements per year:** 500 - 999.

LEGAL NETWORK
600 North Pearl Street, Suite 2100, Dallas TX 75201. 214/777-6400. **Contact:** Manager. **Description:** An executive search firm. **Specializes in the areas of:** Legal.

GEORGE LEHMAN ASSOCIATES INC.
P.O. Box 90881, Houston TX 77290. 281/443-0044. **Contact:** George Lehman, Owner. **Description:** An

executive search firm. **Specializes in the areas of:** Accounting/Auditing; Finance. **Positions commonly filled include:** Accountant.

LEHMAN McLESKEY
98 San Jacinto Boulevard, Suite 615, Austin TX 78701. 512/478-1131. **Fax:** 512/478-1985. **Contact:** Gene Parker, Research Director. **E-mail address:** mail@ lmsearch.com. **World Wide Web address:** http://www. lmsearch.com. **Description:** An executive search firm operating on a retainer basis. **Specializes in the areas of:** Banking; Communications; Electronics; Finance; Manufacturing; Technical.

LOEWENSTEIN & ASSOCIATES
5847 San Felipe, Suite 1250, Houston TX 77057-3009. 713/952-1840. **Toll-free phone:** 800/486-0152. **Fax:** 713/952-4534. **Contact:** Recruiter. **E-mail address:** loewenst@worldnet.att.net. **Description:** An executive search firm. **Specializes in the areas of:** Computer Science/Software; Consulting; Engineering; Industrial; Management; Marketing; Sales; Technical. **Positions commonly filled include:** Chemical Engineer; Computer Programmer; Industrial Engineer; Mechanical Engineer; MIS Specialist; Services Sales Representative; Software Engineer; Systems Analyst. **Average salary range of placements:** More than $50,000. **Number of placements per year:** 1 - 49.

M.H. LOGAN & ASSOCIATES
5641 Yale Boulevard, Suite 102, Dallas TX 75206. 214/706-0558. **Contact:** Manager. **Description:** An executive search firm. **Specializes in the areas of:** Restaurant.

LUCAS FINANCIAL STAFFING
12655 North Central Expressway, Suite 730, Dallas TX 75243. 972/490-0011. **Fax:** 972/991-4144. **Contact:** Andrea Jennings, Regional Manager. **E-mail address:** lucaslfs@aol.com. **Description:** An executive search firm operating on both retainer and contingency bases. The firm also provides some contract placements. **Specializes in the areas of:** Accounting/Auditing; Finance. **Positions commonly filled include:** Accountant; Budget Analyst; CFO; Controller; Credit Manager; EDP Specialist; Finance Director; Financial Analyst; Systems Analyst. **Benefits available to temporary workers:** 401(k); Medical Insurance; Paid Vacation. **Corporate headquarters location:** Atlanta GA. **Average salary range of placements:** $30,000 - $50,000. **Number of placements per year:** 200 - 499.

MH EXECUTIVE SEARCH GROUP
P.O. Box 868068, Plano TX 75086. 972/578-1511. **Contact:** Recruiter. **E-mail address:** Txpkgjobs@ mhgroup.com. **World Wide Web address:** http://www. mhgroup.com. **Description:** An executive search firm. **Specializes in the areas of:** Packaging. **Corporate headquarters location:** Palm Harbor FL.

MANAGEMENT RECRUITERS INTERNATIONAL
317 South Friendswood Drive, Friendswood TX 77546. 281/996-0008. **Fax:** 281/996-5449. **Contact:** Manager. **Description:** An executive search firm operating on a contingency basis. **Specializes in the areas of:** Engineering; Food; Health/Medical; Industrial; Manufacturing. **Positions commonly filled include:** Chemical Engineer; Chemist; Civil Engineer; Electrical/Electronics Engineer; Environmental Engineer; Food Scientist/Tech.; General Mgr.; Health Services Mgr.; Human Resources Mgr.; Industrial Engineer; Industrial Production Mgr.; Materials Engineer; Mechanical Engineer; Medical Records Tech.; Metallurgical Engineer; Occupational Therapist; Operations/Production Mgr.; Petroleum Engineer; Pharmacist; Physical Therapist; Physician; Physicist; Psychologist; Recreational Therapist; Registered Nurse; Respiratory Therapist; Social Worker; Speech-Language Pathologist; Surgical Tech. **Corporate headquarters location:** Cleveland OH. **Other U.S. locations:** Nationwide. **Average salary range of placements:** More than $50,000. **Number of placements per year:** 1 - 49.

MANAGEMENT RECRUITERS INTERNATIONAL
15150 Preston Road, Suite 300, Dallas TX 75248. 972/991-4500. **Contact:** George Buntrock, Owner. **Description:** An executive search firm. **Specializes in the areas of:** Accounting/Auditing; Administration; Computer Science/Software; Engineering; Food; General Management; Health/Medical; Paper; Retail; Technical. **Positions commonly filled include:** Ceramics Engineer; Chemical Engineer; Computer Programmer; Customer Service Rep.; Electrical/Electronics Engineer; General Manager; Health Services Manager; Industrial Engineer; Industrial Production Manager; Materials Engineer; Mechanical Engineer; Metallurgical Engineer; Operations/Production Manager; Pharmacist; Physical Therapist; Purchasing Agent/Manager; Quality Control Supervisor; Registered Nurse; Software Engineer; Speech-Language Pathologist; Systems Analyst; Transportation/Traffic Specialist. **Corporate headquarters location:** Cleveland OH. **Other U.S. locations:** Nationwide. **Number of placements per year:** 1 - 49.

MANAGEMENT RECRUITERS INTERNATIONAL
1360 Post Oak Boulevard, Suite 2110, Houston TX 77056. 713/850-9850. **Fax:** 713/850-1429. **Contact:** Rich Bolls, Manager. **Description:** An executive search firm. **Specializes in the areas of:** Accounting/Auditing; Administration; Advertising; Architecture/Construction; Banking; Communications; Computer Hardware/ Software; Construction; Design; Electrical; Engineering; Finance; Food; General Management; Health/Medical; Industrial; Insurance; Legal; Manufacturing; Personnel/ Labor Relations; Procurement; Publishing; Retail; Sales; Technical; Textiles; Transportation. **Corporate headquarters location:** Cleveland OH. **Other U.S. locations:** Nationwide.

MANAGEMENT RECRUITERS INTERNATIONAL
1001 West Randol Mill Road, Arlington TX 76012. 817/469-6161. **Contact:** Bob Stoessel, Manager. **Description:** An executive search firm. **Specializes in the areas of:** Accounting/Auditing; Administration; Advertising; Architecture/Construction; Banking; Communications; Computer Hardware/Software; Design; Electrical; Engineering; Finance; Food; General Management; Health/Medical; Insurance; Legal; Manufacturing; Operations Management; Personnel/ Labor Relations; Procurement; Publishing; Retail; Sales; Technical; Textiles; Transportation. **Corporate headquarters location:** Cleveland OH. **Other U.S. locations:** Nationwide.

MANAGEMENT RECRUITERS INTERNATIONAL
1250 South Capital of Texas Highway, Building 3, Suite 650, Austin TX 78746. 512/327-8292. **Contact:** Manager. **Description:** An executive search firm. **Specializes in the areas of:** Advertising; Biotechnology; Health/Medical; High-Tech; Pharmaceuticals. **Corporate headquarters location:** Cleveland OH. **Other U.S. locations:** Nationwide.

MANAGEMENT RECRUITERS INTERNATIONAL
7550 Interstate Highway 10 West, Suite 300, San Antonio TX 78229. 210/525-1800. **Contact:** Manager. **Description:** An executive search firm. **Specializes in the areas of:** Food; Manufacturing. **Corporate headquarters location:** Cleveland OH. **Other U.S. locations:** Nationwide.

MANAGEMENT RECRUITERS INTERNATIONAL
8700 Crownhill Boulevard, Suite 701, San Antonio TX 78209. 210/829-8666. **Fax:** 210/822-2218. **Contact:** Manager. **E-mail address:** mrisatx@swbell.net. **Description:** An executive search firm. **Specializes in the areas of:** Food; Manufacturing. **Corporate headquarters location:** Cleveland OH. **Other U.S. locations:** Nationwide.

MANAGEMENT RECRUITERS INTERNATIONAL
3309 67th Street, Suite 5, Lubbock TX 79413. 806/780-6789. **Contact:** Manager. **Description:** An executive search firm. **Specializes in the areas of:** Engineering;

Health/Medical; Marketing. **Corporate headquarters location:** Cleveland OH. **Other U.S. locations:** Nationwide.

MANAGEMENT RECRUITERS INTERNATIONAL
494 South Seguin, New Braunfels TX 78130. 830/629-6291. **Contact:** Jim Rice, Manager. **Description:** An executive search firm. **Specializes in the areas of:** Insurance. **Corporate headquarters location:** Cleveland OH. **Other U.S. locations:** Nationwide.

MANAGEMENT RECRUITERS OF CHAMPIONS
14614 Falling Creek Drive, Suite 214, Houston TX 77068. 281/580-6020. **Fax:** 281/580-6029. **Contact:** Gary Akin, President. **E-mail address:** mrichamp@swbell.net. **World Wide Web address:** http://www.mrichampions.com. **Description:** An executive search firm operating on both retainer and contingency bases. Management Recruiters of Champions focuses on the areas of benefits administration/consulting and engineering design. **Specializes in the areas of:** Administration; Engineering; Food; Health/Medical; Manufacturing. **Positions commonly filled include:** Account Rep.; Administrative Manager; Applications Engineer; Design Engineer; Electrical/Electronics Engineer; Manufacturing Engineer; Mechanical Engineer; Operations Manager; Production Manager; Project Manager; Sales Engineer; Sales Rep. **Corporate headquarters location:** Cleveland OH. **Other U.S. locations:** Nationwide. **Average salary range of placements:** $30,000 - $50,000. **Number of placements per year:** 1 - 49.

MANAGEMENT RECRUITERS OF CLEAR LAKE
2200 Space Park Drive, Suite 420, Houston TX 77058. 281/335-0363. **Fax:** 281/335-0362. **Contact:** Len Bird, President. **Description:** An executive search firm. **Specializes in the areas of:** Engineering; Health/Medical; Manufacturing. **Positions commonly filled include:** Accountant/Auditor; Agricultural Engineer; Biomedical Engineer; Ceramics Engineer; Chemical Engineer; Chemist; Civil Engineer; Electrical/Electronics Engineer; Financial Analyst; Industrial Production Manager; Materials Engineer; Mechanical Engineer; Metallurgical Engineer; Mining Engineer; Occupational Therapist; Operations/Production Manager; Petroleum Engineer; Physical Therapist; Software Engineer. **Corporate headquarters location:** Cleveland OH. **Number of placements per year:** 50 - 99.

MANAGEMENT RECRUITERS OF DALLAS
13101 Preston Road, Suite 560, Dallas TX 75240. 972/788-1515. **Fax:** 972/701-8242. **Contact:** Robert S. Lineback, General Manager. **Description:** An executive search firm operating on both retainer and contingency bases. **Specializes in the areas of:** Accounting/Auditing; Administration; Advertising; Architecture/Construction; Banking; Communications; Computer Hardware/Software; Design; Electrical; Engineering; Finance; Food; General Management; Health/Medical; Insurance; Legal; Manufacturing; Operations Management; Personnel/Labor Relations; Procurement; Publishing; Retail; Sales; Technical; Transportation. **Positions commonly filled include:** Accountant/Auditor; Actuary; Administrative Mgr.; Aerospace Engineer; Agricultural Engineer; Bank Officer/Manager; Biochemist; Biological Scientist; Biomedical Engineer; Branch Manager; Chemical Engineer; Chemist; Civil Engineer; Clinical Lab Tech.; Computer Programmer; Design Engineer; Designer; Dietician/Nutritionist; EEG Technologist; EKG Tech.; Electrical/Electronics Engineer; Emergency Medical Technician; Environmental Engineer; Financial Analyst; Food Scientist/Technologist; General Manager; Health Services Manager; Human Resources Specialist; Industrial Engineer; Licensed Practical Nurse; Management Analyst/Consultant; Management Trainee; Manufacturer's/Wholesaler's Sales Rep.; Mechanical Engineer; Medical Records Technician; Metallurgical Engineer; Mining Engineer; MIS Specialist; Multimedia Designer; Nuclear Engineer; Nuclear Medicine Technologist; Occupational Therapist; Operations/Production Manager; Petroleum Engineer; Pharmacist;

Physical Therapist; Physician; Physicist; Purchasing Agent/Manager; Quality Control Supervisor; Radiological Technologist; Registered Nurse; Respiratory Therapist; Restaurant/Food Service Mgr.; Science Technologist; Securities Sales Rep.; Services Sales Rep.; Software Engineer; Structural Engineer; Surgical Tech.; Systems Analyst; Telecommunications Manager; Transportation/Traffic Specialist; Underwriter/Assistant Underwriter. **Corporate headquarters location:** Cleveland OH. **Other U.S. locations:** Nationwide. **Average salary range of placements:** More than $50,000. **Number of placements per year:** 200 - 499.

MANAGEMENT RECRUITERS OF LBJ PARK/DALLAS
3003 LBJ Freeway, Suite 220E, Dallas TX 75234. 972/488-1133. **Fax:** 972/488-1099. **Contact:** Ray Vlasek, General Manager. **E-mail address:** mrdfw@airmail.net. **Description:** An executive search firm. **Specializes in the areas of:** Engineering; Manufacturing; Software Engineering; Telecommunications. **Positions commonly filled include:** Computer Programmer; Electrical/Electronics Engineer; Mechanical Engineer; MIS Specialist; Software Engineer. **Corporate headquarters location:** Cleveland OH. **Other U.S. locations:** Nationwide. **Number of placements per year:** 50 - 99.

MANAGEMENT RECRUITERS OF LEWISVILLE
1660 South Stemmons, Suite 460, Lewisville TX 75067. 972/434-9612. **Contact:** Manager. **Description:** An executive search firm. **Specializes in the areas of:** Plastics; Sales. **Corporate headquarters location:** Cleveland OH. **Other U.S. locations:** Nationwide.

MANAGEMENT RECRUITERS OF ROUND ROCK
301 Hesters Crossing Road, Suite 110, Round Rock TX 78681. 512/310-1918. **Fax:** 512/310-8318. **Contact:** Account Executive. **Description:** An executive search firm operating on both retainer and contingency bases. **Specializes in the areas of:** Engineering; Industrial; Manufacturing. **Positions commonly filled include:** Chemical Engineer; Design Engineer; Electrical/Electronics Engineer; Industrial Engineer; Mechanical Engineer; Metallurgical Engineer. **Corporate headquarters location:** Cleveland OH. **Other U.S. locations:** Nationwide. **Average salary range of placements:** $30,000 - $50,000. **Number of placements per year:** 100 - 199.

RAY MARBURGER & ASSOCIATES INC.
9800 Northwest Freeway, Suite 505, Houston TX 77092. 713/683-8798. **Contact:** Ray Marburger, CPA, Senior Consultant. **Description:** An executive search firm that operates on a contingency basis. Founded in 1980. **Specializes in the areas of:** Accounting/Auditing. **Positions commonly filled include:** Accountant/Auditor; Controller; Financial Analyst; Systems Analyst. **Average salary range of placements:** $40,000 - $90,000. **Number of placements per year:** 50 - 99.

MAXWEL, FRAIDE & ASSOCIATES
810 Oakwood Loop, Suite 3B, San Marcos TX 78666. 512/754-8287. **Fax:** 512/392-9697. **Contact:** Manager. **Description:** An executive search firm. **Specializes in the areas of:** Biotechnology; Medical Devices; Pharmaceuticals.

McDUFFY-EDWARDS
3117 Medina Drive, Garland TX 75041. 972/864-1174. **Fax:** 972/864-8559. **Contact:** Tom Edwards, Partner. **E-mail address:** tomedwards@earthlink.net. **World Wide Web address:** http://www.mcduffy-edwards.com. **Description:** An executive search firm that also provides consulting services and seminars. **Specializes in the areas of:** Computer Science/Software; Marketing; Sales; Scientific; Technical. **Positions commonly filled include:** Account Manager; Account Rep.; Customer Service Rep.; General Manager; Internet Services Manager; Management Analyst/Consultant; Market

Research Analyst; Marketing Manager; Marketing Specialist; Operations Manager; Project Manager; Sales Engineer; Sales Executive; Sales Manager; Sales Rep.; Software Engineer; Systems Analyst; Systems Manager; Telecommunications Manager; Vice President of Marketing and Sales. **Average salary range of placements:** More than $50,000. **Number of placements per year:** 50 - 99.

McKINLEY-AREND INTERNATIONAL
3200 Southwest Freeway, Suite 3300, Houston TX 77027-7526. 713/623-6400. **Fax:** 713/975-0022. **Contact:** Jim McKinley, Managing Director. **Description:** An executive search firm operating on a retainer basis. **Specializes in the areas of:** Chemicals; Engineering; Finance; Food; General Management; Industrial; Legal; Manufacturing; Mining; Nonprofit; Personnel/Labor Relations; Sales; Technical; Transportation. **Positions commonly filled include:** Accountant; Biological Scientist; Biomedical Engineer; Board of Directors; Ceramics Engineer; Chemist; Civil Engineer; Electrical/Electronics Engineer; Industrial Engineer; Manufacturing Engineer; Mechanical Engineer; Metallurgical Engineer; Operations/Production Manager; Public Relations Specialist; Quality Control Supervisor; Senior Management. **Number of placements per year:** 100 - 199.

MEDIA EXECUTIVE SEARCH & PLACEMENT
1349 Regal Row, Dallas TX 75247. 214/630-9790. **Fax:** 214/630-9905. **Contact:** David Small, President/CEO. **E-mail address:** dsmall@mediaexecutive.com. **World Wide Web address:** http://www.mediaexecutive.com. **Description:** An executive search firm. **Specializes in the areas of:** Cable TV; Internet Marketing; Media Sales. **Positions commonly filled include:** General Manager; Marketing Manager.

MEDICAL SEARCH SOLUTIONS
15905 Bent Tree Forest Circle, Suite 1065, Dallas TX 75248. 972/490-3778. **Fax:** 972/934-2246. **Contact:** Penny Peters, CPC, Medical Recruiting Specialist. **Description:** An executive search firm. **Specializes in the areas of:** Health/Medical. **Positions commonly filled include:** Administrative Assistant; Administrative Manager; Assistant Manager; Clinical Lab Technician; Controller; Dietician/Nutritionist; EEG Technologist; EKG Tech.; Emergency Medical Technician; Finance Director; Financial Analyst; Health Services Manager; Licensed Practical Nurse; Medical Assistant; Medical Records Technician; Nurse Practitioner; Occupational Therapist; Office Manager; Operations Manager; Pharmacist; Physical Therapist; Physician; Physician Assistant; Radiological Technologist; Recreational Therapist; Registered Nurse; Respiratory Therapist; Speech-Language Pathologist; Surgical Technician. **Average salary range of placements:** $30,000 - $50,000. **Number of placements per year:** 50 - 99.

W. ROBERT MICHAELS & COMPANY
5065 Westheimer Road, Suite 830, Houston TX 77056. 713/965-9175. **Fax:** 713/965-0509. **Contact:** Manager. **Description:** An executive search firm. **Specializes in the areas of:** Construction; Engineering.

NATIONAL HUMAN RESOURCE GROUP
609 Capital Ridge Road, Suite 202, Austin TX 78746. 512/328-4448. **Fax:** 512/328-1696. **Contact:** Vicki Volick, President. **E-mail address:** nhrg@nhrg.com. **Description:** An executive search firm operating on both retainer and contingency bases. The firm also offers technical consulting and contract services. **Specializes in the areas of:** Computer Science/Software. **Positions commonly filled include:** Computer Programmer; MIS Specialist; Multimedia Designer; Systems Analyst. **Average salary range of placements:** More than $50,000. **Number of placements per year:** 1 - 49.

NATIONAL SALES RECRUITERS, INC. (NSR)
P.O. Box 703816, Dallas TX 75370-3816. 972/436-3047. **Toll-free phone:** 800/469-6428. **Fax:** 972/221-6134. **Contact:** Rory Deal, Founder. **E-mail address:**

rory@nsrjobs.com. **World Wide Web address:** http://www.nsrjobs.com. **Description:** An executive search firm. **Specializes in the areas of:** Marketing; Sales; Sales Management.

NATIONWIDE MEDICAL PLACEMENT
11407 Meadow Lake Drive, Houston TX 77077. 281/496-0160. **Contact:** Manager. **Description:** An executive search firm. **Specializes in the areas of:** Health/Medical.

NOLL HUMAN RESOURCE SERVICES
5720 LBJ Freeway, Suite 610, Dallas TX 75240. 972/392-2900. **Toll-free phone:** 800/536-7600. **Fax:** 972/934-3600. **Contact:** Mr. Perry Smith, Dallas Division Manager. **World Wide Web address:** http://www.noll-inc.com. **Description:** An executive search firm operating on both retainer and contingency bases. **Specializes in the areas of:** Logistics; Sales; Transportation. **Positions commonly filled include:** Database Manager; Environmental Engineer; Industrial Engineer; Manufacturing Engineer; Marketing Manager; MIS Specialist; Physician; Registered Nurse; Sales Engineer; Sales Executive; Sales Manager; Sales Rep.; Software Engineer; Systems Analyst; Systems Manager; Telecommunications Manager; Transportation/Traffic Specialist. **Corporate headquarters location:** Omaha NE. **Average salary range of placements:** More than $50,000. **Number of placements per year:** 50 - 99.

ODELL & ASSOCIATES INC.
12700 Park Central Place, Suite 1404, Dallas TX 75251. 972/458-7900. **Fax:** 972/233-1215. **Contact:** Executive Vice President. **Description:** An executive search firm. **Specializes in the areas of:** Accounting/Auditing; Data Processing; Engineering; Finance; Health/Medical; Legal. **Positions commonly filled include:** Accountant/ Auditor; Actuary; Attorney; Computer Programmer; Financial Analyst; Medical Records Technician; Occupational Therapist; Registered Nurse; Respiratory Therapist; Systems Analyst. **Number of placements per year:** 100 - 199.

THE DUNCAN O'DELL GROUP
P.O. Box 1161, La Porte TX 77572. 281/470-1881. **Fax:** 281/470-1880. **Contact:** Jim Hall, Senior Partner. **Description:** An executive search firm that focuses on the placement of manufacturing professionals with three or more years experience. **Specializes in the areas of:** Manufacturing; Personnel/Labor Relations. **Positions commonly filled include:** Buyer; Design Engineer; Electrical/Electronics Engineer; Mechanical Engineer; Metallurgical Engineer. **Average salary range of placements:** More than $50,000. **Number of placements per year:** 50 - 99.

OPPORTUNITY UNLIMITED PERSONNEL CONSULTANTS
2720 West Mockingbird Lane, Dallas TX 75235. 214/357-9196. **Toll-free phone:** 800/969-0888. **Fax:** 214/357-0140. **Contact:** Ms. Jean Crawford, President. **E-mail address:** oui@opportunityunlimited.com. **Description:** An executive search firm operating on a contingency basis. Founded in 1959. **Specializes in the areas of:** Aerospace; Computer Science/Software; Data Processing; Engineering; Scientific; Technical; Telecommunications. **Positions commonly filled include:** Aerospace Engineer; Biomedical Engineer; Computer Programmer; Design Engineer; Electrical/ Electronics Engineer; Mechanical Engineer; Multimedia Designer; Software Engineer; Systems Analyst; Telecommunications Manager. **Number of placements per year:** 200 - 499.

THE PAILIN GROUP PROFESSIONAL SEARCH CONSULTANTS
Center City Plaza, 1412 Main Street, Suite 601, Dallas TX 75202. 214/752-5100. **Fax:** 214/752-6101. **Contact:** David L. Pailin, Sr., Senior Partner. **World Wide Web address:** http://www.pailingroup.com. **Description:** An executive search firm operating on a retainer basis. **Specializes in the areas of:** Accounting/Auditing;

Administration; Advertising; Banking; Computer Science/Software; Economics; Engineering; Environmental; Finance; Food; General Management; Health/Medical; Industrial; Insurance; Legal; Manufacturing; Nonprofit; Personnel/Labor Relations; Retail; Sales; Transportation. **Positions commonly filled include:** Accountant; Administrative Mgr.; Aerospace Engineer; Architect; Attorney; Bank Officer/Mgr.; Budget Analyst; Ceramics Engineer; Civil Engineer; Computer Programmer; Construction Contractor; Cost Estimator; Credit Manager; Customer Service Rep.; Design Engineer; Environmental Engineer; Financial Analyst; General Mgr.; Health Services Mgr.; Human Service Worker; Industrial Engineer; Materials Engineer; Mechanical Engineer; Metallurgical Engineer; Mining Engineer; MIS Specialist; Nuclear Engineer; Petroleum Engineer; Pharmacist; Physician; Quality Control Supervisor; Securities Sales Rep.; Services Sales Rep.; Software Engineer; Statistician; Systems Analyst; Technical Writer/Editor; Telecommunications Manager. **Corporate headquarters location:** This Location. **Average salary range of placements:** More than $50,000. **Number of placements per year:** 100 - 199.

PAN AMERICAN SEARCH
600 Sunland Park Drive, Building 2, Suite 200, El Paso TX 79912. 915/833-9991. **Contact:** Manager. **Description:** An executive search firm. **Specializes in the areas of:** Engineering; Manufacturing.

PATE RESOURCES GROUP
595 Orleans Street, Suite 707, Beaumont TX 77701. 409/833-4514. **Fax:** 409/833-4646. **Contact:** W.L. Pate Jr., CPC, CTS/President. **E-mail address:** pateresgrp@ aol.com. **Description:** An executive search firm operating on both retainer and contingency bases. The firm also offers career/outplacement counseling and contract and temporary placements. **Specializes in the areas of:** Accounting; Administration; Computer Science/Software; Engineering; Finance; Food; General Management; Health/Medical; Industrial; Personnel/ Labor Relations; Sales; Secretarial; Technical. **Positions commonly filled include:** Account Manager; Account Rep.; Accountant/Auditor; Administrative Assistant; Administrative Mgr.; Biochemist; Biological Scientist; Biomedical Engineer; Chemical Engineer; Chemist; CFO; Civil Engineer; Clinical Lab Tech.; Computer Programmer; Construction Contractor; Controller; Credit Mgr.; Customer Service Rep.; Design Engineer; Electrical/Electronics Engineer; Environmental Engineer; Finance Director; Financial Analyst; Food Scientist/ Technologist; General Manager; Graphic Artist; Graphic Designer; Hotel Mgr.; Human Resources Mgr.; Industrial Engineer; Internet Services Mgr.; Management Analyst/ Consultant; Manufacturing Engineer; Market Research Analyst; Marketing Manager; Mechanical Engineer; Metallurgical Engineer; MIS Specialist; Nuclear Engineer; Occupational Therapist; Operations/Production Manager; Paralegal; Petroleum Engineer; Pharmacist; Physical Therapist; Physician; Project Manager; Public Relations Specialist; Purchasing Agent/Manager; Quality Control Supervisor; Registered Nurse; Respiratory Therapist; Sales Engineer; Sales Exec.; Sales Manager; Sales Rep.; Secretary; Software Engineer; Speech-Language Pathologist; Strategic Relations Manager; Structural Engineer; Systems Analyst; Systems Manager; Telecommunications Manager; Transportation/Traffic Specialist; Underwriter/Assistant Underwriter. **Average salary range of placements:** More than $50,000. **Number of placements per year:** 50 - 99.

PEDLEY-RICHARD AND ASSOCIATES, INC.
7719 Wood Hollow, Suite 216, Austin TX 78731. 512/418-8848. **Fax:** 512/418-1236. **Contact:** Sally Pedley, Principal. **E-mail address:** spedley@pedley-richard.com. **World Wide Web address:** http://www.pedley-richard.com. **Description:** An executive search firm. **Specializes in the areas of:** Electronics.

PENCOM SYSTEMS INCORPORATED
9433 Bee Caves Road, Austin TX 78733. 512/263-5555. **Fax:** 512/263-0505. **Contact:** Recruiter. **E-mail**

address: sw-jobs@pencom.com. **World Wide Web address:** http://www.pencom.com. **Description:** An executive search firm that also provides some contract services and systems administration outsourcing. Founded in 1973. **Specializes in the areas of:** Technical. **Corporate headquarters location:** New York NY. **Other U.S. locations:** Los Angeles CA; San Jose CA; Washington DC; Atlanta GA; Chicago IL; Boston MA.

PEOPLE SOURCE EXECUTIVE SEARCH
9200 Old Katy Road, Houston TX 77055. 713/935-3333. **Contact:** William Sonne, CEO/Owner. **Description:** An executive search firm. **Specializes in the areas of:** Information Technology; Scientific.

PERI CORPORATION (PROFESSIONAL EXECUTIVE RECRUITERS)
1701 Gateway Boulevard, Suite 419, Richardson TX 75080. 972/235-3984. **Fax:** 972/437-2017. **Contact:** Ken Roberts, Manager. **E-mail address:** PERI@airmail.net. **Description:** An executive search firm operating on a contingency basis. Client company pays fee. **Specializes in the areas of:** Architecture/Construction; Engineering. **Positions commonly filled include:** Architect; Attorney; CFO; Civil Engineer; Construction Contractor; Electrical/Electronics Engineer; Environmental Engineer; Mechanical Engineer. **Corporate headquarters location:** This Location. **International locations:** Worldwide. **Average salary range of placements:** $50,000 - $100,000. **Number of placements per year:** 50 - 99.

THE PERSONNEL OFFICE
24127 Boerne Stage Road, San Antonio TX 78255-9517. 210/698-0300. **Fax:** 210/698-3299. **Contact:** Manager. **Description:** An executive search firm operating on both retainer and contingency bases. The firm also offers contract and temporary placements. **Specializes in the areas of:** Administration; Computer Science/Software; Engineering; Sales. **Positions commonly filled include:** Accountant/Auditor; Computer Programmer; Customer Service Representative; Database Manager; Design Engineer; Electrical/Electronics Engineer; Environmental Engineer; General Manager; Health Services Manager; Human Resources Manager; Industrial Engineer; Manufacturer's/Wholesaler's Sales Rep.; Manufacturing Engineer; MIS Specialist; Software Engineer; Systems Analyst; Systems Manager; Telecommunications Manager. **Average salary range of placements:** $30,000 - $74,000. **Number of placements per year:** 1000+.

RICK PETERSON & ASSOCIATES
515 North Sam Houston Parkway, Suite 250, Houston TX 77060. 281/591-7777. **Fax:** 281/591-6258. **Contact:** Rick Peterson, President. **Description:** An executive search firm. **Specializes in the areas of:** Finance.

PHOENIX STAFFING
G&A STAFF SOURCING
P.O. Box 791891, San Antonio TX 78279. 210/377-3628. **Fax:** 210/820-0138. **Contact:** Clarke Mosley, Area Manager. **E-mail address:** jcmosley@aol.com. **Description:** An executive search firm that also offers some temporary placements, contract services, and career/outplacement counseling. **Specializes in the areas of:** Accounting/Auditing; Administration; Computer Science/Software; Food; General Management; Industrial; Light Industrial; Manufacturing; Personnel/ Labor Relations; Sales; Secretarial. **Positions commonly filled include:** Account Mgr.; Account Rep.; Accountant; Administrative Assistant; Administrative Manager; Assistant Manager; Blue-Collar Worker Supervisor; Branch Manager; Claim Rep.; Clerical Supervisor; Computer Operator; Computer Programmer; Construction Contractor; Customer Service Rep.; Database Mgr.; Design Engineer; General Mgr.; Human Resources Manager; Industrial Production Manager; Manufacturing Engineer; Marketing Manager; Marketing Specialist; Mechanical Engineer; Operations Manager; Production Mgr.; Sales Exec.; Sales Mgr.; Sales Rep.; Secretary. **Corporate headquarters location:** Houston TX. **Other U.S. locations:** San Diego CA; Austin TX;

Laredo TX. **Average salary range of placements:** $30,000 - $50,000. **Number of placements per year:** 1 - 49.

PIPER-MORGAN PERSONNEL
3355 West Alabama Street, Suite 1120, Houston TX 77098. 713/840-9922. **Fax:** 713/840-9931. **Contact:** Manager. **Description:** An executive search firm. **Specializes in the areas of:** Oil and Gas.

PRACTICE DYNAMICS
11222 Richmond Avenue, Suite 125, Houston TX 77082. 281/531-0911. **Fax:** 281/531-9014. **Contact:** Manager. **Description:** An executive search firm. **Specializes in the areas of:** Health/Medical. **Positions commonly filled include:** Physician; Registered Nurse.

PRENG & ASSOCIATES, INC.
2925 Briar Park, Suite 1111, Houston TX 77042. 713/266-2600. **Fax:** 713/266-3070. **Contact:** David Preng, President. **Description:** An executive search firm. **Specializes in the areas of:** Chemicals; Engineering; Manufacturing; Petrochemical; Pharmaceuticals.

PRESCOTT LEGAL SEARCH
3900 Essex Lane, Suite 1110, Houston TX 77027. 713/439-0911. **Fax:** 713/439-1317. **Contact:** Manager. **Description:** An executive search firm. **Specializes in the areas of:** Legal. **Positions commonly filled include:** Attorney.

PRIMUS ASSOCIATES, L.C.
13915 Burnet Road, Suite 440, Austin TX 78728. 512/246-2266. **Fax:** 512/246-1333. **Contact:** Rebecca Gates, Director. **E-mail address:** info@primusnet.com. **World Wide Web address:** http://www.primusnet.com. **Description:** An executive search firm operating on both retainer and contingency bases. **Specializes in the areas of:** High-Tech. **Corporate headquarters location:** This Location.

PRIORITY SEARCH, INC.
4110 Rio Bravo, Suite 215, El Paso TX 79902. 915/534-4457. **Fax:** 915/544-5368. **Contact:** Nellie Cuaron, President. **E-mail address:** prioritysearch@usa.net. **Description:** An executive search firm operating on a contingency basis. Client company pays fee. **Specializes in the areas of:** Accounting; Administration; Computer Science/Software; Engineering; Finance; General Management; Industrial; Internet Development; Marketing; MIS/EDP; Offshore Operations; Personnel/ Labor Relations; Sales; Transportation. **Positions commonly filled include:** Account Mgr.; Account Rep.; Accountant; Administrative Assistant; Administrative Manager; Applications Engineer; AS400 Programmer Analyst; Assistant Manager; Auditor; Branch Manager; Budget Analyst; Buyer; Chemical Engineer; Chemist; CFO; Computer Animator; Computer Engineer; Computer Programmer; Computer Support Technician; Controller; Cost Estimator; Credit Manager; Customer Service Rep.; Database Administrator; Database Mgr.; Design Engineer; Electrical/Electronics Engineer; Environmental Engineer; Finance Director; Financial Analyst; General Manager; Human Resources Manager; Industrial Engineer; Industrial Production Manager; Internet Services Manager; Manufacturing Engineer; Marketing Manager; Marketing Specialist; Mechanical Engineer; Metallurgical Engineer; MIS Specialist; Multimedia Designer; Network/Systems Administrator; Operations Manager; Production Manager; Project Manager; Purchasing Agent/Manager; Quality Assurance Engineer; Quality Control Supervisor; Sales Engineer; Sales Executive; Sales Manager; Sales Rep.; Software Engineer; SQL Programmer; Systems Analyst; Systems Manager; Transportation/raffic Specialist; Webmaster. **Corporate headquarters location:** This Location. **Average salary range of placements:** $50,000 - $100,000. **Number of placements per year:** 1 - 49.

PRITCHARD & ASSOCIATES
14100 Southwest Freeway, Suite 360, Sugar Land TX 77478. 281/275-4100. **Fax:** 281/275-4152. **Contact:** Manager. **Description:** An executive search firm.

Specializes in the areas of: Computer Hardware/Software.

PROFESSIONAL RECRUITING SOLUTIONS
2425 North Central Expressway, Suite 1000, Richardson TX 75080. 972/907-9100. **Toll-free phone:** 800/564-0293. **Fax:** 972/907-2550. **Contact:** Recruiter. **E-mail address:** mail@prsdallas.com. **World Wide Web address:** http://www.prsdallas.com. **Description:** An executive search firm operating on both retainer and contingency bases. PRS also offers contract placements and recruiting consulting services. **Specializes in the areas of:** High-Tech. **Other area locations:** Houston TX. **Other U.S. locations:** Detroit MI.

PROSEARCH RECRUITING
The River Oaks Towers, 3730 Kirby Drive, Suite 1200, Houston TX 77098. 713/529-3767. **Fax:** 713/528-1762. **Contact:** Recruiter. **E-mail address:** prosearchrtg@ earthlink.net. **World Wide Web address:** http://www. prosearchrecruiting.net. **Description:** An executive search firm. **Specializes in the areas of:** Chemicals; Electronics; Engineering; Industrial; Petrochemical; Telecommunications; Transportation.

QUALITY INFORMATION SERVICE (QIS)
P.O. Box 1559, Whitney TX 76692. 254/694-6319. **Fax:** 254/694-6434. **Contact:** Betty Schatz, Senior Account Manager. **Description:** An executive search firm. **Specializes in the areas of:** Computer Science/Software. **Positions commonly filled include:** Computer Programmer; Database Manager; MIS Specialist; Software Engineer; Systems Analyst; Technical Writer/ Editor. **Number of placements per year:** 50 - 99.

LEA RANDOLPH & ASSOCIATES
10210 North Central Expressway, Suite 216, Dallas TX 75231. 214/987-4415. **Fax:** 214/369-9548. **Contact:** Manager. **Description:** An executive search firm. **Specializes in the areas of:** Health/Medical.

RECRUITING ASSOCIATES
P.O. Box 8473, Amarillo TX 79114. 806/353-9548. **Fax:** 806/353-9540. **Contact:** Mike Rokey, CPC, Owner/Manager. **E-mail address:** mikedr@arn.net. **Description:** An executive search firm operating on a contingency basis. Founded in 1978. **Specializes in the areas of:** Computer Science/Software; Engineering. **Positions commonly filled include:** Accountant/Auditor; Applications Engineer; Computer Operator; Computer Programmer; Database Manager; Design Engineer; Electrical/Electronics Engineer; Mechanical Engineer; MIS Specialist; Software Engineer; Systems Analyst; Technical Writer/Editor. **Benefits available to temporary workers:** 401(k); Medical Insurance. **Average salary range of placements:** $30,000 - $50,000. **Number of placements per year:** 1 - 49.

REDSTONE & ASSOCIATES
1906 Treble Drive, Suite 17, Humble TX 77338. 281/446-5625. **Contact:** Randy Redstone, Owner. **Description:** An executive search firm operating on a retainer basis. **Specializes in the areas of:** Construction; Engineering; Manufacturing; Sales. **Positions commonly filled include:** Accountant/Auditor; Chemical Engineer; Construction Contractor; Cost Estimator; Metallurgical Engineer; Quality Control Supervisor. **International locations:** Worldwide. **Average salary range of placements:** More than $50,000. **Number of placements per year:** 1 - 49.

RESTAURANT RECRUITERS OF AMERICA
3701 Kirby Drive, Suite 814, Houston TX 77098. 713/529-0123. **Toll-free phone:** 888/782-4772. **Fax:** 713/523-5830. **Contact:** F. William Troff, President. **E-mail address:** jobs@restaurantrecruiters.com. **World Wide Web address:** http://www.restaurantrecruiters.com. **Description:** An executive search firm operating on a contingency basis. Client company pays fee. **Specializes in the areas of:** Restaurant. **Positions commonly filled include:** Restaurant/Food Service Manager; Vice President of Operations. **Corporate headquarters**

location: This Location. **Average salary range of placements:** $30,000 - $50,000. **Number of placements per year:** 100 - 199.

RICCIONE & ASSOCIATES INC.
16415 Addison Road, Suite 404, Addison TX 75001. 972/380-6432. **Fax:** 972/407-0659. **Contact:** Nick Riccione, President. **E-mail address:** hitec@ riccione.com. **World Wide Web address:** http://www. riccione.com. **Description:** An executive search firm operating on a contingency basis. The firm also provides some contract placements. **Specializes in the areas of:** Computer Science/Software; Engineering; High-Tech. **Positions commonly filled include:** Computer Programmer; Electrical/Electronics Engineer; Software Engineer; Systems Analyst; Telecommunications Manager. **Average salary range of placements:** More than $50,000. **Number of placements per year:** 50 - 99.

BART ROBERSON & COMPANY, INC.
1445 North Loop West, Suite 800, Houston TX 77008. 713/863-1445. **Contact:** Bart Roberson, Owner. **Description:** An executive search firm operating on both retainer and contingency bases. **Specializes in the areas of:** Accounting/Auditing; Economics; Engineering; Finance; Food; Industrial; Manufacturing; Personnel/Labor Relations; Sales; Technical. **Positions commonly filled include:** Accountant/Auditor; Biochemist; Budget Analyst; Buyer; Chemical Engineer; Chemist; Civil Engineer; Cost Estimator; Credit Mgr.; Design Engineer; Economist; Electrical/Electronics Engineer; Environmental Engineer; Financial Analyst; Geologist/Geophysicist; Health Services Mgr.; Human Resources Specialist; Industrial Engineer; Management Analyst/Consultant; Mechanical Engineer; Metallurgical Eng.; Mining Eng.; Petroleum Engineer; Purchasing Agent/Manager; Quality Control Supervisor; Strategic Relations Manager; Structural Engineer; Systems Analyst. **Average salary range of placements:** More than $50,000. **Number of placements per year:** 200 - 499.

R.A. RODRIGUEZ & ASSOCIATES
10935 Ben Crenshaw, Suite 210, El Paso TX 79935. 915/598-5028. **Contact:** Manager. **Description:** An executive search firm. **Specializes in the areas of:** Manufacturing.

ROMAC INTERNATIONAL
5429 LBJ Freeway, Suite 275, Dallas TX 75240. 972/387-1600. **Contact:** Manager. **Description:** An executive search firm. **Specializes in the areas of:** Accounting/Auditing; Computer Hardware/Software; Engineering; Finance.
Other U.S. locations:
- 8701 North Mopac, Suite 455, Austin TX 78759. 512/345-7473.
- 520 Post Oak Boulevard, Suite 700, Houston TX 77027. 713/439-1077.

ROTH YOUNG EXECUTIVE SEARCH
11999 Katy Freeway, Suite 490, Houston TX 77079. 281/368-8550. **Fax:** 281/368-8560. **Contact:** Rob Gladstone, President. **Description:** An executive search firm operating on both retainer and contingency bases. **Specializes in the areas of:** Advertising; Finance; Food; Manufacturing; Personnel/Labor Relations; Retail; Sales; Transportation. **Positions commonly filled include:** Buyer; Computer Programmer; General Manager; Hotel Manager; Human Resources Specialist; Industrial Engineer; Manufacturer's/Wholesaler's Sales Rep.; Operations/Production Manager; Purchasing Agent/Manager; Restaurant/Food Service Manager; Systems Analyst; Transportation/Traffic Specialist. **Average salary range of placements:** More than $50,000. **Number of placements per year:** 50 - 99.

ROTTMAN GROUP INC.
15851 North Dallas Parkway, Suite 500, Addison TX 75001. 972/518-1330. **Contact:** Manager. **Description:** An executive search firm. **Specializes in the areas of:** Health/Medical.

RUSSELL REYNOLDS ASSOCIATES, INC.
2001 Ross Avenue, Suite 1900, Dallas TX 75201. 214/220-2033. **Fax:** 214/220-3998. **Contact:** Manager. **Description:** An executive search firm. **Specializes in the areas of:** Banking; Chemicals; Health/Medical; Technical.

SABER CONSULTANTS
12519 Ramona, Cypress TX 77429. 281/477-0404. **Contact:** Manager. **Description:** An executive search firm. **Specializes in the areas of:** Architecture/Construction. **Positions commonly filled include:** Construction Contractor; Cost Estimator. **Number of placements per year:** 50 - 99.

SALES CONSULTANTS OF AUSTIN, INC.
2301 South Capital of Texas Highway, Building J-101, Austin TX 87846. 512/328-9955. **Fax:** 512/328-8659. **Contact:** Jay Middlebrook, President. **E-mail address:** scaustin@scaustin.com. **World Wide Web address:** http://www.scaustin.com. **Description:** An executive search firm. **Specializes in the areas of:** Architecture/Construction; Biotechnology; Data Communications; Food; Health/Medical; Information Systems; Information Technology; Marketing; Pharmaceuticals; Sales; Software Training; Telecommunications. **Corporate headquarters location:** Cleveland OH. **Other U.S. locations:** Nationwide.

SALES CONSULTANTS OF HOUSTON
5075 Westheimer, Suite 790, Houston TX 77056-5606. 713/627-0809. **Fax:** 713/622-7285. **Contact:** Jim DeForest, General Manager. **Description:** An executive search firm. **Specializes in the areas of:** Accounting/Auditing; Administration; Advertising; Architecture/Construction; Banking; Communications; Computer Hardware/Software; Construction; Design; Electrical; Engineering; Finance; Food; General Management; Health/Medical; Industrial; Insurance; Legal; Manufacturing; Operations Management; Personnel/Labor Relations; Procurement; Publishing; Retail; Sales; Technical; Textiles; Transportation.

SALES RECRUITERS OF HOUSTON
340 North Sam Houston Parkway East, Suite 263, Houston TX 77060. 281/447-0309. **Fax:** 281/448-0001. **Contact:** Sam Stitt, Executive Recruiter. **Description:** An executive search firm operating on a contingency basis. **Specializes in the areas of:** Sales. **Average salary range of placements:** $30,000 - $50,000. **Number of placements per year:** 50 - 99.

SALINAS & ASSOCIATES PERSONNEL SERVICE
1700 Commerce Street, Dallas TX 75201. 214/747-7878. **Contact:** Gerry Salinas, Owner/Recruiter. **Description:** An executive search firm operating on both retainer and contingency bases. Salinas & Associates also offers contract services and career/outplacement counseling. **Specializes in the areas of:** Accounting/Auditing; Advertising; Banking; Computer Hardware/Software; Fashion; Finance; Personnel/Labor Relations; Sales. **Positions commonly filled include:** Account Manager; Account Rep.; Accountant; Administrative Assistant; Administrative Mgr.; Advertising Clerk; Advertising Exec.; Auditor; Bank Officer/Manager; Budget Analyst; Buyer; Chemist; Claim Rep.; Controller; Counselor; Credit Mgr.; Customer Service Rep.; Database Manager; Human Resources Manager; Market Research Analyst; Marketing Manager; Marketing Specialist; Sales Engineer; Sales Executive; Sales Manager; Secretary. **Corporate headquarters location:** This Location. **Other U.S. locations:** Nationwide. **Average salary range of placements:** Less than $20,000. **Number of placements per year:** 50 - 99.

SANFORD ROSE ASSOCIATES
2222 Western Trails Boulevard, Suite 203, Austin TX 78745. 512/448-9555. **Fax:** 512/448-9567. **Contact:** Manager. **World Wide Web address:** http://www. sanfordrose.com. **Description:** An executive search firm. **Specializes in the areas of:** Electronics; Manufacturing.

R.L. SCOTT ASSOCIATES
222 West Exchange Avenue, Suite 203, Fort Worth TX
76106. 817/877-3622. **Contact:** Randall Scott, President.
Description: An executive search firm operating on both
retainer and contingency bases. **Specializes in the areas
of:** Health/Medical. **Positions commonly filled include:**
Accountant/Auditor; Administrator; CEO; CFO;
Controller; Counselor; Marketing Manager; Medical
Records Technician; Recreational Therapist; Registered
Nurse; Respiratory Therapist; Social Worker; Vice
President of Finance; Vice President of Operations.
Corporate headquarters location: This Location.
Average salary range of placements: More than
$50,000. **Number of placements per year:** 50 - 99.

SEARCH COM, INC.
12680 Hillcrest Road, Suite 101, Dallas TX 75230.
972/490-0300. **Contact:** Susan Abrahamson, President.
E-mail address: susana1@airmail.net. **Description:** An
executive search firm operating on a retainer basis.
Client company pays fee. **Specializes in the areas of:**
Advertising; Art/Design; Health/Medical; Internet
Marketing; Publishing. **Positions commonly filled
include:** Advertising Executive; Database Manager;
Designer; Editor; Graphic Artist; Graphic Designer;
Internet Services Manager; Managing Editor; Market
Research Analyst; Marketing Manager; Marketing
Specialist; Multimedia Designer; Public Relations
Specialist; Technical Writer/Editor; Webmaster.
Average salary range of placements: More than
$50,000. **Number of placements per year:** 1 - 49.

SEARCH NETWORK INTERNATIONAL
12801 North Central Expressway, Suite 260, Dallas TX
75243. 972/934-3950. **Fax:** 972/934-3868. **Contact:**
Manager. **E-mail address:** resumes@snint.com. **World
Wide Web address:** http://www.snint.com.
Description: An executive search firm operating on a
contingency basis. **Specializes in the areas of:**
Accounting/Auditing; Computer Science/Software;
Engineering; Food; Industrial; Manufacturing. **Positions
commonly filled include:** Accountant/Auditor;
Aerospace Engineer; Architect; Biochemist; Biomedical
Engineer; Buyer; Chemical Engineer; Chemist; Civil
Engineer; Computer Programmer; Cost Estimator;
Design Engineer; Designer; Draftsperson; Environmental
Engineer; Financial Analyst; Food Scientist/
Technologist; Geologist/Geophysicist; Industrial
Engineer; Industrial Production Manager; Internet
Services Manager; Mathematician; Mechanical Engineer;
Metallurgical Engineer; Mining Engineer; MIS
Specialist; Multimedia Designer; Operations/Production
Manager; Petroleum Engineer; Public Relations
Specialist; Purchasing Agent/Manager; Quality Control
Supervisor; Software Engineer; Statistician; Structural
Engineer; Systems Analyst; Telecommunications
Manager. **Number of placements per year:** 500 - 999.

SEARCHAMERICA INC.
5908 Meadowcreek Drive, Dallas TX 75248. 972/233-
3302. **Fax:** 972/233-1518. **Contact:** Harvey Weiner,
President. **E-mail address:** searchamerica@aol.com.
Description: An executive search firm that also provides
consultation services to boards of directors. Founded in
1974. **Specializes in the areas of:** Consulting; General
Management; Hotel/Restaurant; Personnel/Labor
Relations. **Average salary range of placements:** More
than $50,000. **Number of placements per year:** 50 - 99.

SELECT STAFF
8200 Nashville Avenue, Suite C109, Lubbock TX 79423.
806/794-5511. **Fax:** 806/794-5869. **Contact:** Manager.
Description: An executive search firm operating on a
contingency basis. **Specializes in the areas of:**
Accounting/Auditing; Administration; Food; General
Management; Personnel/Labor Relations; Retail; Sales;
Secretarial. **Positions commonly filled include:**
Accountant/Auditor; Adjuster; Administrative Manager;
Advertising Clerk; Architect; Attorney; Bank Officer/
Mgr.; Blue-Collar Worker Supervisor; Branch Mgr.;
Brokerage Clerk; Buyer; Chemical Engineer; Civil
Engineer; Claim Rep.; Clerical Supervisor; Counselor;

Credit Mgr.; Customer Service Rep.; Dental Assistant/
Dental Hygienist; Draftsperson; Electrical/Electronics
Engineer; Electrician; Environmental Engineer; General
Mgr.; Health Services Manager; Hotel Manager; Human
Resources Specialist; Human Service Worker; Industrial
Engineer; Landscape Architect; Licensed Practical
Nurse; Manufacturer's/Wholesaler's Sales Rep.; MIS
Specialist; Operations/Production Manager; Paralegal;
Pharmacist; Property and Real Estate Manager; Public
Relations Specialist; Purchasing Agent/Manager; Quality
Control Supervisor; Restaurant/Food Service Manager;
Securities Sales Rep.; Social Worker; Systems Analyst;
Technical Writer/Editor; Telecommunications Manager;
Transportation/Traffic Specialist; Underwriter/Assistant
Underwriter. **Average salary range of placements:**
$20,000 - $29,999. **Number of placements per year:**
500 - 999.

SHAW ASSOCIATES, INC.
1104 Commerce Drive, Richardson TX 75081-2307.
972/480-9400. **Fax:** 972/480-8700. **Contact:** Greg Shaw,
Owner. **E-mail address:** greg@shawassociates.com.
World Wide Web address: http://www.
shawassociates.com. **Description:** An executive search
firm. Founded in 1995. **Specializes in the areas of:**
Biotechnology; Medical Devices; Pharmaceuticals.
Corporate headquarters location: This Location.

MARVIN L. SILCOTT & ASSOCIATES, INC.
5477 Glen Lakes Drive, Dallas TX 75231. 214/369-
7802. **Fax:** 214/369-7875. **Contact:** Marvin L. Silcott,
President. **Description:** An executive search firm
operating on a retainer basis. **Specializes in the areas of:**
Legal. **Positions commonly filled include:** Attorney.
Average salary range of placements: More than
$50,000. **Number of placements per year:** 50 - 99.

SOLUTIONS
Rural Route 3, Box 204B, Leander TX 78641. 512/219-
0224. **Fax:** 512/918-2805. **Contact:** Karen Beall, Owner.
Description: An executive search firm operating on both
retainer and contingency bases. **Specializes in the areas
of:** Health/Medical; Sales. **Positions commonly filled
include:** Administrative Manager; Biomedical Engineer;
Claim Rep.; Customer Service Rep.; Dietician/
Nutritionist; Emergency Medical Tech.; Health Services
Mgr.; Nuclear Medicine Technologist; Occupational
Therapist; Operations/Production Manager; Pharmacist;
Physical Therapist; Physician; Psychologist; Public
Relations Specialist; Quality Control Supervisor;
Radiological Technologist; Recreational Therapist;
Registered Nurse; Respiratory Therapist; Social Worker;
Speech-Language Pathologist. **Number of placements
per year:** 1 - 49.

SPRADLEY LEGAL SEARCH
3131 McKinney Avenue, Suite 490, Dallas TX 75204.
214/969-5900. **Contact:** Manager. **Description:** An
executive search firm. **Specializes in the areas of:**
Legal.

STAFF EXTENSION INTERNATIONAL (SEI)
13612 Midway, Suite 103, Dallas TX 75244. 972/991-
4737. **Fax:** 972/991-5325. **Contact:** Jack R. Williams,
President. **E-mail address:** dallas@staffext.com. **World
Wide Web address:** http://www.staffext.com.
Description: An executive search firm that also provides
some temporary and contract placements. **Specializes in
the areas of:** Accounting/Auditing; Administration;
Computer Science/Software; Engineering; Finance;
General Management; Human Resources;
Manufacturing; Personnel/Labor Relations; Sales;
Technical. **Corporate headquarters location:** This
Location. **Other U.S. locations:** Houston TX. **Number
of placements per year:** 50 - 99.
Other U.S. locations:
• 3300 South Gessner Road, Suite 103, Houston TX
   77063. 713/784-8696.

STEINFIELD & ASSOCIATES
2626 Cole Avenue, Suite 400, Dallas TX 75204.
214/220-0535. **Fax:** 214/665-9535. **Contact:** David

Steinfield, President. **E-mail address:** steinfield@ airmail.net. **Description:** An executive search firm. **Specializes in the areas of:** Accounting/Auditing; Finance; Human Resources. **Positions commonly filled include:** Accounting Supervisor; Auditor; Controller; Financial Mgr.; Human Resources Manager. **Average salary range of placements:** More than $50,000.

R.A. STONE & ASSOCIATES
5495 Beltline Road, Suite 140, Dallas TX 75240. 972/233-0483. **Contact:** Manager. **Description:** An executive search firm. **Specializes in the areas of:** Broadcasting; Health/Medical.

STRAIGHT SOURCE
100 North Central Expressway, Suite 1000, Richardson TX 75080. 972/437-2220. **Fax:** 972/437-2310. **Contact:** Recruiting Manager. **Description:** An executive search firm operating on a retainer basis. **Specializes in the areas of:** Computer Science/Software; Engineering; General Management; Publishing; Sales; Technical. **Positions commonly filled include:** Branch Manager; Computer Programmer; General Manager; Software Engineer; Strategic Relations Manager; Systems Analyst. **Corporate headquarters location:** Dallas TX. **Average salary range of placements:** More than $50,000. **Number of placements per year:** 1 - 49.

STRATFORDGROUP
700 Louisiana, Suite 2250, Houston TX 77002. 713/223-7270. **Toll-free phone:** 800/536-4384. **Fax:** 713/223-7279. **Contact:** Recruiter. **World Wide Web address:** http://www.stratfordgroup.com. **Description:** An executive search firm operating on a retainer basis. **Specializes in the areas of:** Automotive; Consumer Products; Engineering; Entertainment; Finance; Health/ Medical; Human Resources; IT; Manufacturing; Nonprofit; Professional; Retail; Telecommunications; Transportation. **Corporate headquarters location:** Cleveland OH. **Other U.S. locations:** Nationwide.

STRAWN ARNOLD & LEECH, INC.
11402 Bee Caves Road West, Austin TX 78733. 512/263-1131. **Contact:** Manager. **Description:** An executive search firm. **Specializes in the areas of:** Biotechnology; Pharmaceuticals.

TGA COMPANY
P.O. Box 331121, Fort Worth TX 76163. 817/370-0865. **Fax:** 817/292-6451. **Contact:** Tom Green, President. **Description:** An executive search firm. **Specializes in the areas of:** Accounting; Computer Science/Software; Finance; Information Systems; Technical. **Positions commonly filled include:** Accountant; CFO; Controller; Credit Mgr.; Financial Analyst; MIS Specialist; Software Engineer; Systems Analyst. **Average salary range of placements:** More than $50,000. **Number of placements per year:** 50 - 99.

TMP WORLDWIDE
1601 Elm Street, Suite 4150, Dallas TX 75201. 214/754-0019. **Fax:** 214/754-0615. **Contact:** Judy Stubbs, Managing Partner. **World Wide Web address:** http://www.tmpw.com. **Description:** An executive search firm. **Specializes in the areas of:** Biotechnology; Consumer Products; Finance; Health/Medical; Industrial; Pharmaceuticals; Technical. **Corporate headquarters location:** New York NY.
Other U.S. locations:
- 3 Riverway, Suite 1800, Houston TX 77056. 713/843-8600.
- San Jacinto Center, 98 San Jacinto Boulevard, Suite 1400, Austin TX 78701-4039. 512/425-3900.

TRS ONSITE STAFFING
P.O. Box 405, Sugar Land TX 77478-0405. 281/263-3560. **Contact:** Manager. **Description:** An executive search firm. **Specializes in the areas of:** Engineering.

THE TALON GROUP
16801 Addison Road, Suite 255, Addison TX 75001. 972/931-8223. **Fax:** 972/931-8063. **Contact:** Bob Piper,

President. **E-mail address:** talongrp@gte.net. **Description:** An executive search firm operating on a retainer basis. **Specializes in the areas of:** Construction; Housing; Manufacturing; Real Estate. **Positions commonly filled include:** Architect; Chief Financial Officer; Civil Engineer; Construction Superintendent; Controller; Cost Estimator; General Manager; Marketing Manager; MIS Specialist; Operations Manager; Production Manager; Project Manager; Purchasing Agent/Manager; Sales Manager; Vice President. **Average salary range of placements:** More than $50,000. **Number of placements per year:** 50 - 99.

BETTY TANNER EXECUTIVE SEARCH
5539 North Mesa Street, El Paso TX 79912. 915/587-5166. **Fax:** 915/587-5191. **Contact:** Bruce Tanner, General Manager. **Description:** An executive search firm operating on both retainer and contingency bases. The firm also provides career/outplacement counseling. **Specializes in the areas of:** Accounting/Auditing; Computer Science/Software; Engineering; Finance; Health/Medical; Industrial; Manufacturing; Personnel; Labor Relations. **Positions commonly filled include:** Accountant/Auditor; Biomedical Engineer; Budget Analyst; Buyer; Ceramics Engineer; Chemical Engineer; Computer Programmer; Designer; Electrical/Electronics Engineer; Financial Analyst; General Manager; Human Resources Manager; Industrial Engineer; Industrial Production Manager; Manufacturer's/Wholesaler's Sales Rep.; Materials Engineer; Mechanical Engineer; Metallurgical Engineer; Operations/Production Manager; Physical Therapist; Purchasing Agent/Manager; Quality Control Supervisor; Software Engineer; Systems Analyst; Transportation/Traffic Specialist. **Average salary range of placements:** More than $50,000. **Number of placements per year:** 50 - 99.

TECH-NET
14785 Preston Road, Dallas TX 75240-7876. 972/934-3000. **Contact:** Chris Cole, Owner. **Description:** An executive search firm that focuses on the placement of engineers in sales positions that utilize UNIX-based design tools. Founded in 1989. **Specializes in the areas of:** Computer Science/Software; Engineering; Sales; Technical. **Positions commonly filled include:** Aerospace Engineer; Design Engineer; Electrical/ Electronics Engineer; Mechanical Engineer; MIS Specialist; Software Engineer; Technical Representative. **Average salary range of placements:** More than $50,000. **Number of placements per year:** 1 - 49.

TECHNICAL ALLIANCE RECRUITERS
TECHNICAL RESOURCE CONSULTANTS (TRC)
5599 San Felipe Road, Suite 800, Houston TX 77056. 713/965-9251. **Fax:** 713/877-1230. **Contact:** Kyle T. Mosley, Manager. **E-mail address:** opportunities@tar-engineering.com. **World Wide Web address:** http://www.tar-engineering.com. **Description:** An executive search firm. Technical Alliance Recruiters is a division of MAGIC (Management Alliance Group of Independent Companies). Technical Resource Consultants (TRC) (also at this location, 713/965-9975, http://www.trcengineering.com) is an executive search firm, and also a division of MAGIC. **Specializes in the areas of:** Engineering; Executives; Finance; Information Technology.

TECHNICAL STAFF RECRUITERS
5599 San Felipe, Suite 506, Houston TX 77056. 713/965-9305. **Fax:** 713/965-0700. **Contact:** Pari Bagheri, Manager. **E-mail address:** opportunities@tsrjobs.com. **World Wide Web address:** http://www.tsrjobs.com. **Description:** An executive search firm. Technical Staff Recruiters is a division of MAGIC (Management Alliance Group of Independent Companies). **Specializes in the areas of:** Computer Hardware/Software; Electrical; Mechanical. **Positions commonly filled include:** Applications Engineer; Buyer; Controls Engineer; Digital Analyst; Electrical/Electronics Engineer; Engineer; Hardware Engineer; Industrial Engineer; Maintenance Technician; Manufacturing Engineer; Plant Engineer; Project Engineer; Project

Manager; Project Planner; Quality Assurance Engineer; Senior Management; Software Engineer; Support Personnel; Test Engineer.

TECHNICAL STAFFING SOLUTIONS
16775 Addison Road, Suite 240, Addison TX 75001. 972/248-0700. **Fax:** 972/248-1175. **Contact:** Don Fink, Office Manager. **E-mail address:** staff@ technicalstaffing.com. **World Wide Web address:** http://www.technicalstaffing.com. **Description:** An executive search firm that also provides some contract services. **Specializes in the areas of:** Chemicals; Computer Science/Software; Engineering. **Positions commonly filled include:** Applications Engineer; AS400 Programmer Analyst; Chemical Engineer; Chemist; Computer Programmer; Content Developer; Database Administrator; Database Manager; Design Engineer; Environmental Engineer; Internet Services Manager; Mechanical Engineer; Metallurgical Engineer; Multimedia Designer; Network/Systems Administrator; Software Engineer; SQL Programmer; Systems Analyst; Systems Mgr.; Webmaster. **Corporate headquarters location:** This Location. **Other U.S. locations:** Nationwide. **Average salary range of placements:** $50,000 - $100,000. **Number of placements per year:** 100 - 199.

TEXAS PERSONNEL
985 Interstate 10 North, Beaumont TX 77706. 409/892-5000. **Fax:** 409/892-5068. **Contact:** Cliff Heubel, Owner. **Description:** An executive search firm operating on a contingency basis. **Specializes in the areas of:** Banking; Computer Science/Software; Insurance; Sales; Secretarial. **Positions commonly filled include:** Accountant; Automotive Mechanic; Bank Officer/Mgr.; Computer Programmer; Dental Assistant/Dental Hygienist; Manufacturer's/Wholesaler's Sales Rep.; MIS Specialist; Services Sales Rep.; Systems Analyst; Typist/Word Processor. **Number of placements per year:** 100 - 199.

TEXSTAR
P.O. Box 926193, Houston TX 77292-6193. 713/681-2300. **Contact:** Manager. **Description:** An executive search firm. **Specializes in the areas of:** Accounting; Management.

THERAPISTS UNLIMITED
2340 East Trinity Mills Road, Suite 215, Carrollton TX 75006. 972/418-1800. **Contact:** Recruiter. **Description:** An executive search firm that also provides temporary and contract placements. **Specializes in the areas of:** Health/Medical. **Positions commonly filled include:** Physical Therapist; Speech-Language Pathologist. **Average salary range of placements:** More than $50,000. **Number of placements per year:** 50 - 99.

TOTAL PERSONNEL INC.
P.O. Box 28975, Dallas TX 75228. 214/327-1165. **Fax:** 214/328-3061. **Contact:** Sherry Phillips, President. **E-mail address:** hunthead@flash.net. **Description:** An executive search firm operating on both retainer and contingency bases. Client company pays fee. **Specializes in the areas of:** Computer Science/Software; MIS/EDP. **Positions commonly filled include:** Applications Engineer; Architect; AS400 Programmer Analyst; Computer Animator; Computer Engineer; Computer Programmer; Content Developer; Database Administrator; Database Manager; Internet Services Manager; MIS Specialist; Network/Systems Administrator; Software Engineer; SQL Programmer; Systems Analyst; Systems Manager; Webmaster. **Corporate headquarters location:** This Location. **Average salary range of placements:** $50,000 - $100,000. **Number of placements per year:** 1 - 49.

TRICOM GROUP
6363 Woodway Drive, Suite 250, Houston TX 77057-1713. 713/334-2227. **Fax:** 713/334-4030. **Contact:** Recruiter. **World Wide Web address:** http://www.tricom-group.com. **Description:** An executive search firm. **Specializes in the areas of:** High-Tech.

CRAIG TROTMAN & ASSOCIATES
3109 Carlisle Street, Suite 206A, Dallas TX 75204. 214/954-1919. **Contact:** Manager. **Description:** An executive search firm. **Specializes in the areas of:** Consumer Package Goods.

THE URBAN PLACEMENT SERVICE
602 Sawyer Street, Suite 460, Houston TX 77007. 713/880-2211. **Fax:** 713/880-5577. **Contact:** Willie S. Bright, Owner. **E-mail address:** urbanplacement@ msn.com. **Description:** An executive search firm. **Specializes in the areas of:** Accounting; Administration; Computer Science/Software; Engineering; Finance; Food; Industrial; Manufacturing; Personnel/Labor Relations; Technical. **Positions commonly filled include:** Account Manager; Account Rep.; Accountant; Applications Engineer; Broadcast Technician; Buyer; Chemist; CFO; Civil Engineer; Controller; Credit Mgr.; Database Manager; Design Engineer; Economist; Electrical/Electronics Engineer; Environmental Engineer; Finance Director; Financial Analyst; Food Scientist/Technologist; Geologist/Geophysicist; Human Resources Manager; Industrial Engineer; Industrial Production Manager; Manufacturing Engineer; Market Research Analyst; Marketing Manager; Mechanical Engineer; Medical Records Technician; Metallurgical Engineer; MIS Specialist; Production Manager; Project Manager; Purchasing Agent/Manager; Sales Engineer; Sales Exec.; Sales Manager; Sales Representative; Software Engineer; Statistician; Systems Analyst; Systems Manager. **Average salary range of placements:** $30,000 - $50,000. **Number of placements per year:** 1 - 49.

VALPERS INC.
8303 Southwest Freeway, Suite 750, Houston TX 77074. 713/771-9420. **Fax:** 713/771-7924. **Contact:** Manager. **Description:** An executive search firm focusing specifically on the placement of professionals in the industrial valve and fluid flow industries. Valpers operates on both retainer and contingency bases and also provides contract services. **Specializes in the areas of:** Engineering; General Management; Industrial; Manufacturing; Sales; Technical. **Positions commonly filled include:** Customer Service Rep.; Design Engineer; Electrical/Electronics Engineer; General Manager; Human Resources Specialist; Industrial Production Manager; Manufacturer's/Wholesaler's Sales Rep.; Market Research Analyst; Materials Engineer; Mechanical Engineer; Metallurgical Engineer; Nuclear Engineer; Operations/Production Manager; Quality Control Supervisor. **Average salary range of placements:** More than $50,000. **Number of placements per year:** 1 - 49.

DICK VAN VLIET & ASSOCIATES
2401 Fountain View Drive, Suite 322, Houston TX 77057. 713/952-0371. **Contact:** Dick Van Vliet, President. **Description:** An executive search firm operating on a contingency basis. **Specializes in the areas of:** Accounting/Auditing; Administration; Computer Science/Software; Finance; Sales. **Positions commonly filled include:** Accountant/Auditor; Budget Analyst; Credit Manager; Financial Analyst; Human Resources Specialist; MIS Specialist; Systems Analyst. **Average salary range of placements:** $30,000 - $100,000. **Number of placements per year:** 50 - 99.

DENIS P. WALSH & ASSOCIATES, INC.
5402 Bent Bough, Houston TX 77088. 281/931-9121. **Fax:** 281/820-4285. **Contact:** Denis P. Walsh, Jr., President. **Description:** An executive search firm operating on a contingency basis. **Specializes in the areas of:** Chemicals; Engineering; Environmental. **Positions commonly filled include:** Chemical Engineer; Construction Contractor; Cost Estimator; Electrical/Electronics Eng.; Environmental Engineer; Mechanical Engineer. **Number of placements per year:** 1 - 49.

WARDRUP ASSOCIATES
2508 Springpark Way, Suite 300, Richardson TX 75082. 972/437-9333. **Fax:** 972/437-1208. **Contact:** Recruiter. **World Wide Web address:** http://www.wardrup.com.

Description: An executive search firm. **Specializes in the areas of:** Communications; Computer Hardware/Software; Electronics; High-Tech; Information Technology.

WATKINS & ASSOCIATES
6161 Savoy, Suite 1120, Houston TX 77036. 713/777-5261. **Fax:** 713/334-4180. **Contact:** Manager. **Description:** An executive search firm operating on both retainer and contingency bases. **Specializes in the areas of:** Accounting/Auditing; Manufacturing; Oil and Gas; Petrochemical; Sales.

ROBERT WESSON & ASSOCIATES
P.O. Box 902, Addison TX 75001. 972/239-8613. **Contact:** Bob McDermid, Partner. **Description:** An executive search firm. **Specializes in the areas of:** Restaurant. **Positions commonly filled include:** Restaurant/Food Service Manager. **Number of placements per year:** 100 - 199.

WHEELER, MOORE & ELAM COMPANY
14800 Quorum Drive, Suite 200, Dallas TX 75240. 972/386-8806. **Contact:** Dr. Mark Moore, President. **Description:** An executive search firm operating on a retainer basis. The firm also provides career/outplacement counseling services. **Specializes in the areas of:** Accounting/Auditing; Administration; Engineering; Finance; General Management; Legal; Manufacturing; Personnel/Labor Relations; Sales; Technical. **Average salary range of placements:** More than $50,000. **Number of placements per year:** 1 - 49.

WILLIAMS COMPANY
8080 North Central Expressway, Suite 400, Dallas TX 75206. 214/891-6340. **Contact:** Sandy Williams, Manager. **Description:** An executive search firm. **Specializes in the areas of:** Retail.

WINDSOR CONSULTANTS INC.
13201 Northwest Freeway, Suite 704, Houston TX 77040. 713/460-0586. **Fax:** 713/460-0945. **Contact:** Dan Narsh, President. **Description:** An executive search firm operating on both retainer and contingency bases. **Specializes in the areas of:** Food; Health/Medical; Legal; Sales. **Positions commonly filled include:** Attorney; Management Trainee; Manufacturer's/Wholesaler's Sales Rep.; Medical Records Technician; Registered Nurse; Restaurant/Food Service Manager. **Corporate headquarters location:** This Location. **Other U.S. locations:** DC; IL; NY. **Average salary range of placements:** More than $50,000. **Number of placements per year:** 100 - 199.

WITT/KIEFFER, FORD, HADELMAN & LLOYD
2 Lincoln Center, 5420 LBJ Freeway, Suite 460, Dallas TX 75240. 972/490-1370. **Fax:** 972/490-3472. **Contact:** Manager. **World Wide Web address:** http://www. wittkieffer.com. **Description:** Witt/Kieffer, Ford, Hadelman & Lloyd is an executive search firm. **Specializes in the areas of:** Health/Medical. **Other U.S. locations:**
- 10375 Richmond Avenue, Suite 1625, Houston TX 77042. 713/266-6779.

BRUCE G. WOODS EXECUTIVE SEARCH
25 Highland Park Village, Suite 100-171, Dallas TX 75205. 214/522-9888. **Contact:** Bruce Woods, Owner. **World Wide Web address:** http://www. contractexecutives.com/brucegwoods.html. **Description:** A global executive search firm. Founded in 1977. **Specializes in the areas of:** Cable TV; Consulting; Finance; Health/Medical; Manufacturing; Real Estate; Telecommunications; Wireless Communications.

JOHN W. WORSHAM & ASSOCIATES INC.
5701 Woodway Drive, Suite 210, Houston TX 77057. 713/266-3235. **Fax:** 713/266-1334. **Contact:** Manager. **Description:** An executive search firm. **Specializes in the areas of:** Banking.

THE WRIGHT GROUP
9217 Frenchman's Way, Dallas TX 75220. 214/351-1115. **Contact:** Jay J. Wright, President. **Description:** An executive search firm. **Specializes in the areas of:** Advertising; Marketing. **Positions commonly filled include:** Market Research Analyst; Marketing Specialist. **Number of placements per year:** 1 - 49.

R.S. WYATT ASSOCIATES, INC.
P.O. Box 92786, Southlake TX 76092. 817/421-8726. **Fax:** 817/421-1374. **Contact:** Robert S. Wyatt, Ph.D., Principal. **E-mail address:** rswassoc@aol.com. **Description:** An executive search firm operating on a retainer basis. The firm also provides consulting services. **Specializes in the areas of:** Consulting; General Management; Personnel/Labor Relations; Retail. **Positions commonly filled include:** Accountant; Branch Manager; Buyer; Computer Programmer; Credit Manager; Customer Service Rep.; Design Engineer; General Manager; Human Resources Specialist; Industrial Engineer; Management Analyst/Consultant; Public Relations Specialist; Software Engineer; Systems Analyst; Transportation/Traffic Specialist. **Average salary range of placements:** More than $50,000. **Number of placements per year:** 1 - 49.

PERMANENT EMPLOYMENT AGENCIES

ABILENE EMPLOYMENT SERVICE
1290 South Willis Street, Suite 111, Abilene TX 79605. 915/698-0451. **Fax:** 915/690-1242. **Contact:** Vi Ballard, Owner. **Description:** A permanent employment agency. **Specializes in the areas of:** Accounting/Auditing; Banking; Computer Science/Software; General Management; Health/Medical; Insurance; Legal; Manufacturing; Retail; Secretarial; Transportation. **Positions commonly filled include:** Accountant/Auditor; Administrative Manager; Advertising Clerk; Aircraft Mechanic/Engine Specialist; Automotive Mechanic; Bank Officer/Manager; Blue-Collar Worker Supervisor; Branch Manager; Buyer; Clerical Supervisor; Computer Programmer; Cost Estimator; Counselor; Customer Service Representative; Electrician; General Manager; Human Service Worker; Landscape Architect; Medical Records Technician; Operations/Production Manager; Physical Therapist; Property and Real Estate Manager; Quality Control Supervisor; Real Estate Agent; Restaurant/Food Service Manager; Securities Sales Representative; Software Engineer; Systems Analyst; Travel Agent; Typist/Word Processor. **Average salary range of placements:** $20,000 - $29,999. **Number of placements per year:** 1 - 49.

ACCOUNTING ACTION PERSONNEL
3010 LBJ Freeway, Suite 710, Dallas TX 75234. 972/241-1543. **Contact:** Cheryl Bieke, Office Manager. **E-mail address:** acaction@airmail.net. **World Wide Web address:** http://www.gtesupersite.com/acctgaction. **Description:** A permanent employment agency that also provides some temporary placements. **Specializes in the areas of:** Accounting/Auditing; Administration; Finance. **Positions commonly filled include:** Accountant/Auditor; Administrative Assistant; Bookkeeper; Clerk; Credit Manager; Data Entry Clerk; Receptionist; Secretary; Typist/Word Processor.

AUSTIN INSURANCE RECRUITERS
1000 West Bank, 5A-110, Austin TX 78746. 512/329-8815. **Contact:** Manager. **Description:** A permanent employment agency. **Specializes in the areas of:** Insurance.

AUSTIN MEDICAL PERSONNEL
3330 Matlock Road, Suite 210, Arlington TX 76015. 817/335-2433. **Fax:** 817/459-0761. **Contact:** Paula Zimmer, Owner. **E-mail address:** paula@ austinmedical.net. **Description:** A permanent

employment agency. **Specializes in the areas of:** Health/Medical.

AWARE AFFILIATES PERSONNEL SERVICE
1209 Lake Street, Fort Worth TX 76147. 817/870-2591. **Fax:** 817/870-2595. **Contact:** Mike Keeton, President. **Description:** A permanent employment agency. **Specializes in the areas of:** Accounting; Administration; Advertising; Finance; General Management; Health/ Medical; Insurance; Legal; Manufacturing; Nonprofit; Personnel/Labor Relations; Publishing; Retail; Sales; Secretarial; Technical; Transportation. **Positions commonly filled include:** Accountant/Auditor; Adjuster; Administrative Mgr.; Advertising Clerk; Blue-Collar Worker Supervisor; Branch Mgr.; Claim Rep.; Clerical Supervisor; Computer Programmer; Cost Estimator; Counselor; Credit Mgr.; Customer Service Rep.; Editor; Financial Analyst; General Mgr.; Health Services Mgr.; Hotel Mgr.; Human Resources Specialist; Insurance Agent/Broker; Library Tech.; Management Trainee; Manufacturer's/Wholesaler's Sales Rep.; Operations/ Production Manager; Paralegal; Property and Real Estate Manager; Purchasing Agent/Manager; Quality Control Supervisor; Securities Sales Rep.; Services Sales Rep.; Transportation/Traffic Specialist; Travel Agent; Typist/ Word Processor; Underwriter/Assistant Underwriter. **Average salary range of placements:** $30,000 - $49,999. **Number of placements per year:** 200 - 499.

B.G. PERSONNEL SERVICES
P.O. Box 803026, Dallas TX 75380. 972/960-7741. **Contact:** Manager. **Description:** A permanent employment agency. **Specializes in the areas of:** Real Estate.

BABICH & ASSOCIATES, INC.
6030 East Mockingbird Lane, Dallas TX 75206. 214/823-9999. **Contact:** Anthony Beshara, President. **Description:** A permanent employment agency. **Specializes in the areas of:** Accounting; Administration; Clerical; Computer Hardware/Software; Engineering; Finance; Manufacturing; Sales; Technical. **Positions commonly filled include:** Accountant; Administrative Assistant; Agricultural Engineer; Bookkeeper; Ceramics Engineer; Civil Engineer; Computer Programmer; Customer Service Rep.; Data Entry Clerk; EDP Specialist; Electrical/Electronics Engineer; Financial Analyst; General Manager; Human Resources Manager; Industrial Engineer; Mechanical Engineer; Medical Secretary; Metallurgical Engineer; Receptionist; Secretary; Systems Analyst; Typist/Word Processor. **Number of placements per year:** 500 - 999.

BABICH & ASSOCIATES, INC.
One Summit Avenue, Suite 602, Fort Worth TX 76102. 817/336-7261. **Contact:** Anthony Beshara, President. **Description:** A permanent employment agency. **Specializes in the areas of:** Accounting/Auditing; Administration; Clerical; Computer Hardware/Software; Engineering; Manufacturing; Sales; Technical. **Positions commonly filled include:** Accountant; Administrative Assistant; Agricultural Engineer; Bookkeeper; Ceramics Engineer; Civil Engineer; Computer Programmer; Customer Service Representative; Data Entry Clerk; EDP Specialist; Electrical/Electronics Engineer; Financial Analyst; General Manager; Human Resources Manager; Industrial Engineer; Mechanical Engineer; Medical Secretary; Metallurgical Engineer; Receptionist; Sales Rep.; Secretary; Stenographer; Systems Analyst; Typist/Word Processor. **Number of placements per year:** 500 - 999.

BESTSTAFF SERVICES, INC.
3730 Kirby Street, Suite 320, Houston TX 77098. 713/527-8233. **Fax:** 713/527-0813. **Contact:** David Harris, CEO. **Description:** A permanent employment agency that also provides some temporary and contract placements. **Specializes in the areas of:** Advertising; Banking; Engineering; Personnel/Labor Relations; Sales; Secretarial; Technical. **Positions commonly filled include:** Accountant; Administrative Mgr.; Advertising Clerk; Aerospace Engineer; Bank Officer/Manager; Budget Analyst; Chemical Engineer; Civil Engineer; Claim Rep.; Computer Programmer; Design Engineer; Electrical/Electronics Engineer; General Mgr.; Human Resources Specialist; Industrial Engineer; Internet Services Manager; Management Analyst/Consultant; Mechanical Engineer; Property and Real Estate Manager; Quality Control Supervisor; Restaurant/Food Service Mgr.; Securities Sales Rep.; Software Engineer; Structural Engineer; Systems Analyst; Technical Writer/ Editor; Typist/Word Processor. **Benefits available to temporary workers:** Paid Holidays; Paid Vacation; Referral Bonus Plan. **Average salary range of placements:** $30,000 - $50,000. **Number of placements per year:** 100 - 199.

BORDER PROFESSIONAL RECRUITERS
5901 McPherson, Suite 5A, Laredo TX 78041. 956/727-4296. **Contact:** Manager. **Description:** A permanent employment agency that also offers some temporary placements. **Specializes in the areas of:** Clerical; Industrial.

BOTT & ASSOCIATES
P.O. Box 42405, Houston TX 77242-2405. 713/782-9814. **Fax:** 713/782-9817. **Contact:** K.W. Bott, President. **Description:** A permanent employment agency. **Specializes in the areas of:** Engineering. **Positions commonly filled include:** Ceramics Engineer; Chemical Engineer; Civil Engineer; Design Engineer; Environmental Engineer; Industrial Engineer; Manufacturing Engineer; Materials Engineer; Mechanical Engineer; Metallurgical Engineer; Petroleum Engineer; Production Manager; Project Manager; Sales Engineer; Structural Engineer. **Average salary range of placements:** $30,000 - $50,000. **Number of placements per year:** 100 - 199.

BRAINPOWER PERSONNEL AGENCY
4210 50th Street, Suite A, Lubbock TX 79413-3810. 806/795-9444. **Fax:** 806/795-0645. **Contact:** Phil Crenshaw, CPC/Owner. **Description:** A permanent employment agency. **Specializes in the areas of:** Accounting; Administration; Computer Science/ Software; Data Processing; Engineering; Finance; Health/Medical; Sales; Secretarial. **Positions commonly filled include:** Accountant; Computer Programmer; Customer Service Rep.; Electrical/Electronics Engineer; MIS Specialist; Social Worker; Software Engineer. **Average salary range of placements:** $20,000 - $29,999. **Number of placements per year:** 1 - 49.

BROWN & KEENE PERSONNEL
14160 Dallas Parkway, Suite 450, Dallas TX 75240. 972/701-9292. **Contact:** Manager. **Description:** A permanent employment agency. **Specializes in the areas of:** Administration.

BULLOCK PERSONNEL, INC.
16414 San Pedro, Suite 600, San Antonio TX 78232. 210/495-5900. **Contact:** Recruiter. **Description:** A permanent employment agency. **Specializes in the areas of:** Accounting; Administration; Finance; General Management; Legal; Personnel/Labor Relations; Retail; Sales; Secretarial. **Positions commonly filled include:** Accountant; Administrative Manager; Bank Officer/ Manager; Clerical Supervisor; Computer Programmer; Customer Service Rep.; General Manager; Human Resources Specialist; Purchasing Agent/Manager.

COLVIN RESOURCES GROUP
4141 Blue Lake Circle, Suite 140, Dallas TX 75244-5132. 972/788-5114. **Fax:** 972/490-5015. **Contact:** Sheila Bridges, Senior Account Executive. **Description:** A permanent employment agency that also provides temporary placements. **Specializes in the areas of:** Accounting; Architecture/Construction; Banking; Finance; General Management; Health/Medical; Personnel/Labor Relations; Secretarial. **Positions commonly filled include:** Accountant; Budget Analyst; Credit Manager; Financial Analyst; Human Resources Specialist; Property and Real Estate Mgr.; Typist/Word Processor. **Average salary range of placements:** $30,000 - $50,000. **Number of placements per year:** 200 - 499.

CONTINENTAL PERSONNEL SERVICE
6671 Southwest Freeway, Suite 101, Houston TX 77074. 713/771-7181. **Fax:** 713/771-4444. **Contact:** Richard Quinn, Owner. **Description:** A permanent employment agency. **Specializes in the areas of:** Engineering; Health/Medical; Manufacturing; Quantitative Marketing. **Positions commonly filled include:** Chemical Engineer; Civil Engineer; Dentist; Electrical/Electronics Engineer; Environmental Engineer; Factory Worker; Industrial Engineer; Manufacturing Engineer; Mechanical Engineer; Medical Records Technician; Nuclear Engineer; Nurse; Packaging Engineer; Physician; Plant Manager; Quality Control Supervisor; Safety Specialist; Supervisor; Technician; Water/Wastewater Engineer.

CREATIVE STAFFING SERVICES
1533 North Lee Trevino Drive, Suite 200, El Paso TX 79936. 915/591-5111. **Fax:** 915/593-7482. **Contact:** Elizabeth Hill, Office Manager. **Description:** A permanent employment agency that also provides some temporary placements. **Specializes in the areas of:** Accounting; Computer Science/Software; General Management; Industrial; Light Industrial; Nonprofit; Personnel/Labor Relations; Printing; Retail; Sales; Secretarial; Technical; Transportation. **Positions commonly filled include:** Account Mgr.; Account Rep.; Accountant; Administrative Assistant; Advertising Clerk; Blue-Collar Worker Supervisor; Budget Analyst; Buyer; Claim Rep.; Clerical Supervisor; Computer Animator; Computer Operator; Computer Programmer; Controller; Credit Mgr.; Customer Service Rep.; Database Manager; Draftsperson; Electrician; Financial Analyst; General Manager; Human Resources Mgr.; Industrial Engineer; Industrial Production Manager; Management Trainee; Manufacturing Engineer; Marketing Specialist; Medical Records Tech.; MIS Specialist; Operations Mgr.; Paralegal; Production Manager; Purchasing Agent/Mgr.; Quality Control Supervisor; Sales Manager; Sales Rep.; Secretary; Systems Analyst; Technical Writer/Editor; Transportation/Traffic Specialist; Typist/Word Processor. **Benefits available to temporary workers:** Medical Insurance; Paid Holidays; Paid Vacation. **Corporate headquarters location:** This Location. **Average salary range of placements:** $30,000 - $50,000. **Number of placements per year:** 1 - 49.

DH&A (DONICE HALL & ASSOCIATES)
826 Tulane, Houston TX 77007. 713/426-4900. **Contact:** Manager. **Description:** A permanent employment agency. **Specializes in the areas of:** Accounting/ Auditing; Banking.

DALLAS EMPLOYMENT SERVICES, INC.
750 North St. Paul Street, Suite 1180, Dallas TX 75201. 214/954-0700. **Toll-free phone:** 800/954-1666. **Fax:** 214/754-0148. **Contact:** Manager. **E-mail address:** des@des-inc.com. **World Wide Web address:** http://www.des-inc.com. **Description:** A permanent employment agency that also offers temporary placements. **Specializes in the areas of:** Accounting; Administration; Banking; Fashion; Finance; General Management; Health/Medical; Industrial; Insurance; Legal; Marketing; Personnel/Labor Relations; Publishing; Retail; Sales; Secretarial. **Positions commonly filled include:** Accountant; Administrative Assistant; Administrative Manager; Advertising Clerk; Assistant Manager; Budget Analyst; Claim Rep.; Clerical Supervisor; Customer Service Rep.; Financial Analyst; General Manager; Graphic Artist; Human Resources Manager; Management Trainee; Market Research Analyst; Marketing Specialist; Operations Manager; Paralegal; Production Manager; Public Relations Specialist; Sales Rep.; Secretary; Typist/Word Processor; Underwriter/Assistant Underwriter. **Corporate headquarters location:** This Location. **Average salary range of placements:** $20,000 - $50,000. **Number of placements per year:** 200 - 499.

DATA STAFFING CENTRE
2600 South Gessner Street, Suite 304, Houston TX 77063. 713/785-9997. **Fax:** 713/785-5179. **Contact:** Manager. **E-mail address:** opportunities@ datastaffing.com. **World Wide Web address:** http://www.datastaffing.com. **Description:** A permanent placement agency. Data Staffing Centre is a division of MAGIC (Management Alliance Group of Independent Companies). **Specializes in the areas of:** Data Communications; Network Administration; Systems Administration. **Positions commonly filled include:** Database Administrator; Database Manager; LAN/WAN Designer/Developer; UNIX System Administrator.

DATAPRO PERSONNEL CONSULTANTS
13355 Noel Road, Suite 2001, Dallas TX 75240. 972/661-8600. **Fax:** 972/661-1309. **Contact:** Jack Kallison, Owner. **Description:** A permanent employment agency. **Specializes in the areas of:** Computer Programming; Computer Science/Software. **Positions commonly filled include:** Computer Programmer; EDP Specialist; Project Manager; Software Engineer; Systems Analyst; Technical Writer/Editor.

DAYSTAR SERVICES
6750 West Loop South, Suite 140, Bellaire TX 77401. 713/664-1000. **Fax:** 713/664-0286. **Contact:** Manager. **Description:** A permanent employment agency that also provides some temporary placements. **Specializes in the areas of:** Administration; Clerical; Office Support.

DENTAL RESOURCE MANAGEMENT
P.O. Box 17513, Austin TX 78760. 512/462-2959. **Contact:** Kathy Waid, Owner. **Description:** A permanent employment agency. **Specializes in the areas of:** Dental. **Positions commonly filled include:** Dental Assistant/Dental Hygienist. **Average salary range of placements:** $20,000 - $29,999.

DONOVAN & WATKINS
1360 Post Oak Boulevard, Suite 100, Houston TX 77056. 713/968-1700. **Fax:** 713/968-1717. **Contact:** Manager. **Description:** A permanent employment agency that also provides temporary placements. **Specializes in the areas of:** Accounting/Auditing; Administration; Legal.

EVINS PERSONNEL CONSULTANTS
2013 West Anderson Lane, Austin TX 78766. 512/454-9561. **Fax:** 512/483-9191. **Contact:** Manager. **Description:** A permanent employment agency. **Positions commonly filled include:** Accountant/Auditor; Computer Programmer; Customer Service Rep.; Human Resources Manager; Registered Nurse; Typist/Word Processor. **Average salary range of placements:** $20,000 - $29,999. **Number of placements per year:** 500 - 999.
Other U.S. locations:
- 3115 Southwest Boulevard, San Angelo TX 76904-5772. 915/944-2571.
- 209 South Leggett, Abilene TX 79605. 915/677-9153.
- 206 West Avenue B, Killeen TX 76541. 254/526-4161.

EXPRESS PERSONNEL SERVICES
P.O. Box 8136, Waco TX 76714-8136. 254/776-3300. **Toll-free phone:** 800/997-7377. **Fax:** 254/776-4822. **Contact:** Jerry Scofield, Owner. **World Wide Web address:** http://www.express-waco.com. **Description:** A permanent employment agency that also provides some temporary placements. Founded in 1983. **Specializes in the areas of:** Accounting/Auditing; Administration; Architecture/Construction; Banking; Clerical; Computer Hardware/Software; Engineering; Finance; Food; Health/Medical; Insurance; Legal; Manufacturing; Physician Executive; Sales; Secretarial.
Other U.S. locations:
- 3701 South Cooper Street, Suite 250, Arlington TX 76015. 817/468-9118.

FINANCIAL PROFESSIONALS
4100 Spring Valley Road, Suite 307, Dallas TX 75244. 972/991-8999. **Toll-free phone:** 800/856-5599. **Fax:** 972/702-0776. **Contact:** Vice President of Operations. **World Wide Web address:** http://www.fpstaff.net.

Description: A permanent employment agency that also provides temporary placements. **Specializes in the areas of:** Banking; Finance. **Positions commonly filled include:** Accountant; Administrative Assistant; Auditor; Bank Officer/Mgr.; Branch Mgr.; CFO; Controller; Credit Mgr.; Customer Service Rep.; Finance Director; Financial Analyst; Human Resources Mgr.; Operations Manager. **Benefits available to temporary workers:** Medical Insurance; Paid Holidays; Paid Vacation. **Corporate headquarters location:** This Location. **Other area locations:** Fort Worth TX; Houston TX. **Average salary range of placements:** $20,000 - $29,999. **Number of placements per year:** 1 - 49.

GULCO INTERNATIONAL RECRUITING SERVICES
23854 Highway 59 North, Suite 338, Kingwood TX 77339. 281/358-2660. **Fax:** 281/358-2120. **Contact:** Recruiter. **Description:** A permanent employment agency. **Specializes in the areas of:** Engineering; Finance; Health/Medical; Manufacturing; Personnel/ Labor Relations. **Positions commonly filled include:** Accountant; Buyer; Chemical Engineer; Civil Engineer; Computer Programmer; Cost Estimator; Designer; Electrical/Electronics Engineer; Financial Analyst; Geologist/Geophysicist; Health Services Mgr.; Human Resources Manager; Licensed Practical Nurse; Materials Engineer; Mechanical Engineer; Mergers/Acquisitions Specialist; Mining Engineer; Nuclear Engineer; Occupational Therapist; Operations/Production Manager; Petroleum Engineer; Physical Therapist; Physician; Purchasing Agent/Manager; Quality Control Supervisor; RN; Respiratory Therapist; Science Technologist; Software Engineer; Stationary Engineer; Structural Engineer; Surgical Tech.; Systems Analyst; Tech. Writer/ Editor. **Average salary range of placements:** More than $50,000. **Number of placements per year:** 50 - 99.

INFO TEC INC.
14275 Midway Road, Suite 140, Dallas TX 75244-3620. 972/661-8400. **Fax:** 972/490-5964. **Contact:** Kim Pinney, Vice President. **E-mail address:** infotec@ infotec-dfw.com. **World Wide Web address:** http://www.infotec-dfw.com. **Description:** A permanent employment agency that also offers consulting services. **Specializes in the areas of:** Computer Science/Software. **Positions commonly filled include:** Computer Programmer; Management Analyst/Consultant; MIS Specialist; Systems Analyst; Technical Writer/Editor. **Benefits available to temporary workers:** Dental Insurance; Medical Insurance. **Average salary range of placements:** $30,000 - $50,000. **Number of placements per year:** 50 - 99.

JOB SERVICES, INC.
6404 Callaghan Road, San Antonio TX 78229. 210/344-3444. **Contact:** Ike Kelly, President. **Description:** A permanent employment agency. **Specializes in the areas of:** Industrial; Manufacturing. **Positions commonly filled include:** Accountant; Adjuster; Administrative Manager; Advertising Clerk; Automotive Mechanic; Bank Officer/ Mgr.; Blue-Collar Worker Supervisor; Branch Manager; Buyer; Claim Rep.; Clerical Supervisor; Clinical Lab Tech.; Collector; Computer Programmer; Construction Contractor; Cost Estimator; Customer Service Rep.; Dental Assistant/Dental Hygienist; Dental Lab Tech.; Draftsperson; Electrician; Emergency Medical Tech.; General Manager; Hotel Manager; Industrial Engineer; Investigator; Licensed Practical Nurse; Management Trainee; Manufacturer's/Wholesaler's Sales Rep.; Mechanical Engineer; Medical Records Tech.; Paralegal; Physical Therapist; Preschool Worker; Property and Real Estate Manager; Public Relations Specialist; Purchasing Agent/Manager; Quality Control Supervisor; Real Estate Agent; Respiratory Therapist; Restaurant/Food Service Mgr.; Securities Sales Rep.; Services Sales Rep.; Systems Analyst; Travel Agent; Wholesale and Retail Buyer. **Number of placements per year:** 100 - 199.

JOBS, ETC., INC.
1411 11th Street, Huntsville TX 77340. 409/295-5627. **Contact:** Paula Ohendalski, Owner. **Description:** A permanent employment agency. **Positions commonly filled include:** Accountant; Administrative Manager; Advertising Clerk; Bank Officer/Manager; Blue-Collar Worker Supervisor; Branch Mgr.; Budget Analyst; Buyer; Claim Rep.; Clerical Supervisor; Computer Programmer; Construction Contractor; Customer Service Rep.; Dental Assistant/Dental Hygienist; Design Engineer; Draftsperson; Editor; Electrician; Emergency Medical Tech.; General Mgr.; Health Services Manager; Hotel Manager; Human Resources Specialist; Human Service Worker; Industrial Production Mgr.; Landscape Architect; Licensed Practical Nurse; Occupational Therapist; Paralegal; Public Relations Specialist; Purchasing Agent/Manager; Quality Control Supervisor; Radio/TV Announcer/Broadcaster; Real Estate Agent; Registered Nurse; Respiratory Therapist; Restaurant/ Food Service Mgr.; Software Engineer; Systems Analyst; Typist/Word Processor; Video Production Coordinator. **Average salary range of placements:** Less than $20,000. **Number of placements per year:** 500 - 999.

KINDRICK & LUTHER
2200 Post Oak Boulevard, Suite 360, Houston TX 77056. 713/629-5559. **Contact:** Manager. **Description:** A permanent employment agency that also provides temporary placements. **Specializes in the areas of:** Accounting/Auditing.

LRJ STAFFING SERVICES
2010 HK Dodgen Loop, Suite 102, Temple TX 76504. 254/742-1981. **Toll-free phone:** 800/581-1850. **Fax:** 254/774-9675. **Contact:** David Kyle, Branch Manager. **Description:** A permanent employment agency. **Specializes in the areas of:** Computer Science/Software; Engineering; Industrial; Light Industrial; Manufacturing; Personnel/Labor Relations; Publishing; Technical. **Positions commonly filled include:** Blue-Collar Worker Supervisor; Computer Programmer; Customer Service Rep.; Industrial Engineer; Industrial Production Manager; Services Sales Rep.; Systems Analyst; Typist/Word Processor. **Benefits available to temporary workers:** Paid Holidays; Sick Days. **Corporate headquarters location:** Austin TX. **Average salary range of placements:** $20,000 - $29,999. **Number of placements per year:** 50 - 99.

THE LUCAS GROUP
5300 Memorial Drive, Suite 270, Houston TX 77008. 713/864-5588. **Fax:** 713/864-7887. **Contact:** Manager. **Description:** A permanent employment agency that also provides temporary placements. **Specializes in the areas of:** Accounting/Auditing; Finance.

MARQUESS & ASSOCIATES
15441 Knoll Trail Drive, Lockbox 1, Suite 280, Dallas TX 75248. 972/490-5288. **Fax:** 972/490-5004. **Contact:** Terri Marquess, Owner. **Description:** A permanent employment agency. **Specializes in the areas of:** Retail; Sales; Secretarial; Technical. **Positions commonly filled include:** Accountant; Administrative Mgr.; Advertising Clerk; Buyer; Clerical Supervisor; Computer Programmer; Credit Mgr.; Customer Service Rep.; Electrical/Electronics Engineer; Financial Analyst; General Manager; Human Service Worker; Industrial Engineer; Management Trainee; Mechanical Engineer; MIS Specialist; Services Sales Rep.; Software Engineer; Sys. Analyst; Tech. Writer/Editor; Telecommunications Mgr. **Average salary range of placements:** $20,000 - $29,999. **Number of placements per year:** 50 - 99.

MEDTEX STAFFING
8140 Walnut Hill Lane, Suite 610, Dallas TX 75231. 214/368-1456. **Contact:** Office Manager. **Description:** A permanent employment agency. **Specializes in the areas of:** Health/Medical. **Positions commonly filled include:** Nurse.

MORNINGSIDE NANNIES
2020 SW Freeway, Suite 200, Houston TX 77098. 713/526-3989. **Contact:** Patricia Cascio, Owner. **Description:** A permanent employment agency providing live-in, live-out, and part-time childcare positions. Client

company pays fee. **NOTE:** Applicants must have training in child development or references relating to childcare work experience. **Specializes in the areas of:** Child Care, In-Home. **Positions commonly filled include:** Nanny. **Number of placements per year:** 100 - 199.

OFICINA DE EMPLEOS, INC.
5415 Maple Avenue, Suite 112A, Dallas TX 75235-7429. 214/634-0500. **Fax:** 214/634-1001. **Contact:** Robert Wingfield, Jr., Owner. **Description:** A permanent employment agency that places documented workers, primarily from Mexico, in the construction and landscaping industries. **Specializes in the areas of:** General Labor. **Number of placements per year:** 500 - 999.

O'KEEFE & ASSOCIATES
3420 Executive Center Drive, Austin TX 78731. 512/320-9191. **Contact:** Recruiter. **World Wide Web address:** http://www.okeefeassociates.com. **Description:** A permanent employment agency. **Specializes in the areas of:** Administration; Computer Hardware/Software; Engineering. **Positions commonly filled include:** Computer Programmer; Electrical/Electronics Engineer; Software Engineer; Systems Analyst. **Number of placements per year:** 50 - 99.

OMNI CONSORTIUM, INC.
1035 Dairy-Ashford Road, Suite 350, Houston TX 77079. 281/589-6550. **Fax:** 281/589-6822. **Contact:** Manager. **Description:** A permanent employment agency. **Specializes in the areas of:** Education; Health/Medical. **Positions commonly filled include:** Physical Therapist; Teacher/Professor. **Number of placements per year:** 100 - 199.

PERSONNEL CONSULTANTS INC. (PCI)
4620 Fairmont Parkway, Suite 106, Pasadena TX 77504. 281/998-8060. **Fax:** 281/998-7794. **Contact:** Judy Hausler, President. **Description:** A permanent employment agency. **Positions commonly filled include:** Accountant; Blue-Collar Worker Supervisor; Buyer; Chemist; Claim Rep.; Clerical Supervisor; Clinical Lab Tech.; Computer Programmer; Construction and Building Inspector; Construction Contractor; Cost Estimator; Credit Mgr.; Customer Service Rep.; Draftsperson; EEG Technologist; EKG Tech.; EMT; Engineer; Financial Analyst; General Mgr.; Geologist/Geophysicist; Health Services Manager; Human Service Worker; Industrial Production Manager; Insurance Agent/Broker; Licensed Practical Nurse; Manufacturer's/Wholesaler's Sales Rep.; Medical Records Tech.; Paralegal; Physical Therapist; Physician; Property and Real Estate Mgr.; Purchasing Agent/Manager; Registered Nurse; Respiratory Therapist; Services Sales Rep.; Surgical Tech.; Systems Analyst; Technical Writer/Editor; Wholesale and Retail Buyer. **Number of placements per year:** 50 - 99.

PERSONNEL ONE, INC.
TELESOURCE
7520 North MacArthur Boulevard, Suite 120, Irving TX 75063. 972/831-1999. **Fax:** 972/831-8668. **Contact:** Christine Willingham, Branch Manager. **Description:** A permanent employment agency that also provides temporary placements. Telesource (also at this location, 972/831-1115) is a temporary agency that also provides temp-to-perm placements. Client company pays fee. **Specializes in the areas of:** Administration; Computer Science/Software; Personnel/Labor Relations; Secretarial. **Positions commonly filled include:** Administrative Assistant; Clerk; Customer Service Representative; Data Entry Clerk; Mail Distributor; Receptionist; Secretary. **Benefits available to temporary workers:** 401(k); Medical Insurance; Paid Holidays; Paid Vacation. **Corporate headquarters location:** This Location. **Average salary range of placements:** $20,000 - $29,999. **Number of placements per year:** 50 - 99. **Other U.S. locations:**
• 344 West Campbell Road, Richardson TX 75080. 972/234-2000.

• 1200 East Copeland, Suite 102, Arlington TX 76011. 817/265-5401.
• 7515 Greenville Avenue, Suite 800, Dallas TX 75231. 214/361-6000.
• 5400 LBJ Freeway, Suite 120, Dallas TX 75240. 972/982-8500.

PLACEMENTS UNLIMITED
932 North Valley Mills Drive, Waco TX 76710. 254/741-0526. **Fax:** 254/741-0529. **Contact:** Ginger Sharp, President. **Description:** A permanent employment agency. **Specializes in the areas of:** Banking; Industrial; Manufacturing; Secretarial. **Positions commonly filled include:** Accountant/Auditor; Aircraft Mechanic/Engine Specialist; Automotive Mechanic; Blue-Collar Worker Supervisor; Buyer; Clerical Supervisor; Customer Service Rep.; MIS Specialist; Purchasing Agent/Mgr.; Technical Writer/Editor; Typist/Word Processor. **Average salary range of placements:** Less than $20,000. **Number of placements per year:** 100 - 199.

PROFESSIONAL CONCEPTS PERSONNEL
4692 East University Boulevard, Suite 101, Odessa TX 79762. 915/362-9214. **Contact:** Ms. Ruby Bruns, Owner. **Description:** A permanent employment agency. **Positions commonly filled include:** Blue-Collar Worker Supervisor; Branch Manager; Broadcast Technician; Claim Rep.; Clerical Supervisor; Clinical Lab Tech.; Computer Programmer; Construction and Building Inspector; Cost Estimator; Counselor; Credit Manager; Customer Service Rep.; Dental Assistant/Dental Hygienist; Dental Lab Tech.; Designer; Draftsperson; EEG Technologist; EKG Tech.; Electrician; Emergency Medical Tech.; General Mgr.; Health Services Manager; Human Resources Manager; Licensed Practical Nurse; Management Analyst/Consultant; Management Trainee; Manufacturer's/Wholesaler's Sales Rep.; Medical Records Technician; Occupational Therapist; Paralegal; Physical Therapist; Property and Real Estate Manager; Purchasing Agent/Manager; Recreational Therapist; Respiratory Therapist; Services Sales Representative; Social Worker; Surveyor; Systems Analyst; Travel Agent. **Number of placements per year:** 50 - 99.

PROFESSIONS TODAY
2811 South Loop 289, Suite 20, Lubbock TX 79423. 806/745-8595. **Fax:** 806/748-0571. **Contact:** Genell Ward, Owner. **Description:** A permanent employment agency. **Specializes in the areas of:** Accounting/Auditing; Administration; Computer Hardware/Software; Engineering; General Management; Health/Medical; Industrial; Sales; Secretarial. **Positions commonly filled include:** Accountant/Auditor; Administrative Assistant; Bookkeeper; Clerk; Computer Programmer; Customer Service Rep.; Data Entry Clerk; Legal Secretary; Marketing Specialist; Medical Secretary; Receptionist; Sales Representative; Secretary; Typist/Word Processor. **Number of placements per year:** 100 - 199.

QUEST PERSONNEL RESOURCES, INC.
50 Briar Hollow Lane, Suite 510 E, Houston TX 77027-9306. 713/961-0605. **Toll-free phone:** 800/846-6081. **Fax:** 713/961-1857. **Contact:** Cristina M. Tolpo, Branch Manager. **Description:** A permanent employment agency that also provides some temporary placements. **Specializes in the areas of:** Legal; Secretarial. **Positions commonly filled include:** Accountant/Auditor; Accounting Clerk; Administrative Assistant; Clerical Supervisor; Customer Service Rep.; Data Entry Clerk; Human Resources Manager; Paralegal; Receptionist; Typist/Word Processor. **Benefits available to temporary workers:** Paid Vacation. **Average salary range of placements:** $30,000 - $50,000. **Number of placements per year:** 100 - 199.

REMEDY INTELLIGENT STAFFING
8310 Capital of Texas Highway North, Suite 195, Austin TX 78731. 512/502-9000. **Fax:** 512/502-9305. **Contact:** Joe Kilpatrick, Owner. **Description:** A permanent employment agency. **Specializes in the areas of:** Accounting/Auditing; Administration; Advertising; Computer Science/Software; Engineering; Industrial;

Personnel/Labor Relations; Publishing; Retail; Sales; Secretarial; Technical. **Positions commonly filled include:** Accountant/Auditor; Administrative Manager; Advertising Clerk; Bank Officer/Mgr.; Branch Manager; Brokerage Clerk; Budget Analyst; Claim Rep.; Clerical Supervisor; Computer Programmer; Cost Estimator; Credit Mgr.; Customer Service Rep.; Design Engineer; Draftsperson; Electrical/Electronics Engineer; Environmental Engineer; Financial Analyst; General Manager; Human Resources Specialist; Insurance Agent/ Broker; Management Analyst/Consultant; Market Research Analyst; MIS Specialist; Multimedia Designer; Paralegal; Property and Real Estate Manager; Purchasing Agent/Manager; Quality Control Supervisor; Real Estate Agent; Services Sales Representative; Software Engineer; Systems Analyst; Technical Writer/Editor; Telecommunications Manager; Travel Agent. **Benefits available to temporary workers:** 401(k); Dental Insurance; Medical Insurance; Paid Holidays; Paid Vacation. **Corporate headquarters location:** Aliso Viejo CA. **Average salary range of placements:** $30,000 - $50,000. **Number of placements per year:** 1000+.
Other U.S. locations:
• 4225 Wingren Drive, Suite 115, Irving TX 75062. 972/650-2005.

RESOURCE CONNECTION WORKFORCE CENTER
1400 Circle Drive, Suite 100, Fort Worth TX 76119. 817/531-5670. **Fax:** 817/531-6701. **Contact:** Sheila Perry, Program Coordinator. **Description:** A permanent employment agency that also provides career counseling services. **Specializes in the areas of:** Accounting/ Auditing; Administration; Computer Science/Software; Education; Finance; Food; General Management; Health/ Medical; Industrial; Manufacturing; Personnel/Labor Relations; Retail; Sales; Secretarial; Transportation. **Positions commonly filled include:** Accountant/Auditor; Administrative Manager; Automotive Mechanic; Biomedical Engineer; Blue-Collar Worker Supervisor; Budget Analyst; Claim Rep.; Clerical Supervisor; Clinical Lab Tech.; Computer Programmer; Construction and Building Inspector; Counselor; Credit Manager; Customer Service Rep.; Dental Assistant/Dental Hygienist; Draftsperson; Education Administrator; EEG Technologist; EKG Technician; Electrical/Electronics Engineer; Electrician; General Manager; Health Services Manager; Human Resources Specialist; Insurance Agent/ Broker; Librarian; Medical Records Technician; MIS Specialist; Operations/Production Manager; Property and Real Estate Mgr.; Purchasing Agent/Mgr.; Radiological Technologist; Restaurant/Food Service Manager; Securities Sales Rep.; Systems Analyst; Teacher/ Professor; Travel Agent; Typist/Word Processor. **Average salary range of placements:** $20,000 - $29,999. **Number of placements per year:** 200 - 499.

SAY AHHH MEDICAL OFFICE SERVICES
909 West Magnolia Avenue, Suite 8, Fort Worth TX 76104. 817/927-2924. **Contact:** Manager. **Description:** A permanent employment agency that also offers some temporary placements. **Specializes in the areas of:** Health/Medical.

SEEGERS ESTES & ASSOCIATES, INC.
14405 Walters Road, Suite 350, Houston TX 77014-1320. 281/587-8765. **Fax:** 281/587-8778. **Contact:** Recruiter. **Description:** A permanent employment agency **Specializes in the areas of:** Engineering. **Positions commonly filled include:** Chemical Engineer; Electrical/Electronics Engineer; Mechanical Engineer. **Average salary range of placements:** More than $50,000. **Number of placements per year:** 1 - 49.

SNELLING PERSONNEL SERVICES
1169 East 42nd Street, Odessa TX 79762. 915/367-7066. **Fax:** 915/550-7066. **Contact:** Jane Williams, Owner. **Description:** A permanent employment agency. **Specializes in the areas of:** Accounting; Engineering; General Management; Industrial; Sales; Secretarial; Technical. **Positions commonly filled include:** Accountant; Blue-Collar Worker Supervisor; Customer

Service Rep.; Services Sales Rep.; Typist/Word Processor. **Average salary range of placements:** $30,000 - $50,000. **Number of placements per year:** 50 - 99.
Other U.S. locations:
• 146 American Bank Plaza, Corpus Christi TX 78475. 361/883-7903.
• 12801 North Central Expressway, Suite 600, Dallas TX 75243-1725. 972/701-8080.
• 5151 Beltline Road, Suite 365, Dallas TX 75240. 972/934-9030.
• 1925 East Beltline Road, Suite 403, Carrollton TX 75006. 972/242-8575.

STAFF FINDERS
ABACUS ACCOUNTING PERSONNEL
3040 Post Oak Boulevard, Suite 1440, Houston TX 77056. 713/850-9131. **Fax:** 713/850-7714. **Contact:** Manager. **Description:** A permanent employment agency that also provides some temp-to-perm and temporary placements. Abacus Accounting Personnel (also at this location) is a permanent employment agency that also provides some temporary placements. **Specializes in the areas of:** Administration; Secretarial. **Other U.S. locations:**
• 515 West Greens Road, Suite 120, Houston TX 77067. 281/875-5700.

STAFFINGSOLUTIONS
702 West Loop 289, Suite 104, Lubbock TX 79416. 806/788-1500. **Fax:** 806/788-1510. **Contact:** Marka Roark, Branch Manager. **Description:** A permanent employment agency that also provides some temporary placements. Client company pays fee. **Specializes in the areas of:** Clerical; Light Industrial. **Positions commonly filled include:** Data Entry Clerk; Mail Distributor; Order Clerk; Receptionist; Secretary; Shipping and Receiving Clerk; Warehouse/Distribution Worker; Welder. **Benefits available to temporary workers:** 401(k); Medical Insurance; Paid Holidays; Paid Vacation. **Corporate headquarters location:** Irving TX. **Average salary range of placements:** $20,000 - $29,999. **Number of placements per year:** 200 - 499.
Other U.S. locations:
• 8585 North Stemmons Freeway, Suite 104S, Dallas TX 75147. 214/637-6300.

STAFFINGSOLUTIONS/RESOURCEMFG
1200 East Copeland Road, Suite 102, Arlington TX 76011. 817/795-9595. **Fax:** 817/461-4776. **Contact:** Manager. **Description:** StaffingSolutions/ReSourceMFG is a permanent employment agency that also provides temporary placements. Client company pays fee. **Specializes in the areas of:** Electronics. **Positions commonly filled include:** Machinist; Plant Manager; Quality Control Supervisor; Technician; Tool and Die Maker; Warehouse/Distribution Worker; Welder. **Benefits available to temporary workers:** 401(k); Medical Insurance; Paid Holidays; Paid Vacation. **Corporate headquarters location:** Irving TX. **Average salary range of placements:** $20,000 - $29,999. **Number of placements per year:** 200 - 499.
Other U.S. locations:
• 1235 Northwest Highway, Garland TX 75041. 972/271-7303.

STEELE & ASSOCIATES
9525 Katy Freeway, Suite 109, Houston TX 77024. 713/461-5823. **Fax:** 713/461-5886. **Contact:** Manager. **Description:** A permanent employment agency. **Specializes in the areas of:** Administration; Clerical; Insurance.

STEHOUWER & ASSOCIATES
2939 Mossrock, Suite 270, San Antonio TX 78230-5118. 210/349-4995. **Fax:** 210/349-4996. **Contact:** Manager. **Description:** A permanent employment agency that also offers organizational design consulting and psychological profiling. **Specializes in the areas of:** Administration; Art/Design; Computer Science/Software; Engineering; Technical. **Positions commonly filled include:** Aerospace Engineer; Chemical Engineer; Chemist; Civil Engineer;

Computer Programmer; Design Engineer; Mechanical Engineer; MIS Specialist; Software Engineer; Structural Engineer; Systems Analyst. **Average salary range of placements:** More than $50,000.

SUMMIT SEARCH SPECIALISTS

14825 St. Mary's Lane, Suite 275, Houston TX 77079. 281/497-5840. **Fax:** 281/497-5841. **Contact:** David Bunce, Owner. **Description:** A permanent employment agency. **Specializes in the areas of:** Insurance. **Positions commonly filled include:** Accountant; Actuary; Claim Representative; Insurance Agent/Broker; Loss Prevention Specialist; Underwriter/Assistant Underwriter.

TSP PERSONNEL SERVICES, INC.

P.O. Box 266, Paris TX 75461. 903/785-0034. **Fax:** 903/784-0864. **Contact:** Kelley Ferguson, Owner. **Description:** A permanent employment agency that also provides temporary placements. **Specializes in the areas of:** Accounting; Industrial; Light Industrial; Retail; Sales; Secretarial. **Positions commonly filled include:** Bank Officer/Mgr.; Clerical Supervisor; Electrician; Secretary. **Corporate headquarters location:** This Location. **Average salary range of placements:** $20,000 - $29,999. **Number of placements per year:** 200 - 499.

THOMAS OFFICE PERSONNEL SERVICE (TOPS)

3909 Flintridge Drive, Irving TX 75038. 972/252-2660. **Contact:** Margaret Thomas, Co-Founder. **E-mail address:** topsmom@aol.com. **Description:** A permanent employment agency. Client company pays fee. **Specializes in the areas of:** Accounting/Auditing; Administration; General Management; Insurance; Manufacturing; Personnel/Labor Relations; Publishing; Secretarial. **Positions commonly filled include:** Accountant/Auditor; Branch Mgr.; Clerical Supervisor; Customer Service Rep.; General Manager; Human Resources Specialist; Paralegal; Secretary; Typist/Word Processor. **Average salary range of placements:** $20,000 - $35,000. **Number of placements per year:** 1 - 49.

TRAVEL SEARCH NETWORK

12860 Hillcrest Road, Suite 112, Dallas TX 75230-1519. 972/458-1145. **Fax:** 972/490-4790. **Contact:** Gina Tedesco, Vice President of Operations. **Description:** A permanent employment agency that also provides temporary placements. **Specializes in the areas of:** Travel. **Positions commonly filled include:** Travel Agent. **Other U.S. locations:** Houston TX. **Average salary range of placements:** $30,000 - $50,000. **Number of placements per year:** 200 - 499.

TRAVEL SEARCH NETWORK

4615 Post Oak Place, Suite 140, Houston TX 77027. 713/624-7177. **Fax:** 713/624-7178. **Contact:** Manager. **Description:** A permanent employment agency that also provides some temporary placements. **Specializes in the areas of:** Travel.

TRAVELCARE UNLIMITED

2340 Trinity Mills, Suite 215, Carrollton TX 75006. 972/323-3388. **Fax:** 972/446-1920. **Contact:** Manager. **Description:** A permanent employment agency that also provides some temporary placements. **Specializes in the areas of:** Health/Medical. **Positions commonly filled include:** Occupational Therapist; Physical Therapist. **Benefits available to temporary workers:** 401(k); Dental Insurance; Life Insurance; Medical Insurance; Vision Plan. **Corporate headquarters location:** Albuquerque NM. **Average salary range of placements:** More than $50,000. **Number of placements per year:** 100 - 199.

VINSON AND ASSOCIATES

4100 McEwen, Suite 180, Dallas TX 75244. 972/980-8800. **Contact:** Fred Vinson. **Description:** Vinson and Associates is a permanent employment agency that also provides temporary placements. **Specializes in the areas of:** Accounting/Auditing; Banking; Clerical; Finance; Insurance; Legal; Manufacturing; Sales.

TEMPORARY EMPLOYMENT AGENCIES

A-1 PERSONNEL

5800 Corporate Drive, Suite B1, Houston TX 77036-2319. 713/773-2900. **Fax:** 713/773-4325. **Contact:** Sandy Radcliffe, Personnel Representative. **Description:** A temporary agency that also provides some temp-to-perm placements.. **Specializes in the areas of:** Accounting; Administration; Light Industrial; Secretarial. **Positions commonly filled include:** Accountant; Assembler; Clerk; Shipping and Receiving Clerk; Typist/Word Processor; Warehouse/Distribution Worker. **Average salary range of placements:** $16,000 - $29,999. **Number of placements per year:** 200 - 499.

ABC TEMPS INC.

3109 Carlisle Street, Suite 208, Dallas TX 75204. 214/754-7052. **Fax:** 214/954-1525. **Contact:** Regional Manager. **Description:** A temporary agency. **Specializes in the areas of:** Accounting; Manufacturing; Personnel/Labor Relations; Secretarial. **Positions commonly filled include:** Blue-Collar Worker Supervisor; Credit Manager; Customer Service Rep.; Human Resources Specialist; Typist/Word Processor. **Benefits available to temporary workers:** Credit Union; Paid Holidays; Paid Vacation. **Corporate headquarters location:** This Location. **Other U.S. locations:** Fort Worth TX. **Average salary range of placements:** Less than $20,000. **Number of placements per year:** 200 - 499.

ACCLAIM SERVICES, INC.

5445 La Sierra, Suite 317, Dallas TX 75231. 214/750-1818. **Fax:** 214/750-4403. **Contact:** Manager. **Description:** A temporary agency. **Specializes in the areas of:** Network Administration; Software Development; Technical Writing. **Positions commonly filled include:** Management Analyst/Consultant; Software Engineer; Systems Analyst; Technical Writer/Editor; Telecommunications Manager. **Average salary range of placements:** More than $50,000. **Number of placements per year:** 50 - 99.

ACSYS STAFFING

12655 North Central Expressway, Suite 310, Dallas TX 75243. 972/991-3330. **Contact:** Mimi Dykes, Area Manager. **Description:** A temporary agency that also provides some temp-to-perm placements. **Specializes in the areas of:** Accounting; Banking; Computer Science/Software; Engineering; Finance; Insurance; Sales; Scientific; Secretarial; Technical. **Other U.S. locations:** Nationwide.

ACTION PERSONNEL INC.

P.O. Drawer 3309, Texas City TX 77592-3309. 409/935-0111. **Contact:** President. **Description:** A temporary agency. **Specializes in the areas of:** Accounting; Administration; Banking; Computer Science/Software; Finance; General Management; Health/Medical; Industrial; Legal; Personnel/Labor Relations; Sales; Secretarial. **Positions commonly filled include:** Accountant; Administrative Manager; Advertising Clerk; Bank Officer/Manager; Claim Rep.; Clerical Supervisor; Computer Programmer; Credit Mgr.; Customer Service Rep.; Draftsperson; Medical Records Tech.; Paralegal; Public Relations Specialist; Purchasing Agent/Manager; Systems Analyst; Travel Agent; Typist/Word Processor.

ADD-A-TEMP
WOODLANDS EXECUTIVE EMPLOYMENT

25025 North Interstate Highway 45, Suite 300, The Woodlands TX 77380. 281/367-3700. **Toll-free phone:** 800/348-0788. **Fax:** 281/367-8049. **Contact:** Jill Silman, President. **E-mail address:** addatemp@addatemp.com. **World Wide Web address:** http://www.addatemp.com.

Description: A temporary agency. Woodlands Executive Employment (also at this location) is an executive search firm. **Specializes in the areas of:** Accounting; Administration; General Management; Health/Medical; Industrial; Light Industrial; MIS/EDP; Nonprofit; Personnel/Labor Relations; Scientific; Secretarial; Technical. **Positions commonly filled include:** Account Rep.; Accountant; Administrative Assistant; Auditor; Biochemist; Biological Scientist; Biomedical Engineer; Blue-Collar Worker Supervisor; Chemist; CFO; Clerical Supervisor; Clinical Lab Tech.; Computer Operator; Computer Programmer; Consultant; Controller; Customer Service Rep.; EEG Tech.; EKG Tech.; Finance Director; Financial Analyst; General Manager; Human Resources Mgr.; Management Analyst/Consultant; Management Trainee; Marketing Manager; Marketing Specialist; Medical Records Tech.; Nuclear Medicine Tech.; Occupational Therapist; Operations/Production Mgr.; Paralegal; Physical Therapist; Production Mgr.; Project Mgr.; Purchasing Agent/Manager; Quality Control Supervisor; Radiological Technologist; Respiratory Therapist; Sales Mgr.; Sales Rep.; Secretary; Surgical Tech.; Tech. Writer/Editor; Typist/Word Processor. **Benefits available to temporary workers:** Bonus Award/Plan; Dental Insurance; Eye Care; Medical Insurance; Paid Holidays; Prescription Drugs. **Corporate headquarters location:** This Location. **Number of placements per year:** 50 - 99.

ADECCO
5151 Flynn Parkway, Suite 103, Corpus Christi TX 78411-4318. 361/814-2342. **Fax:** 361/814-2346. **Contact:** Pete Van Tassel, Office Supervisor. **Description:** A temporary agency. **Specializes in the areas of:** Banking; Health/Medical; Industrial; Manufacturing; Secretarial. **Positions commonly filled include:** Clerical Supervisor; Computer Programmer; Customer Service Representative; Medical Records Technician; Typist/Word Processor. **Benefits available to temporary workers:** Paid Holidays; Paid Vacation; Referral Bonus Plan. **Corporate headquarters location:** Redwood City CA. **International locations:** Worldwide. **Average salary range of placements:** $20,000 - $29,999. **Number of placements per year:** 500 - 999. **Other U.S. locations:**
• 13831 Northwest Freeway, Suite 430, Houston TX 77040. 713/690-9500.

AQUENT PARTNERS
Heritage Square Tower One, LBJ Freeway, Suite 870, Dallas TX 75244-6013. 972/503-8877. **Toll-free phone:** 877/PARTNER. **Fax:** 972/503-8878. **Contact:** Paul Donaghy, Manager. **E-mail address:** pdonaghy@aquent.com. **World Wide Web address:** http://www.aquentpartners.com. **Description:** A temporary agency that also provides some temp-to-perm, permanent, and contract placements. **Specializes in the areas of:** Administration; Art/Design; Computer Science/Software; Marketing. **Positions commonly filled include:** Computer Animator; Computer Engineer; Computer Operator; Computer Programmer; Computer Support Tech.; Computer Technician; Content Developer; Database Administrator; Database Manager; Desktop Publishing Specialist; Editor; Editorial Assistant; Graphic Artist; Graphic Designer; Internet Services Manager; Managing Editor; MIS Specialist; Multimedia Designer; Network/Systems Administrator; Production Manager; Project Manager; Software Engineer; SQL Programmer; Systems Analyst; Systems Manager; Technical Writer/Editor; Webmaster. **Benefits available to temporary workers:** 401(k); Dental Insurance; Disability Coverage; Medical Insurance. **CEO:** John Chuang.
Other U.S. locations:
• 5599 San Felipe, Suite 750, Houston TX 77056. 713/850-7751.

ATTORNEY RESOURCE, INC.
750 North St. Paul, Suite 540, Dallas TX 75201. 214/922-8050. **Toll-free phone:** 800/324-4828. **Fax:** 214/871-3041. **Contact:** Jennifer Colby, Manager. **E-mail address:** info@attorneyresource.com. **World Wide Web address:** http://www.attorneyresource.com.

Description: A temporary agency that also provides permanent placements. **Specializes in the areas of:** Administration; Legal; Secretarial. **Positions commonly filled include:** Attorney; Legal Secretary; Paralegal. **Benefits available to temporary workers:** Paid Holidays; Paid Vacation; Referral Bonus Plan. **Corporate headquarters location:** This Location. **Other U.S. locations:** Tulsa OK; Austin TX; Fort Worth TX. **Number of placements per year:** 100 - 199.

ANN BEST ELITE TEMPORARIES, INC.
P.O. Box 3683, Texas City TX 77592-3683. 409/933-0095. **Fax:** 409/933-0269. **Contact:** Ann Best, President/Owner. **Description:** A temporary agency. **Specializes in the areas of:** Accounting; Administration; Construction; General Management; Legal; Personnel/Labor Relations; Secretarial. **Positions commonly filled include:** Accountant; Administrative Manager; Blue-Collar Worker Supervisor; Chemical Engineer; Civil Engineer; Clerical Supervisor; Computer Programmer; Construction and Building Inspector; Construction Contractor; Dental Assistant/Dental Hygienist; Electrical/Electronics Engineer; Electrician; General Manager; Human Resources Manager; Human Service Worker; Paralegal; Purchasing Agent/Manager; Recreational Therapist; Systems Analyst; Typist/Word Processor. **Average salary range of placements:** $20,000 - $29,999. **Number of placements per year:** 1 - 49.

BRUCO, INC.
P.O. Box 1214, Pasadena TX 77501. 713/473-9251. **Fax:** 713/473-2456. **Contact:** Stella Walters, Manager. **Description:** A temporary agency that also provides some permanent placements. **Specializes in the areas of:** Accounting/Auditing; Clerical. **Positions commonly filled include:** Administrative Assistant; Computer Operator; Computer Programmer; Customer Service Representative; Purchasing Agent/Manager; Secretary; Typist/Word Processor.

BURNETT PERSONNEL SERVICES
9800 Richmond Avenue, Suite 800, Houston TX 77042. 713/977-4777. **Fax:** 713/977-7533. **Contact:** Sue Burnett, President. **E-mail address:** sue@houston.burnettps.com. **World Wide Web address:** http://www.burnettps.com. **Description:** A temporary agency that also provides some permanent placements. **Specializes in the areas of:** Accounting; Clerical; Computer Science/Software; Legal; Secretarial. **Positions commonly filled include:** Accountant; Administrative Assistant; Computer Programmer; Customer Service Rep.; Data Entry Clerk; Human Resources Manager; Human Resources Specialist; Legal Secretary; MIS Specialist; Office Mgr.; Paralegal; Secretary; Systems Analyst; Telemarketer; Typist/Word Processor. **Corporate headquarters location:** This Location. **Other U.S. locations:** Austin TX; El Paso TX. **Average salary range of placements:** $20,000 - $29,999. **Number of placements per year:** 500 - 999.

BURNETT'S STAFFING, INC.
2710 Avenue E East, Arlington TX 76011. 817/649-7000. **Contact:** Paul W. Burnett, President. **Description:** A temporary agency that also provides temp-to-perm and permanent placements. **Specializes in the areas of:** Administration; MIS/EDP; Secretarial. **Positions commonly filled include:** Accountant; Administrative Assistant; Administrative Manager; Advertising Clerk; Bookkeeper; Claim Rep.; Clerical Supervisor; Computer Operator; Controller; Credit Manager; Customer Service Rep.; Data Entry Clerk; Human Resources Manager; Marketing Specialist; Receptionist; Secretary; Typist/Word Processor; Webmaster. **Benefits available to temporary workers:** Medical Insurance; Paid Holidays; Paid Vacation; Profit Sharing. **Average salary range of placements:** $20,000 - $60,000. **Other U.S. locations:**
• 1431 Greenway, Suite 145, Irving TX 75038. 972/580-3333.

CLAYTON PERSONNEL SERVICES
480 North Sam Houston Parkway East, Suite 140, Houston TX 77060-3521. 281/999-3080. **Fax:** 281/931-

5115. Contact: Brenda James, General Manager. Description: A temporary agency that also provides some temp-to-perm placements. Specializes in the areas of: Accounting; Secretarial. Positions commonly filled include: Account Rep.; Accountant; Administrative Manager; Buyer; Customer Service Rep.; Typist/Word Processor. Benefits available to temporary workers: Dental Insurance; Medical Insurance; Paid Vacation; Referral Bonus Plan. Average salary range of placements: $20,000 - $29,999. Number of placements per year: 1 - 49.

CO-COUNSEL
1221 Lamar, Suite 1210, Houston TX 77010. 713/650-8195. Fax: 713/650-6748. Contact: Operations Supervisor. Description: A temporary agency. Founded in 1988. Specializes in the areas of: Legal. Positions commonly filled include: Attorney; Legal Assistant; Legal Secretary; Librarian; Paralegal. Benefits available to temporary workers: Paid Holidays; Paid Vacation.
Other U.S. locations:
• 600 North Pearl Street, Suite 430, Dallas TX 75201. 214/720-3939.

CONSULTIS
10300 North Central Expressway, Suite 125, Dallas TX 75231. 214/691-8111. Contact: Kim Kent, Resource Coordinator. Description: A temporary agency. Specializes in the areas of: Computer Science/Software; Data Processing; Information Technology; Personnel/Labor Relations; Technical. Positions commonly filled include: Computer Operator; Computer Programmer; Internet Services Mgr.; Library Tech.; MIS Specialist; Multimedia Designer; Software Engineer; Systems Analyst; Technical Writer/Editor; Telecommunications Manager. Average salary range of placements: $30,000 - $50,000. Number of placements per year: 200 - 499.

CONSULTIS OF HOUSTON
5177 Richmond Avenue, Suite 580, Houston TX 77056-6736. 713/623-8355. Fax: 713/623-8357. Contact: Branch Manager. Description: A temporary agency. Specializes in the areas of: Computer Science/Software; Technical. Positions commonly filled include: Computer Programmer; MIS Specialist; Software Engineer; Systems Analyst; Technical Writer/Editor; Telecommunications Manager. Benefits available to temporary workers: 401(k); Bonus Award/Plan; Medical Insurance. Corporate headquarters location: Boca Raton FL. Other U.S. locations: Nationwide. Average salary range of placements: $30,000 - $50,000. Number of placements per year: 100 - 199.

CORBETT PERSONNEL SERVICES
3100 South Gessner, Suite 315, Houston TX 77063. 713/974-3800. Fax: 713/952-8689. Contact: Manager. Description: A temporary agency that also provides some temp-to-perm and permanent placements. Specializes in the areas of: Administration; Clerical; Office Support. Positions commonly filled include: Administrative Assistant; Bookkeeper; Receptionist.

CREDIT UNION EMPLOYMENT RESOURCES
1001 West Loop South, Suite 216, Houston TX 77027. 713/961-4567. Toll-free phone: 800/344-8285. Fax: 713/961-4569. Contact: Manager. Description: A temporary agency that also provides some permanent placements. The agency specializes in providing placements in credit unions. Specializes in the areas of: Accounting/Auditing; Banking. Positions commonly filled include: Accountant/Auditor; Bank Officer/Manager; Credit Manager; Customer Service Rep.; Human Resources Specialist; Internet Services Manager; MIS Specialist; Securities Sales Representative. Average salary range of placements: $20,000 - $29,999. Number of placements per year: 200 - 499.

GAIL DARLING STAFFING
GAIL DARLING'S PROFESSIONAL DESK
25 Butterfield Trail, El Paso TX 79906. 915/772-0077. Contact: Account Manager. Description: A temporary agency. Gail Darling's Professional Desk (also at this location) provides permanent placements. Founded in 1986. Specializes in the areas of: Accounting/Auditing; Administration; Architecture/Construction; Banking; Computer Science/Software; Engineering; Finance; General Management; Industrial; Insurance; Legal; Manufacturing; Personnel/Labor Relations; Publishing; Retail; Secretarial. Positions commonly filled include: Accountant/Auditor; Bank Officer/Mgr.; Budget Analyst; Buyer; Chemical Engineer; Civil Engineer; Clerk; Computer Programmer; Credit Manager; Customer Service Rep.; Economist; Editor; Environmental Engineer; Financial Analyst; General Manager; Human Resources Manager; Industrial Engineer; Industrial Production Manager; Internet Services Manager; Management Analyst/Consultant; Market Research Analyst; Mechanical Engineer; Metallurgical Engineer; Mining Engineer; MIS Specialist; Nuclear Engineer; Operations/Production Manager; Paralegal; Petroleum Engineer; Property and Real Estate Manager; Public Relations Specialist; Purchasing Agent/Manager; Securities Sales Representative; Strategic Relations Manager; Structural Engineer; Surveyor; Systems Analyst; Technical Writer/Editor; Telecommunications Manager; Typist/Word Processor. Average salary range of placements: $20,000 - $29,999.

DEPENDABLE DENTAL STAFFING
18601 LBJ Freeway, Suite 707, Mesquite TX 75150-5600. 972/681-9490. Fax: 972/681-9657. Contact: Karen Houston, Vice President. Description: A temporary agency. Specializes in the areas of: Health/Medical. Positions commonly filled include: Dental Assistant/Dental Hygienist; Dentist. Other U.S. locations: Arlington TX. Average salary range of placements: $30,000 - $50,000. Number of placements per year: 200 - 499.

DIVIDEND STAFFING SERVICES
2107 Kemp Boulevard, Wichita Falls TX 76309. 940/723-0150. Toll-free phone: 800/687-1275. Fax: 940/766-1680. Contact: Bill Palin, President. E-mail address: dividend@dividend-staffing.com. World Wide Web address: http://www.dividend-staffing.com. Description: A temporary agency that also offers temp-to-perm and contract placements. Client company pays fee. Specializes in the areas of: Accounting; Administration; Computer Science/Software; Engineering; Finance; General Management; Health/Medical; Industrial; Light Industrial; Marketing; MIS/EDP; Sales; Scientific; Secretarial; Technical. Positions commonly filled include: Account Mgr.; Account Rep.; Accountant; Administrative Assistant; Administrative Manager; Applications Engineer; Architect; AS400 Programmer Analyst; Assistant Manager; Auditor; Bank Officer/Mgr.; Blue-Collar Worker Supervisor; Branch Manager; Budget Analyst; Buyer; Chemical Engineer; Chemist; CFO; Civil Engineer; Clerical Supervisor; Clinical Lab Technician; Computer Engineer; Computer Operator; Computer Programmer; Computer Support Tech.; Computer Technician; Construction Contractor; Controller; Cost Estimator; Credit Manager; Customer Service Representative; Database Administrator; Database Manager; Draftsperson; Ecologist; Education Administrator; Electrical/Electronics Engineer; Electrician; Environmental Engineer; Finance Director; Financial Analyst; Fund Manager; Graphic Artist; Graphic Designer; Human Resources Manager; Industrial Engineer; Industrial Production Manager; Management Trainee; Manufacturing Engineer; Marketing Manager; Mechanical Engineer; Medical Records Technician; Metallurgical Engineer; MIS Specialist; Multimedia Designer; Network/Systems Administrator; Occupational Therapist; Paralegal; Physical Therapist; Physician; Production Manager; Project Manager; Purchasing Agent/Manager; Quality Assurance Engineer; Quality Control Supervisor; Registered Nurse; Sales Engineer; Sales Manager; Sales Rep.; Secretary; Social Worker; Software Engineer; Statistician; Systems Analyst; Systems Mgr.; Technical Writer/Editor; Transportation/Traffic Specialist; Typist/Word Processor; Underwriter/Assistant Underwriter. Benefits available to temporary

workers: Cafeteria Plan. **Corporate headquarters location:** This Location. **Other U.S. locations:** Dallas TX. **Average salary range of placements:** $20,000 - $29,999. **Number of placements per year:** 200 - 499.

DRIVING FORCE, INC.
2030 Las Vegas Trail, Fort Worth TX 76108. 817/246-7113. **Contact:** G. Wayne Brown, Sr., President. **Description:** A temporary agency. **Specializes in the areas of:** Transportation. **Positions commonly filled include:** Driver. **Benefits available to temporary workers:** Credit Union; Dental Insurance; Life Insurance; Medical Insurance. **Other U.S. locations:** Abilene TX; Austin TX; Dallas TX; Houston TX; San Antonio TX. **Average salary range of placements:** $30,000 - $50,000. **Number of placements per year:** 1 - 49.

ESPRIT TEMPORARY SERVICES
P.O. Box 35443, Dallas TX 75235. 214/631-3832. **Fax:** 214/638-2908. **Contact:** Recruiter. **Description:** A temporary agency. **Specializes in the areas of:** Administration; Customer Service; General Labor; Secretarial. **Positions commonly filled include:** Administrative Assistant; Administrative Manager; Blue-Collar Worker Supervisor; Computer Operator; Electrician; Human Resources Manager; Industrial Production Manager; Paralegal; Typist/Word Processor. **Benefits available to temporary workers:** Dental Insurance; Medical Insurance; Paid Vacation. **Average salary range of placements:** $30,000 - $50,000. **Number of placements per year:** 200 - 499.

FIRSTWORD STAFFING SERVICES
10000 North Central Expressway, Suite 118, Dallas TX 75231. 214/360-0020. **Fax:** 214/360-9206. **Contact:** JoLynne Pratt, Recruiting. **Description:** A temporary agency. **Specializes in the areas of:** Computer Science/Software; Personnel/Labor Relations; Secretarial; Technical. **Positions commonly filled include:** Claim Rep.; Clerical Supervisor; Computer Programmer; Cost Estimator; Customer Service Rep.; Electronics Technician; Paralegal; Typist/Word Processor. **Benefits available to temporary workers:** Dental Insurance; Medical Insurance; Paid Holidays; Paid Vacation; Referral Bonus Plan. **Corporate headquarters location:** Charlotte NC. **Average salary range of placements:** $20,000 - $29,999.

HIREKNOWLEDGE
13500 Midway Road, Suite 205, Dallas TX 75244. 972/385-9269. **Toll-free phone:** 800/937-3622. **Fax:** 972/385-1750. **Contact:** Recruiter. **World Wide Web address:** http://www.hireknowledge.com. **Description:** A temporary agency that also offers some permanent placements. Client company pays fee. **Specializes in the areas of:** Advertising; Art/Design; Computer Science/Software; Internet Development; Internet Marketing; MIS/EDP; Printing; Publishing. **Positions commonly filled include:** Applications Engineer; AS400 Programmer Analyst; Computer Animator; Computer Engineer; Computer Graphics Specialist; Computer Operator; Computer Programmer; Computer Scientist; Computer Support Technician; Computer Technician; Content Developer; Database Administrator; Database Manager; Editor; Editorial Assistant; Graphic Artist; Graphic Designer; Internet Services Manager; Managing Editor; MIS Specialist; Multimedia Designer; Network/Systems Administrator; Software Engineer; Systems Analyst; Systems Manager; Technical Writer/Editor; Webmaster. **Benefits available to temporary workers:** 401(k); Direct Deposit; Health Benefits; Vacation Pay. **Corporate headquarters location:** Providence RI. **Other U.S. locations:** Nationwide. **Average salary range of placements:** $30,000 - $49,999. **Number of placements per year:** 200 - 499.

IMPRIMIS STAFFING SOLUTIONS
5550 LBJ Freeway, Suite 100, Dallas TX 75240. 972/419-1631. **Fax:** 972/419-1970. **Contact:** Recruiter. **World Wide Web address:** http://www.imprimis-group.com. **Description:** A temporary agency that also

offers some permanent placements. **Specializes in the areas of:** Accounting/Auditing; Administration; Clerical; Computer Science/Software; Finance; Insurance; Legal; Nonprofit; Personnel/Labor Relations; Secretarial. **Positions commonly filled include:** Accountant/Auditor; Administrative Assistant; Auditor; Clerical Supervisor; Computer Operator; Customer Service Representative; Graphic Artist; Human Resources Specialist; MIS Specialist; Sales Representative; Software Engineer; Typist/Word Processor. **Benefits available to temporary workers:** 401(k); Medical Insurance; Paid Holidays; Paid Vacation. **Other U.S. locations:** Fort Worth TX. **Average salary range of placements:** $20,000 - $29,999. **Number of placements per year:** 1000+.

INSURANCE TEMPORARY SERVICES, INC.
2777 Stemmons Freeway, Suite 946, Dallas TX 75207. 214/638-7777. **Fax:** 214/634-8500. **Contact:** Susie Lowry, President. **Description:** A temporary agency. **Specializes in the areas of:** Insurance. **Positions commonly filled include:** Adjuster; Claim Representative; Customer Service Representative; Typist/Word Processor.

INTERSEARCH ASSOCIATES, INC.
5100 Westheimer Road, Suite 460, Houston TX 77056-5507. 713/960-0444. **Fax:** 713/460-1411. **Contact:** Manager. **Description:** A temporary agency that also provides some permanent placements. **Specializes in the areas of:** Accounting/Auditing; Banking; Finance; Mortgage; Personnel/Labor Relations. **Positions commonly filled include:** Accountant/Auditor; Bank Officer/Manager; Claim Representative; Computer Programmer; Customer Service Representative; Human Resources Specialist; Management Trainee; MIS Specialist; Systems Analyst. **Benefits available to temporary workers:** Paid Holidays; Paid Vacation. **Average salary range of placements:** $30,000 - $50,000. **Number of placements per year:** 200 - 499.

KELLY SCIENTIFIC RESOURCES
18601 LBJ Freeway, Suite 140, Mesquite TX 75150-5629. 972/279-3265. **Contact:** Branch Manager. **World Wide Web address:** http://www.kellyscientific.com. **Description:** A temporary agency for scientific professionals. **Specializes in the areas of:** Biomedical; Biotechnology; Chemicals; Environmental; Food; Petrochemical; Pharmaceuticals.
Other U.S. locations:
- 13831 NW Freeway, Suite 640, Houston TX 77040. 713/690-2155.

KELLY SERVICES, INC.
1800 Teague Drive, Suite 100, Sherman TX 75090. 903/893-7777. **Contact:** Sandi Key, Branch Manager. **Description:** A temporary agency. **Specializes in the areas of:** Accounting/Auditing; Banking; Clerical; Computer Hardware/Software; Engineering; Finance; Health/Medical; Legal; Manufacturing; Secretarial; Technical; Transportation.
Other U.S. locations:
- 1616 South Kentucky, Building D, Suite 110, Amarillo TX 79102. 806/355-9696.

LINK STAFFING SERVICES
1800 Bering Drive, Suite 800, Houston TX 77057. 713/784-4400. **Toll-free phone:** 800/848-5465. **Fax:** 713/784-4454. **Contact:** Ted Long, Vice President. **Description:** A temporary agency. **Specializes in the areas of:** Food; General Management; Industrial; Manufacturing. **Positions commonly filled include:** Automotive Mechanic; Blue-Collar Worker Supervisor; Construction and Building Inspector; Draftsperson; Electrician; Industrial Production Manager. **Benefits available to temporary workers:** Dental Insurance; Medical Insurance. **Average salary range of placements:** $30,000 - $50,000. **Number of placements per year:** 1000+.

MANPOWER TEMPORARY SERVICES
12225 Greenville Avenue, Suite 495, Dallas TX 75243. 972/699-9337. **Contact:** W.H. Wilson, Area Manager.

World Wide Web address: http://www.manpower.com. **Description:** A temporary agency that also provides some permanent placements. **Specializes in the areas of:** Data Processing; Light Industrial; Office Support; Technical; Travel. **Benefits available to temporary workers:** Life Insurance; Medical Insurance; Paid Holidays; Paid Vacation; Referral Bonus Plan; Stock Purchase; Training. **Number of placements per year:** 1000+.
Other U.S. locations:
- 8303 North Mopac Expressway, Suite 220-B, Austin TX 78759. 512/343-2141.
- 5402 South Staples Street, Suite 103, Corpus Christi TX 78411. 361/991-1196.
- 440 Louisiana Street, Suite 470, Houston TX 77002. 713/228-3131.

NORRELL SERVICES
6117 Richmond Avenue, Suite 222, Houston TX 77057. 281/484-5500. **Contact:** Area Manager. **Description:** A temporary agency that also provides some contract placements. Client company pays fee. **Specializes in the areas of:** Accounting; Administration; Finance; MIS/EDP; Personnel/Labor Relations; Scientific; Secretarial; Technical. **Positions commonly filled include:** Administrative Assistant; Auditor; Chief Financial Officer; Clerical Supervisor; Controller; Customer Service Representative; Human Resources Manager; Secretary; Telecommunications Manager; Typist/Word Processor. **Benefits available to temporary workers:** 401(k); Health Benefits; Medical Insurance; Stock Purchase. **Corporate headquarters location:** Atlanta GA. **Other U.S. locations:** Nationwide. **International locations:** Canada; Puerto Rico. **Average salary range of placements:** $20,000 - $29,999. **Number of placements per year:** 1000+.

OLSTEN STAFFING SERVICES
40 Northeast Loop 410, Suite 430, San Antonio TX 78216. 210/349-9911. **Fax:** 210/349-5702. **Contact:** Faye Ripper, Recruiter. **Description:** A temporary agency. Founded in 1950. **Specializes in the areas of:** Accounting; Administration; Computer Science/ Software; Engineering; Industrial; Legal; Light Industrial; Marketing; MIS/EDP; Sales; Secretarial; Technical. **Positions commonly filled include:** Accountant; Administrative Assistant; Blue-Collar Worker Supervisor; Buyer; Chemical Engineer; Chemist; Civil Engineer; Clerical Supervisor; Clinical Lab Technician; Computer Operator; Customer Service Rep.; Design Engineer; Draftsperson; Electrical/Electronics Engineer; Human Resources Manager; Industrial Engineer; Manufacturing Engineer; Mechanical Engineer; MIS Specialist; Paralegal; Purchasing Agent/ Manager; Quality Control Supervisor; Sales Rep.; Secretary; Software Engineer; Systems Analyst; Technical Writer/Editor; Typist/Word Processor; Underwriter/Assistant Underwriter. **Benefits available to temporary workers:** Daycare Assistance; Dental Insurance; Medical Insurance; Referral Bonus Plan. **Corporate headquarters location:** Melville NY. **International locations:** Worldwide. **Average salary range of placements:** Less than $20,000. **Number of placements per year:** 1000+.
Other U.S. locations:
- 4002 Beltline Road, Suite 150, Lockbox 6, Addison TX 75001. 972/789-0100.

P.H.R. (PROFESSIONAL HEALTHCARE RESOURCES)
2825 Wilcrest, Suite 420, Houston TX 77042. 713/785-6931. **Fax:** 713/785-3821. **Contact:** Manager. **Description:** A temporary agency that also provides some permanent placements. **Specializes in the areas of:** Health/Medical. **Positions commonly filled include:** Pharmacist.

PRIORITY PERSONNEL, INC.
312 West Hopkins Street, San Marcos TX 78666. 512/392-2323. **Fax:** 512/396-2366. **Contact:** Placement Manager. **Description:** A temporary agency. Founded in 1994. **Specializes in the areas of:** Accounting/Auditing;

Administration; Industrial; Manufacturing; Secretarial. **Positions commonly filled include:** Automotive Mechanic; Blue-Collar Worker Supervisor; Clerical Supervisor; Electrician; Landscape Architect; Management Trainee; Mechanical Engineer; Quality Control Supervisor; Services Sales Rep.; Typist/Word Processor. **Average salary range of placements:** Less than $20,000. **Number of placements per year:** 1000+.

PRO STAFF PERSONNEL SERVICES
14755 Preston Road, Suite 120, Dallas TX 75240. 972/239-8800. **Toll-free phone:** 800/938-9675. **Fax:** 972/239-4600. **Contact:** Katherine Tolsch, Branch Manager. **World Wide Web address:** http://www. prostaff.com. **Description:** A temporary agency that also provides some permanent placements. **Specializes in the areas of:** Accounting/Auditing; Advertising; Computer Science/Software; Engineering; Finance; Light Industrial; Manufacturing; Sales; Secretarial; Technical. **Positions commonly filled include:** Accountant/Auditor; Administrative Manager; Advertising Clerk; Bank Officer/Manager; Blue-Collar Worker Supervisor; Branch Manager; Brokerage Clerk; Budget Analyst; Claim Rep.; Clerical Supervisor; Computer Programmer; Cost Estimator; Design Engineer; Electrical/Electronics Engineer; Financial Analyst; General Manager; Human Resources Specialist; Industrial Engineer; Industrial Production Manager; Management Analyst/Consultant; Management Trainee; Manufacturer's/Wholesaler's Sales Rep.; Market Research Analyst; Mechanical Engineer; MIS Specialist; Operations/Production Manager; Purchasing Agent/Manager; Quality Control Supervisor; Services Sales Representative; Software Engineer; Systems Analyst; Technical Writer/Editor; Typist/Word Processor; Underwriter/Assistant Underwriter. **Benefits available to temporary workers:** 401(k); Medical Insurance; Paid Holidays; Paid Vacation. **Corporate headquarters location:** Minneapolis MN. **Average salary range of placements:** $20,000 - $29,999. **Number of placements per year:** 1000+.
Other U.S. locations:
- 122 West John Carpenter Freeway, Suite 515, Irving TX 75039. 972/650-1500.

RESOURCE STAFFING
1360 Post Oak Boulevard, Suite 745, Houston TX 77056. 713/621-9895. **Fax:** 713/621-8832. **Contact:** Lisa Duncan, Staffing Manager. **E-mail address:** staffing@onramp.net. **World Wide Web address:** http://www.restaff.com. **Description:** A temporary agency that also provides temp-to-perm placements. Founded in 1988. **Specializes in the areas of:** Accounting/Auditing; Administration; Banking; Computer Science/Software; Finance; Legal; Personnel/ Labor Relations; Sales; Secretarial. **Positions commonly filled include:** Accountant/Auditor; Computer Programmer; Credit Manager; Customer Service Representative; Human Resources Specialist; Internet Services Manager; MIS Specialist; Multimedia Designer; Software Engineer; Systems Analyst; Technical Writer/Editor; Typist/Word Processor. **Benefits available to temporary workers:** Paid Holidays; Referral Bonus Plan. **Other area locations:** Dallas TX. **Average salary range of placements:** $20,000 - $29,999. **Number of placements per year:** 1 - 49.

RESPIRATORY STAFFING SPECIALISTS INC.
310 East Interstate 30, Suite 310, Garland TX 75043. 972/226-5421. **Toll-free phone:** 800/758-3275. **Fax:** 972/226-0323. **Contact:** Carla DeWitt, President. **Description:** A temporary agency. **Specializes in the areas of:** Health/Medical. **Positions commonly filled include:** Respiratory Therapist. **Average salary range of placements:** $20,000 - $29,999. **Number of placements per year:** 1 - 49.

RESTAURANT SERVERS, INC.
P.O. Box 32, Colleyville TX 76034-0032. 214/350-1166. **Fax:** 214/350-0454. **Contact:** Manager. **Description:** A temporary agency that also provides contract services in event management and food protection management. Restaurant Servers also provides training and consulting

services. **Specializes in the areas of:** Food. **Positions commonly filled include:** Blue-Collar Worker Supervisor; Education Administrator; Management Trainee; Registered Nurse; Restaurant/Food Service Mgr. **Average salary range of placements:** Less than $20,000. **Number of placements per year:** 200 - 499.

SOS STAFFING SERVICE
1111 Airport Freeway, Suite 215, Irving TX 75062. 972/870-9662. **Contact:** Manager. **Description:** A temporary agency that also provides some permanent placements. **Specializes in the areas of:** Administration; Industrial; Manufacturing; Personnel/Labor Relations; Secretarial. **Positions commonly filled include:** Accountant/Auditor; Automotive Mechanic; Blue-Collar Worker Supervisor; Buyer; Claim Rep.; Clerical Supervisor; Computer Programmer; Cost Estimator; Credit Manager; Customer Service Rep.; Design Engineer; Draftsperson; Hotel Manager; Human Service Worker; Landscape Architect; Mechanical Engineer; Operations/Production Manager; Purchasing Agent/Mgr.; Restaurant/Food Service Manager; Telecommunications Manager; Travel Agent; Typist/Word Processor. **Benefits available to temporary workers:** Paid Holidays; Paid Vacation. **Number of placements per year:** 100 - 199.

ANNE SADOVSKY & COMPANY
7557 Rambler Road, Suite 1454, Dallas TX 75231. 214/692-9300. **Fax:** 214/692-9823. **Contact:** Manager. **Description:** A temporary agency. **Specializes in the areas of:** Housing; Sales. **Average salary range of placements:** $20,000 - $29,999. **Number of placements per year:** 1000+.

SELECT STAFF
3700 North 10th Street, Suite 300, McAllen TX 78501. 956/631-8367. **Fax:** 956/630-4502. **Contact:** Supervisor. **Description:** A temporary agency. **Specializes in the areas of:** Accounting/Auditing; Banking; Health/Medical; Industrial; Insurance; Legal; Manufacturing; Retail; Sales; Secretarial; Technical. **Positions commonly filled include:** Accountant/Auditor; Claim Rep.; Clerical Supervisor; Customer Service Rep.; Electrician; Environmental Engineer; Management Trainee; Medical Records Technician; Paralegal; Quality Control Supervisor; Real Estate Agent; Services Sales Representative; Surveyor; Typist/Word Processor. **Corporate headquarters location:** This Location. **Other U.S. locations:** Brownsville TX; Harlinger TX. **Average salary range of placements:** Less than $20,000. **Number of placements per year:** 1000+.

SPECIAL COUNSEL
AMICUS LEGAL STAFFING INC.
1412 Main Street, Suite 205, Dallas TX 75202. 214/698-0200. **Contact:** Manager. **Description:** A temporary agency that also provides some permanent placements and executive searches. **Specializes in the areas of:** Legal.

TRC STAFFING SERVICES INC.
1300 Summit Avenue, Suite 634, Fort Worth TX 76102. 817/335-1550. **Contact:** Operations Manager. **E-mail address:** trc@onramp.net. **Description:** A temporary agency that also provides some temp-to-perm placements. Founded in 1990. **Specializes in the areas of:** Clerical; Industrial; Manufacturing; Secretarial; Technical. **Positions commonly filled include:** Accountant; Buyer; Chemist; Claim Representative; Computer Programmer; Customer Service Rep.; Paralegal; Systems Analyst; Technical Writer/Editor. **Benefits available to temporary workers:** Medical Insurance; Paid Holidays; Paid Vacation. **Corporate headquarters location:** Atlanta GA. **Number of placements per year:** 1000+.

TEMPORARY RESOURCES, INC.
P.O. Box 3024, Midland TX 79702-3024. 915/684-0527. **Fax:** 915/684-0836. **Contact:** Patricia de Little, President. **Description:** A temporary agency. **Specializes in the areas of:** Personnel/Labor Relations; Secretarial. **Positions commonly filled include:** Accountant/Auditor;

Administrative Manager; Advertising Clerk; Bank Officer/Manager; Branch Manager; Brokerage Clerk; Buyer; Claim Rep.; Clerical Supervisor; Customer Service Rep.; Draftsperson; General Manager; Health Services Mgr.; Internet Services Manager; Management Trainee; Manufacturer's/Wholesaler's Sales Rep.; Market Research Analyst; Medical Records Technician; Paralegal; Quality Control Supervisor; Radio/TV Announcer/Broadcaster; Reporter; Securities Sales Representative; Services Sales Representative; Travel Agent; Typist/Word Processor; Underwriter/Assistant Underwriter. **Benefits available to temporary workers:** Bonus Award/Plan; Medical Insurance; Paid Vacation. **Average salary range of placements:** Less than $20,000. **Number of placements per year:** 1000+.

TODAYS LEGAL STAFFING
700 North Pearl Street, Suite 350, Dallas TX 75201. 214/754-0700. **Toll-free phone:** 800/693-1514. **Contact:** Tom Gardner, Group Manager. **World Wide Web address:** http://www.todays.com. **Description:** A temporary agency that also provides some permanent placements. **Specializes in the areas of:** Legal; Secretarial. **Positions commonly filled include:** Attorney; Paralegal; Typist/Word Processor. **Other U.S. locations:** Nationwide. **Average salary range of placements:** $30,000 - $50,000. **Number of placements per year:** 200 - 499.

TODAYS OFFICE STAFFING
4100 Alpha Road, Suite 215, Dallas TX 75244-4332. 972/788-4435. **Fax:** 972/233-6388. **Contact:** Manager. **World Wide Web address:** http://www.todays.com. **Description:** A temporary agency. **Specializes in the areas of:** Accounting/Auditing; Computer Science/Software; Legal; Personnel/Labor Relations; Sales. **Positions commonly filled include:** Clerical Supervisor; Financial Analyst; Human Resources Specialist; Human Service Worker. **Benefits available to temporary workers:** Paid Holidays; Paid Vacation. **Corporate headquarters location:** 18111 Preston Road, Suite 700, Dallas TX 75252. **Other U.S. locations:** Nationwide. **Number of placements per year:** 1000+.

TODAYS STAFFING
18111 Preston Road, Suite 700, Dallas TX 75252. 972/380-9380. **Fax:** 972/713-4196. **Contact:** Manager. **World Wide Web address:** http://www.todays.com. **Description:** A temporary agency. **Specializes in the areas of:** Accounting/Auditing; Banking; Legal; Secretarial. **Positions commonly filled include:** Accountant/Auditor; Administrative Manager; Advertising Clerk; Attorney; Brokerage Clerk; Claim Representative; Computer Programmer; Customer Service Representative; Paralegal; Typist/Word Processor. **Benefits available to temporary workers:** 401(k); Paid Holidays; Paid Vacation. **Corporate headquarters location:** This Location. **Average salary range of placements:** Less than $20,000. **Number of placements per year:** 1000+.
Other U.S. locations:
• 1900 West Loop South, Suite 110, Houston TX 77027. 713/621-9880.

VOLT SERVICES GROUP OF DALLAS
9330 LBJ Freeway, Suite 1060, Dallas TX 75243-9946. 972/690-8358. **Contact:** Office Manager. **Description:** A temporary agency. **Specializes in the areas of:** Clerical; Computer Hardware/Software; Engineering; Manufacturing; Personnel/Labor Relations; Technical.

WESTAFF
16479 North Dallas Parkway, Suite 110, Dallas TX 75248. 972/713-9900. **Toll-free phone:** 800/GET-A-JOB. **Fax:** 972/713-8305. **Contact:** Cassidy Fletcher, Staff Recruiter. **World Wide Web address:** http://www.westaff.com. **Description:** A temporary agency. Client company pays fee. **Specializes in the areas of:** Administration. **Positions commonly filled include:** Accountant; Computer Support Technician; Computer Technician. **Benefits available to temporary workers:** Direct Deposit; Health Benefits.

Corporate headquarters location: Walnut Creek CA. **Other U.S. locations:** Nationwide. **Number of placements per year:** 1000+.

WESTAFF
323 East Las Colinas Boulevard, Irving TX 75039-5556. 972/831-8833. **Fax:** 972/831-8856. **Contact:** Staffing Coordinator. **World Wide Web address:** http://www.westaff.com. **Description:** A temporary agency. **Specializes in the areas of:** Industrial;

Personnel/Labor Relations; Sales; Secretarial; Technical. **Positions commonly filled include:** Blue-Collar Worker Supervisor; Customer Service Representative; Human Resources Specialist; Management Trainee; Services Sales Representative. **Benefits available to temporary workers:** 401(k); Medical Insurance; Paid Holidays; Paid Vacation. **Corporate headquarters location:** Walnut Creek CA. **Other U.S. locations:** Nationwide. **Number of placements per year:** 1000+.

CONTRACT SERVICES FIRMS

A-R-C (ALTERNATIVE RESOURCES CORP.)
1800 West Loop South, Suite 1660, Houston TX 77027. 713/871-9900. **Fax:** 713/871-9038. **Contact:** Manager. **World Wide Web address:** http://www.alrc.com. **Description:** A contract services firm. **Specializes in the areas of:** Information Technology; Technical. **Positions commonly filled include:** MIS Specialist; Technical Writer/Editor.
Other U.S. locations:
• 15770 North Dallas Parkway, Suite 400, Dallas TX 75248. 972/934-0505.

ABACUS TECHNICAL SERVICES
2201 North Central Expressway, Suite 180, Richardson TX 75080. 972/644-4105. **Contact:** Manager. **Description:** A contract services firm. **Specializes in the areas of:** Technical. **Positions commonly filled include:** Computer Programmer.

ADECCO/TAD TECHNICAL SERVICES
4300 Alpha Road, Suite 100, Dallas TX 75244. 972/980-0510. **Contact:** Manager. **Description:** A contract services firm.

ARCHITECTURAL CAREER NETWORK (ACN)
12337 Jones Road, Suite 200, Houston TX 77070. 713/464-3838. **Fax:** 713/464-3893. **Contact:** Jim Jackson, Owner. **Description:** A contract services firm. **Specializes in the areas of:** Architecture/Construction; Engineering. **Positions commonly filled include:** Architect; Construction Contractor; Designer; Draftsperson; Interior Designer; Landscape Architect.

B&M ASSOCIATES, INC.
AIR & SPACE DIVISION
2925 LBJ Freeway, Suite 278, Dallas TX 75234. 972/241-8408. **Toll-free phone:** 800/745-9675. **Fax:** 972/241-4363. **Contact:** Division Manager. **World Wide Web address:** http://www.bmanet.com. **Description:** A contract services firm. **Specializes in the areas of:** Aerospace; Computer Science/Software; Engineering; Industrial; Personnel/Labor Relations; Scientific; Technical. **Positions commonly filled include:** Applications Engineer; Biochemist; Buyer; Civil Engineer; Computer Operator; Computer Programmer; Design Engineer; Draftsperson; Electrician; Environmental Engineer; Graphic Artist; Graphic Designer; Internet Services Manager; Manufacturing Engineer; Mechanical Engineer; Metallurgical Engineer; MIS Specialist; Multimedia Designer; Operations Manager; Project Manager; Purchasing Agent/Manager; Quality Control Supervisor; Software Engineer; Systems Analyst; Systems Manager; Technical Writer/Editor; Telecommunications Manager; Webmaster. **Benefits available to temporary workers:** 401(k); Medical Insurance; Paid Holidays; Paid Vacation. **Corporate headquarters location:** Boston MA. **Other U.S. locations:** San Diego CA; Santa Ana CA; Manchester NH; Vienna VA. **Average salary range of placements:** More than $50,000. **Number of placements per year:** 1000+.

BELCAN TECHNICAL SERVICES
3333 Earhart Drive, Suite 120, Carrollton TX 75006. 972/239-0405. **Contact:** Michelle Williams, Team Leader. **World Wide Web address:** http://www.belcan.com. **Description:** A contract services firm.

Specializes in the areas of: Administration; Engineering. **Positions commonly filled include:** Aerospace Engineer; Applications Engineer; Buyer; Chemical Engineer; Civil Engineer; Computer Animator; Computer Operator; Computer Programmer; Cost Estimator; Database Manager; Design Engineer; Designer; Draftsperson; Electrical/Electronics Engineer; Environmental Engineer; Graphic Artist; Graphic Designer; Human Resources Specialist; Industrial Engineer; Mechanical Engineer; MIS Specialist; Multimedia Designer; Project Manager; Quality Control Supervisor; Software Engineer; Structural Engineer; Systems Analyst; Systems Manager; Technical Writer/Editor; Telecommunications Manager. **Benefits available to temporary workers:** 401(k); Medical Insurance; Paid Holidays; Paid Vacation. **Corporate headquarters location:** Cincinnati OH. **Other U.S. locations:** Nationwide. **Average salary range of placements:** More than $50,000. **Number of placements per year:** 200 - 499.

BUTLER INTERNATIONAL
914 Royal Lane, Irving TX 75063. 817/355-9655. **Contact:** Manager. **Description:** A contract services firm. **Specializes in the areas of:** Aerospace; Computer Science/Software; Engineering; Food; Industrial; Manufacturing; Personnel/Labor Relations; Technical. **Positions commonly filled include:** Aircraft Mechanic/Engine Specialist; Budget Analyst; Buyer; Chemical Engineer; Chemist; Civil Engineer; Clinical Lab Technician; Computer Programmer; Cost Estimator; Customer Service Rep.; Design Engineer; Designer; Draftsperson; Editor; Electrician; Environmental Engineer; Industrial Engineer; Mechanical Engineer; MIS Specialist; Petroleum Engineer; Software Engineer; Structural Engineer; Systems Analyst; Technical Writer/Editor; Telecommunications Manager. **Benefits available to temporary workers:** Paid Holidays; Paid Vacation. **Corporate headquarters location:** Montvale NJ. **Number of placements per year:** 200 - 499.

CDI CORPORATION
9101 Burnet Rd, Suite 103, Austin TX 78758. 512/837-1073. **Fax:** 512/832-9568. **Contact:** Manager. **World Wide Web address:** http://www.cdicorp.com. **Description:** A contract services firm. **Specializes in the areas of:** Engineering; Technical. **Corporate headquarters location:** Philadelphia PA. **Other U.S. locations:** Nationwide. **International locations:** Worldwide.

CDI ENGINEERING CORPORATION
1810 Laurel Avenue, Beaumont TX 77701. 409/835-5290. **Fax:** 409/835-5586. **Contact:** Manager. **World Wide Web address:** http://www.cdicorp.com. **Description:** A contract services firm. **Specializes in the areas of:** Engineering; Technical. **Corporate headquarters location:** Philadelphia PA. **Other U.S. locations:** Nationwide. **International locations:** Worldwide.

CDI TELECOMMUNICATIONS
2425 North Central Expressway, Suite 101, Richardson TX 75080. 972/480-8333. **Contact:** Branch Manager. **E-mail address:** richardson@cdicorp.com. **World Wide Web address:** http://www.cdicorp.com. **Description:** A contract services firm. **Specializes in the areas of:**

Telecommunications. **Corporate headquarters location:** Philadelphia PA. **Other U.S. locations:** Nationwide. **Number of placements per year:** 1000+.

CARLTECH
24 Greenway Plaza, Suite 1204, Houston TX 77046. 713/629-5700. **Toll-free phone:** 800/324-5050. **Fax:** 713/629-4209. **Contact:** Manager. **E-mail address:** carltech@firstnethou.com. **Description:** A contract services firm. **Specializes in the areas of:** Computer Science/Software; Engineering; Technical. **Positions commonly filled include:** Chemical Engineer; Civil Engineer; Computer Programmer; Design Engineer; Designer; Draftsperson; Electrical/Electronics Engineer; Environmental Engineer; Mechanical Engineer; MIS Specialist; Software Engineer; Structural Engineer; Systems Analyst. **Benefits available to temporary workers:** 401(k); Paid Vacation. **Average salary range of placements:** $30,000 - $50,000. **Number of placements per year:** 100 - 199.

CERTIFIED PERSONNEL SERVICE INC.
1600 Strawberry Street, Pasadena TX 77502. 713/477-0321. **Toll-free phone:** 800/234-8054. **Fax:** 713/477-2194. **Contact:** Tom Warren, President. **Description:** A contract services firm. **Specializes in the areas of:** Accounting; Architecture/Construction; Computer Science/Software; Engineering; Industrial; Manufacturing; Personnel/Labor Relations; Secretarial. **Positions commonly filled include:** Accountant/Auditor; Chemical Engineer; Chemist; Civil Engineer; Computer Programmer; Construction and Building Inspector; Construction Contractor; Cost Estimator; Counselor; Design Engineer; Designer; Draftsperson; Electrical/ Electronics Engineer; Electrician; Human Resources Specialist; Mechanical Engineer; Purchasing Agent/ Manager; Software Engineer; Stationary Engineer; Systems Analyst; Technical Writer/Editor. **Benefits available to temporary workers:** 401(k); Medical Insurance; Paid Holidays; Paid Vacation. **Average salary range of placements:** $30,000 - $50,000. **Number of placements per year:** 1000+.

COMFORCE INFORMATION TECHNOLOGIES
15305 Dallas Parkway, Suite 250, Lockbox 19, Addison TX 75001. 972/866-5100. **Contact:** Manager. **Description:** A contract services firm. **Specializes in the areas of:** Computer Science/Software.

CONTRACT DESIGN PERSONNEL
2225 East Randol Mill Road, Suite 223, Arlington TX 76011. 817/640-6119. **Fax:** 817/640-6256. **Contact:** Stan Baker, Director of Recruiting Operations. **Description:** A contract services firm. **Specializes in the areas of:** Engineering; High-Tech; Multimedia; Technical. **Positions commonly filled include:** Aerospace Engineer; Architect; Chemical Engineer; Civil Engineer; Computer Programmer; Design Engineer; Designer; Draftsperson; Electrical/Electronics Engineer; Environmental Engineer; Industrial Engineer; Mechanical Engineer; Metallurgical Engineer; Mining Engineer; Multimedia Designer; Nuclear Engineer; Petroleum Engineer; Software Engineer; Structural Engineer; Systems Analyst; Technical Writer/Editor. **Benefits available to temporary workers:** Paid Holidays. **Number of placements per year:** 100 - 199.

DESIGN QUEST INC.
P.O. Box 6555, Tyler TX 75711. 903/561-6241. **Fax:** 903/534-9170. **Contact:** Louie Adams, Recruiter. **Description:** A contract services firm. **Specializes in the areas of:** Engineering; Personnel/Labor Relations. **Positions commonly filled include:** Chemical Engineer; Civil Eng.; Design Engineer; Designer; Draftsperson; Electrical/Electronics Eng.; Industrial Eng.; Mechanical Engineer; Petroleum Engineer; Structural Engineer. **Average salary range of placements:** More than $50,000. **Number of placements per year:** 100 - 199.

EDP CONTRACT SERVICES
4500 Fuller Drive, Suite 405, Irving TX 75038. 972/650-8384. **Contact:** Manager. **Description:** A contract

services firm. **Specializes in the areas of:** Computer Hardware/Software; Technical.

FOCUS POINT, INC.
13201 Northwest Freeway, Suite 520, Houston TX 77040. 713/939-7644. **Fax:** 713/939-7355. **Contact:** Manager. **Description:** A contract services firm. **Specializes in the areas of:** Computer Science/Software; Engineering; Industrial; Manufacturing; Technical. **Positions commonly filled include:** Aerospace Engineer; Architect; Biomedical Engineer; Branch Mgr.; Buyer; Ceramics Engineer; Chemical Engineer; Chemist; Civil Engineer; Computer Programmer; Construction Contractor; Cost Estimator; Design Engineer; Designer; Draftsperson; Electrical/Electronics Engineer; Environmental Engineer; General Mgr.; Geologist/ Geophysicist; Human Resources Specialist; Industrial Engineer; Industrial Production Manager; Internet Services Manager; Materials Engineer; Mechanical Engineer; Metallurgical Engineer; Mining Engineer; MIS Specialist; Multimedia Designer; Nuclear Engineer; Petroleum Engineer; Purchasing Agent/Manager; Quality Control Supervisor; Science Technologist; Software Engineer; Structural Engineer; Surveyor; Systems Analyst; Technical Writer/Editor; Telecommunications Manager. **Benefits available to temporary workers:** Paid Holidays. **Corporate headquarters location:** Dallas TX. **Average salary range of placements:** $30,000 - $50,000. **Number of placements per year:** 100 - 199.

HALL KINION
901 Mopac Expressway, Suite 343, Austin TX 78746. **Toll-free phone:** 888/871-4254. **Fax:** 512/306-8060. **Contact:** Manager. **E-mail address:** au2resume@ hallkinion.com. **World Wide Web address:** http://www. hallkinion.com. **Description:** A contract services firm that also provides some permanent placements. **Specializes in the areas of:** Computer Hardware/ Software; Information Systems; Information Technology; Internet Development; Network Administration; Quality Assurance; Systems Administration; Systems Design; Technical Writing.
Other U.S. locations:
- 1600 North Carolina Boulevard, Suite 2300, Richardson TX 75080.
- 3040 Post Oak Boulevard, Suite 440, Houston TX 77056.
- 8911 Capital of Texas Highway, Suite 3310, Austin TX 78759.

HEALTHCARE PROVIDERS
8700 Commerce Park Drive, Suite 102, Houston TX 77036. 713/778-0114. **Fax:** 713/981-8936. **Contact:** Manager. **Description:** A contract services firm that provides placements in hospitals. **Specializes in the areas of:** Health/Medical. **Positions commonly filled include:** Respiratory Therapist.

L.K. JORDAN & ASSOCIATES
321 Texan Trail, Suite 100, Corpus Christi TX 78411. 361/814-9700. **Contact:** Recruiter. **Description:** A contract services firm. **Specializes in the areas of:** Accounting; Administration; Engineering; Industrial; Secretarial. **Positions commonly filled include:** Accountant; Administrative Manager; Branch Manager; Chemical Engineer; Civil Engineer; Clerical Supervisor; Computer Programmer; Design Engineer; Financial Analyst; Human Resources Specialist; Mechanical Engineer; MIS Specialist; Pharmacist; Purchasing Agent/ Manager; Registered Nurse; Services Sales Rep.; Software Engineer; Structural Engineer; Systems Analyst; Typist/Word Processor. **Average salary range of placements:** $30,000 - $50,000. **Number of placements per year:** 100 - 199.

KADCO CONTRACT DESIGN CORPORATION
3100 Wilcrest Drive, Suite 230, Houston TX 77042. 713/780-2424. **Fax:** 713/784-2838. **Contact:** Jacqueline Kyle, President. **Description:** A contract services firm. **Specializes in the areas of:** Engineering. **Positions commonly filled include:** Architect; Buyer; Chemical

Engineer; Chemist; Civil Engineer; Construction and Building Inspector; Cost Estimator; Design Engineer; Designer; Draftsperson; Electrical/Electronics Engineer; Environmental Engineer; Mechanical Engineer; Metallurgical Engineer; Petroleum Engineer; Purchasing Agent/Manager; Quality Control Supervisor; Radiological Technologist; Structural Engineer. **Benefits available to temporary workers:** 401(k); Medical Insurance; Paid Vacation. **Average salary range of placements:** More than $50,000. **Number of placements per year:** 100 - 199.

PROFESSIONAL SEARCH CONSULTANTS (PSC)
5151 San Felipe, Suite 420, Houston TX 77056. 713/960-9215. **Fax:** 713/960-1172. **Contact:** Manager. **Description:** A contract services firm. **Specializes in the areas of:** Accounting; Computer Science/Software; Engineering; Finance; General Management; Health/ Medical; Information Technology; Manufacturing; Personnel/Labor Relations; Sales; Technical. **Positions commonly filled include:** Accountant; Attorney; Budget Analyst; Chemical Engineer; Computer Programmer; Construction Contractor; Cost Estimator; Design Engineer; EEG Technologist; EKG Tech.; Electrical/ Electronics Engineer; Environmental Engineer; Financial Analyst; General Manager; Geologist/Geophysicist; Human Resources Specialist; Industrial Engineer; Industrial Production Manager; Market Research Analyst; Materials Engineer; Mechanical Engineer; Metallurgical Engineer; MIS Specialist; Multimedia Designer; Occupational Therapist; Operations/Production Manager; Petroleum Engineer; Physician; Recreational Therapist; Registered Nurse; Software Engineer; Structural Engineer; Systems Analyst; Telecommunications Manager. **Average salary range of placements:** More than $50,000. **Number of placements per year:** 50 - 99.

REHABWORKS
9535 Forest Lane, Suite 114, Dallas TX 75243. 972/480-8034. **Contact:** Manager. **Description:** RehabWorks is one of two contract rehabilitation companies owned by Horizon Healthcare Corporation. Together, Community Rehabilitation Center and RehabWorks provide occupational, speech, and physical therapy services to patients in nursing homes and geriatric units at hospitals through 276 contracts, covering approximately 31,000 beds. **Specializes in the areas of:** Health/Medical.

ROBERT SHIELDS & ASSOCIATES
P.O. Box 890723, Houston TX 77289-0723. 281/488-7961. **Toll-free phone:** 800/423-5383. **Fax:** 281/486-1496. **Contact:** Manager. **E-mail address:** itjobs@ aol.com. **Description:** A contract services firm. **Specializes in the areas of:** Computer Science/Software; Engineering. **Positions commonly filled include:** Chemical Engineer; Computer Programmer; MIS Specialist; Software Engineer; Systems Analyst. **Average salary range of placements:** More than $50,000. **Number of placements per year:** 100 - 199.

TECHNICAL CAREERS
12750 Merit Drive, Suite 1430, Park Central VII, Lockbox 56, Dallas TX 75251. 972/991-9424. **Fax:** 972/851-0651. **Contact:** Cary Tobolka, President. **E-mail address:** tobolka@technicalcareers.com. **World Wide Web address:** http://www.technicalcareers.com. **Description:** A contract services firm. Founded in 1978. **Specializes in the areas of:** Computer Science/Software; Engineering; Industrial; Manufacturing; Personnel/Labor Relations; Technical. **Positions commonly filled include:** Aerospace Engineer; Agricultural Engineer; Chemical Engineer; Civil Engineer; Computer Programmer; Design Engineer; Designer; Electrical/ Electronics Engineer; Environmental Engineer; Human Resources Specialist; Industrial Engineer; Industrial Production Manager; Internet Services Manager; Management Analyst/Consultant; Manufacturer's/ Wholesaler's Sales Rep.; Mechanical Engineer; Metallurgical Engineer; MIS Specialist; Multimedia Designer; Nuclear Engineer; Purchasing Agent/Manager; Quality Control Supervisor; Science Technologist;

Software Engineer; Structural Engineer; Systems Analyst; Telecommunications Manager. **Benefits available to temporary workers:** Dental Insurance; Life Insurance; Medical Insurance; Retirement Plan. **Corporate headquarters location:** This Location. **Other area locations:** Addison TX. **Other U.S. locations:** San Diego CA. **Average salary range of placements:** More than $50,000. **Number of placements per year:** 100 - 199.

TRIPLEX COMPUTER CORPORATION
P.O. Box 1949, Sugar Land TX 77487-1949. 281/240-6263. **Fax:** 281/491-0440. **Contact:** Manager. **E-mail address:** triplex@triplexcomputer.com. **World Wide Web address:** http://www.triplexcomputer.com. **Description:** A contract services firm that also provides permanent placements. **Specializes in the areas of:** Computer Science/Software; Information Technology.

UNIVERSAL REHABILITATION SERVICES, INC.
P.O. Box 691689, Houston TX 77269-1689. 281/820-9462. **Fax:** 281/820-0769. **Contact:** Ron McCreight, Executive Director. **Description:** A contract services firm that provides personnel to health care facilities and home health agencies. **Positions commonly filled include:** Occupational Therapist; Physical Therapist; Social Worker; Speech-Language Pathologist. **Average salary range of placements:** More than $50,000. **Number of placements per year:** 100 - 199.

VOLT SERVICES GROUP
1800 St. James Place, Suite 204, Houston TX 77056-4109. 713/626-8658. **Fax:** 713/626-8660. **Contact:** Erika Martinez, Branch Manager. **E-mail address:** voltexas@ ix.netcom.com. **Description:** A contract services firm. **Specializes in the areas of:** Engineering; Industrial; Manufacturing; Technical. **Positions commonly filled include:** Chemical Engineer; Chemist; Civil Engineer; Clinical Lab Technician; Computer Programmer; Construction Contractor; Cost Estimator; Design Engineer; Designer; Draftsperson; Electrical/Electronics Engineer; Environmental Engineer; Geologist/ Geophysicist; Industrial Engineer; Internet Services Manager; Mechanical Engineer; Mining Engineer; MIS Specialist; Petroleum Engineer; Software Engineer; Structural Engineer; Systems Analyst; Technical Writer/ Editor. **Benefits available to temporary workers:** 401(k); Medical Insurance; Paid Holidays; Paid Vacation. **Corporate headquarters location:** New York NY. **Number of placements per year:** 100 - 199. **Other U.S. locations:**
- 275 West Campbell Road, Suite 211, Richardson TX 75080. 972/669-0458.

THE WHITAKER COMPANIES, INC.
820 Gessner, Suite 1400, Houston TX 77024. 713/465-1500. **Fax:** 713/932-2525. **Contact:** Bruce Whitaker, President. **E-mail address:** whitadm@whitakercos.com. **World Wide Web address:** http://www. whitakercos.com. **Description:** A contract services firm that also provides executive searches on both retainer and contingency bases. Client company pays fee. **Specializes in the areas of:** Computer Science/Software; Engineering; Health/Medical; MIS/EDP; Scientific; Technical. **Positions commonly filled include:** Chemical Engineer; Chemist; Civil Engineer; Computer Engineer; Computer Programmer; Content Developer; Database Administrator; Database Manager; Design Engineer; Electrical/Electronics Engineer; Environmental Engineer; Geologist/Geophysicist; Internet Services Manager; Mechanical Engineer; MIS Specialist; Network/Systems Administrator; Nurse Practitioner; Physician; Physician Assistant; Software Engineer; SQL Programmer; Systems Analyst; Systems Manager; Webmaster. **Benefits available to temporary workers:** 401(k); Dental Insurance; Medical Insurance; Paid Holidays. **Corporate headquarters location:** This Location. **Other area locations:** Austin TX; Dallas TX. **Other U.S. locations:** Vincennes IN. **Average salary range of placements:** More than $100,000. **Number of placements per year:** 200 - 499.

H.L. YOH COMPANY
3730 Kirby Drive, Suite 810, Houston TX 77098.
713/524-5111. **Fax:** 713/524-2232. **Contact:** Doug
Walsh, Manager. **Description:** A contract services firm.
Specializes in the areas of: Administration;
Architecture/Construction; Computer Hardware/
Software; Engineering; Manufacturing; Personnel/Labor
Relations; Technical. **Positions commonly filled
include:** Aerospace Engineer; Architect; Buyer;
Chemical Engineer; Chemist; Civil Engineer;
Commercial Artist; Computer Operator; Computer
Programmer; Data Entry Clerk; Draftsperson; Driver;
Editor; EDP Specialist; Electrical/Electronics Engineer;
Human Resources Manager; Industrial Designer;
Industrial Engineer; Manufacturing Engineer;
Mechanical Engineer; Metallurgical Engineer; MIS
Specialist; Operations/Production Manager; Purchasing
Agent/Manager; Quality Control Supervisor; Reporter;
Software Engineer; Systems Analyst; Technical
Illustrator; Tech. Writer/Editor; Technician; Typist/Word
Processor. **Number of placements per year:** 200 - 499.

H.L. YOH COMPANY
13601 Preston Road, Suite 1020E, Dallas TX 75240.
972/239-9875. **Contact:** Manager. **Description:** A
contract services firm. **Specializes in the areas of:**
Architecture/Construction; Computer Hardware/
Software; Engineering; Manufacturing; Technical.

H.L. YOH COMPANY
7800 Shoal Creek Boulevard, Suite 129 South, Austin
TX 78757. 512/302-3373. **Contact:** Manager.
Description: A contract services firm. **Specializes in the
areas of:** High-Tech.

CAREER/OUTPLACEMENT COUNSELING FIRMS

ALLEN & ASSOCIATES
4099 McEwen, Suite 150, Dallas TX 75244. 972/385-
7112. **Toll-free phone:** 800/562-7214. **Fax:** 972/788-
2131. **Contact:** Manager. **World Wide Web address:**
http://www.allenandassociates.com. **Description:** A
career/outplacement counseling firm. **Corporate
headquarters location:** Maitland FL.
Other U.S. locations:
• 5444 Westheimer Boulevard, Suite 1967, Houston
TX 77056. 713/960-9603.

FAIRCHILD BARKLEY & ASSOCIATES
15770 Dallas Parkway, Suite 1000, Dallas TX 75248.
972/387-4800. **Fax:** 972/386-5210. **Contact:** R.J.
Porter, President. **Description:** Fairchild Barkley &
Associates is a career/outplacement counseling firm.
Positions commonly filled include: Accountant/
Auditor; Administrative Manager; Aerospace
Engineer; Agricultural Engineer; Architect; Bank
Officer/Manager; Biochemist; Biomedical Engineer;
Branch Manager; Budget Analyst; Chemical Engineer;
Civil Engineer; Claim Representative; Clerical
Supervisor; Computer Programmer; Cost Estimator;
Credit Manager; Customer Service Representative;
Design Engineer; Economist; Environmental Engineer;
Industrial Engineer; Management Analyst/Consultant;
MIS Specialist; Operations/Production Manager;
Petroleum Engineer; Public Relations Specialist;
Restaurant/Food Service Manager; Services Sales
Representative; Structural Engineer; Systems Analyst;
Telecommunications Manager. **Average salary range
of placements:** More than $50,000. **Number of
placements per year:** 100 - 199.

EXECUTIVE SEARCH FIRMS

ACCOUNTANTS EXECUTIVE SEARCH
170 South Main Street, Suite 550, Salt Lake City UT
84101. 801/328-3338. **Fax:** 801/328-3324. **Contact:**
Manager. **Description:** An executive search firm.
Specializes in the areas of: Accounting.

ACCOUNTSTAFF
5353 South 960 East, Suite 230, Murray UT 84117.
801/892-2002. **Contact:** Manager. **Description:** An
executive search firm. **Specializes in the areas of:**
Accounting/Auditing.

DHR INTERNATIONAL INC.
4001 South 700th East, Salt Lake City UT 84107.
801/263-7033. **Fax:** 801/263-7038. **Contact:** Manager.
Description: An executive search firm.

DEECO INTERNATIONAL
P.O. Box 57033, Salt Lake City UT 84157. 801/261-
3326. **Fax:** 801/261-3955. **Contact:** Dee McBride,
Manager. **Description:** An executive search firm
operating on both retainer and contingency bases.
Specializes in the areas of: Computer Science/Software;
Health/Medical; Sales; Technical. **Positions commonly
filled include:** Biomedical Engineer; Chemical Engineer;
Design Engineer; Market Research Analyst; Marketing
Manager; Mechanical Engineer; Product Manager; Sales
Engineer; Sales Executive; Sales Manager; Sales
Representative; Software Engineer. **Average salary
range of placements:** More than $50,000. **Number of
placements per year:** 1 - 49.

EXECUTIVE SEARCH GROUP
1042 Fort Union Boulevard, Suite 224, Midvale UT
84047. 801/364-3500. **Fax:** 801/944-2474. **Contact:**
Manager. **E-mail address:** searchgroup@sisna.com.
Description: An executive search firm. **Specializes in
the areas of:** High-Tech; Manufacturing.

F-O-R-T-U-N-E PERSONNEL CONSULTANTS
1536 North Woodland Park Drive, Suite 200, Layton UT
84041. 801/775-0444. **Fax:** 801/775-0447. **Contact:**
Manager. **Description:** An executive search firm.
Specializes in the areas of: Engineering. **Corporate
headquarters location:** New York NY. **Other U.S.
locations:** Nationwide.

**ROBERT HALF INTERNATIONAL
ACCOUNTEMPS**
50 West Broadway, Suite 500, Salt Lake City UT 84101.
801/364-5500. **Fax:** 801/364-3585. **Contact:** Recruiter.
World Wide Web address: http://www.roberthalf.com.
Description: An executive search firm. Accountemps
(also at this location) provides temporary accounting
placements. **Specializes in the areas of:** Accounting/
Auditing; Administration; Finance; Secretarial. **Positions
commonly filled include:** Account Manager;
Administrative Assistant; Administrative Manager;
Auditor; Bank Officer/Manager; Controller; Cost
Estimator; Credit Manager; Customer Service
Representative; Finance Director; Financial Analyst;
Secretary; Typist/Word Processor. **Benefits available to
temporary workers:** Dental Insurance; Medical
Insurance; Paid Holidays; Paid Vacation; Vision
Insurance. **Corporate headquarters location:** Menlo
Park CA. **International locations:** Worldwide. **Average
salary range of placements:** $30,000 - $50,000.
Number of placements per year: 50 - 99.

**ROBERT HALF INTERNATIONAL
ACCOUNTEMPS**
7090 South Union Park Avenue, Suite 240, Midvale UT
84047. 801/569-9400. **Contact:** Manager. **World Wide
Web address:** http://www.roberthalf.com. **Description:**
An executive search firm. Accountemps (also at this
location) provides temporary placements. **Specializes in
the areas of:** Accounting/Auditing. **Corporate**

headquarters location: Menlo Park CA. **Other U.S.
locations:** Nationwide.

KEYSEARCH INTERNATIONAL
P.O. Box 910370, St. George UT 84791-0370. 435/634-
1196. **Fax:** 435/634-1195. **Contact:** Deborah Keys,
President. **Description:** An executive search firm.
Specializes in the areas of: Transportation.

KI-TECH EXECUTIVE SEARCH
400 West 900 North, Building #10, North Salt Lake UT
84054. 801/544-3214. **Fax:** 801/544-4030. **Contact:** Jim
Mellos, Recruiter. **E-mail address:** jim@ki-tech.com.
World Wide Web address: http://www.ki-tech.com.
Description: An executive search firm.

**MANAGEMENT RECRUITERS INTERNATIONAL
SALES CONSULTANTS**
759 East 800 North, Orem UT 84097. 801/434-9265. **Fax:**
801/434-9535. **Contact:** Jerry Johnson, Manager/Owner.
Description: An executive search firm. **Specializes in the
areas of:** Food; Industrial Sales and Marketing;
Manufacturing. **Corporate headquarters location:**
Cleveland OH. **Other U.S. locations:** Nationwide.

MANAGEMENT RECRUITERS OF OGDEN
533 26th Street, Suite 203B, Ogden UT 84401. 801/621-
1777. **Fax:** 801/621-1788. **Contact:** Jerry Manning,
Manager. **Description:** An executive search firm operating
on a contingency basis. Founded in 1994. **Specializes in
the areas of:** Engineering; General Management;
Industrial; Manufacturing; Publishing. **Positions commonly
filled include:** Aerospace Engineer; Design Engineer;
Designer; Draftsperson; Electrical/Electronics Engineer;
Environmental Engineer; Human Resources Manager;
Industrial Engineer; Management Analyst/Consultant;
Materials Engineer; Mechanical Engineer; Quality Control
Supervisor; Statistician; Structural Engineer. **Corporate
headquarters location:** Cleveland OH. **Other U.S.
locations:** Nationwide. **Average salary range of
placements:** $30,000 - $50,000. **Number of placements
per year:** 1 - 49.

MANAGEMENT RECRUITERS OF PROVO
1933 North 1120 West, Provo UT 84604. 801/375-0777.
Fax: 801/375-5757. **Contact:** Larry J. Massung, General
Manager. **E-mail address:** gen_mgr@recruitr.com.
Description: An executive search firm. Founded in 1994.
Specializes in the areas of: Automation/Robotics;
Electronics; Manufacturing; Telecommunications.
Positions commonly filled include: Computer
Programmer; Design Engineer; Product Manager; Sales
Manager; Software Engineer. **Corporate headquarters
location:** Cleveland OH. **Other U.S. locations:**
Nationwide. **International locations:** Worldwide. **Average
salary range of placements:** More than $50,000. **Number
of placements per year:** 50 - 99.

**MANAGEMENT RECRUITERS OF SALT LAKE
CITY**
6600 South 1100 East, Suite 520, Salt Lake City UT 84121.
801/264-9800. **Fax:** 801/264-9807. **Contact:** Recruiter. **E-
mail address:** jobsusa@mrislc.com. **World Wide Web
address:** http://www.mrislc.com. **Description:** An
executive search firm operating on both retainer and
contingency bases. **Specializes in the areas of:**
Accounting/Auditing; Administration; Banking; Biology;
Computer Science/Software; Engineering; Finance; General
Management; Health/Medical; Industrial; Sales; Technical.
Positions commonly filled include: Account Manager;
Account Representative; Accountant; Applications
Engineer; Auditor; Biomedical Engineer; Chemical
Engineer; Chief Financial Officer; Civil Engineer;
Computer Programmer; Controller; Database Manager;
Design Engineer; Electrical/Electronics Engineer; Finance
Director; Financial Analyst; General Manager; Human
Resources Manager; Industrial Engineer; Industrial

Production Manager; Internet Services Manager; Manufacturing Engineer; Market Research Analyst; Marketing Manager; Marketing Specialist; Mechanical Engineer; MIS Manager; Multimedia Designer; Online Content Specialist; Operations Manager; Production Manager; Project Manager; Sales Engineer; Sales Representative; Software Engineer; Systems Analyst; Systems Manager; Technical Writer/Editor; Telecommunications Manager; Vice President. **Corporate headquarters location:** Cleveland OH. **Other U.S. locations:** Nationwide.

MILLENNIAL GROUP
925 Executive Park Drive, Suite D, Salt Lake City UT 84117. 801/265-8055. **Fax:** 801/265-8053. **Contact:** Manager. **Description:** An executive search firm. **Specializes in the areas of:** Information Technology; Telecommunications.

PRINCE, PERELSON & ASSOCIATES
19 East 200 South, Suite 1000, Salt Lake City UT 84111. 801/532-1000. **Contact:** Manager. **Description:** An executive search firm. **Specializes in the areas of:** Engineering; Manufacturing.

PROFESSIONAL RECRUITERS INC.
220 East 3900 South, Suite 9, Salt Lake City UT 84107. 801/268-9940. **Contact:** Manager. **Description:** Professional Recruiters Inc. is an executive search firm. **Specializes in the areas of:** Computer Programming; Finance; Health/Medical.

ROMAC INTERNATIONAL
505 East 200 South, Suite 300, Salt Lake City UT 84102. 801/328-0011. **Fax:** 801/994-0024. **Contact:** Manager. **Description:** An executive search firm. **Specializes in the areas of:** Accounting/Auditing; Computer Hardware/Software; Finance; Information Technology.

STM ASSOCIATES
230 South 500 East, Suite 500, Salt Lake City UT 84102. 801/531-6500. **Fax:** 801/531-6062. **Contact:** Recruiter. **Description:** An executive search firm.

SALES CONSULTANTS
428 East Winchester Street, Suite 210, Salt Lake City UT 84107. 801/263-2400. **Fax:** 801/263-2477. **Contact:** Manager. **Description:** An executive search firm. **Specializes in the areas of:** Computer Hardware/Software; Sales. **Corporate headquarters location:** Cleveland OH. **Other U.S. locations:** Nationwide.

SANFORD ROSE ASSOCIATES
8941 Upper Lando Lane, Park City UT 84098. 435/647-9755. **Fax:** 435/647-9069. **Contact:** Recruiter. **World Wide Web address:** http://www.sanfordrose.com. **Description:** An executive search firm. **Other U.S. locations:** Nationwide.

THE SHARKEY GROUP
8893 Willow Green Drive, Sandy UT 84093. 801/943-6002. **Contact:** Cindy Sharkey, Owner. **Description:** An executive search firm.

TOP JOBS
385 East 800 South Street, Orem UT 84097. 801/426-4600. **Fax:** 801/226-8393. **Contact:** Manager. **Description:** A generalist executive search firm.

TROUT & ASSOCIATES INC.
EXECUSEARCH
248 West Cottage Avenue, Salt Lake City UT 84070. 801/576-1547. **Toll-free phone:** 800/965-1527. **Fax:** 801/576-1541. **Contact:** Barton Jeffs, Manager. **Description:** Trout & Associates Inc. is a generalist executive search firm operating on a retainer basis. ExecuSearch (also at this location) is a generalist executive search firm operating on a contingency basis. Founded in 1973. Client company pays fee. **Corporate headquarters location:** This Location. **International locations:** Japan. **Average salary range of placements:** $50,000 - $100,000. **Number of placements per year:** 50 - 99.

UPGRADE ASSOCIATES RECRUITERS
P.O. Box 58279, Salt Lake City UT 84158. 801/583-1000. **Fax:** 801/583-9999. **Contact:** Manager. **Description:** An executive search firm. **Specializes in the areas of:** Information Systems.

PERMANENT EMPLOYMENT AGENCIES

CULVER STAFFING RESOURCES
2970 South Main Street, Salt Lake City UT 84115. 801/467-0300. **Fax:** 801/467-0385. **Contact:** Manager. **Description:** A permanent employment agency.

EXPRESS PERSONNEL SERVICES
56 East 7800 South, Midvale UT 84047. 801/255-1441. **Fax:** 801/255-1488. **Contact:** Recruiter. **Description:** A permanent employment agency that also provides some temporary placements.

THE NANNY CONNECTION
1231 South 425 West, Bountiful UT 84010. 801/295-6496. **Contact:** Director. **Description:** A permanent employment agency. **Specializes in the areas of:**

Nannies. **Positions commonly filled include:** Nanny. **Number of placements per year:** 100 - 199.

SNELLING PERSONNEL SERVICES
1030 Atherton Drive, Suite 202, Salt Lake City UT 84123. 801/268-8444. **Fax:** 801/268-8796. **Contact:** Recruiter. **Description:** A permanent employment agency that also provides temporary placements.

YOUR JOB CONNECTION
1399 South 700 East, Suite 4, Salt Lake City UT 84105. 801/486-0583. **Contact:** Manager. **Description:** A permanent employment agency. **Specializes in the areas of:** Clerical; Office Support.

TEMPORARY EMPLOYMENT AGENCIES

FRANKLIN-NEWBERY ENGINEERING
655 East 4500 South, Suite 102, Murray UT 84107. 801/261-3282. **Contact:** Manager. **Description:** A temporary agency. Client company pays fee. **Specializes in the areas of:** Engineering; Scientific; Technical. **Positions commonly filled include:** Administrative Assistant; Architect; Chemical Engineer; Chemist; Civil Engineer; Clinical Lab Technician; Computer Engineer; Construction Contractor; Cost Estimator; Design Engineer; Draftsperson; Electrical/Electronics Engineer; Environmental Engineer; Geologist/Geophysicist; Industrial Engineer; Manufacturing Engineer; Mechanical Engineer; Metallurgical Engineer;

MIS Specialist; Project Manager; Purchasing Agent/Manager; Quality Assurance Engineer; Secretary. **Corporate headquarters location:** Broomall PA. **Average salary range of placements:** $30,000 - $49,999. **Number of placements per year:** 50 - 99.

INTERMOUNTAIN STAFFING RESOURCES
P.O. Box 65157, Salt Lake City UT 84165. 801/467-6565. **Fax:** 801/467-5090. **Contact:** Mark Holland, President. **Description:** A temporary agency that also provides permanent placements. **Specializes in the areas of:** Accounting/Auditing; Engineering; Finance;

Personnel/Labor Relations; Secretarial; Technical. **Positions commonly filled include:** Accountant; Administrative Manager; Aerospace Engineer; Blue-Collar Worker Supervisor; Branch Manager; Budget Analyst; Claim Rep.; Clerical Supervisor; Computer Programmer; Credit Manager; Customer Service Rep.; Design Engineer; Draftsperson; Electrical Engineer; Electrician; General Manager; Human Resources Manager; Industrial Production Manager; Management Trainee; Mechanical Engineer; Operations/Production Manager; Purchasing Agent/Manager; Services Sales Rep.; Structural Engineer; Systems Analyst. **Benefits available to temporary workers:** 401(k); Cafeteria; Paid Holidays; Paid Vacation. **Corporate headquarters location:** This Location. **Other U.S. locations:** Phoenix AZ; Denver CO; Boise ID; Las Vegas NV. **Average salary range of placements:** $30,000 - $50,000. **Number of placements per year:** 1000+.

MANPOWER TECHNICAL SERVICES
859 West South Jordan Parkway, Suite 110, South Jordan UT 84095. 801/264-1198. **Fax:** 801/262-9598. **Contact:** Manager. **E-mail address:** techjobs@utah-inter.net. **Description:** A temporary agency. **Specializes in the areas of:** Computer Science/Software; Engineering; Manufacturing. **Positions commonly filled include:** Aerospace Engineer; Biomedical Engineer; Civil Engineer; Computer Programmer; Design Engineer; Designer; Draftsperson; Electrical/Electronics Engineer; Environmental Engineer; Industrial Engineer; Quality Control Supervisor; Software Engineer; Structural Engineer; Surveyor; Systems Analyst; Technical Writer/Editor; Telecommunications Manager; Transportation/Traffic Specialist. **Benefits available to temporary workers:** Medical Insurance; Paid Holidays; Paid Vacation. **Corporate headquarters location:** Milwaukee WI. **Other U.S. locations:** Nationwide. **Average salary range of placements:** $30,000 - $50,000. **Number of placements per year:** 200 - 499.

OLSTEN STAFFING SERVICES
5434 South 1900 West, Suite 6, Roy UT 84067. 801/825-0500. **Fax:** 801/825-0555. **Contact:** Branch Manager. **Description:** A temporary agency that also offers permanent placement. **Specializes in the areas of:** Accounting/Auditing; Engineering; Industrial; Manufacturing; Personnel/Labor Relations; Secretarial; Technical. **Positions commonly filled include:** Accountant/Auditor; Administrative Manager; Aerospace Engineer; Blue-Collar Worker Supervisor; Buyer; Clerical Supervisor; Counselor; Customer Service Representative; Draftsperson; Electrical/Electronics Engineer; General Manager; Human Resources Manager; Industrial Engineer; Industrial Production Manager; Management Trainee; Manufacturer's/Wholesaler's Sales Rep.; Mechanical Engineer; Purchasing Agent/Manager; Quality Control Supervisor; Restaurant/Food Service Manager; Securities Sales Representative; Services Sales Representative; Structural Engineer; Systems Analyst. **Benefits available to temporary workers:** Medical Insurance; Paid Vacation; Referral Bonus Plan. **Corporate headquarters location:** Melville NY. **Average salary range of placements:** Less than $20,000. **Number of placements per year:** 1000+.

PEAK STAFFING
284 East 4500 South, Murray UT 84107. 801/264-1212. **Fax:** 801/264-1277. **Contact:** Manager. **Description:** A temporary agency that also offers temp-to-perm placements. **Specializes in the areas of:** Manufacturing. **Positions commonly filled include:** Blue-Collar Worker Supervisor; Design Engineer; Draftsperson; Electrical/Electronics Engineer; Industrial Engineer; Industrial Production Manager; Manufacturer's/Wholesaler's Sales Rep.; Materials Engineer; Mechanical Engineer; MIS Specialist; Operations/Production Manager; Purchasing Agent/Manager; Quality Control Supervisor. **Average salary range of placements:** $20,000 - $29,999. **Number of placements per year:** 200 - 499.

SYSTEMS WEST
136 South Main Street, Suite A-300, Salt Lake City UT 84101. 801/364-7900. **Fax:** 801/364-9700. **Contact:** Jason Halverson, Recruiter. **Description:** A temporary agency. **Specializes in the areas of:** Computer Science/Software; Legal. **Positions commonly filled include:** Attorney; Computer Programmer; Systems Analyst. **Number of placements per year:** 100 - 199.

CONTRACT SERVICES FIRMS

CDI CORPORATION
P.O. Box 3686, Salt Lake City UT 84122. **Toll-free phone:** 800/536-8624. **Fax:** 801/521-8611. **Contact:** Steve Simonson, Recruiter. **E-mail address:** saltlakecity@cdicorp.com. **World Wide Web address:** http://www.cdicorp.com. **Description:** A contract services firm. **Positions commonly filled include:** Civil Engineer; Computer Programmer; Draftsperson; Materials Engineer; MIS Specialist; Software Engineer; Structural Engineer; Systems Analyst; Technical Writer. **Corporate headquarters location:** Philadelphia PA. **Average salary range of placements:** $30,000 - $50,000. **Number of placements per year:** 500 - 999.

HALL KINION
Eagle Gate Plaza, 60 East South Temple, Suite 2050, Salt Lake City UT 84111. **Toll-free phone:** 888/665-2225. **Fax:** 801/322-2205. **Contact:** Manager. **E-mail address:** utresme@hallkinion.com. **World Wide Web address:** http://www.hallkinion.com. **Description:** A contract services firm that also provides some permanent placements. **Specializes in the areas of:** High-Tech; Information Systems; Information Technology; Internet Development; Network Administration; Quality Assurance; Systems Administration; Systems Design.

LUND, FALKNER & BROWN
4505 Wasatch Boulevard, Suite 100, Salt Lake City UT 84124. 801/272-9800. **Toll-free phone:** 877/FALKNER. **Fax:** 801/277-9442. **Contact:** Manager. **World Wide Web address:** http://www.lfb.com. **Description:** A contract services firm for *Fortune* 1000 companies.

VOLT SERVICES GROUP
1100 East 6600 South, Suite 260, Salt Lake City UT 84121. 801/264-9970. **Fax:** 801/264-8632. **Contact:** Charisse Brunner, Recruiter. **E-mail address:** jobs@voltslc.com. **World Wide Web address:** http://www.volt.com. **Description:** A contract services firm. The agency focuses on placing high-level computer professionals. **Specializes in the areas of:** Engineering. **Positions commonly filled include:** Computer Operator; Computer Programmer; Database Manager; Draftsperson; Electrical Engineer; Mechanical Engineer; MIS Manager; Software Engineer; Systems Analyst; Systems Manager; Technical Writer; Telecommunications Manager; Webmaster. **Benefits available to temporary workers:** Dental Insurance; Medical Insurance; Paid Holidays; Vacation Pay. **Corporate headquarters location:** Orange CA. **Average salary range of placements:** $30,000 - $50,000. **Number of placements per year:** 200 - 499.

◆ V E R M O N T ◆

DUNHILL SEARCH OF VERMONT
P.O. Box 204, Warren VT 05674. 802/496-0115. **Toll-free phone:** 800/511-2934. **Fax:** 802/496-0116. **Contact:** Herb Hauser, President. **Description:** An executive search firm operating on a contingency basis. **Specializes in the areas of:** Accounting; Finance; MIS/EDP. **Positions commonly filled include:** Accountant; Auditor; Budget Analyst; Chief Financial Officer; Controller; Financial Analyst. **Other U.S. locations:** Nationwide. **Average salary range of placements:** $50,000 - $100,000. **Number of placements per year:** 50 - 99.

ECKLER PERSONNEL NETWORK (EPN)
P.O. Box 549, Woodstock VT 05091. 802/457-1605. **Toll-free phone:** 800/522-1605. **Contact:** Mr. G.K. Eckler, President. **Description:** An executive search firm operating on both retainer and contingency bases. **Specializes in the areas of:** Administration; Computer Science/Software; Information Technology. **Positions commonly filled include:** Computer Programmer; Internet Services Manager; MIS Specialist; Multimedia Designer; Software Engineer; Systems Analyst. **Average salary range of placements:** More than $50,000. **Number of placements per year:** 50 - 99.

MANAGEMENT RECRUITERS OF BURLINGTON
187 St. Paul Street, Suite 4, Burlington VT 05401. 802/865-0541. **Contact:** Alan Nyhan, Manager. **Description:** An executive search firm operating on both retainer and contingency bases. **Specializes in the areas of:** Banking; Computer Programming; Finance; Information Systems; Investment. **Corporate headquarters location:** Cleveland OH. **Other U.S. locations:** Nationwide.

MARKETSEARCH ASSOCIATES
P.O. Box 462, Williston VT 05495. 802/434-2460. **Contact:** Manager. **Description:** An executive search firm. **Specializes in the areas of:** Sales.

NATIONAL EXECUTIVE SEARCH
201 Allison Run, White River Junction VT 05001. 802/295-8796. **Fax:** 802/296-2086. **Contact:** Bill Chellong, President. **Description:** An executive search firm. **Specializes in the areas of:** Engineering; Environmental; Transportation.

O'CONNOR SEARCH ASSOCIATES, INC.
35 Maple Street, Bristol VT 05443. 802/453-6370. **Fax:** 802/453-6371. **Contact:** Manager. **Description:** An executive search firm. **Specializes in the areas of:** Computer Programming; Engineering; Quality Assurance.

CANDIS PERRAULT ASSOCIATES INC.
109 Covington Lane, Shelburne VT 05482. 802/985-1017. **Contact:** Manager. **Description:** Candis Perrault Associates is an executive search firm. **Specializes in the areas of:** Finance.

J. R. PETERMAN ASSOCIATES, INC.
1250 Waterbury Road, Stowe VT 05672. 802/253-6304. **Fax:** 802/253-6314. **Contact:** Manager. **Description:** An executive search firm. **Specializes in the areas of:** Insurance.

TECHNOLOGY GROUP PARTNERS
156 College Street, Burlington VT 05403. 802/865-9191. **Fax:** 802/660-9939. **Contact:** Manager. **Description:** An executive search firm. **Specializes in the areas of:** Wire and Cable.

THE TETON GROUP
70 South Winooski Avenue, Burlington VT 05401. 888/721-9700. **Contact:** Recruiter. **E-mail address:** info@thetetongroup.com. **World Wide Web address:** http://www.thetetongroup.com. **Description:** An executive search firm. **Specializes in the areas of:** Sales; Software Development.

JAY TRACEY ASSOCIATES
19A Central Street, Woodstock VT 05091. 802/457-4200. **Fax:** 802/457-4114. **Contact:** Jay Tracey, Owner. **Description:** An executive search firm. Client company pays fee. **Specializes in the areas of:** Engineering; Factory Automation; Industrial; Marketing; Sales. **Positions commonly filled include:** Account Manager; Computer Engineer; Electrical/Electronics Engineer; Mechanical Engineer; Sales Engineer; Sales Executive; Sales Manager; Sales Representative; Software Engineer. **Average salary range of placements:** $50,000 - $100,000.

VOLL ASSOCIATES
133 Heritage Lane, Shelburne VT 05482. 802/985-8605. **Contact:** Manager. **Description:** An executive search firm. **Specializes in the areas of:** Finance; Insurance.

EMPLOYMENT AND TRAINING RESOURCE CENTER
25 Main Street, Springfield VT 05156. 802/885-2167. **Contact:** Manager. **Description:** A permanent employment agency. **Positions commonly filled include:** Accountant/Auditor; Administrative Assistant; Bank Officer/Manager; Bookkeeper; Civil Engineer; Clerk; Computer Operator; Computer Programmer; Construction Trade Worker; Data Entry Clerk; Draftsperson; Driver; Electrical/Electronics Engineer; Factory Worker; Hotel Manager; Human Resources Manager; Industrial Designer; Industrial Engineer; Insurance Agent/Broker; Legal Secretary; Light Industrial Worker; Mechanical Engineer; Medical Secretary; Nurse; Purchasing Agent/Manager; Quality Control Supervisor; Receptionist; Sales Representative; Secretary; Typist/Word Processor. **Number of placements per year:** 500 - 999.

TECHNICAL CONNECTION INC.
P.O. Box 1402, Burlington VT 05402. 802/658-8324. **Contact:** Christopher Johnson, Director. **Description:** A permanent employment agency. Founded in 1986. **Specializes in the areas of:** Computer Science/Software; Engineering; Scientific; Technical. **Positions commonly filled include:** Architect; Computer Operator; Computer Programmer; Design Engineer; Draftsperson; Electrical/Electronics Engineer; Environmental Engineer; Food Scientist/Technologist; Geologist/Geophysicist; Human Resources Manager; Manufacturing Engineer; Mechanical Engineer; Metallurgical Engineer; MIS Manager; Pharmacist; Sales Engineer; Systems Analyst. **Corporate headquarters location:** This Location. **Other U.S. locations:** Albany NY. **Average salary range of placements:** $30,000 - $50,000. **Number of placements per year:** 50 - 99.

TEMPORARY EMPLOYMENT AGENCIES

ADECCO
9 Church Street, P.O. Box 536, Arlington VT 05250. 802/375-9956. **Contact:** Branch Manager. **Description:** A temporary agency that also provides some temp-to-perm and permanent placements. **Specializes in the areas of:** Manufacturing; Office Support.

ADECCO
100 Dorset Street, Suite 14, South Burlington VT 05403. 802/658-5007. **Contact:** Manager. **Description:** A temporary agency. **Specializes in the areas of:** Administration; Clerical; Personnel/Labor Relations.

HARMON PERSONNEL SERVICES, INC.
50 Elliott Street, Brattleboro VT 05301. 802/254-8639. **Contact:** Manager. **Description:** A temporary agency. **Specializes in the areas of:** Administration; Bookkeeping; Clerical; Data Entry; Light Industrial.

THE PERSONNEL CONNECTION
272 South Main Street, Rutland VT 05701. 802/773-3737. **Fax:** 802/773-3424. **Contact:** Manager. **Description:** A temporary agency that also provides temp-to-perm placements. **Specializes in the areas of:** Administration; General Labor; Office Support.

PERSONNEL DEPARTMENT INC.
1234 Williston Road, South Burlington VT 05403. 802/865-4243. **Contact:** Office Manager. **Description:** A temporary agency. **Specializes in the areas of:** Accounting/Auditing; Computer Science/Software; Engineering; Finance; Industrial; Manufacturing; Personnel/Labor Relations; Secretarial; Technical. **Positions commonly filled include:** Accountant/Auditor; Administrative Manager; Aerospace Engineer; Architect; Blue-Collar Worker Supervisor; Chemical Engineer; Civil Engineer; Claim Representative; Clerical Supervisor; Computer Programmer; Construction Contractor; Cost Estimator; Credit Manager; Customer Service Representative; Design Engineer; Designer; Draftsperson; Electrical/Electronics Engineer; Electrician; Environmental Engineer; Financial Analyst; Human Resources Specialist; Industrial Engineer; Industrial Production Manager; Insurance Agent/Broker; Internet Services Manager; Mechanical Engineer; MIS Specialist; Multimedia Designer; Nuclear Engineer; Petroleum Engineer; Quality Control Supervisor; Science Technologist; Software Engineer; Structural Engineer; Surveyor; Systems Analyst; Technical Writer/Editor; Telecommunications Manager; Transportation/Traffic Specialist; Typist/Word Processor. **Benefits available to temporary workers:** Medical Insurance; Paid Holidays; Paid Vacation. **Corporate headquarters location:** This Location. **Other area locations:** St. Albans VT. **Number of placements per year:** 1000+.

TRIAD TEMPORARY SERVICES, INC.
P.O. Box 789, Williston VT 05495. 802/864-8255. **Physical address:** 19 Commerce Street, Williston VT. **Toll-free phone:** 800/894-8455. **Fax:** 802/864-0046. **Contact:** Stan Grandfield, President. **Description:** A temporary agency. Founded in 1986. **Specializes in the areas of:** Banking; Computer Science/Software; Food; Industrial; Retail; Sales; Secretarial. **Positions commonly filled include:** Accountant/Auditor; Administrative Manager; Architect; Attorney; Civil Engineer; Claim Representative; Clerical Supervisor; Computer Programmer; Customer Service Representative; Designer; Electrical/Electronics Engineer; Hotel Manager; Human Resources Specialist; Human Service Worker; Industrial Engineer; Management Trainee; Mechanical Engineer; MIS Specialist; Operations/Production Manager; Purchasing Agent/Manager; Restaurant/Food Service Manager; Services Sales Representative; Software Engineer; Systems Analyst; Technical Writer/Editor; Transportation/Traffic Specialist; Typist/Word Processor. **Benefits available to temporary workers:** Paid Holidays; Paid Vacation. **Average salary range of placements:** Less than $20,000. **Number of placements per year:** 1000+.

WESTAFF
187 St. Paul Street, Burlington VT 05401. 802/862-4282. **Fax:** 802/862-4555. **Contact:** Branch Manager. **Description:** A temporary agency that also provides some permanent placements. **Specializes in the areas of:** Clerical; Light Industrial; Office Support; Secretarial; Technical.

EXECUTIVE SEARCH FIRMS

A LA CARTE INTERNATIONAL
3330 Pacific Avenue, Suite 500, Virginia Beach VA 23451-2997. 757/425-6111. **Toll-free phone:** 800/446-3037. **Fax:** 757/425-8507. **Contact:** Michael J. Romaniw, President. **E-mail address:** alacarte@ wedofood.com. **World Wide Web address:** http://www.wedofood.com. **Description:** An executive search firm operating on a retainer basis. The firm specializes in sales, marketing, and general management placements in the food manufacturing, retail, food service, and ingredient industries. Client company pays fee. **Specializes in the areas of:** Food; General Management; Marketing; Retail; Sales. **Positions commonly filled include:** Marketing Manager; Marketing Specialist; Operations Manager; Production Manager; Project Manager; Sales Manager; Vice President of Marketing and Sales. **Corporate headquarters location:** This Location. **Other U.S. locations:** CA. **Average salary range of placements:** $50,000 - $100,000. **Number of placements per year:** 1 - 49.

ABBTECH STAFFING SERVICES
101 East Holly Avenue, Sterling VA 20164. 703/450-5252. **Contact:** Manager. **Description:** An executive search firm. **NOTE:** Jobseekers should send resumes to Abbtech Staffing Services, Dulles International Airport, P.O. Box 20098, Washington DC 20041. **Specializes in the areas of:** Technical.

ABILITY RESOURCES, INC.
716 Church Street, Alexandria VA 22314. 703/548-6400. **Contact:** Noel L. Ruppert, President. **Description:** An executive search firm. **Specializes in the areas of:** Accounting/Auditing; Defense Industry; Economics; Engineering; Finance; General Management; Nonprofit; Technical. **Positions commonly filled include:** Accountant/Auditor; Economist; Engineer; Financial Analyst; General Manager; Management Analyst/ Consultant; Mathematician; Operations/Production Manager; Statistician; Systems Analyst. **Number of placements per year:** 1 - 49.

ACCENT PERSONNEL INC.
4907 Fitzhugh Avenue, Suite 202, Richmond VA 23230. 804/359-9416. **Contact:** Manager. **Description:** An executive search firm.

ACCOUNTANTS EXECUTIVE SEARCH
ACCOUNTANTS ON CALL
8000 Towers Crescent Drive, Suite 825, Vienna VA 22182. 703/448-7500. **Contact:** Recruiter. **Description:** An executive search firm. Accountants On Call (also at this location) is a temporary agency. **Specializes in the areas of:** Accounting/Auditing; Finance. **Positions commonly filled include:** Accountant/Auditor; Budget Analyst; Credit Manager; Financial Analyst.

ACCOUNTANTS EXECUTIVE SEARCH
ACCOUNTANTS ON CALL
6800 Paragon Place, Suite 200, Richmond VA 23230. 804/225-0200. **Fax:** 804/225-0217. **Contact:** Manager. **Description:** An executive search firm. Accountants On Call (also at this location) is a temporary agency that also provides some temp-to-perm placements. **Specializes in the areas of:** Accounting/Auditing; Banking; Finance.

ACCOUNTING SOLUTIONS
4164 Virginia Beach Boulevard, Suite 205, Virginia Beach VA 23452. 757/431-9675. **Contact:** Manager. **Description:** An executive search firm. **Specializes in the areas of:** Accounting.

ACSYS INC.
7100 Forest Avenue, Suite 101, Richmond VA 23226. 804/282-6300. **Fax:** 804/282-6792. **Recorded jobline:** 804/282-1177. **Contact:** MIS Director. **World Wide Web address:** http://www.acsysinc.com. **Description:** An executive search firm. Founded in 1978. **Specializes in the areas of:** Accounting/Auditing; Administration; Computer Science/Software; Finance; Information Systems; Secretarial. **Corporate headquarters location:** This Location.

ACSYS INC.
8300 Greensboro Drive, Suite 720, McLean VA 22102. 703/827-5990. **Contact:** Manager. **World Wide Web address:** http://www.acsysinc.com. **Description:** An executive search firm. **Specializes in the areas of:** Accounting/Auditing; Finance; Information Technology. **Corporate headquarters location:** Richmond VA.

ACTION RECRUITERS INC.
Timbrook Square Shopping Center, 8800 Timberlake Road, Lynchburg VA 24502. 804/237-0908. **Contact:** Manager. **Description:** An executive search firm.

ADAMS SOURCES
P.O. Box 70634, Richmond VA 23255. 804/282-5674. **Toll-free phone:** 800/927-6716. **Fax:** 804/282-5675. **Contact:** Zack Adams, Recruiter. **Description:** An executive search firm. **Specializes in the areas of:** Accounting/Auditing; Administration; Advertising; Banking; Engineering; Personnel/Labor Relations. **Positions commonly filled include:** Accountant/Auditor; Advertising Executive; Bank Officer/Manager; Controller; Design Engineer; Electrician; Human Resources Manager; Management Analyst/Consultant; Manufacturing Engineer; MIS Specialist; Sales Executive; Sales Manager; Sales Rep.; Systems Analyst. **Average salary range of placements:** $30,000 - $50,000. **Number of placements per year:** 1 - 49.

ADVANCED RECRUITING SERVICE
P.O. Box 742, Quinton VA 23141. 804/328-9700. **Fax:** 804/737-2708. **Contact:** Manager. **Description:** An executive search firm. **Specializes in the areas of:** Health/Medical.

THE ALEXIS GROUP, INC.
P.O. Box 241, Midlothian VA 23113. 804/744-7992. **Fax:** 804/744-1795. **Contact:** Manager. **E-mail address:** webmaster@thealexisgroup.com. **World Wide Web address:** http://www.thealexisgroup.com. **Description:** An executive search firm operating on a retainer basis. Founded in 1996. Client company pays fee. **Specializes in the areas of:** Automotive; Chemicals; Construction; Electronics; Finance; Health/Medical; Industrial; Manufacturing; Marketing; Retail; Transportation.

ALLIANCE GROUP
P.O. Box 935, Lexington VA 24450. 540/261-2260. **Contact:** Reed Ferguson, Principal. **Description:** An executive search firm. **Specializes in the areas of:** Engineering. **Positions commonly filled include:** Chemical Engineer; Civil Engineer; Environmental Engineer; Geologist/Geophysicist; Materials Engineer; Mechanical Engineer; Structural Engineer. **Average salary range of placements:** More than $50,000. **Number of placements per year:** 1 - 49.

APEX SYSTEMS, INC.
7617 Little River Turnpike, Suite 110, Annandale VA 22003. 703/256-2000. **Fax:** 703/256-2182. **Contact:** Manager. **Description:** An executive search firm. **Specializes in the areas of:** Technical.

BARNES & ASSOCIATES RETAIL SEARCH
P.O. Box 36556, Richmond VA 23235. 804/379-8264. **Fax:** 804/379-8379. **Contact:** William Barnes, President. **Description:** An executive search firm. **Specializes in the areas of:** Fashion; Gen. Management; Personnel; Retail. **Positions commonly filled include:** Branch Manager; Buyer; General Manager; Human Resources

Specialist; Management Trainee; MIS Specialist; Operations/Production Manager; Purchasing Agent/Manager; Transportation/Traffic Specialist. **Average salary range of placements:** More than $50,000. **Number of placements per year:** 1 - 49.

THE BEST AGENCY
2905 Lamkin Way, Charlottesville VA 22911. 804/978-7748. **Fax:** 804/978-7387. **Contact:** James N. Best, President. **Description:** An executive search firm that places senior management professionals in the hotel industry. **Positions commonly filled include:** Accountant/Auditor; Hotel Manager. **Average salary range of placements:** More than $50,000. **Number of placements per year:** 1 - 49.

BIO EXEC & ASSOCIATES
6700 Weaver Avenue, McLean VA 22101. 703/827-9703. **Fax:** 703/827-9704. **Contact:** Manager. **Description:** An executive search firm. **Specializes in the areas of:** Biotechnology; Pharmaceuticals.

BRAULT & ASSOCIATES LTD.
18417 Island Lanier Square, Leesburg VA 20176. 703/771-0270. **Fax:** 703/771-0200. **Contact:** Manager. **Description:** An executive search firm. **Specializes in the areas of:** High-Tech.

NORMAN BROADBENT INTERNATIONAL
1801 Robert Fulton Drive, Suite 400, Reston VA 20191. 703/758-3528. **Fax:** 703/758-3594. **Contact:** Manager. **World Wide Web address:** http://www.nbisearch.com. **Description:** An executive search firm. **Specializes in the areas of:** Entertainment; Finance; New Media; Technical; Telecommunications. **Other U.S. locations:** CA; GA; IL; NY.

CAR-VIR INC.
2226 Commerce Parkway, Virginia Beach VA 23454. 757/631-1116. **Fax:** 757/631-1780. **Contact:** Recruiter. **Description:** An executive search firm. **Specializes in the areas of:** Pharmaceuticals.

CAREER MARKET CONSULTANTS
1092 Lastin Road, Suite 202, Virginia Beach VA 23451. 757/428-8888. **Contact:** Manager. **Description:** An executive search firm. **Specializes in the areas of:** Hotel/Restaurant; Technical.

CAREER REGISTRY
1600 East Little Creek Road, Suite 322, Norfolk VA 23518. 757/480-2757. **Contact:** Manager. **Description:** An executive search firm operating on both contingency and retainer bases. **Specializes in the areas of:** Engineering; Manufacturing. **Positions commonly filled include:** Accountant/Auditor; Biomedical Engineer; Chemical Engineer; Computer Programmer; Electrical/ Electronics Engineer; Electrician; Environmental Engineer; Industrial Engineer; Mechanical Engineer; Software Engineer; Systems Analyst.

CERTIFIED PLACEMENT ASSOCIATES INC.
2807 North Purham Road, Suite 105, Richmond VA 23294. 804/270-1770. **Contact:** Manager. **Description:** An executive search firm. **Specializes in the areas of:** Technical.

CHELSEA RESOURCE GROUP, INC.
46842 Graham Cove Square, Sterling VA 20165. 703/404-3489. **Fax:** 703/406-1253. **Contact:** Manager. **E-mail address:** chelsearesourcegroup@erols.com. **World Wide Web address:** http://www. chelsearesourcegroup.com. **Description:** An executive search firm. **Specializes in the areas of:** Data Processing; Software Development; Systems Programming.

CHRISTIAN & TIMBERS, INC.
8000 Towers Crescent Drive, Suite 1350, Vienna VA 22182. 703/448-1700. **Fax:** 703/448-1740. **Contact:** Recruiter. **Description:** An executive search firm. **Specializes in the areas of:** Aerospace; Biotechnology;

Consumer Products; Defense Industry; Finance; Information Technology; Medical Devices; Professional.

CLANCY ASSOCIATES
2082 Winchester Road, Delaplane VA 20144. 540/592-3386. **Contact:** Manager. **Description:** An executive search firm operating on a retainer basis.

S.R. CLARKE, INC.
3554 Chain Bridge Road, Suite 201, Fairfax VA 22030. 703/934-4200. **Fax:** 703/934-4201. **Contact:** Manager. **Description:** An executive search firm.

CONTEC SEARCH, INC.
5803 Stone Ridge Drive, Centerville VA 20120. 703/968-0477. **Fax:** 703/968-0064. **Contact:** Brian Canatsey, President. **World Wide Web address:** http://www.contecsearch.com. **Description:** An executive search firm operating on a contingency basis. **Specializes in the areas of:** Computer Science/Software; Finance; Health/Medical; Manufacturing. **Positions commonly filled include:** Computer Programmer; Database Manager; Financial Analyst; Systems Analyst; Systems Manager. **Average salary range of placements:** More than $50,000. **Number of placements per year:** 50 - 99.

CORPORATE CONNECTION LTD.
7202 Glen Forest Drive, Richmond VA 23226. 804/288-8844. **Contact:** Manager. **Description:** An executive search firm. **Specializes in the areas of:** Accounting/ Auditing; Administration; Banking; Computer Science/ Software; Engineering; Finance; General Management; Industrial; Insurance; Legal; Manufacturing; Nonprofit; Personnel/Labor Relations; Publishing; Retail; Sales; Secretarial; Technical. **Positions commonly filled include:** Accountant; Adjuster; Administrative Manager; Advertising Clerk; Aerospace Engineer; Agricultural Engineer; Aircraft Mechanic/Engine Specialist; Bank Officer/Manager; Biological Scientist; Biomedical Engineer; Blue-Collar Worker Supervisor; Branch Manager; Brokerage Clerk; Budget Analyst; Buyer; Chemical Engineer; Chemist; Civil Engineer; Claim Rep.; Clerical Supervisor; Clinical Lab Technician; Computer Programmer; Construction Contractor; Cost Estimator; Credit Manager; Customer Service Rep.; Design Engineer; Designer; Draftsperson; Electrical/ Electronics Engineer; Environmental Engineer; Financial Analyst; General Manager; Human Resources Manager; Industrial Engineer; Industrial Production Manager; Insurance Agent/Broker; Librarian; Library Tech.; Management Analyst/Consultant; Management Trainee; Manufacturer's/Wholesaler's Sales Rep.; Market Research Analyst; Mechanical Engineer; Medical Records Tech.; Metallurgical Engineer; Mining Engineer; Property and Real Estate Manager; Public Relations Specialist; Purchasing Agent/Manager; Quality Control Supervisor; Restaurant/Food Service Manager; Securities Sales Rep.; Services Sales Rep.; Software Engineer; Structural Engineer; Systems Analyst; Transportation/Traffic Specialist; Travel Agent; Typist/Word Processor; Underwriter; Urban/Regional Planner. **Average salary range of placements:** $30,000 - $50,000. **Number of placements per year:** 200 - 499.

CURRAN ASSOCIATES
2241-H Tacketts Mill Drive, Lakeridge VA 22192. 703/492-8000. **Toll-free phone:** 800/497-0497. **Fax:** 703/492-8008. **Contact:** David Curran, President. **Description:** An executive search firm that also provides career/outplacement counseling services. **Specializes in the areas of:** Food. **Positions commonly filled include:** Assistant Manager; General Manager; Management Trainee; Operations Manager; Production Manager; Restaurant/Food Service Manager; Sales Exe.; Sales Rep. **Average salary range of placements:** $30,000 - $50,000. **Number of placements per year:** 50 - 99.

DAHL MORROW INTERNATIONAL
20 South King Street, Suite 200, Leesburg VA 20175. 703/779-5600. **Fax:** 703/779-5678. **Contact:** Barbara Steinem, Principal. **E-mail address:** dmi@dahl-

morrowintl.com. **World Wide Web address:** http://www.dahl-morrowintl.com. **Description:** An executive search firm operating on a retainer basis. **Specializes in the areas of:** Computer Operations; Data Communications; Information Systems; Information Technology; Telecommunications.

BETH DAISEY ASSOCIATES
1800 Diagonal Road, Suite 600, Alexandria VA 22314. 703/751-2328. **Contact:** Manager. **Description:** An executive search firm. **Specializes in the areas of:** Travel.

DINTE RESOURCES INC.
8300 Greensboro Drive, Suite 880, McLean VA 22102. 703/448-3300. **Fax:** 703/448-0215. **Contact:** Recruiter. **Description:** A generalist executive search firm.

DONMAC ASSOCIATES
P.O. Box 2541, Reston VA 20195. 703/620-2866. **Fax:** 703/620-2867. **Contact:** Connie Andersen, President. **Description:** An executive search firm. **Specializes in the areas of:** Computer Science/Software; Data Processing; Engineering. **Positions commonly filled include:** Computer Programmer; Electrical/Electronics Engineer; Software Engineer; Systems Analyst. **Number of placements per year:** 50 - 99.

DUNHILL PROFESSIONAL SEARCH
8100 Three Chopt Road, Suite 133, Richmond VA 23229. 804/282-2216. **Fax:** 804/282-5682. **Contact:** P. Frank Lassiter, President. **Description:** An executive search firm operating on both retainer and contingency bases. **Specializes in the areas of:** Banking; Engineering. **Positions commonly filled include:** Bank Officer/Manager; Chemical Engineer; Design Engineer; Industrial Engineer; Mechanical Engineer; Securities Sales Representative; Trust Officer. **Average salary range of placements:** $50,000 - $130,000. **Number of placements per year:** 1 - 49.

DURILL & ASSOCIATES
7200 Glen Forest Drive, Suite 306, Richmond VA 23226. 804/282-0595. **Contact:** Manager. **Description:** An executive search firm. **Specializes in the areas of:** Finance.

EFFECTIVE STAFFING INC.
2305 Colts Brook Drive, Reston VA 20191. 703/742-9300. **Fax:** 703/742-9747. **Contact:** Mike Millard, President. **Description:** An executive search firm operating on a contingency basis. The firm also provides some temporary placements and contract services. **Specializes in the areas of:** Accounting/Auditing; Administration; Banking; Computer Science/Software; Finance; General Management; Legal; Personnel/Labor Relations; Publishing; Sales; Secretarial; Technical. **Positions commonly filled include:** Accountant/Auditor; Administrative Manager; Bank Officer/Manager; Branch Manager; Broadcast Technician; Budget Analyst; Computer Programmer; Counselor; Customer Service Rep.; Design Engineer; Economist; Education Administrator; Financial Analyst; General Manager; Health Services Manager; Human Resources Specialist; Human Service Worker; Management Analyst/ Consultant; Market Research Analyst; Medical Records Technician; MIS Specialist; Multimedia Designer; Occupational Therapist; Operations/Production Manager; Paralegal; Physical Therapist; Quality Control Supervisor; Registered Nurse; Services Sales Rep.; Technical Writer/Editor; Telecommunications Manager. **Average salary range of placements:** More than $50,000. **Number of placements per year:** 1 - 49.

EXECUTIVE CAREER SEARCH
P.O. Box 480, Lightfoot VA 23090-0480. 757/564-3013. **Fax:** 757/564-1736. **Contact:** Manager. **E-mail address:** headhunter@widomaker.com. **Description:** An executive search firm. **Specializes in the areas of:** Construction.

EXECUTIVE RECRUITERS OF FAIRFAX
1907 Clarks Glen Place, Vienna VA 22182. 703/556-9580. **Contact:** Joe Segal, President. **Description:** An executive search firm. **Specializes in the areas of:** Food; Hotel/Restaurant. **Positions commonly filled include:** Hotel Manager; Restaurant/Food Service Manager. **Number of placements per year:** 50 - 99.

EXECUTIVE SALES SEARCH
8232 Ammonett Drive, Richmond VA 23235. 804/560-7327. **Fax:** 804/560-7564. **Contact:** David W. Bell, President. **E-mail address:** Info@headhunter-sales.com. **World Wide Web address:** http://www.headhunter-sales.com. **Description:** An executive search firm operating on a contingency basis. The firm also provides contract services. **Specializes in the areas of:** Sales. **Positions commonly filled include:** Account Manager; Account Representative; Advertising Executive; Branch Manager; General Manager; Management Analyst/Consultant; Manufacturer's/Wholesaler's Sales Rep.; Marketing Manager; Marketing Specialist; Sales Engineer; Sales Executive; Sales Manager; Sales Representative. **Average salary range of placements:** More than $50,000. **Number of placements per year:** 100 - 199.

EXECUTIVE TRANSITIONS INTERNATIONAL
1655 North Fort Myers Drive, Suite 1150, Arlington VA 22209. 703/243-3838. **Contact:** Manager. **Description:** An executive search firm.

FGI
1595 Spring Hill Road, Suite 350, Vienna VA 22182. 703/847-0010. **Contact:** Manager. **Description:** An executive search firm. **Specializes in the areas of:** Aerospace; Defense Industry; High-Tech; Telecommunications.

FINANCIAL CONNECTIONS
5008 Andrea Avenue, Annandale VA 22003. 703/425-4240. **Fax:** 703/323-6919. **Contact:** Manager. **Description:** An executive search firm. **Specializes in the areas of:** Finance.

FLORES FINANCIAL SERVICE
500 North Washington Street, Alexandria VA 22314. 703/748-1200. **Fax:** 703/739-9805. **Contact:** Manager. **Description:** An executive search firm. **Specializes in the areas of:** Finance.

F-O-R-T-U-N-E PERSONNEL CONSULTANTS
112 West Main Street, Suite 1, Berryville VA 22611. 540/955-0500. **Fax:** 540/955-0518. **Contact:** Manager. **Description:** An executive search firm. **Specializes in the areas of:** Banking; Engineering; Finance; Logistics; Materials; Purchasing. **Corporate headquarters location:** New York NY. **Other U.S. locations:** Nationwide.

WAYNE GARBER & ASSOCIATES, INC.
144 Maple Avenue East, Vienna VA 22180. 703/242-6507. **Fax:** 703/242-6409. **Contact:** Manager. **E-mail address:** ExecSearch@wgainc.com. **World Wide Web address:** http://www.wgainc.com. **Description:** An executive search firm operating on a retainer basis. Founded in 1995. **Specializes in the areas of:** Aerospace; Consulting; Defense Industry; Engineering; Finance; Government; Health/Medical; Information Systems; Manufacturing; Telecommunications.

GLASSMAN ASSOCIATES INC.
6603 Anthony Crest Square, McLean VA 22101. 703/442-8866. **Contact:** Manager. **Description:** An executive search firm.

GRAHAM ASSOCIATES
P.O. Box 7345, Roanoke VA 24019. 540/362-8851. **Contact:** Bill Graham, Manager. **Description:** An executive search firm. **Specializes in the areas of:** Engineering.

HERB GRETZ ASSOCIATES
1206 Laskin Road, Suite 201, Virginia Beach VA 23451. 757/422-8952. **Fax:** 757/422-1189. **Contact:** Manager. **Description:** An executive search firm. **Specializes in the areas of:** Medical Sales and Marketing.

B.H. GRINER & ASSOCIATES
450 Maple Avenue East, Suite 303, Vienna VA 22180. 703/242-9804. **Contact:** Manager. **Description:** A generalist executive search firm.

THE GUILD CORPORATION
8260 Greensboro Drive, Suite 200, McLean VA 22102. 703/761-4023. **Fax:** 703/761-4024. **Contact:** William J. Joyce, Principal. **E-mail address:** staffing@guildcorp.com. **World Wide Web address:** http://www.guildhome.com. **Description:** An executive search firm operating on both retainer and contingency bases. **Specializes in the areas of:** Administration; Computer Science/Software; Engineering. **Positions commonly filled include:** Computer Programmer; Customer Service Representative; Design Engineer; Electrical/Electronics Engineer; Internet Services Manager; Management Analyst/Consultant; MIS Specialist; Software Engineer; Telecommunications Manager. **Average salary range of placements:** More than $50,000. **Number of placements per year:** 200 - 499.

HALBRECHT & COMPANY, INC.
10195 Main Street, Suite L, Fairfax VA 22031. 703/359-2880. **Contact:** Thomas J. Maltby, Director. **Description:** An executive search firm operating on both retainer and contingency bases. **Specializes in the areas of:** Administration; Computer Science/Software; Technical. **Positions commonly filled include:** Actuary; Computer Programmer; EDP Specialist; Electrical/Electronics Engineer; Internet Services Manager; Management Analyst/Consultant; Mathematician; Software Engineer; Statistician; Systems Analyst. **Other U.S. locations:** Greenwich CT. **Number of placements per year:** 50 - 99.

ROBERT HALF INTERNATIONAL ACCOUNTEMPS
1100 Wilson Boulevard, Suite 900, Arlington VA 22209. 703/243-3600. **Contact:** Manager. **World Wide Web address:** http://www.roberthalf.com. **Description:** An executive search firm. Accountemps (also at this location) provides temporary placements. OfficeTeam (also at this location, 703/528-1010) provides both temporary and permanent placements. **Specializes in the areas of:** Accounting/Auditing. **Positions commonly filled include:** Accountant/Auditor; Bookkeeper; Data Entry Clerk; EDP Specialist; Financial Analyst. **Corporate headquarters location:** Menlo Park CA. **Other U.S. locations:** Nationwide. **Number of placements per year:** 200 - 499.

ROBERT HALF INTERNATIONAL ACCOUNTEMPS
4101 Cox Road, Suite 300, Glen Allen VA 23060. 804/965-9600. **Contact:** Manager. **World Wide Web address:** http://www.roberthalf.com. **Description:** An executive search firm. Accountemps (also at this location) provides temporary placements. **Specializes in the areas of:** Accounting/Auditing. **Corporate headquarters location:** Menlo Park CA. **Other U.S. locations:** Nationwide.

HAMILTON GROUP, INC.
9403 Lagovista Court, Great Falls VA 22066. 703/759-9201. **Fax:** 703/759-9203. **Contact:** James Lawrence, Partner. **E-mail address:** jim@hamiltongroup.com. **World Wide Web address:** http://www.hamiltongroup.com. **Description:** An executive search firm operating on a retainer basis. **Specializes in the areas of:** High-Tech; Manufacturing; Telecommunications.

HASLOWE PERSONNEL
5622 Columbia Pike, Baileys Crossroads VA 22041. 703/820-0020. **Contact:** Manager. **Description:** An executive search firm. **Specializes in the areas of:** Finance; Retail; Sales.

HEIDRICK & STRUGGLES
8000 Towers Crescent Drive, Suite 555, Vienna VA 22182. 703/761-4830. **Fax:** 703/761-4831. **Contact:** Manager. **Description:** An executive search firm. **Specializes in the areas of:** Technical.

INFORMATION SPECIALISTS COMPANY, INC.
P.O. Box 55313, Virginia Beach VA 23471-5313. 757/460-7790. **Fax:** 757/460-7886. **Contact:** Hugo E. Schluter, CPC/Senior Vice President. **Description:** An executive search firm operating on a contingency basis. Client company pays fee. **Specializes in the areas of:** Computer Science/Software; Engineering; Scientific; Technical. **Positions commonly filled include:** Biomedical Engineer; Chemical Engineer; Chemist; Civil Engineer; Computer Engineer; Computer Technician; Design Engineer; Electrical/Electronics Engineer; Environmental Engineer; Geologist/Geophysicist; Manufacturing Engineer; Mechanical Engineer; Metallurgical Engineer; Systems Analyst. **Average salary range of placements:** $50,000 - $100,000. **Number of placements per year:** 1 - 49.

INFOTECH SEARCH GROUP LIMITED
1517 Hearthglow Lane, Richmond VA 23233. 804/741-4506. **Fax:** 804/741-2108. **Contact:** Manager. **Description:** An executive search firm. **Specializes in the areas of:** Information Technology.

INTERIM FINANCIAL SOLUTIONS STRATFORDGROUP
1750 Tysons Boulevard, Suite 260, McLean VA 22102. 703/790-1100. **Fax:** 703/790-1123. **Contact:** Ron Sall, Director. **World Wide Web address:** http://www.interim.com. **Description:** An executive search firm that also provides some temporary placements and contract services. StratfordGroup (also at this location; 703/442-5280; http://www.stratfordgroup.com) is an executive search firm. Founded in 1985. **Specializes in the areas of:** Accounting; Computer Science/Software; Finance; Personnel/Labor Relations; Sales; Technical. **Positions commonly filled include:** Accountant/Auditor; Budget Analyst; Computer Programmer; Customer Service Rep.; Financial Analyst; General Manager; Human Resources Specialist; Management Analyst/Consultant; MIS Specialist; Services Sales Rep.; Software Engineer; Systems Analyst; Technical Writer/Editor; Telecommunications Manager; Typist/Word Processor. **Average salary range of placements:** More than $50,000. **Number of placements per year:** 500 - 999.

VERNE JOHNSON & ASSOCIATES
11250 Roger Bacon Drive, Suite 205, Reston VA 20190. 703/834-6270. **Fax:** 703/834-6322. **Contact:** Verne Johnson, Owner. **E-mail address:** vjarecruit@aol.com. **Description:** An executive search firm. **Specializes in the areas of:** Packaging; Plastics.

A.T. KEARNEY EXECUTIVE SEARCH
333 John Carlyle Street, Alexandria VA 22314. 703/739-4624. **Contact:** Manager. **Description:** An executive search firm. **Corporate headquarters location:** Chicago IL. **International locations:** Worldwide.

KINCANNON & REED
2106-C Gallows Road, Vienna VA 22182. 703/761-4046. **Fax:** 703/790-1533. **Contact:** Manager. **E-mail address:** office@krsearch.com. **World Wide Web address:** http://www.krsearch.com. **Description:** An executive search firm operating on a retainer basis. **Specializes in the areas of:** Agri-Business; Biotechnology; Food.

KOGEN PERSONNEL
125 Danville Avenue, Colonial Heights VA 23834. 804/526-0870. **Fax:** 804/526-0869. **Contact:** Manager. **Description:** An executive search firm that also provides some temporary placements. **Specializes in the areas of:** Computer Science/Software; Engineering; Food; General

Management; Retail; Sales; Technical. **Positions commonly filled include:** Accountant/Auditor; Administrative Manager; Attorney; Bank Officer/ Manager; Biological Scientist; Blue-Collar Worker Supervisor; Branch Manager; Buyer; Chemist; Claim Rep.; Clerical Supervisor; Computer Programmer; Construction and Building Inspector; Counselor; Credit Manager; Customer Service Rep.; Draftsperson; Economist; Education Administrator; Electrical/ Electronics Engineer; Electrician; Financial Analyst; Food Scientist/Technologist; General Manager; Health Services Manager; Hotel Manager; Human Resources Manager; Industrial Engineer; Industrial Production Manager; Insurance Agent/Broker; Landscape Architect; Librarian; Library Tech.; Licensed Practical Nurse; Management Analyst/Consultant; Management Trainee; Manufacturer's/Wholesaler's Sales Rep.; Mechanical Engineer; Medical Records Technician; Paralegal; Pharmacist; Physical Therapist; Physician; Property and Real Estate Manager; Public Relations Specialist; Purchasing Agent/Manager; Quality Control Supervisor; Radio/TV Announcer/Broadcaster; Radiological Technologist; Real Estate Agent; Recreational Therapist; Registered Nurse; Reporter; Respiratory Therapist; Restaurant/Food Service Manager; Science Technologist; Securities Sales Rep.; Services Sales Rep.; Social Worker; Sociologist; Software Engineer; Surveyor; Systems Analyst; Teacher/Professor; Technical Writer/ Editor; Telecommunications Manager; Transportation/ Traffic Specialist; Travel Agent; Typist/Word Processor; Underwriter/Assistant Underwriter; Veterinarian. **Average salary range of placements:** $20,000 - $29,999. **Number of placements per year:** 100 - 199.

KORN/FERRY INTERNATIONAL
8045 Leesburg Pike, Suite 540, Vienna VA 22182. 703/761-7020. **Fax:** 703/761-7023. **Contact:** Manager. **World Wide Web address:** http://www.kornferry.com. **Description:** An executive search firm. **Corporate headquarters location:** Los Angeles CA. **International locations:** Worldwide.

LARSON KATZ & YOUNG
4515 Daly Drive, Suite N, Chantilly VA 20151. 703/631-3881. **Fax:** 703/631-3882. **Contact:** Area Manager. **Description:** Larson Katz & Young is an executive search firm. **Specializes in the areas of:** Health/Medical; Information Systems.

LEE STAFFING RESOURCES
703 Thimble Shoals Boulevard, Suite B-1, Newport News VA 23606. 757/873-0792. **Fax:** 757/873-0087. **Contact:** Karen Ellis, Recruiter. **Description:** An executive search firm operating on both retainer and contingency bases. **Specializes in the areas of:** Accounting; Administration; Advertising; Art/Design; Engineering; Finance; Food; General Management; Industrial; Legal; Manufacturing; Personnel/Labor Relations; Retail; Sales; Secretarial; Technical. **Positions commonly filled include:** Accountant/Auditor; Actuary; Adjuster; Administrative Manager; Aerospace Engineer; Agricultural Engineer; Aircraft Mechanic/Engine Specialist; Attorney; Bank Officer/Manager; Biochemist; Biological Scientist; Biomedical Engineer; Blue-Collar Worker Supervisor; Branch Manager; Buyer; Chemical Engineer; Chemist; Civil Engineer; Clerical Supervisor; Clinical Lab Technician; Computer Programmer; Construction and Building Inspector; Construction Contractor; Cost Estimator; Counselor; Credit Manager; Customer Service Rep.; Design Engineer; Designer; Draftsperson; Economist; Electrical/Electronics Engineer; Electrician; Environmental Engineer; Financial Analyst; Food Scientist/Technologist; General Manager; Health Services Manager; Hotel Manager; Human Resources Specialist; Human Service Worker; Industrial Engineer; Industrial Production Manager; Insurance Agent/Broker; Internet Services Manager; Management Analyst/Consultant; Management Trainee; Manufacturer's/Wholesaler's Sales Rep.; Market Research Analyst; Mechanical Engineer; Metallurgical Engineer; Mining Engineer; MIS Specialist; Multimedia Designer; Operations/Production Manager; Paralegal;

Petroleum Engineer; Property and Real Estate Manager; Public Relations Specialist; Purchasing Agent/Manager; Quality Control Supervisor; Real Estate Agent; Restaurant/Food Service Manager; Services Sales Rep.; Software Engineer; Stationary Engineer; Statistician; Strategic Relations Manager; Structural Engineer; Surveyor; Systems Analyst; Technical Writer/Editor; Telecommunications Manager; Typist/Word Processor; Underwriter/Assistant Underwriter. **Other area locations:** Chesapeake VA. **Number of placements per year:** 1000+.

LEE STAFFING RESOURCES
2006 Old Greenbriar Road, Suite 5, Chesapeake VA 23320. 757/420-8011. **Contact:** Manager. **Description:** An executive search firm. **Other area locations:** Newport News VA.

MSI INTERNATIONAL
1612 Washington Plaza North, Reston VA 20190. **Toll-free phone:** 800/557-1674. **Contact:** Manager. **World Wide Web address:** http://www.msi-intl.com. **Description:** An executive search firm. **Specializes in the areas of:** Banking; Health/Medical; Industrial Sales and Marketing; Information Technology.

CAROL MADEN GROUP RECRUITING
2019 Cunningham Drive, Suite 218, Hampton VA 23666. 757/827-9010. **Contact:** Manager. **Description:** An executive search firm. **Specializes in the areas of:** Computer Science/Software; Engineering; Technical.

MANAGEMENT RECRUITERS INTERNATIONAL
45571 Shepherd Drive, Suite 101A, Sterling VA 20164. 703/430-3700. **Fax:** 703/430-7997. **Contact:** Account Executive. **Description:** An executive search firm. **Specializes in the areas of:** Engineering; Health/Medical. **Positions commonly filled include:** Chemical Engineer. **Corporate headquarters location:** Cleveland OH. **Other U.S. locations:** Nationwide.

MANAGEMENT RECRUITERS INTERNATIONAL
4560 South Boulevard, Suite 250, Virginia Beach VA 23452. 757/490-0331. **Contact:** Manager. **Description:** An executive search firm. **Specializes in the areas of:** Health/Medical; Marketing; Sales. **Corporate headquarters location:** Cleveland OH. **Other U.S. locations:** Nationwide.

MANAGEMENT RECRUITERS INTERNATIONAL
2511 Memorial Avenue, Suite 202, Lynchburg VA 24501. 804/528-1611. **Contact:** Manager. **Description:** An executive search firm. **Specializes in the areas of:** Accounting/Auditing; Engineering; Finance. **Corporate headquarters location:** Cleveland OH. **Other U.S. locations:** Nationwide.

MANAGEMENT RECRUITERS INTERNATIONAL
2 Pidgeon Hill Drive, Suite 430, Sterling VA 20165. 703/450-9001. **Fax:** 703/450-9010. **Contact:** Manager. **Description:** An executive search firm. **Specializes in the areas of:** Telecommunications. **Corporate headquarters location:** Cleveland OH. **Other U.S. locations:** Nationwide.

MANAGEMENT RECRUITERS INTERNATIONAL
1039 Sterling Road, Suite 202, Herndon VA 20170. 703/467-9111. **Fax:** 703/467-9115. **Contact:** Manager. **Description:** An executive search firm. **Specializes in the areas of:** Information Systems; Information Technology. **Corporate headquarters location:** Cleveland OH. **Other U.S. locations:** Nationwide.

MANAGEMENT RECRUITERS INTERNATIONAL - THE RICHMOND GROUP
6620 West Broad Street, Suite 406, Richmond VA 23230. 804/285-2071. **Fax:** 804/282-4990. **Contact:** Manager. **Description:** A generalist executive search firm. **Corporate headquarters location:** Cleveland OH. **Other U.S. locations:** Nationwide.

MANAGEMENT RECRUITERS OF CHARLOTTESVILLE
2114 Angus Road, Suite 235, Charlottesville VA 22901. 804/293-0800. **Contact:** Manager. **Description:** A generalist executive search firm. **Corporate headquarters location:** Cleveland OH. **Other U.S. locations:** Nationwide.

MANAGEMENT RECRUITERS OF McLEAN OFFICEMATES5
6849 Old Dominion Drive, Suite 225, McLean VA 22101. 703/442-4842. **Contact:** Howard Reitkopp, Manager. **Description:** An executive search firm. **Specializes in the areas of:** Accounting/Auditing; Administration; Advertising; Banking; Communications; Computer Hardware/Software; Design; Electrical; Engineering; Finance; Food; General Management; Health/Medical; Insurance; Operations Management; Personnel/Labor Relations; Procurement; Publishing; Technical; Transportation. **Corporate headquarters location:** Cleveland OH. **Other U.S. locations:** Nationwide.

MANAGEMENT RECRUITERS INTERNATIONAL OF ROANOKE
1950 Electric Road, Suite B, Roanoke VA 24018. 540/989-1676. **Contact:** Paul Sharp, Manager. **Description:** An executive search firm. **Specializes in the areas of:** Accounting; Manufacturing; Marketing; Operations Management; Procurement; Sales; Scientific; Technical. **Positions commonly filled include:** Account Manager; Account Rep.; Accountant; Chemist; Chief Financial Officer; Controller; Operations Manager; Sales Manager; Sales Rep. **Corporate headquarters location:** Cleveland OH. **Other U.S. locations:** Nationwide. **Average salary range of placements:** $50,000 - $100,000. **Number of placements per year:** 1 - 49.

THE McCORMICK GROUP
1440 Central Park Avenue, Suite 207, Fredericksburg VA 22401. 540/786-9777. **Fax:** 540/786-9355. **Contact:** William J. McCormick, President. **Description:** An executive search firm. **Specializes in the areas of:** Biology; Computer Science/Software; Engineering; Health/Medical; Insurance; Legal; Personnel/Labor Relations; Retail; Sales; Technical. **Positions commonly filled include:** Accountant/Auditor; Architect; Attorney; Biological Scientist; Civil Engineer; Computer Programmer; Cost Estimator; Design Engineer; Designer; Editor; EEG Technologist; Electrical/Electronics Engineer; Environmental Engineer; Financial Analyst; Health Services Manager; Human Resources Specialist; Licensed Practical Nurse; Management Analyst/Consultant; MIS Specialist; Multimedia Designer; Physical Therapist; Physician; Public Relations Specialist; Services Sales Rep.; Software Engineer; Systems Analyst; Technical Writer/Editor. **Corporate headquarters location:** This Location. **Other U.S. locations:** Jacksonville FL; Boston MA; Kansas City MO; Arlington VA. **Average salary range of placements:** More than $50,000. **Number of placements per year:** 1 - 49.

THE McCORMICK GROUP
1400 Wilson Boulevard, Suite 100, Arlington VA 22209. 703/841-1700. **Contact:** Manager. **Description:** An executive search firm. **Corporate headquarters location:** Fredericksburg VA. **Other U.S. locations:** Jacksonville FL; Boston MA; Kansas City MO.

MARVIN MELTZER ASSOCIATES
2121 Jamieson Avenue, Suite 1001, Alexandria VA 22314. 703/836-9398. **Fax:** 703/836-1236. **Contact:** Marvin Meltzer, President. **Description:** An executive search firm. **Specializes in the areas of:** Health/Medical.

CHARLES F. MENG & ASSOCIATES
4501 Arlington Boulevard, Arlington VA 22203. 703/522-1465. **Fax:** 703/522-7336. **Contact:** Charles Meng, Owner. **E-mail address:** ChasMeng@aol.com.

Description: An executive search firm. **Specializes in the areas of:** Education; Nonprofit.

JOHN MICHAEL ASSOCIATES
102 Elden Street, Suite 12, Herndon VA 20170. 703/471-6300. **Contact:** Manager. **Description:** An executive search firm. **NOTE:** Jobseekers should send resumes to John Michael Associates, Dulles International Airport, P.O. Box 17130, Washington DC 20041. **Specializes in the areas of:** Legal.

MICROLINK
8381 Old Courthouse Road, Vienna VA 22182. 703/556-4440. **Fax:** 703/556-4495. **Contact:** Manager. **Description:** An executive search firm. **Specializes in the areas of:** Information Technology.

NATIONAL BANKING NETWORK (NBN)
2628 Barrett Street, Virginia Beach VA 23452. 757/463-5766. **Fax:** 757/340-0826. **Contact:** Manager. **Description:** An executive search firm. **Specializes in the areas of:** Banking.

JAMES E. NAUGHTON LTD.
1573 Quail Point Road, Virginia Beach VA 23454. 757/481-6695. **Fax:** 757/481-6950. **Contact:** James Naughton, President. **E-mail address:** jenaughton@aol.com. **World Wide Web address:** http://members.aol.com/jenaughton/index.html. **Description:** An executive search firm. **Specializes in the areas of:** Automation/Robotics.

NET SYSTEMS SUPPORT
1100 Herndon Parkway, Suite 205, Herndon VA 20170. 703/471-6330. **Fax:** 703/471-0813. **Contact:** Manager. **Description:** An executive search firm.

OERTH ASSOCIATES, INC.
601 King Street, 4th Floor, Alexandria VA 22314. 703/739-1348. **Fax:** 703/739-1349. **Contact:** Lorraine C. Oerth, President. **Description:** An executive search firm. **Specializes in the areas of:** Construction; Real Estate. **Positions commonly filled include:** Construction Manager; Estimator; Property and Real Estate Manager; Superintendent. **Number of placements per year:** 100 - 199.

OMEGA SYSTEMS
1206 Laskin Road, Suite 201, Virginia Beach VA 23451. 757/437-1800. **Fax:** 757/437-7737. **Contact:** Manager. **E-mail address:** OmegaJobs@aol.com. **World Wide Web address:** http://www.topechelon.com/omegasystems. **Description:** An executive search firm. **Specializes in the areas of:** Chemicals; Industrial; Manufacturing.

PAGE-WHEATCROFT
1555 King Street, Suite 300, Alexandria VA 22314. 703/836-9695. **Fax:** 703/836-9733. **Contact:** Manager. **Description:** An executive search firm operating on a retainer basis. **Specializes in the areas of:** Legal; Technical.

PAUL-TITTLE ASSOCIATES, INC.
1485 Chain Bridge Road, Suite 304, McLean VA 22101. 703/442-0500. **Fax:** 703/893-3871. **Contact:** David M. Tittle, President. **E-mail address:** pta@paul-tittle.com. **Description:** An executive search firm operating on a retainer basis. **Specializes in the areas of:** Accounting; Engineering; Finance; Information Technology; Internet Development; Marketing; MIS/EDP; Network Administration; Sales; Telecommunications. **Average salary range of placements:** More than $100,000. **Number of placements per year:** 100 - 199.

PENCOM SYSTEMS INCORPORATED
1851 Alexander Bell Drive, Suite 350, Reston VA 20191. 703/860-2222. **Fax:** 703/860-9419. **Contact:** Manager. **World Wide Web address:** http://www.pencom.com. **Description:** An executive search firm. **Specializes in the areas of:** Technical. **Corporate**

headquarters location: New York NY. **Other U.S. locations:** Austin TX.

PLACEMENT PROFESSIONALS, INC.
P.O. Box 29772, Richmond VA 23242. 804/741-1246. **Fax:** 804/740-3841. **Contact:** Manager. **Description:** A generalist executive search firm.

PROCUREMENT SOLUTIONS INC.
1313 West Hills Lane, Reston VA 20190. 703/742-9661. **Fax:** 703/742-9662. **Contact:** Chuck Bates, President. **E-mail address:** chuck@erols.com. **Description:** An executive search firm operating on a contingency basis. This firm also offers some temporary and contract placements. Client company pays fee. **Specializes in the areas of:** Procurement. **Positions commonly filled include:** Attorney; Buyer; Contract Admin.; Procurement Specialist; Purchasing Agent; Vice President. **Corporate headquarters location:** This Location. **Average salary range of placements:** $30,000 - $100,000. **Number of placements per year:** 1 - 49.

PROFESSIONAL CONNECTIONS
714 Waters Drive, Virginia Beach VA 23462. 757/467-4460. **Fax:** 757/474-1458. **Contact:** Manager. **Description:** An executive search firm.

PROFESSIONAL SEARCH PERSONNEL
4900 Leesburg Pike, Suite 402, Alexandria VA 22302-1103. 703/671-0010. **Contact:** Chuck Cherel, Owner/Manager. **Description:** An executive search firm operating on both retainer and contingency bases. **Specializes in the areas of:** Accounting; Administration; Architecture/Construction; Banking; Biology; Computer Hardware/Software; Engineering; Finance; Health/Medical; Industrial; Personnel/Labor Relations; Technical. **Positions commonly filled include:** Accountant; Actuary; Aerospace Engineer; Architect; Bank Officer/Manager; Biological Scientist; Biomedical Engineer; Buyer; Chemical Engineer; Chemist; Computer Programmer; Cost Estimator; Credit Manager; Design Engineer; Designer; Draftsperson; Electrical/Electronics Engineer; Environmental Engineer; Financial Analyst; Geologist/Geophysicist; Human Resources Manager; Industrial Engineer; Internet Services Manager; Manufacturer's/Wholesaler's Sales Rep.; Mechanical Engineer; Metallurgical Engineer; MIS Specialist; Nuclear Engineer; Occupational Therapist; Petroleum Engineer; Physical Therapist; Quality Control Supervisor; Respiratory Therapist; Securities Sales Representative; Software Engineer; Systems Analyst. **Average salary range of placements:** More than $50,000. **Number of placements per year:** 50 - 99.

QUEST WORLD, INC.
9537 Oakenshaw Drive, Manassas VA 20110. 703/392-7385. **Fax:** 703/392-7808. **Contact:** Manager. **Description:** An executive search firm. **Specializes in the areas of:** Restaurant.

RECRUITING OPTIONS, INC. (ROI)
111 Fairway Lane, Suite 100, Staunton VA 24401. 540/248-2300. **Fax:** 540/248-5530. **Contact:** Manager. **E-mail address:** mail@recruitingoptions.net. **World Wide Web address:** http://www.recruitingoptions.net. **Description:** An executive search firm. **Specializes in the areas of:** Human Resources. **Average salary range of placements:** $100,000.

RECRUITING RESOURCES INC.
13813 Village Mill Drive, Midlothian VA 23113. 804/794-1813. **Contact:** Manager. **Description:** An executive search firm. **Specializes in the areas of:** Computer Programming; Engineering; Manufacturing; Technical.

RELIANCE STAFFING SERVICES
751 Thimble Shoals Boulevard, Suite E, Newport News VA 23606. 757/873-6644. **Fax:** 757/873-2341. **Contact:** Recruiter. **Description:** An executive search firm. **Positions commonly filled include:** Accountant/Auditor; Advertising Clerk; Automotive Mechanic; Blue-Collar Worker Supervisor; Computer Programmer; Design Engineer; Designer; Draftsperson; Electrical/Electronics Engineer; Electrician; Human Resources Specialist; Industrial Engineer; Paralegal; Purchasing Agent/Manager; Software Engineer; Structural Engineer; Systems Analyst; Technical Writer/Editor; Typist/Word Processor. **Corporate headquarters location:** Chesapeake VA. **Other area locations:** Suffolk VA; Virginia Beach VA. **Number of placements per year:** 500 - 999.

ROMAC INTERNATIONAL
11240 Waples Mill Road, Suite 301, Fairfax VA 22030. 703/345-3000. **Fax:** 703/293-9715. **Contact:** Manager. **Description:** An executive search firm. **Specializes in the areas of:** Human Resources.

ROMAC INTERNATIONAL
8045 Leesburg Pike, Suite 200, Vienna VA 22182. 703/790-5610. **Fax:** 703/790-1331. **Contact:** Recruiter. **World Wide Web address:** http://www.romac.com. **Description:** An executive search firm operating on both retainer and contingency bases. Client company pays fee. **Specializes in the areas of:** Accounting; Administration; Computer Science/Software; Engineering; Finance; Information Technology; Secretarial. **Positions commonly filled include:** Account Manager; Account Rep.; Accountant; Adjuster; Administrative Assistant; Administrative Manager; Applications Engineer; AS400 Programmer Analyst; Auditor; Budget Analyst; Chief Financial Officer; Computer Engineer; Computer Tech.; Content Developer; Controller; Cost Estimator; Credit Manager; Database Administrator; Database Manager; Finance Director; Financial Analyst; Human Resources Manager; Secretary; Software Engineer; SQL Programmer; Systems Analyst; Systems Manager. **Benefits available to temporary workers:** Language Training. **Corporate headquarters location:** Tampa FL. **Average salary range of placements:** $20,000 - $100,000. **Number of placements per year:** 1000+.

SEARCH & RECRUIT INTERNATIONAL
4455 South Boulevard, Virginia Beach VA 23452. 757/490-3151. **Toll-free phone:** 800/880-JOBS. **Fax:** 757/497-6503. **Contact:** Manager. **E-mail address:** contact@searchandrecruit.com. **World Wide Web address:** http://www.searchandrecruit.com. **Description:** An executive search firm. **Specializes in the areas of:** Engineering; Food; Industrial; Manufacturing; Publishing. **Positions commonly filled include:** Chemical Engineer; Computer Programmer; Design Engineer; Draftsperson; Electrical/Electronics Engineer; Electrician; Environmental Engineer; General Manager; Mechanical Engineer; MIS Specialist; Quality Control Supervisor; Software Engineer; Technical Writer/Editor; Telecommunications Manager. **Average salary range of placements:** $30,000 - $50,000. **Number of placements per year:** 200 - 499.

SEARCH CONNECTION
1430 Spring Hill Road, Suite 100, McLean VA 22102. 703/288-0900. **Contact:** Manager. **E-mail address:** clientresp@searchconnection.com. **World Wide Web address:** http://www.search-consultants.com. **Description:** An executive search firm. **Specializes in the areas of:** Accounting; Finance; Health/Medical; Information Systems.

SEARCH CONSULTANTS, INC.
2535 Sharmar Road, Roanoke VA 24018. 540/776-3114. **Contact:** Manager. **Description:** An executive search firm. **Specializes in the areas of:** Health/Medical.

SOUDER & ASSOCIATES
P.O. Box 71, Bridgewater VA 22812. 540/828-2365. **Fax:** 540/828-2851. **Contact:** E.G. Souder, President. **Description:** An executive search firm. **Specializes in the areas of:** Engineering; Food; Manufacturing; Personnel; Sales. **Positions commonly filled include:** Buyer; Ceramics Engineer; Chemical Engineer; Design Engineer; Electrical Engineer; Environmental Engineer; Food Scientist; General Manager; Human Resources

Specialist; Industrial Engineer; Industrial Production Manager; Materials Engineer; Mechanical Engineer; Metallurgical Engineer; MIS Specialist; Restaurant Manager. **Average salary range of placements:** More than $50,000. **Number of placements per year:** 50 - 99.

STRATEGIC SEARCH, INC.
5206 Markel Road, Suite 302, Richmond VA 23230. 804/285-6100. **Fax:** 804/285-6182. **Contact:** Dorrie Steinberg, President. **Description:** An executive search firm. **Specializes in the areas of:** Computer Science/Software; Manufacturing; MIS/EDP; Personnel/ Labor Relations; Technical; Telecommunications. **Positions commonly filled include:** Administrator; Business Analyst; Computer Engineer; Computer Programmer; Human Resources Specialist; Purchasing Agent/Manager; Systems Analyst; Systems Manager. **Average salary range of placements:** $30,000 - $50,000. **Number of placements per year:** 50 - 99.

BILLIE SUMMERS & ASSOCIATES
10024 Purcell Road, Richmond VA 23228. 804/262-6800. **Contact:** Manager. **Description:** An executive search firm. **Specializes in the areas of:** Sales.

THE TALLEY GROUP
600 Lee Highway, Verona VA 24482. 540/248-7009. **Fax:** 540/248-7046. **Contact:** John Burkhill, President. **E-mail address:** talley@cfw.com. **World Wide Web address:** http://www.talley-group.com. **Description:** An executive search firm operating on both retainer and contingency bases. **Specializes in the areas of:** Accounting; Banking; Computer Science; Engineering; Finance; Food; Human Resources; Industrial; Info. Systems; Light Industrial; Manufacturing; Personnel; Printing; Publishing; Retail; Sales; Scientific; Technical. **Positions commonly filled include:** Accountant; Auditor; Chemical Engineer; CFO; Computer Programmer; Controller; Cost Estimator; Database Manager; Design Engineer; Draftsperson; Electrical Engineer; Environmental Engineer; Financial Analyst; Food Scientist; Human Resources Manager; Industrial Engineer; Industrial Production Manager; Management Trainee; Manufacturing Engineer; Marketing Manager; Mechanical Engineer; Metallurgical Engineer; MIS Specialist; Operations Manager; Production Manager; Project Manager; Purchasing Agent/Manager; Quality Control Supervisor; Sales Engineer; Sales Manager; Software Engineer; Systems Analyst; Systems Manager. **Number of placements per year:** 1 - 49.

TASKFORCE OF VIRGINIA, INC.
PRG - PROFESSIONAL RESOURCES GROUP
969 Waverly Village Road, Fredericksburg VA 22407. 540/785-6666. **Contact:** Bart D. Mix, President. **E-mail address:** bart@taskforce1.com. **World Wide Web address:** http://www.taskforce1.com. **Description:** An executive search firm operating on a contingency basis. **NOTE:** Inquiries for PRG (also at this location) should be addressed to Rachel Witt, Director of Operations. **Specializes in the areas of:** Accounting; Administration; General Labor; General Management; Industrial; Manufacturing; Secretarial. **Positions commonly filled include:** Accountant; Blue-Collar Worker Supervisor; Branch Manager; Budget Analyst; Buyer; Claim Rep.; Computer Programmer; Customer Service Rep.; Dental Assistant/Hygienist; Draftsperson; Education Admin.; Electrician; Financial Analyst; General Manager; Health Services Manager; Human Resources Specialist; Industrial Production Manager; Internet Services Manager; Manufacturer's/Wholesaler's Sales Rep.; MIS Specialist; Operations Manager; Paralegal; Physical Therapist; Public Relations Specialist; Quality Control Supervisor; Sales Rep.; Software Engineer; Systems

Analyst; Telecomm. Manager. **Benefits available to temporary workers:** Paid Holidays; Paid Vacation. **Average salary range of placements:** $30,000 - $50,000. **Number of placements per year:** 1 - 49.

TELECOM RECRUITERS
P.O. Box 223284, Chantilly VA 20153. 703/620-4096. **Fax:** 703/620-2973. **Contact:** Manager. **E-mail address:** info@telecom-recruiters.com. **World Wide Web address:** http://www.telecom-recruiters.com. **Description:** An executive search firm. **Specializes in the areas of:** Telecommunications.

TRAINING DYNAMICS
2010 Corporate Ridge, Suite 700, McLean VA 22102. 703/734-0014. **Contact:** Manager. **Description:** A generalist executive search firm.

U.S. SEARCH
712 West Broad Street, Suite 3, Falls Church VA 22046. 703/448-1900. **Fax:** 703/448-1907. **Contact:** Arnie Hiller, President. **E-mail address:** ahsearch@aol.com. **Description:** An executive search firm operating on both retainer and contingency bases. The firm focuses on the composite materials, plastics, specialty chemicals, packaging, and plastics/rubber processing equipment industries. **Specializes in the areas of:** Engineering; General Management; Manufacturing; Sales; Technical. **Positions commonly filled include:** Account Manager; Account Representative; Chemist; Manufacturing Engineer; Marketing Analyst; Marketing Specialist; Materials Engineer; Sales Engineer; Sales Executive; Sales Manager; Sales Representative; Vice President of Marketing. **Average salary range of placements:** More than $50,000. **Number of placements per year:** 1 - 49.

LAWRENCE VEBER ASSOCIATES
507 Tozewell Avenue, Cape Charles VA 23310. 757/331-4676. **Fax:** 757/331-2348. **Contact:** Larry Veber, President. **Description:** An executive search firm operating on both contingency and retainer bases. **Specializes in the areas of:** Food; Health/Medical; Retail. **Positions commonly filled include:** Computer Programmer; MIS Specialist; Physical Therapist; Physician; Systems Analyst. **Average salary range of placements:** More than $50,000. **Number of placements per year:** 1 - 49.

WARREN, MORRIS & MADISON, LTD.
4108 Holly Road, Virginia Beach VA 23451. 757/425-9950. **Fax:** 757/425-9936. **Contact:** Manager. **World Wide Web address:** http://www.wmmltd.com. **Description:** An executive search firm. **Specializes in the areas of:** Telecommunications. **Corporate headquarters location:** Del Mar CA. **Other U.S. locations:** Durham NH; Portsmouth NH.

WAYNE ASSOCIATES INC. (WAI)
2628 Barrett Street, Virginia Beach VA 23452. 757/340-0555. **Contact:** Robert Cozzens, Owner. **E-mail address:** wai@infi.net. **Description:** An executive search firm operating on retainer and contingency bases. **Specializes in the areas of:** Chemicals; Engineering; Manufacturing; Sales. **Positions commonly filled include:** Biological Scientist; Chemical Engineer; Chemist; Design Engineer; Draftsperson; Mechanical Engineer. **Average salary range of placements:** $30,000 - $50,000.

WEST & ASSOCIATES
8348 Burkes Mill Drive, James Store VA 23128. 804/693-7478. **Fax:** 804/693-7523. **Contact:** Donna West, Owner. **Description:** An executive search firm. **Specializes in the areas of:** Chemicals; Paper.

PERMANENT EMPLOYMENT AGENCIES

A CHOICE NANNY
1911 Fort Myer Drive, Arlington VA 22209. 703/525-2229. **Contact:** Manager. **Description:** A permanent

employment agency. **Specializes in the areas of:** Nannies. **Other U.S. locations:** FL; MD; NJ.

A+ PERSONNEL
5339 Virginia Beach Boulevard, Suite 201, Virginia Beach VA 23462. 757/456-5347. **Contact:** Manager. **Description:** A permanent employment agency. Specializes in the areas of: Office Support.

ACCESS ENTERPRISES INC.
1608 Spring Hill Road, Suite 210, Vienna VA 22182. 703/442-9004. **Contact:** Manager. **Description:** A permanent employment agency. Specializes in the areas of: Accounting/Auditing; Data Processing; Engineering; Secretarial.

NANCY ALLEN ASSOCIATES, INC.
1730 North Lynn Street, Suite 603, Rosslyn VA 22209. 703/247-4222. **Fax:** 703/247-4181. **Contact:** Polly Ann Frye, Senior Partner. **E-mail address:** naa@patriot.net. **World Wide Web address:** http://www.nancyallen.com. **Description:** A permanent employment agency. Client company pays fee. Specializes in the areas of: Accounting; Administration; Advertising; Banking; Finance; Legal; Marketing; MIS/EDP; Nonprofit; Personnel/Labor Relations; Sales; Secretarial. Positions commonly filled include: Account Rep.; Accountant; Administrative Assistant; Advertising Clerk; Advertising Exec.; Controller; Customer Service Rep.; Database Administrator; Database Manager; Desktop Publishing Specialist; Editorial Assistant; Finance Director; Graphic Artist; Graphic Designer; Human Resources Manager; Marketing Manager; Marketing Specialist; MIS Specialist; Network/Systems Administrator; Paralegal; Public Relations Specialist; Systems Analyst. **Average salary range of placements:** $30,000 - $49,999. **Number of placements per year:** 200 - 499.

ALPHA OMEGA RESOURCES INC.
Forest Professional Park, 1019 Vista Park Drive, Suite A, Forest VA 24551. 804/385-8640. **Fax:** 804/385-0192. **Contact:** Ben Livesay, President. **Description:** A permanent employment agency. Specializes in the areas of: Accounting; Administration; Computer Science/ Software; Engineering; Finance; Food; General Management; Health/Medical; Industrial; Insurance; Manufacturing; Personnel/Labor Relations; Publishing; Sales; Secretarial; Technical; Transportation. Positions commonly filled include: Accountant Administrative Manager; Architect; Attorney; Branch Manager; Buyer; Computer Programmer; Customer Service Rep.; Design Engineer; Electrical/Electronics Engineer; Environmental Engineer; General Manager; Human Resources Specialist; Industrial Engineer; Industrial Production Manager; Insurance Agent/Broker; Internet Services Manager; Manufacturer's/Wholesaler's Sales Rep.; Mechanical Engineer; MIS Specialist; Operations/ Production Manager; Paralegal; Physician; Public Relations Specialist; Quality Control Supervisor; Services Sales Rep.; Software Engineer; Typist/Word Processor. **Number of placements per year:** 1000+.

ARDELLE ASSOCIATES
AA TEMPS
7002 Little River Turnpike, Suite N, Annandale VA 22003. 703/642-9125. **Contact:** Manager. **Description:** A permanent employment agency. AA Temps (also at this location) provides temporary placements. Specializes in the areas of: Accounting/Auditing; Bookkeeping; Data Processing; Office Support.

ATLANTIC RESOURCE GROUP
5511 Staples Mill Road, Suite 100, Richmond VA 23228. 804/262-4400. **Contact:** Manager. **Description:** A permanent employment and consulting firm that also provides temporary placements for information technology professionals with at least 18 months of experience. Specializes in the areas of: Information Technology.

AUSTIN ASSOCIATES MEDICAL PERSONNEL
1760 Reston Parkway, Suite 304, Reston VA 20190. 703/736-0500. **Contact:** Manager. **Description:** A permanent employment agency. Specializes in the areas of: Health/Medical.

BETATECH INC.
344 Maple Avenue West, Suite 182, Vienna VA 22180. 703/276-0039. **Fax:** 703/276-1666. **Contact:** Manager. **World Wide Web address:** http://www. betatechinc.com. **Description:** A permanent employment agency that provides placements in the commercial software industry.

BUCKLER CAREERS, INC.
1701 Euclid Avenue, Suite K, Bristol VA 24201. 540/466-3318. **Fax:** 540/466-6894. **Contact:** Ann McLain, Owner. **Description:** A permanent employment agency. Specializes in the areas of: Accounting/ Auditing; Banking; Computer Science/Software; Fashion; Finance; General Management; Health/Medical; Legal; Personnel/Labor Relations; Publishing; Retail; Sales; Secretarial. Positions commonly filled include: Accountant/Auditor; Administrative Assistant; Bank Officer/Manager; Bookkeeper; Clerk; Computer Operator; Computer Programmer; Credit Manager; Customer Service Rep.; Data Entry Clerk; Factory Worker; General Manager; Insurance Agent/Broker; Medical Secretary; Nurse; Operations/Production Manager; Purchasing Agent/Manager; Quality Control Supervisor; Receptionist; Sales Representative; Secretary; Stenographer; Typist/Word Processor. **Number of placements per year:** 200 - 499.

CAREER DEVELOPMENT
108 North Payne Street, Alexandria VA 22314. 703/548-3400. **Contact:** Manager. **Description:** A permanent employment agency that provides placements for junior officers who have left the military. Specializes in the areas of: Military.

CORE PERSONNEL
2070 Chain Bridge Road, Suite G55, Vienna VA 22182. 703/556-9610. **Contact:** Harvey Silver, President. **Description:** A permanent employment agency. Specializes in the areas of: Computer Hardware/ Software. Positions commonly filled include: Administrative Assistant; Clerk; Computer Programmer; Customer Service Rep.; EDP Specialist; Legal Secretary; Medical Secretary; Receptionist; Sales Rep.; Secretary; Stenographer; Systems Analyst; Typist/Word Processor.

CURZON STAFFING
1434 Duke Street, Alexandria VA 22314. 703/836-4403. **Fax:** 703/836-0514. **Contact:** Consultant. **World Wide Web address:** http://www.curzonstaff.com. **Description:** A permanent employment agency that also provides some temporary and temp-to-perm placements. Client company pays fee. Specializes in the areas of: Accounting/Auditing; Administration; Clerical; Customer Service; Data Processing; Executives; Human Resources; Management. **Average salary range of placements:** $30,000 - $49,999. **Number of placements per year:** 200 - 499.

CAROL DAY AND ASSOCIATES
2105 Electric Road SW, Roanoke VA 24018. 540/989-2831. **Fax:** 540/989-5910. **Contact:** Carol Day, Owner. **E-mail address:** carolday@roanoke.infi.net. **World Wide Web address:** http://www.virtualroanoke. com/carolday. **Description:** A permanent employment agency. Specializes in the areas of: Marketing; Sales. Positions commonly filled include: Account Rep.; Accountant; Administrative Assistant; Advertising Exec.; AS400 Programmer Analyst; Claim Rep.; Computer Programmer; Controller; Credit Manager; Customer Service Rep.; Database Administrator; Database Manager; Design Engineer; Financial Analyst; Human Resources Manager; Management Trainee; Manufacturing Engineer; Marketing Manager; Mechanical Engineer; Network/Systems Administrator; Project Manager; Sales Engineer; Sales Executive; Sales Manager; Sales Rep.; Secretary; Software Engineer; Systems Analyst; Typist/Word Processor. **Corporate headquarters location:** This Location. **Average salary range of placements:** $50,000 - $100,000. **Number of placements per year:** 50 - 99.

DOW PERSONNEL
291 Independence Boulevard, Suite 240, Virginia Beach VA 23462-5481. 757/499-7065. Contact: Manager. Description: A permanent employment agency. Specializes in the areas of: Accounting; Banking; Economics; Finance; Food; General Management; Insurance; Manufacturing; Retail; Sales; Secretarial. Positions commonly filled include: Account Manager; Administrative Manager; Bank Officer/Manager; Branch Manager; Broadcast Technician; Claim Representative; Clerical Supervisor; Computer Programmer; Credit Manager; Customer Service Rep.; Electrician; Financial Analyst; General Manager; Human Resources Specialist; Insurance Agent/Broker; Management Trainee; Medical Records Tech.; Public Relations Specialist; Restaurant/Food Service Manager; Services Sales Representative. Average salary range of placements: $20,000 - $29,999. Number of placements per year: 100 - 199.

ENTEGEE
3601 West Hundred Road, Suite 102, Chester VA 23831. 804/768-9564. Contact: Manager. Description: A permanent employment agency that also offers temporary placements. Specializes in the areas of: Technical.

HEADWAY CORPORATE STAFFING
4525 South Boulevard, Suite 203, Virginia Beach VA 23452. 757/518-0550. Fax: 757/518-1736. Contact: Jeanie Hurrell, Manager. Description: A permanent employment agency. Specializes in the areas of: Accounting; Administration; Computer Science/Software; Industrial; Legal; Personnel/Labor Relations; Sales; Secretarial; Technical. Positions commonly filled include: Accountant; Claim Rep.; Clerical Supervisor; Credit Manager; Customer Service Rep.; Draftsperson; Human Resources Manager; MIS Specialist; Paralegal; Typist/Word Processor. Benefits available to temporary workers: 401(k); Life Insurance; Paid Holidays; Paid Vacation. Average salary range of placements: $20,000 - $29,999. Number of placements per year: 1000+.

HISPANIC COMMITTEE OF VIRGINIA
5827 Columbia Pike, 2nd Floor, Falls Church VA 22041. 703/671-5666. Fax: 703/671-2325. Contact: Rito Berrto Luis, Job Developer. Description: A private, nonprofit, permanent employment agency. Specializes in the areas of: Education; Food; Retail; Sales; Secretarial. Positions commonly filled include: Accountant; Administrative Manager; Advertising Clerk; Automotive Mechanic; Blue-Collar Worker Supervisor; Claim Rep.; Clerical Supervisor; Construction and Building Inspector; Design Engineer; Designer; Editor; Education Administrator; Electrician; Emergency Medical Technician; Financial Analyst; Food Scientist/Technologist; Health Services Manager; Hotel Manager; Human Resources Specialist; Human Service Worker; Landscape Architect; Management Trainee; Manufacturer's/Wholesaler's Sales Rep.; Paralegal; Preschool Worker; Property and Real Estate Manager; Psychologist; Public Relations Specialist; Purchasing Agent/Manager; Radio/TV Announcer/Broadcaster; Real Estate Agent; Registered Nurse; Reporter; Restaurant/Food Service Manager; Services Sales Rep.; Social Worker; Teacher/Professor; Travel Agent; Typist/Word Processor. Average salary range of placements: $20,000 - $29,999. Number of placements per year: 200 - 499.

INTERIM TECHNOLOGY CONSULTING
1651 Old Meadow Road, Suite 105, McLean VA 22102-4308. 703/917-7800. Contact: Recruiter. Description: A permanent employment agency. Specializes in the areas of: Administration; Computer Hardware/Software; Defense Industry; Engineering; Military; Technical. Positions commonly filled include: Account Rep.; Computer Operator; Computer Programmer; Computer Scientist; Customer Service Rep.; Database Manager; Electrical/Electronics Engineer; MIS Specialist; Operations/Production Manager; Software Engineer; Systems Analyst; Technical Writer/Editor. Number of placements per year: 200 - 499.

SUSAN MILLER & ASSOCIATES, INC.
4216 Evergreen Lane, Suite 122, Annandale VA 22003. 703/642-1901. Contact: Manager. Description: A permanent employment agency. Specializes in the areas of: Accounting/Auditing; Office Support; Secretarial. Positions commonly filled include: Administrative Assistant; Executive Assistant; Legal Secretary; Office Manager; Receptionist.

NANNY DIMENSIONS
10408 Towlston Road, Fairfax VA 22030. 703/691-0334. Contact: Recruiter. Description: A permanent employment agency. Specializes in the areas of: Child Care, In-Home; Eldercare, In-Home. Positions commonly filled include: Nanny. Benefits available to temporary workers: Dental Insurance; Medical Insurance. Average salary range of placements: Less than $20,000. Number of placements per year: 100 - 199.

PAE PLACEMENT
1601 North Kent Street, Suite 900, Arlington VA 22209. 703/243-2701. Contact: Manager. Description: A permanent employment agency. Specializes in the areas of: Bilingual; International Executives.

SENIOR EMPLOYMENT RESOURCES (SER)
4201 John Marr Drive, Suite 236, Annandale VA 22003. 703/750-1936. Fax: 703/750-0269. Contact: Executive Director. Description: A permanent employment agency that places individuals who are over the age of 50. Positions commonly filled include: Accountant/Auditor; Administrative Assistant; Architect; Bookkeeper; Clerk; Computer Programmer; Credit Manager; Customer Service Representative; Data Entry Clerk; Draftsperson; Executive Assistant; Industrial Designer; Industrial Engineer; Legal Secretary; Medical Secretary; Public Relations Specialist; Purchasing Agent/Manager; Receptionist; Sales Representative; Typist/Word Processor. Number of placements per year: 200 - 499.

HELEN R. SKINNER ASSOCIATES INC.
8237 Idylwood Road, Vienna VA 22182. 703/847-0091. Contact: Manager. Description: A permanent employment agency. Specializes in the areas of: High-Tech.

SNELLING PERSONNEL SERVICES
45 West Boscawen Street, Winchester VA 22601. 540/667-1911. Fax: 540/667-0505. Contact: Manager. Description: A permanent employment agency that also provides temporary placements. Specializes in the areas of: Accounting/Auditing; Administration; Art/Design; Banking; Education; Engineering; Food; Health/Medical; Legal; Manufacturing; Personnel/Labor Relations; Publishing; Retail; Sales; Secretarial; Technical. Positions commonly filled include: Accountant/Auditor; Administrative Manager; Aerospace Engineer; Attorney; Bank Officer/Manager; Branch Manager; Buyer; Ceramics Engineer; Chemical Engineer; Civil Engineer; Computer Programmer; Electrical/Electronics Engineer; Health Services Manager; Hotel Manager; Human Resources Manager; Industrial Engineer; Industrial Production Manager; Library Technician; Management Trainee; Manufacturer's/Wholesaler's Sales Rep.; Materials Engineer; Mechanical Engineer; Metallurgical Engineer; Occupational Therapist; Paralegal; Purchasing Agent/Manager; Registered Nurse; Respiratory Therapist; Services Sales Rep.; Systems Analyst; Teacher/Professor; Typist/Word Processor; Wholesale and Retail Buyer. Corporate headquarters location: Dallas TX. Number of placements per year: 100 - 199.

SNELLING PERSONNEL SERVICES
8614 Westwood Center Drive, Suite 640, Vienna VA 22182. 703/448-0050. Fax: 703/448-3770. Contact: Palmer Suk, Manager. E-mail address: psuk@snellingva.com. World Wide Web address: http://www.snelling.com/vienna. Description: A permanent employment agency that also provides temporary and contract placements. Specializes in the areas of: Administration; Banking; Computer Science/Software;

Engineering; Sales; Secretarial; Technical. **Positions commonly filled include:** Administrative Assistant; Bookkeeper; Clerk; Computer Programmer; Customer Service Rep.; MIS Specialist; Receptionist; Sales Rep.; Secretary; Systems Analyst; Telemarketer. **Corporate headquarters location:** Dallas TX.

SNELLING PERSONNEL SERVICES
2817 North Parham Road, Suite 5A, Richmond VA 23294. 804/965-9500. **Fax:** 804/965-9533. **Contact:** Manager. **Description:** A permanent employment agency. **Specializes in the areas of:** Advertising; Finance; Industrial; Legal; Personnel/Labor Relations; Sales. **Positions commonly filled include:** Accountant; Clerical Supervisor; Customer Service Rep.; Paralegal; Services Sales Rep.; Typist/Word Processor. **Benefits available to temporary workers:** Medical Insurance; Paid Holidays. **Corporate headquarters location:** Dallas TX. **Average salary range of placements:** Less than $20,000. **Number of placements per year:** 200 - 499.

STAT EMPLOYMENT SERVICES
506 Westwood Office Park, Fredericksburg VA 22401. 540/373-2200. **Fax:** 540/373-5386. **Contact:** Cindy Duffer Matern, Vice President. **Description:** A permanent employment agency that also provides some temporary placements. **Specializes in the areas of:** Accounting; Computer Science/Software; Engineering; General Management; Industrial; Legal; Manufacturing; Personnel/Labor Relations; Secretarial. **Positions commonly filled include:** Accountant/Auditor; Blue-Collar Worker Supervisor; Budget Analyst; Civil Engineer; Clerical Supervisor; Computer Programmer; Construction Contractor; Credit Manager; Customer Service Representative; Dental Assistant/Dental Hygienist; Draftsperson; Electrical/Electronics Engineer; Emergency Medical Technician; General Manager; Human Resources Specialist; Industrial Engineer; Industrial Production Manager; Mechanical Engineer; Operations/Production Manager; Paralegal; Public Relations Specialist; Systems Analyst. **Benefits available to temporary workers:** Medical Insurance. **Average salary range of placements:** $20,000 - $29,999. **Number of placements per year:** 200 - 499.

TECHNICAL SEARCH CORPORATION
804 Moorefield Park Drive, Suite 103, Richmond VA 23236. 804/323-3000. **Fax:** 804/330-9378. **Contact:** Manager. **Description:** A permanent employment agency. **Specializes in the areas of:** Computer Science/Software. **Positions commonly filled include:** Computer Programmer; Software Engineer; Systems Analyst. **Number of placements per year:** 50 - 99.

TEMPORARY EMPLOYMENT AGENCIES

ACCOUNTING ASSETS INC.
8330 Boone Boulevard, Suite 745, Vienna VA 22182. 703/883-2123. **Contact:** Manager. **Description:** A temporary agency that also provides some permanent placements. **Specializes in the areas of:** Accounting/Auditing; Bookkeeping.

ACCUSTAFF
1310 Braddock Place, Suite 110, Alexandria VA 22314. 703/549-5055. **Contact:** Manager. **Description:** A temporary agency that also provides some permanent placements. **Specializes in the areas of:** Clerical; Personnel/Labor Relations. **Positions commonly filled include:** Administrative Assistant; Bookkeeper; Clerk; Computer Operator; Data Entry Clerk; Legal Secretary; Medical Secretary; Receptionist; Secretary; Stenographer; Typist/Word Processor.

ADVANTAGE STAFFING
620 Herndon Parkway, Suite 110, Herndon VA 20170. 703/904-9092. **Contact:** Manager. **Description:** A temporary agency. **Specializes in the areas of:** Health/Medical; Information Technology; Nonprofit; Secretarial. **Positions commonly filled include:** Customer Service Rep.; Editor; Internet Services Manager; Multimedia Designer; Paralegal; Technical Writer/Editor; Typist/Word Processor. **Benefits available to temporary workers:** Medical Insurance; Paid Holidays; Paid Vacation; Profit Sharing. **Corporate headquarters location:** Stamford CT. **Other U.S. locations:** DC; MD; NY; PA. **Average salary range of placements:** $30,000 - $50,000. **Number of placements per year:** 1000+.

CONSULTIS
12120 Sunset Hills Road, Suite 120, Reston VA 20190. 703/481-3334. **Fax:** 703/481-3335. **Contact:** Skip Goodwillie, Branch Manger. **World Wide Web address:** http://www.consultis.com. **Description:** A temporary agency. **Specializes in the areas of:** Administration; Computer Science/Software. **Positions commonly filled include:** MIS Specialist; Software Engineer. **Average salary range of placements:** $30,000 - $50,000. **Number of placements per year:** 100 - 199.

EMPLOYMENT ENTERPRISES
TEMPORARY SOLUTIONS
10328 Battleview Parkway, Manassas VA 20109. 703/361-2220. **Fax:** 703/368-2640. **Contact:** Recruiter. **Description:** A temporary agency. **Specializes in the areas of:** Accounting; Administration; Banking; General Management; Industrial; Manufacturing; Personnel/Labor Relations; Retail; Secretarial. **Positions commonly filled include:** Accountant; Administrative Manager; Bank Officer/Manager; Blue-Collar Worker Supervisor; Clerical Supervisor; Computer Programmer; Customer Service Rep.; Financial Analyst; General Manager; Human Resources Specialist; Human Service Worker; MIS Specialist; Paralegal; Property and Real Estate Manager; Public Relations Specialist; Services Sales Rep.; Technical Writer/Editor; Typist/Word Processor. **Corporate headquarters location:** This Location. **Number of placements per year:** 1000+.

EXPRESS PERSONNEL SERVICES
2155 Electric Road, Suite B, Roanoke VA 24018. 540/776-8729. **Fax:** 540/776-5437. **Contact:** Joe Farmer, Owner. **Description:** A temporary agency. **Specializes in the areas of:** Administration; Computer Science/Software; Manufacturing; Personnel/Labor Relations; Secretarial. **Positions commonly filled include:** Accountant; Administrative Manager; Blue-Collar Worker Supervisor; Branch Manager; Claim Rep.; Clerical Supervisor; Computer Programmer; Credit Manager; Customer Service Rep.; Draftsperson; General Manager; Human Resources Manager; Human Service Worker; Industrial Engineer; Industrial Production Manager; Management Analyst/Consultant; Management Trainee; Market Research Analyst; Operations/Production Manager; Paralegal; Property and Real Estate Manager; Public Relations Specialist; Purchasing Agent/Manager; Quality Control Supervisor; Restaurant/Food Service Manager; Software Engineer; Systems Analyst; Typist/Word Processor; Underwriter/Assistant Underwriter. **Average salary range of placements:** $20,000 - $29,999.

KELLY SERVICES, INC.
3232 Riverside Drive, Danville VA 24540. 804/791-1597. **Contact:** A. Fulcher, Supervisor. **Description:** A temporary agency. **Specializes in the areas of:** Computer Science/Software; Secretarial. **Positions commonly filled include:** Administrative Assistant; Marketing Specialist; Secretary; Typist/Word Processor. **Average salary range of placements:** Less than $20,000. **Number of placements per year:** 200 - 499.

MANPOWER TEMPORARY SERVICES
8300 Greensboro Drive, Suite L-1, McLean VA 22102. 703/821-0101. **Contact:** Recruitment. **Description:** A

temporary agency. **Specializes in the areas of:** Clerical; Personnel/Labor Relations; Word Processing. **Positions commonly filled include:** Administrative Assistant; Bookkeeper; Clerk; Customer Service Rep.; Data Entry Clerk; Legal Secretary; Secretary; Stenographer; Technical Writer/Editor; Typist/Word Processor. **Corporate headquarters location:** Milwaukee WI. **Number of placements per year:** 1000+.

MANPOWER TEMPORARY SERVICES
2300 Fall Hill Avenue, Suite 203, Fredericksburg VA 22401. 540/373-7801. **Fax:** 540/373-8106. **Contact:** Manager. **Description:** A temporary agency. **Specializes in the areas of:** Industrial; Insurance; Manufacturing; Sales; Secretarial. **Positions commonly filled include:** Claim Rep.; Clerical Supervisor; Customer Service Rep.; Industrial Engineer; Insurance Agent/Broker. **Benefits available to temporary workers:** Medical Insurance; Paid Holidays; Paid Vacation. **Corporate headquarters location:** Milwaukee WI. **Average salary range of placements:** $20,000 - $29,999. **Number of placements per year:** 1000+.

MANPOWER TEMPORARY SERVICES
1051 East Cary Street, Suite 102, Richmond VA 23219. 804/780-1800. **Contact:** Branch Manager. **Description:** A temporary agency. **Specializes in the areas of:** Office Support; Technical; Word Processing. **Positions commonly filled include:** Accountant; Accounting Clerk; Administrative Assistant; Assembler; Biological Scientist; Bookkeeper; Chemist; Computer Programmer; Customer Service Rep.; Designer; Desktop Publishing Specialist; Electrician; Inspector/Tester/Grader; Inventory Control Specialist; Machine Operator; Packaging/Processing Worker; Painter; Proofreader; Receptionist; Research Assistant; Secretary; Systems Analyst; Technical Writer/Editor; Telemarketer; Typist/Word Processor. **Corporate headquarters location:** Milwaukee WI. **Number of placements per year:** 1000+.

NORRELL SERVICES
5827 Gaskins Road, Richmond VA 23233. 804/346-3500. **Contact:** Heike Smith, Area Services Manager. **Description:** A temporary agency. **Specializes in the areas of:** Accounting; Administration; Advertising; Banking; Computer Hardware/Software; Engineering; Finance; Food; General Management; Manufacturing; Personnel/Labor Relations; Sales; Secretarial; Technical. **Positions commonly filled include:** Accountant/Auditor; Administrative Manager; Architect; Biological Scientist; Biomedical Engineer; Blue-Collar Worker Supervisor; Branch Manager; Budget Analyst; Buyer; Chemical Engineer; Chemist; Civil Engineer; Claim Rep.; Clerical Supervisor; Clinical Lab Tech.; Computer Programmer; Cost Estimator; Customer Service Rep.; Design Engineer; Designer; Draftsperson; Editor; Electrical/Electronics Engineer; Electrician; Environmental Engineer; Financial Analyst; General Manager; Human Resources Manager; Human Service Worker; Industrial Engineer; Industrial Production Manager; Internet Services Manager; Management Trainee; Mechanical Engineer; Medical Records Technician; Metallurgical Engineer; MIS Specialist; Multimedia Designer; Operations/Production Manager; Paralegal; Purchasing Agent/Manager; Quality Control Supervisor; Restaurant/Food Service Manager; Services Sales Rep.; Software Engineer; Statistician; Structural Engineer; Systems Analyst; Typist/Word Processor. **Benefits available to temporary workers:** 401(k); Dental Insurance; Medical Insurance; Paid Holidays; Paid Vacation. **Average salary range of placements:** $20,000 - $29,999. **Number of placements per year:** 1000+.

NORRELL SERVICES
1109 Eden Way North, Chesapeake VA 23320-2765. 757/436-3446. **Fax:** 757/436-4080. **Contact:** Manager. **Description:** A temporary agency that also provides some temp-to-perm placements and some managed staffing and call center services. **Specializes in the areas of:** Administration; Clerical; Light Industrial; Technical.

NORTHERN VIRGINIA TEMPORARIES, INC.
7700 Leesburg Pike, Suite 218, Falls Church VA 22043. 703/761-4357. **Fax:** 703/556-0494. **Contact:** Larry Gwensberg, President. **Description:** A temporary agency that also provides some permanent placements, executive searches, contract services, and career/outplacement counseling. **Specializes in the areas of:** Sales; Secretarial. **Positions commonly filled include:** Sales Executive; Sales Representative; Secretary; Technical Writer/Editor. **Average salary range of placements:** $30,000 - $50,000.

OLSTEN STAFFING SERVICES
12350 Jefferson Avenue, Suite 100, Newport News VA 23602. 757/881-9760. **Toll-free phone:** 800/967-5669. **Contact:** Manager. **Description:** A temporary agency. **Specializes in the areas of:** Accounting; Computer Science/Software; General Management; Industrial; Legal; Manufacturing; Personnel/Labor Relations; Secretarial; Technical. **Positions commonly filled include:** Accountant; Administrative Manager; Advertising Clerk; Blue-Collar Worker Supervisor; Branch Manager; Buyer; Counselor; Credit Manager; Customer Service Rep.; Human Resources Specialist; Human Service Worker; Library Technician; Paralegal; Purchasing Agent/Manager. **Benefits available to temporary workers:** Paid Vacation. **Average salary range of placements:** Less than $20,000. **Number of placements per year:** 500 - 999.

PRINTING PROFESSIONALS INC.
630 North Washington Street, Alexandria VA 22314. 703/549-5627. **Contact:** Manager. **Description:** A temporary agency that also provides some permanent placements. **Specializes in the areas of:** Publishing.

REMEDY INTELLIGENT STAFFING
144 Business Park Drive, Suite 104, Virginia Beach VA 23462-6527. 757/490-8367. **Fax:** 757/499-4713. **Contact:** President. **Description:** A temporary agency. **Specializes in the areas of:** Accounting; Administration; Banking; Computer Science/Software; Health/Medical; Legal; Personnel/Labor Relations; Secretarial; Technical. **Positions commonly filled include:** Accountant/Auditor; Administrative Manager; Claim Rep.; Clerical Supervisor; Computer Programmer; Customer Service Rep.; Education Administrator; Electrical/Electronics Engineer; Human Resources Specialist; Human Service Worker; Medical Records Technician; MIS Specialist; Paralegal; Systems Analyst; Telecommunications Manager; Typist/Word Processor. **Benefits available to temporary workers:** 401(k); Life Insurance; Medical Insurance. **Number of placements per year:** 500 - 999.

DON RICHARD ASSOCIATES
4701 Columbus Street, Suite 102, Virginia Beach VA 23462. 757/518-8600. **Contact:** Manager. **World Wide Web address:** http://www.dravb.com. **Description:** A temporary agency that also provides some temp-to-perm and permanent placements. **Specializes in the areas of:** Accounting; Bookkeeping; Human Resources; Information Technology; Office Support; Sales. **Corporate headquarters location:** Richmond VA.

TAC STAFFING SERVICES
2095 Chain Bridge Road, Vienna VA 22182. 703/893-5260. **Contact:** Manager. **Description:** A temporary agency. **Specializes in the areas of:** Banking; Clerical; Nonprofit. **Positions commonly filled include:** Bookkeeper; Clerk; Data Entry Clerk; Legal Secretary; Receptionist; Secretary; Typist/Word Processor. **Number of placements per year:** 1000+.

TEAM PLACEMENT SERVICE, INC.
4 Skyline Place, 5113 Leesburg Pike, Suite 510, Falls Church VA 22041. 703/820-8618. **Toll-free phone:** 800/495-6767. **Fax:** 703/820-3368. **Contact:** Tara Weinstein, Recruiter. **Description:** A temporary agency that also provides permanent placements. **Specializes in the areas of:** Health/Medical. **Positions commonly filled include:** Administrative Assistant; Administrative Manager; Biochemist; Biological Scientist; Chemist;

Dental Assistant/Dental Hygienist; Dentist; EKG Tech.; Licensed Practical Nurse; Medical Assistant; Medical Secretary; RN. **Benefits available to temporary workers:** 401(k); Medical Insurance; Paid Vacation. **Average salary range of placements:** $30,000 - $50,000. **Number of placements per year:** 200 - 499.

TECH/AID OF VIRGINIA
2095 Chain Bridge Road, Suite 300, Vienna VA 22182. 703/893-6444. **Contact:** Manager. **Description:** A temporary agency. **Specializes in the areas of:** Architecture/Construction; Cable TV; Computer Hardware/Software; Engineering; Manufacturing; Technical. **Positions commonly filled include:** Aerospace Engineer; Architect; Buyer; Ceramics Engineer; Chemical Engineer; Civil Engineer; Draftsperson; Electrical/Electronics Engineer; Estimator; Industrial Designer; Industrial Engineer; Manufacturing Engineer; Mechanical Engineer; Metallurgical Engineer; Mining Engineer; Operations/Production Manager; Petroleum Engineer; Purchasing Agent/Manager; Quality Control Supervisor; Technical Writer/Editor; Technician. **Number of placements per year:** 1000+.

TELESEC CORESTAFF
1800 Diagonal Road, Suite 140, Alexandria VA 22314. 703/518-2301. **Fax:** 703/518-2305. **Contact:** Manager. **World Wide Web address:** http://www.telesec.com. **Description:** A temporary agency. **Specializes in the areas of:** Finance; Nonprofit; Secretarial. **Positions commonly filled include:** Administrative Assistant; Administrative Manager; Advertising Clerk; Computer Operator; Customer Service Rep.; Database Manager; Graphic Artist; Secretary; Technical Writer/Editor; Typist/Word Processor. **Benefits available to temporary workers:** Credit Union; Direct Deposit; Medical Insurance; Paid Vacation. **Average salary range of placements:** $20,000 - $29,999. **Number of placements per year:** 50 - 99.

TEMPORARIES NOW
7700 Little River Turnpike, Suite 300, Annandale VA 22003-2406. 703/914-9100. **Contact:** Manager. **Description:** A temporary agency. **Specializes in the areas of:** Clerical; Office Support; Personnel/Labor Relations; Secretarial; Word Processing. **Positions commonly filled include:** Customer Service Rep.; Human Resources Specialist; Marketing Specialist; Technical Writer/Editor; Typist/Word Processor. **Benefits available to temporary workers:** Credit Union; Dental Insurance; Medical Insurance; Paid Holidays; Paid Vacation; Vision Insurance. **Average**

salary range of placements: $20,000 - $29,999. **Number of placements per year:** 1000+.

TEMPWORLD STAFFING SERVICES
1593 Spring Hill Road, Suite 110, Vienna VA 22182. 703/448-8000. **Fax:** 703/448-8060. **Contact:** Beth Aopin, Staffing Coordinator. **Description:** A temporary agency. **Specializes in the areas of:** Accounting; Computer Science/Software; Finance; Office Support; Personnel/Labor Relations; Retail; Sales; Secretarial. **Positions commonly filled include:** Administrative Assistant; Administrative Manager; Blue-Collar Worker Supervisor; Branch Manager; Customer Service Rep.; Graphic Artist; Graphic Designer; Human Resources Specialist; Multimedia Designer; Purchasing Agent/Manager; Services Sales Rep.; Technical Writer/Editor; Typist/Word Processor. **Benefits available to temporary workers:** 401(k); Paid Vacation. **Corporate headquarters location:** Atlanta GA. **Average salary range of placements:** $20,000 - $29,999. **Number of placements per year:** 500 - 999.

TEMPWORLD STAFFING SERVICES
1801 Reston Parkway, Suite 102, Reston VA 20190. 703/435-7474. **Contact:** Michelle Cascade, Manager. **Description:** A temporary agency. **Specializes in the areas of:** Administration; Secretarial. **Positions commonly filled include:** Customer Service Rep. **Corporate headquarters location:** Atlanta GA. **Average salary range of placements:** $20,000 - $29,999. **Number of placements per year:** 500 - 999.

WESTAFF
2190 Pimmit Drive, Suite 202, Falls Church VA 22043. 703/448-9500. **Fax:** 703/448-9555. **Contact:** Manager. **World Wide Web address:** http://www.westaff.com. **Description:** A temporary agency. **Specializes in the areas of:** Administration; Clerical; Office Support; Secretarial. **Benefits available to temporary workers:** Medical Insurance; Paid Holidays; Paid Vacation. **Corporate headquarters location:** Walnut Creek CA. **Average salary range of placements:** $20,000 - $29,999. **Number of placements per year:** 1000+.

WESTAFF
800 East Main Street, Suite 160, Wytheville VA 24382. 540/223-1896. **Contact:** Manager. **World Wide Web address:** http://www.westaff.com. **Description:** A temporary agency that also provides temp-to-perm placements. **Specializes in the areas of:** General Management; Industrial; Manufacturing. **Corporate headquarters location:** Walnut Creek CA.

CONTRACT SERVICES FIRMS

B&M ASSOCIATES
7700 Leesburg Pike, Suite 204, Falls Church VA 22043. 703/448-9675. **Contact:** Manager. **Description:** A contract services firm. **Specializes in the areas of:** Computer Science/Software; Information Systems; Technical.

BSC
8500 Leesburg Pike, Suite 407, Vienna VA 22182. 703/821-3500. **Contact:** President. **Description:** A contract services firm that also provides career/outplacement counseling. **Specializes in the areas of:** Engineering; General Management. **Positions commonly filled include:** Accountant; Actuary; Adjuster; Administrative Manager; Advertising Clerk; Aerospace Engineer; Agricultural Engineer; Aircraft Mechanic/Engine Specialist; Architect; Attorney; Automotive Mechanic; Bank Officer/Manager; Biochemist; Biological Scientist; Biomedical Engineer; Blue-Collar Worker Supervisor; Branch Manager; Broadcast Tech.; Brokerage Clerk; Budget Analyst; Construction and Building Inspector; Construction Contractor; Cost Estimator; Draftsperson; Electrical/Electronics Engineer; MIS Specialist; Multimedia Designer; Transportation/Traffic Specialist.

BRADFORD COMPANY
P.O. Box 366, Waynesboro VA 22980. 540/949-6992. **Fax:** 540/949-6996. **Contact:** Patricia L. Cabe, Manager. **Description:** A contract services firm. **Specializes in the areas of:** Clerical; Light Industrial; Production; Secretarial. **Positions commonly filled include:** Administrative Assistant; Computer Operator; Customer Service Representative; Design Engineer; Draftsperson; Electrician; Medical Records Technician; Production Worker; Secretary; Typist/Word Processor. **Corporate headquarters location:** This Location. **Average salary range of placements:** Less than $30,000. **Number of placements per year:** 100 - 199.

BUTLER SERVICE GROUP INC.
6707 Old Dominion Drive, Suite 305, McLean VA 22101. 703/883-3900. **Contact:** Manager. **Description:** A contract services firm.

CDI CORPORATION
14121 Parke Long Court, Suite 200, Chantilly VA 20151. 703/222-0700. **Fax:** 703/222-0704. **Contact:** Manager. **World Wide Web address:** http://www.cdicorp.com. **Description:** A contract services firm. **Specializes in the areas of:** Computer Science/Software;

Engineering; Technical. **Positions commonly filled include:** Aerospace Engineer; Architect; Biochemist; Biological Scientist; Biomedical Engineer; Buyer; Chemical Engineer; Chemist; Civil Engineer; Computer Programmer; Design Engineer; Draftsperson; Editor; Electrical/Electronics Engineer; Environmental Engineer; Geologist/Geophysicist; Industrial Engineer; Internet Services Manager; Mathematician; Mechanical Engineer; MIS Specialist; Multimedia Designer; Science Technologist; Software Engineer; Systems Analyst; Technical Writer/Editor; Telecommunications Manager. **Benefits available to temporary workers:** 401(k); Medical Insurance; Paid Holidays; Paid Vacation. **Corporate headquarters location:** Philadelphia PA. **Average salary range of placements:** More than $50,000. **Number of placements per year:** 500 - 999.

CADWORKS, INC.
1506 Willow Lawn Drive, Suite 207, Richmond VA 23230. 804/288-2233. **Fax:** 804/285-8256. **Contact:** Client Services Manager. **Description:** A contract services firm. **Specializes in the areas of:** Architecture/Construction; Computer Science/Software; Engineering; Personnel/Labor Relations; Technical. **Positions commonly filled include:** Chemical Engineer; Chemist; Civil Engineer; Design Engineer; Designer; Draftsperson; Electrician; Industrial Engineer; Materials Engineer; Mechanical Engineer; Multimedia Designer; Science Technologist; Software Engineer; Structural Engineer; Technical Writer/Editor. **Benefits available to temporary workers:** Medical Insurance. **Average salary range of placements:** $30,000 - $50,000. **Number of placements per year:** 50 - 99.

DPS, INC.
751-K Thimble Shoals Boulevard, Newport News VA 23606-3563. 757/873-3371. **Toll-free phone:** 800/328-3371. **Fax:** 757/873-3670. **Contact:** Recruiter. **E-mail address:** dpsjobs@dpsjobs.com. **Description:** A contract services firm that provides government contracts to health care professionals. **Specializes in the areas of:** Health/Medical. **Positions commonly filled include:** Dental Assistant/Dental Hygienist; Dentist; Licensed Practical Nurse; Medical Records Technician; Pharmacist; Physical Therapist; Radiological Technologist; Registered Nurse; Respiratory Therapist.

EDP
2095 Chain Bridge Road, Vienna VA 22182. 703/893-2400. **Contact:** Manager. **Description:** A contract services firm. **Specializes in the areas of:** Computer Hardware/Software. **Positions commonly filled include:** Computer Operator; Computer Programmer; EDP Specialist; MIS Specialist; Systems Analyst; Technical Writer/Editor. **Number of placements per year:** 1000+.

HALL KINION
7918 Jones Beach Drive, Suite 200, McLean VA 22102. 703/821-2700. **Fax:** 703/821-8827. **Contact:** Manager. **E-mail address:** varesume@hallkinion.com. **World Wide Web address:** http://www.hallkinion.com. **Description:** A contract services firm that also provides some permanent placements. **Specializes in the areas of:** Information Systems; Information Technology; Internet Development; Network Administration; Quality Assurance; Systems Administration; Systems Design; Technical Writing.

STRATEGIC STAFFING, INC.
SSI TECHNICAL SERVICES DIVISION
1420 Prince Street, Suite 100, Alexandria VA 22314. 703/739-8898. **Fax:** 703/739-8199. **Contact:** Mari Torres, Senior Staffing Director. **E-mail address:** ssistaff@aol.com. **Description:** A contract services firm. **Specializes in the areas of:** Administration; Computer Science/Software; Engineering; Network Administration; Systems Administration. **Positions commonly filled include:** Computer Programmer; MIS Specialist; Systems Analyst; Technical Writer/Editor; Telecommunications Manager. **Average salary range of placements:** $30,000 - $50,000. **Number of placements per year:** 50 - 99.

VANTAGE HUMAN RESOURCE SERVICES INC.
2300 Clarendon Boulevard, Suite 1109, Arlington VA 22201. 703/247-4100. **Fax:** 703/247-4102. **Contact:** Mary Ann Wilkinson, CPC/President. **Description:** A contract services firm providing personnel to federal agencies. The firm also provides career counseling. **Specializes in the areas of:** Personnel/Labor Relations. **Positions commonly filled include:** Administrative Assistant; Consultant; Counselor; Human Resources Manager; Management Analyst/Consultant; Operations Manager; Project Manager. **Average salary range of placements:** $30,000 - $50,000. **Number of placements per year:** 1 - 49.

H.L. YOH COMPANY
P.O. Box 36801, Richmond VA 23235. 804/560-2811. **Contact:** Manager. **Description:** A contract services firm. **Specializes in the areas of:** Information Technology.

CAREER/OUTPLACEMENT COUNSELING FIRMS

A PRIVATE RESUME SERVICE
2728 Colonial Avenue, Suite 110, Roanoke VA 24015. 540/981-0209. **Contact:** Manager. **Description:** A resume writing service.

BW CUSTOM RESUMES
18 Clarke Road, Richmond VA 23226. 804/359-1065. **Fax:** 804/359-4150. **Contact:** Betty H. Williams, Certified Professional Resume Writer. **Description:** A resume writing and career counseling firm.

ERICH NORD ASSOCIATES
6801 Whittier Avenue, Suite 201, McLean VA 22101. 703/556-9505. **Fax:** 703/556-9505. **Contact:** Joan Wikstrom, Principal. **Description:** A resume and career/outplacement counseling firm. **Corporate headquarters location:** This Location. **Average salary range of placements:** $50,000 - $100,000. **Number of placements per year:** 100 - 199.

RESUMES & MORE!
919-B East Market Street, Charlottesville VA 22902. 804/296-1777. **Fax:** 804/296-1231. **Contact:** Ariel MacLean, Owner/Operator. **E-mail address:** ariel@resumesandmore.com. **Description:** A resume writing service. **Number of placements per year:** 100 - 199.

ACCOUNTANTS EXECUTIVE SEARCH
ACCOUNTANTS ON CALL
601 Union Street, Suite 1625, Seattle WA 98101. 206/467-0700. **Fax:** 206/467-9986. **Contact:** Manager. **Description:** An executive search firm. Accountants On Call (also at this location) is a temporary agency. **Specializes in the areas of:** Accounting; Finance.

ACCOUNTING PARTNERS
500 108th Avenue NE, Suite 1640, Bellevue WA 98004. 425/450-1990. **Fax:** 425/450-1056. **Contact:** Manager. **Description:** An executive search firm. **Specializes in the areas of:** Accounting/Auditing; Finance. **Other area locations:** Seattle WA.

ACCOUNTING PARTNERS
700 Fifth Avenue, Suite 6150, Seattle WA 98104. 206/621-9070. **Fax:** 206/521-0990. **Contact:** Recruiter. **Description:** An executive search firm. **Specializes in the areas of:** Accounting; Finance. **Other area locations:** Bellevue WA.

ACCOUNTING QUEST
101 Stewart Street, Suite 1000, Seattle WA 98101. 206/441-5600. **Fax:** 206/441-5656. **Contact:** Jennifer Sollom, Project Manager. **E-mail address:** jennifers@accountingquest.com. **World Wide Web address:** http://www.accountingquest.com. **Description:** An executive search firm operating on a contingency basis. Accounting Quest also offers contract, temporary, and permanent placements. Client company pays fee. **Specializes in the areas of:** Accounting; Finance; Tax. **Other U.S. locations:** Phoenix AZ; Denver CO; Portland OR. **Average salary range of placements:** $50,000 - $100,000. **Number of placements per year:** 200 - 499.

ALMOND & ASSOCIATES
P.O. Box 6124, Federal Way WA 98063-6124. 206/721-1111. **Contact:** John Almond, President. **Description:** An executive search firm that places upper-level managers. Almond & Associates also provides some temporary office support placements.

ANCHOR ASSOCIATES, INC.
160 NW Gilman Boulevard, Suite 104, Issaquah WA 98027. 425/837-1355. **Fax:** 425/837-1715. **Contact:** Pamela Gotham, President/CEO. **E-mail address:** pamela@anchr.com. **Description:** An executive search firm that operates on both retainer and contingency bases. Anchor Associates, Inc. also offers some contract placements. **Specializes in the areas of:** Industrial; Manufacturing; Telecommunications. **Average salary range of placements:** $50,000 - $100,000. **Number of placements per year:** 100 - 199.

ROD ASHER ASSOCIATES
411 108th Avenue NE, Suite 2050, Bellevue WA 98004. 425/646-1030. **Contact:** Manager. **Description:** An executive search firm. **Specializes in the areas of:** Computer Hardware/Software.

AXXA CORPORATION
U.S. Bank Centre Building, 1420 Fifth Avenue, 22nd Floor, Seattle WA 98101. 206/224-3555. **Fax:** 206/447-0784. **Contact:** Recruiter. **E-mail address:** service@axxa.com. **World Wide Web address:** http://www.axxa.com. **Description:** An executive search firm. **Specializes in the areas of:** Consulting; Information Technology; Software Development; Technical. **Positions commonly filled include:** Developmental Specialist; Internet Specialist; Operations Manager; Product Specialist; Project Manager; Systems Engineer; Technical Representative.

BEHRENS AND COMPANY
P.O. Box 157, Easton WA 98925. 509/656-0284. **Fax:** 509/656-2298. **Contact:** Rick Behrens, President. **E-mail address:** rick@behrensco.com. **World Wide Web address:** http://www.behrensco.com. **Description:** An executive search firm operating on both retainer and contingency bases. Behrens and Company focuses on placements in the food and packaging machinery industries. **Specializes in the areas of:** Engineering; Industrial; Manufacturing; Sales. **Positions commonly filled include:** Branch Manager; Design Engineer; Electrical/Electronics Engineer; General Manager; Industrial Production Manager; Manufacturer's/Wholesaler's Sales Rep.; Mechanical Engineer; Operations/Production Manager. **Average salary range of placements:** More than $50,000. **Number of placements per year:** 50 - 99.

BELL & ASSOCIATES
2519 East Beaver Lake Drive SE, Issaquah WA 98029. 425/641-3231. **Fax:** 425/641-3250. **Contact:** Manager. **Description:** An executive search firm. **Specializes in the areas of:** Medical Sales and Marketing.

KEN BENSON & ASSOCIATES
P.O. Box 2429, Lynnwood WA 98036. 425/745-8080. **Fax:** 425/745-3626. **Contact:** Ken Benson, Owner. **Description:** An executive search firm.

BERKANA INTERNATIONAL
18907 Forest Park Drive NE, Seattle WA 98155. 206/361-1633. **Fax:** 206/547-3843. **Contact:** Manager. **E-mail address:** resume@headhunters.com. **World Wide Web address:** http://www.headhunters.com. **Description:** An executive search firm operating on a retainer basis. **Specializes in the areas of:** Computer Science/Software; High-Tech. **Positions commonly filled include:** Computer Programmer; Electrical/Electronics Engineer; General Manager; Internet Services Manager; Multimedia Designer; Software Engineer; Strategic Relations Manager; Technical Writer/Editor; Telecommunications Manager; Video Production Coordinator. **Average salary range of placements:** More than $50,000. **Number of placements per year:** 1 - 49.

BIXLER GROUP
11502 NE 34th Avenue, Suite D, Vancouver WA 98686. 360/574-7995. **Fax:** 360/576-0189. **Contact:** Manager. **E-mail address:** bixlergrp@worldaccessnet.com. **Description:** An executive search firm. **Specializes in the areas of:** Data Processing; Engineering; Software Development; Technical.

BLACK & DEERING
1605 116th Avenue NE, Suite 211, Bellevue WA 98004. 425/646-0905. **Contact:** Manager. **Description:** An executive search firm. **Specializes in the areas of:** Health/Medical.

T.M. CAMPBELL COMPANY
1111 Third Avenue, Suite 2500, Seattle WA 98101. 206/583-8355. **Fax:** 206/780-1705. **Contact:** Manager. **Description:** An executive search firm. **Specializes in the areas of:** Government; Nonprofit; Professional; Technical.

SALLY CAPLAN & ASSOCIATES
1420 NW Gilman Boulevard, Suite 2292, Issaquah WA 98027. 425/557-0015. **Fax:** 425/557-0017. **Contact:** Sally Caplan, Owner. **Description:** An executive search firm. **Specializes in the areas of:** Software Development.

THE CAREER CLINIC, INC.
6920 220th Street SW, Suite 107, Mountlake Terrace WA 98043. 425/673-1994. **Contact:** Jane Ray Wilkinson, President. **E-mail address:** info@careerclinic.com. **World Wide Web address:** http://www.careerclinic.com. **Description:** An executive

search firm operating on a contingency basis. The firm also provides temporary placements. Founded in 1967. **Specializes in the areas of:** Administration; Architecture/Construction; Banking; Computer Science/ Software; Engineering; Food; General Management; Industrial; Insurance; Legal; Manufacturing; Retail; Sales; Secretarial; Technical; Transportation. **Positions commonly filled include:** Accountant/Auditor; Administrative Assistant; Administrative Manager; Applications Engineer; Architect; Assistant Manager; Attorney; Auditor; Budget Analyst; Chief Financial Officer; Civil Engineer; Claim Representative; Computer Animator; Computer Operator; Computer Programmer; Construction Contractor; Controller; Cost Estimator; Credit Manager; Customer Service Representative; Database Manager; Design Engineer; Electrical/Electronics Engineer; Finance Director; Financial Analyst; Fund Manager; General Manager; Graphic Artist; Graphic Designer; Human Resources Manager; Insurance Agent/Broker; Internet Services Manager; Management Trainee; Manufacturing Engineer; Mechanical Engineer; MIS Specialist; Operations Manager; Paralegal; Production Manager; Project Manager; Public Relations Specialist; Purchasing Agent/Manager; Quality Control Supervisor; Sales Engineer; Sales Manager; Sales Representative; Secretary; Software Engineer; Statistician. **Number of placements per year:** 50 - 99.

CAREER SPECIALISTS INC.
155 108th Avenue NE, Suite 200, Bellevue WA 98004. 425/455-0582. **Contact:** Manager. **Description:** An executive search firm.

ROBERT COLE ASSOCIATES
1001 Fourth Avenue, Suite 3200, Seattle WA 98154. 206/285-3925. **Fax:** 206/283-5722. **Contact:** Bob Cole, Owner. **Description:** An executive search firm. **Specializes in the areas of:** Health/Medical.

CONSUMER CONNECTION
400 108th Avenue NE, Suite 600, Bellevue WA 98004. 425/455-2770. **Fax:** 425/454-1702. **Contact:** Recruiter. **Description:** An executive search firm. **Specializes in the areas of:** Consumer Products; Human Resources; Logistics; Marketing; Sales.

KIM FINCH COOK EXECUTIVE RECRUITER
8350 164th Avenue NE, Suite 302, Redmond WA 98052. 425/882-3000. **Fax:** 425/882-4890. **Contact:** Kim Cook, Owner. **Description:** An executive search firm. **Specializes in the areas of:** Accounting; Finance; Human Resources.

CORBETT & ASSOCIATES
1215 South Central Avenue, Suite 204A, Kent WA 98032. 253/854-1906. **Fax:** 253/854-1485. **Contact:** Recruiter. **Description:** An executive search firm. **Specializes in the areas of:** Health/Medical; Pharmaceuticals.

JUDITH CUSHMAN & ASSOCIATES
1125 12th Avenue NW, Suite B-1A, Issaquah WA 98027. 425/392-8660. **Fax:** 425/391-9190. **Contact:** Judith Cushman, President. **E-mail address:** jcushman@jc-a.com. **World Wide Web address:** http://www.jc-a.com. **Description:** An executive search firm that operates on a retainer basis. Founded in 1981. **Positions commonly filled include:** Public Relations Specialist. **Average salary range of placements:** More than $50,000. **Number of placements per year:** 1 - 49.

DEMETRIO & ASSOCIATES
12835 Bellevue Redmond Road, Suite 130, Bellevue WA 98005. 425/451-3373. **Fax:** 425/451-3371. **Contact:** Recruiter. **Description:** An executive search firm. **Specializes in the areas of:** Engineering; High-Tech; Marketing; Sales; Software Development.

DEVON JAMES ASSOCIATES
12356 Northup Way, Suite 118, Bellevue WA 98005. 425/885-3050. **Contact:** Manager. **Description:** An executive search firm. **Specializes in the areas of:** High-Tech.

EXECUTIVE RECRUITERS
600 108th Avenue NE, Suite 242, Bellevue WA 98004. 206/447-7404. **Contact:** Manager. **Description:** An executive search firm. **Specializes in the areas of:** Computer Hardware/Software; Computer Science/ Software; Wireless Communications.

RENEE FELDMAN & ASSOCIATES
8533 Second Avenue NE, Seattle WA 98115. 206/527-0980. **Contact:** Renee Feldman, Owner. **Description:** An executive search firm. **Specializes in the areas of:** Chemicals; Industrial; Management; Packaging; Plastics; Sales; Technical.

L.W. FOOTE COMPANY
THE BRIGHTON GROUP
110 110th Avenue NE, Suite 603, Bellevue WA 98004-5840. 425/451-1660. **Fax:** 425/451-1535. **Contact:** Leland W. Foote, President. **E-mail address:** email@lwfoote.com. **World Wide Web address:** http://www.lwfoote.com. **Description:** An executive search firm. The Brighton Group (also at this location) is an outplacement counseling services firm. **Specializes in the areas of:** Consumer Products; Health/Medical; High-Tech; Manufacturing; Retail. **Average salary range of placements:** More than $100,000.

F-O-R-T-U-N-E PERSONNEL CONSULTANTS OF EAST SEATTLE
11661 SE First Street, Suite 202, Bellevue WA 98005. 425/450-9665. **Fax:** 425/450-0357. **Contact:** Daniel Chin, President. **E-mail address:** info@ fortuneseattle.com. **World Wide Web address:** http://www.fortuneseattle.com. **Description:** An executive search firm operating on a contingency basis. Client company pays fee. **Specializes in the areas of:** Engineering; Health/Medical; Industrial. **Positions commonly filled include:** Biomedical Engineer; Design Engineer; Draftsperson; Electrical/ Electronics Engineer; Human Resources Manager; Industrial Engineer; Industrial Production Manager; Manufacturing Engineer; Mechanical Engineer; Metallurgical Engineer; Operations Manager; Production Manager; Project Manager; Quality Assurance Engineer; Sales Engineer; Vice President. **Corporate headquarters location:** New York NY. **Other U.S. locations:** Nationwide. **Average salary range of placements:** $50,000 - $100,000. **Number of placements per year:** 1 - 49.

FREEMAN STAFFING, INC.
P.O. Box 1770, Marysville WA 98270. 360/653-8992. **Fax:** 360/653-8271. **Contact:** Recruiter. **Description:** An executive search firm. **Specializes in the areas of:** Paper.

GORMAN CONSULTING SERVICE
3323 St. Andrew's Court NE, Tacoma WA 98422. 253/927-8786. **Fax:** 253/927-4346. **Contact:** Perry Gorman, Owner. **Description:** An executive search firm. **Specializes in the areas of:** Distribution; Manufacturing.

HRA INSURANCE STAFFING
11100 NE Eighth Street, Suite 600, Bellevue WA 98004. 425/451-4007. **Contact:** Cyndie Boe, General Manager. **Description:** An executive search firm operating on both retainer and contingency bases. **Specializes in the areas of:** Insurance. **Positions commonly filled include:** Adjuster; Branch Manager; Insurance Agent/Broker; Underwriter. **Number of placements per year:** 1 - 49.

HAGEL & COMPANY
1019 Pacific Avenue, Suite 1418, Tacoma WA 98402. 253/572-2439. **Fax:** 253/383-4022. **Contact:** Recruiter. **Description:** An executive search firm.

ROBERT HALF INTERNATIONAL
ACCOUNTEMPS
601 Union Street, Suite 4300, Seattle WA 98101. 206/749-0960. **Contact:** Manager. **World Wide Web**

executive search firm. **Specializes in the areas of:** High-Tech.

address: http://www.roberthalf.com. **Description:** An executive search firm. Accountemps (also at this location) provides temporary accounting placements. **Specializes in the areas of:** Accounting/Auditing. **Corporate headquarters location:** Menlo Park CA. **Other U.S. locations:** Nationwide.

N.G. HAYES COMPANY
P.O. Box 184, Medina WA 98039. 425/453-1313. **Fax:** 425/453-3057. **Contact:** Nelia Hayes, President. **Description:** N.G. Hayes Company is an executive search firm. **Specializes in the areas of:** Computer Science/Software; Marketing; Sales. **Positions commonly filled include:** Computer Programmer; Software Engineer; Systems Analyst. **Number of placements per year:** 1 - 49.

HEADDEN & ASSOCIATES
777 108th Avenue NE, Suite 600, Bellevue WA 98004. 425/451-2427. **Contact:** Manager. **Description:** An executive search firm.

HOUSER MARTIN MORRIS (HMM)
110 110th Avenue NE, Suite 503, Bellevue WA 98004. 425/453-2700. **Fax:** 425/453-8726. **Contact:** Bob Holert, President. **E-mail address:** hmmjobs@houser.com. **World Wide Web address:** http://www.houser.com. **Description:** An executive search firm operating on both retainer and contingency bases. Founded in 1974. **Specializes in the areas of:** Accounting/Auditing; Administration; Computer Science/Software; Engineering; Finance; Legal; MIS/EDP; Personnel/Labor Relations; Sales. **Positions commonly filled include:** Attorney; Chief Financial Officer; Computer Operator; Computer Programmer; Controller; Electrical/Electronics Engineer; Finance Director; General Manager; Human Resources Manager; Industrial Engineer; Insurance Agent/Broker; Intellectual Property Lawyer; Manufacturing Engineer; Marketing Manager; Mechanical Engineer; MIS Specialist; Operations Manager; Production Manager; Purchasing Agent/Manager; Quality Control Supervisor; Sales Executive; Sales Manager; Sales Representative; Software Engineer; Systems Analyst; Systems Manager; Telecommunications Manager; Underwriter/Assistant Underwriter. **Average salary range of placements:** More than $50,000. **Number of placements per year:** 100 - 199.

HUMAN RESOURCES INC.
451 SW 10th Street, Suite 112, Renton WA 98055. 425/228-2289. **Fax:** 425/228-3513. **Contact:** Matt Rogers, Manager. **E-mail address:** hrrenton@accessone.com. **Description:** Human Resources Inc. is an executive search firm that also provides temporary and contract placements. Founded in 1994. **Specializes in the areas of:** Accounting/Auditing; General Management; Legal; Personnel/Labor Relations; Sales; Secretarial. **Positions commonly filled include:** Accountant/Auditor; Blue-Collar Worker Supervisor; Budget Analyst; Claim Representative; Computer Programmer; Counselor; Credit Manager; Customer Service Representative; Dental Assistant/Dental Hygienist; Education Administrator; General Manager; Hotel Manager; Insurance Agent/Broker; Internet Services Manager; Management Analyst/Consultant; Manufacturer's/ Wholesaler's Sales Representative; Medical Records Technician; MIS Specialist; Operations/Production Manager; Paralegal; Property and Real Estate Manager; Public Relations Specialist; Quality Control Supervisor; Real Estate Agent; Reporter; Restaurant/Food Service Manager; Services Sales Representative; Teacher/ Professor; Technical Writer/Word Processor; Telecommunications Manager; Transportation/Traffic Specialist; Travel Agent; Typist/Word Processor; Underwriter/Assistant Underwriter. **Corporate headquarters location:** Bellevue WA. **Other area locations:** Auburn WA; Mercer Island WA; Olympia WA; Tacoma WA. **Average salary range of placements:** $20,000 - $29,999. **Number of placements per year:** 200 - 499.

HURD SIEGEL & ASSOCIATES
1111 Third Avenue, Suite 2880, Seattle WA 98101. 206/622-4282. **Contact:** Manager. **Description:** An executive search firm.

HYGUN GROUP, INC.
P.O. Box 4063, Bellevue WA 98009. 425/644-8011. **Fax:** 425/644-8065. **Contact:** Manager. **E-mail address:** office@hygun.com. **World Wide Web address:** http://www.hygun.com. **Description:** An executive search firm. **Specializes in the areas of:** Engineering; Scientific. **Corporate headquarters location:** Marietta GA.

JENSEN & COOPER
411 108th Avenue NE, Suite 250, Bellevue WA 98004. 425/637-5656. **Fax:** 425/637-5657. **Contact:** Recruiter. **Description:** Jensen & Cooper is a generalist executive search firm.

THE JOBS COMPANY
8900 East Sprague Avenue, Spokane WA 99212-2927. 509/928-3151. **Fax:** 509/928-3168. **Contact:** Mr. Hager, Manager. **Description:** An executive search firm. Founded in 1973. **Specializes in the areas of:** Accounting/Auditing; Administration; Computer Science/Software; Engineering; General Management; Health/Medical; Personnel/Labor Relations; Publishing; Retail; Sales; Secretarial; Technical. **Positions commonly filled include:** Accountant/Auditor; Adjuster; Administrative Manager; Advertising Clerk; Automotive Mechanic; Biological Scientist; Biomedical Engineer; Blue-Collar Worker Supervisor; Branch Manager; Broadcast Technician; Brokerage Clerk; Budget Analyst; Buyer; Chemist; Claim Representative; Clerical Supervisor; Clinical Lab Technician; Computer Programmer; Construction and Building Inspector; Construction Contractor; Cost Estimator; Counselor; Credit Manager; Dental Assistant/Dental Hygienist; Dental Lab Technician; Designer; Draftsperson; Editor; EEG Technologist; EKG Technician; Electrical/Electronics Engineer; Electrician; Emergency Medical Technician; Financial Analyst; Financial Services Sales Representative; General Manager; Health Services Manager; Hotel Manager; Human Resources Manager; Industrial Engineer; Industrial Production Manager; Licensed Practical Nurse; Management Trainee; Manufacturer's/Wholesaler's Sales Representative; Mechanical Engineer; Medical Records Technician; Metallurgical Engineer; Nuclear Medicine Technologist; Occupational Therapist; Paralegal; Purchasing Agent/Manager; Quality Control Supervisor; Registered Nurse; Reporter; Respiratory Therapist; Restaurant/Food Service Manager; Securities Sales Representative; Services Sales Representative; Software Engineer; Stationary Engineer; Structural Engineer; Surgical Technician; Systems Analyst; Technical Writer/Editor; Telecommunications Manager; Typist/Word Processor.

KAMISAR LEGAL SEARCH, INC.
1509 Queen Anne Avenue North, Suite 298, Seattle WA 98109. 425/392-1969. **Fax:** 425/557-0080. **Contact:** Gordon Kamisar, Owner. **E-mail address:** gkamisar@sprynet.com. **World Wide Web address:** http://www.seattlesearch.com. **Description:** An executive search firm. **Specializes in the areas of:** Legal. **Positions commonly filled include:** Attorney.

KERRY-BEN KELLY EXECUTIVE SEARCH
6574 153rd Avenue SE, Bellevue WA 98006. 425/653-0506. **Fax:** 425/653-1625. **Contact:** Recruiter. **Description:** An executive search firm. **Specializes in the areas of:** Internet Development; Retail.

KIRKBRIDE ASSOCIATES INC.
915 118th Avenue SE, Bellevue WA 98005. 425/453-5256. **Fax:** 425/453-5257. **Contact:** Manager. **Description:** Kirkbride Associates Inc. is an executive search firm. **Specializes in the areas of:** Engineering; Sales.

GARY KOKENSPARGER & ASSOCIATES
800 Bellevue Way NE, Suite 400, Bellevue WA 98004.
425/637-2836. **Fax:** 425/333-5600. **Contact:** Gary
Kokensparger, Owner. **Description:** An executive search
firm. **Specializes in the areas of:** Information Systems;
Information Technology.

KORN/FERRY INTERNATIONAL
600 University Suite, Suite 3428, Seattle WA 98101.
206/447-1834. **Fax:** 206/447-9261. **Contact:** Manager.
World Wide Web address: http://www.kornferry.com.
Description: An executive search firm that provides
placements for upper-level managers. **Corporate
headquarters location:** Los Angeles CA. **Average
salary range of placements:** More than $50,000.

KOSSUTH & ASSOCIATES
800 Bellevue Way NE, Suite 400, Bellevue WA 98004.
425/450-9050. **Fax:** 425/450-0513. **Contact:** Jane
Kossuth, President. **Description:** An executive search
firm. **Specializes in the areas of:** Communications;
Computer Science/Software; General Management;
Sales; Technical. **Positions commonly filled include:**
Computer Programmer; General Manager; Public
Relations Specialist; Software Engineer; Systems
Analyst; Technical Writer/Editor. **Number of
placements per year:** 50 - 99.

RUSSELL A. LAGER & ASSOCIATES
P.O. Box 60111, Seattle WA 98160. 206/448-2616.
Contact: Russell Lager, Owner. **Description:** An
executive search firm. **Specializes in the areas of:**
Consumer Package Goods.

LAWRENCE & ASSOCIATES
P.O. Box 6059, Kent WA 98064. 253/630-4939.
Contact: Manager. **Description:** An executive search
firm. **Specializes in the areas of:** Accounting/Auditing;
Finance.

MCE TECHNICAL SEARCH
4204 Meridian Street, Suite 101, Bellingham WA 98226.
360/671-5221. **Contact:** Manager. **Description:** An
executive search firm. **Specializes in the areas of:**
Technical.

MANAGEMENT RECRUITERS INTERNATIONAL
703 Broadway, Suite 695, Vancouver WA 98660.
360/695-4688. **Contact:** Manager. **Description:** An
executive search firm. **Specializes in the areas of:** High-
Tech; Medical Sales and Marketing. **Corporate
headquarters location:** Cleveland OH. **Other U.S.
locations:** Nationwide.

MANAGEMENT RECRUITERS INTERNATIONAL
2633A Parkmont Lane SW, Olympia WA 98502.
360/357-9996. **Contact:** Manager. **Description:** An
executive search firm. **Specializes in the areas of:**
Engineering; Health/Medical. **Corporate headquarters
location:** Cleveland OH. **Other U.S. locations:**
Nationwide.

MANAGEMENT RECRUITERS OF EVERETT
1727 East Marine View Drive, Suite B, Everett WA
98201. 425/303-0335. **Fax:** 425/303-0495. **Contact:**
John McElroy, Manager. **Description:** An executive
search firm. **Specializes in the areas of:** Engineering.
Corporate headquarters location: Cleveland OH.
Other U.S. locations: Nationwide.

MANAGEMENT RECRUITERS OF LAKEWOOD
6124 Motor Avenue SW, Tacoma WA 98499. 253/582-
8488. **Fax:** 253/582-8526. **Contact:** Manager.
Description: An executive search firm. **Specializes in
the areas of:** Biotech; Health/Medical; Information
Systems; I.T.; Pharmaceuticals; Telecommunications.
Corporate headquarters location: Cleveland OH.
Other U.S. locations: Nationwide.

MANAGEMENT RECRUITERS OF LYNNWOOD
19109 36th Avenue West, Suite 100, Lynnwood WA
98036. 425/778-1212. **Fax:** 425/778-7840. **Contact:** Bud

Naff, Owner. **Description:** An executive search firm
operating on a contingency basis. **Specializes in the
areas of:** Engineering; Health/Medical; Technical.
Positions commonly filled include: Biological Scientist;
Biomedical Engineer; Chemical Engineer; Chemist; Civil
Engineer; Clinical Lab Technician; Electrical/Electronics
Engineer; Geologist/Geophysicist; Industrial Engineer;
Licensed Practical Nurse; Mechanical Engineer; Medical
Records Technician; Meteorologist; Mining Engineer;
Nuclear Engineer; Occupational Therapist; Physical
Therapist; Physician; Radiological Technologist;
Registered Nurse; Transportation/Traffic Specialist.
Corporate headquarters location: Cleveland OH.
Other U.S. locations: Nationwide. **Average salary
range of placements:** More than $50,000. **Number of
placements per year:** 50 - 99.

**MANAGEMENT RECRUITERS OF MERCER
ISLAND**
9725 SE 36th Street, Suite 312, Mercer Island WA
98040-3896. 206/232-0204. **Fax:** 206/232-6172.
Contact: James J. Dykeman, Manager. **Description:** An
executive search firm. **Specializes in the areas of:**
Apparel; Computer Science/Software; Design; Electrical;
Engineering; Footwear; General Management;
Manufacturing; Operations Management;
Pharmaceuticals; Retail; Sales; Technical. **Corporate
headquarters location:** Cleveland OH. **Other U.S.
locations:** Nationwide. **Number of placements per
year:** 100 - 199.

**MANAGEMENT RECRUITERS OF NORTH
TACOMA**
2114 Pacific Avenue, Suite 115, Tacoma WA 98402.
253/572-7542. **Toll-free phone:** 800/779-1502. **Fax:**
253/572-7872. **Contact:** Bill Saylor, President/Manager.
E-mail address: mrint@msn.com. **Description:** An
executive search firm operating on both retainer and
contingency bases. **Specializes in the areas of:**
Administration; Computer Science/Software. **Positions
commonly filled include:** Applications Engineer;
Computer Operator; Computer Programmer; Database
Manager; Design Engineer; MIS Manager; MIS
Specialist; Sales Engineer; Software Engineer; Systems
Analyst; Systems Manager; Technical Writer/Editor.
Corporate headquarters location: Cleveland OH.
Other U.S. locations: Nationwide. **Average salary
range of placements:** More than $50,000. **Number of
placements per year:** 1 - 49.

MANAGEMENT RECRUITERS OF SEATTLE
2510 Fairview Avenue East, Seattle WA 98102-3216.
Toll-free phone: 800/237-6562. **Fax:** 206/328-3256.
Contact: Jamie Owen, Manager. **Description:** An
executive search firm operating on both retainer and
contingency bases. **Specializes in the areas of:**
Administration; Computer Science/Software;
Engineering; Food; General Management;
Manufacturing; Retail; Sales; Technical. **Positions
commonly filled include:** Aerospace Engineer;
Biochemist; Biological Scientist; Biomedical Engineer;
Branch Manager; Chemical Engineer; Chemist; Civil
Engineer; Computer Programmer; Design Engineer;
Designer; Electrical/Electronics Engineer; General
Manager; Industrial Engineer; Management
Analyst/Consultant; Manufacturer's/Wholesaler's Sales
Rep.; Mechanical Engineer; MIS Specialist; Multimedia
Designer; Operations/Production Manager; Quality
Control Supervisor; Restaurant/Food Service Manager;
Science Technologist; Services Sales Representative;
Software Engineer; Structural Engineer; Systems
Analyst; Telecommunications Manager. **Corporate
headquarters location:** Cleveland OH. **Other U.S.
locations:** Nationwide. **Average salary range of
placements:** More than $50,000. **Number of
placements per year:** 1 - 49.

MANAGEMENT RECRUITERS OF SPOKANE
316 West Boone Avenue, Suite 370, Spokane WA
99201. 509/324-3333. **Contact:** Manager. **Description:**
An executive search firm. **Specializes in the areas of:**
Banking; Computer Hardware/Software; Engineering;

Finance; Health/Medical; Pharmaceuticals. **Corporate headquarters location:** Cleveland OH. **Other U.S. locations:** Nationwide.

MANAGEMENT RECRUITERS OF TACOMA
2709 Jahn Avenue NW, Suite H-11, Gig Harbor WA 98335. 253/858-9991. **Contact:** Dennis Johnson, Manager. **Description:** An executive search firm. **Specializes in the areas of:** Accounting/Auditing; Administration; Advertising; Architecture/Construction; Banking; Communications; Computer Science/Software; Design; Electrical; Engineering; Finance; Food; General Management; Health/Medical; Insurance; Legal; Manufacturing; Operations Management; Personnel/ Labor Relations; Procurement; Publishing; Retail; Sales; Technical; Textiles; Transportation. **Positions commonly filled include:** Occupational Therapist; Physical Therapist; Speech-Language Pathologist. **Corporate headquarters location:** Cleveland OH. **Other U.S. locations:** Nationwide. **Number of placements per year:** 1 - 49.

MANAGEMENT SOLUTIONS
1809 Seventh Avenue, Suite 408, Seattle WA 98101. 206/344-6222. **Fax:** 206/344-8108. **Contact:** Manager. **Description:** An executive search firm. **Specializes in the areas of:** Accounting; Engineering; Finance; Human Resources; Information Technology.

MARITIME RECRUITERS
P.O. Box 260, Mercer Island WA 98040. 206/232-6041. **Contact:** Manager. **Description:** An executive search firm. **Specializes in the areas of:** Maritime.

JOHN MASON & ASSOCIATES
P.O. Box 3823, Bellevue WA 98009. 425/453-1608. **Fax:** 425/451-9214. **Contact:** John Mason, Manager. **World Wide Web address:** http://members.aol. com/masonsail/. **Description:** An executive search firm that places mid- to senior-level management professionals and provides human resources consulting for small to mid-size companies. Client company pays fee. **Specializes in the areas of:** Computer Science/ Software; Engineering; Finance; General Management; Internet Development; Internet Marketing; Personnel/ Labor Relations. **Positions commonly filled include:** Design Engineer; Electrical/Electronics Engineer; General Manager; Human Resources Manager; Manufacturer's/Wholesaler's Sales Rep.; Mechanical Engineer; MIS Specialist; Software Engineer; Structural Engineer; Systems Analyst; Telecommunications Manager. **Corporate headquarters location:** This Location. **Average salary range of placements:** $50,000 - $100,000. **Number of placements per year:** 50 - 99.

McINTIRE & CARR
P.O. Box 1176, Issaquah WA 98027. 425/391-9320. **Fax:** 425/391-9374. **Contact:** Merlin McIntire, Owner/Manager. **E-mail address:** mlm@halcyon.com. **Description:** An executive search firm. **Specializes in the areas of:** Sales. **Average salary range of placements:** More than $50,000. **Number of placements per year:** 50 - 99.

MILLER & MILLER EXECUTIVE SEARCH
401 Park Place, Suite 207, Kirkland WA 98033. 425/822-3145. **Contact:** Manager. **Description:** An executive search firm. **NOTE:** Jobseekers should call before sending a resume. **Specializes in the areas of:** Biomedical; Biotechnology.

MORGAN PALMER MORGAN & HILL
P.O. Box 13353, Burton WA 98013. 206/463-5721. **Contact:** Manager. **Description:** Morgan Palmer Morgan & Hill is an executive search firm. **Specializes in the areas of:** Finance.

THE OLDANI GROUP
188 106th Avenue NE, Suite 420, Bellevue WA 98004. 425/451-3938. **Fax:** 425/453-6786. **Contact:** Manager. **E-mail address:** searches@theoldanigroup.com. **World Wide Web address:** http://www.theoldanigroup.com. **Description:** An executive search firm. Founded in 1980.

OPUS CORPORATION
777 108th Avenue NE, Suite 2070, Bellevue WA 98004. 425/688-1904. **Fax:** 425/688-1957. **Contact:** Recruiter. **Description:** An executive search firm. **Specializes in the areas of:** Computer Science/Software.

ORION RESOURCES
1411 Fourth Avenue, Suite 1410, Seattle WA 98101. 206/382-8400. **Fax:** 206/382-9111. **Contact:** Recruiter. **Description:** An executive search firm. **Specializes in the areas of:** Accounting; Finance; Information Technology.

PMR MANAGEMENT RESOURCES
14130 SE 171st Way, Suite D301, Renton WA 98058. 206/510-7298. **Contact:** Manager. **E-mail address:** pmresources@msn.com. **Description:** An executive search firm. **Specializes in the areas of:** Construction.

PACE STAFFING NETWORK
2275 116th Avenue NE, Suite 200, Bellevue WA 98004. 425/454-1075. **Fax:** 425/646-4087. **Contact:** Manager. **World Wide Web address:** http://www. pacestaffing.com. **Description:** An executive search firm and full-service staffing agency. **Specializes in the areas of:** Computer Programming; Customer Service; Health/Medical; Manufacturing; Marketing; Office Support; Sales; Technical Writing. **Corporate headquarters location:** This Location. **Other area locations:** Fife WA; Kent WA; Mill Creek WA; Redmond WA; Seattle WA.

PACE STAFFING NETWORK
606 120th Avenue NE, Suite D104, Bellevue WA 98004. 425/455-9611. **Fax:** 425/646-7950. **Contact:** Recruiter. **World Wide Web address:** http://www. pacestaffing.com. **Description:** An executive search firm and full-service staffing agency. **Specializes in the areas of:** Computer Programming; Customer Service; Health/Medical; Manufacturing; Marketing; Office Support; Sales; Technical Writing. **Corporate headquarters location:** Bellevue WA. **Other area locations:** Bellevue WA; Fife WA; Kent WA; Mill Creek WA; Redmond WA; Seattle WA.

PACE STAFFING NETWORK
5580 Pacific Highway East, Suite E, Fife WA 98424-2500. 253/922-5508. **Fax:** 253/922-5703. **Contact:** Recruiter. **World Wide Web address:** http://www. pacestaffing. com. **Description:** An executive search firm and full-service staffing agency. **Specializes in the areas of:** Computer Programming; Customer Service; Health/Medical; Manufacturing; Marketing; Office Support; Sales; Technical Writing. **Corporate headquarters location:** Bellevue WA. **Other area locations:** Bellevue WA; Kent WA; Mill Creek WA; Redmond WA; Seattle WA.

PACE STAFFING NETWORK
19011 West Valley Highway, Suite A105, Kent WA 98032. 425/251-1200. **Fax:** 425/251-1934. **Contact:** Recruiter. **World Wide Web address:** http://www. pacestaffing.com. **Description:** An executive search firm and full-service staffing agency. **Specializes in the areas of:** Computer Programming; Customer Service; Health/Medical; Manufacturing; Marketing; Office Support; Sales; Technical Writing. **Corporate headquarters location:** Bellevue WA. **Other area locations:** Bellevue WA; Fife WA; Mill Creek WA; Redmond WA; Seattle WA.

PACE STAFFING NETWORK
16000 Bothell-Everett Highway, Suite 1000, Mill Creek WA 98012. 425/338-5416. **Fax:** 425/338-7834. **Contact:** Recruiter. **World Wide Web address:** http://www. pacestaffing.com. **Description:** An executive search firm and full-service staffing agency. **Specializes in the areas of:** Computer Programming; Customer Service;

Health/Medical; Manufacturing; Marketing; Office Support; Sales; Technical Writing. **Corporate headquarters location:** Bellevue WA. **Other area locations:** Bellevue WA; Fife WA; Kent WA; Redmond WA; Seattle WA.

PACE STAFFING NETWORK
15337 NE 90th Street, Redmond WA 98052. 425/558-3544. **Fax:** 425/558-3653. **Contact:** Recruiter. **World Wide Web address:** http://www.pacestaffing.com. **Description:** An executive search firm. **Specializes in the areas of:** Computer Programming; Customer Service; Health/Medical; Manufacturing; Marketing; Office Support; Sales; Technical Writing. **Corporate headquarters location:** Bellevue WA. **Other area locations:** Bellevue WA; Fife WA; Kent WA; Mill Creek WA; Seattle WA.

PACE STAFFING NETWORK
720 Third Avenue, Suite 2220, Seattle WA 98104. 206/623-1050. **Fax:** 206/467-8379. **Contact:** Recruiter. **World Wide Web address:** http://www.pacestaffing. com. **Description:** An executive search firm and full-service staffing agency. **Specializes in the areas of:** Computer Programming; Customer Service; Health/Medical; Manufacturing; Marketing; Office Support; Sales; Technical Writing. **Corporate headquarters location:** Bellevue WA. **Other area locations:** Bellevue WA; Fife WA; Kent WA; Mill Creek WA; Redmond WA.

PACIFIC LAW RECRUITERS
1424 Fourth Avenue, Suite 915, Seattle WA 98101. 206/625-0654. **Contact:** Manager. **Description:** An executive search firm. **Specializes in the areas of:** Legal.

PACIFIC PERSONNEL GROUP
2146 Westlake Avenue North, Seattle WA 98109. 206/284-5961. **Fax:** 206/284-5963. **Contact:** Marlaine Kirsch, Managing Principal. **Description:** An executive search firm operating on a contingency basis. **Specializes in the areas of:** Insurance. **Positions commonly filled include:** Account Representative; Accountant/Auditor; Adjuster; Claim Representative; Customer Service Representative; General Manager; Insurance Agent/Broker; Operations Manager; Sales Manager; Underwriter/Assistant Underwriter. **Average salary range of placements:** $30,000 - $50,000. **Number of placements per year:** 50 - 99.

PARKER PROFESSIONAL SEARCH
1420 Fifth Avenue, Suite 1450, Seattle WA 98101. 206/223-8991. **Fax:** 206/223-8227. **Contact:** Diane Daniel, Recruiter. **World Wide Web address:** http://www.parkerservices.com. **Description:** An executive search firm. Parker Professional Search is a division of Parker Services, Inc., which offers staffing, consulting, and skills training services. **Specializes in the areas of:** Finance; Human Resources; Information Technology; Marketing.

PASSAGE & ASSOCIATES
1001 Fourth Avenue, Suite 3200, Seattle WA 98154. 206/622-3330. **Contact:** Manager. **Description:** An executive search firm.

PEOPLE INCORPORATED
P.O. Box 157, Redmond WA 98073. 425/556-5151. **Fax:** 425/836-3114. **Contact:** Manager. **Description:** A generalist executive search firm.

PERSONNEL CONSULTANTS INC.
14042 NE Eighth Street, Suite 201, Bellevue WA 98007. 425/641-0657. **Contact:** Larry L. Dykes, Owner/President. **Description:** An executive search firm. **Specializes in the areas of:** Insurance; Sales. **Positions commonly filled include:** Actuary; Adjuster; Claim Representative; Collector; Insurance Agent/Broker; Investigator; Securities Sales Representative; Underwriter/Assistant Underwriter. **Number of placements per year:** 1 - 49.

PERSONNEL UNLIMITED INC.
West 25 Nora, Spokane WA 99205. 509/326-8880. **Fax:** 509/326-0112. **Contact:** Gary P. Desgrosellier, President. **Description:** An executive search firm. **Specializes in the areas of:** Accounting/Auditing; Administration; Clerical; Computer Science/Software; Engineering; Finance; Food; General Management; Health/Medical; Insurance; Legal; Manufacturing; Personnel/Labor Relations; Sales; Secretarial. **Positions commonly filled include:** Accountant/Auditor; Adjuster; Administrative Worker/Clerk; Agricultural Engineer; Bank Officer/Manager; Bookkeeper; Buyer; Ceramics Engineer; Chemical Engineer; Civil Engineer; Claim Representative; Clerical Supervisor; Collector; Computer Operator; Computer Programmer; Credit Manager; Customer Service Representative; Data Entry Clerk; Draftsperson; EDP Specialist; Electrical/Electronics Engineer; Financial Analyst; Food Scientist/Technologist; General Manager; Health Services Manager; Hotel Manager; Industrial Engineer; Investigator; Legal Secretary; Management Trainee; Manufacturer's/Wholesaler's Sales Rep.; Marketing Specialist; Materials Engineer; Mechanical Engineer; Medical Records Technician; Medical Secretary; Metallurgical Engineer; MIS Specialist; Operations/Production Manager; Public Relations Specialist; Purchasing Agent/Manager; Quality Control Supervisor; Receptionist; Registered Nurse; Secretary; Services Sales Representative; Statistician; Stenographer; Structural Engineer; Systems Analyst; Technical Writer/Editor; Technician; Travel Agent; Typist/Word Processor; Underwriter/Assistant Underwriter. **Number of placements per year:** 500 - 999.

PILON MANAGEMENT COMPANY
1809 Seventh Avenue, Suite 1010, Seattle WA 98101. 206/682-6465. **Fax:** 206/682-6468. **Contact:** Manager. **Description:** An executive search firm. **Specializes in the areas of:** Engineering; High-Tech; Manufacturing.

POWER CONVERSION INTERNATIONAL
120 West Dayton Street, Suite B6, Edmonds WA 98020. 425/771-3373. **Fax:** 425/771-3204. **Contact:** Manager. **Description:** An executive search firm. **Specializes in the areas of:** Electronics.

PRIOR/MARTECH ASSOCIATES, INC.
16000 Christensen Road, Suite 310, Seattle WA 98188. 206/242-1141. **Fax:** 206/242-1255. **Contact:** Manager. **Description:** An executive search firm that also offers management consulting. Founded in 1961.

PRO-ACTIVE CONSULTANTS
4395 South Discovery Road, Port Townsend WA 98368. 360/379-1500. **Fax:** 360/379-0104. **Contact:** Manager. **Description:** An executive search firm. **Specializes in the areas of:** Engineering; Wireless Communications.

PRO/SEARCH
8900 East Sprague Avenue, Spokane WA 99212. 509/928-3151. **Fax:** 509/928-3168. **Contact:** Manager. **Description:** A generalist executive search firm. Pro/Search is a division of Jobs Company.

ROI INTERNATIONAL
16040 Christensen Road, Suite 316, Seattle WA 98188. 206/248-5000. **Fax:** 206/248-5005. **Contact:** Manager. **E-mail address:** roi@roi-intl.com. **World Wide Web address:** http://www.roi-intl.com. **Description:** An executive search firm. Founded in 1993. **Specializes in the areas of:** Telecommunications.

REFFETT & ROBERTI & ASSOCIATES
10900 NE Fourth Street, Suite 2300, Bellevue WA 98004. 425/637-2993. **Contact:** Manager. **Description:** An executive search firm.

RICHARDS, WILLIAMS & ASSOCIATES
6232 76th Drive SE, Snohomish WA 98290. 425/672-3260. **Fax:** 425/334-9065. **Contact:** Manager. **Description:** An executive search firm.

RIGEL EXECUTIVE SEARCH
1611 116th Avenue NE, Bellevue WA 98004. 425/646-4990. **Fax:** 425/646-3058. **Contact:** Rita Ashley, President. **Description:** An executive search firm. **Specializes in the areas of:** Computer Science/Software. **Average salary range of placements:** More than $50,000. **Number of placements per year:** 50 - 99.

ROMAC INTERNATIONAL
500 108th Avenue NE, Suite 1780, Bellevue WA 98004. 425/454-6400. **Fax:** 425/688-0154. **Contact:** Manager. **Description:** An executive search firm. **Specializes in the areas of:** Computer Hardware/Software; Finance; Information Technology.

ROTH YOUNG EXECUTIVE SEARCH - SEATTLE
P.O. Box 3307, Bellevue WA 98009. 425/455-2141. **Fax:** 425/455-0067. **Contact:** David Salzberg, President. **E-mail address:** rothyoung@wolfenet.com. **World Wide Web address:** http://www.rothyoungseattle.com. **Description:** An executive search firm operating on both retainer and contingency bases. Roth Young Executive Search focuses on placing individuals in senior and mid-level management positions. Client company pays fee. **Specializes in the areas of:** Food; General Management; Industrial; Light Industrial; Marketing; Sales. **Positions commonly filled include:** Account Manager; Account Representative; Chief Financial Officer; Controller; Finance Director; Financial Analyst; Food Scientist/Technologist; General Manager; Human Resources Manager; Industrial Engineer; Industrial Production Manager; Manufacturing Engineer; Market Research Analyst; Marketing Manager; Marketing Specialist; Operations Manager; Production Manager; Quality Assurance Engineer; Quality Control Supervisor; Sales Executive; Sales Manager; Sales Representative; Vice President of Marketing. **Average salary range of placements:** $50,000 - $100,000. **Number of placements per year:** 50 - 99.

BARBARA RUHL & ASSOCIATES
15 Diamond S Ranch, Bellevue WA 98004. 425/452-9182. **Contact:** Manager. **Description:** An executive search firm. **Specializes in the areas of:** Finance; Mortgage.

SANDER ASSOCIATES
2011 Market Street, Kirkland WA 98033. 425/827-6446. **Fax:** 425/827-4283. **Contact:** Patti Jones, Owner. **Description:** An executive search firm operating on both retainer and contingency bases. **Specializes in the areas of:** Health/Medical. **Positions commonly filled include:** Clinician; Physician. **Number of placements per year:** 1 - 49.

SUSAN SCHOOS & ASSOCIATES
140 Lakeside Avenue, Suite 220, Seattle WA 98122. 206/324-4942. **Contact:** Manager. **Description:** An executive search firm. **Specializes in the areas of:** Construction; Engineering; Manufacturing.

SCHRENZEL TECHNICAL STAFFING
16526 161st Avenue Southeast, Renton WA 98058. 425/271-4700. **Fax:** 425/271-4722. **Contact:** Ben Schrenzel, Owner. **Description:** An executive search firm. **Specializes in the areas of:** High-Tech.

SCHULTZ GROUP INC.
401 Parkplace Center, Suite 207, Kirkland WA 98033. 425/822-1726. **Contact:** Manager. **Description:** An executive search firm. **Specializes in the areas of:** Information Systems.

SEATTLE RECRUITERS
1001 Fourth Avenue, Suite 3200, Seattle WA 98154. 206/467-6617. **Contact:** Manager. **Description:** An executive search firm. **Specializes in the areas of:** Legal.

SMALL BUSINESS SOLUTIONS INC.
4511 100th Street East, Tacoma WA 98446. 253/537-1040. **Fax:** 253/531-7323. **Contact:** Manager.

Description: An executive search firm. Founded in 1986. **Specializes in the areas of:** Accounting/Auditing; Computer Science/Software. **Positions commonly filled include:** Accountant/Auditor. **Average salary range of placements:** $20,000 - $29,999. **Number of placements per year:** 1 - 49.

WILSON SMITH ASSOCIATES
P.O. Box 12463, Mill Creek WA 98082-0463. 425/486-2900. **Fax:** 425/806-9107. **Contact:** Wilson Smith, Founder. **E-mail address:** info@wilsonsmith.com. **World Wide Web address:** http://www.wilsonsmith.com. **Description:** An executive search firm. Founded in 1999. **Specializes in the areas of:** Biotechnology; Engineering; Finance; High-Tech; Internet Development; Manufacturing; Marketing; Software Development.

SNELLING PERSONNEL
4301 South Pine Street, Suite 91, Tacoma WA 98409. 253/473-1800. **Fax:** 253/471-3060. **Contact:** Manager. **Description:** An executive search firm. **Specializes in the areas of:** Administration; Technical.

SNELLING PERSONNEL SERVICES
2101 Fourth Avenue, Suite 1330, Seattle WA 98121. 206/441-8895. **Fax:** 206/448-5373. **Contact:** Sue and Tom Truscott, Owners/Managers. **E-mail address:** snelling@serv.net. **World Wide Web address:** http://www.snelling.com/seattle. **Description:** An executive search firm operating on a contingency basis. Founded in 1966. **Specializes in the areas of:** Accounting/Auditing; Administration; Computer Science/Software; Finance; Marketing; Sales; Secretarial. **Positions commonly filled include:** Account Manager; Account Representative; Accountant; Administrative Assistant; Assistant Manager; Auditor; Branch Manager; Budget Analyst; Chief Financial Officer; Claim Representative; Clerical Supervisor; Computer Animator; Computer Operator; Computer Programmer; Controller; Credit Manager; Customer Service Representative; Database Manager; Finance Director; Financial Analyst; Marketing Manager; MIS Specialist; Multimedia Designer; Paralegal; Production Manager; Project Manager; Sales Engineer; Sales Executive; Sales Manager; Sales Representative; Secretary; Software Engineer; Systems Analyst; Systems Manager; Technical Writer/Editor; Typist/Word Processor; Underwriter/Assistant Underwriter; Webmaster. **Corporate headquarters location:** Dallas TX. **Other U.S. locations:** Nationwide. **Average salary range of placements:** $30,000 - $50,000. **Number of placements per year:** 200 - 499.

STEVEN & ASSOCIATES
1412 NE 152nd Avenue, Vancouver WA 98684. 360/896-6375. **Fax:** 360/896-6498. **Contact:** Manager. **Description:** An executive search firm. **NOTE:** This firm does not accept unsolicited resumes. Please only respond to advertised openings. **Specializes in the areas of:** Paper.

SUSAN STONEBERG EXECUTIVE SEARCH
8350 164th Avenue NE, Suite 303, Redmond WA 98052. 425/882-4862. **Contact:** Manager. **Description:** An executive search firm. **Positions commonly filled include:** Sales Manager; Sales Representative.

STRAIN PERSONNEL SPECIALISTS
2101 Ninth Avenue, Suite 204, Seattle WA 98121. 206/382-1588. **Fax:** 206/622-1572. **Contact:** Joe Strain, CPC, Partner. **Description:** An executive search firm operating on a retainer basis. Strain Personnel Specialists also provides some contract placements. **Specializes in the areas of:** Administration; Computer Science/Software; Engineering; Manufacturing; Personnel/Labor Relations; Technical. **Positions commonly filled include:** Computer Programmer; Design Engineer; Human Resources Manager; Internet Services Manager; Mathematician; MIS Specialist; Multimedia Designer; Science Technologist; Software Engineer; Systems Analyst; Technical Writer/Editor;

Telecommunications Manager. **Average salary range of placements:** More than $50,000. **Number of placements per year:** 50 - 99.

STRATEGIC RESOURCES
1607 116th Avenue NE, Suite 104, Bellevue WA 98004. 425/688-1151. **Fax:** 425/688-1272. **Contact:** Manager. **E-mail address:** info@strategicresources.com. **World Wide Web address:** http://www.strategicresources.com. **Description:** An executive search firm operating on a contingency basis. **Specializes in the areas of:** Advertising; Apparel; Casinos; Communications; Entertainment; Food; Legal; Marketing; Retail; Textiles.

STRATFORDGROUP
320 180th Avenue Northeast, Suite 600, Bellevue WA 98004. 425/462-7272. **Toll-free phone:** 800/536-4384. **Fax:** 425/462-0752. **Contact:** Recruiter. **World Wide Web address:** http://www.stratfordgroup.com. **Description:** An executive search firm operating on a retainer basis. Founded in 1997. **Specializes in the areas of:** Automotive; Consumer Products; Engineering; Entertainment; Finance; Health/Medical; Human Resources; Information Technology; Manufacturing; Nonprofit; Professional; Retail; Telecommunications; Transportation. **Corporate headquarters location:** Cleveland OH. **Other U.S. locations:** Nationwide.

TECHNICAL RESOURCE GROUP
9922 East Montgomery Street, Suite 5, Spokane WA 99206. 509/534-5208. **Toll-free phone:** 800/975-9000. **Contact:** Manager. **Description:** An executive search firm operating on both retainer and contingency bases. **Specializes in the areas of:** Administration; Engineering; Health/Medical; Personnel/Labor Relations. **Positions commonly filled include:** Actuary; Civil Engineer; Cost Estimator; Dental Assistant/Dental Hygienist; Engineer; Health Services Manager; Information Specialist; Occupational Therapist; Pharmacist; Physical Therapist; Physician; Speech-Language Pathologist; Systems Analyst; Telecommunications Manager. **Number of placements per year:** 50 - 99.

JAMES M. THOMAS & ASSOCIATES
3221 26th Avenue West, Seattle WA 98199. 206/283-9246. **Fax:** 206/285-1026. **Contact:** James Thomas, Owner. **Description:** An executive search firm. **Specializes in the areas of:** Health/Medical.

THOMPSON & ASSOCIATES
2448 76th Avenue SE, Suite 212, Mercer Island WA 98040. 206/236-0153. **Contact:** Manager. **Description:** An executive search firm. **Specializes in the areas of:** Computer Programming; High-Tech. **Positions commonly filled include:** Computer Programmer.

THOMSON, SPONAR & ADAMS, INC. (TSA)
10116 36th Avenue Court SW, Suite 200, Lakewood WA 98499. 253/588-1216. **Fax:** 253/588-2528. **Contact:** Frank Adams, President. **E-mail address:** tsa@tsacareers.com. **World Wide Web address:** http://www.tsacareers.com. **Description:** An executive search firm operating on both retainer and contingency bases. TSA primarily provides placements in the high-energy physics and superconductivity fields, as well as in cryogenics and electronics. **Specializes in the areas of:** Engineering; Scientific; Technical. **Positions commonly filled include:** Applications Engineer; Chemical Engineer; Design Engineer; Electrical/Electronics Engineer; General Manager; Industrial Engineer; Manufacturing Engineer; Mechanical Engineer; Metallurgical Engineer; Operations Manager; Project Manager; Quality Control Supervisor. **Other area locations:** Bellevue WA. **Average salary range of placements:** More than $50,000. **Number of placements per year:** 1 - 49.

THE TRIAD GROUP
12505 Bel-Red Road, Suite 208, Bellevue WA 98005. 425/454-0282. **Contact:** Manager. **Description:** An

executive search firm. **Specializes in the areas of:** Computer Science/Software.

TULLY/WOODMANSEE INTERNATIONAL
524 Sixth Avenue West, Suite 210, Seattle WA 98119. 206/285-9200. **Fax:** 206/285-9299. **Contact:** Manager. **Description:** A generalist executive search firm.

VILLENEUVE ASSOCIATES, INC. (VAI)
U.S. Bank Centre, 1420 Fifth Avenue, 22nd Floor, Seattle WA 98101. 425/836-8445. **Fax:** 425/868-7658. **Contact:** Cheryl Meyers, Manager, Recruiting & Resources. **E-mail address:** vai@vaisearch.com. **World Wide Web address:** http://www.vaisearch.com. **Description:** An executive search firm operating on a retainer basis and serving the retail, e-commerce, and food service industries. VAI also provides clients with succession planning, placement, and retention strategies across all disciplines. **Specializes in the areas of:** Food; Retail. **Corporate headquarters location:** This Location. **Other U.S. locations:** New York NY. **Number of placements per year:** 1000+.

WALDRON & COMPANY
101 Stewart Street, Suite 1200, Seattle WA 98101. 206/441-4144. **Contact:** Manager. **Description:** An executive search firm. **Specializes in the areas of:** Nonprofit.

R.A. WARD & ASSOCIATES
203 Bellevue Way NE, Suite 492, Bellevue WA 98004-5721. 800/639-8127. **Contact:** Recruiter. **E-mail address:** info@raward.com. **World Wide Web address:** http://www.raward.com. **Description:** An executive search firm. **Specializes in the areas of:** Health/Medical; Information Technology.

THE WASHINGTON FIRM
2 Nickerson Street, Courtyard Suite, Seattle WA 98109. 206/284-4800. **Fax:** 206/284-8844. **Contact:** Manager. **Description:** An executive search firm operating on a retainer basis. **Specializes in the areas of:** Administration; Computer Science/Software; General Management; Health/Medical; Nonprofit; Personnel/Labor Relations. **Positions commonly filled include:** Applications Engineer; Chief Financial Officer; Controller; Database Manager; Finance Director; Financial Analyst; General Manager; Human Resources Manager; Marketing Manager; MIS Specialist; Multimedia Designer; Online Content Specialist; Property and Real Estate Manager; Sales Executive; Sales Manager; Software Engineer; Structural Engineer; Systems Analyst; Technical Writer/Editor. **Average salary range of placements:** More than $50,000. **Number of placements per year:** 100 - 199.

WHITTALL MANAGEMENT GROUP
P.O. Box 3709, Federal Way WA 98063-3709. 253/874-0710. **Fax:** 253/952-2918. **Contact:** Manager. **Description:** An executive search firm operating on both retainer and contingency bases. **Specializes in the areas of:** Computer Science/Software; Engineering; Food; General Management; Industrial; Manufacturing; Personnel/Labor Relations; Sales; Technical. **Positions commonly filled include:** Computer Programmer; Construction Contractor; Design Engineer; Electrical/Electronics Engineer; Electrician; Environmental Engineer; Forester/Conservation Scientist; General Manager; Human Resources Manager; Industrial Engineer; Industrial Production Manager; Mechanical Engineer; MIS Specialist; Operations/Production Manager; Quality Control Supervisor; Software Engineer; Structural Engineer; Systems Analyst. **Average salary range of placements:** More than $50,000. **Number of placements per year:** 50 - 99.

WILLIAMS RECRUITING
16336 NE 81st Street, Redmond WA 98052. 425/869-7775. **Fax:** 425/869-1849. **Contact:** Gail Williams, President. **Description:** An executive search firm operating on both retainer and contingency bases. **Specializes in the areas of:** Biology; Engineering;

Health/Medical. **Positions commonly filled include:** Assistant Manager; Biochemist; Biological Scientist; Biomedical Engineer; Chemist; Database Manager; Design Engineer; Electrical/Electronics Engineer; General Manager; Marketing Manager; Mechanical Engineer; Operations Manager; Physician; Quality Control Supervisor; Statistician. **Average salary range of placements:** More than $50,000. **Number of placements per year:** 50 - 99.

WINSEARCH
900 Washington Street, Suite 800, Vancouver WA 98660. 206/343-0222. **Contact:** Manager. **Description:** An executive search firm. **Specializes in the areas of:** Computer Science/Software.

WOODRUFF ASSOCIATES
2450 Sixth Avenue South, Seattle WA 98134. 206/622-9634. **Fax:** 206/622-4149. **Contact:** Manager. **Description:** An executive search firm. **Specializes in the areas of:** Food; Wholesaling.

PERMANENT EMPLOYMENT AGENCIES

A.S.A.P. EMPLOYMENT SERVICES
4181 Wheaton Way, Suite 1, Bremerton WA 98310. 360/479-4310. **Contact:** Ralph and Roberta I. Long, Owners. **Description:** A permanent employment agency that also provides temporary placements. **Positions commonly filled include:** Accountant/Auditor; Administrative Worker/Clerk; Advertising Clerk; Bank Officer/Manager; Bookkeeper; Buyer; Civil Engineer; Claim Representative; Computer Operator; Computer Programmer; Credit Manager; Customer Service Representative; Data Entry Clerk; Draftsperson; Editor; EDP Specialist; Electrical/Electronics Engineer; General Manager; Hotel Manager; Industrial Engineer; Legal Secretary; Manufacturer's/Wholesaler's Sales Rep.; Mechanical Engineer; Medical Secretary; Nurse; Public Relations Specialist; Purchasing Agent/Manager; Quality Control Supervisor; Receptionist; Reporter; Secretary; Services Sales Representative; Stenographer; Systems Analyst; Technical Writer/Editor; Technician. **Number of placements per year:** 200 - 499.

ABLE PERSONNEL AGENCY
NT Office Building, North 4407 Division, Suite 625, Spokane WA 99207. 509/487-2734. **Contact:** William (Jay) Kinzer, Owner/Manager. **Description:** A permanent employment agency. Able Personnel Agency serves Spokane, eastern Washington, and northern Idaho. **Specializes in the areas of:** Accounting/Auditing; Clerical; Engineering; Finance; Sales. **Positions commonly filled include:** Accountant/Auditor; Administrative Worker/Clerk; Bookkeeper; Buyer; Claim Representative; Credit Manager; Customer Service Representative; Data Entry Clerk; Draftsperson; General Manager; Legal Secretary; Manufacturer's/Wholesaler's Sales Rep.; Marketing Specialist; Medical Secretary; Purchasing Agent/Manager; Receptionist; Secretary; Services Sales Representative; Stenographer; Typist/Word Processor. **Number of placements per year:** 50 - 99.

ACCUSTAFF
1000 Second Avenue, Suite 1700, Seattle WA 98104. 206/583-2711. **Fax:** 206/583-2725. **Contact:** B. Joy Pierson, CPC/CTS, Manager. **Description:** A permanent employment agency that also offers some temporary placements.

ACCUSTAFF
15 South Grady Way, Suite 422, Renton WA 98055. 425/204-9466. **Contact:** Manager. **Description:** A permanent employment agency. **Specializes in the areas of:** Light Industrial. **Other area locations:** Bellevue WA; Seattle WA.

ADAMS & ASSOCIATES
701 Fifth Avenue, Suite 3700, Seattle WA 98104. 206/447-9200. **Toll-free phone:** 800/597-6266. **Fax:** 206/447-9525. **Contact:** Marizol Ortiz, Branch Manager. **E-mail address:** seattle@adamsandassoc.com. **World Wide Web address:** http://www.adamsandassoc.com. **Description:** A permanent employment agency that also offers some temporary placements. Client company pays fee. **Specializes in the areas of:** Administration; Marketing; Sales; Secretarial. **Positions commonly filled include:** Account Representative; Accountant; Administrative Assistant; Administrative Manager;

Advertising Clerk; Assistant Manager; Blue-Collar Worker Supervisor; Branch Manager; Clerical Supervisor; Computer Operator; Computer Support Technician; Controller; Credit Manager; Customer Service Representative; Database Administrator; Database Manager; General Manager; Graphic Artist; Graphic Designer; Management Trainee; Marketing Specialist; Production Manager; Sales Representative; Secretary; Technical Writer/Editor; Typist/Word Processor. **Corporate headquarters location:** This Location. **Other area locations:** Bellevue WA. **Other U.S. locations:** Anchorage AK; Portland OR. **Average salary range of placements:** $20,000 - $49,999.

ASHFORD CLARK PERSONNEL
4215 198th Street SW, Suite 102, Lynnwood WA 98036. 425/774-9822. **Contact:** Manager. **Description:** A permanent employment agency.

ASPEN PERSONNEL SERVICES, INC.
2900 North Nevada Street, Spokane WA 99207. 509/624-4858. **Contact:** Manager. **Description:** A permanent employment agency that also provides temporary placements.

BUSINESS CAREERS
600 108th Avenue NE, Suite 246, Bellevue WA 98004. 206/447-7411. **Fax:** 425/462-5217. **Contact:** Manager. **Description:** A permanent placement agency. **Specializes in the areas of:** Accounting/Auditing; Office Support; Sales.

BUSINESS CAREERS
1001 Fourth Avenue, Suite 928, Seattle WA 98154. 206/447-7474. **Contact:** Manager. **Description:** A permanent employment agency. **Specializes in the areas of:** Accounting/Auditing; Office Support; Sales.

BUSINESS CAREERS
15 South Grady Way, Suite 333, Renton WA 98055. 206/447-7433. **Contact:** Manager. **Description:** A permanent employment agency. **Specializes in the areas of:** Accounting/Auditing; Office Support; Sales.

BUSINESS CAREERS
1019 Pacific Avenue, Suite 1716, Tacoma WA 98402. 253/383-1881. **Contact:** Manager. **Description:** A permanent employment agency. **Specializes in the areas of:** Accounting/Auditing; Office Support; Sales.

CMS (CONSTRUCTION MANAGEMENT SERVICES)
40 Lake Bellevue, Suite 100, Bellevue WA 98005. 425/868-2211. **Contact:** Mark Mannon, Owner. **Description:** A permanent employment agency. **Specializes in the areas of:** Construction. **Positions commonly filled include:** Civil Engineer; Construction and Building Inspector; Cost Estimator. **Average salary range of placements:** $30,000 - $50,000. **Number of placements per year:** 50 - 99.

CAREER SERVICES
677 George Washington Way, Richland WA 99352-4208. 509/946-0643. **Contact:** Bob and Jean B. McKee, Owners. **Description:** A permanent employment agency that also provides temporary placements. **Specializes in the areas of:** Accounting/Auditing; Industrial;

Professional; Sales; Secretarial; Technical; Word Processing. **Number of placements per year:** 50 - 99.

HALLMARK SERVICES
1904 Third Avenue, Suite 819, Seattle WA 98101. 206/587-5360. **Contact:** Delores Gohndrone, Owner. **Description:** A permanent employment agency. **Specializes in the areas of:** Clerical; Legal. **Positions commonly filled include:** Administrative Worker/Clerk; Receptionist; Secretary; Stenographer; Typist/Word Processor. **Number of placements per year:** 1 - 49.

HOSPITALITY EMPLOYMENT SERVICE
12308 East Broadway Avenue, Spokane WA 99216. 509/922-1187. **Fax:** 509/922-4647. **Contact:** Frank Pierson, Owner. **Description:** A permanent employment agency. **Specializes in the areas of:** Food. **Average salary range of placements:** Less than $20,000. **Number of placements per year:** 500 - 999.

HUMAN RESOURCES INC.
9725 SE 36th Street, Suite 100, Mercer Island WA 98040. 206/236-8094. **Fax:** 206/236-7658. **Contact:** Sheri Hervey, Vice President. **E-mail address:** hrmercer@accessone.com. **Description:** A permanent employment agency that also provides some temporary placements. Client company pays fee. **Specializes in the areas of:** Accounting; Administration; Secretarial. **Positions commonly filled include:** Accountant; Administrative Assistant; Controller; Customer Service Representative; Human Resources Manager; Secretary; Typist/Word Processor. **Other U.S. locations:** Auburn WA; Olympia WA; Renton WA; Tacoma WA. **Average salary range of placements:** $20,000 - $49,999. **Number of placements per year:** 500 - 999.

HUMAN RESOURCES INC.
2 Auburn Way North, Suite 102, Auburn WA 98002. 253/804-3477. **Contact:** Manager. **Description:** A permanent employment agency that also provides some temporary placements. **Other area locations:** Mercer Island WA; Olympia WA; Renton WA; Tacoma WA.

JOBS UNLIMITED
870 SW 136th Street, Seattle WA 98166. 206/243-8225. **Fax:** 206/244-2767. **Contact:** Donna Lenox, Manager. **Description:** A permanent employment agency. **Specializes in the areas of:** Industrial; Light Industrial; Marketing; Sales; Transportation. **Positions commonly filled include:** Accountant/Auditor; Aerospace Engineer; Aircraft Mechanic/Engine Specialist; Automotive Mechanic; Blue-Collar Worker Supervisor; Construction and Building Inspector; Construction Contractor; Customer Service Representative; Draftsperson; Driver; Electrical/Electronics Engineer; Electrician; Industrial Engineer; Industrial Production Manager; Mechanical Engineer; Operations/Production Manager; Quality

Control Supervisor; Secretary. **Number of placements per year:** 1000+.

MACROSEARCH
MACROSTAFF
13353 Bel Red Road, Suite 206, Bellevue WA 98005. 425/641-7252. **Fax:** 425/641-0969. **Contact:** Manager. **Description:** A permanent employment agency. Macrostaff (also at this location) is a contract services firm. **Specializes in the areas of:** Information Systems; Software Engineering. **Corporate headquarters location:** This Location.

MACROSEARCH
MACROSTAFF
621 Woodland Square Loop, Suite 6, Lacey WA 98503. 360/459-2699. **Fax:** 360/459-2109. **Contact:** Lynne Durrell, Manager. **World Wide Web address:** http://www.macrosearch.com. **Description:** A permanent employment agency. Macrostaff (also at this location) is a contract services firm. Client company pays fee. **Specializes in the areas of:** Computer Science/Software. **Positions commonly filled include:** Computer Animator; Computer Operator; Computer Programmer; Database Manager; Design Engineer; Information Systems Director; Internet Services Manager; MIS Specialist; Multimedia Designer; Software Engineer; Systems Analyst; Systems Manager; Technical Writer/Editor; Telecommunications Manager. **Benefits available to temporary workers:** Dental Insurance; Life Insurance; Medical Insurance. **Corporate headquarters location:** Bellevue WA. **Average salary range of placements:** More than $50,000. **Number of placements per year:** 1 - 49.

JACK PORTER & ASSOCIATES
24119 SE 18th Place, Issaquah WA 98029. 425/392-9252. **Fax:** 425/391-9107. **Contact:** Jack Porter, President. **Description:** A permanent employment agency. **Specializes in the areas of:** Engineering; Manufacturing. **Positions commonly filled include:** Aerospace Engineer; Agricultural Engineer; Biochemist; Biological Scientist; Biomedical Engineer; Chemical Engineer; Chemist; Civil Engineer; Construction Contractor; Cost Estimator; Design Engineer; Electrical/Electronics Engineer; Environmental Engineer; Food Scientist/Technologist; General Manager; Geologist/Geophysicist; Industrial Engineer; Industrial Production Manager; Management Trainee; Manufacturer's/Wholesaler's Sales Rep.; Mathematician; Mechanical Engineer; Mining Engineer; MIS Specialist; Operations/Production Manager; Petroleum Engineer; Quality Control Supervisor; Science Technologist; Software Engineer; Stationary Engineer; Statistician; Structural Engineer; Systems Analyst; Telecommunications Manager. **Number of placements per year:** 1 - 49.

TEMPORARY EMPLOYMENT AGENCIES

ACCOUNTANTS INC.
1420 Fifth Avenue, Suite 1711, Seattle WA 98101. 206/621-0111. **Fax:** 206/621-0285. **Contact:** Manager. **E-mail address:** seattle@accountantsinc.com. **World Wide Web address:** http://www.accountantsinc.com. **Description:** Accountants Inc. is a temporary agency that also offers some permanent placements. **Specializes in the areas of:** Accounting; Finance. **Corporate headquarters location:** Burlingame CA. **Other area locations:** Bellevue WA. **Other U.S. locations:** Nationwide.

ACCOUNTANTS INC.
500 108th Avenue NE, Suite 2350, Bellevue WA 98004. 425/454-4111. **Fax:** 425/454-4906. **Contact:** Manager. **E-mail address:** bellevue@accountantsinc.com. **World Wide Web address:** http://www.accountantsinc.com. **Description:** Accountants Inc. is a temporary agency that also offers some permanent placements. **Specializes in the areas of:** Accounting; Finance. **Corporate**

headquarters location: Burlingame CA. **Other area locations:** Seattle WA. **Other U.S. locations:** Nationwide.

AQUENT PARTNERS
1525 Fourth Avenue, Suite 500, Seattle WA 98101-1607. 206/622-2800. **Toll-free phone:** 877/PARTNER. **Fax:** 206/622-6426. **Contact:** Tom Linde, Manager. **E-mail address:** tlinde@aquent.com. **World Wide Web address:** http://www.aquentpartners.com. **Description:** A temporary agency that provides placements for creative, Web, and technical professionals. Aquent Partners also provides some temp-to-perm, permanent, and contract placements. **Specializes in the areas of:** Administration; Art/Design; Computer Science/Software; Marketing. **Positions commonly filled include:** Computer Animator; Computer Engineer; Computer Operator; Computer Programmer; Computer Support Technician; Computer Technician; Content Developer; Database Administrator; Database Manager; Desktop

Publishing Specialist; Editor; Editorial Assistant; Graphic Artist; Graphic Designer; Internet Services Manager; Managing Editor; MIS Specialist; Multimedia Designer; Network/Systems Administrator; Production Manager; Project Manager; Software Engineer; SQL Programmer; Systems Analyst; Systems Manager; Technical Writer/Editor; Webmaster. **Benefits available to temporary workers:** 401(k); Dental Insurance; Disability Coverage; Medical Insurance. **CEO:** John Chuang.

COMPREHENSIVE STAFFING RESOURCES INC. dba TECHSTAFF
720 Olive Way, Suite 1510, Seattle WA 98101. 206/382-5555. **Fax:** 206/382-5556. **Contact:** Manager. **Description:** A temporary agency. **Specializes in the areas of:** Administration; Architecture/Construction; Computer Science/Software; Engineering; Personnel/Labor Relations; Technical; Transportation. **Positions commonly filled include:** Architect; Civil Engineer; Computer Programmer; Construction and Building Inspector; Design Engineer; Designer; Draftsperson; Electrical/Electronics Engineer; Environmental Engineer; Forester/Conservation Scientist; Geologist/Geophysicist; Industrial Engineer; Internet Services Manager; Landscape Architect; Mechanical Engineer; MIS Specialist; Multimedia Designer; Software Engineer; Structural Engineer; Surveyor; Systems Analyst; Technical Writer/Editor; Urban/Regional Planner. **Benefits available to temporary workers:** 401(k); Paid Holidays; Referral Bonus Plan. **Average salary range of placements:** $30,000 - $50,000. **Number of placements per year:** 100 - 199.

CONMARKE USA INC.
18717 76th Avenue West, Suite I, Lynnwood WA 98037-4111. 425/712-1948. **Toll-free phone:** 800/417-8168. **Fax:** 425/712-7087. **Contact:** Ed Clendenning, President. **Description:** A temporary agency. **Specializes in the areas of:** Engineering. **Positions commonly filled include:** Cost Estimator; Design Engineer; Designer; Draftsperson; Electrical/Electronics Engineer. **Benefits available to temporary workers:** 401(k). **Average salary range of placements:** $30,000 - $50,000. **Number of placements per year:** 50 - 99.

COOPER PERSONNEL
1411 Fourth Avenue, Suite 1327, Seattle WA 98101. 206/583-0722. **Fax:** 206/223-4093. **Contact:** Bonnie Cooper, CPC/Owner. **Description:** A temporary agency that also provides some permanent placements. **Specializes in the areas of:** Administration; Legal; Secretarial. **Positions commonly filled include:** Administrative Assistant; Clerical Supervisor; Computer Operator; Customer Service Representative; Database Manager; Legal Secretary; Paralegal; Purchasing Agent/Manager; Receptionist; Secretary; Typist/Word Processor. **Average salary range of placements:** $20,000 - $29,999. **Number of placements per year:** 200 - 499.

CREATIVE ASSETS
101 Yesler Way, Suite 200, Seattle WA 98104. 206/682-6005. **Fax:** 206/682-5830. **Contact:** Kelly Rust, Recruiter. **World Wide Web address:** http://www.creativeassets.com. **Description:** A temporary agency that also provides permanent and contract placements. **Specializes in the areas of:** Art/Design; Publishing. **Positions commonly filled include:** Designer; Internet Services Manager; Multimedia Designer; Technical Writer/Editor; Video Production Coordinator. **Benefits available to temporary workers:** Medical Insurance. **Other U.S. locations:** Los Angeles CA; San Francisco CA; Denver CO; Portland OR. **Number of placements per year:** 500 - 999.

EXPRESS PERSONNEL SERVICES
222 South Washington Street, Spokane WA 99201. 509/747-6011. **Fax:** 509/747-8930. **Contact:** Manager. **Description:** A temporary agency that also provides some permanent placements. **Specializes in the areas of:** Accounting/Auditing; Computer Science/Software; General Management; Insurance; Personnel/Labor Relations. **Positions commonly filled include:** Accountant/Auditor; Adjuster; Architect; Attorney; Blue-Collar Worker Supervisor; Branch Manager; Credit Manager; Designer; Draftsperson. **Corporate headquarters location:** Oklahoma City OK. **Other U.S. locations:** Nationwide. **Average salary range of placements:** $20,000 - $29,999. **Number of placements per year:** 1000+.

EXPRESS PERSONNEL SERVICES
230 North Mission Street, Wenatchee WA 98801. 509/662-5187. **Fax:** 509/662-5285. **Contact:** Gene Anderson, President. **Description:** A temporary agency. **Specializes in the areas of:** Accounting/Auditing; Engineering; Food; Health/Medical; Industrial; Manufacturing; Sales; Secretarial. **Positions commonly filled include:** Accountant/Auditor; Agricultural Engineer; Automotive Mechanic; Bank Officer/Manager; Branch Manager; Buyer; Chemist; Clerical Supervisor; Computer Programmer; Construction Contractor; Cost Estimator; Customer Service Representative; Dental Assistant/Dental Hygienist; Draftsperson; EEG Technologist; EKG Technician; Electrician; Emergency Medical Technician; Food Scientist/Technologist; General Manager; Industrial Production Manager; Insurance Agent/Broker; Licensed Practical Nurse; Management Trainee; Manufacturer's/Wholesaler's Sales Rep.; Mechanical Engineer; Medical Records Technician; Metallurgical Engineer; Occupational Therapist; Operations/Production Manager; Physical Therapist; Quality Control Supervisor; Recreational Therapist; Registered Nurse; Respiratory Therapist; Restaurant/Food Service Manager; Securities Sales Representative; Surgical Technician; Typist/Word Processor. **Benefits available to temporary workers:** Medical Insurance; Paid Holidays; Paid Vacation. **Other U.S. locations:** Nationwide. **Average salary range of placements:** $20,000 - $29,999. **Number of placements per year:** 1000+.

EXPRESS PERSONNEL SERVICES
4027 Hoyt Avenue, Suite 101A, Everett WA 98201. 425/339-8400. **Contact:** Manager. **Description:** A temporary agency that also provides permanent placements and career/outplacement counseling services. **Specializes in the areas of:** Accounting/Auditing; Advertising; Banking; Computer Science/Software; Insurance; Legal; Manufacturing; Personnel/Labor Relations; Publishing; Secretarial; Technical. **Positions commonly filled include:** Blue-Collar Worker Supervisor; Claim Representative; Clerical Supervisor; Credit Manager; Customer Service Representative; Human Resources Specialist; Public Relations Specialist; Purchasing Agent/Manager; Quality Control Supervisor; Software Engineer; Systems Analyst; Typist/Word Processor. **Benefits available to temporary workers:** Medical Insurance; Paid Holidays; Paid Vacation. **Other U.S. locations:** Nationwide. **Average salary range of placements:** Less than $20,000. **Number of placements per year:** 1000+.

GUIDANCE SERVICES INC.
1010 South 336th Street, Suite 122, Federal Way WA 98003. 253/838-2401. **Contact:** Manager. **Description:** A temporary agency. **Specializes in the areas of:** Accounting/Auditing; Banking; Finance; Legal; Manufacturing; Personnel/Labor Relations; Secretarial. **Positions commonly filled include:** Accountant/Auditor; Administrative Manager; Attorney; Branch Manager; Claim Representative; Clerical Supervisor; Credit Manager; Customer Service Representative; Financial Analyst; General Manager; Health Services Manager; Human Resources Specialist; Medical Records Technician; Paralegal. **Other U.S. locations:** AZ; NY; OR; VA. **Number of placements per year:** 200 - 499.

KELLY SERVICES, INC.
703 Broadway, Suite 102, Vancouver WA 98660. 360/699-5337. **Fax:** 360/737-0489. **Contact:** Manager.

World Wide Web address: http://www.
kellyservices.com. **Description:** A temporary agency.
Founded in 1946. **Specializes in the areas of:**
Administration; Industrial; Light Industrial;
Manufacturing; Personnel/Labor Relations; Sales;
Secretarial; Technical. **Positions commonly filled
include:** Accountant/Auditor; Clerical Supervisor;
Customer Service Representative; Typist/Word
Processor. **Benefits available to temporary workers:**
Paid Holidays; Paid Vacation. **Corporate headquarters
location:** Troy MI. **Other U.S. locations:** Nationwide.
Average salary range of placements: $20,000 -
$29,999. **Number of placements per year:** 500 - 999.

KELLY SERVICES, INC.
16040 Christensen Road, Suite 205, Seattle WA 98188.
206/243-7409. **Toll-free phone:** 800/591-9455. **Contact:**
Manager. **World Wide Web address:**
http://www.kellyservices.com. **Description:** A temporary
agency. **Specializes in the areas of:** Administration;
Computer Science/Software; Insurance; Manufacturing;
Personnel/Labor Relations; Secretarial; Technical.
Positions commonly filled include: Accountant/Auditor;
Administrative Manager; Blue-Collar Worker
Supervisor; Claim Representative; Clerical Supervisor;
Computer Programmer; Customer Service
Representative; Draftsperson; Human Resources
Specialist; Industrial Production Manager; MIS
Specialist; Software Engineer; Systems Analyst;
Technical Writer/Editor; Typist/Word Processor.
Benefits available to temporary workers: Paid
Holidays; Paid Vacation. **Corporate headquarters
location:** Troy MI. **Other U.S. locations:** Nationwide.
Average salary range of placements: Less than
$20,000. **Number of placements per year:** 1000+.

KELLY SERVICES, INC.
1735 Cedardale Road, Suite A400, Mount Vernon WA
98274. 360/424-4858. **Toll-free phone:** 800/863-6238.
Contact: Manager. **World Wide Web address:**
http://www.kellyservices.com. **Description:** A temporary
agency that also provides contract services. **Specializes
in the areas of:** Accounting/Auditing; Administration;
Computer Science/Software; Finance; Food; General
Management; Industrial; Insurance; Personnel/Labor
Relations; Retail; Secretarial; Technical. **Positions
commonly filled include:** Accountant/Auditor;
Administrative Manager; Blue-Collar Worker
Supervisor; Claim Representative; Clerical Supervisor;
Computer Programmer; Customer Service
Representative; Electrician; Human Resources Specialist;
Management Trainee; MIS Specialist; Restaurant/Food
Service Manager; Software Engineer; Systems Analyst;
Technical Writer/Editor; Typist/Word Processor.
Benefits available to temporary workers: Paid
Holidays; Paid Vacation. **Corporate headquarters
location:** Troy MI. **Other U.S. locations:** Nationwide.
Average salary range of placements: Less than
$20,000. **Number of placements per year:** 500 - 999.

LABOR READY, INC.
1222 Tacoma Avenue South, Tacoma WA 98402.
253/383-8909. **Contact:** Manager. **Description:** A
temporary agency. **Specializes in the areas of:**
Construction; Manufacturing. **Other U.S. locations:**
Natiowide.

MANPOWER TEMPORARY SERVICES
1420 Fifth Avenue, Suite 1750, Seattle WA 98101.
206/583-0880. **Contact:** Branch Manager. **Description:**
A temporary agency. **Specializes in the areas of:**
Industrial; Office Support; Technical; Word Processing.
Positions commonly filled include: Accountant/Auditor;
Accounting Clerk; Administrative Manager; Assembler;
Biological Scientist; Bookkeeper; Chemist; Computer
Operator; Customer Service Representative; Designer;
Desktop Publishing Specialist; Electrician; Inventory
Control Specialist; Machine Operator; Materials
Manager; Order Clerk; Packaging Manager; Records
Manager; Research Assistant; Secretary; Software
Engineer; Stenographer; Systems Analyst; Technical
Writer/Editor; Telemarketer; Typist/Word Processor.

Benefits available to temporary workers: Life
Insurance; Medical Insurance; Paid Holidays; Paid
Vacation. **Corporate headquarters location:**
Milwaukee WI. **International locations:** Worldwide.
Number of placements per year: 1000+.

MANPOWER TEMPORARY SERVICES
10049 Kitsap Mall Boulevard NW, Suite 108, Silverdale
WA 98383. 360/698-2592. **Fax:** 360/698-7369. **Contact:**
Linda Patterson, Branch Manager. **World Wide Web
address:** http://www.manpower.com. **Description:** A
temporary agency. **Specializes in the areas of:**
Accounting/Auditing; Administration; Computer
Science/Software; Industrial; Insurance; Legal; Light
Industrial; Personnel/Labor Relations; Retail; Sales;
Secretarial; Transportation. **Positions commonly filled
include:** Accountant/Auditor; Administrative Assistant;
Administrative Manager; Buyer; Clerical Supervisor;
Customer Service Representative; Database Manager;
Editorial Assistant; Human Resources Manager;
Paralegal; Sales Executive; Sales Manager; Sales
Representative; Secretary; Typist/Word Processor.
Benefits available to temporary workers: Life
Insurance; Medical Insurance; Paid Holidays; Paid
Vacation; Stock Purchase. **Corporate headquarters
location:** Milwaukee WI. **International locations:**
Worldwide.

**NORTHWEST TEMPORARY & STAFFING
SERVICES, INC.**
50 116th Avenue SE, Bellevue WA 98004. 425/453-
2310. **Fax:** 425/451-9285. **Contact:** Valerie Nickles,
Area Manager. **World Wide Web address:**
http://www.ntss.com. **Description:** A temporary agency.
Specializes in the areas of: Accounting/Auditing;
General Management; Health/Medical; Industrial; Legal;
Light Industrial; Marketing; Retail; Sales; Secretarial;
Technical. **Positions commonly filled include:**
Accountant; Administrative Assistant; Administrative
Manager; Auditor; Blue-Collar Worker Supervisor;
Budget Analyst; Buyer; Chief Financial Officer; Claim
Representative; Clerical Supervisor; Computer Operator;
Credit Manager; Customer Service Manager; Database
Manager; Editorial Assistant; Finance Director; Financial
Analyst; General Manager; Human Resources Manager;
Librarian; Management Trainee; Operations Manager;
Paralegal; Production Manager; Project Manager;
Purchasing Agent/Manager; Quality Control Supervisor;
Sales Representative; Secretary; Typist/Word Processor.
Benefits available to temporary workers: 401(k);
Bonus Award/Plan; Paid Holidays; Paid Vacation.
Corporate headquarters location: Portland OR.
Average salary range of placements: $20,000 -
$29,999. **Number of placements per year:** 1000+.

OLSTEN STAFFING SERVICES
19115 West Valley Highway, Suite H110, Kent WA
98032. 425/656-4199. **Contact:** Manager. **Description:**
A temporary agency. **Specializes in the areas of:**
Administration; Computer Science/Software;
Manufacturing; Personnel/Labor Relations; Secretarial.
Positions commonly filled include: Administrative
Manager; Claim Rep.; Clerical Supervisor; Computer
Programmer; Customer Service Representative; Human
Resources Specialist; Industrial Production Manager;
Management Trainee; Manufacturer's/Wholesaler's Sales
Rep.; Medical Records Technician; MIS Specialist;
Operations/Production Manager; Systems Analyst;
Technical Writer/Editor; Typist/Word Processor.
Corporate headquarters location: Melville NY.
International locations: Worldwide. **Number of
placements per year:** 1000+.

OLSTEN STAFFING SERVICES
601 Union Street, Suite 732, 2 Union Square, Seattle WA
98101. 206/441-2962. **Fax:** 206/464-1711. **Contact:**
Manager. **Description:** A temporary agency. **Specializes
in the areas of:** Administration; Industrial;
Manufacturing; Personnel/Labor Relations; Secretarial.
Positions commonly filled include: Blue-Collar Worker
Supervisor; Customer Service Representative; Services
Sales Representative; Typist/Word Processor. **Benefits**

available to temporary workers: Paid Vacation; Referral Bonus Plan. **Corporate headquarters location:** Melville NY. **Number of placements per year:** 1000+.

RESOURCE MANAGEMENT INTERNATIONAL
15 South Grady Way, Suite 421, Renton WA 98055. 425/226-3000. **Contact:** Manager. **Description:** A temporary agency. **Specializes in the areas of:** Art/Design; Computer Science/Software; Engineering. **Positions commonly filled include:** Aerospace Engineer; Agricultural Engineer; Aircraft Mechanic/ Engine Specialist; Architect; Buyer; Chemical Engineer; Chemist; Civil Engineer; Computer Programmer; Cost Estimator; Design Engineer; Designer; Draftsperson; Editor; Electrical/Electronics Engineer; Electrician; Environmental Engineer; Geologist/Geophysicist; Industrial Engineer; Industrial Production Manager;

Mechanical Engineer; Metallurgical Engineer; Mining Engineer; Nuclear Medicine Technologist; Quality Control Supervisor; Software Engineer; Structural Engineer; Systems Analyst; Technical Writer/Editor; Telecommunications Manager; Typist/Word Processor. **Benefits available to temporary workers:** 401(k); Medical Insurance; Paid Holidays; Paid Vacation. **Average salary range of placements:** More than $50,000. **Number of placements per year:** 100 - 199.

WOODS & ASSOCIATES
1221 Second Avenue, Suite 330, Seattle WA 98101. 206/623-2930. **Fax:** 206/623-1216. **Contact:** Manager. **Description:** A temporary agency that also provides permanent placements. **NOTE:** Please call for an appointment before sending a resume. **Specializes in the areas of:** Legal.

CONTRACT SERVICES FIRMS

CDI CORPORATION (WEST)
104 South Freya, Yellow Flag Building, Spokane WA 99202. 509/535-6852. **Fax:** 509/536-4333. **Contact:** Robin Lovejoy, Branch Manager. **World Wide Web address:** http://www.cdicorp.com. **Description:** A contract services firm. **Specializes in the areas of:** Aerospace; Chemicals; Communications; Computer Hardware/Software; Electronics; Manufacturing; Medical Technology; Mining; Paper; Transportation. **Positions commonly filled include:** Computer Programmer; Designer; Draftsperson; Engineer; Systems Analyst; Technical Illustrator; Technical Writer/Editor; Technician. **Corporate headquarters location:** Philadelphia PA. **Other U.S. locations:** Nationwide. **International locations:** Worldwide. **Average salary range of placements:** $30,000 - $50,000. **Number of placements per year:** 500 - 999.

CTS INTERNATIONAL
11100 NE Eighth Street, Suite 510, Bellevue WA 98004. 425/451-0051. **Contact:** Manager. **Description:** A contract services firm. **Specializes in the areas of:** Aerospace; Computer Hardware/Software.

COMFORCE TECHNICAL SERVICES, INC.
P.O. Box 97003, Redmond WA 98073-9703. 425/883-2233. **Toll-free phone:** 800/398-2432. **Fax:** 800/643-5474. **Contact:** Manager. **Description:** A contract services firm. **Specializes in the areas of:** High-Tech; Technical.

COMFORCE TECHNICAL SERVICES, INC.
4905 Pacific Highway East, Suite 2A, Tacoma WA 98424. 253/922-9119. **Fax:** 253/922-9274. **Contact:** Manager. **Description:** A contract services firm. **Specializes in the areas of:** Technical.

HALL KINION
2825 Eastlake Avenue East, Suite 120, Seattle WA 98102. **Toll-free phone:** 888/270-6008. **Fax:** 206/726-8833. **Contact:** Manager. **E-mail address:** searesume@hallkinion.com. **World Wide Web address:**

http://www.hallkinion.com. **Description:** A contract services firm that also provides some permanent placements. **Specializes in the areas of:** Information Systems; Information Technology; Internet Development; Network Administration; Quality Assurance; Systems Administration; Systems Design; Technical Writing. **Other area locations:** Bellevue WA.

HALL KINION
3001 112th Avenue NE, Bellevue WA 98004. **Fax:** 425/889-5985. **Contact:** Manager. **E-mail address:** waresume@hallkinion.com. **World Wide Web address:** http://www.hallkinion.com. **Description:** A contract services firm that also provides some permanent placements. **Specializes in the areas of:** Computer Hardware/Software; Information Systems; Information Technology; Internet Development; Network Administration; Quality Assurance; Systems Administration; Systems Design; Technical Writing. **Other area locations:** Seattle WA.

TECHNISOURCE
8440 154th Avenue NE, Building M, Bellevue WA 98052. 425/883-6612. **Fax:** 425/497-1044. **Contact:** Manager. **World Wide Web address:** http://www.tsrc.net. **Description:** A contract services firm. **Specializes in the areas of:** Administration; Computer Science/Software; High-Tech; Technical.

H.L. YOH COMPANY
705 Main Street, Suite 201, Vancouver WA 98660. 360/696-2644. **Contact:** Manager. **Description:** A contract services firm. **Specializes in the areas of:** Computer Hardware/Software; High-Tech. **Other area locations:** Seattle WA.

H.L. YOH COMPANY
130 Andover Park East, Suite 304, Seattle WA 98188. 206/241-0549. **Contact:** Manager. **Description:** A contract services firm. **Other area locations:** Vancouver WA.

CAREER/OUTPLACEMENT COUNSELING FIRMS

CAREER IMPROVEMENT GROUP, INC. (CIG)
10900 NE Eighth Street, Suite 900, Bellevue WA 98004. 425/451-7996. **Contact:** Manager. **E-mail address:** cig@accessone.com. **Description:** A career/outplacement counseling firm. Founded in 1982. **Other U.S. locations:** Seattle WA.

CAREER IMPROVEMENT GROUP, INC. (CIG)
4010 Stoneway North, Suite 200, Seattle WA 98103. 206/545-1155. **Contact:** Manager. **E-mail address:**

cig@accessone.com. **Description:** A career/outplacement counseling firm. Founded in 1982. **Other U.S. locations:** Bellevue WA.

PACIFIC ASSOCIATES
2200 Sixth Avenue, Suite 260, Seattle WA 98121. 206/728-8826. **Contact:** Manager. **Description:** A career/outplacement counseling firm that also offers training programs.

EXECUTIVE SEARCH FIRMS

CAPITOL EXECUTIVE RESOURCES
Board of Trade Building, 12th Street, Wheeling WV 26003. 304/232-6065. **Fax:** 304/232-2257. **Contact:** Manager. **Description:** A full-service executive search firm that also offers temp-to-perm placements.

CAPITOL EXECUTIVE RESOURCES
714 1/2 Lee Street, Suite 6, Charleston WV 25301. 304/343-6640. **Contact:** Manager. **Description:** An executive search firm.

DUNHILL PROFESSIONAL SEARCH
P.O. Box 547, Charleston WV 25322. 304/340-4260. **Fax:** 304/340-4262. **Contact:** Manager. **Description:** An executive search firm. **Specializes in the areas of:** Engineering; Health/Medical; Sales.

MANAGEMENT RECRUITERS INTERNATIONAL
3983 Teays Valley Road, Hurricane WV 25526. 304/757-4399. **Fax:** 304/757-4398. **Contact:** Harry Ray, Account Executive. **Description:** An executive search firm for the power and utilities industries.

MANAGEMENT RECRUITERS OF CHARLESTON
1587 East Washington Street, Charleston WV 25311. 304/344-5632. **Fax:** 304/344-5639. **Contact:** Tony Oliverio, President. **Description:** An executive search firm operating on both retainer and contingency bases.

Client company pays fee. **Specializes in the areas of:** Chemicals; Electrical; Engineering. **Positions commonly filled** include: Electrical/Electronics Engineer. **Corporate headquarters location:** Cleveland OH. **Other U.S. locations:** Nationwide. **Average salary range of placements:** $50,000 - $100,000. **Number of placements per year:** 50 - 99.

MANAGEMENT RECRUITERS OF MORGANTOWN
1714 Mileground Road, Morgantown WV 26505. 304/284-8500. **Fax:** 304/284-8985. **Contact:** Manager. **Description:** An executive search firm. **Specializes in the areas of:** Health/Medical.

PRO MED NATIONAL STAFFING OF WICHITA FALLS, INC.
1501 Brook Avenue, Suite B, Wichita Falls WV 76301. 940/723-0372. **Fax:** 940/723-0375. **Contact:** Manager. **Description:** An executive search firm. **Specializes in the areas of:** Health/Medical.

SANFORD ROSE ASSOCIATES (SRA)
510 29th Street, Vienna WV 26105. 304/295-7080. **Fax:** 304/295-7099. **Contact:** Sid Mitchell, President. **World Wide Web address:** sravwv@aol.com. **Description:** An executive search firm. **Specializes in the areas of:** Manufacturing.

PERMANENT EMPLOYMENT AGENCIES

KEY PERSONNEL, INC.
1124 Fourth Avenue, Suite 300, Huntington WV 25701. 304/529-3377. **Contact:** Recruiter. **Description:** A permanent employment agency. Founded in 1975. **Specializes in the areas of:** Accounting/Auditing; Banking; Computer Science/Software; Engineering; Finance; Food; General Management; Health/Medical; Industrial; Manufacturing; Personnel/Labor Relations; Sales; Technical; Transportation. **Positions commonly filled include:** Accountant/Auditor; Adjuster; Bank Officer/Manager; Branch Manager; Chemical Engineer; Claim Representative; Cost Estimator; Credit Manager; Customer Service Representative; Health Services Manager; Human Resources Specialist; Industrial Engineer; Manufacturer's/Wholesaler's Sales Rep.; Mechanical Engineer; MIS Specialist; Purchasing Agent/Manager; Quality Control Supervisor; Restaurant/Food Service Manager; Services Sales

Representative; Systems Analyst; Transportation/Traffic Specialist; Underwriter/Assistant Underwriter. **Average salary range of placements:** $30,000 - $50,000. **Number of placements per year:** 50 - 99.

QUANTUM RESOURCES
P.O. Box 1751, Parkersburg WV 26102. 304/428-8028. **Contact:** Cindy Miller, Technical Recruiter. **Description:** A permanent employment agency that also provides some temporary placements. **Specializes in the areas of:** Clerical; Computer Hardware/Software; Engineering; Industrial.

UNITED TALENT PERSONNEL
428 Broad Street, Charleston WV 25301. 304/345-1515. **Contact:** Manager. **Description:** A permanent employment agency that also provides some temporary placements.

TEMPORARY EMPLOYMENT AGENCIES

EXTRA SUPPORT STAFFING
1217-A Garfield Avenue, Parkersburg WV 26101. 304/485-5200. **Fax:** 304/485-5212. **Contact:** Charlotte King, Manager. **Description:** A temporary agency that also provides some permanent placements. **Specializes in the areas of:** Accounting/Auditing; Banking; Finance; General Management; Industrial; Light Industrial; Manufacturing; Personnel/Labor Relations; Sales; Secretarial. **Positions commonly filled include:** Accountant; Administrative Manager; Advertising Clerk; Blue-Collar Worker Supervisor; Branch Manager; Human Resources Specialist; Paralegal; Teacher/ Professor; Typist/Word Processor. **Benefits available to temporary workers:** Paid Holidays; Paid Vacation. **Average salary range of placements:** Less than $20,000. **Number of placements per year:** 1000+.

KELLY SERVICES, INC.
611 Virginia Street East, Charleston WV 25301. 304/345-4840. **Fax:** 304/342-4734. **Contact:** Branch

Manager. **Description:** A temporary agency. **Specializes in the areas of:** Clerical; Food; General Labor; Light Industrial; Office Support; Technical. **Other U.S. locations:** Nationwide.

SNELLING PERSONNEL SERVICES
3624 MacCorkle Avenue SE, Charleston WV 25304. 304/925-1818. **Fax:** 304/925-1877. **Contact:** Recruiting. **Description:** A temporary employment agency that also provides permanent placements. Client company pays fee. **Specializes in the areas of:** Accounting; Administration; Computer Science/Software; Industrial; Legal; Light Industrial; Marketing; Personnel/Labor Relations; Sales; Secretarial. **Positions commonly filled include:** Accounting Clerk; Administrative Assistant; Blue-Collar Worker Supervisor; Clerical Supervisor; Legal Secretary; Paralegal; Receptionist; Sales Representative; Secretary. **Average salary range of placements:** $20,000 - $29,999. **Number of placements per year:** 200 - 499.

CONTRACT SERVICES FIRMS

BELCAN TECHNICAL SERVICES
116 West Washington Street, Suite 3E, Charles Town WV 25414. 304/725-6691. **Fax:** 304/728-1189. **Contact:** Howard Myers, Manager. **Description:** A contract services firm. **Specializes in the areas of:** Construction; Engineering. **Positions commonly filled include:** Civil Engineer; Design Engineer; Draftsperson; Project Manager. **Benefits available to temporary workers:** 401(k); Medical Insurance; Paid Holidays; Paid Vacation. **Other U.S. locations:** IN; OH. **Average salary range of placements:** $30,000 - $50,000. **Number of placements per year:** 100 - 199.

CDI CORPORATION
1012 Kanawha Boulevard, 4th Floor, Charleston WV 25301. **Toll-free phone:** 800/527-2527. **Fax:** 304/345-3995. **Contact:** Manager. **World Wide Web address:** http://www.cdicorp.com. **Description:** A contract services firm. **Specializes in the areas of:** Computer Science/Software; Technical. **Corporate headquarters location:** Philadelphia PA. **Other U.S. locations:** Nationwide. **International locations:** Worldwide.

CDI ENGINEERING GROUP
2 Smiley Drive, St. Albans WV 25177. 304/755-8201. **Contact:** Manager. **World Wide Web address:** http://www.cdicorp.com. **Description:** A contract services firm. **Specializes in the areas of:** Engineering. **Corporate headquarters location:** Philadelphia PA. **Other U.S. locations:** Nationwide. **International locations:** Worldwide.

EXECUTIVE SEARCH FIRMS

**ACCOUNTANTS EXECUTIVE SEARCH
ACCOUNTANTS ON CALL**
3333 North Mayfair Road, Suite 213, Milwaukee WI
53222. 414/278-0001. **Fax:** 414/771-2586. **Contact:**
Manager. **Description:** An executive search firm.
Accountants On Call (also at this location) is a temporary
agency.

ACTION SEARCH CONSULTANTS
3090 Hermans Road, New Franken WI 54229. 920/866-
2342. **Fax:** 920/866-2855. **Contact:** Jim Rakun,
President. **E-mail address:** jrakun@aol.com.
Description: An executive search firm. **Specializes in
the areas of:** Engineering. **Positions commonly filled
include:** Chemical Engineer; Electrical/Electronics
Engineer; Human Resources Manager; Industrial
Engineer; Industrial Production Manager; Manufacturing
Engineer; Mechanical Engineer; Metallurgical Engineer;
Operations Manager; Production Manager; Project
Manager; Purchasing Agent/Manager; Quality Control
Supervisor; Sales Engineer; Sales Executive; Sales
Manager; Sales Representative; Software Engineer.
Corporate headquarters location: Green Bay WI.
Number of placements per year: 1 - 49.

THE AMBROSE GROUP
306 North Milwaukee Street, Suite 301, Milwaukee WI
53202. 414/273-8244. **Fax:** 414/273-8250. **Contact:**
Manager. **Description:** An executive search firm.
Specializes in the areas of: Engineering; Human
Resources; Purchasing; Sales.

BARNES DEVELOPMENT GROUP
1017 West Glen Oaks Lane, Suite 108, Mequon WI
53092. 414/241-8468. **Fax:** 414/241-8438. **Contact:**
Roanne Barnes, Co-Principal. **Description:** A generalist
executive search firm operating on a retainer basis.

BENSTON & ASSOCIATES
216 North Green Bay Road, Suite 211, Thiensville WI
53092. 262/236-4005. **Fax:** 262/242-5212. **Contact:**
Jerry Benston, Jr., President. **Description:** An executive
search firm. **Specializes in the areas of:** Banking;
Engineering; Finance; Information Systems;
Manufacturing.

CAREER RECRUITERS
16655 West Bluemound Road, Suite 235-C, Brookfield
WI 53005. 262/784-0595. **Fax:** 262/797-0853. **Contact:**
Don Schoberg, Owner. **E-mail address:** cr@
execpc.com. **Description:** An executive search firm.
Specializes in the areas of: Computer Science/Software.
Positions commonly filled include: Computer
Programmer; MIS Specialist; Software Engineer;
Systems Analyst. **Average salary range of placements:**
More than $50,000. **Number of placements per year:** 1
- 49.

CAREER RESOURCES
P.O. Box 98, Onalaska WI 54650. 608/783-6307. **Fax:**
608/783-6302. **Contact:** Chris M. Jansson, CPC/Owner.
Description: An executive search firm. **Specializes in
the areas of:** Accounting/Auditing; Administration;
Computer Science/Software; Finance; Personnel/Labor
Relations. **Positions commonly filled include:**
Accountant/Auditor; Bank Officer/Manager; Computer
Programmer; Financial Analyst; Human Resources
Manager; MIS Manager; Systems Analyst.

CAREERTRAC EMPLOYMENT SERVICES INC.
135 West Wells Street, Suite 518, Milwaukee WI 53203-
1807. 414/224-8722. **Fax:** 414/224-7080. **Contact:**
Cindy Johnson, President. **Description:** An executive
search firm. **Specializes in the areas of:**
Accounting/Auditing; Administration; Banking; Finance;
Legal; Personnel/Labor Relations; Sales. **Positions
commonly filled include:** Accountant/Auditor;

Administrative Manager; Attorney; Branch Manager;
Buyer; Clerical Supervisor; Credit Manager; Financial
Manager; General Manager; Human Resources Manager;
Insurance Agent/Broker; MIS Manager;
Operations/Production Manager; Paralegal; Public
Relations Specialist; Purchasing Agent/Manager; Quality
Control Supervisor; Systems Analyst. **Average salary
range of placements:** $20,000 - $29,999. **Number of
placements per year:** 100 - 199.

CONSTRUCTION SEARCH SPECIALISTS
115 Fifth Avenue, Suite 501, La Crosse WI 54601.
608/784-4711. **Fax:** 608/784-4904. **Contact:** Tamara
Watters, Vice President. **E-mail address:**
css@csssearch.com. **Description:** An executive search
firm operating on a contingency basis. **Specializes in the
areas of:** Architecture/Construction; Engineering.
Positions commonly filled include: Architect; Chief
Financial Officer; Civil Engineer; Construction
Contractor; Cost Estimator; Design Engineer;
Draftsperson; Electrician; Environmental Engineer;
Mechanical Engineer; Project Manager. **Corporate
headquarters location:** This Location. **Average salary
range of placements:** More than $50,000. **Number of
placements per year:** 1 - 49.

CORPORATE SEARCH INC.
P.O. Box 1808, Waukesha WI 53187-1808. 262/542-
6260. **Fax:** 262/542-1236. **Contact:** Joseph Cali,
President. **Description:** An executive search firm.
Specializes in the areas of: Engineering; Manufacturing.
Positions commonly filled include: Buyer; Chemical
Engineer; Design Engineer; Electrical/Electronics
Engineer; Environmental Engineer; Human Resources
Manager; Mechanical Engineer; Metallurgical Engineer;
Purchasing Agent/Manager; Software Engineer;
Structural Engineer. **Number of placements per year:**
50 - 99.

DHR INTERNATIONAL INC.
300 North Corporate Drive, Suite 290, Brookfield WI
53045. 414/879-0850. **Toll-free phone:** 800/861-7676.
Fax: 414/879-0855. **Contact:** Manager. **Description:** An
executive search firm. DHR International is a division of
EPS Solutions. **Specializes in the areas of:** Engineering;
Operations Management. **Other U.S. locations:**
Nationwide.

DATA PROCESSING SEARCH
West 62 North, 244 Washington Avenue, Cedarburg WI
53012. 262/375-4644. **Fax:** 262/375-5506. **Contact:**
Manager. **Description:** An executive search firm.
Specializes in the areas of: Data Processing;
Information Systems; Information Technology.

DELTA RECRUITING
108 East Lakeview Avenue, Madison WI 53716.
608/224-3981. **Toll-free phone:** 877/954-1571. **Fax:**
608/223-1483. **Contact:** Pamela Jahn, Owner. **E-mail
address:** pjahn@chorus.net. **Description:** An executive
search firm. **Specializes in the areas of:**
Telecommunications.

DIECK MUELLER GROUP
1500 North Casaloma Drive, Suite 409, Appleton WI
54915. 920/733-8500. **Fax:** 920/733-8818. **Contact:**
Daniel W. Dieck, President. **E-mail address:**
execsearch@dieckmueller.com. **Description:** An
executive search firm. **Specializes in the areas of:**
Engineering; Finance; General Management; Marketing;
Personnel/Labor Relations; Publishing; Sales. **Positions
commonly filled include:** Account Manager; Chief
Financial Officer; Controller; Environmental Engineer;
Finance Director; Financial Analyst; Human Resources
Manager; Manufacturing Engineer; Marketing Manager;
Marketing Specialist; MIS Specialist; Operations
Manager; Production Manager; Public Relations

Specialist; Purchasing Agent/Manager; Quality Control Supervisor; Sales Engineer; Sales Executive; Sales Manager; Vice President of Finance; Vice President of Marketing and Sales. **Average salary range of placements:** More then $50,000. **Number of placements per year:** 50 - 99.

DOMRES PROFESSIONAL SEARCH
P.O. Box 103, Coleman WI 54112. 715/735-1943. **Contact:** Terry A. Domres, Principal. **Description:** An executive search firm that focuses on providing placements in the pulp, paper, and related industries. **Positions commonly filled include:** Accountant/Auditor; Blue-Collar Worker Supervisor; Chemical Engineer; Computer Programmer; Electrical/Electronics Engineer; Environmental Engineer; Health Services Manager; Human Resources Manager; Mechanical Engineer; MIS Manager; Purchasing Agent/Manager; Quality Control Supervisor. **Number of placements per year:** 1 - 49.

J.M. EAGLE PARTNERS
11514 North Port Washington Road, Suite 105, Mequon WI 53092. 262/241-1400. **Fax:** 262/241-4745. **Contact:** Jerry Moses, President. **Description:** An executive search firm. **Specializes in the areas of:** Computer Science/Software; Diagnostic Imaging; Engineering; Finance; General Management; Health/Medical; Manufacturing; Personnel/Labor Relations; Sales; Technical. **Number of placements per year:** 1000+.

EGAN & ASSOCIATES
128 South Sixth Avenue, West Bend WI 53095. 262/335-0707. **Fax:** 262/335-0625. **Contact:** Manager. **Description:** An executive search firm. **Specializes in the areas of:** Manufacturing.

ENGINEERING PLACEMENT SPECIALISTS
P.O. Box 416, Elcho WI 54428. 715/275-5322. **Contact:** Manager. **Description:** An executive search firm operating on a contingency basis. **Specializes in the areas of:** Engineering.

EXECUTIVE PLACEMENT & CAREER SERVICES CAREER CONNECTIONS INC.
2825 North Mayfair Road, Suite 110, Milwaukee WI 53222. 414/778-2200. **Contact:** Manager. **Description:** An executive search firm. Career Connections Inc. (also at this location) provides temp-to-perm placements. **Specializes in the areas of:** Engineering; Industrial; Manufacturing. **Positions commonly filled include:** Engineer.

EXECUTIVE RECRUITERS, INC.
P.O. Box 44704, Madison WI 53744. 608/833-4004. **Fax:** 608/833-4774. **Contact:** Manager. **Description:** An executive search firm. Founded in 1979. **Specializes in the areas of:** Data Processing; Engineering; Manufacturing; Technical. **Positions commonly filled include:** Electrical/Electronics Engineer; Environmental Engineer; Industrial Engineer; Manufacturing Engineer; Materials Engineer; Mechanical Engineer; Metallurgical Engineer; Operations Manager; Software Engineer. **Average salary range of placements:** More than $50,000.

EXECUTIVE RESOURCE INC.
P.O. Box 356, Hartland WI 53029. 262/369-2540. **Fax:** 262/369-2558. **Contact:** Duane Strong, President. **Description:** An executive search firm. **Specializes in the areas of:** Accounting; Banking; Engineering; Finance; General Management; Industrial; Light Industrial; Personnel/Labor Relations; Scientific; Technical. **Positions commonly filled include:** Accountant; Auditor; Bank Officer/Manager; Buyer; Chief Financial Officer; Controller; Credit Manager; Design Engineer; Electrical/Electronics Engineer; Fund Manager; General Manager; Human Resources Manager; Industrial Engineer; Industrial Production Manager; Manufacturing Engineer; Mechanical Engineer; Operations Manager; Purchasing Agent/Manager; Quality Control Supervisor. **Corporate headquarters location:** This Location. **Other U.S. locations:**

Nationwide. **Average salary range of placements:** More than $50,000. **Number of placements per year:** 50 - 99.

EXECUTIVE SEARCH & PLACEMENT
1227 Menomonie Street, Eau Claire WI 54703. 715/836-7057. **Fax:** 715/836-7067. **Contact:** Dennis Burkart, Owner. **Description:** A generalist executive search firm.

FINANCIAL MANAGEMENT PERSONNEL
P.O. Box 215, Brookfield WI 53008. 262/784-9630. **Fax:** 262/569-1910. **Contact:** John Higgins, Owner. **Description:** An executive search firm. **Specializes in the areas of:** Accounting/Auditing; Finance; Manufacturing. **Positions commonly filled include:** Accountant/Auditor; Budget Analyst; Credit Manager; Financial Analyst. **Number of placements per year:** 1 - 49.

FLORES FINANCIAL SERVICES
314 Sage Street, Suite 100, Lake Geneva WI 53147-1931. 262/248-2771. **Fax:** 262/248-2562. **Contact:** Robert C. Flores, President. **E-mail address:** rflores007@aol.com. **Description:** An executive search firm. **Specializes in the areas of:** Banking; Economics; Finance; General Management; Investment. **Positions commonly filled include:** Bank Officer/Manager; Economist; Financial Analyst. **Average salary range of placements:** More than $50,000. **Number of placements per year:** 50 - 99.

FOGEC CONSULTANTS, INC.
P.O. Box 28806, Milwaukee WI 53228. 414/427-0690. **Fax:** 414/427-0691. **Contact:** Tom Fogec, Owner. **E-mail address:** tfogec@execpc.com. **Description:** An executive search firm. **Specializes in the areas of:** Accounting; Finance; Food; Human Resources.

FOODSTAFF 2000, INC.
9875 South Franklin Drive, Franklin WI 53132. 414/421-2000. **Fax:** 414/421-6000. **Contact:** Chuck Nolan, President/CEO. **E-mail address:** recruiter@foodstaff2000.com. **World Wide Web address:** http://www.foodstaff2000.com. **Description:** An executive search firm. **Specializes in the areas of:** Engineering; Food; Personnel/Labor Relations; Sales; Technical; Transportation. **Positions commonly filled include:** Accountant/Auditor; Agricultural Engineer; Biological Scientist; Buyer; Computer Programmer; Electrical/Electronics Engineer; Food Scientist/Technologist; General Manager; Human Resources Manager; Industrial Engineer; Mechanical Engineer; Operations/Production Manager; Purchasing Agent/Manager; Restaurant/Food Service Manager; Systems Analyst. **Other U.S. locations:** Scottsdale AZ. **Number of placements per year:** 200 - 499.

F-O-R-T-U-N-E PERSONNEL CONSULTANTS
15300 West Capitol Drive, Suite 201, Brookfield WI 53005. 414/790-6720. **Fax:** 414/790-6721. **Contact:** Manager. **E-mail address:** resume@fpcmilwaukee.com. **Description:** An executive search firm. **Specializes in the areas of:** Purchasing. **Corporate headquarters location:** New York NY. **Other U.S. locations:** Nationwide.

GENEVA FINANCIAL GROUP
P.O. Box 1093, Lake Geneva WI 53147. 414/249-1690. **Fax:** 414/249-1691. **Contact:** Manager. **Description:** An executive search firm. **Specializes in the areas of:** Finance.

GIELOW ASSOCIATES, INC.
705 East Silver Spring Drive, Milwaukee WI 53217. 414/964-4121. **Fax:** 414/964-6410. **Contact:** Manager. **Description:** A generalist executive search firm.

GLOBAL INSIGHTS, INC.
12645 West Burleigh Road, Brookfield WI 53005. 414/782-6365. **Fax:** 414/782-7416. **Contact:** Manager. **Description:** An executive search firm. **Specializes in the areas of:** Engineering; Information Technology.

HR INC.
1017 West Glen Oaks Lane, Mequon WI 53092-3371. 262/241-8588. **Fax:** 262/241-4690. **Contact:** Mr. Sunny Mehta, President. **E-mail address:** hrinc@execpc.com. **World Wide Web address:** http://www.hrincorp.com. **Description:** An executive search firm. Founded in 1984. **Positions commonly filled include:** Buyer; Chemical Engineer; Chemist; Cost Estimator; Design Engineer; Electrical/Electronics Engineer; General Manager; Human Resources Manager; Industrial Engineer; Industrial Production Manager; Management Analyst/Consultant; Mechanical Engineer; MIS Manager; Operations/Production Manager; Purchasing Agent/Manager; Quality Control Supervisor. **Number of placements per year:** 50 - 99.

THE H S GROUP, INC.
2611 Libal Street, Green Bay WI 54301. 920/432-7444. **Fax:** 920/436-2966. **Contact:** Manager. **Description:** An executive search firm. **Specializes in the areas of:** Engineering; Human Resources; Information Systems; Information Technology; Insurance; Manufacturing; Marketing; Purchasing; Sales.

ROBERT HALF INTERNATIONAL ACCOUNTEMPS
411 East Wisconsin Avenue, Suite 2150, Milwaukee WI 53202. 414/271-4253. **Contact:** Manager. **World Wide Web address:** http://www.roberthalf.com. **Description:** An executive search firm. Accountemps (also at this location) provides temporary placements. **Specializes in the areas of:** Accounting/Auditing. **Corporate headquarters location:** Menlo Park CA. **Other U.S. locations:** Nationwide.

HEALTHCARE RECRUITERS INTERNATIONAL
P.O. Box 247, Oconomowoc WI 53066. 608/274-4475. **Contact:** Manager. **Description:** An executive search firm. **Specializes in the areas of:** Health/Medical.

THE HUNTER CORPORATION
W4822 South Pearl Lake Road, Red Granite WI 54970. 920/566-4490. **Contact:** Manager. **Description:** An executive search firm. **Specializes in the areas of:** Manufacturing; Mechanical.

HUNTER MIDWEST
250 Regency Court, Brookfield WI 53045. 262/641-9600. **Fax:** 262/641-0600. **Contact:** Office Manager. **Description:** An executive search firm that focuses on placing IS professionals with AS400, PC, LAN, or UNIX backgrounds. **NOTE:** A minimum of one year of experience is required. The firm does not place recent college graduates. **Specializes in the areas of:** Computer Science/Software; MIS/EDP; Network Administration; Systems Administration. **Positions commonly filled include:** Computer Programmer; Network Administrator. **Number of placements per year:** 50 - 99.

INTERNATIONAL SEARCH
P.O. Box 381, Green Bay WI 54305-0381. 920/437-8055. **Toll-free phone:** 800/276-8319. **Fax:** 920/437-0343. **Contact:** Michael Wingers, Owner. **Description:** An executive search firm. **Specializes in the areas of:** Accounting/Auditing; Computer Science/Software. **Positions commonly filled include:** Accountant/Auditor; Computer Programmer; Systems Analyst; Systems Manager. **Average salary range of placements:** $30,000 - $50,000. **Number of placements per year:** 1 - 49.

JANSSEN & COMPANY
P.O. Box 5393, De Pere WI 54115. 920/336-9889. **Fax:** 920/983-9755. **Contact:** Dan Janssen, Owner. **Description:** A generalist executive search firm.

KGA INC.
1320 Greenway Terrace, Suite 1, Brookfield WI 53005. 262/786-5209. **Fax:** 262/786-7961. **Contact:** Keith Gunkel, Owner. **Description:** An executive search firm operating on a retained basis. **Specializes in the areas**

of: Human Resources. **Average salary range of placements:** $40,000 and up.

KENT MARK PERSONNEL
N802 County Road North, Wisconsin Dells WI 53965. 608/253-9705. **Contact:** Manager. **Description:** An executive search firm.

KOEHLER & COMPANY
700 Pilgrim Parkway, Suite 104, Elm Grove WI 53122. 262/796-8010. **Fax:** 262/796-8788. **Contact:** Manager. **Description:** An executive search firm. **Specializes in the areas of:** Manufacturing; Mechanical; Metals.

KORDUS CONSULTING GROUP
1470 East Standish Place, Milwaukee WI 53217-1958. 414/228-7979. **Fax:** 414/228-1080. **Contact:** Ms. Lee Walther Kordus, President. **E-mail address:** kcginc@aol.com. **Description:** An executive search firm. **Specializes in the areas of:** Advertising; Food; Marketing; Public Relations. **Positions commonly filled include:** Account Manager; Advertising Executive; Graphic Artist; Graphic Designer; Market Research Analyst; Marketing Manager; Marketing Specialist; Product Manager; Public Relations Specialist. **Average salary range of placements:** More than $50,000. **Number of placements per year:** 1 - 49.

MAGLIO & COMPANY
450 North Sunny Slope Road, Suite 130, Brookfield WI 53005. 262/784-6020. **Fax:** 262/784-6046. **Contact:** Manager. **Description:** An executive search firm. **Specializes in the areas of:** Engineering; Manufacturing; Marketing; Sales.

MANAGEMENT RECRUITERS INTERNATIONAL
1711 Woolsey Street, Delavan WI 53115. 262/728-8886. **Fax:** 262/728-8894. **Contact:** Dean Sanderson, Owner. **Description:** An executive search firm. **Specializes in the areas of:** Accounting; Finance; Human Resources. **Corporate headquarters location:** Cleveland OH. **Other U.S. locations:** Nationwide.

MANAGEMENT RECRUITERS INTERNATIONAL
11611 West North Avenue, Suite 201, Wauwatosa WI 53226. 414/607-3677. **Fax:** 414/607-3666. **Contact:** Manager. **E-mail address:** mri-milw@execpc.com. **World Wide Web address:** http://www. mricareercenter.com. **Description:** An executive search firm. **Corporate headquarters location:** Cleveland OH. **Other U.S. locations:** Nationwide.

MANAGEMENT RECRUITERS INTERNATIONAL
20 East Milwaukee Street, Suite 304, Janesville WI 53545. 608/752-2125. **Contact:** Manager. **Description:** An executive search firm. **Specializes in the areas of:** Health/Medical; Manufacturing. **Corporate headquarters location:** Cleveland OH. **Other U.S. locations:** Nationwide.

MANAGEMENT RECRUITERS INTERNATIONAL
W175N11163 Stonewood Drive, Suite 105, Germantown WI 53022. 262/532-0400. **Fax:** 262/532-0402. **Contact:** Manager. **Description:** An executive search firm. **Specializes in the areas of:** Engineering; Medical Devices. **Corporate headquarters location:** Cleveland OH.

MANAGEMENT RECRUITERS INTERNATIONAL
735 North Water Street, Suite 1228, Milwaukee WI 53202. 414/226-2420. **Toll-free phone:** 800/783-2430. **Fax:** 414/226-2421. **Contact:** Manager. **E-mail address:** mrimke@execpc.com. **Description:** An executive search firm. **Specializes in the areas of:** Banking; Consumer Products; Finance; Information Technology; Marketing; Medical Devices; Pharmaceuticals; Purchasing; Telecommunications. **Corporate headquarters location:** Cleveland OH. **Other U.S. locations:** Nationwide.

MANAGEMENT RECRUITERS INTERNATIONAL COMPUSEARCH OF WAUSAU
3309 Terrace Court, Wausau WI 54401-3952. 715/842-1750. **Fax:** 715/842-1741. **Contact:** Laurie L. Prochnow, President. **Description:** An executive search firm. **Specializes in the areas of:** Administration; Computer Science/Software; Information Systems; MIS/EDP. **Positions commonly filled include:** Chief Financial Officer; Computer Operator; Computer Programmer; Database Manager; MIS Specialist; Project Manager; Systems Analyst; Telecommunications Manager; Webmaster. **Corporate headquarters location:** Cleveland OH. **Average salary range of placements:** More than $50,000. **Number of placements per year:** 1 - 49.

MANAGEMENT RECRUITERS INTERNATIONAL (MILWAUKEE WEST)
13000 West Bluemound Road, Suite 310, Elm Grove WI 53122-2655. 262/797-7500. **Fax:** 262/797-7515. **Contact:** Manager. **E-mail address:** mrmilw@aol.com. **Description:** An executive search firm. **Specializes in the areas of:** Information Technology; MIS/EDP; Pharmaceuticals. **Positions commonly filled include:** Auditor; Database Manager; Internet Services Manager; Quality Control Supervisor; Systems Analyst; Systems Manager. **Corporate headquarters location:** Cleveland OH. **Other U.S. locations:** Nationwide. **Average salary range of placements:** $30,000 - $50,000. **Number of placements per year:** 50 - 99.

MANAGEMENT RECRUITERS OF APPLETON COMPUSEARCH
911 North Lynndale Drive, Appleton WI 54914. 920/731-5221. **Contact:** Russ Hanson, Manager. **Description:** An executive search firm. **Specializes in the areas of:** Accounting/Auditing; Administration; Architecture/Construction; Communications; Computer Hardware/Software; Electrical; Engineering; Finance; General Management; Manufacturing; Operations Management; Personnel/Labor Relations; Publishing; Technical; Textiles; Transportation. **Corporate headquarters location:** Cleveland OH.

MANAGEMENT RECRUITERS OF GREEN BAY
375 AMF Court, Green Bay WI 54313. 920/434-8770. **Contact:** Manager. **Description:** An executive search firm. Client company pays fee. **Specializes in the areas of:** Accounting/Auditing; Administration; Advertising; Architecture/Construction; Banking; Communications; Computer Hardware/Software; Electrical; Engineering; Finance; Food; General Management; Health/Medical; Insurance; Legal; Manufacturing; Operations Management; Personnel/Labor Relations; Publishing; Technical; Transportation. **Corporate headquarters location:** Cleveland OH. **Other U.S. locations:** Nationwide. **Average salary range of placements:** $50,000 - $100,000. **Number of placements per year:** 100 - 199.

MANAGEMENT RECRUITERS OF JOHNSON CREEK
202 Village Walk Lane, Suite A, Johnson Creek WI 53038. 920/699-4010. **Contact:** Manager. **Description:** An executive search firm. **Corporate headquarters location:** Cleveland OH. **Other U.S. locations:** Nationwide.

MANAGEMENT RECRUITERS OF LAKE WISCONSIN
609 A North Main Street, Lodi WI 53555. 608/592-2151. **Fax:** 608/592-2133. **Contact:** Manager. **Description:** An executive search firm. **Specializes in the areas of:** Insurance; Manufacturing. **Corporate headquarters location:** Cleveland OH. **Other U.S. locations:** Nationwide.

MANAGEMENT RECRUITERS OF MILWAUKEE SALES CONSULTANTS
1333 West Town Square Road, Mequon WI 53092. 414/241-1600. **Contact:** Tim Lawler, President. **E-mail address:** mr/sc@mri-execsearch.com. **World Wide**

Web address: http://www.recruiters-jobs.com. **Description:** An executive search firm. **Specializes in the areas of:** Accounting/Auditing; Administration; Architecture/Construction; Banking; Communications; Computer Hardware/Software; Electrical; Engineering; Finance; Food; General Management; Health/Medical; Legal; Manufacturing; Operations Management; Personnel/Labor Relations; Publishing; Sales; Technical; Transportation. **Positions commonly filled include:** Account Manager; Account Representative; Accountant; Administrative Manager; Applications Engineer; Architect; Attorney; Auditor; Bank Officer/Manager; Biochemist; Biomedical Engineer; Branch Manager; Budget Analyst; Chemical Engineer; Chemist; Chief Financial Officer; Civil Engineer; Construction Contractor; Controller; Cost Estimator; Credit Manager; Customer Service Representative; Database Manager; Design Engineer; Electrical/Electronics Engineer; Environmental Engineer; Finance Director; Financial Analyst; Fund Manager; General Manager; Human Resources Manager; Industrial Engineer; Industrial Production Manager; Internet Services Manager; Manufacturing Engineer; Marketing Manager; Marketing Specialist; Mechanical Engineer; Metallurgical Engineer; MIS Manager; Operations Manager; Production Manager; Purchasing Agent/Manager; Quality Control Supervisor; Sales Engineer; Sales Executive; Sales Manager; Sales Representative; Secretary; Software Engineer; Systems Analyst; Systems Manager; Telecommunications Manager; Transportation/Traffic Specialist; Typist/Word Processor; Underwriter/Assistant Underwriter. **Corporate headquarters location:** Cleveland OH. **Other U.S. locations:** Nationwide. **International locations:** Worldwide. **Average salary range of placements:** More than $50,000. **Number of placements per year:** 100 - 199.

MANAGEMENT RECRUITERS OF MILWAUKEE (SOUTH)
5307 South 92nd Street, Suite 125, Hales Corners WI 53130. 414/529-8020. **Contact:** Office Manager. **Description:** An executive search firm. **Specializes in the areas of:** Accounting/Auditing; Administration; Advertising; Architecture/Construction; Banking; Communications; Computer Hardware/Software; Electrical; Engineering; Finance; Food; General Management; Health/Medical; Insurance; Legal; Manufacturing; Operations Management; Personnel/Labor Relations; Publishing; Technical; Transportation. **Corporate headquarters location:** Cleveland OH.

MANAGEMENT RECRUITERS OF STEVENS POINT INC.
1117-W County Road DB, Mosinee WI 54455. 715/341-4900. **Fax:** 715/341-4992. **Contact:** Brad Barick, President. **E-mail address:** mri@coredcs.com. **World Wide Web address:** http://www.mrinet.com. **Description:** An executive search firm operating on both retainer and contingency bases. The firm also offers some contract services. **Specializes in the areas of:** Computer Science/Software; Insurance; Safety. **Positions commonly filled include:** Claim Representative; Computer Programmer; Environmental Engineer; Insurance Agent/Broker; MIS Manager; Software Engineer; Systems Analyst; Underwriter/Assistant Underwriter. **Corporate headquarters location:** Cleveland OH. **Number of placements per year:** 1 - 49.

MARBL CONSULTANTS
One Park Plaza, 11270 West Park Place, Suite 270, Milwaukee WI 53224. 414/359-5627. **Fax:** 414/359-5620. **Contact:** Allan Adzima, President. **E-mail address:** marblcons@aero.net (text only). **Description:** An executive search firm operating on both retainer and contingency bases. **Specializes in the areas of:** Administration; Computer Science/Software; Engineering; General Management; Personnel/Labor Relations; Technical. **Positions commonly filled include:** Administrative Manager; Buyer; Computer Programmer; Consultant; Controller; Database Manager; Design Engineer; Electrical/Electronics Engineer; Financial Analyst; General Manager; Human Resources

Manager; Industrial Engineer; Industrial Production Manager; Manufacturing Engineer; Mechanical Engineer; Metallurgical Engineer; MIS Manager; Operations Manager; Production Manager; Project Manager; Purchasing Agent/Manager; Quality Control Supervisor; Sales Engineer; Software Engineer; Systems Analyst; Systems Manager; Telecommunications Manager; Transportation/Traffic Specialist; Video Editor. **Average salary range of placements:** More than $50,000. **Number of placements per year:** 100 - 199.

McMILLAN & ASSOCIATES
2314 North Grand View Boulevard, Suite 310, Waukesha WI 53188. 262/549-3333. **Fax:** 520/752-0126. **Contact:** Walter McMillan, Founder. **E-mail address:** waltmc@execpc.com. **Description:** An executive search firm operating on a contingency basis. Founded in 1998. **NOTE:** E-mail contact is preferred. **Specializes in the areas of:** Information Technology. **Positions commonly filled include:** Network Engineer; Webmaster. **Average salary range of placements:** $60,000 and up. **Number of placements per year:** 1 - 49.

THE MICHAEL DAVID GROUP
117 North Milwaukee Street, Port Washington WI 53074. 262/268-1750. **Fax:** 262/268-1753. **Contact:** Mike Eskra, Director. **E-mail address:** tmdg@aol.com. **Description:** An executive search firm operating on a retainer basis. Client company pays fee. **Specializes in the areas of:** Engineering; General Management; Personnel/Labor Relations. **Positions commonly filled include:** Chemical Engineer; Chemist; General Manager; Human Resources Manager; Industrial Production Manager; Management Analyst/Consultant; Operations Manager; Production Manager; Vice President of Operations. **Average salary range of placements:** $50,000 - $100,000. **Number of placements per year:** 1 - 49.

NAGLE COMPANY
11514 North Port Washington Road, Mequon WI 53092. 262/241-5350. **Fax:** 262/241-5713. **Contact:** Jim Nagle, Owner. **Description:** An executive search firm. **Specializes in the areas of:** Metals.

THE PACIFIC FIRM
338 West Main Street, Waukesha WI 53186. 414/524-8200. **Fax:** 414/521-2748. **Contact:** Manager. **Description:** An executive search firm. **Specializes in the areas of:** Technical. **Corporate headquarters location:** Berkeley CA.

PACKAGING PERSONNEL COMPANY
W1405 Beach Court, Oostburg WI 53070. 920/564-6361. **Fax:** 920/564-6362. **Contact:** Manager. **Description:** An executive search firm. **Specializes in the areas of:** Packaging.

PLACEMENT SOLUTIONS
W270 S3979 Heather Drive, Waukesha WI 53189. 262/542-2250. **Fax:** 262/542-7373. **Contact:** Mary Sue Short, President. **E-mail address:** msshort@execpc.com. **Description:** An executive search firm operating on a contingency basis. The firm focuses on the placement of accounting personnel. **Specializes in the areas of:** Accounting/Auditing. **Positions commonly filled include:** Accountant; Auditor; Chief Financial Officer; Controller; Financial Analyst; Tax Specialist. **Other U.S. locations:** New York NY.

PRAIRIE ENGINEERING
P.O. Box 165, DeForest WI 53532. 608/846-7600. **Fax:** 608/846-7601. **Contact:** Steve Cary, Senior Recruiter. **World Wide Web address:** http://www.prairie-engineering.com. **Description:** An executive search firm. **Specializes in the areas of:** Computer Science/Software; Engineering. **Positions commonly filled include:** Computer Programmer; Software Engineer; Systems Analyst; Technical Writer/Editor. **Average salary range of placements:** $30,000 - $125,000. **Number of placements per year:** 1 - 49.

PROFESSIONAL RESOURCE SERVICES
1825 Lone Oak Circle West, Brookfield WI 53045. 262/782-6901. **Toll-free phone:** 800/729-5746. **Fax:** 414/938-0681. **Contact:** Manager. **World Wide Web address:** http://www.prs2000.com. **Description:** Professional Resource Services is an executive search firm. **Specializes in the areas of:** Computer Science/Software; Information Systems. **Positions commonly filled include:** Computer Programmer; Software Engineer; Systems Analyst. **Average salary range of placements:** $30,000 - $50,000. **Number of placements per year:** 1 - 49.

QTI PROFESSIONAL STAFFING
702 East Washington Avenue, Madison WI 53703. 608/232-2650. **Fax:** 608/663-4830. **Contact:** Recruiter. **Description:** An executive search firm. QTI also provides some temporary and contract placements. **Specializes in the areas of:** Accounting; Computer Operations; Electronics; Engineering; Human Resources.

QUIRK-CORPORON & ASSOCIATES, INC.
1229 North Jackson Street, Milwaukee WI 53202. 414/271-8711. **Fax:** 414/224-9472. **Contact:** Chuck Corporon, President. **Description:** An executive search firm. **Specializes in the areas of:** Banking; Health/Medical; Insurance; Sales. **Positions commonly filled include:** Accountant/Auditor; Actuary; Adjuster; Branch Manager; Claim Representative; Customer Service Representative; Health Services Manager; Insurance Agent/Broker; Physical Therapist; Physician; Registered Nurse; Underwriter/Assistant Underwriter. **Number of placements per year:** 1 - 49.

RANKIN GROUP LIMITED
W1800 County Road B, Genoa City WI 53128. 414/279-5005. **Fax:** 414/279-6705. **Contact:** Manager. **Description:** An executive search firm. **Specializes in the areas of:** Banking; Investment.

CHARLES C. RAY ASSOCIATES INC.
1200 West Sierra Lane, Mequon WI 53092. 262/241-4150. **Contact:** Charles Ray, Owner. **Description:** An executive search firm that provides placements for individuals with experience in the medical device industry. **Specializes in the areas of:** Medical Sales and Marketing.

RECRUITING RESOURCES INC.
123 South Sixth Avenue, West Bend WI 53095. 262/338-2370. **Contact:** Manager. **Description:** An executive search firm. **Specializes in the areas of:** Food; Sales.

RIVERWOOD CONSULTING
N611 County Road Z, Eau Galle WI 54737. 715/283-4922. **Fax:** 715/283-4926. **Contact:** Manager. **Description:** An executive search firm. **Specializes in the areas of:** Manufacturing.

ROMAC INTERNATIONAL
1233 North Mayfair Road, Suite 300, Milwaukee WI 53226. 414/774-6700. **Fax:** 414/774-8155. **Contact:** Manager. **Description:** An executive search firm. The divisions at this location include Source EDP, Source Finance, and Accountant Source Temps. **Specializes in the areas of:** Accounting/Auditing; Computer Hardware/Software; Finance; Information Technology. **Corporate headquarters location:** Tampa FL.

ROTH YOUNG EXECUTIVE SEARCH
5215 North Ironwood Road, Suite 201, Milwaukee WI 53217. 414/962-7684. **Contact:** Manager. **Description:** An executive search firm. **Specializes in the areas of:** Food. **Corporate headquarters location:** New York NY. **Other U.S. locations:** Nationwide.

ROWBOTTOM & ASSOCIATES
7707 Menomonee River Parkway, Wauwatosa WI 53213-2632. 414/475-1974. **Fax:** 414/475-5038. **Contact:** Mark Rowbottom, Owner. **E-mail address:** rowbottom@execpc.com. **Description:** An executive

search firm. **Specializes in the areas of:** Computer Science/Software; Information Systems. **Positions commonly filled include:** Computer Programmer; Internet Services Manager; MIS Manager; Software Engineer; Systems Analyst; Telecommunications Manager. **Average salary range of placements:** $30,000 - $50,000. **Number of placements per year:** 100 - 199.

SALES CONSULTANTS OF MADISON
1818 Parmenter Street, Suite 202, Middleton WI 53562. 608/836-5566. **Fax:** 608/836-1906. **Contact:** Bill Schultz, Owner. **E-mail address:** schultzy@mrimadison.com. **World Wide Web address:** http://www.mrimadison.com. **Description:** An executive search firm. **Specializes in the areas of:** Computer Hardware/Software; Insurance; Marketing; Sales. **Corporate headquarters location:** Cleveland OH. **Other U.S. locations:** Nationwide.

SALES SEARCH
8200 Brown Deer Road, Milwaukee WI 53223. 414/365-3651. **Contact:** Manager. **Description:** An executive search firm. **Specializes in the areas of:** Sales.

SALES SPECIALISTS, INC.
614 West Brown Deer Road, Suite 300, Milwaukee WI 53217. 414/228-8810. **Fax:** 414/228-8815. **Contact:** Jeff Berg, Vice President. **Description:** An executive search firm. **Specializes in the areas of:** Computer Science/Software; Food; General Management; Health/Medical; Industrial; Sales. **Positions commonly filled include:** Branch Manager; Customer Service Representative; General Manager; Landscape Architect; Management Trainee; Manufacturer's/Wholesaler's Sales Rep.; Operations/Production Manager; Securities Sales Representative; Services Sales Representative; Software Engineer; Systems Analyst; Telecommunications Manager. **Average salary range of placements:** More than $50,000. **Number of placements per year:** 50 - 99.

SANFORD ROSE ASSOCIATES - JANESVILLE
15 West Milwaukee Street, Suite 207, Janesville WI 53545. 608/757-8060. **Fax:** 608/757-8061. **Contact:** Bill Dowell, President. **E-mail address:** wedowell@aol.com. **World Wide Web address:** http://www.sanfordrose.com. **Description:** An executive search firm. **Specializes in the areas of:** Aerospace; Electronics; Manufacturing; Telecommunications.

SCHULTZ PERSONNEL
115 6th Street, Wausau WI 54403. 715/845-2212. **Fax:** 715/845-7373. **Contact:** Tom Schultz, Owner. **E-mail address:** tom@allstarnetwork.com. **World Wide Web address:** http://www.allstarnetwork.com. **Description:** A generalist executive search firm. Schultz Personnel is a division of All Star Network, LLC.

STAFF DEVELOPMENT CORPORATION
10400 West North Avenue, Suite 160, Wauwatosa WI 53226. 414/256-3688. **Fax:** 414/256-3699. **Contact:** Mary Krueger, President. **Description:** An executive search firm operating on a retainer basis. Founded in 1990. **Specializes in the areas of:** Health/Medical. **Positions commonly filled include:** EEG Technologist; EKG Technician; Emergency Medical Technician; Health Services Manager; Licensed Practical Nurse;

Occupational Therapist; Pharmacist; Physical Therapist; Physician; Registered Nurse; Respiratory Therapist; Social Worker. **Average salary range of placements:** More than $50,000. **Number of placements per year:** 100 - 199.

T.E.M. ASSOCIATES
P.O. Box 5243, De Pere WI 54115. 920/339-8055. **Fax:** 920/339-6177. **Contact:** Terri E. McCracken, President. **Description:** An executive search firm operating on a contingency basis. T.E.M. Associates primarily places professionals in the pulp, paper, and converting industries. Founded in 1994. **Specializes in the areas of:** Engineering; Manufacturing; Sales. **Positions commonly filled include:** Design Engineer; Designer; Electrical/Electronics Engineer; Environmental Engineer; Industrial Engineer; Industrial Production Manager; Market Research Analyst; Mechanical Engineer; Operations/Production Manager; Purchasing Agent/Manager; Quality Control Supervisor. **Number of placements per year:** 1 - 49.

TMP WORLDWIDE
401 East Host Drive, Lake Geneva WI 53147-2500. 262/249-5200. **Fax:** 262/249-5210. **Contact:** Michael J. Corey, Senior Partner. **World Wide Web address:** http://www.tmpw.com. **Description:** An executive search firm. **Specializes in the areas of:** Biotechnology; Consumer Products; Finance; Health/Medical; Industrial; Pharmaceuticals; Technical. **Corporate headquarters location:** New York NY. **Other U.S. locations:** Nationwide.

U.S. TECH FORCE INC.
485 South Military Road, Fond du Lac WI 54935. 920/922-5000. **Toll-free phone:** 800/230-0505. **Fax:** 920/922-0060. **Contact:** Ron Deabler, Manager. **Description:** An executive search firm operating on a contingency basis. Founded in 1990. **Specializes in the areas of:** Architecture/Construction; Engineering; Industrial; Manufacturing; Office Support; Publishing; Secretarial. **Positions commonly filled include:** Blue-Collar Worker Supervisor; Buyer; Clerical Supervisor; Design Engineer; Draftsperson; Industrial Engineer; Industrial Production Manager; Mechanical Engineer; Metallurgical Engineer; Purchasing Agent/Manager; Quality Control Supervisor; Typist/Word Processor. **Corporate headquarters location:** This Location. **Other area locations:** Appleton WI. **Number of placements per year:** 100 - 199.

UNIVERSAL DESIGN CORPORATION
3256 South 92nd Street, Suite 1, Milwaukee WI 53227. 414/329-0651. **Contact:** Manager. **Description:** An executive search firm. **Specializes in the areas of:** Engineering.

THE URSO GROUP
8000 Excelsior Drive, Suite 201, Madison WI 53717. 608/441-9880. **Contact:** Joe Urso, Managing Partner. **Description:** An executive search firm.

WOJDULA & ASSOCIATES
700 RayOVac Drive, Suite 204, Madison WI 53711. 608/271-2000. **Fax:** 608/271-7475. **Contact:** Manager. **Description:** A generalist executive search firm.

PERMANENT EMPLOYMENT AGENCIES

ABR EMPLOYMENT SERVICES
1521 Metro Drive, Suite 204, Schofield WI 54476. 715/355-7711. **Toll-free phone:** 800/715-0064. **Fax:** 715/355-4486. **Contact:** Carol Howard, Branch Manager. **E-mail address:** scho@abrjobs.com. **World Wide Web address:** http://www.abrjobs.com. **Description:** A permanent employment agency that also provides some temporary placements. Client company pays fee. **Specializes in the areas of:** Accounting; Administration; Engineering; Finance; Light Industrial;

Scientific; Secretarial; Technical. **Positions commonly filled include:** Accountant; Administrative Assistant; Advertising Clerk; AS400 Programmer Analyst; Auditor; Blue-Collar Worker Supervisor; Branch Manager; Civil Engineer; Claim Representative; Clerical Supervisor; Computer Operator; Computer Programmer; Computer Support Technician; Computer Technician; Controller; Customer Service Representative; Database Administrator; Database Manager; Design Engineer; Draftsperson; Electrical/Electronics Engineer;

Electrician; Human Resources Manager; Manufacturing Engineer; MIS Specialist; Network/Systems Administrator; Paralegal; Production Manager; Purchasing Agent/Manager; Quality Control Supervisor; Secretary; Systems Analyst; Transportation/Traffic Specialist; Typist/Word Processor; Underwriter/Assistant Underwriter. **Corporate headquarters location:** This Location. **Average salary range of placements:** $20,000 - $29,999. **Number of placements per year:** 200 - 499.

AMERICAN TECHNICAL SERVICES, INC.
16535 West Bluemound Road, Suite 100, Brookfield WI 53005-5936. 262/789-0505. **Contact:** Manager. **Description:** A permanent employment agency that also provides some permanent and contract placements. Founded in 1991. **Specializes in the areas of:** Engineering; Manufacturing; Office Support; Publishing. **Positions commonly filled include:** Design Engineer; Designer; Draftsperson; Electrician; Industrial Engineer; Mechanical Engineer; Purchasing Agent/Manager; Structural Engineer; Technical Writer/Editor. **Number of placements per year:** 500 - 999.

ARGUS TECHNICAL SERVICES
2339 West Wisconsin Avenue, Appleton WI 54914. 920/731-7703. **Fax:** 920/731-1886. **Contact:** Manager. **Description:** A permanent employment agency. **Specializes in the areas of:** Architecture/Construction; Computer Science/Software; Engineering; Industrial; Manufacturing; Personnel/Labor Relations; Technical. **Positions commonly filled include:** Aerospace Engineer; Architect; Biomedical Engineer; Chemical Engineer; Civil Engineer; Computer Programmer; Designer; Draftsperson; Electrical/Electronics Engineer; Electrician; General Manager; Industrial Engineer; Landscape Architect; Mechanical Engineer; Metallurgical Engineer; Production Manager; Quality Control Supervisor; Software Engineer; Stationary Engineer; Structural Engineer; Surveyor; Technical Writer/Editor; Urban/Regional Planner.

ASSOCIATED SECRETARIAL
7635 West Bluemound Road, Milwaukee WI 53213-3500. 414/476-4333. **Fax:** 414/476-4330. **Contact:** Mary Scheele, Owner. **Description:** A permanent employment agency. **Specializes in the areas of:** Office Support. **Average salary range of placements:** $20,000 - $29,999. **Number of placements per year:** 50 - 99.

AUSTRIA AUSTRIA AND ASSOCIATES
P.O. Box 17682, Milwaukee WI 53217. 414/247-1865. **Contact:** Roger Austria, President. **Description:** A permanent employment agency. Founded in 1983. **Specializes in the areas of:** Engineering; General Management; Health/Medical; Manufacturing; Personnel/Labor Relations; Technical. **Positions commonly filled include:** Accountant/Auditor; Administrative Manager; Aerospace Engineer; Agricultural Engineer; Bank Officer/Manager; Buyer; Ceramics Engineer; Chemical Engineer; Chemist; Civil Engineer; Design Engineer; Education Administrator; EEG Technologist; EKG Technician; Electrical/Electronics Engineer; Emergency Medical Technician; Environmental Engineer; Financial Analyst; Food Scientist/Technologist; Forester/Conservation Scientist; General Manager; Geologist/Geophysicist; Health Services Manager; Hotel Manager; Human Resources Manager; Human Service Worker; Industrial Engineer; Industrial Production Manager; Licensed Practical Nurse; Management Analyst/Consultant; Management Trainee; Manufacturer's/Wholesaler's Sales Rep.; Market Research Analyst; Materials Engineer; Mathematician; Mechanical Engineer; Medical Records Technician; Metallurgical Engineer; Mining Engineer; Nuclear Engineer; Nuclear Medicine Technologist; Occupational Therapist; Operations/Production Manager; Petroleum Engineer; Pharmacist; Physical Therapist; Physician; Physicist; Psychologist; Public Relations Specialist; Purchasing Agent/Manager; Quality Control Supervisor; Recreational Therapist; Registered Nurse; Respiratory Therapist; Science Technologist; Social Worker;

Sociologist; Statistician; Strategic Relations Manager; Structural Engineer; Surgical Technician; Technical Writer/Editor; Telecommunications Manager; Transportation/Traffic Specialist; Travel Agent. **Average salary range of placements:** $30,000 - $50,000. **Number of placements per year:** 50 - 99.

CONCORD STAFF SOURCE INC.
735 North Water Street, Suite 185, Milwaukee WI 53202. 414/291-6180. **Fax:** 414/272-3852. **Contact:** Jamey Morgan, President. **Description:** A permanent employment agency. **Specializes in the areas of:** Computer Science/Software; Health/Medical. **Positions commonly filled include:** Computer Programmer; MIS Specialist; Occupational Therapist; Pharmacist; Physician; Radiological Technologist; Registered Nurse; Respiratory Therapist; Software Engineer; Speech-Language Pathologist; Systems Analyst; Systems Manager. **Average salary range of placements:** More than $50,000. **Number of placements per year:** 100 - 199.

DUNHILL OF GREEN BAY
336 South Jefferson Street, Green Bay WI 54301. 920/432-2977. **Contact:** Office Manager. **Description:** A permanent employment agency. **Specializes in the areas of:** Data Processing; Engineering; Manufacturing; Sales. **Positions commonly filled include:** Engineer; Sales Representative; Typist/Word Processor.

DUNHILL STAFFING SYSTEMS
735 North Water Street, Suite 105, Milwaukee WI 53202. 414/298-2000. **Contact:** Manager. **Description:** A permanent employment agency that also provides some temporary placements. **Specializes in the areas of:** Accounting/Auditing; Administration; Secretarial. **Positions commonly filled include:** Accountant/Auditor; Budget Analyst; Butcher; Clerical Supervisor; Computer Programmer; Credit Manager; Customer Service Representative; Financial Analyst; Human Resources Manager; Insurance Agent; MIS Specialist; Paralegal; Software Engineer; Systems Analyst; Typist/Word Processor; Underwriter/Assistant Underwriter. **Number of placements per year:** 200 - 499.

EAGLE TECHNOLOGY GROUP INC.
11575 Theo Trecker Way, West Allis WI 53214. 414/453-9545. **Toll-free phone:** 800/964-9675. **Fax:** 414/453-9720. **Contact:** Kathy Davis, Vice President. **E-mail address:** info@eagletechnologygroup. com. **World Wide Web address:** http://www. eagletechnologygroup.com. **Description:** A permanent employment agency that also provides some contract placements. **Specializes in the areas of:** Computer Science/Software; Engineering; Industrial; Scientific; Technical. **Positions commonly filled include:** Architect; Biomedical Engineer; Blue-Collar Worker Supervisor; Branch Manager; Chemical Engineer; Chemist; Civil Engineer; Clinical Lab Technician; Computer Animator; Computer Programmer; Database Manager; Design Engineer; Draftsperson; Electrical Engineer; Electrician; Environmental Engineer; Graphic Artist; Graphic Designer; Human Resources Manager; Industrial Engineer; Industrial Production Manager; Internet Services Manager; Management Analyst/Consultant; Manufacturing Engineer; Mechanical Engineer; MIS Manager; Multimedia Designer; Production Manager; Purchasing Agent; Quality Control Supervisor; Sales Engineer; Software Engineer; Systems Analyst; Systems Manager; Technical Writer; Telecommunications Manager. **Benefits available to temporary workers:** Company Pharmacy; Dental Insurance; Disability Coverage; Life Insurance; Medical Insurance; Paid Holidays; Vacation Pay. **Corporate headquarters location:** This Location. **Other U.S. locations:** Nationwide. **Average salary range of placements:** More than $50,000. **Number of placements per year:** 1000+.

EMPLOYABILITY
136 West Grand Avenue, Suite 101, Beloit WI 53511-6259. 608/365-9090. **Fax:** 608/365-9062. **Contact:** Vicki

Schmuck, Office Manager. **Description:** A permanent employment agency. **Specializes in the areas of:** Industrial; Manufacturing; Secretarial; Technical. **Positions commonly filled include:** Blue-Collar Worker Supervisor; Clerical Supervisor; Customer Service Representative; General Manager; Industrial Production Manager; Operations/Production Manager; Quality Control Supervisor; Services Sales Representative; Typist/Word Processor. **Benefits available to temporary workers:** Bonus Award/Plan; Paid Holidays. **Corporate headquarters location:** Rockford IL. **Other area locations:** Delavan WI; Janesville WI. **Other U.S. locations:** Belvidere IL; Oregon IL. **Average salary range of placements:** $20,000 - $29,999. **Number of placements per year:** 500 - 999.

EPIC SKILLED & INDUSTRIAL

10701 West North Avenue, Suite 100, Milwaukee WI 53226. 414/476-8050. **Fax:** 414/771-4848. **Contact:** George Mathews, Office Manager. **Description:** A permanent employment agency. Client company pays fee. **Specializes in the areas of:** Industrial; Manufacturing. **Positions commonly filled include:** Machine Operator; Precision Assembler; Shipping and Receiving Clerk; Tool and Die Maker. **Benefits available to temporary workers:** Medical Insurance; Paid Vacation. **Average salary range of placements:** $20,000 - $29,999. **Number of placements per year:** 200 - 499.

FOOD & DRUG PROFESSIONALS INC.

420 East Lake Street, Horicon WI 53032. 920/485-4100. **Fax:** 920/485-2444. **Contact:** Carl Fausett, CPC/President. **Description:** A permanent employment agency. **Specializes in the areas of:** Food; Pharmaceuticals. **Positions commonly filled include:** Agricultural Engineer; Chemical Engineer; Designer; Draftsperson; Electrical/Electronics Engineer; Food Scientist/Technologist; Industrial Engineer; Mechanical Engineer; Science Technologist. **Number of placements per year:** 50 - 99.

LEGAL PLACEMENT SERVICES, INC.
PERSONNEL SPECIALISTS

161 West Wisconsin Avenue, Suite 3189, Milwaukee WI 53203. 414/276-6689. **Fax:** 414/276-1418. **Contact:** Ian Hamilton, Executive Vice President. **E-mail address:** psips@execpc.com. **Description:** A permanent employment agency that also provides some temporary placements. **Specializes in the areas of:** Accounting; Legal. **Positions commonly filled include:** Account Manager; Accountant; Administrative Assistant; Administrative Manager; Advertising Executive; Applications Engineer; AS400 Programmer Analyst; Attorney; Bank Officer/Manager; Branch Manager; Budget Analyst; Chief Financial Officer; Civil Engineer; Computer Animator; Computer Engineer; Computer Operator; Computer Programmer; Computer Scientist; Computer Support Technician; Computer Technician; Content Developer; Controller; Credit Manager; Customer Service Representative; Database Administrator; Database Manager; Design Engineer; Environmental Engineer; Financial Analyst; General Manager; Human Resources Manager; Industrial Engineer; Intellectual Property Lawyer; Internet Services Manager; Librarian; Manufacturing Engineer; Marketing Manager; Mechanical Engineer; Metallurgical Engineer; MIS Specialist; Multimedia Designer; Network/Systems Administrator; Nurse Practitioner; Operations Manager; Paralegal; Production Manager; Public Relations Specialist; Purchasing Agent/Manager; Quality Assurance Engineer; Quality Control Supervisor; Sales Engineer; Sales Executive; Sales Manager; Sales Representative; Secretary; Software Engineer; SQL Programmer; Systems Analyst; Systems Manager; Typist/Word Processor; Webmaster. **Average salary range of placements:** $50,000 - $100,000. **Number of placements per year:** 100 - 199.

MACPROS, INC.

122 Green Bay Road, Thiensville WI 53092. 262/512-1700. **Fax:** 262/512-1708. **Contact:** Manager. **Description:** A permanent employment agency that also provides some temporary placements. **Specializes in the areas of:** Advertising; Art/Design; Publishing; Sales. **Positions commonly filled include:** Computer Graphics Specialist. **Number of placements per year:** 50 - 99.

N.E.W. CONTRACTING SERVICES, INC.

P.O. Box 2239, Green Bay WI 54306-2239. 920/431-4400. **Fax:** 920/431-4404. **Contact:** Blaise Krautkramer, President. **Description:** A permanent employment agency that also provides some temporary and contract placements. Client company pays fee. **Specializes in the areas of:** Administration; Industrial; Light Industrial; Personnel/Labor Relations; Printing; Publishing; Secretarial. **Positions commonly filled include:** Account Manager; Account Representative; Accountant; Administrative Assistant; Assistant Manager; Auditor; Bank Officer/Manager; Blue-Collar Worker Supervisor; Buyer; Claim Representative; Clerical Supervisor; Computer Operator; Computer Programmer; Computer Support Technician; Computer Technician; Construction Contractor; Controller; Cost Estimator; Credit Manager; Customer Service Representative; Desktop Publishing Specialist; Draftsperson; Electrician; General Manager; Graphic Artist; Human Resources Manager; Industrial Engineer; Management Analyst/Consultant; Management Trainee; Mechanical Engineer; Paralegal; Production Manager; Project Manager; Purchasing Agent/Manager; Quality Assurance Engineer; Sales Engineer; Sales Executive; Sales Manager; Sales Representative; Secretary; Technical Writer/Editor; Typist/Word Processor. **Benefits available to temporary workers:** Dental Insurance; Medical Insurance. **Corporate headquarters location:** This Location. **Other area locations:** Appleton WI; Oconto WI. **Average salary range of placements:** Less than $20,000. **Number of placements per year:** 1000+.

PLACEMENTS OF RACINE INC.

222 Main Street, Suite 101, Racine WI 53403. 262/637-9355. **Contact:** Office Manager. **Description:** A permanent employment agency. **Specializes in the areas of:** Accounting/Auditing; Administration; Clerical; Computer Hardware/Software; Engineering; Finance; Manufacturing; Sales. **Positions commonly filled include:** Accountant/Auditor; Agricultural Engineer; Bookkeeper; Buyer; Computer Programmer; Credit Manager; Customer Service Representative; Draftsperson; EDP Specialist; Electrical/Electronics Engineer; Financial Analyst; Industrial Engineer; Legal Secretary; Marketing Specialist; Mechanical Engineer; Medical Secretary; Metallurgical Engineer; MIS Specialist; Purchasing Agent/Manager; Quality Control Supervisor; Receptionist; Sales Representative; Secretary; Stenographer; Systems Analyst; Technical Writer/Editor; Technician; Typist/Word Processor. **Number of placements per year:** 50 - 99.

PROFESSIONAL ENGINEERING PLACEMENTS

11941 West Rawson Avenue, Franklin WI 53132. 414/427-1700. **Fax:** 414/427-8080. **Contact:** Patty Wiza, President. **E-mail address:** proeng33@aol.com. **World Wide Web address:** http://www.proengineer.com. **Description:** A permanent employment agency. **Specializes in the areas of:** Computer Science/Software; Engineering; Industrial. **Positions commonly filled include:** Computer Programmer; Design Engineer; Draftsperson; Electrical/Electronics Engineer; Industrial Engineer; Manufacturing Engineer; Mechanical Engineer; Production Manager; Project Manager; Quality Control Supervisor; Sales Engineer; Software Engineer. **Average salary range of placements:** $30,000 - $50,000. **Number of placements per year:** 50 - 99.

SAUVE COMPANY, LTD.

P.O. Box 337, Amherst WI 54406. 715/824-2502. **Fax:** 715/824-2192. **Contact:** Gordy Sauve, President. **Description:** A permanent employment agency specializing in food manufacturing with an emphasis on the dairy industry. **Specializes in the areas of:** Engineering; Food; General Management. **Positions commonly filled include:** Accountant; Biological

Scientist; Blue-Collar Worker Supervisor; Buyer; Chemical Engineer; Chemist; Civil Engineer; Controller; Customer Service Representative; Dietician/Nutritionist; Electrical/Electronics Engineer; Environmental Engineer; Food Scientist/Technologist; General Manager; Industrial Engineer; Industrial Production Manager; Management Trainee; Manufacturing Engineer; Operations Manager; Production Manager; Purchasing Agent/Manager; Quality Control Supervisor; Vice President of Operations. **Corporate headquarters location:** This Location. **Average salary range of placements:** $30,000 - $50,000. **Number of placements per year:** 1 - 49.

SEEK INC.
P.O. Box 148, Grafton WI 53024-0148. 262/377-8888. **Toll-free phone:** 800/975-6464. **Fax:** 262/377-2760. **Contact:** Carol Schneider, CPC/CEO. **E-mail address:** info@seekcareers.com. **World Wide Web address:** http://www.seekcareers.com. **Description:** A permanent employment agency that also provides some temporary placements. **Specializes in the areas of:** Accounting; Information Technology; Light Industrial; Office Support; Technical. **Corporate headquarters location:** This Location. **Other area locations:** Fond du Lac WI; Milwaukee WI; Oshkosh WI; Sheboygan WI; West Bend WI.

SEEK INC.
17 Forest Avenue, Suite 116, Fond du Lac WI 54935. 920/924-7886. **Toll-free phone:** 800/221-6407. **Fax:** 920/924-7896. **Contact:** Manager. **Description:** A permanent employment agency that also provides some temporary placements. Founded in 1971. **Specializes in the areas of:** Engineering; Industrial; Secretarial. **Positions commonly filled include:** Accountant/Auditor; Administrative Manager; Blue-Collar Worker Supervisor; Clerical Supervisor; Computer Programmer; Customer Service Representative; Electrical/Electronics Engineer; General Manager; Industrial Engineer; Industrial Production Manager; Mechanical Engineer; MIS Specialist; Multimedia Designer; Operations/Production Manager; Software Engineer; Systems Analyst; Typist/Word Processor. **Benefits available to temporary workers:** Bonus Award/Plan; Medical Insurance. **Corporate headquarters location:** Grafton WI. **Other area locations:** Milwaukee WI; Oshkosh WI; Sheboygan WI; West Bend WI. **Average salary range of placements:** $20,000 - $29,999. **Number of placements per year:** 200 - 499.

SHORE PERSONNEL
342 West Main Street, Waukesha WI 53186-4613. 262/544-6166. **Fax:** 262/544-4847. **Contact:** Dave Shore, Owner. **Description:** A permanent employment agency that also provides some temp-to-perm placements. **Specializes in the areas of:** Industrial. **Positions commonly filled include:** Accountant/Auditor; Automotive Mechanic; Blue-Collar Worker Supervisor; Human Resources Manager; Typist/Word Processor. **Corporate headquarters location:** Greenfield WI. **Average salary range of placements:** Less than $20,000.

TOM SLOAN & ASSOCIATES INC.
P.O. Box 50, Watertown WI 53094. 920/261-8890. **Fax:** 920/261-6357. **Contact:** Tom Sloan, President. **Description:** A permanent employment agency. **Specializes in the areas of:** Engineering; Food; General Management; Sales; Technical. **Positions commonly**

filled include: Account Manager; Account Representative; Accountant; Applications Engineer; Chemical Engineer; Chemist; Chief Financial Officer; Controller; Design Engineer; Electrical/Electronics Engineer; Environmental Engineer; Food Scientist/Technologist; General Manager; Human Resources Manager; Industrial Engineer; Industrial Production Manager; Manufacturing Engineer; Marketing Manager; Mechanical Engineer; Operations Manager; Production Manager; Project Manager; Purchasing Agent/Manager; Quality Control Supervisor; Sales Engineer; Sales Executive; Sales Manager; Sales Representative. **Average salary range of placements:** More than $50,000. **Number of placements per year:** 100 - 199.

TECHSTAFF
11270 West Park Place, Suite 460, Milwaukee WI 53224-3624. 414/359-4444. **Fax:** 414/359-4949. **Contact:** Jeff Moerke, Recruiter. **E-mail address:** recruiter@techstaff.com. **World Wide Web address:** http://www.techstaff.com. **Description:** A permanent employment agency that also provides some temporary placements. **Specializes in the areas of:** Engineering; Manufacturing; Technical. **Positions commonly filled include:** Chemical Engineer; Civil Engineer; Computer Programmer; Draftsperson; Electrical/Electronics Engineer; Environmental Engineer; Industrial Engineer; Industrial Production Manager; Mechanical Engineer; MIS Specialist; Purchasing Agent/Manager; Quality Control Supervisor; Software Engineer; Structural Engineer; Systems Analyst; Technical Writer/Editor. **Benefits available to temporary workers:** 401(k); Dental Insurance; Medical Insurance; Paid Holidays; Paid Vacation. **Other U.S. locations:** CA; FL; IA; IL; MI. **Average salary range of placements:** $30,000 - $50,000. **Number of placements per year:** 200 - 499.

TEMTEC CORPORATION
3927 South Howell Avenue, Milwaukee WI 53207. 414/769-3620. **Fax:** 414/769-3630. **Contact:** Dan Salem, General Manager. **Description:** A permanent employment agency that also provides some temporary placements.

WORK CONNECTION
1045 West Clairemont Avenue, Eau Claire WI 54701-6104. 715/836-9675. **Fax:** 715/836-7974. **Contact:** Cindi Jones, Office Manager. **Description:** A permanent employment agency that also provides some temporary placements. Founded in 1986. **Specializes in the areas of:** Accounting/Auditing; Banking; Personnel/Labor Relations; Publishing; Retail; Sales; Secretarial; Technical; Transportation. **Positions commonly filled include:** Accountant/Auditor; Administrative Manager; Biochemist; Blue-Collar Worker Supervisor; Chemical Engineer; Chemist; Clinical Lab Technician; Credit Manager; Customer Service Representative; Dental Assistant/Dental Hygienist; Dietician/Nutritionist; Electrical/Electronics Engineer; Electrician; Food Scientist/Technologist; Human Resources Manager; Management Trainee; Paralegal; Preschool Worker; Purchasing Agent/Manager; Quality Control Supervisor; Restaurant/Food Service Manager; Systems Analyst; Typist/Word Processor. **Benefits available to temporary workers:** Medical Insurance. **Corporate headquarters location:** Minneapolis MN. **Other U.S. locations:** Nationwide. **Number of placements per year:** 1000+.

TEMPORARY EMPLOYMENT AGENCIES

ADTEC STAFFING
3330 University Avenue, Suite 330, Madison WI 53705. 608/231-3210. **Contact:** Manager. **Description:** A temporary agency that also provides some permanent placements. **Specializes in the areas of:** Clerical; Computer Hardware/Software; Light Industrial; Secretarial.

CROWN SERVICES
10625 West North Avenue, Suite 102, Milwaukee WI 53226. 414/475-7409. **Contact:** Office Manager. **Description:** A temporary agency. **Specializes in the areas of:** Accounting/Auditing; Banking; Clerical; Engineering; Finance; Insurance; Legal; Manufacturing; Personnel/Labor Relations. **Positions commonly filled**

include: Accountant; Administrative Assistant; Advertising Clerk; Bookkeeper; Claim Rep.; Computer Operator; Computer Programmer; Construction Trade Worker; Customer Service Rep.; Data Entry Clerk; Driver; Factory Worker; Legal Secretary; Receptionist; Sales Rep.; Secretary; Typist/Word Processor. **Number of placements per year:** 1000+.

CUSTOM CARE
2317 International Lane, Madison WI 53704. 608/244-4377. **Contact:** Director of Operations. **Description:** A temporary agency. Founded in 1992. **Specializes in the areas of:** Health/Medical. **Positions commonly filled include:** Certified Nurses Aide; Dental Assistant/Dental Hygienist; Dietician/Nutritionist; Licensed Practical Nurse; Registered Nurse. **Benefits available to temporary workers:** Paid Holidays; Paid Vacation. **Average salary range of placements:** $20,000 - $29,999. **Number of placements per year:** 500 - 999.

ENVIROSTAFF, INC.
19601 West Bluemound Road, Suite 100, Brookfield WI 53045. 262/938-6853. **Contact:** Manager. **Description:** A temporary agency providing personnel to environmental consultants, laboratories, and remediation companies. **NOTE:** Jobseekers are asked to call and speak to a recruiter before sending a resume. **Specializes in the areas of:** Biology; Engineering; Food; Industrial; Manufacturing. **Positions commonly filled include:** Biochemist; Biological Scientist; Chemical Engineer; Chemist; Civil Engineer; Clinical Lab Technician; Construction and Building Inspector; Construction Engineer; Design Engineer; Designer; Environmental Engineer; Forester/Conservation Scientist; Geologist/ Geophysicist; Industrial Engineer; Metallurgical Engineer; Mining Engineer; Nuclear Engineer; Petroleum Engineer; Quality Control Supervisor; Science Technologist; Structural Engineer; Surveyor; Transportation/Traffic Specialist. **Corporate headquarters location:** Minneapolis MN. **Average salary range of placements:** $20,000 - $29,999. **Number of placements per year:** 200 - 499.

GREENFIELD REHABILITATION AGENCY
7517 West Coldspring Road, Greenfield WI 53220-2814. **Toll-free phone:** 800/704-4724x23. **Fax:** 414/327-5411. **Contact:** Lisa Slattery, Recruiter. **Description:** A temporary agency. Greenfield Rehabilitation Agency also provides contract services to skilled nursing facilities, as well as temporary rehabilitation services. Founded in 1966. **Specializes in the areas of:** Health/Medical. **Positions commonly filled include:** Occupational Therapist; Physical Therapist; Speech-Language Pathologist. **Benefits available to temporary workers:** Education Assistance; Paid Vacation. **Corporate headquarters location:** This Location.

HATCH STAFFING SERVICES
18900 West Bluemound Road, Suite 29, Brookfield WI 53045. 262/789-8384. **Contact:** Manager. **Description:** A temporary agency that also provides some temp-to-perm and permanent placements. **Specializes in the areas of:** Administration; Customer Service; Information Technology; Management; Sales.

INTERIM PERSONNEL
2310 South Green Bay Road, Racine WI 53406. 262/633-7725. **Fax:** 262/633-7783. **Contact:** Lori Krezinski, Branch Manager. **Description:** A temporary agency that also provides some permanent placements. Founded in 1946. **Specializes in the areas of:** Manufacturing; Personnel/Labor Relations; Sales; Secretarial. **Positions commonly filled include:** Customer Service Representative; Human Resources Manager; Quality Control Supervisor; Typist/Word Processor. **Other U.S. locations:** Nationwide. **Average salary range of placements:** Less than $20,000. **Number of placements per year:** 500 - 999.

LANDMARK THE STAFFING RESOURCE
2100 Riverside Drive, Green Bay WI 54301. 920/437-3130. **Fax:** 920/431-3433. **Contact:** Branch Manager.

World Wide Web address: http://www.lanmrk.com. **Description:** A temporary agency. Specializes in the areas of: Accounting/Auditing; Banking; Secretarial. **Positions commonly filled include:** Accountant/Auditor; Bank Officer/Manager; Credit Manager; Customer Service Representative; Human Resources Manager; Services Sales Representative; Underwriter/Assistant Underwriter. **Benefits available to temporary workers:** 401(k); Medical Insurance; Paid Holidays; Profit Sharing. **Corporate headquarters location:** Appleton WI. **Other area locations:** Neenah WI; Oshkosh WI.

LANDMARK THE STAFFING RESOURCE
10 College Avenue, Suite 311, Appleton WI 54911-5759. 920/731-3130. **Toll-free phone:** 800/750-2528. **Fax:** 920/731-4974. **Contact:** Staffing Supervisor. **E-mail address:** landmark@lanmrk.com. **World Wide Web address:** http://www.lanmrk.com. **Description:** A temporary agency. **Specializes in the areas of:** Accounting/Auditing; Insurance; Office Support; Personnel/Labor Relations; Secretarial. **Positions commonly filled include:** Account Representative; Accountant; Adjuster; Administrative Assistant; Auditor; Budget Analyst; Claim Representative; Clerical Supervisor; Computer Operator; Controller; Cost Estimator; Customer Service Representative; Database Manager; Editorial Assistant; Financial Analyst; Graphic Artist; Graphic Designer; Marketing Specialist; Paralegal; Purchasing Agent/Manager; Sales Representative; Secretary. **Benefits available to temporary workers:** 401(k); Dental Insurance; Medical Insurance; Paid Holidays; Paid Vacation; Profit Sharing. **Corporate headquarters location:** This Location. **Other area locations:** Green Bay WI; Neenah WI; Oshkosh WI.

MANPOWER TEMPORARY SERVICES
2797 Prairie Avenue, Suite 28, Beloit WI 53511-2288. 608/362-1330. **Fax:** 608/362-0585. **Contact:** Dorothy Farrey, Service Representative. **Description:** A temporary agency. **Specializes in the areas of:** Data Processing; Industrial; Manufacturing; Personnel/Labor Relations; Secretarial. **Positions commonly filled include:** Typist/Word Processor. **Benefits available to temporary workers:** Life Insurance; Medical Insurance; Paid Holidays; Paid Vacation. **Corporate headquarters location:** Milwaukee WI. **Other U.S. locations:** Nationwide. **Average salary range of placements:** Less than $20,000. **Number of placements per year:** 100 - 199.

MEDTEAMS
725 American Avenue, Waukesha WI 53188. 262/544-2573. **Toll-free phone:** 800/326-2011x2573. **Fax:** 262/544-4943. **Contact:** Judith Haeberle, Executive Director. **Description:** A temporary agency. Founded in 1987. **Specializes in the areas of:** Health/Medical. **Positions commonly filled include:** Licensed Practical Nurse; Nuclear Medicine Technologist; Occupational Therapist; Physical Therapist; Registered Nurse; Speech-Language Pathologist.

NORRELL STAFFING SERVICES, INC.
3333 North Mayfair Road, Suite 106, Milwaukee WI 53222. 414/476-2777. **Fax:** 414/476-8110. **Contact:** Manager. **Description:** A temporary agency that also provides permanent placements. **Specializes in the areas of:** Administration; Industrial; Secretarial. **Positions commonly filled include:** Administrative Manager; Clerical Supervisor. **Benefits available to temporary workers:** Dental Insurance; Medical Insurance; Paid Holidays; Paid Vacation; Vision Plan. **Corporate headquarters location:** Atlanta GA. **Other U.S. locations:** Nationwide.

OLSTEN STAFFING SERVICES
7500 Green Bay Road, Kenosha WI 53142. 262/697-5140. **Contact:** Branch Manager. **Description:** A temporary agency. **Specializes in the areas of:** Accounting/Auditing; Administration; Banking; Engineering; Finance; General Management; Industrial; Manufacturing; Nonprofit; Personnel/Labor Relations.

Positions commonly filled include: Accountant/Auditor; Bank Officer/Manager; Blue-Collar Worker Supervisor; Chemical Engineer; Chemist; Clinical Lab Technician; Computer Programmer; Draftsperson; Paralegal; Typist/Word Processor. Benefits available to temporary workers: Medical Insurance; Training. Corporate headquarters location: Melville NY. International locations: Worldwide. Average salary range of placements: $20,000 - $29,999. Number of placements per year: 1000+.

OLSTEN STAFFING SERVICES
2147 Brackett Avenue, Eau Claire WI 54701. 715/834-7555. Fax: 715/834-8041. Contact: Christina Cota, Office Manager. Description: A temporary agency. Specializes in the areas of: Accounting; Administration; Computer Science/Software; Engineering; Finance; Industrial; Insurance; Legal; Light Industrial; Printing; Publishing; Secretarial; Technical. Positions commonly filled include: Account Rep.; Accountant; Administrative Assistant; Administrative Manager; Applications Engineer; Clerical Supervisor; Computer Operator; Computer Programmer; Controller; Cost Estimator; Customer Service Rep.; Design Engineer; Draftsperson; Electrical Engineer; Environmental Engineer; Financial Analyst; Graphic Artist; Graphic Designer; Human Resources Manager; Industrial Engineer; Manufacturing Engineer; Mechanical Engineer; MIS Manager; Operations Manager; Paralegal; Production Manager; Project Manager; Purchasing Agent/Manager; Quality Control Supervisor; Sales Engineer; Secretary; Software Engineer; Systems Analyst; Systems Manager; Technical Writer/Editor; Typist/Word Processor. Benefits available to temporary workers: Medical Insurance; Paid Holidays; Paid Vacation. Corporate headquarters location: Melville NY. International locations: Worldwide. Average salary range of placements: $20,000 - $29,999. Number of placements per year: 500 - 999.

OLSTEN STAFFING SERVICES
1017 East Avenue South, La Crosse WI 54601. 608/782-1100. Fax: 608/782-7080. Contact: Jeanne Barr, Regional Sales Manager. Description: A temporary agency that also provides some permanent placements. Specializes in the areas of: Accounting/Auditing; Administration; Manufacturing; Publishing; Secretarial. Positions commonly filled include: Accountant/Auditor; Clerical Supervisor; Computer Programmer; Cost Estimator; Customer Service Representative; Market Research Analyst; Operations/Production Manager; Services Sales Representative; Typist/Word Processor. Corporate headquarters location: Melville NY. International locations: Worldwide. Average salary

range of placements: Less than $20,000. Number of placements per year: 1000+.

SITE PERSONNEL SERVICES, INC.
TRAINOR/FRANK & ASSOCIATES, INC.
16550 West Lisbon Road, Menomonee Falls WI 53051. 262/783-5181. Fax: 262/783-7905. Contact: Amy Reger, Manager. E-mail address: tsacsi@execpc.com. World Wide Web address: http://www.tsacsi.com. Description: A certified minority-owned temporary agency that also provides some permanent placements. Trainor/Frank & Associates (also at this location) is an executive search firm. Specializes in the areas of: Administration; Computer Science/Software; Engineering; Industrial; Light Industrial; Technical; Transportation. Positions commonly filled include: Applications Engineer; Architect; Buyer; Chemical Engineer; Chemist; Civil Engineer; Computer Programmer; Draftsperson; Electrical/Electronics Engineer; Electrician; Environmental Engineer; Graphic Designer; Human Resources Manager; Industrial Engineer; Industrial Production Manager; Manufacturing Engineer; Marketing Manager; Mechanical Engineer; Metallurgical Engineer; MIS Specialist; Operations Manager; Project Manager; Purchasing Agent/Manager; Quality Control Supervisor; Sales Engineer; Software Engineer; Systems Analyst; Technical Writer/Editor; Transportation/Traffic Specialist. Benefits available to temporary workers: Paid Holidays. Corporate headquarters location: This Location. Other U.S. locations: Boulder CO; Tampa FL; Minneapolis MN; Cincinnati OH. Average salary range of placements: $30,000 - $50,000. Number of placements per year: 200 - 499.

TEMPS PLUS STAFFING SERVICES, INC.
7001 West Greenfield Avenue, West Allis WI 53214. 414/475-7300. Toll-free phone: 800/969-1470. Fax: 414/475-9119. Contact: Jim Watters, Vice President. E-mail address: jim9116w@aol.com. Description: A temporary agency that also provides some permanent placements. Founded in 1987. Specializes in the areas of: Administration; Banking; Computer Science/Software; Secretarial; Technical. Positions commonly filled include: Administrative Assistant; Certified Nurses Aide; Claim Representative; Computer Operator; Computer Programmer; Licensed Practical Nurse; MIS Specialist; Registered Nurse; Typist/Word Processor. Benefits available to temporary workers: Bonus Award/Plan; Credit Union; Medical Insurance; Paid Vacation. Corporate headquarters location: This Location. Other area locations: Kenosha WI; Shorewood WI. Other U.S. locations: Minneapolis MN. Average salary range of placements: $20,000 - $29,999. Number of placements per year: 500 - 999.

CONTRACT SERVICES FIRMS

ADECCO/TAD TECHNICAL SERVICES
261 North Casaloma Drive, Appleton WI 54913. 920/739-1500. Fax: 920/739-5921. Contact: Ken Depperman, Manager. Description: A contract services firm. Specializes in the areas of: Computer Science; Engineering; Industrial; Manufacturing; Technical. Positions commonly filled include: Architect; Computer Programmer; Construction Contractor; Construction Manager; Design Engineer; Designer; Draftsperson; Electrical Engineer; Industrial Engineer; Mechanical Engineer; MIS Specialist; Quality Control Supervisor; Software Engineer; Structural Engineer; Systems Analyst; Technical Illustrator; Technical Writer. Benefits available to temporary workers: 401(k); Bonus Award/Plan; Paid Holidays; Paid Vacation. Corporate headquarters location: Cambridge MA. Average salary range of placements: $30,000 - $50,000. Number of placements per year: 200 - 499.

AEROTEK, INC.
400 South Executive Drive, Suite 201, Brookfield WI 53005-4215. Toll-free phone: 800/726-1899. Fax:

262/785-9441. Contact: Senior Recruiter. Description: A contract services firm. Specializes in the areas of: Computer Science/Software; Engineering; Industrial; Technical; Telecommunications. Positions commonly filled include: Chemical Engineer; Civil Engineer; Computer Programmer; Design Engineer; Designer; Draftsperson; Electrical/Electronics Engineer; Electrician; Industrial Engineer; Mechanical Engineer; Metallurgical Engineer; Software Engineer; Structural Engineer; Systems Analyst; Technical Writer/Editor. Benefits available to temporary workers: 401(k); Medical Insurance. Corporate headquarters location: Baltimore MD. Other U.S. locations: Nationwide. Average salary range of placements: $30,000 - $50,000. Number of placements per year: 1000+.

INTERIM TECHNOLOGY
440 Science Drive, Suite 102, Madison WI 53711. 608/233-8201. Fax: 608/233-8416. Contact: Tami Sailing, Associate Technical Specialist. E-mail address: techstaff_madison@compuserve.com. World Wide Web address: http://www.interim.com. Description: A

contract services firm. Interim Technology is a strategic partner of *Fortune* 1000 companies providing supplemental staffing solutions to support data center operations, telecommunications, help desks, client/server and applications development and maintenance, and advanced technology training. **Specializes in the areas of:** Computer Science/Software; Personnel/Labor Relations; Scientific; Technical. **Positions commonly filled include:** Computer Operator; Computer Programmer; Database Manager; Internet Services Manager; MIS Specialist; Software Engineer; Systems Analyst; Technical Writer/Editor. **Corporate headquarters location:** Fort Lauderdale FL. **Other U.S. locations:** Nationwide. **Average salary range of placements:** $30,000 - $50,000. **Number of placements per year:** 100 - 199.

MIDWEST PARALEGAL SERVICES, INC.
312 East Wisconsin Avenue, Suite 410, Milwaukee WI 53202. 414/276-3007. **Contact:** Director. **Description:** A contract services firm. **Positions commonly filled include:** Paralegal.

PDS TECHNICAL SERVICES
2830 Ramada Way, Suite 204, Green Bay WI 54304. 920/499-9943. **Toll-free phone:** 800/333-1389. **Fax:** 920/499-9067. **Contact:** Sue VanPay, Branch Manager. **E-mail address:** greenbay_wi@pdstech.com. **World Wide Web address:** http://www.pdstech.com. **Description:** A contract services firm that also provides permanent placements. **Specializes in the areas of:** Engineering; Information Systems; Manufacturing; Technical. **Corporate headquarters location:** Irving TX.

POLLAK AND SKAN GROUP
13400 Bishops Lane, Suite 300, Brookfield WI 53005-6220. 262/784-3399. **Toll-free phone:** 800/472-9423. **Fax:** 262/784-1913. **Contact:** Pete Dikanovic, Branch Manager. **E-mail address:** milinfo@pscts.com. **World Wide Web address:** http://www.pscts.com. **Description:** A contract services firm. Founded in 1951. **Specializes in the areas of:** Computer Science/Software; Engineering; Scientific; Technical. **Positions commonly filled include:** Architect; Buyer; Chemical Engineer; Civil Engineer; Computer Operator; Computer Programmer; Database Manager; Design Engineer; Draftsperson; Electrical/Electronics Engineer; Industrial Engineer; Manufacturing Engineer; Mechanical Engineer; Project Manager; Purchasing Agent/Manager; Quality Control Supervisor; Software Engineer; Technical Writer/Editor; Webmaster. **Benefits available to temporary workers:** 401(k); Bonus Award/Plan; Dental Insurance; Life Insurance; Medical Insurance; Paid Holidays. **Corporate headquarters location:** Elk Grove Village IL. **Other U.S. locations:** FL; GA; IN;

MI; NC; SC; TX. **Average salary range of placements:** More than $50,000. **Number of placements per year:** 200 - 499.

RCM TECHNOLOGIES
1595 East Allouez Avenue, Green Bay WI 54311. 920/465-3933. **Contact:** Manager. **Description:** A contract services firm. **Specializes in the areas of:** Engineering; Information Systems.

RCM TECHNOLOGIES
8899 North 60th Street, Milwaukee WI 53224. **Toll-free phone:** 800/686-2819. **Fax:** 414/362-8880. **Contact:** Manager. **Description:** A contract services firm. **Specializes in the areas of:** High-Tech.

TECHNOLOGY CONSULTING CORPORATION
N-16 West 23233, Stone Ridge Drive, Waukesha WI 53188. 262/650-6500. **Fax:** 262/650-6530. **Contact:** Recruiting. **World Wide Web address:** http://www.tcc-usa.com. **Description:** A contract services firm. **Specializes in the areas of:** Computer Hardware/Software; High-Tech; Technical. **Positions commonly filled include:** Applications Engineer; Internet Services Manager; MIS Specialist; Systems Analyst. **Other area locations:** Green Bay WI; Madison WI. **Other U.S. locations:** Chicago IL.

THE WATERSTONE GROUP, INC.
1025 West Glen Oaks Lane, Suite 108, Mequon WI 53092. 262/241-8315. **Toll-free phone:** 800/291-3837. **Fax:** 262/241-8349. **Contact:** Manager. **Description:** A technical contract services firm. Founded in 1994. **Specializes in the areas of:** Computer Science/Software; Engineering; Manufacturing; Technical. **Positions commonly filled include:** Architect; Biological Scientist; Chemical Engineer; Civil Engineer; Computer Programmer; Cost Estimator; Design Engineer; Designer; Draftsperson; Electrical/Electronics Engineer; Environmental Engineer; Industrial Engineer; Landscape Architect; Mechanical Engineer; MIS Specialist; Operations/Production Manager; Purchasing Agent/Manager; Quality Control Supervisor; Software Engineer; Structural Engineer; Systems Analyst; Technical Writer/Editor. **Benefits available to temporary workers:** 401(k); Dental Insurance; Life Insurance; Medical Insurance. **Corporate headquarters location:** This Location. **Other area locations:** Green Bay WI. **Average salary range of placements:** $30,000 - $50,000. **Number of placements per year:** 200 - 499.

THE WATERSTONE GROUP, INC.
1331 North Road, Green Bay WI 54313. 920/494-7727. **Contact:** Manager. **Description:** A contract services firm. **Specializes in the areas of:** Technical. **Corporate headquarters location:** Mequon WI.

CAREER/OUTPLACEMENT COUNSELING FIRMS

AT YOUR SERVICE
111 South Pine Street, Burlington WI 53105. 262/763-8467. **Contact:** Carol DeMarco, Owner. **Description:** A career/outplacement counseling firm.

BERNARD HALDANE ASSOCIATES
15800 West Bluemound Road, Suite 320, Brookfield WI 53005. 262/784-2266. **Contact:** Manager. **Description:** A career/outplacement counseling firm.

OVER 50 EMPLOYMENT SERVICES, INC.
10 South Baldwin, Madison WI 53703. 608/255-5585. **Fax:** 608/255-5781. **Contact:** Office Manager. **Description:** A career counseling firm for Dane County residents over the age of 50. The agency provides testing, assessments, job placements, resume counseling, interview skills training, and transitional and follow-up career counseling. **Positions commonly filled include:** Accountant/Auditor; Advertising Clerk; Blue-Collar

Worker Supervisor; Buyer; Counselor; Food Scientist/Technologist; Forester/Conservation Scientist; Health Services Manager; Hotel Manager; Human Resources Manager; Insurance Agent/Broker; Librarian; Management Trainee; Manufacturer's/Wholesaler's Sales Rep.; Property and Real Estate Manager; Public Relations Specialist; Services Sales Representative; Social Worker; Technical Writer/Editor. **Number of placements per year:** 200 - 499.

SUMMIT CAREER SERVICES
3833 County Road A, Rosholt WI 54473. 715/677-6955. **Toll-free phone:** 800/693-8072. **Fax:** 715/677-6944. **Contact:** Marie Keenen Manshein, Owner/President. **Description:** A resume writing and career/outplacement counseling firm. The firm also provides critiques, interview assistance, and job search advice. Summit Career Services also offers an online resume database and Internet services.

◆ W Y O M I N G ◆

EXECUTIVE SEARCH FIRMS

GRI PARTNERS, INC.
3510 North Lake Creek Drive, Jackson WY 83001. 307/733-5483. **Fax:** 307/733-5668. **Contact:** Gene Masciocchi, President. **E-mail address:** gene@ gripartners.com. **World Wide Web address:** http://www.gripartners.com. **Description:** An executive search firm. **Specializes in the areas of:** Communications.

JDO ASSOCIATES
1218 East Pershing Boulevard, PMB 1021, Cheyenne WY 82001. 307/634-0959. Fax: 307/637-2828. **Contact:** Duane Olesen, President. **E-mail address:** duane@jdoassoc.com. **Description:** An executive search firm operating on both retainer and contingency bases. **Specializes in the areas of:** Automotive; Construction; Defense Industry. **Positions commonly filled include:** Construction Contractor; Marketing Manager; Marketing Specialist. **Corporate headquarters location:** This Location. **Average salary range of placements:** $50,000 - $100,000. **Number of placements per year:** 50 - 99.

MANAGEMENT RECRUITERS OF CHEYENNE
1008 East 21st Street, Cheyenne WY 82001. 307/635-8731. **Fax:** 307/635-6653. **Contact:** Manager. **Description:** An executive search firm operating on a contingency basis. Founded in 1978. **Specializes in the areas of:** Communications; Computer Hardware/Software; Design; Electrical; Engineering; Manufacturing. **Positions commonly filled include:** Design Engineer; Draftsperson; Electrical/Electronics Engineer; Industrial Engineer; Industrial Production Manager; Materials Engineer; Mechanical Engineer; Metallurgical Engineer; Quality Control Supervisor; Software Engineer. **Corporate headquarters location:** Cleveland OH. **Other U.S. locations:** Nationwide. **Average salary range of placements:** More than $50,000. **Number of placements per year:** 50 - 99.

PEAK PERFORMANCE CONSULTING, LLC
P.O. Box 54, Banner WY 82832. 307/683-3096. **Fax:** 307/683-3095. **Contact:** Manager. **Description:** An executive search firm. **Specializes in the areas of:** Advertising; Sales; Systems Design.

SPECTRA ASSOCIATES
P.O. Box 667, Laramie WY 82073. 307/742-4688. **Fax:** 307/742-4681. **Contact:** Manager. **World Wide Web address:** http://www.spectra-assoc.com/Jobs.htm. **Description:** An executive search firm specializing in AS/400 positions. **Specializes in the areas of:** Computer Programming.

PERMANENT EMPLOYMENT AGENCIES

THE EMPLOYMENT PLACE
P.O. Box 6776, Cheyenne WY 82003-8776. 307/632-0534. **Contact:** Recruiting. **E-mail address:** tep@juno.com. **Description:** A state-operated permanent employment agency that places applicants in full-time positions worldwide. The Employment Place's two divisions focus on agricultural and general employment. **Specializes in the areas of:** Agriculture; Computer Hardware/Software; Food; Office Support.

EMPLOYMENT RESOURCES
P.O. Box 1610, Riverton WY 82501. 307/856-9231. **Fax:** 307/856-3468. **Contact:** Manager. **Description:** A state-operated, permanent employment agency.

EMPLOYMENT RESOURCES
P.O. Box 1448, Gillette WY 82717. 307/682-9313. **Fax:** 307/686-2975. **Contact:** Manager. **Description:** A state-operated permanent employment agency.

SENIOR COMMUNITY EMPLOYMENT SERVICE
22 West Works Street, Sheridan WY 82801. 307/674-4447. **Fax:** 307/674-4448. **Contact:** Harvey Finch, Project Director. **Description:** A permanent employment agency that trains and assists people age 55 and older. **Positions commonly filled include:** Certified Nurses Aide; Clerical Supervisor; Computer Operator; Daycare Worker; Electrician; Secretary; Typist/Word Processor. **Average salary range of placements:** Less than $20,000. **Number of placements per year:** 1 - 49.

TEMPORARY EMPLOYMENT AGENCIES

EXPRESS PERSONNEL SERVICES
2205 East Pershing Boulevard, Cheyenne WY 82001. 307/634-1635. **Fax:** 307/638-0493. **Contact:** Manager. **Description:** A temporary agency that also provides permanent placements. **Specializes in the areas of:** Clerical; Light Industrial; Retail; Sales. **Other U.S. locations:** Nationwide.

INDEX BY SPECIALIZATION

Goodwin Personnel, *Perm Agcy*
Robert Half Intl/Accountemps, *Exec Srch*
Information Systems Consulting
    Corporation, *Exec Srch*
Initial Staffing Services, *Perm Agcy*
Intellimark, *Temp Agcy*
Interim Personnel, *Temp Agcy*
Job Store Staffing, *Perm Agcy*
JobSearch, *Temp Agcy*
Kelly Services, Inc., *Temp Agcy*
National Affirmative Action Career
    Network, Inc., *Exec Srch*
Norrell Interim, *Temp Agcy*
Office Specialists Inc., *Temp Agcy*
Placement Professionals, *Exec Srch*
Real Estate Personnel, *Exec Srch*
Romac International, *Exec Srch*
SOS Staffing Services, *Temp Agcy*
Sales Conslt, *Exec Srch*
Snelling Personnel Svcs., *Exec Srch*
Star Personnel Service, *Exec Srch*
Stivers Temporary Personnel, *Temp Agcy*
Temporary Accounting Pers., *Temp Agcy*
Todays Temporary, *Temp Agcy*
Two Degrees, *Exec Srch*
WSI Personnel Svc, *Perm Agcy*

Connecticut

Access Financial, *Exec Srch*
Accountants Executive Search/
    Accountants on Call, *Exec Srch*
Admiral Staffing Services, *Temp Agcy*
Blackwood Associate, *Exec Srch*
Bohan & Bradstreet, *Perm Agcy*
Burke & Assc/Westfield Grp, *Exec Srch*
Buxbaum/Rink Consulting, *Exec Srch*
Thomas Byrne Associates, *Perm Agcy*
The Cambridge Group Ltd., *Exec Srch*
Charter Personnel Services, *Exec Srch*
Corporate Staffing Solutions, *Temp Agcy*
Diversified Emp. Svcs., *Perm Agcy*
Dunhill of New Haven/Dunhill Search
    International, *Perm Agcy*
EDP, *Contract Svc*
Employment Opportunities, *Perm Agcy*
Executive Register Inc., *Exec Srch*
Financial Careers, *Exec Srch*
Robert Half Intl/Accountemps, *Exec Srch*
Harbor Associates, *Exec Srch*
Hipp Waters Prof. Search, *Exec Srch*
Impact Personnel, Inc., *Temp Agcy*
Intertec Personnel, *Temp Agcy*
Jobsource, *Perm Agcy*
Judlind Employment Svcs., *Perm Agcy*
Mngmt. Rcrtrs. of Norwalk, *Exec Srch*
Management Search, *Exec Srch*
Manpower, Inc., *Temp Agcy*
McIntyre Associates, *Temp Agcy*
The McKnight Group, *Exec Srch*
Office Services of CT, *Perm Agcy*
PRH Management, Inc., *Exec Srch*
Paramount Resources, *Perm Agcy*
Pascale & LaMorte, LLC, *Exec Srch*
Q.S.I., *Perm Agcy*
Resource Associates, *Perm Agcy*
Romac International, *Exec Srch*
Howard W. Smith Associates, *Exec Srch*
Velen Associates, *Perm Agcy*
Westaff, *Temp Agcy*
Workforce One, *Perm Agcy*

Delaware

Caldwell Staffing Services, *Perm Agcy*
Financial Search & Staffing, *Exec Srch*
J.B. Groner Exec. Search, *Exec Srch*
Robert Half Intl/Accountemps, *Exec Srch*
E.W. Hodges & Associates, *Exec Srch*
Independent National Search &
    Associates (INS), *Exec Srch*
The Placers, Inc., *Temp Agcy*

Dist. of Columbia

Accountants Executive Search/
    Accountants on Call, *Exec Srch*
AccuStaff, *Perm Agcy*
ACSYS Inc., *Exec Srch*
GKA Resources, LLC, *Exec Srch*
Hire Standard Staffing, *Perm Agcy*
NRI Legal Resources/NRI Accounting
    Resources, *Temp Agcy*
Norrell Services, *Temp Agcy*
TempWorld Staffing Svcs., *Temp Agcy*
Woodside Emp. Conslt, *Perm Agcy*

Florida

AAA Employment, *Perm Agcy*
Able Body Corp. Services, *Contract Svc*
Accountants Express, *Perm Agcy*
Active Professionals, *Exec Srch*
Adecco, *Temp Agcy*
Alpha Pers./Alpha Temps, *Perm Agcy*
Ambiance Personnel, *Perm Agcy*
Availability, Inc., *Perm Agcy*
Brickell Pers. Conslt, *Exec Srch*
Career Planners, *Perm Agcy*
Careers USA, *Temp Agcy*
CareerXchange, *Perm Agcy*
Carrier's Career Service, Inc.,
    Career/Outplacement
Custom Staffing, Inc., *Temp Agcy*
DGA Personnel Group, *Exec Srch*
Steven Douglas Associates, *Exec Srch*
Dunhill Professional Search, *Exec Srch*
Employers' Assistant, *Temp Agcy*
En-Data Corporation, *Contract Svc*
Ethan Allen Pers. Placement, *Exec Srch*
Farwell Group Inc., *Exec Srch*
Future Force Personnel, *Temp Agcy*
Gimbel & Associates, *Exec Srch*
HR Professional Conslt, *Exec Srch*
Robert Half Intl/Accountemps, *Exec Srch*
Hastings & Hastings Personnel Conslt,
    Temp Agcy
Interim Financial Solutions, *Exec Srch*
Interim Personnel, *Temp Agcy*
R.H. Larsen & Associates, *Exec Srch*
Mngmt. Rcrtrs. International, *Exec Srch*
Mngmt. Rcrtrs. of Tallahassee, *Exec Srch*
Norrell Services Inc., *Temp Agcy*
Office Ours, *Temp Agcy*
Office Specialists, *Temp Agcy*
Olsten Financial Staffing, *Temp Agcy*
Olsten Professional Staffing, *Temp Agcy*
Olsten Staffing Services, *Temp Agcy*
OMNIpartners, *Exec Srch*
O'Quin Personnel, *Temp Agcy*
PMC&L Associates, *Perm Agcy*
Pearce & Associates, *Exec Srch*
Personnel Center, *Perm Agcy*
Priority Search, *Exec Srch*
Pro Staff, *Temp Agcy*
Pulp & Paper Intnl., *Exec Srch*
Linda Robins & Associates, *Temp Agcy*
Romac International, *Exec Srch*
The Ryan Charles Group, *Exec Srch*
Sales Conslt, Inc., *Exec Srch*
Sanford Rose Associates, *Exec Srch*
Doug Sears & Associates, *Exec Srch*
Secretaries Unlimited, *Temp Agcy*
Shaver Employment Agency, *Perm Agcy*
Staff Leasing Group, *Contract Svc*
Staffing Now, *Temp Agcy*
The Stewart Search Group, *Exec Srch*
TRC Staffing Services, *Temp Agcy*
Todays Temporary, *Temp Agcy*
Uniquest International, *Exec Srch*
Victoria & Assoc. Pers. Svcs, *Perm Agcy*
Terry M. Weiss & Associates, *Exec Srch*

Georgia

A-OK Personnel, *Perm Agcy*
A.D. & Assoc. Exec. Search, *Exec Srch*
Access Personnel Svcs., *Perm Agcy*
Accountants & Bookkeepers Personnel,
    Exec Srch
Accountants Executive Search/
    Accountants On Call, *Exec Srch*
Accountants Inc., *Temp Agcy*
Accountants One, *Perm Agcy*
Accounting Resource Temps, *Temp Agcy*
Michael Alexander Group, *Exec Srch*
Augusta Staffing Assoc., *Perm Agcy*
Basilone-Oliver Exec. Search, *Exec Srch*
Bell Oaks Company, *Exec Srch*
Boreham International, *Exec Srch*
The Bowers Group, Inc., *Exec Srch*
Bradshaw & Associates, *Exec Srch*
Business Professional Group, *Perm Agcy*
Career Placements, *Perm Agcy*
Catalina Human Resources, *Perm Agcy*
Corporate Image Group, *Exec Srch*
Corporate Search Conslt, *Exec Srch*
Dunhill Prof. Search, *Exec Srch*
Elite Staffing Services, *Temp Agcy*
Executive Placement Svcs., *Perm Agcy*
Express Personnel Svcs., *Perm Agcy*

Fox-Morris Associates, *Exec Srch*
Hall Management Group, *Exec Srch*
ISC of Atlanta/International Career
    Continuation, *Exec Srch*
Kelly Services, Inc., *Temp Agcy*
Kenzer Corp. of Georgia, *Exec Srch*
Lowderman & Associates, *Exec Srch*
Lucas Group, *Exec Srch*
Mngmt. Rcrtrs. of Atlanta, *Exec Srch*
Manpower Temp. Svcs., *Temp Agcy*
New Boston Select, *Temp Agcy*
Office Specialists, *Temp Agcy*
OfficeMates5/DayStar Temporary
    Services, *Temp Agcy*
Olsten Staffing Services, *Temp Agcy*
Personnel Opportunities, *Exec Srch*
Priority 1 Staffing Svcs., *Temp Agcy*
Quality Employment Svc, *Temp Agcy*
Randstad Staffing Svcs., *Temp Agcy*
Don Richard Associates, *Exec Srch*
Romac International, *Exec Srch*
Southern Emp. Service, *Perm Agcy*
Staffing Resources, *Perm Agcy*
StaffMark, *Temp Agcy*
Temporary Specialties, *Temp Agcy*
Toar Consulting, *Exec Srch*
Westaff, *Temp Agcy*

Hawaii

Altres Staffing, *Temp Agcy*
Dunhill Prof. Staffing, *Exec Srch*
Executive Search World, *Exec Srch*
Mngmt Search & Consulting, *Exec Srch*
Olsten Staffing Services, *Temp Agcy*
Riders Personnel Svcs., *Contract Svc*
Select Staffing Services, *Temp Agcy*

Idaho

Horne/Brown Intnl., *Exec Srch*

Illinois

A.B.A. Placements/A.B.A. Temp., *Perm
    Agcy*
ASI (Access Search Inc.), *Exec Srch*
ASI Staffing Service, *Perm Agcy*
Abbott Smith Associates, *Exec Srch*
The Ability Group, *Exec Srch*
B.J. Abrams & Associates, *Exec Srch*
Account Pros, *Exec Srch*
Accountants Executive Search/
    Accountants On Call, *Exec Srch*
Accurate Personnel Inc., *Perm Agcy*
Adecco, *Temp Agcy*
Affiliated Pers. Conslt, *Perm Agcy*
American Engineering, *Exec Srch*
Armstrong-Hamilton Assoc., *Exec Srch*
E.J. Ashton & Associates, *Exec Srch*
Availability, Inc., *Perm Agcy*
Banner Personnel Svc., *Perm Agcy*
Barrett Partners, *Exec Srch*
Bell Personnel Inc., *Perm Agcy*
Bevelle & Associates, Inc., *Exec Srch*
Burling Group Ltd., *Exec Srch*
CFR Executive Search, *Exec Srch*
C.S. Global Partners, *Exec Srch*
CareerLink USA, Inc., *Exec Srch*
Carson Mngmt. Assoc., *Contract Svc*
Casey Services, Inc., *Exec Srch*
CEMCO Ltd., *Exec Srch*
Chicago Financial Search, *Exec Srch*
D. Clesen Company, *Exec Srch*
Corporate Staffing, Inc./Proven
    Performers, *Perm Agcy*
Diener & Associates Inc., *Exec Srch*
Dunhill Staffing Svcs., *Temp Agcy*
Dynamic People, *Temp Agcy*
Eastman & Associates, *Exec Srch*
Elsko Executive Search, *Exec Srch*
The Esquire Staffing Grp, *Perm Agcy*
Eve Recruiters Ltd., *Perm Agcy*
Executive Financial Conslt, *Exec Srch*
Executive Placement Conslt, *Exec Srch*
Executive Referral Svc., *Exec Srch*
Express Personnel Svcs., *Temp Agcy*
Fellows Placement, *Temp Agcy*
Financial Search Corp., *Exec Srch*
F-O-R-T-U-N-E Pers. Conslts, *Exec Srch*
Furst Staffing Services, *Temp Agcy*
General Emp. Ent., *Perm Agcy*
David Gomez & Assoc., *Exec Srch*
Robert Half Intl/Accountemps, *Exec Srch*
Human Resource Connection, *Perm Agcy*
IZS Executive Search, *Exec Srch*

Executive Recruiters Intnl, *Exec Srch*
Express Personnel Svcs., *Temp Agcy*
F-O-R-T-U-N-E Pers. Conslts, *Exec Srch*
Joseph Goldring & Assoc., *Exec Srch*
Robert Half Intl/Accountemps, *Exec Srch*
William Howard Agency, *Contract Svc*
Kelly Technical Services, *Contract Svc*
Key Personnel, *Perm Agcy*
Mngmt. Rcrtrs. International, *Exec Srch*
Manpower Tech. Services, *Contract Svc*
Office Staffing Recruiting, *Exec Srch*
Olsten Prof. Staffing, *Temp Agcy*
Professional Personnel Conslt
    International, *Exec Srch*
ProSearch, Inc., *Exec Srch*
Romac International, *Perm Agcy*
Smith Professional Search, *Exec Srch*
Sullivan & Associates, *Exec Srch*
TEA Inc., *Perm Agcy*
Trillium Staffing, *Temp Agcy*
Troy Tech Services, *Contract Svc*
Unlimited Staffing Solns, *Contract Svc*
Wing Tips and Pumps, *Exec Srch*
Wise Personnel Services, *Perm Agcy*
Wood Personnel Services/Wood
    Temporary Staffing, *Perm Agcy*
Workforce, Inc., *Temp Agcy*

Minnesota

Abby Blu Inc., *Temp Agcy*
Accountants Exchange., *Exec Srch*
Accountants Executive Search/
    Accountants On Call, *Exec Srch*
Accountants Placement Registry, Inc.,
    Exec Srch
Advance Personnel Resources, *Exec Srch*
Alternative Staffing, Inc., *Perm Agcy*
Bradley & Associates, *Exec Srch*
Certified Accounting Pros, *Exec Srch*
Diversified Employment Inc., *Perm Agcy*
Financial Staff Recruiters, *Perm Agcy*
Gleason Dale Keene & Assoc., *Exec Srch*
Robert Half Intl/Accountemps, *Exec Srch*
Hayden Search Group, *Exec Srch*
T.H. Hunter, Inc., *Exec Srch*
Mngmt. Rcrtrs. of Minneapolis/
    Sales Conslt, *Exec Srch*
Midwest Staffing Svcs., *Temp Agcy*
C.A. Moore & Associates, *Exec Srch*
Thomas Moore Inc., *Temp Agcy*
Romac International, *Exec Srch*
Sathe & Assoc., *Exec Srch*
Secretary & Accounting Svc, *Perm Agcy*
Jeane Thorne Inc., *Temp Agcy*
Whitney Prof. Staffing, *Temp Agcy*
Working Relationships, *Perm Agcy*

Mississippi

The CPI Group, *Exec Srch*
Capitol Staffing Solutions, *Perm Agcy*
Coats & Coats Personnel, *Perm Agcy*
EPSCO Personnel Svc., *Temp Agcy*
Mngmt. Rcrtrs. International, *Exec Srch*
Norrell Staffing Services, *Temp Agcy*
Opportunities Unlimited, *Exec Srch*
Personnel Unlimited, *Exec Srch*
Service Specialists Ltd., *Perm Agcy*
Jim Woodson & Associates, *Exec Srch*

Missouri

ABC Emp. Service, *Perm Agcy*
Accountants Executive Search/
    Accountants On Call, *Exec Srch*
Accounting Career Conslt, *Exec Srch*
Advanced Careers, *Exec Srch*
Bestemps Inc., *Perm Agcy*
Bottom Line Prof. Svcs., *Contract Svc*
Burns Emp. Service, *Exec Srch*
Business Personnel Svcs., *Temp Agcy*
Crown Services, Inc., *Temp Agcy*
Deck & Decker, *Perm Agcy*
Employer Advantage, *Exec Srch*
ExecuSearch, Inc., *Exec Srch*
ExecuTemps, Inc., *Temp Agcy*
First Place Executive Search/Deck &
    Decker Personnel, *Exec Srch*
F-O-R-T-U-N-E Pers. Conslts, *Exec Srch*
Robert Half Intl/Accountemps, *Exec Srch*
Huey Enterprises, *Exec Srch*
Information Systems Consulting
    Corporation, *Exec Srch*
JoDoc Enterprises, *Temp Agcy*
Linde Group, *Perm Agcy*

Mngmt. Rcrtrs. of Kansas City, *Exec
    Srch*
Mngmt. Rcrtrs. of Springfield, *Exec Srch*
Mngmt. Rcrtrs. of St. Louis/
    Sales Conslt, *Exec Srch*
Manpower Temp. Svcs., *Temp Agcy*
OfficeMates5 (OM5), *Exec Srch*
Romac International, *Exec Srch*
Sales Recruiters, Inc., *Exec Srch*
Search Professionals, *Exec Srch*
Westaff, *Contract Svc*

Montana

Express Personnel Svcs., *Temp Agcy*
LC Staffing Service, *Perm Agcy*

Nebraska

Accounting Resources, *Perm Agcy*
Adecco, *Temp Agcy*
Compusearch of Lincoln, *Exec Srch*
Corporate Recruiters, Ltd./Health Service
    Professionals, *Exec Srch*
Donna's Office Service, *Contract Svc*
Eggers Company, *Perm Agcy*
Robert Half Intl/Accountemps, *Exec Srch*
Hansen Emp. Svc., *Exec Srch*
Kelly Services, Inc., *Temp Agcy*
Mngmt. Rcrtrs. of Omaha/
    OfficeMates5, *Exec Srch*

Nevada

Accountants Inc., *Temp Agcy*
Adecco, *Perm Agcy*
Flowers Exec. Search Group, *Exec Srch*
Robert Half Intnl./Accountemps/
    OfficeTeam, *Exec Srch*
Initial Staffing Services, *Perm Agcy*

New Hampshire

Able 1 Staffing, *Exec Srch*
Advanced Recruiting & Consulting, *Exec
    Srch*
Allstaff, *Perm Agcy*
Barclay Personnel Systems, *Exec Srch*
Career Connections, Inc., *Perm Agcy*
Central NH Emp. Svcs., *Perm Agcy*
Cheshire Emp. Service, *Temp Agcy*
Curtis Associates, *Exec Srch*
Dubois & Company, *Exec Srch*
Kelly Services, Inc., *Temp Agcy*
Key Partners, Inc., *Perm Agcy*
Kogen Personnel, *Perm Agcy*
Mngmt. Rcrtrs. Intl., *Exec Srch*
Manpower Temp. Svcs., *Temp Agcy*
National Emp. Service Corp., *Perm Agcy*
Professional Recruiters, *Perm Agcy*
R.G.T. Associates, Inc., *Exec Srch*
Resource Recruiting/Contemporary
    Accountants, *Perm Agcy*
Surge Resources Inc., *Contract Svc*
TAC Staffing Services, *Temp Agcy*
Thomas & Kavanaugh, *Temp Agcy*
Venture Profiles Corp., *Exec Srch*

New Jersey

A+ Personnel Placement, *Perm Agcy*
A Professional Edge,
    Career/Outplacement
AES Associates, *Exec Srch*
Abbott Associates Inc., *Exec Srch*
Accountants Executive Search/
    Accountants On Call, *Exec Srch*
Accountants Prof. Search, *Exec Srch*
Advanced Personnel Svc., *Perm Agcy*
Raymond Alexander Assoc., *Perm Agcy*
Allstaff Resources, Inc., *Perm Agcy*
American Staffing Resources, *Perm Agcy*
The Ascher Group, *Exec Srch*
BAI Personnel Solutions, *Perm Agcy*
Blake & Assoc. Exec. Search, *Exec Srch*
Bowman & Company, *Exec Srch*
Broad Waverly & Assoc., *Exec Srch*
Career Center, Inc., *Perm Agcy*
Career Management Grp., *Exec Srch*
Careers USA, *Perm Agcy*
Careerworks, *Exec Srch*
Dunhill Prof. Search, *Exec Srch*
Ellis Career Conslt/Career Search
    Associates, *Exec Srch*
Executive Search, Inc., *Exec Srch*
Express Personnel Svcs., *Perm Agcy*
Foster Associates, *Exec Srch*
Gibson Martin Consulting, *Exec Srch*
Globe Emp. Agency, *Perm Agcy*

Grant Franks & Assoc., *Exec Srch*
Robert Half Intl/Accountemps, *Exec Srch*
Holm Personnel Conslt, *Exec Srch*
The Howard Group, Ltd., *Exec Srch*
Hreshko Consulting Grp., *Exec Srch*
Hughes & Podesla Personnel, *Perm Agcy*
Impact Personnel, Inc., *Perm Agcy*
Insearch Inc., *Exec Srch*
Integro Staffing Services, *Temp Agcy*
Inter-Regional Exec. Search, *Exec Srch*
Joule Staffing Services, *Contract Svc*
Kelly Services, Inc., *Temp Agcy*
Joseph Keyes Associates, *Perm Agcy*
MJE Recruiters, Inc., *Exec Srch*
Mngmt. Rcrtrs. of Passaic Cty, *Exec Srch*
Mngmt. Rcrtrs. of Sparta, *Exec Srch*
Mngmt. Rcrtrs./OfficeMates5 of Union
    County, *Exec Srch*
Manpower Tech. Svcs., *Contract Svc*
Martin Personnel Service, *Exec Srch*
Miller Resources, *Perm Agcy*
Norrell Services, *Temp Agcy*
OfficeMates5/DayStar Temporary
    Services, *Perm Agcy*
Olsten Staffing Services, *Temp Agcy*
Orion Consulting, Inc., *Exec Srch*
Solomon Page Group, *Exec Srch*
Park Avenue Personnel, *Perm Agcy*
The Penmor Group, *Exec Srch*
Personnel Plus/Temps Plus, *Perm Agcy*
Pomerantz Staffing Svcs., *Perm Agcy*
Premier Personnel Group, *Exec Srch*
Princeton Exec. Search, *Exec Srch*
Protocall Business Staffing Services,
    Temp Agcy
Ready Pers./Ready Temps, *Perm Agcy*
Jeff Rich Associates, *Exec Srch*
Rochester Systems Inc., *Exec Srch*
Romac International, *Exec Srch*
Rosenthal Associates Intnl, *Exec Srch*
Rotator Staffing Svcs., *Contract Svc*
Rylan Forbes Consulting, *Exec Srch*
S-H-S of Cherry Hill, *Perm Agcy*
R.S. Sadow Associates, *Exec Srch*
Sales Conslt, *Exec Srch*
Sanford Rose Associates, *Exec Srch*
Selective Personnel, *Perm Agcy*
Arline Simpson Assoc. , *Perm Agcy*
Snelling Personnel Svcs., *Perm Agcy*
Source One Personnel, *Perm Agcy*
The Stelton Group, Inc., *Exec Srch*
Temporary Excellence, *Temp Agcy*
UNITEMP Temp. Personnel, *Temp Agcy*
J. Vincent Associates, *Exec Srch*
Winston Staffing Svcs., *Temp Agcy*
Winters & Ross, *Perm Agcy*
Claire Wright Associates, *Perm Agcy*

New Mexico

Albuquerque Personnel, *Perm Agcy*
Excel Staffing Cos., *Perm Agcy*
Robert Half Intl/Accountemps, *Exec Srch*
Henderson Black and Co., *Exec Srch*
Sanderson Emp. Svc., *Perm Agcy*
Santa Fe Services, *Temp Agcy*
Snelling Search, *Exec Srch*

New York

A-L Associates, Inc., *Exec Srch*
AJC Search, *Exec Srch*
Accountants Choice Personnel, *Exec Srch*
Accountants Executive Search/
    Accountants On Call, *Exec Srch*
Accounting & Computer Personnel,
    Perm Agcy
AccuStaff Incorporated, *Temp Agcy*
Adam Personnel, Inc., *Perm Agcy*
Merrill Adams Assoc., *Career/
    Outplacement*
Adecco, *Temp Agcy*
Advice Personnel, *Exec Srch*
Alite Associates, *Exec Srch*
Franklin Allen Conslt, *Exec Srch*
AMESgroup, *Exec Srch*
April International, *Exec Srch*
Asher Personnel Conslt, *Perm Agcy*
Auto Careers, *Perm Agcy*
Bartl & Evins, *Exec Srch*
Benson Associates, *Exec Srch*
Bevan Resources, *Perm Agcy*
Bevlin Personnel Inc., *Perm Agcy*
Branthover Associates, *Exec Srch*
E.E. Brooke Inc., *Perm Agcy*

Barton Personnel Systems, *Exec Srch*
Basilone-Oliver Exec. Search, *Exec Srch*
Bon Temps Staffing Services, *Temp Agcy*
Brackin & Sayers Assoc., *Exec Srch*
Bradley Prof. Services, *Perm Agcy*
Career Concepts Staffing Svcs, *Exec Srch*
Cawley Associates, *Exec Srch*
Charley's Personnel Staffing, *Temp Agcy*
Joseph Conahan Exec. Recruiters, *Exec Srch*
CoreStaff Inc., *Temp Agcy*
P. Robert Dann, *Exec Srch*
Dunhill Prof. Search, *Exec Srch*
Dunn Associates, *Exec Srch*
EDP Contract Services, *Contract Svc*
Eden & Associates, Inc., *Exec Srch*
Executive Avail-A-Search, *Exec Srch*
Financial Industry Staffing Company, *Perm Agcy*
Fox-Morris Associates, *Exec Srch*
HRS/TND Associates, *Exec Srch*
Robert Half Intl/Accountemps, *Exec Srch*
The Hastings Group, *Exec Srch*
Hoskins Hains Associates, *Exec Srch*
Human Assets Inc., *Temp Agcy*
J-Rand Search, *Exec Srch*
Nancy Jackson Inc., *Exec Srch*
Kenneth James Associates, *Exec Srch*
Jefferson-Ross Associates, *Exec Srch*
Mark Joseph Associates, *Perm Agcy*
Kathy Karr Personnel, *Perm Agcy*
Blair Kershaw Associates, *Exec Srch*
Marsetta Lane Temp. Svcs., *Temp Agcy*
Mngmt. Rcrtrs./CompuSearch, *Exec Srch*
Mngmt. Rcrtrs. of Reading/
    Career Sentinel, Inc., *Exec Srch*
Mastersearch, *Exec Srch*
Metropolitan Personnel, *Temp Agcy*
The Morris Group, *Exec Srch*
National Computerized Employment
    Service Inc., *Exec Srch*
Norrell Services, *Temp Agcy*
Olsten Financial Staffing, *Temp Agcy*
Olsten Staffing Services, *Temp Agcy*
LaMonte Owens, Inc., *Exec Srch*
Pancoast Temp. Svcs., *Temp Agcy*
Penn Search, *Exec Srch*
Pratt Personnel Services, *Temp Agcy*
Rice Cohen International, *Exec Srch*
Rittenhouse Exec. Search, *Exec Srch*
Romac International, *Exec Srch*
SHS Associates, Inc., *Exec Srch*
SHS International, *Exec Srch*
Snelling Personnel Svcs., *Temp Agcy*
Spectrum Conslt, Inc./Retail Recruiters, *Exec Srch*
Strauss Personnel Svc., *Perm Agcy*
TRC Staffing Services, *Temp Agcy*
TAC Staffing Services, *Temp Agcy*
W.G. Tucker & Assoc., *Exec Srch*
Uni-Temp Temp. Svc., *Temp Agcy*
Vogue Personnel Inc., *Exec Srch*
Woldoff Associates, *Exec Srch*
Yorktowne Personnel, *Exec Srch*

Rhode Island
Accountants Executive Search/
    Accountants On Call, *Exec Srch*
Accounting Resources, *Exec Srch*
Colony Personnel Assoc., *Temp Agcy*
Daley & Associates Inc., *Exec Srch*
Dorra Search Inc., *Exec Srch*
Kelly Services, Inc., *Temp Agcy*
Albert G. Lee & Assoc., *Exec Srch*
Mngmt. Rcrtrs. International, *Exec Srch*
Norrell Services, *Temp Agcy*
Qualified Resources, *Temp Agcy*
Spectra Temps/Tracey Assoc, *Temp Agcy*
TAC Staffing Services, *Temp Agcy*

South Carolina
Accel Temp. Services, *Temp Agcy*
Carolina Personnel Svcs., *Temp Agcy*
Dunhill Prof. Search, *Exec Srch*
Financial Search Assoc., *Exec Srch*
Ford & Associates, *Exec Srch*
F-O-R-T-U-N-E Pers. Conslts of
    Columbia, *Exec Srch*
Harvey Personnel, Inc., *Perm Agcy*
Mngmt. Rcrtrs. of Columbia, *Exec Srch*
Mngmt. Rcrtrs. of Rock Hill, *Exec Srch*
Miller & Associates, *Exec Srch*
PRL & Associates, Inc., *Perm Agcy*

John Shell Associates, *Exec Srch*
Smith Temps/Smith Pers., *Temp Agcy*
Snelling Personnel Svcs., *Perm Agcy*
Southern Recruiters & Conslt, Inc., *Exec Srch*
StaffingSolutions, *Temp Agcy*

South Dakota
Alternative Human Resources
    Development, *Perm Agcy*
Careers Unlimited, *Perm Agcy*
Key Staffing, *Temp Agcy*
Mngmt. Rcrtrs. of Sioux Falls, *Exec Srch*
Olsten Staffing Services, *Temp Agcy*
Snelling Personnel Service, *Perm Agcy*

Tennessee
Accountants & Bookkeepers, *Exec Srch*
Accountants Executive Search/
    Accountants On Call, *Exec Srch*
Accounting Solutions, *Temp Agcy*
Arvie Personnel Services, *Perm Agcy*
Austin-Allen Company, *Exec Srch*
Career Professionals, Inc., *Exec Srch*
Carroll & Associates, *Exec Srch*
Cook Associates International, *Exec Srch*
Corporate Image Group, *Exec Srch*
F-O-R-T-U-N-E Pers. Conslts, *Exec Srch*
Gateway Grp. Personnel, *Temp Agcy*
Robert Half Intl/Accountemps, *Exec Srch*
Hamilton-Ryker Co., *Temp Agcy*
Randall Howard & Assoc., *Exec Srch*
Dorothy Johnson's Career Conslt, *Exec Srch*
Kelly Services, Inc., *Temp Agcy*
Madison Personnel, *Perm Agcy*
Mngmt. Rcrtrs. International, *Exec Srch*
Manpower, Inc., *Temp Agcy*
The Morgan Group, *Exec Srch*
Olsten Staffing Services, *Temp Agcy*
Personnel Link, *Exec Srch*
Questar Partners Inc., *Exec Srch*
Rasmussen & Assoc., *Perm Agcy*
Snelling Personnel Svcs., *Perm Agcy*
StaffingSolutions, *Perm Agcy*
StaffMark, *Exec Srch*
Wood Personnel Svcs., *Perm Agcy*

Texas
A-1 Personnel, *Temp Agcy*
ABC Temps Inc., *Temp Agcy*
Abilene Emp. Service, *Perm Agcy*
Accountants Executive Search/
    Accountants On Call, *Exec Srch*
Accounting Action Personnel, *Perm Agcy*
ACSYS Inc., *Temp Agcy*
Action Personnel Inc., *Temp Agcy*
Add-A-Temp/Woodlands Executive
    Employment, *Temp Agcy*
Agri-Associates, *Exec Srch*
American Resources, *Exec Srch*
Audit Professionals Intnl., *Exec Srch*
Austin Group, *Exec Srch*
Aware Affiliates Pers. Svc., *Perm Agcy*
Babich & Associates, *Perm Agcy*
Baldwin & Company, *Exec Srch*
Ann Best Elite Temps., *Temp Agcy*
Borrel Personnel, *Exec Srch*
Brainpower Pers. Agency, *Perm Agcy*
Bridge Personnel, *Exec Srch*
Brooklea & Associates, *Exec Srch*
Bruco, Inc., *Temp Agcy*
Bullock Personnel, Inc., *Perm Agcy*
Bundy-Stewart Associates, *Exec Srch*
Burnett Personnel Svcs., *Temp Agcy*
Certified Personnel Svc., *Contract Svc*
Champion Personnel Svc., *Exec Srch*
Clayton Personnel Svcs., *Temp Agcy*
Colvin Resources Group, *Perm Agcy*
Creative Staffing Svcs., *Perm Agcy*
Credit Union Employment Resources,
    Inc., *Temp Agcy*
DH&A, *Perm Agcy*
Dallas Emp. Services, *Perm Agcy*
The Danbrook Group, *Exec Srch*
Gail Darling Staffing/Gail Darling's
    Professional Desk, *Temp Agcy*
Dividend Staffing Svcs., *Temp Agcy*
Donovan & Watkins, *Perm Agcy*
Dunhill Prof. Search, *Exec Srch*
Executeam, *Exec Srch*
Express Personnel Svcs., *Perm Agcy*
Financial Search Conslt, *Exec Srch*

Robert Half Intnl./RHI Mngmt.
    Resources, *Exec Srch*
Hedman & Associates, *Exec Srch*
Imprimis Staffing Solutions, *Temp Agcy*
Information Systems Consulting
    Corporation, *Exec Srch*
InterSearch Associates, *Temp Agcy*
L.K. Jordan & Assoc., *Contract Svc*
Kane & Associates, Inc., *Exec Srch*
Kelly Services, Inc., *Temp Agcy*
Key People Inc., *Exec Srch*
Kindrick & Luther, *Perm Agcy*
George Lehman Assoc., *Exec Srch*
Lucas Financial Staffing, *Exec Srch*
The Lucas Group, *Perm Agcy*
Mngmt. Rcrtrs. International, *Exec Srch*
Manpower Temp. Svcs., *Temp Agcy*
Ray Marburger & Assoc., *Exec Srch*
Norrell Services, *Temp Agcy*
Odell & Associates Inc., *Exec Srch*
Olsten Staffing Services, *Temp Agcy*
The Pailin Group Professional Search
    Conslt, *Exec Srch*
Pate Resources Group, *Exec Srch*
Phoenix Staffing/G&A Staff Sourcing,
    Exec Srch
Priority Personnel, Inc., *Temp Agcy*
Priority Search, Inc., *Exec Srch*
Pro Staff Accounting Svcs., *Temp Agcy*
Pro Staff Personnel Svcs., *Temp Agcy*
Professional Search Conslt (PSC),
    Contract Svc
Professions Today, *Perm Agcy*
Remedy Intelligent Staffing, *Perm Agcy*
Resource Connection Workforce Center,
    Perm Agcy
Resource Staffing, *Temp Agcy*
Bart Roberson & Co., *Exec Srch*
Romac International, *Exec Srch*
Sales Conslt of Houston, *Exec Srch*
Salinas & Assoc. Pers. Svc., *Perm Agcy*
Search Network Intnl., *Exec Srch*
Select Staff, *Temp Agcy*, *Exec Srch*
Snelling Personnel Services, *Perm Agcy*
Staff Extension Intnl., *Exec Srch*
Steinfield & Associates, *Exec Srch*
TGA Company, *Exec Srch*
TSP Personnel Services, *Perm Agcy*
Betty Tanner Exec. Search, *Exec Srch*
TexStar, *Exec Srch*
Thomas Office Pers. Svc., *Perm Agcy*
Todays Office Staffing, *Temp Agcy*
Todays Staffing, *Temp Agcy*
The Urban Placement Svc, *Exec Srch*
Dick Van Vliet & Assoc., *Exec Srch*
Vinson and Associates, *Perm Agcy*
Watkins & Associates, *Exec Srch*
Wheeler, Moore & Elam Co., *Exec Srch*

Utah
Accountants Exec. Search, *Exec Srch*
AccountStaff, *Exec Srch*
Robert Half Intl/Accountemps, *Exec Srch*
Intermountain Staffing Resources, *Temp Agcy*
Mngmt. Rcrtrs. of Salt Lake City, *Exec Srch*
Olsten Staffing Services, *Temp Agcy*
Romac International, *Exec Srch*

Vermont
Dunhill Search of Vermont, *Exec Srch*
Personnel Dept., *Temp Agcy*

Virginia
Ability Resources, Inc., *Exec Srch*
Access Enterprises Inc., *Perm Agcy*
Accountants Executive Search/
    Accountants On Call, *Exec Srch*
Accounting Assets Inc., *Perm Agcy*
Accounting Solutions, *Exec Srch*
ACSYS Inc., *Exec Srch*
Adams Sources, *Exec Srch*
Nancy Allen Associates, *Perm Agcy*
Alpha Omega Resources, *Perm Agcy*
Ardelle Assoc./AA Temps, *Perm Agcy*
Buckler Careers, Inc., *Perm Agcy*
Corporate Connection, *Exec Srch*
Curzon Staffing, *Perm Agcy*
Dow Personnel, *Perm Agcy*
Effective Staffing Inc., *Exec Srch*
Employment Enterprises/Temporary
    Solutions, *Temp Agcy*

Job Store Staffing, *Perm Agcy*
JobSearch, *Temp Agcy*
Kelly Services, Inc., *Temp Agcy*
Mngmt. Rcrtrs. International, *Exec Srch*
Manpower International, *Temp Agcy*
Office Specialists Inc., *Temp Agcy*
Olsten Staffing Services, *Temp Agcy*
Sales Conslt of Denver, *Exec Srch*
Snelling Personnel Svcs., *Exec Srch*
Southwest Technical Conslt, Inc.,
  Contract Svc
Stivers Temporary Pers., *Temp Agcy*
TPM Staffing Service, *Perm Agcy*
Tech Staffing, *Temp Agcy*
Todays Temporary, *Temp Agcy*
Triad Conslt, *Exec Srch*
WSI Personnel Service, *Perm Agcy*
Woodmoor Group, *Exec Srch*

Connecticut

Aquent Partners, *Temp Agcy*
Bohan & Bradstreet, *Perm Agcy*
Charter Personnel Services, *Exec Srch*
Cheney Associates, *Exec Srch*
Corporate Staffing Solutions, *Temp Agcy*
Data Trends Inc., *Exec Srch*
Development Systems, Inc., *Exec Srch*
Dunhill of New Haven/Dunhill Search
  International, *Perm Agcy*
Hallmark Totaltech, Inc., *Exec Srch*
J.G. Hood Associates, *Perm Agcy*
Impact Personnel, Inc., *Temp Agcy*
Intertec Personnel, *Temp Agcy*
Jobsource, *Perm Agcy*
Judlind Emp. Services, *Perm Agcy*
Mngmt. Rcrtrs. of Norwalk, *Exec Srch*
McIntyre Associates, *Temp Agcy*
New England Personnel, *Perm Agcy*
Office Services of CT, *Perm Agcy*
Pascale & LaMorte, LLC, *Exec Srch*
Edward J. Pospesil & Co., *Exec Srch*
United Personnel Services, *Temp Agcy*
Westaff, *Temp Agcy*

Delaware

Caldwell Staffing Svcs., *Perm Agcy*
J.B. Groner Exec. Search, *Exec Srch*
E.W. Hodges & Associates, *Exec Srch*
Personal Placements Inc., *Perm Agcy*
The Placers, Inc., *Temp Agcy*

Dist. of Columbia

AccuStaff, *Perm Agcy*
ACSYS Inc., *Exec Srch*
Aquent Partners, *Temp Agcy*
Career Blazers Pers. Svc., *Perm Agcy*
NRI Legal Resources/NRI Accounting
  Resources, *Temp Agcy*
NRI Staffing Resources, *Temp Agcy*
Norrell Services, *Temp Agcy*
Positions Inc., *Perm Agcy*
Tangent Corporation, *Exec Srch*
Temporary Staffing, Inc., *Temp Agcy*
TempWorld Staffing Svcs, *Temp Agcy*
TRAK Staffing, *Perm Agcy*

Florida

AAA Employment, *Perm Agcy*
Able Body Corporate Svcs., *Contract Svc*
Ablest Staffing Services, *Temp Agcy*
Adecco, *Temp Agcy*
American Recruiters, *Exec Srch*
Aquent Partners, *Temp Agcy*
Availability, Inc., *Perm Agcy*
Balcor Associates, *Exec Srch*
Belmont Training & Employment
  Center, *Perm Agcy*
Brickell Pers. Conslt, *Exec Srch*
B²D Technical Services, *Contract Svc*
Career Planners, Inc., *Perm Agcy*
Careers USA, *Temp Agcy*
Computer Plus Staffing Solutions, Inc.,
  Temp Agcy
Criterion Executive Search, *Exec Srch*
Custom Staffing, Inc., *Temp Agcy*
DGA Personnel Group, *Exec Srch*
Decision Conslt Inc., *Perm Agcy*
Employers' Assistant, Inc., *Temp Agcy*
Ethan Allen Pers. Placement, *Exec Srch*
Executive Directions Inc., *Perm Agcy*
Five Star Temporary, *Temp Agcy*
Future Force Personnel, *Temp Agcy*
Gimbel & Associates, *Exec Srch*

Hastings & Hastings Personnel Conslt,
  Temp Agcy
Janus Career Services, *Perm Agcy*
Kelly Services, Inc., *Temp Agcy*
R.H. Larsen & Associates, *Exec Srch*
Mngmt. Rcrtrs. International, *Exec Srch*
Mankuta Gallagher & Assoc., *Exec Srch*
Norrell Services Inc., *Temp Agcy*
Olsten Staffing Services, *Temp Agcy*
Pro Staff, *Temp Agcy*
The Reserves Network, *Temp Agcy*
Robinson & Associates, *Exec Srch*
The Ryan Charles Group, *Exec Srch*
Sales Conslt of Fort Lauderdale, Inc.,
  Exec Srch
Sanford Rose Associates, *Exec Srch*
Doug Sears & Associates, *Exec Srch*
Shaver Employment Agency, *Perm Agcy*
Snelling Personnel Svcs., *Temp Agcy*
Snyder Executive Search, *Exec Srch*
Staffing Now, *Temp Agcy*
Staffing Solutions By Personnel One,
  Perm Agcy
The Stewart Search Group, *Exec Srch*
System One Services, *Contract Svc*
TRC Staffing Services, *Temp Agcy*
TempSolutions, Inc., *Temp Agcy*
Uniquest International, Inc., *Exec Srch*
Victoria & Assoc. Pers. Svcs, *Perm Agcy*

Georgia

A-OK Personnel, *Perm Agcy*
A.D. & Assoc. Exec. Search, *Exec Srch*
Access Personnel Services, *Perm Agcy*
Aquent Partners, *Temp Agcy*
Augusta Staffing Assoc., *Perm Agcy*
Bell Oaks Company, *Exec Srch*
Boreham International, *Exec Srch*
Catalina Human Resources, *Perm Agcy*
Comprehensive Search, *Exec Srch*
Corporate Search Conslt, *Exec Srch*
Elite Staffing Services, *Temp Agcy*
Express Personnel Svcs., *Perm Agcy*
First Pro, *Temp Agcy*
Lowderman & Associates, *Exec Srch*
Mngmt. Rcrtrs. of Atlanta, *Exec Srch*
Manpower Temp. Svcs., *Temp Agcy*
Mission Corps International/Helping
  Hands Temporary Svc, *Temp Agcy*
Norrell Services Inc., *Temp Agcy*
Office Specialists, *Temp Agcy*
Olsten Staffing Services, *Temp Agcy*
Perimeter Placement, *Exec Srch*
Randstad Staffing Svcs., *Temp Agcy*
Software Search, *Exec Srch*
Southern Emp. Service, *Perm Agcy*
Staffing Resources, *Perm Agcy*
StaffMark, *Temp Agcy*
TRC Staffing Services, *Temp Agcy*
TRI Staffing, *Temp Agcy*
Taurion Corporation, *Exec Srch*
TriTech Associates, *Exec Srch*
WPPS Software Staffing, *Temp Agcy*

Hawaii

Altres Staffing, *Temp Agcy*
Dunhill Prof. Staffing of HI, *Exec Srch*
Executive Search World, *Exec Srch*
Olsten Staffing Services, *Temp Agcy*
Riders Personnel Services, *Contract Svc*

Idaho

Horne/Brown International, *Exec Srch*
Manpower Temp. Svcs., *Temp Agcy*

Illinois

A.B.A. Placements/A.B.A. Temporaries,
  Perm Agcy
The Ability Group, *Exec Srch*
Adecco, *Temp Agcy*
Advantage Personnel Inc., *Exec Srch*
Aquent Partners, *Temp Agcy*
E.J. Ashton & Associates, *Exec Srch*
Assured Staffing, *Temp Agcy*
Availability, Inc., *Perm Agcy*
Barry Personnel Resources, *Perm Agcy*
Bell Personnel Inc., *Perm Agcy*
CES Associates, *Exec Srch*
CareerLink USA, Inc., *Exec Srch*
Carson Mngmt. Assoc., *Contract Svc*
Computer Futures Exchange, *Exec Srch*
Corporate Staffing, Inc./Proven
  Performers, *Perm Agcy*
Davis Staffing, Inc., *Temp Agcy*

Diener & Associates Inc., *Exec Srch*
Dynamic Search Systems, *Exec Srch*
Eve Recruiters Ltd., *Perm Agcy*
Express Personnel Svcs., *Temp Agcy*
Fellows Placement, *Temp Agcy*
General Emp. Enterprises, *Perm Agcy*
General Employment Enterprises,
  Inc./Triad Personnel, *Perm Agcy*
David Gomez & Assoc., *Exec Srch*
Human Resource Connection, *Perm Agcy*
Innovative Systems Group, *Exec Srch*
Interim Personnel, *Contract Svc*
InterStaff, *Temp Agcy*
Raymond Karson Assoc., *Exec Srch*
Kunzer Associates, Ltd., *Exec Srch*
Arlene Leff & Associates, *Exec Srch*
Mack & Associates, Ltd., *Temp Agcy*
Magnum Search, *Exec Srch*
Mngmt. Rcrtrs. International, *Exec Srch*
Michael David Associates, *Perm Agcy*
The Murphy Group, *Perm Agcy*
NJW & Associates, Inc., *Temp Agcy*
National Search, *Exec Srch*
OfficeMates5 (OM5), *Perm Agcy*
OfficeTeam, *Temp Agcy*
Olsten Staffing Services, *Temp Agcy*
PS Inc., *Perm Agcy*
Parker Cromwell & Assoc., *Exec Srch*
Personnel Connections, *Perm Agcy*
Pillar Personnel, *Temp Agcy*
Pro Staff Personnel Svcs., *Temp Agcy*
ProSearch Plus, *Exec Srch*
Redell Search, Inc., *Exec Srch*
Remedy Intelligent Staffing, *Temp Agcy*
Right Services Inc., *Temp Agcy*
The Ryan Charles Group, *Exec Srch*
Sales Conslt of Chicago, *Exec Srch*
Snelling Personnel Services, *Temp Agcy*,
  Perm Agcy
Snyder & Associates Inc., *Temp Agcy*
TDF Corporation, *Contract Svc*
Roy Talman & Associates, *Exec Srch*
Tech. Recruiting Conslt, *Exec Srch*
Temporary Associates, *Temp Agcy*
West Personnel Service, *Perm Agcy*
Working World Inc., *Temp Agcy*
World Employment Svc., *Perm Agcy*

Indiana

Adecco, *Temp Agcy*
Adecco/TAD Tech. Svcs., *Contract Svc*
Artisan Staffing, *Temp Agcy*
Canis Major/HR Quest, *Exec Srch*
The Consulting Forum, *Exec Srch*
Corporate Staffing Resources (CSR),
  Temp Agcy
Execusearch, *Exec Srch*
Interim Personnel, *Temp Agcy*
Job Placement Service, *Perm Agcy*
Mngmt. Rcrtrs. Intl., *Exec Srch*
Management Services, *Exec Srch*
Oakwood International Inc., *Exec Srch*
OfficeMates5 (OM5)/DayStar Temporary
  Services, *Perm Agcy*
P.R.C., *Exec Srch*
QCI Technical Staffing, *Contract Svc*
The Registry Inc., *Perm Agcy*
H.L. Yoh Company, *Contract Svc*

Iowa

Burton Placement Services, *Exec Srch*
Byrnes & Rupkey, Inc., *Exec Srch*
CSI Employment, *Exec Srch*
Career Search Associates, *Exec Srch*
Helping Hands Temp. Svc., *Temp Agcy*
Kelly Services, Inc., *Temp Agcy*
Mngmt. Rcrtrs. International, *Exec Srch*
McGladrey Search Group, *Exec Srch*
Pratt-Younglove, Inc., *Perm Agcy*
Salem Management Inc., *Temp Agcy*
Rudy Salem Staffing Svcs, *Temp Agcy*
Staff Management, Inc., *Contract Svc*
Nate Viall & Associates, *Perm Agcy*

Kansas

Arwood & Associates, *Exec Srch*
Business Specialists, *Perm Agcy*
Dunhill Staffing Systems, *Temp Agcy*
Mngmt. Rcrtrs. of Overland Park/Sales
  Conslt /OfficeMates5, *Exec Srch*
Morgan Hunter Corporate Search, *Exec
  Srch*

New Mexico
Albuquerque Personnel, *Perm Agcy*
Excel Staffing Companies, *Perm Agcy*
Marcia Owen Associates, *Exec Srch*

New York
Accounting & Computer Personnel, *Perm Agcy*
AccuStaff Incorporated, *Temp Agcy*
Merrill Adams Associates, *Career/Outplacement*
Adecco, *Temp Agcy*
Franklin Allen Conslt, *Exec Srch*
AMESgroup, *Exec Srch*
April Tech. Recruiting, *Perm Agcy*
Aquent Partners, *Temp Agcy*
Bartl & Evins, *Exec Srch*
Berkel Associates, Inc., *Exec Srch*
Bevan Resources, *Perm Agcy*
Bevlin Personnel Inc., *Perm Agcy*
Branthover Associates, *Exec Srch*
E.E. Brooke Inc., *Perm Agcy*
Brookville Staffing Svcs., *Perm Agcy*
Career Objectives Pers., *Temp Agcy*
Carlile Personnel Agency, *Perm Agcy*
Compu-Tech Personnel, *Exec Srch*
Dapexs Conslt Inc., *Exec Srch*
Seth Diamond Associates, *Exec Srch*
Dunhill Staffing Systems of Buffalo, *Temp Agcy*
Eden Staffing, *Perm Agcy*
Alexander Edwards Intnl., *Exec Srch*
Employment Recruiters Agency, *Perm Agcy*
Euromonde, Inc., *Temp Agcy*
Execu/Search Group, *Exec Srch*
Executive Directions Inc., *Exec Srch*
Extra Help Emp. Svc., *Temp Agcy*
Fanning Personnel, *Exec Srch*
C.R. Fletcher Associates, *Exec Srch*
Forum Temporary Svcs., *Temp Agcy*
Ronnie Gale Pers. Corp., *Exec Srch*
Graphic Techniques, Inc., *Temp Agcy*
Headway Corp. Staffing, *Perm Agcy*
F.P. Healy & Company, *Exec Srch*
Hunter Mac & Associates, *Perm Agcy*
Hunter Placement Inc., *Exec Srch*
Huntington Pers. Conslt, *Exec Srch*
Information Syst. Staffing, *Contract Svc*
Innovations Associates, *Perm Agcy*
Island Search Group Inc., *Perm Agcy*
Joseph Associates Inc., *Exec Srch*
KLK Personnel, *Perm Agcy*
KPA Staffing Group, Inc., *Exec Srch*
The Kay Group of Fifth Ave., *Exec Srch*
Kelly Services, Inc., *Temp Agcy*
Fred Koffler Associates, *Exec Srch*
Ktech Systems Group, *Perm Agcy*
Lake Associates, *Exec Srch*
John Lawrence & Assoc., *Exec Srch*
The MVP Group, *Exec Srch*
Magill Associates, Inc., *Exec Srch*
Mngmt. Rcrtrs. of Orange Cty, *Exec Srch*
Mentortech, *Exec Srch*
Metropolitan Pers. Syst., *Exec Srch*
Milazzo Associates, Inc., *Perm Agcy*
Nationwide Pers. Grp., *Perm Agcy*
Noah Associates, *Perm Agcy*
Norrell Staffing Services, *Temp Agcy*
Olsten Staffing Services, *Temp Agcy*
Optimal Resources, *Exec Srch*
Arthur Pann Associates, *Exec Srch*
Parsons, Anderson & Gee, *Perm Agcy*
Personnel Services Center, *Exec Srch*
P.G. Prager Search Assoc., *Exec Srch*
Pro Search Associates, Inc., *Exec Srch*
Professional Support Inc., *Exec Srch*
Quest Organization, *Exec Srch*
Recruitment Intnl. Group, *Exec Srch*
Rem Resources, Inc., *Perm Agcy*
Fran Rogers Personnel, *Perm Agcy*
S.W. Management, *Exec Srch*
SearchAmerica Inc., *Exec Srch*
Sigma Staffing, *Perm Agcy*
Snelling Personnel Svcs., *Perm Agcy*
Staff By Manning, Ltd., *Perm Agcy*
Staff Managers, *Temp Agcy*
Stamm Personnel Agency, *Perm Agcy*
Strategic Recruiting, *Exec Srch*
Superior Concepts, *Contract Svc*
Techno-Trac Systems, Inc., *Exec Srch*
United Staffing Systems, *Temp Agcy*

Charles Wanner Associates, *Exec Srch*
Weber Mngmt. Conslt, *Exec Srch*
Wehn Associates, Inc., *Exec Srch*
Werbin Assoc. Exec. Search, *Exec Srch*
Westaff, *Temp Agcy*
Westchester Emp. Agency, *Perm Agcy*
Winston Staffing Services, *Exec Srch*

North Carolina
Accurate Staffing Conslt, *Exec Srch*
ACSYS, *Perm Agcy*
Action Staffing Group, *Temp Agcy*
Advanced Pers. Resources, *Exec Srch*
AmeriPro Search, Inc., *Exec Srch*
Anderson & Daniel Personnel Associates, *Perm Agcy*
Andrews & Associates, *Exec Srch*
COMFORCE Tech. Svcs., *Contract Svc*
Express Personnel Svcs., *Temp Agcy*
Five Star Staffing, Inc., *Temp Agcy*
Granite Personnel Service, *Perm Agcy*
Robert Half Intl/Accountemps, *Exec Srch*
Interim Personnel, Inc., *Temp Agcy*
Kelly Services, Inc., *Temp Agcy*
MKR Pers. Solutions, *Contract Svc*
Mngmt. Rcrtrs. International, *Exec Srch*
Moffitt International, Inc., *Exec Srch*
Norrell Services, *Temp Agcy*
Olsten Staffing Services, *Temp Agcy*
Pro Staff Personnel Svc., *Perm Agcy*
Quality Temporary Svcs., *Temp Agcy*
Romac International, *Exec Srch*
Sales Conslt, *Exec Srch*
Sanford Rose Associates, *Exec Srch*
Snelling Personnel Svcs., *Perm Agcy*
Sparks Personnel Services, *Exec Srch*
The Underwood Group, *Perm Agcy*
USA Staffing, *Perm Agcy*
Youngblood Staffing, *Perm Agcy*

North Dakota
Career Connection, *Exec Srch*
Olsten Staffing Services/Expressway Personnel, *Temp Agcy*

Ohio
Accountants Executive Search/Accountants on Call, *Exec Srch*
AccuStaff, *Temp Agcy*
Adecco, *Temp Agcy*
Adecco/TAD Tech. Svcs., *Contract Svc*
All Star Personnel, Inc., *Perm Agcy*
AllTech Resources, Inc., *Exec Srch*
Aquent Partners, *Temp Agcy*
J.B. Brown & Associates, *Exec Srch*
CBS Personnel Services, *Perm Agcy*
Champion Personnel Syst., *Perm Agcy*
Combined Resources Inc., *Exec Srch*
J.D. Cotter Search, *Exec Srch*
Data Bank Corporation, *Exec Srch*
Eastern Personnel Svcs, *Perm Agcy*
Enterprise Search Assoc., *Perm Agcy*
Executech, *Exec Srch*
Fenzel Milar Associates, *Exec Srch*
Russ Hadick & Associates, *Exec Srch*
Hahn & Associates, Inc., *Exec Srch*
Hammann & Associates, Inc., *Exec Srch*
Hite Executive Search/Hite Management Conslt, Inc., *Exec Srch*
KBK Management Assoc., *Exec Srch*
Mngmt. Rcrtrs. International, *Exec Srch*
Marvel Conslt Inc., *Exec Srch*
Masterson Personnel, Inc./Masterson Temporary Services, *Perm Agcy*
Messina Management Syst., *Exec Srch*
Northcoast Personnel, *Exec Srch*
Olsten Prof. Staffing Services, *Exec Srch*
Olsten Staffing Services, *Temp Agcy*
Jerry Paul Associates, *Perm Agcy*
Providence Pers. Conslt, *Exec Srch*
Romac International, *Exec Srch*
Sales Conslt, *Exec Srch*
Sanford Rose Associates, *Exec Srch*
Sterling Pers. Resources, *Exec Srch*
J.P. Walton & Associates, *Exec Srch*

Oklahoma
Ameri Resource, *Exec Srch*
Cherokee Temps, Inc., *Temp Agcy*
Robert Half Intl/Accountemps, *Exec Srch*
Key Temporary Personnel, *Temp Agcy*
Mngmt. Rcrtrs. International, *Exec Srch*
Terry Neese Pers. Agency, *Temp Agcy*
StaffMark, *Temp Agcy*

Oregon
APA Employment Agency, *Exec Srch*
Adams Temporaries, *Temp Agcy*
Aquent Partners, *Temp Agcy*
Barrett Business Services, *Temp Agcy*
Corporate Careers Inc., *Temp Agcy*
Executives Worldwide, *Exec Srch*
Express Personnel Services, *Exec Srch*
Initial Staffing Services, *Perm Agcy*
Kelly Services, Inc., *Temp Agcy*
Mngmt. Rcrtrs. of Portland/OfficeMates5, *Exec Srch*
Northwest Temporary & Staffing Services, *Temp Agcy*
Office Careers Inc., *Perm Agcy*
Triad Technology Group, *Perm Agcy*
Woodworth Intnl. Group, *Exec Srch*

Pennsylvania
AAP Inc., *Temp Agcy*
Adecco, *Temp Agcy*
All Staffing Inc., *Perm Agcy*
Allegheny Personnel Svcs, *Temp Agcy*
Anita's Careers, Inc., *Exec Srch*
Aquent Partners, *Temp Agcy*
Aquent Partners, *Temp Agcy*
Ashley Search Conslt, *Exec Srch*
Bon Temps Staffing Svcs, *Temp Agcy*
T.W. Boris Associates, *Exec Srch*
CDI Information Services, *Contract Svc*
Career Concepts Staffing Svcs, *Exec Srch*
Career Quest Confidential, *Exec Srch*
Charley's Pers. Staffing, *Temp Agcy*
CoreStaff Inc., *Temp Agcy*
J. Croyle & Associates, *Perm Agcy*
P. Robert Dann, *Exec Srch*
Robert J. DePaul & Assoc., *Exec Srch*
Dunn Associates, *Exec Srch*
EDP Contract Services, *Contract Svc*
Eden & Associates, Inc., *Exec Srch*
Execu-Search, *Exec Srch*
Executive Avail-A-Search, *Exec Srch*
Financial Industry Staffing Company, *Perm Agcy*
Merrill Grumer Assoc., *Perm Agcy*
HRS/TND Associates, Inc., *Exec Srch*
The Hastings Group, *Exec Srch*
The Hobart West Group, *Temp Agcy*
Human Assets Inc., *Temp Agcy*
Impact Search & Strategy, *Exec Srch*
Interim Personnel, *Temp Agcy*
J-Rand Search, *Exec Srch*
Nancy Jackson Inc., *Exec Srch*
Kenneth James Associates, *Exec Srch*
Jefferson-Ross Associates, *Exec Srch*
Kathy Karr Personnel, *Perm Agcy*
London Personnel Svcs., *Perm Agcy*
Mngmt. Rcrtrs. International, *Exec Srch*
Mastersearch, *Exec Srch*
J. McManus Associates, *Perm Agcy*
Metropolitan Personnel, *Temp Agcy*
OfficeTeam, *Temp Agcy*
Olsten Staffing Services, *Temp Agcy*
LaMonte Owens, Inc., *Exec Srch*
Pancoast Temp. Svcs., *Temp Agcy*
Quest Systems, Inc., *Perm Agcy*
Romac International, *Exec Srch*
Select Personnel, Inc., *Perm Agcy*
Snelling Personnel Svcs., *Temp Agcy*
Spectrum Conslt, Inc./Retail Recruiters, *Exec Srch*
TRC Staffing Services, *Temp Agcy*
Terry Taylor & Associates, *Exec Srch*
W.G. Tucker & Associates, *Exec Srch*
Uni-Temp Temp. Svc., *Temp Agcy*
Vogue Personnel Inc., *Exec Srch*

Rhode Island
Capitol Personnel Inc., *Temp Agcy*
Colony Personnel Assoc., *Temp Agcy*
Dorra Search Inc., *Exec Srch*
Initial Staffing Services, *Perm Agcy*
Kelly Services, Inc., *Temp Agcy*
Albert G. Lee & Assoc., *Exec Srch*
Mngmt. Rcrtrs. International, *Exec Srch*
Norrell Services, *Temp Agcy*
Personnel People, Inc., *Perm Agcy*
Pro Staff Personnel Svcs., *Temp Agcy*
Qualified Resources, *Temp Agcy*

South Carolina
F-O-R-T-U-N-E Pers. Conslts of Columbia, *Exec Srch*

Manchester Inc., *Exec Srch*
Meads & Associates, *Exec Srch*
The Ryan Charles Group, *Exec Srch*
Sales Conslt, *Exec Srch*
Staffing Now, *Temp Agcy*
The Stewart Search Group, *Exec Srch*
Temp-Art, *Temp Agcy*

Georgia

Ad Options Inc., *Perm Agcy*
Business Prof. Group, *Perm Agcy*
Comprehensive Search Grp, *Exec Srch*
Creative Search, *Exec Srch*
Elite Staffing Services, *Temp Agcy*
Kenzer Corporation of GA, *Exec Srch*
Mngmt. Rcrtrs. International, *Exec Srch*
Randstad Staffing Svcs., *Temp Agcy*
Staffing Resources, *Perm Agcy*
WPPS Software Staffing, *Temp Agcy*
Westaff, *Temp Agcy*

Hawaii

Select Staffing Services, *Temp Agcy*

Illinois

Accurate Recruiting Inc., *Perm Agcy*
Bell Personnel Inc., *Perm Agcy*
Caprio & Associates Inc., *Exec Srch*
CareerLink USA, Inc., *Exec Srch*
Corporate Staffing, Inc./Proven
  Performers, *Perm Agcy*
Diener & Associates Inc., *Exec Srch*
The Eastwood Group, *Exec Srch*
The Esquire Staffing Grp., *Perm Agcy*
Eve Recruiters Ltd., *Perm Agcy*
Executive Search Intnl., *Exec Srch*
David Gomez & Assoc., *Exec Srch*
Cathy Hurless Executive Recruiting,
  Exec Srch
InterStaff, *Temp Agcy*
Kunzer Associates, Ltd., *Exec Srch*
Arlene Leff & Associates, *Exec Srch*
Mngmt. Rcrtrs. International, *Exec Srch*
McCullum Associates, *Temp Agcy*
Media Staffing Network, *Temp Agcy*
Juan Menefee & Assoc., *Exec Srch*
Michael David Associates, *Perm Agcy*
The Murphy Group, *Perm Agcy*
OfficeMates5 (OM5), *Perm Agcy*
The Ryan Charles Group, *Exec Srch*
SHS, Inc., *Exec Srch*
Snelling Personnel Svcs., *Perm Agcy*
World Employment Svc., *Perm Agcy*

Indiana

Artisan Staffing, *Temp Agcy*
Execusearch, *Exec Srch*
Job Placement Service, *Perm Agcy*
Mngmt. Rcrtrs. of Richmond, *Exec Srch*
OfficeMates5 (OM5)/DayStar Temporary
  Services, *Exec Srch*

Iowa

Mngmt. Rcrtrs. International, *Exec Srch*

Kansas

Business Specialists, *Perm Agcy*
Mngmt. Rcrtrs. of Overland Park/Sales
  Conslt/OfficeMates5, *Exec Srch*

Kentucky

Angel Group International, *Exec Srch*

Louisiana

Mngmt. Rcrtrs. of Metairie/Sales Conslt
  of Metairie, *Exec Srch*
Talley & Assoc/Talley Temps, *Exec Srch*

Maine

Career Management Assoc., *Exec Srch*

Maryland

Executive Placement Assoc., *Exec Srch*
HireKnowledge, *Temp Agcy*
Mngmt. Rcrtrs. International, *Exec Srch*
Placement Associates, *Exec Srch*
Sales Conslt, *Exec Srch*
TAC Staffing Services, *Temp Agcy*
Winston Search, Inc., *Exec Srch*

Massachusetts

Alden and Clark, Inc., *Temp Agcy*
Brattle Temps, *Temp Agcy*
Campbell Associates, *Exec Srch*
Cleary Conslt Inc., *Perm Agcy*
Corporate Staffing Solns., *Temp Agcy*
Derby Associates Inc., *Perm Agcy*

Fanning Personnel, *Perm Agcy*
Ford & Ford Exec. Search, *Exec Srch*
HireKnowledge, *Temp Agcy*
Lake Conslt, *Exec Srch*
John Leonard Pers. Assoc., *Perm Agcy*
Mngmt. Rcrtrs. International, *Exec Srch*
Pile and Company, *Exec Srch*
Pro Staff, *Temp Agcy*
Professional Staffing Grp, *Perm Agcy*
Sales Conslt, *Exec Srch*
Selectemps, *Temp Agcy*
Snelling Personnel Svcs., *Perm Agcy*
Spectra Professional Search/Spectra
  Temps, *Perm Agcy*
Stone & Youngblood, *Exec Srch*
TAC Staffing Services, *Temp Agcy*
Tricor Associates, *Temp Agcy*
The Ward Group, *Exec Srch*

Michigan

Express Personnel Svcs., *Temp Agcy*
Graphic Arts Marketing Associates, *Exec
  Srch*
William Howard Agency, *Contract Svc*
Mngmt. Rcrtrs. International, *Exec Srch*
Roth Young Pers. Services, *Exec Srch*

Minnesota

Abby Blu Inc., *Temp Agcy*
Diversified Employment, *Perm Agcy*
Gerdes Singer & Assoc., *Exec Srch*
Graphic Staffing Inc., *Temp Agcy*
Hayden & Associates, *Exec Srch*
T.H. Hunter, Inc., *Exec Srch*
JFK Search, *Exec Srch*
Eric Kercheval & Assoc., *Exec Srch*
Mngmt. Rcrtrs. of Minneapolis/
  Sales Conslt, *Exec Srch*
Resource Search, *Exec Srch*

Mississippi

EPSCO Personnel Service, *Temp Agcy*
Mississippi State Emp. Svcs., *Perm Agcy*

Missouri

Jay Alexander & Assoc., *Perm Agcy*
Business Personnel Svcs., *Temp Agcy*
HireKnowledge, *Temp Agcy*
Huey Enterprises, *Exec Srch*
Kirdonn Group, *Perm Agcy*
LandAJob, *Perm Agcy*
Charles Luntz & Assoc., *Exec Srch*
Mngmt. Rcrtrs. International, *Exec Srch*
OfficeMates5 (OM5), *Exec Srch*

Nebraska

Compusearch of Lincoln, *Exec Srch*
Mngmt. Rcrtrs. of Omaha/
  OfficeMates5, *Exec Srch*

Nevada

Initial Staffing Services, *Perm Agcy*
NTR, *Exec Srch*
Sales Staffing Specialists, *Perm Agcy*

New Hampshire

Barrett & Company, *Exec Srch*
Cheshire Emp. Svc., *Temp Agcy*
Mngmt. Rcrtrs. International, *Exec Srch*
Sales Conslt, *Exec Srch*

New Jersey

A Professional Edge,
  Career/Outplacement
Advanced Personnel Svc., *Perm Agcy*
Blake & Assoc. Exec. Srch, *Exec Srch*
Career Center, Inc., *Perm Agcy*
Ellis Career Conslt/Career Search
  Associates, *Exec Srch*
Express Personnel Svcs., *Perm Agcy*
Flextime Solutions, Inc., *Perm Agcy*
Horizon Graphics Pers., *Perm Agcy*
Impact Personnel, Inc., *Perm Agcy*
Kelly Services, Inc., *Temp Agcy*
Mngmt. Rcrtrs. International, *Exec Srch*
OfficeMates5 (OM5)/DayStar Temporary
  Services, *Perm Agcy*
Orion Consulting, Inc., *Exec Srch*
Premier Personnel Group, *Perm Agcy*
Salem Associates, *Exec Srch*
Sales Conslt of Sparta, *Exec Srch*
Arline Simpson Assoc., *Perm Agcy*
Trout Associates, Inc., *Exec Srch*
Winston Staffing Services, *Temp Agcy*
Claire Wright Associates, *Perm Agcy*

New Mexico

Albuquerque Personnel, *Perm Agcy*
Santa Fe Services, *Temp Agcy*

New York

Accounting & Computer Personnel,
  Perm Agcy
AccuStaff Incorporated, *Temp Agcy*
Merrill Adams Associates,
  Career/Outplacement
Adecco, *Temp Agcy*
Adept Tech Recruiting, *Exec Srch*
AMESgroup, *Exec Srch*
Analytic Recruiting Inc., *Exec Srch*
Asher Pers. Conslt, *Perm Agcy*
Benson Associates, *Exec Srch*
Bornholdt Shivas & Friends, *Exec Srch*
Branthover Associates, *Exec Srch*
CDI Corporation, *Contract Svc*
CGR Staffing Services, *Temp Agcy*
Seth Diamond Associates, *Exec Srch*
Maggi Dolan Placement, *Perm Agcy*
Eden Staffing, *Perm Agcy*
Alexander Edwards Intnl., *Exec Srch*
Employment Recruiters Agency, *Perm
  Agcy*
Euromonde, Inc., *Temp Agcy*
Freelance Advancers, Inc., *Temp Agcy*
Graphics For Hire, Inc., *Perm Agcy*
Gundersen Partners L.L.C., *Exec Srch*
HireKnowledge, *Temp Agcy*
Ruth Hirsch Associates, *Exec Srch*
Hot Bear/De Bella Productions and
  Editorial Temps, *Temp Agcy*
Innovations Associates, *Perm Agcy*
Island Search Group Inc., *Perm Agcy*
KLK Personnel, *Perm Agcy*
The Kay Group of Fifth Ave., *Exec Srch*
Fred Koffler Associates, *Exec Srch*
John Lawrence & Assoc., *Exec Srch*
Mngmt. Rcrtrs. of Gramercy, *Exec Srch*
Manpower Temp. Svcs., *Temp Agcy*
Media Staffing Network, *Temp Agcy*
Morgan-Murray Personnel/M&M Top
  Temps, *Temp Agcy*
Noble & Associates, *Exec Srch*
Olsten Financial Staffing, *Temp Agcy*
Optimal Resources, *Exec Srch*
Preferred Professionals, *Temp Agcy*
Redwood Partners, *Exec Srch*
Rem Resources, Inc., *Perm Agcy*
Ribolow Associates, *Perm Agcy*
Salem Associates, *Exec Srch*
SearchAmerica Inc., *Exec Srch*
Swing Shift, *Temp Agcy*
Hillary Taylor Personnel, *Perm Agcy*
TemPositions, Inc., *Temp Agcy*
Trebor, Weldon, Lawrence, Levine, *Exec
  Srch*
United Personnel Agency, *Perm Agcy*
Vintage Resources, Inc., *Exec Srch*
Don Waldron & Assoc., *Perm Agcy*
Werbin Assoc. Exec. Search, *Exec Srch*
S.R. Wolman Associates, *Exec Srch*

North Carolina

Kelly Services, Inc., *Temp Agcy*
Mngmt. Rcrtrs. International, *Exec Srch*
Olsten Staffing Services, *Temp Agcy*
Sales Conslt, *Exec Srch*
Sparks Personnel Services, *Exec Srch*

North Dakota

Olsten Staffing Services/Expressway
  Personnel, *Temp Agcy*

Ohio

Adecco, *Temp Agcy*
J.B. Brown & Associates, *Exec Srch*
Champion Personnel Syst., *Perm Agcy*
Combined Resources Inc., *Exec Srch*
Eastern Personnel Svcs., *Perm Agcy*
Fristoe & Carleton, *Exec Srch*
Hite Executive Search/Hite Management
  Conslt, Inc., *Exec Srch*
Ives & Associates, Inc., *Exec Srch*
Mngmt. Rcrtrs. International, *Exec Srch*
Providence Pers. Conslt, *Exec Srch*
Sales Conslt, *Exec Srch*
Sanker & Associates, *Temp Agcy*

Oklahoma

Express Personnel Services, *Exec Srch*
Key Temporary Personnel, *Temp Agcy*

Massachusetts

Cyr Associates, Inc., *Exec Srch*
Ford & Ford Exec. Search, *Exec Srch*
Mngmt. Rcrtrs. International, *Exec Srch*
Sales Conslt, *Exec Srch*
SearchNet, *Contract Svc*
TAD Staffing Services, *Temp Agcy*
TASA International, *Exec Srch*

Michigan

Mngmt. Rcrtrs. International, *Exec Srch*

Minnesota

Mngmt. Rcrtrs. of Minneapolis/
Sales Conslt, *Exec Srch*
Roth Young Exec. Recruiters, *Exec Srch*

Missouri

Mngmt. Rcrtrs. International, *Exec Srch*
OfficeMates5 (OM5), *Exec Srch*

Nebraska

Compusearch of Lincoln, *Exec Srch*
Mngmt. Rcrtrs. of Omaha/
OfficeMates5, *Exec Srch*

New Hampshire

Clayman Management Svc, *Exec Srch*
Reid and Company, *Exec Srch*
Sales Conslt, *Exec Srch*

New Jersey

A Professional Edge, *Career/
Outplacement*
Career Center, Inc., *Perm Agcy*
Career Management Intnl., *Exec Srch*
Horizon Graphics Pers., *Perm Agcy*
Impact Personnel, Inc., *Perm Agcy*
Mngmt. Rcrtrs. International, *Exec Srch*
Solomon Page Group, Inc., *Exec Srch*
Ken Rose Associates, *Exec Srch*
SK Assoc./Career Conslt, *Exec Srch*
Sales Conslt of Sparta, *Exec Srch*
Temporary Excellence, *Temp Agcy*
Winston Staffing Services, *Temp Agcy*

New York

Adam Personnel, Inc., *Perm Agcy*
Adecco, *Temp Agcy*
Asher Personnel Conslt, *Perm Agcy*
Neail Behringer Conslt, *Exec Srch*
C.C. Burke, Ltd., *Exec Srch*
Seth Diamond Assoc., *Exec Srch*
Eden Staffing, *Perm Agcy*
Employment Recruiters Agency, *Perm
Agcy*
Euromonde, Inc., *Temp Agcy*
Fanning Personnel, *Exec Srch*
KLK Personnel, *Perm Agcy*
Kaufman Associates Ltd., *Exec Srch*
Koltnow & Company, *Exec Srch*
Levine Hirshorn & Assoc., *Exec Srch*
Manpower Temp. Svcs., *Temp Agcy*
Optimal Resources, *Exec Srch*
Quest Organization, *Exec Srch*
Recruitment Intnl. Group, *Exec Srch*
Rem Resources, Inc., *Perm Agcy*
Hillary Taylor Personnel, *Perm Agcy*
United Staffing Systems, *Temp Agcy*
Winston Staffing Services, *Exec Srch*
S.R. Wolman Associates, *Exec Srch*

North Carolina

A First Resource, *Exec Srch*
Adkins & Associates, *Exec Srch*
Amcell Associates, *Exec Srch*
Ayers & Associates, Inc., *Exec Srch*
Forbes Temp. Staffing, *Temp Agcy*
Mngmt. Rcrtrs. International, *Exec Srch*
Myers & Associates, *Perm Agcy*
Nagel Executive Search, *Exec Srch*
Sales Conslt, *Exec Srch*
Sickenberger Associates, *Exec Srch*
Sparks Personnel Services, *Exec Srch*
USA Staffing, *Perm Agcy*
Randy Walley Associates, *Exec Srch*

North Dakota

Olsten Staffing Services/Expressway
Personnel, *Temp Agcy*

Ohio

Mngmt. Rcrtrs. International, *Exec Srch*
Sales Conslt, *Exec Srch*

Oklahoma

Mngmt. Rcrtrs. International, *Exec Srch*

Oregon

Mngmt. Rcrtrs. of Portland/
OfficeMates5 of Portland, *Exec Srch*

Pennsylvania

Ashley Search Conslt, *Exec Srch*
CoreStaff Inc., *Temp Agcy*
J. Croyle & Associates, *Perm Agcy*
Eden & Associates, Inc., *Exec Srch*
HRS/TND Associates, Inc., *Exec Srch*
Mngmt. Rcrtrs. International, *Exec Srch*
Manchester Inc., *Career/Outplacement*
Kenn Spinrad Inc., *Exec Srch*

Rhode Island

Creative Input, Inc., *Exec Srch*
Mngmt. Rcrtrs. International, *Exec Srch*

South Carolina

ASAP Search & Recruiters, *Perm Agcy*
Mngmt. Rcrtrs. International, *Exec Srch*
The Stroman Company, *Perm Agcy*

Tennessee

Mngmt. Rcrtrs. International, *Exec Srch*

Texas

Carpenter & Associates, *Exec Srch*
Dallas Employment Svcs., *Perm Agcy*
Kenzer Corporation, *Exec Srch*
Mngmt. Rcrtrs. International, *Exec Srch*
Sales Conslt, *Exec Srch*
Salinas & Assoc Pers. Svc., *Exec Srch*

Virginia

Barnes & Assoc. Retail Srch, *Exec Srch*
Buckler Careers, Inc., *Perm Agcy*

Washington

Mngmt. Rcrtrs. International, *Exec Srch*
Strategic Resources, *Exec Srch*

Wisconsin

Mngmt. Rcrtrs. of Appleton/
Compusearch, *Exec Srch*

ARCHITECTURE/CONSTRUCTION

Alabama

Locke & Associates, *Exec Srch*
Mngmt. Rcrtrs. International, *Exec Srch*
Seatec, Inc., *Contract Svc*

Arizona

Adecco/TAD Tech. Svcs., *Temp Agcy*
C.S. Associates, LLC, *Exec Srch*
COMFORCE Tech. Svcs., *Contract Svc*
Crown Technical Service, *Contract Svc*
Mngmt. Rcrtrs. of Scottsdale, *Exec Srch*
Norrell Interim Services, *Temp Agcy*
PDS Technical Services, *Contract Svc*
Taylor Design Recruiting, *Exec Srch*
Tech/Aid of Arizona, *Perm Agcy*

Arkansas

Mngmt. Rcrtrs., *Exec Srch*
Penmac Personnel Service, *Perm Agcy*

California

Bullis & Company, Inc., *Exec Srch*
Business Systems Support, *Perm Agcy*
C-E Search, *Exec Srch*
CDI Technical Services, *Temp Agcy*
CT Personnel Services, *Perm Agcy*
California Search Agency, *Exec Srch*
Contractors Labor Pool, *Temp Agcy*
Douglas Dorflinger & Assoc., *Exec Srch*
Fay Tech Services, *Perm Agcy*
Goldstein & Associates, *Temp Agcy*
Gould Personnel Services, *Perm Agcy*
Griffith & Associates, *Exec Srch*
Harmeling & Associates, *Exec Srch*
Industrial Services Co., *Temp Agcy*
Interim Personnel, *Temp Agcy*
International Staffing Conslt, *Exec Srch*
Klein & Associates, *Temp Agcy*
J.H. Lindell & Company, *Exec Srch*
The London Associates, *Exec Srch*
Mngmt. Rcrtrs. International, *Exec Srch*
Rowland Associates, *Exec Srch*
Santa Barbara Staffing, *Perm Agcy*
Search West of Ontario, *Exec Srch*
TECH/AID, *Temp Agcy*
Thor Temporary Services, *Temp Agcy*
Truex Associates, *Exec Srch*
Westaff, *Temp Agcy*

Colorado

Career Forum, Inc., *Exec Srch*
Chuck's Contract Labor Service,
Contract Svc
Eagle Valley Temps, *Temp Agcy*
JobSearch, *Temp Agcy*
Mngmt. Rcrtrs. of Colorado Springs,
Exec Srch
Manpower International., *Temp Agcy*
Payroll Principals, Inc., *Perm Agcy*
Pendleton Resources, *Exec Srch*
Real Estate Personnel, *Exec Srch*
Sales Conslt, *Exec Srch*
Terry Personnel, *Perm Agcy*
Todays Temporary, *Temp Agcy*
York & Associates, *Exec Srch*

Connecticut

Intertec Personnel, *Temp Agcy*
Mngmt. Rcrtrs. of Norwalk, *Exec Srch*
Quality Control Recruiters, *Exec Srch*
Tech/Aid, *Temp Agcy*

Delaware

Hornberger Mngmt. Co., *Exec Srch*

Dist. of Columbia

ACSYS Staffing, *Exec Srch*
HireKnowledge, *Temp Agcy*

Florida

Able Body Corporate Svcs., *Contract Svc*
Academy Design & Technical Services,
Inc., *Contract Svc*
Active Professionals, *Exec Srch*
Career Planners, Inc., *Perm Agcy*
Construction Resources Grp., *Exec Srch*
DGA Personnel Group, *Exec Srch*
Gulf Coast Associates, *Exec Srch*
R.H. Larsen & Associates, *Exec Srch*
Mngmt. Rcrtrs. International, *Exec Srch*
Manchester Inc., *Exec Srch*
Pro-Team Services, Inc., *Exec Srch*
Sales Conslt, Inc., *Exec Srch*
Shaver Emp. Agency, *Perm Agcy*
Specialized Search Assoc., *Exec Srch*
TRC Staffing Services, *Temp Agcy*
TechStaff, *Contract Svc*

Georgia

Claremont-Branan, Inc., *Perm Agcy*
Comprehensive Search Grp, *Exec Srch*
Corporate Search Conslt, *Exec Srch*
ISC of Atlanta/International Career
Continuation, *Exec Srch*
MSI International, *Exec Srch*
Mngmt. Rcrtrs. of Atlanta, *Exec Srch*
The Shepard Group, Inc., *Exec Srch*
WPPS Software Staffing, *Temp Agcy*

Hawaii

Altres Staffing, *Temp Agcy*
Dunhill Prof. Staffing of HI, *Exec Srch*
Executive Search World, *Exec Srch*
Sales Conslt, *Exec Srch*

Idaho

Manpower Temp. Svcs., *Temp Agcy*

Illinois

American Contract Svcs., *Contract Svc*
B-W and Associates, Inc., *Perm Agcy*
Burling Group Ltd., *Exec Srch*
Carter Associates, *Exec Srch*
Cook Associates, Inc., *Exec Srch*
Corporate Environment, *Exec Srch*
Executive Referral Svcs., *Exec Srch*
Jerry L. Jung Company, *Exec Srch*
Mngmt. Rcrtrs. International, *Exec Srch*
McCullum Associates, *Temp Agcy*
OfficeMates5 (OM5), *Perm Agcy*
Omega Technical Corp., *Contract Svc*
Strategic Resources Unlimited, *Exec Srch*

Indiana

Adecco/TAD Tech. Svcs., *Contract Svc*
Execusearch, *Exec Srch*
Job Placement Service, *Perm Agcy*
Mngmt. Rcrtrs. of Richmond, *Exec Srch*
OM5/DayStar Temp. Svcs., *Exec Srch*
Technetics Corporation, *Contract Svc*

Iowa

Byrnes & Rupkey, Inc., *Exec Srch*
Helping Hands Temp. Svc., *Temp Agcy*
The Human Resource Grp, *Exec Srch*
Mngmt. Rcrtrs. International, *Exec Srch*

Arkansas
Mngmt. Rcrtrs., *Exec Srch*

California
A.S.A.P. Emp. Service, *Perm Agcy*
Answers Unlimited, *Temp Agcy*
Aquent Partners, *Temp Agcy*
Art Links Staffing, *Perm Agcy*
CDI Technical Services, *Temp Agcy*
Career Quest Intnl, *Contract Svc*
Corporate Search, *Exec Srch*
Creative Assets, *Temp Agcy*
Fastek Technical Services, *Perm Agcy*
F-O-R-T-U-N-E Pers. Conslts, *Exec Srch*
Full Service Temporaries, *Temp Agcy*
Goldstein & Associates, *Temp Agcy*
HireKnowledge, *Temp Agcy*
Larkin Group, *Exec Srch*
Musick & Associates, *Exec Srch*
Professional Recruiters, *Exec Srch*
Santa Barbara Staffing, *Perm Agcy*
TRC Staffing Services, *Perm Agcy*
TECH/AID, *Temp Agcy*
Visuals, *Perm Agcy*

Colorado
Aquent Partners, *Temp Agcy*
Sales Conslt, *Exec Srch*

Connecticut
Admiral Staffing Services, *Temp Agcy*
Aquent Partners, *Temp Agcy*
Computer Graphics Rsrc., *Temp Agcy*

Dist. of Columbia
Aquent Partners, *Temp Agcy*
Goodwin & Company, *Exec Srch*
Graphic Mac, *Temp Agcy*
HireKnowledge, *Temp Agcy*

Florida
AAA Employment, *Perm Agcy*
Aquent Partners, *Temp Agcy*
B²D Technical Services, *Contract Svc*
Temp-Art, *Temp Agcy*
TempSolutions, Inc., *Temp Agcy*

Georgia
Ad Options Inc., *Perm Agcy*
Aquent Partners, *Temp Agcy*
Claremont-Branan, Inc., *Perm Agcy*
Comprehensive Search Group, *Exec Srch*
Kreisler & Associates, *Exec Srch*

Illinois
Aquent Partners, *Temp Agcy*
Bloom, Gross & Assoc., *Exec Srch*
Carson Mngmt Associates, *Contract Svc*
Diener & Associates Inc., *Exec Srch*
The Eastwood Group, *Exec Srch*
David Gomez & Assoc., *Exec Srch*
InterStaff, *Temp Agcy*
Kunzer Associates, Ltd., *Exec Srch*
MacIntyre Emp. Service, *Perm Agcy*
Mngmt. Rcrtrs. International, *Exec Srch*
James C. Pappas & Assoc., *Exec Srch*
ProSearch Plus, *Exec Srch*

Indiana
Artisan Staffing, *Temp Agcy*

Iowa
Mngmt. Rcrtrs. International, *Exec Srch*

Kansas
Mngmt. Rcrtrs. of Overland Park/Sales
    Conslt /OfficeMates5, *Exec Srch*
White Associates/TemTech, *Exec Srch*

Kentucky
Angel Group International, *Exec Srch*

Louisiana
Keenan Staffing Inc., *Temp Agcy*
Mngmt. Rcrtrs. of Metairie/Sales Conslt
    of Metairie, *Exec Srch*

Maryland
HireKnowledge, *Temp Agcy*
Mngmt. Rcrtrs. International, *Exec Srch*

Massachusetts
Alden and Clark, Inc., *Temp Agcy*
Aquent Partners, *Temp Agcy*
CDI Corporation, *Contract Svc*
Cyr Associates, Inc., *Exec Srch*
Derby Associates Inc., *Perm Agcy*
Ford & Ford Exec. Search, *Exec Srch*
HireKnowledge, *Temp Agcy*

National Engineering Svc., *Temp Agcy*
Need Pers. Placement, *Temp Agcy*
Stone & Youngblood, *Exec Srch*
Summit Technical Svcs., *Temp Agcy*

Michigan
AE Employment Services, *Perm Agcy*
Aquent Partners, *Temp Agcy*
Career Quest, Inc., *Exec Srch*
Design & Engineering Svc., *Temp Agcy*
Dynamic Personnel, *Contract Svc*
Entech Personnel Svcs., *Temp Agcy*
Graphic Arts Marketing Associates, *Exec
    Srch*
William Howard Agency, *Contract Svc*
Kelly Technical Services, *Contract Svc*
Key Personnel, *Perm Agcy*
Mngmt. Rcrtrs. International, *Exec Srch*
Resource Technologies Corp., *Perm Agcy*
Technical Prof. Svc., *Perm Agcy*

Minnesota
Aquent Partners, *Temp Agcy*
Design Pers. Resources, *Temp Agcy*
Discovery Personnel, Inc., *Exec Srch*
Diversified Employment, *Perm Agcy*
Graphic Staffing Inc., *Temp Agcy*
Mngmt. Rcrtrs. of Minneapolis/
    Sales Conslt, *Exec Srch*
Resource Search, *Exec Srch*

Missouri
HireKnowledge, *Temp Agcy*
Mngmt. Rcrtrs. International, *Exec Srch*
OfficeMates5 (OM5), *Exec Srch*

Montana
LC Staffing Service, *Perm Agcy*

Nebraska
Compusearch of Lincoln, *Exec Srch*
Mngmt. Rcrtrs. of Omaha/
    OfficeMates5, *Exec Srch*

Nevada
Flowers Exec. Search Grp, *Exec Srch*

New Hampshire
Allstaff, *Perm Agcy*
Sales Conslt, *Exec Srch*
Surge Resources Inc., *Contract Svc*
Technical Emp. Svcs., *Contract Svc*

New Jersey
AES Associates, *Exec Srch*
Blake & Assoc. Exec. Srch, *Exec Srch*
Sandra Grundfest, Ed.D.,
    Career/Outplacement
Horizon Graphics Pers., *Perm Agcy*
Mayfair Services, *Perm Agcy*
Orion Consulting, Inc., *Exec Srch*
Sales Conslt of Sparta, *Exec Srch*
Sharp Technical Services, *Contract Svc*

New Mexico
CDI Technical Services, *Contract Svc*

New York
Accounting & Computer Personnel,
    Perm Agcy
Aquent Partners, *Temp Agcy*
Bornholdt Shivas & Friends, *Exec Srch*
CGR Staffing Services, *Temp Agcy*
Maggi Dolan Placement, *Perm Agcy*
Freelance Advancers, Inc., *Temp Agcy*
Graphics For Hire, Inc., *Perm Agcy*
HireKnowledge, *Temp Agcy*
Ruth Hirsch Associates, *Exec Srch*
Hot Bear/De Bella Productions and
    Editorial Temps, *Temp Agcy*
Innovations Associates, *Perm Agcy*
Lloyd Staffing, *Perm Agcy*
Morgan-Murray Personnel/M&M Top
    Temps, *Temp Agcy*
K.A. Nowack Career Specialists, *Perm
    Agcy*
S.R. Wolman Associates, *Exec Srch*

North Carolina
Executive Staffing Group, *Exec Srch*
The Furniture Agency Inc., *Exec Srch*
Mngmt. Rcrtrs. International, *Exec Srch*
PCS, *Contract Svc*
Sales Conslt, *Exec Srch*

North Dakota
Olsten Staffing Services/Expressway
    Personnel, *Temp Agcy*

Ohio
Aquent Partners, *Temp Agcy*
Combined Resources Inc., *Exec Srch*
Employment Solutions Group, *Exec Srch*
Mngmt. Rcrtrs. International, *Exec Srch*
Olsten Prof. Staffing Svcs., *Exec Srch*
RDS, Inc., *Contract Svc*
Sales Conslt, *Exec Srch*
Sanker & Associates, *Temp Agcy*
J.P. Walton & Associates, *Exec Srch*

Oregon
Aquent Partners, *Temp Agcy*
Mngmt. Rcrtrs. of Portland/
    OfficeMates5, *Exec Srch*

Pennsylvania
Aquent Partners, *Temp Agcy*
CDI Corporation, *Contract Svc*
CoreStaff Inc., *Temp Agcy*
Kay Henry Incorporated, *Exec Srch*
HireKnowledge, *Temp Agcy*
Mngmt. Rcrtrs. International, *Exec Srch*
Olsten Staffing Services, *Temp Agcy*

Rhode Island
Mngmt. Rcrtrs. International, *Exec Srch*
Summit Technical Svcs., *Contract Svc*
Tech/Aid of Rhode Island, *Contract Svc*

South Carolina
Mngmt. Rcrtrs. International, *Exec Srch*
TCG Search, *Exec Srch*

Tennessee
The LYNN Grp, HLF Inc., *Exec Srch*

Texas
Aquent Partners, *Temp Agcy*
Brooklea & Associates, *Exec Srch*
HireKnowledge, *Temp Agcy*
Houston Creative Connections, *Exec Srch*
Mngmt. Rcrtrs. International, *Exec Srch*
Pro Staff Personnel Svcs., *Temp Agcy*
Sales Conslt, *Exec Srch*
Search Com, Inc., *Exec Srch*
Stehouwer & Associates, *Perm Agcy*

Virginia
Lee Staffing Resources, *Exec Srch*
Mngmt. Rcrtrs. of McLean/
    OfficeMates5, *Exec Srch*
Snelling Personnel Svcs., *Perm Agcy*

Washington
Aquent Partners, *Temp Agcy*
Creative Assets, *Temp Agcy*
Mngmt. Rcrtrs. International, *Exec Srch*
Resource Mngmt Intnl., *Temp Agcy*

Wisconsin
MacPros, Inc., *Perm Agcy*

Wyoming
Mngmt. Rcrtrs. of Cheyenne, *Exec Srch*

AUTOMOTIVE

Alabama
F-O-R-T-U-N-E Pers. Conslts, *Exec Srch*
Mngmt. Rcrtrs. of Daphne/Sales Conslt,
    Exec Srch

Arizona
Clifford & Associates, *Perm Agcy*
Dealer Connection, *Perm Agcy*

Arkansas
Sanford Rose Associates, *Exec Srch*

California
Automotive Career Placement
    Counselors (ACPC), *Exec Srch*
Cathy Dunn's Assoc Pers Svc, *Perm Agcy*

Colorado
Automotive Mngmt Careers, *Exec Srch*
Woodmoor Group, *Exec Srch*

Florida
F-O-R-T-U-N-E Pers. Conslts, *Exec Srch*

Georgia
Hall Management Group, *Exec Srch*
Parker, McFadden Assoc., *Exec Srch*

Illinois
F-O-R-T-U-N-E Pers. Conslts, *Exec Srch*
Sanford Rose Associates, *Exec Srch*
The Stanton Group, Inc., *Exec Srch*
Ray White Associates, *Exec Srch*

Farwell Group Inc., *Exec Srch*
Five Star Temporary Inc., *Temp Agcy*
Future Force Personnel, *Temp Agcy*
Gimbel & Associates, *Exec Srch*
Hastings & Hastings Personnel Conslt, *Temp Agcy*
Kelly Services, Inc., *Temp Agcy*
R.H. Larsen & Associates, *Exec Srch*
Mngmt. Rcrtrs. International, *Exec Srch*
Manchester Inc., *Exec Srch*
Olsten Financial Staffing, *Temp Agcy*
Olsten Staffing Services, *Temp Agcy*
Linda Robins & Assoc., *Temp Agcy*
Gene Rogers Associates, *Exec Srch*
Romac International, *Exec Srch*
Sales Conslt, *Exec Srch*
Sanford Rose Associates, *Exec Srch*
Doug Sears & Associates, *Exec Srch*
Shaver Emp. Agency, *Perm Agcy*
Staffing Now, *Temp Agcy*
Victoria & Assoc. Pers. Svcs, *Perm Agcy*

Georgia

Access Personnel Svcs., *Perm Agcy*
Michael Alexander Group, *Exec Srch*
Bell Oaks Company, *Exec Srch*
Catalina Human Resources, *Perm Agcy*
Elite Staffing Service, *Temp Agcy*
Express Personnel Svcs., *Perm Agcy*
Horizons Staffing, *Perm Agcy*
ISC of Atlanta/International Career Continuation, *Exec Srch*
Kenzer Corporation of GA, *Exec Srch*
MSI International, *Exec Srch*
Mngmt. Rcrtrs. International, *Exec Srch*
Manpower Temp. Svcs., *Temp Agcy*
New Boston Select, *Perm Agcy*
Norrell Corporation, *Temp Agcy*
Office Specialists, *Temp Agcy*
Olsten Staffing Services, *Temp Agcy*
Priority 1 Staffing Svcs., *Temp Agcy*
Randstad Staffing Svcs., *Temp Agcy*
Sanford Rose Associates, *Exec Srch*
Southern Emp. Service, *Perm Agcy*
TRC Staffing Services, *Temp Agcy*
Toar Consulting, *Exec Srch*
WPPS Software Staffing, *Temp Agcy*
Workman & Associates, *Exec Srch*

Hawaii

Altres Staffing, *Temp Agcy*
Dunhill Prof. Staffing of HI, *Exec Srch*
Executive Search World, *Exec Srch*

Idaho

F-O-R-T-U-N-E Pers. Conslts, *Exec Srch*
Horne/Brown International, *Exec Srch*

Illinois

A.B.A. Placements/A.B.A. Temporaries, *Perm Agcy*
ASI Staffing Service, Inc., *Perm Agcy*
Abbott Smith Associates, *Exec Srch*
Account Pros, *Exec Srch*
Accountants Executive Search/ Accountants On Call, *Exec Srch*
Accurate Personnel Inc., *Perm Agcy*
Adecco, *Temp Agcy*
Armstrong-Hamilton Assoc., *Exec Srch*
Availability, Inc., *Perm Agcy*
The Bankers Group, *Exec Srch*
Barrett Partners, *Exec Srch*
Bell Personnel Inc., *Perm Agcy*
Bevelle & Associates, Inc., *Exec Srch*
CCS Group, *Exec Srch*
CareerLink USA, Inc., *Exec Srch*
Casey Services, Inc., *Perm Agcy*
CEMCO Ltd., *Exec Srch*
Chicago Financial Search, *Exec Srch*
Cogan Personnel Services, *Exec Srch*
CompuPro, *Exec Srch*
Computer Futures Exchange, *Exec Srch*
Contemporary Services, *Exec Srch*
Cook Associates, Inc., *Exec Srch*
Crown Personnel, *Perm Agcy*
Davis Staffing, Inc., *Temp Agcy*
Diener & Associates Inc., *Exec Srch*
Dunhill Staffing Services, *Temp Agcy*
The Eastwood Group, *Exec Srch*
The Esquire Staffing Grp, *Perm Agcy*
Fellows Placement, *Exec Srch*
Financial Search Corp., *Exec Srch*
Furst Staffing Services, *Temp Agcy*
Gnodde Associates, *Exec Srch*

David Gomez & Assoc., *Exec Srch*
HKA Mortgage Staffing & Training, *Perm Agcy*
Robert Half Intl/Accountemps, *Exec Srch*
Human Resource Connection, *Perm Agcy*
Interim Financial Staffing, *Exec Srch*
InterStaff, *Temp Agcy*
Interviewing Conslt, *Perm Agcy*
Kennedy & Company, *Exec Srch*
Kingsley Emp. Svc., *Perm Agcy*
Kingston/Zak Inc., *Exec Srch*
Kunzer Associates, Ltd., *Exec Srch*
Mngmt. Rcrtrs. International, *Exec Srch*
Manning & Associates, *Exec Srch*
Manpower Temp. Svcs., *Temp Agcy*
Merit Personnel Inc., *Exec Srch*
Michael David Associates, *Perm Agcy*
The Murphy Group, *Perm Agcy*
OfficeMates5 (OM5), *Perm Agcy*
Olsten Staffing Services, *Temp Agcy*
Personnel Connections, *Perm Agcy*
Personnel Placement Conslt, *Perm Agcy*
Professional Research Svcs., *Exec Srch*
Profile Temp. Service, *Temp Agcy*
ProSearch Plus, *Exec Srch*
Remedy Intelligent Staffing, *Temp Agcy*
Right Services Inc., *Temp Agcy*
Romac International, *Exec Srch*
Sales Conslt, *Exec Srch*
Sanford Rose Associates, *Exec Srch*
J.R. Scott & Associates, *Exec Srch*
Smith Hanley Associates, *Exec Srch*
Snelling Personnel Svcs., *Perm Agcy*
Staffing Conslt Inc., *Perm Agcy*
Stivers Temporary Pers., *Temp Agcy*
Roy Talman & Associates, *Exec Srch*
Temporary Associates, *Temp Agcy*
K. David Umlauf Executive Search Conslt, *Exec Srch*
World Employment Svc., *Perm Agcy*

Indiana

Bill Caldwell Emp. Service, *Perm Agcy*
Crowe, Chizek and Co., *Perm Agcy*
Crown Temporary Svcs., *Temp Agcy*
Execusearch, *Exec Srch*
Life Employment Service, *Perm Agcy*
Mngmt. Rcrtrs. International, *Exec Srch*
Morley Group, *Exec Srch*
OfficeMates5 (OM5)/DayStar Temporary Services, *Exec Srch*
Perry Personnel Plus, *Perm Agcy*

Iowa

Burton Placement Services, *Exec Srch*
Byrnes & Rupkey, Inc., *Exec Srch*
Helping Hands Temp. Svc., *Temp Agcy*
The Human Resource Grp., *Exec Srch*
McGladrey Search Group, *Exec Srch*
Personnel, Inc., *Exec Srch*
Pratt-Younglove, Inc., *Perm Agcy*
Premier Search Group, *Exec Srch*
Sedona Staffing Services, *Exec Srch*

Kansas

Bossler-Hix Financial Careers, *Perm Agcy*
Business Specialists, *Perm Agcy*
Century, *Exec Srch*
Dunhill of Wichita, *Perm Agcy*
Ida Group, *Exec Srch*
Mngmt. Rcrtrs. of Overland Park/Sales Conslt /OfficeMates5, *Exec Srch*
Smith Brown & Jones, *Exec Srch*

Kentucky

Angel Group International, *Exec Srch*
C.M. Management Svcs., *Perm Agcy*
Engineering & Exec. Inc., *Exec Srch*
Precision Staffing, Inc., *Perm Agcy*
Professional Search Conslt, *Exec Srch*

Louisiana

Keenan Staffing Inc., *Temp Agcy*
MSI Physicians, *Exec Srch*
Mngmt. Rcrtrs. of Metairie/Sales Conslt of Metairie, *Exec Srch*
Snelling Personnel Svcs., *Exec Srch*
Talley & Associates, Inc./Talley Temporaries, *Exec Srch*

Maine

Accomplished Prof., *Temp Agcy*
Career Management Assoc., *Exec Srch*

Executive Search of New England, *Exec Srch*

Maryland

Accountants Executive Search/ Accountants On Call, *Exec Srch*
Administration Pers Svcs., *Perm Agcy*
Atlas Personnel Agency, *Perm Agcy*
Brandjes Associates, *Exec Srch*
Dunhill of Rockville, In., *Perm Agcy*
The Hanover Group, *Exec Srch*
Mngmt. Rcrtrs. International, *Exec Srch*
TAC Staffing Services, *Temp Agcy*
White Ridgely Associates, Inc., *Career/Outplacement*

Massachusetts

Accurate Staffing Svcs., *Temp Agcy*
Aerotek, Inc., *Contract Svc*
Arthur-Blair Associates, *Perm Agcy*
Campbell Associates, *Exec Srch*
Cleary Conslt Inc., *Perm Agcy*
Computer Security Placement, *Exec Srch*
Davis Companies, *Temp Agcy*
Derby Associates Inc., *Perm Agcy*
Discovery Personnel Inc., *Perm Agcy*
Eastwood Pers. Assoc., *Exec Srch*
Greene & Company, *Exec Srch*
JNB Associates, Inc., *Exec Srch*
Johnson & Hill Staffing Svc., *Temp Agcy*
Kingston-Dwight Assoc., *Perm Agcy*
L&L Assoc. & Temps., *Temp Agcy*
Lane Employment Svc., *Perm Agcy*
John Leonard Pers. Assoc., *Perm Agcy*
Mngmt. Rcrtrs. International, *Exec Srch*
Manpower Temp. Svcs., *Temp Agcy*
Anthony Michael & Co., *Exec Srch*
Olsten Financial Staffing, *Exec Srch*
Open Syst. Technologies, *Perm Agcy*
Remedy Intelligent Staffing, *Temp Agcy*
Resources Objectives Inc., *Exec Srch*
Romac International, *Perm Agcy*
Sales Conslt, *Exec Srch*
Scott-Wayne Associates, *Perm Agcy*
Selected Executives Inc., *Exec Srch*
Selectemps, *Temp Agcy*
Snelling Personnel, *Exec Srch*
Spectra Professional Search/Spectra Temps, *Perm Agcy*
Straube Associates, *Exec Srch*
TAD Staffing Services, *Temp Agcy*
Technical Personnel Svcs., *Perm Agcy*

Michigan

Accountants One Inc., *Perm Agcy*
Accountemps/OfficeTeam, *Temp Agcy*
Advance Employment, *Exec Srch*
The Advantage Group, *Exec Srch*
Benford & Associates, *Exec Srch*
Career Quest, Inc., *Perm Agcy*
Entech Personnel Svcs., *Temp Agcy*
ExecuQuest, Inc., *Exec Srch*
Express Personnel Svcs., *Temp Agcy*
Robert Half Intl/Accountemps, *Exec Srch*
Harvey Hohauser & Assoc., *Exec Srch*
William Howard Agency, *Contract Svc*
Mngmt. Rcrtrs. International, *Exec Srch*
Office Staffing Recruiting, *Exec Srch*
Olsten Prof. Staffing, *Temp Agcy*
ProSearch, Inc., *Exec Srch*
TEA Inc., *Perm Agcy*
Trillium Staffing, *Temp Agcy*
Wing Tips and Pumps, Inc., *Exec Srch*

Minnesota

Abby Blu Inc., *Temp Agcy*
Employment Advisors, *Perm Agcy*
T.H. Hunter, Inc., *Exec Srch*
Mngmt. Rcrtrs. of Minneapolis/ Sales Conslt, *Exec Srch*
Thomas Moore Inc., *Temp Agcy*
Sathe & Assoc. Exec. Srch, *Exec Srch*
Jeane Thorne Inc., *Temp Agcy*
Ultimate Search Unlimited/Temps Unlimited, *Perm Agcy*

Mississippi

EPSCO Personnel Service, *Temp Agcy*
Service Specialists Ltd., *Perm Agcy*

Missouri

Business Personnel Svcs., *Temp Agcy*
Crown Services, Inc., *Temp Agcy*
Employer Advantage, *Exec Srch*

Sales Conslt, *Exec Srch*
Tech/Aid of Ohio, *Perm Agcy*

Oklahoma

Ameri Resource, *Exec Srch*
BancSearch, Inc., *Exec Srch*
Banker Personnel Service, *Exec Srch*
Robert Half Intl/Accountemps, *Exec Srch*
Key Temporary Personnel, *Temp Agcy*
Mngmt. Rcrtrs. International, *Exec Srch*
Manpower Temp. Svcs., *Temp Agcy*
Terry Neese Pers. Agency, *Temp Agcy*
Prospective Pers. Svc., Inc., *Exec Srch*
StaffMark, *Temp Agcy*

Oregon

Express Personnel Services, *Exec Srch*
Initial Staffing Services, *Perm Agcy*
Mngmt. Rcrtrs. of Portland/
OfficeMates5, *Exec Srch*
Robert E. Pfaendler & Assoc., *Exec Srch*

Pennsylvania

Accountants Exec. Search, *Exec Srch*
Allegheny Pers. Services, *Temp Agcy*
Basilone-Oliver Exec. Srch, *Exec Srch*
Charley's Pers. Staffing, *Temp Agcy*
Computer Prof. Unlimited, *Perm Agcy*
CoreStaff Inc., *Temp Agcy*
Robert J. DePaul & Assoc., *Exec Srch*
EDP Contract Services, *Contract Svc*
Financial Ind. Staffing Co., *Perm Agcy*
Fox-Morris Associates, *Exec Srch*
HRS/TND Associates, Inc., *Exec Srch*
The Hastings Group, *Exec Srch*
Human Assets Inc., *Temp Agcy*
J-Rand Search, *Exec Srch*
Nancy Jackson Inc., *Exec Srch*
Kenneth James Associates, *Exec Srch*
Jefferson-Ross Associates, *Exec Srch*
Kathy Karr Personnel, *Perm Agcy*
Mngmt. Rcrtrs. International, *Exec Srch*
Manchester Inc., *Career/Outplacement*
Olsten Financial Staffing, *Temp Agcy*
LaMonte Owens, Inc., *Exec Srch*
Pancoast Temp. Svcs., *Temp Agcy*
SHS International, *Exec Srch*
Strauss Personnel Service, *Perm Agcy*
TAC Staffing Services, *Temp Agcy*
W.G. Tucker & Associates, *Exec Srch*
Vogue Personnel Inc., *Exec Srch*

Rhode Island

Aquidneck Emp. Svc., *Perm Agcy*
Mngmt. Rcrtrs. International, *Exec Srch*
Norrell Services, *Temp Agcy*
Pro-Search, Inc., *Exec Srch*
TAC Staffing Services, *Temp Agcy*

South Carolina

Jerman Personnel Svcs., *Temp Agcy*
Mngmt. Rcrtrs. International, *Exec Srch*
PRL & Associates, Inc., *Perm Agcy*

South Dakota

Careers Unlimited, *Perm Agcy*
Mngmt. Rcrtrs. of Sioux Falls, *Exec Srch*
Metro Personnel Service, *Perm Agcy*
MidWest Recruiters (MIR), *Exec Srch*
Olsten Staffing Services, *Temp Agcy*
Snelling Personnel Svc., *Perm Agcy*

Tennessee

Amenity Staffing, *Temp Agcy*
Gateway Group Personnel, *Temp Agcy*
Mngmt. Rcrtrs. International, *Exec Srch*
Norrell Services, *Temp Agcy*
Snelling Personnel Svcs., *Perm Agcy*
StaffingSolutions, *Perm Agcy*

Texas

Abilene Employment Svc., *Perm Agcy*
ACSYS Staffing, *Temp Agcy*
Action Personnel Inc., *Temp Agcy*
Adecco, *Temp Agcy*
American Resources, *Exec Srch*
Marilyn Austin & Associates Personnel
Services, *Exec Srch*
Best/World Associates, *Exec Srch*
BestStaff Services, Inc., *Perm Agcy*
Colvin Resources Group, *Perm Agcy*
Credit Union Employment Resources,
Inc., *Temp Agcy*
DH&A, *Perm Agcy*
Dallas Employment Svcs., *Perm Agcy*
The Danbrook Group, *Exec Srch*

Gail Darling Staffing/Gail Darling's
Professional Desk, *Temp Agcy*
Dunhill Prof. Search, *Exec Srch*
Evins Personnel Conslt, *Perm Agcy*
The Exec. Consulting Group, *Exec Srch*
Express Personnel Svcs., *Perm Agcy*
Financial Professionals, *Perm Agcy*
Abel M. Gonzalez & Assoc., *Exec Srch*
Robert Half International/RHI
Management Resources, *Exec Srch*
InterSearch Associates, *Temp Agcy*
Kelly Services, Inc., *Temp Agcy*
Lehman McLeskey, *Exec Srch*
Mngmt. Rcrtrs. International, *Exec Srch*
Manpower Temp. Svcs., *Temp Agcy*
The Pailin Group Professional Search
Conslt, *Exec Srch*
Placements Unlimited, *Perm Agcy*
Resource Staffing, *Temp Agcy*
Russell Reynolds Assoc., *Exec Srch*
Sales Conslt, *Exec Srch*
Salinas & Assoc Pers Svc, *Perm Agcy*
Select Staff, *Temp Agcy*
Texas Personnel, *Exec Srch*
Todays Staffing, *Temp Agcy*
Vinson and Associates, *Perm Agcy*
John W. Worsham & Assoc., *Exec Srch*

Utah

Mngmt. Rcrtrs. of Salt Lake City, *Exec Srch*

Vermont

Mngmt. Rcrtrs. of Burlington, *Exec Srch*
Triad Temporary Services, *Temp Agcy*

Virginia

Accountants Executive Search/
Accountants On Call, *Exec Srch*
Adams Sources, *Exec Srch*
Nancy Allen Associates, *Perm Agcy*
Buckler Careers, Inc., *Perm Agcy*
Corporate Connection Ltd., *Exec Srch*
Dow Personnel, *Perm Agcy*
Dunhill Prof. Search, *Exec Srch*
Effective Staffing Inc., *Exec Srch*
Employment Enterprises/Temporary
Solutions, *Temp Agcy*
F-O-R-T-U-N-E Pers. Conslts, *Exec Srch*
MSI International, *Exec Srch*
Mngmt. Rcrtrs. of McLean/
OfficeMates5, *Exec Srch*
National Banking Network, *Exec Srch*
Norrell Services, *Temp Agcy*
Professional Search Pers., *Exec Srch*
Remedy Intelligent Staffing, *Temp Agcy*
Snelling Personnel Svcs., *Perm Agcy*
TAC Staffing Services, *Temp Agcy*
The Talley Group, *Exec Srch*

Washington

The Career Clinic, Inc., *Exec Srch*
Express Personnel Svcs., *Temp Agcy*
Guidance Services Inc., *Temp Agcy*
Mngmt. Rcrtrs. International, *Exec Srch*

West Virginia

Extra Support Staffing, *Temp Agcy*
Key Personnel, Inc., *Perm Agcy*

Wisconsin

Benston & Associates, *Exec Srch*
Careertrac Emp. Services, *Exec Srch*
Crown Services, *Temp Agcy*
Executive Resource Inc., *Exec Srch*
Flores Financial Services, *Exec Srch*
Landmark, Staff Resource, *Temp Agcy*
Mngmt. Rcrtrs. International, *Exec Srch*
Olsten Staffing Services, *Temp Agcy*
Quirk-Corporon & Assoc., *Exec Srch*
Rankin Group Limited, *Exec Srch*
Temps Plus Staffing Svcs., *Temp Agcy*
Work Connection, *Perm Agcy*

BILINGUAL

California
Norrell Temporary Services, *Temp Agcy*

New Jersey
Winters & Ross, *Perm Agcy*

New York
April International, *Exec Srch*

Virginia
PAE Placement, *Perm Agcy*

BIOLOGY

Arizona
Amer. Career Grp, *Career/Outplacement*

California
Apropos Emp. Agency, *Perm Agcy*
Biosource Technical Svc., *Contract Svc*
CDI Technical Services, *Temp Agcy*
California Search Agency, *Exec Srch*
Culver Personnel Services, *Perm Agcy*
Fastek Technical Services, *Perm Agcy*
F-O-R-T-U-N-E Pers. Conslts of Beverly
Hills, *Exec Srch*
Kelly IT Resources, *Temp Agcy*
John Kurosky & Assoc., *Exec Srch*
Lab Support Inc., *Temp Agcy*
Mngmt. Rcrtrs. of Laguna Hills, *Exec
Srch*
Med Exec International, *Exec Srch*
Med Quest, *Exec Srch*
Medical Exec. Recruiters, *Exec Srch*
National Search Associates, *Exec Srch*
Ortman Recruiting Intnl., *Exec Srch*
The Proven Edge Executive Recruiters,
Exec Srch
Edward Rast and Company, *Exec Srch*
Sanford Rose Associates, *Exec Srch*
Santa Barbara Staffing, *Perm Agcy*
TECH/AID, *Temp Agcy*
TechniQuest, *Exec Srch*
Unisearch, *Exec Srch*
United Staffing Solutions, *Exec Srch*

Colorado
Lab Support, Inc., *Temp Agcy*

Connecticut
Charter Personnel Services, *Exec Srch*
Mngmt. Rcrtrs. International, *Exec Srch*
Quality Control Recruiters, *Exec Srch*

Delaware
E.W. Hodges & Associates, *Exec Srch*

Florida
AAA Employment, *Perm Agcy*
Mngmt. Rcrtrs. of Plant City, *Exec Srch*
Mankuta Gallagher & Assoc., *Exec Srch*
Pro-Team Services, Inc., *Exec Srch*

Georgia
F-O-R-T-U-N-E Pers. Conslts of
Atlanta/Alternastaff, *Exec Srch*
ISC of Atlanta/International Career
Continuation, *Exec Srch*
Mngmt. Rcrtrs. International, *Exec Srch*

Illinois
Diener & Associates Inc., *Exec Srch*
Pelichem Associates, *Exec Srch*

Kansas
Smith Brown & Jones, *Exec Srch*

Louisiana
Talley & Associates, Inc./Talley
Temporaries, *Exec Srch*

Maryland
Sanford Rose Associates, *Exec Srch*

Massachusetts
Ability Search of New England, *Perm
Agcy*
Aerotek, Inc., *Contract Svc*
The Environmental Careers
Organization, *Contract Svc*
Human Resource Conslt, *Perm Agcy*
Lab Support Inc., *Temp Agcy*
Need Pers. Placement, *Temp Agcy*
Selectemps, *Temp Agcy*
Snelling Personnel, *Exec Srch*
Stone Consulting Group & Legal Search
Specialists, *Exec Srch*
Winfield Associates, *Exec Srch*

Michigan
Healthcare Recruiters Intnl, *Exec Srch*
Professional Advancement Institute, *Exec
Srch*
RCM Technologies, *Contract Svc*

Minnesota
Agri-Business Services, *Exec Srch*
T.H. Hunter, Inc., *Exec Srch*
Northland Emp. Services, *Exec Srch*

Washington
Mngmt. Rcrtrs. of Lakewood, *Exec Srch*
Miller & Miller Exec. Search, *Exec Srch*
Wilson Smith Associates, *Exec Srch*

Wisconsin
TMP Worldwide, *Exec Srch*

BOOKKEEPING

Arizona
Accounting & Finance Pers., *Exec Srch*

California
Cathy Dunn's Assc Pers Svcs, *Perm Agcy*
Anita R. Johnson & Assoc., *Temp Agcy*
LINK Business & Pers. Services/LINK
  Career Center, *Career/Outplacement*

Connecticut
PRH Management, Inc., *Exec Srch*
Velen Associates, *Perm Agcy*

Dist. of Columbia
Snelling Personnel Svcs., *Exec Srch*

Florida
PMC&L Associates, Inc., *Exec Srch*

Georgia
Don Richard Associates, *Exec Srch*

Indiana
The Registry Inc., *Perm Agcy*

Maryland
ACSYS Staffing, *Exec Srch*
Salsbury & Assoc. Pers., *Temp Agcy*

Michigan
Accountants Connection, *Exec Srch*
Accountants Support Service
  Corporation, *Temp Agcy*
Day Personnel, Inc., *Perm Agcy*

Minnesota
Whitney Prof. Staffing, *Temp Agcy*

New York
Mar-El Emp. Agency, *Exec Srch*

North Carolina
The Greer Group, *Perm Agcy*

Ohio
CBS Personnel Services, *Perm Agcy*
Champion Personnel Syst., *Perm Agcy*

Tennessee
Accountants & Bookkeepers, *Exec Srch*

Vermont
Harmon Personnel Svcs., *Temp Agcy*

Virginia
Accounting Assets Inc., *Temp Agcy*
Ardelle Assoc./AA Temps, *Perm Agcy*
Don Richard Associates, *Temp Agcy*

BROADCASTING

Alabama
VIP Personnel, Inc., *Perm Agcy*

Arizona
Amer. Career Grp, *Career/Outplacement*
Stivers Temporary Pers., *Temp Agcy*

California
Chaitin & Associates, *Exec Srch*
Culver Personnel Services, *Perm Agcy*
The London Associates, *Exec Srch*
London Temporary Svcs., *Temp Agcy*
Tom Pezman & Associates, *Exec Srch*
Truex Associates, *Exec Srch*

Colorado
JobSearch, *Temp Agcy*
Todays Temporary, *Temp Agcy*

Florida
Olsten Staffing Services, *Temp Agcy*

Georgia
Elite Staffing Services, *Temp Agcy*

Illinois
Media Staffing Network, *Temp Agcy*
SHS, Inc., *Exec Srch*
Search Source, *Exec Srch*

Maryland
Sales Conslt, *Exec Srch*

Massachusetts
Selectemps, *Temp Agcy*
Stone & Youngblood, *Exec Srch*

Michigan
Graphic Arts Marketing Associates, *Exec Srch*

Mississippi
Recruitment & Training Programs of
  Mississippi, Inc., *Perm Agcy*

Missouri
Jay Alexander & Assoc., *Perm Agcy*

New Jersey
T.J. Koellhoffer & Assoc., *Exec Srch*

New Mexico
Albuquerque Personnel, *Perm Agcy*

New York
Accounting & Computer Personnel,
  Perm Agcy
Adecco, *Temp Agcy*
Benson Associates, *Exec Srch*
Fanning Personnel, *Exec Srch*
Island Search Group Inc., *Perm Agcy*
KLK Personnel, *Perm Agcy*
Media Staffing Network, *Temp Agcy*
Morgan-Murray Personnel/M&M Top
  Temps, *Temp Agcy*
Rem Resources, Inc., *Perm Agcy*
SearchAmerica Inc., *Exec Srch*
Sunny Bates Associates, *Exec Srch*
United Personnel Agency, *Perm Agcy*
Volt Services Group, *Contract Svc*
Westaff, *Temp Agcy*

Ohio
Champion Personnel Syst., *Perm Agcy*

Texas
R.A. Stone & Associates, *Exec Srch*

BROKERAGE/INVESTMENT

California
Active Search and Placement, *Exec Srch*
Christian & Timbers, *Exec Srch*
Ryan, Miller & Associates, *Exec Srch*
Sanford Rose Associates, *Exec Srch*
D.M. Stone Pro Staffing, *Exec Srch*

Florida
Benson & Associates, *Exec Srch*
Gene Rogers Associates, *Exec Srch*

Georgia
Workman & Associates, *Exec Srch*

Illinois
Chicago Financial Search, *Exec Srch*
The Esquire Staffing Grp, *Perm Agcy*
J.R. Scott & Associates, *Exec Srch*
T. Vincent & Associates, *Exec Srch*

Indiana
Johnson Brown Associates, *Exec Srch*

Massachusetts
Diversified Mngmt. Resources, *Exec Srch*
Fanning Personnel, *Perm Agcy*
Mark Stranberg and Assoc., *Exec Srch*

Missouri
Information Systems Consulting
  Corporation, *Exec Srch*

New Jersey
Butterfass Pepe & McCallan, *Exec Srch*
MJE Recruiters, Inc., *Exec Srch*
J. White & Company, *Exec Srch*

New York
Advisors' Search Group, *Exec Srch*
Alite Associates, Inc., *Exec Srch*
Career Concepts, Inc., *Perm Agcy*
Colton Partnership, *Exec Srch*
Cross Staffing, *Perm Agcy*
The Goldman Group, Inc./Goldman +
  Bell, LLC, *Exec Srch*
Kensington Group, Inc., *Exec Srch*
Lloyd Staffing, *Perm Agcy*
The Parks Group Inc., *Exec Srch*
Personnel Consulting Assoc., *Exec Srch*
Redstone Affiliates, *Exec Srch*
Tyler Search Conslt, *Exec Srch*
Vance Personnel, *Perm Agcy*

North Carolina
Sockwell & Associates, *Exec Srch*

Vermont
Mngmt. Rcrtrs. of Burlington, *Exec Srch*

Wisconsin
Flores Financial Services, *Exec Srch*
Rankin Group Limited, *Exec Srch*

BUSINESS SERVICES

Colorado
BankTemps, Inc., *Temp Agcy*

Florida
The Butlers Company/Insurance
  Recruiters, *Exec Srch*
Environmental Health & Safety Search
  Associates (EH&S), *Exec Srch*
Novacare Employee Svcs, *Contract Svc*
Summit Exec. Srch. Conslt, *Exec Srch*

Georgia
Executive Placement Svcs, *Perm Agcy*
Mngmt. Rcrtrs. of Savannah, *Exec Srch*
Norred & Associates Inc., *Perm Agcy*

Hawaii
Sales Conslt, *Exec Srch*

Illinois
Retail Staffers, Inc., *Exec Srch*

Indiana
Canis Major/HR Quest, *Exec Srch*

Maryland
Charter Business Services, *Perm Agcy*

Massachusetts
Office Specialists, *Temp Agcy*

Nevada
StaffMark, *Exec Srch*
Doug Stumpf Associates, *Exec Srch*

New Hampshire
Individual Emp. Services, *Perm Agcy*

New Jersey
Sandra Grundfest, *Career/Outplacement*

New York
Computech Career Search, *Exec Srch*

Ohio
Downing & Downing, *Exec Srch*

Oklahoma
Dunhill Personnel of Northeast Tulsa,
  Inc., *Exec Srch*

Pennsylvania
Jerry Goldberg & Assoc., *Perm Agcy*
Protocall Business Staffing, *Temp Agcy*

Rhode Island
Unified Mngmt. Corp., *Contract Svc*

Wisconsin
Mngmt. Rcrtrs. of Stevens Point Inc.,
  Exec Srch

CHEMICALS

Alabama
F-O-R-T-U-N-E Pers. Conslts, *Exec Srch*
Hughes & Associates, *Exec Srch*
Mngmt. Rcrtrs. International, *Exec Srch*
Personnel Connection, *Exec Srch*

Arizona
H&M Recruiters, *Exec Srch*
TSS Consulting, Ltd., *Exec Srch*

Arkansas
Mngmt. Rcrtrs., *Exec Srch*

California
Boyle Ogata, *Exec Srch*
Christian & Timbers, *Exec Srch*
Keifer Professional Search, *Exec Srch*
Kelly Scientific Resources, *Temp Agcy*
Mngmt. Rcrtrs. of Encino, *Exec Srch*
The Proven Edge Executive Recruiters,
  Exec Srch

Colorado
The Bridge, *Exec Srch*
Kelly Scientific Resources, *Temp Agcy*
Mngmt. Rcrtrs. of Denver-Downtown,
  Inc., *Exec Srch*
Woodmoor Group, *Exec Srch*

CHILD CARE, IN-HOME/NANNIES

CLERICAL

O'Brien Emp. Svcs., *Temp Agcy*
Olsten Staffing Services, *Temp Agcy*
Pips Personnel Services, *Perm Agcy*
Premier Staffing, *Perm Agcy*
Prestige Personnel Svc., *Perm Agcy*
Pyramid Placement, *Perm Agcy*
Remedy Intelligent Staffing, *Temp Agcy*
David Sharp & Associates, *Perm Agcy*
Snelling Personnel Inc., *Perm Agcy*
Stivers Temporary Pers., *Temp Agcy*
TAC Staffing Services, *Temp Agcy*
Thor Temporary Services, *Temp Agcy*
Tustin Personnel Services, *Perm Agcy*
Westaff, *Temp Agcy*
Western Labor Leasing, *Contract Svc*
Wollborg-Michelson Personnel Service,
    Perm Agcy

Colorado
Absolute Staffing Solns., *Perm Agcy*
Add Staff, Inc., *Perm Agcy*
Adecco, *Temp Agcy*
Aspen Personnel Services, *Perm Agcy*
Eagle Valley Temps, *Temp Agcy*
Goodwin Personnel, Inc., *Perm Agcy*
Kelly Services, Inc., *Temp Agcy*
Payroll Principals, Inc., *Perm Agcy*
Staff Works, *Temp Agcy*
Terry Personnel, *Perm Agcy*

Connecticut
Charter Personnel Services, *Exec Srch*
Employment Opportunities, *Perm Agcy*
Manpower, Inc., *Temp Agcy*
The McKnight Group, *Exec Srch*
Westaff, *Temp Agcy*

Delaware
Barrett Business Services, *Perm Agcy*

Dist. of Columbia
Snelling Personnel Svcs., *Exec Srch*
Temporary Staffing, Inc., *Temp Agcy*

Florida
AccuStaff Incorporated, *Temp Agcy*
Availability, Inc., *Perm Agcy*
DGA Personnel Group, *Exec Srch*
Impact Personnel, *Perm Agcy*
Kelly Services, Inc., *Temp Agcy*
Manpower Temp. Svcs., *Temp Agcy*
Norrell Services Inc., *Temp Agcy*
Office Ours, *Temp Agcy*
Office Specialists, *Temp Agcy*
PMC&L Associates, Inc., *Perm Agcy*
Staffing Now, *Temp Agcy*
TRC Staffing Services, *Temp Agcy*
Todays Temporary, *Temp Agcy*

Georgia
Access Personnel Services, *Perm Agcy*
Kelly Services, Inc., *Temp Agcy*
Norrell Corporation, *Temp Agcy*

Hawaii
Olsten Staffing Services, *Temp Agcy*
Riders Personnel Services, *Contract Svc*

Idaho
Snelling Personnel Svcs., *Perm Agcy*
Volt Technical Services, *Contract Svc*

Illinois
Availability, Inc., *Perm Agcy*
Banner Personnel Service, *Perm Agcy*
Champion Staffing, *Perm Agcy*
Davis Staffing, Inc., *Temp Agcy*
Fellows Placement, *Temp Agcy*
Furst Staffing Services, *Temp Agcy*
Initial Staffing, *Perm Agcy*
Interviewing Conslt, *Temp Agcy*
The Murphy Group, *Perm Agcy*
Paige Personnel Services, *Perm Agcy*
Pillar Personnel, *Temp Agcy*
Snelling Personnel Svcs., *Perm Agcy*
Snyder & Associates Inc., *Temp Agcy*
Stivers Temporary Pers., *Temp Agcy*

Indiana
Adecco, *Perm Agcy*
Angola Personnel Svcs., *Perm Agcy*
Crown Temporary Svcs, *Temp Agcy*
Data Access Grp, *Perm Agcy*
Pat Day Personnel Inc., *Perm Agcy*
Dunhill Staffing Systems, *Temp Agcy*
Employment Plus, *Temp Agcy*
Express Personnel, *Temp Agcy*

Morley Group, *Exec Srch*
Norrell Services, Inc., *Temp Agcy*
Pyramids Personnel Grp., *Perm Agcy*
The Registry Inc., *Perm Agcy*
Time Services, Inc., *Perm Agcy*

Iowa
Cambridge Careers, *Perm Agcy*
Personnel, Inc., *Exec Srch*
Salem Management Inc., *Temp Agcy*
Rudy Salem Staffing Svcs, *Temp Agcy*
Sedona Staffing Services, *Exec Srch*

Kansas
Key Staffing, *Temp Agcy*
Manpower Temp. Svcs., *Temp Agcy*

Kentucky
C.M. Management Svcs., *Perm Agcy*
Precision Staffing, Inc., *Perm Agcy*
Superior Office Support, *Perm Agcy*
Temporary Professionals, *Temp Agcy*

Louisiana
Interim Personnel, *Temp Agcy*
Manpower, Inc., *Temp Agcy*
Professional Temporaries, *Temp Agcy*
Westaff, *Temp Agcy*

Maine
Express Personnel Service, *Perm Agcy*

Maryland
Administration Pers. Svcs., *Perm Agcy*
Careers III, Inc., *Perm Agcy*
Dunhill of Rockville, Inc., *Perm Agcy*
TAC Staffing Services, *Temp Agcy*

Massachusetts
Abbot Pers. Consulting Svcs., *Perm Agcy*
Anodyne Corporation, *Temp Agcy*
Kelly Services, Inc., *Temp Agcy*
Lane Employment Svc., *Perm Agcy*
Molari, Inc., *Temp Agcy*
New Boston Select Staffing, *Temp Agcy*
New Perspectives Pers., *Temp Agcy*
Office Specialists, *Temp Agcy*
Pomerantz Staffing Svcs., *Temp Agcy*
TAD Staffing Services, *Temp Agcy*

Michigan
Advance Employment, *Exec Srch*
Beacon Services Inc., *Exec Srch*
Davis-Smith Med. Emp. Svc., *Perm Agcy*
Diversified Recruiters, *Perm Agcy*
Manpower, Inc., *Temp Agcy*

Minnesota
Alternative Staffing, Inc., *Perm Agcy*
Lynn Temporary, *Temp Agcy*
NER, Inc., *Exec Srch*

Mississippi
AAA Employment, *Exec Srch*
Capitol Staffing Solutions, *Perm Agcy*
Express Personnel Service, *Perm Agcy*
Opportunities Unlimited, *Perm Agcy*

Missouri
Business Personnel Svcs., *Temp Agcy*
Crown Services, Inc., *Temp Agcy*
LandAJob, *Perm Agcy*
B. Loehr Temporaries, *Temp Agcy*

Montana
Express Personnel Svcs., *Temp Agcy*
Manpower Temp. Svcs., *Temp Agcy*

Nebraska
Ameri Search Inc., *Perm Agcy*
Donna's Office Service, *Contract Svc*
Kelly Services, Inc., *Temp Agcy*
Odyssey Group, *Exec Srch*

Nevada
Manpower Temp. Svcs., *Temp Agcy*
Nevada Business Services (NBS),
    Career/Outplacement
StaffMark, *Exec Srch*

New Hampshire
Able 1 Staffing, *Exec Srch*
Allstaff, *Perm Agcy*
Kelly Services, Inc., *Temp Agcy*
R.G.T. Associates, Inc., *Exec Srch*
TAC Staffing Services, *Temp Agcy*

New Jersey
Career Center, Inc., *Perm Agcy*
Citizens Emp. Svcs., *Perm Agcy*

Miller Resources, *Perm Agcy*
Personnel Plus/Temps Plus, *Perm Agcy*
Selective Personnel, *Perm Agcy*
Winters & Ross, *Perm Agcy*

New Mexico
Norrell Staffing Services, *Temp Agcy*
Sanderson Emp. Service, *Perm Agcy*

New York
Adecco, *Temp Agcy*
Cross Staffing, *Perm Agcy*
Initial Staffing Services, *Perm Agcy*
Kelly Services, Inc., *Temp Agcy*
Joseph T. Maloney and Associates, Inc.,
    Perm Agcy
Manpower Temp. Svcs., *Temp Agcy*
Nesco Service Company, *Temp Agcy*
Sloan Staffing Services, *Perm Agcy*
TAC Staffing Services, *Temp Agcy*

North Carolina
Graham & Associates, *Perm Agcy*
Granite Personnel Service, *Perm Agcy*
The Greer Group, *Perm Agcy*
Interim Personnel, Inc., *Temp Agcy*
Mega Force, *Perm Agcy*
Norrell Services, *Temp Agcy*
Olsten Staffing Services, *Temp Agcy*
Personnel Svcs. Unlimited, *Temp Agcy*

North Dakota
Interim Personnel, *Perm Agcy*

Ohio
Adecco, *Temp Agcy*
Belcan Staffing Services, *Temp Agcy*
CBS Personnel Services, *Perm Agcy*
Champion Personnel Syst., *Perm Agcy*
Crown Temporary Svcs., *Temp Agcy*
Manpower Temp. Svcs., *Temp Agcy*
Norrell Services, Inc., *Temp Agcy*
Olsten Staffing Services, *Temp Agcy*

Oklahoma
Manpower Temporary Services, *Temp Agcy*

Oregon
Adams & Assoc. Pers., *Perm Agcy*
Adams Temporaries, *Temp Agcy*
Employment Trends, *Temp Agcy*
Express Personnel Services, *Exec Srch*

Pennsylvania
AAP Inc., *Temp Agcy*
Adecco, *Temp Agcy*
Capital Area Temp. Svcs., *Temp Agcy*
J. Croyle & Associates, *Perm Agcy*
Executive Avail-A-Search, *Exec Srch*
Kenneth James Associates, *Exec Srch*
Kathy Karr Personnel, *Perm Agcy*
Mastersearch, *Exec Srch*
Olsten Staffing Services, *Temp Agcy*
Powers Personnel, *Perm Agcy*
Pratt Personnel Services, *Temp Agcy*
TAC Staffing Services, *Temp Agcy*

Rhode Island
Accountants Executive Search/
    Accountants On Call, *Exec Srch*
Initial Staffing Services, *Perm Agcy*
Kelly Services, Inc., *Temp Agcy*
Personnel People, Inc., *Perm Agcy*
Pro Staff Personnel Svcs., *Temp Agcy*
TAC Staffing Services, *Temp Agcy*

South Carolina
Carolina Personnel Svcs., *Temp Agcy*

South Dakota
Olsten Staffing Services, *Temp Agcy*

Tennessee
Arvie Personnel Services, *Perm Agcy*
Madison Personnel, *Perm Agcy*
Norrell Services, *Temp Agcy*
Piercy Employment Svcs., *Perm Agcy*

Texas
Babich & Associates, Inc., *Perm Agcy*
Border Prof. Recruiters, *Perm Agcy*
Bruco, Inc., *Temp Agcy*
Burnett Personnel Svcs., *Temp Agcy*
Burnett's Staffing, Inc., *Temp Agcy*
Corbett Pers. Services, *Temp Agcy*
DayStar Services, *Perm Agcy*
Executeam, *Exec Srch*

Full Service Temporaries, *Temp Agcy*
GenevaGroup International, *Exec Srch*
Robert Half Intl/Accountemps, *Exec Srch*
Hall Kinion, *Contract Svc*
Hutton Barnes & Assoc., *Exec Srch*
Cindy Jackson Search Intl., *Exec Srch*
Aaron Jensen Associates, *Exec Srch*
London Temporary Svcs., *Temp Agcy*
MIS Search, *Exec Srch*
MS Data Service Corp., *Perm Agcy*
Mngmt. Rcrtrs. International, *Exec Srch*
Management Solutions Inc., *Exec Srch*
Richard Maries Staffing Ctr., *Perm Agcy*
J.M. Meredith & Associates, *Exec Srch*
James Moore & Associates, *Exec Srch*
National Career Choices, *Exec Srch*
Optimum Exec. Search, *Exec Srch*
Protocol Search & Selection, *Exec Srch*
RGA Associates, *Exec Srch*
Remedy Caller Access, *Temp Agcy*
Romac International Corp., *Exec Srch*
Larry Rosenthal & Assoc., *Exec Srch*
Rowland Associates, *Exec Srch*
Royal Staffing Services, *Exec Srch*
SMC Group, *Exec Srch*
Penni Safford & Assoc., *Exec Srch*
Schweichler Associates, *Exec Srch*
Search West, *Exec Srch*
Search West of Ontario, *Exec Srch*
Spectrawest, *Exec Srch*
Strategic Alternatives, *Exec Srch*
Fred Stuart Consulting/Personnel
  Services, *Perm Agcy*
Sunday & Associates, Inc., *Perm Agcy*
TECH/AID, *Temp Agcy*
Thor Temporary Services, *Temp Agcy*
Trend Western Tech. Corp., *Temp Agcy*
Larry Wade & Associates, *Exec Srch*
Weldon Edwards, *Exec Srch*
Westaff, *Temp Agcy*

Colorado

The Ardent Group, *Exec Srch*
Daniels & Patterson Corporate Search,
  Inc., *Exec Srch*
EDP Recruiting Services, *Exec Srch*
F-O-R-T-U-N-E Pers. Conslts, *Exec Srch*
Hall Kinion, *Contract Svc*
Info Syst. Consulting Corp., *Exec Srch*
Premier Consulting, *Exec Srch*
Sales Conslt, *Exec Srch*
Technical Staff Recruiters, *Exec Srch*
J.Q. Turner & Associates, *Exec Srch*
H.L. Yoh Company, *Contract Svc*

Connecticut

Andex Executive Search, *Exec Srch*
Baldwin Associates Inc., *Exec Srch*
Brandywine Retained Ventures, Inc.,
  Exec Srch
Development Systems, Inc., *Exec Srch*
McIntyre Associates, *Exec Srch*
Romac International, *Exec Srch*
Wallace Associates, *Exec Srch*

Delaware

Proview Resources Inc., *Exec Srch*
H.L. Yoh Company, *Contract Svc*

Dist. of Columbia

Pace-Careers, Inc., *Exec Srch*

Florida

Active Professionals, *Exec Srch*
DGA Personnel Group, *Exec Srch*
Decision Conslt Inc., *Perm Agcy*
F-O-R-T-U-N-E Pers. Conslts, *Exec Srch*
Bob Graham & Associates, *Exec Srch*
Innotech Global Resources, *Exec Srch*
F.P. Lennon Associates, *Exec Srch*
Mngmt. Rcrtrs. of Tallahassee, *Exec Srch*
Romac International, *Exec Srch*
Sales Conslt, *Exec Srch*

Georgia

Apex Systems Inc./41 Perimeter Center
  East, *Exec Srch*
Augusta Staffing Assoc., *Perm Agcy*
The Bowers Group, Inc., *Exec Srch*
Bradshaw & Associates, *Exec Srch*
Business Professional Grp, *Perm Agcy*
Dunhill Prof. Search, *Exec Srch*
Fox-Morris Associates, *Exec Srch*
Mngmt. Rcrtrs. of Atlanta, *Exec Srch*
Manpower Temp. Svcs., *Temp Agcy*

Personnel Opportunities, *Exec Srch*
Quest Systems, Inc., *Perm Agcy*
Rita Corporation, *Exec Srch*
SCI Recruiters, *Exec Srch*
Southern Emp. Service, *Perm Agcy*

Hawaii

Select Staffing Services, *Temp Agcy*

Idaho

Diversified Data Systems, *Exec Srch*

Illinois

Advancement Inc., *Exec Srch*
Availability, Inc., *Perm Agcy*
William J. Blender & Assoc., *Exec Srch*
Executive Search Network, *Exec Srch*
General Employment Enterprises, Inc./
  Triad Personnel, *Perm Agcy*
Hall Kinion, *Contract Svc*
HunterSoft.com, Inc., *Exec Srch*
Network Search Inc., *Exec Srch*
Quantum Professional Search/Quantum
  Staffing Services, *Exec Srch*
Sales Conslt, *Exec Srch*
Snelling Personnel Svcs., *Perm Agcy*
Stone Enterprises, Ltd., *Exec Srch*
Wills & Company, Inc., *Perm Agcy*

Indiana

Execusearch, *Exec Srch*
Mngmt. Rcrtrs. of Richmond, *Exec Srch*
OfficeMates5 (OM5)/DayStar Temporary
  Services, *Exec Srch*
Romac International, *Exec Srch*
H.L. Yoh Company, *Contract Svc*

Iowa

Executive Resources, *Exec Srch*
Mngmt. Rcrtrs. International, *Exec Srch*
Personnel, Inc., *Exec Srch*

Kansas

Dunhill of Wichita, *Perm Agcy*
Dunhill Staffing Systems, *Temp Agcy*
Mngmt. Rcrtrs. of Overland Park/Sales
  Conslt/OfficeMates5, *Exec Srch*
Manpower Temp. Svcs., *Temp Agcy*
Romac International, *Exec Srch*

Kentucky

Access Computer Careers, *Perm Agcy*
Angel Group International, *Exec Srch*
C.M. Mngmt. Services, *Perm Agcy*
Computer Career Conslt, *Perm Agcy*
Houck Career Conslt, *Perm Agcy*
Snelling Personnel Svcs., *Perm Agcy*

Louisiana

Mngmt. Rcrtrs. of Metairie/Sales Conslt
  of Metairie, *Exec Srch*
The Pollak and Skan Grp., *Contract Svc*
Snelling Personnel Svcs, *Exec Srch*

Maryland

Administration Pers. Svcs., *Perm Agcy*
Columbia Consulting, *Exec Srch*
A.G. Fishkin and Assoc., *Exec Srch*
J.R. Associates, *Perm Agcy*
Mngmt. Rcrtrs. International, *Exec Srch*
Nations Exec. Search Grp., *Exec Srch*
Romac International, *Exec Srch*
Sales Conslt, *Exec Srch*
Tech/Aid of Maryland, *Temp Agcy*
Tri-Serv Inc., *Perm Agcy*

Massachusetts

Ambit Technology, *Contract Svc*
Blaney Executive Search, *Exec Srch*
Diversified Communications Group,
  Exec Srch
Enginuity Search Inc., *Exec Srch*
Entegee, *Perm Agcy*
F-O-R-T-U-N-E Pers. Conslts, *Exec Srch*
General Computer Resources (GCR),
  Temp Agcy
Hall Kinion, *Contract Svc*
Lake Conslt, *Exec Srch*
Lane Employment Svc., *Perm Agcy*
John Leonard Pers. Assoc., *Perm Agcy*
The Littleton Group, *Exec Srch*
Mngmt. Rcrtrs. International, *Exec Srch*
New Dimensions in Tech., *Exec Srch*
E.S. Rando Associates, *Perm Agcy*
Romac International, *Exec Srch*
Louis Rudzinsky Assoc., *Exec Srch*
Sales & Marketing Search, *Exec Srch*

Sales Conslt, *Exec Srch*
TAD Staffing Services, *Temp Agcy*
Tech/Aid, *Contract Svc*
Tesmer Allen Associates, *Perm Agcy*
H.L. Yoh Company, *Contract Svc*

Michigan

Appnet, *Contract Svc*
Career Search Inc., *Exec Srch*
William Howard Agency, *Contract Svc*
Ludot Personnel, *Perm Agcy*
Mngmt. Rcrtrs. International, *Exec Srch*
Sales Conslt, *Exec Srch*
Sales Executives Inc., *Perm Agcy*
TAC Automotive Group, *Contract Svc*

Minnesota

Alternative Staffing, Inc., *Perm Agcy*
Mngmt. Rcrtrs. of Minneapolis/
  Sales Conslt, *Exec Srch*
NER, Inc., *Exec Srch*
Pioneer Search, Inc., *Exec Srch*
Romac International, *Exec Srch*
Twin City Search, *Exec Srch*

Mississippi

The CPI Group, *Exec Srch*
Opportunities Unlimited, *Perm Agcy*

Missouri

Information Systems Consulting
  Corporation, *Exec Srch*
Mngmt. Rcrtrs. International, *Exec Srch*
OfficeMates5 (OM5), *Exec Srch*
Raiche & Associates, Inc., *Exec Srch*

Nebraska

Compusearch of Lincoln, *Exec Srch*
Mngmt. Rcrtrs./OfficeMates5, *Exec Srch*
Reliable National Personnel Conslt, *Exec
  Srch*

Nevada

Adecco, *Perm Agcy*
Manpower Temp. Svcs., *Temp Agcy*

New Hampshire

Able 1 Staffing, *Exec Srch*
Mngmt. Rcrtrs. International, *Exec Srch*
R.G.T. Associates, Inc., *Exec Srch*
Tech/Aid of NH, *Perm Agcy*
Technical Directions, Inc., *Perm Agcy*

New Jersey

Alta Associates, *Exec Srch*
Capstone Associates, *Exec Srch*
Careers First, Inc., *Perm Agcy*
Carter/MacKay Personnel, *Exec Srch*
Express Personnel Svcs., *Perm Agcy*
Impact Personnel, Inc., *Perm Agcy*
Paul Kull & Company, *Exec Srch*
Mngmt. Rcrtrs. International, *Exec Srch*
Manpower Tech. Svcs., *Contract Svc*
Mayfair Services, *Perm Agcy*
Diedre Moire Corporation, *Exec Srch*
Pomerantz Staffing Svcs., *Perm Agcy*
Romac International, *Exec Srch*
Anthony Ryan Associates, *Exec Srch*
Selective Personnel, *Perm Agcy*
The Stelton Group, Inc., *Exec Srch*
Stewart/Laurence Assoc., *Exec Srch*
Worlco Computer Resources, *Exec Srch*
Claire Wright Associates, *Perm Agcy*

New Mexico

Sanderson Emp. Svc., *Perm Agcy*

New York

Eden Staffing, *Perm Agcy*
Gateway Search Inc., *Exec Srch*
Information Syst Resources, *Exec Srch*
Joseph Associates Inc., *Exec Srch*
David Lawrence Assoc., *Exec Srch*
National Engineering Search, *Exec Srch*
Response Staffing Services, *Exec Srch*
Romac International, *Exec Srch*

North Carolina

Forbes Temp. Staffing, *Temp Agcy*
Graham & Associates, *Perm Agcy*
Robert Half Intl/Accountemps, *Exec Srch*
Mngmt. Rcrtrs. International, *Exec Srch*
Morgan Group, *Exec Srch*
The Nolan Group, Inc., *Exec Srch*
Sales Conslt, *Exec Srch*

Ohio

Adecco/TAD Tech. Svcs, *Contract Svc*

Aztech Recruitment Co., *Exec Srch*
The Bren Group, *Exec Srch*
CDI Corporation, *Contract Svc*
COMFORCE Tech. Svcs., *Contract Svc*
Computech Corporation, *Exec Srch*
DVA Consulting, *Contract Svc*
Paul Dicken Associates, *Contract Svc*
Electronic Power Source, *Exec Srch*
General Emp. Enterprises, *Perm Agcy*
Hall Kinion, *Contract Svc*
Mngmt. Rcrtrs. International, *Exec Srch*
PDS Technical Services, *Contract Svc*
Professional Search, *Exec Srch*
Sales Conslt, *Exec Srch*
SearchAmerica Inc., *Exec Srch*
Snelling Personnel Svcs., *Perm Agcy*
Spectra International, *Exec Srch*
Stivers Temp. Personnel, *Temp Agcy*
TSS Consulting, Ltd., *Exec Srch*
Taylor Design Recruiting, *Temp Agcy*
Volt Technical Services, *Contract Svc*
H.L. Yoh Company, *Contract Svc*

Arkansas
Executive Rec. Agency, *Exec Srch*
Foster Professional Search, *Exec Srch*
Spencer Careers, *Exec Srch*
Turnage Emp. Svc. Group, *Exec Srch*

California
A Permanent Success Employment
Service, *Perm Agcy*
ABA Staffing, Inc., *Exec Srch*
Access IT Resources, *Contract Svc*
ACCESS Technology, *Exec Srch*
AccuStaff Incorporated, *Perm Agcy*
Advanced Tech. Conslt, *Exec Srch*
Advantage Personnel Inc., *Perm Agcy*
Affordable Exec. Recruiters, *Exec Srch*
Allied Search, Inc., *Exec Srch*
Alpha-Net Consulting Grp, *Exec Srch*
Amtec Engineering Corp., *Perm Agcy*
Ankenbrandt Group, *Exec Srch*
Answers Unlimited, *Temp Agcy*
Apple One Emp. Services, *Perm Agcy*
Apropos Emp. Agency, *Perm Agcy*
Aquent Partners, *Temp Agcy*
Aran Rock, *Exec Srch*
AROSE Recruiting Co., *Temp Agcy*
Arrowstaff Services, Inc., *Perm Agcy*
Associated Software Conslt, Inc., *Temp
Agcy*
Astra West Pers. Services, *Perm Agcy*
B&M Associates Inc., *Temp Agcy*
The Badger Group, *Exec Srch*
Robert Beech Inc., *Exec Srch*
Edward Bell Associates, *Perm Agcy*
Harvey Bell & Associates, *Exec Srch*
Blue, Garni & Company, *Exec Srch*
Bozich & Cruz, *Exec Srch*
BridgeGate LLC, *Exec Srch*
Bullis & Company, Inc., *Exec Srch*
Business Systems Support, *Perm Agcy*
CDI Technical Services, *Temp Agcy*
CN Associates, *Exec Srch*
CT Personnel Services, *Perm Agcy*
California Job Connection, *Perm Agcy*
California Search Agency, *Exec Srch*
Career Quest Intnl., *Contract Svc*
Choice Personnel, *Perm Agcy*
Christian & Timbers, *Exec Srch*
CLARIA Corporation, *Exec Srch*
Coast To Coast Exec. Srch, *Exec Srch*
Computer Network Resources, *Exec Srch*
Computer Prof. Unlimited, *Exec Srch*
Corestaff Services, *Perm Agcy*
Corporate Search, *Exec Srch*
Crossroads Staffing Svc., *Temp Agcy*
The Culver Group, *Exec Srch*
Culver Personnel Services, *Perm Agcy*
Culver Staffing Resources, *Temp Agcy*
Daley Consulting & Search, *Exec Srch*
Data Center Personnel, *Exec Srch*
Dependable Employment Agency
Network, *Perm Agcy*
Drake Office Overload, *Temp Agcy*
Dynamic Synergy Corp., *Exec Srch*
EDP Contract Services, *Contract Svc*
Eagle Search Associates, *Exec Srch*
Eastridge Infotech, *Perm Agcy*
Essential Solutions, Inc., *Perm Agcy*
Excel Technical Services, *Exec Srch*
Executive Dynamics, Inc., *Exec Srch*

Executive Resource Syst., *Exec Srch*
Executive Search Conslt, *Exec Srch*
Fastek Technical Services, *Perm Agcy*
Fay Tech Services, *Perm Agcy*
Neil Fink & Associates, *Exec Srch*
Fisher & Associates, *Exec Srch*
Pat Franklyn Associates, *Temp Agcy*
GPL Engineering, *Perm Agcy*
Dianne Gauger & Assoc., *Exec Srch*
General Emp. Enterprises, *Perm Agcy*
Goldstein & Associates, *Temp Agcy*
The Goodman Group, *Exec Srch*
Gorelick & Associates, *Exec Srch*
Gould Personnel Services, *Perm Agcy*
Grant & Associates, *Exec Srch*
Hall Kinion, *Contract Svc*
HireKnowledge, *Temp Agcy*
Impact, Inc., *Exec Srch*
Initial Staffing Services, *Perm Agcy*
International Staffing Conslt, *Exec Srch*
Alan Israel Exec. Search, *Exec Srch*
Jackson Personnel, *Perm Agcy*
John Anthony & Assoc., *Exec Srch*
Kabl Ability Network, *Exec Srch*
Keifer Professional Search, *Exec Srch*
Klein & Associates, *Temp Agcy*
Klenin Group, *Exec Srch*
John Kurosky & Assoc., *Exec Srch*
Lander International, *Exec Srch*
Lending Personnel Svcs., *Exec Srch*
Lifter & Associates, *Exec Srch*
LINK Business & Pers. Services/LINK
Career Center, *Career/Outplacement*
The London Associates, *Exec Srch*
Maciejewski & Associates, *Perm Agcy*
Mngmt. Rcrtrs. International, *Exec Srch*
Management Solutions Inc., *Exec Srch*
Manpower Staffing Svcs., *Temp Agcy*
Brad Marks International, *Exec Srch*
Martin Staffing Resources, *Perm Agcy*
Mason Concepts, *Exec Srch*
Master Search, *Exec Srch*
Mata & Associates, *Exec Srch*
K.E. McCarthy & Assoc., *Exec Srch*
Medical Exec. Recruiters, *Exec Srch*
Mesa International, *Exec Srch*
Micro Track Temp. Svcs., *Temp Agcy*
Milestone Prof. Search, *Exec Srch*
Mindsource Software Engineers, Inc.,
Contract Svc
Multax Systems, Inc., *Perm Agcy*
Murray Enterprises Staffing Services,
Inc., *Temp Agcy*
Musick & Associates, *Exec Srch*
National Resources, *Exec Srch*
National Search Associates, *Exec Srch*
Nelson Human Resource Solutions, *Perm
Agcy*
New Venture Development, *Exec Srch*
Newport Strategic Search, *Exec Srch*
Norrell Temporary Svcs., *Temp Agcy*
Bren Norris Associates, *Contract Svc*
Omni Express Temps, *Temp Agcy*
Online Professional Search, *Exec Srch*
Pacific Search Group, *Exec Srch*
Pasona Pacific, *Temp Agcy*
Peden & Associates, *Exec Srch*
Personnel Strategies Inc., *Exec Srch*
Presidio Personnel, *Temp Agcy*
Pro Staff Personnel Svcs., *Perm Agcy*
Professional Search Inc., *Exec Srch*
ProSearch & Associates, *Exec Srch*
The Proven Edge Executive Recruiters,
Exec Srch
James Randall & Assoc., *Exec Srch*
Edward Rast and Company, *Exec Srch*
Raycor Search, *Exec Srch*
Renoir Staffing Services, *Perm Agcy*
Ritter & Associates, *Exec Srch*
Romac International, *Exec Srch*
SAI, *Exec Srch*
S.R. & Associates, *Exec Srch*
Sanford Rose Associates, *Exec Srch*
Santa Barbara Staffing, *Perm Agcy*
Select Personnel Services, *Temp Agcy*
Sharf, Woodward & Assoc., *Perm Agcy*
David Sharp & Associates, *Perm Agcy*
Sharp Personnel & Search, *Exec Srch*
Sierra Technology Corp., *Contract Svc*
Splaine & Associates Inc., *Exec Srch*
Adele Steinmetz Exec. Search, *Exec Srch*
Strategic Staffing, Inc., *Temp Agcy*

Sun Personnel Services, *Temp Agcy*
System One, *Perm Agcy*
Systematics Agency Inc., *Perm Agcy*
Systems Careers, *Exec Srch*
Systems Research Group, *Exec Srch*
TLC Staffing, *Temp Agcy*
TRC Staffing Services, *Perm Agcy*
TAC Engineering Resources, *Temp Agcy*
Technical Search Conslt, *Exec Srch*
Technology Locator, *Contract Svc*
TechSearch, *Perm Agcy*
Teleforce International, *Exec Srch*
Telford, Adams, & Alexander, *Exec Srch*
TOD Staffing, *Temp Agcy*
Today Personnel Services, *Perm Agcy*
Trattner Network, *Perm Agcy*
Trendtec Inc., *Temp Agcy*
Triple-J Services, *Exec Srch*
United Staffing Solutions, *Exec Srch*
Visuals, *Perm Agcy*
Volt Svcs. Grp, *Contract Svc*, *Temp Agcy*
Weldon Edwards, *Exec Srch*
Westaff, *Temp Agcy*
Western Tech. Resources, *Exec Srch*
Your People Professionals, *Perm Agcy*
Zeiger & Associates, *Exec Srch*
Amy Zimmerman & Assoc., *Perm Agcy*

Colorado
ATA Staffing, *Temp Agcy*
Ahrnsbrak and Associates, *Perm Agcy*
Aquent Partners, *Temp Agcy*
The Bridge, *Exec Srch*
Career Connections, *Exec Srch*
Career Forum, Inc., *Exec Srch*
Career Marketing Assoc., *Exec Srch*
Carlson, Bentley Assoc., *Exec Srch*
Casey Services, Inc. (CSI), *Exec Srch*
Daniels & Patterson Corporate Search,
Inc., *Exec Srch*
F-O-R-T-U-N-E Pers. Conslts, *Exec Srch*
GeoSearch, Inc., *Exec Srch*
Robert Half Intl/Accountemps, *Exec Srch*
Hall Kinion, *Contract Svc*
Hallmark Personnel Syst., *Exec Srch*
Healthcare Recruiters Of The Rockies,
Inc., *Exec Srch*
I.J. & Associates, Inc., *Exec Srch*
Initial Staffing Services, *Perm Agcy*
Integrity Network Inc., *Exec Srch*
Intellimark, *Temp Agcy*
Interim Personnel, *Temp Agcy*
JobSearch, *Temp Agcy*
Kelly IT Resources, *Temp Agcy*
Kelly Services, Inc., *Temp Agcy*
Mngmt. Rcrtrs. of Denver-Downtown,
Inc., *Exec Srch*
Manpower International, *Temp Agcy*
Miller Denver, *Exec Srch*
Pendleton Resources, *Exec Srch*
The Pinnacle Source, *Exec Srch*
Professional Search and Placement, *Exec
Srch*
Romac International, *Exec Srch*
Snelling Personnel Svcs., *Exec Srch*
Southwest Technical Conslt, *Contract
Svc*
Star Personnel Service, *Exec Srch*
Tech Staffing, *Temp Agcy*
Todays Temporary, *Temp Agcy*
Triad Conslt, *Exec Srch*
J.Q. Turner & Associates, *Exec Srch*
Welzig, Lowe & Assoc., *Exec Srch*

Connecticut
Abraham & London, Ltd., *Exec Srch*
Adecco/TAD Tech. Svcs., *Contract Svc*
Andex Executive Search, *Exec Srch*
Aquent Partners, *Temp Agcy*
BA Staffing, Inc., *Perm Agcy*
Bohan & Bradstreet, *Perm Agcy*
The Cambridge Group Ltd., *Exec Srch*
Charter Personnel Services, *Exec Srch*
Chaves & Associates, *Exec Srch*
Corporate Staffing Solns., *Temp Agcy*
Data Pros, *Perm Agcy*
Data Trends Inc., *Exec Srch*
EDP Contract Services, *Contract Svc*
Employment Opportunities, *Perm Agcy*
Executive Register Inc., *Exec Srch*
Hall Kinion, *Contract Svc*
Hallmark Totaltech, Inc., *Exec Srch*
Hipp Waters Prof. Search, *Exec Srch*

Hire Logic, *Temp Agcy*
J.G. Hood Associates, *Perm Agcy*
Infonet LLC, *Exec Srch*
Intertec Personnel, *Temp Agcy*
W.R. Lawry, Inc., *Perm Agcy*
Lutz Associates, *Exec Srch*
Mngmt. Rcrtrs. International, *Exec Srch*
Maxwell-Marcus Staffing Conslt, *Exec Srch*
McIntyre Associates, *Temp Agcy*
McLaughlin Personnel, *Temp Agcy*
PRH Management, Inc., *Exec Srch*
Pascale & LaMorte, LLC, *Exec Srch*
Edward J. Pospesil & Co., *Exec Srch*
Q.S.I., *Perm Agcy*
Resource Associates, *Perm Agcy*
Romac International, *Exec Srch*
Siger & Associates, LLC, *Exec Srch*
Super Systems, Inc., *Exec Srch*
Tech/Aid, *Temp Agcy*
Technical Search, *Exec Srch*
Westaff, *Temp Agcy*
Workforce One, *Perm Agcy*

Delaware
J.B. Groner Exec. Search, *Exec Srch*

Dist. of Columbia
ACSYS Staffing, *Exec Srch*
Aquent Partners, *Temp Agcy*
C Associates, *Exec Srch*
GKA Resources, LLC, *Exec Srch*
HireKnowledge, *Temp Agcy*
Norrell Services, *Temp Agcy*

Florida
AAA Employment, *Perm Agcy*
Able Body Corporate Services, Inc., *Contract Svc*
Academy Design & Technical Services, Inc., *Contract Svc*
Alpha Pers./Alpha Temps, *Perm Agcy*
Aquent Partners, *Temp Agcy*
Arcus Staffing Resources, *Contract Svc*
Availability, Inc., *Perm Agcy*
Bales-Waugh Group, *Exec Srch*
Belmont Training & Employment Center, *Perm Agcy*
Brickell Pers. Conslt, *Exec Srch*
B²D Technical Services, *Contract Svc*
Capital Data, Inc., *Exec Srch*
Career Planners, Inc., *Exec Srch*
Colli Associates of Tampa, *Exec Srch*
Computer Express Intl., *Contract Svc*
Computer Plus Staffing Solutions, *Temp Agcy*
Consultis Inc., *Temp Agcy*
Criterion Exec. Search, *Exec Srch*
Donbar Service Corp., *Temp Agcy*
En-Data Corporation, *Contract Svc*
Ethan Allen Pers. Placement, *Perm Agcy*
Executive Directions Inc., *Perm Agcy*
Farwell Group Inc., *Exec Srch*
Future Force Personnel, *Temp Agcy*
Gallin Associates, *Exec Srch*
Gimbel & Associates, *Perm Agcy*
HR Prof. Conslt, *Exec Srch*
Hall Kinion, *Contract Svc*
Hastings & Hastings Personnel Conslt, *Temp Agcy*
Keys Employment Agency, *Exec Srch*
R.H. Larsen & Associates, *Exec Srch*
Mngmt. Rcrtrs. International, *Exec Srch*
Mankuta Gallagher & Assoc., *Exec Srch*
Norrell Technical Services, *Perm Agcy*
Olsten Professional Staffing, *Temp Agcy*
Olsten Staffing Services, *Temp Agcy*
O'Quin Personnel, *Temp Agcy*
Pro-Team Services, Inc., *Exec Srch*
Jack Richman & Assoc., *Exec Srch*
Doug Sears & Associates, *Exec Srch*
Shaver Emp. Agency, *Perm Agcy*
Snelling Personnel Svcs., *Temp Agcy*
Snyder Executive Search, *Exec Srch*
Staffing Now, *Temp Agcy*
Staffing Solutions by Personnel One, *Perm Agcy*
Strategic Staffing Solns., *Contract Svc*
Strategy Resources Inc., *Perm Agcy*
System One Services, *Contract Svc*
TRC Staffing Services, *Temp Agcy*
TechStaff, *Contract Svc*
TempSolutions, Inc., *Temp Agcy*

Georgia
Ablest, *Exec Srch*
Aquent Partners, *Temp Agcy*
Arjay & Associates, *Exec Srch*
Boreham International, *Exec Srch*
The Bowers Group, Inc., *Exec Srch*
Business Prof. Group, *Perm Agcy*
Catalina Human Resources, *Perm Agcy*
Coast to Coast, *Temp Agcy*
Commonwealth Conslt, *Exec Srch*
Comprehensive Search Grp, *Exec Srch*
Computer Search Assoc., *Exec Srch*
Computer Tech. Search/Data Mngmt. & Staff Recruiters, *Exec Srch*
Corporate Search Conslt, *Exec Srch*
Elite Staffing Services, *Temp Agcy*
Executive Strategies, Inc., *Exec Srch*
Express Personnel Svcs., *Perm Agcy*
H&A Consulting, *Exec Srch*
Hall Management Group, *Exec Srch*
JES Search Firm, Inc., *Perm Agcy*
Leader Institute, Inc., *Exec Srch*
Mngmt. Rcrtrs. International, *Exec Srch*
Mission Corps International/Helping Hands Temp. Service, *Temp Agcy*
Olsten Prof. Staffing, *Perm Agcy*
Priority 1 Staffing Svcs., *Temp Agcy*
Randstad Staffing Svcs., *Temp Agcy*
Sales Opportunities, *Exec Srch*
Sanford Rose Associates, *Exec Srch*
Snelling Personnel Svcs., *Exec Srch*
Software Search, *Exec Srch*
Taurion Corporation, *Exec Srch*
Tennant & Associates, *Exec Srch*
WPPS Software Staffing, *Temp Agcy*
Westaff, *Temp Agcy*

Hawaii
Altres Staffing, *Temp Agcy*
Dunhill Prof. Staffing of HI, *Exec Srch*
Executive Search World, *Exec Srch*
Maresca and Associates, *Exec Srch*

Illinois
Abbott Smith Associates, *Exec Srch*
The Ability Group, *Exec Srch*
Accord Inc., *Exec Srch*
Adecco, *Temp Agcy*
Advanced Clinical/Advanced Personnel, *Contract Svc*
Advancement Inc., *Exec Srch*
Affiliated Pers. Conslt, *Perm Agcy*
Alternative Resources Corporation, *Contract Svc*
American Engineering Co., *Exec Srch*
Aquent Partners, *Temp Agcy*
E.J. Ashton & Assoc., *Exec Srch*
B.D.G. Software Network, *Exec Srch*
Bell Personnel Inc., *Perm Agcy*
Britannia, *Exec Srch*
Business Syst. of America, *Exec Srch*
CES Associates, *Exec Srch*
C.R.T., Inc., *Exec Srch*
CareerLink USA, Inc., *Exec Srch*
Carson Mngmt Associates, *Contract Svc*
Cemco Systems, *Exec Srch*
Chicago Financial Search, *Exec Srch*
CompuPro, *Exec Srch*
Computer Futures Exchange, *Exec Srch*
Computer Search Group, *Exec Srch*
Consultis Inc., *Temp Agcy*
Dataquest Inc., *Exec Srch*
Dunhill Professional Search of Rolling Meadows, *Exec Srch*
Dunhill Staffing Services of Chicago, *Temp Agcy*
Dynamic Search Systems, *Exec Srch*
EDP Contract Services, *Contract Svc*
Executive Concepts Inc., *Exec Srch*
Executive Search Intnl., *Exec Srch*
Express Personnel Svcs., *Temp Agcy*
First Chair Technologies, *Exec Srch*
First Search, Inc., *Exec Srch*
Furst Staffing Services, *Temp Agcy*
General Emp. Enterprises, *Perm Agcy*
David Gomez & Assoc., *Exec Srch*
Hall Kinion, *Contract Svc*
E.J. Howe & Associates, *Exec Srch*
Interim Personnel, *Contract Svc*
Interviewing Conslt, *Perm Agcy*
Johnson Personnel Co., *Exec Srch*
Jerry L. Jung Company, *Exec Srch*
Raymond Karson Assoc., *Exec Srch*

Kenneth Nicholas & Assoc., *Exec Srch*
Kunzer Associates, Ltd., *Exec Srch*
Arlene Leff & Associates, *Exec Srch*
Mngmt. Rcrtrs. International, *Exec Srch*
Richard Marks & Assoc., *Exec Srch*
Paul May & Associates, *Exec Srch*
M.W. McDonald & Assoc., *Exec Srch*
Mullins & Associates, *Perm Agcy*
The Murphy Group, *Perm Agcy*
National Search, *Exec Srch*
Network Resource Group, *Perm Agcy*
Nu-Way Search, *Exec Srch*
OfficeMates5 (OMS), *Perm Agcy*
Olsten Staffing Services, *Temp Agcy*
Omega Technical Corp., *Contract Svc*
Omni One, *Perm Agcy*
PS Inc., *Perm Agcy*
Personnel Connections, *Perm Agcy*
The Pollak and Skan Grp., *Contract Svc*
Professional Search Center, *Exec Srch*
Redell Search, Inc., *Exec Srch*
Remedy Intelligent Staffing, *Temp Agcy*
Responsive Search Inc., *Exec Srch*
Right Services Inc., *Temp Agcy*
Search Dynamics Inc., *Exec Srch*
Sevcor International, Inc., *Exec Srch*
Shannonwood Staffers, *Temp Agcy*
Smith Scott & Associates, *Exec Srch*
Snelling Personnel Svcs., *Perm Agcy*
Synergistics Associates, *Exec Srch*
Systems One, Ltd., *Exec Srch*
TDF Corporation, *Contract Svc*
TSC Mngmt. Svcs. Grp., *Exec Srch*
Roy Talman & Associates, *Exec Srch*
Technical Recruiting Conslt, *Exec Srch*
Walsh & Company, *Perm Agcy*
West Personnel Service, *Perm Agcy*
Wilson-Douglas-Jordan, *Exec Srch*
Working World Inc., *Temp Agcy*
World Employment Svc., *Perm Agcy*

Indiana
Adecco/TAD Tech. Svcs., *Contract Svc*
Alpha Rae Personnel, Inc., *Perm Agcy*
Artisan Staffing, *Temp Agcy*
Bill Caldwell Emp. Svc., *Perm Agcy*
Canis Major/HR Quest, *Exec Srch*
Career Conslt, Inc./O.I. Partners, *Perm Agcy*
Careers Unlimited Inc., *Exec Srch*
CompuSearch, *Exec Srch*
The Consulting Forum, *Exec Srch*
Corporate Staffing Resources (CSR), *Temp Agcy*
Dunhill Staffing Systems, *Temp Agcy*
Employment Recruiters, *Perm Agcy*
Job Placement Service, *Perm Agcy*
Kendall & Davis Resources, *Perm Agcy*
The Mallard Group, *Exec Srch*
Mngmt. Rcrtrs. International, *Exec Srch*
Management Services, *Exec Srch*
Manpower Tech. Svcs., *Temp Agcy*
Mays & Associates Inc., *Perm Agcy*
Oakwood International Inc., *Exec Srch*
QCI Technical Staffing, *Contract Svc*
Quiring Associates, Inc., *Perm Agcy*
The Registry Inc., *Perm Agcy*
Search Force/Data Force, *Exec Srch*
Technetics Corporation, *Contract Svc*
Unique, Inc., *Exec Srch*
Wimmer Temporaries and Direct Placement, *Temp Agcy*

Iowa
Atkinson Search & Placement, *Exec Srch*
Brei & Associates, Inc., *Perm Agcy*
Burton Placement Services, *Exec Srch*
Byrnes & Rupkey, Inc., *Exec Srch*
Cambridge Careers, *Perm Agcy*
Helping Hands Temp. Svc., *Temp Agcy*
Kelly Services, Inc., *Temp Agcy*
Mngmt. Rcrtrs. International, *Exec Srch*
Manpower Professional, *Contract Svc*
Pratt-Younglove, Inc., *Contract Svc*
Staff Management, Inc., *Contract Svc*
TechStaff, Inc., *Temp Agcy*
Nate Viall & Associates, *Perm Agcy*

Kansas
Business Specialists, *Perm Agcy*
Computer Professionals, *Contract Svc*
Foster Design Company, *Contract Svc*
Key Staffing, *Temp Agcy*
MegaForce Ltd., *Perm Agcy*

Morgan Hunter Corporate Search, *Exec Srch*
Rollheiser & Associates, *Perm Agcy*
Stonebuner Associates, *Exec Srch*
U.S.A. Business Systems, *Exec Srch*
White Associates/TemTech, *Exec Srch*

Kentucky
Access Computer Careers, *Perm Agcy*
BJM & Associates, Inc., *Contract Svc*
Manpower Inc., *Temp Agcy*
Karen Marshall Associates, *Exec Srch*
Romac International, *Contract Svc*

Louisiana
Ascent Consulting Group, *Temp Agcy*
Clertech Group, Inc., *Exec Srch*
Frazee Recruiting Conslt, *Exec Srch*
MSI Physicians, *Exec Srch*
Mngmt. Rcrtrs., *Exec Srch*
Manpower, Inc., *Temp Agcy*
Snelling Personnel Svcs., *Exec Srch*
Talley & Associates, Inc./Talley Temporaries, *Exec Srch*
Westaff, *Temp Agcy*

Maine
Accomplished Prof., *Temp Agcy*
Bonney Staffing & Training Centers, *Perm Agcy*
Executive Search of New England, *Exec Srch*
Maine Staffing Services, *Temp Agcy*

Maryland
Atlas Personnel Agency, *Perm Agcy*
Caplan/Gross Associates, *Exec Srch*
Computer Temporaries, *Temp Agcy*
DanSources Tech. Svcs., *Contract Svc*
Echelon Service Co., *Contract Svc*
Employer Employee Exchange, Inc. (EEE), *Exec Srch*
Marge Fox Pers. Services, *Temp Agcy*
HireKnowledge, *Temp Agcy*
JDG Associates Limited, *Exec Srch*
Mngmt. Rcrtrs. International of Baltimore/Timonium/Sales Conslt of Baltimore, *Exec Srch*
Opportunity Search Inc., *Exec Srch*
Professional Pers. Svcs., *Perm Agcy*
Quest Systems, Inc., *Perm Agcy*
Sales Conslt, *Exec Srch*
Seek International, Inc., *Exec Srch*
Sudina Search Inc., *Exec Srch*
TCM Enterprises, *Exec Srch*
TAC Engineering Resources, *Temp Agcy*
Technical Talent Locators, *Perm Agcy*
Vey Mark Associates, Inc., *Exec Srch*
Virtual Staffing Services, *Perm Agcy*

Massachusetts
ABA Personnel, Inc., *Temp Agcy*
Aardvark Systems & Programming, *Exec Srch*
Abbott's of Boston, Inc., *Exec Srch*
Ability Search of New England, *Perm Agcy*
Accurate Staffing Svcs., *Perm Agcy*
Aquent Partners, *Temp Agcy*
Architechs, *Exec Srch*
B&M Associates, *Temp Agcy*
Boston Professional Search, *Exec Srch*
Boston Search Group, *Exec Srch*
Campbell Associates, *Exec Srch*
Michael Cantor Associates, *Exec Srch*
Carter/MacKay, *Exec Srch*
Centor Personnel, *Perm Agcy*
Ciak Associates, *Exec Srch*
Clear Point Conslt, *Exec Srch*
Cleary Conslt Inc., *Perm Agcy*
Computer Express Intl., *Contract Svc*
Computer Security Placement, *Exec Srch*
Robert H. Davidson Assoc., Inc./Exec. and Prof. Resume Service, *Exec Srch*
Derby Associates Inc., *Perm Agcy*
Derek Associates, *Exec Srch*
Digital Arts Group, *Contract Svc*
Diversity Associates, *Exec Srch*
Dunhill Staffing Systems, *Temp Agcy*
EDI Specialists, Inc., *Contract Svc*
The Environmental Careers Organization, *Contract Svc*
Fanning Personnel, *Perm Agcy*
Ford & Ford Exec. Search, *Exec Srch*

F-O-R-T-U-N-E Pers. Conslts, *Exec Srch*
General Computer Resources (GCR), *Temp Agcy*
HM Associates, *Exec Srch*
Hall Kinion, *Contract Svc*
EM Heath & Company, *Exec Srch*
High Tech Ventures, *Exec Srch*
HireKnowledge, *Temp Agcy*
Human Resource Conslt, *Perm Agcy*
IT Resources, *Perm Agcy*
William James Associates, *Perm Agcy*
Kelly Services, Inc., *Temp Agcy*
The Koteen Associates, *Exec Srch*
Locke Associates Engineering Recruiters, *Exec Srch*
Lynx Inc., *Contract Svc*
Manpower Temp. Svcs., *Temp Agcy*
McDevitt Associates, *Exec Srch*
Micro Tech Professionals, *Temp Agcy*
Morgan & Associates, *Exec Srch*
Nationwide Business Svc., *Perm Agcy*
Navin Group, *Exec Srch*
Need Pers. Placement, *Temp Agcy*
New Dimensions in Tech., *Exec Srch*
New England Search, Inc., *Exec Srch*
Norrell Staffing Services, *Contract Svc*
Open Syst. Technologies, *Perm Agcy*
The Pickwick Group, Inc., *Exec Srch*
Norman Powers Associates, *Exec Srch*
Pro Staff, *Temp Agcy*
Professional Placement Consulting Group (PPCG), *Exec Srch*
Progressive Search Assoc., *Exec Srch*
ProSearch, Inc., *Exec Srch*
J.E. Ranta Associates, *Exec Srch*
Reardon Associates, Inc., *Perm Agcy*
Remedy Intelligent Staffing, *Temp Agcy*
The Renaissance Network, *Exec Srch*
Resources Objectives Inc., *Exec Srch*
Romac International, *Perm Agcy*
Sales & Marketing Search, *Exec Srch*
George D. Sandel Associates, *Perm Agcy*
Selected Executives Inc., *Exec Srch*
Selectemps, *Temp Agcy*
L.A. Silver Associates, *Exec Srch*
Snelling Personnel, *Exec Srch*
Snelling Personnel Svcs., *Perm Agcy*
Stone & Youngblood, *Exec Srch*
Stone Consulting Group & Legal Search Specialists, *Exec Srch*
Straube Associates, *Exec Srch*
Summit Tech. Services, *Temp Agcy*
Tech Resource Inc., *Contract Svc*
Technical Personnel Svcs., *Perm Agcy*
Total Technical Services, *Perm Agcy*
S.B. Webster & Associates, *Exec Srch*

Michigan
AE Employment Services, *Perm Agcy*
AJM Professional Services, *Exec Srch*
Acro ASI, *Contract Svc*
Action Management Corp., *Perm Agcy*
Adecco/TAD Tech. Svcs., *Contract Svc*
Advance Employment, *Exec Srch*
Advanced Resources of MI, *Contract Svc*
Alternative Staff, Inc., *Contract Svc*
American Computer Svc., *Exec Srch*
Aquent Partners, *Temp Agcy*
Argus & Associates, *Contract Svc*
Aucon L.L.C., *Exec Srch*
Barman Staffing Solns., *Temp Agcy*
Career Associates Inc., *Perm Agcy*
Career Quest, Inc., *Perm Agcy*
Clark & Hartman Prof. Srch, *Perm Agcy*
Collins & Associates, *Perm Agcy*
Corporate Business Svcs., *Perm Agcy*
Corporate Solutions, *Exec Srch*
Corporate Staffing Resources, *Perm Agcy*
Dynamic Personnel, *Contract Svc*
Entech Personnel Svcs., *Temp Agcy*
Executech, Inc., *Exec Srch*
Executive & Med. Recruiters, *Exec Srch*
Executive Recruiters Intnl., *Exec Srch*
Joseph Goldring & Assoc., *Exec Srch*
Robert Half International, *Exec Srch*
The Hallman Group Inc., *Exec Srch*
Harper Associates, *Exec Srch*
Healthcare Recruiters Intl., *Exec Srch*
IBA Search, *Exec Srch*
Job Fair Network of MI, *Perm Agcy*
Kelly Technical Services, *Contract Svc*
Key Personnel, *Perm Agcy*

Mngmt. Rcrtrs. International, *Exec Srch*
Manpower Tech. Svcs., *Contract Svc*
METROSTAFF, *Exec Srch*
Nationwide Career Network, *Perm Agcy*
Office Staffing Recruiting, *Exec Srch*
Open Page Search Services/Open Page Insurance Search, *Exec Srch*
Preferred Emp. Planning, *Perm Agcy*
Professional Personnel Conslt International, *Exec Srch*
Professional Resource Associates, Inc., *Contract Svc*
ProSearch, Inc., *Exec Srch*
Resource Technologies Corp., *Perm Agcy*
Romac International, *Perm Agcy*
Sales Conslt, *Exec Srch*
Search Plus International, *Exec Srch*
Sharrow & Associates Inc., *Exec Srch*
Source Technology LLC, *Exec Srch*
Sterling Field Associates, *Exec Srch*
Sygnetics Inc., *Temp Agcy*
Technical Prof. Svc., *Exec Srch*
Thomas & Assoc. of MI, *Exec Srch*
Trillium Staffing, *Temp Agcy*
Troy Tech Services, *Contract Svc*
Unlimited Staffing Solns., *Contract Svc*
Henry Welker & Assoc., *Exec Srch*
Wing Tips and Pumps, Inc., *Exec Srch*
Wise Personnel Services, *Perm Agcy*
Wood Personnel Services/Wood Temporary Staffing, *Perm Agcy*
Workforce, Inc., *Temp Agcy*
H.L. Yoh Company, *Contract Svc*

Minnesota
Abby Blu Inc., *Temp Agcy*
Aquent Partners, *Temp Agcy*
Bartz Rogers & Partners, *Perm Agcy*
Computer Employment, *Exec Srch*
Computer Personnel, *Exec Srch*
Enterprise Search Services, *Exec Srch*
Gateway Search Inc., *Exec Srch*
Hall Kinion, *Contract Svc*
T.H. Hunter, Inc., *Exec Srch*
Lynn Temporary, *Temp Agcy*
Manpower Technical, *Contract Svc*
Northland Emp. Svcs., *Exec Srch*
Nycor Search Inc., *Exec Srch*
Quantum Consulting & Placement, *Exec Srch*
RCM Technologies, *Exec Srch*
Regency Recruiters, Inc., *Exec Srch*
Romac International, *Exec Srch*
Search Specialists, *Exec Srch*
Staff Connection, Inc., *Exec Srch*
Sysdyne Corporation, *Contract Svc*
Systems Search, Inc., *Exec Srch*
Total Search, *Exec Srch*
H.L. Yoh Company, *Contract Svc*

Mississippi
Coats & Coats Personnel, *Perm Agcy*
EPSCO Personnel Service, *Temp Agcy*
Service Specialists Ltd., *Perm Agcy*

Missouri
Jay Alexander & Assoc., *Perm Agcy*
Austin Nichols/RCM, *Temp Agcy*
Bottom Line Prof. Svcs., *Contract Svc*
Bradford & Galt Consulting Services, *Perm Agcy*
Burns Employment Svc., *Exec Srch*
Business Personnel Svcs., *Temp Agcy*
Deck & Decker Emp. Svc., *Perm Agcy*
Employer Advantage, *Exec Srch*
ExecuTemps, Inc., *Temp Agcy*
First Place Executive Search/Deck & Decker Personnel, *Exec Srch*
Gruen & Associates, Inc., *Exec Srch*
Robert Half of Kansas City Inc./ Accountemps, *Temp Agcy*
HireKnowledge, *Temp Agcy*
JRL Executive Recruiters, *Exec Srch*
Kirdonn Group, *Perm Agcy*
Knoche EDP Connection, *Contract Svc*
Lloyd, Martin & Assoc., *Exec Srch*
Mngmt. Rcrtrs. International, *Exec Srch*
Manpower Temp. Svcs., *Temp Agcy*
Pinnacle Executive Group, *Exec Srch*
The Riverbend Group, *Exec Srch*
Romac International, *Exec Srch*
Sales Recruiters, Inc., *Exec Srch*
Westaff, *Contract Svc*

Parenica & Company, *Exec Srch*
Professional Pers. Assoc., *Perm Agcy*
REP & Associates, *Perm Agcy*
Romac International, *Exec Srch*
Sales Conslt, *Exec Srch*
Sanford Rose Associates, *Exec Srch*
Snelling Personnel Svcs., *Perm Agcy*
Sparks Personnel Services, *Exec Srch*
The Underwood Group, *Perm Agcy*
USA Staffing, *Perm Agcy*
David Weinfeld Group, *Exec Srch*
Woods-Hoyle, Inc., *Perm Agcy*
H.L. Yoh Company, *Contract Svc*

North Dakota
Career Connection, *Exec Srch*
Dunhill Prof. Search, *Exec Srch*
Olsten Staffing Services/Expressway
   Personnel, *Temp Agcy*
Snelling Personnel Svcs., *Exec Srch*

Ohio
Accountants Executive Search/
   Accountants on Call, *Exec Srch*
AccuStaff, *Temp Agcy*
Advancement LLC, *Contract Svc*
All Star Personnel, Inc., *Perm Agcy*
Alliance Technical Svcs., *Contract Svc*
AllTech Resources, Inc., *Exec Srch*
American Business Personnel Services,
   Inc., *Perm Agcy*
Aquent Partners, *Temp Agcy*
Belcan Technical Svcs., *Contract Svc*
N.L. Benke & Associates, *Perm Agcy*
J.B. Brown & Associates, *Exec Srch*
CBS Personnel Services, *Perm Agcy*
Clopton's Placement Svc., *Perm Agcy*
Combined Resources Inc., *Exec Srch*
Continental Search Assoc., *Exec Srch*
Corporate Research Consulting Group
   Inc., *Exec Srch*
DLD Technical Services, *Contract Svc*
Data Bank Corporation, *Exec Srch*
Eastern Personnel Svcs., *Perm Agcy*
Executive Search Ltd., *Exec Srch*
Fenzel Milar Associates, *Exec Srch*
Fitzpatrick & Associates, *Exec Srch*
Frederick-Lehmann & Associates/
   Temporarily Yours, *Exec Srch*
Gayhart & Associates, *Exec Srch*
Hammann & Associates, *Exec Srch*
J.D. Hersey & Associates, *Exec Srch*
ITS Technical Staffing, *Exec Srch*
KBK Management Assoc., *Exec Srch*
Kelly Services, Inc., *Temp Agcy*
R.E. Lowe Associates, *Perm Agcy*
Mngmt. Rcrtrs. International, *Exec Srch*
Manpower Temp. Svcs., *Temp Agcy*
Marvel Conslt Inc., *Exec Srch*
Messina Management Syst., *Exec Srch*
Midland Conslt, *Exec Srch*
Myers & Associates, *Exec Srch*
Newcomb-Desmond & Assoc., *Exec Srch*
North Peak Group, *Exec Srch*
North Star Resources, *Contract Svc*
Olsten Prof. Staffing Svcs., *Exec Srch*
Olsten Staffing Services, *Temp Agcy*
Palmer Temps/The Palmer Group, *Temp
   Agcy*
Paragon Recruiting Officials, *Exec Srch*
Recruiting Services Inc., *Exec Srch*
RecruitMasters, *Exec Srch*
Romac International, *Exec Srch*
S&P Solutions, *Contract Svc*
Sanford Rose Associates, *Exec Srch*
Selective Search Assoc., *Perm Agcy*
Shafer Jones Associates, *Exec Srch*
Tabb & Associates, *Exec Srch*
Teamwork U.S.A., *Contract Svc*
Teknon Emp. Resources, *Exec Srch*
Vector Technical Inc., *Perm Agcy*
WRS, Ltd., *Exec Srch*

Oklahoma
Ameri Resource, *Exec Srch*
Bradley Group, *Exec Srch*
Express Personnel Services, *Exec Srch*
Express Personnel Services/RWJ &
   Associates, *Perm Agcy*
Terry Neese Pers. Agency, *Temp Agcy*
Sundance Group, *Exec Srch*

Oregon
API Employment Agency, *Perm Agcy*

Aquent Partners, *Temp Agcy*
The Brentwood Group Ltd, *Exec Srch*
D. Brown & Associates, *Exec Srch*
Executives Worldwide, *Exec Srch*
Express Personnel Services, *Exec Srch*
First Choice Personnel, *Perm Agcy*
Hackenschmidt, Weaver & Fox, Inc.,
   Exec Srch
Hall Kinion, *Contract Svc*
Initial Staffing Services, *Perm Agcy*
Nationwide Personnel Recruiting &
   Consulting Inc., *Exec Srch*
Northwest Temporary & Staffing
   Services, *Temp Agcy*
Search Northwest Assoc., *Exec Srch*
Uniforce Staffing Svcs., *Contract Svc*
Woodworth Intnl. Group, *Exec Srch*

Pennsylvania
AA Staffing Solutions, *Contract Svc*
Advance Recruiting Svcs., *Exec Srch*
All Staffing Inc., *Perm Agcy*
Aquent Partners, *Temp Agcy*
Basilone-Oliver Exec. Srch, *Exec Srch*
T.W. Boris Associates, *Exec Srch*
Bradley Professional Svcs, *Perm Agcy*
CDI Information Services, *Contract Svc*
CMIS, *Exec Srch*
Career Concepts Staffing Svcs, *Exec Srch*
Career Quest Confidential, *Exec Srch*
Charley's Pers. Staffing, *Temp Agcy*
Computer Pros. Unlimited, *Perm Agcy*
CoreStaff Inc., *Temp Agcy*
Robert J. DePaul & Assoc., *Exec Srch*
Financial Industry Staffing Company,
   Perm Agcy
F-O-R-T-U-N-E Pers. Conslts, *Exec Srch*
General Emp./Triad Pers., *Perm Agcy*
J.H. Glass & Associates, *Exec Srch*
HRS/TND Associates, Inc., *Exec Srch*
Garrick Hall & Associates, *Exec Srch*
Hayes Associates, *Exec Srch*
HireKnowledge, *Temp Agcy*
The Hobart West Group, *Perm Agcy*
IMC International, Inc., *Contract Svc*
Interactive Search Assoc., *Exec Srch*
Interim Personnel, *Temp Agcy*
J-Rand Search, *Exec Srch*
Nancy Jackson Inc., *Exec Srch*
Jefferson-Ross Associates, *Exec Srch*
Clifton Johnson Assoc., *Exec Srch*
Keynote Systems Inc., *Temp Agcy*
Lawrence Personnel, *Exec Srch*
Main Line Personnel Svc., *Perm Agcy*
Robert McClure Ltd., *Exec Srch*
J. McManus Associates, *Perm Agcy*
Metropolitan Personnel, *Temp Agcy*
National Computerized Employment
   Service Inc., *Exec Srch*
Olsten Staffing Services, *Temp Agcy*
LaMonte Owens, Inc., *Exec Srch*
Pancoast Temp. Services, *Temp Agcy*
Professional Resource Group, Inc.,
   Contract Svc
Quest Systems, Inc., *Perm Agcy*
RHI Consulting, *Contract Svc*
Rice Cohen International, *Exec Srch*
SHS International, *Exec Srch*
Select Personnel, Inc., *Perm Agcy*
Snelling Personnel Svcs., *Temp Agcy*
Suburban Placement Svc., *Exec Srch*
Systems Personnel Inc., *Exec Srch*
TRC Staffing Services, *Temp Agcy*
TECH/AID of PA, *Contract Svc*
C.D. Warner & Associates, *Exec Srch*

Rhode Island
Dorra Search Inc., *Exec Srch*
Kelly Services, Inc., *Temp Agcy*
Norrell Services, *Temp Agcy*
On Line Staff Inc., *Temp Agcy*
PKS Associates, Inc., *Exec Srch*

South Carolina
Accel Temporary Svcs., *Temp Agcy*
Aide Inc. Design Services, *Contract Svc*
CDI IT Services, *Contract Svc*
Companion Emp. Svcs., *Perm Agcy*
Mngmt. Rcrtrs. International, *Exec Srch*
Miller & Associates, *Exec Srch*
PRL & Associates, Inc., *Perm Agcy*
Smith Temps/Smith Pers., *Temp Agcy*
Snelling Personnel Svcs., *Perm Agcy*

Southern Recruiters & Conslt, Inc., *Exec
   Srch*

South Dakota
Availability Emp. Svcs., *Temp Agcy*
Key Staffing, *Temp Agcy*
Mngmt. Rcrtrs. of Sioux Falls, *Exec Srch*
Regency Recruiting, Inc., *Exec Srch*
Staff Search, *Exec Srch*

Tennessee
A-1 Staffing & Personnel, *Temp Agcy*
American Tech. Assoc., *Contract Svc*
Anderson McIntyre Pers. Svcs, *Exec Srch*
Cook Associates Intnl., *Exec Srch*
Eagle Systems, *Perm Agcy*
Engineer One, Inc., *Perm Agcy*
Express Personnel Svcs., *Perm Agcy*
Robert Half Intl/Accountemps, *Exec Srch*
Hamilton-Ryker Co., *Temp Agcy*
Hester & Associates, *Exec Srch*
J&D Resources (JDR), *Exec Srch*
Kelly Services, Inc., *Temp Agcy*
Madison Personnel, *Perm Agcy*
Mngmt. Rcrtrs. International, *Exec Srch*
Manpower, Inc., *Temp Agcy*
W.R. McLeod & Assoc., *Contract Svc*
Snelling Personnel Svcs., *Perm Agcy*
Software Resource Conslt Inc., *Exec Srch*
StaffingSolutions, *Perm Agcy*

Texas
Abilene Employment Svc., *Perm Agcy*
Ackerman Johnson Inc., *Exec Srch*
ACSYS Staffing, *Temp Agcy*
Action Personnel Inc., *Temp Agcy*
Albrecht & Associates Executive Search,
   Exec Srch
American Resources, *Exec Srch*
Aquent Partners, *Temp Agcy*
B&M Associates, Inc., *Contract Svc*
R. Gaines Baty Associates, *Exec Srch*
Best/World Associates, *Exec Srch*
Bilson & Hazel International/Hazel
   Staffing, *Exec Srch*
Brainpower Pers. Agency, *Perm Agcy*
Bridge Personnel, *Exec Srch*
Bundy-Stewart Associates, *Exec Srch*
Burnett Personnel Svcs., *Temp Agcy*
Butler International, *Contract Svc*
C.G. & Company, *Exec Srch*
CAD Technology, Inc., *Exec Srch*
CarlTech, *Contract Svc*
Certified Personnel Svc., *Contract Svc*
COMFORCE Info. Tech., *Contract Svc*
Computer Prof. Unlimited, *Exec Srch*
Consultis, *Temp Agcy*
Consultis of Houston, *Temp Agcy*
Corporate Search Inc., *Exec Srch*
Creative Staffing Services, *Perm Agcy*
Gail Darling Staffing/Gail Darling's
   Professional Desk, *Temp Agcy*
Data Staffing Centre, *Perm Agcy*
Datapro Pers. Conslt, *Perm Agcy*
Dividend Staffing Svcs., *Temp Agcy*
EDP Computer Services, *Exec Srch*
The Elsworth Group, *Exec Srch*
Express Personnel Svcs., *Perm Agcy*
FirstWord Staffing Svcs., *Temp Agcy*
Focus Point, Inc., *Contract Svc*
Robert Half International/RHI
   Management Resources, *Exec Srch*
Hall Kinion, *Contract Svc*
HireKnowledge, *Temp Agcy*
Imprimis Staffing Solns., *Temp Agcy*
Info Tec Inc., *Perm Agcy*
Inside Track, *Exec Srch*
Intratech Resource Group, *Exec Srch*
Kahn Richards & Assoc., *Exec Srch*
Key People Inc., *Exec Srch*
Kristan Intnl. Exec. Search, *Exec Srch*
LRJ Staffing Services, *Perm Agcy*
Loewenstein & Associates, *Exec Srch*
Mngmt. Rcrtrs. International, *Exec Srch*
Manpower Temp. Svcs., *Temp Agcy*
McDuffy-Edwards, *Exec Srch*
National Human Resource Group, *Exec
   Srch*
Olsten Staffing Services, *Temp Agcy*
Opportunity Unlimited Personnel Conslt,
   Exec Srch
The Pailin Group Professional Search
   Conslt, *Exec Srch*

Texas
Craig Trotman & Assoc., *Exec Srch*

Washington
Russell A. Lager & Assoc., *Exec Srch*

CONSUMER PRODUCTS

California
Battalia Winston Intnl., *Exec Srch*
Buff & Associates, *Exec Srch*
Christian & Timbers, *Exec Srch*
Coast To Coast Exec. Srch, *Exec Srch*
Hollander Horizon Intnl., *Exec Srch*
Resource Perspectives, Inc., *Exec Srch*
TMP Executive Resources, *Exec Srch*
TMP Worldwide, *Exec Srch*

Connecticut
Brandywine Retained Ventures, Inc.,
  Exec Srch
Quality Control Recruiters, *Exec Srch*
TMP Worldwide, *Exec Srch*

Florida
Manchester Inc., *Exec Srch*
TMP Worldwide, *Exec Srch*
Wilson & Associates Intnl., *Exec Srch*

Georgia
Mngmt. Rcrtrs. of Atlanta, *Exec Srch*
TMP Worldwide, *Exec Srch*

Illinois
Battalia Winston Intnl., *Exec Srch*
TMP Worldwide, *Exec Srch*

Massachusetts
Battalia Winston Intnl., *Exec Srch*
The Onstott Group, *Exec Srch*
TMP Worldwide, *Exec Srch*
TASA International, *Exec Srch*
Xavier Associates, Inc., *Exec Srch*

Nebraska
Lincoln Group Inc., *Exec Srch*

New Hampshire
Clayman Management Svc, *Exec Srch*
Linford E. Stiles Assoc., *Exec Srch*

New Jersey
Battalia Winston Intnl., *Exec Srch*
William Bell Associates, *Exec Srch*
Rosenthal Associates Intnl., *Exec Srch*
The Stelton Group, Inc., *Exec Srch*
Yoh Scientific, *Perm Agcy*

New York
Asher Pers. Conslt, *Perm Agcy*
Battalia Winston Intnl., *Exec Srch*
The Dartmouth Group, *Exec Srch*
Kaufman Associates Ltd., *Exec Srch*
Tina Lane Personnel, Inc., *Perm Agcy*
Levine Hirshorn & Assoc., *Exec Srch*
Mngmt. Rcrtrs./Compusearch, *Exec Srch*
Pro/TECH Nationwide Staffing, Inc.,
  Exec Srch
Rosenthal Assoc. Intnl., *Exec Srch*
StratfordGroup, *Exec Srch*
TMP Worldwide, *Exec Srch*

North Carolina
A First Resource, *Exec Srch*
Ariail & Associates, *Exec Srch*
Fox-Morris Associates, *Exec Srch*
The Furniture Agency Inc., *Exec Srch*
S. Greene & Co./The Triad, *Exec Srch*
Mngmt. Rcrtrs. International, *Exec Srch*
StratfordGroup, *Exec Srch*

Ohio
R. Green & Associates, *Exec Srch*
StratfordGroup, *Exec Srch*

Pennsylvania
Dunn Associates, *Exec Srch*
Norcon Associates, Inc., *Exec Srch*
StratfordGroup, *Exec Srch*

South Carolina
Mngmt. Rcrtrs. International, *Exec Srch*

Texas
Executive Search Intnl., *Exec Srch*
Kristan Intnl. Exec. Search, *Exec Srch*
Austin McGregor Intnl., *Exec Srch*
StratfordGroup, *Exec Srch*
TMP Worldwide, *Exec Srch*

Virginia
Christian & Timbers, Inc., *Exec Srch*

Washington
Consumer Connection, *Exec Srch*
L.W. Foote Company/The Brighton
  Group, *Exec Srch*
StratfordGroup, *Exec Srch*

Wisconsin
Mngmt. Rcrtrs. International, *Exec Srch*
TMP Worldwide, *Exec Srch*

CUSTOMER SERVICE

California
Complete Staffing Resources, *Perm Agcy*

Delaware
Network Personnel, *Temp Agcy*

Florida
Custom Staffing, Inc., *Temp Agcy*

Georgia
Access Personnel Services, *Perm Agcy*
TAC Staffing Services, *Temp Agcy*
TempWorld Staffing Svcs, *Temp Agcy*

Illinois
Ablest Staffing Services, *Temp Agcy*

Kentucky
The Executive Advantage, *Exec Srch*

Maine
Pro Search, Inc., *Exec Srch*

Maryland
Sparks Personnel Services, *Temp Agcy*

Massachusetts
Diversified Communications Group,
  Exec Srch
Olsten Staffing Services, *Temp Agcy*

Minnesota
Employment Advisors, *Perm Agcy*
Employment Advisors/Staff It Personnel
  Services, *Perm Agcy*

New York
Crandall Associates, Inc., *Exec Srch*
TeleManagement Search, *Exec Srch*

Texas
Esprit Temporary Svcs., *Temp Agcy*
HR Search, *Exec Srch*

Virginia
Curzon Staffing, *Perm Agcy*

Washington
PACE Staffing Network, *Exec Srch*

Wisconsin
Hatch Staffing Services, *Temp Agcy*

DATA COMMUNICATIONS

California
Adler-Brown Associates, *Exec Srch*
Schweichler Associates, *Exec Srch*

Florida
F-O-R-T-U-N-E Pers. Conslts, *Exec Srch*

Georgia
Delta Resource Group, *Exec Srch*

Illinois
Advancement Inc., *Exec Srch*
Corporate Conslt, *Exec Srch*

Maryland
A.G. Fishkin and Assoc., *Exec Srch*
Sales Conslt, *Exec Srch*

Massachusetts
Bowdoin Group, *Exec Srch*
Carter/MacKay, *Exec Srch*
Diversified Comm. Group, *Exec Srch*
Franklin Intnl. Search, *Exec Srch*
Sales & Marketing Search, *Exec Srch*

New Jersey
Access Systems, *Exec Srch*
Carter/MacKay Personnel, *Exec Srch*
Common Agenda, *Exec Srch*
Mngmt. Rcrtrs. Intnl., *Exec Srch*
Softrix, Inc., *Exec Srch*

New York
Huntington Pers. Conslt, *Exec Srch*

North Carolina
MKR Pers. Solutions, *Contract Svc*
The Nolan Group, Inc., *Exec Srch*

Ohio
Fitzpatrick & Associates, *Exec Srch*
Teknon Emp. Resources, *Exec Srch*

Pennsylvania
Lawrence Personnel, *Exec Srch*

Texas
Data Staffing Centre, *Perm Agcy*
Sales Conslt, *Exec Srch*

Virginia
Dahl Morrow International, *Exec Srch*

DATA PROCESSING

Alaska
Manpower Temp. Svcs., *Temp Agcy*

Arizona
AccuStaff Incorporated, *Perm Agcy*
Computer Strategies, Inc., *Perm Agcy*
Manpower Tech. Svcs., *Temp Agcy*

California
AW Data Processing Pers., *Perm Agcy*
Colt Syst. Prof. Pers. Services, *Perm
  Agcy*
Complete Staffing Resources, *Perm Agcy*
Curphey & Malkin Assoc., *Exec Srch*
Daley Consulting & Search, *Exec Srch*
Drake Office Overload, *Temp Agcy*
Manpower Staffing Svcs., *Temp Agcy*

Colorado
Adecco, *Temp Agcy*
Carlson, Bentley Assoc., *Exec Srch*
Staff Works, *Temp Agcy*

Connecticut
Bohan & Bradstreet, *Perm Agcy*
Career Prospects, *Exec Srch*

Florida
Careers USA, *Temp Agcy*
Dunhill Prof. Search, *Exec Srch*
En-Data Corporation, *Contract Svc*
F-O-R-T-U-N-E Pers. Conslts, *Exec Srch*
Manpower Temp. Svcs., *Temp Agcy*
PMC&L Associates, Inc., *Perm Agcy*
Personnel Center, *Perm Agcy*

Georgia
Apex Systems Inc./41 Perimeter Center
  East, *Exec Srch*
The Bowers Group, Inc., *Exec Srch*
Bradshaw & Associates, *Exec Srch*
Data Processing Services, *Exec Srch*
H&A Consulting, *Exec Srch*
Manpower Temp. Svcs., *Temp Agcy*
Norrell Services Inc., *Temp Agcy*
Taurion Corporation, *Exec Srch*

Illinois
DRC & Associates, *Exec Srch*
Data Career Center, Inc., *Exec Srch*
The Esquire Staffing Grp., *Perm Agcy*
Grice Holdener & Assoc., *Exec Srch*
Select Search Inc., *Exec Srch*
Wills & Company, Inc., *Perm Agcy*

Indiana
Alpha Rae Personnel, Inc., *Perm Agcy*
Century Personnel Inc., *Perm Agcy*
Excellence In Search, *Exec Srch*
Unique, Inc., *Exec Srch*

Iowa
City & National Staffing/Recruiting
  Company, *Perm Agcy*
Executive Resources, *Exec Srch*
McGladrey Search Group, *Exec Srch*
Staffing Edge, *Perm Agcy*

Kansas
Hensler & Associates, *Exec Srch*
Metro Information Svcs., *Contract Svc*
Romac International, *Exec Srch*
Search Conslt, Inc., *Exec Srch*
Stoneburner Associates, *Exec Srch*
U.S.A. Business Systems, *Exec Srch*

Maryland
Adecco, *Temp Agcy*
F-O-R-T-U-N-E Pers. Conslts, *Exec Srch*

Minnesota
T.H. Hunter, Inc., *Exec Srch*

Nebraska
Hansen Employment Svc., *Exec Srch*

New Hampshire
Ntnl. Emp. Service Corp., *Perm Agcy*
Surge Resources Inc., *Contract Svc*

New Jersey
A Professional Edge,
 Career/Outplacement
Advanced Personnel Svc., *Perm Agcy*
BAI Personnel Solutions, *Perm Agcy*
Blake & Assoc. Exec. Srch, *Exec Srch*
OfficeMates5 (OM5)/DayStar Temporary
 Services, *Perm Agcy*

New York
AJC Search, *Exec Srch*
Accounting & Computer Personnel,
 Perm Agcy
Merrill Adams Associates,
 Career/Outplacement
Analytic Recruiting Inc., *Exec Srch*
Corporate Careers, Inc., *Exec Srch*
Fred Koffler Associates, *Exec Srch*
Milazzo Associates, Inc., *Perm Agcy*
Morgan-Murray Personnel/M&M Top
 Temps, *Temp Agcy*
Nowack Career Specialists, *Perm Agcy*
S.W. Management, *Exec Srch*
SearchAmerica Inc., *Exec Srch*
Werbin Assoc. Exec. Srch., *Exec Srch*

North Carolina
Mngmt. Rcrtrs. of Raleigh, *Exec Srch*
Olsten Staffing Services, *Temp Agcy*

North Dakota
Olsten Staffing Services/Expressway
 Personnel, *Temp Agcy*

Ohio
Combined Resources Inc., *Exec Srch*

Pennsylvania
Basilone-Oliver Exec. Srch, *Exec Srch*
The Hastings Group, *Exec Srch*
United Employment, *Perm Agcy*

Rhode Island
Norrell Services, *Temp Agcy*

Texas
Austin Group, *Exec Srch*
Pailin Grp. Prof. Srch. Conslt, *Exec Srch*
Bart Roberson & Company, *Exec Srch*

Virginia
Ability Resources, Inc., *Exec Srch*
Dow Personnel, *Perm Agcy*

Wisconsin
Flores Financial Services, *Exec Srch*

EDUCATION

Arizona
Amer. Career Grp, *Career/Outplacement*

California
Harvey Bell & Associates, *Exec Srch*
Dependable Emp Agcy Ntwk, *Perm Agcy*
MacNaughton Associates, *Exec Srch*
TRC Staffing Services, *Perm Agcy*
Trans U.S., Inc., *Perm Agcy*
UAW Labor Employment and Training
 Corporation, *Perm Agcy*
United Staffing Solutions, *Exec Srch*
Volt Services Group, *Temp Agcy*

Colorado
JobSearch, *Temp Agcy*
Kelly Services, Inc., *Temp Agcy*

Connecticut
Admiral Staffing Services, *Temp Agcy*

Delaware
Franklin Consulting Group, *Exec Srch*

Dist. of Columbia
Goodwin & Company, *Exec Srch*
R.H. Perry & Associates, *Exec Srch*

Florida
Belmont Training & Employment
 Center, *Perm Agcy*
Employers' Assistant, Inc., *Temp Agcy*

Georgia
Mission Corps International/Helping
 Hands Temp. Service, *Temp Agcy*
Randstad Staffing Svcs., *Temp Agcy*

Idaho
Magic Valley Rehabilitation Services,
 Inc., *Career/Outplacement*

Illinois
CES Associates, *Exec Srch*

Iowa
Helping Hands Temp. Svc., *Temp Agcy*

Maine
At Work Personnel Svc., *Temp Agcy*

Maryland
American Service Tech., *Contract Svc*
TAC Staffing Services, *Temp Agcy*

Massachusetts
Auerbach Associates, *Exec Srch*
Brattle Temps, *Temp Agcy*
Carney, Sandoe and Assoc., *Exec Srch*
Educational Mngmt. Network, *Exec Srch*
In Search of Nanny Inc., *Perm Agcy*
Johnson & Hill Staffing Svc., *Temp Agcy*
Kelly Services, Inc., *Temp Agcy*
TAC Staffing Services, *Temp Agcy*

Michigan
William Howard Agency, *Contract Svc*
Michigan Indian Employment and
 Training Services, *Perm Agcy*
Sullivan & Associates, *Exec Srch*

Mississippi
Mississippi State Emp. Svcs., *Perm Agcy*
Recruitment & Training Programs of
 Mississippi, Inc., *Perm Agcy*

Missouri
Burns Emp. Service, *Exec Srch*
Business Personnel Svcs., *Temp Agcy*
Educational Placement Svc., *Perm Agcy*
Employer Advantage, *Exec Srch*

Nevada
Initial Staffing Services, *Perm Agcy*
Nevada Business Services (NBS),
 Career/Outplacement

New Hampshire
Allstaff, *Perm Agcy*
Surge Resources Inc., *Contract Svc*

New Jersey
G.A. Agency, *Perm Agcy*
Sandra Grundfest, Ed.D.,
 Career/Outplacement
Joule Staffing Services, *Contract Svc*

New York
AARP Foundation/Senior Employment
 Program, *Perm Agcy*
Merrill Adams Associates,
 Career/Outplacement
Alexander Edwards Intnl., *Exec Srch*
John Lawrence & Assoc., *Exec Srch*
Metropolitan Pers. Syst., *Exec Srch*
Superior Concepts, *Contract Svc*

North Carolina
Sockwell & Associates, *Exec Srch*

North Dakota
Green Thumb, Inc.,
 Career/Outplacement
Olsten Staffing Services/Expressway
 Personnel, *Temp Agcy*

Pennsylvania
CoreStaff Inc., *Temp Agcy*
TAC Staffing Services, *Temp Agcy*

Rhode Island
TAC Staffing Services, *Temp Agcy*

Texas
Kelly Scientific Resources, *Temp Agcy*
OMNI Consortium, Inc., *Perm Agcy*
Resource Connection Workforce Center,
 Perm Agcy

Virginia
Hispanic Committee of VA, *Perm Agcy*
Charles F. Meng & Assoc., *Exec Srch*
Snelling Personnel Svcs., *Perm Agcy*

ELDERCARE, IN-HOME

California
F-O-R-T-U-N-E Pers. Conslts., *Exec
 Srch*

Delaware
Wilmington Senior Center/Employment
 Services, *Perm Agcy*

Maryland
F-O-R-T-U-N-E Pers. Conslts, *Exec Srch*

Massachusetts
Arbor Associates, *Temp Agcy*

Michigan
A Nanny Network Inc., *Perm Agcy*
Birmingham Lakeland Association of
 Caregivers, *Temp Agcy*

Montana
Heartland Nannies & Companions/
 Heartland Caregivers, *Contract Svc*

New Jersey
Capitol Search, *Perm Agcy*
Neighborhood Nannies, *Perm Agcy*

New York
All Home Svcs. Agency, *Perm Agcy*

Oregon
Auntie Fay Domestic Agency, *Perm
 Agcy*

Virginia
Nanny Dimensions, *Perm Agcy*

ELECTRICAL

Alabama
Mngmt. Rcrtrs. International, *Exec Srch*

Arizona
Mngmt. Rcrtrs. of Scottsdale, *Exec Srch*

Arkansas
Mngmt. Rcrtrs., *Exec Srch*

California
Christian & Timbers, *Exec Srch*
F-O-R-T-U-N-E Pers. Conslts, *Exec Srch*
GPL Engineering, *Perm Agcy*
Mngmt. Rcrtrs. International, *Exec Srch*

Colorado
Dunhill of Fort Collins, *Exec Srch*
Mngmt. Rcrtrs. of Colorado Springs,
 Exec Srch
Sales Conslt, *Exec Srch*

Connecticut
Mngmt. Rcrtrs. of Norwalk, *Exec Srch*
Matrix Search Inc., *Perm Agcy*

Florida
Affinity Executive Search, *Exec Srch*
F-O-R-T-U-N-E Pers. Conslts, *Exec Srch*
Mngmt. Rcrtrs. of Tallahassee, *Exec Srch*
Sales Conslt, *Exec Srch*

Georgia
Mngmt. Rcrtrs. International, *Exec Srch*

Illinois
Mngmt. Rcrtrs. International, *Exec Srch*
OfficeMates5 (OM5), *Perm Agcy*

Indiana
Execusearch, *Exec Srch*
Mngmt. Rcrtrs. of Richmond, *Exec Srch*
OfficeMates5 (OM5)/DayStar Temporary
 Services, *Exec Srch*

Iowa
Mngmt. Rcrtrs. International, *Exec Srch*

Kansas
Corporate Resources, *Exec Srch*
Mngmt. Rcrtrs. of Overland Park/Sales
 Conslt/OfficeMates5, *Exec Srch*

Kentucky
Angel Group International, *Exec Srch*

Louisiana
Clertech Group, Inc., *Exec Srch*
Mngmt. Rcrtrs./Sales Conslt, *Exec Srch*

Maryland
F-O-R-T-U-N-E Pers. Conslts, *Exec Srch*
Mngmt. Rcrtrs. International, *Exec Srch*
Sales Conslt, *Exec Srch*

Arrowstaff Services, Inc., *Perm Agcy*
Astra West Pers. Svcs., *Perm Agcy*
B&M Associates Inc., *Temp Agcy*
The Badger Group, *Exec Srch*
Thomas Beck Inc., *Exec Srch*
Harvey Bell & Associates, *Exec Srch*
Blue, Garni & Company, *Exec Srch*
Brandenburg Smith & Assoc., *Exec Srch*
Bryson Myers Company, *Exec Srch*
Bullis & Company, Inc., *Exec Srch*
Business Systems Support, *Perm Agcy*
CDI Technical Services, *Temp Agcy*
CN Associates, *Exec Srch*
CT Personnel Services, *Perm Agcy*
California Search Agency, *Exec Srch*
California Search Conslt, *Exec Srch*
Career Advantage, *Exec Srch*
Wayne Chamberlain & Assoc., *Exec Srch*
Coast Personnel, *Temp Agcy*
Corestaff Services, *Perm Agcy*
Corporate Search, *Exec Srch*
Corporate Technology Inc., *Exec Srch*
Crossroads Staffing Svc., *Temp Agcy*
The Culver Group, *Exec Srch*
Culver Personnel Services, *Perm Agcy*
Drake Office Overload, *Temp Agcy*
Dunhill of San Francisco, *Exec Srch*
Dunhill Prof. Search, *Exec Srch*
EDP Contract Services, *Contract Svc*
Engineering Tech. Svc., *Temp Agcy*
Essential Solutions, Inc., *Perm Agcy*
Executive Directions, *Exec Srch*
Executive Resource Syst., *Exec Srch*
Executive Search Conslt, *Exec Srch*
Fastek Technical Services, *Perm Agcy*
Fay Tech Services, *Perm Agcy*
Fisher & Associates, *Exec Srch*
Fisher Pers. Mngmt. Svcs., *Exec Srch*
F-O-R-T-U-N-E Pers. Conslts, *Exec Srch*
Fresquez and Associates, *Exec Srch*
GPL Engineering, *Perm Agcy*
Garnett Staffing, *Temp Agcy*
Dianne Gauger & Assoc., *Exec Srch*
Global Resources Ltd., *Exec Srch*
Grant & Associates, *Exec Srch*
Griffith & Associates, *Exec Srch*
Harley Associates, *Exec Srch*
HealthCare Recruiters, *Exec Srch*
Impact, Inc., *Exec Srch*
Independent Resource Syst., *Exec Srch*
Industrial Services Co., *Temp Agcy*
Interim Personnel, *Temp Agcy*
International Search Conslt, *Perm Agcy*
International Staffing Conslt, *Exec Srch*
Interstate Recruiters Corp., *Exec Srch*
JPM International, *Exec Srch*
Jerome & Company, *Exec Srch*
John Anthony & Assoc., *Exec Srch*
Keifer Professional Search, *Exec Srch*
Kelly IT Resources, *Temp Agcy*
Klein & Associates, *Temp Agcy*
Kuhn Med-Tech, *Exec Srch*
John Kurosky & Assoc., *Exec Srch*
London Temporary Svcs., *Temp Agcy*
MK Technical Services, *Temp Agcy*
Mngmt. Rcrtrs. International, *Exec Srch*
Management Solutions Inc., *Exec Srch*
Manpower Staffing Svcs., *Temp Agcy*
Markar Associates, *Exec Srch*
Master Search, *Exec Srch*
Med Quest, *Exec Srch*
Mesa International, *Exec Srch*
Milestone Prof. Search, *Exec Srch*
Monroe Personnel Services/Temptime, *Perm Agcy*
Morgen Design Inc., *Contract Svc*
Multax Systems, Inc., *Perm Agcy*
Multisearch Recruiters, *Exec Srch*
Murray Enterprises Staffing Services, Inc., *Temp Agcy*
National Career Choices, *Exec Srch*
Nelson Human Resource Solutions, *Perm Agcy*
Network Resource Group, *Exec Srch*
New Venture Development, *Exec Srch*
Nyborg-Dow Associates, *Exec Srch*
Omni Express Temps, *Temp Agcy*
Ortman Recruiting Intnl., *Exec Srch*
Pasona Pacific, *Temp Agcy*
Power 2000+, *Exec Srch*
Princeton Corporate Conslt, *Exec Srch*
Pro Staff Personnel Svcs., *Perm Agcy*

Professional Recruiters, *Exec Srch*
Professional Search Inc., *Exec Srch*
ProFound, *Perm Agcy*
Pyramid Placement, *Perm Agcy*
Questemps, *Temp Agcy*
Remedy Caller Access, *Temp Agcy*
Remedy Intelligent Staffing, *Temp Agcy*
Resource Perspectives, Inc., *Exec Srch*
Richmar Associates Inc., *Temp Agcy*
Riley-Cole, *Exec Srch*
Ritter & Associates, *Exec Srch*
Romac International, *Exec Srch*
Larry Rosenthal & Assoc., *Exec Srch*
Rowland Associates, *Exec Srch*
Royal Staffing Services, *Exec Srch*
Sanford Rose Associates, *Exec Srch*
Santa Barbara Staffing, *Perm Agcy*
The Search Group, *Exec Srch*
The Search Network, *Exec Srch*
Search West, *Exec Srch*
Search West of Ontario, *Exec Srch*
Select Personnel Services, *Temp Agcy*
Sierra Technology Corp., *Contract Svc*
Software Engineering Solutions, *Contract Svc*
Southwest Search Assoc., *Exec Srch*
Adele Steinmetz Exec. Search, *Exec Srch*
Sun Personnel Services, *Temp Agcy*
System One, *Perm Agcy*
TLC Staffing, *Temp Agcy*
T.R. Employment Agency, *Perm Agcy*
TRC Staffing Services, *Perm Agcy*
TECH/AID, *Temp Agcy*
Technical Search Conslt, *Exec Srch*
TechniQuest, *Exec Srch*
Technology Locator, *Contract Svc*
TechSource, *Contract Svc*
Techstaff West Inc., *Exec Srch*
Teleforce International, *Exec Srch*
Trattner Network, *Perm Agcy*
Trend Western Tech. Corp., *Temp Agcy*
Trendtec Inc., *Temp Agcy*
Triple-J Services, *Exec Srch*
The Truman Agency, *Perm Agcy*
Tustin Personnel Services, *Perm Agcy*
Unisearch, *Exec Srch*
United Staffing Solutions, *Exec Srch*
Vaughan & Co. Exec. Srch, *Exec Srch*
Volt Svcs Grp, *Contract Svc, Temp Agcy*
Westaff, *Temp Agcy*
Western Tech. Resources, *Exec Srch*
S.R. Wilson Inc., *Exec Srch*
H.L. Yoh Company, *Contract Svc*
Your People Professionals, *Perm Agcy*
Don Zee Associates, *Exec Srch*

Colorado

Ahrnsbrak and Associates, *Perm Agcy*
The Bridge, *Exec Srch*
CDI Corporation, *Contract Svc*
Career Forum, Inc., *Exec Srch*
Career Marketing Assoc., *Exec Srch*
Careers Limited, *Exec Srch*
Clockwise Partners, *Exec Srch*
Dunhill of Fort Collins, *Exec Srch*
Dunhill Pers. of Boulder, *Exec Srch*
F-O-R-T-U-N-E Pers. Conslts of Denver, *Exec Srch*
GeoSearch, Inc., *Exec Srch*
Gimble & Nicol Exec. Search, *Exec Srch*
Hallmark Personnel Syst., *Exec Srch*
Initial Staffing Services, *Perm Agcy*
Intellimark, *Temp Agcy*
JobSearch, *Temp Agcy*
Kelly IT Resources, *Temp Agcy*
Kelly Services, Inc., *Temp Agcy*
Mngmt. Rcrtrs. International, *Exec Srch*
Manpower International, *Temp Agcy*
Martinez & Hromada Associates, Inc., *Contract Svc*
Miller Denver, *Exec Srch*
National Affirmative Action Career Network, Inc., *Exec Srch*
Olsten Staffing Services, *Temp Agcy*
Pendleton Resources, *Exec Srch*
Real Estate Personnel, *Exec Srch*
Romac International, *Exec Srch*
Sales Conslt, *Exec Srch*
Snelling Personnel Svcs., *Exec Srch*
Southwest Technical Conslt, Inc., *Contract Svc*
Star Personnel Service, *Exec Srch*

Tech Staffing, *Temp Agcy*
Technical Recruiters of Colorado Springs, *Exec Srch*
Todays Temporary, *Temp Agcy*
J.Q. Turner & Associates, *Exec Srch*
Welzig, Lowe & Assoc., *Exec Srch*
Woodmoor Group, *Exec Srch*
H.L. Yoh Company, *Contract Svc*

Connecticut

Adecco/TAD Tech. Svcs., *Contract Svc*
Admiral Staffing Services, *Temp Agcy*
Availability of Hartford, *Perm Agcy*
Blackwood Associates Inc., *Exec Srch*
Bohan & Bradstreet, *Perm Agcy*
Cahill Associates, *Exec Srch*
Charter Personnel Services, *Exec Srch*
Cheney Associates, *Exec Srch*
Cupples Consulting Svcs., *Exec Srch*
Data Pros, *Perm Agcy*
Diversified Emp. Svcs., *Perm Agcy*
Dunhill of New Haven/Dunhill Search International, *Perm Agcy*
EDP Contract Services, *Contract Svc*
Employment Opportunities, *Perm Agcy*
Engineering Resource Recruiters, *Exec Srch*
Executive Register Inc., *Exec Srch*
Fox Ridge Services, Inc., *Temp Agcy*
Friedman Associates, *Exec Srch*
Hallmark Totaltech, Inc., *Exec Srch*
Hire Logic, *Temp Agcy*
J.G. Hood Associates, *Perm Agcy*
Human Resource Conslt, *Exec Srch*
JAT, Ltd., *Perm Agcy*
The La Pointe Group Inc., *Exec Srch*
W.R. Lawry, Inc., *Perm Agcy*
Lineal Recruiting Svcs., *Perm Agcy*
Lutz Associates, *Exec Srch*
MJF Associates, *Exec Srch*
Mngmt. Rcrtrs. International, *Exec Srch*
Management Search, *Exec Srch*
Matrix Search Inc., *Perm Agcy*
Maxwell-Marcus Staffing Conslt, *Exec Srch*
New England Personnel, *Perm Agcy*
Office Services of CT, *Perm Agcy*
PRH Management, Inc., *Exec Srch*
Barry Persky & Co., *Exec Srch*
Quality Control Recruiters, *Exec Srch*
Romac International, *Exec Srch*
Russo Staffing Inc., *Exec Srch*
Stewart Associates, *Exec Srch*
Tech/Aid, *Temp Agcy*
Technical Search, *Exec Srch*
Technical Staffing Solns., *Temp Agcy*
Wallace Associates, *Exec Srch*
Westaff, *Temp Agcy*

Delaware

DW Technologies, *Contract Svc*
Elliott Davis & Associates, *Exec Srch*
F-O-R-T-U-N-E Pers. Conslts, *Exec Srch*
J.B. Groner Exec. Search, *Exec Srch*
E.W. Hodges & Associates, *Exec Srch*
Independent National Search & Associates (INS), *Exec Srch*
H.L. Yoh Company, *Contract Svc*

Dist. of Columbia

GKA Resources, LLC, *Exec Srch*
Norrell Services, *Temp Agcy*
Pace-Careers, Inc., *Exec Srch*

Florida

AAA Employment, *Perm Agcy*
Able Body Corporate Svcs., *Contract Svc*
Academy Design & Technical Services, Inc., *Contract Svc*
Active Professionals, *Exec Srch*
American Recruiters, *Exec Srch*
Atlantic Prof. Recruiters, *Exec Srch*
Availability, Inc., *Perm Agcy*
The Brand Company, Inc., *Exec Srch*
B²D Technical Services, *Contract Svc*
CDI Corporation, *Contract Svc*
Cantrell & Associates, *Exec Srch*
Caradyne Group, *Exec Srch*
Career Planners, Inc., *Perm Agcy*
Chase-Gardner Exec. Srch, *Exec Srch*
Colli Associates of Tampa, *Exec Srch*
Criterion Executive Search, *Exec Srch*
DGA Personnel Group, *Exec Srch*
Donbar Service Corp., *Temp Agcy*

White Associates/TemTech, *Exec Srch*
Wyatt & Associates Inc., *Contract Svc*

Kentucky

Angel Group International, *Exec Srch*
BJM & Associates, Inc., *Contract Svc*
C.M. Management Svcs., *Perm Agcy*
Compton & Associates, *Exec Srch*
F-O-R-T-U-N-E Pers. Consults, *Exec Srch*
J.E.M. & Associates, Inc., *Temp Agcy*
Kolok Enterprises, *Exec Srch*
Kovac Berrins AG Inc., *Exec Srch*
Mngmt. Rcrtrs. International, *Exec Srch*
Manpower Inc., *Temp Agcy*
Manufacturing Associates, *Exec Srch*
Professional Search, *Exec Srch*
Snelling Personnel Svcs., *Perm Agcy*
Weller-Wooley & Assoc., *Exec Srch*

Louisiana

Accounting Personnel Conslt/STAT Resources, *Perm Agcy*
CDI Engineering Group, *Contract Svc*
Clertech Group, Inc., *Exec Srch*
Delta Personnel, *Perm Agcy*
Dunhill of Baton Rouge, *Exec Srch*
Dunhill Pers. Search, *Exec Srch*
Frazee Recruiting Conslt, *Exec Srch*
Interim Personnel, *Temp Agcy*
Mngmt. Rcrtrs. International, *Exec Srch*
The Pollak and Skan Grp., *Contract Svc*
River Region Personnel, *Exec Srch*
Snelling Personnel Svcs., *Exec Srch*
Talley & Associates, Inc./Talley Temporaries, *Exec Srch*
Technical & Prof. Sources, *Exec Srch*
Universal Personnel, *Contract Svc*

Maine

Career Management Assoc., *Exec Srch*
Global Engineers, Inc., *Contract Svc*
Goodrich Consulting, *Exec Srch*
Maine Staffing Services, *Temp Agcy*
Paper Industry Recruitment, *Perm Agcy*
The Porter Hamel Group, *Exec Srch*
Recruiting Professionals, *Exec Srch*

Maryland

Cemcon International Inc., *Perm Agcy*
Chesapeake Consulting Group, *Exec Srch*
Corporate Resources, *Exec Srch*
Cross Country Conslt, Inc./Fallstaff Search, *Exec Srch*
Echelon Service Co., *Contract Svc*
Employer Employee Exchange, Inc. (EEE), *Exec Srch*
F-O-R-T-U-N-E Pers. Conslts, *Exec Srch*
JDG Associates Limited, *Exec Srch*
J.R. Associates, *Perm Agcy*
Mngmt. Rcrtrs. International, *Exec Srch*
Sales Conslt, *Exec Srch*
Sanford Rose Associates, *Exec Srch*
TCM Enterprises, *Exec Srch*
TAC Engineering Resources, *Temp Agcy*
Tech/Aid of Maryland, *Temp Agcy*
Technical Talent Locators, *Perm Agcy*
Tri-Serv Inc., *Perm Agcy*
Vey Mark Associates, Inc., *Exec Srch*
Virtual Staffing Services, *Perm Agcy*
Winston Search, Inc., *Exec Srch*

Massachusetts

ABA Personnel, Inc., *Temp Agcy*
Abbott's of Boston, Inc., *Exec Srch*
Ability Search of New England, *Perm Agcy*
Aerotek, Inc., *Contract Svc*
Ansara, Bickford, & Fiske, *Exec Srch*
Applied Resources Inc., *Exec Srch*
Architechs, *Exec Srch*
B&M Associates, *Temp Agcy*
Bell Oaks Company, *Exec Srch*
Brady Employment Svc., *Perm Agcy*
CDI Corporation, *Contract Svc*
Construction Directory, *Perm Agcy*
Robert H. Davidson Assoc., Inc./Exec. and Prof. Resume Service, *Exec Srch*
Derby Associates Inc., *Perm Agcy*
Digital Arts Group, *Contract Svc*
Diversity Associates, *Exec Srch*
Diversity Search Specialists, *Exec Srch*
Dunhill Staffing Systems, *Temp Agcy*
EM Heath & Company, *Exec Srch*

EMSI (Engineering Management Support, Inc.), *Temp Agcy*
Enginuity Search Inc., *Exec Srch*
Entegee, *Perm Agcy*
The Environmental Careers Organization, *Contract Svc*
F-O-R-T-U-N-E Pers. Conslts of Topsfield, *Exec Srch*
Gilreath Weatherby Inc., *Exec Srch*
A. Greenstein & Company, *Exec Srch*
HM Associates, *Exec Srch*
Human Resource Conslt, *Perm Agcy*
Hunter Associates, *Perm Agcy*
S.D. Kelly & Associates, *Exec Srch*
Lake Conslt, *Exec Srch*
Lane Employment Svc., *Perm Agcy*
John Leonard Pers. Assoc., *Perm Agcy*
The Littleton Group, *Exec Srch*
Locke Associates Engineering Recruiters, *Exec Srch*
Mngmt. Rcrtrs. International, *Exec Srch*
Management Search, Inc., *Exec Srch*
Master Search, *Exec Srch*
McCormick Group, *Exec Srch*
McDevitt Associates, *Exec Srch*
Micro Tech Conslt, *Temp Agcy*
Micro Tech Professionals, *Temp Agcy*
Morgan & Associates, *Exec Srch*
National Engineering Svc, *Temp Agcy*
Nationwide Business Svc., *Perm Agcy*
Need Pers. Placement, *Temp Agcy*
New Dimensions in Tech., *Exec Srch*
New England Recruiters, *Exec Srch*
New England Search, Inc., *Exec Srch*
D.P. Parker & Associates, *Exec Srch*
Norman Powers Associates, *Exec Srch*
Propos Associates, Inc., *Perm Agcy*
Remedy Intelligent Staffing, *Temp Agcy*
Romac Intl., *Perm Agcy, Exec Srch*
Louis Rudzinsky Assoc., *Exec Srch*
Sales Conslt, *Exec Srch*
George D. Sandel Assoc., *Perm Agcy*
Selected Executives Inc., *Exec Srch*
Snelling Personnel, *Exec Srch*
Stone Consulting Group & Legal Search Specialists, *Exec Srch*
Straube Associates, *Exec Srch*
Summit Technical Svcs., *Temp Agcy*
TAD Staffing Services, *Temp Agcy*
Tech/Aid, *Contract Svc*
Technical Personnel Svcs., *Perm Agcy*
Tesmer Allen Associates, *Perm Agcy*
Total Technical Services, *Perm Agcy*
United Prof. Placement, *Exec Srch*
Van/Grace Associates, Inc., *Exec Srch*
Vanguard Executive Svcs., *Exec Srch*
Winfield Associates, *Exec Srch*
H.L. Yoh Company, *Contract Svc*

Michigan

AE Employment Services, *Perm Agcy*
Acro ASI, *Contract Svc*
Action Management Corp., *Perm Agcy*
Adecco/TAD Tech. Svcs., *Contract Svc*
Advance Associates, *Exec Srch*
Advance Employment, *Exec Srch*
Advance Personnel of MI, *Exec Srch*
Allegheny Search Assoc., *Exec Srch*
Appnet, *Contract Svc*
Argus & Associates, *Contract Svc*
Associates, *Exec Srch*
Aucon L.L.C., *Exec Srch*
Barman Staffing Solns., *Temp Agcy*
Beacon Services Inc., *Exec Srch*
Benford & Associates, *Exec Srch*
CDI Corporation, *Contract Svc*
Career Associates Inc., *Perm Agcy*
Carmac Exec. Recruiting, *Exec Srch*
Case & Company, *Exec Srch*
Coastal Development, Inc., *Exec Srch*
Contract Professionals, *Perm Agcy*
Corporate Business Svcs, *Perm Agcy*
Corporate Staffing Resources, *Perm Agcy*
Davidson, Laird & Assoc., *Exec Srch*
Day Personnel, Inc., *Perm Agcy*
Design & Engineering Svc., *Temp Agcy*
Dickson Associates Inc., *Exec Srch*
Diversified Recruiters, *Perm Agcy*
Dynamic Personnel, *Contract Svc*
Gene Ellefson & Assoc., *Exec Srch*
Engineering Professionals, *Perm Agcy*
Entech Personnel Svcs., *Temp Agcy*

ExecuSearch of Southwest Michigan, *Perm Agcy*
Executech, Inc., *Exec Srch*
Executive & Med. Recruiters, *Exec Srch*
Executive & Tech. Pers., *Exec Srch*
Executive Recruiters Intnl., *Exec Srch*
Express Personnel Svcs., *Temp Agcy*
F-O-R-T-U-N-E Pers. Consltns, *Exec Srch*
GBL Resources Inc., *Exec Srch*
Giacomin Group Inc., *Exec Srch*
Joseph Goldring & Assoc., *Exec Srch*
The Hallman Group Inc., *Exec Srch*
Healthcare Recruiters Intl., *Exec Srch*
Harvey Hohauser & Assoc., *Exec Srch*
William Howard Agency, *Contract Svc*
IBA Search, *Exec Srch*
Job Fair Network of MI, *Perm Agcy*
Kelly Technical Services, *Contract Svc*
Key Personnel, *Perm Agcy*
Ludot Personnel, *Perm Agcy*
Mngmt. Rcrtrs. International, *Exec Srch*
Manpower Tech. Svcs., *Contract Svc*
METROSTAFF, *Exec Srch*
Lou Michaels Associates, *Exec Srch*
Darnell Mitchell & Assoc., *Exec Srch*
Nationwide Career Network, *Perm Agcy*
Office Staffing Recruiting, *Exec Srch*
Parr Search, *Exec Srch*
Preferred Emp. Planning, *Perm Agcy*
Professional Advancement Institute, *Exec Srch*
Professional Personnel Conslt International, *Exec Srch*
Professional Resource Associates, Inc., *Contract Svc*
RC Engineering and Management Services, Inc., *Contract Svc*
RCM Technologies, *Contract Svc*
Resource Tech. Corp., *Perm Agcy*
Romac International, *Perm Agcy*
Roth Young Personnel Services of Detroit, Inc., *Exec Srch*
Sales Conslt, *Exec Srch*
Sanford Rose Associates, *Exec Srch*
Search Plus International, *Exec Srch*
Selective Recruiting Assoc., *Exec Srch*
Sharrow & Associates Inc., *Exec Srch*
Snelling Search, *Perm Agcy*
Source Technology LLC, *Exec Srch*
Sygnetics Inc., *Temp Agcy*
TAC Automotive Group, *Contract Svc*
Technical Prof. Svc., *Perm Agcy*
Temporary Tech. Svcs, *Temp Agcy*
Thomas & Assoc. of MI, *Exec Srch*
Trillium Staffing, *Temp Agcy*
Troy Tech Services, *Contract Svc*
Unlimited Staffing Solns, *Contract Svc*
Vectech Pharmaceuticals Conslt, *Perm Agcy*
Weliver & Associates, *Exec Srch*
Henry Welker & Assoc., *Exec Srch*
Wing Tips and Pumps, Inc., *Exec Srch*
Wise Personnel Services, *Perm Agcy*
Wood Personnel Services/Wood Temporary Staffing, *Perm Agcy*
Workforce, Inc., *Temp Agcy*

Minnesota

Advantage International, *Exec Srch*
Agri-Business Services, *Exec Srch*
Answer Personnel Service, *Temp Agcy*
Bradley & Associates, *Exec Srch*
Bright Search, *Exec Srch*
CDI Corporation, *Contract Svc*
Charles Dahl Associates, *Exec Srch*
Dietrich & Associates, *Exec Srch*
Discovery Personnel, *Exec Srch*
Diversified Employment, *Perm Agcy*
Execu-Tech Search Inc., *Exec Srch*
Roger G. Gilmer & Assoc., *Exec Srch*
HR Services of Plymouth, *Exec Srch*
T.H. Hunter, Inc., *Exec Srch*
Jackley Search Conslt, *Exec Srch*
George Konik Assoc., *Contract Svc*
Lynn Temporary, *Temp Agcy*
Mngmt. Rcrtrs. of Minneapolis/ Sales Conslt, *Exec Srch*
Manpower Technical, *Contract Svc*
NER, Inc., *Exec Srch*
Northland Emp. Services, *Exec Srch*
Nycor Search Inc., *Exec Srch*
Olsten Staffing Services, *Temp Agcy*

Recruitment Group, *Exec Srch*
Ritta Professional Search, *Exec Srch*
Rosenthal Assoc. Intnl., *Exec Srch*
Sales Search, Ltd./Executive Resume Service, *Exec Srch*
SearchAmerica, Inc., *Exec Srch*
Sharp Placement Prof., *Exec Srch*
Snelling Personnel Svcs., *Perm Agcy*
Staff Managers, *Temp Agcy*
StratfordGroup, *Exec Srch*
Superior Concepts, *Contract Svc*
Thorsen Associates, Inc., *Exec Srch*
Todd Arro, Inc., *Exec Srch*
Volt Services Group, *Contract Svc*
Weber Mngmt Conslt, *Exec Srch*
Westaff, *Temp Agcy*
Westchester Emp. Agency, *Perm Agcy*
H.L. Yoh Company, *Temp Agcy*

North Carolina

A First Resource, *Exec Srch*
Accurate Staffing Conslt, *Exec Srch*
Action Staffing Group, *Temp Agcy*
Active Search Recruiters, *Exec Srch*
Advanced Prof. Resources, *Exec Srch*
Alpha Omega Exec. Search, *Exec Srch*
American Quality Staffing, *Exec Srch*
AmeriPro Search, Inc., *Exec Srch*
Anderson & Daniel Pers., *Perm Agcy*
Arjay & Associates, *Exec Srch*
Atchison & Associates, *Exec Srch*
Ayers & Associates, Inc., *Exec Srch*
Bennett Allen & Assoc., *Exec Srch*
CDI IT Services, *Contract Svc*
Career Search Inc., *Exec Srch*
Paul Day & Associates, *Exec Srch*
Eastern Search Group, *Exec Srch*
Engineering Management Staff Recruiters, *Exec Srch*
Environmental Recruiting Services (ERS), *Exec Srch*
Executive Connections, *Exec Srch*
Executive Recruitment Specialists, Inc., *Exec Srch*
Executive Staffing Group, *Exec Srch*
Express Personnel Svcs., *Temp Agcy*
D.D. Fayling Associates, *Exec Srch*
F-O-R-T-U-N-E Pers. Conslts, *Exec Srch*
The Furniture Agency Inc., *Exec Srch*
Glovier & Associates, *Exec Srch*
Graham & Associates, *Perm Agcy*
The Greer Group, *Perm Agcy*
Highlander Search, *Exec Srch*
Kelly Services, Inc., *Temp Agcy*
Mngmt. Rcrtrs. International, *Exec Srch*
Mark III Personnel Inc., *Exec Srch*
Merrick & Moore, *Exec Srch*
Moffitt International, Inc., *Exec Srch*
Morgan Group, *Exec Srch*
Myers & Associates, *Perm Agcy*
Olsten Staffing Services, *Temp Agcy*
The Perkins Group, *Exec Srch*
Professional Pers, Assoc., *Perm Agcy*
SENC Technical Services, *Contract Svc*
Sales Conslt, *Exec Srch*
Sanford Rose Associates, *Exec Srch*
Search Conslt Worldwide Inc., *Exec Srch*
Sickenberger Associates, *Exec Srch*
Snelling Personnel Svcs., *Perm Agcy*
Sparks Personnel Services, *Exec Srch*
Stewart Greene & Company/The Triad, *Exec Srch*
StratfordGroup, *Exec Srch*
Technical Associates, *Exec Srch*
The Underwood Group, *Perm Agcy*
USA Staffing, *Perm Agcy*
Volt Technical Services, *Contract Svc*
David Weinfeld Group, *Exec Srch*
Will/Staff Personnel Svcs, *Temp Agcy*
Wilson Personnel Inc., *Exec Srch*
H.L. Yoh Company, *Contract Svc*

North Dakota

Career Connection, *Exec Srch*
Dunhill Prof. Search, *Exec Srch*
Olsten Staffing Services/Expressway Personnel, *Temp Agcy*

Ohio

Adecco/TAD Tech. Svcs., *Contract Svc*
Advancement LLC, *Contract Svc*
Alliance Technical Svcs., *Contract Svc*
American Bus. Pers. Svcs., *Perm Agcy*

Baldwin & Associates, *Exec Srch*
Belcan Technical Svcs., *Contract Svc*
Bradley-Pierce Personnel, *Perm Agcy*
J.B. Brown & Associates, *Exec Srch*
CBS Personnel Services, *Perm Agcy*
Career Specialists Inc., *Exec Srch*
Clopton's Placement Svc., *Perm Agcy*
Combined Resources Inc., *Exec Srch*
Continental Search Assoc., *Exec Srch*
Corell Associates, *Perm Agcy*
J.D. Cotter Search, Inc., *Exec Srch*
Cross-Jordan Corporation, *Exec Srch*
Crown Temp. Services, *Temp Agcy*
DLD Technical Services, *Contract Svc*
Alan N. Daum & Assoc., *Perm Agcy*
Tonia Deal Conslt, *Exec Srch*
Pete DeLuke & Associates, *Exec Srch*
Eastern Personnel Svcs., *Perm Agcy*
Elite Resources Group, *Exec Srch*
Executech, *Exec Srch*
Executive Connection, *Exec Srch*
Executive Directions, *Exec Srch*
Executive Search Ltd., *Exec Srch*
Fenzel Milar Associates, *Exec Srch*
Fitzpatrick & Associates, *Exec Srch*
Flex-Tech Prof. Services, *Contract Svc*
F-O-R-T-U-N-E Pers. Conslts, *Exec Srch*
Gayhart & Associates, *Exec Srch*
Global Resources Group, *Contract Svc*
H.L. Goehring & Assoc., *Exec Srch*
Griffiths & Associates, *Exec Srch*
Guthoff & Associates, *Exec Srch*
Russ Hadick & Associates, *Exec Srch*
Hahn & Associates, Inc., *Exec Srch*
Hite Executive Search/Hite Management Conslt, Inc., *Exec Srch*
ITS Technical Staffing, *Exec Srch*
Industrial Personnel, *Exec Srch*
Interim Personnel, *Temp Agcy*
KBK Management Assoc., *Exec Srch*
R.E. Lowe Associates, *Perm Agcy*
Mngmt. Rcrtrs. International, *Exec Srch*
Marvel Conslt Inc., *Exec Srch*
Messina Mngmt. Systems, *Exec Srch*
Miami Professional Search, *Exec Srch*
Midland Conslt, *Exec Srch*
Minority Executive Search, *Exec Srch*
Myers & Associates, *Exec Srch*
Newcomb-Desmond & Assoc., *Exec Srch*
North American Tech. Svcs., *Temp Agcy*
North Star Resources, *Contract Svc*
Northcoast Personnel, *Exec Srch*
Olsten Prof. Staffing Svcs., *Exec Srch*
Pak/Teem Tech. Services, *Contract Svc*
Patterson Personnel, *Exec Srch*
Professional Restaffing, *Perm Agcy*
Providence Pers. Conslt, *Exec Srch*
Quality Plus, *Exec Srch*
RDS, Inc., *Contract Svc*
Bill Reber & Associates, *Exec Srch*
Resource Techne Group, *Exec Srch*
SJR & Associates, *Exec Srch*
Sales Conslt, *Exec Srch*
Sanford Rose Associates, *Exec Srch*
Search Technology, *Exec Srch*
Selective Search Assoc., *Perm Agcy*
Shafer Jones Associates, *Exec Srch*
Sterling Personnel Resources, *Exec Srch*
StratfordGroup, *Exec Srch*
Tabb & Associates, *Exec Srch*
Talent Research Corp., *Exec Srch*
Teamwork U.S.A., *Contract Svc*
Tech/Aid of Ohio, *Perm Agcy*
Technical Recruiting Svcs., *Exec Srch*
Technical Search Assoc., *Exec Srch*
Technical/Mngmt. Res., *Perm Agcy*
Teknon Emp. Resources, *Exec Srch*
Fred C. Tippel and Assoc., *Exec Srch*
Vector Technical Inc., *Perm Agcy*
J.P. Walton & Associates, *Exec Srch*
Warner & Associates, Inc., *Perm Agcy*
World Search, *Exec Srch*
H.L. Yoh Company, *Contract Svc*

Oklahoma

Ameri Resource, *Exec Srch*
Career Concepts, *Exec Srch*
Executive Resources Grp., *Exec Srch*
Express Personnel Services/RWJ & Associates, *Temp Agcy*
Holbrook Associates, *Exec Srch*
JDL & Associates, *Exec Srch*

Key Temporary Personnel, *Temp Agcy*
Mngmt. Rcrtrs. International, *Exec Srch*
Terry Neese Pers. Agency, *Temp Agcy*
Phillips & Associates, *Exec Srch*
Reality Group, *Exec Srch*
Sooner Placement Service, *Perm Agcy*
John Wylie Associates, *Exec Srch*

Oregon

Barrett Business Services, *Temp Agcy*
CDI Technical Services, *Contract Svc*
Corporate Builders, Inc., *Exec Srch*
Executives Worldwide, *Exec Srch*
Express Personnel Services, *Exec Srch*
Hackenschmidt, Weaver & Fox, Inc., *Exec Srch*
Robert William James & Associates, *Exec Srch*
Mngmt. Rcrtrs. of Portland/ OfficeMates5, *Exec Srch*
National Eng. Search, *Exec Srch*
Nationwide Personnel Recruiting & Consulting Inc., *Exec Srch*
Sanford Rose Associates, *Exec Srch*
Search Northwest Assoc., *Exec Srch*
Stephenson & Stephenson, *Exec Srch*
Triad Technology Group, *Perm Agcy*
Uniforce Staffing Svcs., *Contract Svc*
Wolf Environmental Grp., *Exec Srch*
Woodworth Intnl. Group, *Exec Srch*

Pennsylvania

AA Staffing Solutions, *Contract Svc*
Action Personnel Services, *Perm Agcy*
J.N. Adams & Associates, *Exec Srch*
Advanced Tech. Resources, *Exec Srch*
Alexander Personnel Assoc., *Exec Srch*
American Search Assoc., *Exec Srch*
Anita's Careers, Inc., *Exec Srch*
Arrow Search Conslt, *Exec Srch*
Ashley Search Conslt, *Exec Srch*
Atomic Personnel, Inc., *Exec Srch*
Barr Associates, *Exec Srch*
Barton Personnel Systems, *Exec Srch*
Bender & Assoc. Intnl., *Exec Srch*
T.W. Boris Associates, *Exec Srch*
Bradley Professional Svcs, *Perm Agcy*
CDI Corporation, *Contract Svc*
CDI Information Services, *Contract Svc*
Career Concepts Staffing Svcs, *Exec Srch*
Career Quest Confidential, *Exec Srch*
Charley's Personnel Staffing, *Temp Agcy*
R. Christine Associates, *Exec Srch*
Consearch, *Exec Srch*
CoreStaff Inc., *Temp Agcy*
Corporate Mngmt. Svcs., *Exec Srch*
DiCenzo Personnel Specialists, *Exec Srch*
Dunn Associates, *Exec Srch*
EDP Contract Services, *Contract Svc*
Eden & Associates, Inc., *Exec Srch*
Executive Avail-A-Search, *Exec Srch*
Fox-Morris Associates, *Exec Srch*
The GMW Group, Inc., *Exec Srch*
Gateway Resources Inc., *Exec Srch*
J.H. Glass & Associates, *Exec Srch*
Jerry Goldberg & Assoc., *Perm Agcy*
H-Tech Inc., *Contract Svc*
HRS/TND Associates, Inc., *Exec Srch*
The Hastings Group, *Exec Srch*
Hoskins Hains Associates, *Exec Srch*
IMC International, Inc., *Contract Svc*
Interactive Search Assoc., *Exec Srch*
J-Rand Search, *Exec Srch*
JK Resources, *Exec Srch*
Nancy Jackson Inc., *Exec Srch*
Clifton Johnson Assoc., *Exec Srch*
Kathy Karr Personnel., *Perm Agcy*
Katron Inc., *Exec Srch*
Blair Kershaw Associates, *Exec Srch*
Lawrence Personnel, *Exec Srch*
Robert Lohrke Associates, *Exec Srch*
Main Line Personnel Svc., *Perm Agcy*
Mngmt. Rcrtrs. International, *Exec Srch*
Mngmt. Rcrtrs./CompuSearch, *Exec Srch*
Mngmt. Rcrtrs. of Reading/ CAREER SENTINEL, *Exec Srch*
Mngmt. Rcrtrs. of West Chester, Inc., *Exec Srch*
George R. Martin Exec. Srch, *Exec Srch*
Robert McClure Ltd., *Exec Srch*
McNichol & Associates, *Exec Srch*
B. Paul Mickey & Assoc., *Exec Srch*
John Morrow & Associates, *Exec Srch*

Index by Specialization/669

National Computerized Employment
Service Inc., *Exec Srch*
Olsten Staffing Services, *Temp Agcy*
LaMonte Owens, Inc., *Exec Srch*
Pratt Personnel Services, *Temp Agcy*
Prestige Personnel, *Exec Srch*
Probe Technology, *Exec Srch*
ProSearch, Inc., *Exec Srch*
Alan Raeburn Conslt, *Exec Srch*
SHS International, *Exec Srch*
Sanford Rose Associates, *Exec Srch*
Select Personnel, Inc., *Perm Agcy*
Singmaster Personnel Svc, *Perm Agcy*
Snelling Personnel Services, *Temp Agcy,
Exec Srch*
Kenn Spinrad Inc., *Exec Srch*
Stewart Associates, *Exec Srch*
StratfordGroup, *Exec Srch*
Strongin Technical Enterprises of
Pennsylvania, Inc., *Perm Agcy*
Suber & McAuley Tech. Srch, *Exec Srch*
TECH/AID of PA, *Contract Svc*
Tell/Com Recruiters, *Exec Srch*
Tops Temporaries Inc., *Temp Agcy*
Triangle Assoc. Intnl., *Perm Agcy*
United Employment, *Perm Agcy*
Virtual Workplace, Inc., *Temp Agcy*
C.D. Warner & Associates, *Exec Srch*
Whittlesey & Associates, *Exec Srch*
H.L. Yoh Company, *Contract Svc*
Yorktowne Personnel, *Exec Srch*

Rhode Island
Colony Personnel Assoc., *Temp Agcy*
Daley & Associates Inc., *Exec Srch*
Johnson & Tregar Assoc., *Perm Agcy*
Kelly Services, Inc., *Temp Agcy*
Albert G. Lee & Assoc., *Exec Srch*
Lybrook Associates, Inc., *Exec Srch*
Mngmt. Rcrtrs. International, *Exec Srch*
Norrell Services, *Temp Agcy*
On Line Staff Inc., *Temp Agcy*
PKS Associates, Inc., *Exec Srch*
Alan J. Price Associates, *Exec Srch*
Sullivan & Cogliano, *Exec Srch*
Summit Tech. Services, *Contract Svc*
Tech/Aid of Rhode Island, *Contract Svc*

South Carolina
ASAP Search & Recruiters, *Perm Agcy*
Accel Temp. Services, *Temp Agcy*
Aide Inc. Design Services, *Contract Svc*
David Anthony Conslt, *Exec Srch*
Bock & Associates, *Exec Srch*
CDI Corporation, *Contract Svc*
Corporate Solutions, *Exec Srch*
Dunhill Prof. Search, *Exec Srch*
Edmonds Personnel Inc., *Exec Srch*
Engineering Pers. Network, *Exec Srch*
Ford & Associates, *Exec Srch*
F-O-R-T-U-N-E Pers. Conslts of
Charleston, *Exec Srch*
F-O-R-T-U-N-E Pers. Conslts of
Columbia, *Exec Srch*
Harvey Personnel, Inc., *Perm Agcy*
Mngmt. Rcrtrs. of Columbia, *Exec Srch*
Mngmt. Rcrtrs. of Orangeburg, *Exec
Srch*
Mngmt. Rcrtrs. of Rock Hill, *Exec Srch*
Miller & Associates, *Exec Srch*
PRL & Associates, Inc., *Perm Agcy*
Phelps Personnel, *Perm Agcy*
Phillips Resource Group, *Exec Srch*
Rand Company, *Exec Srch*
Snelling Personnel Svcs., *Perm Agcy*
Southern Recruiters & Conslt, Inc., *Exec
Srch*
The Stroman Company, *Perm Agcy*
Technical South Inc., *Temp Agcy*

South Dakota
Key Staffing, *Temp Agcy*
Mngmt. Rcrtrs. of Sioux Falls, *Exec Srch*
Snelling Personnel Svc., *Perm Agcy*

Tennessee
A-1 Staffing & Personnel, *Temp Agcy*
Amenity Staffing, *Temp Agcy*
American Tech. Assoc., *Contract Svc*
Austin-Allen Company, *Exec Srch*
Baker & Baker Emp. Svc., *Exec Srch*
Career Professionals, Inc., *Exec Srch*
Cook Assoc. International, *Exec Srch*
Corporate Image Group, *Exec Srch*

Dunhill of Memphis, Inc., *Perm Agcy*
Engineer One, Inc., *Perm Agcy*
Express Personnel Svcs., *Perm Agcy*
F-O-R-T-U-N-E Pers. Conslts, *Exec Srch*
Hamilton-Ryker Co., *Perm Agcy*
Hester & Associates, *Exec Srch*
The LYNN Group, *Exec Srch*
Madison Personnel, *Perm Agcy*
Mngmt. Rcrtrs. International, *Exec Srch*
Mngmt. Rcrtrs. of Brentwood/
Sales Conslt, *Exec Srch*
Mngmt. Rcrtrs. of Chattanooga, *Exec
Srch*
Mngmt. Rcrtrs. of Lenoir City, *Exec Srch*
Manpower, Inc., *Temp Agcy*
Olsten Staffing Services, *Temp Agcy*
Personnel Link, *Exec Srch*
Rasmussen & Associates, *Perm Agcy*
Snelling Personnel Svcs., *Perm Agcy*
Software Resource Conslt Inc., *Exec Srch*
Technical Resource Assoc., *Exec Srch*
Wood Personnel Services, *Perm Agcy*

Texas
Ackerman Johnson Inc., *Exec Srch*
ACSYS Staffing, *Temp Agcy*
Adecco, *Temp Agcy*
Agri-Associates, *Exec Srch*
Albrecht & Assoc. Exec. Srch, *Exec Srch*
American Resources, *Exec Srch*
Architectural Career Network (ACN),
Contract Svc
Atwood Prof. Search, *Exec Srch*
Austin Group, *Exec Srch*
B&M Associates, Inc., *Contract Svc*
Babich & Associates, Inc., *Perm Agcy*
Belcan Tech. Services, *Contract Svc*
Benchmark Professionals, *Exec Srch*
Best/World Associates, *Exec Srch*
BestStaff Services, Inc., *Perm Agcy*
Boles & Associates, *Exec Srch*
Bond & Associates, *Exec Srch*
Bott & Associates, *Perm Agcy*
Brainpower Pers. Agency, *Perm Agcy*
Bundy-Stewart Associates , *Exec Srch*
Butler International, *Contract Svc*
CDI Corporation, *Contract Svc*
CDI Engineering Corp., *Contract Svc*
C.G. & Company, *Exec Srch*
CAD Technology, Inc., *Exec Srch*
CarlTech, *Contract Svc*
Certified Personnel Svc., *Contract Svc*
Champion Personnel Svc., *Contract Svc*
Computer Prof. Unlimited, *Exec Srch*
Continental Personnel Svc, *Perm Agcy*
Contract Design Personnel, *Contract Svc*
Gail Darling Staffing/Gail Darling's
Professional Desk, *Temp Agcy*
Design Quest Inc., *Contract Svc*
Dividend Staffing Svcs., *Temp Agcy*
C. Michael Dixon Assoc., *Exec Srch*
Dunhill Prof. Search, *Exec Srch*
The Elsworth Group, *Exec Srch*
The Energists, *Exec Srch*
Engineering Management Staff
Recruiters, *Exec Srch*
Express Personnel Svcs., *Perm Agcy*
Focus Point, Inc., *Contract Svc*
FoodPro Recruiters, Inc., *Exec Srch*
F-O-R-T-U-N-E Pers. Conslts, *Exec Srch*
Gulco Intl. Recruiting Svcs., *Perm Agcy*
Houston Creative Conn., *Exec Srch*
Inside Track, *Exec Srch*
L.K. Jordan & Associates, *Contract Svc*
Joseph Chris Partners, *Exec Srch*
KADCO Contract Design, *Contract Svc*
Kelly Scientific Resources, *Temp Agcy*
Kelly Services, Inc., *Temp Agcy*
LRJ Staffing Services, *Perm Agcy*
Loewenstein & Associates, *Exec Srch*
Mngmt. Rcrtrs. International, *Exec Srch*
Manpower Temp. Svcs., *Temp Agcy*
McKinley-AREND Intnl., *Exec Srch*
W. Robert Michaels & Co., *Exec Srch*
Odell & Associates Inc., *Exec Srch*
O'Keefe & Associates, *Perm Agcy*
Olsten Staffing Services, *Temp Agcy*
Opportunity Unlimited Personnel Conslt,
Exec Srch
The Pailin Group Professional Search
Conslt, *Exec Srch*
Pan American Search, *Exec Srch*
Pate Resources Group, *Exec Srch*

PERI Corporation, *Exec Srch*
The Personnel Office, *Exec Srch*
Preng & Associates, Inc., *Exec Srch*
Priority Search, Inc., *Exec Srch*
Pro Staff Personnel Svcs., *Temp Agcy*
Professional Search Conslt, *Contract Svc*
Professions Today, *Perm Agcy*
ProSearch Recruiting, *Exec Srch*
Recruiting Associates, *Exec Srch*
Redstone & Associates, *Exec Srch*
Remedy Intelligent Staffing, *Perm Agcy*
Riccione & Associates Inc., *Exec Srch*
Bart Roberson & Company, *Exec Srch*
Romac International, *Exec Srch*
Sales Conslt of Houston, *Exec Srch*
Search Network Intnl., *Exec Srch*
Seegers Estes & Assoc., *Perm Agcy*
Robert Shields & Assoc., *Contract Svc*
Snelling Personnel Svcs., *Perm Agcy*
Staff Extension Intnl., *Exec Srch*
Stehouwer & Associates, *Perm Agcy*
Straight Source, *Exec Srch*
StratfordGroup, *Exec Srch*
TRS Onsite Staffing, *Exec Srch*
Betty Tanner Exec. Search, *Exec Srch*
Tech-Net, *Exec Srch*
Technical Alliance Recruiters, *Exec Srch*
Technical Careers, *Contract Svc*
Technical Staffing Solutions, *Exec Srch*
The Urban Placement Svc., *Exec Srch*
Valpers Inc., *Exec Srch*
Volt Svcs. Group, *Temp Agcy*
Denis P. Walsh & Assoc., *Exec Srch*
Wheeler, Moore & Elam, *Exec Srch*
The Whitaker Companies, *Contract Svc*
H.L. Yoh Company, *Contract Svc*

Utah
F-O-R-T-U-N-E Pers. Conslts, *Exec Srch*
Franklin-Newbery Engineering, *Temp
Agcy*
Intermountain Staffing Resources, *Temp
Agcy*
Mngmt. Rcrtrs. of Ogden, *Exec Srch*
Mngmt. Rcrtrs. of Salt Lake City, *Exec
Srch*
Manpower Tech. Services, *Temp Agcy*
Olsten Staffing Services, *Temp Agcy*
Prince, Perelson & Assoc., *Exec Srch*
Volt Services Group, *Contract Svc*

Vermont
National Executive Search, *Exec Srch*
O'Connor Search Assoc., *Exec Srch*
Personnel Department, *Temp Agcy*
Technical Connection Inc., *Perm Agcy*
Jay Tracey Associates, *Exec Srch*

Virginia
Ability Resources, Inc., *Exec Srch*
Access Enterprises Inc., *Perm Agcy*
Adams Sources, *Exec Srch*
Alliance Group, *Exec Srch*
Alpha Omega Resources, *Perm Agcy*
BSC, *Contract Svc*
CDI Corporation, *Contract Svc*
Cadworks, Inc., *Contract Svc*
Career Registry, *Exec Srch*
Corporate Connection Ltd., *Exec Srch*
Donmac Associates, *Exec Srch*
Dunhill Prof. Search, *Exec Srch*
F-O-R-T-U-N-E Pers. Conslts, *Exec Srch*
Wayne Garber & Assoc., *Exec Srch*
Graham Associates, *Exec Srch*
The Guild Corporation, *Exec Srch*
Information Specialists Co., *Exec Srch*
Interim Tech. Consulting, *Perm Agcy*
Kogen Personnel, *Exec Srch*
Lee Staffing Resources, *Exec Srch*
Carol Maden Grp. Recruiting, *Exec Srch*
Mngmt. Rcrtrs. International, *Exec Srch*
Mngmt. Rcrtrs. of McLean/
OfficeMates5, *Exec Srch*
The McCormick Group, *Exec Srch*
Norrell Services, *Temp Agcy*
Paul-Tittle Associates, Inc., *Exec Srch*
Professional Search Personnel, *Exec Srch*
Recruiting Resources Inc., *Exec Srch*
Romac International, *Exec Srch*
Search & Recruit Intnl., *Exec Srch*
Snelling Personnel Svcs., *Perm Agcy*
Souder & Associates, *Exec Srch*
STAT Emp. Services, *Perm Agcy*
Strategic Staffing, Inc., *Contract Svc*

The Talley Group, *Exec Srch*
Tech/Aid of Virginia, *Temp Agcy*
U.S. Search, *Exec Srch*
Wayne Associates, *Exec Srch*

Washington

Able Personnel Agency, *Perm Agcy*
Behrens and Company, *Exec Srch*
Bixler Group, *Exec Srch*
The Career Clinic, Inc., *Exec Srch*
Comprehensive Staffing Resources Inc., *Temp Agcy*
Conmarke USA Inc., *Temp Agcy*
Demetrio & Associates, *Exec Srch*
Express Personnel Services, *Temp Agcy*
F-O-R-T-U-N-E Pers. Conslts of East Seattle, *Exec Srch*
Houser Martin Morris, *Exec Srch*
Hygun Group, Inc., *Exec Srch*
The Jobs Company, *Exec Srch*
Kirkbride Associates Inc., *Exec Srch*
Mngmt. Rcrtrs. International, *Exec Srch*
Management Solutions, *Exec Srch*
John Mason & Associates, *Exec Srch*
Personnel Unlimited Inc., *Exec Srch*
Pilon Management, *Exec Srch*
Jack Porter & Associates, *Perm Agcy*
Pro-Active Conslt, *Exec Srch*
Resource Mngmt. Intnl., *Temp Agcy*
Susan Schoos & Associates, *Exec Srch*
Wilson Smith Associates, *Exec Srch*
Strain Personnel Specialists, *Exec Srch*
StratfordGroup, *Exec Srch*
Technical Resource Group, *Exec Srch*
Thomson, Sponar & Adams, *Exec Srch*
Whittall Mngmt. Group, *Exec Srch*
Williams Recruiting, *Exec Srch*

West Virginia

Belcan Tech. Services, *Contract Svc*
CDI Engineering Group, *Contract Svc*
Dunhill Prof. Search, *Exec Srch*
Key Personnel, Inc., *Perm Agcy*
Mngmt. Rcrtrs. of Charleston, *Exec Srch*
Quantum Resources, *Perm Agcy*

Wisconsin

ABR Emp. Services, *Perm Agcy*
Action Search Conslt, *Exec Srch*
Adecco/TAD Tech. Svcs., *Contract Svc*
Aerotek, Inc., *Contract Svc*
The Ambrose Group, *Exec Srch*
American Tech. Services, *Perm Agcy*
Argus Technical Services, *Perm Agcy*
Austria Austria & Assoc., *Perm Agcy*
Benston & Associates, *Exec Srch*
Construction Search Specialists, *Exec Srch*
Corporate Search Inc., *Exec Srch*
Crown Services, *Temp Agcy*
DHR International Inc., *Exec Srch*
Dieck Mueller Group, *Exec Srch*
Dunhill of Green Bay, *Perm Agcy*
J.M. Eagle Partners, *Exec Srch*
Eagle Technology Group, *Perm Agcy*
Engineering Placement Specialists, *Exec Srch*
EnviroStaff, Inc., *Temp Agcy*
Executive Placement & Career Svcs./ Career Connections, *Exec Srch*
Executive Recruiters, Inc., *Exec Srch*
Executive Resource Inc., *Exec Srch*
FoodStaff 2000, Inc., *Exec Srch*
Global Insights, Inc., *Exec Srch*
The H S Group, Inc., *Exec Srch*
Maglio & Company, *Exec Srch*
Mngmt. Rcrtrs. International, *Exec Srch*
MARBL Conslt, *Exec Srch*
The Michael David Group, *Exec Srch*
Olsten Staffing Services, *Temp Agcy*
PDS Technical Services, *Contract Svc*
Placements of Racine Inc., *Perm Agcy*
The Pollak and Skan Grp., *Contract Svc*
Prairie Engineering, *Exec Srch*
Professional Engineering Placements, *Perm Agcy*
QTI Professional Staffing, *Exec Srch*
RCM Technologies, *Contract Svc*
Sauve Company, Ltd., *Perm Agcy*
SEEK Inc., *Exec Srch*
Site Personnel Services/Trainor/Frank & Associates, Inc., *Temp Agcy*
Tom Sloan & Assoc., *Perm Agcy*

T.E.M. Associates, *Exec Srch*
Techstaff, *Perm Agcy*
U.S. Tech Force Inc., *Exec Srch*
Universal Design Corp., *Exec Srch*
The Waterstone Group, *Contract Svc*

Wyoming

Mngmt. Rcrtrs. of Cheyenne, *Exec Srch*

ENTERTAINMENT

California

BDP Mngmt. Consulting Grp, *Exec Srch*
Business Systems Support, *Perm Agcy*
Dunhill Exec. Search of L.A., *Exec Srch*
Executive Temps, *Temp Agcy*
Larkin Group, *Exec Srch*
Brad Marks International, *Exec Srch*

Florida

Manchester Inc., *Exec Srch*

Georgia

Executive Placement Svcs, *Perm Agcy*

Illinois

Mngmt. Rcrtrs. of Rockford, *Exec Srch*

Nevada

Career Dev. Assoc., *Exec Srch*

New Jersey

Huff Associates, *Exec Srch*

New York

Norman Broadbent Intnl., *Exec Srch*
Fanning Personnel, *Exec Srch*
Landover Associates, Inc., *Exec Srch*
StratfordGroup, *Exec Srch*

North Carolina

StratfordGroup, *Exec Srch*

Ohio

Richard Johns Career Conslt, *Perm Agcy*
StratfordGroup, *Exec Srch*

Oregon

Mesa International, *Exec Srch*

Pennsylvania

Manchester Inc., *Career/Outplacement*
StratfordGroup, *Exec Srch*

Texas

StratfordGroup, *Exec Srch*

Virginia

Norman Broadbent Intnl., *Exec Srch*

Washington

Strategic Resources, *Exec Srch*
StratfordGroup, *Exec Srch*

ENVIRONMENTAL

California

JPM International, *Exec Srch*
Kelly Scientific Resources, *Temp Agcy*

Colorado

ATA Staffing, *Temp Agcy*
The Bridge, *Exec Srch*
Kelly Scientific Resources, *Temp Agcy*

Connecticut

Management Search, *Exec Srch*

Dist. of Columbia

Goodwin & Company, *Exec Srch*

Florida

Environmental Health & Safety Search Associates (EH&S), *Exec Srch*

Georgia

Kelly Scientific Resources, *Temp Agcy*
Mngmt. Rcrtrs. of Savannah, *Exec Srch*

Illinois

Corporate Environment, Limited, *Exec Srch*

Maine

F-O-R-T-U-N-E Pers. Conslts of Bangor, *Exec Srch*
Recruiting Professionals, *Exec Srch*

Maryland

Kelly Scientific Resources, *Temp Agcy*

Massachusetts

Michael Anthony Associates, *Exec Srch*
Robert H. Davidson Assoc., *Exec Srch*

Derek Associates, *Exec Srch*
Executive Search NE, *Exec Srch*
Locke Assoc. Eng. Recruiters, *Exec Srch*

Michigan

Executive Recruiters Intnl., *Exec Srch*
Kelly Scientific Resources, *Temp Agcy*

Minnesota

EnviroStaff, Inc., *Temp Agcy*

Mississippi

The CPI Group, *Exec Srch*

Missouri

Kelly Scientific Resources, *Temp Agcy*

New Jersey

R.W. Apple & Associates, *Exec Srch*
Gary S. Bell Associates, *Exec Srch*
Robert Drexler Associates, *Exec Srch*
Huff Associates, *Exec Srch*
Kelly Scientific Resources, *Temp Agcy*
Rosenthal Assoc. Intnl., *Exec Srch*
Sales Conslt of Ocean, *Exec Srch*
Will-Cox Associates, *Exec Srch*

New Mexico

Butler Service Group, *Contract Svc*

New York

Rosenthal Assoc. Intnl., *Exec Srch*

North Carolina

Environmental Rec. Svcs., *Exec Srch*
Mark III Personnel Inc., *Exec Srch*

Ohio

North Peak Group, *Exec Srch*

Oklahoma

Holbrook Associates, *Exec Srch*

Oregon

Wolf Environmental Grp., *Exec Srch*

Pennsylvania

Jerry Goldberg & Assoc., *Perm Agcy*
Virtual Workplace, *Temp Agcy*

South Carolina

Engineering Pers. Network, *Exec Srch*

Texas

Kelly Scientific Resources, *Temp Agcy*
Pailin Grp. Prof. Srch Conslt., *Exec Srch*
Denis P. Walsh & Assoc., *Exec Srch*

Vermont

National Executive Search, *Exec Srch*

EXECUTIVES

Alaska

Alaska Executive Search, *Exec Srch*
Olsten Staffing Services, *Temp Agcy*

California

Battalia Winston Intnl., *Exec Srch*
Colt Sys. Prof. Pers. Services, *Perm Agcy*
Full Service Temporaries, *Temp Agcy*
Job Link Inc., *Exec Srch*
Kabl Ability Network, *Exec Srch*
Mixtec Group, *Exec Srch*
National Career Choices, *Exec Srch*
Rusher, Loscavio, & LoPresto, *Exec Srch*
Tax Exec. Search, *Exec Srch*

Colorado

Leading Edge Med. Search, *Exec Srch*

Connecticut

Dunhill of New Haven, *Perm Agcy*

Florida

Center for Career Decisions, *Career/ Outplacement*
PMC&L Associates, Inc., *Perm Agcy*

Georgia

B.A. Associates Inc., *Exec Srch*
Bell Oaks Company, *Exec Srch*
Boreham International, *Exec Srch*
The Diversified Search Cos., *Exec Srch*
National Restaurant Search, *Exec Srch*
Reeder & Associates, Ltd., *Exec Srch*
TriTech Associates, *Exec Srch*

Illinois

Battalia Winston Intnl., *Exec Srch*
Ronald B. Hanson & Assoc., *Exec Srch*

Star Personnel Service, *Exec Srch*
Temporary Accounting Pers., *Temp Agcy*
Todays Temporary, *Temp Agcy*
Two Degrees, *Exec Srch*
Woodmoor Group, *Exec Srch*

Connecticut

Ryan Abbott Search Assoc., *Exec Srch*
Access Financial, *Exec Srch*
Admiral Staffing Services, *Temp Agcy*
Advanced Placement Inc., *Temp Agcy*
Bohan & Bradstreet, *Perm Agcy*
Brandywine Retained Ventures, Inc., *Exec Srch*
Burke and Associates/The Westfield Group, *Exec Srch*
Buxbaum/Rink Consulting, *Exec Srch*
Thomas Byrne Associates, *Perm Agcy*
The Cambridge Group Ltd., *Exec Srch*
Corporate Staffing Solutions, *Temp Agcy*
Dunhill of New Haven, *Perm Agcy*
EDP Contract Services, *Contract Svc*
Executive Register Inc., *Exec Srch*
Financial Careers, *Exec Srch*
Financial Executive Search, *Exec Srch*
Robert Half Intl/Accountemps, *Exec Srch*
Harbor Associates, *Exec Srch*
Hipp Waters Prof. Search, *Exec Srch*
Impact Personnel, Inc., *Temp Agcy*
Intertec Personnel, *Temp Agcy*
Judlind Emp. Svcs., *Perm Agcy*
Mngmt. Rcrtrs. International, *Exec Srch*
McIntyre Associates, *Temp Agcy*
The McKnight Group, *Exec Srch*
Merry Emp. Group, *Perm Agcy*
Office Services of CT, *Perm Agcy*
PRH Management, Inc., *Exec Srch*
Paramount Resources, *Perm Agcy*
Pascale & LaMorte, LLC, *Exec Srch*
Barry Persky & Co., *Exec Srch*
Q.S.I., *Perm Agcy*
Resource Associates, *Perm Agcy*
Romac International, *Exec Srch*
Siger & Associates, LLC, *Exec Srch*
Howard W. Smith Assoc., *Exec Srch*
Strategic Executives, Inc., *Exec Srch*
Super Systems, Inc., *Exec Srch*
TMP Worldwide, *Exec Srch*
Velen Associates, *Perm Agcy*
Westaff, *Temp Agcy*
Workforce One, *Perm Agcy*
Bob Wright Recruiting, *Exec Srch*

Delaware

Caldwell Staffing Svcs., *Perm Agcy*
DW Technologies, *Contract Svc*
Elliott Davis & Associates, *Exec Srch*
J.B. Groner Exec. Search, *Exec Srch*
E.W. Hodges & Associates, *Exec Srch*
Personal Placements Inc., *Perm Agcy*
The Placers, Inc., *Temp Agcy*

Dist. of Columbia

Accountants Executive Search/ Accountants on Call, *Exec Srch*
ACSYS Staffing, *Exec Srch*
Career Blazers Pers. Service, *Perm Agcy*
GKA Resources, LLC, *Exec Srch*
Goodwin & Company, *Exec Srch*
NRI Legal Resources/NRI Accounting Resources, *Temp Agcy*
Norrell Services, *Temp Agcy*

Florida

AAA Employment, *Perm Agcy*
Able Body Corporate Svcs., *Contract Svc*
Accountants Express, *Perm Agcy*
Active Professionals, *Exec Srch*
Ash & Assoc. Exec. Search, *Exec Srch*
Availability, Inc., *Perm Agcy*
Balcor Associates, *Exec Srch*
Brickell Pers. Conslt, *Exec Srch*
Career Planners, Inc., *Perm Agcy*
Carrier's Career Service, Inc., *Career/Outplacement*
Corporate Advisors, Inc., *Exec Srch*
Corporate Search Conslt, *Exec Srch*
DGA Personnel Group, *Exec Srch*
Steven Douglas Associates, *Exec Srch*
Ethan Allen Pers. Placement, *Exec Srch*
Farwell Group Inc., *Exec Srch*
First Recruiters Group Inc., *Exec Srch*
Gimbel & Associates, *Exec Srch*
Global Tech. Resources, *Exec Srch*

Robert Half Intl/Accountemps, *Exec Srch*
Hastings & Hastings Personnel Conslt, *Temp Agcy*
Janus Career Services, *Perm Agcy*
R.H. Larsen & Associates, *Exec Srch*
Mngmt. Rcrtrs. International, *Exec Srch*
Mngmt. Rcrtrs. of Orlando/ Winter Park, *Exec Srch*
Mngmt. Rcrtrs. of St. Petersburg, *Exec Srch*
Mngmt. Rcrtrs. of Tallahassee, *Exec Srch*
Manchester Inc., *Exec Srch*
Office Specialists, *Temp Agcy*
Olsten Financial Staffing, *Temp Agcy*
Olsten Staffing Services, *Temp Agcy*
OMNIpartners, *Exec Srch*
Personnel Center, *Perm Agcy*
Priority Search, *Exec Srch*
Linda Robins & Assoc., *Temp Agcy*
Robinson & Associates, *Exec Srch*
Romac International, *Exec Srch*
Ropes Associates, Inc., *Exec Srch*
The Ryan Charles Group, *Exec Srch*
Sales Conslt of Fort Lauderdale, Inc., *Exec Srch*
Sanford Rose Associates, *Exec Srch*
Doug Sears & Associates, *Exec Srch*
Staffing Now, *Temp Agcy*
The Stewart Search Group, *Exec Srch*
Sun Personnel West, *Exec Srch*
Suncoast Group, *Perm Agcy*
TMP Worldwide, *Exec Srch*
Todays Temporary, *Temp Agcy*
Uniquest International, Inc., *Exec Srch*
Victoria & Assoc. Personnel Svcs., *Perm Agcy*

Georgia

A-OK Personnel, *Perm Agcy*
A.D. & Assoc. Exec. Search, *Exec Srch*
Accountants & Bookkeepers Personnel, *Exec Srch*
Accountants Executive Search/ Accountants On Call, *Exec Srch*
Accountants Inc., *Temp Agcy*
Michael Alexander Group, *Exec Srch*
Basilone-Oliver Exec. Search, *Exec Srch*
Bell Oaks Company, *Exec Srch*
The Bowers Group, Inc., *Exec Srch*
Bradshaw & Associates, *Exec Srch*
Business Prof. Group, *Perm Agcy*
Catalina Human Resources, *Perm Agcy*
Corporate Image Group, *Exec Srch*
Corporate Search Conslt, *Exec Srch*
The Diversified Search Cos., *Exec Srch*
Dunhill Prof. Search, *Exec Srch*
Elite Staffing Services, *Temp Agcy*
Executive Placement Svcs, *Perm Agcy*
Executive Resource Group, *Exec Srch*
Express Personnel Svcs., *Perm Agcy*
Fox-Morris Associates, *Exec Srch*
ISC of Atlanta/International Career Continuation, *Exec Srch*
Lowderman & Associates, *Exec Srch*
Lucas Group, *Exec Srch*
Mngmt. Rcrtrs. International, *Exec Srch*
More Personnel Services, *Perm Agcy*
New Boston Select, *Perm Agcy*
Olsten Staffing Services, *Temp Agcy*
PRI/Invesearch, *Exec Srch*
Perimeter Placement, *Exec Srch*
Priority 1 Staffing Svcs., *Temp Agcy*
Randstad Staffing Svcs., *Temp Agcy*
Don Richard Associates, *Exec Srch*
Romac International, *Exec Srch*
Sanford Rose Associates, *Exec Srch*
Southern Prof. Recruiters, *Exec Srch*
TMP Worldwide, *Exec Srch*
Toar Consulting, *Exec Srch*
TriTech Associates, *Exec Srch*
WPPS Software Staffing, *Temp Agcy*
Westaff, *Temp Agcy*

Hawaii

Dunhill Prof. Staffing of HI, *Exec Srch*
Executive Search World, *Exec Srch*
Management Search & Consulting, Inc., *Exec Srch*

Idaho

F-O-R-T-U-N-E Pers. Conslts, *Exec Srch*
Horne/Brown International, *Exec Srch*
Lost Dutchman Search, *Exec Srch*

Illinois

ASI (Access Search Inc.), *Exec Srch*
Account Pros, *Exec Srch*
Accountants Executive Search/ Accountants On Call, *Exec Srch*
Advanced Personnel, Inc., *Perm Agcy*
American Engineering Co., *Exec Srch*
Armstrong-Hamilton Assoc., *Exec Srch*
E.J. Ashton & Assoc., *Exec Srch*
Availability, Inc., *Perm Agcy*
The Bankers Group, *Exec Srch*
Banner Personnel Service, *Perm Agcy*
Barrett Partners, *Exec Srch*
Battalia Winston Intnl., *Exec Srch*
Bell Personnel Inc., *Perm Agcy*
Burling Group Ltd., *Exec Srch*
CFR Executive Search , *Exec Srch*
C.S. Global Partners, *Exec Srch*
CareerLink USA, Inc., *Exec Srch*
Carson Mngmt. Assoc., *Contract Svc*
Casey Services, Inc., *Perm Agcy*
CEMCO Ltd., *Exec Srch*
Chicago Financial Search, *Exec Srch*
D. Clesen Company, *Exec Srch*
Coffou Partners, Inc., *Exec Srch*
Cogan Personnel Svcs., *Exec Srch*
Computer Futures Exch., *Exec Srch*
Contemporary Services, *Exec Srch*
Diener & Associates Inc., *Exec Srch*
Dunhill Staffing Svcs., *Temp Agcy*
Eastman & Associates, *Exec Srch*
The Eastwood Group, *Exec Srch*
Elsko Executive Search, *Exec Srch*
The Esquire Staffing Grp., *Perm Agcy*
Eve Recruiters Ltd., *Perm Agcy*
Executive Directions, *Exec Srch*
Executive Fin. Conslt, *Exec Srch*
Executive Options Ltd., *Exec Srch*
Executive Placement Conslt, *Exec Srch*
Executive Referral Svcs., *Exec Srch*
Express Personnel Svcs., *Temp Agcy*
Fellows Placement, *Temp Agcy*
Financial Search Corp., *Exec Srch*
F-O-R-T-U-N-E Pers. Conslts, *Exec Srch*
Furst Staffing Services, *Temp Agcy*
General Emp. Enterprises, *Perm Agcy*
Gnodde Associates, *Exec Srch*
David Gomez & Assoc., *Exec Srch*
HKA Mortgage Staffing & Training, *Perm Agcy*
Robert Half Intl/Accountemps, *Exec Srch*
Human Resource Connection, *Perm Agcy*
IZS Executive Search, *Exec Srch*
Interim Financial Staffing, *Exec Srch*
Interim Personnel, *Contract Svc*
InterStaff, *Temp Agcy*
ITEX Executive Search, *Exec Srch*
Raymond Karson Assoc., *Exec Srch*
Kennedy & Company, *Exec Srch*
Kenneth Nicholas & Assoc., *Exec Srch*
Kenzer Corporation, *Exec Srch*
Kingsley Emp. Service, *Perm Agcy*
Kingston/Zak Inc., *Exec Srch*
Kunzer Associates, Ltd., *Exec Srch*
Arlene Leff & Associates, *Exec Srch*
Lyons & Associates, *Exec Srch*
Magnum Search, *Exec Srch*
Mngmt. Rcrtrs. International, *Exec Srch*
Mngmt. Rcrtrs./OfficeMates5, *Exec Srch*
Mngmt. Rcrtrs. of Elgin, Inc., *Exec Srch*
Michael David Associates, *Perm Agcy*
The Murphy Group, *Perm Agcy*
National Search, *Exec Srch*
OfficeMates5 (OM5), *Perm Agcy*
PS Inc., *Perm Agcy*
Parker Cromwell & Assoc., *Exec Srch*
Pratzer & Partners, *Exec Srch*
Profile Temp. Service, *Temp Agcy*
ProSearch Plus, *Exec Srch*
Remedy Intelligent Staffing, *Temp Agcy*
Right Services Inc., *Temp Agcy*
Romac International, *Exec Srch*
The Ryan Charles Group, *Exec Srch*
Sanford Rose Associates, *Exec Srch*
J.R. Scott & Associates, *Exec Srch*
Smith Hanley Associates, *Exec Srch*
Snelling Personnel Svcs., *Perm Agcy*
Snelling Search, *Exec Srch*
Stivers Temporary Personnel, *Temp Agcy*
Strategic Resources Unltd., *Exec Srch*
TMP Worldwide, *Exec Srch*
Roy Talman & Associates, *Exec Srch*

OfficeMates5 (OM5), *Exec Srch*
Pinnacle Executive Group, *Exec Srch*
Romac International, *Exec Srch*
Sales Recruiters, Inc., *Exec Srch*
Search Professionals, *Exec Srch*

Nebraska
Express Personnel, *Exec Srch*
Hansen Employment Svc., *Exec Srch*
Mngmt. Rcrtrs. International, *Exec Srch*
Outsource II, Inc., *Temp Agcy*
Reliable National Personnel Conslt, *Exec Srch*
Sales Conslt of Omaha, *Exec Srch*

Nevada
Accountants Inc., *Temp Agcy*
Flowers Exec. Search Grp., *Exec Srch*
Initial Staffing Services, *Perm Agcy*
The Resource Network, *Exec Srch*
Sales Staffing Specialists, *Perm Agcy*
StaffMark, *Perm Agcy*

New Hampshire
Able 1 Staffing, *Exec Srch*
Advanced Recruiting & Consulting, *Exec Srch*
Allstaff, *Perm Agcy*
Central NH Emp. Services, *Perm Agcy*
Cheshire Emp. Svc., *Temp Agcy*
Kelly Services, Inc., *Temp Agcy*
Mngmt. Rcrtrs. International, *Exec Srch*
National Emp. Svc. Corp., *Perm Agcy*
R.G.T. Associates, Inc., *Exec Srch*
Sales Conslt of Nashua-Manchester, *Exec Srch*
STAT Search, *Exec Srch*
Surge Resources Inc., *Contract Svc*
TAC Staffing Services, *Temp Agcy*
Venture Profiles Corp., *Exec Srch*

New Jersey
A+ Personnel Placement, *Perm Agcy*
A Professional Edge, *Career/Outplacement*
ABC Nationwide Emp., *Perm Agcy*
AES Group, *Exec Srch*
ALS Group, *Exec Srch*
Abbott Associates Inc., *Exec Srch*
Accountants Executive Search/Accountants On Call, *Exec Srch*
Advanced Personnel Svc., *Perm Agcy*
Raymond Alexander Assoc., *Perm Agcy*
Allen Associates, Inc., *Perm Agcy*
Allstaff Resources, Inc., *Perm Agcy*
Anderson Wright Assoc., *Exec Srch*
The Ascher Group, *Exec Srch*
BAI Personnel Solutions, *Perm Agcy*
Battalia Winston Intnl., *Exec Srch*
Blake & Assoc. Exec. Srch, *Exec Srch*
Bowman & Company LLP, *Exec Srch*
Career Center, Inc., *Perm Agcy*
Career Management Grp., *Exec Srch*
Career Management Intnl., *Exec Srch*
Careerworks, *Exec Srch*
Clark Davis Associates, *Exec Srch*
Cox Darrow & Owens, *Exec Srch*
Dunhill Professional Srch, *Exec Srch*
Ellis Career Conslt/Career Search Associates, *Exec Srch*
Executive Search, Inc., *Exec Srch*
Financial Accounting & Management, *Exec Srch*
Flextime Solutions, Inc., *Perm Agcy*
Foster Associates, *Exec Srch*
The Foster McKay Group, *Exec Srch*
Gibson Martin Consulting, *Exec Srch*
Sandra Grundfest, *Career/Outplacement*
Robert Half Intl/Accountemps, *Exec Srch*
Hinckley Associates, *Exec Srch*
The Howard Group, Ltd., *Exec Srch*
Hreshko Consulting Group, *Exec Srch*
Hughes & Podesla Pers., *Perm Agcy*
Impact Personnel, Inc., *Perm Agcy*
Insearch Inc., *Exec Srch*
Integro Staffing Services, *Temp Agcy*
Inter-Regional Exec. Srch, *Exec Srch*
Kelly Services, Inc., *Temp Agcy*
Joseph Keyes Associates, *Perm Agcy*
MJE Recruiters, Inc., *Exec Srch*
Major Conslt, *Exec Srch*
Mngmt. Rcrtrs./OfficeMates5, *Exec Srch*
Mngmt. Rcrtrs. of Bridgewater, *Exec Srch*

Mngmt. Rcrtrs. of Passaic County, *Exec Srch*
Mngmt. Rcrtrs. of Sparta, *Exec Srch*
Manpower Tech. Svcs., *Contract Svc*
McMahon Associates, *Exec Srch*
The Melville Group, Inc., *Exec Srch*
Diedre Moire Corporation, *Exec Srch*
Norrell Services, *Temp Agcy*
Northeastern Financial Conslt, *Exec Srch*
OfficeMates5 (OM5)/DayStar Temporary Services, *Perm Agcy*
Orion Consulting, Inc., *Exec Srch*
PLC Associates, *Exec Srch*
Solomon Page Group, Inc., *Exec Srch*
Park Avenue Personnel, *Perm Agcy*
The Pennmor Group, *Exec Srch*
Premier Personnel Group, *Perm Agcy*
Princeton Search Partners, *Exec Srch*
Ready Pers./Ready Temps, *Perm Agcy*
Remedy Intelligent Staffing, *Temp Agcy*
Jeff Rich Associates, *Exec Srch*
Romac International, *Exec Srch*
Rosenthal Assoc. Intnl., *Exec Srch*
Rylan Forbes Consulting Grp., *Exec Srch*
R.S. Sadow Associates, *Exec Srch*
Salem Associates, *Exec Srch*
Sales Conslt of Morris County, *Exec Srch*
Sales Conslt of Sparta, *Exec Srch*
Sanford Rose Associates, *Exec Srch*
Selective Personnel, *Perm Agcy*
Arline Simpson Assoc., *Perm Agcy*
SkuppSearch, Inc., *Exec Srch*
Snelling Personnel Svcs., *Perm Agcy*
The Staffing Group, *Exec Srch*
Stewart/Laurence Assoc., *Exec Srch*
Temporary Excellence, *Temp Agcy*
Thomas & Associates, *Exec Srch*
Trout Associates, Inc., *Exec Srch*
Tucker Associates, *Exec Srch*
UNITEMP Temp. Pers., *Temp Agcy*
J. Vincent Associates, *Exec Srch*
J. White & Company, *Exec Srch*
Winston Staffing Services, *Temp Agcy*
Winters & Ross, *Perm Agcy*
Claire Wright Associates, *Perm Agcy*
Michael D. Zinn & Assoc., *Exec Srch*

New Mexico
Albuquerque Personnel, *Perm Agcy*
CDI Technical Services, *Contract Svc*
Creative Financial Staffing, *Exec Srch*
Excel Staffing Companies, *Perm Agcy*
Snelling Search, *Exec Srch*

New York
A-L Associates, Inc., *Exec Srch*
AJC Search, *Exec Srch*
Accountants Executive Search/Accountants On Call, *Exec Srch*
Accounting & Computer Personnel, *Perm Agcy*
AccuStaff Incorporated, *Temp Agcy*
Merrill Adams Assoc., *Career/Outplacement*
Adecco, *Temp Agcy*
Advantage Resumes of NY, *Career/Outplacement*
Advice Personnel, *Exec Srch*
Alite Associates, Inc., *Exec Srch*
Franklin Allen Conslt, *Exec Srch*
AMESgroup, *Exec Srch*
Analytic Recruiting Inc., *Exec Srch*
Asher Pers. Conslt, *Perm Agcy*
Auto Careers, *Perm Agcy*
Bartl & Evins, *Exec Srch*
Battalia Winston Intnl., *Exec Srch*
Benson Associates, *Exec Srch*
Bevan Resources, *Perm Agcy*
Bevlin Personnel Inc., *Perm Agcy*
Branthover Associates, *Exec Srch*
Norman Broadbent Intnl., *Exec Srch*
E.E. Brooke Inc., *Exec Srch*
Brookville Staffing Svcs., *Perm Agcy*
CK Resources, *Exec Srch*
Career Blazers Pers. Svc., *Perm Agcy*
Career Concepts, Inc., *Perm Agcy*
Carlile Personnel Agency, *Perm Agcy*
Chriss Careers Ltd., *Exec Srch*
Compu-Tech Personnel, *Exec Srch*
Concorde Search, *Perm Agcy*
Conspectus Inc., *Exec Srch*
The Cornell Group, *Exec Srch*
Corporate Careers, Inc., *Exec Srch*

Corporate Search Inc., *Exec Srch*
Cromwell Partners Inc., *Exec Srch*
D&L Associates, Inc., *Exec Srch*
Dapexs Conslt Inc., *Exec Srch*
The Denison Group, *Exec Srch*
Seth Diamond Associates, *Exec Srch*
Drummond Associates, *Exec Srch*
EDP Contract Services, *Contract Svc*
ETR Technology Center, *Exec Srch*
Eden Staffing, *Perm Agcy*
Irwin Edwards Recruiters, *Exec Srch*
Alexander Edwards Intnl., *Exec Srch*
Mark Elzweig Company, *Exec Srch*
Employment Recruiters Agency, *Perm Agcy*
The Employment Store/TES Technical, *Exec Srch*
Euromoed, Inc., *Temp Agcy*
Execu/Search Group, *Exec Srch*
Executive Image, *Exec Srch*
Executive Resources Ltd., *Exec Srch*
Executive Search Conslt International, *Exec Srch*
Fanning Personnel, *Exec Srch*
Filcro Personnel, *Perm Agcy*
C.R. Fletcher Associates, *Exec Srch*
Forray Associates, Inc., *Exec Srch*
Forum Temporary Svcs., *Temp Agcy*
Frontrunner Search, Ltd., *Exec Srch*
GT Solutions, Inc., *Exec Srch*
Gardiner, Townsend & Assoc., *Exec Srch*
Gruen Resources, Inc., *Exec Srch*
Gundersen Partners L.L.C., *Exec Srch*
The Haas Associates, Inc., *Exec Srch*
Haesloop and Hegarty, *Temp Agcy*
Headway Corp. Staffing, *Perm Agcy*
Hessel Associates, Inc., *Exec Srch*
The Horizon Group, *Exec Srch*
Hudson Search Conslt, *Exec Srch*
Hunter Mac & Associates, *Perm Agcy*
Hunter Placement Inc., *Exec Srch*
Interspace Interactive Inc., *Exec Srch*
Ivana Legal Services, Inc., *Exec Srch*
KLK Personnel, *Perm Agcy*
KPA Staffing Group, Inc., *Exec Srch*
A.T. Kearney Inc., *Exec Srch*
Kingsbury Wax Bova, *Exec Srch*
Fred Koffler Associates, *Exec Srch*
Kramer Exec. Resources, *Exec Srch*
Ktech Systems Group, *Perm Agcy*
Lake Associates, *Exec Srch*
Landover Associates, Inc., *Exec Srch*
Tina Lane Personnel, Inc., *Perm Agcy*
John Lawrence & Assoc., *Exec Srch*
Lloyd Staffing, *Perm Agcy*
M.B. Inc. Exec. Search, *Exec Srch*
The MVP Group, *Exec Srch*
Magill Associates, Inc., *Exec Srch*
Joseph T. Maloney and Associates, Inc., *Perm Agcy*
Mngmt. Rcrtrs. International, *Exec Srch*
Manpower Temp. Svcs., *Temp Agcy*
Mar-El Emp. Agency, *Exec Srch*
Marcus & Associates, *Exec Srch*
Maximum Management, *Exec Srch*
McLaughlin Resources, *Exec Srch*
Milazzo Associates, Inc., *Perm Agcy*
Morgan-Murray Personnel/M&M Top Temps, *Temp Agcy*
Mortgage Pers of America, *Perm Agcy*
Neal Management, Inc., *Exec Srch*
New York-New York Pers., *Exec Srch*
Noah Associates, *Perm Agcy*
Norrell Staffing Services, *Temp Agcy*
K.A. Nowack Career Specialists, *Perm Agcy*
Olsten Financial Staffing, *Temp Agcy*
Olsten Staffing Services, *Temp Agcy*
Optimal Resources, *Exec Srch*
OTEC Inc., *Perm Agcy*
Parker Clark Executive Recruitment, *Exec Srch*
The Parks Group Inc., *Exec Srch*
Parsons, Anderson & Gee, *Perm Agcy*
Pathway Executive Search, *Exec Srch*
Paywise Inc., *Temp Agcy*
Peak Search Inc., *Exec Srch*
Pendleton James Assoc., *Exec Srch*
Personnel Consulting Assoc., *Exec Srch*
P.G. Prager Search Assoc., *Exec Srch*
Pro Search Associates, Inc., *Exec Srch*
Quest Organization, *Exec Srch*

Accounting Action Pers., *Perm Agcy*
ACSYS Staffing, *Temp Agcy*
Action Personnel Inc., *Temp Agcy*
Agri-Associates, *Exec Srch*
American Resources, *Exec Srch*
Audit Professionals Intnl., *Exec Srch*
Marilyn Austin & Associates Personnel
  Services, *Exec Srch*
Aware Affiliates Pers., *Perm Agcy*
B.G.A. & Associates, *Exec Srch*
Babich & Associates, Inc., *Perm Agcy*
Baldwin & Company, *Exec Srch*
R. Gaines Baty Assoc., *Exec Srch*
Best/World Associates, *Exec Srch*
Borrel Personnel, *Exec Srch*
Brainpower Pers. Agency, *Perm Agcy*
Bridge Personnel, *Exec Srch*
Brooklea & Associates, *Exec Srch*
Bullock Personnel, Inc., *Perm Agcy*
Colvin Resources Group, *Perm Agcy*
Dallas Employment Svcs., *Perm Agcy*
The Danbrook Group, *Exec Srch*
Gail Darling Staffing/Gail Darling's
  Professional Desk, *Temp Agcy*
Dividend Staffing Svcs., *Temp Agcy*
Dunhill Professional Srch, *Exec Srch*
The Exec. Consulting Group, *Exec Srch*
Express Personnel Svcs., *Perm Agcy*
Financial Professionals, *Perm Agcy*
Financial Srch Conslt, *Exec Srch*
Gulco Intnl. Recruiting Svcs., *Perm Agcy*
Robert Half International/RHI Mngmt.
  Resources, *Exec Srch*
Hedman & Associates, *Exec Srch*
Herndon & Associates, *Exec Srch*
Imprimis Staff Solutions, *Temp Agcy*
InterSearch Associates, *Temp Agcy*
Kane & Associates, Inc., *Exec Srch*
Kelly Services, Inc., *Temp Agcy*
George Lehman Associates, *Exec Srch*
Lehman McLeskey, *Exec Srch*
Lucas Financial Staffing, *Exec Srch*
The Lucas Group, *Perm Agcy*
Mngmt. Rcrtrs. International, *Exec Srch*
McKinley-AREND Intl., *Exec Srch*
Norrell Services, *Temp Agcy*
Odell & Associates Inc., *Exec Srch*
The Pailin Group Professional Search
  Conslt, *Exec Srch*
Pate Resources Group, *Exec Srch*
Rick Peterson & Assoc., *Exec Srch*
Priority Search, Inc., *Exec Srch*
Pro Staff Personnel Svcs., *Temp Agcy*
Professional Search Conslt (PSC),
  Contract Svc
Resource Connection Workforce Center,
  Perm Agcy
Resource Staffing, *Temp Agcy*
Bart Roberson & Company, *Exec Srch*
Romac International, *Exec Srch*
Roth Young Exec. Search, *Exec Srch*
Salinas & Assoc. Pers Svc., *Exec Srch*
Staff Extension Intnl., *Exec Srch*
Steinfield & Associates, *Exec Srch*
StratfordGroup, *Exec Srch*
TGA Company, *Exec Srch*
TMP Worldwide, *Exec Srch*
Betty Tanner Exec. Search, *Exec Srch*
Technical Alliance Recruiters, *Exec Srch*
The Urban Placement Svc., *Exec Srch*
Dick Van Vliet & Assoc., *Exec Srch*
Vinson and Associates, *Perm Agcy*
Wheeler, Moore & Elam, *Exec Srch*
Bruce G. Woods Exec Srch, *Exec Srch*

Utah
Robert Half Intl/Accountemps, *Exec Srch*
Intermountain Staffing Resources, *Temp
  Agcy*
Mngmt. Rcrtrs. of Salt Lake City, *Exec
  Srch*
Professional Recruiters, *Exec Srch*
Romac International, *Exec Srch*

Vermont
Dunhill Search of Vermont, *Exec Srch*
Mngmt. Rcrtrs. of Burlington, *Exec Srch*
Candis Perrault Associates, *Exec Srch*
Personnel Department, *Temp Agcy*
Voll Associates, *Exec Srch*

Virginia
Ability Resources, Inc., *Exec Srch*

Accountants Executive Search/
  Accountants On Call, *Temp Agcy*
ACSYS Inc., *Exec Srch*
The Alexis Group, Inc., *Exec Srch*
Nancy Allen Associates, *Perm Agcy*
Alpha Omega Resources, *Perm Agcy*
Norman Broadbent Intnl., *Exec Srch*
Buckler Careers, Inc., *Perm Agcy*
Christian & Timbers, Inc., *Exec Srch*
Contec Search, Inc., *Exec Srch*
Corporate Connection Ltd., *Exec Srch*
Dow Personnel, *Perm Agcy*
Durill & Associates, *Exec Srch*
Effective Staffing Inc., *Exec Srch*
Financial Connections, *Exec Srch*
Flores Financial Service, *Exec Srch*
F-O-R-T-U-N-E Pers. Conslts, *Exec Srch*
Wayne Garber & Assoc., *Exec Srch*
Haslowe Personnel, *Exec Srch*
Interim Financial Solutions/
  StratfordGroup, *Exec Srch*
Lee Staffing Resources, *Exec Srch*
Mngmt. Rcrtrs. International, *Exec Srch*
Norrell Services, *Temp Agcy*
Paul-Tittle Associates, Inc., *Exec Srch*
Professional Search Pers., *Exec Srch*
Romac International, *Exec Srch*
Search Connection, *Exec Srch*
Snelling Personnel Svcs., *Perm Agcy*
The Talley Group, *Exec Srch*
Telesec Corestaff, *Temp Agcy*
TempWorld Staffing Svcs, *Temp Agcy*

Washington
Able Personnel Agency, *Perm Agcy*
Accountants Inc., *Temp Agcy*
Accounting Partners, *Exec Srch*
Accounting Quest, *Exec Srch*
Kim Finch Cook Exec Rec., *Exec Srch*
Guidance Services Inc., *Temp Agcy*
Houser Martin Morris, *Exec Srch*
Kelly Services, Inc., *Temp Agcy*
Lawrence & Associates, *Exec Srch*
Mngmt. Rcrtrs. of Spokane, *Exec Srch*
Mngmt. Rcrtrs. of Tacoma, *Exec Srch*
Management Solutions, *Exec Srch*
John Mason & Associates, *Exec Srch*
Morgan Palmer Morgan & Hill, *Exec
  Srch*
Orion Resources, *Exec Srch*
Parker Professional Search, *Exec Srch*
Personnel Unlimited Inc., *Exec Srch*
Romac International, *Exec Srch*
Barbara Ruhl & Associates, *Exec Srch*
Wilson Smith Associates, *Exec Srch*
Snelling Personnel Svcs., *Exec Srch*
StratfordGroup, *Exec Srch*

West Virginia
Extra Support Staffing, *Temp Agcy*
Key Personnel, Inc., *Perm Agcy*

Wisconsin
ABR Employment Svcs., *Perm Agcy*
Benston & Associates, *Exec Srch*
Career Resources, *Exec Srch*
Careertrac Emp. Svcs., *Exec Srch*
Crown Services, *Temp Agcy*
Dieck Mueller Group, *Exec Srch*
J.M. Eagle Partners, *Exec Srch*
Executive Resource Inc., *Exec Srch*
Financial Mngmt. Pers., *Exec Srch*
Flores Financial Services, *Exec Srch*
Fogec Conslt, Inc., *Exec Srch*
Geneva Financial Group, *Exec Srch*
Mngmt. Rcrtrs. International, *Exec Srch*
Olsten Staffing Services, *Temp Agcy*
Placements of Racine Inc., *Perm Agcy*
Romac International, *Exec Srch*
TMP Worldwide, *Exec Srch*

FOOD

Alabama
Labor Finders, *Temp Agcy*
Mngmt. Rcrtrs. International, *Exec Srch*
WorkForce Enterprises, *Temp Agcy*

Alaska
Alaska Dept. of Labor and Workforce
  Development, *Perm Agcy*

Arizona
Amer. Career Grp, *Career/Outplacement*

Executemps, Inc., *Exec Srch*
FoodStaff 2000, Inc., *Exec Srch*
Mngmt. Rcrtrs. of Scottsdale, *Exec Srch*
Weinman & Associates, *Exec Srch*

Arkansas
Mngmt. Rcrtrs., *Exec Srch*

California
Alpha-Net Consulting Grp, *Exec Srch*
Apple One Emp. Svcs., *Perm Agcy*
BSA Personnel Center, *Perm Agcy*
Biosource Technical Svc., *Contract Svc*
The Black Leopard, *Exec Srch*
Bristol Associates, *Exec Srch*
California Search Agency, *Exec Srch*
Career Advantage, *Exec Srch*
Career Quest Intnl., *Contract Svc*
Coast To Coast Exec. Srch, *Exec Srch*
Marlene Critchfield Co., *Perm Agcy*
Crossroads Staffing Svc., *Temp Agcy*
Culver Personnel Services, *Perm Agcy*
Culver Staffing Resources, *Temp Agcy*
Dunhill Professional Srch, *Exec Srch*
Ethos Consulting, Inc., *Exec Srch*
Finesse Personnel Assoc., *Exec Srch*
Fisher Pers. Mngmt Svcs, *Exec Srch*
Fresquez and Associates, *Exec Srch*
Garnett Staffing, *Temp Agcy*
Gorelick & Associates, *Exec Srch*
Griffith & Associates, *Exec Srch*
Hollander Horizon Intnl., *Exec Srch*
Fred L. Hood & Associates, *Exec Srch*
Interim Personnel, *Temp Agcy*
Kelly Scientific Resources, *Temp Agcy*
John Kurosky & Assoc., *Exec Srch*
Lab Support Inc./Healthcare Financial
  Staffing, *Temp Agcy*
Mngmt. Rcrtrs. International, *Exec Srch*
Mesa International, *Exec Srch*
Mixtec Group, *Exec Srch*
M.O.R.E. Emp. Svcs., *Perm Agcy*
National Hospitality Recs., *Exec Srch*
Nesco Service Company, *Perm Agcy*
Ortman Recruiting Intnl., *Exec Srch*
Pacific Search Group, *Exec Srch*
Resource Perspectives, Inc., *Exec Srch*
Riley-Cole, *Exec Srch*
Royal Staffing Services, *Exec Srch*
Avery Schlueter Ex. Srch, *Exec Srch*
Search West, *Exec Srch*
Search West of Ontario, *Exec Srch*
Steinbrun Hughes & Assoc., *Exec Srch*
Thor Temporary Services, *Temp Agcy*
Triple-J Services, *Exec Srch*
Unisearch, *Exec Srch*
United Staffing Solutions, *Exec Srch*
Your People Professionals, *Perm Agcy*

Colorado
Chuck's Contract Labor, *Contract Svc*
Dunhill Personnel, *Exec Srch*
Executives By Sterling, *Exec Srch*
Hallmark Personnel Syst., *Exec Srch*
Info Syst. Consulting, *Exec Srch*
JobSearch, *Temp Agcy*
Kelly Scientific Resources, *Temp Agcy*
Mngmt. Rcrtrs. of Colorado Springs,
  Exec Srch
National Affirmative Action Career
  Network, Inc., *Exec Srch*
SOS Staffing Services, *Temp Agcy*
Sales Conslt, *Exec Srch*
TPM Staffing Service, *Perm Agcy*
Woodmoor Group, *Exec Srch*
Woodstone Consulting Co., *Exec Srch*

Connecticut
Admiral Staffing Services, *Temp Agcy*
Employment Opps., *Perm Agcy*
Mngmt. Rcrtrs. of Norwalk, *Exec Srch*
Office Services of CT, *Perm Agcy*
Barry Persky & Co., *Exec Srch*
Quality Control Recruiters, *Exec Srch*
Snyder & Company, *Exec Srch*
Bob Wright Recruiting, *Exec Srch*
Yankee Hospitality Search, *Exec Srch*

Delaware
The Placers, Inc., *Temp Agcy*
Wilmington Senior Center/Employment
  Services, *Perm Agcy*

Florida
AAA Employment, *Perm Agcy*

Accounting & Computer Personnel, *Perm Agcy*
Merrill Adams Associates, *Career/Outplacement*
Adecco, *Temp Agcy*
Alfus Group, *Exec Srch*
Franklin Allen Conslt, *Exec Srch*
Beishline Executive Search, *Exec Srch*
Bornholdt Shivas & Friends, *Exec Srch*
Corporate Careers, Inc., *Exec Srch*
Eden Staffing, *Perm Agcy*
Elliot Associates Inc., *Exec Srch*
The Kay Grp. of 5th Ave., *Exec Srch*
Lab Support Inc., *Temp Agcy*
John Lawrence & Assoc., *Exec Srch*
Lloyd Staffing, *Perm Agcy*
Mngmt. Rcrtrs. of Orange Cty, *Exec Srch*
Mngmt. Rcrtrs. of Upper Westchester, Inc., *Exec Srch*
Marshall-Alan Associates, *Exec Srch*
Metropolitan Pers. Syst., *Exec Srch*
Mickler Associates Inc., *Exec Srch*
Morgan-Murray Personnel/M&M Top Temps, *Temp Agcy*
Olsten Financial Staffing, *Temp Agcy*
Parsons, Anderson & Gee , *Perm Agcy*
Phoenix Emp. Agency, *Perm Agcy*
Remedy Intelligent Staffing, *Temp Agcy*
Roth Young of Long Island, *Exec Srch*
Sales Conslt, *Exec Srch*
Stafkings Personnel Syst., *Temp Agcy*
Superior Concepts, *Contract Svc*
Trebor, Weldon, Lawrence, Levine, *Exec Srch*
Weber Mngmt Conslt, *Exec Srch*
Westaff, *Temp Agcy*

North Carolina
Forbes Temp. Staffing, *Temp Agcy*
F-O-R-T-U-N-E Pers. Conslts of Raleigh, Inc., *Perm Agcy*
Interim Personnel, Inc., *Temp Agcy*
Linden Group Inc., *Exec Srch*
Mngmt. Rcrtrs. International, *Exec Srch*
Sales Conslt, *Exec Srch*
Waddy R. Thomson Assoc., *Exec Srch*
USA Staffing, *Perm Agcy*
Winston Personnel Group, *Temp Agcy*

North Dakota
Olsten Staffing Services/Expressway Personnel, *Temp Agcy*

Ohio
Adecco, *Temp Agcy*
Adecco/TAD Tech. Svcs, *Contract Svc*
Choice Personnel/LaGrange & Associates, *Exec Srch*
Continental Search Assoc., *Exec Srch*
J.D. Cotter Search, Inc., *Exec Srch*
Alan N. Daum & Assoc., *Perm Agcy*
Eastern Personnel Svcs, *Perm Agcy*
Executive Connection, *Exec Srch*
Graduate Conslt, *Perm Agcy*
Griffiths & Associates, *Exec Srch*
Ives & Associates, Inc., *Exec Srch*
Mngmt. Rcrtrs. International, *Exec Srch*
Professional Restaffing of OH, *Perm Agcy*
Sales Conslt, *Exec Srch*
Tabb & Associates, *Exec Srch*
The Target HR Cos., *Temp Agcy*
Temporarily Yours Placement, *Temp Agcy*

Oklahoma
Ameri Resource, *Exec Srch*
Express Personnel Services, *Exec Srch*
Food Manufacturing Conslt, *Exec Srch*
Mngmt. Rcrtrs. International, *Exec Srch*

Oregon
Express Personnel Services, *Exec Srch*
Mngmt. Rcrtrs./OfficeMates5, *Exec Srch*
Sanford Rose Associates, *Exec Srch*
Smith & Laue, *Exec Srch*

Pennsylvania
American Search Assoc., *Exec Srch*
Atomic Personnel, Inc., *Exec Srch*
Caliber Associates, *Exec Srch*
Career Concepts Staff Svcs., *Exec Srch*
Charley's Personnel Staffing, *Temp Agcy*
CoreStaff Inc., *Temp Agcy*
J. Croyle & Associates, *Perm Agcy*

Eden & Associates, Inc., *Exec Srch*
HRS/TND Associates, Inc., *Exec Srch*
The Hastings Group, *Exec Srch*
Hire Solutions, *Exec Srch*
Hospitality Services, *Perm Agcy*
J-Rand Search, *Exec Srch*
M.K. & Associates, *Exec Srch*
Mngmt. Rcrtrs./CompuSearch, *Exec Srch*
Mngmt. Rcrtrs. of West Chester, Inc., *Exec Srch*
Manchester Inc., *Career/Outplacement*
Norcon Associates, Inc., *Exec Srch*
Olsten Staffing Services, *Temp Agcy*
Pittsburgh Placement Svc, *Perm Agcy*
R.H.A. Exec. Pers. Services, *Exec Srch*
Rice Cohen International, *Exec Srch*
Spectrum Conslt, Inc./Retail Recruiters, *Exec Srch*
TRC Staffing Services, *Temp Agcy*
Uni-Temp Temp. Svc., *Temp Agcy*
United Employment, *Perm Agcy*
Whittlesey & Associates, *Exec Srch*
Yorktowne Personnel, *Exec Srch*

Rhode Island
Albert G. Lee & Assoc., *Exec Srch*
Lybrook Associates, Inc., *Exec Srch*
Mngmt. Rcrtrs. International, *Exec Srch*
Norrell Services, *Temp Agcy*

South Carolina
Accel Temporary Svcs., *Temp Agcy*
Mngmt. Rcrtrs. of Columbia, *Exec Srch*
Mngmt. Rcrtrs. of Rock Hill, *Exec Srch*
Smith Temps/Smith Pers., *Temp Agcy*

South Dakota
Agra Placements, Ltd., *Exec Srch*
Careers Unlimited, *Perm Agcy*
Mngmt. Rcrtrs. of Sioux Falls, *Exec Srch*

Tennessee
A-1 Staffing & Personnel, *Temp Agcy*
Amenity Staffing, *Temp Agcy*
Engineer One, Inc., *Perm Agcy*
Mngmt. Rcrtrs./Sales Conslt, *Exec Srch*
Manpower, Inc., *Temp Agcy*
W.R. McLeod & Assoc., *Exec Srch*
Personnel Link, *Exec Srch*
Quest International, *Exec Srch*

Texas
Ackerman Johnson Inc., *Exec Srch*
Agri-Associates, *Exec Srch*
American Resources, *Exec Srch*
Best/World Associates, *Exec Srch*
Butler International, *Contract Svc*
Corporate Search Inc., *Exec Srch*
Craig Search, *Exec Srch*
DKS & Associates, *Exec Srch*
Dunhill Professional Srch, *Exec Srch*
Executive Search Intnl., *Exec Srch*
Express Personnel Svcs., *Perm Agcy*
FoodPro Recruiters, Inc., *Exec Srch*
Abel M. Gonzalez & Assoc., *Exec Srch*
Info Syst. Consulting, *Exec Srch*
Kelly Scientific Resources, *Temp Agcy*
Kenzer Corporation, *Exec Srch*
Link Staffing Services, *Temp Agcy*
Mngmt. Rcrtrs. International, *Exec Srch*
McKinley-AREND Intnl., *Exec Srch*
The Pailin Group Professional Search Conslt, *Exec Srch*
Pate Resources Group, *Exec Srch*
Phoenix Staffing/G&A Staff Sourcing, *Exec Srch*
Resource Connection Workforce Center, *Perm Agcy*
Restaurant Servers, Inc., *Temp Agcy*
Bart Roberson & Company, *Exec Srch*
Roth Young Exec. Search, *Exec Srch*
Sales Conslt, *Exec Srch*
Search Network Intnl., *Exec Srch*
Select Staff, *Exec Srch*
Snelling Personnel Svcs., *Perm Agcy*
The Urban Placement Svc., *Exec Srch*
Windsor Conslt Inc., *Exec Srch*

Utah
Mngmt. Rcrtrs./Sales Conslt, *Exec Srch*

Vermont
Triad Temporary Services, *Temp Agcy*

Virginia
A La Carte International, *Exec Srch*

Alpha Omega Resources, *Perm Agcy*
Curran Associates, *Exec Srch*
Dow Personnel, *Perm Agcy*
Executive Recruiters, *Exec Srch*
Hispanic Committee of VA, *Perm Agcy*
Kincannon & Reed, *Exec Srch*
Kogen Personnel, *Exec Srch*
Lee Staffing Resources, *Exec Srch*
Mngmt. Rcrtrs./OfficeMates5, *Exec Srch*
Norrell Services, *Temp Agcy*
Search & Recruit Intnl., *Exec Srch*
Snelling Personnel Svcs., *Perm Agcy*
Souder & Associates, *Exec Srch*
The Talley Group, *Exec Srch*
Lawrence Veber Assoc., *Exec Srch*

Washington
The Career Clinic, Inc., *Exec Srch*
Express Personnel Svcs., *Temp Agcy*
Hospitality Emp. Service, *Perm Agcy*
Kelly Services, Inc., *Temp Agcy*
Mngmt. Rcrtrs. of Seattle, *Exec Srch*
Mngmt. Rcrtrs. of Tacoma, *Exec Srch*
Personnel Unlimited Inc., *Exec Srch*
Roth Young Exec. Srch, *Exec Srch*
Strategic Resources, *Exec Srch*
Villeneuve Associates, Inc., *Exec Srch*
Whittall Management Group, *Exec Srch*
Woodruff Associates, *Exec Srch*

West Virginia
Kelly Services, Inc., *Temp Agcy*
Key Personnel, Inc., *Perm Agcy*

Wisconsin
EnviroStaff, Inc., *Temp Agcy*
Fogec Conslt, Inc., *Exec Srch*
Food & Drug Pros, *Perm Agcy*
FoodStaff 2000, Inc., *Exec Srch*
Kordus Consulting Group, *Exec Srch*
Mngmt. Rcrtrs./Sales Conslt, *Exec Srch*
Recruiting Resources Inc., *Exec Srch*
Roth Young Exec. Search, *Exec Srch*
Sales Specialists, Inc., *Exec Srch*
Sauve Company, Ltd., *Perm Agcy*
Tom Sloan & Associates, *Perm Agcy*

Wyoming
The Employment Place, *Perm Agcy*

GENERAL LABOR

Alaska
Chugach North Tech. Svc., *Temp Agcy*

California
Complete Staffing Resources, *Perm Agcy*
Pyramid Placement, *Perm Agcy*
Wollborg-Michelson Pers., *Perm Agcy*

Colorado
Aspen Personnel Services, *Perm Agcy*
Chuck's Contract Labor, *Contract Svc*

Florida
Able Body Corp. Svcs., *Contract Svc*

Hawaii
ASAP Express, *Contract Svc*

Maryland
Adecco, *Temp Agcy*

Massachusetts
Pendleton James Assoc., *Exec Srch*

New York
Pendleton James Assoc., *Exec Srch*

North Carolina
StaffMark, *Temp Agcy*

Ohio
Belcan Staffing Services, *Temp Agcy*

Oklahoma
StaffMark, *Temp Agcy*

Texas
Esprit Temporary Svcs., *Temp Agcy*
Oficina de Empleos, Inc., *Perm Agcy*

Vermont
The Personnel Connection, *Temp Agcy*

Virginia
Taskforce of VA/PRG - Professional Resources Group, *Exec Srch*

West Virginia
Kelly Services, Inc., *Temp Agcy*

GENERAL MANAGEMENT

Alabama
F-O-R-T-U-N-E Pers. Conslts, *Exec Srch*
Healthcare Recruiters of AL, *Exec Srch*
Mngmt. Rcrtrs. International, *Exec Srch*
Sanford Rose Assoc., *Exec Srch*
VIP Personnel, Inc., *Perm Agcy*

Arizona
Amer. Career Grp, *Career/Outplacement*
Andrews, Stevens & Associates, *Contract Svc*
COMFORCE Tech. Svcs., *Contract Svc*
Construction Secretaries, *Perm Agcy*
Dealer Connection, *Perm Agcy*
Fishel HR Assoc., *Exec Srch*
Kerry's Referrals, *Perm Agcy*
Mngmt. Rcrtrs. of Scottsdale, *Exec Srch*
Spectra International, *Exec Srch*

Arkansas
Mngmt. Rcrtrs., *Exec Srch*
Moore & Associates, *Exec Srch*
Premier Staffing, Inc., *Temp Agcy*
Sanford Rose Associates, *Exec Srch*
Snelling Search, *Exec Srch*
Turnage Emp. Svc. Grp., *Exec Srch*
Utopia, Inc., *Exec Srch*

California
A.S.A.P. Emp. Svc., *Perm Agcy*
AW Data Processing Pers., *Perm Agcy*
Affordable Exec. Recruiters, *Exec Srch*
Allied Search, Inc., *Exec Srch*
Alpha-Net Consulting Grp, *Exec Srch*
Answers Unlimited, *Temp Agcy*
Apple One Emp. Svcs, *Perm Agcy*
Apropos Emp. Agency, *Perm Agcy*
Astra West Pers. Svcs., *Perm Agcy*
Bsa Personnel Center, *Perm Agcy*
The Badger Group, *Exec Srch*
Harvey Bell & Associates, *Exec Srch*
Bennett & Company Consulting Group, *Exec Srch*
Bialla and Associates, Inc., *Exec Srch*
Blue, Garni & Company, *Exec Srch*
Bradford Staff, Inc., *Temp Agcy*
BridgeGate LLC, *Exec Srch*
Brooks Associates, *Exec Srch*
Bullis & Company, Inc., *Exec Srch*
Business Systems Support, *Perm Agcy*
California Search Agency, *Exec Srch*
Career Quest Intnl., *Contract Svc*
Corestaff Services, *Perm Agcy*
Marlene Critchfield Co., *Perm Agcy*
Crossroads Staffing Svc., *Temp Agcy*
The Culver Group, *Exec Srch*
Culver Personnel Services, *Perm Agcy*
Culver Staffing Resources, *Temp Agcy*
Desert Personnel Service, Inc./Desert Temps, *Perm Agcy*
Robert W. Dingman Co., *Exec Srch*
Douglas Personnel Assoc., *Exec Srch*
Drake Office Overload, *Temp Agcy*
Dunhill of San Francisco, *Exec Srch*
Ethos Consulting, Inc., *Exec Srch*
Express Personnel Svcs., *Temp Agcy*
Finesse Personnel Assoc., *Exec Srch*
Fisher & Associates, *Exec Srch*
Fisher Pers. Mngmt. Svcs, *Exec Srch*
F-O-R-T-U-N-E Pers. Conslts, *Exec Srch*
Fresquez and Associates, *Exec Srch*
Garnett Staffing, *Temp Agcy*
Dianne Gauger & Assoc., *Exec Srch*
Global Resources Ltd., *Exec Srch*
Goldstein & Associates, *Temp Agcy*
Gorelick & Associates, *Exec Srch*
Gould Personnel Services, *Perm Agcy*
Grant & Associates, *Exec Srch*
Herrerias & Associates, *Exec Srch*
Interactive Search Network, *Exec Srch*
Interim Personnel, *Temp Agcy*
Jerome & Company, *Exec Srch*
JAA Employment Agency, *Perm Agcy*
John Anthony & Assoc., *Exec Srch*
Kabl Ability Network, *Exec Srch*
Kuhn Med-Tech, *Exec Srch*
John Kurosky & Assoc., *Exec Srch*
Lending Personnel Svcs., *Exec Srch*
The London Associates, *Exec Srch*
Madden Associates, *Exec Srch*
Mngmt. Rcrtrs. International, *Exec Srch*

Manpower Staffing Svcs., *Temp Agcy*
K.E. McCarthy & Assoc., *Exec Srch*
Milestone Pro Search, *Exec Srch*
Musick & Associates, *Exec Srch*
Nelson HR Solutions, *Perm Agcy*
Nesco Service Company, *Perm Agcy*
Network Resource Group, *Exec Srch*
Norsell & Associates, Inc., *Exec Srch*
Paar & Associates, *Exec Srch*
Pacific Search Group, *Exec Srch*
Pasona Pacific, *Temp Agcy*
Power 2000+, *Exec Srch*
Premier Personnel Svcs., *Temp Agcy*
Presidio Personnel, *Temp Agcy*
PrideStaff, *Temp Agcy*
Pro Staff Personnel Svcs., *Perm Agcy*
Professional Recruiters, *Exec Srch*
The Proven Edge Exec. Recruiters, *Exec Srch*
Edward Rast and Company, *Exec Srch*
Remedy Caller Access, *Temp Agcy*
Remedy Intelligent Staffing, *Temp Agcy*
Resource Perspectives, Inc., *Exec Srch*
Riley-Cole, *Exec Srch*
Ritter & Associates, *Exec Srch*
Rusher, Loscavio, and LoPresto, *Exec Srch*
Sanford Rose Associates, *Exec Srch*
Santa Barbara Staffing, *Perm Agcy*
Select Personnel Services, *Temp Agcy*
David Sharp & Associates, *Perm Agcy*
Steinbrun, Hughes and Assoc., *Exec Srch*
Fred Stuart Consulting/Personnel Services, *Perm Agcy*
T.R. Employment Agency, *Perm Agcy*
Teleforce International, *Exec Srch*
Telford, Adams, & Alexander, *Exec Srch*
Today Personnel Services, *Perm Agcy*
Truex Associates, *Exec Srch*
The Truman Agency, *Perm Agcy*
Unisearch, *Exec Srch*
United Staffing Solutions, *Exec Srch*
Vaughan & Co. Exec. Srch, *Exec Srch*
Walker & Torrente, *Exec Srch*
Westaff, *Temp Agcy*
Western Labor Leasing, *Contract Svc*
Wollborg-Michelson Personnel Svc., *Perm Agcy*
Your People Professionals, *Perm Agcy*
Zeiger & Associates, *Exec Srch*

Colorado
Ahrnsbrak and Associates, *Perm Agcy*
Career Forum, Inc., *Exec Srch*
Casey Services, Inc. (CSI), *Exec Srch*
Dunhill Personnel, *Exec Srch*
Intellimark, *Temp Agcy*
JobSearch, *Perm Agcy*
Kelly Services, Inc., *Temp Agcy*
Mngmt. Rcrtrs. of Colorado Springs, *Exec Srch*
Real Estate Personnel, *Exec Srch*
SOS Staffing Services, *Temp Agcy*
Sales Conslt, *Exec Srch*
Star Personnel Service, *Exec Srch*
Todays Temporary, *Temp Agcy*
Julie West & Associates, *Exec Srch*

Connecticut
Admiral Staffing Services, *Temp Agcy*
Advanced Placement Inc., *Temp Agcy*
Bohan & Bradstreet, *Perm Agcy*
Buxbaum/Rink Consulting, *Exec Srch*
Cahill Associates, *Exec Srch*
The Cambridge Group Ltd., *Exec Srch*
Charter Personnel Services, *Exec Srch*
Corporate Staffing Solutions, *Temp Agcy*
Cupples Consulting Svcs., *Exec Srch*
Flynn Hannock, Inc., *Exec Srch*
W.R. Lawry, Inc., *Perm Agcy*
MJF Associates, *Exec Srch*
Mngmt. Rcrtrs. of Norwalk, *Exec Srch*
Maxwell-Marcus Staff Conslt, *Exec Srch*
McIntyre Associates, *Temp Agcy*
Office Services of CT, *Perm Agcy*
PRH Management, Inc., *Exec Srch*
Barry Persky & Co., *Exec Srch*
Wallace Associates, *Exec Srch*
Westaff, *Temp Agcy*
Bob Wright Recruiting, *Exec Srch*

Delaware
F-O-R-T-U-N-E Pers. Conslts, *Exec Srch*
J.B. Groner Exec. Search, *Exec Srch*

E.W. Hodges & Associates, *Exec Srch*
Independent National Search & Associates (INS), *Exec Srch*
The Placers, Inc., *Temp Agcy*

Dist. of Columbia
Career Blazers Pers. Svc., *Perm Agcy*
GKA Resources, LLC, *Exec Srch*
NRI Staffing Resources, *Temp Agcy*
Savoy Partners Ltd., *Exec Srch*
Tangent Corporation, *Exec Srch*

Florida
AAA Employment, *Perm Agcy*
Able Body Corp. Svcs., *Contract Svc*
Active Professionals, *Exec Srch*
Adecco, *Temp Agcy*
American Recruiters, *Exec Srch*
Ash & Assoc. Exec. Srch, *Exec Srch*
Availability, Inc., *Perm Agcy*
Bales-Waugh Group, *Exec Srch*
Belmont Training & Employment Center, *Perm Agcy*
The Brand Company, Inc., *Exec Srch*
CareerXchange, *Temp Agcy*
Carrier's Career Service, Inc., *Career/Outplacement*
Employers' Assistant, Inc., *Temp Agcy*
Ethan Allen Pers. Placement, *Exec Srch*
First Recruiters Group Inc., *Exec Srch*
Five Star Temporary Inc., *Temp Agcy*
F-O-R-T-U-N-E Pers. Conslts, *Exec Srch*
Janus Career Services, *Exec Srch*
Just Management Services, *Exec Srch*
R.H. Larsen & Associates, *Exec Srch*
Mngmt. Rcrtrs. International, *Exec Srch*
Manpower Temp. Svcs., *Temp Agcy*
OMNIpartners, *Exec Srch*
PMC&L Associates, Inc., *Perm Agcy*
Pro-Team Services, Inc., *Exec Srch*
The Ryan Charles Group, *Exec Srch*
Sales Conslt, Inc., *Exec Srch*
Sanford Rose Associates, *Exec Srch*
Doug Sears & Associates, *Exec Srch*
Shaver Emp. Agency, *Perm Agcy*
Staffing Now, *Temp Agcy*
The Stewart Search Group, *Exec Srch*
Sun Personnel West, *Exec Srch*
Suncoast Group, *Perm Agcy*
TRC Staffing Services, *Temp Agcy*

Georgia
A.D. & Assoc. Exec. Srch, *Exec Srch*
Augusta Staffing Assoc., *Perm Agcy*
B.A. Associates Inc., *Exec Srch*
Bell Oaks Company, *Exec Srch*
Boreham International, *Exec Srch*
Bradshaw & Associates, *Exec Srch*
Corporate Srch Conslt, *Exec Srch*
Elite Staffing Services, *Temp Agcy*
Executive Placement Svcs, *Perm Agcy*
Executive Strategies, Inc., *Exec Srch*
Express Personnel Svcs., *Perm Agcy*
First Pro, *Temp Agcy*
ISC of Atlanta/International Career Continuation, *Exec Srch*
Kenzer Corporation of GA, *Exec Srch*
Lowderman & Associates, *Exec Srch*
MSI International, *Exec Srch*
Bob Maddox Associates, *Exec Srch*
Mngmt. Rcrtrs. International, *Exec Srch*
Manpower Temp. Svcs., *Temp Agcy*
More Personnel Services, *Perm Agcy*
National Pers. Recruiters, *Exec Srch*
RIF (Resources in Food), *Exec Srch*
Randstad Staffing Svcs., *Temp Agcy*
P.J. Reda & Assoc., Inc., *Exec Srch*
Sanford Rose Associates, *Exec Srch*
Sondra Search, *Exec Srch*
Southern Emp. Svc., *Perm Agcy*

Hawaii
Dunhill Pro Staffing of HI, *Exec Srch*
Executive Search World, *Exec Srch*
Management Srch & Conslt, *Exec Srch*
Maresca and Associates, *Exec Srch*

Idaho
Horne/Brown International, *Exec Srch*
Idaho Dept. of Employment/Jobservice, *Perm Agcy*

Illinois
ASI Staffing Service, Inc., *Perm Agcy*
B.J. Abrams & Associates, *Exec Srch*

American Technical Srch, *Exec Srch*
Armstrong-Hamilton Assoc., *Exec Srch*
Banner Personnel Service, *Perm Agcy*
Bevelle & Associates, Inc., *Exec Srch*
Burling Group Ltd., *Exec Srch*
CareerLink USA, Inc., *Exec Srch*
Carson Mngmt. Assoc., *Contract Svc*
Cast Metals Personnel Inc., *Exec Srch*
Champion Staffing, *Perm Agcy*
CompuPro, *Exec Srch*
Cook Associates, Inc., *Exec Srch*
Corporate Environment, *Exec Srch*
Diener & Associates Inc., *Exec Srch*
Executive Referral Svcs., *Exec Srch*
Express Personnel Svcs., *Temp Agcy*
Fellows Placement, *Temp Agcy*
David Gomez & Assoc., *Exec Srch*
HR Connection, *Perm Agcy*
InterStaff, *Temp Agcy*
Interviewing Conslt, *Perm Agcy*
Irwin & Wagner, Inc., *Exec Srch*
Raymond Karson Assoc., *Exec Srch*
Kunzer Associates, Ltd., *Exec Srch*
Arlene Leff & Associates, *Exec Srch*
Lyons & Associates, *Exec Srch*
Magnum Search, *Exec Srch*
Mngmt. Rcrtrs. International, *Exec Srch*
Marsteller Wilcox Assoc., *Exec Srch*
The Murphy Group, *Perm Agcy*
NJW & Associates, Inc., *Temp Agcy*
National Search, *Exec Srch*
OfficeMates5 (OM5), *Perm Agcy*
James C. Pappas & Assoc., *Exec Srch*
Parker Cromwell & Assoc., *Exec Srch*
Pelichem Associates, *Exec Srch*
Personnel Connections, *Perm Agcy*
Personnel Placement Conslt, *Perm Agcy*
Patricia Pocock & Assoc., *Exec Srch*
Professional Research Svcs, *Exec Srch*
RPh On The Go, USA, *Temp Agcy*
Remedy Intelligent Staffing, *Temp Agcy*
Retail Staffers, Inc., *Exec Srch*
Right Services Inc., *Temp Agcy*
Ritt-Ritt and Associates, *Exec Srch*
The Robinson Group, *Exec Srch*
The Ryan Charles Group, *Exec Srch*
SHS, Inc., *Exec Srch*
Sanford Rose Associates, *Exec Srch*
Select Staffing, *Perm Agcy*
SelectAbility, Inc., *Perm Agcy*
Ralph Smith & Associates, *Exec Srch*
Snelling Personnel Svcs., *Perm Agcy*
Strategic Resources Unlimited, *Exec Srch*
Ron Sunshine Associates, *Exec Srch*
Thirty Three Pers. Ctr., *Perm Agcy*
Voigt Associates, *Exec Srch*
West Personnel Service, *Perm Agcy*
Working World Inc., *Temp Agcy*
World Employment Svc., *Perm Agcy*

Indiana
Bill Caldwell Emp. Svc., *Perm Agcy*
Careers Unlimited Inc., *Exec Srch*
Corporate Staffing Resources (CSR),
 Temp Agcy
Employment Recruiters, *Perm Agcy*
Execusearch, *Exec Srch*
Job Placement Service, *Perm Agcy*
Lange & Associates, Inc., *Exec Srch*
Life Employment Service, *Perm Agcy*
Mngmt. Rcrtrs. International, *Exec Srch*
Management Support Svcs, *Exec Srch*
Oakwood International Inc., *Exec Srch*
OM5/DayStar Temp. Services, *Exec Srch*
Perry Personnel Plus, *Perm Agcy*
Quality Search, *Exec Srch*
Unique, Inc., *Exec Srch*
Wimmer Temporaries and Direct
 Placement, *Temp Agcy*

Iowa
Burton Placement Services, *Exec Srch*
Byrnes & Rupkey, Inc., *Exec Srch*
CSI Employment, *Exec Srch*
Helping Hands Temps, *Temp Agcy*
The Human Resource Grp, *Exec Srch*
Mngmt. Rcrtrs. International, *Exec Srch*
McGladrey Search Group, *Exec Srch*
Personnel, Inc., *Exec Srch*
Pratt-Younglove, Inc., *Perm Agcy*
Salem Management Inc., *Temp Agcy*
Rudy Salem Staffing Svcs, *Temp Agcy*
Sanford Rose Associates, *Exec Srch*

Kansas
Business Specialists, *Perm Agcy*
Mngmt. Rcrtrs. /Sales Conslt/OM5, *Exec Srch*
Stoneburner Associates, *Exec Srch*
White Associates/TemTech, *Exec Srch*

Kentucky
Angel Group International, *Exec Srch*
Kovac Berrins AG Inc., *Exec Srch*
Mngmt. Rcrtrs. of Richmond, *Exec Srch*
Manufacturing Associates, *Exec Srch*
Romac International, *Exec Srch*

Louisiana
Delta Personnel, *Perm Agcy*
Frazee Recruiting Conslt, *Exec Srch*
Mngmt. Rcrtrs. of Metairie/Sales Conslt
 of Metairie, *Exec Srch*
Sanford Rose Associates, *Exec Srch*
Talley & Associates, Inc./Talley
 Temporaries, *Exec Srch*

Maine
Accomplished Pros, *Temp Agcy*
At Work Personnel Svc., *Temp Agcy*
Bonney Staffing & Training Centers,
 Perm Agcy
Career Management Assoc., *Exec Srch*
Executive Search, *Exec Srch*

Maryland
Brindisi Search, *Exec Srch*
Caplan/Gross Associates, *Exec Srch*
Chesapeake Consulting Group, *Exec Srch*
JDG Associates Limited, *Exec Srch*
Mngmt. Rcrtrs. of Annapolis, *Exec Srch*
Mngmt. Rcrtrs. of Frederick/
 OfficeMates5, *Exec Srch*
Tom McCall & Assoc., *Perm Agcy*
Sales Conslt, *Exec Srch*
TCM Enterprises, *Exec Srch*
Winston Search, Inc., *Exec Srch*

Massachusetts
ABA Personnel, Inc., *Temp Agcy*
Ability Search, *Perm Agcy*
Aerotek, Inc., *Contract Svc*
The Alpha Group, *Temp Agcy*
Bell Oaks Company, *Exec Srch*
Brady Employment Svc, *Perm Agcy*
Cyr Associates, Inc., *Exec Srch*
F-O-R-T-U-N-E Pers. Conslts of
 Topsfield, *Exec Srch*
Gilreath Weatherby Inc., *Exec Srch*
A. Greenstein & Company, *Exec Srch*
Johnson & Hill Staff. Svc, *Temp Agcy*
Lake Conslt, *Exec Srch*
The Littleton Group, *Exec Srch*
Mngmt. Rcrtrs. International, *Exec Srch*
Master Search, *Exec Srch*
McDevitt Associates, *Exec Srch*
Need Pers. Placement, *Temp Agcy*
New Dimensions in Technology, Inc.
 (NDT), *Exec Srch*
New England Search, Inc., *Exec Srch*
The Onstott Group, *Exec Srch*
D.P. Parker & Associates, *Exec Srch*
Pro Staff, *Temp Agcy*
Quality Pers./Quality Temps, *Perm Agcy*
Sales Conslt, *Exec Srch*
Search International, *Exec Srch*
Snelling Personnel, *Exec Srch*
Stone & Youngblood, *Exec Srch*
Straube Associates, *Exec Srch*
Volt Services Group, *Temp Agcy*
S.B. Webster & Associates, *Exec Srch*

Michigan
Action Mngmt. Corp., *Perm Agcy*
Alternative Staff, Inc., *Contract Svc*
Associates, *Exec Srch*
Aucon L.L.C., *Exec Srch*
Barman Staff Solutions, *Temp Agcy*
Beacon Services Inc., *Exec Srch*
Career Quest, Inc., *Perm Agcy*
Case & Company, *Exec Srch*
Coastal Development, Inc., *Exec Srch*
Cole's Paper Industry Recruiters, Inc.,
 Exec Srch
Corporate Business Svcs., *Exec Srch*
Corporate Staff Resources, *Perm Agcy*
Day Personnel, Inc., *Perm Agcy*
Entech Personnel Svcs., *Temp Agcy*
ExecuQuest, Inc., *Exec Srch*

Missouri (right column continuation of Michigan heading area)
Executive & Tech. Pers., *Exec Srch*
Executive Recruiters Intnl., *Exec Srch*
Express Personnel Svcs., *Temp Agcy*
F-O-R-T-U-N-E Pers. Conslts, *Exec Srch*
Giacomin Group Inc., *Exec Srch*
Joseph Goldring & Assoc., *Exec Srch*
HR Employment Svcs., *Perm Agcy*
Kelly Technical Services, *Contract Svc*
Lambert International, *Exec Srch*
Mngmt. Rcrtrs. International, *Exec Srch*
Lou Michaels Associates, *Exec Srch*
Office Staffing Recruiting, *Exec Srch*
Preferred Emp. Planning, *Perm Agcy*
Sales Conslt, *Exec Srch*
Sales Executives Inc., *Perm Agcy*
Sanford Rose Associates, *Exec Srch*
Search Plus International, *Exec Srch*
Source Technology LLC, *Exec Srch*
Technical Pro Svc., *Perm Agcy*
Thomas & Assoc. of MI, *Exec Srch*
Trillium Staffing, *Temp Agcy*
Henry Welker & Assoc., *Exec Srch*
Workforce, Inc., *Temp Agcy*

Minnesota
Abby Blu Inc., *Temp Agcy*
Advance Pers. Resources, *Exec Srch*
Agri-Business Services, *Exec Srch*
Bright Search/Pro Staffing, *Exec Srch*
Discovery Personnel, Inc., *Exec Srch*
Diversified Employment, *Perm Agcy*
Employment Advisors, *Perm Agcy*
Employment Advisors/Staff It Personnel
 Services, *Perm Agcy*
Gleason Dale Keene & Assoc., *Exec Srch*
Heinze & Associates, *Exec Srch*
Mngmt. Rcrtrs./Sales Conslt, *Exec Srch*
Metro Hospitality Conslt, *Perm Agcy*
Nycor Search Inc., *Exec Srch*
Professional Recruiters, *Exec Srch*
Resource Search, *Exec Srch*
Sathe & Assoc. Exec. Srch, *Exec Srch*
Ultimate Search Unlimited/Temps
 Unlimited, *Perm Agcy*
Working Relationships, *Perm Agcy*

Mississippi
AAA Employment, *Exec Srch*
The CPI Group, *Exec Srch*
Coats & Coats Personnel, *Perm Agcy*
EPSCO Personnel Service, *Temp Agcy*
Recruitment & Training Programs of
 Mississippi, Inc., *Perm Agcy*

Missouri
ABC Employment Svc., *Perm Agcy*
Advanced Careers, *Exec Srch*
Bottom Line Pro Svcs., *Contract Svc*
Business Personnel Svcs., *Temp Agcy*
Jim Crumpley & Assoc., *Exec Srch*
Debbon Recruiting Group, *Exec Srch*
Deck & Decker Emp. Svc., *Perm Agcy*
Employer Advantage, *Exec Srch*
F-O-R-T-U-N-E Pers. Conslts, *Exec Srch*
Huey Enterprises, *Exec Srch*
JoDoc Enterprises, *Temp Agcy*
Charles Luntz & Assoc., *Exec Srch*
Mngmt. Rcrtrs. of Kansas City, *Exec Srch*
Mngmt. Rcrtrs. of Springfield, *Exec Srch*
Mngmt. Rcrtrs. of St. Louis, *Exec Srch*
Manpower Temp. Svcs., *Temp Agcy*
OfficeMates5 (OM5), *Exec Srch*
Olsten Staffing Services, *Temp Agcy*

Montana
Caria Resources, Inc., *Exec Srch*
LC Staffing Service, *Perm Agcy*

Nebraska
Business Professions, Inc., *Perm Agcy*
Compusearch of Lincoln, *Exec Srch*
Corporate Recruiters, Ltd./Health Service
 Professionals, *Exec Srch*
Express Personnel, *Exec Srch*
Hansen Employment Svc., *Exec Srch*
Mngmt. Rcrtrs. /OfficeMates5, *Exec Srch*
Noll HR Services, *Exec Srch*
Outsource II, Inc., *Temp Agcy*

Nevada
Flowers Exec. Srch. Grp., *Exec Srch*
Nevada Business Services (NBS),
 Career/Outplacement

Whittlesey & Associates, *Exec Srch*
Yorktowne Personnel, *Exec Srch*

Rhode Island

Colony Personnel Assoc., *Temp Agcy*
Johnson & Tregar Assoc., *Perm Agcy*
Kelly Services, Inc., *Temp Agcy*
Albert G. Lee & Assoc., *Exec Srch*
Mngmt. Rcrtrs. International, *Exec Srch*
Norrell Services, *Temp Agcy*
PKS Associates, Inc., *Exec Srch*
The Schattle Group, *Exec Srch*

South Carolina

Accel Temporary Svcs., *Temp Agcy*
F-O-R-T-U-N-E Pers. Conslts of
  Columbia, *Exec Srch*
Harvey Personnel, Inc., *Perm Agcy*
Mngmt. Rcrtrs. of Columbia, *Exec Srch*
Mngmt. Rcrtrs. of Rock Hill, *Exec Srch*
PRL & Associates, Inc., *Perm Agcy*
Sanford Rose Associates, *Exec Srch*
Smith Temps/Smith Pers., *Temp Agcy*
Southern Recruiters & Conslt, Inc., *Exec
  Srch*
The Stroman Company, *Perm Agcy*
TCG Search, *Exec Srch*

South Dakota

Careers Unlimited, *Perm Agcy*
Key Staffing, *Temp Agcy*

Tennessee

A-1 Staffing & Personnel, *Temp Agcy*
Anderson McIntyre Pers Svcs., *Exec Srch*
Express Personnel Svcs., *Perm Agcy*
Grant & Associates Inc., *Exec Srch*
HR Group, *Exec Srch*
Hamilton-Ryker Co., *Temp Agcy*
Hester & Associates, *Exec Srch*
Randall Howard & Assoc., *Exec Srch*
Dorothy Johnson's Career Conslt, *Exec
  Srch*
Just Management Service, *Exec Srch*
Mngmt. Rcrtrs. International, *Exec Srch*
Mngmt. Rcrtrs. of Brentwood/Sales
  Conslt of Brentwood, *Exec Srch*
Manpower, Inc., *Temp Agcy*
W.R. McLeod & Associates, *Exec Srch*
The Morgan Group, *Exec Srch*
Olsten Staffing Services, *Temp Agcy*
Rasmussen & Associates, *Perm Agcy*
Snelling Personnel Svcs., *Perm Agcy*
Technical Resource Assoc., *Exec Srch*

Texas

ABA Executive Search, *Exec Srch*
Abilene Employment Svc, *Perm Agcy*
Ackerman Johnson Inc., *Exec Srch*
Action Personnel Inc., *Temp Agcy*
Add-A-Temp/Woodlands Executive
  Employment, *Temp Agcy*
Advanced Syst. Consulting, *Exec Srch*
Agri-Associates, *Exec Srch*
American Resources, *Exec Srch*
Aware Affiliates Pers. Svc., *Perm Agcy*
Ann Best Elite Temps, *Temp Agcy*
Boles & Associates, *Exec Srch*
Bullock Personnel, Inc., *Perm Agcy*
Champion Personnel Svc., *Exec Srch*
Colvin Resources Group, *Perm Agcy*
Creative Staffing Services, *Perm Agcy*
Dallas Employment Svcs., *Perm Agcy*
The Danbrook Group, *Exec Srch*
Gail Darling Staffing/Gail Darling's
  Professional Desk, *Temp Agcy*
Dividend Staffing Svcs., *Temp Agcy*
Dunhill Pro Search, *Exec Srch*
The Elsworth Group, *Exec Srch*
The Energists, *Exec Srch*
Evins Personnel Conslt of Killeen, Inc.,
  Perm Agcy
Express Personnel Svcs., *Perm Agcy*
Abel M. Gonzalez & Assoc., *Exec Srch*
Haragan Associates, *Exec Srch*
Joseph Chris Partners, *Exec Srch*
Kenzer Corporation, *Exec Srch*
Kristan Intnl. Exec. Search, *Exec Srch*
Link Staffing Services, *Temp Agcy*
Loewenstein & Associates, *Exec Srch*
Mngmt. Rcrtrs. International, *Exec Srch*
McKinley-AREND Intnl., *Exec Srch*
The Pailin Group Professional Search
  Conslt, *Exec Srch*

Pate Resources Group, *Exec Srch*
Phoenix Staffing/G&A Staff Sourcing,
  Exec Srch
Priority Search, Inc., *Exec Srch*
Professional Search Conslt (PSC),
  Contract Svc
Professions Today, *Perm Agcy*
Resource Connection Workforce Center,
  Perm Agcy
Sales Conslt, *Exec Srch*
SearchAmerica Inc., *Exec Srch*
Select Staff, *Exec Srch*
Snelling Personnel Svcs., *Perm Agcy*
Staff Extension Intnl., *Exec Srch*
StaffingSolutions/ReSourceMFG, *Perm
  Agcy*
Straight Source, *Exec Srch*
TexStar, *Exec Srch*
Thomas Office Pers. Svc., *Perm Agcy*
Valpers Inc., *Exec Srch*
Wheeler, Moore & Elam Co., *Exec Srch*
R.S. Wyatt Associates, Inc., *Exec Srch*

Utah

Mngmt. Rcrtrs. of Ogden, *Exec Srch*
Mngmt. Rcrtrs. of Salt Lake City, *Exec
  Srch*

Virginia

A La Carte International, *Exec Srch*
Ability Resources, Inc., *Exec Srch*
Alpha Omega Resources, *Perm Agcy*
BSC, *Contract Svc*
Barnes & Assoc. Retail Srch, *Exec Srch*
Buckler Careers, Inc., *Perm Agcy*
Corporate Connection Ltd., *Exec Srch*
Curzon Staffing, *Perm Agcy*
Dow Personnel, *Perm Agcy*
Effective Staffing Inc., *Exec Srch*
Employment Enterprises/Temporary
  Solutions, *Temp Agcy*
Kogen Personnel, *Exec Srch*
Lee Staffing Resources, *Exec Srch*
Mngmt. Rcrtrs./OfficeMates5, *Exec Srch*
Norrell Services, *Temp Agcy*
Olsten Staffing Services, *Temp Agcy*
STAT Employment Svcs., *Perm Agcy*
Taskforce of VA/PRG - Professional
  Resources Group, *Exec Srch*
U.S. Search, *Exec Srch*
Westaff, *Temp Agcy*

Washington

The Career Clinic, Inc., *Exec Srch*
Express Personnel Svcs., *Temp Agcy*
Renee Feldman & Assoc., *Exec Srch*
Human Resources Inc., *Exec Srch*
The Jobs Company, *Exec Srch*
Kelly Services, Inc., *Temp Agcy*
Kossuth & Associates, *Exec Srch*
Mngmt. Rcrtrs. of Mercer Island, *Exec
  Srch*
Mngmt. Rcrtrs. of Seattle, *Exec Srch*
Mngmt. Rcrtrs. of Tacoma, *Exec Srch*
John Mason & Associates, *Exec Srch*
Northwest Temporary & Staffing
  Services, Inc., *Temp Agcy*
Personnel Unlimited Inc., *Exec Srch*
Roth Young Exec. Srch, *Exec Srch*
The Washington Firm, *Exec Srch*
Whittall Mngmt Group, *Exec Srch*

West Virginia

Extra Support Staffing, *Temp Agcy*
Key Personnel, Inc., *Perm Agcy*

Wisconsin

Austria Austria & Assoc., *Perm Agcy*
Dieck Mueller Group, *Exec Srch*
J.M. Eagle Partners, *Exec Srch*
Executive Resource Inc., *Exec Srch*
Flores Financial Services, *Exec Srch*
Hatch Staffing Services, *Temp Agcy*
Mngmt. Rcrtrs. of Appleton/
  Compusearch, *Exec Srch*
Mngmt. Rcrtrs. of Green Bay, *Exec Srch*
Mngmt. Rcrtrs. of Milwaukee/
  Sales Conslt, *Exec Srch*
MARBL Conslt, *Exec Srch*
The Michael David Group, *Exec Srch*
Olsten Staffing Services, *Temp Agcy*
Sales Specialists, Inc., *Exec Srch*
Sauve Company, Ltd., *Perm Agcy*
Tom Sloan & Associates, *Perm Agcy*

GOVERNMENT

California

Dunhill Exec Search of LA, *Exec Srch*
Hughes Perry & Associates, *Exec Srch*
Mahoney Brewer Assoc., *Exec Srch*

Dist. of Columbia

Goodwin & Company, *Exec Srch*

Florida

Manchester Inc., *Exec Srch*
Romac International, *Exec Srch*

Illinois

Kingston/Zak Inc., *Exec Srch*

Maryland

Charter Business Svcs., *Perm Agcy*

New Mexico

Mercer Group, *Exec Srch*

New York

Alexander Edwards Intnl., *Exec Srch*
SearchAmerica Inc., *Exec Srch*

North Carolina

Executive Recruitment Specialists, Inc.,
  Exec Srch

Pennsylvania

Keynote Systems Inc., *Temp Agcy*
Manchester Inc., *Career/Outplacement*

Virginia

Wayne Garber & Assoc., *Exec Srch*

Washington

T M Campbell Company, *Exec Srch*

GRAPHIC ARTS

California

Magenta Group, *Exec Srch*
Pacific Placement Group, *Temp Agcy*

Dist. of Columbia

Graphic Mac, *Temp Agcy*

Florida

Manchester Inc., *Exec Srch*

Illinois

Advancement Inc., *Exec Srch*
Cook Associates, Inc., *Exec Srch*
Lyons & Associates, *Exec Srch*
Mngmt. Rcrtrs. of Elgin, Inc., *Exec Srch*

Massachusetts

Pro Staff, *Temp Agcy*

New York

Beaver Personnel, Inc., *Perm Agcy*

Ohio

Dave Arnold & Associates, *Exec Srch*

Oregon

Creative Assets, *Temp Agcy*

Pennsylvania

Manchester Inc., *Career/Outplacement*
Sanford Rose Associates, *Exec Srch*

Tennessee

Sanford Rose Assoc., *Exec Srch*

Texas

Key People Inc., *Exec Srch*

HEALTH/MEDICAL

Alabama

EAI Health Care Staffing, *Temp Agcy*
Employment Conslt, *Perm Agcy*
Executive Staffing Inc., *Perm Agcy*
Healthcare Recruiters of AL, *Exec Srch*
Mngmt. Rcrtrs. International, *Exec Srch*
Snelling Personnel Svcs., *Perm Agcy,
  Exec Srch*
VIP Personnel, Inc., *Perm Agcy*

Alaska

Alaska Executive Search, *Exec Srch*

Arizona

Amer. Career Grp, *Career/Outplacement*
Arizona Medical Exchange, *Perm Agcy*
BJB Medical Associates, *Exec Srch*
Cizek Associates Inc., *Exec Srch*
EAI Healthcare Staffing Solutions, *Temp
  Agcy*
Favorite Nurses Inc., *Temp Agcy*

Human Resource Network, *Perm Agcy*
Mngmt. Rcrtrs. of Scottsdale, *Exec Srch*
Pearson & Associates, Inc., *Exec Srch*
Sales Conslt, *Exec Srch*
Marjorie Starr & Assoc., *Exec Srch*
Stivers Temporary Pers., *Temp Agcy*
Witt/Kieffer, Ford, Hadelman & Lloyd, *Exec Srch*

Arkansas
Mngmt. Rcrtrs., *Exec Srch*
Search Associates, *Exec Srch*
Turnage Emp. Svc. Grp., *Exec Srch*

California
ABA Staffing, Inc., *Exec Srch*
ARI International, *Exec Srch*
Allied Search, Inc., *Exec Srch*
Apple One Emp. Svcs., *Perm Agcy*
Apropos Emp. Agency, *Perm Agcy*
Assured Personnel Svcs., *Perm Agcy*
Astra West Pers. Svcs., *Perm Agcy*
Bsa Personnel Center, *Perm Agcy*
Battalia Winston Intnl., *Exec Srch*
Harvey Bell & Associates, *Exec Srch*
Bristol Associates, *Exec Srch*
Bryson Myers Company, *Exec Srch*
CRI Professional Search, *Exec Srch*
Career Quest Intnl., *Contract Svc*
Carlson & Associates, *Exec Srch*
Coast To Coast Exec. Srch, *Exec Srch*
The Culver Group, *Exec Srch*
Culver Personnel Services, *Perm Agcy*
Culver Staffing Resources, *Temp Agcy*
DEC Healthcare Pers., *Temp Agcy*
DNA Medical Search, *Exec Srch*
Dental Plus Medical, *Temp Agcy*
Robert W. Dingman Co., *Exec Srch*
Drake Office Overload, *Temp Agcy*
Dunhill Exec. Srch of LA, *Exec Srch*
Cathy Dunn's Associated Personnel Services Inc., *Perm Agcy*
Eaton & Associates, *Exec Srch*
Ensearch Mngmt. Conslt, *Exec Srch*
Ethos Consulting, Inc., *Exec Srch*
Executive Medical Search, *Exec Srch*
Faithful Support Systems, *Temp Agcy*
F-O-R-T-U-N-E Pers. Conslts, *Exec Srch*
Garrison-Randall Inc., *Exec Srch*
Goldstein & Associates, *Temp Agcy*
The Goodman Group, *Exec Srch*
Gould Personnel Services, *Perm Agcy*
Griffith & Associates, *Exec Srch*
Healthcare Exec. Recruiters, *Exec Srch*
HealthCare Recruiters of LA, *Exec Srch*
HealthCare Recruiters of Orange County, *Exec Srch*
HealthCare Recruiters of San Diego, *Exec Srch*
Bruce Henry Associates, *Exec Srch*
Initial Staffing Services, *Perm Agcy*
Intech Summit Group, Inc., *Exec Srch*
Interim Personnel, *Temp Agcy*
Interstate Recruiters Corp., *Exec Srch*
JPM International, *Exec Srch*
Johnston Associates, *Exec Srch*
Kenneth, George, & Assoc., *Exec Srch*
Kuhn Med-Tech, *Exec Srch*
John Kurosky & Assoc., *Exec Srch*
Lab Support Inc., *Temp Agcy*
Leinow Associates, *Exec Srch*
Lewis & Blank Intnl., *Exec Srch*
The London Associates, *Exec Srch*
London Temporary Svcs., *Temp Agcy*
MacNaughton Associates, *Exec Srch*
Judy Madrigal & Assoc., *Exec Srch*
Mahoney Brewer Assoc., *Exec Srch*
Mngmt. Rcrtrs. International, *Exec Srch*
Richard Maries Staff Ctr., *Perm Agcy*
Sabine McManus & Assoc., *Exec Srch*
Med Exec International, *Exec Srch*
Med Quest, *Exec Srch*
Medical Exec. Recruiters, *Exec Srch*
Medical Financial Svcs., *Contract Svc*
Medical Staff Unlimited, *Perm Agcy*
Mixtec Group, *Exec Srch*
M.O.R.E. Emp. Svcs., *Perm Agcy*
National Staffing by Noelle & Associates, *Exec Srch*
Nurses International, *Perm Agcy*
O'Brien Emp. Svcs., *Temp Agcy*
Olsten Staffing Services, *Temp Agcy*
On Assignment, Inc., *Temp Agcy*

Pacific Search Group, *Exec Srch*
Paster & Associates, *Exec Srch*
Physicians Search Assoc., *Exec Srch*
Premier Nursing Service, *Perm Agcy*
Princeton Corporate Conslt, *Exec Srch*
Quality Imaging Services, *Contract Svc*
R$_x$ Relief, *Temp Agcy*
Edward Rast and Company, *Exec Srch*
Remedy Caller Access, *Temp Agcy*
Sampson Medical Search, *Exec Srch*
Sanford Rose Associates, *Exec Srch*
Search West, *Exec Srch*
David Sharp & Associates, *Perm Agcy*
Sharp Personnel & Search, *Exec Srch*
Staff Seekers, *Exec Srch*
Star Med Staff, *Temp Agcy*
Stivers Temporary Pers., *Temp Agcy*
TMP Executive Resources, *Exec Srch*
TMP Worldwide, *Exec Srch*
TRC Staffing Services, *Perm Agcy*
Telford, Adams, & Alexander, *Exec Srch*
Thor Temporary Services, *Temp Agcy*
Thornton Associates, *Exec Srch*
Trans U.S., Inc., *Perm Agcy*
UAW Labor Employment and Training Corporation, *Perm Agcy*
Unisearch, *Exec Srch*
United Staffing Solutions, *Exec Srch*
K.K. Walker Professional Recruitment, *Exec Srch*
Westaff, *Temp Agcy*
Western Tech. Resources, *Exec Srch*
WestPacific National Srch, *Exec Srch*
Witt/Kieffer, Ford, Hadelman & Lloyd, *Exec Srch*

Colorado
American Med. Recruiters, *Exec Srch*
Casey Services, Inc. (CSI), *Exec Srch*
F-O-R-T-U-N-E Pers. Conslts of Denver, *Exec Srch*
Goodwin Personnel, Inc., *Perm Agcy*
Healthcare Recruiters Of The Rockies, Inc., *Exec Srch*
Initial Staffing Services, *Perm Agcy*
Interim Personnel, *Temp Agcy*
JobSearch, *Temp Agcy*
Leading Edge Medical Search, *Exec Srch*
Mngmt. Rcrtrs. of Colorado, *Exec Srch*
Mngmt. Rcrtrs. of Colorado Springs, *Exec Srch*
Medical Pers. Resources, *Perm Agcy*
Office Specialists Inc., *Temp Agcy*
Sales Conslt, *Exec Srch*
Surgical Associated Svcs., *Perm Agcy*
WSI Personnel Service, *Perm Agcy*
The Westminster Group, *Exec Srch*

Connecticut
Admiral Staffing Services, *Temp Agcy*
Anderson Group, *Exec Srch*
Blackwood Associates Inc., *Exec Srch*
Bonnell Associates Ltd., *Exec Srch*
CPH Staffing & Consulting, *Temp Agcy*
The Cambridge Group Ltd., *Exec Srch*
Charter Personnel Services, *Exec Srch*
Drew Pro Recruiters, *Exec Srch*
Employment Opps., *Perm Agcy*
Higbee Associates, *Exec Srch*
Intertec Personnel, *Temp Agcy*
The La Pointe Group Inc., *Exec Srch*
MRG Search & Placement, *Exec Srch*
Mngmt. Rcrtrs. International, *Exec Srch*
Napolitano & Wulster, *Perm Agcy*
New England Personnel, *Perm Agcy*
Barry Persky & Co., *Exec Srch*
Quality Control Recruiters, *Exec Srch*
Siger & Associates, LLC, *Exec Srch*
Howard W. Smith Assoc., *Exec Srch*
Snyder & Company, *Exec Srch*
TMP Worldwide, *Exec Srch*
Vezan Associates, *Exec Srch*
Wallace Associates, *Exec Srch*
Weatherby Health Care, *Exec Srch*

Delaware
J.B. Groner Exec. Search, *Exec Srch*
Healthcare Network, *Exec Srch*

Dist. of Columbia
AccuStaff, *Perm Agcy*
Goodwin & Company, *Exec Srch*
Medical Personnel Svcs., *Perm Agcy*
Trifax Corporation, *Perm Agcy*

Florida
AAA Employment, *Perm Agcy*
ATS Health Services, *Perm Agcy*
All Medical Personnel, *Temp Agcy*
American Recruiters, *Exec Srch*
Availability, Inc., *Perm Agcy*
Bales-Waugh Group, *Exec Srch*
Careers Unlimited, Inc., *Exec Srch*
Carrier's Career Service, Inc., *Career/Outplacement*
Contract Health Pros, *Contract Svc*
DGA Personnel Group, *Exec Srch*
Dunhill Pro Search, *Exec Srch*
Employers' Assistant, Inc., *Temp Agcy*
The Eye Group, *Exec Srch*
Five Star Temporary Inc., *Temp Agcy*
Gimbel & Associates, *Exec Srch*
Healthcare Recruiters of Central Florida, *Exec Srch*
Janus Career Services, *Perm Agcy*
Mngmt. Rcrtrs. International, *Exec Srch*
Manchester Inc., *Exec Srch*
National Medical Recruiting & Consulting, INC., *Exec Srch*
Olsten Staffing Services, *Temp Agcy*
Perfect Search Inc., *Exec Srch*
Physician Exec. Mngmt. Ctr., *Exec Srch*
Linda Robins & Assoc., *Temp Agcy*
Robinson & Associates, *Exec Srch*
Roth Young of Tampa Bay, *Exec Srch*
Sales Conslt, *Exec Srch*
Sea-change, Inc., *Exec Srch*
Search Masters Intnl., *Exec Srch*
Doug Sears & Associates, *Exec Srch*
Snelling Personnel Svcs., *Temp Agcy*
Staffing Now, *Temp Agcy*
The Stewart Search Grp., *Exec Srch*
Summit Health Care, Inc., *Exec Srch*
Sun Personnel West, *Exec Srch*
TMP Worldwide, *Exec Srch*
Uniquest International, Inc., *Exec Srch*
Weatherby Health Care, *Exec Srch*
Weber & Company/Mngmt. Rcrtrs. International, *Exec Srch*

Georgia
A-OK Personnel, *Perm Agcy*
Catalina HR, *Perm Agcy*
Corporate Image Group, *Exec Srch*
Corporate Srch Conslt, *Exec Srch*
DDS Staffing Resources, *Perm Agcy*
The Diversified Srch Cos., *Exec Srch*
Dunhill Pro Search, *Exec Srch*
Elite Medical Search, *Exec Srch*
Elite Staffing Services, *Temp Agcy*
Executive Resource Group, *Exec Srch*
Executive Strategies, Inc., *Exec Srch*
William Halderson Assoc., *Exec Srch*
Healthcare Financial Staffing/Lab Support, *Temp Agcy*
Healthcare Recruiters Intnl, *Exec Srch*
ISC of Atlanta/International Career Continuation, *Exec Srch*
JJ&H Ltd./Jacobson Assoc., *Exec Srch*
Lowderman & Associates, *Exec Srch*
MAU, Inc., *Perm Agcy*
MSI International, *Exec Srch*
Mngmt. Rcrtrs. of Atlanta, *Exec Srch*
Med Pro Personnel, *Exec Srch*
Medical Search of America, *Exec Srch*
Olsten Staffing Services, *Temp Agcy*
Personnel Opportunities, *Exec Srch*
Randstad Staffing Svcs., *Temp Agcy*
P.J. Reda & Associates, *Exec Srch*
Reeder & Associates, Ltd., *Exec Srch*
Scott George & Associates, *Exec Srch*
Snelling Personnel Svcs., *Exec Srch*
Southern Pro Recruiters, *Exec Srch*
Staffing Resources, *Perm Agcy*
TMP Worldwide, *Exec Srch*
Thorne Consulting, *Exec Srch*
Tyler & Company, *Exec Srch*
Witt/Kieffer, Ford, Hadelman & Lloyd, *Exec Srch*

Hawaii
ASAP Express, *Contract Svc*
Altres Staffing, *Temp Agcy*
Executive Search World, *Exec Srch*
Lam Assoc. Physician Search, *Exec Srch*
Management Search & Consulting, Inc., *Exec Srch*
Maresca and Associates, *Exec Srch*

Riders Personnel Services, *Contract Svc*
Sales Conslt, *Exec Srch*

Idaho
Horne/Brown International, *Exec Srch*
Idaho Dept. of Employment/Jobservice, *Perm Agcy*

Illinois
B.J. Abrams & Associates, *Exec Srch*
American Medical Pers., *Perm Agcy*
E.J. Ashton & Associates, *Exec Srch*
B-W and Associates, Inc., *Perm Agcy*
Battalia Winston Intnl., *Exec Srch*
Burling Group Ltd., *Exec Srch*
CES Associates, *Exec Srch*
CEMCO Ltd., *Exec Srch*
Chatterton & Associates, *Exec Srch*
Cook Associates, Inc., *Exec Srch*
Corp Staff/Proven Prfrmrs., *Perm Agcy*
Diener & Associates Inc., *Exec Srch*
Dynamic People, *Temp Agcy*
The Eastwood Group, *Exec Srch*
The Esquire Staffing Grp, *Perm Agcy*
Executive Referral Svcs., *Exec Srch*
Fellows Placement, *Temp Agcy*
Furst Staffing Services, *Temp Agcy*
Healthcare Recruiters Intnl, *Exec Srch*
Healthcare Training & Placement, *Temp Agcy*
Hersher & Associates, Ltd., *Exec Srch*
Highland Group, *Exec Srch*
Jacobson Assoc./Insurance Staffers, *Exec Srch*
Raymond Karson Assoc., *Exec Srch*
Kingston/Zak Inc., *Exec Srch*
Kunzer Associates, Ltd., *Exec Srch*
Arlene Leff & Associates, *Exec Srch*
The MBP Group, *Exec Srch*
Mngmt. Rcrtrs. International, *Exec Srch*
Manpower Temp. Svcs., *Temp Agcy*
Medical Tech. Placements, *Temp Agcy*
National Search, *Exec Srch*
OfficeMates5 (OM5), *Perm Agcy*
Peak Pro Health Service, *Perm Agcy*
RPh On The Go, USA, *Temp Agcy*
Relief Medical Services, *Temp Agcy*
Remedy Intelligent Staffing, *Temp Agcy*
Right Services Inc., *Temp Agcy*
David Rowe & Associates, *Exec Srch*
SHS, Inc., *Exec Srch*
Sanford Rose Associates, *Exec Srch*
Smith Hanley Associates, *Exec Srch*
The Stanton Group, Inc., *Exec Srch*
Stivers Temporary Pers., *Temp Agcy*
TMP Worldwide, *Exec Srch*
U.S. Medical Placements, *Perm Agcy*
Witt/Kieffer, Ford, Hadelman & Lloyd, *Exec Srch*
World Employment Svc., *Perm Agcy*

Indiana
Bill Caldwell Emp. Svc., *Perm Agcy*
Canis Major/HR Quest, *Exec Srch*
Century Personnel Inc., *Perm Agcy*
The Curare Group, Inc., *Exec Srch*
Dental Medical Power, *Perm Agcy*
Dunhill of Brown County, *Exec Srch*
Excellence In Search, *Exec Srch*
Execusearch, *Exec Srch*
HMO Executive Search, *Exec Srch*
Keith Hayes & Associates, *Exec Srch*
Mngmt. Rcrtrs. of Richmond, *Exec Srch*
Morley Group, *Exec Srch*
OM5/DayStar Temp. Services, *Exec Srch*
Quiring Associates, Inc., *Perm Agcy*
The Registry Inc., *Perm Agcy*
Romac International, *Exec Srch*
StaffMark Medical Staffing, *Temp Agcy*
Strategic Resource Mngmt, *Exec Srch*

Iowa
Byrnes & Rupkey, Inc., *Exec Srch*
Cambridge Careers, *Perm Agcy*
Helping Hands Temps, *Temp Agcy*
Mngmt. Rcrtrs. International, *Exec Srch*
Premier Search Group, *Exec Srch*
Quality Recruiters Inc., *Exec Srch*
Staff Management, Inc., *Contract Svc*
Tri-State Nurse Enterprises, *Temp Agcy*

Kansas
Brinkman & Associates, *Exec Srch*
Business Specialists, *Perm Agcy*

Century, *Exec Srch*
Health Search, Inc., *Exec Srch*
Kelly Assisted Living Svcs., *Temp Agcy*
Mngmt. Rcrtrs./Sales Conslt/OM5, *Exec Srch*
Peterson Group, *Exec Srch*
Preferred Med. Placement, *Perm Agcy*
Sherriff & Associates, *Exec Srch*
B.E. Smith Associates, *Exec Srch*
Stoneburner Associates, *Exec Srch*
White Associates/TemTech, *Exec Srch*

Kentucky
Angel Group International, *Exec Srch*
Engineering & Exec. Srch, *Exec Srch*
F.C.S., *Exec Srch*
Healthcare Recruiters Intnl, *Exec Srch*
Precision Staffing, Inc., *Perm Agcy*

Louisiana
Graham Search Group, *Exec Srch*
Hale & Associates, *Exec Srch*
Healthcare Recruiters Intnl, *Exec Srch*
Keenan Staffing Inc., *Temp Agcy*
MSI Physicians, *Exec Srch*
Mngmt. Rcrtrs. International, *Exec Srch*
Medforce, *Perm Agcy*
Medi-Lend Nursing Svcs., *Perm Agcy*
Premier Staffing, Inc., *Temp Agcy*
Shiell Personnel, *Perm Agcy*
Snelling Personnel Svcs., *Exec Srch*
Talley & Associates, Inc./Talley Temporaries, *Exec Srch*
Westaff, *Temp Agcy*
X Techs, *Temp Agcy*

Maine
At Work Personnel Svc., *Temp Agcy*
Career Management Assoc., *Exec Srch*

Maryland
Caplan/Gross Associates, *Exec Srch*
F-O-R-T-U-N-E Pers. Conslts, *Exec Srch*
HealthCare Recruiters of the Mid-Atlantic, *Exec Srch*
Mngmt. Rcrtrs. of Annapolis, *Exec Srch*
Mngmt. Rcrtrs. of Frederick/OfficeMates5, *Exec Srch*
Mngmt. Rcrtrs. of Washington, DC, *Exec Srch*
Mark Hofmeister & Associates Executive Recruiters, *Exec Srch*
NRI Healthcare, *Temp Agcy*
Sales Conslt, *Exec Srch*
Sanford Rose Associates, *Exec Srch*
Search Connection, *Exec Srch*
Sudina Search Inc., *Exec Srch*
TAC Staffing Services, *Temp Agcy*
Universal Healthcare Placements, *Exec Srch*
White Ridgely Associates, Inc., *Career/Outplacement*
Witt/Kieffer, Ford, Hadelman & Lloyd, *Exec Srch*

Massachusetts
A.S.I. Temps/Michael Ward Assoc., *Temp Agcy*
Abbott's of Boston, Inc., *Exec Srch*
Accurate Staffing Svcs., *Perm Agcy*
Anodyne Corporation, *Temp Agcy*
Michael Anthony Assoc., *Exec Srch*
Auerbach Associates, *Exec Srch*
Nathan Barry & Associates, *Exec Srch*
Battalia Winston Intnl., *Exec Srch*
Bowdoin Group, *Exec Srch*
Brattle Temps, *Temp Agcy*
Breitner Clark & Hall, *Exec Srch*
CEC Associates, *Exec Srch*
Cleary Conslt Inc., *Perm Agcy*
Robert H. Davidson Assoc./Exec. & Pro Resume Svc., *Exec Srch*
DeLuca & Associates, *Exec Srch*
Directions Medical Group, *Exec Srch*
The Diversified Srch Cos., *Exec Srch*
Dunhill Staffing Systems, *Temp Agcy*
Fitzgerald Associates, *Exec Srch*
F-O-R-T-U-N-E Pers. Conslts, *Exec Srch*
Healthcare Recruiters Intnl, *Exec Srch*
Human Resource Conslt, *Perm Agcy*
Johnson & Hill Staff Svc., *Temp Agcy*
Kelly Services, Inc., *Temp Agcy*
L&L Assoc & Temps, *Temp Agcy*
John Leonard Pers. Assoc., *Perm Agcy*

Mngmt. Rcrtrs. International, *Exec Srch*
Manpower Temp. Svcs., *Temp Agcy*
Medical Bureau, *Exec Srch*
Molari, Inc., *Temp Agcy*
Navin Group, *Exec Srch*
P.A.R. Associates Inc., *Exec Srch*
Pendleton James Assoc., *Exec Srch*
Phillips & Associates, *Exec Srch*
The Pickwick Group, Inc., *Exec Srch*
Pro Staff, *Temp Agcy*
Professional Staff Group, *Perm Agcy*
E.S. Rando Associates, *Perm Agcy*
Russell Reynolds Assoc., *Exec Srch*
Sales Conslt, *Exec Srch*
George D. Sandel Assoc., *Perm Agcy*
Snelling Personnel, *Exec Srch*
Stone & Youngblood, *Exec Srch*
Straube Associates, *Exec Srch*
TMP Worldwide, *Exec Srch*
TAD Staffing Services, *Temp Agcy*
TASA International, *Exec Srch*
Travcorps, *Temp Agcy*
Winfield Associates, *Exec Srch*
Witt/Kieffer, Ford, Hadelman & Lloyd, *Exec Srch*

Michigan
Acton Sell Associates, *Exec Srch*
AEGIS Group, *Exec Srch*
Beacon Services Inc., *Exec Srch*
Catalyst Health Care Group, *Exec Srch*
Circlewood Search Group, *Exec Srch*
Entech Personnel Svcs., *Temp Agcy*
Express Personnel Svcs., *Temp Agcy*
F-O-R-T-U-N-E Pers. Conslts., *Exec Srch*
Genesys Health Personnel, *Exec Srch*
Joseph Goldring & Assoc., *Exec Srch*
Harper Associates, *Exec Srch*
Health Care Professionals, *Perm Agcy*
Healthcare Recruiters Intnl, *Exec Srch*
William Howard Agency, *Contract Svc*
Mngmt. Rcrtrs. International, *Exec Srch*
MedMatch, *Exec Srch*
METROSTAFF, *Exec Srch*
Nationwide Career Network, *Perm Agcy*
Nustar Temporary Svcs., *Temp Agcy*
Olsten Pro Staffing, *Temp Agcy*
Premier Healthcare Recruiters, *Exec Srch*
Professional Advancement Institute, *Exec Srch*
Professional Personnel Conslt International, *Exec Srch*
Roth Young Pers. Svcs., *Exec Srch*
Sales Conslt, *Exec Srch*
Sales Executives Inc., *Perm Agcy*
Sharrow & Associates Inc., *Exec Srch*
Snelling Search, *Perm Agcy*
Sterling Field Associates, *Exec Srch*
Sullivan & Associates, *Exec Srch*
Vectech Pharmaceuticals Conslt, *Perm Agcy*
Wing Tips and Pumps, Inc., *Exec Srch*

Minnesota
Bright Search/Pro Staffing, *Exec Srch*
Erspamer Associates, *Exec Srch*
Fogarty & Associates, *Exec Srch*
Health Pers. Options, *Temp Agcy*
Healthcare Recruiters, *Exec Srch*
Hilleren & Associates, *Exec Srch*
T.H. Hunter, Inc., *Exec Srch*
Johnson Associates, *Temp Agcy*
Mngmt. Rcrtrs./Sales Conslt, *Exec Srch*
MedSearch Corporation, *Exec Srch*
Resource Search, *Exec Srch*
Roth Young Exec. Recs., *Exec Srch*
Ultimate Search Unlimited/Temps Unlimited, *Temp Agcy*

Mississippi
Compass Group, Inc., *Exec Srch*
EPSCO Personnel Service, *Temp Agcy*
Recruitment & Training Programs of Mississippi, Inc., *Perm Agcy*

Missouri
AnesTemps, Inc., *Temp Agcy*
Burns Employment Svc., *Exec Srch*
Business Personnel Svcs., *Temp Agcy*
Deck & Decker Emp. Svc, *Perm Agcy*
Employer Advantage, *Exec Srch*
Healthcare Recruiters Intnl, *Exec Srch*
Insurance Overload Syst., *Temp Agcy*

Mngmt. Rcrtrs./OfficeMates5, *Exec Srch*
Northwest Temporary & Staffing
Services, *Temp Agcy*
Provider Management, *Exec Srch*
Search & Recruiting Specialist, *Exec Srch*
Woodworth Intnl. Group, *Exec Srch*

Pennsylvania

AAP Inc., *Temp Agcy*
Advent Associates, *Exec Srch*
All Staffing Inc., *Perm Agcy*
Allegheny Personnel Svcs, *Temp Agcy*
Barton Personnel Syst., *Exec Srch*
Bradley Professional Svcs, *Perm Agcy*
Caliber Associates, *Exec Srch*
Career Quest Confidential, *Exec Srch*
Charley's Pers. Staffing, *Temp Agcy*
CoreStaff Inc., *Temp Agcy*
DPSI Medical, *Exec Srch*
P. Robert Dann, *Exec Srch*
Delta ProSearch, *Exec Srch*
Robert J. DePaul & Assoc., *Exec Srch*
The Diversified Srch Cos., *Exec Srch*
Garrick Hall & Associates, *Exec Srch*
Hallmark Personnel Inc./Abel Temps, *Perm Agcy*
The Hastings Group, *Exec Srch*
Healthcare Recruiters Intnl, *Exec Srch*
The Hobart West Group, *Perm Agcy*
Interactive Search Assoc., *Exec Srch*
Interim Healthcare, *Perm Agcy*
J-Rand Search, *Exec Srch*
Nancy Jackson Inc., *Exec Srch*
Jefferson-Ross Assoc., *Exec Srch*
Keynote Systems Inc., *Temp Agcy*
Mngmt. Rcrtrs. International, *Exec Srch*
Mngmt. Rcrtrs. of Bucks County, Inc., *Exec Srch*
Mngmt. Rcrtrs./CompuSearch, *Exec Srch*
Mngmt. Rcrtrs. of Pittsburgh-North, Inc., *Exec Srch*
Manchester Inc., *Career/Outplacement*
Mastersearch, *Exec Srch*
Norcon Associates, Inc., *Exec Srch*
Orion Delta Group Ltd., *Exec Srch*
LaMonte Owens, Inc., *Exec Srch*
PRN Conslt, *Perm Agcy*
Physician Billing Solutions, *Perm Agcy*
Probe Technology, *Exec Srch*
Protocall Bus. Staffing, *Temp Agcy*
Rice Cohen International, *Exec Srch*
Roth Young Pers. Svcs., *Perm Agcy*
SPC F-O-R-T-U-N-E, *Exec Srch*
Spectrum Conslt, Inc./Retail Recruiters, *Exec Srch*
Daniel Stern & Associates, *Exec Srch*
StratfordGroup, *Exec Srch*
TRC Staffing Services, *Temp Agcy*
TAC Staffing Services, *Temp Agcy*
Terry Taylor & Associates, *Exec Srch*
Uni-Temp Temp. Svc., *Temp Agcy*
United Staffing Services, *Temp Agcy*
Vogue Personnel Inc., *Exec Srch*
Whittlesey & Associates, *Exec Srch*

Rhode Island

Kelly Services, Inc., *Temp Agcy*
Albert G. Lee & Assoc., *Exec Srch*
Mngmt. Rcrtrs. International, *Exec Srch*
Sullivan & Cogliano, *Exec Srch*
TAC Staffing Services, *Temp Agcy*
Westminster Group, *Exec Srch*

South Carolina

Columbia Health Care Svcs., *Exec Srch*
Columbus Intnl. Group, *Exec Srch*
F-O-R-T-U-N-E Pers. Conslts, *Exec Srch*
Health Care Search Assoc., *Exec Srch*
Health Force, *Temp Agcy*
Mngmt. Rcrtrs. of Aiken, *Exec Srch*
Mngmt. Rcrtrs. of Anderson, *Exec Srch*
Mngmt. Rcrtrs. of Columbia, *Exec Srch*
Mngmt. Rcrtrs. of Rock Hill, *Exec Srch*
Southern Recruiters & Conslt, Inc., *Exec Srch*
StaffingSolutions, *Temp Agcy*

South Dakota

Interim Healthcare, *Contract Svc*
Olsten Staffing Services, *Temp Agcy*

Tennessee

A-1 Staffing & Personnel, *Temp Agcy*

Anderson McIntyre Pers. Svcs, *Exec Srch*
Angel Medical Pers. Pool, *Temp Agcy*
C.J. Staffing Services, *Contract Svc*
Cook Associates Intnl., *Exec Srch*
Corporate Image Group, *Exec Srch*
Gateway Group Personnel, *Temp Agcy*
H R Group, *Exec Srch*
Health Staff, *Temp Agcy*
Healthcare Recruiters, *Exec Srch*
Mngmt. Rcrtrs./Sales Conslt, *Exec Srch*
Manpower, Inc., *Temp Agcy*
W.R. McLeod & Assoc., *Exec Srch*
Medical & Dental Resources, *Exec Srch*
PIRC, *Exec Srch*
Personnel Link, *Exec Srch*
Physician Placement Svc., *Exec Srch*
Snelling Personnel Svcs., *Perm Agcy*

Texas

Abilene Employment Svc, *Perm Agcy*
Action Personnel Inc., *Temp Agcy*
Add-A-Temp/Woodlands Executive Employment, *Temp Agcy*
Adecco, *Temp Agcy*
Albrecht & Assoc. Exec. Srch, *Exec Srch*
Marilyn Austin & Associates Personnel Services, *Exec Srch*
Austin Medical Personnel, *Perm Agcy*
Aware Affiliates Pers. Svc, *Perm Agcy*
Kaye Bassman Intnl. Corp., *Exec Srch*
Benchmark Professionals, *Exec Srch*
BioSource International, *Exec Srch*
Bond & Associates, *Exec Srch*
Borrel Personnel, *Exec Srch*
Brainpower Pers. Agency, *Perm Agcy*
Brooklea & Assoc., *Exec Srch*
CAP Associates, *Exec Srch*
Colvin Resources Group, *Perm Agcy*
Continental Pers. Service, *Perm Agcy*
Dallas Employment Svcs., *Perm Agcy*
Dependable Dental Staffing, *Temp Agcy*
Dividend Staffing Svcs., *Temp Agcy*
John A. Domino & Assoc., *Exec Srch*
Dunhill Pro Search, *Exec Srch*
EAI Healthcare Staffing Solutions, *Exec Srch*
Express Personnel Svcs., *Temp Agcy*
Gulco Intl Recruiting Svcs., *Perm Agcy*
H.P.R. Health Staff, *Exec Srch*
Haragan Associates, *Exec Srch*
Health Network USA, *Exec Srch*
Health Professionals, *Exec Srch*
Healthcare Providers, *Contract Svc*
Healthcare Recruiters, *Exec Srch*
Horn & Associates, *Exec Srch*
Innovative Staff Search, *Exec Srch*
Kelly Services, Inc., *Temp Agcy*
Korn/Ferry International, *Exec Srch*
Mngmt. Rcrtrs. International, *Exec Srch*
Medical Search Solutions, *Exec Srch*
MedTex Staffing, *Perm Agcy*
Nationwide Med. Placement, *Exec Srch*
Odell & Associates Inc., *Exec Srch*
OMNI Consortium, Inc., *Perm Agcy*
P.H.R., *Temp Agcy*
The Pailin Group Professional Search Conslt, *Exec Srch*
Pate Resources Group, *Exec Srch*
Practice Dynamics, *Exec Srch*
Professional Search Conslt, *Contract Svc*
Professions Today, *Perm Agcy*
Lea Randolph & Assoc., *Exec Srch*
RehabWorks, *Contract Svc*
Resource Connection Workforce Center, *Perm Agcy*
Respiratory Staffing Specialists Inc., *Temp Agcy*
Rottman Group Inc., *Exec Srch*
Russell Reynolds Assoc., *Exec Srch*
Sales Conslt, *Exec Srch*
Say Ahhh Med. Office Svcs., *Perm Agcy*
R.L. Scott Associates, *Exec Srch*
Search Com, Inc., *Exec Srch*
Select Staff, *Temp Agcy*
Snelling Personnel Svcs., *Perm Agcy*
Solutions, *Exec Srch*
R.A. Stone & Associates, *Exec Srch*
StratfordGroup, *Exec Srch*
TMP Worldwide, *Exec Srch*
Betty Tanner Exec. Search, *Exec Srch*
Therapists Unlimited, *Exec Srch*
TravelCare Unlimited, *Perm Agcy*

The Whitaker Companies, *Contract Svc*
Windsor Conslt Inc., *Exec Srch*
Witt/Kieffer, Ford, Hadelman & Lloyd, *Exec Srch*
Bruce Woods Exec. Srch, *Exec Srch*

Utah

Deeco International, *Exec Srch*
Mngmt. Rcrtrs. of Salt Lake City, *Exec Srch*
Professional Recruiters, *Exec Srch*

Virginia

Advanced Recruiting Svc, *Exec Srch*
Advantage Staffing, *Temp Agcy*
The Alexis Group, Inc., *Exec Srch*
Alpha Omega Resources, *Perm Agcy*
Austin Assoc. Med. Pers., *Perm Agcy*
Buckler Careers, Inc., *Perm Agcy*
Contec Search, Inc., *Exec Srch*
DPS, Inc., *Contract Svc*
Wayne Garber & Assoc., *Exec Srch*
Larson Katz & Young, *Exec Srch*
MSI International, *Exec Srch*
Mngmt. Rcrtrs. International, *Exec Srch*
The McCormick Group, *Exec Srch*
Marvin Meltzer Associates, *Exec Srch*
Professional Search Pers., *Exec Srch*
Remedy Intelligent Staffing, *Temp Agcy*
Search Connection, *Exec Srch*
Search Conslt, Inc., *Exec Srch*
Snelling Personnel Svcs., *Perm Agcy*
Team Placement Service, *Temp Agcy*
Lawrence Veber Assoc., *Exec Srch*

Washington

Black & Deering, *Exec Srch*
Robert Cole Associates, *Exec Srch*
Corbett & Associates, *Exec Srch*
Express Personnel Svcs., *Temp Agcy*
L.W. Foote Co./The Brighton Group, *Exec Srch*
F-O-R-T-U-N-E Pers. Conslts of East Seattle, *Exec Srch*
The Jobs Company, *Exec Srch*
Mngmt. Rcrtrs. International, *Exec Srch*
Northwest Temporary & Staffing Services, Inc., *Temp Agcy*
PACE Staffing Network, *Exec Srch*
Personnel Unlimited Inc., *Exec Srch*
Sander Associates, *Exec Srch*
StratfordGroup, *Exec Srch*
Technical Resource Group, *Exec Srch*
James M. Thomas & Assoc, *Exec Srch*
R.A. Ward & Associates, *Exec Srch*
The Washington Firm, *Exec Srch*
Williams Recruiting, *Exec Srch*

West Virginia

Dunhill Pro Search, *Exec Srch*
Key Personnel, Inc., *Exec Srch*
Mngmt. Rcrtrs. of Morgantown, *Exec Srch*
Pro Med National Staffing of Wichita Falls, Inc., *Exec Srch*

Wisconsin

Austria Austria & Assoc., *Perm Agcy*
Concord Staff Source Inc., *Perm Agcy*
Custom Care, *Temp Agcy*
J.M. Eagle Partners, *Exec Srch*
Greenfield Rehab Agency, *Temp Agcy*
Healthcare Recruiters Intnl, *Exec Srch*
Mngmt. Rcrtrs. International, *Exec Srch*
Medteams, *Temp Agcy*
Quirk-Corporon & Assoc., *Exec Srch*
Sales Specialists, Inc., *Exec Srch*
Staff Development Corp., *Exec Srch*
TMP Worldwide, *Exec Srch*

HIGH-TECH

Arizona

Bartholdi & Company, *Exec Srch*
Corporate Dynamix, *Exec Srch*
DVA Consulting, *Contract Svc*
TSS Consulting, Ltd., *Exec Srch*

California

Amtec Engineering Corp., *Perm Agcy*
BDP Mngmt. Consulting Grp., *Exec Srch*
Deborah Bishop & Assoc., *Exec Srch*
Boyle Ogata, *Exec Srch*
Brandenburg Smith & Assoc, *Exec Srch*
CLARIA Corporation, *Exec Srch*

Ohio

Hospitality ProServices, *Exec Srch*
Richard Johns Career Conslt, *Perm Agcy*
Jerry Paul Associates, *Perm Agcy*

Pennsylvania

Roth Young Personnel Services, *Exec Srch*

South Carolina

Hospitality Recruiters, *Exec Srch*

South Dakota

Snelling Personnel Services, *Perm Agcy*

Tennessee

Bishop Placement Service, *Exec Srch*
Quest International, *Exec Srch*

Texas

ACTION Recruiting Svcs., *Exec Srch*
Alpha Resource Group, *Exec Srch*
Burgeson Hospitality Search, *Exec Srch*
Elliot Associates Inc., *Exec Srch*
Executive Restaurant Search/Pinnacle Search Group, *Exec Srch*
Ken Herst Hotel Executive Search and Consulting, *Exec Srch*
M.H. Logan & Associates, *Exec Srch*
Restaurant Recruiters, *Exec Srch*
SearchAmerica Inc., *Exec Srch*
Robert Wesson & Assoc., *Exec Srch*

Virginia

Career Market Conslt, *Exec Srch*
Executive Recruiters, *Exec Srch*

INDUSTRIAL

Alabama

Aerotek, Inc., *Perm Agcy*
Mary Cheek & Associates, *Exec Srch*
Clark Personnel Service, *Exec Srch*
Employment Conslt, *Perm Agcy*
F-O-R-T-U-N-E Pers. Conslts, *Exec Srch*
Labor Finders, *Temp Agcy*
J.L. Small Associates, *Exec Srch*
VIP Personnel, Inc., *Perm Agcy*
WorkForce Enterprises, *Temp Agcy*

Alaska

Manpower Temp. Svcs., *Temp Agcy*

Arizona

Adecco/TAD Tech. Svcs., *Temp Agcy*
Amer. Career Grp, *Career/Outplacement*
Dan Bolen & Associates, *Exec Srch*
CDI Corporation, *Contract Svc*
Devau Human Resources, *Temp Agcy*
H&M Recruiters, *Exec Srch*
Manpower Tech. Svcs., *Temp Agcy*
Stivers Temporary Pers., *Temp Agcy*

Arkansas

Turnage Emp. Svc. Group, *Exec Srch*
Utopia, Inc., *Exec Srch*

California

AccuStaff Incorporated, *Temp Agcy*
Alfano Temp. Personnel, *Temp Agcy*
Alpha-Net Consulting Grp, *Exec Srch*
Apple One Emp. Svcs., *Perm Agcy*
Apropos Emp. Agency, *Perm Agcy*
Battalia Winston Intnl., *Exec Srch*
Best Temporary Service, *Temp Agcy*
CDI Technical Services, *Temp Agcy*
California Job Connection, *Perm Agcy*
California Search Agency, *Exec Srch*
Career Quest Intnl., *Contract Svc*
Wayne Chamberlain & Assoc., *Exec Srch*
Corestaff Services, *Perm Agcy*
Crossroads Staffing Svc., *Temp Agcy*
Culver Personnel Services, *Perm Agcy*
Drake Office Overload, *Temp Agcy*
Dunhill of San Francisco, *Exec Srch*
Employment Svc Agency, *Perm Agcy*
Fisher Pers. Mngmt. Svcs., *Exec Srch*
F-O-R-T-U-N-E Pers. Conslts, *Exec Srch*
Dianne Gauger & Assoc., *Exec Srch*
Global Resources Ltd., *Exec Srch*
Griffith & Associates, *Exec Srch*
Industrial Services Co., *Temp Agcy*
Interim Personnel, *Temp Agcy*
International Staff Conslt, *Exec Srch*
Intertec Personnel, *Temp Agcy*
JPM International, *Exec Srch*

Jerome & Company, *Exec Srch*
Keifer Professional Search, *Exec Srch*
Klein & Associates, *Temp Agcy*
John Kurosky & Assoc., *Exec Srch*
Lab Support Inc., *Temp Agcy*
Lab Support Inc./Healthcare Financial Staffing, *Temp Agcy*
MK Tech. Services, Inc., *Temp Agcy*
Mngmt. Rcrtrs. International, *Exec Srch*
Manpower Staffing Svcs., *Temp Agcy*
Multisearch Recruiters, *Exec Srch*
Murray Enterprises Staffing Services, Inc., *Temp Agcy*
Nelson HR Solutions, *Perm Agcy*
Norrell Temp. Svcs., *Temp Agcy*
Omni Express Temps, *Temp Agcy*
Ortman Recruiting Intnl., *Exec Srch*
Premier Personnel Svcs., *Temp Agcy*
Premier Staffing, *Perm Agcy*
Presidio Personnel, *Temp Agcy*
PrideStaff, *Temp Agcy*
Pro Staff Personnel Svcs., *Perm Agcy*
Questemps, *Temp Agcy*
Remedy Caller Access, *Temp Agcy*
Remedy Intelligent Staffing, *Temp Agcy*
Resource Perspectives, Inc., *Exec Srch*
Riley-Cole, *Exec Srch*
San Diego Pers. & Emp., *Temp Agcy*
Santa Barbara Staffing, *Perm Agcy*
Select Personnel Services, *Temp Agcy*
Sierra Technology Corp., *Contract Svc*
Spectrum Personnel, *Temp Agcy*
Sun Personnel Services, *Temp Agcy*
TMP Worldwide, *Exec Srch*
T.R. Employment Agency, *Perm Agcy*
TECH/AID, *Temp Agcy*
Temps Unlimited, Inc., *Temp Agcy*
Trendtec Inc., *Temp Agcy*
United Staffing Solutions, *Exec Srch*
Vaughan & Co. Exec. Srch., *Exec Srch*
Volt Services Group, *Temp Agcy*
Westaff, *Temp Agcy*
Work Load Inc., *Temp Agcy*

Colorado

Aspen Personnel Services, *Perm Agcy*
Career Forum, Inc., *Exec Srch*
Intellimark, *Temp Agcy*
JobSearch, *Temp Agcy*
Kelly Services, Inc., *Temp Agcy*
Labor Ready, Inc., *Temp Agcy*
Manpower International, *Temp Agcy*
Olsten Staffing Services, *Temp Agcy*
SOS Staffing Services, *Temp Agcy*
Star Personnel Service, *Exec Srch*
Tech Staffing, *Temp Agcy*
Todays Temporary, *Temp Agcy*
J.Q. Turner & Associates, *Exec Srch*
Woodmoor Group, *Exec Srch*

Connecticut

Admiral Staffing Services, *Temp Agcy*
Bohan & Bradstreet, *Perm Agcy*
Cahill Associates, *Exec Srch*
Charter Personnel Services, *Exec Srch*
Corporate Staff Solutions, *Temp Agcy*
Hallmark Totaltech, Inc., *Exec Srch*
Hire Logic, *Perm Agcy*
J.G. Hood Associates, *Perm Agcy*
Human Resource Conslt, *Exec Srch*
Lutz Associates, *Exec Srch*
MJF Associates, *Exec Srch*
Mngmt. Rcrtrs. International, *Exec Srch*
Office Services, *Perm Agcy*
Barry Persky & Co., *Exec Srch*
Quality Control Recruiters, *Exec Srch*
TMP Worldwide, *Exec Srch*
Technical Staff Solutions, *Temp Agcy*
Westaff, *Temp Agcy*

Delaware

J.B. Groner Exec. Search, *Exec Srch*
E.W. Hodges & Associates, *Exec Srch*
Norris & Roberts Ltd., *Exec Srch*
The Placers, Inc., *Temp Agcy*

Dist. of Columbia

Manpower, *Temp Agcy*
Norrell Services, *Temp Agcy*

Florida

AAA Employment, *Perm Agcy*
Able Body Corp. Svcs., *Contract Svc*

Academy Design & Tech. Svcs., *Contract Svc*
Active Professionals, *Exec Srch*
Adecco, *Temp Agcy*
The Brand Company, Inc., *Exec Srch*
Colli Associates of Tampa, *Exec Srch*
DGA Personnel Group, *Exec Srch*
Donbar Service Corp., *Temp Agcy*
Employers' Assistant, Inc., *Temp Agcy*
Environmental Health & Safety Search Associates (EH&S), *Exec Srch*
Ethan Allen Pers. Placement, *Exec Srch*
Five Star Temporary Inc., *Temp Agcy*
F-O-R-T-U-N-E Pers. Conslts, *Exec Srch*
Kay Concepts, *Exec Srch*
Kelly Services, Inc., *Temp Agcy*
Mngmt. Rcrtrs. International, *Exec Srch*
Manchester Inc., *Exec Srch*
Manpower Temp. Svcs., *Temp Agcy*
Norrell Services Inc., *Temp Agcy*
Norrell Technical Services, *Exec Srch*
Priority Search, *Exec Srch*
Pro-Team Services, Inc., *Exec Srch*
The Reserves Network, *Temp Agcy*
The Ryan Charles Group, *Exec Srch*
Sales Conslt, Inc., *Exec Srch*
Doug Sears & Assoc., *Exec Srch*
Staffing Now, *Temp Agcy*
Summit Exec. Search Conslt, *Exec Srch*
Sun Personnel West, *Exec Srch*
System One Services, *Contract Svc*
TMP Worldwide, *Exec Srch*

Georgia

All-Star Temp. & Emp. Svcs, *Temp Agcy*
Anderson Industrial Assoc., *Exec Srch*
Arjay & Associates, *Exec Srch*
Augusta Staffing Assoc., *Perm Agcy*
B.A. Associates Inc., *Exec Srch*
Comprehensive Search Grp, *Exec Srch*
Corporate Srch Conslt, *Exec Srch*
Express Personnel Svcs., *Perm Agcy*
F-O-R-T-U-N-E Pers. Conslts of Atlanta/Alternastaff, *Exec Srch*
ISC of Atlanta/International Career Continuation, *Exec Srch*
Job Shop Inc., *Exec Srch*
Kelly Services, Inc., *Temp Agcy*
MSI International, *Exec Srch*
Mngmt. Rcrtrs. of Atlanta, *Exec Srch*
Mngmt. Rcrtrs. of Marietta, *Exec Srch*
Mngmt. Rcrtrs. of Savannah, *Exec Srch*
Norred & Associates Inc., *Perm Agcy*
Parker, McFadden Assoc., *Exec Srch*
Priority 1 Staffing Svcs., *Temp Agcy*
Quality Employment Svc, *Temp Agcy*
Randstad Staffing Svcs., *Temp Agcy*
Sondra Search, *Exec Srch*
Southern Emp. Svc., *Perm Agcy*
TMP Worldwide, *Exec Srch*
Todays Emp. Solutions, *Perm Agcy*
Westaff, *Temp Agcy*

Hawaii

ASAP Express, *Contract Svc*
Altres Staffing, *Temp Agcy*
Dunhill Pro Staffing, *Exec Srch*
Kelly Services, Inc., *Temp Agcy*
Olsten Staffing Services, *Temp Agcy*

Idaho

Intermountain Staffing Resources, *Perm Agcy*

Illinois

A.B.A. Placements/A.B.A. Temporaries, *Perm Agcy*
The Ability Group, *Exec Srch*
Ablest Staffing Services, *Temp Agcy*
Accurate Personnel Inc., *Perm Agcy*
Adecco, *Temp Agcy*
American Contract Svcs., *Contract Svc*
American Tech. Search, *Exec Srch*
Assured Staffing, *Temp Agcy*
Banner Personnel Service, *Perm Agcy*
Battalia Winston Intnl., *Exec Srch*
Britannia, *Exec Srch*
Burling Group Ltd., *Exec Srch*
CareerLink USA, Inc., *Exec Srch*
Cast Metals Personnel Inc., *Exec Srch*
Cook Associates, Inc., *Exec Srch*
Corporate Environment, *Exec Srch*
Cumberland Group, *Exec Srch*
Diener & Associates Inc., *Exec Srch*

New Hampshire

Affordable Solutions, *Contract Svc*
Barclay Personnel Syst., *Exec Srch*
Chaucer Group, *Exec Srch*
Kelly Services, Inc., *Temp Agcy*
Manpower Temp. Svcs., *Temp Agcy*
National Emp. Svc. Corp., *Perm Agcy*
Preferred Resource Group, *Exec Srch*
Sales Conslt, *Exec Srch*
Surge Resources Inc., *Contract Svc*

New Jersey

Advanced Personnel Svc., *Perm Agcy*
Allstaff Resources, Inc., *Perm Agcy*
American Staff Resources, *Perm Agcy*
Battalia Winston Intnl., *Exec Srch*
Berman & Larson, *Perm Agcy*
Blake & Assoc. Exec. Srch, *Exec Srch*
Careers USA, *Perm Agcy*
Citizens Emp. Svcs., *Perm Agcy*
Cox Darrow & Owens, *Exec Srch*
M.T. Donaldson Assoc., *Exec Srch*
Dynamic Recruiters Inc., *Exec Srch*
Ellis Career Conslt/Career Search
  Associates, *Exec Srch*
Express Personnel Svcs., *Perm Agcy*
Hughes & Podesla Pers., *Perm Agcy*
Impact Personnel, Inc., *Perm Agcy*
Joule Staffing Services, *Contract Svc*
Kaye Personnel Inc., *Temp Agcy*
Joseph Keyes Associates, *Perm Agcy*
Mngmt. Rcrtrs./OfficeMates5, *Exec Srch*
Mayfair Services, *Perm Agcy*
OMNE Staffing Services, *Temp Agcy*
Orion Consulting, Inc., *Exec Srch*
Pomerantz Staffing Svcs., *Perm Agcy*
Protocall Bus. Staff Svcs., *Temp Agcy*
Rotator Staffing Svcs., *Contract Svc*
R.S. Sadow Associates, *Exec Srch*
Sales Conslt, *Exec Srch*
Robert Scott Associates, *Exec Srch*
Summit Group, Inc., *Exec Srch*
Michael D. Zinn & Assoc., *Exec Srch*

New Mexico

Albuquerque Personnel, *Perm Agcy*
CDI Technical Services, *Contract Svc*
Manpower, Inc., *Temp Agcy*
Trambley The Recruiter, *Perm Agcy*

New York

AARP Foundation/Senior Employment
  Program, *Perm Agcy*
ATS Reliance, Inc., *Contract Svc*
Accounting & Computer Personnel,
  Perm Agcy
Merrill Adams Associates, *Career/
  Outplacement*
Adecco/TAD Tech. Svcs, *Contract Svc*
Arrow Emp. Agency, *Perm Agcy*
Battalia Winston Intnl., *Exec Srch*
Beishline Executive Search, *Exec Srch*
Bestemp Temporary Svcs., *Temp Agcy*
Bos Business Conslt, *Exec Srch*
Burns Personnel, *Exec Srch*
Carlile Personnel Agency, *Perm Agcy*
Corporate Careers, Inc., *Exec Srch*
Corporate Moves, Inc., *Exec Srch*
Frank Cuomo & Assoc., *Exec Srch*
Eden Staffing, *Perm Agcy*
Exek Recruiters Ltd., *Exec Srch*
Extra Help Emp. Svcs., *Temp Agcy*
Graphic Techniques, Inc., *Temp Agcy*
The Haas Associates, Inc., *Exec Srch*
Hart-Merrell Personnel, *Exec Srch*
Interim Personnel, *Temp Agcy*
Kirk-Mayer, *Contract Svc*
Fred Koffler Associates, *Exec Srch*
Lab Support Inc., *Temp Agcy*
Lake Associates, *Exec Srch*
John Lawrence & Assoc., *Exec Srch*
Mngmt. Rcrtrs. of Orange Cty, *Exec Srch*
Mngmt. Rcrtrs. of St. Lawrence County,
  Exec Srch
Mngmt. Rcrtrs. of Suffolk, *Exec Srch*
Manpower Temp. Svcs., *Temp Agcy*
Metro Resources of Rochester Inc., *Temp
  Agcy*
Metropolitan Pers. Syst., *Exec Srch*
Morgan-Murray Personnel/M&M Top
  Temps, *Temp Agcy*
Noah Associates, *Perm Agcy*
Olsten Financial Staffing, *Temp Agcy*

Olsten Staffing Services, *Temp Agcy*
Parsons, Anderson & Gee, *Perm Agcy*
Pendleton James Assoc., *Exec Srch*
Phoenix Emp. Agency, *Perm Agcy*
Recruitment Intnl. Group, *Exec Srch*
Remedy Intelligent Staffing, *Temp Agcy*
Sales Search/Exec. Resume Svc., *Exec
  Srch*
SearchAmerica Inc., *Exec Srch*
Staff Managers, *Temp Agcy*
Stafkings Personnel Syst., *Temp Agcy*
Superior Concepts, *Contract Svc*
TMP Worldwide, *Exec Srch*
Thorsen Associates, Inc., *Exec Srch*
Todd Arro, Inc., *Exec Srch*
Volt Services Group, *Contract Svc*
Weber Mngmt Conslt, *Exec Srch*
Westaff, *Temp Agcy*
Westchester Emp. Agency, *Perm Agcy*
Michael D. Zinn & Assoc., *Exec Srch*

North Carolina

A First Resource, *Exec Srch*
Accurate Staffing Conslt, *Exec Srch*
Action Staffing Group, *Temp Agcy*
Active Search Recruiters, *Exec Srch*
Alpha Omega Exec. Srch, *Exec Srch*
AmeriPro Search, Inc., *Exec Srch*
Atchison & Associates, *Exec Srch*
Ayers & Associates, Inc., *Exec Srch*
Barrett Business Services, *Temp Agcy*
Caldwell Pers. Services, *Perm Agcy*
Eastern Search Group, *Exec Srch*
Executive Staffing Group, *Exec Srch*
F-O-R-T-U-N-E Pers. Conslts, *Exec Srch*
The Furniture Agency Inc., *Exec Srch*
Interim Personnel, Inc., *Temp Agcy*
The Jobs Market, Inc., *Perm Agcy*
Kelly Services, Inc., *Temp Agcy*
Mngmt. Rcrtrs. International/
  Sales Conslt, *Exec Srch*
McCain Employment Svc, *Temp Agcy*
Myers & Associates, *Perm Agcy*
Olsten Staffing Services, *Temp Agcy*
The Perkins Group, *Exec Srch*
Professional Pers. Assoc., *Perm Agcy*
Quality Temp. Services, *Temp Agcy*
Sanford Rose Assoc., *Exec Srch*
Search Conslt Worldwide Inc., *Exec Srch*
Snelling Personnel Svcs., *Perm Agcy*
Sparks Personnel Svcs., *Exec Srch*
Waddy R. Thomson Assoc., *Exec Srch*
USA Staffing, *Perm Agcy*
Winston Personnel Group, *Temp Agcy*
Youngblood Staffing, *Perm Agcy*

North Dakota

Career Connection, *Exec Srch*
Olsten Staffing Services/Expressway
  Personnel, *Temp Agcy*

Ohio

AccuStaff, *Temp Agcy*
Adecco/TAD. Svcs, *Contract Svc*
Alliance Technical Svcs., *Contract Svc*
Dave Arnold & Assoc., *Exec Srch*
Belcan Technical Svcs., *Contract Svc*
CBS Personnel Services, *Perm Agcy*
Combined Resources Inc., *Exec Srch*
Continental Search Assoc., *Exec Srch*
Corell Associates, *Perm Agcy*
Custom Staffing, Inc., *Temp Agcy*
DLD Technical Services, *Contract Svc*
Eastern Personnel Svcs., *Perm Agcy*
Elite Resources Group, *Exec Srch*
Executech, *Exec Srch*
Executive Connection, *Exec Srch*
Executive Search Ltd., *Exec Srch*
F.L.A.G., *Exec Srch*
Flex-Tech Prof. Svcs., *Contract Svc*
F-O-R-T-U-N-E Pers. Conslts, *Exec Srch*
Frederick-Lehmann & Associates/
  Temporarily Yours, *Exec Srch*
Gayhart & Associates, *Exec Srch*
Global Resources Group, *Contract Svc*
H.L. Goehring & Assoc., *Exec Srch*
Griffiths & Associates, *Exec Srch*
ITS Technical Staffing, *Exec Srch*
Interim Personnel, *Temp Agcy*
Anne Jones Staffing, Inc., *Perm Agcy*
KBK Management Assoc., *Exec Srch*
A.T. Kearney Exec. Search, *Exec Srch*
Kelly Services, Inc., *Temp Agcy*

Mngmt. Rcrtrs. International, *Exec Srch*
Manpower Temp. Svcs., *Temp Agcy*
Marvel Conslt Inc., *Exec Srch*
Masterson Personnel, Inc./Masterson
  Temporary Services, *Perm Agcy*
Messina Management Syst., *Exec Srch*
Miami Professional Search, *Exec Srch*
Midland Conslt, *Exec Srch*
Nesco Service Company, *Temp Agcy*
Newcomb-Desmond & Assoc., *Exec Srch*
Northcoast Personnel, *Exec Srch*
Professional Emp. Svcs., *Perm Agcy*
Professional Restaffing, *Perm Agcy*
Providence Pers. Conslt, *Exec Srch*
RDS, Inc., *Contract Svc*
Resource Techne Group, *Exec Srch*
Revere Associates, *Exec Srch*
Sales Conslt, *Exec Srch*
Tabb & Associates, *Exec Srch*
The Target HR Cos., Inc., *Temp Agcy*
Teamwork U.S.A., *Contract Svc*
Technical Recruiting Svcs., *Exec Srch*
Technical/Mngmt. Resources, *Perm Agcy*
Temporarily Yours Placement, *Temp
  Agcy*
Tradesman International, *Contract Svc*
Vector Technical Inc., *Perm Agcy*
J.P. Walton & Associates, *Exec Srch*

Oklahoma

Ameri Resource, *Exec Srch*
Cherokee Temps, Inc., *Temp Agcy*
Express Personnel Services/RWJ &
  Associates, *Temp Agcy*
Key Temporary Personnel, *Temp Agcy*
StaffMark, *Temp Agcy*

Oregon

APA Employment Agency, *Exec Srch*
API Employment Agency, *Perm Agcy*
Barrett Business Services, *Temp Agcy*
Employment Trends, *Temp Agcy*
Executives Worldwide, *Exec Srch*
Express Personnel Services, *Exec Srch*
Hackenschmidt, Weaver & Fox, Inc.,
  Exec Srch
Kelly Services, Inc., *Temp Agcy*
Manpower Temp. Svcs., *Temp Agcy*
Nationwide Personnel Recruiting &
  Consulting Inc., *Exec Srch*
Northwest Temporary & Staffing
  Services, *Temp Agcy*
Quest Temporary Svcs., *Temp Agcy*
Specialized Search Co., *Exec Srch*
Uniforce Staffing Svcs., *Contract Svc*

Pennsylvania

AA Staffing Solutions, *Contract Svc*
Action Personnel Services, *Perm Agcy*
Alexander Personnel Assoc, *Exec Srch*
All Staffing Inc., *Perm Agcy*
Allegheny Personnel Svcs, *Temp Agcy*
American Search Assoc., *Exec Srch*
Atomic Personnel, Inc., *Exec Srch*
Basilone-Oliver Exec. Srch, *Exec Srch*
CDI Corporation, *Contract Svc*
Career Concepts Staff Svcs, *Exec Srch*
CoreStaff Inc., *Temp Agcy*
Dunn Associates, *Exec Srch*
Fox-Morris Associates, *Exec Srch*
Jerry Goldberg & Assoc., *Perm Agcy*
HRS/TND Associates, Inc., *Exec Srch*
Garrick Hall & Associates, *Exec Srch*
The Hastings Group, *Exec Srch*
Hobbie Personnel Svcs., *Temp Agcy*
IMC International, Inc., *Contract Svc*
Interim Personnel, *Temp Agcy*
J-Rand Search, *Exec Srch*
JK Resources, *Exec Srch*
Clifton Johnson Assoc., *Exec Srch*
Kathy Karr Personnel, *Perm Agcy*
London Personnel Svcs., *Perm Agcy*
Manpower Temp. Svcs., *Temp Agcy*
Robert McClure Ltd., *Exec Srch*
B. Paul Mickey & Assoc., *Exec Srch*
The Morris Group, *Exec Srch*
National Computerized Employment
  Service Inc., *Exec Srch*
Norcon Associates, Inc., *Exec Srch*
Norrell Services, *Temp Agcy*
Olsten Staffing Services, *Temp Agcy*
Probe Technology, *Exec Srch*
Protocall Bus. Staffing, *Temp Agcy*

Humbert Group, *Exec Srch*
Mngmt. Rcrtrs. International, *Exec Srch*

Kansas
Effective Search Inc., *Exec Srch*
Manpower Technical, *Perm Agcy*
WESSYX, *Exec Srch*

Kentucky
Mngmt. Rcrtrs. International, *Exec Srch*
Superior Office Support, *Perm Agcy*

Louisiana
Mngmt. Rcrtrs. International, *Exec Srch*

Maine
Pro Search, Inc., *Exec Srch*
Win Win Solutions, *Exec Srch*

Maryland
Columbia Consulting, *Exec Srch*
Computer Management, *Exec Srch*
Search Connection, *Exec Srch*

Massachusetts
Architechs, *Exec Srch*
CDI Corporation, *Contract Svc*
Hall Kinion, *Contract Svc*
Hoffman Recruiters, *Exec Srch*
Management Search, Inc., *Exec Srch*
McCormick Group, *Exec Srch*
E.S. Rando Assoc., *Perm Agcy*

Michigan
AJM Professional Services, *Exec Srch*
Account Ability Now, *Perm Agcy*
Dickson Associates Inc., *Exec Srch*
Info. Syst. Exec. Recruiters, *Exec Srch*
Sullivan & Associates, *Exec Srch*
Troy Tech Services, *Contract Svc*

Minnesota
ESP Systems Professionals, *Exec Srch*
Emerging Tech. Search, *Exec Srch*
Fairfax Group, *Exec Srch*
Hall Kinion, *Contract Svc*

Missouri
Gruen & Associates, Inc., *Exec Srch*
Lloyd, Martin & Assoc., *Exec Srch*
Pinnacle Executive Group, *Exec Srch*

Montana
Caria Resources, Inc., *Exec Srch*

New Hampshire
Access Data Personnel, *Exec Srch*
Exeter 2100, *Perm Agcy*

New Jersey
AES Associates, *Exec Srch*
Berman & Larson, *Perm Agcy*
Carnegie Associates, *Exec Srch*
Data Search Network, *Exec Srch*
A. Davis Grant & Co., *Exec Srch*
The Dowd Group, *Exec Srch*
Executive Registry Inc., *Exec Srch*
Global Search, Inc., *Exec Srch*
Hall Kinion, *Contract Svc*
Hreshko Consulting Group, *Exec Srch*
M.R. Group, Inc., *Exec Srch*
Mngmt. Rcrtrs. of New Providence, *Exec Srch*
On Target Search, *Exec Srch*
Softsearch Exec. Recs., *Exec Srch*
J. Vincent Associates, *Exec Srch*

New York
Audit Data Search Ltd., *Exec Srch*
Brian Associates, Inc., *Exec Srch*
CDI Corporation, *Contract Svc*
Cavan Systems, Ltd., *Exec Srch*
Computer Resources Corp., *Exec Srch*
D&L Associates, Inc., *Exec Srch*
Hall Kinion, *Contract Svc*
Ktech Systems Group, *Perm Agcy*
Pro Search Associates, Inc., *Exec Srch*
SearchAmerica Inc., *Exec Srch*
Setford-Shaw-Najarian Assoc., *Exec Srch*

North Carolina
Hall Kinion, *Contract Svc*
Mngmt. Rcrtrs. International, *Exec Srch*

Ohio
Career Enterprises, *Exec Srch*
Executive Search Ltd., *Exec Srch*
W.A. Hill & Associates, *Exec Srch*
ITS Technical Staffing, *Exec Srch*

North Peak Group, *Exec Srch*
K.J. Phillips Associates, *Exec Srch*
Sanford Rose Associates, *Exec Srch*
Sterling Pers. Resources, *Exec Srch*
True North Conslt, *Exec Srch*

Oklahoma
Advanced Recruiting Inc., *Exec Srch*

Oregon
D. Brown & Associates, *Exec Srch*
Computer Recruiters/Creative Data Corporation, *Exec Srch*
Hall Kinion, *Contract Svc*

Pennsylvania
Advent Associates, *Exec Srch*
Dunhill Prof. Search, *Exec Srch*
Fox-Morris Associates, *Exec Srch*
Mngmt. Rcrtrs. International, *Exec Srch*
Romac International, *Exec Srch*
Terry Taylor & Associates, *Exec Srch*
Technical Search Services, *Exec Srch*

Rhode Island
Careers Unlimited, *Perm Agcy*
Furlong Professional Svcs., *Exec Srch*

South Carolina
Corporate Solutions, *Exec Srch*

Tennessee
Pittman Group, *Exec Srch*
Wood Personnel Services, *Perm Agcy*

Texas
Audit Professionals Intnl., *Exec Srch*
Bridge Personnel, *Exec Srch*
EDP Computer Services, *Exec Srch*
Hall Kinion, *Contract Svc*
Sales Conslt, *Exec Srch*
TGA Company, *Exec Srch*

Utah
Hall Kinion, *Contract Svc*
Upgrade Assoc. Recruiters, *Exec Srch*

Vermont
Mngmt. Rcrtrs. of Burlington, *Exec Srch*

Virginia
ACSYS Inc., *Exec Srch*
B&M Associates, *Contract Svc*
Dahl Morrow International, *Exec Srch*
Wayne Garber & Assoc., *Exec Srch*
Hall Kinion, *Contract Svc*
Larson Katz & Young, *Exec Srch*
Mngmt. Rcrtrs. International, *Exec Srch*
Search Connection, *Exec Srch*
The Talley Group, *Exec Srch*

Washington
Hall Kinion, *Contract Svc*
Gary Kokensparger & Assoc., *Exec Srch*
Macrosearch/Macrostaff, *Perm Agcy*
Mngmt. Rcrtrs. of Lakewood, *Exec Srch*
Schultz Group Inc., *Exec Srch*

Wisconsin
Benston & Associates, *Exec Srch*
Data Processing Search, *Exec Srch*
The H S Group, Inc., *Exec Srch*
Mngmt. Rcrtrs./Compusearch, *Exec Srch*
PDS Technical Services, *Contract Svc*
Professional Resource Svcs, *Exec Srch*
RCM Technologies, *Contract Svc*
Rowbottom & Associates, *Exec Srch*

INFORMATION TECHNOLOGY

Alabama
Langford Search, *Exec Srch*
Prosearch, *Exec Srch*
Sanford Rose Associates, *Exec Srch*

Arizona
Hall Kinion, *Contract Svc*
McEvoy & Johnson Assoc., *Perm Agcy*
Romac International, *Exec Srch*
SearchAmerica Inc., *Exec Srch*
TSS Consulting, Ltd., *Exec Srch*
H.L. Yoh Company, *Contract Svc*

Arkansas
EDP Staffing Solutions, *Exec Srch*
Seatec, *Contract Svc*

California
AROSE Recruiting Co., *Temp Agcy*
B&M Associates Inc., *Temp Agcy*

Career Conslt Intnl., *Exec Srch*
Christian & Timbers, *Exec Srch*
Computer Network Resources, *Exec Srch*
General Emp. Enterprises, *Perm Agcy*
InfoSYS, *Exec Srch*
Lifter & Associates, *Exec Srch*
Mngmt. Rcrtrs. of Roseville, *Exec Srch*
Management Solutions Inc., *Exec Srch*
Planting & Associates, *Exec Srch*
Premier Resources, *Exec Srch*
RJ Associates, *Exec Srch*
Romac International, *Exec Srch*
Sampson Medical Search, *Exec Srch*
TechSource, *Contract Svc*
Techstaff West Inc., *Exec Srch*
H.L. Yoh Company, *Contract Svc*

Colorado
Alexander Group, *Exec Srch*
Careers Limited, *Exec Srch*
Hall Kinion, *Contract Svc*
Interim Technology, *Contract Svc*

Connecticut
Cheney Associates, *Exec Srch*
Data Careers, *Exec Srch*
Hall Kinion, *Contract Svc*
Huntington Group, *Exec Srch*
Infonet LLC, *Exec Srch*
The La Pointe Group Inc., *Exec Srch*
Pascale & LaMorte, LLC, *Exec Srch*
Romac International, *Exec Srch*
H.L. Yoh Co./Yoh Information Technology Assoc., *Contract Svc*

Delaware
DW Technologies, *Contract Svc*
The Placers, Inc., *Temp Agcy*
Prof. Rec. Conslt, *Perm Agcy*

Florida
American Recruiters, *Exec Srch*
First Recruiters Group Inc., *Exec Srch*
F-O-R-T-U-N-E Pers. Conslts, *Exec Srch*
Hall Kinion, *Contract Svc*
Mngmt. Rcrtrs. International, *Exec Srch*
Sanford Rose Associates, *Exec Srch*
System One Services, *Contract Svc*

Georgia
Bell Oaks Company, *Exec Srch*
Cobb George Exec. Search, *Exec Srch*
Comforce Brannon & Tully, *Exec Srch*
Comms People, *Contract Svc*
Computer Tech. Search/Data Mngmt. & Staff Recruiters, *Exec Srch*
Delta Resource Group, *Exec Srch*
Executive Strategies, Inc., *Exec Srch*
The GateKeepers Intnl., *Exec Srch*
Leader Institute, Inc., *Exec Srch*
PRI/Invesearch, *Exec Srch*
Romac International, *Exec Srch*
SCI Recruiters, *Exec Srch*
The Shepard Group, Inc., *Exec Srch*
Sondra Search, *Exec Srch*
Technical Alliance Group, *Exec Srch*
Think Resources, *Contract Svc*
TriTech Associates, *Exec Srch*
Tyler Technical Staffing, *Perm Agcy*
Van Zant Resource Group, *Perm Agcy*

Illinois
Alternative Rsrcs. Corp., *Contract Svc*
Barry Pers. Resources, *Perm Agcy*
Beta Technologies, *Exec Srch*
Career Placements, Inc., *Exec Srch*
Coffou Partners, Inc., *Exec Srch*
Computer Search Group, *Exec Srch*
Hall Kinion, *Contract Svc*
Hamilton Grey Exec. Srch, *Exec Srch*
K-Force, *Exec Srch*
Pratzer & Partners, *Exec Srch*
Pro Staff Personnel Svcs., *Temp Agcy*
Pro-Tech Search Inc., *Exec Srch*
Professional Search Center, *Exec Srch*
Quest Enterprises, Ltd., *Exec Srch*
Recruitment Network, *Exec Srch*
Smith Scott & Associates, *Exec Srch*
Texcel, Inc., *Exec Srch*
Wilson-Douglas-Jordan, *Exec Srch*

Indiana
Johnson Brown Associates, *Exec Srch*

Arkansas

Mngmt. Rcrtrs., *Exec Srch*
Premier Staffing, Inc., *Temp Agcy*
Snelling Search, *Exec Srch*
Turnage Emp. Svc. Group, *Exec Srch*

California

ABA Staffing, Inc., *Exec Srch*
A.S.A.P. Emp. Svc., *Perm Agcy*
Actuarial Search Assoc., *Exec Srch*
Amato & Assoc. of CA, *Exec Srch*
Answers Unlimited, *Temp Agcy*
Apropos Emp. Agency, *Perm Agcy*
Associated Software Conslt, Inc., *Temp Agcy*
Astra West Pers. Svcs., *Perm Agcy*
Bsa Personnel Center, *Perm Agcy*
Blackhawk Advantage, *Exec Srch*
Business Systems Support, *Perm Agcy*
CRI Professional Search, *Exec Srch*
California Mngmt. Search, *Exec Srch*
Career Quest Intnl., *Contract Svc*
Champagne Personnel, *Temp Agcy*
Choice Personnel, *Perm Agcy*
Christian & Timbers, *Exec Srch*
Claimsearch/The Srch Grp, *Exec Srch*
Computer Network Resources, *Exec Srch*
Crossroads Staffing Svc., *Temp Agcy*
The Culver Group, *Exec Srch*
Culver Personnel Services, *Perm Agcy*
Culver Staffing Resources, *Temp Agcy*
Daco Recruiting Inc., *Exec Srch*
Dependable Employment Agency Network, *Perm Agcy*
E.C. International, *Exec Srch*
Finesse Personnel Assoc., *Exec Srch*
GM Management Services, *Exec Srch*
Goldstein & Associates, *Temp Agcy*
The Goodman Group, *Exec Srch*
Gould Personnel Services, *Perm Agcy*
Interim Personnel, *Temp Agcy*
JPM International, *Exec Srch*
Jackson Personnel, *Perm Agcy*
Jatinen & Associates, *Exec Srch*
John Anthony & Assoc., *Exec Srch*
Lending Personnel Svcs., *Exec Srch*
Lifter & Associates, *Exec Srch*
London Temporary Svcs., *Temp Agcy*
Mngmt. Rcrtrs. International, *Exec Srch*
Medical Staff Unlimited, *Perm Agcy*
Musick & Associates, *Exec Srch*
Nelson HR Solutions, *Perm Agcy*
O'Crowley & O'Toole Exec. Search, *Exec Srch*
Olsten Staffing Services, *Temp Agcy*
Pacific Recruiting Offices, *Exec Srch*
Pacific Search Group, *Exec Srch*
Pasona Pacific, *Temp Agcy*
Premier Personnel Svcs., *Temp Agcy*
Presidio Personnel, *Temp Agcy*
Pro Staff Personnel Svcs., *Perm Agcy*
Pryor & Associates, *Perm Agcy*
Remedy Caller Access, *Temp Agcy*
The Rogan Group, *Exec Srch*
Rusher, Loscavio, and LoPresto, *Exec Srch*
Santa Barbara Staffing, *Perm Agcy*
Search West, *Exec Srch*
Search West of Ontario, *Exec Srch*
Sharp Personnel & Search, *Exec Srch*
Stivers Temporary Pers., *Temp Agcy*
Stone & Associates, *Exec Srch*
D.M. Stone Pro Staffing, *Exec Srch*
TRC Staffing Services, *Perm Agcy*
Telford, Adams, & Alexander, *Exec Srch*
Thor Temporary Services, *Temp Agcy*
TOD Staffing, *Temp Agcy*
Today Personnel Services, *Perm Agcy*
Trans U.S., Inc., *Perm Agcy*
Truex Associates, *Exec Srch*
United Staffing Solutions, *Exec Srch*
Volt Services Group, *Temp Agcy*
Your People Professionals, *Perm Agcy*

Colorado

Adecco, *Temp Agcy*
Ahrnsbrak and Assoc., *Perm Agcy*
Careers Limited, *Exec Srch*
Initial Staffing Services, *Perm Agcy*
JobSearch, *Temp Agcy*
Manpower Intnl. Inc., *Temp Agcy*
Peak Ltd., *Exec Srch*
SOS Staffing Services, *Temp Agcy*

Sales Conslt, *Exec Srch*
Stivers Temporary Pers., *Temp Agcy*

Connecticut

Admiral Staffing Services, *Temp Agcy*
Andrews & Mahon, *Exec Srch*
Thomas Byrne Associates, *Perm Agcy*
Clifford Garzone Assoc., *Exec Srch*
Corporate Staff Solutions, *Temp Agcy*
Data Pros, *Perm Agcy*
EDP Contract Services, *Contract Svc*
Harvard Aimes Group, *Exec Srch*
Hipp Waters Prof. Search, *Exec Srch*
Mngmt. Rcrtrs. of Norwalk, *Exec Srch*
The McKnight Group, *Exec Srch*
Office Services of CT, *Perm Agcy*
Howard W. Smith Associates, *Exec Srch*
Westaff, *Temp Agcy*

Delaware

Caldwell Staffing Services, *Perm Agcy*
J.B. Groner Executive Search, *Exec Srch*
The Placers, Inc., *Temp Agcy*

Dist. of Columbia

GKA Resources, LLC, *Exec Srch*
Norrell Services, *Temp Agcy*

Florida

AAA Employment, *Perm Agcy*
Active Professionals, *Exec Srch*
American Recruiters, *Exec Srch*
The Butlers Company/Insurance Recruiters, *Exec Srch*
Careers Unlimited, Inc., *Exec Srch*
Carrier's Career Service, Inc., *Career/Outplacement*
Criterion Executive Search, *Exec Srch*
Executive Career Strategies, *Exec Srch*
Gans, Gans & Associates, *Perm Agcy*
Hastings & Hastings Personnel Conslt, *Temp Agcy*
International Insurance Conslt, Inc., *Exec Srch*
LaMorte Search Assoc., *Exec Srch*
Lear & Associates, *Exec Srch*
Mngmt. Rcrtrs. International, *Exec Srch*
Manchester Inc., *Exec Srch*
Olsten Staffing Services, *Temp Agcy*
OMNIpartners, *Exec Srch*
Priority Search, *Exec Srch*
Linda Robins & Assoc., *Temp Agcy*
The Ryan Charles Group, *Exec Srch*
Sales Conslt, *Exec Srch*
Doug Sears & Assoc., *Exec Srch*
Snelling Personnel Svcs., *Temp Agcy*
Staffing Now, *Temp Agcy*
TRC Staffing Services, *Temp Agcy*
Todays Temporary, *Temp Agcy*
Uniquest International, Inc., *Temp Agcy*

Georgia

Bell Oaks Company, Inc., *Exec Srch*
Bridgers & Associates, *Exec Srch*
Corporate Image Group, *Exec Srch*
Elite Staffing Services, *Temp Agcy*
Executive Resource Group, *Exec Srch*
Fellows Students Assoc., *Exec Srch*
International Insurance Pers., *Perm Agcy*
JJ&H Ltd./Jacobson Assoc., *Exec Srch*
MSI International, *Exec Srch*
The Malcolm Group, Inc., *Perm Agcy*
Mngmt. Rcrtrs. of Atlanta, *Exec Srch*
More Personnel Svcs., *Perm Agcy*
Olsten Staffing Services, *Temp Agcy*
Personnel Opportunities Inc., *Exec Srch*
Priority 1 Staffing Svcs., *Temp Agcy*
Randstad Staffing Svcs., *Temp Agcy*
Rollins Search Group, *Exec Srch*
Staffing Resources, *Perm Agcy*
TRC Staffing Services, *Temp Agcy*
Temporary Specialties, *Temp Agcy*

Hawaii

Executive Search World, *Exec Srch*

Idaho

Horne/Brown International, *Exec Srch*
Idaho Department of Employment/Jobservice, *Perm Agcy*

Illinois

A.B.A. Placements/A.B.A. Temporaries, *Perm Agcy*
Account Pros, *Exec Srch*
American Medical Pers., *Perm Agcy*

E.J. Ashton & Associates, *Exec Srch*
The Bankers Group, *Exec Srch*
Bell Personnel Inc., *Perm Agcy*
Burling Group Ltd., *Exec Srch*
CareerLink USA, Inc., *Exec Srch*
Cogan Pers. Services, Inc., *Exec Srch*
Cook Associates, Inc., *Exec Srch*
Dynamic People, *Temp Agcy*
The Esquire Staffing Grp, *Perm Agcy*
Executive Directions, *Exec Srch*
Executive Search Conslt, *Exec Srch*
Fellows Placement, *Temp Agcy*
Financial Search Corporation, *Exec Srch*
F-O-R-T-U-N-E Pers. Conslts, *Exec Srch*
Furst Staffing Services, *Temp Agcy*
Godfrey Personnel Inc., *Exec Srch*
David Gomez & Assoc., *Exec Srch*
Hallmark Personnel Inc., *Perm Agcy*
Ronald B. Hanson & Assoc., *Exec Srch*
Hersher & Associates, Ltd., *Exec Srch*
Human Resource Connection, *Perm Agcy*
InterStaff, *Temp Agcy*
Interviewing Conslt, *Perm Agcy*
Jacobson Associates/Insurance Staffers, *Exec Srch*
Raymond Karson Associates, *Exec Srch*
Kinderis & Loercher Group, *Exec Srch*
Kingston/Zak Inc., *Exec Srch*
Arlene Leff & Associates, *Exec Srch*
Mngmt. Rcrtrs. International, *Exec Srch*
Manpower Temp. Svcs., *Temp Agcy*
The Murphy Group, *Perm Agcy*
National Search, *Exec Srch*
Olsten Staffing Services, *Temp Agcy*
Parker Cromwell & Assoc., *Exec Srch*
Personnel Connections, *Perm Agcy*
Professional Research Svcs., *Exec Srch*
Profile Temporary Svc., *Temp Agcy*
Remedy Intelligent Staffing, *Temp Agcy*
Right Services Inc., *Temp Agcy*
SC International, *Exec Srch*
J.R. Scott & Associates, *Exec Srch*
Sevcor International, Inc., *Exec Srch*
D.W. Simpson & Co., *Exec Srch*
Smith Hanley Associates, *Exec Srch*
Snelling Personnel Svcs., *Perm Agcy*
Staffing Conslt Inc., *Perm Agcy*
The Stanton Group, Inc., *Exec Srch*
Stivers Temporary Pers., *Temp Agcy*
VG & Associates, *Perm Agcy*
Waterford Executive Group, *Exec Srch*
Working World Inc., *Temp Agcy*
World Employment Svc., *Perm Agcy*

Indiana

Canis Major, Inc./HR Quest, *Exec Srch*
Crown Temporary Svcs., *Temp Agcy*
Execusearch, *Exec Srch*
Insurance People, *Exec Srch*
Job Placement Service, *Perm Agcy*
Mngmt. Rcrtrs. of Richmond, *Exec Srch*
OfficeMates5 (OM5)/DayStar Temporary Services, *Exec Srch*
Sanford Rose Associates, *Exec Srch*

Iowa

Byrnes & Rupkey, Inc., *Exec Srch*
Drake-Brennan, Inc., *Exec Srch*
Executive Resources, *Exec Srch*
Helping Hands Temps, *Temp Agcy*
Mngmt. Rcrtrs. International/Compusearch, *Exec Srch*
Mid America Search, *Exec Srch*
Premier Search Group, *Exec Srch*
Snelling Personnel, *Exec Srch*
Staff Management, Inc., *Contract Svc*
Staffing Edge, *Perm Agcy*

Kansas

Arwood & Associates, *Exec Srch*
Blackwell Associates, *Exec Srch*
Business Specialists, *Perm Agcy*
Mngmt. Rcrtrs. International, *Exec Srch*
Mngmt. Rcrtrs./Sales Conslt/OfficeMates5, *Exec Srch*
Morgan Hunter Corp. Search, *Exec Srch*
Winn Group, *Exec Srch*

Kentucky

Angel Group International, *Exec Srch*
Mngmt. Rcrtrs. International, *Exec Srch*
Precision Staffing, Inc., *Perm Agcy*
Temporary Professionals, *Temp Agcy*

Mngmt. Rcrtrs. International/ Newtown Consulting Grp, *Exec Srch*
Mngmt. Rcrtrs. of Delaware County/CompuSearch, *Exec Srch*
Manchester Inc., *Career/Outplacement*
J. McManus Associates, *Exec Srch*
The Morris Group, *Exec Srch*
Olsten Staffing Services, *Temp Agcy*
Pancoast Temp. Svcs., *Temp Agcy*
Physician Billing Solutions, *Perm Agcy*
Questor Conslt, Inc., *Exec Srch*
SHS International, *Exec Srch*
TRC Staffing Services, *Temp Agcy*
TAC Staffing Services, *Temp Agcy*
Uni-Temp Temp. Svc., *Temp Agcy*
Vogue Personnel Inc., *Exec Srch*

Rhode Island
Careers Unlimited, *Perm Agcy*
Daley & Associates Inc., *Exec Srch*
Mngmt. Rcrtrs. International, *Exec Srch*
Norrell Services, *Temp Agcy*
TAC Staffing Services, *Temp Agcy*

South Carolina
Mngmt. Rcrtrs. of Columbia, *Exec Srch*
Mngmt. Rcrtrs. of Rock Hill, *Exec Srch*
Sales Conslt of Mount Pleasant, *Exec Srch*
Smith Temps/Smith Pers., *Temp Agcy*

South Dakota
Mngmt. Rcrtrs. of Sioux Falls, *Exec Srch*
MidWest Recruiters (MIR), *Exec Srch*
Olsten Staffing Services, *Temp Agcy*

Tennessee
A-1 Staffing & Personnel, *Temp Agcy*
Cook Associates Intnl., *Exec Srch*
Corporate Image Group, *Exec Srch*
Leeds and Leeds, *Exec Srch*
Mngmt. Rcrtrs./Sales Conslt, *Exec Srch*
Norrell Services, *Temp Agcy*
Personnel Link, *Exec Srch*
Shiloh Careers Intnl., *Perm Agcy*
Snelling Personnel Svcs., *Perm Agcy*

Texas
Abilene Employment Svc., *Perm Agcy*
ACSYS Staffing, *Temp Agcy*
Austin Insurance Recruiters, *Perm Agcy*
Aware Affiliates Pers. Svc., *Perm Agcy*
Bundy-Stewart Assoc., *Exec Srch*
Daher & Associates Insurance Search Specialists, Inc., *Exec Srch*
Dallas Employment Svcs., *Perm Agcy*
The Danbrook Group, *Exec Srch*
Gail Darling Staffing/Gail Darling's Professional Desk, *Temp Agcy*
Express Personnel Svcs., *Perm Agcy*
Imprimis Staff Solutions, *Temp Agcy*
Insurance Search, *Exec Srch*
Insurance Temp. Svcs., *Temp Agcy*
Kelly Services, Inc., *Temp Agcy*
Mngmt. Rcrtrs. International, *Exec Srch*
The Pailin Group Professional Search Conslt, *Exec Srch*
Sales Conslt, *Exec Srch*
Select Staff, *Temp Agcy*
Snelling Personnel Svcs., *Perm Agcy*
Steele & Associates, *Perm Agcy*
Summit Srch Specialists, *Perm Agcy*
Texas Personnel, *Exec Srch*
Thomas Office Pers. Svc., *Perm Agcy*
Vinson and Associates, *Perm Agcy*

Vermont
J. R. Peterman Assoc., *Exec Srch*
Voll Associates, *Exec Srch*

Virginia
Alpha Omega Resources, *Perm Agcy*
Corporate Connection Ltd., *Exec Srch*
Dow Personnel, *Perm Agcy*
Mngmt. Rcrtrs./OfficeMates5, *Exec Srch*
Manpower Temp. Svcs., *Temp Agcy*
The McCormick Group, *Exec Srch*

Washington
The Career Clinic, Inc., *Exec Srch*
Express Personnel Svcs., *Temp Agcy*
HRA Insurance Staffing, *Exec Srch*
Kelly Services, Inc., *Temp Agcy*
Mngmt. Rcrtrs. of Tacoma, *Exec Srch*
Manpower Temp. Svcs., *Temp Agcy*
Pacific Personnel Group, *Exec Srch*

Personnel Conslt Inc., *Exec Srch*
Personnel Unlimited Inc., *Exec Srch*

Wisconsin
Crown Services, *Temp Agcy*
The H S Group, Inc., *Exec Srch*
Landmark, The Staffing Resource, *Temp Agcy*
Mngmt. Rcrtrs. of Green Bay, *Exec Srch*
Mngmt. Rcrtrs. of Lake Wisconsin, *Exec Srch*
Mngmt. Rcrtrs. of Milwaukee, *Exec Srch*
Mngmt. Rcrtrs. of Stevens Point, *Exec Srch*
Olsten Staffing Services, *Temp Agcy*
Quirk-Corporon & Assoc., *Exec Srch*
Sales Conslt of Madison, *Exec Srch*

INTERNET DEVELOPMENT

Arizona
Amer. Career Grp, *Career/Outplacement*
The Bren Group, *Exec Srch*
Hall Kinion, *Contract Svc*
Taylor Design Recruiting, *Temp Agcy*

California
ACCESS Technology, *Exec Srch*
Arrowstaff Services, Inc., *Perm Agcy*
The Badger Group, *Exec Srch*
BridgeGate LLC, *Exec Srch*
EDP Contract Services, *Contract Svc*
Essential Solutions, Inc., *Perm Agcy*
GenevaGroup International, *Exec Srch*
Hall Kinion, *Contract Svc*
HireKnowledge, *Temp Agcy*
Maciejewski & Associates, *Perm Agcy*
Reed Group, LLC, *Exec Srch*
Schweichler Associates Inc., *Exec Srch*
Splaine & Associates Inc., *Exec Srch*
TRC Staffing Services, *Perm Agcy*
Amy Zimmerman & Assc, *Perm Agcy*

Colorado
Hall Kinion, *Contract Svc*
Mngmt. Rcrtrs., Inc., *Exec Srch*

Connecticut
The Cambridge Group Ltd., *Exec Srch*
Hall Kinion, *Contract Svc*
Hallmark Totaltech, Inc., *Exec Srch*
Infonet LLC, *Exec Srch*

Dist. of Columbia
GKA Resources, LLC, *Exec Srch*
HireKnowledge, *Temp Agcy*

Florida
Hall Kinion, *Contract Svc*
Pro-Team Services, Inc., *Exec Srch*
Strategy Resources Inc., *Perm Agcy*

Georgia
Elite Staffing Services, *Temp Agcy*
TriTech Associates, *Exec Srch*

Illinois
William J. Blender & Assoc., *Exec Srch*
CompuPro, *Exec Srch*
Hall Kinion, *Contract Svc*
Macro Resources, *Exec Srch*
Paul May & Associates, *Exec Srch*
Network Resource Group, *Perm Agcy*

Louisiana
Mngmt. Rcrtrs., *Exec Srch*

Maryland
HireKnowledge, *Temp Agcy*

Massachusetts
Fanning Personnel, *Perm Agcy*
Hall Kinion, *Contract Svc*
HireKnowledge, *Temp Agcy*
Morency Associates, *Exec Srch*
Nationwide Business Svc., *Perm Agcy*
Remedy Intelligent Staffing, *Temp Agcy*
The Renaissance Network, *Exec Srch*

Michigan
Clark & Hartman Prof. Srch, *Perm Agcy*
Kelly Technical Services, *Contract Svc*
Troy Tech Services, *Contract Svc*

Minnesota
Hall Kinion, *Contract Svc*

Missouri
Austin Nichols/RCM, *Temp Agcy*
HireKnowledge, *Temp Agcy*

Montana
Caria Resources, Inc., *Exec Srch*

New Hampshire
CCSI Inc., *Perm Agcy*

New Jersey
BAI Personnel Solutions, *Perm Agcy*
Global Resources Group, *Exec Srch*
Hall Kinion, *Contract Svc*
The Howard Group, Ltd., *Exec Srch*
Lancaster Assc/Swan Grp., *Exec Srch*
Search EDP Inc., *Exec Srch*
Stewart/Laurence Associates, *Exec Srch*

New Mexico
Excel Staffing Companies, *Perm Agcy*

New York
AZR Inc., *Exec Srch*
Adecco/TAD Tech. Svcs., *Contract Svc*
Adept Tech Recruiting, *Exec Srch*
Advantage Resumes of New York, *Career/Outplacement*
Alpha Health Svcs. Corp., *Exec Srch*
C.C. Burke, Ltd., *Exec Srch*
Execu/Search Group, *Exec Srch*
Fifth Avenue Exec. Staffing, *Exec Srch*
Hall Kinion, *Contract Svc*
HireKnowledge, *Temp Agcy*
Landover Associates, Inc., *Exec Srch*
Olsten Financial Staffing, *Temp Agcy*
Phoenix Search Group, *Exec Srch*
Quantum Personnel Agency, *Exec Srch*
RCM Technologies, Inc., *Perm Agcy*
Total Computer People Inc., *Exec Srch*

North Carolina
Hall Kinion, *Contract Svc*

Ohio
Mngmt. Rcrtrs., *Exec Srch*

Oregon
Hall Kinion, *Contract Svc*

Pennsylvania
Computer Professionals, Inc., *Exec Srch*
HireKnowledge, *Temp Agcy*

Texas
E*OnLine Learning Recs., *Exec Srch*
Hall Kinion, *Contract Svc*
HireKnowledge, *Temp Agcy*
Priority Search, Inc., *Exec Srch*

Utah
Hall Kinion, *Contract Svc*

Virginia
Hall Kinion, *Contract Svc*
Paul-Tittle Associates, Inc., *Exec Srch*

Washington
Hall Kinion, *Contract Svc*
Kerry-Ben Kelly Exec. Srch, *Exec Srch*
John Mason & Associates, *Exec Srch*
Wilson Smith Associates, *Exec Srch*

INTERNET MARKETING

Arizona
Amer. Career Grp, *Career/Outplacement*
The Bren Group, *Exec Srch*
Taylor Design Recruiting, *Temp Agcy*

California
BridgeGate LLC, *Exec Srch*
Christian & Timbers, *Exec Srch*
CLARIA Corporation, *Exec Srch*
Drummer Personnel, Inc., *Exec Srch*
GenevaGroup International, *Exec Srch*
HireKnowledge, *Temp Agcy*
Interactive Search Network, *Exec Srch*
Reed Group, LLC, *Exec Srch*
Splaine & Associates Inc., *Exec Srch*

Dist. of Columbia
GKA Resources, LLC, *Exec Srch*
HireKnowledge, *Temp Agcy*

Florida
F.P. Lennon Associates, *Exec Srch*

Georgia
Elite Staffing Services, *Temp Agcy*

Bevelle & Associates, Inc., *Exec Srch*
CareerLink USA, Inc., *Exec Srch*
Chicago Legal Search, Ltd., *Exec Srch*
Cook Associates, Inc., *Exec Srch*
Credentia Inc., *Exec Srch*
Diener & Associates Inc., *Exec Srch*
Dynamic People, *Temp Agcy*
Early Cochran & Olson, *Exec Srch*
The Esquire Staffing Grp, *Perm Agcy*
Eve Recruiters Ltd., *Perm Agcy*
First Attorney Conslt, *Exec Srch*
General Counsel Corporation, *Exec Srch*
HR Search, *Perm Agcy*
Human Resource Connection, *Perm Agcy*
InterStaff, *Temp Agcy*
Law Corps Legal Staffing, *Temp Agcy*
Major Hagen & Africa, *Exec Srch*
Mngmt. Rcrtrs. International/
  Sales Conslt, *Exec Srch*
Manpower Temp. Svcs., *Temp Agcy*
Michael David Assoc., *Perm Agcy*
NJW & Associates, Inc., *Exec Srch*
OfficeMates5 (OM5), *Perm Agcy*
Olsten Staffing Services, *Temp Agcy*
Personnel Placement Conslt, *Perm Agcy*
Vera L. Rast Partners, *Exec Srch*
Remedy Intelligent Staffing, *Temp Agcy*
Right Services Inc., *Temp Agcy*
Keith Ross & Associates, Inc., *Exec Srch*
Seville Temporary Svcs., *Temp Agcy*
Snelling Personnel Svcs., *Temp Agcy*
Stivers Temporary Pers., *Temp Agcy*
Templeton & Associates, *Perm Agcy*
Verdin Associates, *Exec Srch*
Anne Violante & Associates, *Exec Srch*
Robert Whitfield Associates, *Exec Srch*
Philip Wieland & Associates, *Exec Srch*
Working World Inc., *Temp Agcy*
World Employment Svc., *Perm Agcy*

Indiana

Alpha Rae Personnel, Inc., *Perm Agcy*
Crown Temp. Services, *Temp Agcy*
Execusearch, *Exec Srch*
Job Placement Service, *Perm Agcy*
Mngmt. Rcrtrs. of Richmond, *Exec Srch*
Management Support Svcs., *Exec Srch*
OfficeMates5 (OM5)/DayStar Temporary
  Services, *Exec Srch*
Olsten Staffing Services, *Temp Agcy*
The Registry Inc., *Perm Agcy*
Unique, Inc., *Exec Srch*

Iowa

Burton Placement Services, *Exec Srch*
Helping Hands Temps, *Temp Agcy*
Mngmt. Rcrtrs. International/
  Compusearch, *Exec Srch*
Personnel, Inc., *Exec Srch*
Pratt-Younglove, Inc., *Perm Agcy*

Kansas

Business Specialists, *Perm Agcy*
Jag & Assoc Attorney Search, *Exec Srch*
Legal Search Associates, *Exec Srch*
LegalTEMPS of Kansas, Inc., *Temp Agcy*
Mngmt. Rcrtrs./Sales Conslt/
  OfficeMates5, *Exec Srch*
Manpower Temp. Svcs., *Temp Agcy*
Westaff, *Temp Agcy*
Wichita Bar Association Legal Placement
  Service, *Perm Agcy*

Kentucky

Angel Group International, *Exec Srch*
The Legal Edge, Inc./The Professional
  Edge, Inc., *Temp Agcy*
Precision Staffing, Inc., *Perm Agcy*
Professional Srch Conslt, *Exec Srch*

Louisiana

Mngmt. Rcrtrs./Sales Conslt., *Exec Srch*
Olsten Staffing Services/Briggs Legal
  Staffing, *Temp Agcy*
Special Counsel, *Temp Agcy*
Talley & Associates, Inc./Talley
  Temporaries, *Exec Srch*
Westaff, *Temp Agcy*

Maine

At Work Personnel Svc., *Temp Agcy*

Maryland

Caplan/Gross Associates, Inc., *Exec Srch*
Charter Business Services, *Perm Agcy*

F-O-R-T-U-N-E Pers. Conslts, *Exec Srch*
Graham Staffing Services, *Perm Agcy*
Mngmt. Rcrtrs. of Annapolis, *Exec Srch*
Mngmt. Rcrtrs. of Frederick/
  OfficeMates5, *Exec Srch*
Sigman & Summerfield Associates, Inc.,
  Perm Agcy
Special Counsel, *Temp Agcy*
TAC Staffing Services, *Temp Agcy*

Massachusetts

A.S.I. Temps/Michael Ward Associates,
  Temp Agcy
Ability Search, *Perm Agcy*
Attorney Special Assignment Placement/
  Paralegal Resource Ctr, *Temp Agcy*
Boston Professional Search, *Exec Srch*
Bostonian Personnel Co., *Perm Agcy*
Center for Professional Development in
  the Law, *Career/Outplacement*
Cleary Conslt Inc., *Perm Agcy*
Corporate Staff Solutions, *Temp Agcy*
Diversity Search Specialists, *Exec Srch*
Dunhill Staffing Systems, *Temp Agcy*
Fanning Personnel, *Perm Agcy*
Gillard Associates, *Perm Agcy*
Interim Personnel, *Temp Agcy*
Johnson & Hill Staff Svc, *Temp Agcy*
Kelly Services, Inc., *Temp Agcy*
Kennison & Assoc., *Temp Agcy*
L&L Associates & Temps, *Temp Agcy*
John Leonard Pers. Assoc., *Perm Agcy*
Mngmt. Rcrtrs. International, *Exec Srch*
Manpower Temp. Svcs., *Temp Agcy*
McCormick Group, *Exec Srch*
New England Legal Search, *Exec Srch*
New England Personnel, *Perm Agcy*
Professional Staffing Grp, *Perm Agcy*
Resources Objectives Inc., *Exec Srch*
Routhier Placement Specialists, *Perm
  Agcy*
Sales Conslt, *Exec Srch*
Selectemps, *Temp Agcy*
Snelling Personnel, *Exec Srch*
Special Counsel, *Temp Agcy*
Spectra Professional Search/Spectra
  Temps, *Perm Agcy*
Volt Services Group, *Temp Agcy*
Wallace Law Registry, *Temp Agcy*

Michigan

Beacon Services Inc., *Exec Srch*
Brookside Consulting Group, *Exec Srch*
Express Personnel Svcs., *Temp Agcy*
F-O-R-T-U-N-E Pers. Conslts, *Exec Srch*
William Howard Agency, *Contract Svc*
Legal Search & Management, *Exec Srch*
Mngmt. Rcrtrs. International, *Exec Srch*
Personnel At Law, Inc., *Temp Agcy*
Sharrow & Associates Inc., *Exec Srch*
Snelling Personnel Services/Bryant
  Bureau, *Perm Agcy*
T.M.S. Associates, *Exec Srch*
Trillium Staffing, *Temp Agcy*
Wing Tips and Pumps, Inc., *Exec Srch*

Minnesota

Abby Blu Inc., *Temp Agcy*
Alternative Staffing, Inc., *Perm Agcy*
Bright Search/Prof. Staffing, *Exec Srch*
The Esquire Group, *Exec Srch*
T.H. Hunter, Inc., *Exec Srch*
Interim Legal Profs., *Temp Agcy*
Howard Lieberman & Assoc., *Exec Srch*
Mngmt. Rcrtrs./Sales Conslt, *Exec Srch*
Midwest Staffing Svcs., *Temp Agcy*
C.A. Moore & Assoc., *Exec Srch*
Ultimate Search Unlimited/Temps
  Unlimited, *Perm Agcy*

Mississippi

Capitol Staffing Solutions, *Perm Agcy*
EPSCO Personnel Svc., *Temp Agcy*
Recruitment & Training Programs of
  Mississippi, Inc., *Perm Agcy*

Missouri

Aaron Consulting, Inc., *Exec Srch*
Bottom Line Prof. Svcs., *Contract Svc*
Business Personnel Svcs., *Temp Agcy*
Crown Services, Inc., *Temp Agcy*
ExecuTemps, Inc., *Temp Agcy*
Huey Enterprises, *Exec Srch*

Huntress Real Estate Exec. Search, *Exec
  Srch*
JoDoc Enterprises, *Temp Agcy*
Mngmt. Rcrtrs. of Kansas City, *Exec
  Srch*
Mngmt. Rcrtrs. of Springfield, *Exec Srch*
Mngmt. Rcrtrs. of St. Louis, *Exec Srch*
Manpower Temp. Svcs., *Temp Agcy*
OfficeMates5 (OM5), *Exec Srch*

Montana

Express Personnel Svcs., *Temp Agcy*
Kelly Services, Inc., *Temp Agcy*

Nebraska

Compusearch of Lincoln, *Exec Srch*
Corporate Recruiters, Ltd./Health Service
  Professionals, *Exec Srch*
Donna's Office Service, *Contract Svc*
Mngmt. Rcrtrs. of Omaha/
  OfficeMates5 of Omaha, *Exec Srch*

Nevada

Flowers Exec. Search Grp., *Exec Srch*
Initial Staffing Services, *Perm Agcy*

New Hampshire

Able 1 Staffing, *Exec Srch*
Allstaff, *Perm Agcy*
Barclay Personnel Systems, *Exec Srch*
Career Connections, Inc., *Perm Agcy*
Central NH Emp. Svcs., *Perm Agcy*
Emerald Legal Search, *Perm Agcy*
Kogen Personnel, *Perm Agcy*
Mngmt. Rcrtrs. International, *Exec Srch*
Manpower Temp. Svcs., *Temp Agcy*
Resource Recruiting/Contemporary
  Accountants, *Perm Agcy*

New Jersey

A+ Personnel Placement, *Perm Agcy*
ABC Nationwide Emp., *Perm Agcy*
AV Search Conslt, *Exec Srch*
Advanced Personnel Svc., *Perm Agcy*
BAI Personnel Solutions, *Perm Agcy*
Blake & Assoc. Exec. Search, *Exec Srch*
Executive Search, Inc., *Exec Srch*
Express Personnel Svcs., *Perm Agcy*
Foster Associates, *Exec Srch*
Sandra Grundfest, *Career/Outplacement*
Haley Stuart, Inc., *Exec Srch*
Impact Personnel, Inc., *Perm Agcy*
Integro Staffing Services, *Temp Agcy*
Joule Staffing Services, *Contract Svc*
L&K Associates, *Exec Srch*
Law Pros Legal Placement Svcs., *Exec
  Srch*
OfficeMates5 (OM5)/DayStar Temporary
  Services, *Exec Srch*
Orion Consulting, Inc., *Exec Srch*
Solomon Page Group, Inc., *Exec Srch*
Florence Pape Legal Search, *Exec Srch*
Pat's Secretarial Service, *Temp Agcy*
Premier Personnel Group, *Perm Agcy*
James F. Robinson Professional
  Recruiter, *Exec Srch*
Romac International, *Exec Srch*
Sales Conslt of Sparta, *Exec Srch*
Sanford Rose Associates, *Exec Srch*
Selective Personnel, *Perm Agcy*
Arline Simpson Assoc., *Perm Agcy*
Snelling Personnel Svcs., *Perm Agcy*
Topaz Attorney Search, *Exec Srch*
UNITEMP Temp. Pers., *Temp Agcy*
Winston Staffing Services, *Temp Agcy*
Winters & Ross, *Perm Agcy*
Claire Wright Associates, *Perm Agcy*

New Mexico

Albuquerque Personnel, *Perm Agcy*
Excel Staffing Companies, *Perm Agcy*
Santa Fe Services, *Temp Agcy*

New York

A-L Associates, Inc., *Exec Srch*
AJC Search, *Exec Srch*
AM & PM Temps Inc., *Temp Agcy*
Accounting & Computer Personnel,
  Perm Agcy
AccuStaff Incorporated, *Temp Agcy*
Adam Personnel, Inc., *Perm Agcy*
Merrill Adams Associates, *Career/
  Outplacement*
Asher Pers. Conslt, *Perm Agcy*
D. Bacal & Associates, *Exec Srch*

Seattle Recruiters, *Exec Srch*
Strategic Resources, *Exec Srch*
Woods & Associates, *Temp Agcy*

West Virginia
Snelling Personnel Svcs., *Temp Agcy*

Wisconsin
Careertrac Employment Svcs., *Exec Srch*
Crown Services, *Temp Agcy*
Legal Placement Services, Inc./Personnel Specialists, *Perm Agcy*
Mngmt. Rcrtrs. of Green Bay, *Exec Srch*
Mngmt. Rcrtrs. of Milwaukee/ Sales Conslt, *Exec Srch*
Olsten Staffing Services, *Temp Agcy*

LIGHT INDUSTRIAL

Alaska
Manpower Temp. Svcs., *Temp Agcy*

Arizona
Devau Human Resources, *Temp Agcy*
Electronic Power Source, *Exec Srch*

California
Best Temporary Service, *Temp Agcy*
Career Quest Intnl., *Contract Svc*
COMFORCE Tech. Svcs., *Contract Svc*
Complete Staff Resources, *Perm Agcy*
Culver Personnel Services, *Perm Agcy*
Full Service Temporaries, *Temp Agcy*
Interim Personnel, *Temp Agcy*
Intertec Design, Inc., *Perm Agcy*
Kelly Services, Inc., *Temp Agcy*
Klein & Associates, *Temp Agcy*
Manpower Staffing Svcs., *Temp Agcy*
Nelson HR Solutions, *Perm Agcy*
Ortman Recruiting Intnl., *Exec Srch*
PrideStaff, *Temp Agcy*
Pyramid Placement, *Perm Agcy*
ReliStaff, *Perm Agcy*
Remedy Intelligent Staffing, *Temp Agcy*
Santa Barbara Staffing, *Temp Agcy*
Select Personnel Services, *Temp Agcy*
Adele Steinmetz Exec. Srch, *Exec Srch*
TRC Staffing Services, *Temp Agcy, Perm Agcy*
TAC Staffing Services, *Temp Agcy*
Today Personnel Services, *Perm Agcy*
Western Labor Leasing, *Contract Svc*
Your People Professionals, *Perm Agcy*

Colorado
Absolute Staff Solutions, *Perm Agcy*
Executive Career Conslt, *Exec Srch*
Goodwin Personnel, Inc., *Perm Agcy*
Job Store Staffing, *Perm Agcy*
Kelly Services, Inc., *Temp Agcy*
Payroll Principals, Inc., *Perm Agcy*
TPM Staffing Service, *Perm Agcy*

Connecticut
Charter Personnel Services, *Exec Srch*
Quality Control Recruiters, *Exec Srch*
United Personnel Services, *Temp Agcy*

Dist. of Columbia
Adecco, *Temp Agcy*

Florida
AccuStaff Incorporated, *Temp Agcy*
Careers USA, *Temp Agcy*
Kelly Services, Inc., *Temp Agcy*
Mngmt. Rcrtrs. of Lake Cty, *Exec Srch*
Manpower Temp. Svcs., *Temp Agcy*
Olsten Staffing Services, *Temp Agcy*
Pro Staff, *Temp Agcy*
Victoria & Assoc. Pers. Svcs., *Perm Agcy*

Georgia
Elite Staffing Services, *Temp Agcy*
Express Personnel Svcs., *Perm Agcy*
Kelly Services, Inc., *Temp Agcy*
Manpower Temp. Svcs., *Temp Agcy*
Randstad Staffing Svcs., *Temp Agcy*
Westaff, *Temp Agcy*

Hawaii
Altres Staffing, *Temp Agcy*
Olsten Staffing Services, *Temp Agcy*

Idaho
Manpower Temporary Services, *Temp Agcy*

Illinois
A.B.A. Placements/A.B.A. Temporaries, *Perm Agcy*
Ablest Staffing Services, *Temp Agcy*
Adecco, *Temp Agcy*
CareerLink USA, Inc., *Exec Srch*
Davis Staffing, Inc., *Temp Agcy*
Interim Personnel, *Contract Svc*
Parker Cromwell & Assoc., *Exec Srch*
Quantum Professional Search/Quantum Staffing Services, *Exec Srch*
Staffing Conslt Inc., *Perm Agcy*

Indiana
Angola Personnel Svcs., *Perm Agcy*
Dunhill Staffing Systems, *Temp Agcy*
Employment Plus, *Temp Agcy*
Personnel Management, *Temp Agcy*
Personnel Partners, *Perm Agcy*
Pro Resources, *Perm Agcy*

Iowa
CSI Employment, *Exec Srch*
Kelly Services, Inc., *Temp Agcy*
Salem Management Inc., *Temp Agcy*
Rudy Salem Staffing Svcs, *Temp Agcy*

Kansas
Key Staffing, *Temp Agcy*

Kentucky
Manpower Inc., *Temp Agcy*
Precision Staffing, Inc., *Perm Agcy*
Staffing Alternatives, *Temp Agcy*

Louisiana
Frazee Recruiting Conslt, *Exec Srch*
Professional Temporaries, *Temp Agcy*
Westaff, *Temp Agcy*

Maine
Bonney Staffing & Training Centers, *Perm Agcy*
Maine Staffing Svcs, *Temp Agcy*

Maryland
Adecco, *Temp Agcy*
Interim Personnel, *Temp Agcy*

Massachusetts
ABA Personnel, Inc., *Temp Agcy*
The Alpha Group, *Temp Agcy*
Kelly Services, Inc., *Temp Agcy*
L&L Associates & Temps, *Temp Agcy*
Manpower Temp. Svcs., *Temp Agcy*
New Boston Select Staffing, *Temp Agcy*
Pomerantz Staffing Svcs., *Temp Agcy*
Quality Pers./Quality Temps, *Perm Agcy*
Remedy Intelligent Staffing, *Temp Agcy*
Selectemps, *Temp Agcy*
TAD Staffing Services, *Temp Agcy*
Volt Services Group, *Temp Agcy*
The Work Place, *Career/Outplacement*

Michigan
Advance Employment, *Exec Srch*
Alternative Staff, Inc., *Contract Svc*
Barman Staff Solutions, *Temp Agcy*
Entech Personnel Svcs., *Temp Agcy*
Mngmt. Rcrtrs. International, *Exec Srch*
Manpower, Inc., *Temp Agcy*
Snelling Personnel Svcs., *Perm Agcy*

Minnesota
Advantage Personnel Inc., *Perm Agcy*

Mississippi
EPSCO Personnel Svc., *Temp Agcy*

Missouri
Deck & Decker Emp. Svc, *Perm Agcy*
Huntress Real Estate Executive Search, *Exec Srch*
JoDoc Enterprises, *Temp Agcy*
Manpower Temp. Svcs., *Temp Agcy*

Montana
Kelly Services, Inc., *Temp Agcy*
LC Staffing Service, *Perm Agcy*
Manpower Temp. Svcs., *Temp Agcy*

Nebraska
Hansen Employment Service, *Exec Srch*

Nevada
Flowers Exec. Search Group, *Exec Srch*

New Hampshire
Allstaff, *Perm Agcy*
Kelly Services, Inc., *Temp Agcy*

Manpower Temp. Svcs., *Temp Agcy*
Olsten Staffing Services, *Temp Agcy*
TAC Staffing Services, *Temp Agcy*

New Jersey
American Staff Resources, *Perm Agcy*
Broad Waverly & Associates, *Exec Srch*
Joule Industrial Contractors, *Contract Svc*
Mngmt. Rcrtrs. of Bay Head, *Exec Srch*
Norrell Services, *Temp Agcy*
OMNE Staffing Svcs., *Temp Agcy*
Pomerantz Staffing Svcs., *Perm Agcy*

New Mexico
CDI Technical Services, *Contract Svc*
Excel Staffing Companies, *Perm Agcy*
Norrell Staffing Services, *Temp Agcy*

New York
AccuStaff Incorporated, *Temp Agcy*
Contract Specialties Grp., *Contract Svc*
Group Agency, Inc., *Perm Agcy*
Hart-Merrell Personnel, *Exec Srch*
Initial Staffing Services, *Perm Agcy*
Kelly Services, Inc., *Temp Agcy*
Manpower Temp. Svcs., *Temp Agcy*
Nesco Service Company, *Temp Agcy*
Olsten Staffing Services, *Temp Agcy*
Sales Search, Ltd./Executive Resume Service, *Exec Srch*
Sigma Staffing, *Perm Agcy*
Westaff, *Temp Agcy*
H.L. Yoh Company, *Temp Agcy*

North Carolina
Action Staffmasters, *Temp Agcy*
Caldwell Personnel Svcs., *Perm Agcy*
F-O-R-T-U-N-E Pers. Conslts of Charlotte, *Exec Srch*
Interim Personnel, Inc., *Temp Agcy*
Mngmt. Rcrtrs. of Kinston, *Exec Srch*
Manpower, Inc., *Temp Agcy*
Norrell Services, *Temp Agcy*
USA Staffing, *Perm Agcy*
Westaff, *Perm Agcy*

North Dakota
Interim Personnel, *Perm Agcy*

Ohio
Adecco/TAD Tech. Svcs., *Contract Svc*
Belcan Staffing Services, *Temp Agcy*
Career Connections, Inc., *Temp Agcy*
Manpower Temp. Svcs., *Temp Agcy*
Masterson Personnel, Inc./Masterson Temporary Services, *Temp Agcy*
Olsten Staffing Services, *Temp Agcy*
Pak/Teem Technical Svcs, *Contract Svc*
Personalized Placement, *Exec Srch*
Tabb & Associates, *Exec Srch*
Tandem Staffing, *Temp Agcy*

Oklahoma
Dow Personnel Inc., *Temp Agcy*
Key Temporary Personnel, *Temp Agcy*
Terry Neese Pers. Agency, *Temp Agcy*
StaffMark, *Temp Agcy*

Oregon
Adams Temporaries, *Temp Agcy*
Barrett Business Svcs., *Temp Agcy*
Employment Trends, *Temp Agcy*
Express Personnel Services, *Exec Srch*
Kelly Services, Inc., *Temp Agcy*
Northwest Temporary & Staffing Services, *Temp Agcy*
Uniforce Staffing Svcs., *Temp Agcy*

Pennsylvania
American Staff Resources, *Temp Agcy*
Bon Temps Staffing Svcs., *Temp Agcy*
CoreStaff Inc., *Temp Agcy*
Interim Personnel of Lehigh Valley PA, Inc., *Temp Agcy*
London Personnel Svcs., *Perm Agcy*
Manpower Temp. Svcs., *Temp Agcy*
Metropolitan Personnel, *Temp Agcy*
Norrell Services, *Temp Agcy*
Olsten Staffing Services, *Temp Agcy*
Pratt Personnel Services, *Temp Agcy*
Snelling Personnel Svcs., *Temp Agcy*
Whittlesey & Associates, Inc., *Exec Srch*

Rhode Island
Capitol Personnel Inc., *Temp Agcy*
Central 2000 Emp. Agency, *Exec Srch*

TECH/AID, *Temp Agcy*
Telford, Adams, & Alexander, *Exec Srch*
Temps Unlimited, Inc., *Temp Agcy*
Thor Temporary Services, *Temp Agcy*
TOD Staffing, *Temp Agcy*
Trendtec Inc., *Temp Agcy*
The Truman Agency, *Perm Agcy*
Tustin Personnel Services, *Temp Agcy*
United Staffing Solutions, *Exec Srch*
Volt Services Group, *Temp Agcy*
Westaff, *Temp Agcy*
Don Zee Associates, *Exec Srch*

Colorado
Absolute Staffing Solutions, *Perm Agcy*
Aspen Personnel Services, *Perm Agcy*
The Bridge, *Exec Srch*
Chuck's Contract Labor Svc., *Contract Svc*
COREStaff Services, *Perm Agcy*
F-O-R-T-U-N-E Pers. Conslts, *Exec Srch*
Intellimark, *Temp Agcy*
Interim Personnel, *Temp Agcy*
JobSearch, *Temp Agcy*
Kelly IT Resources, *Temp Agcy*
Labor Ready, Inc., *Temp Agcy*
Mngmt. Rcrtrs. of Colorado Springs, *Exec Srch*
Mngmt. Rcrtrs. of Golden Hill, *Exec Srch*
Manpower International Inc., *Temp Agcy*
Miller Denver, *Exec Srch*
National Affirmative Action Career Network, Inc., *Exec Srch*
Olsten Staffing Services, *Temp Agcy*
SOS Staffing Services, *Temp Agcy*
Sales Conslt of Denver, *Exec Srch*
Star Personnel Service, Inc., *Exec Srch*
Tech Staffing, *Temp Agcy*
Terry Personnel, *Perm Agcy*
Todays Temporary, *Temp Agcy*
J.Q. Turner & Associates, *Exec Srch*
Woodmoor Group, *Exec Srch*

Connecticut
Admiral Staffing Services, *Temp Agcy*
Anderson Group, *Exec Srch*
Andrews & Mahon, *Exec Srch*
Thomas Byrne Associates, *Perm Agcy*
Cahill Associates, *Exec Srch*
Charter Personnel Services, *Temp Agcy*
Corporate Staffing Solutions, *Temp Agcy*
Cupples Consulting Services, *Exec Srch*
Diversified Emp. Svcs., *Perm Agcy*
EDP Contract Services, *Contract Svc*
Employment Opportunities, *Perm Agcy*
Executive Register Inc., *Exec Srch*
Fox Ridge Services, Inc., *Temp Agcy*
Hire Logic, *Temp Agcy*
J.G. Hood Associates, *Perm Agcy*
JAT, Ltd., *Perm Agcy*
Lutz Associates, *Exec Srch*
MJF Associates, *Exec Srch*
Mngmt. Rcrtrs. International, *Exec Srch*
Management Search, *Exec Srch*
Office Services of CT, *Perm Agcy*
Barry Persky & Co., *Exec Srch*
Quality Control Recruiters, *Exec Srch*
Tech/Aid, *Temp Agcy*
Technical Staffing Solutions, *Temp Agcy*
Wallace Associates, *Exec Srch*
Ward Liebelt & Associates, *Exec Srch*
Westaff, *Temp Agcy*
Workforce One, *Perm Agcy*

Delaware
F-O-R-T-U-N-E Pers. Conslts, *Exec Srch*
J.B. Groner Executive Search, *Exec Srch*
E.W. Hodges & Associates, *Exec Srch*
The Placers, Inc., *Temp Agcy*

Florida
AAA Employment, *Perm Agcy*
Able Body Corporate Svcs., *Contract Svc*
Academy Design & Tech. Svcs., *Contract Svc*
Active Professionals, *Exec Srch*
Adecco, *Temp Agcy*
Alpha Pers./Alpha Temps, *Perm Agcy*
American Recruiters, *Exec Srch*
Atlantic Prof. Recruiters, *Exec Srch*
The Brand Company, Inc., *Exec Srch*
Career Planners, Inc., *Perm Agcy*
Chase-Gardner Exec. Search, *Exec Srch*

Colli Associates of Tampa, *Exec Srch*
Corporate Advisors, Inc., *Exec Srch*
Criterion Executive Search, *Exec Srch*
DGA Personnel Group, Inc., *Exec Srch*
Donbar Service Corporation, *Temp Agcy*
Ethan Allen Pers. Placement, *Exec Srch*
Five Star Temporary Inc., *Temp Agcy*
F-O-R-T-U-N-E Pers. Conslts, *Exec Srch*
Future Force Personnel, *Temp Agcy*
Gulf Coast Associates (GCA), *Exec Srch*
Interim Personnel, *Temp Agcy*
Just Management Services, *Exec Srch*
Kelly Services, Inc., *Temp Agcy*
R.H. Larsen & Assoc., *Exec Srch*
Mngmt. Rcrtrs. International, *Exec Srch*
Mankuta Gallagher & Assoc., *Exec Srch*
Norrell Technical Services, *Exec Srch*
Olsten Staffing Services, *Temp Agcy*
Pulp & Paper International, *Exec Srch*
Linda Robins & Associates, *Perm Agcy*
The Ryan Charles Group, *Exec Srch*
Sales Conslt, Inc., *Exec Srch*
Doug Sears & Associates, *Exec Srch*
Shaver Employment Agency, *Perm Agcy*
Snelling Personnel Services, *Temp Agcy*
Staffing Now, *Temp Agcy*
Summit Exec. Search Conslt, *Exec Srch*
Sun Personnel West, *Exec Srch*
TRC Staffing Services, *Temp Agcy*
TechStaff, *Contract Svc*
Wilson & Associates Intnl., *Exec Srch*

Georgia
Advanced Resumes, *Career/Outplacement*
Anderson Industrial Assoc., *Exec Srch*
Arjay & Associates, *Exec Srch*
Augusta Staffing Associates, *Perm Agcy*
Bell Oaks Company, *Exec Srch*
Bradshaw & Associates, *Exec Srch*
Comprehensive Search Grp., *Exec Srch*
Corporate Image Group, *Exec Srch*
Corporate Search Conslt, *Exec Srch*
Dunhill Professional Search, *Exec Srch*
Durham Staffing Inc., *Temp Agcy*
Express Personnel Services, *Perm Agcy*
F-O-R-T-U-N-E Pers. Conslts of Atlanta/Alternastaff, *Exec Srch*
Fox-Morris Associates, *Exec Srch*
Hall Management Group, *Exec Srch*
Hines Recruiting Association, *Exec Srch*
ISC of Atlanta/International Career Continuation, *Exec Srch*
Job Shop Inc., *Exec Srch*
Kelly Services, Inc., *Temp Agcy*
Kenzer Corp. of Georgia, *Exec Srch*
Kreisler & Associates, *Exec Srch*
MAU, Inc., *Perm Agcy*
Mngmt. Rcrtrs. International/Sales Conslt, *Exec Srch*
Manpower Temp. Svcs., *Temp Agcy*
Personnel Opportunities Inc., *Exec Srch*
Pro-Tech Inc., *Exec Srch*
Quality Employment Service, *Temp Agcy*
Randstad Staffing Services, *Temp Agcy*
Sanford Rose Associates, *Exec Srch*
The Shepard Group, Inc., *Exec Srch*
Southern Employment Svc., *Perm Agcy*
StaffMark, *Temp Agcy*
Temporary Specialties, *Temp Agcy*
Toar Consulting, *Exec Srch*
Warren Executive Services, *Exec Srch*
Westaff, *Temp Agcy*

Hawaii
Dunhill Prof. Staffing of HI, *Exec Srch*

Idaho
Horne/Brown International, *Exec Srch*
Idaho Department of Employment/Jobservice, *Perm Agcy*

Illinois
The Ability Group, *Exec Srch*
B.J. Abrams & Associates, *Exec Srch*
Accord Inc., *Exec Srch*
Adecco, *Temp Agcy*
Advanced Technical Search, *Exec Srch*
American Engineering Co., *Exec Srch*
American Technical Search, *Exec Srch*
Assured Staffing, *Temp Agcy*
B-W and Associates, Inc., *Perm Agcy*
Banner Personnel Service, *Perm Agcy*
Britannia, *Exec Srch*

Burling Group Ltd., *Exec Srch*
CareerLink USA, Inc., *Exec Srch*
Carson Management Assoc, *Contract Svc*
Cook Associates, Inc., *Exec Srch*
Corporate Environment, Ltd., *Exec Srch*
Ned Dickey & Associates, Inc./Dickey Staffing Solutions, *Exec Srch*
Express Personnel Services, *Temp Agcy*
Fellows Placement, *Temp Agcy*
F-O-R-T-U-N-E Pers. Conslts, *Exec Srch*
Furst Staffing Services, *Temp Agcy*
David Gomez & Associates, *Exec Srch*
Human Resource Connection, *Perm Agcy*
J.C.G. Limited, Inc., *Perm Agcy*
Johnson Personnel Company, *Exec Srch*
Jerry L. Jung Company, Inc., *Exec Srch*
Raymond Karson Associates, *Exec Srch*
Kenzer Corporation, *Exec Srch*
Kingston/Zak Inc., *Exec Srch*
Evie Kreisler Associates Inc., *Exec Srch*
Kunzer Associates, Ltd., *Exec Srch*
Magnum Search, *Exec Srch*
Mngmt. Rcrtrs. International/Sales Conslt, *Exec Srch*
Manufacturing Resources, *Exec Srch*
Manufacturing Search Co., *Exec Srch*
Manufacturing Tech. Search, *Exec Srch*
Marsteller Wilcox Associates, *Exec Srch*
Mathey Services, *Exec Srch*
R. Michaels & Associates, *Exec Srch*
Michaels & Moere, Ltd., *Exec Srch*
The Murphy Group, *Perm Agcy*
New Directions, Inc., *Exec Srch*
OfficeMates5 (OM5), *Perm Agcy*
Olsten Staffing Services, *Temp Agcy*
Omni Search Ltd., *Exec Srch*
James C. Pappas & Assoc., *Exec Srch*
Pelichem Associates, *Exec Srch*
The Pollak and Skan Grp., *Contract Svc*
Prestige Employment Svcs., *Perm Agcy*
Professional Research Svcs., *Exec Srch*
Profile Temporary Service, *Temp Agcy*
Remedy Intelligent Staffing, *Temp Agcy*
Right Services Inc., *Temp Agcy*
The Robinson Group, *Exec Srch*
Search Dynamics Inc., *Exec Srch*
SelectAbility, Inc., *Perm Agcy*
Ralph Smith & Associates, *Exec Srch*
Snelling Personnel Services, *Perm Agcy*
Stivers Temporary Pers., *Temp Agcy*
Stone Enterprises, Ltd., *Exec Srch*
Ron Sunshine Associates, *Exec Srch*
Systems Research Inc., *Perm Agcy*
Technical Rec. Conslt, *Exec Srch*
Technical Search, *Exec Srch*
Texcel, Inc., *Exec Srch*
Valentine & Associates, *Exec Srch*
Working World Inc., *Temp Agcy*
World Employment Service, *Perm Agcy*
Xagas & Associates, *Exec Srch*

Indiana
Adecco/TAD Tech. Svcs., *Contract Svc*
Alexander & Associates, *Exec Srch*
Angola Personnel Services, *Perm Agcy*
Bill Caldwell Emp. Svc., *Perm Agcy*
Canis Major, Inc./HR Quest, *Exec Srch*
Career Conslt/O.I. Partners, *Perm Agcy*
Careers Unlimited Inc., *Exec Srch*
Chevigny Personnel Agency, *Exec Srch*
Corporate Staff Resources, *Temp Agcy*
Crowe, Chizek and Company, *Perm Agcy*
Crown Temp. Svcs., *Temp Agcy*
Dunhill Staffing Systems, *Temp Agcy*
Employment Recruiters Inc., *Perm Agcy*
Execusearch, *Exec Srch*
F-O-R-T-U-N-E Pers. Conslts, *Exec Srch*
The Hart Line Inc., *Exec Srch*
Job Placement Service Inc., *Perm Agcy*
Krise Professional Pers. Svcs, *Perm Agcy*
The Mallard Group, *Exec Srch*
Mngmt. Rcrtrs. International, *Exec Srch*
Management Services, *Exec Srch*
Mayhall Search Group Inc., *Exec Srch*
Mays & Associates Inc., *Perm Agcy*
Miller Personnel, *Exec Srch*
Morley Group, *Exec Srch*
Norrell Services, Inc., *Temp Agcy*
Norrell Staffing Services, *Temp Agcy*
Oakwood International Inc., *Exec Srch*
OfficeMates5 (OM5)/DayStar Temporary Services, *Exec Srch*

Mngmt. Rcrtrs. of Kansas City, *Exec Srch*
Mngmt. Rcrtrs. of Springfield, *Exec Srch*
Mngmt. Rcrtrs. of St. Louis, *Exec Srch*
Manpower Temp. Svcs., *Temp Agcy*
J. Miles Personnel Services, *Exec Srch*
OfficeMates5 (OM5), *Exec Srch*
Gordon A. Smith & Assoc., *Exec Srch*
Workforce, Inc., *Temp Agcy*

Montana
LC Staffing Service, *Temp Agcy*

Nebraska
Compusearch of Lincoln, *Exec Srch*
Corporate Recruiters, Ltd./Health Service Professionals, *Exec Srch*
Eggers Company, *Perm Agcy*
Express Personnel, *Exec Srch*
Hahn Technical Staffing, *Exec Srch*
Kelly Services, Inc., *Temp Agcy*
Mngmt. Rcrtrs./OfficeMates5, *Exec Srch*
Professional Recruiters Inc., *Perm Agcy*
Staffing Services, *Perm Agcy*

Nevada
Initial Staffing Services, *Perm Agcy*

New Hampshire
Affordable Solutions, *Contract Svc*
Availability Contract Svc., *Contract Svc*
Central NH Emp. Svcs., *Perm Agcy*
Chaucer Group, *Exec Srch*
Cheshire Employment Svc., *Temp Agcy*
Dubois & Company, *Exec Srch*
Enterprise Technologies, *Exec Srch*
Mainstay Staffing, *Exec Srch*
Mngmt. Rcrtrs. International, *Exec Srch*
National Emp. Service Corp., *Perm Agcy*
Pelham Professional Group, *Temp Agcy*
Preferred Resource Group, *Exec Srch*
R.G.T. Associates, Inc., *Exec Srch*
Resource Recruiting/Contemporary Accountants, *Perm Agcy*
Linford E. Stiles Associates, *Exec Srch*
Surge Resources Inc., *Contract Svc*
TAC Staffing Services, *Temp Agcy*
Tech/Aid of New Hampshire, *Perm Agcy*
Technical Needs, *Exec Srch*

New Jersey
A+ Personnel Placement, *Perm Agcy*
ABC Nationwide Emp., *Perm Agcy*
Advanced Personnel Service, *Perm Agcy*
R.P. Barone Associates, *Exec Srch*
Gary S. Bell Associates, Inc., *Exec Srch*
Blake & Assoc. Exec. Search, *Exec Srch*
Brett Associates, *Exec Srch*
Career Center, Inc., *Perm Agcy*
Careers USA, *Perm Agcy*
Careerworks, *Exec Srch*
Citizens Employment Svcs., *Perm Agcy*
Cox Darrow & Owens, Inc., *Exec Srch*
M.T. Donaldson Associates, *Exec Srch*
Dreier Consulting, *Exec Srch*
Ellis Career Conslt/Career Search Associates, *Exec Srch*
Express Personnel Services, *Perm Agcy*
F-O-R-T-U-N-E Pers. Conslts of Menlo Park, *Exec Srch*
Grant Franks & Associates, *Exec Srch*
Harris Executive Search, *Exec Srch*
Hreshko Consulting Group, *Exec Srch*
Huff Associates, *Exec Srch*
Hughes & Podesla Personnel, *Perm Agcy*
Impact Personnel, Inc., *Perm Agcy*
J.M. Joseph Associates, *Exec Srch*
Joule Staffing Services, *Contract Svc*
Kaye Personnel Inc., *Temp Agcy*
Joseph Keyes Associates, *Perm Agcy*
Kiley, Owen & McGovern, *Exec Srch*
Paul Kull & Company, *Exec Srch*
Lab Support Inc., *Temp Agcy*
Mngmt. Rcrtrs. of Bay Head, *Exec Srch*
Mngmt. Rcrtrs. of Medford, *Exec Srch*
Manpower Tech. Services, *Contract Svc*
Mayfair Services, *Perm Agcy*
Orion Consulting, Inc., *Exec Srch*
Price Baker Search, *Exec Srch*
Protocall Bus. Staff Svcs., *Temp Agcy*
RCE Associates, *Exec Srch*
Ramming & Associates, Inc., *Exec Srch*
Rochester Systems Inc., *Exec Srch*
Romac International, *Exec Srch*

Rosenthal Associates Intnl., *Exec Srch*
Rylan Forbes Consulting Grp, *Exec Srch*
S-H-S of Cherry Hill, *Perm Agcy*
R.S. Sadow Associates, *Exec Srch*
Sales Conslt, *Exec Srch*
Sales Conslt of Sparta, *Exec Srch*
Robert Scott Associates, *Exec Srch*
Selective Personnel, *Perm Agcy*
The Stelton Group, Inc., *Exec Srch*
Summit Group, Inc., *Exec Srch*
TRS Staffing Solutions, Inc., *Temp Agcy*
Will-Cox Associates, *Exec Srch*
Claire Wright Associates, *Perm Agcy*

New Mexico
Albuquerque Personnel, Inc., *Perm Agcy*
Butler Service Group, *Contract Svc*
Norrell Staffing Services, *Temp Agcy*

New York
APA Search, *Exec Srch*
ATS Reliance, Inc., *Contract Svc*
Accounting & Computer Personnel, *Perm Agcy*
Merrill Adams Associates, *Career/Outplacement*
Adecco, *Temp Agcy*
April Technical Recruiting, *Perm Agcy*
Arrow Employment Agency, *Perm Agcy*
Bestemp Temporary Svcs., *Temp Agcy*
Bornholdt Shivas & Friends, *Exec Srch*
Bos Business Conslt, *Exec Srch*
Branthover Associates, *Exec Srch*
Burns Personnel, *Exec Srch*
CDI Corporation, *Contract Svc*
Carlile Personnel Agency, *Perm Agcy*
Colton Partnership, *Exec Srch*
Corporate Careers, Inc., *Exec Srch*
Corporate Search Inc., *Exec Srch*
Frank Cuomo & Associates, *Exec Srch*
The Dartmouth Group, *Exec Srch*
Seth Diamond Associates, *Exec Srch*
Dymanex Search Inc., *Exec Srch*
EDP Contract Services, *Contract Svc*
Employment Recruiters Agency, *Perm Agcy*
Extra Help Employment Svc, *Temp Agcy*
F-O-R-T-U-N-E Pers. Conslts, *Exec Srch*
Graphic Techniques, Inc., *Temp Agcy*
The Haas Associates, Inc., *Exec Srch*
F.P. Healy & Company Inc., *Exec Srch*
Kelly Services, Inc., *Temp Agcy*
Kirk-Mayer, *Contract Svc*
Fred Koffler Associates, *Exec Srch*
Lab Support Inc., *Temp Agcy*
Lake Associates, *Exec Srch*
John Lawrence & Associates, *Exec Srch*
Levine Hirshorn & Assoc., *Exec Srch*
Mngmt. Rcrtrs. of Nassau Inc., *Exec Srch*
Mngmt. Rcrtrs. of Orange Cty, *Exec Srch*
Mngmt. Rcrtrs. of Utica/Rome, *Exec Srch*
Manpower Temp. Svcs., *Temp Agcy*
Metro Resources of Rochester, *Temp Agcy*
Metropolitan Personnel Syst., *Exec Srch*
Mickler Associates, *Exec Srch*
Morgan-Murray Personnel/M&M Top Temps, *Temp Agcy*
Noah Associates, *Perm Agcy*
Norris Emp. Conslt, *Perm Agcy*
Olsten Staffing Services, *Temp Agcy*
Parsons, Anderson and Gee, *Perm Agcy*
Phoenix Emp. Agency, *Perm Agcy*
Pro/TECH Nationwide Staff, *Temp Agcy*
ROI Associates Inc., *Exec Srch*
Remedy Intelligent Staffing, *Temp Agcy*
Staff Managers, *Temp Agcy*
Staffing Services, *Exec Srch*
StratfordGroup, *Exec Srch*
Superior Concepts, *Contract Svc*
Taylor Jordan Associates, *Exec Srch*
Thorsen Associates, Inc., *Exec Srch*
Weber Mngmt. Conslt, *Exec Srch*
Werbin Assoc. Exec. Search, *Exec Srch*
Westchester Emp. Agency, *Perm Agcy*
H.L. Yoh Company, *Temp Agcy*

North Carolina
Accountants Executive Search/
Accountants On Call, *Exec Srch*
Accurate Staffing Conslt, *Exec Srch*
Action Staffing Group, *Temp Agcy*

Active Search Recruiters, *Exec Srch*
Advanced Pers. Resources, *Exec Srch*
Advanced Prof. Resources, *Exec Srch*
Amcell Associates, *Exec Srch*
AmeriPro Search, Inc., *Exec Srch*
Atchison & Associates, Inc., *Exec Srch*
Ayers & Associates, Inc., *Exec Srch*
Barrett Business Services, *Temp Agcy*
Career Search Inc., *Exec Srch*
Cline, Jobe & Associates, *Exec Srch*
Ellis Associates, Inc., *Exec Srch*
Executive Connections, *Exec Srch*
Executive Recruitment Specialists, Inc., *Exec Srch*
Executive Staffing Group, *Exec Srch*
D.D. Fayling Associates, Inc., *Exec Srch*
F-O-R-T-U-N-E Pers. Conslts, *Exec Srch*
Fox-Morris Associates, *Exec Srch*
The Furniture Agency Inc., *Exec Srch*
Glovier & Associates, *Exec Srch*
Graham & Associates, *Perm Agcy*
Highlander Search, *Exec Srch*
Interim Personnel, Inc., *Temp Agcy*
The Jobs Market, Inc., *Perm Agcy*
Kelly Services, Inc., *Temp Agcy*
Mngmt. Rcrtrs. International/
Sales Conslt, *Exec Srch*
Manpower, Inc., *Temp Agcy*
McCain Emp. Service, *Temp Agcy*
Merrick & Moore, *Exec Srch*
Myers & Associates, *Perm Agcy*
Olsten Staffing Services, *Temp Agcy*
The Perkins Group, *Exec Srch*
Personnel Svcs. Unlimited, *Temp Agcy*
Professional Pers. Assoc., *Perm Agcy*
Quality Temporary Services, *Temp Agcy*
Sanford Rose Associates, *Exec Srch*
Snelling Personnel Services, *Perm Agcy*
Sparks Personnel Services, *Exec Srch*
Stewart Greene & Co./The Triad, *Exec Srch*
StratfordGroup, *Exec Srch*
Waddy R. Thomson Assoc., *Exec Srch*
Volt Technical Services, *Contract Svc*
Wilson Personnel Inc., *Exec Srch*
Winston Personnel Group, *Temp Agcy*
Youngblood Staffing, *Perm Agcy*

North Dakota
Career Connection, *Exec Srch*
Olsten Staffing Services/Expressway Personnel, *Temp Agcy*

Ohio
AccuStaff, *Temp Agcy*
Adecco, *Temp Agcy*
Adecco/TAD Tech. Svcs., *Contract Svc*
Alliance Technical Svcs., *Contract Svc*
Dave Arnold & Assoc., *Exec Srch*
Baldwin & Associates, *Exec Srch*
Bason Associates Inc., *Exec Srch*
Belcan Technical Services, *Contract Svc*
Bowden & Company, *Exec Srch*
Bradley-Pierce Personnel, *Perm Agcy*
J.B. Brown & Associates, *Exec Srch*
CBS Personnel Services, *Perm Agcy*
Career Specialists Inc., *Exec Srch*
Combined Resources Inc., *Exec Srch*
Continental Search Assoc., *Exec Srch*
Corell Associates, *Perm Agcy*
J.D. Cotter Search, Inc., *Exec Srch*
Crown Temp. Svcs., *Temp Agcy*
Custom Staffing, Inc., *Temp Agcy*
Alan N. Daum & Associates, *Perm Agcy*
Eastern Personnel Services, *Perm Agcy*
Executech, *Exec Srch*
Executive Connection, *Exec Srch*
Executive Search Ltd., *Exec Srch*
Fenzel Milar Associates, *Exec Srch*
Flex-Tech Prof. Svcs., *Contract Svc*
Gayhart & Associates, *Exec Srch*
Global Resources Group, *Contract Svc*
H.L. Goehring & Associates, *Exec Srch*
R. Green & Associates, *Exec Srch*
Griffiths & Associates, *Exec Srch*
Guthoff & Associates, *Exec Srch*
Russ Hadick & Associates, *Exec Srch*
Hite Executive Search/Hite Management Conslt, Inc., *Exec Srch*
ITS Technical Staffing, *Exec Srch*
Interim Personnel, *Temp Agcy*
Ives & Associates, Inc., *Exec Srch*
Kelly Services, Inc., *Temp Agcy*

Watkins & Associates, *Exec Srch*
Wheeler, Moore & Elam Co., *Exec Srch*
Bruce G. Woods Exec Search, *Exec Srch*
H.L. Yoh Company, *Contract Svc*

Utah

Executive Search Group, *Exec Srch*
Mngmt. Rcrtrs. International/
Sales Conslt, *Exec Srch*
Manpower Tech. Services, *Temp Agcy*
Olsten Staffing Services, *Temp Agcy*
Peak Staffing, *Temp Agcy*
Prince, Perelson & Assoc., *Exec Srch*

Vermont

Adecco, *Temp Agcy*
Personnel Department Inc., *Temp Agcy*

Virginia

The Alexis Group, Inc., *Exec Srch*
Alpha Omega Resources Inc., *Perm Agcy*
Bradford Company, *Contract Svc*
Career Registry, *Exec Srch*
Contec Search, Inc., *Exec Srch*
Corporate Connection Ltd., *Exec Srch*
Dow Personnel, *Perm Agcy*
Emp Enterprises/Temp Solutions, *Temp Agcy*
Express Personnel Services, *Temp Agcy*
Wayne Garber & Assoc., *Exec Srch*
Hamilton Group, Inc., *Exec Srch*
Lee Staffing Resources, *Exec Srch*
Mngmt. Rcrtrs. International of Roanoke, *Exec Srch*
Manpower Temp. Services, *Temp Agcy*
Norrell Services, *Temp Agcy*
Olsten Staffing Services, *Temp Agcy*
Omega Systems, *Exec Srch*
Recruiting Resources Inc., *Exec Srch*
Search & Recruit Intnl., *Exec Srch*
Snelling Personnel Services, *Perm Agcy*
Souder & Associates, *Exec Srch*
STAT Employment Services, *Perm Agcy*
Strategic Search, Inc., *Exec Srch*
The Talley Group, *Exec Srch*
Taskforce of Virginia/PRG - Professional
Resources Group, *Exec Srch*
Tech/Aid of Virginia, *Temp Agcy*
U.S. Search, *Exec Srch*
Wayne Associates Inc., *Exec Srch*
Westaff, *Temp Agcy*

Washington

Anchor Associates, Inc., *Exec Srch*
Behrens and Company, *Exec Srch*
CDI Corporation (West), *Contract Svc*
The Career Clinic, Inc., *Exec Srch*
Express Personnel Services, *Temp Agcy*
L.W. Foote Co./Brighton Grp, *Exec Srch*
Gorman Consulting Service, *Exec Srch*
Guidance Services Inc., *Temp Agcy*
Kelly Services, Inc., *Temp Agcy*
Labor Ready, Inc., *Temp Agcy*
Mngmt. Rcrtrs. of Mercer Island, *Exec Srch*
Mngmt. Rcrtrs. of Seattle, *Exec Srch*
Mngmt. Rcrtrs. of Tacoma, *Exec Srch*
Olsten Staffing Services, *Temp Agcy*
PACE Staffing Network, *Exec Srch*
Personnel Unlimited Inc., *Exec Srch*
Pilon Management Company, *Exec Srch*
Jack Porter & Associates, *Perm Agcy*
Susan Schoos & Associates, *Exec Srch*
Wilson Smith Associates, *Exec Srch*
Strain Personnel Specialists, *Exec Srch*
StratfordGroup, *Exec Srch*
Whittall Management Group, *Exec Srch*

West Virginia

Extra Support Staffing, *Temp Agcy*
Key Personnel, Inc., *Perm Agcy*
Sanford Rose Associates, *Exec Srch*

Wisconsin

Adecco/TAD Tech. Svcs., *Contract Svc*
American Technical Services, *Perm Agcy*
Argus Technical Services, *Perm Agcy*
Austria Austria & Associates, *Perm Agcy*
Benston & Associates, *Exec Srch*
Corporate Search Inc., *Exec Srch*
Crown Services, *Temp Agcy*
Dunhill of Green Bay, *Perm Agcy*
J.M. Eagle Partners, *Exec Srch*
Egan & Associates, *Exec Srch*
Employability, *Perm Agcy*

EnviroStaff, Inc., *Temp Agcy*
Epic Skilled & Industrial, *Perm Agcy*
Executive Placement & Career Services/
Career Connections Inc., *Exec Srch*
Executive Recruiters, Inc., *Exec Srch*
Financial Mngmt. Personnel, *Exec Srch*
The HS Group, Inc., *Exec Srch*
The Hunter Corporation, *Exec Srch*
Interim Personnel, *Temp Agcy*
Koehler & Company, *Exec Srch*
Maglio & Company, *Exec Srch*
Mngmt. Rcrtrs./Compusearch, *Exec Srch*
Manpower Temp. Services, *Temp Agcy*
Olsten Staffing Services, *Temp Agcy*
PDS Technical Services, *Contract Svc*
Placements of Racine Inc., *Perm Agcy*
Riverwood Consulting, *Exec Srch*
Sanford Rose Associates, *Exec Srch*
T.E.M. Associates, *Exec Srch*
Techstaff, *Perm Agcy*
U.S. Tech Force Inc., *Exec Srch*
The Waterstone Group, *Contract Svc*

Wyoming

Mngmt. Rcrtrs. of Cheyenne, *Exec Srch*

MARITIME

Alabama

Marine Jobs, Inc., *Perm Agcy*

Florida

CTI Group, *Perm Agcy*
Passport Marine, *Perm Agcy*

Louisiana

Rhema Employment Agency, *Exec Srch*

Rhode Island

Spectrum Business Associates, *Exec Srch*

Washington

Maritime Recruiters, *Exec Srch*

MARKETING

Alabama

Healthcare Recruiters, *Exec Srch*

Alaska

Manpower Temp. Services, *Temp Agcy*
Olsten Staffing Services, *Temp Agcy*

Arizona

Amer. Career Grp, *Career/Outplacement*
Aquent Partners, *Temp Agcy*
The Bren Group, *Exec Srch*
COMFORCE Tech. Svcs., *Contract Svc*
Taylor Design Recruiting, *Temp Agcy*

Arkansas

Executive Recruiters Agency, *Exec Srch*

California

A Permanent Success Emp. Svc., *Perm Agcy*
Aquent Partners, *Temp Agcy*
Astra West Personnel Svcs., *Perm Agcy*
BDP Mngmt Consulting Grp., *Exec Srch*
The Badger Group, *Exec Srch*
Bast & Associates, Inc., *Exec Srch*
Beck/Eastwood Recruitment Solutions, *Exec Srch*
BridgeGate LLC, *Exec Srch*
Bristol Associates, *Exec Srch*
California Search Agency, *Exec Srch*
Career Quest International, *Contract Svc*
J. Carson & Associates, *Exec Srch*
Wayne Chamberlain & Assoc, *Exec Srch*
Champagne Personnel, *Temp Agcy*
The Culver Group, *Exec Srch*
Drummer Personnel, Inc., *Exec Srch*
Dunhill of San Francisco, *Exec Srch*
F-O-R-T-U-N-E Pers. Conslts, *Exec Srch*
Dianne Gauger & Associates, *Exec Srch*
Global Resources Ltd., *Exec Srch*
Fred L. Hood & Associates, *Exec Srch*
Interactive Search Network, *Exec Srch*
International Staff Conslt, *Exec Srch*
K&M International, Inc., *Exec Srch*
Karsch/Card, *Exec Srch*
Mngmt. Rcrtrs. International, *Exec Srch*
Manpower Staffing Services, *Temp Agcy*
Mesa International, *Exec Srch*
New Venture Development, *Exec Srch*
Ortman Recruiting Intnl., *Exec Srch*

Pacific Search Group, *Exec Srch*
Power 2000+, *Exec Srch*
Premier Personnel Services, *Temp Agcy*
Premier Staffing, *Perm Agcy*
Proven Edge Exec Recruiters, *Exec Srch*
ReliStaff, *Perm Agcy*
Remedy Intelligent Staffing, *Temp Agcy*
Resource Perspectives, Inc., *Exec Srch*
Ricci Lee Associates, Inc., *Exec Srch*
Rusher, Loscavio, and LoPresto, *Exec Srch*
Sales Profs. Pers. Svcs., *Exec Srch*
Select Personnel Services, *Temp Agcy*
Solution Marketing, *Exec Srch*
Strategic Alternatives, *Exec Srch*
Systems Research Group, *Exec Srch*
T.R. Employment Agency, *Exec Srch*
TRC Staffing Services, Inc., *Perm Agcy*
UAW Labor Employment and Training
Corporation, *Perm Agcy*
Unisearch, *Exec Srch*
Vaughan & Co. Exec. Search, *Exec Srch*
Weldon Edwards, *Exec Srch*
WestPacific National Search, *Exec Srch*
Your People Professionals, *Perm Agcy*
Amy Zimmerman & Assoc., *Perm Agcy*

Colorado

Ahrnsbrak and Assoc., *Perm Agcy*
Aquent Partners, *Temp Agcy*
Career Connections, *Exec Srch*
Executive Career Conslt, *Exec Srch*
Executives By Sterling, Inc., *Exec Srch*
Kelly Services, Inc., *Temp Agcy*

Connecticut

Abraham & London, Ltd., *Exec Srch*
Anderson Group, *Exec Srch*
Aquent Partners, *Temp Agcy*
Flynn Hannock, Inc., *Exec Srch*
Harris Heery Executive Resource Conslt, *Exec Srch*
MJF Associates, *Exec Srch*
The McKnight Group, *Exec Srch*
Strategic Executives, Inc., *Exec Srch*
Super Systems, Inc., *Exec Srch*
TSW Associates, LLC, *Exec Srch*
Wittlan Group, *Exec Srch*

Delaware

Personal Placements Inc., *Perm Agcy*

Dist. of Columbia

ACSYS Inc., *Exec Srch*
Aquent Partners, *Temp Agcy*
GKA Resources, LLC, *Exec Srch*
Pace-Careers, Inc., *Exec Srch*
TRAK Staffing, *Perm Agcy*

Florida

AccuStaff Incorporated, *Temp Agcy*
American Recruiters, *Exec Srch*
Aquent Partners, *Temp Agcy*
Carrier's Career Service, Inc., *Career/Outplacement*
Corporate Advisors, Inc., *Exec Srch*
First Recruiters Group Inc., *Exec Srch*
F-O-R-T-U-N-E Pers. Conslts, *Exec Srch*
Kay Concepts, *Exec Srch*
Mngmt. Rcrtrs. of Jensen Beach, Inc., *Exec Srch*
OmniSearch Inc., *Exec Srch*
O'Quin Personnel, *Temp Agcy*
Priority Search, *Exec Srch*
Sanford Rose Associates, *Exec Srch*
Snelling Personnel Services, *Temp Agcy*
Snyder Executive Search, *Exec Srch*
The Stewart Search Group, *Exec Srch*
Strategic Staffing Solutions, *Contract Svc*
Strategy Resources Inc., *Perm Agcy*

Georgia

Ad Options Inc., *Perm Agcy*
Aquent Partners, *Temp Agcy*
Bell Oaks Company, *Exec Srch*
Business Professional Group, *Perm Agcy*
Corporate Image Group, *Exec Srch*
Dunhill Professional Search, *Exec Srch*
Elite Staffing Services, *Temp Agcy*
Executive Placement Svcs., *Perm Agcy*
Hire Intellect Inc., *Temp Agcy*
National Personnel Recruiters, *Exec Srch*
Randstad Staffing Services, *Temp Agcy*
Sanford Rose Associates, *Exec Srch*
TriTech Associates, *Exec Srch*

Mngmt. Rcrtrs. of Reading/
   CAREER SENTINEL, *Exec Srch*
Metropolitan Personnel, Inc., *Temp Agcy*
Alan Raeburn Conslt, *Exec Srch*
SHS Associates, Inc., *Exec Srch*
SPC F-O-R-T-U-N-E, *Exec Srch*
Sanford Rose Associates, *Exec Srch*
Snelling Personnel Services, *Temp Agcy*
Spectrum Conslt, Inc./Retail Recruiters,
   Exec Srch
Todays Temporary, *Temp Agcy*
W.G. Tucker & Associates, *Exec Srch*
Vogue Personnel Inc., *Exec Srch*
C.D. Warner & Associates, *Exec Srch*

Rhode Island
Career Conslt, *Exec Srch*
Greene Pers. Conslt, *Exec Srch*
Kelly Services, Inc., *Temp Agcy*
Lou Ricci Associates, *Exec Srch*
Sales Conslt, *Exec Srch*
Sullivan & Cogliano, *Exec Srch*

South Carolina
Mngmt. Rcrtrs. of Greenville/
   Sales Conslt, *Exec Srch*
Sales Conslt, *Exec Srch*
Smith Temps/Smith Pers., *Temp Agcy*

South Dakota
Availability Emp. Svcs., *Temp Agcy*
Key Staffing, *Temp Agcy*

Tennessee
Corporate Image Group, *Exec Srch*
Kelly Services, Inc., *Temp Agcy*
Mngmt. Rcrtrs./Sales Conslt, *Exec Srch*
Questar Partners Inc., *Exec Srch*
Sanford Rose Associates, *Exec Srch*
StaffMark, *Exec Srch*

Texas
Alexander & Company, *Exec Srch*
American Resources, *Exec Srch*
Aquent Partners, *Temp Agcy*
Buckley Group, *Exec Srch*
Continental Personnel Svc., *Perm Agcy*
Dallas Employment Services, *Perm Agcy*
Dividend Staffing Services, *Temp Agcy*
Executive Search Intnl., *Exec Srch*
Hunter & Michaels, *Exec Srch*
Loewenstein & Associates, *Exec Srch*
Mngmt. Rcrtrs. International, *Exec Srch*
McDuffy-Edwards, *Exec Srch*
National Sales Recruiters, *Exec Srch*
Olsten Staffing Services, *Temp Agcy*
Priority Search, Inc., *Exec Srch*
Sales Conslt of Austin, *Exec Srch*
Snelling Personnel Services, *Perm Agcy*
The Wright Group, *Exec Srch*

Utah
Deeco International, *Exec Srch*

Vermont
Jay Tracey Associates, *Exec Srch*

Virginia
A La Carte International, *Exec Srch*
The Alexis Group, Inc., *Exec Srch*
Nancy Allen Associates, Inc., *Perm Agcy*
Carol Day and Associates, *Perm Agcy*
Mngmt. Rcrtrs. International, *Exec Srch*
Paul-Tittle Associates, Inc., *Exec Srch*

Washington
Adams & Associates, *Perm Agcy*
Aquent Partners, *Temp Agcy*
Consumer Connection, *Exec Srch*
Demetrio & Associates, *Exec Srch*
N.G. Hayes Company, *Exec Srch*
Jobs Unlimited, *Perm Agcy*
Northwest Temporary & Staffing
   Services, Inc., *Temp Agcy*
PACE Staffing Network, *Exec Srch*
Parker Professional Search, *Exec Srch*
Roth Young Exec. Search, *Exec Srch*
Wilson Smith Associates, *Exec Srch*
Snelling Personnel Services, *Exec Srch*
Strategic Resources, *Exec Srch*

West Virginia
Snelling Personnel Services, *Temp Agcy*

Wisconsin
Dieck Mueller Group, *Exec Srch*
The H S Group, Inc., *Exec Srch*

Kordus Consulting Group, *Exec Srch*
Maglio & Company, *Exec Srch*
Mngmt. Rcrtrs. International, *Exec Srch*
Sales Conslt, *Exec Srch*

MEDICAL DEVICES

California
Boyle Ogata, *Exec Srch*
Christian & Timbers, *Exec Srch*
F-O-R-T-U-N-E Pers. Conslts, *Exec Srch*
Lewis & Blank International, *Exec Srch*
Med Exec International, *Exec Srch*
Sanford Rose Associates, *Exec Srch*
TechniQuest, *Exec Srch*

Colorado
Leading Edge Medical Srch, *Exec Srch*

Connecticut
Quality Control Recruiters, *Exec Srch*

Florida
F-O-R-T-U-N-E Pers. Conslts, *Exec Srch*
Mngmt. Rcrtrs. International, *Exec Srch*

Georgia
F-O-R-T-U-N-E Pers. Conslts of
   Atlanta/Alternastaff, *Exec Srch*
Hall Management Group, *Exec Srch*

Illinois
Sanford Rose Associates, *Exec Srch*

Louisiana
Shiell Personnel, *Perm Agcy*

Maine
The Haystack Group, *Exec Srch*

Maryland
F-O-R-T-U-N-E Pers. Conslts, *Exec Srch*

New Jersey
The Stelton Group, Inc., *Exec Srch*

New York
Mngmt. Rcrtrs. of Woodbury/
   Compusearch, *Exec Srch*

Oregon
F-O-R-T-U-N-E Pers. Conslts, *Exec Srch*
Heartbeat Medical, *Exec Srch*

Pennsylvania
Mngmt. Rcrtrs. of Pittsburgh-North, Inc.,
   Exec Srch
Mngmt. Rcrtrs. of Reading/
   CAREER SENTINEL, *Exec Srch*
Norcon Associates, Inc., *Exec Srch*

Tennessee
Shaw Associates, Inc., *Exec Srch*

Texas
Maxwel, Fraide & Associates, *Exec Srch*
Shaw Associates, Inc., *Exec Srch*

Virginia
Christian & Timbers, Inc., *Exec Srch*

Wisconsin
Mngmt. Rcrtrs. International, *Exec Srch*

MEDICAL SALES AND MARKETING

Arizona
Marjorie Starr & Associates, *Exec Srch*

Colorado
Health Industry Conslt, Inc./
   MedQuest Associates, *Exec Srch*

Florida
F-O-R-T-U-N-E Pers. Conslts, *Exec Srch*
OmniSearch Inc., *Exec Srch*

Georgia
Sondra Search, *Exec Srch*

Illinois
Giovannini Associates, *Exec Srch*
Krezowski & Company, *Perm Agcy*
Medical Recruiters, *Exec Srch*
Sanford Rose Associates, *Exec Srch*

Kansas
Network, *Exec Srch*

Louisiana
Sanford Rose Associates, *Exec Srch*

Michigan
Executive & Med. Recruiters, *Exec Srch*

Minnesota
Healthcare Recruiters, *Exec Srch*

New Jersey
Ridgewood Intermediaries, *Exec Srch*

New York
Harbrowe, Inc., *Perm Agcy*

North Carolina
Hunkler Medical Associates, *Exec Srch*

Ohio
J. Joseph & Associates, *Exec Srch*

Pennsylvania
Century Associates, *Exec Srch*

Texas
Otis Faulkner & Associates, *Exec Srch*

Virginia
Herb Gretz Associates, *Exec Srch*

Washington
Bell & Associates, *Exec Srch*
Mngmt. Rcrtrs. International, *Exec Srch*

Wisconsin
Charles C. Ray Associates, *Exec Srch*

MEDICAL TECHNOLOGY

Arizona
Sales Conslt, *Exec Srch*

Colorado
F-O-R-T-U-N-E Pers. Conslts of Denver,
   Exec Srch

Massachusetts
Carter/MacKay, *Exec Srch*
Diversified Communications Group,
   Exec Srch
F-O-R-T-U-N-E Pers. Conslts, *Exec Srch*
Scientific Resources, *Exec Srch*

Minnesota
Erspamer Associates, *Exec Srch*
NER, Inc., *Exec Srch*

Montana
F-O-R-T-U-N-E Pers. Conslts, *Exec Srch*

New Hampshire
F-O-R-T-U-N-E Pers. Conslts, *Exec Srch*

New Jersey
Dreier Consulting, *Exec Srch*
F-O-R-T-U-N-E Pers. Conslts, *Exec Srch*

Washington
CDI Corporation (West), *Contract Svc*

METALS

Florida
F-O-R-T-U-N-E Pers. Conslts, *Exec Srch*
Mngmt. Rcrtrs. of Lake Cty, *Exec Srch*
Manchester Inc., *Exec Srch*

Illinois
Magnum Search, *Exec Srch*

Indiana
National Recruiting Service, *Exec Srch*

Michigan
Mngmt. Rcrtrs. of Grand Rapids, *Exec
   Srch*
Sullivan & Associates, *Exec Srch*

Minnesota
Palesch & Associates, Inc., *Perm Agcy*

Missouri
Dunhill Personnel System, *Exec Srch*

Nebraska
Harrison Moore Inc., *Exec Srch*

New Jersey
Will-Cox Associates, *Exec Srch*

North Carolina
Advanced Prof. Resources, *Exec Srch*

Ohio
KBK Management Assoc., *Exec Srch*

Oregon
Search Northwest Associates, *Exec Srch*

Merrill Grumer Associates, *Perm Agcy*
HireKnowledge, *Temp Agcy*
Interactive Search Associates, *Exec Srch*
London Personnel Services, *Perm Agcy*
Olsten Staffing Services, *Temp Agcy*
Sanford Rose Associates, *Exec Srch*
Select Personnel, Inc., *Perm Agcy*
Systems Personnel Inc., *Exec Srch*
W.G. Tucker & Associates, *Exec Srch*
Vogue Personnel Inc., *Exec Srch*

Rhode Island
Daley & Associates Inc., *Exec Srch*
The Schattle Group, *Exec Srch*

South Carolina
Southern Recruiters & Conslt, *Exec Srch*

South Dakota
Key Staffing, *Temp Agcy*

Tennessee
Advanced Computer Careers, *Perm Agcy*
Gateway Group Personnel, *Temp Agcy*

Texas
Add-A-Temp/Woodlands Executive
    Employment, *Temp Agcy*
American Resources, *Exec Srch*
R. Gaines Baty Associates, *Exec Srch*
Burnett's Staffing, Inc., *Temp Agcy*
Dividend Staffing Services, *Temp Agcy*
F-O-R-T-U-N-E Pers. Conslts, *Exec Srch*
Hedman & Associates, *Exec Srch*
HireKnowledge, *Temp Agcy*
Norrell Services, *Temp Agcy*
Olsten Staffing Services, *Temp Agcy*
Priority Search, Inc., *Exec Srch*
Total Personnel Inc., *Exec Srch*
The Whitaker Companies, *Contract Svc*

Vermont
Dunhill Search of Vermont, *Exec Srch*

Virginia
Nancy Allen Associates, Inc., *Perm Agcy*
Paul-Tittle Associates, Inc., *Exec Srch*
Strategic Search, Inc., *Exec Srch*

Washington
Houser Martin Morris, *Exec Srch*

Wisconsin
Hunter Midwest, *Exec Srch*
Mngmt. Rcrtrs. International/
    Compusearch of Wausau, *Exec Srch*
Mngmt. Rcrtrs. International (Milwaukee
    West), *Exec Srch*

MULTIMEDIA

California
Aquent Partners, *Temp Agcy*
Art Links Staffing, *Perm Agcy*
Larkin Group, *Exec Srch*
Edward Rast and Company, *Exec Srch*

Illinois
Advancement Inc., *Exec Srch*

Massachusetts
New Dimensions in Tech., *Exec Srch*
Pro Staff, *Temp Agcy*

New Jersey
Rosenthal Associates Intnl., *Exec Srch*

New York
Cavan Systems, Ltd., *Exec Srch*
Rosenthal Assoc. Intnl., *Exec Srch*

Texas
Alexander & Company, *Exec Srch*
Contract Design Personnel, *Contract Svc*

NETWORK ADMINISTRATION

Arizona
Hall Kinion, *Contract Svc*

California
Hall Kinion, *Contract Svc*
Keifer Professional Search, *Exec Srch*
Mindsource Software Engineers,
    Contract Svc
PC Personnel, *Contract Svc*
PeopleWare Tech. Resources, *Contract
    Svc*
Schweichler Associates Inc., *Exec Srch*
Smartsource Incorporated, *Contract Svc*

Colorado
Hall Kinion, *Contract Svc*

Connecticut
Hall Kinion, *Contract Svc*

Dist. of Columbia
Pace-Careers, Inc., *Exec Srch*

Georgia
Executive Strategies, Inc., *Exec Srch*

Illinois
Hall Kinion, *Contract Svc*

Massachusetts
F-O-R-T-U-N-E Pers. Conslts, *Exec Srch*
Hall Kinion, *Contract Svc*
New Dimensions, *Exec Srch*

Minnesota
Hall Kinion, *Contract Svc*

Mississippi
The CPI Group, *Exec Srch*

New Hampshire
Barros Associates, *Perm Agcy*
Professional Recruiters Inc., *Perm Agcy*

New Jersey
Hall Kinion, *Contract Svc*
SnellingSearch, *Exec Srch*

New York
Hall Kinion, *Contract Svc*
Huntington Pers. Conslt, *Exec Srch*

North Carolina
Hall Kinion, *Contract Svc*

Ohio
Recruiting Services Inc., *Exec Srch*

Oregon
Hall Kinion, *Contract Svc*

Pennsylvania
Computer Professionals, Inc., *Exec Srch*
I/S Computer Services, Inc., *Exec Srch*
F.P. Lennon Associates, *Exec Srch*

Texas
Acclaim Services, Inc., *Temp Agcy*
Data Staffing Centre, *Perm Agcy*
Hall Kinion, *Contract Svc*

Utah
Hall Kinion, *Contract Svc*

Virginia
Hall Kinion, *Contract Svc*
Paul-Tittle Associates, Inc., *Exec Srch*
Strategic Staffing, Inc./SSI Technical
    Services Division, *Contract Svc*

Washington
Hall Kinion, *Contract Svc*

Wisconsin
Hunter Midwest, *Exec Srch*

NONPROFIT

Alabama
VIP Personnel, Inc., *Perm Agcy*

Arizona
Amer. Career Grp, *Career/
    Outplacement*
Cizek Associates Inc., *Exec Srch*
Stivers Temporary Personnel, *Temp Agcy*

California
ABA Staffing, Inc., *Exec Srch*
Answers Unlimited, *Temp Agcy*
Battalia Winston Intnl., *Exec Srch*
Bennett & Co Consult Grp, *Exec Srch*
Blue Moon Personnel Inc., *Temp Agcy*
Business Systems Support, *Perm Agcy*
Career Quest International, *Contract Svc*
Champagne Personnel, *Temp Agcy*
The Culver Group, *Exec Srch*
Dunhill Exec. Search of LA, *Exec Srch*
Goldstein & Associates, *Temp Agcy*
Gould Personnel Services, *Perm Agcy*
Intertec Design, Inc., *Perm Agcy*
Kabl Ability Network, *Exec Srch*
Klein & Associates, *Temp Agcy*
The London Associates, *Exec Srch*
London Temporary Services, *Temp Agcy*
MacNaughton Associates, *Exec Srch*
Presidio Personnel, *Temp Agcy*

Pro Staff Personnel Services, *Perm Agcy*
Edward Rast and Company, *Exec Srch*
Royal Staffing Services, *Exec Srch*
Rusher, Loscavio, and LoPresto, *Exec
    Srch*
Santa Barbara Staffing, *Perm Agcy*
TRC Staffing Services, Inc., *Perm Agcy*
The Forest Group, *Exec Srch*
UAW Labor Employment and Training
    Corporation, *Perm Agcy*
Your People Professionals, *Perm Agcy*

Colorado
A to Z Business Services, *Perm Agcy*
JobSearch, *Temp Agcy*
National Affirmative Action Career
    Network, Inc., *Exec Srch*
Todays Temporary, *Temp Agcy*

Connecticut
EDP Contract Services, *Contract Svc*

Delaware
J.B. Groner Executive Search, *Exec Srch*

Dist. of Columbia
ACSYS Inc., *Exec Srch*
Hire Standard Staffing, *Perm Agcy*
K.M.S. Associates, *Perm Agcy*
Morrison Associates, *Exec Srch*
Tangent Corporation, *Exec Srch*

Florida
AAA Employment, *Perm Agcy*
Alpha Pers./Alpha Temps, *Perm Agcy*
TRC Staffing Services, *Temp Agcy*

Georgia
The Diversified Srch Cos., *Exec Srch*
Elite Staffing Services, *Temp Agcy*
Bob Maddox Associates, *Exec Srch*
Mission Corps International/Helping
    Hands Temporary Svc., *Temp Agcy*
Olsten Staffing Services, *Temp Agcy*
WPPS Software Staffing, *Temp Agcy*

Hawaii
Alu Like Inc., *Career/Outplacement*

Idaho
Magic Valley Rehabilitation Services,
    Inc., *Career/Outplacement*

Illinois
AARP Foundation/Senior Community
    Service Emp. Program, *Perm Agcy*
Battalia Winston Intnl., *Exec Srch*
CareerLink USA, Inc., *Exec Srch*
InterStaff, *Temp Agcy*
Personnel Placement Conslt, *Perm Agcy*
Remedy Intelligent Staffing, *Temp Agcy*
Right Services Inc., *Temp Agcy*
Staffing Conslt Inc., *Perm Agcy*
Tuft & Associates, *Exec Srch*

Indiana
Job Placement Service Inc., *Perm Agcy*
Quiring Associates, Inc., *Perm Agcy*

Iowa
Helping Hands Temp. Svc., *Temp Agcy*
Iowa Workforce Develop Ctr, *Perm Agcy*

Kansas
Business Specialists, *Perm Agcy*
Key Staffing, *Temp Agcy*

Louisiana
Port City Enterprises, *Career/
    Outplacement*

Maine
Career Management Assoc., *Exec Srch*

Maryland
Caplan/Gross Associates, Inc., *Exec Srch*
JDG Associates Limited, *Exec Srch*
Sigman & Summerfield Assc, *Perm Agcy*
TAC Staffing Services, *Temp Agcy*

Massachusetts
Auerbach Associates, *Exec Srch*
Battalia Winston Intnl., *Exec Srch*
Brattle Temps, *Temp Agcy*
The Diversified Srch Cos., *Exec Srch*
Educational Mngmt. Network, *Exec Srch*
Fanning Personnel, *Perm Agcy*
Kelly Services, Inc., *Temp Agcy*
Mass Temps Inc., *Temp Agcy*
Pendleton James Associates, *Exec Srch*

OFFICE SUPPORT

Joan Leslie Personnel, Inc., *Perm Agcy*
S-H-S of Cherry Hill, *Perm Agcy*
Winters & Ross, *Perm Agcy*

New Mexico
Manpower, Inc., *Temp Agcy*
Norrell Staffing Services, *Temp Agcy*

New York
AccuStaff Incorporated, *Temp Agcy*
Asher Personnel Conslt, *Perm Agcy*
Career Blazers Pers. Svc., *Perm Agcy*
Chriss Careers Ltd., *Perm Agcy*
Group Agency, Inc., *Perm Agcy*
Harbrowe, Inc., *Perm Agcy*
Manpower Temp. Services, *Temp Agcy*
Mar-El Employment Agency, *Exec Srch*
Olsten Staffing Services, *Temp Agcy*
P.G. Prager Search Assoc., *Exec Srch*
Sloan Staffing Services, *Perm Agcy*
TAC Staffing Services, *Temp Agcy*
TemPositions, Inc., *Temp Agcy*
Winston Staffing Services, *Exec Srch*

North Carolina
Forbes Temporary Staffing, *Temp Agcy*
The Greer Group, *Perm Agcy*
Manpower, Inc., *Temp Agcy*
Mega Force, *Perm Agcy*
Norrell Services, *Temp Agcy*
Snelling Personnel Services, *Perm Agcy*

Ohio
CBS Personnel Services, *Perm Agcy*
Manpower Temp. Services, *Temp Agcy*
Snelling Personnel Services, *Temp Agcy*

Oregon
Adams Temporaries, *Temp Agcy*
Manpower Temp. Services, *Temp Agcy*

Pennsylvania
AAP Inc., *Temp Agcy*
Alexander Personnel Assoc., *Exec Srch*
Marsetta Lane Temp. Svcs., *Temp Agcy*
Manpower Temp. Services, *Temp Agcy*
Olsten Staffing Services, *Temp Agcy*

Rhode Island
Kelly Services, Inc., *Temp Agcy*
Kennedy Personnel Services, *Exec Srch*
Office Specialists, *Temp Agcy*

South Dakota
Alternative HR Development, *Perm Agcy*

Tennessee
Manpower, Inc., *Temp Agcy*
Quarles Kelly Associates, *Exec Srch*
Questar Partners Inc., *Exec Srch*
StaffingSolutions, *Perm Agcy*

Texas
Corbett Personnel Services, *Temp Agcy*
DayStar Services, *Perm Agcy*
Executeam, *Exec Srch*
HR Search, *Exec Srch*
Manpower Temp. Services, *Temp Agcy*

Utah
Your Job Connection, *Perm Agcy*

Vermont
Adecco, *Temp Agcy*
The Personnel Connection, *Temp Agcy*
Westaff, *Temp Agcy*

Virginia
A+ Personnel, *Perm Agcy*
Ardelle Assoc./AA Temps, *Perm Agcy*
Manpower Temp. Services, *Temp Agcy*
Susan Miller & Assoc., *Perm Agcy*
Don Richard Associates, *Perm Agcy*
Temporaries Now, *Temp Agcy*
TempWorld Staffing Svcs., *Temp Agcy*
Westaff, *Temp Agcy*

Washington
Business Careers, *Perm Agcy*
Manpower Temp. Services, *Temp Agcy*
PACE Staffing Network, *Exec Srch*

West Virginia
Kelly Services, Inc., *Temp Agcy*

Wisconsin
American Technical Services, *Perm Agcy*
Associated Secretarial, *Perm Agcy*
Landmark, The Staff Resource, *Temp Agcy*

SEEK Inc., *Perm Agcy*
U.S. Tech Force Inc., *Exec Srch*

Wyoming
The Employment Place, *Perm Agcy*

OIL AND GAS

California
Triple-J Services, *Exec Srch*

Colorado
Welzig, Lowe & Associates, *Exec Srch*
Woodmoor Group, *Exec Srch*

Minnesota
NER, Inc., *Exec Srch*

Nebraska
Power Brokers, LLC, *Exec Srch*

New Mexico
RLR Resources, *Exec Srch*

Oklahoma
Sooner Placement Service, *Perm Agcy*
U.S. Gas Search, *Exec Srch*

Texas
ABA Executive Search, *Exec Srch*
Atwood Professional Search, *Exec Srch*
Denson & Associates, *Exec Srch*
The Energists, *Exec Srch*
Energy Personnel, *Exec Srch*
Kelly Scientific Resources, *Temp Agcy*
Korn/Ferry International, *Exec Srch*
Piper-Morgan Personnel, *Exec Srch*
Watkins & Associates, *Exec Srch*

OPERATIONS MANAGEMENT

Alabama
Mngmt. Rcrtrs. International, *Exec Srch*

Arkansas
Mngmt. Rcrtrs., *Exec Srch*
Sanford Rose Associates, *Exec Srch*

California
Jason Best Agency, *Perm Agcy*
Marvin Laba & Associates, *Exec Srch*
Mngmt. Rcrtrs. International, *Exec Srch*
Strategic Alternatives, *Exec Srch*

Colorado
Mngmt. Rcrtrs. of Colorado Springs, *Exec Srch*
Sales Conslt of Denver, *Exec Srch*
Woodstone Consulting Co., *Exec Srch*

Connecticut
Mngmt. Rcrtrs. of Norwalk, *Exec Srch*
Mngmt. Rcrtrs. of Winsted, *Exec Srch*

Florida
F-O-R-T-U-N-E Pers. Conslts, *Exec Srch*
Mngmt. Rcrtrs. of St. Petersburg, *Exec Srch*
Mngmt. Rcrtrs. of Tallahassee, *Exec Srch*
Sales Conslt, *Exec Srch*
Sanford Rose Associates, *Exec Srch*

Georgia
Bell Oaks Company, *Exec Srch*
Mngmt. Rcrtrs. of Atlanta, *Exec Srch*

Illinois
Corporate Environment, Ltd., *Exec Srch*
Executive Search Link, Ltd., *Exec Srch*
Mngmt. Rcrtrs. International/
Sales Conslt, *Exec Srch*
OfficeMates5 (OM5), *Perm Agcy*
Sanford Rose Associates, *Exec Srch*

Indiana
Mngmt. Rcrtrs. of Richmond, *Exec Srch*

Iowa
Mngmt. Rcrtrs. International/
CompuSearch, *Exec Srch*

Kansas
Mngmt Rcrts/Sales Cnsl/OM5, *Exec Srch*
Talent Scouts Inc. (TSI), *Perm Agcy*

Kentucky
Angel Group International, *Exec Srch*
F-O-R-T-U-N-E Pers. Conslts, *Exec Srch*

Louisiana
Mngmt. Rcrtrs. of Metairie/Sales Conslt of Metairie, *Exec Srch*

Maine
F-O-R-T-U-N-E Pers. Conslts of Bangor, *Exec Srch*

Maryland
Mngmt. Rcrtrs. of Annapolis, *Exec Srch*
Mngmt. Rcrtrs. of Frederick/
OfficeMates5, *Exec Srch*

Massachusetts
Bell Oaks Company, *Exec Srch*
Mngmt. Rcrtrs. International, *Exec Srch*
Reardon Associates, Inc., *Perm Agcy*
Sales Conslt, *Exec Srch*

Michigan
Christopher Associates, *Exec Srch*
Mngmt. Rcrtrs. International, *Exec Srch*

Minnesota
Mngmt. Rcrtrs./Sales Conslt, *Exec Srch*

Missouri
Mngmt. Rcrtrs. of Kansas City, *Exec Srch*
Mngmt. Rcrtrs. of Springfield, *Exec Srch*
Mngmt. Rcrtrs. of St. Louis, *Exec Srch*
OfficeMates5 (OM5), *Exec Srch*

Nebraska
Compusearch of Lincoln, *Exec Srch*
Mngmt. Rcrtrs. of Omaha/
OfficeMates5 of Omaha, *Exec Srch*

Nevada
The Resource Network, *Exec Srch*

New Hampshire
Mngmt. Rcrtrs. International, *Exec Srch*
Resource Recruiting/Contemporary
Accountants, *Perm Agcy*
Sales Conslt, *Exec Srch*

New Jersey
Diedre Moire Corporation, *Exec Srch*
Orion Consulting, Inc., *Exec Srch*
Sales Conslt of Sparta, *Exec Srch*

New York
Staff By Manning, Ltd., *Perm Agcy*
Stamm Personnel Agency, *Perm Agcy*

North Carolina
Management Advisors Intnl., *Exec Srch*
Mngmt. Rcrtrs. International/
Sales Conslt, *Exec Srch*

Ohio
Ives & Associates, Inc., *Exec Srch*
Mngmt. Rcrtrs. International, *Exec Srch*
Sales Conslt, *Exec Srch*

Oregon
Mngmt. Rcrtrs. of Portland/
OfficeMates5 of Portland, *Exec Srch*

Pennsylvania
Mngmt. Rcrtrs./CompuSearch, *Exec Srch*

Rhode Island
Mngmt. Rcrtrs. International, *Exec Srch*

South Carolina
Mngmt. Rcrtrs. of Columbia, *Exec Srch*
Mngmt. Rcrtrs. of Rock Hill, *Exec Srch*
Sanford Rose Associates, *Exec Srch*

Tennessee
Mngmt. Rcrtrs./Sales Conslt, *Exec Srch*

Texas
Hyman & Associates, *Exec Srch*
Mngmt. Rcrtrs. International, *Exec Srch*
Sales Conslt of Houston, *Exec Srch*

Virginia
Mngmt. Rcrtrs. of McLean/
OfficeMates5, *Exec Srch*
Mngmt. Rcrtrs. International of Roanoke, *Exec Srch*

Washington
Mngmt. Rcrtrs. of Mercer Island, *Exec Srch*
Mngmt. Rcrtrs. of Tacoma, *Exec Srch*

Wisconsin
DHR International Inc., *Exec Srch*
Mngmt. Rcrtrs. of Appleton/
Compusearch, *Exec Srch*
Mngmt. Rcrtrs. of Milwaukee/
Sales Conslt, *Exec Srch*

Sun Personnel Services, *Temp Agcy*
TRC Staffing Services, Inc., *Perm Agcy*
TLC Staffing, *Temp Agcy*
Teleforce International, *Exec Srch*
Telford, Adams, & Alexander, *Exec Srch*
Temps Unlimited, Inc., *Temp Agcy*
TOD Staffing, *Temp Agcy*
Today Personnel Services, *Perm Agcy*
Truex Associates, *Exec Srch*
The Truman Agency, *Perm Agcy*
Tustin Personnel Services, *Perm Agcy*
UAW Labor Employment and Training
  Corporation, *Perm Agcy*
United Staffing Solutions, *Exec Srch*
Volt Services Group, *Temp Agcy*
Westaff, *Temp Agcy*
The Windsor Group, *Perm Agcy*
Your People Professionals, *Perm Agcy*
Amy Zimmerman & Assoc., *Perm Agcy*

Colorado

BankTemps, Inc., *Temp Agcy*
The Bridge, *Exec Srch*
CORE Staff Services, *Perm Agcy*
Dunhill Personnel of Boulder, *Exec Srch*
Executemps, Inc., *Temp Agcy*
Hallmark Personnel Systems, *Exec Srch*
Initial Staffing Services, *Perm Agcy*
JobSearch, *Temp Agcy*
Kelly Services, Inc., *Temp Agcy*
Labor Ready, Inc., *Temp Agcy*
Mngmt. Rcrtrs. of Colorado Springs,
  Exec Srch
Manpower International Inc., *Temp Agcy*
Martinez & Hromada Associates, Inc.,
  Contract Svc
National Affirmative Action Career
  Network, Inc., *Exec Srch*
Norrell Interim, *Temp Agcy*
Office Specialists Inc., *Temp Agcy*
Olsten Staffing Services, *Temp Agcy*
SOS Staffing Services, *Temp Agcy*
Sales Conslt of Denver, *Exec Srch*
Snelling Personnel Services, *Exec Srch*
Star Personnel Service, Inc., *Exec Srch*
Stivers Temporary Personnel, *Temp Agcy*
Tech Staffing, *Temp Agcy*
Todays Temporary, *Temp Agcy*
The Woodstone Conslt Co., *Exec Srch*

Connecticut

Advanced Placement Inc., *Temp Agcy*
Bohan & Bradstreet, *Perm Agcy*
Burke and Associates/The Westfield
  Group, *Exec Srch*
Buxbaum/Rink Consulting, *Exec Srch*
CPH Staffing & Consulting, *Temp Agcy*
Cahill Associates, *Exec Srch*
Corporate Staffing Solutions, *Temp Agcy*
Development Systems, Inc., *Exec Srch*
Dunhill of New Haven/Dunhill Search
  International, *Perm Agcy*
EDP Contract Services, *Contract Svc*
Employment Opportunities, *Perm Agcy*
Flynn Hannock, Inc., *Exec Srch*
Goodrich & Sherwood Assoc., *Exec Srch*
J.G. Hood Associates, *Perm Agcy*
Human Resource Conslt, *Exec Srch*
Impact Personnel, Inc., *Temp Agcy*
Intertec Personnel, *Temp Agcy*
Mngmt. Rcrtrs. of Norwalk, *Exec Srch*
McIntyre Associates, *Temp Agcy*
The McKnight Group, *Exec Srch*
Barry Persky & Co., *Exec Srch*
Howard W. Smith Associates, *Exec Srch*
Westaff, *Temp Agcy*
Workforce One, *Perm Agcy*

Delaware

J.B. Groner Executive Search, *Exec Srch*
E.W. Hodges & Associates, *Exec Srch*
HRdirect Incorporated, *Perm Agcy*
Independent National Search &
  Associates (INS), *Exec Srch*
Personal Placements Inc., *Perm Agcy*
The Placers, Inc., *Temp Agcy*

Dist. of Columbia

Career Blazers Pers. Service, *Perm Agcy*
Trifax Corporation, *Perm Agcy*

Florida

AAA Employment, *Perm Agcy*
Able Body Corporate Svcs., *Contract Svc*

AccuStaff Incorporated, *Temp Agcy*
Active Professionals, *Exec Srch*
Alpha Per./Alpha Temps, *Perm Agcy*
Ash & Assoc. Exec. Search, *Exec Srch*
Availability, Inc., *Perm Agcy*
Balcor Associates, *Exec Srch*
The Brand Company, Inc., *Exec Srch*
Career Planners, Inc., *Perm Agcy*
CareerXchange, *Temp Agcy*
Carrier's Career Service, Inc.,
  Career/Outplacement
Chase-Gardner Exec. Search, *Exec Srch*
Computer Plus Staffing Solutions, Inc.,
  Temp Agcy
Employers' Assistant, Inc., *Temp Agcy*
Ethan Allen Pers. Placement, *Exec Srch*
Farwell Group Inc., *Exec Srch*
First Recruiters Group Inc., *Exec Srch*
Five Star Temporary Inc., *Temp Agcy*
F-O-R-T-U-N-E Pers. Conslts, *Exec Srch*
Future Force Personnel, *Temp Agcy*
Gallin Associates, *Exec Srch*
HR Professional Conslt, *Exec Srch*
Hastings & Hastings Personnel Conslt,
  Temp Agcy
Interim Financial Solutions, *Exec Srch*
Janus Career Services, *Exec Srch*
Kelly Services, Inc., *Temp Agcy*
R.H. Larsen & Associates, *Exec Srch*
Mngmt. Rcrtrs. International, *Exec Srch*
Mngmt. Rcrtrs. of Tallahassee, *Exec Srch*
Manpower Temp. Services, *Temp Agcy*
NPF Associates Ltd., Inc., *Exec Srch*
Norrell Technical Services, *Exec Srch*
Olsten Staffing Services, *Temp Agcy*
The Ryan Charles Group, Inc., *Exec Srch*
Sales Conslt of Fort Lauderdale, Inc.,
  Exec Srch
Search Enterprises South, Inc., *Exec Srch*
Doug Sears & Associates, *Exec Srch*
Staffing Now, *Temp Agcy*
Staffing Solutions by Personnel One,
  Perm Agcy
TRC Staffing Services, *Temp Agcy*
Todays Temporary, *Temp Agcy*
Tower Conslt, Ltd., *Exec Srch*
Velkin Personnel Services, *Perm Agcy*

Georgia

Augusta Staffing Associates, *Perm Agcy*
Bell Oaks Company, *Exec Srch*
Boreham International, *Exec Srch*
Bradshaw & Associates, *Exec Srch*
R.A. Clark Consulting, *Exec Srch*
Corporate Image Group, *Exec Srch*
Corporate Search Conslt, *Exec Srch*
Dunhill Professional Search, *Exec Srch*
Dynamic People, *Temp Agcy*
Elite Staffing Services, *Temp Agcy*
Executive Strategies, Inc., *Exec Srch*
Express Personnel Services, *Perm Agcy*
Fox-Morris Associates, *Exec Srch*
The HR Group, Inc., *Exec Srch*
Hall Management Group, *Exec Srch*
ISC of Atlanta/International Career
  Continuation, *Exec Srch*
Job Shop Inc., *Exec Srch*
Kelly Services, Inc., *Temp Agcy*
Kenzer Corp. of Georgia, *Exec Srch*
Lowderman & Associates, *Exec Srch*
Mngmt. Rcrtrs. of Atlanta, *Exec Srch*
Mngmt. Rcrtrs. of Marietta, *Exec Srch*
New Boston Select, *Perm Agcy*
Olsten Staffing Services, *Temp Agcy*
Priority 1 Staffing Services, *Temp Agcy*
Randstad Staffing Services, *Temp Agcy*
P.J. Reda & Associates, Inc., *Exec Srch*
PRI /Invesearch, *Exec Srch*
Southern Employment Svc., *Perm Agcy*
Staffing Resources, *Perm Agcy*
StaffMark, *Temp Agcy*
TRC Staffing Services, *Temp Agcy*
TRI Staffing, *Temp Agcy*
Temporary Specialties, *Temp Agcy*
Todays Emp. Solutions, *Perm Agcy*
WPPS Software Staffing, *Temp Agcy*
Westaff, *Temp Agcy*

Hawaii

Executive Search World, *Exec Srch*
Maresca and Associates, *Exec Srch*
Olsten Staffing Services, *Temp Agcy*

Idaho

Horne/Brown International, *Exec Srch*
Intermountain Staffing Resources, *Perm
  Agcy*
Manpower Temp. Services, *Temp Agcy*

Illinois

A.B.A. Placements/A.B.A. Temporaries,
  Perm Agcy
ASI Staffing Service, Inc., *Perm Agcy*
Abbott Smith Associates, *Exec Srch*
The Ability Group, *Exec Srch*
B.J. Abrams & Associates, *Exec Srch*
Accurate Recruiting Inc., *Perm Agcy*
Adecco, *Temp Agcy*
Affiliated Pers. Conslt, *Perm Agcy*
Armstrong-Hamilton Assoc., *Exec Srch*
Assured Staffing, *Temp Agcy*
Banner Personnel Service, *Perm Agcy*
Barry Personnel Resources, *Perm Agcy*
Bevelle & Associates, Inc., *Exec Srch*
Burling Group Ltd., *Exec Srch*
CareerLink USA, Inc., *Exec Srch*
Carson Mngmt. Assoc., *Contract Svc*
Coffou Partners, Inc., *Exec Srch*
Corporate Staffing, Inc./Proven
  Performers, *Perm Agcy*
Ned Dickey & Associates, Inc./Dickey
  Staffing Solutions, *Exec Srch*
Diener & Associates Inc., *Exec Srch*
Dynamic People, *Temp Agcy*
Eastman & Associates, *Exec Srch*
The Esquire Staffing Group, *Perm Agcy*
Executive Referral Services, *Exec Srch*
Express Personnel Services, *Temp Agcy*
Fellows Placement, *Temp Agcy*
David Gomez & Associates, *Exec Srch*
HR Search, *Perm Agcy*
Human Resource Connection, *Perm Agcy*
Interim Pers., *Contract Svc, Temp Agcy*
InterStaff, *Temp Agcy*
Johnson Personnel Company, *Exec Srch*
Raymond Karson Associates, *Exec Srch*
Kenneth Nicholas & Assoc., *Exec Srch*
Kunzer Associates, Ltd., *Exec Srch*
Mack & Associates, Ltd., *Temp Agcy*
Magnum Search, *Exec Srch*
Mngmt. Rcrtrs. International/Sales
  Conslt, *Exec Srch*
Mngmt. Rcrtrs. of Des Plaines/
  OfficeMates5 Personnel, *Exec Srch*
Manpower Temp. Services, *Temp Agcy*
Marsteller Wilcox Associates, *Exec Srch*
Medical Tech. Placements, *Temp Agcy*
Juan Menefee & Associates, *Exec Srch*
Merit Personnel Inc., *Perm Agcy*
Michael David Associates, *Perm Agcy*
The Murphy Group, *Perm Agcy*
NJW & Associates, Inc., *Temp Agcy*
National Search, *Exec Srch*
Norrell Services, *Temp Agcy*
Olsten Staffing Services, *Temp Agcy*
The Opportunities Group, *Perm Agcy*
PS Inc., *Perm Agcy*
Parker Cromwell & Assoc., *Exec Srch*
Personnel Connections Inc., *Perm Agcy*
Personnel Placement Conslt, *Perm Agcy*
Professional Research Svcs., *Exec Srch*
ProSearch Plus, *Exec Srch*
Remedy Intelligent Staffing, *Temp Agcy*
Retail Staffers, Inc., *Exec Srch*
Right Services Inc., *Temp Agcy*
Ritt-Ritt and Associates, *Exec Srch*
SC International, *Exec Srch*
Select Staffing, *Perm Agcy*
Seville Temporary Services, *Temp Agcy*
Snelling Personnel Services, *Perm Agcy*
Staffing Conslt Inc., *Perm Agcy*
Stivers Temporary Personnel, *Temp Agcy*
Strategic Resources Unlimited, *Exec Srch*
Thirty Three Personnel Ctr., *Perm Agcy*
Working World Inc., *Temp Agcy*
World Employment Service, *Perm Agcy*

Indiana

Angola Personnel Services, *Perm Agcy*
Canis Major, Inc./HR Quest, *Exec Srch*
Corporate Staff Resources, *Temp Agcy*
Crown Temp. Svcs., *Temp Agcy*
Dunhill of Brown County, *Exec Srch*
Execusearch, *Exec Srch*

Career Center, Inc., *Perm Agcy*
Career Management Group, *Exec Srch*
Career Management Intnl., *Exec Srch*
Careers USA, *Perm Agcy*
Careerworks, *Exec Srch*
Cox Darrow & Owens, Inc., *Exec Srch*
Dean-Wharton Associates, *Exec Srch*
M.T. Donaldson Associates, *Exec Srch*
Dunhill Professional Search, *Exec Srch*
Ellis Career Conslt/Career Search Associates, *Exec Srch*
Executive Search, Inc., *Exec Srch*
F-O-R-T-U-N-E Pers. Conslts of Menlo Park, *Exec Srch*
Fox-Morris Associates, *Exec Srch*
Goodrich & Sherwood Assoc, *Exec Srch*
HRD Conslt, Inc., *Exec Srch*
Holm Personnel Conslt, *Exec Srch*
Hughes & Podesla Personnel, *Perm Agcy*
ITC Personnel Services, *Temp Agcy*
J.M. Joseph Associates, *Exec Srch*
Joule Staffing Services, *Contract Svc*
Karras Personnel Inc., *Exec Srch*
Kaye Personnel Inc., *Temp Agcy*
Major Conslt, *Exec Srch*
Mngmt. Rcrtrs. International, *Exec Srch*
Mayfair Services, *Perm Agcy*
OfficeMates5 (OM5)/DayStar Temporary Services, *Perm Agcy*
Northeastern Financial Conslt, *Exec Srch*
OMNE Staffing Svcs., *Temp Agcy*
Orion Consulting, Inc., *Exec Srch*
Park Avenue Personnel, *Perm Agcy*
The Penmor Group, *Exec Srch*
Personnel Plus/Temps Plus, *Perm Agcy*
Pomerantz Staffing Services, *Perm Agcy*
Premier Personnel Group, *Perm Agcy*
Princeton Executive Search, *Exec Srch*
Recruitment Alternatives, *Perm Agcy*
Rosenthal Associates Intnl., *Exec Srch*
Robert Scott Associates, *Exec Srch*
S-H-S of Cherry Hill, *Perm Agcy*
Search Conslt, Inc., *Exec Srch*
Selective Personnel, *Perm Agcy*
Snelling Personnel Services, *Perm Agcy*
The Stelton Group, Inc., *Exec Srch*
TRS Staffing Solutions, Inc., *Temp Agcy*
Temporary Excellence Inc., *Temp Agcy*
UNITEMP Temporary Pers., *Temp Agcy*
Winston Staffing Services, *Temp Agcy*
Winters & Ross, *Perm Agcy*

New Mexico
Albuquerque Personnel, Inc., *Perm Agcy*
CDI Technical Services, *Contract Svc*
Excel Staffing Companies, *Perm Agcy*
Mngmt Resource Consulting, *Exec Srch*

New York
AARP Foundation/Senior Employment Program, *Perm Agcy*
Accounting & Computer Personnel, *Perm Agcy*
AccuStaff Incorporated, *Temp Agcy*
Merrill Adams Associates, *Career/Outplacement*
Adecco, *Temp Agcy*
Franklin Allen Conslt, *Exec Srch*
Asher Personnel Conslt, *Perm Agcy*
Beishline Executive Search, *Exec Srch*
Berkel Associates, Inc., *Exec Srch*
Bevlin Personnel Inc., *Perm Agcy*
Bornholdt Shivas & Friends, *Exec Srch*
Branthover Associates, *Exec Srch*
E.E. Brooke Inc., *Perm Agcy*
Brookville Staffing Services, *Perm Agcy*
Burns Personnel, *Exec Srch*
CK Resources, *Exec Srch*
Canny, Bowen Inc., *Exec Srch*
Career Concepts, Inc., *Perm Agcy*
Career Objectives Personnel, *Temp Agcy*
Carlile Personnel Agency, *Perm Agcy*
Chriss Careers Ltd., *Exec Srch*
Colton Partnership, *Exec Srch*
Concorde Search, *Perm Agcy*
Corporate Careers, Inc., *Exec Srch*
Corporate Search Inc., *Exec Srch*
Dental Placement Plus, *Temp Agcy*
Seth Diamond Associates, *Exec Srch*
EDP Contract Services, *Contract Svc*
Eden Staffing, *Perm Agcy*
Employment Recruiters Agency, *Perm Agcy*

Euromonde, Inc., *Temp Agcy*
Fanning Personnel, *Exec Srch*
C.R. Fletcher Associates, *Exec Srch*
Gardiner, Townsend & Assoc, *Exec Srch*
Goodrich & Sherwood Assoc, *Exec Srch*
Gundersen Partners L.L.C., *Exec Srch*
Haesloop and Hegarty, *Temp Agcy*
Headway Corporate Staffing, *Perm Agcy*
Healthsearch Group, *Exec Srch*
Hunter Mac & Associates, *Perm Agcy*
Hunter Placement Inc., *Exec Srch*
Interspace Interactive Inc., *Temp Agcy*
Island Search Group Inc., *Perm Agcy*
KLK Personnel, *Perm Agcy*
KPA Staffing Group, Inc., *Exec Srch*
The Kay Grp. of Fifth Avenue, *Exec Srch*
Kelly Services, Inc., *Temp Agcy*
Lab Support Inc., *Temp Agcy*
Lake Associates, *Exec Srch*
John Lawrence & Associates, *Exec Srch*
The MVP Group, *Exec Srch*
Magill Associates, Inc., *Exec Srch*
Joseph T. Maloney & Assoc, *Exec Srch*
Manpower Temp. Services, *Temp Agcy*
Media Staffing Network, *Temp Agcy*
Mentortech, *Exec Srch*
Metro Resources of Rochester, *Temp Agcy*
Metro Support Group, *Perm Agcy*
Metropolitan Personnel Syst., *Exec Srch*
Milazzo Associates, Inc., *Perm Agcy*
Morgan-Murray Personnel/M&M Top Temps, *Temp Agcy*
Noah Associates, *Perm Agcy*
Noble & Associates, *Exec Srch*
Norrell Staffing Services, *Temp Agcy*
Norris Emp. Conslt, *Perm Agcy*
Nowack Career Specialists, *Perm Agcy*
Olsten Staffing Services, *Temp Agcy*
Optimal Resources, *Exec Srch*
OTEC Inc., *Perm Agcy*
The Parks Group Inc., *Exec Srch*
Parsons, Anderson & Gee, *Perm Agcy*
Paxton Resources Inc., *Exec Srch*
Personnel Consulting Assoc., *Exec Srch*
P.G. Prager Search Assoc., *Exec Srch*
Professional Support Inc., *Exec Srch*
Quest Organization, *Exec Srch*
Recruitment Intnl. Group, *Exec Srch*
Rem Resources, *Exec Srch*
Remedy Intelligent Staffing, *Temp Agcy*
Rosenthal Assoc. Intnl., *Exec Srch*
Alexander Ross Associates, *Perm Agcy*
Roth Young of Long Island, *Exec Srch*
S.W. Management, *Exec Srch*
SearchAmerica Inc., *Exec Srch*
Sharp Placement Profs., *Exec Srch*
Sporn Group Inc., *Exec Srch*
Staff By Manning, Ltd., *Perm Agcy*
Staff Managers, *Temp Agcy*
Staffing Services, *Exec Srch*
StratfordGroup, *Exec Srch*
Superior Concepts, *Contract Svc*
Tempo Services, Inc., *Temp Agcy*
Temporary Resource Center, *Temp Agcy*
TemPositions, Inc., *Temp Agcy*
United Personnel Agency, *Perm Agcy*
Vantage Staffing Services, *Temp Agcy*
Weber Mngmt. Conslt, *Exec Srch*
Westaff, *Temp Agcy*
Westchester Emp. Agency, *Perm Agcy*
Westfield Associates, Inc., *Exec Srch*
Winston Staffing Services, *Exec Srch*
S.R. Wolman Associates, Inc., *Exec Srch*
Woodbury Personnel, *Perm Agcy*

North Carolina
A First Resource, *Exec Srch*
Accurate Staff Conslt, *Exec Srch*
Action Staffing Group, *Temp Agcy*
Advanced Pers. Resources, *Exec Srch*
Alpha Omega Exec. Search, *Exec Srch*
AmeriPro Search, Inc., *Exec Srch*
Anderson & Daniel Pers. Assoc., *Perm Agcy*
Ayers & Associates, Inc., *Exec Srch*
Career Search Inc., *Exec Srch*
Executive Connections, *Exec Srch*
Executive Staffing Group, *Exec Srch*
D.D. Fayling Associates, Inc., *Exec Srch*
F-O-R-T-U-N-E Pers. Conslts, *Exec Srch*
Fox-Morris Associates, *Exec Srch*

Graham & Associates, *Perm Agcy*
Interim Personnel, Inc., *Temp Agcy*
The Jobs Market, Inc., *Perm Agcy*
Kelly Services, Inc., *Temp Agcy*
Mngmt. Rcrtrs. International/Sales Conslt, *Exec Srch*
Mark III Personnel Inc., *Exec Srch*
McCain Employment Svc., *Temp Agcy*
Moffitt International, Inc., *Exec Srch*
Olsten Staffing Services, *Temp Agcy*
Parenica & Company, *Exec Srch*
The Perkins Group, *Exec Srch*
Professional Pers. Assoc., *Perm Agcy*
Quality Temporary Services, *Temp Agcy*
Sparks Personnel Services, *Exec Srch*
StaffMark, *Temp Agcy*
StratfordGroup, *Exec Srch*
Summit Occupational Staff, *Exec Srch*
USA Staffing, *Perm Agcy*
Youngblood Staffing, *Perm Agcy*

North Dakota
Career Connection, *Exec Srch*
Green Thumb, *Career/Outplacement*
Olsten Staffing Services/Expressway Personnel, *Temp Agcy*

Ohio
AccuStaff, *Temp Agcy*
Adecco, *Temp Agcy*
N.L. Benke & Associates, *Perm Agcy*
Bradley-Pierce Personnel, *Perm Agcy*
J.B. Brown & Associates, *Exec Srch*
CBS Personnel Services, *Perm Agcy*
Career Specialists Inc., *Exec Srch*
Champion Personnel System, *Perm Agcy*
Combined Resources Inc., *Exec Srch*
Continental Search Assoc., *Exec Srch*
J.D. Cotter Search, Inc., *Exec Srch*
Crown Temp. Svcs., *Temp Agcy*
Dankowski and Associates, *Exec Srch*
Pete DeLuke & Associates, *Exec Srch*
Eastern Personnel Services *Perm Agcy*
Executech, *Exec Srch*
Executive Search Ltd., *Exec Srch*
Flex-Tech Prof. Svcs., *Contract Svc*
Gayhart & Associates, *Exec Srch*
Global Resources Group, *Contract Svc*
H.L. Goehring & Associates, *Exec Srch*
Griffiths & Associates, *Exec Srch*
Guthoff & Associates, *Exec Srch*
Russ Hadick & Associates, *Exec Srch*
Hahn & Associates, Inc., *Exec Srch*
Hite Executive Search/Hite Management Conslt, Inc., *Exec Srch*
ITS Technical Staffing, *Exec Srch*
Interim Personnel, *Temp Agcy*
Ives & Associates, Inc., *Exec Srch*
KBK Management Assoc., *Exec Srch*
Kelly Services, Inc., *Temp Agcy*
Mngmt. Rcrtrs. International, *Exec Srch*
Manpower Temp. Services, *Temp Agcy*
Marvel Conslt Inc., *Exec Srch*
Miami Professional Search, *Exec Srch*
Minority Executive Search, *Exec Srch*
Newcomb-Desmond & Assoc, *Exec Srch*
Norrell Services, Inc., *Temp Agcy*
Olsten Prof. Staff Svcs., *Exec Srch*
Palmer Temps/Palmer Grp, *Temp Agcy*
Professional Restaffing, *Perm Agcy*
Providence Pers. Conslt, *Exec Srch*
Quality Plus, *Exec Srch*
Quality Source, Inc., *Exec Srch*
Bill Reber & Associates, Inc., *Exec Srch*
RecruitMasters of Cincinnati, *Exec Srch*
Resource Techne Group, *Exec Srch*
Sales Conslt, *Exec Srch*
Shafer Jones Associates, *Exec Srch*
StratfordGroup, *Exec Srch*
The Target HR Cos., *Temp Agcy*
Teamwork U.S.A., *Contract Svc*
Tech/Aid of Ohio, *Perm Agcy*
Temporarily Yours Placement, *Temp Agcy*
Tradesman International, *Contract Svc*

Oklahoma
Ameri Resource, *Exec Srch*
Cherokee Temps, Inc., *Temp Agcy*
Express Personnel Services, *Exec Srch*
Interim Personnel, *Temp Agcy*
Key Temporary Personnel, *Temp Agcy*
National Recruiters, *Exec Srch*

Houser Martin Morris (HMM), *Exec Srch*
Human Resources Inc., *Exec Srch*
The Jobs Company, *Exec Srch*
Kelly Services, Inc., *Temp Agcy*
Mngmt. Rcrtrs. of Tacoma, *Exec Srch*
Management Solutions, *Exec Srch*
Manpower Temp. Services, *Temp Agcy*
John Mason & Associates, *Exec Srch*
Olsten Staffing Services, *Temp Agcy*
Parker Professional Search, *Exec Srch*
Personnel Unlimited Inc., *Exec Srch*
Strain Personnel Specialists, *Exec Srch*
StratfordGroup, *Exec Srch*
Technical Resource Group, *Exec Srch*
The Washington Firm, *Exec Srch*
Whittall Management Group, *Exec Srch*

West Virginia

Extra Support Staffing, *Temp Agcy*
Key Personnel, Inc., *Perm Agcy*
Snelling Personnel Services, *Temp Agcy*

Wisconsin

The Ambrose Group, *Exec Srch*
Argus Technical Services, *Perm Agcy*
Austria Austria and Assoc., *Perm Agcy*
Career Resources, *Exec Srch*
Careertrac Employment Svcs., *Exec Srch*
Crown Services, *Temp Agcy*
Dieck Mueller Group, *Exec Srch*
J.M. Eagle Partners, *Exec Srch*
Executive Resource Inc., *Exec Srch*
Fogec Conslt. Inc., *Exec Srch*
FoodStaff 2000, Inc., *Exec Srch*
The H S Group, Inc., *Exec Srch*
Interim Personnel, *Temp Agcy*
Interim Technology, *Contract Svc*
KGA Inc., *Exec Srch*
Landmark, The Staffing Resource, *Temp Agcy*
Mngmt. Rcrtrs., *Exec Srch*
Manpower Temp. Services, *Temp Agcy*
MARBL Conslt, *Exec Srch*
The Michael David Group, *Exec Srch*
N.E.W. Contracting Svcs., *Perm Agcy*
Olsten Staffing Services, *Temp Agcy*
QTI Professional Staffing, *Exec Srch*
Work Connection, *Perm Agcy*

PHARMACEUTICALS

Arizona

Search Masters International, *Exec Srch*

California

Bench International Search, *Exec Srch*
Biosource Tech. Service, *Contract Svc*
Boyle Ogata, *Exec Srch*
Christian & Timbers, *Exec Srch*
COMFORCE Tech. Svcs., *Contract Svc*
F-O-R-T-U-N-E Pers. Conslts, *Exec Srch*
Kelly Scientific Resources, *Temp Agcy*
Jeff Kroh Associates, *Exec Srch*
Lewis & Blank International, *Exec Srch*
Mngmt. Rcrtrs. International, *Exec Srch*
Med. Exec. International, *Exec Srch*
Med Quest, *Exec Srch*
Medical Executive Recruiters, *Exec Srch*
National Career Choices, *Exec Srch*
Norsell & Associates, *Exec Srch*
Paster & Associates, *Exec Srch*
The Proven Edge Exec. Recs., *Exec Srch*
Sampson Medical Search, *Exec Srch*
Sanford Rose Associates, *Exec Srch*
TMP Executive Resources, *Exec Srch*
TMP Worldwide, *Exec Srch*

Colorado

F-O-R-T-U-N-E Pers. Conslts, *Exec Srch*
Sales Conslt of Denver, *Exec Srch*

Connecticut

Ryan Abbott Search Assoc., *Exec Srch*
Brandywine Retained Ventures, *Exec Srch*
Charter Personnel Services, *Exec Srch*
Mngmt. Rcrtrs. International, *Exec Srch*
C.A. McInnis & Associates, *Exec Srch*
TMP Worldwide, *Exec Srch*
H.L. Yoh Company/Yoh Information Technology Associates, *Contract Svc*

Delaware

DW Technologies, *Contract Svc*
The Franklin Company, *Exec Srch*

Florida

Ash & Assoc. Exec. Search, *Exec Srch*
Contract Health Profs., *Contract Svc*
F-O-R-T-U-N-E Pers. Conslts, *Exec Srch*
Mngmt. Rcrtrs. of Plant City, *Exec Srch*
Mngmt. Rcrtrs. of Tallahassee, *Exec Srch*
Manchester Inc., *Exec Srch*
OmniSearch Inc., *Exec Srch*
The Stewart Search Group, *Exec Srch*
TMP Worldwide, *Exec Srch*
Zackrison Associates Inc., *Exec Srch*

Georgia

F-O-R-T-U-N-E Pers. Conslts of Atlanta/Alternastaff, *Exec Srch*
Kelly Scientific Resources, *Temp Agcy*
Mngmt. Rcrtrs. of Atlanta, *Exec Srch*
TMP Worldwide, *Exec Srch*

Hawaii

Sales Conslt of Honolulu, *Exec Srch*

Illinois

Corporate Environment, Ltd., *Exec Srch*
Executive Referral Svcs., *Exec Srch*
Kelly Scientific Resources, *Temp Agcy*
Mngmt. Rcrtrs. International, *Exec Srch*
OfficeMates5 (OM5), *Perm Agcy*
TMP Worldwide, *Exec Srch*
Texcel, Inc., *Exec Srch*
Voigt Associates, *Exec Srch*

Indiana

Execusearch, *Exec Srch*
Keith Hayes & Associates, *Exec Srch*
Mngmt. Rcrtrs. of Richmond, *Exec Srch*
OfficeMates5 (OM5)/DayStar Temporary Services, *Exec Srch*

Kansas

The Chase Group, *Exec Srch*
Network, *Exec Srch*

Louisiana

Shiell Personnel, *Perm Agcy*

Maine

The Haystack Group, *Exec Srch*

Maryland

F-O-R-T-U-N-E Pers. Conslts, *Exec Srch*
Mngmt. Rcrtrs. of Annapolis, *Exec Srch*
Mngmt. Rcrtrs. of Frederick/OfficeMates5, *Exec Srch*
Sales Conslt, *Exec Srch*

Massachusetts

Carter/MacKay of Framingham, *Exec Srch*
F-O-R-T-U-N-E Pers. Conslts, *Exec Srch*
Mngmt. Rcrtrs. International, *Exec Srch*
Sales Conslt, *Exec Srch*
Scientific Resources, *Exec Srch*
J. Robert Scott, *Exec Srch*
TMP Worldwide, *Exec Srch*
TASA International, *Exec Srch*

Michigan

Kelly Scientific Resources, *Temp Agcy*
Professional Advancement Institute, *Exec Srch*
Roth Young Personnel Services of Detroit, Inc., *Exec Srch*
Vectech Pharmaceuticals Conslt, *Perm Agcy*

Minnesota

Hilleren & Associates, *Exec Srch*
Kelly Scientific Resources, *Temp Agcy*
Mngmt. Rcrtrs./Sales Conslt, *Exec Srch*

Missouri

Jim Crumpley & Associates, *Exec Srch*
Debbon Recruiting Group, *Exec Srch*
Kelly Scientific Resources, *Temp Agcy*
Mngmt. Rcrtrs. of Kansas City, *Exec Srch*
Mngmt. Rcrtrs. of Springfield, *Exec Srch*
Mngmt. Rcrtrs. of St. Louis, *Exec Srch*

Montana

F-O-R-T-U-N-E Pers. Conslts, *Exec Srch*

Nebraska

Lincoln Group Inc., *Exec Srch*

New Hampshire

F-O-R-T-U-N-E Pers. Conslts, *Exec Srch*

New Jersey

Anderson Wright Associates, *Exec Srch*
Andos Associates Inc., *Exec Srch*
Arc Medical and Prof. Pers., *Temp Agcy*
Gary S. Bell Associates, Inc., *Exec Srch*
Besen Associates, *Exec Srch*
Blau Mancino & Associates, *Exec Srch*
The Bonner Group, *Exec Srch*
Bradin Search Group, *Exec Srch*
Brissenden, McFarland, Fuccella & Reynolds, Inc., *Exec Srch*
CPS Technical Placements, *Perm Agcy*
CSA Associates, *Exec Srch*
Carter/MacKay Personnel Inc., *Exec Srch*
Ken Clark International, *Exec Srch*
Clinforce, *Exec Srch*
Robert Drexler Associates, *Exec Srch*
Dynamic Recruiters Inc., *Exec Srch*
E&A Recruiters, *Exec Srch*
Eagle Research Inc., *Exec Srch*
Evergreen Personnel Service, *Exec Srch*
F-O-R-T-U-N-E Pers. Conslts, *Exec Srch*
W.N. Garbarini & Associates, *Exec Srch*
The Harrison Group, *Exec Srch*
Huff Associates, *Exec Srch*
KDC Group, *Exec Srch*
Kelly Scientific Resources, *Temp Agcy*
Mngmt. Rcrtrs. of Medford, *Exec Srch*
Merlin International Inc., *Exec Srch*
Mufson Associates, *Exec Srch*
Orion Consulting, Inc., *Exec Srch*
Rosenthal Associates Intnl., *Exec Srch*
Ruderfer & Company, *Exec Srch*
Salem Associates, *Exec Srch*
Shifrin-Fischer Group, Inc., *Exec Srch*
Phyllis Solomon Exec. Search, *Exec Srch*
Spectrum Scientific Recruiters, *Exec Srch*
Stewart/Laurence Associates, *Exec Srch*
Janet Stoakes Associates Inc., *Exec Srch*
Target Pros, Inc., *Exec Srch*
Thomas & Associates, *Exec Srch*
Worksource 2000, Inc., *Exec Srch*
Yoh Scientific, *Perm Agcy*
Yoh Scientific/H. L. Yoh Company, *Contract Svc*
Michael D. Zinn & Associates, *Exec Srch*

New York

The Dartmouth Group, *Exec Srch*
Gardiner, Townsend & Assoc., *Exec Srch*
The Hampton Group, *Exec Srch*
Lake Associates, *Exec Srch*
Mngmt. Rcrtrs./Compusearch, *Exec Srch*
The Neil Michael Group, *Exec Srch*
Pharmaceutical Recruiters, *Exec Srch*
Pro/TECH Nationwide Staff, *Exec Srch*
Rosenthal Assoc. Intnl., *Exec Srch*
Salem Associates, *Exec Srch*
Staffing Services, *Exec Srch*
TMP Worldwide, *Exec Srch*
Michael D. Zinn & Associates, *Exec Srch*

North Carolina

Amcell Associates, *Exec Srch*
S.L. Collins Associates, *Exec Srch*
Ellis Associates, Inc., *Exec Srch*
Mngmt. Rcrtrs. of Greensboro, *Exec Srch*
Moffitt International, Inc., *Exec Srch*
Office Specialists, *Temp Agcy*

Oregon

F-O-R-T-U-N-E Pers. Conslts, *Exec Srch*

Pennsylvania

Delta ProSearch, *Exec Srch*
Impact Search & Strategy, *Exec Srch*
Mngmt. Rcrtrs. of Reading/CAREER SENTINEL, INC., *Exec Srch*
Manchester Inc., *Career/Outplacement*
George R. Martin Exec. Srch, *Exec Srch*
Mastersearch, *Exec Srch*
Norcon Associates, Inc., *Exec Srch*
Triangle Associates Intnl., *Perm Agcy*

Rhode Island

Albert G. Lee & Associates, *Exec Srch*
Lybrook Associates, Inc., *Exec Srch*

South Carolina

F-O-R-T-U-N-E Pers. Conslts, *Exec Srch*
Mngmt. Rcrtrs. of Anderson, *Exec Srch*

Tennessee

Frye/Joure & Associates, Inc., *Exec Srch*

Mngmt. Rcrtrs. International/Sales
Conslt, *Exec Srch*
McCullum Associates Inc., *Temp Agcy*
The Murphy Group, *Perm Agcy*
OfficeMates5 (OM5), *Perm Agcy*
Parker Cromwell & Assoc., *Exec Srch*
Remedy Intelligent Staffing, *Temp Agcy*
Sanford Rose Associates, *Exec Srch*
Staffing Conslt Inc., *Perm Agcy*
VG & Associates, *Perm Agcy*

Indiana
Artisan Staffing, *Temp Agcy*
Execusearch, *Exec Srch*
Mngmt. Rcrtrs. of Richmond, *Exec Srch*
OfficeMates5 (OM5)/DayStar Temporary
Services, *Exec Srch*
Unique, Inc., *Exec Srch*

Iowa
Burton Placement Services, *Exec Srch*
Helping Hands Temps, *Temp Agcy*
Mngmt. Rcrtrs. International/
Compusearch, *Exec Srch*
Premier Search Group, *Exec Srch*

Kansas
Business Specialists, *Perm Agcy*
Key Staffing, *Temp Agcy*
Mngmt. Rcrtrs. of Fort Scott, *Exec Srch*
Mngmt. Rcrtrs. of Overland Park/Sales
Conslt /OfficeMates5, *Exec Srch*
Stoneburner Associates, Inc., *Exec Srch*
Westaff, *Temp Agcy*

Kentucky
Angel Group International, *Exec Srch*
Graphic Arts Emp. Svc., *Perm Agcy*

Louisiana
Mngmt. Rcrtrs. of Metairie/Sales Conslt
of Metairie, *Exec Srch*
Talley & Associates, Inc./Talley
Temporaries, *Exec Srch*

Maine
Career Management Assoc., *Exec Srch*

Maryland
Caplan/Gross Associates, Inc., *Exec Srch*
HireKnowledge, *Temp Agcy*
Mngmt. Rcrtrs. of Annapolis, *Exec Srch*
Mngmt. Rcrtrs. of Frederick/
OfficeMates5, *Exec Srch*
Sales Conslt, *Exec Srch*
TAC Staffing Services, *Temp Agcy*

Massachusetts
Ability Search, *Perm Agcy*
Alden and Clark, Inc., *Temp Agcy*
Brattle Temps, *Temp Agcy*
Clear Point Conslt, *Exec Srch*
Ford & Ford Exec. Search, *Exec Srch*
HireKnowledge, *Temp Agcy*
Kingsbury Wax Bova, *Exec Srch*
Lake Conslt, *Exec Srch*
Mngmt. Rcrtrs. International, *Exec Srch*
Mass Temps Inc., *Temp Agcy*
Morency Associates, *Exec Srch*
Need Personnel Placement, *Temp Agcy*
Pro Staff, *Temp Agcy*
Professional Staffing Group, *Perm Agcy*
Sales Conslt, *Exec Srch*
Selectemps, *Temp Agcy*
Snelling Personnel Services, *Perm Agcy*
Stone & Youngblood, *Exec Srch*
TAC Staffing Services, *Temp Agcy*
TAD Staffing Services, *Temp Agcy*

Michigan
Executive Recruiters Intnl., *Exec Srch*
Express Personnel Services, *Temp Agcy*
Graphic Arts Marketing Assc, *Exec Srch*
William Howard Agency, *Contract Svc*
John Lawrence Group, *Exec Srch*
Mngmt. Rcrtrs. Intnl., *Exec Srch*
Snelling Personnel Services/Bryant
Bureau, *Perm Agcy*
Sullivan & Associates, *Exec Srch*
Trillium Staffing, *Temp Agcy*
Unlimited Staffing Solutions, Inc.,
Contract Svc
Workforce, Inc., *Temp Agcy*

Minnesota
Advance Personnel Resources, *Exec Srch*
Alternative Staffing, Inc., *Perm Agcy*

Diversified Employment Inc., *Perm Agcy*
Graphic Staffing Inc., *Temp Agcy*
T.H. Hunter, Inc., *Exec Srch*
Susan Lee & Associates, *Exec Srch*
Lynn Temporary, *Temp Agcy*
Mngmt. Rcrtrs./Sales Conslt, *Exec Srch*
Manpower Technical, *Contract Svc*
NER, Inc., *Exec Srch*
G.J. Nienhaus & Associates, *Exec Srch*
Olsten Staffing Services, *Temp Agcy*

Mississippi
EPSCO Personnel Service, *Temp Agcy*

Missouri
Jay Alexander & Associates, *Perm Agcy*
Business Personnel Services, *Temp Agcy*
Employer Advantage, *Exec Srch*
F-O-R-T-U-N-E Pers. Conslts, *Exec Srch*
HireKnowledge, *Temp Agcy*
Kirdonn Group, *Perm Agcy*
LandAJob, *Perm Agcy*
Charles Luntz & Associates, *Exec Srch*
Mngmt. Rcrtrs. of Kansas City, *Exec
Srch*
Mngmt. Rcrtrs. of Springfield, *Exec Srch*
Mngmt. Rcrtrs. of St. Louis, *Exec Srch*
Manpower Temp. Services, *Temp Agcy*
National Physician Placement Svcs.,
Exec Srch
OfficeMates5 (OM5), *Exec Srch*

Nebraska
Compusearch of Lincoln, *Exec Srch*
Mngmt. Rcrtrs. of Omaha/OfficeMates5
of Omaha, *Exec Srch*
Sales Conslt of Omaha, *Exec Srch*

Nevada
Flowers Exec. Search Group, *Exec Srch*
Initial Staffing Services, *Perm Agcy*
Labor Finders, *Temp Agcy*

New Hampshire
Able 1 Staffing, *Exec Srch*
Career Profiles, *Exec Srch*
Cheshire Employment Svc., *Temp Agcy*
Dubois & Company, *Exec Srch*
Mngmt. Rcrtrs. Intnl., *Exec Srch*
Sprout/Standish, Inc., *Exec Srch*

New Jersey
Allstaff Resources, Inc., *Perm Agcy*
Blake & Assoc. Exec. Search, *Exec Srch*
Express Personnel Services, *Perm Agcy*
Flextime Solutions, Inc., *Perm Agcy*
Horizon Graphics Personnel, *Perm Agcy*
Impact Personnel, Inc., *Perm Agcy*
Kaye Personnel Inc., *Temp Agcy*
Joseph Keyes Associates, *Perm Agcy*
Al Londino & Associates, *Exec Srch*
Mngmt. Rcrtrs. of Passaic Cty, *Exec Srch*
Mayfair Services, *Perm Agcy*
OfficeMates5 (OM5)/DayStar Temporary
Services, *Perm Agcy*
R.S. Sadow Associates, *Exec Srch*
Sales Conslt, *Exec Srch*
Arline Simpson Associates, *Perm Agcy*

New Mexico
Albuquerque Personnel, Inc., *Perm Agcy*

New York
Accounting & Computer Personnel,
Perm Agcy
AccuStaff Incorporated, *Temp Agcy*
Merrill Adams Associates, *Career/
Outplacement*
Adecco, *Temp Agcy*
AMESgroup, *Exec Srch*
Ariel Associates, *Exec Srch*
Beaver Personnel, Inc., *Perm Agcy*
Berardi & Associates, *Exec Srch*
Bornholdt Shivas & Friends, *Exec Srch*
Branthover Associates, *Exec Srch*
E.E. Brooke Inc., *Perm Agcy*
CGR Staffing Services, *Temp Agcy*
Canny, Bowen Inc., *Exec Srch*
Career Objectives Personnel, *Temp Agcy*
Corporate Careers, Inc., *Exec Srch*
Cross Hill Partners L.L.C., *Exec Srch*
Bert Davis Executive Search, *Exec Srch*
Seth Diamond Associates Inc., *Exec Srch*
Maggi Dolan Placement, *Perm Agcy*
EDP Contract Services, *Contract Svc*
Euromonde, Inc., *Temp Agcy*

Freelance Advancers, Inc., *Temp Agcy*
Graphics For Hire, Inc., *Perm Agcy*
Hart-Merrell Personnel, *Exec Srch*
HireKnowledge, *Temp Agcy*
Hot Bear/De Bella Productions and
Editorial Temps, *Temp Agcy*
Howard-Sloan-Koller Group, *Exec Srch*
Lloyd Staffing, *Perm Agcy*
Mngmt. Rcrtrs. of Gramercy, *Exec Srch*
Manpower Temp. Services, *Temp Agcy*
Olsten Staffing Services, *Temp Agcy*
Lynne Palmer Exec. Recruitment, *Exec
Srch*
Parsons, Anderson & Gee, *Perm Agcy*
Rem Resources, Inc., *Perm Agcy*
Remedy Intelligent Staffing, *Temp Agcy*
Ribolow Associates, *Perm Agcy*
Sales Conslt, *Exec Srch*
Sunny Bates Associates, *Exec Srch*
United Personnel Agency, *Perm Agcy*

North Carolina
Action Staffmasters, *Temp Agcy*
Advanced Pers. Resources, *Exec Srch*
Amcell Associates, *Exec Srch*
Beta Consulting Service, *Exec Srch*
Kelly Services, Inc., *Temp Agcy*
Mngmt. Rcrtrs. International/Sales
Conslt, *Exec Srch*
Nationwide Recruiters, *Exec Srch*
Olsten Staffing Services, *Temp Agcy*
PCS, *Contract Svc*
Sanford Rose Associates, *Exec Srch*
USA Staffing, *Perm Agcy*

North Dakota
Olsten Staffing Services/Expressway
Personnel, *Temp Agcy*

Ohio
AccuStaff, *Temp Agcy*
Adecco/TAD Tech. Svcs., *Contract Svc*
Dave Arnold & Associates, *Exec Srch*
Champion Personnel System, *Perm Agcy*
Choice Pers./LaGrange & Assoc., *Exec
Srch*
Executech, *Exec Srch*
Executive Directions, *Exec Srch*
F-O-R-T-U-N-E Pers. Conslts, *Exec Srch*
H.L. Goehring & Associates, *Exec Srch*
Mngmt. Rcrtrs. International, *Exec Srch*
Midland Conslt, *Exec Srch*
Olsten Prof. Staffing Services, *Exec Srch*
Sales Conslt, *Exec Srch*
Sanker & Associates, *Temp Agcy*
Tech/Aid of Ohio, *Perm Agcy*
Temporarily Yours Placement, *Temp
Agcy*

Oklahoma
Ameri Resource, *Exec Srch*
Express Personnel Services, *Exec Srch*
Mngmt. Rcrtrs. International, *Exec Srch*
StaffMark, *Temp Agcy*

Oregon
Mngmt. Rcrtrs./OfficeMates5, *Temp Agcy*
Quest Temporary Services, *Temp Agcy*
Uniforce Staffing Services, *Temp Agcy*

Pennsylvania
American Search Associates, *Exec Srch*
Anita's Careers, Inc., *Exec Srch*
CoreStaff Inc., *Temp Agcy*
EDP Contract Services, *Contract Svc*
HireKnowledge, *Temp Agcy*
Nancy Jackson Inc., *Exec Srch*
Mngmt. Rcrtrs./CompuSearch, *Exec Srch*
Manchester Inc., *Career/Outplacement*
Olsten Staffing Services, *Temp Agcy*
Pratt Personnel Services, *Temp Agcy*
SHS International, *Exec Srch*
Sanford Rose Associates, *Exec Srch*
TAC Staffing Services, Inc., *Temp Agcy*
Uni-Temp Temporary Svc., *Temp Agcy*
Gordon Wahls Exec. Search, *Exec Srch*

Rhode Island
Mngmt. Rcrtrs. International, *Exec Srch*
Norrell Services, *Temp Agcy*
TAC Staffing Services, *Temp Agcy*

South Carolina
Jerman Personnel Services, *Temp Agcy*
Mngmt. Rcrtrs. of Columbia, *Exec Srch*
Mngmt. Rcrtrs. of Rock Hill, *Exec Srch*

Tennessee
A-1 Staffing & Personnel, *Temp Agcy*
Cook Associates International, *Exec Srch*
Mngmt. Rcrtrs./Sales Conslt, *Exec Srch*
Mngmt. Rcrtrs. of Franklin, *Exec Srch*
Mngmt. Rcrtrs. of Knoxville, *Exec Srch*
W.R. McLeod & Associates, *Exec Srch*
Rasmussen & Associates, *Perm Agcy*
Sanford Rose Associates, *Exec Srch*

Texas
Aware Affiliates Pers. Svc., *Perm Agcy*
Creative Staffing Services, *Perm Agcy*
Dallas Employment Services, *Perm Agcy*
Gail Darling Staffing/Gail Darling's
  Professional Desk, *Temp Agcy*
Dunhill Prof. Search, *Exec Srch*
EPPA, Inc., *Exec Srch*
Express Personnel Services, *Perm Agcy*
HireKnowledge, *Temp Agcy*
Houston Creative Connections, *Exec Srch*
Key People Inc., *Exec Srch*
LRJ Staffing Services, *Perm Agcy*
Mngmt. Rcrtrs. International, *Exec Srch*
Remedy Intelligent Staffing, *Perm Agcy*
Sales Conslt of Houston, *Exec Srch*
Search Com, Inc., *Exec Srch*
Straight Source, *Exec Srch*
Thomas Office Pers. Svc., *Perm Agcy*

Utah
Mngmt. Rcrtrs. of Ogden, *Exec Srch*

Virginia
Alpha Omega Resources Inc., *Perm Agcy*
Buckler Careers, Inc., *Perm Agcy*
Corporate Connection Ltd., *Exec Srch*
Effective Staffing Inc., *Exec Srch*
Mngmt. Rcrtrs. of McLean/
  OfficeMates5, *Exec Srch*
Printing Professionals Inc., *Temp Agcy*
Search & Recruit Intnl., *Exec Srch*
Snelling Personnel Services, *Perm Agcy*
The Talley Group, *Exec Srch*

Washington
Creative Assets, *Temp Agcy*
Express Personnel Services, *Temp Agcy*
The Jobs Company, *Exec Srch*
Mngmt. Rcrtrs. of Tacoma, *Exec Srch*

Wisconsin
American Technical Services, *Perm Agcy*
Dieck Mueller Group, *Exec Srch*
MacPros, Inc., *Perm Agcy*
Mngmt. Rcrtrs. of Appleton/
  Compusearch, *Exec Srch*
Mngmt. Rcrtrs. of Green Bay, *Exec Srch*
Mngmt. Rcrtrs./Sales Conslt, *Exec Srch*
N.E.W. Contracting Services, *Perm Agcy*
Olsten Staffing Services, *Temp Agcy*
U.S. Tech Force Inc., *Exec Srch*
Work Connection, *Perm Agcy*

PROCUREMENT

Alabama
Mngmt. Rcrtrs. International, *Exec Srch*

Arizona
Mngmt. Rcrtrs. of Scottsdale, *Exec Srch*

Arkansas
Mngmt. Rcrtrs., *Exec Srch*

California
Mngmt. Rcrtrs. International, *Exec Srch*

Colorado
Mngmt. Rcrtrs. of Colorado Springs,
  Exec Srch
Sales Conslt of Denver, *Exec Srch*

Connecticut
Mngmt. Rcrtrs. of Norwalk, *Exec Srch*

Florida
Mngmt. Rcrtrs. of Tallahassee, *Exec Srch*
Sales Conslt, *Exec Srch*

Georgia
Mngmt. Rcrtrs. of Atlanta, *Exec Srch*

Illinois
Mngmt. Rcrtrs. International/Sales
  Conslt, *Exec Srch*
OfficeMates5 (OM5), *Perm Agcy*

Indiana
Execusearch, *Exec Srch*

Mngmt. Rcrtrs. of Richmond, *Exec Srch*
OfficeMates5 (OM5)/DayStar Temporary
  Services, *Exec Srch*

Iowa
Mngmt. Rcrtrs. International/
  Compusearch, *Exec Srch*

Kansas
Mngmt. Rcrtrs./Sales Conslt/
  OfficeMates5, *Exec Srch*

Kentucky
Angel Group International, *Exec Srch*

Louisiana
Mngmt. Rcrtrs. of Metairie/Sales Conslt
  of Metairie, *Exec Srch*

Maryland
Mngmt. Rcrtrs. of Annapolis, *Exec Srch*
Mngmt. Rcrtrs. of Frederick/
  OfficeMates5, *Exec Srch*

Massachusetts
Mngmt. Rcrtrs. International, *Exec Srch*
Sales Conslt, *Exec Srch*

Michigan
Mngmt. Rcrtrs. International, *Exec Srch*

Minnesota
Mngmt. Rcrtrs./Sales Conslt, *Exec Srch*

Missouri
Mngmt. Rcrtrs. of Kansas City, *Exec
  Srch*
Mngmt. Rcrtrs. of Springfield, *Exec Srch*
Mngmt. Rcrtrs. of St. Louis, *Exec Srch*
OfficeMates5 (OM5), *Exec Srch*

Montana
Caria Resources, Inc., *Exec Srch*

Nebraska
Compusearch of Lincoln, *Exec Srch*
Mngmt. Rcrtrs. of Omaha/OfficeMates5
  of Omaha, *Exec Srch*

New Hampshire
Mngmt. Rcrtrs. Intnl., *Exec Srch*
Sales Conslt, *Exec Srch*

New Jersey
Mngmt. Rcrtrs. of Passaic Cty, *Exec Srch*
Orion Consulting, Inc., *Exec Srch*
Sales Conslt of Sparta, *Exec Srch*

North Carolina
Mngmt. Rcrtrs. International, *Exec Srch*
Sales Conslt, *Exec Srch*

Ohio
Mngmt. Rcrtrs. International, *Exec Srch*
Sales Conslt, *Exec Srch*

Oregon
Mngmt. Rcrtrs./OfficeMates5, *Exec Srch*

Pennsylvania
Mngmt. Rcrtrs./CompuSearch, *Exec Srch*

Rhode Island
Mngmt. Rcrtrs. International, *Exec Srch*

South Carolina
Mngmt. Rcrtrs. of Columbia, *Exec Srch*
Mngmt. Rcrtrs. of Rock Hill, *Exec Srch*

Texas
Mngmt. Rcrtrs. International, *Exec Srch*
Sales Conslt of Houston, *Exec Srch*

Virginia
Mngmt. Rcrtrs. of McLean/
  OfficeMates5, *Exec Srch*
Mngmt. Rcrtrs. Intnl. of Roanoke, *Exec
  Srch*
Procurement Solutions Inc., *Exec Srch*

Washington
Mngmt. Rcrtrs. of Tacoma, *Exec Srch*

PUBLIC RELATIONS

California
Ricci Lee Associates, Inc., *Exec Srch*
Solution Marketing, *Exec Srch*

Dist. of Columbia
Goodwin & Company, *Exec Srch*

Illinois
Bloom, Gross & Associates, *Exec Srch*

Massachusetts
Chaloner Associates, *Exec Srch*
Professional Staffing Group, *Perm Agcy*
The Ward Group, *Exec Srch*

New Jersey
Flextime Solutions, Inc., *Perm Agcy*
Mngmt. Rcrtrs. International of Morris
  County, *Exec Srch*
Rosenthal Associates Intnl., *Exec Srch*

New York
Adecco, *Temp Agcy*
Cantor Concern, *Exec Srch*
Toby Clark Associates, Inc., *Exec Srch*
The Fry Group Inc., *Exec Srch*
The Goldman Group, Inc./Goldman +
  Bell, LLC, *Exec Srch*
Arnold Huberman Associates, *Exec Srch*
Paxton Resources Inc., *Exec Srch*
Ribolow Associates, *Perm Agcy*
Spring Associates, Inc., *Exec Srch*
Strategic Recruiting, *Exec Srch*

Pennsylvania
Brackin & Sayers Associates, *Exec Srch*
Kay Henry Incorporated, *Exec Srch*

Rhode Island
Greene Personnel Conslt, *Exec Srch*

Texas
Alexander & Company, *Perm Agcy*

Wisconsin
Kordus Consulting Group, *Exec Srch*

PURCHASING

Florida
F-O-R-T-U-N-E Pers. Conslts, *Exec Srch*
McMillan Associates, Inc., *Exec Srch*

Georgia
Bell Oaks Company, *Exec Srch*

Kentucky
Compton & Associates, *Exec Srch*

Maine
F-O-R-T-U-N-E Pers. Conslts of Bangor,
  Exec Srch

Massachusetts
Aerotek, Inc., *Contract Svc*
Bell Oaks Company, *Exec Srch*
Cyr Associates, Inc., *Exec Srch*

Michigan
F-O-R-T-U-N-E Pers. Conslts, *Exec Srch*

New Hampshire
GFI Prof. Staffing Svcs., *Temp Agcy*

New Jersey
F-O-R-T-U-N-E Pers. Conslts, *Exec Srch*

New York
CK Resources, *Exec Srch*
Pro/TECH Nationwide Staff, *Exec Srch*

North Carolina
Career Search Inc., *Exec Srch*

Ohio
Tonia Deal Conslt, *Exec Srch*

Texas
FoodPro Recruiters, Inc., *Exec Srch*

Virginia
F-O-R-T-U-N-E Pers. Conslts, *Exec Srch*

Wisconsin
The Ambrose Group, *Exec Srch*
F-O-R-T-U-N-E Pers. Conslts, *Exec Srch*
The HS Group, Inc., *Exec Srch*
Mngmt. Rcrtrs. Intnl. (MRI), *Exec Srch*

QUALITY ASSURANCE

Alabama
Allgood Associates, *Exec Srch*

Arizona
Hall Kinion, *Contract Svc*

California
F-O-R-T-U-N-E Pers. Conslts, *Exec Srch*
Hall Kinion, *Contract Svc*
Med Exec International, *Exec Srch*

Colorado
Hall Kinion, *Contract Svc*

Connecticut
Hall Kinion, *Contract Svc*
Quality Control Recruiters, *Exec Srch*

Florida
F-O-R-T-U-N-E Pers. Conslts, *Exec Srch*
F-O-R-T-U-N-E Pers. Conslts of Jacksonville, *Exec Srch*
Hall Kinion, *Contract Svc*

Georgia
Bell Oaks Company, *Exec Srch*
F-O-R-T-U-N-E Pers. Conslts of Atlanta/Alternastaff, *Exec Srch*
SCI Recruiters, *Exec Srch*

Illinois
F-O-R-T-U-N-E Pers. Conslts, *Exec Srch*
Hall Kinion, *Contract Svc*

Maine
The Haystack Group, *Exec Srch*

Massachusetts
Bell Oaks Company, *Exec Srch*
F-O-R-T-U-N-E Pers. Conslts, *Exec Srch*
Gilreath Weatherby Inc., *Exec Srch*
Hall Kinion, *Contract Svc*
Interactive Software Placement, Inc. (ISPI), *Perm Agcy*
Quality Search, *Exec Srch*

Michigan
F-O-R-T-U-N-E Pers. Conslts, *Exec Srch*
Mngmt. Rcrtrs. International, *Exec Srch*

Minnesota
Hall Kinion, *Contract Svc*
Mngmt. Rcrtrs. of Rochester, *Exec Srch*

Mississippi
The CPI Group, *Exec Srch*

New Jersey
Hall Kinion, *Contract Svc*
Rosenthal Associates Intnl., *Exec Srch*
The Stelton Group, Inc., *Exec Srch*

New York
Hall Kinion, *Contract Svc*
Huntington Pers. Conslt, *Exec Srch*
Pro/TECH Nationwide Staff, *Exec Srch*
Rosenthal Assoc. Intnl., *Exec Srch*
Bob Ross Exec. Search Corp., *Exec Srch*

North Carolina
Hall Kinion, *Contract Svc*

Oklahoma
Holbrook Associates, *Exec Srch*

Oregon
Hall Kinion, *Contract Svc*

Pennsylvania
J.N. Adams & Associates Inc., *Exec Srch*

South Carolina
Ford & Associates, *Exec Srch*
F-O-R-T-U-N-E Pers. Conslts of Columbia, *Exec Srch*
Health Care Search Assoc., *Exec Srch*
Sanford Rose Associates, *Exec Srch*

Texas
F-O-R-T-U-N-E Pers. Conslts of San Antonio, *Exec Srch*
Hall Kinion, *Contract Svc*

Utah
Hall Kinion, *Contract Svc*

Vermont
O'Connor Search Associates, *Exec Srch*

Virginia
Hall Kinion, *Contract Svc*

Washington
Hall Kinion, *Contract Svc*

REAL ESTATE

Arizona
Amer. Career Grp, *Career/Outplacement*
Mngmt. Rcrtrs. of Scottsdale, *Exec Srch*

California
Bsa Personnel Center, *Perm Agcy*
Brennan Associates, *Exec Srch*
Dunhill Exec. Search of LA, *Exec Srch*
J.H. Lindell & Company, *Exec Srch*

Madden Associates, *Exec Srch*
Mngmt. Rcrtrs. of Encino, *Exec Srch*
Management Solutions Inc., *Exec Srch*
Olsten Staffing Services, *Temp Agcy*
Bob Poline Associates Inc., *Exec Srch*
Renoir Staffing Services Inc., *Perm Agcy*
Ryan, Miller & Associates, *Exec Srch*
Search West, *Exec Srch*
Telford, Adams, & Alexander, *Exec Srch*
Thor Temporary Services, *Temp Agcy*

Florida
Manchester Inc., *Exec Srch*
Pearce & Associates, *Exec Srch*
Ropes Associates, Inc., *Exec Srch*

Georgia
Dorothy Long Search, *Exec Srch*
Mngmt. Rcrtrs. of Atlanta, *Exec Srch*

Illinois
CEMCO Ltd., *Exec Srch*
Contemporary Services, *Exec Srch*
Corporate Staffing, Inc./Proven Performers, *Perm Agcy*
Diener & Associates Inc., *Exec Srch*
Eve Recruiters Ltd., *Perm Agcy*
Kingston/Zak Inc., *Exec Srch*
Mack & Associates, Ltd., *Temp Agcy*
Pratzer & Partners, *Exec Srch*
M. Rector & Associates, *Exec Srch*
Sanford Rose Associates, *Exec Srch*
David Saxner & Associates, *Exec Srch*
Stivers Temporary Personnel, *Temp Agcy*

Indiana
Execusearch, *Exec Srch*
Mngmt. Rcrtrs. of Richmond, *Exec Srch*
OfficeMates5 (OM5)/DayStar Temporary Services, *Exec Srch*
The Registry Inc., *Perm Agcy*

Massachusetts
Attorney Special Assignment Placement/Paralegal Resource Ctr., *Temp Agcy*
Fanning Personnel, *Perm Agcy*
Professional Staffing Group, *Perm Agcy*
Sales Conslt, *Exec Srch*

Michigan
Executive Recruiters Intnl., *Exec Srch*
William Howard Agency, *Contract Svc*
Mngmt. Rcrtrs. of Birmingham, *Exec Srch*
Sharrow & Associates Inc., *Exec Srch*
Sullivan & Associates, *Exec Srch*

Minnesota
Mngmt. Rcrtrs./Sales Conslt, *Exec Srch*

Missouri
Huntress Real Estate Executive Search, *Exec Srch*
Mngmt. Rcrtrs. of Kansas City, *Exec Srch*
Mngmt. Rcrtrs. of Springfield, *Exec Srch*
Mngmt. Rcrtrs. of St. Louis, *Exec Srch*
OfficeMates5 (OM5), *Exec Srch*

Nebraska
Compusearch of Lincoln, *Exec Srch*

New Jersey
Mngmt. Rcrtrs. of Passaic Cty, *Exec Srch*
Sales Conslt of Sparta, *Exec Srch*

New York
Gruen Resources, Inc., *Exec Srch*
Island Search Group Inc., *Perm Agcy*
Tina Lane Personnel, Inc., *Perm Agcy*
Lloyd Staffing, *Perm Agcy*
MacInnis, Ward & Associates, *Exec Srch*
E.J. Rhodes Executive Search, *Exec Srch*
Staffing Services, *Exec Srch*

North Carolina
Sockwell & Associates, *Exec Srch*

Ohio
Belcan Technical Services, *Contract Svc*
J.D. Hersey & Associates, *Exec Srch*
Mngmt. Rcrtrs. International, *Exec Srch*

Oklahoma
Mngmt. Rcrtrs. International, *Exec Srch*

Pennsylvania
Mngmt. Rcrtrs. of Bucks Cty., *Exec Srch*
Manchester Inc., *Career/Outplacement*

K. Maxin & Associates, *Exec Srch*
Specialty Conslt Inc., *Exec Srch*

Texas
B.G. Personnel Services, *Perm Agcy*
Borrel Personnel, *Exec Srch*
Bundy-Stewart Associates, *Exec Srch*
Joseph Chris Partners, *Exec Srch*
The Talon Group, *Exec Srch*
Bruce G. Woods Exec. Search, *Exec Srch*

Virginia
Oerth Associates, Inc., *Exec Srch*

RESEARCH AND DEVELOPMENT

California
F-O-R-T-U-N-E Pers. Conslts, *Exec Srch*
Mngmt. Rcrtrs. of San Luis Obispo, *Exec Srch*
Strategic Alternatives, *Exec Srch*

Connecticut
William Willis Worldwide, *Exec Srch*

Florida
F-O-R-T-U-N-E Pers. Conslts, *Exec Srch*

Georgia
F-O-R-T-U-N-E Pers. Conslts of Atlanta/Alternastaff, *Exec Srch*

Illinois
Hufford Associates, *Exec Srch*
Sanford Rose Associates, *Exec Srch*

Maine
F-O-R-T-U-N-E Pers. Conslts, *Exec Srch*
The Haystack Group, *Exec Srch*

Maryland
F-O-R-T-U-N-E Pers. Conslts, *Exec Srch*
Wallach Associates, Inc., *Exec Srch*

Massachusetts
Aerotek, Inc., *Contract Svc*

Michigan
Sullivan & Associates, *Exec Srch*

New Jersey
Anderson Wright Associates, *Exec Srch*
The Harrison Group, *Exec Srch*
Management Catalysts, *Exec Srch*
Diedre Moire Corporation, *Exec Srch*
PLC Associates, *Exec Srch*

New York
Stamm Personnel Agency, *Perm Agcy*
Techno-Trac Systems, Inc., *Exec Srch*

Pennsylvania
Probe Technology, *Exec Srch*

Texas
FoodPro Recruiters, Inc., *Exec Srch*

RETAIL

Alabama
Labor Finders, *Temp Agcy*
Mngmt. Rcrtrs. International, *Exec Srch*
Millman Search Group Inc., *Exec Srch*
WorkForce Enterprises, *Temp Agcy*

Arizona
Amer. Career Grp, *Career/Outplacement*
Clifford & Associates, *Perm Agcy*
Dealer Connection, *Perm Agcy*
Devau Human Resources, *Temp Agcy*
Spectra International, *Exec Srch*
Stivers Temporary Personnel, *Temp Agcy*

Arkansas
Mngmt. Rcrtrs., *Exec Srch*

California
ABA Staffing, Inc., *Exec Srch*
Allard Associates, *Exec Srch*
Allied Search, Inc., *Exec Srch*
Bsa Personnel Center, *Perm Agcy*
Career Quest International, *Contract Svc*
Chaitin & Associates, *Exec Srch*
Christian & Timbers, *Exec Srch*
Corestaff Services, *Perm Agcy*
The Culver Group, *Exec Srch*
Culver Personnel Services, *Perm Agcy*
Dominguez Metz & Assoc., *Exec Srch*
Douglas Personnel Associates, *Exec Srch*
Ethos Consulting, Inc., *Exec Srch*

Merrill Adams Associates, *Career/Outplacement*
Adecco, *Temp Agcy*
Franklin Allen Conslt, *Exec Srch*
Amherst Personnel Group, *Perm Agcy*
Asher Personnel Conslt, *Perm Agcy*
Neail Behringer Conslt, *Exec Srch*
Bornholdt Shivas & Friends, *Exec Srch*
Seth Diamond Associates Inc., *Exec Srch*
Eden Staffing, *Perm Agcy*
Alexander Edwards Intnl., *Exec Srch*
Elliot Associates Inc., *Exec Srch*
Evie Kreisler & Associates, *Exec Srch*
John Lawrence & Associates, *Exec Srch*
Levine Hirshorn & Associates, *Exec Srch*
Levy-Kerson, *Exec Srch*
Mngmt. Rcrtrs. of Orange Cty, *Exec Srch*
Metropolitan Personnel Syst., *Exec Srch*
Herbert Mines Associates, *Exec Srch*
Morgan-Murray Personnel/M&M Top Temps, *Temp Agcy*
Noble & Associates, *Exec Srch*
Olsten Financial Staffing, *Temp Agcy*
Olsten Staffing Services, *Temp Agcy*
Pendleton James Associates, *Exec Srch*
Personnel Services Center, *Exec Srch*
Retail Recruiters Inc., *Exec Srch*
Roth Young of Long Island, *Exec Srch*
StratfordGroup, *Exec Srch*
Wehinger Services, *Perm Agcy*
Westaff, *Temp Agcy*
Westchester Emp. Agency, *Perm Agcy*
S.R. Wolman Associates, Inc., *Exec Srch*
Woodbury Personnel, *Perm Agcy*

North Carolina
Mngmt. Rcrtrs. International, *Exec Srch*
Quality Temporary Services, *Temp Agcy*
Sales Conslt, *Exec Srch*
StratfordGroup, *Exec Srch*
Waddy R. Thomson Assoc., *Exec Srch*
USA Staffing, *Perm Agcy*

North Dakota
Green Thumb, *Career/Outplacement*
Olsten Staffing Services/Expressway Personnel, *Temp Agcy*

Ohio
Bason Associates Inc., *Exec Srch*
CBS Personnel Services, *Perm Agcy*
Combined Resources Inc., *Exec Srch*
Eastern Personnel Services, *Perm Agcy*
Employment Solutions Group, *Exec Srch*
Graduate Conslt, *Perm Agcy*
George Gum & Associates, *Exec Srch*
Richard Johns Career Conslt, *Perm Agcy*
Mngmt. Rcrtrs. International, *Exec Srch*
Sales Conslt, *Exec Srch*
StratfordGroup, *Exec Srch*
Temporarily Yours Placement, *Temp Agcy*

Oklahoma
Mngmt. Rcrtrs. International, *Exec Srch*

Oregon
Initial Staffing Services, *Perm Agcy*
Mngmt. Rcrtrs. of Portland/OfficeMates5 of Portland, *Exec Srch*
Mesa International, *Exec Srch*
Uniforce Staffing Services, *Temp Agcy*

Pennsylvania
All Staffing Inc., *Perm Agcy*
Ashley Search Conslt, *Exec Srch*
Basilone-Oliver Exec. Search, *Exec Srch*
CoreStaff Inc., *Temp Agcy*
J. Croyle & Associates, Inc., *Perm Agcy*
Robert J. DePaul & Assoc., *Exec Srch*
Eden & Associates, Inc., *Exec Srch*
HRS/TND Associates, Inc., *Exec Srch*
Human Assets Inc., *Temp Agcy*
Interactive Search Associates, *Exec Srch*
Mngmt. Rcrtrs./CompuSearch, *Exec Srch*
Manchester Inc., *Career/Outplacement*
R.H.A. Executive Pers. Svcs., *Exec Srch*
Roth Young Personnel Svcs., *Exec Srch*
Spectrum Conslt, Inc./Retail Recruiters, *Exec Srch*
StratfordGroup, *Exec Srch*

Rhode Island
Colony Personnel Associates, *Temp Agcy*
Albert G. Lee & Associates, *Exec Srch*

Mngmt. Rcrtrs. International, *Exec Srch*
Norrell Services, *Temp Agcy*

South Carolina
Mngmt. Rcrtrs. of Columbia, *Exec Srch*
Mngmt. Rcrtrs. of Rock Hill, *Exec Srch*

Tennessee
A-1 Staffing & Personnel, *Temp Agcy*
Bishop Placement Service, *Exec Srch*
Cornerstone Emp. Svcs., *Perm Agcy*
Mngmt. Rcrtrs. of Brentwood/Sales Conslt of Brentwood, *Exec Srch*
Mngmt. Rcrtrs. of Knoxville, *Exec Srch*
W.R. McLeod & Associates, *Exec Srch*

Texas
Abilene Employment Service, *Perm Agcy*
Aware Affiliates Pers. Svc., *Perm Agcy*
Bullock Personnel, Inc., *Perm Agcy*
Carpenter & Associates, *Exec Srch*
Corporate Search Inc., *Exec Srch*
Creative Staffing Services, *Perm Agcy*
Dallas Employment Services, *Perm Agcy*
Gail Darling Staffing/Gail Darling's Professional Desk, *Temp Agcy*
Evins Personnel Conslt, *Perm Agcy*
Kenzer Corporation, *Exec Srch*
Evie Kreisler & Associates, *Exec Srch*
Mngmt. Rcrtrs. International, *Exec Srch*
Mngmt. Rcrtrs. of Dallas, *Exec Srch*
Marquess & Associates, *Perm Agcy*
The Pailin Group Professional Search Conslt, *Exec Srch*
Remedy Intelligent Staffing, *Perm Agcy*
Resource Connection Workforce Center, *Perm Agcy*
Roth Young Executive Search, *Exec Srch*
Sales Conslt of Houston, *Exec Srch*
Select Staff, *Temp Agcy, Exec Srch*
StratfordGroup, *Exec Srch*
TSP Personnel Services, Inc., *Perm Agcy*
Williams Company, *Exec Srch*
R.S. Wyatt Associates, Inc., *Exec Srch*

Vermont
Triad Temporary Services, *Temp Agcy*

Virginia
A La Carte International, *Exec Srch*
The Alexis Group, Inc., *Exec Srch*
Barnes & Assoc. Retail Srch, *Exec Srch*
Buckler Careers, Inc., *Perm Agcy*
Corporate Connection Ltd., *Perm Agcy*
Dow Personnel, *Perm Agcy*
Employment Enterprises/Temporary Solutions, *Temp Agcy*
Haslowe Personnel, *Exec Srch*
Hispanic Committee of VA, *Perm Agcy*
Kogen Personnel, *Exec Srch*
Lee Staffing Resources, *Exec Srch*
The McCormick Group, *Exec Srch*
Snelling Personnel Services, *Perm Agcy*
The Talley Group, *Exec Srch*
TempWorld Staffing Svcs., *Temp Agcy*
Lawrence Veber Associates, *Exec Srch*

Washington
The Career Clinic, Inc., *Exec Srch*
L.W. Foote Company/The Brighton Group, *Exec Srch*
The Jobs Company, *Exec Srch*
Kerry-Ben Kelly Exec. Search, *Exec Srch*
Kelly Services, Inc., *Temp Agcy*
Mngmt. Rcrtrs. of Mercer Island, *Exec Srch*
Mngmt. Rcrtrs. of Seattle, *Exec Srch*
Mngmt. Rcrtrs. of Tacoma, *Exec Srch*
Manpower Temp. Services, *Temp Agcy*
Northwest Temp & Staff Svc, *Temp Agcy*
Strategic Resources, *Exec Srch*
StratfordGroup, *Exec Srch*
Villeneuve Associates, Inc., *Exec Srch*

Wisconsin
Work Connection, *Perm Agcy*

Wyoming
Express Personnel Services, *Temp Agcy*

SALES AND MARKETING

Alabama
Clark Pers. Svc. of Mobile, *Exec Srch*
Employment Conslt, *Perm Agcy*
Healthcare Recruiters, *Exec Srch*

Mngmt. Rcrtrs. International, *Exec Srch*
Sanford Rose Associates, *Exec Srch*
Snelling Pers. Svcs., *Perm Agcy, Exec Srch*
VIP Personnel, Inc., *Perm Agcy*
WorkForce Enterprises, *Temp Agcy*

Alaska
Olsten Staffing Services, *Temp Agcy*

Arizona
Amer. Career Grp, *Career/Outplacement*
Andrews, Stevens & Associates, *Contract Svc*
The Bren Group, *Exec Srch*
Clifford & Associates, *Perm Agcy*
Mngmt. Rcrtrs. of Scottsdale, *Exec Srch*
Norrell Interim Services, *Temp Agcy*
Sales Conslt, *Exec Srch*
Saxon Associates, *Exec Srch*
Snelling Personnel Services, *Perm Agcy*
Spectra International, *Exec Srch*
Staff One Search, *Exec Srch*
Marjorie Starr & Associates, *Exec Srch*
Stivers Temporary Personnel, *Temp Agcy*
Taylor Design Recruiting, *Temp Agcy*

Arkansas
Executive Recruiters Agency, *Exec Srch*
Mngmt. Rcrtrs., *Exec Srch*
Premier Staffing, Inc., *Temp Agcy*
Turnage Emp. Svc. Grp., *Exec Srch*

California
A Permanent Success Employment Service, *Perm Agcy*
ABA Staffing, Inc., *Exec Srch*
A.S.A.P. Employment Svc., *Perm Agcy*
AccuStaff Inc., *Temp Agcy, Perm Agcy*
Act 1 Personnel Services, *Perm Agcy*
Advantage Personnel Inc., *Perm Agcy*
Affordable Exec. Recruiters, *Exec Srch*
Agriesti & Associates, *Exec Srch*
Alert Staffing, *Exec Srch*
Alpha-Net Consulting Group, *Exec Srch*
Ankenbrandt Group, *Exec Srch*
Apple One Emp. Services, *Perm Agcy*
Apropos Emp. Agency, *Perm Agcy*
Astra West Personnel Svcs., *Exec Srch*
Automotive Career Placement Counselors (ACPC), *Exec Srch*
The Badger Group, *Exec Srch*
Barnes & Associates, *Exec Srch*
Thomas Beck Inc., *Exec Srch*
Beck/Eastwood Recruitment Solutions, *Exec Srch*
Robert Beech Inc., *Exec Srch*
Harvey Bell & Associates, *Exec Srch*
Bennett & Co Consulting Grp, *Exec Srch*
Bialla and Associates, Inc., *Exec Srch*
The Black Leopard, *Exec Srch*
BridgeGate LLC, *Exec Srch*
Brooks Associates, *Exec Srch*
Business Systems Support, *Perm Agcy*
C&C Associates, *Exec Srch*
CN Associates, *Exec Srch*
California Job Connection, *Perm Agcy*
California Search Agency, *Exec Srch*
Career Advantage, *Exec Srch*
Career Quest International, *Contract Svc*
Chaitin & Associates, *Exec Srch*
Wayne Chamberlain & Assoc., *Exec Srch*
Champagne Personnel, *Temp Agcy*
Coast To Coast Exec. Search, *Exec Srch*
Computer Network Resources, *Exec Srch*
Corestaff Services, *Perm Agcy*
Corporate Dynamix, *Exec Srch*
Cory Associates Agency Inc., *Exec Srch*
Marlene Critchfield Co., *Perm Agcy*
The Culver Group, *Exec Srch*
Culver Personnel Services, *Perm Agcy*
Curphey & Malkin Associates, *Exec Srch*
Robert W. Dingman Co., *Exec Srch*
Drake Office Overload, *Temp Agcy*
Drummer Personnel, Inc., *Exec Srch*
Dunhill Prof. Srch Inc., *Exec Srch*
Dynamic Synergy Corp., *Exec Srch*
Eagle Search Associates, *Exec Srch*
Ethos Consulting, Inc., *Exec Srch*
Executive Group West, *Exec Srch*
Executive Resource Systems, *Exec Srch*
Fastek Technical Services, *Perm Agcy*

Bell Oaks Company, *Exec Srch*
Boreham International, *Exec Srch*
Bradshaw & Associates, *Exec Srch*
Business Professional Group, *Perm Agcy*
Career Placements, *Perm Agcy*
Catalina Human Resources, *Perm Agcy*
Commonwealth Conslt, *Exec Srch*
Comprehensive Search Group, *Exec Srch*
Corporate Image Group, *Exec Srch*
Corporate Search Conslt, *Exec Srch*
Dunhill Professional Search, *Exec Srch*
Elite Staffing Services, *Temp Agcy*
Express Personnel Services, *Perm Agcy*
First Pro, *Temp Agcy*
Fox-Morris Associates, *Exec Srch*
ISC of Atlanta/International Career
  Continuation, *Exec Srch*
Kenzer Corp. of Georgia, *Exec Srch*
Kreisler & Associates, *Exec Srch*
MSI International, *Exec Srch*
Mngmt. Rcrtrs. International, *Exec Srch*
Manpower Temp. Services, *Temp Agcy*
Mission Corps International/Helping
  Hands Temp. Service, *Temp Agcy*
More Personnel Services Inc., *Perm Agcy*
National Personnel Recruiters, *Exec Srch*
Olsten Staffing Services, *Temp Agcy*
Omni Recruiting, *Exec Srch*
Perimeter Placement, *Exec Srch*
Personalized Mngmt. Assoc., *Exec Srch*
Personnel Opportunities Inc., *Exec Srch*
Priority 1 Staffing Services, *Temp Agcy*
Randstad Staffing Services, *Temp Agcy*
Rowland, Mountain & Assoc., *Exec Srch*
Sales Opportunities, *Exec Srch*
Sanford Rose Associates, *Exec Srch*
Snelling Personnel Services, *Exec Srch*
Sondra Search, *Exec Srch*
Southern Employment Svc., *Perm Agcy*
Staffing Resources, *Perm Agcy*
StaffMark, *Temp Agcy*
TRC Staffing Services, *Temp Agcy*
TempWorld Staffing Svcs., *Temp Agcy*
WPPS Software Staffing, *Temp Agcy*
Westaff, *Temp Agcy*

Hawaii
Dunhill Prof. Staffing of HI, *Exec Srch*
Executive Search World, *Exec Srch*
Kelly Services, Inc., *Temp Agcy*
Sales Conslt of Honolulu, *Exec Srch*

Idaho
Horne/Brown International, *Exec Srch*
Idaho Department of Employment/
  Jobservice, *Perm Agcy*
Mngmt. Rcrtrs. of Boise, Inc., *Exec Srch*
Snelling Personnel Services, *Perm Agcy*

Illinois
A.B.A. Placements/A.B.A. Temporaries,
  Perm Agcy
ASI Staffing Service, Inc., *Perm Agcy*
Abbott Smith Associates, *Exec Srch*
B.J. Abrams & Associates, *Exec Srch*
Accurate Recruiting Inc., *Perm Agcy*
Adecco, *Temp Agcy*
Advantage Personnel Inc., *Exec Srch*
Affiliated Pers. Conslt, *Perm Agcy*
American Engineering Co., *Exec Srch*
Armstrong-Hamilton Assoc., *Exec Srch*
Availability, Inc., *Perm Agcy*
Banner Personnel Service, *Perm Agcy*
Bell Personnel Inc., *Perm Agcy*
Bloom, Gross & Associates, *Exec Srch*
Britannia, *Exec Srch*
Brooke Chase Associates, Inc., *Exec Srch*
CareerLink USA, Inc., *Exec Srch*
Carson Mngmt. Assoc., *Contract Svc*
Coffou Partners, Inc., *Exec Srch*
CompuPro, *Exec Srch*
Corporate Conslt, *Exec Srch*
Corporate Environment, Ltd., *Exec Srch*
Cumberland Group, *Exec Srch*
Diener & Associates Inc., *Exec Srch*
Dunhill Staffing Svcs. of Chicago, *Temp Agcy*
Dynamic People, *Temp Agcy*
Eastman & Associates, *Exec Srch*
The Eastwood Group, *Exec Srch*
The Esquire Staffing Group, *Perm Agcy*
Executive Referral Services, *Exec Srch*
Executive Search Intnl., *Exec Srch*

Express Personnel Services, *Temp Agcy*
Fellows Placement, *Temp Agcy*
First Search, Inc., *Exec Srch*
David Gomez & Associates, *Exec Srch*
Healthcare Recruiters Intnl., *Exec Srch*
Hufford Associates, *Exec Srch*
Human Resource Connection, *Perm Agcy*
InterStaff, *Temp Agcy*
Interviewing Conslt, *Perm Agcy*
Irwin & Wagner, Inc., *Exec Srch*
Raymond Karson Associates, *Exec Srch*
Kenneth Nicholas & Assoc., *Exec Srch*
Kunzer Associates, Ltd., *Exec Srch*
Arlene Leff & Associates, *Exec Srch*
Lomack Agency Inc., *Temp Agcy*
Lyons & Associates, *Exec Srch*
Mngmt. Rcrtrs. International/Sales
  Conslt, *Exec Srch*
Richard Marks & Associates, *Exec Srch*
Marsteller Wilcox Associates, *Exec Srch*
M.W. McDonald & Assoc., *Exec Srch*
Media Staffing Network, *Temp Agcy*
Juan Menefee & Associates, *Exec Srch*
Midwest Consulting Corp., *Exec Srch*
The Murphy Group, *Perm Agcy*
NJW & Associates, Inc., *Temp Agcy*
National Search, *Exec Srch*
OfficeMates5 (OM5), *Perm Agcy*
Olsten Staffing Services, *Temp Agcy*
PS Inc., *Perm Agcy*
Parker Cromwell & Assoc., *Exec Srch*
Pelichem Associates, *Exec Srch*
Personnel Connections Inc., *Perm Agcy*
Patricia Pocock & Associates, *Exec Srch*
Prestige Employment Svcs., *Perm Agcy*
Professional Research Svcs., *Exec Srch*
ProSearch Plus, *Exec Srch*
Quantum Professional Search/Quantum
  Staffing Services, *Exec Srch*
Recruitment Network, *Exec Srch*
Remedy Intelligent Staffing, *Temp Agcy*
Retail Staffers, Inc., *Exec Srch*
Right Services Inc., *Temp Agcy*
The Robinson Group, *Exec Srch*
The Ryan Charles Group, Inc., *Exec Srch*
SHS, Inc., *Exec Srch*
Sales Conslt of Chicago, *Exec Srch*
Sanford Rose Associates, *Exec Srch*
Shannonwood Staffers, Inc., *Temp Agcy*
Ralph Smith & Associates, *Exec Srch*
Snelling Personnel Services, *Temp Agcy,
  Perm Agcy*
Snelling Search, *Exec Srch*
Staffing Conslt Inc., *Perm Agcy*
Staffing Team International, *Temp Agcy*
Stern Prof Srch & Conslt, *Exec Srch*
Strategic Resources Unlimited, *Exec Srch*
Stone Enterprises, Ltd., *Exec Srch*
Temporary Associates, *Temp Agcy*
VG & Associates, *Perm Agcy*
Walsh & Company, *Perm Agcy*
Watters & Byrd, Inc., *Perm Agcy*
West Personnel Service, *Perm Agcy*
Ray White Associates, *Exec Srch*
Working World Inc., *Temp Agcy*
World Employment Service, *Perm Agcy*

Indiana
A.B.S., *Exec Srch*
Alpha Rae Personnel, Inc., *Perm Agcy*
Bill Caldwell Emp. Svc., *Perm Agcy*
Corporate Staff Resources, *Temp Agcy*
Pat Day Personnel Inc., *Perm Agcy*
Employment Recruiters Inc., *Perm Agcy*
Execusearch, *Exec Srch*
Job Placement Service Inc., *Perm Agcy*
Johnson Brown Associates, *Exec Srch*
Key Sales Personnel, *Exec Srch*
Lange & Associates, Inc., *Exec Srch*
Life Employment Service, *Perm Agcy*
The Mallard Group, *Exec Srch*
Mngmt. Rcrtrs. International/Sales
  Conslt, *Exec Srch*
Management Services, *Exec Srch*
Management Support Svcs., *Exec Srch*
Mayhall Search Group Inc., *Exec Srch*
Oakwood International Inc., *Exec Srch*
OfficeMates5 (OM5)/DayStar Temporary
  Services, *Exec Srch*
Perry Personnel Plus, *Perm Agcy*
Quiring Associates, Inc., *Perm Agcy*
Reach Consulting Group, *Exec Srch*

Sales Search, *Exec Srch*
Snelling Personnel Services, *Perm Agcy*
Unique, Inc., *Exec Srch*
Warrick County Employment & Training
  Center, *Career/Outplacement*

Iowa
Bryant Bureau, *Perm Agcy*
Burton Placement Services, *Exec Srch*
Byrnes & Rupkey, Inc., *Exec Srch*
Cambridge Careers, *Perm Agcy*
Drake-Brennan, Inc., *Exec Srch*
Executive Resources, *Exec Srch*
Helping Hands Temp. Svc., *Temp Agcy*
Kelly Services, Inc., *Temp Agcy*
Mngmt. Rcrtrs. International/
  Compusearch, *Exec Srch*
McGladrey Search Group, *Exec Srch*
Personnel, Inc., *Exec Srch*
Pratt-Younglove, Inc., *Perm Agcy*
Premier Search Group, *Exec Srch*
Salem Management Inc., *Temp Agcy*
Rudy Salem Staffing Svcs, *Temp Agcy*
Snelling Personnel, *Exec Srch*
Staffing Edge, *Perm Agcy*

Kansas
Business Specialists, *Perm Agcy*
Execu-Search International, *Exec Srch*
Key Staffing, *Temp Agcy*
Mngmt. Rcrtrs./Sales Conslt/
  OfficeMates5, *Exec Srch*
Smith Brown & Jones, *Exec Srch*
Stoneburner Associates, Inc., *Exec Srch*
Talent Scouts Inc. (TSI), *Perm Agcy*
White Associates/TemTech, *Exec Srch*

Kentucky
Angel Group International, *Exec Srch*
Belcan Staffing & Prof. Svcs., *Exec Srch*
C.M. Management Services, *Perm Agcy*
The Executive Advantage, *Exec Srch*
Kovac Berrins AG Inc., *Exec Srch*
Professional Srch Conslt, *Exec Srch*
Sales Conslt, *Exec Srch*
Snelling Personnel Services, *Perm Agcy*

Louisiana
Ascent Consulting Group, *Temp Agcy*
Delta Personnel, *Perm Agcy*
Keenan Staffing Inc., *Temp Agcy*
Mngmt. Rcrtrs. of Metairie/Sales Conslt
  of Metairie, *Exec Srch*
Mngmt. Rcrtrs. of St. Tammany, *Exec
  Srch*
Shiell Personnel, *Perm Agcy*
Snelling Personnel Services, *Exec Srch*
Talley & Associates, Inc./Talley
  Temporaries, *Exec Srch*
Technical & Prof. Sources, *Exec Srch*

Maine
At Work Personnel Service, *Temp Agcy*
Career Management Assoc., *Exec Srch*
Exec. Search of New England, *Exec Srch*
F-O-R-T-U-N-E Pers. Conslts of Bangor,
  Exec Srch
Goodrich Consulting, *Exec Srch*
Pro Search, Inc., *Exec Srch*

Maryland
Administration Pers. Svcs., *Perm Agcy*
Auto Careers, *Exec Srch*
Caplan/Gross Associates, Inc., *Exec Srch*
Chesapeake Consulting Group, *Exec Srch*
Comprehensive Search Group, *Exec Srch*
Employer Employee Exchange, *Exec
  Srch*
A.G. Fishkin and Associates, *Exec Srch*
J.R. Associates, *Perm Agcy*
The Jonathan Ladd Company, *Perm Agcy*
Ken Leiner Associates, Inc., *Exec Srch*
Mngmt. Rcrtrs. International/Sales Conslt
  of Baltimore, *Exec Srch*
Mngmt. Rcrtrs. of Annapolis, *Exec Srch*
Mngmt. Rcrtrs. of Frederick/
  OfficeMates5, *Exec Srch*
Tom McCall & Associates, *Perm Agcy*
Nations Exec. Search Group, *Exec Srch*
Porter Group Inc., *Exec Srch*
Seek International, Inc., *Exec Srch*
Sparks Personnel Services, *Temp Agcy*
TCM Enterprises, *Exec Srch*
TAC Staffing Services, *Temp Agcy*

Executive Exchange Corp., *Exec Srch*
Executive Search, Inc., *Exec Srch*
Express Personnel Services, *Perm Agcy*
Flextime Solutions, Inc., *Perm Agcy*
Lawrence Glaser Associates, *Exec Srch*
Global Resources Group, *Exec Srch*
Headhunters Exec. Search, *Exec Srch*
Holm Personnel Conslt, *Exec Srch*
The Howard Group, Ltd., *Exec Srch*
Hreshko Consulting Group, *Exec Srch*
Hughes & Podesla Personnel, *Perm Agcy*
Impact Personnel, Inc., *Perm Agcy*
Insearch Inc., *Exec Srch*
Inter-Regional Exec. Search, *Exec Srch*
J.M. Joseph Associates, *Exec Srch*
Key Employment, *Exec Srch*
Kiley, Owen & McGovern, *Exec Srch*
Paul Kull & Company, *Exec Srch*
M.R. Group, Inc., *Exec Srch*
Major Conslt, *Exec Srch*
Mngmt. Rcrtrs. International, *Exec Srch*
Normyle/Erstling Health Search Group,
  Exec Srch
OfficeMates5 (OM5)/DayStar Temporary
  Services, *Perm Agcy*
Olsten Staffing Services, *Temp Agcy*
Orion Consulting, Inc., *Exec Srch*
PR Management Conslt, *Exec Srch*
Park Avenue Personnel, *Perm Agcy*
Personnel Plus/Temps Plus, *Perm Agcy*
Philadelphia Search Group, *Exec Srch*
Pomerantz Staffing Services, *Perm Agcy*
Premier Personnel Group, *Perm Agcy*
Rosenthal Associates Intnl., *Exec Srch*
The Russell Group Inc., *Exec Srch*
S-H-S of Cherry Hill, *Perm Agcy*
Salem Associates, *Exec Srch*
Sales Conslt, *Exec Srch*
Selective Personnel, *Perm Agcy*
Shifrin-Fischer Group, Inc., *Exec Srch*
Arline Simpson Associates, *Perm Agcy*
Snelling Personnel Services, *Perm Agcy*
Source One Personnel, *Perm Agcy*
The Stelton Group, Inc., *Exec Srch*
Stewart/Laurence Associates, *Exec Srch*
Temporary Excellence Inc., *Temp Agcy*
Tschudin Inc., *Exec Srch*
Don Waldron & Associates, *Perm Agcy*
Winston Staffing Services, *Temp Agcy*
Worlco Computer Resources, *Exec Srch*
Claire Wright Associates, *Perm Agcy*

New Mexico

Albuquerque Personnel, Inc., *Perm Agcy*
Roadrunner Personnel, Inc., *Exec Srch*
Sanderson Employment Svc., *Perm Agcy*
Snelling Search, *Exec Srch*

New York

AJC Search, *Exec Srch*
APA Search, *Exec Srch*
Aadams Personnel Agency, *Temp Agcy*
Accounting & Computer Personnel,
  Perm Agcy
AccuStaff Incorporated, *Temp Agcy*
Merrill Adams Associates, *Career/
  Outplacement*
Adecco, *Temp Agcy*
Advantage Resumes of New York,
  Career/Outplacement
Franklin Allen Conslt, *Exec Srch*
Ames O'Neill Associates Inc., *Exec Srch*
Amherst Personnel Group, , *Perm Agcy*
Ariel Associates, *Exec Srch*
Arrow Employment Agency, *Perm Agcy*
Asher Personnel Conslt, *Perm Agcy*
Auto Careers, *Perm Agcy*
Beishline Executive Search, *Exec Srch*
Benson Associates, *Exec Srch*
Bestemp Temporary Svcs., *Temp Agcy*
Bornholdt Shivas & Friends, *Exec Srch*
Branthover Associates, *Exec Srch*
Brian Associates, Inc. (BAI), *Exec Srch*
C.C. Burke, Ltd., *Exec Srch*
CFI Resources Inc., *Exec Srch*
CGR Staffing Services, *Temp Agcy*
Canny, Bowen Inc., *Exec Srch*
Career Blazers Personnel Svc, *Perm Agcy*
Carlile Personnel Agency, *Perm Agcy*
Carter/MacKay, *Exec Srch*
Concorde Search, *Perm Agcy*
Corporate Careers, Inc., *Exec Srch*
Corporate Moves, Inc., *Exec Srch*

Corporate Search Inc., *Exec Srch*
Crandall Associates, Inc., *Exec Srch*
Cross Hill Partners L.L.C., *Exec Srch*
Frank Cuomo & Associates, *Exec Srch*
The Dartmouth Group, *Exec Srch*
Seth Diamond Associates Inc., *Exec Srch*
Alexander Edwards Intnl., *Exec Srch*
Efco Conslt, Inc., *Exec Srch*
The Employment Store/TES Technical,
  Exec Srch
C.R. Fletcher Associates, *Exec Srch*
Forray Associates, Inc., *Exec Srch*
Ronnie Gale Personnel Corp., *Exec Srch*
Gundersen Partners L.L.C., *Exec Srch*
Harbrowe, Inc., *Perm Agcy*
Hart-Merrell Personnel, *Exec Srch*
Hawkes-Peers & Company, *Exec Srch*
F.P. Healy & Company Inc., *Exec Srch*
Innovations Associates, *Perm Agcy*
Interspace Interactive Inc., *Exec Srch*
Island Search Group Inc., *Perm Agcy*
JDC Associates, *Perm Agcy*
KPA Staffing Group, Inc., *Exec Srch*
The Kay Group of Fifth Ave., *Exec Srch*
Kelly Services, Inc., *Temp Agcy*
Fred Koffler Associates, *Exec Srch*
Lake Associates, *Exec Srch*
John Lawrence & Associates, *Exec Srch*
Lloyd Staffing, *Perm Agcy*
M.B. Inc. Executive Search, *Exec Srch*
Magill Associates, Inc., *Exec Srch*
Joseph T. Maloney & Assoc., *Perm Agcy*
Mngmt. Rcrtrs. International, *Exec Srch*
Manpower Temp. Services, *Temp Agcy*
Media Staffing Network, *Temp Agcy*
Mentortech, *Exec Srch*
Metropolitan Personnel Syst., *Exec Srch*
Mickler Associates Inc., *Exec Srch*
Milazzo Associates, Inc., *Perm Agcy*
Morgan-Murray Personnel/M&M Top
  Temps, *Temp Agcy*
Natek Corporation, *Exec Srch*
Network Dynamics, *Exec Srch*
Noah Associates, *Perm Agcy*
Noble & Associates, *Exec Srch*
Norrell Staffing Services, *Temp Agcy*
Nowack Career Specialists, *Perm Agcy*
Olsten Staffing Services, *Temp Agcy*
Optimal Resources, *Exec Srch*
Parsons, Anderson and Gee, *Perm Agcy*
Personnel Services Center, *Exec Srch*
P.G. Prager Search Associates, *Exec Srch*
Professional Corporate Search, *Exec Srch*
Rand Thompson Conslt/Merlin Temps,
  Exec Srch
Recruitment Intnl. Group, *Exec Srch*
Redwood Partners, *Exec Srch*
Rem Resources, Inc., *Perm Agcy*
Beth Richman Associates, *Perm Agcy*
Rosenthal Assoc. Intnl., *Exec Srch*
Roth Young of Long Island, *Exec Srch*
Salem Associates, *Exec Srch*
Sales Careers, *Exec Srch*
Sales Conslt, *Exec Srch*
Sales Recruiters International, *Exec Srch*
Sales Search, Ltd./Executive Resume
  Service, *Exec Srch*
SearchAmerica Inc., *Exec Srch*
Sharp Placement Profs., *Exec Srch*
Snelling Personnel Services, *Perm Agcy*
Sporn Group Inc., *Exec Srch*
Staff Managers, *Temp Agcy*
Staffing Services, *Exec Srch*
Stamm Personnel Agency, *Perm Agcy*
Superior Concepts, *Contract Svc*
Taylor Search Associates, *Exec Srch*
TeleManagement Search, *Exec Srch*
Tempo Services, Inc., *Perm Agcy*
Todd Arro, Inc., *Exec Srch*
Trebor, Weldon, Lawrence, Levine, *Exec
  Srch*
Vintage Resources, Inc., *Exec Srch*
Weber Mngmt. Conslt, *Exec Srch*
Westaff, *Temp Agcy*
Westchester Emp. Agency, *Perm Agcy*
S.R. Wolman Associates, Inc., *Exec Srch*

North Carolina

Active Search Recruiters, *Exec Srch*
Advanced Pers. Resources, *Exec Srch*
AmeriPro Search, Inc., *Exec Srch*
Bullington Associates, *Exec Srch*

Carter/MacKay of Cary, *Exec Srch*
Executive Staffing Group, *Exec Srch*
Express Personnel Services, *Temp Agcy*
D.D. Fayling Associates, Inc., *Exec Srch*
Fox-Morris Associates, *Exec Srch*
Glovier & Associates, *Exec Srch*
Granite Personnel Service, *Perm Agcy*
The Jobs Market, Inc., *Perm Agcy*
Kelly Services, Inc., *Temp Agcy*
Mngmt. Rcrtrs. International/Sales
  Conslt, *Exec Srch*
Manpower, Inc., *Temp Agcy*
McCain Employment Svc., *Temp Agcy*
Moffitt International, Inc., *Exec Srch*
Olsten Staffing Services, *Temp Agcy*
The Perkins Group, *Exec Srch*
Quality Temporary Services, *Temp Agcy*
Remedy Intelligent Staffing, *Perm Agcy*
SGI (Sports Group Intnl.), *Exec Srch*
Sanford Rose Associates, *Exec Srch*
Sickenberger Associates, *Exec Srch*
Snelling Personnel Services, *Perm Agcy*
Sparks Personnel Services, *Exec Srch*
S. Greene & Co./The Triad, *Exec Srch*
USA Staffing, *Perm Agcy*
David Weinfeld Group, *Exec Srch*
Youngblood Staffing, *Perm Agcy*

North Dakota

Olsten Staffing Services/Expressway
  Personnel, *Temp Agcy*
Snelling Personnel Services, *Exec Srch*

Ohio

Adecco, *Temp Agcy*
AllTech Resources, Inc., *Exec Srch*
Dave Arnold & Associates, *Exec Srch*
Richard L. Bencin & Assoc., *Perm Agcy*
J.B. Brown & Associates, *Exec Srch*
Buckman-Enochs & Assoc., *Exec Srch*
CBS Personnel Services, *Perm Agcy*
Choice Personnel/LaGrange &
  Associates, *Exec Srch*
Combined Resources Inc., *Exec Srch*
Continental Search Associates, *Exec Srch*
Corporate Directions Group, *Perm Agcy*
Corporate Research Consulting Group
  Inc., *Exec Srch*
J.D. Cotter Search, Inc., *Exec Srch*
Dunhill Prof. Search, *Exec Srch*
Eastern Personnel Services, *Perm Agcy*
Executech, *Exec Srch*
Executive Directions, *Exec Srch*
F.L.A.G., *Exec Srch*
Flex-Tech Prof. Services, *Contract Svc*
Fristoe & Carleton, *Exec Srch*
H.L. Goehring & Associates, *Exec Srch*
Griffiths & Associates, *Exec Srch*
J.D. Hersey & Associates, *Exec Srch*
Hite Executive Search/Hite Management
  Conslt, Inc., *Exec Srch*
Initial Staffing Services, *Temp Agcy*
Ives & Associates, Inc., *Exec Srch*
J. Joseph & Associates, *Exec Srch*
Richard Kader & Associates, *Exec Srch*
Laughlin & Associates, *Exec Srch*
Leith & Associates, *Exec Srch*
Mngmt. Rcrtrs. International, *Exec Srch*
Manpower Temp. Services, *Temp Agcy*
Marvel Conslt Inc., *Exec Srch*
Messina Management Syst., *Exec Srch*
Miami Professional Search, *Exec Srch*
Midland Conslt, *Exec Srch*
Minority Executive Search, *Exec Srch*
National Register, *Exec Srch*
North American Tech. Svcs., *Temp Agcy*
Olsten Prof. Staffing Services, *Exec Srch*
Palmer Temps/Palmer Group, *Temp Agcy*
Jerry Paul Associates, *Perm Agcy*
Personalized Placement, *Exec Srch*
Professional Emp. Svcs., *Perm Agcy*
Professional Restaffing, *Perm Agcy*
Providence Pers. Conslt, *Exec Srch*
Bill Reber & Associates, Inc., *Exec Srch*
RecruitMasters of Cincinnati, *Exec Srch*
Sales Conslt, *Exec Srch*
Sanford Rose Associates, *Exec Srch*
Tabb & Associates, *Exec Srch*
The Target HR Cos., *Temp Agcy*
Temporarily Yours Placement, *Temp
  Agcy*
J.P. Walton & Associates, *Exec Srch*

Executive Sales Search, *Exec Srch*
Haslowe Personnel, *Exec Srch*
Headway Corporate Staffing, *Perm Agcy*
Hispanic Committee of VA, *Perm Agcy*
Interim Financial Solutions/
StratfordGroup, *Exec Srch*
Kogen Personnel, *Exec Srch*
Lee Staffing Resources, *Exec Srch*
Mngmt. Rcrtrs. International, *Exec Srch*
MSI International, *Exec Srch*
Manpower Temp. Services, *Temp Agcy*
The McCormick Group, *Exec Srch*
Norrell Services, *Temp Agcy*
Northern Virginia Temps, *Temp Agcy*
Paul-Tittle Associates, Inc., *Exec Srch*
Don Richard Associates, *Temp Agcy*
Snelling Personnel Services, *Perm Agcy*
Souder & Associates, *Exec Srch*
Billie Summers & Associates, *Exec Srch*
The Talley Group, *Exec Srch*
TempWorld Staffing Svcs., *Temp Agcy*
U.S. Search, *Exec Srch*
Wayne Associates Inc. (WAI), *Exec Srch*

Washington

Able Personnel Agency, *Perm Agcy*
Adams & Associates, *Perm Agcy*
Behrens and Company, *Exec Srch*
Business Careers, *Perm Agcy*
The Career Clinic, Inc., *Exec Srch*
Career Services, *Perm Agcy*
Consumer Connection, *Exec Srch*
Demetrio & Associates, *Exec Srch*
Express Personnel Services, *Temp Agcy*
Renee Feldman & Associates, *Exec Srch*
N.G. Hayes Company, *Exec Srch*
Houser Martin Morris (HMM), *Exec Srch*
Human Resources Inc., *Exec Srch*
The Jobs Company, *Exec Srch*
Jobs Unlimited, *Perm Agcy*
Kelly Services, Inc., *Temp Agcy*
Kirkbride Associates Inc., *Exec Srch*
Kossuth & Associates, *Exec Srch*
Mngmt. Rcrtrs., *Exec Srch*
Mngmt. Rcrtrs. of Seattle, *Exec Srch*
Mngmt. Rcrtrs. of Tacoma, *Exec Srch*
Manpower Temp. Services, *Temp Agcy*
McIntire & Carr, *Exec Srch*
Northwest Temp & Staff Svc, *Temp Agcy*
PACE Staffing Network, *Exec Srch*
Personnel Conslt Inc., *Exec Srch*
Personnel Unlimited Inc., *Exec Srch*
Roth Young Exec. Search, *Exec Srch*
Snelling Personnel Services, *Exec Srch*
Whittall Management Group, *Exec Srch*

West Virginia

Dunhill Professional Search, *Exec Srch*
Extra Support Staffing, *Temp Agcy*
Key Personnel, Inc., *Perm Agcy*
Snelling Personnel Services, *Temp Agcy*

Wisconsin

The Ambrose Group, *Exec Srch*
Careertrac Employment Svcs., *Exec Srch*
Dieck Mueller Group, *Exec Srch*
Dunhill of Green Bay, *Exec Srch*
J.M. Eagle Partners, *Exec Srch*
FoodStaff 2000, Inc., *Exec Srch*
The H S Group, Inc., *Exec Srch*
Hatch Staffing Services, *Temp Agcy*
Interim Personnel, *Temp Agcy*
MacPros, Inc., *Perm Agcy*
Maglio & Company, *Exec Srch*
Mngmt. Rcrtrs./Sales Conslt, *Exec Srch*
Placements of Racine Inc., *Perm Agcy*
Quirk-Corporon & Associates, *Exec Srch*
Recruiting Resources Inc., *Exec Srch*
Sales Search, *Exec Srch*
Sales Specialists, Inc., *Exec Srch*
Tom Sloan & Associates Inc., *Exec Srch*
T.E.M. Associates, *Exec Srch*
Work Connection, *Perm Agcy*

Wyoming

Express Personnel Services, *Temp Agcy*
Peak Performance Consulting, *Exec Srch*

SECRETARIAL

Alabama

Dunhill of South Birmingham, *Exec Srch*
Employment Conslt, *Perm Agcy*
Initial Staffing, *Perm Agcy*

Labor Finders, *Temp Agcy*
Placers, Inc., *Perm Agcy*
VIP Personnel, Inc., *Perm Agcy*
WorkForce Enterprises, *Temp Agcy*

Alaska

Elite Employment Service, *Temp Agcy*
Olsten Staffing Services, *Temp Agcy*
Professional Business Svc., *Temp Agcy*

Arizona

AccuStaff Incorporated, *Temp Agcy*
Clifford & Associates, *Perm Agcy*
Construction Secretaries, *Perm Agcy*
Devau Human Resources, *Temp Agcy*
Insurance Support Services, *Temp Agcy*
Kerry's Referrals, *Perm Agcy*
Retiree Skills Inc., *Temp Agcy*
Saxon Associates, *Exec Srch*
Snelling Personnel Services, *Perm Agcy*
Staff One Search, *Exec Srch*
Stivers Temporary Personnel, *Temp Agcy*

Arkansas

Premier Staffing, Inc., *Temp Agcy*
SEARK Business Services, *Temp Agcy*
Turnage Emp. Svc. Group, *Exec Srch*

California

A Permanent Success Employment
Service, *Perm Agcy*
ABA Staffing, Inc., *Exec Srch*
AccuStaff Inc., *Temp Agcy*, *Perm Agcy*
Act 1 Personnel Services, *Perm Agcy*
Advantage Personnel Inc., *Perm Agcy*
Alert Staffing, *Exec Srch*
Alpha-Net Consulting Group, *Exec Srch*
Answers Unlimited, *Temp Agcy*
Apple One Emp. Services, *Perm Agcy*
Apropos Emp. Agency, *Perm Agcy*
Assured Personnel Services, *Perm Agcy*
Astra West Personnel Svcs., *Perm Agcy*
Bsa Personnel Center, *Perm Agcy*
Edward Bell Associates, *Exec Srch*
Blaine & Associates, *Temp Agcy*
Bradford Staff, Inc., *Temp Agcy*
Business Systems Support, *Perm Agcy*
CDI Information Services, *Contract Svc*
CT Personnel Services, *Perm Agcy*
California Job Connection, *Perm Agcy*
Career Images, *Temp Agcy*
Champagne Personnel, *Temp Agcy*
Choice Personnel, *Perm Agcy*
Complete Staffing Resources, *Perm Agcy*
Corestaff Services, *Perm Agcy*
Crossroads Staffing Service, *Temp Agcy*
Culver Personnel Services, *Perm Agcy*
Culver Staffing Resources, *Temp Agcy*
Dependable Employment Agency
Network, *Perm Agcy*
Desert Personnel Service, Inc./Desert
Temps, *Perm Agcy*
Drake Office Overload, *Temp Agcy*
Cathy Dunn Assoc Pers Svcs, *Perm Agcy*
Employment Service Agency, *Perm Agcy*
Express Personnel Services, *Temp Agcy*
Faithful Support Systems, *Temp Agcy*
Finesse Personnel Associates, *Exec Srch*
Pat Franklyn Associates Inc., *Temp Agcy*
Garnett Staffing, *Temp Agcy*
Goldstein & Associates, *Temp Agcy*
Gould Personnel Services, *Perm Agcy*
Hall Kinion, *Contract Svc*
Initial Staffing Services, *Perm Agcy*
Interim Personnel, *Temp Agcy*
Intertec Design, Inc., *Perm Agcy*
Intertec Personnel, *Temp Agcy*
Jackson Personnel, *Perm Agcy*
Jason Best Agency, *Perm Agcy*
John Anthony & Associates, *Exec Srch*
Kelly IT Resources, *Temp Agcy*
Kelly Services, Inc., *Temp Agcy*
Klein & Associates, *Temp Agcy*
Leigh & Associates, *Temp Agcy*
LINK Bus. & Personnel Services/LINK
Career Center, *Career/Outplacement*
The London Associates, *Exec Srch*
London Temporary Services, *Temp Agcy*
Manpower Staffing Services, *Temp Agcy*
Richard Maries Staffing Ctr., *Perm Agcy*
Martin Staffing Resources, *Perm Agcy*
Medical Staff Unlimited, *Perm Agcy*
Monroe Pers Svcs/Temptime, *Perm Agcy*

Murray Enterprises Staffing Services,
Inc., *Temp Agcy*
Nelson Staffing Solutions, *Perm Agcy*
Nesco Service Company, *Perm Agcy*
Norrell Temporary Services, *Temp Agcy*
OfficeMates5 (OM5)/DayStar Temporary
Services, *Temp Agcy*
Olsten Staffing Services, *Temp Agcy*
Personalized Placement Agency, *Temp
Agcy*
Premier Personnel Services, *Temp Agcy*
Presidio Personnel, *Temp Agcy*
Prestige Personnel Service, *Perm Agcy*
PrideStaff, *Temp Agcy*
Pro Staff Personnel Services, *Perm Agcy*
ProSearch & Associates, *Exec Srch*
Protocol Search & Selection, *Exec Srch*
Quality Imaging Services, *Contract Svc*
Questemps, *Temp Agcy*
ReliStaff, *Perm Agcy*
Remedy Caller Access, *Temp Agcy*
Remedy Intelligent Staffing, *Temp Agcy*
Royal Staffing Services, *Exec Srch*
San Diego Pers. & Emp., *Temp Agcy*
Santa Barbara Staffing, *Perm Agcy*
Select Personnel Services, *Temp Agcy*
David Sharp & Associates, *Perm Agcy*
Sharp Personnel & Search, *Exec Srch*
Snelling Personnel Inc., *Perm Agcy*
Spectrum Personnel, *Temp Agcy*
Strategic Staffing, Inc., *Temp Agcy*
Sun Personnel Services, *Temp Agcy*
TLC Staffing, *Temp Agcy*
TRC Staff Svcs., *Temp Agcy*, *Perm Agcy*
TAC Staffing Services, *Temp Agcy*
Temps Unlimited, Inc., *Temp Agcy*
Thomas Staffing, *Temp Agcy*
Thor Temporary Services, *Temp Agcy*
TOD Staffing, *Temp Agcy*
Today Personnel Services, *Temp Agcy*
Trans U.S., Inc., *Perm Agcy*
Truex Associates, *Exec Srch*
The Truman Agency, *Perm Agcy*
UAW Labor Employment and Training
Corporation, *Perm Agcy*
United Staffing Solutions, *Exec Srch*
Volt Services Group, *Temp Agcy*
Westaff, *Temp Agcy*
The Windsor Group, *Perm Agcy*
Wollborg-Michelson Pers. Svc., *Perm
Agcy*
Your People Professionals, *Perm Agcy*
Amy Zimmerman & Assoc., *Perm Agcy*

Colorado

A to Z Business Services, *Perm Agcy*
Absolute Staffing Solutions, *Perm Agcy*
Adecco, *Temp Agcy*
Ahrnsbrak and Associates, *Perm Agcy*
BankTemps, Inc., *Temp Agcy*
Career Connections, *Exec Srch*
Casey Services, Inc. (CSI), *Exec Srch*
CORESttaff Services, *Perm Agcy*
Eagle Valley Temps, *Temp Agcy*
Executemps, Inc., *Temp Agcy*
Robert Half Intl/Accountemps, *Exec Srch*
Initial Staffing Services, *Temp Agcy*
Interim Personnel, *Temp Agcy*
JobSearch, *Temp Agcy*
Kelly IT Resources, *Temp Agcy*
Kelly Services, Inc., *Temp Agcy*
Manpower International Inc., *Temp Agcy*
Norrell Interim, *Temp Agcy*
Office Specialists Inc., *Temp Agcy*
Olsten Staffing Services, *Temp Agcy*
SOS Staffing Services, *Temp Agcy*
Snelling Personnel Services, *Exec Srch*
Stivers Temporary Personnel, *Temp Agcy*
TPM Staffing Service, *Perm Agcy*
Terry Personnel, *Perm Agcy*
Todays Temporary, *Temp Agcy*

Connecticut

Admiral Staffing Services, *Temp Agcy*
Advanced Placement Inc., *Temp Agcy*
Charter Personnel Services, *Exec Srch*
Corporate Staffing Solutions, *Temp Agcy*
Diversified Emp. Services, *Perm Agcy*
Employment Opportunities, *Temp Agcy*
Hallmark Totaltech, Inc., *Exec Srch*
Impact Personnel, Inc., *Temp Agcy*
Intertec Personnel, *Temp Agcy*
Jobsource, *Perm Agcy*

Franklin-Pierce Associates, *Perm Agcy*
Interim Personnel, *Temp Agcy*
Johnson & Hill Staffing Svc., *Temp Agcy*
Kelly Services, Inc., *Temp Agcy*
Kennison & Associates, Inc., *Temp Agcy*
L&L Associates & Temps, *Temp Agcy*
Lane Employment Service, *Perm Agcy*
John Leonard Pers. Assoc., *Perm Agcy*
Manpower Temp. Services, *Temp Agcy*
Mass Temps Inc., *Temp Agcy*
Need Personnel Placement, *Temp Agcy*
New Boston Select Staffing, *Temp Agcy*
New England Personnel, Inc., *Perm Agcy*
New Perspectives Personnel, *Temp Agcy*
Norrell Staffing Services, *Contract Svc*
Office Specialists, *Temp Agcy*
OfficeTeam/Robert Half Intl, *Temp Agcy*
Olsten Staffing Services, *Temp Agcy*
Pomerantz Staffing Services, *Temp Agcy*
Pro Staff, *Temp Agcy*
Propos Associates, Inc., *Perm Agcy*
Quality Pers./Quality Temps, *Perm Agcy*
Reardon Associates, Inc., *Perm Agcy*
Remedy Intelligent Staffing, *Temp Agcy*
Routhier Plcmnt. Specialists, *Perm Agcy*
Selectemps, *Temp Agcy*
Selective Office Staffing, *Perm Agcy*
The Skill Bureau, Inc., *Perm Agcy*
Snelling Personnel, *Exec Srch*
Snelling Personnel Services, *Perm Agcy*
Spectra Professional Search/Spectra
   Temps, *Perm Agcy*
TAC Staffing Services, *Temp Agcy*
TAD Staffing Services, *Temp Agcy*
Tech Resource Inc., *Contract Svc*
Total Services, Inc. (TTS), *Perm Agcy*
Tricor Associates, *Temp Agcy*
Unlimited Opportunities of New
   England, Inc., *Temp Agcy*
Volt Services Group, *Temp Agcy*
The Work Place, *Career/Outplacement*

Michigan
Accountemps/OfficeTeam, *Temp Agcy*
Alternative Staff, Inc., *Contract Svc*
Career Quest, Inc., *Perm Agcy*
Davidson, Laird & Associates, *Exec Srch*
Day Personnel, Inc., *Perm Agcy*
Dynamic People, *Temp Agcy*
Entech Personnel Services, *Temp Agcy*
Executive Recruiters Intnl., *Exec Srch*
Express Personnel Services, *Temp Agcy*
Harper Associates, *Exec Srch*
William Howard Agency, *Contract Svc*
Human Resources Emp. Svcs, *Perm Agcy*
Interim Personnel, *Temp Agcy*
Kelly Services, Inc., *Temp Agcy*
METROSTAFF, *Exec Srch*
Nationwide Career Network, *Perm Agcy*
Nustar Temporary Services, *Temp Agcy*
Office Staffing Recruiting, *Exec Srch*
Permanent Staff Company, *Perm Agcy*
Personnel At Law, Inc., *Temp Agcy*
Preferred Emp. Planning, *Perm Agcy*
Prof. Pers. Conslt Intnl., *Exec Srch*
Search Plus International, *Exec Srch*
Snelling Personnel Services/Bryant
   Bureau, *Perm Agcy*
Sygnetics Inc., *Temp Agcy*
TRC Staffing Services, *Temp Agcy*
TEA Inc., *Perm Agcy*
Total Employee Mngmt., *Temp Agcy*
Trillium Staffing, *Temp Agcy*
Troy Tech Services, *Contract Svc*
Unlimited Staffing Solns., *Contract Svc*
Workforce, Inc., *Temp Agcy*

Minnesota
Abby Blu Inc., *Temp Agcy*
Alternative Staffing, Inc., *Perm Agcy*
Diversified Employment Inc., *Perm Agcy*
Express Personnel Services, *Perm Agcy*
Lynn Temporary, *Temp Agcy*
Manpower Temp. Services, *Temp Agcy*
Midwest Staffing Services, *Temp Agcy*
Romac International, *Exec Srch*
Secretary & Accounting Svcs., *Perm
   Agcy*
Temp Force, *Temp Agcy*
Jeane Thorne Inc., *Temp Agcy*
Ultimate Search Unlimited/Temps
   Unlimited, *Perm Agcy*
Working Relationships Inc., *Perm Agcy*

Mississippi
AAA Employment, *Exec Srch*
Capitol Staffing Solutions, *Perm Agcy*
Coats & Coats Personnel, *Perm Agcy*
Columbus Personnel Inc., *Temp Agcy*
EPSCO Personnel Service, *Temp Agcy*
Laborchex Companies, *Perm Agcy*
Recruitment & Training Programs of
   Mississippi, Inc., *Perm Agcy*
Service Specialists Ltd., *Perm Agcy*

Missouri
Adecco, *Temp Agcy*
Bestemps Inc., *Perm Agcy*
Business Personnel Services, *Temp Agcy*
Employer Advantage, *Exec Srch*
Executaries by Gray, *Exec Srch*
ExecuTemps, Inc., *Temp Agcy*
Interim Personnel, *Temp Agcy*
JoDoc Enterprises, *Temp Agcy*
LandAJob, *Perm Agcy*
Manpower Temp. Services, *Temp Agcy*
National Physician Placement Services,
   Exec Srch
Olsten Staffing Services, *Temp Agcy*
Snelling Personnel Services, *Temp Agcy*
Workforce, Inc., *Temp Agcy*

Montana
Express Personnel Services, *Temp Agcy*
Kelly Services, Inc., *Temp Agcy*
LC Staffing Service, *Perm Agcy*

Nebraska
Adecco, *Temp Agcy*
Corporate Recruiters, Ltd./Health Service
   Professionals, *Exec Srch*
Donna's Office Service, *Contract Svc*
Express Personnel, *Exec Srch*
Kelly Services, Inc., *Temp Agcy*
Noll Human Resource Svcs., *Exec Srch*
Outsource II, Inc., *Temp Agcy*

Nevada
Initial Staffing Services, *Perm Agcy*
Manpower Temp. Services, *Temp Agcy*
Nevada Bus. Svcs., *Career/Outplacement*

New Hampshire
Able 1 Staffing, *Exec Srch*
Barclay Personnel Systems, *Exec Srch*
Career Connections, Inc., *Perm Agcy*
Central NH Emp. Services, *Perm Agcy*
Cheshire Employment Svc., *Temp Agcy*
Kelly Services, Inc., *Temp Agcy*
Key Partners, Inc., *Perm Agcy*
Manpower Temp. Services, *Temp Agcy*
Pelham Professional Group, *Temp Agcy*
Resource Recruiting/Contemporary
   Accountants, *Perm Agcy*
TAC Staffing Services, *Temp Agcy*

New Jersey
A+ Personnel Placement, *Perm Agcy*
A Professional Edge, *Career/
   Outplacement*
ABC Nationwide Emp., *Perm Agcy*
Advanced Personnel Service, *Perm Agcy*
Allen Associates, Inc., *Perm Agcy*
Allstaff Resources, Inc., *Perm Agcy*
American Staffing Resources, *Perm Agcy*
Angelord Inc., *Temp Agcy*
The Ascher Group, *Exec Srch*
BAI Personnel Solutions, *Perm Agcy*
Blake & Assoc. Exec. Search, *Exec Srch*
Career Management Group, *Exec Srch*
Careers USA, *Perm Agcy*
Dunhill Professional Search, *Exec Srch*
Executive Search, Inc., *Exec Srch*
Express Personnel Services, *Perm Agcy*
Globe Employment Agency, *Perm Agcy*
Holm Personnel Conslt, *Exec Srch*
ITC Personnel Services, *Temp Agcy*
Impact Personnel, Inc., *Perm Agcy*
Integro Staffing Services, *Temp Agcy*
Joule Staffing Services, *Contract Svc*
Kaye Personnel Inc., *Temp Agcy*
Kelly Services, Inc., *Temp Agcy*
Mngmt. Rcrtrs./OfficeMates5 of Union
   County, *Exec Srch*
McDermott Resources Inc., *Exec Srch*
Miller Resources, *Perm Agcy*
Norrell Services, *Temp Agcy*
OfficeMates5 (OM5)/DayStar Temporary
   Services, *Perm Agcy*

OMNE Staffing Services, *Temp Agcy*
Park Avenue Personnel, *Perm Agcy*
Pat's Secretarial Service, *Temp Agcy*
Pomerantz Staffing Services, *Perm Agcy*
Premier Personnel Group, *Perm Agcy*
Protocall Bus. Staffing Svcs., *Temp Agcy*
Remedy Intelligent Staffing, *Temp Agcy*
Rotator Staffing Services, *Contract Svc*
Arline Simpson Associates, , *Perm Agcy*
Snelling Personnel Services, *Perm Agcy*
TRS Staffing Solutions, Inc., *Temp Agcy*
Temporary Excellence Inc., *Temp Agcy*
UNITEMP Temporary Pers., *Temp Agcy*
Winston Staffing Services, *Temp Agcy*
Winters & Ross, *Perm Agcy*

New Mexico
Albuquerque Personnel, Inc., *Perm Agcy*
CDI Technical Services, *Contract Svc*
Excel Staffing Companies, *Perm Agcy*
Sanderson Employment Svc., *Perm Agcy*
Santa Fe Services, *Temp Agcy*
Snelling Search, *Exec Srch*

New York
AARP Foundation/Senior Employment
   Program, *Perm Agcy*
AM & PM Temps Inc., *Temp Agcy*
Aadams Personnel Agency, *Temp Agcy*
AccuStaff Incorporated, *Temp Agcy*
Adam Personnel, Inc., *Perm Agcy*
Adecco, *Temp Agcy*
Advice Personnel, *Exec Srch*
AMESgroup, *Exec Srch*
Arrow Employment Agency, *Perm Agcy*
Asher Personnel Conslt, *Perm Agcy*
Auto Careers, *Perm Agcy*
Berkel Associates, Inc., *Exec Srch*
Bestemp Temporary Svcs., *Temp Agcy*
Bevan Resources, *Perm Agcy*
Bevlin Personnel Inc., *Perm Agcy*
The British Connection, *Perm Agcy*
Brookville Staffing Services, *Perm Agcy*
Burns Personnel, *Exec Srch*
Career Blazers Personnel Svc, *Perm Agcy*
Career Objectives Personnel, *Temp Agcy*
Corporate Search Inc., *Exec Srch*
Seth Diamond Associates Inc., *Exec Srch*
Maggi Dolan Placement, Inc., *Perm Agcy*
Dunhill Staffing Systems, *Temp Agcy*
Eden Staffing, *Perm Agcy*
Emp. Recruiters Agency, *Perm Agcy*
Emp. Store/TES Technical, *Exec Srch*
Euromonde, Inc., *Temp Agcy*
Execu/Search Group, *Exec Srch*
Fanning Personnel, *Exec Srch*
Filcro Personnel, *Perm Agcy*
Finest Employment Agency, *Perm Agcy*
Forum Temporary Services, *Temp Agcy*
Friedman Emp. Agency, Inc., *Perm Agcy*
Ronnie Gale Personnel Corp., *Exec Srch*
Graphic Techniques, Inc., *Temp Agcy*
Haesloop and Hegarty, *Temp Agcy*
Harbrowe, Inc., *Perm Agcy*
Hart-Merrell Personnel, *Exec Srch*
Headway Corporate Staffing, *Perm Agcy*
Hunter Mac & Associates, *Perm Agcy*
Hunter Placement Inc., *Exec Srch*
Ideal Personnel, *Perm Agcy*
Interim Personnel, *Temp Agcy*
Island Search Group Inc., *Perm Agcy*
JDC Associates, *Perm Agcy*
Josef Group Personnel, *Perm Agcy*
KPA Staffing Group, Inc., *Exec Srch*
Kelly Services, Inc., *Temp Agcy*
Magill Associates, Inc., *Exec Srch*
Manpower Temp. Services, *Temp Agcy*
Mar-El Employment Agency, *Exec Srch*
Lynn Marshall Pers. Agency, *Perm Agcy*
Metro Resources, *Temp Agcy*
Metro Support Group, *Perm Agcy*
Metropolitan Personnel Syst., *Exec Srch*
Milazzo Associates, Inc., *Perm Agcy*
Morgan-Murray Personnel/M&M Top
   Temps, *Temp Agcy*
New York-New York Pers., *Temp Agcy*
Norrell Staffing Services, *Temp Agcy*
Nowack Career Specialists, *Perm Agcy*
Olsten Staffing Services, *Temp Agcy*
Optimal Resources, *Exec Srch*
Paywise Inc., *Temp Agcy*
Personnel Services Center, *Exec Srch*
Adele Poston Agency, *Perm Agcy*

P.G. Prager Search Associates, *Exec Srch*
Preferred Professionals, *Temp Agcy*
Rand Thompson Conslt/Merlin Temps, *Exec Srch*
Rem Resources, Inc., *Perm Agcy*
Remedy Intelligent Staffing, *Temp Agcy*
Republic Emp. Agency, *Perm Agcy*
Response Staffing Services, *Exec Srch*
Ribolow Associates, *Perm Agcy*
Beth Richman Associates, *Perm Agcy*
S.W. Management, *Exec Srch*
Sigma Staffing, *Perm Agcy*
Sloan Staffing Services, *Perm Agcy*
Snelling Personnel Services, *Perm Agcy*
Staff By Manning, Ltd., *Perm Agcy*
Staff Managers, *Temp Agcy*
Stamm Personnel Agency, *Perm Agcy*
Strategic Recruiting, *Exec Srch*
Swing Shift, *Temp Agcy*
Hillary Taylor Personnel, *Perm Agcy*
Tempo Services, Inc., *Perm Agcy*
Temporary Resource Center, *Temp Agcy*
TemPositions, Inc., *Temp Agcy*
Unique Support Services, *Temp Agcy*
United Personnel Agency, *Perm Agcy*
United Staffing Systems, *Temp Agcy*
Vance Personnel, *Perm Agcy*
Vantage Staffing Services, *Temp Agcy*
Westaff, *Temp Agcy*
Westfield Associates, Inc., *Exec Srch*
H.L. Yoh Company, *Temp Agcy*

North Carolina

Accurate Staffing Conslt, *Exec Srch*
Action Staffing Group, *Temp Agcy*
Action Staffmasters, *Temp Agcy*
Advanced Pers. Resources, *Exec Srch*
Anderson & Daniel Pers., *Perm Agcy*
Barrett Business Services, *Temp Agcy*
Caldwell Personnel Services, *Perm Agcy*
Executive Staffing Group, *Exec Srch*
Express Personnel Services, *Temp Agcy*
Interim Personnel, Inc., *Temp Agcy*
The Jobs Market, Inc., *Temp Agcy*
Kelly Services, Inc., *Temp Agcy*
Manpower, Inc., *Temp Agcy*
McCain Employment Svc., *Temp Agcy*
Norrell Services, *Temp Agcy*
Office Specialists, *Temp Agcy*
Olsten Staffing Services, *Temp Agcy*
Pro Staff Personnel Services, *Perm Agcy*
Quality Temporary Services, *Temp Agcy*
Remedy Intelligent Staffing, *Perm Agcy*
Snelling Personnel Services, *Perm Agcy*
Sparks Personnel Services, *Exec Srch*
StaffMark, *Temp Agcy*
Summit Occupational Staffing, *Exec Srch*
USA Staffing, *Temp Agcy*
Westaff, *Perm Agcy*
Will/Staff Personnel Svcs., *Temp Agcy*
Youngblood Staffing, *Perm Agcy*

North Dakota

Olsten Staffing Services/Expressway Personnel, *Temp Agcy*

Ohio

AccuStaff, *Temp Agcy*
Adecco, *Temp Agcy*
Belcan Staffing Services, *Temp Agcy*
CBS Personnel Services, *Perm Agcy*
Career Connections, Inc., *Temp Agcy*
Champion Personnel System, *Perm Agcy*
Custom Staffing, Inc., *Temp Agcy*
Eastern Personnel Services, *Perm Agcy*
Elite Personnel Agency, *Perm Agcy*
Exact Personnel Specialists, *Perm Agcy*
Initial Staffing Services, *Temp Agcy*
Anne Jones Staffing, Inc., *Perm Agcy*
Kelly Services, Inc., *Temp Agcy*
Manpower Temp. Services, *Temp Agcy*
Masterson Personnel, Inc./Masterson Temporary Services, *Perm Agcy*
Messina Management Syst., *Exec Srch*
Palmer Temps/Palmer Group, *Temp Agcy*
Professional Restaffing, Inc., *Perm Agcy*
Quality Plus, *Exec Srch*
Quality Source, Inc., *Exec Srch*
The Target HR Companies, *Temp Agcy*
Temporarily Yrs. Placement, *Temp Agcy*

Oklahoma

Ameri Resource, *Exec Srch*
Cherokee Temps, Inc., *Temp Agcy*

Dow Personnel Inc., *Temp Agcy*
Express Personnel Services, *Exec Srch*
Robert Half Intl/Accountemps, *Exec Srch*
Interim Personnel, *Temp Agcy*
Key Temporary Personnel, *Temp Agcy*
Terry Neese Pers. Agency, *Temp Agcy*
Sooner Placement Service, *Temp Agcy*
StaffMark, *Temp Agcy*

Oregon

Barrett Business Services, *Temp Agcy*
Corporate Careers Inc., *Perm Agcy*
Employment Trends, LLC, *Temp Agcy*
Express Personnel Services, *Exec Srch*
Initial Staffing Services, *Perm Agcy*
Kelly Services, Inc., *Temp Agcy*
Northwest Temp & Staff Svc, *Temp Agcy*
Office Careers Inc., *Perm Agcy*
Quest Temporary Services, *Temp Agcy*
Uniforce Staffing Services, *Temp Agcy*

Pennsylvania

AA Staffing Solutions, Inc., *Contract Svc*
Adecco, *Temp Agcy*
Alexander Personnel Assoc., *Exec Srch*
All Staffing Inc., *Perm Agcy*
Allegheny Personnel Svcs., *Temp Agcy*
Anita's Careers, Inc., *Exec Srch*
Becker Personnel, *Perm Agcy*
Career Quest Confidential, *Exec Srch*
Charley's Personnel Staffing, *Temp Agcy*
CoreStaff Inc., *Temp Agcy*
J. Croyle & Associates, Inc., *Perm Agcy*
DiCenzo Personnel Specialists, *Exec Srch*
Dunhill Professional Search, *Exec Srch*
Merrill Grumer Associates, *Perm Agcy*
Hallmark Pers./Abel Temps, *Perm Agcy*
The Hobart West Group, *Perm Agcy*
Hobbie Personnel Services, *Temp Agcy*
Human Assets Inc., *Temp Agcy*
Interim Personnel, *Temp Agcy*
Nancy Jackson Inc., *Exec Srch*
Kenneth James Associates, *Exec Srch*
Kathy Karr Personnel, Inc., *Perm Agcy*
Kelly Services, Inc., *Temp Agcy*
Marsetta Lane Temp. Svcs., *Temp Agcy*
Legal Search, *Temp Agcy*
London Personnel Services, *Perm Agcy*
J. McManus Associates, *Perm Agcy*
Metropolitan Personnel, Inc., *Temp Agcy*
Norrell Services, *Temp Agcy*
Olsten Staffing Services, *Temp Agcy*
Pancoast Temporary Svcs., *Temp Agcy*
The Placers, Inc., *Temp Agcy*
Powers Personnel, *Perm Agcy*
Pratt Personnel Services, *Temp Agcy*
R.H.A. Exec. Pers. Services, *Exec Srch*
SHS International, *Exec Srch*
Strauss Personnel Service, *Perm Agcy*
TRC Staffing Services, *Temp Agcy*
TAC Staffing Services, Inc., *Temp Agcy*
Todays Temporary, *Temp Agcy*
Tops Temporaries Inc., *Temp Agcy*
Uni-Temp Temporary Svc., *Temp Agcy*
Vogue Personnel Inc., *Exec Srch*
Williford & Associates/Williford Legal Support Services, *Temp Agcy*

Rhode Island

Aquidneck Employment Svc., *Perm Agcy*
Capitol Personnel Inc., *Temp Agcy*
Colony Personnel Associates, *Temp Agcy*
Kelly Services, Inc., *Temp Agcy*
Norrell Services, *Temp Agcy*
Occupations Unlimited, Inc., *Perm Agcy*
Qualified Resources, *Temp Agcy*
Spectra Temps/Tracey Assoc, *Temp Agcy*

South Carolina

Accel Temporary Services, *Temp Agcy*
Carolina Personnel Services, *Temp Agcy*
Charles Foster Staffing, Inc., *Temp Agcy*
Jerman Personnel Services, *Temp Agcy*
Smith Temps/Smith Pers., *Temp Agcy*
Snelling Personnel Services, *Perm Agcy*
StaffingSolutions, *Temp Agcy*
StaffMark, *Temp Agcy*

South Dakota

Key Staffing, *Temp Agcy*
Snelling Personnel Service, *Perm Agcy*

Tennessee

A-1 Staffing & Personnel, *Temp Agcy*
Amenity Staffing, *Temp Agcy*

Anderson McIntyre Pers. Svcs, *Exec Srch*
Arvie Personnel Services, *Perm Agcy*
Gateway Group Personnel, *Temp Agcy*
Kelly Services, Inc., *Temp Agcy*
Manpower, Inc., *Temp Agcy*
W.R. McLeod & Associates, *Exec Srch*
Norrell Services, *Temp Agcy*
Olsten Staffing Services, *Temp Agcy*
Personnel Link, *Exec Srch*
Piercy Employment Services, *Perm Agcy*
Quarles Kelly Associates, *Exec Srch*

Texas

A-1 Personnel, *Temp Agcy*
ABC Temps Inc., *Temp Agcy*
Abilene Employment Service, *Perm Agcy*
ACSYS Inc., *Temp Agcy*
Action Personnel Inc., *Temp Agcy*
Add-A-Temp/Woodlands Executive Employment, *Temp Agcy*
Adecco, *Temp Agcy*
Attorney Resource, Inc., *Temp Agcy*
Aware Affiliates Pers. Svc., *Perm Agcy*
Ann Best Elite Temporaries, *Temp Agcy*
BestStaff Services, Inc., *Perm Agcy*
Brainpower Pers. Agency, *Perm Agcy*
Brooklea & Associates, Inc., *Exec Srch*
Bullock Personnel, Inc., *Perm Agcy*
Burnett Personnel Services, *Temp Agcy*
Burnett's Staffing, Inc., *Temp Agcy*
Certified Personnel Svc., *Contract Svc*
Clayton Personnel Services, *Temp Agcy*
Colvin Resources Group, *Perm Agcy*
Creative Staffing Services, *Perm Agcy*
Dallas Employment Services, *Perm Agcy*
Gail Darling Staffing/Gail Darling's Professional Desk, *Temp Agcy*
Dividend Staffing Services, *Temp Agcy*
Esprit Temporary Services, *Temp Agcy*
Evins Personnel Conslt, *Perm Agcy*
Executeam, *Exec Srch*
Express Personnel Services, *Perm Agcy*
FirstWord Staffing Services, *Temp Agcy*
Robert Half International/Management Resources, *Exec Srch*
Imprimis Staffing Solutions, *Temp Agcy*
L.K. Jordan & Associates, *Contract Svc*
Kelly Services, Inc., *Temp Agcy*
Key People Inc., *Exec Srch*
Manpower Temp. Services, *Temp Agcy*
Marquess & Associates, *Perm Agcy*
Norrell Services, *Temp Agcy*
Olsten Staffing Services, *Temp Agcy*
Pate Resources Group, *Exec Srch*
Personnel One, Inc., *Perm Agcy*
Phoenix Staffing/G&A Staff Sourcing, *Exec Srch*
Placements Unlimited, *Perm Agcy*
Priority Personnel, Inc., *Temp Agcy*
Pro Staff Personnel Services, *Temp Agcy*
Professions Today, *Perm Agcy*
Quest Personnel Resources, *Perm Agcy*
Remedy Intelligent Staffing, *Perm Agcy*
Resource Connection Workforce Center, *Perm Agcy*
Resource Staffing, *Temp Agcy*
SOS Staffing Service, *Temp Agcy*
Select Staff, *Temp Agcy, Exec Srch*
Snelling Personnel Services, *Perm Agcy*
Staff Finders/Abacus Accounting Personnel, *Perm Agcy*
TRC Staffing Services Inc., *Temp Agcy*
TSP Personnel Services, Inc., *Perm Agcy*
Temporary Resources, Inc., *Temp Agcy*
Texas Personnel, *Exec Srch*
Thomas Office Pers. Svc., *Perm Agcy*
Todays Legal Staffing, *Temp Agcy*
Todays Staffing, *Temp Agcy*
Westaff, *Temp Agcy*

Utah

Robert Half Intl/Accountemps, *Exec Srch*
Intermountain Staffing Rsrc, *Temp Agcy*
Olsten Staffing Services, *Temp Agcy*

Vermont

Personnel Department Inc., *Temp Agcy*
Triad Temporary Svcs., *Temp Agcy*
Westaff, *Temp Agcy*

Virginia

Access Enterprises Inc., *Perm Agcy*
ACSYS Inc., *Exec Srch*
Advantage Staffing, *Temp Agcy*

Nancy Allen Associates, Inc., *Perm Agcy*
Alpha Omega Resources Inc., *Perm Agcy*
Bradford Company, *Contract Svc*
Buckler Careers, Inc., *Perm Agcy*
Corporate Connection Ltd., *Exec Srch*
Dow Personnel, *Perm Agcy*
Effective Staffing Inc., *Exec Srch*
Employment Enterprises/Temporary
    Solutions, *Temp Agcy*
Express Personnel Services, *Temp Agcy*
Headway Corporate Staffing, *Perm Agcy*
Hispanic Committee of VA, *Perm Agcy*
Kelly Services, Inc., *Temp Agcy*
Lee Staffing Resources, *Exec Srch*
Manpower Temp. Services, *Temp Agcy*
Susan Miller & Associates, *Perm Agcy*
Norrell Services, *Temp Agcy*
Northern Virginia Temps, *Temp Agcy*
Olsten Staffing Services, *Temp Agcy*
Remedy Intelligent Staffing, *Temp Agcy*
Romac International, *Exec Srch*
Snelling Personnel Services, *Perm Agcy*
STAT Employment Services, *Perm Agcy*
Taskforce of Virginia/PRG, *Exec Srch*
Telesec Corestaff, *Temp Agcy*
Temporaries Now, *Temp Agcy*
TempWorld Staffing Svcs., *Temp Agcy*
Westaff, *Temp Agcy*

Washington
Adams & Associates, *Perm Agcy*
The Career Clinic, Inc., *Exec Srch*
Career Services, *Perm Agcy*
Cooper Personnel, *Temp Agcy*
Express Personnel Services, *Temp Agcy*
Guidance Services Inc., *Temp Agcy*
Human Resources Inc., *Exec Srch*
The Jobs Company, *Exec Srch*
Kelly Services, Inc., *Temp Agcy*
Manpower Temp. Services, *Temp Agcy*
Northwest Temporary & Staffing
    Services, Inc., *Temp Agcy*
Olsten Staffing Services, *Temp Agcy*
Personnel Unlimited Inc., *Temp Agcy*
Snelling Personnel Services, *Exec Srch*

West Virginia
Extra Support Staffing, *Temp Agcy*
Snelling Personnel Services, *Temp Agcy*

Wisconsin
ABR Employment Services, *Perm Agcy*
ADTEC Staffing, *Temp Agcy*
Dunhill Staffing Systems, *Perm Agcy*
Employability, *Perm Agcy*
Interim Personnel, *Temp Agcy*
Landmark, The Staffing Rsrc, *Temp Agcy*
Manpower Temp. Services, *Temp Agcy*
N.E.W. Contracting Services, *Perm Agcy*
Norrell Staffing Services, *Temp Agcy*
Olsten Staffing Services, *Temp Agcy*
SEEK Inc., *Perm Agcy*
Temps Plus Staffing Svcs., *Temp Agcy*
U.S. Tech Force Inc., *Exec Srch*
Work Connection, *Perm Agcy*

SOFTWARE DEVELOPMENT

California
Larkin Group, *Exec Srch*
Maciejewski & Associates, *Perm Agcy*
National Career Choices, *Exec Srch*
PeopleWare Tech. Resources, Inc.,
    Contract Svc
Systems Careers, *Exec Srch*

Illinois
The Stanton Group, Inc., *Exec Srch*

Massachusetts
Aerotek, Inc., *Contract Svc*
Hoffman Recruiters, *Exec Srch*
Interactive Software Placement, Inc.
    (ISPI), *Perm Agcy*
KM Associates, *Exec Srch*

Michigan
Sullivan & Associates, *Exec Srch*

Minnesota
Search Specialists, *Exec Srch*

Mississippi
Compass Group, Inc., *Exec Srch*

Montana
Caria Resources, *Exec Srch*

New Hampshire
Bell Quest Associates, *Exec Srch*
Zymac Inc./EDA Plus, *Exec Srch*

New Jersey
Shifrin-Fischer Group, Inc., *Exec Srch*
Sonimax Corporation, *Exec Srch*
Stewart/Laurence Associates, *Exec Srch*

New Mexico
Henderson Black and Co., *Exec Srch*

New York
Huntington Pers. Conslt, *Exec Srch*
Network Dynamics, *Exec Srch*

Ohio
FWC Conslt, *Perm Agcy*

Tennessee
Exec-U-Tech Recruiting Svcs, *Exec Srch*
Mngmt. Rcrtrs./Sales Conslt, *Exec Srch*

Texas
Acclaim Services, Inc., *Temp Agcy*
Borrel Personnel, *Exec Srch*

Vermont
The Teton Group, *Exec Srch*

Virginia
Chelsea Resource Group, Inc., *Exec Srch*

Washington
Axxa Corporation, *Exec Srch*
Bixler Group, *Exec Srch*
Sally Caplan & Associates, *Exec Srch*
Demetrio & Associates, *Exec Srch*
Wilson Smith Associates, *Exec Srch*

SOFTWARE ENGINEERING

California
Advanced Tech. Conslt, *Exec Srch*
Spectrawest, *Exec Srch*
TAC Engineering Resources, *Temp Agcy*

Colorado
F-O-R-T-U-N-E Pers. Conslts, *Exec Srch*
Tech. Resource Conslt, *Exec Srch*

Georgia
Emergin Technology Search, *Exec Srch*

Indiana
Alpha Rae Personnel, Inc., *Perm Agcy*

Iowa
Staffing Edge, *Perm Agcy*

Maryland
F-O-R-T-U-N-E Pers. Conslts, *Exec Srch*
Nations Exec. Search Group, *Exec Srch*

Massachusetts
Intellimark, *Exec Srch*
Interactive Software Plcmnt., *Perm Agcy*
Lynx Inc., *Contract Svc*
New Dimensions in Tech., *Exec Srch*
E.S. Rando Associates, Inc., *Perm Agcy*

Michigan
Sullivan & Associates, *Exec Srch*

Minnesota
Custom Search Inc., *Exec Srch*
Lee Marsh & Associates, *Exec Srch*

New York
Huntington Pers. Conslt, *Exec Srch*
Landover Associates, Inc., *Exec Srch*
Daniel F. Reilly and Assoc., *Exec Srch*

Oregon
VanderHouwen & Associates, *Exec Srch*

Pennsylvania
Advanced Tech. Resources, *Exec Srch*

Texas
Mngmt. Rcrtrs. of LBJ Park/Dallas, *Exec
    Srch*

Washington
Macrosearch/Macrostaff, *Perm Agcy*

TAX

Arizona
Accounting Quest, *Exec Srch*

California
Accountants Executive Search/
    Accountants On Call, *Exec Srch*

Singer Strouse, *Exec Srch*
Tax Executive Search, Inc., *Exec Srch*

Colorado
Accounting Quest, *Exec Srch*
Two Degrees, *Exec Srch*

Connecticut
Access Financial, *Exec Srch*

Florida
Terry M. Weiss & Associates, *Exec Srch*

Georgia
Lucas Group, *Exec Srch*

Illinois
ITEX Executive Search, *Exec Srch*
The Robinson Group, *Exec Srch*
Stone Enterprises, Ltd., *Exec Srch*
Two Degrees, *Exec Srch*

Michigan
Accountants Support Service Corp.,
    Temp Agcy

Minnesota
Whitney Prof. Staffing, *Temp Agcy*

New York
Advice Personnel, *Exec Srch*
Corporate Search Inc., *Exec Srch*
RCM Technologies, Inc., *Perm Agcy*

Oklahoma
TaxSearch Incorporated, *Exec Srch*

Oregon
Accounting Quest, *Exec Srch*

Texas
Austin Group, *Exec Srch*
Kane & Associates, Inc., *Exec Srch*

Washington
Accounting Quest, *Exec Srch*

TECHNICAL AND SCIENTIFIC

Alabama
Mary Cheek & Assoc., *Exec Srch*
Dunhill of South Birmingham, *Exec Srch*
Healthcare Recruiters of AL, *Exec Srch*
Mngmt. Rcrtrs. International, *Exec Srch*
Mngmt. Rcrtrs. of North AL, *Exec Srch*
Seatec, Inc., *Contract Svc*

Alaska
Alaska Department of Labor and
    Workforce Development, *Perm Agcy*
Alaska Executive Search, *Exec Srch*
Manpower Temp. Services, *Temp Agcy*
Olsten Staffing Services, *Temp Agcy*

Arizona
Adecco/TAD Technical Svcs, *Temp Agcy*
Amer. Career Grp, *Career/
    Outplacement*
Aztech Recruitment Company, *Exec Srch*
CDI Corporation, *Contract Svc*
Circuit Technology Search, *Exec Srch*
Cizek Associates Inc., *Exec Srch*
COMFORCE Tech. Svcs., *Contract Svc*
Devau Human Resources, *Temp Agcy*
General Emp. Enterprises, *Perm Agcy*
H&M Recruiters, *Exec Srch*
Hunter Technical Services, *Exec Srch*
Mngmt. Rcrtrs. of Scottsdale, *Exec Srch*
PDS Technical Services, *Contract Svc*
Priority Staffing, Inc., *Perm Agcy*
Snelling Personnel Services, *Perm Agcy*
Spectra International, *Exec Srch*
Stivers Temporary Personnel, *Temp Agcy*
Tech/Aid of Arizona, *Perm Agcy*
Volt Technical Services, *Contract Svc*

Arkansas
Executive Recruiters Agency, *Exec Srch*
Mngmt. Rcrtrs., *Exec Srch*
SEARK Business Services, *Temp Agcy*
StaffMark, *Temp Agcy*
Turnage Emp. Service Group, *Exec Srch*

California
ABA Staffing, Inc., *Exec Srch*
ACS Technology Solutions, *Perm Agcy*
A.S.A.P. Employment Svc., *Perm Agcy*
ACCESS Technology, *Exec Srch*
AccuStaff Incorporated, *Temp Agcy*
Adecco/TAD Tech. Svcs., *Perm Agcy*

Southern Research Services, *Exec Srch*
System One Services, *Contract Svc*
TMP Worldwide, *Exec Srch*
Technisource, *Contract Svc*
TechStaff, *Contract Svc*
TempSolutions, Inc., *Temp Agcy*
The Witt Group, *Exec Srch*

Georgia
A.D. & Assoc. Exec. Search, *Exec Srch*
Anderson Industrial Assoc., *Exec Srch*
Apex Systems Inc./41 Perimeter Center East, *Exec Srch*
Business Professional Group, *Perm Agcy*
Catalina Human Resources, *Perm Agcy*
Coast to Coast, *Temp Agcy*
Corporate Search Conslt, *Exec Srch*
Data Processing Services, Inc., *Exec Srch*
Dunhill Professional Search, *Exec Srch*
Elite Staffing Services, *Temp Agcy*
Express Personnel Services, *Perm Agcy*
Hall Management Group, *Exec Srch*
Job Shop Inc., *Exec Srch*
Kelly Services, Inc., *Temp Agcy*
MSI International, *Exec Srch*
Mngmt. Rcrtrs. International, *Exec Srch*
Manpower Temporary Svcs., *Temp Agcy*
Office Specialists, *Temp Agcy*
Olsten Professional Staffing, *Perm Agcy*
Olsten Staffing Services, *Temp Agcy*
Pro-Tech Inc., *Exec Srch*
Randstad Staffing Services, *Temp Agcy*
Rollins Search Group, *Exec Srch*
Sanford Rose Associates, *Exec Srch*
StaffMark, *Temp Agcy*
TMP Worldwide, *Exec Srch*
Technical Associates, *Contract Svc*
Think Resources, *Contract Svc*
Westaff, *Temp Agcy*

Hawaii
ASAP Express, *Contract Svc*
Altres Staffing, *Temp Agcy*
Dunhill Prof. Staffing of HI, *Exec Srch*
Executive Search World, *Exec Srch*
Olsten Staffing Services, *Temp Agcy*

Idaho
Snelling Personnel Services, *Perm Agcy*
Volt Technical Services, *Contract Svc*

Illinois
The Ability Group, *Exec Srch*
Accord Inc., *Exec Srch*
Adecco, *Temp Agcy*
Advanced Technical Search, *Exec Srch*
Alternative Resources Corporation, *Contract Svc*
American Contract Svcs., *Contract Svc*
American Engineering Co., *Exec Srch*
American Technical Search, *Exec Srch*
Availability, Inc., *Perm Agcy*
Banner Personnel Service, *Perm Agcy*
Battalia Winston International, *Exec Srch*
Britannia, *Exec Srch*
Burling Group Ltd., *Exec Srch*
CDI Corporation, *Contract Svc*
CareerLink USA, Inc., *Exec Srch*
Carson Mngmt. Assoc., *Contract Svc*
Consultis Inc., *Temp Agcy*
Corporate Environment, Ltd., *Exec Srch*
Diener & Associates Inc., *Exec Srch*
Electronic Search Inc., *Exec Srch*
Eve Recruiters Ltd., *Perm Agcy*
Executive Search Network, *Exec Srch*
Express Personnel Services, *Temp Agcy*
First Search, Inc., *Exec Srch*
General Emp. Enterprises, *Perm Agcy*
HT Associates, *Exec Srch*
Hersher & Associates, Ltd., *Exec Srch*
Interim Personnel, *Contract Svc*
Raymond Karson Associates, *Exec Srch*
Kunzer Associates, Ltd., *Exec Srch*
Magnum Search, *Exec Srch*
Mngmt. Rcrtrs. International, *Exec Srch*
Marsteller Wilcox Assoc., *Exec Srch*
Mathey Services, *Exec Srch*
Paul May & Associates, *Exec Srch*
M.W. McDonald & Assoc., *Exec Srch*
Medical Tech. Placements, *Temp Agcy*
R. Michaels & Associates, *Exec Srch*
The Murphy Group, *Perm Agcy*
National Search, *Exec Srch*
OfficeMates5 (OM5), *Perm Agcy*

Omega Technical Corp., *Contract Svc*
Omni One, *Perm Agcy*
Omni Search Ltd., *Exec Srch*
James C. Pappas & Associates, *Exec Srch*
Pelichem Associates, *Exec Srch*
Patricia Pocock & Associates, *Exec Srch*
The Pollak and Skan Grp., *Contract Svc*
Remedy Intelligent Staffing, *Temp Agcy*
Search Dynamics Inc., *Exec Srch*
Search Enterprises, *Exec Srch*
Select Search Inc., *Exec Srch*
SelectAbility, Inc., *Perm Agcy*
Sevcor International, Inc., *Exec Srch*
Snelling Personnel Services, *Perm Agcy*
Staffing Team International, *Temp Agcy*
Systems Research Inc., *Perm Agcy*
TMP Worldwide, *Exec Srch*
TSC Management Svcs. Grp., *Exec Srch*
Working World Inc., *Temp Agcy*
World Employment Service, *Perm Agcy*
Xagas & Associates, *Exec Srch*

Indiana
Adecco/TAD Tech. Svcs., *Contract Svc*
Alliance Group Tech., *Contract Svc*
Angola Personnel Services, *Perm Agcy*
Belcan Technical Services, *Contract Svc*
Career Conslt, Inc./O.I. Partners, *Perm Agcy*
Century Personnel Inc., *Perm Agcy*
Corporate Staffing Resources (CSR), *Temp Agcy*
Dunhill of Brown County, *Exec Srch*
Dunhill Staffing Systems, *Temp Agcy*
Employment Plus, *Temp Agcy*
Execusearch, *Exec Srch*
Johnson Brown Associates, *Exec Srch*
Kelly Services, Inc., *Temp Agcy*
Mngmt. Rcrtrs. International/Sales Conslt, *Exec Srch*
Management Services, *Exec Srch*
Management Support Svcs., *Exec Srch*
Manpower Technical Svcs., *Temp Agcy*
Oakwood International Inc., *Exec Srch*
OfficeMates5 (OM5)/DayStar Temporary Services, *Exec Srch*
Personnel Plus, Inc., *Exec Srch*
QCI Technical Staffing, *Contract Svc*
Quality Search, *Exec Srch*
Reliable Technical Services, *Perm Agcy*
Technetics Corporation, *Contract Svc*
Time Services, Inc., *Perm Agcy*
Try Temps Inc., *Temp Agcy*
Wimmer Temporaries and Direct Placement, *Temp Agcy*
H.L. Yoh Company, *Contract Svc*

Iowa
Burton Placement Services, *Exec Srch*
Byrnes & Rupkey, Inc., *Exec Srch*
CDI Corporation, *Contract Svc*
Drake-Brennan, Inc., *Exec Srch*
Mngmt. Rcrtrs. International, *Exec Srch*
Personnel, Inc., *Exec Srch*
Premier Search Group, *Exec Srch*
Snelling Personnel, *Exec Srch*
Staff Management, Inc., *Contract Svc*
TechStaff, Inc., *Temp Agcy*

Kansas
Business Specialists, *Perm Agcy*
CDI Corporation Midwest, *Contract Svc*
Corporate Resources, *Exec Srch*
Dunhill of Wichita, *Perm Agcy*
Foster Design Company, *Contract Svc*
Ida Group, *Exec Srch*
Mngmt. Rcrtrs. of Overland Park/Sales Conslt/OfficeMates5, *Exec Srch*
Manpower Technical, *Perm Agcy*
Manpower Temp. Services, *Temp Agcy*
J.T. Nelson & Associates, *Perm Agcy*
Spencer Reed Tech. Group, *Exec Srch*
Stoneburner Associates, Inc., *Exec Srch*
White Associates/TemTech, *Exec Srch*
H.L. Yoh Company, *Contract Svc*

Kentucky
Angel Group International, *Exec Srch*
C.M. Management Services, *Perm Agcy*
Manpower Inc., *Temp Agcy*
Precision Staffing, Inc., *Perm Agcy*
Professional Search, *Exec Srch*
Snelling Personnel Services, *Perm Agcy*

Louisiana
Career Personnel Conslt, *Exec Srch*
Clertech Group, Inc., *Exec Srch*
Dunhill of Baton Rouge, *Exec Srch*
Dunhill Professional Search, *Exec Srch*
Frazee Recruiting Conslt, *Exec Srch*
Interim Personnel, *Temp Agcy*
Mngmt. Rcrtrs. of Metairie/Sales Conslt of Metairie, *Exec Srch*
Mngmt. Rcrtrs. of St. Tammany, *Exec Srch*
Manpower, Inc., *Temp Agcy*
Professional Temporaries, *Temp Agcy*
River Region Personnel, Inc., *Exec Srch*
Talley & Associates, Inc./Talley Temporaries, *Exec Srch*
TECH 2000 Services & Staffing, Inc., *Temp Agcy*
Universal Personnel, *Contract Svc*
Westaff, *Temp Agcy*

Maine
Adecco/TAD Tech. Svcs., *Contract Svc*
Bonney Staffing & Training Centers, *Perm Agcy*
Express Personnel Service, *Perm Agcy*
Global Engineers, Inc., *Contract Svc*

Maryland
Caplan/Gross Associates, Inc., *Exec Srch*
Charter Business Services, *Perm Agcy*
Chesapeake Consulting Group, *Exec Srch*
DanSources Tech. Services, *Contract Svc*
Echelon Service Company, *Contract Svc*
Employer Employee Exchange, *Exec Srch*
A.G. Fishkin and Associates, *Exec Srch*
Graham Staffing Services, *Perm Agcy*
J.R. Associates, *Perm Agcy*
Ken Leiner Associates, Inc., *Exec Srch*
Mngmt. Rcrtrs. of Annapolis, *Exec Srch*
Mngmt. Rcrtrs. of Frederick/OfficeMates5, *Exec Srch*
Mark Hoefmeister & Associates Executive Recruiters, *Exec Srch*
Sales Conslt, *Exec Srch*
Sanford Rose Associates, *Exec Srch*
TCM Enterprises, *Exec Srch*
TAC Engineering Resources, *Temp Agcy*
Tech/Aid of Maryland, *Temp Agcy*
Technical Talent Locators, *Perm Agcy*
Tri-Serv Inc., *Perm Agcy*
Virtual Staffing Services, *Perm Agcy*

Massachusetts
ABA Personnel, Inc., *Temp Agcy*
Abbott's of Boston, Inc., *Exec Srch*
Ability Srch of New England, *Perm Agcy*
Aerotek, Inc., *Contract Svc*
B&M Associates, *Temp Agcy*
Battalia Winston International, *Exec Srch*
CDI Corporation, *Contract Svc*
Corporate Growth Resources, *Exec Srch*
Digital Arts Group, *Contract Svc*
Diversified Comm. Group, *Exec Srch*
Diversity Associates, *Exec Srch*
Diversity Search Specialists, *Exec Srch*
EMSI, *Temp Agcy*
Entegee, *Perm Agcy*
The Environmental Careers Organization, *Contract Svc*
HM Associates, *Exec Srch*
Hoffman Recruiters, *Exec Srch*
Interim Technology, *Contract Svc*
Kelly Services, Inc., *Temp Agcy*
Lake Conslt, *Exec Srch*
The Littleton Group, *Exec Srch*
Lynx Inc., *Contract Svc*
Mngmt. Rcrtrs. International, *Exec Srch*
Manpower Temp. Services, *Temp Agcy*
Master Search, *Exec Srch*
Micro-Comm Exec. Search, *Exec Srch*
National Engineering Svc., *Temp Agcy*
Nationwide Business Service, *Perm Agcy*
Need Personnel Placement, *Temp Agcy*
Norrell Staffing Services, *Contract Svc*
Open Systems Technologies, *Perm Agcy*
Pendleton James Associates, *Exec Srch*
Pomerantz Staffing Services, *Temp Agcy*
Pro Staff, *Temp Agcy*
Progressive Search Associates, *Exec Srch*
Propos Associates, Inc., *Perm Agcy*
J.E. Ranta Associates, *Exec Srch*

Career Circuit, *Career/Outplacement*
Carlile Personnel Agency, *Perm Agcy*
Colton Partnership, *Exec Srch*
Contract Specialties Group, *Contract Svc*
Corporate Careers, Inc., *Exec Srch*
The Dartmouth Group, *Exec Srch*
Maggi Dolan Placement, Inc., *Perm Agcy*
Dymanex Search Inc., *Exec Srch*
EDP Contract Services, *Contract Svc*
The Employment Store/TES Technical, *Exec Srch*
Execu/Search Group, *Exec Srch*
Exek Recruiters Ltd., *Exec Srch*
Gardiner, Townsend & Assoc., *Exec Srch*
Graphic Techniques, Inc., *Temp Agcy*
Hampshire Associates, Inc., *Perm Agcy*
Information Syst. Resources, *Exec Srch*
Irene Kane Personnel, *Exec Srch*
Kelly Services, Inc., *Temp Agcy*
Fred Koffler Associates, *Exec Srch*
Ktech Systems Group, Inc., *Perm Agcy*
Lab Support Inc., *Temp Agcy*
Lake Associates, *Exec Srch*
Landover Associates, Inc., *Exec Srch*
Magill Associates, Inc., *Exec Srch*
Mngmt. Rcrtrs. of Nassau Inc., *Exec Srch*
Manpower Tech. Services, *Temp Agcy*
Manpower Temp. Services, *Temp Agcy*
Mar-El Employment Agency, *Exec Srch*
Metro Resources of Rochester Inc., *Temp Agcy*
Metropolitan Pers. Systems, *Exec Srch*
Milazzo Associates, Inc., *Perm Agcy*
Morgan-Murray Personnel/M&M Top Temps, *Temp Agcy*
Natek Corporation, *Exec Srch*
Nesco Service Company, *Temp Agcy*
Network Dynamics, *Exec Srch*
Noah Associates, *Perm Agcy*
Norrell Staffing Services, *Temp Agcy*
K.A. Nowack Career Specialists, *Perm Agcy*
Olsten Staffing Services, *Temp Agcy*
Parsons, Anderson and Gee, *Perm Agcy*
Pathway Executive Search., *Exec Srch*
Pencom Systems Incorporated, *Exec Srch*
Pendleton James Associates, *Exec Srch*
RCM Technologies, Inc., *Perm Agcy*
RHI Consulting, *Exec Srch*
Recruitment International Grp, *Exec Srch*
Fran Rogers Personnel, *Perm Agcy*
Sales Search, Ltd./Executive Resume Service, *Exec Srch*
Sharp Placement Pros., *Exec Srch*
Snelling Personnel Services, *Perm Agcy*
Staff Managers, *Temp Agcy*
Staffing Solutions USA, Inc., *Temp Agcy*
Superior Concepts, *Contract Svc*
Sutton Staffing, *Exec Srch*
TMP Worldwide, *Exec Srch*
Venture Resources, *Exec Srch*
Charles Wanner Associates, *Exec Srch*
Wayne Group Ltd., *Exec Srch*
Westaff, *Temp Agcy*
Westchester Emp. Agency, *Perm Agcy*
H.L. Yoh Company, *Temp Agcy*
Michael D. Zinn & Associates, *Exec Srch*

North Carolina
A First Resource, *Exec Srch*
Accurate Staffing Conslt, *Exec Srch*
Action Staffing Group, *Temp Agcy*
Alpha Omega Exec. Search, *Exec Srch*
American Quality Staffing, *Exec Srch*
AmeriPro Search, Inc., *Exec Srch*
Anderson & Daniel Personnel Associates, *Perm Agcy*
Arjay & Associates, *Exec Srch*
Atchison & Associates, Inc., *Exec Srch*
CDI IT Services, *Contract Svc*
COMFORCE Tech. Svcs., *Contract Svc*
Creative Resource Systems, *Exec Srch*
Eastern Search Group, *Exec Srch*
Ellis Associates, Inc., *Exec Srch*
Executive Staffing Group, *Exec Srch*
Express Personnel Services, *Temp Agcy*
Forbes Temporary Staffing, *Temp Agcy*
F-O-R-T-U-N-E Pers. Conslts of Charlotte, *Exec Srch*
Graham & Associates, *Perm Agcy*
Granite Personnel Service, *Perm Agcy*
Information Systems Pros., *Exec Srch*

Interim Personnel, Inc., *Temp Agcy*
Kelly Services, Inc., *Temp Agcy*
Mngmt. Rcrtrs. International, *Exec Srch*
Mark III Personnel Inc., *Exec Srch*
Merrick & Moore, *Exec Srch*
Moffitt International, Inc., *Exec Srch*
Olsten Staffing Services, *Temp Agcy*
PCS, *Contract Svc*
Quality Temporary Services, *Temp Agcy*
Romac International, *Exec Srch*
SENC Technical Services, *Contract Svc*
Sales Conslt, *Exec Srch*
Snelling Personnel Services, *Perm Agcy*
Sockwell & Associates, *Exec Srch*
StaffMark, *Temp Agcy*
USA Staffing, *Perm Agcy*
Volt Technical Services, *Contract Svc*
Wilson Personnel Inc., *Exec Srch*

North Dakota
Career Connection, *Exec Srch*
Olsten Staffing Services/Expressway Personnel, *Temp Agcy*

Ohio
Adecco/TAD Tech. Svcs., *Contract Svc*
Advancement LLC, *Contract Svc*
Alliance Tech. Services, *Contract Svc*
AllTech Resources, Inc., *Exec Srch*
Dave Arnold & Associates, *Exec Srch*
Baldwin & Associates, *Exec Srch*
Belcan Technical Services, *Contract Svc*
CBS Personnel Services, *Perm Agcy*
Career Enterprises, *Exec Srch*
Clopton's Placement Service, *Perm Agcy*
Corell Associates, *Perm Agcy*
Cross-Jordan Corporation, *Exec Srch*
Custom Staffing, Inc., *Temp Agcy*
DLD Technical Services, *Contract Svc*
Data Bank Corporation, *Exec Srch*
Alan N. Daum & Associates, *Perm Agcy*
Tonia Deal Conslt, *Exec Srch*
Eastern Personnel Services, *Perm Agcy*
Elite Resources Group, *Exec Srch*
Executech, *Exec Srch*
Executive Directions, *Exec Srch*
Executive Search Ltd., *Exec Srch*
F.L.A.G., *Exec Srch*
Fitzpatrick & Associates, *Exec Srch*
Frederick-Lehmann & Associates/Temporarily Yours, *Exec Srch*
Gayhart & Associates, *Exec Srch*
Global Resources Group, *Contract Svc*
Griffiths & Associates, *Exec Srch*
Russ Hadick & Associates, *Exec Srch*
Health Care Advantage, *Exec Srch*
Hite Executive Search/Hite Management Conslt, Inc., *Exec Srch*
ITS Technical Staffing, *Exec Srch*
Interim Personnel, *Temp Agcy*
KBK Management Associates, *Exec Srch*
Mngmt. Rcrtrs. International, *Exec Srch*
Manpower Temp. Services, *Temp Agcy*
Minority Executive Search, *Exec Srch*
North Star Resources, *Contract Svc*
Olsten Prof. Staffing Services, *Exec Srch*
Personalized Placement, *Exec Srch*
Professional Emp. Services, *Perm Agcy*
Providence Pers. Conslt, *Exec Srch*
Quality Plus, *Exec Srch*
RDS, Inc., *Contract Svc*
S&P Solutions, *Contract Svc*
Sales Conslt, *Exec Srch*
Sanford Rose Associates, *Exec Srch*
Tabb & Associates, *Exec Srch*
Talent Research Corporation, *Exec Srch*
The Target Human Resource Companies, Inc., *Temp Agcy*
Teamwork U.S.A., *Contract Svc*
Tech/Aid of Ohio, *Perm Agcy*
Technical Recruiting Services, *Exec Srch*
Temporarily Yours Placement, *Temp Agcy*
Fred C. Tippel and Associates, *Exec Srch*
Vector Technical Inc., *Perm Agcy*

Oklahoma
Ameri Resource, *Exec Srch*
Express Personnel Services, *Exec Srch*
Huddleston Associates, *Exec Srch*
Key Temporary Personnel, *Temp Agcy*
Mngmt. Rcrtrs. International, *Exec Srch*
John Wylie Associates, Inc., *Exec Srch*

Oregon
APA Employment Agency, *Exec Srch*
CDI Technical Services, *Contract Svc*
Executives Worldwide, Inc., *Exec Srch*
Express Personnel Services, *Exec Srch*
Initial Staffing Services, *Perm Agcy*
Kelly Services, Inc., *Temp Agcy*
Mngmt. Rcrtrs. of Portland/OfficeMates5 of Portland, *Exec Srch*
Manpower Temp. Services, *Temp Agcy*
Nationwide Personnel Recruiting & Consulting Inc. (NPRC), *Exec Srch*
Uniforce Staffing Services, *Contract Svc*
Volt Services Group, *Contract Svc*
Woodworth Intnl. Group, *Exec Srch*

Pennsylvania
AA Staffing Solutions, Inc., *Contract Svc*
Alexander Personnel Assoc., *Exec Srch*
American Staffing Resources, *Temp Agcy*
Atomic Personnel, Inc., *Exec Srch*
T.W. Boris Associates, *Exec Srch*
Bradley Professional Svcs., *Perm Agcy*
CDI Corporation, *Contract Svc*
Career Concepts Staffing Svcs, *Exec Srch*
Career Quest Confidential, *Exec Srch*
Century Associates, *Exec Srch*
R. Christine Associates, *Exec Srch*
CoreStaff Inc., *Temp Agcy*
EDP Contract Services, *Contract Svc*
Executive Avail-A-Search, *Exec Srch*
Fox-Morris Associates, *Exec Srch*
J.H. Glass & Associates, *Exec Srch*
Jerry Goldberg & Associates, *Perm Agcy*
HRS/TND Associates, Inc., *Exec Srch*
Hobbie Personnel Services, *Temp Agcy*
IMC International, Inc., *Contract Svc*
Interim Personnel, *Temp Agcy*
J-Rand Search, *Exec Srch*
JK Resources, *Exec Srch*
Kelly Services, Inc., *Temp Agcy*
Blair Kershaw Associates, *Exec Srch*
Lab Support Inc., *Temp Agcy*
Robert Lohrke Associates, *Exec Srch*
London Personnel Services, *Perm Agcy*
Main Line Personnel Service, *Perm Agcy*
Mngmt. Rcrtrs./CompuSearch, *Exec Srch*
Manpower Temp. Services, *Temp Agcy*
George R. Martin Exec. Srch, *Exec Srch*
Robert McClure Ltd., *Exec Srch*
The Morris Group, *Exec Srch*
National Computerized Employment Service Inc., *Exec Srch*
Norrell Services, *Temp Agcy*
Olsten Staffing Services, *Temp Agcy*
LaMonte Owens, Inc., *Exec Srch*
Prestige Personnel, *Exec Srch*
Probe Technology, *Exec Srch*
Quest Systems, Inc., *Perm Agcy*
R.H.A. Executive Pers. Svcs., *Exec Srch*
Romac International, *Exec Srch*
SHS International, *Exec Srch*
SPC F-O-R-T-U-N-E, *Exec Srch*
Sanford Rose Associates, *Exec Srch*
Strongin Technical Enterprises of Pennsylvania, Inc., *Perm Agcy*
Suber & McAuley Technical Search, *Exec Srch*
Systems Personnel Inc., *Exec Srch*
TECH/AID of PA, *Contract Svc*
Texcel, Inc., *Exec Srch*
Uni-Temp Temp. Service, *Temp Agcy*
Virtual Workplace, Inc., *Temp Agcy*
Whittlesey & Associates, Inc., *Exec Srch*
Witthauer Associates Ltd., *Exec Srch*
Yorktowne Personnel, *Exec Srch*

Rhode Island
Colony Personnel Associates, *Temp Agcy*
Kelly Services, Inc., *Temp Agcy*
Albert G. Lee & Associates, *Exec Srch*
Lybrook Associates, Inc., *Exec Srch*
Mngmt. Rcrtrs. International, *Exec Srch*
Norrell Services, *Temp Agcy*
Nugent Associates, *Exec Srch*
Occupations Unlimited, Inc., *Perm Agcy*
On Line Staff Inc., *Temp Agcy*
PKS Associates, Inc., *Exec Srch*
Summit Technical Services, *Contract Svc*

South Carolina
Accel Temporary Services, *Temp Agcy*
Bock & Associates, *Exec Srch*

Florida
Active Wireless Inc., *Exec Srch*
Ash & Assoc. Exec. Search, *Exec Srch*
Caradyne Group, *Exec Srch*
COMFORCE, *Contract Svc*
F-O-R-T-U-N-E Pers. Conslts, *Exec Srch*
Mngmt. Rcrtrs. International, *Exec Srch*
Manchester Inc., *Exec Srch*
The Stewart Search Group, *Exec Srch*
Uniquest International, Inc., *Exec Srch*

Georgia
Bell Oaks Company, *Exec Srch*
Corporate Resources, Inc., *Exec Srch*
Delta Resource Group, *Exec Srch*
Executive Strategies, Inc., *Exec Srch*
Tennant & Associates, *Exec Srch*
Think Resources, *Contract Svc*
Van Zant Resource Group, *Perm. Agcy*

Hawaii
Executive Support Hawaii, *Perm Agcy*

Illinois
Advancement Inc., *Exec Srch*
Bonner & Stricklin & Assoc., *Exec Srch*
Bratland & Associates, *Exec Srch*
COMFORCE Telecom, *Contract Svc*
Corporate Conslt, *Exec Srch*
Data Career Center, Inc., *Exec Srch*
First Search, Inc., *Exec Srch*
Manpower Temp. Services, *Temp Agcy*
SHS, Inc., *Exec Srch*
Sales Conslt of Chicago, *Exec Srch*
Search Source, *Exec Srch*
The Stanton Group, Inc., *Exec Srch*
Stone Enterprises, Ltd., *Exec Srch*

Indiana
Unique, Inc., *Exec Srch*

Iowa
F-O-R-T-U-N-E Pers. Conslts., *Exec Srch*
Humbert Group, *Exec Srch*

Maine
Mountain Ltd., *Exec Srch*

Maryland
Corporate Resources, *Exec Srch*
A.G. Fishkin and Associates, *Exec Srch*
F-O-R-T-U-N-E Pers. Conslts, *Exec Srch*
Sales Conslt, *Exec Srch*

Massachusetts
Aerotek, Inc., *Contract Svc*
Bell Oaks Company, *Exec Srch*
Bowdoin Group, *Exec Srch*
Carter/MacKay, *Exec Srch*
Franklin International Search, *Exec Srch*
HM Associates, *Exec Srch*
New Dimensions in Tech., *Exec Srch*
Professional Placement Consulting Group (PPCG), *Exec Srch*
Sales & Marketing Search, *Exec Srch*
L.A. Silver Associates, *Exec Srch*
TASA International, *Exec Srch*

Michigan
Advanced Resources of MI, *Contract Svc*
Business Trends, Inc., *Perm Agcy*
Sales Conslt, *Exec Srch*
Sullivan & Associates, *Exec Srch*

Minnesota
Add On Staffing Solutions, *Exec Srch*

Missouri
Information Systems Consulting Corporation, *Exec Srch*
Sanford Rose Associates, *Exec Srch*

Montana
Caria Resources, Inc., *Exec Srch*

Nebraska
Sales Conslt of Omaha, *Exec Srch*

Nevada
Sales Staffing Specialists, *Perm Agcy*

New Hampshire
Linford E. Stiles Associates, *Exec Srch*
Warren, Morris & Madison, *Exec Srch*

New Jersey
Baker Scott & Company, *Exec Srch*
Common Agenda, *Exec Srch*
The Dowd Group, *Exec Srch*

Dreier Consulting, *Exec Srch*
E&A Associates, *Exec Srch*
Huff Associates, *Exec Srch*
Kiley, Owen & McGovern, *Exec Srch*
L&K Associates, *Exec Srch*
M.R. Group, Inc., *Exec Srch*
Madison Executive Search, *Exec Srch*
Mngmt. Rcrtrs. International of Morris County, *Exec Srch*
Rosenthal Associates Intnl., *Exec Srch*
Shifrin-Fischer Group, *Exec Srch*
SnellingSearch, *Exec Srch*
Softrix, Inc., *Exec Srch*
The Stelton Group, Inc., *Exec Srch*
Telequest Communications, *Exec Srch*

New Mexico
Manpower, Inc., *Temp Agcy*

New York
Norman Broadbent Intnl., *Exec Srch*
CK Resources, *Exec Srch*
COMFORCE Telecom, *Contract Svc*
Executive Exchange, *Exec Srch*
Gardiner, Townsend & Assoc., *Exec Srch*
Huntington Pers. Conslt, *Exec Srch*
Manpower Temp. Services, *Temp Agcy*
National Field Service Corp., *Perm Agcy*
Resource Services, Inc., *Exec Srch*
Rosenthal Assoc. Intnl., *Exec Srch*
Sales Conslt, *Exec Srch*
StratfordGroup, *Exec Srch*

North Carolina
COMFORCE Telecom, *Contract Svc*
Paul Day & Associates, *Exec Srch*
mf Branch Associates, *Exec Srch*
MKR Personnel Solutions, *Contract Svc*
Sales Conslt of Concord, *Exec Srch*
StratfordGroup, *Exec Srch*
David Weinfeld Group, *Exec Srch*

Ohio
Fitzpatrick & Associates, *Exec Srch*
Guthoff & Associates, *Exec Srch*
StratfordGroup, *Exec Srch*
Teknon Emp. Resources, Inc., *Exec Srch*

Oklahoma
Mngmt. Rcrtrs. International, *Exec Srch*

Pennsylvania
Advanced Tech. Resources, *Exec Srch*
D'Elia & Associates, Inc., *Exec Srch*
Eclectic International, *Exec Srch*
Lawrence Personnel, *Exec Srch*
Mngmt. Rcrtrs. International, *Exec Srch*
Manchester Inc., *Career/Outplacement*
Manpower Temp. Services, *Temp Agcy*
StratfordGroup, *Exec Srch*
Terry Taylor & Associates, *Exec Srch*
Tell/Com Recruiters, *Exec Srch*

Rhode Island
Pro-Search, Inc., *Exec Srch*

South Carolina
Columbus Intnl. Group, *Exec Srch*

Tennessee
Mngmt. Rcrtrs. of Chattanooga-Brainerd/Sales Conslt, *Exec Srch*
Software Resource Conslt, *Exec Srch*

Texas
Bundy-Stewart Associates, *Exec Srch*
CDI Telecommunications, *Contract Svc*
Eissler & Associates, *Exec Srch*
Information Systems Consulting Corporation, *Exec Srch*
Inside Track, *Exec Srch*
Mngmt. Rcrtrs. of LBJ Park/Dallas, *Exec Srch*
Opportunity Unlimited Personnel Conslt, *Exec Srch*
ProSearch Recruiting, *Exec Srch*
Sales Conslt of Austin, *Exec Srch*
StratfordGroup, *Exec Srch*
Bruce G. Woods Exec. Search, *Exec Srch*

Utah
Mngmt. Rcrtrs. of Provo, *Exec Srch*

Virginia
Norman Broadbent Intnl., *Exec Srch*
Dahl Morrow International, *Exec Srch*
FGI, *Exec Srch*
Wayne Garber & Associates, *Exec Srch*

Hamilton Group, Inc., *Exec Srch*
Mngmt. Rcrtrs. International, *Exec Srch*
Paul-Tittle Associates, Inc., *Exec Srch*
Strategic Search, Inc., *Exec Srch*
Telecom Recruiters, *Exec Srch*
Warren, Morris & Madison, *Exec Srch*

Washington
Anchor Associates, Inc., *Exec Srch*
Mngmt. Rcrtrs. of Lakewood, *Exec Srch*
ROI International, *Exec Srch*
StratfordGroup, *Exec Srch*

Wisconsin
Aerotek, Inc., *Contract Svc*
Delta Recruiting, *Exec Srch*
Mngmt. Rcrtrs. Intnl. (MRI), *Exec Srch*
Sanford Rose Associates, *Exec Srch*

TRANSPORTATION

Alabama
Clark Pers. Service of Mobile, *Exec Srch*
Labor Finders, *Temp Agcy*
Mngmt. Rcrtrs. International, *Exec Srch*
Mngmt. Rcrtrs. of North AL, *Exec Srch*

Arizona
Amer. Career Grp, *Career/Outplacement*
The Bren Group, *Exec Srch*
Clifford & Associates, *Perm Agcy*
Dealer Connection, *Perm Agcy*
Mngmt. Rcrtrs. of Scottsdale, *Exec Srch*
Spectra International, *Exec Srch*
Taylor Design Recruiting, *Temp Agcy*

Arkansas
Mngmt. Rcrtrs., *Exec Srch*
Penmac Personnel Service, *Perm Agcy*
Snelling Search, *Exec Srch*

California
Alpha-Net Consulting Group, *Exec Srch*
Apropos Emp. Agency, *Perm Agcy*
Blue, Garni & Company, *Exec Srch*
Business Systems Support, *Perm Agcy*
CDS Staffing Services, *Contract Svc*
California Search Agency, *Exec Srch*
Career Quest International, *Contract Svc*
Complete Staffing Resources, *Perm Agcy*
The Culver Group, *Exec Srch*
Culver Personnel Services, *Perm Agcy*
Drake Office Overload, *Temp Agcy*
Ethos Consulting, Inc., *Exec Srch*
Fisher Personnel Mngmt Svcs, *Exec Srch*
Garnett Staffing, *Temp Agcy*
International Staffing Conslt, *Exec Srch*
LeBlanc & Associates, *Exec Srch*
Mngmt. Rcrtrs. Inland Empire Agency, *Exec Srch*
Mngmt. Rcrtrs. International, *Exec Srch*
Edward Rast and Company, *Exec Srch*
Scott-Thaler Associates, Inc., *Exec Srch*
Thor Temporary Services, *Temp Agcy*
The Truman Agency, *Perm Agcy*
Westaff, *Temp Agcy*
Work Load Inc., *Temp Agcy*

Colorado
F-O-R-T-U-N-E Pers. Conslts, *Exec Srch*
Information Systems Consulting Corporation, *Exec Srch*
JobSearch, *Temp Agcy*
Labor Ready, Inc., *Temp Agcy*
SOS Staffing Services, *Temp Agcy*
Sales Conslt of Denver, *Exec Srch*
Todays Temporary, *Temp Agcy*
Woodmoor Group, *Exec Srch*

Connecticut
Admiral Staffing Services, *Temp Agcy*
Brandywine Retained Ventures, Inc., *Exec Srch*
Mngmt. Rcrtrs. of Norwalk, *Exec Srch*
Barry Persky & Co., *Exec Srch*

Delaware
Independent National Search & Associates (INS), *Exec Srch*

Florida
AAA Employment, *Perm Agcy*
Able Body Corporate Svcs., *Contract Svc*
Ambiance Personnel Inc., *Perm Agcy*
DGA Personnel Group, Inc., *Exec Srch*
F-O-R-T-U-N-E Pers. Conslts, *Exec Srch*
Mngmt. Rcrtrs. of Tallahassee, *Exec Srch*

Manchester Inc., *Exec Srch*
OMNIpartners, *Exec Srch*
Sales Conslt of Fort Lauderdale, Inc., *Exec Srch*

Georgia
A-OK Personnel, *Perm Agcy*
All-Star Temp. & Emp. Svcs, *Temp Agcy*
Boreham International, *Exec Srch*
Dunhill Professional Search, *Exec Srch*
Mngmt. Rcrtrs. International/Sales Conslt, *Exec Srch*
Mngmt. Rcrtrs. of Atlanta, *Exec Srch*
Mngmt. Rcrtrs. of Marietta, *Exec Srch*
Randstad Staffing Services, *Temp Agcy*

Hawaii
Executive Search World, *Exec Srch*

Illinois
Bevelle & Associates, Inc., *Exec Srch*
CareerLink USA, Inc., *Exec Srch*
J.C.G. Limited, Inc., *Perm Agcy*
Mngmt. Rcrtrs. International, *Exec Srch*
John R. O'Connor & Assoc., *Exec Srch*
OfficeMates5, *Perm Agcy*
Parker Cromwell & Assoc., *Exec Srch*
Staffing Team International, *Temp Agcy*
Stivers Temporary Personnel, *Temp Agcy*
Strand Associates, Inc., *Perm Agcy*

Indiana
Execusearch, *Exec Srch*
Mngmt. Rcrtrs. of Richmond, *Exec Srch*
OM5/DayStar Temp. Services, *Exec Srch*
Personnel Plus, Inc., *Exec Srch*
Warrick County Emp. & Training Center, *Career/Outplacement*

Iowa
Mngmt. Rcrtrs. International, *Exec Srch*
Sanford Rose Associates, *Exec Srch*

Kansas
Mngmt. Rcrtrs. of Overland Park/Sales Conslt/OfficeMates5, *Exec Srch*
Smith Brown & Jones, *Exec Srch*

Kentucky
Angel Group International, *Exec Srch*

Louisiana
Mngmt. Rcrtrs. of Metairie/Sales Conslt of Metairie, *Exec Srch*
Talley & Associates, Inc./Talley Temporaries, *Exec Srch*

Maine
At Work Personnel Service, *Temp Agcy*
F-O-R-T-U-N-E Pers. Conslts of Bangor, *Exec Srch*

Maryland
American Service Tech., *Contract Svc*
Mngmt. Rcrtrs. of Annapolis, *Exec Srch*
Mngmt. Rcrtrs. of Frederick/OfficeMates5, *Exec Srch*
TAC Staffing Services, *Temp Agcy*

Massachusetts
Derek Associates, *Exec Srch*
Endicott & Colby/Placement Company, *Temp Agcy*
Mngmt. Rcrtrs. International, *Exec Srch*
Sales Conslt, *Exec Srch*

Michigan
Associates, *Exec Srch*
Beacon Services Inc., *Exec Srch*
Day Personnel, Inc., *Perm Agcy*
Executive Recruiters Intnl., *Exec Srch*
William Howard Agency, *Contract Svc*
Job Fair Network of MI, *Perm Agcy*
Mngmt. Rcrtrs. International, *Exec Srch*
METROSTAFF, *Exec Srch*
Nustar Temporary Services, *Temp Agcy*
Thomas & Associates of MI, *Exec Srch*
Unlimited Staffing Solutions, Inc., *Contract Svc*

Minnesota
Advance Personnel Resources, *Exec Srch*
Mngmt. Rcrtrs. of Minneapolis/Sales Conslt, *Exec Srch*

Mississippi
The CPI Group, *Exec Srch*
EPSCO Personnel Service *Temp Agcy*

Recruitment & Training Programs of Mississippi, *Perm Agcy*

Missouri
Agri-Tech Personnel, Inc., *Exec Srch*
Business Personnel Services, *Temp Agcy*
The Christiansen Group, *Exec Srch*
Employer Advantage, *Exec Srch*
Information Systems Consulting Corporation, *Exec Srch*
Mngmt. Rcrtrs. of Kansas City, *Exec Srch*
Mngmt. Rcrtrs. of Springfield, *Exec Srch*
Mngmt. Rcrtrs. of St. Louis/Sales Conslt, *Exec Srch*
Mngmt. Rcrtrs. of St. Louis, *Exec Srch*
Manpower Temp. Services, *Temp Agcy*
J. Miles Personnel Services, *Exec Srch*
OfficeMates5 (OM5), *Exec Srch*

Nebraska
Compusearch of Lincoln, *Exec Srch*
Corporate Recruiters, Ltd./Health Service Professionals, *Exec Srch*
Express Personnel, *Exec Srch*
Hansen Employment Service, *Exec Srch*
Mngmt. Rcrtrs. of Omaha/OfficeMates5, *Exec Srch*
Noll Human Resource Svcs., *Exec Srch*
Sales Conslt of Omaha, *Exec Srch*

Nevada
Flowers Exec. Search Group, *Exec Srch*
Mngmt. Rcrtrs. of Lake Tahoe, NV, *Exec Srch*

New Hampshire
Able 1 Staffing, *Exec Srch*
Futures, Inc., *Exec Srch*
Mngmt. Rcrtrs. Intnl., *Exec Srch*
National Employment Service Corporation, *Perm Agcy*
TAC Staffing Services, *Temp Agcy*

New Jersey
Advance Positions Inc., *Exec Srch*
Robert Drexler Associates, *Exec Srch*
Dynamic Quality Search, *Exec Srch*
Ellis Career Conslt/Career Search Associates, *Exec Srch*
Mngmt. Rcrtrs. of Bridgewater, *Exec Srch*
Mngmt. Rcrtrs. of Passaic Cty, *Exec Srch*
Mayfair Services, *Perm Agcy*
OfficeMates5/DayStar Temporary Services, *Perm Agcy*
Orion Consulting, Inc., *Exec Srch*
Sales Conslt of Sparta, *Exec Srch*
Sparta Group, *Exec Srch*
Summit Group, Inc., *Exec Srch*

New Mexico
Albuquerque Personnel, Inc., *Perm Agcy*
CDI Technical Services, *Contract Svc*

New York
APA Search, *Exec Srch*
Canny, Bowen Inc., *Exec Srch*
Gardiner, Townsend & Assoc., *Exec Srch*
R.I. James Inc., *Exec Srch*
Kirk-Mayer, *Contract Svc*
Mngmt. Rcrtrs. of Orange Cty, *Exec Srch*
Metropolitan Personnel Syst., *Exec Srch*
Noah Associates, *Perm Agcy*
StratfordGroup, *Exec Srch*
Tyler Search Conslt, *Exec Srch*
Yours In Travel Pers. Agcy, *Perm Agcy*

North Carolina
Anderson & Daniel Pers., *Perm Agcy*
F-O-R-T-U-N-E Pers. Conslts, *Exec Srch*
Interim Personnel, Inc., *Temp Agcy*
The Jobs Market, *Perm Agcy*
Mngmt. Rcrtrs. International, *Exec Srch*
Olsten Staffing Services, *Temp Agcy*
Sales Conslt of High Point, *Exec Srch*
StratfordGroup, *Exec Srch*
Waddy R. Thomson Assoc., *Exec Srch*
USA Staffing, *Perm Agcy*

North Dakota
Olsten Staffing Services/Expressway Personnel, *Temp Agcy*

Ohio
Adecco/TAD Tech. Svcs., *Contract Svc*
CBS Personnel Services, *Perm Agcy*

Choice Personnel/LaGrange & Associates, *Exec Srch*
Tonia Deal Conslt, *Exec Srch*
Eastern Personnel Services, *Perm Agcy*
Elite Resources Group, *Exec Srch*
Ives & Associates, Inc., *Exec Srch*
Leith & Associates, *Exec Srch*
Mngmt. Rcrtrs. International, *Exec Srch*
Marvel Conslt Inc., *Exec Srch*
Minority Executive Search, *Exec Srch*
National Register of Akron, *Exec Srch*
National Register of Toledo, *Exec Srch*
North American Tech. Svcs., *Temp Agcy*
Providence Pers. Conslt, *Exec Srch*
Quality Plus, *Exec Srch*
Sales Conslt, *Exec Srch*
Speer & Associates, *Exec Srch*
StratfordGroup, *Exec Srch*

Oklahoma
Mngmt. Rcrtrs. International, *Exec Srch*

Oregon
Barrett Business Services, *Temp Agcy*
Mngmt. Rcrtrs. of Portland/OfficeMates5, *Exec Srch*
Woodworth Intnl. Group, *Exec Srch*

Pennsylvania
CDI Corporation, *Contract Svc*
CoreStaff Inc., *Temp Agcy*
Eden & Associates, Inc., *Exec Srch*
IMC International, Inc., *Contract Svc*
J-Rand Search, *Exec Srch*
Kathy Karr Personnel, *Perm Agcy*
Mngmt. Rcrtrs./CompuSearch, *Exec Srch*
Mngmt. Rcrtrs. of Reading/CAREER SENTINEL, *Exec Srch*
Manchester Inc., *Career/Outplacement*
R.H.A. Exec. Pers. Services, *Exec Srch*
StratfordGroup, *Exec Srch*
TAC Staffing Services, *Temp Agcy*
W.G. Tucker & Associates, *Exec Srch*

Rhode Island
Mngmt. Rcrtrs. International, *Exec Srch*
Norrell Services, *Temp Agcy*
Sullivan & Cogliano, *Exec Srch*
TAC Staffing Services, *Temp Agcy*

South Carolina
F-O-R-T-U-N-E Pers. Conslts, *Exec Srch*
F-O-R-T-U-N-E Pers. Conslts of Columbia, *Exec Srch*
Mngmt. Rcrtrs. of Columbia, *Exec Srch*
Mngmt. Rcrtrs. of Rock Hill, *Exec Srch*
Snelling Personnel Services, *Perm Agcy*

Tennessee
Express Personnel Services, *Perm Agcy*
Mngmt. Rcrtrs. of Brentwood/Sales Conslt, *Exec Srch*
Mngmt. Rcrtrs. of Knoxville, *Exec Srch*
Personnel Link, *Exec Srch*

Texas
Abilene Employment Service, *Perm Agcy*
American Resources, *Exec Srch*
Aware Affiliates Pers. Svc., *Perm Agcy*
Creative Staffing Services, *Perm Agcy*
Driving Force, Inc., *Temp Agcy*
The Elsworth Group, *Exec Srch*
FoodPro Recruiters, Inc., *Exec Srch*
Information Systems Consulting Corporation, *Exec Srch*
Kelly Services, Inc., *Temp Agcy*
Mngmt. Rcrtrs. International, *Exec Srch*
Mngmt. Rcrtrs. of Dallas, *Exec Srch*
McKinley-AREND Intnl., *Exec Srch*
Noll Human Resource Svcs., *Exec Srch*
Pailin Grp. Prof. Srch Conslt, *Exec Srch*
Priority Search, Inc., *Exec Srch*
ProSearch Recruiting, *Exec Srch*
Resource Connection Workforce Center, *Perm Agcy*
Roth Young Executive Search, *Exec Srch*
Sales Conslt of Houston, *Exec Srch*
StratfordGroup, *Exec Srch*

Utah
Keysearch International, *Exec Srch*

Vermont
National Executive Search, *Exec Srch*

Virginia
The Alexis Group, Inc., *Exec Srch*

Alpha Omega Resources Inc., *Perm Agcy*
Mngmt. Rcrtrs. of McLean/
OfficeMates5, *Exec Srch*

Washington
CDI Corporation (West), *Contract Svc*
The Career Clinic, Inc., *Exec Srch*
Comprehensive Staffing Resources Inc.,
Temp Agcy
Jobs Unlimited, *Perm Agcy*
Mngmt. Rcrtrs. of Tacoma, *Exec Srch*
Manpower Temp. Services, *Temp Agcy*
StratfordGroup, *Exec Srch*

West Virginia
Key Personnel, *Perm Agcy*

Wisconsin
FoodStaff 2000, Inc., *Exec Srch*
Mngmt. Rcrtrs. of Appleton/
Compusearch, *Exec Srch*
Mngmt. Rcrtrs. of Green Bay, *Exec Srch*
Mngmt. Rcrtrs. of Milwaukee/
Sales Conslt, *Exec Srch*
Mngmt. Rcrtrs. of Milwaukee (South),
Exec Srch
Site Personnel Services, Inc./
Trainor/Frank & Assoc., *Temp Agcy*
Work Connection, *Perm Agcy*

TRAVEL

Arizona
The Bren Group, *Exec Srch*

Florida
Madison Travel Careers Unlimited, *Perm Agcy*

Georgia
Executive Strategies, Inc., *Exec Srch*

Massachusetts
Travel Career Network, Ltd., *Perm Agcy*
Travel Industry Conslt, *Perm Agcy*

New Jersey
Yours In Travel Pers. Agcy., *Perm Agcy*

New York
Allegheny Travel Services, *Perm Agcy*
Yours In Travel Pers. Agcy., *Perm Agcy*

Texas
Manpower Temp. Services, *Temp Agcy*
Travel Search Network, *Perm Agcy*

Virginia
Beth Daisey Associates, *Exec Srch*

WHOLESALING

California
Evie Kreisler & Associates, *Exec Srch*
Rollins & Assoc. Pers. Svc., *Exec Srch*

Georgia
Boreham International, *Exec Srch*

Illinois
Kenzer Corporation, *Exec Srch*

New York
Tyler Search Conslt, *Exec Srch*

Washington
Woodruff Associates, *Exec Srch*

WIRELESS COMMUNICATIONS

California
Cohen Associates, *Exec Srch*
Harley Associates, *Exec Srch*
LaCosta & Associates, *Exec Srch*
Tom Pezman & Associates, *Exec Srch*
Schweichler Associates Inc., *Exec Srch*
Warren, Morris & Madison, *Exec Srch*

Florida
Active Wireless Inc., *Exec Srch*
Caradyne Group, *Exec Srch*
Mngmt. Rcrtrs., *Exec Srch*

Georgia
Sanford Rose Associates, *Exec Srch*

Illinois
Advancement Inc., *Exec Srch*
National Search, *Exec Srch*

Maryland
A.G. Fishkin & Associates, *Exec Srch*

New Jersey
Advanced Technology Search, *Exec Srch*
Electronic Search Inc., *Exec Srch*
Mngmt. Rcrtrs. Intnl., *Exec Srch*
Pennington Consulting Group, *Exec Srch*

North Carolina
mf Branch Associates, *Exec Srch*

Tennessee
Software Resource Consltnts, *Exec Srch*

Texas
Bruce G. Woods Exec. Search, *Exec Srch*

Washington
Executive Recruiters, *Exec Srch*
Pro-Active Conslt, *Exec Srch*

WORD PROCESSING

Arizona
Manpower Tech. Services, *Temp Agcy*

California
CDI Information Services, *Contract Svc*
Complete Staffing Resources, *Perm Agcy*
Jason Best Agency, *Perm Agcy*
Manpower Staffing Services, *Temp Agcy*
Norrell Temporary Services, *Temp Agcy*
Remedy Intelligent Staffing, *Temp Agcy*
Wollborg-Michelson Personnel Service,
Perm Agcy

Colorado
Adecco, *Temp Agcy*
Staff Works, *Temp Agcy*

Dist. of Columbia
Manpower, *Temp Agcy*

Florida
Custom Staffing, Inc., *Temp Agcy*
Manpower Temp. Services, *Temp Agcy*
Office Specialists, *Temp Agcy*

Georgia
TempWorld Staffing Svcs., *Temp Agcy*

Illinois
The Esquire Staffing Group, *Perm Agcy*
Manpower Temp. Services, *Temp Agcy*
The Murphy Group, *Perm Agcy*
Pillar Personnel, *Temp Agcy*
Prestige Employment Svcs., *Perm Agcy*
Tempfleet, *Temp Agcy*
Thirty Three Pers. Center, *Perm Agcy*
West Personnel Service, *Perm Agcy*

Indiana
Adecco, *Temp Agcy*
Interim Personnel, *Temp Agcy*

Kentucky
BJM & Associates, Inc., *Contract Svc*

Maryland
Adecco, *Temp Agcy*

Massachusetts
Campbell Associates, *Exec Srch*
Endicott & Colby/Placement Company,
Temp Agcy
Manpower Temp. Services, *Temp Agcy*
Office Specialists, *Temp Agcy*
The Skill Bureau, Inc., *Perm Agcy*

Michigan
Manpower, Inc., *Temp Agcy*

Minnesota
Manpower Temp. Services, *Temp Agcy*

Missouri
Manpower Temp. Services, *Temp Agcy*

Nevada
Manpower Temp. Services, *Temp Agcy*

New Hampshire
Manpower Temp. Services, *Temp Agcy*

New Mexico
Manpower, Inc., *Temp Agcy*

New York
Filcro Personnel, *Perm Agcy*
Initial Staffing Services, *Perm Agcy*
Manpower Temp. Services, *Temp Agcy*
United Personnel Agency, *Perm Agcy*

Ohio
Belcan Staffing Services, *Temp Agcy*
Champion Personnel System, *Perm Agcy*
Manpower Temp. Services, *Temp Agcy*

Oregon
Manpower Temp. Services, *Temp Agcy*

Pennsylvania
Marsetta Lane Temp. Svcs., *Temp Agcy*
Manpower Temp. Services, *Temp Agcy*

Tennessee
Manpower, Inc., *Temp Agcy*

Texas
Manpower Temp. Services, *Temp Agcy*

Virginia
Manpower Temp. Svcs., *Temp Agcy*
Temporaries Now, *Temp Agcy*

Washington
Career Services, *Perm Agcy*
Manpower Temp. Svcs., *Temp Agcy*

BOSSLER-HIX FINANCIAL CAREERS • 241
THE BOSTIC GROUP, INC. • 528
THE BOSTON CAREER LINK • 296
BOSTON PROF. SEARCH • 269
BOSTON SEARCH GROUP • 269
BOSTONIAN PERSONNEL • 281
BOTT & ASSOCIATES • 565
BOTTOM LINE PROF. SVCS. • 345
BOULEWARE & ASSOC. • 186
BOVE ASSOCIATES INC. • 366
BOWDEN & COMPANY • 462
BOWDOIN GROUP • 269
THE BOWERS GROUP, INC. • 160
BOWERS THOMAS • 34
BOWMAN & COMPANY LLP • 366
BOWMAN & MARSHALL • 241
BOWMAN ASSOCIATES • 34
BOYDEN • 34, 129, 186, 335, 366, 400, 499
BOYDEN GLOBAL EXEC. SEARCH • 298
BOYLE & ASSOCIATES • 320
BOYLE OGATA • 34
BOZICH & CRUZ • 34
BRACK HUNTER CORP. • 239
BRACKIN & SAYERS ASSOC. • 500
BRADEN RESUME SOL. • 545
BRADFORD & GALT CONSULTING SERVICES • 341
BRADFORD COMPANY • 135
BRADFORD ONE STOP CAREER CENTER • 148
BRADFORD STAFF, INC. • 82
BRADIN SEARCH GROUP • 366
BRADLEY & ASSOCIATES • 320
BRADLEY GROUP • 486
BRADLEY PERS. CNSLTS. • 11
BRADLEY PROF. SERVICES • 512
BRADLEY-PIERCE PERS. • 476
BRADY EMP. SERVICE • 281
THE BRADY GROUP, INC. • 160
BRAINPOWER PERS. AGY. • 565
MF BRANCH ASSOCIATES • 447
THE BRAND COMPANY • 135
J.W. BRANDENBURG & ASSOC. • 462
BRANDENBURG SMITH & ASSOC. • 34
BRANDJES ASSOCIATES • 258
BRANDYWINE RETAINED VENTURES, INC. • 113
BRANTHOVER ASSOCIATES • 400
BRATLAND & ASSOCIATES • 186
BRATTLE TEMPS • 287
BRAULT & ASSOCIATES • 586
BREEN PERSONNEL, INC. • 11
BREI & ASSOCIATES, INC. • 234
BREITNER CLARK & HALL • 269
THE BREN GROUP • 17
BREN NORRIS ASSOC. • 97
BRENNAN ASSOCIATES • 34
THE BRENTWOOD GRP. • 366, 491
BRETT ASSOCIATES • 366
BRIAN ASSOCIATES, INC. • 400
BRICKELL PERS. CNSLTS. • 135
THE BRIDGE • 100
BRIDGE PERSONNEL • 548
BRIDGECREEK & ASSOC. • 34
BRIDGEGATE LLC • 34
BRIDGERS & ASSOCIATES • 160
BRIGHT SEARCH • 320
THE BRIMEYER GROUP • 325
BRINDISI SEARCH • 258
BRINKMAN & ASSOCIATES • 238
BRISSENDEN, McFARLAND, FUCCELLA & REYNOLDS • 366
BRISTOL ASSOCIATES • 34
BRITANNIA • 186
THE BRITISH CONNECTION • 424
BROAD WAVERLY & ASSOC. • 366
NORMAN BROADBENT INTNL. • 400, 586
BROOK-BLAIR LTD. • 34
BROOKDALE SEARCH ASSOC. • 367
BROOKE CHASE ASSOC. • 186
E.E. BROOKE INC. • 424
BROOKLEA & ASSOC. • 548
BROOKS ASSOCIATES • 34
BROOKSIDE CONSULTING GRP • 298
BROOKVILLE STAFFING SVCS. • 424
BROWARD-DOBBS INC. • 160
A.J. BROWN & ASSOCIATES • 35

D. BROWN & ASSOCIATES • 491
J.B. BROWN & ASSOCIATES • 462
KEN BROWN & COMPANY • 335
BROWN & KEENE PERS. • 565
THOMAS E. BROWN CAREER PLANNING • 345
BRUCO, INC. • 571
D. BRUSH & ASSOCIATES • 548
BRYANT & COMPANY • 443
D.F. BRYANT & COMPANY • 238
BRYANT BUREAU • 234
BRYSON MYERS COMPANY • 35
B²D TECHNICAL SERVICES • 156
BUCKINGHAM PERS. SVC. • 281
BUCKLER CAREERS, INC. • 593
BUCKLEY GROUP • 367, 548
BUCKMAN-ENOCHS & ASSOC. • 463
BUCKNER & ASSOCIATES • 129
BUFF & ASSOCIATES • 35
BULLINGTON ASSOCIATES • 443
BULLIS & COMPANY, INC. • 35
BULLOCK & COMPANY • 486
BULLOCK PERSONNEL, INC. • 565
BUNDY-STEWART ASSOC. • 548
BURGEON HOSPITALITY SEARCH • 548
BURGESS ASSOCIATES • 238
BURKE AND ASSOCIATES • 113
C.C. BURKE, LTD. • 400
BURLING GROUP LTD. • 186
BURLINGTON WELLS OF SOUTHERN FLORIDA • 135
BURNETT PERS. SVCS. • 571
BURNETT'S STAFFING, INC. • 571
BURNS EMPLOYMENT SVC. • 336
BURNS PERSONNEL • 400
DAVID S. BURT ASSOC. • 347
BURTON PLCMT.SVCS. • 187, 232
BUSINESS AND PROF. CNSLTS. • 35
BUSINESS CAREERS • 607
BUSINESS CONTROL SYSTEMS • 126
BUSINESS PERS. SVCS. • 343
BUSINESS PROF. GROUP • 170
BUSINESS PROFESSIONS • 351
BUSINESS SPECIALISTS • 241
BUSINESS SYSTEMS OF AMERICA, INC. • 187
BUSINESS SYSTS. SUPPORT • 69
BUSINESS TRENDS, INC. • 308
BUTLER INTNL. • 391,576
BUTLER SVC. GROUP • 396, 597
BUTLER-McCALL GROUP • 444
THE BUTLERS COMPANY • 135
BUTTERFASS PEPE & McCALLAN • 367
BUXBAUM/RINK CONSULTING • 113
BUZHARDT ASSOCIATES • 332
THOMAS BYRNE GROUP • 120
BYRNES & RUPKEY, INC. • 232
BYRON LEONARD INTNL. • 48

C

C ASSOCIATES • 129
C&C ASSOCIATES • 35
C-E SEARCH • 35
CBA • 35
CBS PERSONNEL SERVICES • 476
CCS GROUP • 187
CCSI INC. • 359
CDI CORP. • 24, 112, 156, 219, 236, 242, 294, 317, 329, 345, 361, 391, 439, 521, 534, 576, 582, 597, 611, 613
CDI ENG. GRP. • 253, 576, 613
CDI IT SERVICES • 458, 534
CDI INFORMATION SVCS • 95, 521
CDI INFORMATION SYSTS. • 545
CDI TECH. SVCS. • 83, 396, 458, 497
CDI TELECOMM. • 576
CDS STAFFING SERVICES • 95
CEC ASSOCIATES • 269
CEO • 160
CEO SERVICES • 367
CES ASSOCIATES • 187
CFI RESOURCES INC. • 400
CFR EXECUTIVE SEARCH • 187
C.G. & COMPANY • 548
CGR STAFFING SERVICES • 433
CGS PERSONNEL • 353
C.J. STAFFING SERVICES • 545
CK RESOURCES • 400

CKR ASSOCIATES • 367
C.M. MANAGEMENT SVCS. • 246
CMIS • 500
CMS • 607
CMS MANAGEMENT SVCS. • 230
CMS PERSONNEL SERVICES • 160
CN ASSOCIATES • 35
CP RESUMES, INC. • 459
CPH STAFFING & CONSULTING, LLC • 123
THE CPI GROUP • 332
CPS TECH. PLACEMENTS • 384
CQ PERSONNEL • 281
C.R. ASSOCIATES • 35
CRI PROFESSIONAL SEARCH • 35
C.R.T., INC. • 187
C.S. ASSOCIATES, LLC • 17
C.S. GLOBAL PARTNERS • 187
CSA ASSOCIATES • 367
CSI EMPLOYMENT • 232
CT GROUP • 401
CT PERSONNEL SERVICES • 69
CTI GROUP • 148
CTS INTERNATIONAL • 611
CAD TECHNOLOGY, INC. • 549
CADWORKS, INC. • 598
CAHILL ASSOCIATES • 114
BILL CALDWELL EMP. SVC. • 225
CALDWELL PERS. SVCS. • 452
CALDWELL STAFFING SVCS • 127
CALIBER ASSOCIATES • 500
CALIFORNIA JOB CONNECTION • 70
CALIFORNIA MNGMNT SEARCH • 35
CALIFORNIA SEARCH AGY. • 35
CALIFORNIA SEARCH CNSLTS. • 35
CALLAN & ASSOCIATES • 187
CALVERT ASSOCIATES INC. • 308
CAMBRIDGE CAREERS • 234
CAMBRIDGE GROUP • 114, 238
CAMERON BROWN & ASSOC. • 160
CAMPBELL ASSOCIATES • 269
T.M. CAMPBELL COMPANY • 599
CANIS MAJOR, INC. • 221
CANNY, BOWEN INC. • 401
J.P. CANON ASSOCIATES • 401
CANON BROWER • 35
MICHAEL CANTOR ASSOC. • 269
CANTOR CONCERN • 401
CANTRELL & ASSOCIATES • 135
CAP ASSOCIATES • 549
CAPITAL AREA TEMP. SVCS. • 516
CAPITAL DATA, INC. • 135
CAPITAL FINANCE RECRUITING • 367
CAPITOL EXEC. RESOURCES • 612
CAPITOL PERSONNEL INC. • 525
CAPITOL SEARCH • 129, 384
CAPITOL STAFFING SOL. • 332
SALLY CAPLAN & ASSOC. • 599
CAPLAN/GROSS ASSOC. • 258
CAPRIO & ASSOCIATES INC. • 187
CAPSTONE ASSOCIATES • 367
CAR-VIR INC. • 586
CARADYNE GROUP • 135
CARDINAL PERS. CONSULTING • 444
CAREER & VOCATIONAL COUNSELING • 267
CAREER ADVANTAGE • 35
CAREER ASSOCIATES INC. • 308
CAREER BLAZERS PERSONNEL SERVICE • 131, 424
CAREER CENTER, INC. • 384
CAREER CHANGERS & CO. • 267
CAREER CHOICE, INC. • 135
CAREER CIRCUIT • 441
THE CAREER CLINIC, INC. • 599
CAREER CONCEPTS • 347, 424, 486
CAREER CONCEPTS STAFFING SERVICES • 500
CAREER CONNECTIONS • 100, 101, 360, 460, 480
CAREER CONSULTANTS • 226, 523
CAREER CONSULTANTS INTNL. • 36
CAREER COUNSELING INC. • 244
CAREER DEVELOPMENT • 593
CAREER DEV. ASSOCIATES • 353
CAREER DEV. SERVICES • 441
CAREER DIRECTIONS • 319
CAREER ENTERPRISES • 463
CAREER FINDERS • 234
CAREER FORUM, INC. • 101

T

JobBank List Service
Custom-Designed For Your Job Search

Generated by the same editors who bring you the nationally renowned *JobBank* series, the electronic *JobBank List Service* is a compilation of company information that is important to you. Our huge database is updated year-round to ensure that our data is as accurate as possible. Our company information is available to you by e-mail or on disk in ASCII delimited text format.

Whether you're looking for a small company to work for, or a large corporation to do business with, *JobBank List Service* can help! *JobBank List Service* is not mass-produced for the general public; it is built for *you* through a personal consultation with a member of the *JobBank* staff.

While other services offer their company information on pre-generated disk or CD-ROM, we construct the data explicitly to match your criteria. Your *JobBank* consultant will work with you to find the company information that applies to your specific job search needs. Criteria for companies or employment agencies can be specified geographically, by industry, by occupation, or any variation or combination you can imagine... you decide.

With the most current information on companies in more than thirty industries, jobseekers, recruiters, and businesses alike will find the *JobBank List Service* the perfect solution to their personal and professional needs. Industries covered include:

- *Accounting and Management Consulting*
- *Advertising, Marketing, and Public Relations*
- *Aerospace*
- *Apparel, Fashion & Textiles*
- *Architecture, Construction, and Engineering*
- *Arts, Entertainment, Sports, & Recreation*
- *Automotive*
- *Banking/Savings and Loans*
- *Biotechnology, Pharmaceuticals & Scientific R&D*
- *Charities and Social Services*
- *Chemicals/Rubber & Plastics*

- *Communications: Telecommunications & Broadcasting*
- *Computer Hardware, Software, and Services*
- *Educational Services*
- *Electronic/Industrial Electrical Equipment*
- *Environmental & Waste Management Services*
- *Fabricated/Primary Metals & Products*
- *Financial Services*
- *Food & Beverages/Agriculture*
- *Government*
- *Health Care: Services,*

  Equipment & Products
- *Hotels & Restaurants*
- *Insurance*
- *Manufacturing*
- *Mining/Gas/Petroleum/Energy Related*
- *Paper & Wood Products*
- *Printing and Publishing*
- *Real Estate*
- *Retail*
- *Stone, Glass, Clay, and Concrete Products*
- *Transportation*
- *Utilities*
- *Miscellaneous Wholesaling and many others*

- NO MINIMUM ORDER — NO ORDER IS TOO SMALL!
- THOUSANDS OF PRIVATE & PUBLIC COMPANIES IN <u>ALL</u> 50 STATES & DC
- THOUSANDS OF EMPLOYMENT SERVICES
- EACH LISTING INCLUDES THE SAME TYPE OF DETAILED CONTACT & BUSINESS INFORMATION OFFERED IN THE *JOBBANK* BOOK SERIES
- STANDING ORDER DISCOUNTS ARE AVAILABLE

Contact a *JobBank* staff member now for your individual consultation
and pricing information.
E-mail: jobbank@adamsonline.com
Phone: 800/872-5627 x5317 (in MA: 781/767-8100 x5317)
Fax: 781/767-2055

Other Adams Media Books

The Adams Electronic Job Search Almanac 2000

Uncover thousands of jobs in minutes using your own computer! This comprehensive guide features hundreds of online resources available through commercial online services, the World Wide Web, newsgroups, and more. *The Adams Electronic Job Search Almanac 2000* also includes a selection of company joblines, advice on posting an electronic resume, and strategies for researching companies on the Internet. The book also features information on a variety of job-hunting software. 5½" x 8½", 312 pages, paperback, $10.95. ISBN: 1-58062-221-6, ISSN: 1099-016X

The JobBank Series

There are 30 *JobBank* books, each providing extensive, up-to-date employment information on hundreds of the largest employers in each job market. The #1 best-selling series of employment directories, the *JobBank* series has been recommended as an excellent place to begin your job search by the *New York Times*, the *Los Angeles Times*, the *Boston Globe*, and the *Chicago Tribune*. *JobBank* books have been used by millions of people to find jobs. Titles available:

The Atlanta JobBank • *The Austin/San Antonio JobBank* • *The Boston JobBank* • *The Carolina JobBank* • *The Chicago JobBank* • *The Connecticut JobBank* • *The Dallas-Fort Worth JobBank* • *The Denver JobBank* • *The Detroit JobBank* • *The Florida JobBank* • *The Houston JobBank* • *The Indiana JobBank* • *The Las Vegas JobBank* • *The Los Angeles JobBank* • *The Minneapolis-St. Paul JobBank* • *The Missouri JobBank* • *The New Jersey JobBank* • *The Metropolitan New York JobBank* • *The Ohio JobBank* • *The Greater Philadelphia JobBank* • *The Phoenix JobBank* • *The Pittsburgh JobBank* • *The Portland JobBank* • *The San Francisco Bay Area JobBank* • *The Seattle JobBank* • *The Tennessee JobBank* • *The Virginia JobBank* • *The Metropolitan Washington DC JobBank* • *The JobBank Guide to Computer & High-Tech Companies ($17.95)* • *The JobBank Guide to Health Care Companies ($17.95)*

EACH JOBBANK BOOK IS 6" X 9¼", OVER 300 PAGES, PAPERBACK, $16.95.
For ISBNs and ISSNs, please visit http://www.careercity.com/booksoftware/jobbank.asp

JobBank List Service: If you are interested in variations of this information in electronic format for sales or job search mailings, please call 800-872-5627 x5317, or e-mail us at jobbank@adamsonline.com.

Available Wherever Books Are Sold

If you cannot find these titles at your favorite retail outlet, you may order them directly from the publisher. BY PHONE: Call 1-800-872-5627. We accept Visa, Mastercard, and American Express. $4.95 will be added to your total order for shipping and handling. BY MAIL: Write out the full titles of the books you'd like to order and send payment, including $4.95 for shipping and handling, to: Adams Media Corporation, 260 Center Street, Holbrook, MA 02343. U.S.A. 30-day money-back guarantee. BY FAX: 800-872-5628. BY E-MAIL: jobbank@adamsonline.com. *Discounts available for standing orders.*

Visit our exciting job and career site at http://www.careercity.com

Other Adams Media Books

The Adams Cover Letter Almanac

The Adams Cover Letter Almanac is the most detailed cover letter resource in print, containing 600 cover letters used by real people to win real jobs. It features complete information on all types of letters, including networking, "cold," broadcast, and follow-up. In addition to advice on how to avoid fatal cover letter mistakes, the book includes strategies for people changing careers, relocating, recovering from layoff, and more. ISBN 1-55850-497-4. $5^1/_2$" x $8^1/_2$", 736 pages, paperback, $12.95.

The Adams Resume Almanac

This almanac features detailed information on resume development and layout, a review of the pros and cons of various formats, an exhaustive look at the strategies that will definitely get a resume noticed, and 600 sample resumes in dozens of career categories. *The Adams Resume Almanac* is the most comprehensive, thoroughly researched resume guide ever published. ISBN 1-55850-358-7. $5^1/_2$" x $8^1/_2$", 768 pages, paperback, $10.95.

The Adams Jobs Almanac

Updated annually, *The Adams Jobs Almanac* includes names and addresses of over 7,000 U.S. employers; information on which positions each company commonly fills; industry forecasts; geographical cross-references; employment prospects in all 50 states; and advice on preparing resumes and cover letters and standing out at interviews. $5^1/_2$" x $8^1/_2$", 952 pages, paperback, $16.95. ISBN: 1-58062-220-8, ISSN: 1072-592X

If you are interested in variations of the Jobs Almanac information in electronic format for sales or job search mailings, please call 800-872-5627 x5317, or e-mail us at jobbank@adamsonline.com

Available Wherever Books Are Sold

If you cannot find these titles at your favorite retail outlet, you may order them directly from the publisher. BY PHONE: Call 1-800-872-5627. We accept Visa, Mastercard, and American Express. $4.95 will be added to your total order for shipping and handling. BY MAIL: Write out the full titles of the books you'd like to order and send payment, including $4.95 for shipping and handling, to: Adams Media Corporation, 260 Center Street, Holbrook, MA 02343. U.S.A. 30-day money-back guarantee. BY FAX: 800-872-5628. BY E-MAIL: jobbank@adamsonline.com. *Discounts available for standing orders.*

Visit our exciting job and career site at http://www.careercity.com

Other Adams Media Books

The Adams Cover Letter Almanac and Disk
Writing cover letters has never been easier! *FastLetter*™
software includes: a choice of dynamic opening sentences,
effective following paragraphs, and sure-fire closings; a
complete word processing program so you can customize your
letter in any way you choose; and a tutorial that shows you
how to make your cover letter terrific. Windows compatible.
ISBN 1-55850-619-5. $5\frac{1}{2}$" x $8\frac{1}{2}$", 752 pages, *FastLetter*™
software included (one $3\frac{1}{2}$" disk), trade paperback, $19.95.

The Adams Resume Almanac and Disk
Create a powerful resume in minutes! *FastResume*™ software
includes: a full range of resume styles and formats; ready-to-use
action phrases that highlight your skills and experience; a tutorial
that shows you how to make any resume terrific; and a full word
processor with ready-made layout styles. Windows compatible.
ISBN 1-55850-618-7. $5\frac{1}{2}$" x $8\frac{1}{2}$", 786 pages, *FastResume*™
software included (one $3\frac{1}{2}$" disk), trade paperback, $19.95.

The Adams Job Interview Almanac and CD-ROM
Beat the competition with The Adams Job Interview Almanac & CD-ROM!
The Adams Job Interview Almanac includes answers and dis-
cussions for over 1,800 interview questions. There are 100 complete job interviews for all fields, industries, and career levels.
Also included is valuable information on handling stress interviews, strategies for second and third interviews, and negotiat-
ing job offers.

The *Adams Job Interview CD-ROM* features over 300 video
and 200 audio clips to guide you through an interview. Decide
how many questions you want to answer and go one-on-one with
one of the world's top experts on job interviewing. Stuck? Expert
advice is just a click away. ISBN 1-55850-709-4. $5\frac{1}{2}$" x $8\frac{1}{2}$", 840 pages,
Adams Job Interview Pro software included (one CD-ROM), trade paperback, $19.95.

Available Wherever Books Are Sold

If you cannot find these titles at your favorite retail outlet, you may order them directly from
the publisher. BY PHONE: Call 1-800-872-5627. We accept Visa, Mastercard, and American
Express. $4.95 will be added to your total order for shipping and handling. BY MAIL: Write
out the full titles of the books you'd like to order and send payment, including $4.95 for
shipping and handling, to: Adams Media Corporation, 260 Center Street, Holbrook, MA
02343. U.S.A. 30-day money-back guarantee. BY FAX: 800-872-5628. BY E-MAIL:
jobbank@adamsonline.com. *Discounts available for standing orders.*

Visit our exciting job and career site at http://www.careercity.com

From the publishers of the *JobBank* and *Knock'em Dead* books

Visit our Web Site: www.careercity.com

...free access to tens of thousands of current job openings plus the most comprehensive career info on the web today!

- Current job listings at top employers in all professions

- Descriptions and hot links to 27,000 major US employers

- Free resume posting gets noticed by top hiring companies

- Access to thousands of executive search firms and agencies

- Comprehensive salary surveys cover all fields

- Directories of associations and other industry resources

- Hundreds of articles on getting started, changing careers, job interviews, resumes, cover letters and more

Post your resume at CareerCity and have the job offers come to you!

It's fast, free and easy to post your resume at CareerCity—and you'll get noticed by hundreds of leading employers in all fields.